DRAPER'S book of

QUOTATIONS FOR THE CHRISTIAN WORLD

Edythe **Draper**

TYNDALE HOUSE PUBLISHERS, INC.
WHEATON, ILLINOIS

Poetry by Luci Shaw is used by permission of Harold Shaw Publishers (Wheaton, IL) and is reprinted from the following books: *Listen to the Green* © 1971, *Postcard from the Shore* © 1985, *A Widening Light: Poems of the Incarnation* © 1984, *The Secret Trees* © 1976, and *The Sighting* © 1981.

Library of Congress Cataloging-in-Publication Data

Draper, Edythe.
   [Book of quotations for the Christian world]
   Draper's book of quotations for the Christian world / Edythe
Draper.
      p.   cm.
   ISBN 0-8423-5109-4
   1. Quotations, English.   2. Theology—Quotations, maxims, etc.
I. Title. II. Title: Book of quotations for the Christian world.
PN6081.D7   1992
082—dc20   91-35165

Printed in the United States of America

99 98 97 96 95 94 93 92
9   8   7   6   5   4   3   2   1

CONTENTS

A tribute to

HARRY VERPLOEGH

An incurable quotations anthologist

who provided me with many of the resources
needed to produce this work. The depth and
breadth of this book would not have been possible
without his help. More important, he never fails to
be a source of inspiration. We both relish searching
for those quotations that deserve to be set apart,
reflected upon, and passed along.

EDYTHE DRAPER

LIST OF TOPICS

A
Ability
Abortion
Abuse
Acceptance
Accomplishment
Accountability
Achievement
Action
Activity
Addiction
Adversity
Adversity/Prosperity
Advice
Affliction
Age
Agnosticism
Alcohol
Ambition
Angels
Anger
Anxiety
Apathy
Apology
Appearance
Appreciation
Argument
Arrogance
Ascension
Asceticism
Aspiration
Atheism
Atonement
Attitude
Authority

B
Baptism
Beatitudes
Beauty
Beginnings
Behavior
Belief
Benediction
Benevolence
Betrayal
Bible
Bible Personalities
Bible/Psalms
Birth
Blessings
Body
Books
Boredom
Born Again
Brokenness
Brotherhood
Burdens
Burnout

C
Certainty
Change
Character
Charity
Cheerfulness
Children
Choice
Christianity
Christians
Christmas

Church
Circumstances
Civil Rights
Clergy
Comfort
Commandments
Commitment
Compassion
Complaint
Compliment
Compromise
Conceit
Confession
Confidence
Confidentiality
Conflict
Conformity
Conscience
Consciousness
Consecration
Consequences
Consistency
Contemplation
Contempt
Contentment
Controversy
Conversation
Conversion
Conviction
Courage
Courtesy
Cowardice
Creation
Creation/Evolution
Creativity

Creeds
Crime
Crisis
Criticism
Cross
Crucifixion
Cynicism

D
Day
Death
Death/Last Words
Deceit
Decisions
Deeds
Defeat
Democracy
Dependability
Depression
Desires
Despair
Destiny
Determination
Devil
Difficulties
Dignity
Diligence
Disappointment
Discernment
Discipleship
Discipline
Discontent
Discouragement
Discretion
Discussion

A

ABILITY

1 Abilities are like tax deductions—we use them or we lose them.
SAM JENNINGS

2 Everyone excels in something in which another fails.
LATIN PROVERB

3 God does not ask about our ability or our inability, but our availability.

4 God does not require that each individual shall have capacity for everything.
RICHARD ROTHE (1799–1867)

5 God's gifts are meted out according to the taker, not according to the giver.
MEISTER ECKHART (C. 1260–C. 1327)

6 God's gifts put man's best dreams to shame.
ELIZABETH BARRETT BROWNING
(1806–1861)

7 Great talents have some admirers, but few friends.

8 It is not a question of our equipment, but of our poverty; not what we bring with us, but what he puts in us; not our natural virtues, our strength of character, our knowledge, our experience; all that is of no avail. . . . God can do nothing with people who think they will be of use to him.
OSWALD CHAMBERS (1874–1917)

9 It is not my ability, but my response to God's ability, that counts.
CORRIE TEN BOOM (1892–1983)

10 The disillusionment with our own abilities is, perhaps, one of the most important things that can ever happen to us.
TIM HANSEL

11 The presence of Christ brings us his power and ability to use our limited resources in his limitless ways.
REBECCA MANLEY PIPPERT

12 These are gifts from God arranged by infinite wisdom, notes that make up the scores of creation's loftiest symphony, threads that compose the master tapestry of the universe.
A. W. TOZER (1897–1963)

13 Use your own mind, then rely upon God.
ARABIAN PROVERB

14 When it is a question of God's
almighty Spirit, never say "I can't."
OSWALD CHAMBERS (1874–1917)

ABORTION

15 Abortion stops a beating heart.
—Theme of West Virginians for Life
state convention

16 For us murder is once for all forbidden; so even the child in the womb . . .
is not lawful for us to destroy. To forbid birth is only quicker murder. . . .
The fruit is always present in the seed.
TERTULLIAN (C. 160–AFTER 220)

17 How would you like to be that baby
inside the womb of a woman who isn't
sure she wants you to live any longer?
CHARLES R. SWINDOLL (1934–   )

18 I believe this society will one day look
back at the horror of abortion, and
critics will ask, "Where was the
church?"
JOEL REITER

19 I do not believe in abortion. But I will
prefer to counsel a woman who has
had a legal abortion rather than to
bury one who has had an illegal one. I
have done both.
ALBERT DEMOS

20 I have a right to free speech, but not to
shout "fire" in a theater. A person's
right to anything stops when it injures
or kills another living human. Should
any civilized nation give to one citizen
the absolute right to kill another to
solve that first person's personal problem?
JOHN WILKE

21 I will not give a woman an instrument
to procure abortion.
HIPPOCRATES (C. 460–C. 377 B.C.)

22 It's haunting me. I can't get it out of
my mind. . . . I helped murder somebody and I can't sleep.
—Linda Johnson, after being forced to
witness an abortion and package
the aborted baby for use as evidence

23 We are fighting abortion by adoption.
We have sent word to the clinics, to
the hospitals, to the police stations.
"Please do not destroy the child. We
will take the child."
MOTHER TERESA OF CALCUTTA (1910–   )

24 We cannot treat the human embryo as
cheap and worthless without passing
judgment on all human life, including
our own.
MONICA FURLONG

25 What would God have done if Mary
and Joseph had decided to have an
abortion?

ABUSE

26 A beast does not know that he is a
beast, and the nearer a man gets to
being a beast, the less he knows it.
GEORGE MACDONALD (1824–1905)

27 All cruelty springs from weakness.
LUCIUS ANNAEUS SENECA (C. 4 B.C.–A.D. 65)

28 Cruelty is a detested sport that owes
its pleasures to another's pain.
WILLIAM COWPER (1731–1800)

29 Cruelty isn't softened by tears, it feeds
on them.
PUBLILIUS SYRUS (FIRST CENTURY B.C.)

30 Man's inhumanity to man
Makes countless thousands mourn.
ROBERT BURNS (1759–1796)

31 Men are the only animals who devote
themselves assiduously to making one
another unhappy.
H. L. MENCKEN (1880–1956)

32 More than 90 percent of all the prisoners in our American prisons have been
abused as children.
JOHN POWELL

ACCEPTANCE

33 Acceptance says, "True, this is my situation at the moment. I'll look unblinkingly at the reality of it. But I'll also
open my hands to accept willingly
whatever a loving Father sends."
CATHERINE WOOD MARSHALL (1914–1983)

34 For after all, the best thing one can do when it's raining is to let it rain.
HENRY WADSWORTH LONGFELLOW (1807–1882)

35 If the Giver gives you a hill to plough, don't level it.
ARABIAN PROVERB

36 If you have no power to prevail over someone, leave it to God.
ARABIAN PROVERB

37 It ain't no use to grumble and complain,
It's just as easy to rejoice;
When God sorts out the weather and sends rain,
Why, rain's my choice.
JAMES WHITCOMB RILEY (1849–1916)

38 Let us take things as we find them. Let us not attempt to distort them into what they are not. We cannot make facts. All our wishing cannot change them. We must use them.
CARDINAL JOHN HENRY NEWMAN (1801–1890)

39 My child, it will be better for you if you accept my decisions without complaint. Do not ask me to defend my actions or to explain why one person is favored and another seems slighted. The answers to these questions go far beyond your comprehension.
THOMAS À KEMPIS (C. 1380–1471)

40 One already wet does not feel the rain.
TURKISH PROVERB

41 Resignation is putting God between ourselves and our troubles.
MADAME ANNE SOPHIE SOYMANOV SWETCHINE (1782–1857)

42 Resignation is the rarest sort of courage.
GUSTAVE DROZ

43 Since the house is on fire, let us warm ourselves.
ITALIAN PROVERB

44 There is no good in arguing with the inevitable. The only argument available with an east wind is to put on your overcoat.
JAMES RUSSELL LOWELL (1819–1891)

45 When you are outraged by somebody's impudence, ask yourself at once, "Can the world exist without impudent people?" It cannot; so do not ask for impossibilities.
MARCUS AURELIUS ANTONINUS (121–180)

46 You are not accepted by God because you deserve to be, or because you have worked hard for him; but because Jesus died for you.
COLIN URQUHART (1940–   )

ACCOMPLISHMENT

47 Ancient of Days! except thou deign
Upon the finished task to smile,
The workman's hand hath toiled in vain,
To hew the rock and rear the pile.
WILLIAM CULLEN BRYANT (1794–1878)

48 Are you in earnest? Seize this very minute! What you can do, or dream you can, begin it. Boldness has genius, power and magic in it. Only engage, and then the mind grows heated. Begin, and then the work will be completed.
JOHANN WOLFGANG VON GOETHE (1749–1832)

49 At the day of judgment we shall not be asked what we have read but what we have done.
THOMAS À KEMPIS (C. 1380–1471)

50 Being able to do something well is one of life's great joys.
FRANK TYGER

51 Determine never to be idle. . . . It is wonderful how much may be done if we are always doing.
THOMAS JEFFERSON (1743–1826)

52 Do what you can with what you have where you are.
THEODORE ROOSEVELT (1858–1919)

53 Efficiency is enhanced not by what we accomplish but more often by what we relinquish.
CHARLES R. SWINDOLL (1934–   )

54 Every job is a self-portrait of the person who did it.

55 God will not demand more from you than you can do. Whatever God asks

of you, he will give you the strength
to do.
ERWIN W. LUTZER (1941–)

56 Great is the art of beginning, but
greater is the art of ending.
HENRY WADSWORTH LONGFELLOW
(1807–1882)

57 He who begins many things finishes
but few.
ITALIAN PROVERB

58 He who cannot do something big can
do something small in a big way.

59 He who moves a mountain starts by
carrying away small stones.

60 If we prune back that part of our activity which is not really fruitful in the
Holy Spirit, we find that we do less,
but accomplish more.
JOHN MICHAEL TALBOT

61 Lord, grant that I may always desire
more than I can accomplish.
MICHELANGELO (1475–1564)

62 Men are much more apt to agree in
what they do than in what they think.
JOHANN WOLFGANG VON GOETHE
(1749–1832)

63 No matter what a man does, no matter how successful he seems to be in
any field, if the Holy Spirit is not the
chief energizer of his activity, it will all
fall apart when he dies.
A. W. TOZER (1897–1963)

64 The difference between something
good and something great is attention
to detail.
CHARLES R. SWINDOLL (1934–)

65 The virtue of deeds lies in completing
them.
ARABIAN PROVERB

66 The world is moving so fast these days
that the man who says it can't be done
is generally interrupted by someone
doing it.
ELBERT GREEN HUBBARD (1856–1915)

67 Thinking well is wise; planning well,
wiser; doing well wisest and best of all.
PERSIAN PROVERB

68 Unless you try to do something
beyond what you have already mastered, you will never grow.
RONALD E. OSBORN

69 Well done is better than well said.
BENJAMIN FRANKLIN (1706–1790)

ACCOUNTABILITY

70 A person may cause evil to others not
only by his actions but by his inaction,
and in either case he is justly accountable to them for the injury.
JOHN STUART MILL (1806–1873)

71 Life is like a cash register in that every
account, every thought, every deed,
like every sale, is registered and
recorded.
ARCHBISHOP FULTON J. SHEEN (1895–1979)

72 My Spirit searches the deep things of
the heart. I not only taste the fruit, I
test the soundness of the tree. I do not
look at the leaves, but examine the
roots. I behold not the shape of the
tree, but test the heart.
FRANCES J. ROBERTS

73 The sins ye do by two and two, ye
must pay for, one by one.
RUDYARD KIPLING (1865–1936)

74 What difference does it make to you
what someone else becomes, or says,
or does? You do not need to answer
for others, only for yourself.
THOMAS À KEMPIS (C. 1380–1471)

ACHIEVEMENT

75 A bell doesn't ring on its own—if
someone doesn't pull or push it, it will
remain silent.
PLAUTUS (C. 254–184 B.C.)

76 A ship in a harbor is safe, but that's
not what ships are built for.

77 A strong man must have something difficult to do.
JOHN STUART BLACKIE (1809–1895)

78 Doing becomes the natural overflow
of being when the pressure within is
stronger than the pressure without.
LOIS LEBAR

79 Every calling is great when greatly pursued.
OLIVER WENDELL HOLMES (1809–1894)

80 Four steps to achievement: Plan purposefully, prepare prayerfully, proceed positively, pursue persistently.
WILLIAM ARTHUR WARD (1812–1882)

81 Give me a person who says, "This one thing I do, and not these fifty things I dabble in."
DWIGHT LYMAN MOODY (1837–1899)

82 I'm a slow walker, but I never walk back.
ABRAHAM LINCOLN (1809–1865)

83 It is not enough to aim: you must hit.
ITALIAN PROVERB

84 It is very easy to overestimate the importance of our own achievements in comparison with what we owe others.
DIETRICH BONHOEFFER (1906–1945)

85 No great achievement is possible without persistent work.
BERTRAND ARTHUR WILLIAM RUSSELL (1872–1970)

86 Nothing will ever be attempted if all possible objections must be first overcome.
SAMUEL JOHNSON (1709–1784)

87 Only those who dare to fail greatly can ever achieve greatly.

88 Sitting on a tack is often more useful than having an idea; at least it makes you get up and do something about it.

89 Some men dream of worthy accomplishments, while others stay awake and do them.

90 The airplane, the atomic bomb, and the zipper have cured me of any tendency to state that a thing can't be done.
R. L. DUFFUS

91 The greatest works are done by the ones. The hundreds do not often do much, the companies never; it is the units, the single individuals, that are the power and the might.
CHARLES HADDON SPURGEON (1834–1892)

92 The roots of true achievement lie in the will to become the best that you can become.
HAROLD TAYLOR

93 The world is divided into people who do things and people who get the credit; try to belong to the first class—there's far less competition.
DWIGHT WHITNEY MORROW (1873–1931)

94 There is no gathering the rose without being pricked by the thorns.

95 What people say you cannot do, you try and find that you can.
HENRY DAVID THOREAU (1817–1862)

96 Whatever is worth doing at all, is worth doing well.
LORD CHESTERFIELD (1694–1773)

97 Where would you be if God took away all your Christian work? Too often it is our Christian work that is worshiped and not God.
OSWALD CHAMBERS (1874–1917)

ACTION

98 A Christian should always remember that the value of his good works is not based on their number and excellence, but on the love of God which prompts him to do these things.
SAINT JOHN OF THE CROSS (1542–1591)

99 A dog barks when his master is attacked. I would be a coward if I saw that God's truth is attacked and yet would remain silent.
JOHN CALVIN (1509–1564)

100 A few dozen act while millions stand impotent.
JOHN FOWLES (1926–)

101 A thousand words will not leave so deep an impression as one deed.
HENRIK IBSEN (1828–1906)

102 All glory comes from daring to begin.

103 All our actions take
Their hues from the complexion of the heart,
As landscapes their variety from light.
W. T. BACON (1812–1881)

104 Christian action is not of ourselves; it is the spirit of Christ operating in our lives.

105 Every action of our lives touches on some chord that will vibrate in eternity.
EDWIN HUBBEL CHAPIN (1814–1880)

106 I am only one,
But still I am one.
I cannot do everything,
But still I can do something;
And because I cannot do everything
I will not refuse to do the something
   that I can do.
EDWARD EVERETT HALE (1822–1909)

107 If you sit down at set of sun
And count the acts that you have done,
And, counting, find one self-denying
   deed, one word
That eased the heart of him who
   heard—
One glance most kind,
That fell like sunshine where it went—
Then you may count that day well
   spent.
GEORGE ELIOT (1819–1880)

108 Let a good man do good deeds with the same zeal that the evil man does bad ones.
THE BELZER RABBI

109 Resolved, never to do anything which I should be afraid to do if it were the last hour of my life.
JONATHAN EDWARDS (1703–1758)

110 Some people are content not to do mean actions; I want to become incapable of a mean thought or feeling.
GEORGE MACDONALD (1824–1905)

111 We have a shortage of effective Christian action at the real centers of national influence because of misplaced Christian energy, misplaced Christian money—and misplaced Christians.
MCCANDLISH PHILLIPS

ACTIVITY

112 Activity itself proves nothing: the ant is praised, the mosquito swatted.

113 Apart from God every activity is merely a passing whiff of insignificance.
ALFRED NORTH WHITEHEAD (1861–1947)

114 Beware of the barrenness of a busy life.

115 In an effort to get the work of the Lord done we often lose contact with the Lord of the work and quite literally wear our people out as well. I have heard more than one pastor boast that his church was a "live" one, pointing to the printed calendar as a proof—something on every night and several meetings during the day. Of course this proves nothing except that the pastor and the church are being guided by a bad spiritual philosophy. A great many of these time-consuming activities are useless and others plain ridiculous.
A. W. TOZER (1897–1963)

116 It is not enough to be busy; so are the ants. The question is: What are we busy about?
HENRY DAVID THOREAU (1817–1862)

117 It is possible to be so active in the service of Christ as to forget to love him.
P. T. FORSYTH (1848–1921)

118 Many a person who thinks he's a human dynamo is probably more like an electric fan.

119 More people would live to a ripe old age if they weren't too busy providing for it.

120 Much of our activity these days is nothing more than a cheap anesthetic to deaden the pain of an empty life.

121 Our Adversary majors in three things: noise, hurry and crowds. If he can keep us engaged in "muchness" and "manyness," he will rest satisfied.
RICHARD J. FOSTER (1942–   )

122 Purposeless activity may be a phase of death.
PEARL S. BUCK (1892–1973)

123 Study the poise and quietness of Christ. His task and responsibility might well have driven a man out of his mind. But he was never in a hurry,

never impressed by numbers, never a
slave of the clock.
J. B. PHILLIPS (1906–1982)

124 The activities we do for God are secondary. God is looking for people who
long for communication with him.
ERWIN W. LUTZER (1941–   )

125 The depths of our spirituality does not
depend upon changing the things we
do, but in doing for God what we ordi-
narily do for ourselves.
BROTHER LAWRENCE OF THE
RESURRECTION (C. 1605–1691)

126 The people who are always desperately active are a nuisance; it is
through the saints who are one with
him that God is doing things all the
time. The broken and the jaded and
the twisted are being ministered to by
God through the saints who are not
overcome by their own panic, who
because of their oneness with him are
absolutely at rest, consequently he can
work through them.
OSWALD CHAMBERS (1874–1917)

127 Today, through an overplus of Christian activities, Jesus Christ is being
dethroned and Christian wits and wisdom are taking his place.
OSWALD CHAMBERS (1874–1917)

128 We haven't the time to take our time.
EUGÈNE IONESCO (1912–   )

129 We hurt people by being too busy. Too
busy to notice their needs. Too busy to
drop that note of comfort or encouragement or assurance of love. Too
busy to listen when someone needs to
talk. Too busy to care.
BILLY GRAHAM (1918–   )

130 We of the nervous West are victims of
the philosophy of activism tragically
misunderstood. Getting and spending,
going and returning, organizing and
promoting, buying and selling, working and playing—this alone constitutes
living. If we are not making plans or
working to carry out plans already
made, we feel that we are failures, that
we are sterile, unfruitful eunuchs, parasites on the body of society. The gospel
of work, as someone has called it, has

crowded out the gospel of Christ in
many Christian churches.
A. W. TOZER (1897–1963)

ADDICTION

131 All gluttons have one thing in common: they don't believe in eating on an
empty stomach.

132 Gluttons dig their graves with their
teeth.
JEWISH PROVERB

133 Gluttony is an emotional escape, a
sign that something is eating us.
PETER DEVRIES (C. 1910–   )

134 If drug use isn't a sin, I don't know
what it is. We've seen treatment programs run by churches that are every
bit as effective as very expensive medical programs . . . If it's a spiritual problem, then the recovery should take
place as much in churches as in hospitals.
WILLIAM BENNETT

135 Only 5 percent of the [drug and alco-
hol] addicts in America live on skid
row. Many attend our churches regularly. Addicts are good actors and
actresses, and our congregations are
filled with actors and actresses.
NELSON PRICE

ADVERSITY

136 A gem is not polished without rubbing, nor a man made perfect without
trials.
CHINESE PROVERB

137 A good pilot is best tried in a storm.

138 A kick in the teeth may be the best
thing in the world for you.
WALT DISNEY (1901–1966)

139 A saint's life is in the hands of God as
a bow and arrow in the hands of an
archer. God is aiming at something the
saint cannot see; he stretches and
strains, and every now and again the
saint says: "I cannot stand any more."
But God does not heed; he goes on
stretching until his purpose is in sight,

then he lets fly. We are here for God's designs, not for our own.
OSWALD CHAMBERS (1874–1917)

140 Adversities do not make a man frail; they show what sort of man he is.
THOMAS À KEMPIS (C. 1380–1471)

141 Adversity can either destroy or build up, depending on our chosen response.
TIM HANSEL

142 Adversity introduces a man to himself.

143 Adversity is the diamond dust heaven polishes its jewels with.
ARCHBISHOP ROBERT LEIGHTON (1611–1684)

144 Adversity is the first path to truth.
LORD GEORGE NOEL GORDON BYRON (1788–1824)

145 Adversity is the trial of principle. Without it a man hardly knows whether he is honest or not.
HENRY FIELDING (1707–1754)

146 Adversity makes a man wise, not rich.
JOHN RAY (1627–1705)

147 Adversity reveals genius, prosperity conceals it.
HORACE (65–8 B.C.)

148 All that a man bears for God's sake, God makes light and sweet for him.
MEISTER ECKHART (C. 1260–C. 1327)

149 An hour of pain is as long as a day of pleasure.

150 Aromatic plants bestow
No spicy fragrance while they grow;
But crushed or trodden to the ground
Diffuse their sweetness all around.
OLIVER GOLDSMITH (1730–1774)

151 As sure as ever God puts his children in the furnace, he will be in the furnace with them.
CHARLES HADDON SPURGEON (1834–1892)

152 Ask not that all troubles end, for when troubles end, life ends too.

153 Bad is called good when worse happens.

154 Acceptance of what has happened is the first step to overcoming the consequences of any misfortune.
WILLIAM JAMES (1842–1910)

155 Beethoven composed his deepest music after becoming totally deaf. Pascal set down his most searching observations about God, man, life and death in brief intervals of release from a prostrating illness.
ROBERT J. MCCRACKEN (1904–1973)

156 Calamity is the perfect glass wherein we truly see and know ourselves.
SIR WILLIAM DAVENANT (1606–1668)

157 Calamity is virtue's opportunity.
LUCIUS ANNAEUS SENECA (C. 4 B.C.–A.D. 65)

158 Calamity: the test of integrity.
SAMUEL RICHARDSON (1689–1761)

159 Christ made no promise that those who followed him in his plan of re-establishing life on its proper basic principles would enjoy a special immunity from pain and sorrow—nor did he himself experience such immunity. He did, however, promise enough joy and courage, enough love and confidence in God to enable those who went his way to do far more than survive.
J. B. PHILLIPS (1906–1982)

160 Count each affliction, whether light or grave, God's messenger sent down to thee; do thou with courtesy receive him.
AUBREY THOMAS DE VERE (1814–1902)

161 Cripple him, and you have a Sir Walter Scott. Lock him in a prison cell, and you have a John Bunyan. Bury him in the snows of Valley Forge, and you have a George Washington. Raise him in abject poverty, and you have an Abraham Lincoln. Strike him down in infantile paralysis, and he becomes Franklin Roosevelt. Deafen him, and you have a Ludwig van Beethoven. Have him or her born black in a society filled with racial discrimination, and you have a Booker T. Washington, a Marian Anderson, a George Washington Carver. . . . Call him a slow learner, "retarded," and write him off an uneducable, and you have an Albert Einstein.
TED W. ENGSTROM (1916–   )

162 Crosses are ladders that lead to heaven.

163 Every wise workman takes his tools away from the work from time to time that they may be ground and sharpened; so does the only-wise Jehovah take his ministers oftentimes away into darkness and loneliness and trouble, that he may sharpen and prepare them for harder work in his service.
ROBERT MURRAY McCHEYNE (1813–1843)

164 For God to explain a trial would be to destroy its purpose . . . calling forth simple faith and implicit obedience.
ALFRED EDERSHEIM (1825–1889)

165 God could have kept Daniel out of the lions' den . . . he could have kept Paul and Silas out of jail . . . he could have kept the three Hebrew children out of the fiery furnace . . . but God has never promised to keep us out of hard places . . . what he has promised is to go with us through every hard place, and to bring us through victoriously.
MERV ROSELL

166 God does not offer us a way out of the testings of life. He offers us a way through, and that makes all the difference.
W. T. PURKISER

167 God never answers the why, because the person who asks why doesn't really want an explanation; he wants an argument!
ROBERT HAROLD SCHULLER (1926–)

168 God often puts us in situations that are too much for us so that we will learn that no situation is too much for him.
ERWIN W. LUTZER (1941–)

169 God only is holy; he alone knows how to lead his children in the paths of holiness. Even though there are clouds around, and your way seems dark, he is directing all, and what seems a hindrance will prove a blessing since he wills it.
JEAN NICOLAS GROU (1731–1803)

170 God promises a safe landing but not a calm passage.

171 God tests us so that we might stand; the devil tests us that we might stumble.
ADRIAN ROGERS

172 God will not look you over for medals, degrees, or diplomas, but for scars.
ELBERT GREEN HUBBARD (1856–1915)

173 Great and small suffer the same mishaps.
BLAISE PASCAL (1623–1662)

174 Happiness is like a sunbeam which the least shadow intercepts, while adversity is often as the rain of spring.
CHINESE PROVERB

175 Have you not learned great lessons from those who reject you, and brace themselves against you? Or who treat you with contempt, or dispute the passage with you?
WALT WHITMAN (1819–1892)

176 He said not,
Thou shall not be tempested,
Thou shall not be travailed,
Thou shall not be afflicted,
But he said,
Thou shall not be overcome.
JULIAN OF NORWICH (C. 1342–AFTER 1413)

177 He who sees the calamity of other people finds his own calamity light.
ARABIAN PROVERB

178 How often we look upon God as our last and feeblest resource! We go to him because we have nowhere else to go. And then we learn that the storms of life have driven us, not upon the rocks, but into the desired haven.
GEORGE MACDONALD (1824–1905)

179 I wondered why the years have flown
Unto my hand
Cling weaker, sadder ones who walk alone—
I understand.

180 If God sends us on stony paths, he will provide us with strong shoes.
ALEXANDER MACLAREN (1826–1910)

181 If we can enter into our trials and temptations, our spiritual darkness and dry spells, with an attitude of gratitude, they will cease to be horrible

experiences from which we try to run away.
JOHN MICHAEL TALBOT

182 If we had no winter, the spring would not be so pleasant; if we did not sometimes taste of adversity, prosperity would not be so welcome.
ANNE BRADSTREET (C. 1612–1672)

183 If you carry the cross willingly, it will carry you. If you are forced against your will to carry the cross, then you make it difficult for yourself, adding to your load. No matter what attitude you have, you must bear the burden. If you manage to throw away one cross, you will certainly find another, and it may be even heavier.
THOMAS À KEMPIS (C. 1380–1471)

184 If your every human plan and calculation has miscarried, if, one by one, human props have been knocked out, and doors have shut in your face, take heart. God is trying to get a message through to you, and the message is: "Stop depending on inadequate human resources. Let me handle the matter."
CATHERINE WOOD MARSHALL (1914–1983)

185 It doesn't matter how great the pressure is. What really matters is where the pressure lies—whether it comes between you and God or whether it presses you nearer his heart.
JAMES HUDSON TAYLOR (1832–1905)

186 It is a misery to be born, a pain to live, a trouble to die.
BERNARD OF CLAIRVAUX (1090–1153)

187 It is good for us that we sometimes have sorrows and adversities, for they often make a man lay to heart that he is only a stranger and sojourner, and may not put his trust in any worldly thing. It is good that we sometimes endure contradictions and are hardly and unfairly judged when we do and mean what is good. For these things help us to be humble and shield us from vainglory.
THOMAS À KEMPIS (C. 1380–1471)

188 It is not true to say that God wants to teach us something in our trials. In every cloud he brings, God wants us to unlearn something. God's purpose in the cloud is to simplify our belief until our relationship to him is exactly that of a child. God uses every cloud which comes in our physical life, in our moral or spiritual life, or in our circumstances, to bring us nearer to him, until we come to the place where our Lord Jesus Christ lived, and we do not allow our hearts to be troubled.
OSWALD CHAMBERS (1874–1917)

189 It is trial that proves one thing weak and another strong. A house built on the sand is in fair weather just as good as if builded on a rock. A cobweb is as good as the mightiest cable when there is no strain upon it.
HENRY WARD BEECHER (1813–1887)

190 It takes a rough stone to sharpen the edge.

191 Life is literally filled with God-appointed storms. These squalls surge across everyone's horizon. We all need them.
CHARLES R. SWINDOLL (1934–)

192 Life is short and full of blisters.
AMERICAN NEGRO PROVERB

193 Little minds are tamed and subdued by misfortune; but great minds rise above it.
WASHINGTON IRVING (1783–1859)

194 Look upon adversities as adventures.
ROBERT HAROLD SCHULLER (1926–)

195 Misfortune is an occasion to demonstrate character.
LUCIUS ANNAEUS SENECA (C. 4 B.C.–A.D. 65)

196 Misfortunes come on wings and depart on foot.

197 Neither usefulness nor duty is God's ultimate purpose. His aim is to bring out the message of the gospel, and if that can only be done by his "bruising" me, why shouldn't he?
OSWALD CHAMBERS (1874–1917)

198 No man is fit to comprehend heavenly things who hath not resigned himself to suffer adversities for Christ.
THOMAS À KEMPIS (C. 1380–1471)

199 No pain, no palm; no thorns, no throne; no gall, no glory; no cross, no crown.
WILLIAM PENN (1644–1718)

200 One is given strength to bear what happens to one, but not the one hundred and one different things that might happen.
C. S. LEWIS (1898–1963)

201 One's attitude toward a handicap determines its impact on his life.
JAMES C. DOBSON (1936–)

202 Problems are the cutting edge that distinguishes between success and failure. Problems . . . create our courage and our wisdom. It is only because of problems that we grow mentally and spiritually.
M. SCOTT PECK (1936–)

203 Rebuke is cruel in adversity.
LATIN PROVERB

204 Rejection is the sand in the oyster, the irritant that ultimately produces the pearl.
BURKE WILKINSON

205 Remember the teakettle: when it's up to its neck in hot water, it sings.

206 Some oysters are never wounded . . . and those who seek for gems toss them aside, fit only for stew.
CHARLES R. SWINDOLL (1934–)

207 Storms make oaks take deeper root.

208 Sweet are the uses of adversity.
WILLIAM SHAKESPEARE (1564–1616)

209 The greater the difficulty, the more glory in surmounting it. Skillful pilots gain their reputation from storms and tempests.
EPICURUS (341–270 B.C.)

210 The longer we dwell on our misfortunes, the greater is their power to harm us.

211 The marathons—the relentless, incessant, persistent, continual tests that won't go away—ah, these are the ones that bruise but build character.
CHARLES R. SWINDOLL (1934–)

212 The roots grow deep when the winds are strong.
CHARLES R. SWINDOLL (1934–)

213 The same boiling water that hardens the egg will soften the carrot.

214 The tests of life are to make, not break us. Trouble may demolish a man's business but build up his character. The blow at the outer man may be the greatest blessing to the inner man. If God, then, puts or permits anything hard in our lives, be sure that the real peril, the real trouble, is that we shall lose if we flinch or rebel.
MALTBIE D. BABCOCK (1858–1901)

215 There are disasters to be faced by the one who is in real fellowship with the Lord Jesus Christ. God has never promised to keep us immune from trouble. He says, "I will be with him in trouble," which is a very different thing.
OSWALD CHAMBERS (1874–1917)

216 There are no crown wearers in heaven who were not cross bearers here below.
CHARLES HADDON SPURGEON (1834–1892)

217 There is always someone worse off than yourself.
AESOP (FL. C. 550 B.C.)

218 There is no education like adversity.
BENJAMIN DISRAELI (1804–1881)

219 There is no situation so chaotic that God cannot from that situation create something that is surpassingly good. He did it at the creation. He did it at the cross. He is doing it today.
BISHOP HANDLEY CARR GLYN MOULE (1841–1920)

220 Times of general calamity and confusion have ever been productive of the greatest minds. The purest ore is produced from the hottest furnace, and the brightest thunderbolt is elicited from the darkest storm.
CHARLES CALEB COLTON (1780–1832)

221 To mourn adversity multiplies the misfortune. It is not hypocrisy to rejoice in distress. It is obedience.
FRANCES J. ROBERTS

222 Tough times never last, but tough people do.
ROBERT HAROLD SCHULLER (1926–   )

223 Trial is God's alchemy by which the dross is left in the crucible, the baser metals are transmuted, and the character is enriched with gold.
WILLIAM MORLEY PUNSHON (1824–1881)

224 Trials are medicines which our gracious and wise physician prescribes because we need them; and he proportions the frequency and weight of them to what the case requires. Let us trust in his skill and thank him for his prescription.
JOHN NEWTON (1725–1807)

225 Tribulation: God's fastest road to patience, character, hope, confidence, and genuine love.
BILL GOTHARD

226 Virtue flourishes in misfortune.
GERMAN PROVERB

227 Virtue is like precious odors—most fragrant when they are incensed or crushed.
FRANCIS BACON (1561–1626)

228 We are always in the forge, or on the anvil; by trials God is shaping us for higher things.
HENRY WARD BEECHER (1813–1887)

229 We bring God to the bar of our judgment and say hard things about him: "Why does God bring thunderclouds and disasters when we want green pastures and still waters?" Bit by bit we find, behind the clouds, the Father's feet; behind the lightning, an abiding day that has no night; behind the thunder a still, small voice that comforts with a comfort that is unspeakable.
OSWALD CHAMBERS (1874–1917)

230 We contradict the Lord to his face when we say: It is hard, it is difficult; we cannot, we are men; we are encompassed with fragile flesh. O blind madness! O unholy audacity! We charge the God of all knowledge with a twofold ignorance, that he does not seem to know what he has made nor what he has commanded, as though, forgetting the human weakness of which he is himself the author, he imposed laws upon man which he cannot endure.
PELAGIUS (C. 354–AFTER 418)

231 What does not destroy me makes me stronger.
FRIEDRICH WILHELM NIETZSCHE (1844–1900)

232 What though my joys and comforts die?
The Lord my Savior liveth;
What though the darkness gather round?
Songs in the night he giveth;
No storm can shake my inmost calm,
While to that refuge clinging;
Since Christ is Lord of heaven and earth,
How can I keep from singing?
ROBERT LOWRY

233 What we call adversity, God calls opportunity.

234 When compassed about on every side with tribulations, remember that it is the way of the saints, through which they passed to the kingdom of heaven. Learn to comfort thyself also, because that in this thou art made like unto Christ Jesus, thy Lord; and return thanks, if thou art in any small degree able to repay this to him. For I say unto thee that it is a greater merit in thee to suffer affliction patiently than to perform good works.
THOMAS À KEMPIS (C. 1380–1471)

235 When the work presses, and the battle thickens, and the day seems long in coming, it is good for the heart to remember that the present conflict is with defeated foes, and that there is no room for question as to the final issue, for the Man of Nazareth is not only seated in the place of authority, he carries forward the work of active administration.
G. CAMPBELL MORGAN (1863–1945)

236 When you get into a tight place and everything goes against you till it seems as though you could not hold on a minute longer, never give up, for that is just the place and time that the tide will turn.
HARRIET BEECHER STOWE (1811–1896)

237 Wherever souls are being tried and ripened, in whatever commonplace and homely way, there God is hewing out the pillars for his temple.
PHILLIPS BROOKS (1835–1893)

238 Worship God in the difficult circumstances, and when he chooses, he will alter them in two seconds.
OSWALD CHAMBERS (1874–1917)

239 You fight dandelions all weekend, and late Monday afternoon there they are, pert as all get out in full and gorgeous bloom, pretty as can be, thriving as only dandelions can in the face of adversity.
HAL BORLAND (1900–1978)

240 You need a few splinters in your thumb. They may help you forget the worries in your head.
CHARLES R. SWINDOLL (1934–   )

ADVERSITY/PROSPERITY

241 If adversity hath killed his thousands, prosperity hath killed his ten thousands; therefore adversity is to be preferred. The one deceives, the other instructs; the one is miserably happy, the other happily miserable; and therefore many philosophers have voluntarily sought adversity and commend it in their precepts.
ROBERT BURTON (1577–1640)

242 Prosperity is a great teacher; adversity is a greater. Possession pampers the mind; privation trains and strengthens it.
WILLIAM HAZLITT (1778–1830)

243 Prosperity is the blessing of the Old Testament, adversity is the blessing of the New which carries the greater benediction and the clearer revelation of God's favor.
FRANCIS BACON (1561–1626)

244 There is in every heart a spark of heavenly fire which lies dormant in the broad daylight of prosperity, but which kindles up and beams and blazes in the dark hour of adversity.
WASHINGTON IRVING (1783–1859)

245 We become wiser by adversity; prosperity destroys our appreciation of the right.
LUCIUS ANNAEUS SENECA (C. 4 B.C.–A.D. 65)

246 Stars may be seen from the bottom of a deep well when they cannot be discerned from the top of a mountain.
CHARLES HADDON SPURGEON (1834–1892)

247 Prosperity is not without many fears and distastes; adversity is not without comforts and hopes.
FRANCIS BACON (1561–1626)

248 Prosperity is the blessing of the Old Testament; adversity is the blessing of the New.
FRANCIS BACON (1561–1626)

249 There are many men who appear to be struggling against adversity, and yet are happy; but yet more, who, although abounding in wealth, are miserable.
CORNELIUS TACITUS (C. 56–C. 120)

250 We can stand affliction better than we can prosperity, for in prosperity we forget God.
DWIGHT LYMAN MOODY (1837–1899)

ADVICE

251 A new broom sweeps clean, but the old brush knows all the corners.
IRISH PROVERB

252 Advice is like snow; the softer it falls, the longer it dwells upon and the deeper it sinks into the mind.
SAMUEL TAYLOR COLERIDGE (1772–1834)

253 As to advice be wary; if honest, it is also criticism.
DAVID GRAYSON (1870–1946)

254 Be not angry that you cannot make others as you wish them to be since you cannot make yourself as you wish to be.
THOMAS À KEMPIS (C. 1380–1471)

255 Every light casts a shadow; in everything we do for the good of a person's soul we run in some degree the risk of taking God's place there.
PAUL TOURNIER (1898–1986)

256 Every piece of advice conceals a veiled criticism, unless it has been asked for.
PAUL TOURNIER (1898–1986)

257 Four eyes see more than two.

258 Give neither counsel nor salt until you are asked for it.

259 I not only use all the brains I have but all I can borrow.
WOODROW WILSON (1856–1924)

260 Keeping from falling is better than helping up.

261 None so deaf as those who will not hear.
MATTHEW HENRY (1662–1714)

262 One man does not see everything.
GREEK PROVERB

263 One of our severest lessons comes from the stubborn refusal to see that we must not interfere in other people's lives. It takes a long time to realize the danger of being an amateur providence, that is, interfering with God's order for others.
OSWALD CHAMBERS (1874–1917)

264 Seek counsel of him who makes you weep, and not of him who makes you laugh.
ARABIAN PROVERB

265 The better advice is, the harder it is to take.

266 The pope and a peasant know more between them than the pope alone.
ITALIAN PROVERB

267 The right to criticize must be earned, even if the advice is constructive in nature.
JAMES C. DOBSON (1936–   )

268 There are two kinds of light—the glow that illumines, and the glare that obscures.
JAMES GROVER THURBER (1894–1961)

269 To know the road ahead, ask those coming back.
CHINESE PROVERB

270 We are better persuaded by the reasons we discover ourselves than by those given to us by others.
BLAISE PASCAL (1623–1662)

271 When you shoot an arrow of truth, dip its point in honey.
ARABIAN PROVERB

272 Words are like medicine; they should be measured with care for an overdose may hurt.
JEWISH PROVERB

273 Write down the advice of him who loves you, though you do not like it.
ITALIAN PROVERB

AFFLICTION

274 Affliction is able to drown out every earthly voice . . . but the voice of eternity within a man it cannot drown. When by the aid of affliction all irrelevant voices are brought to silence, it can be heard, this voice within.
SØREN AABYE KIERKEGAARD (1813–1855)

275 Affliction is God's shepherd dog to drive us back to the fold.

276 Affliction, like the iron-smith, shapes as it smites.

277 Afflictions are but the shadow of God's wings.
GEORGE MACDONALD (1824–1905)

278 Afflictions make the heart more deep, more experimental, more knowing and profound, and so, more able to hold, to contain, and beat more.
JOHN BUNYAN (1628–1688)

279 All your fingernails grow with inconvenient speed except the broken one.
OGDEN NASH (1902–1971)

280 As in nature and in the arts, so in grace: it is rough treatment that gives souls, as well as stones, their luster. The more the diamond is cut, the brighter it sparkles, and in what seems hard dealings God has no end in view but to perfect our graces.
THOMAS GUTHRIE (1803–1873)

281 As out of Jesus' affliction came a new sense of God's love and a new basis for love between men, so out of our affliction we may grasp the splendor of God's love and how to love one another. Thus the consummation of the two commandments was on Golgo-

tha; and the Cross is, at once, their
image and their fulfillment.
MALCOLM MUGGERIDGE (1903–1990)

282 As the sea is subject to storm and tempests, so is every man in the world.
JOHN DONNE (1572–1631)

283 By afflictions God is spoiling us of
what otherwise might have spoiled us.
When he makes the world too hot for
us to hold, we let it go.
SIR JOHN POWELL (1633–1696)

284 Calamity is the perfect glass wherein
we truly see and know ourselves.
SIR WILLIAM DAVENANT (1606–1668)

285 God has many sharp cutting instruments and rough files for the polishing
of his jewels; and those he especially
loves and means to make the most
resplendent, he often uses his tools
upon.
ARCHBISHOP ROBERT LEIGHTON
(1611–1684)

286 God ne'er afflicts us more than our
        desert,
Though he may seem to overact his
        part
Sometimes he strikes us more than
        flesh can bear
But yet still less than grace can suffer
here.
ROBERT HERRICK (1591–1674)

287 God's ways seem dark, but, soon
        or late,
They touch the shining hills of day.
JOHN GREENLEAF WHITTIER (1807–1892)

288 Good when he gives, supremely good,
Nor less when he denies,
E'en crosses from his sovereign hand
Are blessings in disguise.
JAMES HERVEY (1714–1758)

289 If God has made your cup sweet,
drink it with grace. If he has made it
bitter, drink it in communion with him.
OSWALD CHAMBERS (1874–1917)

290 Men think that God is destroying
them when he is tuning them.
HENRY WARD BEECHER (1813–1887)

291 On the top of those very billows
which look as if they would overwhelm us walks the Son of God.
OSWALD CHAMBERS (1874–1917)

292 Open thy gate of mercy, gracious God!
My soul flies through these wounds to
seek out thee.
WILLIAM SHAKESPEARE (1564–1616)

293 Take the cross he sends as it is, and
not as you imagine it to be.
CORNELIA AUGUSTA PEACOCK CONNELLY
(1809–1879)

294 The flame will not corrode or blacken
gold, for fire burns it pure and clean,
and gives it a shining color.
SAINT MECHTHILD OF MAGDEBURG
(C. 1210–C. 1280)

295 The Lord gets his best soldiers out of
the highlands of affliction.
CHARLES HADDON SPURGEON (1834–1892)

296 The only way to meet affliction is to
pass through it solemnly, slowly, with
humility and faith, as the Israelites
passed through the sea. Then its very
waves of misery will divide and
become to us a wall, on the right side
and on the left, until the gulf narrows
before our eyes and we land safe on
the opposite shore.
DINAH MARIA MULOCK CRAIK
(1826–1887)

297 There are disasters to be faced by the
one who is in real fellowship with the
Lord Jesus Christ. God has never
promised to keep us immune from
trouble. He says, "I will be with him
in trouble," which is a very different
thing.
OSWALD CHAMBERS (1874–1917)

298 This is the blessing of affliction to
those who will lie still and not struggle
in a cowardly or a resentful way. It is
God speaking to Job out of the whirlwind, and saying, "In the sunshine
and the warmth you cannot meet me;
but in the hurricane and the darkness
when wave after wave has swept
down and across the soul, you shall

see my form and hear my voice and know that your Redeemer lives."
FREDERICK WILLIAM ROBERTSON (1816–1853)

299 Turn your scars into stars.
ROBERT HAROLD SCHULLER (1926–   )

300 When I am in the cellar of affliction, I look for the Lord's choicest wines.
SAMUEL RUTHERFORD (1600–1661)

301 When it is dark enough, men see the stars.
RALPH WALDO EMERSON (1803–1882)

302 When our faith, hope, and love ends, God's begins.
CHRIS ANDERSON

303 Who in this mortal life would see
The Light that is beyond all light,
Beholds it best by going forth
Into the darkness of the night.
ANGELUS SILESIUS (1624–1677)

AGE

304 Age appears to be best in four things: old wood best to burn, old wine to drink, old friends to trust, and old authors to read.
FRANCIS BACON (1561–1626)

305 Age: the only thing that comes to us without effort.

306 And when youth's gone
As men count going, twixt us two alone,
Still let me be Thy little child
Left learning at Thy knee.

307 Forty is the old age of youth; fifty is the youth of old age.
FRENCH PROVERB

308 How are you desirous at the same time to live to old age, and at the same time not to see the death of any person whom you love?
EPICTETUS (C. 55–C. 135)

309 How old do you think you'd be if you didn't know your age?

310 In youth we learn; in age we understand.
MARIE EBNER-ESCHENBACH (1830–1916)

311 Manhood in the Christian life is a better thing than boyhood because it is a riper thing; and old age ought to be a brighter and a calmer and a more serene thing than manhood.
FREDERICK WILLIAM ROBERTSON (1816–1853)

312 The average life span of a woman is constantly increasing, thus enabling her to stay twenty-nine much longer.

313 The young feel tired at the end of an action; the old at the beginning.
T. S. ELIOT (1888–1965)

314 There are four signs of approaching age: baldness, bifocals, bridges, and bulges!
E. STANLEY JONES (1884–1973)

315 We are always the same age inside.
GERTRUDE STEIN (1874–1946)

AGNOSTICISM

316 In the Garden of Paradise, man hid from God in the garden; now man hides within himself.
ARCHBISHOP FULTON J. SHEEN (1895–1979)

317 Most people have some sort of religion—at least they know what church they're staying away from.
JOHN ERSKINE (1509–1591)

318 The agnostic's prayer: "O God, if there is a God, save my soul, if I have a soul."
JOSEPH ERNEST RENAN (1823–1892)

319 The everlasting perhaps.
FRANCIS THOMPSON (1859–1907)

320 When agnosticism has done its withering work in the mind of man, the mysteries remain as before; all that has been added to them is a settled despair.
VINCENT MCNABB (1868–1943)

ALCOHOL

321 'Tis not the drinking that is to be blamed but the excess.
JOHN SELDEN (1584–1654)

322 A drinker has a hole under his nose that all his money runs into.
THOMAS FULLER (1654–1734)

323 Alcohol does not drown care, but
waters it and makes it grow faster.
BENJAMIN FRANKLIN (1706–1790)

324 An alcoholic never feels fit as a fiddle
because he is always as tight as a drum.

325 Drink has
Drained more blood
Hung more crepe
Sold more houses
Plunged more people into bankruptcy
Armed more villains
Slain more children
Snapped more wedding rings
Defiled more innocence
Blinded more eyes
Twisted more limbs
Dethroned more reason
Wrecked more manhood
Dishonored more womanhood
Broken more hearts
Blasted more lives
Driven more to suicide, and
Dug more graves than any other poi-
soned scourge that ever swept its
death-dealing waves across the
world.
EVANGELINE CORY BOOTH (1865–1950)

326 Drinking is the refuge of the weak; it
is crutches for lame ducks.
E. STANLEY JONES (1884–1973)

327 Drunkenness is nothing else but a voluntary madness.
LUCIUS ANNAEUS SENECA (C. 4 B.C.–A.D. 65)

328 Drunkenness is temporary suicide; the
happiness that it brings is merely negative, a momentary cessation of unhappiness.
BERTRAND ARTHUR WILLIAM RUSSELL
(1872–1970)

329 Drunkenness is the ruin of a person. It
is premature old age. It is temporary
death.
SAINT BASIL (C. 330–379)

330 First the man—takes the drink, then
the drink—takes the man.
JAPANESE PROVERB

331 I am the greatest criminal in history.
I have killed more men than have
fallen in all the wars of all the world.
I have turned men into brutes.

I have made millions of homes
unhappy.
I have changed many promising
young men into hopeless parasites.
I destroy the weak and weaken the
strong.
I make the wise man a fool and I
ensnare the innocent.
I have ruined millions and shall try to
ruin millions more.
I am alcohol.
H. W. GIBSON

332 O God, that men should put an enemy
in their mouths to steal away their
brains; that we should, with joy, pleas-
ance, revel and applause, transform
ourselves into beasts!
WILLIAM SHAKESPEARE (1564–1616)

333 Some of the domestic evils of drunkenness are houses without windows, gardens without fences, fields without
tillage, barns without roofs, children
without clothing, principles, morals,
or manners.
BENJAMIN FRANKLIN (1706–1790)

334 The drunken man is a living corpse.
SAINT JOHN CHRYSOSTOM (C. 347–407)

335 The man who drinks to drown his sorrow is trying to put out a fire with oil.

336 The sight of a drunkard is a better sermon against that vice than the best
that was ever preached on the subject.
JOHN FAUCIT SAVILLE (1783–1853)

337 Wine is a turncoat; first a friend, and
then an enemy.
THOMAS FULLER (1608–1661)

AMBITION

338 All ambitions are lawful except those
which climb upward on the miseries of
others.
JOSEPH CONRAD (1857–1924)

339 Ambition destroys its possessor.
TALMUD

340 Ambition is greed for power.
CHARLES CALEB COLTON (1780–1832)

341 Ambition is ruthless; any person that
it cannot use it throws aside.

342 Ambition is the grand enemy of all
peace.
JOHN COWPER POWYS (1872–1963)

343 Ambition is to become a foreman so
you can get paid for watching other
people work.

344 Ambition: a mental condition that
compels one to work one's self to
death in order to live.

345 However high we reach, we are never
satisfied.
NICCOLÒ MACHIAVELLI (1469–1527)

346 I charge thee, fling away ambition: By
that sin fell the angels.
WILLIAM SHAKESPEARE (1564–1616)

347 In our natural life our ambitions are
our own. In the Christian life we have
no aim of our own, and God's aim
looks like missing the mark because
we are too shortsighted to see what he
is aiming at.
OSWALD CHAMBERS (1874–1917)

348 Most people would succeed in small
things if they were not troubled with
great ambitions.
HENRY WADSWORTH LONGFELLOW
(1807–1882)

349 Personal ambition and empire building
are hindering the spread of the gospel.
JOHN R. W. STOTT (1921–)

350 The fruit of the Spirit is not push,
drive, climb, grasp, and trample.
Don't let the rat-racing world keep
you on its treadmill. There is a legitimate place for blood, sweat, and tears;
but it should have its roots in the call
of God, not in the desire to get ahead.
Life is more than a climb to the top of
the heap.
RICHARD J. FOSTER (1942–)

351 The Lord frustrates our plans, shatters
our purposes, lets us see the wreck of
all our hopes, and whispers to us, "It's
not your work I wanted, but you."

352 You cannot be anything if you want to
be everything.
SOLOMON SCHECHTER (1847–1915)

353 You may get to the very top of the ladder and find it has not been leaning
against the right wall.
A. RAINE

ANGELS

354 An angel is a spiritual creature created
by God without a body for the service
of Christendom and of the church.
MARTIN LUTHER (1483–1546)

355 Angels are bright still, though the
brightest fell.
WILLIAM SHAKESPEARE (1564–1616)

356 Angels guard you when you walk with
Me. What better way could you
choose?
FRANCES J. ROBERTS

357 Angels see only the light, and devils
only the darkness.
JAKOB BÖHME (1575–1624)

358 Around our pillows golden ladders
rise,
And up and down the skies,
With winged sandals shod,
The angels come and go, the Messen-
gers of God!
RICHARD HENRY STODDARD (1825–1903)

359 Cherubim, seraphim, all the angelic
host as they are described in Scripture,
have a wild and radiant power that
often takes us by surprise. They are
not always gentle. They bar the
entrance to Eden, so that we may
never return home. They send plagues
upon the Egyptians. They are messengers of God. They are winds. They are
flames of fire. They are young men
dressed in white.
MADELEINE L'ENGLE (1918–)

360 Christians should never fail to sense
the operation of angelic glory. It forever eclipses the world of demonic
powers, as the sun does a candle's
light.
BILLY GRAHAM (1918–)

361 Hush! my dear, lie still and slumber,
Holy angels guard thy bed.
Heavenly blessings without number
Gently falling on thy head.
ISAAC WATTS (1674–1748)

362 Millions of spiritual creatures walk the
earth
Unseen, both when we wake, and
when we sleep:
All these with ceaseless praise his
works behold
Both day and night.
JOHN MILTON (1608–1674)

363 The angels are the dispensers and
administrators of the divine beneficence toward us; they regard our
safety, undertake our defense, direct
our ways, and exercise a constant solicitude that no evil befall us.
JOHN CALVIN (1509–1564)

364 The earth is to the sun what man is to
the angels.
VICTOR HUGO (1802–1885)

365 The stars shine on brightly while
Adam and Eve pursue their way into
the far wilderness. There is a sound
through the silence, as of the falling
tears of an angel.
ELIZABETH BARRETT BROWNING
(1806–1861)

366 There stands an angel by every man as
soon as he is born to guide him
through the mystery of life.
GREEK PROVERB

367 When angels come, the devils leave.
ARABIAN PROVERB

ANGER

368 A man who can't control his temper is
like a city without defenses.
JEWISH PROVERB

369 An angry man opens his mouth and
shuts his eyes.
CATO THE ELDER (234–149 B.C.)

370 Anger can be an expensive luxury.
ITALIAN PROVERB

371 Anger is a weed; hate is the tree.
SAINT AUGUSTINE OF HIPPO (354–430)

372 Anger is quieted by a gentle word just
as fire is quenched by water.
JEAN PIERRE CAMUS (1584–1652)

373 Anybody can become angry—that is
easy; but to be angry with the right
person, and to the right degree, and at
the right time, and for the right purpose, and in the right way—that is not
within everybody's power and is not
easy.
ARISTOTLE (384–322 B.C.)

374 Arrows pierce the body, but harsh
words pierce the soul.
SPANISH PROVERB

375 Control yourself! Anger is only one letter short of danger.

376 Do not do to others that which would
anger you if others did it to you.
ISOCRATES (436–338 B.C.)

377 Don't fly into a rage unless you are
prepared for a rough landing.

378 Don't get angry at the person who acts
in ways that displease you. Give him
the smile he lacks. Spread the sunshine
of your Lord's limitless love.
JONI EARECKSON TADA

379 Doomed are the hotheads! Unhappy
are they who lose their cool and are
too proud to say, "I'm sorry."
ROBERT HAROLD SCHULLER (1926–)

380 Father expected a good deal of God.
He didn't actually accuse God of inefficiency, but when he prayed, his tone
was loud and angry, like that of a dissatisfied guest in a carelessly managed
hotel.
CLARENCE SHEPARD DAY, JR. (1874–1935)

381 He that would be angry and sin not
must not be angry with anything but
sin.
THOMAS SECKER (1693–1768)

382 He who kicks up a storm should
expect rough sailing.

383 Heat not so hot a furnace for your
antagonist that you burn yourself.

384 Hitting the ceiling is the worst way to
get up in the world.

385 Hot heads and cold hearts never
solved anything.
BILLY GRAHAM (1918–)

386 I was angry with my friend.
I told my wrath, my wrath did end.
I was angry with my foe.
I told it not, my wrath did grow.
WILLIAM BLAKE (1757–1827)

387 I was angry, for I had no shoes. Then I met a man who had no feet.
CHINESE PROVERB

388 It is easier to swallow angry words than to have to eat them.

389 It is raging; the dust is blown high; who shall put out the flame?
ARABIAN PROVERB

390 Malice never spoke well.
WILLIAM CAMDEN (1551–1623)

391 People who fly into a rage always make a bad landing.
WILL ROGERS (1879–1935)

392 Satan's most successful maneuver in churches and Christian organizations is to get people angry at one another, to attack and insult our brothers and sisters, thus splitting the body of Christ.
JAMES C. DOBSON (1936–   )

393 Sharp words make more wounds than surgeons can heal.

394 So long as a man is angry he cannot be in the right.
CHINESE PROVERB

395 Speak when you are angry and you will make the best speech you will ever regret.
AMBROSE GWINNETT BIERCE (1842–C. 1914)

396 The continuance of anger is hatred.
FRANCIS QUARLES (1592–1644)

397 The greatest remedy for anger is delay.
LUCIUS ANNAEUS SENECA (C. 4 B.C.–A.D. 65)

398 The man who loses his temper quickest is the one who finds it quickest. The man you need to beware of is not the man who flares up, but the man who smoulders, who is vindictive and harbors vengeance.
OSWALD CHAMBERS (1874–1917)

399 The reason fat people are generally good-natured is that it takes them so long to get mad clear through.

400 The seducer of thought. No man can think clearly when his fists are clenched.
GEORGE JEAN NATHAN (1882–1958)

401 The wrath of God is as pure as the holiness of God. When God is angry he is perfectly angry. When he is displeased there is every reason he should be.
  We tend to think of anger as sin; but sometimes it is sinful not to be angry. It is unthinkable that God would not be purely and perfectly angry with sin.
STUART BRISCOE

402 To reply to a nasty remark with another nasty remark is like trying to remove dirt with mud.

403 Two heads are better than one, but not when they are soreheads.

404 Two things a man should never be angry at: what he can help, and what he cannot help.

405 When anger enters the mind, wisdom departs.
THOMAS À KEMPIS (C. 1380–1471)

406 When anger was in Cain's heart, murder was not far off.
PHILIP HENRY (1631–1696)

407 When angry, take a lesson from technology; always count down before blasting off.

408 When I am angry I can write, pray, and preach well, for then my whole temperament is quickened, my understanding sharpened, and all mundane vexations and temptations depart.
MARTIN LUTHER (1483–1546)

ANXIETY

409 Anxiety does not empty tomorrow of its sorrows but only empties today of its strength.
CHARLES HADDON SPURGEON (1834–1892)

410 Anxiety is a thin stream of fear trickling through the mind. If encouraged, it cuts a channel into which all other thoughts are drained.
ARTHUR SOMERS ROCHE

411 Anxiety is not only a pain which we must ask God to assuage but also a weakness we must ask him to par-

don—for he's told us to take no care for the morrow.
C. S. LEWIS (1898–1963)

412 Anxiety is the interest paid on trouble before it is due.
WILLIAM RALPH INGE (1860–1954)

413 Anxiety is the natural result when our hopes are centered in anything short of God and his will for us.
BILLY GRAHAM (1918–)

414 Anxiety springs from the desire that things should happen as we wish rather than as God wills.

415 Do not look forward to what may happen tomorrow; the same everlasting Father, who cares for you today, will take care of you tomorrow, and every day. Either he will shield you from suffering or he will give you unfailing strength to bear it.
SAINT FRANCIS OF SALES (1567–1622)

416 Fretfulness springs from a determination to get my own way.
OSWALD CHAMBERS (1874–1917)

417 God never built a Christian strong enough to carry today's duties and tomorrow's anxieties piled on top of them.
THEODORE LEDYARD CUYLER (1822–1909)

418 If your heart is troubled, you are not living up to your belief.
OSWALD CHAMBERS (1874–1917)

419 Lord Jesus, make my heart sit down.
AFRICAN PROVERB

420 Man's world has become a nervous one, encompassed by anxiety. God's world is other than this; always balanced, calm, and in order.
FAITH BALDWIN (1893–1978)

421 Man, like the bridge, was designed to carry the load of the moment, not the combined weight of a year at once.
WILLIAM ARTHUR WARD (1812–1882)

422 O Lord Jesus Christ, who has told us not to be anxious, we trust ourselves and our loved ones to thy loving care, knowing that round about and underneath are the everlasting arms, and praying thee to give us now and always that peace which the world can-

not give, nor take away, but which comes only from the Father and from thee, our Savior and Friend.

423 One cannot remove anxiety by arguing it away.
PAUL JOHANNES OSKAR TILLICH (1886–1965)

424 The beginning of anxiety is the end of faith; and the beginning of true faith is the end of anxiety.
GEORGE MULLER (1805–1898)

425 There is the danger and the temptation to you of drawing your minds into your business and clogging them with it; so that ye can hardly do anything to the service of God, but there will be crying, "My business, my business"; and your minds will go into the things, and not over the things. . . . And then, if the Lord God cross you, and stop you by sea and land, and take your goods and customs from you, that your minds should not be cumbered, then that mind that is cumbered will fret, being out of the power of God.
GEORGE FOX (1624–1691)

APATHY

426 Mourn not the dead that in the cool
        earth lie
But rather mourn the apathetic throng
The cowed and the meek
Who see the world's great anguish and
        its wrong
And dare not speak.
RALPH CHAPLIN (1887–1961)

427 Where apathy is the master, all men are slaves.

APOLOGY

428 An apology is saying the right thing after doing the wrong thing.

429 Humble pie is the only pastry that's never tasty.

APPEARANCE

430 All is not gold that glitters.
DAVID GARRICK (1717–1779)

431 Do not judge men by mere appearances; for the light laughter that bubbles on the lip often mantles over the depths of sadness, and the serious look may be the sober veil that covers a divine peace and joy.
EDWIN HUBBELL (1814–1880)

432 Don't judge a tree by its bark.
FRENCH PROVERB

433 It takes a great deal of energy to maintain an appearance of greatness, more than the really great are able to spare.
VAN WYCK BROOKS (1886–1963)

434 Of all the things you wear, your expression is the most important.
JANET LANE

435 The face is the portrait of the mind.
CICERO (106–43 B.C.)

436 The world is a looking glass and gives back to every man the reflection of his own face.
WILLIAM MAKEPEACE THACKERAY (1811–1863)

APPRECIATION

437 Appreciation is a wonderful thing: it makes what is excellent in others belong to us as well.
VOLTAIRE (1694–1778)

438 Cow to Maine farmer: "Thank you for a warm hand on a cold morning."

439 It is human nature to grumble at having to get up early in the morning—until the day comes when you can't get up.

440 The deepest principle of human nature is the craving to be appreciated.
WILLIAM JAMES (1842–1910)

441 The difference between appreciation and flattery? That is simple. One is sincere and the other insincere. One comes from the heart out; the other from the teeth out. One is unselfish; the other selfish. One is universally admired; the other is universally condemned.
DALE CARNEGIE (1888–1955)

442 The question is not what a man can scorn, or disparage, or find fault with, but what he can love and value and appreciate.
JOHN RUSKIN (1819–1900)

443 To be really enjoyed, sleep, health, and wealth must be interrupted.
JOHANN PAUL FRIEDRICH RICHTER (1763–1825)

444 When the well's dry, we know the worth of water.
BENJAMIN FRANKLIN (1706–1790)

ARGUMENT

445 Behind every argument is someone's ignorance.
LOUIS D. BRANDEIS (1856–1941)

446 Many an argument holds no more water than a newborn puppy.

447 Never argue with another: remember he too has a right to his own stupid opinion.

448 The less sound a man's argument, the louder he talks.

ARROGANCE

449 A know-it-all always seems to have the solution to every problem right in the hollow of his head.

450 A smart aleck knows everything, except how to keep others from thinking him a fool.

451 Arrogance has its own built-in misery. The arrogant person may offend others, but he hurts himself more.
BILLY GRAHAM (1918–   )

452 Nobody roots for Goliath.
WILL CHAMBERLAIN

453 When two know-it-alls get together, why do they always disagree?

454 All the people like us are We, And everyone else is They.
RUDYARD KIPLING (1865–1936)

455 I like snobs. A snob has to spend so much time being a snob that he has little time left to meddle with you.
WILLIAM CUTHBERT FAULKNER (1897–1962)

456 Nothing is so shallow as dogmatism.
RALPH WALDO EMERSON (1803–1882)

457 The word *snob* belongs to the sourgrape vocabulary.
LOGAN PEARSALL SMITH (1865–1946)

458 Where men are the most sure and arrogant, they are usually the most mistaken.
DAVID HUME (1711–1776)

ASCENSION

459 At his ascension our Lord entered
heaven, and he keeps the door open
for humanity to enter.
OSWALD CHAMBERS (1874–1917)

460 If upward you can soar and let God
have his way,
Then this has in your spirit become
Ascension Day.
ANGELUS SILESIUS (1624–1677)

461 Jesus departed from our sight that he
might return to our heart. He
departed, and behold, he is here.
SAINT AUGUSTINE OF HIPPO (354–430)

462 The Ascension placed Jesus Christ
back in the glory which he had with
the Father before the world was. The
Ascension, not the Resurrection, is the
completion of the Transfiguration.
OSWALD CHAMBERS (1874–1917)

463 Where every angel as he sings
Keeps time with his applauding wings.
JOSEPH BEAUMONT (1615–1699)

ASCETICISM

464 A man cannot shut out what is inside
by cutting himself off from the outside. Jesus Christ was not a solitary
man.
OSWALD CHAMBERS (1874–1917)

465 Asceticism is the passion of giving up
things and is recognizable in a life not
born again of the Spirit of God. It is
all very well if it ends in giving up the
one thing God wants us to give up,
viz., our right to ourselves, but if it
does not end there, it will do endless
damage to the life.
OSWALD CHAMBERS (1874–1917)

466 If there is no element of asceticism in
our lives, if we give free rein to the
desires of the flesh . . . we shall find it
hard to train for the service of Christ.
DIETRICH BONHOEFFER (1906–1945)

467 The black shadow of asceticism spread
over the sky of the Puritan Fathers.
Given two coats, they chose the ugliest
one. Given two colors for the woman's
garb, they chose the saddest and
somberest. Given two roads, they
chose the one that held the most
thorns and cutting rocks. Given two
forms of fear and self-denial, they
took both. The favorite text of asceticism is "deny yourself." The favorite
color of asceticism is black; its favorite
music, a dirge; its favorite hour is midnight; its favorite theme is a
tombstone. The mistake of asceticism
is in thinking that it has a moral value.
NEWELL DWIGHT HILLIS (1858–1929)

ASPIRATION

468 The heavens are as deep as our aspirations are high.
HENRY DAVID THOREAU (1817–1862)

469 The true worth of a man is to be measured by the objects he pursues.
MARCUS AURELIUS ANTONINUS (121–180)

470 There is not a heart but has its
moments of longing, yearning for
something better, nobler, holier than it
knows now.
HENRY WARD BEECHER (1813–1887)

471 We are not to make the ideas of contentment and aspiration quarrel, for
God made them fast friends. A man
may aspire and yet be quite content
until it is time to rise; and both flying
and resting are but parts of one contentment. The very fruit of the gospel
is aspiration. It is to the heart what
spring is to the earth, making every
root, and bud, and bough desire to be
more.
HENRY WARD BEECHER (1813–1887)

ATHEISM

472 An atheist cannot find God for the same reason a thief cannot find a policeman.

473 An atheist is a man who believes himself an accident.
FRANCIS THOMPSON (1859–1907)

474 An atheist is a man without any invisible means of support.
JOHN BUCHAN (1875–1940)

475 Atheism is rather in the lip than in the heart of man.
FRANCIS BACON (1561–1626)

476 Atheists put on a false courage and alacrity in the midst of their darkness and apprehensions, like children who, when they fear to go into the dark, will sing or whistle to keep up their courage.
ALEXANDER POPE (1688–1744)

477 By night an atheist half believes in God.
EDWARD YOUNG (1683–1765)

478 Every effort to prove there is no God is in itself an effort to reach for God.
CHARLES EDWARD LOCKE

479 Few men are so obstinate in their atheism that a pressing danger will not compel them to the acknowledgment of a divine power.
PLATO (C. 428–348 B.C.)

480 I am an atheist, thank God!

481 I was . . . living, like so many atheists or antitheists, in a whirl of contradictions. I maintained that God did not exist. I was also very angry with God for not existing. I was equally angry with him for creating a world.
C. S. LEWIS (1898–1963)

482 If man ever appears as a consummate ass, it's when he denies the existence of God.
BILLY SUNDAY (1862–1935)

483 No one is so much alone in the universe as a denier of God. With an orphaned heart, which has lost the greatest of fathers, he stands mourning by the immeasurable corpse of the universe.
JOHANN PAUL FRIEDRICH RICHTER (1763–1825)

484 Nobody talks so constantly about God as those who insist there is no God.
HEYWOOD BROUN (1888–1939)

485 People who tell me there is no God are like a six-year-old boy saying there is no such thing as passionate love—they just haven't experienced it.
WILLIAM ALFRED

486 Some are atheists only in fair weather.
THOMAS FULLER (1654–1734)

487 The number one cause of atheism is Christians. Those who proclaim God with their mouths and deny him with their life-styles is what an unbelieving world finds simply unbelievable.
KARL RAHNER (1904–1984)

488 The worst moment for the atheist is when he is really thankful and has nobody to thank.
DANTE GABRIEL ROSSETTI (1828–1882)

489 There are no atheists in foxholes.
WILLIAM THOMAS CUMMINGS (1903–1944)

490 Those who hope for no other life are dead even for this.
JOHANN WOLFGANG VON GOETHE (1749–1832)

491 Were every man on earth to become atheist, it could not affect God in any way. He is what he is in himself without regard to any other. To believe in him add nothing to his perfections; to doubt him takes nothing away.
A. W. TOZER (1897–1963)

492 What reason have atheists for saying that we cannot rise again? Which is the more difficult, to be born, or to rise again? That what has never been, should be, or that what has been should be again? Is it more difficult to come into being than to return to it?
BLAISE PASCAL (1623–1662)

493 Really, a young atheist cannot guard his faith too carefully. Dangers lie in wait for him on every side. You must not do, you must not even try to do, the will of the Father unless you are

prepared to "know of the doctrine."
. . . For the first time I examined
myself with a seriously practical purpose. And there I found what appalled
me; a zoo of lusts, a bedlam of ambitions, a nursery of fears, a harem of
fondled hatreds. My name was legion.
C. S. LEWIS (1898–1963)

ATONEMENT

494 A great many people are trying to
make peace, but that has already been
done. God has not left it for us to do;
all we have to do is to enter into it.
DWIGHT LYMAN MOODY (1837–1899)

495 He left his Father's throne above,
So free, so infinite his grace!
Emptied himself of all but love,
And bled for Adam's helpless race.
CHARLES WESLEY (1707–1788)

496 The Old Testament Hebrew word that
we translate *atonement* means literally
"to cover up." The animal sacrifices
were intended to "cover" a man's sins.
In the New Testament, however, the
meaning of atoning sacrifice is conveyed by the word *expiate,* which
means "to put away." The blood that
Jesus shed in our behalf on the cross at
Calvary does not merely cover up our
sin, it puts away our sin as though it
had never been committed.
T. W. WILSON

497 When Jesus Christ shed his blood on
the cross, it was not the blood of a
martyr, or the blood of one man for
another; it was the life of God poured
out to redeem the world.
OSWALD CHAMBERS (1874–1917)

498 When we are filled with the Holy
Spirit, he unites us body, soul, and
spirit with God until we are one with
God even as Jesus was. This is the
meaning of the Atonement—at-one-
ment with God.
OSWALD CHAMBERS (1874–1917)

ATTITUDE

499 At any moment in life we have the
option to choose an attitude of gratitude, a posture of grace, a commitment to joy.
TIM HANSEL

500 Attitudes are capable of making the
same experience either pleasant or
painful.
JOHN POWELL

501 Attitudes determine our actions, for
good or bad.

502 Be careful for nothing, prayerful for
everything, thankful for anything.
DWIGHT LYMAN MOODY (1837–1899)

503 God . . . gives me the freedom to acknowledge my negative attitudes
before him but not the freedom to act
them out because they are as destructive for me as they are for the other
person.
REBECCA MANLEY PIPPERT

504 If you don't learn to laugh at trouble,
you won't have anything to laugh at
when you're old.
ED HOWE (1853–1937)

505 If your daily life seems poor, do not
blame it; blame yourself, tell yourself
that you are not poet enough to call
forth its riches.
RAINER MARIA RILKE (1875–1926)

506 It all depends on how we look at
things, and not how they are in themselves.
CARL GUSTAV JUNG (1875–1961)

507 It isn't your problems that are bothering you. It is the way you are looking
at them.
EPICTETUS (C. 55–C. 135)

508 It's not what happens to me that matters most; it's how I react to what happens to me.
ROBERT HAROLD SCHULLER (1926–   )

509 My attitude determines whether grief
causes a disease in me or a glorious
and everlasting reward.
S. I. MCMILLEN

510 People can alter their lives by altering
their attitudes.
WILLIAM JAMES (1842–1910)

511 The best thing to give to your enemy is
forgiveness; to an opponent, tolerance;

to a friend, your heart; to your child, a good example; to your father, deference; to your mother, conduct that will make her proud of you; to yourself, respect; to all men, charity.
ARTHUR JAMES BALFOUR (1848–1930)

512 The mind is its own place, and in itself can make a heaven of hell, a hell of heaven.
JOHN MILTON (1608–1674)

513 The Sermon on the Mount cuts across differences of temperament and variations in capacity. It outlines the kind of character which is possible for any man, gifted or relatively ungifted, strong or weak, clever or slow. Once more we find Christ placing his finger, not upon the externals, but upon the vital internal attitude.
J. B. PHILLIPS (1906–1982)

514 The way in which you endure that which you must endure is more important than the crisis itself.
SAM RUTIGLIANO (1932–)

515 The world is a looking-glass and gives back to every man the reflection of his own face. Frown at it, and it in turn will look sourly at you; laugh at it, and with it, and it is a jolly, kind companion.
WILLIAM MAKEPEACE THACKERAY (1811–1863)

516 There is very little difference in people, but that little difference makes a big difference. The little difference is attitude. The big difference is whether it is positive or negative.
W. CLEMENT STONE (1902–)

517 Think of it as being easy, and it shall be easy. Think of it as being difficult, and it shall be difficult.
ARABIAN PROVERB

518 We awaken in others the same attitude of mind we hold toward them.
ELBERT GREEN HUBBARD (1856–1915)

519 We who lived in the concentration camps can remember the men who walked through the huts comforting others, giving away their last piece of bread. They may have been few in number, but they offer sufficient proof that everything can be taken from a man but one thing: the last of his freedoms—to choose one's attitude in any given set of circumstances, to choose one's own way.
VIKTOR E. FRANKL (1905–)

520 What is this pain? It is the birth pang of a new attitude trying to be born.
ROBERT HAROLD SCHULLER (1926–)

521 With the right attitude, all the problems in the world will not make you a failure. With the wrong mental attitude, all the help in the world will not make you a success.
WARREN DEATON

522 Your living is determined not so much by what life brings to you as by the attitude you bring to life; not so much by what happens to you as by the way your mind looks at what happens. Circumstances and situations do color life, but you have been given the mind to choose what the color shall be.
JOHN HOMER MILLER (1722–1791)

AUTHORITY

523 Authority is God-ordained, but authoritarianism and raw power, in almost all forms, is dangerous.
JAMES C. DOBSON (1936–)

524 If you accept the authority of Jesus in your life, then you accept the authority of his words.
COLIN URQUHART (1940–)

525 Our world is fast becoming a madhouse, and the inmates are trying to run the asylum. It is a strange time when the patients are writing the prescriptions, the students are threatening to run the schools, the children to manage the homes, and church members—not the Holy Spirit—to direct the churches.
VANCE HAVNER

526 Self-chosen authority is an impertinence. Jesus said that the great ones in this world exercise authority but that in his kingdom it is not so; no one exercises authority over another because in his kingdom the king is ser-

vant of all. If a saint tries to exercise authority, it is a proof that he is not rightly related to Jesus Christ.
OSWALD CHAMBERS (1874–1917)

527 Who overcomes by force, hath overcome but half his foe.
JOHN MILTON (1608–1674)

B

BAPTISM

528 Baptism points back to the work of God, and forward to the life of faith.
J. ALICE MOTYER

529 In baptism, the Christian is born. His old self is buried and the new self emerges. Whether in the case of infants or adults, baptism signifies this more as a promise than as an actually fulfilled fact. The direction is indicated rather than the arrival.
FRIEDRICH REST (1913–)

BEATITUDES

530 Beatitudes, just by virtue of having been spoken by him, have enriched our mortal existence beyond imagining, putting a yeast of love into the unlively dough of human greed and human spite and human willfulness, so that it can rise marvellously.
MALCOLM MUGGERIDGE (1903–1990)

531 If you were to take the sum total of all authoritative articles ever written by the most qualified of psychologists and psychiatrists on the subject of mental hygiene—if you were to combine them and refine them and cleave out the excess verbiage—if you were to take the whole of the meat and none of the parsley, and if you were to have these unadulterated bits of pure scientific knowledge concisely expressed by the most capable of living poets, you would have an awkward and incomplete summation of the Sermon on the Mount. And it would suffer immeasurably through comparison. For nearly two thousand years the Christian world has been holding in its hands the complete answer to its restless and fruitless yearnings. Here . . . rests the blueprint for successful human life with optimism, mental health, and contentment.
J. T. FISHER

532 The Peoples Beatitudes
Happy are the pushers for they get on in the world.
Happy are the hard-boiled for they never let life hurt them.

Happy are they who complain for they get their own way in the end.

Happy are the blasé for they never worry over their sins.

Happy are the slave drivers for they get results.

Happy are the knowledgeable men of the world for they know their way around.

Happy are the troublemakers for they make people take notice of them.
J. B. PHILLIPS (1906–1982)

533 We hear it said that Jesus Christ taught nothing contrary to common sense. Everything Jesus Christ taught was contrary to common sense. Not one thing in the Sermon on the Mount is common sense. The basis of Christianity is neither common sense nor rationalism.
OSWALD CHAMBERS (1874–1917)

BEAUTY

534 A thing of beauty is a joy forever;
Its loveliness increases; it will never
Pass into nothingness. . . .
JOHN KEATS (1795–1821)

535 Beauty is God's handwriting—a wayside sacrament. Welcome it in every fair face, in every fair sky, in every fair flower, and thank God for it as a cup of blessing.
RALPH WALDO EMERSON (1803–1882)

536 Beauty, unaccompanied by virtue, is as a flower without perfume.
FRENCH PROVERB

537 God's fingers can touch nothing but to mould it into loveliness.
GEORGE MACDONALD (1824–1905)

538 The beautiful can have but one source . . . God.
ARTHUR SCHOPENHAUER (1788–1860)

539 The best part of beauty is that which no picture can express.
FRANCIS BACON (1561–1626)

540 The perception of beauty is a moral test.
HENRY DAVID THOREAU (1817–1862)

BEGINNINGS

541 Beginning is half done.
ROBERT HAROLD SCHULLER (1926–   )

542 I have learned one important thing in my life—how to begin again.
SAM KEEN

543 If well thou hast begun, go on foreright;
It is the end that crowns us, not the fight.
ROBERT HERRICK (1591–1674)

544 The beginning is the most important part of the work.
PLATO (C. 428–348 B.C.)

545 The first step is the hardest.
MARIE DE VICHY-CHAMROND (1697–1780)

BEHAVIOR

546 A good example is the tallest kind of preaching.
AFRICAN CHIEF

547 All I do ought to be founded on a perfect oneness with [God], not a self-willed determination to be godly.
OSWALD CHAMBERS (1874–1917)

548 All people smile in the same language.

549 Always imitate the behavior of the winners when you lose.
GEORGE MEREDITH (1828–1909)

550 Be civil to all; sociable to many; familiar with few; friend to one; enemy to none.
BENJAMIN FRANKLIN (1706–1790)

551 Be such a man, and live such a life, that if every man were such as you, and every life such as yours, this earth would be God's paradise.
PHILLIPS BROOKS (1835–1893)

552 Behave toward everyone as if receiving a great guest.
CONFUCIUS (C. 551–479 B.C.)

553 Behavior is the mirror in which everyone shows his image.
JOHANN WOLFGANG VON GOETHE (1749–1832)

554 Conduct is an unspoken sermon.
HENRI FRÉDÉRIC AMIEL (1821–1881)

555 Determine a plan of action in the morning, and then evaluate yourself at night. How have you behaved today? What were your words, your deeds, your thoughts?
THOMAS À KEMPIS (C. 1380–1471)

556 Do every act in thy life as if it were the last.
MARCUS AURELIUS ANTONINUS (121–180)

557 Don't be too sweet, lest you be eaten up; don't be too bitter, lest you be spewed out.
JEWISH PROVERB

558 Environmental influences, in themselves, will not account for the behavior we observe in our fellowman. There is something else . . . something from within . . . that also operates to make us who we are.
JAMES C. DOBSON (1936–)

559 Four things a man must learn to do
If he would make his record true:
To think without confusion clearly
To love his fellowmen sincerely
To act from honest motives purely
To trust in God and heaven securely.
HENRY VAN DYKE (1852–1933)

560 I cannot hear what you say for the thunder of what you are.
AFRICAN PROVERB

561 I have always tried to be good—it's very demanding!
BENNY ANDERSEN

562 If things go on as they have, imagine the horrifying things the children of the next generation will have to do to shock their parents.

563 If we judge our conduct by Christ and his desire to please the Father, we will solve many decisions regarding behavior.
ERWIN W. LUTZER (1941–)

564 If you love the good that you see in another, make it your own.
POPE GREGORY THE GREAT (540–604)

565 It would scarcely be necessary to expound doctrine if our lives were radiant enough. If we behaved like true Christians, there would be no pagans.
POPE JOHN XXIII (1881–1963)

566 Jesus taught, first, that a man's business is to do the will of God; second, that God takes upon himself the care of that man; third, therefore, that a man must never be afraid of anything; and so, fourth, be left free to love God with all his heart, and his neighbor as himself.
GEORGE MACDONALD (1824–1905)

567 Make no distinction in your conduct between small things and great.
WILLIAM TAYLOR (1821–1902)

568 Our Lord lived his life . . . to give us the normal standard for our lives.
OSWALD CHAMBERS (1874–1917)

569 Resolved, to live with all my might while I do live. Resolved, never to lose one moment of time, to improve it in the most profitable way I can. Resolved, never to do anything which I should despise or think meanly in another. Resolved, never to do anything out of revenge. Resolved, never to do anything which I should be afraid to do if it were the last hour of my life.
JONATHAN EDWARDS (1703–1758)

570 The best thing to give your enemy is forgiveness; to an opponent, tolerance; to a friend, your heart; to your child, a good example; to a father, deference; to your mother, conduct that will make her proud of you; to yourself, respect; to all men, charity.
ARTHUR JAMES BALFOUR (1848–1930)

571 The chastising lesson . . . first, not to make private assumptions from public conduct, and second, if we have to judge, let our judgments be provisional, not ultimate. We do not really know why people do what they do, even when we are close to them—and sometimes especially because we are close to them.
SYDNEY J. HARRIS (1917–1986)

572 The least movement affects all nature; the entire sea changes because of a rock. Thus, in grace, the least action

affects everything by its consequences; therefore everything is important.

In each action we must look beyond the action at our past, present, and future state, and at others whom it affects, and see the relations of all those things. And then we shall be very cautious.
BLAISE PASCAL (1623–1662)

573 The mark of a man is how he treats a person who can be of no possible use to him.

574 The modern attitude is, "Father, forgive us for we know not what we are doing—and please don't tell us!"
ERWIN W. LUTZER (1941–)

575 The world takes its notions of God from the people who say that they belong to God's family. They read us a great deal more than they read the Bible. They see us; they only hear about Jesus Christ.
ALEXANDER MACLAREN (1826–1910)

576 Walk softly, speak tenderly, pray fervently. Do not run up stairs, do not run down God's people.
T. J. BACH

577 What if God arranged things so that we would experience a mild jolt of pain with every sin, or a tickle of pleasure with every act of virtue? Sort of a divine behavior modification, if you will. Would you obey because you loved God? I don't think so. I think you'd obey simply because you desired pleasure and not pain.
JONI EARECKSON TADA

578 Whatever a man does he must do first in his mind.
ALBERT SZENT-GYÖRGYI VON NAGYRAPOLT (1893–)

579 When we are tempted to begin a statement with "If people would only . . . ," it is good to keep in mind that "people" is an abstraction standing for "I and thou," and that at least half the responsibility for human conduct rests upon the "I."
SYDNEY J. HARRIS (1917–1986)

580 You cannot add to the peace and good will of the world if you fail to create

an atmosphere of harmony and love right where you live and work.
THOMAS DREIER (1884–)

BELIEF

581 As a man believes, so he is.

582 Belief is truth held in the mind; faith is fire in the heart.
JOSEPH FORT NEWTON (1880–1950)

583 Believe to the end, even if all men go astray and you are left the only one faithful; bring your offering even then and praise God in your loneliness.
FYODOR MIKHAYLOVICH DOSTOYEVSKI (1821–1881)

584 Believe what you do believe and stick to it, but don't profess to believe more than you intend to stick to. If you say you believe God is love, stick to it though all Providence becomes a pandemonium shouting that God is cruel to allow what he does.
OSWALD CHAMBERS (1874–1917)

585 God takes and God keeps the initiative. God alone can make a man a believer. Our part is to accept or reject his initiative.
JOHN POWELL

586 I am not afraid of those tender and scrupulous consciences who are ever cautious of professing and believing too much. If they are sincerely wrong, I forgive their errors and respect their integrity. The men I am afraid of are those who believe everything, subscribe to everything, and vote for everything.
WILLIAM DAVIES SHIPLEY (1745–1826)

587 If all things are possible with God, then all things are possible to him who believes in him.
CORRIE TEN BOOM (1892–1983)

588 If you believe what you like in the gospel, and reject what you don't like, it is not the gospel you believe, but yourself.
SAINT AUGUSTINE OF HIPPO (354–430)

589 It is a great thing to be a believer, but easy to misunderstand what the New Testament means by it. It is not that

we believe Jesus Christ can do things, or that we believe in a plan of salvation. It is that we believe him; whatever happens we will hang on to the fact that he is true. If we say, "I am going to believe he will put things right," we shall lose our confidence when we see things go wrong.
OSWALD CHAMBERS (1874–1917)

590 It is as absurd to argue men, as to torture them, into believing.
CARDINAL JOHN HENRY NEWMAN (1801–1890)

591 It is doubtful whether any sense of tragedy is compatible with the belief in God.
GEORGE ORWELL (1903–1950)

592 It is easy to say we believe in God as long as we remain in the little world we choose to live in; but get out into the great world of facts, the noisy world where people are absolutely indifferent to you, where your message is nothing more than a crazy tale belonging to a bygone age, can you believe God there?
OSWALD CHAMBERS (1874–1917)

593 It is so hard to believe because it is so hard to obey.
SØREN AABYE KIERKEGAARD (1813–1855)

594 Just as no one can go to hell or heaven for me, so no one can believe for me and so no one can open or close heaven or hell for me, and no one can drive me either to believe or disbelieve.
MARTIN LUTHER (1483–1546)

595 Man prefers to believe what he prefers to be true.
FRANCIS BACON (1561–1626)

596 Mock on, mock on, Voltaire, Rousseau; Mock on, mock on; 'tis all in vain! You throw the sand against the wind, And the wind blows it back again.
WILLIAM BLAKE (1757–1827)

597 No man ever believes with a true and saving faith unless God inclines his heart; and no man when God does incline his heart can refrain from believing.
BLAISE PASCAL (1623–1662)

598 Our beliefs in a rich future life are of little importance unless we coin them into a rich present life.
THOMAS DREIER (1884–)

599 The greatest proof of Christianity for others is not how far a man can logically analyze his reasons for believing, but how far in practice he will stake his life on his belief.
T. S. ELIOT (1888–1965)

600 The unbelieving mind would not be convinced by any proof, and the worshiping heart needs none.
A. W. TOZER (1897–1963)

601 Theological beliefs may get one into a church, but not into the kingdom of heaven.
STANLEY I. STUBER

602 To believe everything is too much, to believe nothing is not enough.
GERMAN PROVERB

603 To believe in God is to believe in someone who will always be far beyond us, who will forever be presenting a new aspect of himself to us.
LOUIS EVELY (1910–)

604 To believe in God is to know that all the rules will be fair—and that there will be many surprises!
SISTER CORITA

605 To believe only possibilities is not faith, but mere philosophy.
SIR THOMAS BROWNE (1605–1682)

606 To believe with certainty, we must begin with doubting.
STANISLAW J. LEC (1909–1966)

607 To one who thinks, life is comedy. To one who feels, life is tragedy. To one who believes, life is victory.

608 To those who believe, no explanation is necessary. To those who do not believe, no explanation is possible.
FRANZ WERFEL (1890–1945)

609 Understanding is the reward of faith. Therefore seek not to understand that you may believe, but believe that you may understand.
SAINT AUGUSTINE OF HIPPO (354–430)

610 We are inclined to believe those whom we do not know because they have never deceived us.
SAMUEL JOHNSON (1709–1784)

611 We blunder when we tell people they must believe certain things about Jesus Christ; a man cannot believe until he knows him, then belief is spontaneous and natural.
OSWALD CHAMBERS (1874–1917)

612 We can prove our faith by our committal to it, and in no other way. Any belief that does not command the one who holds it is not a real belief; it is a pseudo belief only. And it might shock some of us profoundly if we were brought suddenly face to face with our beliefs and forced to test them in the fires of practical living.
A. W. TOZER (1897–1963)

613 What a man accomplishes depends on what he believes.

614 What I believe about God is the most important thing about me.
A. W. TOZER (1897–1963)

615 Who . . . has ever seen an idea? . . . Who has ever seen love? . . . Who has ever seen faith? . . . The real things in the world are the invisible spiritual realities. Is it so difficult, then, to believe in God?
CHARLES TEMPLETON (1915–)

616 You never know how much you really believe anything until its truth or falsehood becomes a matter of life and death to you.
C. S. LEWIS (1898–1963)

617 Faith and thought belong together, and believing is impossible without thinking.
JOHN R. W. STOTT (1921–)

BENEDICTION

618 Be thou the rainbow to the storm of life,
The evening beam that smiles the clouds away,
And tints tomorrow with prophetic ray!
LORD GEORGE NOEL GORDON BYRON (1788–1824)

619 Bless all who worship thee, from the rising of the sun unto the going down of the same. Of thy goodness, give us; with thy love, inspire us; by thy spirit, guide us; by thy power, protect us; in thy mercy, receive us now and always.

620 The splendor, the love, and the strength of God be upon us.
C. S. LEWIS (1898–1963)

BENEVOLENCE

621 Be grateful to the beggar; he gives you the chance to do good.
JEWISH PROVERB

622 Bread for myself is a material question; bread for my neighbor is a spiritual question.
JACQUES MARITAIN (1882–1973)

623 Do not wait for extraordinary circumstances to do good actions; try to use ordinary situations.
JOHANN PAUL FRIEDRICH RICHTER (1763–1825)

624 In this world it is not what we take up but what we give up that makes us rich.
HENRY WARD BEECHER (1813–1887)

625 My piece of bread only belongs to me when I know that everyone else has a share and that no one starves while I eat.
LEO TOLSTOY (1828–1910)

626 The best portions of a good man's life—His little, nameless, unremembered acts Of kindness and love.
WILLIAM WORDSWORTH (1770–1850)

627 Who gives to the poor, lends to God.
SPANISH PROVERB

BETRAYAL

628 A man may betray Jesus Christ by speaking too many words, and he may betray him through keeping his mouth shut.
OSWALD CHAMBERS (1874–1917)

629 Does not he to whom you betray another . . . know that you will at another time do as much for him?
MICHEL EYQUEM DE MONTAIGNE (1533–1592)

630 To say the truth, so Judas kiss'd his
    Master,
    And cried, "All hail," whereas he
    meant all harm.
    WILLIAM SHAKESPEARE (1564–1616)

631 When you betray somebody else, you
    also betray yourself.
    ISAAC BASHEVIS SINGER (1904–1991)

BIBLE

632 A Bible that's falling apart probably
    belongs to someone who isn't.
    CHRISTIAN JOHNSON

633 A bit of the Book in the morning,
    To order my onward way.
    A bit of the Book in the evening,
    To hallow the end of the day.
    MARGARET SANGSTER (1838–1912)

634 A glory gilds the sacred page,
    Majestic like the sun;
    It gives a light to every age,
    It gives, but borrows none.
    WILLIAM COWPER (1731–1800)

635 A loving Personality dominates the
    Bible, walking among the trees of the
    garden and breathing fragrance over
    every scene. Always a living Person is
    present, speaking, pleading, loving,
    working, and manifesting himself
    whenever and wherever his people
    have the receptivity necessary to
    receive the manifestation.
    A. W. TOZER (1897–1963)

636 A man who loves his wife will love her
    letters and her photographs because
    they speak to him of her. So if we love
    the Lord Jesus, we shall love the Bible
    because it speaks to us of him.
    JOHN R. W. STOTT (1921–)

637 A new world will arise out of the reli-
    gious mists when we approach our
    Bible with the idea that it is . . . a
    book which is now speaking.
    A. W. TOZER (1897–1963)

638 A real book is not one that we read,
    but one that reads us.
    W. H. AUDEN (1907–1973)

639 A single line in the Bible has consoled
    me more than all the books I have ever
    read.
    IMMANUEL KANT (1724–1804)

640 A thorough knowledge of the Bible is
    worth more than a college education.
    THEODORE ROOSEVELT (1858–1919)

641 All things desirable to men are con-
    tained in the Bible.
    ABRAHAM LINCOLN (1809–1865)

642 Any single verse of the Bible, taken in
    isolation, may actually be dangerous
    to your spiritual health. Every part of
    it must be read in relation to the
    whole message.
    LOUIS CASSELS (1922–1974)

643 As in paradise, God walks in the Holy
    Scriptures, seeking man.
    SAINT AMBROSE (C. 340–397)

644 Be astounded that God should have
    written to us.
    ANTONY OF EGYPT (C. 251–356)

645 Born in the East and clothed in Orien-
    tal form and imagery, the Bible walks
    the ways of all the world with familiar
    feet and enters land after land to find
    its own everywhere. It has learned to
    speak in hundreds of languages to the
    heart of man. It comes into the palace
    to tell the monarch that he is a servant
    of the Most High, and into the cottage
    to assure the peasant that he is a son
    of God. Children listen to its stories
    with wonder and delight, and wise
    men ponder them as parables of life.
    HENRY VAN DYKE (1852–1933)

646 Centuries of experience have tested the
    Bible. It has passed through critical
    fires no other volume has suffered,
    and its spiritual truth has endured the
    flames and come out without so much
    as the smell of burning.
    W. E. SANGSTER

647 Christ is the master; the Scriptures are
    only the servant.
    MARTIN LUTHER (1483–1546)

648 Come, Holy Ghost, for moved by thee
    The prophets wrote and spoke;
    Unlock the truth, thyself the key,
    Unseal the sacred book.
    JOHN CALVIN (1509–1564)

649 Do you know a book that you are willing to put under your head for a pillow when you are dying? Very well; that is the book you want to study when you are living. There is only one such book in the world.
JOSEPH COOK (1838–1901)

650 Every Christian must refer always and everywhere to the Scriptures for all his choices, becoming like a child before it, seeking in it the most effective remedy against all his various weaknesses, and not daring to take a step without being illuminated by the divine rays of those words.
POPE JOHN PAUL II (1920–   )

651 Father made me learn so many Bible verses every day that by the time I was eleven years of age, I had learned about three fourths of the Old Testament and all of the New by heart.
JOHN MUIR (1838–1914)

652 One controlling, guiding, unifying mind must have been operative through all the weary ages to produce out of such composite elements a result so wonderfully unique, uplifting, and unfathomable as the Bible; and that mind in the nature of things could not have been human.
WILLIAM EWART GLADSTONE (1809–1898)

653 Give the Bible to the people, unadulterated, pure, unaltered, unexplained, uncheapened, and then see it work through the whole nature. It is very difficult indeed for a man or for a boy who knows the Scriptures ever to get away from it. It follows him like the memory of his mother. It haunts him like an old song. It reminds him like the word of an old and revered teacher. It forms a part of the warp and woof of his life.
WOODROW WILSON (1856–1924)

654 God did not write a book and send it by messenger to be read at a distance by unaided minds. He spoke a book and lives in his spoken words, constantly speaking his words and causing the power of them to persist across the years.
A. W. TOZER (1897–1963)

655 God the Father is the giver of Holy Scripture; God the Son is the theme of Holy Scripture; and God the Spirit is the author, authenticator, and interpreter of Holy Scripture.
J. I. PACKER (1926–   )

656 God's Book is packed full of overwhelming riches; they are unsearchable—the more we have the more there is to have.
OSWALD CHAMBERS (1874–1917)

657 He was great on texts, the doctor was. When he had a point to prove, he'd just go through the Bible and drive all the texts ahead of him like a flock of sheep; and then, if there was a text that seemed against him, why, he'd come out with his Greek and Hebrew and kind of chase it around a spell, just as you see a fellow chase a contrary bell-weather, and make him jump the fence after the rest. I tell you, there wasn't no text in the Bible that could stand against the doctor when his blood was up.
HARRIET BEECHER STOWE (1811–1896)

658 He who hath heard the Word of God can bear his silences.
SAINT IGNATIUS OF LOYOLA (1491–1556)

659 How petty are the books of the philosophers with all their pomp compared with the Gospels!
JEAN JACQUES ROUSSEAU (1712–1778)

660 However powerful and learned he may be, the Bible always sets man face to face with God, reminding him thus of his frailty and his weakness.
PAUL TOURNIER (1898–1986)

661 I am sorry for men who do not read the Bible every day. I wonder why they deprive themselves of the strength and the pleasure.
WOODROW WILSON (1856–1924)

662 I discover an arrant laziness in my soul. For when I am to read a chapter in the Bible, before I begin I look where it ends. And if it ends not on the same side, I cannot keep my hands

from turning over the leaf, to measure the length on the other side; if it swells to many verses, I begin to grudge. Surely my heart is not rightly affected. Were I truly hungry after heavenly food, I would not complain of meat. Scourge, Lord, this laziness of my soul; make the reading of your Word, not a penance, but a pleasure to me; so I may esteem that chapter in your Word the best which is the longest.
SIR THOMAS FULLER (1608–1661)

663 I know the Bible is inspired because it finds me at a greater depth of my being than any other book.
SAMUEL TAYLOR COLERIDGE (1772–1834)

664 I never had any doubt about it being of divine origin . . . point out to me any similar collection of writings that has lasted for as many thousands of years and is still a best-seller, world-wide. It had to be of divine origin.
RONALD WILSON REAGAN (1911–)

665 I never knew all there was in the Bible until I spent those years in jail. I was constantly finding new treasures.
JOHN BUNYAN (1628–1688)

666 I read my Bible to know what people ought to do, and my newspaper to know what they are doing.
CARDINAL JOHN HENRY NEWMAN (1801–1890)

667 I study my Bible as I gather apples. First, I shake the whole tree that the ripest might fall. Then I shake each limb, and when I have shaken each limb, I shake each branch and every twig. Then I look under every leaf.
MARTIN LUTHER (1483–1546)

668 I use the Scripture, not as an arsenal, to be resorted to only for arms and weapons . . . but as a matchless temple, where I delight to be to contemplate the beauty, the symmetry and the magnificence of the structure.
ROBERT BOYLE (1627–1691)

669 I was reading the Bible in many different languages, and I saw that it cannot really be translated, the real meaning cannot be given in another language. It is only in Hebrew that you feel the full meaning of it—all the associations which a different word has.
DAVID BEN-GURION (1886–1973)

670 In all my perplexities and distresses, the Bible has never failed to give me light and strength.
ROBERT EDWARD LEE (1807–1870)

671 In teaching me the way to live, it taught me how to die.
GEORGE POPE MORRIS (1802–1864)

672 In the Bible there is no twilight, but intense light and intense darkness.
OSWALD CHAMBERS (1874–1917)

673 In the case of Shakespeare the dependence is so obvious as to have obtained from Emerson the verdict, "Shakespeare leans upon the Bible." His mind is saturated with Scripture. He thinks naturally in terms of Scripture. These are the marks of one who has read and absorbed the Bible. Indeed, so close is the resemblance of Shakespeare to the Bible in quality and tone that memory sometimes stumbles and we ask, "Is this from the one or the other?" To take the Bible out of Shakespeare would leave not merely a great gap—it would leave a deep wound in the side. The Bible is woven in with the very texture of the immortal plays. If the Bible were lost, much of its language and incident, together with much of its spirit, would be preserved to us in Shakespeare.
EDGAR W. WORK

674 In the Old Testament the new lies hidden, in the New Testament the old is laid open.
SAINT AUGUSTINE OF HIPPO (354–430)

675 It ain't those parts of the Bible that I can't understand that bother me, it is the parts that I do understand.
MARK TWAIN (1835–1910)

676 It is a profound source of literary stimulation, both because of its majestic prose, and because of its ideas.
STUART CHASE (1888–1985)

677 It is impossible to mentally or socially enslave a Bible-reading people.
HORACE GREELEY (1811–1872)

678 It is not possible ever to exhaust the mind of the Scriptures. It is a well that has no bottom.
SAINT JOHN CHRYSOSTOM (C. 347–407)

679 Its critics, who claimed it to be filled with forgery, fiction, and unfulfilled promises, are finding that the difficulties lie with themselves, and not the Bible. Greater and more careful scholarship has shown that apparent contradictions were caused by incorrect translations rather than divine inconsistencies. It was man and not the Bible that needed correcting. It is the blueprint of the Master Architect.
BILLY GRAHAM (1918–)

680 Its light is like the body of heaven in its clearness; its vastness like the bosom of the sea; its variety like scenes of nature.
CARDINAL JOHN HENRY NEWMAN (1801–1890)

681 Make it the first morning business of your life to understand some part of the Bible clearly, and make it your daily business to obey it in all that you do understand.
JOHN RUSKIN (1819–1900)

682 My deepest regret, on reaching threescore years and ten, is that I have not devoted more time to the study of the Bible. Still in less than nineteen years I have gone through the New Testament in Chinese fifty-five times.
JONATHAN GOFORTH (1859–1936)

683 My own experience is that the Bible is dull when I am dull. When I am really alive, and set in upon the text with a tidal pressure of living affinities, it opens, it multiplies discoveries, and reveals depths even faster than I can note them. The worldly spirit shuts the Bible; the Spirit of God makes it a fire, flaming out all meanings and glorious truths.
HORACE BUSHNELL (1802–1876)

684 No one ever graduates from Bible study until he meets the author face to face.
E. T. HARRIS

685 Nobody ever outgrows Scripture; the book widens and deepens with our years.
CHARLES HADDON SPURGEON (1834–1892)

686 Once you and I are face to face with the Word of God . . . we can only accept or reject it. Jesus becomes the two-edged sword that cuts right down the middle, dividing us into believers and nonbelievers.
JOHN POWELL

687 One of the many divine qualities of the Bible is this: that it does not yield its secrets to the irreverent and censorious.
J. I. PACKER (1926–)

688 One who uses the Bible as his guide never loses his sense of direction.

689 Other books were given for our information, the Bible was given for our transformation.

690 Read the Bible. Free gift inside.

691 Scripture is far higher and wider than our need.
CARDINAL JOHN HENRY NEWMAN (1801–1890)

692 Sin will keep you from this book. This book will keep you from sin.
DWIGHT LYMAN MOODY (1837–1899)

693 Some people unfortunately try to reduce the great mystery to an absurd kind of magic. They open the Bible at random, stab their fingers at a verse, and expect therein to find God's instant answer to whatever is troubling them at that moment. The notion that divine guidance is dispensed in such a mechanical, penny-in-the-slot manner is an insult to God and puts the Bible on a par with a ouija board.
LOUIS CASSELS (1922–1974)

694 The amazing wealth of the Bible is precisely what makes it a difficult book to study.
PAUL TOURNIER (1898–1986)

695 The Bible contains more of my little philosophy than all the libraries I have seen; and such parts of it as I cannot

reconcile to my little philosophy, I postpone for future investigation.
JOHN ADAMS (1735–1826)

696 The Bible deals with terrors and upsets, with . . . all that the devil can do, and yet all through there is the uncrushable certainty that in the end everything will be all right.
OSWALD CHAMBERS (1874–1917)

697 The Bible does not thrill, the Bible nourishes. Give time to the reading of the Bible, and the recreating effect is as real as that of fresh air physically.
OSWALD CHAMBERS (1874–1917)

698 The Bible furnishes the only fitting vehicle to express the thoughts that overwhelm us when contemplating the stellar universe.
ORMSBY M. MITCHELL (1809–1862)

699 The Bible grows more beautiful as we grow in our understanding of it.
JOHANN WOLFGANG VON GOETHE (1749–1832)

700 The Bible has been the Magna Charta of the poor and oppressed.
THOMAS HENRY HUXLEY (1825–1895)

701 The Bible has meant a great deal to me always, not only for the spiritual values it asserts, but for many other reasons—the beauty of its poetry, the fact that it is the most human book or collection of books ever written, containing the story of all human weaknesses and strength. I enjoy it also because it contains nearly all the great stories that have been written and rewritten many times and because it contains the Ten Commandments, which provide the best formula ever set down by which people can live together in civilized justice and understanding. It is unquestionably the greatest of books and the whole compendium of human experience in the real world as well as in the spiritual one.
LOUIS BROMFIELD (1896–1956)

702 The Bible holds up before us ideals that are within sight of the weakest and the lowliest, and yet so high that the best and the noblest are kept with their faces turned ever upward.
WILLIAM JENNINGS BRYAN (1860–1925)

703 The Bible is . . . the bedrock foundation of all our literature and, therefore, if you want to know anything, the Bible is where you must go to find it. . . . It is too big for systems, it comprehends man and all his thoughts. . . . a great gallery of superb human portraits.
THOMAS LANSING MASSON (1866–1934)

704 The Bible is a letter from God with our personal address on it.
SØREN AABYE KIERKEGAARD (1813–1855)

705 The Bible is a living book, an ever-enlarging book.
JAMES G. K. MCCLURE (1848–1932)

706 The Bible is a page torn out of the great volume of human life; torn by the hand of God and annotated by his Spirit.
JOSEPH PARKER (1830–1902)

707 The Bible is a stream wherein the elephant may swim and the lamb may wade.
POPE GREGORY THE GREAT (540–604)

708 The Bible is a supernatural book and can be understood only by supernatural aid.
A. W. TOZER (1897–1963)

709 The Bible is a universe of revelation facts which have no meaning for us until we are born from above; when we are born again we see in it what we never saw before. We are lifted into the realm where Jesus lives and we begin to see what he sees.
OSWALD CHAMBERS (1874–1917)

710 The Bible is a vein of pure gold, unalloyed by quartz or any earthly substance. This is a star without a speck; a sun without a blot; a light without darkness; a moon without its paleness; a glory without a dimness. O Bible! It cannot be said of any other book that it is perfect and pure; but of thee we can declare all wisdom is gathered up in thee, without a particle of folly. This is the judge that ends the strife, where wit and reason fail. This is the

book untainted by any error; but is pure, unalloyed, perfect truth.
CHARLES HADDON SPURGEON (1834–1892)

711 The Bible is a window in this prison-world through which we may look into eternity.
TIMOTHY DWIGHT (1752–1817)

712 The Bible is alive, it speaks to me; it has feet, it runs after me; it has hands, it lays hold on me.
MARTIN LUTHER (1483–1546)

713 The Bible is God's chart for you to steer by, to keep you from the bottom of the sea, and to show you where the harbour is, and how to reach it without running on rocks and bars.
HENRY WARD BEECHER (1813–1887)

714 The Bible is like a telescope. If a man looks through his telescope, then he sees worlds beyond; but if he looks at his telescope, then he does not see anything but that. The Bible is a thing to be looked through, to see that which is beyond.
PHILLIPS BROOKS (1835–1893)

715 The Bible is meant to be bread for our daily use, not just cake for special occasions.

716 The Bible is my church. It is always open, and there is my High Priest ever waiting to receive me. There I have my confessional, my thanksgiving, my psalm of praise, a field of promises, and a congregation of whom the world is not worthy—prophets and apostles, and martyrs and confessors—in short, all I can want, there I find.
CHARLOTTE ELLIOTT (1789–1871)

717 The Bible is such excellent medicine.
S. I. MCMILLEN

718 The Bible is the constitution of Christianity.
BILLY GRAHAM (1918–)

719 The Bible is the most thought-suggesting book in the world. No other deals with such grand themes.
HERRICK JOHNSON (1832–1913)

720 The Bible is the only thing that can combat the devil. Quote the Scriptures and the devil will run . . . use the Scriptures like a sword and you'll drive temptation away.
BILLY GRAHAM (1918–)

721 The Bible never deals with the domains our human minds delight to deal with. The Bible deals with heaven and hell, good and bad, God and the devil, right and wrong, salvation and damnation; we like to deal with things in-between.
OSWALD CHAMBERS (1874–1917)

722 The Bible redirects my will, cleanses my emotions, enlightens my mind, and quickens my total being.
E. STANLEY JONES (1884–1973)

723 The Bible shows how the world progresses. It begins with a garden, but ends with a holy city.
PHILLIPS BROOKS (1835–1893)

724 The Bible treats us as human life does—roughly.
OSWALD CHAMBERS (1874–1917)

725 The Bible was never intended to be a book for scholars and specialists only. From the very beginning it was intended to be everybody's book, and that is what it continues to be.
F. F. BRUCE (1910–1990)

726 The Bible—banned, burned, beloved. More widely read, more frequently attacked than any other book in history. Generations of intellectuals have attempted to discredit it; dictators of every age have outlawed it and executed those who read it. Yet soldiers carry it into battle believing it more powerful than their weapons. Fragments of it smuggled into solitary prison cells have transformed ruthless killers into gentle saints.
CHARLES COLSON (1931–)

727 The Bible? That's the Book.
The Book indeed,
The Book of books;
On which who looks,
As he should do, aright,
Shall never need
Wish for a better light
To guide him in the night.
GEORGE HERBERT (1593–1633)

728 The book to read is not the one which thinks for you, but the one that makes you think. No other book in the world equals the Bible for that.
JAMES MCCOSH (1811–1894)

729 The devil is not afraid of the Bible that has dust on it.

730 The empire of Caesar is gone; the legions of Rome are smouldering in the dust; the avalanches that Napoleon hurled upon Europe have melted away; the prince of the Pharaohs is fallen; the pyramids they raised to be their tombs are sinking every day in the desert sands; Tyre is a rock for bleaching fisherman's nets; Sidon has scarcely left a wreck behind; but the Word of God still survives. All things that threatened to extinguish it have only aided it; and it proves every day how transient is the noblest monument that men can build, how enduring is the least word that God has spoken.
ALBERT BAIRD CUMMINS (1850–1926)

731 The Good Book—one of the most remarkable euphemisms ever coined.
ASHLEY MONTAGU (1905–   )

732 The gospel is not merely a book—it is a living power—a book surpassing all others. I never omit to read it, and every day with the same pleasure. The gospel possesses a secret virtue, a mysterious efficacy, a warmth which penetrates and soothes the heart. One finds in meditating upon it that which one experiences in contemplating the heavens. The gospel is not a book; it is a living being, with an action, a power, which invades everything that opposes its extension.
NAPOLEON BONAPARTE (1769–1821)

733 The highest earthly enjoyments are but a shadow of the joy I find in reading God's Word.
LADY JANE GREY (1537–1554)

734 The Holy Bible is an abyss. It is impossible to explain how profound it is, impossible to explain how simple it is.
ERNEST HELLO (1828–1885)

735 The Holy Scriptures tell us what we could never learn any other way: they tell us what we are, who we are, how we got here, why we are here and what we are required to do while we remain here.
A. W. TOZER (1897–1963)

736 The incongruity of the Bible with the age of its birth; its freedom from earthly mixtures; its original, unborrowed, solitary greatness; the suddenness with which it broke forth amidst the general gloom; these, to me, are strong indications of its divine descent: I cannot reconcile them with a human origin.
WILLIAM ELLERY CHANNING (1780–1842)

737 The most learned, acute, and diligent student cannot, in the longest life, obtain an entire knowledge of the Bible. The more deeply he works the mine, the richer and more abundant he finds the ore; new light continually beams from this source of heavenly knowledge, to direct the conduct, and illustrate the work of God and the ways of men; and he will at last leave the world confessing, that the more he studied the Scriptures, the fuller conviction he had of his own ignorance, and of their inestimable value.
SIR WALTER SCOTT (1771–1832)

738 The mystery of the Bible should teach us, at one and the same time, our nothingness and our greatness, producing humility and animating hope.
HENRY DUNDAS MELVILLE (1742–1811)

739 The New Testament holds up a strong light by which a man can read even the small print of his soul.
JOHN A. HUTTON (1868–1947)

740 The perfection of human expression was achieved when the world was younger: The Song of Songs, which is Solomon's, the Book of Psalms, the Revelation of St. John the Divine.
FANNIE HURST (1889–1968)

741 The sacred page is not meant to be the end, but only the means toward the end, which is knowing God himself.
A. W. TOZER (1897–1963)

742 The Scriptures teach us the best way of living, the noblest way of suffering, and the most comfortable way of dying.
JOHN FLAVEL (1627–1691)

743 The third chapter of Genesis is undoubtedly the most important chapter in the whole Bible. It is the only chapter which, if we could conceive it as being withdrawn, would leave all the rest of Scripture unintelligible. Take away this chapter and you take away the key of knowledge to all the rest of the Bible.
ARCHBISHOP RICHARD CHENEVIX TRENCH (1807–1886)

744 There came a time in my life when I doubted the divinity of the Scriptures, and I resolved as a lawyer and a judge I would try the book as I would try anything in the courtroom, taking evidence for and against. It was a long, serious, and profound study; and using the same principles of evidence in this religious matter as I always do in secular matters, I have come to the decision that the Bible is a supernatural book, that it has come from God, and that the only safety for the human race is to follow its teachings.
SALMON P. CHASE (1808–1873)

745 There's far more truth in the book of Genesis than in the quantum theory.
MALCOLM MUGGERIDGE (1903–1990)

746 This little book—it has said everything there is to be said. Everything is implied and anticipated in it. Whatever one should like to put into words has already been said in it.
MORDECAI OBADIAH (1810–1882)

747 To me the memorizing of Scripture has been an unfailing help in doubt, anxiety, sorrow, and all the countless vicissitudes and problems of life. I believe in it enough to have devoted many, many hours to stowing away passages where I can neither leave them behind me nor be unable to get at them.
SIR WILFRED THOMASON GRENFELL (1865–1940)

748 Trying to absorb the depths of the Bible is like trying to mop up the ocean floor with a sponge.

749 We find the Bible difficult because we try to read it as we would read any other book, and it is not the same as any other book.
A. W. TOZER (1897–1963)

750 What a book! Great and wide as the world, rooted in the abysmal depths of creation and rising aloft into the blue mysteries of heaven. Sunrise and sunset, promise and fulfillment, birth and death, the whole human drama, everything is in this book. It is the book of books, Biblia.
HEINRICH HEINE (1797–1856)

751 Why do they put the Gideon Bibles only in the bedrooms, where its usually too late, and not in the barroom downstairs?
CHRISTOPHER DARLINGTON MORLEY (1890–1957)

752 Without the present illumination of the Holy Spirit, the Word of God must remain a dead letter to every man, no matter how intelligent or well-educated he may be. . . . It is just as essential for the Holy Spirit to reveal the truth of Scripture to the reader today as it was necessary for him to inspire the writers in their day.
WILLIAM LAW (1686–1761)

753 You can learn more about human nature by reading the Bible than by living in New York.
WILLIAM LYON PHELPS (1865–1943)

754 You cannot criticize the New Testament. It criticizes you.
JOHN JAY CHAPMAN (1862–1933)

BIBLE PERSONALITIES

755 The heroes of the Bible are people who discovered something in God and in themselves which was a mixture of the majestic and the ordinary, the divine and the human.
TIM HANSEL

756 Adam should have been adamant.

757 Adam switched off from God's design. Instead of maintaining his dependence on God, he took his rule over himself and thereby introduced sin into the world.
OSWALD CHAMBERS (1874–1917)

758 Adam was created to be the friend and companion of God; he was to have dominion over all the life in the air and earth and sea, but one thing he was not to have dominion over, and that was himself.
OSWALD CHAMBERS (1874–1917)

759 No man ever got so much out of a surgical operation as Adam did.

760 Originally one, he has fallen, and, breaking up . . . he has filled the whole earth with the pieces.
SAINT AUGUSTINE OF HIPPO (354–430)

761 There is a charm about the forbidden that makes it unspeakably desirable. It was not that Adam ate the apple for the apple's sake, but because it was forbidden.
MARK TWAIN (1835–1910)

762 It wasn't an apple from the tree that started the trouble in the Garden of Eden; it was the pair on the ground.

763 Silence, O sinner, stop! Accuse not Eve and Adam.
   Without that incident, it's you who would have done it.
ANGELUS SILESIUS (1624–1677)

764 Caleb? Every new sunrise introduced another reminder that his body and rocking chair weren't made for each other. While his peers were yawning, Caleb was yearning.
CHARLES R. SWINDOLL (1934–   )

765 The most enjoyable way to follow a vegetable diet is to let the cow eat it and take yours in roast beef.

766 David swung. And God made his point. Anyone who underestimates what God can do with the ordinary has rocks in his head.
MAX L. LUCADO (1955–   )

767 Remember Eutychus who fell asleep during Paul's sermon and fell out of the window? Could planning worship save nodding slaves from broken necks?
CALVIN MILLER

768 "Such a thing never entered my head before," said Goliath when struck by the shot from David.

769 The Lord could not be on Jacob's side until he had been disabled and learned to use other weapons than those of his own wrestling.
ALFRED EDERSHEIM (1825–1889)

770 Jeremiah refutes the popular, modern notion that the end of religion is an integrated personality, freed of its fears, its doubts, and its frustrations. Certainly Jeremiah was no integrated personality. It is doubtful if to the end of his tortured existence he ever knew the meaning of the word *peace*. . . . If Jeremiah had been integrated, it would have been at the cost of ceasing to be Jeremiah! A man at peace simply could not be a Jeremiah. Spiritual health is good; mental assurance is good. But the summons of faith is neither to an integrated personality nor to the laying by of all questions, but to the dedication of personality—with all its fears and questions—to its duty and destiny under God.
JOHN BRIGHT (1811–1889)

771 Job feels the rod yet blesses God.

772 Job flings at God one riddle, God flings back at Job a hundred riddles, and Job is at peace; he is comforted with conundrums.
G. K. CHESTERTON (1874–1936)

773 Seeing God, Job forgets all he wanted to say, all he thought he would say if he could but see him.
GEORGE MACDONALD (1824–1905)

774 Jonah felt down in the mouth when the great fish swallowed him.

775 Still as of old
   Men by themselves are priced—
   For thirty pieces Judas sold
   Himself, not Christ.
HESTER H. CHOLMONDELEY

776 Ah foolish woman!
   who must always be,

A sight more strange
   than that she turn'd to see!
ABRAHAM COWLEY (1618–1667)

777 Methuselah lived nine hundred and
sixty-nine years without a bathtub,
without a toothbrush; he was never x-
rayed, manicured, or had his appendix
removed.
HARRY COLLINS SPILLMAN

778 By Nebo's lonely mountain,
On this side Jordan's wave,
In a vale in the land of Moab,
There lies a lonely grave;
But no man built that sepulcher,
And no man saw it e'er,
For the angels of God upturned the sod
And laid the dead man there.
CECIL FRANCES ALEXANDER (1818–1895)

779 Moses was a great lawgiver: keeping
the Ten Commandments short and to
the point shows he was no ordinary
lawyer.

780 Wise Nicodemus saw such light
As made him know his God by night.
HENRY VAUGHAN (1622–1695)

781 I don't believe Noah could have
rounded up all the animals in one herd
without the skunk causing a stampede.
WILL ROGERS (1879–1935)

782 Majorities mean nothing: during the
Flood only one man knew enough to
get out of the rain.

783 Noah told his sons to go easy on the
fishing bait. He only had two worms.

784 Noah was the best financier in the
Bible. He floated his stock while the
whole world was in liquidation.

785 Why didn't Noah swat those two flies
when he had the chance?

786 Because it was not politically expedient, none of the three judges resolved
Paul's case. Felix walked the fence like
a cat, Festus found Paul to be as irritating as a festering sore, and Agrippa
failed to get a grip on the situation.

787 Medical materialism finished up Saint
Paul by calling his vision on the road
of Damascus "A discharging lesion of
the occipital cortex, he being an epilep-
tic."
WILLIAM JAMES (1842–1910)

788 Peter often looked more like a sandpile than a rock.
JOHN POWELL

789 Samson with his strong body had a
weak head or he would not have laid
it in a harlot's lap.
BENJAMIN FRANKLIN (1706–1790)

790 Samson was strong. One day he was
out in a field, and a lion came, roared
and sprang at him, and Samson turned
around and took the lion's jaws in his
bare hand and ripped his head open.
Now, that takes a pretty good man to
do that. Tarzan couldn't even do that—
he had to have a knife!
BILLY GRAHAM (1918–   )

791 Samson was the most popular actor in
the Bible. He brought the house down.

792 Samson's weakness was his fondness
for showing off his strength.

793 There's nothing worse than a homemade haircut—look what it did for
Samson!

794 Solomon got whatever he wanted,
especially when it came to symbols of
power and status. Gradually, he
depended less on God and more on
the props around him: the world's largest harem, a house twice the size of the
temple, an army well stocked with
chariots, a strong economy.
PHILIP YANCEY (1949–   )

795 Solomon was famous for his wisdom,
not because he knew everything, but
because he knew how little he knew.

BIBLE/PSALMS

796 Psalms: a "Little Bible" since it contains, set out in the briefest and most
beautiful form, all that is to be found
in the whole Bible.
MARTIN LUTHER (1483–1546)

797 Psalms: the songs of the human soul,
timeless and universal.
THEODORE H. ROBINSON

798 The book of Psalms contains the
whole music of the heart of man,
swept like a harp by the hand of his
Maker. In it are gathered the lyrical
burst of his tenderness, the moan of
his penitence, the pathos of his sorrow,
the triumph of his victory, the despair
of his defeat, the firmness of his confidence, the rapture of his assured hope.
ROWLAND E. PROTHERO (1851–1937)

799 The Psalms are the anatomy of the soul.
JOHN CALVIN (1509–1564)

800 The Psalms: a mirror in which each
man sees the motions of his own soul.
ROWLAND E. PROTHERO (1851–1937)

801 The Twenty-third Psalm is the nightingale of the psalms. It is small, of a
homely feather, singing shyly out of
obscurity; but it has filled the air of
the whole world with melodious joy.
HENRY WARD BEECHER (1813–1887)

BIRTH

802 A baby is an inestimable blessing and
bother.
MARK TWAIN (1835–1910)

803 A rose with all its sweetest leaves yet
folded.
LORD GEORGE NOEL GORDON BYRON
(1788–1824)

804 A sweet new blossom of humanity,
fresh fallen from God's own home to
flower on earth.
GERALD MASSEY (1828–1907)

805 Baby: Unwritten history! Unfathomed
mystery!
JOSIAH GILBERT HOLLAND (1819–1881)

806 Every moment dies a man,
Every moment one is born.
ALFRED, LORD TENNYSON (1809–1892)

807 Little arms and legs dangle aimlessly
in four directions, appearing to be
God's afterthoughts.
JAMES C. DOBSON (1936–   )

808 My mother groaned! my father wept.
Into the dangerous world I leapt;
Helpless, naked, piping loud,
Like a fiend hid in a cloud.
WILLIAM BLAKE (1757–1827)

809 Not in utter nakedness,
But trailing clouds of glory do we come
From God, who is our home.
WILLIAM WORDSWORTH (1770–1850)

810 Nothing begins, and nothing ends,
That is not paid with moan;
For we are born in other's pain,
And perish in our own.
FRANCIS THOMPSON (1859–1907)

811 Our birth is nothing but our death
begun.
EDWARD YOUNG (1683–1765)

812 Our birth made us mortal, our death
will make us immortal.
ENGLISH PROVERB

813 Some are born to sweet delight,
Some are born to endless night.
WILLIAM BLAKE (1757–1827)

814 Some folks pray for a boy, and some
For a golden-haired girl to come;
Some think there is more joy
Wrapped up in the smile of a little boy,
While others think the silky curls
And plump pink cheeks of a little girl
Bring more bliss to the old home place,
Than a small boy's little freckled face.
Now which is better, I can't say
If the Lord should ask me to choose
    today,
If he should put in a call for me
And say: "Now what shall your
    order be,
A boy or a girl? I have both in store—"
I'd say with one of my broadest grins,
"Send either one, if it can't be twins."

815 The birth of every new baby is God's
vote of confidence in the future of
man.
IMOGENE FEY

816 The first handshake in life is the greatest of all: the clasp of an infant around
the finger of a parent.

817 Why is it that we rejoice at a birth and
grieve at a funeral? It is because we
are not the person involved.
MARK TWAIN (1835–1910)

BLESSINGS

818 A person who is to be happy must actively enjoy his blessings.
CICERO (106–43 B.C.)

819 All that is required to make men unmindful of what they owe to God for any blessing is that they should receive that blessing often and regularly.
RICHARD WHATELY (1787–1863)

820 Every misery I miss is a new blessing.
IZAAK WALTON (1593–1683)

821 God particularly pours out his blessings upon those who know how much they need him.
ROBERT HAROLD SCHULLER (1926–   )

822 If you don't get everything you want, think of the things you don't get that you don't want.
OSCAR WILDE (1854–1900)

823 In the kingdom of the blind the one-eyed man is king.
DESIDERIUS ERASMUS (C. 1466–1536)

824 It would be a blessing if each human being were striken blind and deaf for a few days at some time during his adult life. Darkness would make him more appreciative of sight; silence would teach him the joys of sound.
HELEN ADAMS KELLER (1880–1968)

825 Never look at what you have lost; look at what you have left.
ROBERT HAROLD SCHULLER (1926–   )

826 Never undertake anything for which you wouldn't have the courage to ask the blessings of heaven.
GEORG CHRISTOPH LICHTENBERG (1742–1799)

827 Once it was the blessing, now it is the Lord.
ALBERT BENJAMIN SIMPSON (1843–1919)

828 Reflect upon your present blessings of which every man has many; not on your past misfortunes of which all men have some.
CHARLES DICKENS (1812–1870)

829 The best things are nearest: breath in your nostrils, light in your eyes, flowers at your feet, duties at your hand, the path of God just before you.
ROBERT LOUIS BALFOUR STEVENSON (1850–1894)

830 The greatest blessing we ever get from God is to know that we are destitute spiritually.
OSWALD CHAMBERS (1874–1917)

831 The Lord gives his blessing when he finds the vessel empty.
THOMAS À KEMPIS (C. 1380–1471)

832 Unwelcomed visitors sometimes bring unexpected blessings.

BODY

833 A human being: an ingenious assembly of portable plumbing.
CHRISTOPHER DARLINGTON MORLEY (1890–1957)

834 Body: not a home but an inn—and that only briefly.
LUCIUS ANNAEUS SENECA (C. 4 B.C.–A.D. 65)

835 God always locates his spiritual revelations in a physical body. The great God became Incarnate in flesh and blood; the great thoughts of God became crystallized in words.
OSWALD CHAMBERS (1874–1917)

836 O God, may we so value our bodies and minds that we never mar them. May we not be tricked into bad habits by publicity and advertisements that deliberately mislead, or by the desire for easy applause, or by the fear of being thought narrow. But may we be sturdy and upright in our thinking and our behavior, and treat our bodies as the temple of thy Spirit.
SID G. HODGES

837 Our body is the most gracious gift God has given us, and that if we hand over the mainspring of our life to God we can work out in our bodily life all that he works in. It is through our bodily lives that Satan works and, thank God, it is through our bodily lives that God's Spirit works. God gives us his grace and his Spirit; he puts right all that was wrong, he does not suppress

it nor counteract it, but readjusts the whole thing; then begins our work.
OSWALD CHAMBERS (1874–1917)

838 Our body is to be the temple of the Holy Ghost, the medium for manifesting the marvellous disposition of Jesus Christ.
OSWALD CHAMBERS (1874–1917)

839 Thank God we are not going to be angels, we are going to be something tenfold better. By the redemption of Jesus Christ there is a time coming when our bodies will be in the image of God.
OSWALD CHAMBERS (1874–1917)

840 The Bible, instead of ignoring the fact that we have a body, exalts it.
OSWALD CHAMBERS (1874–1917)

841 The body is matter, but it is God's creation . . . when it is neglected or scoffed at, God himself is insulted.
MICHEL QUOIST (1921–   )

842 The body: a marvelous machine . . . a chemical laboratory, a powerhouse. Every movement, voluntary or involuntary, full of secrets and marvels.
THEODOR HERZL (1860–1904)

843 The brain and the body are pure mechanisms, there is nothing spiritual about them; they are the machines we use to express our personality.
OSWALD CHAMBERS (1874–1917)

844 The ear tends to be lazy, craves the familiar, and is shocked by the unexpected; the eye, on the other hand, tends to be impatient, craves the novel, and is bored by repetition.
W. H. AUDEN (1907–1973)

845 The ears and eyes are the doors and windows of the soul.
JOSEPH JOUBERT (1754–1824)

846 The human body is probably the most amazing example of teamwork anywhere. Every part needs the other. When the stomach is hungry, the eyes spot the hamburger. The nose smells the onions, the feet run to the snack stand, the hands douse the burger with mustard and shove it back into the mouth, where it goes down to the stomach. Now that's cooperation!
JONI EARECKSON TADA

847 We have a bodily machine which we must regulate. God does not regulate it for us. Until we learn to bring the bodily machine into harmony with God's will, there will be friction, and the friction is a warning that part of the machine is not in working order.
OSWALD CHAMBERS (1874–1917)

848 We have to treat the body as the servant of Jesus Christ: when the body says, "Sit," and he says, "Go," go! When the body says, "Eat," and he says, "Fast," fast! When the body says, "Yawn," and he says, "Pray," pray!
OSWALD CHAMBERS (1874–1917)

BOOKS

849 A book is like a garden carried in the pocket.
CHINESE PROVERB

850 A good book is not one that we read, but one that reads us.
W. H. AUDEN (1907–1973)

851 All that mankind has done, thought, gained or been; it is lying as in magic perservation in the pages of books.
THOMAS CARLYLE (1795–1881)

852 Children don't read to find their identity, to free themselves from guilt, to quench the thirst for rebellion or to get rid of alienation. They have no use for psychology. They detest sociology. They still believe in God, the family, angels, devils, witches, goblins, logic, clarity, punctuation, and other such obsolete stuff. . . . When a book is boring, they yawn openly. They don't expect their writer to redeem humanity, but leave to adults such childish illusions.
ISAAC BASHEVIS SINGER (1904–1991)

853 Never lend books—nobody ever returns them; the only books I have in my library are those which people have lent me.
ANATOLE FRANCE (1844–1924)

854 Next to acquiring good friends, the best acquisition is that of a good book.
CHARLES CALEB COLTON (1780–1832)

855 No entertainment is so cheap as reading, nor any pleasure so lasting.
LADY MARY WORTLEY MONTAGU (1689–1762)

856 Read not to contradict and confute, nor to believe and take for granted, nor to find talk and discourse—but to weigh and consider.
FRANCIS BACON (1561–1626)

857 Readers may be divided into four classes: 1. Sponges, who absorb all they read and return it nearly in the same state, only a little dirtied. 2. Sandglasses, who retain nothing and are content to get through a book for the sake of getting through the time. 3. Stainbags, who retain merely the dregs of what they read. 4. Mogul diamonds, equally rare and valuable, who profit by what they read, and enable others to profit by it, also.
SAMUEL TAYLOR COLERIDGE (1772–1834)

858 Reading—the nice and subtle happiness of reading. . . . This joy not dulled by age, this polite and unpunished vice, this selfish, serene, lifelong intoxication.
LOGAN PEARSALL SMITH (1865–1946)

859 Some books are to be tasted, others to be swallowed, and some few to be chewed and digested.
FRANCIS BACON (1561–1626)

860 The man who does not read good books has no advantage over the man who cannot read at all.
MARK TWAIN (1835–1910)

861 The reading of all good books is like a conversation with the finest men of past centuries.
RENÉ DESCARTES (1596–1650)

862 The things you read will fashion you by slowly conditioning your mind.
A. W. TOZER (1897–1963)

863 To read without reflecting is like eating without digesting.
EDMUND BURKE (1729–1797)

BOREDOM

864 Boredom has made more gamblers than greed, more drunkards than thirst, and perhaps as many suicides as despair.
CHARLES CALEB COLTON (1780–1832)

865 Boredom: the consciousness of a barren, meaningless existence.
ERIC HOFFER (1902–1983)

866 Boredom: what happens when we lose contact with the universe.
JOHN CIARDI (1916–1986)

867 Somehow or other, and with the best intentions, we have shown the world the typical Christian in the likeness of a crashing and rather ill-natured bore—and this in the name of one who assuredly never bored a soul in those thirty-three years during which he passed through the world like a flame.
DOROTHY L. SAYERS (1893–1957)

868 There are no uninteresting things; there are only uninterested people.
G. K. CHESTERTON (1874–1936)

869 We all denounce bores, but while we do so, let us remember that there is nobody who isn't a bore to somebody.
JOHN ALFRED SPENDER (1862–1942)

870 What a bore it is, waking up in the morning always the same person. I wish I were unflinching and emphatic and had big, bushy eyebrows and a message for the age. I wish I were a deep thinker or a great ventriloquist.
LOGAN PEARSALL SMITH (1865–1946)

871 When people are bored, it is primarily with their own selves.
ERIC HOFFER (1902–1983)

BORN AGAIN

872 Everything that is born of God is no shadowy work. God will not bring forth a dead fruit, a lifeless and powerless work, but a living, new man must be born from the living God.
JOHANN ARNDT (1555–1621)

873 In the natural world it is impossible to be made all over again, but in the spiri-

tual world it is exactly what Jesus
Christ makes possible.
OSWALD CHAMBERS (1874–1917)

874 No human birth can compare to the
supernatural birth of a child of God.
JAMES MONTGOMERY BOICE

875 The egg's no chick by falling from
the hen,
Nor man a Christian till he's born
again.
JOHN BUNYAN (1628–1688)

876 The first time we're born, as children,
human life is given to us; and when we
accept Jesus as our Savior, it's a new
life. That's what "born again" means.
JIMMY CARTER (1924–)

877 There are two spirits abroad in the
earth: the spirit that works in the children of disobedience and the Spirit of
God. These two can never be reconciled in time or in eternity. The spirit
that dwells in the once-born is forever
opposed to the Spirit that inhabits the
heart of the twice-born.
A. W. TOZER (1897–1963)

878 Though Christ a thousand times in
Bethlehem be born,
If he's not born in thee, thy soul is still
forlorn.
ANGELUS SILESIUS (1624–1677)

879 You must be born again. This is not a
command, it is a foundation fact. The
characteristic of the new birth is that I
yield myself so completely to God that
Christ is formed in me.
OSWALD CHAMBERS (1874–1917)

880 Your whole nature must be re-born,
your passions, and your affections,
and your aims, and your conscience,
and your will must all be bathed in a
new element and reconsecrated to
your Maker and, the last not the least,
your intellect.
CARDINAL JOHN HENRY NEWMAN
(1801–1890)

BROKENNESS

881 Brokenness is not revival; it is a vital
and indispensable step toward it.
ARTHUR WALLIS (1928–)

882 Deliverance can come to us only by
the defeat of our old life. Safety and
peace come only after we have been
forced to our knees. God rescues us by
breaking us, by shattering our strength
and wiping out our resistance.
A. W. TOZER (1897–1963)

883 God can never make us wine if we
object to the fingers he uses to crush
us with. If God would only use his
own fingers and make us broken
bread and poured out wine in a special
way! But when he uses someone
whom we dislike, or some set of circumstances to which we said we
would never submit, and makes those
the crushers, we object.
OSWALD CHAMBERS (1874–1917)

884 God creates out of nothing. Therefore
until a man is nothing, God can make
nothing out of him.
MARTIN LUTHER (1483–1546)

885 God is a Specialist at making something useful and beautiful out of something broken and confused.
CHARLES R. SWINDOLL (1934–)

886 God salvages the individual by liquidating him and then raising him again to
newness of life.
A. W. TOZER (1897–1963)

887 God will make us broken bread and
poured out wine to feed and nourish
others.
OSWALD CHAMBERS (1874–1917)

888 God will never plant the seed of his
life upon the soil of a hard, unbroken
spirit. He will only plant that seed
where the conviction of his Spirit has
brought brokenness, where the soil
has been watered with the tears of
repentance as well as the tears of joy.
ALAN REDPATH (1907–1989)

889 He can give us a crop in one year that
will make up for ten.
D. MARTYN LLOYD-JONES (1899–1981)

890 How does God take a Christian who
lives one-half inch from hell and make
him live one-half inch from heaven? It
is not easy. There is a price to be paid.
The divine Surgeon must be permitted
to use his scalpel to cut, cleanse, and

break, so healing can take place. In fact, such spiritual surgery is more painful than physical surgery. God doesn't use an anesthetic; he doesn't do his work while we are asleep. God can take any brokenhearted believer and make him or her a radiant, loving person. But when he performs such "heart operations," his children are wide awake.
ERWIN W. LUTZER (1941–)

891 How else but through a broken heart may Lord Christ enter in?
OSCAR WILDE (1854–1900)

892 Human beings are only bearable when the last defenses of their egos are down; when they stand, helpless and humbled, before the awful circumstances of their being. It is only thus that the point of the cross becomes clear, and the point of the cross is the point of life.
MALCOLM MUGGERIDGE (1903–1990)

893 If God is going to bless me, he must condemn and blast out of my being what he cannot bless.
OSWALD CHAMBERS (1874–1917)

894 If you . . . begin to find that the Holy Spirit is scrutinizing you, let his searchlight go straight down, and he will not only search you, he will put everything right that is wrong; he will make the past as though it had never been.
OSWALD CHAMBERS (1874–1917)

895 In love's service only broken hearts will do.
ROBERT HAROLD SCHULLER (1926–)

896 It appears as if God were sometimes most unnatural; we ask him to bless our lives and bring benedictions, and what immediately follows turns everything into actual ruin. The reason is that before God can make the heart into a garden of the Lord, he has to plough it, and that will take away a great deal of natural beauty.
OSWALD CHAMBERS (1874–1917)

897 Lord, I'm at the end
Of all my resources.

Child, you're just at the beginning of Mine.
RUTH HARMS CALKIN (1918–)

898 The only things that are improved by breaking are the hearts of sinners.

899 We must be broken into life.
CHARLES E. RAVEN

900 You fathom the depth of My own heart only to the extent that your heart is broken and your inmost consciousness torn asunder by the pain of grief.
FRANCES J. ROBERTS

BROTHERHOOD

901 A jeweled pivot on which our lives must turn is the deep realization that every person we meet in the course of a day is a dignified, essential human soul and that we are being guilty of gross inhumanity when we snub or abuse him.
JOSHUA LOTH LIEBMAN (1907–1948)

902 Brotherhood is not only a generous impulse but a divine command.
HARRY S TRUMAN (1884–1972)

903 Brotherhood: helping yourself by helping others.
ELBERT GREEN HUBBARD (1856–1915)

904 Brotherhood: to live, think, and suffer with the men of your time, as one of them.
HENRI DE LUBAC (1896–)

905 Help your brother's boat across, and lo, your own has reached the shore.

906 However wretched a fellow mortal may be, he is still a member of our common species.
LUCIUS ANNAEUS SENECA (C. 4 B.C.–A.D. 65)

907 Human blood is all one color.
SIR THOMAS FULLER (1608–1661)

908 I am not born for one corner; the whole world is my native land.
LUCIUS ANNAEUS SENECA (C. 4 B.C.–A.D. 65)

909 If all good people were clever,
And all clever people were good,
The world would be nicer than ever
We thought that it possibly could.
But somehow, 'tis seldom or never

The two hit it off as they should;
The good are so harsh to the clever,
The clever so rude to the good.
ELIZABETH WORDSWORTH (1840–1932)

910 If any little love of mine may make a
    life the sweeter,
    If any little care of mine may make a
    friend's the fleeter,
    If any little lift may ease the burden of
    another,
    God give me love and care and
    strength to help my toiling brother.

911 In Christ there is no east or west,
    In him no south or north,
    But one great fellowship of love
    Throughout the whole wide earth.
    JOHN OXENHAM (1861–1941)

912 It's silly to go on pretending that
    under the skin we are all brothers. The
    truth is more likely that under the skin
    we are all cannibals, assassins, trai-
    tors, liars, hypocrites, poltroons.
    HENRY MILLER (1891–1980)

913 Jesus throws down the dividing preju-
    dices of nationality and teaches univer-
    sal love, without distinction of race,
    merit, or rank. A man's neighbor is
    everyone that needs help.
    JOHN CUNNINGHAM GEIKIE (1826–1906)

914 Keep Jesus Christ in your hearts and
    you will recognize his face in every
    human being. You will want to help
    him out in all his needs: the needs of
    your brothers and sisters.
    POPE JOHN PAUL II (1920–   )

915 Oh, east is east and west is west,
    and never the twain shall meet,
    Till earth and sky stand presently
    at God's great judgment seat.
    But there is neither east nor west,
    border, nor breed, nor birth,
    When two strong men stand face to
    face,
    though they come from the ends of the
    earth!
    RUDYARD KIPLING (1865–1936)

916 The Christian life was not meant to
    live in a solitude forever, nor is it
    suited to it. It is a social life. All its
    movements suggest and prophesy a

brotherhood. That brotherhood of
believers is the Christian church.
PHILLIPS BROOKS (1835–1893)

917 The same heart beats in every human
    breast.

918 The will is the strong blind man who
    carries on his shoulders the lame man
    who can see.
    ARTHUR SCHOPENHAUER (1788–1860)

919 There is a destiny that makes us
    brothers;
    None goes his way alone:
    All that we send into the lives of
    others
    Comes back into our own.
    EDWIN MARKHAM (1852–1940)

920 There is no brotherhood of man with-
    out the fatherhood of God.
    HENRY MARTYN FIELD (1822–1907)

921 To know that all men are brothers is
    not only to know that all men are
    alike, but to know that all men are dif-
    ferent.
    ROBERT BURNS (1759–1796)

922 We cannot possibly let ourselves get
    frozen into regarding everyone we do
    not know as an absolute stranger.
    ALBERT SCHWEITZER (1875–1965)

923 We must learn to live together as
    brothers or perish together as fools.
    MARTIN LUTHER KING, JR. 1929–1968

924 What is brotherhood? Brotherhood is
    giving to others the rights you want to
    keep for yourself . . . giving to the indi-
    vidual in another group the same dig-
    nity, the same full appreciation that
    you want to have yourself.
    EVERETT R. CLINCHY (1896–   )

925 Without faith in the fatherhood of
    God, people have a pretty hard time
    being brotherly. They drift off into
    hate societies, or more often, into the
    society of the indifferent.
    EDWIN T. DAHLBERG (1892–1986)

926 Yes, you'd know him for a heathen
    If you judged him by the hide,
    But bless you, he's my brother,
    For he's just like me inside.
    ROBERT FREEMAN (1878–1940)

BURDENS

927 A burden shared is a lighter load.

928 God gives the shoulder according to the burden.
GERMAN PROVERB

929 I do not pray for a lighter load, but for a stronger back.
PHILLIPS BROOKS (1835–1893)

930 I have read in Plato and Cicero sayings that are very wise and very beautiful; but I never read in either of them: "Come unto me all ye that labour and are heavy laden."
SAINT AUGUSTINE OF HIPPO (354–430)

931 Life has burdens that no one can escape. Christianity does not remove the load: it teaches us how to bear the burdens that fall rightfully to us.

932 Money and time are the heaviest burdens of life. Unhappiest are those who have more of either than they know how to use.
SAMUEL JOHNSON (1709–1784)

933 Most churches have little emphasis on bearing one another's burdens. Indeed, the people do not know one another's burdens even exist, let alone be concerned enough to bear them.
ERWIN W. LUTZER (1941–)

934 No burden is too heavy when it is carried with love.

935 No man ever sank under the burden of the day. It is when tomorrow's burden is added to the burden of today that the weight is more than a man can bear. Never load yourself so. If you find yourself so loaded, at least remember this: it is your own doing, not God's. He begs you to leave the future to him, and mind the present.
GEORGE MACDONALD (1824–1905)

936 The truest help we can render an afflicted man is not to take his burden from him, but to call out his best strength that he may be able to bear the burden.
PHILLIPS BROOKS (1835–1893)

937 We must distinguish between the burden-bearing that is right and the burden-bearing that is wrong. We ought never to bear the burden of sin or doubt, but there are burdens placed on us by God which he does not intend to lift off. He wants us to roll them back on him.
OSWALD CHAMBERS (1874–1917)

BURNOUT

938 Beware of Christian activities instead of Christian being. The reason workers come to stupendous collapses is that their work is the evidence of a heart that evades facing the truth of God for itself—"I have no time for prayer, for Bible study, I must be always at it."
OSWALD CHAMBERS (1874–1917)

939 Collapse in the Christian life is seldom a blowout; it is usually a slow leak.
PAUL E. LITTLE

940 It is impossible to get exhausted in work for God. We get exhausted because we try to do God's work in our own way.
OSWALD CHAMBERS (1874–1917)

941 It is our best work that God wants, not the dregs of our exhaustion. I think he must prefer quality to quantity.
GEORGE MACDONALD (1824–1905)

942 Taking out without putting in soon comes to the bottom.

943 The bow too tensely strung is easily broken.
PUBLILIUS SYRUS (FIRST CENTURY B.C.)

944 Work without a love relationship spells burnout.
LLOYD JOHN OGILVIE (1930–)

945 You're through. Finished. Burned out. Used up. You've been replaced . . . forgotten. That's a lie!
CHARLES R. SWINDOLL (1934–)

C

CERTAINTY

946 Ah, what a dusty answer gets the soul
when hot for certainties in this our life!
GEORGE MEREDITH (1828–1909)

947 Change and decay in all around I see:
O thou who changest not,
    abide with me.
HENRY FRANCIS LYTE (1793–1847)

948 Earth changes, but thy soul and God
stand sure.
ROBERT BROWNING (1812–1889)

949 Guessing turns to certainty when the
mind of man and the Spirit of God
meet.
WILLIAM BARCLAY (1907–1978)

950 If we begin with certainties, we shall
end in doubts; but if we begin with
doubts, and are patient in them, we
shall end in certainties.
FRANCIS BACON (1561–1626)

951 It is not certain that everything is
uncertain.
BLAISE PASCAL (1623–1662)

952 Security is never the friend of faith. It
is peril that produces steadfastness.

When the church is secure, she gains
too many freedoms. She enjoys the
freedom to doubt, the freedom to
major on minor issues and the freedom to indulge herself in community
acceptance.
CALVIN MILLER

953 There are very few certainties that
touch us all in this mortal experience,
but one of the absolutes is that we will
experience hardship and stress at some
point.
JAMES C. DOBSON (1936–)

954 There is nothing certain in a man's life
but that he must lose it.
OWEN MEREDITH (1831–1891)

955 What an imperturbable certainty there
is about the man who is in contact
with the real God!
OSWALD CHAMBERS (1874–1917)

956 When I was young I was sure of everything; in a few years, having been mistaken a thousand times, I was not half
so sure of most things as I was before;
at present, I am hardly sure of any-

thing but what God has revealed to me.
JOHN WESLEY (1703–1791)

CHANGE

957 An Eastern monarch once charged his wise men to invent him a sentence to be ever in view, and which should be true and appropriate in all times and situations. They presented him with the words: "And this, too, shall pass away." How much it expresses! How chastening in the hour of pride! How consoling in the depths of affliction!
ABRAHAM LINCOLN (1809–1865)

958 Be not the first by whom the new are tried,
Nor yet the last to lay the old aside.
ALEXANDER POPE (1688–1744)

959 Change is the handmaiden nature requires to do her miracles with.
MARK TWAIN (1835–1910)

960 Change is the nursery of music, joy, life, and eternity.
JOHN DONNE (1572–1631)

961 Christians are supposed not merely to endure change, nor even to profit by it, but to cause it.
HARRY EMERSON FOSDICK (1878–1969)

962 Every day we are changing, every day we are dying.
SAINT JEROME (C. 374–420)

963 Every end is a new beginning.
ROBERT HAROLD SCHULLER (1926–   )

964 Everyone thinks of changing the world, but no one thinks of changing himself.
LEO TOLSTOY (1828–1910)

965 Everything changes but change itself.
JOHN FITZGERALD KENNEDY (1917–1963)

966 Everything in life that we really accept undergoes a change. So suffering must become love.
KATHERINE MANSFIELD (1888–1923)

967 He would not change the ground whereon I stood;
He would not take the bad and make it good;

He would not part the waters of the sea—
The only thing that he would change was me.
BRELAND

968 If we try to resist loss and change or to hold on to blessings and joy belonging to a past which must drop away from us, we postpone all the new blessings awaiting us on a higher level and find ourselves left in a barren, bleak winter of sorrow and loneliness.
HANNAH HURNARD (1905–1990)

969 If you're going through difficult times today, hold steady. It will change soon. If you are experiencing smooth sailing and easy times now, brace yourself. It will change soon. The only thing you can be certain of is change.
JAMES C. DOBSON (1936–   )

970 In this life we will encounter hurts and trials that we will not be able to change; we are just going to have to allow them to change us.
RON LEE DAVIS

971 Keep changing. When you're through changing, you're through.
BRUCE FAIRFIELD BARTON (1886–1967)

972 Nothing is really important in life, not even the relationships that blossom in a healthy home. In time, we must release our grip on everything we hold dear.
JAMES C. DOBSON (1936–   )

973 O Lord! my heart is sick,
Sick of this everlasting change;
And life runs tediously quick
Through its unresting race and varied range:
Change finds no likeness to itself in thee,
And wakes no echo in thy mute eternity.
FREDERICK WILLIAM FABER (1814–1863)

974 Once in Persia reigned a king
Who upon his signet ring
Graved a maxim true and wise,
Which if held before the eyes
Gave him counsel at a glance
Fit for every change and chance.

Solemn words, and these are they:
"Even this shall pass away."
THEODORE TILTON (1835–1907)

975 People can cry much easier than they
can change.
JAMES BALDWIN (1924–   )

976 The dogmas of the quiet past are inadequate to the stormy present. The occasion is piled high with difficulty, and
we must rise with the occasion. As our
case is new, so we must think anew
and act anew. We must disenthrall ourselves.
ABRAHAM LINCOLN (1809–1865)

977 The immutability of God appears in
its most perfect beauty when viewed
against the mutability of men. In God
no change is possible; in men change is
impossible to escape. Neither the man
is fixed nor his world, and he and it
are in constant flux.
A. W. TOZER (1897–1963)

978 The old order changeth, yielding place
    to new,
And God fulfills himself in many ways.
ALFRED, LORD TENNYSON (1809–1892)

979 The president of today is the postage
stamp of tomorrow.

980 The reasonable man adapts himself to
the world: the unreasonable one persists in trying to adapt the world to
himself. Therefore all progress
depends on the unreasonable man.
GEORGE BERNARD SHAW (1856–1950)

981 Today is not yesterday. We ourselves
change. How then, can our works and
thoughts, if they are always to be the
fittest, continue always the same.
Change, indeed, is painful, yet ever
needful; and if memory have its force
and worth, so also has hope.
THOMAS CARLYLE (1795–1881)

982 We live in a moment of history where
change is so speeded up that we begin
to see the present only when it is
already disappearing.
R. D. LAING (1927–   )

983 Weep not that the world changes—did
it keep a stable, changeless state, it
were a cause indeed to weep.
WILLIAM CULLEN BRYANT (1794–1878)

984 When I came to believe in Christ's
teaching, I ceased desiring what I had
wished for before. The direction of my
life, my desires, became different.
What was good and bad had changed
places.
LEO TOLSTOY (1828–1910)

985 You cannot step twice into the same
river, for other waters are continually
flowing on.
HERACLITUS (C. 540–C. 480 B.C.)

CHARACTER

986 A bad tree does not yield good apples.
DANISH PROVERB

987 A credible message needs a credible
messenger because charisma without
character is catastrophe.
PETER KUZMIC

988 A crooked stick will have a crooked
shadow.

989 A lizard on a cushion will still seek
leaves.
RUSSIAN PROVERB

990 A man is what he is—not what he
used to be.
JEWISH PROVERB

991 A man never discloses his own character so clearly as when he describes
another's.
JOHANN PAUL FRIEDRICH RICHTER
(1763–1825)

992 A man shows his character by what he
laughs at.
GERMAN PROVERB

993 Be not angry that you cannot make
others as you wish them to be since
you cannot make yourself as you wish
to be.
THOMAS À KEMPIS (C. 1380–1471)

994 Be what thou seemest! Live thy creed!
HORATIUS BONAR (1808–1889)

995 Cast off everything that is not yourself.
PERSIUS (34–62)

996 Character builds slowly, but it can be torn down with incredible swiftness.
FAITH BALDWIN (1893–1978)

997 Character gives splendor to youth and awe to wrinkled skin and gray hairs.
RALPH WALDO EMERSON (1803–1882)

998 Character in a saint means the disposition of Jesus Christ persistently manifested.
OSWALD CHAMBERS (1874–1917)

999 Character is always lost when a high ideal is sacrificed on the altar of conformity and popularity.
CHARLES R. SWINDOLL (1934–)

1000 Character is distilled out of our daily confrontation with temptation, out of our regular response to the call of duty. It is formed as we learn to cherish principles and to submit to self-discipline. Character is the sum total of all the little decisions, the small deeds, the daily reactions to the choices that confront us. Character is not obtained instantly. We have to mold and hammer and forge ourselves into character. It is a distant goal to which there is no shortcut.
SIDNEY GREENBERG

1001 Character is like a tree and reputation like its shadow. The shadow is what we think of it; the tree is the real thing.
ABRAHAM LINCOLN (1809–1865)

1002 Character is not made in a crisis—it is only exhibited.
ROBERT FREEMAN (1878–1940)

1003 Character is simply habit long continued.
PLUTARCH (C. 46–AFTER 119)

1004 Character is that which can do without success.
RALPH WALDO EMERSON (1803–1882)

1005 Character is what you are in the dark.
DWIGHT LYMAN MOODY (1837–1899)

1006 Do not eat garlic and you will not smell of garlic.
ARABIAN PROVERB

1007 Eccentricity has always abounded when and where strength of character has abounded; and the amount of eccentricity in a society has usually been proportional to genius, mental vigor, and moral courage.
JOHN STUART MILL (1806–1873)

1008 Every human being is intended to have a character of his own; to be what no other is, and to do what no other can do.
CHANNING POLLOCK (1880–1946)

1009 Expedients are for the hour; principles for the ages.
HENRY WARD BEECHER (1813–1887)

1010 Fame is vapor, popularity an accident, riches take wings. Only one thing endures and that is character.
HORACE GREELEY (1811–1872)

1011 Go put your creed into your deed, nor speak with double tongue.
RALPH WALDO EMERSON (1803–1882)

1012 God alters our disposition, but he does not make our character. When God alters my disposition, the first thing the new disposition will do is to stir up my brain to think along God's line. As I begin to think, begin to work out what God has worked in, it will become character. Character is consolidated thought. God makes me pure in heart; I must make myself pure in conduct.
OSWALD CHAMBERS (1874–1917)

1013 God does not pass out packages of spiritual victory sent special delivery to the person who requests them. Your sin cost him the death of his Son; he is not about to hand out spiritual bandages. He uses your struggles to give you a thorough housecleaning, reorganize your priorities, and make you dependent on his grace. There are no cheap, easy miracles. You must want spiritual freedom, not merely for your own sake, but for God's sake as well.
ERWIN W. LUTZER (1941–)

1014 God does not supply us with character, he gives us the life of his Son, and we can either ignore him and refuse to obey him, or we can so obey him, so bring every thought and imagination into captivity, that the life of Jesus is manifested in our mortal flesh. It is not a question of being saved from

hell, but of being saved in order to manifest the Son of God in our mortal flesh. Our responsibility is to keep ourselves fit to manifest him.
OSWALD CHAMBERS (1874–1917)

1015 God has a program of character development for each one of us. He wants others to look at our lives and say, "He walks with God, for he lives like Christ."
ERWIN W. LUTZER (1941–   )

1016 God is more concerned about our character than our comfort. His goal is not to pamper us physically but to perfect us spiritually.
PAUL W. POWELL

1017 Human improvement is from within outward.
JAMES ANTHONY FROUDE (1818–1894)

1018 I would be true, for there are those
    who trust me;
  I would be pure, for there are those
    who care;
  I would be strong, for there is much to
    suffer;
  I would be brave, for there is much to
    dare.
  I would be friend of all—the foe, the
    friendless;
  I would be giving, and forget the gift,
  I would be humble, for I know my
    weakness,
  I would look up, and laugh, and love,
    and lift.
HOWARD ARNOLD WALTER (1883–1918)

1019 I've seen the difference character makes in individual football players. Give me a choice between an outstanding athlete with poor character and a lesser athlete of good character, and I'll choose the latter every time. The athlete with good character will often perform to his fullest potential and be a successful football player, while the outstanding athlete with poor character will usually fail to play up to his potential and often won't even achieve average performance.
TOM LANDRY (1924–   )

1020 If I take care of my character, my reputation will take care of itself.
DWIGHT LYMAN MOODY (1837–1899)

1021 If not seemly, do it not; if not true, say it not.
GREEK PROVERB

1022 If the deal isn't good for the other party, it isn't good for you.
B. C. FORBES

1023 If you think about what you ought to do for other people, your character will take care of itself.
WOODROW WILSON (1856–1924)

1024 In education everything is built up on difficulty, there is always something to overcome. And this is true in the spiritual world. If the world, the flesh, and the devil have knocked you out once, get up and face them again, and again, until you have done with them. That is how character is made in the spiritual domain as well as in the natural.
OSWALD CHAMBERS (1874–1917)

1025 It is better to be hated for what you are than loved for what you are not.
ANDRÉ GIDE (1869–1951)

1026 It is easy to be nice, even to an enemy, from lack of character.
DAG HAMMARSKJÖLD (1905–1961)

1027 It is not the brains that matter most, but that which guides them—the character, the heart, generous qualities, progressive ideas.
FYODOR MIKHAYLOVICH DOSTOYEVSKI (1821–1881)

1028 It is with trifles, and when he is off guard, that a man best reveals his character.
ARTHUR SCHOPENHAUER (1788–1860)

1029 More is at stake than your personal victory. Conflict is the main ingredient in God's character development program.
ERWIN W. LUTZER (1941–   )

1030 Most of man's psychological makeup is probably due to his body: when his body dies, all that will fall off him, and the real central man, the thing that chose, that made the best or the worst out of this material, will stand

naked. All sorts of nice things which we thought our own, but which were really due to a good digestion, will fall off some of us; all sorts of nasty things which were due to complexes or bad health will fall off others. We shall then, for the first time, see everyone as he really was. There will be surprises.
C. S. LEWIS (1898–1963)

1031 Not in the clamor of the crowded street,
Not in the shouts and plaudits of the throng,
But in ourselves, are triumph and defeat.
HENRY WADSWORTH LONGFELLOW (1807–1882)

1032 Our echoes roll from soul to soul and grow forever and forever.
ALFRED, LORD TENNYSON (1809–1892)

1033 Our outward imperfections are a reminder of God's priorities. He is concerned with character, not the deception of outward beauty.
ERWIN W. LUTZER (1941–   )

1034 Personality has the power to open many doors, but character keeps them open.

1035 Reputation is what folks think you are. Personality is what you seem to be. Character is what you really are.
ALFRED ARMAND MONTAPERT

1036 Reputation is what men and women think of us. Character is what God and the angels know of us.
THOMAS PAINE (1737–1809)

1037 Right is right, even if everyone is against it; and wrong is wrong, even if everyone is for it.
WILLIAM PENN (1644–1718)

1038 Show me the man you honor, and I will know what kind of a man you are.
THOMAS CARLYLE (1795–1881)

1039 So live that you would not mind selling your pet parrot to the town gossip.
WILL ROGERS (1879–1935)

1040 Some people strengthen the society just by being the kind of people they are.
JOHN W. GARDNER (1912–   )

1041 Sow a thought and you reap an act;
Sow an act and you reap a habit;
Sow a habit and you reap a character;
Sow a character and you reap a destiny.
SAMUEL SMILES (1812–1904)

1042 Talent is nurtured in solitude; character is formed in the stormy billows of the world.
JOHANN WOLFGANG VON GOETHE (1749–1832)

1043 The best thing to give to your enemy is forgiveness; to an opponent, tolerance; to a friend, your heart; to your child, a good example; to a father, deference; to your mother, conduct that will make her proud of you; to yourself, respect; to all men, charity.
ARTHUR JAMES BALFOUR (1848–1930)

1044 The expression of Christian character is not good doing, but God-likeness. If the Spirit of God has transformed you within, you will exhibit divine characteristics in your life, not good human characteristics. God's life in us expresses itself as God's life, not as human life trying to be godly. The secret of a Christian is that the supernatural is made natural in him by the grace of God, and the experience of this works out in the practical details of life, not in times of communion with God.
OSWALD CHAMBERS (1874–1917)

1045 The highest reward for man's toil is not what he gets for it, but what he becomes by it.
JOHN RUSKIN (1819–1900)

1046 The lions didn't eat Daniel because he was grit and backbone.

1047 The measure of a man's real character is what he would do if he knew he never would be found out.
THOMAS BABINGTON MACAULAY (1800–1859)

1048 The most fatiguing activity in the world is the drive to seem other than you are; it is less exhausting to become what you want to be than to maintain a facade.
SYDNEY J. HARRIS (1917–1986)

1049 The most important part of us is the part that no one ever sees.
ERWIN W. LUTZER (1941–)

1050 The revelation of God to me is determined by my character, not by God's. If I am mean, that is how God will appear to me. 'Tis because I am mean, thy ways so oft look mean to me.
OSWALD CHAMBERS (1874–1917)

1051 There is a difference between one who does right because of his own conscience and him who is kept from wrongdoing because of the presence of others.

1052 There is a kind of character in thy life, That to the observer doth thy history Fully unfold.
WILLIAM SHAKESPEARE (1564–1616)

1053 To judge a man's character by only one of its manifestations is like judging the sea by a jugful of its water.
PAUL ELDRIGE

1054 Unless the vessel is clean, what you pour into it turns sour.
LATIN PROVERB

1055 Very few people in this world would care to listen to the real defense of their own characters. The real defense, the defense which belongs to the Day of Judgment, would make such damaging admissions, would clear away so many artificial virtues, would tell such tragedies of weakness and failure, that a man would sooner be misunderstood and censured by the world than exposed to that awful and merciless eulogy.
G. K. CHESTERTON (1874–1936)

1056 We live in deeds, not years; in thoughts, not breaths; in feelings, not in figures on a dial. We should count time by heartthrobs. He most lives who thinks most, feels the noblest, acts the best.
PHILIP JAMES BAILEY (1816–1902)

1057 We must never put character in the place of faith. Our character can never be meritorious before God; we stand before God on the basis of his grace.

Character is the evidence that we are built on the right foundation.
OSWALD CHAMBERS (1874–1917)

1058 What lies behind us and what lies before us are tiny matters compared to what lies within us.
RALPH WALDO EMERSON (1803–1882)

1059 What we have to be is what we are.
THOMAS MERTON (1915–1968)

1060 What we stand up for proves what our character is like. If we stand up for our reputation, it is a sign it needs standing up for! God never stands up for his saints, they do not need it. The devil tells lies about men, but no slander on earth can alter a man's character.
OSWALD CHAMBERS (1874–1917)

1061 What you are thunders so loud that I cannot hear what you say to the contrary.
RALPH WALDO EMERSON (1803–1882)

1062 What you possess in the world will be found at the day of your death to belong to someone else, but what you are will be yours forever.
HENRY VAN DYKE (1852–1933)

1063 When the fight begins within himself, A man's worth something.
ROBERT BROWNING (1812–1889)

1064 When the Spirit of God moves into a man's heart, he will make that man generous, but he will never make a fool out of him. He will make the man happy, but he will never make him silly. He may make him sad with the woe and the weight of the world's grief, but he will never let him become a gloomy cynic. The Holy Spirit will make him warmhearted and responsive, but he will never cause him to do things of which he will be ashamed later.
A. W. TOZER (1897–1963)

1065 When we see men of worth, we should think of becoming like them; when we see men of a contrary character, we

should turn inward and examine ourselves.
FRANÇOIS ALEXANDRE FRÉDÉRIC, DUC DE LA ROCHEFOUCAULD-LIANCOURT (1747–1827)

1066 When wealth is lost, nothing is lost;
When health is lost, something is lost;
When character is lost, all is lost!
GERMAN PROVERB

1067 You are not a better person because you are praised; neither are you any worse if somebody denigrates you. God knows what you are. People consider actions, but God evaluates intentions.
THOMAS À KEMPIS (C. 1380–1471)

1068 You are only what you are when no one is looking.
ROBERT C. EDWARDS

1069 You can't make a good cloak out of bad cloth.
SPANISH PROVERB

1070 You cannot carve rotten wood.
CHINESE PROVERB

1071 You cannot dream yourself into a character; you must hammer and forge yourself one.
JAMES ANTHONY FROUDE (1818–1894)

1072 I stand before my neighbors on my character; but in heaven I have no standing myself at all. I stand there in the character of my Savior.
PAUL DANIEL RADER (1879–1938)

CHARITY

1073 Charity is helping a man to help himself.
MOSES MAIMONIDES (1135–1204)

1074 Charity is money put to interest in the other world.
ROBERT SOUTHEY (1774–1843)

1075 Charity is never lost. It may meet with ingratitude, or be of no service to those on whom it was bestowed, yet it ever does a work of beauty and grace upon the heart of the giver.
CONYERS MIDDLETON (1683–1750)

1076 Charity is the scope of all God's commands.
SAINT JOHN CHRYSOSTOM C. 347–407

1077 If you haven't got any charity in your heart, you have the worse kind of heart trouble.
BOB HOPE (1903–   )

1078 In charity there is no excess.
FRANCIS BACON (1561–1626)

1079 In faith and hope the world will disagree,
But all mankind's concern is charity.
ALEXANDER POPE (1688–1744)

1080 Never to judge rashly; never to interpret the actions of others in an ill-sense, but to compassionate their infirmities, bear their burdens, excuse their weaknesses, and make up for their defects—to hate their imperfections, but love themselves, this is the true spirit of charity.
NICHOLAS CAUSSIN (1583–1651)

1081 The charity that hastens to proclaim its good deeds ceases to be charity and is only pride and ostentation.
WILLIAM HUTTON (1723–1815)

1082 The highest exercise of charity is charity toward the uncharitable.
J. S. BUCKMINSTER

1083 This only is charity, to do all that we can.
JOHN DONNE (1572–1631)

1084 True charity is the desire to be useful to others without thought of recompense.
EMANUEL SWEDENBORG (1688–1772)

1085 What is charity?
It's silence when your words would hurt
It's patience when your neighbor's hurt
It's deafness when scandal flows
It's thoughtfulness for another's woes
It's promptness when a stern duty calls
It's courage when misfortune falls.

CHEERFULNESS

1086 Burdens become light when cheerfully borne.
OVID (43 B.C.–A.D. 17)

1087 Cheerfulness and contentment are great beautifiers and are famous preservers of good looks.
CHARLES DICKENS (1812–1870)

1088 Cheerfulness in most cheerful people is the rich and satisfying result of strenuous discipline.
EDWIN PERCY WHIPPLE (1819–1886)

1089 Cheerfulness is health; its opposite, melancholy, is disease.
THOMAS CHANDLER HALIBURTON (1796–1865)

1090 Cheerfulness is no sin, nor is there any grace in a solemn cast of countenance.
JOHN NEWTON (1725–1807)

1091 Cheerfulness is the atmosphere in which all things thrive.
JOHANN PAUL FRIEDRICH RICHTER (1763–1825)

1092 Cheerfulness keeps up a kind of daylight in the mind and fills it with a steady and perpetual serenity.
JOSEPH ADDISON (1672–1719)

1093 Cheerfulness removes the rust from the mind, lubricates our inward machinery, and enables us to do our work with fewer creaks and groans.

1094 Cheerfulness: a habit of the mind . . . fixed and permanent.
JOSEPH ADDISON (1672–1719)

1095 Cheerfulness: the habit of looking at the good side of things.
WILLIAM BERNARD ULLANTHORNE (1806–1889)

1096 I wonder many times that ever a child of God should have a sad heart, considering what the Lord is preparing for him.
SAMUEL RUTHERFORD (1600–1661)

1097 If I can put one thought of rosy sunset into the life of any man or woman, I shall feel that I have worked with God.
GEORGE MACDONALD (1824–1905)

1098 Keep your face to the sunshine and you cannot see the shadow.
HELEN ADAMS KELLER (1880–1968)

1099 Wondrous is the strength of cheerfulness and its power of endurance—the cheerful man will do more in the same time, will do it better, will persevere in it longer, than the sad or sullen.
THOMAS CARLYLE (1795–1881)

CHILDREN

1100 A child between eighteen and thirty-six months of age is a sheer delight, but he can also be utterly maddening. He is inquisitive, short-tempered, demanding, cuddly, innocent, and dangerous at the same time. I find it fascinating to watch him run through his day, seeking opportunities to crush things, flush things, kill things, spill things, fall off things, eat horrible things—and think up ways to rattle his mother.
JAMES C. DOBSON (1936–   )

1101 A child's suffering can be very real and very deep and all the worse since a child has neither the wisdom nor the resources of mature men and women. His misery fills the whole of his world, leaving no space for other things. He has only emotions with no cynicism or resignation to dull the edges of his jealousy or suffering. Those people who think of adolescence as a happy, carefree time either possess deficient emotions or inadequate memories.
LOUIS BROMFIELD (1896–1956)

1102 A rose can say I love you,
Orchids can enthrall,
But a weed bouquet in a chubby fist,
Oh my, that says it all!

1103 A spoiled child never loves its mother.
SIR HENRY TAYLOR (1800–1886)

1104 A world without children is a world without newness, regeneration, color, and vigor.
JAMES C. DOBSON (1936–   )

1105 All children talk with integrity up to about the age of five, when they fall victim to the influences of the adult world and mass entertainment. It is then they begin, all unconsciously, to become plausible actors. The product of this process is known as maturity, or you and me.
CLIFTON FADIMAN (1904–   )

1106 Childhood: that happy period when nightmares occur only during sleep.

1107 Children are God's apostles, day by day sent forth to preach of love, and hope, and peace.
JAMES RUSSELL LOWELL (1819–1891)

1108 Children are like clocks; they must be allowed to run.
JAMES C. DOBSON (1936–)

1109 Children are natural mimics who act like their parents in spite of every attempt to teach them good manners.

1110 Children are not casual guests in our home. They have been loaned to us temporarily for the purpose of loving them and instilling a foundation of values on which their future lives will be built.
JAMES C. DOBSON (1936–)

1111 Children begin by loving their parents. As they grow older they judge them; sometimes they forgive them.
OSCAR WILDE (1854–1900)

1112 Children have never been very good at listening to their elders, but they have never failed to imitate them.
JAMES BALDWIN (1924–)

1113 Children in a family are like flowers in a bouquet: there's always one determined to face in an opposite direction from the way the arranger desires.
MARCELENE COX

1114 Children learn what they observe.
If children live with criticism, they learn to condemn and be judgmental.
If children live with hostility, they learn to be angry and fight.
If children live with ridicule, they learn to be shy and withdrawn.
If children live with shame, they learn to feel guilty.
If children live with tolerance, they learn to be patient.
If children live with encouragement, they learn confidence.
If children live with praise, they learn to appreciate.
If children live with fairness, they learn justice.
If children live with security, they learn to have faith.
If children live with approval, they learn to like themselves.
If children live with acceptance and friendship, they learn to find love in the world.
DOROTHY KNOLTE

1115 Children must be valued as our most priceless possession.
JAMES C. DOBSON (1936–)

1116 Children possess an uncanny ability to cut to the core of the issue, to expose life to the bone, and strip away the barnacles that cling to the hull of our too sophisticated pseudo-civilization. One reason for this, I believe, is that children have not mastered our fine art of deception that we call "finesse." Another is that they are so "lately come from God" that faith and trust are second nature to them. They have not acquired the obstructions to faith that come with education; they possess instead unrefined wisdom, a gift from God.
GLORIA GAITHER

1117 Gentle Jesus, meek and mild,
Look upon a little child,
Pity my simplicity,
Suffer me to come to thee.
CHARLES WESLEY (1707–1788)

1118 Give me the children until they are seven and anyone may have them afterwards.
SAINT FRANCIS XAVIER (1506–1552)

1119 How sharper than a serpent's tooth it is
To have a thankless child!
WILLIAM SHAKESPEARE (1564–1616)

1120 In praise of little children I will say
God first made man, then found a better way
For woman, but his third way was the best.
Of all created things, the loveliest
And most divine are children.
WILLIAM CANTON

1121 Kids are not a short-term loan, they are a long-term investment!

1122 Know you what it is to be a child? . . .
It is to believe in love, to believe in

loveliness, to believe in belief; it is to be so little that the elves can reach to whisper in your ear; it is to turn pumpkins into coaches, and mice into horses, lowness into liftiness, and nothing into everything, for each child has its fairy godmother in its soul.
FRANCIS THOMPSON SHELLEY (1859–1927)

1123 Sleep, my child, and peace attend thee,
All through the night;
Guardian angels God will lend thee,
All through the night;
Soft the drowsy hours are creeping,
Hill and dale in slumber steeping,
Love alone his watch is keeping—
All through the night.
OLD WELSH AIR

1124 The childhood shows the man
As morning shows the day.
JOHN MILTON (1608–1674)

1125 The difficult child is the child who is unhappy. He is at war with himself; and in consequence, he is at war with the world.
A. S. NEILL

1126 The little world of childhood with its familiar surroundings is a model of the greater world. The more intensively the family has stamped its character upon the child, the more it will tend to feel and see its earlier miniature world again in the bigger world of adult life. Naturally, this is not a conscious, intellectual process.
CARL GUSTAV JUNG (1875–1961)

1127 The Lord made Adam from the dust of the earth, but when the first toddler came along, he added electricity!

1128 The most deprived children are those who have to do nothing in order to get what they want.
SYDNEY J. HARRIS (1917–1986)

1129 The toddler is the world's most hard-nosed opponent of law and order.
JAMES C. DOBSON (1936–)

1130 There are millions of Americans who are clever and fearless . . . they are four years old.

1131 There are no illegitimate children—only illegitimate parents.
LEON R. YANKWICH (1888–)

1132 Unlike grown-ups, children have little need to deceive themselves.
JOHANN WOLFGANG VON GOETHE (1749–1832)

1133 We can hardly be surprised if children feel fairly soon that they have outgrown the "tender Shepherd" and find their heroes elsewhere.
J. B. PHILLIPS (1906–1982)

1134 What a child is taught on Sunday, he will remember on Monday.
WELSH PROVERB

1135 When childhood dies, its corpses are called adults and they enter society, one of the politer names of hell.
BRIAN ALDISS (1925–)

1136 William daily reenacts the feeding of the 5,000. We give him one small rice cake, and when he's finished, we clean up twelve baskets full of the remnants.
KENNETH L. DRAPER (1957–)

CHOICE

1137 Be entirely tolerant or not at all; follow the good path or the evil one. To stand at the crossroads requires more strength than you possess.
HEINRICH HEINE (1797–1856)

1138 Choose to love—rather than hate
Choose to smile—rather than frown
Choose to build—rather than destroy
Choose to persevere—rather than quit
Choose to praise—rather than gossip
Choose to heal—rather than wound
Choose to give—rather than grasp
Choose to act—rather than delay
Choose to forgive—rather than curse
Choose to pray—rather than despair.

1139 God always gives his very best to those who leave the choice with him.
JAMES HUDSON TAYLOR (1832–1905)

1140 God asks no one whether he will accept life. This is not the choice. The only choice you have as you go through life is how you will live it.
BERNARD MELTZER

1141 God gave us a free choice because there is no significance to love that knows no alternative.
JAMES C. DOBSON (1936–   )

1142 God has no need of marionettes. He pays men the compliment of allowing them to live without him if they choose. But if they live without him in this life, they must also live without him in the next.
LEON MORRIS

1143 God regenerates us and puts us in contact with all his divine resources, but he cannot make us walk according to his will.
OSWALD CHAMBERS (1874–1917)

1144 In darkness there is no choice. It is light that enables us to see the differences between things; and it is Christ who gives us light.
AUGUSTUS W. HARE (1792–1834)

1145 It is this way. The Lord, he is always voting for a man; and the devil, he is always voting against him. Then the man himself votes and that breaks the tie.

1146 No man need stay the way he is.
HARRY EMERSON FOSDICK (1878–1969)

1147 One day there came along that silent shore,
While I my net was casting in the sea,
A Man who spoke as never man before,
I followed him; new life began in me.
Mine was the boat, but his the voice,
And his the call, yet mine the choice.
GEORGE MACDONALD (1824–1905)

1148 One's philosophy is not best expressed in words; it is expressed in the choices one makes. . . . In the long run, we shape our lives and we shape ourselves. The process never ends until we die. And the choices we make are ultimately our responsibility.
ELEANOR ROOSEVELT (1884–1962)

1149 Our destiny is not determined for us, but it is determined by us. Man's free will is part of God's sovereign will. We have freedom to take which course we choose, but not freedom to determine the end of that choice. God makes clear what he desires, we must choose, and the result of the choice is not the inevitableness of law, but the inevitableness of God.
OSWALD CHAMBERS (1874–1917)

1150 The choices of time are binding in eternity.
JACK MACARTHUR

1151 The crossroads are down here: which way to pull the rein? The left brings you but loss, the right nothing but gain.
ANGELUS SILESIUS (1624–1677)

1152 The difficulty in life is the choice.
GEORGE MOORE (1852–1933)

1153 The disciple who is in the condition of abiding in Jesus is in the will of God, and his apparent free choices are God's foreordained decrees. Mysterious? Logically absurd? But a glorious truth to a saint.
OSWALD CHAMBERS (1874–1917)

1154 The teachings of Christ reveal him to be a realist in the finest meaning of that word. Nowhere in the Gospels do we find anything visionary or overoptimistic. He told his hearers the whole truth and let them make up their minds. He might grieve over the retreating form of an inquirer who could not face up to the truth, but he never ran after him to try to win him with rosy promises. He would have men follow him, knowing the cost, or he would let them go their ways.
A. W. TOZER (1897–1963)

1155 To every soul there openeth
A high way and a low;
And every man decideth
Which way his soul shall go.
JOHN OXENHAM (1861–1941)

1156 We put one foot on God's side and one on the side of human reasoning; then God widens the space until we either drop down in between or jump on to one side or the other.
OSWALD CHAMBERS (1874–1917)

1157 When you have to make a choice and don't make it, that is in itself a choice.
WILLIAM JAMES (1842–1910)

1158 Where there is no choice, we do well to make no difficulty.
GEORGE MACDONALD (1824–1905)

1159 Whoever is on God's side is on the winning side and cannot lose; whoever is on the other side is on the losing side and cannot win. Here there is no chance, no gamble. There is freedom to choose which side we shall be on but no freedom to negotiate the results of the choice once it is made. By the mercy of God we may repent a wrong choice and alter the consequences by making a new and right choice. Beyond that we cannot go.
A. W. TOZER (1897–1963)

1160 You can't do anything about the length of your life, but you can do something about its width and depth.
EVAN ESAR

CHRISTIANITY

1161 "Crucified" is the only really definitive adjective by which to describe the Christian life.
J. FURMAN MILLER

1162 A great deal of what passes for current Christianity consists in denouncing other people's vices and faults.
HENRY H. WILLIAMS

1163 Apart from Christ the life of man is a broken pillar, the race of man an unfinished pyramid. One by one in sight of eternity all human ideals fall short; one by one before the open grave all hopes dissolve.
HENRY DRUMMOND (1851–1897)

1164 Christianity can be condensed into four words: admit, submit, commit, and transmit.
SAMUEL WILBERFORCE (1805–1873)

1165 Christianity does not teach a doctrine of weakness. But the strength it gives a man is quite different from his natural strength. It is a God-directed strength, doing what God wills. It wins great victories, but they are only over evil and self, not the destructive victories that are won over others.
PAUL TOURNIER (1898–1986)

1166 Christianity has made martyrdom sublime, and sorrow triumphant.
EDWIN HUBBEL CHAPIN (1814–1880)

1167 Christianity is a battle—not a dream.
WENDELL PHILLIPS (1811–1884)

1168 Christianity is an invitation to true living, and its truth is only endorsed by actual experience. When a man becomes a committed Christian, he sooner or later sees the falsity, the illusions, and the limitations of the humanist geocentric way of thinking. He becomes (sometimes suddenly, but more often gradually) aware of a greatly enhanced meaning in life and of a greatly heightened personal responsibility. Beneath the surface of things as they seem to be, he can discern a kind of cosmic conflict in which he is now personally and consciously involved. He has ceased to be a spectator or a commentator and a certain small part of the battlefield is his alone. He also becomes aware . . . of the forces ranged against him.
J. B. PHILLIPS (1906–1982)

1169 Christianity is bread for daily use, not cake for special occasions.

1170 Christianity is more than a doctrine. It is Christ himself.
THOMAS MERTON (1915–1968)

1171 Christianity is more than a list of don'ts.
ERWIN W. LUTZER (1941–)

1172 Christianity is neither a creed nor a ceremonial, but life vitally connected with a loving Christ.
JOSIAH STRONG (1847–1916)

1173 Christianity is neither contemplation nor action. It is participation. Contemplation is looking at God as if he were an object. But if you participate in God in the sense that you let yourself be penetrated by him, you will go to the cross like him, you will go to work like him, you will clean shoes, do the washing up and the cooking, all like him. You cannot do otherwise because you will have become part of him. You will do what he loves to do.
LOUIS EVELY (1910–)

1174 Christianity is not "an idea in the air." It is feet on the ground going God's way.
FREDERICK W. BRINK

1175 Christianity is not a religion, it is a relationship.
ROBERT B. THIEME

1176 Christianity is not devotion to work, or to a cause, or a doctrine, but devotion to a person, the Lord Jesus Christ.
OSWALD CHAMBERS (1874–1917)

1177 Christianity is the good man's text; his life, the illustration.
JOSEPH PARRISH THOMPSON (1819–1879)

1178 Christianity is the land of beginning again.
W. A. CRISWELL (1909–)

1179 Christianity is the power of God in the soul of man.
ROBERT BOYD MUNGER (1910–)

1180 Christianity isn't only going to church on Sunday. It is living twenty-four hours of every day with Jesus Christ.
BILLY GRAHAM (1918–)

1181 Christianity seems at first to be all about morality, all about duties and rules and guilt and virtue, yet it leads you on, out of all that, into something beyond. One has a glimpse of a country where they do not talk of those things, except perhaps as a joke. Everyone there is filled full with what we should call goodness as a mirror is filled with light. But they do not call it goodness. They do not call it anything. They are not thinking of it. They are too busy looking at the source from which it comes.
C. S. LEWIS (1898–1963)

1182 Christianity takes for granted the absence of any self-help and offers a power which is nothing less than the power of God.
A. W. TOZER (1897–1963)

1183 Christianity taught men that love is worth more than intelligence.
JACQUES MARITAIN (1882–1973)

1184 Christianity, if false, is of no importance, and, if true, of infinite impor-tance. The one thing it cannot be is moderately important.
C. S. LEWIS (1898–1963)

1185 Christianity. We cannot speak against it without anger, nor speak for it without love.
JOSEPH JOUBERT (1754–1824)

1186 Churchianity is an organization; Christianity is an organism.
OSWALD CHAMBERS (1874–1917)

1187 Civil society was renovated in every part by the teachings of Christianity. In the strength of that renewal, the human race was lifted up to better things. Nay, it was brought back from death to life.
POPE LEO XIII (1810–1903)

1188 Critics often complain that, if the world is in its present state after nineteen centuries of Christianity, then it cannot be a very good religion. They make two mistakes. In the first place Christianity—the real thing—has never been accepted on a large scale and has therefore never been in a position to control "the state of the world," though its influence has been far from negligible. In the second place, they misunderstand the nature of Christianity. It is not to be judged by its success or failure to reform the world which rejects it. It is a revelation of the true way of living, the way to know God, the way to live life of eternal quality.
J. B. PHILLIPS (1906–1982)

1189 Deity indwelling men! That, I say, is Christianity!
A. W. TOZER (1897–1963)

1190 Enemy-occupied territory—that is what this world is. Christianity is the story of how the rightful king has landed, you might say landed in disguise, and is calling us all to take part in a great campaign of sabotage. When you go to church, you are really listening in to the secret wireless from our friends: that is why the enemy is so anxious to prevent us from going.

He does it by playing on our conceit
and laziness and intellectual snobbery.
C. S. LEWIS (1898–1963)

1191 Evil repay with good, if wronged do
      no one slight,
Thank for ingratitude, that is the
      Christian life.
ANGELUS SILESIUS (1624–1677)

1192 God has never had on his side a majority of men and women. He does not
need a majority to work wonders in
history, but he does need a minority
fully committed to him and his purpose.
ERNEST FREMONT TITTLE (1885–1949)

1193 God is no fonder of intellectual slackers than of any other slackers. If you
are thinking of becoming a Christian, I
warn you you are embarking on something which is going to take the whole
of you, brains and all. But, fortunately, it works the other way round.
Anyone who is honestly trying to be a
Christian will soon find his intelligence being sharpened. One of the reasons why it needs no special education
to be a Christian is that Christianity is
an education itself. That is why an
uneducated believer like Bunyan was
able to write a book that has
astonished the whole world.
C. S. LEWIS (1898–1963)

1194 God's demands are so great that only
he can supply what he demands.
ERWIN W. LUTZER (1941–   )

1195 He is no fool who gives what he cannot keep to gain what he cannot lose.
JIM ELLIOT (1927–1956)

1196 He who shall introduce into public
affairs the principles of primitive Christianity will change the face of the
world.
BENJAMIN FRANKLIN (1706–1790)

1197 I believe in Christianity as I believe
that the sun has risen not only because
I see it but because by it I see everything else.
C. S. LEWIS (1898–1963)

1198 I believe it to be a grave mistake to
present Christianity as something

charming and popular with no offense
in it.
DOROTHY L. SAYERS (1893–1957)

1199 I have now disposed of all my property to my family. There is one thing
more I wish I could give them and that
is the Christian religion. If they had
that, and I had not given them one shilling, they would have been rich; and if
they had not that, and I had given
them all the world, they would be
poor.
PATRICK HENRY (1736–1799)

1200 I know some muddle-headed Christians have talked as if Christianity
thought that sex, or the body, or pleasure, were bad in themselves. But they
were wrong. Christianity is almost the
only one of the great religions which
thoroughly approves of the body—
which believes that matter is good,
that God himself once took on a
human body, that some kind of body
is going to be given to us even in
heaven and is going to be an essential
part of our happiness, our beauty, and
our energy. Christianity has glorified
marriage more than any other religion;
and nearly all the greatest love poetry
in the world has been produced by
Christians.
C. S. LEWIS (1898–1963)

1201 If Christianity has never disturbed us,
we have not yet learned what it is.
SIR WILLIAM TEMPLE (1628–1699)

1202 If Christianity were small enough for
our understanding, it would not be
large enough for our needs.

1203 In science we have been reading only
the notes to a poem; in Christianity we
find the poem itself.
C. S. LEWIS (1898–1963)

1204 Is your Christianity ancient history or
current events?
SAMUEL M. SHOEMAKER (1893–1963)

1205 It is . . . startling to discover how
many people there are who heartily
dislike and despise Christianity without having the faintest notion what it
is. If you tell them, they cannot believe
you. . . . They simply cannot believe

that anything so interesting, so exciting, and so dramatic can be the ortho-
dox creed of the church.
DOROTHY L. SAYERS (1893–1957)

1206 It is absurd to call Christianity a system of nonresistance; the great doctrine of Christianity is resistance "unto
blood" against sin.
OSWALD CHAMBERS (1874–1917)

1207 It is human to demand justice; it is
Christian to give it. It is human to
keep what one has; it is Christian to
share it.
E. W. CROSS

1208 It is no fault of Christianity that a hypocrite falls into sin.
SAINT JEROME (C. 374–420)

1209 It is unnatural for Christianity to be
popular.
BILLY GRAHAM (1918–)

1210 Jesus invited us, not to a picnic, but to
a pilgrimage; not to a frolic, but to a
fight. He offered us, not an excursion,
but an execution. Our Savior said that
we would have to be ready to die to
self, sin, and the world.
BILLY GRAHAM (1918–)

1211 Let us not be shocked by the suggestion that there are disadvantages to
the life in Christ. There most certainly
are. Abel was murdered, Joseph was
sold into slavery, Daniel was thrown
into the den of lions, Stephen was
stoned to death, Paul was beheaded,
and a noble army of martyrs was put
to death by various painful methods
all down the long centuries. And
where the hostility did not lead to
such violence (and mostly it did not
and does not) the sons of this world
nevertheless managed to make it tough
for the children of God in a thousand
cruel ways.
A. W. TOZER (1897–1963)

1212 Mother Teresa sees it differently.
When I asked her once what was the
difference, in her eyes, between the
welfare services and what her Missionaries of Charity do, she said that welfare workers do for an idea, a social
purpose, what she and the Missionar-

ies of Charity do for a person. What
we will do for a person is quite different from what we will do as a duty to
the society we live in, or in fulfillment
of a social idea or ideal.
MALCOLM MUGGERIDGE (1903–1990)

1213 My chief reason for choosing Christianity was because the mysteries were
incomprehensible. What's the point of
revelation if we could figure it out ourselves? If it were wholly comprehensible, then it would be just another
philosophy.
MORTIMER JEROME ADLER 1902–)

1214 My experience is that Christianity dis-
pels more mystery than it involves.
With Christianity it is twilight in the
world; without it, night.
MADAME ANNE SOPHIE SOYMANOV
SWETCHINE (1782–1857)

1215 No kingdom has ever had as many
civil wars as the kingdom of Christ.
CHARLES DE SECONDAT MONTESQUIEU
(1689–1755)

1216 One of the greatest attractions of
Christianity to me is its sheer absurdity. I love all those crazy sayings in the
New Testament—which, incidentally,
turn out to be literally true—about
how fools and illiterates and children
understand what Jesus was talking
about better than the wise, the
learned, and the venerable; about how
the poor, not the rich, are blessed, the
meek, not the arrogant, inherit the
earth, and the pure in heart, not the
strong in mind, see God.
MALCOLM MUGGERIDGE (1903–1990)

1217 One of the marks of a certain type of
bad man is that he cannot give up a
thing himself without wanting every
one else to give it up. That is not the
Christian way. An individual Christian
may see fit to give up all sorts of
things for special reasons—marriage,
or meat, or beer, or the cinema; but
the moment he starts saying the things
are bad in themselves, or looking
down his nose at other people who do
use them, he has taken the wrong turning.
C. S. LEWIS (1898–1963)

1218 Prosperity has often been fatal to
Christianity, but persecution never.
AMISH BISHOP

1219 Religion is humans trying to work
their way to God through good works.
Christianity is God coming to men
and women through Jesus Christ offering them a relationship with himself.
JOSH MCDOWELL

1220 The Christian faith has not been tried
and found wanting. It has been found
difficult and left untried.
G. K. CHESTERTON (1874–1936)

1221 The Christian life is never automatic.
ERWIN W. LUTZER (1941–)

1222 The Christian life is not a way out, but
a way through life.
BILLY GRAHAM (1918–)

1223 The Christian life is stamped all
through with impossibility. Human
nature cannot come anywhere near
what Jesus Christ demands, and any
rational being facing his demands honestly, says, "It can't be done, apart
from a miracle." Exactly.
OSWALD CHAMBERS (1874–1917)

1224 The Christian religion is like a vast
cathedral with dimly lighted windows:
standing without, you see no beauty
nor can you possibly imagine any.
Standing within, every ray of light
reveals a harmony of splendor.
NATHANIEL HAWTHORNE (1804–1864)

1225 The constant challenge in this life we
call Christian is the translation of all
we believe to be true into our day-
to-day life-style.
TIM HANSEL

1226 The deeper Christian life . . . is the
willingness to quit trying to use the
Lord for our ends and to let him work
in us for his glory.
A. W. TOZER (1897–1963)

1227 The greatest test of Christianity is the
wear and tear of daily life. It is like the
shining of silver, the more it is rubbed
the brighter it grows.
OSWALD CHAMBERS (1874–1917)

1228 The primary declaration of Christianity is not "This do!" but "This happened!"
EVELYN UNDERHILL (1875–1941)

1229 The purpose of Christianity is not to
avoid difficulty, but to produce a character adequate to meet it when it
comes. It does not make life easy;
rather it tries to make us great enough
for life.
JAMES L. CHRISTENSEN (1922–)

1230 The simplicity which is in Christ is
rarely found among us. In its stead are
programs, methods, organizations,
and a world of nervous activities
which occupy time and attention.
A. W. TOZER (1897–1963)

1231 The Spirit-filled life is not a special,
deluxe edition of Christianity. It is part
and parcel of the total plan of God for
his people.
A. W. TOZER (1897–1963)

1232 There have been, and still are, religions which are concerned with the
worship of a god or gods, but which
have no influence on man's behavior
toward man. Christianity is not like
this. The fact that the infinite God
focused himself in a man is the best
proof that God cares about people. In
the teaching of that man, Jesus Christ,
we find repeated again and again, an
insistence on love to God and love to
men being inseparably linked. He vio-
lently denounced those who divorced
religion from life. He had no use at all
for those who put up a screen of elaborate ceremonial and long prayers, and
exploited their fellowmen behind it.
J. B. PHILLIPS (1906–1982)

1233 There is no greater and more dangerous enemy of Christianity than all that
makes it small and narrow.
HENRI HUVELIN (1838–1910)

1234 There is no provision for a "privileged
class" in genuine Christianity.
J. B. PHILLIPS (1906–1982)

1235 There is simply no room for passivity
in the Christian faith. Life in Christ is
one long string of action verbs: grow
. . . praise . . . love . . . learn . . .

stretch ... reach ... put on ... put off ... press on ... follow ... hold ... cleave ... run ... weep ... produce ... stand ... fight.
JONI EARECKSON TADA

1236 To hold on to the plough while wiping our tears—this is Christianity.
WATCHMAN NEE (1903–1972)

1237 To lift up the hands in prayer gives God glory, but a man with a dungfork in his hand, a woman with a slop pail, gives him glory too. He is so great that all things give him glory if you mean they should.
GERARD MANLEY HOPKINS (1844–1889)

1238 To the corruptions of Christianity I am indeed, opposed; but not to the genuine precepts of Jesus himself. I am a Christian in the only sense in which he wished anyone to be; sincerely attached to his doctrines in preference to all others; ascribing to himself every human excellence; and believing he never claimed any other.
THOMAS JEFFERSON (1743–1826)

1239 To try to find a common ground between the message of the cross and man's fallen reason is to try the impossible, and if persisted in must result in an impaired reason, a meaningless cross, and a powerless Christianity.
A. W. TOZER (1897–1963)

1240 Unless we love God we cannot love our neighbor, and, correspondingly, unless we love our neighbor we cannot love God. Once again, there has to be a balance; Christianity is a system of such balanced obligations—to God and Caesar, to flesh and spirit, to God and our neighbor and so on. Happy the man who strikes the balance justly; to its imbalance are due most of our miseries and misfortunes, individual as well as collective.
MALCOLM MUGGERIDGE (1903–1990)

1241 We do not have to give up our reason, our intelligence, our knowledge, our faculty to judge, nor our emotions, our likes, our desires, our instincts, our conscious and unconscious aspirations, but rather to place them all in God's hands, so that he may direct, stimulate, fertilize, develop, and use them.
PAUL TOURNIER (1898–1986)

1242 Whatever is benevolent is right; whatever is malevolent or indifferent is wrong. This is the radical simplicity of the gospel's ethnic, even though it can lead situationally to the most complicated, headaching, heartbreaking calculations and gray rather than black and white decisions.
JOSEPH FLETCHER

CHRISTIANS

1243 A child of God should be a visible beatitude for joy and happiness, and a living doxology for gratitude and adoration.
CHARLES HADDON SPURGEON (1834–1892)

1244 Being a Christian means taking risks: risking that our love will be rejected, misunderstood, or even ignored.
REBECCA MANLEY PIPPERT

1245 Every Christian occupies some kind of pulpit and preaches some kind of sermon everyday.

1246 A Christian has God's honor at stake.
OSWALD CHAMBERS (1874–1917)

1247 A Christian is a living sermon whether or not he preaches a word.

1248 A Christian is
a mind through which Christ thinks;
a heart through which Christ loves;
a voice through which Christ speaks;
a hand through which Christ helps.

1249 A Christian is an oak flourishing in winter.
THOMAS TRAHERNE (C. 1637–1674)

1250 A Christian is never in a state of completion but always in the process of becoming.
MARTIN LUTHER (1483–1546)

1251 A Christian is not one who withdraws but one who infiltrates.
BILL GLASS

1252 A Christian is salt, and salt is the most concentrated thing known. Salt preserves wholesomeness and prevents

decay. It is a disadvantage to be salt. Think of the action of salt on a wound. If you get salt into a wound, it hurts, and when God's children are amongst those who are "raw" toward God, their presence hurts. The man who is wrong with God is like an open wound, and when "salt" gets in, it causes annoyance and distress and he is spiteful and bitter. The disciples of Jesus preserve society from corruption; the "salt" causes excessive irritation which spells persecution for the saint.
OSWALD CHAMBERS (1874–1917)

1253 A Christian is someone who shares the sufferings of God in the world.
DIETRICH BONHOEFFER (1906–1945)

1254 A Christian is the keyhole through which other folk see God.
ROBERT E. GIBSON

1255 A Christian is the most free of all, and subject to none; a Christian is the most dutiful servant of all, subject to everyone.
MARTIN LUTHER (1483–1546)

1256 A Christian is what he is not by ecclesiastical manipulation but by the new birth. He is a Christian because of a Spirit which dwells in him.
A. W. TOZER (1897–1963)

1257 A Christian life based on feeling is headed for a gigantic collapse.
ERWIN W. LUTZER (1941–)

1258 A Christian life is not an imitation but a reproduction of the life of Christ.
HENRY VAN DYKE (1852–1933)

1259 A devout man . . . sets eternity against time; and chooses rather to be forever great in the presence of God when he dies than to have the greatest share of worldy pleasure while he lives.
WILLIAM LAW (1686–1761)

1260 A genuine Christian is like a good watch. He has an open face, busy hands, is made of pure gold, is well-regulated, and is full of good works.

1261 A God-intoxicated man.
NOVALIS (1772–1801)

1262 A large measure of disappointment with God stems from disillusionment with other Christians.
PHILIP YANCEY (1949–)

1263 A maid, after she had been confirmed, was asked how she knew she was a Christian. "Because," she replied, "now I do not sweep the dirt under the rugs."
JOHN H. MILLER (1722–1791)

1264 A man's spiritual health is exactly proportional to his love for God.
C. S. LEWIS (1898–1963)

1265 A real Christian is an odd number anyway. He feels supreme love for one whom he has never seen, talks familiarly every day to someone he cannot see, expects to go to heaven on the virtue of another, empties himself in order to be full, admits he is wrong so he can be declared right, goes down in order to get up, is strongest when he is weakest, richest when he is poorest, and happiest when he feels worst. He dies so he can live, forsakes in order to have, gives away so he can keep, sees the invisible, hears the inaudible, and knows that which passes knowledge.
A. W. TOZER (1897–1963)

1266 A vital fringe benefit of being a Christian is the tremendous sense of identity that grows out of knowing Jesus Christ.
JAMES C. DOBSON (1936–)

1267 As his child, you are entitled to his kingdom,
The warmth, the peace, and the power of his presence,
The wisdom, the insight, and the guidance of his Spirit,
The goodness, the joy, and every supreme expression of his love.

1268 Be to the world a sign that while we as Christians do not have all the answers, we do know and care about the questions.
BILLY GRAHAM (1918–)

1269 Being a Christian is more than just an instantaneous conversion—it is a daily

process whereby you grow to be more and more like Christ.
BILLY GRAHAM (1918–)

1270 Christ cannot live his life today in this world without our mouth, without our eyes, without our going and coming, without our heart. When we love, it is Christ loving through us. This is Christianity.
LEON JOSEPH SUENENS (1904–)

1271 Christ chose an image that was familiar when he said to his disciples: "You are the salt of the earth." This was his conception of their mission—their influence. They were to cleanse and sweeten the world in which they lived, to keep it from decay, and to give a new and more wholesome flavor to human existence. Their characters were not to be passive, but active.

There is no use in saving salt for heaven. It will not be needed there. Its mission is to permeate, season, and purify things on earth.
HENRY VAN DYKE (1852–1933)

1272 Christian, are you a fool? You trust eternity
Yet cling with body and soul to temporality.
ANGELUS SILESIUS (1624–1677)

1273 Christians can be like a sack of marbles—unfeeling, unloving, just *clacking* against each other as they go through life. Or, they can be *caring* people—like a sack of grapes pressing together to provide a soft loving place to cushion and comfort each other from the hard crushes of life.
CHARLES R. SWINDOLL (1934–)

1274 Christians may not see eye to eye, but they should walk arm in arm.

1275 Christians must see and hear something for themselves if they are to escape religious stultification. Effete catchwords cannot save them. Meanings are expressed in words, but it is one of the misfortunes of life that words tend to persist long after their meanings have departed with the result that thoughtless men and

women believe they have the reality because they have the word for it.
A. W. TOZER (1897–1963)

1276 Christians often ignore any thought of walking by the Spirit because they think they are not good enough. Their life is too filled with fleshly struggles. But that's like refusing to accept medicine until you get well and feel worthy of it!
ERWIN W. LUTZER (1941–)

1277 Christians should be in the vanguard. The church of Jesus Christ is the most universal body in the world today. All we need to do is truly obey the One we rightly worship. But to obey will mean to follow. And he lives among the poor and oppressed, seeking justice for those in agony.
RONALD J. SIDER

1278 Dost thou see a soul with the image of God in him? Love him, love him. Say to thyself, "This man and I must go to heaven together someday."
JOHN BUNYAN (1628–1688)

1279 Every believer is God's miracle.
PHILIP JAMES BAILEY (1816–1902)

1280 Faith makes a Christian; life proves a Christian; trials confirm a Christian; and death crowns a Christian.
JOHANN GEORG CHRISTIAN HOPFNER (1765–1827)

1281 Fearless devotion to Jesus Christ ought to mark the saint today, but more often it is devotion to our set that marks us. We are more concerned about being in agreement with Christians than about being in agreement with God.
OSWALD CHAMBERS (1874–1917)

1282 Following Christ is a hard, rugged life. There is nothing easy or sissy about it.
BILLY GRAHAM (1918–)

1283 For the Christian, to do wrong, is to wound his Friend.
WILLIAM TEMPLE (1881–1944)

1284 God calls us to live a life we cannot live, so that we must depend on him for supernatural ability. We are called

to do the impossible, to live beyond
our natural ability.
ERWIN W. LUTZER (1941–)

1285 God entrusted his reputation to ordinary people. Yet in some way invisible to us, those ordinary people filled with the Spirit are helping to restore the universe to its place under the reign of God. At our repentance, the angels rejoice. By our prayers, mountains are moved.
PHILIP YANCEY (1949–)

1286 Going to church doesn't make you a Christian any more than going to a garage makes you an automobile.
BILLY SUNDAY (1862–1935)

1287 How long does it take to become a Christian? A moment—and a lifetime.
LOUIS CASSELS (1922–1974)

1288 If a man cannot be a Christian in the place where he is, he cannot be a Christian anywhere.
HENRY WARD BEECHER (1813–1887)

1289 If Christ lives in us, controlling our personalities, we will leave glorious marks on the lives we touch. Not because of us but because of him.
EUGENIA PRICE (1916–)

1290 If you accept this gospel and become Christ's man, you will stumble on wonder upon wonder, and every wonder true.
BRENDAN (C. 486–578)

1291 If you are trying to be a Christian, it is a sure sign you are not one.
OSWALD CHAMBERS (1874–1917)

1292 If you were arrested for being a Christian, would there be enough evidence to convict you?
DAVID OTIS FULLER

1293 It is a bad world, an incredibly bad world. But I have discovered in the midst of it a quiet and holy people who have learned a great secret. They have found a joy which is a thousand times better than any pleasure of our sinful life. They are despised and persecuted, but they care not. They are masters of their souls. They have

overcome the world. These people are the Christians—and I am one of them.
SAINT CYPRIAN (200–258)

1294 It is an interesting thing that when he wants to get up, the Christian always starts down, for God's way is always down, even though that is contrary to common sense. It is also contrary to the finest wisdom on the earth, because the foolish things of God are wiser than anything on this earth.
A. W. TOZER (1897–1963)

1295 It is one thing to go through a crisis grandly, and another thing to go through every day glorifying God when there is no witness, no limelight, no one paying the remotest attention to us.
OSWALD CHAMBERS (1874–1917)

1296 It is strange that we rarely notice the other side of this truth: that God also visits his children with the usual problems common to all the sons of men. The Christian will feel the heat on a sweltering day; the cold will bite into his skin as certainly as into that of his unsaved neighbor; he will be affected by war and peace, booms, and depressions, without regard to his spiritual state. To believe otherwise is to go beyond the Scriptures and to falsify the experience of the saints in every age.
A. W. TOZER (1897–1963)

1297 It may be all right for angels to spend their time in visions and meditation, but if I am a Christian, I find God in the ordinary occurrences of my life.
OSWALD CHAMBERS (1874–1917)

1298 Let not it be imagined that the life of a good Christian must be a life of melancholy and gloominess; for he only resigns some pleasures to enjoy others infinitely better.
BLAISE PASCAL (1623–1662)

1299 Look in, and see Christ's chosen saint
In triumph wear his Christlike chain;
No fear lest he should swerve or faint;
His life is Christ, his death is gain.
JOHN KEBLE (1792–1866)

1300 Many Christians are staking their reputations on church attendance, religious activity, social fellowship, sessions of singing—because in all of these things they are able to lean on one another. They spend a lot of time serving as religious props for one another in Christian circles.
A. W. TOZER (1897–1963)

1301 Many of us who profess to be Christians are so busy with the mechanics of our religion that we have no time left for the spiritual part of it.
WILLIAM B. MARTIN

1302 Mediocre—most Christians are mediocre!
A. W. TOZER (1897–1963)

1303 Most Christians would be better pleased if the Lord did not inquire into their personal affairs too closely. They want him to save them, keep them happy, and take them to heaven at last, but not to be too inquisitive about their conduct or service.
A. W. TOZER (1897–1963)

1304 Much of our difficulty as seeking Christians stems from our unwillingness to take God as he is and adjust our lives accordingly.
A. W. TOZER (1897–1963)

1305 Now that I am a Christian I do have moods in which the whole thing looks very improbable; but when I was an atheist, I had moods in which Christianity looked terribly probable.
C. S. LEWIS (1898–1963)

1306 Once you say the yes of faith to Jesus and accept his blueprint for the fullness of life, the whole world can no longer revolve around you, your needs, your gratifications; you'll have to revolve around the world, seeking to bandage its wounds, loving dead men into life, finding the lost, wanting the unwanted, and leaving far behind all the selfish, parasitical concerns which drain our time and energies.
JOHN POWELL

1307 Our greatest need today is not more Christianity but more true Christians. The world can argue against Christianity as an institution, but there is no convincing argument against a person who, through the Spirit of God, has been made Christlike.
BILLY GRAHAM (1918–   )

1308 Our Lord calls to no special work; he calls to himself.
OSWALD CHAMBERS (1874–1917)

1309 People who think that once they are converted all will be happy, have forgotten Satan.
D. MARTYN LLOYD-JONES (1899–1981)

1310 Pliny: I will banish thee. Christian: Thou canst not, for the whole world is my Father's house. Pliny: I will slay thee. Christian: Thou canst not, for my life is hid with Christ in God. Pliny: I will take away thy treasures. Christian: Thou canst not, for my treasure is in heaven. Pliny: I will drive thee away from men, and thou wilt have no friends. Christian: Thou canst not, for I have a Friend from whom thou canst never separate me.
PLINY THE ELDER (23–79)

1311 Remember who your ruler is. Don't forget his daily briefing.
CARL F. H. HENRY (1913–   )

1312 So many people think themselves no longer capable to be Christians because they are unchaste, weak, and backsliding. But in fact there is a far greater number of people who will never be Christians because they think themselves just, honorable, and pure.
LOUIS EVELY (1910–   )

1313 Some Christians are like candles: they glow with a warmth that draws people to them. Then again, you have the flashlight sort of believers who seem to be able to look right through you. Christians with the gift of teaching remind me of reliable, steady light bulbs—dispelling darkness, showing things for what they truly are. Then there are the laser-types, cutting right through the tomfoolery and getting things done. Searchlight people have a way of leading others out of darkness

and guiding and directing them back to safety.
JONI EARECKSON TADA

1314 Some churches seem filled with people who can tell you the day and the hour of their conversion but who live as if God were dead.
RICHARD OWEN ROBERTS (1931–)

1315 Some seem to think our Lord said, "You are the sugar of the earth," meaning that gentleness and winsomeness without curativeness is the ideal of the Christian.
OSWALD CHAMBERS (1874–1917)

1316 Take the case of a sour old maid, who is a Christian, but cantankerous. On the other hand, take some pleasant and popular fellow, but who has never been to church. Who knows how much more cantankerous the old maid might be if she were not a Christian, and how much more likeable the nice fellow might be if he were a Christian? You can't judge Christianity simply by comparing the product in those two people; you would need to know what kind of raw material Christ was working on in both cases.
C. S. LEWIS (1898–1963)

1317 The assured Christian is more motion than notion, more work than word, more life than lip, more hand than tongue.
THOMAS BENTON BROOKS (1608–1680)

1318 The average Christian these days is a harmless enough thing. God knows. He is a child wearing with considerable self-consciousness the harness of the warrior; he is a sick eaglet that can never mount up with wings; he is a spent pilgrim who has given up the journey and sits with a waxy smile trying to get what pleasure he can from sniffing the wilted flowers he has plucked by the way.
A. W. TOZER (1897–1963)

1319 The best tests of my Christian growth occur in the mainstream of life, not in the quietness of my study.
CHARLES R. SWINDOLL (1934–)

1320 The Christian is not one who has gone all the way with Christ. None of us has. The Christian is one who has found the right road.
CHARLES L. ALLEN (1913–)

1321 The Christian is strong or weak depending upon how closely he has cultivated the knowledge of God.
A. W. TOZER (1897–1963)

1322 The Christian should resemble a fruit tree, not a Christmas tree! For the gaudy decorations of a Christmas tree are only tied on, whereas fruit grows on a fruit tree.
JOHN R. W. STOTT (1921–)

1323 The Christian who has the smile of God needs no status symbols.
LEONARD RAVENHILL (1867–1942)

1324 The initiative of the saint is not toward self-realization, but toward knowing Jesus Christ. The spiritual saint never believes circumstances to be haphazard, or thinks of his life as secular and sacred; he sees everything he is dumped down in as the means of securing the knowledge of Jesus Christ.
OSWALD CHAMBERS (1874–1917)

1325 The man who is poor in spirit is the man who has realized that things mean nothing, and that God means everything.
WILLIAM BARCLAY (1907–1978)

1326 The ordinary Christian knows and understands more about life than the greatest philosopher who is not a Christian.
D. MARTYN LLOYD-JONES (1899–1981)

1327 The people of God are not merely to mark time, waiting for God to step in and set right all that is wrong. Rather, they are to model the new heaven and new earth, and by so doing awaken longings for what God will someday bring to pass.
PHILIP YANCEY (1949–)

1328 The Scriptures give four names to Christians—saints, for their holiness; believers, for their faith; brethren, for their love; disciples for their knowledge.
ANDREW FULLER (1754–1815)

1329 The servant of God has a good master.
BLAISE PASCAL (1623–1662)

1330 The ship's place is in the sea, but God pity the ship when the sea gets into it. The Christian's place is in the world, but God pity the Christian if the world gets the best of him.

1331 The way we act behind the wheel is far more indicative of our walk with God than the way we act praying in a pew or smiling over a well-marked Bible.
CHARLES R. SWINDOLL (1934–)

1332 The well-defined spiritual life is not only the highest life, but it is also the most easily lived. The whole cross is more easily carried than the half. It is the man who tries to make the best of both worlds who makes nothing of either. And he who seeks to serve two masters misses the benediction of both. But he who has taken his stand, who has drawn a boundary-line sharp and deep about his religious life, who has marked off all beyond as forever forbidden ground to him, finds the yoke easy and the burden light. For this forbidden environment comes to be as if it were not. . . . And the balm of death numbing his lower nature releases him for the scarce disturbed communion of a higher life. So even here to die is gain.
HENRY DRUMMOND (1851–1897)

1333 The world does need changing, society needs changing, the nation needs changing, but we never will change it until we ourselves are changed.
BILLY GRAHAM (1918–)

1334 The world is glad of an excuse not to listen to the gospel message, and the inconsistencies of Christians is made the excuse.
OSWALD CHAMBERS (1874–1917)

1335 The world says, "What can't be cured must be endured." Christians say, "What can't be cured can be enjoyed."
JONI EARECKSON TADA

1336 There are many who agree with God in principle but not in practice.
RICHARD OWEN ROBERTS (1931–)

1337 There are religious sects whose witnesses are willing to go to jail, to be pushed around, to be lampooned for the sake of a miserable, twisted doctrine! But in our Christian ranks, we prefer to be respectable and smooth.
A. W. TOZER (1897–1963)

1338 There is a division as high as heaven and as deep as hell between the Christian and the world.
OSWALD CHAMBERS (1874–1917)

1339 There is nothing so refreshing as to watch a new Christian before he has heard too many sermons and watched too many Christians.
A. W. TOZER (1897–1963)

1340 We are called to be God's transmitters, to be completely separated from all thoughts which are contrary to his thinking, so that we may transmit his thoughts to others.
HANNAH HURNARD (1905–1990)

1341 We are never sure where a true Christian may be found. One thing we do know: the more like Christ he is, the less likely it will be that a newspaper reporter will be seeking him out.
A. W. TOZER (1897–1963)

1342 We are not criticized for being Christians, but for not being Christian enough.
LEON JOSEPH SUENENS (1904–)

1343 We are not evangelicals, or fundamentalists, or charismatics, or ecumenists, or Catholics, or Protestants; we are children of God.
STEPHEN D. WATKINS

1344 We don't have to be supersaints, just thirsty sinners.
ERWIN W. LUTZER (1941–)

1345 We get no deeper into Christ than we allow him to get into us.
JOHN HENRY JOWETT (1864–1923)

1346 We must not think of ourselves as ordinary people. We are not natural men; we are born again. God has given us his Holy Spirit.
D. MARTYN LLOYD-JONES (1899–1981)

1347 We often find that we were better persons just after our conversion than we are after many years of being a Christian. Every day that passes should make us more like Christ, but we tend to grow cooler rather than warmer.
THOMAS À KEMPIS (C. 1380–1471)

1348 We were chaff, now we are wheat;
We were dross, now we are gold;
We were ravens, now we are sheep;
We were thorns, now we are grapes;
We were thistles, now we are lilies;
We were strangers, now we are citizens;
We were harlots, now we are virgins;
Hell was our inheritance, now heaven is our possession;
We were children of wrath, now we are sons of mercy;
We were bondslaves to Satan, now we are heirs of God and co-heirs with Jesus Christ.
JAMES BISSE

1349 What gets me into the kingdom, from Christ's own statement, is not saying, "Lord, Lord," but acting "Lord, Lord."
JIM ELLIOT (1927–1956)

1350 What, dear Clement, is a Christian to do when we have so much that we feel so little need of Christ.
CALVIN MILLER

1351 When Christians meet . . . to take counsel together, their purpose is not— or should not be—to ascertain what is the mind of the majority, but what is the mind of the Holy Spirit—something which may be quite different.
MARGARET HILDA THATCHER (1925–   )

1352 When Christians say the Christ-life is in them, they do not mean simply something mental or moral. When they speak of being "in Christ" or of Christ being "in them," this is not simply a way of saying that they are thinking about Christ or copying him. They mean that Christ is actually operating through them; that the whole mass of Christians are the physical organism through which Christ acts—that we are his fingers and muscles, the cells of his body.
C. S. LEWIS (1898–1963)

1353 When the world is at its worst, Christians must be at their best.
PROVERB

1354 You are the light of the world, but the switch must be turned on.
AUSTIN ALEXANDER LEWIS

1355 You cannot have Christian principles without Christ.
DOROTHY L. SAYERS (1893–1957)

1356 [Christians] don't work in order to go to heaven; they work because they are going to heaven. Arrogance and fear are replaced with gratitude and joy.
MAX L. LUCADO (1955–   )

CHRISTMAS

1357 Ah! dearest Jesus, Holy Child,
Make thee a bed, soft, undefiled,
Within my heart, that it may be
A quiet chamber kept for thee.
MARTIN LUTHER (1483–1546)

1358 Are you willing to stoop down and consider the needs and desires of little children; to remember the weaknesses and loneliness of people who are growing old; to stop asking how much your friends love you, and to ask yourself whether you love them enough; to bear in mind the things that other people have to bear on their hearts; to trim your lamp so that it will give more light and less smoke, and to carry it in front so that your shadow will fall behind you; to make a grave for your ugly thoughts and a garden for your kindly feelings, with the gate open? Are you willing to do these things for a day? Then you are ready to keep Christmas!
HENRY VAN DYKE (1852–1933)

1359 Christmas began in the heart of God. It is complete only when it reaches the heart of man.

1360 Christmas is based on an exchange of gifts: the gift of God to man—his Son; and the gift of man to God—when we first give ourselves to God.
VANCE HAVNER

1361 Christmas is not a date. It is a state of mind.
MARY ELLEN CHASE (1887–1973)

1362 Christmas is the day that holds all time together.
ALEXANDER SMITH (1830–1867)

1363 Give the earth to Christ,
A little boy of heavenly birth,
But far from home today,
Comes down to find his ball, the earth
That sin has cast away.
O comrades, let us one and all
Join in to get him back his ball.
JOHN BANNISTER TABB (1845–1909)

1364 God grant you the light in Christmas, which is faith; the warmth of Christmas, which is love; the radiance of Christmas, which is purity; the righteousness of Christmas, which is justice; the belief in Christmas, which is truth; the all of Christmas, which is Christ.
WILDA ENGLISH

1365 How proper it is that Christmas should follow Advent. For him who looks toward the future, the manger is situated on Golgotha, and the cross has already been raised in Bethlehem.
DAG HAMMARSKJÖLD (1905–1961)

1366 It is Christmas every time you let God love others through you . . . yes, it is Christmas every time you smile at your brother and offer him your hand.
MOTHER TERESA OF CALCUTTA (1910–   )

1367 Let us . . . make a compact that, if we are both alive next year, whenever we write to one another it shall not be at Christmastime. That period is becoming a sort of nightmare to me—it means endless quill-driving!
C. S. LEWIS (1898–1963)

1368 Oh! the million Christmas mornings
When you'd lie, a babe again,
Beneath a million million trees
And hear the countless tongues chanting your name.
Ah . . . will they remember crimson
Dripping from the iron nails
And will they pray, and will they know
A whiter white than snow?
KEITH PATMAN

1369 Once in the year and only once, the whole world stands still to celebrate the advent of a life. Only Jesus claims this worldwide, undying remembrance.

1370 Or consider Christmas—could Satan in his most malignant mood have devised a worse combination of graft plus bunkum than the system whereby several hundred million people get a billion or so gifts for which they have no use, and some thousands of shop clerks die of exhaustion while selling them, and every other child in the Western world is made ill from over-eating—all in the name of the lowly Jesus?
UPTON BEALL SINCLAIR (1878–1968)

1371 Some say that ever 'gainst that season comes
Wherein our Savior's birth is celebrated,
The bird of dawning singeth all night long;
And then, they say, no spirit dare stir abroad;
The nights are wholesome; then no planets strike,
No fairy takes, nor witch hath power to charm,
So hallow'd and so gracious is the time.
WILLIAM SHAKESPEARE (1564–1616)

1372 Thanks be to God for his unspeakable Gift—
indescribable
inestimable
incomparable
inexpressible
precious beyond words.
LOIS LEBAR

1373 The simple shepherds heard the voice of an angel and found their Lamb; the wise men saw the light of a star and found their Wisdom.
ARCHBISHOP FULTON J. SHEEN (1895–1979)

1374 Though Christ a thousand times in Bethlehem be born,
If he's not born in thee thy soul is still forlorn.
ANGELUS SILESIUS (1624–1677)

1375 We rejoice in the light,
And we echo the song
That comes down through the night
From the heavenly throng.
Ay! we shout to the lovely evangel
    they bring,
And we greet in his cradle our Savior
    and King.
JOSIAH GILBERT HOLLAND (1819–1881)

1376 What can I give him,
Poor as I am?
If I were a shepherd,
I would bring a lamb;
If I were a wise man,
I would do my part;
Yet what I can I give him—
Give my heart.
CHRISTINA GEORGINA ROSSETTI
(1830–1894)

CHURCH

1377 "Where is the church at 11:25 on
Monday morning?" The church then
is in the dentist's office, in the automobile sales room and repair shop, and
out in the truck. It is in the hospital, in
the classroom, and in the home. It is in
the offices, insurance, law, real estate,
whatever it is. That is where the
church is, wherever God's people are.
They are doing what they ought to be
doing. They are honoring God, not
just while they worship in a building
but out there.
ARTHUR H. DEKRUYTER (1926–)

1378 A Christian church is a body or collection of persons, voluntarily associated
together, professing to believe what
Christ teaches, to do what Christ
enjoins, to imitate his example, cherish
his spirit, and make known his gospel
to others.
R. F. SAMPLE

1379 A church is a hospital for sinners, not
a museum for saints.
L. L. NASH

1380 A church that is soundly rooted cannot be destroyed, but nothing can save
a church whose root is dried up. No
stimulation, no advertising campaigns,
no gifts of money and no beautiful edifice can bring back life to the rootless
tree.
A. W. TOZER (1897–1963)

1381 All our Lord succeeded in doing during his life on earth was to gather
together a group of fishermen—the
whole church of God and the enterprise of our Lord on earth in a fishing
boat!
OSWALD CHAMBERS (1874–1917)

1382 An inscription over a church door:
This is the house of God. This is the
gate of heaven. (This door is locked in
the winter months).

1383 As long as you notice, and have to
count the steps, you are not yet dancing but only learning to dance. A good
shoe is a shoe you don't notice. Good
reading becomes possible when you
need not consciously think about eyes,
or light, or print, or spelling. The perfect church service would be one we
were almost unaware of; our attention
would have been on God.
C. S. LEWIS (1898–1963)

1384 Before the service speak to God. During the service let God speak to you.
After the service speak with your
neighbor.

1385 Biblically the church is an organism
not an organization—a movement, not
a monument. It is not a part of the
community; it is a whole new community. It is not an orderly gathering; it is
a new order with new values, often in
sharp conflict with the values of the
surrounding society.
CHARLES COLSON (1931–)

1386 Big doesn't necessarily mean better.
Sunflowers aren't better than violets.
EDNA FERBER (1887–1968)

1387 Church unity is internal; church
union, external. The former is the
result of spiritual and organic growth;
the latter is to a great extent the product of the organizing activity of men.
LOUIS BERKHOF (1873–1957)

1388 Church-goers are like coals in a fire.
When they cling together, they keep

the flame aglow; when they separate, they die out.
BILLY GRAHAM (1918–)

1389 Church: the only place where someone speaks to me . . . and I do not have to answer back.
CHARLES DE GAULLE (1890–1970)

1390 Churches: Soulariums
P. K. THOMAJAN

1391 Everytime I pass a church
I stop in for a visit,
So when I'm carried in
The Lord won't say,
"Who is it?"

1392 God fully expects the church of Jesus Christ to prove itself a miraculous group in the very midst of a hostile world. Christians of necessity must be in contact with the world but in being and spirit ought to be separated from the world—and as such, we should be the most amazing people in the world.
A. W. TOZER (1897–1963)

1393 God never intended his church to be a refrigerator in which to preserve perishable piety. He intended it to be an incubator in which to hatch converts.
F. LINCICOME

1394 I like the silent church before the service begins better than any preaching.
RALPH WALDO EMERSON (1803–1882)

1395 I love thy church, O God!
Her walls before thee stand,
Dear as the apple of thine eye,
And graven on thy hand.
TIMOTHY DWIGHT (1752–1817)

1396 If after kirk ye bide a wee,
There's some would like to speak to ye;
If after kirk ye rise and flee,
We'll all seem cold and stiff to ye.
The one that's in the seat wi' ye,
Is stranger here than you, may be;
All here hae got their fears and cares—
Add you your soul unto our prayers;
Be you our angel unawares.

1397 If the person who doesn't attend church because hypocrites do were consistent, he wouldn't attend anything.
OLIN MILLER

1398 In her voyage across the ocean of this world, the church is like a great ship being pounded by the waves of life's different stresses. Our duty is not to abandon ship but to keep her on her course.
SAINT BONIFACE (680–C. 754)

1399 In the average church service the most real thing is the shadowy unreality of everything. The worshiper sits in a state of suspended mentation; a kind of dreamy numbness creeps upon him; he hears words, but they do not register, he cannot relate them to anything on his own life level. . . . It does not affect anything in his everyday life. He is aware of no power, no presence, no spiritual reality.
A. W. TOZER (1897–1963)

1400 In the church of God two opposite dangers are to be recognized and avoided: they are a cold heart and a hot head.
A. W. TOZER (1897–1963)

1401 In what strange quarries and stoneyards the stones for the celestial wall are being hewn! Out of the hillsides of humiliated pride; deep in the darkness of crushed despair; in the fretting and dusty atmosphere of little cares; in the hard cruel contacts that man has with man; wherever souls are being tried and ripened, in whatever commonplace and homely ways— there God is hewing out the pillars for his temple.
PHILLIPS BROOKS (1835–1893)

1402 It is not with the motes from one's neighbor's eye that the house of God can be built, but with the beams that one takes out of one's own.
ANDRÉ GIDE (1869–1951)

1403 It is scarcely possible in most places to get anyone to attend a meeting where the only attraction is God. One can only conclude that God's professed children are bored with him, for they must be wooed to meeting with a stick of striped candy in the form of religious movies, games, and refreshments.
A. W. TOZER (1897–1963)

1404 It matters not how spiritual a church may profess to be, if souls are not saved, something is radically wrong, and the professed spirituality is simply a false experience, a delusion of the devil. People who are satisfied to meet together simply to have a good time among themselves are far away from God. Real spirituality always has an outcome.
OSWALD J. SMITH (B. 1889)

1405 It may take a crucified church to bring a crucified Christ before the eyes of the world.
WILLIAM E. ORCHARD (1877–1955)

1406 It seems to me a significant, if not a positively ominous, thing that the words *program* and *programming* occur so frequently in the language of the church these days.
A. W. TOZER (1897–1963)

1407 Market-driven churches? Whatever happened to gospel-driven churches?
WALTER B. SHURDEN

1408 Mrs. Chapman had her church for supper Monday evening.

1409 Much of the church is caught up in the success mania of American society. Often more concerned with budgets and building programs than with the body of Christ, the church places more emphasis on growth than on repentance. Suffering, sacrifice, and service have been preempted by success and self-fulfillment.
CHARLES COLSON (1931–)

1410 Never before has the church had so many degrees yet so little temperature.
VANCE HAVNER

1411 No church or other association truly thrives unless struggles and differences are alive within it.
GEORGE MACAULAY TREVELYAN (1876–1962)

1412 No other organization on the face of the earth is charged with the high calling to which the church is summoned: to confront men with Jesus Christ.
J. W. HYDE

1413 One hundred religious persons knit into a unity by careful organization do not constitute a church any more than eleven dead men make a football team.
A. W. TOZER (1897–1963)

1414 One of American Christianity's most serious evils may be the sin of sermon listening. We hear, but we do not act. God is not basically interested in our listening to sermons. He wants us to be living sermons. The church is intended to be a vibrant, redeeming community of compassion, service, love, and worship. It is not a fraternity of fans of the faith.
BEAM

1415 One of the advantages of pure congregational singing is that you can join in the singing whether you have a voice or not. The disadvantage is that your neighbor can do the same.
CHARLES DUDLEY WARNER (1829–1900)

1416 One sees the structure and says, "What a great church." The other sees the Savior and says, "What a great Christ!"
MAX L. LUCADO (1955–)

1417 Church signboard: Open on Sunday. Come early for a back seat.

1418 Our business is not to do something for the church, but to do something with it.
JOSEPH FORT NEWTON (1880–1950)

1419 Persecution has not crushed the church; power has not beaten it back; time has not abated its forces; and what is most wonderful of all, the abuses of its friends have not shaken its stability.
HORACE BUSHNELL (1802–1876)

1420 Protestantism is divided into more than 200 different groups. It would take a microscope to find the reasons—which in most cases have been forgotten.
JOHN SUTHERLAND BONNELL

1421 Some folks would close the churches because there still is sin—would they also stop medical research because there still are diseases?

1422 The atmosphere of our churches is becoming so man-centered and entertainment-oriented that the saints now must be amused and not amazed.
DONALD LLEWELLYN ROBERTS

1423 The average church has so much machinery and so little oil of the Holy Spirit that it squeaks like a threshing machine when you start it up in the fall after it has been out in the field all year.
BILLY SUNDAY (1862–1935)

1424 The chief trouble with the church is that you and I are in it.
CHARLES H. HEIMSATH (1894–)

1425 The Christian church is a society of sinners. It is the only society in the world in which membership is based upon the single qualification that the candidate shall be unworthy of membership.
CHARLES CLAYTON MORRISON (1874–1966)

1426 The church as a whole must be concerned with both evangelism and social action. It is not a case of either-or; it is both-and. Anything less is only a partial gospel, not the whole counsel of God.
ROBERT D. DEHAAN

1427 The church does not draw people in; it sends them out. It does not settle into a comfortable niche, taking its place alongside the Rotary, the Elks, and the country club. Rather, the church is to make society uncomfortable. Like yeast, it unsettles the mass around it, changing it from within. Like salt, it flavors and preserves that into which it vanishes.
CHARLES COLSON (1931–)

1428 The church does not lead the world nor echo it; she confronts it. Her note is the supernatural note.
OSWALD CHAMBERS (1874–1917)

1429 The church exists for those outside it.
WILLIAM TEMPLE (1881–1944)

1430 The church has been, and is, open to a great deal of criticism, but it has made a great deal of hard-won progress. It is, at any rate, trying to carry out the divine plan, and insofar as it is working along the lines of real truth and real love it cannot, of course, fail—anymore than God can cease to exist.
J. B. PHILLIPS (1906–1982)

1431 The church has lasted for a phenomenal length of time—longer, certainly, than any comparable institution.
MALCOLM MUGGERIDGE (1903–1990)

1432 The church has many critics but no rivals.

1433 The church is a force for good in a world bombarded with evil. It is a force for love in a world buried with hatred. It is a force for peace in a world torn with violence.
C. NEIL STRAIT

1434 The church is a workshop, not a dormitory.
ALEXANDER MACLAREN (1826–1910)

1435 The church is like a bank—the more you put into it, the more interest you have in it.

1436 The church is looking for better methods; God is looking for better men.
EDWARD MCKENDREE BOUNDS (1835–1913)

1437 The church is not a gallery for the exhibition of eminent Christians, but a school for the education of imperfect ones.
HENRY WARD BEECHER (1813–1887)

1438 The church is the only thing that is going to make the terrible world we are coming to endurable; the only thing that makes the church endurable is that it is somehow the body of Christ and that on this we are fed. It seems to be a fact that you have to suffer as much from the church as for it, but if you believe in the divinity of Christ, you endure it.
FLANNERY O'CONNOR (1925–1964)

1439 The church should consist of communities of loving defiance. Instead it consists largely of comfortable clubs of conformity. A far-reaching reformation of the church is a prerequisite if it

is to commit itself to Jesus' mission of liberating the oppressed.
RONALD J. SIDER

1440 The church was not designed to be a reservoir, ever-receiving and retaining for itself God's spiritual blessings, but rather a conduit, conveying them on and out to others everywhere.
ROBERT HALL GLOVER (1871–1947)

1441 The church with no great anguish on its heart has no great music on its lips.
KARL BARTH (1886–1968)

1442 The church, like most institutions of our society, is scared and is anxious to ingratiate itself with people, rather than to tell them the truth.
MALCOLM MUGGERIDGE (1903–1990)

1443 The enemies of Christ are triumphant, Christianity is a failure, they say, and the church of God herself looks on in pain at the shortcomings in her midst. But lo, at length from the very heart of the shadows appears the majestic figure of Jesus, his countenance is as the sun shineth in his strength, around those wounds in brow and side and hands and feet—those wounds which shelter countless thousands of broken hearts—are healing rays.
OSWALD CHAMBERS (1874–1917)

1444 The holiest moment of the church service is the moment when God's people—strengthened by preaching and sacrament—go out of the church door into the world to be the church. We don't go to church; we are the church.
ERNEST SOUTHCOTT

1445 The New Testament does not envisage solitary religion; some kind of regular assembly for worship and instruction is everywhere taken for granted in the Epistles. So we must be regular practicing members of the church. Of course we differ in temperament. Some (like you—and me) find it more natural to approach God in solitude; but we must go to church as well. For the church is not a human society of people united by their natural affinities, but the body of Christ, in which

all members, however different (and he rejoices in their differences and by no means wishes to iron them out) must share the common life, complementing and helping one another precisely by their differences.
C. S. LEWIS (1898–1963)

1446 The problem is not hostility to the church; it is indifference. For many the church is simply irrelevant; it is not even worth criticizing, it is simply to be ignored.
WILLIAM BARCLAY (1907–1978)

1447 There is not a home church and a foreign church; it is all one great work.
OSWALD CHAMBERS (1874–1917)

1448 There is one church here, so I go to it. On Sunday mornings I quit the house and wander down the hill to the white frame church in the firs. On a big Sunday there might be twenty of us there; often I am the only person under sixty and feel as though I'm on an archaeological tour of Soviet Russia. The members are of mixed denominations; the minister is a Congregationalist and wears a white shirt. The man knows God. Once, in the middle of the long pastoral prayer of intercession for the whole world—for the gift of wisdom to its leaders, for hope and mercy to the grieving and pained, succor to the oppressed, and God's grace to all—in the middle of this he stopped and burst out, "Lord, we bring you these same petitions every week." After a shocked pause, he continued reading the prayer. Because of this, I like him very much.
ANNIE DILLARD (1945–)

1449 We are producing Christian activities faster than we are producing Christian experience and Christian faith.
JOHN RALEIGH MOTT (1865–1955)

1450 We ask the leaf, "Are you complete in yourself?" and the leaf answers, "No, my life is in the branches." We ask the branch, and the branch answers, "No, my life is in the trunk." We ask the trunk, and it answers, "No, my life is in the root." We ask the root, and it answers, "No, my life is in the trunk

and the branches and the leaves. Keep the branches stripped of leaves and I shall die." So it is with the great tree of being. Nothing is completely and merely individual.
EDWARD EVERETT (1794–1865)

1451 We do not find in the gospel, that Christ has provided for the uniformity of churches, but only for their unity.
ROGER WILLIAMS

1452 We do not want, as the newspapers say, a church that will move with the world. We want a church that will move the world.
G. K. CHESTERTON (1874–1936)

1453 Went to church today, and was not greatly depressed.
ROBERT LOUIS BALFOUR STEVENSON (1850–1894)

1454 What would my church be like if every member were just like me?

1455 When I first became a Christian, about fourteen years ago, I thought that I could do it on my own, by retiring to my rooms and reading theology, and I wouldn't go to the churches and gospel halls . . . I disliked very much their hymns, which I considered to be fifth-rate poems set to sixth-rate music. But as I went on I saw the great merit of it. I came up against different people of quite different outlooks and different education, and then gradually my conceit just began peeling off. I realized that the hymns (which were just sixth-rate music) were, nevertheless, being sung with devotion and benefit by an old saint in elastic-side boots in the opposite pew, and then you realize that you aren't fit to clean those boots.
C. S. LEWIS (1898–1963)

1456 When the church fails to break the [cultural] barrier, both sides lose. Those who need the gospel message of hope and the reality of love, don't get it, and the isolated church keeps evangelizing the same people over and over until its only mission finally is to entertain itself.
CHARLES COLSON (1931–)

1457 When the church transcends culture, it can transform culture. In the Dark Ages, reform did not arise from the state but from communities of those who remained uncompromising in a compromising age.
CHARLES COLSON (1931–)

1458 Wherever the Word of God is preached and heard, there a church of God exists, even if it swarms with many faults.
JOHN CALVIN (1509–1564)

1459 When you go to church, you should actively seek something. You must not go like an empty basket, waiting passively to be filled.
ROGER WILLIAM RIIS

1460 Somehow the pressures of modern society were making it increasingly difficult for us to live by the values we had been taught. We thought our church should constitute a community of believers capable of withstanding these pressures, yet it seemed to go along with things as they were instead of encouraging an alternative. The "pillars" of the church seemed as severely trapped by material concerns and alienation as most non-Christians we knew.
DAVID JACKSON (1944–)

CIRCUMSTANCES

1461 Accept equally all God's gifts, whether they are light or darkness. Treat fruitfulness and barrenness the same way. Whether it be weakness or strength, sweetness or bitterness, temptation, distraction, pain, weariness, uncertainty or blessing, all should be received as equal from the Lord's hand.
MADAME JEANNE MARIE DE LA MOTHE GUYON (1648–1717)

1462 Accusing the times is but excusing ourselves.
SIR THOMAS FULLER (1608–1661)

1463 As the water shapes itself to the vessel that contains it, so a wise man adapts himself to circumstances.
CONFUCIUS (C. 551–479 B.C.)

1464 Blessed are those who see the hand of God in the haphazard, inexplicable, and seemingly senseless circumstances of life.
ERWIN W. LUTZER (1941–)

1465 Everything that God brings into our life is directed to one purpose: that we might be conformed to the image of Christ.
ERWIN W. LUTZER (1941–)

1466 Everything that happens to me can help me along in my Christian life.
E. STANLEY JONES (1884–1973)

1467 Firmly entrenched within every human being lies a most deceptive presupposition, namely, that circumstances and other people are responsible for our responses in life.
ERWIN W. LUTZER (1941–)

1468 He does not need to transplant us into a different field, but right where we are, with just the circumstances that surround us, he makes his sun to shine and his dew to fall upon us, and transforms the very things that were before our greatest hindrances into the chiefest and most blessed means of our growth. No difficulties in your case can baffle him. No dwarfing of your growth in years that are past, no apparent dryness of your inward springs of life, no crookedness or deformity in any of your past development, can in the least mar the perfect work that he will accomplish, if you will only put yourselves absolutely into his hands and let him have his own way with you.
HANNAH WHITHALL SMITH (1832–1911)

1469 If you can't change circumstances, change the way you respond to them.
TIM HANSEL

1470 In spring no one thinks of the snow that fell last year.
SWEDISH PROVERB

1471 It is misleading to imagine that we are developed in spite of our circumstances, we are developed because of them. It is mastery in circumstances that is needed, not mastery over them.
OSWALD CHAMBERS (1874–1917)

1472 It is never the big things that disturb us, but the trivial things. Do I believe in the circumstances that are apt to bother me just now, that Jesus Christ is not perplexed at all? If I do, his peace is mine. If I try to worry it out, I obliterate him and deserve what I get.
OSWALD CHAMBERS (1874–1917)

1473 It is through accepting the circumstances that come to us in life that self is crucified.
HANNAH HURNARD (1905–1990)

1474 Man is not the creature of circumstances, circumstances are the creatures of men. We are free agents, and man is more powerful than matter.
BENJAMIN DISRAELI (1804–1881)

1475 Nothing with God can be accidental.
HENRY WADSWORTH LONGFELLOW (1807–1882)

1476 Read not the times. Read the eternities.
HENRY DAVID THOREAU (1817–1862)

1477 Some of us can only hear God in the thunder of revivals or in public worship; we have to learn to listen to God's voice in the ordinary circumstances of life.
OSWALD CHAMBERS (1874–1917)

1478 The wise adapt themselves to circumstances, as water molds itself to the pitcher.
CHINESE PROVERB

1479 To a good man nothing that happens is evil.
GREEK PROVERB

1480 To be independent of God is ultimately to be dependent on circumstances—and a victim of circumstances.
RICHARD C. HALVERSON (1916–)

1481 We talk about "circumstances over which we have no control." None of us have control over our circumstances, but we are responsible for the way we pilot ourselves in the midst of things as they are.
OSWALD CHAMBERS (1874–1917)

CIVIL RIGHTS

1482 After all, there is but one race—humanity.
GEORGE MOORE (1852–1933)

1483 At the heart of racism is the religious assertion that God made a creative mistake when he brought some people into being.
FRIEDRICH OTTO HERTZ

1484 Hear him, ye Senates, hear this truth sublime: He who allows oppression shares the crime.
ERASMUS DARWIN (1731–1802)

1485 I want to be the white man's brother, not his brother-in-law.
MARTIN LUTHER KING, JR. (1929–1968)

1486 Jesus has a family in an interracial neighborhood called heaven.

1487 Keep not thou silent, O God! Sit no longer blind, Lord God, deaf to our prayer and dumb to our dumb suffering. Surely thou, too, art not white, O Lord, a pale, bloodless, heartless thing.
W. E. B. DU BOIS (1868–1963)

1488 Motives and forces behind racism are anti-Christ, denying that man is made in the divine image.
TREVOR HUDDLESTON (1913–)

1489 Nothing in scriptural revelation precludes an evangelical and a secular humanist from standing together against race discrimination.
CARL F. H. HENRY (1913–)

1490 Race prejudice is as thorough a denial of the Christian God as atheism.
HARRY EMERSON FOSDICK (1878–1969)

1491 Skin color does not matter to God, for he is looking upon the heart. . . . When men are standing at the foot of the cross, there are no racial barriers.
BILLY GRAHAM (1918–)

1492 The church must be a sample of the kind of humanity within which . . . economic and racial differences are surmounted. Only then will she have anything to say to the society that surrounds her about how those differences must be dealt with. Otherwise her preaching to the world a standard of reconciliation which is not her own experience will be neither honest nor effective.
JOHN HOWARD YODER

1493 The grass is still green. The lawns are as neat as ever. The same birds are still in the trees. I guess it didn't occur to them to leave just because we moved in.
MAHALIA JACKSON (1911–1972)

1494 There are many humorous things in the world; among them the white man's notion that he is less savage than the other savages.
MARK TWAIN (1835–1910)

1495 To remain neutral in a situation where the laws of the land virtually criticized God for having created men of color, was the sort of thing I could not, as a Christian, tolerate.
ALBERT JOHN LUTHULI (1898–1967)

CLERGY

1496 A minister may fill his pews, his communion roll, the mouths of the public, but what that minister is on his knees in secret before God Almighty, that he is and no more.
JOHN OWEN (1616–1683)

1497 People expect the clergy to have the grace of a swan, the friendliness of a sparrow, the strength of an eagle and the night hours of an owl—and some people expect such a bird to live on the food of a canary.
EDWARD JEFFREY

1498 People expect their priest to have the skill in sermon composition of Knox, the oratorical power of Churchill, the personal charm of a film star, the tact of royalty, the hide of a hippo, the adminstrative ability of Lord Nuffield, the wisdom of Socrates and the patience of Job.
GEOFFREY GRAY

1499 The word *layman* has crept into our vocabulary to describe the laity, that is, the vast majority of Christians who do not belong to the "professional" minis-

try known as the clergy. The use of this distinction has crippled the impact of the church on the world. Thousands of Christians have shirked their God-given responsibilities because they expect their pastor, minister, or priest (or whatever designation their church adopts) to perform all spiritual functions. The minister is expected to execute his duties so well that the people need not have any meaningful involvement in the church of Jesus Christ. The more competent the minister, the better, so that fewer requirements fall on the shoulders of the congregation.
ERWIN W. LUTZER (1941–)

1500 The world looks at ministers out of the pulpit to know what they mean when in it.
RICHARD CECIL (1748–1810)

COMFORT

1501 All human comfort is vain and short.
THOMAS À KEMPIS (C. 1380–1471)

1502 Be still, my soul: the Lord is on thy side;
Bear patiently the cross of grief or pain;
Leave to thy God to order and provide;
In every change he faithful will remain.
Be still, my soul; thy best, thy heavenly Friend
Through thorny ways leads to a joyful end.
KATHARINA VON SCHLEGEL (B. 1697)

1503 God does not comfort us to make us comfortable, but to make us comforters.
JOHN HENRY JOWETT (1817–1893)

1504 God does not leave us comfortless, but we have to be in dire need of comfort to know the truth of his promise. It is in time of calamity . . . in days and nights of sorrow and trouble that the presence, the sufficiency, and the sympathy of God grow very sure and very wonderful.
Then we find out that the grace of God is sufficient for all our needs, for every problem, and for every difficulty, for every broken heart, and for every human sorrow.
PETER MARSHALL (1902–1949)

1505 God is closest to those whose hearts are broken.
JEWISH PROVERB

1506 How shall we comfort those who weep? By weeping with them.
FATHER YELCHANINOV

1507 How sweet the name of Jesus sounds In a believer's ear!
It soothes his sorrows,
   heals his wounds,
And drives away his fear!
JOHN NEWTON (1725–1807)

1508 It is not difficult to be independent of human comfort when we have God's comfort. It is a great thing, an extremely great thing, to be able to live without both human and divine comfort.
THOMAS À KEMPIS (C. 1380–1471)

1509 Let me come in where you are weeping, friend,
And let me take your hand.
I, who have known a sorrow such as yours,
Can understand.
Let me come in—I would be very still Beside you in your grief;
I would not bid you cease your weeping, friend,
Tears bring relief.
Let me come in—I would only breathe a prayer,
And hold your hand,
For I have known a sorrow such as yours,
And understand.
GRACE NOLL CROWELL

1510 Oh! there is never sorrow of heart That shall lack a timely end,
If but to God we turn, and ask Of him to be our friend!
WILLIAM WORDSWORTH (1770–1850)

1511 One reason a dog is such a comfort when you're downcast is that he doesn't ask to know why.

1512 Thank you, Father, for these tears that have carried me to the depth of your love. How could I have known your fullness without the emptiness, your acceptance without the rejection, your forgiveness without my failure, our

togetherness without that dreadful
loneliness. You have brought me to
Gethsemane, and oh, the joy of finding you already there! Amen.
BONNIE BARROWS THOMAS

1513 Those who can sit in silence with their
fellowman, not knowing what to say
but knowing that they should be there,
can bring new life in a dying heart.
Those who are not afraid to hold a
hand in gratitude, to shed tears in
grief, and to let a sigh of distress arise
straight from the heart can break
through paralyzing boundaries and
witness the birth of a new fellowship,
the fellowship of the broken.
HENRI J. M. NOUWEN

1514 When the house doth sigh and weep,
And the world is drowned in sleep,
Yet mine eyes the watch do keep,
Sweet Spirit comfort me!
ROBERT HERRICK (1591–1674)

1515 Why does God bring thunderclouds
and disasters when we want green pastures and still waters? Bit by bit we
find, behind the clouds, the Father's
feet; behind the lightning, an abiding
day that has no night; behind the thunder, a still, small voice that comforts
with a comfort that is unspeakable.
OSWALD CHAMBERS (1874–1917)

1516 You don't have to be alone in your
hurt! Comfort is yours. Joy is an
option. And it's all been made possible
by your Savior. He went without comfort so that you might have it. He post-
poned joy so that you might share in
it. He willingly chose isolation so that
you might never be alone in your hurt
and sorrow.
JONI EARECKSON TADA

COMMANDMENTS

1517 Christ's deeds and examples are commandments of what we should do.
JOHN WYCLIFFE (C. 1330–1384)

1518 Ever since the Ten Commandments
were given, legislators have been busy
passing millions of laws trying to
enforce them.

1519 God does all before he asks us to do
anything.
R. W. BARBOUR (1900–)

1520 God is an omniscient Creator who
knows which rules are best for mankind; and these moral laws are a reflection of his nature, imposed on a
universe which he created—a universe
which functions best when his laws
are obeyed.
ERWIN W. LUTZER (1941–)

1521 God's commands are made to the life
of his Son in us, not to our human
nature; consequently all that God tells
us to do is always humanly difficult;
but it becomes divinely easy immediately we obey because our obedience
has behind it all the onmipotent power
of the grace of God.
OSWALD CHAMBERS (1874–1917)

1522 God's restrictions were given to show
us more keenly our need of him.
ERWIN W. LUTZER (1941–)

1523 Most people believe that the Christian
commandments (e.g., to love one's
neighbor as oneself) are intentionally a
little too severe, like putting the clock
half an hour ahead to make sure of
not being late in the morning.
SØREN AABYE KIERKEGAARD (1813–1855)

1524 No man can break any of the Ten
Commandments. He can only break
himself against them.
G. K. CHESTERTON (1874–1936)

1525 The commandments can never be kept
while there is a strife to keep them; the
man is overwhelmed in the weight of
their broken pieces. It needs a . . .
power of life, not of struggle; the
strength of love, not the effort of duty.
GEORGE MACDONALD (1824–1905)

1526 The commandments were given irrespective of human ability or inability
to keep them; then when Jesus Christ
came, instead of doing what we all too
glibly say he did—put something easier before men, he made it a hundred-

fold more difficult because he goes behind the law to the disposition.
OSWALD CHAMBERS (1874–1917)

1527 The commandments were given with the inexorable awfulness of Almighty God; and the subsequent history of the people is the record of how they could not keep them.
OSWALD CHAMBERS (1874–1917)

1528 The commands of God are all designed to make us more happy than we can possibly be without them.
THOMAS WILSON (1663–1735)

1529 The eleventh commandment: Thou shalt not be found out.
GEORGE JOHN WHYTE-MELVILLE (1821–1878)

1530 The law reflects God's holiness; it is a plumbline that shows us that we are crooked.
ERWIN W. LUTZER (1941–   )

1531 Thou no gods shalt have but me.
Before no idol bow the knee.
Take not the name of God in vain.
Dare not the Sabbath Day profane.
Give to thy parents honor due.
Take heed that thou no murder do.
Abstain from words and deeds
   unclean.
Steal not, for thou by God art seen.
Tell no willful lie and love it.
What is thy neighbor's do not covet.
—The Ten Commandments in Rhyme

COMMITMENT

1532 Commitment without reflection is fanaticism in action. But reflection without commitment is the paralysis of all action.
JOHN MACKAY

1533 He is no fool who gives what he cannot keep to gain what he cannot lose.
JIM ELLIOT (1927–1956)

1534 He who lightly assents will seldom keep his word.
CHINESE PROVERB

1535 Jesus did not say, "Come to me and get it over with." He said, "If any man would come after me, let him take up his cross daily and follow me." *Daily*

is the key word. Our commitment to Christ, however genuine and whole-hearted it may be today, must be renewed tomorrow . . . and the day after that . . . and the day after that . . . until the path comes at last to the river.
LOUIS CASSELS (1922–1974)

1536 Say, "Yes," Son. I need your yes as I needed Mary's yes to come to earth, For it is I who must do your work, it is I who must live in your family, it is I who must be in your neighborhood, and not you. For it is my look that penetrates, and not yours; my words that carry weight, and not yours; my life that transforms, and not yours. Give all to me, abandon all to me. I need your yes to be united with you and to come down to earth, I need your yes to continue saving the world.
MICHEL QUOIST (1921–   )

1537 Sometimes a man imagines that he will lose himself if he gives himself, and keep himself if he hides himself. But the contrary takes place with terrible exactitude.
ERNEST HELLO (1828–1885)

1538 Thine am I, I was born for thee,
What wouldst thou, Master, make
   of me?
Give me death or give me life
Give health or give infirmity
Give honor or give obloquy
Give peace profound or daily strife,
Weakness or strength add to my life;
Yes, Lord, my answer still shall be
What wilt thou, Master, have of me?
SAINT TERESA OF AVILA (1515–1582)

1539 Tomorrrow I keep for God. Today I give to God.
FRANCES J. ROBERTS

1540 What does God require? Everything!
ERWIN W. LUTZER (1941–   )

COMPASSION

1541 Christianity demands a level of caring that transcends human inclinations.
ERWIN W. LUTZER (1941–   )

1542 Compassion means justice.
MEISTER ECKHART (C. 1260–C. 1327)

1543 God's care will carry you so you can carry others.
ROBERT HAROLD SCHULLER (1926–)

1544 Hearin' is one thing and listenin' is another.
WILLIAM FREND DEMORGAN (1839–1917)

1545 If I had known what trouble you were bearing;
What griefs were in the silence of your face;
I would have been more gentle and more caring,
And tried to give you gladness for a space.
MARY CAROLYN DAVIES

1546 Let us not underestimate how hard it is to be compassionate. Compassion is hard because it requires the inner disposition to go with others to the place where they are weak, vulnerable, lonely, and broken. But this is not our spontaneous response to suffering. What we desire most is to do away with suffering by fleeing from it or finding a quick cure for it.
HENRI J. M. NOUWEN

1547 Man may dismiss compassion from his heart, but God will never.
WILLIAM COWPER (1731–1800)

1548 Man's sorrows often will not let me sleep.
HENRIETTE ROLAND HOLST (1869–1952)

1549 Never interfere with God's providential dealings with other souls. Be true to God yourself and watch.
OSWALD CHAMBERS (1874–1917)

1550 Quaker to a burglar: "Friend, I would do thee no harm for the world, but thou standest where I am about to shoot."

1551 Regardless of how we define Christ's separation from the world, one fact is clear: he did not separate himself from human beings and their needs. Nor did he limit his concern to the spiritual part of man's personality.
ERWIN W. LUTZER (1941–)

1552 Teach me to feel another's woe,
To hide the fault I see;
That mercy I to others show,
That mercy show to me.
ALEXANDER POPE (1688–1744)

1553 The dew of compassion is a tear.
LORD GEORGE NOEL GORDON BYRON (1788–1824)

1554 Why stand we here trembling around calling on God for help, and not ourselves, in whom God dwells, stretching a hand to save the falling man?
WILLIAM BLAKE (1757–1827)

COMPLAINT

1555 A grouch always looks as if he were weaned on a pickle.

1556 Complain to one who can help you.
YUGOSLAVIAN PROVERB

1557 Complainers are the greatest persecutors.
SAMUEL BUTLER (1612–1680)

1558 Complaining about our lot in life might seem quite innocent in itself, but God takes it personally.
ERWIN W. LUTZER (1941–)

1559 Don't complain; the more you complain about things the more things you will have to complain about.
E. STANLEY JONES (1884–1973)

1560 Grumbling is the death of love.
MARLENE DIETRICH (1901–)

1561 If Christians spent as much time praying as they do grumbling, they would have nothing to grumble about.

1562 It's the worst wheel of the wagon that screeches the loudest.
SPANISH PROVERB

1563 Murmur at nothing: if our ills are irreparable, it is ungrateful; if remediless, it is in vain. A Christian builds his fortitude on a better foundation than stoicism; he is pleased with everything that happens because he knows it could not happen unless it had first pleased God, and that which pleases him must be the best.
CHARLES CALEB COLTON (1780–1832)

1564 Some people are always grumbling because roses have thorns; I am thankful that thorns have roses.
ALPHONSE KARR (1808–1890)

1565 The wrong was his who wrongfully complained.
WILLIAM COWPER (1731–1800)

1566 There are many ways to get ulcers but the most common is mountain-climbing over molehills.

1567 When we are discontented with ourselves, we complain about others.
PAUL TOURNIER (1898–1986)

1568 When you ask some people how they are, they expect you to listen to the details.

1569 Whenever you find yourself disposed to uneasiness or murmuring at anything that is the effect of God's providence, look upon yourself as denying either the wisdom or goodness of God.
WILLIAM LAW (1686–1761)

COMPLIMENT

1570 A compliment is a gift, not to be thrown away carelessly unless you want to hurt the giver.
ELEANOR HAMILTON

1571 A compliment is verbal sunshine.
ROBERT ORBEN

1572 An acquaintance that begins with a compliment is sure to develop into a real friendship.
OSCAR WILDE (1854–1900)

1573 I can live for two months on a good compliment.
MARK TWAIN (1835–1910)

1574 If you would reap praise, sow the seeds; Gentle words and useful deeds.
BENJAMIN FRANKLIN (1706–1790)

1575 The most delicate compliment is to treat the person with whom you are talking as an exception to all rules.
SAMUEL MCCHORD CROTHERS (1857–1927)

1576 To be trusted is a greater compliment than to be loved.
GEORGE MACDONALD (1824–1905)

1577 What are compliments? They are things you say to people when you don't know what else to say.
CONSTANCE JONES (1848–1922)

COMPROMISE

1578 A term compatible with anything and everything is meaningless.
ERWIN W. LUTZER (1941–   )

1579 Compromise is but the sacrifice of one right or good in the hope of retaining another—too often ending in the loss of both.
TRYON EDWARDS (1809–1894)

1580 Compromise makes a good umbrella but a poor roof; it is a temporary expedient.
JAMES RUSSELL LOWELL (1819–1891)

1581 He who lives all his life trying to please and appease everyone dies in sadness.
ARABIAN PROVERB

1582 People talk about the middle of the road as though it were unacceptable. Actually, all human problems, excepting morals, come into the gray areas. Things are not all black and white. There have to be compromises. The middle of the road is all of the usable surface. The extremes, right and left, are in the gutters.
DWIGHT D. EISENHOWER (1890–1969)

1583 Please all, and you will please none.
AESOP (FL. C. 550 B.C.)

1584 The swift wind of compromise is a lot more devastating than the sudden jolt of misfortune.
CHARLES R. SWINDOLL (1934–   )

CONCEIT

1585 A vain man can never be utterly ruthless; he wants to win applause and therefore he accommodates himself to others.
JOHANN WOLFGANG VON GOETHE (1749–1832)

1586 Conceit is a weird disease—it makes everybody sick except the guy who has it. Or like the mother whale told her

baby, "When you get to the surface and start to blow, that's when you get harpooned!"
JAMES C. DOBSON (1936–   )

1587 Don't think yourself so big that other people look small.
CONFUCIUS (C. 551–479 B.C.)

1588 No one likes a skunk because it puts on such awful airs.

1589 Self-admiration is so demanding that little is left over for others.

1590 To admire ourselves as we are is to have no wish to change. And with those who don't want to change, the soul is dead.
WILLIAM BARCLAY (1907–1978)

1591 When a man is wrapped up in himself, he makes a pretty small package.
JOHN RUSKIN (1819–1900)

CONFESSION

1592 A fault confessed is a new virtue added to a man.
JAMES S. KNOWLES (1784–1862)

1593 A man should never be ashamed to own he has been in the wrong, which is but saying, in other words, that he is wiser today than he was yesterday.
ALEXANDER POPE (1688–1744)

1594 A man who confesses his sins in the presence of a brother knows that he is no longer alone with himself; he experiences the presence of God in the reality of the other person. As long as I am by myself in the confession of my sins everything remains in the dark, but in the presence of a brother the sin has to be brought into the light.
DIETRICH BONHOEFFER (1906–1945)

1595 Confession is necessary for fellowship. Sin builds a barrier between us and God.
ERWIN W. LUTZER (1941–   )

1596 Confession is to bring to light the unknown, the unconscious darkness, and the underdeveloped creativity of our deeper layers.
FRITZ KUNKEL

1597 Confession, which means to agree with God regarding our sin, restores our fellowship. It is a form of discipline which God requires.
ERWIN W. LUTZER (1941–   )

1598 Explaining is half confessing.
MARQUIS OF HALIFAX (1633–1695)

1599 For a good confession three things are necessary: an examination of conscience, sorrow, and a determination to avoid sin.
ALPHONSUS LUGUORI

1600 For him who confesses, shams are over and realities have begun.
WILLIAM JAMES (1842–1910)

1601 Forgiveness is always free. But that doesn't mean that confession is always easy. Sometimes it is hard. Incredibly hard. It is painful (sometimes literally) to admit our sins and entrust ourselves to God's care.
ERWIN W. LUTZER (1941–   )

1602 In confession . . . we open our lives to healing, reconciling, restoring, uplifting grace of him who loves us in spite of what we are.
LOUIS CASSELS (1922–1974)

1603 It is not wrong actions which require courage to confess, so much as those which are ridiculous and foolish.
JEAN-JACQUES ROUSSEAU (1712–1778)

1604 Two grave dangers threaten all confession: too little and too much. Beware lest your concern for propriety and pride keep you from confessing those sins the public deserves to hear about. Likewise, beware that your earnestness in making all things right before God does not play into the hands of the great deceiver who would love to turn your confession of sin into an inducement for another to sin.
RICHARD OWEN ROBERTS (1931–   )

CONFIDENCE

1605 Confidence in the natural world is self-reliance, in the spiritual world it is God-reliance.
OSWALD CHAMBERS (1874–1917)

1606 Confidence is a plant of slow growth.
ENGLISH PROVERB

1607 Confidence is keeping your chin up; overconfidence is sticking your neck out.

1608 God wants us to be victors, not victims; to grow, not grovel; to soar, not sink; to overcome, not to be overwhelmed.
WILLIAM ARTHUR WARD (1812–1882)

1609 I felt so young, so strong, so sure of God.
ELIZABETH BARRETT BROWNING (1806–1861)

1610 If your security is based on something that can be taken away from you—you will constantly be on a false edge of security.
TIM HANSEL

1611 Our confidence in Christ does not make us lazy, negligent, or careless, but, on the contrary, it awakens us, urges us on, and makes us active in living righteous lives and doing good. There is no self-confidence to compare with this.
ULRICH ZWINGLI (1484–1531)

1612 They can conquer who believe they can.
JOHN DRYDEN (1631–1700)

1613 When once a saint puts his confidence in the election of God, no tribulation or affliction can ever touch that confidence. When we realize that there is no hope of deliverance in human wisdom, or in human rectitude, or in anything that we can do . . . this is the finest cure for spiritual degeneration or spiritual sulks.
OSWALD CHAMBERS (1874–1917)

CONFIDENTIALITY

1614 A secret is best kept by keeping the secret of its being a secret.

1615 A secret's safe 'twixt you, me, and the gatepost.
ROBERT BROWNING (1812–1889)

1616 Keeping a secret is like trying to smuggle daylight past a rooster.

1617 Three may keep a secret if two of them are dead.
BENJAMIN FRANKLIN (1706–1790)

1618 To keep your secret is wisdom; but to expect others to keep it is foolish.
SAMUEL JOHNSON (1709–1784)

1619 To whom you tell your secrets, to him you resign your liberty.
SPANISH PROVERB

CONFLICT

1620 A house divided against itself cannot stand.
ABRAHAM LINCOLN (1809–1865)

1621 All things are born through strife.
HERACLITUS (C. 540–C. 480 B.C.)

1622 As sure as there is will versus will, there must be punch versus punch.
OSWALD CHAMBERS (1874–1917)

1623 He that wrestles with us strengthens our nerves and sharpens our skill. Our antagonist is our helper.
EDMUND BURKE (1729–1797)

1624 Honest differences are often a healthy sign of progress.
MAHATMA GANDHI (1869–1948)

1625 Luther arose and threw the apple of discord into the world.
DESIDERIUS ERASMUS (C. 1466–1536)

1626 Opposition inflames the enthusiast, never converts him.
JOHANN FRIEDRICH VON SCHILLER (1759–1805)

1627 The best way to keep people from jumping down your throat is to keep your mouth shut.

1628 The harder the conflict, the more glorious the triumph.
THOMAS PAINE (1737–1809)

1629 The more the Holy Spirit reigns within, the more intensified becomes the conflict.
FRANCES J. ROBERTS

1630 The only competition worthy of a wise man is with himself.
WASHINGTON ALLSTON (1779–1843)

1631 There are other important things in life besides conflict, but there are not

many other things so inevitably interesting. The very saints interest us most when we think of them as engaged in a conflict with the devil.
ROBERT STAUGHTON LYND (1892–1970)

1632 Whatever we have achieved in character we have achieved through conflict.
J. WALLACE HAMILTON

1633 You are but a poor soldier of Christ if you think you can overcome without fighting, and suppose you can have the crown without the conflict.
SAINT JOHN CHRYSOSTOM C. 347–407

CONFORMITY

1634 Are we driven people, propelled by the winds of our times, pressed to conform or compete? Or are we called people, the recipients of the gracious beckoning of Christ when he promises to make us into something?
GORDON MACDONALD (1939–)

1635 Conformity is one of the most fundamental dishonesties of all. When we reject our specialness, water down our God-given individuality and uniqueness, we begin to lose our freedom. The conformist is in no way a free man. He has to follow the herd.
NORMAN VINCENT PEALE (1898–)

1636 I don't like these cold, precise, perfect people who, in order not to speak wrong never speak at all, and in order not to do wrong never do anything.
HENRY WARD BEECHER (1813–1887)

1637 I wonder if it ain't just cowardice instead of generosity that makes us give tips.
WILL ROGERS (1879–1935)

1638 In the land of the naked, people are ashamed of clothes.
RUSSIAN PROVERB

1639 Man is a gregarious animal, and much more so in his mind than in his body. He may like to go alone for a walk, but he hates to stand alone in his opinions.
GEORGE SANTAYANA (1863–1952)

1640 Most people are other people. Their thoughts are someone else's opinions, their lives a mimicry, their passions a quotation.
OSCAR WILDE (1854–1900)

1641 Nothing is more rare in any man than an act of his own.
RALPH WALDO EMERSON (1803–1882)

1642 One of the great American myths is that we are a nation of rugged individualists. We really have ourselves fooled at this point. In truth, we are a nation of social cowards. A major proportion of our energy is expended in trying to be like everyone else, cringing in fear of true individuality.
JAMES C. DOBSON (1936–)

1643 Our wretched species is so made that those who walk on the well-trodden path always throw stones at those who are showing a new road.
VOLTAIRE (1694–1778)

1644 The crow tried to emulate the partridge's gait, but he forgot his own.
ARABIAN PROVERB

1645 The popular image of the man of God as a smiling, congenial, asexual religious mascot whose handshake is always soft and whose head is always bobbing in the perpetual yes of universal acquiescence is not the image found in the Scriptures of truth.
A. W. TOZER (1897–1963)

1646 To deny self is to become a nonconformist. The Bible tells us not to be conformed to this world either physically or intellectually or spiritually.
BILLY GRAHAM (1918–)

1647 We become independent of our fear of social judgment and the disapproval of men in proportion to our dependence on God.
PAUL TOURNIER (1898–1986)

1648 We think according to inclinations, speak according to learning and opinions, but act according to custom.
FRANCIS BACON (1561–1626)

1649 We would know mankind better if we were not so anxious to resemble one another.
JOHANN WOLFGANG VON GOETHE (1749–1832)

CONSCIENCE

1650 A bad conscience embitters the sweetest comforts; a good one sweetens the bitterest crosses.

1651 A bad conscience is a snake in one's heart.
JEWISH PROVERB

1652 A conscience void of offense before God and man is an inheritance for eternity.
DANIEL WEBSTER (1782–1852)

1653 A good conscience can sleep in the mouth of a cannon.
THOMAS WATSON (C. 1557–1592)

1654 A good conscience is a continual feast.
FRANCIS BACON (1561–1626)

1655 A good conscience is a soft pillow.
PROVERB

1656 A guilty conscience is a hell on earth and points to one beyond.

1657 A man could not have anything upon his conscience if God did not exist, for the relationship between the individual and God, the God-relationship, is the conscience, and that is why it is so terrible to have even the least thing upon one's conscience, because one is immediately conscious of the infinite weight of God.
SØREN AABYE KIERKEGAARD (1813–1855)

1658 A person of honor would prefer to lose his honor rather than lose his conscience.
MICHEL EYQUEM DE MONTAIGNE (1533–1592)

1659 A quiet conscience sleeps in thunder.

1660 A scar on the conscience is the same as a wound.
PUBLILIUS SYRUS (FIRST CENTURY B.C.)

1661 A sleeping pill will never take the place of a clear conscience.
EDDIE CANTOR (1892–1964)

1662 An uneasy conscience is a hair in the mouth.
MARK TWAIN (1835–1910)

1663 And I know of the future judgment
How dreadful so'er it be
That to sit alone with my conscience
Would be judgment enough for me.
CHARLES WILLIAM STUBBS (1845–1912)

1664 And I will place within them as a guide
My Umpire Conscience, whom if they will hear,
Light after light well us'd they shall attain,
And to the end persisting, safe arrive.
JOHN MILTON (1608–1674)

1665 Conscience gets a lot of credit that belongs to cold feet.

1666 Conscience is a sacred sanctuary where God alone may enter as judge.
HUGO FÉLICITÉ ROBERT DE LAMENNAIS (1782–1854)

1667 Conscience is a thousand witnesses.
PROVERB

1668 Conscience is a three-pointed thing in my heart that turns around when I do something wrong, and the points hurt a lot. But if I keep doing bad, the points eventually wear off, and then it doesn't hurt any more.

1669 Conscience is a walkie-talkie set by which God speaks to us.
JAMES J. METCALF

1670 Conscience is God's presence in man.
EMANUEL SWEDENBORG (1688–1772)

1671 Conscience is the inner voice which warns us that someone may be looking.
H. L. MENCKEN (1880–1956)

1672 Conscience is the still small voice that makes you feel still smaller.
JAMES A. SANAKER

1673 Conscience is the true vicar of Christ in the soul; a prophet in its information; a monarch in its preemptoriness; a priest in its blessings or anathemas, according as we obey or disobey it.
CARDINAL JOHN HENRY NEWMAN (1801–1890)

1674 Conscience is thoroughly well bred and soon leaves off talking to those who do not wish to hear it.
SAMUEL BUTLER (1612–1680)

1675 Conscience is, in most men, an anticipation of the opinion of others.
SIR HENRY TAYLOR (1800–1886)

1676 Conscience reigns, but it does not govern.
PAUL VALERY (1871–1945)

1677 Conscience warns us as a friend before
it punishes us as a judge.
KING LESZCZYNSKI STANISLAW I
(1677–1766)

1678 Conscience: my accomplice.
HYMAN MAXWELL BERSTON

1679 Cowardice asks, Is it safe? Expediency
asks, Is it politic? Vanity asks, Is it
popular? Conscience asks, Is it right?
WILLIAM MORLEY PUNSHON (1824–1881)

1680 Even the voice of conscience
undergoes mutation.
STANISLAW J. LEC (1909–1966)

1681 Great tranquillity has he who cares neither for praise nor criticism. He will
be content whose conscience is pure.
You are not more holy if you are
praised; nor more worthless if you are
criticized. What you are, that you are;
words cannot make you greater than
what you are in the sight of God.
THOMAS À KEMPIS (C. 1380–1471)

1682 He had a mania for washing and disin-
fecting himself. . . . For him the only
danger came from the microbes which
attacked the body. He had not studied
the microbe of conscience which eats
into the soul.
ANAÏS NIN (1903–1977)

1683 He that has light within his own clear
breast
May sit i' the center and enjoy bright
day;
But he that hides a dark soul and foul
thoughts
Benighted walks under the midday sun.
JOHN MILTON (1608–1674)

1684 His gain is loss;
For he that wrongs his friends
Wrongs himself more,
And ever has about him a silent court
and jury

And himself, the prisoner at the bar
Ever condemned.
ALFRED, LORD TENNYSON (1809–1892)

1685 I desire so to conduct the affairs of
this administration that if at the end,
when I come to lay down the reins of
power, I have lost every other friend
on earth, I shall at least have one
friend left, and that friend shall be
down inside of me.
—Reply to Missouri Committee of
Seventy
ABRAHAM LINCOLN (1809–1865)

1686 If conscience smite thee once, it is an
admonition; if twice, it is a condemnation.
NATHANIEL HAWTHORNE (1804–1864)

1687 In vain we call old notions fudge,
And bend our conscience to our
dealing;
The Ten Commandments will not
budge,
And stealing will continue stealing.
JAMES RUSSELL LOWELL (1819–1891)

1688 It is not sufficient for a Christian to
walk in the light of his conscience; he
must walk in a sterner light, in the
light of the Lord.
OSWALD CHAMBERS (1874–1917)

1689 Let dictatorship not serve as an alibi
for our conscience. We have failed to
fight for right, for justice, for goodness; as a result we must fight against
wrong, against injustice, against evil.
ABRAHAM J. HESCHEL (1907–1972)

1690 Living with a conscience is like driving
a car with the brakes on.
BUDD SCHULBERG

1691 Most of us follow our conscience as
we follow a wheelbarrow. We push it
in front of us in the direction we want
to go.
BILLY GRAHAM (1918–)

1692 My conscience is captive to the word
of God.
MARTIN LUTHER (1483–1546)

1693 Now, Jessie, there is some beauty and
some goodness in everything God has
made, and he who has a pure conscience is like one looking into a clear

stream; he sees it all; while him who has a bad conscience, all things look as you say they did in the muddy stream—black and ugly.
MARY McINTOSH (1803–1878)

1694 O Conscience, into what abyss of fears
And horrors hast thou driv'n me;
Out of which I find no way,
From deep to deeper plung'd!
JOHN MILTON (1608–1674)

1695 Oh! Conscience! Conscience! Man's most faithful friend,
Him canst thou comfort, ease, relieve, defend:
But if he will thy friendly checks forego,
Thou art, oh! woe for me, his deadliest foe!
GEORGE CRABBE (1754–1832)

1696 Only the heart without a stain knows perfect ease.
GERMAN PROVERB

1697 Our consciences take no notice of pain inflicted on others until it reaches a point where it gives pain to us.
MARK TWAIN (1835–1910)

1698 The conscience is a built-in feature
That haunts the sinner, helps the preacher.
Some sins it makes us turn and run from,
But most it simply takes the fun from.
RICHARD ARMOUR

1699 The conscience is an imperfect mental faculty. There are times when it condemns us for mistakes and human frailties that can't be avoided; at other times it will remain silent in the face of indescribable wickedness.
JAMES C. DOBSON (1936–)

1700 The disease of an evil conscience is beyond the practice of all the physicians of all countries in the world.
WILLIAM EWART GLADSTONE (1809–1898)

1701 The importance of conscience is eternal, like love.
PABLO CASALS (1876–1973)

1702 The man who has a guilty secret in his life is a lonely man.
JAMES DENNEY (1856–1917)

1703 The only tyrant I accept in this world is the still voice within.
MAHATMA GANDHI (1869–1948)

1704 The whole conscience begins to unravel if a single stitch drops. One single sin makes a hole you can put your head through.
CHARLES BUXTON (1823–1871)

1705 The world has achieved brilliance without conscience. Ours is a world of nuclear giants and ethical infants.
OMAR NELSON BRADLEY (1893–1981)

1706 There is another man within me that is angry with me.
SIR THOMAS BROWNE (1605–1682)

1707 To sit alone with my conscience will be judgment enough for me.
CHARLES WILLIAM STUBBS (1845–1912)

1708 Trust that man in nothing who has not a conscience in everything.
LAURENCE STERNE (1713–1768)

1709 Two things fill the mind with ever new and increasing wonder and awe—the starry heavens above me and the moral law within me.
IMMANUEL KANT (1724–1804)

CONSCIOUSNESS

1710 Earth's crammed with heaven,
And every common bush afire with God;
But only he who sees, takes off his shoes—
The rest sit round it and pluck blackberries. . . .
ELIZABETH BARRETT BROWNING (1806–1861)

1711 He who knows himself best esteems himself least.
HENRY GEORGE BOHN (1796–1884)

1712 Immense hidden powers seem to lurk in the unconscious depths of even the most common man—indeed, of all people without exception. It is these powers, when put under pressure, that are responsible for all great creative efforts. The men who make history are those who—consciously or unconsciously—turn the switch on the inner switchboards of human character.

Pour out all your fears and anxieties, malicious joy and greed and hatred, and you will be astonished at the terrific amount of power which is pent up in your unconscious mind. We can release this power and transform it from negative into positive power, only by bringing into the open, into the light of consciousness, and by accepting ourselves as we are even though the mountains of doubts seem to crush us. This is the principle of honesty. And it is clear that it can be applied only if connected with the principle of faith.
FRITZ KUNKEL

1713 It is easier for us to get to know God than to know our own soul . . . God is nearer to us than our own soul, for he is the ground in which it stands . . . So if we want to know our own soul and enjoy its fellowship, it is necessary to seek it in our Lord God.
JULIAN OF NORWICH (C. 1342–AFTER 1413)

1714 Many of us are on the borders of consciousness—consciously serving, consciously devoted to God; all that is immature. The first stages of spiritual life are passed in conscientious carefulness; the mature life is lived in unconscious consecration.
OSWALD CHAMBERS (1874–1917)

1715 Men resemble great deserted palaces: the owner occupies only a few rooms and has closed-off wings where he never ventures.
FRANÇOIS MAURIAC (1885–1970)

1716 Nothing happens that is not significant if you can only see the significance.
CHRISTOPHER WILLIAM BRADSHAW ISHERWOOD (1904–1986)

1717 Nothing so distasteful to man as to go the way which leads him to himself.
HERMANN HESSE (1877–1962)

1718 Suffering is the sole origin of consciousness.
FYODOR MIKHAYLOVICH DOSTOYEVSKI (1821–1881)

1719 What we need is not a false peace which enables us to evade the impli-cable light of judgment, but the grace courageously to accept the bitter truth that is revealed to us; to abandon our inertia, our egotism and submit entirely to the demands of the Spirit.
THOMAS MERTON (1915–1968)

CONSECRATION

1720 Consecration is handing God a blank sheet to fill in with your name signed at the bottom.
M. H. MILLER (1904–   )

1721 Consecration is not wrapping one's self in a holy web in the sanctuary and then coming forth after prayer and twilight meditation and saying, "There, I am consecrated." Consecration is going out into the world where God Almighty is and using every power for his glory. It is taking all advantages as trust funds.
HENRY WARD BEECHER (1813–1887)

1722 Consecration is the narrow, lonely way to overflowing love. We are not called upon to live long on this planet, but we are called upon to be holy at any and every cost. If obedience costs you your life, then pay it.
OSWALD CHAMBERS (1874–1917)

1723 It does not take great men to do great things; it only takes consecrated men.
PHILLIPS BROOKS (1835–1893)

1724 Our reservations are the damnations of our consecrations.
WILLIAM BOOTH (1829–1912)

1725 You give but little when you give of your possessions. It is when you give yourself that you truly give.
KAHLIL GIBRAN (1883–1931)

CONSEQUENCES

1726 All that we send into the lives of others comes back into our own.
EDWIN MARKHAM (1852–1940)

1727 As ye sow, so shall ye reap, unless of course you are an amateur gardener.

1728 Every beginning is a consequence—every beginning ends something.
PAUL VALERY (1871–1945)

1729 Everyone constructs his own bed of
nails.
D. SUTTEN

1730 God does not pay weekly, but he pays
at the end.
DUTCH PROVERB

1731 If a man gets drunk and goes out and
breaks his leg so that it must be ampu-
tated, God will forgive him if he asks
it, but he will have to hop around on
one leg all his life.
DWIGHT LYMAN MOODY (1837–1899)

1732 If lawyers are disbarred and clergymen
are defrocked, doesn't it follow that
electricians can be delighted; musi-
cians, denoted; cowboys, deranged;
tree surgeons, debarked; and dry cleaners, depressed?
VIRGINIA OSTMAN

1733 If we walk in the woods, we must feed
mosquitoes.
RALPH WALDO EMERSON (1803–1882)

1734 Many a have and have-not of today
are the did and did-not of yesterday.

1735 No man is rich enough to buy back his
past.
OSCAR WILDE (1854–1900)

1736 Of one ill, come many.
PROVERB

1737 The thorns which I have reap'd are of
the tree I planted; they have torn me,
and I bleed. I should have known
what fruit would spring from such
seed.
LORD GEORGE NOEL GORDON BYRON
(1788–1824)

1738 The way many a driver speeds through
traffic, you'd think he was late for his
accident.

1739 The wheel is come full circle.
WILLIAM SHAKESPEARE (1564–1616)

1740 We get in return exactly what we give.
Incredible echoes mirror our actions to
an emphatic degree, sometimes in
greater measure than we give.
CHARLES R. SWINDOLL (1934–   )

1741 We sifted them with a coarse sieve, but
they did it to us with a fine sieve.
ARABIAN PROVERB

1742 Sow a thought and you reap an act;
Sow an act and you reap a habit;
Sow a habit and you reap a character;
Sow a character and you reap a destiny.
SAMUEL SMILES (1812–1904)

1743 What's got badly, goes badly.
IRISH PROVERB

1744 You cannot unscramble eggs.
PROVERB

CONSISTENCY

1745 Consistency is contrary to nature, contrary to life. The only completely consistent people are the dead.
ALDOUS HUXLEY (1894–1963)

1746 Consistency is the quality of a stagnant mind.
JOHN FRENCH SLOAN (1871–1951)

1747 Consistency requires you to be as ignorant today as you were a year ago.
BERNARD BERENSON (1865–1959)

1748 Consistency, thou art a jewel.
PROVERB

1749 Consistency:
It's the jewel worth wearing;
It's the anchor worth weighing;
It's the thread worth weaving;
It's the battle worth winning.
CHARLES R. SWINDOLL (1934–   )

1750 From the darkness round the cross
there rings out this voice so sure that
God is love. In him there is no caprice
and no changeableness. Do what you
will to him, however you may hurt
and disappoint him and break his
heart, you cannot alter his essential
nature.
ARTHUR JOHN GOSSIP

1751 He does not believe who does not live
according to his belief.
SIR THOMAS FULLER (1608–1661)

1752 How seldom we weigh our neighbor
in the same balance with ourselves.
THOMAS À KEMPIS (C. 1380–1471)

CONTEMPLATION

1753 Being has ceased to have much appeal
for people, and doing engages almost

everyone's attention. Modern Christians lack symmetry. They know almost nothing about the inner life.
A. W. TOZER (1897–1963)

1754 Christ was the greatest contemplative that ever lived, yet he was ever at the service of men.
JAN VAN RUYSBROECK (1293–1381)

1755 Contemplation involves all of life. It is a twenty-four-hour-a-day job.
RICHARD J. FOSTER (1942–)

1756 Contemplation is like sleep in the arms of God.
BERNARD OF CLAIRVAUX (1090–1153)

1757 Deep within us all there is an amazing inner sanctuary of the soul, a holy place, a divine center, a speaking voice, to which we may continuously return. Eternity is at our hearts, pressing upon our time-torn lives, warming us with intimations of an astounding destiny, calling us home unto itself. . . . It is a seed stirring to life if we do not choke it. . . . Here is the slumbering Christ, stirring to be awakened, to become the soul we clothe in earthly form and action.
THOMAS R. KELLY (1893–1941)

1758 Dispose our soul for tranquility, O God, that the loving knowledge of contemplation may the more grow and the soul will feel it and relish it more than all other things whatever; because it brings with it peace and rest, sweetness and delight, without trouble.
SAINT JOHN OF THE CROSS (1542–1591)

1759 I admire people who are suited to the contemplative life, but I am not one of them. They can sit inside themselves like honey in a jar and just be. It's wonderful to have someone like that around, you always feel you can count on them. You can go away and come back, you can change your mind and your hairdo and your politics, and when you get through doing all these upsetting things, you look around and there they are, just the way they were, just being.
ELIZABETH JANEWAY (1913–)

1760 If we hope to move beyond the superficialities of our culture—including our religious culture—we must be willing to go down into the recreating silences, into the inner world of contemplation.
RICHARD J. FOSTER (1942–)

1761 In proportion as our inward life fails, we go more constantly and desperately to the post office. You may depend on it, that poor fellow who walks away with the greatest number of letters, proud of his extensive correspondence, has not heard from himself this long while.
HENRY DAVID THOREAU (1817–1862)

1762 Learn less and contemplate more.
RENÉ DESCARTES (1596–1650)

1763 Only to sit and think of God,
Oh what a joy it is!
To think the thought, to breathe the name
Earth has no higher bliss.
FREDERICK WILLIAM FABER (1814–1863)

1764 The active life is such that it begins and ends on earth. The contemplative life, however, may indeed begin on earth, but it will continue without end into eternity. This is because the contemplative life is Mary's part which shall never be taken away.

1765 True contemplation is not a psychological trick but a theological grace.
THOMAS MERTON (1915–1968)

1766 Unite contemplation with action. They are not contradictory and incompatible, but mutually helpful to each other. Contemplation will strengthen for action, and action sends us back to contemplation, and thus the inner and outer life will be harmoniously developed.
SAMUEL FOOTE (1720–1777)

1767 When plunging into the darkness which is above the intellect, we pass not merely into brevity of speech, but even into absolute silence, of thoughts as well as of words.
DIONYSIUS (C. FIFTH CENTURY)

CONTEMPT

1768 Many can bear adversity, but few contempt.
ENGLISH PROVERB

1769 Never point a finger of scorn at another, for in so doing you are pointing three fingers of scorn at your own self.
BURMESE PROVERB

1770 Sarcasm is the weapon of the weak man; the word literally means to tear flesh from the bone.
OSWALD CHAMBERS (1874–1917)

1771 The arrows of sarcasm are barbed with contempt.
WASHINGTON GLADDEN (1836–1918)

CONTENTMENT

1772 'Tis better to be lowly born,
And range with humble lives
    in content,
Than to be perked up in a glistering
    grief,
And wear a golden sorrow.
WILLIAM SHAKESPEARE (1564–1616)

1773 A contented man is the one who enjoys the scenery along the detours.

1774 A contented mind is a continual feast.
PROVERB

1775 A wise man cares not for what he cannot have.
GEORGE HERBERT (1593–1633)

1776 As there is no worldly gain without some loss, so there is no worldly loss without some gain. If thou hast lost thy wealth, thou hast lost some trouble with it. If thou art degraded from thy honor, that art likewise freed from the stroke of envy. If sickness hath blurred thy beauty, it hath delivered thee from pride. Set the allowance against the loss and thou shalt find no loss great.
FRANCIS QUARLES (1592–1644)

1777 Be content with the strength you've got.
ARABIAN PROVERB

1778 Better a handful of dry dates and content therewith than to own the Gate of Peacocks and be kicked in the eye by a broody camel.
ARABIAN PROVERB

1779 Content is the philosopher's stone that turns all it touches into gold.
PROVERB

1780 Contentment consists not in great wealth but in few wants.
EPICTETUS (C. 55–C. 135)

1781 Contentment is an inexhaustible treasure.
ARABIAN PROVERB

1782 Contentment is not happiness. An oyster may be contented.
CHRISTIAN NESTELL BOVEE (1820–1904)

1783 Contentment is not the fulfillment of what you want, but the realization of how much you already have.

1784 Contentment is realizing that God has already given me everything I need for my present happiness.
BILL GOTHARD

1785 Contentment is understanding that if I am not satisfied with what I have, I will never be satisfied with what I want.
BILL GOTHARD

1786 Do not anxiously hope for that which is not yet come; do not vainly regret what is already past.
PROVERB

1787 Enjoy your own life without comparing it with that of another.
MARQUIS DE CONDORCET (1743–1794)

1788 Everything has its wonders, even darkness and silence.
HELEN ADAMS KELLER (1880–1968)

1789 For after all, the best thing one can do when it's raining is to let it rain.
HENRY WADSWORTH LONGFELLOW (1807–1882)

1790 God's thoughts, his will, his love, his judgments are all man's home. To think his thoughts, to choose his will, to love his loves, to judge his judgments, and thus to know that he is in us, is to be at home.
GEORGE MACDONALD (1824–1905)

1791 Great tranquillity of heart is his who cares for neither praise nor blame.
THOMAS À KEMPIS (C. 1380–1471)

1792 Handsome is not what is handsome, but what pleases.
YIDDISH PROVERB

1793 He is a wise man who does not grieve for the things which he has not, but rejoices for those which he has.
EPICTETUS (C. 55–C. 135)

1794 He is richest who is content with the least.
SOCRATES (470–399 B.C.)

1795 He is well paid that is well satisfied.
WILLIAM SHAKESPEARE (1564–1616)

1796 He who desires nothing will always be free.
E. R. LEFEBVRE LABOULAYE (1811–1883)

1797 He who is content can never be ruined.
CHINESE PROVERB

1798 He who is contented need not lie nor flatter.

1799 He who wants little always has enough.
JOHANN GEORG ZIMMERMAN (1728–1795)

1800 I am always content with what happens, for what God chooses is better than what I choose.
EPICTETUS (C. 55–C. 135)

1801 I don't want to own anything that won't fit into my coffin.
FRED ALLEN (1894–1956)

1802 I was too ambitious in my deed,
And thought to distance all men
in success,
Till God came to me, marked the
place, and said,
"Ill doer, henceforth keep within this
line,
Attempting less than others"—and I
stand
And work among Christ's little ones,
content.
ELIZABETH BARRETT BROWNING
(1806–1861)

1803 If finding God's way in the suddenness of storms makes our faith grow broad, then trusting God's wisdom in the

"dailyness" of living makes it grow deep. And strong.
CHARLES R. SWINDOLL (1934–   )

1804 If we have not quiet in our minds, outward comfort will do no more for us than a golden slipper on a gouty foot.
JOHN BUNYAN (1628–1688)

1805 If you are not satisfied with a little, you will not be satisfied with much.

1806 It is right to be contented with what we have, but never with what we are.
SIR JAMES MACKINTOSH (1765–1832)

1807 Joy of life seems to me to arise from a sense of being where one belongs. . . . All the discontented people I know are trying sedulously to be something they are not, to do something they cannot do. Contentment, and indeed usefulness, comes as the infallible result of great acceptances, great humilities—of not trying to make ourselves this or that (to conform to some dramatized version of ourselves), but of surrendering ourselves to the fullness of life—of letting life flow through us.
DAVID GRAYSON (1870–1946)

1808 My crown is in my heart, not on my
head;
Not deck'd with diamonds and Indian
stones,
Nor to be seen: my crown is call'd
content;
A crown it is that seldom kings enjoy.
WILLIAM SHAKESPEARE (1564–1616)

1809 Nine requisites for contented living:
Health enough to make work a plea-
sure;
Wealth enough to support your needs;
Strength to battle with difficulties
and overcome them;
Grace enough to confess your sins
and forsake them;
Patience enough to toil until some
good is accomplished;
Charity enough to see some good in
your neighbor;
Love enough to move you to be use-
ful and helpful to others;
Faith enough to make real the things
of God;

Hope enough to remove all anxious
fears concerning the future.
JOHANN WOLFGANG VON GOETHE
(1749–1832)

1810 O what a happy soul am I!
Although I cannot see,
I am resolved that in this world
Contented I will be;
How many blessings I enjoy
That other people don't!
To weep and sigh because I'm blind,
I cannot, and I won't.
FANNY CROSBY (1820–1915)

1811 Since we have loaves, let us not look
for cakes.
SPANISH PROVERB

1812 Sweet are the thoughts that savour of
content;
The quiet mind is richer than a crown.
ROBERT GREENE (1558–1592)

1813 The children of Israel did not find in
the manna all the sweetness and
strength they might have found in it;
not because the manna did not contain
them, but because they longed for
other meat.
SAINT JOHN OF THE CROSS (1542–1591)

1814 The contented man is never poor, the
discontented never rich.
GEORGE ELIOT (1819–1880)

1815 There is a great difference between
being occupied with God who gives us
the contentment, and being busied
with the contentment which God
gives us.
SAINT FRANCIS OF SALES (1567–1622)

1816 There is a sense in which a man looking at the present in the light of the
future, and taking his whole being into
account, may be contented with his
lot: that is Christian contentment. But
if a man has come to that point where
he is so content that he says, "I do not
want to know any more, or do anymore, or be anymore," he is in a state
in which he ought to be changed into
a mummy!
HENRY WARD BEECHER (1813–1887)

1817 They took away what should have
been my eyes,
(But I remembered Milton's Paradise)

They took away what should have
been my ears,
(Beethoven came and wiped away my
tears)
They took away what should have
been my tongue,
(But I had talked with God when I
was young)
He would not let them take away my
soul,
Possessing that, I still possess the
whole.
HELEN ADAMS KELLER (1880–1968)

1818 To have what we want is riches; but to
be able to do without is power.
GEORGE MACDONALD (1824–1905)

1819 True contentment is a real, even an
active, virtue—not only affirmative
but creative. It is the power of getting
out of any situation all there is in it.
G. K. CHESTERTON (1874–1936)

1820 We shall be made truly wise if we be
made content; content not only with
what we can understand, but content
with what we do not understand—the
habit of mind which theologians call,
and rightly, faith in God.
CHARLES KINGSLEY (1819–1875)

1821 Whatever comes, let's be content
withall:
Among God's blessings there is
no one small.
ROBERT HERRICK (1591–1674)

1822 When life isn't the way you like, like it
the way it is.
JEWISH PROVERB

CONTROVERSY

1823 If a cause be good, the most violent
attack of its enemies will not injure it
so much as an injudicious defense of it
by its friends.
CHARLES CALEB COLTON (1780–1832)

1824 No great advance has ever been made
in science, politics, or religion, without
controversy.
LYMAN BEECHER (1775–1863)

1825 No man can be a Christian without
being a controversialist.
CHARLES HADDON SPURGEON (1834–1892)

1826 The devil loves to fish in troubled waters.
JOHN TRAPP

1827 When a thing ceases to be a subject of controversy, it ceases to be a subject of interest.
WILLIAM HAZLITT (1778–1830)

CONVERSATION

1828 A bore is a person who uses his mouth to talk while you use yours to yawn.

1829 A bore is always giving you twice as many details as you want to hear.

1830 A chatterbox keeps on talking while trying to think of something to say.

1831 A judicious silence is always better than truth spoken without charity.
PHILIP MANN

1832 A wise old owl sat on an oak,
The more he saw the less he spoke;
The less he spoke the more he heard;
Why aren't we like that wise old bird?
EDWARD H. RICHARDS

1833 Actions don't always speak louder than words—your tongue can undo everything you do.

1834 And 'tis remarkable that they
Talk most who have the least to say.
MATTHEW PRIOR (1664–1721)

1835 As long as a word remains unspoken, you are its master; once you utter it, you are its slave.
SOLOMON BEN GABIROL (C. 1020–1070)

1836 Better to remain silent and be thought a fool than to speak out and remove all doubt.
ABRAHAM LINCOLN (1809–1865)

1837 Blessed is the man who, having nothing to say, abstains from giving us wordy evidence of the fact.
GEORGE ELIOT (1819–1880)

1838 Conversation is but carving!
Give no more to every guest
Than he's able to digest.
Give him always of the prime,
And but little at a time.
Carve to all but just enough,
Let them neither starve nor stuff,
And that you may have your due,
Let your neighbor carve for you.
JONATHAN SWIFT (1667–1745)

1839 Conversation is more often likely to be an attempt at deliberate evasion, deliberate confusion, rather than communication. We're all cheats and liars, really.
JAMES JONES (1921–)

1840 Do you know that conversation is one of the greatest pleasures in life? But it wants leisure.
WILLIAM SOMERSET MAUGHAM (1874–1965)

1841 Don't knock the weather—without it, how would we start conversations?

1842 Examine what is said, not him who speaks.
ARABIAN PROVERB

1843 Give every man thy ear, but few thy voice.
WILLIAM SHAKESPEARE (1564–1616)

1844 Good words are worth much and cost little.
PROVERB

1845 Great minds talk about ideas; mediocre minds talk about things; small minds talk about other people.

1846 Great talkers are never great doers.
PROVERB

1847 He that speaks much is much mistaken.
PROVERB

1848 He who speaks, sows; who listens, reaps.
RUSSIAN PROVERB

1849 He whose conversation lacks depth makes up for it in length.
PROVERB

1850 Her tongue is so long she can seal an envelope after she puts it in the mailbox.

1851 I don't like to talk much with people who always agree with me. It is amusing to coquette with an echo for a little while, but one soon tires of it.
THOMAS CARLYLE (1795–1881)

1852 If nobody ever said anything unless he knew what he was talking about, what

a ghastly hush would descend upon
the earth!
SIR ALAN PATRICK HERBERT (1890–1971)

1853 If you add a word a day to your vocabulary, at the end of the year your
friends will wonder who you think
you are.

1854 If you keep your mouth shut, the flies
won't get in.
SPANISH PROVERB

1855 If you your lips would keep from slips,
Five things observe with care;
Of whom you speak, to whom you
    speak,
And how and when and where.
If you your ears would save from jeers,
These things keep mildly hid;
Myself and I, and mine and my,
And how I do and did.

1856 It is easier to look wise than to talk
wisely.
SAINT AMBROSE (C. 340–397)

1857 Listening is a magnetic and strange
thing, a creative force. The friends
who listen to us are the ones we move
toward, and we want to sit in their
radius. When we are listened to, it creates us, makes us unfold and expand.
KARL AUGUSTUS MENNINGER
(1893–1990)

1858 Man has been given two ears and only
one tongue that he might listen twice
as much as he speaks.
WALTER COLTON (1797–1851)

1859 Many a man's tongue has broken his
nose.
SPANISH PROVERB

1860 Men of few words are the best men.
WILLIAM SHAKESPEARE (1564–1616)

1861 More have repented speech than
silence.
PROVERB

1862 Never hold anyone by the button, or
the hand, in order to be heard out; for
if people are unwilling to hear you,
better hold your tongue than them.
LORD CHESTERFIELD (1694–1773)

1863 Never say more than is necessary.
RICHARD BRINSLEY SHERIDAN (1751–1816)

1864 Not to answer is one kind of answer.
JEWISH PROVERB

1865 Nothing is often a good thing to say.
WILL DURANT (1885–1981)

1866 O boy, hold thy tongue. Silence has
many advantages.
MENANDER (342–292 B.C.)

1867 Recipe for being a bore: drown your
tales in details.

1868 She talks so much that when she came
home from a Florida vacation, her
tongue was sunburned.

1869 Silence is foolish if we are wise, but
wise if we are foolish.
CHARLES CALEB COLTON (1780–1832)

1870 Silence is more eloquent than words.
THOMAS CARLYLE (1795–1881)

1871 Silence is one great art of conversation.
WILLIAM HAZLITT (1778–1830)

1872 Some people are such bores they give
even an aspirin a headache.

1873 Speaking without thinking is shooting
without aiming.
SIR WILLIAM GURNEY BENHAM
(1859–1944)

1874 Speech is silver; silence is golden.
GERMAN PROVERB

1875 Take a tip from nature: your ears
aren't made to shut, but your mouth is.

1876 The ability to speak several languages
is an asset, but the ability to keep your
mouth shut in one language is priceless.
PROVERB

1877 The man who remarks that it goes
without saying, goes right ahead and
says it anyway.

1878 The secret of success in conversation is
to be able to disagree without being
disagreeable.

1879 The stillest tongue can be the truest
friend.
PROVERB

1880 The tongue is located only inches
away from the brain, but it often
sounds as if it were miles away.

1881 The tongue is not steel, yet it cuts.
GEORGE HERBERT (1593–1633)

1882 The tongue is our most powerful weapon of manipulation. A frantic stream of words flows from us because we are in a constant process of adjusting our public image. We fear so deeply what we think other people see in us, so we talk in order to straighten out their understanding.
RICHARD J. FOSTER (1942–)

1883 The voice is a second face.
GERARD BAUER (1888–1967)

1884 To avoid trouble, breathe through the nose. It keeps the mouth shut.

1885 To do all the talking and not be willing to listen is a form of greed.
DEMOCRITUS OF ABDERA
(C. 460–C. 370 B.C.)

1886 To talk much and arrive nowhere is the same as climbing a tree to catch a fish.
CHINESE PROVERB

1887 Two things indicate weakness: to be silent when it is proper to speak, and to speak when it is proper to be silent.
PERSIAN PROVERB

1888 We make more enemies by what we say than friends by what we do.
SPANISH PROVERB

1889 Well-timed silence has more eloquence than speech.
MARTIN FARQUHAR TUPPER (1810–1889)

1890 What the heart did think, the tongue would click.
PROVERB

1891 When you speak, remember God is one of your listeners.

1892 Your chances of blowing it are directly proportional to the amount of time you spend with your mouth open. Try closing it for a while.
CHARLES R. SWINDOLL (1934–)

CONVERSION

1893 A man can accept what Christ has done without knowing how it works; indeed he certainly won't know how it works until he's accepted it.
C. S. LEWIS (1898–1963)

1894 A turn involves two things: it involves a terminus a quo and a terminus ad quem. It involves a turning from something and a turning toward something.
WILLIAM BARCLAY (1907–1978)

1895 Conversion is a deep work—a heart work. It goes throughout the man, throughout the mind, throughout the members, throughout the entire life.
JOSEPH ALLEINE (1634–1668)

1896 Conversion is so simple that the smallest child can be converted, but it is also so profound that theologians throughout history have pondered the depth of its meaning.
BILLY GRAHAM (1918–)

1897 Conversion may occur in an instant, but the process of coming from sinfulness into a new life can be a long and arduous journey.
CHARLES COLSON (1931–)

1898 Conversion simply means turning around.
VINCENT MCNABB (1868–1943)

1899 Every story of conversion is the story of a blessed defeat.
C. S. LEWIS (1898–1963)

1900 For one man conversion means the slaying of the beast within him; in another it brings the calm of conviction to an unquiet mind; for a third it is the entrance into a larger liberty and a more abundant life; and yet again it is the gathering into one of the forces of a soul at war with itself.
GEORGE JACKSON (1785–1861)

1901 He who made us also remade us.
SAINT AUGUSTINE OF HIPPO (354–430)

1902 In what way, or by what manner of working God changes a soul from evil to good—how he impregnates the barren rock with priceless gems and gold—is, to the human mind, an impenetrable mystery.
SAMUEL TAYLOR COLERIDGE (1772–1834)

1903 It is not necessary that we should be able to tell where or how we have been converted, but it is important

that we should be able to tell that we are converted.
DWIGHT LYMAN MOODY (1837–1899)

1904 It is true that the convert has laid upon him an obligation like no obligation in all the world because he has been loved with a love like no other love in the world; but the convert has also been given a peace like none in the world, for he knows that God loves him, not for what he is, but for what God is.
WILLIAM BARCLAY (1907–1978)

1905 Jesus Christ burst from the grave and exploded in my heart.
DONNA HOSFORD

1906 My life collided with me. Christ, the master adjuster, investigated and cancelled my policy. Then he gave me his.
MARILYN BARTLETT

1907 No man ever really comes to himself without meeting God somewhere along the way.
ROY L. SMITH

1908 The sincere convert is not one man at church and another at home. He is not a saint on his knees and a cheat in his shop. He will not tithe mint and cummin, and neglect mercy and judgment.
JOSEPH ALLEINE (1634–1668)

1909 We should think of conversion, not as the acceptance of a particular creed, but as a change of heart.
HELEN ADAMS KELLER (1880–1968)

1910 With your calling and your crying you broke through my deafness. Your shining and your splendor drove out my blindness.
SAINT AUGUSTINE OF HIPPO (354–430)

CONVICTION

1911 Martyrdom has always been a proof of the intensity, never of the correctness of a belief.
ARTHUR SCHNITZLER (1862–1931)

1912 Never, for sake of peace and quiet, deny your own experience or convictions.
DAG HAMMARSKJÖLD (1905–1961)

1913 The enemies a person makes by taking a stand will have more respect for him than the friends he makes by being on the fence.
PROVERB

1914 The great thing in this world is not so much where we stand, as in what direction we are moving.
OLIVER WENDELL HOLMES (1809–1894)

COURAGE

1915 'Tis nothing for a man to hold up his head in a calm; but to maintain his post when all others have quitted their ground and there to stand upright when other men are beaten down is divine.
LUCIUS ANNAEUS SENECA (C. 4 B.C.–A.D. 65)

1916 A great deal of talent is lost in this world for want of a little courage.
SYDNEY SMITH (1771–1845)

1917 A man without courage is a knife without an edge.
BENJAMIN FRANKLIN (1706–1790)

1918 And having thus chosen our course, let us renew our trust in God and go forward without fear and with manly hearts.
ABRAHAM LINCOLN (1809–1865)

1919 Courage is fear that has said its prayers.
DOROTHY BERNARD

1920 Courage is resistance to fear, mastery of fear, not absence of fear.
MARK TWAIN (1835–1910)

1921 Do not ask the Lord for a life free from grief, instead ask for courage that endures.

1922 Far better it is to dare mighty things, to win glorious triumphs, even though checkered by failure, than to take rank with those poor spirits who neither enjoy much nor suffer much because they live in the gray twilight that knows not victory nor defeat.
THEODORE ROOSEVELT (1858–1919)

1923 Fear can keep a man out of danger, but courage can support him in it.
SIR THOMAS FULLER (1608–1661)

1924 Have plenty of courage. God is stronger than the devil. We are on the winning side.
JOHN JAY CHAPMAN (1862–1933)

1925 Here I stand; I can do no other. God help me. Amen!
—Speech at the Diet of Worms, April 18, 1521
MARTIN LUTHER (1483–1546)

1926 I am only one, but I am one.
I can't do everything, but
I can do something.
And what I can do, I ought to do.
And what I ought to do, by the
Grace of God, I shall do.
EDWARD EVERETT HALE (1822–1909)

1927 I do not ask to walk smooth paths
Nor bear an easy load,
I pray for strength and fortitude
To climb the rock-strewn road.
Give me such courage I can scale
The hardest peaks alone,
And transform every stumbling block
Into a stepping-stone.
GAIL BROOK BURKET

1928 It takes guts to leave the ruts.
ROBERT HAROLD SCHULLER (1926–)

1929 Never undertake anything for which you wouldn't have the courage to ask the blessings of heaven.
GEORG CHRISTOPH LICHTENBERG (1742–1799)

1930 No man can answer for his courage who has never been in danger.
FRANÇOIS, DUC DE LA ROCHEFOUCAULD (1813–1913)

1931 Noah was a brave man to sail in a wooden boat with two termites.

1932 One man with courage makes a majority.
ANDREW JACKSON (1767–1845)

1933 Renew the courage that prevails,
The steady faith that never fails,
And makes us stand in every fight
Firm as a fortress to defend the right.
HENRY VAN DYKE (1852–1933)

1934 Some have been thought brave because they were afraid to run away.
SIR THOMAS FULLER (1608–1661)

1935 Take courage. We walk in the wilderness today and in the Promised Land tomorrow.
DWIGHT LYMAN MOODY (1837–1899)

1936 The Bible is a first-hand story of goose-bump courage in very ordinary people who were invaded by the living God.
TIM HANSEL

1937 The coward seeks release from pressure. The courageous pray for strength.
FRANCES J. ROBERTS

1938 The test of courage comes when we are in the minority; the test of tolerance when we are in the majority.
RALPH WASHINGTON SOCKMAN (1889–1970)

1939 Those who have courage to love should have courage to suffer.
ANTHONY TROLLOPE (1815–1882)

1940 Why not go out on a limb? Isn't that where the fruit is?
FRANK SCULLY

1941 You needn't go to war to test your courage—have your teeth fixed.
ED HOWE (1853–1937)

COURTESY

1942 A polite man is one who listens with interest to things he knows about when they are told to him by a person who knows nothing about them.
PHILLIPE DE MORNAY (1549–1623)

1943 It's better to be last in the traffic lane than first in the funeral procession.
PROVERB

1944 Nothing is ever lost by courtesy. It is the cheapest of the pleasures; costs nothing and conveys much. It pleases him who gives and him who receives, and thus, like mercy, it is twice blessed.
ERASTUS WIMAN

1945 Politeness goes far, yet costs nothing.
SAMUEL SMILES (1812–1904)

1946 Politeness is like an air cushion: there may be nothing in it, but it eases our jolts wonderfully.
SAMUEL JOHNSON (1709–1784)

1947 We must be as courteous to a man as we are to a picture which we are will-

ing to give the advantage of a good light.
RALPH WALDO EMERSON (1803–1882)

COWARDICE

1948 Fear has its use but cowardice has none.
MAHATMA GANDHI (1869–1948)

1949 Many would be cowards if they have courage enough.
SIR THOMAS FULLER (1608–1661)

1950 There are several good protections against temptations, but the surest is cowardice.
MARK TWAIN (1835–1910)

1951 We all live in the protection of certain cowardices which we call our principles.
MARK TWAIN (1835–1910)

CREATION

1952 A handful of the earth to make God's image!
ELIZABETH BARRETT BROWNING (1806–1861)

1953 A house testifies that there was a builder, a dress that there was a weaver, a door that there was a carpenter; so our world by its existence proclaims its Creator, God.
RABBI AKIBA BEN JOSEPH (C. 40–135)

1954 A human being: an ingenious assembly of portable plumbing.
CHRISTOPHER DARLINGTON MORLEY (1890–1957)

1955 All created things are but the crumbs which fall from the table of God.
SAINT JOHN OF THE CROSS (1542–1591)

1956 All God's great works are silent. They are not done amid rattle of drums and flare of trumpets. Light as it travels makes no noise, utters no sound to the ear. Creation is a silent process; nature rose under the Almighty hand without clang or clamor, or noises that distract and disturb.
ANDREW MARTIN FAIRBAIRN (1838–1912)

1957 All the world in a grain of sand; all the universe too. If I could understand a

grain of sand, I should understand everything.
MALCOLM MUGGERIDGE (1903–1990)

1958 Could blind chance create symmetry and rhythm and light and color and melody? Or begin with the mathematics of the universe? The great mathematicians—Euclid, Newton, Einstein—did not create mathematical order; they uncovered the truth that was already there.
HARRY EMERSON FOSDICK (1878–1969)

1959 Everything is a thought of Infinite God. And in studying the movements of the solar system, or the composition of an ultimate cell arrested in a crystal, developed in a plant; in tracing the grains of phosphorus in the brain of man; or in the powers, and action thereof—I am studying the thought of the Infinite God.
THEODORE PARKER (1810–1860)

1960 God has four ways of making a human body. He can create one without the agency of either man or woman as he did when he made Adam out of the dust of the ground. Then God can form a body through the agency of just a man as he did when he formed Eve from the rib taken from Adam's side. A third way is through the agency of both a man and a woman. This is the common way, the way we have received our bodies. But God can also form a body through the agency of just a woman, and that is the way our Lord received his body—born of a virgin.
R. I. HUMBRED

1961 God must have made some parts of creation for sheer fun—how else would you account for the kangaroo?
G. K. CHESTERTON (1874–1936)

1962 I repent me of the ignorance wherein I ever said that God made man out of nothing: there is no nothing out of which to make anything; God is all in all, and he made us out of himself. He who is parted from God has no original nothingness with which to take refuge.
GEORGE MACDONALD (1824–1905)

1963 In the vast and the minute we see
The unambiguous footsteps of the God
Who gives its luster to an insect's wing
And wheels his throne upon the
        whirling worlds.
WILLIAM COWPER (1731–1800)

1964 Let us study the visible creation as we
will; take the anatomy of the smallest
animal; look at the smallest grain of
corn that is planted in the earth, and
the manner in which its germ produces
and multiplies; observe attentively the
rose-bud, how carefully it opens to the
sun and closes at its setting; and we
shall see more skill and design than in
all the works of man.
FRANÇOIS FÉNELON (1651–1715)

1965 Man is heaven's masterpiece.
FRANCIS QUARLES (1592–1644)

1966 My heart is awed within me when I
        think
Of the great miracle that still goes on,
In silence, round me—the perpetual
        work
Of thy creation, finished, yet renewed
        forever.
Written on thy works I read
The lesson of thy own eternity.
WILLIAM CULLEN BRYANT (1794–1878)

1967 Open, ye heavens, your living doors;
        let in
The great Creator from his work
        return'd
Magnificent, his six days' work,
        a world!
JOHN MILTON (1608–1674)

1968 The created world is but a small parenthesis in eternity.
SIR THOMAS BROWNE (1605–1682)

1969 The creation of a thousand forests is
in one acorn.
RALPH WALDO EMERSON (1803–1882)

1970 The Creator of the earth is the owner
of it.
JOHN WOOLMAN (1720–1772)

1971 The extravagant gesture is the very
stuff of creation. After the one extravagant gesture of creation in the first
place, the universe has continued to
deal exclusively in extravagances, flinging intricacies and colossi down aeons

of emptiness, heaping profusions on
profligacies with ever fresh vigor. The
whole show has been on fire from the
word go!
ANNIE DILLARD (1945–)

1972 The Genesis account of creation is
brief, giving evidence of having been
intended only as a prologue to the
more important human drama.
SOLOMON GOLDMAN (1893–1953)

1973 The glory of creation is in its infinite
diversity.

1974 The universe seems to have been
designed by a pure mathematician.
SIR JAMES HOPWOOD JEANS (1877–1946)

1975 The world is the immeasurable totality
of energies and forms, a tissue of relations extending into ever-increasing
enormity and withdrawing into ever-
decreasing minuteness. All this was
thought, willed, and realized by God.
Nothing was supplied for him, neither
models nor matter. And all these forms
and arrangements, so full of truth,
which science strives unceasingly to
penetrate, only to see again and again
that they continue into the vast
unknown; this profusion of value and
meaning which ever and ever again
impinges upon the human mind yet
can never be fathomed—God has
made them.
ROMANO GUARDINI (1885–1968)

1976 The world was built in order
And the atoms march in tune.
RALPH WALDO EMERSON (1803–1882)

1977 The world we inhabit must have had
an origin; that origin must have con-
sisted in a cause; that cause must have
been intelligent; that intelligence must
have been supreme; and that supreme,
which always was and is supreme, we
know by the name of God.
NIKITA IVANOVICH PANIN (1718–1783)

1978 To say that God is Creator is another
way of saying that he is Father; had he
not been Father, he would not have
been Creator. It was being Father that
made him want to create. Because he
was infinitely pleased in his Son, he
wanted sons, and it was in the image

of his Son that he made the world. His creation was an overflowing of love and delight.
LOUIS EVELY (1910–   )

1979 What can be more foolish than to think that all this rare fabric of heaven and earth could come by chance, when all the skill of science is not able to make an oyster.
JEREMY TAYLOR (1613–1667)

1980 What is there more natural, and yet more magnificent, what is easier to conceive and more in accord with human reason, than the Creator descending into the primordial night to make light with a word?
FRANÇOIS RENÉ, VICOMTE DE CHATEAUBRIAND (1768–1848)

1981 When God conceived the world, that was poetry. He formed it, and that was sculpture. He colored it, and that was painting. He peopled it with living beings, and that was the grand, divine, eternal drama.
DAVID BELASCO (1853–1931)

1982 When God scooped up a handful of dust,
And spit on it, and molded the shape of man,
And blew a breath into it and told it to walk—
That was a great day.
CARL SANDBURG (1878–1967)

1983 Whoever considers the study of anatomy, I believe will never be an atheist.
EDWARD HERBERT (1583–1648)

1984 Wonderful and vast as is the universe, man is greater. The universe does not know that it exists; man does. The universe is not free to act; man is.
MARTIN J. SCOTT

CREATION/EVOLUTION

1985 I don't believe your own bastard theory of evolution either; I believe it's pure jackass nonsense.
BILLY SUNDAY (1862–1935)

1986 It shall be unlawful for any teacher in any of the universities, normals, and all other public schools of the State which are supported in whole or in part by the public school funds of the State, to teach any theory that denies the story of the divine creation of man as taught in the Bible, and to teach instead that man has descended from a lower order of animals.
—Tennessee Legislature Act, March 21, 1925. Repealed, May 17, 1967

1987 So far, evolution has been nothing but staggering from one error to the other.
HENRIK IBSEN (1828–1906)

1988 Some call it evolution, and others call it God.
W. H. CARRUTH (1859–1924)

1989 That the universe was formed by a fortuitous concourse of atoms, I will no more believe than that the accidental jumbling of the alphabet would fall into a most ingenious treatise of philosophy.
JONATHAN SWIFT (1667–1745)

1990 The evolutionists seem to know everything about the missing link except the fact that it is missing.
G. K. CHESTERTON (1874–1936)

1991 What shall we say of the intelligence . . . of those who distinguish between fishes and reptiles and birds, but put a man with an immortal soul in the same circle with the wolf, the hyena, and the skunk?
WILLIAM JENNINGS BRYAN (1860–1925)

1992 There is no more reason to believe that man descended from an inferior animal than there is to believe that a stately mansion has descended from a small cottage.
WILLIAM JENNINGS BRYAN (1860–1925)

CREATIVITY

1993 A true work of art is but a shadow of divine perfection.
MICHELANGELO (1475–1564)

1994 Adam was the only man who, when he said a good thing, knew that nobody had said it before him.
MARK TWAIN (1835–1910)

1995 Art is the gift of God and must be used for his glory. That in art is highest which aims at this.
MICHELANGELO (1475–1564)

1996 As soon as any art is pursued with a view of money, then farewell, in ninety-nine cases out of a hundred, all hope of genuine good work.
SAMUEL BUTLER (1835–1902)

1997 Creative force, like a musical composer, goes on unweariedly repeating a simple air or theme, now high, now low, in solo, in chorus, ten thousand times reverberated till it fills earth and heaven with the chant.
RALPH WALDO EMERSON (1803–1882)

1998 Creative men and women are in the church. Some express their art through music, the only art fully accepted by the church. But others sit quietly alone; waiting to be affirmed, encouraged, supported. They are waiting for the body of Christ to understand and find room for the novel, the film, the play, the masterpiece ruminating within that could reach beyond the subculture and challenge the basic assumptions of our secular age and point the world toward ultimate truth.
MAX McLEAN

1999 Creativity is the basic attribute of God, identical with his uniqueness.
HERMANN COHEN (1842–1918)

2000 Don't expect anything original from an echo.

2001 Everything has been thought of before, the problem is to think of it again.
JOHANN WOLFGANG VON GOETHE (1749–1832)

2002 God is our Creator. God made us in his image and likeness. Therefore we are creators. . . . The joy of creativeness should be ours.
DOROTHY MAY DAY (1897–1980)

2003 High heels were invented by somebody who was kissed on the forehead.
CHRISTOPHER MARLEY

2004 I invent nothing. I rediscover.
AUGUSTE RODIN (1840–1917)

2005 Imagination is more important than knowledge.
ALBERT EINSTEIN (1879–1955)

2006 Imitation is the sincerest form of flattery.
CHARLES CALEB COLTON (1780–1832)

2007 In creating, the only hard thing's to begin;
A grass-blade's no easier to make than an oak.
JAMES RUSSELL LOWELL (1819–1891)

2008 It is better to fail in originality than to succeed in imitation.
HERMAN MELVILLE (1819–1891)

2009 No work noble or lastingly good can come of emulation any more than of greed: I think the motives are spiritually the same.
GEORGE MACDONALD (1824–1905)

2010 Nothing is ordinary if you know how to use it.
WILLIAM WOLCOTT

2011 Originality does not consist in saying what no one has ever said before, but in saying exactly what you think yourself.
JAMES STEPHENS (1882–1950)

2012 Originality, I fear, is too often only undetected and frequently unconscious plagiarism.
WILLIAM RALPH INGE (1860–1954)

2013 Oscar Wilde put it this way: "An idea that isn't dangerous is hardly worth calling an idea at all." It's the shock part, the frightening part, the unknown element that makes an idea an idea in the first place. If you feel comfortable with it from the very first, take another look. It's probably not an idea.

2014 Overmuch organization in Christian work is always in danger of killing God-born originality; it keeps us conservative, makes our hands feeble.
OSWALD CHAMBERS (1874–1917)

2015 Painting, better than any other means, enables us to see the humility of the saints, the constancy of the martyrs, the purity of the virgins, the beauty of the angels, the love and charity with

which the seraphim burn. It raises and transports mind and soul beyond the stars, and leaves us to contemplate the eternal sovereignty of God.
VITTORIO COLONNA (1490–1547)

2016 Photography records the gamut of feelings written on the human face, the beauty of the earth and skies that man has inherited, and the wealth and confusion man has created. It is a major force in explaining man to man.
EDWARD JEAN STEICHEN (1879–1973)

2017 Poems are made by fools like me,
But only God can make a tree.
JOYCE KILMER (1886–1918)

2018 Satisfaction is felt not by those who take and make demands but by those who give and make sacrifices. In them alone the energy of life does not fail, and this is precisely what is meant by creativity.
NIKOLAI ALEKSANDROVICH BERDYAEV (1874–1948)

2019 The ideas I stand for are not mine. I borrowed them from Socrates. I swiped them from Chesterfield. I stole them from Jesus. And I put them in a book. If you don't like their rules, whose would you use?
DALE CARNEGIE (1888–1955)

2020 The world is brimming with happy thoughts just waiting to be discovered.

2021 We enjoy lovely music, beautiful paintings, a thousand intellectual delicacies, but we have no idea of their cost to those who invented them, in sleepless nights, tears, spasmodic laughter, rashes, asthmas, epilepsies, and the fear of death.
MARCEL PROUST (1871–1922)

2022 When I am finishing a picture, I hold some God-made object up to it—a rock, a flower, the branch of a tree or my hand—as a kind of final test. If the painting stands up beside a thing man cannot make, the painting is authentic. If there's a clash between the two, it is bad art.
MARC CHAGALL (1887–1985)

2023 When you think about it, for sheer bulk there's more art done with Crayolas than with anything else. There must be billions of sheets of paper in every country in the world, in billions of boxes and closets and attics and cupboards, covered with billions of pictures in crayon. The imagination of the human race poured out like a river.
ROBERT FULGHUM

2024 Without this playing with fantasy no creative work has ever yet come to birth. The debt we owe to the play of imagination is incalculable.
CARL GUSTAV JUNG (1875–1961)

CREEDS

2025 A Christian is to be consistent only to the life of the Son of God in him, not consistent to hard and fast creeds.
OSWALD CHAMBERS (1874–1917)

2026 A creed is the road or street. It is very good as far as it goes, but if it doesn't take us to Christ it is worthless.
DWIGHT LYMAN MOODY (1837–1899)

2027 Brother, the creed would stifle me that shelters you.
KARLE WILSON BAKER

2028 Faithfully faithful to every trust,
Honestly honest in every deed,
Righteously righteous and justly just;
This is the whole of the good man's creed.

2029 Human hopes and human creeds
Have their root in human needs.
EUGENE FITCH WARE 1841–1911

2030 If you have a Bible creed, it is well; but is it filled out and inspired by Christian love?
J. F. BRODIE

2031 The only creed that is worth twopence to you is not a creed that you tried to take over from your grandfather. The only creed that is going to be worth anything to you is the creed you built up out of your own experience of Christ.
LESLIE D. WEATHERHEAD (1893–1976)

2032 The proper question to be asked about any creed is not "Is it pleasant?" but "Is it true?"
DOROTHY L. SAYERS (1893–1957)

2033 Volumes of angry controversy have been poured out about the Christian creeds, under the impression that they represent, not statement of facts, but arbitrary edicts. The conditions of salvation, for instance, are discussed as though they were conditions for membership in some fantastic club like the Red-Headed League.
DOROTHY L. SAYERS (1893–1957)

CRIME

2034 Crime is inherent in human nature; the germ is in every man.
H. B. IRVING

2035 He sins as much who holds the bag as he who puts into it.
FRENCH PROVERB

2036 He who holds the ladder is as bad as the thief.
GERMAN PROVERB

2037 He who profits by a crime commits it.
PROVERB

2038 Punishment hardens and numbs, it produces concentration, it sharpens the consciousness of alienation, it strengthens the power of resistance.
FRIEDRICH WILHELM NIETZSCHE (1844–1900)

2039 Purposelessness is the fruitful mother of crime.
CHARLES HENRY PARKHURST (1842–1933)

2040 So many are the shapes of crime.
VIRGIL A. KRAFT

2041 What man was ever content with one crime?
JUVENAL (C. 60–C. 127)

CRISIS

2042 After crises crush sufficiently, God steps in to comfort and teach.
CHARLES R. SWINDOLL (1934–   )

2043 Crises and deadlocks have at least this advantage, that they force us to think.
JAWAHARLAL NEHRU (1889–1964)

2044 Crises refine life. In them you discover what you are.
ALLAN K. CHALMERS

2045 Genuine love demands toughness in moments of crisis.
JAMES C. DOBSON (1936–   )

2046 Growth in the Christian life depends on obedience in times of crisis.
JAMES C. DOBSON (1936–   )

2047 In crisis the most daring course is often the safest.
HENRY KISSINGER (1923–   )

2048 The Chinese symbols for *crisis* are identical to those for the word *opportunity*. Literally translated it reads, "Crisis is an opportunity riding the dangerous wind." View crises as opportunities, and stumbling blocks as stepping-stones to the stars.
DENIS WAITLEY

CRITICISM

2049 A faultfinder is a person with a bad memory who never remembers the good, or a person with a good memory who always remembers the bad.

2050 A malignant deity, called Critisism . . . At her right hand sat Ignorance, her father and husband, blind with age; at her left, Pride, her mother, dressing her up in scraps of paper she herself had torn. There was Opinion, her sister, light of foot, hoodwinked, and headstrong, yet giddy and perpetually turning. About her played her children, Noise and Impudence, Dullness and Vanity, Positiveness, Pedantry, and Ill-Manners. The goddess herself had claws like a cat, her head, and ears, and voice resembled those of an ass; her teeth fallen out before, her eyes turned inward, as if she also looked only upon herself; her diet was the overflowing of her own gall.
JONATHAN SWIFT (1667–1745)

2051 A sharp word cuts deeper than a
weapon.
PROVERB

2052 And so it criticized each flower,
This supercilious seed;
Until it woke one summer hour,
And found itself a weed.
MILDRED HOWELLS (1872–1966)

2053 Boredom, after all, is a form of criticism.
WILLIAM PHILLIPS

2054 By seeing the tremendous blossoming
which a person can experience when
surrounded by love and confidence,
when he does not feel judged, we can
measure the stifling power of other
people's criticism.
PAUL TOURNIER (1898–1986)

2055 Criticism is futile because it puts a
man on the defensive and usually
makes him strive to justify himself.
Criticism is dangerous because it
wounds a man's precious pride, hurts
his sense of importance, and arouses
his resentment.
DALE CARNEGIE (1888–1955)

2056 Criticism leaves you with the flattering
unction that you are a superior person. It is impossible to develop the
characteristics of a saint and maintain
a critical attitude.
OSWALD CHAMBERS (1874–1917)

2057 Criticism, like rain, should be gentle
enough to nourish a man's growth
without destroying his roots.
FRANK A. CLARK

2058 Do not remove a fly from your friend's
forehead with a hatchet.
CHINESE PROVERB

2059 Find the grain of truth in criticism—
chew it and swallow it.
D. SUTTEN

2060 He has the right to criticize who has
the heart to help.
ABRAHAM LINCOLN (1809–1865)

2061 He who criticizes another needs himself to be outstanding.
PLAUTUS (C. 254–184 B.C.)

2062 He who sifts people with a coarse
sieve shall find people sifting him with
a very fine one.
ARABIAN PROVERB

2063 He who wants to blame finds the
sugar sour.
GERMAN PROVERB

2064 If it's very painful for you to criticize
your friends—you're safe in doing it.
But if you take the slightest pleasure in
it—that's the time to hold your tongue.
ALICE DUER MILLER (1874–1942)

2065 If your brother is a donkey, what are
you?

2066 It is harder to avoid censure than to
gain applause, for this may be done by
one great or wise action in an age; but
to escape censure a man must pass his
whole life without saying or doing one
ill or foolish thing.
DAVID HUME (1711–1776)

2067 It is much easier to be critical than to
be correct.
BENJAMIN DISRAELI (1804–1881)

2068 Man who beef too much find himself
in stew.
CHINESE PROVERB

2069 Nagging is a form of continual criticism whereby the same complaint is
repeated over and over.
MORRIS CHALFANT

2070 No man can justly censure or condemn another because no man truly
knows another.
SIR THOMAS BROWNE (1605–1682)

2071 On facing criticism: If what they are
saying about you is true, mend your
ways. If it isn't true, forget it, and go
on and serve the Lord.
H. A. IRONSIDE (1876–1951)

2072 One should examine oneself for a very
long time before thinking of condemning others.
JEAN BAPTISTE MOLIÈRE (1622–1673)

2073 People who are always pointing fingers rarely hold out their hands.

2074 Silence is sometimes the severest criticism.
CHARLES BUXTON (1823–1871)

2075 The camel never sees its own hump; but its neighbor's hump is ever before its eyes.
ARABIAN PROVERB

2076 The faultfinder is a person who has one sharp eye for faults, and one blind eye for virtues.

2077 The faults of others are like headlights of an approaching car—they always seem more glaring than our own.

2078 The Holy Ghost alone is in the true position of a critic; he is able to show what is wrong without wounding and hurting.
OSWALD CHAMBERS (1874–1917)

2079 The sieve says to the needle, "You have a hole in your head."
INDIAN PROVERB

2080 They blame the man who is silent, they blame the man who speaks too much, and they blame the man who speaks too little.
ANTISTHENES (C. 445–C. 365 B.C.)

2081 They condemn what they do not understand.
CICERO (106–43 B.C.)

2082 To avoid criticism, do nothing, say nothing, be nothing.
ELBERT GREEN HUBBARD (1856–1915)

2083 To speak ill of others is a dishonest way of praising ourselves.
WILL DURANT (1885–1981)

2084 When we persecute and hurt the children of God, we are but persecuting God and hurting ourselves far more.
ALBERT BENJAMIN SIMPSON (1843–1919)

2085 You may find hundreds of faultfinders among professed Christians; but all their criticism will not lead one solitary soul to Christ. I never preached a sermon yet that I could not pick to pieces, and find fault with. I feel that Jesus Christ ought to have a far better representative than I am. But I have lived long enough to discover that there is nothing perfect in this world. If you are to wait till you find a perfect preacher, or perfect meetings, I am afraid you will have to wait till the millennium arrives. What we want is to be looking up to Christ. Let us be done with faultfinding.
DWIGHT LYMAN MOODY (1837–1899)

2086 You should not say it is not good. You should say you do not like it; then you're perfectly safe.
JAMES ABBOT MCNEILL WHISTLER (1834–1903)

CROSS

2087 A man who is always on the cross, just piece after piece, cannot be happy in that process. But when that man takes his place on the cross with Jesus Christ once and for all, and commends his spirit to God, lets go of everything and ceases to defend himself—sure, he has died, but there is a resurrection that follows!
A. W. TOZER (1897–1963)

2088 Carry the cross patiently and with perfect submission and in the end it shall carry you.
THOMAS À KEMPIS (C. 1380–1471)

2089 God . . . will treat us without pity because he desires to raise us without measure—just as he did with his own Son on the cross!
A. W. TOZER (1897–1963)

2090 God gives us the cross, and then the cross gives us God.
MADAME JEANNE MARIE DE LA MOTHE GUYON (1648–1717)

2091 I don't pray that you may be delivered from your troubles; rather, I pray that God will give you the strength and patience to bear them. Comfort yourself with him who nails you to the cross. He will let you go when he is ready. Happy are those who suffer with him.
BROTHER LAWRENCE OF THE RESURRECTION (C. 1605–1691)

2092 If the cross suited us, it would no longer be a cross, and if we refuse those that hurt us, we will refuse all crosses. The cross which God sends us must of necessity always be humiliating, painful, paralyzing, difficult. The cross is precisely what hurts us in that

place where we are most disarmed and vulnerable.
LOUIS EVELY (1910–)

2093 If we are wise, we will do what Jesus said: endure the cross and despise its shame for the joy that is set before us. To do this is to submit the whole pattern of our life to be destroyed and built again in the power of an endless life. And we shall find that it is more than poetry, more than sweet hymnody and elevated feeling. The cross will cut into our lives where it hurts worst, sparing neither us nor our carefully cultivated reputation. It will defeat us and bring our selfish life to an end.
A. W. TOZER (1897–1963)

2094 If your love for the Lord is pure, you will love him as much on Calvary as on Mt. Tabor.
MADAME JEANNE MARIE DE LA MOTHE GUYON (1648–1717)

2095 If you put fine grapes into the winepress, there will come out a delicious juice; our souls, in the winepress of the cross, give out juice which nourishes and strengthens.
SAINT JEAN BAPTISTE MARIE VIANNEY (1786–1859)

2096 In the cross is health, in the cross is life, in the cross is protection from enemies, in the cross is heavenly sweetness, in the cross strength of mind, in the cross joy of the Spirit, in the cross the height of virtue, in the cross perfection of holiness. There is no health of the soul, no hope of eternal life, save in the cross.
THOMAS À KEMPIS (C. 1380–1471)

2097 Let us remember that when we talk of rending the veil, we are speaking in a figure, and the thought of it is poetical, almost pleasant; but in actuality there is nothing pleasant about it. In human experience that veil is made of living spiritual tissue; it is composed of the sentient, quivering stuff of which our whole being consist, and to touch it is to touch us where we feel pain. To tear it away is to injure us, to hurt us and make us bleed. . . . That is what

the cross did to Jesus, and it is what the cross would do to every man to set him free. Let us beware of tinkering with our inner life in hope ourselves to rend the veil. God must do everything for us. Our part is to yield and trust.
A. W. TOZER (1897–1963)

2098 May I be willing, Lord, to bear
Daily my cross for thee;
Even thy cup of grief to share,
Thou hast borne all for me.
JENNIE EVELYN HUSSEY (1874–1958)

2099 My God, I have never thanked thee for my thorn. I have thanked thee a thousand times for my roses, but not once for my thorn. I have been looking forward to a world where I shall get compensation for my cross, but I have never thought of my cross as itself a present glory. Thou divine Love, whose human path has been perfected through sufferings, teach me the glory of my cross, teach me the value of my thorn.
GEORGE MATHESON (1842–1906)

2100 No powers can separate us from God's love in Christ. Unmasked, revealed in their true nature, they have lost their mighty grip on men. The cross has disarmed them: wherever it is preached, the unmasking and disarming of the Powers takes place.
HENDRIK BERKHOF

2101 Nothing in my hand I bring,
Simply to thy cross I cling.
AUGUSTUS MONTAGUE TOPLADY (1740–1778)

2102 Our Lord promised a cross and scars, not medals, down here. The honors are given out later.
VANCE HAVNER

2103 The believer's cross is no longer any and every kind of suffering, sickness, or tension, the bearing of which is demanded. The believer's cross must be, like his Lord's, the price of his social nonconformity. It is not, like sickness or catastrophe, an inexplicable, unpredictable suffering; it is the end of a path freely chosen after counting the cost. . . . It is the social reality

of representing in an unwilling world the Order to come.
JOHN HOWARD YODER

2104 The cross is "I" crossed out.

2105 The cross is always ready, everywhere in wait for you. You cannot escape it wherever you run, for wherever you go, you carry yourself with you and will always find yourself. Turn yourself upwards, turn yourself inwards—everywhere you will find the cross, everywhere you must hold tight to patience if you will have inward peace and earn an everlasting crown.
THOMAS À KEMPIS (C. 1380–1471)

2106 The cross is rough, and it is deadly, but it is effective.
A. W. TOZER (1897–1963)

2107 The cross is the pain involved in doing the will of God.
OSWALD CHAMBERS (1874–1917)

2108 The cross of Jesus Christ is a revelation; our cross is an experience.
OSWALD CHAMBERS (1874–1917)

2109 The cross would not be a cross to us if it destroyed in us only the unreal and the artificial. It is when it goes on to slay the best in us that its cruel sharpness is felt.
A. W. TOZER (1897–1963)

2110 The greatest of all crosses is self—if we die in part every day, we shall have but little to do on the last. These little daily deaths will destroy the power of the final dying.
FRANÇOIS FÉNELON (1651–1715)

2111 The man with a cross no longer controls his destiny; he lost control when he picked up his cross. That cross immediately became to him an all-absorbing interest, an overwhelming interference. No matter what he may desire to do, there is but one thing he can do; that is, move on toward the place of crucifixion.
A. W. TOZER (1897–1963)

2112 The way to bliss lies not on beds of down,
And he that has no cross deserves no crown.
FRANCIS QUARLES (1592–1644)

2113 There is no escaping the cross. You will feel either pain in your body or tribulation in your spirit. Sometimes you will feel deserted by God. Sometimes your neighbor will trouble you. Quite frankly, you will sometimes be a burden to yourself. As long as God wants you to bear it, there can be no remedy for your suffering because there are some vital lessons you need to learn.
THOMAS À KEMPIS (C. 1380–1471)

2114 To resist one's cross is to make it heavier.
HENRI FRÉDÉRIC AMIEL (1821–1881)

2115 To take up the cross means that you take your stand for the Lord Jesus no matter what it costs.
BILLY GRAHAM (1918–)

2116 We all know that a Christian must bear the cross. In theory we are all prepared to accept one. But you will no doubt have noticed that the cross that comes our way is never the right one. The cross we bear (our health, our face, our circumstances, our family, our stupid job, our failure—or our stupid success) always seem to us to be intolerable, mean, humiliating, harmful. . . . Desperately we call for another, a cross made to our own size, a cross which will be bearable, spiritual, elevating, beneficial to ourselves and to others.
LOUIS EVELY (1910–)

2117 We must do something about the cross, and one of two things only we can do—flee it or die upon it.
A. W. TOZER (1897–1963)

2118 What does the apotheosis of the cross mean, if not the death of death, the defeat of sin, the beatification of martyrdom, the raising to the skies of voluntary sacrifice, the defiance of pain?
HENRI FRÉDÉRIC AMIEL (1821–1881)

2119 What is the cross? It is a minus turned into a plus.
ROBERT HAROLD SCHULLER (1926–)

2120 When Christ brings his cross, he brings his presence; and where he is,

none is desolate, and there is no room for despair. As he knows his own, so he knows how to comfort them, using sometimes the very grief itself, and straining it to a sweetness of peace unattainable by those ignorant of sorrow.
ELIZABETH BARRETT BROWNING (1806–1861)

2121 Yesterday I hung on the cross with Christ; today I am glorified with him; yesterday I was dying with him; today I am brought to life with him; yesterday I was buried with him; today I rise with him. Let us become like Christ, since Christ also became like us. Let us become gods for him, since he became man for us.
GREGORY OF NYSSA (C. 335–C. 394)

CRUCIFIXION

2122 All heaven is interested in the cross of Christ, all hell terribly afraid of it, while men are the only beings who more or less ignore its meaning.
OSWALD CHAMBERS (1874–1917)

2123 Before lambs bled in Egypt, One was given.
Before the worm tore Eden, pain was faced.
Somewhere, before earth's cornerstone was placed,
a hammer crashed in heaven—nails were driven.
KEITH PATMAN

2124 Calvary is the place of decision. It is the eternal sword, erected to divide men into two classes, the saved and the lost.
BILLY GRAHAM (1918–)

2125 Calvary means "the place of a skull" and that is where our Lord is always crucified, in the culture and intellect of men.
OSWALD CHAMBERS (1874–1917)

2126 Christ did not die a martyr. He died— infinitely more humbly—a common criminal.
SIMONE WEIL (1909–1943)

2127 Christ in his weakest hour performed his greatest work—dying on the cross to redeem mankind.

2128 For him to see me mended I must see him torn.
LUCI SHAW (1928–)

2129 God proved his love on the cross. When Christ hung, and bled, and died it was God saying to the world—I love you.
BILLY GRAHAM (1918–)

2130 God sat in silence while the sins of the world were placed upon his Son. Was it right? No. Was it fair? No. Was it love? Yes. In a world of injustice, God once and for all tipped the scales in the favor of hope.
MAX L. LUCADO (1955–)

2131 I argue that the cross be raised again at the center of the marketplace as well as on the steeple of the church. . . . that Jesus was not crucified in a cathedral between two candles, but on a cross between two thieves; on the town garbage heap; at a crossroads so cosmopolitan that they had to write his title in Hebrew and Latin and in Greek; at the kind of place where cynics talk smut, and thieves curse, and soldiers gamble. Because that is where he died. And that is what he died about . . . that is where churchmen should be and what churchmen should be about.
GEORGE MACLEOD

2132 In surgery I cut delicately, using scalpel blades that slice through one layer of tissue at a time, to expose the intricacies of nerves and blood vessels and tiny bones and tendons and muscles inside. I know well what crucifixion must have done to a human hand.
    Roman executioners drove their spikes through the wrist, right through the carpel tunnel that houses finger-controlling tendons and the median nerve. . . . Later, his weight hung from them, tearing more tissue, releasing more blood. Has there ever been a more helpless image than that of the Son of God hanging paralyzed from a tree? The disciples, who had hoped he was the

Messiah, cowered in the darkness or
drifted away.
PAUL BRAND

2133 In the cross of Christ I glory,
Towering o'er the wrecks of time;
All the light of sacred story
Gathers round its head sublime.
SIR JOHN BOWRING (1792–1872)

2134 It costs God nothing, so far as we
know, to create nice things: but to convert rebellious wills cost him crucifixion.
C. S. LEWIS (1898–1963)

2135 Love's as hard as nails,
Love is nails:
Blunt, thick, hammered through
The medial nerves of One
Who, having made us, knew
The thing he had done,
Seeing (with all that is)
Our cross, and his.
C. S. LEWIS (1898–1963)

2136 O my Savior, make me see
How dearly thou hast paid for me.
RICHARD CRASHAW (C. 1613–1649)

2137 One thing at least can be said with certainty about the crucifixion of Christ;
it was manifestly the most famous
death in history. No other death has
aroused one hundredth part of the
interest, or been remembered with one
hundredth part of the intensity and
concern.
MALCOLM MUGGERIDGE (1903–1990)

2138 Oneness with Christ means to be identified with Christ, identified with him
in crucifixion. But we must go on to
be identified with him in resurrection
as well, for beyond the cross is resurrection and the manifestation of his
presence.
A. W. TOZER (1897–1963)

2139 Suffering love, the cross, stands at the
heart of the church.
T. Z. KOO

2140 The Bible says that God himself
accepted the responsibility for sin; the
cross is the proof that he did. It cost
Jesus Christ to the last drop of blood
to deal with the vast evil of the world.
OSWALD CHAMBERS (1874–1917)

2141 The blood of Christ may seem to be a
grim, repulsive subject to those who
do not realize its true significance, but
to those who have accepted his
redemption and have been set free
from sin's chains, the blood of Christ
is precious.
BILLY GRAHAM (1918–)

2142 The blood that from the Lord's
beloved wounds does flow
Is the most precious dew he will on us
bestow.
ANGELUS SILESIUS (1624–1677)

2143 The cross for the first time revealed
God in terms of weakness and lowliness and suffering; even, humanly
speaking, of absurdity. He was seen
thenceforth in the image of the most
timid, most gentle, and most vulnerable of all living creatures—a lamb.
Agnus Dei!
MALCOLM MUGGERIDGE (1903–1990)

2144 The cross has revealed to good men
that their goodness has not been good
enough.
JOHANN H. SCHROEDER (1642–1704)

2145 The cross is a picture of violence, yet
the key to peace, a picture of suffering,
yet the key to healing, a picture of
death, yet the key to life.
DAVID WATSON (1933–1984)

2146 The cross is a way of life; the way of
love meeting all hate with love, all evil
with good, all negatives with positives.
RUFUS MOSELEY

2147 The cross is real wood, the nails are
real iron, the vinegar truly tastes bitter,
and the cry of desolation is live, not
recorded.
MALCOLM MUGGERIDGE (1903–1990)

2148 The cross is the crystallized point in
history where eternity merges with
time.
OSWALD CHAMBERS (1874–1917)

2149 The cross is the ladder to heaven.
THOMAS DRAXE (D. 1618)

2150 The cross is where history and life, legend and reality, time and eternity, intersect. There, Jesus is nailed forever to

show us how God could become a
man and a man become God.
MALCOLM MUGGERIDGE (1903–1990)

2151 The cross of Christ destroyed the equation religion equals happiness.
DIETRICH BONHOEFFER (1906–1945)

2152 The cross of Christ is Christ's glory.
Man seeks to win his glory by the sacrifice of others—Christ by the sacrifice
of himself. Men seek to get crowns of
gold—he sought a crown of thorns.
Men think that glory lies in being
exalted over others—Christ thought
that his glory did lie in becoming "a
worm and no man," a scoff and
reproach among all that beheld him.
He stooped when he conquered; and
he counted that the glory lay as much
in the stooping as in the conquest.
CHARLES HADDON SPURGEON (1834–1892)

2153 The cross of Christ is God's last and
endless word. There the prince of this
world is judged, there sin is killed, and
pride is done to death, there lust is frozen, and self-interest slaughtered, not
one can get through.
OSWALD CHAMBERS (1874–1917)

2154 The cross of Christ, on which he was
extended, points, in the length of it, to
heaven and earth, reconciling them
together; and in the breadth of it, to
former and following ages, as being
equally salvation to both.
SAMUEL RUTHERFORD (1600–1661)

2155 The cross of Jesus Christ is not the
cross of a martyr, but the door
whereby God keeps open house for
the universe.
OSWALD CHAMBERS (1874–1917)

2156 The cross . . . reveals the vast difference between a god who proves himself through power and One who
proves himself through love.
PHILIP YANCEY (1949–)

2157 The cross stands high above the opinions of men, and to that cross all opinions must come at last for judgment.
A. W. TOZER (1897–1963)

2158 The cross strikes at the root of the tree
rather than simply the branches.
ERWIN W. LUTZER (1941–)

2159 The Crucifixion, however else we may
interpret it, accuses human nature,
accuses all of us in the very things that
we think are our righteousness. . . .
Our attitude to the Crucifixion must
be that of self-identification with the
rest of human nature—we must say,
"We did it"; and the inability to adopt
something of the same attitude in the
case of twentieth-century events has
caused our phenomenal failure to deal
with the problem of evil.
HERBERT BUTTERFIELD (1900–)

2160 The death of Jesus goes away down
underneath the deepest, vilest sin that
human nature ever committed. Every
pious mood must be stripped off when
we stand before the cross.
OSWALD CHAMBERS (1874–1917)

2161 The death of Jesus is the only entrance
into the life he lived. We cannot get
into his life by admiring him, or by
saying what a beautiful life his was, so
pure and holy. To dwell only on his
life would drive us to despair. We
enter into his life by means of his
death. Until the Holy Spirit has had
his way with us spiritually, the death
of Jesus Christ is an insignificant
thing, and we are amazed that the
New Testament should make so much
of it.
OSWALD CHAMBERS (1874–1917)

2162 The hands of Christ
Seem very frail
For they were broken
By a nail.
But only they
Reach heaven at last
Whom these frail, broken
Hands hold fast.
JOHN RICHARD MORELAND (1880–1947)

2163 The love on the cross is not what God
suddenly became but what God
always was and ever shall be.
WILLIAM BARCLAY (1907–1978)

2164 The passion of our Lord did not end
on the cross
By night and also day he suffers still
for us.
ANGELUS SILESIUS (1624–1677)

2165 The purpose of the cross is to repair the irreparable.
ERWIN W. LUTZER (1941–   )

2166 The sovereignty of Christ from the cross is a new sovereignty. It has destroyed forever the formula that might is right. It has put to shame the self-assertion of false heroism. It has surrounded with imperishable dignity the completeness of sacrifice. It has made clear to the pure heart that the prerogative of authority is wider service. The divine King rules forever by dying.
BROOKE FOSS WESTCOTT (1825–1901)

2167 The symbol of God's nature is the cross, whose arms stretch out to limitless reaches.
OSWALD CHAMBERS (1874–1917)

2168 The world crucified Jesus because they couldn't stand him! There was something in him that rebuked them, and they hated him for it and finally crucified him.
A. W. TOZER (1897–1963)

2169 The world's one and only remedy is the cross.
CHARLES HADDON SPURGEON (1834–1892)

2170 There is an amazing sanity in Jesus Christ that shakes the foundations of death and hell, no panic, absolute dominant mastery over everything— such a stupendous mastery that he let men take his strength from him.
OSWALD CHAMBERS (1874–1917)

2171 They mocked and railed on him and smote him, they scourged and crucified him. . . . He was executed by a corrupt church, a timid politician, and a fickle proletariat led by professional agitators. His executioners made vulgar jokes about him, called him filthy names, taunted him, smacked him in the face, flogged him with the cat, and hanged him on the common gibbet—a bloody, dusty, sweaty, and sordid business.
    If you show people that, they are shocked. So they should be. If that does not shock them, nothing can. If the mere

representation of it has an air of irreverence, what is to be said about the deed?
DOROTHY L. SAYERS (1893–1957)

2172 Through his death on the cross Jesus Christ not only readjusts a man in conscience and heart to God, he does something grander, he imparts to him the power to do all God wants, he presences him with divinity, the Holy Spirit, so that he is garrisoned from within, and enabled to live without blame before God.
OSWALD CHAMBERS (1874–1917)

2173 To make a valentine God took two
      shafts of wood
And on that wood in love and anguish
      placed his Son,
Who gave his heart that mine might
Be made new.
ELEANOR WHITESIDES

2174 To ten men who talk about the character of Jesus there is only one who will talk about his cross.
OSWALD CHAMBERS (1874–1917)

2175 We go to Calvary to learn how we may be forgiven, and to learn how to forgive others, to intercede on their behalf, to join the noble band of intercessors.
S. J. REID

CYNICISM

2176 A cynic can chill and dishearten with a single word.
RALPH WALDO EMERSON (1803–1882)

2177 A cynic is a man who, when he smells flowers, looks around for a coffin.
H. L. MENCKEN (1880–1956)

2178 A cynic is not merely one who reads bitter lessons from the past; he is one who is prematurely disappointed in the future.
SYDNEY J. HARRIS (1917–1986)

2179 A cynic looks at life with a magnifying glass.
FORRESTER BARRINGTON

2180 Cynicism is an unpleasant way of saying the truth.
LILLIAN HELLMAN (1905–1984)

2181 Cynicism—the intellectual cripple's substitute for intelligence.
RUSSELL LYNES

2182 Don't be cynical. There'll be deaths and disappointments and failures. When they come, you meet them. Nobody promises you a good time or an easy time.
JAMES GOULD COZZENS (1903–1978)

2183 I hate cynicism a great deal and worse than I do the devil; unless, perhaps, the two were the same thing.
ROBERT LOUIS BALFOUR STEVENSON (1850–1894)

2184 Jesus Christ never trusted human nature, yet he was never cynical, never in despair about any man, because he trusted absolutely in what the grace of God could do in human nature.
OSWALD CHAMBERS (1874–1917)

2185 Never, never, never be a cynic, even a gentle one. Never help out a sneer, even at the devil.
VACHEL LINDSAY (1879–1931)

2186 Sour godliness is the devil's religion.
JOHN WESLEY (1703–1791)

2187 The cynic is one who never sees a good quality in a man and never fails to see a bad one. He is the human owl, vigilant in darkness and blind to light, mousing for vermin and never seeing noble game. The cynic puts all human actions into two classes—openly bad and secretly bad.
HENRY WARD BEECHER (1813–1887)

2188 Watch what people are cynical about, and one can often discover what they lack.
HARRY EMERSON FOSDICK (1878–1969)

2189 What is a cynic? A man who knows the price of everything and the value of nothing.
OSCAR WILDE (1854–1900)

D

DAY

2190 A day is a miniature eternity.
RALPH WALDO EMERSON (1803–1882)

2191 A day is a span of time no one is wealthy enough to waste.

2192 Each day comes bearing its gifts, Untie the ribbons.
ANN RUTH SCHABACKER

2193 Each day is a little life.
ARTHUR SCHOPENHAUER (1788–1860)

2194 Every day is a day of reckoning.
JOHN W. GARDNER (1912–)

2195 Every day is a messenger of God.
RUSSIAN PROVERB

2196 Every ordinary day given to God and touched by God is a sacrament.
BERTHA MUNRO

2197 Normal day, let me be aware of the treasure you are. Let me learn from you, love you, savor you, bless you before you depart. Let me not pass you by in quest of some rare and perfect tomorrow. Let me hold you while I may for it will not always be so. One day I shall dig my nails into the earth, or bury my face in the pillow, or stretch myself taut, or raise my hands to the sky, and want, more than all the world, your return.
MARY JEAN IRION

2198 So here hath been dawning
Another blue day;
Think, wilt thou let it
Slip useless away?
THOMAS CARLYLE (1795–1881)

2199 The cock crows, but daybreak is from God.
ARABIAN PROVERB

2200 The day will happen whether or not you get up.
JOHN CIARDI (1916–1986)

2201 Unwrap the hidden beauties in an ordinary day.
GERHARD E. FROST

2202 What a day may bring a day may take away.
SIR THOMAS FULLER (1608–1661)

DEATH

2203 . . . Sustained and soothed
By an unfaltering trust, approach thy grave,

Like one that wraps the drapery of his
    couch
About him, and lies down to pleasant
    dreams.
WILLIAM CULLEN BRYANT (1794–1878)

2204 A corpse is something like the cover of
an old book, its contents torn out, and
stript of its lettering and gilding . . .
yet the work itself shall not be lost, for
it will appear once more in a new and
more beautiful edition.
BENJAMIN FRANKLIN (1706–1790)

2205 A funeral among men is a wedding
feast among the angels.
KAHLIL GIBRAN (1883–1931)

2206 A good man never dies—
In worthy deed and prayer
And helpful hands, and honest eyes,
If smiles or tears be there;
Who lives for you and me—
Lives for the world he tries
To help—he lives eternally.
A good man never dies.
JAMES WHITCOMB RILEY (1849–1916)

2207 A grave, wherever found, preaches a
short and pithy sermon to the soul.
NATHANIEL HAWTHORNE (1804–1864)

2208 A man I know found out last year he
had terminal cancer. He was a doctor
and knew about dying, and he didn't
want to make his family and friends
suffer through that with him. So he
kept his secret. And died. Everybody
said how brave he was to bear his suffering in silence and not tell everybody, and so on and so forth. But
privately his family and friends said
how angry they were that he didn't
need them, didn't trust their strength.
And it hurt that he didn't say good-
bye.
ROBERT FULGHUM

2209 A man should be mourned at his birth,
not at his death.
CHARLES DE SECONDAT MONTESQUIEU
(1689–1755)

2210 A man's dying is more the survivor's
affair than his own.
THOMAS MANN (1875–1955)

2211 A single death is a tragedy, a million
deaths is a statistic.
JOSEPH STALIN (1879–1953)

2212 A sudden death is but a sudden joy.

2213 After sixty years the stern sentence of
the burial service seems to have a
meaning that one did not notice in former years. There begins to be something personal about it.
OLIVER WENDELL HOLMES (1809–1894)

2214 Ah Christ, that it were possible
For one short hour to see
The souls we loved, that they might
    tell us
What and where they be.
ALFRED, LORD TENNYSON (1809–1892)

2215 All days travel toward death, the last
one reaches it.
MICHEL EYQUEM DE MONTAIGNE
(1533–1592)

2216 All mankind is of one Author, and is
one volume; when one man dies, one
chapter is not torn out of the book,
but translated into a better language;
and every chapter must be so translated; God employs several translators;
some pieces are translated by age,
some by sickness, some by war, some
by justice; but God's hand is in every
translation, and his hand shall bind up
all our scattered leaves again for that
library where every book shall lie open
to one another.
JOHN DONNE (1572–1631)

2217 All our finite eyes could tell us
Was the sadness and the gloom,
All the emptiness and silence
Of the sorrow-striken room;
But we could not see the welcome,
Could not hear the angels sing,
Nor the shouts of exultation
As the pilgrim entered in.
F. NORMAN BARRINGTON

2218 And come he slow, or come he fast,
It is but Death who comes at last.
SIR WALTER SCOTT (1771–1832)

2219 And thou, most kind and gentle death,
Waiting to hush our latest breath;
O Praise Him—Alleluia!
Thou leadest home the child of God

And Christ our Lord the way hath
  trod.
SAINT FRANCIS OF ASSISI (C. 1181–1226)

2220 And what is so intricate, so entangling
  as death? Who ever got out of a wind-
  ing sheet?
JOHN DONNE (1572–1631)

2221 Angels, joyful to attend,
  Hov'ring, round thy pillow bend;
  Wait to catch the signal giv'n,
  And escort thee quick to heav'n.
  Saints in glory perfect made,
  Wait thy passage through the shade;
  Ardent for thy coming o'er,
  See, they throng the blissful shore.
AUGUSTUS MONTAGUE TOPLADY
(1740–1778)

2222 Anyone not coming to be a dead one
  before coming to be an old one comes
  to be an old one and comes then to be
  a dead one as any old one comes to be
  a dead one.
GERTRUDE STEIN (1874–1946)

2223 Are we willing to not run away from
  the pain, to not get busy when there is
  nothing to do and instead stand rather
  in the face of death together with
  those who grieve?
HENRI J. M. NOUWEN

2224 As a well-spent day brings happy
  sleep, so life well used brings happy
  death.
LEONARDO DA VINCI (1452–1519)

2225 As the mother's womb holds us for
  nine months, making us ready, not for
  the womb itself, but for life, just so,
  through our lives, we are making ourselves ready for another birth. . . .
  Therefore, look forward without fear
  to that appointed hour—the last hour
  of the body, but not of the soul. . . .
  That day, which you fear as being the
  end of all things, is the birthday of
  your eternity.
LUCIUS ANNAEUS SENECA (C. 4 B.C.–A.D. 65)

2226 As to death, we can experience it but
  once and are all apprentices when we
  come to it.
MICHEL EYQUEM DE MONTAIGNE
(1533–1592)

2227 At death we cross from one territory
  to another, but we'll have no trouble
  with visas. Our representative is
  already there, preparing for our
  arrival. As citizens of heaven, our
  entrance is incontestable.
ERWIN W. LUTZER (1941–)

2228 Be near me, Lord, when dying;
  O show thy cross to me;
  And, for my succour flying,
  Come, Lord to set me free;
  These eyes, new faith receiving,
  From thee shall never move;
  For he who dies believing
  Dies safely through thy love.
BERNARD OF CLAIRVAUX (1090–1153)

2229 Be still prepared for death
  And death or life shall thereby be the
    sweeter.
WILLIAM SHAKESPEARE (1564–1616)

2230 Because I could not stop for death
  He kindly stopped for me;
  The carriage held but just ourselves
  And immortality.
EMILY ELIZABETH DICKINSON (1830–1886)

2231 Because through death alone we
    become liberated,
  I say it is the best of all the things
    created.
ANGELUS SILESIUS (1624–1677)

2232 By all standards, death is the most
  dreaded event. Our society will pay
  any price to prolong life. Just one
  more month, or even another day. Perhaps our desire to postpone death
  reflects our dissatisfaction with God's
  ultimate purpose. Remember, his work
  isn't finished until we are glorified.
  Most of us would like to see God's
  work remain half finished. We're glad
  we are called and justified, but we're
  not too excited about being glorified.
ERWIN W. LUTZER (1941–)

2233 By turns we catch the fatal breath and
  die.
ALEXANDER POPE (1688–1744)

2234 Christ taught an astonishing thing
  about physical death: not merely that
  it is an experience robbed of its terror,
  but that as an experience it does not
  exist at all. To "sleep in Christ,"

"depart and be with Christ," "fall asleep,"—these are the expressions the New Testament uses. It is high time the "icy river," "the gloomy portal," "the bitter pains," and all the rest of the melancholy images were brought face to face with the fact: Jesus Christ has abolished death.
J. B. PHILLIPS (1906–1982)

2235 Coffin: a container small enough for bums, large enough for presidents.

2236 Coffin: a room without a door or a skylight.
ELBERT GREEN HUBBARD (1856–1915)

2237 Come lovely and soothing death,
Undulate round the world, serenely arriving, arriving,
In the day, in the night, to all, to each,
Sooner or later, delicate death.
WALT WHITMAN (1819–1892)

2238 Death and taxes are inevitable.
THOMAS CHANDLER HALIBURTON (1796–1865)

2239 Death cancels everything but truth.

2240 Death has an amazing power of altering what a man desires because death profoundly affects his outlook.
OSWALD CHAMBERS (1874–1917)

2241 Death has got something to be said for it:
There's no need to get out of bed for it;
Wherever you may be,
They bring it to you, free.
KINGSLEY AMIS (1922–)

2242 Death is a camel that lies down at every door.
PERSIAN PROVERB

2243 Death is an awfully big adventure.
SIR JAMES M. BARRIE (1860–1937)

2244 Death is as necessary to the constitution as sleep, we shall rise refreshed in the morning.
BENJAMIN FRANKLIN (1706–1790)

2245 Death is but a sharp corner near the beginning of life's procession down eternity.
JOHN AYSCOUGH (1858–1928)

2246 Death is God's delightful way of giving us life.
OSWALD CHAMBERS (1874–1917)

2247 Death is merely moving from one home to another.
THE KOTZKER RABBI (1787–1859)

2248 Death is nature's way of telling you to slow down.

2249 Death is not a journeying into an unknown land; it is a voyage home. We are going not to a strange country, but to our Father's house, and among our kith and kin.
JOHN RUSKIN (1819–1900)

2250 Death is not death if it raises us in a moment from darkness into light, from weakness into strength, from sinfulness into holiness.
CHARLES KINGSLEY (1819–1875)

2251 Death is not death if it rids us of doubt and fear, of chance and change, of space and time, and all which space and time bring forth and then destroy.
CHARLES KINGSLEY (1819–1875)

2252 Death is not extinguishing the light; it is only putting out the lamp because the dawn has come.
SIR RABINDRANATH TAGORE (1861–1941)

2253 Death is not the end; it is only a new beginning. Death is not the master of the house; he is only the porter at the King's lodge, appointed to open the gate and let the King's guests into the realm of eternal day.
JOHN HENRY JOWETT (1864–1923)

2254 Death is not the greatest loss in life. The greatest loss is what dies inside us while we live.
NORMAN COUSINS (1912–)

2255 Death is psychologically as important as birth. . . . Shrinking away from it is something unhealthy and abnormal which robs the second half of life of its purpose.
CARL GUSTAV JUNG (1875–1961)

2256 Death is the end of labor, entry into rest.
WILLIAM ALEXANDER

2257 Death is the flowering of life, the consummation of union with God.

2258 Death is the grand leveller.
SIR THOMAS FULLER (1608–1661)

2259 Death is the great adventure beside
which moon landings and space trips
pale into insignificance.
JOSEPH BAYLY (1920–1986)

2260 Death is the Liberator of him whom
freedom cannot release, the Physician
of him whom medicine cannot cure,
and the Comforter of him whom time
cannot console.
CHARLES CALEB COLTON (1780–1832)

2261 Death is the opening of a more subtle
life. In the flower, it sets free the perfume; in the chrysalis, the butterfly; in
man, the soul.
JULIETTE ADAM (1836–1936)

2262 Death keeps no calendar.
SIR THOMAS FULLER (1608–1661)

2263 Death may be free—but it costs a life.
JEWISH PROVERB

2264 Death opens unknown doors. It is
most grand to die.
JOHN MASEFIELD (1878–1967)

2265 Death takes no bribes.
BENJAMIN FRANKLIN (1706–1790)

2266 Death to the Christian is the funeral of
all his sorrows and evils, and the resurrection of all his joys.
AUGHEY

2267 Death's but a path that must be trod,
If man would ever pass to God.
THOMAS PARNELL (1679–1718)

2268 Death's truer name
Is "Onward," no discordance in the
roll
And march of that eternal harmony
Whereto the world beats time.
ALFRED, LORD TENNYSON (1809–1892)

2269 Death, death; O amiable lovely death!
WILLIAM SHAKESPEARE (1564–1616)

2270 Death, the gate of life.
BERNARD OF CLAIRVAUX (1090–1153)

2271 Death, the grisly terror.
JOHN MILTON (1608–1674)

2272 Death, to a good man, is but passing
through a dark entry, out of one little
dusky room of his Father's house into
another that is fair and large, lightsome and glorious, and divinely entertaining.
MCDONALD CLARKE (1798–1842)

2273 Death—the last sleep? No, it is the
final awakening.
SIR WALTER SCOTT (1771–1832)

2274 Death: a punishment to some, to some
a gift, and to many a favor.
LUCIUS ANNAEUS SENECA (C. 4 B.C.–A.D. 65)

2275 Death: when man is put to bed with a
shovel.

2276 Death: when the soul shall emerge
from its sheath.
MARCUS AURELIUS ANTONINUS (121–180)

2277 Down you mongrel, Death! Back into
your kennel!
EDNA ST. VINCENT MILLAY (1892–1950)

2278 Each departed friend is a magnet that
attracts us to the next world.
JOHANN PAUL FRIEDRICH RICHTER
(1763–1825)

2279 Every man knows he will die, but no
one wants to believe it.
JEWISH PROVERB

2280 Every man must do two things alone;
he must do his own believing and his
own dying.
MARTIN LUTHER (1483–1546)

2281 Every moment dies a man,
Every moment one is born.
ALFRED, LORD TENNYSON (1809–1892)

2282 Everybody wants to go to heaven, but
nobody wants to die.
JOE LOUIS (1914–   )

2283 Fear not that your life shall come to
an end, but rather fear that it shall
never have a beginning.
CARDINAL JOHN HENRY NEWMAN
(1801–1890)

2284 For each of us there comes a moment
when death takes us by the hand and
says—it is time to rest, you are tired,
lie down and sleep.
WILL HAY (1888–1949)

2285 For restful death I cry.
WILLIAM SHAKESPEARE (1564–1616)

2286 God buries his workmen but carries
on his work.
CHARLES WESLEY (1707–1788)

2287 God calls our loved ones,
But we lose not wholly
What he hath given;
They live on earth
In thought and deed
As truly in his heaven.
JOHN GREENLEAF WHITTIER (1807–1892)

2288 God's eternity and man's mortality
join to persuade us that faith in Jesus
Christ is not optional.
A. W. TOZER (1897–1963)

2289 God's finger touched him, and he slept.
ALFRED, LORD TENNYSON (1809–1892)

2290 Golden lads and girls all must,
As chimney-sweepers, come to dust.
WILLIAM SHAKESPEARE (1564–1616)

2291 Good-bye, proud world! I'm going
home;
Thou art not my friend, and I'm not
thine.
RALPH WALDO EMERSON (1803–1882)

2292 Grass grows at last above all graves.
JULIA C. R. DORR (1825–1913)

2293 Has this world been so kind to you
that you would leave it with regret?
There are better things ahead than any
we leave behind.
C. S. LEWIS (1898–1963)

2294 He who does not fear death has no
fear of threats.
PIERRE CORNEILLE (1606–1684)

2295 Here's death, twitching my ear:
"Live," says he, "for I'm coming."
VIRGIL (70–19 B.C.)

2296 His maker kissed his soul away,
And laid his flesh to rest.
ISAAC WATTS (1674–1748)

2297 How strange this fear of death is! We
are never frightened at a sunset.
GEORGE MACDONALD (1824–1905)

2298 How wonderful is Death,
Death and his brother Sleep.
PERCY BYSSHE SHELLEY (1792–1822)

2299 I acquiesce in my death with complete
willingness, uncolored by hesitation;
how foolish to cling to life when God
has ordained otherwise!
JORGE MANRIQUE (C. 1440–1479)

2300 I am afraid of dying—but being dead,
oh yes, that to me is often an appealing prospect.
KÄTHE SCHMIDT KOLLWITZ (1867–1945)

2301 I am ready at any time. Do not keep
me waiting.
JOHN BROWN (1715–1766)

2302 I am ready to meet my Maker.
Whether my Maker is prepared for the
great ordeal of meeting me is another
matter.
—Winston Churchill on his 75th
birthday

2303 I cannot forgive my friends for dying; I
do not find these vanishing acts of
theirs at all amusing.
LOGAN PEARSALL SMITH (1865–1946)

2304 I go from a corruptible to an incorruptible crown, where no disturbance can
have place.
CHARLES I, KING OF ENGLAND (1600–1649)

2305 I have talked to doctors and nurses
who have held the hands of dying
people, and they say that there is as
much difference between the death of
a Christian and a non-Christian as
there is between heaven and hell.
BILLY GRAHAM (1918–   )

2306 I look forward to it with an intense
and reverent curiosity.
CHARLES KINGSLEY (1819–1875)

2307 I look upon life as a gift from God. I
did nothing to earn it. Now that the
time is coming to give it back, I have
no right to complain.
JOYCE CARY (1888–1957)

2308 I never knew what joy was until I gave
up pursuing happiness, or cared to live
until I chose to die. For these two discoveries I am beholden to Jesus.
MALCOLM MUGGERIDGE (1903–1990)

2309 I shall die, but that is all that I shall do
for Death; I am not on his payroll.
EDNA ST. VINCENT MILLAY (1892–1950)

2310 I shall not live 'till I see God; and
when I have seen him, I shall never die.
JOHN DONNE (1572–1631)

2311 I think funerals are barbaric and miserable. Everything connected with
them—the black, the casket, the shiny

hearse, the sepulchral tones of the preacher—is destructive to true memory.
MARY MANNES (1904–)

2312 I'm not afraid to die, honey. In fact, I'm kind of looking forward to it. I know the Lord has his arms wrapped around this big, fat sparrow.
ETHEL WATERS (1896–1977)

2313 I'm not afraid to die. I just don't want to be there when it happens.
WOODY ALLEN (1937–)

2314 If death be terrible, the fault is not in death, but thee.

2315 If we really think that home is elsewhere and that this life is a "wandering to find home," why should we not look forward to the arrival?
C. S. LEWIS (1898–1963)

2316 If you submit to God's will, everything, including the time of your death, is under God's supervision.
ERWIN W. LUTZER (1941–)

2317 If you treat your friend shabbily while he lives, you have no right to try to even up matters by whining over him when he is dead.
JOSEPH F. BERRY (1856–)

2318 In my end is my beginning.
MARY STUART (1542–1587)

2319 Is this the end? I know it cannot be, Our ships shall sail upon another sea; New islands yet shall break upon our sight, New continents of love and truth and might.
JOHN WHITE CHADWICK (1840–1904)

2320 It is as natural to die as to be born.

2321 It is in dying that we are born to eternal life.
SAINT FRANCIS OF ASSISI (C. 1181–1226)

2322 Jesus audaciously abolished death, transforming it from a door that slammed to, into one that opened to whoever knocked.
MALCOLM MUGGERIDGE (1903–1990)

2323 Jesus Christ alone is qualified to guide us into the vast unknown. Since he is the only one who has returned from the grave, he tells us accurately about life after death.
ERWIN W. LUTZER (1941–)

2324 Leaves have their time to fall, And flowers to wither at the northwind's breath, And stars to set—but all, Thou hast all seasons for thine own, O Death!
FELICIA HEMANS (1793–1835)

2325 Let dissolution come when it will, it can do the Christian no harm, for it will be but a passage out of a prison into a palace; out of a sea of troubles into a haven of rest; out of a crowd of enemies into an innumerable company of true, loving and faithful friends; out of shame, reproach and contempt, into exceeding great and eternal glory.
JOHN BUNYAN (1628–1688)

2326 Let me die As the leaves die, Gladly.
D. C. CLAUSSEN

2327 Let us not lament too much the passing of our friends. They are not dead, but simply gone before us along the road which all must travel.
ANTIPHANES (C. 388–C. 311 B.C.)

2328 Life is real! Life is earnest! And the grave is not its goal; Dust thou art, to dust returneth, Was not spoken of the soul.
HENRY WADSWORTH LONGFELLOW (1807–1882)

2329 Like as the waves make toward the pebbled shore, So do our minutes hasten to their end.
WILLIAM SHAKESPEARE (1564–1616)

2330 Like pilgrims to th' appointed place we tend: The world's an inn, and death the journey's end.
JOHN DRYDEN (1631–1700)

2331 Lord Jesus, you died to help me die. Take my life. I draw no protective line around anything that needs to go.
FRANÇOIS FÉNELON (1651–1715)

2332 Lord, grant that my last hour may be
my best hour.
OLD ENGLISH PRAYER

2333 Lord, look out for me when I die.
Make it a good experience.
SAINT FRANCIS OF SALES (1567–1622)

2334 Memorial service: farewell party for
someone who has already left.
ROBERT BYRNE

2335 Men fear death as children fear to go
in the dark; and as that natural fear in
children is increased with tales, so is
the other.
FRANCIS BACON (1561–1626)

2336 Men fear death because they refuse to
understand it. But the way a man dies
is more important than death itself.
Fine dying is a man's privilege, for that
man can himself control. We cannot
influence death, but we can influence
the style of our departure. Men surprise themselves by the fashion in
which they face this death: some more
proudly and more valiantly than ever
they dared imagine; and some in
abject terror.
CYRUS L. SULZBERGER (1858–1932)

2337 My name is Death; the last best friend
am I.
ROBERT SOUTHEY (1774–1843)

2338 Nature herself gives us courage. . . .
Death is not to be feared. It is a friend.
No man dies before his hour. The time
you leave behind was no more yours
than that which was before your birth
and concerneth you no more. Make
room for others as others have done
for you. Like a full-fed guest, depart to
rest. . . . The profit of life consists not
in the space, but in the use. Some man
hath lived long that has had a short
life. . . .
     Depart then without fear out of this
world even as you came into it. The
same way you came from death to life,
return from life to death. Yield your
torch to others as in a race. Your death
is but a piece of the world's order, but a
parcel of the world's life.
MICHEL EYQUEM DE MONTAIGNE
(1533–1592)

2339 Never send to know for whom the bell
tolls; it tolls for thee.
JOHN DONNE (1572–1631)

2340 No man ever repented of being a
Christian on his death bed.
HANNAH MORE (1745–1833)

2341 Nothing is so certain as death, and
nothing is so uncertain as the hour of
death.
SAINT AUGUSTINE OF HIPPO (354–430)

2342 Nothing seems worse to a man than
his death, and yet it may be the height
of his good luck.
IRISH PROVERB

2343 Now we face a paradox: on the one
hand nothing in the world is more precious than one single human person;
on the other hand nothing in the
world is more squandered, more
exposed to all kinds of dangers, than
the human being—and this condition
must be. What is the meaning of this
paradox? It is perfectly clear. We have
here a sign that man knows very well
that death is not an end, but a beginning. . . . Life is changed, life is not
taken away.
JACQUES MARITAIN (1882–1973)

2344 O how small a portion of earth will
hold us when we are dead, who ambitiously seek after the whole world
while we are living.
PHILIP II (382–336 B.C.)

2345 Of all the thoughts of God that are
Borne inward into souls afar,
Along the Psalmist's music deep,
Now tell me if there any is,
For gift or grace, surpassing this—
"He giveth his beloved sleep!"
ELIZABETH BARRETT BROWNING
(1806–1861)

2346 Of course, I do not want to go—this is
a mighty interesting world, and I'm
having a mighty good time in it. But I
am no more afraid of going than of
going through the door of this study.
For I know that I shall then have a
spiritual body to do with as I please,
and I won't have to worry about the

aches and pains of this poor physical body.
OZORA S. DAVIS

2347 Oh well, no matter what happens, there's always death.
NAPOLEON BONAPARTE (1769–1821)

2348 Oh, what a sign it is of evil life
When death's approach is seen
so terrible.
WILLIAM SHAKESPEARE (1564–1616)

2349 Old men go to death; death comes to young men.

2350 On the day of death, when my bier is on the move, do not suppose that I have any pain at leaving this world. Do not weep for me, say not, "Alas, alas!" You will fall into the devil's snare—that would indeed be alas! When you see my hearse, say not, "Parting, parting!" That time there will be for me union and encounter. When you commit me to the grave, say not, "Farewell, farewell!" For the grave is a veil over the reunion of paradise. Having seen the going-down, look upon the coming-up; how should setting impair the sun and the moon? To you it appears as setting, but it is a rising; the tomb appears as a prison, but it is release for the soul. What seed ever went down into the earth which did not grow? Why do you doubt so regarding the human seed?
JALAL AL-DIN AR-RUMI (C. 1207–1273)

2351 One can survive everything nowadays except death.
OSCAR WILDE (1854–1900)

2352 One consolation of death is that it is also the end of your taxes.

2353 One may live as a conqueror, a king, or a magistrate; but he must die a man. The bed of death brings every human being to his pure individuality, to the intense contemplation of that deepest and most solemn of all relations—the relation between the creature and his Creator.
DANIEL WEBSTER (1782–1852)

2354 One must always have one's boots on and be ready to go.
MICHEL EYQUEM DE MONTAIGNE (1533–1592)

2355 One of the great lessons the fall of the leaf teaches is this: Do your work well and then be ready to depart when God shall call.
TRYON EDWARDS (1809–1894)

2356 One short sleep past, we wake eternally, and death shall be no more: death, thou shalt die.
JOHN DONNE (1572–1631)

2357 One who longs for death is miserable, but more miserable is he who fears it.
JULIUS WILHELM ZINCGREF (1591–1635)

2358 Our Lord makes little of physical death, but he makes much of moral and spiritual death.
OSWALD CHAMBERS (1874–1917)

2359 Our valleys may be filled with foes and tears; but we can lift our eyes to the hills to see God and the angels, heaven's spectators, who support us according to God's infinite wisdom as they prepare our welcome home.
BILLY GRAHAM (1918–   )

2360 Out of the finite darkness,
Into the infinite light.
LOUISE CHANDLER MOULTON (1835–1908)

2361 Pale Death, with impartial step, knocks at the poor man's cottage and at the palaces of kings.
HORACE (65–8 B.C.)

2362 People living deeply have no fear of death.
ANAÏS NIN (1903–1977)

2363 Revenge triumphs over death. Love slights it. Honor aspires to it. Grief flys to it. Fear preoccupies it.
FRANCIS BACON (1561–1626)

2364 Shall I doubt my Father's mercy?
Shall I think of death as doom,
Or the stepping o'er the threshold
To a bigger, brighter room?
ROBERT FREEMAN (1878–1940)

2365 Sleep on, beloved, sleep, and take thy rest;
Lay down thy head upon thy Savior's breast;

We love thee well, but Jesus loves thee
   best—
Good night! Good night! Good night!
SARAH DOUDNEY (1843–1926)

2366 So he passed over, and all the trumpets
sounded for him on the other side.
JOHN BUNYAN (1628–1688)

2367 Someday you will read in the papers
that D. L. Moody of East Northfield is
dead. Don't you believe a word of it.
At that moment I shall be more alive
than now. I shall have gone up higher,
that is all—out of this old clay tene-
ment into a house that is immortal; a
body that death cannot touch, that sin
cannot taint, a body fashioned like
unto his glorious body. That which is
born of the flesh may die. That which
is born of the spirit will live forever.
DWIGHT LYMAN MOODY (1837–1899)

2368 Sunset and evening star,
   And one clear call for me!
And may there be no moaning at
   the bar
When I put out to sea . . .
For tho' from out our bourne of Time
   and Place
The flood may bear me far,
I hope to see my Pilot face to face
When I have crossed the bar.
ALFRED, LORD TENNYSON (1809–1892)

2369 Take care of your life and the Lord
will take care of your death.
GEORGE WHITEFIELD (1714–1770)

2370 Teach me to live, that I may dread
The grave as little as my bed.
BISHOP THOMAS KEN (1637–1711)

2371 The Angel of Death has been abroad
throughout the land; you may almost
hear the beating of his wings.
JOHN BRIGHT (1811–1889)

2372 The believer is freed from death as a
curse. The nature of death is taken
away, and therefore the name is
changed. It is but called a sleep, and a
sleep in Christ, and a gathering to our
fathers, a change, a departing. Death
is the godly man's wish, the wicked
man's fear.
SAMUEL BOLTON (1606–1654)

2373 The certainty that he who went
through death, who restored the connection between nature and the spiritual world, changes death to win a
triumph, a triumph that is awaiting us
like the warrior who is going toward a
certain victory. Although I want to live
and labor as long as God lets me, I
consider the moment of my death as
the most precious of my life.
FRIEDRICH WILHELM JOSEPH
VON SCHELLING (1775–1854)

2374 The crooked paths look straighter as
we approach the end.
JOHANN PAUL FRIEDRICH RICHTER
(1763–1825)

2375 The fear of death is ingrafted in the
common nature of all men, but faith
works it out of Christians.
VAVASOR POWELL

2376 The fear of death is worse than death.
ROBERT BURTON (1577–1640)

2377 The grave is but the threshold of eternity.
ROBERT SOUTHEY (1774–1843)

2378 The hour of departure has arrived,
and we go our ways—I to die, and you
to live. Which is better only God
knows.
SOCRATES (470–399 B.C.)

2379 The last words of Noah Webster probably were: zyme, zymosis, and
zymurgy.

2380 The lilies of the field whose bloom is
   brief;
We are as they;
Like them we fade away
As doth a leaf.
CHRISTINA GEORGINA ROSSETTI
(1830–1894)

2381 The man who dies out of Christ is said
to be lost, and hardly a word in the
English tongue expresses his condition
with greater accuracy. He has squandered a rare fortune and at the last he
stands for a fleeting moment and
looks around, a moral fool, a wastrel
who has lost in one overwhelming and
irrecoverable loss, his soul, his life, his

peace, his total, mysterious personality, his dear and everlasting all.
A. W. TOZER (1897–1963)

2382 The only ultimate disaster that can befall us is to feel ourselves at home on this earth.
MALCOLM MUGGERIDGE (1903–1990)

2383 The pain is brief, but the joy eternal!
JOHANN FRIEDRICH VON SCHILLER (1759–1805)

2384 The rich, the poor, the great, the small
Are levell'd. Death confounds 'em all.
JOHN GAY (1685–1732)

2385 The seed dies into a new life and so does man.
GEORGE MACDONALD (1824–1905)

2386 The statistics on death are quite impressive. One out of one people die.
GEORGE BERNARD SHAW (1856–1950)

2387 The stroke of death is as a lover's pinch,
Which hurts and is desired.
WILLIAM SHAKESPEARE (1564–1616)

2388 The undiscover'd country from whose bourn
No traveller returns.
WILLIAM SHAKESPEARE (1564–1616)

2389 The world recedes; it disappears;
Heav'n opens on my eyes; my ears
With sound seraphic ring:
Lend, lend your wings! I mount! I fly!
O grave! Where is thy victory?
O death! Where is thy sting?
ALEXANDER POPE (1688–1744)

2390 There are no dead people, Lord.
There are only the living, on earth and beyond.
Death exists, Lord,
But it's nothing but a moment,
A second, a step,
The step from provisional to permanent,
From temporal to eternal.
As in the death of the child the adolescent is born,
From the caterpillar emerges the butterfly,
From the grain the full-blown sheath.
MICHEL QUOIST (1921–)

2391 There is no death. Only a change of worlds.
CHIEF SEATTLE

2392 There is no death.
What seems so is transition;
This life of mortal breath
Is but the suburb of the life elysian,
Whose portal we call death.
She is not dead—the child of our affection—
But gone unto that school
Where she no longer needs our poor protection,
And Christ himself doth rule.
HENRY WADSWORTH LONGFELLOW (1807–1882)

2393 There is only one way to be born and a thousand ways to die.
SERBIAN PROVERB

2394 There was a time when I dreaded the thought of moving. I have enjoyed this house, and in many ways it has been pleasant. But I know I will soon have to leave it, so recently I've been consulting the blueprints of my future residence. The more I study God's Word, the more I'm overwhelmed by the advantages of that new home. So much so, that I'm getting eager to go to be with the one who is preparing that place for me in the Father's mansions. Somehow this old crumbling house is losing its appeal.
M. R. DEHAAN (1891–1965)

2395 There were some who said that a man at the point of death was more free than all others, because death breaks every bond, and over the dead the united world has no power.
FRANÇOIS FÉNELON (1651–1715)

2396 There's no dying by proxy.
FRENCH PROVERB

2397 There's one thing that keeps surprising you about stormy old friends after they die—their silence.
BEN HECHT (1894–1964)

2398 These eyes, new faith receiving,
From Jesus shall not move;
For he who dies believing,
Dies safely, through thy love.
BERNARD OF CLAIRVAUX (1090–1153)

2399 Think of stepping on shore and finding it heaven! Of taking hold of a
hand and finding it God's! Of breathing a new air and finding it celestial
air! Of feeling invigorated and finding
it immortality! Of passing from storm
and stress to a perfect calm! Of waking and finding it home!

2400 This world is the land of the dying; the
next is the land of the living.
TRYON EDWARDS (1809–1894)

2401 Those who live in the Lord never see
each other for the last time.
GERMAN PROVERB

2402 Thou know'st 'tis common; all that
lives must die,
Passing through nature to eternity.
WILLIAM SHAKESPEARE (1564–1616)

2403 Though too much valour may our
fortunes try,
To live in fear of death is many times
to die.
LOPE DE VEGA (1562–1635)

2404 Vital spark of heav'nly flame!
Quit, oh quit, this mortal frame:
Trembling, hoping, ling'ring, flying,
Oh the pain, the bliss of dying.
ALEXANDER POPE (1688–1744)

2405 We all labor against our own cure; for
death is the cure for all diseases.
SIR THOMAS BROWNE (1605–1682)

2406 We are but tenants, and . . . shortly
the great Landlord will give us notice
that our lease has expired.
JOSEPH JEFFERSON (1774–1832)

2407 There are, aren't there, only three
things we can do about death: to
desire it, to fear it, or to ignore it.
C. S. LEWIS (1898–1963)

2408 We go to the grave of a friend, saying,
"A man is dead." But angels throng
about him, saying, "A man is born."
CHRISTIAN SHRIVER GOTTHOLD (C. 1700)

2409 We picture death as coming to
destroy; let us rather picture Christ as
coming to save. We think of death as
ending; let us rather think of life as
beginning, and that more abundantly.
We think of parting; let us think of
meeting. We think of doing away; let

us think of arriving. And as the voice
of death whispers, "You must go from
earth," let us hear the voice of Christ
saying, "You are but coming to me!"
NORMAN MACLEOD (1812–1872)

2410 We should teach our children to think
no more of their bodies when dead
than they do of their hair when cut
off, or of their old clothes when they
have done with them.
GEORGE MACDONALD (1824–1905)

2411 We understand death for the first time
when he puts his hand upon one
whom we love.
ANNE-LOUISE-GERMAINE DE STAËL
(1766–1817)

2412 Weep if you must,
Parting is here—
But life goes on,
So sing as well.
JOYCE GRENFELL (1910–1979)

2413 What a scandal it would cause if an
undertaker gave way to cheerfulness
and whistled at his work!
ED HOWE (1853–1937)

2414 What is the Lord saying? There's only
one message: "Trust me. Even when
you don't understand and can't comprehend: trust me!"
—E. V. HILL on the death of his wife

2415 What we call death was to him only
emigration, and I care not where he
now tarries. He is doing God's will,
and more alive than ever he was on
earth.
AMELIA EDITH BARR (1831–1919)

2416 When a man dies, he clutches in his
hands only that which he has given
away in his lifetime.
JEAN JACQUES ROUSSEAU (1712–1778)

2417 When a man knows he is to be hanged
in a fortnight, it concentrates his mind
wonderfully.
SAMUEL JOHNSON (1709–1784)

2418 When all is done, say not my day
is o'er,
And that thro' night I seek a dimmer
shore:
Say rather that my morn has just
begun—

I greet the dawn and not a setting sun,
When all is done.
PAUL LAURENCE DUNBAR (1872–1906)

2419 When asked what he thought would
happen to him when he died, the man
replied, "I suppose I shall inherit eternal bliss, but I wish you wouldn't talk
about such unpleasant subjects."

2420 When death, the great reconciler, has
come, it is never our tenderness that
we regret, but our severity.
GEORGE ELIOT (1819–1880)

2421 When I die, I should like to slip out of
the room without fuss—for what matters is not what I am leaving, but
where I am going.
WILLIAM BARCLAY (1907–1978)

2422 When I go down to the grave I can
say, like so many others, I have finished my work; but I cannot say I have
finished my life. My day's work will
begin the next morning. My tomb is
not a blind alley. It is a thoroughfare.
It closes in the twilight to open in the
dawn.
VICTOR HUGO (1802–1885)

2423 When I look upon the tombs of the
great, every emotion of envy dies in
me; when I read the epitaphs of the
beautiful, every inordinate desire goes
out; when I meet with the grief of parents upon a tombstone, my heart melts
with compassion; when I see the
tombs of the parents themselves, I consider the vanity of grieving for those
whom we must quickly follow; when I
see kings lying by those who deposed
them, when I consider rival wits
placed side by side, or the holy men
that divided the world with their contests and disputes, I reflect with sorrow and astonishment on the little
competitions, factions, and debates of
mankind.
JOSEPH ADDISON (1672–1719)

2424 When our parents are living, we feel
that they stand between us and death;
when they go, we move to the edge of
the unknown.
R. I. FITZHENRY

2425 When the friends we love the best
Lie in their churchyard bed,
We must not cry too bitterly
Over the happy dead.
CECIL FRANCES ALEXANDER (1818–1895)

2426 When the landscape darkens and the
trembling pilgrim comes to the Valley
of the Shadow, he is not afraid to
enter: he takes the rod and staff of
Scripture in his hand; he says to friend
and comrade, "Good-bye; we shall
meet again;" and comforted by that
support, he goes toward the lonely
pass as one who walks through darkness into light.
HENRY VAN DYKE (1852–1933)

2427 Whoso lives the holiest life is fittest far
to die.
MARGARET PRESTON (1820–1897)

2428 Why dost thou fear thy last day? It
contributes no more to thy death than
does every other day. The last step
does not cause the lassitude: it declares
it. All days journey toward death; the
last arrives there.
MICHEL EYQUEM DE MONTAIGNE
(1533–1592)

2429 Why is it that we rejoice at a birth and
grieve at a funeral? It is because we
are not the person involved.
MARK TWAIN (1835–1910)

2430 Wouldn't you think a man a prize fool
if he burst into tears because he didn't
live a thousand years ago? A man is as
much a fool for shedding tears because
he isn't going to be alive a thousand
years from now.
LUCIUS ANNAEUS SENECA (C. 4 B.C.–A.D. 65)

2431 You can't die, for you are linked to the
permanent life of God through Jesus
Christ.
J. B. PHILLIPS (1906–1982)

2432 You have laughed God out of your
schools, out of your books, and out of
your life, but you cannot laugh him
out of your death.
DAGOBERT RUNES

2433 Young men may die, old men must.
ENGLISH PROVERB

DEATH/LAST WORDS

2434 Ah, Jesus!
CHARLES V, KING OF FRANCE (1338–1380)

2435 As I lie here on the brink of the eternal world, I want to tell you that you need have no fear for the integrity of those who have the direction of this great movement. God is with them. I would gladly have stayed here a little longer to have pushed forward the war, and to have taken part in the special effort for a hundred thousand souls just inaugurated by the General, but I shall hear of their ingathering as surely, and rejoice in it as fully, in the country whither I am going. Good-bye. I will meet you in the morning.
CATHERINE BOOTH (1829–1890)

2436 Doctor, I die hard but I am not afraid to go.
GEORGE WASHINGTON (1732–1799)

2437 Earth recedes, heaven opens. I've been through the gates! Don't call me back . . . if this is death, it's sweet. Dwight! Irene! I see the children's faces.
[Dwight and Irene were his dead grandchildren.]
DWIGHT LYMAN MOODY (1837–1899)

2438 Eighty-six years I have served him, and he has done me no wrong. How can I blaspheme my King who has saved me?
—To his executioners
SAINT POLYCARP (D. C. 167)

2439 Glory, hallelujah! Glory, hallelujah! I am with the Lord! Glory, ready, go!
—From the scaffold
CHARLES J. GUITEAU (1841–1882)

2440 I am not dying. I am entering into life.
THERESE OF LISIEUX (1873–1897)

2441 I have been dying for twenty years, now I am going to live.
JAMES DRUMMOND BURNS

2442 I have been everything and everything is nothing. A little urn will contain all that remains of one for whom the whole world was too little.
LUCIUS SEPTIMIUS SEVERUS (146–211)

2443 I have lost a world of time! Had I one year more, it should be spent in perus-ing David's Psalms and Paul's Epistles. Mind the world less and God more.
CLAUDIUS SALMASIUS (1588–1653)

2444 I shall hear in heaven.
LUDWIG VAN BEETHOVEN (1770–1827)

2445 I surely must be going now, my strength sinks so fast. What glory! The angels are waiting for me!
THOMAS BATEMAN

2446 I will stick to Christ as a burr to a top-coat.
KATIE LUTHER

2447 I would give worlds, if I had them, that Age of Reason had not been published. O Lord, help me! Christ, help me! O God what have I done to suffer so much? But there is no God! But if there should be, what will become of me hereafter? Stay with me, for God's sake! Send even a child to stay with me, for it is hell to be alone. If ever the devil had an agent, I have been that one.
THOMAS PAINE (1737–1809)

2448 Joy!
HANNAH MORE (1745–1833)

2449 Like as thy arms, Lord Jesus Christ, were stretched out upon the cross, even so receive me with the out-stretched arms of thy mercy.
MARY STUART (1542–1587)

2450 Lord, I am coming as fast as I can.
—From the scaffold
WILLIAM LAUD (1573–1645)

2451 See how pure the sky is, there is not a single cloud. Don't you see that God is waiting for me?
JEAN JACQUES ROUSSEAU (1712–1778)

2452 Standing as I do in view of God and eternity, I realize that patriotism is not enough. I must have no hatred or bitterness toward anyone.
EDITH CAVELL (1865–1915)

2453 This is the last of earth! I am content.
JOHN QUINCY ADAMS (1767–1848)

2454 Turn up the lights; I don't want to go home in the dark.
O. HENRY (1862–1910)

2455 Weep not for me, but for yourselves.
JOHN BUNYAN (1628–1688)

2456 What a beautiful day!
EMPEROR OF RUSSIA ALEXANDER I
(1777–1825)

2457 What is life? It is the flash of a firefly
in the night. It is the breath of a buffalo in the wintertime. It is the little
shadow which runs across the grass
and loses itself in the sunset.
CROWFOOT OF THE BLACKFEET
(1821–1890)

2458 Why fear death? It is the most beautiful adventure in life.
CHARLES FROHMAN (1860–1915)

2459 Wonderful, wonderful, this death.
WILLIAM ETTY (1787–1849)

DECEIT

2460 A clean glove often hides a dirty hand.

2461 A handsome shoe often pinches the
foot.
FRENCH PROVERB

2462 A whitewashed crow soon shows
black again.
CHINESE PROVERB

2463 Dirty water does not wash clean.
DANISH PROVERB

2464 Faces we see, hearts we know not.
SPANISH PROVERB

2465 Half the work that is done in the
world is to make things appear what
they are not.
E. R. BEADLE (1812–1879)

2466 He who will sell a blind horse praises
the feet.
GERMAN PROVERB

2467 Ill-gotten gains never prosper.
FRENCH PROVERB

2468 It is an awful hour when the first
necessity of hiding anything comes.
The whole life is different thenceforth.
When there are questions to be feared
and eyes to be avoided and subjects
that must not be touched, then the
bloom of life is gone.
PHILLIPS BROOKS (1835–1893)

2469 Knot in de plank will show through de
whitewash.
AMERICAN NEGRO PROVERB

2470 O what may a man within him hide,
Though angel on the outward side!
WILLIAM SHAKESPEARE (1564–1616)

2471 The easiest person to deceive is one's
own self.
EDWARD GEORGE BULWER-LYTTON
(1803–1873)

2472 The handsomest flower is not the
sweetest.

2473 The kiss of an enemy is full of deceit.

2474 The sun discovers the filth under the
white snow.

2475 There's no getting white flour out of a
coal sack.

2476 To tell a lie might help you to have
lunch, but not to have supper.
ARABIAN PROVERB

2477 We are experts at deceiving others and
ourselves too!
ERWIN W. LUTZER (1941–)

2478 When a rogue kisses you, count your
teeth.
HEBREW PROVERB

2479 When the fox preaches, look to your
geese.
GERMAN PROVERB

2480 You can fool some of the people all of
the time, and all of the people some of
the time, but you cannot fool all of the
people all the time.
ABRAHAM LINCOLN (1809–1865)

2481 You fool me once, shame on you. You
fool me twice, shame on me.
CHINESE PROVERB

2482 You k'n hide de fier, but what you
guine do wid de smoke? [You can hide
the fire, but what are you going to do
with the smoke?]
JOEL CHANDLER HARRIS (1848–1908)

2483 Our fine art of deception that we call
finesse.
GLORIA GAITHER

DECISIONS

2484 If we are ever in doubt about what to do, it is a good rule to ask ourselves what we shall wish on the morrow that we had done.
SIR JOHN LUBBOCK (1834–1913)

2485 Men must be decided on what they will not do, and then they are able to act with vigor in which they ought to do.
MENG-TZU (C. 371–C. 289 B.C.)

2486 No one learns to make right decisions without being free to make wrong ones.
KENNETH SOLLITT

2487 Not to decide is to decide.
HARVEY COX (1929–   )

2488 Nothing is so exhausting as indecision and nothing is so futile.
BERTRAND ARTHUR WILLIAM RUSSELL (1872–1970)

2489 Once to every man and nation comes the moment to decide,
In the strife of truth and falsehood, for the good or evil side.
JAMES RUSSELL LOWELL (1819–1891)

2490 The phrase "Decide for Christ" which we so frequently hear is too often an emphasis on the thing our Lord never trusted. Our Lord never asks us to decide for him: he asks us to yield to him—a very different matter.
OSWALD CHAMBERS (1874–1917)

2491 There is a time when we must firmly choose the course we will follow, or the relentless drift of events will make the decision.
HERBERT V. PROCHNOW

2492 Tough decision: when to discard a toothbrush.

2493 When God says today, the devil says tomorrow.
GERMAN PROVERB

2494 You are facing a dilemma; you are not quite sure which of two decisions to make. Apply the test of universality. Suppose your personal decision should become a universal custom, would it

bring the world happiness or unhappiness?
JOSEPH R. SIZOO

DEEDS

2495 A good man makes no noise over a good deed, but passes on to another as a vine to bear grapes again in season.
MARCUS AURELIUS ANTONINUS (121–180)

2496 All of this world will soon have passed away. But God will remain, and you, whatever you have become, good or bad. Your deeds now are the seedcorn of eternity. Each single act, in each day, good or bad, is a portion of that seed. Each day adds some line, making you more or less like him, more or less capable of his love.
EDWARD BOUBERIE PUSEY (1800–1882)

2497 Give me the ready hand rather than the ready tongue.
GIUSEPPE GARIBALDI (1807–1882)

2498 Heaven ne'er helps the man who will not help himself.
SOPHOCLES (C. 496–406 B.C.)

2499 How far that little candle throws his beams!
So shines a good deed in a naughty world.
WILLIAM SHAKESPEARE (1564–1616)

2500 I am only one, but still I am one;
I cannot do everything,
but still I can do something;
and because I cannot do everything,
I will not refuse to do
the something that I can do.
EDWARD EVERETT HALE (1822–1909)

2501 If any man hopes to do a deed without God's knowledge, he errs.
PINDAR (C. 522–438 B.C.)

2502 It isn't the thing you do;
It's the thing you leave undone,
Which gives you a bit of heartache
At the setting of the sun.
MARGARET SANGSTER (1838–1912)

2503 Little deeds of kindness, little words of love,
Make our earth an Eden like the heaven above.
JULIA A. FLETCHER CARNEY (1823–1908)

2504 Noble deeds that are concealed are most esteemed.
BLAISE PASCAL (1623–1662)

2505 The smallest good deed is better than the grandest intention.

2506 The whole worth of a kind deed lies in the love that inspires it.
TALMUD

DEFEAT

2507 Defeat is a school in which truth always grows strong.
HENRY WARD BEECHER (1813–1887)

2508 Defeat may serve as well as victory
To shake the soul and let the glory out.
When the great oak is straining in the wind
The boughs drink in new beauty, and the trunk
Sends down a deeper root on the windward side.
Only the soul that knows the mighty grief
Can know the mighty rapture. Sorrows come
To stretch out spaces in the heart for joy.
EDWIN MARKHAM (1852–1940)

2509 Defeat should never be a source of discouragement but rather a fresh stimulus.
ROBERT SOUTH (1634–1716)

2510 He gains most who is defeated, since he learns most.
SYDNEY J. HARRIS (1917–1986)

2511 It is defeat that turns bone to flint, and gristle to muscle, and makes men invincible, and formed those heroic natures that are now in ascendency in the world. Do not then be afraid of defeat. You are never so near to victory as when defeated in a good cause.
HENRY WARD BEECHER (1813–1887)

2512 It's not the giants who defeat us, but the mosquitoes.
GAGE SPINDLER

2513 Men stumble over pebbles, never over mountains.
CHINESE PROVERB

2514 There are some defeats more triumphant than victories.
MICHEL EYQUEM DE MONTAIGNE (1533–1592)

2515 To lose is to learn.

2516 Victory finds a hundred fathers, but defeat is an orphan.
COUNT GALEAZZO CIANO (1903–1944)

2517 What is defeat? Nothing but education, nothing but the first step to something better.
WENDELL PHILLIPS (1811–1884)

2518 When the frustration of my helplessness seemed greatest, I discovered God's grace was more than sufficient. And after my imprisonment, I could look back and see how God used my powerlessness for his purpose. What he has chosen for my most significant witness was not my triumphs or victories, but my defeat.
CHARLES COLSON (1931–   )

2519 The kingdom of God is a kingdom of paradox, where through the ugly defeat of a cross, a holy God is utterly glorified. Victory comes through defeat; healing through brokenness; finding self through losing self.
CHARLES COLSON (1931–   )

DEMOCRACY

2520 As I would not be a slave, so I would not be a master. This expresses my idea of democracy. Whatever differs from this, to the extent of the difference, is no democracy.
ABRAHAM LINCOLN (1809–1865)

2521 Democracy . . . is the only form of government that is founded on the dignity of man, not the dignity of some men, of rich men, of educated men, or of white men, but of all men. Its sanction is not the sanction of force, but the sanction of human nature.
ROBERT MAYNARD HUTCHINS (1899–1977)

2522 Democracy assumes that there are extraordinary possibilities in ordinary people.
HARRY EMERSON FOSDICK (1878–1969)

2523 Democracy is an attempt to apply the principles of the Bible to a human society.
WALLACE SPEERS

2524 Democracy is the very child of Jesus' teachings of the infinite worth of every personality.
FRANCIS JOHN MCCONNELL (1871–1953)

2525 Democracy is the worst form of government. It is the most inefficient, the most clumsy, the most unpractical. . . . It reduces wisdom to impotence and secures the triumph of folly, ignorance, clap-trap and demagogy. . . . Yet democracy is the only form of social order admissible because it is the only one consistent with justice.
ROBERT BRIFFAULT (1876–1948)

2526 Democracy means not "I am as good as you are," but "You are as good as I am."
THEODORE PARKER (1810–1860)

2527 I believe in democracy because it releases the energies of every human being.
WOODROW WILSON (1856–1924)

2528 Man's capacity for justice makes democracy possible, but man's inclination to injustice makes democracy necessary.
REINHOLD NIEBUHR (1892–1971)

2529 The real democratic idea is, not that every man shall be on a level with every other, but that every one shall have liberty, without hindrance, to be what God made him.
HENRY WARD BEECHER (1813–1887)

DEPENDABILITY

2530 An acre of performance is worth the whole world of promise.
JAMES HOWELL (C. 1594–1666)

2531 Be slow to promise, quick to perform.

2532 Deeds are fruits, words are but leaves.
ENGLISH PROVERB

2533 Dependability: fulfilling what I agreed to do even though it requires unexpected sacrifices.
BILL GOTHARD

2534 Do little things now; so shall big things come to thee by and by asking to be done.
PERSIAN PROVERB

2535 He loses his thanks who promises and delays.

2536 If a link is broken, the whole chain breaks.
YIDDISH PROVERB

2537 Talking is easy, action difficult.
SPANISH PROVERB

DEPRESSION

2538 Abide with me—fast falls the eventide;
The darkness deepens: Lord, with me abide;
When other helpers fail, and comforts flee,
Help of the helpless, O abide with me.
HENRY FRANCIS LYTE (1793–1847)

2539 Cheer up—only a dentist has to look down in the mouth.

2540 Cloudless days are fine, but remember: some pottery gets pretty fragile sitting in the sun day after day after day.
CHARLES R. SWINDOLL (1934–   )

2541 Darkness is more productive of sublime ideas than light.
EDMUND BURKE (1729–1797)

2542 Don't brood: you're a human being, not a hen.

2543 Every man has a rainy corner in his life.
JOHANN PAUL FRIEDRICH RICHTER (1763–1825)

2544 Every mile is two in winter.

2545 Give no place to despondency. God's designs regarding you, and his methods of bringing about these designs, are infinitely wise.
MADAME JEANNE MARIE DE LA MOTHE GUYON (1648–1717)

2546 God sends nothing but what can be borne.
ITALIAN PROVERB

2547 If a person at the time of these darknesses observes closely, he will see clearly how little the appetites and faculties are distracted with useless and

harmful things and how secure he is from vainglory, from pride and presumption, from an empty and false joy, and from many other evils. By walking in darkness the soul not only avoids going astray but advances rapidly, because it thus gains the virtues.
SAINT JOHN OF THE CROSS (1542–1591)

2548 If there be a hell upon earth it is to be found in a melancholy man's heart.
ROBERT BURTON (1577–1640)

2549 Into each life some rain must fall, Some days must be dark and dreary.
HENRY WADSWORTH LONGFELLOW (1807–1882)

2550 It takes both the rain and the sunshine to make a rainbow.

2551 Lead, kindly Light, amid th' encircling gloom;
Lead thou me on.
The night is dark, and I am far from home;
Lead thou me on.
Keep thou my feet; I do not ask to see
The distant scene—one step enough for me.
CARDINAL JOHN HENRY NEWMAN (1801–1890)

2552 Most of the shadows of this life are caused by standing in one's own sunshine.
RALPH WALDO EMERSON (1803–1882)

2553 Night, you are for a man more nourishing than bread and wine.
CHARLES PÉGUY (1873–1914)

2554 O guiding night! O night more lovely than the dawn!
SAINT JOHN OF THE CROSS (1542–1591)

2555 Only eyes washed by tears can see clearly.
LOUIS L. MANN

2556 Recognize the dark night for what it is. Be grateful that God is lovingly drawing you away from every distraction so that you can see him. Rather than chafing and fighting, become still and wait.
RICHARD J. FOSTER (1942–)

2557 Reconcile yourself to wait in this darkness as long as is necessary, but still go on longing after him whom you love. For if you are to feel him in this life, it must always be in this cloud in this darkness.
THE CLOUD OF UNKNOWING (1370)

2558 The best cure for an empty day or a longing heart is to find people who need you. Look, the world is full of them.

2559 The best way to cheer yourself up is to try to cheer somebody else up.
MARK TWAIN (1835–1910)

2560 The stars are constantly shining, but often we do not see them until the dark hours.
EARL RINEY

2561 There is a melancholy that stems from greatness of mind.
SÉBASTIEN ROCH NICOLAS CHAMFORT (1741–1794)

2562 They feared as they entered the cloud. Is there anyone save Jesus only in your cloud? If so, it will get darker; you must get into the place where there is no one save Jesus only.
OSWALD CHAMBERS (1874–1917)

2563 Those who are the happiest are not necessarily those for whom life has been easiest. Emotional stability is an attitude. It is refusing to yield to depression and fear, even when black clouds float overhead. It is improving that which can be improved and accepting that which is inevitable.
JAMES C. DOBSON (1936–)

2564 We ought to praise God even when we do not feel like it. Praising him takes away the blues and restores us to normal.
HAROLD LINDSELL (1913–)

2565 When you see your appetites darkened, your inclinations dry and constrained, your faculties incapacitated for any interior exercise, do not be afflicted; think of this as a grace . . . God takes you by the hand and guides you in darkness, as though you were blind, along a way and to a place you know not. You would never have suc-

ceeded in reaching this place no matter how good your eyes and your feet.
SAINT JOHN OF THE CROSS (1542–1591)

DESIRES

2566 A man's heart is right when he wills what God wills.
SAINT THOMAS AQUINAS (1225–1274)

2567 Desire himself runs out of breath,
And getting, doth but gain his death.
SIR WALTER RALEIGH (1554–1618)

2568 God will either give you what you ask, or something far better.
ROBERT MURRAY MCCHEYNE (1813–1843)

2569 If a man could have half his wishes, he would double his troubles.
BENJAMIN FRANKLIN (1706–1790)

2570 In this world there are only two tragedies. One is not getting what one wants, and the other is getting it.
OSCAR WILDE (1854–1900)

2571 Man finds it hard to get what he wants because he does not want the best; God finds it hard to give because he would give the best and man will not take it.
GEORGE MACDONALD (1824–1905)

2572 To want what you want, you must want what your want leads to.
FRENCH PROVERB

2573 We would often be sorry if our wishes were gratified.
AESOP (FL. C. 50 B.C.)

DESPAIR

2574 At the edge of despair dawns a clarity in which one is almost happy.
JEAN ANOUILH (1910–)

2575 Beware of desperate steps; the darkest day,
Lived till tomorrow, will have passed away.
WILLIAM COWPER (1731–1800)

2576 But what am I? An infant crying in the night;
An infant crying for the light,
And with no language but a cry.
ALFRED, LORD TENNYSON (1809–1892)

2577 Despair doubles our strength.
ENGLISH PROVERB

2578 Despair is a frightful queerness . . . that there is no way out, or around, or through the impasse. It is the end.
H. G. WELLS (1866–1946)

2579 Despair is an evil counselor.
SIR WALTER SCOTT (1771–1832)

2580 Despair is the damp of hell as joy is the serenity of heaven.
JOHN DONNE (1572–1631)

2581 Despair itself, if it goes on long enough, can become a kind of sanctuary in which one settles down and feels at ease.
CHARLES AUGUSTIN SAINTE-BEUVE (1804–1869)

2582 God be praised, that to believing souls
Gives light in darkness, comfort in despair!
WILLIAM SHAKESPEARE (1564–1616)

2583 God harden me against myself,
This coward with pathetic voice
Who craves for ease, and rest, and joys.
Myself, arch-traitor to myself
My hollowest friend, my deadliest foe,
My clog whatever road I go.
Yet One there is can curb myself,
Can roll the strangling load from me,
Break off the yoke and set me free.
CHRISTINA GEORGINA ROSSETTI (1830–1894)

2584 He that despairs degrades God.
OWEN FELLTHAM (C. 1602–1668)

2585 He that is fallen cannot help him that is down.

2586 He who despairs wants love and faith, for faith, hope, and love are three torches which blend their life together, nor does the one shine without the other.
PIETRO METASTASIS (1698–1782)

2587 I have no wit, no words, no tears;
My heart within me like a stone
Is numbed too much for hopes or fears;
Look right, look left, I dwell alone;
I lift mine eyes, but dimmed with grief
No everlasting hills I see;
My life is in the falling leaf

O Jesus, quicken me.
CHRISTINA GEORGINA ROSSETTI
(1830–1894)

2588 I remember, I remember
The house where I was born,
The little window where the sun
Came peeping in at morn;
He never came a wink too soon
Nor brought too long a day;
But now, I often wish the night
Had borne my breath away.
THOMAS HOOD (1799–1845)

2589 I turned to speak to God
About the world's despair;
But to make bad matters worse
I found God wasn't there.
ROBERT FROST (1874–1963)

2590 I would say to my soul, O my soul,
this is not the place of despair; this is
not the time to despair in. As long as
mine eyes can find a promise in the
Bible, as long as there is a moment left
me of breath or life in this world, so
long will I wait or look for mercy, so
long will I fight against unbelief and
despair.
JOHN BUNYAN (1628–1688)

2591 If at any time you feel disposed again
to say, "It is enough," and that you
can bear of the burden of life no
longer, do as Elijah did, flee into the
silence of solitude, and sit under—not
the juniper tree—but under that tree
whereon the incarnate Son of God was
made a curse for you.
FRIEDRICH WILHELM KRUMMACHER
(1796–1868)

2592 If you get gloomy, just take an hour
off and sit and think how much better
this world is than hell. Of course, it
won't cheer you up much if you expect
to go there.
DON MARQUIS (1878–1937)

2593 If you should temporarily lose your
sense of well-being, don't be too quick
to despair. With humility and patience,
wait for God who is able to give you
back even more comfort. There is
nothing novel about this to those who
are familiar with God's ways. The
great saints and ancient prophets fre-

quently experienced the alternation of
up and down, joy and sorrow.
THOMAS À KEMPIS (C. 1380–1471)

2594 In a really dark night of the soul it is
always three in the morning, day after
day.
F. SCOTT FITZGERALD (1896–1940)

2595 It is impossible for that man to despair
who remembers that his Helper is
omnipotent.
JEREMY TAYLOR (1613–1667)

2596 It is when we are out of options that
we are most ready for God's surprises.
MAX L. LUCADO (1955–)

2597 Life begins on the other side of despair.
JEAN PAUL SARTRE (1905–1980)

2598 Life is a bridge of groans across a
stream of tears.
PHILIP JAMES BAILEY (1816–1902)

2599 Life is not as idle ore
But iron dug from central gloom,
And heated hot with burning fears,
And dipt in baths of hissing tears,
And battered with the shocks of doom
To shape and use.
ALFRED, LORD TENNYSON (1809–1892)

2600 Lord, it is dark! Lord, are you there in
my darkness? Where are you, Lord?
Do you love me still? I haven't wearied
you? Lord, answer me! Answer! It is
so dark!
MICHEL QUOIST (1921–)

2601 Never despair, but if you do, work on
in despair.
EDMUND BURKE (1729–1797)

2602 Never fear shadows. They simply
mean there's a light shining somewhere.
RUTH E. RENKEL

2603 O God! O God!
How weary, stale, flat and unprofitable
Seem to me all the uses of this world.
WILLIAM SHAKESPEARE (1564–1616)

2604 O man, cleave close to God and mean
but him alone,
Then agony and toil a paradise
become.
ANGELUS SILESIUS (1624–1677)

2605 Only those who see themselves as utterly destitute can fully appreciate the grace of God.
ERWIN W. LUTZER (1941–)

2606 Play it down and pray it up.
ROBERT HAROLD SCHULLER (1926–)

2607 Surrendering to despair is man's favorite pastime. God offers a better plan, but it takes effort to grab it and faith to claim it.
CHARLES R. SWINDOLL (1934–)

2608 "The dark night of the soul" is not something bad or destructive. On the contrary it is an experience to be welcomed as a sick person might welcome a surgery that promises health and well-being. The purpose of the darkness is not to punish or afflict us. It is to set us free.
RICHARD J. FOSTER (1942–)

2609 The lives that are getting stronger are lives in the desert, deep-rooted in God.
OSWALD CHAMBERS (1874–1917)

2610 The mass of men lead lives of quiet desperation.
HENRY DAVID THOREAU (1817–1862)

2611 There is a weeping in the world, as though our dear Lord were dead; and the leaden shadows that descend on us oppress us with the weight of the tomb.
ELSE LASKER-SCHULER (1876–1945)

2612 What is this darkness? What is its name? Call it an aptitude for sensitivity. Call it a rich sensitivity which will make you whole. Call it your potential for vulnerability.
MEISTER ECKHART (C. 1260–C. 1327)

2613 When a man gets to despair, he knows that all his thinking will never get him out, he will only get out by the sheer creative effort of God; consequently, he is in the right attitude to receive from God that which he cannot gain for himself.
OSWALD CHAMBERS (1874–1917)

2614 When you get into a tight place and everything goes against you, 'til it seems you could not hold on a minute longer, never give up then, for that is just the place and time that the tide will turn.
HARRIET BEECHER STOWE (1811–1896)

2615 When you get to the end of your rope, tie a knot and hang on.

2616 Who will not grieve when deprived of hope?
GIACOMO LEOPARDI (1798–1837)

DESTINY

2617 And God gives to every man
The virtue, temper, understanding, taste,
That lifts him into life, and lets him fall
Just in the niche he was ordained to fill.
WILLIAM COWPER (1731–1800)

2618 Ask of the devil, use magic—still you cannot turn any human being from his destiny.
JEAN DE LA FONTAINE (1621–1695)

2619 Destiny is a tyrant's authority for crime and a fool's excuse for failure.
AMBROSE GWINNETT BIERCE (1842–C. 1914)

2620 Destiny waits in the hand of God, not in the hands of statesmen.
T. S. ELIOT (1888–1965)

2621 The destiny of every human being depends on his relationship to Jesus Christ. It is not on his relationship to life, or on his service or his usefulness, but simply and solely on his relationship to Jesus Christ.
OSWALD CHAMBERS (1874–1917)

2622 The tissue of the Life to be
We weave with colors all our own,
And in the field of Destiny
We reap as we have sown.
JOHN GREENLEAF WHITTIER (1807–1892)

2623 Whatever befalls you was preordained for you from eternity.
MARCUS AURELIUS ANTONINUS (121–180)

DETERMINATION

2624 A man in earnest finds means, or if he cannot find, creates them.
WILLIAM ELLERY CHANNING (1780–1842)

2625 A thick skin is a gift from God.
KONRAD ADENAUER (1876–1967)

2626 Earnestness is not by any means everything; it is very often a subtle form of
pious self-idolatry because it is
obsessed with the method and not
with the Master.
OSWALD CHAMBERS (1874–1917)

2627 Every noble work is at first impossible.
THOMAS CARLYLE (1795–1881)

2628 I will go anywhere—provided it be
forward.
DAVID LIVINGSTONE (1813–1873)

2629 If you don't invest much, defeat
doesn't hurt and winning is not exciting.
DICK VERMEIL

2630 Recognizing that our cause is, and will
be, combated by mighty, determined
and relentless forces, we will, trusting
in him who is the Prince of Peace,
meet argument with argument, misjudgment with patience, denunciations
with kindness, and all our difficulties
and dangers with prayer.
FRANCES ELIZABETH CAROLINE
WILLARD (1839–1898)

2631 The difference between the impossible
and the possible lies in a man's determination.
TOMMY LASORDA (1927–   )

2632 The will is the strong blind man who
carries on his shoulders the lame man
who can see.
ARTHUR SCHOPENHAUER (1788–1860)

2633 When faced with a mountain, I will
not quit! I will keep on striving until I
climb over, find a pass through, tunnel
underneath . . . or simply stay and
turn the mountain into a gold mine,
with God's help.
ROBERT HAROLD SCHULLER (1926–   )

2634 Where the willingness is great, the difficulties cannot be great.
NICCOLÒ MACHIAVELLI (1469–1527)

2635 Will is power.
GERMAN PROVERB

DEVIL

2636 'Gainst the logic of the devil
Human logic strives in vain.
ADAM LINDSAY GORDON (1833–1870)

2637 A sort of creeping comes over my skin
when I hear the devil quote Scripture.
SIR WALTER SCOTT (1771–1832)

2638 And in he came with eyes of flame,
The devil, to fetch the dead;
And all the church with his presence
glowed
Like a fiery furnace red.
ROBERT SOUTHEY (1774–1843)

2639 And them all the Lord transformed to
devils,
Because they his deed and word
Would not revere.
CAEDMON (D. C. 680)

2640 Anything the devil does is always done
well!
CHARLES BAUDELAIRE (1821–1867)

2641 At the devil's booth are all things sold,
Each ounce of dross costs its ounce of
gold;
For a cap and bells our lives we pay,
Bubbles we buy with a whole soul's
tasking:
'Tis heaven alone that is given away,
'Tis only God may be had for the ask-
ing;
No price is set on the lavish summer;
June may be had by the poorest comer.
JAMES RUSSELL LOWELL (1819–1891)

2642 Confusion is the dust raised by the feet
of the devil.
FRANCES J. ROBERTS

2643 Devil: the strongest and fiercest spirit
that fought in heaven, now fiercer by
despair.
JOHN MILTON (1608–1674)

2644 Everything the devil does, God overreaches to serve his own purpose.
OSWALD CHAMBERS (1874–1917)

2645 He must have a long spoon that shall
eat with the devil.
WILLIAM SHAKESPEARE (1564–1616)

2646 He that serves God for money will
serve the devil for better wages.
SIR ROGER L'ESTRANGE (1616–1704)

2647 He who will fight the devil with his own weapons must not wonder if he finds him an overmatch.
ROBERT SOUTH (1634–1716)

2648 His method of working is to present us with the magnificent set-up, hoping he shall not use either our brains or our spiritual faculties to penetrate the illusion. He is playing for sympathy; therefore he is much better served by exploiting our virtues than by appealing to our lower passions; consequently, it is when the devil looks most noble and reasonable that he is most dangerous.
DOROTHY L. SAYERS (1893–1957)

2649 I am a great enemy to flies. When I have a good book, they flock upon it and parade up and down upon it and soil it. 'Tis just the same with the devil. When our hearts are purest, he comes and soils them.
MARTIN LUTHER (1483–1546)

2650 I believe in the devil for three reasons:
  1. The Bible plainly says he exists.
  2. I see his work everywhere.
  3. Great scholars have recognized his existence.
BILLY GRAHAM (1918–)

2651 I call'd the devil, and he came
And with wonder his form did I
  closely scan;
He is not ugly, and is not lame,
But really a handsome and charming
  man.
A man in the prime of life is the devil,
Obliging, a man of the world, and civil
A diplomatist too, well skill'd in
  debate,
He talks quite glibly of church and
  state.
HEINRICH HEINE (1797–1856)

2652 I sought only for the heart of God, therein to hide myself from the tempestuous storms of the devil.
JAKOB BÖHME (1575–1624)

2653 I'm not running from the devil, the devil is running from me.
CARLTON PEARSON

2654 If you don't open the door to the devil, he goes away.

2655 Illusion is the dust the devil throws in the eyes of the foolish.
MIMA ANTRIM (B. 1861)

2656 In heaven he scorns to serve, so now in hell he reigns.
JOHN FLETCHER (1579–1625)

2657 It is easy to bid the devil to be your guest, but difficult to get rid of him.
DANISH PROVERB

2658 Man, wrap yourself in God,
  abscond into his light;
I swear that you will thus
  escape the devil's sight.
ANGELUS SILESIUS (1624–1677)

2659 Order governs the world. The devil is the author of confusion.
JONATHAN SWIFT (1667–1745)

2660 Our adversary is a master strategist, forever fogging up our minds with smokescreens.
CHARLES R. SWINDOLL (1934–)

2661 Our songs and psalms sorely vex and grieve the devil, whereas our passions and impatiences, our complainings and cryings, our "Alas" and "Woe is me" please him well, so that he laughs in his fist. He takes delight in tormenting us, especially when we confess, praise, preach, and laud Christ.
MARTIN LUTHER (1483–1546)

2662 Satan fails to speak of the remorse, the futility, the loneliness, and the spiritual devastation which go hand in hand with immorality.
BILLY GRAHAM (1918–)

2663 Satan rocks the cradle when we sleep at our devotions.
JOSEPH HALL (1574–1656)

2664 Satan watches for those vessels that sail without a convoy.
GEORGE SWINNOCK (D. 1673)

2665 Satan's friendship reaches to the prison door.
TURKISH PROVERB

2666 Satan; so call him now, his former
  name
Is heard no more in heaven.
JOHN MILTON (1608–1674)

2667 Since the beginning of all times, men have perpetrated horrors against one another. It is the devil in them, but the devil would have no power over men if God did not allow it. Could he not, if he so willed, quell this revolution with his word? Must we not rather bow to his will and try to realize that something great, something good, something, at any rate, that is in accordance with the great scheme of the universe must in the end come out of all this sorrow?
BARONESS EMMUSKA ORCZY (1865–1947)

2668 Sometimes the devil is a gentleman.
PERCY BYSSHE SHELLEY (1792–1822)

2669 Speak boldly, and speak truly. Shame the devil!
JOHN FLETCHER (1579–1625)

2670 The devil always leaves a stink behind him.

2671 The devil and me, we don't agree; I hate him; and he hates me.
SALVATION ARMY HYMN

2672 The devil can cite Scripture for his purpose.
WILLIAM SHAKESPEARE (1564–1616)

2673 The devil cannot lord it over those who are servants of God with their whole heart and who place their hope in him. The devil can wrestle with but not overcome them.
SHEPHERD OF HERMAS (C. 155)

2674 The devil comes to us in our hour of darkness, but we do not have to let him in. And we do not have to listen either.
JEWISH PROVERB

2675 The devil does not tempt unbelievers and sinners who are already his own.
THOMAS À KEMPIS (C. 1380–1471)

2676 The devil doesn't know how to sing, only how to howl.
FRANCIS THOMPSON (1859–1907)

2677 The devil entangles youth with beauty, the miser with gold, the ambitious with power, the learned with false doctrine.
HENRY GEORGE BOHN (1796–1884)

2678 The devil has one good quality, that he will flee if we resist him. Though cowardly, it is safety for us.
TRYON EDWARDS (1809–1894)

2679 The devil has power to suggest evil, but he was not given the power to compel you against your will.
SAINT CYRIL (C. 315–386)

2680 The devil has three children: pride, falsehood, and envy.
WELSH PROVERB

2681 The devil hath power to assume a pleasing shape.
WILLIAM SHAKESPEARE (1564–1616)

2682 The devil is a bully, but when we stand in the armor of God he cannot harm us; if we tackle him in our own strength, we are soon done for; but if we stand with the strength and courage of God, he cannot gain one inch of way at all.
OSWALD CHAMBERS (1874–1917)

2683 The devil is making his pitch!
BILLY GRAHAM (1918–   )

2684 The devil is not afraid of the Bible that has dust on it.

2685 The devil is not always at one door.

2686 The devil is perfectly willing for a person to profess Christianity, so long as he doesn't practice it.

2687 The devil paints himself black, but we see him rose-colored.
FINNISH PROVERB

2688 The devil too loves man, but not for man's sake—for his own. He loves man out of egotism, to aggrandize himself, to extend his power.
LUDWIG ANDREAS FEUERBACH (1804–1872)

2689 The devil tries to shake truth by pretending to defend it.
TERTULLIAN (C. 160–AFTER 220)

2690 The devil was piqu'd such saintship to behold
And longed to tempt him like good Job of old;
But Satan now is wiser than of yore,
And tempts by making rich, not making poor.
ALEXANDER POPE (1688–1744)

2691 The devil wrestles with God, and the field of battle is the human heart.
FYODOR MIKHAYLOVICH DOSTOYEVSKI (1821–1881)

2692 The devil's best ruse is to persuade us that he does not exist.
CHARLES BAUDELAIRE (1821–1867)

2693 The devil's boots don't creak.
SCOTTISH PROVERB

2694 The devil's ever kind to his own.
ALEXANDER BROME (1620–1666)

2695 The devil's most devilish when respectable.
ELIZABETH BARRETT BROWNING (1806–1861)

2696 The devil's snare does not catch you unless you are first caught by the devil's bait.
SAINT AMBROSE (C. 340–397)

2697 The devil, that old stager . . . who leads Downward, perhaps, but fiddles all the way!
ROBERT BROWNING (1812–1889)

2698 The media have, indeed, provided the devil with perhaps the greatest opportunity accorded him since Adam and Eve were turned out of the Garden of Eden.
MALCOLM MUGGERIDGE (1903–1990)

2699 The method of the evil one is to obscure himself behind some other object of worship.
G. CAMPBELL MORGAN (1863–1945)

2700 The serpent—subtlest beast of all the field.
JOHN MILTON (1608–1674)

2701 The whole world has been booby-trapped by the devil, and the deadliest trap of all is the religious one.
A. W. TOZER (1897–1963)

2702 We cannot stand against the wiles of the devil by our wits. The devil only comes along the line that God understands, not along the lines we understand, and the only way we can be prepared for him is to do what God tells us, stand complete in his armor, indwelt by his Spirit, in complete obedience to him.
OSWALD CHAMBERS (1874–1917)

2703 We must not so much as taste of the devil's broth, lest at last he brings us to eat of his beef.
THOMAS HALL (1610–1665)

2704 What the devil wanted of Jesus . . . was, essentially, to involve him in the exigencies of power, thereby neutralizing his gospel of love, and leaving mankind still at the devil's mercy.
MALCOLM MUGGERIDGE (1903–1990)

2705 When you close your eyes to the devil, be sure that it is not a wink.
JOHN C. KULP (1921–)

2706 Where the devil can't go he sends his grandmother.
GERMAN PROVERB

2707 Where the devil cannot put his head he puts his tail.
ITALIAN PROVERB

DIFFICULTIES

2708 A gem is not polished without rubbing, nor a man made perfect without trials.
CHINESE PROVERB

2709 All sunshine makes the desert.
ARABIAN PROVERB

2710 All things are difficult before they are easy.

2711 An obstacle is often an unrecognized opportunity.

2712 Be of good courage, all is before you, and time passed in the difficult is never lost. . . . What is required of us is that we love the difficult and learn to deal with it. In the difficulties are the friendly forces, the hands that work on us.
RAINER MARIA RILKE (1875–1926)

2713 Believing God's promises the Christian is taken through difficulties of every shape and size—and arrives safely.
RICHARD C. HALVERSON (1916–)

2714 Difficulties are God's errands and when we are sent upon them we should consider it proof of God's confidence, as a compliment of God.
HENRY WARD BEECHER (1813–1887)

2715 Difficulties are meant to rouse, not discourage. The human spirit is to grow strong by conflict.
WILLIAM ELLERY CHANNING (1780–1842)

2716 Difficulty and joy are mutual friends.
TIM HANSEL

2717 Difficulty is a severe instructor.
EDMUND BURKE (1729–1797)

2718 Difficulty is the excuse history never accepts.
SAMUEL GRAFTON

2719 Difficulty is the nurse of greatness—a harsh nurse, who roughly rocks her foster-children into strength and athletic proportion.
WILLIAM JENNINGS BRYAN (1860–1925)

2720 Each problem is a God-appointed instructor.
CHARLES R. SWINDOLL (1934–)

2721 God does not do what false Christianity makes out—keep a man immune from trouble. God says, "I will be with him in trouble."
OSWALD CHAMBERS (1874–1917)

2722 God never gives strength for tomorrow, or for the next hour, but only for the strain of the moment. . . . The saint is hilarious when he is crushed with difficulties because the thing is so ludicrously impossible to anyone but God.
OSWALD CHAMBERS (1874–1917)

2723 Good when he gives, supremely good, Nor less when he denies.
E'en crosses from his sovereign hand Are blessings in disguise.
JAMES HERVEY (1714–1758)

2724 Great pains cause us to forget the small ones.
GERMAN PROVERB

2725 Great trials seem to be a necessary preparation for great duties.
EDWARD THOMSON (1810–1870)

2726 I always view problems as opportunities in work clothes.
HENRY J. KAISER (1882–1967)

2727 I used to tell my troubles to everyone I knew, and the more I told my troubles the more my troubles grew.

2728 I've had my trials and troubles. The Lord has given me both vinegar and honey, but he has given me the vinegar with a teaspoon and the honey with a ladle.
BILLY BRAY

2729 If it weren't for obstacles, we'd never know whether we really want something or merely think we do.

2730 If there were no difficulties there would be no triumphs.
B. C. FORBES

2731 If you see difficulties, you are not looking at Jesus Christ.

2732 In divine things there is no prudence which is not bold. It must live and work in the dark as briskly as in the light. It must be gay, playing blithely with difficulties; for difficulties are the stone out of which all God's houses are built.
FREDERICK WILLIAM FABER (1814–1863)

2733 In front a precipice, behind a wolf.
LATIN PROVERB

2734 In time of trouble go not out of yourself to seek for aid; for the whole benefit of trial consists in silence, patience, rest, and resignation. In this condition divine strength is found for the hard warfare because God himself fights for the soul.
MIGUEL DE MOLINOS (1628–1696)

2735 It is difficulties that show what men are.
EPICTETUS (C. 55–C. 135)

2736 It is in this whole process of meeting and solving problems that life has meaning.
M. SCOTT PECK (1936–)

2737 It is not the outward storms and stresses of life that defeat and disrupt personality, but its inner conflicts and miseries. If a man is happy and stable at heart, he can normally cope, even with zest, with difficulties that lie outside his personality.
J. B. PHILLIPS (1906–1982)

2738 Life's difficulties force us to break through the superficiality to the deeper life within.
TIM HANSEL

2739 Many men owe the grandeur of their lives to their tremendous difficulties.
CHARLES HADDON SPURGEON (1834–1892)

2740 Misunderstanding cannot thwart the good purposes of God.

2741 Nothing will ever be attempted if all possible objections must be first overcome.
SAMUEL JOHNSON (1709–1784)

2742 Stand still . . . and refuse to retreat. Look at it as God looks at it and draw upon his power to hold up under the blast.
CHARLES R. SWINDOLL (1934–   )

2743 Take a lesson from tea: its real strength comes out when it gets into hot water.

2744 Take everything that comes into your life as being from the hand of God, not from the hand of man.
MADAME JEANNE MARIE DE LA MOTHE GUYON (1648–1717)

2745 Take those road hazards—the potholes, ruts, detours, and all the rest— as evidence that you're on the right route. It's when you find yourself on that big, broad, easy road that you ought to worry.
JONI EARECKSON TADA

2746 The chief pang of most trials is not so much the actual suffering itself as our own spirit of resistance to it.
JEAN NICOLAS GROU (1731–1803)

2747 The course of true anything never does run smooth.
SAMUEL BUTLER (1612–1680)

2748 The difficulties of life are intended to make us better, not bitter.

2749 The distance is nothing; it is only the first step that is difficult.
MARQUISE DU DEFFAND (1697–1780)

2750 The great thing, if one can, is to stop regarding all the unpleasant things as interruptions of one's own or real life. The truth is of course that what one calls the interruptions are precisely one's real life—the life God is sending one day by day. What one calls one's real life is a phantom of one's own imagination.
C. S. LEWIS (1898–1963)

2751 The greater the difficulty the more glory in surmounting it.
EPICURUS (341–270 B.C.)

2752 The most magnificent opportunities come into our lives disguised as problems.
JOHN POWELL

2753 There are two ways to handle difficulties: change the situation or change yourself.

2754 There is no uphill without a downhill.
ARABIAN PROVERB

2755 There is nothing so bad that good may not come of it.
SPANISH PROVERB

2756 There is nothing so easy but that it becomes difficult when you do it with reluctance.
TERENCE (C. 186–C. 159 B.C.)

2757 Things which come to us easily have no significance. Satisfaction comes when we do something which is difficult; when there is sacrifice involved.
BARRY MORRIS GOLDWATER (1909–   )

2758 Undertake something that is difficult; it will do you good. Unless you try to do something beyond what you have already mastered, you will never grow.
RONALD E. OSBORN

DIGNITY

2759 Dignity does not consist in possessing honors, but in deserving them.
ARISTOTLE (384–322 B.C.)

2760 Dignity is like a perfume; those who use it are scarcely conscious of it.
QUEEN CHRISTINA OF SWEDEN (1626–1689)

2761 Dignity never savors of artificiality or affectation. It never struts or poses. Dignity never struggles to be dignified. The man of inborn and natural dignity has too much respect for his dignity to stand upon it. He who is inordinately

anxious to appear dignified usually walks on stilts to make himself seem bigger than he really is.
F. W. BOREHAM

2762 No race can prosper till it learns that there is as much dignity in tilling a field as in writing a poem.
BOOKER T. WASHINGTON (1856–1915)

2763 Recognize, O Christian, thy dignity.
SAINT LEO X (1475–1521)

2764 True dignity abides with him alone
Who, in the silent hour of inward thought,
Can still suspect, and still revere himself,
In lowliness of heart.
WILLIAM WORDSWORTH (1770–1850)

2765 True dignity is never gained by place, and never lost when honors are withdrawn.
PHILIP MASSINGER (1583–1640)

2766 If man is not ready to risk his life, where is his dignity?
ANDRÉ MALRAUX (1901–1976)

2767 Where is there dignity unless there is honesty?
MARCUS TULLIUS CICERO (106–43 B. C.)

DILIGENCE

2768 Avoid the last minute rush: do it yesterday.

2769 Be first in the field and the last to the couch.
CHINESE PROVERB

2770 Doing things by halves is worthless. It may be the other half that counts.

2771 Earnestness commands the respect of mankind. A wavering, vacillating, dead-and-alive Christian does not get the respect of the church or of the world.
JOHN HALL (1829–)

2772 Even a mosquito doesn't get a slap on the back until he starts working.

2773 Everything requires effort: the only thing you can achieve without it is failure.

2774 God wishes each of us to work as hard as we can, holding nothing back but giving ourselves to the utmost, and when we can do no more, that is the moment when the hand of divine providence is stretched out to us and takes over.
DON ORIONE (1872–1940)

2775 I think and think for months, for years; ninety-nine times the conclusion is false, but the hundredth time I am right.
ALBERT EINSTEIN (1879–1955)

2776 If a man has good corn, or wood, or boards, or pigs, to sell, or can make better chairs or knives, crucibles, or church organs than anybody else, you will find a broad, hard-beaten road to his house, though it be in the woods.
RALPH WALDO EMERSON (1803–1882)

2777 If a man is called to be a streetsweeper, he should sweep streets even as Michelangelo painted, or Beethoven composed music, or Shakespeare wrote poetry. He should sweep streets so well that all the hosts of heaven and earth will pause to say: "Here lived a great streetsweeper who did his job well."
MARTIN LUTHER KING, JR. (1929–1968)

2778 If God is diligent, surely we ought to be diligent in doing our duty to him. Think how patient and how diligent God has been with us!
OSWALD CHAMBERS (1874–1917)

2779 In doing what we ought we deserve no praise.
SAINT AUGUSTINE OF HIPPO (354–430)

2780 Keep your heart with all diligence and God will look after the universe.
A. W. TOZER (1897–1963)

2781 Make hay while the sun shines.
MIGUEL DE CERVANTES (1547–1616)

2782 Make the most of yourself for that is all there is to you.
RALPH WALDO EMERSON (1803–1882)

2783 Measure a thousand times and cut once.
TURKISH PROVERB

2784 No one ever attains very eminent success by simply doing what is required of him; it is the amount and excellence of what is over and above the required that determines the greatness of ultimate distinction.
CHARLES KENDALL ADAMS (1835–1902)

2785 Rest satisfied with doing well, and leave others to talk of you as they please.
PYTHAGORAS (C. 580–C. 500 B.C.)

2786 Take a lesson from the clock; it passes the time by keeping its hands busy.

2787 Take care of the minutes and the hours will take care of themselves.
LORD CHESTERFIELD (1694–1773)

2788 The average person puts only 25 percent of his energy and ability into his work.
ANDREW CARNEGIE (1835–1919)

2789 The leading rule for a man of every calling is diligence; never put off until tomorrow what you can do today.
ABRAHAM LINCOLN (1809–1865)

2790 Through every rift of discovery some seeming anomaly drops out of the darkness, and falls, a golden link into the great chain of order.
EDWIN HUBBEL CHAPIN (1814–1880)

2791 Whatsoever we beg of God, let us also work for it.
JEREMY TAYLOR (1613–1667)

2792 Who guards his post, no matter where,
Believing God must need him there,
Although but lowly toil it be,
Has risen to nobility.
EDGAR ALBERT GUEST (1881–1959)

DISAPPOINTMENT

2793 Blessed is he who expects nothing, for he shall never be disappointed.
ALEXANDER POPE (1688–1744)

2794 Disappointment is often the salt of life.
THEODORE PARKER (1810–1860)

2795 Disappointment, parent of despair.
JOHN KEATS (1795–1821)

2796 Disappointments that come not by our own fault, they are the trials or corrections of heaven; and it is our own fault if they prove not to our advantage.
WILLIAM PENN (1644–1718)

2797 Every cloud has a silver lining.
ENGLISH PROVERB

2798 Have some of your carefully created castles been washed away? Mine have. Several times along my life's journey, I had nowhere to turn except into my heavenly Father's arms. There I remained quiet, soaking up his love for as long as I needed. Then I saw his hand begin a new creation for my life, a new direction, a new service for him and his kingdom. Waves need not always destroy. We must allow our heavenly Father to use them to redirect our lives.
JEAN OTTO

2799 If you expect perfection from people, your whole life is a series of disappointments, grumblings, and complaints. If, on the contrary, you pitch your expectations low, taking folks as the inefficient creatures which they are, you are frequently surprised by having them perform better than you had hoped.
BRUCE FAIRFIELD BARTON (1886–1967)

2800 Out of every disappointment there is treasure. Satan whispers, "All is lost." God says, "Much can be gained."
FRANCES J. ROBERTS

2801 There are no disappointments to those whose wills are buried in the will of God.
FREDERICK WILLIAM FABER (1814–1863)

2802 When life becomes all snarled up, offer it to our Lord and let him untie the knots.
RICHARDSON WRIGHT (1885–)

DISCERNMENT

2803 A man of correct insight among those who are duped and deluded resembles one whose watch is right while all the clocks in the town give the wrong time. He alone knows the correct time, but of what use is this to him? The

whole world is guided by the clocks that show the wrong time.
ARTHUR SCHOPENHAUER (1788–1860)

2804 Beware of allowing the discernment of wrong in another to blind you to the fact that you are what you are by the grace of God.
OSWALD CHAMBERS (1874–1917)

2805 Discernment is God's call to intercession, never to faultfinding.
CORRIE TEN BOOM (1892–1983)

2806 Don't pour away the water you are travelling with because of a mirage.
ARABIAN PROVERB

2807 He who wants to know people should study their excuses.
FRIEDRICH HEBBEL (1813–1863)

2808 See not evil in others and good in yourself, but the good in the other and the failings in yourself.
THE BERDICHEVER RABBI (1740–1809)

2809 Those who are in the heavenly places see God's counsels in what to the wisdom of the world is arrogant stupidity.
OSWALD CHAMBERS (1874–1917)

2810 Where the river is deepest, it makes the least noise.
ITALIAN PROVERB

2811 You must look into people as well as at them.
LORD CHESTERFIELD (1694–1773)

DISCIPLESHIP

2812 "I will make the place of my feet glorious"—among the poor, the devil-possessed, the mean, the decrepit, the selfish, the sinful, the misunderstood—that is where Jesus went, and that is exactly where he will take you if you are his disciple.
OSWALD CHAMBERS (1874–1917)

2813 "It is enough for the disciple that he be as his Master." At first sight this looks like an enormous honor: to be "as his Master" is marvelous glory—is it? Look at Jesus as he was when he was here, it was anything but glory. He was easily ignorable, saving to those who knew him intimately; to the

majority of men he was "as a root out of a dry ground." For thirty years he was obscure, then for three years he went through popularity, scandal, and hatred; he succeeded in gathering a handful of fishermen as disciples, one of whom betrayed him, one denied him, and all forsook him; and he says, "It is enough for you to be like that." The idea of evangelical success, church prosperity, civilized manifestation, does not come into it at all.
OSWALD CHAMBERS (1874–1917)

2814 Christ died for me. What am I doing for him?

2815 Conversion without discipleship is openly implied in much of our evangelical teaching. It has become strangely possible to be Christ's without taking up the cross.
C. D. ALEXANDER

2816 Did you ever stop to ask what a yoke is really for? Is it to be a burden to the animal which wears it? It is just the opposite. It is to make its burden light. Attached to the oxen in any other way than by a yoke the plough would be intolerable. Worked by means of a yoke it is light. A yoke is not an instrument of torture; it is an instrument of mercy. It is not a malicious contrivance for making work hard; it is a gentle device to make hard labor light. It is not meant to give pain, but to save pain. And yet men speak of the yoke of Christ as if it were a slavery and look upon those who wear it as objects of compassion.
JOHN DRUMMOND (1851–1897)

2817 Discipleship and salvation are two different things: a disciple is one who, realizing the meaning of the atonement, deliberately gives himself up to Jesus Christ in unspeakable gratitude.
OSWALD CHAMBERS (1874–1917)

2818 Discipleship means discipline. The disciple is one who has come with his ignorance, superstition, and sin to find learning, truth, and forgiveness from the Savior. Without discipline we are not disciples.
VICTOR RAYMOND EDMAN (1900–1967)

2819 If we were willing to learn the meaning of real discipleship and actually to become disciples, the church in the West would be transformed and the resultant impact on society would be staggering.
DAVID WATSON (1933–1984)

2820 If you want to remain a full-orbed grape, you must keep out of God's hands for he will crush you. Wine cannot be had in any other way.
OSWALD CHAMBERS (1874–1917)

2821 In every Christian's heart there is a cross and a throne, and the Christian is on the throne till he puts himself on the cross; if he refuses the cross, he remains on the throne. Perhaps this is at the bottom of the backsliding and worldliness among gospel believers today. We want to be saved, but we insist that Christ do all the dying. No cross for us, no dethronement, no dying. We remain king within the little kingdom of Mansoul and wear our tinsel crown with all the pride of a Caesar; but we doom ourselves to shadows and weakness and spiritual sterility.
A. W. TOZER (1897–1963)

2822 In the initial stages of discipleship you get "stormy weather," then you lose the nightmare of your own separate individuality and become part of the personality of Christ, and the thought of yourself never bothers you anymore because you are taken up with your relationship to God.
OSWALD CHAMBERS (1874–1917)

2823 It never cost a disciple anything to follow Jesus: to talk about cost when you are in love with someone is an insult.
OSWALD CHAMBERS (1874–1917)

2824 It seems amazingly difficult to put on the yoke of Christ, but immediately we do put it on, everything becomes easy.
OSWALD CHAMBERS (1874–1917)

2825 James the brother of Jesus and James the son of Zebedee preach and are killed by mobs in Jerusalem; Matthew is slain with a sword in Ethiopia; Philip is hanged in Phrygia; Bartholomew flayed alive in Armenia. Andrew is crucified in Achaia, Thomas is run through with a lance in East India, Thaddeus is shot to death with arrows, a cross goes up in Persia for Simon the Zealot, and another in Rome for Peter. Matthias is beheaded; only John escapes a martyr's grace.
FRANK S. MEAD (1898–1982)

2826 Jesus Christ always talked about discipleship with an "if." We are at perfect liberty to toss our spiritual head and say, "No, thank you, that is a bit too stern for me," and the Lord will never say a word, we can do exactly what we like. He will never plead, but the opportunity is there, "If . . ."
OSWALD CHAMBERS (1874–1917)

2827 Jesus Christ didn't commit the gospel to an advertising agency; he commissioned disciples.
JOSEPH BAYLY (1920–1986)

2828 Jesus has many lovers of the heavenly kingdom, but few bearers of his cross. He has many desirous of consolation, but few of tribulation. He finds many companions of his table, but few of his abstinence. All desire to rejoice with him, few are willing to endure anything for him, or with him. Many follow Jesus to the breaking of bread, but few to the drinking of the cup. Many reverence his miracles, few follow the ignominy of his cross. Many love Jesus so long as no adversities befall them, many praise and bless him so long as they receive any consolations from him; but if Jesus hides himself and leaves them but a little while, they fall either into complaining or into too much dejection of mind.
THOMAS À KEMPIS (C. 1380–1471)

2829 Let him make our lives narrow; let him make them intense; let him make them absolutely his!
OSWALD CHAMBERS (1874–1917)

2830 Not what the disciple says in public prayer, not what he preaches from pulpit or platform, not what he writes on paper or in letters, but what he is in his heart which God alone knows,

determines God's revelation of himself to him. Character determines revelation.
OSWALD CHAMBERS (1874–1917)

2831 Our Lord's conception of discipleship is not that we work for God, but that God works through us; he uses us as he likes; he allots our work where he chooses.
OSWALD CHAMBERS (1874–1917)

2832 Salvation is free, but discipleship costs everything we have.
BILLY GRAHAM (1918–   )

2833 The great stumbling block in the way of some people being disciples is that they are gifted, so gifted that they won't trust God.
OSWALD CHAMBERS (1874–1917)

2834 The walk of a disciple is gloriously difficult, but gloriously certain.
OSWALD CHAMBERS (1874–1917)

2835 The world has yet to see what God can do with and for and through and in a man who is fully and wholly consecrated to Christ.
HENRY VARLEY

2836 There is a difference between devotion to principles and devotion to a person. Hundreds of people today are devoting themselves to phases of truth, to causes. Jesus Christ never asks us to devote ourselves to a cause or a creed; he asks us to devote ourselves to him.
OSWALD CHAMBERS (1874–1917)

2837 We should live our lives as though Christ were coming this afternoon.
JIMMY CARTER (1924–   )

2838 We talk about the joys and comforts of salvation; Jesus Christ talks about taking up the cross and following him.
OSWALD CHAMBERS (1874–1917)

DISCIPLINE

2839 A stern discipline pervades all nature, which is a little cruel that it may be very kind.
EDMUND SPENSER (1552–1599)

2840 Batter my heart, three-personed God; for, you

As yet but knock, breathe, shine, and seek to mend;
That I may rise, and stand, o'erthrow me, and bend
Your force, to break, blow, burn and make me new.
JOHN DONNE (1572–1631)

2841 Better be pruned to grow than cut up to burn.
JOHN TRAPP

2842 Discipline is a proof of our sonship.
ERWIN W. LUTZER (1941–   )

2843 Do not consider painful what is good for you.
EURIPIDES (C. 484–406 B.C.)

2844 God brings problems and struggles into our lives so that we will not stray from the main road. He is not angry with us but disciplines us so that we can mature spiritually.
ERWIN W. LUTZER (1941–   )

2845 God does not discipline us to subdue us, but to condition us for a life of usefulness and blessedness.
BILLY GRAHAM (1918–   )

2846 God takes deliberate time with us, he does not hurry . . . we can only appreciate his point of view by a long discipline.
OSWALD CHAMBERS (1874–1917)

2847 God, who truly loves, will chastise well.

2848 It is one thing to praise discipline; another to submit to it.
MIGUEL DE CERVANTES (1547–1616)

2849 Let God put you on his wheel and whirl you as he likes. . . . Don't lose heart in the process.
OSWALD CHAMBERS (1874–1917)

2850 Look upon your chastenings as God's chariots sent to carry your soul into the high places of spiritual achievement.
HANNAH WHITHALL SMITH (1832–1911)

2851 Never console the one who pines under My chastening lest you become an obstacle to his spiritual growth.
FRANCES J. ROBERTS

2852 No horse gets anywhere until he is harnessed. No steam or gas ever drives anything until it is confined. No Niagara is ever turned into light and power until it is tunneled. No life ever grows great until it is focused, dedicated, disciplined.
HARRY EMERSON FOSDICK (1878–1969)

2853 No pain, no palm; no thorns, no throne; no gall, no glory; no cross, no crown.
WILLIAM PENN (1644–1718)

2854 Rebukes ought not to have a grain more of salt than of sugar.

2855 Reprove thy friend privately; commend him publicly.
SOLON (C. 630–C. 560 B.C.)

2856 The culture of the sanctified life is often misunderstood. The discipline of that life consists of suffering, loneliness, patience, and prayer. Many who started with the high ecstasy of vision have ended in the disasters of shallowness!
OSWALD CHAMBERS (1874–1917)

2857 Those whose lives are filled with tragedy are not necessarily more sinful than those who seem to live in uninterrupted comfort. Job experienced calamity, not because he was wicked, but because he was righteous.
ERWIN W. LUTZER (1941–)

2858 We ought as much to pray for a blessing upon our daily rod as upon our daily bread.
JOHN OWEN (1616–1683)

2859 When it is God's will to plague a man, a mouse can bite him to death.
DUTCH PROVERB

DISCONTENT

2860 A man's discontent is his worst evil.
GEORGE HERBERT (1593–1633)

2861 All the wants which disturb human life, which make us uneasy to ourselves, quarrelsome with others, and unthankful to God, which weary us in vain labors and foolish anxieties, which carry us from project to project, from place to place in a poor pursuit of we don't know what, are the wants which neither God nor nature, nor reason hath subjected us to, but are solely infused into us by pride, envy, ambition, and covetousness.
WILLIAM LAW (1686–1761)

2862 Beware of ambition—it can drive you into a lot of work.

2863 Discontent follows ambition like a shadow.
HENRY H. HASKINS

2864 Discontent is the first step in the progress of a man or a nation.
OSCAR WILDE (1854–1900)

2865 Discontent is the source of trouble, but also of progress.
BERTHOLD AUERBACH (1812–1882)

2866 Half the world is unhappy because it can't have the things that are making the other half unhappy.

2867 If you don't get everything you want, think of the things you don't get that you don't want.
OSCAR WILDE (1854–1900)

2868 It is not the man who has too little, but the man who craves more, who is poor.
LUCIUS ANNAEUS SENECA (C. 4 B.C–A.D. 65)

2869 Our desires always increase with our possessions. The knowledge that something remains yet unenjoyed impairs our enjoyment of the good before us.
SAMUEL JOHNSON (1709–1784)

2870 Restlessness and discontent are the necessities of progress.
THOMAS ALVA EDISON (1847–1931)

2871 Show me a thoroughly satisfied man— and I will show you a failure.
THOMAS ALVA EDISON (1847–1931)

2872 The ass went seeking for horns and lost his ears.
ARABIAN PROVERB

2873 The grass is always greener in the next lawn, and the traffic always moves faster in the next lane.

2874 The poorest man in the world is the one who is always wanting more than he has.

2875 The world owes all its onward impulses to men ill at ease. The happy man inevitably confines himself within ancient limits.
NATHANIEL HAWTHORNE (1804–1864)

2876 There are two kinds of discontent in this world: the discontent that works, and the discontent that wrings its hands. The first gets what it wants, and the second loses what it has. There's no cure for the first but success; and there's no cure at all for the second.
GORDON GRAHAM

2877 There's no place like home—except Florida, Mexico, and Europe.

2878 Those who want much are always much in need.
HORACE (65–8 B.C.)

DISCOURAGEMENT

2879 Discouragement comes when we insist on having our own way.
OSWALD CHAMBERS (1874–1917)

2880 Discouragement is disenchanted egotism.
GIUSEPPE MAZZINI (1805–1872)

2881 He that is down need fear no fall, He that is low, no pride.
JOHN BUNYAN (1628–1688)

2882 I could lie down like a tired child, And weep away the life of care Which I have borne and yet must bear.
PERCY BYSSHE SHELLEY (1792–1822)

2883 In times of dryness and desolation we must be patient, and wait with resignation the return of consolation, putting our trust in the goodness of God. We must animate ourselves by the thought that God is always with us, that he only allows this trial for our greater good, and that we have not necessarily lost his grace because we have lost the taste and feeling of it.
SAINT IGNATIUS OF LOYOLA (1491–1556)

2884 Jonah felt down in the mouth when the great fish swallowed him.

2885 Never doubt in the dark what God told you in the light.
VICTOR RAYMOND EDMAN (1900–1967)

2886 One of my great encouragements is to be friends with those who were personally acquainted with A. W. Tozer. This man, who knew God so intimately, had days when he was so discouraged he felt he could not continue as a minister. A man who instructed thousands in the deep things of God often felt he was a miserable failure.
ERWIN W. LUTZER (1941–)

2887 We should not be upset when unexpected and upsetting and discouraging things happen. God in his wisdom means to make something of us which we have not yet attained and is dealing with us accordingly.
J. I. PACKER (1926–)

2888 When we yield to discouragment, it is usually because we give too much thought to the past or to the future.
THERESE OF LISIEUX (1873–1897)

DISCRETION

2889 A foolish man tells a woman to stop talking, but a wise man tells her that her mouth is extremely beautiful when her lips are closed.

2890 A word out of season may mar a whole lifetime.
GREEK PROVERB

2891 Be civil to all; sociable to many; familiar with few; friend to one; enemy to none.
BENJAMIN FRANKLIN (1706–1790)

2892 Discretion is leaving a few things unsaid.
ELBERT GREEN HUBBARD (1856–1915)

2893 Discretion is putting two and two together and keeping your mouth shut.

2894 Discretion is seeing as much as you ought, not as much as you can.
MICHEL EYQUEM DE MONTAIGNE (1533–1592)

2895 Discretion is the salt, and fancy the sugar of life; the one preserves, the other sweetens it.
CHRISTIAN NESTELL BOVEE (1820–1904)

2896 If thou art a master, be sometimes blind; if a servant, sometimes deaf.
SIR THOMAS FULLER (1608–1661)

2897 It takes two years to learn to talk and seventy years to learn to keep your mouth shut.

2898 Much that may be thought cannot wisely be said.

2899 Speak less than thou knowest.
WILLIAM SHAKESPEARE (1564–1616)

DISCUSSION

2900 A man has a right to unrestricted liberty of discussion.
PERCY BYSSHE SHELLEY (1792–1822)

2901 Discussion is an exchange of knowledge; argument an exchange of ignorance.
ROBERT QUILLEN (1887–1948)

2902 Free and fair discussion will ever be found the firmest friend to truth.
GEORGE CAMPBELL (1719–1796)

2903 He that is not open to conviction is not qualified for discussion.
RICHARD WHATELY (1787–1863)

2904 Whoever is afraid of submitting a question to the test of free discussion is more in love with his own opinion than with truth.
THOMAS WATSON (C. 1557–1592)

DISHONESTY

2905 A jug is never carried under one's coat for an honest reason.
LATIN PROVERB

2906 Cleaning a blot with a blotted finger makes a greater blot.
CHINESE PROVERB

2907 Corruption is a tree,
    whose branches are
Of an unmeasurable length:
    they spread
Ev'rywhere.
FRANCIS BEAUMONT (1584–1616)

2908 Dishonesty is a scorpion that will sting itself to death.
PERCY BYSSHE SHELLEY (1792–1822)

2909 He is most cheated who cheats himself.
DANISH PROVERB

2910 He who knows the truth but keeps silent is like him who tells lies.
ARABIAN PROVERB

2911 He who purposely cheats his friend would cheat his God.
JOHANN KASPAR LAVATER (1741–1801)

2912 He who steals an egg will steal a camel.
ARABIAN PROVERB

2913 Tongue double brings trouble.

2914 Unfaithfulness in the keeping of an appointment is dishonesty. You may as well borrow a person's money as his time.
HORACE MANN (1796–1859)

2915 When you say that you agree with a thing in principle, you mean that you have not the slightest intention of carrying it out in practice.
OTTO EDUARD LEOPOLD VON BISMARCK (1815–1898)

2916 Yes, even I am dishonest. Not in many ways, but in some. Forty-one, I think it is.
MARK TWAIN (1835–1910)

DISRESPECT

2917 Insolence is pride when her mask is pulled off.

2918 Insults are like bad coins; we cannot help their being offered to us, but we need not take them.
CHARLES HADDON SPURGEON (1834–1892)

DIVORCE

2919 Divorce and adultery invaded the church . . . creating an epidemic-like atmosphere. Rationalization reigned supreme.
CHARLES R. SWINDOLL (1934–)

2920 Divorce is a hash made of domestic scraps.
ED WYNN

2921 Divorce is an easy escape, many think. But . . . the guilt and loneliness they experience can be even more tragic than living with their problem.
BILLY GRAHAM (1918–)

2922 Divorce is disengagement for trivial reasons because the couple married for trivial reasons.

2923 Divorce is the sacrament of adultery.
FRENCH PROVERB

2924 God made marriage an indissoluble contract; the world today has made it a scrap of paper to be torn up at the whim of the participants.
CARDINAL GEORGE WILLIAM MUNDELEIN (1872–1939)

2925 I have such hatred of divorce that I prefer bigamy to divorce.
MARTIN LUTHER (1483–1546)

2926 Most divorces are not bad marriages, just poorly prepared marriages.
JIM TALLEY

2927 So many persons who think divorce a panacea for every ill find out when they try it that the remedy is worse than the disease.
DOROTHY DIX (1870–1951)

2928 We have put men on the moon but have not found a solution for moral decay. We have made gigantic strides in medicine but cannot stop the alarming number of divorces and the near dissolution of the family unit.
ERWIN W. LUTZER (1941–)

DOUBT

2929 Beware of doubt—faith is the subtle chain that binds us to the infinite.
ELIZABETH OAKES SMITH (1806–1893)

2930 Christ never failed to distinguish between doubt and unbelief. Doubt is can't believe; unbelief is won't believe. Doubt is honesty; unbelief is obstinacy. Doubt is looking for light; unbelief is content with darkness.
JOHN DRUMMOND (1851–1897)

2931 Clouds of doubt are created when the warm, moist air of our expectations meets the cold air of God's silence.

The problem is not as much in God's silence as it is in your ability to hear.
MAX L. LUCADO (1955–)

2932 Doubt is a pain too lonely to know that faith is his twin brother.
KAHLIL GIBRAN (1883–1931)

2933 Doubt is not always a sign that a man is wrong; it may be a sign that he is thinking.
OSWALD CHAMBERS (1874–1917)

2934 Doubt is the beginning, not the end, of wisdom.
GEORGE ILES

2935 Doubt is the disease of this inquisitive, restless age. It is the price we pay for our advanced intelligence and civilization—the dim night of our resplendent day. But as the most beautiful light is born of darkness, so the faith that springs from conflict is often the strongest and the best.
BILLY GRAHAM (1918–)

2936 Doubt is the hammer that breaks the windows clouded with human fancies and lets in the pure light.
GEORGE MACDONALD (1824–1905)

2937 Doubt is not the opposite of faith; it is one element of faith.
PAUL JOHANNES OSKAR TILLICH (1886–1965)

2938 Doubt makes the mountain which faith moves.

2939 Doubt sees the obstacles; faith sees the way.
Doubt sees the darkest night; faith sees the day.
Doubt dreads to take a step; faith soars on high;
Doubt questions, "Who believes?" Faith answers, "I."

2940 Every step toward Christ kills a doubt. Every thought, word, and deed for him carries you away from discouragement.
THEODORE LEDYARD CUYLER (1822–1909)

2941 God has never turned away the questions of a sincere searcher.
MAX L. LUCADO (1955–)

2942 I respect faith but doubt is what gets
you an education.
WILSON MIZNER (1876–1933)

2943 If a man begins with certainties, he
shall end in doubts; but if he begins
with doubts, he shall end in certainties.
FRANCIS BACON (1561–1626)

2944 If a man doubts his way, Satan is
always ready to help him to a new set
of opinions.
LYDIA MARIA CHILD (1802–1880)

2945 If I stoop
Into the dark, tremendous sea of cloud,
It is but for a time: I press God's lamp
Close to my breast; its splendor, soon
     or late,
Will pierce the gloom: I shall emerge
     one day.
ROBERT BROWNING (1812–1889)

2946 If one regards oneself as a sceptic, it is
well from time to time to be sceptical
about one's scepticism.
SIGMUND FREUD (1856–1939)

2947 If you pray for bread and bring no basket to carry it, you prove the doubting
spirit, which may be the only hindrance to the boon you ask.
DWIGHT LYMAN MOODY (1837–1899)

2948 In our constant struggle to believe we
are likely to overlook the simple fact
that a bit of healthy disbelief is sometimes as needful as faith to the welfare
of our souls.
A. W. TOZER (1897–1963)

2949 It need not discourage us if we are full
of doubts. Healthy questions keep
faith dynamic. Unless we start with
doubts we cannot have a deep-rooted
faith. One who believes lightly and
unthinkingly has not much of a belief.
He who has a faith which is not to be
shaken has won it through blood and
tears—has worked his way from
doubt to truth as one who reaches a
clearing through a thicket of brambles
and thorns.
HELEN ADAMS KELLER (1880–1968)

2950 It's a healthy thing now and then to
hang a question mark on the things
you have long taken for granted.
BERTRAND ARTHUR WILLIAM RUSSELL
(1872–1970)

2951 Modest doubt is call'd
The beacon of the wise.
WILLIAM SHAKESPEARE (1564–1616)

2952 Skepticism is the first step toward
truth.
DENIS DIDEROT (1713–1784)

2953 Skepticism, riddling the faith of yesterday, prepares the way for the faith of
tomorrow.
ROMAIN ROLLAND (1866–1944)

2954 The good must be doubted to be
defended.
ERIC SIEPMANN

2955 The stupid are cocksure and the intelligent full of doubt.
BERTRAND ARTHUR WILLIAM RUSSELL
(1872–1970)

2956 There are two ways to slide easily
through life: to believe everything or
to doubt everything, both ways save
us from thinking.
ALFRED HABDANK SKARBEK KORZYBSKI
(1879–1950)

2957 There lives more faith in honest doubt,
Believe me, than in half the creeds.
ALFRED, LORD TENNYSON (1809–1892)

2958 To believe greatly, it's necessary to
doubt greatly.
MALCOLM MUGGERIDGE (1903–1990)

2959 We all know of Christians who say
that they have never doubted. Their
lives seem so pale, so far off from the
heroic adventure that is faith. The
most fruitful believers tell us shamedly
of the inner battles that have torn
them between doubt and faith. And
the great Bible characters from Abraham or Moses right through Jacob, Jeremiah, Peter, and Paul all show us
their conflict-filled lives, their revolts
against heaven, their refusals to adapt
to a God who was too demanding of
them. They show us as well their reconciliation to that God. God loves

those who don't give in without a
fight!
PAUL TOURNIER (1898–1986)

2960 When the mind doubts, a feather
sways it to and fro.
TERENCE (C. 186–C. 159 B.C.)

2961 When you really see Jesus, I defy you
to doubt him.
OSWALD CHAMBERS (1874–1917)

2962 Whoso draws nigh to God one step
through doubtings dim, God will
advance a mile in blazing light to him.

2963 Without somehow destroying me in
the process, how could God reveal
himself in a way that would leave no
room for doubt? If there were no
room for doubt, there would be no
room for me.
FREDERICK BUECHNER (1926–   )

DREAMS

2964 When a dream enslaves a man,
A dream of the vast untrod,
A dream that says, "Strike out with
me, strike out or part with God,"
It is something
To test the stuff of your rough-hewn
faith
And the fibre of your soul.
PERCY R. HAYWARD

2965 All men whilst they are awake are in
one common world; but each of them,
when he is asleep, is in a world of his
own.
PLUTARCH (C. 46–AFTER 119)

2966 Dreams are the touchstones of our
characters. For in dreams we but act a
part which must have been learned
and rehearsed in our waking hours.

Our truest life is when we are in
dreams awake.
HENRY DAVID THOREAU (1817–1862)

2967 Dreams are true interpreters of our
inclinations; but there is art required
to sort and understand them.
MICHEL EYQUEM DE MONTAIGNE
(1533–1592)

2968 Every dream reveals a psychological
structure, full of significance. . . . The
dream is not meaningless, not absurd
. . . it is a perfectly valid phenomenon,
actually a . . . disguised fulfillment of a
suppressed wish.
SIGMUND FREUD (1856–1939)

2969 Our heart oft times wakes when we
sleep, and God can speak to that,
either by words, by proverbs, by signs
and similitudes, as well as if one was
awake.
JOHN BUNYAN (1628–1688)

2970 Sleep is often the only occasion in
which man cannot silence his conscience; but the tragedy of it is that
when we do hear our conscience speak
in sleep, we cannot act, and that,
when able to act, we forget what we
knew in our dream.
ERICH FROMM (1900–1980)

2971 The dream is the small hidden door in
the deepest and most intimate sanctum
of the soul, which opens into that primeval cosmic night that was soul long
before there was a conscious ego and
will be soul far beyond what a conscious ego could ever reach.
CARL GUSTAV JUNG (1875–1961)

2972 This whole creation is essentially subjective, and the dream is the theater
where the dreamer is at once scene,
actor, prompter, stage manager,
author, audience, and critic.
CARL GUSTAV JUNG (1875–1961)

E

EARTH

2973 Earth, with her thousand voices,
praises God.
SAMUEL TAYLOR COLERIDGE (1772–1834)

2974 Oh, earth, you're too wonderful for
anybody to realize you.
THORNTON NIVEN WILDER (1897–1975)

2975 The only ultimate disaster that can
befall us . . . is to feel ourselves to be
at home here on earth. As long as we
are aliens we cannot forget our true
homeland.
MALCOLM MUGGERIDGE (1903–1990)

2976 The poetry of earth is never dead;
The poetry of earth is ceasing never.
JOHN KEATS (1795–1821)

EASTER

2977 'Twas Easter Sunday. The
full-blossomed trees
Filled all the air with fragrance and
with joy.
HENRY WADSWORTH LONGFELLOW
(1807–1882)

2978 Because he lives I can face tomorrow,
Because he lives all fear is gone.
Because I know he holds the future,
And life is worth the living,
Just because he lives.
WILLIAM AND GLORIA GAITHER

2979 But because he was once emptied I am
each day refilled;
My spirit-arteries pulse with the vital
red of love;
Poured out, it is his life that now
pumps through my own heart's
core.
He bled, and died, and I have been
transfused.
LUCI SHAW (1928–)

2980 Fools! For I also had my hour;
One far fierce hour, and sweet:
There was a shout about my ears,
And palms before my feet.
G. K. CHESTERTON (1874–1936)

2981 Ride on! Ride on in majesty!
In lowly pomp ride on to die;
Bow thy meek head to mortal pain,
Then take, O God, thy power and
reign.
HENRY HART MILMAN (1791–1868)

2982 Spring bursts today,
　　For Christ is risen and all the earth's at
　　　play.
　　CHRISTINA GEORGINA ROSSETTI
　　(1830–1894)

2983 The Easter bunny never rose again.
　　S. RICKLY CHRISTIAN (1953–　)

2984 The seed of God stirred, shoved, and
　　sprouted. The ground trembled, and
　　the rock of the tomb tumbled. And the
　　flower of Easter blossomed.
　　MAX L. LUCADO (1955–　)

2985 Tomb, thou shalt not hold him longer;
　　Death is strong, but life is stronger;
　　Stronger than the dark, the light;
　　Stronger than the wrong, the right;
　　Faith and hope triumphant say,
　　Christ will rise on Easter Day.
　　PHILLIPS BROOKS (1835–1893)

2986 Welcome happy morning, age to age
　　　shall say;
　　Hell today is vanquished, heaven is
　　　won today.
　　SAINT VENANTIUS HONORIUS
　　CLEMENTIANUS FORTUNATUS OF POITIERS
　　(C. 530–C. 610)

ECUMENISM

2987 Evangelicals are not the only Chris-
　　tians. There are those who share with
　　us a firm belief in historic, supernatu-
　　ral Christianity, who worship Christ
　　as Lord and Savior, who take a high
　　view of Scripture, yet who may not
　　use all our terminology and who hold
　　a view of the church and the ministry
　　different from ours. They too are
　　Christians; and from some of them we
　　have much to learn.
　　FRANK E. GAEBELEIN (B. 1899)

2988 Jesus Christ is the unique and total
　　incarnation of truth, the only way, the
　　only life, and yet we betray his spirit
　　of love when we build a wall between
　　Buddhists, Jews, or Muslims and our-
　　selves. He is our only Master, and yet
　　without betraying him we can learn
　　from the Greek philosophers, the sages
　　of India, the philosophers of China, or
　　the sacred text of ancient Egypt.
　　PAUL TOURNIER (1898–1986)

2989 None understand better the nature of
　　real distinction than those who have
　　entered into unity.
　　JOHANN TAULER (C. 1300–1361)

2990 The ecumenical movement brings back
　　a vivid childhood memory of about
　　twenty people reeling out the pub
　　door. They all had their arms around
　　each other's shoulders, because if they
　　didn't they would fall down.
　　MALCOLM MUGGERIDGE (1903–1990)

EDUCATION

2991 'Tis education forms the common mind
　　As the twig is bent the tree's inclined.
　　ALEXANDER POPE (1688–1744)

2992 A little learning is a dangerous thing.
　　ALEXANDER POPE (1688–1744)

2993 A teacher affects eternity; he can never
　　tell where his influence stops.
　　HENRY BROOKS ADAMS (1838–1918)

2994 And still they gazed, and still the
　　　wonder grew,
　　That one small head should carry all it
　　　knew.
　　OLIVER GOLDSMITH (1730–1774)

2995 Anyone who stops learning is old,
　　whether at twenty or eighty.

2996 Crafty men condemn studies, simple
　　men admire them, and wise men use
　　them.
　　FRANCIS BACON (1561–1626)

2997 Education . . . has produced a vast
　　population able to read but unable to
　　distinguish what is worth reading.
　　GEORGE MACAULAY TREVELYAN
　　(1876–1962)

2998 Education and scholarship may enable
　　a man to put things well, but they will
　　never give him insight. Insight comes
　　only from a pureheartedness in work-
　　ing out the will of God.
　　OSWALD CHAMBERS (1874–1917)

2999 Education is a method whereby one
　　acquires a higher grade of prejudices.
　　LAURENCE J. PETER (1919–　)

3000 Education is a progressive discovery of
　　our own ignorance.
　　WILL DURANT (1885–1981)

3001 Education is a social process. Education is growth. Education is not preparation for life; education is life itself.
JOHN DEWEY (1859–1952)

3002 Education is not the filling of a pail, but the lighting of a fire.
WILLIAM BUTLER YEATS (1865–1939)

3003 Education is useless without the Bible.
NOAH WEBSTER (1758–1843)

3004 Education teaches us how little man yet knows, how much he has still to learn.
SIR JOHN LUBBOCK (1834–1913)

3005 Education without religion, as useful as it is, seems rather to make man a more clever devil.
C. S. LEWIS (1898–1963)

3006 Education, like neurosis, begins at home.
MILTON R. SAPIRSTEIN (1914–)

3007 Faith is greater than learning.
MARTIN LUTHER (1483–1546)

3008 I am always ready to learn, but I do not always like being taught.
SIR WINSTON CHURCHILL (1874–1965)

3009 I am still learning.
MICHELANGELO (1475–1564)

3010 If a man empties his purse in his head, no man can take it away from him.
BENJAMIN FRANKLIN (1706–1790)

3011 If it's heads, I go to bed. If it's tails, I stay up. If it stands on edge, I study.

3012 If you think education is expensive—try ignorance.
DEREK BOK

3013 Integrity without knowledge is weak and useless, and knowledge without integrity is dangerous and dreadful.
SAMUEL JOHNSON (1709–1784)

3014 It is a great nuisance that knowledge can only be acquired by hard work.
WILLIAM SOMERSET MAUGHAM (1874–1965)

3015 It is better to learn late than never.
PUBLILIUS SYRUS (FIRST CENTURY B.C.)

3016 It is no profit to have learned well if you neglect to do well.
PUBLILIUS SYRUS (FIRST CENTURY B.C.)

3017 It is of primordial importance to learn more every year than the year before. After all, what is education but a process by which a person begins to learn how to learn?
PETER USTINOV (1921–)

3018 Many learned men, with all the rich furniture of their brain, live and die slaves to the spirit of this world.
WILLIAM LAW (1686–1761)

3019 Most people are mirrors, merely reflecting the mood and emotions of the times; few are windows, bringing light to bear on the dark corners, where troubles fester; and the whole purpose of education is to turn mirrors into windows.
SYDNEY J. HARRIS (1917–1986)

3020 Oh, that one could learn to learn in time!
ENRIQUE SOLARI

3021 Perception of ideas rather than the storing of them should be the aim of education. The mind should be an eye to see with rather than a bin to store facts in. The man who has been taught by the Holy Spirit will be a seer rather than a scholar. The difference is that the scholar sees and the seer sees through; and that is a mighty difference indeed.
A. W. TOZER (1897–1963)

3022 Scholarship should follow faith, not guide it or intrude upon it. I am, after all, beyond human comprehension and I do things you cannot understand.
THOMAS À KEMPIS (C. 1380–1471)

3023 See some good picture—in nature, if possible, or on a canvas—hear a page of the best music, or read a great poem every day. You will always find a free half hour for one or the other, and at the end of the year your mind will shine with such an accumulation of jewels as will astonish even yourself.
HENRY WADSWORTH LONGFELLOW (1807–1882)

3024 Sixty years ago I knew everything; now I know nothing.
WILL DURANT (1885–1981)

3025 So far as the university is concerned, I have no patience with piety alone—I want the most rigorous intellectual training, I want the perfection of the mind; equally, I have no patience with reason alone—I want the salvation of the soul, I want the fear of the Lord, I want at least neutrality with respect to the knowledge of Jesus Christ.
CHARLES HABIB MALIK (1906–   )

3026 The best teacher is not one who crams the most into a pupil, but who gets the most out of one. Education is a process not of stuffing people, like sausage into a casing, but of eliciting from people the potentialities hidden even from themselves.
SYDNEY J. HARRIS (1917–1986)

3027 The greatest danger besetting American evangelical Christianity is the danger of anti-intellectualism. The mind as to its greatest and deepest reaches is not cared for enough. This cannot take place apart from profound immersion for a period of years in the history of thought and spirit. People are in a hurry to get out of the university and start earning money or serving the church or preaching the gospel. They have no idea of the infinite value of spending years of leisure in conversing with the greatest minds and souls of the past, and thereby ripening and sharpening and enlarging their powers of thinking. The result is that the arena of creative thinking is abdicated and vacated to the enemy.
CHARLES HABIB MALIK (1906–   )

3028 The man who is too old to learn was probably always too old to learn.
HENRY H. HASKINS

3029 The more we learn the more we realize how little we know.
R. BUCKMINSTER FULLER (1895–1983)

3030 The most important things in life we need to learn are precisely those things that cannot be taught.
SYDNEY J. HARRIS (1917–1986)

3031 The most worthwhile form of education is the kind that puts the educator inside you, as it were, so that the appetite for learning persists long after the external pressure for grades and degrees has vanished. Otherwise you are not educated; you are merely trained.
SYDNEY J. HARRIS (1917–1986)

3032 The surest way to corrupt a young man is to teach him to esteem more highly those who think alike than those who think differently.
FRIEDRICH WILHELM NIETZSCHE (1844–1900)

3033 The wisest mind has something yet to learn.
GEORGE SANTAYANA (1863–1952)

3034 Today one has to pass more tests to get into college than dad had to pass to get out.

3035 We must educate people in what nobody knew yesterday, and prepare in our schools for what no one knows yet but what some people must know tomorrow.
MARGARET MEAD (1901–1978)

3036 What can the poor church, even at its best, do; what can evangelization, even at its most inspired do; what can the poor family, even at its purest and noblest, do if the children spend between fifteen and twenty years of their life, and indeed the most formative period of their life, in school and college, in an atmosphere of formal denial of any relevance of God and spirit and soul and faith to the formation of their mind? The enormity of what is happening is beyond words.
CHARLES HABIB MALIK (1906–   )

3037 What greater work is there than training the mind and forming the habits of the young?
SAINT JOHN CHRYSOSTOM (C. 347–407)

3038 What sculpture is to a block of marble, education is to the human soul. The philosopher, the saint, the hero, the wise and the good, or the great, very often lie hid and concealed in a plebeian, which a proper education might have disinterred and brought to light.
JOSEPH ADDISON (1672–1719)

3039 When will we teach our children in school what they are? We should say to each of them: Do you know what you are? You are a marvel. You are unique. In all of the world there is no other child exactly like you. In the millions of years that have passed there has never been another child like you. And look at your body—what a wonder it is! Your legs, your arms, your cunning fingers, the way you move! You may become a Shakespeare, a Michelangelo, a Beethoven. You have the capacity for anything. Yes, you are a marvel. And when you grow up, can you then harm another who is, like you, a marvel?
PABLO CASALS (1876–1973)

3040 Who among the evangelicals can stand up to the great secular or naturalistic or atheistic scholars on their own terms of scholarship and research? Who among the evangelical scholars is quoted as a normative source by the greatest secular authorities on history or philosophy or psychology or sociology or politics? Does your mode of thinking have the slightest chance of becoming the dominant mode of thinking in the great universities of Europe and America which stamp your entire civilization with their own spirit and ideas?
CHARLES HABIB MALIK (1906–   )

3041 Whom, then, do I call educated? First, those who control circumstances instead of being mastered by them, those who meet all occasions manfully and act in accordance with intelligent thinking, those who are honorable in all dealings, who treat good-naturedly persons and things that are disagreeable; and furthermore, those who hold their pleasures under control and are not overcome by misfortune; finally, those who are not spoiled by success.
SOCRATES (469–399 B.C.)

ELECTION

3042 "I have chosen you." Keep that note of greatness in your creed. It is not

that you have got God, but that he has got you. Why is God at work in me, bending, breaking, moulding, doing just as he chooses? For one purpose only—that he may be able to say, "This is my man, my woman."
OSWALD CHAMBERS (1874–1917)

3043 Election is ascribed to God the Father, sanctification to the Spirit, and reconciliation to Jesus Christ. . . . The Son cannot die for them whom the Father never elected, and the Spirit will never sanctify them whom the Father hath not elected nor the Son redeemed.
THOMAS MANTON (1620–1677)

3044 God did not choose us because we were worthy, but by choosing us he makes us worthy.
THOMAS WATSON (C. 1557–1592)

3045 Many are called but most are frozen in corporate or collective cold, these are the stalled who choose not to be chosen except to be bought and sold.
LEE CARROLL PIEPER

3046 The elect are whosoever will; the non-elect are whosoever won't.
HENRY WARD BEECHER (1813–1887)

3047 This doctrine affords comfort: thy unworthiness may dismay thee, but remember that thy election depends not upon thy worthiness but upon the will of God.
ELNATHAN PARR

3048 When God elects us, it is not because we are handsome.
JOHN CALVIN (1509–1564)

EMOTIONS

3049 Both my body and my emotions were given to me, and it is as futile for me to condemn myself for feeling scared, insecure, selfish, or revengeful as it is for me to get mad at myself for the size of my feet. I am not responsible for my feelings but for what I do with them.
HUGH PRATHER

3050 By starving emotions we become humorless, rigid, and stereotyped; by repressing them we become literal,

reformatory, and holier-than-thou; encouraged, they perfume life; discouraged, they poison it.
JOSEPH COLLINS (1866–1950)

3051 Don't bother much about your feelings. When they are humble, loving, brave, give thanks for them; when they are conceited, selfish, cowardly, ask to have them altered. In neither case are they you, but only a thing that happens to you. What matters is your intentions and your behavior.
C. S. LEWIS (1898–1963)

3052 Emotion cannot be cut out of life. No intelligent person would think of saying, "Let's do away with all emotion." Some critics are suspicious of any conversion that does not take place in a refrigerator. There are many dangers in false emotionalism, but that does not rule out true emotion and depth of feeling. Emotion may vary in religious experience. Some people are stoical and others are demonstrative, but the feeling will be there. There is going to be a tug at the heart.
BILLY GRAHAM (1918–)

3053 Emotion is the chief source of all becoming-conscious. There can be no transforming of darkness into light and of apathy into movement without emotion.
CARL GUSTAV JUNG (1875–1961)

3054 Emotion: ah! Let us never be one of those who treat lightly one of the words that most deserve reverence.
CHARLES DU BOS (1882–1939)

3055 Emotions should be servants, not masters—or at least not tyrants.
ROBERT H. BENSON (1871–1914)

3056 In every one of us the deepest emotions are constantly caused by some absurdly trivial thing, or by nothing at all. Conversely, the great things in our lives—the true occasions for wrath, anguish, rapture, what not—very often leave us quite calm.
SIR MAX BEERBOHM (1872–1956)

3057 Nobility grows out of contained emotion.
GEORGES BRAQUE (1882–1963)

3058 The experience of the whole gamut of emotions is a part of the human condition, the inheritance of every man.
JOHN POWELL

3059 Thoughts too deep to be expressed, And too strong to be suppressed.
GEORGE WITHER (1588–1667)

3060 We allow our emotions to arise so that they can be identified. We make the necessary adjustments in the light of our own ideals and hopes for growth. We change.
JOHN POWELL

3061 We do not bury our emotions dead; they remain alive in our subconscious minds and intestines to hurt and trouble us.
JOHN POWELL

3062 When emotions are allowed to illuminate our inner selves, they can tell us things we never knew about ourselves.
JOHN POWELL

EMPATHY

3063 A generous heart feels others' ill as if it were responsible for them.
LUC DE CLAPIERS, MARQUIS DE VAUVENARGUES (1715–1747)

3064 Among those who stand, do not sit; Among those who sit, do not stand; Among those who laugh, do not weep; Among those who weep, do not laugh.
JEWISH PROVERB

3065 Bring thy soul and interchange with mine.
JOHANN FRIEDRICH VON SCHILLER (1759–1805)

3066 Discouraged people don't need critics. They hurt enough already. They don't need more guilt or piled-on distress. They need encouragement. They need a refuge. A willing, caring, available someone.
CHARLES R. SWINDOLL (1934–)

3067 Do not speak of your own happiness to one who is unhappy.

3068 Empathy is your pain in my heart.
HALFORD E. LUCCOCK (1885–1960)

3069 Fragile and delicate are the feelings of most who seek our help. They need to sense we are there because we care . . . not just because it's our job.
CHARLES R. SWINDOLL (1934–)

3070 I don't want to be insensitive, but to hurt where other people hurt, nor to say I know how you feel, but to say God knows and I'll try if you'll be patient with me, and meanwhile I'll be quiet.
JOSEPH BAYLY (1920–1986)

3071 I never ask the wounded person how he feels; I myself become the wounded person.
WALT WHITMAN (1819–1892)

3072 If you can't help your friend with money, help him at least with a sigh.
YIDDISH PROVERB

3073 Instead of putting others in their place, try putting yourself in their place.

3074 Never elated while one man's oppress'd. Never dejected while another's bless'd.
ALEXANDER POPE (1688–1744)

3075 No man is a good physician who has never been sick.
ARABIAN PROVERB

3076 Said a wise man to one in deep sorrow, "I did not come to comfort you; God only can do that; but I did come to say how deeply and tenderly I feel for you in your affliction."
TRYON EDWARDS (1809–1894)

3077 The capacity to care gives life its deepest significance.
PABLO CASALS (1876–1973)

3078 To understand any living thing you must creep within and feel the beating of its heart.
W. MACNEILE DIXON

3079 Understanding a person does not mean condoning; it only means that one does not accuse him as if one were God or a judge placed above him.
ERICH FROMM (1900–1980)

3080 We tend to look at caring as an attitude of the strong toward the weak, of the powerful toward the powerless, of the haves toward the havenots. . . . Still, when we honestly ask ourselves which persons in our lives mean the most to us, we often find that it is those who, instead of giving much advice, solutions, or cures, have chosen rather to share our pain and touch our wounds with a gentle and tender hand. The friend who can be silent with us in a moment of despair or confusion, who can stay with us in an hour of grief and bereavement, who can tolerate not-knowing, not-curing, not-healing and face with us the reality of our powerlessness, that is the friend who cares.
HENRI J. M. NOUWEN

3081 When men are animated by the love of Christ, they feel united, and the needs, sufferings, and joys of others are felt as their own.
POPE JOHN XXIII (1881–1963)

EMPLOYMENT

3082 A dairymaid can milk cows to the glory of God.
MARTIN LUTHER (1483–1546)

3083 A few years ago to work ten hours a day was called economic slavery. Today it is called moonlighting.

3084 A servant that is diligent, honest, and good,
Must sing at his work like a bird in the wood.

3085 Absence of occupation is not rest, A mind quite vacant is a mind distress'd.
WILLIAM COWPER (1731–1800)

3086 An astronaut is the only man who runs around in circles—and gets somewhere.

3087 Duty does not have to be dull. Love can make it beautiful and fill it with life.
THOMAS MERTON (1915–1968)

3088 Each individual has his own kind of living assigned to him by the Lord as a sort of sentry post.
JOHN CALVIN (1509–1564)

3089 Few men ever drop dead from over-work, but many quietly curl up and die because of undersatisfaction.
SYDNEY J. HARRIS (1917–1986)

3090 Give us, oh, give us, the man who sings at his work! He will do more in the same time, he will do it better, he will persevere longer. One is scarcely sensible of fatigue while he marches to music.
THOMAS CARLYLE (1795–1881)

3091 God gives every bird its food, but he does not throw it into the nest.
JOSIAH GILBERT HOLLAND (1819–1881)

3092 God gives no linen, but flax to spin.
GERMAN PROVERB

3093 God gives the birds their food, but they must fly for it.
DUTCH PROVERB

3094 God says, "Rise up and I shall rise with you." He does not say, "Sleep and I shall feed you."
ARABIAN PROVERB

3095 Heaven is the Christian's vocation and therefore he counts all earthly employ-ments as avocations.
SIR THOMAS FULLER (1608–1661)

3096 If a man does only what is required of him, he is a slave. If a man does more than is required of him, he is a free man.
CHINESE PROVERB

3097 If the Almighty had ever made a set of men that should do all the eating and none of the work, he would have made them with mouths only and no hands; and if he had ever made another class that he intended should do all the work and no eating, he would have made them with hands only and no mouths.
ABRAHAM LINCOLN (1809–1865)

3098 If you don't want to work, you have to work to earn enough money so that you won't have to work.
OGDEN NASH (1902–1971)

3099 If you would have good servants, see that you be a good master.

3100 In doing what we ought we deserve no praise, it is our duty.
SAINT AUGUSTINE OF HIPPO (354–430)

3101 In order that people may be happy in their work, these three things are needed: they must be fit for it, they must not do too much of it, and they must have a sense of success in it.
JOHN RUSKIN (1819–1900)

3102 Labor is but refreshment from repose.

3103 Labor: a powerful medicine.
SAINT JOHN CHRYSOSTOM (C. 347–407)

3104 Monday-through-Friday employment is pure, it's sacred—just as sacred as your Sunday activities.
CHARLES R. SWINDOLL (1934–)

3105 Never fall out with your bread and butter.
ENGLISH PROVERB

3106 No life can be dreary when work is delight.
FRANCES RIDLEY HAVERGAL (1836–1879)

3107 No one can make a real masterpiece of life until he sees something infinitely greater in his vocation than bread and butter and shelter.
ORISON SWETT MARDEN

3108 No person who is enthusiastic about his work has anything to fear from life.
SAMUEL GOLDWYN (1882–1974)

3109 Nothing is more dangerous than dis-continued labor; it is habit lost. A habit easy to abandon, difficult to resume.
VICTOR HUGO (1802–1885)

3110 Nothing is particularly hard if you divide it into small jobs.
HENRY FORD (1863–1947)

3111 Nothing is work unless you would rather be doing something else.
SIR JAMES M. BARRIE (1860–1937)

3112 Oh, let us love our occupations,
Bless the squire and his relations,
Live upon our daily rations,
And always know our proper stations.
CHARLES DICKENS (1812–1870)

3113 Our forefathers succeeded because their goal was not material wealth alone but glory to God. Their mun-

dane work was as sacred as the frontier parson's. They believed whatever they did was God ordained.
TOM HAGGAI

3114 People used to need rest after work; today they need exercise.

3115 Plough deep while sluggards sleep, and you shall have corn to sell and keep.

3116 Quality workmanship is not expensive; it's priceless!

3117 Spin carefully—spin prayerfully, but leave the thread to God.

3118 The dictionary is the only place where success comes before work.

3119 The highest reward of a man's labor is not what he gets for it, but what it does for him.
JOHN RUSKIN (1819–1900)

3120 The outstanding mistake of the employer is his failure to realize that he is dealing with human material.
ROGER WARD BABSON (1875–1967)

3121 The perfect job: the responsibility of an office boy, the hours of an absentee, and the income of an executive.

3122 There is no future in any job. The future lies in the man who holds the job.
GEORGE CRANE

3123 There is no work better than another to please God; to pour water, to wash dishes, to be a cobbler, or an apostle, all is one; to wash dishes and to preach is all one, as touching the deed, to please God.
WILLIAM TYNDALE (C. 1494–1536)

3124 We work to become, not to acquire.
ELBERT GREEN HUBBARD (1856–1915)

3125 When you are working for others, let it be with the same zeal as if it were for yourself.
CONFUCIUS (C. 551–479 B.C.)

3126 Work is easy—for those who like to work.
JEWISH PROVERB

3127 Work should be looked upon, not as a necessary drudgery to be undergone for the purpose of making money, but as a way of life in which the nature of man should find its proper exercise and delight and so fulfill itself to the glory of God.
DOROTHY L. SAYERS (1893–1957)

ENCOURAGEMENT

3128 A good word costs no more than a bad one.
ENGLISH PROVERB

3129 Apt words have power to assuage
The tumors of a troubled mind
And are as balm to fester'd wounds.
JOHN MILTON (1608–1674)

3130 Correction does much, but encouragement does more. Encouragement after censure is as the sun after a shower.
JOHANN WOLFGANG VON GOETHE (1749–1832)

3131 Don't point a finger—hold out a helping hand.

3132 Don't rely on the broken reed of human support.
ASHER BEN JEHIEL (1250–1327)

3133 Encouragement is oxygen to the soul.
GEORGE M. ADAMS (1878–1962)

3134 He climbs highest who helps another up.
ZIG ZIGLAR

3135 How many people stop because so few say, "Go!"
CHARLES R. SWINDOLL (1934–)

3136 Is anyone happier because you passed his way? Does anyone remember that you spoke to him today?

3137 It's so nice to get flowers while you can still smell the fragrance.
LENA HORNE (1917–)

3138 More people fail for lack of encouragement than for any other reason.

3139 Strengthen me by sympathizing with my strength, not my weakness.
AMOS BRONSON ALCOTT (1799–1888)

3140 Tell a man he is brave, and you help him to become so.
THOMAS CARLYLE (1795–1881)

3141 The deepest principle in human nature is the craving to be appreciated.
WILLIAM JAMES (1842–1910)

3142 The men who are lifting the world upward and onward are those who encourage more than criticize.
ELISABETH HARRISON

3143 The small change of human happiness lies in the unexpected friendly word.

3144 We blossom under praise like flowers in sun and dew; we open, we reach, we grow.
GERHARD E. FROST

3145 We cannot hold a torch to light another's path without brightening our own.
BEN SWEETLAND

3146 When a person is down in the world, an ounce of help is better than a pound of preaching.
EDWARD GEORGE BULWER-LYTTON (1803–1873)

ENDURANCE

3147 American pioneers in their covered wagons endured many hardships while traveling westward into the setting sun, the worst being their lack of sunglasses.

3148 Enjoy when you can and endure when you must.
JOHANN WOLFGANG VON GOETHE (1749–1832)

3149 Endurance is not just the ability to bear a hard thing, but to turn it into glory.
WILLIAM BARCLAY (1907–1978)

3150 Not in the achievement, but in the endurance of the human soul does it show its divine grandeur and its alliance with the infinite God.
EDWIN HUBBEL CHAPIN (1814–1880)

3151 Nothing great was ever done without much enduring.
CATHERINE OF SIENA (1347–1380)

3152 Patient endurance is the perfection of charity.
SAINT AMBROSE (C. 340–397)

3153 To endure is greater than to dare; to tire out hostile fortune; to be daunted by no difficulty; to keep heart when all have lost it; to go through intrigue spotless; to forego even ambition when the end is gained—who can say this is not greatness.
WILLIAM MAKEPEACE THACKERAY (1811–1863)

3154 What can't be cured must be endured.
ROBERT BURTON (1577–1640)

ENEMIES

3155 A wise man gets more use from his enemies than a fool from his friends.
BALTASAR GRACIÁN Y MORALES (1601–1658)

3156 Better is the enemy of good.
ITALIAN PROVERB

3157 Beware of no man more than of yourself; we carry our worst enemies within us.
CHARLES HADDON SPURGEON (1834–1892)

3158 Do not fear when your enemies criticize you. Beware when they applaud.
VO DONG GIANG

3159 Even the mean man has his value. You can learn from him how not to live.

3160 He that wrestles with us strengthens our nerves, and sharpens our skill. Our antagonist is our helper.
EDMUND BURKE (1729–1797)

3161 If we could read the secret history of our enemies, we should find in each man's life sorrow and suffering enough to disarm all hostility.
HENRY WADSWORTH LONGFELLOW (1807–1882)

3162 It is my rule, from experience, to remember my friend may become my enemy, and my enemy my friend.
SOPHOCLES (C. 496–406 B.C.)

3163 It is never wise to underestimate an enemy. We look upon the enemy of our souls as a conquered foe, so he is, but only to God, not to us.
OSWALD CHAMBERS (1874–1917)

3164 Love your enemies, for they tell you your faults.
BENJAMIN FRANKLIN (1706–1790)

3165 Man's chief enemy is his own unruly nature and the dark forces pent up within him.
ERNEST JONES (1879–1958)

3166 Men who walk in the ways of God would not grieve the hearts even of their enemies.
SA'DI (THIRTEENTH CENTURY)

3167 Never cease loving a person and never give up hope for him, for even the Prodigal Son who had fallen most low could still be saved. The bitterest enemy and also he who was your friend could again be your friend; love that has grown cold can kindle again.
SØREN AABYE KIERKEGAARD (1813–1855)

3168 Our real enemies are the people who make us feel so good that we are slowly, but inexorably, pulled down into the quicksand of smugness and self-satisfaction.
SYDNEY J. HARRIS (1917–1986)

3169 Pay attention to your enemies for they are the first to discover your mistakes.
ANTISTHENES (C. 445–C. 365 B.C.)

3170 The safe and sure way to destroy an enemy is to make him your friend.

3171 Two enemies are two potential friends who don't know each other.

3172 We should conduct ourselves toward our enemy as if he were one day to be our friend.
CARDINAL JOHN HENRY NEWMAN (1801–1890)

3173 Yet is every man his greatest enemy, and . . . his own executioner.
SIR THOMAS BROWNE (1605–1682)

3174 You have no enemies, you say?
Alas! my friend, the boast is poor—
He who has mingled in the fray
Of duty, that the brave endure,
Must have made foes! If you have none,
Small is the work that you have done;
You've hit no traitor on the hip;
You've dashed no cup from perjured lip;
You've never turned the wrong to right—
You've been a coward in the fight!
CHARLES MACKAY (1814–1889)

3175 Your reactions to your enemy can hurt you more than your enemy can.
HANNAH HURNARD (1905–1990)

ENTHUSIASM

3176 A man can succeed at almost anything for which he has unlimited enthusiasm.
CHARLES M. SCHWAB (1862–1939)

3177 Enthusiasm makes ordinary people extraordinary.
NORMAN VINCENT PEALE (1898–   )

3178 Every great and commanding movement in the annals of the world is the triumph of enthusiasm. Nothing great was ever achieved without it.
RALPH WALDO EMERSON (1803–1882)

3179 Exuberance is beauty.
WILLIAM BLAKE (1757–1827)

3180 God wants no wallflowers; all must join the dance.
GERHARD E. FROST

3181 Nothing is so easy but it becomes difficult when done reluctantly.
LATIN PROVERB

3182 Spirit-filled souls are ablaze for God. They love with a love that glows. They believe with a faith that kindles. They serve with a devotion that consumes. They hate sin with a fierceness that burns. They rejoice with a joy that radiates. Love is perfected in the fire of God.
SAMUEL CHADWICK (1832–1917)

3183 The worst bankrupt in the world is the man who has lost his enthusiasm.
H. W. ARNOLD

3184 There seems to be a chilling fear of holy enthusiasm among the people of God. We try to tell how happy we are—but we remain so well-controlled that there are very few waves of glory experienced in our midst.
A. W. TOZER (1897–1963)

3185 Think excitement, talk excitement, act out excitement, and you are bound to become an excited person. Life will take on a new zest, deeper interest and greater meaning. You can think, talk, and act yourself into dullness or into monotony or into unhappiness. By the same process you can build up inspiration, excitement, and a surging depth of joy.
NORMAN VINCENT PEALE (1898–   )

3186 Wherever you are, be all there. Live to the hilt every situation you believe to be the will of God.
JIM ELLIOT (1927–1956)

3187 Wherever you go, go with your whole heart.
CONFUCIUS (C. 551–479 B.C.)

3188 Enthusiasm is the element of success in everything. It is the light that leads and the strength that lifts men on and up in the great struggles of scientific pursuits and of professional labor. It robs endurance of difficulty and makes pleasure of duty.
BISHOP DOANE (1832–1913)

3189 Acquire enthusiasm; you can't be enthusiastic and unhappy at the same time.

ENVIRONMENT

3190 Ah, how unjust to nature and himself
Is thoughtless, thankless, inconsistent man!
EDWARD YOUNG (1683–1765)

3191 All of creation God gives to humankind to use. If this privilege is misused, God's justice permits creation to punish humanity.
SAINT HILDEGARDE OF BINGEN (1098–1179)

3192 Every flower of the field, every fibre of a plant, every particle of an insect carries with it the impress of its Maker and can—if duly considered—read us lectures of ethics or divinity.
SIR THOMAS POPE BLOUNT (1649–1697)

3193 Everything is perfect coming from the hands of the Creator, everything degenerates in the hands of man.
JEAN JACQUES ROUSSEAU (1712–1778)

3194 I shot an arrow in the air—and it stuck.

3195 It is God's world still. It has been given to man not absolutely, but in trust, that man may work out in it the will of God; given—may we not say?—just as a father gives a child a corner of his great garden, and says, "There, that is yours; now cultivate it."
PHILLIPS BROOKS (1835–1893)

3196 Let us permit nature to have her way; she understands her business better than we do.
MICHEL EYQUEM DE MONTAIGNE (1533–1592)

3197 Man is a complex being; he makes deserts bloom and lakes die.
GIL STERN

3198 Nature, to be commanded, must be obeyed.
FRANCIS BACON (1561–1626)

3199 The ground is holy, being even as it came from the Creator. Keep it, guard it, care for it, for it keeps men, guards men, cares for men. Destroy it and man is destroyed.
ALAN STEWART PATON (1903–   )

3200 The laws given in the Bible include a scheme for the treatment of the earth. . . . Leviticus 25 is the great classic on the rights of the earth.
OSWALD CHAMBERS (1874–1917)

3201 The pagans do not know God and love only the earth. The Jews know the true God and love only the earth. The Christians know the true God and do not love the earth.
BLAISE PASCAL (1623–1662)

3202 The sun, the moon, and the stars would have disappeared long ago had they happened to be within reach of predatory human hands.
HAVELOCK ELLIS (1859–1939)

3203 The world is disgracefully managed; one hardly knows to whom to complain.
RONALD FIRBANK (1886–1926)

3204 There is a sufficiency in the world for man's need, but not for man's greed.
MAHATMA GANDHI (1869–1948)

3205 We are told that when Jehovah created the world, he saw that it was good. What would he say now?
GEORGE BERNARD SHAW (1856–1950)

ENVY

3206 A person is truly great when he is not envious of his rival's success.

3207 As rust corrupts iron, so envy corrupts
man.
ANTISTHENES (C. 445–C. 365 B.C.)

3208 Don't envy the man who has everything: he probably has an ulcer too.

3209 Envy eats nothing but its own heart.
GERMAN PROVERB

3210 Envy is a kind of praise.
JOHN GAY (1685–1732)

3211 Envy is impotent, numbed with fear,
never ceasing in its appetite, and it
knows no gratification but endless self
torment. It has the ugliness of a
trapped rat, which gnaws its own foot
in an effort to escape.
ANGUS WILSON (1913–   )

3212 Envy is like a disease—it consumes the
soul.
JEWISH PROVERB

3213 Envy is like a fly that passes all a
body's sounder parts and dwells upon
the sores.
GEORGE CHAPMAN (C. 1559–1634)

3214 Envy shoots at others and wounds herself.
SIR THOMAS FULLER (1608–1661)

3215 Envy slays itself by its own arrows.
GREEK PROVERB

3216 Envy's a coal come hissing hot from
hell.
PHILIP JAMES BAILEY (1816–1902)

3217 Envy: the green sickness.
WILLIAM SHAKESPEARE (1564–1616)

3218 Happiness vanishes when envy
appears.
JEWISH PROVERB

3219 He who envies another admits his own
inferiority.

3220 How bitter a thing it is to look into
happiness through another man's eyes.
WILLIAM SHAKESPEARE (1564–1616)

3221 If we did but know how little some
enjoy of the great things that they possess, there would not be much envy in
the world.
EDWARD YOUNG (1683–1765)

3222 Our envy always lasts longer than the
happiness of those we envy.
FRANÇOIS, DUC DE LA ROCHEFOUCAULD
(1613–1680)

3223 The only thing more disturbing than a
friend with a noisy old car is a friend
with a quiet new one.

3224 Too many Christians envy the sinners
their pleasure and the saints their joy
because they don't have either one.
MARTIN LUTHER (1483–1546)

EQUALITY

3225 All men are by nature equal, made of
the same earth by the same Creator,
and however we deceive ourselves, as
dear to God is the poor peasant as the
mighty prince.
PLATO (C. 428–348 B.C.)

3226 All men are equal in the presence of
death.
PUBLILIUS SYRUS (FIRST CENTURY B.C.)

3227 God who rules this earth
Gave life to every race;
He chose its day of birth,
The color of its face;
So none may claim superior grade
Within the family he's made.
RICHARD G. JONES

3228 I don't look down upon royalty, the
wealthy, and the socially elect; they'd
be just as good as anybody else if they
had an equal chance.
WILL ROGERS (1879–1935)

3229 I dream of a day when there will be
better understanding among people.
When I sing, I don't want them to see
that my face is black; I don't want
them to see that my face is white—I
want them to see my soul. And that is
colorless.
MARIAN ANDERSON (1902–   )

3230 I recognize no rights but human
rights—I know nothing of men's rights
and women's rights; for in Christ Jesus
there is neither male nor female. It is
my solemn conviction that, until this
principal of equality is recognized and
embodied in practice, the church can

do nothing effectual for the permanent reformation of the world.
ANGELINA GRIMKÉ (1805–1879)

3231 I'm not denyin' the women are foolish: God Almighty made 'em to match the men.
GEORGE ELIOT (1819–1880)

3232 If God were to send two angels to earth, the one to occupy a throne, and the other to clean a road, they would each regard their employments as equally distinguished and equally happy.
FREDERICK WILLIAM FABER (1814–1863)

3233 If this is God's world, there are no unimportant people.
GEORGE THOMAS

3234 If you meet those of different race and color to yourself . . . think of them as different colored roses growing in the beautiful garden of humanity and rejoice to be among them.
ABDU'L-BAHA (1884–1921)

3235 In celebration the high and the mighty regain their balance, and the weak and lowly receive new stature. Who can be high or low at the festival of God?
RICHARD J. FOSTER (1942–   )

3236 In God's sight there are only two classes of people, those who are in Christ and those who are outside of him. And all those who are in Christ are accepted equally; there are no grades of perfection with God.
ERWIN W. LUTZER (1941–   )

3237 In the gates of eternity the black hand and the white hold each other with an equal clasp.
HARRIET BEECHER STOWE (1811–1896)

3238 It is only in love that the unequal can be made equal.
SØREN AABYE KIERKEGAARD (1813–1855)

3239 Male and female are not contenders for supremacy, but each the complement of the other. Both equal, yet each with his own station and role.
BILLY GRAHAM (1918–   )

3240 No race can prosper until it learns that there is as much dignity in tilling a field as in writing a poem.
BOOKER T. WASHINGTON (1856–1915)

3241 Oh, east is east, and west is west,
   and never the twain shall meet,
Till earth and sky stand presently
   at God's great judgment seat;
But there is neither east nor west,
   border, nor breed, nor birth,
When two strong men stand face to
   face, though they come from the
   ends of the earth!
RUDYARD KIPLING (1865–1936)

3242 Only as children of God are we equal; all other claims to equality—social, economic, racial, intellectual, sexual— only serve in practice to intensify inequality. For this reason your commandment to love our fellowmen follows after, and depends upon, the commandment to love God. How marvelous is the love thus attained—the faces looming up, young and old, sullen and gay, beautiful and plain, clever and stupid, black, pink and grey; all brothers and sisters, all equally dear!
MALCOLM MUGGERIDGE (1903–1990)

3243 The Lord so constituted everybody that no matter what color you are you require the same amount of nourishment.
WILL ROGERS (1879–1935)

3244 The passion for equality produces uniformity which produces mediocrity.
ALEXIS TOCQUEVILLE (1805–1859)

3245 The sole equality on earth is death.
PHILIP JAMES BAILEY (1816–1902)

3246 We hold these truths to be self-evident— that all men are created equal; that they are endowed by their Creator with certain unalienable rights, that among these are life, liberty, and the pursuit of happiness. That to secure these rights, governments are instituted among men, deriving their just powers from the consent of the governed.
—The Declaration of Independence 1776

3247 What makes equality such a difficult business is that we only want it with our superiors.
HENRY FRANÇOIS BECQUE (1837–1899)

3248 You are just as important as the next person, but no more important.
DANIEL WEBSTER (1782–1852)

ERROR

3249 A man should never be ashamed to own he has been in the wrong, which is but saying that he is wiser today than he was yesterday.
ALEXANDER POPE (1688–1744)

3250 An error is the more dangerous, the more truth it contains.
HENRI FRÉDÉRIC AMIEL (1821–1881)

3251 Error is a hardy plant; it flourishes in every soil.
MARTIN FARQUHAR TUPPER (1810–1889)

3252 Error is discipline through which we advance.
WILLIAM ELLERY CHANNING (1780–1842)

3253 Error is just as important a condition of life as truth.
CARL GUSTAV JUNG (1875–1961)

3254 Errors to be dangerous must have a great deal of truth mingled with them. It is only from this alliance that they can ever obtain an extensive circulation.
SYDNEY SMITH (1771–1845)

3255 Errors, like straws, upon the surface flow;
He who would search for pearls must dive below.
JOHN DRYDEN (1631–1700)

3256 Every absurdity has a champion to defend it, for error is always talkative.
OLIVER GOLDSMITH (1730–1774)

3257 From the errors of others a wise man corrects his own.
PUBLILIUS SYRUS (FIRST CENTURY B.C.)

3258 Ignorance is content to stand still, with her back to the truth; but error is more presumptuous and proceeds in the wrong direction. Ignorance has no light, but error follows a false one.
CHARLES CALEB COLTON (1780–1832)

3259 It is easier to perceive error than truth, for error lies on the surface and is easily seen, truth lies in the depth where few are willing to search for it.
JOHANN WOLFGANG VON GOETHE (1749–1832)

3260 It is the nature of every man to err, but only the fool perseveres in error.
CICERO (106–43 B.C.)

3261 Men prefer a prosperous error to an afflicted truth.
JEREMY TAYLOR (1613–1667)

3262 Sometimes we may learn more from a man's errors than from his virtues.
HENRY WADSWORTH LONGFELLOW (1807–1882)

3263 To err is human, but when the eraser wears out ahead of the pencil, you're overdoing it.
JOSH JENKINS

3264 Who errs and mends, to God himself commends.
MIGUEL DE CERVANTES (1547–1616)

ETERNITY

3265 All that is not eternal is eternally out of date.
C. S. LEWIS (1898–1963)

3266 Eternity has no gray hairs! The flowers fade, the heart withers, man grows old and dies, the world lies down in the sepulchre of ages, but time writes no wrinkles on the brow of eternity.
REGINALD HEBER (1783–1826)

3267 Eternity is the ocean; time is the wave.
MAURICE MAETERLINCK (1862–1949)

3268 Eternity looks grander and kinder if time grows meaner and more hostile.
THOMAS CARLYLE (1795–1881)

3269 Eternity stands always fronting God; a stern colossal image, with blind eyes, and grand dim lips that murmur evermore, "God—God—God!"
ELIZABETH BARRETT BROWNING (1806–1861)

3270 Eternity will not be long enough to learn all he is, or to praise him for all he has done, but then, that matters

not; for we shall be always with him, and we desire nothing more.
FREDERICK WILLIAM FABER (1814–1863)

3271 Eternity! thou pleasing, dreadful thought!
JOSEPH ADDISON (1672–1719)

3272 He who has no vision of eternity will never get a true hold of time.
THOMAS CARLYLE (1795–1881)

3273 High up in the north in the land called Svithjod, there stands a rock. It is one hundred miles high and one hundred miles wide. Once every thousand years a little bird comes to this rock to sharpen its beak. When the rock has thus been worn away, then a single day of eternity will have gone by.
HENDRICK WILLEM VAN LOON (1882–1944)

3274 How completely satisfying to turn from our limitations to a God who has none. Eternal years lie in his heart. For him time does not pass, it remains; and those who are in Christ share with him all the riches of limitless time and endless years.
A. W. TOZER (1897–1963)

3275 I can't help it, the idea of the infinite torments me.
ALFRED DE MUSSET (1810–1857)

3276 I saw eternity the other night
Like a great ring of pure and endless light.
HENRY VAUGHAN (1622–1695)

3277 I thank thee, O Lord, that thou hast so set eternity within my heart that no earthly thing can ever satisfy me wholly.
JOHN BAILLIE (1741–1806)

3278 In eternity everything is just beginning.
ELIAS CANETTI (1905–)

3279 In the presence of eternity, the mountains are as transient as the clouds.
ROBERT GREEN INGERSOLL (1833–1899)

3280 Learn to hold loosely all that is not eternal.
AGNES MAUDE ROYDEN (1876–1956)

3281 Live near to God, and all things will appear little to you in comparison with eternal realities.
ROBERT MURRAY MCCHEYNE (1813–1843)

3282 Man does not know what to do with this life, yet wants another one which will last forever.
ANATOLE FRANCE (1844–1924)

3283 None can comprehend eternity but the eternal God. Eternity is an ocean, whereof we shall never see the shore; it is a deep, where we can find no bottom; a labyrinth from whence we cannot extricate ourselves and where we shall ever lose the door.
THOMAS BOSTON (1676–1732)

3284 The created world is but a small parenthesis in eternity.
SIR THOMAS BROWNE (1605–1682)

3285 The eternal silence of these infinite spaces terrifies me.
BLAISE PASCAL (1623–1662)

3286 The only alternative to eternal life is eternal punishment.
HARRY W. POST (1909–)

3287 The thought of eternity consoles for the shortness of life.
CHRÉTIEN GUILLAUME DE LAMOIGNON DE MALESHERBES (1721–1794)

3288 The time will come when every change shall cease,
The quick revolving wheel shall rest in peace:
No summer then shall glow, nor winter freeze;
Nothing shall be to come, and nothing past,
But an eternal now shall ever last.
PETRARCH (1304–1374)

3289 The tissue of the Life to be
We weave with colors all our own,
And in the field of Destiny
We reap as we have sown.
JOHN GREENLEAF WHITTIER (1807–1892)

3290 There is a hint of the everlasting in the vastness of the sea.
J. B. PHILLIPS (1906–1982)

3291 They that love beyond the world cannot be separated by it. Death cannot kill what never dies, nor can spirits

ever be divided that love and live in
the same divine principle.
WILLIAM PENN (1644–1718)

3292 This was the strength of the first Christians, that they lived not in one world
only, but in two, and found in consequence not tension alone, but power,
the vision of a world unshaken and
unshakable.
HARRY EMERSON FOSDICK (1878–1969)

3293 We have all eternity to celebrate our
victories, but only one short hour
before sunset in which to win them.
ROBERT MOFFAT (1795–1883)

3294 When ten thousand times ten thousand times ten thousand years have
passed, eternity will have just begun.
BILLY SUNDAY (1862–1935)

3295 When you look at a mountain, imagine in your hearts how long would it
be before that mountain should be
removed by a little bird coming but
once every thousand years, and carrying away but one grain of the dust of
it at once: the mountain would at
length be removed that way, and
brought to an end; but eternity will
never end. Suppose with respect to all
the mountains of the earth, no, with
respect to the whole globe itself: the
grains of dust of which the whole of it
is made up are not infinite; and therefore the last grain would, at length,
come to be carried away, as above: yet
eternity would be, in effect, but beginning.
THOMAS BOSTON (1676–1732)

EVANGELISM

3296 Angels cannot preach the gospel, only
beings such as Paul and you and I can
preach the gospel.
OSWALD CHAMBERS (1874–1917)

3297 Are we as willing to go into debt for
the work of God as we are for a vacation to Hawaii?
ERWIN W. LUTZER (1941–)

3298 Be to the world a sign that while we as
Christians do not have all the answers,

we do know and care about the questions.
BILLY GRAHAM (1918–)

3299 Being an extrovert isn't essential to
evangelism—obedience and love are.
REBECCA MANLEY PIPPERT

3300 Christ calls men to carry a cross; we
call them to have fun in his name. He
calls them to forsake the world; we
assure them that if they but accept
Jesus the world is their oyster. He calls
them to suffer; we call them to enjoy
all the bourgeois comfort modern civilization affords. He calls them to self-
abnegation and death; we call them to
spread themselves like green bay trees
or perchance even to become stars in a
pitiful fifth-rate religious zodiac. He
calls them to holiness; we call them to
a cheap and tawdry happiness that
would have been rejected with scorn
by the least of the Stoic philosophers.
A. W. TOZER (1897–1963)

3301 Christianity is the only world religion
that is evangelical in the sense of sharing good news with others. Islam converts by force; Buddhism, without the
benefit of a theology; Hinduism
doesn't even try.
MORTIMER JEROME ADLER (1902–)

3302 Christianity spread rapidly during the
first century because all Christians saw
themselves as responsible for disseminating the gospel.
ERWIN W. LUTZER (1941–)

3303 Christians and non-Christians have
something in common: We're both
uptight about evangelism.
REBECCA MANLEY PIPPERT

3304 Evangelism applies a supernatural remedy for the need of the world.
FARIS WHITESELL

3305 Evangelism is a cross in the heart of
God.
LEIGHTON FORD

3306 For one man who can introduce
another to Jesus Christ by the way he
lives and by the atmosphere of his life,
there are a thousand who can only
talk jargon about him.
OSWALD CHAMBERS (1874–1917)

3307 Give a man a dollar, and you cheer his heart. Give him a dream, and you challenge his heart. Give him Christ, and you change his heart.

3308 God is not saving the world; it is done. Our business is to get men and women to realize it.
OSWALD CHAMBERS (1874–1917)

3309 How many people have you made homesick for God?
OSWALD CHAMBERS (1874–1917)

3310 I am convinced that people are open to the Christian message if it is seasoned with authority and proclaimed as God's own Word.
BILLY GRAHAM (1918–)

3311 I just want to lobby for God.
BILLY GRAHAM (1918–)

3312 I look upon all the world as my parish.
JOHN WESLEY (1703–1791)

3313 If you live by the same values and priorities [Jesus] had, you will find evangelism happening naturally. It becomes a life-style and not a project.
REBECCA MANLEY PIPPERT

3314 If you want your neighbor to know what Christ will do for him, let the neighbor see what Christ has done for you.
HENRY WARD BEECHER (1813–1887)

3315 Instead of telling people to give up things, we are safer to tell them to "seek first the kingdom of God," and then they will get new things and better things, and the old things will drop off by themselves.
JOHN DRUMMOND (1851–1897)

3316 Jesus . . . wants us to see that the neighbor next door or the people sitting next to us on a plane or in a classroom are not interruptions to our schedule. They are there by divine appointment. Jesus wants us to see their needs, their loneliness, their longings, and he wants to give us the courage to reach out to them.
REBECCA MANLEY PIPPERT

3317 Mass communication can aid in personal evangelism and the development of Christians, but it cannot be a substitute for the world seeing the truth lived through us.
ERWIN W. LUTZER (1941–)

3318 Men look for better methods, but God looks for better men.
ERWIN W. LUTZER (1941–)

3319 Nothing will convince and convict those around us like the peaceful and positive way you and I respond to our twentieth century hurts and distress. The unbelieving world—your neighbors, the guy at the gas station, the postman, the lady at the cleaners, your boss at work—is observing the way we undergo our trials.
JONI EARECKSON TADA

3320 Our prayers for the evangelization of the world are only bitter irony so long as we only give our lip service and draw back from the sacrifice of ourselves.
M. FRANÇOIS GOILLARD

3321 Our task is to live our personal communion with Christ with such intensity as to make it contagious.
PAUL TOURNIER (1898–1986)

3322 People say that it is so hard to bring Jesus Christ and present him before the lives of men today. Of course it is, it is so hard that it is impossible except by the power of the indwelling Holy Ghost.
OSWALD CHAMBERS (1874–1917)

3323 Should first my lamp spread light and purest rays bestow
The oil must then from you, my dearest Jesus, flow.
ANGELUS SILESIUS (1624–1677)

3324 Show me that you are redeemed, and I will believe in your Redeemer.
FRIEDRICH WILHELM NIETZSCHE (1844–1900)

3325 Taking the gospel to people wherever they are—death row, the ghetto, or next door—is frontline evangelism. Frontline love. It is our one hope for breaking down barriers and for restoring the sense of community, of caring for one another, that our decadent,

impersonalized culture has sucked out of us.
CHARLES COLSON (1931–   )

3326 The camera follows a young woman as she makes her way through the stands to an area set aside for repentance and conversion. But Jesus' stories imply that far more may be going on out there: beyond that stadium scene, in a place concealed from all camera lenses, a great party has erupted, a gigantic celebration in the unseen world.
PHILIP YANCEY (1949–   )

3327 The Christian is called upon to be the partner of God in the work of the conversion of men.
WILLIAM BARCLAY (1907–1978)

3328 The church has many tasks but only one mission.
ARTHUR PRESTON

3329 The church is under orders. Evangelistic inactivity is disobedience.
JOHN R. W. STOTT (1921–   )

3330 The minister lives behind a "stained-glass curtain." The layman has opportunities for evangelism which a minister will never have.
JAMES McCORD (1919–   )

3331 The people of Jesus' day thought holy men were unapproachable. But Jesus' work was in the marketplace. He made people feel welcome, and that they had a place. His life was a constant demonstration that there were only two things that really mattered in this life—God and people. They were the only things that lasted forever.
REBECCA MANLEY PIPPERT

3332 The salvation of a single soul is more important than the production or preservation of all the epics and tragedies in the world.
C. S. LEWIS (1898–1963)

3333 The trouble is that the whole "accept Christ"attitude is likely to be wrong. It shows Christ applying to us rather than us to him. It makes him stand hat-in-hand awaiting our verdict on him, instead of our kneeling with troubled hearts awaiting his verdict on us. It

may even permit us to accept Christ by an impulse of mind or emotions, painlessly, at no loss to our ego and no inconvenience to our usual way of life.
A. W. TOZER (1897–1963)

3334 The way from God to a human heart is through a human heart.
SAMUEL DICKEY GORDON (1859–1936)

3335 To accept Christ is to know the meaning of the words "as he is, so are we in this world." We accept his friends as our friends, his enemies as our enemies, his ways as our ways, his rejection as our rejection, his cross as our cross, his life as our life and his future as our future.
    If this is what we mean when we advise the seeker to accept Christ, we had better explain it to him. He may get into deep spiritual trouble unless we do.
A. W. TOZER (1897–1963)

3336 To be a witness does not consist of engaging in propaganda or in stirring people up. It means to live in such a way that one's life would not make sense if God did not exist.
EMMANUEL SUHARD (1874–1949)

3337 We cannot be content with an evangelism which does not lead to the drawing of converts into the church, nor with a church order whose principle of cohesion is a superficial social camaraderie instead of a spiritual fellowship with the Father and with his Son, Jesus Christ.
JOHN R. W. STOTT (1921–   )

3338 We preach to men as if they were conscious they were dying sinners, they are not; they are having a good time.
OSWALD CHAMBERS (1874–1917)

3339 What makes us Christians shrug our shoulders when we ought to be flexing our muscles? What makes us apathetic in a day when there are loads to lift, a world to be won and captives to be set free? Why are so many bored when the times demand action?
BILLY GRAHAM (1918–   )

3340 When God is seeking a person, he will not allow my fear, my feeling of intimidation or my lack of knowledge or

experience to prevent that person from finding him.
REBECCA MANLEY PIPPERT

3341 When social action is mistaken for evangelism, the church has ceased to manufacture its own blood cells and is dying of leukemia.
SHERWOOD WIRT

3342 While some weep, as they do now, I'll fight; while little children go hungry, I'll fight; while men go to prison, in and out, in and out, as they do now, I'll fight; while there is a drunkard left, while there is a poor, lost girl upon the streets, where there remains one dark soul without the light of God—I'll fight! I'll fight to the very end!
WILLIAM BOOTH (1829–1912)

3343 Winning the world to Christ means winning individuals.
ERWIN W. LUTZER (1941–)

3344 Witnessing is not a spare-time occupation or a once-a-week activity. It must be a quality of life. You don't go witnessing, you are a witness.
DAN GREENE

3345 You never know till you try to reach them how accessible men are; but you must approach each man by the right door.
HENRY WARD BEECHER (1813–1887)

EVIL

3346 A person may cause evil to others not only by his actions but by his inaction.
JOHN STUART MILL (1806–1873)

3347 Alas, then the sun goes in again, and we are back in the kingdom of fantasy, where it is goodness that is flat and boring, and evil that is varied and attractive, profound, intriguing and full of charm.
MALCOLM MUGGERIDGE (1903–1990)

3348 All spirits are enslaved which serve things evil.
PERCY BYSSHE SHELLEY (1792–1822)

3349 Because the designs of God's providence are deeply hidden and his judgment as great deeps, it happens that some, seeing that all the evils which

men do go unpunished, rashly conclude that human affairs are not governed by God's providence or even that all crimes are committed because God so wills. "Both errors are impious," says St. Augustine, "especially the latter."
ROBERT BELLARMINE (1542–1621)

3350 Even in evil, that dark cloud that hangs over creation, we discern rays of light and hope and gradually come to see, in suffering and temptation, proofs and instruments of the sublimest purposes of wisdom and love.
WILLIAM ELLERY CHANNING (1780–1842)

3351 Everything evil is revenge.
OTTO WEININGER (1880–1903)

3352 Everything is filthy to him who has filthy hands.
BERTOLT BRECHT (1898–1956)

3353 Evil being the root of mystery, pain is the root of knowledge.
SIMONE WEIL (1909–1943)

3354 Evil can never be undone, but only purged and redeemed.
DOROTHY L. SAYERS (1893–1957)

3355 Evil enters like a needle and spreads like an oak tree.
ETHIOPIAN PROVERB

3356 Evil gains are the equivalent of disaster.
HESIOD (EIGHTH CENTURY B.C.)

3357 Evil has no substance of its own, but is only the defect, excess, perversion, or corruption of that which has substance.
CARDINAL JOHN HENRY NEWMAN (1801–1890)

3358 Evil is here? That's work for us to do.
ISRAEL ZANGWILL (1864–1926)

3359 Evil is ready for anything.
FRENCH PROVERB

3360 Evil is sweet in the beginning but bitter in the end.
TALMUD

3361 Evil is that which God does not will.
EMIL BRUNNER (1889–1966)

3362 Evil is the real problem in the hearts and minds of men. It is not a problem of physics but of ethics. It is easier to

denature plutonium than to denature the evil spirit of man.
ALBERT EINSTEIN (1879–1955)

3363 Evil is wrought by want of thought as well as want of heart.
THOMAS HOOD (1799–1845)

3364 Evil means subtraction, deprivation, failure.
MARTIN C. D'ARCY (1888–1976)

3365 Evil must go somewhere. . . . The exorcism of evil is forever an uncertain affair.
PAUL TOURNIER (1898–1986)

3366 Evil often triumphs, but never conquers.
JOSEPH ROUX (1834–1886)

3367 Evil people have a kind of enamorment with their own will. When there is a conflict between their conscience and their will, it is the conscience which has to go. They are extraordinarily willful people and extraordinarily controlling people.
M. SCOTT PECK (1936–   )

3368 Evil unchecked grows, evil tolerated poisons the whole system.
JAWAHARLAL NEHRU (1889–1964)

3369 Father of Light! how blind is he
Who sprinkles the altar he rears to thee
With the blood and tears of humanity!
JOHN GREENLEAF WHITTIER (1807–1892)

3370 God created free beings, beings endowed with the terrible power of retreating from reality into nothingness if they so willed—for, once again, evil is privation, nonbeing, emptiness—and Satan is simply the first of those beings to choose this path.
GERALD VANN (1906–1963)

3371 God is so powerful that he can direct any evil to a good end.
SAINT THOMAS AQUINAS (1225–1274)

3372 God would never permit evil if he could not bring good out of evil.
THOMAS WATSON (C. 1557–1592)

3373 He who digs a pit for his brother to fall into shall fall into it himself.
ARABIAN PROVERB

3374 He who passively accepts evil is as much involved in it as he who helps to perpetrate it. He who accepts evil without protesting against it is really co-operating with it.
MARTIN LUTHER KING, JR. (1929–1968)

3375 How exhausting it is to be evil!
BERTOLT BRECHT (1898–1956)

3376 I do not fear the explosive power of the atom bomb. What I fear is the explosive power of evil in the human heart.
ALBERT EINSTEIN (1879–1955)

3377 If evil did not make its dwelling in man, it would be much more evil than it is. Evil cannot be an evil as it wills to be because it is tied to man. Because it is in man, a watch is kept on evil. In man, the image of God, evil is constricted; it is there under custody as in a prison. The destructive power of evil would be unlimited if it were on earth alone, unsheltered by God's image. The earth is saved from destruction because, in God's image, a watch is kept upon evil.
MAX PICARD (1888–1965)

3378 If evil is not something directly willed by God and not something wholly outside of his control, but something in his good world which he has temporarily permitted to exist while he calls for volunteers to oppose and correct it, then the task of overcoming evil is never a hopeless one.
WALTER MARSHALL HORTON (1895–1966)

3379 Indifference to evil is more insidious than evil itself; it is more universal, more contagious, more dangerous.
ABRAHAM J. HESCHEL (1907–1972)

3380 It is bad to lean against a falling wall.
DANISH PROVERB

3381 It is far easier to meet an evil in the open and defeat it in fair combat in people's minds, than to drive it underground and have no hold on it or proper approach to it. Evil flourishes far more in the shadows than in the light of day.
JAWAHARLAL NEHRU (1889–1964)

3382 It is important that human beings should not overlook the danger of the evil lurking within them. It is unfortunately only too real, which is why psychology must insist on the reality of evil and must reject any definition that regards it as insignificant or actually nonexistent.
CARL GUSTAV JUNG (1875–1961)

3383 Many have puzzled themselves about the origin of evil. I am content to observe that there is evil, and that there is a way to escape from it, and with this I begin and end.
JOHN NEWTON (1725–1807)

3384 Most of the greatest evils that man has inflicted upon man have come through people feeling quite certain about something which, in fact, was false.
BERTRAND ARTHUR WILLIAM RUSSELL (1872–1970)

3385 No evil which is done to us can harm us ultimately, for it will be compensated for by God himself.
HANNAH HURNARD (1905–1990)

3386 No man chooses evil because it is evil; he only mistakes it for happiness, the good he seeks.
MARY WOLLSTONECRAFT (1759–1797)

3387 No matter how many people steal, stealing remains wrong. No matter how many people are corrupt, corruption remains wrong. No matter how many people betray public trust, that action remains wrong. The fact that any misdeed becomes popular does not make it permissible. The problem of evil is not solved by multiplication.
SIDNEY GREENBERG

3388 Nonresistence to evil which takes the form of paying no attention to it is a way of promoting it.
JOHN DEWEY (1859–1952)

3389 Of evil grain, no good seed can come.
ENGLISH PROVERB

3390 Of two evils, choose neither.
CHARLES HADDON SPURGEON (1834–1892)

3391 Of two evils, pass up the first, and turn down the other.

3392 One no averts seventy evils.
INDIAN PROVERB

3393 One does evil enough when one does nothing good.
GERMAN PROVERB

3394 One may smile, and smile, and be a villain.
WILLIAM SHAKESPEARE (1564–1616)

3395 Our greatest pretences are built up, not to hide the evil and the ugly in us, but our emptiness.

3396 People do not need Satan to recruit them to evil. They are quite capable of recruiting themselves.
M. SCOTT PECK (1936–   )

3397 The evil for which we punish others is of the same substance as the evil in our own thinking and feeling.
DAVID ABRAHAMSEN

3398 The existence of evil here below, far from disproving the reality of God, is the very thing that reveals him in his truth.
SIMONE WEIL (1909–1943)

3399 The existence of evil is not so much an obstacle to faith in God as a proof of God's existence, a challenge to turn toward that in which love triumphs over hatred, union over division, and eternal life over death.
NIKOLAI ALEKSANDROVICH BERDYAEV (1874–1948)

3400 The fight for our planet, physical and spiritual, a fight of cosmic proportions, is not a vague matter of the future; it has already started. The forces of evil have begun their decisive offensive. You can feel their pressure, yet your screens and publications are full of prescribed smiles and raised glasses. What is the joy about?
ALEXANDER ISAYEVICH SOLZHENITSYN (1918–   )

3401 The greater the evil, the greater the opportunity to fashion out of it everlasting good.
HANNAH HURNARD (1905–1990)

3402 The only thing necessary for the triumph of evil is for good men to do nothing.
EDMUND BURKE (1729–1797)

3403 The snake stood up for evil in the Garden.
ROBERT FROST (1874–1963)

3404 The soul itself its awful witness is. Say not in evil doing, "No one sees."
JOHN GREENLEAF WHITTIER (1807–1892)

3405 There are a thousand hacking at the branches of evil to one who is striking at the root.
HENRY DAVID THOREAU (1817–1862)

3406 There is a devil—a spirit of evil in us tugging at us to make us animals rather than angels.
MALCOLM MUGGERIDGE (1903–1990)

3407 There is nothing evil in matter itself. Evil lies in the spirit. Evils of the heart, of the mind, of the soul, of the spirit— these have to do with man's sin, and the only reason the human body does evil is because the human spirit uses it to do evil.
A. W. TOZER (1897–1963)

3408 They that know no evil will suspect none.
BEN JONSON (1572–1637)

3409 Thinking evil is the same as doing it.
GREEK PROVERB

3410 To great evils we submit; we resent little provocations.
WILLIAM HAZLITT (1778–1830)

3411 To ignore evil is to become an accomplice to it.
MARTIN LUTHER KING, JR. (1929–1968)

3412 We are likely to believe the worst about another because the capacity for evil is so pronounced in ourselves.
LOUIS NIZER (1902–   )

3413 We cannot do evil to others without doing it to ourselves.
JOSEPH FRANCOIS EDUARD DESMAHIS (1722–1761)

3414 We have to carry on the struggle against the evil that is in mankind, not by judging others, but by judging ourselves. Struggle with oneself and veracity toward oneself are the means by which we influence others.
ALBERT SCHWEITZER (1875–1965)

3415 We must never feel that God will, through some breathtaking miracle or a wave of the hand, cast evil out of the world. As long as we believe this, we will pray unanswerable prayers and ask God to do things that he will never do. The belief that God will do everything for a man is as untenable as the belief that man can do everything for himself.
MARTIN LUTHER KING, JR. (1929–1968)

3416 We who live beneath a sky still streaked with the smoke of crematoria, have paid a high price to find out that evil is really evil.
FRANÇOIS MAURIAC (1885–1970)

3417 Weeds always flourish.
DESIDERIUS ERASMUS (1466–1539)

3418 When God sends us evil, he sends with it the weapon to conquer it.
PAUL VINCENT CARROLL (1900–1968)

3419 When the snake is dead, his venom is dead.
FRENCH PROVERB

EXAGGERATION

3420 A windbag is one who can blow up a one-minute experience into a two-hour description.

3421 Exaggeration is an offshoot of lying.
BALTASAR GRACIÁN Y MORALES (1601–1658)

3422 Hypochondriacs get more talk out of a minor pain than others can get out of a major operation.

3423 Love and hatred are natural exaggerators.
JEWISH PROVERB

3424 The angler caught a fish so big, he dislocated both shoulders describing it.

3425 To exaggerate invariably weakens the point of what we have to say.
FRENCH PROVERB

3426 You can't tell: maybe a fish goes home and lies about the size of the man he got away from.

EXAMPLE

3427 A good example is the best sermon.
SIR THOMAS FULLER (1608–1661)

3428 A person who lives right, and is right, has more power in his silence than another has by words.
PHILLIPS BROOKS (1835–1893)

3429 Always do right. This will surprise some people and astonish the rest.
MARK TWAIN (1835–1910)

3430 Example is a lesson that all men can read.
GILBERT WEST

3431 Example is not the main thing in influencing others—it is the only thing.
ALBERT SCHWEITZER (1875–1965)

3432 Example is the most powerful rhetoric.
THOMAS BENTON BROOKS (1608–1680)

3433 Fewer things are harder to put up with than the annoyance of a good example.
MARK TWAIN (1835–1910)

3434 He who gives to me teaches me to give.
DANISH PROVERB

3435 I'd rather see a sermon
    than hear one any day;
I'd rather one should walk with me
    than merely tell the way.
EDGAR ALBERT GUEST (1881–1959)

3436 If you try to improve one person by being a good example, you're improving two. If you try to improve someone without being a good example, you won't improve anybody.
JAMES H. THOM

3437 If you want your neighbor to see what Christ will do for him, let him see what Christ has done for you.
HENRY WARD BEECHER (1813–1887)

3438 Keep yourself clean and bright—you are the window through which the world sees God.

3439 Let him that would move the world first move himself.
SOCRATES (470–399 B.C.)

3440 Live to explain thy doctrine by thy life.
MATTHEW PRIOR (1664–1721)

3441 Lives of great men all remind us
We can make our lives sublime,
And, departing, leave behind us
Footprints on the sands of time.
HENRY WADSWORTH LONGFELLOW (1807–1882)

3442 Man is a creature that is led more by patterns than by precepts.
GEORGE SWINNOCK (D. 1673)

3443 More depends on my walk than talk.
DWIGHT LYMAN MOODY (1837–1899)

3444 Never has a man who has bent himself been able to make others straight.
MENG-TZU (C. 371–C. 289 B.C.)

3445 No man is so insignificant as to be sure his example can do no harm.
EDWARD HYDE (1609–1674)

3446 No person is absolutely unnecessary, one can always serve as a horrible example.

3447 None preaches better than the ant, and she says nothing.
BENJAMIN FRANKLIN (1706–1790)

3448 Nothing is so infectious as example.
CHARLES KINGSLEY (1819–1875)

3449 Of all commentaries on the Scriptures, good examples are the best.
JOHN DONNE (1572–1631)

3450 One example is worth a thousand arguments.
THOMAS CARLYLE (1795–1881)

3451 People seldom improve when they have no other model but themselves to copy.
OLIVER GOLDSMITH (1730–1774)

3452 Search thine own heart.
What paineth thee
In others, in thyself may be.
JAMES RUSSELL LOWELL (1819–1891)

3453 So act that your principle of action might safely be made a law for the whole world.
IMMANUEL KANT (1724–1804)

3454 The busy bee teaches two lessons: one is not to be idle, and the other is not to get stung.

3455 There are two ways of spreading light; to be a candle, or the mirror that reflects it.
EDITH WHARTON (1862–1937)

3456 We can do more good by being good than in any other way.
ROWLAND HILL (1744–1833)

3457 We reform others unconsciously when we act uprightly.
MADAME ANNE SOPHIE SOYMANOV SWETCHINE (1782–1857)

3458 We taught him to steal, and the first thing he did was to try it on us.
ARABIAN PROVERB

3459 Well done is better than well said.
BENJAMIN FRANKLIN (1706–1790)

3460 What can't be done by advice can often be done by example.

3461 What should not be heard by little ears, should not be said by big mouths.

3462 You can preach a better sermon with your life than with your lips.
OLIVER GOLDSMITH (1730–1774)

EXCELLENCE

3463 Aim at perfection in everything, though in most things it is unattainable; however, they who aim at it, and persevere, will come much nearer to it than those whose laziness and despondency make them give it up as unattainable.
LORD CHESTERFIELD (1694–1773)

3464 All excellence involves discipline and tenacity of purpose.
JOHN W. GARDNER (1912–)

3465 All things excellent are as difficult as they are rare.
BENEDICT SPINOZA (1632–1677)

3466 Good is not good where better is expected.
SIR THOMAS FULLER (1608–1661)

3467 Hit the ball over the fence and you can take your time going around the bases.
JOHN W. RAPER

3468 If I had given you any parting advice it would, I think, all have been comprised in this one sentence: to live up always to the best and highest you know.
HANNAH WHITHALL SMITH (1832–1911)

3469 There is a canyon of difference between doing your best to glorify God and doing whatever it takes to glorify yourself. The quest for excellence is a mark of maturity. The quest for power is childish.
MAX L. LUCADO (1955–)

3470 Those who attain to any excellence spend life in some one single pursuit, for excellence is not often gained on easier terms.
SAMUEL JOHNSON (1709–1784)

3471 To get the best out of a man go to what is best in him.
DANIEL CONSIDINE

3472 True excellence is rarely found; even more rarely is it cherished.
JOHANN WOLFGANG VON GOETHE (1749–1832)

EXCUSES

3473 An alibi is the proof that you did do what you didn't do so that others will think you didn't do what you did.

3474 An excuse is worse and more terrible than a lie; for an excuse is a lie guarded.
ALEXANDER POPE (1688–1744)

3475 He who excuses himself accuses himself.
GABRIEL MEURIER (1530–1601)

3476 Rationalization: It's what we do when we substitute false explanations for true reasons . . . when we cloud our actual motives with a smoke screen of nice-sounding excuses.
CHARLES R. SWINDOLL (1934–)

3477 The greatest excuse given to me by people in every country for not becoming Christians is the division among Christians today.
BILLY GRAHAM (1918–)

3478 You may often make excuses for another, never for yourself.
PUBLILIUS SYRUS (FIRST CENTURY B.C.)

EXISTENCE

3479 As soon as high consciousness is reached, the enjoyment of existence is entwined with pain, frustration, loss, tragedy.
ALFRED NORTH WHITEHEAD (1861–1947)

3480 Every luxury must be paid for, and everything is a luxury, starting with being in the world.
CESARE PAVESE (1908–1950)

3481 God is not greater for our being, nor would he be less if we did not exist. That we do exist is altogether of God's free determination, not by our desert nor by divine necessity.
A. W. TOZER (1897–1963)

3482 I am wrapped in mortality, my flesh is a prison, my bones the bars of death. What is mortality but the things related to the body, which dies. What is immortality but the things related to the spirit, which lives eternally. What is the joy of heaven but improvement of the things of the spirit. What are the pains of hell but ignorance and bodily lust, idleness and devastation of the things of the spirit.
WILLIAM BLAKE (1757–1827)

3483 I took one draught of life
I'll tell you what I paid
Precisely an existence
The market price, they said.
EMILY ELIZABETH DICKINSON (1830–1886)

3484 Man can only find meaning for his existence in something outside himself.
VIKTOR E. FRANKL (B. 1905)

3485 My life has been brought to an impasse, I loathe existence. . . . One sticks one's finger into the soil to tell by the smell in what land one is: I stick my finger into existence—it smells of nothing. Where am I? What is this thing called the world? What does this word mean? Who is it that has lured me into the thing and now leaves me there? Who am I? How did I come into the world? Why was I not consulted, why not made acquainted with its manners and customs . . .? How did I obtain an interest in it? Is it not a voluntary concern? And if I am to be compelled to take part in it, where is the director? Whither shall I turn with my complaint?
SØREN AABYE KIERKEGAARD (1813–1855)

3486 No power of genius has ever yet had the smallest success in explaining existence.
THOMAS CARLYLE (1795–1881)

3487 One's life is a heavy price to pay for being born.
HENRIK IBSEN (1828–1906)

3488 The higher the hill that you climb, the bigger, the wider the vista that presents itself. The nearer you get to comprehending the true nature of our existence, the more possibility there is of being skeptical about our capacity to express that understanding.
MALCOLM MUGGERIDGE (1903–1990)

3489 We are, because God is.
EMANUEL SWEDENBORG (1688–1772)

3490 We existed before the foundation of the world; because we were destined to be in him, we preexisted in the sight of God.
CLEMENT OF ALEXANDRIA (C. 150–C. 215)

3491 We mostly spend our lives conjugating three verbs: "to want," "to have," and "to do," forgetting that these verbs have no significance except as they are included in the verb "to be."
EVELYN UNDERHILL (1875–1941)

3492 What a towering mound of sin rises from one small word—to be!
HENRIK IBSEN (1828–1906)

EXISTENTIALISM

3493 The accepted philosophy of today is existentialism, which, in its popular form, emphasizes meaningful experience as the criterion for truth. Facts are considered irrelevant, except insofar as they "turn us on." Jesus is popular in some groups, not necessarily because he is the only way to God, but because "you can get high on him," as the lapel buttons suggest. Many who have tried Christ have become disillusioned because they didn't get high, as they had expected. In terms of sheer thrills, some other substitute might do just as well. At least for a while.
ERWIN W. LUTZER (1941–   )

3494 The central preoccupation of existentialism can be defined in one phrase: the stature of man. Is he a god or a worm?
COLIN HENRY WILSON (1931–)

3495 The Sarte brand . . . is an atheist who sees man as helpless, flung without knowing why or how into a world he cannot understand, endowed with liberty . . . which he may betray but which he cannot deny, to make his way as best he can in fear and trembling, in uncertainty and anguish.
JOHN BROWN (1715–1766)

EXPECTATION

3496 'Tis expectation makes a blessing dear, Heaven were not heaven, if we knew what it were.
SIR JOHN SUCKLING (1609–1642)

3497 As a man gets wiser, he expects less, and probably gets more than he expects.
JOSEPH FARRELL

3498 Before we set our hearts too much upon anything, let us examine how happy those are who already possess it.
FRANÇOIS, DUC DE LA ROCHEFOUCAULD (1613–1680)

3499 Blessed is he who expects nothing, for he shall never be disappointed.
ALEXANDER POPE (1688–1744)

3500 Do not anticipate trouble, or worry about what may never happen. Keep in the sunlight.
BENJAMIN FRANKLIN (1706–1790)

3501 Every day cannot be a feast of lanterns.
CHINESE PROVERB

3502 I cannot change yesterday. I can only make the most of today and look with hope toward tomorrow.

3503 Keep your eye on the ball, your ear to the ground, and your shoulder to the wheel. Now—in that position—try working.

3504 Men expect too much, do too little.
ALLEN TATE (1899–1979)

3505 Men have a trick of coming up to what is expected of them, good or bad.
JACOB AUGUST RIIS (1849–1914)

3506 Nothing is so good as it seems beforehand.
GEORGE ELIOT (1819–1880)

3507 Our expectation of what the human animal can learn, can do, can be, remains remarkably low and timorous.
GEORGE B. LEONARD

3508 The hours we pass with happy prospects in view are more pleasing than those crowned with fruition.
OLIVER GOLDSMITH (1730–1774)

3509 There is something new every day if you look for it.
HANNAH HURNARD (1905–1990)

3510 Those who dwell continually upon their expectations are apt to become oblivious to the requirements of their actual situation.
CHARLES SANDERS PIERCE (1831–1914)

3511 What a wonderful world this would be if we all did as well today as we expect to do tomorrow.

EXPERIENCE

3512 A burnt child dreads the fire.
ENGLISH PROVERB

3513 All we need to experience is that we have "passed out of death into life." What we need to know takes all time and eternity.
OSWALD CHAMBERS (1874–1917)

3514 Deep experience is never peaceful.
HENRY JAMES (1843–1916)

3515 Every experience God gives us, every person he puts in our lives, is the perfect preparation for the future that only he can see.
CORRIE TEN BOOM (1892–1983)

3516 Experience dulls the edges of all our dogmas.
GILBERT AIMÉ MURRAY (1866–1957)

3517 Experience enables you to recognize a mistake when you make it again.
FRANKLIN P. JONES

3518 Experience is a comb that nature gives to men when they are bald.

3519 Experience is a costly school, yet some learn no other way.
BENJAMIN FRANKLIN (1706–1790)

3520 Experience is a dim lamp which only lights the one who bears it.
LOUIS FERDINAND CÉLINE (1894–1961)

3521 Experience is a good school, but the fees are high.
HEINRICH HEINE (1797–1856)

3522 Experience is a hard teacher because she gives the test first, the lessons afterwards.
VERNON SANDERS LAW

3523 Experience is a jewel, and it had need be so, for it is often purchased at an infinite rate.
WILLIAM SHAKESPEARE (1564–1616)

3524 Experience is never limited, and it is never complete; it is an immense sensibility, a kind of huge spider web of the finest silken threads suspended in the chamber of consciousness and catching every air-borne particle in its tissue.
HENRY JAMES (1843–1916)

3525 Experience is never the ground of our trust, it is the gateway to the One whom we trust.
OSWALD CHAMBERS (1874–1917)

3526 Experience is not always the kindest of teachers, but it is the best.
SPANISH PROVERB

3527 Experience is not what happens to you. It is what you do with what happens to you.
ALDOUS HUXLEY (1894–1963)

3528 Experience is that which makes a person better or bitter.
SAMUEL LEVENSON

3529 Experience is the extract of suffering.
ARTHUR HELPS (1813–1875)

3530 Experience is the mother of truth; and by experience we learn wisdom.
WILLIAM SHIPPEN, JR. (1736–1808)

3531 Experience is the name people give to their mistakes.
OSCAR WILDE (1854–1900)

3532 Experience is the one thing you can't get for nothing.
OSCAR WILDE (1854–1900)

3533 Experience is what you get when you didn't get what you wanted.

3534 Few men are worthy of experience. The majority let it corrupt them.
JOSEPH JOUBERT (1754–1824)

3535 He who has not believed will not experience, and he who has not experienced will not understand; for just as experiencing a thing is better than hearing about it, so knowledge that stems from experience outweighs knowledge derived through hearsay.
SAINT ANSELM (C. 1033–1109)

3536 He who has once burnt his mouth always blows his soup.
GERMAN PROVERB

3537 It's not the same to talk of bulls as to be in the bullring.
SPANISH PROVERB

3538 Nor deem the irrevocable past
As wholly wasted, wholly vain
If, rising on its wrecks, at last
To something nobler we attain.
HENRY WADSWORTH LONGFELLOW (1807–1882)

3539 Nothing ever becomes real until it is experienced—even a proverb is no proverb to you till your life has illustrated it.
JOHN KEATS (1795–1821)

3540 One thorn of experience is worth a whole wilderness of warning.
JAMES RUSSELL LOWELL (1819–1891)

3541 Only he who has travelled the road knows where the holes are deep.
CHINESE PROVERB

3542 Only the wearer knows where the shoe pinches.
ENGLISH PROVERB

3543 Practice is the best of all instructors.
PUBLILIUS SYRUS (FIRST CENTURY B.C.)

3544 The snare of experiences is that we keep coming back to the shore when God wants to get us out into the deeps.
OSWALD CHAMBERS (1874–1917)

3545 The things we have to learn before we can do them, we learn by doing.
ARISTOTLE (384–322 B.C.)

3546 The years teach much which the days never knew.
RALPH WALDO EMERSON (1803–1882)

3547 Today is yesterday's pupil.
SIR THOMAS FULLER (1608–1661)

3548 Truth divorced from experience will always dwell in doubt.
HENRY KRAUSE

3549 We cannot afford to forget any experience, even the most painful.
DAG HAMMARSKJÖLD (1905–1961)

3550 We must guard against grounding our spiritual commitment on the quicksands of fluctuating experiences. Experience (yes, even revival experience) must be constantly tested and verified by the objective truths of the Word of God.
ERWIN W. LUTZER (1941–)

3551 We should be careful to get out of an experience only the wisdom that is in it—and stop there; lest we be like the cat that sits down on a hot stove lid. She will never sit down on a hot stove lid again—and that is well; but also she will never sit down on a cold one anymore.
MARK TWAIN (1835–1910)

3552 You cannot acquire experience by making experiments. You cannot create experience. You must undergo it.
ALBERT CAMUS (1913–1960)

EXTREMISM

3553 Be not the first by whom the new are tried,
Nor yet the last to lay the old aside.
ALEXANDER POPE (1688–1744)

3554 Extremes, though contrary, have the like effects. Extreme heat kills, and so extreme cold; extreme love breeds satiety, and so extreme hatred; and too violent rigor tempts chastity, as does too much license.
GEORGE CHAPMAN (C. 1559–1634)

3555 Mistrust the man who finds everything good, the man who finds everything evil, and still more, the man who is indifferent to everything.
JOHANN KASPAR LAVATER (1741–1801)

3556 The desire of power in excess caused angels to fall; the desire of knowledge in excess caused man to fall; but in charity is no excess, neither can man or angels come into danger by it.
FRANCIS BACON (1561–1626)

3557 There is no better example of extremism than the haughtiness of humility.
RALPH WALDO EMERSON (1803–1882)

3558 Thus each extreme to equal danger tends,
Plenty, as well as want, can sep'rate friends.
ABRAHAM COWLEY (1618–1667)

3559 Too much noise deafens us; too much light blinds us; too great a distance, or too much of proximity equally prevents us from being able to see; too long or too short a distance obscures our knowledge of a subject; too much of truth stuns us.
BLAISE PASCAL (1623–1662)

3560 What is new is not necessarily needed and what is old is not automatically obsolete.
HARRY G. MENDELSON

EYE

3561 An eye can threaten like a loaded and levelled gun, or it can insult like hissing or kicking; or, in its altered mood, by beams of kindness, it can make the heart dance for joy.
RALPH WALDO EMERSON (1803–1882)

3562 Man was created with two eyes, so that with one he may see God's greatness, and with the other his own lowliness.
SHMUEL YOSEF AGNON (1888–1970)

3563 Man's eyes have great power, for they convey the soul.
MICHEL QUOIST (1921–)

3564 Men are born with two eyes but only one tongue, in order that they should see twice as much as they say.
CHARLES CALEB COLTON (1780–1832)

3565 Men of cold passions have quick eyes.
NATHANIEL HAWTHORNE (1804–1864)

3566 One's eyes are what one is, one's mouth what one becomes.
JOHN GALSWORTHY (1867–1933)

3567 The eyes are more exact witnesses than the ears.
HERACLITUS (C. 540–C. 480 B.C.)

3568 The eyes tell what the heart means.
JUDAH L. LAZEROV

3569 The face is the mirror of the mind; and eyes, without speaking, confess the secrets of the heart.
SAINT JEROME (C. 342–420)

FACE

3570 A pleasant face is a silent recommendation.
PUBLILIUS SYRUS (FIRST CENTURY B.C.)

3571 In people's eyes I read pages of malice and vice.
MIKHAIL YURYEVICH LERMONTOV (1814–1841)

3572 Keep your face to the sunshine and you cannot see the shadow.
HELEN ADAMS KELLER (1880–1968)

3573 Of all the things you wear, your expression is the most important.
JANET LANE

3574 The face is the mirror of the mind; and eyes, without speaking, confess the secrets of the heart.
SAINT JEROME (C. 342–420)

3575 Trust not too much to an enchanting face.
VIRGIL (70–19 B.C.)

FACTS

3576 Don't fight a fact, deal with it.
HUGH PRATHER

3577 Facts are facts and will not disappear on account of your likes.
JAWAHARLAL NEHRU (1889–1964)

3578 Facts are stubborn things.
ALAIN-RENÉ LESAGE (1668–1747)

3579 Facts do not cease to exist because they are ignored.
ALDOUS HUXLEY (1894–1963)

FAILURE

3580 A failure is a person who has blundered but is not able to cash in on the experience.
ELBERT GREEN HUBBARD (1856–1915)

3581 A failure is not someone who has tried and failed; it is someone who has given up trying and resigned himself to failure; it is not a condition, but an attitude.
SYDNEY J. HARRIS (1917–1986)

3582 A failure, within God's purpose, is no longer really a failure. Thus the cross, the supreme failure, is at the same time the supreme triumph of God,

since it is the accomplishment of the purpose of salvation.
PAUL TOURNIER (1898–1986)

3583 A stumble may prevent a fall.
SIR THOMAS FULLER (1608–1661)

3584 Any man may make a mistake; none but a fool will persist in it.
CICERO (106–43 B.C.)

3585 Better a fall than not to climb.

3586 Beware of succumbing to failure as inevitable; make it the stepping-stone to success.
OSWALD CHAMBERS (1874–1917)

3587 Failure is an invitation to have recourse to God.
ANTONIN DALMACE SERTILLANGES

3588 Failure is not falling down; it is remaining there when you have fallen.

3589 Failure is not the worst thing in the world. The worst is not to try.

3590 Failure isn't fatal.

3591 Failure teaches success.

3592 Fall seven times, stand up eight.
JAPANESE PROVERB

3593 Great accomplishments are often attempted but only occasionally reached. Those who reach them are usually those who missed many times before. Failures are only temporary tests to prepare us for permanent triumphs.
CHARLES R. SWINDOLL (1934–)

3594 He who has never failed cannot be great. Failure is the true test of greatness.
HERMAN MELVILLE (1819–1891)

3595 I'd rather attempt to do something great and fail than attempt to do nothing and succeed.
ROBERT HAROLD SCHULLER (1926–)

3596 I've never met a person, I don't care what his condition is, in whom I could not see possibilities. I don't care how much a man may consider himself a failure, I believe in him, for he can change the thing that is wrong in his life any time he is ready and prepared to do it. Whenever he develops the

desire, he can take away from his life the thing that is defeating it. The capacity for reformation and change lies within.
PRESTON BRADLEY (1888–1983)

3597 If at first you don't succeed, relax; you're just like the rest of us.

3598 If you have made mistakes, even serious mistakes, there is always another chance for you. And supposing you have tried and failed again and again, you may have a fresh start any moment you choose, for this thing that we call "failure" is not the falling down, but the staying down.
MARY PICKFORD (1892–)

3599 If you've never stubbed your toe, you're probably standing still.

3600 In great attempts it is glorious even to fail.

3601 It is defeat which educates us.
RALPH WALDO EMERSON (1803–1882)

3602 It is often the failure who is the pioneer in new lands, new undertakings, and new forms of expression.
ERIC HOFFER (1902–1983)

3603 It is very difficult to be humble if you are always successful, so God chastises us with failure at times in order to humble us, to keep us in a state of humility.
D. MARTYN LLOYD-JONES (1899–1981)

3604 It's the nature of God to make something out of nothing; therefore, when anyone is nothing, God may yet make something of him.
MARTIN LUTHER (1483–1546)

3605 Jesus Christ's life was an absolute failure from every standpoint but God's.
OSWALD CHAMBERS (1874–1917)

3606 Make kindling out of a fallen tree.
SPANISH PROVERB

3607 Many of life's failures are men who did not realize how close they were to success when they gave up.

3608 More men fail through lack of purpose than lack of talent.
BILLY SUNDAY (1862–1935)

3609 No amount of falls will really undo us if we keep picking ourselves up each time. We shall of course be very muddy and tattered children by the time we reach home. . . . It is when we notice the dirt that God is most present in us; it is the very sign of his presence.
C. S. LEWIS (1898–1963)

3610 Not failure, but low aim, is a crime.
JAMES RUSSELL LOWELL (1819–1891)

3611 Notice the difference between what happens when a man says to himself, "I have failed three times," and what happens when he says, "I am a failure."
S. I. HAYAKAWA

3612 Often the doorway to success is entered through the hallway of failure.
ERWIN W. LUTZER (1941–)

3613 Often we assume that God is unable to work in spite of our weaknesses, mistakes, and sins. We forget that God is a specialist; he is well able to work our failures into his plans.
ERWIN W. LUTZER (1941–)

3614 Only those who see themselves as utterly destitute can fully appreciate the grace of God.
ERWIN W. LUTZER (1941–)

3615 Our Father in heaven . . . help us to see that it is better to fail in a cause that will ultimately succeed than to succeed in a cause that will ultimately fail.
PETER MARSHALL (1902–1949)

3616 Our mistakes won't irreparably damage our lives unless we let them.
JAMES E. SWEANEY

3617 Simon Peter, the Rock, very often looked more like a sandpile than a rock.
JOHN POWELL

3618 Stumblers who give up are a dime a dozen. In fact, they're useless. Stumblers who get up are rare. In fact, they're priceless.
CHARLES R. SWINDOLL (1934–)

3619 The formula for failure: try to please everybody.
HERBERT BAYARD SWOPE (1882–1958)

3620 The glory is not in never failing, but in rising every time you fail.
CHINESE PROVERB

3621 The human soul, beaten down, overwhelmed, faced by complete failure and ruin, can still rise up against unbearable odds and triumph.
HAROLD RUSSELL

3622 The only real mistake is the one from which we learn nothing.
JOHN POWELL

3623 The past cannot be changed, but our response to it can be.
ERWIN W. LUTZER (1941–)

3624 The person who succeeds is not the one who holds back, fearing failure, nor the one who never fails . . . but rather the one who moves on in spite of failure.
CHARLES R. SWINDOLL (1934–)

3625 The probability that we may fail in the struggle should not deter us from the support of a cause we believe to be just.
ABRAHAM LINCOLN (1809–1865)

3626 There are some defeats more triumphant than victories.
MICHEL EYQUEM DE MONTAIGNE (1533–1592)

3627 There's no defeat, in truth, save from within;
Unless you're beaten there, you're bound to win.
HENRY AUSTIN

3628 Those who have failed miserably are often the first to see God's formula for success.
ERWIN W. LUTZER (1941–)

3629 Through God turn our endings into beginnings.

3630 We learn wisdom from failure much more than from success. We often discover what will do, by finding out what will not do, and probably he who never made a mistake never made a discovery.
SAMUEL SMILES (1812–1904)

3631 We mount to heaven mostly on the ruins of our cherished schemes, finding our failures were successes.
AMOS BRONSON ALCOTT (1799–1888)

3632 What seems to be the end may really be a new beginning.

3633 When you feel that all is lost, sometimes the greatest gain is ready to be yours.
THOMAS À KEMPIS (C. 1380–1471)

3634 Whether we stumble or whether we fall, we must only think of rising again and going on in our course.
FRANÇOIS FÉNELON (1651–1715)

3635 Who falls for love of God shall rise a star.
BEN JONSON (1572–1637)

3636 You don't drown by falling in the water, you drown by staying there.

3637 You must appreciate failure to appreciate success.
CHINESE PROVERB

FAITH

3638 A Christian who walks by faith accepts all circumstances from God. He thanks God when everything goes good, when everything goes bad, and for the "blues" somewhere in-between. He thanks God whether he feels like it or not.
ERWIN W. LUTZER (1941–   )

3639 A faith that cannot survive collision with the truth is not worth many regrets.
ARTHUR C. CLARKE (1917–   )

3640 A faith that hasn't been tested can't be trusted.
ADRIAN ROGERS

3641 A man can accept what Christ has done without knowing how it works; indeed, he certainly won't know how it works until he's accepted it.
C. S. LEWIS (1898–1963)

3642 A man who has faith must be prepared not only to be a martyr, but to be a fool.
G. K. CHESTERTON (1874–1936)

3643 A perfect faith would lift us absolutely above fear.
GEORGE MACDONALD (1824–1905)

3644 And all is well, tho faith and form
Be sundered in the night of fear;
Well roars the storm to those that hear
A deeper voice across the storm.
ALFRED, LORD TENNYSON (1809–1892)

3645 Better a baffled faith than no faith at all.
ALBERT CORNELIUS KNUDSON (1873–1953)

3646 Beware of worshiping Jesus as the Son of God and professing your faith in him as the Savior of the world, while you blaspheme him by the complete evidence in your daily life that he is powerless to do anything in and through you.
OSWALD CHAMBERS (1874–1917)

3647 Can a faith that does nothing be called sincere?
JEAN RACINE (1639–1699)

3648 Christian faith is a grand cathedral, with divinely pictured windows. Standing without, you see no glory, nor can imagine any. But standing within, every ray of light reveals a harmony of unspeakable splendors.
NATHANIEL HAWTHORNE (1804–1864)

3649 Dark as my path may seem to others, I carry a magic light in my heart. Faith, the spiritual strong searchlight, illumines the way, and although sinister doubts lurk in the shadow, I walk unafraid toward the enchanted wood where the foliage is always green, where joy abides, where nightingales nest and sing, and where life and death are one in the presence of the Lord.
HELEN ADAMS KELLER (1880–1968)

3650 Don't be afraid to take a big step. You can't cross a chasm in two small jumps.
DAVID LLOYD GEORGE (1863–1945)

3651 Doubt is not the opposite of faith; it is one element of faith.
PAUL JOHANNES OSKAR TILLICH (1886–1965)

3652 Eternal life does not begin with death; it begins with faith.
SAMUEL M. SHOEMAKER (1893–1963)

3653 Every man lives by faith, the non-believer as well as the saint; the one by faith in natural laws and the other by faith in God.
A. W. TOZER (1897–1963)

3654 Faith and love are apt to be spasmodic in the best minds. Men live on the brink of mysteries and harmonies into which they never enter, and with their hand on the doorlatch they die outside.
RALPH WALDO EMERSON (1803–1882)

3655 Faith builds a bridge across the gulf of death.
EDWARD YOUNG (1683–1765)

3656 Faith can put a candle in the darkest night.
MARGARET SANGSTER (1838–1912)

3657 Faith does not mean believing without evidence. It means believing in realities that go beyond sense and sight—for which a totally different sort of evidence is required.
JOHN BAILLIE (1741–1806)

3658 Faith does not struggle; faith lets God do it all.
CORRIE TEN BOOM (1892–1983)

3659 Faith does not wish, hope, or desire—faith receives.
ORD MORROW

3660 Faith does nothing alone—nothing of itself, but everything under God, by God, through God.
WILLIAM STOUGHTON (1631–1701)

3661 Faith draws the poison from every grief, takes the sting from every loss, and quenches the fire of every pain; and only faith can do it.
JOSIAH GILBERT HOLLAND (1819–1881)

3662 Faith for my deliverance is not faith in God. Faith means, whether I am visibly delivered or not, I will stick to my belief that God is love. There are some things only learned in a fiery furnace.
OSWALD CHAMBERS (1874–1917)

3663 Faith grows only in the dark. You've got to trust him when you can't trace him. That's faith.
LYELL RADER

3664 Faith has never yet outstripped the bounty of the Lord.

3665 Faith has no merit where human reason supplies the proof.
POPE GREGORY THE GREAT (C. 540–604)

3666 Faith in an all-seeing and personal God elevates the soul, purifies the emotions, sustains human dignity, and lends poetry, nobility, and holiness to the commonest state, condition, and manner of life.
JUAN VALERA Y ALCALÁ GALIANO (1824–1905)

3667 Faith in faith is faith astray.
A. W. TOZER (1897–1963)

3668 Faith in God is a terrific venture in the dark.
OSWALD CHAMBERS (1874–1917)

3669 Faith in God is like believing a man can walk over Niagara Falls on a tightrope while pushing a wheelbarrow. Trust in God is like getting into the wheelbarrow! To believe God can do something miraculous is one thing; to risk his willingness to do it in your life is another.
JAMES C. DOBSON (1936–   )

3670 Faith instructs us in the depths of God. Faith stands above any human system, no matter how valid; it is concerned with the revealed data, with that glory which cannot be named by any human name, yet has desired to make itself known to us in words which all may understand.
JACQUES MARITAIN (1882–1973)

3671 Faith is . . . doing the right thing regardless of the consequences, knowing God will turn the ultimate effect to good.
PAMELA REEVE

3672 Faith is . . . refusing to feel guilty over past confessed sins when God, the Judge, has sovereignly declared me "pardoned."
PAMELA REEVE

3673 Faith is a . . . form of knowledge which transcends the intellect.
MALCOLM MUGGERIDGE (1903–1990)

3674 Faith is a gift but you can ask for it.

3675 Faith is a higher faculty than reason.
PHILIP JAMES BAILEY (1816–1902)

3676 Faith is a reasoning trust, a trust which reckons thoughtfully and confidently upon the trustworthiness of God.
JOHN R. W. STOTT (1921–   )

3677 Faith is a refusal to panic.
D. MARTYN LLOYD-JONES (1899–1981)

3678 Faith is a strong power, mastering any difficulty in the strength of the Lord who made heaven and earth.
CORRIE TEN BOOM (1892–1983)

3679 Faith is an activity; it is something that has to be applied.
CORRIE TEN BOOM (1892–1983)

3680 Faith is an affirmation and an act That bids eternal truth be fact.
SAMUEL TAYLOR COLERIDGE (1772–1834)

3681 Faith is an inner conviction of being overwhelmed by God.
GUSTAF AULÉN (1879–1978)

3682 Faith is believing where we cannot prove.
ALFRED, LORD TENNYSON (1809–1892)

3683 Faith is blind—except upward. It is blind to impossibilities and deaf to doubt. It listens only to God.
SAMUEL DICKEY GORDON (1859–1936)

3684 Faith is deliberate confidence in the character of God whose ways you cannot understand at the time.
OSWALD CHAMBERS (1874–1917)

3685 Faith is for that which lies on the other side of reason. Faith is what makes life bearable, with all its tragedies and ambiguities and sudden, startling joys.
MADELEINE L'ENGLE (1918–   )

3686 Faith is like love. It cannot be forced.
ARTHUR SCHOPENHAUER (1788–1860)

3687 Faith is not a sense, nor sight, nor reason, but taking God at his Word.
ARTHUR BENONI EVANS (1781–1854)

3688 Faith is not a thing which one loses, we simply cease to shape our lives by it.
GEORGES BERNANOS (1888–1948)

3689 Faith is not an easy virtue; but, in the broad world of man's total voyage through time to eternity, faith is not only a gracious companion, but an essential guide.
THEODORE M. HESBURGH (1917–   )

3690 Faith is not anti-intellectual. It is an act of man that reaches beyond the limits of our five senses.
BILLY GRAHAM (1918–   )

3691 Faith is not believing that God can, but that God will!
ABRAHAM LINCOLN (1809–1865)

3692 Faith is not merely you holding on to God—it is God holding on to you.
E. STANLEY JONES (1884–1973)

3693 Faith is not shelter against difficulties, but belief in the face of all contradictions.
PAUL TOURNIER (1898–1986)

3694 Faith is the antiseptic of the soul.
WALT WHITMAN (1819–1892)

3695 Faith is the bird that sings when the dawn is still dark.
SIR RABINDRANATH TAGORE (1861–1941)

3696 Faith is the capacity to trust God while not being able to make sense out of everything.
JAMES KOK

3697 Faith is the daring of the soul to go farther than it can see.
WILLIAM NEWTON CLARKE (1841–1912)

3698 Faith is the possibility which belongs to men in God, in God himself, and only in God, when all human possibilities have been exhausted.
KARL BARTH (1886–1968)

3699 Faith is the root of works. A root that produces nothing is dead.
THOMAS WILSON (1663–1735)

3700 Faith is the subtle chain Which binds us to the infinite; the voice Of a deep life within, that will remain Until we crowd it thence.
ELIZABETH OAKES SMITH (1806–1893)

3701 Faith is to believe what we do not see; and the reward of this faith is to see what we believe.
SAINT AUGUSTINE OF HIPPO (354–430)

3702 Faith knows itself to be weak and uncertain, and yet, like the reed it will survive the storm better than the proud oak. It knows that in this world it can never penetrate all the unfathomable mysteries of God, and yet, however tiny the light it receives from him, this is the only light that can really show it the way.
PAUL TOURNIER (1898–1986)

3703 Faith laughs at the shaking of the spear; unbelief trembles at the shaking of a leaf, unbelief starves the soul; faith finds food in famine and a table in the wilderness.
ROBERT CECIL (1563–1612)

3704 Faith makes the discords of the present the harmonies of the future.
ROBERT COLLYER (1823–1912)

3705 Faith makes the uplook good, the outlook bright, the inlook favorable, and the future glorious.
VICTOR RAYMOND EDMAN (1900–1967)

3706 Faith makes things possible—it does not make them easy.

3707 Faith means being grasped by a power that is greater than we are, a power that shakes us and turns us, and transforms and heals us. Surrender to this power is faith.
PAUL JOHANNES OSKAR TILLICH (1886–1965)

3708 Faith means believing in advance what will only make sense in reverse.
PHILIP YANCEY (1949–)

3709 Faith never knows where it is being led, but it loves and knows the one who is leading.
OSWALD CHAMBERS (1874–1917)

3710 Faith never means gullibility. The man who believes everything is as far from God as the man who refuses to believe anything.
A. W. TOZER (1897–1963)

3711 Faith on a full stomach may be simply contentment—but if you have it when you're hungry, it's genuine.
FRANK A. CLARK

3712 Faith says, "I cannot believe that he who has brought me so far is going to let me down at this point. It is impossible; it would be inconsistent with the character of God."
D. MARTYN LLOYD-JONES (1899–1981)

3713 Faith sees the invisible, believes the unbelievable, and receives the impossible.
CORRIE TEN BOOM (1892–1983)

3714 Faith walking in the dark with God only prays him to clasp its hand more closely, does not even ask him for the lifting of the darkness.
PHILLIPS BROOKS (1835–1893)

3715 Faith wears everyday clothes and proves herself in life's ordinary situations.
BERTHA MUNRO

3716 Faith will lead you where you cannot walk. Reason has never been a mountain climber.
E. W. KENYON

3717 Faith, mighty faith, the promise sees,
And looks to that alone;
Laughs at impossibilities,
And cries it shall be done.
CHARLES WESLEY (1707–1788)

3718 Fold the arms of your faith and wait in quietness until the light goes up in your darkness. Fold the arms of your faith, I say, but not of your action. Think of something you ought to do, and go do it. Heed not your feelings. Do your work.
GEORGE MACDONALD (1824–1905)

3719 For each of us the time is surely coming when we shall have nothing but God. Health and wealth and friends and hiding places will all be swept away, and we shall have only God. To the man of pseudo faith that is a terrifying thought, but to real faith it is one of the most comforting thoughts the heart can entertain.
A. W. TOZER (1897–1963)

3720 For they conquer who believe they can.
VIRGIL (70–19 B.C.)

3721 God . . . cannot believe for us. Faith is
a gift of God . . . but whether or not
we shall act upon that faith lies altogether within our own power. We may
or we may not, as we choose.
A. W. TOZER (1897–1963)

3722 God comes to us, not only to give us
peace, but also to disturb us. Inner
restlessness and disquiet can well be
God sowing the first seeds of faith in
the human heart.
JOHN POWELL

3723 God needs no one, but when faith is
present, he works through anyone.
A. W. TOZER (1897–1963)

3724 Granted that faith cannot be proved,
what harm will come to you if you
gamble on its truth and it proves false?
. . . If you gain, you gain all; if you
lose, you lose nothing.
BLAISE PASCAL (1623–1662)

3725 Great faith is not the faith that walks
always in the light and knows no darkness, but the faith that perseveres in
spite of God's seeming silences.
FATHER ANDREW

3726 He who claims never to have doubted
does not know what faith is, for faith
is forged through doubt.
PAUL TOURNIER (1898–1986)

3727 He who feeds his faith will starve his
doubts to death.

3728 He who has lost faith, what has he left
to live on?
PUBLILIUS SYRUS (FIRST CENTURY B.C.)

3729 He who loses money loses much. He
who loses a friend loses more. But he
who loses faith loses all.
SPANISH PROVERB

3730 Human misery is too great for men to
do without faith.
HEINRICH HEINE (1797–1856)

3731 I am so made that worry and anxiety
are sand in the machinery of life: faith
is oil.
E. STANLEY JONES (1884–1973)

3732 I believe in the sun even when it is not
shining;
I believe in love even when I do not
feel it;
I believe in God even when he is silent.

3733 I do not understand the digestive system, but I eat. I don't understand all
about our respiratory system, but I
continue to breathe. So it is with faith.
BILLY GRAHAM (1918–   )

3734 I do not want merely to possess a
faith; I want a faith that possesses me.
CHARLES KINGSLEY (1819–1875)

3735 I prayed for faith and thought that
some day faith would come down and
strike me like lightning. But faith did
not seem to come. One day I read in
the tenth chapter of Romans, "Faith
cometh by hearing, and hearing by the
Word of God." I had up to this time
closed my Bible and prayed for faith. I
now opened my Bible and began to
study, and faith has been growing ever
since.
DWIGHT LYMAN MOODY (1837–1899)

3736 If a blade of grass can grow in a concrete walk and a fig tree in the side of
the mountain cliff, a human being
empowered with an invincible faith
can survive all odds the world can
throw against his tortured soul.
ROBERT HAROLD SCHULLER (1926–   )

3737 If faith is the gaze of the heart at God,
and if this gaze is but the raising of the
inward eyes to meet the all-seeing eyes
of God, then it follows that it is one of
the easiest things possible to do. It
would be like God to make the most
vital thing easy and place it within the
range of possibility for the weakest
and poorest of us.
A. W. TOZER (1897–1963)

3738 If faith without works is dead, then
conviction without action is worthless.
JAY HUDSON

3739 If I stoop
Into a dark tremendous sea of cloud,
It is but for a time; I press God's lamp
Close to my breast; its splendor, soon
or late,

Will pierce the gloom: I shall emerge
some day.
ROBERT BROWNING (1812–1889)

3740 If it can be verified, we don't need
faith.
MADELEINE L'ENGLE (1918–   )

3741 If you can't turn your faith into the
vernacular, then either you don't understand it or you don't believe it.
C. S. LEWIS (1898–1963)

3742 If you examined a hundred people
who had lost their faith in Christianity, I wonder how many of them
would turn out to have been reasoned
out of it by honest argument? Do not
most people simply drift away?
C. S. LEWIS (1898–1963)

3743 In natural matters faith follows evidence and is impossible without it, but
in the reality of the spirit, faith precedes understanding; it does not follow it. The natural man must know in
order to believe; the spiritual man
must believe in order to know.
A. W. TOZER (1897–1963)

3744 In the early years of Christian experience he often meets our needs in striking ways in order to strengthen and
confirm our new and weak faith. But
the more experience of his goodness
and faithfulness we have, the more he
is able to test and develop our faith by
teaching us long-suffering and the
assurance to wait patiently.
HANNAH HURNARD (1905–1990)

3745 Is it possible to become free from ourselves without faith in the living God?
RICHARD ROTHE (1799–1867)

3746 It gives me a deep, comforting sense
that "things seen are temporal and
things unseen are eternal."
HELEN ADAMS KELLER (1880–1968)

3747 It is cynicism and fear that freeze life;
it is faith that thaws it out, releases it,
sets it free.
HARRY EMERSON FOSDICK (1878–1969)

3748 It is faith that brings power, not
merely praying and weeping and struggling, but believing, daring to believe

the written Word with or without feeling.
CATHERINE BOOTH (1829–1890)

3749 It is never our merit God looks at but
our faith. If there is only one strand of
faith amongst all the corruption
within us, God will take hold of that
one strand.
OSWALD CHAMBERS (1874–1917)

3750 It is the heart which is aware of God,
and not reason. That is what faith is:
God perceived intuitively by the heart,
not by reason.
MALCOLM MUGGERIDGE (1903–1990)

3751 It is the trial of our faith that is precious. If we go through the trial, there
is so much wealth laid up in our heavenly banking account to draw upon
when the next test comes.
OSWALD CHAMBERS (1874–1917)

3752 It takes real faith to begin to live the
life of heaven while still upon the
earth, for this requires that we rise
above the law of moral gravitation
and bring to our everyday living the
high wisdom of God. And since this
wisdom is contrary to that of the
world, conflict is bound to result.
This, however, is a small price to pay
for the inestimable privilege of following Christ.
A. W. TOZER (1897–1963)

3753 It will not save me to know that Christ
is a Savior; but it will save me to trust
him to be my Savior. I shall not be
delivered from the wrath to come by
believing that his atonement is sufficient; but I shall be saved by making
that atonement my trust, my refuge,
and my all. The pith, the essence of
faith lies in this—a casting oneself on
the promise.
CHARLES HADDON SPURGEON (1834–1892)

3754 Knowledge of things divine escapes us
through want of faith.
GREEK PROVERB

3755 Let us have faith that right makes
might, and in that faith let us to the
end dare to do our duty as we understand it.
ABRAHAM LINCOLN (1809–1865)

3756 Like the roots of a plant, faith must seek greater depth or be subject to the law of death.
JOHN POWELL

3757 Little faith will bring your soul to heaven; great faith will bring heaven to your soul.
CHARLES HADDON SPURGEON (1834–1892)

3758 Most of us go through life praying a little, planning a little, jockeying for position, hoping but never being quite certain of anything, and always secretly afraid that we will miss the way. This is a tragic waste of truth and never gives rest to the heart.

There is a better way. It is to repudiate our own wisdom and take instead the infinite wisdom of God. Our insistence upon seeing ahead is natural enough, but it is a real hindrance to our spiritual progress. God has charged himself with full responsibility for our eternal happiness and stands ready to take over the management of our lives the moment we turn in faith to him.
A. W. TOZER (1897–1963)

3759 Most people are brought to faith in Christ, not by argument for it, but by exposure to it.
SAMUEL M. SHOEMAKER (1893–1963)

3760 My faith has no bed to sleep upon but omnipotency.
SAMUEL RUTHERFORD (1600–1661)

3761 My most cherished possession I wish I could leave you is my faith in Jesus Christ, for with him and nothing else you can be happy, but without him and with all else you'll never be happy.
PATRICK HENRY (1736–1799)

3762 Never doubt in the dark what God told you in the light.
VICTOR RAYMOND EDMAN (1900–1967)

3763 Never put a question mark where God has put a period.
JOHN R. RICE (1895–1980)

3764 No Christian has ever been known to recant on his deathbed.
C. M. WARD

3765 No coward soul is mine,
No trembler in the world's storm--
    troubled sphere;
I see heaven's glories shine,
And faith shines equal, arming me
    from fear.
EMILY BRONTË (1818–1848)

3766 No man can create faith in himself. Something must happen to him which Luther calls "the divine work in us," which changes us, gives us new birth, and makes us completely different people in heart, spirit, mind, and all our powers.
COUNT NIKOLAUS LUDWIG
VON ZINZENDORF (1700–1760)

3767 Nothing before, nothing behind;
The steps of faith
Fall on the seeming void, and find
The rock beneath.
JOHN GREENLEAF WHITTIER (1807–1892)

3768 O for a faith that will not shrink
Tho' pressed by every foe
That when in danger knows no fear,
In darkness feels no doubt.
WILLIAM H. BATHURST

3769 One of the ways that our faith expresses itself is by our ability to be still, to be present, and not to panic or lose perspective. God still does his best work in the most difficult of circumstances.
TIM HANSEL

3770 One result of the unbelief of our day is the tragedy of trying to live a maximum life on a minimum faith.
RUFUS MATTHEW JONES (1863–1948)

3771 Our faith grows by expression. If we want to keep our faith, we must share it. We must act.
BILLY GRAHAM (1918–   )

3772 Our faith is a light, kindly coming from our endless day that is our Father God.
JULIAN OF NORWICH (C. 1342–AFTER 1413)

3773 People only think a thing's worth believing in if it's hard to believe.
ARMIGER BARCLAY

3774 Put your faith to the test of life and see whether it will not justify your confidence. If God be really what our faith

assumes, we shall find him unifying our thinking, satisfying our sense of beauty or of wonder, opening out to us an enlarging and enfranchising life.
WILLIAM ADAMS BROWN (1865–1943)

3775 Real true faith is man's weakness leaning on God's strength.
DWIGHT LYMAN MOODY (1837–1899)

3776 Reason does not prove to us that God exists, but neither does it prove he cannot exist.
MIGUEL DE UNAMUNO (1864–1936)

3777 Reason saw not till faith sprung the light.
JOHN DRYDEN (1631–1700)

3778 Talk faith. The world is better off without
    Your uttered ignorance and morbid doubt.
    If you have faith in God, or man, or self,
    Say so. If not, push back upon the shelf
    Of silence all your thoughts, till faith shall come;
    No one will grieve because your lips are dumb.
ELLA WHEELER WILCOX (1850–1919)

3779 Teach me, O God, not to torture myself, not to make a martyr out of myself through stifling reflection, but rather teach me to breathe deeply in faith.
SØREN AABYE KIERKEGAARD (1813–1855)

3780 That man is perfect in faith who can come to God in the utter dearth of his feelings and his desires, without a glow or an aspiration, with the weight of low thoughts, failures, neglects, and wandering forgetfulness, and say to him, "Thou art my refuge because thou art my home."
GEORGE MACDONALD (1824–1905)

3781 The Almighty does nothing without reason though the frail mind of man cannot explain the reason.
SAINT AUGUSTINE OF HIPPO (354–430)

3782 The Bible's accounts show that miracles—dramatic, show-stopping miracles like many of us still long for—simply do not foster deep faith.
PHILIP YANCEY (1949–)

3783 The Christian does not begin with what the human intellect has discovered. The Christian begins with what God has revealed.
WILLIAM BARCLAY (1907–1978)

3784 The Christian faith engages the profoundest problems the human mind can entertain and solves them completely and simply by pointing to the Lamb of God.
A. W. TOZER (1897–1963)

3785 The Christian faith is a revolutionary faith. It demands a complete change of attitude. But in some revolutions the aim of the revolution is that those who have been underneath get on top, whereas in this one those who have been proud put themselves underneath.
MICHAEL GRIFFITHS

3786 The difference between faith and works is just this: In the case of faith, God does it; in the case of works, we try to do it ourselves; and the difference is measured simply by the distance between the infinite and the finite, the Almighty God and a helpless worm.
ALBERT BENJAMIN SIMPSON (1843–1919)

3787 The faith that will shut the mouths of lions must be more than a pious hope that they will not bite.

3788 The greatness of God rouses fear within us, but his goodness encourages us not to be afraid of him. To fear and not be afraid—that is the paradox of faith.
A. W. TOZER (1897–1963)

3789 The kind of faith God values seems to develop best when everything fuzzes over, when God stays silent, when the fog rolls in.
PHILIP YANCEY (1949–)

3790 The larger the God we know, the larger will be our faith. The secret of power in our lives is to know God and expect great things from him.
ALBERT BENJAMIN SIMPSON (1843–1919)

3791 The man without faith is a walking corpse.
POPE XYSTUS I (C. 150)

3792 The principal part of faith is patience.
GEORGE MACDONALD (1824–1905)

3793 The road that leads us to the living
God, the God of the heart, and that
leads us back to him when we have
left him for the lifeless god of logic is
the road of faith, not of rational or
mathematical conviction.
MIGUEL DE UNAMUNO (1864–1936)

3794 The senses see the action of the creatures; faith sees the action of God.
JEAN PIERRE DE CAUSSADE (1675–1751)

3795 The smallest seed of faith is better
than the largest fruit of happiness.
HENRY DAVID THOREAU (1817–1862)

3796 The witness of the church is most effective when she declares rather than
explains, for the gospel is addressed
not to reason but to faith.
A. W. TOZER (1897–1963)

3797 There are three kinds of faith in
Christ:
1. Struggling faith, like a man in deep
water desperately swimming.
2. Clinging faith, like a man hanging
to the side of a boat.
3. Resting faith, like a man safely
within the boat (and able to reach out
with a hand to help someone else get in).
DWIGHT LYMAN MOODY (1837–1899)

3798 They can conquer who believe they
can.
RALPH WALDO EMERSON (1803–1882)

3799 Those who don't keep faith with God,
won't keep it with man.
DUTCH PROVERB

3800 Through this dark and stormy night
Faith beholds a feeble light
Up the blackness streaking;
Knowing God's own time is best,
In a patient hope I rest
For the full day-breaking!
JOHN GREENLEAF WHITTIER (1807–1892)

3801 To believe on Christ is initial faith; to
receive him is appropriating faith; to
understand him is intelligent faith; to
assimilate him is active faith.
CORNELIUS WOELFKIN (1859–1928)

3802 To believe only possibilities is not
faith, but philosophy.
SIR THOMAS BROWNE (1605–1682)

3803 To choose what is difficult all one's
days as if it were easy, that is faith.
W. H. AUDEN (1907–1973)

3804 To have faith is to believe the task
ahead of us is never as great as the
Power behind us.

3805 To me, faith means not worrying.
JOHN DEWEY (1859–1952)

3806 To seek proof is to admit doubt, and
to obtain proof is to render faith superfluous.
A. W. TOZER (1897–1963)

3807 True faith acts on supernatural facts
and gets supernatural results.
DONALD GREY BARNHOUSE (1895–1960)

3808 True faith commits us to obedience.
A. W. TOZER (1897–1963)

3809 True faith is never found alone; it is
accompanied by expectation.
C. S. LEWIS (1898–1963)

3810 True faith needs neither evidence nor
research.
JEWISH PROVERB

3811 Understanding is the reward of faith.
Therefore seek not to understand that
you may believe, but believe that you
may understand.
SAINT AUGUSTINE OF HIPPO (354–430)

3812 We human beings instinctively regard
the seen world as the "real" world and
the unseen world as the "unreal"
world, but the Bible calls for almost
the opposite. Through faith, the
unseen world increasingly takes shape
as the real world and sets the course
for how we live in the seen world.
PHILIP YANCEY (1949–   )

3813 We live by Faith; but Faith is not the
slave
Of text and legend. Reason's voice and
God's,
Nature's and Duty's never are at odds.
JOHN GREENLEAF WHITTIER (1807–1892)

3814 We may well know that there is a God
without knowing what he is. By faith

we know his existence; in glory we shall know his nature.
BLAISE PASCAL (1623–1662)

3815 We never test the resources of God until we attempt the impossible.
F. B. MEYER (1847–1929)

3816 We should act with as much energy as those who expect everything from themselves, and we should pray with as much earnestness as those who expect everything from God.
CHARLES CALEB COLTON (1780–1832)

3817 What is faith, unless it is to believe what you do not see?
SAINT AUGUSTINE OF HIPPO (354–430)

3818 When outward strength is broken, faith rests on the promises. In the midst of sorrow, faith draws the sting out of every trouble and takes out the bitterness from every affliction.
ROBERT CECIL (1563–1612)

3819 When the Master of earth, sea, and skies calls the shots, things happen.
CHARLES R. SWINDOLL (1934–   )

3820 Where can one find faith? In some hour of desperate need it will be born within just when we are "at the end of the rope."

3821 Where reason cannot wade there faith may swim.
THOMAS WATSON (C. 1557–1592)

3822 Without Christ, not one step; with him, anywhere!
DAVID LIVINGSTONE (1813–1873)

3823 Without faith it is impossible to please God, but not all faith pleases God.
A. W. TOZER (1897–1963)

3824 Without faith man becomes sterile, hopeless, and afraid to the very core of his being.
ERICH FROMM (1900–1980)

3825 Workless faith God never regards, Faithless work God never rewards.
D. L. HOOD

3826 Works without faith are like a fish without water: it wants the element it should live in. A building without a basis cannot stand; faith is the founda-

tion, and every good action is as a stone laid.
OWEN FELLTHAM (C. 1602–1668)

3827 You can do very little with faith, but you can do nothing without it.
NICHOLAS MURRAY BUTLER (1862–1947)

3828 You can't pump up faith out of your own heart. Whenever faith is starved in your soul, it is because you are not in contact with Jesus; get in contact with him, and lack of faith will go in two seconds.
OSWALD CHAMBERS (1874–1917)

3829 You do right when you offer faith to God; you do right when you offer works. But if you separate the two, then you do wrong. For faith without works is dead; and lack of charity in action murders faith, just as Cain murdered Abel, so that God cannot respect your offering.
BERNARD OF CLAIRVAUX (1090–1153)

3830 The whole trouble with a man of little faith is that he does not think. He allows circumstances to bludgeon him . . . The Bible is full of logic, and we must never think of faith as something purely mystical. We do not just sit down in an armchair and expect marvellous things to happen to us. That is not Christian faith. Christian faith is essentially thinking.
D. MARTYN LLOYD-JONES (1899–1981)

FAITH/BELIEF

3831 At the root of the Christian life lies belief in the invisible. The object of the Christian's faith is unseen reality.
A. W. TOZER (1897–1963)

FAITH/DOUBT

3832 There lives more faith in honest doubt, believe me, than in half the creeds.
ALFRED, LORD TENNYSON (1809–1892)

FAITH/HOPE

3833 Faith has to do with things that are
not seen, and hope with things that
are not in hand.
SAINT THOMAS AQUINAS (1225–1274)

FAITH/HOPE/LOVE

3834 By faith we are led, not against reason
but beyond reason, to the knowledge
of God in himself and therefore of ourselves. By hope we are kept young of
heart; for it teaches us to trust in God,
to work with all our energy but to
leave the future to him; it gives us poverty of spirit and so saves us from
solicitude. And by love we are not told
about God, we are brought to him.
GERALD YANN (1906–1963)

3835 Faith has to do with the basis, the
ground on which we stand. Hope is
reaching out for something to come.
Love is just being there and acting.
EMIL BRUNNER (1889–1966)

3836 Faith is the key to fit the door of hope,
but there is no power anywhere like
love for turning it.
ELAINE EMANS

3837 Faith is the root; hope is the stem; love
the perfect flower. You may have faith
without hope, and hope without love;
but you cannot have love apart from
faith and hope.
F. B. MEYER (1847–1929)

3838 The best things in life are free, are they
not? The air we breathe is not sold by
the cubic foot. The water that flows
crystal clear from the mountain stream
is free for the taking. Love is free, faith
is free, hope is free.
BILLY GRAHAM (1918–)

FAITH/LOVE

3839 Faith, like light, should always be
simple and unbending; while love, like
warmth, should beam forth on every
side and bend to every necessity of our
brethren.
MARTIN LUTHER (1483–1546)

FAITH/REASON

3840 God does not expect us to submit our
faith to him without reason, but the
very limits of reason make faith a
necessity.
SAINT AUGUSTINE OF HIPPO (354–430)

3841 If the work of God could be comprehended by reason, it would be no
longer wonderful, and faith would
have no merit if reason provided proof.
POPE GREGORY THE GREAT (540–604)

3842 Faith and sight are set in opposition to
each other in Scripture, but not faith
and reason. . . . True faith is essentially reasonable because it trusts in
the character and the promises of
God. A believing Christian is one
whose mind reflects and rests on these
certitudes.
JOHN R. W. STOTT (1921–)

FAITHFULNESS

3843 Faithfulness in little things is a big
thing.
SAINT JOHN CHRYSOSTOM (C. 347–407)

3844 Faithfulness is consecration in overalls.
EVELYN UNDERHILL (1875–1941)

3845 He who is faithful over a few things is
a lord of cities. It does not matter
whether you preach in Westminster
Abbey, or teach a ragged class, so you
be faithful. The faithfulness is all.
GEORGE MACDONALD (1824–1905)

3846 If we are correct and right in our
Christian life at every point, but refuse
to stand for the truth at a particular
point where the battle rages—then we
are traitors to Christ.
MARTIN LUTHER (1483–1546)

3847 Is your place a small place?
Tend it with care!—He set you there.
Is your place a large place?
Guard it with care!—He set you there.
Whate'er your place, it is
Not yours alone, but his
Who set you there.
JOHN OXENHAM (1861–1941)

3848 Watch where Jesus went. The one dominant note in his life was to do his

Father's will. His is not the way of wisdom or of success, but the way of faithfulness.
OSWALD CHAMBERS (1874–1917)

3849 When men cease to be faithful to their God, he who expects to find them so to each other will be much disappointed.
GEORGE HORNE (1730–1792)

FAME

3850 Avoid shame, but do not seek glory—nothing so expensive as glory.
SYDNEY SMITH (1771–1845)

3851 Fame is a fickle food
Upon a shifting plate.
EMILY ELIZABETH DICKINSON (1830–1886)

3852 Fame usually comes to those who are thinking about something else.
OLIVER WENDELL HOLMES (1809–1894)

3853 Fame, like flame, is harmless until you start inhaling it.
O. A. BATTISTI

3854 God is not impressed with celebrities or those who would like to be. He is impressed by only one man—Christ. And only those who accept Christ by faith receive God's approval.
ERWIN W. LUTZER (1941–)

3855 I had the world, and it wasn't nothin'.
MUHAMMAD ALI (1942–)

3856 It is better to be a nobody who accomplishes something than a somebody who accomplishes nothing.

3857 Men think highly of those who rise rapidly in the world; whereas nothing rises quicker than dust, straw, and feathers.
AUGUST W. HARE (1792–1834)

3858 Popularity is a crime from the moment it is sought; it is only a virtue where men have it whether they will or no.
MARQUIS OF HALIFAX (1633–1695)

3859 Popularity? It's glory's small change.
VICTOR HUGO (1802–1885)

3860 Seeking to perpetuate one's name on earth is like writing on the sand by the seashore; to be perpetual it must be written on eternal shores.
DWIGHT LYMAN MOODY (1837–1899)

3861 The best of men are still sinners. If we take pride in the "greats" of this world, we have a warped view of God's values. He chooses the base, the lowly, and the unknown.
ERWIN W. LUTZER (1941–)

3862 What is fame? An empty bubble.
JAMES GRAINGER (1721–1766)

FAMILY

3863 A family is a place where principles are hammered and honed on the anvil of everyday living.
CHARLES R. SWINDOLL (1934–)

3864 A family is a unit composed not only of children, but of men, women, an occasional animal, and the common cold.
OGDEN NASH (1902–1971)

3865 A happy family is but an earlier heaven.
SIR JOHN BOWRING (1792–1872)

3866 A sweater is a knitted garment worn by a child when his mother feels cold.

3867 A teenager waits impatiently to grow up and become his own boss—then he gets married.

3868 Civilization varies with the family, and the family with civilization. Its highest and most complete realization is found where enlightened Christianity prevails; where woman is exalted to her true and lofty place as equal with the man; where husband and wife are one in honor, influence, and affection, and where children are a common bond of care and love. This is the idea of a perfect family.
WILLIAM AIKMAN (1682–1731)

3869 Govern a small family as you would cook a small fish, very gently.
CHINESE PROVERB

3870 How sharper than a serpent's tooth it is
To have a thankless child!
WILLIAM SHAKESPEARE (1564–1616)

3871 I believe the family was established long before the church, and my duty is to my family first. I am not to neglect my family.
DWIGHT LYMAN MOODY (1837–1899)

3872 If your father and mother, your sister and brother, if the very cat and dog in the house, are not happier for your being Christian, it is a question whether you really are.
JAMES HUDSON TAYLOR (1832–1905)

3873 Infidelity and marital conflict are cancers that gnaw on the soul of mankind, twisting and warping innocent family members who can only stand and watch.
JAMES C. DOBSON (1936–   )

3874 Insanity is hereditary: you can get it from your children.
SAMUEL LEVENSON

3875 It is impossible to overstate the need for prayer in the fabric of family life.
JAMES C. DOBSON (1936–   )

3876 Many have forgotten the value of characteristics and activities which identify the family as unique and different. They are called "traditions."
JAMES C. DOBSON (1936–   )

3877 No other structure can replace the family. Without it, our children have no moral foundation. Without it, they become moral illiterates whose only law is self.
CHARLES COLSON (1931–   )

3878 Nobody's family can hang out the sign Nothing the Matter Here.
CHINESE PROVERB

3879 Nothing stops a family quarrel more quickly than the arrival of an unexpected guest.

3880 Ordained by God as the basic unit of human organization, the family is . . . the first school of human instruction. Parents take small, self-centered monsters, who spend much of their time screaming defiantly and hurling peas on the carpet, and teach them to share, to wait their turn, to respect others' property. These lessons translate into respect for others, self-

restraint, obedience to law—in short, into the virtues of individual character that are vital to a society's survival.
CHARLES COLSON (1931–   )

3881 Our very nature is acquired within families: we are not self-reared after the fashion of Tarzan. The human family lacking, there would cease to be a human nature. Doubtlessly some race resembling in outward aspect the extinct homo sapiens would survive for a time. But you and I would feel little kinship with these . . . degenerate caricatures of human beings among whom families had ceased to exist.
RUSSELL KIRK (1918–   )

3882 Out of the mouths of babes come words we shouldn't have said in the first place.

3883 Parents have lots of trouble solving their children's problems, and children have even more trouble solving their parents' problems.

3884 Raising children is not unlike a long-distance race in which the contestants must learn to pace themselves. . . . That is the secret of winning.
JAMES C. DOBSON (1936–   )

3885 The child says nothing but what is heard by the fire.

3886 The dark, uneasy world of family life—where the greatest can fail and the humblest succeed.
RANDALL JARRELL (1914–1965)

3887 The family circle is the supreme conductor of Christianity.
HENRY DRUMMOND (1851–1897)

3888 The family is the most basic unit of government. As the first community to which a person is attached and the first authority under which a person learns to live, the family establishes society's most basic values.
CHARLES COLSON (1931–   )

3889 The family you come from isn't as important as the family you're going to have.
RING LARDNER (1885–1933)

3890 The family, grounded on marriage freely contracted, monogamous and

indissoluble, is and must be considered the first and essential cell of human society.
POPE JOHN XXIII (1881–1963)

3891 The father should treat his son as a guest, the son should treat his father as a host.

3892 The first half of our lives is ruined by our parents and the second half by our children.
CLARENCE S. DARROW (1857–1938)

3893 The first part of your life your parents learn to stand you, and the last part you learn to stand them.

3894 The future of the church and the future of humanity depend in great part on parents and on the family life they build in their homes. The family is the true measure of the greatness of a nation, just as the dignity of individuals is the true measure of civilization.
POPE JOHN PAUL II (1920–)

3895 The greatest benefits God has conferred on human life, fatherhood, motherhood, childhood, home, become the greatest curse if Jesus Christ is not the head.
OSWALD CHAMBERS (1874–1917)

3896 The tempo of life is growing faster: a college student used to write home for money; nowadays he calls collect.

3897 The thing that impresses me most about North America is the way parents obey their children.
EDWARD VIII, DUKE OF WINDSOR (1894–1972)

3898 There is never much trouble in any family where the children hope someday to resemble their parents.
WILLIAM LYON PHELPS (1865–1943)

3899 There's not much practical Christianity in the man who lives on better terms with angels and seraphs than with his children, servants, and neighbors.
HENRY WARD BEECHER (1813–1887)

3900 We have careful thought for the stranger,
And smiles for the sometime guest,
But oft for our own the bitter tone,

Though we love our own the best.
MARGARET SANGSTER (1838–1912)

3901 We must strengthen our commitment to model strong families ourselves, to live by godly priorities in a culture where self so often supersedes commitment to others. And as we not only model but assertively reach out to help others, we must realize that even huge societal problems are solved one person at a time.
CHARLES COLSON (1931–)

3902 We never know the love of the parent until we become parents ourselves.
HENRY WARD BEECHER (1813–1887)

3903 When teenagers get money, they want a car. When they get a car, they want money.

3904 Work can be used as a defensive shield. There are men who bring work home every evening so as to have an excuse for not entering into any serious conversation with their wives or children. Others barricade themselves behind the newspaper as soon as they get home, pretending to be deeply absorbed in it when their wives try to tell them of their troubles.
PAUL TOURNIER (1898–1986)

3905 Youth begins when one objects to parents having their own way.

3906 Youth begins when your parents whom you highly regarded have somehow become greatly retarded.

FANATICISM

3907 A fanatic is one who can't change his mind and won't change the subject.
SIR WINSTON CHURCHILL (1874–1965)

3908 Fanaticism consists in redoubling your effort when you have forgotten your aim.
GEORGE SANTAYANA (1863–1952)

3909 Fanaticism is the false fire of an overheated mind.
WILLIAM COWPER (1731–1800)

3910 Scratch a fanatic and you find a wound that never healed.
WILLIAM NORTH JAYME (1925–)

3911 What is fanaticism today is the fashionable creed tomorrow, and trite as the multiplication table a week after.
WENDELL PHILLIPS (1811–1884)

FATHER

3912 A father once took his little boy on his lap and described what a Christian was. When he was through, the little boy asked a question that pierced his father's heart: "Daddy, have I ever seen one?"

3913 A father who teaches his children responsibility provides them with a fortune.

3914 A father who whipped his son for swearing, and swore himself while he whipped him, did more harm by his example than good by his correction.
SIR THOMAS FULLER (1608–1661)

3915 A good father will leave his imprint on his daughter for the rest of her life.
JAMES C. DOBSON (1936–)

3916 Authentic men aren't afraid to show affection, release their feelings, hug their children, cry when they're sad, admit it when they're wrong, and ask for help when they need it.
CHARLES R. SWINDOLL (1934–)

3917 Becoming a father is easy enough, but being one can be rough.
WILHELM BUSCH (1832–1908)

3918 Can't you see the Creator of the universe, who understands every secret, every mystery . . . sitting patiently and listening to a four-year-old talk to him? That's a beautiful image of a father.
JAMES C. DOBSON (1936–)

3919 Fathering is a marathon, not a sprint.
PAUL L. LEWIS (1944–)

3920 I'm left with the memory of a child who said with his eyes, "Could you be a daddy to me?"
JAMES C. DOBSON (1936–)

3921 If he's wealthy and prominent, and you stand in awe of him, call him "Father." If he sits in his shirt sleeves and suspenders at a ball game and picnic, call him "Pop." If he wheels the baby carriage and carries bundles meekly, call him "Papa" (with the accent on the first syllable). If he belongs to a literary circle and writes cultured papers, call him "Papa" (with the accent on the last syllable).

If, however, he makes a pal of you when you're good and is too wise to let you pull the wool over his loving eyes when you're not; if, moreover, you're quite sure no other fellow you know has quite so fine a father, you may call him "Dad."
WILLIAM BUEL FRANKLIN (1823–1903)

3922 It is easier for a father to have children than for children to have a real father.
POPE JOHN XXIII (1881–1963)

3923 One father is worth more than a hundred schoolmasters.
GEORGE HERBERT (1593–1633)

3924 One of the best legacies a father can leave his children is to love their mother.
C. NEIL STRAIT

3925 The acid test of a father's leadership is not in the realm of his social skills, his public relations, his managerial abilities at the office, or how well he handles himself before the public. It is in the home.
CHARLES R. SWINDOLL (1934–)

3926 The father in praising the son extols himself.
CHINESE PROVERB

3927 The father's most important responsibility is to communicate the real meaning of Christianity to his children.
JAMES C. DOBSON (1936–)

3928 When I was a boy of fourteen, my father was so ignorant I could hardly stand to have the old man around. But when I got to be twenty-one, I was astonished at how much the old man had learned in seven years.
MARK TWAIN (1835–1910)

3929 You don't need to be right all the time. Your child wants a man for a father, not a formula. He wants real parents,

real people, capable of making mistakes without moping about it.
C. D. WILLIAMS

FAULTS

3930 'Tis a great confidence in a friend to tell him your faults; greater to tell him his.
BENJAMIN FRANKLIN (1706–1790)

3931 A fault which humbles a man is of more use to him than a good action which puffs him up.
THOMAS WILSON (1663–1735)

3932 A person's defect may also serve as a source of strength for the total personality, just as metallurgists deliberately build defects into their crystals to improve their strength. (Indeed, by sticking defects into perfect crystals, solid-state physics has given us the semiconductor, which revolutionized modern technology.)
SYDNEY J. HARRIS (1917–1986)

3933 Almost all our faults are more pardonable than the methods we resort to to hide them.
FRANÇOIS, DUC DE LA ROCHEFOUCAULD (1613–1680)

3934 And ofttimes excusing of a fault
Doth make the fault the worse by the excuse.
WILLIAM SHAKESPEARE (1564–1616)

3935 Commune with your own selves, for the kingdom of God is within you. See with whom ye associate, with whom ye readily stay; and examine the reasons and the tendency to all evil habits. For if a man gives way to a fault for a year or two, that fault takes such deep root in his heart, that he can scarcely overcome it with all his might.
JOHANN TAULER (C. 1300–1361)

3936 Condemn the fault, and not the actor of it.
WILLIAM SHAKESPEARE (1564–1616)

3937 Dare to be true:
Nothing can need a lie;
A fault, which needs it most, grow two thereby.
GEORGE HERBERT (1593–1633)

3938 Deal with the faults of others as gently as with your own.
CHINESE PROVERB

3939 Do not think of the faults of others but of what is good in them and faulty in yourself.
SAINT TERESA OF AVILA (1515–1582)

3940 Do not think of your faults; still less of others' faults; in every person who comes near you look for what is good and strong: honor that; rejoice in it; and, as you can, try to imitate it; and your faults will drop off, like dead leaves, when their time comes.
JOHN RUSKIN (1819–1900)

3941 I prefer a comfortable vice to a virtue that bores.
MOLIÈRE (1622–1673)

3942 I will chide no heathen in the world but myself
Against whom I know most faults.
WILLIAM SHAKESPEARE (1564–1616)

3943 If the best man's faults were written on his forehead, he would draw his hat over his eyes.
THOMAS GRAY (1716–1771)

3944 If we had no faults of our own, we would not take so much pleasure in noticing those of others.
FRANÇOIS, DUC DE LA ROCHEFOUCAULD (1613–1680)

3945 If you are pleased at finding faults, you are displeased at finding perfections.
JOHANN KASPAR LAVATER (1741–1801)

3946 If you feel you have no faults, that makes another one.

3947 Most people are careful drivers; every time they have an accident, it's the other driver's fault.

3948 Never love unless you can
bear with all the faults of man.
THOMAS CAMPION (1567–1620)

3949 No man is perfect unless he admits his faults. But if he has faults to admit, how can he be perfect?

3950 Some people excuse their faults; others abandon them.

3951 The brightest of all things, the sun, has its spots.

3952 The greatest fault is to be conscious of none.
THOMAS CARLYLE (1795–1881)

3953 There is so much good in the worst
of us,
And so much bad in the best of us,
That it hardly behooves any of us
To talk about the rest of us.
EDWARD WALLIS HOCH (1849–1925)

3954 They see nothing but faults who look for nothing else.
SIR THOMAS FULLER (1608–1661)

3955 Think not those faithful who praise all thy words and actions; but those who kindly reprove thy faults.
SOCRATES (470–399 B.C.)

3956 We acknowledge our faults in order to repair by our sincerity the damage they have done us in the eyes of others.
FRANÇOIS, DUC DE LA ROCHEFOUCAULD (1613–1680)

3957 We have a bat's eyes for our own faults, and an eagle's for the faults of others.
JAMES L. GORDON

3958 What once were vices are now manners.
LUCIUS ANNAEUS SENECA (C. 4 B.C–A.D. 65)

3959 You will find it less easy to uproot faults, than to choke them by gaining virtues.
JOHN RUSKIN (1819–1900)

FEAR

3960 A good scare is worth more than good advice.
ED HOWE (1853–1937)

3961 Anxiety has its use, stimulating us to seek with keener longing for that security where peace is complete and unassailable.
SAINT AUGUSTINE OF HIPPO (354–430)

3962 Do the thing you fear and the death of fear is certain.
RALPH WALDO EMERSON (1803–1882)

3963 Extreme fear can neither fight nor fly.
WILLIAM SHAKESPEARE (1564–1616)

3964 Fear always springs from ignorance.
RALPH WALDO EMERSON (1803–1882)

3965 Fear imprisons, faith liberates; fear paralyzes, faith empowers; fear disheartens, faith encourages; fear sickens, faith heals; fear makes useless, faith makes serviceable—and, most of all, fear puts hopelessness at the heart of life, while faith rejoices in its God.
HARRY EMERSON FOSDICK (1878–1969)

3966 Fear is tax that conscience pays to guilt.
GEORGE SEWELL (D. 1726)

3967 Fear is the sand in the machinery of life.
E. STANLEY JONES (1884–1973)

3968 Fear knocked at the door. Faith answered. No one was there.

3969 Fear makes the wolf bigger than he is.
GERMAN PROVERB

3970 Fear of God can deliver us from the fear of man.
JOHN WITHERSPOON (1723–1794)

3971 Fear. His modus operandi is to manipulate you with the mysterious, to taunt you with the unknown. Fear of death, fear of failure, fear of God, fear of tomorrow—his arsenal is vast. His goal? To create cowardly, joyless souls. He doesn't want you to make the journey to the mountain. He figures if he can rattle you enough, you will take your eyes off the peaks and settle for a dull existence in the flatlands.
MAX L. LUCADO (1955–)

3972 God incarnate is the end of fear; and the heart that realizes that he is in the midst . . . will be quiet in the midst of alarm.
F. B. MEYER (1847–1929)

3973 God planted fear in the soul as truly as he planted hope or courage. It is a kind of bell or gong which rings the mind into quick life on the approach of danger. It is the soul's signal for rallying.
HENRY WARD BEECHER (1813–1887)

3974 God's never missed the runway
through all the centuries of fearful fog.
CHARLES R. SWINDOLL (1934–)

3975 He who fears death cannot enjoy life.
SPANISH PROVERB

3976 He who fears to suffer, suffers from
fear.
FRENCH PROVERB

3977 I fear God, yet am not afraid of him.
SIR THOMAS BROWNE (1605–1682)

3978 I, a stranger and afraid
In a world I never made.
A. E. HOUSMAN (1859–1936)

3979 It is better to die of hunger, so that
you be free from pain and from fear,
than to live in plenty and be troubled
in mind.
EPICTETUS (C. 55–C. 135)

3980 It is the fear of everything new which
gives personal and social life its stability and the framework of habits without which all is confusion.
PAUL TOURNIER (1898–1986)

3981 Many a man threatens while he
quakes for fear.

3982 Many of our fears are tissue-paper
thin, and a single courageous step
would carry us clear through them.
BRENDAN FRANCIS

3983 My father had never lost his temper
with us, never beaten us, but we had
for him that feeling often described as
fear, which is something quite different
and far deeper than alarm. . . . One
does not fear God because he is terrible, but because he is literally the soul
of goodness and truth, because to do
him wrong is to do wrong to some
mysterious part of oneself, and one
does not know exactly what the consequence may be.
JOYCE CARY (1888–1957)

3984 Nothing in life is to be feared. It is
only to be understood.
MARIE CURIE (1867–1934)

3985 Only he who can say, "The Lord is the
strength of my life," can say, "Of
whom shall I be afraid?"
ALEXANDER MACLAREN (1826–1910)

3986 Our Lord cannot endure that any who
love him should be worried, for fear is
painful. Thus St. John says: "Love
casteth out fear." Love cannot put up
with either fear or pain, and so, to
grow in love is to diminish in fear, and
when one has become a perfect lover,
fear has gone out of him altogether.
    At the beginning of a good life, how-
ever, fear is useful. It is love's gateway. A
punch or an awl makes a hole for the
thread with which a shoe is sewed . . .
and a bristle is put on the thread to get
it through the hole, but when the thread
does bind the shoe together, the bristle is
out. So fear leads love at first, and when
love has bound us to God, fear is done
away.
MEISTER ECKHART (C. 1260–C. 1327)

3987 Relinquishment of burdens and fears
begins where adoration and worship
of God become the occupation of the
soul.
FRANCES J. ROBERTS

3988 Shame arises from the fear of men,
conscience from the fear of God.
SAMUEL JOHNSON (1709–1784)

3989 Taking a new step, uttering a new
word, is what people fear the most.
FYODOR MIKHAYLOVICH DOSTOYEVSKI
(1821–1881)

3990 The adventurous life is not one
exempt from fear, but on the contrary
one that is lived in full knowledge of
fears of all kinds, one in which we go
forward in spite of our fears.
PAUL TOURNIER (1898–1986)

3991 The cure for fear is faith.
NORMAN VINCENT PEALE (1898–)

3992 The only power which can resist the
power of fear is the power of love.
ALAN STEWART PATON (1903–)

3993 The only sure way to take fear out of
living is to keep a respectful fear of
God in our lives, which means to maintain a reverent attitude toward his
place and influence. This brand of fear
is a healthy ingredient, a deterrent to
want, a spur to courage and confi-

dence, an insurance against loss, and source of comfort and understanding.
EUGENE ASA CARR (1830–1910)

3994 The remarkable thing about fearing God is that when you fear God, you fear nothing else, whereas if you do not fear God, you fear everything else.
OSWALD CHAMBERS (1874–1917)

3995 The right fear is the fear of losing God.
MEISTER ECKHART (C. 1260–C. 1327)

3996 The wicked is a coward, and is afraid of everything; of God, because he is his enemy; of Satan, because he is his tormentor; of God's creatures, because they, joining with their Maker, fight against him; of himself, because he bears about with him his own accuser and executioner. The godly man contrarily is afraid of nothing; not of God, because he knows him as his best friend, and will not hurt him; not of Satan, because he cannot hurt him; not of afflictions, because he knows they come from a loving God, and end in his good; not of the creatures, since "the very stones in the field are in league with him"; not of himself, since his conscience is at peace.
JOSEPH HALL (1574–1656)

3997 The wise man in the storm prays to God, not for safety from danger, but for deliverance from fear. It is the storm within which endangers him, not the storm without.
RALPH WALDO EMERSON (1803–1882)

3998 There are moments when everything goes well; don't be frightened, it won't last.
JULES RENARD (1864–1910)

3999 This is a wise, sane Christian faith: that a man commit himself, his life, and his hopes to God; that God undertakes the special protection of that man; that therefore that man ought not to be afraid of anything.
GEORGE MACDONALD (1824–1905)

4000 Those who loved to be feared, fear to be loved.
SAINT FRANCIS OF SALES (1567–1622)

4001 To be feared is to fear: no one has been able to strike terror into others

and at the same time enjoy peace of mind.
LUCIUS ANNAEUS SENECA (C. 4 B.C.–A.D. 65)

4002 To the man who is afraid everything rustles.
SOPHOCLES (C. 496–406 B.C.)

4003 Tommy's tears and Mary's fears
Will make them old before their years.

4004 We fear something before we hate it; a child who fears noises becomes a man who hates noises.
CYRIL CONNOLLY (1903–1974)

4005 We master fear through faith—faith in the worthwhileness of life and the trustworthiness of God; faith in the meaning of our pain and our striving, and confidence that God will not cast us aside but will use each one of us as a piece of priceless mosaic in the design of his universe.
JOSHUA LOTH LIEBMAN (1907–1948)

4006 Whatever you fear (or supremely respect) the most you will serve.
REBECCA MANLEY PIPPERT

4007 When I think of us human beings, it seems to me that we have a lot of nerve to make fun of the ostrich.
HEYWOOD BROUN (1888–1939)

4008 Where man can find no answer, he will find fear.
NORMAN COUSINS (1912–)

4009 Who lives in fear will never be a free man.
HORACE (65-8 B. C.)

4010 You can discover what your enemy fears most by observing the means he uses to frighten you.
ERIC HOFFER (1902–1983)

FEELINGS

4011 A Christian life based on feeling is headed for a gigantic collapse.
ERWIN W. LUTZER (1941–)

4012 Before we can feel the deepest tenderness for others, we must feel the deepest tenderness of God.
EMILY MORGAN

4013 Don't bother much about your feelings. When they are humble, loving,

brave, give thanks for them; when they are conceited, selfish, cowardly, ask to have them altered. In neither case are they you, but only a thing that happens to you. What matters is your intentions and your behavior.
C. S. LEWIS (1898–1963)

4014 It is terribly amusing how many different climates of feeling one can go though in one day.
ANNE MORROW LINDBERGH (1906–)

4015 Most Christians understand that salvation comes by faith, apart from feelings. But they think that the Spirit-controlled life requires some type of mystical experience—a feeling, a surge of power, or being overcome by waves of love. Those experiences are usually not around when you need them. What you need is spiritual power, independent of feelings, experiences, or circumstances. That comes when we give each day to God and anticipate his blessing.
ERWIN W. LUTZER (1941–)

4016 No natural feelings are high or low, holy or unholy, in themselves. They are all holy when God's hand is on the rein. They all go bad when they . . . make themselves into false gods.
C. S. LEWIS (1898–1963)

4017 Our generation is characterized by a craze for subjective experience. Our society has placed an inordinate emphasis on feeling good.
ERWIN W. LUTZER (1941–)

4018 Respect in yourself the oscillations of feeling: they are your life and your nature; a wiser than you made them.
HENRI FRÉDÉRIC AMIEL (1821–1881)

4019 There is no feeling in a human heart that exists in that heart alone—which is not, in some form or degree, in every heart.
GEORGE MACDONALD (1824–1905)

FELLOWSHIP

4020 Be united with other Christians. A wall with loose bricks is not good. The bricks must be cemented together.
CORRIE TEN BOOM (1892–1983)

4021 Before thee in humility, with thee in faith, in thee in peace.
DAG HAMMARSKJÖLD (1905–1961)

4022 For the early Christians, koinonia was not the frilly "fellowship" of church-sponsored, biweekly bowling parties. It was not tea, cookies, and sophisticated small talk in Fellowhip Hall after the sermon. It was an almost unconditional sharing of their lives with the other members of Christ's body.
RONALD J. SIDER

4023 Human fellowship can go to great lengths, but not all the way. Fellowship with God can go to all lengths.
OSWALD CHAMBERS (1874–1917)

4024 In a dream I walked with God through the deep places of creation; past walls that receded and gates that opened, through hall after hall of silence, darkness, and refreshment—the dwelling place of souls acquainted with light and warmth—until, around me, was an infinity into which we all flowed together and lived anew, like the rings made by raindrops falling upon wide expanses of calm dark waters.
DAG HAMMARSKJÖLD (1905–1961)

4025 It seems stupid to me that fellowship must be limited to the narrow ranks of predictable personalities clad in "acceptable" attire.
CHARLES R. SWINDOLL (1934–)

4026 No man is an island, entire of itself; every man is a piece of the continent, a part of the main.
JOHN DONNE (1572–1631)

4027 The only basis for real fellowship with God and man is to live out in the open with both.
ROY HESSION

4028 We are all strings in the concert of his joy.
JAKOB BÖHME (1575–1624)

4029 What happens when God grants the gift of genuine Christian fellowhip? Deep, joyful sharing replaces the polite prattle typically exchanged by Christians on Sunday morning. Sisters and brothers begin to discuss the things that really matter to them. They disclose their inner fears, their areas of peculiar temptation, their deepest joys.
RONALD J. SIDER

FINANCES

4030 A budget is a detailed record of how you managed to spend more than you earned.

4031 About the only thing you can do on a shoestring nowadays is trip.

4032 Before you borrow money from a friend, decide which you need more.

4033 Better go to bed supperless than rise in debt.

4034 Cheer up: birds have bills too, but they keep on singing.

4035 Don't borrow trouble: borrow money and trouble will come of its own accord.

4036 Economy: save money in one store so you can spend it in another.

4037 Feel for others—in your pocket.
CHARLES HADDON SPURGEON (1834–1892)

4038 He who borrows sells his freedom.
GERMAN PROVERB

4039 O money, money, money! I often stop to wonder how thou canst go out so fast when thou comest in so slowly.
OGDEN NASH (1902–1971)

4040 People come to poverty in two ways: accumulating debts and paying them off.
JEWISH PROVERB

4041 Some shoppers imitate General Custer—the only word they say is "charge."

4042 There are still a few things you can get for a quarter—pennies, nickels, and dimes.

4043 Who goeth a borrowing
Goeth a sorrowing.
THOMAS TUSSER (C. 1524–1580)

4044 Without debt, without care.
ITALIAN PROVERB

FLATTERY

4045 A flatterer doesn't sufficiently value either himself or others.
JEAN DE LA BRUYÈRE (1645–1696)

4046 A flatterer is a man that tells you your opinion and not his own.

4047 Flatterers look like friends as wolves resemble dogs.

4048 Flattery corrupts both the receiver and giver.
EDMUND BURKE (1729–1797)

4049 Flattery: a mouth that praises and a hand that kills.
ARABIAN PROVERB

4050 He is sweet as salt in your mouth.

4051 Men seldom flatter without a purpose; and they who listen to such music may expect to pay the piper.
AESOP (FL. C. 550 B.C.)

4052 Treachery lurks in honeyed words.
DANISH PROVERB

4053 We recognize that flattery is poison, but its perfume intoxicates us.
MARQUIS DE LA GRANGE

4054 When flatterers meet, the devil goes to dinner.
ETHIOPIAN PROVERB

FLEXIBILITY

4055 Better to bend than break.
SCOTTISH PROVERB

4056 We cannot direct the wind, but we can adjust the sails.

4057 Who would be constant in happiness must often change.
CHINESE PROVERB

FOOL

4058 A fool wanders; the wise man travels.

4059 A narrow mind and a wide mouth usually go together.

4060 Fools rush in where angels fear to tread.
ALEXANDER POPE (1688–1744)

4061 Give him but rope enough and he'll hang himself.

4062 He fled from the rain and sat down under the drainpipe.
ARABIAN PROVERB

4063 He who makes himself an ass must not take it ill if men ride him.

4064 Outside noisy, inside empty.
CHINESE PROVERB

4065 Some are wise, and some are otherwise.

4066 The empty vessel makes the greatest sound.
WILLIAM SHAKESPEARE (1564–1616)

4067 The fool has his answer on the edge of his tongue.
ARABIAN PROVERB

FORGIVENESS

4068 A retentive memory is a good thing, but the ability to forget is the true token of greatness.
ELBERT GREEN HUBBARD (1856–1915)

4069 Alas! if my best Friend, who laid down his life for me, were to remember all the instances in which I have neglected him, and to plead them against me in judgment, where should I hide my guilty head in the day of recompense? I will pray, therefore, for blessings on my friends, even though they cease to be so, and upon my enemies, though they continue such.
WILLIAM COWPER (1731–1800)

4070 An injury is much sooner forgiven than an insult.
LORD CHESTERFIELD (1694–1773)

4071 As we grow in wisdom, we pardon more freely.
ANNE-LOUISE-GERMAINE DE STAËL (1766–1817)

4072 As we practice the work of forgiveness we discover more and more that forgiveness and healing are one.
AGNES SANFORD

4073 Doing an injury puts you below your enemy; revenging one makes you even with him; forgiving it sets you above him.

4074 For the sake of one good action a hundred evil ones should be forgotten.
CHINESE PROVERB

4075 Forgiveness is a funny thing—it warms the heart and cools the sting.
WILLIAM ARTHUR WARD (1812–1882)

4076 Forgiveness is a required course.
CHARLES R. SWINDOLL (1934–   )

4077 Forgiveness is man's deepest need and highest achievement.
HORACE BUSHNELL (1802–1876)

4078 Forgiveness is not an occasional act, it is a permanent attitude.
MARTIN LUTHER KING, JR. (1929–1968)

4079 Forgiveness is not that stripe which says, "I will forgive, but not forget." It is not to bury the hatchet with the handle sticking out of the ground, so you can grasp it the minute you want it.
DWIGHT LYMAN MOODY (1837–1899)

4080 Forgiveness is the fragrance that the flower leaves on the heel of the one who crushed it.
MARK TWAIN (1835–1910)

4081 Forgiveness ought to be like a cancelled note—torn in two and burned up, so that it never can be shown against one.
HENRY WARD BEECHER (1813–1887)

4082 God will forgive me; that is his business.
HEINRICH HEINE (1797–1856)

4083 Good to forgive;
Best, to forget!
ROBERT BROWNING (1812–1889)

4084 He that demands mercy, and shows none, ruins the bridge over which he himself is to pass.
THOMAS ADAMS (1612–1653)

4085 He who forgives ends the quarrel.
AFRICAN PROVERB

4086 Humanity is never so beautiful as when praying for forgiveness or when forgiving another.
JOHANN PAUL FRIEDRICH RICHTER (1763–1825)

4087 If God forgives us, we must forgive ourselves. Otherwise it is almost like setting up ourselves as a higher tribunal than him.
C. S. LEWIS (1898–1963)

4088 If God were not willing to forgive sin, heaven would be empty.
GERMAN PROVERB

4089 It is cheaper to pardon than to resent. Forgiveness saves the expense of anger, the cost of hatred.
HANNAH MORE (1745–1833)

4090 It is in pardoning that we are pardoned.
SAINT FRANCIS OF ASSISI (C. 1181–1226)

4091 It is necessary to repent for years in order to efface a fault in the eyes of men; a single tear suffices with God.
FRANÇOIS RENÉ, VICOMTE DE CHATEAUBRIAND (1768–1848)

4092 Know all and you will pardon all.
THOMAS À KEMPIS (C. 1380–1471)

4093 Life lived without forgiveness becomes a prison.
WILLIAM ARTHUR WARD (1812–1882)

4094 Making peace requires action:
sometimes crossing the street when the
    light is red
swimming upstream
getting bruised
maybe dying.
JEAN JANZEN

4095 Never does the human soul appear so strong as when it foregoes revenge and dares to forgive an injury.
EDWIN HUBBEL CHAPIN (1814–1880)

4096 Only one petition in the Lord's Prayer has any condition attached to it. It is the petition for forgiveness.
SIR WILLIAM TEMPLE (1628–1699)

4097 Regard as enormous the little wrong you did to others, and as trifling the great wrong done to you.
TALMUD

4098 The heaviest load any man carries on his back is a pack of grudges.

4099 The more a man knows, the more he forgives.
CATHERINE II OF RUSSIA (1729–1796)

4100 The voice of sin is loud, but the voice of forgiveness is louder.
DWIGHT LYMAN MOODY (1837–1899)

4101 They who forgive most shall be most forgiven.
PHILIP JAMES BAILEY (1816–1902)

4102 To return evil for good is devilish; to return good for good is human; but to return good for evil is godlike.

4103 We achieve inner health only through forgiveness—the forgiveness not only of others but also of ourselves.
JOSHUA LOTH LIEBMAN (1907–1948)

4104 We all agree that forgiveness is a beautiful idea until we have to practice it.
C. S. LEWIS (1898–1963)

4105 We hand folks over to God's mercy and show none ourselves.
GEORGE ELIOT (1819–1880)

4106 We pardon to the degree that we love.
FRANÇOIS, DUC DE LA ROCHEFOUCAULD (1813–1913)

4107 When God pardons, he consigns the offense to everlasting forgetfulness.
MERV ROSELL

4108 When you forgive you in no way change the past—but you sure do change the future.
BERNARD MELTZER

4109 You must choose to forgive whoever has wronged you. Forgiveness is not an emotion, it is a decision of the will.
ERWIN W. LUTZER (1941–)

4110 Christians aren't perfect—just forgiven.

FREEDOM

4111 A free will is not the liberty to do whatever one likes, but the power of doing whatever one sees ought to be

done, even in the very face of otherwise overwhelming impulse. There lies freedom indeed.
GEORGE MACDONALD (1824–1905)

4112 A person can be free even within prison walls. Freedom is something spiritual. Whoever has once had it, can never lose it. There are some people who are never free outside a prison. The body can be bound with chains, the spirit never. One's thoughts are free.
BERTOLT BRECHT (1898–1956)

4113 A wise man, though he be a slave, is at liberty; though a fool rule, he is in slavery.
SAINT AMBROSE (C. 340–397)

4114 Ay, call it holy ground,
The soil where first they trod!
They have left unstained what there they found—
Freedom to worship God.
—on the landing of the Pilgrim Fathers
FELICIA HEMANS (1793–1835)

4115 Be not intimidated . . . by any terrors, from publishing with the utmost freedom whatever can be warranted by the laws of your country; nor suffer yourselves to be wheedled out of your liberty by any pretenses of politeness, delicacy, or decency. These, as they are often used, are but three different names for hypocrisy, chicanery, and cowardice.
JOHN ADAMS (1735–1826)

4116 Christianity promises to make men free; it never promises to make them independent.
WILLIAM RALPH INGE (1860–1954)

4117 Creation, which seems like pure freedom, involves limitation. . . . Rebellion, which also seems like freedom, involves limitation as well.
PHILIP YANCEY (1949–)

4118 Find me the men on earth who care
Enough for faith or creed today
To seek a barren wilderness
For simple liberty to pray.
HELEN MARIA FISKE HUNT JACKSON (1830–1885)

4119 Free at last, free at last. Thank God Almighty, I'm free at last.
—Inscription on the gravestone of Martin Luther King, Jr. (1929–1968)

4120 Free will, though it makes evil possible, is also the only thing that makes possible any love or goodness or joy worth having. A world of automata— of creatures that worked like machines—would hardly be worth creating. The happiness which God designs for his higher creatures is the happiness of being freely, voluntarily united to him and to each other in an ecstasy of love and delight compared with which the most rapturous love between a man and a woman on this earth is mere milk and water. And for that they must be free.
C. S. LEWIS (1898–1963)

4121 Freedom comes by filling your mind with God's thoughts.
ERWIN W. LUTZER (1941–)

4122 Freedom does not mean I am able to do whatever I want to do. That's the worst kind of bondage. Freedom means I have been set free to become all that God wants me to be, to achieve all that God wants me to achieve, to enjoy all that God wants me to enjoy.
WARREN W. WIERSBE (1929–)

4123 Freedom! A fine word when rightly understood. What freedom would you have? What is the freedom of the most free? To act rightly!
JOHANN WOLFGANG VON GOETHE (1749–1832)

4124 Freethinkers are those who are willing to use their minds without prejudice and without fearing to understand things that clash with their own customs, privileges, or beliefs. This state of mind is not common, but it is essential for right thinking; where it is absent, discussion is apt to become worse than useless.
LEO TOLSTOY (1828–1910)

4125 From his imprisonment my freedoms grow, find wings.
Part of his body, I transcend this flesh.

From his sweet silence my mouth sings.
Out of his dark I glow.
LUCI SHAW (1928–)

4126 God forces no one, for love cannot
compel, and God's service is a thing of
perfect freedom.
HANS DENK

4127 God has laid upon man the duty of
being free, of safeguarding freedom of
spirit, no matter how difficult that
may be, or how much sacrifice and suffering it may require.
NIKOLAI ALEKSANDROVICH BERDYAEV
(1874–1948)

4128 God has so constituted us that there
must be a free willingness on our part.
This power is at once the most fearful
and the most glorious power.
OSWALD CHAMBERS (1874–1917)

4129 God in no way hinders his creatures in
their struggle for development. Not
only does the sun shine upon the just
and the unjust; God lets the rebellious
shake their fists at him, and even deny
his existence, as freely as the devout
adore and praise him.
GEDDES MACGREGOR (1909–)

4130 God never forces man, never sets a
limit to man's freedom.
NIKOLAI ALEKSANDROVICH BERDYAEV
(1874–1948)

4131 He that is good is free, though he is a
slave; he that is evil is a slave, though
he be a king.
SAINT AUGUSTINE OF HIPPO (354–430)

4132 If God thinks this state of war in the
universe a price worth paying for free
will—that is, for making a live world
in which creatures can do real good or
harm and something of real importance can happen, instead of a toy
world which only moves when he
pulls the strings—then we may take it
it is worth paying.
C. S. LEWIS (1898–1963)

4133 If man lost his liberty, he would be disqualified for membership in the kingdom of God. Not even God could
build a society of love out of puppets
or robots. Therefore, he never defeats

himself by taking away freedom of
choice from man.
KIRBY PAGE (1890–1957)

4134 If the truth be mighty, and God all-
powerful, his children need not fear
that disaster will follow freedom of
thought.
FRANÇOIS FÉNELON (1651–1715)

4135 If we can understand the mind of God
at all, we must thrill at his willingness
to release men from the limitations of
the animal world and give them the
right to seek and rebel.
GERALD A. KENNEDY (1907–)

4136 Jesus blew everything apart, and when
I saw where the pieces landed, I knew
I was free.
GEORGE BURMAN FOSTER (1858–1918)

4137 Men must be governed by God or they
will be ruled by tyrants.
WILLIAM PENN (1644–1718)

4138 No man is free who is a slave to the
flesh.
LUCIUS ANNAEUS SENECA (C. 4 B.C.–A.D. 65)

4139 No man is free who is not master of
himself.
EPICTETUS (C. 55–C. 135)

4140 O Thou, to whose all-searching sight
The darkness shineth as the light!
Search, prove my heart; it pants for
    Thee.
Oh, burst these bonds, and set it free!
GERHARD TERSTEEGEN (1697–1769)

4141 Proclaim liberty throughout all the
inhabitants thereof.
—Leviticus 25:10, inscription on the
    Liberty Bell at Philadelphia

4142 The basic test of freedom is perhaps
less in what we are free to do than in
what we are free not to do.
ERIC HOFFER (1902–1983)

4143 The cause of freedom is the cause of
God!
WILLIAM LISLE BOWLES (1762–1850)

4144 The first duty of every soul is to find
not its freedom but its Master.
P. T. FORSYTH (1848–1921)

4145 The free man is he who does not fear to go to the end of his thought.
WILLIAM BLAKE (1757–1827)

4146 The God who gave us life, gave us liberty at the same time.
THOMAS JEFFERSON (1743–1826)

4147 The important thing about a man is not where he goes when he is compelled to go, but where he goes when he is free to go where he will.
A. W. TOZER (1897–1963)

4148 The only lasting treasure is spiritual; the only perfect freedom is serving God.
MALCOLM MUGGERIDGE (1903–1990)

4149 The world is full of wickedness and misery precisely because it is based on freedom—yet that freedom constitutes the whole dignity of man and of his world. Doubtless at the price of its repudiation, evil and suffering could be abolished, and the world forced to be "good" and "happy," but man would have lost his likeness to God, which primarily resides in his freedom.
NIKOLAI ALEKSANDROVICH BERDYAEV (1874–1948)

4150 There are two freedoms: the false, where man is free to do what he likes; the true, where a man is free to do what he ought.
CHARLES KINGSLEY (1819–1875)

4151 This is liberty: to know that God alone matters.
DONALD HAUKEY (1874–1917)

4152 We are only free when the Son sets us free; but we are free to choose whether or not we will be made free.
OSWALD CHAMBERS (1874–1917)

4153 We find freedom when we find God; we lose it when we lose him.
PAUL E. SCHERER (1892–   )

4154 We have in our hands the most potent weapon God has ever given man— freedom of speech. But with this great freedom must go a strong sense of responsibility for what we say.
BILLY GRAHAM (1918–   )

4155 What is freedom? Freedom is the right to choose: the right to create for oneself the alternatives of choice. Without the possibility of choice and the exercise of choice a man is not a man but a member, an instrument, a thing.
ARCHIBALD MACLEISH (1892–1982)

4156 When the Athenians finally wanted not to give to society, but for society to give to them, when the freedom they wished for was freedom from responsibility, then Athens ceased to be free.
EDWARD GIBBON (1737–1794)

4157 When we let freedom ring, when we let it ring from every village and every hamlet, and every state and every city, we will be able to speed up that day when all God's children, black men and white men, Jews and Gentiles, Protestants and Catholics, will be able to join hands and sing in the words of that old Negro spiritual, "Free at last! Free at last! Thank God Almighty, we are free at last!"
—Lincoln Memorial Speech, 1963
MARTIN LUTHER KING, JR. (1929–1968)

4158 Without free will, man would not be created "in the image of God." With it, he has the power to defy God's wishes and to bring misery on himself and others.
C. S. LEWIS (1898–1963)

4159 Worldy people imagine that the saints must find it difficult to live with so many restrictions, but the bondage is with the world, not with the saints. There is no such thing as freedom in the world, and the higher we go in the social life the more bondage there is.
OSWALD CHAMBERS (1874–1917)

4160 Christian life, then, is liberty, the liberation of the person from the trammels imposed by external influences. It is the rising of the sap from within. It is life under God's leadership. It is a balance between prayer and action: between the dialogue in which his creative inspiration is sought, and the bold and confident affirmation of self, in which the inspiration received is put into practice.
PAUL TOURNIER (1898–1986)

FRIENDS

4161 To find a friend one must close one eye; to keep him, two.
NORMAN DOUGLAS (1868–1952)

4162 A faithful friend is an image of God.

4163 A faithful friend is one of life's greatest assets.

4164 A foe to God was ne'er true friend to man,
Some sinister intent taints all he does.
EDWARD YOUNG (1683–1765)

4165 A friend is a person with whom I may think aloud.
RALPH WALDO EMERSON (1803–1882)

4166 A friend is never known until a man have need.
JOHN HEYWOOD (C. 1497–1580)

4167 A friend is one who comes in when the whole world has gone out.

4168 A friend is one who knows all about you and likes you just the same.
ELBERT GREEN HUBBARD (1856–1915)

4169 A friend is one who
knows you as you are
understands where you've been
accepts who you've become
and still, gently invites you to grow.

4170 A friend is one who makes me do my best.
OSWALD CHAMBERS (1874–1917)

4171 A friend is one who warns you.
ARABIAN PROVERB

4172 A friend is someone who understands your past, believes in your future, and accepts you today just the way you are.

4173 A friend is someone with whom you dare to be yourself.
C. RAYMOND BERAN

4174 A friend is:
a push when you've stopped
a word when you're lonely
a guide when you're searching
a smile when you're sad
a song when you're glad.

4175 A friend will joyfully sing with you when you are on the mountaintop, and silently walk beside you through the valley.

4176 A friend you have to buy won't be worth what you pay for him.
GEORGE D. PRENTICE (1802–1870)

4177 A real friend is not so much someone you feel free to be serious with as someone you feel free to be silly with.
SYDNEY J. HARRIS (1917–1986)

4178 A real friend is one who helps us to think our noblest thoughts, put forth our best efforts, and to be our best selves.

4179 A real friend warms you by his presence, trusts you with his secrets, and remembers you in his prayers.

4180 A true friend is forever a friend.
GEORGE MACDONALD (1824–1905)

4181 After the friendship of God, a friend's affection is the greatest treasure here below.

4182 Chide a friend in private and praise him in public.
SOLON (C. 630–C. 560 B.C.)

4183 Cover the blemishes and excuse the failings of a friend; draw a curtain before his stains, display his perfection; bury his weakness in silence, proclaim his virtues on the housetop.
ROBERT SOUTH (1634–1716)

4184 Few delights can equal the mere presence of one whom we trust utterly.
GEORGE MACDONALD (1824–1905)

4185 Friends who understand each other speak with words sweet and strong which emerge from their hearts like the fragrance of orchids.
CONFUCIUS (C. 551–479 B.C.)

4186 Friends—and I mean real friends—reserve nothing; the property of one belongs to the other.
EURIPIDES (C. 484–406 B.C.)

4187 He who has many friends, has none.
ARISTOTLE (384–322 B.C.)

4188 Hold a true friend with both your hands.
AFRICAN PROVERB

4189 If instead of a gem, or even a flower, we should cast the gift of a loving

thought into the heart of a friend, that would be giving as the angels give.
GEORGE MACDONALD (1824–1905)

4190 Insomuch as anyone pushes you nearer to God, he or she is your friend.

4191 It is better to keep a friend from falling than to help him up.

4192 It is one mark of a friend that he makes you wish to be at your best while you are with him.
HENRY VAN DYKE (1852–1933)

4193 It takes a long time to grow an old friend.
JOHN LEONARD (1939–   )

4194 Judge yourself by the friends you choose.

4195 My friend peers in on me with merry Wise face, and though the sky stays dim,
The very light of day, the very Sun's self comes in with him.
ALGERNON CHARLES SWINBURNE (1837–1909)

4196 No problem is ever as dark when you have a friend to face it with you.

4197 Old friends, old scenes will lovelier be As more of heav'n in each we see.
JOHN KEBLE (1792–1866)

4198 On the choice of friends Our good or evil name depends.
JOHN GAY (1685–1732)

4199 Strange that I did not know him then, That friend of mine.
I did not even show him then One friendly sign . . .
I would have rid the earth of him Once, in my pride.
I never knew the worth of him Until he died.
EDWIN ARLINGTON ROBINSON (1869–1935)

4200 The best mirror is an old friend.
GEORGE HERBERT (1593–1633)

4201 The dearest friend on earth is a mere shadow compared with Jesus Christ.
OSWALD CHAMBERS (1874–1917)

4202 The fingers of God touch your life when you touch a friend.
MARY DAWN HUGHES

4203 The happiest miser on earth is the man who saves up every friend he can make.
ROBERT EMMET SHERWOOD (1896–1955)

4204 The most agreeable of all companions is a simple, frank person, without any high pretensions to an oppressive greatness—one who loves life and understands the use of it; obliging alike at all hours; above all, of a golden temper, and steadfast as an anchor. For such an one we gladly exchange the greatest genius, the most brilliant wit, the profoundest thinker.
GOTTHOLD EPHRAIM LESSING (1729–1781)

4205 The only way to have a friend is to be one.
RALPH WALDO EMERSON (1803–1882)

4206 The ornaments of our house are the friends who frequent it.
RALPH WALDO EMERSON (1803–1882)

4207 The sight of you is good for sore eyes.
JONATHAN SWIFT (1667–1745)

4208 There is no friend like an old friend Who has shared our morning days,
No greeting like his welcome,
No homage like his praise.
OLIVER WENDELL HOLMES (1809–1894)

4209 Three firm friends,
more sure than day and night,
Himself, his Maker,
and the angel Death.
SAMUEL TAYLOR COLERIDGE (1772–1834)

4210 What can wound more deeply than a false friend?
SOPHOCLES (C. 496–406 B.C.)

4211 What is a friend? A single soul dwelling in two bodies.
ARISTOTLE (384–322 B.C.)

4212 Wherever you are, it is your friends who make your world.
WILLIAM JAMES (1842–1910)

4213 You can always tell a real friend: when you've made a fool of yourself, he doesn't feel you've done a permanent job.
LAURENCE J. PETER (1919–   )

4214 You cannot say that you are friendless when Christ has said, "Henceforth I

call you not servants . . . but I have
called you friends."
BILLY GRAHAM (1918–)

FRIENDSHIP

4215 A friend to everybody and to nobody
is the same thing.
SPANISH PROVERB

4216 Anyone with a heart full of friendship
has a hard time finding enemies.

4217 Be a friend. You don't need glory.
Friendship is a simple story.
Pass by trifling errors blindly,
Gaze on honest effort kindly,
Cheer the youth who's bravely trying,
Pity him who's sadly sighing;
Just a little labor spend
On the duties of a friend.
EDGAR ALBERT GUEST (1881–1959)

4218 Be courteous to all, but intimate with
few, and let those few be well tried
before you give them your confidence.
True friendship is a plant of slow
growth and must undergo and withstand the shocks of adversity.
GEORGE WASHINGTON (1732–1799)

4219 Better fare hard with good men than
feast it with bad.
SIR THOMAS FULLER (1608–1661)

4220 Blessed are they who have the gift of
making friends, for it is one of God's
best gifts. It involves many things, but
above all, the power of going out of
one's self and appreciating whatever is
noble and loving in another.
THOMAS HUGHES (1822–1896)

4221 Cheerful company shortens the miles.
GERMAN PROVERB

4222 Convey thy love to thy friends, as an
arrow to the mark, to stick there; not
as a ball against the wall to rebound
back to thee. That friendship will not
continue to the end that is begun for
an end.
FRANCIS QUARLES (1592–1644)

4223 Do not keep the alabaster boxes of
your love and tenderness sealed up
until your friends are dead. Fill their
lives with sweetness. Speak approving,
cheering words while their ears can

hear them and while their hearts can
be thrilled by them.
HENRY WARD BEECHER (1813–1887)

4224 Don't lead me; I may not follow. Don't
walk behind me, I may not lead. Walk
beside me and be my friend.

4225 Every man should keep a fair-sized
cemetery in which to bury the faults of
his friends.
HENRY WARD BEECHER (1813–1887)

4226 Fly with the eagles! Don't run around
with the Henny Pennys who are looking up chanting, "The sky is falling!"
Your best friends should be individuals who are the "No problem, it's just
little, temporary inconvenience" type.
DENIS WAITLEY

4227 Four things are the property of friendship: love and affection, security and
joy. And four things must be tried in
friendship: faith, intention, discretion,
and patience. Indeed, as the sage says,
all men would lead a happy life if only
two tiny words were taken from them,
mine and thine.
SAINT AILRED OF RIEVAULX (1109–1167)

4228 Friendship adds a brighter radiance to
prosperity and lightens the burden of
adversity by dividing and sharing it.

4229 Friendship doubles our joy and divides
our grief.

4230 Friendship flourishes at the fountain
of forgiveness.
WILLIAM ARTHUR WARD (1812–1882)

4231 Friendship is a plant which must often
be watered.
GERMAN PROVERB

4232 Friendship is a sheltering tree.

4233 Friendship is a spiritual thing. It is independent of matter or space or time.
That which I love in my friend is not
that which I see. What influences me
in my friend is not his body, but his
spirit.
JOHN DRUMMOND (1851–1897)

4234 Friendship is in loving rather than in
being loved.
ROBERT SEYMOUR BRIDGES (1844–1930)

4235 Friendship is like money, easier made than kept.
SAMUEL BUTLER (1612–1680)

4236 Friendship is one of the sweetest joys of life. Many might have failed beneath the bitterness of their trial had they not found a friend.
CHARLES HADDON SPURGEON (1834–1892)

4237 Friendship is usually treated as a tough and everlasting thing which will survive all manner of bad treatment. But it may die in an hour of a single unwise word; its conditions of existence are that it should be dealt with delicately and tenderly. It is a plant and not a roadside thistle. We must not expect our friend to be above humanity.
OUIDA (1839–1908)

4238 Friendship ought never to conceal what it thinks.
SAINT JEROME (C. 374–C. 420)

4239 Friendship without self-interest is rare and beautiful.
JAMES FRANCIS BYRNES (1879–1972)

4240 Friendship, of itself a holy tie,
Is made more sacred by adversity.
JOHN DRYDEN (1631–1700)

4241 Friendships form among people who strengthen one another.
FRANKLIN OWEN

4242 Go slowly to the entertainment of thy friends, but quickly to their misfortunes.

4243 God evidently does not intend us all to be rich, or powerful, or great, but he does intend us all to be friends.
RALPH WALDO EMERSON (1803–1882)

4244 He who ceases to be your friend never was a good one.

4245 He who looks for advantage out of friendship strips it of all its nobility.
LUCIUS ANNAEUS SENECA (C. 4 B.C.–A.D. 65)

4246 He who seeks a faultless friend is friendless.
TURKISH PROVERB

4247 I am simply not mature enough to enter into true friendship unless I realize that I cannot judge the intention or motivation of another. I must be humble and sane enough to bow before the complexity and mystery of a human being.
JOHN POWELL

4248 I love you for what you are, but I love you yet more for what you are going to be. I love you not so much for your realities as for your ideals. I pray for your desires that they may be great, rather than for your satisfactions, which may be so hazardously little. You are going forward toward something great. I am on the way with you, and therefore I love you.
CARL SANDBURG (1878–1967)

4249 If a man does not make new acquaintances as he advances through life, he will soon find himself alone. A man, sir, must keep his friendships in constant repair.
SAMUEL JOHNSON (1709–1784)

4250 If the world is cold, make it your business to build fires.
HORACE TRAUBEL

4251 If we would build on a sure foundation in friendship, we must love our friends for their sake rather than for our own.
CHARLOTTE BRONTË (1816–1855)

4252 It is best to be with those in time we hope to be with in eternity.
SIR THOMAS FULLER (1608–1661)

4253 Jesus wasn't afraid to associate with anyone!
BILLY GRAHAM (1918–   )

4254 Life is partly what we make it and partly what it is made by the friends we choose.
CHINESE PROVERB

4255 Like cuttlefish we conceal ourselves, we darken the atmosphere in which we move; we are not transparent. I pine for one to whom I can speak my first thoughts; thoughts which represent me truly, which are no better and no worse than I; thoughts which have the bloom on them, which alone can be sacred or divine.
HENRY DAVID THOREAU (1817–1862)

4256 No camel route is long, with good company.
TURKISH PROVERB

4257 No man is useless while he has a friend.
ROBERT LOUIS BALFOUR STEVENSON (1850–1894)

4258 No one is rich enough to do without a neighbor.
DANISH PROVERB

4259 Not many sounds in life, and I include all urban and rural sounds, exceed in interest a knock at the door.
CHARLES LAMB (1775–1834)

4260 Oh, the comfort, the inexpressible comfort of feeling safe with a person, having neither to weigh thoughts nor measure words, but pouring them all right out, just as they are, chaff and grain together; certain that a faithful hand will take and sift them, keep what is worth keeping, and then with the breath of kindness blow the rest away.
DINAH MARIA MULOCK CRAIK (1826–1887)

4261 Only solitary men know the full joys of friendship. Others have their families, but to a solitary and an exile his friends are everything.
WILLA SIBERT CATHER (1873–1947)

4262 Promises may get friends, but it is performance that must nurse and keep them.
OWEN FELLTHAM (C. 1602–1668)

4263 Rare as is true love, true friendship is still rarer.
FRANÇOIS, DUC DE LA ROCHEFOUCAULD (1613–1680)

4264 Real friends don't care if your socks don't match.

4265 Real friends have a great time doing absolutely nothing together.

4266 Real friends know that you have a good reason for being three days late picking them up at the bus station.

4267 Real friendship is shown in times of trouble; prosperity is full of friends.
EURIPIDES (C. 484–406 B.C.)

4268 Silences make the real conversations between friends. Not the saying, but the never needing to say is what counts.
MARGARET LEE RUNBECK

4269 Such is friendship that through it we love places and seasons; for as bright bodies emit rays to a distance, and flowers drop their sweet leaves on the ground around them, so friends impart favor even to the places where they dwell. With friends even poverty is pleasant. Words cannot express the joy which a friend imparts; they only can know who have experienced that joy. A friend is dearer than the light of heaven, for it would be better for us that the sun were extinguished than that we should be without friends.
SAINT JOHN CHRYSOSTOM C. 347–407

4270 Tell me with whom thou art found, and I will tell thee who thou art.
JOHANN WOLFGANG VON GOETHE (1749–1832)

4271 The comfort of having a friend may be taken away, but not that of having had one.
LUCIUS ANNAEUS SENECA (C. 4 B.C.–A.D. 65)

4272 The essence of a perfect friendship is that each friend reveals himself utterly to the other, flings aside his reserves, and shows himself for what he truly is.
ROBERT H. BENSON (1871–1914)

4273 The firmest friendships have been formed in mutual adversity, as iron is most strongly united by the fiercest flame.
CHARLES CALEB COLTON (1780–1832)

4274 The friendship that can cease has never been real.
SAINT JEROME (C. 374–C. 420)

4275 The glory of friendship is not the outstretched hand, nor the kindly smile nor the joy of companionship; it is the spiritual inspiration that comes to me when he discovers that someone else believes in him and is willing to trust him.
RALPH WALDO EMERSON (1803–1882)

4276 The highest privilege there is, is the privilege of being allowed to share

another's pain. You talk about your pleasures to your acquaintances; you talk about your troubles to your friends.
FATHER ANDREW

4277 The highest sign of friendship is that of giving another the privilege of sharing your inner thought. It is a personal gift in which there is self-commitment.
PAUL TOURNIER (1898–1986)

4278 The impulse of love that leads us to the doorway of a friend is the voice of God within.
AGNES SANFORD

4279 The wise man seeks a friend with qualities which he himself lacks.
JEREMY TAYLOR (1613–1667)

4280 The world is so empty if one thinks only of mountains, rivers, and cities, but to know someone here and there who thinks and feels with us and who, though distant, is close to us in spirit, makes the earth a garden.
JOHANN WOLFGANG VON GOETHE (1749–1832)

4281 There are those who pass like ships in the night.
Who meet for a moment, then sail out of sight
With never a backward glance of regret;
Folks we know briefly then quickly forget.
Then there are friends who sail together
Through quiet waters and stormy weather
Helping each other through joy and through strife.
And they are the kind who give meaning to life.

4282 There is a magnet in your heart that will attract true friends. That magnet is unselfishness, thinking of others first . . . when you learn to live for others, they will live for you.
PARAMAHANSA YOGANANDA

4283 There is an inverse ratio between quantity and quality: When I see someone who is "everybody's friend," I tend to doubt that he or she is anyone's friend very deeply.
SYDNEY J. HARRIS (1917–1986)

4284 There is no wilderness like a life without friends.
BALTASAR GRACIÁN Y MORALES (1601–1658)

4285 There's a special kind of freedom friends enjoy. Freedom to share innermost thoughts, to ask a favor, to show their true feelings. The freedom to simply be themselves.

4286 Those who have resources within themselves, who can dare to live alone, who want friends the least, best know how to prize them the most. No company is far preferable to bad; we are more apt to catch the vices of others than their virtues. Disease is far more contagious than health.
CHARLES CALEB COLTON (1780–1832)

4287 To a friend's house the road is never long.
DUTCH PROVERB

4288 To friendship every burden is light.

4289 To speak painful truth through loving words is friendship.
HENRY WARD BEECHER (1813–1887)

4290 Too many of us stay walled up because we are afraid of being hurt. We are afraid to care too much for fear that the other person does not care at all.
ELEANOR ROOSEVELT (1884–1962)

4291 True friends have no solitary joy or sorrow.
WILLIAM ELLERY CHANNING (1780–1842)

4292 True friendship is like sound health, the value of it is seldom known until it be lost.
CHARLES CALEB COLTON (1780–1832)

4293 True happiness consists not in the multitude of friends, but in the worth and choice.
BEN JONSON (1572–1637)

4294 Unless you make allowances for your friend's foibles, you betray your own.
PUBLILIUS SYRUS (FIRST CENTURY B.C.)

4295 Unshared joy is an unlighted candle.

4296 Warmth, friendliness and a gentle touch are always stronger than force and fury.
DENIS WAITLEY

4297 We can never replace a friend. When a man is fortunate enough to have several, he finds they are all different. No one has a double in friendship.
JOHANN FRIEDRICH VON SCHILLER (1759–1805)

4298 What is love? two souls and one flesh. Friendship? two bodies and one soul.
JOSEPH ROUX (1834–1886)

4299 What sweetness is left in life if you take away friendship? Robbing life of friendship is like robbing the world of the sun.
CICERO (106–43 B.C.)

4300 When a friend dies, part of yourself dies too.
JOHN IRVINE

4301 When there are friends, there is wealth.
LATIN PROVERB

4302 Where hearts are true, few words will do.

4303 Winning has always meant much to me, but winning friends has meant the most.
MILDRED "BABE" DIDRIKSON (1872–1966)

4304 With merry company, the dreary way is endured.
SPANISH PROVERB

4305 You can hardly make a friend in a year, but you can lose one in an hour.
CHINESE PROVERB

4306 You can make more friends in two months by becoming interested in other people than you can in two years by trying to get other people interested in you.
DALE CARNEGIE (1888–1955)

FULFILLMENT

4307 A pure, honest, and stable spirit is not distracted by a lot of activity. He does everything to honor God and is at rest within himself. He seeks to be free from all selfishness.
THOMAS À KEMPIS (C. 1380–1471)

4308 Fulfillment comes as a by-product of our love for God. And that satisfaction is better than we ever imagined. God can make the pieces of this world's puzzle fit together; he helps us view the world from a new perspective.
ERWIN W. LUTZER (1941–)

4309 God's restrictions not only hold us down, but they also hold us up. We will never achieve fulfillment unless he is in control.
ERWIN W. LUTZER (1941–)

4310 People can meet superficial needs. But only God can meet our deep needs.
FORRESTER BARRINGTON

4311 Until we have learned to be satisfied with fellowship with God, until he is our rock and our fortress, we will be restless with our place in the world.
ERWIN W. LUTZER (1941–)

4312 You have made us for yourself and our hearts are restless until they rest in you.
SAINT AUGUSTINE OF HIPPO (354–430)

FUTURE

4313 A wonderful way is the King's Highway;
It runs through the nightland up to the day;
From the wonderful was, by the wonderful is,
To the still more wonderful is to be.
JOHN MASEFIELD (1878–1967)

4314 God will not permit man to have a knowledge of things to come; for if man had a foresight of his prosperity, he would become arrogant and careless; and if he had an understanding of his adversity, he would become listless and despairing.
SAINT AUGUSTINE OF HIPPO (354–430)

4315 I want to do away with everything behind man, so that there is nothing to see when he looks back. I want to take

him by the scruff of his neck and turn his face toward the future!
LEONID NIKOLAYEVICH ANDREYEV (1871–1919)

4316 I've read the last page of the Bible. It's all going to turn out all right.
BILLY GRAHAM (1918–   )

4317 It is bad enough to know the past; it would be intolerable to know the future.
WILLIAM SOMERSET MAUGHAM (1874–1965)

4318 Many live in dread of what is coming. Why should we? The unknown puts adventure into life. It gives us something to sharpen our souls on. The unexpected around the corner gives a sense of anticipation and surprise. Thank God for the unknown future. If we saw all good things which are coming to us, we would sit down and degenerate. If we saw all the evil things, we would be paralyzed. How merciful God is to lift the curtain on today; and as we get strength today to meet tomorrow, then to lift the curtain on the morrow. He is a considerate God.
E. STANLEY JONES (1884–1973)

4319 No man ever sank under the burden of the day. It is when tomorrow's burden is added to the burden of today that the weight is more than a man can bear. Never load yourself so. If you find yourself so loaded, at least remember this: it is your own doing, not God's. He begs you to leave the future to him, and mind the present.
GEORGE MACDONALD (1824–1905)

4320 The best thing about the future is that it comes only one day at a time.
ABRAHAM LINCOLN (1809–1865)

4321 The Christian's future is still before him. I will give you time to smile at that because it sounds like a self-evident bromide if ever one was uttered. But I assure you that it is not a self-evident banality; it is rather a proof that we ought to ponder soberly the fact that many Christians already have their future behind them. Their glory

is behind them. . . . They are always lingering around the cold ashes of yesterday's burned-out campfire. Their testimonies indicate it, their outlook and their uplook reveal it, and their downcast look betrays it! Above all, their backward look indicates it. I always get an uneasy feeling when I find myself with people who have nothing to discuss but the glories of the days that are past.
A. W. TOZER (1897–1963)

4322 The crosses which we make for ourselves by a restless anxiety as to the future are not crosses which come from God. We show want of faith in him by our false wisdom, wishing to forestall his arrangements, and struggling to supplement his providence by our own providence. The future is not yet ours; perhaps it never will be. If it comes, it may come wholly different from what we have foreseen. Let us shut our eyes, then, to that which God hides from us, and keeps in reserve in the treasures of his deep counsels. Let us worship without seeing; let us be silent; let us abide in peace.
FRANÇOIS FÉNELON (1651–1715)

4323 The future has a habit of suddenly and dramatically becoming the present.
ROGER WARD BABSON (1875–1967)

4324 The future is a convenient place for dreams.
ANATOLE FRANCE (1844–1924)

4325 The future is an opportunity yet unmet, a path yet untraveled, a life yet unlived. But how the future will be lived, what opportunities will be met, what paths traveled, depends on the priorities and purposes of life today.
C. NEIL STRAIT

4326 The future is purchased by the present.
SAMUEL JOHNSON (1709–1784)

4327 The future is something which everyone reaches at the rate of sixty minutes an hour, whatever he does, whoever he is.
C. S. LEWIS (1898–1963)

4328 The future isn't what it used to be.

4329 The possibility of the future far exceeds the accomplishment of the past. We review the past with the common sense, but we anticipate the future with transcendental senses.
HENRY DAVID THOREAU (1817–1862)

4330 The veil that covers the face of futurity is woven by the hand of mercy.
SIR HENRY BULWER (1801–1872)

4331 Trust no future, howe'er pleasant!
Let the dead past bury its dead!
Act—act in the living present!
Heart within and God o'erhead!
HENRY WADSWORTH LONGFELLOW (1807–1882)

4332 Very soon, all of us will be living in the electronic village hooked up to a huge computer, and we will be able to know what everybody else in the world thinks. The majority opinion will become law in that hour.
FRANCIS AUGUST SCHAEFFER (1912–1984)

4333 We should all be concerned about the future because we will have to spend the rest of our lives there.
CHARLES FRANKLIN KETTERING (1876–1958)

4334 When all else is lost, the future still remains.
CHRISTIAN NESTELL BOVEE (1820–1904)

4335 While time lasts there will always be a future, and that future will hold both good and evil since the world is made to that mingled pattern.
DOROTHY L. SAYERS (1893–1957)

4336 Who could stand to see a whole week before it was lived?
C. NEIL STRAIT

4337 You have not measured your fingers with God's, therefore you cannot know the future.

G

GAIN/LOSS

4338 Profit? Loss?
Who shall declare this good, that ill?
When good and ill so intertwine
But to fulfill the vast design
Of an omniscient will?
When seeming gain but turns to loss,
When earthly treasure proves but
   dross,
And what seemed loss but turns again
To high, eternal gain?
JOHN OXENHAM (1861–1941)

4339 Sometimes the best gain is to lose.
GEORGE HERBERT (1593–1633)

4340 To gain that which is worth having, it
may be necessary to lose everything
else.
BERNADETTE DEVLIN (1947–)

4341 Was anything real ever gained without
sacrifice of some kind?
ARTHUR HELPS (1813–1875)

4342 Without sacrifice there is no resurrection. Nothing grows and blooms save
by giving.
ANDRÉ GIDE (1869–1951)

4343 You must lose a fly to catch a trout.
GEORGE HERBERT (1593–1633)

GENEROSITY

4344 A bit of fragrance always clings to the
hand that gives you roses.
CHINESE PROVERB

4345 A generous action is its own reward.
WILLIAM WALSH (1663–1708)

4346 A generous man forgets what he gives
and remembers what he receives.

4347 A happy spirit takes the grind out of
giving. The grease of gusto frees the
gears of generosity.
CHARLES R. SWINDOLL (1934–)

4348 A man there was, and they called him
   mad;
The more he gave, the more he had.
JOHN BUNYAN (1628–1688)

4349 All we can hold in our cold dead
hands is what we have given away.

4350 Alms never make poor.
ENGLISH PROVERB

4351 As the purse is emptied, the heart is filled.
VICTOR HUGO (1802–1885)

4352 Every gift which is given, even though it be small, is great if given with affection.
PINDAR (C. 522–438 B.C.)

4353 Generosity is giving more than you can, and pride is taking less than you need.
KAHLIL GIBRAN (1883–1931)

4354 Give and spend, and God will send.
HENRY GEORGE BOHN (1796–1884)

4355 Give unto all, lest he whom thou deny'st
May chance to be no other man but Christ.
ROBERT HERRICK (1591–1674)

4356 Give what you have. To someone it may be better than you dare to think.
HENRY WADSWORTH LONGFELLOW (1807–1882)

4357 Giving is a joy if we do it in the right spirit. It all depends on whether we think of it as "What can I spare?" or as "What can I share?"
ESTHER YORK BURKHOLDER

4358 Giving is the thermometer of love.

4359 God does not need our money. But you and I need the experience of giving it.
JAMES C. DOBSON (1936–)

4360 God's arithmetic: love, joy, and peace multiply when you divide with others.

4361 He gives twice who gives quickly.
ENGLISH PROVERB

4362 He that does good to another does good to himself.
LUCIUS ANNAEUS SENECA (C. 4 B.C.–A.D. 65)

4363 He that gives should never remember, he that receives should never forget.
TALMUD

4364 He who bestows his goods upon the poor,
Shall have as much again, and ten times more.
JOHN BUNYAN (1628–1688)

4365 He who gives what he would as readily throw away, gives without gen-

erosity; for the essence of generosity is in self-sacrifice.
SIR HENRY TAYLOR (1800–1886)

4366 If you are not generous with a meager income, you will never be generous with abundance.
HAROLD NYE

4367 If you loan your breeches, don't cut off the buttons.
IRISH PROVERB

4368 It is better to give one shilling than to lend a pound.
ENGLISH PROVERB

4369 Let us give according to our incomes, lest God make our incomes match our gifts.
PETER MARSHALL (1902–1949)

4370 Not he who has much is rich, but he who gives much.
ERICH FROMM (1900–1980)

4371 Not how much we give, but what we do not give, is the test of our Christianity.
OSWALD CHAMBERS (1874–1917)

4372 Rich gifts prove poor when givers prove unkind.
WILLIAM SHAKESPEARE (1564–1616)

4373 Some kinds of charity are like that of the man who cast his bread upon the waters while he was seasick.

4374 That man may last, but never lives,
Who much receives, but nothing gives,
Whom none can love, whom none can thank,
Creation's blot, creation's blank.
THOMAS GIBBONS (1720–1785)

4375 The hand that gives is above the hand that takes.
TURKISH PROVERB

4376 The hand that gives, gathers.
ENGLISH PROVERB

4377 The man who leaves money to charity in his will is only giving away what no longer belongs to him.
VOLTAIRE (1694–1778)

4378 The test of generosity is not how much you give, but how much you have left.

4379 Two mites, two drops (yet all her
      house and land),
    Falls from a steady heart, though
      trembling hand;
    The other's wanton wealth foams
      high, and brave,
    The other cast away, she only gave.
    —The Widow's Mite
    RICHARD CRASHAW (C. 1613–1649)

4380 We are never more like God than
     when we give.
     CHARLES R. SWINDOLL (1934–   )

4381 We make a living by what we get; we
     make a life by what we give.
     SIR WINSTON CHURCHILL (1874–1965)

4382 What brings joy to the heart is not so
     much the friend's gift as the friend's
     love.
     SAINT AILRED OF RIEVAULX (1109–1167)

4383 What I kept, I lost; what I spent, I
     had; what I gave, I have.
     PERSIAN PROVERB

4384 What is a true gift? One for which
     nothing is expected in return.
     CHINESE PROVERB

4385 When the hand ceases to scatter, the
     heart ceases to pray.
     IRISH PROVERB

4386 When you give to God, you discover
     that God gives to you.

4387 When you give, take to yourself no
     credit for generosity unless you deny
     yourself something in order that you
     may give.
     SIR HENRY TAYLOR (1800–1886)

4388 You do not have to be rich to be gener-
     ous. If he has the spirit of true generos-
     ity, a pauper can give like a prince.
     CORINNE U. WELLS

GENIUS

4389 Every man of genius sees the world at
     a different angle from his fellows, and
     there is his tragedy.
     HAVELOCK ELLIS (1859–1939)

4390 Everything great in the world comes
     from neurotics. They alone have
     founded our religions and composed
     our masterpieces. Never will the world

know all it owes to them nor all that
they have suffered to enrich it.
MARCEL PROUST (1871–1922)

4391 Genius is one percent inspiration and
     99 percent perspiration.
     THOMAS ALVA EDISON (1847–1931)

4392 Genius is only great patience.
     GEORGES LOUIS LECLERC DE BUFFON
     (1707–1788)

4393 Good sense travels on the well-worn
     paths; genius, never. And that is why
     the crowd, not altogether without rea-
     son, is so ready to treat great men as
     lunatics.
     CESARE LOMBROSO (1836–1909)

4394 If we are to have genius, we must put
     up with the inconvenience of genius, a
     thing the world will never do; it wants
     geniuses, but would like them just like
     other people.
     GEORGE MOORE (1852–1933)

4395 Men of genius are often dull and inert
       in society; as the blazing meteor,
     When it descends to earth, is only a
       stone.
     HENRY WADSWORTH LONGFELLOW
     (1807–1882)

4396 The Holy Spirit is stronger than genius.
     MARTIN LUTHER (1483–1546)

4397 The public is wonderfully tolerant.
     They forgive everything except genius.
     OSCAR WILDE (1854–1900)

4398 There is no great genius without a mix-
     ture of madness.
     ARISTOTLE (384–322 B.C.)

4399 What then is genius? Could it be that
     a genius is a man haunted by the
     Speaking Voice, laboring and striving
     like one possessed to achieve ends
     which he only vaguely understands?
     A. W. TOZER (1897–1963)

4400 When a true genius appears in this
     world, you may know him by the sign
     that the dunces are all in confederacy
     against him.
     JONATHAN SWIFT (1667–1745)

GENTLENESS

4401 Feelings are everywhere . . . be gentle.
J. MASAI

4402 In our rough-and-rugged individualism, we think of gentleness as weakness, being soft, and virtually spineless. Not so! . . . Gentleness includes such enviable qualities as having strength under control, being calm and peaceful when surrounded by a heated atmosphere, emitting a soothing effect on those who may be angry or otherwise beside themselves, and possessing tact and gracious courtesy that causes others to retain their self-esteem and dignity. . . . Instead of losing, the gentle gain. Instead of being ripped off and taken advantage of, they come out ahead!
CHARLES R. SWINDOLL (1934–   )

4403 Power can do by gentleness what violence fails to accomplish.
LATIN PROVERB

4404 The best soldiers are not warlike.
LAO-TSE (C. 604–C. 531 B.C.)

4405 There is nothing stronger than gentleness.

GLORY

4406 Avoid shame, but do not seek glory. Nothing is so expensive as glory.
SYDNEY SMITH (1771–1845)

4407 Glory avoids those who chase after it and is endowed on many who did not try to pursue it.
JEWISH PROVERB

4408 Glory is perfected grace.
MEISTER ECKHART (C. 1260–C. 1327)

4409 Glory. Lovelier to desire than to possess.
JOSEPH JOUBERT (1754–1824)

4410 Godliness is no longer valued, except for the very old or the very dead. The saintly souls are forgotten in the whirl of religious activity. The noisy, the self-assertive, the entertaining are sought after and rewarded in every way, with gifts, crowds, offerings, and publicity. The Christlike, the self-forgetting, the other-worldly are jostled aside to make room for the latest converted playboy who is usually not too well converted and still very much of a playboy.
A. W. TOZER (1897–1963)

4411 How lucky he is who can obliterate the pursuit of glory, that useless aim which thwarts his happiness.
MARQUIS DE RACAN (1589–1670)

4412 Life, the world, pleasure and glory are but nothing, smoke, shadow, and pain.
ANTONIO MIRA DE AMESCUA (1574–1644)

4413 Our great honor lies in being just what Jesus was and is. To be accepted by those who accept him, rejected by all who reject him, loved by those who love him and hated by everyone who hates him. What greater glory could come to any man?
A. W. TOZER (1897–1963)

4414 Real glory springs from the silent conquest of ourselves.
JOSEPH PARRISH THOMPSON (1819–1879)

4415 Sad as glory itself.
NAPOLEON BONAPARTE (1769–1821)

4416 The deed is everything, the glory naught.
JOHANN WOLFGANG VON GOETHE (1749–1832)

4417 The greater the difficulty, the greater the glory.
CICERO (106–43 B.C.)

4418 The road to glory is not strewn with flowers.
JEAN DE LA FONTAINE (1621–1695)

4419 The snake pulled back the curtain to the throne room and invited Eve to take a seat. Put on the crown. Pick up the scepter. Put on the cape. See how it feels to have power. See how it feels to have a name. See how it feels to be in control! Eve swallowed the hook. The temptation to be like God eclipsed her view of God.
MAX L. LUCADO (1955–   )

GOALS

4420 Ah, but a man's reach should exceed
   his grasp,
   Or what's a heaven for?
   ROBERT BROWNING (1812–1889)

4421 Climb every mountain, ford every
   stream,
   Follow every rainbow, 'til you find
   your dream.
   OSCAR HAMMERSTEIN (1895–1960)

4422 Everyone should have a goal for which
   he is willing to exchange a piece of his
   life.
   CARLYLE BOEHME

4423 If it's going to be, it's up to me.
   ROBERT HAROLD SCHULLER (1926–)

4424 It's not enough to be busy . . . the question is: What are we busy about?
   HENRY DAVID THOREAU (1817–1862)

4425 Jesus knew where he had come from,
   why he was here, and what he was
   supposed to accomplish. He came
   down from heaven, not to do his own
   will, but the will of the Father. That
   determination controlled every decision he made.
       As a result, he was not distracted
   with trivia. He was never in a hurry, for
   he knew his Father would not give a
   task without the time to do it. Christ
   was not driven by crises, feeling he must
   heal everyone in Israel. He could say, "It
   is finished," even when many people
   were still bound by demons and twisted
   by disease. What mattered ultimately
   was not the number of people healed or
   fed, but whether the Father's will was
   being done. His clearly defined goals
   simplified his decisions.
   ERWIN W. LUTZER (1941–)

4426 Life without a goal is like entering a
   jewel mine and coming out with
   empty hands.
   JAPANESE PROVERB

4427 More men fail through lack of purpose than through lack of talent.
   BILLY SUNDAY (1862–1935)

4428 My goal is God himself, not joy nor
   peace,
   Nor even blessing, but himself, my
   God;
   'Tis his to lead me there, not mine, but
   his—
   At any cost, dear Lord, by any road!
   F. BROOK

4429 Nothing is more terrible than activity
   without insight.
   THOMAS CARLYLE (1795–1881)

4430 Obstacles are those frightful things
   you see when you take your eyes off
   the goal.
   HANNAH MORE (1745–1833)

4431 One half of knowing what you want is
   knowing what you must give up
   before you get it.
   SIDNEY COE HOWARD (1891–1939)

4432 One ship drives east and another west,
   with the self-same winds that blow;
   'tis the set of the sails and not the gales
   that determines where they go.
   Like the winds of the sea are the ways
   of fate, as we voyage along through
   life;
   'tis the set of a soul that decides its
   goal—and not the calm or the strife.
   ELLA WHEELER WILCOX (1850–1919)

4433 Our plans miscarry because they have
   no aim. When a man does not know
   what harbor he is making for, no wind
   is the right wind.
   LUCIUS ANNAEUS SENECA (C. 4 B.C.–A.D. 65)

4434 The great thing in the world is not so
   much where we stand, as in what
   direction we are moving.
   OLIVER WENDELL HOLMES (1809–1894)

4435 The journey of a thousand miles
   begins with one step.
   LAO-TSE (C. 604–C. 531 B.C.)

4436 The man without a purpose is like a
   ship without a rudder—a waif, a nothing, a no man.
   THOMAS CARLYLE (1795–1881)

4437 The vast neurotic misery of the world
   could be termed a neuroses of emptiness. Men cut themselves off from the
   root of their being, from God, and
   then life turns empty, inane, meaningless, without purpose. So when God
   goes, goal goes. When goal goes,

meaning goes. When meaning goes, value goes, and life turns dead on our hands.
CARL GUSTAV JUNG (1875–1961)

4438 What is important is not where you come from but where you are going.
BERNIE RHODES

4439 Year by year we are becoming better equipped to accomplish the things we are striving for. But what are we actually striving for?
BERTRAND DE JOUVENAL (1903–   )

4440 You can't drive straight on a twisting lane.
RUSSIAN PROVERB

GOD

4441 'Tis God gives skill, but not without men's hands: he could not make Antonio Stradivari's violins without Antonio.
GEORGE ELIOT (1819–1880)

4442 A man can no more diminish God's glory by refusing to worship him than a lunatic can put out the sun by scribbling the word *darkness* on the walls of his cell.
C. S. LEWIS (1898–1963)

4443 Faith reposes on the character of God, and if we believe that God is perfect, we must conclude that his ways are perfect also.
A. W. TOZER (1897–1963)

4444 God builds the nest of the blind bird.
TURKISH PROVERB

4445 God delays but doesn't forget.
SPANISH PROVERB

4446 God does well what he does.
FRENCH PROVERB

4447 God doesn't care so much about being analyzed. Mainly, he wants to be loved.
PHILIP YANCEY (1949–   )

4448 God doesn't reveal his grand design. He reveals himself.
FREDERICK BUECHNER (1926–   )

4449 God feels the pulse and then prescribes the medicine.
ARABIAN PROVERB

4450 God gives every bird his food, but he does not throw it into the nest.
JOSIAH GILBERT HOLLAND (1819–1881)

4451 God gives his wrath by weight, and without weight, his mercy.

4452 God has no need of his creatures, but everything created has need of him.
MEISTER ECKHART (C. 1260–C. 1327)

4453 God has no stones to throw.
ARABIAN PROVERB

4454 God is a God of emotion, and if he observes mathematics, it is mathematics set to music, and his figures are written, not in white chalk on blackboards, but by a finger of sunlight on walls of jasmine and trumpet-creeper.
THOMAS DE WITT TALMAGE (1832–1902)

4455 God is beauty.
SAINT FRANCIS OF ASSISI (C. 1181–1226)

4456 God is never in a hurry, but he is always on time.

4457 God is the beyond in the midst of our life.
DIETRICH BONHOEFFER (1906–1945)

4458 God is the great reality. His resources are available and endless. His promises are real and glorious, beyond our wildest dreams.
J. B. PHILLIPS (1906–1982)

4459 God is the light in my darkness, the voice in my silence.
HELEN ADAMS KELLER (1880–1968)

4460 God is the silent partner in all great enterprises.
ABRAHAM LINCOLN (1809–1865)

4461 God is too kind to do anything cruel, too wise to make a mistake, too deep to explain himself.
CHARLES R. SWINDOLL (1934–   )

4462 God never tells us what he is going to do, he reveals who he is.
OSWALD CHAMBERS (1874–1917)

4463 God passes through the thicket of the world, and wherever his glance falls he turns all things to beauty.
SAINT JOHN OF THE CROSS (1542–1591)

4464 God squeezes but he never chokes.
MEXICAN PROVERB

4465 God the Father is both far away and near at hand; his voice is, at once, deafening in its thunderousness, and too still and small to be easily audible.
MALCOLM MUGGERIDGE (1903–1990)

4466 God wets you with his rain, but he also dries you with his sun.

4467 God who needs no one has in sovereign condescension stooped to work by and in and through his obedient children.
A. W. TOZER (1897–1963)

4468 God will inevitably appear to disappoint the man who is attempting to use him as a convenience, a prop, or a comfort for his own plans. God has never been known to disappoint the man who is sincerely wanting to cooperate with his own purposes.
J. B. PHILLIPS (1906–1982)

4469 God's creative method is movement, change, continuing search, ongoing inquiry. Those who seek are rewarded.
JOHN M. TEMPLETON

4470 God's promises are sealed to us, but not dated.
SUSANNA WESLEY (1669–1742)

4471 God's treasure is like an infinite ocean, and yet a little wave of emotion, passing with the moment, is enough for many.
BROTHER LAWRENCE OF THE RESURRECTION (C. 1605–1691)

4472 God: All other beings are distinguished by their shadow, but he is distinguished by his light.
JOSEPH JOUBERT (1754–1824)

4473 He demands so much that only he can supply what he demands!
ERWIN W. LUTZER (1941–)

4474 He is the poet of the world, with tender patience leading it by his vision of truth, beauty, and goodness.
ALFRED NORTH WHITEHEAD (1861–1947)

4475 He loses nothing who loses not God.

4476 He that so much for you did do,
Will do yet more.
THOMAS WASHBOURNE (1606–1687)

4477 His wisdom is sublime;
His heart profoundly kind;
God never is before his time
And never is behind.
J. J. LYNCH

4478 I do not find God hard to live with.
A. W. TOZER (1897–1963)

4479 If God is God, he's big and generous and magnificent.
J. B. PHILLIPS (1906–1982)

4480 If God lived on earth, people would break his windows.
JEWISH PROVERB

4481 In his will is our peace.
DANTE ALIGHIERI (1265–1321)

4482 In the vast and the minute we see
The unambiguous footsteps of the God,
Who gives its lustre to an insect's wing
And wheels his throne upon the whirling worlds.
WILLIAM COWPER (1731–1800)

4483 It takes all time and eternity to know God.
OSWALD CHAMBERS (1874–1917)

4484 Less is more. God is in the details.
MES VAN DER ROHE

4485 No rain, no mushrooms. No God, no world.
AFRICAN PROVERB

4486 Nothing in all creation is so like God as stillness.
MEISTER ECKHART (C. 1260–C. 1327)

4487 Only God can put the touch on something that changes it from the common place to something special, different, and apart.
R. C. SPROUL (1939–)

4488 Outside of God, there is nothing but nothing.
MEISTER ECKHART (C. 1260–C. 1327)

4489 People grow up with all sorts of notions of what God is like. They may see God as an Enemy, or a Policeman, or even an Abusive Parent. Or perhaps they do not see God at all and only hear his silence. Because of Jesus, however, we no longer have to wonder how God feels or what he is like.

When in doubt, we can look at Jesus to correct our blurry vision.
PHILIP YANCEY (1949–)

4490 Safe in Jehovah's keeping,
Safe in temptation's hour.
Safe in the midst of perils,
Kept by Almighty power.
Safe when the tempest rages,
Safe though the night be long;
E'en when my sky is darkest
God is my strength and song.
SIR ROBERT ANDERSON (1841–1918)

4491 Simply reading the Bible, I encountered not a misty vapor but an actual Person. A Person as unique and distinctive and colorful as any person I know. God has deep emotions; he feels delight and frustration and anger.
PHILIP YANCEY (1949–)

4492 The Almighty does nothing without reason, though the frail mind of man cannot explain the reason.
SAINT AUGUSTINE OF HIPPO (354–430)

4493 The characteristics of God Almighty are mirrored for us in Jesus Christ. Therefore if we want to know what God is like, we must study Jesus Christ.
OSWALD CHAMBERS (1874–1917)

4494 The Christian does not understand God in terms of love; he understands love in terms of God as seen in Christ.
JOSEPH FLETCHER

4495 The failure of rationalism is that it tries to find a place for God in its picture of the world. But God . . . is rather the canvas on which the picture is painted, or the frame in which it is set.
WILLIAM RALPH INGE (1860–1954)

4496 The favorite place of God is in the heart of man.
JEWISH PROVERB

4497 The finger of God never leaves identical fingerprints.
STANISLAW J. LEC (1909–1966)

4498 The hardness of God is kinder than the softness of men and his compulsion is our liberation.
C. S. LEWIS (1898–1963)

4499 The less theorizing you do about God the more receptive you are to his inpouring.
MEISTER ECKHART (C. 1260–C. 1327)

4500 The Lord may not come when you want him, but he's always going to be there on time.
LOU GOSSETT, JR.

4501 The rich man at his castle,
The poor man at his gate,
God made them, high or lowly,
And ordered their estate.
CECIL FRANCES ALEXANDER (1818–1895)

4502 The sun makes not the day, but thee.
SIR THOMAS BROWNE (1605–1682)

4503 The word *God* is a theology in itself, indivisibly one, inexhaustibly various.
CARDINAL JOHN HENRY NEWMAN (1801–1890)

4504 There are some again to whom the idea of a God perfect as they could imagine him in love and devotion and truth, seems, they say, too good to be true: such have not yet perceived that no God anything less than absolutely glorious in loveliness would be worth believing in, or such as the human soul could believe in.
GEORGE MACDONALD (1824–1905)

4505 There is a God! the sky his presence snares,
His hand upheaves the billows in their mirth,
Destroys the mighty, yet the humble spares
And with contentment crowns the thought of worth.
CHARLOTTE SAUNDERS CUSHMAN (1816–1876)

4506 There is in God, some say, a deep but dazzling darkness.
HENRY VAUGHAN (1622–1695)

4507 To accept the will of God never leads to the miserable feeling that it is useless to strive anymore. God does not ask for the dull, weak, sleepy acquiescence of indolence. He asks for something vivid and strong. He asks us to cooperate with him, actively willing what he wills, our only aim his glory.
AMY CARMICHAEL (1867–1951)

4508 To believe in God is to know that all
the rules will be fair—and that there
will be wonderful surprises!
SISTER CORITA

4509 We can seek God and find him! God is
knowable, touchable, hearable, seeable, with the mind, the hands, the
ears, and eyes of the inner man.
A. W. TOZER (1897–1963)

4510 Were the works of God readily understandable by human reason, they
would be neither wonderful nor
unspeakable.
THOMAS À KEMPIS (C. 1380–1471)

4511 What I believe about God is the most
important thing about me.
A. W. TOZER (1897–1963)

4512 What idea could we have of God without the sky?
GEORGE MACDONALD (1824–1905)

4513 What is impossible to God? Not that
which is difficult to his power, but that
which is contrary to his nature.
SAINT AMBROSE (C. 340–397)

4514 What then is God? Of the universe he
is the final end; as to election, he is salvation; as to himself, he hath knowledge. What is God? Omnipotent will,
virtue of highest benevolence, light
eternal, reason unchangeable, highest
blessedness; creator of minds to
receive of his own fulness, imparting
to them life to be conscious of him,
prompting them to desire him, enlarging them to receive him, fitting them
to be worthy of him, enkindling them
with zeal, aiding them to yield fruit,
directing them to equity, fashioning
them to benevolence, tempering them
for wisdom, strengthening them for
virtue, visiting them for consolation,
illuminating them for knowledge.
BERNARD OF CLAIRVAUX (1090–1153)

4515 When the need is highest, God is
nighest.
HEBREW PROVERB

4516 When we have nothing left but God,
then you become aware that God is
enough.
AGNES MAUDE ROYDEN (1876–1956)

4517 Where there is faith, there is love;
Where there is love, there is peace;
Where there is peace, there is God;
And where there is God, there is no
need.
LEO TOLSTOY (1828–1910)

4518 Wherever I go—only thou!
Wherever I stand—only thou!
Just thou; again thou; always thou!
Thou, thou, thou!
When things are good—thou!
When things are bad—thou! thou!
thou!
HASIDIC SONG

4519 Who has God, has all; who has him
not, has less than nothing.

4520 Why indeed must God be a noun?
Why not a verb—the most active and
dynamic of all?
MARY DALY (1928–   )

4521 Within one of his hours, God is able
to fulfill all his designs.
ARABIAN PROVERB

4522 Without God the world would be a
maze without a clue.
WOODROW WILSON (1856–1924)

4523 The God that holds you over the pit of
hell, much as one holds a spider, or
some loathsome insect over the fire,
abhors you, and is dreadfully provoked; his wrath toward you burns
like fire . . . he is of purer eyes than to
bear to have you in his sight; you are
ten thousand times more abominable
in his eyes, than the most hateful
venemous serpent is in ours. You have
offended him infinitely more than ever
a stubborn rebel did his prince; and
yet it is nothing but his hand that
holds you from falling into the fire
every moment.
JONATHAN EDWARDS (1703–1758)

GOD AND MAN

4524 A little from God is better than a great
deal from men. What is from men is
uncertain and is often lost and tumbled over and over by men; but what

is from God is fixed as a nail in a sure place.
JOHN BUNYAN (1628–1688)

4525 A wise old proverb says, "God comes to see us without a bell": that is, as there is no screen or ceiling between our heads and the infinite heavens, so is there no bar or wall in the soul, where man, the effect, ceases, and God, the cause, begins. The walls are taken away.
RALPH WALDO EMERSON (1803–1882)

4526 As I stand over the insect crawling amid the pine needles on the forest floor and endeavoring to conceal itself from my sight, and ask myself why it will cherish those humble thoughts and hide its head from me who might, perhaps, be its benefactor and impart to its race some cheering information, I am reminded of the greater Benefactor and Intelligence that stands over me the human insect.
HENRY DAVID THOREAU (1817–1862)

4527 Before we were born, God was God, the Lord God Almighty! He has never needed us. None of our human talents and abilities are significant to him. But he needs our love and wants our love!
A. W. TOZER (1897–1963)

4528 By his first work God gave me to myself; and by the next he gave himself to me. And when he gave himself, he gave me back myself that I had lost.
BERNARD OF CLAIRVAUX (1090–1153)

4529 Every soul belongs to God and exists by his pleasure. God being who and what he is, and we being who and what we are, the only thinkable relation between us is one of full lordship on his part and complete submission on ours. We owe him every honor that it is in our power to give him.
A. W. TOZER (1897–1963)

4530 Give me the greedy heart and the little creeping treasons,
Give me the proud heart and the blind, obstinate eyes;
Give me the shallow heart, and the vain lust, and the folly;

Give me the coward heart and the spiritless refusals;
Give me the confused self that you can do nothing with;
I can do something.
DOROTHY L. SAYERS (1893–1957)

4531 God and man exist for each other and neither is satisfied without the other.
A. W. TOZER (1897–1963)

4532 God bought man here with his heart's blood expense,
And man sold God here for base thirty pence.
ROBERT HERRICK (1591–1674)

4533 God can no more do without us than we can do without him.
MEISTER ECKHART (C. 1260–C. 1327)

4534 God comes padding after me like a Hound of Heaven.
MALCOLM MUGGERIDGE (1903–1990)

4535 God created man because God loves and wanted an object to love. He created man so that he could return his love.
BILLY GRAHAM (1918–   )

4536 God does all before he asks us to do anything; he redeems before he enjoins; and only the redeemed can truly keep his commandments.
R. W. BARBOUR (1900–   )

4537 God does not communicate things to us so much as he just is himself in us. We are the vessels, the containers, so that the first work after the new birth is to cultivate the habit of receptivity.
NORMAN GRUBB

4538 God does not die on the day when we cease to believe in a personal Deity, but we die on the day when our lives cease to be illumined by the steady radiance, renewed daily, of a wonder, the source of which is beyond all reason.
DAG HAMMARSKJÖLD (1905–1961)

4539 God does not expect us to imitate Jesus Christ. He expects us to allow the life of Jesus to be manifested.
OSWALD CHAMBERS (1874–1917)

4540 God has his own secret stairway into every heart.

4541 God himself is made rich by man's
necessity.
GEORGE MACDONALD (1824–1905)

4542 God is he without whom one cannot
live.
LEO TOLSTOY (1828–1910)

4543 God is not a cosmic bellboy for whom
we can press a button to get things.
HARRY EMERSON FOSDICK (1878–1969)

4544 God is to us like the sky to a small
bird, which cannot see its outer limits
and cannot reach its distant horizons,
but can only lose itself in the greatness
and immensity of the blueness.
JOHN POWELL

4545 God must love the common man; he
made so many of them.
ABRAHAM LINCOLN (1809–1865)

4546 God often visits us, but most of the
time we are not at home.
POLISH PROVERB

4547 God said, "Let us make man in our
image," and man said, "Let us make
God in our image."
DOUGLAS WILLIAM JERROLD (1803–1857)

4548 God to the blessed is an ever-joyful
guest
And to the damned he is a burden in
excess.
ANGELUS SILESIUS (1624–1677)

4549 God wants to come to his world, but
he wants to come to it through man.
This is the mystery of our existence,
the superhuman chance of mankind.
MARTIN BUBER (1878–1965)

4550 God will be our compensation for
every sacrifice we have made.
F. B. MEYER (1847–1929)

4551 Hollywood has not yet recognized
what truly tingles the spine, buckles
the knees, quakes the heart, and turns
bones into jelly. To meet God is a terrifying adventure.
TERRY LINDVALL

4552 If God does not know what is best for
us, who would?
ERWIN W. LUTZER (1941–   )

4553 If you say that man is too little for
God to speak to him, you must be
very big to be able to judge.
BLAISE PASCAL (1623–1662)

4554 In commanding us to glorify him, God
is inviting us to enjoy him.
C. S. LEWIS (1898–1963)

4555 It is your relationship to God which
fits you to live on the earth in the right
way, not necessarily the successful
way. Sometimes you will have the
worst of it for doing right.
OSWALD CHAMBERS (1874–1917)

4556 Job felt the hand of destruction upon
him, and he felt the hand of preservation too; and it was all one hand; this
is God's method, and his alone, to preserve by destroying.
JOHN DONNE (1572–1631)

4557 Let each man think himself an act of
God, his mind a thought of God, his
life a breath of God.
PHILIP JAMES BAILEY (1816–1902)

4558 Let us bring what is our own, God
will supply the rest.
SAINT JOHN CHRYSOSTOM (C. 347–407)

4559 Live near to God and so all things will
appear to you little in comparison
with eternal realities.
ROBERT MURRAY MCCHEYNE (1813–1843)

4560 Man calls it an accident; God calls it
an abomination. Man calls it a blunder; God calls it a blindness. Man calls
it a defect; God calls it a disease. Man
calls it a chance; God calls it a choice.
Man calls it an error; God calls it an
enmity. Man calls it a fascination; God
calls it a fatality. Man calls it an infirmity; God calls it an iniquity. Man
calls it a luxury; God calls it a leprosy.
Man calls it a liberty; God calls it lawlessness. Man calls it a trifle; God calls
it a tragedy. Man calls it a mistake;
God calls it a madness. Man calls it a
weakness; God calls it willfulness.

4561 My child, I have need of nothing. I
desire only your love. Give me this
first and whatever service may follow,
you will then do with light feet and a
heart set free.
FRANCES J. ROBERTS

4562 No man ever wanted anything so much as God wants to make the soul aware of him. God is ever ready, but we are so unready. God is in, we are out; God is at home, we are strangers.
MEISTER ECKHART (C. 1260–C. 1327)

4563 Of the building of life, God is the architect and man is the contractor. God has one plan and man has another. Is it strange that there are clashings and collisions?
HENRY WARD BEECHER (1813–1887)

4564 So necessary is our friendship to God that he approaches us and asks us to be his friends.
MEISTER ECKHART (C. 1260–C. 1327)

4565 The Engineer of the universe has made me part of his whole design.
LEIGH NYGARD

4566 The glory of God is man fully alive.
SAINT IRENAEUS (C. 130–C. 200)

4567 The highest standard God has is himself, and it is up to God to make a man as good as he is himself; and it is up to me to let him do it.
OSWALD CHAMBERS (1874–1917)

4568 The wrong concept of God leads to the wrong concept of sin, self, and salvation.
RICHARD OWEN ROBERTS (1931–)

4569 There is an Arm that never tires, When human strength gives way.
GEORGE MATHESON (1842–1906)

4570 Think of the enormous leisure of God! He never is in a hurry. We are in such a frantic hurry. We get down before God and pray, then we get up and say, "It is all done now," and in the light of the glory of the vision we go forth to do the thing. But it is not real, and God has to take us into the valley and put us through fires and floods to batter us into shape, until we get into the condition in which he can trust us with the reality of his recognition of us.
OSWALD CHAMBERS (1874–1917)

4571 To know man we must begin with God.
A. W. TOZER (1897–1963)

4572 Two men please God—who serves him with all his heart because he knows him; who seeks him with all his heart because he knows him not.
NIKITA IVANOVICH PANIN (1718–1783)

4573 We pursue God because, and only because, he has first put an urge within us that spurs us to the pursuit.
A. W. TOZER (1897–1963)

4574 What does God require? Everything!
ERWIN W. LUTZER (1941–)

4575 Whate'er we leave to God, God does And blesses us.
HENRY DAVID THOREAU (1817–1862)

4576 When God measures a man, he puts the tape around the heart, not the head.

4577 When he says to your disturbed, distracted, restless soul or mind, "Come unto me," he is saying, come out of the strife and doubt and struggle of what is at the moment where you stand, into that which was and is and is to be—the eternal, the essential, the absolute.
PHILLIPS BROOKS (1835–1893)

4578 God knows us through and through. Not the most secret thought, which we most hide from ourselves, is hidden from him. As then we come to know ourselves through and through, we come to see ourselves more as God sees us, and then we catch some little glimpse of his designs with us, how each ordering of his providence, each check to our desires, each failure of our hopes, is just fitted for us, and for something in our own spiritual state, which others know not of, and which, till then, we knew not. Until we come to this knowledge, we must take all in faith, believing, though we know not, the goodness of God toward us.
EDWARD BOUBERIE PUSEY (1800–1882)

GOD/ATTRIBUTES

4579 All of God's acts are consistent with all of his attributes. No attribute contradicts any other, but all harmonize and blend into each other in the infi-

nite abyss of the Godhead. All that God does agrees with all that God is, and being and doing are one in him. The familiar picture of God as often torn between his justice and his mercy is altogether false to the facts. To think of God as inclining first toward one and then toward another of his attributes is to imagine a God who is unsure of himself, frustrated and emotionally unstable, which of course is to say that the one of whom we are thinking is not the true God at all but a weak, mental reflection of him badly out of focus.
A. W. Tozer (1897–1963)

4580 All that which we call the attributes of God are only so many human ways of our conceiving that abyssal All which can neither be spoken nor conceived by us. And this way of thinking and speaking of God is suitable to our capacities, has its good use, and helps to express our adoration of him and his perfections. . . . Omnipotent love, inconceivable goodness, is that unity of God which we can neither conceive, as it is in itself, nor divide into this or that.
William Law (1686–1761)

4581 Do we want to contemplate his power? We see it in the immensity of the creation. Do we want to contemplate his wisdom? We see it in the unchangeable order by which the incomprehensible whole is governed. Do we want to contemplate his munificence? We see it in the abundance with which he fills the earth. Do we want to contemplate his mercy? We see it in his not withholding that abundance even from the unthankful.
Thomas Paine (1737–1809)

4582 God is spirit and to him magnitude and distance have no meaning. To us they are useful as analogies and illustrations, so God refers to them when speaking down to our limited understanding.
A. W. Tozer (1897–1963)

4583 If God is self-existent, he must be also self-sufficient; and if he has power, he,

being infinite, must have all power. If he possesses knowledge, his infinitude assures us that he possesses all knowledge. Similarly, his immutability presuppose his faithfulness. If he is unchanging, it follows that he could not be unfaithful, since that would require him to change. Any failure within the divine character would argue imperfection and, since God is perfect, it could not occur. Thus the attributes explain each other and prove that they are but glimpses the mind enjoys of the absolutely perfect Godhead.
A. W. Tozer (1897–1963)

4584 The attributes of God, though intelligible to us on their surface yet, for the very reason that they are infinite, transcend our comprehension, when they are dwelt upon, when they are followed out, and can only be received by faith.
Cardinal John Henry Newman (1801–1890)

4585 There are innumerable definitions of God because his manifestations are innumerable. They overwhelm me . . . stun me.
Mahatma Gandhi (1869–1948)

GOD/CHANGELESS

4586 All but God is changing day by day.
Charles Kingsley (1819–1875)

4587 God is not affected by our mutability; our changes do not alter him. When we are restless, he remains serene and calm; when we are low, selfish, mean, or dispirited, he is still the unalterable I Am. The same yesterday, today, and forever, in whom is no variableness, neither shadow of turning. What God is in himself, not what we may chance to feel him in this or that moment to be, that is our hope.
Frederick William Robertson (1816–1853)

4588 Let nothing disturb thee,
Let nothing affright thee.
All things are passing.
God never changes.

Patience gains all things.
Who has God wants nothing.
God alone suffices.
SAINT TERESA OF AVILA (1515–1582)

4589 The law of mutation belongs to a
fallen world, but God is immutable,
and in him men of faith find eternal
permanence.
A. W. TOZER (1897–1963)

4590 What peace it brings to the Christian's
heart to realize that our heavenly
Father never differs from himself. In
coming to him at any time we need
not wonder whether we shall find him
in a receptive mood. He is always
receptive to misery and need, as well
as to love and faith. He does not keep
office hours nor set aside periods
when he will see no one. Neither does
he change his mind about anything.
Today, this moment, he feels toward
his creatures, toward babies, toward
the sick, the fallen, the sinful, exactly
as he did when he sent his only begot-
ten Son into the world to die for mankind.
A. W. TOZER (1897–1963)

4591 With God, Abram's day and this day
are the same.
A. W. TOZER (1897–1963)

GOD/CREATOR

4592 A thousand worlds which roll around
us brightly,
Thee in their orbits bless;
Ten thousand suns which shine above
us nightly,
Proclaim thy righteousness.
Thou didst create the world—'twas
thy proud mandate
That woke it unto day;
And the same power that measured,
weighed, and spanned it,
Shall bid that world decay.
SIR JOHN BOWRING (1792–1872)

4593 All the vastness of astronomy—and
space—and systems of suns, carried in
their computation to the farthest that
figures are able, and then multiplied in
geometrical progression ten thousand
billion fold, do no more than symbol-

ize the reflection of the reflection, of
the spark thrown off a spark, from
some emanation of God.
MARK TWAIN (1835–1910)

4594 God's whole boundless and beautiful
world is the breath of one eternal idea,
the thought of one eternal God.
VISSARION GRIGOREVICH BELINSKI
(1811–1848)

4595 God: the uncreated Creator of everything.
SIMON GRUENBERG

4596 He paints the wayside flower,
He lights the evening star.
JANE MONTGOMERY CAMPBELL
(1817–1879)

4597 It is so impossible for the world to
exist without God that if God should
forget it, it would immediately cease
to be.
SØREN AABYE KIERKEGAARD (1813–1855)

4598 Thou dost preserve the stars from
wrong;
And the most ancient heavens,
through thee, are fresh and strong.
WILLIAM WORDSWORTH (1770–1850)

4599 To me it seems as if when God conceived the world, that was poetry; he
formed it, and that was sculpture; he
colored it, and that was painting; he
peopled it with living beings, and that
was the grand, divine, eternal drama.
EMMA STEBBINS (1816–1876)

GOD/ETERNITY

4600 God dwells in eternity, but time dwells
in God. He has already lived all our
tomorrows as he has lived all our yesterdays.
A. W. TOZER (1897–1963)

4601 God is and that not in time but in eternity, motionless, timeless, changeless
eternity, that has no before or after;
and being One, he fills eternity with
one now and so really is.
PLUTARCH (C. 46–AFTER 119)

4602 I cannot tell where God begins, still
less where he ends. But my belief is bet-

ter expressed if I say that there is no end to God's beginning.
ANDRÉ GIDE (1869–1951)

4603 I know nothing of his having created matter, bodies, spirits, or the world. The idea of creation confounds me and surpasses my conception, though I believe as much of it as I am able to conceive. But I know that God has formed the universe and all that exists, in the most consummate order. He is doubtless eternal, but I am incapacitated to conceive an idea of eternity. All that I can conceive is, that he existed before all things, that he exists with them and will exist after them, if they should ever have an end.
JEAN JACQUES ROUSSEAU (1712–1778)

4604 In God there is no was or will be, but a continuous and unbroken is. In him history and prophecy are one and the same.
A. W. TOZER (1897–1963)

4605 No age can heap its outward years on thee, dear God! Thou art, thyself, thine own eternity.
FREDERICK WILLIAM FABER (1814–1863)

GOD/EXISTENCE

4606 As the existence of hunger presupposes the existence of bread, and the existence of a fiddle that of music, so the longing for God and awareness of God which characterizes all these mystical experiences presupposes his existence.
MALCOLM MUGGERIDGE (1903–1990)

4607 Back of all, above all, before all is God; first in sequential order, above in rank and station, exalted in dignity and honor.
A. W. TOZER (1897–1963)

4608 Drop to your knees beside the wide road,
And pick up a stone to turn in your hand.
Now make one like it—seed of the earth—
Then if you succeed, tell me there's no God.
Take clay and dust, and fashion a child

With wistful brown eyes and breath in its lungs;
Make flesh-warm lips, a brain, and red blood—
Then, if you succeed, tell me there's no God.
CARRIE ESTHER HAMMILL

4609 God does not belong to the class of existing things . . . not that he has no existence, but that he is above all existing things, nay even above existence itself.
SAINT JOHN OF DAMASCUS (C. 700–C. 760)

4610 God exists in himself and of himself. His being he owes to no one. His substance is indivisible. He has no parts but is single in his unitary being.
A. W. TOZER (1897–1963)

4611 God is more truly imagined than expressed, and he exists more truly than is imagined.
SAINT AUGUSTINE OF HIPPO (354–430)

4612 God is within all things, but not included; outside all things, but not excluded; above all things, but not beyond their reach.
POPE GREGORY THE GREAT (540–604)

4613 *Origin* is a word that can apply only to things created. When we think of anything that has origin, we are not thinking of God. God is self-existent, while all created things necessarily originated somewhere at some time. Aside from God, nothing is self-caused.
A. W. TOZER (1897–1963)

4614 The human mind, being created, has an understandable uneasiness about the Uncreated. We do not find it comfortable to allow for the presence of One who is wholly outside of the circle of our familiar knowledge. We tend to be disquieted by the thought of One who does not account to us for his being, who is responsible to no one, who is self-existent, self-dependent, and self-sufficient.
A. W. TOZER (1897–1963)

GOD/FAITHFULNESS

4615 God does not desert those who serve him, even if they are called upon to give up all material wealth and a regular income.
PAUL TOURNIER (1898–1986)

4616 God's decree is the very pillar and basis on which the saints' perseverance depends. That decree ties the knot of adoption so fast, that neither sin, death, nor hell, can break it asunder.
THOMAS WATSON (C. 1557–1592)

4617 God's investment in us is so great he could not possibly abandon us.
ERWIN W. LUTZER (1941–)

4618 I looked up to the heavens once more, and the quietness of the stars seemed to reproach me. "We are safe up here," they seemed to say, "we shine, fearless and confident, for the God who gave the primrose its rough leaves to hide it from the blast of uneven spring, hangs us in the awful hollows of space. We cannot fall out of his safety. Lift up your eyes on high, and behold!"
GEORGE MACDONALD (1824–1905)

4619 If God maintains sun and planets in bright and ordered beauty he can keep us.
F. B. MEYER (1847–1929)

4620 In God's faithfulness lies eternal security.
CORRIE TEN BOOM (1892–1983)

4621 Let a man go away or come back: God never leaves. He is always at hand and if he cannot get into your life, still he is never farther away than the door.
MEISTER ECKHART (C. 1260–C. 1327)

4622 Lord, help me to remember that nothing is going to happen to me today that you and I cannot handle.

4623 Though Christians be not kept altogether from falling, yet they are kept from falling altogether.
WILLIAM SECKER (C. 1650)

4624 We do not seek God—God seeks us.
FREDERICK WILLIAM ROBERTSON (1816–1853)

4625 We plough the fields and scatter
The good seed on the land,
But it is fed and watered
By God's Almighty hand.
JANE MONTGOMERY CAMPBELL (1817–1879)

4626 When God calls a man, he does not repent of it. God does not, as many friends do, love one day, and hate another; or as princes, who make their subjects favorites, and afterwards throw them into prison. This is the blessedness of a saint; his condition admits of no alternation. God's call is founded upon his decree, and his decree is immutable. Acts of grace cannot be reversed. God blots out his people's sins, but not their names.
THOMAS WATSON (C. 1557–1592)

4627 When you are at the end of your rope, God is there to catch you—but not before.
ERWIN W. LUTZER (1941–)

4628 Whoever falls from God's right hand
Is caught into his left.
EDWIN MARKHAM (1852–1940)

GOD/FATHERHOOD

4629 Be content to be a child, and let the Father proportion out daily to thee what light, what power, what exercises, what straits, what fears, what troubles he sees fit for thee.
ISAAC PENINGTON (1616–1679)

4630 Our heavenly Father never takes anything from his children unless he means to give them something better.
GEORGE MUELLER

4631 The proper study of a Christian is the Godhead. The highest science, the loftiest speculation, the mightiest philosophy which can ever engage the attention of a child of God is the name, the person, the work, the doings, and the existence of the great God whom he calls his Father.
CHARLES HADDON SPURGEON (1834–1892)

4632 Trying to build the brotherhood of man without the fatherhood of God is

like trying to make a wheel without a hub.
IRENE DUNNE (1904–)

GOD/FORGIVENESS

4633 God does not wish us to remember what he is willing to forget.
GEORGE ARTHUR BUTTRICK (1892–1980)

4634 God will forgive me; that's his business.
HEINRICH HEINE (1797–1856)

4635 Our God has a big eraser.
BILLY ZEOLI

4636 Rock of Ages, cleft for me,
Let me hide myself in thee.
AUGUSTUS MONTAGUE TOPLADY
(1740–1778)

4637 The most marvelous ingredient in the forgiveness of God is that he also forgets, the one thing a human being can never do. Forgetting with God is a divine attribute; God's forgiveness forgets.
OSWALD CHAMBERS (1874–1917)

4638 When God pardons, he consigns the offense to everlasting forgetfulness.
MERV ROSELL

GOD/GOODNESS

4639 God is so good that he only awaits our desire to overwhelm us with the gift of himself.
FRANÇOIS FÉNELON (1651–1715)

4640 God knows best what is best. Why then should we question him?

4641 God's blessings steal into life noiselessly. They are neither self-proclaiming nor even self-announcing.
HENRY WARD BEECHER (1813–1887)

4642 I see the wrong that round me lies,
I feel the guilt within;
I hear, with groan and travail-cries,
The world confess its sin.
Yet, in the maddening maze of things,
And tossed by storm and flood,
To one fixed trust my spirit clings:
I know that God is good!
JOHN GREENLEAF WHITTIER (1807–1892)

4643 It is part of the kindness of God that amid all the change there are things we can always count on. The unfailing regularity of the seasons and the reliability of nature; the glory of the stars, the innocence of morning; the healing power of time and the sustaining power of hope; the heart's yearning for love and the soul's hunger for prayer; the endless quest for truth and the stubborn struggle for justice; the restless urge to create and the valiant will to overcome—these are some of the things we can count on. These are the things that hold in a slippery world.
SIDNEY GREENBERG

4644 The goodness of God knows how to use our disordered wishes and actions, often lovingly turning them to our advantage while always preserving the beauty of his order.
BERNARD OF CLAIRVAUX (1090–1153)

4645 The Infinite Goodness has such wide arms that it takes whatever turns to it.
DANTE ALIGHIERI (1265–1321)

4646 The Lord's goodness surrounds us at every moment. I walk through it almost with difficulty, as through thick grass and flowers.
R. W. BARBOUR (1900–)

4647 There are no days when God's fountain does not flow.
RICHARD OWEN ROBERTS (1931–)

4648 Think of how good God is! He gives us the physical, mental, and spiritual ability to work in his kingdom, and then he rewards us for doing it!
ERWIN W. LUTZER (1941–)

4649 To the frightened, God is friendly; to the poor in spirit, he is forgiving; to the ignorant, considerate; to the weak, gentle; to the stranger, hospitable.
A. W. TOZER (1897–1963)

GOD/GRACE

4650 God is no faultfinder, always looking for things to condemn in us. He estimates us at our best, not our worst.

4651 God's grace turns out men and women with a strong family likeness to Jesus Christ, not milksops.
OSWALD CHAMBERS (1874–1917)

4652 Grace is the good pleasure of God that inclines him to bestow benefits upon the undeserving. It is a self-existent principle inherent in the divine nature and appears to us as a self-caused propensity to pity the wretched, spare the guilty, welcome the outcast, and bring into favor those who were before under just disapprobation. Its use to us sinful men is to save us and makes us sit together in heavenly places to demonstrate to the ages the exceeding riches of God's kindness to us in Christ Jesus.
A. W. TOZER (1897–1963)

4653 Lord
I crawled
across the barrenness
to you
with my empty cup
uncertain
in asking
any small drop
of refreshment.
If only
I had known you
better
I'd have come
running
with a bucket.
NANCY SPIEGELBERG

4654 Man is born broken. He lives by mending. The grace of God is glue.
EUGENE GLADSTONE O'NEILL (1888–1953)

4655 Men may flee from the sunlight to dark and musty caves of the earth, but they cannot put out the sun. So men may in any dispensation despise the grace of God, but they cannot extinguish it.
A. W. TOZER (1897–1963)

4656 The grace of God is infinite and eternal. As it had no beginning, so it can have no end, and being an attribute of God, it is as boundless as infinitude.
A. W. TOZER (1897–1963)

GOD/HOLINESS

4657 God is compelled to conceal himself in a measure from the natural world, for the divine illumination would blind the eyes of mortal man were it to shine upon him in full strength.
L. S. THORNTON

4658 God is holy with an absolute holiness that knows no degrees, and this he cannot impart to his creatures. But there is a relative and contingent holiness which he shares with angels and seraphim in heaven and with redeemed men on earth as their preparation for heaven. This holiness God can and does impart to his children. He shares it with them by imputation and by impartation, and because he has made it available to them through the blood of the Lamb, he requires it of them.
A. W. TOZER (1897–1963)

4659 How dread are thine eternal years,
O everlasting Lord!
By prostrate spirits day and night
Incessantly adored!
How beautiful, how beautiful
The sight of thee must be,
Thine endless wisdom, boundless
power,
And awful purity!
FREDERICK WILLIAM FABER (1814–1863)

4660 It is not the constant thought of their sins, but the vision of the holiness of God that makes the saints aware of their own sinfulness.
ARCHBISHOP ANTHONY BLOOM (1914–)

4661 There is a danger of forgetting that the Bible reveals, not first the love of God, but the intense, blazing holiness of God, with his love as the center of that holiness.
OSWALD CHAMBERS (1874–1917)

GOD/INCOMPREHENSIBLE

4662 A comprehended God is no God at all.
GERHARD TERSTEEGEN (1697–1769)

4663 Do not try to imagine God, or you will have an imaginary God.
A. W. TOZER (1897–1963)

4664 God cannot come to me in any way
but his own way, and his way is often
insignificant and unobtrusive.
OSWALD CHAMBERS (1874–1917)

4665 God is beyond our ken—infinite,
immense, and his real greatness is
known to himself alone. Our mind is
too limited to understand him.
MARCUS M. FELIX

4666 God is more truly imagined than
expressed, and he exists more truly
than he is imagined.
SAINT AUGUSTINE OF HIPPO (354–430)

4667 God is the being . . . that may properly
only be addressed, not expressed.
MARTIN BUBER (1878–1965)

4668 God makes shoes upside down.
ARABIAN PROVERB

4669 God the Father is both far away and
near at hand; his voice is, at once, deafening in its thunderousness, and too
still and small to be easily audible.
MALCOLM MUGGERIDGE (1903–1990)

4670 God's actual divine essence and his
will, administration and works—are
absolutely beyond all human thought,
human understanding or wisdom; in
short, that they are and ever will be
incomprehensible, inscrutable, and
altogether hidden to human reason.
MARTIN LUTHER (1483–1546)

4671 God: That which has no definition.
JOSEPH ALBO (C. 1380–C. 1435)

4672 Hail, Father! Whose creating call
Unnumber'd worlds attend;
Jehovah! comprehending all,
Whom none can comprehend.
SAMUEL WESLEY (1691–1739)

4673 How can we little crawling creatures,
so utterly helpless as he has made us,
how can we possibly measure his greatness, his boundless love, his infinite
compassion, such that he allows man
insolently to deny him, wrangle about
him, and cut the throat of his fellowmen? How can we measure the greatness of God who is so forgiving, so
divine?
MAHATMA GANDHI (1869–1948)

4674 How haphazard God seems, not sometimes but always. God's ways turn
man's thinking upside down.
OSWALD CHAMBERS (1874–1917)

4675 If the mind of God as discovered to us
in his Word and works is so vast and
deep, what must his mind be in all its
undisclosed resources in the infinity
and eternity of its existence?
JOHN BATE (SEVENTEENTH CENTURY)

4676 In vain our haughty reason swells,
For nothing's found in thee
But boundless inconceivables
And vast eternity.
ISAAC WATTS (1674–1748)

4677 Incomprehensible? But because you
cannot understand a thing, it does not
cease to exist.
BLAISE PASCAL (1623–1662)

4678 Only God is permanently interesting.
Other things we may fathom, but he
outtops our thought and can neither
be demonstrated nor argued down.
JOSEPH FORT NEWTON (1880–1950)

4679 Only to our intellect is God incomprehensible; not to our love.
THE CLOUD OF UNKNOWING (1370)

4680 Our concepts of measurement
embrace mountains and men, atoms
and stars, gravity, energy, numbers,
speed, but never God. We cannot
speak of measure or amount or size or
weight and at the same time be speaking of God, for these tell of degrees
and there are no degrees in God. All
that he is he is without growth or addition or development.
A. W. TOZER (1897–1963)

4681 Our safest eloquence concerning him
is our silence, when we confess without confession that his glory is inexplicable, his greatness above our capacity
and reach.
RICHARD HOOKER (1554–1600)

4682 The element of paradox comes into all
religious thought and statement
because God cannot be comprehended
in any human words or in any of the
categories of our finite thought.
DONALD BAILLIE (1887–1854)

4683 The humility of God is a hard thing to accept and believe.
J. B. PHILLIPS (1906–1982)

4684 The infinity of God is not mysterious, it is only unfathomable—not concealed, but incomprehensible. It is a clear infinity—the darkness of the pure, unsearchable sea.
JOHN RUSKIN (1819–1900)

4685 Then alone do we know God truly, when we believe that God is far beyond all that we can possibly think of God.
SAINT THOMAS AQUINAS (1225–1274)

4686 There is ever a beyond of mystery; for the more we know, the more we wonder.
GEORGE TYRRELL (1861–1909)

4687 Though we can know that God is, we cannot know what God is.
SAINT AUGUSTINE OF HIPPO (354–430)

4688 We cannot always understand the ways of Almighty God—the crosses which he sends us, the sacrifices which he demands of us. . . . But we accept with faith and resignation his holy will with no looking back to what might have been, and we are at peace.
ROSE FITZGERALD KENNEDY (1890–)

4689 We demand proof of God, forgetting that if we could prove God he would be within the compass of our rationalities, and then our logical mind would be our own grotesque God.
GEORGE ARTHUR BUTTRICK (1892–1980)

4690 We know God but as men born blind know the fire, they know that there is such a thing as fire, for they feel it warm them, but what it is they know not. So, that there is a God we know, but what he is we know little, and indeed we can never search him out to perfection; a finite creature can never fully comprehend that which is infinite.
THOMAS MANTON (1620–1677)

4691 We know God easily, if we do not constrain ourselves to define him.
JOSEPH JOUBERT (1754–1824)

4692 What is God? The universal intelligence. What is God did I say? All that you see and all that you cannot see. His greatness exceeds the bounds of thought. He is all in all. He is at once within and without his works.
LUCIUS ANNAEUS SENECA (C. 4 B.C.–A.D. 65)

4693 You may know God, but not comprehend him.
RICHARD BAXTER (1615–1691)

GOD/INFINITE

4694 Before there was an earth at all, or sun, or stars in the splashed heavens, before matter came into being, for endless eternities before, as Genesis puts it in four initial words, "In the beginning God," he has seen kingdoms and civilizations and earths and solar systems rise and wane. He, and he alone, knows the secret of history, the meaning of the mystery called time. Shall he not know the hearts of men and women?
BERNARD IDDINGS BELL (1886–1958)

4695 God being who he is, the inheritance we receive from him is limitless—it is all of the universe.
A. W. TOZER (1897–1963)

4696 God has in himself all power to defend you, all wisdom to direct you, all mercy to pardon you, all grace to enrich you, all righteousness to clothe you, all goodness to supply you, and all happiness to crown you.
THOMAS BENTON BROOKS (1608–1680)

4697 God hears the footsteps of an ant.
MADAME JEANNE MARIE DE LA MOTHE GUYON (1648–1717)

4698 God is a light that is never darkened; an unwearied life that cannot die; a fountain always flowing; a garden of life; a seminary of wisdom; a radical beginning of all goodness.
FRANCIS QUARLES (1592–1644)

4699 God is ever giving to his children, yet has not less.
THOMAS WATSON (C. 1557–1592)

4700 God is greater than mind itself. His greatness cannot be conceived. Nay,

could we conceive of his greatness he would be less than the human mind which could form the conception. He is greater than all language, and no statement can express him.
ANTIPOPE NOVATIAN (D. 258)

4701 God is not in the slightest degree baffled or bewildered by what baffles and bewilders us . . . he is either a present help or he is not much help at all.
J. B. PHILLIPS (1906–1982)

4702 God's infinitude places him so far above our knowing that a lifetime spent in cultivating the knowledge of him leaves as much yet to learn as if we had never begun.
A. W. TOZER (1897–1963)

4703 Infinitude can belong to but One. There can be no second.
A. W. TOZER (1897–1963)

4704 Our minds do and always will emotionally speculate on the unknowable, on what lies behind nature, the mysterious and miraculous adjustment conditioning all things. We shall never know, never find out, and this it is which constitutes the "glory and poetry of God," just as the poetry and glory of our lives is that we do not know from moment to moment what is coming.
JOHN GALSWORTHY (1867–1933)

4705 The Infinite has sowed his name in the heavens in glowing stars, but on the earth . . . in tender flowers.
JOHANN PAUL FRIEDRICH RICHTER (1763–1825)

4706 The word *infinite* describes what is unique, it can have no modifiers. We do not say "more unique" or "very infinite." Before infinitude we stand silent.
A. W. TOZER (1897–1963)

4707 The world appears very little to a soul that contemplates the greatness of God.
BROTHER LAWRENCE OF THE RESURRECTION (C. 1605–1691)

4708 There is a glory which thou canst not see,

There is a music which thou canst not hear;
But if the spaces of Infinity
Unrolled themselves unto thine eye and ear,
Thou wouldst behold the crystal dome above
Lighted with living splendors, and the sound
Of their great voices uttering endless love
Would sink forever thro' the vast profound.
FREDERICK TENNYSON (1807–1898)

4709 To him no high, no low, no great, no small; he fills, he bounds, connects, and equals all.
ALEXANDER POPE (1688–1744)

4710 To say that God is infinite is to say that he is measureless. Measurement is the way created things have of accounting for themselves. It describes limitations, imperfections, and cannot apply to God. Weight describes the gravitational pull of the earth upon material bodies; distance describes intervals between bodies in space; length means extension in space, and there are other familiar measurements such as those for liquid, energy, sound, light, and numbers for pluralities. We also try to measure abstract qualities, and speak of great or little faith, high or low intelligence, large or meager talents. Is it not plain that all this does not and cannot apply to God? . . . He is above all this, outside of it, beyond it.
A. W. TOZER (1897–1963)

4711 What, but God? Inspiring God!
Who boundless Spirit all,
And unremitting Energy, pervades,
Adjusts, sustains, and agitates the whole.
JAMES THOMSON (1700–1748)

4712 Ye storms howl out his greatness; let your thunders roll like drums in the march of God's armies! Let your lightning write his name in fire on the midnight darkness; let the illimitable void of space become one mouth for song; and let the unnavigated ether, through its shoreless depths, bear through the

infinite remote the name of him whose goodness endureth forever!
CHARLES HADDON SPURGEON (1834–1892)

GOD/JUDGE

4713 God judges a man, not by the point he has reached, but by the way he is facing; not by distance, but by direction.
JAMES S. STEWART (1896–)

4714 God will not look you over for medals, degrees, or diplomas, but for scars.
ELBERT GREEN HUBBARD (1856–1915)

4715 He has sounded forth the trumpet that shall never call retreat
He is sifting out the hearts of men before his judgment seat.
JULIA WARD HOWE (1819–1910)

4716 Heaven is above all yet; there sits a judge
That no king can corrupt.
WILLIAM SHAKESPEARE (1564–1616)

4717 If God dealt with people today as he did in the days of Ananias and Sapphira, every church would need a morgue in the basement.
VANCE HAVNER

4718 In the day when all men will stand before God, the significant question for each of us will no longer be what we think of Christ, but what he thinks of us.
ELVA J. HOOVER

4719 Jesus, thy blood and righteousness
My beauty are, my glorious dress;
'Midst flaming worlds, in these arrayed,
With joy shall I lift up my head.
Bold shall I stand in thy great day;
For who aught to my charge shall lay?
Fully absolved through these I am—
From sin and fear, from guilt and shame.
COUNT NIKOLAUS LUDWIG
VON ZINZENDORF (1700–1760)

4720 Nobody can judge men but God, and we can hardly obtain a higher or more reverent view of God than that which represents him to us as judging men with perfect knowledge, unperplexed certainty, and undisturbed compassion.
FREDERICK WILLIAM FABER (1814–1863)

4721 The judgment of God is the reaping that comes from sowing and is evidence of the love of God, not proof of his wrath. The penalty of an evil harvest is not God's punishment; it is the consequence of defying the moral order which in love he maintains as the only environment in which maturity of fellowship and communion can be achieved.
KIRBY PAGE (1890–1957)

GOD/JUSTICE

4722 Even God attributes to himself avarice, jealousy, anger; and these are virtues as well as kindness, pity, constancy.
BLAISE PASCAL (1623–1662)

4723 God of all mercy is a God unjust.
EDWARD YOUNG (1683–1765)

4724 God's compassion flows out of his goodness, and goodness without justice is not goodness. God spares us because he is good, but he could not be good if he were not just.
A. W. TOZER (1897–1963)

4725 God's justice and love are one. Infinite justice must be infinite love.
FREDERICK WILLIAM ROBERTSON
(1816–1853)

4726 God's justice stands forever against the sinner in utter severity. The vague and tenuous hope that God is too kind to punish the ungodly has become a deadly opiate for the consciences of millions. It hushes their fears and allows them to practice all pleasant forms of iniquity while death draws every day nearer and the command to repent goes unregarded. As responsible moral beings we dare not so trifle with our eternal future.
A. W. TOZER (1897–1963)

4727 God: A leveler, who renders equal small and great.
JOHANAN HACOHEN

4728 If his justice were such as could be
adjudged just by human reckoning, it
clearly would not be divine; it would
in no way differ from human justice.
But inasmuch as he is the one true
God, wholly incomprehensible and
inaccessible to man's understanding, it
is reasonable, indeed inevitable, that
his justice also should be incomprehensible.
MARTIN LUTHER (1483–1546)

4729 Not only is it right for God to display
anger against sin, I find it impossible
to understand how he could do otherwise.
A. W. TOZER (1897–1963)

4730 Redemptive theology teaches that
mercy does not become effective
toward a man until justice has done its
work.
A. W. TOZER (1897–1963)

GOD/KINGDOM

4731 Everyone wants the kingdom of God,
but few want it first. Everyone wants
high achievement, but few want to pay
the price. Everyone wants God, but
few want to put him first.
CHARLES L. VENABLE

4732 If only we knew how to look at life as
God sees it, we should realize that
nothing is secular in the world, but
that everything contributes to the
building of the kingdom of God.
MICHEL QUOIST (1921–)

4733 In the kingdom of God the surest way
to lose something is to try to protect
it, and the best way to keep it is to let
it go.
A. W. TOZER (1897–1963)

4734 The kingdom of God does not exist
because of your effort or mine. It
exists because God reigns. Our part is
to enter this kingdom and bring our
life under his sovereign will.
T. Z. KOO

4735 When we seek first the kingdom of
God and righteousness, fulfillment
comes as a by-product of our love for
God. And that satisfaction is better

than we ever imagined. God can make
the pieces of this world's puzzle fit
together; he helps us view the world
from a new perspective.
ERWIN W. LUTZER (1941–)

4736 Wherever God rules over the human
heart as King, there is the kingdom of
God established.
PAUL W. HARRISON

GOD/KNOWLEDGE

4737 Acquaint thyself with God,
If thou wouldst taste His works.
Admitted once to his embrace,
Thou shalt perceive that thou wast
blind before.
WILLIAM COWPER (1731–1800)

4738 God cannot be found by thought; he
can only be known through his own
manifestation of himself, and in this
he shows himself to be the absolute
mystery, who can be understood only
through his own self-revelation.
EMIL BRUNNER (1889–1966)

4739 God is not discoverable or demonstrable by purely scientific means, unfortunately for the scientifically-minded.
But that really proves nothing. It simply means that the wrong instruments
are being used for the job.
J. B. PHILLIPS (1906–1982)

4740 God would not be God if he could be
fully known to us, and God would not
be God if he could not be known at all.
H. G. WOOD

4741 It is in silence that God is known, and
through mysteries that he declares himself.
ROBERT H. BENSON (1871–1914)

4742 Nothing will so enlarge the intellect,
nothing so magnify the whole soul of
man, as a devout, earnest, continued
investigation of the great subject of the
Deity.
CHARLES HADDON SPURGEON (1834–1892)

4743 That God can be known by the soul in
tender personal experience while
remaining infinitely aloof from the
curious eyes of reason constitutes a
paradox best described as:

Darkness to the intellect
But sunshine to the heart.
                        —Frederick W. Faber
A. W. TOZER (1897–1963)

4744 The yearning to know what cannot be
known, to comprehend the incomprehensible, to touch and taste the unapproachable, arises from the image of
God in the nature of man. Deep
calleth unto deep, and though polluted
and landlocked by the mighty disaster
theologians call the Fall, the soul
senses its origin and longs to return to
its source.
A. W. TOZER (1897–1963)

4745 There is something exceedingly
improving to the mind in a contemplation of the Divinity. It is a subject so
vast, that all our thoughts are lost in
its immensity; so deep, that our pride
is drowned in its infinity. Other subjects we can compass and grapple
with; in them we feel a kind of self-
content and go our way with the
thought, *Behold, I am wise.* But when
we come to this master-science, finding that our plumb line cannot sound
its depth, and that our eagle eye cannot see its height, we turn away with
the thought that vain man would be
wise, but he is like a wild ass's colt;
and with solemn exclamation, "I am
but of yesterday, and know nothing."
No subject of contemplation will tend
more to humble the mind than
thoughts of God.
CHARLES HADDON SPURGEON (1834–1892)

4746 Who knows? God knows and what he
   knows
Is well and best.
The darkness hideth not from him, but
   glows
Clear as the morning or the evening
   rose
Of east or west.
CHRISTINA GEORGINA ROSSETTI
(1830–1894)

GOD/LOVE

4747 As for that which is beyond your
strength, be absolutely certain that our
Lord loves you, devotedly and individually, loves you just as you are. . . .
Accustom yourself to the wonderful
thought that God loves you with a tenderness, a generosity, and an intimacy
that surpasses all your dreams. Give
yourself up with joy to a loving confidence in God and have courage to
believe firmly that God's action
toward you is a masterpiece of partiality and love. Rest tranquilly in this
abiding conviction.
ABBE HENRI DE TOURVILLE (1842–1903)

4748 Could we with ink the ocean fill,
And were the heav'ns of parchment
   made,
Were every stalk on earth a quill,
And every man a scribe by trade,
To write the love of God above
Would drain the ocean dry,
Nor could the scroll contain the whole,
Though stretch'd from sky to sky.
CHALDEE ODE

4749 Even here and now, whenever the
heart begins to burn with a desire for
God, she is made able to receive the
uncreated light and, inspired and fulfilled by the gifts of the Holy Ghost,
she tastes the joys of heaven. She transcends all visible things and is raised
to the sweetness of eternal life. . . .
Herein truly is perfect love; when all
the intent of the mind, all the secret
working of the heart, is lifted up into
the love of God.
RICHARD ROLLE OF HAMPOLE
(C. 1300–1349)

4750 From God's other known attributes
we may learn much about his love. We
can know, for instance, that because
God is self-existent, his love had no
beginning; because he is eternal, his
love can have no end; because he is
infinite, it has no limit; because he is
holy, it is the quintessence of all spotless purity; because he is immense, his
love is an incomprehensibly vast, bottomless, shoreless sea before which we
kneel in joyful silence and from which
the loftiest eloquence retreats confused
and abashed.
A. W. TOZER (1897–1963)

4751 God carries your picture in his wallet.
TONY CAMPOLO

4752 God does not love us because we are
valuable. We are valuable because
God loves us.
ARCHBISHOP FULTON J. SHEEN (1895–1979)

4753 God hugs you.
SAINT HILDEGARDE OF BINGEN
(1098–1179)

4754 God is love and God is sovereign. His
love disposes him to desire our everlasting welfare, and his sovereignty
enables him to secure it.
A. W. TOZER (1897–1963)

4755 God is love, not, God is loving. God
and love are synonymous. Love is not
an attribute of God, it is God; whatever God is, love is. If your conception
of love does not agree with justice and
judgment and purity and holiness,
then your idea of love is wrong.
OSWALD CHAMBERS (1874–1917)

4756 God loves each of us as if there were
only one of us.
SAINT AUGUSTINE OF HIPPO (354–430)

4757 God soon turns from his wrath, but he
never turns from his love.
CHARLES HADDON SPURGEON (1834–1892)

4758 God! Thou art love! I build my faith
on that!
I know thee, thou hast kept my path
and made
Light for me in the darkness—temper-
ing sorrow,
So that it reached me like a solemn joy;
It were too strange that I should doubt
thy love.
ROBERT BROWNING (1812–1889)

4759 God's love for us is proclaimed with
each sunrise.

4760 God's love is measureless. It is more: it
is boundless. It has no bounds because
it is not a thing but a facet of the essential nature of God. His love is something he is, and because he is infinite,
that love can enfold the whole created
world in itself and have room for ten
thousand times ten thousand worlds
beside.
A. W. TOZER (1897–1963)

4761 He paints the lily of the field,
Perfumes each lily bell;
If he so loves the little flowers,
I know he loves me well.
MARIA STRAUS

4762 Human beings must be known to be
loved, but divine things must be loved
to be known.
BLAISE PASCAL (1623–1662)

4763 I know not where his islands lift
Their fronded palms in air;
I only know I cannot drift
Beyond his love and care.
JOHN GREENLEAF WHITTIER (1807–1892)

4764 I know what you look like. I know
your past. I know your future. I know
your thoughts, even those you try persistently to hide. And you know what?
I love you because you're mine.
STEVE GOODIER

4765 If God loved you as much as you love
him, where would you be?

4766 If literally God is love, then literally
love is God, and we are in all duty
bound to worship love as the only
God there is. If love is equal to God,
then God is only equal to love, and
God and love are identical. Thus we
destroy the concept of personality in
God and deny outright all his attributes save one, and that one we substitute for God.
A. W. TOZER (1897–1963)

4767 If we have got the true love of God
shed abroad in our hearts, we will
show it in our lives. We will not have
to go up and down the earth proclaiming it. We will show it in everything
we say or do.
DWIGHT LYMAN MOODY (1837–1899)

4768 If we need something to buttress us in
the inevitable struggles of life, there is
nothing that can help us more than the
conviction that each one of us is
sought by him who made the Pleiades
and Orion, that each of us is truly
known as no finite men can ever know
us, and that, in spite of our feebleness
and sin, we can become channels of
God's universal love.
D. ELTON TRUEBLOOD (1900–   )

4769 In the very beginning, when this great universe lay in the mind of God, like unborn forests in the acorn-cup; long ere the echoes waked the solitudes, before the mountains were brought forth, and long ere the light flashed through the sky, God loved his chosen creatures.
CHARLES HADDON SPURGEON (1834–1892)

4770 It is but right that our hearts should be on God, when the heart of God is so much on us.
RICHARD BAXTER (1615–1691)

4771 It is the heart which experiences God and not the reason.
BLAISE PASCAL (1623–1662)

4772 Measure not God's love and favor by your own feeling. The sun shines as clearly in the darkest day as it does in the brightest. The difference is not in the sun, but in some clouds.
RICHARD SIBBS (1577–1635)

4773 None of us feels the true love of God till we realize how wicked we are. But you can't teach people that—they have to learn by experience.
DOROTHY L. SAYERS (1893–1957)

4774 Nor can we fall below the arms of God, how lowsoever it be we fall.
WILLIAM PENN (1644–1718)

4775 Nor will God force any door to enter in. He may send a tempest about the house; the wind of his admonishment may burst doors and windows, yea, shake the house to its foundations; but not then, not so, will he enter. The door must be opened by the willing hand ere the foot of Love will cross the threshold. He watches to see the door move from within. Every tempest is but an assault in the siege of love. The terror of God is but the other side of his love; it is love outside, that would be inside—love that knows the house is no house, only a place, until it enter.
GEORGE MACDONALD (1824–1905)

4776 O love of God, how deep and great. Far deeper than man's deepest hate.
CORRIE TEN BOOM (1892–1983)

4777 On the whole, God's love for us is a much safer subject to think about than our love for him. Nobody can always have devout feelings; and even if we could, feelings are not what God principally cares about. Christian love, either toward God or toward man, is an affair of the will. But the great thing to remember is that, though our feelings come and go, his love for us does not.
C. S. LEWIS (1898–1963)

4778 One of the greatest evidences of God's love to those who love him is to send them grace to bear afflictions.

4779 Our only warrant for believing that God cares is that he has communicated this fact to us. It is the key fact about himself which he has chosen to reveal to us, and it is the most comforting fact imaginable.
LOUIS CASSELS (1922–1974)

4780 The love of God is no mere sentimental feeling; it is redemptive power.
CHARLES CLAYTON MORRISON (1874–1966)

4781 The love of God, with arms extended on a cross, bars the way to hell. But if that love is ignored, rejected, and finally refused, there comes a time when love can only weep while man pushes past into the self-chosen alienation which Christ went to the cross to avert.
MICHAEL GREEN (1930–)

4782 The only way God's love makes sense is when it is seen as personal (not mechanical). He doesn't start your stalled car for you; but he comes and sits with you in the snowbank.
ROBERT F. CAPON

4783 The rock of the divine love is deeper down than the human buildings that have been reared upon it.
ALEXANDER MACLAREN (1826–1910)

4784 The springs of love are in God, not in us. It is absurd to look for the love of God in our hearts naturally, it is only there when it has been shed abroad in our hearts by the Holy Spirit.
OSWALD CHAMBERS (1874–1917)

4785 There is no need to plead that the love of God shall fill our heart as though he were unwilling to fill us. He is willing as light is willing to flood a room that is opened to its brightness; willing as water is willing to flow into an emptied channel. Love is pressing round us on all sides like air. Cease to resist, and instantly love takes possession.
AMY CARMICHAEL (1867–1951)

4786 There is nothing you can do to make God love you more! There is nothing you can do to make God love you less! His love is unconditional, impartial, everlasting, infinite, perfect! God is love!

4787 This, this is the God we adore,
Our faithful, unchangeable friend.
Whose love is as great as his power,
And neither knows measure nor end.
JOSEPH HART

4788 We have a God who loves. That means that we have a God who suffers.
J. B. PHILLIPS (1906–1982)

4789 We sometimes fear to bring our troubles to God, because they must seem so small to him who sitteth on the circle of the earth. But if they are large enough to vex and endanger our welfare, they are large enough to touch his heart of love. For love does not measure by a merchant's scales, nor with a surveyor's chain. It has a delicacy which is unknown in any handling of material substances.
R. A. TORREY (1856–1928)

4790 While he strips of everything the souls who give themselves absolutely to him, God gives them something which takes the place of all: his love.
JEAN PIERRE DE CAUSSADE (1675–1751)

4791 Who falls for love of God shall rise a star.
BEN JONSON (1572–1637)

4792 You asked for a loving God; you have one. The great spirit you so lightly invoked, the "lord of terrible aspect," is present; not a senile benevolence that drowsily wishes you to be happy in your own way, not the cold philanthropy of a conscientious magistrate, nor the care of a host who feels responsible for the comfort of his guests, but the consuming fire himself, the Love that made the worlds, persistent as the artist's love for his work and despotic as a man's love for a dog, provident and venerable as a father's love for a child, jealous, inexorable, exacting as love between the sexes.
C. S. LEWIS (1898–1963)

GOD/LOVE FOR

4793 A man's spiritual health is exactly proportional to his love for God.
C. S. LEWIS (1898–1963)

4794 How beautiful, how beautiful
The sight of thee must be,
Thine endless wisdom, boundless power,
And awful purity!
FREDERICK WILLIAM FABER (1814–1863)

4795 I love thee so, I know not how
My transport to control;
Thy love is like a burning fire
Within my very soul.
FREDERICK WILLIAM FABER (1814–1863)

4796 I love, my God, but with no love of mine,
For I have none to give;
I love thee, Lord, but all the love is thine,
For by thy love I live.
MADAME JEANNE MARIE DE LA MOTHE GUYON (1648–1717)

4797 It is always springtime in the heart that loves God.
SAINT JEAN BAPTISTE MARIE VIANNEY (1786–1859)

4798 Love thy God and love him only
And thy breast will ne'er be lonely.
AUBREY THOMAS DE VERE (1814–1902)

4799 Only to sit and think of God,
Oh what a joy it is!
To think the thought, to breathe the name
Earth has no higher bliss.
FREDERICK WILLIAM FABER (1814–1863)

4800 Our love for God is tested by the question of whether we seek him or his gifts.
RALPH WASHINGTON SOCKMAN (1889–1970)

4801 Some people want to see God with their eyes as they see a cow and to love him as they love their cow—they love their cow for the milk and cheese and profit it makes them. This is how it is with people who love God for the sake of outward wealth or inward comfort. They do not rightly love God when they love him for their own advantage. Indeed, I tell you the truth, any object you have on your mind, however good, will be a barrier between you and the inmost truth.
MEISTER ECKHART (C. 1260–C. 1327)

4802 The living God, the human God, is reached, not by the way of reason, but by the way of love and of suffering. It is not possible to know him in order that afterwards we may love him; we must begin by loving him, longing for him, hungering for him, before knowing him.
MIGUEL DE UNAMUNO (1864–1936)

4803 The man who does not love God is really in love with himself, his position, his success, his pleasure. He may be lucky or unlucky, but by no conceivable effort can he accept all that life may bring and turn it to good account. For it may bring him failure and disappointment, ill-health and loss, and "what will the robin do then, poor thing?"
    The man who loves God is in an unassailable position. He has surrendered his own plans to the greater permanent plan of God, the responsibility for which is God's. He asks no favors of God but he does ask for the guiding and the strength of God that, through him, God's will may be achieved. There is nothing now that can happen which cannot be turned into good for him.
J. B. PHILLIPS (1906–1982)

4804 This I know is God's own truth, that pain and troubles and trials and sorrows and disappointments are either

one thing or another. To all who love God they are love tokens from him. To all who do not love God and do not want to love him they are merely a nuisance. Every single pain that we feel is known to God because it is the most loving touch of his hand.
EDWARD ADRIAN WILSON (1872–1912)

4805 Too late loved I thee, O thou Beauty of ancient days, yet ever new! Too late I loved thee! And behold thou wert within, and I abroad, and there I searched for thee; deformed as I was, running after those beauties which thou hast made. Thou wert with me, but I was not with thee. Things held me far from thee—things which, unless they were in thee, were not at all. Thou calledst and shoutedst and didst pierce my deafness. Thou flashedst and shonest and didst dispel my blindness. Thou didst send forth thy fragrance, and I drew in breath and panted for thee. I tasted, and still I hunger and thirst. Thou touchedst me, and I burned for thy peace.
SAINT AUGUSTINE OF HIPPO (354–430)

4806 We must repudiate this great, modern wave of seeking God for his benefits. The sovereign God wants to be loved for himself and honored for himself, but that is only part of what he wants. The other part is that he wants us to know that when we have him, we have everything—we have all the rest.
A. W. TOZER (1897–1963)

4807 We ought to love our Maker for his own sake, without either hope of good or fear of pain.
MIGUEL DE CERVANTES (1547–1616)

GOD/MERCY

4808 God doesn't always smooth the path, but sometimes he puts springs in the wagon.
MARSHALL LUCAS

4809 God excludes none, if they do not exclude themselves.
WILLIAM GUTHRIE (1620–1665)

4810 God expects of us only what he has himself first supplied. He is quick to

mark every simple effort to please him, and just as quick to overlook imperfections when he knows we meant to do his will.
A. W. TOZER (1897–1963)

4811 God giveth his wrath by weight, but his mercy without measure.
SIR THOMAS FULLER (1608–1661)

4812 God hath two wings, which he doth ever move,
The one is mercy, and the next is love;
Under the first the sinners ever trust,
And with the last he still directs the just.
ROBERT HERRICK (1591–1674)

4813 God in his mercy made
The fixed pains of hell.
That misery might be stayed,
God in his mercy made
Eternal bounds and bade
Its waves no further swell.
God in his mercy made
The fixed pains of hell.
C. S. LEWIS (1898–1963)

4814 God works powerfully, but for the most part gently and gradually.
JOHN NEWTON (1725–1807)

4815 God's mercy is boundless, free and, through Jesus Christ our Lord, available to us now in our present situation.
A. W. TOZER (1897–1963)

4816 O God, your mercy is a boundless ocean,
A mere drop suffices for me!
SHARAFUDDIN MANERI
(FOURTEENTH CENTURY)

4817 Our faults are like a grain of sand beside the great mountain of the mercies of God.
SAINT JEAN BAPTISTE MARIE VIANNEY
(1786–1859)

4818 The hardness of God is kinder than the softness of men, and his compulsion is our liberation.
C. S. LEWIS (1898–1963)

4819 When all thy mercies, O my God,
My rising soul surveys,
Transported with the view, I'm lost
In wonder, love, and praise.
JOSEPH ADDISON (1672–1719)

GOD/OMNIPOTENCE

4820 Events of all sorts creep or fly exactly as God pleases.
WILLIAM COWPER (1731–1800)

4821 God has delegated power to his creatures, but being self-sufficient, he cannot relinquish anything of his perfections, and power being one of them, he has never surrendered the least iota of his power. He gives, but he does not give away. All that he gives remains his own and returns to him again. Forever he must remain what he has forever been, the Lord God omnipotent.
A. W. TOZER (1897–1963)

4822 God is never defeated. Though he may be opposed, attacked, resisted, still the ultimate outcome can never be in doubt.
FATHER ANDREW

4823 God's problem is not that God *is not able* to do certain things. God's problem is that God loves. Love complicates the life of God as it complicates every life.
DOUGLAS JOHN HALL

4824 Great as is the power of God, he cannot work in a vacuum or with empty minds or with hearts filled with prejudice.
JAMES MOFFATT (1811–1890)

4825 I recognize
Power passing mine, immeasurable, God.
ROBERT BROWNING (1812–1889)

4826 If we take God's program we can have God's power—not otherwise.
E. STANLEY JONES (1884–1973)

4827 Loud o'er my head, though awful thunders roll,
And vivid lightings flash from pole to pole,
Yet 'tis thy voice, my God, that bids them fly,
Thy arm directs those lightnings through the sky.
SIR WALTER SCOTT (1771–1832)

4828 Nothing, therefore, happens unless the Omnipotent wills it to happen; he

either permits it to happen, or he brings it about himself.
SAINT AUGUSTINE OF HIPPO (354–430)

4829 The church cannot increase God's power, but she can limit it.
WATCHMAN NEE (1903–1972)

4830 We impoverish God's ministry to us the moment we forget he is Almighty; the impoverishment is in us, not in him.
OSWALD CHAMBERS (1874–1917)

4831 Were it not good that evil things should also exist, the omnipotent God would most certainly not allow evil to be. It is just as easy for him not to allow what he does not will, as it is for him to do what he will.
SAINT AUGUSTINE OF HIPPO (354–430)

GOD/OMNIPRESENCE

4832 A philosopher once asked, "Where is God?" The Christian answered, "Let me first ask you, where is he not?"
JOHN ARROWSMITH

4833 A sense of deity is inscribed on every heart.
JOHN CALVIN (1509–1564)

4834 Among so many, can he care?
Can special love be everywhere?
A myriad homes—a myriad ways,
And God's eye over every place?
I asked, my soul bethought of this;
In just that very place of his
Where he hath put and keepeth you,
God hath no other thing to do!
A. D. T. WHITNEY

4835 Begin where we will, God is there first.
A. W. TOZER (1897–1963)

4836 Fountain of life, and all-abounding grace,
Our source, our center, and our dwelling place!
MADAME JEANNE MARIE DE LA MOTHE GUYON (1648–1717)

4837 God comes at last when we think he is farthest off.

4838 God comes to see without ringing the doorbell.
SPANISH PROVERB

4839 God far more dwells in me than if the entire sea
Would in a tiny sponge wholly contained be.
ANGELUS SILESIUS (1624–1677)

4840 God in me, God without! Beyond compare!
A being wholly here and wholly there!
ANGELUS SILESIUS (1624–1677)

4841 God is above, presiding; beneath, sustaining; within, filling.
HILDEBERT OF LAVARDIN (1056–1133)

4842 God is an infinite circle whose center is everywhere and whose circumference is nowhere.
SAINT AUGUSTINE OF HIPPO (354–430)

4843 God is an utterable sigh, planted in the depths of the soul.
JOHANN PAUL FRIEDRICH RICHTER (1763–1825)

4844 God is as present as the air.
MICHAEL HOLLINGS

4845 God is in all things and in every place. There is not a place in the world in which he is not most truly present. Just as birds, wherever they fly, always meet with the air, so we, wherever we go, or wherever we are, always find God present.
SAINT FRANCIS OF SALES (1567–1622)

4846 God is inescapable. He is God only because he is inescapable. And only that which is inescapable is God . . . It is safe to say that a man who has never tried to flee God has never experienced the God who is really God. . . . A god whom we can easily bear, a god from whom we do not have to hide, a god whom we do not hate in moments, a god whose destruction we never desire, is not God at all and has no reality.
PAUL JOHANNES OSKAR TILLICH (1886–1965)

4847 God is not a supernatural interferer; God is the everlasting portion of his people. When a man born from above begins his new life, he meets God at every turn, hears him in every sound, sleeps at his feet, and wakes to find him there.
OSWALD CHAMBERS (1874–1917)

4848 God is over all things, under all things, outside all, within, but not enclosed, without, but not excluded, above, but not raised up, below, but not depressed, wholly above, presiding, wholly without, embracing, wholly within, filling.
HILDEBERT OF LAVARDIN (1056–1133)

4849 God is where he was.

4850 God, surrounding all things, is himself not surrounded.
PHILO JUDAEUS (30 B.C.–40 A.D.)

4851 God, whose center is everywhere and his circumference nowhere, cannot be fitted into a diagram.
EMPEDOCLES (C. 494–C. 430 B.C.)

4852 I am the vase of God, he fills me
    to the brim,
He is the ocean deep, contained I am
    in him.
ANGELUS SILESIUS (1624–1677)

4853 I cannot understand how in the presence of our Lord anyone could go on thinking about himself.
ABBE HENRI DE TOURVILLE (1842–1903)

4854 I know that nothing can exist without you; does that mean that whatever exists contains you? . . . Do the heavens and the earth contain you, since you fill them? Or do you cram them to overflowing? And if you do overflow the universe, into what do you overflow? . . . And then, when you fill all things, do you fill it with your whole being?
SAINT AUGUSTINE OF HIPPO (354–430)

4855 I quarrel with God, fight with him, make up with him, but I am never without him.
ELIE WIESEL

4856 If we cannot find God in your house or in mine, upon the roadside or the margin of the sea; in the bursting seed or opening flower; in the day duty or the night musing; in the general laugh or the secret grief; in the procession of life, ever entering afresh, and solemnly passing by and dropping off; I do not think we should discern him any more on the grass of Eden, or beneath the moonlight of Gethsemane.
JAMES MARTINEAU (1805–1900)

4857 If you don't feel close to God, guess who moved?

4858 In the face of the sun you may see God's beauty; in the fire you may feel his heart warming; in the water his gentleness to refresh you.
JEREMY TAYLOR (1613–1667)

4859 Near, so very near to God,
Nearer I cannot be;
For in the person of his Son
I am as near as he.
CATESBY PAGET (D. 1742)

4860 Nothing is void of God; he himself fills his work.
LUCIUS ANNAEUS SENECA (C. 4 B.C.–A.D. 65)

4861 Open your eyes and the whole world is full of God.
JAKOB BÖHME (1575–1624)

4862 Speak to him, thou, for he hears, and
    Spirit with Spirit can meet—
Closer is he than breathing, and nearer
    than hands and feet.
ALFRED, LORD TENNYSON (1809–1892)

4863 The knowledge that we are never alone calms the troubled sea of our lives and speaks peace to our souls.
A. W. TOZER (1897–1963)

4864 The presence of God is a fact of life. St. Paul rightly said of God, "In him we live, and move, and have our being." Jesus said, "The kingdom of God is within you." We may, by defying the purpose of God, insulate ourselves from that presence. We may, by unrepented sin, cut off the sense of God because we are clouded by a sense of guilt. We may, through no fault of our own, be unable to sense the God who is all about us. But the fact remains that he is with us all the time.
J. B. PHILLIPS (1906–1982)

4865 The presence of God's glory is in heaven; the presence of his power on earth; the presence of his justice in hell; and the presence of his grace with his people. If he deny us his powerful presence, we fall into nothing; if he deny us his gracious presence, we fall

into sin; if he deny us his merciful presence, we fall into hell.
JOHN MASON (1706–1773)

4866 This is well-nigh the greatest of discoveries a man can make, that God is not confined in churches, but that the streets are sacred because his presence is there, that the marketplace is one of his abiding places, and ought, therefore, to be a sanctuary.
R. C. GILLIE (B.1865)

4867 Thou, O God, who art unchangeable. Thou art always and invariably to be found and always to be found unchanged. Whether in life or in death, no one journeys so far afield that thou art not to be found by him, that thou art not there, thou who art everywhere.
SØREN AABYE KIERKEGAARD (1813–1855)

4868 Though God be everywhere present, yet he is present to you in the deepest and most central part of the soul.
WILLIAM LAW (1686–1761)

4869 To me remains not place nor time;
My country is in every clime;
I can be calm and free from care
On any shore, since God is there.
MADAME JEANNE MARIE DE LA MOTHE GUYON (1648–1717)

4870 We do not need to go "somewhere" to find God, any more than the fish needs to soar to find the ocean or the eagle to plunge to find the air.
RUFUS MATTHEW JONES (1863–1948)

4871 We may ignore, but we can nowhere evade, the presence of God. The world is crowded with him. He walks everywhere incognito.
C. S. LEWIS (1898–1963)

4872 We never do anything so secretly but that it is in the presence of two witnesses: God and our own conscience.
BENJAMIN WHICHCOTE (1609–1683)

4873 Were I a preacher, I should preach above all other things the practice of the presence of God. Were I a teacher,

I should advise all the world to it; so necessary do I think it, and so easy.
BROTHER LAWRENCE OF THE RESURRECTION (C. 1605–1691)

4874 When God makes his presence felt through us, we are like the burning bush; Moses never took any heed what sort of bush it was—he only saw the brightness of the Lord.
GEORGE ELIOT (1819–1880)

4875 Whether invoked or not, God will be present.
—Inscription carved on the lintel of his house
C. G. JUNG (1875–1961)

4876 Within thy circling power I stand;
On every side I find thy hand;
Awake, asleep, at home, abroad,
I am surrounded still with God.
ISAAC WATTS (1674–1748)

4877 Without thy presence, wealth are bags of cares;
Wisdom, but folly; joy, disquiet sadness;
Friendship is treason, and delights are snares;
Pleasure's but pain, and mirth but pleasing madness.
FRANCIS QUARLES (1592–1644)

4878 You need not cry very loud; he is nearer to us than we think.
BROTHER LAWRENCE OF THE RESURRECTION (C. 1605–1691)

GOD/OMNISCIENCE

4879 Before God created the universe, he already had you in mind.
ERWIN W. LUTZER (1941–   )

4880 Don't play games with God—first, because you shouldn't; second, because he won't let you.
JEWISH PROVERB

4881 God knows instantly and effortlessly all matter and all matters, all mind and every mind, all spirit and all spirits, all being and every being, all creaturehood and all creatures, every plurality and all pluralities, all law and every law, all relations, all causes, all thoughts, all mysteries, all enigmas, all

feeling, all desires, every unuttered secret, all thrones and dominions, all personalities, all things visible and invisible in heaven and in earth, motion, space, time, life, death, good, evil, heaven, and hell.
A. W. TOZER (1897–1963)

4882 God's foreknowledge of what he will do does not necessitate him to do.
STEPHEN CHARNOCK (1628–1680)

4883 Homer with his honeyed lips sang of the bright sun's clear light; yet the sun cannot burst with his feeble rays the bowels of the earth or the depths of the sea. Not so with the Creator of his great sphere. No masses of earth can block his vision as he looks over all. With one glance of his intelligence, he sees all that has been, that is, and that is to come.
ANICIUS MANLIUS SEVERINUS BOETHIUS (c. 480–524)

4884 How unutterably sweet is the knowledge that our heavenly Father knows us completely. No talebearer can inform on us, no enemy can make an accusation stick; no forgotten skeleton can come tumbling out of some hidden closet to abash us and expose our past; no unsuspected weakness in our characters can come to light to turn God away from us, since he knew us utterly before we knew him and called us to himself in the full knowledge of everything that was against us.
A. W. TOZER (1897–1963)

4885 Is God all-wise? Then the darkest providences have meaning. We will set ourselves as God's interpreters, and because we cannot make straight lines out of our crooked lot, we think that God has turned our life into inextricable confusion. The darkest hours in our life have some intent, and it is really not needful that we should know all at once what that intent is. Let us keep within our own little sphere, and live a day at a time, and breathe a breath at a time, and be content with one pulsation at a time, and

interpretation will come when God pleases, and as he pleases.
JOSEPH PARKER (1830–1902)

4886 The remarkable thing about the way in which people talk about God, or about their relation to God, is that it seems to escape them completely that God hears what they are saying. A man says, "At the moment I have not the time or the necessary recollection to think about God, but later on perhaps." Or better still a young man says, "I am too young now; first of all I will enjoy life—and then." Would it be possible to talk like that if one realized that God heard one?
SØREN AABYE KIERKEGAARD (1813–1855)

4887 Though men may spin their cunning schemes—God knows who shall lose or win.
HITOPADESA

4888 What can escape the eye of God, all seeing,
Or deceive his heart, omniscient?
JOHN MILTON (1608–1674)

4889 When, by the reception of the Holy Spirit, I begin to realize that God knows all the deepest possibilities there are in me, knows all the eccentricities of my being, I find that the mystery of myself is solved by this besetting God.
OSWALD CHAMBERS (1874–1917)

GOD/PATIENCE

4890 Even bein' Gawd ain't a bed of roses.
MARC CONNELLY (1890–1980)

4891 God is the only being who can afford to be misunderstood. He deliberately stands aside and lets himself be slandered and misrepresented; he never vindicates himself.
OSWALD CHAMBERS (1874–1917)

4892 God is very patient. It took him years to teach me to say two words: "Lord, anything!"
A. DOUGLAS BROWN

4893 God's love for poor sinners is very wonderful, but God's patience with ill-natured saints is a deeper mystery.
HENRY DRUMMOND (1851–1897)

4894 He who hears himself cursed and remains silent becomes a partner of God—for does not the Lord hear nations blame him, yet remain silent.
MIDRASH

4895 Judge from your own feelings how God, with his infinite sensibility, must feel when he sees men rising up against their fellowmen; performing gross deeds of cruelty on every hand; waging wars that cause blood to flow like rivers throughout the globe, when, in short, he sees them devastating society by every infernal mischief that their ingenuity can invent.
HENRY WARD BEECHER (1813–1887)

4896 Our ground of hope is that God does not weary of mankind.
RALPH WASHINGTON SOCKMAN (1889–1970)

4897 Sometimes a nation abolishes God, but fortunately God is more tolerant.
HERBERT V. PROCHNOW

GOD/PURPOSE

4898 All revolutions, from the beginning of the world to the end of it, are but the various parts of the same scheme, all conspiring to bring to pass that great event which the great Creator and Governor of the world has ultimately in view.
JONATHAN EDWARDS (1703–1758)

4899 God lets himself be pushed out of the world on to the cross. He is weak and powerless in the world, and that is precisely the way, the only way, in which he is with us and helps us. Matthew makes it quite clear that Christ helps us, not by virtue of his omnipotence, but by virtue of his weakness and suffering.
DIETRICH BONHOEFFER (1906–1945)

4900 God perseveres in speaking to us in his own language. God speaks to us in this language that we do not know and do not want to learn, he speaks to us of acceptance, of sacrifice, of renunciation, of his plan, so vast in scale, so unimaginably bold, so improbably generous, the plan by which he wills to save us, us and the world.
LOUIS EVELY (1910–)

4901 I can hardly recollect a single plan of mine, of which I have not since seen reason to be satisfied that, had it taken place in season and circumstance just as I proposed, it would, humanly speaking, have proved my ruin; or at least it would have deprived me of the greater good the Lord had designed for me.
JOHN NEWTON (1725–1807)

4902 In spite of all appearances to the contrary, God has a plan for this bankrupt world. He still has something in store for it. This dark, satanic earth, drowned in blood and tears, this earth of ours, he still wants as a theatre for his grace and glorious direction.
HELMUT THIELICKE (1908–1986)

4903 Nothing in this world is without meaning.
A. W. TOZER (1897–1963)

4904 Only when God hath brought to light all the hidden things of darkness, whosoever were the actors therein, will it be seen that wise and good were all his ways, that he saw through the thick cloud, and governed all things by the wise counsels of his own will, that nothing was left to chance, or the caprice of men, but God disposed all strongly and sweetly, and wrought all into one connected chain of justice, mercy, and truth.
JOHN WESLEY (1703–1791)

4905 When I consider the short duration of my life, swallowed up in the eternity before and after, the little space which I fill, and even can see, engulfed in the infinite immensity of spaces of which I am ignorant, and which knows me not, I am frightened, and am astonished at being here rather than there; for there is no reason why here rather than there, why now rather than then. Who has put me here? By

whose order and direction have this place and time been allotted to me?
BLAISE PASCAL (1623–1662)

GOD/REVELATION

4906 God hides nothing. His very work from the beginning is revelation—a casting aside of veil after veil, a showing unto men of truth after truth. On and on from fact divine he advances, until at length in his Son Jesus he unveils his very face.
GEORGE MACDONALD (1824–1905)

4907 God reveals himself unfailingly to the thoughtful seeker.
HONORÉ DE BALZAC (1799–1850)

4908 Instead of complaining that God has hidden himself, you should give him thanks for having revealed so much of himself.
BLAISE PASCAL (1623–1662)

4909 It was said, sneeringly, by someone that if a clam could conceive of God, it would conceive of him in the shape of a great, big clam. Naturally. And if God has revealed himself to clams, it could only be under conditions of perfect clamhood, since any other manifestation would be wholly irrelevant to clam nature.
DOROTHY L. SAYERS (1893–1957)

4910 Man cannot seek God, unless God himself teaches him; nor find him, unless he reveals himself. The believer does not seek to understand that he may believe, but he believes that he may understand, for unless he believed he would not understand.
SAINT ANSELM (C. 1033–1109)

4911 Revelation is God's word, creation his work, the Spirit sole seer and interpreter of both.
AMOS BRONSON ALCOTT (1799–1888)

GOD/SATAN

4912 God seeks comrades and claims love; the devil seeks slaves and claims obedience.
SIR RABINDRANATH TAGORE (1861–1941)

4913 God's country begins where men love to serve their fellows; the devil's country begins where men eat men.
WALTER RAUSCHENBUSCH (1861–1918)

4914 God's truth judges created things out of love, and Satan's truth judges them out of envy and hatred.
DIETRICH BONHOEFFER (1906–1945)

4915 The devil has nothing to say about the will of God. For he hates this will and categorically refuses to do its bidding. He refuses to stand under God. He stands outside—as we see—as the cunning observer, the mischief-maker and intriguer.
HELMUT THIELICKE (1908–1986)

4916 The whole history of the world is discovered to be but a contest between the wisdom of God and the cunning of Satan and fallen men. The outcome of the contest is not in doubt.
A. W. TOZER (1897–1963)

4917 There are two great forces at work in the world today: the unlimited power of God and the limited power of Satan.
CORRIE TEN BOOM (1892–1983)

4918 There is no neutral ground in the universe: every square inch, every split second, is claimed by God and counterclaimed by Satan.
C. S. LEWIS (1898–1963)

GOD/SEARCH FOR

4919 God is never found accidentally.
A. W. TOZER (1897–1963)

4920 God will have all, or none;
    serve him, or fall
Down before Baal, Bel, or Belial;
Either be hot or cold.
    God doth despise,
Abhor, and spew out all neutralities.
ROBERT HERRICK (1591–1674)

4921 I sought him in a great cathedral, dim
With age, where oft-repeated prayers
    arise,
But caught no glimpse of him.
I sought him then atop a lonely hill,
Like Moses once, but though I
    scanned the skies,
My search was fruitless still.

There was a little home where grief
    and care
Had bred but courage, love, and val-
    iant will,
I sought—and found him there.
ANNE MARRIOTT

4922 If thou intend not nor seek nothing
else but the pleasing of God and the
profit of thy neighbor thou shalt have
inward liberty.
THOMAS À KEMPIS (C. 1380–1471)

4923 If we seek God for our own good and
profit, we are not seeking God.
MEISTER ECKHART (C. 1260–C. 1327)

4924 We are not forced to take wings to
find him, but have only to seek solitude and to look within ourselves. You
need not be overwhelmed with confusion before so kind a Guest, but with
utter humility, talk to him as to your
Father; ask for what you want as from
a father.
SAINT TERESA OF AVILA (1515–1582)

4925 Whoso draws nigh to God one step
    through doubtings dim,
God will advance a mile in blazing
    light to him.

4926 You travel wide and far to scout and
    see and search;
If God you fail to see, you have noth-
    ing observed.
ANGELUS SILESIUS (1624–1677)

GOD/SOVEREIGNTY

4927 At first laying down, as a fact
    fundamental,
That nothing with God can be
    accidental.
HENRY WADSWORTH LONGFELLOW
(1807–1882)

4928 Chance does nothing that has not been
prepared beforehand.
ALEXIS TOCQUEVILLE (1805–1859)

4929 Divine love can admit no rival.
JOHANN TAULER (C. 1300–1361)

4930 God casts the die, not the dice.
ALBERT EINSTEIN (1879–1955)

4931 God did not abolish the fact of evil; he
transformed it. He did not stop the
Crucifixion; he rose from the dead.
DOROTHY L. SAYERS (1893–1957)

4932 God does not tell us what he is going
to do, he reveals who he is.
OSWALD CHAMBERS (1874–1917)

4933 God governs in the affairs of men; and
if a sparrow cannot fall to the ground
without his notice, neither can a kingdom rise without his aid.
BENJAMIN FRANKLIN (1706–1790)

4934 God governs the world, and we have
only to do our duty wisely and leave
the issue to him.
JOHN JAY CHAPMAN (1862–1933)

4935 God is and all is well.
JOHN GREENLEAF WHITTIER (1807–1892)

4936 God is good and God is light,
In this faith I rest secure,
Evil can but serve the right,
Over all shall love endure.
JOHN GREENLEAF WHITTIER (1807–1892)

4937 God is never in a panic, nothing can
be done that he is not absolute Master
of, and no one in earth or heaven can
shut a door he has opened, nor open a
door he has shut. God alters the inevitable when we get in touch with him.
OSWALD CHAMBERS (1874–1917)

4938 God will have the last word, and it
will be good.
ROBERT HAROLD SCHULLER (1926–   )

4939 God's calling the shots. He's running
the show. Either he's in full control or
he's off his throne.
CHARLES R. SWINDOLL (1934–   )

4940 God, so great an artificer in great
things, is not less great in small things.
SAINT AUGUSTINE OF HIPPO (354–430)

4941 He treasures up his bright designs,
And works his sovereign will.
WILLIAM COWPER (1731–1800)

4942 I have lived, sir, a long time, and the
longer I live the more convincing
proof I see of this truth—that God
governs the affairs of men.
BENJAMIN FRANKLIN (1706–1790)

4943 If God doesn't approve, a fly doesn't move.
JEWISH PROVERB

4944 If God willed it, brooms would shoot.
JEWISH PROVERB

4945 It is for us to make the effort. The result is always in God's hands.
MAHATMA GANDHI (1869–1948)

4946 Man cannot cover what God would reveal.
THOMAS CAMPBELL (1733–1795)

4947 Man drives, but it is God who holds the reins.
JEWISH PROVERB

4948 Nothing that happens in the world happens by chance. God is a God of order. Everything is arranged upon definite principles and never at random.
JOHN DRUMMOND (1851–1897)

4949 That the Almighty does make use of human agencies and directly intervenes in human affairs is one of the plainest statements in the Bible. I have had so many evidences of his direction, so many instances when I have been controlled by some other power than my own will, that I cannot doubt that this power comes from above.
ABRAHAM LINCOLN (1809–1865)

4950 The Almighty has his own purposes.
ABRAHAM LINCOLN (1809–1865)

4951 The only sovereign I recognize is he who sets fire to the suns and, with one blow of his hand, can send the worlds rolling in space.
FRANÇOIS RENÉ, VICOMTE DE CHATEAUBRIAND (1768–1848)

4952 The right of God's sovereignty is derived from his omnipotence.
THOMAS HOBBES (1588–1679)

4953 Things do not happen in this world—they are brought about.
WILL HAYS

4954 Thou lovest, without passion; art jealous, without anxiety; repentest, yet grievest not; art angry, yet serene; changest thy works, thy purpose unchanged; receivest again what thou findest, yet didst never lose; never in need, yet rejoicing in gains; never covetous, yet exacting usury. Thou receivest over and above, that thou mayest owe; and who hath ought that is not thine?
SAINT AUGUSTINE OF HIPPO (354–430)

4955 To discuss the authority of Almighty God seems a bit meaningless, and to question it would be absurd. Can we imagine the Lord God of Hosts having to request permission of anyone or to apply for anything to a higher body? To whom would God go for permission? Who is higher than the Highest? Who is mightier than the Almighty? Whose position antedates that of the Eternal? At whose throne would God kneel? Where is the greater one to whom he must appeal?
A. W. TOZER (1897–1963)

4956 We are all dangerous folk without God's controlling hand.
WILLIAM WARD AYER (1891–1985)

4957 We may say what we like, but God does allow the devil, he does allow sin, he does allow bad men to triumph and tyrants to rule, and these things either make us fiends or they make us saints. It depends entirely on the relationship we are in toward God.
OSWALD CHAMBERS (1874–1917)

4958 What God does not choose to give, you cannot take.
JEWISH PROVERB

4959 What God will, no frost can kill.

4960 What, but God? Inspiring God!
Who, boundless Spirit all,
And unremitting Energy, pervades,
Adjusts, sustains, and agitates the
    whole.
JAMES THOMSON (1700–1748)

4961 Who of us can see, behind chance and in chance, God? Who of us can see the finger of God in the weather?
OSWALD CHAMBERS (1874–1917)

GOD/VOICE

4962 A voice in the wind I do not know;
A meaning on the face of the high hills
Whose utterance I cannot comprehend.

A something is behind them: that is God.
GEORGE MACDONALD (1824–1905)

4963 If he has spoken, why is the universe not convinced?
PERCY BYSSHE SHELLEY (1792–1822)

4964 If you keep watch over your hearts, and listen for the voice of God and learn of him, in one short hour you can learn more from him than you could learn from man in a thousand years.
JOHANN TAULER (C. 1300–1361)

4965 It never frightened a Puritan when you bade him stand still and listen to the speech of God. His closet and his church were full of reverberations of the awful, gracious, beautiful voice for which he listened.
DANIEL BREVINT (1616–1695)

4966 The voice of God is a friendly voice. No one need fear to listen to it unless he has already made up his mind to resist it.
A. W. TOZER (1897–1963)

4967 The voice of the subconscious argues with you, tries to convince you; but the inner voice of God does not argue, does not try to convince you. It just speaks and it is self-authenticating.
E. STANLEY JONES (1884–1973)

4968 There is hardly ever a complete silence in our soul. God is whispering to us well nigh incessantly. Whenever the sounds of the world die out in the soul, or sink low, then we hear these whisperings of God. He is always whispering to us, only we do not always hear because of the noise, hurry, and distraction which life causes as it rushes on.
FREDERICK WILLIAM FABER (1814–1863)

4969 You know no disturbing voice? God never points out for you a pathway altogether different from the one you had planned? Then, my brother, you are living still in the land of slavery, in the land of darkness.
G. CAMPBELL MORGAN (1863–1945)

GOD/WILL

4970 I find doing the will of God leaves me no time for disputing about his plans.
GEORGE MACDONALD (1824–1905)

4971 I want what God wants, that's why I am so merry.
SAINT FRANCIS OF ASSISI (C. 1181–1226)

4972 In great contests each party claims to act in accordance with the will of God. Both may be, and one must be, wrong. God cannot be for and against the same thing at the same time.
ABRAHAM LINCOLN (1809–1865)

4973 In his will is our peace.
DANTE ALIGHIERI (1265–1321)

4974 It is not by seeking more fertile regions where toil is lighter—happier circumstances free from difficult complications and troublesome people—but by bringing the high courage of a devout soul, clear in principle and aim, to bear upon what is given to us, that we brighten our inward light, lead something of a true life, and introduce the kingdom of heaven into the midst of our earthly day. If we cannot work out the will of God where God has placed us, then why has he placed us there?
JAMES H. THOM

4975 Like anybody I would like to live a long life. Longevity has its place. But I'm not concerned about that now. I just want to do God's will. And he's allowed me to go up to the mountain. I've looked over, and I've seen the Promised Land.
MARTIN LUTHER KING, JR. (1929–1968)

4976 Not as I will, but as thou wilt. To be able to say these words and truly mean them is the highest point we can ever hope to attain. Then, indeed, we have broken out of time's hard shell to breathe, not its stale air, but the fresh, exhilarating atmosphere of eternity.
MALCOLM MUGGERIDGE (1903–1990)

4977 O Will, that willest good alone,
Lead thou the way, thou guidest best;
A silent child, I follow on,
And trusting lean upon thy breast.
And if in gloom I see thee not,

I lean upon thy love unknown;
In me thy blessed will is wrought,
If I will nothing of my own.
GERHARD TERSTEEGEN (1697–1769)

4978 Self-will should be so completely
poured out of the vessel of the soul
into the ocean of the will of God, that
whatever God may will, that at once
the soul should will; and that whatever God may allow, that the soul
should at once willingly embrace,
whether it may be in itself sweet or bitter.
LOUIS DE BLOIS

4979 Teach us to care and not to care;
Teach us to sit still;
Even among these rocks,
Our peace in his will.
T. S. ELIOT (1888–1965)

4980 The center of God's will is our only
safety.
BETSIE TEN BOOM (1885–1944)

4981 There are no disappointments to those
whose wills are buried in the will of
God.
FREDERICK WILLIAM FABER (1814–1863)

4982 To walk out of his will is to walk into
nowhere.
C. S. LEWIS (1898–1963)

4983 To will the will of God in himself and
for himself and concerning himself is
the highest possible condition of a
man.
GEORGE MACDONALD (1824–1905)

4984 We need to remember that we cannot
train ourselves to be Christians; we
cannot discipline ourselves to be
saints; we cannot bend ourselves to
the will of God: we have to be broken
to the will of God.
OSWALD CHAMBERS (1874–1917)

GOD/WISDOM

4985 All is best, though we oft doubt
What the unsearchable dispose
Of Highest Wisdom brings about.
JOHN MILTON (1608–1674)

4986 As a blind man has no idea of colors,
so have we no idea of the manner by
which the all-wise God perceives and
understands all things.
SIR ISAAC NEWTON (1642–1727)

4987 God never put anyone in a place too
small to grow in.
HENRIETTA CORNELIA MEARS (1890–1963)

4988 God's gifts put man's best dreams to
shame.
ELIZABETH BARRETT BROWNING
(1806–1861)

4989 To know the reasons which have
moved God to choose this order of the
universe, to permit sin, to dispense his
salutary grace in a certain manner—
this passes the capacity of a finite
mind, above all when such a mind has
not come into the joy of the vision of
God.
BARON GOTTFRIED WILHELM VON LEIBNIZ
(1646–1716)

4990 Too wise to err, too good to be
unkind,
Are all the movements of the eternal
mind.
JOHN EAST

4991 What God sends is better than what
men ask for.

GOD/WORKS

4992 "I believe in God the Father Almighty,
Maker of heaven and earth." What
does this mean? I believe that God has
made me and all creatures; that he has
given and still preserves to me my
body and soul, eyes, ears, and all my
members, my reason and all my
senses; also clothing and shoes, meat
and drink, house and home, wife and
child, land, cattle and all my goods;
that he richly and daily provides me
with all that I need for this body and
life, protects me against all danger and
guards and keeps me from all evil; and
all this purely out of fatherly, divine
goodness and mercy, without merit or
worthiness in me; for all of which I am
in duty bound to thank and praise, to
serve and obey him.
MARTIN LUTHER (1483–1546)

4993 God is the most unique being, all his works are unique, this angel, this man, this sun, this stone; in short, nothing can be found that is not a unique thing.
PIERRE GASSENDI (1592–1655)

4994 I used to ask God to help me. Then I asked if I might help him. I ended up by asking him to do his work through me.
JAMES HUDSON TAYLOR (1832–1905)

4995 If we miss seeing God in his works we deprive ourselves of the sight of a royal display of wisdom and power so elevating, so ennobling, so awe-inspiring as to make all attempts at description futile. Such a sight the angels behold day and night forever and ask nothing more to make them perpetually satisfied.
A. W. TOZER (1897–1963)

4996 What God does, he does well.
JEAN DE LA FONTAINE (1621–1695)

GOD/WRATH

4997 I believe in a God of absolute and unbounded love, therefore I believe in a loving anger of his which will and must devour and destroy all that is decayed, monstrous, abortive in the universe.
CHARLES KINGSLEY (1819–1875)

4998 Many would like religion as a sort of lightning rod to their houses to ward off, by and by, the bolts of divine wrath.
HENRY WARD BEECHER (1813–1887)

4999 The best way to understand the doctrine of the wrath of God is to consider the alternatives. The alternative is not love; since rightly considered love and wrath are only the obverse and reverse of the same thing . . . the alternative to wrath is neutrality—neutrality in the conflict of the world . . . to live in such a world would be a nightmare. It is only the doctrine of the wrath of God, of his irreconcilable hostility to all evil, which makes human life tolerable in such a world as ours.
STEPHEN NEILL

5000 The hardness of God is kinder than the softness of men, and his compulsion is our liberation.
C. S. LEWIS (1898–1963)

GOLDEN RULE

5001 Christ turned the world's accepted standards upside down. It was the poor, not the rich, who were blessed; the weak, not the strong, who were to be esteemed; the pure in heart, not the sophisticated and the worldly, who understood what life was about. Righteousness, not power or money or sensual pleasure, should be man's pursuit. We should love our enemies, bless them that curse us, do good to them that hate us, and pray for them that despitefully use us, in order that we may be worthy members of a human family whose father is in heaven.
MALCOLM MUGGERIDGE (1903–1990)

5002 Do not do to others what angers you if done to you by others.
ISOCRATES (436–338 B.C.)

5003 Do not that to thy neighbor that thou wouldst not suffer from him.
—Haeckel, The Riddle of the Universe, believes Pittacus was the first to utter the Golden Rule.
PITTACUS OF LESBOS (C. 650–C. 570 B.C.)

5004 Every man takes care that his neighbor does not cheat him. But a day comes when he begins to care that he does not cheat his neighbor. Then all goes well.
RALPH WALDO EMERSON (1803–1882)

5005 The Golden Rule would reconcile capital and labor, all political contention and uproar, all selfishness and greed.
JOSEPH PARKER (1830–1902)

5006 Treat your inferiors as you would be treated by your betters.
LUCIUS ANNAEUS SENECA (C. 4 B.C.–A.D. 65)

5007 We have committed the Golden Rule to memory; let us now commit it to life.
EDWIN MARKHAM (1852–1940)

5008 What you do not want others to do to you, do not do to others.
CONFUCIUS (C. 551–479 B.C.)

5009 When we and ours have it in our
power to do for you and yours what
you and yours have done for us and
ours, then we and ours will do for you
and yours what you and yours have
done for us and ours.
OLD ENGLISH TOAST

GOOD/EVIL

5010 A good end cannot sanctify evil
means; nor must we ever do evil that
good may come of it.
WILLIAM PENN (1644–1718)

5011 An evil soul producing holy witness
Is like a villain with a smiling cheek,
A goodly apple rotten at the heart.
WILLIAM SHAKESPEARE (1564–1616)

5012 As soon as men decide that all means
are permitted to fight an evil, then their
good becomes indistinguishable from
the evil that they set out to destroy.
CHRISTOPHER DAWSON (1889–1970)

5013 As there is much beast and some devil
in man, so is there some angel and
some God in him. The beast and the
devil may be conquered, but in this life
never destroyed.
SAMUEL TAYLOR COLERIDGE (1772–1834)

5014 Evil is whatever dehumanizes. Humanness is the realization of love, self-
awareness, empathy toward others,
inner peace, ecstatic joy, and a host of
other fruits of the Spirit. Whenever
personal relationships, vocational
activities, play, and religious life
develop these qualities in us there is
good. And whenever personal relationships, vocational activities, play, and
religious life diminish our humanness,
there is evil. God is at work through
the former. Satan is at work in the latter.
TONY CAMPOLO

5015 Evil minds change good to their own
nature.
PERCY BYSSHE SHELLEY (1792–1822)

5016 God has set a Savior against sin, a
heaven against a hell, light against
darkness, good against evil, and the
breadth and length and depth and

height of grace that is in himself for
my good, against all the power and
strength and subtlety of every enemy.
JOHN BUNYAN (1628–1688)

5017 God himself would not permit evil in
this world if good did not come of it.
SAINT THOMAS AQUINAS (1225–1274)

5018 God judged it better to bring good out
of evil than to suffer no evil to exist.
SAINT AUGUSTINE OF HIPPO (354–430)

5019 God makes all things good; man
meddles with them and they become
evil.
JEAN JACQUES ROUSSEAU (1712–1778)

5020 God would never have created a single
angel—not even a single man—whose
future wickedness he foresaw, unless,
at the same time, he knew of the good
which could come out of this evil. It
was as though he meant the harmony
of history, like the beauty of a poem,
to be enriched by antithetical elements.
SAINT AUGUSTINE OF HIPPO (354–430)

5021 Good and evil both increase at compound interest. That is why the little
decisions you and I make every day
are of such infinite importance. The
smallest good act today is the capture
of a stategic point from which, a few
months later, you may be able to go
on to victories you never dreamed of.
An apparently trivial indulgence in
lust or anger today is the loss of a
ridge or railway line or bridgehead
from which the enemy may launch an
attack otherwise impossible.
C. S. LEWIS (1898–1963)

5022 Good has but one enemy, the evil; but
the evil has two enemies, the good and
itself.
JOHANNES VON MULLER (1752–1809)

5023 Good is a principle of totality, of
coherence, of meaning; evil is a principle of fragmentariness, of incoherence,
of mockery. Hence there is no immanent logic in evil; evil is the Satan that
laughs at logic.
EDGAR SHEFFIELD BRIGHTMAN (1884–1953)

5024 Good is all that serves life, evil is all
that serves death. Good is reverence
for life . . . and all that enhances life.

Evil is all that stifles life, narrows it down, cuts it to pieces.
ERICH FROMM (1900–1980)

5025 Good is that which makes for unity; evil is that which makes for separateness.
ALDOUS HUXLEY (1894–1963)

5026 He that is good is free, though he is a slave; he that is evil is a slave, though he be a king.
SAINT AUGUSTINE OF HIPPO (354–430)

5027 If there is a God, whence come evils? But whence comes good, if there is none?
ANICIUS MANLIUS SEVERINUS BOETHIUS (C. 480–524)

5028 Impure thoughts will not stand against pure words, and prayers, and deeds. Little doubts will not avail against great certainties. Fix your affections on things above, and then you will be less and less troubled by the cares, the temptations, the troubles of things on earth.
ARTHUR PENRHYN STANLEY (1815–1881)

5029 In the face of evil there are three kinds of souls: there are those who do evil and deny that there is evil and call it good (John 16:2). There are also those who see evil in others, but not in themselves, and who flatter their own virtue by criticizing the sinful (Matthew 7:5). Finally, there are those who carry the burden of another's woe and sin as their own.
ARCHBISHOP FULTON J. SHEEN (1895–1979)

5030 It is the law of our humanity that man must know good through evil. No great principle ever triumphed but through much evil. No man ever progressed to greatness and goodness but through great mistakes.
FREDERICK WILLIAM ROBERTSON (1816–1853)

5031 It would no doubt have been well if the world had altogether refrained from evil; yet, the evil having occurred, the opportunity appears to make out of that evil a still more noble

good; the second Adam is greater than the first Adam could ever have been.
DOROTHY L. SAYERS (1893–1957)

5032 Let no man be sorry he has done good, because others have done evil! If a man has acted right, he has done well, though alone; if wrong, the sanction of all mankind will not justify him.
HENRY FIELDING (1707–1754)

5033 Life eternal is the supreme good, death eternal the supreme evil.
SAINT AUGUSTINE OF HIPPO (354–430)

5034 Life in itself is neither good nor an evil; it is the scene of good and evil.
LUCIUS ANNAEUS SENECA (C. 4 B.C.–A.D. 65)

5035 No deed that sets an evil example can bring joy to the doer.
JUVENAL (C. 60–C. 127)

5036 Nothing out of its place is good and nothing in its place is bad.
WALT WHITMAN (1819–1892)

5037 One of the dangers with focusing on the subject of evil is that you can lose your bearings. Perhaps the mystery of human evil isn't as great or magnificent as the extraordinary mystery of human goodness.
M. SCOTT PECK (1936–   )

5038 Right here let us make it plain, that each individual is either a sinner or a saint. It is impossible to be both; it is impossible to be neutral; there is no halfway business in God. Either you are the child of the Lord or you are serving the devil—there is no middle territory.
AIMEE SEMPLE MCPHERSON (1890–1944)

5039 Sweetest things turn sourest by their deeds;
Lilies that fester smell far worse than weeds.
WILLIAM SHAKESPEARE (1564–1616)

5040 The confession of evil works is the first beginning of good works.
SAINT AUGUSTINE OF HIPPO (354–430)

5041 The difference between a good person and a bad person (and each of us, naturally, is a little of both) is really very simple at bottom: the good person

loves people and uses things, while the bad person loves things and uses people.
SYDNEY J. HARRIS (1917–1986)

5042 The difference between those whom the world esteems as good and those whom it condemns as bad is, in many cases, little else than that the former have been better sheltered from temptation.

5043 The evil that men do lives after them;
The good is oft interred with their bones.
WILLIAM SHAKESPEARE (1564–1616)

5044 The fundamental idea of good is thus: that it consists in preserving life, in favoring it, in wanting to bring it to its highest value; and evil consists in destroying life, doing it injury, hindering its development.
ALBERT SCHWEITZER (1875–1965)

5045 The good are like one another and friends to one another and . . . the bad, as is often said of them, are never at unity with one another or with themselves. They are passionate and restless, and anything which is at variance and enmity with itself is not likely to be in union or harmony with any other thing.
PLATO (C. 428–348 B.C.)

5046 The inward attitude of the man who loves God is so different that, without breaking any of the rules that he himself has made, God is able to bring good to that man even out of evil and pain.
J. B. PHILLIPS (1906–1982)

5047 The power of choosing good and evil is within the reach of all.
ORIGEN (C. 185–C. 254)

5048 The worst and best are both inclined
To snap like vixens at the truth.
But, O, beware the middle mind
That purrs and never shows a tooth!
ELINOR HOYT WYLIE (1885–1928)

5049 To a good man nothing that happens is evil.
PLATO (C. 428–348 B.C.)

5050 We cannot love good if we do not hate evil.
SAINT JEROME (C. 374–C. 420)

5051 Whence my ability to wish evil and to refuse the good? Who placed this in me and planted the seedling of bitterness in me, since my whole being is from my most sweet God?
SAINT AUGUSTINE OF HIPPO (354–430)

5052 While time lasts there will always be a future, and that future will hold both good and evil, since the world is made to that mingled pattern.
DOROTHY L. SAYERS (1893–1957)

5053 Wicked men obey from fear; good men from love.
ARISTOTLE (384–322 B.C.)

GOODNESS

5054 A good heart is better than all the heads in the world.
EDWARD GEORGE BULWER-LYTTON (1803–1873)

5055 All our goodness is a loan; God is the owner.
SAINT JOHN OF THE CROSS (1542–1591)

5056 Concealed goodness is a sort of vice.

5057 Do all the good you can, to all the people you can, in all the ways you can, as often as ever you can, as long as you can.
CHARLES HADDON SPURGEON (1834–1892)

5058 Do not wait for extraordinary circumstances to do good. Try to use ordinary situations.
JOHANN PAUL FRIEDRICH RICHTER (1763–1825)

5059 God cannot accept goodness from me. He can only accept my badness, and he will give me the solid goodness of the Lord Jesus in exchange for it.
OSWALD CHAMBERS (1874–1917)

5060 God has a lively, profound interest in man's being good; he wills that man should be good, happy—for without goodness there is no happiness.
LUDWIG ANDREAS FEUERBACH (1804–1872)

5061 Good works never erase guilt.
ERWIN W. LUTZER (1941–   )

5062 Good, the more communicated, more abundant grows.
JOHN MILTON (1608–1674)

5063 Goodness consists not in the outward things we do, but in the inward thing we are.
EDWIN HUBBEL CHAPIN (1814–1880)

5064 Goodness is like praise to God.
ARABIAN PROVERB

5065 Goodness is love in action, love with its hand to the plow, love with the burden on its back, love following his footsteps who went about continually doing good.
JAMES HAMILTON (1814–1867)

5066 Goodness is something so simple: always live for others, never to seek one's advantage.
DAG HAMMARSKJÖLD (1905–1961)

5067 Goodness is uneventful. It does not flash, it glows.
DAVID GRAYSON (1870–1946)

5068 Great works do not always lie in our way, but every moment we may do little ones excellently, that is, with great love.
SAINT FRANCIS OF SALES (1567–1622)

5069 He that does good to another man does also good to himself; not only in the consequence, but in the very act of doing it. The consciousness of well-doing is an ample reward.
LUCIUS ANNAEUS SENECA (C. 4 B.C.–A.D. 65)

5070 He who receives a good turn should never forget it; he who does one should never remember it.
PIERRE CHARRON (1541–1603)

5071 He who waits to do a great deal of good at once, will never do anything.
SAMUEL JOHNSON (1709–1784)

5072 I will speak ill of no man, and speak all the good I know of everybody.
BENJAMIN FRANKLIN (1706–1790)

5073 In the end the good will triumph.
EURIPIDES (C. 484–406 B.C.)

5074 It is goodness, not greatness, that will do you good.

5075 It is not enough to do good. One must do it in the right way.
JOHN MORLEY (1838–1923)

5076 Learn the luxury of doing good.
OLIVER GOLDSMITH (1730–1774)

5077 Look for strength in people, not weakness; for good, not evil. Most of us find what we search for.
J. WILBUR CHAPMAN (1859–1918)

5078 Many individuals have, like uncut diamonds, shining qualities beneath a rough exterior.
JUVENAL (C. 60–C. 127)

5079 Real goodness does not attach itself merely to this life—it points to another world. Political or professional reputation cannot last forever, but a conscience void of offense before God and man is an inheritance for eternity.
DANIEL WEBSTER (1782–1852)

5080 That which is striking and beautiful is not always good, but that which is good is always beautiful.
NINON DE L'ENCLOS (1620–1705)

5081 The good have no need of an advocate.
PHOCION (C. 402–318 B.C.)

5082 The good man is his own friend.
SOPHOCLES (C. 496–406 B.C.)

5083 The good you do is not lost, though you forget it.

5084 The heart of a good man is the sanctuary of God.
ANNE-LOUISE-GERMAINE DE STAËL (1766–1817)

5085 To get good is animal; to do good is human; to be good is divine.
JAMES MARTINEAU (1805–1900)

5086 We always love what is good or what we think is good; it is in our judgment of what is good that we can make mistakes.
JEAN JACQUES ROUSSEAU (1712–1778)

5087 We must first be made good before we can do good; we must first be made just, before our works can please God. When we are justified by faith in Christ, then come good works.
HUGH LATIMER (C. 1485–1555)

GOSPEL

5088 A purely social gospel is like a body without a soul—it is a corpse. A purely personal gospel is like a soul without a body—it is a ghost. But put them both together and you have a man.
E. STANLEY JONES (1884–1973)

5089 Because it was the message of God to humanity, the gospel could only reveal itself in the simplest of garments.
ADOLF DEISSMANN (1866–1937)

5090 Brown bread and the gospel is good fare.
PURITANS

5091 *Euangelion* (which we call *gospel*) is a Greek word, and signifies good, merry, glad, and joyful tydings, that makes a mans heart glad, and makes him sing, dance, and leap for joy.
WILLIAM TYNDALE (C. 1494–1536)

5092 Humble and self-forgetting we must be always, but diffident and apologetic about the gospel, never.
JAMES S. STEWART (1896–)

5093 No one is excluded from the gospel, but many are excluded by the gospel.
KARL BARTH (1886–1968)

5094 Talk about the question of the day! There is but one question and that is the gospel. It can and will correct everything needing correction. All men at the head of great movements are Christian men. During the many years I was in the cabinet I was brought into association with sixty master minds, and all but five of them were Christians. My only hope for the world is in bringing the human mind into contact with divine revelation.
WILLIAM EWART GLADSTONE (1809–1898)

5095 The glory of the gospel is its freedom.
A. W. TOZER (1897–1963)

5096 The glory of the gospel is that when the church is absolutely different from the world, she invariably attracts it.
D. MARTYN LLOYD-JONES (1899–1981)

5097 The gospel is like a fresh, mild, and cool air in the extreme heat of sum-mer, a solace and comfort in the anguish of the conscience.
MARTIN LUTHER (1483–1546)

5098 The gospel is neither a discussion nor a debate. It is an announcement.
PAUL STROMBERG REES (1900–)

5099 The gospel is not made to dominate the world. It's the grain of sand that upsets the world's machinery. One can't inhale its fragrance and be content to leave everything the way it is.
JEAN SULLIVAN

5100 The gospel is not so much a demand as it is an offer, an offer of new life to man by the grace of God.
E. STANLEY JONES (1884–1973)

5101 The gospel to me is simply irresistible.
BLAISE PASCAL (1623–1662)

5102 The nature of the gospel is that it divides.
RICHARD OWEN ROBERTS (1931–)

5103 The shifting systems of false religion are continually changing their places; but the gospel of Christ is the same forever. While other false lights are extinguished, this true light ever shines.
THEODORE LEDYARD CUYLER (1822–1909)

5104 The social gospel needs a theology to make it effective; but theology needs the social gospel to vitalize it.
WALTER RAUSCHENBUSCH (1861–1918)

5105 The words of our Lord, "Think not that I came to cast peace on the earth: I came not to cast peace, but a sword," are a description of what happens when the gospel is preached—upset, conviction, concern, and confusion.
OSWALD CHAMBERS (1874–1917)

5106 The world has many religions; it has but one gospel.
GEORGE OWEN

5107 There are two things to do about the gospel—believe it and behave it.
SUSANNA WESLEY (1669–1742)

5108 There is nothing attractive about the gospel to the natural man; the only man who finds the gospel attractive is the man who is convicted of sin.
OSWALD CHAMBERS (1874–1917)

5109 To make the message interesting, relevant, and palatable to the world, the message of the gospel is often diluted when it is prepared for popular consumption. Some Christian singing groups are so concerned about being inoffensive that even believers can scarcely find a clear biblical message in the songs.
ERWIN W. LUTZER (1941–)

5110 We can learn nothing of the gospel except by feeling its truths. There are some sciences that may be learned by the head, but the science of Christ crucified can only be learned by the heart.
CHARLES HADDON SPURGEON (1834–1892)

5111 We say that Jesus preached the gospel, but he did more. He came that there might be a gospel to preach.
OSWALD CHAMBERS (1874–1917)

GOSSIP

5112 A gossip is one who talks to you about others; a bore is one who talks to you about himself; and a brilliant conversationalist is one who talks to you about yourself.
LISA KIRK

5113 A gossip speaks ill of all and all of her.

5114 A gossip usually makes a mountain out of a molehill by adding some dirt.

5115 A secret between two is a secret of God; a secret among three is everybody's secret.
FRENCH PROVERB

5116 A small leak will sink a great ship.

5117 A statement once let loose cannot be caught by four horses.
JAPANESE PROVERB

5118 A tongue can be a dangerous weapon.
JEWISH PROVERB

5119 A wound caused by words is more painful than a wound caused by an arrow.
ARABIAN PROVERB

5120 Be busy, but not a busybody!
SPANISH PROVERB

5121 Dirt is matter in the wrong place.
LORD PALMERSTON (1784–1865)

5122 Don't meddle with that which does not concern you.
PLAUTUS (C. 254–184 B.C.)

5123 Eavesdroppers never hear any good of themselves.
FRENCH PROVERB

5124 Fie! What a spendthrift he is of his tongue!
WILLIAM SHAKESPEARE (1564–1616)

5125 First thing in the morning she brushes her teeth and sharpens her tongue.

5126 From a man's mouth you can tell what he is.
ZOHAR (THIRTEENTH CENTURY)

5127 Gossip can estrange the closest friends.
JEWISH PROVERB

5128 Gossip is always a personal confession either of malice or imbecility.
JOSIAH GILBERT HOLLAND (1819–1881)

5129 Gossip is like mud thrown against a clean wall: it may not stick, but it leaves a mark.

5130 Gossip is nature's telephone.
SHOLEM ALEICHEM (1859–1916)

5131 Gossip is the lack of a worthy theme.
ELBERT GREEN HUBBARD (1856–1915)

5132 Gossip is the sort of smoke that comes from the dirty tobacco pipes of those who diffuse it; it proves nothing but the bad taste of the smoker.
GEORGE ELIOT (1819–1880)

5133 Gossip is what no one claims to like but what everybody enjoys.
JOSEPH CONRAD (1857–1924)

5134 Gossip is worse than fighting.
ARABIAN PROVERB

5135 Gossip leads to criticism, and criticism kills love.
CORRIE TEN BOOM (1892–1983)

5136 Gossip: social sewage.
GEORGE MEREDITH (1828–1909)

5137 Gossips and talebearers set on fire all the houses they enter.

5138 Hating anything in the way of ill-natured gossip ourselves, we are always grateful to those who do it for us and do it well.
H. H. MUNRO (1870–1916)

5139 He who gossips to you will gossip about you.
ARABIAN PROVERB

5140 He who hunts for flowers will find flowers; and he who loves weeds may find weeds.
HENRY WARD BEECHER (1813–1887)

5141 How can we expect another to keep our secret if we cannot keep it ourselves?
FRANÇOIS, DUC DE LA ROCHEFOUCAULD (1613–1680)

5142 I know nothing swifter in life than the voice of rumor.
PLAUTUS (C. 254–184 B.C.)

5143 I would rather play with the forked lightning, or take in my hands living wires with their fiery current, than speak a reckless word against any servant of Christ, or idly repeat the slanderous darts which thousands of Christians are hurling on others, to the hurt of their own souls and bodies.
ALBERT BENJAMIN SIMPSON (1843–1919)

5144 If there is a person to whom you feel dislike, that is the person of whom you ought never to speak.
RICHARD CECIL (1748–1810)

5145 Ill words are bellows to a slackening fire.

5146 Lord, remind us often that a gossip's mouth is the devil's mailbag.
WELSH PROVERB

5147 Nature invented the nose for breathing and smelling, but human nature added a new one: sticking it into other people's business.

5148 Never believe anything bad about anybody unless you positively know it to be true; never tell even that unless you feel that it is absolutely necessary—and remember that God is listening while you tell it.
HENRY VAN DYKE (1852–1933)

5149 Never tell evil of a man, if you do not know it for certainty, and if you know it for a certainty, then ask yourself, "Why should I tell it?"
JOHANN KASPAR LAVATER (1741–1801)

5150 None are so fond of secrets as those who do not mean to keep them.
CHARLES CALEB COLTON (1780–1832)

5151 Only a baby is admired for opening his mouth and putting his foot into it.

5152 Plastic surgeons can do almost anything with a nose, except keep it out of other people's business.

5153 Rumor is a great traveler.

5154 Scandal should be treated as you treat mud on your clothes. If you try and deal with it while it is wet, you rub the mud into the texture, but if you leave it till it is dry, you can flick it off with a touch, it is gone without a trace. Leave scandal alone, never touch it.
OSWALD CHAMBERS (1874–1917)

5155 She told him it was terrible to hear such things as he told her and to please go ahead.
GEORGE ADE (1866–1944)

5156 Shun the inquisitive, for you will be sure to find him leaky.
HORACE BUSHNELL (1802–1876)

5157 Speak to me—not of me!
ROBERT BROWNING (1812–1889)

5158 Talebearers are just as bad as the talemakers.

5159 The only time people dislike gossip is when you gossip about them.
WILL ROGERS (1879–1935)

5160 The sewing circle—the Protestant confessional, where each one confesses, not her own sins, but the sins of her neighbors.
CHARLES B. FAIRBANKS

5161 The tongue is but three inches long, yet it can kill a man six feet high.
JAPANESE PROVERB

5162 There is so much good in the worst of us,
And so much bad in the best of us,
That it hardly behooves any of us
To talk about the rest of us.
EDWARD WALLIS HOCH (1849–1925)

5163 There's only one thing as difficult as unscrambling an egg, and that's unspreading a rumor.

5164 We cannot control the evil tongues of others; but a good life enables us to disregard them.
CATO THE ELDER (234–149 B.C.)

5165 What you don't see with your eyes, don't invent with your mouth.
JEWISH PROVERB

5166 Where there is least heart there is most tongue.
ITALIAN PROVERB

5167 You make no repute for yourself when you publish another's secret fault.
PERSIAN PROVERB

GOVERNMENT

5168 A government big enough to give you everything you want is a government big enough to take from you everything you have.
GERALD R. FORD (1913–)

5169 Although church and state stand separate, the political order cannot be renewed without theological virtues working upon it. . . . It is from the church that we receive our fundamental postulates of order, justice, and freedom, applying them to our civil society.
RUSSELL KIRK (1918–)

5170 Christianity introduced no new forms of government, but a new spirit which totally transformed the old ones.
LORD ACTON (1834–1902)

5171 Congress is so strange. A man gets up to speak and says nothing. Nobody listens, then everybody disagrees.
BORIS MARSHALOV

5172 Democracy is a form of government where you can say what you think even if you don't think.

5173 Democracy is a process by which the people are free to choose the man who will get the blame.

5174 Do you not know, my son, with what little understanding the world is ruled?
POPE JULIUS III (1487–1555)

5175 God does not take the responsibility for the existence of the rebellious "powers that be" or for their shape or identity; they already are. . . . He

orders them, brings them into line, [and] by his permissive government he lines them up with his purpose.
JOHN HOWARD YODER

5176 God governs the world, and we have only to do our duty wisely and leave the issue to him.
JOHN JAY (1745–1829)

5177 Government originated as an ordinance of God. It is, in one sense, God's response to the nature of the people themselves. While it cannot redeem the world or be used as a tool to establish the kingdom of God, civil government does set the boundaries for human behavior. The state is not a remedy for sin, but a means to restrain it.
CHARLES COLSON (1931–)

5178 He who shall introduce into public affairs the principles of primitive Christianity will change the face of the world.
BENJAMIN FRANKLIN (1706–1790)

5179 I now leave, not knowing when, or whether ever, I may return, with a task before me greater than that which rested upon Washington. Without the assistance of that Divine Being who ever attended him I cannot succeed. With that assistance I cannot fail. Trusting in him who can go with me, and remain with you, and be everywhere for good, let us confidently hope that all will yet be well. To his care commending you, as I hope in your prayers you will commend me, I bid you an affectionate farewell.
—Farewell address at Springfield, Illinois, upon leaving to become president
ABRAHAM LINCOLN (1809–1865)

5180 In politics, a week is a very long time.
HAROLD WILSON

5181 It is impossible to rightly govern the world without God and the Bible.
GEORGE WASHINGTON (1732–1799)

5182 It is out of the question that there should be a Christian government even over one land . . . since the wicked always outnumber the good. Hence a man who would venture to

govern . . . with the gospel would be like a shepherd who should place in one fold wolves, lions, eagles, and sheep together and let them freely mingle.
MARTIN LUTHER (1483–1546)

5183 No person who shall deny the being of God, or the truth of the Christian religion, shall be capable of holding any office or place of trust or profit.
—Constitution,
State of North Carolina, 1836

5184 One of the greatest delusions in the world is the hope that the evils in this world are to be cured by legislation.
—Speech in the House of Representatives, 1886
THOMAS BRACKETT REED (1839–1902)

5185 Politics is the gizzard of society, full of gut and gravel.
HENRY DAVID THOREAU (1817–1862)

5186 Politics is the science of how who gets what, when, and why.
SIDNEY HILLMAN (1887–1946)

5187 That government is best which governs least.
—Masthead slogan of the Democratic Review

5188 The Bible is the rock upon which our republic rests.
ANDREW JACKSON (1767–1845)

5189 The foundation of our society and of our government rests so much on the teachings of the Bible that it would be difficult to support them if faith in these teachings should cease.
CALVIN COOLIDGE (1872–1933)

5190 The hope of the nation is not in its forms of government, not in the wisdom and equity of its executive, nor in the justice and purity of its administration, so much as in the elevation and redemption of individual character among its people.
BISHOP HENRY CODMAN POTTER (1834–1908)

5191 The majority is the best way because it is visible and has strength to make

itself obeyed. Yet it is the opinion of the least able.
BLAISE PASCAL (1623–1662)

5192 The more laws and order are made prominent, the more thieves and robbers there will be.
LAO-TSE (C. 604–C. 531 B.C.)

5193 The penalty that good men pay for not being interested in politics is to be governed by men worse than themselves.
PLATO (C. 428–348 B.C.)

5194 The perpetual irony of government is that rule by the majority is fairest, but minorities are almost always in the right.
SYDNEY J. HARRIS (1917–1986)

5195 There can be no good government without law and order; nor that without authority; nor that without justice; nor that without God.
EDWARD GIBBON (1737–1794)

5196 We have no government armed in power capable of contending with human passions unbridled by morality and religion. . . . Our constitution was made only for a moral and religious people. It is wholly inadequate for the government of any other.
JOHN ADAMS (1735–1826)

5197 What was the conduct of Shadrach, Meshach and Abednego? . . . Did these men do right in disobeying the law of their sovereign? Let their miraculous deliverance from the burning fiery furnace answer.
ANGELINA GRIMKÉ (1805–1879)

5198 When they call the roll in the Senate, the senators do not know whether to answer "present" or "not guilty."
THEODORE ROOSEVELT (1858–1919)

5199 With malice toward none; with charity for all; with firmness in the right, as God gives us to see the right, let us strive on to finish the work we are in; to bind up the nation's wounds; to care for him who shall have borne the battle, and for his widow and his orphan—to do all which may achieve and cherish a just and lasting peace among ourselves and with all nations.
ABRAHAM LINCOLN (1809–1865)

GRACE

5200 A man is never so truly and intensely himself as when he is most possessed by God. It is impossible to say where, in the spiritual life, the human will leaves off and divine grace begins.
WILLIAM RALPH INGE (1860–1954)

5201 A man must completely despair of himself in order to become fit to obtain the grace of Christ.
MARTIN LUTHER (1483–1546)

5202 A state of mind that sees God in everything is evidence of growth in grace and a thankful heart.
CHARLES G. FINNEY (1792–1875)

5203 Abounding sin is the terror of the world, but abounding grace is the hope of mankind.
A. W. TOZER (1897–1963)

5204 All men who live with any degree of serenity live by some assurance of grace.
REINHOLD NIEBUHR (1892–1971)

5205 As heat is opposed to cold, and light to darkness, so grace is opposed to sin.
THOMAS BENTON BROOKS (1608–1680)

5206 As mercy is God's goodness confronting human misery and guilt, so grace is his goodness directed toward human debt and demerit.
A. W. TOZER (1897–1963)

5207 As the earth can produce nothing unless it is fertilized by the sun, so we can do nothing without the grace of God.
SAINT JEAN BAPTISTE MARIE VIANNEY (1786–1859)

5208 Christ is no Moses, no exactor, no giver of laws, but a giver of grace, a Savior; he is infinite mercy and goodness, freely and bountifully given to us.
MARTIN LUTHER (1483–1546)

5209 For grace is given not because we have done good works, but in order that we may be able to do them.
SAINT AUGUSTINE OF HIPPO (354–430)

5210 Grace abounds only when there is genuine repentance and we cannot . . . simultaneously will sin and repentance since this involves a contradiction in terms.
DOROTHY L. SAYERS (1893–1957){?}

5211 Grace binds you with far stronger cords than the cords of duty or obligation can bind you. Grace is free, but when once you take it, you are bound forever to the Giver and bound to catch the spirit of the Giver. Like produces like. Grace makes you gracious, the Giver makes you give.
E. STANLEY JONES (1884–1973)

5212 Grace can pardon our ungodliness and justify us with Christ's righteousness; it can put the Spirit of Jesus Christ within us; it can help us when we are down; it can heal us when we are wounded; it can multiply pardons, as we through frailty multiply transgressions.
JOHN BUNYAN (1628–1688)

5213 Grace comes into the soul, as the morning sun into the world; first a dawning, then a light; and at last the sun in his full and excellent brightness.
THOMAS ADAMS (1612–1653)

5214 Grace does not destroy nature, it perfects it.
SAINT THOMAS AQUINAS (1225–1274)

5215 Grace grows best in winter.
SAMUEL RUTHERFORD (1600–1661)

5216 Grace is a certain beginning of glory in us.
SAINT THOMAS AQUINAS (1225–1274)

5217 Grace is an energy; not a mere sentiment; not a mere thought of the Almighty; not even a word of the Almighty. It is as real an energy as the energy of electricity. It is a divine energy; it is the energy of the divine affection rolling in plenteousness toward the shores of human need.
BENJAMIN JOWETT (1817–1893)

5218 Grace is but glory begun, and glory is but grace perfected.
JONATHAN EDWARDS (1703–1758)

5219 Grace is God himself, his loving energy at work within his church and within our souls.
EVELYN UNDERHILL (1875–1941)

5220 Grace is love that cares and stoops
and rescues.
JOHN R. W. STOTT (1921–   )

5221 Grace is the central invitation to life
and the final word. It's the beckoning
nudge and the overwhelming, undeserved mercy that urges us to change
and grow, and then gives us the power
to pull it off.
TIM HANSEL

5222 Grace is the love that gives, that loves
the unlovely and the unlovable.
OSWALD C. HOFFMANN

5223 He giveth more grace when the
burdens grow greater,
He sendeth more strength when the
labors increase;
To added affliction he addeth his
mercy,
To multiplied trials,
His multiplied peace.
ANNIE JOHNSON FLINT (1862–1932)

5224 He who has not felt what sin is in the
Old Testament knows little what grace
is in the New. He who has not trembled in Moses, and wept in David, and
wondered in Isaiah will rejoice little in
Matthew, rest little in John. He who
has not suffered under the Law will
scarcely hear the glad sound of the gospel.
R. W. BARBOUR (1900–   )

5225 I need thy presence every passing hour;
What but thy grace can foil the tempt-
er's power?
HENRY FRANCIS LYTE (1793–1847)

5226 If God wants you to do something,
he'll make it possible for you to do it,
but the grace he provides comes only
with the task and cannot be stockpiled
beforehand. We are dependent on him
from hour to hour, and the greater our
awareness of this fact, the less likely
we are to faint or fail in a crisis.
LOUIS CASSELS (1922–1974)

5227 In the Bible there are three distinctive
meanings of grace; it means the mercy
and active love of God; it means the
winsome attractiveness of God; it

means the strength of God to overcome.
CHARLES L. ALLEN (1913–   )

5228 That is the mystery of grace: it never
comes too late.
FRANÇOIS MAURIAC (1885–1970)

5229 The burden of life is from ourselves,
its lightness from the grace of Christ
and the love of God.
WILLIAM BERNARD ULLANTHORNE
(1806–1889)

5230 The growth of grace is like the polishing of metals. There is first an opaque
surface; by and by you see a spark
darting out, then a strong light; till at
length it sends back a perfect image of
the sun that shines upon it.
EDWARD PAYSON (1783–1827)

5231 The law detects, grace alone conquers
sin.
SAINT AUGUSTINE OF HIPPO (354–430)

5232 The law tells me how crooked I am.
Grace comes along and straightens me
out.
DWIGHT LYMAN MOODY (1837–1899)

5233 The motive and purpose behind the
law . . . is to make it clear exactly how
much you must do and no more.
Grace refuses to put a ceiling or a
floor on concern for the neighbor.
JOSEPH FLETCHER

5234 There, but for the grace of God, goes
John Bradford.
—On seeing a condemned man
JOHN BRADFORD (C. 1510–1555)

5235 They travel lightly whom God's grace
carries.
THOMAS À KEMPIS (C. 1380–1471)

5236 To be able to live peaceably with hard
and perverse persons, or with the disorderly, or with such as go contrary to
us, is a great grace.
THOMAS À KEMPIS (C. 1380–1471)

5237 We cannot "psychologize" the grace of
God. God's actions are outside and
above our human sciences.
JOHN POWELL

5238 When the mask of self-righteousness
has been torn from us and we stand
stripped of all our accustomed

defenses, we are candidates for God's generous grace.
ERWIN W. LUTZER (1941–   )

GRATITUDE

5239 A grateful thought toward heaven is of itelf a prayer.
GOTTHOLD EPHRAIM LESSING (1729–1781)

5240 A true Christian is a man who never for a moment forgets what God has done for him in Christ, and whose whole comportment and whole activity have their root in the sentiment of gratitude.
JOHN BAILLIE (1741–1806)

5241 Do not cut down the tree that gives you shade.
ARABIAN PROVERB

5242 Gratitude is a duty which ought to be paid, but which none have a right to expect.
JEAN JACQUES ROUSSEAU (1712–1778)

5243 Gratitude is a seasoning for all seasons.

5244 Gratitude is born in hearts that take time to count up past mercies.
CHARLES EDWARD JEFFERSON (1860–1937)

5245 Gratitude is one of the least articulate of the emotions, especially when it is deep.
FELIX FRANKFURTER (1882–1965)

5246 Gratitude is the heart's memory.
FRENCH PROVERB

5247 Gratitude is the sign of noble souls.
AESOP (FL. C. 550 B.C.)

5248 Gratitude to God makes even a temporal blessing a taste of heaven.
WILLIAM ROMAINE (1714–1795)

5249 How happy a person is depends upon the depth of his gratitude.
JOHN MILLER (1923–1961)

5250 I have found the least gratitude from those families in which I had performed the greatest services.
BENJAMIN RUSH (1746–1813)

5251 I have learned silence from the talkative, toleration from the intolerant, and kindness from the unkind; yet strange, I am ungrateful to those teachers.
KAHLIL GIBRAN (1883–1931)

5252 If a man carries his cross beautifully and makes it radiant with glory of a meek and gentle spirit, the time will come when the things that now disturb will be the events for which he will most of all give gratitude to God.

5253 If gratitude is due from children to their earthly parent, how much more is the gratitude of the great family of men due to our Father in heaven.
HOSEA BALLOU (1771–1852)

5254 If you discern [God's] love in every moment of happiness, you will multiply a thousandfold your capacity to fully enjoy your blessings.
FRANCES J. ROBERTS

5255 Ingratitude is always a form of weakness. I have never known a man of real ability to be ungrateful.
JOHANN WOLFGANG VON GOETHE (1749–1832)

5256 It is not the services we render them, but the services they render us that attaches people to us.
LABICHE ET MARTIN (1815–1888)

5257 It is only with gratitude that life becomes rich.
DIETRICH BONHOEFFER (1906–1945)

5258 Pride slays thanksgiving, but a humble mind is the soil out of which thanks naturally grows. A proud man is seldom a grateful man; he never thinks he gets as much as he deserves.
HENRY WARD BEECHER (1813–1887)

5259 So much has been given to me, I have no time to ponder over that which has been denied.
HELEN ADAMS KELLER (1880–1968)

5260 Swift gratitude is the sweetest.
GREEK PROVERB

5261 The best way to show my gratitude to God is to accept everything, even my problems, with joy.
MOTHER TERESA OF CALCUTTA (1910–   )

5262 The gratitude of most men is but a secret desire of receiving greater benefits.
FRANÇOIS, DUC DE LA ROCHEFOUCAULD (1613–1680)

5263 There is as much greatness of mind in acknowledging a good turn, as in doing it.
LUCIUS ANNAEUS SENECA (C. 4 B.C.–A.D. 65)

5264 Those who wish to sing always find a song.
SWEDISH PROVERB

5265 Thou hast given so much to me
Give one thing more—a grateful heart:
Not thankful when it pleaseth me,
As if thy blessings had spare days,
But such a heart whose pulse may be
Thy praise.
GEORGE HERBERT (1593–1633)

5266 Too great haste to repay an obligation is a kind of ingratitude.
FRANÇOIS, DUC DE LA ROCHEFOUCAULD (1613–1680)

5267 Two kinds of gratitude: the sudden kind we feel for what we take, the larger kind we feel for what we give.
EDWIN ARLINGTON ROBINSON (1869–1935)

5268 When it comes to life, the critical thing is whether you take things for granted or take them with gratitude.
G. K. CHESTERTON (1874–1936)

5269 When the heart is full, the eyes overflow.
SHOLEM ALEICHEM (1859–1916)

5270 When the heart is full, the lips are silent.

5271 You will receive a double portion of joy when you recognize My love coming to you through the kindness of others and when you learn to express your gratitude both to them and to Me.
FRANCES J. ROBERTS

GREATNESS

5272 A great man shows his greatness by the way he treats little men.
THOMAS CARLYLE (1795–1881)

5273 A great man's foolish sayings pass for wise ones.

5274 A quiet life is characteristic of great men; their pleasures have not been of the sort that would look exciting to the outward eye.
BERTRAND ARTHUR WILLIAM RUSSELL (1872–1970)

5275 All greatness is unconscious.
SIR WALTER SCOTT (1771–1832)

5276 Goodness is not tied to greatness, but greatness is tied to goodness.
GREEK PROVERB

5277 Great hopes make great men.
SIR THOMAS FULLER (1608–1661)

5278 Great men are meteors designed to burn so that the earth may be lighted.
NAPOLEON BONAPARTE (1769–1821)

5279 Great men never know they are great.
CHINESE PROVERB

5280 Great men stand like solitary towers in the city of God.
HENRY WADSWORTH LONGFELLOW (1807–1882)

5281 Great minds have purposes, others have wishes. Little minds are tamed and subdued by misfortune; but great minds rise above it.
WASHINGTON IRVING (1783–1859)

5282 Great spirits have always encountered violent opposition from mediocre minds.
ALBERT EINSTEIN (1879–1955)

5283 Greatness is a matter, not of size, but of quality, and it is within the reach of everyone of us. Greatness lies in the faithful performance of whatever duties life places upon us and in the generous performance of the small acts of kindness that God has made possible for us. There is greatness in patient endurance; in unyielding loyalty to a goal; in resistance to the temptation to betray the best we know; in speaking up for the truth when it is assailed; in steadfast adherence to vows given and promises made.
SIDNEY GREENBERG

5284 Greatness lies, not in being strong, but in the right use of strength.
HENRY WARD BEECHER (1813–1887)

5285 He is genuinely great who considers himself small and cares nothing about high honors.
THOMAS À KEMPIS (C. 1380–1471)

5286 He was such a great man that I have forgotten his faults.
VISCOUNT HENRY ST. JOHN BOLINGBROKE (1678–1751)

5287 It is a rough road that leads to the heights of greatness.
LUCIUS ANNAEUS SENECA (C. 4 B.C.–A.D. 65)

5288 Lives of great men all remind us
We can make our lives sublime,
And, departing, leave behind us
Footprints on the sands of time.
HENRY WADSWORTH LONGFELLOW (1807–1882)

5289 No saint, no hero, no discoverer, no prophet, no leader ever did his work cheaply and easily, comfortably and painlessly, and no people was ever great which did not pass through the valley of the shadow of death on its way to greatness.
WALTER LIPPMANN (1889–1974)

5290 Nothing can make a man truly great but being truly good and partaking of God's holiness.
MATTHEW HENRY (1662–1714)

5291 Really great men have a curious feeling that the greatness is not in them but through them.
JOHN RUSKIN (1819–1900)

5292 Serve a great man and you will know what sorrow is.

5293 The beginning of greatness is to be little; the increase of greatness is to be less; the perfection of greatness is to be nothing.
DWIGHT LYMAN MOODY (1837–1899)

5294 The great man is he who does not lose his child's heart.
MENG-TZU (C. 371–C. 289 B.C.)

5295 The great of this world are those who simply loved God more than others did.
A. W. TOZER (1897–1963)

5296 The greater a man is, the more distasteful is praise and flattery to him.
JOHN BURROUGHS (1837–1921)

5297 The greatest man is he who chooses the right with invincible resolution, who resists the sorest temptations from within and without, who bears the heaviest burdens cheerfully, who is calmest in storms and most fearless under menace and frowns, whose reliance on truth, virtue, on God, is most unfaltering; and is this a greatness which is apt to make a show, or which is most likely to abound in conspicuous station?
WILLIAM ELLERY CHANNING (1780–1842)

5298 The greatest truths are the simplest—and so are the greatest men.
AUGUSTUS JOHN CUTHBERT HARE (1834–1903)

5299 The Greek picture of a great man is the picture of a man who is conscious of nothing so much as of his own superiority, a man to whom a confession of need would be a confession of failure. The blessings of the Christian view are for the man conscious of his own poverty, the man sad for his own sins, the man hungry for a goodness which he is sadly conscious that he does not possess.
WILLIAM BARCLAY (1907–1978)

5300 The more one approaches great men, the more one finds that they are men.
BERNARD MANNES BARUCH (1870–1965)

5301 The saints have their power, their glory, their victory, their lustre, and need no worldly or intellectual greatness. . . . God is enough for them.
BLAISE PASCAL (1623–1662)

5302 The world's great men have not commonly been great scholars.
OLIVER WENDELL HOLMES (1809–1894)

5303 There is a melancholy that stems from greatness of mind.
SÉBASTIEN ROCH NICOLAS CHAMFORT (1741–1794)

5304 There is the great man who makes every man feel small, but the really great man is the man who makes every man feel great.
G. K. CHESTERTON (1874–1936)

5305 To be great is to be misunderstood.
RALPH WALDO EMERSON (1803–1882)

5306 True greatness is measured by the degree to which one's life and work emblazon the character and ministry of Jesus Christ.
MARK JORDAN

5307 We are always glad when a great man reassures us of his humanity by possessing a few peculiarities.
ANDRÉ MAUROIS (1885–1967)

5308 Which would you prefer? To be king of the mountain for a day? Or to be a child of God for eternity?
MAX L. LUCADO (1955–)

5309 Whosoever would be great in this world, Jesus was always telling them, is small; and whoever, through his sense of God's greatness, realizes his own smallness, becomes spiritually great.
MALCOLM MUGGERIDGE (1903–1990)

5310 You can be great when you are in good fortune; only in misfortune can you be sublime.
JOHANN FRIEDRICH VON SCHILLER (1759–1805)

GREED

5311 A miser is ever in want.
GREEK PROVERB

5312 Avarice and happiness never saw each other, how then should they become acquainted?
BENJAMIN FRANKLIN (1706–1790)

5313 Covetousness has for its mother unlawful desire, for its daughter injustice, and for its friend violence.
ARABIAN PROVERB

5314 Grasp all, lose all.

5315 He who insists upon having all will have to give up all.
ARABIAN PROVERB

5316 He who seeks more than he needs hinders himself from enjoying what he has.
HEBREW PROVERB

5317 If your desires be endless, your cares will be too.

5318 It is not necessity but abundance which produces greed.
MICHEL EYQUEM DE MONTAIGNE (1533–1592)

5319 No gain satisfies a greedy mind.
LATIN PROVERB

5320 Once upon a time money swore solemnly that nobody who did not love it should have it.

5321 One of the weaknesses of our age is inability to distinguish needs from greeds.
DON ROBINSON

5322 Poverty wants much; greed, everything.
PUBLILIUS SYRUS (FIRST CENTURY B.C.)

5323 Some of us will take all God has to give us while we take good care not to give him anything back.
OSWALD CHAMBERS (1874–1917)

5324 The covetous man is ever in want.
HORACE BUSHNELL (1802–1876)

5325 The covetous man pines in plenty, like Tantalus up to the chin in water, and yet thirsty.
THOMAS ADAMS (C. 1640)

5326 The earth provides enough for every man's need but not for every man's greed.
MAHATMA GANDHI (1869–1948)

5327 The greed of gain has no time or limit to its capaciousness. Its one object is to produce and consume. It has pity neither for beautiful nature nor for living human beings. It is ruthlessly ready without a moment's hesitation to crush beauty and life out of them, molding them into money.
SIR RABINDRANATH TAGORE (1861–1941)

5328 Thinking to get at once all the gold the goose could give, he killed it and opened it only to find—nothing.
AESOP (FL. 550 B.C.)

5329 What he has is no more use to the miser than what he has not.
LATIN PROVERB

GRIEF

5330 A suppressed grief chokes and seethes within, multiplying its strength.
OVID (43 B.C.–A.D. 17)

5331 Count each affliction, whether light or grave,
God's messenger sent down to thee; do thou
With courtesy receive him . . .
Grief should be
Like joy, majestic, equable, sedate;
Confirming, cleansing, raising, making free;
Strong to consume small troubles; to commend
Great thoughts, grave thoughts, thoughts lasting to the end.
AUBREY THOMAS DE VERE (1814–1902)

5332 Deep is the plowing of grief! But often-times less would not suffice for the agriculture of God.
THOMAS DE QUINCEY (1785–1859)

5333 Give sorrow words. The grief that does not speak whispers the o'erfraught heart and bids it break.
WILLIAM SHAKESPEARE (1564–1616)

5334 Grief can be your servant, helping you to feel more compassion for others who hurt.
ROBERT HAROLD SCHULLER (1926–)

5335 Grief is a very antisocial state.
PENELOPE MORTIMER (1918–)

5336 Grief is itself a medicine.
WILLIAM COWPER (1731–1800)

5337 Grief is the agony of an instant; the indulgence of grief, the blunder of a life.
BENJAMIN DISRAELI (1804–1881)

5338 Grief knits two hearts in closer bonds than happiness ever can, and common suffering is a far stronger link than common joy.
ALPHONSE-MARIE-LOUIS DE PRAT DE LAMARTINE (1790–1869)

5339 Grief may be joy misunderstood.
ELIZABETH BARRETT BROWNING (1806–1861)

5340 Happiness is beneficial for the body, but it is grief that develops the powers of the mind.
MARCEL PROUST (1871–1922)

5341 He that conceals his grief finds no remedy for it.
TURKISH PROVERB

5342 I am not mad; I would to heaven I were!
For then, 'tis like I should forget myself;
O, if I could, what grief should I forget!
WILLIAM SHAKESPEARE (1564–1616)

5343 If you bottle grief up, you'll never soften it.
HEBREW PROVERB

5344 In grief nothing "stays put." One keeps on emerging from a phase, but it always recurs. Round and round. Everything repeats. Am I going in circles, or dare I hope I am on a spiral?
C. S. LEWIS (1898–1963)

5345 It is foolish to tear one's hair in grief, as if grief could be lessened by baldness.
CICERO (106–43 B.C.)

5346 Let tears flow of their own accord: their flowing is not inconsistent with inward peace and harmony.
LUCIUS ANNAEUS SENECA (C. 4 B.C.–A.D. 65)

5347 Light griefs can speak; but deeper ones are dumb.
LATIN PROVERB

5348 My grief lies all within;
And these external manners of laments
Are merely shadows to the unseen grief
That swells with silence in the tortured soul.
WILLIAM SHAKESPEARE (1564–1616)

5349 O sacred sorrow, he who knows not thee,
Knows not the best emotions of the heart,
Those tender tears that humanize the soul,
The sign that charms, the pang that gives delight.
HIGH THOMSON KERR (1871–1950)

5350 On the wings of time grief flies away.
JEAN DE LA FONTAINE (1621–1695)

5351 One can bear grief, but it takes two to
be glad.
ELBERT GREEN HUBBARD (1856–1915)

5352 Only when grief finds its work done
can God dispense us from it. Trial
then only stops when it is useless; that
is why it scarcely ever stops.
HENRI FRÉDÉRIC AMIEL (1821–1881)

5353 Pleasure and pain are opposites: when
you share grief, you decrease it; when
you share joy, you increase it.

5354 The great thing with unhappy times is
to take them bit by bit, hour by hour,
like an illness. It is seldom the present,
the exact present, that is unbearable.
C. S. LEWIS (1898–1963)

5355 The greatest griefs are those we cause
ourselves.
SOPHOCLES (C. 496–406 B.C.)

5356 The love of the cross must swallow up
our personal grief.
MEISTER ECKHART (C. 1260–C. 1327)

5357 The more grief inflicted upon you, the
better fitted you are to appreciate joy.
More often than not the so-called negatives are assets. There cannot be a
front with a back, and up without a
down, a cold without heat, a love without hate.
CADLE CALL

5358 There is no grief which time does not
lessen and soften.
CICERO (106–43 B.C.)

5359 There is only one being who can satisfy the last aching abyss of the human
heart, and that is the Lord Jesus Christ.
OSWALD CHAMBERS (1874–1917)

5360 These things are beautiful beyond
belief;
The pleasant weakness that comes
after pain,
The radiant greenness that comes
after rain,
The deepened faith that follows
after grief,
And the awakening to love again.

5361 To weep is to make less the depth of
grief.
WILLIAM SHAKESPEARE (1564–1616)

5362 We are healed of grief only when we
express it to the full.
CHARLES R. SWINDOLL (1934–)

GROWTH

5363 All growth that is not toward God is
growing to decay.
GEORGE MACDONALD (1824–1905)

5364 As long as you're green, you're growing. As soon as you're ripe, you start
to rot.

5365 Be not afraid of growing slowly, be
afraid only of standing still.
CHINESE PROVERB

5366 Growth is demanding and may seem
dangerous, for there is loss as well as
gain in growth.
MAY SARTON (B. 1912)

5367 Measure your growth in grace by your
sensitiveness to sin.
OSWALD CHAMBERS (1874–1917)

5368 The sun warmed the upturned earth
that day. The small seed placed in the
furrow to grow shrank instead and
softened inside as the outside wrinkled. The earth grew dark and damp
and cold. Shriveling hurt until the sun
drew forth from the ache a leaf.
CLAIRE PEDRETTI

5369 We can never be lilies in the garden
unless we have spent time as bulbs in
the dark, totally ignored.
OSWALD CHAMBERS (1874–1917)

GUIDANCE

5370 A deeply spiritual (though misin-
formed) missionary I know used to
pray for special guidance about the
most trivial matters. She would even
try to decide whether it was God's will
that she wash her hair on a given evening. She was right in understanding
that God is interested in the mundane
affairs of life, but she was wrong in
believing that she always needed a special sign. Obviously she was a mental

wreck. She did not realize that the will of God is simply living in obedience to whatever lies ahead. His guidance is not mysterious. In short, if your hair needs washing, wash it!
ERWIN W. LUTZER (1941–)

5371 A glimpse of the next three feet of road is more important and useful than a view of the horizon.
C. S. LEWIS (1898–1963)

5372 Abraham did not know the way, but he knew the Guide.
LEE ROBERSON

5373 All heaven is waiting to help those who will discover the will of God and do it.
J. ROBERT ASHCROFT (1878–1958)

5374 Be simple; take our Lord's hand and walk through things.
FATHER ANDREW

5375 Be thou a bright flame before me,
Be thou a guiding star above me,
Be thou a smooth path below me,
And be a kindly Shepherd behind me,
Today, tonight and forever.
ALEXANDER CARMICHAEL

5376 Before us is a future all unknown, a path untrod;
Beside us a friend well loved and known—
That friend is God.

5377 Behind the dim unknown standeth God within the shadow, keeping watch above his own.
JAMES RUSSELL LOWELL (1819–1891)

5378 Blind unbelief is sure to err,
And scan his work in vain;
God is his own interpreter,
And he will make it plain.
WILLIAM COWPER (1731–1800)

5379 Christ leads me through no darker rooms than he went through before.
RICHARD BAXTER (1615–1691)

5380 Deep in your heart it is not guidance that you want as much as a guide.
JOHN WHITE

5381 Everywhere, O Truth, dost thou give audience to all who ask counsel of thee, and at once answerest all, though on manifold matters they ask thy coun-

sel. Clearly dost thou answer, though all do not clearly hear.
SAINT AUGUSTINE OF HIPPO (354–430)

5382 Follow the river and you will find the sea.
FRENCH PROVERB

5383 From thee, great God, we spring, to thee we tend,
Path, motive, guide, original, and end.
SAMUEL JOHNSON (1709–1784){?}

5384 God Almighty, to reserve to himself the sole right of instructing us, and to prevent our solving the difficulties of our own being, has hid the knot so high, or, to speak more properly, so low, that we cannot reach it.
BLAISE PASCAL (1623–1662)

5385 God calls each of us in secret to make certain sacrifices which always involve a risk, even though it may differ from person to person. God speaks to the crowd, but his call comes to individuals, and through their personal obedience he acts. He does not promise them success, or even final victory in this life. The goal of the adventure to which he commits them is in heaven. God does not promise that he will protect them from trials, from material cares, from sickness, from physical or moral suffering. He promises only that he will be with them in all these trials, and that he will sustain them if they remain faithful to him.
PAUL TOURNIER (1898–1986)

5386 God does not play hide-and-seek.
ERWIN W. LUTZER (1941–)

5387 God gives to every man the virtue, temper, understanding, taste that lifts him into life and lets him fall just in the niche he was ordained to fall.
WILLIAM COWPER (1731–1800)

5388 God has led. God will lead. God is leading!
RICHARD C. HALVERSON (1916–)

5389 God is an ever-present Spirit guiding all that happens to a wise and holy end.
DAVID HUME (1711–1776)

5390 God is more concerned about keeping us in his will than we are to be kept in it!
ERWIN W. LUTZER (1941–   )

5391 God knows what he's about. If he has you sidelined, out of the action for awhile, he knows what he's doing. You just stay faithful . . . stay flexible . . . stay available . . . stay humble, like David with his sheep (even after he had been anointed king!).
CHARLES R. SWINDOLL (1934–   )

5392 God leads us step by step, from event to event. Only afterwards, as we look back over the way we have come and reconsider certain important moments in our lives in the light of all that has followed them, or when we survey the whole progress of our lives, do we experience the feeling of having been led without knowing it, the feeling that God has mysteriously guided us.
PAUL TOURNIER (1898–1986)

5393 God made the moon as well as the sun; and when he does not see fit to grant us the sunlight, he means us to guide our steps by moonlight.
RICHARD WHATELY (1787–1863)

5394 God shall be my hope, my stay, my guide, and lantern to my feet.
WILLIAM SHAKESPEARE (1564–1616)

5395 God speaks to us unceasingly through the events of our life, through the firmness with which he negates our petty human ordering of it, through the regularity with which he disappoints our plans and our attempts to escape, through his endless defeat of all our calculations by which we hoped to become able to do without him. And little by little he tames us, he draws us into relationship with him. Then one day, when we are helpless on a bed, stopped dead by some reverse, isolated by some misfortune, crushed by a sense of our own powerlessness, one day he brings us to the point of resigning ourselves to listening to his language, to admitting his presence, to recognizing his will. And we realize then that he had always been speaking to us.
LOUIS EVELY (1910–   )

5396 God wants to bring us beyond the point where we need signs to discern his guiding hand. Satan cannot counterfeit the peace of God or the love of God dwelling in us. When Christ's abiding presence becomes our guide, then guidance becomes an almost unconscious response to the gentle moving of his Holy Spirit within us.
BOB MUMFORD

5397 God wills us to tread the hidden paths of grace in faith only; and so he only gives us just such light as we need for the present moment. It is not his will that we should see before us or around us, but he never fails to grant such light as makes it impossible for us to lose our way so long as we follow his leading.
JEAN NICOLAS GROU (1731–1803)

5398 God would not have created us without a specific plan in mind.
ERWIN W. LUTZER (1941–   )

5399 God's heavenly plan doesn't always make earthly sense.
CHARLES R. SWINDOLL (1934–   )

5400 God's might to direct me,
God's power to protect me,
God's wisdom for learning,
God's eye for discerning,
God's ear for my hearing,
God's Word for my clearing.
SAINT PATRICK (C. 389–C. 461)

5401 God's order comes in the haphazard, and never according to our scheming and planning. God takes a great delight in breaking up our programs.
OSWALD CHAMBERS (1874–1917)

5402 God's permission means there is no shadow of doubt on the horizon of consciousness; when there is, wait.
OSWALD CHAMBERS (1874–1917)

5403 God's plan, like lilies pure and white, unfold. We must not tear the close-shut leaves apart. Time will reveal the calyxes of gold.
MARY RILEY SMITH (1842–1927)

5404 God's way becomes plain when we
start walking in it.
ROY L. SMITH

5405 God's will is good, acceptable and perfect. We need not fear it.
ERWIN W. LUTZER (1941–)

5406 God's will is not an itinerary but an
attitude.
ANDREW DHUSE

5407 Have you come to the Red Sea place
in your life
Where, in spite of all you can do,
There is no way out, there is no way
back,
There is no other way but through?
ANNIE JOHNSON FLINT (1862–1932)

5408 He guides me and the bird.
In his good time!
ROBERT BROWNING (1812–1889)

5409 However far you go, it is not much
use if it is not in the right direction.
WILLIAM BARCLAY (1907–1978)

5410 I am satisfied that when the Almighty
wants me to do or not to do any particular thing, he finds a way of letting
me know it.
ABRAHAM LINCOLN (1809–1865)

5411 I believe the will of God prevails;
Without him all human reliance is
vain;
Without the assistance of that divine
being I cannot succeed;
With that assistance I cannot fail.
I believe I am a humble instrument in
the hands of our heavenly Father;
I desire that all my works and acts be
according to his will;
And that it may be so, I give thanks to
the Almighty and seek his aid.
—Formulated by Carl Sandburg from
The War Years
ABRAHAM LINCOLN (1809–1865)

5412 I dare not choose my lot
I would not if I might
Choose thou for me, my God
So shall I walk aright.
HORATIUS BONAR (1808–1889)

5413 I faced a future all unknown,
No opening could I see,
I heard without the night wind moan,

The days were dark to me—
I cannot face it all alone
O be thou near to me!
JOHN OXENHAM (1861–1941)

5414 I know not where his islands lift
Their fronded palms in air;
I only know I cannot drift
Beyond his love and care.
JOHN GREENLEAF WHITTIER (1807–1892)

5415 I listened—quiet and still,
there came a voice:
"This path is mine, not thine;
I made the choice.
Dear child, this service will
be best for thee and me
If thou wilt simply trust and
leave the end with me."
And so we travel on.

5416 I never really look for anything. What
God throws my way comes. I wake up
in the morning and whichever way
God turns my feet, I go.
PEARL MAE BAILEY (1918–)

5417 I said to the man who stood at the
gate of the year:
"Give me a light that I may tread
safely into the Unknown."
And he replied: "Go out into the dark-
ness and put your hand
Into the hand of God. That shall be to
you better than light
And safer than a known way."
MINNIE LOUISE HASKINS (1875–1957)

5418 I shall not fear the battle
If thou art by my side,
Nor wander from the pathway
If thou wilt be my guide.
JOHN E. BODE

5419 I would rather walk with God in the
dark than go alone in the light.
MARY GARDINER BRAINARD (C. 1860)

5420 I'll go where you want me to go, dear
Lord,
O'er mountain, or plain, or sea;
I'll say what you want me to say, dear
Lord,
I'll be what you want me to be.
MARY ELIZABETH BROWN (1842–1917)

5421 If God shuts one door, he opens
another.
IRISH PROVERB

5422 If the light is red or even yellow,
you're wise to let God hold you back.
CHARLES R. SWINDOLL (1934–   )

5423 If we read the Old Testament prophets
we see that sometimes . . . the will of
God is that everything should be
destroyed, that the cup of sin be
drained to the dregs, so as to make
possible a resurrection. We find it hard
to understand the detours along which
God takes us, and it is often only afterwards that we see that we had to go
that way.
PAUL TOURNIER (1898–1986)

5424 It is better to ask the way ten times
than to take the wrong road once.
JEWISH PROVERB

5425 It is one thing to know how God
thinks, it is quite another to want
what he wants.
JOHN WHITE

5426 Jesus does it all, and I do nothing, I
hold, and know from experience that
the kingdom of heaven is within us.
Our Lord needs neither books nor
teachers in order to guide our souls.
He, the teacher of teachers, gives his
guidance noiselessly. I have never
heard him speak, and yet I know that
he is within me. At every moment he
instructs me and guides me. And whenever I am in need of it, he enlightens
me afresh.
THERESE OF LISIEUX (1873–1897)

5427 Just walk on uninterruptedly and very
quietly; if God makes you run, he will
enlarge your heart.
SAINT FRANCIS OF SALES (1567–1622)

5428 Lead us, heavenly Father, lead us
O'er the world's tempestuous sea;
Guard us, guide us, keep us, feed us,
For we have no help but thee;
Yet possessing every blessing
If our God our Father be.
JAMES EDMESTON (1791–1867)

5429 Lead, kindly Light, amid the encircling
gloom
Lead thou me on!
The night is dark, and I am far from
home;
Lead thou me on!

Keep thou my feet; I do not ask to see
The distant scene; one step enough
for me.
CARDINAL JOHN HENRY NEWMAN
(1801–1890)

5430 Learn your lessons well in the schoolroom of obscurity. God is preparing
you as his chosen arrow. As yet your
shaft is hidden in his quiver, in the
shadows . . . but at the precise
moment at which it will tell with the
greatest effect, he will reach for you
and launch you to that place of his
appointment.
CHARLES R. SWINDOLL (1934–   )

5431 Let him lead thee blindfold onwards,
Love needs not to know;
Children whom the Father leadeth
Ask not where they go.
GERHARD TERSTEEGEN (1697–1769)

5432 Man makes plans; God changes them.
JEWISH PROVERB

5433 Men give advice; God gives guidance.
LEONARD RAVENHILL (1867–1942)

5434 Not for one single day
Can I discern my way,
But this I surely know—
Who gives the day,
Will show the way,
So I securely go.
JOHN OXENHAM (1861–1941)

5435 Obedience to revealed truth guarantees guidance in matters unrevealed.
ERWIN W. LUTZER (1941–   )

5436 Often God has to shut a door in our
face so that he can subsequently open
the door through which he wants us to
go.
CATHERINE WOOD MARSHALL (1914–1983)

5437 One night a man had a dream. He
dreamed he was walking along the
beach with the Lord. Across the sky
flashed scenes from his life. For each
scene, he noticed two sets of footprints
in the sand: one belonging to him, and
the other to the Lord.
   When the last scene of his life flashed
before him, he looked back at the footprints in the sand. He noticed that many
times along the path of his life there was
only one set of footprints. He also

noticed that it happened at the very lowest and saddest times in his life.

This really bothered him and he questioned the Lord about it. "Lord, you said that once I decided to follow you, you'd walk with me all the way. But I have noticed that during the most troublesome times in my life, there is only one set of footprints. I don't understand why, when I needed you most, you would leave me."

The Lord replied, "My son, my precious child, I love you and I would never leave you. During your times of trial and suffering, when you see only one set of footprints, it was then that I carried you."

5438 Only a God who knows all things and who has infinite wisdom could draft a plan that would anticipate virtually every situation, every sin, every failure.
ERWIN W. LUTZER (1941–)

5439 Signs are given to us because God meets us on the level where we operate. . . . In guidance when God shows us a sign, it doesn't mean we've received the final answer. A sign means we're on the way.
BOB MUMFORD

5440 Simply wait upon him. So doing, we shall be directed, supplied, protected, corrected, and rewarded.
VANCE HAVNER

5441 Take the woman who, in a moment of perplexity, opens her Bible at random, and happens to light upon a passage which exactly meets her need; she sees in it a direct personal message from God. She is in danger of magic if on another occasion she uses the same means and imagines that she is certain to find God's reply to her new problem in some verse thus chosen.
PAUL TOURNIER (1898–1986)

5442 Thank God you don't have to be flawless to be blessed! You need to have a big heart that desires and wants the will of God more than anything else in the world. You need also to have an eye single to his glory.
A. W. TOZER (1897–1963)

5443 That which is often asked of God, is not so much his will and way, as his approval of our way.
S. F. SMILEY

5444 The circumstances of our daily life are to us an infallible indication of God's will, when they concur with the inward promptings of the Spirit and with the Word of God. So long as they are stationary, wait. When you must act, they will open, and a way will be made through oceans and rivers, wastes and rocks.
F. B. MEYER (1847–1929)

5445 The Holy Spirit expects us to take seriously the answers he has already provided, the light he has already shed; and he does not expect us to plead for things that have already been denied.
PAUL E. LITTLE

5446 The one striking thing about following is we must not find our own way, for when we take the initiative, we cease to follow. In the natural world everything depends upon our taking the initiative, but if we are followers of God, we cannot take the initiative, we cannot choose our own work or say what we will do; we have not to find our way at all, we have just to follow.
OSWALD CHAMBERS (1874–1917)

5447 The only way to know is to will to do God's will.
OSWALD CHAMBERS (1874–1917)

5448 The Pilot knows the unknown seas, And he will bring us through.
JOHN OXENHAM (1861–1941)

5449 The process involved in redirecting our lives is often painful, slow, and even confusing. Occasionally it seems unbearable.
CHARLES R. SWINDOLL (1934–)

5450 The ways of Providence cannot be reasoned out by the finite mind. I cannot fathom them, yet seeking to know them is the most satisfying thing in all the world.
SELMA OTTILIANA LOVISA LAGERLÖF (1858–1940)

5451 The will of God is either a burden we
carry or a power which carries us.
CORRIE TEN BOOM (1892–1983)

5452 The wind of God is always blowing
. . . but you must hoist your sail.
FRANÇOIS FÉNELON (1651–1715)

5453 The wrong way always seems the
more reasonable.
GEORGE MOORE (1852–1933)

5454 There are in everyone's life certain connections, twists, and turns which pass
awhile under the category of chance,
but at the last, well examined, prove
to be the very hand of God.
SIR THOMAS BROWNE (1605–1682)

5455 There are two kinds of people: those
who say to God, "Thy will be done,"
and those to whom God says, "All
right, then, have it your way."
C. S. LEWIS (1898–1963)

5456 Thy way, not mine, O Lord,
However dark it be!
Lead me by thine own hand,
Choose out the path for me.
Not mine, not mine the choice,
In things great or small;
Be thou my guide, my strength,
My wisdom and my all!
HORATIUS BONAR (1808–1889)

5457 Trust the past to the mercy of God,
the present to his love, and the future
to his providence.
SAINT AUGUSTINE OF HIPPO (354–430)

5458 We are so mysterious in personality.
There are so many forces at work in
and about us which we cannot calculate or cope with, that if we refuse to
take the guidance of Jesus Christ, we
may, and probably shall be, deluded
by supernatural forces far greater than
ourselves.
OSWALD CHAMBERS (1874–1917)

5459 We cannot get behind the before of
birth or the after of death; therefore
the wise man is the one who trusts the
wisdom of God, not his own wits.
OSWALD CHAMBERS (1874–1917)

5460 We must wait for God, long, meekly,
in the wind and wet, in the thunder
and lightning, in the cold and the
dark. Wait, and he will come. He
never comes to those who do not wait.
He does not go their road. When he
comes, go with him, but go slowly, fall
a little behind; when he quickens his
pace, be sure of it before you quicken
yours. But when he slackens, slacken
at once; and do not be slow only, but
silent, very silent, for he is God.
FREDERICK WILLIAM FABER (1814–1863)

5461 When a train goes through a tunnel
and it gets dark, you don't throw
away your ticket and jump off. You sit
still and trust the engineer.
CORRIE TEN BOOM (1892–1983)

5462 When God shuts a door, he opens a
window.
JOHN RUSKIN (1819–1900)

5463 When we are rightly related to God,
life is full of spontaneous joyful uncertainty and expectancy—we do not
know what God is going to do next;
he packs our life with surprises.
OSWALD CHAMBERS (1874–1917)

5464 When you are rightly related to God,
it is a life of freedom and liberty and
delight; you are God's will and all
your commonsense decisions are his
will for you unless he checks. You
decide things in perfect delightful
friendship with God, knowing that if
your decisions are wrong he will
always check. When he checks, stop at
once.
OSWALD CHAMBERS (1874–1917)

5465 When you walk with God, you get
where he's going.

5466 Whenever ecstasies or visions of God
unfit us for practical life, they are danger signals that the life is on the wrong
track.
OSWALD CHAMBERS (1874–1917)

5467 Whenever we are faced with a crucial
decision, our generation has been
taught to ask, What's in it for me?
Will it give me pleasure? Profit? Security? Fulfillment? We are not necessarily opposed to God; we just fit him in
wherever he is able to help us. The
idea that our wills should be subjected
to his control, even when our personal

ambitions are at stake, is not easy to accept. We can assent mentally to God's control, but in practice, we might still spend our lives pleasing ourselves.
ERWIN W. LUTZER (1941–   )

5468 Where God has put a period, do not change it to a question mark.
T. J. BACH

5469 Who brought me hither
Will bring me hence; no other guide I seek.
JOHN MILTON (1608–1674)

5470 With God, go over the sea—without him, not over the threshold.
RUSSIAN PROVERB

5471 You say, "Where goest thou?" I cannot tell,
And still go on. If but the way be straight,
I cannot go amiss: before me lies
Dawn and the day: the night behind me: that
Suffices me: I break the bounds: I see,
And nothing more; believe and nothing less.
My future is not one of my concerns.
VICTOR HUGO (1802–1885)

GUILT

5472 A guilty conscience is a hidden enemy.
INDIAN PROVERB

5473 A guilty conscience needs no accuser.

5474 All those people weighed down by the obsessive fear of "doing something wrong," or who utter so many prayers that their very number suggests that the utterer has his doubts about their being heard, are not a very good advertisement for the way of God.
PAUL TOURNIER (1898–1986)

5475 Every guilty person is his own hangman.
LUCIUS ANNAEUS SENECA (C. 4 B.C.–A.D. 65)

5476 From the body of one guilty deed
a thousand ghostly fears and haunting thoughts proceed.
WILLIAM WORDSWORTH (1770–1850)

5477 Guilt suggested by the judgment of men is a false guilt if it does not receive inner support by a judgment of God.
PAUL TOURNIER (1898–1986)

5478 He who does what he should not shall feel what he would not.

5479 How guilt, once harbour'd in the conscious breast,
Intimidates the brave, degrades the rest.
SAMUEL JOHNSON (1709–1784)

5480 Keep clear of concealment, keep clear of the need of concealment. It is an awful hour when the first necessity of hiding anything comes. The whole life is different thenceforth. When there are questions to be feared and eyes to be avoided and subjects which must not be touched, then the bloom of life is gone.
PHILLIPS BROOKS (1835–1893)

5481 Love bade me welcome; yet my soul drew back,
Guilty of dust and sin.
GEORGE HERBERT (1593–1633)

5482 My case is bad, Lord, be my advocate,
My sin is red; I'm under God's arrest.
EDWARD TAYLOR (C. 1645–1729)

5483 No creature that deserved redemption would need to be redeemed.
C. S. LEWIS (1898–1963)

5484 No one can be caught in a place he does not visit.
DANISH PROVERB

5485 Psychiatrists require many sessions to relieve a patient of guilt feelings which have made him sick in body and mind; Jesus' power of spiritual and moral persuasion was so overwhelming that he could produce the same effect just by saying: Thy sins be forgiven thee.
MALCOLM MUGGERIDGE (1903–1990)

5486 Regret is an appalling waste of energy; you can't build on it. It's only good for wallowing in.
KATHERINE MANSFIELD (1888–1923)

5487 Religion without guilt just tries to make God a big "pal" of man.
A. W. TOZER (1897–1963)

5488 Suspicion always haunts the guilty
mind;
The thief doth fear each bush an
officer.
WILLIAM SHAKESPEARE (1564–1616)

5489 The act of sin may pass, and yet the
guilt remains.
SAINT THOMAS AQUINAS (1225–1274)

5490 The guilty is he who merely meditates
a crime.
CONTE VITTORIO ALFIERI (1749–1803)

5491 The purpose of being guilty is to
bring us to Jesus. Once we are there,
then its purpose is finished. If we continue to make ourselves guilty—to
blame ourselves—then that is sin in
itself.
CORRIE TEN BOOM (1892–1983)

5492 There smites nothing so sharp, nor
smelleth so sour
As shame.
WILLIAM LANGLAND (C. 1330–C. 1400)

5493 We have no choice but to be guilty.
God is unthinkable if we are innocent.
ARCHIBALD MACLEISH (1892–1982)

5494 Whoever profits by the crime is guilty
of it.
FRENCH PROVERB

H

HABITS

5495 A habit cannot be tossed out the window; it must be coaxed down the stairs a step at a time!
MARK TWAIN (1835–1910)

5496 Habit is a shirt made of iron.
CZECH PROVERB

5497 Habits are cobwebs at first, then become cables.

5498 Habits are servants that regulate your sleep, your work and your thought.
ELBERT GREEN HUBBARD (1856–1915)

5499 Sow an act and you reap a habit.
Sow a habit and you reap a character.
Sow a character and you reap a destiny.
SAMUEL SMILES (1812–1904)

5500 The chains of habit are too weak to be felt until they are too strong to be broken.
SAMUEL JOHNSON (1709–1784)

5501 The second half of a man's life is made up of the habits he acquired during the first half.
FYODOR MIKHAYLOVICH DOSTOYEVSKI (1821–1881)

5502 The strength of a man's virtue should not be measured by his special exertions, but by his habitual acts.
BLAISE PASCAL (1623–1662)

5503 We are creatures of habit. Old cranks have practiced all their lives, just as old saints have likewise practiced all their lives.
JOHN POWELL

HAPPINESS

5504 A frowning face repels. A smile reaches out and attracts. Don't fence it in . . . loosen up . . . smile!
CHARLES R. SWINDOLL (1934–)

5505 All who joy would win must share it. Happiness was born a twin.
LORD GEORGE NOEL GORDON BYRON (1788–1824)

5506 Cherish all your happy moments: they make a fine cushion for old age.
CHRISTOPHER DARLINGTON MORLEY (1890–1957)

5507 Do not look back on happiness or dream of it in the future. You are only

sure of today; do not let yourself be
cheated out of it.
HENRY WARD BEECHER (1813–1887)

5508 Gaiety is often the reckless ripple over
depths of despair.
EDWIN HUBBEL CHAPIN (1814–1880)

5509 Give us, oh, give us, the man who
sings at his work! He will do more in
the same time, he will do it better, he
will persevere longer. One is scarcely
aware of fatigue while he marches to
music.
THOMAS CARLYLE (1795–1881)

5510 God cannot give us happiness and
peace apart from himself, because it is
not there. There is no such thing.
C. S. LEWIS (1898–1963)

5511 God has charged himself with full
responsibility for our eternal happiness and stands ready to take over the
management of our lives.
A. W. TOZER (1897–1963)

5512 Happiness and intelligence are rarely
found in the same person.
WILLIAM FEATHER (B. 1889)

5513 Happiness doesn't depend on the
actual number of blessings we manage
to scratch from life, but on our
attitude toward them.
ALEXANDER ISAYEVICH SOLZHENITSYN
(1918–)

5514 Happiness held is the seed; happiness
shared is the flower.

5515 Happiness is a matter of my attitude.
Happiness begins in the head.
JOHN POWELL

5516 Happiness is a perfume you cannot
pour on others without getting a few
drops on yourself.
RALPH WALDO EMERSON (1803–1882)

5517 Happiness is a thing that comes and
goes, it can never be an end in itself.
Holiness, not happiness, is the end of
man.
OSWALD CHAMBERS (1874–1917)

5518 Happiness is as a butterfly, which,
when pursued, is always just beyond
our grasp, but which, if you will sit
down quietly, may alight upon you.
NATHANIEL HAWTHORNE (1804–1864)

5519 Happiness is like the bluebird of
Maeterlinck: try to catch it and it loses
its color. It's like trying to hold water
in your hands. The more you squeeze
it, the more it runs away.
MICHELANGELO ANTONIONI (1912–)

5520 Happiness is neither within us only, or
without us; it is the union of ourselves
with God.
BLAISE PASCAL (1623–1662)

5521 Happiness is not a question of having
or not having problems.
ROBERT HAROLD SCHULLER (1926–)

5522 Happiness is not a reward, it is a consequence.
ROBERT GREEN INGERSOLL (1833–1899)

5523 Happiness is not a state to arrive at,
but a manner of traveling.
MARGARET LEE RUNBECK

5524 Happiness is not having what you
want, but wanting what you have.
RABBI HYMAN SCHACHTEL (1907–)

5525 Happiness is not in doing what one
likes, but liking what one has to do.
SIR JAMES M. BARRIE (1860–1937)

5526 Happiness is not the absence of conflict, but the ability to cope with it.

5527 Happiness is the light on the water.
The water is cold and dark and deep.
WILLIAM MAXWELL

5528 Happiness is the spiritual experience
of living every minute with love, grace,
and gratitude.
DENIS WAITLEY

5529 Have your heart right with Christ, and
he will visit you often, and so turn
weekdays into Sundays, meals into sacraments, homes into temples, and
earth into heaven.
CHARLES HADDON SPURGEON (1834–1892)

5530 I can say that I never knew what joy
was until I gave up pursuing happiness, or care to live until I chose to
die. For these two discoveries I am
beholden to Jesus.
MALCOLM MUGGERIDGE (1903–1990)

5531 I thought God's purpose was to make
me full of happiness and joy. It is, but

it is happiness and joy from God's standpoint, not from mine.
OSWALD CHAMBERS (1874–1917)

5532 If you don't enjoy what you have now, how can you be happier with more?

5533 If you don't have a little bit of heartache, how do you know when you're happy?
JANE POWELL

5534 If you have to move even ten inches from where you are now in order to be happy, you never will be.
TIM HANSEL

5535 If you think of this world as a place intended simply for our happiness, you find it quite intolerable: think of it as a place of training and correction, and it's not so bad.
C. S. LEWIS (1898–1963)

5536 If your happiness depends on what somebody else says, you have a problem.
RICHARD BACH

5537 It is a barren life that holds only happiness.
FRANCES J. ROBERTS

5538 It is not the level of prosperity that makes for happiness but the kinship of heart to heart and the way we look at the world. Both attitudes are within our power, so that a man is happy so long as he chooses to be happy, and no one can stop him.
ALEXANDER ISAYEVICH SOLZHENITSYN (1918–)

5539 Many people are extremely happy, but are absolutely worthless to society.
CHARLES GOW

5540 Men can only be happy when they do not assume that the object of life is happiness.
GEORGE ORWELL (1903–1950)

5541 Men who are unhappy, like men who sleep badly, are always proud of the fact.
BERTRAND ARTHUR WILLIAM RUSSELL (1872–1970)

5542 Much happiness is overlooked because it doesn't cost anything.
OSCAR WILDE (1854–1900)

5543 No man should desire to be happy who is not at the same time holy. He should spend his efforts in seeking to know and do the will of God, leaving to Christ the matter of how happy he shall be.
A. W. TOZER (1897–1963)

5544 No matter how fair the sun shines, Still it must set.
FERDINAND RAIMUND (1790–1836)

5545 No one truly knows happiness who has not suffered.
HENRI FRÉDÉRIC AMIEL (1821–1881)

5546 O what a happy soul am I!
Although I cannot see,
I am resolved that in this world
Contented I will be.
FANNY CROSBY (1820–1915)

5547 O, how bitter a thing it is to look into happiness through another man's eyes!
WILLIAM SHAKESPEARE (1564–1616)

5548 Of all the different purposes set before mankind, the most disastrous is surely "the pursuit of happiness," slipped into the American Declaration of Independence along with "life and liberty" as an unalienable right, almost accidentally, at the last moment. Happiness is like a young deer, fleet and beautiful. Hunt him, and he becomes a poor frantic quarry; after the kill, a piece of stinking flesh.
MALCOLM MUGGERIDGE (1903–1990)

5549 One of the most persistent and widely believed delusions is that one person can make another happy. You cannot confer on me the fullness of life. That has to be my choice.
JOHN POWELL

5550 Pleasure-seeking is a barren business; happiness is never found till we have the grace to stop looking for it, and to give our attention to persons and matters external to ourselves.
J. I. PACKER (1926–)

5551 Seek for happiness and you will never find it. Seek righteousness and you will discover you are happy. It will be there without your knowing it, without your seeking it.
D. MARTYN LLOYD-JONES (1899–1981)

5552 Success is getting what you want; happiness is wanting what you get.

5553 The doctrine of man's inalienable right to happiness is anti-God and anti-Christ, and its wide acceptance by society tells us a lot about that same society.
A. W. TOZER (1897–1963)

5554 The end of life is not to be happy nor to achieve pleasure and avoid pain, but to do the will of God, come what may.
MARTIN LUTHER KING, JR. (1929–1968)

5555 The greatest happiness you can have is knowing that you do not necessarily require happiness.
WILLIAM SAROYAN (1908–1981)

5556 The happiness of life is made up of minute fractions—the little soon forgotten charities of a kiss or smile, a kind look, a heartfelt compliment, and the countless infinitesimals of pleasurable and genial feeling.
SAMUEL TAYLOR COLERIDGE (1772–1834)

5557 The Lord will happiness divine
On contrite hearts bestow:
Then tell me, gracious God, is mine
A contrite heart, or no?
WILLIAM COWPER (1731–1800)

5558 The pursuit of happiness is a most ridiculous phrase: if you pursue happiness you'll never find it.
CHARLES PERCY SNOW (1905–1980)

5559 The search for happiness is one of the chief sources of unhappiness.
ERIC HOFFER (1902–1983)

5560 The sole cause of man's unhappiness is that he does not know how to stay quietly in his room.
BLAISE PASCAL (1623–1662)

5561 The way to happiness—Keep your heart free from hate, your mind from worry, live simply, expect little, give much.

5562 The word *happiness* comes from the same root as the word *happening*, suggesting that happiness is circumstantial.
TIM HANSEL

5563 There is no cosmetic for beauty like happiness.
MARGUERITE COUNTESS OF BLESSINGTON (1789–1849)

5564 They alone are truly happy who are seeking to be righteous. Put happiness in the place of righteousness and you will never get it.
D. MARTYN LLOYD-JONES (1899–1981)

5565 Those who are content with themselves are in the utmost danger of never knowing that happiness for which they were created.
WILLIAM LAW (1686–1761)

5566 Those who chase happiness run away from contentment.
HASIDIC SAYING

5567 Those who decide to use leisure as a means of mental development, who love good music, good books, good pictures, good plays, good company, good conversation—who are they? They are the happiest people in the world.
WILLIAM LYON PHELPS (1865–1943)

5568 True happiness is of a retired nature, and an enemy to pomp and noise; it arises, in the first place, from the enjoyment of one's self; and in the next, from the friendship and conversation of a few select companions.
JOSEPH ADDISON (1672–1719)

5569 We have no more right to consume happiness without producing it than to consume wealth without producing it.
GEORGE BERNARD SHAW (1856–1950)

5570 We try to be our own masters as if we had created ourselves. Then we hopelessly strive to invent some sort of happiness for ourselves outside of God, apart from God. And out of that hopeless attempt has come human history . . . the long, terrible story of man trying to find something other than God which will make him happy.
C. S. LEWIS (1898–1963)

5571 What we loosely call happiness is more a disposition than an attainment.
SYDNEY J. HARRIS (1917–1986)

5572 When a man is happy he does not hear the clock strike.
GERMAN PROVERB

5573 When one door of happiness closes another opens; but often we look so long at the closed door that we do not see the one which has been opened for us.
HELEN ADAMS KELLER (1880–1968)

5574 Where your pleasure is, there is your treasure. Where your treasure is, there is your heart. Where your heart is, there is your happiness.
SAINT AUGUSTINE OF HIPPO (354–430)

5575 You say that this world to you seems drained of its sweets! I don't know what you call sweet. Honey and the honeycomb, roses and violets, are yet in the earth.
    The sun and moon yet reign in heaven, and the stars keep up their pretty twinklings. Meats and drinks, sweet sights and sweet smells, a country walk, spring and autumn, follies and repentance, quarrels and reconcilements have all a sweetness by turns. Good humor and good nature, friends at home that love you, and friends abroad that miss you—you possess all these things, and more innumerable, and these are all sweet things. You may extract honey from everything.
CHARLES LAMB (1775–1834)

HASTE

5576 God made time, but man made haste.
IRISH PROVERB

5577 Haste: breathless for no reason and busy doing nothing.
PHAEDRUS (C. 15 B.C.–A.D. 50)

5578 Hasten slowly.
AUGUSTUS CAESAR (63 B.C.–A.D. 14)

5579 Hurry is not of the devil; it is the devil.
CARL GUSTAV JUNG (1875–1961)

5580 Impulse manages all things badly.
LATIN PROVERB

5581 In divine things there is never hurry, and hurry is not a divine thing.
FATHER ANDREW

5582 Make haste slowly.
SUETONIUS (C. 69–AFTER 122)

5583 Nothing should be done in haste except catching fleas.
SCOTTISH PROVERB

5584 People in a hurry cannot think, cannot grow, nor can they decay. They are preserved in a state of perpetual puerility.
ERIC HOFFER (1902–1983)

5585 Plenty of people miss their share of happiness, not because they never found it, but because they didn't stop to enjoy it.
WILLIAM FEATHER (1889–   )

5586 Rashness and haste make all things insecure.
SIR JOHN DENHAM (1615–1669)

5587 Slow me down, Lord; I am going too fast.
I can't see my brother when he's walking past.
I miss a lot of good things day by day;
I don't know a blessing when it comes my way.

5588 Take time for all things: great haste makes great waste.
BENJAMIN FRANKLIN (1706–1790)

5589 The man who hasn't time to stop at a railroad crossing always finds time to attend his funeral.

5590 We move through life in such a distracted way that we do not even take the time and rest to wonder if any of the things we think, say, or do are *worth* thinking, saying, or doing.
HENRI J. M. NOUWEN

5591 What's the use of hurrying when there's a perfectly good day coming tomorrow that hasn't even been touched.

5592 Whoever is in a hurry shows that the thing he is about is too big for him.
LORD CHESTERFIELD (1694–1773)

HATRED

5593 Folks never understand the folks they hate.
JAMES RUSSELL LOWELL (1819–1891)

5594 Had I gone my own way and not gotten to know God or accepted him as a part of my life, I think that I would have been a very belligerent individual, full of hate and bitterness.
ANITA BRYANT (1940–)

5595 Hatred is blind as well as love.
SIR THOMAS FULLER (1608–1661)

5596 Hatred is like burning down your own house to get rid of a rat.
HARRY EMERSON FOSDICK (1878–1969)

5597 Hatred is like fire; it makes even light rubbish deadly.
GEORGE ELIOT (1819–1880)

5598 Hatred is self-punishment.
HOSEA BALLOU (1771–1852)

5599 If I hate or despise any one man in the world, I hate something which God cannot hate, and despise that which he loves.
WILLIAM LAW (1686–1761)

5600 If you hate a person, you hate something in him that is part of yourself. What isn't part of ourselves doesn't disturb us.
HERMANN HESSE (1877–1962)

5601 Life has taught me that it is not for our faults that we are disliked and even hated, but for our qualities.
BERNARD BERENSON (1865–1959)

5602 Love blinds us to faults, but hatred blinds us to virtues.
MOSES BEN JACOB IBN EZRA (C. 1135)

5603 Violent hatred sinks us below those we hate.
FRENCH PROVERB

HEALTH

5604 Fear less, hope more;
Eat less, chew more;
Whine less, breathe more;
Hate less, love more;
And all good things are yours.
SWEDISH PROVERB

5605 From the bitterness of disease man learns the sweetness of health.
SPANISH PROVERB

5606 He who formed our frame
Made man a perfect whole
And made the body's health
Depend upon the soul.

5607 Health and cheerfulness mutually beget each other.
JOSEPH ADDISON (1672–1719)

5608 Health and wealth wean us of our need for Christ.
CALVIN MILLER

5609 Health is better than wealth.
ENGLISH PROVERB

5610 I have prayed hundreds, if not thousands, of times for the Lord to heal me—and he finally healed me of the need to be healed.
TIM HANSEL

5611 I treated him, God cured him.
AMBROISE PARÉ (1517–1590)

5612 It has been scientifically proven that worry, discord, and melancholy undermine health. Good spirits make for good digestion. Cheerfulness costs nothing; yet is beyond price.
B. C. FORBES

5613 Malignity of soul often dwells in diseased bodies.
JOHANN FRIEDRICH VON SCHILLER (1759–1805)

5614 Our Father yet heals the spirit of amputees—even when they will not grow legs. And, once the spirit is healed, the legs can be done without.
CALVIN MILLER

5615 Prescription for a happier and healthier life: resolve to slow your pace; learn to say no gracefully; resist the temptation to chase after more pleasures, hobbies, and more social entanglements; then "hold the line" with the tenacity of a tackle for a professional football team.
JAMES C. DOBSON (1936–)

5616 Psychotherapy will put a Band-Aid on the gash; but for healing, men's lives must be changed from within.
RAYMOND J. LARSON

5617 The best of healers is good cheer.
PINDAR (C. 522–438 B.C.)

5618 Those obsessed with health are not healthy; the first requisite of good

health is a certain calculated carelessness about oneself.
SYDNEY J. HARRIS (1917–1986)

5619 Youth thinks nothing of health, and
age thinks of nothing but.

HEART

5620 A heart in every thought renewed
    And full of love divine,
Perfect and right and pure and good,
A copy, Lord, of thine.
CHARLES WESLEY (1707–1788)

5621 God has two dwellings: one in heaven,
and the other in a meek and thankful
heart.
IZAAK WALTON (1593–1683)

5622 It is only with the heart that one can
see rightly; what is essential is invisible
to the eye.
ANTOINE DE SAINT-EXUPÉRY (1900–1944)

5623 Sighs are the natural language of the
heart.
THOMAS SHADWELL (C. 1642–1692)

5624 The secret of your own heart you can
never know; but you can know him
who knows its secret.
GEORGE MACDONALD (1824–1905)

5625 The widest thing in the universe is not
space; it is the potential capacity of the
human heart. Being made in the image
of God, it is capable of almost unlimited extension in all directions. And
one of the world's greatest tragedies is
that we allow our hearts to shrink
until there is room in them for little
beside ourselves.
A. W. TOZER (1897–1963)

5626 To my God, a heart of flame; to my
fellowmen, a heart of love; to myself,
a heart of steel.
SAINT AUGUSTINE OF HIPPO (354–430)

5627 We cough to clear our throats. We
sigh to clear our hearts.
T. S. MATTHEWS

5628 You can't reason with your heart; it
has its own laws, and thumps about
things which the intellect scorns.
MARK TWAIN (1835–1910)

HEAVEN

5629 A continual looking forward to the
eternal world is not a form of escapism or wishful thinking, but one of the
things a Christian is meant to do. It
does not mean that we are to leave the
present world as it is. If you read history, you will find that the Christians
who did the most for the present
world were just those who thought
most of the next.
C. S. LEWIS (1898–1963)

5630 Aim at heaven and you get earth
thrown in. Aim at earth and you get
neither.
C. S. LEWIS (1898–1963)

5631 All the scriptural imagery (harps,
crowns, gold, etc.) is, of course, a
merely symbolical attempt to express
the inexpressible. Musical instruments
are mentioned because for many
people (not all) music is the thing
known in the present life which most
strongly suggests ecstasy and infinity.
Crowns are mentioned to suggest the
fact that those who are united with
God in eternity share his spendor and
power and joy. Gold is mentioned to
suggest the timelessness of heaven
(gold does not rust) and the precious-
ness of it. People who take these symbols literally might as well think that
when Christ told us to be like doves,
he meant that we were to lay eggs.
C. S. LEWIS (1898–1963)

5632 Anyone can devise a plan by which
good people may go to heaven. Only
God can devise a plan whereby sinners, who are his enemies, can go to
heaven.
LEWIS SPERRY CHAFER (1871–1952)

5633 Beyond this vale of tears
There is a life above
Unmeasured by the flight of years
And all that life is love.
JAMES MONTGOMERY

5634 By heaven we understand a state of
happiness infinite in degree and endless in duration.
BENJAMIN FRANKLIN (1706–1790)

5635 Come, Lord, when grace has made me
meet
Thy blessed face to see;
For if thy work on earth be sweet
What will thy glory be!
My knowledge of that life is small
The eye of faith is dim;
But 'tis enough that Christ knows all
And I shall be with him.
RICHARD BAXTER (1615–1691)

5636 Earth breaks up, time drops away,
In flows heaven, with its new day.
ROBERT BROWNING (1812–1889)

5637 Earth has no sorrow that heaven cannot heal.
THOMAS MOORE (1779–1852)

5638 Faith is the Christian's foundation,
hope is his anchor, death is his harbor,
Christ is his pilot, and heaven is his
country.
JEREMY TAYLOR (1613–1667)

5639 God is the author, men are only the
players. These grand pieces which are
played upon earth have been composed in heaven.
HONORÉ DE BALZAC (1799–1850)

5640 Great Spirit, give to me
A heaven not so large as yours
But large enough for me.
EMILY ELIZABETH DICKINSON (1830–1886)

5641 He that will enter into paradise must
come with the right key.
SIR THOMAS FULLER (1608–1661)

5642 Heaven begins where sin ends.
THOMAS ADAMS (1612–1653)

5643 Heaven is a place prepared for those
who are prepared for it.

5644 Heaven is not a resting place, where
men may sleep out an eternity; there
they rest not day nor night, but their
work is their rest and continual recreation, and toil and weariness have no
place there. They rest there in God,
who is the center of their souls. Here
they find the completion or satisfaction of all their desires, having the full
enjoyment of God and uninterrupted
communion with him.
THOMAS BOSTON (1676–1732)

5645 Heaven is not a reward for "being a
good boy" but is the continuation and
expansion of a quality of life which
begins when a man's central confidence is transferred from himself to
God.
J. B. PHILLIPS (1906–1982)

5646 Heaven is the perfectly ordered and
harmonious enjoyment of God and of
one another in God.
SAINT AUGUSTINE OF HIPPO (354–430)

5647 Heaven is the place where questions
and answers become one.
ELIE WIESEL

5648 Heaven would hardly be heaven if we
could define it.
WILLIAM EDWARD BIEDERWOLF
(1867–1939)

5649 Heaven-gates are not so highly arch'd
As princes' palaces; they that enter
there
Must go upon their knees.
JOHN WEBSTER (1782–1852)

5650 Hell is God's justice; heaven is his
love; earth, his long-suffering.

5651 How far away is heaven? It is not so
far as some imagine. It wasn't very far
from Daniel. It was not so far off that
Elijah's prayer and those of others
could not be heard there. Men full of
the Spirit can look right into heaven.
DWIGHT LYMAN MOODY (1837–1899)

5652 I would not give one moment of
heaven for all the joys and riches of
the world, even if it lasted for thousands and thousands of years.
MARTIN LUTHER (1483–1546)

5653 I'm not going to heaven because I've
preached to great crowds of people.
I'm going to heaven because Christ
died on that cross. None of us are
going to heaven because we're good.
And we're not going to heaven
because we've worked. We're not
going to heaven because we pray and
accept Christ. We're going to heaven
because of what he did on the cross.
All I have to do is receive him. And it's
so easy to receive Christ that millions
stumble over its sheer simplicity.
BILLY GRAHAM (1918–   )

5654 If a person does not enjoy the worship and services of the Lord, he no doubt would be out of place in heaven.
A. G. HOBBS, JR.

5655 If I ever reach heaven, I expect to find three wonders there: first, to meet some I had not thought to see there; second, to miss some I had expected to see there; and third, the greatest wonder of all, to find myself there.
JOHN NEWTON (1725–1807)

5656 If you read history, you will find that the Christians who did most for the present world were just those who thought most of the next. The apostles themselves, who set on foot the conversion of the Roman Empire, the great men who built up the Middle Ages, the English evangelicals who abolished the slave trade, all left their mark on earth, precisely because their minds were occupied with heaven. It is since Christians have largely ceased to think of the other world that they have become so ineffective in this.
C. S. LEWIS (1898–1963)

5657 In heaven it is always autumn. His mercies are ever in their maturity.
JOHN DONNE (1572–1631)

5658 In heaven, to be even the least is a great thing, for all will be great.
THOMAS À KEMPIS (C. 1380–1471)

5659 It is not darkness you are going to, for God is light. It is not lonely, for Christ is with you. It is not an unknown country, for Christ is there.
CHARLES KINGSLEY (1819–1875)

5660 John Bunyan was once asked a question about heaven which he could not answer because the matter was not revealed in the Scriptures. He advised the inquirer to live a holy life, then go and see.
JOHN BUNYAN (1628–1688)

5661 Lord, I've been active all my life. This idea of eternal rest frightens me. The beatific something-or-other they talk about in sermons doesn't mean a thing to me. I shall be thoroughly miserable

if all I have to do is to gaze and gaze. Isn't there anything to do in heaven?
DAVID HEAD

5662 No man can resolve himself into heaven.
DWIGHT LYMAN MOODY (1837–1899)

5663 No man was ever scared into heaven.
SIR THOMAS FULLER (1608–1661)

5664 One path leads to Paradise, but a thousand lead to hell.
JEWISH PROVERB

5665 The bottom line is in heaven.
EDWIN HERBERT LAND (1909–   )

5666 The early Christians were so much in that other world that nothing which happened to them in this one seemed very important.
HANNAH HURNARD (1905–1990)

5667 The highest bliss in heaven (save God) shall surely be
Hearts opened to each other in pure transparency.
ANGELUS SILESIUS (1624–1677)

5668 The man who is seriously convinced that he deserves to go to hell is not likely to go there, while the man who believes that he is worthy of heaven will certainly never enter that blessed place.
A. W. TOZER (1897–1963)

5669 The Promised Land always lies on the other side of a wilderness.
HAVELOCK ELLIS (1859–1939)

5670 There is a land of pure delight,
Where saints immortal reign;
Infinite day excludes the night,
And pleasures banish pain.
ISAAC WATTS (1674–1748)

5671 There is not a Quaker or a Baptist, a Presbyterian or an Episcopalian, a Catholic or a Protestant in heaven; on entering the gate, we leave those badges of schism behind.
THOMAS JEFFERSON (1743–1826)

5672 Think of yourself just as a seed patiently wintering in the earth; waiting to come up a flower in the Gardener's good time, up into the real world, the real waking. I suppose that our whole present life, looked back on from there, will seem only a drowsy

half-waking. We are here in the land of dreams. But cock-crow is coming.
C. S. LEWIS (1898–1963)

5673 Though we live on earth we have already established legal residence in heaven.
ERWIN W. LUTZER (1941–)

5674 To believe in heaven is not to run away from life; it is to run toward it.
JOSEPH D. BLINCO

5675 To get to heaven, turn right and keep straight.

5676 Today I am one day nearer home than ever before. One day nearer the dawning when the fog will lift, mysteries clear, and all question marks straighten up into exclamation points! I shall see the King!
VANCE HAVNER

5677 We talk about heaven being so far away. It is within speaking distance to those who belong there.
DWIGHT LYMAN MOODY (1837–1899)

5678 We thank God for having created this world, and praise him for having made another, quite different one, where the wrongs of this one are corrected.
ANATOLE FRANCE (1844–1924)

5679 When once our heav'nly-guided soul shall climb,
Then all this earthly grossness quit,
Attir'd with stars, we shall forever sit,
Triumphing over death and chance and thee, O Time.
JOHN MILTON (1608–1674)

5680 When you speak of heaven, let your face light up. When you speak of hell—well, then your everyday face will do.
CHARLES HADDON SPURGEON (1834–1892)

5681 You will get to heaven by accepting Christ as Savior, but by accepting Christ as Lord you will bring heaven down to yourself.
JORDAN C. KHAN

5682 You'll get pie in the sky when you die.
JOE HILL (1879–1915)

HELL

5683 All hope abandon, ye who enter here.
DANTE ALIGHIERI (1265–1321)

5684 Damnation: continual dying.
JOHN DONNE (1572–1631)

5685 Even as in heaven there will be most perfect charity, so in hell there will be the most perfect hate.
SAINT THOMAS AQUINAS (1225–1274)

5686 God will never send anybody to hell. If man goes to hell, he goes by his own free choice. Hell was created for the devil and his angels, not for man. God never meant that man should go there.
BILLY GRAHAM (1918–)

5687 Hell is full of the ungrateful.

5688 Hell is paved with good intentions.
JAMES BOSWELL (1740–1795)

5689 Hell is the highest reward that the devil can offer you for being a servant of his.
BILLY SUNDAY (1862–1935)

5690 Hell is truth seen too late.
TRYON EDWARDS (1809–1894)

5691 Hell is where everyone is doing his own thing. Paradise is where everyone is doing God's thing.
THOMAS HOWARD

5692 Hell is where no one has anything in common with anybody else except the fact that they all hate one another and cannot get away from one another and from themselves.
THOMAS MERTON (1915–1968)

5693 Hell, madame, is to love no longer.
GEORGES BERNANOS (1888–1948)

5694 I had ambition, by which sin
The angels fell;
I climbed, and step by step, O Lord,
Ascended into hell.
WILLIAM HENRY DAVIES (1871–1940)

5695 If you insist on having your own way, you will get it. Hell is the enjoyment of your own way forever.
DANTE ALIGHIERI (1265–1321)

5696 Teeth will be provided for those who do not have teeth.

5697 The essence of hell is complete separation from God, and that is the ultimate disaster.
W. R. MATTHEWS (1818–1909)

5698 The gnashing of teeth . . . despair, when men see themselves abandoned by God.
MARTIN LUTHER (1483–1546)

5699 The one principle of hell is, "I am my own."
GEORGE MACDONALD (1824–1905)

5700 The pain of punishment will be without the fruit of penitence; weeping will be useless, and prayer ineffectual. Too late they will believe in eternal punishment who would not believe in eternal life.
SAINT CYPRIAN (200–258)

5701 The road to hell is easy to travel.
BION (FL. C. 100 B.C.)

5702 The safest road to hell is the gradual one—the gentle slope, soft underfoot, without sudden turnings, without milestones, without signposts.
C. S. LEWIS (1898–1963)

5703 There are harps in heaven, but cymbals in hell.
IRISH PROVERB

5704 There are no fans in hell.
ARABIAN PROVERB

5705 We must picture hell as a state where everyone is perpetually concerned about his own dignity and advancement, where everyone has a grievance, and where everyone lives the deadly serious passions of envy, self-importance, and resentment.
C. S. LEWIS (1898–1963)

5706 What do the damned endure, but despair?
WILLIAM CONGREVE (1670–1729)

5707 What is hell? The suffering that comes from the consciousness that one is no longer able to love.
FYODOR MIKHAYLOVICH DOSTOYEVSKI (1821–1881)

HISTORY

5708 A historian is a prophet in reverse.
AUGUST WILHELM VON SCHLEGEL (1767–1845)

5709 All history is incomprehensible without Christ.
JOSEPH ERNEST RENAN (1823–1892)

5710 Christ is the great central fact in the world's history. To him everything looks forward or backward. All the lines of history converge upon him. All the great purposes of God culminate in him. The greatest and most momentous fact which the history of the world records is the fact of his birth.
CHARLES HADDON SPURGEON (1834–1892)

5711 God raised up Jesus, not simply to give credence to man's immemorial hopes of life beyond the grave, but to shatter history and remake it by a cosmic, creative event, ushering in a new age and a new dimension of existence.
J. S. STEWART (1896–   )

5712 History is a story written by the finger of God.
C. S. LEWIS (1898–1963)

5713 History is an endless repetition of the wrong way of living.
LAWRENCE DURRELL (1912–   )

5714 History is too fragile and indeterminate a structure to contain Jesus; like—using the imagery of one of his own parables—the old wineskins into which new wine cannot be put, or like the worn cloth which cannot be patched with new. How shabby, how patched and repatched, how threadbare and faded this fabric of history is, compared with the ever-renewed, gleaming and glistening garment of truth!
MALCOLM MUGGERIDGE (1903–1990)

5715 History teaches us the mistakes we are going to make.

5716 Jesus Christ is everywhere; he is behind everything we see if only we have eyes to see him; and he is the Lord of history if only we penetrate deep enough beneath the surface.
CHARLES HABIB MALIK (1906–   )

5717 Jesus Christ was not a man who twenty centuries ago lived on this earth for thirty-three years and was crucified; he was God Incarnate, manifested at one point of history. All before looked forward to that point; all since look back to it. The presentation of this fact produces what no other fact in the whole of history could produce: the miracle of God at work in human souls.
OSWALD CHAMBERS (1874–1917)

5718 Looking for Jesus in history is as futile as trying to invent a yardstick that will measure infinity, or a clock that will tick through eternity. God molds history to his purposes, revealing in it the fearful symmetry which is his language in conversing with men; but history is no more than the clay in which he works.
MALCOLM MUGGERIDGE (1903–1990)

5719 Man writes histories; goodness is silent. History is, indeed, little more than the register of the crimes, follies, and misfortunes of mankind.
EDWARD GIBBON (1737–1794)

5720 Many great events have been touched off by very small agencies, but who could possibly have divined the total redirection of history that would follow the arrival of thirteen men—Jesus and his twelve disciples—in Jerusalem for the Feast of the Passover round about A.D. 33, in the reign of the Emperor Tiberius?
MALCOLM MUGGERIDGE (1903–1990)

5721 No revolution that has ever taken place in society can be compared to that which has been produced by the words of Jesus Christ.
MARK HOPKINS (1802–1887)

5722 Providence is like a curious piece of arras, made up of thousands of shreds, which single we know not what to make of, but put together they present us with a beautiful history.
JOHN FLAVEL (C. 1627–1691)

5723 Skepticism has not founded empires, established principles, or changed the world's heart. The great doers of history have always been men of faith.
EDWIN HUBBEL CHAPIN (1814–1880)

5724 The concern to know where history is going is not an idle philosophical curiosity. It is a necessary expression of the conviction that God has worked in past history and has promised to continue thus to be active among men. If God is the kind of God-active-in-history of whom the Bible speaks, then concern for the course of history is itself not an illegitimate or an irrelevant concern.
JOHN HOWARD YODER

5725 The most important events in every age never reach the history books.
C. S. LEWIS (1898–1963)

5726 The most outstanding record that is graven on the scroll of time is the date of the birth of Jesus Christ. No issued document is legal, no signed check is valid, and no business receipt is of value unless it bears the statistical reference to this great historic event.
HOMER G. RHEA, JR.

5727 The name of Jesus is not so much written as plowed into the history of the world.
RALPH WALDO EMERSON (1803–1882)

5728 The nature of Christ's existence is mysterious, I admit; but this mystery meets the wants of man. Reject it and the world is an inexplicable riddle; believe it, and the history of our race is satisfactorily explained.
NAPOLEON BONAPARTE (1769–1821)

5729 The story of how Jesus came into the world, what he said and did there, and how he left the world while still remaining in it, has, it is safe to say, been more told, mulled over, analyzed, and expounded and illustrated, than any other in human history.
MALCOLM MUGGERIDGE (1903–1990)

5730 Throughout history, truth has been considered a form of dementia, and those who have turned away from fantasy and fixed their eyes on reality, judged insane.
MALCOLM MUGGERIDGE (1903–1990)

5731 What a story a redwood stump could tell, with its 2000 rings of annual growth. One of the outermost rings carries us back to the landing of the Pilgrims. Count back from there: 1600, 1500, 1400, 1100—you are still only at the First Crusade. Keep on counting, year by year. Your eyes will be sore and strained before you get back to the year when Alaric was sacking a fallen humbled Rome. And yet this proud, this lusty American tree was already a strong young giant. When it was a sapling the Chinese were inventing paper. When it was a hopeful shoot, Pompeii, the pride of pagan pleasure cities, was buried under the ashes of Vesuvius. As the seed sprouted, Christ was born in Bethlehem.
DONALD CULROSS PEATTIE

5732 What Satan put into the heads of our remote ancestors was the idea that they could "be like gods"—could set up on their own as if they had created themselves—be their own masters—invent some sort of happiness for themselves outside God, apart from God. And out of that hopeless attempt has come nearly all that we call human history—money, poverty, ambition, war, prostitution, classes, empires, slavery—the long terrible story of man trying to find something other than God which will make him happy.
C. S. LEWIS (1898–1963)

5733 Who could possibly be harmed or impoverished, from the point of view of knowing and loving and worshiping Jesus Christ, if he knew something authentic about St. Ignatius of Antioch, or St. John Chrysostom, or St. Basil the Great, or St. Ephrem, or St. Augustine, or St. Thomas Aquinas, or St. Teresa of Avila? I assure you these are among the greatest Christians of all time, and Protestants will not be polluted if they steep themselves in them.
CHARLES HABIB MALIK (1906–)

HOLINESS

5734 *Holy* has the same root as wholly, it means complete. A man is not complete in spiritual stature if all his mind, heart, soul, and strength are not given to God.
R. J. STEWART

5735 A holy life is a voice; it speaks when the tongue is silent and is either a constant attraction or a perpetual reproof.
ARCHBISHOP ROBERT LEIGHTON (1611–1684)

5736 A holy life is not an ascetic, or gloomy, or solitary life, but a life regulated by divine truth and faithful in Christian duty. It is living above the world while we are still in it.
TRYON EDWARDS (1809–1894)

5737 A holy life will produce the deepest impression. Lighthouses blow no horns; they only shine.
DWIGHT LYMAN MOODY (1837–1899)

5738 Although we become Christians instantaneously by faith in Christ, knowing God and developing faith is a gradual process. There are no shortcuts to maturity. It takes time to be holy.
ERWIN W. LUTZER (1941–)

5739 Holiness has love for its essence, humility for its clothing, the good of others as its employment, and the honor of God as its end.
NATHANAEL EMMONS (1745–1840)

5740 Holiness in a human being is only manifested by antagonism.
OSWALD CHAMBERS (1874–1917)

5741 Holiness is a fire whose outgoing warmth pervades the universe.
PLOTINUS (205–270)

5742 Holiness is inwrought by the Holy Spirit, not because we have suffered, but because we have surrendered.
RICHARD SHELLEY TAYLOR

5743 Holiness is not exemption from conflict, but victory through conflict.
G. CAMPBELL MORGAN (1863–1945)

5744 Holiness is not freedom from temptation, but power to overcome temptation.
G. CAMPBELL MORGAN (1863–1945)

5745 Holiness is not inability to sin, but ability not to sin.
G. CAMPBELL MORGAN (1863–1945)

5746 Holiness is not the end of progress, but deliverance from standing still.
G. CAMPBELL MORGAN (1863–1945)

5747 Holiness is the symmetry of the soul.
PHILIP HENRY (1631–1696)

5748 Holiness means something more than the sweeping away of the old leaves of sin; it means the life of Jesus developed in us.
I. LILIAS TROTTER

5749 Holy is the way God is. To be holy he does not conform to a standard. He is that standard. He is absolutely holy with an infinite, incomprehensible fullness of purity that is incapable of being other than it is. Because he is holy, all his attributes are holy; that is, whatever we think of as belonging to God must be thought of as holy.
A. W. TOZER (1897–1963)

5750 How little people know who think that holiness is dull. When one meets the real thing . . . it is irresistible. If even 10 percent of the world's population had it, would not the whole world be converted and happy before a year's end?
C. S. LEWIS (1898–1963)

5751 If only ten among us be righteous, the ten will become twenty, the twenty fifty, the fifty a hundred, the hundred a thousand, and the thousand will become the entire city. As when ten lamps are kindled, a whole house may easily be filled with light; so it is with the progress of spiritual things. If but ten among us lead a holy life, we shall kindle a fire which shall light up the entire city.
SAINT JOHN CHRYSOSTOM (C. 347–407)

5752 It is quite true to say, "I can't live a holy life," but you can decide to let Jesus make you holy.
OSWALD CHAMBERS (1874–1917)

5753 It is time for us Christians to face up to our responsibility for holiness. Too often we say we are "defeated" by this or that sin. No, we are not defeated; we are simply disobedient. It might be well if we stopped using the terms *victory* and *defeat* to describe our progress in holiness. Rather we should use the terms *obedience* and *disobedience*.
JERRY BRIDGES

5754 Our progress in holiness depends on God and ourselves—on God's grace and on our will to be holy.
MOTHER TERESA OF CALCUTTA (1910–   )

5755 Saying yes to God means saying no to things that offend his holiness.
A. MORGAN DERHAM

5756 Spring cleaning should begin with the head and end with the heart.

5757 The destined end of man is not happiness, nor health, but holiness. God's one aim is the production of saints. He is not an eternal blessing machine for men; he did not come to save men out of pity; he came to save men because he had created them to be holy.
OSWALD CHAMBERS (1874–1917)

5758 The essence of true holiness is conformity to the nature and will of God.
SAMUEL LUCAS (1818–1868)

5759 The greatest miracle that God can do today is to take an unholy man out of an unholy world, and make that man holy and put him back into that unholy world and keep him holy in it.
LEONARD RAVENHILL (1867–1942)

5760 The holier a man is, the less he is understood by men of the world.
CARDINAL JOHN HENRY NEWMAN (1801–1890)

5761 The holiest person is . . . one who is most conscious of what sin is.
OSWALD CHAMBERS (1874–1917)

5762 The holy man is not one who cannot sin. A holy man is one who will not sin.
A. W. TOZER (1897–1963)

5763 The holy man is the most humble man you can meet.
OSWALD CHAMBERS (1874–1917)

5764 The inward stirring and touching of God makes us hungry and yearning; for the Spirit of God hunts our spirit, and the more it touches it, the greater our hunger and our craving.
JAN VAN RUYSBROECK (1293–1381)

5765 The old word for *holy* in the German language, *heilig,* also means healthy. And so *heilbronn* means holy-well, or healthy-well. You could not get any better definition of what *holy* really is than healthy—completely healthy.
THOMAS CARLYLE (1795–1881)

5766 The serene, silent beauty of a holy life is the most powerful influence in the world, next to the might of the Spirit of God.
BLAISE PASCAL (1623–1662)

5767 The true Christian ideal is not to be happy but to be holy.
A. W. TOZER (1897–1963)

5768 There is no detour to holiness. Jesus came to the resurrection through the cross, not around it.
LEIGHTON FORD

5769 Things that are holy are revealed only to men who are holy.
HIPPOCRATES (C. 460–C. 377 B.C.)

5770 When God purifies the heart by faith, the market is sacred as well as the sanctuary.
MARTIN LUTHER (1483–1546)

5771 When godliness is produced in you from the life that is deep within you— then that godliness is real, lasting and the genuine essence of the Lord.
MADAME JEANNE MARIE DE LA MOTHE GUYON (1648–1717)

HOLY SPIRIT

5772 Before we can be filled with the Spirit, the desire to be filled must be all-consuming. It must be for the time the biggest thing in the life, so acute, so intrusive as to crowd out everything else. The degree of fullness in any life accords perfectly with the intensity of true desire. We have as much of God as we actually want.
A. W. TOZER (1897–1963)

5773 Beware of being in bondage to yourself or to other people. Oppression and depression never come from the Spirit of God. He never oppresses, he convicts and comforts.
OSWALD CHAMBERS (1874–1917)

5774 Breathe on me, breath of God;
Fill me with life anew,
That I may love what thou dost love,
And do what thou wouldst do.
EDWIN HATCH (1835–1889)

5775 Call the Comforter by the term you think best—Advocate, Helper, Paraclete, the word conveys the indefinable blessedness of his sympathy; an inward invisible kingdom that causes the saint to sing through every night of sorrow. This Holy Comforter represents the ineffable motherhood of God.
OSWALD CHAMBERS (1874–1917)

5776 Do you want to be filled with a Spirit who, though he is like Jesus in his gentleness and love, will nevertheless demand to be Lord of your life? Are you willing to let your personality be taken over by another, even if that other be the Spirit of God himself? If the Spirit takes charge of your life he will expect unquestioning obedience in everything. He will not tolerate in you the self-sins even though they are permitted and excused by most Christians. . . . You will find the Spirit to be in sharp opposition to the easy ways of the world and of the mixed multitude within the precincts of religion. He will be jealous over you for good. He will not allow you to boast or swagger or show off. He will take the direction of your life away from you. He will reserve the right to test you, to discipline you, to chasten you for your soul's sake. He may strip you of many of those borderline pleasures which other Christians enjoy but which are to you a source of refined evil. Through it all he will enfold you in a love so vast, so mighty, so all-embracing, so wondrous that your

very losses will seem like gains and your small pains like pleasure.
A. W. Tozer (1897–1963)

5777 Every time we say, "I believe in the Holy Spirit," we mean that we believe that there is a living God able and willing to enter human personality and change it.
J. B. Phillips (1906–1982)

5778 God commands us to be filled with the Spirit, and if we are not filled, it is because we are living beneath our privileges.
Dwight Lyman Moody (1837–1899)

5779 God does not fill with his Holy Spirit those who believe in the fullness of the Spirit, or those who desire him, but those who obey him.
F. B. Meyer (1847–1929)

5780 He who is plenteously provided for from within needs but little from without.
Johann Wolfgang von Goethe (1749–1832)

5781 I have often, myself, sat in darkness, and cried aloud for the Holy Spirit to deliver me from the fantasies that gather round a parched soul like flies round a rotting carcass in the desert. Likewise, I have sat tongue-tied, crying out to be given utterance, and delivered from the apprehensions that afflict the earth-bound. And never, ultimately, in vain. Jesus' promise is valid; the Comforter needs only to be summoned. The need is the call, the call is the presence, and the presence is the Comforter, the Spirit of Truth.
Malcolm Muggeridge (1903–1990)

5782 If the Holy Ghost is indwelling a man or woman, no matter how sweet, how beautiful, how Christlike they are, the lasting thought you go away with is— what a wonderful being the Lord Jesus Christ is.
Oswald Chambers (1874–1917)

5783 If we are full of pride and conceit and ambition and self-seeking and pleasure and the world, there is no room for the Spirit of God, and I believe many a man is praying to God to fill him when he is full already with something else.
Dwight Lyman Moody (1837–1899)

5784 If we seek the baptism of the Holy Ghost in order that God may make us great servants of his, we shall never receive anything. God baptizes us with the Holy Ghost that he may be all in all.
Oswald Chambers (1874–1917)

5785 It is extraordinary how things fall off from a man like autumn leaves once he comes to the place where there is no rule but that of the personal domination of the Holy Spirit.
Oswald Chambers (1874–1917)

5786 It would take a theologian with a fine-toothed comb to find the Holy Spirit recognizably present with power in much of our ecclesiastical routine.
Samuel M. Shoemaker (1893–1963)

5787 Living one day in the Spirit is worth more than a thousand lived in the flesh.
Richard Owen Roberts (1931–   )

5788 Ocean, wide flowing ocean,
Thou of uncreated love
A sea which can contract itself
Within my narrow heart.
Frederick William Faber (1814–1863)

5789 The baptism of the Holy Ghost does not mean that we are put into some great and successful venture for God, but that we are a satisfaction to Jesus wherever we are placed.
Oswald Chambers (1874–1917)

5790 The baptism of the Holy Ghost makes us witnesses to Jesus, not wonder-workers. The witness is not to what Jesus does, but to what he is.
Oswald Chambers (1874–1917)

5791 The Bible teaches—and Christian experience abundantly confirms—that the works of the Holy Spirit are unpredictable and by no means confined to the institutional church. Even the most narrow-minded Christian must admit, on occasion, that the Holy Spirit seems to be working in and through people who do not consciously profess faith in Christ. This should not sur-

prise anyone who has read the New Testament. Jesus was always consorting with sinners, to the horror of pious types who thought he should have been exclusively concerned with them.
LOUIS CASSELS (1922–1974)

5792 The biggest blessing in your life was when you came to the end of trying to be a Christian, the end of reliance on natural devotion, and were willing to come as a pauper and receive the Holy Spirit.
OSWALD CHAMBERS (1874–1917)

5793 The great idea is not that we are at work for God, but that he is at work in us . . . that he is working out a strong family likeness to his Son in us.
OSWALD CHAMBERS (1874–1917)

5794 The great King, immortal, invisible, the divine person called the Holy Ghost, the Holy Spirit: it is he that quickens the soul, or else it would lie dead forever; it is he that makes it tender, or else it would never feel; it is he that imparts efficacy to the Word preached, or else it could never reach farther than the ear; it is he who breaks the heart; it is he who makes it whole.
CHARLES HADDON SPURGEON (1834–1892)

5795 The Holy Ghost destroys my personal private life and turns it into a thoroughfare for God.
OSWALD CHAMBERS (1874–1917)

5796 The Holy Spirit cannot be located as a guest in a house. He invades everything.
OSWALD CHAMBERS (1874–1917)

5797 The Holy Spirit descended upon me in a manner that seemed to go through me, body and soul. I could feel the impression like a wave of electricity going through and through me. Indeed, it seemed to come in waves and waves of liquid love . . . like the very breath of God . . . it seemed to fan me like immense wings.
CHARLES G. FINNEY (1792–1875)

5798 The Holy Spirit does not obliterate a man's personality; he lifts it to its highest use.
OSWALD CHAMBERS (1874–1917)

5799 The Holy Spirit is composer and conductor. He gives each member of the worshiping congregation sounds—which he weaves together in heavenly harmony.

5800 The Spirit of God first imparts love; he next inspires hope, and then gives liberty; and that is about the last thing we have in many of our churches.
DWIGHT LYMAN MOODY (1837–1899)

5801 The Spirit of God has the habit of taking the words of Jesus out of their scriptural setting and putting them into the setting of our personal lives.
OSWALD CHAMBERS (1874–1917)

5802 The Spirit's control will replace sin's control. His power is greater than the power of all your sin.
ERWIN W. LUTZER (1941–)

5803 The Spirit-filled life is no mystery revealed to a select few, no goal difficult of attainment. To trust and to obey is the substance of the whole matter.
VICTOR RAYMOND EDMAN (1900–1967)

5804 The word *Comforter* as applied to the Holy Spirit needs to be translated by some vigorous term. Literally, it means "with strength." Jesus promised his followers that "The Strengthener" would be with them. This promise is no lullaby for the fainthearted. It is a blood transfusion for courageous living.
E. PAUL HOVEY (1908–)

5805 There is one thing we cannot imitate: we cannot imitate being full of the Holy Ghost.
OSWALD CHAMBERS (1874–1917)

5806 To the church, Pentecost brought light, power, joy. There came to each illumination of mind, assurance of heart, intensity of love, fullness of power, exuberance of joy. No one needed to ask if they had received the Holy Ghost. Fire is self-evident. So is power!
SAMUEL CHADWICK (1832–1917)

5807 "Tongues" is a heart language. As a baby lies in his mother's arms and babbles to his mother—they both understand what he means. So we lie in God's arms and babble to him. And we both understand.
JOHN HARPER

5808 We have substituted relativity for reality, psychology for prayer, an inferiority complex for sin, social control for family worship, autosuggestion for conversion, reflex action for revelation, the spirit of the wheels for the power of the Spirit.
HIGH THOMSON KERR (1871–1950)

5809 When the Spirit illuminates the heart, then a part of the man sees which never saw before; a part of him knows which never knew before, and that with a kind of knowing which the most acute thinker cannot imitate. He knows now in a deep and authoritative way, and what he knows needs no reasoned proof. His experience of knowing is above reason, immediate, perfectly convincing and inwardly satisfying.
A. W. TOZER (1897–1963)

5810 Wherever the Son of God goes, the winds of God are blowing, the streams of living water are flowing, and the sun of God is smiling.
HELMUT THIELICKE (1908–1986)

5811 Why is it when you speak to the modern church about Pentecost that cold shivers go up and down the spines of cultured people?
E. STANLEY JONES (1884–1973)

HOME

5812 A good laugh is sunshine in a house.
WILLIAM MAKEPEACE THACKERAY (1811–1863)

5813 A home is no home unless it contains food and fire for the mind as well as for the body.
MARGARET FULLER (1810–1850)

5814 A little house well filled, a little field well tilled, a little wife well willed, are great riches.
BENJAMIN FRANKLIN (1706–1790)

5815 A man travels the world over in search of what he needs and returns home to find it.
GEORGE MOORE (1852–1933)

5816 A palace without affection is a poor hovel, and the meanest hut with love in it is a palace for the soul.
ROBERT GREEN INGERSOLL (1833–1899)

5817 A world of care without,
A world of strife shut out,
A world of love shut in.
DORA GREENWELL

5818 America's future will be determined by the home and the school. The child becomes largely what he is taught; hence we must watch what we teach, and how we live.
JANE ADDAMS (1860–1935)

5819 Anyone can build a house: we need the Lord for the creation of a home.
JOHN HENRY JOWETT (1864–1923)

5820 Better a hundred enemies outside the house than one inside.
ARABIAN PROVERB

5821 Better the cottage where one is merry than the palace where one weeps.
CHINESE PROVERB

5822 Charity begins at home but should not end there.

5823 Christ is the head of this house,
The unseen guest at every meal,
The unseen listener to every conversation.

5824 Christ moves among the pots and pans.
SAINT TERESA OF AVILA (1515–1582)

5825 Every meal shared in love is a feast.

5826 God walks among the pots and pipkins.
LATIN PROVERB

5827 He is the happiest, be he king or peasant, who finds peace in his home.
JOHANN WOLFGANG VON GOETHE (1749–1832)

5828 He that has not rest at home is in the world's hell.
TURKISH PROVERB

5829 Home is a place where the great are small, and the small are great.

5830 Home is not where you live but where they understand you.
CHRISTIAN MORGENSTERN (1871–1914)

5831 Home is the place where, when you have to go there, they have to take you in.
ROBERT FROST (1874–1963)

5832 Home is where life makes up its mind. It is there—with fellow family members—we hammer out our convictions on the anvil of relationships. It is there we cultivate the valuable things in life, like attitudes, memories, beliefs, and most of all, character.
CHARLES R. SWINDOLL (1934–   )

5833 Home, a place that our feet may leave, but not our hearts.

5834 Home, the spot of earth supremely best,
A dearer, sweeter spot than all the rest.
ROBERT MONTGOMERY (1807–1855)

5835 Home: the best security of civilization.
BENJAMIN DISRAELI (1804–1881)

5836 Home: the strength of a nation.
LYDIA HUNTLEY SIGOURNEY (1791–1865)

5837 Home: where each lives for the other and all live for God.

5838 If there is any good in you, it should show itself first in your own household.
ARABIAN PROVERB

5839 If your home is unbearable, maybe you're the bear.

5840 Many who have gold in the house are looking for copper outside.
RUSSIAN PROVERB

5841 Men build bridges and throw railroads across deserts, yet the job of sewing on a button is beyond them.
HEYWOOD BROUN (1888–1939)

5842 Of all modern notions the worst is this: that domesticity is dull. Inside the home, they say, is dead decorum and routine; outside is adventure and variety. But the truth is that the home is the only place of liberty, the only spot on earth where a man can alter arrangements suddenly, make an experiment, or indulge in a whim. The home is not the one tame place in a world of adventure; it is the one wild place in a world of rules and set tasks.
G. K. CHESTERTON (1874–1936)

5843 One does not love a place the less for having suffered in it.
JANE AUSTEN (1775–1817)

5844 Our home joys are the most delightful earth affords, and the joy of parents in their children is the most holy joy of humanity. It makes their hearts pure and good; it lifts men up to their Father in heaven.
JOHANN HEINRICH PESTALOZZI (1746–1827)

5845 Pity the home where everyone is the head.
JEWISH PROVERB

5846 Praise will transform the humblest dwelling to a hallowed heaven.
FRANCES J. ROBERTS

5847 Sad is the home where the hen crows and the cock is silent.
SPANISH PROVERB

5848 Six things are requisite to create a happy home. Integrity must be the architect and tidiness the upholsterer. It must be warmed by affection, lighted up with cheerfulness; and industry must be the ventilator, renewing the atmosphere and bringing in fresh salubrity day by day; whole over all, as a protecting canopy and glory, nothing will suffice except the blessing of God.
JAMES HAMILTON (1814–1867)

5849 Strength of character may be acquired at work, but beauty of character is learned at home. There the affections are trained. There the gentle life reaches us, the true heaven life.
HENRY DRUMMOND (1851–1897)

5850 The Christian home is the Master's workshop where the processes of character-molding are silently,

lovingly, faithfully and successfully carried on.
RICHARD MONCKTON MILNES (1809–1885)

5851 The crown of the home is godliness;
The beauty of the home is order;
The glory of the home is hospitality;
The blessing of the home is contentment.
HENRY VAN DYKE (1852–1933)

5852 The family circle is the supreme conductor of Christianity.
HENRY DRUMMOND (1851–1897)

5853 The family should be a closely knit group. The home should be a self-contained shelter of security; a kind of school where life's basic lessons are taught; a kind of church where God is honored; a place where wholesome recreation and simple pleasures are enjoyed.
BILLY GRAHAM (1918–   )

5854 The home is God's built-in training facility.
CHARLES R. SWINDOLL (1934–   )

5855 The right temperature at home is maintained by warm hearts, not by hotheads.

5856 The voice of parents is the voice of gods, for to their children they are heaven's lieutenants.
WILLIAM SHAKESPEARE (1564–1616)

5857 The woman who creates and sustains a home and under whose hands children grow up to be strong and pure men and women is a creator second only to God.
HELEN MARIA FISKE HUNT JACKSON (1830–1885)

5858 There is no synthetic replacement for a decent home life. Our high crime rate, particularly among juveniles, is directly traceable to a breakdown in moral fiber—to the disintegration of home and family life. Religion and home life are supplementary. Each strengthens the other. It is seldom that a solid and wholesome home life can be found in the absence of religious inspiration.
J. EDGAR HOOVER (1895–1972)

5859 We give people a box in the suburbs, it's called a house, and every night they sit in it staring at another box, in the morning they run off to another box called an office, and at the weekends they get into another box, on wheels this time, and grope their way through endless traffic jams.
CAROLINE KELLY

5860 What God gives, and what we take,
'Tis a gift for Christ his sake:
Be the meal of beans and peas,
God be thank'd for those, and these.
Have we flesh, or have we fish.
All are fragments from his dish.
ROBERT HERRICK (1591–1674)

5861 What we desire our children to become, we must endeavor to be before them.
ANDREW COMBE (1797–1847)

5862 When home is ruled according to God's Word, angels might be asked to stay with us, and they would not find themselves out of their element.
CHARLES HADDON SPURGEON (1834–1892)

HONESTY

5863 A commentary of the times is that the word *honesty* is now preceded by *old-fashioned.*
LARRY WOLTERS

5864 A frank talk is good soap for hearts.
ARABIAN PROVERB

5865 A guileless mind is a great treasure; it is worth any price.
A. W. TOZER (1897–1963)

5866 An honest man is not the worse because a dog barks at him.
DANISH PROVERB

5867 To be honest as this world goes, is to be one man picked out of a thousand.
WILLIAM SHAKESPEARE (1564–1616)

5868 Being entirely honest with oneself is a good exercise.
SIGMUND FREUD (1856–1939)

5869 Candor is always a double-edged sword; it may heal or it may separate.
WILHELM STEKEL

5870 Candor is the brightest gem of criticism.
BENJAMIN DISRAELI (1804–1881)

5871 Friends, if we be honest with ourselves, we shall be honest with each other.
GEORGE MACDONALD (1824–1905)

5872 He has but one word.

5873 Honesty consists of the unwillingness to lie to others; maturity, which is equally hard to attain, consists of the unwillingness to lie to oneself.
SYDNEY J. HARRIS (1917–1986)

5874 Honesty has a beautiful and refreshing simplicity about it. No ulterior motives. No hidden meanings. An absence of hypocrisy, duplicity, political games, and verbal superficiality. As honesty and real integrity characterize our lives, there will be no need to manipulate others.
CHARLES R. SWINDOLL (1934–   )

5875 Honesty is a fine jewel, but much out of fashion.
SIR THOMAS FULLER (1608–1661)

5876 Honesty is looking painful truths in the face.
AUBREY THOMAS DE VERE (1814–1902)

5877 Honesty is often in the wrong.
LUCAN (39–65)

5878 Honesty is praised, but left to shiver.
JUVENAL (C. 60–C. 127)

5879 Honesty is the first chapter of the book of wisdom.
THOMAS JEFFERSON (1743–1826)

5880 How desperately difficult it is to be honest with oneself. It is much easier to be honest with other people.
EDWARD WHITE BENSON (1829–1896)

5881 I hope I shall always possess firmness and virtue enough to maintain what I consider the most enviable of all titles, the character of an honest man.
GEORGE WASHINGTON (1732–1799)

5882 I love you more today than yesterday. Yesterday, you really got on my nerves!

5883 Openness is to wholeness as secrets are to sickness.
BARBARA JOHNSON

5884 People who are brutally honest get more satisfaction out of the brutality than out of the honesty.
RICHARD J. NEEDHAM

5885 Princes and lords are but the breath of kings,
An honest man's the noblest work of God.
ROBERT BURNS (1759–1796)

5886 "Real isn't how you are made" said the Skin Horse. "It's a thing that happens to you. . . . When you are Real, you don't mind being hurt. . . . It doesn't happen all at once. It takes a long time. That's why it doesn't often happen to people who break easily, or have sharp edges, or who have to be carefully kept. Generally, by the time you are Real, most of your hair has been loved off, and your eyes drop out, and you get loose in the joints and very shabby. But these things don't matter at all because once you are real you can't be ugly, except to people who don't understand.
MARGERY WILLIAMS

5887 Say what you have to say, not what you ought. Any truth is better than make-believe.
HENRY DAVID THOREAU (1817–1862)

5888 Some of the finest cheating in the world has been done under the guise of honesty.
HENRY H. CRANE

5889 The more honesty a man has, the less he affects the air of a saint.
JOHANN KASPAR LAVATER (1741–1801)

5890 [Jesus] knows we are sinners and there will be people that we do not like and that do not like us. The issue as a Christian is not to *pretend* that we love everything that moves and breathes. That would be phony and hypocritical. Jesus does not tell us to pretend they are friends either. Rather he asks that we acknowledge the fact that they are enemies without pretense and yet to respond to them with love, not hate or bitterness.
REBECCA MANLEY PIPPERT

HONOR

5891 Christians have fallen into the habit of accepting the noisiest and most notorious among them as the best and the greatest. They too have learned to equate popularity with excellence, and in open defiance of the Sermon on the Mount they have given their approval, not to the meek, but to the self-assertive; not to the mourner, but to the self-assured; not to the pure in heart who see God, but to the publicity hunter who seeks headlines.
A. W. TOZER (1897–1963)

5892 He who seeks only for applause from without has all his happiness in another's keeping.

5893 It is a worthier thing to deserve honor than to possess it.

5894 It is the Lord's sovereign right to demote as well as to promote . . . and we seldom know why he chooses whom.
CHARLES R. SWINDOLL (1934–   )

5895 No person was ever honored for what he received; honor has been the reward for what he gave.
CALVIN COOLIDGE (1872–1933)

5896 Our own heart, and not other men's opinions, form true honor.
SAMUEL TAYLOR COLERIDGE (1772–1834)

5897 Seniority in the kingdom of God does not imply superiority.
ERWIN W. LUTZER (1941–   )

5898 The honors of this world: what are they but puff, and emptiness, and peril of falling?
SAINT AUGUSTINE OF HIPPO (354–430)

5899 The louder he talked of his honor, the faster we counted our spoons.
RALPH WALDO EMERSON (1803–1882)

5900 To esteem everything is to esteem nothing.
MOLIÈRE (1622–1673)

5901 When one seeks the honor that comes from God only, he will take the withholding of the honor that comes from men very quietly indeed.
GEORGE MACDONALD (1824–1905)

HOPE

5902 'Tis always morning somewhere.
HENRY WADSWORTH LONGFELLOW (1807–1882)

5903 As long as matters are really hopeful, hope is a mere flattery or platitude; it is only when everything is hopeless that hope begins to be a strength. Like all the Christian virtues, it is as unreasonable as it is indispensable.
G. K. CHESTERTON (1874–1936)

5904 Behind the cloud the starlight lurks, Through showers the sunbeams fall; For God, who loveth all his works Has left his hope with all!
JOHN GREENLEAF WHITTIER (1807–1892)

5905 Blessed is he who expects nothing for he shall never be disappointed.
ALEXANDER POPE (1688–1744)

5906 Dark things reach out toward brightness.
EUGENIO MONTALE (1896–1981)

5907 Do not look forward to the changes and chances of this life in fear; rather look to them with full hope that, as they arise, God, whose you are, will deliver you out of them. He is your Keeper. He has kept you hitherto. Hold fast to his dear hand, and he will lead you safely through all things; and, when you cannot stand, he will bear you in his arms. Do not look forward to what may happen tomorrow. Our Father will either shield you from suffering, or he will give you strength to bear it.
SAINT FRANCIS OF SALES (1567–1622)

5908 God's gifts put man's best dreams to shame.
ELIZABETH BARRETT BROWNING (1806–1861)

5909 He that lives in hope dances without a fiddle.

5910 He who has health has hope; and he who has hope has everything.
ARABIAN PROVERB

5911 Hope for the best; get ready for the worst; then take what God chooses to send.

5912 Hope has a thick skin and will endure many a blow; it will put on patience as a vestment, it will wade through a sea of blood, it will endure all things if it be of the right kind, for the joy that is set before it. Hence patience is called "patience of hope," because it is hope that makes the soul exercise patience and long-suffering under the cross, until the time comes to enjoy the crown.
JOHN BUNYAN (1628–1688)

5913 Hope humbly then; with trembling pinions soar;
Wait the great teacher death, and God adore.
What future bliss he gives not thee to know,
But gives that hope to be thy blessing now,
Hope springs eternal in the human breast;
Man never is, but always to be blessed.
ALEXANDER POPE (1688–1744)

5914 Hope in the Lord, but exert yourself.
RUSSIAN PROVERB

5915 Hope is a good breakfast, but it is a bad supper.
FRANCIS BACON (1561–1626)

5916 Hope is a more gentle name for fear.
LETITIA ELIZABETH LANDON (1802–1838)

5917 Hope is a vigorous principle; it sets the head and heart to work and animates a man to do his utmost.
JEREMY COLLIER (1650–1726)

5918 Hope is an adventure, a going forward—a confident search for a rewarding life.
KARL AUGUSTUS MENNINGER (1893–1990)

5919 Hope is an echo, hope ties itself yonder, yonder.
CARL SANDBURG (1878–1967)

5920 Hope is faith holding out its hands in the dark.
GEORGE ILES

5921 Hope is grief's best music.
HENRY GEORGE BOHN (1796–1884)

5922 Hope is like the clouds: some pass by, others bring rain.

5923 Hope is like the sun, which, as we journey toward it, casts the shadow of our burden behind us.
SAMUEL SMILES (1812–1904)

5924 Hope is the last thing that dies in man, and although it be exceedingly deceitful, yet it is of this good use to us, that while we are traveling through life it conducts us in an easier and more pleasant way to our journey's end.
FRANÇOIS, DUC DE LA ROCHEFOUCAULD (1613–1680)

5925 Hope is the major weapon against the suicide impulse.
KARL AUGUSTUS MENNINGER (1893–1990)

5926 Hope is the physician of every misery.
IRISH PROVERB

5927 Hope is wishing for a thing to come true; faith is believing that it will come true.
NORMAN VINCENT PEALE (1898–)

5928 Hope looks for the good in people instead of harping on the worst in them. Hope opens doors where despair closes them. Hope discovers what can be done instead of grumbling about what cannot be done. Hope draws its power from a deep trust in God and the basic goodness of mankind. Hope "lights a candle" instead of "cursing the darkness." Hope regards problems, small or large, as opportunities. Hope cherishes no illusions, nor does it yield to cynicism.

5929 Hope means expectancy when things are otherwise hopeless.
G. K. CHESTERTON (1874–1936)

5930 Hope not only bears up the mind under sufferings but makes her rejoice in them.
JOSEPH ADDISON (1672–1719)

5931 Hope thinks nothing difficult; despair tells us that difficulty is unsurmountable.
ISAAC WATTS (1674–1748)

5932 Hope! Of all ills that men endure,
The only cheap and universal cure!
Thou captive's freedom, and thou sick man's health,

Thou lover's victory, and thou beggar's
wealth!
ABRAHAM COWLEY (1618–1667)

5933 Hope, the balm and lifeblood of the
soul.
JOHN ARMSTRONG (1709–1779)

5934 How deceitful hope may be, yet she
carries us on pleasantly to the end of
life.
FRANÇOIS, DUC DE LA ROCHEFOUCAULD
(1613–1680)

5935 If it were not for hope the heart would
break.
ENGLISH PROVERB

5936 In the kingdom of hope there is no
winter.
RUSSIAN PROVERB

5937 In the presence of hope, faith is born.
ROBERT HAROLD SCHULLER (1926–   )

5938 Life with Christ is an endless hope,
without him a hopeless end.

5939 Make us thy mountaineers
We would not linger on the lower
    slope,
Fill us afresh with hope,
O God of hope.
AMY CARMICHAEL (1867–1951)

5940 O hope! Dazzling, radiant hope! What
a change thou bringest to the hopeless;
brightening the darkened paths, and
cheering the lonely way.
AIMEE SEMPLE MCPHERSON (1890–1944)

5941 Our hope lies, not in the man we put
on the moon, but in the Man we put
on the cross.
DON BASHAM

5942 Sad soul, take comfort nor forget
The sunrise never failed us yet.
CELIA THAXTER (1835–1894)

5943 The hopeful man sees success where
others see failure, sunshine where
others see shadows and storm.
ORISON SWETT MARDEN

5944 The march of providence is so slow
and our desires so impatient; the work
of progress is so immense and our
means of aiding it so feeble; the life of
humanity is so long, that of the individual so brief, that we often see only
the ebb of the advancing wave and are
thus discouraged. It is history that
teaches us to hope.
ROBERT EDWARD LEE (1807–1870)

5945 The resurrection of Jesus Christ is our
hope today. It is our assurance that we
have a living Savior to help us live as
we should now, and that when, in the
end, we set forth on that last great
journey, we shall not travel an
uncharted course, but rather we shall
go on a planned voyage—life to death
to eternal living.
RAYMOND MACKENDREE

5946 The word *hope* I take for faith; and
indeed hope is nothing else but the
constancy of faith.
JOHN CALVIN (1509–1564)

5947 The word which God has written on
the brow of every man is *hope*.
VICTOR HUGO (1802–1885)

5948 There is more hope for a self-convicted sinner than there is for a self--
conceited saint.

5949 We hope vaguely but dread precisely.
PAUL VALERY (1871–1945)

5950 We promise according to our hopes
and perform according to our fears.
FRANÇOIS, DUC DE LA ROCHEFOUCAULD
(1613–1680)

HOPELESSNESS

5951 Hopelessness is anticipated defeat.
KARL THEODOR JASPERS (1883–1969)

5952 Naked to earth was I brought—
Naked to earth I descend.
Why should I labor for nought,
Seeing how naked the end?
PALLADAS (C. 400)

5953 There are no hopeless situations.
There are only people who have
grown hopeless about them.
CLARE BOOTHE LUCE (1903–1987)

5954 When you are at the end of your rope,
God is there to catch you—but not
before.
ERWIN W. LUTZER (1941–   )

5955 When you say a situation or a person is hopeless, you are slamming the door in the face of God.
CHARLES L. ALLEN (1913–)

HOSPITALITY

5956 Fish and visitors smell in three days.
BENJAMIN FRANKLIN (1706–1790)

5957 Hospitality is a test for godliness because those who are selfish do not like strangers (especially needy ones) to intrude upon their private lives. They prefer their own friends who share their life-style. Only the humble have the necessary resources to give of themselves to those who could never give of themselves in return.
ERWIN W. LUTZER (1941–)

5958 Hospitality is one form of worship.
JEWISH PROVERB

5959 If the world seems cold to you, kindle fires to warm it.

5960 When there is room in the heart there is room in the house.
DANISH PROVERB

5961 Who practices hospitality entertains God himself.

HUMAN RIGHTS

5962 He who allows the oppression shares the crime.

5963 If human beings were as wise as animals, the only creature they would segregate is the skunk.

5964 Resistance to tyrants is obedience to God.

5965 The principles of the Bible are the groundwork of human freedom.
HORACE GREELEY (1811–1872)

HUMANITY

5966 All mankind is of one Author and is one volume; when one man dies, one chapter is not torn out of the book but translated into a better language; and every chapter must be so translated; God employs several translators; some pieces are translated by age, some by sickness, some by war, some by justice; but God's hand is in every translation; and his hand shall bind up all our scattered leaves again for that library where every book shall lie open to one another.
JOHN DONNE (1572–1631)

5967 Every human person is an aristocrat. Every human person is noble and of royal blood, born from the intimate depths of the divine nature and the divine wilderness.
MEISTER ECKHART (C. 1260–C. 1327)

5968 Human nature is like a drunk peasant. Lift him into the saddle on one side, over he topples on the other side.
MARTIN LUTHER (1483–1546)

5969 Humanity never stands still; it advances or retreats.
AUGUSTE BLANQUI (1805–1881)

5970 Humanity, let us say, is like people packed in an automobile that is travelling downhill without lights at terrific speed and driven by a four-year-old child. The signposts along the way are all marked Progress.
LORD DUNSANY (1906–)

5971 If you treat men the way they are, you never improve them. If you treat them the way you want them to be, you do.
JOHANN WOLFGANG VON GOETHE (1749–1832)

5972 It is easier to love humanity as a whole than to love one's neighbor.
ERIC HOFFER (1902–1983)

5973 It is human nature to think wisely and act foolishly.
ANATOLE FRANCE (1844–1924)

5974 It's a funny thing, this human nature! It clings to a man with such persistance.
HENRIK IBSEN (1828–1906)

5975 Man is trampled by the same forces he has created.
JUANA FRANCES

5976 Never underestimate the ability of human beings to get themselves tangled up.
A. W. TOZER (1897–1963)

5977 No one can resign from the human race.
FREDERIC KELLER STAMM

5978 No two human beings have made, or ever will make, exactly the same journey in life.
SIR ARTHUR KEITH (1866–1955)

5979 Our humanity were a poor thing were it not for the divinity that stirs within us.
FRANCIS BACON (1561–1626)

5980 Our true nationality is mankind.
H. G. WELLS (1866–1946)

5981 That which man has received from God, that which makes him different from the animals, his spirituality, his mind, his soul, whatever name we give it, is not described in the Bible as a thing, a part of man, a substance, but as a breath, a movement, an impulse, an echo of God's voice.
PAUL TOURNIER (1898–1986)

5982 The human race, to which so many of my readers belong, has been playing at children's games from the beginning and will probably do it till the end, which is a nuisance for the few people who grow up.
G. K. CHESTERTON (1874–1936)

5983 The stork in the sky knows her seasons, the ocean tide rolls in on schedule, snow always covers the high mountains, but human beings are like nothing else in nature. God cannot control them. Yet he cannot simply thrust them aside either. He cannot get humanity out of his mind.
PHILIP YANCEY (1949–)

5984 There are only two or three human stories, and they go on repeating themselves as fiercely as if they had never happened before.
WILLA SIBERT CATHER (1873–1947)

5985 We are all alike—on the inside.
MARK TWAIN (1835–1910)

5986 We are all beggars, each in his own way.
MARK TWAIN (1835–1910)

5987 We must learn to live together as brothers or perish together as fools.
MARTIN LUTHER KING, JR. (1929–1968)

5988 You must not lose faith in humanity. Humanity is an ocean; if a few drops of the ocean are dirty, the ocean does not become dirty.
MAHATMA GANDHI (1869–1948)

HUMILITY

5989 A man can counterfeit love, he can counterfeit faith, he can counterfeit hope and all the other graces, but it is very difficult to counterfeit humility.
DWIGHT LYMAN MOODY (1837–1899)

5990 After crosses and losses, men grow humbler and wiser.
BENJAMIN FRANKLIN (1706–1790)

5991 Always take the lowest place, and the highest will be given to you, for high structures require a solid foundation. The greatest, in the judgment of God, are the least in their own opinion; the more worthy they are, the more humility will be seen in them.
THOMAS À KEMPIS (C. 1380–1471)

5992 Because Christ Jesus came to the world clothed in humility, he will always be found among those who are clothed with humility. He will be found among the humble people.
A. W. TOZER (1897–1963)

5993 Being humble involves the willingness to be reckoned a failure in everyone's sight but God's.
ROY M. PEARSON (1914–)

5994 Common sense shines with a double lustre when set in humility.
WILLIAM PENN (1644–1718)

5995 Courage, brother! Do not stumble, Though thy path be as dark as night; There's a star to guide the humble, Trust in God and do the right.
NORMAN MACLEOD (1812–1872)

5996 Do you wish people to think well of you? Don't speak well of yourself.
BLAISE PASCAL (1623–1662)

5997 Do you wish to be great? Then begin by being humble. Do you desire to construct a vast and lofty fabric? Think first about the foundations of humility.

The higher your structure is to be, the deeper must be its foundation.
SAINT AUGUSTINE OF HIPPO (354–430)

5998 Don't be so humble. You're not that great.
GOLDA MEIR (1898–1978)

5999 Forget others' faults by remembering your own.

6000 He is not laughed at, that laughs at himself first.

6001 He that is down needs fear no fall,
He that is low, no pride;
He that is humble ever shall
Have God to be his guide.
JOHN BUNYAN (1628–1688)

6002 He who knows himself best esteems himself least.
HENRY GEORGE BOHN (1796–1884)

6003 He who takes his rank lightly raises his own dignity.
HEBREW PROVERB

6004 He whose garments are the whitest will best perceive the spots upon them. He whose crown shines the brightest will know when he has lost a jewel. He who gives the most light to the world will always be able to discover his own darkness.
CHARLES HADDON SPURGEON (1834–1892)

6005 Humility is a divine veil that covers our good deeds and hides them from our eyes.
CLIMACUS SAINT JOHN (570–649)

6006 Humility is a most strange thing. The moment that you think you have acquired it is just the moment you have lost it.
BERNARD MELTZER

6007 Humility is a necessary prerequisite for grace. When you are humiliated, grace is on the way. It is only the one who can see the value of being humbled that is completely righteous. The humble person has changed humiliation into humility.
BERNARD OF CLAIRVAUX (1090–1153)

6008 Humility is never gained by seeking it. The more we pursue it the more dis-

tant it becomes. To think we have it is sure evidence that we don't.
RICHARD J. FOSTER (1942–   )

6009 Humility is nothing but truth, while pride is nothing but lying.
VINCENT DE PAUL (1580–1660)

6010 Humility is perfect quietness of heart. It is to have no trouble. It is never to be fretted or irritated or sore or disappointed. It is to expect nothing, to wonder at nothing that is done to me. It is to be at rest when nobody praises me and when I am blamed or despised. It is to go in and shut the door and kneel to my Father in secret, and be at peace as in the deep sea of calmness when all around and above is trouble.
ANDREW MURRAY (1828–1917)

6011 Humility is recognizing that God and others are responsible for the achievements in my life.
BILL GOTHARD

6012 Humility is strong—not bold; quiet—not speechless; sure—not arrogant.
ESTELLE SMITH

6013 Humility is the exhibition of the spirit of Jesus Christ and is the touchstone of saintliness.
OSWALD CHAMBERS (1874–1917)

6014 Humility is to make a right estimate of one's self.
CHARLES HADDON SPURGEON (1834–1892)

6015 Humility, that low, sweet root
From which all heavenly virtues shoot.
THOMAS MOORE (1779–1852)

6016 I swear 'tis better to be lowly born,
And range with humble lives in content,
Than to be perked up in a glistering grief,
And wear a golden sorrow.
WILLIAM SHAKESPEARE (1564–1616)

6017 I used to think that God's gifts were on shelves one above the other and that the taller we grew in Christian character the more easily we could reach them. I now find that God's gifts are on shelves one beneath the other

and that it is not a question of growing taller but of stooping lower.
F. B. MEYER (1847–1929)

6018 I've never known a person whom I thought was truly filled with the Holy Spirit who went out and bragged about it or sought to draw attention to himself.
BILLY GRAHAM (1918–)

6019 It is no great thing to be humble when you are brought low; but to be humble when you are praised is a great and rare attainment.
BERNARD OF CLAIRVAUX (1090–1153)

6020 It was pride that changed angels into devils; it is humility that makes men as angels.
SAINT AUGUSTINE OF HIPPO (354–430)

6021 It's a good idea to begin at the bottom in everything except in learning to swim.

6022 Lighthouses don't ring bells and fire cannon to call attention to their shining; they just shine on.

6023 Most of us must be content to be as though we had not been, to be found in the register of God, not in the record of man.
SIR THOMAS BROWNE (1605–1682)

6024 Nothing sets a person so much out of the devil's reach as humility.
JONATHAN EDWARDS (1703–1758)

6025 "Poor in spirit" refers, not precisely to humility, but to an attitude of dependence on God and detachment from earthly supports.
RONALD ARBUTHNOTT KNOX (1888–1957)

6026 Pride is the cold mountain peak, sterile and bleak; humility is the quiet valley fertile and abounding in life, and peace lives there.
ANNE AUSTIN (1921–)

6027 Pride kills thanksgiving, but a humble mind is the soil out of which thanks naturally grows. A proud man is seldom a grateful man, for he never thinks he gets as much as he deserves.
HENRY WARD BEECHER (1813–1887)

6028 Soft is the music that would charm forever

The flower of sweetest smell is shy and lowly.
WILLIAM WORDSWORTH (1770–1850)

6029 The boughs that bear most hang lowest.

6030 The Christian is like the ripening corn: the riper he grows, the more lowly he bends his head.
THOMAS GUTHRIE (1803–1873)

6031 The easiest way to dignity is humility.
ENGLISH PROVERB

6032 The first test of a truly great man is his humility. I do not mean by humility, doubt of his own power. But really great men have a curious feeling that the greatness is not in them, but through them. And they see something divine in every other man and are endlessly, foolishly, incredibly merciful.
JOHN RUSKIN (1819–1900)

6033 The humble man receives praise the way a clean window takes the light of the sun. The truer and more intense the light is, the less you see of the glass.
THOMAS MERTON (1915–1968)

6034 The path of humility is the path to glory.
ROBERT HAROLD SCHULLER (1926–)

6035 The proud man counts his newspaper clippings; the humble man his blessings.
ARCHBISHOP FULTON J. SHEEN (1895–1979)

6036 The tumult and the shouting dies,
The captains and the kings depart,
Still stands the ancient sacrifice,
A humble and a contrite heart.
RUDYARD KIPLING (1865–1936)

6037 The way to be humble is not to stoop until you are smaller than yourself but to stand at your real height against some higher nature that will show you how small your greatness is.
PHILLIPS BROOKS (1835–1893)

6038 There is nothing more awful than conscious humility; it is the most satanic type of pride.
OSWALD CHAMBERS (1874–1917)

6039 They that know God will be humble;
they that know themselves cannot be
proud.
JOHN FLAVEL (1627–1691)

6040 Thy home is with the humble, Lord!
The simple are thy rest;
Thy lodging is in childlike hearts;
Thou makest there thy rest.
FREDERICK WILLIAM FABER (1814–1863)

6041 True humility makes no pretence of
being humble and scarcely ever utters
words of humility.
SAINT FRANCIS OF SALES (1567–1622)

6042 We can be humble only when we
know that we are God's children, of
infinite value and eternally loved.
MADELEINE L'ENGLE (1918–   )

6043 When your work speaks for itself,
don't interrupt.
HENRY J. KAISER (1882–1967)

6044 Wisdom is oftentimes nearer when we
stoop than when we soar.
WILLIAM WORDSWORTH (1770–1850)

HYPOCRISY

6045 A bad man is worse when he pretends
to be a saint.
FRANCIS BACON (1561–1626)

6046 A man who hides behind the hypocrite
is smaller than the hypocrite.
WILLIAM EDWARD BIEDERWOLF
(1867–1939)

6047 A Pharisee is a man who prays publicly and preys privately.
DON MARQUIS (1878–1937)

6048 As for conforming outwardly, and living your own life inwardly, I do not
think much of that.
HENRY DAVID THOREAU (1817–1862)

6049 Better be a sinner than a hypocrite.
DANISH PROVERB

6050 Don't stay away from church because
there are so many hypocrites. There's
always room for one more.
ARTHUR R. ADAMS (B. 1861)

6051 Hypocrisy is the homage that vice
pays to virtue.
FRANÇOIS, DUC DE LA ROCHEFOUCAULD
(1613–1680)

6052 Hypocrisy: prejudice with a halo.
AMBROSE GWINNETT BIERCE
(1842–C. 1914)

6053 Hypocrites in the church? Yes, and in
the lodge, and at home. Don't hunt
through the church for a hypocrite.
Go home and look in the glass. Hypocrites? Yes. See that you make the number one less.
BILLY SUNDAY (1862–1935)

6054 I will have nought to do with a man
who can blow hot and cold with the
same breath.
AESOP (FL. C. 550 B.C.)

6055 If the devil ever laughs, it must be at
hypocrites; they are the greatest dupes
he has.
CHARLES CALEB COLTON (1780–1832)

6056 If we are not concentrated, we affect a
great many attitudes; but when we
"set our faces unto the Lord God," all
affectation is gone—the religious pose,
the devout pose, the pious pose, all go
instantly when we determine to concentrate; our attention is so concentrated that we have no time to wonder
how we look.
OSWALD CHAMBERS (1874–1917)

6057 It is easier to wear a mask. An ugly
face is sometimes better than a real
one. Thus are we afraid to show each
other who we really are.
CALVIN MILLER

6058 One foot cannot stand on two boats.
CHINESE PROVERB

6059 One may smile, and smile, and be a villain.
WILLIAM SHAKESPEARE (1564–1616)

6060 Our virtues are frequently but vices
disguised.
FRANÇOIS, DUC DE LA ROCHEFOUCAULD
(1613–1680)

6061 Outside show is a poor substitute for
inner worth.
AESOP (FL. C. 550 B.C.)

6062 Some churches train their greeters and
ushers to smile, showing as many teeth
as possible. But I can sense that kind
of display—and when I am greeted by
a man who is smiling because he has

been trained to smile, I know I am shaking the flipper of a trained seal.
A. W. TOZER (1897–1963)

6063 The most exhausting thing in life is being insincere.
ANNE MORROW LINDBERGH (1906–)

6064 The world is glad of an excuse not to listen to the gospel message, and the inconsistencies of Christians is the excuse.
OSWALD CHAMBERS (1874–1917)

6065 There must be something farcical and fraudulent in the kind of pietism that preaches from villas in the west end to slums in the east end about mansions in heaven.
A. C. CRAIG (1888–)

6066 We are not hypocrites in our sleep.
WILLIAM HAZLITT (1778–1830)

6067 We are so accustomed to wearing a disguise before others that we are unable to recognize ourselves.
FRANÇOIS, DUC DE LA ROCHEFOUCAULD (1613–1680)

6068 We are split spiritual personalities. We swear allegiance to one set of principles and live by another.

We extol self-control and practice self-indulgence.

We proclaim brotherhood and harbor prejudice.

We laud character but strive to climb to the top at any cost.

We erect houses of worship, but our shrines are our places of business and recreation.

We are suffering from a distressing cleavage between the truths we affirm and the values we live by. Our souls are the battlegrounds for civil wars, but we are trying to live serene lives in houses divided against themselves.
MELVIN F. WHEATLEY

6069 We play the game; God keeps the score.
ERWIN W. LUTZER (1941–)

6070 With one hand he put
A penny in the urn of poverty
And with the other took a shilling out.
ROBERT POLLOK (1798–1827)

IDOLATRY

6071 Idolatry is not only the adoration of images . . . but also trust in one's own righteousness, works and merits, and putting confidence in riches and power.
MARTIN LUTHER (1483–1546)

6072 Idolatry: trusting people, possessions or positions to do for me what only God can do.
BILL GOTHARD

6073 O senseless man who cannot make a worm, and yet makes gods by dozens.
MICHEL EYQUEM DE MONTAIGNE (1533–1592)

6074 The dearest idol I have known,
Whate'er that idol be,
Help me to tear it from thy throne,
And worship only thee.
WILLIAM COWPER (1731–1800)

6075 The essence of idolatry is the entertainment of thoughts about God that are unworthy of him.
A. W. TOZER (1897–1963)

6076 Whatever a man seeks, honors, or exalts more than God, is idolatry.
WILLIAM BERNARD ULLANTHORNE (1806–1889)

6077 Whenever we take what God has done and put it in the place of himself, we become idolators.
OSWALD CHAMBERS (1874–1917)

IGNORANCE

6078 Chance is a name for our ignorance.
SIR LESLIE STEPHENS (1832–1904)

6079 Everybody is ignorant, only on different subjects.
WILL ROGERS (1879–1935)

6080 I have never met a man so ignorant that I couldn't learn something from him.
GALILEO GALILEI (1564–1642)

6081 Ignorance is the necessary condition of life itself. If we knew everything, we could not endure existence for a single hour.
ANATOLE FRANCE (1844–1924)

6082 Nothing is so firmly believed as that which is least known.
LORD FRANCIS JEFFREY (1773–1850)

6083 The trouble ain't that people are ignorant: it's that they know so much that ain't so.
JOSH BILLINGS (1818–1885)

6084 There is nothing more frightful than ignorance in action. Alternate translation: Nothing is so terrible as activity without thought.
JOHANN WOLFGANG VON GOETHE (1749–1832)

ILLNESS

6085 Before you can cure the diseases of the body, you must cure the diseases of the soul—greed, ignorance, prejudice, and intolerance.
PAUL EHRLICH (1854–1915)

6086 Every sick person is faced with the problem of the meaning of things. . . . "What is God saying to me through this?" is their constant question. That is the meaning of things. It is to ask myself what God is saying through that star that I am looking at, through this friend who is speaking to me, through this difficulty that is holding me up, or through this trouble that befalls me. Once awake to this way of thinking, one discovers the true savor of life. Everything becomes throbbing with interest.
PAUL TOURNIER (1898–1986)

6087 Make sickness itself a prayer.
SAINT FRANCIS OF SALES (1567–1622)

6088 Sickness shows us what we are.
LATIN PROVERB

6089 The chamber of sickness is the chapel of devotion.
ENGLISH PROVERB

IMMORTALITY

6090 Everything science has taught me—and continues to teach me—strengthens my belief in the continuity of our spiritual existence after death.
WERNHER VON BRAUN (1912–1977)

6091 Faith is positive, enriching life in the here and now. Doubt is negative, robbing life of glow and meaning. So though I do not understand immortality, I choose to believe.
WEBB B. GARRISON (1919–   )

6092 God is making the world, and the show is so grand and beautiful and exciting I have never been able to study any other. Nor do I fret about this ignorance of future life, being willing to take one world at a time, since the Lord of this is also Lord of every other. And surely none who has enjoyed God's glory and goodness on earth need look forward to any other without boundless trust and a thankful heart.
JOHN MUIR (1838–1914)

6093 He sins against this life who slights the next.
EDWARD YOUNG (1683–1765)

6094 I am fully convinced that the soul is indestructible and that its activities will continue through eternity. It is like the sun, which, to our eyes, seems to set in night; but it has really gone to diffuse its light elsewhere.
JOHANN WOLFGANG VON GOETHE (1749–1832)

6095 If the Father deigns to touch with divine power the cold and pulseless heart of the buried acorn and to make it burst forth from its prison walls, will he leave neglected in the earth the soul of man made in the image of his Creator?
WILLIAM JENNINGS BRYAN (1860–1925)

6096 In our sad condition, our only consolation is the expectancy of another life. Here below all is incomprehensible.
MARTIN LUTHER (1483–1546)

6097 Life is eternal; and love is immortal; and death is only a horizon, and a horizon is nothing save the limit of our sight.
ROSSITER WORTHINGTON RAYMOND (1840–1918)

6098 Life is the childhood of our immortality.
JOHANN WOLFGANG VON GOETHE (1749–1832)

6099 Live as if you expect to live forever, but plan as if you expect to enter the hereafter tomorrow.
SOLOMON BEN GABIROL (C. 1020–1070)

6100 Millions long for immortality who do not know what to do with themselves on a rainy Sunday afternoon.
SUSAN ERTZ

6101 No man is prosperous whose immortality is forfeited. No man is rich to whom the grave brings eternal bankruptcy. No man is happy upon whose path there rests but a momentary glimmer of light, shining out between clouds that are closing over him in darkness forever.
HENRY WARD BEECHER (1813–1887)

6102 Only you can prove immortality to yourself, for it is not a demonstration or a proposition. It is, and must forever be, a deep conviction or instinct.
NORMAN VINCENT PEALE (1898–)

6103 Seems it strange that thou shouldst live forever? Is it less strange that thou shouldst live at all?
EDWARD YOUNG (1683–1765)

6104 Surely God would not have created such a being as man . . . to exist only for a day! No, no, man was made for immortality.
ABRAHAM LINCOLN (1809–1865)

6105 The best proof of immortality rests not so much in demonstrating the continuance of life as in sharing here and now the life of God.
CHARLES F. WISHART

6106 The few little years we spend on earth are only the first scene in a divine drama that extends on into eternity.
EDWIN MARKHAM (1852–1940)

6107 The first requisite for immortality is death.
STANISLAW J. LEC (1909–1966)

6108 The glory of the star, the glory of the sun—we must not lose either in the other. We must not be so full of the hope of heaven that we cannot do our work on the earth; we must not be so lost in the work of the earth that we shall not be inspired by the hope of heaven.
PHILLIPS BROOKS (1835–1893)

6109 There is no death.
They only truly live
Who pass into the life beyond, and see
This earth is but a school preparative
For higher ministry.
JOHN OXENHAM (1861–1941)

6110 We are like deep sea divers moving slowly and clumsily in the dim twilight of the depths, and we have our work to do. But this is not our element, and the relief of the diver in coming back to fresh air and sunlight and the sight of familiar faces is but a poor picture of the unspeakable delight with which we shall emerge from our necessary imprisonment into the loveliness and satisfaction of our true home.
J. B. PHILLIPS (1906–1982)

6111 We only see a little of the ocean,
A few miles distance from the rocky shore;
But oh! out there beyond—beyond the eyes' horizon
There's more—there's more.
We only see a little of God's loving,
A few rich treasures from his mighty store;
But oh! out there beyond—beyond our life's horizon
There's more—there's more.

6112 When God measures men in the next world, he will not put the tape about their head; he will put it about their heart.
HENRY WARD BEECHER (1813–1887)

IMPATIENCE

6113 From housework to heights of prayer . . . hurry and impatience are sure marks of the amateur.
EVELYN UNDERHILL (1875–1941)

6114 Hasty climbers have sudden falls.

6115 I have not so great a struggle with my vices, great and numerous as they are, as I have with my impatience.
JOHN CALVIN (1509–1564)

6116 What is destructive is impatience,
haste, expecting too much too fast.
MAY SARTON (B. 1912)

6117 With thoughtless and impatient hands
we tangle up the plans the Lord hath
wrought.

INCARNATION

6118 A spider spins her silver still
    within your darkened stable shed:
In asterisks her webs are spread
    to ornament your manger bed.
LUCI SHAW (1928–)

6119 Advent. The coming of quiet joy.
Arrival of radiant light in our darkness.

6120 Breath, mouth, ears, eyes
    he is curtailed who overflowed all
        skies, all years.
Older than eternity, now he is new.
Now native to earth as I am,
    nailed to my poor planet,
    caught that I might be free.
LUCI SHAW (1928–)

6121 Christ did not only come into our
flesh, but also into our condition, into
the valley and shadow of death, where
we were, and where we are, as we are
sinners.
JOHN BUNYAN (1628–1688)

6122 Filling the world he lies in a manger.
SAINT AUGUSTINE OF HIPPO (354–430)

6123 For lo! the world's great Shepherd
    now is born,
A blessed babe, an infant full of power.
EDMUND BOLTON (C. 1575–C. 1633)

6124 Girded for war, humility his mighty
    dress,
He moves into the battle wholly weap-
    onless.
MADELEINE L'ENGLE (1918–)

6125 God became man; the divine Son
became a Jew; the Almighty appeared
on earth as a helpless human baby,
unable to do more than lie and stare
and wriggle and make noises, needing
to be fed and changed and taught to
talk like any other child. And there
was no illusion or deception in this:

the babyhood of the Son of God was a
reality. The more you think about it,
the more staggering it gets. Nothing in
fiction is so fantastic as is this truth of
the Incarnation.
J. I. PACKER (1926–)

6126 God clothed himself in vile man's flesh
so he might be weak enough to suffer.
JOHN DONNE (1572–1631)

6127 God plans and engineers a personal
visit to his own world and the reaction
of the world is to get rid of him.
J. B. PHILLIPS (1906–1982)

6128 God, who had fashioned time and
space in a clockwork of billions of
suns and stars and moons, in the form
of his beloved Son became a human
being like ourselves. On the micro-
scopic midge of planet he remained for
thirty-three years. He became a real
man, and the only perfect one. While
continuing to be the true God, he was
born in a stable and lived as a work-
ingman and died on a cross. He came
to show us how to live, not for a few
years but eternally.
FULTON OURSLER (1949–)

6129 Hark, hark, the wise eternal Word
Like a weak infant cries,
In form of servant is the Lord,
And God in cradle lies.
T. PESTEL (1584–1659)

6130 He clothed himself with our lowliness
in order to invest us with his grandeur.
RICHARDSON WRIGHT (1885–)

6131 He stretched skin over spirit
like a rubber glove,
aligning Trinity with bone,
twining through veins
until Deity square-knotted flesh.
MARJORIE MADDOX PHIFER

6132 His life is the highest and the holiest
entering in at the lowliest door.
OSWALD CHAMBERS (1874–1917)

6133 I saw a stable, low and very bare,
A little child in a manger.
The oxen knew him, had him in their
    care,
To men he was a stranger.

The safety of the world was lying
there,
And the world's danger.
MARY COLERIDGE (1861–1907)

6134 I'll wrap him warm with love,
well as I'm able,
in my heart stable.
LUCI SHAW (1928–)

6135 In the humanity of Jesus, God was
truly speaking our language.
JOHN POWELL

6136 Jesus' coming is the final and unanswerable proof that God cares.
WILLIAM BARCLAY (1907–1978)

6137 No one could ever have found God; he
gave himself away.
MEISTER ECKHART (C. 1260–C. 1327)

6138 Prepare the way! A God, a God appears
A God, a God! the vocal hills reply,
The rocks proclaim th' approaching
Deity
Lo, earth receives him from the bend-
ing skies!
ALEXANDER POPE (1688–1744)

6139 Quiet he lies
whose vigor hurled
a universe.
LUCI SHAW (1928–)

6140 Run, shepherds run, and solemnize his
birth
This is that night—no, day, grown
great with bliss,
In which the power of Satan broken is.
WILLIAM HENRY DRUMMOND (1854–1907)

6141 Shine out, O Blessed Star,
Promise of the dawn;
Glad tidings send afar,
Christ the Lord is born.

6142 Small-folded in a warm dim female
space—
the Word stern-sentenced to be nine
months dumb—
infinity walled in a womb until the
next enormity—
the Mighty, after submission to a
woman's pains
helpless on a barn-bare floor
first-tasting bitter earth.
LUCI SHAW (1928–)

6143 Swift fly the years, and rise th'
expected morn!
Oh spring to light, auspicious Babe, be
born!
ALEXANDER POPE (1688–1744)

6144 The Christian faith is founded upon
. . . a well attested sober fact of history; that quietly, but with deliberate
purpose, God himself has visited this
little planet.
J. B. PHILLIPS (1906–1982)

6145 The coming of Christ by way of a
Bethlehem manger seems strange and
stunning. But when we take him out
of the manger and invite him into our
hearts, then the meaning unfolds and
the strangeness vanishes.
C. NEIL STRAIT

6146 The coming of Jesus into the world is
the most stupendous event in human
history.
MALCOLM MUGGERIDGE (1903–1990)

6147 The shepherds didn't ask God if he
was sure he knew what he was doing.
Had the angel gone to the theologians,
they would have first consulted their
commentaries. Had he gone to the
elite, they would have looked around
to see if anyone was watching. Had he
gone to the successful, they would
have first looked at their calendars.
So he went to the shepherds. Men
who didn't have a reputation to protect
or an ax to grind or a ladder to climb.
Men who didn't know enough to tell
God that angels don't sing to sheep and
that messiahs aren't found wrapped in
rags and sleeping in a feed trough.
MAX L. LUCADO (1955–)

6148 Through the black space of death to
baby life
Came God, planting the secret genes
of God.
CHAD WALSH

6149 Today,
A shed that's thatched
(Yet straws can sing)
Holds God.
CLEMENT PAMAN (C. 1660)

6150 Trumpets! Lightnings!
The earth trembles!
But into the virgin's womb
thou didst descend with noiseless tread.
AGATHIAS SCHOLASTICUS

6151 We know how God would act if he
were in our place—he has been in our
place.
A. W. TOZER (1897–1963)

6152 We saw thee in thy balmy nest,
Bright dawn of our eternal day!
We saw thee; and we blest the sight,
We saw thee by thine own sweet light.
—The Nativity
RICHARD CRASHAW (C. 1613–1649)

6153 Welcome, all wonders in one sight!
Eternity shut in a span.
Summer in winter. Day in night.
Heaven in earth, and God in man.
Great little one! whose all-embracing
birth
Lifts earth to heaven, stoops heaven to
earth.
RICHARD CRASHAW (C. 1613–1649)

6154 What a terrific moment in history that
was . . . when men first saw their God
in the likeness of the weakest, mildest
and most defenseless of all living creatures!
MALCOLM MUGGERIDGE (1903–1990)

6155 When is the time for love to be born?
The inn is full on the planet earth,
And by greed and pride the sky is
torn—
Yet Love still takes the risk of birth.
MADELEINE L'ENGLE (1918–   )

6156 Yet if we celebrate, let it be
that he
has invaded our lives with purpose.
LUCI SHAW (1928–   )

INDIFFERENCE

6157 A wrongdoer is often a man who has
left something undone, not always one
who has done something.
MARCUS AURELIUS ANTONINUS (121–180)

6158 Do not be afraid of enemies; the worst
they can do is to kill you. Do not be
afraid of friends; the worst they can
do is betray you. Be afraid of the indifferent; they do not kill or betray. But
only because of their silent agreement,
betrayal and murder exist on earth.
BRUNO YASIENSKI

6159 Hardening of the heart ages people
more quickly than hardening of the
arteries.

6160 It takes little effort to watch a man
carry a load.
CHINESE PROVERB

6161 Most of us have no real loves and no
real hatreds. Blessed is love, less
blessed is hatred, but thrice accursed is
that indifference which is neither one
nor the other.
MARK RUTHERFORD (1831–1913)

6162 Nonchalance is the art of looking like
an owl when you have acted like an
ass.

6163 The greatest evil today is the lack of
love and charity, the terrible indifference toward one's neighbor who lives
at the roadside assaulted by exploitation, corruption, poverty, and disease.
MOTHER TERESA OF CALCUTTA (1910–   )

6164 The worst sin toward our fellow creatures is not to hate them, but to be
indifferent to them.
GEORGE BERNARD SHAW (1856–1950)

6165 There is nothing harder than the softness of indifference.
JUAN MONTALVO (1832–1889)

INDIVIDUALITY

6166 Are the fingers of your hand all alike?
ARABIAN PROVERB

6167 Carry your own lantern, and you need
not fear the dark.
JEWISH PROVERB

6168 Cultivate your own capabilities, your
own style. Appreciate the members of
your family for who they are, even
though their outlook or style may be
miles different from yours. Rabbits
don't fly. Eagles don't swim. Ducks
look funny trying to climb. Squirrels
don't have feathers. Stop comparing.
There's plenty of room in the forest.
CHARLES R. SWINDOLL (1934–   )

6169 Each of the redeemed shall forever know and praise some one aspect of the divine beauty better than any other creature can. Why else were individuals created, but that God, loving all infinitely, should love each differently? . . . If all experience God in the same way and returned him an identical worship, the song of the church triumphant would have no symphony, it would be like an orchestra in which all the instruments played the same note. . . . Heaven is a city and a body because the blessed remain eternally different. . . . For doubtless the continually successful, yet never completed, attempt by each soul to communicate its vision to all others . . . is also among the ends for which the individual was created.
C. S. LEWIS (1898–1963)

6170 Every human being is intended to have a character of his own; to be what no others are, and to do what no other can do.
WILLIAM ELLERY CHANNING (1780–1842)

6171 Every man carries his kingdom within, and no one knows what is taking place in another's kingdom. "No one understands me!" Of course they don't, each one of us is a mystery. There is only one who understands you, and that is God.
OSWALD CHAMBERS (1874–1917)

6172 Every man is a volume if you know how to read him.
WILLIAM ELLERY CHANNING (1780–1842)

6173 Every man knows well enough that he is a unique being, only once on this earth; and by no extraordinary chance will such a marvelously picturesque piece of diversity in unity as he is ever be put together a second time.
FRIEDRICH WILHELM NIETZSCHE (1844–1900)

6174 Every shoe fits not every foot.

6175 Every single person has one thing that he can do a little better than most people around him, and he has a sacred obligation to himself to find out what that thing is and to do it.

(Most saints, after all, have been men and women, not who soared to heights of achievement, but who sank to depths of service we would not dream of.)
SYDNEY J. HARRIS (1917–1986)

6176 Everything in Christianity that matters is from individual to individual; collectivities belong to the devil and so easily respond to his persuasion. The devil is a demagogue and sloganeer; Jesus was, and is, concerned with individual souls, with the Living Word. What he gives us is truth carried on the wings of love, not slogans carried on the thrust of power.
MALCOLM MUGGERIDGE (1903–1990)

6177 God made our individuality as well as, and a greater marvel than, our dependence; made our apartness from himself, that freedom should bind us divinely dearer to himself, and the freer the man, the stronger the bond that binds him to him who made his freedom.
GEORGE MACDONALD (1824–1905)

6178 God vouchsafes to speak to us one by one, to manifest himself to us one by one, to lead us forward one by one; he gives us something to rely upon that others do not experience, that we cannot convey to others, that we can but use for ourselves.
CARDINAL JOHN HENRY NEWMAN (1801–1890)

6179 God wills a rich harmony, not a colorless uniformity.
HINDU PROVERB

6180 God, our wise and creative Maker, has been pleased to make everyone different and no one perfect. The sooner we appreciate and accept that fact, the deeper we will appreciate and accept one another, just as our Designer planned us.
CHARLES R. SWINDOLL (1934–)

6181 Heresy is only another word for freedom of thought.
GRAHAM GREENE (1904–)

6182 How glorious it is—and also how painful—to be an exception.
ALFRED DE MUSSET (1810–1857)

6183 Human personality and individuality written and signed by God on each human countenance . . . is something altogether sacred, something for the resurrection, for eternal life.
LÉON HENRI MARIE BLOY (1846–1917)

6184 If all men pulled in one direction, the world would keel over.
JEWISH PROVERB

6185 If flies are flies because they fly, and fleas are fleas because they flee, then bees are bees because they be.

6186 If God had wanted me otherwise, he would have created me otherwise.
JOHANN WOLFGANG VON GOETHE (1749–1832)

6187 If God made you a duck saint—you're a duck, friend. Swim like mad, but don't get bent out of shape because you wobble when you run or flap instead of fly. If you're an eagle saint, stop expecting squirrel saints to soar, or rabbit saints to build the same kind of nests you do.
CHARLES R. SWINDOLL (1934–   )

6188 If I try to be like him, who will be like me?

6189 If we wish to make everyone the same, we are discrediting the wisdom of God.
ERWIN W. LUTZER (1941–   )

6190 If you surpass me in eating, I surpass you in sleeping.
AFRICAN PROVERB

6191 If you want to be original, just try being yourself, because God has never made two people exactly alike.
BERNARD MELTZER

6192 In order to be irreplaceable one must always be different.
GABRIELLE COCO CHANEL (1883–1971)

6193 Individuals have as much right to act in the way they decide as we have.
CHARLES WILLIAMS

6194 Insist on yourself; never imitate.
RALPH WALDO EMERSON (1803–1882)

6195 It is easy in the world to live after the world's opinions. It is easy in solitude to live after our own. But the great man is he who in the midst of the crowd keeps with perfect sweetness the independence of solitude.
RALPH WALDO EMERSON (1803–1882)

6196 It is not necessarily the well-adjusted man who makes the world a better place. Certainly Jesus was poorly adjusted to the society in which he lived and moved, but he gave the world such mature insights into human nature that we have not yet grasped their full significance.
WILBUR MCFEELY

6197 It is our uniqueness that gives freshness and vitality to a relationship.
JAMES C. DOBSON (1936–   )

6198 Lights of a thousand stars do not make one moon.

6199 Man by origin is a herd animal. His actions are determined by an instinctive impulse to follow the leader and to have close contact with the other animals around him. A few individuals can stand isolation and say the truth in spite of the danger of losing touch. They are the true heroes of the human race.
ERICH FROMM (1900–1980)

6200 Man is more interesting than men. It's him, not them, whom God made in his image. Each is more precious than all.
ANDRÉ GIDE (1869–1951)

6201 No man should part with his own individuality and become that of another.
WILLIAM ELLERY CHANNING (1780–1842)

6202 No two human beings have made, or ever will make, exactly the same journey in life.
SIR ARTHUR KEITH (1866–1955)

6203 Nobody can be you as effectively as you can.
NORMAN VINCENT PEALE (1898–   )

6204 Nobody else can do the work that God marked out for you.
PAUL LAURENCE DUNBAR ((1872–1906)

6205 One beats the bush and another catches flies.

6206 Thank God for the way he made you. You are special, distinct and unique. You were not made from a common mold.
ERWIN W. LUTZER (1941–   )

6207 The best compliment to a child or a friend is the feeling you give him that he has been set free to make his own inquiries, to come to conclusions that are right for him, whether or not they coincide with your own.
ALISTAIR COOKE (1908–   )

6208 The comparison game is the sure way to a poor self-image.
JOHN POWELL

6209 The crowd is composed of individuals, but it must also be in the power of each one to be what he is: an individual; and no one, no one at all, no one whatsoever is prevented from being an individual unless he prevents himself— by becoming one of the masses.
SØREN AABYE KIERKEGAARD (1813–1855)

6210 The dissenter is every human being at those moments of his life when he resigns momentarily from the herd and thinks for himself.
ARCHIBALD MACLEISH (1892–1982)

6211 The finger of God never leaves the same fingerprint.
STANISLAW J. LEC (1909–1966)

6212 The real man is a maze of a million notes: the label is all one note.
HILAIRE BELLOC (1870–1953)

6213 The reason a polar bear wears a fur coat is because he'd look funny in a woolen one.

6214 The shoe that fits one person pinches another; there is no recipe for living that suits all cases. Each of us carries his own life-form—an indeterminable form which cannot be superseded by any other.
CARL GUSTAV JUNG (1875–1961)

6215 To be nobody but yourself—in a world that is doing its best, night and day, to make you everybody else— means to fight the hardest battle any human being can fight, and never stop fighting.
E. E. CUMMINGS (1894–1962)

6216 To be one's self, and unafraid whether right or wrong, is more admirable than the easy cowardice of surrender to conformity.
IRVING WALLACE (1916–   )

6217 To dream of the person you would like to be is to waste the person you are.

6218 We forfeit three-fourths of ourselves in order to be like other people.
ARTHUR SCHOPENHAUER (1788–1860)

6219 What is originality? It is being one's self and reporting accurately what we see and are.
RALPH WALDO EMERSON (1803–1882)

6220 What to one man is food, to another is rank poison.
LUCRETIUS (C. 96–C. 55 B.C.)

6221 What would the ant do if it had the head of a bull?
GERMAN PROVERB

6222 Whatever crushes individuality is a dictatorship by whatever name it may be called.
JOHN STUART MILL (1806–1873)

6223 Who can say more than this rich praise, that you alone are you?
WILLIAM SHAKESPEARE (1564–1616)

6224 Why is it so many want to be what they're not while what they are is what others want to be?

6225 You cannot put the same shoe on every foot.
PUBLILIUS SYRUS (FIRST CENTURY B.C.)

6226 Your own gift you can present every moment with the cumulative force of a whole life's cultivation; but of the adopted talent of another, you have only an extemporaneous half-expression. That which each can do best none but his Maker can teach him.
RALPH WALDO EMERSON (1803–1882)

INFERIORITY

6227 Exaggerated sensitiveness is an expression of inferiority.
ALFRED ADLER (1870–1937)

6228 No one can make you feel inferior without your consent.
ELEANOR ROOSEVELT (1884–1962)

6229 Self-centeredness is not the result of self-love, but the product of pain, the result of a poor self-image. What may look like an excess of self-love in fact represents an absence of self-love.
JOHN POWELL

6230 There is a luxury in self-reproach. . . . When we blame ourselves, we feel no one has a right to blame us.
OSCAR WILDE (1854–1900)

INFLUENCE

6231 A man leaves all kinds of footprints when he walks through life. Some you can see, like his children and his house. Others are invisible, like the prints he leaves across other people's lives: the help he gives them and what he has said—his jokes, gossip that has hurt others, encouragement. A man doesn't think about it, but everywhere he passes, he leaves some kind of mark.
MARGARET LEE RUNBECK

6232 A river touches places of which its source knows nothing, and Jesus says if we have received of his fullness, however small the visible measure of our lives, out of us will flow the rivers that will bless to the uttermost parts of the earth. We have nothing to do with the outflow.
OSWALD CHAMBERS (1874–1917)

6233 God rarely allows a soul to see how great a blessing he is.
OSWALD CHAMBERS (1874–1917)

6234 I am a part of all that I have met.
ALFRED, LORD TENNYSON (1809–1892)

6235 It is the most natural thing to be like the person you live with most, therefore live most with Jesus Christ.
OSWALD CHAMBERS (1874–1917)

6236 Our lives are shaped by those who love us—and by those who refuse to love us.
JOHN POWELL

6237 So live that your principles might safely be made the law for the whole world.
IMMANUEL KANT (1724–1804)

6238 The entire ocean is affected by a pebble.
BLAISE PASCAL (1623–1662)

6239 The people who influence us are those who have stood unconsciously for the right thing; they are like the stars and the lilies; and the joy of God flows through them.
OSWALD CHAMBERS (1874–1917)

6240 The people who influence you are people who believe in you.
HENRY DRUMMOND (1851–1897)

6241 The radiating influence from one person rightly related to God is incalculable; he may not say much, but you feel different.
OSWALD CHAMBERS (1874–1917)

6242 This learned I from the shadow of a tree,
that to and fro did sway against a wall,
our shadow selves, our influence, may fall
where we can never be.

6243 We are all of us more or less echoes, repeating involuntarily the virtues, the defects, the movements and the character of those among whom we live.
JOSEPH JOUBERT (1754–1824)

6244 We reform others unconsciously when we walk uprightly.
MADAME ANNE SOPHIE SOYMANOV SWETCHINE (1782–1857)

6245 When I think of those who have influenced my life the most, I think not of the great but of the good.
JOHN KNOX (C. 1514–1572)

6246 Whom you would change, you must first love.
MARTIN LUTHER KING, JR. (1929–1968)

6247 Why does one man's yawning make another yawn?
ROBERT BURTON (1577–1640)

6248 Your influence is negative or positive, never neutral.
HENRIETTA CORNELIA MEARS (1890–1963)

INGRATITUDE

6249 Blow, blow, thou winter wind!
Thou art not so unkind
As man's ingratitude.
WILLIAM SHAKESPEARE (1564–1616)

6250 I fear that what will surprise us most,
when we see our Lord, will be the
extent of our own ingratitude.
EDWARD BOUBERIE PUSEY (1800–1882)

6251 I have lost two friends by helping
them to considerable positions in life. I
was able to do a favor for them at a
certain time in life, and I have not got
the friends I had before. We do not
quarrel, but they are not as near as
they were. Does not that sound cynical? It is a fact of life many of you
know. That is how we treat God. We
pray for what we want, but we do not
come back to thank him. It is the sign
of a shallow nature. In life, as we
know, ingratitude is the unfailing
mark of a narrow soul. No great mind
is ever ungrateful, and if we can't be
grateful in other respects, we can at
any rate be grateful to God. And genuine Christianity has always this vital
throb of praise.
JAMES MOFFATT (1811–1890)

6252 Ingratitude is the daughter of pride.

6253 Is not sight a jewel? Is not hearing a
treasure? Is not speech a glory? O my
Lord, pardon my ingratitude, and pity
my dullness who am not sensible of
these gifts.
THOMAS TRAHERNE (C. 1637–1674)

6254 Some people are grateful for the roses;
others grumble at the thorns.

6255 We can be thankful to a friend for a
few acres, or a little money, and yet
for the freedom and command of the
whole earth, and for the great benefits
of our being, our life, health, and reason, we look upon ourselves as under
no obligation.
LUCIUS ANNAEUS SENECA (C. 4 B.C.–A.D. 65)

INJUSTICE

6256 Be strong! It matters not how deep
intrenched the wrong,
How hard the battle goes, the day
how long;
Faint not—fight on!
Tomorrow comes the song.
MALTBIE D. BABCOCK (1858–1901)

6257 Bearing wrong is a glorious part of the
fellowship with Christ's sufferings.
ANDREW MURRAY (1828–1917)

6258 Can it be right to water the tree of
knowledge with blood and stir its
boughs with the gusts of bitter agony,
that we may force its flowers into blossom before their time? . . . Shall I quiet
my heart with the throbs of another
heart? Soothe my nerves with the ago-
nized tension of a system? Live a few
days longer by a century of shrieking
deaths? It were a hellish wrong, a selfish, hateful, violent injustice.
GEORGE MACDONALD (1824–1905)

6259 Delay in justice is injustice.
WALTER SAVAGE LANDOR (1775–1864)

6260 Don't pay much attention to who is
for you and who is against you. This
is your major concern: that God be
with you in everything you do.
THOMAS À KEMPIS (C. 1380–1471)

6261 He who defends an injury is next to
him who commits it.

6262 He who does wrong does wrong
against himself. He who acts unjustly
acts unjustly to himself.
MARCUS AURELIUS ANTONINUS (121–180)

6263 He who injured you is either stronger
or weaker. If he is weaker, spare him;
if he is stronger, spare yourself.
LUCIUS ANNAEUS SENECA (C. 4 B.C.–A.D. 65)

6264 If it were not for injustice, men would
not know justice.
HERACLITUS (C. 540–C. 480 B.C.)

6265 If thou suffer injustice, console thyself;
true unhappiness is in doing it.
DEMOCRITUS OF ABDERA
(C. 460–C. 370 B.C.)

6266 Injustice anywhere is a threat to justice
everywhere.
MARTIN LUTHER KING, JR. (1929–1968)

6267 Injustice is relatively easy to bear; it is
justice that hurts.
H. L. MENCKEN (1880–1956)

6268 Injustice never rules forever.
LUCIUS ANNAEUS SENECA (C. 4 B.C.–A.D. 65)

6269 Injustice, suave, erect, and unconfined,
Sweeps the wide earth, and tramples
o'er mankind—
While prayers to heal her wrongs
move slow behind.
HOMER (C. EIGHTH CENTURY B.C.)

6270 It is good that people sometimes misunderstand us, that they have a poor
opinion of us even when our intentions are good. Our inner life grows
stronger when we are outwardly condemned.
THOMAS À KEMPIS (C. 1380–1471)

6271 It is great wisdom to keep silent when
damaging words are spoken to you.
Turn your attention to God and don't
worry about rumor and slander.
THOMAS À KEMPIS (C. 1380–1471)

6272 Man's capacity for justice makes
democracy possible; but man's inclination to injustice makes democracy necessary.
REINHOLD NIEBUHR (1892–1971)

6273 My ear is pain'd,
My soul is sick with every day's report
Of wrong and outrage with which
earth is fill'd.
WILLIAM COWPER (1731–1800)

6274 O blessed are the patient meek who
quietly suffer wrong.
HANNAH HURNARD (1905–1990)

6275 One more wrong to man, one more
insult to God.
ROBERT BROWNING (1812–1889)

6276 Rather suffer an injustice than commit
one.

6277 There is no human condition into
which the divine presence does not penetrate. This is what the Cross, the most
extreme of all human conditions, tells
us. . . . The certainty of divine participation gives us the courage to endure the
riddle of inequality, although our finite
minds cannot solve it.
PAUL JOHANNES OSKAR TILLICH
(1886–1965)

6278 There is no greater opportunity to
influence our fellowman for Christ
than to respond with love when we
have been unmistakably wronged.
Then the difference between Christian
love and the values of the world are
most brilliantly evident.
JAMES C. DOBSON (1936–)

6279 Those who commit injustice bear the
greatest burden.
HOSEA BALLOU (1771–1852)

6280 To believe that God made many of the
lower creatures merely for prey, or to
be the slaves of a slave and writhe
under the tyrannies of a cruel master
who will not serve his own master;
that he created and is creating an endless succession of them to reap little or
no good of life but its cessation—a
doctrine held by some, and practically
accepted by multitudes—is to believe
in a God who, so far as one portion at
least of his creation is concerned, is a
demon.
GEORGE MACDONALD (1824–1905)

6281 To forbear replying to an unjust
reproach, and overlook it with a generous or, if possible, with an entire
neglect of it, is one of the most heroic
acts of a great mind.
JOSEPH ADDISON (1672–1719)

6282 To sin by silence when they should protest makes cowards out of men.
ABRAHAM LINCOLN (1809–1865)

6283 To spare the ravening leopard is an act
of injustice to the sheep.
PERSIAN PROVERB

6284 We hand folks over to God's mercy
and show none ourselves.
GEORGE ELIOT (1819–1880)

6285 We shall have to repent in this generation, not so much for the evil deeds of
the wicked people, but for the appalling silence of the good people.
MARTIN LUTHER KING, JR. (1929–1968)

6286 We shall only resist social injustice and the disintegration of community if justice and mercy prevail in our own common life and social differences have lost their power to divide.
HENDRIK BERKHOF

6287 What power does anyone have to injure you with words? He hurts himself, not you.
THOMAS À KEMPIS (C. 1380–1471)

6288 Your response to a vicious assault can instantly reveal the Christian values by which you live.
JAMES C. DOBSON (1936–   )

INSENSITIVITY

6289 To be blind is bad, but worse is it to have eyes and not to see.
HELEN KELLER (1880–1968)

6290 When a man has lost his shirt, people expect him to roll up his sleeves.

INTEGRITY

6291 A free Christian should act from within with a total disregard for the opinions of others. If a course is right, he should take it because it is right, not because he is afraid not to take it. And if it is wrong, he should avoid it though he lose every earthly treasure and even his very life as a consequence.
A. W. TOZER (1897–1963)

6292 A good name keeps its brightness even in dark days.
LATIN PROVERB

6293 A person who lives right and is right has more power in his silence than another has by words. Character is like bells which ring out sweet notes, and which, when touched—accidentally even—resound with sweet music.
PHILLIPS BROOKS (1835–1893)

6294 And yet, my friend, I would rather that the whole world should be at odds with me, and oppose me, than that I myself should be at odds with myself and contradict myself.
PLATO (C. 428–348 B.C.)

6295 Any man may play his part in the mummery and act the honest man on the scaffolding, but to be right within, in his own bosom, where all is allowed, where all is concealed—there's the point! The next step is to be so in our own home, in our ordinary actions, of which we need render no account to any man, where there is no study, no make-believe.
MICHEL EYQUEM DE MONTAIGNE (1533–1592)

6296 Dear Christ, make one that which we are and that which we appear to be. Be Lord of naked faces.
CALVIN MILLER

6297 Do not look upon the vessel, but upon what it holds.
HEBREW PROVERB

6298 Four things a man must learn to do
If he would make his record true:
To think, without confusion, clearly
To act, from honest motives, purely
To love his fellowman sincerely
To trust in God and heaven securely.
HENRY VAN DYKE (1852–1933)

6299 God give us men! A time like this demands
Strong minds, great hearts, true faith, and ready hands;
Men whom the lust of office does not kill;
Men whom the spoils of office cannot buy;
Men who possess opinions and a will;
Men who have honor; men who will not lie.
JOSIAH GILBERT HOLLAND (1819–1881)

6300 God looks with favor at pure, not full, hands.
LATIN PROVERB

6301 God wants to develop the same character traits in us as exist in Christ. We are to react to the situations of life as Christ did.
ERWIN W. LUTZER (1941–   )

6302 He is rich or poor according to what he is, not according to what he has.
HENRY WARD BEECHER (1813–1887)

6303 I am not bound to win, but I am bound to be true. I am not bound to

succeed, but I am bound to live by the light that I have. I must stand with anybody that stands right, stand with him while he is right, and part with him when he goes wrong.
ABRAHAM LINCOLN (1809–1865)

6304 I desire so to conduct the affairs of this administration that if at the end, when I come to lay down the reins of power, I have lost every other friend on earth, I shall at least have one friend left, and that friend shall be down inside of me.
ABRAHAM LINCOLN (1809–1865)

6305 If I must choose between peace and righteousness, I choose righteousness.
THEODORE ROOSEVELT (1858–1919)

6306 If one can be certain that his principles are right, he need not worry about the consequences.
ROBERT ELLIOTT SPEER (1867–1947)

6307 If the roots are deep, no fear that the wind will uproot the tree.
CHINESE PROVERB

6308 In matters of principle, stand like a rock; in matters of taste, swim with the current.
THOMAS JEFFERSON (1743–1826)

6309 *Integrity* is a good word and those who guide their lives by it will die happy, even though poor.
WILLIAM FEATHER (1889–   )

6310 Integrity is essential if we are to cope with life's difficulties.
EURIPIDES (C. 484–406 B.C.)

6311 Integrity is the first step to true greatness.
CHARLES SIMMONS (1798–1856)

6312 Integrity needs no rules.
ALBERT CAMUS (1913–1960)

6313 It is never "do, do" with the Lord, but "be, be," and he will "do" through you.
OSWALD CHAMBERS (1874–1917)

6314 Jesus Christ is not teaching ordinary integrity, but supernormal integrity, a likeness to our Father in heaven.
OSWALD CHAMBERS (1874–1917)

6315 My worth to God in public is what I am in private.
OSWALD CHAMBERS (1874–1917)

6316 Nothing can come out of a sack but what is in it.
ITALIAN PROVERB

6317 The cross of Christ is in itself an offense to the world; let us take heed that we add no offense of our own.
CHARLES HADDON SPURGEON (1834–1892)

6318 This above all: to thine own self be true,
And it must follow, as the night the day,
Thou canst not then be false to any man.
WILLIAM SHAKESPEARE (1564–1616)

6319 To be persuasive, we must be believable. To be believable, we must be credible. To be credible, we must be truthful.
EDWARD R. MURROW (1908–1965)

6320 What stronger breastplate than a heart untainted.
WILLIAM SHAKESPEARE (1564–1616)

6321 When a Christian jealously guards his secret life with God, his public life will take care of itself.
OSWALD CHAMBERS (1874–1917)

6322 When the fight begins within himself, A man's worth something.
ROBERT BROWNING (1812–1889)

INTELLECT

6323 A smart person isn't really smart until he knows how to get along with fools—which is the chief reason so many intellectuals remain socially powerless and suspect.
SYDNEY J. HARRIS (1917–1986)

6324 I do not feel obliged to believe that that same God who has endowed us with sense, reason, and intellect has intended us to forego their use.
GALILEO GALILEI (1564–1642)

6325 Intellectual sophistication can dry up the wells of spiritual creativity.
HARRY EMERSON FOSDICK (1878–1969)

6326 Intelligence is derived from two words—*inter* and *legere*—*inter* meaning "between" and *legere* meaning "to choose." An intelligent person, therefore, is one who has learned to "choose between." He knows that good is better than evil, that confidence should supersede fear, that love is superior to hate, that gentleness is better than cruelty, forbearance than intolerance, compassion than arrogrance, and that truth has more virtue than ignorance.
J. MARTIN KLOTSCHE

6327 Intelligence must follow faith, never precede it, and never destroy it.
THOMAS À KEMPIS (C. 1380–1471)

6328 It is impossible to find God through the intellectual processes alone. If we try, we end up being ridiculous and foolish.
BILLY GRAHAM (1918–)

6329 Rule your mind or it will rule you.
HORACE (65-8 B. C.)

6330 The intellect is always fooled by the heart.
FRANÇOIS, DUC DE LA ROCHEFOUCAULD (1613–1680)

6331 The voice of the intelligence is soft and weak, said Freud. It is drowned out by the roar of fear. It is ignored by the voice of desire. It is contradicted by the voice of shame. It is hissed away by hate and extinguished by anger. Most of all, it is silenced by ignorance.
KARL AUGUSTUS MENNINGER (1893–1990)

6332 There is no inherent reason why the miner, plowman, and milkmaid should not be an intellectual as the poet, auditor, or schoolteacher.
STUART CHASE (1888–1985)

6333 We should take care not to make the intellect our god; it has, of course, powerful muscles, but no personality.
ALBERT EINSTEIN (1879–1955)

INTENTION

6334 God looks at the intention of the heart rather than the gifts he is offered.
JEAN PIERRE CAMUS (1584–1652)

6335 He who means well is useless unless he does well.
PLAUTUS (C. 254–184 B.C.)

6336 Man considers the actions, but God weighs the intentions.
THOMAS À KEMPIS (C. 1380–1471)

J

JEALOUSY

6337 A jealous man's horns hang in his eyes.

6338 In jealousy there is more self-love than love.
FRANÇOIS, DUC DE LA ROCHEFOUCAULD (1613–1680)

6339 Jealousy is a blister on the heels of friendship.

6340 Jealousy is the foolish child of pride.
PIERRE AUGUSTIN CARON DE BEAUMARCHAIS (1732–1799)

6341 Jealousy is the great exaggerator.
JOHANN FRIEDRICH VON SCHILLER (1759–1805)

6342 Jealousy is the injured lover's hell.
JOHN MILTON (1608–1674)

6343 Jealousy, the jaundice of the soul.
JOHN DRYDEN (1631–1700)

6344 Love is blind; jealousy sees too much.
JEWISH PROVERB

6345 O jealousy! thou magnifier of trifles.
JOHANN FRIEDRICH VON SCHILLER (1759–1805)

6346 O, beware, my lord, of jealousy!
It is the green-ey'd monster which doth mock
The meat it feeds on.
WILLIAM SHAKESPEARE (1564–1616)

6347 Some say that jealousy is love, but I deny it; for though jealousy be procured by love, as ashes are by fire, yet jealousy extinguishes love as ashes smother the flame.
LA REINE DE NAVARRE

6348 The jealous are troublesome to others; a torment to themselves.
WILLIAM PENN (1644–1718)

JESUS CHRIST

6349 A man who can read the New Testament and not see that Christ claims to be more than a man can look all over the sky at high noon on a cloudless day and not see the sun.
WILLIAM EDWARD BIEDERWOLF (1867–1939)

6350 A man who was merely a man and said the sort of things Jesus said wouldn't be a great moral teacher. He'd be either a lunatic—on a level

with a man who says he's a poached egg—or else he'd be the devil of hell. You must make your choice. Either this man was, and is, the Son of God, or else a madman or something worse.
C. S. LEWIS (1898–1963)

6351 Alexander, Caesar, Charlemagne, and myself founded empires; but upon what did we rest the creations of our genius? Upon force. Jesus Christ alone founded his empire upon love, and at this hour millions of men would die for him.
NAPOLEON BONAPARTE (1769–1821)

6352 All his glory and beauty come from within, and there he delights to dwell, his visits there are frequent, his conversations sweet, his comforts refreshing, and his peace passing all understanding.
THOMAS À KEMPIS (C. 1380–1471)

6353 All the armies that ever marched, and all the navies that ever were built, and all the parliaments that ever sat, and all the kings that ever reigned, put together, have not affected the life of man upon this earth as powerfully as has this one solitary life.

6354 All we want in Christ, we shall find in Christ. If we want little, we shall find little. If we want much, we shall find much; but if, in utter helplessness, we cast our all on Christ, he will be to us the whole treasury of God.
HENRY BENJAMIN WHIPPLE (1822–1901)

6355 As the print of the seal on the wax is the express image of the seal itself, so Christ is the express image—the perfect representation—of God.
SAINT AMBROSE (C. 340–397)

6356 Assail'd by scandal and the tongue of strife,
His only answer was, a blameless life.
WILLIAM COWPER (1731–1800)

6357 Because eternity
was closeted in time,
he is my open door
to forever.
LUCI SHAW (1928–)

6358 Because Jesus was not wanted, he was driven to a life of silence, solitude, and simplicity.
CHARLES R. SWINDOLL (1934–)

6359 Besides belonging to eternity, Christ belonged to his times; on the outskirts of a dying civilization he spoke of dying in order to live. Today, when our civilization is likewise dying, his words have the same awe-inspiring relevance as they had then.
MALCOLM MUGGERIDGE (1903–1990)

6360 By a Carpenter mankind was made, and only by that Carpenter can mankind be remade.
DESIDERIUS ERASMUS (C. 1466–1536)

6361 By his first work he gave me to myself; and by the next he gave himself to me. And when he gave himself, he gave me back myself that I had lost.
BERNARD OF CLAIRVAUX (1090–1153)

6362 Caesar was more talked about in his time than Jesus, and Plato taught more science than Christ. People still discuss the Roman ruler and the Greek philosopher, but who nowadays is hotly for Caesar or against him; and who now are the Platonists and the anti-Platonists? There are still people who love him and who hate him. . . . The fury of so many against him is a proof that he is not dead.
GIOVANNI PAPINI (1923–)

6363 Christ . . . combines within himself . . . the qualities of every race.
CHARLES FREER ANDREWS (1871–1940)

6364 Christ as God is the fatherland where we are going. Christ as man is the way by which we go.
SAINT AUGUSTINE OF HIPPO (354–430)

6365 Christ died to save us, not from suffering, but from ourselves; not from injustice, far less than justice, but from being unjust. He died that we might live—but live as he lives, by dying as he died who died to himself.
GEORGE MACDONALD (1824–1905)

6366 Christ either deceived mankind by conscious fraud [regarding an early end of the world], or he was himself deluded,

or he was divine. There is no getting
out of this trilemma.
J. DUNCAN (B. 1870)

6367 Christ has not lost a battle yet—not one.
RICHARD OWEN ROBERTS (1931–   )

6368 Christ has turned all our sunsets into
dawns.
CLEMENT OF ALEXANDRIA (C. 150–C. 215)

6369 Christ himself is living at the heart of
the world; and his total mystery—that
of creation, incarnation, redemption,
and resurrection—embodies and animates all of life and all of history.
MICHEL QUOIST (1921–   )

6370 Christ is full and sufficient for all his
people. He is bread, wine, milk, living
waters, to feed them; he is a garment
of righteousness to cover and adorn
them; a Physician to heal them; a
Counselor to advise them; a Captain
to defend them; a Prince to rule; a
Prophet to teach; a Priest to make
atonement for them; a Husband to
protect; a Father to provide; a Brother
to relieve; a Foundation to support; a
Root to quicken; a Head to guide; a
Treasure to enrich; a Sun to enlighten;
and a Fountain to cleanse.
JOHN SPENCER (1630–1693)

6371 Christ is God acting like God in the
lowly raiments of human flesh.
A. W. TOZER (1897–1963)

6372 Christ is not one of many ways to
approach God, nor is he the best of
several ways; he is the only way.
A. W. TOZER (1897–1963)

6373 Christ is the aperture through which
the immensity and magnificence of
God can be seen.
J. B. PHILLIPS (1906–1982)

6374 Christ is the bread for men's souls. In
him the church has enough to feed the
whole world.
IAN MACLAREN (1850–1907)

6375 Christ made it clear that his coming,
far from meaning peace, meant war.
His message was a fire that would set
society ablaze with division and strife.
BILLY GRAHAM (1918–   )

6376 Christ's life outwardly was one of the
most troubled lives that was ever
lived: tempest and tumult, tumult and
tempest, the waves breaking over it all
the time. But the inner life was a sea of
glass. The great calm was always there.
HENRY DRUMMOND (1851–1897)

6377 Christ's message was revolutionizing;
his words simple, yet profound. And
his words provoked either happy
acceptance or violent rejection. Men
were never the same after listening to
him.
BILLY GRAHAM (1918–   )

6378 Earth grows into heaven, as we come
to live and breathe in the atmosphere
of the Incarnation. Jesus makes heaven
wherever he is.
FREDERICK WILLIAM FABER (1814–1863)

6379 Every character has an inward spring;
let Christ be that spring. Every action
has a keynote; let Christ be that note
to which your whole life is attuned.
HENRY DRUMMOND (1851–1897)

6380 Every passage in the history of our
Lord and Savior is of unfathomable
depth and affords inexhaustible matter
for contemplation. All that concerns
him is infinite, and what we first discern is but the surface of that which
begins and ends in eternity.
CARDINAL JOHN HENRY NEWMAN
(1801–1890)

6381 Feed on Christ, and then go and live
your life, and it is Christ in you that
lives your life, that helps the poor, that
tells the truth, that fights the battle,
and that wins the crown.
PHILLIPS BROOKS (1835–1893)

6382 Follow me: I am the way, the truth,
     and the life.
Without the way there is no going;
Without the truth there is no knowing;
Without the life there is no living.
THOMAS À KEMPIS (C. 1380–1471)

6383 For the Lord Jesus, there was no fellowship in suffering. For the Lord, there
was only the wooden insensitivity of
his disciples—from the first day right
up to the end of his ministry. For him,
there was only that awful climax of iso-

lation on the cross, even to the point of being forsaken by the Father and abandoned to God's blazing wrath.
JONI EARECKSON TADA

6384 From his Bethlehem birth to his death in Jerusalem, Jesus took the road the prophets had marked out, knowing that it would end on Golgotha. If at times he groaned over its ardours, and right at the end asked whether, after all, he might be let off the final sacrifice and left a little longer in a world he must have loved, or he could not have described and explained it so exquisitely, he always returned to his ultimate prayer: Not what I will, but what thou wilt. This was the theme of his life, the essence of the drama he lived out in order to guide all who came after him in the ways of truth; to give us hope in our despair, and light in our darkness, enabling us to look out from time, our prison, on to the mercy of eternity, our liberty.
MALCOLM MUGGERIDGE (1903–1990)

6385 From morning to night keep Jesus in your heart, long for nothing, desire nothing, hope for nothing, but to have all that is within you changed into the spirit and temper of the Holy Jesus.
WILLIAM LAW (1686–1761)

6386 God has himself gone through the whole of human experience, from the trivial irritations of family life and the cramping restrictions of hard work and lack of money to the worst horrors of pain and humiliation, defeat, despair, and death.
DOROTHY L. SAYERS (1893–1957)

6387 God never gave a man a thing to do concerning which it were irreverent to ponder how the Son of God would have done it.
GEORGE MACDONALD (1824–1905)

6388 Had there been a lunatic asylum in the suburbs of Jerusalem, Jesus Christ would infallibly have been shut up in it at the outset of his public career. That interview with Satan on a pinnacle of the Temple would alone have damned him, and everything that hap-

pened after could but have confirmed the diagnosis.
HAVELOCK ELLIS (1859–1939)

6389 He did not come to conquer by force of armies and physical weapons but by love planted in the hearts of individuals.
W. W. MELTON

6390 He has entered little into the depths of our Master's character who does not know that the settled tone of his disposition was a peculiar and subdued sadness.
FREDERICK WILLIAM ROBERTSON (1816–1853)

6391 He is a path, if any be misled;
He is a robe, if any naked be;
If any chance to hunger, he is bread;
If any be a bondman, he is free;
If any be but weak, how strong is he!
To dead men, life is he; to sick men, health;
To blind men, sight; and to the needy, wealth;
A pleasure without loss; a treasure without stealth.
GILES FLETCHER (1584–1623)

6392 He tore through the temple courts like a mad man.
FLAVIUS JOSEPHUS (C. 37–100)

6393 He wrestled with justice, that thou mightest have rest; he wept and mourned, that thou mightest laugh and rejoice; he was betrayed, that thou mightest go free; was apprehended, that thou mightest escape; he was condemned, that thou mightest be justified, and was killed, that thou mightest live; he wore a crown of thorns, that thou mightest wear a crown of glory; and was nailed to the cross with his arms wide open, to show with what freeness all his merits shall be bestowed on the coming soul, and how heartily he will receive it into his bosom.
JOHN BUNYAN (1628–1688)

6394 He wrote no book, and yet his words and prayer
Are intimate on many myriad tongues,
Are counsel everywhere.
THERESE LINDSEY

6395 How widely Jesus had become known is difficult to judge. The Gospels, very naturally, imply that his words and miracles were on everyone's lips, but it is significant that Pilate had never heard of Jesus when he was brought before him, even though it was his business to keep track of agitators and wandering evangelists liable to stir up the excitable populace in his turbulent province.
MALCOLM MUGGERIDGE (1903–1990)

6396 I am much struck with the contrast between Christ's mode of gathering people to himself and the way practiced by Alexander the Great, by Julius Caesar, and by myself. The people have been gathered to us by fear; they were gathered to Christ by love. Alexander, Caesar, and I have been men of war, but Christ was the Prince of Peace. The people have been driven to us; they were drawn to him. In our case there has been forced conscription; in his there was free obedience.
NAPOLEON BONAPARTE (1769–1821)

6397 I am the Way unchangeable; the Truth infallible; the Life everlasting.
THOMAS À KEMPIS (C. 1380–1471)

6398 I cannot row it myself,
My boat on the raging sea;
But beside me sits another,
Who pulls or steers with me;
And I know that we too shall come
into port—
His child and he.
DAN CRAWFORD

6399 I have a great need for Christ; I have a great Christ for my need.
CHARLES HADDON SPURGEON (1834–1892)

6400 I have one passion only: It is he! It is he!
COUNT NIKOLAUS LUDWIG VON ZINZENDORF (1700–1760)

6401 I must know Jesus Christ as Savior before his teaching has any meaning for me other than that of an ideal which leads to despair.
OSWALD CHAMBERS (1874–1917)

6402 If all Jesus Christ came to do was to upset me, make me unfit for my work, upset my friendships and my life, produce disturbance and misery and distress, then I wish he had never come. But that is not all he came to do. He came to lift us up to "the heavenly places" where he is himself. The whole claim of the redemption of Jesus is that he can satisfy the last aching abyss of the human soul, not hereafter only, but here and now.
OSWALD CHAMBERS (1874–1917)

6403 If Jesus Christ is only a teacher, then all he can do is to tantalize us, to erect a standard we cannot attain to; but when we are born again of the Spirit of God, we know that he did not come only to teach us, he came to make us what he teaches we should be.
OSWALD CHAMBERS (1874–1917)

6404 If Jesus Christ were not virgin born, then, of course, he had a human father; if he had a human father, then he inherited the nature of the father; as that father had a nature of sin, then he inherited his nature of sin; then Jesus himself was a lost sinner, and he himself needed a Savior from sin. Deny the virgin birth of Jesus Christ and you paralyze the whole scheme of redemption by Jesus Christ.
I. M. HALDEMAN (1845–1933)

6405 If Jesus Christ were to come today, people would not even crucify him. They would ask him to dinner, and hear what he had to say, and make fun of it.
THOMAS CARLYLE (1795–1881)

6406 If Shakespeare should come into this room, we would all rise; but if Jesus Christ should come in, we would all kneel.
CHARLES LAMB (1775–1834)

6407 If we have never been hurt by a statement of Jesus, it is questionable whether we have ever really heard him speak. Jesus Christ has no tenderness whatever toward anything that is ultimately going to ruin a man for the service of God. If the Spirit of God brings to our mind a word of the Lord that hurts, we may be perfectly certain

there is something he wants to hurt to death.
OSWALD CHAMBERS (1874–1917)

6408 If you wish to be disappointed, look to others. If you wish to be downhearted, look to yourself. If you wish to be encouraged . . . look upon Jesus Christ.
ERICH SAUER

6409 Immortal Love, forever full,
Forever flowing free,
Forever shared, forever whole,
A never-ebbing sea!
JOHN GREENLEAF WHITTIER (1807–1892)

6410 In his life, Christ is an example, showing us how to live. In his death, he is a sacrifice, satisfying for our sins. In his resurrection, he is a conqueror. In his ascension, he is a king. In his intercession, he is a high priest.
MARTIN LUTHER (1483–1546)

6411 In Jesus Christ there was nothing secular and sacred, it was all real, and he makes his disciples like himself.
OSWALD CHAMBERS (1874–1917)

6412 In Jesus we have . . . the holiest man who ever lived, and yet it was the prostitutes and lepers and thieves who adored him, and the religious who hated his guts.
REBECCA MANLEY PIPPERT

6413 In most trials, people are tried for what they have done, but this was not true of Christ's. Jesus was tried for who he was.
JOSH MCDOWELL

6414 Independence is not strength but unrealized weakness and is the very essence of sin. There was no independence in our Lord, the great characteristic of his life was submission to his Father.
OSWALD CHAMBERS (1874–1917)

6415 Is Christ thy advocate to plead thy cause? Art thou his client? Such shall never slide. He never lost his case.
EDWARD TAYLOR (C. 1645–1729)

6416 It is a profound irony that the Son of God visited this planet, and one of the chief complaints against him was that he was not religious enough.
REBECCA MANLEY PIPPERT

6417 It is, in my experience, the people who have never troubled seriously to study the four Gospels who are loudest in their protest that there was no such person as Jesus.
J. B. PHILLIPS (1906–1982)

6418 It was love that kept Jesus from calling 12,000 angels who had already drawn their swords to come to his rescue.
BILLY GRAHAM (1918–   )

6419 It was those luminous words of his, sealed with his death on the cross, that led to his being recognized as God. After all, who but God would have dared to ask of men what he asked of them? Demanding everything and enduring everything, he set in train a great creative wave of love and sacrifice such as the world had never before seen or dreamed of.
MALCOLM MUGGERIDGE (1903–1990)

6420 Jerusalem and Jesus! What a contrast! With what an amazed stare of contempt the personal powers of Jerusalem confronted Jesus, the despised and rejected! Yet he was their Peace for time and eternity, and the things that belonged to their peace were all connected with him.
OSWALD CHAMBERS (1874–1917)

6421 Jesus appeared in Judea in the reign of Tiberius Caesar . . . a very definite personality. One is obliged to say: "Here was a man." This could not have been invented. He was like some terrible moral huntsman digging mankind out of the snug burrows in which they had lived hitherto. For to take him seriously was to enter upon a strange and alarming life, to abandon habits, to control instincts and impulses, and to essay an incredible happiness.
J. B. PHILLIPS (1906–1982)

6422 Jesus Christ always speaks from the source of things; consequently those who deal only with the surface find him an offense.
OSWALD CHAMBERS (1874–1917)

6423 Jesus Christ came into my prison cell last night, and every stone flashed like a ruby.
SAMUEL RUTHERFORD (1600–1661)

6424 Jesus Christ came to do what no human being can do: he came to redeem men, to alter their disposition, to plant in them the Holy Spirit, to make them new creatures. Christianity is not the obliteration of the old, but the transfiguration of the old. Jesus Christ did not come to teach men to be holy, he came to make men holy. His teaching has no meaning for us unless we enter into his life by means of his death. The cross is the great central point.
OSWALD CHAMBERS (1874–1917)

6425 Jesus Christ exhibited a divine paradox of the lion and the lamb. He was the Lion in majesty, rebuking the winds and demons. He was the Lamb in meekness, "who when he was reviled, reviled not again." He was the Lion in power, raising the dead. He was the Lamb in patience who was "brought as a lamb to the slaughter, and as a sheep before her shearers is dumb, so he openeth not his mouth." He was the Lion in authority, "Ye have heard that it hath been said . . . but I say unto you." He was the Lamb in gentleness, "Suffer the little children to come unto me."
OSWALD CHAMBERS (1874–1917)

6426 Jesus Christ had a twofold personality: he was the Son of God revealing what God is like and Son of Man revealing what man is to be like.
OSWALD CHAMBERS (1874–1917)

6427 Jesus Christ is God's everything for man's total need.
RICHARD C. HALVERSON (1916–   )

6428 Jesus Christ is the Completer
of unfinished people
with unfinished work
in unfinished times.
LONA M. FOWLER

6429 Jesus Christ is the divine Physician and Pharmacist, and his prescriptions are never out of balance.
VANCE HAVNER

6430 Jesus Christ is the sternest and the gentlest of Saviors.
OSWALD CHAMBERS (1874–1917)

6431 Jesus Christ never asks anyone to define his position or to understand a creed, but "Who am I to you?" . . . Jesus Christ makes the whole of human destiny depend on a man's relationship to himself.
OSWALD CHAMBERS (1874–1917)

6432 Jesus Christ reveals, not an embarrassed God, not a confused God, not a God who stands apart from the problems, but one who stands in the thick of the whole thing.
OSWALD CHAMBERS (1874–1917)

6433 Jesus Christ served others first; he spoke to those to whom no one spoke; he dined with the lowest members of society; he touched the untouchable. He had no throne, no crown, no bevy of servants or armored guards. A borrowed manger and a borrowed tomb framed his earthly life.
CHARLES COLSON (1931–   )

6434 Jesus Christ set a window in the tiny dark dungeon of the ego in which we all languish, letting in a light, providing a vista, and offering a way of release from the servitude of the flesh and the fury of the will.
MALCOLM MUGGERIDGE (1903–1990)

6435 Jesus Christ was not a conservative.
ERIC HOFFER (1902–1983)

6436 Jesus Christ was not a recluse. He did not cut himself off from society, he was amazingly in and out among the ordinary things of life; but he was disconnected fundamentally from it all. He was not aloof, but he lived in another world. His life was so social that men called him a glutton and a wine-bibber, a friend of publicans and sinners. His detachments were inside toward God.
OSWALD CHAMBERS (1874–1917)

6437 Jesus Christ will be Lord of all or he will not be Lord at all.
SAINT AUGUSTINE OF HIPPO (354–430)

6438 Jesus Christ will never strong-arm his way into your life.
GRADY B. WILSON

6439 Jesus Christ's outward life was densely immersed in the things of the world, yet he was inwardly disconnected. The one irresistible purpose of his life was to do the will of his Father.
OSWALD CHAMBERS (1874–1917)

6440 Jesus Christ's teaching never beats about the bush.
OSWALD CHAMBERS (1874–1917)

6441 Jesus Christ: the condescension of divinity and the exaltation of humanity.
PHILLIPS BROOKS (1835–1893)

6442 Jesus differs from all other teachers; they reach the ear, but he instructs the heart; they deal with the outward letter, but he imparts an inward taste for the truth.
CHARLES HADDON SPURGEON (1834–1892)

6443 Jesus fulfills all the procedures of the prophecies, duly riding into Jerusalem on an ass to the plaudits of the multitude. Only, his victory lies in defeat, his glory in obscurity, his acclaim in ridicule.
MALCOLM MUGGERIDGE (1903–1990)

6444 Jesus had things to say about how we should behave that captivated his listeners and have continued to captivate succeeding generations. This is not because the standards he proposed were lax and easy-going, like today's permissiveness. Far from it. They asked more of his followers than any other teacher ever has . . . not just to refrain from adultery, but to refrain from desiring, which amounts to the same thing, and not just to refrain from killing, but from being angry or calling someone a fool, these being also mortal sins—alas!
MALCOLM MUGGERIDGE (1903–1990)

6445 Jesus is God spelling himself out in language that man can understand.
SAMUEL DICKEY GORDON (1859–1936)

6446 Jesus is God with the skin on.

6447 Jesus is the prophet of the losers' not the victors' camp, the one who proclaims that the first will be last, that the weak are the strong, and the fools are the wise.
MALCOLM MUGGERIDGE (1903–1990)

6448 Jesus leaps in a unique way across the changing centuries because he spoke to the unchanging needs of the heart of man. Jesus speaks to us, not as an antiquated first-century theologian, but as one who knew what was in the heart of man. He expounded no doctrines but lived great life convictions and hence speaks to the living experience of all time.
CLARENCE T. CRAIG

6449 Jesus of Nazareth, without money and arms, conquered more millions than Alexander, Caesar, Muhammad, and Napoleon; without science and learning, he shed more light on things human and divine than all the philosophers and scholars combined; without the eloquence of the school, he spoke words of life such as were never spoken before nor since and produced effects that lie beyond the reach of orator or poet; without writing a single line, he has set more pens in motion and furnished themes for more sermons, orations, discussions, works of art, learned volumes, and sweet songs of praise than the whole army of great men of ancient and modern times.
PHILIP SCHAFF (1819–1893)

6450 Jesus offends men because he lays emphasis on the unseen life, because he speaks of motives rather than of actions.
OSWALD CHAMBERS (1874–1917)

6451 Jesus was . . . a simple rural figure. He talked about the sparrows and the lilies to fishermen and peasants, lepers and outcasts. His radical personalization of all ethical problems is only possible in a village sociology where knowing everyone and having time to treat everyone as a person is culturally an available possibility. The rustic "face-to-face model of social rela-

tions" is the only one he cared about. There is thus in the ethic of Jesus no intention to speak substantially to the problems of complex organization, of institutions and offices, cliques and power and crowds.
JOHN HOWARD YODER

6452 Jesus was a radical. . . . His religion has been so long identified with conservatism—often with conservatism of the obstinate and unyielding sort— that it is almost startling for us sometimes to remember that all of the conservatism of his own times was against him; that it was the young, free, restless, sanguine, progressive part of the people who flocked to him.
PHILLIPS BROOKS (1835–1893)

6453 Jesus' guilt is our innocence; as his captivity is our freedom, and his death our life.
MALCOLM MUGGERIDGE (1903–1990)

6454 Let all be loved for Jesus' sake, but Jesus for himself.
THOMAS À KEMPIS (C. 1380–1471)

6455 Life passes, riches fly away, popularity is fickle, the senses decay, the world changes. One alone is true to us; one alone can be all things to us; one alone can supply our need.
CARDINAL JOHN HENRY NEWMAN (1801–1890)

6456 Little Jesus, was thou shy
Once, and just so small as I?
And what did it feel like to be
Out of heaven, and just like me?
FRANCIS THOMPSON (1859–1907)

6457 Love has a clear eye; but it can see only one thing—it is blind to every interest but that of its Lord; it sees things in the light of his glory and weighs actions in the scales of his honor; it counts royalty but drudgery if it cannot reign for Christ, but it delights in servitude as much as in honor, if it can thereby advance the Master's kingdom; its end sweetens all its means; its object lightens its toil and removes its weariness.
CHARLES HADDON SPURGEON (1834–1892)

6458 Men overlooked a baby's birth
When love unnoticed came to earth;
And later, seeking in the skies,
Passed by a man in workman's guise.
Only children paused to stare
While God Incarnate made a chair.
MARY TATLOW

6459 *Mr. Webster, can you comprehend how Jesus Christ could be both God and man?* No sir, I cannot comprehend it; and I would be ashamed to acknowledge him as my Savior if I could comprehend it. If I could comprehend him, he could be no greater than myself, and such is my conviction of accountability to God, such is my sense of sinfulness before him, and such is my knowledge of my own incapacity to recover myself, that I feel I need a superhuman Savior.
DANIEL WEBSTER (1782–1852)

6460 No one need be downcast, for Jesus is the joy of heaven, and it is his joy to enter into sorrowful hearts.
FREDERICK WILLIAM FABER (1814–1863)

6461 Not only do we know God through Jesus Christ, we only know ourselves through Jesus Christ.
BLAISE PASCAL (1623–1662)

6462 Of all the epithets that could be applied to Christ, mild seems one of the least appropriate.
J. B. PHILLIPS (1906–1982)

6463 Once chosen he's no chance
But certainty.
LUCI SHAW (1928–   )

6464 Once I was visited by someone who told me, in the greatest confidence, that he was Jesus Christ, and that it had been revealed to him that I was the Apostle Paul, my acceptance of this role being my reward for acknowledging my visitor as being indeed Jesus. To get rid of such awkward intruders I easily decided they were mad. Subsequently, I had qualms of conscience, thinking: *Suppose it was Jesus! And I sent him away!* After all, this was just how Jesus would have appeared during his ministry to unbelievers—as a megalomaniac crackpot,

prattling of being God's Son, and authorized to speak on his behalf. Had I lived in the time of Jesus, I fear I should have been among the scoffers and missed the glory of those who heard and saw him and believed.
MALCOLM MUGGERIDGE (1903–1990)

6465 Once it was the blessing,
Now it is the Lord;
Once it was the feeling,
Now it is his Word.
Once his gifts I wanted,
Now the Giver own;
Once I sought for healing,
Now himself alone.
ALBERT BENJAMIN SIMPSON (1843–1919)

6466 Our great High Priest is in glory, exalted above all created angels. But he is the same Jesus we knew in the days of his flesh. He is the same Jesus in heaven as he was on earth, as he was before the world began. The face shining above the brightness of the sun is the face that drew sinners to his feet. The hand that holds the seven stars is the hand that was laid in blessing upon little children. The breast girt about with a golden girdle is the breast upon which the beloved disciple laid his head at the last supper.
A. D. FOREMAN, JR.

6467 Our society has taken Jesus and recreated him in our own cultural image. When I hear Jesus being proclaimed from the television stations across our country, from pulpits hither and yon, he comes across not as the biblical Jesus, not as the Jesus described in the Bible, but as a white, Anglo-Saxon, Protestant Republican. . . . God created us in his image, but we have decided to return the favor and create a God who is in our image.
TONY CAMPOLO

6468 Rest of the weary,
Joy of the sad,
Hope of the dreary,
Light of the glad,
Home of the stranger,
Strength to the end,
Refuge from danger,
Savior and Friend!
JOHN SAMUEL BEWLEY MONSELL
(1811–1875)

6469 Since Jesus died for all men, he might be said to have died even for Judas. The thought so delighted me that I kept on repeating to myself: Jesus died even for Judas! as though I had made some extraordinary discovery. Perhaps in a way I had.
MALCOLM MUGGERIDGE (1903–1990)

6470 The Christ child stood at Mary's knee,
His hair was like a crown,
And all the flowers looked up at him,
And all the stars looked down.
G. K. CHESTERTON (1874–1936)

6471 The cross for the first time revealed God in terms of weakness and lowliness and suffering; even, humanly speaking, of absurdity. He was seen thenceforth in the image of the most timid, most gentle and most vulnerable of all living creatures—a lamb. Agnus Dei!
MALCOLM MUGGERIDGE (1903–1990)

6472 The death of Jesus was not the death of a martyr, it was the revelation of the eternal heart of God.
OSWALD CHAMBERS (1874–1917)

6473 The dying Jesus is the evidence of God's anger toward sin; but the living Jesus is the proof of God's love and forgiveness.
LORENZ EIFERT

6474 The essential teachings of Jesus . . . were literally revolutionary and will always remain so if they are taken seriously.
HERBERT J. MULLER (1905–1967)

6475 The first and also last is solely Christ himself
From him all come to be, in him all comes to rest.
ANGELUS SILESIUS (1624–1677)

6476 The life of Jesus of Nazareth cannot be discussed in the same way as the life of any other man, however famous. Men like Caesar or Napoleon, for example, had a profound effect on their own age and may properly be said to have altered the course

of history, but none of them ever claimed to give the final and definitive explanation of all that has happened, or will happen, in the course of time. Other men, like the Pharaohs of Egypt, have insisted on being worshiped as gods during their lifetime; but no one takes their claims to divinity seriously today. Quite the contrary is true when we consider the life of Jesus.
XAVIER LEON-DUFOUR (1963–)

6477 The Lord appeared in the flesh, that he might arouse us by his teaching, kindle us by his example, redeem us by his death, and renew us by his resurrection.
POPE GREGORY THE GREAT (540–604)

6478 The Lord has turned all our sunsets into sunrise.
CLEMENT OF ALEXANDRIA (C. 150–C. 215)

6479 The miracles of Jesus were the ordinary works of his Father, wrought small and swift that we might take them in.
GEORGE MACDONALD (1824–1905)

6480 The more you know about Christ, the less you will be satisfied with superficial views of him.
CHARLES HADDON SPURGEON (1834–1892)

6481 The most perfect being who has ever trod the soil of this planet was called the Man of Sorrows.
JAMES ANTHONY FROUDE (1818–1894)

6482 The Sermon on the Mount is Christ's biography. Every syllable he had already written down in deeds. The sermon merely translated his life into language.
THOMAS WRIGHT (1810–1877)

6483 The simple record of three short years of active life has done more to regenerate and soften mankind than all the disquisitions of philosophers and all the exhortations of moralists.
WILLIAM EDWARD HARTPOLE LECKY (1838–1903)

6484 The Son no more thought of his own goodness than an honest man thinks of his honesty.
GEORGE MACDONALD (1824–1905)

6485 The strange thing about Jesus is that you can never get away from him.

6486 The teaching of Jesus Christ does not appear at first to be what it is. At first it appears to be beautiful and pious and lukewarm; but before long it becomes a ripping and tearing torpedo which splits to atoms every preconceived notion a man ever had.
OSWALD CHAMBERS (1874–1917)

6487 The teachings of Christ alone can solve our personal difficulties and the world's problems. Every man is a miniature world. Christ enters that world to heal its wounds. We know that all the various schemes of world reconstruction from the beginning of history to our time have failed. Christ's method of making a better world by making better men alone succeeds.
MAX I. REICH

6488 The Transfiguration was the "Great Divide" in the life of our Lord. He stood there in the perfect, spotless holiness of his manhood; then he turned his back on the glory and came down from the Mount to be identified with sin.
OSWALD CHAMBERS (1874–1917)

6489 The whole life of Christ was a continual passion; others die martyrs, but Christ was born a martyr. He found a Golgotha (where he was crucified) even in Bethlehem, where he was born; for to his tenderness then, the straws were almost as sharp as the thorns after, and the manger as uneasy at first as his cross at last. His birth and his death were but one continual act, and his Christmas Day and his Good Friday are but the evening and morning of one and the same day.
JOHN DONNE (1572–1631)

6490 There is no discovery of the truth of Christ's teaching, no unanswerable inward endorsement of it, without committing oneself to his way of life.
J. B. PHILLIPS (1906–1982)

6491 There is one source of power that is stronger than every disappointment, bitterness or ingrained mistrust, and

that power is Jesus Christ, who
brought forgiveness and reconciliation
to the world.
POPE JOHN PAUL II (1920–   )

6492 They should have known that he was
God. His patience should have proved
that to them.
TERTULLIAN (C. 160–AFTER 220)

6493 Thinking of Jesus, I suddenly understand that I know nothing, and for
some reason begin to laugh
hilariously, which brings me to the
realization that I understand everything I need to understand.
MALCOLM MUGGERIDGE (1903–1990)

6494 To become like Christ is the only thing
in the world worth caring for, the
thing before which every ambition of
man is folly and all lower achievement
vain. Those only who make this quest
the supreme desire and passion of
their lives can even begin to hope to
reach it.
JOHN DRUMMOND (1851–1897)

6495 To forsake Christ for the world is to
leave a treasure for a trifle . . . eternity
for a moment, reality for a shadow.
WILLIAM JENKYN

6496 To tear your name from this world
would shake it to its foundations.
JOSEPH ERNEST RENAN (1823–1892)

6497 To the dead he sayeth: Arise!
To the living: Follow me!
And that voice still soundeth on
From the centuries that are gone,
To the centuries that shall be!
HENRY WADSWORTH LONGFELLOW
(1807–1882)

6498 True have his promises been; not one
has failed. I want none beside him. In
life he is my life, and in death he shall
be the death of death; in poverty,
Christ is my riches; in sickness, he
makes my bed; in darkness, he is my
star, and in brightness, he is my sin; he
is the manna of the camp in the wilderness, and he shall be the new corn of
the host when they come to Canaan.
Jesus is to me all grace and no wrath,

all truth and no falsehood; and of
truth and grace he is full, infinitely full.
CHARLES HADDON SPURGEON (1834–1892)

6499 Unspeakably wise,
He is wisely speechless.
SAINT AUGUSTINE OF HIPPO (354–430)

6500 Virtually all the miracles attributed to
Jesus are directly associated with some
lesson he was trying to teach or some
insight he wanted to give to his disciples. The real question to be asked
about any miracle is not how it happened but why: what was God saying
to us in this significant act?
LOUIS CASSELS (1922–1974)

6501 We are taken up with interesting
details; Jesus Christ was not. His insulation was on the inside, not the outside; his dominating interest was hid
with God. His kingdom was on the
inside; consequently he took the ordinary social life of his time in a most
unobtrusive way. His life externally
was oblivious of details; he spent his
time with publicans and sinners and
did the things that were apparently
unreligious. But one thing he never
did—he never contaminated his inner
kingdom.
OSWALD CHAMBERS (1874–1917)

6502 We get no deeper into Christ than we
allow him to get into us.
JOHN HENRY JOWETT (1864–1923)

6503 We marvel, not that he performed
miracles, but rather that he performed
so few. He who could have stormed
the citadels of men with mighty battalions of angels, let men spit upon him
and crucify him.
OSWALD CHAMBERS (1874–1917)

6504 We must not have Christ Jesus, the
Lord of Life, put any more in the
stable amongst the horses and asses,
but he must now have the best chamber.
GEORGE FOX (1624–1691)

6505 We shall never understand anything of
our Lord's preaching and ministry
unless we continually keep in mind
what exactly and exclusively his
errand was in this world. Sin was his

errand in this world, and it was his only errand. He would never have been in this world, either preaching or doing anything else, but for sin. He could have done everything else for us without coming down into this world at all; everything else but take away our sin.
ALEXANDER WHYTE (1836–1921)

6506 We should all like life to be free from suffering, and our love to be free from pain. But there is no true love without suffering. So the highest love of all, the love of Christ for men, showed unforgettably how deeply he must suffer in order to bring men to himself.
J. B. PHILLIPS (1906–1982)

6507 What Christ had to say was too simple to be grasped, too truthful to be believed.
MALCOLM MUGGERIDGE (1903–1990)

6508 What stands out most . . . in the picture of Jesus is his aloneness. . . . Free of family, he remained alone. He had neither wife nor children. He never clung to any of the companions of his youth, his colleagues, the friends with whom he talked at the doors of the towns he passed. He did not enter into any part, nor any faction. He was not an Essene, not a Pharisee, he would not let himself be classified. He was a solitary man.
JOSÉ COMBLIN

6509 Whatever he laid aside to come to us, to whatever limitations, for our sake, he stooped his regal head, he dealt with the things about him in such lordly, childlike manner as made it clear they were not strange to him, but the things of his father.
GEORGE MACDONALD (1824–1905)

6510 When he came, there was no light. When he left, there was no darkness.

6511 When Jesus Christ utters a word, he opens his mouth so wide that it embraces all heaven and earth, even though that word be but in a whisper.
MARTIN LUTHER (1483–1546)

6512 When Jesus is present, all is good and nothing seems difficult; but when Jesus is absent, all is hard.
THOMAS À KEMPIS (C. 1380–1471)

6513 When Jesus turned water into wine at the wedding feast in Cana of Galilee, he was only performing quickly the slow miracle occurring year by year in vineyards.
MALCOLM MUGGERIDGE (1903–1990)

6514 When Jesus walked on earth, he was a man acting like God: but equally wonderful is it that he was also God acting like himself in man and in a man.
A. W. TOZER (1897–1963)

6515 When we try to understand Jesus Christ's teaching with our heads, we get into a fog. What Jesus Christ taught is only explainable to the personality of the mind in relation to the personality of Jesus Christ. It is a relationship of life, not of intellect.
OSWALD CHAMBERS (1874–1917)

6516 Wherever [Jesus] went he produced a crisis. He compelled individuals to decide, to make a choice. In fact, he struck me as the most crisis-producing individual I had ever encountered. . . . Nearly everyone clashed with Jesus, whether they loved him or hated him.
REBECCA MANLEY PIPPERT

6517 Who stumbles upon Christ (who is a granite stone)
Lies shattered; grasp him and be led securely home.
ANGELUS SILESIUS (1624–1677)

6518 Why is it that you can talk about God and nobody gets upset, but as soon as you mention Jesus, people often want to stop the conversation? Why have men and women down through the ages been divided over the question, Who is Jesus?
JOSH MCDOWELL

6519 With infinite love and compassion our Lord understood the human predicament. He had deep empathy with people; he saw their needs, their weaknesses, their desires, and their hurts. He understood and was concerned for people. Every word he

spoke was uttered because he saw a
need for that word in some human
life. His concern was always to uplift
and never to tear down, to heal and
never hurt, to save and not condemn.
CHARLES L. ALLEN (1913–)

6520 You are wisdom
You are peace
You are beauty
You are eternal life.
SAINT FRANCIS OF ASSISI (C. 1181–1226)

6521 You can have it all—everything—on
the wire called Jesus Christ. That wire
will never snap. Not for a lifetime.
Not for eternity.
CHARLES R. SWINDOLL (1934–)

6522 You can read a much more detailed
and intimate account of the thoughts
and teachings of Marcus Aurelius who
lived at roughly the same time. But,
although many have admired him, his
influence upon human life is not one-
ten-millionth part of that of the One
of whom, alas, we know so little.
J. B. PHILLIPS (1906–1982)

6523 You never get to the end of Christ's
words. There is something in them
always behind. They pass into proverbs; they pass into laws; they pass
into doctrines; they pass into consolations; but they never pass away, and
after all the use that is made of them
they are still not exhausted.
ARTHUR PENRHYN STANLEY (1815–1881)

JOY

6524 For the heart
That finds joy
In small things,
In all things
Each day is
A wonderful gift.

6525 God works continually, a thousand
joys he would
Pour into you at once, if suffer it you
could.
ANGELUS SILESIUS (1624–1677)

6526 Great joys, like griefs, are silent.
SHACKERLEY MARMION (1603–1639)

6527 Happiness depends on what happens;
joy does not.
OSWALD CHAMBERS (1874–1917)

6528 Happiness is a feeling. Joy is an
attitude. A posture. A position. A
place.
TIM HANSEL

6529 Happiness is caused by things that happen around me, and circumstances
will mar it; but joy flows right on
through trouble; joy flows on through
the dark; joy flows in the night as well
as in the day; joy flows all through persecution and opposition. It is an
unceasing fountain bubbling up in the
heart; a secret spring the world can't
see and doesn't know anything about.
The Lord gives his people perpetual
joy when they walk in obedience to
him.
DWIGHT LYMAN MOODY (1837–1899)

6530 I cannot choose to be strong, but I can
choose to be joyful. And when I am
willing to do that, strength will follow.
TIM HANSEL

6531 I have met people so empty of joy that
when I clasped their frosty fingertips it
seemed as if I were shaking hands with
a northeast storm. Others there are
whose hands have sunbeams in them,
so that their grasp warms my heart. It
may be only the clinging touch of a
child's hand, but there is as much
potential sunshine in it for me as there
is in a loving glance for others.
HELEN ADAMS KELLER (1880–1968)

6532 I have no understanding of a long-
faced Christian. If God is anything, he
must be joy.
JOE E. BROWN (1892–1973)

6533 I know not how God will dispose of
me. I am always happy. All the world
suffers; and I, who deserve the severest
discipline, feel joys so continual and so
great that I can scarce contain them.
BROTHER LAWRENCE OF THE RESURRECTION
(C. 1605–1691)

6534 If you have no joy in your religion,
there's a leak in your Christianity
somewhere.
BILLY SUNDAY (1862–1935)

6535 It is a poor heart that never rejoices.

6536 Joy has something within itself that is beyond joy and sorrow. This something is called blessedness . . . is asked for and promised in the Bible. It makes the joy of life possible in pleasure and pain, in happiness and unhappiness, in ecstasy and sorrow. Where there is joy, there is fulfillment. And where there is fulfillment, there is joy.
PAUL JOHANNES OSKAR TILLICH (1886–1965)

6537 Joy is a positive thing: in joy one does not only feel secure, but something goes out from oneself to the universe, a warm, positive effluence of love.
RICHARD HOOKER (1554–1600)

6538 *Joy* is distinctly a Christian word and a Christian thing. It is the reverse of happiness. Happiness is the result of what happens of an agreeable sort. Joy has its springs deep down inside. And that spring never runs dry, no matter what happens. Only Jesus gives that joy. He had joy, singing its music within, even under the shadow of the cross.
SAMUEL DICKEY GORDON (1859–1936)

6539 Joy is magnified when shared.
TIM HANSEL

6540 Joy is never in our power, and pleasure is. I doubt whether anyone who has tasted joy would ever, if both were in his power, exchange it for all the pleasure in the world.
C. S. LEWIS (1898–1963)

6541 Joy is not in things; it is in us.
RICHARD WAGNER (1813–1883)

6542 Joy is peace dancing and peace is joy at rest.
F. B. MEYER (1847–1929)

6543 Joy is sorrow inside out;
Grief remade again.
HANNAH HURNARD (1905–1990)

6544 Joy is that deep settled confidence that God is in control in every area of my life.
PAUL SAILHAMER

6545 Joy is the echo of God's life within us.
JOSEPH COLUMBA MARMION (1858–1923)

6546 Joy is the gigantic secret of the Christian.
G. K. CHESTERTON (1874–1936)

6547 Joy is the great note all through the Bible.
OSWALD CHAMBERS (1874–1917)

6548 Joy is the most infallible sign of the presence of God.
LÉON HENRI MARIE BLOY (1846–1917)

6549 Joy is the serious business of heaven.
C. S. LEWIS (1898–1963)

6550 Joy is to behold God in everything.
JULIAN OF NORWICH (C. 1342–AFTER 1413)

6551 Joys divided are increased.
JOSIAH GILBERT HOLLAND (1819–1881)

6552 Man cannot find true essential joy anywhere but in his relationship to God.
OSWALD CHAMBERS (1874–1917)

6553 No sky is heavy if the heart be light.

6554 Oh the joy of that life with God and in God and for God!
OSWALD CHAMBERS (1874–1917)

6555 One joy dispels a hundred cares.
CHINESE PROVERB

6556 Our level of joy (and therefore strength and healing) is directly proportional to our level of acceptance.
TIM HANSEL

6557 Real joy is sorrow accepted and transformed.
HANNAH HURNARD (1905–1990)

6558 Silence is the perfectest herald of joy;
I were but little happy if I could say how much.
WILLIAM SHAKESPEARE (1564–1616)

6559 The heart that is to be filled to the brim with holy joy must be held still.
GEORGE SEATON BOWES (C. 1875)

6560 The joy of the heart colors the face.

6561 The joy that you give to others
Is the joy that comes back to you.
JOHN GREENLEAF WHITTIER (1807–1892)

6562 The most profound joy has more of gravity than of gaiety in it.
MICHEL EYQUEM DE MONTAIGNE (1533–1592)

6563 The Stoic bears, the Epicurean seeks to enjoy, the Buddhist and Hindu stand

apart disillusioned; the Muslim submits, but only the Christian exults.
E. STANLEY JONES (1884–1973)

6564 The word *joy* is too great and grand to be confused with the superficial things we call happiness.
KIRBY PAGE (1890–1957)

6565 There are joys which long to be ours. God sends ten thousand truths, which come about us like birds seeking inlet; but we are shut up to them, and so they bring us nothing, but sit and sing awhile upon the roof and then fly away.
HENRY WARD BEECHER (1813–1887)

6566 This is the secret of joy. We shall no longer strive for our own way, but commit ourselves, easily and simply, to God's way, acquiesce in his will, and in so doing find our peace.
EVELYN UNDERHILL (1875–1941)

6567 Those who bring sunshine to the lives of others cannot keep it from themselves.
SIR JAMES M. BARRIE (1860–1937)

6568 True joy is not a thing of moods, not a capricious emotion, tied to fluctuating experiences. It is a state and condition of the soul. It survives through pain and sorrow and, like a subterranean spring, waters the whole life. It is intimately allied and bound up with love and goodness, and so is deeply rooted in the life of God.
RUFUS MATTHEW JONES (1863–1948)

6569 We all long for heaven where God is, but we have it in our power to be in heaven with him right now—to be happy with him at this very moment. But being happy with him now means:
loving as he loves,
helping as he helps,
giving as he gives,
serving as he serves,
rescuing as he rescues,
being with him for all the
    twenty-four hours,
touching him in his distressing
    disguise.
MOTHER TERESA OF CALCUTTA (1910–)

6570 We are all strings in the concert of God's joy.
JAKOB BÖHME (1575–1624)

6571 You and I were created for joy, and if we miss it, we miss the reason for our existence. . . . If our joy is honest joy, it must somehow be congruous with human tragedy. This is the test of joy's integrity: is it compatible with pain? . . . Only the heart that hurts has a right to joy.
LEWIS B. SMEDES

JUDGMENT

6572 Do not condemn your neighbor; you do not know what you would have done in his place.

6573 Do not judge a man until you know his whole story.

6574 Don't judge any man until you have walked two moons in his moccasins.
INDIAN PROVERB

6575 Don't judge anyone harshly until you yourself have been through his experiences.
JOHANN WOLFGANG VON GOETHE (1749–1832)

6576 Examine the contents, not the bottle.
TALMUD

6577 Forebear to judge, for we are sinners all.
WILLIAM SHAKESPEARE (1564–1616)

6578 He who judges others condemns himself.
ENGLISH PROVERB

6579 I am not judged by the light I have, but by the light I have refused to accept.
OSWALD CHAMBERS (1874–1917)

6580 If you say that man is too little for God to speak to him, you must be very big to be able to judge.
BLAISE PASCAL (1623–1662)

6581 Judge a tree from its fruit; not from the leaves.
EURIPIDES (C. 484–406 B.C.)

6582 Jumping to conclusions seldom leads to happy landings.

6583 Man judges from a partial view.
None ever yet his brother knew;
The eternal eye that sees the whole
May better read the darkened soul,
And find, to outward sense denied,
The flower upon its inmost side!
JOHN GREENLEAF WHITTIER (1807–1892)

6584 Most people judge men only by their
success.
FRANÇOIS, DUC DE LA ROCHEFOUCAULD
(1613–1680)

6585 No man can justly censure or condemn another because no man truly
knows another.
SIR THOMAS BROWNE (1605–1682)

6586 No man is condemned for anything he
has done: he is condemned for continuing to do wrong. He is condemned for
not coming out of the darkness, for
not coming to the light.
GEORGE MACDONALD (1824–1905)

6587 One cool judgment is worth a thousand hasty councils. The thing to do is
to supply light and not heat.
WOODROW WILSON (1856–1924)

6588 Only judge when you have heard all.
GREEK PROVERB

6589 Our concept of time makes it necessary for us to speak of the Day of Judgment; in reality, it is a summary court
in perpetual session.
FRANZ KAFKA (1883–1924)

6590 Remind the religious phony that the
splinter within your eye is between
you and your Lord, and to pay attention to the tree trunk in his own eye.
CHARLES R. SWINDOLL (1934–)

6591 Such was the rule of life! I worked my
best, subject to ultimate judgment;
God's, not man's.
ROBERT BROWNING (1812–1889)

6592 The archer who overshoots misses as
well as he who falls short.

6593 The more one judges, the less one
loves.
HONORÉ DE BALZAC (1799–1850)

6594 The unsurrendered Christian stands
condemned for what he does not do
more than for what he does.
BILLY GRAHAM (1918–)

6595 To judge wisely, we must know how
things appear to the unwise.
GEORGE ELIOT (1819–1880)

6596 We judge ourselves by our motives
and others by their actions.
DWIGHT WHITNEY MORROW (1873–1931)

6597 When one knows oneself well, one is
not desirous of looking into the faults
of others.
JOHN MOSCHUS (C. 550–619)

6598 When rattling bones together fly
From the four corners of the sky.
JOHN DRYDEN (1631–1700)

6599 While we are coldly discussing a man's
career, sneering at his mistakes, blaming his rashness, and labelling his opinions—"Evangelical and narrow," or
"Latitudinarian and Pantheistic," or
"Anglican and supercilious"—that
man, in his solitude, is perhaps shedding hot tears because his sacrifice is a
hard one, because strength and
patience are failing him to speak the
difficult word and do the difficult deed.
GEORGE ELIOT (1819–1880)

6600 You can be certain of this: when the
Day of Judgment comes, we shall not
be asked what we have read, but what
we have done; not how well we have
spoken, but how well we have lived.
THOMAS À KEMPIS (C. 1380–1471)

6601 You should not say it is not good. You
should say you do not like it; and then
you're perfectly safe.
JAMES ABBOT MCNEILL WHISTLER
(1834–1903)

JUSTICE

6602 A good cause will fear no judge.
LATIN PROVERB

6603 An injury to one is the concern of all.

6604 By largely ignoring the central biblical
teaching that God is on the side of the
poor, our theology has been profoundly unorthodox. The Bible has
just as much to say about this doctrine
as it does about Jesus' resurrection.
And yet we insist on the Resurrection
as a criterion of orthodoxy and largely
ignore the equally prominent biblical

teaching that God is on the side of the poor and the oppressed.
RONALD J. SIDER

6605 Corn can't expect justice from a court composed of chickens.
AFRICAN PROVERB

6606 Don't hear one and judge two.
GREEK PROVERB

6607 God's mill grinds slow, but sure.
GEORGE HERBERT (1593–1633)

6608 He injures good men who spare the wicked.
PUBLILIUS SYRUS (FIRST CENTURY B.C.)

6609 If we do justice to our brother even though we may not like him, we will come to love him; but if we do injustice to him because we do not love him, we will come to hate him.
JOHN RUSKIN (1819–1900)

6610 It is impossible to be just if one is not generous.
JOSEPH ROUX (D. 1794)

6611 Justice delayed is justice denied.
WILLIAM EWART GLADSTONE (1809–1898)

6612 Justice is nothing other than love working out its problems.
JOSEPH FLETCHER

6613 Justice is truth in action.
BENJAMIN DISRAELI (1804–1881)

6614 Justice to be justice must be much more than justice. Love is the law of our condition, without which we can no more render justice than a man can keep a straight line, walking in the dark.
GEORGE MACDONALD (1824–1905)

6615 Let us have faith that right makes might, and in that faith let us to the end dare to do our duty as we understand it.
ABRAHAM LINCOLN (1809–1865)

6616 Man's capacity for justice makes democracy possible, but man's inclination to injustice makes democracy necessary.
REINHOLD NIEBUHR (1892–1971)

6617 One hour of justice is worth a hundred of prayer.
ARABIAN PROVERB

6618 One man's word is no man's word; we should quietly hear both sides.
JOHANN WOLFGANG VON GOETHE (1749–1832)

6619 Only through an inner spiritual transformation do we gain the strength to fight vigorously the evils of the world in a humble and loving spirit. The transformed nonconformist, moreover, never yields to the passive sort of patience which is an excuse to do nothing.
MARTIN LUTHER KING, JR. (1929–1968)

6620 People become house builders through building houses, harp players through playing the harp. We become just by doing things which are just.
ARISTOTLE (384–322 B.C.)

6621 Right predominates, nothing prevails against it.
ARABIAN PROVERB

6622 Silence is the freedom to let our justification rest entirely with God.
RICHARD J. FOSTER (1942–   )

6623 The Christian's goal is not power but justice. We are to seek to make the institutions of power just, without being corrupted by the process necessary to do this.
CHARLES COLSON (1931–   )

6624 The just hand is a precious ointment.
LATIN PROVERB

6625 The pearl of justice is found in the heart of mercy.
CATHERINE OF SIENA (1347–1380)

6626 The probability that we may fail in the struggle should not deter us from the support of a cause we believe to be just.
ABRAHAM LINCOLN (1809–1865)

6627 To sin by silence when they should protest makes cowards of men.
ABRAHAM LINCOLN (1809–1865)

6628 Truth is justice's handmaid; freedom is its child, peace is its companion; safety walks in its steps; victory follows in its train; it is the brightest emanation from the gospel; it is an attribute of God.
SYDNEY SMITH (1771–1845)

6629 We will not be satisfied until justice rolls down like waters, and righteousness like a mighty stream.
MARTIN LUTHER KING, JR. (1929–1968)

6630 [God's] freedom from bias does not mean that he maintains neutrality in the struggle for justice. He is indeed on the side of the poor! The Bible clearly and repeatedly teaches that God is at work in history casting down the rich and exalting the poor because frequently the rich are wealthy precisely because they have oppressed the poor or have neglected to aid the needy. God also sides with the poor because of their special vulnerability.
RONALD J. SIDER

JUSTIFICATION

6631 God does not justify us because we are worthy, but by justifying us makes us worthy.
THOMAS WATSON (C. 1557–1592)

6632 Justification means "just-as-if-I-never-sinned."

6633 The doctrine of justification is the foundation that supports all of the other benefits we receive from Christ.
ERWIN W. LUTZER (1941–)

6634 To say that God justifies the ungodly means quite simply that God in his amazing love treats the sinner as if he was a good man. Again, to put it very simply, God loves us, not for anything that we are, but for what he is.
WILLIAM BARCLAY (1907–1978)

K

KINDNESS

6635 Be kind; everyone you meet is fighting
a hard battle.
IAN MACLAREN (1850–1907)

6636 Can you ever remember a time when
you regretted having said a kind word?

6637 Do all the good you can,
By all the means you can,
In all the ways you can,
In all the places you can,
At all the times you can,
To all the people you can,
As long as ever you can.

6638 Forget injuries, never forget kindnesses.
CHINESE PROVERB

6639 Hatred and anger are powerless when
met with kindness.

6640 Have you had a kindness shown?
Pass it on;
'Twas not given for thee alone,
Pass it on;
Let it travel down the years,
Let it wipe another's tears,
'Till in heaven the deed appears—
Pass it on.
HENRY BURTON (1840–1930)

6641 He was so benevolent, so merciful a
man that he would have held an
umbrella over a duck in a shower of
rain.
DOUGLAS WILLIAM JERROLD (1803–1857)

6642 I expect to pass through life but once.
If therefore, there be any kindness that
I can show, or any good thing I can do
to any fellow being, let me do it now,
and not defer or neglect it, as I shall
not pass this way again.
STEPHEN GRELLET (1773–1855)

6643 It is easier to catch flies with honey
than with vinegar.
ENGLISH PROVERB

6644 Keep what is worth keeping—
And with a breath of kindness
Blow the rest away.
DINAH MARIA MULOCK CRAIK
(1826–1887)

6645 Kind words are the music of the
world. They have a power that seems
to be beyond natural causes, as if they
were some angel's song that had lost
its way and come on earth. It seems as
if they could almost do what in reality
God alone can do—soften the hard

and angry hearts of men. No one was ever corrected by a sarcasm—crushed, perhaps, if the sarcasm was clever enough, but drawn nearer to God, never.
FREDERICK WILLIAM FABER (1814–1863)

6646 Kind words don't wear out the tongue.
DANISH PROVERB

6647 Kind words toward those you daily meet,
Kind words and actions right,
Will make this life of ours most sweet,
Turn darkness into light.
ISAAC WATTS (1674–1748)

6648 Kindness has converted more sinners than zeal, eloquence, or learning.
FREDERICK WILLIAM FABER (1814–1863)

6649 Kindness in words creates confidence. Kindness in thinking creates profoundness. Kindness in giving creates love.
LAO-TSE (C. 604–C. 531 B.C.)

6650 Kindness is a language the dumb can speak, the deaf can hear, and the blind can see.

6651 Kindness is like a rose, which though easily crushed and fragile, yet speaks a language of silent power.
FRANCES J. ROBERTS

6652 Kindness is love in work clothes.

6653 Kindness is loving people more than they deserve.
JOSEPH JOUBERT (1754–1824)

6654 Kindness is the sunshine in which virtue grows.

6655 Kindness will always attract kindness.
SOPHOCLES (C. 496–406 B.C.)

6656 Life is made up, not of great sacrifices or duties, but of little things, in which smiles and kindness and small obligations win and preserve the heart.
HUMPHREY DAVY (1778–1829)

6657 Life is mostly froth and bubble,
Two things stand like stone—
Kindness in another's trouble,
Courage in your own.
ADAM LINDSAY GORDON (1833–1870)

6658 Life is short and we have not too much time for gladdening the hearts of those who are traveling the dark way with us. Oh, be swift to love! Make haste to be kind!
HENRI FRÉDÉRIC AMIEL (1821–1881)

6659 Little drops of water, little grains of sand,
Make the mighty ocean and the pleasant land.
Little deeds of kindness, little words of love,
Help to make earth happy like the heaven above.
JULIA A. FLETCHER CARNEY (1823–1908)

6660 Make a rule and pray to God to help you to keep it, never, if possible, to lie down at night without being able to say: "I have made one human being at least a little wiser, or a little happier, or at least a little better this day."
CHARLES KINGSLEY (1819–1875)

6661 One kind act will teach more love of God than a thousand sermons.

6662 One kind word can warm three winter months.
JAPANESE PROVERB

6663 Speak your kind words soon, for you never know how soon it will be too late.

6664 The best portions of a good man's life—
His little, nameless, unremembered acts
Of kindness and love.
WILLIAM WORDSWORTH (1770–1850)

6665 The greatest thing a man can do for his heavenly Father is to be kind to some of his other children.
HENRY DRUMMOND (1851–1897)

6666 The heart benevolent and kind
The most resembles God.
ROBERT BURNS (1759–1796)

6667 The kindest are those who forgive and forget.

6668 The sun makes ice melt; kindness causes misunderstanding, mistrust, and hostility to evaporate.
ALBERT SCHWEITZER (1875–1965)

6669 There is a grace of kind listening, as well as a grace of kind speaking.
FREDERICK WILLIAM FABER (1814–1863)

6670 This world is but the vestibule of eternity. Every good thought or deed touches a chord that vibrates in heaven.

6671 What time is it?
Time to do well,
Time to live better,
Give up that grudge,
Answer that letter,
Speak the kind word
To sweeten a sorrow,
Do that kind deed
You would leave 'till tomorrow.

6672 Wise sayings often fall on barren ground; but a kind word is never thrown away.
ARTHUR HELPS (1813–1875)

6673 You are best to yourself when you are good to others.

6674 You may be sorry that you spoke,
sorry you stayed or went,
Sorry you won or lost,
Perhaps, sorry so much was spent.
But as you go through life, you'll find
you're never sorry you were kind.

KNOWLEDGE

6675 A man can accept what Christ has done without knowing how it works; indeed, he certainly won't know how it works until he's accepted it.
C. S. LEWIS (1898–1963)

6676 A scrap of knowledge about sublime things is worth more than any amount about trivialities.
SAINT THOMAS AQUINAS (1225–1274)

6677 All we know is still infinitely less than all that still remains unknown.
WILLIAM HARVEY (1578–1657)

6678 As knowledge increases, wonder deepens.
CHARLES MORGAN (1894–1958)

6679 By our anti-intellectualism, in which we either refuse or cannot be bothered to listen to God's Word, we may be storing up for ourselves the judgment of Almighty God. . . . God has constituted us thinking beings; he has treated us as such by communicating with us in words; he has renewed us in Christ and given us the mind of Christ; and he will hold us responsible for the knowledge we have.
JOHN R. W. STOTT (1921–   )

6680 Far more crucial than what we know or do not know is what we do not want to know.
ERIC HOFFER (1902–1983)

6681 For the attainment of divine knowledge we are directed to combine a dependence on God's Spirit with our own researches. Let us, then, not presume to separate what God has thus united.
CHARLES SIMEON (1759–1836)

6682 He that boasts of his own knowledge proclaims his ignorance.

6683 He who asks a question is a fool for five minutes; he who does not ask a question remains a fool forever.
CHINESE PROVERB

6684 I am not young enough to know everything.
SIR JAMES M. BARRIE (1860–1937)

6685 I can stand what I know. It's what I don't know that frightens me.
FRANCES NEWTON

6686 I keep six honest serving men
(They taught me all I knew);
Their names are What and Why
and When
And How and Where and Who.
RUDYARD KIPLING (1865–1936)

6687 If I only had three years to serve the Lord, I would spend two of them studying and preparing.
DONALD GREY BARNHOUSE (1895–1960)

6688 It is better to ask some of the questions than to know all of the answers.
JAMES GROVER THURBER (1894–1961)

6689 It is in knowledge that a man is most haunted with a sense of inevitable limitation.
JOSEPH FARRELL

6690 Knowledge and wisdom, far from
being one,
Have ofttimes no connection.
Knowledge dwells

In heads replete with thoughts of other
    men,
Wisdom in minds attentive to their
    own.
WILLIAM COWPER (1731–1800)

6691 Knowledge begins with wondering. Set
a child to wondering and you have put
him on the road to understanding.
SAMUEL PIERPONT LANGLEY (1834–1906)

6692 Knowledge comes, but wisdom lingers.
ALFRED, LORD TENNYSON (1809–1892)

6693 Knowledge is indispensable to Christian life and service. If we do not use
the mind that God has given us, we
condemn ourselves to spiritual superficiality and cut ourselves off from
many of the riches of God's grace. . . .
Knowledge is given us to be used, to
lead us to higher worship, greater
faith, deeper holiness, better service.
JOHN R. W. STOTT (1921–)

6694 Knowledge is power, but the unnecessary display of it is weakness.

6695 Knowledge is proud that he has
learned so much; wisdom is humble
that he knows no more.
WILLIAM COWPER (1731–1800)

6696 Knowledge of nature and atheism are
incompatible. To know nature is to
know that there must be a God.
EDWARD GEORGE BULWER-LYTTON
(1803–1873)

6697 Man knows much more than he understands.
ALFRED ADLER (1870–1937)

6698 Man, if he compare himself with all
that he can see, is at the Zenith of
Power; but if he compare himself with
all that he can conceive, he is at the
Nadir of Weakness.
CHARLES CALEB COLTON (1780–1832)

6699 Our knowledge, compared with
God's, is ignorance.
SAINT AUGUSTINE OF HIPPO (354–430)

6700 Strange how much you've got to know
before you know how little you know.

6701 The first temptation that came to . . .
us was the promise of learning and
knowledge.
MICHEL EYQUEM DE MONTAIGNE
(1533–1592)

6702 The larger the island of knowledge,
the longer the shoreline of wonder.
RALPH WASHINGTON SOCKMAN
(1889–1970)

6703 The silly question is the first intimation of some totally new development.
ALFRED NORTH WHITEHEAD (1861–1947)

6704 The true knowledge of God will result,
not in our being puffed up with conceit at how knowledgeable we are, but
in our falling on our faces before God
in sheer wonder and crying, "O the
depth of the riches and wisdom and
knowledge of God! How unsearchable
are his judgments and how unscrut-
able his ways!" Whenever our knowledge becomes dry or leaves us cold,
something has gone wrong.
JOHN R. W. STOTT (1921–)

6705 There are three things that only God
knows: the beginning of things, the
cause of things, and the end of things.
WELSH PROVERB

6706 There is no absolute knowledge. All
information is imperfect. We have to
treat it with humility.
SIR D. W. BROGAN (1900–1974)

6707 Things human must be known to be
loved; things divine must be loved to
be known.
BLAISE PASCAL (1623–1662)

6708 Those who would know much and
love little, will remain ever at the
beginning of a godly life. . . . Simple
love, with even but little knowledge,
can do great things.
SAINT MECHTHILD OF MAGDEBURG
(C. 1210–C. 1280)

6709 We do not know one millionth of one
percent about anything.
THOMAS ALVA EDISON (1847–1931)

6710 We owe almost all our knowledge not
to those who have agreed but to those
who have differed.
CHARLES CALEB COLTON (1780–1832)

6711 Where there is much desire to learn, there of necessity will be much arguing, much writing, many opinions; for opinion in good men is but knowledge in the making.
JOHN MILTON (1608–1674)

6712 Where there is much light, the shadow is deep.
JOHANN WOLFGANG VON GOETHE (1749–1832)

KNOWLEDGE/DOUBTS

6713 Half our doubts and fears arise from dim perceptions of the real nature of Christ's gospel. . . . The root of a happy religion is clear, distinct, well-defined knowledge of Jesus Christ.
JOHN CHARLES RYLE (1816–1900)

KNOWLEDGE/FAITH

6714 If assurance is the child of faith, faith is the child of knowledge, the sure knowledge of Christ and of the gospel.
JOHN R. W. STOTT (1921–   )

L

LAUGHTER

6715 A sense of humor is the pole that adds balance to our steps as we walk the tightrope of life.

6716 Always laugh when you can; it is cheap medicine.
LORD GEORGE NOEL GORDON BYRON (1788–1824)

6717 He who laughs—lasts.

6718 Humor is the sunshine of the mind.
EDWARD GEORGE BULWER-LYTTON (1803–1873)

6719 Humor makes all things tolerable.
HENRY WARD BEECHER (1813–1887)

6720 If you don't learn to laugh at trouble, you won't have anything to laugh at when you're old.
ED HOWE (1853–1937)

6721 If you're not allowed to laugh in heaven, I don't want to go there.
MARTIN LUTHER (1483–1546)

6722 It is often just as sacred to laugh as it is to pray.
CHARLES R. SWINDOLL (1934–)

6723 It is the heart that is not yet sure of its God that is afraid to laugh in his presence.
GEORGE MACDONALD (1824–1905)

6724 Laugh out loud. That helps flush out the nervous system.
CHARLES R. SWINDOLL (1934–)

6725 Laughing 100 times a day works the heart as much as exercising for ten minutes on a rowing machine.

6726 Laughing is the sensation of feeling good all over and showing it principally in one spot.
JOSH BILLINGS (1818–1885)

6727 Laughter adds richness, texture, and color to otherwise ordinary days. It is a gift, a choice, a discipline, and an art.
TIM HANSEL

6728 Laughter and weeping are the two intensest forms of human emotion, and these profound wells of human emotion are to be consecrated to God.
OSWALD CHAMBERS (1874–1917)

6729 Laughter is a sacred sound to our God.
TIM HANSEL

6730 Laughter is a tranquilizer with no side effects.
ARNOLD GLASGOW

6731 Laughter is God's hand on a troubled world.

6732 Laughter is the contentment of God.
JOHANN WEISS (1818–1879)

6733 Laughter is the most beautiful and beneficial therapy God ever granted humanity.
CHARLES R. SWINDOLL (1934–   )

6734 Laughter is the music of life.
SIR WILLIAM OSLER (1849–1919)

6735 Laughter is the sun that drives winter from the human face.

6736 Laughter or tears, both derive from God.
SOPHOCLES (C. 496–406 B.C.)

6737 Man alone can smile and laugh.
ERIC HOFFER (1902–1983)

6738 Mirth is God's medicine. Everybody ought to bathe in it. Grim care, moroseness, anxiety—all this rust of life ought to be scoured off by the oil of mirth.
HENRY WARD BEECHER (1813–1887)

6739 Mirth is the sweet wine of human life. It should be offered sparkling with zestful life unto God.
HENRY WARD BEECHER (1813–1887)

6740 On this hapless earth
There's small sincerity of mirth,
And laughter oft is but an art
To drown the outcry of the heart.
HARTLEY COLERIDGE (1796–1849)

6741 One laugh = 3 Tbsp. oat bran

6742 Perhaps I know best why it is man alone who laughs; he alone suffers so deeply that he had to invent laughter.
FRIEDRICH WILHELM NIETZSCHE (1844–1900)

6743 Please, Lord, teach us to laugh again; but God, don't ever let us forget that we cried.
BILL WILSON

6744 That day is lost on which one has not laughed.
FRENCH PROVERB

6745 What sunshine is to flowers, smiles are to humanity.
JOSEPH ADDISON (1672–1719)

6746 When you're laughing, your attention is focused. You can't do anything else. Everything else, whether it's depression or stress, stops.
ROBERT LEONE

6747 With the fearful strain that is on me night and day, if I did not laugh I should die.
ABRAHAM LINCOLN (1809–1865)

6748 You don't stop laughing because you grow old, you grow old because you stop laughing.

LAZINESS

6749 A lazy man is a workshop for Satan.
ARABIAN PROVERB

6750 A lazy sheep thinks its wool heavy.

6751 A man grows most tired while standing still.
CHINESE PROVERB

6752 Absence of occupation is not rest. A mind quite vacant is a mind distressed.
WILLIAM COWPER (1731–1800)

6753 Activity is a blessing, laziness wears you out.
ARABIAN PROVERB

6754 An idle brain is the devil's workshop.
ENGLISH PROVERB

6755 Don't loaf away your time and depend on the Lord for your daily bread; he isn't running a bakery.

6756 He slept beneath the moon,
He basked beneath the sun;
He lived a life of going-to-do,
And died with nothing done.
—Epitaph written for himself
JAMES ALBERY (1838–1889)

6757 He who kills time kills opportunities.

6758 He's willing to swallow but too lazy to chew.
RUSSIAN PROVERB

6759 Hunger is a suitable comrade for the work-shy.
HESIOD (EIGHTH CENTURY B.C.)

6760 Idle hours breed wandering thoughts.
LUCIAN (C. 125–C. 190)

6761 Idleness is a sort of suicide.
LORD CHESTERFIELD (1694–1773)

6762 Idleness: the devil's pillow.
DANISH PROVERB

6763 If I rest, I rust.
MARTIN LUTHER (1483–1546)

6764 In idleness there is perpetual despair.
THOMAS CARLYLE (1795–1881)

6765 Iron rusts from disuse, stagnant water
loses its purity and in cold weather
becomes frozen; even so inaction saps
the vigor of the mind.
LEONARDO DA VINCI (1452–1519)

6766 It cost the devil little trouble to catch
the lazy man.
GERMAN PROVERB

6767 It is better to wear out than to rust out.
GEORGE WHITEFIELD (1714–1770)

6768 Laziness travels so slowly that poverty
soon overtakes him.
BENJAMIN FRANKLIN (1706–1790)

6769 Laziness: resting before you get tired.
JULES RENARD (1864–1910)

6770 Men are naturally tempted by the
devil, but an idle man tempts the devil.
SPANISH PROVERB

6771 Our nature lies in movement; absolute
rest is death.
BLAISE PASCAL (1623–1662)

6772 Satan finds mischief for idle hands
to do.
ARABIAN PROVERB

6773 Some people are like blisters—they
don't show up until the work is done.

6774 The Bible doesn't promise loaves to
the loafer.

6775 The hardest work of all is to do nothing.
JEWISH PROVERB

6776 The lazy man does not, will not, cannot pray, for prayer demands energy.
EDWARD MCKENDREE BOUNDS
(1835–1913)

6777 The tongue of idle persons is never
idle.

6778 The way to be nothing is to do nothing.
NATHANIEL HOWE (1764–1837)

6779 There are hazards in anything one
does, but there are greater hazards in
doing nothing.
SHIRLEY WILLIAMS (1930–   )

6780 Though the fool waits, the day does
not.
FRENCH PROVERB

6781 Too much rest is rust.
SIR WALTER SCOTT (1771–1832)

6782 You can't get warm on another's fur
coat.
YIDDISH PROVERB

6783 You cannot get to the top by sitting on
your bottom.

6784 You cannot kill time without injury to
eternity.
HENRY DAVID THOREAU (1817–1862)

LEADERSHIP

6785 A true and safe leader is likely to be
one who has no desire to lead but is
forced into a position of leadership by
the inward pressure of the Holy Spirit
and the press of the external situation.
A. W. TOZER (1897–1963)

6786 Any fool can govern with a stick in his
hand. I could govern that way. It is not
God's way.
GEORGE BERNARD SHAW (1856–1950)

6787 Do not follow where the path may
lead. Go instead where there is no
path and leave a trail.

6788 Dost thou wish to rise? Begin by
descending. You plan a tower that
shall pierce the clouds? Lay first the
foundation of humility.
SAINT AUGUSTINE OF HIPPO (354–430)

6789 Eagles don't flock. You have to find
them one at a time.

6790 God give us men. A time like this
demands
Strong minds, great hearts, true faith
and ready hands!
Men whom the lust of office does not
kill,

Men whom the spoils of office cannot
buy,
Men who possess opinions and a will,
Men who love honor, men who will
not lie.
JOSIAH GILBERT HOLLAND (1819–1881)

6791 He who has confidence in himself will
lead the rest.
HORACE BUSHNELL (1802–1876)

6792 He who has learned to obey will know
how to command.
SOLON (C. 630–C. 560 B.C.)

6793 He who would be a good leader must
be prepared to deny himself much.
JOHANN WOLFGANG VON GOETHE
(1749–1832)

6794 I believe it might be accepted as a
fairly reliable rule of thumb that the
man who is ambitious to lead is disqualified as a leader.
A. W. TOZER (1897–1963)

6795 I use not only all the brains I have, but
all I can borrow.
WOODROW WILSON (1856–1924)

6796 If we work upon marble, it will perish.
If we work upon brass, time will
efface it. If we rear temples, they will
crumble to dust. But if we work upon
men's immortal minds, if we imbue
them with high principles, with the
just fear of God and love of their
fellowmen, we engrave on those tab-
lets something which no time can
efface and which will brighten to all
eternity.
DANIEL WEBSTER (1782–1852)

6797 If you can't face the music, you'll
never get to lead the band.

6798 Leaders are ordinary people with
extraordinary determination.

6799 Leadership: The art of getting someone else to do something you want
done because he wants to do it.
DWIGHT D. EISENHOWER (1890–1969)

6800 Let not thy will roar when thy power
can but whisper.
SIR THOMAS FULLER (1608–1661)

6801 Never follow the crowd if you want
the crowd to follow you.

6802 No one deserves the right to lead without first persevering through pain and
heartache and failure.
CHARLES R. SWINDOLL (1934–)

6803 Of a good leader, who talks little,
When his work is done, his aim ful-
filled,
They will say, "We did this ourselves."
LAO-TSE (C. 604–C. 531 B.C.)

6804 One of the marks of true greatness is
the ability to develop greatness in
others.
J. C. MACAULAY

6805 The time to be right is when everyone
else is wrong.

6806 To be a chief of people is to serve them.
ARABIAN PROVERB

6807 Trust men and they will be true to
you; treat them gently and they will
show themselves great.
RALPH WALDO EMERSON (1803–1882)

6808 Two captains in one boat make it sink.
ARABIAN PROVERB

LEGALISM

6809 Be aware that rigidity imprisons.
MADELEINE L'ENGLE (1918–)

6810 Believers who are motivated by legalism are always anxious to know what
is expected of them. They want to do
only what is necessary to make themselves look respectable. They crave specific rules so they can know precisely
how to behave. They plod along hoping that someday their efforts will pay
off. According to the New Testament
such people are legalists; they are
using the law to establish their righteousness.
ERWIN W. LUTZER (1941–)

6811 Christ's answer to legalism is that
external obedience to the moral law
must be coupled with a corresponding
inner attitude of love and honesty.
Christ's teaching was not intended to
abrogate obedience to the moral law,
but to add to its intended spirit.
ERWIN W. LUTZER (1941–)

6812 He who makes the law his standard is obligated to perform all its precepts, for to break one commandment is to break the law. He who lives by faith and love is not judged on that basis, but by a standard infinitely higher and at the same time more attainable.
JOSEPH FLETCHER

6813 I cannot keep count of the number of people in whom religion, the love of God and the desire to serve him, or even a quite secular ideal of perfection, lead only to a life of sterility, sadness, and anxiety. The fear of sinning has killed all their spontaneity. The subtle analysis of their conscience has taken the place of that childlike simplicity of heart that Christ demands. All joy has been replaced by the pursuit of duty. They have come to the point of doing nothing that gives them pleasure, as if God, who loves us, never required any but disagreeable things of us! They make incredible efforts but win no victories. They are always comparing themselves with those they look upon as their betters.
PAUL TOURNIER (1898–1986)

6814 Legalism is self-righteousness. It is the belief that God is satisfied with our attempt to obey a moral code.
ERWIN W. LUTZER (1941–)

6815 Legalists keep the law for self-glory, or to merit some reward; they do not keep it because it expresses the desire of their heart.
ERWIN W. LUTZER (1941–)

6816 Principles or maxims or general rules are illuminators. But they are not directors.
JOSEPH FLETCHER

6817 Rigidity is the trademark of legalism, the archenemy of any church on the move. Let legalism have enough rope, and there will be a lynching of all new ideas, fresh thinking, and innovative programs.
CHARLES R. SWINDOLL (1934–)

6818 Rigidity restrains creativity, thus blocking progress. Threatened by risk and the possibility of failure, it clips the future's wings—then later criticizes it for not flying.
CHARLES R. SWINDOLL (1934–)

6819 Rules blunt the appetite for Christ. Joy intrigues.
CALVIN MILLER

6820 Situation ethics puts people at the center of concern, not things. Obligation is to persons, not to objects. The legalist is a what asker (What does the law say?); the situationist is a who seeker (Who is to be helped?). That is, situationists are personalistic.
JOSEPH FLETCHER

6821 Some of the most virtuous men in the world are also the bitterest and most unhappy because they have unconsciously come to believe that all their happiness depends on their being more virtuous than other men.
THOMAS MERTON (1915–1968)

6822 Some persons think they have to look like a hedgehog to be pious.
BILLY SUNDAY (1862–1935)

6823 The bite of legalism spreads paralyzing venom into the body of Christ. Its poison blinds our eyes, dulls our edge, and arouses pride in our hearts. Soon our love is eclipsed as it turns into a mental clipboard with a long checklist.
CHARLES R. SWINDOLL (1934–)

6824 There are people who do not want us to be free. They don't want us to be free before God, accepted just as we are by his grace. They don't want us to be free to express our faith originally and creatively in the world. They . . . insist that all look alike, talk alike and act alike, thus validating one another's worth. Without being aware of it we become anxious about what others will say about us, obsessively concerned about what others think we should do. We no longer live the good news but anxiously try to memorize and recite the script that someone else has assigned to us. We may be secure, but we will not be free.
EUGENE PETERSON

6825 There's a little Pharisee in all of us. Harmful though it is, we find a lot of

security in our iron bars and solid walls. . . . Tragically, this ball-and-chain mentality keeps us from giving ourselves in fresh, innovative ways to others.
CHARLES R. SWINDOLL (1934–)

6826 We make the world miserable in measuring each other by our own moral maxims.
CALVIN MILLER

6827 What Protestantism has gained by its simplicity, it has lost through its rigidity, its puritanical insistence on moral rules.
JOSEPH FLETCHER

LEISURE

6828 "Holy leisure" refers to a sense of balance in the life, an ability to be at peace through the activities of the day, an ability to rest and take time to enjoy beauty, an ability to pace ourselves.
RICHARD J. FOSTER (1942–)

6829 A poor life this if, full of care,
we have no time to stand and stare.
WILLIAM HENRY DAVIES (1871–1940)

6830 And then there is time in which to be, simply to be, that time in which God quietly tells us who we are and who he wants us to be. It is then that God can take our emptiness and fill it up with what he wants, and drain away the business with which we inevitably get involved in the dailiness of human living.
MADELEINE L'ENGLE (1918–)

6831 Beware of the barrenness of a busy life.

6832 For fast-acting relief, try slowing down.
LILY TOMLIN (1939–)

6833 If you are losing your leisure, look out! You may be losing your soul.
LOGAN PEARSALL SMITH (1865–1946)

6834 Leisure is the mother of philosophy.
THOMAS HOBBES (1588–1679)

6835 People who cannot find time for recreation are obliged sooner or later to find time for illness.
JOHN WANAMAKER (1838–1922)

6836 Planning a vacation: take along half as much baggage and twice as much money.

6837 Recreation is not the highest kind of enjoyment; but in its time and place it is quite as proper as prayer.
S. IRENAEUS PRIME (1812–1885)

6838 Roughing it: a cabin without television.

6839 Take rest; a field that has rested gives a bountiful crop.
OVID (43 B.C.–A.D. 17)

6840 Vacation: getting into the pink by going into the red.

6841 Vacationeer: the person who looks forward all year to vacation and then returns with mosquito bites over poison ivy on top of sunburn.

6842 We do not know a nation until we know its pleasures of life, just as we do not know a man until we know how he spends his leisure. It is when a man ceases to do the things he has to do and does the things he likes to do, that the character is revealed. It is when the repressions of society and business are gone and when the goads of money and fame and ambition are lifted, that we see the inner man, his real self.
LIN YÜ-T'ANG (1895–1976)

LIE/LYING

6843 A half truth is a whole lie.
YIDDISH PROVERB

6844 A liar isn't believed even when he speaks the truth.
GERMAN PROVERB

6845 A lie is the refuge of weakness. The man of courage is not afraid of the truth.
J. C. MACAULAY

6846 A lie travels around the world while truth is putting her boots on.
FRENCH PROVERB

6847 All lies are not told—some are lived.
ARNOLD GLASGOW

6848 All sin is a kind of lying.
SAINT AUGUSTINE OF HIPPO (354–430)

6849 Falsehoods not only disagree with truths, but usually quarrel among themselves.
DANIEL WEBSTER (1782–1852)

6850 He who tells a lie is forced to invent twenty more to maintain it.
ALEXANDER POPE (1688–1744)

6851 It is almost always through fear of being criticized that people tell lies.
PAUL TOURNIER (1898–1986)

6852 It is better to be lied about than to lie.

6853 Lies can be so furbished and disguised in gorgeous wrappings that not a soul would recognize their skinny carcasses.
HENRIK IBSEN (1828–1906)

6854 Much speaking and lying are cousins.
GERMAN PROVERB

6855 No man has a good enough memory to make a successful liar.
ABRAHAM LINCOLN (1809–1865)

6856 One lie gives birth to another.
TERENCE (C. 186–C. 159 B.C.)

6857 Sin has many tools, but a lie is the handle that fits them all.
OLIVER WENDELL HOLMES (1809–1894)

6858 The cruelest lies are often told in silence.
ROBERT LOUIS BALFOUR STEVENSON (1850–1894)

6859 The essence of lying is in deception, not in words; a lie may be told by silence, by equivocation, by the accent on a syllable, by a glance of the eye attaching a peculiar significance to a sentence.
JOHN RUSKIN (1819–1900)

6860 The rope of a lie is short.
ARABIAN PROVERB

6861 This is the punishment of a liar: he is not believed, even when he speaks the truth.

6862 Who lies for you will lie against you.
AFRICAN PROVERB

6863 You can best reward a liar by believing nothing of what he says.
ARISTIPPUS (C. 435–366 B.C.)

LIE/TRUTH

6864 A lie stands on one leg, truth on two.
BENJAMIN FRANKLIN (1706–1790)

6865 Falsehood is always first. Truth arrives last, limping along on time's arm.
BALTASAR GRACIÁN Y MORALES (1601–1658)

6866 Sometimes it is easier to see clearly into the liar than into the man who tells the truth. Truth, like light, blinds. Falsehood, on the contrary, is a beautiful twilight that enhances every object.
ALBERT CAMUS (1913–1960)

6867 Truth exists, only falsehood has to be invented.
GEORGES BRAQUE (1882–1963)

6868 Truth lies within a little and certain compass, but error is immense.
VISCOUNT HENRY ST. JOHN BOLINGBROKE (1678–1751)

6869 Truth may walk around naked, but lies should be clothed.
JEWISH PROVERB

6870 We swallow wholeheartedly any lie that flatters us, but sip reluctantly at any truth we find harsh.
DENIS DIDEROT (1713–1784)

LIFE

6871 A journey of a thousand miles must begin with a single step.
LAO-TSE (C. 604–C. 531 B.C.)

6872 A man who cannot
Resolve upon a moment's notice
To live his own life
Forever lives
A slave to others.
GOTTHOLD EPHRAIM LESSING (1729–1781)

6873 A single event can awaken within us a stranger totally unknown to us. To live is to be slowly born.
ANTOINE DE SAINT-EXUPÉRY (1900–1944)

6874 All of life is a war.
JEWISH PROVERB

6875 And why should mortals fear to tread
the pathway to their future home?
EMILY BRONTË (1818–1848)

6876 Any idiot can face a crisis—it's this
day-to-day living that wears you out.
ANTON PAVLOVICH CHEKHOV (1860–1904)

6877 Anytime the going seems easy, better
check to see if you're going downhill.

6878 Art thou in misery, brother? Then I
pray
Be comforted. Thy grief shall pass
away.
Art thou elated? Ah, be not too gay;
Temper thy joy: this, too, shall pass
away.
Art thou in danger? Still let reason
sway,
And cling to hope: this, too, shall pass
away.
Tempted are thou? In all thine anguish
lay
One truth to heart: this, too, shall pass
away.
Do rays of loftier glory round thee
play?
Kinglike art thou? This, too, shall pass
away!
PAUL HAMILTON HAYNE (1830–1886)

6879 As soon as there is life, there is danger.
RALPH WALDO EMERSON (1803–1882)

6880 At any innocent tea table we may easily hear a man say, "Life is not worth
living." We regard it as we regard the
statement that it is a fine day; nobody
thinks that it can possibly have any
serious effect on the man or on the
world. And yet if that utterance were
really believed, the world would stand
on its head. Murderers would be given
medals for saving men from life; fire-
men would be denounced for keeping
men from death; poisons would be
used as medicines; doctors would be
called in when people were well.
G. K. CHESTERTON (1874–1936)

6881 Be strong! We are not here
To play, to dream, to drift.
We have hard work to do
And loads to lift.
Shun not the struggle;
Face it—'tis God's gift.

6882 Be such a man, and live such a life,
That if every man were such as you,
And every life a life like yours,
This earth would be God's Paradise.
PHILLIPS BROOKS (1835–1893)

6883 Count it the greatest sin to prefer life
to honor, and for the sake of living to
lose what makes life worth living.
JUVENAL (C. 60–C. 127)

6884 Death is more universal than life;
everyone dies, but not everyone lives.
A. SACHS

6885 Does the road wind uphill all the way?
Yes, to the very end.
Will the day's journey take the whole
long day?
From morn to night, my friend.
CHRISTINA GEORGINA ROSSETTI
(1830–1894)

6886 Dost thou love life? Then do not
squander time; for that's the stuff life
is made of.
BENJAMIN FRANKLIN (1706–1790)

6887 Every day should be passed as if it
were to be our last.
PUBLILIUS SYRUS (FIRST CENTURY B.C.)

6888 Every man's life is a plan of God.
HORACE BUSHNELL (1802–1876)

6889 Every moment of this strange and
lovely life from dawn to dusk is a miracle. Somewhere, always, a rose is
opening its petals to the dawn. Somewhere, always, a flower is fading in
the dusk.
BEVERLEY NICHOLS (1899–1983)

6890 Every uphill has its downhill.
JEWISH PROVERB

6891 Fear not that thy life shall come to an
end, but rather fear that it shall never
have a beginning.
CARDINAL JOHN HENRY NEWMAN
(1801–1890)

6892 Finding, following, keeping, struggling,
Is He sure to bless?
Saints, apostles, prophets, martyrs,
Answer, "Yes."
JOHN MASON NEALE (1818–1866)

6893 God asks no man whether he will accept life. That is not the choice. You must take it. The only question is how.
HENRY WARD BEECHER (1813–1887)

6894 God has given to man a short time here upon earth, and yet upon this short time eternity depends.
JEREMY TAYLOR (1613–1667)

6895 God held my life and your life like flowers in his hand.
AGNES MIEGEL (1879–1964)

6896 God loves life; he invented it.
PAUL TOURNIER (1898–1986)

6897 God never develops one part of our being at the expense of the other; spirit, soul, and body are kept in harmony.
OSWALD CHAMBERS (1874–1917)

6898 He only is advancing in life whose heart is getting softer, whose blood warmer, whose brain quicker, whose spirit is entering into living peace.
JOHN RUSKIN (1819–1900)

6899 He who lives to live forever, never fears dying.
WILLIAM PENN (1644–1718)

6900 Hold sacred every experience.
FRANCES J. ROBERTS

6901 How endless is that volume which God hath written of the world! Every creature is a letter, every day a new page.
JOSEPH HALL (1574–1656)

6902 How to compose your life: pursue, keep up with, circle round and round your life, as a dog does his master's chaise. Do what you love. Know your own bone; gnaw at it, bury it, unearth it, and gnaw it still.
HENRY DAVID THOREAU (1817–1862)

6903 However mean your life is, meet it and live it; do not shun and call it hard names. It is not so bad as you are. It looks poorest when you are richest. The faultfinder will find faults even in Paradise. Love your life.
HENRY DAVID THOREAU (1817–1862)

6904 Human life is but a series of footnotes to a vast, obscure unfinished masterpiece.
VLADIMIR VLADIMIROVICH NABOKOV (1899–1977)

6905 Human life resembles iron. When you use it, it wears out. When you don't, rust consumes it.
CATO THE ELDER (234–149 B.C.)

6906 I asked God for all things so I could enjoy life. He gave me life so I could enjoy all things.

6907 I believe that life is given us so we may grow in love, and I believe that God is in me as the sun is in the color and fragrance of a flower—the Light in my darkness, the Voice in my silence.
HELEN ADAMS KELLER (1880–1968)

6908 I count life just a stuff
   To try the soul's strength on.
ROBERT BROWNING (1812–1889)

6909 I count that part of my life lost which I spent not in communion with God, or in doing good.
JOHN DONNE (1572–1631)

6910 I desire to have both heaven and hell ever in my eye, while I stand on this isthmus of life, between two boundless oceans.
JOHN WESLEY (1703–1791)

6911 I fall upon the thorns of life! I bleed!
PERCY BYSSHE SHELLEY (1792–1822)

6912 I find that many Christians are in trouble about the future; they think they will not have grace enough to die by. It is much more important that we should have grace enough to live by. It seems to me that death is of very little importance in the meantime. When the dying hour comes, there will be dying grace; but you do not require dying grace to live by.
DWIGHT LYMAN MOODY (1837–1899)

6913 I have four things to learn in life:
   To think clearly without hurry or confusion;
   To love everybody sincerely;

To act in everything with the
   highest motives;
To trust in God unhesitatingly.
HELEN ADAMS KELLER (1880–1968)

6914 I have lived,
And seen God's hand thro a lifetime,
And all was for best.
ROBERT BROWNING (1812–1889)

6915 I have one foot in heaven and one foot
on earth, and the foot on earth is on a
banana peel.
MALCOLM MUGGERIDGE (1903–1990)

6916 I know not what the future hath
Of marvel or surprise,
Assured alone that life or death
His mercy underlies.

I know not where his islands lift
Their fronded palms in air;
I only know I cannot drift
Beyond his love and care.

And so beside the silent sea
I wait the muffled oar;
No harm from him can come to me
On ocean or on shore.
JOHN GREENLEAF WHITTIER (1807–1892)

6917 I laugh and shout for life is good,
Though my feet are set in silent ways.
HELEN ADAMS KELLER (1880–1968)

6918 I simply believe that there is a mystery
of the ordinary, that the commonplace
is full of wonder, and that this life that
we call Christian is different from
what we think it is. It is infinitely more
subtle, more powerful, more dangerous, more magnificent, more exciting,
more humorous, more delicious, more
adventurous, more involved, and more
troublesome than most of us think.
TIM HANSEL

6919 I will consider my earthly existence to
have been wasted unless I can recall a
loving family, a consistent investment
in the lives of people, and an earnest
attempt to serve the God who made
me.
JAMES C. DOBSON (1936–)

6920 I will not just live my life. I will not
just spend my life. I will invest my life.
HELEN ADAMS KELLER (1880–1968)

6921 If God has work for me to do, I cannot die.
HENRY MARTYN FIELD (1822–1907)

6922 If I can stop one heart from breaking,
I shall not live in vain;
If I can ease one life the aching,
Or cool one pain,
Or help one fainting robin
Unto his nest again,
I shall not live in vain.
EMILY ELIZABETH DICKINSON (1830–1886)

6923 If life be long I will be glad,
That I may long obey;
If short—yet why should I be sad
To soar to endless day?
RICHARD BAXTER (1615–1691)

6924 If we fully comprehended the brevity
of life, our greatest desire would be to
please God and to serve one another.
JAMES C. DOBSON (1936–)

6925 If you find yourself loving any pleasure better than your prayers, and any
book better than the Bible, any house
better than the house of God, any
table better than the Lord's Table, any
person better than Christ, any indulgence better than the hope of heaven—
take alarm!
THOMAS GUTHRIE (1803–1873)

6926 If you want to die happily, learn to
live; if you would live happily, learn to
die.
CELIO CALCAGNINI (1479–1551)

6927 In infinite time, in infinite matter, in
infinite space is formed a bubble-
organism, and that bubble lasts a
while and bursts; and that bubble is
me.
LEO TOLSTOY (1828–1910)

6928 In the morning of life, work; in the
midday give counsel; in the evening
pray.
HESIOD (EIGHTH CENTURY B.C.)

6929 In this world I am a stranger. I don't
belong here. I am straying here for a
bit and it's a very nice place, an interesting place, but I don't belong here.
MALCOLM MUGGERIDGE (1903–1990)

6930 Inch by inch life's a cinch.
Yard by yard life is hard.

6931 Is life so wretched? Isn't it rather your hands which are too small, your vision which is muddied? You are the one who must grow up.
DAG HAMMARSKJÖLD (1905–1961)

6932 Is life worth living?
Aye, with the best of us,
Heights of us, depths of us,
Life is the test of us!
CORINNE ROOSEVELT ROBINSON
(1861–1933)

6933 It is not how many years we live, but what we do with them.
EVANGELINE CORY BOOTH (1865–1950)

6934 It is the familiar that usually eludes us in life. What is before our nose is what we see last.
WILLIAM BARRETT (1914–   )

6935 It is with life as with a play; what matters is not how long it is, but how good it is.
LUCIUS ANNAEUS SENECA (C. 4 B.C.–A.D. 65)

6936 It's a funny old world—a man's lucky if he gets out of it alive.
W. C. FIELDS (1880–1946)

6937 Just as a planet rushing through space is only a comet on its way to destruction until it is caught by some central sun and begins to revolve around that sun as its center and its life; so my life is an aimless comet burning itself out in its own self-will, till it finds the pull and attractive of Christ's love, halts its deadly way, and forever revolves around him, its central sun and life.
E. STANLEY JONES (1884–1973)

6938 Let all live as they would die.

6939 Let us face life as it is, not as we feel it ought to be, for it never will be what it ought to be until the kingdom of this world is become the kingdom of our Lord, and of his Christ.
OSWALD CHAMBERS (1874–1917)

6940 Life can never be wholly dark or wholly futile once the key to its meaning is in our hands.
J. B. PHILLIPS (1906–1982)

6941 Life can only be understood backwards; but it must be lived forwards.
SØREN AABYE KIERKEGAARD (1813–1855)

6942 Life has taught me to think, but thinking has not taught me to live.
ALEXANDER IVANOVICH HERZEN
(1812–1870)

6943 Life is a bridge.
ARABIAN PROVERB

6944 Life is a glorious opportunity, if it is used to condition us for eternity. If we fail in this, though we succeed in everything else, our life will have been a failure.
BILLY GRAHAM (1918–   )

6945 Life is a great book of which those who never stir from home read only a page.

6946 Life is a great bundle of little things.
OLIVER WENDELL HOLMES (1809–1894)

6947 Life is a hard fight, a struggle, a wrestling with the principle of evil, hand to hand, foot to foot. Every inch of the way is disputed. The night is given us to take breath and to pray, to drink deep at the fountain of power. The day, to use the strength that has been given us, to go forth to work with it till the evening.
FLORENCE NIGHTINGALE (1820–1910)

6948 Life is a hereditary disease.

6949 Life is a mirror: if you frown at it, it frowns back; if you smile, it returns the greeting.
WILLIAM MAKEPEACE THACKERAY
(1811–1863)

6950 Life is a one-way street.
BERNARD BERENSON (1865–1959)

6951 Life is a predicament that precedes death.
HENRY JAMES (1843–1916)

6952 Life is a sentence man has to serve for being born.
PEDRO CALDERÓN DE LA BARCA
(1600–1681)

6953 Life is a test that has more questions than answers.

6954 Life is a tragedy for those who feel, and a comedy for those who think.
JEAN DE LA BRUYÈRE (1645–1696)

6955 Life is a tumble-about thing of ups and downs.
BENJAMIN DISRAELI (1804–1881)

6956 Life is a voyage that's homeward bound.
HERMAN MELVILLE (1819–1891)

6957 Life is an event at which you arrive after it has begun and depart from before it has ended.

6958 Life is but a day at most.
ROBERT BURNS (1759–1796)

6959 Life is but a dewdrop on the lotus leaf.
SIR RABINDRANATH TAGORE (1861–1941)

6960 Life is dust, which frugal nature lends man for an hour.
EDWARD YOUNG (1683–1765)

6961 Life is easier than you think—
All you have to do is:
Accept the impossible,
Do without the indispensible,
Bear the intolerable and
Be able to smile at anything.

6962 Life is either a daring adventure or nothing.
HELEN ADAMS KELLER (1880–1968)

6963 Life is ever
Since man was born,
Licking honey
From a thorn.
LOUIS GINSBERG

6964 Life is half spent before we know what it is.
GEORGE HERBERT (1593–1633)

6965 Life is like a library owned by an author. In it are a few books that he wrote himself, but most of them were written for him.
HARRY EMERSON FOSDICK (1878–1969)

6966 Life is like music; it must be composed by ear, feeling, and instinct, not by rule.
SAMUEL BUTLER (1612–1680)

6967 Life is like playing a violin solo in public and learning the instrument as one goes on.
SAMUEL BUTLER (1612–1680)

6968 Life is like the life of a fly in a room filled with a hundred boys, each armed with a fly swatter.
H. L. MENCKEN (1880–1956)

6969 Life is made up of sobs, sniffles, and smiles, with sniffles predominating.
O. HENRY (1862–1910)

6970 Life is not a matter of extent but of content.
STEPHEN SAMUEL WISE (1874–1949)

6971 Life is not an exact science, it is an art.
SAMUEL BUTLER (1612–1680)

6972 Life is not lost by dying! Life is lost minute by minute, day by dragging day, in all the thousand, small, uncaring ways.
STEPHEN VINCENT BENÉT (1898–1943)

6973 Life is not the wick or the candle—it is the burning.

6974 Life is one long process of getting tired.
SAMUEL BUTLER (1612–1680)

6975 Life is painting a picture, not doing a sum.
OLIVER WENDELL HOLMES, JR.
(1841–1935)

6976 Life is rather like a tin of sardines—we are all looking for the key.
ALAN BENNETT

6977 Life is really simple, but men insist on making it complicated.
CONFUCIUS (C. 551–479 B.C.)

6978 Life is the preparation, the training ground, the place where God begins his work of making us into what he wants us to be. But it is not our home.
J. B. PHILLIPS (1906–1982)

6979 Life is the soul's nursery—its training place for the destinies of eternity.
WILLIAM MAKEPEACE THACKERAY
(1811–1863)

6980 Life is to be, to do, to do without, and to depart.
JOHN MORLEY (1838–1923)

6981 Life is warfare.
LUCIUS ANNAEUS SENECA (C. 4 B.C.–A.D. 65)

6982 Life is what happens to us while we are making other plans.
THOMAS LA MANCE

6983 Life isn't what you want, but it's what
you've got.
BARBARA JOHNSON

6984 Life isn't logical or sensible or orderly.
Life is a mess most of the time. And
theology must be lived in the midst of
that mess.
CHARLES COLSON (1931–)

6985 Life must be sacramental. For God,
the life which he has created as a manifold thing can have but different
aspects, facets of one diamond reflecting the light. Fundamentally, there is
no distinction between spiritual work
and material work.
HENRY VAN ETTEN

6986 Life was a funny thing that happened
to me on the way to the grave.
QUENTIN CRISP (1908–)

6987 Life with Christ has not always been
easy, but it has never been dull.
LLOYD JOHN OGILVIE (1930–)

6988 Life without conflict is impossible.
OSWALD CHAMBERS (1874–1917)

6989 Life would be infinitely happier if we
could only be born at the age of eighty
and gradually approach eighteen.
MARK TWAIN (1835–1910)

6990 Life's a pudding full of plums.
SIR W. S. GILBERT (1836–1911)

6991 Life's a short summer—man is but a
flower.
SAMUEL JOHNSON (1709–1784)

6992 Life's a tough proposition, and the
first hundred years are the hardest.
WILSON MIZNER (1876–1933)

6993 Life's but a shadow of a bird in flight.
TALMUD

6994 Life's but a walking shadow,
    a poor player
That struts and frets his hour
    upon the stage.
WILLIAM SHAKESPEARE (1564–1616)

6995 Life's mysteries are for our worship;
its sorrows for our trust; its perils for
our courage; its temptations for our
faith.
JAMES MARTINEAU (1805–1900)

6996 Life: the cheapest bargain. You get it
for nothing.
JEWISH PROVERB

6997 Little self-denials, little honesties, little
passing words of sympathy, little
nameless acts of kindness, little silent
victories over favorite temptations—
these are the silent threads of gold
which, when woven together, gleam
out so brightly in the pattern of life
that God approves.
FREDERIC WILLIAM FARRAR (1831–1903)

6998 Live out your life in its full meaning; it
is God's life.
JOSIAH ROYCE (1855–1916)

6999 Living each day as if it were our only
day makes for a total life lived at full
potential.
LLOYD JOHN OGILVIE (1930–)

7000 Living is learning the meaning of
words. That does not mean the long
ten syllable words we have to look up
in the dictionary. The really great
words to master are short ones—
work, love, hope, joy, pain, home,
child, life, death.
HALFORD E. LUCCOCK (1885–1960)

7001 Love your life, poor as it is. You may
have pleasant, thrilling, glorious hours
even in a poorhouse. The setting sun is
reflected from the windows of the
almshouse as bright as from the rich
man's abode.
HENRY DAVID THOREAU (1817–1862)

7002 Man enters each stage of life as a
novice.
SÉBASTIEN ROCH NICOLAS CHAMFORT
(1741–1794)

7003 My life is like a broken bowl,
A broken bowl that cannot hold
One drop of water for my soul
Or cordial in the searching bold
Cast in the fire the perished thing
Melt and remould it, till it be
A royal cup for him, my King:
O Jesus, drink of me.
CHRISTINA GEORGINA ROSSETTI
(1830–1894)

7004 No man has a right to lead such a life
of contemplation as to forget in his
own ease the service due to his

neighbor; nor has any man a right to be so immersed in active life as to neglect the contemplation of God.
SAINT AUGUSTINE OF HIPPO (354–430)

7005 Nor do I regret that I have lived, since I have so lived that I think I was not born in vain, and I quit life as if it were an inn, not a home.
CICERO (106–43 B.C.)

7006 O God, since thou hast shut me up in this world, I will do the best I can, without fear or favor. When my task is done, let me out!
MARY H. CATHERWOOD (1847–1901)

7007 O Life! thou art a galling load,
Along a rough, a weary road,
To wretches such as I!
ROBERT BURNS (1759–1796)

7008 O Lord, let me not live to be useless.
JOHN WESLEY (1703–1791)

7009 Ofttimes the test of courage is to live rather than to die.
CONTE VITTORIO ALFIERI (1749–1803)

7010 Oh, how daily life is!
JULES LAFORGUE (1860–1887)

7011 On the day I first really believed in God, for the first time life made sense to me and the world had meaning.
DAG HAMMARSKJÖLD (1905–1961)

7012 Once we truly know that life is difficult—once we truly understand and accept it—then life is no longer difficult.
M. SCOTT PECK (1936–)

7013 One life—a little gleam of time between two eternities.
THOMAS CARLYLE (1795–1881)

7014 Our Father refreshes us on the journey with some pleasant inns but will not encourage us to mistake them for home.
C. S. LEWIS (1898–1963)

7015 Our life is scarce the twinkle of a star in God's eternal day.
BAYARD TAYLOR (1825–1878)

7016 Our lives are a manifestation of what we think about God.

7017 Our lives are albums written through With good or ill, with false or true;

And as the blessed angels turn
The pages of our years,
God grant they read the good with smiles,
And blot the ill with tears!
JOHN GREENLEAF WHITTIER (1807–1892)

7018 Pythagoras used to say life resembles the Olympic Games; a few men strain their muscles to carry off a prize; others bring trinkets to sell to the crowd for a profit; and some there are who seek no further advantage than to look at the show and see how and why everything is done.
MICHEL EYQUEM DE MONTAIGNE (1533–1592)

7019 Reason thus with life:
If I do lose thee,
I do lose a thing
That none but fools would keep.
WILLIAM SHAKESPEARE (1564–1616)

7020 Recipe for a long life: be careful not to exceed the feed limit.

7021 Reckon not upon a long life: think every day the last.
SIR THOMAS BROWNE (1605–1682)

7022 Religion can offer a man a burial service, but Christ offers every man new, abundant and everlasting life.
WILMA REED

7023 Sometimes life is like going through a car wash on a bicycle.

7024 The acts of this life are the destiny of the next.

7025 Man does not know what to do with this life, yet wants another one which will last forever.
ANATOLE FRANCE (1844–1924)

7026 The belief that youth is the happiest time of life is founded upon a fallacy. The happiest person is the person who thinks the most interesting thoughts, and we grow happier as we grow older.
WILLIAM LYON PHELPS (1865–1943)

7027 The glory of God, and, as our only means to glorifying him, the salvation of human souls, is the real business of life.
C. S. LEWIS (1898–1963)

7028 The great majority of men exist but do not live.
BENJAMIN DISRAELI (1804–1881)

7029 The greatest moments of your life are those when through all the confusion God got a message through to you plain and certain.
BERTHA MUNRO

7030 The least of things with a meaning is worth more in life than the greatest of things without it.
CARL GUSTAV JUNG (1875–1961)

7031 The leaves of life keep falling one by one.
OMAR KHAYYÁM (C. 1048–1122)

7032 The life that is unexamined is not worth living.
PLATO (C. 428–348 B.C.)

7033 The man who has no inner life is a slave to his surroundings.
HENRI FRÉDÉRIC AMIEL (1821–1881)

7034 The most important thing in life is to live your life for something more important than your life.
WILLIAM JAMES (1842–1910)

7035 The price and the glory of a mortal's life is that "we never arrive; we are always on the way."
D. ELTON TRUEBLOOD (1900–   )

7036 The rule that governs my life is this: Anything that dims my vision of Christ, or takes away my taste for Bible study, or cramps my prayer life, or makes Christian work difficult, is wrong for me, and I must, as a Christian, turn away from it.
J. WILBUR CHAPMAN (1859–1918)

7037 The seven ages of man: spills, drills, thrills, bills, ills, pills, wills.
RICHARD J. NEEDHAM

7038 The shallow amenities of life, eating and drinking, walking and talking, are all ordained by God.
OSWALD CHAMBERS (1874–1917)

7039 The things that count most in life are usually the things that cannot be counted.
BERNARD MELTZER

7040 The time to be alarmed in life is when all things are undisturbed.
OSWALD CHAMBERS (1874–1917)

7041 The tombstones of some people should read: Died at thirty, buried at sixty.
NICHOLAS MURRAY BUTLER (1862–1947)

7042 The tragedy of life is not that it ends so soon, but that we wait so long to begin it.
W. M. LEWIS

7043 The wailing of the newborn infant is mingled with the dirge for the dead.
LUCRETIUS (C. 96–C. 55 B.C.)

7044 The weariness, the fever, and the fret
Here, where men sit and hear each
    other groan.
JOHN KEATS (1795–1821)

7045 The web of our life is of a mingled yarn, good and ill together.
WILLIAM SHAKESPEARE (1564–1616)

7046 The whole course of the life is upset by failure to put God where he belongs.
A. W. TOZER (1897–1963)

7047 The world is a ladder for some to go up and some down.
ITALIAN PROVERB

7048 The world is very lovely,
O my God, I thank thee that I live!
ALEXANDER SMITH (1830–1867)

7049 There are always plenty of seats available in the subway; the trouble is, people are always sitting on them.

7050 There are but three events in a man's life: birth, life, and death. He is not conscious of being born, he dies in pain, and he forgets to live.
JEAN DE LA BRUYÈRE (1645–1696)

7051 There are things in life which are irreparable; there is no road back to yesterday.
OSWALD CHAMBERS (1874–1917)

7052 There is an eternity behind and an eternity before, and this little speck in the center, however long, is but a minute.
JOHN BROWN (1715–1766)

7053 There is more to life than increasing its speed.
MAHATMA GANDHI (1869–1948)

7054 There is no cure for birth and death save to enjoy the interval.
GEORGE SANTAYANA (1863–1952)

7055 There is no life so humble that, if it be true and genuinely human and obedient to God, it cannot reflect his light. There is no life so meager that the greatest and wisest can afford to despise it. We cannot know at what moment it may flash forth with the life of God.
PHILLIPS BROOKS (1835–1893)

7056 There is no music in a rest, but there is the making of music in it. In our whole life-melody the music is broken off here and there by rests, and we foolishly think we have come to the end of the theme. God sends a time of forced leisure, sickness, disappointed plans, frustrated efforts, and makes a sudden pause in the choral hymn of our lives; and we lament that our voices must be silent, and our part missing in the music which ever goes up to the ear of the Creator. How does the musician read the rest? See him beat the time with unvarying count and catch up the next note true and steady, as if no breaking place had come between.

   Not without design does God write the music of our lives. Be it ours to learn the tune, and not to be dismayed at the rests. They are not to be slurred over, not to be omitted, not to destroy the melody, not to change the keynote. If we look up, God himself will beat the time for us. With the eye on him, we shall strike the next note full and clear. If we sadly say to ourselves, there is no music in a rest, let us not forget there is the making of music in it. The making of music is often a slow and painful process in this life. How patiently God works to teach. How long he waits for us to learn the lesson.
JOHN RUSKIN (1819–1900)

7057 There is not one life . . . which is not so near to God that whatever touches it touches him with sorrow or with joy.
PHILLIPS BROOKS (1835–1893)

7058 There is nothing permanent except change.
GREEK PROVERB

7059 There is nothing terrible in life for the man who realizes that there is nothing terrible in death.
EPICURUS (341–270 B.C.)

7060 There will come one day a personal and direct touch from God when every tear and perplexity, every oppression and distress, every suffering and pain, and wrong and injustice will have a complete and ample and overwhelming explanation.
OSWALD CHAMBERS (1874–1917)

7061 There's many a battle fought daily the world knows nothing about.
PHOEBE CARY (1824–1871)

7062 There's nothing certain in this world; today we are on top, tomorrow we're at the bottom of the ladder.
DENIS DIDEROT (1713–1784)

7063 Think of the totality of all being, and what a mite of it is yours; think of all time and the brief fleeting instant of it that is allotted to yourself; think of destiny, and how puny a part of it you are.
MARCUS AURELIUS ANTONINUS (121–180)

7064 This world is the land of the dying; the next is the land of the living.
TRYON EDWARDS (1809–1894)

7065 To err is human, to repent divine, to persist devilish.
BENJAMIN FRANKLIN (1706–1790)

7066 To live is to fight, to suffer, and to love.
ELIZABETH LESEUR (1866–1914)

7067 To live long, it is necessary to live slowly.
CICERO (106–43 B.C.)

7068 To live remains an art that everyone must learn and that no one can teach.
HAVELOCK ELLIS (1859–1939)

7069 To understand the world and to like it are two things not easy to reconcile.
GEORGE SAVILE (1633–1695)

7070 To what shall I compare this life of ours? Even before I can say, "It is like a lightning flash or a dewdrop," it is no more.
SENGAI

7071 To yield is to be preserved whole. To be bent is to become straight. To be empty is to be full. To be worn out is to be renewed. To have little is to possess. To have plenty is to be perplexed.
LAO-TSE (C. 604–C. 531 B.C.)

7072 We are afraid to accept what is given to us; we are in compulsive self-seclusion toward our world. We try to escape life instead of controlling it.
PAUL JOHANNES OSKAR TILLICH (1886–1965)

7073 We are all making a crown for Jesus out of these daily lives of ours, either a crown of golden, divine love, studded with gems of sacrifice and adoration, or a thorny crown, filled with the cruel briars of unbelief, or selfishness, and sin, and placing it upon his brow.
AIMEE SEMPLE MCPHERSON (1890–1944)

7074 We are all serving a life-sentence in the dungeon of life.
CYRIL CONNOLLY (1903–1974)

7075 We are born crying, live complaining, and die disappointed.
SIR THOMAS FULLER (1608–1661)

7076 We are in the world as words are in a book. Each generation is like a line, a phrase.
JOSEPH JOUBERT (1754–1824)

7077 We are in this life as it were in another man's house. . . . Heaven is our home, the world is our inn.
PAUL GERHARDT (1607–1676)

7078 We can have both heaven and hell in this world.
JEWISH PROVERB

7079 We live as we dream—alone.
JOSEPH CONRAD (1857–1924)

7080 We live less than the time it takes to blink an eye, if we measure our lives against eternity. . . . I learned a long time ago that a blink of an eye in itself is nothing. But the eye that blinks, that is something. A span of life is nothing. But the man who lives that span, he is something. He can fill that tiny span with meaning, so its quality is immeasurable though its quantity may be insignificant.
CHAIM POTOK (1929–)

7081 We may not prefer a world in which sorrow always seems to be so close to joy; in which heartbreak always seems so close to happiness; in which doubt always seems to be so close to faith. But this is the kind of world we're in.
JEROLD SAVORY

7082 What is life? It is the flash of a firefly in the night.
CROWFOOT OF THE BLACKFEET (1821–1890)

7083 What is our life more than a short day in which the sun hardly rises before it is lost in the utter darkness of the cold night?
ANDRES FERNANDES DE ANDRADA (1600)

7084 When I consider the short duration of my life, swallowed up in the eternity before and after, the little space that I fill and even can see, engulfed in the infinite immensity of spaces of which I am ignorant and which know me not, I am frightened and am astonished at being here rather than there; for there is no reason why here rather than there, why now rather than then. Who has put me here? By whose order and direction have this place and time been allotted to me? . . . The eternal silence of these infinite spaces terrifies me.
BLAISE PASCAL (1623–1662)

7085 When we finally turn into heaven's doorway and see him waiting at the open door, the long drive won't seem so long at all.
JONI EARECKSON TADA

7086 Who knows but life be that which men call death,
And death what men call life?
EURIPIDES (C. 484–406 B.C.)

7087 Whoso does not see that genuine life is a battle and a march has poorly read his origin and his destiny.
LYDIA MARIA CHILD (1802–1880)

7088 Why all this toil for triumphs of an hour?
What tho' we wade in wealth, or soar in fame?
Earth's highest station ends in "Here he lies,"
And "dust to dust" concludes her noblest song.
OWEN D. YOUNG (1874–1962)

7089 Why are we so fond of a life that begins with a cry and ends with a groan?
MARY, COUNTESS OF WARWICK

7090 Why is life so tragic; so like a little strip of pavement over an abyss. I look down; I feel giddy; I wonder how I am ever to walk to the end.
VIRGINIA WOOLF (1882–1941)

7091 Why wish for the privilege of living your past life again? You begin a new one every morning.
ROBERT QUILLEN (1887–1948)

7092 With renunciation life begins.
AMELIA EDITH BARR (1831–1919)

7093 With the goodness of God to desire our highest welfare, the wisdom of God to plan it, and the power of God to achieve it, what do we lack?
A. W. TOZER (1897–1963)

7094 Without Christ life is as the twilight with dark night ahead; with Christ it is the dawn of morning with the light and warmth of full day ahead.
PHILIP SCHAFF (1819–1893)

7095 You can't do anything about the length of your life, but you can do something about its width and depth.
EVAN ESAR

7096 You must either conquer the world or the world will conquer you. You must be either master or slave.
CARDINAL JOHN HENRY NEWMAN (1801–1890)

7097 Youth is a blunder, manhood a struggle, old age a regret.
BENJAMIN DISRAELI (1804–1881)

LIFE/THOUGHTS

7098 God is more real to me than any thought or thing or person. I feel him in the sunshine or rain; and all mingled with a delicious restfulness most nearly describes my feelings. I talk to him as to a companion in prayer and praise, and our communion is delightful. He answers me again and again, often in words so clearly spoken that it seems my outer ear must have carried the tone, but generally in strong mental impressions. Usually a text of Scripture, unfolding some new view of him and his love for me, and care for my safety. . . . That he is mine and I am his never leaves me; it is an abiding joy. Without it life would be a blank, a desert, a shoreless, trackless waste.
WILLIAM JAMES (1842–1910)

7099 I am no more of a Christian than Pilate was . . . and yet, like Pilate, I greatly prefer Jesus of Nazareth to Amos or Caiaphas; and I am ready to admit that I see no way out of the world's misery but the way that would have been found by his will.
GEORGE BERNARD SHAW (1856–1950)

7100 I have now reigned above fifty years in victory and peace, beloved by my subjects, dreaded by my enemies, and respected by my allies. Riches and honors, power and pleasure, have waited on my call, nor does any earthly blessing appear to be wanting for my felicity. In this situation, I have diligently numbered the days of pure and genuine happiness that have fallen to my lot: they amount to fourteen.
ABD-AL-RAHMAN III (912–961)

7101 It is the great mystery of human life that old grief passes gradually into quiet, tender joy. The mild serenity of age takes the place of the riotous blood of youth. I bless the rising sun each day, and, as before, my heart sings to meet it, but now I love even more its setting, its long slanting rays and the soft, tender, gentle memories that come with them, the dear images from the whole of my long, happy life—and over all the divine truth, soft-

ening, reconciling, forgiving! My life is
ending, I know that well, but every
day that is left me I feel how my
earthly life is in touch with a new infinite, unknown, but approaching life,
the nearness of which sets my soul
quivering with rapture, my mind glowing, and my heart weeping with joy.
FYODOR MIKHAYLOVICH DOSTOYEVSKI
(1821–1881)

7102 Shall I tell you what supported me
through all these years of exile, among
a people whose language I could not
understand and whose attitude toward
me was always uncertain and often
hostile? It was this: "Lo, I am with
you always even unto the end of the
world."
DAVID LIVINGSTONE (1813–1873)

7103 They will kill me if they please, but
they will never, never tear the living
Christ from my heart.
GIROLAMO SAVONAROLA (1452–1498)

7104 Today I entered on my eighty-second
year and found myself just as strong to
labor and as fit for any exercise of
body or mind as I was forty years ago.
I do not impute this to second causes,
but to the Sovereign Lord of all. It is
he who bids the sun of life stand still,
so long as it pleases him. I am as
strong at eighty-one as I was at twenty-
one; but abundantly more healthy,
being a stranger to the headache,
toothache, and other bodily disorders
that attended me in my youth. We can
only say, "The Lord reigneth!" While
we live, let us live to him!
JOHN WESLEY (1703–1791)

7105 What a blessedness when I came to the
knowledge that I had been looking in
the wrong place, when I found that victory, sanctification, deliverance, purity,
holiness—all must be found in Christ
Jesus himself, not in some formula.
When I claimed Jesus just for himself,
it became easy and the glory came to
my life.
ALBERT BENJAMIN SIMPSON (1843–1919)

LIGHT

7106 Darkness is my point of view, my right
to myself; light is God's point of view.
OSWALD CHAMBERS (1874–1917)

7107 I don't have to light all the world, but
I do have to light my part.

7108 Light is above us, and color around
us; but if we have not light and color
in our eyes, we shall not perceive them
outside us.
JOHANN WOLFGANG VON GOETHE
(1749–1832)

7109 Light! Nature's resplendent robe;
Without whose vesting beauty
All were wrapt in gloom.
FRANCIS THOMPSON SHELLEY (1859–1927)

7110 Light, even though it passes through
pollution, is not polluted.
SAINT AUGUSTINE OF HIPPO (354–430)

LISTENING

7111 A good listener is not only popular
everywhere, but after awhile he knows
something.
WILSON MIZNER (1876–1933)

7112 God has given man one tongue but
two ears that we may hear twice as
much as we speak.

7113 It takes a great man to make a good
listener.
ARTHUR HELPS (1813–1875)

7114 Know how to listen, and you will
profit even from those who talk
badly.
PLUTARCH (C. 46–AFTER 119)

7115 One of the best ways to demonstrate
God's love is to listen to people.
BRUCE LARSEN

LITTLE

7116 A little thing in hand is worth more
than a great thing in prospect.
AESOP (FL. C. 550 B.C.)

7117 Do little things as if they were great
because of the majesty of the Lord
Jesus Christ who dwells in you.
BLAISE PASCAL (1623–1662)

7118 God does not want us to do extraordinary things; he wants us to do the ordinary things extraordinarily well.
CHARLES GORE (1853–1932)

7119 Great events, we often find,
On little things depend,
And very small beginnings
Have oft a mighty end.

7120 It is better to have a little than nothing.
PUBLILIUS SYRUS (FIRST CENTURY B.C.)

7121 There is nothing small in the service of God.
SAINT FRANCIS OF SALES (1567–1622)

LONELINESS

7122 A crowd is not company.

7123 Bear patiently your exile and the dryness of your mind. The time will come when I will make you forget these painful moments and you will enjoy inward quietness. I will open the Bible for you and you will be thrilled by your new understanding of my truth.
THOMAS À KEMPIS (C. 1380–1471)

7124 Cannot the heart in the midst of crowds feel frightfully alone?
CHARLES LAMB (1775–1834)

7125 Didst thou give me this inescapable loneliness so that it would be easier for me to give thee all?
DAG HAMMARSKJÖLD (1905–1961)

7126 Essentially loneliness is the knowledge that one's fellow human beings are incapable of understanding one's condition and therefore are incapable of bringing the help most needed.
HUBERT VAN ZELLER

7127 For each, God has a different response. With every man he has a secret—the secret of a new name. In every man there is a loneliness, an inner chamber of peculiar life into which God only can enter.
GEORGE MACDONALD (1824–1905)

7128 If you are afraid of loneliness, don't marry.
ANTON PAVLOVICH CHEKOV

7129 It is one thing to go through a crisis grandly, and another thing to go through every day glorifying God when nobody is paying any attention to you.
OSWALD CHAMBERS (1874–1917)

7130 It is strange to be known so universally and yet be so lonely.
ALBERT EINSTEIN (1879–1955)

7131 Language has created the word *loneliness* to express the pain of being alone, and the word *solitude* to express the glory of being alone.
PAUL JOHANNES OSKAR TILLICH (1886–1965)

7132 Loneliness and the feeling of being uncared for and unwanted are the greatest poverty.
MOTHER TERESA OF CALCUTTA (1910–)

7133 Loneliness can be conquered only by those who can bear solitude.
PAUL JOHANNES OSKAR TILLICH (1886–1965)

7134 Loneliness eats into the soul.
JEWISH PROVERB

7135 Loneliness is a great price to pay for independence.

7136 Loneliness is the first thing that God's eye nam'd not good.
JOHN MILTON (1608–1674)

7137 Loneliness, far from being a rare and curious phenomenon, peculiar to myself and to a few other solitary men, is the central and inevitable fact of human existence.
THOMAS CLAYTON WOLFE (1900–1938)

7138 Most of the world's great souls have been lonely.
A. W. TOZER (1897–1963)

7139 People are lonely because they build walls instead of bridges.
JOSEPH FORT NEWTON (1880–1950)

7140 Pray that your loneliness may spur you into finding something to live for, great enough to die for.
DAG HAMMARSKJÖLD (1905–1961)

7141 Shakespeare, Leonardo da Vinci, Benjamin Franklin, and Lincoln . . . were not afraid of being lonely because they

knew that was when the creative
mood in them would work.
CARL SANDBURG (1878–1967)

7142 So lonely 'twas that God himself
Scarce seemed there to be.
SAMUEL TAYLOR COLERIDGE (1772–1834)

7143 The deepest need of man is the need to
overcome his separateness, to leave the
prison of his aloneness.
ERICH FROMM (1900–1980)

7144 The essential loneliness is an escape
from an inescapable God.
WALTER FARRELL (1902–1951)

7145 The loneliness you get by the sea is personal and alive. It doesn't subdue you
and make you feel abject. It's a stimulating loneliness.
ANNE MORROW LINDBERGH (1906–)

7146 The soul hardly ever realizes it, but
whether he is a believer or not, his
loneliness is really a homesickness for
God.
HUBERT VAN ZELLER

7147 There is none more lonely than the
man who loves only himself.
MOSES BEN JACOB IBN EZRA (C. 1135)

7148 We're all sentenced to solitary confinement inside our own skins, for life.
TENNESSEE WILLIAMS (1914–1983)

7149 What loneliness is more lonely than
distrust?
GEORGE ELIOT (1819–1880)

7150 Women and men in the crowd meet
and mingle,
Yet with itself every soul standeth
single.
ALICE CARY (1820–1871)

7151 You come into the world alone and
you go out of the world alone. Yet it
seems to me you are more alone while
living than even going and coming.
EMILY CARR (1871–1945)

LORD'S PRAYER

7152 In the Lord's Prayer the first petition is
for daily bread. No one can worship
God or love his neighbor on an empty
stomach.
WOODROW WILSON (1856–1924)

7153 The Lord's Prayer may be committed
to memory quickly, but it is slowly
learnt by heart.
JOHN FREDERICK DENISON MAURICE
(1805–1872)

7154 The Lord's Prayer, for a succession of
solemn thought, for fixing the attention upon a few great points, for suitableness to every condition, for
sufficiency, for conciseness without
obscurity, for the weight and real
importance of its petition, is without
equal or rival.
WILLIAM PALEY (1743–1805)

7155 The prayer "Thy Kingdom come," if
we only knew, is asking God to conduct a major operation.
GEORGE ARTHUR BUTTRICK (1892–1980)

7156 What deep mysteries are contained in
the Lord's Prayer. How many and
great they are! They are expressed in a
few words, but they are rich in spiritual power so that nothing is left out;
every petition and prayer we have to
make is included. It is a compendium
of heavenly doctrine.
SAINT CYPRIAN (200–258)

LOVE

7157 A wise lover values not so much the
gift of the lover as the love of the giver.
THOMAS À KEMPIS (C. 1380–1471)

7158 Agape love is . . . profound concern
for the well-being of another, without
any desire to control that other, to be
thanked by that other, or to enjoy the
process.
MADELEINE L'ENGLE (1918–)

7159 Alas, oh, love is dead! How could it
perish thus?
No one has cared for it: It simply
died of frost.
ANGELUS SILESIUS (1624–1677)

7160 Anticipation is more delightful than
realization in love.
PAULUS SILENTIARIUS (C. A.D. 560)

7161 Better to have loved and lost than not
to have loved at all.
LUCIUS ANNAEUS SENECA (C. 4 B.C.–A.D. 65)

7162 Can there be a love which does not make demands on its object?
CONFUCIUS (C. 551–479 B.C.)

7163 Charity sees the need, not the cause.
GERMAN PROVERB

7164 Christian love links love of God and love of neighbor in a twofold Great Commandment from which neither element can be dropped, so sin against neighbor through lack of human love is sin against God.
GEORGIA HARKNESS (1891–1979)

7165 Duty does not have to be dull. Love can make it beautiful and fill it with life.
THOMAS MERTON (1915–1968)

7166 Erotic and philia love are emotional. Christian love [agape] is an attitude, not feeling.
JOSEPH FLETCHER

7167 Every love has its own force; and it cannot lie idle in the soul of the lover. Love must draw the soul on. Do you, then, wish to know the character of a love? See where it leads.
SAINT AUGUSTINE OF HIPPO (354–430)

7168 Faith, like light, should always be simple and unbending; while love, like warmth, should beam forth on every side and bend to every necessity of our brethren.
MARTIN LUTHER (1483–1546)

7169 Forgetting oneself is not a refinement of love. It is a first condition of love.
LEON JOSEPH SUENENS (1904–)

7170 Give me such love for God and men as will blot out all hatred and bitterness.
DIETRICH BONHOEFFER (1906–1945)

7171 God hears no sweeter music than the cracked chimes of the courageous human spirit ringing in imperfect acknowledgment of his perfect love.
JOSHUA LOTH LIEBMAN (1907–1948)

7172 God loved the world. Go thou and do likewise.
ERWIN W. LUTZER (1941–)

7173 God proved his love on the cross. When Christ hung, and bled, and died, it was God saying to the world, "I love you."
BILLY GRAHAM (1918–)

7174 He prayeth best, who loveth best
All things both great and small;
For the dear God who loveth us,
He made and loveth all.
SAMUEL TAYLOR COLERIDGE (1772–1834)

7175 He that falls in love with himself will have no rivals.
BENJAMIN FRANKLIN (1706–1790)

7176 He who knows he is loved can be content with a piece of bread, while all the luxuries of the world cannot satisfy the craving of the lonely.
FRANCES J. ROBERTS

7177 He who loves something mentions it very often.
ARABIAN PROVERB

7178 Holding a beggar's child
Against my heart,
Through blinding tears I see
That as I love the tiny, piteous thing,
So God loves me!
TOYOHIKO KAGAWA (1888–1960)

7179 Hope is like a harebell, trembling from
its birth;
Love is like a rose, the joy of all the
earth;
Faith is like a lily, lifted high and white,
Love is like a lovely rose; the world's
delight.
Harebells and sweet lilies show a
thornless growth,
But the rose with all its thorns excels
them both.
CHRISTINA GEORGINA ROSSETTI
(1830–1894)

7180 Human things must be known to be loved: but divine things must be loved to be known.
BLAISE PASCAL (1623–1662)

7181 I don't want to explain the difference between eros and philos and agape but to love.
JOSEPH BAYLY (1920–1986)

7182 I have decided to stick with love. Hate is too great a burden to bear.
MARTIN LUTHER KING, JR. (1929–1968)

7183 I love you, not because you're perfect, but because you're so perfect for me.

7184 I must ask if there is any person in my life whose growth and happiness is as real or more real to me than my own. If so, love has truly entered my life.
JOHN POWELL

7185 I never knew how to worship until I knew how to love.
HENRY WARD BEECHER (1813–1887)

7186 If God is love, he is, by definition, something more than mere kindness. And it appears, from all the records, that though he has often rebuked us and condemned us, he has never regarded us with contempt. He has paid us the intolerable compliment of loving us, in the deepest, most tragic, most inexorable sense.
C. S. LEWIS (1898–1963)

7187 If my interest in the work of others is cool . . . then I know nothing of Calvary love.
AMY CARMICHAEL (1867–1951)

7188 If souls can suffer alongside, and I hardly know it . . . then I know nothing of Calvary love.
AMY CARMICHAEL (1867–1951)

7189 If you have love in your heart, you always have something to give.

7190 If you have love, you are not only going to think no evil, you're going to take your tongue and have it nailed to the cross so that you bless instead of curse.
BILLY GRAHAM (1918–   )

7191 If you love, you will suffer, and if you do not love, you do not know the meaning of a Christian life.
AGATHA CHRISTIE (1891–1976)

7192 If you would be loved, love and be lovable.

7193 If your love be pure, simple, and well ordered, you shall be free from bondage.
THOMAS À KEMPIS (C. 1380–1471)

7194 Immature love says: "I love you because I need you." Mature love says: "I need you because I love you."
ERICH FROMM (1900–1980)

7195 In comparison with a loving human being, everything else is worthless.
HUGH MACLENNAN (1907–   )

7196 In necessary things, unity; in doubtful things, liberty; in all things, charity.
RICHARD BAXTER (1615–1691)

7197 In real love you want the other person's good. In romantic love you want the other person.
MARGARET ANDERSON (1893–1973)

7198 In the triangle of love between ourselves, God, and other people, is found the secret of existence, and the best foretaste, I suspect, that we can have on earth of what heaven will probably be like.
SAMUEL M. SHOEMAKER (1893–1963)

7199 It is astonishing how little one feels poverty when one loves.
JOHN BULVER (C. 1654)

7200 It is not love that produces jealousy— it is selfishness.
JUSTICE WALLINGTON

7201 Jesus redefines the meaning of love for neighbor; it means love for any man in need.
GEORGE ELDON LADD (1911–1982)

7202 Joy is love exalted; peace is love in repose; long-suffering is love enduring; gentleness is love in society; goodness is love in action; faith is love on the battlefield; meekness is love in school; and temperance is love in training.
DWIGHT LYMAN MOODY (1837–1899)

7203 Let love be purified, and all the rest will follow. A pure love is thus, indeed, the panacea for all the ills of the world.
HENRY DAVID THOREAU (1817–1862)

7204 Life bears love's cross, death brings love's crown.
DINAH MARIA MULOCK CRAIK (1826–1887)

7205 Life is the flower of which love is the honey.
VICTOR HUGO (1802–1885)

7206 Life minus love equals zero!

7207 Love accepts people as they are; love can take insults without ill will.
ERWIN W. LUTZER (1941–   )

7208 Love alone is capable of uniting living beings in such a way as to complete and fulfill them, for it alone takes them and joins them by what is deepest in themselves.
PIERRE TEILHARD DE CHARDIN (1881–1955)

7209 Love can hope where reason would despair.
LORD GEORGE LYTTELTON (1709–1773)

7210 Love can make any place agreeable.
ARABIAN PROVERB

7211 Love cannot be inactive; its life is a ceaseless effort to know, to feel, and to realize the boundless treasures hidden within its depths. This is its insatiable desire.
JAN VAN RUYSBROECK (1293–1381)

7212 Love comforteth like sunshine after rain.
WILLIAM SHAKESPEARE (1564–1616)

7213 Love cures people—both the ones who give it and the ones who receive it.
KARL AUGUSTUS MENNINGER (1893–1990)

7214 Love does not analyze its object.
HENRY DAVID THOREAU (1817–1862)

7215 Love does not consist in gazing at each other but in looking together in the same direction.
ANTOINE DE SAINT-EXUPÉRY (1900–1944)

7216 Love does not dominate; it cultivates.
JOHANN WOLFGANG VON GOETHE (1749–1832)

7217 Love doesn't just sit there, like a stone; it has to be made, like bread; remade all the time, made new.
URSULA K. LEGUIN (1929–   )

7218 Love ever gives,
Forgives, outlives,
And ever stands
With open hands.
And while it lives,
It gives.
For this is love's prerogative—
O give, and give, and give.
JOHN OXENHAM (1861–1941)

7219 Love every day. Each one is so short and they are so few.
NORMAN VINCENT PEALE (1898–   )

7220 Love feels no burden, thinks nothing of trouble, attempts what is above its strength, pleads no excuse of impossibility; for it thinks all things lawful for itself, and all things possible. It is therefore able to undertake all things, and warrants them to take effect, where he who does not love, would faint and lie down.
THOMAS À KEMPIS (C. 1380–1471)

7221 Love for the Lord is not an ethereal, intellectual, dreamlike thing; it is the intensest, the most vital, the most passionate love of which the human heart is capable.
OSWALD CHAMBERS (1874–1917)

7222 Love gives itself; it is not bought.
HENRY WADSWORTH LONGFELLOW (1807–1882)

7223 Love has power to give in a moment what toil can scarcely reach in an age.
JOHANN WOLFGANG VON GOETHE (1749–1832)

7224 Love in its essence is spiritual fire.
EMANUEL SWEDENBORG (1688–1772)

7225 Love is . . . the gift of oneself.
JEAN ANOUILH (1910–   )

7226 Love is a gift from God.

7227 Love is a great beautifier.
LOUISA MAY ALCOTT (1832–1888)

7228 Love is a mixture of honey and bitterness.
CISTELLARIA (250–184 B.C.)

7229 Love is a symbol of eternity. It wipes out all sense of time, destroying all memory of a beginning and all fear of an end.
ANNE-LOUISE-GERMAINE DE STAËL (1766–1817)

7230 Love is a tender plant; when properly nourished, it becomes sturdy and enduring, but neglected it will soon wither and die.
HUGH B. BROWN

7231 Love is an action, an activity. It is not a feeling.
M. SCOTT PECK (1936–   )

7232 Love is demonstrably superior to money, not only on a sentimental plane, but even on a computable basis: The more money you give away, the less you have, but the more love you give away, the more comes back to you.
SYDNEY J. HARRIS (1917–1986)

7233 Love is difficult to sustain, not because it is a positive emotion, but because it is a complex one. Hate is easy to maintain for a lifetime because it is a simple one. Love might be compared to the building of a tall and elaborate sandcastle, taking many hours of painstaking effort, cooperation, balance, and persistence; and hate might be compared to the foot that comes along and with one vicious or thoughtless kick destroys in a moment what has been built up.
SYDNEY J. HARRIS (1917–1986)

7234 Love is friendship set to music.
ROBERT POLLOK (1798–1827)

7235 Love is higher than the other gifts in value; love is the one gift open to every member of the church. It is not dependent on ability, popularity, or shrewdness. The greatest path is open to the least of travelers.
ERWIN W. LUTZER (1941–   )

7236 Love is like a friendship caught on fire. In the beginning a flame, very pretty, often hot and fierce but still only light and flickering. As love grows older, our hearts mature and our love becomes as coals, deep-burning and unquenchable.
BRUCE LEE

7237 Love is like a magnet is, it draws me into God,
And what is greater still, it pulls God into death.
ANGELUS SILESIUS (1624–1677)

7238 Love is like the five loaves and two fishes. It doesn't start to multiply until you give it away.

7239 Love is most free when it is offered in spite of suffering, of injustice, and of death.
ARCHIBALD MACLEISH (1892–1982)

7240 Love is my decision to make your problem my problem.
ROBERT HAROLD SCHULLER (1926–   )

7241 Love is never lost. If not reciprocated it will flow back and soften and purify the heart.
WASHINGTON IRVING (1783–1859)

7242 Love is not affectionate feeling, but a steady wish for the loved person's ultimate good as far as it can be obtained.
C. S. LEWIS (1898–1963)

7243 Love is not getting, but giving.
HENRY VAN DYKE (1852–1933)

7244 Love is not the work of the Holy Spirit, it is the Holy Spirit—working in us. God is love, he doesn't merely have it or give it; he gives himself—to all men, to all sorts and conditions.
JOSEPH FLETCHER

7245 Love is something so divine,
Description would but make it less;
'Tis what I feel, but can't define,
'Tis what I know, but can't express.
BEILBY PORTEUS (1731–1808)

7246 Love is swift, pure, tender, joyful, and pleasant. Love is strong, patient, faithful, prudent, long-suffering, vigorous, and never self-seeking. For when a man is self-seeking, he abandons love. Love is watchful, humble, and upright. Love is not fickle and sentimental, nor is it intent on vanities. It is sober, pure, steadfast, quiet, and guarded in all the senses. Love is submissive and obedient to superiors, mean and contemptible in its own sight, devoted and thankful to God, trusting and hoping in him even when not enjoying his sweetness; for none can live in love without suffering.
THOMAS À KEMPIS (C. 1380–1471)

7247 Love is the fairest bloom in God's garden.

7248 Love is the fire of life; it either consumes or purifies.

7249 Love is the greatest gift one person can give another.

7250 Love is the medicine for the sickness of the world.
KARL AUGUSTUS MENNINGER (1893–1990)

7251 Love is the one ingredient of which our world never tires and of which there is never an abundance. It is needed in the marketplace and in the mansions. It is needed in the ghettos and in the governments. It is needed in homes, in hospitals, and in individual hearts. The world will never outgrow its need for love.
C. NEIL STRAIT

7252 Love is the one treasure that multiplies by division. It is the one gift that grows bigger the more you take from it. It is the one business in which it pays to be an absolute spendthrift. You can give it away, throw it away, empty your pockets, shake the basket, turn the glass upside down, and tomorrow you will have more than ever.

7253 Love is the only service that power cannot command and money cannot buy.

7254 Love is the only true freedom. It lets us cast off our false exteriors and be our real selves.
SUSAN POLIS SCHUTZ

7255 Love is the subtlest force in the world.
MAHATMA GANDHI (1869–1948)

7256 Love is the wine that gladdens the heart of man.
ISAAC OF NINEVEH (SEVENTH CENTURY)

7257 Love isn't like a reservoir. You'll never drain it dry. It's much more like a natural spring. The longer and the farther it flows, the stronger and the deeper and the clearer it becomes.
EDDIE CANTOR (1892–1964)

7258 Love isn't love until you give it away.

7259 Love looks through a telescope; envy, through a microscope.
JOSH BILLINGS (1818–1885)

7260 Love makes a subtle man out of a crude one, it gives eloquence to the mute; it gives courage to the cowardly, and makes the idle quick and sharp.
JUAN RUTZ (1283–1350)

7261 Love makes all hard hearts gentle.
GEORGE HERBERT (1593–1633)

7262 Love makes everything lovely; hate concentrates itself on the one thing hated.
GEORGE MACDONALD (1824–1905)

7263 Love makes the whole difference between an execution and a martyrdom.
EVELYN UNDERHILL (1875–1941)

7264 Love makes those young whom age doth chill,
And whom he finds young, keeps young still.
PETER CARTWRIGHT (1611–1643)

7265 Love must be learned again and again; there is no end to it. Hate needs no instruction, but waits only to be provoked.
KATHERINE ANNE PORTER (1890–1980)

7266 Love overlooks defects.
ARABIAN PROVERB

7267 Love people, not things.

7268 Love produces a certain flowering of the whole personality that nothing else can achieve.
IVAN SERGEYEVICH TURGENEV (1818–1883)

7269 Love puts the fun in together . . . the sad in apart . . . the hope in tomorrow . . . the joy in a heart.

7270 Love rules his kingdom without a sword.
ROBERT HERRICK (1591–1674)

7271 Love seeks not limits but outlets.

7272 Love slays what we have been that we may be what we were not.
SAINT AUGUSTINE OF HIPPO (354–430)

7273 Love will ask much more of us than the law could ever require. True love can never say, "I have done enough. I have now fulfilled all my obligations." Love is restless, drives us on. Love asks us to walk many miles not demanded by justice or legalism.
JOHN POWELL

7274 Love's business is not to play favorites or to find friends or to "fall" for some one-and-only. It plays the field, universalizes its concern, has a social interest, is no respecter of persons.
JOSEPH FLETCHER

7275 Love, not law, is the greatest cleanser.
MADELEINE L'ENGLE (1918–)

7276 Love: in tennis, nothing; in life, everything.
FRANK TYGER

7277 Loving, like prayer, is a power as well
as a process. It's curative. It is creative.
ZONA GALE (1874–1938)

7278 Man's love is of man's life a thing apart,
'Tis woman's whole existence.
LORD GEORGE NOEL GORDON BYRON
(1788–1824)

7279 No cord or cable can draw so forcibly,
or bind so fast, as love can do with a
single thread.
ROBERT BURTON (1577–1640)

7280 No one could have had a more sensitive love in human relationship than
Jesus; and yet he says there are times
when love to father and mother must
be hatred in comparison to our love
for him.
OSWALD CHAMBERS (1874–1917)

7281 Nobody will know what you mean by
saying that "God is love" unless you
act it as well.
LAWRENCE PEARSALL JACKS (1860–1955)

7282 Not where I breathe, but where I love,
I live.
ROBERT SOUTHWELL (C. 1561–1595)

7283 Nothing is sweeter than love, nothing
stronger, nothing higher, nothing
wider, nothing more pleasant, nothing
fuller or better in heaven or on
earth. . . . A lover flies, runs,
rejoices. . . . Love often knows no limits but is fervent beyond measure.
Love feels no burden, thinks nothing
of labors, attempts what is above its
strength, pleads no excuse of impossibility. . . . Though wearied, it is not
tired; though pressed, it is not straitened; though alarmed, it is not confounded; but as a lively flame and
burning torch, it forces its way
upwards and passes securely through
all.
THOMAS À KEMPIS (C. 1380–1471)

7284 O Brother Man, fold to thy heart thy
brother;

Where pity dwells, the peace of God is
there;
To worship rightly is to love each
other,
Each smile a hymn, each kindly deed a
prayer.
JOHN GREENLEAF WHITTIER (1807–1892)

7285 O love, resistless in thy might, thou
triumphest even over gold!
SOPHOCLES (C. 496–406 B.C.)

7286 Old age can love God better than a
doctor of theology can.
SAINT BONAVENTURE (1221–1274)

7287 One cannot love his neighbor unless
he loves God.
ERWIN W. LUTZER (1941–)

7288 Our Lord does not care so much for
the importance of our works as for the
love with which they are done.
SAINT TERESA OF AVILA (1515–1582)

7289 Plant a word of love heart-deep in a
person's life. Nurture it with a smile
and a prayer, and watch what happens.
MAX L. LUCADO (1955–)

7290 Respect is what we owe; love is what
we give.
PHILIP JAMES BAILEY (1816–1902)

7291 Riches take wings, comforts vanish,
hope withers away, but love stays with
us. God is love.
LEW WALLACE (1827–1905)

7292 So long as we love, we serve. So long
as we are loved by others, I would
almost say we are indispensable; and
no man is useless while he has a friend.
ROBERT LOUIS BALFOUR STEVENSON
(1850–1894)

7293 Suffering is the true cement of love.
PAUL SABATIER (1858–1928)

7294 Take away love and our earth is a
tomb.
ROBERT BROWNING (1812–1889)

7295 Tell me how much you know of the
sufferings of your fellowmen, and I
will tell you how much you have loved
them.
HELMUT THIELICKE (1908–1986)

7296 Tell me whom you love, and I will tell you what you are.
ARSENE HOUSSAYE (1815–1896)

7297 Tennis is one of the few pastimes where love means nothing.

7298 The alphabet of love consists of avowals and consents.

7299 The difference between duty and love is that the first represents Sinai and the second represents Calvary.
RICHARD BRAUNSTEIN (B. 1885)

7300 The eyes of love see in every other person not one but two persons: the wounded and angry, the good and gifted.
JOHN POWELL

7301 The first duty of love is to listen.
PAUL JOHANNES OSKAR TILLICH (1886–1965)

7302 The heart that loves is always young.

7303 The love of wealth makes bitter men; the love of God, better men.
W. L. HUDSON (D. 1904)

7304 The love that Christ commands is not easy, even for people who are blessed with great natural warmth of heart. And it is not impossible, even for those of us who tend to be crabby and short-tempered. For Christian love is not a vague feeling of affection for someone. It is rather a condition of the heart and will that causes us to seek the welfare of others—including people we don't particularly like, and even people who have done us wrong.
LOUIS CASSELS (1922–1974)

7305 The most revolutionary statement in history is "Love thine enemy."
ELDRIDGE CLEAVER (1935–)

7306 The night has a thousand eyes,
And the day but one;
Yet the light of the bright world dies
With the dying sun.
The mind has a thousand eyes,
And the heart but one;
Yet the light of a whole life dies
When love is done.
FRANCIS WILLIAM BOURDILLON (1852–1921)

7307 The norm or measure by which any thought or action is to be judged a success or failure, right or wrong, is love.
JOSEPH FLETCHER

7308 The one thing we can never get enough of is love. And the one thing we never give enough of is love.
HENRY MILLER (1891–1980)

7309 The rose is sweetest wash'd with morning dew,
And love is loveliest when embalm'd in tears.
SIR WALTER SCOTT (1771–1832)

7310 The soul is not where it lives but where it loves.

7311 The way to love anything is to realize that it might be lost.
G. K. CHESTERTON (1874–1936)

7312 The word love is a swampy one, a semantic confession:
1. See it now! Uncensored! Love in the raw.
2. I just love that hat! Isn't it absolutely divine.
3. Do you promise to love, honor, and obey?
4. Aw, come on—just this once—prove your love.
5. I love strawberries, but they give me a rash.
JOSEPH FLETCHER

7313 The world does not understand theology or dogma, but it understands love and sympathy.
DWIGHT LYMAN MOODY (1837–1899)

7314 There is no surprise more magical than the surprise of being loved. It is the finger of God on a man's shoulder.
CHARLES MORGAN (1894–1958)

7315 There is nothing so loyal as love.
ALICE CARY (1820–1871)

7316 There is only one being who loves perfectly, and that is God, yet the New Testament distinctly states that we are to love as God does; so the first step is obvious. If ever we are going to have perfect love in our hearts we must have the very nature of God in us.
OSWALD CHAMBERS (1874–1917)

7317 There is only one kind of love, but there are a thousand imitations.
HUGH LATIMER (C. 1485–1555)

7318 They are the true disciples of Christ, not who know most, but who love most.
FREDERICH SPANHEIM THE ELDER (1600–1649)

7319 They that love beyond the world cannot be separated. Death cannot kill what never dies. Nor can spirits ever be divided that love and live in the same divine principle; the root and record of their friendship. Death is but crossing the world, as friends do the seas, they live in one another still.
WILLIAM PENN (1644–1718)

7320 This is charity, to do all, all that we can.
JOHN DONNE (1572–1631)

7321 Those who do not love their fellow beings live unfruitful lives.
PERCY BYSSHE SHELLEY (1792–1822)

7322 Those who tease you love you.
JEWISH PROVERB

7323 To be able to say how much you love is to love little.
PETRARCH (1304–1374)

7324 To love as Christ loves is to let our love be a practical and not a sentimental thing.
SIR CHARLES VILLIERS STANFORD (1852–1924)

7325 To love for the sake of being loved is human, but to love for the sake of loving is angelic.
ALPHONSE-MARIE-LOUIS DE PRAT DE LAMARTINE (1790–1869)

7326 To love is to admire with the heart; to admire is to love with the mind.
THÉOPHILE GAUTIER (1811–1872)

7327 To love is to give one's time. We never give the impression that we care when we are in a hurry. To exercise a spiritual ministry means to take time. If we want to save our time for more important matters than a soul, we are but tradesmen.
PAUL TOURNIER (1898–1986)

7328 True love is always costly.
BILLY GRAHAM (1918–)

7329 Vulnerability, attachment, uprooting, tenderness, interest, anxiety, expectation, anguish—all these are nothing else but love. It all strips, it all causes suffering.
LOUIS EVELY (1910–)

7330 We are shaped and fashioned by what we love.
JOHANN WOLFGANG VON GOETHE (1749–1832)

7331 We do not live under a law of the jungle, an eye for an eye, a tooth for a tooth. We have a new law: Love one another as I have loved you.
JOHN POWELL

7332 We don't love qualities, we love a person; sometimes by reason of their defects as well as their qualities.
JACQUES MARITAIN (1882–1973)

7333 We like someone because. We love someone although.
HENRI DE MONTHERLANT (1896–)

7334 We must spiritually renounce all other loves for love of God or at least so hold them in subordination to this that we are ready to forego them for its sake; yet when we find God, or, rather, when we know ourselves as found of him, we find in and with him all the loves which for his sake we had foregone.
SIR WILLIAM TEMPLE (1628–1699)

7335 What does love look like? It has hands to help others. It has feet to hasten to the poor and needy. It has eyes to see misery and want. It has ears to hear the sighs and sorrows of men. That is what love looks like.
SAINT AUGUSTINE OF HIPPO (354–430)

7336 What we love we shall grow to resemble.
BERNARD OF CLAIRVAUX (1090–1153)

7337 Whatever else love may ask of us, it does not ask us to be doormats or compulsive pleasers or peace-at-any-price persons. The primary gift of love is the offering of one's most honest

self through one's most honest self-disclosure.
JOHN POWELL

7338 Whatever you love most, be it sports, pleasure, business, or God, that is your god!
BILLY GRAHAM (1918–)

7339 When we reflect on the meaning of love, we see that it is to the heart what the summer is to the farmer's year. It brings to harvest all the loveliest flowers of the soul.
BILLY GRAHAM (1918–)

7340 When you come to Jesus Christ and accept him as your Lord and Savior, he gives you a supernatural love that allows you to love your enemy whom you normally would not love.
BILLY GRAHAM (1918–)

7341 Where love is not, there can be no pleasures.
RUSSIAN PROVERB

7342 Where love reigns, the very joy of heaven itself is felt.
HANNAH HURNARD (1905–1990)

7343 Where love rules, there is no will to power; and where power predominates, there love is lacking.
CARL GUSTAV JUNG (1875–1961)

7344 Where there is no love, put love in, and you will draw out love.
SAINT JOHN OF THE CROSS (1542–1591)

7345 While faith makes all things possible, it is love that makes all things easy.

7346 With all thy faults, I love thee still.
WILLIAM COWPER (1731–1800)

7347 With the knowledge of God comes love.
CATHERINE OF SIENA (1347–1380)

7348 Without distinction, without calculation, without procrastination, love. Lash it upon the poor, where it is very easy; especially upon the rich, who often need it most; most of all, upon our equals, where it is very difficult, and for whom perhaps we each do least of all.
HENRY DRUMMOND (1851–1897)

7349 Would not the carrying out of one single commandment of Christ, "Love one another," change the whole aspect of the world and sweep away prisons and workhouses, and envying and strife, and all the strongholds of the devil? Two thousand years have nearly passed, and people have not yet understood that one single command of Christ, "Love one another!"
MAX MULLER (1823–1900)

7350 You can give without loving, but you cannot love without giving.
AMY CARMICHAEL (1867–1951)

7351 You cannot love a fellow creature till you love God.
C. S. LEWIS (1898–1963)

7352 You learn to speak by speaking, to study by studying, to run by running, to work by working; and just so you learn to love God and man by loving. Begin as a mere apprentice, and the very power of love will lead you on to become a master of the art.
SAINT FRANCIS OF SALES (1567–1622)

LUST

7353 Love can wait and worship endlessly; lust says, "I must have it at once."
OSWALD CHAMBERS (1874–1917)

7354 Lust and reason are enemies.
SOLOMON BEN GABIROL (C. 1020–1070)

7355 Lust is felt even by fleas and lice.
MARTIN LUTHER (1483–1546)

7356 Lust is like rot in the bones.
JEWISH PROVERB

7357 Lust's effect is tempest after sun.
WILLIAM SHAKESPEARE (1564–1616)

7358 Lust, at its height, does not know shame.
MARQUIS OF HALIFAX (1633–1695)

7359 We use for passions the stuff that has been given to us for happiness.
JOSEPH JOUBERT (1754–1824)

7360 You can get a large audience together for a strip-tease act—that is, to watch a girl undress on the stage. Now suppose you came to a country where you could fill a theatre by simply bringing

a covered plate on to the stage and then slowly lifting the cover so as to let everyone see, just before the lights went out, that it contained a mutton chop or a bit of bacon, would you not think that in that country something had gone wrong with the appetite for food? And would not anyone who had grown up in a different world think there was something equally queer about the state of the sex instinct among us?
C. S. LEWIS (1898–1963)

LUXURY

7361 Comfort comes as a guest, lingers to become a host, and stays to enslave.
LEE BICKMORE (1908–   )

7362 Luxury is more deadly than any foe.
JUVENAL (C. 60–C. 127)

7363 Luxury makes a man so soft that it is hard to please him and easy to trouble him; so that his pleasures at last become his burden. Luxury is a nice master, hard to be pleased.
HENRY MACKENZIE (1745–1831)

7364 On the soft bed of luxury most kingdoms have died.
EDWARD YOUNG (1683–1765)

7365 Possessions, outward success, publicity, luxury—to me these have always been contemptible. I believe that a simple and unassuming manner of life is best for everyone, best for both the body and the mind.
ALBERT EINSTEIN (1879–1955)

M

MAN

7366 A man's true value consists in his likeness to God. What gives value to his thoughts, his feelings, and his actions is the extent to which they are inspired by God, the extent to which they express the thought, the will, and the acts of God.
PAUL TOURNIER (1898–1986)

7367 A walking chemical factory driven by instincts of hunger and sex.
HENRY SLOANE COFFIN (1877–1954)

7368 As the generation of leaves, so is that of men.
HOMER (C. EIGHTH CENTURY B.C.)

7369 Below the surface-stream, shallow and light
Of what we say we feel—below the stream
As light of what we think we feel—there flows
With noiseless current strong, obscure and deep
The central stream of what we are indeed.
MATTHEW ARNOLD (1822–1888)

7370 Beneath you and external to you lies the entire created universe. Yes, even the sun, the moon, and the stars. They are fixed above you, splendid in the firmament, yet they cannot compare to your exalted dignity as a human being.

7371 But trailing clouds of glory do we come
From God, who is our home.
WILLIAM WORDSWORTH (1770–1850)

7372 Each man appears for a little while to laugh and weep, to work and play, and then to go to make room for those who shall follow him in the never-ending cycle.
A. W. TOZER (1897–1963)

7373 Every man I meet is my superior in some way. In that, I learn from him.
RALPH WALDO EMERSON (1803–1882)

7374 Every man knows well enough that he is a unique being, only once on this earth; and by no extraordinary chance will such a marvelously picturesque piece of diversity in unity as he is, ever be put together a second time.
FRIEDRICH WILHELM NIETZSCHE (1844–1900)

7375 Every other animal can, at his will, wear on his face the expression he pleases. He is not obligated to smile if he has a mind to weep. When he does not wish to see his fellows, he does not see them. While man is the slave of everything and everybody!
MARIE KONSTANTINOVNA BASHKIRTSEFF (1860–1884)

7376 Everyone is a moon and has a dark side, which he never shows to anybody.
MARK TWAIN (1835–1910)

7377 Everyone's different. The five fingers are not all the same.
ARABIAN PROVERB

7378 God looks at a man's heart before he looks at a man's brains.
JEWISH PROVERB

7379 God was smart when he made man. He made six holes in the head for information to go in, and only one for it to come out.
WALLACE JOHNSON

7380 Great men never feel great. Small men never feel small.

7381 He is of the earth, but his thoughts are with the stars. Mean and petty his wants and desires; yet they serve a soul exalted with grand, glorious aims—with immortal longings—with thoughts that sweep the heavens, and wander through eternity. A pigmy standing on the outward crest of this small planet, his far-reaching spirit stretches outward to the infinite, and there alone finds rest.
THOMAS CARLYLE (1795–1881)

7382 Human beings themselves are wild animals when they are born—more helpless than other species, but by no means more tame. If they seem tamer, it is only because they are brought up in that way. Don't you realize if you can tame boys, you can tame almost anything? Wild horses from the range can be tamed quickly in a few weeks, but it takes years of patience and effort to tame young human beings.
CLARENCE SHEPARD DAY, JR. (1874–1935)

7383 Humanity moves between the two poles of simplicity and complexity. People who have the sort of mind that sees only one side to every question tend toward vigorous action. They succeed in everything they do because they do not stop to split hairs and have abounding confidence in their own abilities. . . . On the other hand, those with subtle and cultivated minds tend to get lost in a maze of fine distinctions. They always see how complicated things really are, so that their powers of persuasion are nil. . . . It is only very few who manage to combine both tendencies, and in my view a lively Christian faith is the best precondition for the accomplishment of this miracle because it gives both profound understanding and simplicity of heart.
PAUL TOURNIER (1898–1986)

7384 I am a little world made cunningly Of elements, and an angelic sprite.
JOHN DONNE (1572–1631)

7385 I am greater than the stars for I know that they are up there, and they do not know that I am down here.
SIR WILLIAM TEMPLE (1628–1699)

7386 I am my own heaven and hell!
JOHANN FRIEDRICH VON SCHILLER (1759–1805)

7387 I am one individual on a small planet in a little solar system in one of the galaxies.
ROBERTO ASSAGIOLI

7388 I have never seen a greater miracle or monster than myself.
MICHEL EYQUEM DE MONTAIGNE (1533–1592)

7389 If individuals live only seventy years, then a state, or a nation, or a civilization which may last for a thousand years is more important than an individual. But if Christianity is true, then the individual is not only more important but incomparably more important, for he is everlasting and the life of a state or a civilization, compared with his, is only a moment.
C. S. LEWIS (1898–1963)

7390 If man could be crossed with the cat, it would improve man, but it would deteriorate the cat.
MARK TWAIN (1835–1910)

7391 In great matters men show themselves as they wish to be seen; in small matters, as they are.
GAMALIEL BRADFORD (1863–1932)

7392 In nature a repulsive caterpillar turns into a lovely butterfly. But with human beings it is the other way around: a lovely butterfly turns into a repulsive caterpillar.
ANTON PAVLOVICH CHEKHOV (1860–1904)

7393 It is easier to know mankind than man individually.
FRANÇOIS, DUC DE LA ROCHEFOUCAULD (1613–1680)

7394 It is good to know what a man is, and also what the world takes him for. But you do not understand him until you have learnt how he understands himself.
FRANCIS HERBERT BRADLEY (1846–1924)

7395 It is man's dignity to stand upright, his face toward the stars and not toward the earth like the beasts, for he is the most exalted of all God's works.
THE CLOUD OF UNKNOWING (1370)

7396 It is not a world out of joint that makes our problem but the shipwrecked soul in it. It is Hamlet, not his world, that is wrong.
P. T. FORSYTH (1848–1921)

7397 It is not starvation, not microbes, not cancer, but man himself who is mankind's greatest danger.
CARL GUSTAV JUNG (1875–1961)

7398 Man differs from the animals in that he asks himself questions. He asks them about the world and about himself, about the meaning of things, the meaning of disease and healing, life and death. He is conscious of his weakness, of his responsibility, and of his shortcomings, and he asks himself if there is any way out. I know that it is in fact God who puts these questions to him, that it is God who is speaking to him, even though he may not realize it.
PAUL TOURNIER (1898–1986)

7399 Man enters each stage of life as a novice.
SÉBASTIEN ROCH NICOLAS CHAMFORT (1741–1794)

7400 Man has two great spiritual needs. One is for forgiveness. God answered it at Calvary. The other is for goodness. God answered it at Pentecost.
BILLY GRAHAM (1918–   )

7401 Man is a constant puzzle.
WALT WHITMAN (1819–1892)

7402 Man is a peculiar, puzzling paradox, groping for God and hoping to hide from him at the same time.
WILLIAM ARTHUR WARD (1812–1882)

7403 Man is an abyss, and I turn giddy when I look down into it.
GEORGE BÜCHNER (1813–1837)

7404 Man is an animal that makes bargains; no other animal does this—no dog exchanges bones with another.
ADAM SMITH (1723–1790)

7405 Man is an inexhaustible mystery. He fits into none of our categories of thought.
PAUL TOURNIER (1898–1986)

7406 Man is but a reed, the weakest in nature, but he is a thinking reed.
BLAISE PASCAL (1623–1662)

7407 Man is God's risk.
PHILIP YANCEY (1949–   )

7408 Man is the greatest miracle and the greatest problem on this earth.
DAVID SARNOFF (1891–1971)

7409 Man is the miracle of miracles, the great inscrutable mystery of God.
THOMAS CARLYLE (1795–1881)

7410 Man is the only animal of which I am thoroughly and cravenly afraid. I have never thought much of the courage of a lion tamer. Inside the cage he is at least safe from other men. There is less harm in a well-fed lion. It has no ideals, no sect, no party, no nation, no class: in short, no reason for destroying anything it does not want to eat.
GEORGE BERNARD SHAW (1856–1950)

7411 Man is the only animal that blushes. Or needs to.
MARK TWAIN (1835–1910)

7412 Man is the only animal that knows nothing and can learn nothing without being taught. He can neither speak nor walk nor eat, nor do anything at the prompting of nature, but only weep.
PLINY THE ELDER (23–79)

7413 Man is the only animal that laughs and weeps, for he is the only animal that knows the difference between what things are and what they ought to be.
WILLIAM HAZLITT (1778–1830)

7414 Man's conquest of nature has been astonishing. His failure to conquer human nature has been tragic.
JULIUS MARK

7415 Man's unique agony as a species consists in his perpetual conflict between the desire to stand out and the need to blend in.
SYDNEY J. HARRIS (1917–1986)

7416 Man—a reasoning rather than a reasonable animal.
ALEXANDER HAMILTON (1757–1804)

7417 Man: the glory, jest, and riddle of the world.
ALEXANDER POPE (1688–1744)

7418 Men are but children of a larger growth.
JOHN DRYDEN (1631–1700)

7419 Men are like wine. Some turn to vinegar, but the best improve with age.
C. E. M. JOAD (1891–1953)

7420 Men are very queer animals—a mixture of horse-nervousness, ass-stubbornness, and camel-malice.
THOMAS HENRY HUXLEY (1825–1895)

7421 Men have never been good, they are not good, they never will be good.
KARL BARTH (1886–1968)

7422 No man safely travels who loves not to rest at home. No man safely talks but he who loves to listen. No man safely rules but he who loves to be subject. No man safely commands but he who loves to obey.
THOMAS À KEMPIS (C. 1380–1471)

7423 Not, how did he die? But, how did he live?

Not, what did he gain? But what did he give?

These are the merits to measure the worth

Of a man as man, regardless of birth.

Not, what was his station? But, had he a heart?

And how did he play his God-given part?

Was he ever ready with word or good cheer

To bring a smile, to banish a tear?

Not, what was his church? Nor, what was his creed?

But, had he befriended those really in need?

Not, what did the sketch in the newspaper say?

But, how many were sorry when he passed away?

7424 Numberless are the world's wonders, but none more wonderful than man.
SOPHOCLES (C. 496–406 B.C.)

7425 Show a man his failures without Jesus, and the result will be found in the roadside gutter. Give a man religion without reminding him of his filth, and the result will be arrogance in a three-piece suit.
MAX L. LUCADO (1955–)

7426 That man is to be feared who fears not God.
TURKISH PROVERB

7427 The finest clothing made is a person's own skin.
MARK TWAIN (1835–1910)

7428 The most important thing about the individual is his isolation; we're all isolated in our minds; where we come in touch with other people is through our affections, our sympathies, our animosities; we don't even know ourselves well enough to tell another person exactly what we are.
JOYCE CARY (1888–1957)

7429 The natural view and the Bible view of man are different: the natural point of view is that man is a great being in the

making, his achievements are a wonderful promise of what he is going to be; the Bible point of view is that man is a magnificent ruin of what God designed him to be.
OSWALD CHAMBERS (1874–1917)

7430 The spirit in man is the candle of the Lord, lighted by God and lighting men to God.
BENJAMIN WHICHCOTE (1609–1683)

7431 The truth of a man is first and foremost what he hides.
ANDRÉ MALRAUX (1901–1976)

7432 The world is beautiful, but has a disease called man.
FRIEDRICH WILHELM NIETZSCHE (1844–1900)

7433 There is no indispensable man.
WOODROW WILSON (1856–1924)

7434 There is no man so good, who, were he to submit all his thoughts and actions to the laws, would not deserve hanging ten times in his life.
MICHEL EYQUEM DE MONTAIGNE (1533–1592)

7435 To find the point where hypothesis and fact meet; delicate equilibrium between dream and reality; the place where fantasy and earthy things are metamorphosed into a work of art; the hour when faith in the future becomes knowledge of the past;
   To lay down one's power for others in need;
   To shake off the old ordeal and get ready for the new;
   To question, knowing that never can the full answer be found;
   To accept uncertainties quietly, even our incomplete knowledge of God;
   This is what man's journey is about, I think.
LILLIAN SMITH (1897–1966)

7436 Vaguely at first, then more distinctly, I realized that man is an eternal stranger on this planet.
ERIC HOFFER (1902–1983)

7437 We are not made of iron, we are not like rocks, we are mortal men full of fragility.
JOHN CALVIN (1509–1564)

7438 We can never know who or what we are till we know at least something of what God is.
A. W. TOZER (1897–1963)

7439 What a chimera, then, is man! What a novelty! What a monster, what a chaos, what a contradiction, what a prodigy!
BLAISE PASCAL (1623–1662)

7440 What is man? A foolish baby,
Vainly strives, and fights, and frets.
Demanding all, deserving nothing,
One small grave is what he gets.
THOMAS CARLYLE (1795–1881)

7441 Whatever you may be sure of, be sure of this, that you are dreadfully like other people.
JAMES RUSSELL LOWELL (1819–1891)

7442 When faith is lost,
When honor dies,
The man is dead!
JOHN GREENLEAF WHITTIER (1807–1892)

7443 Whenever two people meet there are really six people present. There is each man as he sees himself, each man as the other person sees him, and each man as he really is.
WILLIAM JAMES (1842–1910)

7444 Why is it that, in spite of all the mirrors in the world, no one really knows what he looks like?
ARTHUR SCHOPENHAUER (1788–1860)

7445 Man is nothing but dust, and he is always throwing it in someone's eyes.

MAN AND GOD

7446 A man without God is not like a cake without raisins; he is like the cake without the flour and milk.
ARCHBISHOP FULTON J. SHEEN (1895–1979)

7447 A thousand voices clamor for our attention, and a thousand causes vie for our support. But until we have learned to be satisfied with fellowship with God, until he is our rock and our fortress, we will be restless with our place in the world.
ERWIN W. LUTZER (1941–)

7448 Ah! for a vision of God!
For a mighty grasp of the real,
Feet firm based on granite in place of
crumbling sand!
RODEN NOEL (1834–1894)

7449 Ancient of Days! Except thou deign
Upon the finished tasks to smile,
The workman's hand hath toiled in
vain,
To hew the rock and rear the pile.
WILLIAM CULLEN BRYANT (1794–1878)

7450 And what kind of habitation pleases
God? What must our natures be like
before he can feel at home within us?
He asks nothing but a pure heart and
a single mind. He asks no rich panel-
ing, no rugs from the Orient, no art
treasures from afar. He desires but sincerity, transparency, humility, and
love. He will see to the rest.
A. W. TOZER (1897–1963)

7451 As a choir of singers encircling the
leader may for a time have their attention drawn from him and so sing out
of tune, yet when they turn to him
they sing in perfect harmony; so do we
encircle God. But near as he is to us,
we often do not look toward him.
When we do turn to him, our utmost
wish is crowned, our souls have rest,
our song is no longer a discord but a
hymn divine.
PLOTINUS (205–270)

7452 At cool of day, with God I walk
My garden's grateful shade;
I hear his voice among the trees
And I am not afraid.

7453 Before us is a future all unknown, a
path untrod;
Beside us a friend well loved and
known—
That friend is God.

7454 Father! replenish with thy grace this
longing heart of mine;
Make it thy quiet dwelling place, thy
sacred inmost shrine!
ANGELUS SILESIUS (1624–1677)

7455 Finding God is really letting God find
us; for our search for him is simply
surrender to his search for us.
HARRY EMERSON FOSDICK (1878–1969)

7456 Fountain of good, all blessing flows
From thee; no want thy fullness knows;
What but thyself canst thou desire?
Yet, self-sufficient as thou art,
Thou dost desire my worthless heart;
This, only this, dost thou require.
JOHANN SCHEFFLER (1624–1677)

7457 Friendship with God means that there
is now something of the nature of God
in a man on which God can base his
friendship.
OSWALD CHAMBERS (1874–1917)

7458 Give me a pure heart—that I may see
thee;
A humble heart—that I may hear thee,
A heart of love—that I may serve thee,
A heart of faith—that I may abide in
thee.
DAG HAMMARSKJÖLD (1905–1961)

7459 God designed the human machine to
run on himself. He himself is the fuel
our spirits were designed to burn, or
the food our spirits were designed to
feed on. There is no other. That is why
it is just no good asking God to make
us happy in our own way.
C. S. LEWIS (1898–1963)

7460 God has no grandchildren; either you
know him firsthand or you do not
know him at all.

7461 God is always previous, God is always
there first, and if you have any desire
for God and for the things of God, it
is God himself who put it there.
A. W. TOZER (1897–1963)

7462 God is my being, my me, my strength,
my beatitude, my good, my delight.
CATHERINE OF GENOA (1447–1510)

7463 God is so vastly wonderful, so utterly
and completely delightful that he can,
without anything other than himself,
meet and overflow the deepest
demands of our total nature, mysterious and deep as that nature is.
A. W. TOZER (1897–1963)

7464 He that is false to God can never be
true to man.
BARON WILLIAM CECIL BURGHLEY
(1520–1598)

7465 He that is made in the image of God
must know him or be desolate.
GEORGE MACDONALD (1824–1905)

7466 He who knows about depth knows
about God.
PAUL JOHANNES OSKAR TILLICH
(1886–1965)

7467 He who offers to God a second place
offers him no place.
JOHN RUSKIN (1819–1900)

7468 How great a God we need; and how
much greater is our God than our
greatest need.

7469 I am a single drop; how can it be
That God, the whole ocean, floweth
into me?
ANGELUS SILESIUS (1624–1677)

7470 I am as rich as God; there's nothing
anywhere
That I with him (believe it!) do not
share.
ANGELUS SILESIUS (1624–1677)

7471 I am not concerned whether God is on
my side or not, but I am concerned
whether I am on God's side.
ABRAHAM LINCOLN (1809–1865)

7472 I began to draw near to the believers
among the poor, simple, and ignorant,
the pilgrims, monks, and peasants.
The more I contemplated the lives of
these simple folk, the more deeply was
I convinced of the reality of their faith,
which I perceived to be a necessity for
them, for it alone gave life a meaning
and made it worth living. The more I
learned of these men of faith, the more
I liked them and the easier I felt it so
to live. . . . Still I did not find him
whom I sought. . . . I realized that the
conception of God was not God himself. I felt that I had only truly lived
when I believed in God. God is life.
Live to seek God, and life will not be
without him. The light that then shone
never left me. . . . I came to know that
God is all we need.
LEO TOLSTOY (1828–1910)

7473 I came to love you late, O Beauty so
ancient and new; I came to love you
late. You were within me and I was
outside, where I rushed about wildly
searching for you like some monster
loose in your beautiful world. You
were with me, but I was not with you.
You called me, you shouted to me, you
wrapped me in your splendor, you sent
my blindness reeling. You gave out
such a delightful fragrance, and I drew
it in and came breathing hard after
you. I tasted and it made me hunger
and thirst; you touched me, and I
burned to know your peace.
SAINT AUGUSTINE OF HIPPO (354–430)

7474 I fear no foe with thee at hand to bless,
Ills have no weight, and tears no bitter-
ness.
HENRY FRANCIS LYTE (1793–1847)

7475 I soar and rise
Up to the skies,
Leaving the world their day,
And in my flight,
For the true light
Go searching all the way.
HENRY VAUGHAN (1622–1695)

7476 If God be my friend, I cannot be
wretched.
OVID (43 B.C.–A.D. 17)

7477 If God should give my soul all he ever
made or might make, apart from himself, and giving it, he stayed away even
by as much as a hairbreadth, my soul
would not be satisfied.
MEISTER ECKHART (C. 1260–C. 1327)

7478 If I forget,
Yet God remembers! If these hands of
mine
Cease from their clinging, yet the
hands divine
Hold me so firmly that I cannot fall;
And if sometimes I am too tired to call
For him to help me, then he reads the
prayer
Unspoken in my heart, and lifts my
care.
ROBERT BROWNING (1812–1889)

7479 If man is not made for God, why is he
happy only in God? If man is made for
God, why is he opposed to God?
BLAISE PASCAL (1623–1662)

7480 If there be good in what I wrought,
Thy hand compelled it, Master, thine—
Where I have failed to meet thy thought

I know, through thee, the blame was
   mine.
RUDYARD KIPLING (1865–1936)

7481 If we fail to emphasize that we can glorify God, we raise the whole question
of whether men are significant at all.
We begin to lose our humanity as soon
as we begin to lose the emphasis that
what we do makes a difference.
FRANCIS AUGUST SCHAEFFER (1912–1984)

7482 If you are never alone with God, it is
not because you are too busy; it is
because you don't care for him, don't
like him. And you had better face the
facts.
AL-GHAZZALI (1058–1111)

7483 If you are not governed by God, you
will be ruled by tyrants.
WILLIAM PENN (1644–1718)

7484 If you ask me how I believe in God,
how God creates himself in me and
reveals himself to me, my answer may
perhaps provoke your smiles or laughter and even scandalize you. I believe in
God as I believe in my friends because I
feel the breath of his affection, feel his
invisible and tangible hand drawing me,
leading me, grasping me.
MIGUEL DE UNAMUNO (1864–1936)

7485 Is there any greater need than that we
get to grips with the living God, that
we understand the discipline of God,
that we learn the truth of God, that
we accept the will of God, that we fulfill the purpose of God, that we know
the resources of God, that we realize
the power of God, and that we radiate
the peace and love of God?
TRAVERS V. JEFFERS

7486 It does not matter where he places me
or how. That is rather for him to consider than for me. For the easiest positions he must give grace; and in the
most difficult his grace is sufficient.
So, if God places me in great perplexity, must he not give me much guidance? In positions of great difficulty,
much grace? In circumstances of great
pressure and trial, much strength? As
to work, mine was never so plentiful,
so responsible, or so difficult; but the

weight and strain are all gone. His
resources are mine, for he is mine.
JAMES HUDSON TAYLOR (1832–1905)

7487 It is absurd to try and put God into a
definition; if I can define God, I am
greater than God.
OSWALD CHAMBERS (1874–1917)

7488 It is an overwhelming experience to
fall into the hands of the living God,
to be invaded to the depths of one's
being by his presence, to be without
warning wholly uprooted from all
earth-born securities and assurances,
and to be blown by a tempest of unbelievable power which leaves one's old
proud self utterly, utterly defenseless.
THOMAS R. KELLY (1893–1941)

7489 It is astonishing that I—dust, ash, and
   mud—
May on familiar terms be with the
   highest God.
ANGELUS SILESIUS (1624–1677)

7490 It is only when man wishes the impossible that he remembers God. To
obtain that which is possible he turns
to fellowmen.
LEV SHESTOV (1866–1938)

7491 It is quite natural and inevitable that,
if we spend sixteen hours daily of our
waking lives in thinking about the
affairs of the world and five minutes
in thinking about God and our souls,
this world will seem two hundred
times more real to us than God.
WILLIAM RALPH INGE (1860–1954)

7492 Lord, thou mighty River, all-knowing,
   all-seeing,
And I like a little fish in thy great
   waters,
How shall I sound thy depths?
How shall I reach thy shores?
NANAK (1469–1539)

7493 Man cannot break the laws of God, he
can only break himself against them.
G. K. CHESTERTON (1874–1936)

7494 Man does not know himself truly
except as he knows himself confronted
by God. Only in that confrontation
does he become aware of his full stature and freedom and of the evil in him.
REINHOLD NIEBUHR (1892–1971)

7495 Man does what he can, and God what
he will.
JOHN RAY (1627–1705)

7496 Man has been created a God addict.
KARL STERN

7497 Man is the greatest marvel in the universe—not because his heart beats 40
million times a year, driving the blood-
stream a distance of over 60,000 miles;
not because of the wonderful mechanism of eye and ear; not because of his
conquest over disease and the lengthen-
ing of human life; but because man
alone has the capacity to walk and
talk with God.

7498 Man rides and God holds the reins.
YIDDISH PROVERB

7499 Man, whether he likes it or not, is a
being forced by his nature to seek
some higher authority.
JOSÉ ORTEGA Y GASSET (1883–1955)

7500 Many of us are not thirsty for God
because we have quenched our thirst
at other fountains!
ERWIN W. LUTZER (1941–   )

7501 Men look for better methods, but God
looks for better men.
ERWIN W. LUTZER (1941–   )

7502 Misplaced zeal is zeal for God rather
than zeal of God.
WILLIAM LEROY PETTINGILL (1866–1950)

7503 My times are in thy hand,
My God, I wish them there;
My life, my friends, my soul I leave
Entirely to thy care.
WILLIAM FREEMAN LLOYD (1627–1717)

7504 Naught but God can satisfy the soul.
PHILIP JAMES BAILEY (1816–1902)

7505 No church or priest can stand between
God and man.
MARTIN LUTHER (1483–1546)

7506 No distant Lord have I,
Loving afar to be;
Made flesh for me, he cannot rest
Until he rests in me.
Brother in joy and pain,
Bone of my bone was he,
Now—intimacy closer still,
He dwells himself in me.
MALTBIE D. BABCOCK (1858–1901)

7507 O for a closer walk with God,
A calm and heavenly frame,
A light to shine upon the road
That leads me to the Lamb!
WILLIAM COWPER (1731–1800)

7508 O greedy men, what will satisfy you if
God himself will not?
BLAISE PASCAL (1623–1662)

7509 Once we come into simple relationship
with God, he can put us where he
pleases, and we are not even conscious
of where he puts us. All we are conscious of is an amazing simplicity of
life that seems to be a haphazard life
externally.
OSWALD CHAMBERS (1874–1917)

7510 One on God's side is a majority.
WENDELL PHILLIPS (1811–1884)

7511 Our humanity were a poor thing were
it not for the divinity that stirs within
us.
FRANCIS BACON (1561–1626)

7512 Our nature hungers for God even
when it broke with him long ago, perhaps the more intensely the longer ago
it was. It experiences a sort of famine.
But the devil rides it and spurs it on,
to distract it from its own need. He
changes its hunger into haste. That is
why people today are in such a hurry.
Their speed is to distract their hunger.
LOUIS EVELY (1910–   )

7513 Our pursuit of God is successful just
because he is forever seeking to manifest himself to us.
A. W. TOZER (1897–1963)

7514 Reach up as far as you can, and God
will reach down all the way.
JOHN HEYL VINCENT (1832–1920)

7515 Relying on God has to begin all over
again every day as if nothing had yet
been done.
C. S. LEWIS (1898–1963)

7516 So it is that men sigh on, not knowing
what the soul wants, but only that it
needs something. Our yearnings are
homesickness for heaven. Our sighings
are sighings for God just as children
that cry themselves to sleep away from
home and sob in their slumber, not

knowing that they sob for their parents. The soul's inarticulate moanings are the affections, yearning for the Infinite, and having no one to tell them what it is that ails them.
HENRY WARD BEECHER (1813–1887)

7517 So many are busy "using" God. Use God to get a job. Use God to give us safety. Use God to give us peace of mind. Use God to obtain success in business. Use God to provide heaven at last.
A. W. TOZER (1897–1963)

7518 Some people talk about finding God— as if he could get lost.

7519 Spare not the stroke! Do with us as thou wilt!
Let there be naught unfinished, broken, marred;
Complete thy purpose, that we may become
Thy perfect image, O our God and Lord!
HORATIUS BONAR (1808–1889)

7520 That's best which God sends.
'Twas his will: it is mine.
OWEN MEREDITH (1831–1891)

7521 The center of me is always and eternally a terrible pain—a curious wild pain—a searching for something beyond what the world contains, something transfigured and infinite—the beatific vision—God—I do not find it, I do not think it is to be found—but the love of it is my life—it's like passionate love for a ghost.
BERTRAND ARTHUR WILLIAM RUSSELL (1872–1970)

7522 The closer one gets to the light, the more the imperfections show.

7523 The man who has lost contact with God lives on the same dead-end street as the man who denies him.
MILTON A. MARCY

7524 The more complete our sense of need, the more satisfactory is our dependence on God.
OSWALD CHAMBERS (1874–1917)

7525 The most important thought I ever had was that of my individual responsibility to God.
DANIEL WEBSTER (1782–1852)

7526 The people who related to God best— Abraham, Moses, David, Isaiah, Jeremiah—treated him with startling familiarity. They talked to God as if he were sitting in a chair beside them, as one might talk to a counselor, a boss, a parent, or a lover. They treated him like a person.
PHILIP YANCEY (1949–)

7527 The soul alone, like a neglected harp,
Grows out of tune and needs a hand divine.
Dwell thou within it, tune and touch the chords
Till every note and string shall answer thine.
HARRIET BEECHER STOWE (1811–1896)

7528 The soul is a never ending sigh after God.
THEODORE CHRISTLIEB (1833–1889)

7529 The tendency of the world is down— God's path is up.
DWIGHT LYMAN MOODY (1837–1899)

7530 The world is not a prison house but a kind of spiritual kindergarten where millions of bewildered infants are trying to spell God with the wrong blocks.
EDWIN ARLINGTON ROBINSON (1869–1935)

7531 The yearning to know what cannot be known, to comprehend the incomprehensible, to touch and taste the unapproachable, arises from the image of God in the nature of man.
A. W. TOZER (1897–1963)

7532 There are many avenues of attractiveness to God. Some are drawn to him through his beauty, others to his peace, and still others are attracted by his power.
JOHN POWELL

7533 There are two reasons for loving God: no one is more worthy of our love, and no one can return more in response to our love.
BERNARD OF CLAIRVAUX (1090–1153)

7534 There is a God within us, and we glow
when he stirs us.
OVID (43 B.C.–A.D. 17)

7535 There is a native, elemental homing
instinct in our souls that turns us to
God as naturally as the flower turns to
the sun.
RUFUS MATTHEW JONES (1863–1948)

7536 There is no thought, feeling, yearning,
or desire, however low, trifling, or vulgar we may deem it, which, if it affects
our real interest or happiness, we may
not lay before God and be sure of his
sympathy. His nature is such that our
often coming does not tire him. The
whole burden of the whole life of
every man may be rolled onto God
and not weary him, though it has wearied the man.
HENRY WARD BEECHER (1813–1887)

7537 They never sought in vain that sought
the Lord aright.
ROBERT BURNS (1759–1796)

7538 Thirst must be quenched! If our
desires are not met by God, we will
quickly find something else to alleviate
our thirst.
ERWIN W. LUTZER (1941–)

7539 Thou art the God of the early mornings, the God of the late-at-nights, the
God of the mountain peaks, the God
of the sea; but, my God, my soul has
further horizons than the early mornings, deeper darkness than the nights
of earth, higher peaks than any mountain, greater depths than any sea can
know. My God, thou art the God of
these, be my God!
OSWALD CHAMBERS (1874–1917)

7540 To be brought within the zone of
God's voice is to be profoundly altered.
OSWALD CHAMBERS (1874–1917)

7541 To be with God, there is no need to be
in church. We may make an oratory of
our heart wherein to retire from time
to time to converse with him in meekness, humility, and love. Everyone is
capable of such familiar conversation
with God, some more, some less.
BROTHER LAWRENCE OF THE RESURRECTION
(C. 1605–1691)

7542 To fall in love with God is the greatest
of all romances! To seek him is the
greatest of all adventures! To find him
is the greatest human achievement.
RAPHAEL SIMON

7543 To get at the core of God at his greatest, one must first get into the core of
himself at the least, for no one can
know God who has not first known
himself. Go to the depths of the soul,
the secret place of the Most High, to
the roots, to the heights; for all that
God can do is focused there.
MEISTER ECKHART (C. 1260–C. 1327)

7544 To have found God is not an end in
itself but a beginning.
FRANZ ROSENZWEIG (1886–1929)

7545 To have God for our mother and
father and guardian, shall this not
deliver us from griefs and fears?
EPICTETUS (C. 55–C. 135)

7546 To know God is at once the easiest
and the most difficult thing in the
world.
A. W. TOZER (1897–1963)

7547 To see God is the highest aspiration of
man and has preoccupied the rarest
human spirits at all times. Seeing God
means understanding, seeing into the
mystery of things.
MALCOLM MUGGERIDGE (1903–1990)

7548 True understanding of God comes
only after the heart has ceased to
reach to human beings as a source of
life and help. As you recognize Me as
your source, you immediately become
a channel and dispenser of life, and
need look to no other.
FRANCES J. ROBERTS

7549 Two men please God—who serves him
with all his heart because he knows
him; who seeks him with all his heart
because he knows him not.
NIKITA IVANOVICH PANIN (1718–1783)

7550 We are all strings in the concert of
God's joy; the spirit from his mouth
strikes the note and tune of our strings.
JAKOB BÖHME (1575–1624)

7551 We are called to an everlasting preoccupation with God.
A. W. TOZER (1897–1963)

7552 We are not our own, anymore than what we possess is our own. We did not make ourselves; we cannot be supreme over ourselves. We cannot be our own masters. We are God's property by creation, by redemption, by regeneration.
CARDINAL JOHN HENRY NEWMAN (1801–1890)

7553 We are the fuel, the fire is the love of God; we are the channel, the tide is his perpetual flow of grace.
RICHARDSON WRIGHT (1885–)

7554 We are the wire, God is the current. Our only power is to let the current pass through us.
CARLO CARRETTO (1910–)

7555 We are, because God is.
EMANUEL SWEDENBORG (1688–1772)

7556 We dare not think that God is absent or daydreaming. The do-nothing God. He's not tucked away in some far corner of the universe, uncaring, unfeeling, unthinking . . . uninvolved. Count on it—God intrudes in glorious and myriad ways.
JONI EARECKSON TADA

7557 We have not to do with a God who is off there above the sky, who can deal with us only through the violation of physical law. We have instead a God in whom we live and move and are, whose being opens into ours and ours into his, who is the very life of our lives, the matrix of our personality; and there is no separation between us unless we make it ourselves.
RUFUS MATTHEW JONES (1863–1948)

7558 We never better enjoy ourselves than when we most enjoy God.
BENJAMIN WHICHCOTE (1609–1683)

7559 We play the game; God keeps the score.
ERWIN W. LUTZER (1941–)

7560 We please God most, not by frantically trying to make ourselves good, but by throwing ourselves into his arms with all our imperfections, and believing that he understands everything and loves us still.

7561 We say that there are millions of people who never think of God, but we don't know; we can never really know. It appears like that, but we can never tell. One gets some very strange surprises. I firmly believe that there is a divine light in every human being ever born or to be born.
MALCOLM MUGGERIDGE (1903–1990)

7562 We should find God in what we do know, not in what we don't; not in problems still outstanding, but in those we have already solved . . . God cannot be used as a stopgap.
DIETRICH BONHOEFFER (1906–1945)

7563 What comes into our minds when we think about God is the most important thing about us.
A. W. TOZER (1897–1963)

7564 What God in his sovereignty may yet do on a world scale I do not claim to know: but what he will do for the plain man or woman who seeks his face I believe I do know and can tell others. Let any man turn to God in earnest, let him begin to exercise himself unto godliness, let him seek to develop his powers of spiritual receptivity by trust and obedience and humility, and the results will exceed anything he may have hoped in his leaner and weaker days.
A. W. TOZER (1897–1963)

7565 What I want is not more certainty about you . . . but to be more certain in you.
SAINT AUGUSTINE OF HIPPO (354–430)

7566 What in me is dark
Illumine, what is low raise and support;
That to the height of this great argument
I may assert eternal Providence,
And justify the ways of God to men.
JOHN MILTON (1608–1674)

7567 What is our reason for saying in sorrow that God does not heed us, when we ourselves do not heed him? What

is our reason for muttering that God
does not look down toward earth,
when we ourselves do not look up
toward heaven?
SALVIANUS (FIFTH CENTURY)

7568 What reward therefore shall I give the
Lord for all the benefits that he has
done to me? By his first work he gave
me to myself; and by the next he gave
himself to me. And when he gave himself, he gave me back myself that I had
lost.
BERNARD OF CLAIRVAUX (1090–1153)

7569 When I am with God
My fear is gone
In the great quiet of God.
My troubles are as the pebbles on the
road,
My joys are like the everlasting hills.
WALTER RAUSCHENBUSCH (1861–1918)

7570 When we have exhausted our store of
endurance,
When our strength has failed ere the
day is half done,
When we reach the end of our
hoarded resources,
Our Father's full giving is only begun.
His love has no limit, his grace has no
measure,
His power no boundary known unto
men;
For out of his infinite riches in Jesus
He giveth, and giveth, and giveth
again.
ANNIE JOHNSON FLINT (1862–1932)

7571 When we take to ourselves the place
that is God's, the whole course of our
lives is out of joint.
A. W. TOZER (1897–1963)

7572 Who fathoms the eternal thought?
Who talks of scheme and plan?
The Lord is God! He needeth not
The poor device of man.
JOHN GREENLEAF WHITTIER (1807–1892)

7573 Whosoever walks toward God one
cubit, God runs toward him twain.
JEWISH PROVERB

7574 Why and how is God to be loved?
God himself is the reason why; with-
out limit is how.
BERNARD OF CLAIRVAUX (1090–1153)

7575 Wide is our mouth and
our hands reach always
upward
Need is our name
Giving
is Yours.
LUCI SHAW (1928–   )

7576 Without God we cannot; without us
he will not.
SAINT AUGUSTINE OF HIPPO (354–430)

7577 Yet, self-sufficient as thou art,
Thou dost desire my worthless heart;
This, only this, dost thou require.
JOHANN SCHEFFLER (1624–1677)

7578 You awake us to delight in your
praise; for you have made us for yourself, and our heart is restless until it
rests in you.
SAINT AUGUSTINE OF HIPPO (354–430)

7579 You called me, Lord, you called, you
shouted, you terrified me, you compelled my deaf ears to hear you, you
struck me down, beat me, overpowered my hard heart, you sweetened
and softened and dispelled my bitterness.
AELRED GRAHAM (1909–   )

7580 Your God is too small.
J. B. PHILLIPS (1906–1982)

MANIPULATION

7581 A fortune-teller always foretells a
bright future for others in order to
make a brighter future for herself.

7582 Beware of a manipulator: he shakes
your hand one minute and pulls your
leg the next.

7583 Beware the opportunist: he has no use
for people he cannot use.

7584 I would have praised you more had
you praised me less.
LOUIS XIV (1638–1715)

7585 Man is the only animal that can
remain on friendly terms with the victims he intends to eat until he eats
them.
SAMUEL BUTLER (1612–1680)

7586 Many men know how to flatter, few men know how to praise.
WENDELL PHILLIPS (1811–1884)

7587 The worst tumble of all is when you fall over your own bluff.

MARRIAGE

7588 A bridegroom is a man who spends a lot of money on a new suit that nobody notices.

7589 A deaf husband and a blind wife are always a happy couple.
FRENCH PROVERB

7590 A good husband makes a good wife.

7591 A good marriage is not one where perfection reigns: it is a relationship where a healthy perspective overlooks a multitude of "unresolvables."
JAMES C. DOBSON (1936–)

7592 A good wife makes a good husband.

7593 A happy marriage is the union of two good forgivers.
ROBERT QUILLEN (1887–1948)

7594 A man too good for the world is no good for his wife.
JEWISH PROVERB

7595 A marriage is like a long trip in a tiny rowboat: if one passenger starts to rock the boat, the other has to steady it; otherwise they will go to the bottom together.
DAVID ROBERT REUBEN (1933–)

7596 A successful marriage demands a divorce; a divorce from your own self-love.
PAUL FROST (1938–)

7597 A successful marriage is an edifice that must be rebuilt every day.
ANDRÉ MAUROIS (1885–1967)

7598 A successful marriage is not a gift; it is an achievement.
ANN LANDERS (1918–)

7599 A wife is not a guitar; you can't play on her and then hang her on the wall.
RUSSIAN PROVERB

7600 An ideal wife is any woman who has an ideal husband.

7601 And they lived happily ever after is one of the most tragic sentences in literature. It is tragic because it tells a falsehood about life and has led countless generations of people to expect something from human existence that is not possible on this fragile, failing, imperfect earth.
JOSHUA LOTH LIEBMAN (1907–1948)

7602 As you would have a daughter, so choose a wife.
ITALIAN PROVERB

7603 Be to her virtues very kind;
Be to her faults a little blind.
MATTHEW PRIOR (1664–1721)

7604 Better be half hang'd, than ill wed.

7605 Better to break the engagement than the marriage.

7606 By all means, marry. If you get a good wife, you will become very happy. If you get a bad one, you will become a philosopher.
SOCRATES (470–399 B.C.)

7607 Centenarians seldom marry, probably because they are old enough to know better.

7608 Chains do not hold a marriage together. It is threads, hundreds of tiny threads that sew people together through the years.
SIMONE SIGNORET (1921–1985)

7609 Choose neither a wife nor linen by candlelight.
SPANISH PROVERB

7610 Choose your wife by ear rather than by eye.

7611 Dogs are quick to show their affection. They never pout, they never bear a grudge. They never run away from home when mistreated. They never complain about their food. They never gripe about the way the house is kept. They are chivalrous and courageous, ready to protect their mistress at the risk of their lives. They love children, and no matter how noisy and boisterous they are, the dog loves every minute of it. In fact, a dog is still competition for a husband. Perhaps if we husbands imitated a few of our

dog's virtues, life with our family might be more amiable.
BILLY GRAHAM (1918–)

7612 Don't marry for money; you can borrow it cheaper.
SCOTTISH PROVERB

7613 Even if marriages are made in heaven, man has to be responsible for the maintenance.

7614 Extreme independence is as destructive to a relationship as total dependence.
JAMES C. DOBSON (1936–)

7615 Getting married is easy. Staying married is more difficult. Staying happily married for a lifetime should rank among the fine arts.
ROBERTA FLACK

7616 He who does not honor his wife dishonors himself.
SPANISH PROVERB

7617 Husbands and wives should constantly guard against overcommitment. Even worthwhile and enjoyable activities become damaging when they consume the last ounce of energy or the remaining free moments in the day.
JAMES C. DOBSON (1936–)

7618 Husbands are in heaven whose wives chide not.

7619 I'd trade my fortune for just one happy marriage.
J. PAUL GETTY (1892–1976)

7620 If your wife is small, stoop down and whisper in her ear.
JEWISH PROVERB

7621 It is as absurd to say that a man can't love one woman all the time as it is to say that a violinist needs several violins to play the same piece of music.
HONORÉ DE BALZAC (1799–1850)

7622 It is not marriage that fails, it is people that fail.
HARRY EMERSON FOSDICK (1878–1969)

7623 It takes two to make a marriage a success and only one to make it a failure.
HERBERT SAMUEL

7624 Keep your eyes wide open before marriage, half shut afterwards.

7625 Knit your hearts with an unslipping knot.
WILLIAM SHAKESPEARE (1564–1616)

7626 Knowing when to say nothing is 50 percent of tact and 90 percent of marriage.
SYDNEY J. HARRIS (1917–1986)

7627 Let the wife make her husband glad to come home and let him make her sorry to see him leave.
MARTIN LUTHER (1483–1546)

7628 Life is full of troubles and most of them are man-maid.

7629 Love is blind, but marriage restores its sight.
GEORG CHRISTOPH LICHTENBERG (1742—1799)

7630 Love is not a state, it is a movement. Personal contact is not a state, but a fleeting movement that must be ceaselessly rediscovered. Marriage is not a state, but a movement—a boundless adventure.
PAUL TOURNIER (1898–1986)

7631 Love is one long sweet dream, and marriage is the alarm clock.

7632 Marriage cannot make anyone happier who does not bring the ingredients for happiness into it.
SYDNEY J. HARRIS (1917–1986)

7633 Marriage does not make us better, any more than it makes us worse; it merely intensifies what is already there, for good and for bad.
SYDNEY J. HARRIS (1917–1986)

7634 Marriage halves our griefs, doubles our joys, and quadruples our expenses.

7635 Marriage has in it less of beauty, but more of safety, than the single life; it has more care, but less danger; it is more merry, and more sad; it is fuller of sorrows, and fuller of joys; it lies under more burdens, but it is supported by all the strengths of love, and charity, and those burdens are delightful.
JEREMY TAYLOR (1613–1667)

7636 Marriage is a desperate thing.
JOHN SELDEN (1584–1654)

7637 Marriage is a perpetual test of character.

7638 Marriage is adventure, not an achievement.
DAVID A. SEAMANDS

7639 Marriage is heaven or hell.
GERMAN PROVERB

7640 Marriage is like a cage; one sees the birds outside desperate to get in, and those inside equally desperate to get out.
MICHEL EYQUEM DE MONTAIGNE (1533–1592)

7641 Marriage is not for a moment; it is for a lifetime. It requires long and serious preparation. It is not to be leaped into, but entered with solemn steps of deliberation. For one of the most intimate and difficult of human relationships is that of marriage.

Infinitely rewarding at its best, unspeakably oppressive at its worst, marriage offers the uttermost extremes of human happiness and human bondage—with all the lesser degrees of felicity and restraint in-between.
GINA CERMINARA

7642 Marriage is that relation between man and woman in which the independence is equal, the dependence mutual, and the obligation reciprocal.
LOUIS K. ANSPACHER

7643 Marriage may be an institution, but it is not a reform school.

7644 Marriage resembles a pair of shears, so joined that they cannot be separated; often moving in opposite directions, yet always punishing any one who comes between them.
SYDNEY SMITH (1771–1845)

7645 Marriage with peace is this world's paradise; with strife, this life's purgatory.

7646 Married life is a marathon. . . . It is not enough to make a great start toward long-term marriage. You will need the determination to keep plugging. . . . Only then will you make it to the end.
JAMES C. DOBSON (1936–)

7647 Married life offers no panacea—if it is going to reach its potential, it will require an all-out investment by both husband and wife.
JAMES C. DOBSON (1936–)

7648 More and more young people are . . . too impatient to make the adjustments that marriage inevitably entails. They cannot wait to learn the tolerance that marriage always demands. They don't have the time to achieve the understanding that never comes quickly. They have not been taught that while love may come suddenly, happiness is a distant goal to which there is no shortcut.
SIDNEY GREENBERG

7649 My wife is an angel.
You are lucky, my wife is still living.

7650 Pray one hour before going to war,
Two hours before going to sea,
Three hours before getting married.

7651 She is but half a wife who is not a friend.
WILLIAM PENN (1644–1718)

7652 Success in marriage is more than finding the right person: it is being the right person.
ROBERT BROWNING (1812–1889)

7653 Successful marriage is always a triangle: a man, a woman, and God.
CECIL MYERS

7654 The Christian is supposed to love his neighbor, and since his wife is his nearest neighbor, she should be his deepest love.
MARTIN LUTHER (1483–1546)

7655 The man who is forever criticizing his wife's judgment never seems to question her choice of a husband.

7656 The man who would rather play golf than eat should marry the woman who would rather shop than cook.

7657 There is no perfect marriage for there are no perfect people.
FRENCH PROVERB

7658 There's no marrying in heaven; that's why it's heaven.

7659 Think of all the squabbles Adam and
Eve must have had in the course of
their nine hundred years. Eve would
say, "You ate the apple," and Adam
would retort, "You gave it to me."
MARTIN LUTHER (1483–1546)

7660 Those who marry mostly to escape an
unhappy home soon find that they
have just added one more to the total
number.
SYDNEY J. HARRIS (1917–1986)

7661 To marry a woman for her beauty is
like buying a house for its paint.

7662 Try praising your wife even if it does
frighten her at first.
BILLY SUNDAY (1862–1935)

7663 Variability is one of the virtues of a
woman. It obviates the crude requirements of polygamy. If you have one
good wife you are sure to have a spiritual harem.
G. K. CHESTERTON (1874–1936)

7664 When a marriage works, nothing on
earth can take its place.
HELEN GAHAGAN DOUGLAS

7665 When I was a young man, I vowed
never to marry until I found the ideal
woman. Well, I found her—but, alas,
she was waiting for the ideal man.
ROBERT SCHUMANN (1810–1856)

7666 When marriage becomes a solution for
loneliness . . . it rarely satisfies.
STEVE GOODIER

7667 When will there be an end of marrying? I suppose, when there is an end of
living.
TERTULLIAN (C. 160–AFTER 220)

7668 Where there's marriage without love,
there will be love without marriage.
BENJAMIN FRANKLIN (1706–1790)

7669 Who of us is mature enough for offspring before the offspring themselves
arrive? The value of marriage is not
that adults produce children but that
children produce adults.
PETER DE VRIES (C. 1910–   )

7670 You see roses; he sees thorns. You see
God vacuuming the sky; he sees God
dumping the vacuum bag. You're planning the next party, and he's worrying
about all the trash the party will
make; in fact, he worries about all the
trash in the whole world, plus the
shortage of water, the national debt,
and any number of other serious matters.
BARBARA JOHNSON

7671 You'll never see perfection in your
mate, nor will he or she find it in you.
JAMES C. DOBSON (1936–   )

MARTYRDOM

7672 And martyrs, when the joyful crown is
given,
Forget the pain by which they pur-
chased heaven.
—To King James II
GEORGE STEPNEY (1663–1707)

7673 Every step of progress the world has
made has been from scaffold to scaffold, and from stake to stake.
WENDELL PHILLIPS (1811–1884)

7674 If I had ten thousand lives, I could
freely and cheerfully lay down them
all to witness in this matter. By God I
have leaped over a wall; by God I have
run through a troup, and by God I
will get through this death, and he will
make it easy for me.
—From the scaffold
THOMAS HARRISON

7675 It is the cause, and not the death, that
makes the martyr.
NAPOLEON BONAPARTE (1769–1821)

7676 Martyrdom does not end something. It
is only the beginning.
INDIRA GANDHI (1917–   )

7677 Rather let my head stoop to the block
Than these knees bow to any, save to
the God of heaven.
WILLIAM SHAKESPEARE (1564–1616)

7678 The more you mow us down, the
more quickly we grow; the blood of
Christians is fresh seed.
TERTULLIAN (C. 160–AFTER 220)

7679 The tyrant dies and his rule ends, the
martyr dies and his rule begins.
SØREN AABYE KIERKEGAARD (1813–1855)

7680 They never fail who die in a great
cause.
LORD GEORGE NOEL GORDON BYRON
(1788–1824)

7681 To die for a religion is easier than to
live it absolutely.
JORGE LUIS BORGES (1899–1986)

MATURITY

7682 'Tis a mark of great perfection to bear
with the imperfections of others.
ITALIAN PROVERB

7683 A weak person is injured by prosperity; a finer person by adversity; but the
finest by neither.
PAUL FROST (1938–)

7684 God gives you and me the lumber of
our lives, and offers to help us build
from it a cathedral of love and praise.
JOHN POWELL

7685 God never destroys the work of his
own hands, he removes what would
pervert it, that is all. Maturity is the
stage where the whole life has been
brought under the control of God.
OSWALD CHAMBERS (1874–1917)

7686 God offers a tough love that turns us
into sweeter and stronger persons.
ROBERT HAROLD SCHULLER (1926–)

7687 Has any man ever attained to inner
harmony by pondering the experience
of others? Not since the world began!
He must pass through the fire.
NORMAN DOUGLAS (1868–1952)

7688 If only I may grow
firmer,
simpler,
quieter,
warmer.
DAG HAMMARSKJÖLD (1905–1961)

7689 If you are born of God; then in you
God will green;
His godhead is your sap; your beauty
is in him.
ANGELUS SILESIUS (1624–1677)

7690 In the early stages of our Christian
experience we are inclined to hunt in
an overplus of delight for the commandments of our Lord in order to
obey them out of our love for him, but
when that conscious obedience is
assimilated and we begin to mature in
our life with God, we obey his commandments unconsciously, until in the
maturest stage of all we are simply
children of God through whom God
does his will, for the most part unconsciously to us.
OSWALD CHAMBERS (1874–1917)

7691 It's what you learn after you know it
all that counts.

7692 Life is very simple: it merely consists
in learning how to accept the impossible, how to do without the indispensable, how to endure the insupportable.
KATHLEEN NORRIS (B. 1880)

7693 Maturity begins to grow when you
can sense your concern for others outweighing your concern for yourself.
JOHN MACNAUGHTON

7694 Maturity is the ability to be comfortable with people who are not like us.
VIRGIL A. KRAFT

7695 Maturity: among other things—not to
hide one's strength out of fear and,
consequently, live below one's best.
DAG HAMMARSKJÖLD (1905–1961)

7696 Maturity: releasing a dream; allowing
a child space to grow up; letting a
friend have the freedom to be and to
do.
CHARLES R. SWINDOLL (1934–)

7697 One of the marks of spiritual maturity
is the quiet confidence that God is in
control . . . without the need to understand why he does what he does.
CHARLES R. SWINDOLL (1934–)

7698 Receive every inward and outward
trouble, every disappointment, pain,
uneasiness, temptation, darkness, and
desolation, with both thy hands, as a
true opportunity and blessed occasion
of dying to self, and entering into a
fuller fellowship with thy self-denying,
suffering Savior. Look at no inward or
outward trouble in any other view;
reject every other thought about it,
and then every kind of trial and distress will become the blessed day of
thy prosperity. That state is best,

which exerciseth the highest faith in and fullest resignation to God.
WILLIAM LAW (1686–1761)

7699 The flowering of the person is not a state at which we arrive, it is the movement that results from perpetual incompleteness.
PAUL TOURNIER (1898–1986)

7700 The mature believer is a searching believer.
JOHN POWELL

7701 The soul's dark cottage, batter'd and decay'd,
Lets in new light through chinks that Time hath made
Stronger by weakness; wiser men become
As they draw near to their eternal home.
EDMUND WALLER (1606–1687)

7702 The spheres God brings us into are not meant to teach us something but to make us something.
OSWALD CHAMBERS (1874–1917)

7703 The stronger and deeper the roots, the less visible they are.
CHARLES R. SWINDOLL (1934–)

7704 There are no shortcuts to spiritual maturity. It takes time to be holy.
ERWIN W. LUTZER (1941–)

7705 There is no formula to teach us how to arrive at maturity, and there is no grammar for the language of the inner life.
DAG HAMMARSKJÖLD (1905–1961)

7706 Why stay we on earth except to grow?
ROBERT BROWNING (1812–1889)

MEDITATION

7707 Every Christian can elevate himself by meditation . . . silence in the presence of God, in which the soul without being inactive acts no longer except by divine impulse.
MADAME JEANNE MARIE DE LA MOTHE GUYON (1648–1717)

7708 Flee for a little while thy occupations; hide thyself for a time from thy disturbing thoughts. Cast aside now thy burdensome cares, and put away thy toilsome business. Yield room for some little time to God, and rest for a little time in him. Enter the inner chamber of thy mind; shut out all thoughts save that of God and such as can aid thee in seeking him. Speak now, my whole heart! Speak now to God, saying, "I seek thy face; thy face, Lord, will I seek."
SAINT ANSELM (C. 1033–1109)

7709 God discovers himself to babes and hides himself in thick darkness from the wise and the prudent. We must simplify our approach to him. We must strip down to essentials (and they will be found to be blessedly few). We must put away all effort to impress and come with the guileless candor of childhood. If we do this, without doubt God will quickly respond.
A. W. TOZER (1897–1963)

7710 Half an hour's listening is essential except when you are very busy. Then a full hour is needed.
SAINT FRANCIS OF SALES (1567–1622)

7711 I cannot be the man I should be without times of quietness. Stillness is an essential part of growing deeper.
CHARLES R. SWINDOLL (1934–)

7712 I neglect God and his angels for the noise of a fly, for the rattling of the coach, for the whining of a door.
JOHN DONNE (1572–1631)

7713 If we bring our minds back again and again to God, we shall be gradually giving the central place to God, not only in our inner selves, but in our practical everyday lives.
PAUL TOURNIER (1898–1986)

7714 If we really want some things to count, if we genuinely desire some depth to emerge, some impact to be made, some profound and enduring investment to cast a comforting shadow across another's life, it is essential that we slow down . . . at times, stop completely. And think. Now . . . not later.
CHARLES R. SWINDOLL (1934–)

7715 If, like the lake that has the boon
Of cradling the little moon
Above the hill,
I want the Infinite to be
Reflected undisturbed in me,
I must be still.
EDNA BECKER

7716 It is easier to walk six miles to hear a
sermon than to spend one quarter of
an hour in meditating on it when I
come home.
PHILIP HENRY (1631–1696)

7717 Meditation is the soul's chewing.
WILLIAM GRIMSHAW (1708–1763)

7718 Only in quiet waters things mirror
themselves undistorted. Only in a
quiet mind is adequate perception of
the world.
HANS MARGOLIUS

7719 Our pursuit of God is successful just
because he is forever seeking to manifest himself to us.
A. W. TOZER (1897–1963)

7720 The holiest of all holidays are those
kept by ourselves in silence and apart:
the secret anniversaries of the heart.
HENRY WADSWORTH LONGFELLOW
(1807–1882)

7721 The lost art of the twentieth century is
meditation. Meditation is disciplined
thought, focused on a single object or
Scripture for a period of time.
CHARLES R. SWINDOLL (1934–)

7722 There is such a thing as a sacred idleness.
GEORGE MACDONALD (1824–1905)

7723 Think often on God, by day, by night,
in your business, and even in your
diversions. He is always near you and
with you; leave him not alone. You
would think it rude to leave a friend
alone who came to visit you; why,
then, must God be neglected?
BROTHER LAWRENCE OF THE
RESURRECTION (C. 1605–1691)

7724 Waiting upon God is not idleness, but
work which beats all other work to
one unskilled in it.
BERNARD OF CLAIRVAUX (1090–1153)

7725 What we do with our lives outwardly,
how well we care for others, is as
much a part of meditation as what we
do in the quietness and turning
inward. In fact, Christian meditation
that does not make a difference in the
quality of one's outer life is short-
circuited. It may flare for a while, but
unless it results in finding richer and
more loving relationships with other
human beings or in changing conditions in the world that cause human
suffering, the chances are that an individual's prayer activity will fizzle out.
MORTON T. KELSEY

7726 Words are but the shell;
Meditation is the kernel.
BAHYA IBN PAQUDA (1050–1120)

MEEKNESS

7727 Learn the blessedness of the
unoffended in the face of the unexplainable.
AMY CARMICHAEL (1867–1951)

7728 Meek endurance and meek obedience,
the accepting of his dealings, of whatever complexion they are and however they may tear and desolate our
hearts, without murmuring, without
sulking, without rebellion or resistance, is the deepest conception of the
meekness that Christ pronounced
blessed.
ALEXANDER MACLAREN (1826–1910)

7729 Meek—what does it mean? The
answer lies in the word itself:
M—Mighty,
E—Emotionally stable,
E—Educable,
K— Kind.
ROBERT HAROLD SCHULLER (1926–)

7730 Meekness is not weakness.
SIR WILLIAM GURNEY BENHAM
(1859–1944)

MEMORY

7731 Each man's memory is his private literature.
ALDOUS HUXLEY (1894–1963)

7732 God gave us memories that we might have roses in December.
SIR JAMES M. BARRIE (1860–1937)

7733 Memory is the cabinet of imagination, the treasury of reason, the registry of conscience, and the council chamber of thought.
SAINT BASIL (C. 330–379)

7734 Memory is the diary that we all carry about with us.
OSCAR WILDE (1854–1900)

7735 Memory tempers prosperity, mitigates adversity, controls youth, and delights old age.

7736 Nothing fixes a thing so intensely in the memory as the wish to forget it.
MICHEL EYQUEM DE MONTAIGNE (1533–1592)

7737 One thing you will probably remember well is any time you forgive and forget.
FRANKLIN P. JONES

7738 The memory capacity of even an ordinary human mind is fabulous. We may not consider ourselves particularly adept at remembering technical data . . . but consider how many faces we can recognize, how many names call up some past incident, how many words we can spell and define . . . It is estimated that in a lifetime, a brain can store one million billion "bits" of information.
ISAAC ASIMOV (1920–)

MERCY

7739 Every misery that I miss is a new mercy.
IZAAK WALTON (1593–1683)

7740 Mercy comes down from heaven to earth so that man by practicing it may resemble God.
GIAMBATTISTA GIRALDI (1504–1573)

7741 Mercy imitates God and disappoints Satan.
SAINT JOHN CHRYSOSTOM C. 347–407

7742 Mercy is not for them that sin and fear not, but for them that fear and sin not.
THOMAS WATSON (C. 1557–1592)

7743 O Lord, turn not away thy face
From him that lies prostrate,
Lamenting sore his sinful life,
Before thy mercy gate;
Mercy, good Lord, mercy I ask,
This is the total sum;
For mercy, Lord, is all my suit:
Lord, let thy mercy come.
JOHN MARCKANT (1559–1568)

7744 The quality of mercy is not strain'd.
It droppeth as the gentle rain from heaven
Upon the place beneath.
It is twice bless'd:
It blesseth him that gives and him that takes.
WILLIAM SHAKESPEARE (1564–1616)

7745 There's a wideness in God's mercy,
Like the wideness of the sea;
There's a kindness in his justice,
Which is more than liberty.
FREDERICK WILLIAM FABER (1814–1863)

7746 We are going to meet unmerciful good people and unmerciful bad people, unmerciful institutions, unmerciful organizations, and we shall have to go through the discipline of being merciful to the merciless.
OSWALD CHAMBERS (1874–1917)

7747 We do pray for mercy;
And that same prayer doth teach us all to render
The deeds of mercy.
WILLIAM SHAKESPEARE (1564–1616)

7748 We hand folks over to God's mercy and show none ourselves.
GEORGE ELIOT (1819–1880)

7749 When all thy mercies, O my God,
My rising soul surveys,
Transported with the view, I'm lost
In wonder, love, and praise.
JOSEPH ADDISON (1672–1719)

7750 When God's goodness cannot be seen, his mercy can be experienced.
ROBERT HAROLD SCHULLER (1926–)

7751 Whoever falls from God's right hand
Is caught in his left.
EDWIN MARKHAM (1852–1940)

MIND

7752 A chief event of life is the day in which
we have encountered a mind that
startled us.
RALPH WALDO EMERSON (1803–1882)

7753 A humble, ignorant man or woman
depending on the mind of God has an
explanation for things that the rational man without the Spirit of God
never has.
OSWALD CHAMBERS (1874–1917)

7754 A weak mind is like a microscope that
magnifies trifling things but cannot
receive great ones.
LORD CHESTERFIELD (1694–1773)

7755 Don't insult God by telling him he forgot to give you any brains when you
were born. We all have brains, what
we need is work.
OSWALD CHAMBERS (1874–1917)

7756 Few minds wear out, more rust out.
CHRISTIAN NESTELL BOVEE (1820–1904)

7757 If a man lets his garden alone, it very
soon ceases to be a garden; and if a
saint lets his mind alone, it will soon
become a rubbish heap for Satan to
make use of.
OSWALD CHAMBERS (1874–1917)

7758 If it is the will of the Holy Ghost that
we attend to the soul, certainly it is
not his will that we neglect the mind.
CHARLES HABIB MALIK (1906–   )

7759 Man's mind is the Holy of Holies, and
to admit evil thoughts is like setting up
an idol in the temple.
THE BERDICHEVER RABBI (1740–1809)

7760 Mental slavery is mental death, and
every man who has given up his intellectual freedom is the living coffin of
his dead soul.
ROBERT GREEN INGERSOLL (1833–1899)

7761 Merely having an open mind is nothing. The object of opening the mind,
as of opening the mouth, is to shut it
again on something solid.
G. K. CHESTERTON (1874–1936)

7762 Minds are like parachutes. They only
function when they are open.
SIR JAMES DEWAR (1842–1923)

7763 Most people think with their hopes or
fears or wishes rather than with their
minds.
WALTER DURANTY

7764 Occupy your mind with good
thoughts, or the enemy will fill it with
bad ones: unoccupied it cannot be.
SIR THOMAS MORE (1478–1535)

7765 Of all the tyrannies on humankind
The worst is that which persecutes the
mind.
JOHN DRYDEN (1631–1700)

7766 One of the highest and noblest functions of man's mind is to listen to
God's Word, and so to read his mind
and think his thoughts after him.
JOHN R. W. STOTT (1921–   )

7767 Our unconscious is like a vast subterranean factory with intricate machinery
that is never idle, where work goes on
day and night from the time we are
born until the moment of our death.
MILTON R. SAPIRSTEIN (1914–   )

7768 The Christian mind has succumbed to
the secular drift with a degree of weakness and nervelessness unmatched in
Christian history. It is difficult to do
justice in words to the complete loss of
intellectual morale in the twentieth-
century church. One cannot characterize it without having recourse to
language that will sound hysterical
and melodramatic. There is no longer
a Christian mind. There is still, of
course, a Christian ethic, a Christian
practice, and a Christian spirituality. . . . But as a thinking being, the
modern Christian has succumbed to
secularization.
HARRY BLAMIRES

7769 The difference between worldliness
and godliness is a renewed mind.
ERWIN W. LUTZER (1941–   )

7770 The human mind is like an umbrella—
it functions best when open.
WALTER GROPIUS (1883–1969)

7771 The trinity of the mind (memory—
understanding—love) is the image of
God, not because the mind remembers
itself, understands itself, and loves itself,
but rather because it can remember, un-

derstand, and love its Maker. And when it does this, the mind is made wise.
SAINT AUGUSTINE OF HIPPO (354–430)

7772 The unconscious is not just evil by nature, it is also the source of the highest good: not only dark but also light, not only bestial, semihuman, and demonic but superhuman, spiritual, and, in the classical sense of the word, "divine."
CARL GUSTAV JUNG (1875–1961)

7773 To the quiet mind all things are possible. What is the quiet mind? A quiet mind is one that nothing weighs on, nothing worries, which, free from ties and from all self-seeking, is wholly merged into the will of God and dead to its own.
MEISTER ECKHART (C. 1260–C. 1327)

7774 Untilled ground, however rich, will bring forth thistles and thorns; so also the mind of man.
SAINT TERESA OF AVILA (1515–1582)

7775 What the country needs is dirtier fingernails and cleaner minds.
WILL ROGERS (1879–1935)

7776 The human intellect even in its fallen state is an awesome work of God, but it lies in darkness until it has been illuminated by the Holy Spirit. Our Lord has little good to say of the unilluminated mind, but He revels in the mind that has been renewed and enlightened by grace. He always makes the place of His feet glorious; there is scarcely anything on earth more beautiful than a Spirit-filled mind, certainly nothing more wonderful than an alert and eager mind made incandescent by the presence of the indwelling Christ.
A. W. TOZER (1897–1963)

MISSIONS

7777 A missionary is a person who teaches cannibals to say grace before they eat him.

7778 God had an only Son, and he was a missionary and a physician.
DAVID LIVINGSTONE (1813–1873)

7779 I have but one candle of life to burn and would rather burn it out where people are dying in darkness than in a land that is flooded with light.

7780 I look upon foreign missionaries as the scaffolding around a rising building. The sooner it can be dispensed with, the better; or rather, the sooner it can be transferred to other places, to serve the same temporary use, the better.
JAMES HUDSON TAYLOR (1832–1905)

7781 If God calls you to be a missionary, don't stoop to be a king.
JORDON GROOMS

7782 Linguist: a talented person who can make mistakes in more than one language.

7783 Some wish to live within the sound of church and chapel bell. I wish to run a rescue mission within a yard of hell.
CHARLES THOMAS STUDD (1862–1931)

7784 The special person called to do missionary work is every person who is a member of the church of Christ. The call does not come to a chosen few, it is to every one of us.
OSWALD CHAMBERS (1874–1917)

7785 The Spirit of Christ is the spirit of missions, and the nearer we get to him, the more intensely missionary we must become.
HENRY MARTYN (1781–1812)

7786 When the Spirit of God comes into a man, he gives him a worldwide outlook.
OSWALD CHAMBERS (1874–1917)

MISTAKES

7787 All great men make mistakes.
LORD RANDOLPH HENRY SPENCER CHURCHILL (1849–1895)

7788 Anyone may make a mistake; none but a fool will persist in it.
CICERO (106–43 B.C.)

7789 Consider yourself lucky: suppose your mistakes were published every day like those of a ball player.

7790 From the error of others a wise man corrects his own.
PUBLILIUS SYRUS (FIRST CENTURY B.C.)

7791 He is always right who suspects that he makes mistakes.
SPANISH PROVERB

7792 The man who does things makes many mistakes, but he never makes the biggest mistake of all—doing nothing.
BENJAMIN FRANKLIN (1706–1790)

7793 The six mistakes of man:
1. The delusion that personal gain is made by crushing others.
2. The tendency to worry about things that cannot be changed or corrected.
3. Insisting that a thing is impossible because he cannot accomplish it.
4. Refusing to set aside trivial preferences.
5. Neglecting development and refinement of the mind, and not acquiring the habit of reading and study.
6. Attempting to compel others to believe and live as he does.
CICERO (106–43 B.C.)

7794 To make no mistakes is not in the power of man; but from their errors and mistakes the wise and good learn wisdom for the future.
PLUTARCH (C. 46–AFTER 119)

MONEY

7795 A penny will hide the biggest star in the universe if you hold it close enough to your eye.
SAMUEL GRAFTON

7796 Building one's life on a foundation of gold is just like building a house on foundations of sand.
HENRIK IBSEN (1828–1906)

7797 God will not merely judge us on the basis of what we gave but also on the basis of what we did with what we kept for ourselves.
ERWIN W. LUTZER (1941–)

7798 Gold is no balm to a wounded spirit.

7799 He who serves God for money will serve the devil for better wages.
ENGLISH PROVERB

7800 If a man runs after money, he's money-mad; if he keeps it, he's a capitalist; if he spends it, he's a playboy; if he doesn't try to get it, he lacks ambition. If he gets it without working for it, he's a parasite; and if he accumulates it after a lifetime of hard work, people call him a fool who never got anything out of life.
VIC OLIVER

7801 If you make money your god, it will plague you like the devil.
HENRY FIELDING (1707–1754)

7802 If you want to know what a man is really like, take notice how he acts when he loses money.
JEWISH PROVERB

7803 It is not a custom with me to keep money to look at.
GEORGE WASHINGTON (1732–1799)

7804 Jesus talked a great deal about money and the problems it causes man—in fact, one-fifth of all Jesus had to say was about money.
BILLY GRAHAM (1918–)

7805 Money and marriage . . . are the two things that make men and women devils or saints.
OSWALD CHAMBERS (1874–1917)

7806 Money buys everything except love, personality, freedom, immortality.

7807 Money can buy the husk of many things, but not the kernel. It brings you food, but not appetite; medicine, but not health; acquaintances, but not friends; servants, but not faithfulness; days of joy, but not peace and happiness.
HENRIK IBSEN (1828–1906)

7808 Money has never yet made anyone rich.
LUCIUS ANNAEUS SENECA (C. 4 B.C.–A.D. 65)

7809 Money is a good servant, but a dangerous master.
DOMINIQUE BOUHOURS (1628–1702)

7810 Money is an instrument that can buy you everything but happiness and pay your fare to every place but heaven.

7811 Money is emphasized in Scripture simply because our temptation to love it is inexplicably powerful.
ERWIN W. LUTZER (1941–)

7812 Money is like manure: If you spread it around, it does a world of good; but if you pile it up, it stinks to high heaven.

7813 Money is not required to buy one necessity of the soul.
HENRY DAVID THOREAU (1817–1862)

7814 Money never made a man happy yet, nor will it. There is nothing in its nature to produce happiness. The more a man has, the more he wants. Instead of its filling a vacuum, it makes one. If it satisfies one want, it doubles and triples that want another way.
BENJAMIN FRANKLIN (1706–1790)

7815 Money really adds no more to the wise than clothes can to the beautiful.
JEWISH PROVERB

7816 Money will buy a pretty good dog, but it won't buy the wag of his tail.
JOSH BILLINGS (1818–1885)

7817 Mr. Money is a powerful gentleman.
MEXICAN PROVERB

7818 Nothing that is God's is obtainable by money.
TERTULLIAN (C. 160–AFTER 220)

7819 O Lord, the sin,
Done for the things there's money in.
JOHN MASEFIELD (1878–1967)

7820 Riches serve a wise man but command a fool.
ENGLISH PROVERB

7821 Sad is the man who has nothing but money.
JEWISH PROVERB

7822 There are no pockets in a shroud.

7823 To get money is difficult, to keep it more difficult, but to spend it wisely most difficult of all.

7824 When I have any money, I get rid of it as quickly as possible, lest it find a way into my heart.
JOHN WESLEY (1703–1791)

7825 When money speaks, the truth is silent.
RUSSIAN PROVERB

7826 Workers earn it,
spendthrifts burn it,
bankers lend it,
women spend it,
forgers fake it,
taxes take it,
dying leaves it,
heirs receive it,
thrifty save it,
misers crave it,
robbers seize it,
rich increase it,
gamblers lose it . . .
I could use it.
RICHARD ARMOUR

MORALITY

7827 A world of nice people, content in their own niceness, looking no further, turned away from God, would be just as desperately in need of salvation as a miserable world—and might even be more difficult to save.
C. S. LEWIS (1898–1963)

7828 God alone knows all the facts, sets all the goals, and determines morality. Nowhere in Scripture are his principles to be replaced in favor of human calculation. He allows us to play the game; he does not allow us to make the rules.
ERWIN W. LUTZER (1941–)

7829 Morality comes with the sad wisdom of age, when the sense of curiosity has withered.
GRAHAM GREENE (1904–)

7830 Morality does not make a Christian, yet no man can be a Christian without it.
DANIEL WILSON (1778–1858)

7831 Morality is always higher than law.
ALEXANDER ISAYEVICH SOLZHENITSYN (1918–)

7832 Morality is not only correct conduct on the outside, but correct thinking within where only God can see.
OSWALD CHAMBERS (1874–1917)

7833 Morality without religion is a tree without roots; a stream without any spring to feed it; a house built on the sand; a pleasant place to live in till the

heavens grow dark, and the storm begins to beat.
JAMES BOYLAN SHAW (1808–1890)

7834 No nation has ever made any progress in a downward direction. No people ever became great by lowering their standards. No people ever became good by adopting a looser morality. It is not progress when the moral tone is lower than it was. It is not progress when purity is not as sweet. It is not progress when womanhood has lost its fragrance. Whatever else it is, it is not progress!
PETER MARSHALL (1902–1949)

7835 Only he who knows God is truly moral.
FRIEDRICH WILHELM JOSEPH VON SCHELLING (1775–1854)

7836 The most dangerous thing you can do is to take any one impulse of your own nature and set it up as the thing you ought to follow at all costs. There's not one of them that won't make us into devils if we set it up as an absolute guide. You might think love of humanity in general was safe, but it isn't. If you leave out justice, you'll find yourself breaking agreements and faking evidence in trials "for the sake of humanity," and becoming in the end a treacherous man.
C. S. LEWIS (1898–1963)

7837 The new morality and biblical morality part when the problem is raised regarding the content of love. The new moralists think that love must be defined by human beings and tailored to meet each situation; biblical writers hold that love is served by keeping the commandments of God.
ERWIN W. LUTZER (1941–)

7838 The three hardest tasks in the world are neither physical feats nor intellectual achievements, but moral acts: to return love for hate, to include the excluded, and to say, "I was wrong."
SYDNEY J. HARRIS (1917–1986)

7839 There are . . . occasions on which a mother's love for her own children or a man's love for his own country have to be suppressed or they'll lead to unfairness toward other people's children or countries. Strictly speaking, there aren't such things as good and bad impulses. Think of a piano. It has not got two kinds of notes on it, the right notes and the wrong ones. Every single note is right at one time and wrong at another. The moral law isn't any one instinct or any set of instincts: it is something which makes a kind of tune (the tune we call goodness or right conduct) by directing the instincts.
C. S. LEWIS (1898–1963)

7840 There is no moral precept that does not have something inconvenient about it.
DENIS DIDEROT (1713–1784)

MOTHER

7841 A mother is God's deputy on earth.
RACHEL L. VARNHAGEN

7842 A mother understands what a child does not say.
JEWISH PROVERB

7843 An ounce of mother is worth a pound of clergy.
SPANISH PROVERB

7844 Countless times each day a mother does what no one else can do quite as well. She wipes away a tear, whispers a word of hope, eases a child's fear. She teaches, ministers, loves, and nurtures the next generation of citizens. And she challenges and cajoles her kids to do their best and be the best. But no editorials praise these accomplishments—where is the coverage our mothers rightfully deserve?
JAMES C. DOBSON (1936–)
AND GARY L. BAUER (1946–)

7845 God can't always be everywhere, and so he invented mothers.
SIR EDWIN ARNOLD (1832–1904)

7846 In the eyes of its mother every beetle is a gazelle.
AFRICAN PROVERB

7847 Let your home be your parish, your little brood your congregation, your

living room a sanctuary, and your knee a sacred altar.
BILLY GRAHAM (1918–   )

7848 Mother is the name for God in the lips and hearts of little children.
WILLIAM MAKEPEACE THACKERAY (1811–1863)

7849 Motherhood is the greatest privilege of life.
MAY R. COKER

7850 No gift to your mother can ever equal her gift to you—life.

7851 No man is poor who has had a godly mother.
ABRAHAM LINCOLN (1809–1865)

7852 Thank you, God,
For pretending not to notice that one of Your angels is missing and for guiding her to me.
You must have known how much I would need her, so
You turned your head for a minute and allowed her to slip away to me.
Sometimes I wonder what special name you had for her.
I call her "Mother."
BERNICE MADDUX

7853 The child, in the decisive first years of his life, has the experience of his mother as an all-enveloping, protective, nourishing power. Mother is food; she is love; she is warmth; she is earth. To be loved by her means to be alive, to be rooted, to be at home.
ERICH FROMM (1900–1980)

7854 The commonest fallacy among women is that simply having children makes one a mother—which is as absurd as believing that having a piano makes one a musician.
SYDNEY J. HARRIS (1917–1986)

7855 The God to whom little boys say their prayers has a face very like their mother's.
SIR JAMES M. BARRIE (1860–1937)

7856 The most important occupation on earth for a woman is to be a real mother to her children. It does not have much glory to it; there is a lot of grit and grime. But there is no greater

place of ministry, position, or power than that of a mother.
PHIL WHISENHUNT

7857 The mother's heart is the child's schoolroom.
HENRY WARD BEECHER (1813–1887)

7858 The mother-child relationship is paradoxical and, in a sense, tragic. It requires the most intense love on the mother's side, yet this very love must help the child grow away from the mother and to become fully independent.
ERICH FROMM (1900–1980)

7859 When God thought of mother, he must have laughed with satisfaction and framed it quickly—so rich, so deep, so divine, so full of soul, power, and beauty was the conception.
HENRY WARD BEECHER (1813–1887)

7860 Youth fades; love droops; the leaves of friendship fall
A mother's secret love outlives them all.
OLIVER WENDELL HOLMES (1809–1894)

MOTIVATION

7861 God considers not the action, but the spirit of the action.
PETER ABELARD (1079–1142)

7862 God does not care
What good you did
But why you did it.
He does not grade the fruit
But probes the core and tests the root.
ANGELUS SILESIUS (1624–1677)

7863 God strikes at the core of our motivations. He is not interested in merely applying a new coat of paint, imposing a new set of rules. He wants to rebuild our minds and give us new values.
ERWIN W. LUTZER (1941–   )

7864 God values not your deeds, but how they are performed;
He does not view the fruit, only the root and core.
ANGELUS SILESIUS (1624–1677)

7865 It is not what a man does that determines whether his work is sacred or secular, it is why he does it.
A. W. TOZER (1897–1963)

7866 Man sees your actions, but God your motives.
THOMAS À KEMPIS (C. 1380–1471)

7867 Many a solo is sung to show off; many a sermon is preached as an exhibition of talent; many a church is founded as a slap to some other church. Even missionary activity may become competitive, and soul-winning may degenerate into a sort of brush-salesman project to satisfy the flesh.
A. W. TOZER (1897–1963)

7868 Not all people can be driven by the same stick.
ARABIAN PROVERB

7869 Nothing is impossible; there are ways that lead to everything, and if we had sufficient will, we should always have sufficient means. It is often merely for an excuse that we say things are impossible.
FRANÇOIS, DUC DE LA ROCHEFOUCAULD (1613–1680)

7870 When the will is ready, the feet are light.
GEORGE HERBERT (1593–1633)

7871 Where the heart is willing it will find a thousand ways, but where it is unwilling it will find a thousand excuses.

MOTTOS

7872 Burned but not consumed.
—Motto of the Church of Scotland

7873 Fear knocked at the door. Faith answered. No one was there.
—Inscription at Hind's Head Inn, Bray, England

7874 God has breathed and they are dispersed.
—Motto on medal celebrating the victory over the Spanish Armada

7875 Hammer away ye hostile hands!
Your hammers break;
God's anvil stands.
—Motto on the seal of a Waldensian church

7876 The will of God—
Nothing more, nothing less.
—Motto in G. Campbell Morgan's study

7877 To work is to pray.
—Benedictine motto

7878 We believe that the power behind us is greater than the task ahead.
—Motto over a church in Missouri

7879 When Jesus comes, the shadows depart.
—Inscription on Scottish castle wall

MURDER

7880 Blood that has been shed does not rest.
JEWISH PROVERB

7881 He forfeits his own blood that spills another's.
WILLIAM SHAKESPEARE (1564–1616)

7882 Murder isn't that bad. We all die sometime.
—Eleven-year-old British murderess
MARY BELL (1957–   )

MUSIC

7883 A bird doesn't sing because he has an answer—he sings because he has a song.
JOAN ANGLUND

7884 After silence, that which comes nearest to expressing the inexpressible is music.
ALDOUS HUXLEY (1894–1963)

7885 All one's life is music if one touches notes rightly and in time.
JOHN RUSKIN (1819–1900)

7886 Among the first things created was the bird. Why? Because God wanted the world to have music at the start. And this infant world, wrapped in swaddling clothes of light, so beautifully serenaded at the start is to die amid the ringing blast of the archangel's trumpet; so that as the world had music at

the start, it is going to have music at the last.
THOMAS DE WITT TALMAGE (1832–1902)

7887 And the night shall be filled with music,
And the cares that infest the day,
Shall fold their tents like the Arabs,
And as silently steal away.
HENRY WADSWORTH LONGFELLOW (1807–1882)

7888 Anyone who sings the blues has a broken spirit . . . Being oppressed or worried about something and not knowing God, they've sought a way of trying to relieve themselves . . . the blues make you feel moody and sad and make you cry.
MAHALIA JACKSON (1911–1972)

7889 As the music is, so are the people of the country.
TURKISH PROVERB

7890 Blues are the songs of despair, gospel songs are the songs of hope.
MAHALIA JACKSON (1911–1972)

7891 God is its author, and not man. He laid the keynote of all harmonies. He planned all perfect combinations, and he made us so that we would hear and understand.

7892 God is the organist, we are his instrument,
His Spirit sounds each pipe and gives the tone its strength.
ANGELUS SILESIUS (1624–1677)

7893 God made the perfect and complete instrument: the human voice. It gives you personality, individuality, words, and music all in one vehicle.
HARRY VERPLOEGH (1908–   )

7894 He who sings frightens away his ills.
MIGUEL DE CERVANTES (1547–1616)

7895 However desolate, weird, or strange
Life's monody sounds to you,
Before tomorrow the air may change,
And the Great Director of music arrange
A program perfectly new;
A dirge in minor may suddenly be
Turned into a jubilant song of glee.
ELLA WHEELER WILCOX (1850–1919)

7896 I should be sorry, my lord, if I have only succeeded in entertaining them; I wished to make them better.
—To Lord Kinnoull, after the first London performance of Messiah, March 23, 1743
GEORGE FRIDERIC HANDEL (1685–1759)

7897 It's easy to play any musical instrument: all you have to do is touch the right key at the right time, and the instrument will play by itself.
JOHANN SEBASTIAN BACH (1685–1750)

7898 Jazz will endure just as long as people hear it through their feet instead of their brains.
JOHN PHILIP SOUSA (1854–1932)

7899 Let us go singing as far as we go; the road will be less tedious.
VIRGIL A. KRAFT

7900 Music exalts each joy, allays each grief,
Expels diseases, softens every pain,
Subdues the rage of poison and the plague.
JOHN ARMSTRONG (1709–1779)

7901 Music has charms to soothe the savage breast,
To soften rocks, or bend a knotted oak.
WILLIAM CONGREVE (1670–1729)

7902 Music is almost all we have of heaven on earth.
JOSEPH ADDISON (1672–1719)

7903 Music is as seasonable in grief as in joy.
RICHARD HOOKER (1554–1600)

7904 Music is God's best gift to man,
The only art of heaven given to earth,
The only art of earth we take to heaven.
LETITIA ELIZABETH LANDON (1802–1838)

7905 Music is love itself—it is the purest, most ethereal language of passion, showing in a thousand ways all possible changes of color and feeling; and though true in only a single instance, it yet can be understood by thousands of men—who all feel differently.
CARL MARIA VON WEBER (1786–1826)

7906 Music is the child of prayer.
FRANÇOIS RENÉ, VICOMTE DE CHATEAUBRIAND (1768–1848)

7907 Music is the language spoken by angels.
HENRY WADSWORTH LONGFELLOW
(1807–1882)

7908 Music is the medicine of a troubled mind.
WALTER HADDON (1516–1572)

7909 Music is the moonlight in the gloomy night of life.
JOHANN PAUL FRIEDRICH RICHTER
(1763–1825)

7910 Music is the primary weapon used to make the perverse seem glamorous, exciting, and appealing. Music is used to ridicule religion, morality, patriotism, and productivity—while glorifying drugs, destruction, revolution, and sexual promiscuity.
GARY ALLEN

7911 Music the fiercest grief can charm,
And fate's severest rage disarm,
Music can soften pain to ease,
And make despair and madness please;
Our joys below it can improve,
And antedate the bliss above.
ALEXANDER POPE (1688–1744)

7912 Music washes away from the soul the dust of everyday life.
BERTHOLD AUERBACH (1812–1882)

7913 Music, like balm, eases grief's smarting wound.
SAMUEL PORDAGE (1633–1691)

7914 Next to theology I give to music the highest place and honor. Music is the art of the prophets, the only art that can calm the agitations of the soul; it is one of the most magnificent and delightful presents God has given us.
MARTIN LUTHER (1483–1546)

7915 Not without design does God write the music of our lives. Be it ours to learn the time, and not be discouraged at the rests. The making of music is often a slow and painful process in this life.
JOHN RUSKIN (1819–1900)

7916 O Music! thou bringest the receding waves of eternity nearer to the weary soul of man as he stands upon the shore and longs to cross over!
JOHANN PAUL FRIEDRICH RICHTER
(1763–1825)

7917 Oh, surely melody from heaven was sent
To cheer the soul when tired with human strife,
To soothe the wayward heart by sorrow rent,
And soften down the rugged road of life!
HENRY KIRKE WHITE (1785–1806)

7918 One man's music is another's noise.
ERWIN W. LUTZER (1941–   )

7919 Seated one day at the organ,
I was weary and ill at ease,
And my fingers wandered idly
Over the noisy keys.
I do not know what I was playing,
Or what I was dreaming then,
But I struck one chord of music
Like the sound of a great Amen.
ADELAIDE ANN PROCTER (1825–1864)

7920 Songs spring forth weblike from a mind at peace.
OVID (43 B.C.–A.D. 17)

7921 The human soul is a silent harp in God's choir, whose strings need only to be swept by the divine breath to chime in with the harmonies of creation.
HENRY DAVID THOREAU (1817–1862)

7922 The little girl who hears music for the first time cries out: "It's God speaking to us!"
JOSEPH JOUBERT (1754–1824)

7923 The only time that our blessed Lord ever is recorded as having sung is the night that he went out to his death.
ARCHBISHOP FULTON J. SHEEN (1895–1979)

7924 The song is ended, but the melody lingers on.

7925 The trumpet shall be heard on high,
The dead shall live, the living die,
And music shall untune the sky!
JOHN DRYDEN (1631–1700)

7926 The woods would be very silent if no birds sang there except those who sang best.

7927 There's music in the dawning morn,
There's music in the twilight cloud,
There's music in the depth of night,
When the world is still and dim,

And the stars flame out in the
   pomp of light,
Like thrones of the cherubim!
WILLIAM HONE (1780–1842)

7928 Tune me, O Lord, into one harmony
With thee, one full responsive vibrant
   chord;
Unto thy praise, all love and melody,
Tune me, O Lord.
CHRISTINA GEORGINA ROSSETTI
(1830–1894)

7929 What is to reach the heart must come
from above; if it does not come from
thence, it will be nothing but notes,
body without spirit.
LUDWIG VAN BEETHOVEN (1770–1827)

7930 What will a child learn sooner than a
song?
ALEXANDER POPE (1688–1744)

7931 When I think upon my God, my heart
is so full of joy that the notes dance
and leap from my pen; and since God
has given me a cheerful heart, it will
be pardoned me that I serve him with
a cheerful spirit.
FRANZ JOSEPH HAYDN (1732–1809)

7932 When words leave off, music begins.
HEINRICH HEINE (1797–1856)

7933 Who among us has not sought peace
in a song?
VICTOR HUGO (1802–1885)

7934 Words seem to be so ambiguous, so
vague, so easily misunderstandable in
comparison with genuine music,
which fills the soul with things a thousand times better than words.
FELIX MENDELSSOHN-BARTHOLDY
(1809–1847)

7935 Yes, music is the prophet's art;
Among the gifts that God hath sent,
One of the most magnificent!
It calms the agitated heart;
Temptations, evil thoughts, and all
The passions that disturb the soul,
Are quelled by its divine control,
As the evil spirit fled from Saul,
And his distemper was allayed,
When David took his harp and played.
HENRY WADSWORTH LONGFELLOW
(1807–1882)

MYSTERY

7936 A mystery is a fact about which we
cannot know everything, but the
deeper we plunge, the more we learn.
It is a thicket we are in.
LEONARD FEENEY (1898–1978)

7937 A revelation is religious doctrine
viewed on its illuminated side; a mystery is the selfsame doctrine viewed on
the side unilluminated.
CARDINAL JOHN HENRY NEWMAN
(1801–1890)

7938 A thing is not necessarily against reason because it happens to be above it.
CHARLES CALEB COLTON (1780–1832)

7939 I have observed the power of the
watermelon seed. It has the power of
drawing from the ground and through
itself 200,000 times its weight. When
you can tell me how it takes this material and out of it colors an outside surface beyond the imitation of art, and
then forms inside of it a white rind
and within that again a red heart,
thickly inlaid with black seeds, each
one of which in turn is capable of
drawing through itself 200,000 times
its weight—when you can explain to
me the mystery of a watermelon, you
can ask me to explain the mystery of
God.
WILLIAM JENNINGS BRYAN (1860–1925)

7940 In the same sense that everything may
be said to be a mystery, so also may it
be said that everything is a miracle,
and that no one thing is a greater
miracle than another. The elephant,
though larger, is not a greater miracle
than a mite; nor a mountain a greater
miracle than an atom. To an almighty
power it is no more difficult to make
the one than the other, and no more
difficult to make a million worlds than
to make one.
THOMAS PAINE (1737–1809)

7941 In what way, or by what manner of
working, God changes a soul from evil
to good—how he impregnates the barren rock with priceless gems and

gold—is, to the human mind, an impenetrable mystery.
SAMUEL TAYLOR COLERIDGE (1772–1834)

7942 Mystery is but another name for our ignorance; if we were omniscient, all would be perfectly plain.
TRYON EDWARDS (1809–1894)

7943 Oh, the depths of the fathomless deep,
Oh, the riddle and secret of things,
And the voice through the darkness heard,
And the rush of winnowing wings!
SIR LEWIS MORRIS (1833–1907)

7944 Shall we think that with our tiny brains we can unravel the mysteries of him who made the whole vast cosmos? He who causes things to be must smile in great pity when he hears men talking about some day finding out, of their own selves, the secrets of matter, and of life, and of death, and of him.
BERNARD IDDINGS BELL (1886–1958)

7945 We talked of the beauty of the world of God's and of the great mystery of it. Every blade of grass, every insect, ant, and golden bee, all so amazingly know their path, though they have not intelligence, they bear witness to the mystery of God and continually accomplish it themselves.
FYODOR MIKHAYLOVICH DOSTOYEVSKI (1821–1881)

MYSTICISM

7946 For the mystic especially it is important that theology should flourish and good theologians abound, for in the guidance which objective theology supplies lies the mystic's sole certainty of escaping self-delusion.
PHILIP HUGHES (1895–1967)

7947 For what is mysticism? Is it not the attempt to draw near to God, and not by rites or ceremonies, but by inward disposition? Is it not merely a hard word for "the kingdom of heaven is within"? Heaven is neither a place nor a time.
FLORENCE NIGHTINGALE (1820–1910)

7948 Formless and vague and fleeting as it is, the mystical experience is the bedrock of religious faith. In it the soul, acting as a unity with all its faculties, rises above itself and becomes spirit; it asserts its claim to be a citizen of heaven.
THOMAS À KEMPIS (C. 1380–1471)

7949 God draws us in three ways: first, by his creatures; secondly, by his voice in the soul when an eternal truth mysteriously suggests itself, as happens not infrequently in morning sleep; thirdly, without resistance or means, when the will is quite subdued.
JOHANN TAULER (C. 1300–1361)

7950 I have learnt that the place where thou art found unveiled is girt round with the coincidence of contradictories, and this is the wall of paradise wherein thou dost abide, the door whereof is guarded by the proud spirit of Reason, and unless he is vanquished, the way will not be open. Thus 'tis beyond the coincidence of contradictories thou mayst be seen and nowhere this side thereof.
NICHOLAS OF CUSA (1401–1464)

7951 I must speed to my God before all things.
My God, by his nature my Father above,
My Brother in his humanity,
My Bridegroom in his ardent love,
And I his from eternity.
Do you think that his Fire will consume my soul?
He knows how to burn, and then to gently cool.
SAINT MECHTHILD OF MAGDEBURG (C. 1210–C. 1280)

7952 Lord God, I am now a naked soul, and you arrayed all gloriously. We are two in one, we have reached the goal, immortal rapture that cannot die.
Now a blessed silence flows over us. Both have willed it. He is given to her and she to him. What now will happen the soul well knows and therefore I am comforted.
SAINT MECHTHILD OF MAGDEBURG (C. 1210–C. 1280)

7953 My way is very simple. My soul lives on God, by a glance of love between him and myself. By this glance God gives himself to me, and I give myself to him. This is my habitual state, that in which God has placed me. I neither can nor should turn myself from it on account of suffering. This I accept as inseparable from love here below. Love suffers as the voice sings.
LUCIE CHRISTINE (1858–1916)

7954 Mystical means real. It is the intimate quality of the spiritual life.
HENRI J. M. NOUWEN

7955 Mysticism is communion with God.
WILLIAM RALPH INGE (1860–1954)

7956 Mysticism is the art of union with reality.
EVELYN UNDERHILL (1875–1941)

7957 Mysticism is the filling of the consciousness with a content (feeling, thought, desire) through involuntary emergence from the unconscious.
EDUARD VON HARTMANN (1842–1906)

7958 Never can father or mother embrace their child, nor any person embrace another with so much love as God Almighty embraces the rational soul.
ANGELA OF FOLIGNO (C. 1248–1309)

7959 No room is allowed either in the Old or New Testament for mysticism pure and simple because that will mean sooner or later an aloofness from actual life, a kind of contempt expressed or implied by a superior attitude, by occult relationships and finer sensibilities.
OSWALD CHAMBERS (1874–1917)

7960 O my God, let me walk in the way of love which knoweth not how to seek self in anything whatsoever. O sight to be wished, desired and longed for, because once to have seen thee is to have learned all things! Nothing can bring us to this sight but love. O Lord, give this love into my soul, that I may never more live nor breathe, but out of a pure love of thee, my all and only good.
DAME GERTRUDE MORE (1606–1633)

7961 O sweetness of my heart! O life of my soul, joyous resting place of my spirit! O bright and beautiful day of eternity, serene light deep within me! Flowering paradise of my heart! When shall I be wholly thine? When shall I cease to be my own? When shall nothing but thyself live in me? When shall I love thee with the fullest ardour? When shall I be wholly enkindled by the flame of thy love?
SAINT PETER OF ALCÁNTARA (1499–1562)

7962 One of the greatest paradoxes of the mystical life is this: that a man cannot enter into the deepest center of himself and pass through that center into God unless he is able to pass entirely out of himself and empty himself and give himself to other people in the purity of a selfless love.
THOMAS MERTON (1915–1968)

7963 Only on the wings of mysticism can the spirit soar to its full height.
ALEXIS CARREL (1873–1944)

7964 Suddenly I feel myself transformed and changed; it is joy unspeakable. My mind is exhilarated; I lose the memory of past trials; my intelligence is clarified; my desires are satisfied. I grasp something inwardly as with the embracement of love.
HUGH OF ST. VICTOR (1096–1141)

7965 The mystic is too full of God to speak intelligibly to the world.
ARTHUR WILLIAM SYMONS (1865–1945)

7966 The mystic's spirit is sunk and lost in the abyss of Deity and loses the consciousness of all creature distinctions.
JOHANN TAULER (C. 1300–1361)

7967 The soul loves and is loved in return; she seeks and is sought; she calls and is called. But in this, she lifts and is lifted up; she holds and is herself held; she clasps and she is closely embraced, and by the bond of love she unites herself to God, one with one, alone with him.
SAINT THOMAS AQUINAS (1225–1274)

7968 The spirit is submerged and absorbed in the depths of the divine ocean, so that we can exclaim: God is in me.

God is outside of me. God is everywhere round about me.
JOHANN TAULER (C. 1300–1361)

7969 To be a mystic is simply to participate
here and now in that real and eternal
life in the fullest deepest sense which is
possible to man.
EVELYN UNDERHILL (1875–1941)

7970 Unless you lead me, Lord, I cannot
dance.
Would you have me leap and spring?
You yourself, dear Lord, must sing;
So shall I spring into your love,
    from your love to understanding,
    from understanding to delight;
Then soaring far above all human
    thought,
There circling will I stay and taste
    encircling love.
SAINT MECHTHILD OF MAGDEBURG
(C. 1210–C. 1280)

7971 When the soul is purified and made
serene, and the knowledge of Christ
the Lord dawns upon it, its mind
ascends and beholds the majesty of
God, and sees him to be incomprehensible and infinite. When it looks on
high, it sees him as at first, and when
it looks within itself, it sees him there.
When the mind floats on the sea of the
majesty of God and his incomprehensi-
bility, it is amazed and lost in wonder
at the serene majesty of God. And
forthwith the soul becomes humble, so
that if it were possible, when the efful-
gence of God's majesty envelops it, it
would take its place below the whole
creation because of its awe and wondering amazement at the majesty of
God, ineffable, incomprehensible as it
is, beyond the penetration of his servants.
JOHN OF LYCOPOLIS (D. 394)

N

NAIVETE

7972 I cannot spare the luxury of believing that all things beautiful are what they seem.
FITZ-GREENE HALLECK (1790–1867)

7973 Let us believe neither half of the good people tell us of ourselves, nor half the evil they say of others.
J. P. SENN

7974 The great masses of the people . . . will more easily fall victims to a great lie than to a small one.
ADOLF HITLER (1889–1945)

7975 The most positive men are the most naive.
ALEXANDER POPE (1688–1744)

7976 To be naive helps one go through life very smoothly.

7977 To be naive is the man's weakness, but the child's strength.
CHARLES LAMB (1775–1834)

7978 When people are bewildered, they tend to become gullible.
CALVIN COOLIDGE (1872–1933)

7979 You risk just as much in being naive as in being suspicious.
DENIS DIDEROT (1713–1784)

NATION

7980 "My country, right or wrong" is like saying, "My mother, drunk or sober."
G. K. CHESTERTON (1874–1936)

7981 A remarkable thing about George Washington is that he was born on a national holiday.

7982 A thoughtful mind . . . sees not the flag only, but the nation itself . . . the principles, the truths, the history.
HENRY WARD BEECHER (1813–1887)

7983 America is still the land of opportunity: everyone can become a taxpayer.

7984 Any nation that thinks more of its ease and comfort than its freedom will soon lose its freedom; and the ironical thing about it is that it will lose its ease and comfort too.
WILLIAM SOMERSET MAUGHAM (1874–1965)

7985 Give me your tired, your poor,
　　　Your huddled masses, yearning to
　　　　　breathe free,
　　　The wretched refuse of your teeming
　　　　　shore.
　　　Send these, the homeless, tempest-
　　　　　tossed to me,
　　　I lift my lamp beside the golden door!
　　　—Inscription on Statue of Liberty,
　　　　　New York Harbor
　　　EMMA LAZARUS (1849–1887)

7986 God send us men with hearts ablaze,
　　　All truth to love, all wrong to hate;
　　　These are the patriots nations need,
　　　These are the bulwarks of the state.
　　　F. J. GILLMAN

7987 No nation is better than the individu-
　　　als that compose it.
　　　CORDELL HULL (1871–1955)

7988 The strength of a country is the
　　　strength of its religious convictions.
　　　CALVIN COOLIDGE (1872–1933)

7989 The things that are wrong with the
　　　country today are the sum total of all
　　　the things that are wrong with us as
　　　individuals.
　　　CHARLES W. TOBEY

7990 What is largely missing in American
　　　life today is a sense of context, of say-
　　　ing or doing anything that is intended
　　　or even expected to live beyond the
　　　moment. There is no culture in the
　　　world that is so obsessed as ours with
　　　immediacy. In our journalism the triv-
　　　ial displaces the momentous because
　　　we tend to measure the importance of
　　　events by how recently they happened.
　　　We have become so obsessed with
　　　facts that we have lost all touch with
　　　truth.
　　　TED KOPPEL (1940–)

7991 When good people in any country
　　　cease their vigilance and struggle, then
　　　evil men prevail.
　　　PEARL S. BUCK (1892–1973)

7992 With malice toward none; with charity
　　　for all; with firmness in the right, as
　　　God gives us to see the right, let us
　　　strive on to finish the work we are in;
　　　to bind up the nation's wounds; to
　　　care for him who shall have borne the
battle, and for his widow and his
orphan—to do all which may achieve
and cherish a just and lasting peace
among ourselves and with all nations.
ABRAHAM LINCOLN (1809–1865)

NATURE

7993 A man who could make one rose . . .
　　　would be accounted most wonderful;
　　　yet God scatters countless such flow-
　　　ers around us! His gifts are so infinite
　　　that we do not see them.
　　　MARTIN LUTHER (1483–1546)

7994 A voice in the wind I do not know;
　　　A meaning on the face of the high hills
　　　Whose utterance I cannot comprehend,
　　　A something is behind them: that is
　　　　　God.
　　　GEORGE MACDONALD (1824–1905)

7995 All God's great works are silent. They
　　　are not done amid rattles of drums
　　　and flare of trumpets. Light as it trav-
　　　els makes no noise, utters no sound to
　　　the ear. Creation is a silent process;
　　　nature rose under the Almighty hand
　　　without clang or clamor, or noises that
　　　distract and disturb.
　　　ANDREW MARTIN FAIRBAIRN (1838–1912)

7996 Behold! the Holy Grail is found,
　　　Found in each poppy's cup of gold;
　　　And God walks with us as of old.
　　　Behold! the burning bush still burns
　　　For man, whichever way he turns;
　　　And all God's earth is holy ground.
　　　JOAQUIN MILLER (1837–1913)

7997 Does not all nature around me praise
　　　God? If I were silent, I should be an
　　　exception to the universe. Does not
　　　the thunder praise him as it rolls like
　　　drums in the march of the God of
　　　armies? Do not the mountains praise
　　　him when the woods upon their sum-
　　　mits wave in adoration? Does not the
　　　lightning write his name in letters of
　　　fire? Has not the whole earth a voice?
　　　And shall I, can I, silent be?
　　　CHARLES HADDON SPURGEON (1834–1892)

7998 Don't knock the weather; nine-tenths
　　　of the people couldn't start a conversa-
　　　tion if it didn't change once in a while.
　　　KEN HUBBARD (1868–1930)

7999 Earth with her thousand voices praises
God.
SAMUEL TAYLOR COLERIDGE (1772–1834)

8000 Evening after evening in the summer, I
have gone to see the white clover fall
asleep in the meadow. Kneeling and
looking very closely, one sees the two
lower leaves on each stalk gently
approach one another like little hands
that were going to clap but thought
better of it, and at last lie folded quietly as though for prayer. Then the
upper leaf droops, as a child's face
might, until it rests on the others.
Everywhere in the dusk the white clover leaves are sleeping in an attitude of
worship.
MARY WEBB (1881–1927)

8001 Every formula which expresses a law
of nature is a hymn of praise to God.
—Inscription on a bust in the Hall of
Fame
MARIA MITCHELL (1818–1889)

8002 Every morning the sun rises to warm
the earth. If it were to fail to shine for
just one minute, all life on the earth
would die. The rains come to water
the earth. There is fertility in the soil,
life in the seeds, oxygen in the air. The
providence of God is about us in unbelievable abundance every moment. But
so often we just take it for granted.
CHARLES L. ALLEN (1913–)

8003 Flowers are heaven's masterpieces.
DOROTHY PARKER (1893–1967)

8004 Flowers have an expression of countenance as much as man or animals.
Some seem to smile, some have a sad
expression, some are pensive and diffident, others again are plain, honest,
and upright.
HENRY WARD BEECHER (1813–1887)

8005 For the man sound in body and serene
of mind there is no such thing as bad
weather. Every sky has its beauty.
GEORGE ROBERT GISSING (1857–1903)

8006 Go thou and seek the House of Prayer!
I to the woodlands wend, and there,
In lovely nature see the God of love.
ROBERT SOUTHEY (1774–1843)

8007 God Almighty first planted a garden;
and indeed, it is the purest of human
pleasures.
FRANCIS BACON (1561–1626)

8008 God makes the glow worm as well as
the star; the light in both is divine.
GEORGE MACDONALD (1824–1905)

8009 Grant me, O God, the power to see
In every rose, eternity.
In every bud, the coming day;
In every snow, the promised May;
In every storm the legacy
Of rainbows smiling down at me!
VIRGINIA WUERFEL

8010 Great, wide, beautiful, wonderful
world,
With the wonderful water round you
curled,
And the wonderful grass upon your
breast,
World, you are beautifully dressed.
MATTHEW BROWNE (1823–1882)

8011 I am in love with this world . . . I have
climbed its mountains, roamed its forests, sailed its waters, crossed its
deserts, felt the sting of its frosts, the
oppression of its heats, the drench of
its rains, the fury of its winds, and
always have beauty and joy waited
upon my goings and comings.
JOHN BURROUGHS (1837–1921)

8012 I love nature partly because she is not
man, but a retreat from him. None of
his institutions control or pervade her.
There is a different kind of right that
prevails. In her midst I can be glad
with an entire gladness. If this world
were all man, I could not stretch
myself, I should lose all hope. He is
constraint, she is freedom to me. He
makes me wish for another world. She
makes me content with this.
HENRY DAVID THOREAU (1817–1862)

8013 I love to think of nature as an unlimited broadcasting station through
which God speaks to us every hour if
we will only tune in.
GEORGE WASHINGTON CARVER
(C. 1864–1943)

8014 I need not shout my faith. Thrice
eloquent

Are quiet trees and the green listening
　sod;
Hushed are the stars, whose power is
　never spent;
The hills are mute: yet how they speak
　of God!
CHARLES HANSOM TOWNE

8015 I saw the lightning's gleaming rod
Reach forth and write upon the sky
The awful autograph of God.
JOAQUIN MILLER (1837–1913)

8016 I'm glad the sky is painted blue
And the earth is painted green
With such a lot of nice fresh air
All sandwiched in-between.

8017 If you have never heard the mountains
singing, or seen the trees of the field
clapping their hands, do not think
because of that they don't. Ask God to
open your ears so you may hear it and
your eyes so you may see it, because,
though few men ever know it, they do,
my friend, they do.
MCCANDLISH PHILLIPS

8018 In spring I delight you,
In summer I cool you,
In autumn I feed you,
In winter I warm you.
—A tree

8019 In wonder-workings, or some bush
　aflame,
Men look for God and fancy him con-
　cealed;
But in earth's common things he
　stands revealed
While grass and flowers and stars spell
　out his name.
MINOT JUDSON SAVAGE (1841–1918)

8020 Is ditchwater dull? Naturalists with
microscopes have told me that it teems
with quiet fun.
G. K. CHESTERTON (1874–1936)

8021 Miracles are not contrary to nature
but only contrary to what we know
about nature.
SAINT AUGUSTINE OF HIPPO (354–430)

8022 Nature has perfections in order to
show that she is the image of God,
and defects to show that she is only
his image.
BLAISE PASCAL (1623–1662)

8023 Nature in her laws tells of God, but
the message is not too clear. It tells us
nothing of the love and grace of God.
Conscience, in our inmost being, does
tell us of God, but the message is fragmentary. The only place we can find a
clear, unmistakable message is in the
Word of God, which we call the Bible.
BILLY GRAHAM (1918–)

8024 Nature is but a name for an effect,
Whose cause is God.
WILLIAM COWPER (1731–1800)

8025 Nature is the art of God Eternal.
DANTE ALIGHIERI (1265–1321)

8026 Nature with open volume stands,
To spread her Maker's praise abroad;
And every labor of his hands
Shows something worthy of a God.
ISAAC WATTS (1674–1748)

8027 Nature! We are surrounded by her and
locked in her clasp, powerless to leave
her and powerless to come closer to
her. Without asking us or warning us
she takes us up into the whirl of her
dance and hurries on with us until we
are weary and fall from her arms.
JOHANN WOLFGANG VON GOETHE
(1749–1832)

8028 No snowflake ever falls in the wrong
place.
ZENO (335–263 B.C.)

8029 Nothing is without voice; God
　everywhere can hear
Arising from creation his praise and
echo clear.
ANGELUS SILESIUS (1624–1677)

8030 O world, as God has made it!
All is beauty.
ROBERT BROWNING (1812–1889)

8031 Observe God in his works: here
　fountains flow,
Birds sing, beast feed, fish leap, and
　th' earth stands fast:
Above are restless motions, running
　lights,
Vast circling azure, giddly clouds,
　days, nights.
HENRY VAUGHAN (1622–1695)

8032 One is nearer God's heart in a garden
Than anywhere else on earth.
DOROTHY FRANCES GURNEY (1858–1932)

8033 Sunshine is delicious, rain is refreshing, wind braces up, snow is exhilarating. There is no such thing as bad
weather, only different kinds of good
weather.
JOHN RUSKIN (1819–1900)

8034 The best thing is to go from nature's
God down to nature; and if you once
get to nature's God, and believe him,
and love him, it is surprising how easy
it is to hear music in the waves, and
songs in the wild whisperings of the
winds; to see God everywhere in the
stones, in the rocks, in the rippling
brooks, and hear him everywhere, in
the lowing of cattle, in the rolling of
thunder, and in the fury of tempests.
CHARLES HADDON SPURGEON (1834–1892)

8035 The greatest joy in nature is the
absence of man.
BLISS CARMAN (1861–1929)

8036 The groves were God's first temples.
WILLIAM CULLEN BRYANT (1794–1878)

8037 The Infinite has sowed his name in the
heavens in glowing stars, but on the
earth he sowed his name in tender
flowers.
JOHANN PAUL FRIEDRICH RICHTER
(1763–1825)

8038 The landscape belongs to the man
who looks at it.
RALPH WALDO EMERSON (1803–1882)

8039 The lark is up to greet the sun,
The bee is on the wing;
The ant its labor has begun,
The woods with music ring.
JANE TAYLOR (1783–1824)

8040 The more I study nature, the more I
am amazed at the Creator.
LOUIS PASTEUR (1822–1895)

8041 The stillness of nature speaks louder
than a choir of voices.

8042 The tree is full of poetry.
HENRY DAVID THOREAU (1817–1862)

8043 The whole of art is only an imitation
of nature.
LUCIUS ANNAEUS SENECA (C. 4 B.C.–A.D. 65)

8044 The world is charged with the grandeur of God.
GERARD MANLEY HOPKINS (1844–1889)

8045 The world is God's epistle to mankind—his thoughts are flashing upon
us from every direction.
PLATO (C. 428–348 B.C.)

8046 Think of the number of trees and
blades of grass and flowers, the extravagant wealth of beauty no one ever
sees! Think of the sunrises and sunsets
we never look at! God is lavish in
every degree.
OSWALD CHAMBERS (1874–1917)

8047 Touched by a light that hath no name,
A glory never sung,
Aloft on sky and mountain wall
Are God's great pictures hung.
JOHN GREENLEAF WHITTIER (1807–1892)

8048 We see God all around us: the mountains are God's thoughts upheaved, the
rivers are God's thoughts in motion,
the oceans are God's thoughts
imbedded, the dewdrops are God's
thoughts in pearls.
SAM JONES (1847–1906)

8049 What man has written man may read;
But God fills every root and seed
With cryptic words, too strangely set
For mortals to decipher yet.
CHARLES DALMON (1872–   )

8050 Whatever we see, wherever we look,
whether we recognize it as true or not,
we cannot touch or handle the things
of earth and not, in that very moment,
be confronted with the sacraments of
heaven.
C. A. COULSON

8051 When I can go just where I want to go,
There is a copse of birch trees that I
   know;
And, as in Eden, Adam walked with
   God,
When in that quiet aisle my feet have
   trod
I have found peace among the silver
   trees,
Known comfort in the cool kiss of the
   breeze,

Heard music in its whisper, and have known
Most certainly that I was not alone!
FATHER ANDREW

8052 When the oak is felled, the whole forest echoes with its fall, but a hundred acorns are sown in silence by an unnoticed breeze.
THOMAS CARLYLE (1795–1881)

8053 Who has seen the wind?
Neither you nor I;
But when the trees bow down their heads,
The wind is passing by.
CHRISTINA GEORGINA ROSSETTI (1830–1894)

8054 You're a man, you've seen the world—
The beauty and the wonder and the power,
The shape of things, their colors, lights, and shades,
Changes, surprises—and God made it all!
ROBERT BROWNING (1812–1889)

NEIGHBOR

8055 Do not waste time bothering whether you love your neighbor; act as if you do. As soon as we do this we find one of the great secrets. When you are behaving as if you loved someone, you will presently come to love him. If you injure someone you dislike, you will find yourself disliking him more. If you do him a good turn, you will find yourself disliking him less.
C. S. LEWIS (1898–1963)

8056 If my heart is right with God, every human being is my neighbor.
OSWALD CHAMBERS (1874–1917)

8057 If you truly love God, you will love your neighbor. It does not make any difference if he loves you or not.
THOMAS A. JUDGE (1868–1933)

8058 If you want to hear the whole truth about yourself, anger your neighbor.

8059 Looking through the wrong end of a telescope is an injustice to the astronomer, to the telescope, and to the stars; likewise, looking at our neighbor's

faults instead of the attributes gives us an incorrect conception of ourselves, our neighbor, and our God.
WILLIAM ARTHUR WARD (1812–1882)

8060 Love your neighbor, but don't pull down the hedge.
SWISS PROVERB

8061 Some of us . . . think to ourselves, "If I had only been there! How quick I would have been to help the baby. I would have washed his linen. How happy I would have been to go with the shepherds to see the Lord lying in the manger!" Yes, we would! We say that because we know how great Christ is. But if we had been there at that time, we would have done no better than the people of Bethlehem. Why don't we do it now? We have Christ in our neighbor.
MARTIN LUTHER (1483–1546)

8062 The impersonal hand of government can never replace the helping hand of a neighbor.
HUBERT H. HUMPHREY (1911–1978)

8063 The love of our neighbor is the only door out of the dungeon of self.
GEORGE MACDONALD (1824–1905)

8064 The only time to look down on your neighbor is when you are bending over to help.

8065 We are not the better for our Christianity if our neighbor is the worse for it.

8066 We make our friends; we make our enemies; but God makes our next door neighbor. Hence he comes to us clad in all the careless terrors of nature; he is as strange as the stars, as reckless and indifferent as the rain. He is man, the most terrible of the beasts.
G. K. CHESTERTON (1874–1936)

8067 What you wish for your neighbor, that you ask for yourself. If you don't wish his good, you ask for your own death.
ANGELUS SILESIUS (1624–1677)

8068 While the spirit of neighborliness was important on the frontier because neighbors were so few, it is even more

important now because our neighbors
are so many.
LADY BIRD JOHNSON

8069 Your neighbor is the man who is next
to you at the moment, the man with
whom any business has brought you
into contact.
GEORGE MACDONALD (1824–1905)

8070 Your neighbor is the man who needs
you.
ELBERT GREEN HUBBARD (1856–1915)

NEUTRALITY

8071 Neutral men are the devil's allies.
EDWIN HUBBEL CHAPIN (1814–1880)

8072 Neutrality is at times a graver sin than
belligerence.
LOUIS D. BRANDEIS (1856–1941)

8073 Neutrality is evidence of weakness.
LAJOS KOSSUTH (1802–1894)

8074 The hottest places in hell are reserved
for those who, in a period of moral crisis, maintain their neutrality.
DANTE ALIGHIERI (1265–1321)

8075 There is no such thing as being neutral, we are either children of God or
of the devil; we either love or we hate;
the twilight is torn away ruthlessly.
OSWALD CHAMBERS (1874–1917)

8076 We sometimes try to maintain our
moral neutrality by saying that there
are two sides to every question. True
enough, and there are two sides to a
sheet of flypaper, but it makes a big
difference to the fly which side he
chooses.
SIDNEY GREENBERG

NEW YEAR

8077 Another year is dawning;
dear Father, let it be,
In working or in waiting,
another year with thee.
Another year of progress,
another year of praise,
Another year of proving
thy presence all the days.

Another year of service,
of witness for thy love;
Another year of training
for holier work above.
Another year is dawning;
dear Father, let it be,
on earth, or else in heaven, another
year for thee.
FRANCES RIDLEY HAVERGAL (1836–1879)

8078 Even while we sing, he smiles his last,
And leaves our sphere behind.
The good Old Year is with the past,
O be the New as kind!
WILLIAM CULLEN BRYANT (1794–1878)

8079 I see not a step before me as I tread on
another year;
But I've left the past in God's keeping—the future his mercy shall clear;
And what looks dark in the distance
may brighten as I draw near.
MARY GARDINER BRAINARD (C. 1860)

8080 I suppose when we wake on January 1
the world will look the same. But
there is a reminder of the Resurrection
at the start of each new year, each new
decade. That's why I also like sunrises,
Mondays, and new seasons. God
seems to be saying, "With me you can
always start afresh."
ADA LUM

8081 The New Year! And a road that we
must go!
Lord God, you know
Each bog, each rugged hill.
GRACE NOLL CROWELL

8082 The year is closed, the record made,
The last deed done, the last word said,
The memory alone remains
Of all its joys, its griefs, its gains,
And now with purpose full and clear,
We turn to meet another year.
ROBERT BROWNING (1812–1889)

NIGHT

8083 Night conceals a world but reveals a
universe.
ROBERT BROWNING (1812–1889)

8084 Night falls but never breaks, and day
breaks but never falls.

8085 Night is the sabbath of mankind,
     To rest the body and the mind.
     SAMUEL BUTLER (1612–1680)

8086 The day is done, and the darkness
     Falls from the wings of night,

As a feather is wafted downward
From an eagle in his flight.
HENRY WADSWORTH LONGFELLOW
(1807–1882)

O

OBEDIENCE

8087 All heaven is waiting to help those who will discover the will of God and do it.
J. ROBERT ASHCROFT (1878–1958)

8088 All my requests are lost in one, "Father, thy will be done!"
CHARLES WESLEY (1707–1788)

8089 Faith and obedience are bound up in the same bundle. He that obeys God, trusts God; and he that trusts God, obeys God.
CHARLES HADDON SPURGEON (1834–1892)

8090 If for one whole day, quietly and determinedly, we were to give ourselves up to the ownership of Jesus and to obeying his orders, we should be amazed at its close to realize all he had packed into that one day.
OSWALD CHAMBERS (1874–1917)

8091 If God were to remove from us the possibility of disobedience there would be no value in our obedience, it would be a mechanical business.
OSWALD CHAMBERS (1874–1917)

8092 If you desire Christ for a perpetual guest, give him all the keys of your heart; let not one cabinet be locked up from him; give him the range of every room and the key of every chamber.
CHARLES HADDON SPURGEON (1834–1892)

8093 If you have received the Spirit and are obeying him, you find he brings your spirit into complete harmony with God, and the sound of your goings and the sound of God's goings are one and the same.
OSWALD CHAMBERS (1874–1917)

8094 It is not what we do that matters, but what a sovereign God chooses to do through us. God doesn't want our success; he wants us. He doesn't demand our achievements; he demands our obedience.

8095 It is only by obedience that we understand the teaching of God.
OSWALD CHAMBERS (1874–1917)

8096 Justice is the insurance we have on our lives, and obedience is the premium we pay for it.
WILLIAM PENN (1644–1718)

8097 Never think that Jesus commanded a trifle, nor dare to trifle with anything he has commanded.
DWIGHT LYMAN MOODY (1837–1899)

8098 No bliss I seek, but to fulfill
In life, in death, thy lovely will;
No succour in my woes I want,
Except what thou art pleased to grant.
Our days are numbered—let us spare
Our anxious hearts a needless care;
'Tis thine to number out our days,
And ours to give them to thy praise.
MADAME JEANNE MARIE DE LA MOTHE GUYON (1648–1717)

8099 Obedience is not servitude of man to man, but submission to the will of God who governs through the medium of men.
POPE LEO XIII (1810–1903)

8100 Obedience is the eye of the spirit. Failure to obey dims and dulls the spiritual understanding.
SAMUEL DICKEY GORDON (1859–1936)

8101 Obedience is the key that unlocks the door to every profound spiritual experience.
DOROTHY KERIN

8102 Obedience is the key to every door.
GEORGE MACDONALD (1824–1905)

8103 Obedience leads to faith. Live faithfully by the little bit of light you now have, and you will be given more.
LOUIS CASSELS (1922–1974)

8104 Obedience means marching right on whether we feel like it or not. Many times we go against our feelings. Faith is one thing, feeling is another.
DWIGHT LYMAN MOODY (1837–1899)

8105 Obedience to God will mean that some time or other you enter into desolation.
OSWALD CHAMBERS (1874–1917)

8106 Obedience to Jesus Christ is essential, but not compulsory; he never insists on being Master. We feel that if only he would insist, we should obey him. But our Lord never enforces his "thou shalts" and "thou shalt nots"; he never takes means to force us to do what he says. He never coerces. In certain moods we wish he would make us do the thing, but he will not; and in other moods we wish he would leave us alone altogether, but he will not. If we do not keep his commandments, he does not come and tell us we are wrong. We know it, we cannot get away from it.
OSWALD CHAMBERS (1874–1917)

8107 Obedience to revealed truth guarantees guidance in matters unrevealed.
ERWIN W. LUTZER (1941–)

8108 Obey . . . take up your cross . . . deny yourself . . . it all sounds very hard. It is hard. Anyone who tells you differently is peddling spiritual soothing syrup, not real Christianity. And yet, in a strangely paradoxical way, it is also easy. With every cross that we lift in obedience to Christ comes the strength to carry it. It is always a package deal.
LOUIS CASSELS (1922–1974)

8109 One act of obedience is better than one hundred sermons.
DIETRICH BONHOEFFER (1906–1945)

8110 The really important thing in life is not the avoidance of mistakes, but the obedience of faith. By obedience, the man is led step by step to correct his errors, whereas nothing will ever happen to him if he doesn't get going.
PAUL TOURNIER (1898–1986)

8111 The term *obey* would be better expressed by the word *use*. For instance, a scientist uses the laws of nature; that is, he more than obeys them, he causes them to fulfill their destiny in his work. That is exactly what happens in the saint's life. He uses the commands of the Lord, and they fulfill God's destiny in his life.
OSWALD CHAMBERS (1874–1917)

8112 Thirty years of our Lord's life are hidden in these words of the gospel: "He was subject unto them."
JACQUES BÉNIGNE BOSSUET (1627–1704)

8113 To be like Christ. That is our goal, plain and simple. It sounds like a peaceful, relaxing, easy objective. But stop and think. He learned obedience

by the things he suffered. So must we. It is neither easy nor quick nor natural. It is impossible in the flesh, slow in coming, and supernatural in scope. Only Christ can accomplish it within us.
CHARLES R. SWINDOLL (1934–)

8114 Understanding can wait, but obedience cannot.
GEOFFREY GROGAN

8115 We are born subjects, and to obey God is perfect liberty. He that does this shall be free, safe, and happy.
LUCIUS ANNAEUS SENECA (C. 4 B.C.–A.D. 65)

8116 We learn more by five minutes' obedience than by ten years' study.
OSWALD CHAMBERS (1874–1917)

8117 Weighing the pros and cons for and against a statement of Jesus Christ's means that for the time being I refuse to obey him.
OSWALD CHAMBERS (1874–1917)

8118 What we think of, what we know, or what we believe is, in the end, of little consequence. The only thing of consequence is what we do.
JOHN RUSKIN (1819–1900)

8119 When we are obedient, God guides our steps and our stops.
CORRIE TEN BOOM (1892–1983)

OLD AGE

8120 'Tis sweet to grow old in the fear of the Lord,
As life's shadows longer creep.
Till our steps grow slow, and our sun swings low—
He gives his beloved sleep.
JOHN WESLEY (1703–1791)

8121 A description of old age in its frailty: The keepers of the house (arms) and the strong men (legs) are weak and trembling; the grinders cease (teeth) and the windows are darkened (eyesight dimmed), the doors shut (ears are deaf), the grinding low (slow and tedious mastication); the easily startled nerves, and the loss of voice, the inability to climb, and the fear of highway traffic, the whitened hair like the almond tree in blossom when any work seems a burden, and the failing natural desire, all portray the old man nearing the end of his earthly journey.
OSWALD CHAMBERS (1874–1917)

8122 Age is a quality of mind.
If you have left your dreams behind,
If hope is cold,
If you no longer look ahead,
If your ambitions' fires are dead—
Then you are old.
But if from life you take the best,
And if in life you keep the zest,
If love you hold;
No matter how the years go by,
No matter how the birthdays fly—
You are not old.

8123 Age is not important—unless you're a cheese.

8124 An elderly person is a person who is ten years older than you are.

8125 As a white candle
In a holy place,
So is the beauty
Of an aged face.
JOSEPH CAMPBELL (1881–1944)

8126 As long as you can still be disappointed, you are still young.
SARAH CHURCHILL (1914–)

8127 As we get old we become at the same time more foolish and wiser.
FRANÇOIS ALEXANDRE FRÉDÉRIC, DUC DE LA ROCHEFOUCAULD-LIANCOURT (1747–1827)

8128 Between the ages of seventy and eighty-three Commodore Vanderbilt added about 100 million to his fortune.
Kant at seventy-four wrote his *Anthropology, Metaphysics of Ethics,* and *Strife of the Faculties.*
Tintoretto at seventy-four painted the vast *Paradise,* a canvas seventy-four by thirty feet.
Verdi at seventy-four produced his masterpiece, *Otello;* at eighty, *Falstaff;* and at eighty-five, the famous *Ave Maria, Stabat Mater,* and *Te Deum.*
Lamarck at seventy-eight completed his great zoological work, *The Natural History of the Invertebrates.*

Oliver Wendell Holmes at seventy-nine wrote *Over the Teacups*.

Cato at eighty began the study of Greek.

Goethe at eighty completed *Faust*.

Tennyson at eighty-three wrote *Crossing the Bar*.

Titian at ninety-eight painted his historic picture of the *Battle of Lepanto*.

8129 Everyone faces at all times two fateful possibilities: one is to grow older, the other not.

8130 Few people know how to be old.
FRANÇOIS, DUC DE LA ROCHEFOUCAULD (1613–1680)

8131 God gave us memories that we might have roses in December.
SIR JAMES M. BARRIE (1860–1937)

8132 Grow old along with me!
The best is yet to be,
The last of life, for which the first was made:
Our times are in his hand,
Who saith, "A whole I planned,
Youth shows but half; trust God:
See all, nor be afraid!"
ROBERT BROWNING (1812–1889)

8133 I have had just about all I can take of myself.
SAMUEL NATHANIEL BEHRMAN (1893–1973)

8134 I'm deteriorating according to schedule.

8135 If I cannot work or rise from my chair or my bed, love remains to me; I can pray.
WILLIAM CONGREVE (1670–1729)

8136 If only, when one heard
That Old Age was coming
One could bolt the door,
Answer "Not at home"
And refuse to meet him!
KOKINSHU

8137 If wrinkles must be written upon our brows, let them not be written upon the heart. The spirit should not grow old.
JAMES A. GARFIELD (1831–1881)

8138 In old age faith seems to be the most marvelous possession anyone can have.
MALCOLM MUGGERIDGE (1903–1990)

8139 In spite of illness, in spite even of the archenemy sorrow, one can remain alive long past the usual date of disintegration if one is unafraid of change, insatiable in intellectual curiosity, interested in big things, and happy in small ways.
EDITH WHARTON (1862–1937)

8140 In the days of my youth I remembered my God! And he hath not forgotten my age.
ROBERT SOUTHEY (1774–1843)

8141 It is better to show up for work in the kingdom of heaven at sunset than not to show up at all!
ERWIN W. LUTZER (1941–)

8142 John Quincy Adams himself is very well, thank you. But the house he lives in is sadly dilapidated. It is tottering on its foundations. The walls are badly shattered, and the roof is worn. The building trembles with every wind, and I think John Quincy Adams will have to move out of it before long. But he himself is very well.
JOHN QUINCY ADAMS (1767–1848)

8143 Let me grow lovely, growing old—
So many fine things do;
Laces and ivory and gold,
And silks need not be new.
And there is a healing in old trees,
Old streets a glamor hold;
Why may not I, as well as these,
Grow lovely, growing old?
KARLE WILSON BAKER

8144 Live your life and forget your age.
FRANK BERING

8145 Lord, hear our prayer for those who, growing old
Feel that their time of usefulness is told.
Let them still find some little part of play,
Nor feel unwanted at the close of day.

8146 My deafness I endure
To dentures I'm resigned
Bifocals I can manage
But how I miss my mind.

8147 No man loves life as he who's growing old.
SOPHOCLES (C. 496–406 B.C.)

8148 Nothing is more beautiful than cheerfulness in an old face.
JOHANN PAUL FRIEDRICH RICHTER (1763–1825)

8149 O age! Blessed time of life, I salute you even now! Men are afraid of you, but they should love you as the most happy time of life because you are its end. I shall love you as the dawning of the eternal day. I can already see my temples growing white under the touch of your harbingers, and a smile rises to my lips.
LUCIE CHRISTINE (1858–1916)

8150 O harsh old age! How hateful is your reign!
EURIPIDES (C. 484–406 B.C.)

8151 Old age comes from God, old age leads on to God.
PIERRE TEILHARD DE CHARDIN (1881–1955)

8152 Old age is a dreary solitude.
PLATO (C. 428–348 B.C.)

8153 Old age is an illness in itself.
TERENCE (C. 186–C. 159 B.C.)

8154 Old age is an incurable disease.
LUCIUS ANNAEUS SENECA (C. 4 B.C.–A.D. 65)

8155 Old age is an island surrounded by death.
JUAN MONTALVO (1832–1889)

8156 Old age is but a second childhood.
ARISTOPHANES (C. 450–385 B.C.)

8157 Old age is but older children.
LEWIS CARROLL (1833–1898)

8158 Old age is like a plane flying through a storm. Once you're aboard, there's nothing you can do. You can't stop the plane, you can't stop the storm, you can't stop time. So one might as well accept it calmly, wisely.
GOLDA MEIR (1898–1978)

8159 Old age is more to be feared than death.
JUVENAL (C. 60–C. 127)

8160 Old age isn't so bad when you consider the alternative.
MAURICE CHEVALIER (1888–1972)

8161 Old age needs so little but needs that little so much.
MARGARET WILLOUR

8162 Old age puts more wrinkles in our minds than on our faces.
MICHEL EYQUEM DE MONTAIGNE (1533–1592)

8163 Old age, a second child, by nature curs'd
With more and greater evils than the first,
Weak, sickly, full of pains; in ev'ry breath
Railing at life, and yet afraid of death.
CHARLES CHURCHILL (1731–1764)

8164 Old age, though despised, is coveted by all men.
FRENCH PROVERB

8165 Old age: the arctic loneliness of age.
S. WEIR MITCHELL (1829–1914)

8166 Old age: the crown of life, our play's last act.
CICERO (106–43 B.C.)

8167 Old age: twice a child.
CRATINUS (C. 495–C. 420 B.C.)

8168 One thing about getting old is that you can sing in the bathroom while brushing your teeth.

8169 Some people, no matter how old they get, never lose their beauty—they merely move it from their faces into their hearts.

8170 Strength has ever to be made perfect in weakness, and old age is one of the weaknesses in which it is perfected.
GEORGE MACDONALD (1824–1905)

8171 The evening of a well-spent life brings its lamps with it.
JOSEPH JOUBERT (1754–1824)

8172 The fairest and the sweetest rose
In time must fade and beauty lose.

8173 The older the fiddle, the sweeter the tune.
ENGLISH PROVERB

8174 The tree of deepest root is found
Least willing still to quit the ground;
'Twas therefore said by ancient sages
That love of life increased with years,
So much that in our later stages,

When pains grow sharp, and sickness
  rages,
The greatest love of life appears.
HESTER LYNCH THRALE PIOZZI
(1741–1821)

8175 The trouble with growing old is that
you stop feeling your oats and start
feeling your corns.

8176 The unlovely personality that develops
in some senior citizens is not a sudden
onset. It is rather the continuation of
childhood temper tantrums, the elabo-
ration of teenage assertiveness, the further development of middle-aged
orneriness that has not fully developed
into the thorny, sour, and crabbed frustrations of old age.
S. I. McMILLEN

8177 There is more danger of rusting out
than wearing out.
HUMPHREY DAVY ROLLESTON (1862–1944)

8178 To know how to grow old is the master work of wisdom and one of the
most difficult chapters in the great art
of living.
HENRI FRÉDÉRIC AMIEL (1821–1881)

8179 To me, fair friend, you never can be old.
For as you were when first your eye I
  ey'd, such seems your beauty still.
WILLIAM SHAKESPEARE (1564–1616)

8180 We grow neither better nor worse as
we grow old, but more like ourselves.
MAY LAMBERTON BECKER

8181 We must both, I'm afraid, recognize
that, as we grow older, we become like
old cars—more and more repairs and
replacements are necessary. We must
just look forward to the fine new
machines (lastest Resurrection model)
which are waiting for us, we hope, in
the Divine garage.
C. S. LEWIS (1898–1963)

8182 What can be more miserable than that
old age, when it looks back, sees with
great horror what beautiful things it
has neglected, and what foul things it
has embraced: and again, when it
looks forward, sees the last day hanging over its head.
DESIDERIUS ERASMUS (C. 1466–1536)

8183 When men grow virtuous in their old
age, they are merely making a sacrifice
to God of the devil's leavings.
JONATHAN SWIFT (1667–1745)

8184 When you see an old man amiable,
mild, equable, content, and good-
humored, be sure that in his youth he
has been just, generous, and forbearing. In his end he does not lament the
past, nor dread the future; he is like
the evening of a fine day.
ARABIAN PROVERB

8185 Whenever a man's friends begin to
compliment him about looking young,
he may be sure that they think he is
growing old.
WASHINGTON IRVING (1783–1859)

8186 Whoever saw old age not praising
times past and blaming the present?
MICHEL EYQUEM DE MONTAIGNE
(1533–1592)

8187 Winter is on my head, but eternal
spring is in my heart.
VICTOR HUGO (1802–1885)

8188 Wrinkles should merely indicate where
smiles have been.
MARK TWAIN (1835–1910)

8189 You don't grow old; when you cease
to grow, you are old.
CHARLES JUDSON HERRICK (1868–1960)

8190 You really know you're getting old
when you bend over to tie your shoes,
and you wonder what else you can do
while you're down there.

OPINION

8191 All empty souls tend to extreme opinion.
WILLIAM BUTLER YEATS (1865–1939)

8192 An obstinate man does not hold opinions, they hold him.
ALEXANDER POPE (1688–1744)

8193 Do not think of knocking out another
person's brains because he differs in
opinion from you. It would be as rational to knock yourself on the head
because you differ from yourself ten
years ago.
HORACE MANN (1796–1859)

8194 Every new opinion, at its starting, is precisely in a minority of one.
THOMAS CARLYLE (1795–1881)

8195 He that never changes his opinions, never corrects his mistakes, will never be wiser tomorrow than he is today.
TRYON EDWARDS (1809–1894)

8196 I beg you, do not be unchangeable.
Do not believe that you alone can be right.
The man who thinks that,
The man who maintains that only he has the power
To reason correctly, the gift to speak, the soul,
A man like that, when you know him, turns out empty.
SOPHOCLES (C. 496–406 B.C.)

8197 Man is a gregarious animal, and much more so in his mind than in his body. He may like to go alone for a walk, but he hates to stand alone in his opinions.
GEORGE SANTAYANA (1863–1952)

8198 Opinion is that exercise of the human will which helps us to make a decision without information.
JOHN ERSKINE (1509–1591)

8199 Opinions are stronger than armies. Opinions, if they are founded in truth and justice, will in the end prevail against the bayonets of infantry, the fire of artillery, and the charges of calvary.
LORD PALMERSTON (1784–1865)

8200 Private opinion is weak, but public opinion is almost omnipotent.
HARRIET BEECHER STOWE (1811–1896)

8201 Refusing to have an opinion is a way of having one, isn't it?
LUIGI PIRANDELLO (1867–1936)

8202 So many men, so many opinions.
TERENCE (C. 186–C. 159 B.C.)

8203 Some praise at morning what they blame at night,
But always think the last opinion right.
ALEXANDER POPE (1688–1744)

8204 That was excellently observed, say I, when I read a passage in an author where his opinion agrees with mine.
JONATHAN SWIFT (1667–1745)

8205 The feeble tremble before opinion, the foolish defy it, the wise judge it, the skillful direct it.
MADAME ROLAND (1754–1793)

8206 The foolish and the dead alone never change their opinions.
JAMES RUSSELL LOWELL (1819–1891)

8207 Those who never retract, love themselves better than the truth.
JOSEPH JOUBERT (1754–1824)

8208 Where there is much desire to learn, there of necessity will be much arguing, much writing, many opinions; for opinion in good men is but knowledge in the making.
JOHN MILTON (1608–1674)

8209 Whoever fears to submit any question to the test of free discussion, loves his own opinion more than the truth.
THOMAS WATSON (C. 1557–1592)

OPPORTUNITY

8210 A wise man will make more opportunities than he finds.
FRANCIS BACON (1561–1626)

8211 An ostrich with its head in the sand is just as blind to opportunity as to disaster.

8212 Do not wait for extraordinary circumstances to do good; try to use ordinary situations.
JOHANN PAUL FRIEDRICH RICHTER (1763–1825)

8213 Four things come not back: the sped arrow, the spoken word, time past, and the neglected opportunity.
ARABIAN PROVERB

8214 Gather ye rosebuds while ye may, Old time is still a-flying,
And this same flower that smiles today
Tomorrow will be dying.
ROBERT HERRICK (1591–1674)

8215 He that waits for chance is never sure of his dinner.
FRENCH PROVERB

8216 He that will not when he may,
He shall not when he will.
ROBERT MANNING (1288–1338)

8217 Life's great opportunities often open
on the road of daily duties.

8218 Man's extremity is God's opportunity.
JOHN FLAVEL (1627–1691)

8219 Never think you could do something if
only you had a different lot and sphere
assigned you. What you call hindrances, obstacles, discouragements,
are probably God's opportunities.
HORACE BUSHNELL (1802–1876)

8220 No great man ever complains of want
of opportunity.
RALPH WALDO EMERSON (1803–1882)

8221 Opportunities are usually disguised as
hard work, so most people don't recognize them.
ANN LANDERS (1918–)

8222 Seize the day; trust the morrow as
little as possible.
HORACE (65–8 B.C.)

8223 Take a lesson from the mosquito: he
never waits for an opening—he makes
one.

8224 The keen spirit
Seizes the prompt occasion—
Makes the thought
Start into instant action, and at once
Plans and performs, resolves and exe-
cutes.
HANNAH MORE (1745–1833)

8225 The lure of the distant and the difficult
is deceptive. The great opportunity is
where you are.
JOHN BURROUGHS (1837–1921)

8226 There's no use going back for a lost
opportunity—someone else has
already found it.

8227 To recognize opportunity is the difference between success and failure.

8228 We are all faced with a series of great
opportunities brilliantly disguised as
impossible situations.
CHARLES R. SWINDOLL (1934–)

8229 When one door closes, another opens;
but we often look so long and so regretfully upon the closed door that we do
not see the one that has opened for us.
ALEXANDER GRAHAM BELL (1847–1922)

8230 With doubt and dismay you are
smitten,
You think there's no chance for you,
son?
Why the best books haven't been
written,
The best race hasn't been run.
BERTON BRALEY (1882–1966)

OPTIMISM

8231 Accentuate the positive,
Eliminate the negative,
Latch on to the affirmative,
Don't mess with Mr. In-Between.
HAROLD ARLEN AND JOHNNY MERCER

8232 An optimist is a guy who has never
had much experience.
DON MARQUIS (1878–1937)

8233 God's in his heaven
All's right with the world!
ROBERT BROWNING (1812–1889)

8234 I am an optimist. It does not seem too
much use being anything else.
SIR WINSTON CHURCHILL (1874–1965)

8235 Keep your face to the sunshine and
you cannot see the shadow.
HELEN ADAMS KELLER (1880–1968)

8236 Optimism is the madness of maintaining that everything is right when it is
wrong.
VOLTAIRE (1694–1778)

8237 Optimism, apart from a man's belief
and his acceptance of Christianity,
may be healthy-minded, but it is
blinded; when he faces the facts of life
as they are, uncolored by his temperament, despair is the only possible ending for him.
OSWALD CHAMBERS (1874–1917)

8238 Optimists do not wait for improvement; they achieve it.
PAUL WILHELM VON KEPPLER (1852–1926)

8239 Still round the corner there may wait,
A new road, or a secret gate.
J. R. R. TOLKIEN (1892–1973)

8240 There is no danger of developing eye-strain from looking on the bright side.

8241 There is not enough darkness in all the world to put out the light of even one small candle.
ROBERT ALDEN

8242 They can conquer who believe they can.
VIRGIL (70–19 B.C.)

8243 What will be will be well, for what is, is well.
WALT WHITMAN (1819–1892)

OPTIMISM/PESSIMISM

8244 'Twixt the optimist and the pessimist
The difference is droll;
The optimist sees the doughnut
But the pessimist sees the hole.
McLANDBURGH WILSON (1877–1945)

8245 An optimist is a person who sees a green light everywhere, while the pessimist sees only the red light. But the truly wise are color-blind.
ALBERT SCHWEITZER (1875–1965)

8246 An optimist sees a light where there is none, and a pessimist always tries to put it out.

8247 My knowledge is pessimistic, but my willing and hoping are optimistic.
ALBERT SCHWEITZER (1875–1965)

8248 On the whole, I came to the conclusion that the optimist thought everything good except the pessimist, and that the pessimist thought everything bad, except himself.
G. K. CHESTERTON (1874–1936)

8249 The pessimist complains about the wind; the optimist expects it to change; the realist adjusts the sails.
WILLIAM ARTHUR WARD (1812–1882)

8250 The pessimist sees only the tunnel; the optimist sees the light at the end of the tunnel; the realist sees the tunnel and the light—and the next tunnel.
SYDNEY J. HARRIS (1917–1986)

8251 The pessimist sees the difficulty in every opportunity; the optimist sees the opportunity in every difficulty.
LAWRENCE PEARSALL JACKS (1860–1955)

8252 The cross-carrying Christian . . . is both a confirmed pessimist and an optimist the like of which is to be found nowhere else on earth.
A. W. TOZER (1897–1963)

P

PAIN

8253 Adam ate the apple and our teeth still ache.
HUNGARIAN PROVERB

8254 Although today he prunes my twigs with pain,
Yet doth his blood nourish and warm my root:
Tomorrow I shall put forth buds again
And clothe myself with fruit.
CHRISTINA GEORGINA ROSSETTI (1830–1894)

8255 For philosophers, pain is a problem of metaphysics; for stoics, it is an exercise; for mystics, it is an ecstasy; for the religious, a travail meekly to be borne; for clinicians a symptom to be understood and an ill to be relieved.
CHARLES F. W. ILLINGWORTH (1899–)

8256 God uses chronic pain and weakness, along with other afflictions, as his chisel for sculpting our lives. Felt weakness deepens dependence on Christ for strength each day. The weaker we feel, the harder we lean. And the harder we lean, the stronger we grow spiritually, even while our bodies waste away. To live with your "thorn" uncomplainingly—that is, sweet, patient, and free in heart to love and help others, even though every day you feel weak—is true sanctification. It is true healing for the spirit. It is a supreme victory of grace. The healing of your sinful person thus goes forward, even though the healing of your mortal body does not.
J. I. PACKER (1926–)

8257 God whispers to us in our pleasures, speaks in our conscience, but shouts in our pains: it is his megaphone to rouse a deaf world.
C. S. LEWIS (1898–1963)

8258 I believe that all pain is contrary to God's will, absolutely but not relatively. A mother spanking a child would . . . rather cause it this pain than let it go on pulling the cat's tail, but she would like it better if no situation which demands a smack had arisen.
C. S. LEWIS (1898–1963)

8259 If I ever wonder about the appropriate "spiritual" response to pain and suffering, I can note how Jesus responded to his own: with fear and trembling, with loud cries and tears.
PHILIP YANCEY (1949–)

8260 If you come to think about it, physical pain has many singularities. Of all human experiences it is, as long as it lasts, the most absorbing; and it is the only human experience which, when it comes to an end, automatically confers a real if not perhaps a very high kind of happiness. It is also the only experience this side of death which is by its nature solitary. But the oddest thing about it is that despite its intensity, despite its unequalled power over mind and body, when it is over, you cannot really remember it at all.
PETER FLEMING (1907–1971)

8261 Illness is the doctor to whom we pay most heed: to kindness, to knowledge we make promises only; pain we obey.
MARCEL PROUST (1871–1922)

8262 My soul is a dark ploughed field
In the cold rain;
My soul is a broken field
Ploughed by pain.
SARA TEASDALE (1884–1933)

8263 Not to have had pain is not to have been human.
JEWISH PROVERB

8264 Pain and suffering produce a fork in the road. It is not possible to remain unchanged. To let others or circumstances dictate your future is to have chosen. To allow pain to corrode your spirit is to have chosen. And to be transformed into the image of Christ by these difficult and trying circumstances is to have chosen.
TIM HANSEL

8265 Pain can either make us better or bitter.
TIM HANSEL

8266 Pain is inevitable for all of us, but misery is optional.
BARBARA JOHNSON

8267 Pain is life—the sharper, the more evidence of life.
CHARLES LAMB (1775–1834)

8268 Pain is no evil, unless it conquer us.
CHARLES KINGSLEY (1819–1875)

8269 Pain is the deepest thing we have in our nature, and union through pain and suffering has always seemed more real and holy than any other.
ARTHUR HENRY HALLAM (1811–1833)

8270 Pain teaches the luxury of health.
MARTIN FARQUHAR TUPPER (1810–1889)

8271 Pleasure is oft a visitant; but pain
Clings cruelly to us.
JOHN KEATS (1795–1821)

8272 The pain of the mind is worse than the pain of the body.
PUBLILIUS SYRUS (FIRST CENTURY B.C.)

8273 There is no gain without pain.
ROBERT HAROLD SCHULLER (1926–)

8274 There is purpose in pain,
Otherwise it were devilish.
OWEN MEREDITH (1831–1891)

8275 Those who wear the shoe know best where it pinches.
CHARLES HADDON SPURGEON (1834–1892)

8276 We cannot learn without pain.
ARISTOTLE (384–322 B.C.)

8277 We haven't too much pain, we have too little; for through pain we enter into God.
GEORGE BÜCHNER (1813–1837)

8278 When God sees a scar, . . . he creates a star!
ROBERT HAROLD SCHULLER (1926–)

8279 When I enter into my pain rather than run from it, I will find at the center of my pain an amazing insight.
JOHN POWELL

8280 When pain is to be borne, a little courage helps more than much knowledge, a little human sympathy more than much courage, and the least tincture of the love of God more than all.
C. S. LEWIS (1898–1963)

PARENTING

8281 Accept the fact that there will be moments when your children will hate you. This is normal and natural. But how a child handles hate may deter-

mine whether he will go to Harvard or San Quentin.
ANN LANDERS (1918–   )

8282 Be very vigilant over thy child in the April of his understanding, lest the frosts of May nip his blossoms.
FRANCIS QUARLES (1592–1644)

8283 Better a little chiding than a great deal of heartbreak.
WILLIAM SHAKESPEARE (1564–1616)

8284 Better the child should cry than the father.
GERMAN PROVERB

8285 Build me a son, O Lord, who will be strong enough to know when he is weak and brave enough to face himself when he is afraid, one who will be proud and unbending in honest defeat, and humble and gentle in victory.
DOUGLAS MACARTHUR (1880–1964)

8286 Children have more need of models than of critics.
FRENCH PROVERB

8287 Children just don't fit into a "to do" list very well. It takes time to be an effective parent when children are small. It takes time to introduce them to good books. It takes time to fly kites and play punch ball and put together jigsaw puzzles. It takes time to listen.
JAMES C. DOBSON (1936–   )

8288 Children want their parents more than they want the junk we buy them.
JAMES C. DOBSON (1936–   )

8289 Children will invariably talk, eat, walk, think, respond, and act like their parents. Give them a target to shoot at. Give them a goal to work toward. Give them a pattern that they can see clearly, and you give them something that gold and silver cannot buy.
BILLY GRAHAM (1918–   )

8290 Could I climb to the highest place in Athens, I would lift my voice and proclaim: "Fellow citizens, why do you turn and scrape every stone to gather wealth, and take so little care of your

children to whom one day you must relinquish it all?"
SOCRATES (470–399 B.C.)

8291 Direct your efforts more to preparing youth for the path and less to preparing the path for youth.
BENJAMIN BARR LINDSEY (1869–1943)

8292 Discipline and love are not antithetical; one is a function of the other.
JAMES C. DOBSON (1936–   )

8293 Do not try to produce an ideal child; it would find no fitness in this world.
HERBERT SPENCER (1820–1903)

8294 Don't let these parenting years get away from you. Your contributions to your children and grandchildren could rank as your greatest accomplishments in life.
JAMES C. DOBSON (1936–   )

8295 Don't panic even during the storms of adolescence. Better times are ahead.
JAMES C. DOBSON (1936–   )

8296 Ere a child has reached to seven
Teach him all the way to heaven;
Better still the work will thrive
If he learns before he's five.
CHARLES HADDON SPURGEON (1834–1892)

8297 Give a little love to a child and you get a great deal back.
JOHN RUSKIN (1819–1900)

8298 How can one have a sweet fragrance whose father is an onion and whose mother is garlic?
ARABIAN PROVERB

8299 Ideal parenting is modeled after the relationship between God and man.
JAMES C. DOBSON (1936–   )

8300 If a child sees his parents day in and day out living without self-restraint or self-discipline, then he will come in the deepest fibers of his being to believe that that is the way to live.
M. SCOTT PECK (1936–   )

8301 If a child tells a lie, tell him that he has told a lie, but don't call him a liar. If you define him as a liar, you break down his confidence in his own character.
JOHANN PAUL FRIEDERICH (1763–1825)

8302 If it was going to be easy to raise kids, it never would have started with something called labor.

8303 If you love your son, give him plenty of discipline; if you hate him, cram him with dainties.
CHINESE PROVERB

8304 Kids can frustrate and irritate their parents . . . but the rewards of raising them far outweigh the cost. Besides, nothing worth having ever comes cheap.
JAMES C. DOBSON (1936–)

8305 Learning in childhood is like engraving on a rock.
ARABIAN PROVERB

8306 Let every Christian father and mother understand, when their child is three years old, that they have done more than half of all they will ever do for his character.
HORACE BUSHNELL (1802–1876)

8307 Let thy child's first lesson be obedience, and the second will be what thou wilt.
BENJAMIN FRANKLIN (1706–1790)

8308 Let us not fool ourselves—without Christianity, without Christian education, without the principles of Christ inculcated into young life, we are simply rearing pagans.
PETER MARSHALL (1902–1949)

8309 Love your children with all your hearts, love them enough to discipline them before it is too late. . . . Praise them for important things, even if you have to stretch them a bit. Praise them a lot. They live on it like bread and butter, and they need it more than bread and butter.
LAVINA CHRISTENSEN FUGAL

8310 Making the decision to have a child is momentous—it is to decide forever to have your heart go walking around outside your body.
ELIZABETH STONE

8311 Many children are afraid to go to their parents for counsel. Parents many times treat children as children when they often need to be talked to like grown-ups.
BILLY GRAHAM (1918–)

8312 Most parents learn too late that if they castigate, they should castigate the fault and not the child; if you reproach a fault, it can be reformed, but if you attack a personality, it can only defend itself.
SYDNEY J. HARRIS (1917–1986)

8313 Motherhood is full of frustrations and challenges . . . but, eventually they move out.

8314 Mothers and fathers are granted a single decade in which to lay a foundation of values and attitudes that will help their children cope with the future pressures and problems of adulthood.
JAMES C. DOBSON (1936–)

8315 Mothers' darlings make but milksop heroes.

8316 My father was a Methodist and believed in the laying on of hands, and believe me, he really laid them on!
A. W. TOZER (1897–1963)

8317 No job can compete with the responsibility of shaping and molding a new human being.
JAMES C. DOBSON (1936–)

8318 No wonder Cain turned out badly— his parents didn't have a book on child psychology to read.

8319 Oh, what a tangled web do parents weave
When they think that their children are naive.
OGDEN NASH (1902–1971)

8320 Our tendency is to grab and hold our children and not allow them to make mistakes. Then, when they do fail, we jump forward to bail them out and prevent them from learning valuable lessons.
JAMES C. DOBSON (1936–)

8321 Parents can afford to give allowances; what breaks them are the fringe benefits.

8322 Parents should work together as efficiently as two bookends.

8323 Parents who are afraid to put their foot down usually have children who step on their toes.
CHINESE PROVERB

8324 Parents who are always giving their children nothing but the best usually wind up with nothing but the worst.

8325 *Sensitivity* is the key word. It means "tuning in" to the thoughts and feelings of our kids, listening to the cues they give us, and reacting appropriately to what we detect.
JAMES C. DOBSON (1936–)

8326 The ability to say no is perhaps the greatest gift a parent has.

8327 The best way for a child to learn to fear God is to know a real Christian. The best way for a child to learn to pray is to live with a father and mother who know a life of friendship with God and who truly pray.
JOHANN HEINRICH PESTALOZZI 1746–1827)

8328 The fathers eat sour grapes and their children's teeth are set on edge.
ARABIAN PROVERB

8329 The most successful parents are those who have the skill to get behind the eyes of the child, seeing what he sees, thinking what he thinks, feeling what he feels.
JAMES C. DOBSON (1936–)

8330 The mother who spoils her child fattens a serpent.
SPANISH PROVERB

8331 The parent must convince himself that discipline is not something he does to the child; it is something he does for the child.
JAMES C. DOBSON (1936–)

8332 The proper attitude toward a child's disobedience is this: "I love you too much to let you behave like that."
JAMES C. DOBSON (1936–)

8333 The school will teach children how to read, but the environment of the home must teach them what to read. The school can teach them how to think, but the home must teach them what to believe.
CHARLES A. WELLS

8334 To withhold from a child some knowledge—apportioned to his understanding—of the world's sorrows and wrongs is to cheat him of his kinship with humanity.
AGNES REPPLIER (1855–1950)

8335 Today's young generation has grown up for the most part with too little loving discipline. These young people often say their parents hate them. The Bible would bear the kids out, for it says the father who doesn't chasten his son hates his son (Proverbs 13:24). Children somehow know this. They know it takes more love and hard work to discipline them.
ANITA BRYANT (1940–)

8336 We spend the first three years of a child's life teaching him to walk and talk and the next fifteen teaching him to sit down and be quiet!

8337 When you have saved a boy from the possibility of making any mistake, you have also prevented him from developing initiative.
JOHN ERSKINE (1509–1591)

8338 While yielding to loving parental leadership, children are also learning to yield to the benevolent leadership of God himself.
JAMES C. DOBSON (1936–)

PARENTS

8339 A child identifies his parents with God, whether or not the adults want that role.
JAMES C. DOBSON (1936–)

8340 A child tells in the street what its father and mother say at home.

8341 A mother plays a vital role as the primary interpreter of a father's personality, character, and integrity to their children. She can either help them bond together in love, or she can become a wedge that keeps them apart.
JAMES C. DOBSON (1936–)

8342 A suspicious parent makes an artful child.
THOMAS CHANDLER HALIBURTON (1796–1865)

8343 As a parent, you have to establish yourself as the leader early on and then work yourself out of a job thereafter.
JAMES C. DOBSON (1936–)

8344 As the twig is bent, the tree inclines.
VIRGIL (70–19 B.C.)

8345 Every parent is at some time the father of the unreturned prodigal with nothing to do but keep his house open to hope.
JOHN CIARDI (1916–1986)

8346 Every word and deed of a parent is a fibre woven into the character of a child that ultimately determines how that child fits into the fabric of society.
DAVID WILKERSON

8347 I believe I should have been swept by the flood of French infidelity, if it had not been for one thing, the remembrance of the time when my mother used to make me kneel by her side, and taking my little hand in hers, taught me to repeat the Lord's Prayer.
JOHN RANDOLPH (1773–1833)

8348 If you have no prayer life yourself, it is rather a useless gesture to make your child say his prayers every night.
PETER MARSHALL (1902–1949)

8349 Level with your child by being honest. Nobody spots a phony quicker than a child.
MARY MACCRACKEN

8350 Parents are the bones on which children sharpen their teeth.
PETER USTINOV (1921–)

8351 Parents have little time for children and a great vacuum has developed, and into that vacuum is going to move some kind of ideology.
BILLY GRAHAM (1918–)

8352 Parents wonder why the streams are bitter when they themselves have poisoned the fountain.
JOHN LOCKE (1632–1704)

8353 Slow down, parents! What's your rush, anyway? Your children will be gone so quickly, and you will have nothing but blurred memories of those years when they needed you.
JAMES C. DOBSON (1936–)

8354 The accent is on youth, but the stress is on parents.

8355 The parent who does not teach his child to obey is being cruel to him. The habit of implicit obedience to parental authority is the foundation of good citizenship. More than that, it is the foundation of subjection to God's authority.
BILLY GRAHAM (1918–)

8356 The religion of a child depends on what its mother and father are, and not on what they say.
HENRI FRÉDÉRIC AMIEL (1821–1881)

8357 The thing that impresses me most about America is the way parents obey their children.
THE DUKE OF WINDSOR (1894–1972)

8358 The voice of parents is the voice of gods, for to their children they are heaven's lieutenants.
WILLIAM SHAKESPEARE (1564–1616)

8359 There are no illegitimate children— only illegitimate parents.
LEON R. YANKWICH (1888–)

8360 Those who control what young people are taught and what they experience, what they see, hear, think, and believe . . . will determine the future course for the nation.
JAMES C. DOBSON (1936–)

8361 When I think of parents today, I'm reminded of a photograph of an elegantly dressed woman who is holding a cup of coffee. Her little finger is cocked ever so daintily to the side, and her face reveals utter self-confidence. Unfortunately, this woman does not yet know that her slip has collapsed around her feet. The caption reads, "Confidence is what you have before you understand the situation." Indeed!
JAMES C. DOBSON (1936–)

8362 Whenever a child lies, you will always find a severe parent. A lie would have no sense unless the truth were felt to be dangerous.
ALFRED ADLER (1870–1937)

8363 You fathers and you mothers fond, also,
If you have children, be it one or two,
Yours is the burden of their wise guidance
The while they are within your governance.
Beware that not from your own lax living,
Or by your negligence in chastening
They fall and perish; for I dare well say,
If that should chance you'll dearly have to pay.
Under a shepherd soft and negligent
Full many a sheep and lamb by wolf is rent.
GEOFFREY CHAUCER (C. 1342–1400)

PAST

8364 In Christ we can move out of our past into a meaningful present and a breathtaking future.
ERWIN W. LUTZER (1941–)

8365 Nothing is certain except the past.
LUCIUS ANNAEUS SENECA (C. 4 B.C.–A.D. 65)

8366 The past cannot be changed, but our response to it can be.
ERWIN W. LUTZER (1941–)

8367 The past is valuable as a guidepost, but dangerous if used as a hitching post.

8368 There is no past we can bring back by longing for it. There is only an eternal now that builds and creates out of the past something new and better.
JOHANN WOLFGANG VON GOETHE (1749–1832)

8369 There was—and O! how many sorrows crowd
Into these two brief words!
SIR WALTER SCOTT (1771–1832)

8370 These poor Might-Have-Beens,
These fatuous, ineffectual yesterdays!
WILLIAM ERNEST HENLEY (1849–1903)

8371 Through the centuries the people have dreamed of a Golden Age and longed for its return, unconscious that they dream of a day that had never been.
GUY E. SHIPLER

8372 You can never ride on the wave that went out yesterday.
JOHN WANAMAKER (1838–1922)

8373 You can't turn back the clock. But you can wind it up again.
BONNIE PRUDDEN

PAST/PRESENT/FUTURE

8374 Every man's life lies within the present; for the past is spent and done with, and the future is uncertain.
MARCUS AURELIUS ANTONINUS (121–180)

8375 Finish every day and be done with it. You have done what you could. Some blunders and absurdities no doubt crept in; forget them as soon as you can. Tomorrow is a new day; begin it well and serenely and with too high a spirit to be cumbered with your old nonsense. This day is all that is good and fair. It is too dear, with its hopes and invitations, to waste a moment on the yesterdays.
RALPH WALDO EMERSON (1803–1882)

8376 Gratitude looks to the past and love to the present; fear, greed, lust, and ambition look ahead.
C. S. LEWIS (1898–1963)

8377 It is of no use to pray for the old days; stand square where you are and make the present better than any past has been.
OSWALD CHAMBERS (1874–1917)

8378 Look not mournfully into the past. It comes not back again. Wisely improve the present. It is thine. Go forth to meet the shadowy future, without fear and with a manly heart.
HENRY WADSWORTH LONGFELLOW (1807–1882)

8379 Look up and not down; look forward and not back; look out and not in; and lend a hand.
EDWARD EVERETT HALE (1822–1909)

8380 Man spends his life in reasoning on the past, in complaining of the present, in fearing for the future.
ANTOINE DE RIVAROL (1753–1801)

8381 Our continual mistake is that we do not concentrate upon the present day, the actual hour, of our life; we live in the past or in the future; we are continually expecting the coming of some special hour when our life shall unfold itself in its full significance. And we do not observe that life is flowing like water through our fingers, sifting like precious grain from a loosely fastened bag.
FATHER YELCHANINOV

8382 Past and to come seem best; things present worst.
WILLIAM SHAKESPEARE (1564–1616)

8383 Shut out all of your past except that which will help you weather your tomorrows.
SIR WILLIAM OSLER (1849–1919)

8384 The moment passed is no longer; the future may never be; the present is all of which man is the master.
JEAN JACQUES ROUSSEAU (1712–1778)

8385 The past cannot be changed; the future is still in your power.
HUGH LAWSON WHITE (1773–1840)

8386 The present is the period when the future pauses for a short while before becoming the past.

8387 Time is a threefold present: the present as we experience it, the past as a present memory, and the future as a present expectation.
SAINT AUGUSTINE OF HIPPO (354–430)

PATIENCE

8388 "Take your needle, my child, and work at your pattern; it will come out a rose by and by." Life is like that; one stitch at a time taken patiently, and the pattern will come out all right like embroidery.
OLIVER WENDELL HOLMES (1809–1894)

8389 A delay is better than a disaster.

8390 A handful of patience is worth more than a bushel of brains.
DUTCH PROVERB

8391 All comes at the proper time to him who knows how to wait.
SAINT VINCENT DE PAUL (1581–1660)

8392 Be patient with everyone, but above all with yourself.
SAINT FRANCIS OF SALES (1567–1622)

8393 Dear God, please grant me patience. And I want it right now.

8394 Don't jump to conclusions too quickly; many things lie unsolved, and the biggest test of all is that God looks as if he were totally indifferent.
OSWALD CHAMBERS (1874–1917)

8395 God engineers our circumstances as he did those of his Son; all we have to do is to follow where he places us. The majority of us are busy trying to place ourselves. God alters things while we wait for him.
OSWALD CHAMBERS (1874–1917)

8396 God often permits us to be perplexed so that we may learn patience.
T. J. BACH

8397 Have patience! All things are difficult before they become easy.
PERSIAN PROVERB

8398 He that can have patience can have what he wills.
BENJAMIN FRANKLIN (1706–1790)

8399 How poor are they that have not patience! What wound did ever heal but by degrees?
WILLIAM SHAKESPEARE (1564–1616)

8400 Never become irritable while waiting; if you are patient, you'll find that you can wait much faster.

8401 Never cut what you can untie.
JOSEPH JOUBERT (1754–1824)

8402 Never think that God's delays are God's denials. Hold on; hold fast; hold out. Patience is genius.
COMTE GEORGES-LOUIS LECLERC DE BUFFON (1707–1788)

8403 No one will ever know the full depth of his capacity for patience and humility as long as nothing bothers him. It

is only when times are troubled and difficult that he can see how much of either is in him.
SAINT FRANCIS OF ASSISI (C. 1181–1226)

8404 One minute of patience, ten years of peace.
GREEK PROVERB

8405 One moment of patience may prevent disaster; one moment of impatience may ruin a life.
CHINESE PROVERB

8406 Only those who have the patience to do simple things perfectly will acquire the skill to do difficult things easily.
JOHANN FRIEDRICH VON SCHILLER (1759–1805)

8407 Patience achieves more than force.
EDMUND BURKE (1729–1797)

8408 Patience and diligence, like faith, remove mountains.
WILLIAM PENN (1644–1718)

8409 Patience has its limits. Take it too far, and it's cowardice.
GEORGE JACKSON (1785–1861)

8410 Patience is bitter, but its fruit is sweet.
JEAN JACQUES ROUSSEAU (1712–1778)

8411 Patience is the ability to put up with people you'd like to put down.
ULRIKE RUFFERT

8412 Patience is the companion of wisdom.
SAINT AUGUSTINE OF HIPPO (354–430)

8413 Patience is the mother of expectation.
HENRI J. M. NOUWEN

8414 Patience means waiting without anxiety.
SAINT FRANCIS OF SALES (1567–1622)

8415 Patience: accepting a difficult situation without giving God a deadline to remove it.
BILL GOTHARD

8416 Patient waiting is often the highest way of doing God's will.
JEREMY COLLIER (1650–1726)

8417 Please be patient. God isn't finished with me yet.

8418 Teach us, O Lord, the disciplines of patience, for to wait is often harder than to work.
PETER MARSHALL (1902–1949)

8419 The Almighty is working on a great scale and will not be hustled by our peevish impetuosity.
WILLIAM GRAHAM SCROGGIE (1877–1958)

8420 The key to everything is patience. You get the chicken by hatching the egg, not by smashing it open.
ARNOLD GLASGOW

8421 The times we find ourselves having to wait on others may be the perfect opportunities to train ourselves to wait on the Lord.
JONI EARECKSON TADA

8422 There is no such thing as preaching patience into people unless the sermon is so long they have to practice it while they hear. No man can learn patience except by going out into the hurly-burly world and taking life just as it blows. Patience is riding out the gale.
HENRY WARD BEECHER (1813–1887)

8423 To lie down in the time of grief, to be quiet under the stroke of adverse fortune, implies a great strength. But I know of something that implies a strength greater still. It is the power to work under stress, to continue under hardship, to have anguish in your spirit and still perform daily tasks. This is a Christlike thing. The hardest thing is that most of us are called to exercise patience, not in the sick bed, but in the street.
GEORGE MATHESON (1842–1906)

8424 Wait on the Lord in prayer as you sit on the freeway, sharing with him the anxiety of so many jobs to be done in such a short time. Watch your frustrations melt into praise as you sing hymns and choruses for his ears alone.
JONI EARECKSON TADA

8425 We do not obtain the most precious gifts by going in search of them but by waiting for them.
SIMONE WEIL (1909–1943)

8426 We must wait for God, long, meekly, in the wind and wet, in the thunder and lightning, in the cold and the dark. Wait, and he will come. He never comes to those who do not wait.
FREDERICK WILLIAM FABER (1814–1863)

PEACE

8427 A great many people are trying to make peace, but that has already been done. God has not left it for us to do; all we have to do is to enter into it.
DWIGHT LYMAN MOODY (1837–1899)

8428 All men desire peace, but very few desire those things that make for peace.
THOMAS À KEMPIS (C. 1380–1471)

8429 At the heart of the cyclone tearing the sky
And flinging the clouds and the towers by,
Is a place of central calm;
So here in the roar of mortal things,
I have a place where my spirit sings,
In the hollow of God's palm.
EDWIN MARKHAM (1852–1940)

8430 Calm soul of all things! make it mine
To feel, amid the city's jar,
That there abides a peace of thine
Man did not make, and cannot mar!
The will to neither strive nor cry,
The power to feel with others give!
Calm, calm me more! nor let me die
Before I have begun to live.
MATTHEW ARNOLD (1822–1888)

8431 Drop thy still dews of quietness,
Till all our strivings cease;
Take from our souls the strain and stress,
And let our ordered lives confess
The beauty of thy peace.
JOHN GREENLEAF WHITTIER (1807–1892)

8432 Emotional peace and calm come after doing God's will and not before.
ERWIN W. LUTZER (1941–)

8433 Finding God, you have no need to seek peace, for he himself is your peace.
FRANCES J. ROBERTS

8434 First keep the peace within yourself, then you can also bring peace to others.
THOMAS À KEMPIS (C. 1380–1471)

8435 Five great enemies to peace: greed, ambition, envy, anger, and pride.
PETRARCH (1304–1374)

8436 For most men the world is centered in self, which is misery: to have one's world centered in God is peace.
DONALD HANKEY (1874–1917)

8437 God is a tranquil being and abides in a tranquil eternity. So must your spirit become a tranquil and clear little pool, wherein the serene light of God can be mirrored.
GERHARD TERSTEEGEN (1697–1769)

8438 God takes life's pieces and gives us unbroken peace.
W. D. GOUGH

8439 Great tranquility of heart is his who cares for neither praise nor blame.
THOMAS À KEMPIS (C. 1380–1471)

8440 However painful or difficult, or, on the other hand, however inconspicuous or humdrum life may be, the Christian finds his peace in accepting and playing his part in the master plan.
J. B. PHILLIPS (1906–1982)

8441 If there is righteousness in the heart, there will be beauty in the character. If there is beauty in the character, there will be harmony in the home. If there is harmony in the home, there will be order in the nation. If there is order in the nation, there will be peace in the world.
CHINESE PROVERB

8442 If we have not quiet in our minds, outward comfort will do no more for us than a golden slipper on a gouty foot.
JOHN BUNYAN (1628–1688)

8443 In his will is our peace.
DANTE ALIGHIERI (1265–1321)

8444 In life troubles will come which seem as if they never will pass away. The night and storm look as if they would last forever; but the calm and the morning cannot be stayed; the storm in its very nature is transient. The effort of nature, as that of the human heart, ever is to return to its repose, for God is peace.
GEORGE MACDONALD (1824–1905)

8445 In spite of everything I still believe that people are really good at heart. I simply can't build up my hopes on a foun-

dation consisting of confusion, misery, and death. I see the world gradually being turned into a wilderness, I hear the ever-approaching thunder, which will destroy us too. I can feel the sufferings of millions, and yet, if I look up into the heavens, I think that it will all come right, that this cruelty too will end, and that peace and tranquility will return again.
ANNE FRANK (1929–1945)

8446 It is madness for sheep to talk peace with a wolf.
SIR THOMAS FULLER (1608–1661)

8447 It is the spiritually humble who know what peace is.
THOMAS À KEMPIS (C. 1380–1471)

8448 My son, now will I teach thee the way of peace and inward liberty. Be desirous to do the will of another rather than thine own. Choose always to have less rather than more. Seek always the lowest place and to be inferior to everyone. Wish always, and pray, that the will of God may be wholly fulfilled in thee.
THOMAS À KEMPIS (C. 1380–1471)

8449 No sleep can be tranquil unless the mind is at rest.
LUCIUS ANNAEUS SENECA (C. 4 B.C.–A.D. 65)

8450 Nobody studies peace. There are no courses in peace, no examinations, no discoveries, and alas, no advances. We are no farther on the road to peace than were the ancient Greek city-states, and perhaps we're farther away.
SYDNEY J. HARRIS (1917–1986)

8451 Not all my prayers nor sighs nor tears, Can ease my awful load.
Thy work alone, O Christ,
Can ease this weight of sin;
Thy blood alone, O Lamb of God,
Can give me peace within.
HORATIUS BONAR (1808–1889)

8452 Peace cannot be kept by force. It can only be achieved by understanding.
ALBERT EINSTEIN (1879–1955)

8453 Peace does not dwell in outward things, but within the soul; we may preserve it in the midst of the bitterest pain if our will remain firm and sub-

missive. Peace in this life springs from acquiescence, not in an exemption from suffering.
FRANÇOIS FÉNELON (1651–1715)

8454 Peace does not mean the end of all our striving,
Joy does not mean the drying of our tears;
Peace is the power that comes to souls arriving
Up to the light where God himself appears.
Joy is the wine that God is ever pouring
Into the hearts of those who strive with him,
Light'ning their eyes to vision and adoring,
Strength'ning their arms to warfare glad and grim.
GEOFFREY ANKETELL STUDDERT-KENNEDY (1883–1929)

8455 Peace is not an absence of war, it is a virtue, a state of mind, a disposition for benevolence, confidence, justice.
BENEDICT SPINOZA (1632–1677)

8456 Peace is not arbitrary. It must be based upon definite facts. God has all the facts on his side; the world does not. Therefore God, and not the world, can give peace.
BILLY GRAHAM (1918–)

8457 Peace is not made at the council tables, or by treaties, but in the hearts of men.
HERBERT HOOVER (1874–1964)

8458 Peace is not the absence of conflict from life, but the ability to cope with it.

8459 Peace is one of those things, like happiness, which we are sure to miss if we aim at them directly.
DOROTHY L. SAYERS (1893–1957)

8460 Peace is the deliberate adjustment of my life to the will of God.

8461 Peace is when time doesn't matter as it passes by.
MARIA SCHELL

8462 Peace rules the day when Christ rules the mind.

8463 Peace within makes beauty without.
ENGLISH PROVERB

8464 Peace won by compromise is usually a short-lived achievement.
WINFIELD SCOTT (1786–1866)

8465 Peace: the wisp of straw that binds the sheaf of blessings.
JEWISH PROVERB

8466 Quiet minds cannot be perplexed or frightened, but go on in fortune or misfortune at their own private pace, like a clock in a thunderstorm.
ROBERT LOUIS BALFOUR STEVENSON (1850–1894)

8467 Selfishness is a gangrene, eating at the very vitals. Sin is a cancer, poisoning the blood. Peace is the rhythm of our wills with Jesus' love-will.
SAMUEL DICKEY GORDON (1859–1936)

8468 Sowing seeds of peace is like sowing beans. You don't know why it works; you just know it does. Seeds are planted, and topsoils of hurt are shoved away.
MAX L. LUCADO (1955–   )

8469 The soul of peace is love, which . . . comes from the love of God and expresses itself in love for men.
POPE PAUL VI (1897–1978)

8470 The storm was raging. The sea was beating against the rocks in huge, dashing waves. The lightning was flashing, the thunder was roaring, the wind was blowing; but the little bird was sound asleep in the crevice of the rock, its head tucked serenely under its wing. That is peace: to be able to sleep in the storm!

   In Christ we are relaxed and at peace in the midst of the confusions, bewilderments, and perplexities of this life. The storm rages, but our hearts are at rest. We have found peace—at last!
BILLY GRAHAM (1918–   )

8471 The time of business does not differ from the time of prayer; and in the noise and clutter of my kitchen, while several persons are at the same time calling for different things, I possess God in as great tranquility as if I were upon my knees at the Blessed Sacrament.
BROTHER LAWRENCE OF THE RESURRECTION (C. 1605–1691)

8472 To be glad of life because it gives you the chance to love and to work and to play and to look up at the stars—to be satisfied with your possessions but not contented with yourself until you have made the best of them—to despise nothing in the world except falsehood and meanness, and to fear nothing except cowardice—to be governed by your admirations rather than by your disgusts; to covet nothing that is your neighbor's except his kindness of heart and gentleness of manners—to think seldom of your enemies, often of your friends, and every day of Christ—these are little guideposts on the footpath to peace.
HENRY VAN DYKE (1852–1933)

8473 To thee, O God, we turn for peace . . . but grant us too the blessed assurance that nothing shall deprive us of that peace, neither ourselves, nor our foolish earthly desires, nor my wild longings, nor the anxious cravings of my heart.
SØREN AABYE KIERKEGAARD (1813–1855)

8474 True peace is found by man in the depths of his own heart, the dwelling-place of God.
JOHANN TAULER (C. 1300–1361)

8475 Where there is peace, God is.

PEOPLE

8476 A few people think, many think they think, and the rest use clichés so they won't have to think.

8477 A mystery of life is why people will always ask if the empty seat beside you is occupied.

8478 Adults are obsolete children.
DR. SEUSS (1904–1991)

8479 Don't sell people short: you can always find someone ready to carry the stool when there's a piano to be moved.

8480 Men are queer animals—a mixture of horse-nervousness, ass-stubbornness, and camel-malice.
THOMAS HENRY HUXLEY (1825–1895)

8481 People are strange: they want the front of the bus, the back of the church, and the center of attention.

8482 Practical men know where they are, but not always whither they are going; thinkers know whither we are going, but not always where we are.
GEORGE BERNARD SHAW (1856–1950)

8483 There are no ordinary people. You have never met a mere mortal. . . . But it is immortals whom we joke with, work with, marry, snub, and exploit— immortal horrors or everlasting splendors.
C. S. LEWIS (1898–1963)

PERCEPTION

8484 A giant in your eyes may be a dwarf in ours.
MIDRASH

8485 A good general not only sees the way to victory but he also knows when victory is impossible.

8486 A moment's insight is sometimes worth a life's experience.
OLIVER WENDELL HOLMES (1809–1894)

8487 As he that fears God fears nothing else, so he that sees God sees everything else.
JOHN DONNE (1572–1631)

8488 As we begin to focus upon God, the things of the Spirit will take shape before our inner eyes.
A. W. TOZER (1897–1963)

8489 Earth's crammed with heaven
And every common bush afire with God;
But only he who sees takes off his shoes—
The rest sit around it and pluck blackberries.
ELIZABETH BARRETT BROWNING (1806–1861)

8490 Every man is a volume if you know how to read him.
WILLIAM ELLERY CHANNING (1780–1842)

8491 Everybody calls "clear" those ideas that have the same degree of confusion as his own.
MARCEL PROUST (1871–1922)

8492 Everything has its beauty, but not everyone sees it.
CHINESE PROVERB

8493 Eyes that look are common, eyes that see are rare.
J. OSWALD SANDERS

8494 From a man's face I can read his character; if I see him walk, I know his thoughts.
GAIUS PETRONIUS (D. C. 66)

8495 God gives the believer a new set of inner eyes to see what he could not see before, a new set of inner ears to hear what he could not hear before.
JOHN POWELL

8496 If we had a keen vision of all that is ordinary in human life, it would be like hearing the grass grow or the squirrel's heartbeat, and we should die of that roar which is the other side of silence.
GEORGE ELIOT (1819–1880)

8497 If you can evaluate things as they really are, and not as people report them to be, then you are wise, and God is your teacher.
THOMAS À KEMPIS (C. 1380–1471)

8498 It is not raining rain to me,
It's raining daffodils;
In every dimpled drop I see
Wild flowers on distant hills.
ROBERT LOVEMAN (1865–1923)

8499 It is only with the heart that one can see rightly; what is essential is invisible to the eye.
ANTOINE DE SAINT-EXUPÉRY (1900–1944)

8500 It rained so hard that all the pigs got clean, and all the people dirty.
GEORG CHRISTOPH LICHTENBERG (1742–1799)

8501 Many see, but few understand.
JEWISH PROVERB

8502 One may have good eyes and yet see nothing.
ITALIAN PROVERB

8503 The heart has eyes that the brain knows nothing of.
CHARLES HENRY PARKHURST (1842–1933)

8504 The insight that relates us to God arises from purity of heart, not from clearness of intellect.
OSWALD CHAMBERS (1874–1917)

8505 The more a person is in harmony with himself and the more simple he is inwardly, the more he understands intuitively. He receives divine illumination.
THOMAS À KEMPIS (C. 1380–1471)

8506 The tree which moves some to tears of joy is in the eyes of others only a green thing which stands in the way.
WILLIAM BLAKE (1757–1827)

8507 The world is full of untold novelties for him who has the eyes to see them.
THOMAS HENRY HUXLEY (1825–1895)

8508 The world today doesn't make sense, so why should I paint pictures that do?
PABLO RUIZ Y PICASSO (1881–1973)

8509 There's one good thing about tight shoes: they make you forget your other troubles.
JOSH BILLINGS (1818–1885)

8510 Things are seldom what they seem: that's why people mistake education for intelligence, wealth for happiness, and sex for love.

8511 To be blind in the eye is better than to be blind in the heart.
ARABIAN PROVERB

8512 To perceive is to suffer.
ARISTOTLE (384–322 B.C.)

8513 To see ourselves as others see us is a most salutary gift. Hardly less important is the capacity to see others as they see themselves.
ALDOUS HUXLEY (1894–1963)

8514 We see things not as they are, but as we are.

8515 Who has recalled his sense to the interior life

Hears what one cannot say, sees in the darkest night.
ANGELUS SILESIUS (1624–1677)

8516 Worship your heroes from afar; contact withers them.
MADAME NECKER (1766–1841)

8517 Your point of view is everything: the pond is an ocean to a tadpole.

PERFECTION

8518 God demands perfection from his creatures, but if they will ever have it, he himself must supply it. We need not be concerned about how high God's standard is, as long as he meets it for us.
ERWIN W. LUTZER (1941–   )

8519 He who is faultless is lifeless.
JOHN HEYWOOD (C. 1497–C. 1580)

8520 If you check out the life of Jesus you will discover what made him perfect. He did not attain a state of perfection by carrying around in his pocket a list of rules and regulations, or by seeking to conform to the cultural mores of his time. He was perfect because he never made a move without his Father.
TOM SKINNER

8521 It is only imperfection that complains of what is imperfect. The more perfect we are, the more gentle and quiet we become toward the defects of others.
FRANÇOIS FÉNELON (1651–1715)

8522 The divine nature is perfection and to be nearest to the divine nature is to be nearest to perfection.
XENOPHON (C. 431–C. 352 B.C.)

8523 The farther a man knows himself to be from perfection, the nearer he is to it!
GERARD GROOTE (1340–1384)

8524 What is Christian perfection? Loving God with all our heart, mind, soul, and strength.
JOHN WESLEY (1703–1791)

PERSECUTION

8525 It is preferable to have the whole world against thee, than Jesus offended with thee.
THOMAS À KEMPIS (C. 1380–1471)

8526 Perhaps we should start praying that God would make every Christian in Philippi taste so bad that no beast of wholesome palate would ever consider us tasty.
CALVIN MILLER

8527 Persecution often does in this life, what the last great day will do completely—separate the wheat from the tares.
JAMES MILNER (D. 1721)

8528 The martyr cannot be dishonored . . . every burned book or house enlightens the world; every suppressed or expunged word reverberates through the earth from side to side.
RALPH WALDO EMERSON (1803–1882)

8529 The most savage controversies are those about matters as to which there is no good evidence either way. Persecution is used in theology, not in arithmetic.
BERTRAND ARTHUR WILLIAM RUSSELL (1872–1970)

8530 The way of this world is to praise dead saints and persecute living ones.

8531 Where there are sheep, the wolves are never very far away.
PLAUTUS (C. 254–184 B.C.)

8532 Wherever you see persecution, there is more than a probability that truth is on the persecuted side.
HUGH LATIMER (C. 1485–1555)

PERSEVERANCE

8533 All that is necessary to break the spell of inertia and frustration is this: act as if it were impossible to fail. That is the talisman, the formula, the command of right-about-face that turns us from failure toward success.
DOROTHEA BRANDE

8534 Bear in mind, if you are going to amount to anything, that your success does not depend upon the brilliancy and the impetuosity with which you take hold, but upon the everlasting and sanctified bull-doggedness with

which you hang on after you have taken hold.
A. B. MELDRUM

8535 By perseverance the snail reached the ark.

8536 Every noble work is at first impossible.
THOMAS CARLYLE (1795–1881)

8537 Far better it is to dare mighty things, to win glorious triumphs even though checkered by failures, than to rank with those poor spirits who neither enjoy much nor suffer much because they live in the gray twilight that knows not victory or defeat.
THEODORE ROOSEVELT (1858–1919)

8538 Few things are impossible to diligence and skill.
SAMUEL JOHNSON (1709–1784)

8539 Genius, that power that dazzles mortal eyes,
Is oft but perseverance in disguise.
HENRY AUSTIN (1613–   )

8540 God is with those who persevere.
ARABIAN PROVERB

8541 Great souls have wills, feeble ones have only wishes.
CHINESE PROVERB

8542 He that perseveres makes every difficulty an advancement and every contest a victory.
CHARLES CALEB COLTON (1780–1832)

8543 If you stop every time a dog barks, your road will never end.
ARABIAN PROVERB

8544 If your determination is fixed, I do not counsel you to despair. Great works are performed not by strength, but perseverance.
SAMUEL JOHNSON (1709–1784)

8545 It is a great thing to see physical pluck, and greater still to see moral pluck, but the greatest to see of all is spiritual pluck, to see a man who will stand true to the integrity of Jesus Christ no matter what he is going through.
OSWALD CHAMBERS (1874–1917)

8546 Keep the faculty of effort alive in you by a little gratuitous exercise every day. Be systematically ascetic or heroic

in little unnecessary points. Do every day or two something for no other reason than that you would rather not do it, so that when the hour of dire needs draws nigh, it may find you not unnerved and untrained to stand the test.
WILLIAM JAMES (1842–1910)

8547 Little strokes fell great oaks.
BENJAMIN FRANKLIN (1706–1790)

8548 Never give in! Never give in! Never! Never! Never! Never! In anything great or small, large or petty—never give in except to convictions of honor and good sense.
SIR WINSTON CHURCHILL (1874–1965)

8549 Nothing is difficult to those who have the will.

8550 On a long journey even a straw is heavy.
ITALIAN PROVERB

8551 Perseverance can do anything which genius can do, and very many things which it cannot.
HENRY WARD BEECHER (1813–1887)

8552 Perseverance is more prevailing than violence.
PLUTARCH (C. 46–AFTER 119)

8553 Perseverance is the most overrated of traits: if it is unaccompanied by talent, beating your head against a wall is more likely to produce a concussion in the head than a hole in the wall.
SYDNEY J. HARRIS (1917–1986)

8554 Perseverance is the rope that ties the soul to the doorpost of heaven.
FRANCES J. ROBERTS

8555 Press on! Nothing in the world can take the place of perseverance. Talent will not; nothing is more common than unsuccessful men with talent. Genius will not; unrewarded genius is almost a proverb. Education will not; the world is full of educated derelicts.
CALVIN COOLIDGE (1872–1933)

8556 Small drops of water hollow out a stone.
LUCRETIUS (C. 96–C. 55 B.C.)

8557 Strength is the lot but of a few privileged men; but austere perseverance, harsh and continuous, may be employed by the smallest of us and rarely fails in its purpose. Its silent power grows irresistibly greater with time.
JOHANN WOLFGANG VON GOETHE (1749–1832)

8558 'Tis a lesson you should heed,
Try, try again.
If at first you don't succeed,
Try, try again.
Then your courage should appear,
For, if you will persevere,
You will conquer, never fear;
Try, try again.
WILLIAM EDWARD HICKSON (1803–1870)

8559 Unless the clay be well pounded, no pitcher can be made.
LATIN PROVERB

8560 What you are is God's gift to you. What you make of yourself is your gift to him.

8561 With time and patience the mulberry leaf becomes satin.
CHINESE PROVERB

8562 You must scale the mountains if you would view the plain.
CHINESE PROVERB

8563 What we obtain too easy, we value too lightly; it is the cost that gives value.

PERSISTENCE

8564 I hate to be a kicker, I always long for peace,
But the wheel that does the squeaking is the one that gets the grease.

8565 If you're ever tempted to give up, think of Brahms who took seven long years to compose his famous Lullaby. He kept falling asleep at the piano.
ROBERT ORBEN

8566 The heights by great men reached and kept
Were not attained by sudden flight,
ut they, while their companions slept,
Were toiling upward in the night.
HENRY WADSWORTH LONGFELLOW (1807–1882)

8567 The most rewarding things you do in life are often the ones that look like they cannot be done.
ARNOLD PALMER (1929–)

8568 When you get into a tight place and everything goes against you 'til it seems as though you could not hold on a minute longer, never give up then, for that is just the place and time that the tide will turn.
HARRIET BEECHER STOWE (1811–1896)

PERSONALITY

8569 Even the most fervent believer may appear paradoxical, difficult, illogical. . . . It expresses the difficulty inherent in our human condition.
PAUL TOURNIER (1898–1986)

8570 God does what we cannot do. He alters the mainspring and plants in us a totally new disposition.
OSWALD CHAMBERS (1874–1917)

8571 Many times . . . the most irritating characteristic is a by-product of a quality most respected.
JAMES C. DOBSON (1936–)

PERSPECTIVE

8572 A one-eyed man among the blind is a man with full sight.
ARABIAN PROVERB

8573 Better keep yourself clean and bright; you are the window through which you must see the world.
GEORGE BERNARD SHAW (1856–1950)

8574 For everything you have missed, you have gained something else. For everything you gain, you lose something else.
RALPH WALDO EMERSON (1803–1882)

8575 Give me the ability to see good things in unexpected places and talents in unexpected people.

8576 If a laborer were to dream for twelve hours every night that he was a king, I believe he would be almost as happy as a king who should dream for twelve hours every night that he was a laborer.
BLAISE PASCAL (1623–1662)

8577 If dandelions were rare and fragile, people would knock themselves out to pay $14.95 a plant, raise them by hand in greenhouses, and form dandelion societies and all that. But they are everywhere and don't need us and kind of do what they please. So we call them "weeds" and murder them at every opportunity.
ROBERT FULGHUM

8578 If you know I only send what is for your good, you will see all things good and will know it passes through My love as it comes to you.
FRANCES J. ROBERTS

8579 The man who said that work well done never needs doing over has never raked leaves.

8580 The question of common sense, What is it good for? would abolish the rose and be answered triumphantly by the cabbage.
JAMES RUSSELL LOWELL (1819–1891)

8581 There's only one thing worse than a flooded basement and that's a flooded attic.

8582 These are trying times: most of us have to do without the things our parents never heard of.

8583 We see actual things, and we say that we see them, but we never really see them until we see God; when we see God, everything becomes different. It is not the external things that are different, but a different disposition looks through the same eyes as the result of the internal surgery that has taken place.
OSWALD CHAMBERS (1874–1917)

8584 Whether or not a black cat crossing your path brings bad luck depends on whether you are a man or a mouse.

PESSIMISM

8585 A pessimist is a man who looks both ways when he's crossing a one-way street.
LAURENCE J. PETER (1919–)

8586 Strange as it may be, the holiest souls who have ever lived have earned the reputation for being pessimistic.
A. W. TOZER (1897–1963)

8587 The man who thinks must be pessimistic; thinking can never produce optimism.
OSWALD CHAMBERS (1874–1917)

PHILOSOPHY

8588 A philosopher should remind himself, now and then, that he is a particle pontificating on infinity.
WILL DURANT (1885–1981)

8589 Being a philosopher, I have a problem for every solution.
ROBERT ZEND

8590 God created man in his own image, says the Bible. Philosophers reverse the process; they create God in theirs.
GEORG CHRISTOPH LICHTENBERG (1742–1799)

8591 Philosophers are so highly educated that they can take the simplest thing and quickly turn it into something unintelligible.

8592 Philosophy and science have not always been friendly toward the idea of God, the reason being that they are dedicated to the task of accounting for things and are impatient with anything that refuses to give an account of itself.
A. W. TOZER (1897–1963)

8593 Philosophy is a longing after heavenly wisdom.
PLATO (C. 428–348 B.C.)

8594 Philosophy is the science of the limitations of the human mind. When you know philosophy, you know what you cannot know.
JOSEPH RICKABY

8595 Philosophy is the science that considers truth.
ARISTOTLE (384–322 B.C.)

8596 Philosophy should be piecemeal and provisional like science; final truth belongs to heaven, not to this world.
BERTRAND ARTHUR WILLIAM RUSSELL (1872–1970)

8597 What we call philosophy is a complicated method of avoiding all the important problems of life.
KENNETH REXROTH (1905–1982)

PLEASURE

8598 If pleasures are greatest in anticipation, remember that this is also true of trouble.
ELBERT GREEN HUBBARD (1856–1915)

8599 In diving to the bottom of pleasure we bring up more gravel than pearls.
HONORÉ DE BALZAC (1799–1850)

8600 Live while you live, the Epicure would say,
And seize the pleasures of the present day;
Live while you live, the sacred preacher cries,
And give to God each moment as it flies;
Lord, in my view let both united be;
I live in pleasure when I live to thee.
PHILIP DODDRIDGE (1702–1751)

8601 Men pursue pleasure with such breathless haste that they hurry past it.
SØREN AABYE KIERKEGAARD (1813–1855)

8602 Once man believed he could make his own pleasures; now he believes he must pay for them. As if flowers no longer grew in fields and gardens; but only in florists' shops.
JOHN FOWLES (1926–   )

8603 Our loving God wills that we eat, drink, and be merry.
MARTIN LUTHER (1483–1546)

8604 Pleasure is frail like a dewdrop, while it laughs it dies.
SIR RABINDRANATH TAGORE (1861–1941)

8605 Pleasure is our greatest evil or our greatest good.
ALEXANDER POPE (1688–1744)

8606 Pleasure is seldom found where it is sought; our brightest blazes of gladness are kindled by unexpected sparks.
SAMUEL JOHNSON (1709–1784)

8607 The greatest pleasure I know is to do a good action by stealth and to have it found out by accident.
CHARLES LAMB (1775–1834)

8608 The Lord is very jealous over any saint who is utterly abandoned to him. He does not let that believer have any pleasures at all outside of himself.
MADAME JEANNE MARIE DE LA MOTHE GUYON (1648–1717)

8609 The only path to pleasure is in pleasing God.
RICHARD OWEN ROBERTS (1931–)

8610 The river of pleasure, though it flows through lush meadows and beautiful glens, contains no healing for the soul.
BILLY GRAHAM (1918–)

8611 There is no pleasure comparable to not being captivated by any external thing whatever.
THOMAS WILSON (1663–1735)

8612 There is nothing more unexpected and surprising than the arrivals and departures of pleasure. If we find it in one place today, it is vain to seek it there tomorrow. You cannot lay a trap for it.
ALEXANDER SMITH (1830–1867)

8613 We tire of those pleasures we take, but never of those we give.
JOHN PETIT-SENN

8614 When pleasure is the business of life, it ceases to be pleasure.
THOMAS CHANDLER HALIBURTON (1796–1865)

8615 Who bathes in worldly joys swims in a world of fears.

POETRY

8616 Poetry has been to me "its own exceeding great reward"; it has soothed my afflictions; it has multiplied and refined my enjoyments; it has endeared solitude; and it has given me the habit of wishing to discover the good and the beautiful in all that meets and surrounds me.
SAMUEL TAYLOR COLERIDGE (1772–1834)

8617 Poetry is not an assertion of truth, but the making of that truth more real to us.
T. S. ELIOT (1888–1965)

8618 Poetry is the language in which man explores his own amazement.
CHRISTOPHER FRY (1907–)

8619 Poetry is what in a poem makes you laugh, cry, prickle, be silent, makes your toenails twinkle, makes you want to do this or that or nothing, makes you know that you are alone in the unknown world, that your bliss and suffering is forever shared and forever all your own.
DYLAN MARLAIS THOMAS (1914–1953)

8620 Poetry is what makes the invisible appear.
NATHALIE SARRAUTE (1902–)

8621 The most beautiful poems are those filled with despair, and I know of immortal lines that are nothing but sobs.
ALFRED DE MUSSET (1810–1857)

POSSESSIONS

8622 All that we possess is qualified by what we are.
JOHN LANCASTER SPALDING (1840–1916)

8623 All you are unable to give possesses you.
ANDRÉ GIDE (1869–1951)

8624 America has more things than any other nation in the world, and more books on how to find happiness.
W. E. SANGSTER

8625 Every increased possession loads us with a new weariness.
JOHN RUSKIN (1819–1900)

8626 Every possession is a trust.
ROY L. SMITH

8627 Having nothing, nothing can he lose.
WILLIAM SHAKESPEARE (1564–1616)

8628 I have held many things in my hands, and I have lost them all; but whatever I have placed in God's hands, that I still possess.
MARTIN LUTHER (1483–1546)

8629 If a man has spent all his days about some business by which he has got much money, many houses and barns and woodlots, his life has been a failure.
HENRY DAVID THOREAU (1817–1862)

8630 If there were no mixture in your soul, the soul would instantly rush toward

the all-powerful, irresistible God within to be lost in him. But if you are loaded down with many material possessions—or anything else—this attraction is greatly hindered. Many Christians seize some part of this world or some part of the self with so tight a grip that they spend their whole lives making only a snail's progress toward their Center.
MADAME JEANNE MARIE DE LA MOTHE GUYON (1648–1717)

8631 It is because people live in the things they possess instead of in their relationship to God, that God at times seems cruel.
OSWALD CHAMBERS (1874–1917)

8632 Many people cling to their possessions instead of sharing them because they are worried about the future. But is not such an attitude finally unbelief?
RONALD J. SIDER

8633 Materialism is organized emptiness of the spirit.
FRANZ WERFEL (1890–1945)

8634 Materialistic concerns and one-sided values are never sufficient to fill the heart and mind of a human person. A life reduced to the sole dimension of possessions, of consumer goods, of temporal concerns will never let you discover and enjoy the full richness of your humanity. It is only in God—in Jesus, God made man—that you will fully understand what you are.
POPE JOHN PAUL II (1920–)

8635 May we never let the things we can't have, or don't have, or shouldn't have, spoil our enjoyment of the things we do have and can have. As we value our happiness let us not forget it, for one of the greatest lessons in life is learning to be happy without the things we cannot or should not have.
RICHARD L. EVANS

8636 Not what we have, but what we enjoy, constitutes our abundance.
JOHN PETIT-SENN

8637 Possession makes not rich. He is a wealthy man

Who can all that he has, lose without hurt or pain.
ANGELUS SILESIUS (1624–1677)

8638 Theirs is an endless road, a hopeless maze, who seek for goods before they seek for God.
BERNARD OF CLAIRVAUX (1090–1153)

8639 What you don't get, you can't lose.
JEWISH PROVERB

8640 You can't take it with you—a shroud has no pockets.

POSSIBILITIES

8641 A possibility is a hint from God.
SØREN AABYE KIERKEGAARD (1813–1855)

8642 God can do nothing for me until I get to the limit of the possible.
OSWALD CHAMBERS (1874–1917)

8643 Make that possible for me which is impossible by nature.
THOMAS À KEMPIS (C. 1380–1471)

8644 Nothing is impossible; there are ways that lead to everything, and if we had sufficient will, we should always have sufficient means. It is often merely an excuse that we say things are impossible.
FRANÇOIS, DUC DE LA ROCHEFOUCAULD (1613–1680)

8645 Somebody is always doing what somebody else said couldn't be done.

POTENTIAL

8646 A weed is a plant whose virtues have not yet been discovered.
RALPH WALDO EMERSON (1803–1882)

8647 Alas for those who never sing, but die with all their music in them.
OLIVER WENDELL HOLMES (1809–1894)

8648 An atom is the smallest thing in the world which, when split, becomes the biggest.

8649 Bad will be the day for every man when he becomes absolutely content with the life that he is living, with the thoughts that he is thinking, with the deeds that he is doing, when there is not forever beating at the doors of his

soul some great desire to do something larger, which he knows that he was meant and made to do because he is still, in spite of all, the child of God.
PHILLIPS BROOKS (1835–1893)

8650 Cheerios: hula-hoops for ants.

8651 Compared to what we ought to be, we are only half awake.
WILLIAM JAMES (1842–1910)

8652 Do not let what you cannot do interfere with what you can do.
JOHN WOODEN

8653 Every saint has a past and every sinner has a future.
OSCAR WILDE (1854–1900)

8654 God holds us responsible, not for what we have, but for what we could have; not for what we are, but for what we might be.

8655 If seed in the black earth can turn into such beautiful roses, what might not the heart of man become in its long journey toward the stars?
G. K. CHESTERTON (1874–1936)

8656 If you treat a person as he is, he will stay as he is; but if you treat him as if he were what he ought to be and could be, he will become what he ought to be and could be.
JOHANN WOLFGANG VON GOETHE (1749–1832)

8657 Large streams from little fountains flow, Tall oaks from little acorns grow.
DAVID EVERETT

8658 Many individuals have, like uncut diamonds, shining qualities beneath a rough exterior.
JUVENAL (C. 60–C. 127)

8659 Most people live, physically, intellectually, or morally, in a restricted circle of their potential being. They make use of a very small portion of their consciousness and of their soul's resources, much like a man who uses only his little finger. Great emergencies and crises show us how great our resources are.
WILLIAM JAMES (1842–1910)

8660 One machine can do the work of fifty ordinary men. No machine can do the work of one extraordinary man.
ELBERT GREEN HUBBARD (1856–1915)

8661 One of the saddest experiences that can come to a human being is to awaken, gray-haired and wrinkled, near the close of an unproductive career, to the fact that all through the years he has been using only a small part of himself.
V. W. BURROWS

8662 So much God would give . . . so little is received. Why live so beggarly when the riches of heaven are yours for the asking?
FRANCES J. ROBERTS

8663 The atom is proof that it's the little things that count.

8664 The creation of a thousand forests is in one acorn.
RALPH WALDO EMERSON (1803–1882)

8665 The frog in the well knows nothing of the great ocean.
JAPANESE PROVERB

8666 The measure of the depth to which a man can fall is the height to which he can rise.
OSWALD CHAMBERS (1874–1917)

8667 The same stuff that makes the criminal makes the saint.
OSWALD CHAMBERS (1874–1917)

8668 There are no great men in this world, only great challenges which ordinary men rise to meet.
WILLIAM FREDERICK HALSEY, JR. (1882–1959)

8669 There is a great deal of unmapped country within us.

8670 There is a potential hero in every man—and a potential skunk.
OSWALD CHAMBERS (1874–1917)

8671 Wake for shame, my sluggish heart, Wake, and gladly sing thy part: Learn of birds, and springs, and flowers, How to use thy noble powers.
JOHN AUSTIN (1613–1669)

8672 We know what we are, but know not what we may be.
WILLIAM SHAKESPEARE (1564–1616)

8673 Where man sees but withered leaves, God sees sweet flowers growing.
ALBERT LAIGHTON (1829–1887)

POVERTY

8674 Better to be poor than wicked.

8675 Better to be poor and live, than rich and perish.

8676 He is rich enough who is poor with Christ.
SAINT JEROME (C. 374–C. 420)

8677 He who knows how to be poor knows everything.
JULES MICHELET (1798–1874)

8678 It is easy enough to tell the poor to accept their poverty as God's will when you yourself have warm clothes and plenty of food and medical care and a roof over your head and no worry about the rent. But if you want them to believe you—try to share some of their poverty and see if you can accept it as God's will for yourself.
THOMAS MERTON (1915–1968)

8679 It is not poverty so much as pretense that harasses a ruined man—the struggle between a proud mind and an empty purse—the keeping up a hollow show that must soon come to an end. Have the courage to appear poor, and you disarm poverty of its sharpest sting.
ANNA JAMESON (1794–1860)

8680 It is not the man who has too little, but the man who craves more, who is poor.
LUCIUS ANNAEUS SENECA (C. 4 B.C.–A.D. 65)

8681 It is not the rich man only who is under the dominion of things; they too are slaves who, having no money, are unhappy from the lack of it.
GEORGE MACDONALD (1824–1905)

8682 O God! that bread should be so dear, And flesh and blood so cheap!
THOMAS HOOD (1799–1845)

8683 Of all God's creatures, man alone is poor.
THOMAS CARLYLE (1795–1881)

8684 Oh! poverty is a weary thing, 'tis full of grief and pain;
It keepeth down the soul of man, as with an iron chain.
MARY HOWITT (1799–1888)

8685 One Saturday morning as I was beginning to prepare a lecture (on poverty!), a poor man came into my office and asked for five dollars. He was drinking. He had no food, no job, no home. The Christ of the poor confronted me in this man. But I didn't have the time, I said. I had to prepare a lecture on the Christian view of poverty. I did give him a couple of dollars, but that was not what he needed. He needed somebody to talk to, somebody to love him. He needed my time. He needed me. But I was too busy. "Inasmuch as you did it not to the least of these, you did it not. . . ."
RONALD J. SIDER

8686 Poor men need no guards.
JEWISH PROVERB

8687 Poverty is no disgrace to a man, but it is confoundedly inconvenient.
SYDNEY SMITH (1771–1845)

8688 Poverty is not a crime.
LATIN PROVERB

8689 Poverty is the load of some, and wealth is the load of others, perhaps the greater load of the two. Bear the load of your neighbor's poverty, and let him bear with you the load of your wealth. You lighten your load by lightening his.
SAINT AUGUSTINE OF HIPPO (354–430)

8690 Poverty makes people satirical— soberly, sadly, bitterly satirical.
FRISWELL

8691 Pride and laziness are the keys of poverty.
SPANISH PROVERB

8692 The greatest threat to this nation [the United States] and the stability of the entire world is hunger. It's more explosive than all the atomic weaponry pos-

sessed by the big powers. Desperate people do desperate things, and remember that nuclear fission is now in the hands of even developing nations.
RONALD J. SIDER

8693 The poor come to all of us in many forms. Let us be sure that we never turn our backs on them, wherever we may find them. For when we turn our backs on the poor, we turn them on Jesus Christ.
MOTHER TERESA OF CALCUTTA (1910–)

8694 The poor too often turn away, unheard,
From hearts that shut against them with a snap
That will be heard in heaven.
HENRY WADSWORTH LONGFELLOW (1807–1882)

8695 There is no one more happy than the poor man; he expects no change for the worse.
EIPHILUS (320 B.C.)

8696 Unless we drastically reshape both our theology and our entire institutional church life so that the fact that God is on the side of the poor and oppressed becomes as central to our theology and institutional programs as it is in Scripture, we will demonstrate to the world that our verbal commitment to *sola scriptura* is a dishonest ideological support for an unjust, materialistic status quo.
RONALD J. SIDER

8697 We have mistaken the nature of poverty and thought it was economic poverty. No, it is poverty of the soul, deprivation of God's recreating, loving peace.
THOMAS R. KELLY (1893–1941)

8698 We must care for the poor, console them, help them, support their cause. Since Christ willed to be born poor, he chose for himself disciples who were poor. He made himself the servant of the poor and shared their poverty. He went so far as to say that he would consider every deed that helps or

harms the poor as done for or against himself.
SAINT VINCENT DE PAUL (1581–1660)

8699 World poverty is a hundred million mothers weeping . . . because they cannot feed their children.
RONALD J. SIDER

POWER

8700 A giant feels the sting of a bee.
BEN SOLOMON IMMANUEL OF ROME (C. 1270–C. 1330)

8701 A tiny fly can choke a big man.
SOLOMON BEN GABIROL (C. 1020–1070)

8702 Authority intoxicates,
And makes mere sots of magistrates;
The fumes of it invade the brain,
And make men giddy, proud, and vain.
SAMUEL BUTLER (1612–1680)

8703 Being powerful is like being a lady. If you have to tell people you are, you ain't.
JESSE CARR (1901–)

8704 He who has great power should use it lightly.
LUCIUS ANNAEUS SENECA (C. 4 B.C.–A.D. 65)

8705 In order to obtain and hold power a man must love it. Thus the effort to get it is not likely to be coupled with goodness, but with the opposite qualities of pride, craft, and cruelty.
LEO TOLSTOY (1828–1910)

8706 Nearly all men can stand adversity, but if you want to test a man's character, give him power.
ABRAHAM LINCOLN (1809–1865)

8707 O! it is excellent
To have a giant's strength;
But it is tyrannous
To use it like a giant.
WILLIAM SHAKESPEARE (1564–1616)

8708 Patience and gentleness is power.
LEIGH HUNT (1784–1859)

8709 Power can do everything but the most important thing: it cannot control love.
PHILIP YANCEY (1949–)

8710 Power is in tearing human minds to pieces and putting them together again in new shapes of our own choosing.
GEORGE ORWELL (1903–1950)

8711 Power is like saltwater; the more you drink, the thirstier you get.
CHARLES COLSON (1931–)

8712 Power is much more easily manifested in destroying than in creating.
WILLIAM WORDSWORTH (1770–1850)

8713 Power is to be able to do without.
GEORGE MACDONALD (1824–1905)

8714 Power will intoxicate the best hearts, as wine the strongest heads. No man is wise enough, nor good enough to be trusted with unlimited power.
CHARLES CALEB COLTON (1780–1832)

8715 The basic difference between physical and spiritual power is that men use physical power but spiritual power uses men.
JUSTIN WROE NIXON (1886–1958)

8716 The love of liberty is the love of others; the love of power is the love of ourselves.
WILLIAM HAZLITT (1778–1830)

8717 The lure of power can separate the most resolute of Christians from the true nature of Christian leadership, which is service to others. It's difficult to stand on a pedestal and wash the feet of those below.
CHARLES COLSON (1931–)

8718 The lust for power is not rooted in strength but in weakness.
ERICH FROMM (1900–1980)

8719 The sin of the Garden was the sin of power.
RICHARD J. FOSTER (1942–)

8720 There is more power in the open hand than in the clenched fist.

8721 There is no stronger test of a man's character than power and authority.
PLUTARCH (C. 46–AFTER 119)

8722 Without hypocrisy, lying, punishments, prisons, fortresses, and murders, no new power can arise and no existing one hold its own.
LEO TOLSTOY (1828–1910)

PRAISE

8723 A refusal of praise is a desire to be praised twice.
FRANÇOIS, DUC DE LA ROCHEFOUCAULD (1613–1680)

8724 A sacrifice of praise will always cost you something. It will be a difficult thing to do. It requires trading in our pride, our anger, and most valued of all, our human logic. We will be compelled to voice our words of praise firmly and precisely, even as our logic screams that God has no idea what he's doing. Most of the verses written about praise in God's Word were penned by men and women who faced crushing heartaches, injustice, treachery, slander, and scores of other intolerable situations.
JONI EARECKSON TADA

8725 Angels listen for your songs, for your voice rises to the very gates of heaven when you praise Me.
FRANCES J. ROBERTS

8726 Generally we praise with enthusiasm only those who admire us.
FRANÇOIS ALEXANDRE FRÉDÉRIC, DUC DE LA ROCHEFOUCAULD-LIANCOURT (1747–1827)

8727 He who does not praise God while here on earth shall in eternity be dumb.
JAN VAN RUYSBROECK (1293–1381)

8728 He who praises everybody praises nobody.
SAMUEL JOHNSON (1709–1784)

8729 I praise loudly; I blame softly.
CATHERINE II OF RUSSIA (1729–1796)

8730 Make of our hearts a field to raise your praise.
LUCI SHAW (1928–)

8731 Now burst,
all our bell throats!
Toll,
every clapper tongue!
LUCI SHAW (1928–)

8732 O for a thousand tongues to sing my great Redeemer's praise!
CHARLES WESLEY (1707–1788)

8733 On earth join all ye creatures to extol
Him first, him last, him midst, and
without end.
JOHN MILTON (1608–1674)

8734 Praise is more than singing, it's the
saint reflecting the life of Christ.

8735 Praise is the best auxiliary to prayer.
He who most bears in mind what has
been done for him by God will be
most emboldened to ask for fresh gifts
from above.
ANDREW MELVILLE (1545–1622)

8736 Praise to the undeserving is severe satire.
BENJAMIN FRANKLIN (1706–1790)

8737 Receive every day as a resurrection
from death, as a new enjoyment of life
. . . let your joyful heart praise and
magnify so good and glorious a Creator.
WILLIAM LAW (1686–1761)

8738 The fetus of praise grows deep in my
spirit.
EUGENE PETERSON

8739 The meanest, most contemptible kind
of praise is that which first speaks well
of a man, and then qualifies it with a
"but."
HENRY WARD BEECHER (1813–1887)

8740 The sweetest of all sounds is praise.
XENOPHON (C. 431–C. 352 B.C.)

8741 The trouble with most of us is that we
would rather be ruined by praise than
saved by criticism.
NORMAN VINCENT PEALE (1898–)

8742 You awaken us to delight in your
praise; for you have made us for yourself, and our hearts are restless until
they rest in you.
SAINT AUGUSTINE OF HIPPO (354–430)

8743 To the ear of God everything he created makes exquisite music, and man
joined in the paean of praise until he
fell, then there came in the frantic discord of sin. The realization of redemption brings man by way of the minor
note of repentance back into tune with
praise again.
OSWALD CHAMBERS (1874–1917)

8744 We all sin by needlessly disobeying the
apostolic injunction to rejoice as much
as by anything else.
C. S. LEWIS (1898–1963)

8745 What else can I do, a lame old man,
but sing hymns to God?
EPICTETUS (C. 55–C. 135)

8746 When all thy mercies, O my God!
My rising soul surveys,
Transported with the view, I'm lost
In wonder, love, and praise.
JOSEPH ADDISON (1672–1719)

8747 You don't learn to praise in a day, especially since you may have been complaining for years! New habits take
time to develop. But you can begin
today, and practice tomorrow, and the
next day, until it becomes part of you.
ERWIN W. LUTZER (1941–)

PRAYER

8748 "O God, stay with me; let no word
cross my lips that is not your word, no
thoughts enter my mind that are not
your thoughts, no deed ever be done
or entertained by me that is not your
deed. Amen."
    That was my own prayer, and its
form is an exception. That is why I
wrote it down because I don't very often
feel induced to address my Creator in
that sort of way. To me prayer is a sort
of understanding.
MALCOLM MUGGERIDGE (1903–1990)

8749 A Christian is more music
When he prays,
Than spheres, or angel's praises be,
In panegyric alleluias.
JOHN DONNE (1572–1631)

8750 A logical fallacy attends all ingenious
proposals to "test the efficacy of
prayer" by (for example) praying for
the patients in Ward A of a hospital
and leaving Ward B unprayed for, in
order to see which set recovers. Prayer
undertaken in that spirit is not prayer
at all, and it requires a singular naiveté
to imagine that Omniscience could be
so easily bamboozled.
DOROTHY L. SAYERS (1893–1957)

8751 A man prayed, and at first he thought that prayer was talking. But he became more and more quiet until in the end he realized that prayer is listening.
SØREN AABYE KIERKEGAARD (1813–1855)

8752 A man without prayer is like a tree without roots.
POPE PIUS XII (1876–1958)

8753 A prayer in its simplest definition is merely a wish turned Godward.
PHILLIPS BROOKS (1835–1893)

8754 A prayer is not holy chewing gum and you don't have to see how far you can stretch it.
LIONEL BLUE

8755 A single grateful thought raised to heaven is the most perfect prayer.
GOTTHOLD EPHRAIM LESSING (1729–1781)

8756 Adoration is the highest form of prayer.
LOUIS CASSELS (1922–1974)

8757 All men, Socrates, who have any degree of right feeling at the beginning of every enterprise, whether small or great, always call upon God.
PLATO (C. 428–348 B.C.)

8758 All the Christian virtues are locked up in the word *prayer*.
CHARLES HADDON SPURGEON (1834–1892)

8759 Although posture is not important, I find that I am able to express my dependence better on my knees, a sign of our helplessness apart from the divine enablement.
ERWIN W. LUTZER (1941–)

8760 An intercessor means one who is in such vital contact with God and with his fellowmen that he is like a live wire closing the gap between the saving power of God and the sinful men who have been cut off from that power.
HANNAH HURNARD (1905–1990)

8761 An ordinary simple Christian kneels down to say his prayers. . . . But if he is a Christian, he knows that what is prompting him to pray is also God: God, so to speak, inside him. But he also knows that all his real knowledge of God comes through Christ, the man who was God—that Christ is standing beside him, helping him to pray, praying for him. You see what is happening. God is the thing to which he is praying—the goal he is trying to reach. God is also the thing inside him which is pushing him on—the motive power. God is also the road or bridge along which he is being pushed to that goal. So that the whole threefold life of the three-personal Being is actually going on in that ordinary little bedroom where an ordinary man is saying his prayers.
C. S. LEWIS (1898–1963)

8762 Anyone who has ever tried to formulate a private prayer in silence, and in his own heart, will know what I mean by diabolical interference. The forces of evil are in opposition to the will of God. And the nearer a man approaches God's will, the more apparent and stronger and more formidable this opposition is seen to be. It is only when we are going in more or less the same direction as the devil that we are unconscious of any opposition at all.
DAVID BOLT

8763 Anything large enough for a wish to light upon is large enough to hang a prayer on.
GEORGE MACDONALD (1824–1905)

8764 As a physician, I have seen men, after all other therapy had failed, lifted out of disease and melancholy by the serene effort of prayer.
ALEXIS CARREL (1873–1944)

8765 As artists give themselves to their models, and poets to their classical pursuits, so must we addict ourselves to prayer.
CHARLES HADDON SPURGEON (1834–1892)

8766 As it is the business of tailors to make clothes and of cobblers to mend shoes, so it is the business of Christians to pray.
MARTIN LUTHER (1483–1546)

8767 At the profoundest depths in life, men talk not about God but with him.
D. ELTON TRUEBLOOD (1900–)

8768 Be not afraid to pray; to pray is right;
Pray if thou canst with hope, but ever
pray,
Though hope be weak or sick with
long delay;
Pray in the darkness if there be no
light;
And if for any wish thou dare not pray
Then pray to God to cast that wish
away.
EDWARD MC KENDREE BOUNDS
(1835–1913)

8769 Be not forgetful of prayer. Every time
you pray, if your prayer is sincere,
there will be new feeling and new
meaning in it, which will give you
fresh courage, and you will understand that prayer is an education.
FYODOR MIKHAYLOVICH DOSTOYEVSKI
(1821–1881)

8770 Be yourself. Be natural before God.
Do not pretend to emotions you do
not feel. Tell him whatever is on your
heart and mind with whatever words
are most natural to you. You do not
have to speak to him in "religious"
language about "spiritual" matters
only . . . Speak as naturally and as easily as you would to a friend, since God
is just that. . . . This natural expression of yourself at the outset is the
guarantee that you can go on to a creative, free, and mature relationship
with God.
JOHN B. COBURN

8771 Between the humble and contrite heart
and the majesty of heaven, there are
no barriers; the only password is
prayer.
HOSEA BALLOU (1771–1852)

8772 Beware in your prayer, above everything, of limiting God, not only by
unbelief, but by fancying that you
know what he can do.
ANDREW MURRAY (1828–1917)

8773 Beware of placing the emphasis on
what prayer costs us; it cost God everything to make it possible for us to pray.
OSWALD CHAMBERS (1874–1917)

8774 Call on God, but row away from the
rocks.
RALPH WALDO EMERSON (1803–1882)

8775 Careful for nothing, prayerful for
everything, thankful for anything.
DWIGHT LYMAN MOODY (1837–1899)

8776 Certain thoughts are prayers. There
are moments when, whatever be the
attitude of the body, the soul is on its
knees.
VICTOR HUGO (1802–1885)

8777 Communion with God is one thing;
familiarity with God is quite another
thing. I don't even like (and this may
hurt some of your feelings—but they'll
heal) I don't even like to hear God
called "you." *You* is a coloquial
expression. I can call a man *you*, but I
would to call God *thou* and *thee*. Now
I know these are old Elizabethan
words, but I also know that there are
some things too precious to cast
lightly away, and I think that when we
talk to God, we ought to use the pure,
respectful pronouns.
A. W. TOZER (1897–1963)

8778 Deep in my soul the still prayer of
devotion
Unheard by the world, rises silent to
thee.
THOMAS MOORE (1779–1852)

8779 Do not let it be imagined that one must
remain silent about one's feelings of
rebellion in order to enter into dialogue
with God. Quite the opposite is the
truth: it is precisely when one expresses
them that a dialogue of truth begins.
PAUL TOURNIER (1898–1986)

8780 Do not pray for easy lives,
Pray to be stronger men.
Do not pray for tasks equal to your
powers,
Pray for powers equal to your task.
PHILLIPS BROOKS (1835–1893)

8781 Don't ask God for what you think is
good; ask him for what he thinks is
good for you.

8782 Don't bother to give God instructions;
just report for duty.

8783 Don't expect a thousand-dollar answer to a ten-cent prayer.

8784 Don't let your sorrow come higher than your knees.
SWEDISH PROVERB

8785 Don't pray when you feel like it. Have an appointment with the Lord and keep it. A man is powerful on his knees.
CORRIE TEN BOOM (1892–1983)

8786 Each time I pray, I fervently plea, "Lord, make me worthy
To associate with thee."
M. JOAN RARDIN

8787 Even the most devout seem to think they must storm heaven with loud outcries and mighty bellowings or their prayers are of no avail.
A. W. TOZER (1897–1963)

8788 Events and circumstances awaken our religion, as though there were no need to pray to God except in illness and sorrow. As soon as affairs take a turn for the better and the danger is past, our devotion vanishes; the most we think of doing is to thank God for the successful end of our troubles; after a short act of gratitude we forget him and think of nothing but our pleasures. The necessities and accidents of life form the main subject and the actuating motive of the prayers of the ordinary Christian.
JEAN NICOLAS GROU (1731–1803)

8789 Every chain that spirits wear
Crumbles in the breath of prayer.
JOHN GREENLEAF WHITTIER (1807–1892)

8790 Every Christian needs a half hour of prayer each day, except when he is busy, then he needs an hour.
SAINT FRANCIS OF SALES (1567–1622)

8791 Every day we plead in the Lord's Prayer, "Thy will be done!" Yet when his will is done we grumble and are not pleased with it.
MEISTER ECKHART (C. 1260–C. 1327)

8792 Fountain of mercy! Whose pervading eye
Can look within and read what passes there,
Accept my thoughts for thanks; I have no words.

My soul o'erfraught with gratitude, rejects
The aid of language—Lord!—behold my heart.
HANNAH MORE (1745–1833)

8793 Francis of Assisi spent 75 percent of his time in prayer and 25 percent in preaching and apostolic service. Yet we think of him primarily as a preacher. He was so energized by the Spirit of God that he made a significant mark on his world in a small amount of time each day or week.

8794 From three to four each morning— that is my hour. Then I am free from interruption and from the fear of interruption. Each morning I wake at three and live an hour with God. It gives me strength for everything. Without it I would be utterly helpless. I could not be true to my friends, or do my work, or preach the gospel which God has given me for his poor.
TOYOHIKO KAGAWA (1888–1960)

8795 God always answers us in the deeps, never in the shallows of our soul.
AMY CARMICHAEL (1867–1951)

8796 God bestows many things on us out of his liberality, even without our asking for them. But that he wishes to bestow certain things on us at our asking is for the sake of our good, that we may acquire confidence in having recourse to God, and that we may recognize in him the Author of our goods.
SAINT THOMAS AQUINAS (1225–1274)

8797 God has not always answered my prayers. If he had, I would have married the wrong man—several times!
RUTH BELL GRAHAM

8798 God is not a cosmic bellboy for whom we can press a button to get things.
HARRY EMERSON FOSDICK (1878–1969)

8799 God is perfect love and perfect wisdom. We do not pray in order to change his will, but to bring our wills into harmony with his.
SIR WILLIAM TEMPLE (1628–1699)

8800 God never ceases to speak to us, but the noise of the world without and the tumult of our passions within bewilder

us and prevent us from listening to him.
FRANÇOIS FÉNELON (1651–1715)

8801 God puts his ear so closely down to your lips that he can hear your faintest whisper. It is not God away off up yonder; it is God away down here, close up—so close up that when you pray to him, it is more a whisper than a kiss.
THOMAS DE WITT TALMAGE (1832–1902)

8802 God will either give you what you ask, or something far better.
ROBERT MURRAY MCCHEYNE (1813–1843)

8803 God will not do for me what I can do for myself. Prayer must never be regarded as a labor-saving device.
WILLIAM BARCLAY (1907–1978)

8804 God's way of answering the Christian's prayer for more patience, experience, hope, and love often is to put him into the furnace of affliction.
RICHARD CECIL (1748–1810)

8805 Great supplicants have sought the secret place of the Most High, not that they might escape the world, but that they might learn to conquer it.
SAMUEL CHADWICK (1832–1917)

8806 He prayed for strength that he might achieve;
He was made weak that he might obey.
He prayed for wealth that he might do greater things;
He was given infirmity that he might do better things.
He prayed for riches that he might be happy;
He was given poverty that he might be wise.
He prayed for power that he might have the praise of men;
He was given weakness that he might feel the need of God.
He prayed for all things that he might enjoy life;
He was given life that he might enjoy all things.
He received nothing that he asked for—but all that he hoped for.

8807 He prayeth best who loveth best
All things both great and small.
SAMUEL TAYLOR COLERIDGE (1772–1834)

8808 He that prays much by night, his face is fair by day.
ORACLE OF TATSUTA

8809 He who does not pray when the sun shines will not know how to pray when the clouds roll in.

8810 He who fails to pray does not cheat God. He cheats himself.
GEORGE FAILING

8811 He who labors as he prays, lifts his heart to God with his hands.
BERNARD OF CLAIRVAUX (1090–1153)

8812 He who prays as he ought will endeavor to live as he prays.
JOHN OWEN (1616–1683)

8813 How can you expect God to speak in that gentle and inward voice which melts the soul when you are making so much noise with your rapid reflections?
FRANÇOIS FÉNELON (1651–1715)

8814 How marvelous that I, a filthy clod, May yet hold friendly converse with my God!
ANGELUS SILESIUS (1624–1677)

8815 I am convinced that the most outstanding enemy in prayer is the lack of knowledge of what we are in Christ, and of what he is in us, and what he did for us, and of our standing and legal rights before the throne.
E. W. KENYON

8816 I am so busy now that if I did not spend two or three hours each day in prayer, I would not get through the day.
MARTIN LUTHER (1483–1546)

8817 I can tell you that God is alive because I talked with him this morning.
BILLY GRAHAM (1918–   )

8818 I cannot say *our* if religion has no room for others and their needs.
   I cannot say *Father,* if I do not demonstrate this relationship in my daily living.
   I cannot say *who art in heaven* if all my interests and pursuits are on earthly things.

I cannot say *hallowed be thy name* if I, who am called by his name, am not holy.

I cannot say *thy kingdom come* if I am unwilling to give up my own sovereignty and accept the righteous reign of God.

I cannot say *thy will be done* if I am unwilling or resentful of having it in my life.

I cannot say *in earth as it is in heaven* unless I am truly ready to give myself to his service here and now.

I cannot say *give us this day our daily bread* without expending honest effort for it or by ignoring the genuine needs of my fellowmen.

I cannot say *forgive us our trespasses as we forgive those who trespass against us* if I contine to harbor a grudge against anyone.

I cannot say *lead us not into temptation* if I deliberately choose to remain in a situation where I am likely to be tempted.

I cannot say *deliver us from evil* if I am not prepared to fight in the spiritual realm with the weapon of prayer.

I cannot say *thine is the kingdom* if I do not give the King the disciplined obedience of a loyal subject.

I cannot say *thine is the power* if I fear what my neighbors may say or do.

I cannot say *thine is the glory* if I am seeking my own glory first.

I cannot say *forever* if I am too anxious about each day's affairs.

I cannot say *amen* unless I honestly say, "Cost what it may, this is my prayer."

8819 I do not think that prayer is ever evasion, that prayer saves us from having to face things that we do not want to face and that are going to hurt if we face them. Jesus in Gethsemane discovered that there was no evasion of the cross.
WILLIAM BARCLAY (1907–1978)

8820 I don't want to keep a prayer list but to pray, nor agonize to find your will but to obey.
JOSEPH BAYLY (1920–1986)

8821 I have always found praying, in any definite sense, very difficult. Somehow the notion of putting specific requests to God strikes me as unseemly, if not absurd. . . . I can never find anything to say to God except: Thy will be done. If it is true, as St. Paul tells us— and it surely is—that all things work together for good to them that love God, then all that is required of us is that we should love God, and, in loving him, fall in with his purposes.
MALCOLM MUGGERIDGE (1903–1990)

8822 I have been driven many times to my knees by the overwhelming conviction that I had nowhere else to go. My own wisdom, and that of all about me, seemed insufficient for the day.
ABRAHAM LINCOLN (1809–1865)

8823 I have lived to thank God that all my prayers have not been answered.
JEAN INGELOW (1820–1897)

8824 I have not placed reading before praying because I regard it more important, but because, in order to pray aright, we must understand what we are praying for.
ANGELINA GRIMKÉ (1805–1879)

8825 I know not by what methods rare, But this I know: God answers prayer. I know not if the blessing sought Will come in just the guise I thought. I leave my prayer to him alone Whose will is wiser than my own.
ELIZA M. HICKOK

8826 I need to stop talking about prayer— and pray.
BERTHA MUNRO

8827 I sit beside my lonely fire And pray for wisdom yet; For calmness to remember Or courage to forget.
CHARLES HAMILTON AÏDÉ (1826–1906)

8828 I used to think the Lord's Prayer was a short prayer; but, as I live longer, and see more of life, I begin to believe there is no such thing as getting through it. If a man, in praying that prayer, were to be stopped by every word until he had thoroughly prayed it, it would take him a lifetime. "Our

Father"—there would be a wall a hundred feet high in just those two words to most men. If they might say, "Our Tyrant," or "Our Monarch," or even "Our Creator," they could get along with it; but "Our Father"—why, a man is almost a saint who can pray that!

You read, "Thy will be done," and you say to yourself, "O, I can pray that"; and all the time your mind goes round and round in immense circuits and far-off distances; but God is continually bringing the circuits nearer to you, till he says, "How is it about your temper and your pride? How is it about your business and daily life?"

This is a revolutionary petition. It would make many a man's shop and store tumble to the ground to utter it. Who can stand at the end of the avenue along which all his pleasant thoughts and wishes are blossoming like flowers, and send these terrible words, "Thy will be done," crashing down through it? I think it is the most fearful prayer to pray in the world.
HENRY WARD BEECHER (1813–1887)

8829 I wake up in the morning, and I like to begin the day by thinking what life is about, rather than plunging into the sort of things one is going to have to do. So I like to read the Gospels, the Epistles, St. Augustine, the metaphysical poets like George Herbert, whom I consider to be the most exquisite religious poet in the English language. I read a bit, and then my mind dwells on what I've read, and this I consider to be prayer.
MALCOLM MUGGERIDGE (1903–1990)

8830 If God bores you, tell him that he bores you; that you prefer the vilest amusements to his presence; that you only feel at your ease when you are far from him.
FRANÇOIS FÉNELON (1651–1715)

8831 If God were to answer dogs' prayers, it would rain bones.
ARABIAN PROVERB

8832 If I could hear Christ praying for me in the next room, I would not fear a million enemies. Yet distance makes no difference. He is praying for me.
ROBERT MURRAY MCCHEYNE (1813–1843)

8833 If man is man and God is God, to live without prayer is not merely an awful thing; it is an infinitely foolish thing.
PHILLIPS BROOKS (1835–1893)

8834 If the sky falls, hold up your hands.
SPANISH PROVERB

8835 If we knew how to listen to God, we should hear him speaking to us, for God does speak. He speaks in his gospel; he speaks also through life—that new gospel to which we ourselves add a page each day.
MICHEL QUOIST (1921–   )

8836 If you are swept off your feet, it's time to get on your knees.
FREDERICK BECK

8837 If you can beat the devil in the matter of regular daily prayer, you can beat him anywhere. If he can beat you there, he can possibly beat you anywhere.
PAUL DANIEL RADER (1879–1938)

8838 If you pray for another, you will be helped yourself.
JEWISH PROVERB

8839 If you seek your own advantage or blessing through God you are not really seeking God at all.
MEISTER ECKHART (C. 1260–C. 1327)

8840 If you want to know about God, there is only one way to do it: Get down on your knees. The man who thinks only of himself says prayers of petition; he who thinks of his neighbor says prayers of intercession; he who thinks only of loving and serving God says prayers of abandonment to God's will, and that is the prayer of the saints.
ARCHBISHOP FULTON J. SHEEN (1895–1979)

8841 If your day is hemmed with prayer, it is less likely to unravel.

8842 If your knees are shaking, kneel on them.
CHARLES L. ALLEN (1913–   )

8843 In our private prayers and in our public services we are forever asking God to do things that he either has already

done or cannot do because of our unbelief. We plead for him to speak when he has already spoken and is at that very moment speaking. We ask him to come when he is already present and waiting for us to recognize him. We beg the Holy Spirit to fill us while all the time we are preventing him by our doubts.
A. W. TOZER (1897–1963)

8844 In prayer it is better to have a heart without words, than words without a heart.
JOHN BUNYAN (1628–1688)

8845 In the average church we hear the same prayers repeated each Sunday year in and year out with, one would suspect, not the remotest expectation that they will be answered. It is enough, it seems, that they have been uttered. The familiar phrase, the religious tone, the emotionally loaded words have their superficial and temporary effect, but the worshiper is no nearer to God, no better morally, and no surer of heaven than he was before.
A. W. TOZER (1897–1963)

8846 In the morning prayer is the key that opens to us the treasures of God's mercies and blessings; in the evening, it is the key that shuts us up under his protection and safeguard.

8847 Is not prayer precisely of itself peace, silence, strength, since it is a way of being with God?
JACQUES ELLUL

8848 Is prayer your steering wheel or your spare tire?
CORRIE TEN BOOM (1892–1983)

8849 It does not need to be a formal prayer: the most stumbling and broken cry—a sigh, a whisper, anything that tells the heart's loneliness and need and penitence—can find its way to him.
PHILLIPS BROOKS (1835–1893)

8850 It is a terribly serious thing to pray. The real seriousness comes not in the possibility that our prayer may not be answered; the appallingly serious thing is that it may be answered. A real answer to prayer will usually let us in

for more than we ask for. A man prays for strength, for instance, without much thought of the matter, as though strength could be wrapped up in a package like a pound of tea and handed to one. Strength must be grown; it comes from struggle against obstacles. The only way in which a prayer for strength can be answered is by putting a man into a place where he will have to struggle. We ought to take good care before we ask for strength! God may overhear us and answer us. So it is with the frequent prayer that we may have the spirit of Jesus. Many people make that prayer thoughtlessly without realizing that if they really had the spirit of Jesus, it would knock themselves and their whole world upside down.
HALFORD E. LUCCOCK (1885–1960)

8851 It is best to read the weather forecasts before we pray for rain.
MARK TWAIN (1835–1910)

8852 It is futile to pretend that prayer is indispensable to man. Today he gets along very well without it.
JACQUES ELLUL

8853 It is no use to ask God with factitious earnestness for A when our whole mind is in reality filled with the desire for B. We must lay before him what is in us, not what ought to be in us.
C. S. LEWIS (1898–1963)

8854 It is not good that a man should batter day and night at the gate of heaven. Sometimes he can do nothing else, and then nothing else is worth doing; but the very noise of the siege will sometimes drown the still small voice that calls from the open postern.
GEORGE MACDONALD (1824–1905)

8855 It is not that prayer changes God, or awakens in him purposes of love and compassion that he has not already felt. No, it changes us, and therein lies its glory and its purpose.
HANNAH HURNARD (1905–1990)

8856 It is not well for a man to pray cream and live skim milk.
HENRY WARD BEECHER (1813–1887)

8857 It is prayer, meditation, and converse with God that refreshes, restores, and renews the temper of our minds, at all times, under all trials, after all conflicts with the world. By this contact with the world unseen we receive continual accesses of strength. As our day, so is our strength. Without this healing and refreshing of spirit, duties grow to be burdens, the events of life chafe our temper, employments lower the tone of our minds, and we become fretful, irritable, and impatient.
CARDINAL HENRY EDWARD MANNING (1808–1892)

8858 It is said of James, the head of the community in Jerusalem, that the skin of his knees was as hard as a camel's from constantly praying, and that he could pray for days together. To our age that may seem laughable; but one should remember what eloquence and fullness of heart is implied by being able to pray for so long without growing tired, particularly as we have difficulty enough in making a truly heartfelt prayer.
SØREN AABYE KIERKEGAARD (1813–1855)

8859 Jesus Christ carries on intercession for us in heaven; the Holy Ghost carries on intercession in us on earth; and we the saints have to carry on intercession for all men.
OSWALD CHAMBERS (1874–1917)

8860 Jesus often retired to deserted places to pray. We see him spending nights in prayer. When you visit the Holy Land and see the places he prayed, you realize that it took a significant effort for him to get there. He had to leave the crowds that were beginning to inundate him. And it was work to climb a mountain to pray. The Mount of Transfiguration is a difficult mountain to climb.
JOHN MICHAEL TALBOT

8861 Keep praying, but be thankful that God's answers are wiser than your prayers!
WILLIAM CULBERTSON

8862 Kneel before you leap.
GEORGE H. ALLEN

8863 Let one unceasing, earnest prayer
Be, too, for light—for strength to bear
Our portion of the weight of care,
That crushes into dumb despair,
One half the human race.
HENRY WADSWORTH LONGFELLOW (1807–1882)

8864 Let us beware of sublime prayers and of all the lies they make us tell.
LOUIS EVELY (1910–   )

8865 Like art, like music, like so many other disciplines, prayer can only be appreciated when you actually spend time in it. Spending time with the Master will elevate your thinking. The more you pray, the more will be revealed. You will understand. You will smile and nod your head as you identify with others who fight long battles and find great joy on their knees.
JONI EARECKSON TADA

8866 Lord, speak to me that I may speak,
In living echoes of thy tone.
FRANCES RIDLEY HAVERGAL (1836–1879)

8867 Lord, what a change within us one short hour
Spent in thy presence will Avail to make!
What heavy burdens from our bosoms take!
What parched grounds refresh as with a shower!
We kneel, and all around us seems to lower;
We rise, and all, the distant and the near,
Stands forth in sunny outline brave and clear;
We kneel, how weak! We rise, how full of power!
Why, therefore, should we do ourselves this wrong
Or others, that we are not always strong,
That we are ever overborne with care,
That we should ever weak or heartless be,
Anxious or troubled, when with us is prayer,

And joy and strength and courage are
with thee!
ARCHBISHOP RICHARD CHENEVIX TRENCH
(1807–1886)

8868 Many a person is praying for rain
with his tub the wrong side up.
SAM JONES (1847–1906)

8869 More things are wrought by prayer
Than this world dreams of.
ALFRED, LORD TENNYSON (1809–1892)

8870 Most of us have much trouble praying
when we are in little trouble, but we
have little trouble praying when we
are in much trouble.
RICHARD P. COOK

8871 Much of our praying is just asking God
to bless some folks that are ill and to
keep us plugging along. But prayer is
not merely prattle: it is warfare.
ALAN REDPATH (1907–1989)

8872 Neglect of prayer is a guarantee that
we will not be victors.
RICHARD OWEN ROBERTS (1931–)

8873 Never make the blunder of trying to
forecast the way God is going to
answer your prayer.
OSWALD CHAMBERS (1874–1917)

8874 Never wait for fitter time or place to
talk to him. To wait till you go to
church or to your room is to make
him wait. He will listen as you walk.
GEORGE MACDONALD (1824–1905)

8875 No one can say his prayers are poor
prayers when he is using the language
of love.
JOHN MAILLARD

8876 No prayer of adoration will ever soar
higher than a simple cry: "I love you,
God."
LOUIS CASSELS (1922–1974)

8877 O sad estate
Of human wretchedness; so weak is
man,
So ignorant and blind, that did not
God
Sometimes withhold in mercy what
we ask,
We should be ruined at our own
request.
HANNAH MORE (1745–1833)

8878 Of course I prayed—
And did God care?
He cared as much
As on the air
A bird had stamped her foot
And cried, "Give me!"
EMILY ELIZABETH DICKINSON (1830–1886)

8879 Oh, I wish that God had not given me
what I prayed for! It was not so good
as I thought.
JOHANNA SPYRI (1827–1901)

8880 Only when we have knelt before God
can we stand before men.

8881 Our biggest mistake is to think that a
time of prayer is different from any
other time. It is all one.
BROTHER LAWRENCE OF THE
RESURRECTION (C. 1605–1691)

8882 Our God does not always answer our
prayers as we request. But he does for
us, as for our Lord in the Garden; he
strengthens us.
F. B. MEYER (1847–1929)

8883 Our own personal experience can
never be taken as the norm for other
people. What matters is that our
prayers should be living and sincere.
Each of us has his own temperament;
one is more intuitive, another more
logical; one is more intellectual,
another more emotional. The relationship of each with God will be marked
with the stamp of his own particular
temperament.
PAUL TOURNIER (1898–1986)

8884 Our prayer and God's mercy are like
two buckets in a well; while the one
ascends the other descends.
MARK HOPKINS (1802–1887)

8885 Our prayers are only as powerful as
our lives. In the long pull we pray only
as well as we live.
A. W. TOZER (1897–1963)

8886 Our prayers lay the track down which
God's power can come. Like a mighty
locomotive, his power is irresistible,
but it cannot reach us without rails.
WATCHMAN NEE (1903–1972)

8887 People often say to me: "I don't seem
to be able to say my prayers; what

ought I to do?" I reply: "Talk to God as you are talking to me; even more simply, in fact." St. Paul writes that the truest prayer is sometimes a sigh. A sigh can say more than could be contained in many words.
PAUL TOURNIER (1898–1986)

8888 Perfect prayer is that in which he who is praying is unaware that he is praying at all.

8889 Perhaps little praying is worse than no praying. Little praying is a kind of make-believe, a salve for the conscience, a farce and a delusion.
EDWARD MCKENDREE BOUNDS (1835–1913)

8890 Perhaps the most astonishing characteristic of Jesus' praying is that when he prayed for others, he never concluded by saying, "If it be thy will." Nor did the apostles or prophets when they were praying for others. They obviously believed that they knew what the will of God was before they prayed the prayer of faith. They were so immersed in the milieu of the Holy Spirit that when they encountered a specific situation, they knew what should be done. Their praying was so positive that it often took the form of a direct, authoritative command.
RICHARD J. FOSTER (1942–)

8891 Ponder for a moment what great crises would face you if tomorrow all your prayers were answered.
FRANCES J. ROBERTS

8892 Pray as though everything depended on God. Work as though everything depended on you.
SAINT AUGUSTINE OF HIPPO (354–430)

8893 Pray as you can, for prayer doesn't consist of thinking a great deal, but of loving a great deal.
SAINT TERESA OF AVILA (1515–1582)

8894 Pray devoutly, but hammer stoutly.

8895 Pray not for crutches but for wings.
PHILLIPS BROOKS (1835–1893)

8896 Pray not for lighter burdens but for stronger backs.
THEODORE ROOSEVELT (1858–1919)

8897 Pray that your loneliness may spur you into finding something to live for, great enough to die for.
DAG HAMMARSKJÖLD (1905–1961)

8898 Pray to God in the storm—but keep on rowing.
DANISH PROVERB

8899 Pray? Why pray?
What can praying do?
Praying really changes things,
    arranges life anew.
It's good for your digestion,
    gives peaceful sleep at night
And fills the grayest, gloomiest day—
    with rays of glowing light.
HELEN STEINER RICE

8900 Prayer . . . the very highest energy of which the mind is capable.
SAMUEL TAYLOR COLERIDGE (1772–1834)

8901 Prayer and helplessness are inseparable. Only he who is helpless can truly pray. Your helplessness is your best prayer. It calls from your heart to the heart of God with greater effect than all your uttered pleas.
OLE HALLESBY

8902 Prayer begins by talking to God, but it ends by listening to him. In the face of Absolute Truth, silence is the soul's language.
ARCHBISHOP FULTON J. SHEEN (1895–1979)

8903 Prayer can do anything that God can do.
EDWARD MCKENDREE BOUNDS (1835–1913)

8904 Prayer catapults us onto the frontier of the spiritual life.
RICHARD J. FOSTER (1942–)

8905 Prayer changes things? No! Prayer changes people and people change things.

8906 Prayer constantly enlarges our horizon and our person. It draws us out of the narrow limits within which our habits, our past, and our whole personage confine us.
PAUL TOURNIER (1898–1986)

8907 Prayer does not change God, but changes him who prays.
SØREN AABYE KIERKEGAARD (1813–1855)

8908 Prayer does not enable us to do a greater work for God. Prayer is a greater work for God.
THOMAS CHALMERS (1780–1847)

8909 Prayer does not mean that I am to bring God down to my thoughts and my purposes, and bend his government according to my foolish, silly, and sometimes sinful notions. Prayer means that I am to be raised up into feeling, into union and design with him; that I am to enter into his counsel and carry out his purpose fully.
DWIGHT LYMAN MOODY (1837–1899)

8910 Prayer enlarges the heart until it is capable of containing God's gift of himself.
MOTHER TERESA OF CALCUTTA (1910–)

8911 Prayer from a living source
within the will,
And beating up thro'
all the bitter world,
Like fountains of sweet waters
in the sea,
Kept him a living soul.
ALFRED, LORD TENNYSON (1809–1892)

8912 Prayer girds human weakness with divine strength.

8913 Prayer is a ladder on which thoughts mount to God.
ABRAHAM J. HESCHEL (1907–1972)

8914 Prayer is a rare gift, not a popular, ready gift. Prayer is not the fruit of natural talents; it is the product of faith, of holiness, of deeply spiritual character. Men learn to pray as they learn to love. Perfection in simplicity, in humility, in faith—these form its chief ingredients. Novices in these graces are not adept in prayer. It cannot be seized upon by untrained hands; graduates in heaven's highest school of art can alone touch its finest keys, raise its sweetest, highest notes. Fine material and fine finish are requisite. Master workmen are required, for mere journeymen cannot execute the work of prayer.
EDWARD McKENDREE BOUNDS (1835–1913)

8915 Prayer is a shield to the soul, a sacrifice to God, and a scourge to Satan.
JOHN BUNYAN (1628–1688)

8916 Prayer is a supernatural activity.
LOUIS EVELY (1910–)

8917 Prayer is a way of lifting ourselves, of getting a higher look, of transcending self. In prayer one sees life as God sees it, and relates his own little life and his own little needs to the needs and life of humanity.
ROBERT L. KAHN

8918 Prayer is an education.
FYODOR MIKHAYLOVICH DOSTOYEVSKI (1821–1881)

8919 Prayer is battering the gates of heaven with storms of prayer.
ALFRED, LORD TENNYSON (1809–1892)

8920 Prayer is exhaling the spirit of man and inhaling the spirit of God.
EDWIN KEITH

8921 Prayer is God's psychotherapy for his children.
RAPHAEL SIMON

8922 Prayer is identifying oneself with the divine will by the studied renunciation of one's own.
PAUL CLAUDEL (1868–1955)

8923 Prayer is more than words. It's listening, seeing, feeling.
NORMAN VINCENT PEALE (1898–)

8924 Prayer is not a lazy substitute for work. It is not a shortcut to skill or knowledge. And sometimes God delays the answer to our prayer in final form until we have time to build up the strength, accumulate the knowledge, or fashion the character that would make it possible for him to say yes to what we ask.
SAMUEL PEPYS (1633–1703)

8925 Prayer is not an argument with God to persuade him to move things our way, but an exercise by which we are enabled by his Spirit to move ourselves his way.
LEONARD RAVENHILL (1867–1942)

8926 Prayer is not artful monologue
Of voice uplifted from the sod;

It is love's tender dialogue
Between the soul and God.
JOHN RICHARD MORELAND (1880–1947)

8927 Prayer is not flight; prayer is power.
Prayer does not deliver a man from
some terrible situation; prayer enables
a man to face and to master the situation.
WILLIAM BARCLAY (1907–1978)

8928 Prayer is not getting but becoming.
SIDNEY GREENBERG

8929 Prayer is not just informing God of
our needs, for he already knows them.
God does not show himself equally to
all creatures. This does not mean that
he has favorites, that he decides to
help some and to abandon others, but
the difference occurs because it is
impossible for him to manifest himself
to certain hearts under the conditions
they set up. The sunlight plays no
favorites, but its reflection is very different on a lake and on a swamp.
ARCHBISHOP FULTON J. SHEEN (1895–1979)

8930 Prayer is not learned in a classroom
but in the closet.
EDWARD MCKENDREE BOUNDS
(1835–1913)

8931 Prayer is not merely an occasional
impulse to which we respond when we
are in trouble: prayer is a life attitude.
WALTER A. MUELLER

8932 Prayer is not monologue, but dialogue.
God's voice in response to mine is its
most essential part.
ANDREW MURRAY (1828–1917)

8933 Prayer is not overcoming God's reluctance; it is laying hold of his highest
willingness.
ARCHBISHOP RICHARD CHENEVIX TRENCH
(1807–1886)

8934 Prayer is not something we do at a specific time, but something we do all the
time.
RICHARD OWEN ROBERTS (1931–   )

8935 Prayer is not to hear oneself speak, but
to arrive at silence and continue being
silent; to wait till one hears God speak.
SØREN AABYE KIERKEGAARD (1813–1855)

8936 Prayer is putting oneself under God's
influence.
HARRY EMERSON FOSDICK (1878–1969)

8937 Prayer is simple, as simple as a child
making known its wants to its parents.
OSWALD CHAMBERS (1874–1917)

8938 Prayer is the breath of the newborn
soul, and there can be no Christian life
without it.
ROWLAND HILL (1744–1833)

8939 Prayer is the burden of a sigh,
The falling of a tear;
The upward glancing of an eye,
When none but God is near.
JAMES MONTGOMERY

8940 Prayer is the easiest and hardest of all
things; the simplest and the sublimest;
the weakest and the most powerful; its
results lie outside the range of human
possibilities; they are limited only by
the omnipotence of God.
EDWARD MCKENDREE BOUNDS
(1835–1913)

8941 Prayer is the gymnasium of the soul.
SAMUEL MARINUS ZWEMER (1867–1952)

8942 Prayer is the highest use to which
speech can be put.
P. T. FORSYTH (1848–1921)

8943 Prayer is the key of the morning and
the bolt of the night.

8944 Prayer is the link between finite man
and the infinite purposes of God. . . .
To pray in the truest sense means to
put our lives into total conformity
with what God desires.
PAT ROBERTSON (1930–   )

8945 Prayer is the most important thing in
my life. If I should neglect prayer for a
single day, I should lose a great deal of
the fire of faith.
MARTIN LUTHER (1483–1546)

8946 Prayer is the pulse of life.
ANDREW MURRAY (1828–1917)

8947 Prayer is the rope that pulls God and
man together. But it doesn't pull God
down to us: it pulls us up to him.
BILLY GRAHAM (1918–   )

8948 Prayer is the soul's sincere desire
Uttered or unexpressed

The motion of a hidden fire
That trembles in the breast.
JAMES MONTGOMERY

8949 Prayer is weakness leaning on omnipotence.
W. S. BOWDEN

8950 Prayer moves the arm which moves
    the world,
And brings salvation down.
JAMES MONTGOMERY

8951 Prayer provides power, poise, peace, and purpose.

8952 Prayer requires more of the heart than of the tongue.
ADAM CLARKE (1762–1832)

8953 Prayer serves as an edge and border to preserve the web of life from unraveling.
ROBERT HALL (1764–1831)

8954 Prayer, like radium, is a source of luminous self-generating energy. True prayer is a way of life.
ALEXIS CARREL (1873–1944)

8955 Prayerlessness is a sin.
CORRIE TEN BOOM (1892–1983)

8956 Prayers go up and blessings come down.
YIDDISH PROVERB

8957 Quiet waiting before the Lord in prayer will give him a chance to change your mood. The situation may not change, but you will have changed for the better in spite of the situation.
ROBERT A. COOK (1912–1991)

8958 Real prayer is simply being in the presence of God. When I am in trouble, and when I go to my friend, I don't want anything from him except himself. I just want to be with him for a time, to feel his comradeship, his concern, his caring round me and about me, and then to go out to a world warmer because I spent an hour with him. It must be that way with me and God. I must go to him simply for himself.
WILLIAM BARCLAY (1907–1978)

8959 Satan trembles when he sees
The weakest saint upon his knees.
WILLIAM COWPER (1731–1800)

8960 Seven days without prayer makes one weak.
ALLEN E. BARTLETT

8961 Some men will spin out a long prayer telling God who and what he is, or they pray out a whole system of divinity. Some people preach, others exhort the people, till everybody wishes they would stop, and God wishes so, too, most undoubtedly.
CHARLES G. FINNEY (1792–1875)

8962 Some of our shortest prayers are our most effectual ones.
VICTOR RAYMOND EDMAN (1900–1967)

8963 Some people are greedy even when they pray: they expect a thousand-dollar answer to a one-minute prayer.

8964 Some people think God does not like to be troubled with our constant coming and asking. The way to trouble God is not to come at all.
DWIGHT LYMAN MOODY (1837–1899)

8965 Some people's prayers need to be cut off at both ends and set on fire in the middle.
DWIGHT LYMAN MOODY (1837–1899)

8966 Something of my old self—my old, bad life—
And the old Adam in me, rises up,
And will not let me pray.
HENRY WADSWORTH LONGFELLOW (1807–1882)

8967 Take prayer out of the world, and it is as if you had torn asunder the bond that binds humanity to God and had struck dumb the tongue of the child in the presence of his Father.
GUSTAV THEODORE FECHNER (1801–1887)

8968 Talk to him in prayer of all your wants, your troubles, even of the weariness you feel in serving him. You cannot speak too freely, too trustfully to him.
FRANÇOIS FÉNELON (1651–1715)

8969 Talking to men for God is a great thing, but talking to God for men is greater still.
EDWARD MCKENDREE BOUNDS (1835–1913)

8970 Tell God all that is in your heart, as one unloads one's heart to a dear friend. People who have no secrets from each other never want subjects of conversations; they do not weigh their words because there is nothing to be kept back.
FRANÇOIS FÉNELON (1651–1715)

8971 That wisdom must sometimes refuse what ignorance may quite innocently ask seems to be self-evident.
C. S. LEWIS (1898–1963)

8972 The activities we do for God are secondary. Above all else, God is looking for people who long for communication with him.
ERWIN W. LUTZER (1941–   )

8973 The armour is for the battle of prayer. The armour is not to fight in, but to shield us while we pray. Prayer is the battle.
OSWALD CHAMBERS (1874–1917)

8974 The best prayers often have more groans than words.
JOHN BUNYAN (1628–1688)

8975 The Christian on his knees sees more than the philosopher on tiptoe.
DWIGHT LYMAN MOODY (1837–1899)

8976 The closet is not an asylum for the indolent and worthless Christian. It is not a nursery where none but babes belong. It is the battlefield of the church, its citadel, the scene of heroic and unearthly conflicts. The closet is the base of supplies for the Christian and the church. Cut off from it there is nothing left but retreat and disaster. The energy for work, the mastery over self, the deliverance from fear, all spiritual results and graces, are much advanced by prayer. The difference between the strength, the experience, the holiness of Christians is found in the contrast of their praying.
EDWARD MCKENDREE BOUNDS (1835–1913)

8977 The divine wisdom has given us prayer, not as a means whereby to obtain the good things of earth, but as a means whereby we learn to do without them; not as a means whereby we

escape evil, but as a means whereby we become strong to meet it.
FREDERICK WILLIAM ROBERTSON (1816–1853)

8978 The fewer the words the better the prayer.
GERMAN PROVERB

8979 The good unask'd, in mercy grant;
The ill, though ask'd, deny.
JAMES MERRICK (1720–1769)

8980 The holy time is quiet
Breathless with adoration
The gentleness of heaven broods o'er
    the sea;
Listen!
WILLIAM WORDSWORTH (1770–1850)

8981 The immediate person thinks and imagines that when he prays, the important thing, the thing he must concentrate upon, is that God should hear what he is praying for. And yet in the true, eternal sense it is just the reverse: the true relation in prayer is not when God hears what is prayed for, but when the person praying continues to pray until he is the one who hears, who hears what God wills. The immediate person uses many words and makes demands in his prayer; the true man of prayer only attends.
SØREN AABYE KIERKEGAARD (1813–1855)

8982 The man who says his prayers in the evening is a captain posting his sentries. After that, he can sleep.
CHARLES BAUDELAIRE (1821–1867)

8983 The most blessed result of prayer would be to rise thinking, *But I never knew before. I never dreamed . . .* I suppose it was at such a moment that Thomas Aquinas said of all his own theology, "It reminds me of straw."
C. S. LEWIS (1898–1963)

8984 The night is given us to take breath, to pray, to drink deep at the fountain of power. The day, to use the strength which has been given us, to go forth to work with it till the evening.
FLORENCE NIGHTINGALE (1820–1910)

8985 The one concern of the devil is to keep Christians from praying. He fears nothing from prayerless studies,

prayerless work, and prayerless religion. He laughs at our toil, mocks at our wisdom, but trembles when we pray.
SAMUEL CHADWICK (1832–1917)

8986 The only time my prayers are never answered is on the golf course.
BILLY GRAHAM (1918–   )

8987 The potency of prayer hath subdued the strength of fire; it has bridled the rage of lions, hushed anarchy to rest, extinguished wars, appeased the elements, expelled demons, burst the chains of death, expanded the gates of heaven, assuaged diseases, repelled frauds, rescued cities from destruction, stayed the sun in its course, and arrested the progress of the thunderbolt. Prayer is an all-efficient panoply, a treasure undiminished, a mine which is never exhausted, a sky unobscured by clouds, a heaven unruffled by the storm. It is the root, the fountain, the mother of a thousand blessings.
SAINT JOHN CHRYSOSTOM (C. 347–407)

8988 The prayer of the feeblest saint on earth who lives in the Spirit and keeps right with God is a terror to Satan. The very powers of darkness are paralyzed by prayer; no spiritual séance can succeed in the presence of a humble praying saint. No wonder Satan tries to keep our minds fussy in active work till we cannot think in prayer.
OSWALD CHAMBERS (1874–1917)

8989 The prayer preceding all prayers is "May it be the real I who speaks."
C. S. LEWIS (1898–1963)

8990 The reason we must ask God for things he already intends to give us is that he wants to teach us dependence, especially our need for himself.
ERWIN W. LUTZER (1941–   )

8991 The spectacle of a nation praying is more awe-inspiring than the explosion of an atomic bomb. The force of prayer is greater than any possible combination of man-controlled powers because prayer is man's greatest

means of tapping the infinite resources of God.
J. EDGAR HOOVER (1895–1972)

8992 The time of business does not with me differ from the time of prayer; and in the noise and clatter of my kitchen, while several persons are at the same time calling for different things, I possess God in as great tranquility as if I were upon my knees.
BROTHER LAWRENCE OF THE RESURRECTION (C. 1605–1691)

8993 The time to pray is not when we are in a tight spot but as soon as we get out of it.
JOSH BILLINGS (1818–1885)

8994 The wish to pray is a prayer in itself.
GEORGES BERNANOS (1888–1948)

8995 The world is full of faces, black with anger, green with envy, and red with shame, which could be made radiantly white with holiness and spirituality aglow by the transfiguring power of prayer.
SAMUEL HENRY PRICE

8996 There are two doorkeepers to the house of prayer, and Sorrow is more on the alert to open than her grandson Joy.
GEORGE MACDONALD (1824–1905)

8997 There is a communion with God that asks for nothing, yet asks for everything. . . . He who seeks the Father more than anything he can give is likely to have what he asks, for he is not likely to ask amiss.
GEORGE MACDONALD (1824–1905)

8998 There is a vast difference between saying prayers and praying.

8999 There is nothing that makes us love a man so much as praying for him.
WILLIAM LAW (1686–1761)

9000 Thou art coming to a King
Large petitions with thee bring;
For his grace and power are such
None can ever ask too much.
JOHN NEWTON (1725–1807)

9001 To clasp the hands in prayer is the beginning of an uprising against the disorder of the world.
KARL BARTH (1886–1968)

9002 To God we use the simplest, shortest words we can find because eloquence is only air and noise to him.
FREDERICK WILLIAM ROBERTSON (1816–1853)

9003 To lift up the hands in prayer gives God glory, but a man with a dung-fork in his hand, a woman with a slop pail, give him glory, too.
GERARD MANLEY HOPKINS (1844–1889)

9004 To pray "in Jesus' name" means to pray in his spirit, in his compassion, in his love, in his outrage, in his concern. In other words, it means to pray a prayer that Jesus himself might pray.
KENNETH L. WILSON

9005 To pray is to change. Prayer is the central avenue God uses to transform us.
RICHARD J. FOSTER (1942–   )

9006 To pray is to expose the shores of the mind to the incoming tide of God.
RALPH WASHINGTON SOCKMAN (1889–1970)

9007 To pray well is the better half of study.
MARTIN LUTHER (1483–1546)

9008 To pray when one ought to be working is as much a sin as to work when one ought to be praying.
DOROTHY L. SAYERS (1893–1957)

9009 To spend an hour worrying on our knees is not prayer. Indeed, there are times when it is our duty, having committed a problem to God in prayer, to stop praying and to trust and to do the necessary work to arrive at a solution.
OLIVER BARCLAY

9010 To suppose that God could not care for each of us because there are so many people in the world is to place upon him human limitations; but, let us remember, he is God, not man! If he knows our need and seeks to help us, we do not have to give him information, but we do need through prayer to place ourselves in an attitude to be helped.
GEORGIA HARKNESS (1891–1979)

9011 True prayer is born out of brokenness.
FRANCES J. ROBERTS

9012 True prayers are like carrier pigeons: from heaven they came, they are only going home.
CHARLES HADDON SPURGEON (1834–1892)

9013 Trying to be perfect means trying to do your particular best, with the particular graces God has given you. You cannot pray like Saint Teresa anymore than you can sing like Caruso, but how foolish if for that reason you give up trying to pray at all. What God asks of you is that you should do your best, not Saint Teresa's best.
GERALD VANN (1906–1963)

9014 We are ill-taught if we look for results only in the earthlies when we pray. A praying saint performs far more havoc among the unseen forces of darkness than we have the slightest notion of.
OSWALD CHAMBERS (1874–1917)

9015 We are obliged to pray if we are citizens of God's Kingdom. . . . The gospel cannot live, fight, or conquer without prayer—prayer unceasing, instant, and ardent.
EDWARD MCKENDREE BOUNDS (1835–1913)

9016 We are slaves to our gadgets, puppets of our power, and prisoners of our security. The theme of our generation is: "Get more, know more, and do more," instead of "Pray more, be more, and serve more."
BILLY GRAHAM (1918–   )

9017 We are too busy to pray, and so we are too busy to have power. We have a great deal of activity, but we accomplish little; many services but few conversions; much machinery but few results.
R. A. TORREY (1856–1928)

9018 We may pray most when we say least, and we may pray least when we say most.
SAINT AUGUSTINE OF HIPPO (354–430)

9019 We pour out millions of words and never notice that the prayers are not answered.
A. W. TOZER (1897–1963)

9020 We shall never sing, "Gloria in excelsis" except we pray to God *de profundis:* out of the depths must we cry, or we shall never behold glory in the highest.
CHARLES HADDON SPURGEON (1834–1892)

9021 We, on our side, are praying to God to give us victory because we believe we are right; but those on the other side pray him, too, for victory, believing they are right. What must he think of us?
ABRAHAM LINCOLN (1809–1865)

9022 Well spoke that soldier who asked what he would do if he became too weak to cling to Christ, answered, "Then I will pray him to cling to me."
CHRISTINA GEORGINA ROSSETTI (1830–1894)

9023 What we sometimes ask for when we pray to God is that two and two may not make four.
RUSSIAN PROVERB

9024 When God inclines the heart to pray
He hath an ear to hear;
To him there's music in a groan
And beauty in a tear.

9025 When I can neither see, nor hear, nor speak, still I can pray so that God can hear. When I finally pass through the valley of the shadow of death, I expect to pass through it in conversation with him.
SIR WILFRED THOMASON GRENFELL (1865–1940)

9026 When in prayer you clasp your hands, God opens his.
GERMAN PROVERB

9027 When life knocks you to your knees, you're in position to pray.

9028 When our requests are such as honor God, we may ask as largely as we will. The more daring the request, the more glory accrues to God when the answer comes.
A. W. TOZER (1897–1963)

9029 When the Lord wants to lead someone to great faith, he leaves his prayers unheard.
ANDREW MURRAY (1828–1917)

9030 When the outlook is bad, try the uplook.

9031 When we become too glib in prayer, we are most surely talking to ourselves.
A. W. TOZER (1897–1963)

9032 When you cannot pray as you would, pray as you can.
EDWARD MEYRICK GOULBURN (1818–1897)

9033 When you pray, things remain the same, but you begin to be different.
OSWALD CHAMBERS (1874–1917)

9034 Who rises from prayer a better man, his prayer is answered.
GEORGE MEREDITH (1828–1909)

9035 Why is it when we talk to God, we're said to be praying—but when God talks to us, we're schizophrenic?
LILY TOMLIN (1939–   )

9036 You know I say just what I think, and nothing more or less,
And, when I pray, my heart is in my prayer.
I cannot say one thing and mean another
If I can't pray, I will not make-believe.
HENRY WADSWORTH LONGFELLOW (1807–1882)

9037 You shall find this to be God's usual course: not to give his children the taste of his delights till they begin to sweat in seeking after them.
RICHARD BAXTER (1615–1691)

9038 You stand tall when you kneel to pray.

9039 You will find in your "closet of prayer" what you frequently lose when you are out in the world. The more you visit it, the more you will want to return. If you are faithful to your secret place, it will become your closest friend and bring you much comfort. The tears shed there bring cleansing.
THOMAS À KEMPIS (C. 1380–1471)

PRAYERS

9040 And help us, this and every day,
To live more nearly as we pray.
JOHN KEBLE (1792–1866)

9041 Be pleased, O God, to grant unto me
that great freedom of mind that will
enable me to . . . manage the common
affairs of life in such wise as not to
misemploy or neglect the improvement
of my talents; to be industrious without covetousness; diligent without anxiety; as exact in each punctilio of
action as if success were dependent
upon it, and yet so resigned as to leave
all events to thee and still attributing
to thee the praise of every good work.
SUSANNA WESLEY (1669–1742)

9042 Behold my needs which I know not
myself.
FRANÇOIS FÉNELON (1651–1715)

9043 Day by day, dear Lord,
Of thee three things I pray:
To see thee more clearly,
Love thee more dearly,
Follow thee more nearly,
Day by day.
RICHARD OF CHICHESTER (1198–1253)

9044 Dear God, help me get up; I can fall
down by myself.
JEWISH PROVERB

9045 Dear Lord, for all in pain
We pray to thee;
O come and smite again
Thine enemy.
Give to thy servants skill
To soothe and bless,
And to the tired and ill
Give quietness.
And, Lord, to those who know
Pain may not cease,
Come near, that even so
They may have peace.
AMY CARMICHAEL (1867–1951)

9046 Dear Lord, never let me be afraid to
pray for the impossible.
DOROTHY SHELLENBERGER

9047 Direct, control, suggest, this day,
All I design, or do, or say,
That all my powers with all their might,
In thy sole glory may unite.
BISHOP THOMAS KEN (1637–1711)

9048 Father of light, to thee I call;
My soul is dark within.
Thou who canst mark the sparrow's
fall,

Avert the death of sin.
Thou who canst guide the wandering
star,
Who calm'st the elemental war,
Whose mantle is yon boundless sky;
My thoughts, my words, my crimes
forgive,
And, since I soon must cease to live,
Instruct me how to die.
LORD GEORGE NOEL GORDON BYRON
(1788–1824)

9049 Father, I scarcely dare to pray,
So clear I see, now it is done,
How I have wasted half my day,
And left my work but just begun.
HELEN MARIA FISKE HUNT JACKSON
(1830–1885)

9050 Father, in thy mysterious presence
kneeling,
Fain would our souls feel all
thy kindling love;
For we are weak, and need some deep
revealing
Of trust and strength and calmness
from above.
SAMUEL JOHNSON (1709–1784)

9051 Father, let me hold thy hand and like a
child walk with thee down all my
days, secure in thy love and strength.
THOMAS À KEMPIS (C. 1380–1471)

9052 Father, set me free in the glory of thy
will, so that I will only as thou willest.
Thy will be at once thy perfection and
mine. Thou alone art deliverance—
absolute safety from every cause and
kind of trouble that ever existed, anywhere now exists, or ever can exist in
thy universe.
GEORGE MACDONALD (1824–1905)

9053 Father, we thank thee that dark and
uncertain is our future,
Because in darkness and doubt we
must cling more closely to thee.
Father, we thank thee that there will
be pain,
Because through pain we are forced to
clutch at thy hand.
Father, we thank thee that there will
be loneliness,
Because in loneliness thou art more
surely our friend.

Father, we thank thee that there shall
   be death,
Because dying we come unto thee.
JOHN S. HOYLAND (1830–1894)

9054 Fill up that which our lives have left
behind. Undo that which we have
done amiss. Repair the places we have
wasted, bind the hearts we have
wounded. Dry the eyes which we have
flooded. Make the evil we have done
work for good, so that we ourselves
would not know it.
—Prayer for the past

9055 For all that has been, thanks!
For all that shall be, yes!
DAG HAMMARSKJÖLD (1905–1961)

9056 Forgive me my nonsense as I also forgive the nonsense of those who think
they talk sense.
ROBERT FROST (1874–1963)

9057 Give me, O Lord, a steadfast heart,
   which no unworthy affection may
   drag downwards;
Give me an unconquered heart, which
   no tribulation can wear out;
Give me an upright heart, which no
   unworthy purpose may tempt aside.
SAINT THOMAS AQUINAS (1225–1274)

9058 Give us a pure heart
That we may see thee.
A humble heart
That we may hear thee.
A heart of love
That we may serve thee.
A heart of faith
That we may live thee.
DAG HAMMARSKJÖLD (1905–1961)

9059 God of our life, there are days when
the burdens we carry chafe our shoulders and weigh us down; when the
road seems dreary and endless, the
skies grey and threatening; when our
lives have no music in them, and our
hearts are lonely, and our souls have
lost their courage. Flood the path with
light, we beseech thee; turn our eyes to
where the skies are full of promise;
tune our hearts to brave music; give us
the sense of comradeship with heroes
and saints of every age; and so
quicken our spirits that we may be

able to encourage the souls of all who
journey with us on the road of life, to
thy honor and glory.
SAINT AUGUSTINE OF HIPPO (354–430)

9060 God, give us
grace to accept with serenity the things
   that cannot be changed,
courage to change the things which
   should be changed, and the
wisdom to distinguish the one from
   the other.
—Prayer for serenity
REINHOLD NIEBUHR (1892–1971)

9061 Good morning, God, I love you! What
are you up to today? I want to be a
part of it.
NORMAN GRUBB

9062 Grant me grace, O merciful God, to
desire ardently all that is pleasing to
thee, to examine it prudently, to acknowledge it truthfully, and to accomplish it perfectly, for the praise and
glory of thy name. Amen.
—Prayer before study
SAINT THOMAS AQUINAS (1225–1274)

9063 Grant to us, O Lord,
to know that which is worth knowing,
to love that which is worth loving,
to praise that which pleaseth thee
   most,
to esteem that which is most precious
   unto thee, and
to dislike whatsoever is evil in thy eyes.
   Grant us with true judgment to distinguish things that differ, and above
all to search out and to do what is
well pleasing unto thee, through Jesus
Christ our Lord.
THOMAS À KEMPIS (C. 1380–1471)

9064 Grant us, we pray thee, a heart wide
open to all this joy and beauty, and
save our souls from being so steeped
in care, or so darkened by passion,
that we pass heedless and unseeing
when even the thornbush by the wayside is aflame with the glory of God.
WALTER RAUSCHENBUSCH (1861–1918)

9065 Great Spirit, help me never to judge
another until I have walked in his moccasins for two weeks.
—Sioux Indian prayer

9066 I am your servant! Everything I have is yours. But even as I say that, I know you are serving me more than I am serving you. At your command all of the resources of heaven and earth are at my disposal, and even the angels help me.
THOMAS À KEMPIS (C. 1380–1471)

9067 If I am right, thy grace impart
Still in the right to stay;
If I am wrong, O teach my heart
To find that better way!
ALEXANDER POPE (1688–1744)

9068 Let me know myself, O God, that I may know thee.
SAINT AUGUSTINE OF HIPPO (354–430)

9069 Let not that happen which I wish, but that which is right.
MENANDER (342–292 B.C.)

9070 Let truth, light of my heart, and not the shadows within me speak to me! I slid down into that state and was in darkness, but even from there I loved you. I strayed, and yet I remembered you. I heard your voice behind me, telling me to return, but I heard only faintly because of the uproar of the restless. And now I am returning, sweaty and out of breath, to your fountain. Let no one get in my way. I will drink this and I will live it. May I not be my life; I have lived badly on my own. I was my own death. I revive in you. Speak to me; discuss with me. I have believed your books, and their words are full of mystery.
SAINT AUGUSTINE OF HIPPO (354–430)

9071 Lord, either lighten my burden or strengthen my back.
SIR THOMAS FULLER (1608–1661)

9072 Lord, give me faith to live from day to day,
With tranquil heart to do my simple part,
And with my hand in thine just go thy way!
Lord, give me faith to leave it all to thee!
The future is thy gift;
I would not lift

The veil thy love has hung 'twixt it and me.
JOHN OXENHAM (1861–1941)

9073 Lord, give me the wisdom to make stepping-stones out of stumbling blocks.

9074 Lord, help me faithfully to journey along my road, holding my rightful place in the great procession of humanity.
MICHEL QUOIST (1921–   )

9075 Lord, help me live from day to day
In such a self-forgetful way,
That even when I kneel to pray,
My prayer shall be for—others.
CHARLES DELUCENA MEIGS (1792–1869)

9076 Lord, I shall be very busy this day. I may forget thee, but do not thou forget me.
—Prayer before the Battle of Newbury
SIR JACOB ASTELEY (1579–1652)

9077 Lord, it is my chief complaint
That my love is weak and faint;
Yet I love thee, and adore;
O for grace to love thee more!
WILLIAM COWPER (1731–1800)

9078 Lord, let me not live to be useless.
JOHN WESLEY (1703–1791)

9079 Lord, make my life a window for your light to shine through and a mirror to reflect your love to all I meet. Amen.
ROBERT HAROLD SCHULLER (1926–   )

9080 Lord, send me where thou wilt, only go with me; lay on me what thou wilt, only sustain me. Cut any cord but the one that binds me to thy cause, to thy heart.
TITUS COAN

9081 Lord, teach me what I am in thy sight.
EDWARD BOUBERIE PUSEY (1800–1882)

9082 Lord, thy will be done in father, mother, child, in everything and everywhere; without a reserve, without a but, an if, or a limit.
SAINT FRANCIS OF SALES (1567–1622)

9083 Lord, what we know not, teach us.
Lord, what we have not, give us.
Lord, what we are not, make us.
SAINT AUGUSTINE OF HIPPO (354–430)

9084 Make me what thou wouldst have me;
I bargain for nothing; I make no
terms; I seek for no previous information whither thou art taking me; I will
be what thou wilt make me, and all
that thou wilt make me. I say not, I
will follow thee whithersoever thou
goest, for I am weak; but I give myself
to thee to lead me anywhere.
CARDINAL JOHN HENRY NEWMAN
(1801–1890)

9085 Make us, O God, to appreciate our
own privileges. We have full use of our
limbs and strength to move and do as
we will, and so we ask thy blessings
on those who are denied these things.
May our sympathy always go out to
the paralyzed and the handicapped
who cannot share the varied and strenuous joys which makes our lives so
full and happy. Show us how to give
friendship and help to deprived ones,
in the true spirit of Jesus our Lord.
SID G. HEDGES

9086 Lord,
make me an instrument of your peace.
Where there is hatred, let me sow love;
where there is injury, pardon;
where there is doubt, faith;
where there is despair, hope;
where there is darkness, light; and
where there is sadness, joy.
O divine Master,
grant that I may not so much seek
to be consoled as to console;
to be understood as to understand;
to be loved as to love.
For it is in giving that we receive;
it is in pardoning that we are pardoned;
and it is in dying that we are born to
eternal life.
SAINT FRANCIS OF ASSISI (C. 1181–1226)

9087 Merciful God, we confess to you that
we have sinned. We confess the sins
that no one knows and the sins that
everyone knows, the sins that burden
us and the sins that do not bother us
because we are at ease with them. We
confess our sins as a congregation. We
have not loved one another as Christ
loves us. We have not comforted one
another as Christ comforts us. We
have not forgiven one another as we
have been forgiven. We have not given
ourselves in service for the world as
Christ gives himself for us. All gracious God, forgive us. Send to us your
Holy Spirit, that we be strengthened to
live, as by your mercy you call us to
live; through Jesus Christ, our Lord.
Amen.

9088 My Lord, I am ready on the threshold
of this new day to go forth armed with
thy power, seeking adventure on the
high road, to right wrong, to overcome evil, to suffer wounds and
endure pain if need be, but in all
things to serve thee bravely, faithfully,
joyfully, that at the end of the day's
labor, kneeling for thy blessing, thou
mayst find no blot upon my shield.
—Inscribed in Chester Cathedral
KNIGHT'S PRAYER

9089 My soul is too small to accommodate
you. Enlarge it.
SAINT AUGUSTINE OF HIPPO (354–430)

9090 O Father, who hast ordained that in
stern conflict we should find our
strength and triumph over all, withhold not from us the courage by which
alone we can conquer. Still our
tongues of their weak complainings,
steel our hearts against all fear, and in
joyfully accepting the conditions of
our earthly pilgrimage, may we come
to possess our souls and to achieve our
purposed destiny. Amen.

9091 O God unrecognized, whom all thy
works proclaim,
O God, hear these my final words:
If ever I have erred, 'twas searching for
thy law;
My heart may go astray, but it is full
of thee.
VOLTAIRE (1694–1778)

9092 O God, animate us to cheerfulness.
May we have a joyful sense of our
blessings, learn to look on the bright
circumstances of our lot, and maintain
a perpetual contentedness under thy
allotments. Fortify our minds against
disappointment and calamity. Preserve
us from despondency, from yielding to

dejection. Teach us that no evil is intolerable but a guilty conscience, and that nothing can hurt us, if with true loyalty of affection, we keep thy commandments and take refuge in thee; through Jesus Christ our Lord. Amen.
WILLIAM ELLERY CHANNING (1780–1842)

9093 O God, give to all those in the world who seek thee a new understanding of their oneness, that forgetting what divides, they may so explore what unites that the whole world may at last become one family, in love and forbearance and a common joy.
SID G. HEDGES

9094 O God, give us sympathy for those who are deaf. They live in a silent world so remote and so different from ours. We take for granted speech and music and the ceaseless sounds of ordinary life—to them all is silence, they cannot even hear the voices of their dearest friends. We enjoy the song of birds, the splash of water, the rush of wind, the whispering of trees—to them all is silence. Give us sympathy, O God, and an eagerness to take into their silent world imaginative understanding and love, as you would have us do.
SID G. HEDGES

9095 O God, help us not to despise or oppose what we do not understand.
WILLIAM PENN (1644–1718)

9096 O God, help us to be masters of ourselves that we may be servants of others.
SIR ALEC PATERSON

9097 O God, I have tasted thy goodness, and it has both satisfied me and made me thirsty for more. I am painfully conscious of my need of further grace. I am ashamed of my lack of desire. O God, the Triune God, I want to want thee: I long to be filled with longing; I thirst to be made more thirsty still. Show me thy glory, I pray thee, that so I may know thee indeed. Begin in mercy a new work of love within me. Say to my soul, "Rise up, my love, my fair one, and come away." Then give me grace to rise and follow thee

up from this misty lowland where I have wandered so long. In Jesus' name, Amen.
A. W. TOZER (1897–1963)

9098 O Great Spirit!
Thou hast made this lake;
Thou hast also created us as thy children;
Thou art able to make this water calm
Until we have safely passed over.
—Chippewa Indian voyager's prayer

9099 O Lord God, we pray that we may be inspired to nobleness of life in the least things. May we dignify all our daily life. May we set such a sacredness upon every part of our life that nothing shall be trivial, nothing unimportant, and nothing dull, in the daily round.
HENRY WARD BEECHER (1813–1887)

9100 O Lord, forgive me for what I have been, sanctify what I am, and order what I shall be.
FREDERICK MACNUTT

9101 O Lord, let me not henceforth desire health or life, except to spend them for thee, with thee, and in thee. Thou alone knowest what is good for me; do, therefore, what seemeth thee best. Give to me, or take from me; conform my will to thine.
BLAISE PASCAL (1623–1662)

9102 O Lord, our heavenly Father, High and Mighty, King of kings and Lord of lords, who dost from the throne behold all the dwellers on earth and reignest with power supreme and uncontrolled over all kingdoms, empires and governments; look down in mercy we beseech thee on these American States, who had fled to thee from the rod of the oppressor, and thrown themselves on thy gracious protection desiring henceforth to be dependent only on thee. To thee they have appealed for the righteousness of their cause. To thee do they look up for that countenance and support which thou alone canst give. Take them therefore, heavenly Father, under thy nurturing care. Give them wisdom in counsel and valor in the field. Defeat the malicious

designs of our cruel adversaries. Convince them of the unrighteousness of their cause, and if they persist in their sanguinary purpose, O let the voice of thine own unerring justice, sounding in their hearts, constrain them to drop their weapons of war from their unnerved hands in the day of battle.
—First Prayer in Congress, December 17, 1777
REV. J. DUCHE

9103 O Lord, reform thy world—beginning with me.

9104 O Lord, strengthen and support, we entreat thee, all persons unjustly accused or underrated. Comfort them by the ever-present thought that thou knowest the whole truth and wilt, in thine own good time, make their righteousness as clear as the light. Give them grace to pray for such as do them wrong and hear and bless them when they pray; for the sake of Jesus Christ our Lord and Savior. Amen.
CHRISTINA GEORGINA ROSSETTI (1830–1894)

9105 O Lord, support us all the day long, until the shadows lengthen and the evening comes and the busy world is hushed, and the fever of life is over, and our work is done. Then in thy mercy grant us a safe lodging and a holy rest, and peace at last.
CARDINAL JOHN HENRY NEWMAN (1801–1890)

9106 O Lord, we beseech thee to bless and prosper us, gathered here together this day. Grant us reasonableness in all our dealings with each other. Make us large-hearted in helping and generous in criticizing. Keep us from unkind words and unkind silence. Make us quick to understand the needs and feelings of others, and grant that, living in the brightness of thy presence, we may bring thy sunshine into cloudy places, like true followers of Jesus Christ, our Lord.
SID G. HEDGES

9107 O Lord—if there is a Lord;
Save my soul—if I have a soul.
Amen.

—Prayer of a skeptic
JOSEPH ERNEST RENAN (1823–1892)

9108 O thou by whom we come to God—
The Life, the Truth, the Way;
The path of prayer thyself hast trod;
Lord, teach us how to pray.
JAMES MONTGOMERY

9109 O thou my God, stand by me, against all the world. . . . Do thou do it, thou must do it, thou alone. It is indeed not my cause, but thine.
MARTIN LUTHER (1483–1546)

9110 Protect me, my Lord, my boat is so small, and your ocean so big.
—Breton fisherman's prayer

9111 Remind me each day that the race is not always to the swift and that there is more to life than increasing its speed. . . . Slow me down, Lord, and inspire me to send my roots deep into the soil of life's enduring values, that I may grow toward the stars of my greater destiny.
O. L. CRAIN

9112 Teach me, my God and King,
In all things thee to see
And what I do in anything,
To do it as for thee.
GEORGE HERBERT (1593–1633)

9113 Teach us, good Lord, to serve thee as thou deservest;
To give and not to count the cost;
To fight and not to heed the wounds;
To toil and not to seek for rest;
To labor and not to ask for any reward,
Save that of knowing that we do thy will. Amen.
SAINT IGNATIUS OF LOYOLA (1491–1556)

9114 Thank you, Lord, for the sheer joy of wanting to get up and help the world go around.
ROXIE GIBSON

9115 We do not ask that thou wilt keep us safe, but that thou wilt keep us loyal: who for us didst face death unafraid, and dost live and reign forever and ever.

9116 We thank thee for the stars wherewith thou hast spangled the raiment of

darkness, giving beauty to the world when the sun withdraws his light. All this magnificence is but a little sparklet that has fallen from thy presence, thou Central Fire and Radiant Light of all! These are but reflections of thy wisdom, thy power, and thy glory!
THEODORE PARKER (1810–1860)

9117 We thank you, Father, for the richness of your creation! Remind us not to waste it, litter it, or pollute it.

9118 We want rain. We do not propose to dictate unto thee, but our pastures are dry, and the earth is gaping open for rain. The cattle are wandering about and lowing in search of water. Even the little squirrels in the woods are suffering from thirst. Unless thou givest us rain, our cattle will die and our harvests will come to naught. O Lord, send us rain, and send it now! Although to us there is no sign of it, it is an easy thing for thee to do. Send it now, for Christ's sake. Amen.
CHARLES G. FINNEY (1792–1875)

9119 When we are wrong,
Make us willing to change.
And when we are right,
Make us easy to live with.
PETER MARSHALL (1902–1949)

9120 Who can tell what a day may bring forth? Cause us, therefore, gracious God, to live every day as if it were to be our last, for that we know not but it may be such. Cause us to live at present as we shall wish we had done when we come to die.
THOMAS À KEMPIS (C. 1380–1471)

PREACHING

9121 A holy clumsiness is better than a sinful eloquence.
SAINT JEROME (C. 374–C. 420)

9122 A man's nose is a prominent feature on his face, but it is possible to make it so large that eyes and mouth, and everything else are thrown into insignificance, and the drawing is a caricature and not a portrait; so certain important doctrines of the Bible can

be so proclaimed in excess as to throw the rest of the truth into the shade, and the preaching is no longer the gospel in its natural beauty, but a caricature of the truth.
CHARLES HADDON SPURGEON (1834–1892)

9123 A mist in the pulpit does create a fog in the pew.
CHARLES R. SWINDOLL (1934–   )

9124 A New Testament preacher . . . has to be surgical.
OSWALD CHAMBERS (1874–1917)

9125 A pastor needs the tact of a diplomat, the strength of Samson, the patience of Job, the wisdom of Solomon—and a cast-iron stomach.
JAMES STREET (1903–1954)

9126 A preacher is one who leads men from what they want to what they need.
RALPH WASHINGTON SOCKMAN (1889–1970)

9127 A preacher must be both a soldier and a shepherd. He must nournish, defend, and teach; he must have teeth in his mouth and be able to bite and to fight.
MARTIN LUTHER (1483–1546)

9128 A preacher should be a live coal to kindle all the church.
RALPH WALDO EMERSON (1803–1882)

9129 A prepared messenger is more important than a prepared message.
ROBERT BOYD MUNGER (1910–   )

9130 Actors speak of things imaginary as if they were real, while you preachers too often speak of things real as if they were imaginary.
THOMAS BETTERTON (C. 1635–1710)

9131 An ounce of performance is worth more than a pound of preachment.
ELBERT GREEN HUBBARD (1856–1915)

9132 Conduct is the only effective sermon.

9133 Continuous eloquence is tedious.
BLAISE PASCAL (1623–1662)

9134 Eloquence is the power to translate a truth into language perfectly intelligible to the person to whom you speak.
RALPH WALDO EMERSON (1803–1882)

9135 Eloquence is vehement simplicity.
RICHARD CECIL (1748–1810)

9136 Give me one hundred preachers who fear nothing but sin and desire nothing but God, and I care not a straw whether they be clergymen or laymen, such alone will shake the gates of hell and set up the kingdom of God upon the earth.
JOHN WESLEY (1703–1791)

9137 God's Word is as a seed. The seed-thought is one that preachers and evangelists need to remember. We imagine we have to plough the field, sow the seed, reap the grain, bind it into sheaves, put it through the threshing machine, make the bread—all in one discourse.
OSWALD CHAMBERS (1874–1917)

9138 He preaches well who lives well. That's all the divinity I know.
MIGUEL DE CERVANTES (1547–1616)

9139 He that has but one word of God before him, and out of that word cannot make a sermon, can never be a preacher.
MARTIN LUTHER (1483–1546)

9140 His tonus is mono and his tempus is longus.
CALVIN MILLER

9141 I don't like to hear cut-and-dried sermons. When I hear a man preach, I like to see him act as if he were fighting bees.
ABRAHAM LINCOLN (1809–1865)

9142 I have taught you, my dear flock, for above thirty years how to live; and I will show you in a very short time how to die.
SIR EDWIN SANDYS (1561–1629)

9143 I like the silent church before the service begins better than any preaching.
RALPH WALDO EMERSON (1803–1882)

9144 I would have every minister of the gospel address his audience with the zeal of a friend, with the generous energy of a father, and with the exuberant affection of a mother.
FRANÇOIS FÉNELON (1651–1715)

9145 If spiritual pastors are to refrain from saying anything that might ever, by any possibility, be misunderstood by anybody, they will end—as in fact many of them do—by never saying anything worth hearing.
DOROTHY L. SAYERS (1893–1957)

9146 If the man in the pew was trained to think for himself, very soon the man in the pulpit would have to give him something better to think about.
OSWALD CHAMBERS (1874–1917)

9147 If your work is not going to communicate, what good is it?
LAURA J. HOBSON

9148 In order to expound a passage, live in it well beforehand.
OSWALD CHAMBERS (1874–1917)

9149 Interest comes garbed in brevity.
CALVIN MILLER

9150 It is our duty to bark in the house of the Lord.
—Saying of medieval preachers

9151 It is unreasonable for the preacher to hope to please all alike. Let a man stand with his face in what direction he will, he must necessarily turn his back on one-half of the world.

9152 No sermon is of any value, or likely to be useful, which has not the three Rs in it: ruin by the fall, redemption by Christ, and regeneration by the Holy Spirit.
JOHN C. RYLAND (1723–1792)

9153 Of all vocations the Christian ministry is the most sacred, the most exacting, the most humbling.
SIR WILLIAM ROBERTSON NICOLL (1851–1923)

9154 Our Lord's Sermon on the Mount took only about eighteen minutes to preach.
CALVIN MILLER

9155 Paul's preaching usually ended in a riot or in a revival.
ORIN PHILIP GIFFORD (B. 1847)

9156 Preach nothing down but the devil, nothing up but the Christ.
CHARLES HADDON SPURGEON (1834–1892)

9157 Preaching is thirty minutes in which to raise the dead.
JOHN RUSKIN (1819–1900)

9158 Speaking the truth is important; speaking the truth in love is all-important. Truth without love can become a bludgeon to beat the heart out of a church.
W. T. PURKISER

9159 The best sermon is preached by the minister who has a sermon to preach and not by the man who has to preach a sermon.
WILLIAM FEATHER (1889–)

9160 The life-giving preacher is a man of God, whose heart is ever athirst for God, whose soul is following hard after God, whose eye is single to God, and in whom by the power of God's Spirit the flesh and the world have been crucified; his ministry is like the generous flood of a life-giving river. Life-giving preaching costs the preacher much—death to self, crucifixion to the world, the travail of his own soul. Only crucified preaching can give life. Crucified preaching can come only from a crucified man.
EDWARD MCKENDREE BOUNDS (1835–1913)

9161 The preacher must have the heart of a lion, the skin of a hippopotamus, and agility of a greyhound, the patience of a donkey, the wisdom of an elephant, the industry of an ant, and as many lives as a cat.
EDGAR DEWITT JONES (1876–1956)

9162 The test of a preacher is that his congregation goes away saying, not "What a lovely sermon," but, "I will do something!"
SAINT FRANCIS OF SALES (1567–1622)

9163 The world is dying for want, not of good preaching, but of good hearing.
GEORGE DANA BOARDMAN (1801–1831)

9164 The world is my parish.
JOHN WESLEY (1703–1791)

9165 The young preacher preached from his ears and his memory and never a word from his soul.
RALPH WALDO EMERSON (1803–1882)

9166 To love to preach is one thing—to love those to whom we preach, quite another.
RICHARD CECIL (1748–1810)

9167 True eloquence consists in saying all that should be, not all that could be said.
FRANÇOIS, DUC DE LA ROCHEFOUCAULD (1613–1680)

9168 True eloquence does not consist in speech. . . . It must consist in the man, in the subject, and in the occasion. It comes, if it comes at all, like the outbreaking of a fountain from the earth, or the bursting forth of volcanic fires, with spontaneous, original, native force.
DANIEL WEBSTER (1782–1852)

9169 We are not diplomats but prophets, and our message is not a compromise but an ultimatum.
A. W. TOZER (1897–1963)

9170 When I preach I regard neither doctors nor magistrates, of whom I have above forty in the congregation. I have all my eyes on the servant maids and on the children. And if the learned men are not well pleased with what they hear, well, the door is open.
MARTIN LUTHER (1483–1546)

9171 When people sleep in church, maybe it's the preacher who should wake up.

9172 You can preach sociology or psychology or any other kind of ology, but if you leave Jesus Christ out of it, you hit the toboggan slide to hell.
BILLY SUNDAY (1862–1935)

PREDESTINATION

9173 All things move along an appointed path.
LUCIUS ANNAEUS SENECA (C. 4 B.C.–A.D. 65)

9174 God is preparing his heroes; and when the opportunity comes, he can fit them into their places in a moment, and the world will wonder where they came from.
ALBERT BENJAMIN SIMPSON (1843–1919)

9175 God predestines every man to be saved. The devil predestines every man to be damned. Man has the casting vote.

9176 He that is born to be hanged shall never be drowned.

PREJUDICE

9177 A fox should not be on the jury at a goose's trial.
SIR THOMAS FULLER (1608–1661)

9178 A great many people think they are thinking when they are merely rearranging their prejudices.
WILLIAM JAMES (1842–1910)

9179 A man convinced against his will
Is of the same opinion still.
SAMUEL BUTLER (1612–1680)

9180 Bigotry has no head and cannot think; no heart and cannot feel.
DANIEL O'CONNELL (1775–1847)

9181 He flattered himself on being a man without any prejudices, and this pretension itself is a very great prejudice.
ANATOLE FRANCE (1844–1924)

9182 He hears but half who hears one party only.
AESCHYLUS (C. 525–456 B.C.)

9183 Prejudice is being down on something you're not up on.

9184 Prejudice is the child of ignorance.
WILLIAM HAZLITT (1778–1830)

9185 The man who never alters his opinion is like standing water and breeds reptiles of the mind.
WILLIAM BLAKE (1757–1827)

9186 The people who are the most bigoted are the people who have no convictions at all.
G. K. CHESTERTON (1874–1936)

PRIDE

9187 A man is never so proud as when striking an attitude of humility.
C. S. LEWIS (1898–1963)

9188 A proud man is always looking down on things and people; and, of course, as long as you're looking down, you can't see something that's above you.
C. S. LEWIS (1898–1963)

9189 A vain man can never be utterly ruthless; he wants to win applause, and therefore he accommodates himself to others.
JOHANN WOLFGANG VON GOETHE (1749–1832)

9190 Absalom was vain about his hair, therefore was he hanged by his hair.
TALMUD

9191 An egotist is a man whose self-importance makes his mind shrink while his head swells.

9192 And the devil did grin, for his darling sin
Is pride that apes humility.
SAMUEL TAYLOR COLERIDGE (1772–1834)

9193 Be not proud of race, face, place, or grace.
CHARLES HADDON SPURGEON (1834–1892)

9194 Conceit is a strange disease: it makes everyone sick except the person who has it.

9195 Count not thyself better than others, lest perchance thou appear worse in the sight of God, who knoweth what is in man. Be not proud of thy good works, for God's judgments are of another sort than the judgments of man, and what pleaseth man is ofttimes displeasing to him.
THOMAS À KEMPIS (C. 1380–1471)

9196 Don't get stuck inside your own ego because it will become a prison in no time flat—and . . . don't think that "self-realization" will make you happy. That is the way you will end in . . . your own hell.
BARBARA WARD (1914–1981)

9197 Every now and then you meet a man who enjoys the reputation of being the most remarkable person he knows.

9198 God hates those who praise themselves.
SAINT CLEMENT (30–100)

9199 God made us, and God is able to empower us to do whatever he calls us to do. Denying that we can accomplish God's work is not humility; it's the worst kind of pride!
WARREN W. WIERSBE (1929–   )

9200 God sends no one away empty except those who are full of themselves.
DWIGHT LYMAN MOODY (1837–1899)

9201 He doesn't want anyone to make a fuss over him . . . just treat him as they would any other great man.

9202 He is so full of himself that he is quite empty.

9203 He that desires honors, is not worthy of honor.

9204 He that praises himself spatters himself.
GEORGE HERBERT (1593–1633)

9205 He who knows everything has a lot to learn.

9206 He who sings his own praise is usually off key.

9207 He who thinks too much of his virtues bids others think of his vices.

9208 He's suffering from I-dolatry.

9209 If ever a man becomes proud, let him remember that a mosquito preceded him in the divine order of creation.
TALMUD

9210 If you think you know it all, you haven't been listening.

9211 If you're too proud (or too afraid) to admit you are hurting . . . don't be surprised if nobody seems to care.
ROBERT HAROLD SCHULLER (1926–   )

9212 Ignorance and power and pride are a deadly mixture.

9213 In all that surrounds him, the egotist sees only the frame of his own portrait.
JOHN PETIT-SENN

9214 It is only the devil who praises himself.
ARABIAN PROVERB

9215 It is our own ego that makes the ego of others intolerable to us.
FRANÇOIS, DUC DE LA ROCHEFOUCAULD (1613–1680)

9216 It is the lofty pine that by the storm Is oftener tossed; towers fall with heavier crash Which higher soar.
HORACE BUSHNELL (1802–1876)

9217 It's ludicrous for any Christian to believe that he or she is the worthy object of public worship; it would be like the donkey carrying Jesus into Jerusalem believing the crowds were cheering and laying down their garments for him.
CHARLES COLSON (1931–   )

9218 Let me give you the history of pride in three small chapters. The beginning of pride was in heaven. The continuance of pride is on earth. The end of pride is in hell. This history shows how unprofitable it is.
RICHARD NEWTON (1813–1887)

9219 Man thinks he amounts to a great deal, but to a flea or mosquito a human being is merely something good to eat.
DON MARQUIS (1878–1937)

9220 Most of the trouble in the world is caused by people wanting to be important.
T. S. ELIOT (1888–1965)

9221 Most of us can handle a sudden demotion much better than a sizable promotion.
CHARLES R. SWINDOLL (1934–   )

9222 Never blow your own horn—unless you're in an orchestra.

9223 Noise proves nothing. Often a hen who has merely laid an egg cackles as if she had laid an asteroid.
MARK TWAIN (1835–1910)

9224 O God of earth and altar,
Bow down and hear our cry,
Our earthly rulers falter,
Our people drift and die;
The walls of gold entomb us,
The swords of scorn divide:
Take not thy thunder from us,
But take away our pride.
G. K. CHESTERTON (1874–1936)

9225 Oh, why should the spirit of mortal be proud?
Like a swift-flitting meteor, a fast-- flying cloud,
A flash of the lightning, a break of the wave,
He passeth from life to his rest in the grave.
WILLIAM KNOX (1789–1825)

9226 Pride and weakness are Siamese twins.
JAMES RUSSELL LOWELL (1819–1891)

9227 Pride is a form of selfishness.
D. H. LAWRENCE (1885–1930)

9228 Pride is at the bottom of all great mistakes.
JOHN RUSKIN (1819–1900)

9229 Pride is spiritual cancer; it eats the very possibility of love or contentment, or even common sense.
C. S. LEWIS (1898–1963)

9230 Pride is the ground in which all the other sins grow, and the parent from which all the other sins come.
WILLIAM BARCLAY (1907–1978)

9231 Pride, when puffed up, vainly, with many things
Unseasonable, unfitting, mounts the wall,
Only to hurry to that fatal fall.
SOPHOCLES (C. 496–406 B.C.)

9232 Proud people breed sad sorrows for themselves.
EMILY BRONTË (1818–1848)

9233 Quarry the granite rock with razors, or moor the vessel with a thread of silk; then may you hope with such keen and delicate instruments as human knowledge and human reason to contend against the giants of passion and pride.
CARDINAL JOHN HENRY NEWMAN (1801–1890)

9234 Self-complacency and spiritual pride are always the beginning of degeneration. When I begin to be satisfied with where I am spiritually, I begin to degenerate.
OSWALD CHAMBERS (1874–1917)

9235 Self-praise is no recommendation.
LATIN PROVERB

9236 Some men will never ask for information because it implies that they do not know.
CARDINAL HENRY EDWARD MANNING (1808–1892)

9237 Temper gets people into trouble. Pride keeps them there.

9238 The advantage of doing one's praising for oneself is that one can lay it on so thick and exactly in the right places.
SAMUEL BUTLER (1612–1680)

9239 The core of pride is self-rejection.
ERIC HOFFER (1902–1983)

9240 The essential vice, the utmost evil, is pride. Unchastity, anger, greed, drunkenness, and all that, are mere fleabites in comparison. It was through pride that the devil became the devil. Pride leads to every other vice; it is the complete anti-God state of mind.
C. S. LEWIS (1898–1963)

9241 The highest and most lofty trees have the most reason to dread the thunder.
CHARLES ROLLIN

9242 The man who blows his own horn has everyone dodging when he approaches.

9243 The man who thinks too much of himself usually thinks too little of others.

9244 The only animal that can keep his feet on the ground while his head is in the clouds is the giraffe.

9245 The pleasure of pride is like the pleasure of scratching. If there is an itch, one does want to scratch; but it is much nicer to have neither the itch nor the scratch. As long as we have the itch of self-regard we shall want the pleasure of self-approval; but the happiest moments are those when we forget our precious selves and have neither but have everything else (God, our fellow humans, animals, the garden, and the sky) instead.
C. S. LEWIS (1898–1963)

9246 The pride of dying rich raises the loudest laugh in hell.
JOHN FOSTER (1836–1917)

9247 The proud hate pride—in others.
BENJAMIN FRANKLIN (1706–1790)

9248 There is no use our mounting on stilts, for on stilts we must still walk on our own legs. And on the loftiest throne in the world we are still sitting only on our own rump.
MICHEL EYQUEM DE MONTAIGNE (1533–1592)

9249 There is one kind of religion in which the more devoted a man is, the fewer proselytes he makes: the worship of himself.
GEORGE MACDONALD (1824–1905)

9250 There is plenty of sound in an empty barrel.
RUSSIAN PROVERB

9251 There was one who thought himself above me, and he was above me until he had that thought.
ELBERT GREEN HUBBARD (1856–1915)

9252 They are proud in humility, proud in that they are not proud.
ROBERT BURTON (1577–1640)

9253 Things average out: if you think too much of yourself, other people won't.

9254 Though the Bible urges us on to perfection, it gives no encouragement to suppose that perfection is achieved. A man who thinks he is righteous is not righteous . . . for the reason, primarily, that he is full of spiritual pride, the most deadly form that sin can take.
D. ELTON TRUEBLOOD (1900–   )

9255 Too much humility is pride.
GERMAN PROVERB

9256 Two vanities can never love one another.
LORD CHESTERFIELD (1694–1773)

9257 When a wall is cracked and lofty, its fall will be speedy.
CHINESE PROVERB

9258 When someone says you look like a million dollars, don't swell with pride; maybe you do look overtaxed.

9259 You can have no greater sign of a confirmed pride than when you think you are humble enough.
WILLIAM LAW (1686–1761)

PRIORITIES

9260 A man's heart has only enough life in it to pursue one object fully.
CHARLES HADDON SPURGEON (1834–1892)

9261 Be about your Father's business. There will always be plenty of other people occupied with the affairs of the world.
FRANCES J. ROBERTS

9262 Better go to heaven in rags than to hell in embroidery.
ENGLISH PROVERB

9263 Fortune lost, nothing lost;
Courage lost, much lost;
Honor lost, more lost;
Soul lost, all lost.

9264 God first
Others second
Self last.

9265 Have some time for yourself, and some time for your God.
ARABIAN PROVERB

9266 If ants are so busy, how is it that they attend all the picnics?

9267 It's the little things that matter most: what good is a bathtub without a plug?

9268 Jesus has many who love his heavenly kingdom, but few who bear his cross. Many want consolation, but few desire adversity. Many are eager to share Jesus' table, but few will join him in fasting.
THOMAS À KEMPIS (C. 1380–1471)

9269 One great piece of mischief has been done by the modern restriction of the word *temperance* to the question of drink. It helps people to forget that you can be just as intemperate about lots of other things. A man who makes his golf or his motor bicycle the center of his life, or a woman who devotes all her thoughts to clothes or bridge or her dog, is being just as intemperate as someone who gets drunk every evening. Of course, it does not show on the outside so easily: bridge-mania or golf-mania do not make you fall down in the middle of the road. But God is not deceived by externals.
C. S. LEWIS (1898–1963)

9270 Remember the wonderful blessings that come to you each day from the hands of a generous and gracious God, and forget the irritations that would detract from your happiness.
　　Remember the gift of life; forget your aches and pains.
　　Remember the privilege of prayer; forget the negatives that needle you.

Remember the majesty of the mountains; forget the valley of despair.

Remember the friends who encourage; forget the frustrations that discourage.

Remember to forget your losses, setbacks, and defeats.

Don't forget to remember your blessings, your triumphs, and your victories.
WILLIAM ARTHUR WARD (1812–1882)

9271 Remember your possibilities; forget your limitations.

Remember your potentialities; forget your seeming restrictions.

Remember your abilities; forget your disabilities.

Remember your assets; forget your liabilities.

Remember your strengths; forget your weaknesses.

Remember your joys; forget your sorrows.
WILLIAM ARTHUR WARD (1812–1882)

9272 Take glory neither in money, if you have some, nor in influential friends, but in God who gives you everything and above all wants to give you himself.
THOMAS À KEMPIS (C. 1380–1471)

9273 Tell me to what you pay attention, and I will tell you who you are.
JOSÉ ORTEGA Y GASSET (1883–1955)

9274 The desire of love, joy;
the desire of life, peace;
the desire of the soul, heaven.
FIONA MACLEOD (1855–1905)

9275 The main thing is to keep the main thing the main thing!

9276 The Spirit of God alters my dominating desires; he alters the things that matter, and a universe of desires I had never known before suddenly comes on the horizon.
OSWALD CHAMBERS (1874–1917)

9277 What we love to do we find time to do.
JOHN LANCASTER SPALDING (1840–1916)

9278 When a person is renewed from day to day by growing in the knowledge of God, in righteousness, and in the sanctity of truth, that person transfers its love from things temporal to things eternal, from things visible to things intelligible, from things carnal to things spiritual.
SAINT AUGUSTINE OF HIPPO (354–430)

9279 When Jesus said that whosoever shall do the will of God, the same is my brother, and my sister, and mother, he meant simply that now, for the short time remaining to him, his mission was everything, his personal life nothing.
MALCOLM MUGGERIDGE (1903–1990)

9280 When we are right with God, he gives us our desires and aspirations. Our Lord had only one desire, and that was to do the will of his Father, and to have this desire is characteristic of a disciple.
OSWALD CHAMBERS (1874–1917)

9281 Worry less and work more.
Ride less and walk more.
Frown less and laugh more.
Drink less and breathe more.
Eat less and chew more.
Preach less and practice more.

9282 Yet for all God's good will toward us he is unable to grant us our heart's desires till all our desires have been reduced to one.
A. W. TOZER (1897–1963)

PROBLEMS

9283 A problem is an opportunity to prove God.
BERTHA MUNRO

9284 Every solution of a problem is a new problem.
JOHANN WOLFGANG VON GOETHE (1749–1832)

9285 Human problems are never greater than divine solutions.
ERWIN W. LUTZER (1941–)

9286 I would not rob a man of his problems, nor would I have another man rob me of my problems. They are the delight of life, and the whole intellectual world would be stale and unprofitable if we knew everything.
JOHN DRUMMOND (1851–1897)

9287 In times like these, it helps to recall that there have always been times like these.
PAUL HARVEY (1918–)

9288 No problem is too big for God.

9289 Problems are opportunities in work clothes.
HENRY J. KAISER (1882–1967)

9290 Trying to settle a problem with oratory is like attempting to unsnarl a traffic jam by blowing horns.

9291 When you repress or suppress those things that you don't want to live with, you don't really solve the problem because you don't bury the problem dead—you bury it alive. It remains active inside of you.
JOHN POWELL

9292 You must live with people to know their problems, and live with God in order to solve them.
P. T. FORSYTH (1848–1921)

PROCRASTINATION

9293 Later never exists.

9294 A reducing diet is strange: the more you put it off, the more you put on.

9295 Do today what you want to postpone till tomorrow.
ARABIAN PROVERB

9296 He who is not ready today will not be ready tomorrow.
ENGLISH PROVERB

9297 Nothing is so fatiguing as the eternal hanging on of an uncompleted task.
WILLIAM JAMES (1842–1910)

9298 One of these days is none of these days.
HENRY GEORGE BOHN (1796–1884)

9299 Procrastination is the art of keeping up with yesterday.
DON MARQUIS (1878–1937)

9300 Procrastination is the thief of time, but it is much more. It clutters up our lives with an appalling number of half-done things.
CLIFF COLE

9301 There's nothing easier than not being able to find time to do the things you don't want to do.

9302 Tomorrow must be the longest day in the week—judging from the number of things we are going to do then.

9303 Tomorrow, tomorrow, not today, Hear the lazy people say.
CHRISTIAN FELIX WEISSE

9304 What may be done at anytime will be done at no time.
ENGLISH PROVERB

PROFANITY

9305 Profanity fixes the other person's attention on my words rather than my thoughts.
HUGH PRATHER

9306 To curse is to pray to the devil.
GERMAN PROVERB

9307 When I swear, I am being something rather than saying something.
HUGH PRATHER

PROGRESS

9308 All progress has resulted from people who took unpopular positions.
ADLAI E. STEVENSON (1900–1965)

9309 Always night! Never blue skies! Never dawn! We march—but so far we have not progressed an inch! We still dream what Adam dreamt!
VICTOR HUGO (1802–1885)

9310 Every step of progress the world has made has been from scaffold to scaffold, and from stake to stake.
WENDELL PHILLIPS (1811–1884)

9311 Humanity's most valuable assets have been the nonconformists. Were it not for the nonconformists, he who refuses to be satisfied to go along with the continuance of things as they are and insists upon attempting to find new ways of bettering things, the world would have known little progress indeed.
JOSIAH WILLIAM GITT (1884–1973)

9312 If there is no struggle, there is no progress.
FREDERICK AUGUSTUS WASHINGTON
BAILEY DOUGLASS (1817–1895)

9313 Is it progress if a cannibal uses a fork?
STANISLAW J. LEC (1909–1966)

9314 Progress is the mother of problems.
G. K. CHESTERTON (1874–1936)

9315 The reasonable man adapts himself to the world. The unreasonable one persists in trying to adapt the world to himself. Therefore all progress depends on the unreasonable man.
GEORGE BERNARD SHAW (1856–1950)

9316 The rung of a ladder was never meant to rest upon, but only to hold a man's foot long enough to enable him to put the other somewhat higher.
THOMAS HENRY HUXLEY (1825–1895)

9317 What we call progress is the exchange of one nuisance for another nuisance.
HAVELOCK ELLIS (1859–1939)

9318 Without bigots, eccentrics, cranks, and heretics the world would not progress.
GELETT BURGESS (1866–1951)

PROMISES

9319 A man of words and not of deeds is like a garden full of weeds.
ENGLISH PROVERB

9320 From the promise to the deed is a day's journey.
BULGARIAN PROVERB

9321 God is the God of promise. He keeps his word, even when that seems impossible; even when the circumstances seem to point to the opposite.
COLIN URQUHART (1940–)

9322 God makes a promise; faith believes it, hope anticipates it, patience quietly awaits it.

9323 God's promises are like the stars; the darker the night the brighter they shine.
DAVID NICHOLAS

9324 God's promises are, virtually, obligations that he imposes upon himself.
FRIEDRICH WILHELM KRUMMACHER (1796–1868)

9325 He who is slow in making a promise is most likely to be faithful in the performance of it.
JEAN JACQUES ROUSSEAU (1712–1778)

9326 He who promises too much means nothing.
ENGLISH PROVERB

9327 It is better to run the risk of being considered indecisive, better to be uncertain and not promise, than to promise and not fulfill.
OSWALD CHAMBERS (1874–1917)

9328 The big print giveth and the small print taketh away.

9329 The Promised Land always lies on the other side of a wilderness.
HAVELOCK ELLIS (1859–1939)

9330 Vows made in storms are forgotten in calms.

9331 We need to stop long enough to let our feet catch up with our mouths.
BILLY GRAHAM (1918–)

PROPHETS

9332 A prophet is one who knows his times and what God is trying to say to the people of his times.
A. W. TOZER (1897–1963)

9333 Prophets are the beating hearts of the Old Testament.
WALTER RAUSCHENBUSCH (1861–1918)

9334 Scholars can interpret the past; it takes prophets to interpret the present.
A. W. TOZER (1897–1963)

PROSPERITY

9335 Abundance, like want, ruins men.
BENJAMIN FRANKLIN (1706–1790)

9336 Like glass, the brighter the glitter, the more easily broken.
PUBLILIUS SYRUS (FIRST CENTURY B.C.)

9337 Our many advantages do us harm.
LUCIUS ANNAEUS SENECA (C. 4 B.C.–A.D. 65)

9338 Prosperity is good campaigning weather for the devil.
C. S. LEWIS (1898–1963)

9339 Prosperity is more than an economic condition; it is a state of mind.
FREDERICK LEWIS ALLEN (1890–1954)

9340 Prosperity is only an instrument to be used, not a deity to be worshiped.
CALVIN COOLIDGE (1872–1933)

9341 Prosperity is the greatest enemy a man can have.
SAMUEL DANIEL (1562–1619)

9342 The meaning of earthly existence lies, not as we have grown used to thinking, in prospering, but in the development of the soul.
ALEXANDER ISAYEVICH SOLZHENITSYN (1918–)

9343 Things are in the saddle
And ride mankind.
RALPH WALDO EMERSON (1803–1882)

9344 We shall prosper as we learn to do the common things of life in an uncommon way. Let down your buckets where you are.
BOOKER T. WASHINGTON (1856–1915)

PROVISION

9345 Back of the loaf is the snowy flour,
And back of the flour the mill,
And back of the mill is the wheat and the shower,
And the sun and the Father's will.
MALTBIE D. BABCOCK (1858–1901)

9346 Get the spindle ready and God will send the flax.

9347 God feeds even the worm in the earth.
YIDDISH PROVERB

9348 God gives the nuts, but he does not crack them.
GERMAN PROVERB

9349 He who gives us teeth will give us bread.
JEWISH PROVERB

9350 The Lord my pasture shall prepare,
And feed me with a shepherd's care;
His presence shall my wants supply,
And guard me with a watchful eye.
JOSEPH ADDISON (1672–1719)

PSYCHOLOGY

9351 God wills the development of all men. When from time to time he makes them hear his call to self-denial, to renunciation and even self-sacrifice, it is not for their impoverishment but for their enrichment. Christianity is in full accord with psychology. Like psychology, it sees man in continual evolution from a lesser condition to a greater one, from limited freedom to greater freedom, from poor wealth to truer wealth. The gospel of Jesus Christ is nothing if not a gospel of growth. It sets our eyes on a development more complete than any that can be conceived by a psychology confined within the limits of nature. All Christ's calls to detachment are accompanied by promises that point to their real meaning.
PAUL TOURNIER (1898–1986)

9352 One may understand the cosmos, but never the ego; the self is more distant than any star.
G. K. CHESTERTON (1874–1936)

9353 We study everything but ourselves. We pour billions into research of every kind, but in the six thousand years of recorded history we have not learned to live together any better than the ancient Babylonians. All our sociology, our psychology, and our philosophy have penetrated hardly an inch into the inner dynamics of the human organism.
SYDNEY J. HARRIS (1917–1986)

PUNISHMENT

9354 I don't believe in a vindictive God who punishes to get even with us sinners. I do believe that we punish ourselves. When we leave the sunlight of God's love, we grow dark and cold, but this is self-inflicted punishment.
JOHN POWELL

9355 The paradox of punishment is that it works only with those who have retained a sense of justice; for the rest,

it merely evokes resentment and a vow of retaliation.
SYDNEY J. HARRIS (1917–1986)

9356 We are not punished for our sins, but by them.
ELBERT GREEN HUBBARD (1856–1915)

QUARREL

9357 A contentious man will never lack
words.

9358 In quarreling, the truth is always lost.
PUBLILIUS SYRUS (FIRST CENTURY B.C.)

9359 Most quarrels are inevitable at the
time; incredible afterwards.
E. M. FORSTER (1879–1970)

9360 No one damns like a theologian, nor is
any quarrel so bitter as a religious
quarrel.
OSWALD CHAMBERS (1874–1917)

9361 Once again the ministry of the church
will have ceased while we quarrel over
the Prince of Peace.
CALVIN MILLER

9362 Quarrels are the weapons of the weak.
JEWISH PROVERB

9363 I never learn anything talking. I only
learn things when I ask questions.
LOU HOLTZ

9364 It is not every question that deserves
an answer.
PUBLILIUS SYRUS (FIRST CENTURY B.C.)

9365 It is not the answer that enlightens,
but the question.
EUGÈNE IONESCO (1912–   )

9366 There was a time when I had all the
answers. My real growth began when
I discovered that the questions to
which I had the answers were not the
important questions.
REINHOLD NIEBUHR (1892–1971)

QUIETNESS

9367 All the troubles of life come upon us
because we refuse to sit quietly for a
while each day in our room.
BLAISE PASCAL (1623–1662)

9368 Drop thy still dews of quietness,
Till all our strivings cease;
Take from our souls the strain and
stress,
And let our ordered lives confess
The beauty of thy peace.
JOHN GREENLEAF WHITTIER (1807–1892)

9369 God is a tranquil being and abides in a
tranquil eternity. So must your spirit
become a tranquil and clear little pool,

wherein the serene light of God can be mirrored.
GERHARD TERSTEEGEN (1697–1769)

9370 Happiness is the harvest of a quiet eye.
AUSTIN O'MALLEY (1858–1932)

9371 I cannot be the man I should be without times of quietness. Stillness is an essential part of our growing deeper as we grow older.
CHARLES R. SWINDOLL (1934–   )

9372 Only in a quiet mind is adequate perception of the world.
HANS MARGOLIUS

9373 The good and the wise lead quiet lives.
EURIPIDES (C. 484–406 B.C.)

9374 True silence is the rest of the mind and is to the spirit what sleep is to the body, nourishment and refreshment.
WILLIAM PENN (1644–1718)

9375 What sweet delight a quiet life affords.
WILLIAM HAWTHORDEN DRUMMOND (1585–1649)

QUOTATIONS

9376 A proverb is a short sentence based on long experience.
MIGUEL DE CERVANTES (1547–1616)

9377 A proverb is much matter decocted into a few words.
SIR THOMAS FULLER (1608–1661)

9378 Apothegms form a shortcut to much knowledge.
THOMAS HOOD (1799–1845)

9379 By necessity, by proclivity, and by delight we all quote.
RALPH WALDO EMERSON (1803–1882)

9380 Collecting quotations seems a similar occupation to the one practiced by those birds and animals who pick up shiny pebbles, pieces of glass, and paper to line their nests and burrows. They discard one, pick up another, apparently at random, but all with a particular spot in mind. The result is a living place that conforms to their own sensibility and shape. Picking up bright and clever quotations, turning them over, scrutinizing them, and finally placing them in a particular

spot would undoubtedly get a chirp of approval.

9381 Every poem and piece of prose in an anthology is there because the person who compiled the anthology likes it. It is a collector's piece. But behind this obvious fact is another. The compiling of an anthology can be an act of thanksgiving. What would any of us do without the books and poems that help us along our way? The books we return to again and again, the poems we learn by heart and repeat for comfort in sleepless nights? We long to say thank you. In the case of writers who have been dead for several centuries, this can be difficult, but to those who are happily still with us an anthology says—thank you.
ELIZABETH GOUDGE

9382 I quote others, the better to express myself.
MICHEL EYQUEM DE MONTAIGNE (1533–1592)

9383 It is a good thing for an uneducated man to read books of quotations. *Bartlett's Familiar Quotations* is an admirable work, and I studied it intently. The quotations when engraved upon the memory give you good thoughts. They also make you anxious to read the authors and look for more.
SIR WINSTON CHURCHILL (1874–1965)

9384 Pithy sentences are like sharp nails that force truth upon our memory.
DENIS DIDEROT (1713–1784)

9385 Quotations tell us of the inward thoughts and aspirations of men and women, of their struggle with life and death, with ambition, misfortune, evil, grief, of their experience with love and joy, of their sense of humor. They reveal to us that people from ancient times, from the first written utterances, can speak to us today in ways that inspire, inform, comfort, entertain.
JOHN BARTLETT (1820–1905)

9386 The genius, wit, and spirit of a nation are discovered in its proverbs.
FRANCIS BACON (1561–1626)

9387 The only way to read a book of aphorisms without being bored is to open it
at random and, having found something that interests you, close the book
and meditate.
CHARLES JOSEPH, PRINCE DE LIGNE
(1735–1814)

9388 We pay much more attention to a wise
passage when it is quoted, than when
we read it in the original author.
PHILIP G. HAMERTON (1834–1894)

9389 Writers love quotations. They love
quoting someone else's work almost as
much as they love quoting their own.
We consider a well-placed quotation,
whether it be Shakespeare, Twain, or
Groucho Marx, to be one of the signs
of an erudite and educated person. It
lends weight to one's own opinions by
somehow invoking a greater—or at
least more well-known—authority.

R

RAINBOW

9390 A rainbow is heaven's promise in technicolor.

9391 A rainbow is the ribbon nature puts on after washing her hair.
RAMÓN GÓMEZ DE LA SERNA

9392 Mild arch of promise!
ROBERT SOUTHEY (1774–1843)

9393 Rainbow: God's glowing covenant.
HOSEA BALLOU (1771–1852)

RATIONALISM

9394 He was a rationalist, but he had to confess that he liked the ringing of church bells.
ANTON PAVLOVICH CHEKHOV (1860–1904)

9395 The rationalist demands an explanation of everything: The reason I won't have anything to do with God is because I cannot define him. If I can define God, I am greater than the God I define. If I can define love and life, I am greater than they are.
OSWALD CHAMBERS (1874–1917)

9396 The rationalist makes himself his own center, not his Maker; he does not go to God, but he implies that God must come to him.
CARDINAL JOHN HENRY NEWMAN (1801–1890)

9397 There is nothing so irrational as rationalism.
ERICH SAUER

9398 When a rationalist points out sin and iniquity and disease and death and says, "How does God answer that?" you have always a fathomless answer—the Cross of Christ.
OSWALD CHAMBERS (1874–1917)

REALITY

9399 A test of what is real is that it is hard and rough. Joys are found in it, not pleasure. What is pleasant belongs to dreams.
SIMONE WEIL (1909–1943)

9400 How reluctantly the mind consents to reality!
NORMAN DOUGLAS (1868–1952)

9401 I am torn between the desire to think positively or to confront life as it is.
CALVIN MILLER

9402 It is no good asking for a simple religion. After all, real things aren't simple. They look simple, but they're not. The table I'm sitting at looks simple: but ask a scientist to tell you what it's really made of—all about the atoms and how the light waves rebound from them and hit my eye, and what they do to the optic nerve, and what it does to my brain—and, of course, you find that what we call "seeing a table" lands you in mysteries and complications which you can hardly get to the end of. . . .

Reality, in fact, is always something you couldn't have guessed. That's one of the reasons I believe Christianity. . . . It has just that queer twist about it that real things have.
C. S. LEWIS (1898–1963)

9403 Jesus Christ makes us real, not merely sincere.
OSWALD CHAMBERS (1874–1917)

9404 Journalism is pure fantasy, and news is fantasy. Reality belongs to eternity and therefore has no news value.
MALCOLM MUGGERIDGE (1903–1990)

9405 Real life seems to have no plots.
IVY COMPTON BURNETT (1884–1969)

9406 Reality is always more conservative than ideology.
RAYMOND ARON (1905–)

9407 Reality is not only more fantastic than we think, but also much more fantastic than we imagine.
J. B. S. HALDANE (1892–1964)

9408 The difference between life as it is and life as it ought to be is a frightening and distressing bit of reality.
JAMES C. DOBSON (1936–)

9409 The sky is not less blue because the blind man does not see it.
DANISH PROVERB

REASON

9410 A few observations and much reasoning leads to error; many observations and a little reasoning to truth.
ALEXIS CARREL (1873–1944)

9411 All reason and natural investigation ought to follow faith, not to precede, nor to break it. . . . If the works of God were of such sort that they might easily be comprehended by human reason, they should no longer be called wonderful or unspeakable.
THOMAS À KEMPIS (C. 1380–1471)

9412 As sight is in the body, so is reason in the soul.
ARISTOTLE (384–322 B.C.)

9413 God never contradicts reason, he transcends it.
OSWALD CHAMBERS (1874–1917)

9414 Had Mary been filled with reason there'd have been no room for the child.
MADELEINE L'ENGLE (1918–)

9415 He who will not reason is a bigot; he who cannot is a fool; and he who dares not, is a slave.
JOHN DRUMMOND (1851–1897)

9416 In spiritual matters, human reasoning certainly is not in order; other intelligence, other skill and power, are requisite here—something to be granted by God himself and revealed through his Word.
MARTIN LUTHER (1483–1546)

9417 Man is not an angel, whose reason always works perfectly, nor is he a mule whose reason works not at all.
JOSEPH BEN ABBA MARI CASPI (1280–1340)

9418 Neither great poverty, nor great riches, will hear reason.
HENRY FIELDING (1707–1754)

9419 Reason and logic and intellect have to do with the time between birth and death, but they can give no explanation of before birth or after death.
OSWALD CHAMBERS (1874–1917)

9420 Reason can ascertain the profound difficulties of our condition; it cannot remove them.
CARDINAL JOHN HENRY NEWMAN (1801–1890)

9421 Reason's last step is the recognition that there are an infinite number of things that are beyond it.
BLAISE PASCAL (1623–1662)

9422 Reason, as it exists in man, is only our intellectual eye, and that, like the eye, to see, it needs light—to see clearly and far it needs the light of heaven.

9423 The Almighty does nothing without reason though the frail mind of man cannot explain the reason.
SAINT AUGUSTINE OF HIPPO (354–430)

9424 The way the serpent beguiled Eve through his subtlety was by enticing her away from personal faith in God to depend on her reason alone.
OSWALD CHAMBERS (1874–1917)

9425 We are not only endowed with a soul and a will to be saved but also with a reason to be sharpened and satisfied. . . . It is neither a shame nor a sin to discipline and cultivate our reason to the utmost; it is a necessity, it is a duty, it is an honor to do so.
CHARLES HABIB MALIK (1906–)

9426 We cannot enter the kingdom of heaven head first.
OSWALD CHAMBERS (1874–1917)

9427 When man reasons, God laughs.
JEWISH PROVERB

9428 You can save yourself a lot of time and mental agony by recognizing at the outset that you cannot reason your way to a belief in God as a loving Father in heaven.
LOUIS CASSELS (1922–1974)

RECONCILIATION

9429 In God alone can man meet man.
GEORGE MACDONALD (1824–1905)

9430 Never once is God said to be reconciled to man; it is always man who is reconciled to God.
WILLIAM BARCLAY (1907–1978)

9431 Reconciliation is not weakness or cowardice. It demands courage, nobility, generosity, sometimes heroism, an overcoming of oneself rather than of one's adversary.
POPE PAUL VI (1897–1978)

9432 To reconcile man with man and not with God is to reconcile no one at all.
THOMAS MERTON (1915–1968)

REDEMPTION

9433 An understanding of redemption is not necessary to salvation any more than an understanding of life is necessary before we can be born into it.
OSWALD CHAMBERS (1874–1917)

9434 God redeemed the human race when we were spitting in his face, as it were.
OSWALD CHAMBERS (1874–1917)

9435 If I had the wisdom of Solomon, the patience of John, the meekness of Moses, the strength of Samson, the obedience of Abraham, the compassion of Joseph, the tears of Jeremiah, the poetic skill of David, the prophetic voice of Elijah, the courage of Daniel, the greatness of John the Baptist, the endurance and love of Paul, I would still need redemption through Christ's blood, the forgiveness of sin.
R. L. WHEELER

9436 Redemption means that Jesus Christ can put into any man the disposition that ruled his own life.
OSWALD CHAMBERS (1874–1917)

9437 The cross of Jesus Christ and his baptism express the same thing. Our Lord was not a martyr; he was not merely a good man; he was God Incarnate. He came down to the lowest reach of creation in order to bring back the whole human race to God, and in order to do this he must take upon him, as representative man, the whole massed sin of the race.
OSWALD CHAMBERS (1874–1917)

9438 The purpose of Christ's redeeming work was to make it possible for bad

men to become good—deeply, radically, and finally.
A. W. TOZER (1897–1963)

9439 The strangest truth of the gospel is that redemption comes through suffering.
MILO L. CHAPMAN

REGRET

9440 Regret is an appalling waste of energy; you can't build on it; it's only good for wallowing in.
KATHERINE MANSFIELD (1888–1923)

RELATIONSHIPS

9441 A loving person lives in a loving world. A hostile person lives in a hostile world. Everyone you meet is your mirror.
KEN KEYES, JR.

9442 A single arrow is easily broken, but not ten in a bundle.
JAPANESE PROVERB

9443 A stranger is a friend whose acquaintance you haven't made yet.

9444 A wise man gets more use from his enemies than a fool from his friends.
BALTASAR GRACIÀN Y MORALES (1601–1658)

9445 An egotist talks to you about himself, a gossip talks to you about others, and a brilliant conversationalist talks to you about you.

9446 Any deep relationship to another human being requires watchfulness and nourishment; otherwise, it is taken from us. And we cannot recapture it. This is a form of having and not having that is the root of innumerable tragedies.
PAUL JOHANNES OSKAR TILLICH (1886–1965)

9447 Anyone who builds a relationship on less than openness and honesty is building on sand.
JOHN POWELL

9448 Christ was willing to suffer; do you dare to complain? Christ had enemies and detractors; so you want everyone to be your friend and benefactor?
THOMAS À KEMPIS (C. 1380–1471)

9449 Do good to your friend to keep him, to your enemy to gain him.
BENJAMIN FRANKLIN (1706–1790)

9450 Don't expect your neighbor to be better than your neighbor's neighbor.

9451 Every person we meet in the course of a day is a dignified, essential human soul, and we are guilty of gross inhumanity when we snub or abuse him.
JOSHUA LOTH LIEBMAN (1907–1948)

9452 Everyone knows how to say good-bye but not everyone knows when.

9453 Fear that man who fears not God.

9454 God rejoices when one beggar scratches another.
YIDDISH PROVERB

9455 Half the misery in the world comes because one person demands of another a complete understanding, which is absolutely impossible.
OSWALD CHAMBERS (1874–1917)

9456 Have a deaf ear for unkind remarks about others, and a blind eye to trivial faults.
SIR WALTER SCOTT (1771–1832)

9457 He who accepts nothing has nothing to return.
GERMAN PROVERB

9458 He who goes with wolves learns to howl.
SPANISH PROVERB

9459 He who has a thousand friends has not a friend to spare, and he who has one enemy shall meet him everywhere.
ALI BEN ABU TALEB

9460 He who injured you is either stronger or weaker. If he is weaker, spare him; if he is stronger, spare yourself.
LUCIUS ANNAEUS SENECA (C. 4 B.C.–A.D. 65)

9461 Hearts may agree though heads differ.

9462 Heaven's eternal wisdom has decreed that man should ever stand in need of man.
THEOCRITUS (C. 310–250 B.C.)

9463 Human freedom is a precious thing and we react decisively against those who would restrict it or take it from us.
JAMES C. DOBSON (1936–)

9464 I likened you to those I saw you with.
MALTESE PROVERB

9465 If men would consider not so much wherein they differ, as wherein they agree, there would be far less uncharitableness and angry feeling in the world.
JOSEPH ADDISON (1672–1719)

9466 If we knew everything that was ever said about us and at the same time we took every word at face value, we would remain friends with no one.
HUGH PRATHER

9467 If we try to find lasting joy in any human relationship, it will end in vanity, something that passes like a morning cloud. The true joy of a man's life is in his relationship to God.
OSWALD CHAMBERS (1874–1917)

9468 If you approach each new person in a spirit of adventure, you will find yourself endlessly fascinated by the new channels of thought and experience and personality that you encounter.
ELEANOR ROOSEVELT (1884–1962)

9469 If you expect perfection from people, your whole life is a series of disappointments, grumblings, and complaints. If, on the contrary, you pitch your expectations low, taking folks as the inefficient creatures which they are, you are frequently surprised by having them perform better than you had hoped.
BRUCE FAIRFIELD BARTON (1886–1967)

9470 If you expect to find peace in the friendship of any person, you are likely to be disappointed. But if you are intimate with God, the disloyalty or death of a friend will not crush you.
THOMAS À KEMPIS (C. 1380–1471)

9471 If you ride a horse, sit close and tight, If you ride a man, sit easy and light.

9472 If you want enemies, excel others; if you want friends, let others excel you.
CHARLES CALEB COLTON (1780–1832)

9473 It is a foolish sheep that makes the wolf his confessor.

9474 It is best to be with those in time we hope to be with in eternity.
SIR THOMAS FULLER (1608–1661)

9475 It is better to weep with wise men than to laugh with fools.
SPANISH PROVERB

9476 It is impossible to satisfy everyone.
THOMAS À KEMPIS (C. 1380–1471)

9477 Jest with an ass, and he will flap you in the face with his tail.

9478 Leaning too heavily on another person, regardless of how committed he or she seems, is to set ourselves up for disappointment.
JAMES C. DOBSON (1936–)

9479 Let us be first to give a friendship sign, to nod first, smile first, speak first, and if such a thing is necessary—forgive first.

9480 Make happy those who are near, and those who are far will come.
CHINESE PROVERB

9481 Man shall commune with all creatures to his profit, but enjoy God alone. That is why no human being can be a permanent source of happiness to another.
DAG HAMMARSKJÖLD (1905–1961)

9482 Most people are just like cats in that if you rub them the right way, they will purr. But if you rub them the wrong way, they will bite and scratch.
WILLIAM ROSS

9483 My idea of an agreeable person is a person who agrees with me.
BENJAMIN DISRAELI (1804–1881)

9484 One way to get rid of an enemy is to turn him into a friend.

9485 Only the person who has faith in himself is able to be faithful to others.
ERICH FROMM (1900–1980)

9486 Our opinion of others depends far more than we like to think on what we believe their opinion of us is.
SYDNEY J. HARRIS (1917–1986)

9487 Our sociology reflects our theology.
REBECCA MANLEY PIPPERT

9488 Raised voices lower esteem. Hot tempers cool friendships. Loose tongues stretch truth. Swelled heads shrink influence. Sharp words dull respect.
WILLIAM ARTHUR WARD (1812–1882)

9489 See everything; overlook a great deal; correct a little.
POPE JOHN XXIII (1881–1963)

9490 Seek not every quality in one individual.
CONFUCIUS (C. 551–479 B.C.)

9491 Sojourn in every place as if you meant to spend your life there, never omitting an opportunity of doing a kindness, speaking a true word, or making a friend.
JOHN RUSKIN (1819–1900)

9492 Some people can stay longer in an hour than others can in a week.
WILLIAM DEAN HOWELLS (1837–1920)

9493 Sparrows should not dance with cranes; their legs are too short.
DANISH PROVERB

9494 The healthiest relationships are those that breathe—that move out and then move back together.
JAMES C. DOBSON (1936–   )

9495 The injuries we do and those we suffer are seldom weighed in the same scales.
AESOP (FL. C. 550 B.C.)

9496 The man or woman who does not know God demands an infinite satisfaction from other human beings which they cannot give.
OSWALD CHAMBERS (1874–1917)

9497 The more I demand the love of others, the less I deserve that love.
FRANÇOIS FÉNELON (1651–1715)

9498 The real . . . is always checked with failure, imperfection, and even wrong. So instead of biting and devouring one another, let's support individual freedom as we serve one another in love.
CHARLES R. SWINDOLL (1934–   )

9499 The reason a dog has so many friends is that he wags his tail instead of his tongue.

9500 The rotten apple spoils his companions.
BENJAMIN FRANKLIN (1706–1790)

9501 The world is a collection of cogs; each depends on the other.
JEWISH PROVERB

9502 There are areas in our lives where in our effort to be right we may go wrong:
   1. When in our determination to be bold we become brazen.
   2. When in our desire to be frank we become rude.
   3. When in our effort to be watchful we become suspicious.
   4. When we seek to be serious and become somber.
   5. When we mean to be conscientious and become overscrupulous.
A. W. TOZER (1897–1963)

9503 There are some men and women in whose company we are always at our best. All the best stops in our nature are drawn out, and we find a music in our souls never felt before.
WILLIAM HENRY DRUMMOND (1854–1907)

9504 There can be no happiness equal to the joy of finding a heart that understands.
VICTOR ROBINSOLL

9505 There's a great deal of difference between go and let's go.

9506 Those who think they have no need of others become unreasonable.
LUC DE CLAPIERS, MARQUIS DE VAUVENARGUES (1715–1747)

9507 To be right with God has often meant to be in trouble with men.
A. W. TOZER (1897–1963)

9508 To handle yourself, use your head. To handle others, use your heart.
DONALD LAIRD

9509 To his dog, every man is Napoleon; hence the constant popularity of dogs.
ALDOUS HUXLEY (1894–1963)

9510 To live fully, we must learn to use things and love people not love things and use people.
JOHN POWELL

9511 To my God, a heart of flame;
to my fellowmen, a heart of love;
to myself, a heart of steel.
SAINT AUGUSTINE OF HIPPO (354–430)

9512 Unselfishness recognizes infinite variety of types as a delightful thing,
accepts it, acquiesces in it, and enjoys
it.
OSCAR WILDE (1854–1900)

9513 We are born helpless. As soon as we
are fully conscious we discover loneliness. We need others physically, emotionally, intellectually. We need them if
we are to know anything, even ourselves.
C. S. LEWIS (1898–1963)

9514 We are far more liable to catch the
vices than the virtues of our associates.
DENIS DIDEROT (1713–1784)

9515 We are interested in others when they
are interested in us.
PUBLILIUS SYRUS (FIRST CENTURY B.C.)

9516 We often refuse to accept an idea
merely because the tone of voice in
which it has been expressed is unsympathetic to us.
FRIEDRICH WILHELM NIETZSCHE
(1844–1900)

9517 When a dove begins to associate with
crows, its feathers remain white but its
heart grows black.
GERMAN PROVERB

9518 When dealing with people, let us
remember we are not dealing with
creatures of logic. We are dealing with
creatures of emotion, creatures bustling with prejudices and motivated by
pride and vanity.
DALE CARNEGIE (1888–1955)

9519 When one is a stranger to oneself, then
one is estranged from others too.
ANNE MORROW LINDBERGH (1906–   )

9520 When we honestly consider the well-being of others, we become truly rich
in the deepest sense.
DENIS WAITLEY

9521 When you have Christ, you are rich.
He is enough. He will provide everything you need so you won't have to
count on others without him. People

change and fail. You cannot depend
on them. Those that are for you today
may be against you tomorrow. They
are as variable as the wind. But Christ
is eternally faithful.
THOMAS À KEMPIS (C. 1380–1471)

9522 Wherever our life touches yours, we
help or hinder . . . wherever your life
touches ours, you make us stronger or
weaker. . . . There is no escape—man
drags man down, or man lifts man up.
BOOKER T. WASHINGTON (1856–1915)

9523 Write injuries in dust, benefits in marble.
FRENCH PROVERB

9524 You can choose to be a bag of marbles
. . . independent, hard, loud,
unmarked, and unaffected by others.
Or you can be a bag of grapes . . . fragrant, soft, blending, mingling, flowing into one another's lives. Marbles
are made to be counted and kept.
Grapes are made to be bruised and
used. Marbles scar and clank. Grapes
yield and cling.
CHARLES R. SWINDOLL (1934–   )

9525 You can't spell *brothers* without at the
same time spelling *others*.

9526 Your opinion of others is apt to be
their opinion of you.
B. C. FORBES

RELATIVITY

9527 Sit with a pretty girl for an hour, and
it seems like a minute; sit on a hot
stove for a minute, and it seems like
an hour—that's relativity.
ALBERT EINSTEIN (1879–1955)

9528 To a mouse, a cat is a lion.
ALBANIAN PROVERB

RELAXATION

9529 A relaxed, easygoing Christian is miles
more attractive and effective than the
rigid, uptight brother who squeaks
when he walks and whines when he
talks.
CHARLES R. SWINDOLL (1934–   )

9530 Don't hurry, don't worry. You're only here for a short visit. So be sure to stop and smell the flowers.
WALTER C. HAGEN (1892–1969)

9531 I found I could add nearly two hours to my working day by going to bed for an hour after luncheon.
SIR WINSTON CHURCHILL (1874–1965)

9532 Jesus knows we must come apart and rest awhile, or else we may just plain come apart.
VANCE HAVNER

9533 Renewal and restoration are not luxuries. They are essentials. Being alone and resting for a while is not selfish. It is Christlike. Taking your day off each week or rewarding yourself with a relaxing, refreshing vacation is not carnal. It's spiritual. There is absolutely nothing enviable or spiritual about a coronary or a nervous breakdown, nor is an ultrabusy schedule necessarily the mark of a productive life.
CHARLES R. SWINDOLL (1934–   )

9534 The best time to relax is when you don't have time to relax.

9535 Those who do not find time for exercise will have to find time for illness.

9536 You will break the bow if you keep it always bent.
GREEK PROVERB

RELIGION

9537 A man may go to hell with baptismal water upon his face.
JOHN TRAPP

9538 A religion that is small enough for our understanding is not great enough for our need.
ARTHUR JAMES BALFOUR (1848–1930)

9539 God is not interested in organized religion, Catholic or Protestant. He is interested only in what we are.
RICHARD OWEN ROBERTS (1931–   )

9540 I suspect that worse dishonesty and greater injustice are to be found among the champions, lay and cleric, of religious opinions than in any other class.
GEORGE MACDONALD (1824–1905)

9541 It was religion that put Christ on the cross, religion without the indwelling Spirit. It is no use to deny that Christ was crucified by persons who would today be called Fundamentalists.
A. W. TOZER (1897–1963)

9542 Let your religion be less of a theory and more of a love affair.
G. K. CHESTERTON (1874–1936)

9543 Religion . . . is in essence the response of created personalities to the Creating Personality, God.
A. W. TOZER (1897–1963)

9544 Religion beats me. I'm amazed at folk drinking the gospel in and never scratching their heads for questions.
SIEGFRIED LORRAINE SASSOON (1886–1967)

9545 Religion is man's quest for God; the gospel is the Savior God seeking lost men. Religion originates on earth; the gospel originated in heaven. Religion is man-made; the gospel is the gift of God. Religion is the story of what a sinful man tries to do for a holy God; the gospel is the story of what a holy God has done for sinful men. Religion is good views; the gospel is good news.
ROY GUSTAFSON

9546 Religion that is merely ritual and ceremonial can never satisfy. Neither can we be satisfied by a religion that is merely humanitarian or serviceable to mankind. Man's craving is for the spiritual.
SAMUEL M. SHOEMAKER (1893–1963)

9547 Religions are man's search for God; the gospel is God's search for man. There are many religions, but one gospel.
E. STANLEY JONES (1884–1973)

9548 Religious contention is the devil's harvest.
CHARLES FONTAINE (1515–1590)

9549 The opposite of the religious fanatic is not the fanatical atheist but the gentle

cynic, who cares not whether there is a
God or not.
ERIC HOFFER (1902–1983)

9550 The true religion is built upon the
Rock; the rest are tossed upon the
waves of time.
FRANCIS BACON (1561–1626)

9551 There are only two religions that
accept gloom as a fact (I mean by
gloom, sin, anguish, and misery, the
things that make people feel that life is
not worth living) Buddhism and Christianity. Every other religion ignores it.
OSWALD CHAMBERS (1874–1917)

9552 We are allowing too many rivals of
God. We actually have too many gods.
We have too many irons in the fire.
We have too much theology that we
don't understand. We have too much
churchly institutionalism. We have too
much religion. Actually, I guess we just
have too much of too much!
A. W. TOZER (1897–1963)

9553 What religion is he of? Why, he is an
Anythingarian.
JONATHAN SWIFT (1667–1745)

9554 What we need in religion is not new
light, but new sight; not new paths,
but new strength to walk in the old
ones; not new duties, but new strength
from on high to fulfill those that are
plain to us.
TRYON EDWARDS (1809–1894)

RELINQUISHMENT

9555 Better lose the anchor than the whole
ship.
DUTCH PROVERB

9556 Go out and God comes in; die, and
    you live in God,
Be not, it will be he; be still, God's
    plan is wrought.
ANGELUS SILESIUS (1624–1677)

9557 God can do what he likes with the
man who is abandoned to him.
OSWALD CHAMBERS (1874–1917)

9558 God's restrictions not only hold us
down but they also hold us up. We
will never achieve fulfillment unless he
is in control. He did not send his Son

to cramp our life-style but to give us a
much better one.
ERWIN W. LUTZER (1941–   )

9559 I have lost all and found myself.

9560 That we gain heaven, that we are delivered from sin, that we are made useful
to God—these things never enter as
considerations into real abandonment,
which is a personal sovereign preference for Jesus Christ himself.
OSWALD CHAMBERS (1874–1917)

9561 The Lord doesn't want the first place
in my life, he wants all of my life.
HOWARD AMERDING

9562 The more a man denies himself, the
more shall he obtain from God.
HORACE BUSHNELL (1802–1876 B.C.)

9563 The weakest saint can experience the
power of the deity of the Son of God if
he is willing to let go.
OSWALD CHAMBERS (1874–1917)

9564 There is no royal road to becoming a
worker for God. The only way is to let
God in his mighty providence lift the
life by a great tide, or break it from its
moorings in some storm, and in one
way or another get the life out to sea
in reckless abandon to God.
OSWALD CHAMBERS (1874–1917)

9565 Treasures in heaven are laid up only as
treasures on earth are laid down.

9566 While he strips of everything the souls
who give themselves absolutely to
him, God gives them something which
takes the place of all: his love.
JEAN PIERRE DE CAUSSADE (1675–1751)

REMORSE

9567 Nor ear can hear nor tongue can tell
The tortures of that inward hell!
LORD GEORGE NOEL GORDON BYRON
(1788–1824)

9568 O God! O God! that it were possible
To undo things done; to call back yes-
    terday!
That Time could turn up his swift
    sandy glass,

To untell the days, and to redeem
these hours.
THOMAS HEYWOOD (C. 1574–1641)

9569 On how many mornings have I, like
Peter, heard the cock crow thrice with
an aching heart!
MALCOLM MUGGERIDGE (1903–1990)

9570 Only man was endowed with shame.
JEWISH PROVERB

9571 Remorse is the echo of a lost virtue.
EDWARD GEORGE BULWER-LYTTON
(1803–1873)

9572 Remorse is the pain of sin.
THEODORE PARKER (1810–1860)

9573 Remorse is to carry your own accuser
within your breast.

9574 Remorse: beholding heaven and feeling hell.
GEORGE MOORE (1852–1933)

REPENTANCE

9575 An unrepented sin is a continued sin.
CORRIE TEN BOOM (1892–1983)

9576 Death-bed repentance is burning the
candle of life in the service of the
devil, then blowing the snuff in the
face of heaven.
LORENZO DOW (1777–1834)

9577 Fallen man is not simply an imperfect
creature who needs improvement; he
is a rebel who must lay down his
arms. . . . This process of surrender—
this movement full speed astern—is
what Christians call repentance. Now
repentance is no fun at all. It is something much harder than merely eating
humble pie. It means unlearning all
the self-conceit and self-will that we
have been training ourselves into for
thousands of years. It means killing
part of yourself, undergoing a kind of
death.
C. S. LEWIS (1898–1963)

9578 God will take nine steps toward us,
but he will not take the tenth. He will
incline us to repent, but he cannot do
our repenting for us.
A. W. TOZER (1897–1963)

9579 He who repents is angry with himself;
I need not be angry with him.
BENJAMIN WHICHCOTE (1609–1683)

9580 If your sorrow is because of certain
consequences that have come on your
family because of your sin, this is
remorse, not true repentance. If, on
the other hand, you are grieved
because you also sinned against God
and his holy laws, then you are on the
right road.
BILLY GRAHAM (1918–   )

9581 It is one thing to mourn for sin
because it exposes us to hell, and
another to mourn for it because it is
an infinite evil; one thing to mourn for
it because it is injurious to ourselves,
and another thing to mourn for it
because it is wrong and offensive to
God. It is one thing to be terrified;
another, to be humbled.
GARDINER SPRING (1785–1873)

9582 Like the father of the Prodigal Son,
God can see repentance coming a
great way off and is there to meet it,
the repentance is the reconciliation.
DOROTHY L. SAYERS (1893–1957)

9583 Man is born with his face turned away
from God. When he truly repents, he
is turned right round toward God; he
leaves his old life.
DWIGHT LYMAN MOODY (1837–1899)

9584 Never mistake remorse for repentance;
remorse simply puts a man in hell
while he is on earth.
OSWALD CHAMBERS (1874–1917)

9585 No man is ever more than four steps
from God: conviction, repentance, consecration, and faith.
ROY L. SMITH

9586 Penitence does not grow by our looking gloomily on our own badness, but
by looking up to God's loveliness,
God's love for us.
WILLIAM CONGREVE (1670–1729)

9587 Repentance is a key that opens any
lock.
JEWISH PROVERB

9588 Repentance is an attitude rather than a single act.
RICHARD OWEN ROBERTS (1931–   )

9589 Repentance is an ongoing process. One must be forever repentant. It is not enough to once feel sorrow over sin. . . . True repentance affects the whole man and alters the entire life-style.
RICHARD OWEN ROBERTS (1931–   )

9590 Repentance is another way of saying that the bad past is to be considered as the starting point for better things.
DOROTHY L. SAYERS (1893–1957)

9591 Repentance is not a fatal day when tears are shed, but a natal day when, as a result of tears, a new life begins.
ILION T. JONES

9592 Repentance is not self-regarding, but God-regarding. It is not self-loathing, but God-loving.
ARCHBISHOP FULTON J. SHEEN (1895–1979)

9593 Repentance is the golden key that opens the palace of eternity.
JOHN MILTON (1608–1674)

9594 Repentance is the process by which we see ourselves, day by day, as we really are: sinful, needy, dependent people. It is the process by which we see God as he is: awesome, majestic, and holy.
CHARLES COLSON (1931–   )

9595 Repentance is to be sorry enough to quit.

9596 Repentance means the opportunity of a new start, the chance to correct what man had left crooked, to fill that which is wanting in one's life.
ABBA HILLEL SILVER (1893–1963)

9597 Repentance must be something more than mere remorse for sins; it comprehends a change of nature befitting heaven.
LEW WALLACE (1827–1905)

9598 Right actions for the future are the best apologies for wrong ones in the past.
TRYON EDWARDS (1809–1894)

9599 Self-knowledge is the first condition of repentance.
OSWALD CHAMBERS (1874–1917)

9600 Sleep with clean hands, either kept clean all day by integrity or washed clean at night by repentance.
JOHN DONNE (1572–1631)

9601 The difference between true and false repentance lies in this: the man who truly repents cries out against his heart; but the other, as Eve, against the serpent, or something else.
JOHN BUNYAN (1628–1688)

9602 There is one case of death-bed repentance recorded, that of the penitent thief, that none should despair; and only one that none should presume.
SAINT AUGUSTINE OF HIPPO (354–430)

9603 There's no repentance in the grave.
ISAAC WATTS (1674–1748)

9604 To move across from one sort of person to another is the essence of repentance: the liar becomes truthful, the thief, honest, the lewd, pure, the proud, humble.
A. W. TOZER (1897–1963)

9605 To repent is to alter one's way of looking at life; it is to take God's point of view instead of one's own.

9606 When God's people repent and give themselves to God, they will have a song. It will be spontaneous, for what is down in the well will come up in the bucket.
VANCE HAVNER

9607 When prodigals return, great things are done.
A. A. DOWTY (1873–   )

9608 When the soul has laid down its faults at the feet of God, it feels as though it had wings.
EUGÉNIE DE GUÉRIN (1805–1848)

9609 You cannot repent too soon because you do not know how soon it may be too late.
SIR THOMAS FULLER (1608–1661)

REPUTATION

9610 A good name is better than great riches.
MIGUEL DE CERVANTES (1547–1616)

9611 A good name, like good will, is got by many actions and lost by one.
LORD FRANCIS JEFFREY (1773–1850)

9612 A reputation once broken may possibly be repaired, but the world will always keep their eyes on the spot where the crack was.
JOSEPH HALL (1574–1656)

9613 Avoid suspicion: when you're walking through your neighbor's melon patch, don't tie your shoe.
CHINESE PROVERB

9614 Do you wish people to think well of you? Don't speak well of yourself.
BLAISE PASCAL (1623–1662)

9615 Glass, china, and reputation are easily cracked and never well mended.
BENJAMIN FRANKLIN (1706–1790)

9616 It often happens that those of whom we speak least on earth are best known in heaven.
NICHOLAS CAUSSIN (1583–1651)

9617 Life is for one generation, a good name is forever.
JAPANESE PROVERB

9618 Many a man's reputation would not know his character if they met on the street.
ELBERT GREEN HUBBARD (1856–1915)

9619 Men's evil manners live in brass, Their virtues we write in water.
WILLIAM SHAKESPEARE (1564–1616)

9620 No ruins are so irreparable as those of reputation.

9621 Reputation is what men and women think of us. Character is what God and the angels know of us.
THOMAS PAINE (1737–1809)

9622 Reputation, reputation, reputation! O, I have lost my reputation! I have lost the immortal part of myself; and what remains is bestial.
WILLIAM SHAKESPEARE (1564–1616)

9623 Scarce anything about us is just as it seems.
GEORGE MACDONALD (1824–1905)

9624 The broken string may be joined, but a knot will always remain.
ANWAR-I-SUHELI

9625 The reputation of a thousand years may be determined by the conduct of one hour.
JAPANESE PROVERB

9626 What is outside yourself does not convey much worth; Clothes do not make the man, the saddle not the horse.
ANGELUS SILESIUS (1624–1677)

9627 What other people think of me is becoming less and less important; what they think of Jesus because of me is critical.
CLIFF RICHARDS (1940–)

9628 What people say behind your back is your standing in the community.
ED HOWE (1853–1937)

9629 When we try to polish our reputation, we lose it; when we give it to Christ, we gain it.
ERWIN W. LUTZER (1941–)

RESENTMENT

9630 An irritable person is like a hedgehog rolled up the wrong way, tormenting himself with his own prickles.
THOMAS HOOD (1799–1845)

9631 Animosity cloaked in piety is a demon even if it sits in church praising the Creator.
CALVIN MILLER

9632 By bearing old wrongs you provoke new ones.
PUBLILIUS SYRUS (FIRST CENTURY B.C.)

9633 If there is the tiniest grudge in your mind against anyone . . . your spiritual penetration into the knowledge of God stops.
OSWALD CHAMBERS (1874–1917)

9634 If you hug to yourself any resentment against anybody else, you destroy the bridge by which God would come to you.
PETER MARSHALL (1902–1949)

9635 It is never the big things that disturb us, but the trivial things.
OSWALD CHAMBERS (1874–1917)

9636 It's the little things that annoy us; we can sit on a mountain but not on a tack.

9637 Malice has a strong memory.
SIR THOMAS FULLER (1608–1661)

9638 Nothing on earth consumes a man more quickly than resentment.
FRIEDRICH WILHELM NIETZSCHE (1844–1900)

9639 Resentment becomes a black, furry, growling grudge. Grudge . . . starts with a growl. "Grr . . . " Like a bear with bad breath coming out of hibernation.
MAX L. LUCADO (1955–)

9640 There is no torment like the inner torment of an unforgiving spirit. It refuses to be soothed, it refuses to be healed, it refuses to forget.
CHARLES R. SWINDOLL (1934–)

9641 Those who say they will forgive but can't forget, bury the hatchet, but they leave the handle out for immediate use.
DWIGHT LYMAN MOODY (1837–1899)

RESPECT

9642 He removes the greatest ornament of friendship who takes away from it respect.
CICERO (106–43 B.C.)

9643 If you want to be respected, you must respect yourself.
SPANISH PROVERB

9644 Respect is intended to operate on a two-way street.
JAMES C. DOBSON (1936–)

9645 Respect is love in plain clothes.
FRANKIE BYRNE

9646 Respect is what we owe; love is what we give.
PHILIP JAMES BAILEY (1816–1902)

9647 There was no respect for youth when I was young, and now that I am old, there is no respect for age—I missed it coming and going.
J. B. PRIESTLY (1894–1984)

RESPONSIBILITY

9648 Do right, and God's recompense to you will be the power to do more right.
FREDERICK WILLIAM ROBERTSON (1816–1853)

9649 Do the truth you know, and you shall learn the truth you need to know.
GEORGE MACDONALD (1824–1905)

9650 Do today's duty . . . and do not weaken and distract yourself by looking forward to things that you cannot see and could not understand if you saw them.
CHARLES KINGSLEY (1819–1875)

9651 Do your duty and leave the rest to heaven.
PIERRE CORNEILLE (1606–1684)

9652 Don't go around saying the world owes you a living; the world owes you nothing, it was here first.
MARK TWAIN (1835–1910)

9653 Duty done is the soul's fireside.
ROBERT BROWNING (1812–1889)

9654 Duty is ours and events are God's.
ANGELINA GIMKE (1805–1879)

9655 For all your days prepare
And meet them all alike:
When you are the anvil, bear—
When you are the hammer, strike.
EDWIN MARKHAM (1852–1940)

9656 Four things a man must learn to do
If he would make his record true:
To think without confusion clearly
To love his fellowmen sincerely
To act from honest motives purely
To trust in God and heaven securely.
HENRY VAN DYKE (1852–1933)

9657 God gives us the ingredients for our daily bread, but he expects us to do the baking.

9658 God has other work for you, and it waits only the completion of the present task.
FRANCES J. ROBERTS

9659 God never imposes a duty without giving time to do it.
JOHN RUSKIN (1819–1900)

9660 God will hold us responsible as to how well we fulfill our responsibilities to this age and take advantage of our opportunities.

BILLY GRAHAM (1918–   )

9661 I alone am responsible for the wrong I do.

OSWALD CHAMBERS (1874–1917)

9662 I ought, therefore I can.

IMMANUEL KANT (1724–1804)

9663 I slept and dreamed that life was joy, I awoke and saw that life was duty, I acted, and behold duty was joy.

SIR RABINDRANATH TAGORE (1861–1941)

9664 If each one sweeps in front of his own door, the whole street is clean.

JEWISH PROVERB

9665 If you're willing to admit you're all wrong when you are, you're all right.

9666 In doing what we ought we deserve no praise because it is our duty.

SAINT AUGUSTINE OF HIPPO (354–430)

9667 It is thy duty oftentimes to do what thou wouldst not; thy duty, too, to leave undone that thou wouldst do.

THOMAS À KEMPIS (C. 1380–1471)

9668 Keep us, Lord, so awake in the duties of our callings that we may sleep in thy peace and wake in thy glory.

JOHN DONNE (1572–1631)

9669 Man should perform his duties to his fellowmen even as to God.

TALMUD

9670 No man has a right to lead such a life of contemplation as to forget in his own ease the service due to his neighbor; nor has any man a right to be so immersed in active life as to neglect the contemplation of God.

SAINT AUGUSTINE OF HIPPO (354–430)

9671 Our grand business is, not to see what lies dimly at a distance, but to do what lies closely at hand.

THOMAS CARLYLE (1795–1881)

9672 Sin with the multitude, and your responsibility and guilt are as great and as truly personal, as if you alone had done the wrong.

TRYON EDWARDS (1809–1894)

9673 Since you cannot do good to all, you are to pay special regard to those who, by the accidents of time, or place, or circumstances, are brought into closer connection with you.

SAINT AUGUSTINE OF HIPPO (354–430)

9674 Take care of the pennies, the dollars will take care of themselves.

9675 The consciousness of a duty performed gives us music at midnight.

GEORGE HERBERT (1593–1633)

9676 Those things, good Lord, that we pray for, give us also the grace to labor for.

9677 To persevere in one's duty and be silent is the best answer to misrepresentation.

GEORGE WASHINGTON (1732–1799)

9678 We are all fellow passengers on the same planet, and we are all equally responsible for the happiness and the well-being of the world in which we happen to live.

HENDRICK WILLEM VAN LOON (1882–1944)

9679 We are too fond of our own will. We want to be doing what we fancy mighty things; but the great point is to do small things, when called to do them, in a right spirit.

RICHARD CECIL (1748–1810)

9680 When an archer misses the mark, he turns and looks for the fault within himself. Failure to hit the bull's-eye is never the fault of the target.

GILBERT ARLAND

9681 Who escapes a duty, avoids a gain.

THEODORE PARKER (1810–1860)

9682 You would not think any duty small if you yourself were great.

GEORGE MACDONALD (1824–1905)

REST

9683 How shall we rest in God? By giving ourselves wholly to him. If you give yourself by halves, you cannot find full rest; there will ever be a lurking disquiet in that half that is withheld. Martyrs, confessors, and saints have tasted this rest, and "counted themselves happy in that they endured." A countless host of God's faithful ser-

vants have drunk deeply of it under the daily burden of a weary life—dull, commonplace, painful, or desolate. All that God has been to them he is ready to be to you. The heart once fairly given to God, with a clear conscience, a fitting rule of life, and a steadfast purpose of obedience, you will find a wonderful sense of rest coming over you.
JEAN NICOLAS GROU (1731–1803)

9684 Not without design does God write the music of our lives. Be it ours to learn the time, and not be discouraged at the rests. They are not to be slurred over, not to be omitted, not to destroy the melody, not to change the keynote. If we look up, God himself will beat the time for us. With the eye on him, we shall strike the next note full and clear.
JOHN RUSKIN (1819–1900)

9685 Rest and motion, unrelieved and unchecked, are equally destructive.
BENJAMIN NATHAN CARDOZO (1870–1938)

9686 Take rest; a field that has rested gives a bountiful crop.
OVID (43 B.C.–A.D. 17)

9687 There is no music in a rest, but there is the making of music in it.
JOHN RUSKIN (1819–1900)

RESURRECTION

9688 Christianity is a religion of the open tomb.
ROY L. SMITH

9689 Christianity is in its very essence a resurrection religion. The concept of resurrection lies at its heart. If you remove it, Christianity is destroyed.
JOHN R. W. STOTT (1921–)

9690 I danced on a Friday when the sky turned black;
It's hard to dance with the devil on your back.
They buried my body and they thought I'd gone;
But I am the dance and I still go on:
Dance, then, wherever you may be;
I am the Lord of the Dance, said he,

And I'll lead you all, wherever you may be
And I'll lead you all in the dance, said he.
SYDNEY CARTER

9691 If you are irrevocably committed to the proposition that it would have been impossible for Christ to triumph over death, you may as well quit fiddling around the fringes of Christianity, because, as Paul bluntly said, the whole thing stands or falls on the fact of the Resurrection. Either it happened, or it didn't, and if it didn't, Christianity is a gigantic fraud, and the sooner we are quit of it, the better.
LOUIS CASSELS (1922–1974)

9692 Jesus is risen! he shall the world restore!
Awake, ye dead! dull sinners, sleep no more!
JOHN WESLEY (1703–1791)

9693 No person hearing the story of the Resurrection can possibly be any more skeptical of it than were the apostles when they first heard about it. The record shows that Jesus had to go to great lengths to overcome their disbelief. Once he ate an impromptu meal of cold fish and honeycomb—the only food at hand—to demonstrate to one diehard doubter that he wasn't a ghost.
LOUIS CASSELS (1922–1974)

9694 Our Lord has written the promise of the resurrection not in books alone, but in every leaf in springtime.
MARTIN LUTHER (1483–1546)

9695 The best proof that Christ has risen is that he is still alive. And for the immense majority of our contemporaries, the only way of seeing him alive is for us Christians to love one another.
LOUIS EVELY (1910–)

9696 The Gospels do not explain the Resurrection; the Resurrection explains the Gospels. Belief in the Resurrection is not an appendage to the Christian faith; it is the Christian faith.
JOHN S. WHALE

9697 The head that once was crowned with thorns is crowned with glory now.
THOMAS KELLEY (1769–1855)

9698 The same power that brought Christ back from the dead is operative within those who are Christ's. The Resurrection is an ongoing thing.
LEON MORRIS

9699 The stone was rolled away from the door, not to permit Christ to come out, but to enable the disciples to go in.

9700 There is more evidence that Jesus rose from the dead than there is that Julius Caesar ever lived or that Alexander the Great died at the age of thirty-three.
BILLY GRAHAM (1918–)

9701 To renounce all is to gain all; to descend is to rise; to die is to live.
KARL RAHNER (1904–1984)

9702 Whether we are prepared or not to accept the occurrence of the Resurrection as a fact of history, we cannot deny the influence that a belief in it has exercised in the world. We cannot deny that it has brought life and immortality to light as no other belief could conceivably have done; that it has substituted for the fear of death, for a large portion of the human race, that sure and certain knowledge of God which is eternal life; that it has permeated our customs, our literature, and our language with a glory and a hope that could have been derived from no other source.
C. H. ROBINSON

REVELATION

9703 A Christian cannot live by philosophy. Only the light of Christian revelation gives the end as well as the means of life.
JOHN JAY CHAPMAN (1862–1933)

9704 As prayer is the voice of man to God, so revelation is the voice of God to man.
CARDINAL JOHN HENRY NEWMAN (1801–1890)

9705 Every revelation of truth felt with interior savor and spiritual joy is a secret whispering of God in the ear of a pure soul.
WALTER HILTON (1340–1396)

9706 God hides nothing. His very work from the beginning is revelation—a casting aside of veil after veil, a showing to men of truth after truth. On and on from fact divine he advances, until at length in his Son, Jesus, he unveils his very face.
GEORGE MACDONALD (1824–1905)

9707 God manifests himself in his children; consequently the manifestation is seen by others, not by us.
OSWALD CHAMBERS (1874–1917)

9708 God reveals that which it is to our profit to know; but what we are unable to bear he keeps secret.
SAINT JOHN OF DAMASCUS (C. 700–C. 760)

9709 Man cannot cover what God would reveal.
THOMAS CAMPBELL (1733–1795)

9710 Revelation is the record of God's acts in time, his often violent intrusions into human history.
PHILIP SCHARPER

9711 We do not believe that God has added, or ever will add, anything to his revelation in his Son. But we can now see many things in that revelation which could not be seen by those who first received it. Each generation of Christians, and each people to which the Christian gospel is preached, makes its own contribution to the understanding of the riches of Jesus Christ.
C. B. MOSS

REVENGE

9712 "I can forgive, but I cannot forget," is only another way of saying, "I will not forgive."
HENRY WARD BEECHER (1813–1887)

9713 A lawsuit is a machine you go into as a pig and come out of as a sausage.
AMBROSE GWINNETT BIERCE (1842–C. 1914)

9714 A man who studies revenge keeps his own wounds green.
FRANCIS BACON (1561–1626)

9715 By taking revenge, a man is but even with his enemy; but in passing over it, he is superior.
FRANCIS BACON (1561–1626)

9716 Can vengeance be pursued further than death?
WILLIAM SHAKESPEARE (1564–1616)

9717 He who seeks revenge, digs two graves.
CHINESE PROVERB

9718 It is foolish to punish your neighbor by fire when you live next door.
PUBLILIUS SYRUS (FIRST CENTURY B.C.)

9719 Living well is the best revenge.
GEORGE HERBERT (1593–1633)

9720 Men are more prone to revenge injuries than to requite kindnesses.

9721 Men must not turn into bees and kill themselves in stinging others.
FRANCIS BACON (1561–1626)

9722 O Lord, deliver me from this lust of always vindicating myself.
SAINT AUGUSTINE OF HIPPO (354–430)

9723 Revenge in cold blood is the devil's own act and deed.

9724 Revenge is a confession of pain.
LUCIUS ANNAEUS SENECA (C. 4 B.C.–A.D. 65)

9725 Revenge is the pure delight of little minds.
JUVENAL (C. 60–C. 127)

9726 Revenge proves its own executioner.

9727 The best sort of revenge is not to be like him who did the injury.
MARCUS AURELIUS ANTONINUS (121–180)

9728 The smallest revenge will poison the soul.
JEWISH PROVERB

9729 To forget a wrong is mild revenge.
SIR THOMAS FULLER (1608–1661)

9730 When we "get even" with someone, that is literally what we are doing— becoming even with them, that is, descending to their level in vengeance and losing whatever moral advantage we may have had.
SYDNEY J. HARRIS (1917–1986)

REVERENCE

9731 Devotion is not a thing that passes, that comes and goes, as it were, but it is something habitual, fixed, permanent that extends over every instant of life and regulates all our conduct.
DOUGLAS V. STEERE (1901–   )

9732 God is not greater if you reverence him, but you are greater if you serve him.
SAINT AUGUSTINE OF HIPPO (354–430)

9733 He who fears God need fear nothing else, and he who fears not God needs to fear everything else.

9734 Of all the ways of awakening inner reverence in man, the best is the contemplation of the works of God. Their transcendent greatness must inspire awe.
ELIJAH DE VIDAS (SIXTEENTH CENTURY)

9735 Reverence is one of the signs of strength; irreverence one of the surest indications of weakness. No man will rise high who jeers at sacred things.

9736 The fear of God is to be united with the love of God; for love without fear makes men remiss, and fear without love makes them servile and desperate.
JOHANN GERHARD (1582–1637)

REVIVAL

9737 A religious awakening that does not awaken the sleeper to love has roused him in vain.
JESSAMYN WEST (1907–   )

9738 A revival out of balance is soon a revival out of power.
RICHARD OWEN ROBERTS (1931–   )

9739 Evangelism affects the other fellow; revival affects me.
LEONARD RAVENHILL (1867–1942)

9740 Every really spiritual movement is instantly followed by a missionary movement. . . . Given a Wesley in one generation, a Carey in the next is inevitable. . . . As soon as John Wesley caught and communicated to his countrymen the vision of the King in his beauty, Carey arose to carry beatific revelations to the land that were very far off.
F. W. BOREHAM

9741 Jesus Christ is unique, and one cannot be in his presence and not reveal the man he really is. Jesus pulls each person from behind his mask. In the exposure of that bleeding love on the cross, men become what they really are.

You may think you are wonderful until you stand in the presence of the One who is purity itself. It is the pure light of God that pierces a man. You can keep up your pretense of being holy until you stand in that light. Then immediately there is nowhere to hide, all your masks are torn away, all your hollow smiles fade. Revival means to be exposed for what we are. The presence of the Lord is revealing.
BISHOP FESTO KIVENGERE (C. 1920–)

9742 Lord, revive the church—beginning with me.
SAMUEL M. SHOEMAKER (1893–1963)

9743 Prayer is the backbone of a revival. . . . Instead of substituting new ideas such as religious films or social entertainments, why not really try the God-given method for revivals: "Pray without ceasing"?
JOHN W. BASHAM

9744 Revival and the exclusive love of comfortable truths are bitter enemies.
RICHARD OWEN ROBERTS (1931–)

9745 Revival is . . . God revealing himself to man in awful holiness and irresistible power. . . . If we find a revival that is not spoken against, we had better look again to ensure that it is a revival.
ARTHUR WALLIS (1928–)

9746 Revival is a sovereign act of God upon the church whereby he intervenes to lift the situation completely out of human hands and works in extraordinary power.
GEOFFREY R. KING

9747 Revival is always extraordinary.
RICHARD OWEN ROBERTS (1931–)

9748 Revival is God's finger pointed right at me.
WILBERT L. MCLEOD

9749 Revival is the inrush of the Spirit into a body that threatens to become a corpse.
D. M. PANTON

9750 Some preachers don't believe in revivals; neither does the devil.
BILLY SUNDAY (1862–1935)

9751 The purpose of revival is to make God not men, famous; to focus the eyes of the people, not upon human leaders, but upon the Divine Leader; to give glory not to great men but to a great Savior.
RICHARD OWEN ROBERTS (1931–)

9752 There is a sense in which revival is like a prairie fire ignited by a bolt of lightning from the heavens. Without organization, advertising, or even sometimes human leadership, revivals have altered the hearts of men, the social attitudes of millions, and the destinies of nations.
RICHARD OWEN ROBERTS (1931–)

9753 They tell me a revival is only temporary; so is a bath, but it does you good.
BILLY SUNDAY (1862–1935)

RIGHTEOUSNESS

9754 God takes notice of clean hands, not full hands.
LATIN PROVERB

9755 Why did God abolish the law? Its standards reflected his righteousness, but the law as a system was replaced because it was powerless. It could not bring us what we desperately need—righteousness.
ERWIN W. LUTZER (1941–)

RUMOR

9756 Rumor is a pipe blown by surmises, jealousies, conjectures.
WILLIAM SHAKESPEARE (1564–1616)

9757 The flying rumors gather'd as they roll'd;
Scarce any tale was sooner heard than told.
And all who told it added something new.
And all who heard it made enlargement, too.
In every ear it spread, on every tongue it grew.
ALEXANDER POPE (1688–1744)

S

SACRIFICE

9758 Christians are often accused of being morbid when they talk of the joy of sacrificing. I think it is one of the deepest truths of the Christian religion. Far from being a source of sadness, sacrifice is a great joy and source of illumination—perhaps the greatest of all. I also think that to live modestly is always a richer experience because you are living like the majority of people.
MALCOLM MUGGERIDGE (1903–1990)

9759 For anything worth having one must pay the price; and the price is always work, patience, love, self-sacrifice—no paper currency, no promises to pay, but the gold of real service.
JOHN BURROUGHS (1837–1921)

9760 I never made a sacrifice. We ought not to talk of sacrifice when we remember the great sacrifice that he made who left his Father's throne on high to give himself for us.
DAVID LIVINGSTONE (1813–1873)

9761 If Jesus Christ is God and died for me, then no sacrifice can be too great for me to make for him.
CHARLES THOMAS STUDD (1862–1931)

9762 Our notion of sacrifice is the wringing out of us something we don't want to give up, full of pain and agony and distress. The Bible idea of sacrifice is that I give as a love-gift the very best thing I have.
OSWALD CHAMBERS (1874–1917)

9763 Self-sacrifice is never entirely unselfish, for the giver never fails to receive.
DOLORES E. McGUIRE

9764 That which one sacrifices is never lost.
GERMAN PROVERB

SAINTS

9765 A man can be as truly a saint in a factory as in a monastery, and there is as much need of him in the one as in the other.
ROBERT J. McCRACKEN (1904–1973)

9766 A saint . . . has the same spirit, the same judgment, the same will with Christ.
THOMAS WATSON (C. 1557–1592)

9767 A saint is a creature of vast possibilities, knit into shape by the ruling personality of God.
OSWALD CHAMBERS (1874–1917)

9768 A saint is never consciously a saint; a saint is consciously dependent on God.
OSWALD CHAMBERS (1874–1917)

9769 A saint is one the light shines through.

9770 A saint is one who makes goodness attractive.
LAURENCE HOUSMAN (1865–1959)

9771 A saint is one who makes it easy to believe in Jesus.
RUTH BELL GRAHAM

9772 All are not saints that go to church.
BENJAMIN FRANKLIN (1706–1790)

9773 God creates out of nothing—wonderful, you say; yes, to be sure, but he does what is still more wonderful. He makes saints out of sinners.
SØREN AABYE KIERKEGAARD (1813–1855)

9774 God deliver us from sullen saints!
SAINT TERESA OF AVILA (1515–1582)

9775 Great saints have often been great sinners.
COVENTRY KERSEY DIGHTON PATMORE (1823–1896)

9776 Many of the insights of the saint stem from his experiences as a sinner.
ERIC HOFFER (1902–1983)

9777 People who are born even-tempered, placid, and untroubled—secure from violent passions or temptations to evil—those who have never needed to struggle all night with the angel to emerge lame but victorious at dawn, never become great saints.
EVA LEGALLIENEE (1899–)

9778 Sainthood makes it possible for saints to admire everybody else. It gives them a vision that can find good in the most terrible criminals. It delivers them from the burden of judging others, condemning other men.
THOMAS MERTON (1915–1968)

9779 Saints are usually killed by their own people.
ERIC SEVAREID (1912–)

9780 That they are never sated makes all the saints rejoice;
Oh, what a happy hunger! Oh, what a blessed thirst!
ANGELUS SILESIUS (1624–1677)

9781 The most delightful saint is the one who has been chastened through great sorrows.
OSWALD CHAMBERS (1874–1917)

9782 The saint deems it the same: if God lets him lie ill,
He thanks him just as much as he were sound and well.
ANGELUS SILESIUS (1624–1677)

9783 The saint does everything that any other decent person does, only . . . with a totally different motive.
COVENTRY KERSEY DIGHTON PATMORE (1823–1896)

9784 The saint does not call himself a worm because he enjoys being wormy, but because there is simply no other way graphic enough to express the richness of God and the meagreness of men.
MADELEINE L'ENGLE (1918–)

9785 The saint is ever young; amazingly and boisterously young, certain that everything is all right.
OSWALD CHAMBERS (1874–1917)

9786 The saints are always among the unofficial crowd, the crowd that is not noticed, and their one dominant note is Jesus Christ.
OSWALD CHAMBERS (1874–1917)

9787 The tears of saints are more sweet by far Than all the songs of sinners are.
ROBERT HERRICK (1591–1674)

9788 Those saints which God loves best, The devil tempts not least.
ROBERT HERRICK (1591–1674)

9789 We hear, or read, of someone who was "a real saint: he never saw any harm in anyone and never spoke a word against anyone all his life." If this really is Christian saintliness then Jesus Christ was no saint. It is true that he taught men not to sit in judg-

ment upon one another, but he never suggested that they should turn a blind eye to evil or pretend that other people were faultless. He "knew what was in man," as St. John tersely puts it.
J. B. PHILLIPS (1906–1982)

9790 Who is the greatest saint in the world? It is not he who prays most or fasts mosts; it is not he who gives most alms, or is most eminent for temperance, chastity, or justice; but it is he who is always thankful to God, who wills everything that God wills, who receives everything as an instance of God's goodness, and has a heart always ready to praise God for it.
WILLIAM LAW (1686–1761)

9791 Who plumbs the depth of God? Who knows how high the flames?
Who measures length and breadth? The company of saints.
ANGELUS SILESIUS (1624–1677)

SALVATION

9792 A person may go to heaven without health, without riches, without honors, without learning, without friends; but he can never go there without Christ.
JOHN DYER (1699–1757)

9793 Absolute candor is an indispensable requisite to salvation.
A. W. TOZER (1897–1963)

9794 Ah! happy they whose hearts can break And peace of pardon win!
How else may man make straight his plan
And cleanse his soul from sin?
How else but through a broken heart
May the Lord Christ enter in?
OSCAR WILDE (1854–1900)

9795 For a cap and bells our lives we pay, Bubbles we buy with a whole soul's tasking:
'Tis heaven alone that is given away, 'Tis only God may be had for the asking.
JAMES RUSSELL LOWELL (1819–1891)

9796 He who created us without our help will not save us without our consent.
SAINT AUGUSTINE OF HIPPO (354–430)

9797 I remember two things: that I am a great sinner and that Christ is a great Savior.
JOHN NEWTON (1725–1807)

9798 I was a stricken deer that left the herd Long since; with many an arrow deep infixed
My panting side was charged, when I withdrew
To seek a tranquil death in distant shades.
There was I found by One who had himself
Been hurt by the archers. In his side he bore,
And in his hands and feet, the cruel scars.
With gentle force soliciting the darts, He drew them forth, and healed and bade me live.
WILLIAM COWPER (1731–1800)

9799 I would pay any price to be able to say truthfully, "All will be saved." But my reason retorts, "Without their will, or with it?" If I say, "Without their will," I at once perceive a contradiction; how can the supreme voluntary act of self-surrender be involuntary? If I say, "With their will," my reason replies, "How if they will not give in?"
C. S. LEWIS (1898–1963)

9800 In new birth God does three impossible things: the first is to make a man's past as though it had never been; the second, to make a man all over again, and the third, to make a man as certain of God as God is of himself.
OSWALD CHAMBERS (1874–1917)

9801 It is impossible for us to be the children of God naturally, to love our enemies, to forgive, to be holy, to be pure, and it is certainly impossible to us to follow God naturally; consequently the fundamental fact to recognize is that we must be born again.
OSWALD CHAMBERS (1874–1917)

9802 It is not your hold of Christ that saves you, but his hold of you!
CHARLES HADDON SPURGEON (1834–1892)

9803 Just as Christian came up with the cross, his burden loosed from off his shoulders and fell from off his back and began to tumble, and so continued to do till it came to the mouth of the sepulcher, where it fell in, and I saw it no more.
JOHN BUNYAN (1628–1688)

9804 Looking at the wound of sin will never save anyone. What you must do is to look at the remedy.
DWIGHT LYMAN MOODY (1837–1899)

9805 My life, as his,
slips through death's
mesh,
time's bars,
joins hands with heaven,
speaks with stars.
LUCI SHAW (1928–)

9806 Our salvation, thank God, depends much more on his love of us than on our love of him.
FATHER ANDREW

9807 Salvation is . . . bringing back to normal the Creator-creature relation.
A. W. TOZER (1897–1963)

9808 Salvation is a gift you can ask for.

9809 Salvation is moving from living death to deathless life.
JACK ODELL

9810 Salvation is worth working for. It is worth a man's going round the world on his hands and knees, climbing its mountains, crossing its valleys, swimming its rivers, going through all manner of hardship in order to attain it. But we do not get it in that way. It is to him who believes.
DWIGHT LYMAN MOODY (1837–1899)

9811 Salvation means the incoming into human nature of the great characteristics that belong to God.
OSWALD CHAMBERS (1874–1917)

9812 Sin separates, pain isolates, but salvation and comfort unite.
JULIAN OF NORWICH (C. 1342–AFTER 1413)

9813 Someone asked Luther: "Do you feel that you have been forgiven?"
He answered: "No, but I'm as sure as there's a God in heaven.
For feelings come and feelings go, and feelings are deceiving;
My warrant is the Word of God, naught else is worth believing.
Though all my heart should feel condemned for want of some sweet token,
There is One greater than my heart whose Word cannot be broken.
I'll trust in God's unchanging Word till soul and body sever;
For though all things shall pass away, his Word shall stand forever!"
MARTIN LUTHER (1483–1546)

9814 Souls are not saved in bundles.
RALPH WALDO EMERSON (1803–1882)

9815 The knowledge of sin is the beginning of salvation.
EPICURUS (341–270 B.C.)

9816 The temptation to make our relation to God judicial instead of personal is very strong. Believing for salvation has been reduced to a once-done act that requires no further attention.
A. W. TOZER (1897–1963)

9817 The terms for *salvation* in many languages are derived from roots like *salvus, saos, whole, heil,* which all designate health, the opposite of disintegration and disruption. Salvation is healing in the ultimate sense; it is final, cosmic, and individual healing.
PAUL JOHANNES OSKAR TILLICH (1886–1965)

9818 There are too many grandchildren of Christ in the world, those whose parents were Christians, but they aren't. Nowhere in the Bible does God claim grandchildren—just children, born again by faith in Christ.
BOB PIERCE (1914–1976)

9819 There is never any traffic congestion on the straight and narrow path.
HERBERT V. PROCHNOW

9820 There's nothing more irritating than a Savior when you aren't ready to be saved.
D. SUTTEN

9821 This new life impedes us in our natural outlook and ways . . . until the Son of God is formed in us and both the natural and the holy are the same.
OSWALD CHAMBERS (1874–1917)

9822 This world is a great sculptor's shop. We are the statues and there is a rumor going round the shop that some of us are some day going to come to life.
C. S. LEWIS (1898–1963)

9823 Though Christ a thousand times in Bethlehem be born,
If he's not born in thee thy soul is still forlorn.
ANGELUS SILESIUS (1624–1677)

9824 Three things are necessary for the salvation of man: to know what he ought to believe; to know what he ought to desire; and to know what he ought to do.
SAINT THOMAS AQUINAS (1225–1274)

9825 We ain't what we want to be. We ain't what we gonna be. But, thank God, we ain't what we was.
MARTIN LUTHER KING, JR. (1929–1968)

9826 We have been holding the letter of truth while at the same time we have been moving away from it in spirit because we have been preoccupied with what we are saved from rather than what we have been saved to.
A. W. TOZER (1897–1963)

9827 What takes place is an explosion on the inside (a literal explosion, not a theoretical one) that opens all the doors that have been closed and life becomes larger; there is the incoming of a totally new point of view.
OSWALD CHAMBERS (1874–1917)

9828 When you from Sodom flee, the judgment to escape,
Salvation will depend on never looking back.
ANGELUS SILESIUS (1624–1677)

9829 You must picture me alone in that room in Magdalen, night after night, feeling, whenever my mind lifted even for a second from my work, the steady, unrelenting approach of him whom I so earnestly desired not to meet. That which I greatly feared had at last come upon me. In the Trinity Term of 1929 I gave in and admitted that God was God, and knelt and prayed: perhaps, that night, the most dejected and reluctant convert in all England. I did not then see what is now the most shining and obvious thing; the Divine humility which will accept a convert even on such terms. . . . The hardness of God is kinder than the softness of men, and his compulsion is our liberation.
C. S. LEWIS (1898–1963)

SANCTIFICATION

9830 After sanctification, it is difficult to state what your aim in life is because God has taken you up into his purposes.
OSWALD CHAMBERS (1874–1917)

9831 Are we prepared for what sanctification will do? It will cost an intense narrowing of all our interests on earth and an immense broadening of our interest in God.
OSWALD CHAMBERS (1874–1917)

9832 However we may set out on the path of pilgrimage, we spend a lifetime walking it. There are no rest stops, no plateaus at which we can flop down and say that we've gone far enough. At the beginning, God accepts us in all of our sinfulness and selfishness. But this does not mean that he is content to have us remain in that state. We are all, in the New Testament's terrifying phrase, "called to be saints." Our Father knows our weaknesses even better than we do, and he does not expect us to become saints overnight. But he does demand that we keep moving in that direction, or as the good old

Methodist phrase puts it, that we continue "groaning toward perfection."

At each step of the journey, the question that really matters is not whether we are a little farther along than some of our friends and neighbors, but how far we have progressed since yesterday.
LOUIS CASSELS (1922–1974)

9833 Die before you die. There is no chance after.
C. S. LEWIS (1898–1963)

9834 God does not give us power to imitate him; he gives us his very self.
OSWALD CHAMBERS (1874–1917)

9835 How does our will become sanctified? By conforming itself unreservedly to that of God. We will all that he wills, and will nothing that he does not will; we attach our feeble will to that all-powerful will which performs everything. Thus, nothing can ever come to pass against our will; for nothing can happen save that which God wills, and we find in his good pleasure an inexhaustible source of peace and consolation.
FRANÇOIS FÉNELON (1651–1715)

9836 I cannot crucify my old nature, but Christ can and did.
ERWIN W. LUTZER (1941–)

9837 If God has not sanctified us and made us blameless, there is only one reason why he has not—we do not want him to.
OSWALD CHAMBERS (1874–1917)

9838 If I exalt sanctification, I preach people into despair; but if I lift up Jesus Christ, people learn the way to be made holy.
OSWALD CHAMBERS (1874–1917)

9839 In coming to Christ we do not bring our old life up to a higher plane; we leave it at the Cross. The corn of wheat must fall into the ground and die.
A. W. TOZER (1897–1963)

9840 In the first experience of sanctification we lose altogether the consciousness of our own identity, we are absorbed in God; but that is not the final place, it is merely the introduction to a totally new life. We lose our natural identity and consciously gain the identity that Jesus had, and it is when God begins to deal with sanctified souls on that line that darkness sometimes comes and the strange misunderstanding of God's ways.
OSWALD CHAMBERS (1874–1917)

9841 It is the great moment of our lives when we decide that sin must die right out, not be curbed or suppressed or counteracted, but crucified.
OSWALD CHAMBERS (1874–1917)

9842 Sanctification is not a heavy yoke, but a joyful liberation.
CORRIE TEN BOOM (1892–1983)

9843 Sanctification is not something our Lord does in me; sanctification is himself in me.
OSWALD CHAMBERS (1874–1917)

9844 Sanctification means . . . a life of discipline such as nine out of every ten of us will have nothing to do with.
OSWALD CHAMBERS (1874–1917)

9845 The test of sanctification is not our talk about holiness and singing pious hymns; but, what are we like where no one sees us . . . with those who know us best?
OSWALD CHAMBERS (1874–1917)

9846 There are three marks of one who is crucified. One, he is facing in only one direction. Two, he can never turn back. And three, he no longer has any plans of his own.
A. W. TOZER (1897–1963)

9847 Those of you who have never had this experience of sanctification, think! The perfections of Jesus Christ made your entirety! The Lord showing his love, his purity, his holiness through you!
OSWALD CHAMBERS (1874–1917)

9848 To be another than I am, I must abandon that I am.
SAINT JOHN CHRYSOSTOM (C. 347–407)

9849 To be controlled by the Spirit means that we are not controlled by what

happens on the outside but by what is happening on the inside.
ERWIN W. LUTZER (1941–)

9850 We are saved and sanctified for God, not to be specimens in his showroom, but for God to do with us ever as he did with Jesus—make us broken bread and poured out wine as he chooses.
OSWALD CHAMBERS (1874–1917)

9851 When in his mercy God leads a soul in the higher path of sanctification, he begins by stripping it of all self-confidence, and to this end he allows our own schemes to fail, our judgment to mislead us. We grope and totter and make countless mistakes until we learn wholly to mistrust ourselves and to put all our confidence in him.
JEAN NICOLAS GROU (1731–1803)

9852 You know how things look when the sun's beams are on them, the very air then appears full of impurities which, before it came out, were not seen. So it is with our souls. We are full of stains and corruptions, we see them not, they are like the air before the sun shines; but though we see them not, God sees them; he pervades us as the sunbeam.
CARDINAL JOHN HENRY NEWMAN (1801–1890)

SATAN

9853 For a thing to be satanic does not mean that it is abominable and immoral; the satanically-managed man is absolutely self-governed and has no need of God.
OSWALD CHAMBERS (1874–1917)

9854 I believe Satan to exist for two reasons: first, the Bible says so; and second, I've done business with him.
DWIGHT LYMAN MOODY (1837–1899)

9855 No matter how many pleasures Satan offers you, his ultimate intention is to ruin you. Your destruction is his highest priority.
ERWIN W. LUTZER (1941–)

9856 Satan is a chronic grumbler. The Christian ought to be a living doxology.
MARTIN LUTHER (1483–1546)

9857 Satan is quite content for us to make any number of beginnings as long as we never complete anything.
SAINT FRANCIS OF SALES (1567–1622)

9858 Satan must be the most frustrated personality in the universe! His army of demons is compelled to obey Jesus, and whatever the devil does to discourage a Christian, God can use for the Christian's benefit.
BILLY GRAHAM (1918–)

9859 Satan uses the problems of this life to slander God's character; he tries to make us think that all the calamities and miseries and wrongs spring from God.
OSWALD CHAMBERS (1874–1917)

9860 Satan wastes no ammunitions on those who are dead in trespasses and sins.
CORRIE TEN BOOM (1892–1983)

9861 The devil never sleeps, and your flesh is very much alive. Prepare yourself for battle. Surrounding you are enemies that never rest.
THOMAS À KEMPIS (C. 1380–1471)

9862 The devil's most devilish when respectable.
ELIZABETH BARRETT BROWNING (1806–1861)

9863 The infernal serpent; he it was, whose guile,
Stirred up with envy and revenge, deceived
The mother of mankind.
JOHN MILTON (1608–1674)

9864 There is no heaven with a little of hell in it—no plan to retain this or that of the devil in our hearts or our pockets. Out Satan must go, every hair and feather!
GEORGE MACDONALD (1824–1905)

SCIENCE

9865 If the Bible agreed with modern science, it would soon be out of date because, in the very nature of things, modern science is bound to change.
OSWALD CHAMBERS (1874–1917)

9866 In its early stages, science seemed at odds with religion; but this was merely

a token of its immaturity. The more familiar story is that of scientists who become increasingly aware of the mystery of the universe and come to religion through knowledge of the limitations of science. Indeed, how can those who play with the building blocks of the universe, its atoms and electrons and genes, fail to be touched by awe? Every victory of science reveals more clearly a divine design in nature, a remarkable conformity in all things, from the infinitesimal to the infinite.
DAVID SARNOFF (1891–1971)

9867 One thing I have learned in a long life—that all our science, measured against reality, is primitive and childlike.
ALBERT EINSTEIN (1879–1955)

9868 Our scientific power has outrun our spiritual power. We have guided missiles and misguided men.
MARTIN LUTHER KING, JR. (1929–1968)

9869 Science has sometimes been said to be opposed to faith and inconsistent with it. But all science, in fact, rests on a basis of faith, for it assumes the permanence and uniformity of natural laws—a thing which can never be demonstrated.
TRYON EDWARDS (1809–1894)

9870 Science, the sweet talking goddess that but a short time ago smilingly disposed of the Bible as a trustworthy guide and took the world by the hand to lead it into a man-made millennium, has turned out to be a dragon capable of destroying that same world with a flick of her fiery tail.
A. W. TOZER (1897–1963)

9871 Study the sciences in the light of the truth, that is—as before God; for their business is to show the truth, that is to say, God everywhere. Write nothing, say nothing, think nothing that you cannot believe to be true before God.
JOSEPH JOUBERT (1754–1824)

9872 Within the last century man has leaped ahead in scientific achievement but has lagged behind morally, with

the result that he is now technically capable of destroying the world and morally incapable of restraining himself from doing so.
A. W. TOZER (1897–1963)

SEASONS

9873 Each moment of the year has its own beauty . . . a picture which was never seen before and which shall never be seen again.
RALPH WALDO EMERSON (1803–1882)

9874 If winter comes, can spring be far behind?
PERCY BYSSHE SHELLEY (1792–1822)

9875 Nature cannot jump from winter to summer without a spring, or from summer to winter without a fall.

9876 Snowy, flowy, blowy,
Showery, flowery, bowery,
Hoppy, croppy, droppy,
Breezy, sneezy, freezy.
GEORGE ELLIS (1753–1815)

9877 The day is an epitome of the year. The night is the winter, the morning and evening are the spring and fall, and the noon is the summer.
HENRY DAVID THOREAU (1817–1862)

9878 There is no season such delight can bring
As summer, autumn, winter, and the spring.
WILLIAM BROWNE (1591–1643)

9879 You can't beat the weather:
Spring is too rainy and summer's too hot;
Fall is soon over and winter is not.

SEASONS/FALL

9880 O, it sets my heart a clickin'
Like the tickin' of a clock,
When the frost is on the punkin
And the fodder's in the shock.
JAMES WHITCOMB RILEY (1849–1916)

9881 Octembruary: the best month to get married.

9882 September: the month when gardeners put off until October the chores they should have done in August.

9883 Thy bounty shines in autumn unconfined,
And spreads a common feast for all that lives.
JAMES THOMSON (1700–1748)

SEASONS/SPRING

9884 April showers bring May flowers—with the help of spading, fertilizing, planting, watering, and weeding.

9885 Every April God rewrites the book of Genesis.

9886 Flame-flowered, yellow-petalled June.
DON BLANDING

9887 How softly runs the afternoon
Beneath the billowy clouds of June!
C. H. TOWNE

9888 March: a homeowner's favorite: it's time to put away the snow shovel, but not yet time to get out the lawn mower.

9889 No one objects to March coming in like a lion—it's the hanging around like a polar bear that's depressing.
BILL VAUGHAN

9890 Spring is a season that says it with flowers.

9891 Spring is full of sweet days and roses.
GEORGE HERBERT (1593–1633)

9892 Spring is God's way of saying hello.

9893 Spring is winter defrosting.

9894 Spring makes everything young again except man.
JOHANN PAUL FRIEDRICH RICHTER (1763–1825)

9895 Spring unlocks the flowers to paint the laughing soil.
REGINALD HEBER (1783–1826)

9896 Springtime . . . invites you to try out its splendor . . . to believe anew. To realize that the same Lord who renews the trees with buds and blossoms is ready to renew your life with hope and courage.
CHARLES R. SWINDOLL (1934–   )

9897 The forest smiles;
And every sense, and every heart is joy.
JAMES THOMSON (1700–1748)

9898 The glory of the spring how sweet!
The newborn life how glad!
What joy the happy earth to greet,
In new, bright raiment clad!
Divine Redeemer, thee I bless;
I greet thy going forth;
I love thee in the loveliness
Of thy renewed earth.
THOMAS HORNBLOWER GILL

9899 There is no time
Like spring
When life's alive
In everything.
CHRISTINA GEORGINA ROSSETTI (1830–1894)

SEASONS/SUMMER

9900 July: the month when mothers realize why schoolteachers need long summer vacations.

9901 Summer is the season when people get out of the crowded city to get out on the crowded highway.

9902 Summer is the time when it's too hot to do the job that it was too cold to do last winter.

SEASONS/WINTER

9903 If only I could sleep away the winter time!
WALTHER VON DER VOGELWEIDE (1170–1230)

9904 Snow is beautiful—when you are watching the other fellow shovel it.

9905 The snow falls alike upon the just and the unjust, after which the just slips upon the snow the unjust doesn't clear away.

9906 Winter . . . the ideal occasion to slow down. To invest a few extra hours in quiet reverence.
CHARLES R. SWINDOLL (1934–   )

9907 Winter is a disease.
ALFRED DE MUSSET (1810–1857)

SECOND COMING

9908 I do not know how I am going to stay up "in the air" with the Lord; but that is no business of mine.
OSWALD CHAMBERS (1874–1917)

9909 I hope that the day is near at hand when the advent of the great God will appear, for all things everywhere are boiling, burning, moving, falling, sinking, groaning.
MARTIN LUTHER (1483–1546)

9910 Many Christians long for the Rapture, not because of their intense love for the Lord, but because it symbolizes an escape from the distress of our age.
ERWIN W. LUTZER (1941–)

9911 The doctrine of the Second Coming teaches us that we do not and cannot know when the world drama will end. The curtain may be rung down at any moment. . . . This seems to some people intolerably frustrating. . . . We do not know the play. . . . The Author knows. The audience, if there is an audience (if angels and archangels and all the company of heaven fill the pit and the stalls) may have an inkling. . . . When it is over, we may be told. We are led to expect that the Author will have something to say to each of us on the part that each of us has played. The playing it well is what matters infinitely.
C. S. LEWIS (1898–1963)

9912 The only way to wait for the Second Coming is to watch that you do what you should do, so that when he comes is a matter of indifference. It is the attitude of a child, certain that God knows what he is about. When the Lord does come, it will be as natural as breathing. God never does anything hysterical, and he never produces hysterics.
OSWALD CHAMBERS (1874–1917)

9913 The primitive church thought more about the Second Coming of Jesus Christ than about death or about heaven. The early Christians were looking not for a cleft in the ground called a grave but for a cleavage in the sky called Glory. They were watching not for the undertaker but for the uppertaker.
ALEXANDER MACLAREN (1826–1910)

9914 We are not a post-war generation; but a pre-peace generation. Jesus is coming.
CORRIE TEN BOOM (1892–1983)

SELF

9915 "I'm a self-made man, you know," explained a certain magnate of modern business to Dr. Joseph Parker, who immediately replied, "Sir, you have lifted a great load of responsibility from the Almighty."
JOHN BAILLIE (1741–1806)

9916 "Me" is always at the bottom of all sin. It may spell drink, lust, pride, covetousness, self-will; but it is some form of "me."

9917 . . . burdened with the unbearable weight of ourselves.
JOSEPH JOUBERT (1754–1824)

9918 A man wrapped up in himself makes a very small bundle.
BENJAMIN FRANKLIN (1706–1790)

9919 A man's self is his greatest cross.
FRANÇOIS FÉNELON (1651–1715)

9920 And I grow young as I leave my me behind.
DILYS LAING (1906–1960)

9921 Beware of no man more than yourself; we carry our worst enemies with us.
CHARLES HADDON SPURGEON (1834–1892)

9922 Dear Heavenly Father;
I'm working on a puzzle, pure and simple.
It is I.

Dear Searching Child:
Here's the answer to your puzzle, pure and simple.
It is I.
ETHELYN A. SHATTUCK

9923 Don't be ferocious with yourself because that is treating badly a precious (if imperfect) thing which God has made.
EVELYN UNDERHILL (1875–1941)

9924 Every extreme attitude is a flight from the self.
ERIC HOFFER (1902–1983)

9925 Everyone thinks of changing the world, but no one thinks of changing himself.
LEO TOLSTOY (1828–1910)

9926 *Flesh* is the Bible's word for unperfected human nature. Leaving off the *h* and spelling it in reverse we have the world *self*. Flesh is the self-life: it is what we are when we are left to our own devices.
BILLY GRAHAM (1918–   )

9927 From the highest to the lowest, self exists to be abdicated and, by that abdication, becomes the more truly self.
C. S. LEWIS (1898–1963)

9928 God knows, I'm not the thing I should be,
Nor am I even the thing I could be.
ROBERT BURNS (1759–1796)

9929 I am more afraid of my own heart than of the pope and all his cardinals. I have within me the great pope, self.
MARTIN LUTHER (1483–1546)

9930 I have to take care not to settle on the sandbank of selfishness, but to leave all for the Lord to order it. If I then make shipwreck, it will be in the wide sea of God's love, the depths of which are as welcome to me as the surest heaven. But nature fights against the thought of venturing forth we know not where, out of self, into unknown regions.
GERHARD TERSTEEGEN (1697–1769)

9931 I seem to have an awful lot of people inside me.
EDITH EVANS (1888–1976)

9932 If I am half-full of myself, there is no way I can be full of God.
RICHARD OWEN ROBERTS (1931–   )

9933 Inside myself is a place where I live all alone, and that's where you renew your springs that never dry up.
PEARL S. BUCK (1892–1973)

9934 It is not my business to think about myself. My business is to think about God. It is for God to think about me.
SIMONE WEIL (1909–1943)

9935 Lord of himself—that heritage of woe.
LORD GEORGE NOEL GORDON BYRON (1788–1824)

9936 Love hates Self, or that which we call I, because it is a deadly thing and the two of them, Love and Self, cannot well stand together.
JAKOB BÖHME (1575–1624)

9937 Man is always frightened as soon as he realizes that he loses himself by giving himself. It is a terrible feeling, a leap in the dark.
LOUIS EVELY (1910–   )

9938 Men are so possessed by themselves that they have no vacuum into which God's deep water may rise.
THOMAS ERSKINE (1750–1823)

9939 Most of us . . . cannot spend an evening without trying to escape from someone whom we know slightly and find, it seems, an intolerable bore—ourselves.
WILLIAM RALPH INGE (1860–1954)

9940 No, when the fight begins within himself,
A man's worth something.
God stoops o'er his head,
Satan looks up between his feet—both tug—
He's left, himself, in the middle: the soul wakes
And grows.
ROBERT BROWNING (1812–1889)

9941 One of the hardest lessons to learn for a certain type of person—and some never learn it at all—is that when you try to make yourself more, you are actually diminishing yourself.
SYDNEY J. HARRIS (1917–1986)

9942 Self . . . is not to be annihilated, but to be rightly centered in God.
OSWALD CHAMBERS (1874–1917)

9943 Self is one of the toughest plants that grows in the garden of life. It is, in fact, indestructible by any human means. Just when we are sure it is

dead, it turns up somewhere as robust as ever to trouble our peace and poison the fruit of our lives.
A. W. TOZER (1897–1963)

9944 Self is the only prison that can ever bind the soul.
HENRY VAN DYKE (1852–1933)

9945 Self is the opaque veil that hides the face of God from us.
A. W. TOZER (1897–1963)

9946 Self-centeredness of any kind is always a movement away from God and consequently a very serious form of disorder.
PHILIP PARE

9947 She faced the crowd and cried:
I love you all but one,
The one who wears my face.
DILYS LAING (1906–1960)

9948 Somebody's boring me . . . I think it's me.
DYLAN MARLAIS THOMAS (1914–1953)

9949 The greatest burden we have to carry in life is self; the most difficult thing we have to manage is self.
HANNAH WHITHALL SMITH (1832–1911)

9950 The image of myself which I try to create in my own mind in order that I may love myself is very different from the image which I try to create in the minds of others in order that they may love me.
W. H. AUDEN (1907–1973)

9951 The more thou thine own self out of thyself dost throw,
The more will into thee God with his Godhead flow.
ANGELUS SILESIUS (1624–1677)

9952 There is nothing wrong with being individuals; the problem is with the "ism." As a rule, "isms" convert healthy ideas into ideologies. Authority, for example, is a biblical notion; authoritarianism twists that good into a lust for power and repressive control. Community is good; communism is an insidious ideology. Recognition of the individual affirms respect for human dignity and the uniqueness of each person; individualism distorts

that joy of identity into an ego cult of one.
CHARLES COLSON (1931–)

9953 There's only one corner of the universe you can be certain of improving and that's your own self.
ALDOUS HUXLEY (1894–1963)

9954 To be nobody but yourself—in a world that is doing its best, night and day, to make you everybody else— means to fight the hardest battle any human being can fight, and never stop fighting.
E. E. CUMMINGS (1894–1962)

9955 What other dungeon is so dark as one's own heart! What jailer so inexorable as one's self!
NATHANIEL HAWTHORNE (1804–1864)

9956 When you empty yourself, God Almighty rushes in!
A. W. TOZER (1897–1963)

9957 Whenever I look inside myself, I am afraid.
C. E. M. JOAD (1891–1953)

9958 You have but two topics, yourself and me. I am sick of both.
SAMUEL JOHNSON (1709–1784)

SELF-CONTROL

9959 Lord of himself, though not of lands;
And having nothing, yet hath all.
SIR HENRY WOTTON (1568–1639)

9960 Rule lust, temper the tongue, and bridle the belly.

9961 Self-control is the ability to keep cool while someone is making it hot for you.

SELF-DENIAL

9962 All great virtues bear the imprint of self-denial.
WILLIAM ELLERY CHANNING (1780–1842)

9963 In submission we are free to value other people. Their dreams and plans become important to us. We have entered into a new, wonderful, glorious freedom, the freedom to give up our own rights for the good of others. For the first time we can love people

unconditionally. We have given up the right for them to return our love. No longer do we feel that we have to be treated in a certain way. We can rejoice with their successes. We feel genuine sorrow at their failures. It is of little consequence that our plans are frustrated if their plans succeed. We discover that it is far better to serve our neighbor than to have our own way.
RICHARD J. FOSTER (1942–)

9964 The more a man denies himself, the more shall he obtain from God.
HORACE BUSHNELL (1802–1876)

SELF-DISCIPLINE

9965 A compass is narrow-minded—it always points to the magnetic north. It seems that is a very narrow view, but a compass is not broad-minded. If it were, all the ships at sea and all the planes in the air would be in danger. We must discipline ourselves, personally, to fight any deviation from the course Jesus set for us. We cannot be tolerant of any other course. To deviate is to sin.
BILLY GRAHAM (1918–)

9966 Beware of saying, "I haven't time to read the Bible, or to pray"; say rather, "I haven't disciplined myself to do these things."
OSWALD CHAMBERS (1874–1917)

9967 Discipline is the basic set of tools we require to solve life's problems.
M. SCOTT PECK (1936–)

9968 He is strong who conquers others; he is mighty who conquers himself.

9969 I have more trouble with D. L. Moody than with any other man I ever met.
DWIGHT LYMAN MOODY (1837–1899)

9970 It's possible that we—in pursuit of the disciplined life—focus our eyes on larger-than-life goals. We take on three jobs at church. We memorize not only verses, but chapters. We sell the TV or get up at 4:00 A.M. every morning for devotions. . . . But it may be that we've overlooked more immediate and obvious things. We've passed over things like a clean room, or being on time, or curbing our tongue.
JONI EARECKSON TADA

9971 No horse gets anywhere until he is harnessed. No steam or gas ever drives anything until it is confined. No Niagara is ever turned into light and power until it is tunneled. No life ever grows great until it is focused, dedicated, disciplined.
HARRY EMERSON FOSDICK (1878–1969)

9972 People lose weight, not by talking about it, but by keeping their mouths shut.

9973 Rule your mind or it will rule you.
HORACE (65–8 B.C.)

9974 Self-discipline never means giving up anything, for giving up is a loss. Our Lord did not ask us to give up the things of earth, but to exchange them for better things.
ARCHBISHOP FULTON J. SHEEN (1895–1979)

9975 Some people regard discipline as a chore. For me, it is a kind of order that sets me free to fly.
JULIE ANDREWS (1935–)

9976 Voices are saying, "Let it all hang out" and "Tell it like it is" and "Hold nothing back" and "Be open . . . express your feelings without restraint!" It's easy to buy that kind of advice. But when I go to my Bible, I find contrary counsel being marketed.
CHARLES R. SWINDOLL (1934–)

9977 You never will be the person you can be if pressure, tension, and discipline are taken out of your life.
JAMES G. BILKEY

SELF-ESTEEM

9978 A healthy self-image is seeing yourself as God sees you—no more and no less.
JOSH MCDOWELL

9979 A man must learn to forgive himself.
ARTHUR DAVISON FICKE

9980 Acceptance of one's intrinsic worth is the core of the personality. When it collapses, everything else begins to quiver.
JAMES C. DOBSON (1936–)

9981 All I could never be,
All men ignored in me—
This, I was worth to God.
ROBERT BROWNING (1812–1889)

9982 Consider then thyself, O noble soul, and the nobility within thee, for thou art honored above all creatures in that thou art an image of God; . . . thou art destined to greatness!
MEISTER ECKHART (C. 1260–C. 1327)

9983 Do not be awestruck by other people and try to copy them. Nobody can be you as effectively as you can. Remind yourself that God is with you and nothing can defeat him.
NORMAN VINCENT PEALE (1898–)

9984 Every new adjustment is a crisis in self-esteem.
ERIC HOFFER (1902–1983)

9985 He who is able to love himself is able to love others also; he who has learned to overcome self-contempt has overcome his contempt for others.
PAUL JOHANNES OSKAR TILLICH (1886–1965)

9986 He who respects himself is safe from others; he wears a coat of mail that none can pierce.
HENRY WADSWORTH LONGFELLOW (1807–1882)

9987 I am as my Creator made me, and since he is satisfied, so am I.
MINNIE SMITH

9988 If a poll should be taken to name the six greatest men in the world and our names would not be included, we would still have the same privileges in God's world that they would have! We can breathe God's beautiful air, look at his blue sky, gaze into a never-ending array of stars in the night sky. We can stand upon the hard earth and stamp our little feet—and our big feet, too—and know that it will sustain us. We are as much a part of this human race as the greatest men and women.
A. W. TOZER (1897–1963)

9989 If the value of an article is dependent upon the price paid for it, Christ's death made our value skyrocket. Let no one say we are worthless. God is not a foolish speculator; he would never invest in worthless property.
ERWIN W. LUTZER (1941–)

9990 If you were someone else, could you stand yourself?

9991 Let each man think himself an act of God, his mind a thought of God, his life a breath of God.
PHILIP JAMES BAILEY (1816–1902)

9992 Our acceptance before God is complete and secure even when we are disappointed in ourselves.
ERWIN W. LUTZER (1941–)

9993 Self-acceptance is basically a spiritual issue. What it boils down to is this: are we able to thank the Creator for the way he made us? If not, we are casting doubt on his wisdom. If we can thank him, we display our belief that he knows what is best for us. And that will help us accept ourselves—limitations, failures, and all.
ERWIN W. LUTZER (1941–)

9994 Self-esteem is a fragile flower and can be crushed so easily.
JAMES C. DOBSON (1936–)

9995 Self-respect cannot be hunted. It cannot be purchased. It is never for sale. It cannot be fabricated out of public relations. It comes to us when we are alone, in quiet moments, in quiet places, when we suddenly realize that, knowing the good, we have done it; knowing the beautiful, we have served it; knowing the truth, we have spoken it.
WHITNEY GRISWOLD

9996 Sincere self-forgetting, sacrificial service to searching and suffering souls satisfies my self-esteem more than the stimulation of a celebrity status.
ROBERT HAROLD SCHULLER (1926–)

9997 The better the self-image, the larger the capacity for loving.
JOHN POWELL

9998 The mirror shows everyone his best friend.
YIDDISH PROVERB

9999 The most obscure believer, even the least successful among us, can hold his head high, look tomorrow square in the eye and exclaim, "I am special to the God of the universe!" You might not want to honk your horn if you love Jesus, but you could at least put a smile on your face.
ERWIN W. LUTZER (1941–   )

10000 The truest self-respect is not to think of self.
HENRY WARD BEECHER (1813–1887)

10001 The worth of an individual is not ascribed by law . . . it's endowed by the Creator.
JAMES C. DOBSON (1936–   )

10002 There are those who depend on us, watch us, learn from us, take from us. And we never know. Don't sell yourself short. You may never have proof of your importance, but you are more important than you think.
ROBERT FULGHUM

10003 When my sense of self depends on what others say of me, anger is a quite natural reaction to a critical word. And when my sense of self depends on what I can acquire, greed flares up when my desires are frustrated. Thus greed and anger are the brother and sister of a false self, fabricated by the social compulsions of an unredeemed world.
HENRI J. M. NOUWEN

10004 You aren't an accident. You weren't mass-produced. You aren't an assembly-line product. You were deliberately planned, specifically gifted, and lovingly positioned on this earth by the Master Craftsman.
MAX L. LUCADO (1955–   )

SELF-KNOWLEDGE

10005 Beware of no man more than thyself.

10006 God in his wisdom only gives the grace of self-knowledge gradually; if he were to show us our true selves suddenly, we should despair and lose all courage. But as we perceive and conquer the more glaring faults, his gracious light shows us the subtler, more hidden imperfections; and this spiritual process lasts all through life.
JEAN NICOLAS GROU (1731–1803)

10007 It is as hard to see one's self as to look backwards without turning around.
HENRY DAVID THOREAU (1817–1862)

10008 It is not only the most difficult thing to know oneself, but the most inconvenient one, too.
JOSH BILLINGS (1818–1885)

10009 Just stand aside and watch yourself go by. Think of yourself as "he" instead of "I."
STRICKLAND W. GILLILAN (1869–1954)

10010 Know thyself, that thou mayest know God; and know God, that thou mayst love him and be like him. In the one thou art initiated into wisdom; in the other perfected in it.
FRANCIS QUARLES (1592–1644)

10011 Know thyself? If I knew myself, I'd run away.
JOHANN WOLFGANG VON GOETHE (1749–1832)

10012 Most of us do not like to look inside ourselves for the same reason we don't like to open a letter that has bad news.
ARCHBISHOP FULTON J. SHEEN (1895–1979)

10013 Not only do we know God through Jesus Christ, we only know ourselves through Jesus Christ.
BLAISE PASCAL (1623–1662)

10014 Nothing will make us so charitable and tender to the faults of others as, by self-examination, thoroughly to know our own.
FRANÇOIS FÉNELON (1651–1715)

10015 Once we become conscious that we are infinitely more than we can fathom, and infinitely greater in possibility either for good or bad than we can know, we shall be only too glad to hand ourselves over to God.
OSWALD CHAMBERS (1874–1917)

10016 Rules for Self Discovery:
1. What we want most;
2. What we think about most;
3. How we use our money;
4. What we do with our leisure time;
5. The company we enjoy;
6. Who and what we admire;
7. What we laugh at.
A. W. TOZER (1897–1963)

10017 Search thine own heart.
What paineth thee
In others, in thyself may be.
JOHN GREENLEAF WHITTIER (1807–1892)

10018 Self-knowledge grows out of a man's
self-confrontation with God.
DIETRICH VON HILDEBRAND (1889–1977)

10019 Self-knowledge is so critically important to us in our pursuit of God and
his righteousness that we lie under
heavy obligation to do immediately
whatever is necessary to remove the
disguise and permit our real selves to
be known.
A. W. TOZER (1897–1963)

10020 The knowledge of ourselves not only
arouses us to seek God, but also leads
us by the hand to find him.
JOHN CALVIN (1509–1564)

10021 The nausea of being the thing I was
leapt from my throat like sobbing. . . .
DACIA MARAINI (1936–)

10022 To know one's self is the true;
To strive with one's self is the good;
To conquer one's self is the beautiful.
JOSEPH ROUX (1834–1886)

SELF-LOVE

10023 He who is able to love himself is able
to love others also.
PAUL JOHANNES OSKAR TILLICH
(1886–1965)

10024 If you love yourself in such a way that
you compass your own destruction, I
have no wish to see you loving anyone
as much as you love yourself.
SAINT AUGUSTINE OF HIPPO (354–430)

10025 Self-love is a medium of a peculiar
kind; it magnifies everything that is
amiss in others at the same time that it
lessens everything that is amiss in ourselves.
BISHOP JOSEPH BUTLER (1692–1752)

10026 Self-love is a mote in every man's eye.
ENGLISH PROVERB

10027 Self-love pushes and insinuates itself
into everything, while making us
believe it is not there at all.
SAINT FRANCIS OF SALES (1567–1622)

10028 The root of discontent is self-love; the
more self is indulged, the more it
demands.
PROVERB

SELF-PITY

10029 Everyone thinks his sack is the heaviest.
PROVERB

10030 God gave a loaf to every bird—
But just a crumb to me.
EMILY ELIZABETH DICKINSON (1830–1886)

10031 I felt sorry for myself because I had no
shoes—until I met a man who had no
feet.

10032 If you have the whine in you, kick it
out ruthlessly.
OSWALD CHAMBERS (1874–1917)

10033 Our tears so blind our eyes that we
cannot see our mercies.
JOHN FLAVEL (1627–1691)

10034 Self-pity . . . cuddle and nurse it as an
infant and you'll have on your hands
in a brief period of time a beast, a
monster, a raging, coarse brute that
will spread the poison of bitterness
and paranoia throughout your system.
CHARLES R. SWINDOLL (1934–)

10035 The least pain in our little finger gives
us more concern and uneasiness than
the destruction of millions of our fel-
low-beings.
WILLIAM HAZLITT (1778–1830)

10036 When God is weaning a soul from
creatures, from Christian experience,
from teachers and friends, then is the
time that the devil begins the advocacy
of self-pity.
OSWALD CHAMBERS (1874–1917)

SELF-RIGHTEOUSNESS

10037 He who gives to be seen will relieve
none in the dark.
ENGLISH PROVERB

10038 O you who are so good yourself,
So pious and so holy,
You've nought to do but mark and tell
Your neighbors' faults and folly!
ROBERT BURNS (1759–1796)

10039 Self-righteousness is the devil's masterpiece.
THOMAS ADAMS (1612–1653)

10040 They are most deceived that trust the
most in themselves.
QUEEN ELIZABETH I (1533–1603)

10041 While a man rests on his own merits
for acceptance with God, it is of little
consequence whether he be a pagan
idolator, or a proud, ignorant Pharisee. I know not which of the two is
most distant from the kingdom of God.
JAMES MILNER (D. 1721)

SELF-SUFFICIENCY

10042 Might never prays.
BULGARIAN PROVERB

10043 Not irreverently we may say that
God has no easy time of it to smash
the bridgeheads of our clever self-
sufficiency, to break down the fortified
walls of our self-defenses, and capture
the inner stronghold of our pride.
PAUL STROMBERG REES (1900–   )

10044 Nothing blinds the mind to the claims
of Jesus Christ more effectually than a
good, clean-living, upright life based
on self-realization. For a thing to be
satanic does not mean that it is
abominable and immoral. The satanically managed man is moral, upright,
proud, and individual; he is absolutely
self-governed and has no need of God.
OSWALD CHAMBERS (1874–1917)

10045 The greatest of all disorders is to think
we are whole and need no help.
THOMAS WILSON (1663–1735)

SELF/DEATH TO

10046 He best can part with life without a
sigh whose daily living is to daily die.
CHARLES HADDON SPURGEON (1834–1892)

10047 Man, if you live in God, and die to
your own will,
How simple it will be his precepts to
fulfill.
ANGELUS SILESIUS (1624–1677)

10048 To be willing to accept crucifixion
with Christ; to leave all yourself, your
plans and your longings, your abilities
and your possessions, all of them at
the cross so that you only trust and
love and live for Christ, hurts a great
deal. . . . It requires an absolute venture of faith; but beyond it, God says,
"much fruit." And the way to it is
"into the ground and die"—it is the
only way.
L. F. E. WILKINSON

10049 When Christ calls a man, he bids him
come and die.
DIETRICH BONHOEFFER (1906–1945)

10050 You will be dead so long as you refuse
to die.
GEORGE MACDONALD (1824–1905)

SELFISHNESS

10051 "Affluent society" is a euphemism, in
the context of our poverty-stricken
and starvation-ridden world, for selfishness.
JOHN FOWLES (1926–   )

10052 Can a man love God while ignoring
the need of his brother?
FRANCES J. ROBERTS

10053 Christ regarded the self-loving, self-
regarding, self-seeking spirit as the
direct antithesis of real living. His two
fundamental rules for life were that
"love-energy," instead of being turned
in on itself, should go out first to God
and then to other people.
J. B. PHILLIPS (1906–1982)

10054 Glory built on selfish principles is
shame and guilt.
WILLIAM COWPER (1731–1800)

10055 He is a slave of the greatest slave who serves nothing but himself.

10056 He merits no thanks who does a kindness for his own ends.

10057 He sets my house on fire only to roast his eggs.

10058 He suffers most who is most selfish.
CHINESE PROVERB

10059 He who lives only for himself is truly dead to others.
PUBLILIUS SYRUS (FIRST CENTURY B.C.)

10060 He who withholds but a pennyworth of worldly goods from his neighbor, knowing him to be in need of it, is a robber in the sight of God.
MEISTER ECKHART (C. 1260–C. 1327)

10061 Himself is his dungeon.
GEORGE MACDONALD (1824–1905)

10062 I doubt that there has ever been one recorded case of deep and lasting fulfillment reported by a person whose basic mind-set and only question was: What am I getting out of this?
JOHN POWELL

10063 If I really love God, my innate and persistent selfishness will have received its death-blow.
ALEXANDER SMELLIE

10064 If we build to please ourselves, we are building on the sand; if we build for the love of God, we are building on the rock.
OSWALD CHAMBERS (1874–1917)

10065 If you wish to be miserable, think much about yourself; about what you want, what you like, what respect people ought to pay you, and what people think of you.
CHARLES KINGSLEY (1819–1875)

10066 In heaven they scorn to serve, so now in hell they reign.
JOHN FLETCHER (1579–1625)

10067 Living in our selfishness means stopping at human limits and preventing our transformation into divine love.
CARLO CARRETTO (1910–   )

10068 Man is still a super-age-savage, predatory, acquisitive, primarily interested in himself.
EARNEST A. HOOTON (1887–1954)

10069 Men are not against you; they are merely for themselves.
GENE FOWLER (1890–1960)

10070 Most people are good. There aren't very many really evil people. But there are an awful lot of selfish ones.
WALTER CRONKITE (1916–   )

10071 Much of our philanthropy is simply the impulse to save ourselves an uncomfortable feeling.
OSWALD CHAMBERS (1874–1917)

10072 Next to the very young, I suppose the very old are the most selfish.
WILLIAM MAKEPEACE THACKERAY (1811–1863)

10073 No indulgence of passion destroys the spiritual nature so much as respectable selfishness.
GEORGE MACDONALD (1824–1905)

10074 One year of
Self-surrender
Will bring
Larger blessings
Than fourscore
Years of
Selfishness.
HENRY VAN DYKE (1852–1933)

10075 Our-Father-who-art-in-heaven-gimme-gimme-gimme.
CALVIN MILLER

10076 People imagine they are pursuing the glory of God when actually they are only pursuing their own.
BLAISE PASCAL (1623–1662)

10077 People who are self-centered always live in unpleasant surroundings.

10078 Posthumous charities are the very essence of selfishness when bequeathed by those who, when alive, would part with nothing.
CHARLES CALEB COLTON (1780–1832)

10079 Selfishness always aims at creating around it an absolute uniformity of type.
OSCAR WILDE (1854–1900)

10080 Selfishness is never so exquisitely self-ish as when it is on its knees. Self can turn what would otherwise be a pure and powerful prayer into a weak and ineffective one. I may cry loudly to God that the church be restored to her New Testament splendor, and be secretly dreaming that I may be the one to lead her.
A. W. TOZER (1897–1963)

10081 Selfishness is not living as one wishes to live; it is asking others to live as one wishes to live.
OSCAR WILDE (1854–1900)

10082 Selfishness is the enemy of all true affection.
CORNELIUS TACITUS (C. 56–C. 120)

10083 Selfishness turns life into a burden. Unselfishness turns burdens into life!
ROBERT HAROLD SCHULLER (1926–   )

10084 Some people are for seeing God with their eyes, as they can see a cow (which they love for the milk, and for the cheese, and for their own profit.) Thus do all those who love God for the sake of outward riches or of inward comfort; they do not love aright, but seek only themselves and their own advantage.
MEISTER ECKHART (C. 1260–C. 1327)

10085 That man who lives for self alone Lives for the meanest mortal known.
JOAQUIN MILLER (1837–1913)

10086 The church says covetousness is a deadly sin—but does she really think so? Is she ready to found welfare societies to deal with financial immorality as she does with sexual immorality? Do the officials stationed at church doors in Italy to exclude women with bare arms turn anybody away on the grounds that they are too well-dressed to be honest? Do the vigilance committees who complain of suggestive books and plays make any attempt to suppress the literature which suggests that getting on in the world is the chief object in life? Does the church arrange services with bright congregational

singing, for Total Abstainers from Usury?
DOROTHY L. SAYERS (1893–1957)

10087 The philosophy of "me first" has the power to blow our world to pieces, whether applied to marriage, business, or international politics.
JAMES C. DOBSON (1936–   )

10088 The wretch, concentrated all in self, Living, shall forfeit fair renown, And, doubly dying, shall go down To the vile dust from whence he sprung, Unwept, unhonored, and unsung.
SIR WALTER SCOTT (1771–1832)

10089 There is no room for God in the man who is full of himself.
JEWISH PROVERB

10090 This "I" and "mine" causes the whole misery.
VIVEKANANDA (1863–1902)

10091 What we have done for ourselves alone dies with us; what we have done for others and the world remains and is eternal.
ALBERT PIKE (1809–1891)

10092 When all sins are old in us and go upon crutches, covetousness does but then lie in her cradle.
THOMAS DEKKER (C. 1572–C. 1632)

SERMONS

10093 A good example is the best sermon.
SIR THOMAS FULLER (1608–1661)

10094 A good sermon helps people in different ways: some rise from it strengthened, others wake from it refreshed.

10095 A sermon wearies people by its length, seldom by its depth.

10096 Americans are so tense and keyed up that it is impossible even to put them to sleep with a sermon.
NORMAN VINCENT PEALE (1898–   )

10097 Great sermons lead the people to praise the preacher. Good preaching leads the people to praise the Savior.
CHARLES G. FINNEY (1792–1875)

10098 I'd rather see a sermon than hear one any day;

I'd rather one should walk with me
    than merely tell the way.
EDGAR ALBERT GUEST (1881–1959)

10099 I'm a believer, and I try to live a Christian life, but I'd as soon hear a surveyor's book read out, figgers an' all, as try to get any simple truth o' most sermons.
SARAH ORNE JEWETT (1849–1909)

10100 If you stay awake and listen to the sermon at church, it will do you good—you'll sleep better that night.

10101 It is a poor sermon that gives no offense; that neither makes the hearer displeased with himself nor with the preacher.
GEORGE WHITEFIELD (1714–1770)

10102 It takes only fifteen minutes to read the greatest sermon ever preached—and when you have finished it, you will have read a complete summary of all that Jesus taught.
CHARLES L. ALLEN (1913–)

10103 Sermons remain one of the last forms of public discourse where it is culturally forbidden to talk back.
HARVEY COX (1929–)

10104 Some clergy prepare their sermons; others prepare themselves.
SAMUEL WILBERFORCE (1805–1873)

10105 Speak boldly, and speak truly. Shame the devil!
JOHN FLETCHER (1579–1625)

10106 The average person's idea of a good sermon is one that goes over his head—and hits one of his neighbors.
JOURNEYMAN BARBER

10107 The belly hates a long sermon.
SIR THOMAS FULLER (1608–1661)

10108 The half-baked sermon causes spiritual indigestion.
AUSTIN O'MALLEY (1858–1932)

10109 The world's shortest sermon is a traffic sign: Keep Right.

10110 We'll get more from the sermon if we learn the knack of listening like a Christian instead of a critic.

10111 You can preach a better sermon with your life than with your lips.
OLIVER GOLDSMITH (1730–1774)

SERVICE

10112 "Whatsoever" is not necessarily active work. It may be waiting (whether half an hour or half a lifetime), learning, suffering, sitting still. But shall we be less ready for these if any of them are his appointments for today?
FRANCES RIDLEY HAVERGAL (1836–1879)

10113 A candle loses nothing by lighting another candle.
PROVERB

10114 A charge to keep I have,
    A God to glorify;
A never-dying soul to save,
    And fit it for the sky.
CHARLES WESLEY (1707–1788)

10115 A Christian should always remember that the value of his good works is not based on their number and excellence, but on the love of God which prompts him to do these things.
SAINT JOHN OF THE CROSS (1542–1591)

10116 All service ranks the same with God.
ROBERT BROWNING (1812–1889)

10117 Are we jabbering busybodies, so taken up with Christian work that we have no time for the Christ whose work it is, no time for him in the morning, no time for him at night?
OSWALD CHAMBERS (1874–1917)

10118 Attempt great things for God; expect great things from God.
WILLIAM CAREY (1761–1834)

10119 Before the judgment seat of Christ my service will not be judged by how much I have done but by how much of me there is in it. No man gives at all until he has given all. No man gives anything acceptable to God until he has first given himself in love and sacrifice.
A. W. TOZER (1897–1963)

10120 Begin at once; before you venture away from this quiet moment, ask your King to take you wholly into his service, and place all the hours of this

day quite simply at his disposal, and
ask him to make and keep you ready
to do just exactly what he appoints.
Never mind about tomorrow; one day
at a time is enough. Try it today, and
see if it is not a day of strange, almost
curious peace, so sweet that you will
be only too thankful when tomorrow
comes to ask him to take it also.
FRANCES RIDLEY HAVERGAL (1836–1879)

10121 Behold, I do not give lectures or a little
        charity
      When I give, I give myself.
      WALT WHITMAN (1819–1892)

10122 Christ has no hands but our hands
      To do his work today;
      He has no feet but our feet
      To lead men in his way;
      He has no tongues but our tongues
      To tell men how he died;
      He has no help but our help
      To bring them to his side.
      ANNIE JOHNSON FLINT (1862–1932)

10123 Christian action should be defined as
      an action of God mediated through a
      person.
      ARCHBISHOP ANTHONY BLOOM (1914–   )

10124 Christian work is constantly crippled
      by clinging to blessings and traditions
      of the past. God is not the God of yes-
      terday. He is the God of today.
      Heaven forbid that we should go on
      playing religious games in one corner
      when the cloud and fire of God's pres-
      ence have moved to another.
      DAVID WATSON (1933–1984)

10125 Dedicate some of your life to others.
      Your dedication will not be a sacrifice;
      It will be an exhilarating experience.
      THOMAS DOOLEY

10126 Do all the good you can,
      By all the means you can,
      In all the ways you can,
      In all the places you can,
      At all the times you can,
      To all the people you can,
      As long as ever you can.
      JOHN WESLEY (1703–1791)

10127 Do little things as if they were great
      because of the majesty of the Lord
      Jesus Christ who dwells in you; and

do great things as if they were little
and easy because of his omnipotence.
BLAISE PASCAL (1623–1662)

10128 Do what you can, with what you
      have, where you are.
      THEODORE ROOSEVELT (1858–1919)

10129 Doctrine divides but service unites.
      NATHAN SODERBLOM (1866–1931)

10130 Give me the power to live for mankind;
      Make me the mouth for such as can-
        not speak;
      Eyes let me be to groping men and
        blind;
      A conscience to the base; and to the
        weak—
      Let me be hands and feet;
      And to the foolish, mind.
      THEODORE PARKER (1810–1860)

10131 Give me the ready hand rather than
      the ready tongue.
      GIUSEPPE GARIBALDI (1807–1882)

10132 Give others a piece of your heart, not
      a piece of your mind.

10133 Go, labor on; spend and be spent—
      Thy joy to do the Father's will;
      It is the way the Master went;
      Should not the servant tread it still?
      HORATIUS BONAR (1808–1889)

10134 God can do tremendous things
      through people who don't care who
      gets the credit.

10135 God did not write solo parts for very
      many of us. He expects us to be partic-
      ipants in the great symphony of life.
      DONALD TIPPETT

10136 God does not do anything with us,
      only through us.
      OSWALD CHAMBERS (1874–1917)

10137 God does not so much need people to
      do extraordinary things as he needs
      people who do ordinary things extraor-
      dinarily well.
      WILLIAM BARCLAY (1907–1978)

10138 God is always calling on us to do the
      impossible. It helps me to remember
      that anything Jesus did during his life
      here on earth, is something we should
      be able to do, too.
      MADELEINE L'ENGLE (1918–   )

10139 God likes help when helping people.
IRISH PROVERB

10140 God never gave man a thing to do concerning which it were irreverent to ponder how the Son of God would have done it.
GEORGE MACDONALD (1824–1905)

10141 God's main concern is that we are more interested in him than in work for him. Once you are rooted and grounded in Christ the greatest thing you can do is to be. Don't try and be useful; be yourself and God will use you to further his ends.
OSWALD CHAMBERS (1874–1917)

10142 Have thy tools ready; God will find thee work.
CHARLES KINGSLEY (1819–1875)

10143 He profits most who serves best.
—Motto for Rotary International
A. F. SHELDON

10144 He stands erect by bending over the fallen. He rises by lifting others.
ROBERT GREEN INGERSOLL (1833–1899)

10145 He who governed the world before I was born shall take care of it likewise when I am dead. My part is to improve the present moment.
JOHN WESLEY (1703–1791)

10146 He who helps in the saving of others saves himself as well.
HARTMAN VON AUE (C. 1170–C. 1215)

10147 He who labors as he prays, lifts his heart to God with his hands.
BERNARD OF CLAIRVAUX (1090–1153)

10148 He who sees a need and waits to be asked for help is as unkind as if he had refused it.
DANTE ALIGHIERI (1265–1321)

10149 He who serves God has a good master.
TORRIANO (C. 1666)

10150 I am not bound to make the world go right,
But only to discover and to do,
With cheerful heart, the work that
God appoints.
JEAN INGELOW (1820–1897)

10151 I am only one, but I am one.
I cannot do everything, but I can do something.
And what I can do, I ought to do.
And what I ought to do, by the Grace of God, I shall do.
EDWARD EVERETT HALE (1822–1909)

10152 I expect to pass through this world but once; any good thing, therefore, that I can do, or any kindness that I can show to my fellow creatures, let me do it now; let me not defer or neglect it, for I shall not pass this way again.
MARCUS AURELIUS ANTONINUS (121–180)

10153 I used to ask God to help me. Then I asked if I might help him. I ended up by asking him to do his work through me.
JAMES HUDSON TAYLOR (1832–1905)

10154 If I can stop one heart from breaking,
I shall not live in vain;
If I can ease one life the aching,
Or cool one pain,
Or help one fainting robin
Into his nest again,
I shall not live in vain.
EMILY ELIZABETH DICKINSON (1830–1886)

10155 If I cannot do great things, I can do small things in a great way.
JAMES FREEMAN CLARKE (1810–1888)

10156 If I love Jesus Christ, I will serve humanity, though men and women treat me like a doormat.
OSWALD CHAMBERS (1874–1917)

10157 If I were fruitless, it mattered not who commended me; but if I were fruitful, I cared not who did condemn.
JOHN BUNYAN (1628–1688)

10158 If I work for God because I know it brings me the good opinion of those whose good opinion I wish to have, I am a Sadducee.
OSWALD CHAMBERS (1874–1917)

10159 If you are going to live for the service of your fellowmen, you will certainly be pierced through with many sorrows, for you will meet with more base ingratitude from your fellowmen than you would from a dog. You will meet with unkindness and two-facedness, and if your motive is love for your fellowmen, you will be exhausted in the battle of life. But if the main-

spring of your service is love for God, no ingratitude, no sin, no devil, no angel, can hinder you from serving your fellowmen, no matter how they treat you. You can love your neighbor as yourself, not from pity, but from the true centering of yourself in God.
OSWALD CHAMBERS (1874–1917)

10160 If you wish to be a leader you will be frustrated, for very few people wish to be led. If you aim to be a servant, you will never be frustrated.
FRANK F. WARREN

10161 In God's family there is to be one great body of people: servants. In fact, that's the way to the top in his kingdom.
CHARLES R. SWINDOLL (1934–   )

10162 In order to be of service to others we have to die to them; that is, we have to give up measuring our meaning and value with the yardstick of others. To die to our neighbors means to stop judging them, to stop evaluating them, and thus to become free to be compassionate. Compassion can never coexist with judgment because judgment creates the distance, the distinction, which prevents us from really being with the other.
HENRI J. M. NOUWEN

10163 Is your place a small place?
Tend it with care!—He set you there.
Is your place a large place?
Guard it with care!—He set you there.
Whate'er your place, it is
Not yours alone, but his
Who set you there.
JOHN OXENHAM (1861–1941)

10164 It is better to light one small candle than to curse the darkness.
CHINESE PROVERB

10165 It is easy to turn our religious life into a cathedral for beautiful memories, but there are feet to be washed, hard flints to be walked over, people to be fed. Very few of us go there, but that is the way the Son of God went.
OSWALD CHAMBERS (1874–1917)

10166 It is ours to offer what we can, God's to supply what we cannot.
SAINT JEROME (C. 374–C. 420)

10167 It is possible to be so active in the service of Christ as to forget to love him.
P. T. FORSYTH (1848–1921)

10168 Learn the luxury of doing good.
OLIVER GOLDSMITH (1730–1774)

10169 Let not your right hand know what the left is doing.
PROVERB

10170 Life is a lot like tennis—the one who can serve best seldom loses.

10171 Make your life a mission—not an intermission.
ARNOLD GLASGOW

10172 Make yourself necessary to somebody.
RALPH WALDO EMERSON (1803–1882)

10173 Ministry that costs nothing, accomplishes nothing.
JOHN HENRY JOWETT (1864–1923)

10174 No man has a right to lead such a life of contemplation as to forget in his own ease the service due to his neighbor; nor has any man a right to be so immersed in active life as to neglect the contemplation of God.
SAINT AUGUSTINE OF HIPPO (354–430)

10175 No one is useless in this world who lightens the burden of it for anyone else.
CHARLES DICKENS (1812–1870)

10176 Not one thing which you have ever done for God has been lost; not one is lost or ever will be lost.
EDWARD BOUBERIE PUSEY (1800–1882)

10177 Nothing makes one feel so strong as a call for help.
GEORGE MACDONALD (1824–1905)

10178 Our business is not to see what lies dimly at a distance, but to do what lies clearly at hand.
THOMAS CARLYLE (1795–1881)

10179 Our rewards in life will depend on the quality and amount of the contributions we make.
DENIS WAITLEY

10180 Pay attention to the Source and God will look after the outflow.
OSWALD CHAMBERS (1874–1917)

10181 Religious work can be done by natural men without the gifts of the Spirit, and it can be done well and skillfully. But

work designed for eternity can only be done by the eternal Spirit.
A. W. TOZER (1897–1963)

10182 Some Christians refer with smug satisfaction to many years of "faithful service" to the Lord. They are quite sure that they will receive a great reward at the judgment seat of Christ—and, candidly, they think they deserve it. Obviously, they have not understood the words of Christ, that the first shall be last and the last shall be first. Surprises lie ahead!
ERWIN W. LUTZER (1941–   )

10183 Teach me, My God and King,
In all things thee to see;
And what I do in anything,
To do it as for thee!
GEORGE HERBERT (1593–1633)

10184 Teach us, good Lord, to serve thee as thou deservest;
To give and not to count the cost;
To fight and not to heed the wounds;
To toil and not to seek for rest;
To labor and not to ask for any reward,
Save that of knowing that we do thy will. Amen.
SAINT IGNATIUS OF LOYOLA (1491–1556)

10185 The average church member would do well to look in his concordance and see how many columns it takes to list all the "serve," "servant," and "service" references.
VANCE HAVNER

10186 The call of Christ is always a promotion.
A. W. TOZER (1897–1963)

10187 The Christian who tugs on the oars hasn't time to rock the boat.
AUSTIN ALEXANDER LEWIS

10188 The Christian worker must be sent; he must not elect to go.
OSWALD CHAMBERS (1874–1917)

10189 The great use of life is to spend it for something that outlasts it.
WILLIAM JAMES (1842–1910)

10190 The highest service may be prepared for and done in the humblest surroundings. In silence, in waiting, in obscure, unnoticed offices, in years of uneventful, unrecorded duties, the Son of God grew and waxed strong.
—Inscription in the Stanford University Chapel

10191 The noblest service comes from unseen hands,
And the best servant does his work unseen.
OLIVER WENDELL HOLMES (1809–1894)

10192 The power and authority of your service will correspond to your dedication to a hidden life of prayer.

10193 The princes among us are those who forget themselves and serve mankind.
WOODROW WILSON (1856–1924)

10194 The reward for a good deed is to have done it.
PROVERB

10195 The Sea of Galilee and the Dead Sea are made of the same water. It flows down, clear and cool, from the heights of Hermon and the roots of the cedars of Lebanon. The Sea of Galilee makes beauty of it, for the Sea of Galilee has an outlet. It gets to give. It gathers in its riches that it may pour them out again to fertilize the Jordan plain. But the Dead Sea with the same water makes horror. For the Dead Sea has no outlet. It gets to keep.
HARRY EMERSON FOSDICK (1878–1969)

10196 The service that counts is the service that costs.
HOWARD HENDRICKS

10197 The smallest good deed is better than the grandest good intention.
PROVERB

10198 The world is full of two kinds of people: the givers and the takers. The takers eat well—but the givers sleep well.

10199 There are some things that only God can do, and for us to attempt to do them is to waste our efforts; and there are other things that only man can do, and for us to ask God to do them is to waste our prayers.
A. W. TOZER (1897–1963)

10200 There are two ways of spreading light: to be the candle or the mirror that reflects it.
EDITH WHARTON (1862–1937)

10201 There's not a pair of legs so thin, there's not a head so thick,
There's not a hand so weak and white, nor yet a heart so sick,
But it can find some needful job that's crying to be done
For the glory of the Garden glorifieth every one.
RUDYARD KIPLING (1865–1936)

10202 They also serve who only stand and wait.
JOHN MILTON (1608–1674)

10203 They serve God well, who serve his creatures.
CAROLINE SHERIDAN NORTON (1808–1877)

10204 Thine is the seed time: God alone Beholds the end of what is sown;
Beyond our vision weak and dim The harvest time is hid with him.
JOHN GREENLEAF WHITTIER (1807–1892)

10205 Trust God for great things; with your five loaves and two fishes, he will show you a way to feed thousands.
HORACE BUSHNELL (1802–1876)

10206 Victory in service is to be expected from supernaturally born men who are supernaturally delivered, supernaturally sustained, and supernaturally directed. We are thus supernaturally created for a supernatural work which is supernaturally prepared and is to be supernaturally performed.
L. L. LEGTERS

10207 We are here to add what we can to life, not to get what we can from it.
SIR WILLIAM OSLER (1849–1919)

10208 We can do little things for God: I turn the cake that is frying on the pan, for love of him; and that done, if there is nothing else to call me, I prostrate myself in worship before him who has given me grace to work; afterwards I rise happier than a king.
BROTHER LAWRENCE OF THE RESURRECTION (C. 1605–1691)

10209 We do the works, but God works in us the doing of the works.
SAINT AUGUSTINE OF HIPPO (354–430)

10210 We give thee but thine own, Whate'er the gift may be;
All that we have is thine alone, A trust, O Lord, from thee.
WILLIAM WALSHAM HOW (1823–1897)

10211 We have fallen into the temptation of separating ministry from spirituality, service from prayer. Our demon says: "We are too busy to pray; we have too many needs to attend to, too many people to respond to, too many wounds to heal. Prayer is a luxury, something to do during a free hour, a day away from work or on a retreat. . . . " But to think this way is harmful. . . . Service and prayer can never be separated; they are related to each other as the Yin and Yang of the [Chinese] Circle.
HENRI J. M. NOUWEN

10212 When people are serving, life is no longer meaningless.
JOHN W. GARDNER (1912–)

10213 When the heart is right, the feet are swift.
THOMAS JEFFERSON (1743–1826)

10214 When we talk of a man doing anything for God or giving anything to God, I will tell you what it is really like. It is like a small child going to its father and saying, "Daddy, give me sixpence to buy you a birthday present." Of course, the father does, and he is pleased with the child's present.
C. S. LEWIS (1898–1963)

10215 When you are a prince and I am a prince, tell me pray, who will drive the donkeys?
ARABIAN PROVERB

10216 When you find a hurt and heal it, you find a need and fill it.
ROBERT HAROLD SCHULLER (1926–)

10217 When you work for the Lord, the pay may not be so hot, but you can't beat the retirement plan.

10218 You came here to serve, not to rule.
THOMAS À KEMPIS (C. 1380–1471)

10219 You give but little when you give of your possessions. It is when you give of yourself that you truly give.
KAHLIL GIBRAN (1883–1931)

10220 You must live with people to know their problems and live with God in order to solve them.
P. T. FORSYTH (1848–1921)

10221 Without God, we cannot. Without us, God will not.
SAINT AUGUSTINE OF HIPPO (354–430)

SEX

10222 Celibacy: Single blessedness.
WILLIAM SHAKESPEARE (1564–1616)

10223 I am constantly amazed when I talk to young people to learn how much they know about sex and how little about soap.
BILLIE BURKE

10224 In this department of life, as in every other, thrills come at the beginning and do not last. . . . Let the thrill go— let it die away—go on through that period of death into the quieter interest and happiness that follow—and you will find you are living in a world of new thrills.
C. S. LEWIS (1898–1963)

10225 It is with our passions, as it is with fire and water. They are good servants but bad masters.
SIR ROGER L'ESTRANGE (1616–1704)

10226 Man is fire, woman tow; along comes the devil and blows!
SPANISH PROVERB

10227 Most of the so-called sexual incompatibility in marriage springs from the delusion that sex is an activity when it is primarily a relationship; if the relationship is faulty, the activity cannot long be self-sustaining or truly satisfactory.
SYDNEY J. HARRIS (1917–1986)

10228 Of the delights of this world man cares most for sexual intercourse. He will go any length for it—risk fortune, character, reputation, life itself. And what do you think he has done? In a thousand years you would never guess—he has left it out of his heaven! Prayer takes its place.
MARK TWAIN (1835–1910)

10229 Sex for procreation is a marvelous thing, and when one is young passion is a marvelous thing, but not to build on. . . . I don't think any marriage built on sex can possibly last, because sex doesn't last and can't last, and it would be obscene if it did. If there is one thing I completely loathe in the contemporary world it is this unashamed effort to devise means to protract physical desire when in the normal way it has disappeared.
MALCOLM MUGGERIDGE (1903–1990)

10230 Sex is a very holy subject.
GEDDES MACGREGOR (1909–)

10231 Sex is the ersatz or substitute religion of the twentieth century.
MALCOLM MUGGERIDGE (1903–1990)

10232 Sex, like all else between human beings, is never perfect.
THEODORE ISAAC RUBIN

10233 The orgasm has replaced the cross as the focus of longing and the image of fulfillment.
MALCOLM MUGGERIDGE (1903–1990)

10234 The passions are like fire, useful in a thousand ways and dangerous only in one, through their excess.
CHRISTIAN NESTELL BOVEE (1820–1904)

10235 There is a tendency to think of sex as something degrading; it is not, it is magnificent, an enormous privilege, but because of that the rules are tremendously strict and severe.
FRANCIS DEVAS

10236 There is little praise for the consistently sexually controlled single. Too often, it is mixed with granulated pity or powdered condescension. Ironically, while discipline and self-control are encouraged and admired in scholarship, athletics, music, and ministry, their absence is strangely excused in sexual matters. The secular myth has infiltrated the Christian consciousness; our sexual urges are overpowering and irresistible. . . . Chastity is a requisite of Christian singleness. Furthermore,

chastity is possible. There will always be somebody to suggest that such thinking is legalistic, unreasonable, and unlikely to succeed. My reply can only be: "When it's bigger than I am, so is God."
ROSALIE DE ROSSET

10237 There is no getting away from it: the old Christian rule is "Either marriage, with complete faithfulness to your partner, or else total abstinence." Chastity is the most unpopular of our Christian virtues.
C. S. LEWIS (1898–1963)

10238 To read the papers and the magazines you would think we were almost worshiping the female bosom.
BILLY GRAHAM (1918–)

10239 What then is the place and purpose of sex? God intends, as the story of Eve's creation from Adam shows, that the "one flesh" experience should be an expression and a heightening of the partner's sense that, being given to each other, they now belong together, each needing the other for completion and wholeness.
   Children are born from their relationship, but this is secondary: what is basic is the enriching of their relationship itself through their repeated "knowing" of each other as persons who belong to each other exclusively and without reserve.
J. I. PACKER (1926–)

SILENCE

10240 All in me is silent . . . I am immersed in the silence of God.
CATHERINE DE HAECK DOHERTY

10241 And silence, like a poultice, comes
To heal the blows of sound.
OLIVER WENDELL HOLMES (1809–1894)

10242 Be silent about great things; let them grow inside you. Never discuss them; discussion is so limiting and distracting. It makes things grow smaller.
BARON FRIEDRICH VON HÜGEL (1852–1925)

10243 Better silent than stupid.
GERMAN PROVERB

10244 Eloquent silence often is better than eloquent speech.
JEWISH PROVERB

10245 Every man who delights in a multitude of words, even though he says admirable things, is empty within. If you love truth, be a lover of silence. Silence, like the sunlight, will illuminate you in God and will deliver you from the phantoms of ignorance. Silence will unite you to God himself.
ISAAC OF NINEVEH (–C. 700)

10246 Everything true and great grows in silence. Without silence we fall short of reality and cannot plumb the depths of being.
LADISLAUS BOROS

10247 For thy great gift, O Father,
We thank thee today—
The gift of silence;
For the rich, warm, generous silence
We thank thee,
Wherein our souls,
Stunted and shrivelled and starved
In the arid desert of everyday hurry and strain,
May rest, and quietly grow, and expand
Upward to thee.
JOHN S. HOYLAND (1830–1894)

10248 Four things go together: silence, listening, prayer, truth.
HUBERT VAN ZELLER

10249 God far exceeds all words that we can here express;
In silence he is heard, in silence worshiped best.
ANGELUS SILESIUS (1624–1677)

10250 God is the friend of silence. Trees, flowers, grass grow in silence. See the stars, moon, and sun, how they move in silence.
MOTHER TERESA OF CALCUTTA (1910–)

10251 He who does not understand your silence will probably not understand your words.
ELBERT GREEN HUBBARD (1856–1915)

10252 I have shown you the power of silence, how thoroughly it heals and how fully pleasing it is to God. . . . It is by silence that the saints grew. . . . It was because of silence that the power of God dwelt in them; because of silence that the mysteries of God were known to them.
FATHER AMMONAS (C. 350)

10253 In this chatty society, silence has become a very fearful thing. For most people, silence creates itchiness and nervousness. Many experience silence not as full and rich, but as empty and hollow. For them silence is like a gaping abyss which can swallow them up.
HENRI J. M. NOUWEN

10254 It is impossible to live in your inmost being where Christ lives without loving silence.
MADAME JEANNE MARIE DE LA MOTHE GUYON (1648–1717)

10255 It is in silence that God is known, and through mysteries that he declares himself.
ROBERT H. BENSON (1871–1914)

10256 Let thy soul walk slowly in thee,
As a saint in heaven unshod,
For to be alone with silence
Is to be alone with God.
SAMUEL MILLER HAGEMAN

10257 Lord, teach me to silence my own heart that I may listen to the gentle movement of the Holy Spirit within me and sense the depths which are of God.
ELIJAH DE VIDAS
SIXTEENTH CENTURY

10258 Nothing in all creation is so like God as stillness.
MEISTER ECKHART (C. 1260–C. 1327)

10259 One reason we can hardly bear to remain silent is that it makes us feel so helpless. We are so accustomed to relying upon words to manage and control others. If we are silent, who will take control? God will take control; but we will never let him take control until we trust him. Silence is intimately related to trust.
RICHARD J. FOSTER (1942–)

10260 Silence is a friend who will never betray.
CONFUCIUS (C. 551–479 B.C.)

10261 Silence is a great peacemaker.
HENRY WADSWORTH LONGFELLOW (1807–1882)

10262 Silence is but a rich pause in the music of life.
SAROJINI NAIDU (1879–1949)

10263 Silence is deep as eternity. Speech is shallow as time.
THOMAS CARLYLE (1795–1881)

10264 Silence is the brother of acceptance.
ARABIAN PROVERB

10265 Silence is the element in which great things fashion themselves.
THOMAS CARLYLE (1795–1881)

10266 Silence is the universal refuge, the sequel to all dull discourses and all foolish acts, a balm to our every chagrin, as welcome after satiety as after disappointment.
HENRY DAVID THOREAU (1817–1862)

10267 Still waters run deep.
ENGLISH PROVERB

10268 The greatest events are not our noisiest, but our stillest hours.
FRIEDRICH WILHELM NIETZSCHE (1844–1900)

10269 The greatest ideas, the most profound thoughts, and the most beautiful poetry are born from the womb of silence.
WILLIAM ARTHUR WARD (1812–1882)

10270 The mouth keeps silent to hear the heart speak.
ALFRED DE MUSSET (1810–1857)

10271 The present state of the world and the whole of life is diseased. If I were a doctor and were asked for my advice, I should reply: Create silence.
SØREN AABYE KIERKEGAARD (1813–1855)

10272 There are two kinds of people who keep silent. The first is one who has nothing to say, and the other is one who has too much to say.
MADAME JEANNE MARIE DE LA MOTHE GUYON (1648–1717)

10273 There is hardly ever a complete silence in our soul. God is whispering to us well-nigh incessantly. Whenever the sounds of the world die out in the soul, or sink low, then we hear these whisperings of God. He is always whispering to us, only we do not always hear because of the noise, hurry, and the distraction that life causes as it rushes on.
FREDERICK WILLIAM FABER (1814–1863)

10274 There is no utterance for love or death;
Words cannot speak for grief or ecstasy;
They must stand by like impotent pale ghosts
When hearts are blest or stricken verily.
No eloquence is adequate to tell
Of beauty; man is mute as any clod
Of earth before an elemental truth;
He has no word that gives a hint of God.
Silence alone is great enough to hold
A thing so real it never can be told.
ADELAIDE LOVE

10275 These be
Three silent things:
The falling snow . . . the hour
Before the dawn . . . the mouth of one
Just dead.
ADELAIDE CRAPSEY (1878–1914)

10276 With silence one irritates the devil.
BULGARIAN PROVERB

SIMPLICITY

10277 All great things are simple, and many can be expressed in single words: freedom, justice, honor, duty, mercy, hope.
SIR WINSTON CHURCHILL (1874–1965)

10278 If you are absolutely obedient to God, then there is no ambiguity in you and . . . you are mere simplicity before God. . . . One thing there is which all Satan's cunning and all the snares of temptation cannot take by surprise. That is simplicity.
SØREN AABYE KIERKEGAARD (1813–1855)

10279 Make it clear. Make it simple. Emphasize the essentials. Forget about

impressing. Leave some things unsaid. Let the thing be simplified.
CHARLES R. SWINDOLL (1934–   )

10280 Nothing is more simple than greatness; indeed, to be simple is to be great.
RALPH WALDO EMERSON (1803–1882)

10281 Our life is frittered away by detail. . . . Simplicity, simplicity, simplicity!
HENRY DAVID THOREAU (1817–1862)

10282 Pray, God, keep us simple.
WILLIAM MAKEPEACE THACKERAY (1811–1863)

10283 Simplicity of character is the natural result of profound thought.
WILLIAM HAZLITT (1778–1830)

10284 The greatest truths are the simplest, and so are the greatest men.
AUGUST W. HARE (1792–1834)

10285 When a thought is too weak to be expressed simply, simply drop it.
LUC DE CLAPIERS, MARQUIS DE VAUVENARGUES (1715–1747)

10286 Within simplicity lies the sublime.

SIN

10287 A man is first startled by sin; then it becomes pleasing, then easy, then delightful, then frequent, then habitual, then confirmed. The man is impenitent, then obstinate, and then he is damned.
JEREMY TAYLOR (1613–1667)

10288 A scab is a scab, even if you smear honey on it.
YIDDISH PROVERB

10289 A sin is two sins when it is defended.
HENRY SMITH

10290 A sin repeated seems permitted.
JEWISH PROVERB

10291 A thing of bad quality is expensive though you may get it for nothing.
ARABIAN PROVERB

10292 A wrong-doer is often a man who has left something undone, not always one who has done something.
MARCUS AURELIUS ANTONINUS (121–180)

10293 After one vice, a greater follows.
SPANISH PROVERB

10294 All human sin seems so much worse in its consequences than in its intentions.
REINHOLD NIEBUHR (1892–1971)

10295 All sins are attempts to fill voids.
SIMONE WEIL (1909–1943)

10296 All the seven deadly sins are self-destroying, morbid appetites, but in their early stages, at least, lust and gluttony, avarice, and sloth know some gratification, while anger and pride have power, even though that power eventually destroys itself. Envy is impotent, numbed with fear, never ceasing in its appetite, and it knows no gratification, but endless self-torment. It has the ugliness of a trapped rat, which gnaws its own foot in an effort to escape.
ANGUS WILSON (1913–)

10297 Anybody who has once been horrified by the dreadfulness of his own sin that nailed Jesus to the cross will no longer be horrified by even the rankest sins of a brother.
DIETRICH BONHOEFFER (1906–1945)

10298 As virtue is its own reward, so vice is its own punishment.
PROVERB

10299 Christ's death on the cross included a sacrifice for all our sins, past, present, and future. Every sin that you will ever commit has already been paid for. All of our sins were future when Christ died two thousand years ago. There is no sin that you will ever commit that has not already been included in Christ's death.
ERWIN W. LUTZER (1941–)

10300 Christ's definition of sin penetrates far deeper than a list of sins on a membership card. It goes to our inner desire, motivations, and secret thoughts.
ERWIN W. LUTZER (1941–)

10301 Commit a major sin, all lesser sins follow.
FORRESTER BARRINGTON

10302 Disobedience and sin are the same thing, for there is no sin but disobedience.
THEOLOGIA GERMANICA (C. 1350)

10303 Fashions in sin change.
ANNA ROOSEVELT HALSTED (1906–1975)

10304 Fight with your own sin, and let that fight keep you humble and full of sympathy when you go out into the world and strike at the sin of which the world is full.
PHILLIPS BROOKS (1835–1893)

10305 Fix your thought more on the God you desire than on the sin you abhor.
WALTER HILTON (1340–1396)

10306 God does not cause us to sin, but he uses our sins to remind us of our weakness. We are less tempted to judge others, and more understanding when we become well acquainted with the wickedness of our own heart. We then learn how to view others with humility. . . . When we are caught by sin, God uses the experience to teach us about his righteousness and his hatred of sin.
ERWIN W. LUTZER (1941–)

10307 God has nothing to say to the self-righteous.
DWIGHT LYMAN MOODY (1837–1899)

10308 God is a specialist in the sin disease.
ERWIN W. LUTZER (1941–)

10309 He that falls into sin is a man; that grieves at it is a saint; that boasts of it is a devil.
SIR THOMAS FULLER (1608–1661)

10310 He who does not forbid sin when he can, encourages it.
LUCIUS ANNAEUS SENECA (C. 4 B.C.–A.D. 65)

10311 He who has commanded us not to look back when we have put our hands to the plough does as he would have us do—he does not regard the past sins of a soul which seeks his kingdom.
SAINT CYRAN

10312 He who has not felt what sin is in the Old Testament knows little what grace is in the New. He who has not trembled in Moses, and wept in David, and wondered in Isaiah, will rejoice little in Matthew, rest little in John. He who has not suffered under the law will scarcely hear the glad sound of the gos-

pel. He who has not been awakened under the mountain will be little delighted with the cross.
R. W. BARBOUR (1900–)

10313 He who lives in sin and looks for happiness hereafter is like him who sows cockle and thinks to fill his barn with wheat or barley.
JOHN BUNYAN (1628–1688)

10314 Her rash hand in evil hour
Forth reaching to the fruit, she
    plucked, she eat:
Earth felt the wound, and nature from
    her seat,
Sighing through all her works, gave
    signs of woe
That all was lost.
JOHN MILTON (1608–1674)

10315 His face was filled with broken commandments.
JOHN MASEFIELD (1878–1967)

10316 How immense appear to us the sins that we have not committed.
MADAME NECKER (1766–1841)

10317 I enquired what the iniquity was and found it to be no substance but the perversion of the will, turned aside from thee, O God.
SAINT AUGUSTINE OF HIPPO (354–430)

10318 I have fallen, Lord,
Once more.
I can't go on, I'll never succeed.
I am ashamed, I don't dare look at you.
Ask my pardon
And get up quickly.
You see, it's not falling that is the
    worst,
But staying on the ground.
MICHEL QUOIST (1921–)

10319 I see the right, and I approve it too,
Condemn the wrong, and yet the
    wrong pursue.
OVID (43 B.C.–A.D. 17)

10320 I wore vice like a garment; now it is stuck to my skin.
ALFRED DE MUSSET (1810–1857)

10321 If my hangups and negatives are called sin by our Lord, then sin it is.
BOB TURNBULL (1775–1833)

10322 If you want to clear the stream, get the hog out of the spring.
AMERICAN NEGRO PROVERB

10323 In Adam's fall
We sinned all.

10324 It does not matter how small the sins are, provided that their cumulative effect is to edge the man away from the light and out into nothing. Murder is no better than cards if cards can do the trick. Indeed, the safest road to hell is the gradual one—the gentle slope, soft under foot, without sudden turnings, without signposts.
C. S. LEWIS (1898–1963)

10325 It is against himself that everybody sins.
LATIN PROVERB

10326 It is but a step from companionship to slavery when one associates with vice.
HOSEA BALLOU (1771–1852)

10327 It is much easier to repent of sins that we have committed than to repent of those we intend to commit.
JOSH BILLINGS (1818–1885)

10328 It is not only temptation that tries the generous Christian, but at times sin also; he may have a heavy fall, one that he had thought impossible, so deep and strong had seemed his love for the Lord. And having fallen, he is likely to become discouraged. Never before has he understood to such an extent the ugliness of sin—because he has now a greater understanding of the love of God.
    All is grace. This fall will make him realize that he cannot rely on himself at all. It will put him in his place—at the bottom. But with this mistrust of himself must go a greater confidence in God, the Father.
MICHEL QUOIST (1921–)

10329 It is not when we are conscious of our faults that we are the most wicked; on the contrary, we are less so.
FRANÇOIS FÉNELON (1651–1715)

10330 Like a bramble, anyway you grasp it, it hurts.
ARABIAN PROVERB

10331 Love a man even in his sin, for that love is a likeness of the divine love and is the summit of love on earth.
FYODOR MIKHAYLOVICH DOSTOYEVSKI (1821–1881)

10332 Man is the only animal that blushes. Or needs to.
MARK TWAIN (1835–1910)

10333 Man, I can assure you, is a wicked creature.
MOLIÈRE (1622–1673)

10334 Man-like it is to fall into sin,
Fiend-like it is to dwell therein;
Christ-like it is for sin to grieve,
God-like it is all sin to leave.
FRIEDRICH VON LOGAU (1604–1655)

10335 Measure your growth in grace by your sensitiveness to sin.
OSWALD CHAMBERS (1874–1917)

10336 Men never violate the laws of God without suffering the consequences.
LYDIA MARIA CHILD (1802–1880)

10337 Men who could not sin would not be men; they would be good clocks ticking out goodness.
GEORGE ARTHUR BUTTRICK (1892–1980)

10338 Men wish to be saved from the mischiefs of their vices, but not from their vices.
RALPH WALDO EMERSON (1803–1882)

10339 My soul is like a mirror in which the glory of God is reflected, but sin, however insignificant, covers the mirror with smoke.
SAINT TERESA OF AVILA (1515–1582)

10340 Nights of pleasure are short.
ARABIAN PROVERB

10341 No sin is small. No grain of sand is small in the mechanism of a watch.
JEREMY TAYLOR (1613–1667)

10342 O sin, what hast thou done to this fair earth!
R. H. DANA (1815–1882)

10343 Oh, how horrible our sins look when they are committed by someone else.
CHARLES R. SWINDOLL (1934–   )

10344 One leak will sink a ship; and one sin will destroy a sinner.
JOHN BUNYAN (1628–1688)

10345 One reason sin flourishes is that it is treated like a cream puff instead of a rattlesnake.
BILLY SUNDAY (1862–1935)

10346 Only when the axe is put to the tree does the fruit of sin wither.
ERWIN W. LUTZER (1941–   )

10347 Original sin is the malice that is ever flickering within us.
ERIC HOFFER (1902–1983)

10348 Other men's sins are before our eyes; our own behind our backs.
LUCIUS ANNAEUS SENECA (C. 4 B.C.–A.D. 65)

10349 Our sense of sin is in proportion to our nearness to God.
THOMAS D. BERNARD (1750–1818)

10350 People are no longer sinful. They are only immature or underprivileged or frightened or, more particularly, sick.
PHYLLIS MCGINLEY (1905–1977)

10351 We are not punished for our sins, but by them.
ELBERT GREEN HUBBARD (1856–1915)

10352 Shallow natures tremble for a night after their sin, and when they find that the sun rises and men greet them as cordially as before, and that no hand lays hold on them from the past, they think little more of their sin—they do not understand that fatal calm that precedes the storm.
MARCUS DODDS (1834–1909)

10353 Should we all confess our sins to one another, we would all laugh at one another for our lack of originality.
KAHLIL GIBRAN (1883–1931)

10354 Sin . . . presents itself as a most desirable thing.
OSWALD CHAMBERS (1874–1917)

10355 Sin becomes a crime, not against law, but against love; it means not breaking God's law so much as breaking God's heart.
WILLIAM BARCLAY (1907–1978)

10356 Sin causes the cup of blessing to spring a leak.
ERWIN W. LUTZER (1941–   )

10357 Sin does not appear to be irresistible—until you want to be free from it. The

moment you attack it, you are surprised to find that most of its power is hidden.
ERWIN W. LUTZER (1941–)

10358 Sin enough and you will soon be unconscious of sin.
OSWALD CHAMBERS (1874–1917)

10359 Sin has four characteristics: self-sufficiency instead of faith; self-will instead of submission; self-seeking instead of benevolence; self-righteousness instead of humility.
E. PAUL HOVEY (1908–)

10360 Sin is a breach of nature, a death of the soul, a disquiet of the heart, a weakening of power, a blindness of the sense, a sorrow of the spirit, a death of grace, a death of virtue, a death of good works, an aberration of the spirit, a fellowship with the devil, an expulsion of Christianity, a dungeon of hell, a banquet of hell, an eternity of hell.
MEISTER ECKHART (C. 1260–C. 1327)

10361 Sin is an affair of the will. It is not a "vestige of our animal inheritance." That trivial notion comes from an unexamined, too-quickly swallowed doctrine of evolution. Why blame the brute creation? No self-respecting wolf would be guilty of our modern wars.
GEORGE ARTHUR BUTTRICK (1892–1980)

10362 Sin is defiance to the authority of God.
BENJAMIN WHICHCOTE (1609–1683)

10363 Sin is disease, deformity, weakness.
PLATO (C. 428–348 B.C.)

10364 Sin is energy in the wrong channel.
SAINT AUGUSTINE OF HIPPO (354–430)

10365 Sin is essentially a departure from God.
MARTIN LUTHER (1483–1546)

10366 Sin is essentially rebellion against the rule of God.
CHARLES COLSON (1931–)

10367 Sin is fatal in all languages.
ROY L. SMITH

10368 Sin is first a simple suggestion, then a strong imagination, then delight, then assent.
THOMAS À KEMPIS (C. 1380–1471)

10369 Sin is like ice in our pipes—our spiritual lives have been "frozen." There is only one solution, and that is repentance to clear the blockage and restore the flow of the Holy Spirit.
BILLY GRAHAM (1918–)

10370 Sin is not a distance, it is a turning of our gaze in the wrong direction.
SIMONE WEIL (1909–1943)

10371 Sin is not weakness, it is not a disease; it is red-handed rebellion against God and the magnitude of that rebellion is expressed by Calvary.
OSWALD CHAMBERS (1874–1917)

10372 Sin is not wrong doing; it is wrong being, deliberate and emphatic independence of God.
OSWALD CHAMBERS (1874–1917)

10373 Sin is sovereign till sovereign grace dethrones it.
CHARLES HADDON SPURGEON (1834–1892)

10374 Sin is strong and fleet of foot, outrunning everything.
HOMER (C. EIGHTH CENTURY B.C.)

10375 Sin is sweet in the beginning, but bitter in the end.
TALMUD

10376 Sin is the dare of God's justice, the rape of his mercy, the jeer of his patience, the slight of his power, and the contempt of his love.
JOHN BUNYAN (1628–1688)

10377 Sin may be clasped so close we cannot see its ugly face.
ARCHBISHOP RICHARD CHENEVIX TRENCH (1807–1886)

10378 Sin may open bright as the morning, but it will end dark as night.
THOMAS DE WITT TALMAGE (1832–1902)

10379 Sin pays—but it pays in remorse, regret, and failure.
BILLY GRAHAM (1918–)

10380 Sin writes histories; goodness is silent.
JOHANN WOLFGANG VON GOETHE (1749–1832)

10381 Sin. Rub out the first and last letters and you have *I*—or carnal self—the root of sin.

10382 Sinning is nothing but turning from
God one's face
And having turned it thus, turning it
toward death.
ANGELUS SILESIUS (1624–1677)

10383 Sins are like circles in the water when
a stone is thrown into it; one produces
another. When anger was in Cain's
heart, murder was not far off.
PHILIP HENRY (1631–1696)

10384 Some sins we have committed,
Some we have contemplated,
Some we have desired,
Some we have encouraged;
In the case of some we are innocent
only because we did not succeed.
LUCIUS ANNAEUS SENECA (C. 4 B.C.–A.D. 65)

10385 The apple is eaten and the core sticks
in the throat.
CHRISTIAN NESTELL BOVEE (1820–1904)

10386 The best of us are but poor wretches
just saved from shipwreck.
GEORGE ELIOT (1819–1880)

10387 The Bible everywhere takes for granted
Israel's ability to obey the law. Condemnation fell because Israel, having that
ability, refused to obey. They sinned not
out of amiable weakness, but out of
deliberate rebellion against the will of
God. That is the inner nature of sin
always, willful refusal to obey God. But
still men go on trying to get conviction
upon sinners by telling them they
sinned because they could not help it.
A. W. TOZER (1897–1963)

10388 The desire of power in excess caused
angels to fall; the desire of knowledge
in excess caused man to fall.
FRANCIS BACON (1561–1626)

10389 The essence of sin is my claim to my
right to myself.
OSWALD CHAMBERS (1874–1917)

10390 The essence of sin is rebellion against
divine authority.
A. W. TOZER (1897–1963)

10391 The Holy Ghost reveals . . . not only a
depth of possible iniquity that makes
us shudder but a height of holiness of
which we never dreamed.
OSWALD CHAMBERS (1874–1917)

10392 The knowledge of Scripture is no
obstacle to sin.
JEWISH PROVERB

10393 The laughter of sin is as the crackling
of burning thorns.
OSWALD CHAMBERS (1874–1917)

10394 The religious dimension of sin is man's
rebellion against God. The moral and
social dimension of sin is injustice.
REINHOLD NIEBUHR (1892–1971)

10395 The reward of sin is death: that's hard.
CHRISTOPHER MARLOWE (1564–1593)

10396 The seeds of our punishment are sown
at the same time we commit the sin.
HESIOD (EIGHTH CENTURY B.C.)

10397 The sin that shocks God is the thing
which is highly esteemed among men—
self-realization, pride, my right to
myself.
OSWALD CHAMBERS (1874–1917)

10398 The sin you do by two and two you
must pay for one by one!
RUDYARD KIPLING (1865–1936)

10399 The sins of the bedroom are not the
only ones. The sins of the boardroom
should be just as much a matter of
concern.
BISHOP RICHARD HARRIES

10400 The sins of the flesh are bad, but they
are the least bad of all sins. All the
worst pleasures are purely spiritual:
the pleasure of putting other people in
the wrong, of bossing and patronizing
and spoiling sport and backbiting; the
pleasures of power, of hatred.
C. S. LEWIS (1898–1963)

10401 The sins of youth are paid for in old age.
LATIN PROVERB

10402 The Spirit of Jesus is continual forgiveness of sin. He who waits to be righteous before he enters into the Savior's
kingdom, the divine body, will never
enter there.
WILLIAM BLAKE (1757–1827)

10403 The way to Babylon will never bring
you to Jerusalem.
PROVERB

10404 There are only two kinds of men: the
righteous who believe themselves sin-

ners, and the rest, sinners who believe themselves righteous.
BLAISE PASCAL (1623–1662)

10405 There is no minor sin when his justice confronts you, and there is no major sin when his grace confronts you.

10406 Three things sap a man's strength: worry, travel, and sin.
JEWISH PROVERB

10407 To deny the reality of sin or struggle in our lives is to deny God the opportunity of working through our weakness.
REBECCA MANLEY PIPPERT

10408 To fall into sin is human, but to remain in sin is devilish.
GERMAN PROVERB

10409 To forsake sin is to leave it without any thought of returning to it again.
WILLIAM GURNALL (1617–1679)

10410 Vice is a miscalculation of chances, a mistake in estimating the value of pleasures and pains. It is false moral arithmetic.
JEREMY BENTHAM (1748–1832)

10411 Vice repeated, is like the wand'ring wind, Blows dust in others' eyes.
WILLIAM SHAKESPEARE (1564–1616)

10412 Vice stings us even in our pleasures, but virtue consoles us, even in our pains.
WALTER COLTON (1797–1851)

10413 Vices creep in under the name of virtues.
LUCIUS ANNAEUS SENECA (C. 4 B.C.–A.D. 65)

10414 Vices that are familiar we pardon, new ones we rebuke.
PUBLILIUS SYRUS (FIRST CENTURY B.C.)

10415 We are all afflicted with the disease; God is the physician.
ARABIAN PROVERB

10416 We are sinful not merely because we have eaten of the Tree of Knowledge but also because we have not eaten of the Tree of Life.
FRANZ KAFKA (1883–1924)

10417 We are too Christian really to enjoy sinning, and too fond of sinning really to enjoy Christianity. Most of us know perfectly well what we ought to do; our trouble is that we do not want to do it.
PETER MARSHALL (1902–1949)

10418 We can never sin but there will be two witnesses present to observe and register it, our own selves and God.
RALPH VENNING (C. 1621–1674)

10419 We have a strange illusion that mere time cancels sin. I have heard others, and I have heard myself, recounting cruelties and falsehoods committed in boyhood as if they were no concern of the present speaker's, and even with laughter. But mere time does nothing either to the fact or to the guilt of a sin. The guilt is washed out not by time but by repentance and the blood of Christ.
C. S. LEWIS (1898–1963)

10420 We make a ladder of our vices if we trample them underfoot.
SAINT AUGUSTINE OF HIPPO (354–430)

10421 We sin on the installment plan. The bills come in later. But come they will for sin pays handsomely, relentlessly.
ERWIN W. LUTZER (1941–   )

10422 We sin two kinds of sin. We sin one kind of sin as though we trip off the curb, and it overtakes us by surprise. We sin a second kind of sin when we deliberately set ourselves up to fall.
FRANCIS AUGUST SCHAEFFER (1912–1984)

10423 We used to say that we were punished for our sins, as though God were a judge on a bench who passed on the case and meted out penalty. The truth goes far deeper than that. We are not punished *for* our sins, but *by* them. It is our sins themselves that rise to slay us.
ELBERT GREEN HUBBARD (1856–1915)

10424 Whatever weakens your reason, impairs the tenderness of your conscience, obscures your sense of God, and takes off the relish of spiritual things—that to you is sin.
SUSANNA WESLEY (1669–1742)

10425 When God should guide us, we guide ourselves; when he should be our Sovereign, we rule ourselves; the laws which he gives us we find fault with and would correct, and if we had the making of them, we would have made them otherwise; when he should take care of us (and must, or we perish), we

will care for ourselves. . . . We are naturally our own idols.
RICHARD BAXTER (1615–1691)

10426 Who swims in sin shall sink in sorrow.
PROVERB

10427 You may say you are far from hating God; but if you live in sin, you are among God's enemies, you are under Satan's standard and enlisted there. You may not like it, no wonder; you may wish to be elsewhere. But there you are, an enemy to God.
GERARD MANLEY HOPKINS (1844–1889)

SINCERITY

10428 Sincerity is an openness of heart; we find it in very few people.
FRANÇOIS, DUC DE LA ROCHEFOUCAULD (1613–1680)

10429 The devil is sincere, but he is sincerely wrong.
BILLY GRAHAM (1918–   )

10430 The most exhausting thing in life . . . is being insincere.
ANNE MORROW LINDBERGH (1906–   )

10431 Weak persons cannot be sincere.
FRANÇOIS, DUC DE LA ROCHEFOUCAULD (1613–1680)

SINNERS

10432 Don't condemn the sinner! We are, or we were, or we could be as this man is.
—An old abbot to his monks

10433 Forebear to judge, for we are sinners all.
WILLIAM SHAKESPEARE (1564–1616)

10434 God is not merely in the sunshine; God is in the cavern of the man's sin. God is with the sinner wherever he can be.
PHILLIPS BROOKS (1835–1893)

10435 I am thirsty for sin.
ANTONIO MIRA DE AMESCUA (1574–1644)

10436 Man is no helpless invalid left in a valley of total depravity until God pulls him out. Man is rather an upstanding human being whose vision has been impaired by the cataracts of sin and whose soul has been weakened by the

virus of pride, but there is sufficient vision left for him to lift his eyes unto the hills, and there remains enough of God's image for him to turn his weak and sin-battered life toward the Great Physician, the curer of the ravages of sin.
MARTIN LUTHER (1483–1546)

10437 Many of the insights of the saint stem from his experiences as a sinner.
ERIC HOFFER (1902–1983)

10438 My sins don't make me a sinner. They're just the evidence.
S. RICKLY CHRISTIAN (1953–   )

10439 The closer one is to God, the more one feels a sinner.
LOUIS EVELY (1910–   )

10440 The pervasive sinfulness of man becomes evident when contrasted with the radiant holiness of God.
RICHARD J. FOSTER (1942–   )

10441 We are not sinners because we sin; we sin because we are sinners.
R. C. SPROUL (1939–   )

10442 We know we sin; and we're not happy unless there are bigger sinners to point to.
AUBREY MENEN (1912–   )

SLANDER

10443 A lot of molehills become mountains when someone adds a little dirt.
PROVERB

10444 A slip of the foot may be soon recovered; but that of the tongue, perhaps never.
PROVERB

10445 A spark will set a whole city on fire.
ARABIAN PROVERB

10446 A wound heals, but the scar remains.
PROVERB

10447 Close your ear against him who opens his mouth against another. If you receive not his words, they fly back and wound him. If you receive them, they fly forward and wound you.
FRANCIS QUARLES (1592–1644)

10448 Have patience awhile; slanders are not long-lived. Truth is the child of time;

ere long she shall appear to vindicate
thee.
IMMANUEL KANT (1724–1804)

10449 He that filches from me my good
name,
Robs me of that which not enriches
him,
And makes me poor indeed.
WILLIAM SHAKESPEARE (1564–1616)

10450 He that injures one threatens a hundred.
PROVERB

10451 He who blackens others does not
whiten himself.
GERMAN PROVERB

10452 He who flings dirt upon another dirties himself more.
PROVERB

10453 He who is guilty of slander never can
repair it. A false report spreads where
a recantation never reaches, and an
accusation flies faster than a defense.
SAMUEL JOHNSON (1709–1784)

10454 He who plants thorns must never
expect to gather roses.
ARABIAN PROVERB

10455 If nobody took slander in and gave it
lodging, it would starve and die.
ARCHBISHOP ROBERT LEIGHTON
(1611–1684)

10456 If slander be a snake, it is a winged
one—it flies as well as creeps.
DOUGLAS WILLIAM JERROLD (1803–1857)

10457 It isn't necessary to blow out the other
person's light to let your own shine.
PROVERB

10458 Never burn your fingers to snuff
another man's candle.
PROVERB

10459 Never report what may hurt another
unless it be a greater hurt to conceal it.
WILLIAM PENN (1644–1718)

10460 Never tell evil of a man if you do not
know it for a certainty, and if you
know it for a certainty, then ask yourself, "Why should I tell it?"
JOHANN KASPAR LAVATER (1741–1801)

10461 Slander flings stones at itself.
SIR THOMAS FULLER (1608–1661)

10462 Slander is a kind of murder.
SAINT FRANCIS OF SALES (1567–1622)

10463 Slander is a vice that strikes a double
blow, wounding both him that commits and him against whom it is committed.
JACQUES SAURIN (1677–1730)

10464 Slander is answered best with silence.
BEN JONSON (1572–1637)

10465 Slander is like counterfeit money:
many people who would not coin it
circulate it without qualms.
DIANE DE POITIERS

10466 Slander slays three persons: the
speaker, the spoken to, and the spoken
of.
HEBREW PROVERB

10467 Slander—whose edge is sharper than
the sword.
WILLIAM SHAKESPEARE (1564–1616)

10468 Slander: at every word a reputation
dies.
ALEXANDER POPE (1688–1744)

10469 Slanderers are the devil's bellows to
blow up contention.
PROVERB

10470 That abominable tittle-tattle,
The cud eschewed by human cattle.
LORD GEORGE NOEL GORDON BYRON
(1788–1824)

10471 The absent are always in the wrong.
ENGLISH PROVERB

10472 The most dangerous of wild beasts: a
slanderer; of tame ones: a flatterer.
GREEK PROVERB

10473 The tongue breaketh bone, though
itself have none.
PROVERB

10474 The tongue is more to be feared than
the sword.
JAPANESE PROVERB

10475 Trample not on any; there may be
some work of grace there, that you do
not know. The name of God may be
written upon that soul.
SAMUEL TAYLOR COLERIDGE (1772–1834)

10476 We cannot control the evil tongues of others; but a good life enables us to disregard them.
CATO THE ELDER (234–149 B.C.)

10477 When will talkers refrain from evil-speaking? When listeners refrain from evil-hearing.
AUGUST W. HARE (1792–1834)

10478 Whispered insinuations are the rhetoric of the devil.
JOHANN WOLFGANG VON GOETHE (1749–1832)

10479 You can't hold a man down without staying down with him.
BOOKER T. WASHINGTON (1856–1915)

10480 You cannot sink someone else's end of the boat and still keep your own afloat.
CHARLES BROWER

SLEEP

10481 Come, blessed darkness, come and bring thy balm
For eyes grown weary of the garish day!
JULIA C. R. DORR (1825–1913)

10482 It takes more than a soft pillow to insure sound sleep.

10483 It's the worry that gets you, not the loss of sleep.
DALE CARNEGIE (1888–1955)

10484 O bed! O bed! delicious bed! That heaven upon earth to the weary head.
THOMAS HOOD (1799–1845)

10485 O sleep, O gentle sleep,
Nature's soft nurse!
How have I frighted thee,
That thou no more wilt weigh my eyelids down
And steep my senses in forgetfulness?
WILLIAM SHAKESPEARE (1564–1616)

10486 Sleep is God's celestial nurse who croons away our consciousness, and God deals with the unconscious life of the soul in places where only he and his angels have charge. As you retire to rest, give your soul and God a time together, and commit your life to God with a conscious peace for the hours of sleep, and deep and profound developments will

go on in spirit, soul, and body by the kind creating hand of our God.
OSWALD CHAMBERS (1874–1917)

10487 Sleep recreates. The Bible indicates that sleep is not meant only for the recuperation of a man's body, but that there is a tremendous furtherance of spiritual and moral life during sleep.
OSWALD CHAMBERS (1874–1917)

10488 Sleep vanishes before the house of care.
ALBIUS TIBULLUS (C. 55–C. 19 B.C.)

10489 Thank God for sleep!
And, when you cannot sleep,
Still thank him that you live
To lie awake.
JOHN OXENHAM (1861–1941)

10490 Those whose spirits are stirred by the breath of the Holy Spirit go forward even in sleep.
BROTHER LAWRENCE OF THE RESURRECTION (C. 1605–1691)

10491 Tired nature's sweet restorer, balmy sleep!
EDWARD YOUNG (1683–1765)

10492 [Sleep is] so like death. I dare not trust it without my prayers.
SIR THOMAS BROWNE (1605–1682)

SMILE

10493 'Tis easy enough to be pleasant,
When life flows along like a song;
But the man worthwhile is the one who will smile
When everything goes dead wrong.
ELLA WHEELER (1855–1919)

10494 A smile costs nothing but creates much.

10495 A smile is a curve that helps to set things straight.

10496 If you meet a man who has no smile, give him yours.

10497 Most smiles are started by another smile.

10498 Nobody needs a smile as much as those who have none to give.

10499 There are a thousand languages, but a smile speaks them all.

10500 There are many kinds of smiles, each having a distinct character. Some an-

nounce goodness and sweetness, others betray sarcasm, bitterness, and pride; some soften the countenance by their languishing tenderness, others brighten by their spiritual vivacity.
JOHANN KASPAR LAVATER (1741–1801)

10501 They might not need me, yet they might.
I'll let my head be just in sight;
A smile as small as mine might be
Precisely their necessity.
EMILY ELIZABETH DICKINSON (1830–1886)

10502 Wear a smile and have friends; wear a scowl and have wrinkles.
GEORGE ELIOT (1819–1880)

SOCIETY

10503 A good many people fret themselves over the rather improbable speculation that the earth may be blown asunder by nuclear weapons. The grimmer and more immediate prospect is that men and women may be reduced to a sub-human state through limitless indulgence in their own vices—with ruinous consequences to society.
RUSSELL KIRK (1918–   )

10504 All mankind is divided into three classes: those that are immovable, those that are moveable, and those that move.
ARABIAN PROVERB

10505 Each human being is a more complex structure than any social system to which he belongs.
ALFRED NORTH WHITEHEAD (1861–1947)

10506 God has ordained three institutions for the ordering of society: the family for the propagation of life, the state for the preservation of life; and the church for the proclamation of the gospel. These are not just voluntary associations that people can join or not as they see fit; they are organic sources of authority for restraining evil and humanizing society.
CHARLES COLSON (1931–   )

10507 If all hearts were open and all desires known—as they would be if people showed their souls—how many gap-

ings, sighings, clenched fists, knotted brows, broad grins, and red eyes would we see in the marketplace!
THOMAS HARDY (1840–1928)

10508 Indeed, the times smell of sunset.
CHARLES COLSON (1931–   )

10509 It's not that we don't believe in God, we just have too many other things on our minds.
ROBERT HAROLD SCHULLER (1926–   )

10510 Men and nations sink or soar, survive or perish, as they choose to be dominated by sin or righteousness.
A. P. GOUTHEY

10511 No man is an island, entire of itself; every man is a piece of the continent, a part of the main.
JOHN DONNE (1572–1631)

10512 O wisdom of the world! and strength of the world! What are you when matched beside the foolishness and the weakness of the Christian? You are great in resources, manifold in methods, hopeful in prospects; but one thing you have not—and that is peace. You are always tumultuous, restless, apprehensive. You have nothing you can rely upon. You have no rock under your feet. The humblest, feeblest Christian has that which is impossible to you.
CARDINAL JOHN HENRY NEWMAN (1801–1890)

10513 Our civilization is based on the foundation of murder—the first civilization was founded by Cain; and civilized life is a vast, complicated, more or less gilded-over system of murder.
OSWALD CHAMBERS (1874–1917)

10514 Our society is not a community radiant with the love of Christ, but a dangerous network of domination and manipulation in which we can easily get entangled and lose our soul.
HENRI J. M. NOUWEN

10515 Silence isolates us from the crowds that love to pool their misery; an unhappy civilization is always gregarious.
ARCHBISHOP FULTON J. SHEEN (1895–1979)

10516 The custom and fashion of today will be the awkwardness and outrage of

tomorrow—so arbitrary are these transient laws.
ALEXANDRE DUMAS (1802–1870)

10517 The multitude is a fickle master.
F. W. BOREHAM

10518 The trouble with the world is that the stupid are cocksure and the intelligent full of doubt.
BERTRAND ARTHUR WILLIAM RUSSELL (1872–1970)

10519 The whole cockeyed civilization is a series of pricetags hanging out for people to read each other by.
ROSS LOCKRIDGE (1914–1948)

10520 The world is big, its troubles still bigger.
JEWISH PROVERB

10521 The world is horribly disordered and out of joint; it must come under omnipotent surgery before we can expect health.
BILLY SUNDAY (1862–1935)

10522 There are different ways of seeing the city. The statistician sees the city as a social unit, comprising so many parliamentary voters, so many town council wards, so many new housing sites, factories, industrial estates, art galleries, churches, schools. The poet sees the city as a fascinating silhouette against the sky. . . . The moralist sees the city as a microcosm of humanity. . . . When Wordsworth saw the city, he grew lyrical over it. When Carlyle saw the city, he philosophized over it. When Jesus saw the city, he wept over it.
JAMES S. STEWART (1896–)

10523 There are two large sections to society: those with more dinners than appetite, those with more appetite than dinners.
SÉBASTIEN ROCH NICOLAS CHAMFORT (1741–1794)

10524 We are moving toward a world not merely of throwaway products but throwaway friends and marriages.
ALVIN TOFFLER (1928–)

10525 We ought to seek and work for the good of our country. Sometimes we may be called upon to die for it. We are to do it gladly—as unto God. We are to be conscientious in our work as good citizens.
BILLY GRAHAM (1918–)

10526 When we lose our individual independence in the corporateness of a mass movement, we find a new freedom—freedom to hate, bully, lie, torture, murder, and betray without shame and remorse. Herein undoubtedly lies part of the attractiveness of a mass movement.
ERIC HOFFER (1902–1983)

10527 Whether you are king or subject, says Solomon, you cannot find joy in any system of civilized life, or in trade and commerce; for underneath there is a rivalry that stings and bites, and the kindest man will put his heel on his greatest friend. These are not the blind statements of a disappointed man, but statements of facts discerned by the wisest man that ever lived.
OSWALD CHAMBERS (1874–1917)

10528 While human politics is based on the premise that society must be changed in order to change people, in the politics of the kingdom it is people who must be changed in order to change society.
CHARLES COLSON (1931–)

SOLITUDE

10529 'Tis pleasant, through the loopholes of retreat,
To peep at such a world; to see the stir
Of the Great Babel, and not feel the crowd.
WILLIAM COWPER (1731–1800)

10530 'Tis solitude should teach us how to die;
It hath no flatterers; vanity can give
No hollow aid; alone—man with his God must strive.
LORD GEORGE NOEL GORDON BYRON (1788–1824)

10531 A life without a quiet center, easily becomes destructive. When we cling to the results of our actions as our only way of self-identification, then we become possessive and defensive and tend to look at our fellow human

beings more as enemies to be kept at a distance than as friends with whom we share the gifts of life.
HENRI J. M. NOUWEN

10532 Alone with God! It is there that what is hid with God is made known—God's ideals, God's hopes, God's doings.
OSWALD CHAMBERS (1874–1917)

10533 Conversation enriches the understanding, but solitude is the school of genius.
EDWARD GIBBON (1737–1794)

10534 Converse with men makes sharp the glittering wit,
But God to man doth speak in solitude.
JOHN STUART BLACKIE (1809–1895)

10535 Glorious indeed is the world of God around us, but more glorious the world of God within us. There lies the land of song; there lies the poet's native land.
HENRY WADSWORTH LONGFELLOW (1807–1882)

10536 I know that people do not want to be alone with God, but if your longing heart ever finds the living water, it will be alone.
A. W. TOZER (1897–1963)

10537 I never found the companion that was so companionable as solitude.
HENRY DAVID THOREAU (1817–1862)

10538 I weep for what I'm like when I'm alone.
THEODORE ROETHKE (1908–1963)

10539 If we possess inward solitude, we will not fear being alone, for we know that we are not alone. Neither do we fear being with others, for they do not control us. In the midst of noise and confusion we are settled into a deep inner silence.
RICHARD J. FOSTER (1942–   )

10540 In solitude, our heart can slowly take off its many protective devices and can grow so wide and deep that nothing human is strange to it. Then we can become contrite, crushed, and broken, not just by our own sins and failings, but also by the pain of our fellow human beings. Then we can give birth

to a new awareness reaching far beyond the boundaries of our human efforts. And then we who, in our fearful narrow-mindedness, were afraid that we would not have enough food for ourselves, will have to smile.
HENRI J. M. NOUWEN

10541 In solitude, when we are least alone . . .
LORD GEORGE NOEL GORDON BYRON (1788–1824)

10542 In the poverty of solitude all riches are present.
PAUL JOHANNES OSKAR TILLICH (1886–1965)

10543 It is easy in the world to live after the world's opinion; it is easy in solitude to live after your own; but the great man is he who in the midst of the crowd keeps with perfect sweetness the independence of solitude.
RALPH WALDO EMERSON (1803–1882)

10544 It is in lonely solitude that God delivers his best thoughts, and the mind needs to be still and quiet to receive them.
CHARLES R. SWINDOLL (1934–   )

10545 It is in solitude that we discover that being is more important than having, and that we are worth more than the result of our efforts. In solitude we discover that our life is not a possession to be defended, but a gift to be shared. It's there we recognize that the healing words we speak are not just our own, but are given to us; that the love we can express is part of a greater love; and that the new life we bring forth is not a property to cling to, but a gift to be received.
HENRI J. M. NOUWEN

10546 Language has created the word *loneliness* to express the pain of being alone, and the word *solitude* to express the glory of being alone.
PAUL JOHANNES OSKAR TILLICH (1886–1965)

10547 Let him who cannot be alone beware of community. . . . Let him who is not in community beware of being alone. . . . Each by itself has profound pitfalls and perils. One who wants

fellowship without solitude plunges into the void of words and feelings, and one who seeks solitude without fellowship perishes in the abyss of vanity, self-infatuation, and despair.
DIETRICH BONHOEFFER (1906–1945)

10548 Loneliness is inner emptiness. Solitude is inner fulfillment. Solitude is a state of mind and heart.
RICHARD J. FOSTER (1942–)

10549 Not till we have lost the world do we begin to find ourselves.
HENRY DAVID THOREAU (1817–1862)

10550 O solitude! Where are the charms That sages have seen in thy face?
WILLIAM COWPER (1731–1800)

10551 Our primary task in solitude is . . . to keep the eyes of our mind and heart on him who is our divine Savior. Only in the context of grace can we face our sin; only in the place of healing do we dare to show our wounds; only with a single-minded attention to Christ can we give up our clinging fears and face our own true nature. As we come to realize that it is not we who live, but Christ who lives in us, that he is our true self, we can slowly let our compulsions melt away and begin to experience the freedom of the children of God.
HENRI J. M. NOUWEN

10552 People who cannot bear to be alone are the worst company.
ALBERT GUINON

10553 Practice the art of aloneness and you will discover the treasure of tranquility. Develop the art of solitude and you will unearth the gift of serenity.
WILLIAM ARTHUR WARD (1812–1882)

10554 Shall we not shut the door against earthly noise and find that, once the noise is gone, God will roar all about us? It's the silent communion of the closet that best declares his reality.
CALVIN MILLER

10555 Solitude is bearable only with God.
ANDRÉ GIDE (1869–1951)

10556 Solitude is for me a fount of healing which makes my life worth living.

Talking is often a torment for me, and I need many days of silence to recover from the futility of words.
CARL GUSTAV JUNG (1875–1961)

10557 Solitude is often the best society.
PROVERB

10558 Solitude is the furnace of transformation.
HENRI J. M. NOUWEN

10559 Solitude is the soul's best friend.
CHARLES COTTON (1630–1687)

10560 Solitude makes us tougher toward ourselves and tender toward others; in both ways it improves our character.
FRIEDRICH WILHELM NIETZSCHE (1844–1900)

10561 Solitude molds self-righteous people into gentle, caring, forgiving persons who are so deeply convinced of their own great sinfulness and so fully aware of God's even greater mercy that their life itself becomes a ministry. In such a ministry there is hardly any difference left between doing and being. When we are filled with God's merciful presence, we can do nothing other than minister because our whole being witnesses to the light that has come into the darkness.
HENRI J. M. NOUWEN

10562 Solitude shows us the way to let our behavior be shaped, not by the compulsions of the world, but by our new mind, the mind of Christ. Silence prevents us from being suffocated by our wordy world and teaches us to speak the Word of God. Finally, unceasing prayer gives solitude and silence their real meaning. In unceasing prayer, we descend with the mind into the heart. Thus we enter through our heart into the heart of God, who embraces all of history with his eternally creative and recreative love.
HENRI J. M. NOUWEN

10563 Solitude, though it be silent as light, is like light, the mightiest of agencies.
THOMAS DE QUINCEY (1785–1859)

10564 Sometimes God thrusts us out of the crowd into a solitude we did not desire, but which nonetheless takes hold of

us. . . . He wants us to ask the question of truth that may isolate us from most men, and that can be asked only in solitude. He wants us to ask the question of justice that may bring us suffering and death . . . He wants us to break through the ordinary ways of man that may bring disrepute and hatred upon us. . . . He wants us to penetrate to the boundaries of our being, where the mystery of life appears.
PAUL JOHANNES OSKAR TILLICH (1886–1965)

10565 The desert does not mean the absence of men, it means the presence of God.
CARLO CARRETTO (1910–   )

10566 The more powerful and original a mind, the more it will incline toward the religion of solitude.
ALDOUS HUXLEY (1894–1963)

10567 The soul that has been enriched by communion with God will not be dismayed by isolation but will welcome solitude. He will seek not the crowd but the closet, and emerging will never walk alone, for he has unseen companionship.
FRANCES J. ROBERTS

10568 The soul that is growing in holiness is the least lonely when it is most alone.
FATHER ANDREW

10569 The thought,
The deadly thought of solitude.
JOHN KEATS (1795–1821)

10570 This great misfortune—to be incapable of solitude.
JEAN DE LA BRUYÈRE (1645–1696)

10571 To be alone is the fate of all great minds.
ARTHUR SCHOPENHAUER (1788–1860)

10572 To be in company, even with the best, is soon wearisome and dissipating. I love to be alone. I never found the companion that was so companionable as solitude. We are for the most part more lonely when we go abroad among men than when we stay in our chambers.
HENRY DAVID THOREAU (1817–1862)

10573 Unlovely, nay frightful, is the solitude of the soul which is without God in the world—this chill, houseless, fatherless, aimless Cain, the man who hears only the sound of his own footsteps in God's resplendent creation.
RALPH WALDO EMERSON (1803–1882)

10574 We enter the world alone, we leave it alone.
JAMES ANTHONY FROUDE (1818–1894)

10575 We have developed a phobia of being alone. We prefer the most trivial and even obnoxious company, the most meaningless activities, to being alone with ourselves; we seem to be frightened at the prospect of facing ourselves.
ERICH FROMM (1900–1980)

10576 We must show a new generation of nervous, almost frantic, Christians that power lies at the center of the life. Speed and noise are evidences of weakness, not strength. Eternity is silent, time is noisy.
A. W. TOZER (1897–1963)

10577 We're all sentenced to solitary confinement inside our own skins, for life.
TENNESSEE WILLIAMS (1914–1983)

10578 When from our better selves we have too long
Been parted by the hurrying world, and droop,
Sick of its business, of its pleasures tired,
How gracious, how benign, is solitude.
WILLIAM WORDSWORTH (1770–1850)

10579 You cannot become or remain creative without solitude.
PAUL JOHANNES OSKAR TILLICH (1886–1965)

SORROW

10580 A day of sorrow is longer than a month of joy.
CHINESE PROVERB

10581 All our winters are God's:
the winter of our sorrow,
the winter of our unhappiness,
even the winter of our discontent.
GEORGE MACDONALD (1824–1905)

10582 Be still, sad heart, and cease repining;
Behind the clouds is the sun still shining;

Thy fate is the common fate of all,
Into each life some rain must fall,
Some days must be dark and dreary.
HENRY WADSWORTH LONGFELLOW
(1807–1882)

10583 Behind joy and laughter there may be
a temperament, coarse, hard, and callous. But behind sorrow there is
always sorrow. Pain, unlike pleasure,
wears no mask.
OSCAR WILDE (1854–1900)

10584 Christ can do wonders with a broken
heart if given all the pieces.
PROVERB

10585 Come what come may;
Time and the hour runs through the
darkest day.
WILLIAM SHAKESPEARE (1564–1616)

10586 Do not cheat thy heart and tell her,
"Grief will pass away,
Hope for fairer times in future,
And forget today."
Tell her, if you will, that sorrow
Need not come in vain;
Tell her that the lesson taught her
Far outweighs the pain.
ADELAIDE ANN PROCTER (1825–1864)

10587 Do not conceal your sadness from us
under a pretended gaiety! You please
as much by your sorrow as by your
enchanting smile.
GÈRARD LABRUNIE (1808–1855)

10588 Do not rejoice at my grief, for when
mine is old, yours will be new.
SPANISH PROVERB

10589 Earth has no sorrow that heaven cannot heal.
THOMAS MOORE (1779–1852)

10590 Every heart has its own ache.
SIR THOMAS FULLER (1608–1661)

10591 God sometimes washes the eyes of his
children with tears in order that they
may read aright his providence and his
commandments.
THEODORE LEDYARD CUYLER (1822–1909)

10592 He who can look on the loveliness of
the world and share its sorrow, and
realize something of the wonder of
both, is in immediate contact with
divine things, and has got as near to
God's secret as anyone can get.
OSCAR WILDE (1854–1900)

10593 I found more joy in sorrow
Than you could find in joy.
SARA TEASDALE (1884–1933)

10594 I have taken life on the sad side, and it
has helped me to understand many,
many failures, many utter ruins.
HENRI HUVELIN (1838–1910)

10595 I love everything in life, even to be sad.
ARTHUR RUBINSTEIN (1886–1982)

10596 I walked a mile with Pleasure
She chatted all the way;
And left me none the wiser
For all she had to say.
I walked a mile with Sorrow
And ne'er a word said she;
But, oh, the things I learned from her
When Sorrow walked with me.
ROBERT BROWNING HAMILTON
(1812–1889)

10597 In every pang that rends the heart
The Man of Sorrows had a part.
MICHAEL BRUCE

10598 In the Bible, clouds are always connected with God. Clouds are those sorrows or sufferings or providences
without or within our personal lives
which seem to dispute the empire of
God. If there were no clouds we
would not need faith. Seen apart from
God, the clouds or difficulties are accidents, but by those very clouds the
Spirit of God teaches us to walk by
faith.
OSWALD CHAMBERS (1874–1917)

10599 Light cares speak; great ones are silent.
LUCIUS ANNAEUS SENECA (C. 4 B.C.–A.D. 65)

10600 My soul, thou art receiving a music lesson from thy Father. Thou art being
educated for the choir invisible. There
are parts in the symphony that none
can take but thee. Thy Father is training thee for the part the angels cannot
sing, and the school is sorrow. In the
night he is preparing thy song. In the
valley he is tuning thy voice. In the
cloud he is deepening thy chords. In
the rain he is sweetening thy melody.

In the cold he is molding thy expression.
GEORGE MATHESON (1842–1906)

10601 No matter how great a sorrow may be, God has already suffered it.
MEISTER ECKHART (C. 1260–C. 1327)

10602 No one knows the sorrows of another.
JEWISH PROVERB

10603 No one needs to be downcast, for Jesus is the joy of heaven, and it is his joy to enter into sorrowful hearts.
FREDERICK WILLIAM FABER (1814–1863)

10604 No wound, no scar? Yet, as the Master shall the servant be.
AMY CARMICHAEL (1867–1951)

10605 Not every heart that laughs is cheerful.
JEWISH PROVERB

10606 Not until each loom is silent
And the shuttles cease to fly,
Will God unroll the pattern
And explain the reason why.
The dark threads are as needful
In the Weaver's skillful hand
As the threads of gold and silver
For the pattern which he planned.

10607 One can endure sorrow alone, but it takes two to be glad.
ELBERT GREEN HUBBARD (1856–1915)

10608 Our sweetest songs are those
That tell of saddest thought.
PERCY BYSSHE SHELLEY (1792–1822)

10609 Sadness flies away on the wings of time.
JEAN DE LA FONTAINE (1621–1695)

10610 Sorrow . . . can be your servant, helping you to feel more compassion for others who hurt.
ROBERT HAROLD SCHULLER (1926–   )

10611 Sorrow is a fruit. God does not make it grow on limbs too weak to bear it.
VICTOR HUGO (1802–1885)

10612 Sorrow is a sacred thing.
WILLIAM COWPER (1731–1800)

10613 Sorrow is divine. Sorrow reigns on all the thrones of the universe and the crown of all crowns was one of thorns.
HARRIET BEECHER STOWE (1811–1896)

10614 Sorrow is knowledge.
LORD GEORGE NOEL GORDON BYRON (1788–1824)

10615 Sorrow is like a precious treasure, shown only to friends.
AFRICAN PROVERB

10616 Sorrow is our John the Baptist, clad in grim garments, with rough arms, a son of the wilderness, baptizing us with bitter tears, preaching repentance; and behind him comes the gracious, affectionate, healing Lord, speaking peace and joy to the soul.
FREDERIC DAN HUNTINGTON (1819–1904)

10617 Sorrow is the root of all virtue.
MEISTER ECKHART (C. 1260–C. 1327)

10618 Sorrow makes men sincere.
HENRY WARD BEECHER (1813–1887)

10619 Sorrow makes silence her best orator.
ENGLISH PROVERB

10620 Sorrow makes us all children again—destroys all differences of intellect.
RALPH WALDO EMERSON (1803–1882)

10621 Sorrow, like rain, makes roses and mud.
AUSTIN O'MALLEY (1858–1932)

10622 Sorrows are visitors that come without invitation.
CHARLES HADDON SPURGEON (1834–1892)

10623 Sorrows come to stretch out spaces in the heart for joy.
EDWIN MARKHAM (1852–1940)

10624 Sorrows remembered sweeten present joy.
ROBERT POLLOK (1798–1827)

10625 Tears are the showers that fertilize the world.
OWEN MEREDITH (1831–1891)

10626 The deeper that sorrow carves into your being, the more joy you can contain. Joy and sorrow are inseparable.
KAHLIL GIBRAN (1883–1931)

10627 The deeper the sorrow, the less the tongue has to say.
TALMUD

10628 The divine Alchemist can miraculously change a sorrowing heart of lead into

a golden mellowness that sings praises through tears.
S. I. McMILLEN

10629 The longest day will have an end.
PROVERB

10630 The most perfect being who has ever trod the soil of this planet was called the Man of Sorrows.
JAMES ANTHONY FROUDE (1818–1894)

10631 The soul would have no rainbow had the eye no tears.
JOHN VANCE CHENEY (1848–1922)

10632 The stars are constantly shining, but often we do not see them until the dark hours.
EARL RINEY

10633 Then sorrow, touch'd by thee, grows bright
    With more than rapture's ray;
    As darkness shows us worlds of light
    We never saw by day.
THOMAS MOORE (1779–1852)

10634 There are nettles everywhere,
    But smooth green grasses are more common still;
    The blue of heaven is larger than the cloud.
ELIZABETH BARRETT BROWNING (1806–1861)

10635 There are times when God asks nothing of his children except silence, patience, and tears.
CHARLES SEYMOUR ROBINSON (1829–1899)

10636 There can be no rainbow without a cloud and a storm.
JOHN HEYL VINCENT (1832–1920)

10637 There can be poison in the cup of sorrow, but only if we put it there ourselves.
HANNAH HURNARD (1905–1990)

10638 There is a sweet joy that comes to us through sorrow.
CHARLES HADDON SPURGEON (1834–1892)

10639 This world is so full of care and sorrow that it is a gracious debt we owe to one another to discover the bright crystals of delight hidden in somber circumstances and irksome tasks.
HELEN ADAMS KELLER (1880–1968)

10640 Through the portals of sorrow we can enter into the suffering of others. Our human compassion is kindled. Our sympathies are awakened. Grief can also help purge us of pettiness and selfishness. It can elicit from us powers of fortitude and patience.
SIDNEY GREENBERG

10641 To live through a period of stress and sorrow with another human being creates a bond which nothing seems able to break.
ELEANOR ROOSEVELT (1884–1962)

10642 We are never ripe till we have been made so by suffering.
HENRY WARD BEECHER (1813–1887)

10643 We cannot receive ourselves in success, we lose our heads; we cannot receive ourselves in monotony, we grouse; the only way we can find ourselves is in the fires of sorrow. Why it should be so I do not know, but that it is so is true not only in Scripture but in human life.
OSWALD CHAMBERS (1874–1917)

10644 What soap is for the body, tears are for the soul.
JEWISH PROVERB

10645 When some great sorrow, like a mighty river,
    Flows through your life with peace-destroying power,
    And dearest things are swept from sight forever,
    Say to your heart each trying hour:
    "This, too, shall pass away."
LANTA WILSON SMITH

10646 When sorrows come, they come not single spies,
    But in battalions.
WILLIAM SHAKESPEARE (1564–1616)

10647 When you laugh, all see; when you weep, no one sees.
YIDDISH PROVERB

10648 Where there is sorrow, there is holy ground.
OSCAR WILDE (1854–1900)

SOUL

10649 Alas! while the body stands so broad and brawny, must the soul lie blinded, dwarfed, stupefied, almost annihilated? Alas! this was a breath of God, bestowed in heaven, but on earth never to be unfolded!
THOMAS CARLYLE (1795–1881)

10650 All the money you made will never buy back your soul.
BOB DYLAN (1941–)

10651 Apart from God himself, the nearest thing to God is a human soul.
A. W. TOZER (1897–1963)

10652 Be careless in your dress if you must, but keep a tidy soul.
MARK TWAIN (1835–1910)

10653 Beware of believing that the human soul is simple, or that human life is simple. Our relationship to God in Christ is the only simple thing there is. If the devil succeeds in making this relationship complicated, then the human soul and human life will appear to be simple; whereas in reality they are far too complex for us to touch.
OSWALD CHAMBERS (1874–1917)

10654 Everything here but the soul of man is a passing shadow. The only enduring substance is within. When shall we awake to the sublime greatness, the perils, the accountableness, and the glorious destinies of the immortal soul?
WILLIAM ELLERY CHANNING (1780–1842)

10655 If the soul be lost, the man is lost.
JOHN FLAVEL (1627–1691)

10656 It is not the eye that sees the beauty of the heaven, nor the ear that hears the sweetness of music, but the soul.
JEREMY TAYLOR (1613–1667)

10657 Money is not required to buy one necessity of the soul.
HENRY DAVID THOREAU (1817–1862)

10658 Narrow is the mansion of my soul; enlarge thou it, that thou mayst enter in.
SAINT AUGUSTINE OF HIPPO (354–430)

10659 No image but the image of God can fit our soul; every other seal is too narrow, too shallow for it.
JOHN DONNE (1572–1631)

10660 Nothing presented to the soul is simple, and the soul never applies itself simply to any subject. That is why the same thing makes us laugh and cry.
BLAISE PASCAL (1623–1662)

10661 Poor intricated soul!
Riddling, perplexed, labyrinthical soul!
JOHN DONNE (1572–1631)

10662 Self is the only prison that can ever bind the soul.
HENRY VAN DYKE (1852–1933)

10663 The first string that the musician usually touches is the bass, when he intends to put all in tune. God also plays upon this string first when he sets the soul in tune for himself.
JOHN BUNYAN (1628–1688)

10664 The ground of the soul is dark.
MEISTER ECKHART (C. 1260–C. 1327)

10665 The human soul is a silent harp in God's choir whose strings need only to be swept by the divine breath to chime in with the harmonies of creation.
HENRY DAVID THOREAU (1817–1862)

10666 The human soul is God's treasury, out of which he coins unspeakable riches. Thoughts and feelings, desires and yearnings, faith and hope—these are the most precious things which God finds in us.
HENRY WARD BEECHER (1813–1887)

10667 The human soul is so mysterious that in the moment of a great tragedy men get face to face with things they never gave heed to before, and in the moment of death it is extraordinary what takes place in the human heart toward God.
OSWALD CHAMBERS (1874–1917)

10668 The problem of restoring to the world original and eternal beauty is solved by the redemption of the soul.
RALPH WALDO EMERSON (1803–1882)

10669 The production of the soul is the secret of unfathomable depth.
VICTOR HUGO (1802–1885)

10670 The soul can split the sky in two,
And let the face of God shine through.
EDNA ST. VINCENT MILLAY (1892–1950)

10671 The soul is created in a place between time and eternity; with its highest powers it touches eternity, with its lower, time.
MEISTER ECKHART (C. 1260–C. 1327)

10672 The soul is the place where man's supreme and final battles are fought.
ABRAHAM NEUMAN

10673 The soul of man is like the rolling world,
One half in day, the other dipt in night;
The one has music and the flying cloud,
The other, silence and the wakeful stars.
ALEXANDER SMITH (1830–1867)

10674 The soul unto itself
Is an imperial friend,
Or the most agonizing spy
An enemy could send.
EMILY ELIZABETH DICKINSON (1830–1886)

10675 The soul, of origin divine,
God's glorious image, freed from clay,
In heaven's eternal sphere shall shine
A star of day!
ROBERT MONTGOMERY (1807–1855)

10676 The universal language of the human soul has always been "I perish with hunger." This is what fits it for Christ. There is a grandeur in this cry from the depths, which makes its very unhappiness sublime.
JOHN DRUMMOND (1851–1897)

10677 The wealth of a soul is measured by how much it can feel; its poverty by how little.
WILLIAM ROUNSEVILLE ALGER (1822–1905)

10678 Thought is deeper than all speech,
Feeling deeper than all thought;
Souls to souls can never teach
What unto themselves was taught.
CHRISTOPHER PEARSE CRANCH
(1813–1892)

10679 To every man there openeth
A way, and ways, and a way,
The high soul climbs the high way,
The low soul gropes the low,

And in-between on the misty flats,
The rest drift to and fro.
JOHN OXENHAM (1861–1941)

10680 We take excellent care of our bodies, which we have for only a lifetime; yet we let our souls shrivel which we will have for eternity.
BILLY GRAHAM (1918–   )

SPEECH

10681 A word rashly spoken cannot be brought back by a chariot and four horses.
CHINESE PROVERB

10682 I have noticed that nothing I never said ever did me any harm.
CALVIN COOLIDGE (1872–1933)

10683 Jesus . . . says it's murder when we destroy people with our words. It's murder when we put people down and treat them as insignificant.
REBECCA MANLEY PIPPERT

10684 Man's speech is like his life.
PLATO (C. 428–348 B.C.)

10685 Mischief all comes from much opening of the mouth.
CHINESE PROVERB

10686 Nothing is said nowadays that has not been said before.
TERENCE (C. 186–C. 159 B.C.)

10687 One's eyes are what one is, one's mouth what one becomes.
JOHN GALSWORTHY (1867–1933)

10688 Speech is a mighty ruler.
LEONTINI GORGIAS (483–376 B.C.)

10689 Speech is a mirror of the soul; as a man speaks, so is he.
PUBLILIUS SYRUS (FIRST CENTURY B.C.)

10690 Speech is the index of the mind.
LUCIUS ANNAEUS SENECA (C. 4 B.C.–A.D. 65)

10691 When you have nothing to say, say nothing.
CHARLES CALEB COLTON (1780–1832)

SPIRIT

10692 God's thoughts belong to the world of spirit, man's to the world of intellect, and while spirit can embrace intellect,

the human intellect can never comprehend spirit.
A. W. TOZER (1897–1963)

10693 Great men are they who see that the spiritual is stronger than any material force.
RALPH WALDO EMERSON (1803–1882)

10694 If the spirit within us withers, so too will all the world we build around us.
THEODORE ROSZAK (1933–)

10695 The spirit always has conquered the sword.
NAPOLEON BONAPARTE (1769–1821)

10696 The spirit is an inward flame; a lamp the world blows upon but never puts out.
MARGOT ASQUITH

10697 The spirit is not a thing apart . . . it is in every thought and every word and every act.
BENJAMIN NATHAN CARDOZO (1870–1938)

SPIRITUALITY

10698 A spirituality that preaches resignation under official brutalities, servile acquiescence in frustration and sterility, and total submission to organized injustice is one which has lost interest in holiness and remains concerned only with a spurious notion of "order."
THOMAS MERTON (1915–1968)

10699 A vessel that grows as it is filled will never be full. If a bin able to hold a cartload grew while you were dumping your load in it, you could never fill it. The soul is like that: the more it wants the more it is given; the more it receives the more it grows.
MEISTER ECKHART (C. 1260–C. 1327)

10700 Every advance in spiritual life has its corresponding dangers; every step that we rise nearer God increases the depths of the gulf into which we may fall.
ROBERT H. BENSON (1871–1914)

10701 He who believes himself to be far advanced in the spiritual life has not even made a good beginning.
JEAN PIERRE CAMUS (1584–1652)

10702 If our spiritual life does not grow where we are, it will grow nowhere.
OSWALD CHAMBERS (1874–1917)

10703 If you had any idea how much inward peace you would gain for yourself, and how much joy you would bring to others, by devoting yourself single-heartedly to God, you would certainly pay more attention to your spiritual progress.
THOMAS À KEMPIS (C. 1380–1471)

10704 It is a bad thing to be satisfied spiritually.
OSWALD CHAMBERS (1874–1917)

10705 It is right that you should begin again every day. There is no better way to finish the spiritual life than to be ever beginning.
SAINT FRANCIS OF SALES (1567–1622)

10706 Live close to Me, and I will minister to you in secret and do a deep inner work veiled to the eye of man. Others may view the results, but the process will be secret.
FRANCES J. ROBERTS

10707 Many people think that a "spiritual Christian" is mystical, dreamy, impractical, and distant. When he prays, he shifts his voice into a sepulchral tone in tremolo. This kind of unctuous piety is a poor example of true spirituality. To be "spiritually minded" simply means to look at earth from heaven's point of view. The spiritually minded believer makes his decisions on the basis of eternal values and not the passing fads of society.
WARREN W. WIERSBE (1929–)

10708 Our intellect and other gifts have been given to be used for God's greater glory, but sometimes they become the very god for us. That is the saddest part: we are losing our balance when this happens. We must free ourselves to be filled by God. Even God cannot fill what is full.
MOTHER TERESA OF CALCUTTA (1910–)

10709 Spiritual maturity: the quiet confidence that God is in control.
CHARLES R. SWINDOLL (1934–)

10710 Spiritual rose bushes are not like natural rose bushes; with these latter the thorns remain but the roses pass, with the former the thorns pass and the roses remain.
SAINT FRANCIS OF SALES (1567–1622)

10711 *Spirituality* really means "Holy Spirit at work."
LEON JOSEPH SUENENS (1904–)

10712 Spiritually, we never grow old; through the passing of the years we grow so many years young. The characteristic of the spiritual life is its unaging youth, exactly the opposite of the natural life.
OSWALD CHAMBERS (1874–1917)

10713 The concept of spirituality varies among different Christian groups. In some circles the highly vocal person who talks religion continually is thought to be very spiritual; others accept noisy exuberance as a mark of spirituality, and in some churches the man who prays first, longest, and loudest gets a reputation for being the most spiritual man in the assembly.
A. W. TOZER (1897–1963)

10714 The fruits of the Spirit are nothing but the virtues of Christ.
FRIEDRICH ERNST DANIEL SCHLEIERMACHER (1768–1834)

10715 The life of obedience to Jesus Christ means living moment by moment in the Spirit of God, and it will be so different from your former life that you will often be considered strange. In fact, the life in the Spirit is such a different life that some of your former associates will probably discuss the question of whether or not you are mentally disturbed.
A. W. TOZER (1897–1963)

10716 There are not three stages in spiritual life—worship, waiting, and work. Some of us go in jumps like spiritual frogs. We jump from worship to waiting, and from waiting to work. God's idea is that the three should go together. They were always together in the life of our Lord.
OSWALD CHAMBERS (1874–1917)

10717 To put sin out of the life, or to live a separated life, are humanly impossible tasks. That is the work of the Spirit. It is not a matter of human repression of sin, but of divine expulsion.
KENNETH WUEST

10718 True spirituality is as rare as true bestiality in human beings. And those few who achieve it are those who are terribly aware of the perils of spirituality—who know, as the Romans warned us, that a corruption of the best becomes the worst.
SYDNEY J. HARRIS (1917–1986)

10719 True spirituality manifests itself in:
1. The desire to be holy rather than happy.
2. The desire to see the honor of God advanced through his life.
3. The desire to carry his cross.
4. The desire to see everything from God's viewpoint.
5. The desire to die right rather than live wrong.
6. The desire to see others advance at his expense.
7. The desire to make eternity-judgments instead of time-judgments.
A. W. TOZER (1897–1963)

10720 We often put a false barrier between what we call the secular and the sacred, limiting the way that God can touch us and express himself through us.
TIM HANSEL

10721 What we call crises, God ignores; and what God reveals as the great critical moments of a man's life, we look on as humdrum commonplaces. When we become spiritual, we discern that God was in the humdrum commonplace and we never knew it.
OSWALD CHAMBERS (1874–1917)

10722 When a little child becomes conscious of being a little child, the childlikeness is gone; and when a saint becomes conscious of being a saint, something has gone wrong.
OSWALD CHAMBERS (1874–1917)

10723 You can't catch the wind in a net.
CHARLES HADDON SPURGEON (1834–1892)

STEWARDSHIP

10724 All you are unable to give possesses
you.
ANDRÉ GIDE (1869–1951)

10725 As we give, we live.
SIDNEY GREENBERG

10726 Giving is the highest expression of
potency.
ERICH FROMM (1900–1980)

10727 Giving is the secret of a healthy life.
Not necessarily money, but whatever a
man has of encouragement and sympathy and understanding.
JOHN D. ROCKEFELLER, JR. (1874–1960)

10728 Go break to the needy sweet charity's
bread;
"For giving is living," the angel said.
"And must I be giving again and
again?"
My peevish and pitiless answer ran.
"Oh no," said the angel, piercing me
through,
"Just give till the Master stops giving
to you."

10729 God has given us two hands—one to
receive with and the other to give
with. We are not cisterns made for
hoarding; we are channels made for
sharing.
BILLY GRAHAM (1918–)

10730 God will not merely judge us on the
basis of what we gave but also on the
basis of what we did with what we
kept for ourselves.
ERWIN W. LUTZER (1941–)

10731 Have you ever stopped to think that
Christ never gave anyone money? The
riches of the world were his for the
taking and his to give away, yet when
the poor and the hungry came to him,
he didn't give them money, and he
rarely gave them food; he gave them
love and service and the greatest gift
of all—himself.

10732 It is not what we take up, but what we
give up that makes us rich.
HENRY WARD BEECHER (1813–1887)

10733 More important than length of life is
how we spend each day.
MARIA A. FURTADO

10734 The only safe rule is to give more than
we can spare. Our charities should
pinch and hamper us. If we live at the
same level of affluence as other people
who have our level of income, we are
probably giving away too little.
C. S. LEWIS (1898–1963)

10735 The world asks, "How much does he
give?" Christ asks, "Why does he
give?"
JOHN RALEIGH MOTT (1865–1955)

10736 There are three kinds of giving: grudge
giving, duty giving, and thanksgiving.
Grudge giving says, "I hate to," duty
giving says, "I ought to," thanksgiving
says, "I want to." The first comes
from constraint, the second from a
sense of obligation, the third from a
full heart. Nothing much is conveyed
in grudge giving since "the gift without the giver is bare." Something more
happens in duty giving, but there is no
song in it. Thanksgiving is an open
gate into the love of God.
ROBERT N. RODENMAYER

10737 There is no portion of our time that is
our time, and the rest God's; there is
no portion of money that is our
money, and the rest God's money. It is
all his; he made it all, gives it all, and
he has simply trusted it to us for his
service. A servant has two purses, the
master's and his own, but we have
only one.
ADOLPHE MONOD (1800–1856)

10738 Those who give much without sacrifice are reckoned as having given little;
those who give from all their living are
reckoned as having given much. Without that basic understanding, we've
missed the purpose of giving—and
we've missed it by a mile.
ERWIN W. LUTZER (1941–)

10739 Unless you and I commit ourselves to
concrete plans for increasing our giving, I'm afraid God will come one day
and find that we have all died from
suffocating luxury.
EVA DEN HARTOG

10740 Use everything as if it belongs to God.
It does. You are his steward.

10741 We make a living by what we get, but we make a life by what we give.
SIR WINSTON CHURCHILL (1874–1965)

10742 What you give to humanity you get back. Bread cast upon the waters is much more wholesome and nourishing than pie in the sky.
MELVIN JONES (1879–1961)

10743 Whoever is capable of giving is rich.
ERICH FROMM (1900–1980)

STRENGTH

10744 A chain is no stronger than its weakest link.
PROVERB

10745 God . . . is not in the business of helping the humanly strong become stronger; rather he takes the weak and makes them strong in himself.
ERWIN W. LUTZER (1941–)

10746 God gives the shoulder according to the burden.
GERMAN PROVERB

10747 I am not in the whirlwind of activity, but in the still, small voice of communion. Find it, my child, and hold to it, and you will be energized.
FRANCES J. ROBERTS

10748 It is a sign of strength, not of weakness, to admit that you don't know all the answers.
JOHN P. LOUGHRANE

10749 Knowing your own strength is a fine thing. Recognizing your own weakness is even better. What is really bad, what hurts and finally defeats us, is mistaking a weakness for a strength.
SYDNEY J. HARRIS (1917–1986)

10750 Natural strength is often as great a handicap as natural weakness.
HANNAH HURNARD (1905–1990)

10751 No power on earth or in hell can conquer the Spirit of God in a human spirit, it is an inner unconquerableness. If you have the whine in you, kick it out ruthlessly. It is a positive crime to be weak in God's strength.
OSWALD CHAMBERS (1874–1917)

10752 Nothing is so strong as gentleness; nothing so gentle as real strength.
SAINT FRANCIS OF SALES (1567–1622)

10753 O, it is excellent
To have a giant's strength; but it is tyrannous
To use it like a giant.
WILLIAM SHAKESPEARE (1564–1616)

10754 Obstacles in the pathway of the weak become stepping-stones in the pathway of the strong.
THOMAS CARLYLE (1795–1881)

10755 Our strength grows out of our weakness.
RALPH WALDO EMERSON (1803–1882)

10756 So let it be in God's own might
We gird us for the coming fight,
And, strong in him whose cause is ours,
In conflict with unholy powers,
We grasp the weapons he has given,
The light and truth and love of heaven.
JOHN GREENLEAF WHITTIER (1807–1892)

10757 Strenuousness is the open foe of attainment. The strength that wins is calm and has an exhaustless source in its passive depths.
SIR RABINDRANATH TAGORE (1861–1941)

10758 The Lord doesn't promise to give us something to take so we can handle our weary moments. He promises us himself. That is all. And that is enough.
CHARLES R. SWINDOLL (1934–)

10759 The strongest man in the world is he who stands most alone.
HENRIK IBSEN (1828–1906)

10760 The thing we have to watch most of all is our strength, our strong point. We all tend to fail ultimately at our strong point.
D. MARTYN LLOYD-JONES (1899–1981)

10761 The weaker we feel, the harder we lean on God. And the harder we lean, the stronger we grow.
JONI EARECKSON TADA

10762 There is no merit where there is no trial; and until experience stamps the mark of strength, cowards may pass for heroes, and faith for falsehood.
AARON HILL (1685–1750)

10763 Three things sap a man's strength: worry, travel, and sin.
JEWISH PROVERB

10764 They that wait upon the Lord renew their strength. They that wait upon men dissipate their energies.
LEONARD RAVENHILL (1867–1942)

10765 Unguarded strength is double weakness.
OSWALD CHAMBERS (1874–1917)

10766 When a man has no strength, if he leans on God, he becomes powerful.
DWIGHT LYMAN MOODY (1837–1899)

10767 When God is our strength, it is strength indeed; when our strength is our own, it is only weakness.
SAINT AUGUSTINE OF HIPPO (354–430)

10768 When God wants to move a mountain, he does not take a bar of iron, but he takes a little worm. The fact is, we have too much strength. We are not weak enough. It is not our strength that we want. One drop of God's strength is worth more than all the world.
DWIGHT LYMAN MOODY (1837–1899)

10769 You become stronger only when you become weaker. When you surrender your will to God, you discover the resources to do what God requires.
ERWIN W. LUTZER (1941–   )

STUBBORNNESS

10770 None so deaf as those who will not hear.
MATTHEW HENRY (1662–1714)

10771 God's will is hard only when it comes up against our stubbornness, then it is as cruel as a ploughshare and as devastating as an earthquake.
OSWALD CHAMBERS (1874–1917)

10772 She is so determined to get her own way she writes her diary in advance.

10773 The difference between perseverance and obstinacy is that one comes from a strong will, and the other from a strong won't.
HENRY WARD BEECHER (1813–1887)

10774 The three most intractable beasts: the owl, the serpent, and the people.
DEMOSTHENES (384–322 B.C.)

SUCCESS

10775 'Tis man's to fight, but heaven's to give success.
HOMER (C. EIGHTH CENTURY B.C.)

10776 A great many people go through life in bondage to success. They are in mortal dread of failure. I do not have to succeed. I have only to be true to the highest I know—success or failure are in the hands of God.
E. STANLEY JONES (1884–1973)

10777 Better to love God and die unknown than to love the world and be a hero; better to be content with poverty than to die a slave to wealth; better to have taken some risks and lost than to have done nothing and succeeded at it; better to have lost some battles than to have retreated from the war; better to have failed when serving God than to have succeeded when serving the devil. What a tragedy to climb the ladder of success, only to discover that the ladder was leaning against the wrong wall!
ERWIN W. LUTZER (1941–   )

10778 Doing God's will may not always lead to increased popularity, sales, and profits. It didn't in Bible days.
LLOYD CORY

10779 God has not called me to be successful; he has called me to be faithful.
MOTHER TERESA OF CALCUTTA (1910–   )

10780 Have a sincere desire to serve God and mankind, and stop doubting, stop thinking negatively. . . . Simply start living by faith, pray earnestly and humbly, and get into the habit of looking expectantly for the best. . . . When you live on a faith basis, your desire will be only for that which you can ask in God's name. By success, of course, I do not mean that you may become rich, famous, or powerful.
NORMAN VINCENT PEALE (1898–   )

10781 He has achieved success who has lived well, laughed often, and loved much.
BESSIE ANDERSON STANLEY (1879–   )

10782 He who would climb the ladder must begin at the bottom.
ENGLISH PROVERB

10783 How can you say my life is not a success? Have I not for more than sixty years got enough to eat and escaped being eaten?
LOGAN PEARSALL SMITH (1865–1946)

10784 I find praise very embarrassing. Was it not opposition and even persecution that Jesus promised to his disciples?
PAUL TOURNIER (1898–1986)

10785 If A is success in life, then A equals X plus Y plus Z. Work is X, Y is play, and Z is keeping your mouth shut.
ALBERT EINSTEIN (1879–1955)

10786 If I'm such a legend, then why am I so lonely? . . . Let me tell you, legends are all very well if you've got somebody around who loves you.
JUDY GARLAND (1922–1969)

10787 If you wish to travel far and fast, travel light. Take off all your envies, jealousies, unforgiveness, selfishness, and fears.
GLENN CLARK

10788 It is always easy to covet another man's success without envying his labors.

10789 It is the man who has stuck true to God and damned the consequences who will come out the best; whether he has made the best or the worst of himself in this life is another matter.
OSWALD CHAMBERS (1874–1917)

10790 It takes twenty years to be an overnight success.
EDDIE CANTOR (1892–1964)

10791 Let us work as if success depended upon ourselves alone; but with heartfelt conviction that we are doing nothing and God everything.
SAINT IGNATIUS OF LOYOLA (1491–1556)

10792 Most of the shadows of this life are caused by standing in one's own sunshine.
RALPH WALDO EMERSON (1803–1882)

10793 Nature gave men two ends—one to sit on and one to think with. Ever since then man's success or failure has been dependent on the one he uses most.
GEORGE R. KIRKPATRICK (1867–1937)

10794 Not in the clamor of the crowded street,
Not in the shouts and plaudits of the throng,
But in ourselves are triumph and defeat.
HENRY WADSWORTH LONGFELLOW (1807–1882)

10795 Nothing fails like success because we don't learn from it. We learn only from failure.
KENNETH BOULDING

10796 Nothing good is failure and no evil thing success.
PROVERB

10797 Nothing is impossible to the willing heart.
THOMAS HEYWOOD (C. 1574–1641)

10798 Nothing recedes like success.
WALTER WINCHELL (1897–1972)

10799 Six essential qualities that are the key to success: sincerity, personal integrity, humility, courtesy, wisdom, charity.
WILLIAM MENNINGER

10800 Small numbers make no difference to God. There is nothing small if God is in it.
DWIGHT LYMAN MOODY (1837–1899)

10801 Success . . . demands strange sacrifices from those who worship her.
ALDOUS HUXLEY (1894–1963)

10802 Success comes to those who are neither afraid to fail nor discouraged by failures.
PROVERB

10803 Success consecrates the foulest crimes.
LUCIUS ANNAEUS SENECA (C. 4 B.C.–A.D. 65)

10804 Success consists of getting up more times than you fall.
OLIVER GOLDSMITH (1730–1774)

10805 Success in life depends upon the three I's: integrity, intelligence, and industry.
CHARLES RUPERT STOCKARD (1879–1939)

10806 Success is failure turned inside out.

10807 Success is neither fame, wealth, nor power; rather it is seeking, knowing, loving, and obeying God. If you seek, you will know; if you know, you will love; if you love, you will obey.
CHARLES HABIB MALIK (1906–)

10808 Success is to be measured, not by wealth, power, or fame, but by the ratio between what a man is and what he might be.
H. G. WELLS (1866–1946)

10809 Success is to be measured not so much by the position that one has reached in life as by the obstacles that he has overcome while trying to succeed.
BOOKER T. WASHINGTON (1856–1915)

10810 Success, a sort of suicide, is ruin'd by success.
EDWARD YOUNG (1683–1765)

10811 Success—for the glory of God or for your own, for the peace of mankind or for your own?
DAG HAMMARSKJÖLD (1905–1961)

10812 Successful people are those who apply God's remedy for failure.
ERWIN W. LUTZER (1941–)

10813 Sum up the life of Jesus Christ by any other standard than God's, and it is an anticlimax of failure.
OSWALD CHAMBERS (1874–1917)

10814 The figure of the Crucified invalidates all thought which takes success for its standard.
DIETRICH BONHOEFFER (1906–1945)

10815 The measure of our success will be the measure of our ability to help others.
F. B. MEYER (1847–1929)

10816 The men I have seen succeed have always been cheerful and hopeful, who went about their business with a smile on their faces, and took the changes and chance of this mortal life like men. . . . If you wish to be miserable, you must think about yourself; about what you want, what you like, what respect people ought to pay you, what people think of you, and then to you nothing will be pure. You will spoil everything you touch; you will make sin and misery out of everything God sends you; you can be as wretched as you choose.
CHARLES KINGSLEY (1819–1875)

10817 The real demon is success—the anxieties engendered by this quest are relentless, degrading, corroding. What is worse, there is no end to this escalation of desire.
MARY MANNES (1904–)

10818 The secret of success is to do all you can without thought of fame.
PROVERB

10819 The very qualities that have led to man's extraordinary capacity for success are also those most likely to destroy him.
ANTHONY STORR (1920–)

10820 Three qualities vital to success: toil, solitude, prayer.
CARL SANDBURG (1878–1967)

10821 To find his place and fill it is success for a man.
PHILLIPS BROOKS (1835–1893)

10822 To follow, without halt, one aim: there's the secret of success.
ANNA PAVLOVA (1882–1931)

10823 We are not called to be successful in accordance with ordinary standards, but in accordance with a corn of wheat falling into the ground and dying, becoming in that way what it never could be if it were to abide alone.
OSWALD CHAMBERS (1874–1917)

10824 We have nothing whatever to do with what men call success or failure. If God's command is clear, and the constraint of his Spirit is clear, we have nothing to do with the result of our obedience.
OSWALD CHAMBERS (1874–1917)

10825 When I was young, I observed that nine out of every ten things I did were failures, so I did ten times more work.
GEORGE BERNARD SHAW (1856–1950)

10826 When success turns a man's head, he faces failure.
PROVERB

10827 Why should we be in such a desperate haste to succeed and in such desperate enterprises? If a man does not keep

pace with his companions, perhaps it is because he hears a different drummer. Let him step to the music which he hears, however measured or far away.
HENRY DAVID THOREAU (1817–1862)

10828 You don't have to lie awake nights to succeed—just stay awake days.

10829 Your success and happiness lie in you. External conditions are the accidents of life. The great enduring realities are love and service. Joy is the holy fire that keeps our purpose warm and our intelligence aglow. Resolve to keep happy, and your joy and you shall form an invincible host against difficulty.
HELEN ADAMS KELLER (1880–1968)

SUFFERING

10830 A deep distress has humanized my soul.
WILLIAM WORDSWORTH (1770–1850)

10831 A man who fears suffering is already suffering from what he fears.
MICHEL EYQUEM DE MONTAIGNE (1533–1592)

10832 A man who has not suffered, what does he know?
HENRY SUSO (1295–1366)

10833 Accept suffering graciously. When you have reached such a point, all misery will seem sweet and you will relish it for Christ's sake and think that you have discovered paradise on earth. As long as you object to suffering you will be ill at ease. Accept it, and you will find peace.
THOMAS À KEMPIS (C. 1380–1471)

10834 Affliction can be a treasure. Absolutely functional, it triggers life's greatest insights and accomplishments.
FRED GREVE

10835 All thought worth thinking is conceived in the furnace of suffering.
THOMAS CARLYLE (1795–1881)

10836 Are you laying a featherbed for me, No that shall not be;

My Lord was stretched on a hard and painful tree.
SAINT LAWRENCE (C. 258)

10837 Be still, my soul: the Lord is on thy side; Bear patiently the cross of grief or pain; Leave to thy God to order and provide; In every change he faithful will remain.
KATHARINA VON SCHLEGEL

10838 Better to suffer ill, than do ill.
PROVERB

10839 Even as Christ suffers watching our suffering, this price is his price. He's willing to pay to have us desire to be close to him. Willingly he loses us until we find him.
MARGUERITE REISS

10840 Every invalid is a physician.
IRISH PROVERB

10841 Faith in immortality, like belief in God, leaves unanswered the ancient question: Is God unable to prevent suffering, and thus not omnipotent? Or is he able and not willing and thus not merciful? And is he just?
WALTER KAUFMANN (1921–1980)

10842 Flee a thousand leagues from saying, "I was in the right. It was not right for me to suffer this. They had no right to treat me so." God deliver us from all such rights. And when we receive honors, or affection, or kind treatment, let us ask what right we have to them.
SAINT TERESA OF AVILA (1515–1582)

10843 God had one Son on earth without sin, but never one without suffering.
SAINT AUGUSTINE OF HIPPO (354–430)

10844 God is a Master Artist. And there are aspects of your life and character—good, quality things—he wants others to notice. So without using blatant tricks or obvious gimmicks, God brings the cool, dark contrast of suffering into your life. That contrast, laid up against the golden character of Christ within you, will draw attention . . . to him. Light against darkness. Beauty against affliction. Joy against sorrow. A sweet, patient spirit against pain and disappointment—major contrasts that have a way of attracting notice. You are the canvas on which

he paints glorious truths, sharing beauty, and inspiring others. So that people might see him.
JONI EARECKSON TADA

10845 God is a specialist when the anguish is deep. His ability to heal the soul is profound . . . but only those who rely on his wounded Son will experience relief.
CHARLES R. SWINDOLL (1934–)

10846 God will not look you over for medals, degrees, or diplomas, but for scars.
ELBERT GREEN HUBBARD (1856–1915)

10847 God's wisest saints are often people who endure pain rather than escape it.
CHARLES R. SWINDOLL (1934–)

10848 Great souls suffer in silence.
JOHANN FRIEDRICH VON SCHILLER (1759–1805)

10849 Great sufferers do the world's work; a crown of loftiest achievement is a crown of thorns like our Savior's.
THEODORE HERMAN EPP (1907–1985)

10850 He jests at scars that never felt a wound.
WILLIAM SHAKESPEARE (1564–1616)

10851 He who knows how to suffer will enjoy much peace. Such a one is a conqueror of himself and lord of the world, a friend of Christ and an heir of heaven.
THOMAS À KEMPIS (C. 1380–1471)

10852 He who suffers much will know much.
GREEK PROVERB

10853 I can look back at my darkest periods and realize that these were the times when the Lord was holding me closest. But I couldn't see his face because my face was in his breast—crying.
JOHN MICHAEL TALBOT

10854 I love the majesty of human suffering.
ALFRED DE VIGNY (1797–1863)

10855 I owe more to the fire and the hammer and the file than to anything else in my Lord's workshop. I sometimes question whether I have ever learned anything except through the rod. When my schoolroom is darkened, I see most.
CHARLES HADDON SPURGEON (1834–1892)

10856 If God has let you suffer, it is because he sees something good in it.
POPE JOHN PAUL II (1920–)

10857 In suffering one learns to pray best of all.
HAROLD A. BOSLEY (1907–1975)

10858 It is by those who have suffered that the world has been advanced.
LEO TOLSTOY (1828–1910)

10859 It is infinitely easier to suffer with others than to suffer alone. It is infinitely easier to suffer as public heroes than to suffer apart and in ignominy. It is infinitely easier to suffer physical death than to endure spiritual suffering.
DIETRICH BONHOEFFER (1906–1945)

10860 It is nonsense to say that suffering makes saints, it makes some people devils.
OSWALD CHAMBERS (1874–1917)

10861 It is not miserable to be blind; it is miserable to be incapable of enduring blindness.
JOHN MILTON (1608–1674)

10862 It is remarkable with what Christian fortitude and resignation we can bear the suffering of other folks.
JONATHAN SWIFT (1667–1745)

10863 It is suffering and then glory. Not to have the suffering means not to have the glory.
ROBERT CRAWFORD MCQUILKIN (1886–1952)

10864 It is the fire of suffering which will bring forth the gold of godliness.
MADAME JEANNE MARIE DE LA MOTHE GUYON (1648–1717)

10865 It requires more courage to suffer than to die.
NAPOLEON BONAPARTE (1769–1821)

10866 Its way of suffering is the witness which a soul bears to itself.
HENRI FRÉDÉRIC AMIEL (1821–1881)

10867 Jesus did not come to explain away suffering or remove it. He came to fill it with his presence.
PAUL CLAUDEL (1868–1955)

10868 Jesus refuses to swallow the drugged drink normally provided as an act of

compassion to those about to be crucified; he has to be aware of his suffering. His supreme sacrifice, to be valid, must be conscious.
MALCOLM MUGGERIDGE (1903–1990)

10869 Know how sublime a thing it is
To suffer and be strong.
HENRY WADSWORTH LONGFELLOW
(1807–1882)

10870 Knowledge by suffering entereth,
And life is perfected by death.
ELIZABETH BARRETT BROWNING
(1806–1861)

10871 Man can endure almost any suffering if he can see a purpose or meaning in it. Conversely, he will be miserable even amidst great luxury if he cannot relate his life to some larger context which makes it meaningful.
VIKTOR E. FRANKL (B. 1905)

10872 Man, if you only knew the worth of suffering,
You would have chosen it ahead of anything.
ANGELUS SILESIUS (1624–1677)

10873 My life is one great suffering, unknown and incomprehensible to all others.
SØREN AABYE KIERKEGAARD (1813–1855)

10874 No one truly knows happiness who has not suffered.
HENRI FRÉDÉRIC AMIEL (1821–1881)

10875 Nothing great is done without suffering, without humiliation . . . I believe, O my God, that poverty is better than riches, pain better than pleasure, obscurity and contempt better than name, and ignominy and reproach better than honor.
I will never have faith in riches, rank, power, or reputation. I will never set my heart on worldly success or on worldly advantages. I will never wish for what men call the prizes of life.
CARDINAL JOHN HENRY NEWMAN
(1801–1890)

10876 O God, Creator of mankind, I do not aspire to comprehend you or your creation, nor to understand pain or suffering. I aspire only to relieve the pain and suffering of others, and I trust in doing so I may understand more clearly your nature, that you are the Father of all mankind, and that the hairs of my head are numbered.
SAINT FRANCIS OF ASSISI (C. 1181–1226)

10877 O God, men think the heroes of tragedy great, and they admire them. But Abraham's contemporaries could not understand him. What then did he achieve? That he was true to his love. And he who loves God has no need of admiration, no need that others weep for him. He forgets his suffering in love, forgets it so thoroughly that no one even suspects his pain except thee, O God, who sees in secret, and knows the need, and counts the tears, forgetting nothing.
SØREN AABYE KIERKEGAARD (1813–1855)

10878 O God, thy world is dark! The music of the spheres
Is made of sighs and sobs no less than songs, I think.
Man is an atom lost in an endless vale of tears,
A night wherein the good rise and the wicked sink.
VICTOR HUGO (1802–1885)

10879 Oft the cloud which wraps the present hour,
Serves but to brighten all our future days!
JOHN BROWN (1715–1766)

10880 Only Christianity has taught us the true peace and function of suffering. The Stoics tried the hopeless little game of denying its objective reality, or of declaring it a good in itself (which it never is). And the Pessimists attempted to revel in it, as a good to their melancholy, and as something that can no more be transformed than it can be avoided or explained. But Christ came, and he did not really explain it: he did far more. He met it, willed it, transformed it, and he taught us how to do all this, or rather he himself does it through us if we do not hinder the all-healing hands.
BARON FRIEDRICH VON HUGEL
(1852–1925)

10881 Our blood and tears are the oil of the lamp that the Lord makes us carry before the human race.
ALPHONSE-MARIE-LOUIS DE PRAT DE LAMARTINE (1790–1869)

10882 Out of suffering have emerged the strongest souls; the most massive characters are seamed with scars; martyrs have put on their coronation robes glittering with fire, and through their tears have the sorrowful first seen the gates of heaven.
EDWIN HUBBEL CHAPIN (1814–1880)

10883 Pearls are the product of pain . . . a precious, tiny jewel conceived through irritation, born of adversity, nursed by adjustments. Some oysters are never wounded . . . and those who seek for gems toss them aside, fit only for stew.
CHARLES R. SWINDOLL (1934–)

10884 Perhaps we are in a larger process of maturing than we can see from our limited and materialist immersion in our tiny worlds. And if God is in the business of creating a family of sons and daughters who are to have the kind of sensitive wisdom and loving-kindness which can enter men's suffering with them, maybe firsthand experience of evil, of sickness, death, are in some way necessary for all of us Christians.
KEITH MILLER

10885 Remember this: all suffering comes to an end. And whatever you suffer authentically, God has suffered from it first.
MEISTER ECKHART (C. 1260–C. 1327)

10886 Silence in times of suffering is the best.
JOHN DRYDEN (1631–1700)

10887 Sometimes the greatest sermon is silence. A suffering person doesn't need a lecture, he needs a listener.
BILLY GRAHAM (1918–)

10888 Suffering "according to the will of God" raises us to a freedom and felicity that baffles all language to express. The only sufficient language is the language of Scripture.
OSWALD CHAMBERS (1874–1917)

10889 Suffering . . . no matter how multiplied is always individual.
ANNE MORROW LINDBERGH (1906–)

10890 Suffering disappears, but the fact of having suffered remains always with us.
LÉON HENRI MARIE BLOY (1846–1917)

10891 Suffering is . . . an opportunity to experience evil and change it into good.
SAUL BELLOW (1915–)

10892 Suffering is a cleansing fire that clears away triviality and restlessness.
LOUIS E. BISCH

10893 Suffering is a revelation. One discovers things one never discovered before.
OSCAR WILDE (1854–1900)

10894 Suffering is the very best gift God has to give us. He gives it only to his chosen friends.
THERESE OF LISIEUX (1873–1897)

10895 Suffering is too precious to be shared.
EDWARD DAHLBERG

10896 Suffering was a curse from which man fled; now it becomes a purification of the soul, a sacred trial sent by eternal love, a divine dispensation meant to sanctify and ennoble us, an acceptable aid to faith, a strange initiation into happiness.
HENRI FRÉDÉRIC AMIEL (1821–1881)

10897 Suffering, and the inevitable result of suffering, is the only way some of us can learn, and if we are shielded, God will ultimately take the one who interferes by the scruff of the neck and remove him. The fingers that caress a child may also hurt its flesh; it is the power of love that makes them hurt.
OSWALD CHAMBERS (1874–1917)

10898 Supposing you eliminated suffering, what a dreadful place the world would be! I would almost rather eliminate happiness. The world would be the most ghastly place because everything that corrects the tendency of this unspeakable little creature, man, to feel over-important and over-pleased with himself would disappear. He's bad enough now, but he would be

absolutely intolerable if he never suffered. However, we needn't fear that.
MALCOLM MUGGERIDGE (1903–1990)

10899 The avoidance of legitimate suffering means we also avoid the growth that problems demand of us.
CHARLES R. SWINDOLL (1934–)

10900 The door of suffering is wide.
ARABIAN PROVERB

10901 The first thing that Jesus promises is suffering: "I tell you . . . you will be weeping and wailing . . . and you will be sorrowful." But he calls these pains birth pains. And so, what seems a hindrance becomes a way; what seems an obstacle becomes a door; and what seems a misfit becomes a cornerstone. Jesus changes our history from a random series of sad incidents and accidents into a constant opportunity for a change of heart.
HENRI J. M. NOUWEN

10902 The language of heartbreak is not learned in the schools of men but in the furnace of suffering and the crucible of trouble.
VANCE HAVNER

10903 The man who has not tasted the bitter does not know what the sweet is.
JEWISH PROVERB

10904 The more a man loves, the more he suffers.
HENRI FRÉDÉRIC AMIEL (1821–1881)

10905 The only cure for suffering is to face it head on, grasp it round the neck, and use it.
MARY CRAIG (1928–)

10906 The pain of life best buys for us that intimacy with Christ that money is powerless to purchase.
CALVIN MILLER

10907 The peace and joy that belong to deepest suffering are the miracles of faith.
RALPH WALDO EMERSON (1803–1882)

10908 The picture of God in the Bible is of one who suffers, and when the mask is torn off life and we see all its profound and vast misery, the suffering,

sorrowing God is the only one who does not mock us.
OSWALD CHAMBERS (1874–1917)

10909 The real problem is not why some pious, humble, believing people suffer, but why some do not.
C. S. LEWIS (1898–1963)

10910 The saint knows not why he suffers as he does, yet he comprehends with a knowledge that passes knowledge that all is well.
OSWALD CHAMBERS (1874–1917)

10911 The self-centered suffer when others disappoint them. The Christ-centered suffer when they disappoint others.
LEONARD RAVENHILL (1867–1942)

10912 The suffering of man is also the suffering of God.
PAUL TOURNIER (1898–1986)

10913 The "bundle of myrrh" in its bitterness, represents the suffering the Bride will have to endure for the Beloved's sake. Since my conversion I have always gathered this little bouquet of myrrh from among my Lord's persecution and suffering. I pick them from . . . his travel fatigue, his prayers in the night, his temptations when he fasted, his sympathetic tears, the tricks of those who tried to catch them in the things he said. . . . There is wisdom in meditating on these things. When I face adversity, they give me strength. When everything is going well, they keep my perspective in balance.
BERNARD OF CLAIRVAUX (1090–1153)

10914 There are comforts and compensations that one who has not suffered knows nothing of—like the lamps that nobody sees till the tunnel comes.
A. W. BARBOUR

10915 There are those who suffer greatly, and yet, through the recognition that pain can be a thread in the pattern of God's weaving, find the way to a fundamental joy.
ELIZABETH GOUDGE

10916 Those things that hurt, instruct.
BENJAMIN FRANKLIN (1706–1790)

10917 To "suffer as a Christian" is not to be marked peculiar because of your views, or because you will not bend to conventionality; these things are not Christian but ordinary human traits from which all men suffer irrespective of creed or religion or no religion. To "suffer as a Christian" is to suffer because there is an essential difference between you and the world which rouses the contempt of the world and the disgust and hatred of the spirit that is in the world. To "suffer as a Christian" is to have no answer when the world's satire is turned on you, as it was turned on Jesus Christ when he hung upon the cross, when they turned his words into jest and jeer; they will do the same to you. He gave no answer, neither can you.
OSWALD CHAMBERS (1874–1917)

10918 To be able to explain suffering is the clearest indication of never having suffered.
OSWALD CHAMBERS (1874–1917)

10919 Unearned suffering is redemptive.
MARTIN LUTHER KING, JR. (1929–1968)

10920 We all know people who have been made much meaner and more irritable and more intolerable to live with by suffering; it is not right to say that all suffering perfects. It only perfects one type of person—the one who accepts the call of God in Christ Jesus.
OSWALD CHAMBERS (1874–1917)

10921 We are healed of a suffering only by experiencing it to the full.
MARCEL PROUST (1871–1922)

10922 We look on the woes of the world. We hear the whole creation, to use Paul's language, groaning and laboring in pain. We see a few good men vainly striving to help the world into life and light; and in our sense of the awful magnitude of the problem and of our inability to do much, we cry out: "Where's God? How can he bear this? Why doesn't he do something?" And there is but one answer that satisfies: and that is the Incarnation and the Cross. God could not bear it. He has done something. He has done the utmost compatible with moral wisdom. He has entered into the fellowship of our suffering and misery and at infinite cost has taken the world upon his heart.
BORDEN P. BROWNE

10923 We must learn from life how to suffer it.
FRENCH PROVERB

10924 We must never minimize the suffering of another.
BILLY GRAHAM (1918–   )

10925 We, by our sufferings, learn to praise our bliss.
JOHN DRYDEN (1631–1700)

10926 What is the best comfort in suffering and pain? It is that a man should take all things as if he had wished for them and prayed for them. For you would have indeed have wished for them if you had known that all things happen because of, with, and in God's will.
LUCIUS ANNAEUS SENECA (C. 4 B.C.–A.D. 65)

10927 When God is putting his saints through the experience of the millstones, we are apt to want to interfere. Hands off! No saint dare interfere in the discipline of the suffering of another saint.
OSWALD CHAMBERS (1874–1917)

10928 When I consider my crosses, tribulations, and temptations, I shame myself almost to death, thinking what are they in comparison to the sufferings of my blessed Savior, Christ Jesus.
MARTIN LUTHER (1483–1546)

10929 When it is dark enough, men see the stars.
RALPH WALDO EMERSON (1803–1882)

10930 When life is rosy, we may slide by with knowing about Jesus, with imitating him and quoting him and speaking of him. But only in the fellowship of suffering will we know Jesus. We indentify with him at the point of his deepest humiliation. The cross, symbol of his greatest suffering, becomes our personal touch-point with the Lord of the universe.
JONI EARECKSON TADA

10931 When one is in very great pain and fear, it is extremely difficult to pray coherently, and I could only raise my mind in anguish to God and ask for strength to hold on.
SHEILA CASSIDY (1937–   )

10932 When our minds are filled with God, suffering will become full of sweetness and quiet joy.
BROTHER LAWRENCE OF THE
RESURRECTION (C. 1605–1691)

10933 With profound potential for good, suffering can also be a destroyer. Suffering can pull families together, uniting them through hardship, or it can rip them apart in selfishness and bitterness. Suffering can file all the rough edges off your character, or it can further harden you. It all depends. On us. On how we respond.
JONI EARECKSON TADA

10934 You can't have a mountain without valleys.
ERWIN W. LUTZER (1941–   )

10935 You desire to know the art of living, my friend? It is contained in one phrase: make use of suffering.
HENRI FRÉDÉRIC AMIEL (1821–1881)

10936 You rarely hear a man who has been through the real agony of suffering who says he disbelieves in God; it is the one who watches others going through suffering who says he disbelieves in God.
OSWALD CHAMBERS (1874–1917)

10937 Your call to suffering requires strong faith and patience. It means you are called to love with a special intensity.
POPE JOHN PAUL II (1920–   )

10938 The way you and I handle our big and little trials makes the world pause in its frantic, headlong pursuits. Our godly response to those obstacles and perplexities in our lives literally kicks the psychological crutches right out from under the skeptic. The unbeliever can no longer refuse to face the reality of our faith.
JONI EARECKSON TADA

SUICIDE

10939 Doesn't suicide seem a little like going where you haven't been invited?
RICHARD EBERHART (1904–   )

10940 It came over me, blindingly, for the first time in my life, that suicide was a wrong act, was indeed "mortal sin." In that moment, God stopped me. I did not want my life, but I knew I was suddenly forbidden by something outside myself to let it go.
LORAN HURNSCOT (1900–1970)

10941 Man is a prisoner who has no right to open the door of his prison and run away.
PLATO (C. 428–348 B.C.)

10942 My work is done, why wait?
—Suicide note left by Eastman Kodak founder
GEORGE EASTMAN (1854–1932)

10943 Razors pain you,
Rivers are damp,
Acids stain you,
And drugs cause cramp.
Guns aren't lawful,
Nooses give,
Gas smells awful—
You might as well live.
DOROTHY PARKER (1893–1967)

10944 Suicide is the severest form of self-criticism.
LEONARD L. LEVINSON

10945 Suicide is the worst form of murder because it leaves no opportunity for repentance.
JOHN CHURTON COLLINS (1848–1908)

10946 Suicide is to desert from the world's garrison without the express command of him who has placed us here.
MICHEL EYQUEM DE MONTAIGNE
(1533–1592)

10947 There is no suicide for which all society is not responsible.
CYRIL CONNOLLY (1903–1974)

10948 When the blandishments of life are gone,
The coward sneaks to death, the brave live on.
MARCUS VALERIUS MARTIAL (43–104)

SUNDAY

10949 A man's Sunday self and his weekday self are like two halves of a round trip ticket; not good if detached.
LEE H. BRISTOL, JR. (1923–1979)

10950 God, by giving the Sabbath, has given fifty-two springs in every year.
SAMUEL TAYLOR COLERIDGE (1772–1834)

10951 Jesus spoke about the ox in the ditch on the Sabbath. But if your ox gets in the ditch every Sabbath, you should either get rid of the ox or fill up the ditch.
BILLY GRAHAM (1918–   )

10952 Our great-grandfathers called it the holy Sabbath; our grandfathers, the Sabbath; our fathers, Sunday; but today we call it the weekend.

10953 Safely through another week
God has brought us on our way;
Let us now a blessing seek,
Waiting in his courts today.
Day of all the week the best.
Emblem of eternal rest.
JOHN NEWTON (1725–1807)

10954 Sunday clears away the rust of the whole week.
JOSEPH ADDISON (1672–1719)

10955 Sunday is a continual proclamation of the message of Easter: Christ is risen.
GUSTAVE WINGREN

10956 Sunday is the golden clasp that binds together the volume of the week.
HENRY WADSWORTH LONGFELLOW (1807–1882)

10957 Sundays observe! think, when the bells do chime,
'Tis angel's music.
GEORGE HERBERT (1593–1633)

10958 The Lord's Day is a firm foundation on which to build a six-story week.

10959 The Sabbath should be a time when hope is reborn, dreams are rekindled, self-worth restored.
ROBERT HAROLD SCHULLER (1926–   )

10960 This solemn pause, the breathing space of man,
The halt of toil's exhausted caravan—
Comes sweet with music to thy wearied ear;
Rise with its anthems to a holier sphere!
OLIVER WENDELL HOLMES (1809–1894)

10961 You see, God, it's like this: we could attend church more faithfully if your day came at some other time. You have chosen a day that comes at the end of a hard week, and we're all tired out. Not only that, but it's the day following Saturday night, and Saturday night is one time when we feel that we should go out and enjoy ourselves. Often it is after midnight when we reach home, and it is impossible to get up on Sunday morning. We'd like to go to church and know we should; but you have just chosen the wrong day.

SUNSHINE

10962 But yonder comes the powerful King of Day,
Rejoicing in the east.
JAMES THOMSON (1700–1748)

10963 Christ has turned all our sunsets into dawns.
CLEMENT OF ALEXANDRIA (C. 150–C. 215)

10964 Never once since the world began
Has the sun ever stopped his shining.
His face very often we could not see,
And we grumbled at his inconstancy;
But the clouds were really to blame, not he,
For, behind them, he was shining.
And so—behind life's darkest clouds
God's love is always shining.
We veil it at times with our faithless fears,
And darken our sight with our foolish tears,
But in time the atmosphere always clears,
For his love is always shining.
JOHN OXENHAM (1861–1941)

10965 Those who bring sunshine to the lives of others bring sunshine to their own.

SUPERSTITION

10966 Superstition is the poison of the mind.
JOSEPH LEWIS (1889–)

10967 Superstition is the religion of feeble minds.
EDMUND BURKE (1729–1797)

10968 There is but a hairline between truth and superstition.
A. W. TOZER (1897–1963)

SURRENDER

10969 Better in bitterest agony to lie,
Before thy throne,
Than through much increase to be lifted up on high,
And stand alone.
Yet best—the need that broke me at thy feet,
In voiceless prayer,
And cast my chastened heart, a sacrifice complete,
Upon thy care.
JOHN OXENHAM (1861–1941)

10970 God can make you anything you want to be, but you have to put everything in his hands.
MAHALIA JACKSON (1911–1972)

10971 If you don't surrender to Christ, you surrender to chaos.
E. STANLEY JONES (1884–1973)

10972 If you make a compromise with surrender, you can remain interested in the abundant life, all the riches of freedom, love, and peace, but it is the same as looking at a display in a shop window. You look through the window but do not go in and buy. You will not pay the price—surrender.
E. STANLEY JONES (1884–1973)

10973 Make me a captive, Lord,
And then I shall be free;
Force me to render up my sword,
And I shall conqueror be.
I sink in life's alarms
When by myself I stand;
Imprison me within thine arms,
And strong shall be my hand.
GEORGE MATHESON (1842–1906)

10974 Surrender not only what the Lord does to you, but surrender your reaction to what he does.
MADAME JEANNE MARIE DE LA MOTHE GUYON (1648–1717)

10975 The greatness of a man's power is the measure of his surrender.
WILLIAM BOOTH (1829–1912)

10976 The man who surrenders to Christ exchanges a cruel slave driver for a kind and gentle Master whose yoke is easy and whose burden is light.
A. W. TOZER (1897–1963)

10977 The reason why many are still troubled, still seeking, still making little forward progress is because they have not yet come to the end of themselves. We are still giving some of the orders, and we are still interfering with God's working within us.
A. W. TOZER (1897–1963)

10978 The tendency is strong to say, "O God won't be so stern as to expect me to give up that!" but he will; "He won't expect me to walk in the light so that I have nothing to hide," but he will; "He won't expect me to draw on his grace for everything," but he will.
OSWALD CHAMBERS (1874–1917)

10979 To take all that we are and have and hand it over to God may not be easy; but it can be done, and when it is done, the world has in it one less candidate for misery.
PAUL E. SCHERER (1892–)

10980 We say we must do all we can.
Jesus says we must let God do all we can.
OSWALD CHAMBERS (1874–1917)

SYMPATHY

10981 Sympathy is never wasted except when you give it to yourself.
JOHN W. RAPER

10982 Sympathy is your pain in my heart.

10983 Teach me to feel another's woe,
To hide the fault I see;
That mercy I to others show,
That mercy show to me.
ALEXANDER POPE (1688–1744)

T

TACT

10984 If you your lips would keep from slips,
Five things observe with care;
To whom you speak, of whom you
speak,
And how, and when, and where.

10985 Never tell a man you can read him
through and through; most people prefer to be thought enigmas.
MARCHIONESS TOWNSEND

10986 Tact is a kind of mind-reading.
SARAH ORNE JEWETT (1849–1909)

10987 Tact is emotional intelligence.

10988 Tact is giving a person a pat on the
back when you feel like giving him a
kick in the pants.

10989 Tact is the ability to describe others as
they see themselves.
ABRAHAM LINCOLN (1809–1865)

10990 Tact is the knack of making a point
without making an enemy.
HOWARD W. NEWTON

10991 The oil can is mightier than the sword.
EVERETT MCKINLEY DIRKSEN (1896–1969)

10992 We have a head on us for the same reason a pin has: to keep us from going
too far.

TALENT

10993 If you have a talent, use it in every
which way possible. Don't hoard it.
Don't dole it out like a miser. Spend it
lavishly like a millionaire intent on
going broke.
BRENDAN FRANCIS

10994 Talent is God-given; be thankful. Conceit is self-given; be careful.
THOMAS LA MANCE

10995 Talent is like an arm or a leg—use it
or lose it.

10996 Talent is something God gives you;
experience is something you give yourself.
DANIEL LOUIS ROTTINGHANS

10997 The real tragedy of life is not in being
limited to one talent, but in the failure
to use the one talent.
EDGAR W. WORK

TEACHING

10998 A good teacher is one whose ears get as much exercise as his mouth.
PROVERB

10999 A teacher affects eternity; he can never tell where his influence stops.
HENRY GARDINER ADAMS (1812–1881)

11000 A teacher who is attempting to teach without inspiring the pupil with a desire to learn is hammering on cold iron.
HORACE MANN (1796–1859)

11001 Give a man a fish, and he eats for a day; teach him to fish, and he eats for the rest of his life.
CHINESE PROVERB

11002 I love to teach. I love to teach as a painter loves to paint, as a musician loves to play, as a singer loves to sing, as a strong man rejoices to run a race. Teaching is an art—an art so great and so difficult to master that a man or a woman can spend a long life at it without realizing much more than his limitations and mistakes and his distances from the ideal.
WILLIAM LYON PHELPS (1865–1943)

11003 If a teacher fascinates with his doctrine, his teaching never came from God. The teacher sent from God is the one who clears the way to Jesus and keeps it clear; souls forget altogether about him because the vision of Jesus is the only abiding result. When people are attracted to Jesus Christ through you, see always that you stay on God all the time, and their hearts and affections will never stop at you.
OSWALD CHAMBERS (1874–1917)

11004 No teacher should strive to make men think as he thinks, but to lead them to the living Truth, to the Master himself, of whom alone they can learn anything.
GEORGE MACDONALD (1824–1905)

11005 The teacher is like the candle which lights others in consuming itself.
ITALIAN PROVERB

11006 The true teacher defends his pupils against his own personal influence.
AMOS BRONSON ALCOTT (1799–1888)

11007 To discharge the duties of a professor means to be willing to make . . . ideas accessible to anyone, anywhere, at any time. It means to consider scholarship, not as a property, but as a sacrament. . . . It means to be willing to pursue an idea wherever it may lead, not departing from its pursuit for any consideration of gain, prestige, or advantage, until one has found out that the line of thought has run out. . . . It means that if the line of research cannot be compassed within a single lifetime, to be content with doing what one humanly can do, even though it means leaving to others to reap where one has sown.
NORBERT WIENER (1894–1964)

11008 To teach is to learn twice.
JOSEPH JOUBERT (1754–1824)

11009 When I transfer my knowledge, I teach; when I transfer my beliefs, I indoctrinate.
ARTHUR DANTO (1924–   )

11010 You cannot teach a man anything; you can only help him to find it himself.
GALILEO GALILEI (1564–1642)

TEARS

11011 A teardrop on earth summons the King of heaven.
CHARLES R. SWINDOLL (1934–   )

11012 God has a bottle and a book for his people's tears. What was sown as a tear will come up as a pearl.
MATTHEW HENRY (1662–1714)

11013 God washes the eyes by tears until they can behold the invisible land where tears shall come no more.
HENRY WARD BEECHER (1813–1887)

11014 Grief, like a tree, has tears for its fruit.
PHILEMON (C. 363–C. 264 B.C.)

11015 It is such a secret place, the land of tears.
ANTOINE DE SAINT-EXUPÉRY (1900–1944)

11016 It's ironic. In heaven, where I will be able once again to wipe my own tears, I won't have to.
JONI EARECKSON TADA

11017 Tears clean the windows of the soul.
PEARL BARKER

11018 Tears speak more eloquently than ten thousand tongues.
WASHINGTON IRVING (1783–1859)

11019 Tears teach us wisdom no book of philosophy can give us.

11020 Tears: the best gift of God to suffering man.
JOHN KEBLE (1792–1866)

11021 The world!—it is a wilderness
Where tears are hung on every tree.
THOMAS HOOD (1799–1845)

11022 To weep is to make less the depth of grief.
WILLIAM SHAKESPEARE (1564–1616)

11023 We need never be ashamed of our tears, for they are rain upon the blinding dust of earth, overlying our hard hearts.
CHARLES DICKENS (1812–1870)

11024 We should be thankful for our tears; they prepare us for a clearer vision of God.
WILLIAM ARTHUR WARD (1812–1882)

11025 White, black, and yellow men—they all cry salt tears.
CLAUDE AVELINE (1901–)

11026 Tears shed for self are tears of weakness, but tears shed for others are a sign of strength.
BILLY GRAHAM (1918–)

TELEVISION

11027 Delegates to the United Nations are not as important as the people in this room. We're the ones that determine what the people's attitudes are. It's in our hands.
—Speaking to a group of broadcasters
TED TURNER (1938–)

11028 Everything is for the eye these days. The next generation will have eyeballs as big as cantaloupes and no brain at all.
FRED ALLEN (1894–1956)

11029 I find television very educating. Every time somebody turns on the set I go into the other room and read a book.
GROUCHO MARX (1895–1977)

11030 If you want to look at human lunacy at its choicest and best, a course in television advertising would be about right because it is saying things that are so patently ridiculous.
MALCOLM MUGGERIDGE (1903–1990)

11031 Insofar as people . . . make watching TV a habit and take its drama at all seriously, it insinuates chiefly hollow or false values, cheapens the quality of life, muddies rather than clarifies their own experience. . . . Above all, it impoverishes life. It dulls the capacity of people for wonder and awe.
HERBERT J. MULLER (1905–1967)

11032 Of all the inventions of our time TV is likely to prove the most destructive. Whereas nuclear power can only reduce us and our world to a cinder, the camera grinds us down to spiritual dust so fine that a puff of wind scatters it, leaving nothing behind.
MALCOLM MUGGERIDGE (1903–1990)

11033 Television . . . the bland leading the bland.

11034 Television has proved that people will look at anything rather than each other.
ANN LANDERS (1918–)

11035 Television is an invention that permits you to be entertained in your living room by people you wouldn't have in your home.
DAVID FROST (1939–)

11036 Television is chewing gum for the eyes.
FRED ALLEN (1894–1956)

11037 Television is simply automated day dreaming.
LEE LOVINGER

11038 Television relies for its effectiveness on tricks, not perceptiveness, complete with canned laughter, studio applause, special effects, and dawn for dusk—a

medium fated never to get beneath the surface.
MALCOLM MUGGERIDGE (1903–1990)

11039 Television: a nightly national séance.
DANIEL SCHORR (1916–)

11040 Television: radio with eyestrain.

11041 The great droning, giggling body of television is polluting us. Not hopelessly so, for there are many earnest people trying to navigate fine programs to the air, and some do get through. But most of television betrays us. It lies about what this world is like and what it means to be human.
LORING MANDEL

11042 There's not a thing wrong with television that not watching it won't cure.
FRANKLIN P. JONES

11043 TV is another kind of car, a windshield on the world. We climb inside, drive it, and it drives us, and we all go in the same direction, see the same thing. It is more than a mobile home, it is a mobile nation. It has become, then, our common language, our ceremony, our style, our entertainment and anxiety, our sympathetic magic, our way of celebrating, mourning, worshiping. It's flimsy glue, but for the moment it's the only thing holding America together.
JOHN LEONARD (1939–)

11044 TV, while it may threaten to turn every home into a theater, can also turn every parlor into a church.
EDWARD JOHN CARNELL (1919–1967)

11045 You people sit there, night after night. You're beginning to believe this illusion we're spinning here. You're beginning to think the tube is reality and your own lives are unreal. This is mass madness!
HOWARD BEALE

TEMPTATION

11046 'Tis one thing to be tempted,
Another thing to fall.
WILLIAM SHAKESPEARE (1564–1616)

11047 An idle person tempts the devil to tempt him.
PROVERB

11048 Be not a baker if your head be of butter.
SPANISH PROVERB

11049 Better shun the bait than struggle in the snare.
JOHN DRYDEN (1631–1700)

11050 Curiosity is a kernel of the forbidden fruit which still sticks in a man's throat, sometimes to the danger of his choking.
SIR THOMAS FULLER (1608–1661)

11051 Do not bite at the bait of pleasure till you know there is no hook beneath it.
THOMAS JEFFERSON (1743–1826)

11052 Each temptation leaves us better or worse; neutrality is impossible.
ERWIN W. LUTZER (1941–)

11053 Eve, with all the fruits of Eden blest,
Save only one, rather than leave that one unknown,
Lost all the rest.
THOMAS MOORE (1779–1852)

11054 Feather by feather the goose is plucked.
JOHN RAY (1627–1705)

11055 Flee temptation and don't leave a forwarding address.

11056 For every great temptation there will be many small ones. Wolves and bears are more dangerous than flies, but we are bothered most by flies.
SAINT FRANCIS OF SALES (1567–1622)

11057 God delights in our temptations and yet hates them. He delights in them when they drive us to prayer; he hates them when they drive us to despair.
MARTIN LUTHER (1483–1546)

11058 God does not make our choices easier because temptation is his character development curriculum.
ERWIN W. LUTZER (1941–)

11059 God is better served in resisting a temptation to evil than in many formal prayers.
WILLIAM PENN (1644–1718)

11060 God never tempts any man. That is
Satan's business.
BILLY GRAHAM (1918–   )

11061 God tested Abraham. Temptation is
not meant to make us fail; it is meant
to confront us with a situation out of
which we emerge stronger than we
were. Temptation is not the penalty of
manhood; it is the glory of manhood.
WILLIAM BARCLAY (1907–1978)

11062 He must have iron nails that scratches
a bear.
RUSSIAN PROVERB

11063 He that lies with dogs rises with fleas.
PROVERB

11064 He who feeds a wolf strengthens his
enemy.
DANISH PROVERB

11065 He who has no mind to trade with the
devil should keep from his shop.
ROBERT SOUTH (1634–1716)

11066 He who plays with the dust will get
his eyes full of dust.
ARABIAN PROVERB

11067 He who wants to play with a cat
should be able to bear its scratches.
ARABIAN PROVERB

11068 He who would not fall off the precipice must not venture too near the
edge.
FRANCES J. ROBERTS

11069 Her rash hand in evil hour
Forth reaching to the fruit, she
plucked, she eat:
Earth felt the wound, and Nature
from her seat,
Sighing through all her works, gave
signs of woe
That all was lost.
JOHN MILTON (1608–1674)

11070 Honest bread is very well—it's the butter that makes the temptation.
DOUGLAS WILLIAM JERROLD (1803–1857)

11071 However big the whale may be, the
tiny harpoon can rob him of his life.
MALAY PROVERB

11072 If it takes temptation and sin to show
God in his true colors and Satan in

his, something has been saved from
the wreck.
MICHAEL GREEN (1930–   )

11073 It is easier to stay out than to get out.
MARK TWAIN (1835–1910)

11074 It is much easier to repent of sins that
we have committed than to repent of
those we intend to commit.
JOSH BILLINGS (1818–1885)

11075 My temptation has become my
strength, for to the very fight with it I
owe my force.
W. C. GANNETT

11076 My temptations have been my masters
in divinity.
MARTIN LUTHER (1483–1546)

11077 No matter how many pleasures Satan
offers you, his ultimate intention is to
ruin you. Your destruction is his highest priority.
ERWIN W. LUTZER (1941–   )

11078 Oftentimes great and open temptations are the most harmless because
they come with banners flying and
bands playing and all the munitions of
war in full view, so that we know we
are in the midst of enemies that mean
us damage, and we get ready to meet
and resist them. Our peculiar dangers
are those that surprise us and work
treachery in our fort.
HENRY WARD BEECHER (1813–1887)

11079 Our response to temptation is an accurate barometer of our love for God.
ERWIN W. LUTZER (1941–   )

11080 People do not decide to be drunkards,
drug addicts, prostitutes, murderers,
or thieves, but they pitch their tent
toward Sodom, and the powers of evil
overcome them.
JOHN H. EASTWOOD

11081 Pheasants are fools if they invite the
hawk to dinner.
PROVERB

11082 Satan tried to put Jesus Christ on the
way to becoming King of the world
and Savior of men in a way other than
that predetermined by God.
OSWALD CHAMBERS (1874–1917)

11083 Some people are tempted most strongly at the beginning of their spiritual life, others near the end. Some are troubled all their lives. Still others receive only light temptation. Such things are decided by God, and we can trust his wisdom.
THOMAS À KEMPIS (C. 1380–1471)

11084 Step not on the sleeping serpent.
SPANISH PROVERB

11085 Straw should make no pact with fire.
RUSSIAN PROVERB

11086 Temptation is God's magnifying glass; it shows us how much work he has left to do in our lives.
ERWIN W. LUTZER (1941–)

11087 Temptation is not a sin; it is a call to battle.
ERWIN W. LUTZER (1941–)

11088 Temptation is the devil looking through the keyhole; yielding is opening the door and inviting him in.
BILLY SUNDAY (1862–1935)

11089 Temptation provokes me to look upward to God.
JOHN BUNYAN (1628–1688)

11090 Temptation: the fiend at my elbow.
WILLIAM SHAKESPEARE (1564–1616)

11091 Temptations are like tramps. Treat them kindly, and they will return bringing others with them.

11092 Temptations are never so dangerous as when they come to us in a religious garb.
DWIGHT LYMAN MOODY (1837–1899)

11093 Temptations in the life of faith are not accidents; each temptation is part of a plan, a step in the progress of faith.
OSWALD CHAMBERS (1874–1917)

11094 Temptations that find us leaning on God are to our faith like winds that more firmly root the tree.

11095 Temptations, when we first meet them, are as the lion that roared upon Samson; but if we overcome them, the next time we see them we shall find a nest of honey within them.
JOHN BUNYAN (1628–1688)

11096 The devil tempts that he may ruin; God tests that he may crown.
SAINT AMBROSE (C. 340–397)

11097 The greatest of all evils is not to be tempted because there are then grounds for believing that the devil looks upon us as his property.
SAINT JEAN BAPTISTE MARIE VIANNEY (1786–1859)

11098 The man who has never been tempted doesn't know how dishonest he is.
JOSH BILLINGS (1818–1885)

11099 The whole effort—the object—of temptation is to induce us to substitute something else for God. To obscure God.
R. H. STEWART

11100 There are no faults in a thing we want badly.
ARABIAN PROVERB

11101 There is no evil that does not offer inducements. Vices tempt you by the rewards which they offer.
LUCIUS ANNAEUS SENECA (C. 4 B.C.–A.D. 65)

11102 There is no way to kill a man's righteousness but by his own consent.
JOHN BUNYAN (1628–1688)

11103 They said to a mouse, "There is a piece of cheese on the cat's whiskers." She replied, "Yes, the cheese is delicious, but the way to it is risky."
ARABIAN PROVERB

11104 Things forbidden have a secret charm.
CORNELIUS TACITUS (C. 56–C. 120)

11105 Things sweet to taste prove in digestion sour.
WILLIAM SHAKESPEARE (1564–1616)

11106 Those saints which God loves best, The devil tempts not least.
ROBERT HERRICK (1591–1674)

11107 Though this test be not thy choice, It is his—therefore rejoice!
HANNAH HURNARD (1905–1990)

11108 To attempt to resist temptation, abandon bad habits, and control passion in our own strength, is like attempting to check by a spider's thread the progress of a ship.
BENJAMIN WAUGH (1839–1908)

11109 Unless there is within us that which is
above us, we shall soon yield to that
which is about us.
P. T. FORSYTH (1848–1921)

11110 We are no more responsible for the
evil thoughts that pass through our
minds than a scarecrow for the birds
which fly over the seedplot he has to
guard. The sole responsibility in each
case is to prevent them from settling.
JOHN CHURTON COLLINS (1848–1908)

11111 We cannot say no to temptation without saying yes to something far better.
ERWIN W. LUTZER (1941–   )

11112 We have all a propensity to grasp at
forbidden fruit.
LATIN PROVERB

11113 When Eve upon the first of men
The apple pressed, with specious cant,
Oh! what a thousand pities then
That Adam was not Adamant!
THOMAS HOOD (1799–1845)

11114 When in doubt, go home.

11115 When the spider would attack thee, it
extends its web to entangle thee.
AFRICAN PROVERB

11116 When we do ill, the devil tempts us;
when we do nothing, we tempt him.
SIR THOMAS FULLER (1608–1661)

11117 When you fly from temptation, don't
leave a forwarding address.

11118 Where there's smoke there's fire.
PLAUTUS (C. 254–184 B.C.)

11119 While I see many hoofmarks going in,
I see none coming out. It is easier to
get into the enemy's toils than out
again.
AESOP (C. 550 B.C.)

11120 Who hangs himself in the chimney
should not complain of smoke.
GERMAN PROVERB

11121 Who rides a tiger cannot dismount.
CHINESE PROVERB

11122 Why comes temptation, but for man
to meet
And master and make crouch beneath
his foot,
And so be pedestaled in triumph?
ROBERT BROWNING (1812–1889)

TESTIMONY

11123 I do not believe . . . I know.
—When asked if he believed in God
CARL GUSTAV JUNG (1875–1961)

11124 I do not feel that I am the product of
chance, a speck of dust in the universe,
but someone who was expected, prepared, prefigured. In short, a being
whom only a Creator could put here;
and this idea of a creating hand refers
to God.
JEAN PAUL SARTRE (1905–1980)

11125 If my testimony makes anyone wish to
emulate me, it is a mistaken testimony;
it is not a witness to Jesus.
OSWALD CHAMBERS (1874–1917)

11126 Jesus is the foundation of my whole
life. He is my strength. If you have
Jesus in your life, you know it, you
feel it. He's the solid rock you can
stand on every day. There's no problem you can't face if you have the love
of Jesus to strengthen you.
JOHNNY CASH (1932–   )

11127 Like anybody, I would like to live a
long life. Longevity has its place. But
I'm not concerned about that now. I
just want to do God's will. And he's
allowed me to go up to the mountain.
I've looked over, and I've seen the
promised land.
MARTIN LUTHER KING, JR. (1929–1968)

11128 Observers in the full enjoyment of
their bodily senses pity me, but it is
because they do not see the golden
chamber in my life where I dwell
delighted; for, dark as my path may
seem to them, I carry a magic light in
my heart.
HELEN ADAMS KELLER (1880–1968)

11129 So through the clouds of Calvary—
There shines his face, and I believe
that evil dies,
And good lives on, loves on, and conquers all—
All war must end in peace. These
clouds are lies.
They cannot last. The blue sky is the
truth.
For God is Love. Such is my faith,
and such

My reasons for it, and I find them
  strong
Enough. And you? You want to argue?
Well, I can't. It is a choice.
I choose the Christ.
GEOFFREY ANKETELL STUDDERT-KENNEDY
(1883–1929)

11130 When Christ came into my life, I came
about like a well-handled ship.
ROBERT LOUIS BALFOUR STEVENSON
(1850–1894)

11131 Whosoever believeth in him should
not perish. . . . With these words . . .
my sense of inferiority, my fear of
handicaps, dropped away. It meant
that I, a humble Negro girl, had just as
much chance as anybody in the sight
and love of God. These words stored
up a battery of faith and confidence
and determination in my heart which
has not failed me to this day.
MARY MCLEOD BETHUNE (1875–1955)

11132 Winter is on my head, but eternal
spring is in my heart. The nearer I
approach the end, the plainer I hear
around me the immortal symphonies
of the world to come. For half a century I have been writing my thoughts
in prose and verse; but I feel that I
have not said one-thousandth part of
what is in me. When I have gone
down to the grave, I shall have ended
my day's work; but another day will
begin the next morning. Life closes in
the twilight but opens with the dawn.
VICTOR HUGO (1802–1885)

THANKFULNESS

11133 A Christian who walks by faith
accepts all circumstances from God.
He thanks God when everything goes
good, when everything goes bad, and
for the "blues" somewhere in-between. He thanks God whether he
feels like it or not.
ERWIN W. LUTZER (1941–)

11134 A thankless man never does a thankful
deed.
DANISH PROVERB

11135 All that we are comes from God. Give
thanks.

11136 An easy thing, O Power Divine,
To thank thee for these gifts of thine,
For summer's sunshine, winter's snow,
For hearts that kindle, thoughts that
  glow;
But when shall I attain to this—
To thank thee for the things I miss?
THOMAS WENTWORTH STORROW HIGGINSON
(1823–1911)

11137 And let us give thanks for Someone to
thank.
GERHARD E. FROST

11138 And then be thankful; O admire his
  ways,
Who fills the world's unempty'd grana-
  ries!
A thankless feeder is a thief, his feast
A very robbery, himself no guest.
HENRY VAUGHAN (1622–1695)

11139 Cultivate the thankful spirit! It will be
to you a perpetual feast.
JOHN R. MACDUFF (1818–1895)

11140 Do not blame God for having created
the tiger, but thank him for not having
given it wings.
INDIAN PROVERB

11141 Don't be sorry if the bottle is half
empty. Be glad that it is half full.
PROVERB

11142 Even the hen lifteth her head toward
heaven when swallowing her grain.
AFRICAN PROVERB

11143 For all that has been, thanks!
For all that shall be, yes!
DAG HAMMARSKJÖLD (1905–1961)

11144 For three things I thank God every day
of my life: thanks that he has vouchsafed me knowledge of his works;
deep thanks that he has set in my darkness the lamp of faith; deep, deepest
thanks that I have another life to look
forward to—a life joyous with light
and flowers and heavenly song.
HELEN ADAMS KELLER (1880–1968)

11145 From David learn to give thanks for
everything. Every furrow in the book
of Psalms is sown with the seeds of
thanksgiving.
JEREMY TAYLOR (1613–1667)

11146 I can no other answer make but
thanks and ever thanks.
WILLIAM SHAKESPEARE (1564–1616)

11147 I thank God for my handicaps; for,
through them, I have found myself,
my work, and my God.
HELEN ADAMS KELLER (1880–1968)

11148 I thank thee for a daily task to do,
For books that are my ships with
golden wings,
For mighty gifts let others offer
praise—
Lord, I am thanking thee for little
things.

11149 I thank thee, God, and like a child
Rejoice as for a Christmas gift,
That I am living—just alive—
Just for this human face I wear,
That I can see the sun, the sea,
The hills and grass and leafy trees,
And walk beneath the host of stars
And watch the lovely moon above.
MATTHIAS CLAUDIUS (1740–1815)

11150 If men thanked God for good things,
they wouldn't have time to complain
about the bad.
JEWISH PROVERB

11151 If thankfulness arises through prosperity, well and good. But what are you
going to do when the prosperity fails?
If thankfulness springs up through
health, well and good. But what will
you do when disease makes you bedridden? Must you then become glum
or bitter? But now, supposing it is
through our dear Lord Christ that you
cultivate the fine art of thanksgiving,
then what? Then money in the bank,
however useful, does not have me at
its mercy: if I lose it, I can still offer
thanks.
PAUL STROMBERG REES (1900–)

11152 It's only when we choose to give praise
for the rough spots in life that we will
begin to see them from God's perspective. If we don't give thanks in all
things, we are living in unbelief, for we
are assuming that our circumstances
are not controlled by a God who loves
us! I'm not saying that you should give
thanks for sin, but you can thank God

for how he will use that sin to teach, to
rebuke, or to challenge you.
ERWIN W. LUTZER (1941–)

11153 Just the word *thanksgiving* prompts
the spirit of humility. Genuine gratitude to God for his mercy, his abundance, his protection, his smile of
favor. Life simplifies itself.
CHARLES R. SWINDOLL (1934–)

11154 Life without thankfulness is devoid of
love and passion. Hope without thankfulness is lacking in fine perception.
Faith without thankfulness lacks
strength and fortitude. Every virtue
divorced from thankfulness is maimed
and limps along the spiritual road.
JOHN HENRY JOWETT (1864–1923)

11155 May silent thanks at least to God be
given with a full heart;
Our thoughts are heard in heaven.
WILLIAM WORDSWORTH (1770–1850)

11156 O Lord! that lends me life,
Lend me a heart replete with thankful-
ness!
WILLIAM SHAKESPEARE (1564–1616)

11157 One act of thanksgiving when things
go wrong with us is worth a thousand
thanks when things are agreeable to
our inclination.
SAINT JOHN OF AVILA (1500–1569)

11158 Remember the day's blessings; forget
the day's troubles.
PROVERB

11159 Some have meat and cannot eat,
And some would eat that want it;
But we have meat, and we can eat,
And so the Lord be thanked.
ROBERT BURNS (1759–1796)

11160 Thank God every morning when you
get up that you have something to do
that day which must be done, whether
you like it or not.
CHARLES KINGSLEY (1819–1875)

11161 Thank you, dear God
For all you have given me
For all you have taken away from me
For all you have left me.

11162 Thanksgiving . . . invites God to
bestow a second benefit.
ROBERT HERRICK (1591–1674)

11163 There's more and more to be so very grateful for.

11164 Think not on what you lack as much as on what you have.
GREEK PROVERB

11165 Three things for which thanks are due: an invitation, a gift, and a warning.
WELSH PROVERB

11166 We should spend as much time in thanking God for his benefits as we do in asking him for them.
VINCENT DE PAUL (1580–1660)

11167 Were there no God, we would be in this glorious world with grateful hearts and no one to thank.
CHRISTINA GEORGINA ROSSETTI (1830–1894)

11168 When thou hast thanked thy God
For every blessing sent,
What time will then remain
For murmurs or lament?
ARCHBISHOP RICHARD CHENEVIX TRENCH (1807–1886)

11169 When you break your leg, be thankful it isn't your neck.

11170 When you drink from the stream, remember the spring.
CHINESE PROVERB

11171 Who does not thank for little will not thank for much.
PROVERB

11172 Without thy sunshine and thy rain
We could not have the golden grain;
Without thy love we'd not be fed;
We thank thee for our daily bread.

11173 You can learn to give thanks even if you don't feel particularly thankful. If God gives a command, he expects obedience, whether you are in the mood or not. Thankfulness, like forgiveness, is not an emotion. Thankfulness is an intelligent response of gratitude to God.
ERWIN W. LUTZER (1941–)

THANKSGIVING

11174 For each new morning with its light,
Father, we thank thee,
For rest and shelter of the night,
Father, we thank thee,

For health and food, for love and friends,
For everything thy goodness sends,
Father, in heaven, we thank thee.
RALPH WALDO EMERSON (1803–1882)

11175 Heap high the board with plenteous cheer, and gather to the feast,
And toast the sturdy Pilgrim band whose courage never ceased.
Give praise to that All-Gracious One by whom their steps were led,
And thanks unto the harvest's Lord who sends our daily bread.
—The first Thanksgiving Day
ALICE WILLIAMS BROTHERTON

11176 It has seemed to me fit and proper that [the gifts of God] should be solemnly, reverently, and gratefully acknowledged with one heart and one voice by the whole American people. I do, therefore, invite my fellow citizens . . . to set apart and observe the last Thursday of November next as a day of thanksgiving and praise to our beneficent Father who dwelleth in the heavens.
—Thanksgiving proclamation, 1863
ABRAHAM LINCOLN (1809–1865)

11177 Thanksgiving was never meant to be shut up in a single day.
ROBERT CASPAR LINTNER

11178 Thanksgiving, to be truly thanksgiving, is first thanks, then giving.
PROVERB

THEOLOGY

11179 "God knows me" is different from "God is omniscient"; the latter is a mere theological statement; the former is a child of God's most precious possession.
OSWALD CHAMBERS (1874–1917)

11180 A doctrine has practical value only as far as it is prominent in our thoughts and makes a difference in our lives.
A. W. TOZER (1897–1963)

11181 Any doctrine that will not bear investigation is not a fit tenant for the mind of an honest man.
ROBERT GREEN INGERSOLL (1833–1899)

11182 As the grave grows nearer, my theology is growing strangely simple, and it begins and ends with Christ as the only Savior of the lost.
HENRY BENJAMIN WHIPPLE (1822–1901)

11183 Could God pass an examination in theology?
MALCOLM MUGGERIDGE (1903–1990)

11184 Doctrine nails your faith.

11185 Doctrine won't make you happy unless it is translated into life.
HENRY VAN DYKE (1852–1933)

11186 Dogma is nothing more or less than emergency measures to which the church is driven by heresies.
HANS KÜNG (1928–)

11187 Dogma is the ark within which the church floats safely down the floodtide of history.
ALFRED NORTH WHITEHEAD (1861–1947)

11188 Great saints have always been dogmatic. We need a return to a gentle dogmatism that smiles while it stands stubborn and firm on the Word of God.
A. W. TOZER (1897–1963)

11189 If God consistently sent lightning bolts in response to bad doctrine, our planet would sparkle nightly like a Christmas tree.
PHILIP YANCEY (1949–)

11190 If your theology doesn't change your behavior, it will never change your destiny.
CHARLES HADDON SPURGEON (1834–1892)

11191 In theology we must consider the predominance of authority; in philosophy the predominance of reason.
JOHANNES KEPLER (1571–1630)

11192 Let a man go to the grammar school of faith and repentance before he goes to the university of election and predestination.
GEORGE WHITEFIELD (1714–1770)

11193 Let one define his terms and then stick to the definition, and half the differences in philosophy and theology would come to an end.
TRYON EDWARDS (1809–1894)

11194 Many a long dispute among divines may be thus abridged: It is so. It is not so. It is so. It is not so.
BENJAMIN FRANKLIN (1706–1790)

11195 My entire theology can be condensed into four words: "Jesus died for me."
CHARLES HADDON SPURGEON (1834–1892)

11196 My strong advice to you is to soak, soak, soak in philosophy and psychology until you know more of these subjects than ever you need consciously to think. It is ignorance of these subjects on the part of ministers and workers that has brought our evangelical theology to such a sorry plight.
OSWALD CHAMBERS (1874–1917)

11197 Never take the conception of a theologian as infallible; it is simply an attempt to state things.
OSWALD CHAMBERS (1874–1917)

11198 Nothing dies harder than a theological difference.
RONALD ARBUTHNOTT KNOX (1888–1957)

11199 Our theology must become biography.
TIM HANSEL

11200 The best theology is rather a divine life than a divine knowledge.
JEREMY TAYLOR (1613–1667)

11201 The Christian faith is the most exciting drama that ever staggered the imagination of man—and the dogma is the drama.
DOROTHY L. SAYERS (1893–1957)

11202 The theological problems of original sin, origin of evil, predestination, and the like are the soul's mumps and measles and whooping coughs.
RALPH WALDO EMERSON (1803–1882)

11203 The Trinity, the Incarnation, and the Resurrection: your faith and my faith must include these three mysteries. They are difficult to understand. They are not unintelligible—God understands them. But for us there is an element of mystery. The greatest error

anyone can make is to think they can fully understand these three mysteries. It makes a mockery of faith.
MORTIMER JEROME ADLER (1902–)

11204 Theologians are always bothering about the origin of evil, but evil is just natural behavior; it's the origin of human goodness that is really so extraordinary and inexplicable.
KINGSLEY MARTIN

11205 Theological truth is useless until it is obeyed.
A. W. TOZER (1897–1963)

11206 Theology is an attempt to understand the mystery.

11207 Theology is but the science of mind applied to God. As schools change, theology must necessarily change. Truth is everlasting, but our ideas of truth are not. Theology is but our ideas of truth classified and arranged.
HENRY WARD BEECHER (1813–1887)

11208 Theology is that madness gone systematic which tries to crowd God's fullness into a formula and a system.
JOEL BLAU

11209 Theology is the science of religion, an intellectual attempt to systematize the consciousness of God.
OSWALD CHAMBERS (1874–1917)

11210 Theology should be empress, and philosophy and the other arts merely her servants.
MARTIN LUTHER (1483–1546)

11211 Theology teaches us what ends are desirable and what means are lawful, while politics teaches what means are effective.
C. S. LEWIS (1898–1963)

11212 There is no wild beast so ferocious as Christians who differ concerning their faith.
WILLIAM EDWARD HARTPOLE LECKY (1838–1903)

11213 True doctrine is a master key to all the world's problems. With it the world can be taken apart and put together.
ERIC HOFFER (1902–1983)

11214 We can be certain about God, but tentative about theology.
IAN RAMSEY

11215 Your theology is what you are when the talking stops and the action starts.
COLIN MORRIS (1929–)

THOUGHT

11216 A book that agrees with our views may be gratifying to the ego, but it does nothing to develop flexibility of mind or independence of judgment. Moreover, it makes us narrow and rigid in the defense of our most warmly held opinions.
SYDNEY J. HARRIS (1917–1986)

11217 All things are at odds when God lets a thinker loose on this planet.
EDITH HAMILTON (1867–1963)

11218 As long as the devil can keep us terrified of thinking, he will always limit the work of God in our souls.
OSWALD CHAMBERS (1874–1917)

11219 As nothing is more easy than to think, so nothing is more difficult than to think well.
THOMAS TRAHERNE (C. 1637–1674)

11220 As soon as a man does not take his existence for granted, but beholds it as something unfathomably mysterious, thought begins.
ALBERT SCHWEITZER (1875–1965)

11221 Christian thinking is a rare and difficult thing; so many seem unaware that the first great commandment according to our Lord is, "Thou shalt love the Lord thy God . . . with all thy mind."
OSWALD CHAMBERS (1874–1917)

11222 Everything that can be thought at all can be thought clearly. Everything that can be said at all can be said clearly. But not everything that can be thought can be said.
LUDWIG JOSEF JOHAN WITTGENSTEIN (1889–1951)

11223 Good thoughts bear good fruit, bad thoughts bear bad fruit—and man is his own gardener.
JAMES ALLEN

11224 Great thoughts reduced to practice become great acts.
WILLIAM HAZLITT (1778–1830)

11225 If, instead of a gem or even a flower, we could cast the gift of a lovely thought into the heart of a friend, that would be giving as angels give.
GEORGE MACDONALD (1824–1905)

11226 In pagan religions the doctrinal element is at a minimum—the chief thing there is the performance of a ritual. But this is precisely where Christianity distinguishes itself from other religions—it does contain doctrine. It comes to men with definite, positive teaching; it claims to be the truth; it bases religion on knowledge, though a knowledge which is only attainable under moral conditions. . . . A religion divorced from earnest and lofty thought has always, down the whole history of the church, tended to become weak, jejune, and unwholesome; while the intellect, deprived of its rights within religion, has sought its satisfaction without and developed into godless rationalism.
JAMES ORR (1844–1913)

11227 It is hardly an exaggeration to say that many people contrive never once to think for themselves from the cradle to the grave. They may go through the motions of thinking, but in fact they solve all problems either by the dictate of their emotions, or by accepting without enquiry the ruling of some outside authority. Even quite well-informed people do this.
DOROTHY L. SAYERS (1893–1957)

11228 It is well for people who think to change their minds occasionally. For those who do not think, it is best at least to rearrange their prejudices once in a while.
LUTHER BURBANK (1849–1926)

11229 It will take all time and eternity to experience God's thought.
OSWALD CHAMBERS (1874–1917)

11230 Less than 15 per cent of people do any original thinking on any subject. . . .

The greatest torture in the world for most people is to think.
LUTHER BURBANK (1849–1926)

11231 Man is obviously made for thinking. Therein lies all his dignity and his merit.
BLAISE PASCAL (1623–1662)

11232 Men fear thought as they fear nothing else on earth—more than death. Thought is subversive and revolutionary, destructive and terrible; thought is merciless to privilege, established institutions, and comfortable habits; thought is anarchic and lawless, indifferent to authority, careless to the well-tried wisdom of the ages. Thought looks into the pit of hell and is not afraid. Thought is great and swift and free, the light of the world, and the chief glory of man.
BERTRAND ARTHUR WILLIAM RUSSELL (1872–1970)

11233 Most people would die sooner than think; in fact, they do so.
BERTRAND ARTHUR WILLIAM RUSSELL (1872–1970)

11234 No amount of energy will take the place of thought. A strenuous life with its eyes shut is a kind of wild insanity.
HENRY VAN DYKE (1852–1933)

11235 Only when we turn thoughtfully toward what has already been thought will we be turned to use for what must still be thought.
MARTIN HEIDEGGER (1889–1976)

11236 Our most important thoughts are those which contradict our emotions.
PAUL VALERY (1871–1945)

11237 The average man never really thinks from end to end of his life. The mental activity of such people is only a mouthing of clichés. What they mistake for thought is simply repetition of what they have heard. My guess is that well over 80 percent of the human race goes through life without having one single original thought. Whenever a new one appears, the average man shows signs of dismay and resentment.
H. L. MENCKEN (1880–1956)

11238 The Christian method of thinking puts the intellect second, not first; the modern view puts intellect on the throne. God does not sum up a man's worth by his thinking but by the way he expresses his thinking in actual life, that is, by his character.
OSWALD CHAMBERS (1874–1917)

11239 The Christian thinker challenges current prejudices . . . disturbs the complacent . . . obstructs the busy pragmatists . . . questions the very foundations of all about him and . . . is a nuisance.
HARRY BLAMIRES

11240 The first thing that goes when you begin to think is your theology. If you stick too long to a theological point of view, you become stagnant, without vitality.
OSWALD CHAMBERS (1874–1917)

11241 The free man is he who does not fear to go to the end of his thought.
LÉON BLUM (1872–1950)

11242 The history of thought . . . is absurd by what it seeks, great by what it finds.
PAUL VALERY (1871–1945)

11243 The majority of us recognize the necessity of receiving the Holy Spirit for living, but we do not sufficiently recognize the need for drawing on the resources of the Holy Spirit for thinking.
OSWALD CHAMBERS (1874–1917)

11244 The man who idly sits and thinks,
May sow a nobler crop than corn,
For thoughts are seeds of future deeds,
And when God thought—the world
was born!
HARRY ROMAINE

11245 The march of the human mind is slow.
EDMUND BURKE (1729–1797)

11246 The mind grows by what it feeds on.
JOSIAH GILBERT HOLLAND (1819–1881)

11247 The soul is tinged with the color and complexion of its thoughts.
MARCUS AURELIUS ANTONINUS (121–180)

11248 The third-rate mind is only happy when it is thinking with the majority; the second-rate mind is only happy when it is thinking with the minority; and the first-rate mind is only happy when it is thinking.
A. A. MILNE (1882–1956)

11249 The thought of God is never a burden; it is a gentle breeze which bears us up, a hand which supports us and raises us, a light which guides us, and a spirit which vivifies us though we do not feel its working.
FRANCESCO MALAVAL (1627–1719)

11250 The thoughts that come to us are worth more than the ones we seek.
JOSEPH JOUBERT (1754–1824)

11251 The universe is one of God's thoughts.
JOHANN FRIEDRICH VON SCHILLER (1759–1805)

11252 The world does move, and its motive power under God is the fearless thought and speech of those who dare to be in advance of their time—who are sneered at and shunned through their days of struggle as lunatics, dreamers, impracticables, and visionaries; men of crochets, vagaries, and isms.
HORACE GREELEY (1811–1872)

11253 There are few emotions so satisfying as the joy that comes from the act of recognition when we see and identify our own thoughts.
A. W. TOZER (1897–1963)

11254 There are very few original thinkers in the world, or ever have been. The greatest part of those who are called philosophers have adopted the opinions of some who went before them.
DUGALD STEWART (1753–1828)

11255 There is nothing either good or bad, But thinking makes it so.
WILLIAM SHAKESPEARE (1564–1616)

11256 There's something so beautiful in coming on one's very own inmost thoughts in another. In one way it's one of the greatest pleasures one has.
OLIVE SCHREINER (1855–1920)

11257 Think like a man of action; act like a man of thought.
HENRI BERGSON (1859–1941)

11258 Think today, and speak tomorrow.
HENRY GEORGE BOHN (1796–1884)

11259 Thinking in its lower grades is comparable to paper money, and in its higher forms it is a kind of poetry.
HAVELOCK ELLIS (1859–1939)

11260 Thinking is like loving and dying. Each of us must do it for himself.
JOSIAH ROYCE (1855–1916)

11261 Thinking is the magic of the mind.
LORD GEORGE NOEL GORDON BYRON (1788–1824)

11262 Thinking is the talking of the soul with itself.
PLATO (C. 428–348 B.C.)

11263 Thinking is to me the greatest fatigue in the world.
SIR JOHN VANBRUGH (1664–1726)

11264 Thought is always in advance; it can see too far ahead, outstripping our bodies, which are in the present.
ALBERT CAMUS (1913–1960)

11265 Thought is what changes knowledge into energy.
DOROTHY L. SAYERS (1893–1957)

11266 Thought only starts with doubt.
ROGER MARTIN DU GARD (1881–1958)

11267 Thought serves as a mirror: it shows us the ugliness and the beauty within.
SHIRAT YISRAEL MOSES IBN EZRA (1055–1135)

11268 Through space the universe grasps me and swallows me up like a speck; through thought I grasp it.
BLAISE PASCAL (1623–1662)

11269 To do his gracious work God must have the intelligent cooperation of his people. If we would think God's thoughts, we must learn to think continually of God.
A. W. TOZER (1897–1963)

11270 To think is an effort; to think rightly is a great effort, and to think as a Christian ought to think is the greatest effort of a human soul.
OSWALD CHAMBERS (1874–1917)

11271 To think is to see.
LOUIS LAMBERT (1799–1850)

11272 We are all capable of evil thoughts, but only very rarely of evil deeds; we can all do good deeds, but very few of us can think good thoughts.
CESARE PAVESE (1908–1950)

11273 We have no business to limit God's revelations to the bias of the human mind.
OSWALD CHAMBERS (1874–1917)

11274 We have to work out, not our redemption, but our human appreciation of our redemption. We owe it to God that we refuse to have rusty brains.
OSWALD CHAMBERS (1874–1917)

11275 What is the hardest task in the world? To think.
RALPH WALDO EMERSON (1803–1882)

11276 What thought can think, another thought can mend.
ROBERT SOUTHWELL (C. 1561–1595)

11277 What we think about when we are free to think about what we will—that is what we are or will soon become.
A. W. TOZER (1897–1963)

11278 Whatever failures I have known, whatever errors I have committed, whatever follies I have witnessed in private and public life have been the consequences of action without thought.
BERNARD MANNES BARUCH (1870–1965)

11279 Where all think alike, no one thinks very much.
WALTER LIPPMANN (1889–1974)

11280 Where do thoughts go? Into the memory of God.
JOSEPH JOUBERT (1754–1824)

11281 Who can mistake great thoughts? They seize upon the mind—
arrest, and search,
And shake it.
PHILIP JAMES BAILEY (1816–1902)

THOUGHTFULNESS

11282 Give to every other human being the right that you claim for yourself.
ROBERT GREEN INGERSOLL (1833–1899)

11283 I am the inferior of any man whose rights I trample under foot.
ROBERT GREEN INGERSOLL (1833–1899)

11284 Manner may in seven words be found:
Forget yourself and think of those
around.
ARTHUR GUITERMAN (1871–1943)

11285 Mention not a halter in the house of
him that was hanged.
GEORGE HERBERT (1593–1633)

11286 The best way to keep from stepping
on the other fellow's toes is to put
yourself in his shoes.

TIME

11287 'Tis not for man to trifle; life is brief,
And sin is here.
Our age is but the falling of a leaf,
A dropping tear.
We have no time to sport away the
hours;
All must be earnest in the world like
ours.
Not many lives, but only one have we,
Only, only one.
How earnest should that one life be,
That narrow span;
Day after day spent in blessed toil.
HORATIUS BONAR (1808–1889)

11288 All passes; nothing lasts. The moment
that we put our hand upon it, it melts
away like smoke, is gone forever, and
the snake is eating at our heart again;
we see then what we are and what our
lives must come to.
THOMAS CLAYTON WOLFE (1900–1938)

11289 As every thread of gold is valuable, so
is every minute of time.
JOHN MASON (1706–1773)

11290 As if you could kill time without injuring eternity.
HENRY DAVID THOREAU (1817–1862)

11291 By the time we've reached the *w* of
now the *n* is ancient history.
MICHAEL FRAYN (1933–)

11292 Do not walk through time without
leaving worthy evidence of your passage.
POPE JOHN XXIII (1881–1963)

11293 Every moment comes to you pregnant
with a divine purpose; time being so
precious that God deals it out only second by second. Once it leaves your

hands and your power to do with it as
you please, it plunges into eternity, to
remain forever what you made it.
ARCHBISHOP FULTON J. SHEEN (1895–1979)

11294 Gather ye rosebuds while ye may,
Old Time is still aflying,
And this same flower that smiles today,
Tomorrow will be dying.
ROBERT HERRICK (1591–1674)

11295 God dwells in eternity, but time dwells
in God. He has already lived all our
tomorrows as he has lived all our yesterdays.
A. W. TOZER (1897–1963)

11296 God gives me the gift of twenty-four
hours a day; yet he is kind enough to
accept in return the little time I give
back to him.
PAUL TOURNIER (1898–1986)

11297 God has said he will exalt you in due
time, but remember, he is referring to
his time and not yours!
A. W. TOZER (1897–1963)

11298 God is not subject to time.
DOROTHY L. SAYERS (1893–1957)

11299 God's ways seem dark, but, soon or
late,
They touch the shining hills of day;
The evil cannot brook delay,
The good can well afford to wait.
Give ermined knaves their hour of
crime;
Yet have the future grand and great,
The safe appeal of Truth to Time.
JOHN GREENLEAF WHITTIER (1807–1892)

11300 He who neglects the present moment
throws away all he has.
JOHANN FRIEDRICH VON SCHILLER
(1759–1805)

11301 I still find each day too short for all
the thoughts I want to think, all the
walks I want to take, all the books I
want to read, and all the friends I
want to see. The longer I live, the
more my mind dwells upon the beauty
and wonder of the world.
JOHN BURROUGHS (1837–1921)

11302 It is ten o'clock: Thus may we see how
the world wags.
'Tis but an hour ago, since it was nine;

And after an hour more, 'twill be
  eleven;
And so, from hour to hour, we ripe
  and ripe,
And then, from hour to hour, we rot
  and rot,
And thereby hangs a tale.
WILLIAM SHAKESPEARE (1564–1616)

11303 It's up to me to use it.
  I must suffer if I lose it.
  Give account if I abuse it.
  Just a tiny little minute,
  But eternity is in it.

11304 Learn from yesterday;
  Live for today;
  Hope for tomorrow.

11305 Lost time is never found again.
  BENJAMIN FRANKLIN (1706–1790)

11306 Lost, yesterday, somewhere between
  sunrise and sunset, two golden hours,
  each set with sixty diamond minutes.
  No reward is offered for they are gone
  forever.
  HORACE MANN (1796–1859)

11307 Man thinks he loses something—time—
  when he does not do things quickly.
  Yet he does not know what to do with
  the time he gains—except kill it.
  ERICH FROMM (1900–1980)

11308 Misspending a man's time is a kind of
  self-homicide.
  GEORGE SAVILE (1633–1695)

11309 Most people object to the speed of
  light—it arrives too early in the morning.

11310 No wonder time flies—there are so
  many people trying to kill it.

11311 Only eternal values can give meaning
  to temporal ones. Time must be the
  servant of eternity.
  ERWIN W. LUTZER (1941–   )

11312 Spend your time
      in nothing which you know must be
  repented of;
      in nothing on which you might not
  pray for the blessing of God;
      in nothing which you could not
  review with a quiet conscience on your
  dying bed;

in nothing which you might not
safely and properly be found doing if
death should surprise you in the act.
RICHARD BAXTER (1615–1691)

11313 Take care of the minutes, and the
  hours will take care of themselves.
  LORD CHESTERFIELD (1694–1773)

11314 That God appears at time's beginning
  is not too difficult to comprehend, but
  that he appears at the beginning and
  end of time simultaneously is not so
  easy to grasp. Time is known to us by
  a succession of events. . . . Changes
  take place not all at once but in succession, one after the other, and it is the
  relation of "after" to "before" that
  gives us our idea of time. . . . God is
  not compelled so to wait. For him
  everything that will happen has
  already happened.
  A. W. TOZER (1897–1963)

11315 That old bald cheater—Time.
  BEN JONSON (1572–1637)

11316 The highest part of the soul stands
  above time and knows nothing of
  time. In eternity there is neither time
  nor space, neither before nor after;
  everything is present in one fresh-
  springing now.
  MEISTER ECKHART (C. 1260–C. 1327)

11317 The inaudible and noiseless foot of
  time.
  WILLIAM SHAKESPEARE (1564–1616)

11318 The morning hour has gold in its hand.
  BENJAMIN FRANKLIN (1706–1790)

11319 The small moment is the carrier of
  God's most endearing gift. It must not
  be permitted to slip away unsavored
  and unappreciated.
  GERHARD E. FROST

11320 The years come to my door and knock
  and walk away sighing.
  TILLINGHAST

11321 The year
    On the earth,
    Her deathbed, in a shroud of leaves
      dead
    Is lying.
    PERCY BYSSHE SHELLEY (1792–1822)

11322 There is no other time than now with
God, no past and no future.
OSWALD CHAMBERS (1874–1917)

11323 Time converts knowledge into wisdom, energies spent into experience
gained. Time leaves us richer for what
we have had. And time thoughtfully
permits us to use the fire of youth to
drive the engines of age. We can be
young and old at the same time.
SIDNEY GREENBERG

11324 Time crumbles things.
ARISTOTLE (384–322 B.C.)

11325 Time discovers the truth.
LUCIUS ANNAEUS SENECA (C. 4 B.C.–A.D. 65)

11326 Time goes by; reputation increases,
ability declines.
DAG HAMMARSKJÖLD (1905–1961)

11327 Time goes, you say? Ah no! Alas, time
stays, we go.
AUSTIN DOBSON (1840–1921)

11328 Time has a way of insulting the most
beautiful things, and will fade your
rosy cheeks just as he has wrinkled my
brow.
PIERRE CORNEILLE (1606–1684)

11329 Time has no divisions to mark its passage, there is never a thunderstorm or
blare of trumpets to announce the
beginning of a new month or year.
Even when a new century begins, it is
only we mortals who ring bells and
fire off pistols.
THOMAS MANN (1875–1955)

11330 Time has no flight—'tis we who speed
along.
The days and nights are but the same
as when
The earth awoke with the first rush of
song,
And felt the swiftly passing feet of
men.
THOMAS S. COLLIER

11331 Time heals all things—except leaky
faucets.

11332 Time heals what reason cannot.
LUCIUS ANNAEUS SENECA (C. 4 B.C.–A.D. 65)

11333 Time is . . .
Too slow for those who wait,
Too swift for those who fear,
Too long for those who grieve,
Too short for those who rejoice,
But for those who love,
Time is eternity.
HENRY VAN DYKE (1852–1933)

11334 Time is a circus; always packing up
and moving away.
BEN HECHT (1894–1964)

11335 Time is a dressmaker specializing in
alteration.
FAITH BALDWIN (1893–1978)

11336 Time is a physician that heals every
grief.
DIPHILIUS

11337 Time is a precious gift of God; so precious that he only gives it to us
moment by moment.
AMELIA EDITH BARR (1831–1919)

11338 Time is nothing to God.
OSWALD CHAMBERS (1874–1917)

11339 Time is so precious that it is dealt out
to us only in the smallest possible fractions—a tiny moment at a time.
IRISH PROVERB

11340 Time is the deposit each one has in the
bank of God, and no one knows the
balance.
RALPH WASHINGTON SOCKMAN
(1889–1970)

11341 Time never takes time off.
SAINT AUGUSTINE OF HIPPO (354–430)

11342 Time ripens all things. No man is born
wise.
MIGUEL DE CERVANTES (1547–1616)

11343 Time slides through our fingers like a
well-greased string.
JAMES C. DOBSON (1936–   )

11344 Time's glory is to calm contending
kings,
To unmask falsehood and bring truth
to light,
To stamp the seal of time in aged
things,
To wake the morn and sentinel the
night,
To wrong the wronger till he render
right,
To ruinate proud buildings with thy
hours,

And smear with dust their glittering
 golden towers.
WILLIAM SHAKESPEARE (1564–1616)

11345 Time, as he passes us, has a dove's
 wing,
Unsoil'd and swift, and of a silken
 sound.
WILLIAM COWPER (1731–1800)

11346 To the philosopher, time is one of the
fundamental quantities. To the average
man, time has something to do with
dinner.
J. A. VANHORN

11347 Wait for that wisest of all counselors,
Time.
PERICLES (C. 495–429 B.C.)

11348 We all find time to do what we really
want to do.
WILLIAM FEATHER (1889–   )

11349 We can choke God's Word with a
yawn; we can hinder the time that
should be spent with God by remembering we have other things to do. "I
haven't time!" Of course you have
time! Take time, strangle some other
interests, and make time to realize that
the center of power in your life is the
Lord Jesus Christ.
OSWALD CHAMBERS (1874–1917)

11350 We can look backward in time until
the dim past vanishes, then turn and
look into the future until thought and
imagination collapse from exhaustion
and God is at both points, unaffected
by either.
A. W. TOZER (1897–1963)

11351 What, then, is time? If no one asks me,
I know; but if I want to explain it to a
questioner, I do not know.
SAINT AUGUSTINE OF HIPPO (354–430)

11352 Whenever I attempt to frame a simple
idea of time . . . I am lost and em-
brangled in inextricable difficulties.
GEORGE BERKELEY (1685–1753)

11353 Where, except in the present, can the
eternal be met?
C. S. LEWIS (1898–1963)

11354 Winged time glides on insensibly and
deceives us; and there is nothing more
fleeting than years.
OVID (43 B.C.–A.D. 17)

11355 With God one day is as a thousand
years and a thousand years as one day,
which is to say that there is no calendar and no timepiece in the divine
experience, no aging, no getting away
from the beginning, nor approaching
toward the end.
CHARLES HENRY PARKHURST (1842–1933)

11356 You wake up in the morning with
twenty-four hours of the unmanufac-
tured tissue of the universe of your
life. It is yours. It is the most precious
of possessions. No one can take it
from you. It is unstealable. And no
one receives either more or less.
ARNOLD BENNETT (1867–1931)

TITHE

11357 A half dollar isn't supposed to be as
good as a dollar, but it goes to church
more often.

11358 He gives nothing but worthless gold
Who gives from a sense of duty.
JAMES RUSSELL LOWELL (1819–1891)

11359 His alms were money put to interest
In the other world.
ROBERT SOUTHEY (1774–1843)

11360 The quantity of money that one gives
is of little importance. What is important is what one gives. If it is a part of
one's income, then this is not righteousness, goodness, and good faith. If
it is capital that one gives, then everything is in order.
JOHN HOWARD YODER

TODAY

11361 *Now* is the watchword of the wise.
CHARLES HADDON SPURGEON (1834–1892)

11362 Build a little fence of trust
 Around today;
Fill the space with loving deeds,
 And therein stay.
Look not through the sheltering bars
 Upon tomorrow;

God will help thee bear what comes
Of joy or sorrow.
MARY FRANCES BUTTS (1836–1902)

11363 Consider that this day ne'er dawns
again.
DANTE ALIGHIERI (1265–1321)

11364 Each morning puts a man on trial, and
each evening passes judgment.
ROY L. SMITH

11365 Enjoy the blessings of this day, if God
sends them; and the evils of it bear
patiently and sweetly: for this day only
is ours, we are dead to yesterday, and
we are not yet born to the morrow.
JEREMY TAYLOR (1613–1667)

11366 Finish every day and be done with it.
You have done what you could. Some
blunders and absurdities no doubt
have crept in; forget them as soon as
you can. Tomorrow is a new day;
begin it well and serenely and with too
high a spirit to be cumbered with your
old nonsense. This day is all that is
good and fair. It is too dear, with its
hopes and invitations, to waste a
moment on yesterdays.
RALPH WALDO EMERSON (1803–1882)

11367 He who governed the world before I
was born shall take care of it likewise
when I am dead. My part is to
improve the present moment.
JOHN WESLEY (1703–1791)

11368 He who neglects the present moment
throws away all he has.
JOHANN FRIEDRICH VON SCHILLER
(1759–1805)

11369 I've shut the door on yesterday
And thrown the key away—
Tomorrow holds no fears for me,
Since I have found today.
VIVIAN YEISER LARAMORE (1891–   )

11370 If you allot your day and say, "I am
going to give so much time to this, and
so much to that," and God's providence upsets your timetable, what
becomes of your spirituality?
OSWALD CHAMBERS (1874–1917)

11371 It is harder to see today when we are
looking at tomorrow.

11372 Know the true value of time; snatch,
seize, and enjoy every moment of it.
No idleness; no laziness, no procrastination. Never put off till tomorrow
what you can do today.
LORD CHESTERFIELD (1694–1773)

11373 Let us enjoy the fugitive hour. Man
has no harbor, time has no shore, it
rushes on and carries us with it.
ALPHONSE-MARIE-LOUIS DE PRAT
DE LAMARTINE (1790–1869)

11374 Life is a journey, not a destination;
and happiness is not "there" but here;
not tomorrow, but today.
SIDNEY GREENBERG

11375 Live full today, and let no pleasure
pass untasted—
And no transient beauty scorn;
Fill well the storehouse of the soul's
delight
With light of memory—
Who knows? Tomorrow may be—
Night.

11376 One today is worth two tomorrows.
BENJAMIN FRANKLIN (1706–1790)

11377 Since Time is not a person we can over-
take when he is gone, let us honor him
with mirth and cheerfulness of heart
while he is passing.
JOHANN WOLFGANG VON GOETHE
(1749–1832)

11378 The present is the only thing that has
no end.
ERWIN SCHRÖDINGER (1887–1961)

11379 The present, the present is all thou hast
For thy sure possessing;
Like the patriarch's angel hold it fast
Till it gives its blessing.
JOHN GREENLEAF WHITTIER (1807–1892)

11380 There was a wise man in the east
whose constant prayer was that he
might see today with the eyes of
tomorrow.
ALFRED MERCIER (1816–1894)

11381 These are the good old days the next
generation will hear so much about.

11382 Today . . . that special block of time
holding the key that locks out yester-

day's nightmares and unlocks tomorrow's dreams.
CHARLES R. SWINDOLL (1934–   )

11383 Today is the tomorrow you worried about yesterday, and all is well.

11384 Today is yesterday's pupil.
BENJAMIN FRANKLIN (1706–1790)

11385 Today's today. Tomorrow we may be ourselves gone down the drain of eternity.
EURIPIDES (C. 484–406 B.C.)

11386 Trust no future, howe'er pleasant!
Let the dead past bury its dead!
Act—act in the living present!
Heart within and God o'erhead!
HENRY WADSWORTH LONGFELLOW (1807–1882)

11387 We are never content with our lot; the worst time is always the present.
JEAN DE LA FONTAINE (1621–1695)

11388 We cannot put off living until we are ready. The most salient characteristic of life is its coerciveness; it is always urgent, "here and now" without any possible postponement. Life is fired at us point blank.
JOSÉ ORTEGA Y GASSET (1883–1955)

11389 Where is it, this present? It has melted in our grasp, fled ere we could touch it, gone in the instant of becoming.
WILLIAM JAMES (1842–1910)

11390 Yesterday is a canceled check, and tomorrow is a promissory note. But today is cash, ready for us to spend in living.
BARBARA JOHNSON

11391 You say that you will see God and his light someday;
O fool! You never shall, you must see him today.
ANGELUS SILESIUS (1624–1677)

TOLERANCE

11392 A difference of opinion alienates only little minds.
PROVERB

11393 I have seen gross intolerance shown in support of tolerance.
SAMUEL TAYLOR COLERIDGE (1772–1834)

11394 In the world it is called tolerance, but in hell it is called despair . . . the sin that believes in nothing, interferes with nothing, enjoys nothing, hates nothing, finds purpose in nothing, lives for nothing, and remains alive because there is nothing for which it will die.
DOROTHY L. SAYERS (1893–1957)

11395 It is only imperfection that complains of what is imperfect. The more perfect we are, the more gentle and quiet we become toward the defects of others.
FRANÇOIS FÉNELON (1651–1715)

11396 Love thy neighbor, even when he plays the trombone.
JEWISH PROVERB

11397 O God, help us not to despise or oppose what we do not understand.
WILLIAM PENN (1644–1718)

11398 To understand all makes one tolerant.
ANNE-LOUISE-GERMAINE DE STAËL (1766–1817)

11399 Tolerance implies a respect for another person, not because he is wrong or even because he is right, but because he is human.
JOHN COGLEY (1916–1976)

11400 Tolerance is a tremendous virtue, but the immediate neighbors of tolerance are apathy and weakness.
SIR JAMES GOLDSMITH (1933–   )

11401 *Tolerance* is another word for *indifference*.
WILLIAM SOMERSET MAUGHAM (1874–1965)

TOMORROW

11402 To worry about tomorrow is to be unhappy today.
PROVERB

11403 Tomorrow comes to us at midnight very clean. It's perfect when it arrives, and it puts itself in our hands and hopes we've learnt something from yesterday.
JOHN WAYNE (1907–1979)

11404 Tomorrow is the day on which loafers work, fools act sensibly, and people lose the opportunity to accept Christ.

TONGUE

11405 A bridle for the tongue is a necessary piece of furniture.
PROVERB

11406 A sharp tongue is the only edge tool that grows keener with constant use.
WASHINGTON IRVING (1783–1859)

11407 A slip of the foot you may soon recover,
But a slip of the tongue you may never get over.
BENJAMIN FRANKLIN (1706–1790)

11408 Better the feet slip than the tongue.
PROVERB

11409 Birds are entangled by their feet and men by their tongues.
SIR THOMAS FULLER (1608–1661)

11410 By examining the tongue of the patient, physicians find out the diseases of the body, and philosophers the diseases of the mind.
JUSTIN THE MARTYR (C. 100–C. 165)

11411 Confine your tongue, lest it confine you.
PROVERB

11412 Learn to hold thy tongue. Five words cost Zacharias forty weeks' silence.
SIR THOMAS FULLER (1608–1661)

11413 Nothing causes more trouble than the tongue.
JEWISH PROVERB

11414 The great test of a man's character is his tongue.
OSWALD CHAMBERS (1874–1917)

11415 The tongue is a wild beast; once let loose it is difficult to chain.
BALTASAR GRACIÁN Y MORALES (1601–1658)

11416 The tongue is the ambassador of the heart.
JOHN LYLY (C. 1554–1606)

11417 The tongue is the most dangerous of weapons.
JEWISH PROVERB

11418 The tongue is the rudder of our ship.
SIR THOMAS FULLER (1608–1661)

11419 There is danger when a man throws his tongue into high gear before he gets his brain a-going.
C. C. PHELPS

11420 Though your eyelids get heavy and your shoulders, arms, and legs ache with fatigue, your tongue registers no weariness.

11421 To speak kindly does not hurt the tongue.
PROVERB

TRINITY

11422 A popular belief among Christians divides the work of God between the three Persons, giving a specific part to each: creation to the Father, redemption to the Son, and regeneration to the Holy Spirit. This is partly true but not wholly so, for God cannot so divide himself that one Person works while another is inactive. In the Scriptures the three Persons are shown to act in harmonious unity in all the mighty works that are wrought throughout the universe.
A. W. TOZER (1897–1963)

11423 God does not live in isolation—not in the solitude of a single person, but three persons in one essence.
LOUIS EVELY (1910–)

11424 Holiest Trinity, perfect in unity,
Bind in thy love every nation and race;
May we adore thee for time and eternity,
Father, Redeemer, and Spirit of grace.
PATRICK APPLEFORD

11425 In Christianity God is not a static thing—not even a person—but a dynamic, pulsating activity, a life, almost a kind of drama. Almost, if you will not think me irreverent, a kind of dance. The union between the Father and Son is such a live concrete thing that this union itself is a Person. . . . What grows out of the joint life of the Father and Son is a real Person, is, in fact, the Third of the three Persons who are God. The whole dance, or drama, a pattern of this

three-Personal life is to be played out in each one of us or (putting it the other way round) each one of us has got to enter that pattern, take his place in that dance.
C. S. LEWIS (1898–1963)

11426 The Creed confesses three persons as comprehended in one divine essence, each one, however, retaining his distinct personality . . . to the Father we ascribe the work of creation; to the Son the work of redemption; to the Holy Spirit the power to forgive sins, to gladden, to strengthen, to transport from death to life eternal.
MARTIN LUTHER (1483–1546)

11427 The Trinity attributes to the Father those works of the Divinity in which power excels, to the Son those in which wisdom excels, and those in which love excels to the Holy Ghost.
POPE JOHN XXIII (1881–1963)

11428 The Trinity is a mystery which my faith embraces as revealed in the Word, but my reason cannot fathom.
JOHN ARROWSMITH

11429 Timeless, spaceless, single, lonely,
Yet sublimely Three,
Thou art grandly, always, only
God is Unity!
Lone in grandeur, lone in glory,
Who shall tell thy wondrous story?
Awful Trinity!
FREDERICK WILLIAM FABER (1814–1863)

TROUBLE

11430 Better never trouble Trouble
Until Trouble troubles you;
For you only make your trouble
Double-trouble when you do.
DAVID KEPPEL (C. 1846)

11431 Funny thing how trouble acts different on people: it's like hot weather—sours milk but sweetens apples.
JOSEPH C. LINCOLN

11432 God's darkest threatenings are always accompanied with a revelation of the way of escape. The ark is always along with the Flood. Zoar is pointed out when God foretells Sodom's ruin. The

brazen serpent is ever reared where the venomous snakes bite and burn.
ALEXANDER MACLAREN (1826–1910)

11433 He who will live for others shall have great troubles, but they shall seem to him small. He who will live for himself shall have small troubles, but they shall seem to him great.
WILLIAM RALPH INGE (1860–1954)

11434 I am an old man and have known a great many troubles, but most of them never happened.
MARK TWAIN (1835–1910)

11435 I believe in getting into hot water; it keeps you clean.
G. K. CHESTERTON (1874–1936)

11436 If a man could have half his wishes, he would double his troubles.
BENJAMIN FRANKLIN (1706–1790)

11437 If pleasures are greatest in anticipation, remember that this is also true of trouble.
ELBERT GREEN HUBBARD (1856–1915)

11438 If you don't learn to laugh at trouble, you won't have anything to laugh at when you're old.
ED HOWE (1853–1937)

11439 In trouble we may find comfort, though it be only that things might have been worse.
AMELIA EDITH BARR (1831–1919)

11440 Many of our troubles are God dragging us, and they would end if we would stand upon our feet and go whither he would have us.
HENRY WARD BEECHER (1813–1887)

11441 Maybe the Lord lets some people get into trouble because that is the only time they ever think of him.

11442 Most troubles are imaginary: what you think are huge clouds in the sky may be nothing more than dust on your eyelashes.

11443 Never attempt to bear more than one kind of trouble at once. Some people bear three kinds—all they have had, all they have now, and all they expect to have.
EDWARD EVERETT HALE (1822–1909)

11444 No man ever got himself out of trouble until he first admitted he was in trouble.
PROVERB

11445 Nobody knows the trouble I've seen, Nobody knows but Jesus.
NEGRO SPIRITUAL

11446 Oh, a trouble's a ton, or a trouble's an ounce,
Or a trouble is what you make it,
And it isn't the fact that you're hurt that counts,
But only how did you take it?
EDMUND VANCE COOKE (1866–1932)

11447 One leg in the stocks, or two, 'tis all the same.
IRISH PROVERB

11448 One trouble with trouble is that it usually starts out like fun.
PROVERB

11449 Some people are so fond of ill-luck that they run halfway to meet it.
DOUGLAS WILLIAM JERROLD (1803–1857)

11450 Some people go back into the past and rake up all the troubles they ever had, and then they look into the future and anticipate that they will have still more trouble, and then they go reeling and staggering all through life.
DWIGHT LYMAN MOODY (1837–1899)

11451 The Bible nowhere indicates that God withdraws us from the troubles of life. In fact, we become more involved in life's troubles when we come to Christ. But he gives us power to go on with the battle.
BILLY GRAHAM (1918–   )

11452 The Christian under trouble doesn't break up—he breaks out.
E. STANLEY JONES (1884–1973)

11453 The way out of trouble is never as simple as the way in.
ED HOWE (1853–1937)

11454 The whole trouble is that we won't let God help us.
GEORGE MACDONALD (1824–1905)

11455 There are many troubles which you cannot cure by the Bible and the hymnbook but which you can cure by a good perspiration and a breath of fresh air.
HENRY WARD BEECHER (1813–1887)

11456 There are people who are always anticipating trouble, and in this way they manage to enjoy many sorrows that never really happen to them.
JOSH BILLINGS (1818–1885)

11457 There are three kinds of trouble in the world: money, others, yourself.
THOMAS LANSING MASSON (1866–1934)

11458 There's one thing to be said for inviting trouble: it generally accepts.
MAE MALOO

11459 Trouble . . . why do we fear it? Why do we dread ordeal? Every good thing the human race has experienced was trouble for somebody. Our birth was trouble for our mothers. To support us was trouble for our fathers.
LILLIAN SMITH (1897–1966)

11460 Trouble is often the lever in God's hands to raise us up to heaven.
PROVERB

11461 Trouble knocked at the door, but hearing a laugh within hurried away.
BENJAMIN FRANKLIN (1706–1790)

11462 Trouble rides a fast horse.
ITALIAN PROVERB

11463 When in trouble, always hold your chin up—if it does nothing else, it will keep your mouth shut.

11464 When troubles come from God, then naught behooves like patience; but for troubles wrought of men, patience is hard—I tell you it is hard.
JEAN INGELOW (1820–1897)

TRUST

11465 All I have seen teaches me to trust the Creator for all I have not seen.
RALPH WALDO EMERSON (1803–1882)

11466 An ideal method of time management is T-R-U-S-T, putting the pressure it brings back into God's hand.
CHARLES R. SWINDOLL (1934–   )

11467 Courage, brother! do not stumble, Though thy path be dark as night;

There's a star to guide the humble,
Trust in God and do the right.
NORMAN MACLEOD (1812–1872)

11468 God knows, not I, the reason why
His winds of storm drive through my
door;
I am content to live or die
Just knowing this, nor knowing more.
My Father's hand appointing me
My days and ways, so I am free.
MARGARET SANGSTER (1838–1912)

11469 Hush! my dear, lie still and slumber,
Holy angels guard thy bed.
Heavenly blessings without number
Gently falling on thy head.
ISAAC WATTS (1674–1748)

11470 I will not doubt, though all my ships
at sea
Come drifting home with broken
masts and sails;
I shall believe the hand which never
fails,
From seeming evil worketh good to
me.
And, though I weep because those
sails are battered,
Still will I cry, while my best hopes lie
shattered,
"I trust in thee."
ELLA WHEELER WILCOX (1850–1919)

11471 I would rather walk with God in the
dark than go alone in the light.
MARY GARDINER BRAINARD (C. 1860)

11472 If we love Christ much, surely we shall
trust him much.
THOMAS BENTON BROOKS (1608–1680)

11473 It is an equal failing to trust everybody
and to trust nobody.
PROVERB

11474 It is not our trust that keeps us, but
the God in whom we trust who keeps
us.
OSWALD CHAMBERS (1874–1917)

11475 Let us be like a bird for a moment
perched
On a frail branch when he sings;
Though he feels it bend, yet he sings
his song,
Knowing that he has wings.
VICTOR HUGO (1802–1885)

11476 O holy trust! O endless sense of rest!
Like the beloved John
To lay his head upon the Savior's
breast,
And thus to journey on!
HENRY WADSWORTH LONGFELLOW
(1807–1882)

11477 Relying on God has to begin all over
again every day as if nothing had yet
been done.
C. S. LEWIS (1898–1963)

11478 That little bird has chosen his shelter;
above it are the stars and the deep
heaven of worlds; yet he is rocking
himself to sleep without caring for
tomorrow's lodging, calmly clinging to
his little twig and leaving God to think
for him.
MARTIN LUTHER (1483–1546)

11479 The bravery of God in trusting us! It is
a tremendously risky thing to do.
OSWALD CHAMBERS (1874–1917)

11480 The highest pinnacle of the spiritual
life is not happy joy in unbroken sunshine, but absolute and undoubting
trust in the love of God.
A. W. THOROLD

11481 The more we depend on God, the
more dependable we find he is.
CLIFF RICHARDS (1940–)

11482 There is no panic in trust.
BERTHA MUNRO

11483 To be trusted is a greater compliment
than to be loved.
GEORGE MACDONALD (1824–1905)

11484 Trust begets truth.
SIR WILLIAM GURNEY BENHAM
(1859–1944)

11485 Trust God where you cannot trace
him. Do not try to penetrate the cloud
he brings over you; rather look to the
bow that is on it. The mystery is
God's; the promise is yours.
JOHN R. MACDUFF (1818–1895)

11486 Trust involves letting go and knowing
God will catch you.
JAMES C. DOBSON (1936–)

11487 Trustfulness is based on confidence in
God, whose ways I do not understand.

If I did, there would be no need for trust.
OSWALD CHAMBERS (1874–1917)

11488 What we need very badly these days is a company of Christians who are prepared to trust God as completely now as they know they must do at the last day. For each of us the time is coming when we shall have nothing but God. Health and wealth and friends and hiding places will be swept away, and we shall have only God. To the man of pseudo faith that is a terrifying thought, but to real faith it is one of the most comforting thoughts the heart can entertain.
A. W. TOZER (1897–1963)

11489 When you have accomplished your daily task, go to sleep in peace; God is awake.
VICTOR HUGO (1802–1885)

11490 When you have no helpers, see all your helpers in God. When you have many helpers, see God in all your helpers. When you have nothing but God, see all in God. When you have everything, see God in everything. Under all conditions, stay thy heart only on the Lord.
CHARLES HADDON SPURGEON (1834–1892)

TRUTH

11491 A collapsing world is more conducive to understanding the nature of truth than a triumphant world.
MALCOLM MUGGERIDGE (1903–1990)

11492 A half-truth is a dangerous thing, especially if you have got hold of the wrong half.
MYRON F. BOYD

11493 A man can't always be defending the truth; there must be a time to feed on it.
C. S. LEWIS (1898–1963)

11494 About money and sex, it is impossible to be truthful ever. One's ego is too involved.
MALCOLM MUGGERIDGE (1903–1990)

11495 Absolute truth belongs to God alone.
GOTTHOLD EPHRAIM LESSING (1729–1781)

11496 All truth is not to be told at all times.
PROVERB

11497 Although it be with truth thou speakest evil, that also is a crime.
SAINT JOHN CHRYSOSTOM C. 347–407

11498 Better the ugly truth than a beautiful lie.
JEWISH PROVERB

11499 Beware lest you lose the substance by grasping at the shadow.
AESOP (FL. C. 550 B.C.)

11500 Exaggeration is truth that has lost its temper.
KAHLIL GIBRAN (1883–1931)

11501 For the truth-teller and truth-seeker, indeed, the whole world has very little liking. He is always unpopular, and not infrequently his unpopularity is so excessive that it endangers his life. Run your eye back over the list of martyrs, lay and clerical; nine-tenths of them stood accused of nothing worse than honest efforts to find out and announce the truth.
H. L. MENCKEN (1880–1956)

11502 For years it had been my policy not to correct untrue statements about me that appeared in the press. As a rule, the friends whose good opinion you value will not believe ill of you. Your enemies will believe, or profess to believe, evil of you regardless of your denial.
JAMES FRANCIS BYRNES (1879–1972)

11503 Forge thy tongue on an anvil of truth
And what flies up, though it be but a spark,
Shall have weight.
PINDAR (C. 522–438 B.C.)

11504 From the death of the old the new proceeds,
And the life of truth from the death of creeds.
JOHN GREENLEAF WHITTIER (1807–1892)

11505 God gives us the will wherewith to will, and the power to use it, and the help needed to supplement the power . . . but we ourselves must will the truth, and for that the Lord is waiting.
GEORGE MACDONALD (1824–1905)

11506 He who says that some lies are just says no other than that some sins are just, and therefore some things are just which are unjust. What can be more absurd?
SAINT AUGUSTINE OF HIPPO (354–430)

11507 I made him swear he'd always tell me
        nothing but the truth.
I promised him I never would resent it,
No matter how unbearable, how
        harsh, how cruel.
How come he thought I meant it?
JUDITH STAHL VIORST (1931–)

11508 I seem to have been only like a boy playing on the seashore, and diverting myself in now and then finding a smoother pebble or a prettier shell than ordinary, whilst the great ocean of truth lay all undiscovered before me.
SIR ISAAC NEWTON (1642–1727)

11509 If Christ did not speak the truth in all matters, the claims about himself vanish like the idle babbling of a lunatic bent on deceiving the world. Unlike Plato and Aristotle, he could not afford to be wrong—even once.
ERWIN W. LUTZER (1941–)

11510 If you tell the truth, you have infinite power supporting you; but if not, you have infinite power against you.
CHARLES GEORGE GORDON (1833–1885)

11511 In seeking truth you have to get both sides of a story.
WALTER CRONKITE (1916–)

11512 It is contrary to reason for a thirsty person to turn from a pure, sparkling mountain stream to quench his thirst at a stale, putrid cistern—yet that is what the human race does when it rejects God's truth and standards in favor of the devil's impure philosophies.
BILLY GRAHAM (1918–)

11513 It must be Sunday, everybody's telling the truth.
PHOEBE SNOW (1951–)

11514 It requires as much caution to tell the truth as to conceal it.
BALTASAR GRACIÁN Y MORALES (1601–1658)

11515 Let truth, light of my heart, and not the shadows within me speak to me! I slid down into that state and was in darkness, but even from there I loved you. I strayed and yet I remembered you. I heard your voice behind me, telling me to return, but I heard only faintly because of the uproar of the restless. And now I am returning, sweaty and out of breath, to your fountain. Let no one get in my way. I will drink this and I will live it. May I not be my life; I have lived badly on my own. I was my own death. I revive in you. Speak to me; discuss with me. I have believed your books and their words are full of mystery.
SAINT AUGUSTINE OF HIPPO (354–430)

11516 Life is short, but truth works far and lives long; let us speak the truth.
ARTHUR SCHOPENHAUER (1788–1860)

11517 Love the truth though it may do you harm; hate the lie though it may please you.
ARABIAN PROVERB

11518 Man finds God through truth.
JEWISH PROVERB

11519 Man with his burning soul
Has but an hour of breath
To build a ship of truth
In which his soul may sail
Sail on the sea of death
For death takes toll
Of beauty, courage, youth,
Of all but truth.
JOHN MASEFIELD (1878–1967)

11520 No one can bar the road to truth, and to advance its cause I'm ready to accept even death.
ALEXANDER ISAYEVICH SOLZHENITSYN (1918–)

11521 No truths are simple, especially those of Scripture. But as we pursue them and participate in them more fully, they begin to reveal to us a life deeper and more integrated than we ever could have known otherwise.
TIM HANSEL

11522 Old truths are always new to us if they come to us with the smell of heaven upon them.
JOHN BUNYAN (1628–1688)

11523 Our world is so exceedingly rich in delusions that a truth is priceless.
CARL GUSTAV JUNG (1875–1961)

11524 Philosophy seeks the truth, theology finds it, religion possesses it.
GIOVANNI PICO DELLA MIRANDOLA (1463–1494)

11525 Plato, three hundred years before Christ, predicted that if ever the truly good man were to appear, the man who would tell the truth, he would have his eyes gouged out and in the end be crucified. That risk was once taken, in its fullest measure. The Man appeared. He told the world the truth—about itself—and even made the preposterous claim: "I am the Truth." As Plato foresaw, the Man was crucified.
ELIZABETH ELLIOT

11526 Rather than love, than money, than fame, give me truth.
HENRY DAVID THOREAU (1817–1862)

11527 Seek the truth
Listen to the truth
Teach the truth
Love the truth
Abide by the truth
And defend the truth
Unto death.
JOHN HUSS (C. 1370–1415)

11528 Soak and soak and soak continually in the one great truth of which you have had a vision; take it to bed with you, sleep with it, rise up in the morning with it, continually bring your imagination into captivity to it, and slowly and surely as the months and years go by God will make you one of his specialists in that particular truth.
OSWALD CHAMBERS (1874–1917)

11529 Spiritual truth is discernable only to a pure heart, not to a keen intellect. It is not a question of profundity of intellect, but of purity of heart.
OSWALD CHAMBERS (1874–1917)

11530 The city of truth cannot be built on the swampy ground of scepticism.
ALBERT SCHWEITZER (1875–1965)

11531 The Cross is God's truth about us, and therefore it is the only power which can make us truthful. When we know the Cross, we are no longer afraid of the truth.
DIETRICH BONHOEFFER (1906–1945)

11532 The devil sometimes speaks the truth.
HENRY GLAPTHORNE (1610–1643)

11533 The devil tries to shake truth by pretending to defend it.
TERTULLIAN (C. 160–AFTER 220)

11534 The grave of one who dies for the truth is holy ground.
GERMAN PROVERB

11535 The greatest friend of truth is time, her greatest enemy is prejudice, and her constant companion is humility.
CHARLES CALEB COLTON (1780–1832)

11536 The man who finds a truth lights a torch.
ROBERT GREEN INGERSOLL (1833–1899)

11537 The man who speaks the truth is always at ease.
PERSIAN PROVERB

11538 The more men suppress the truth of God which they know, the more futile, even senseless, they become in their thinking.
JOHN R. W. STOTT (1921–   )

11539 The old faiths light their candles all about,
But burly Truth comes by and puts them out.
LIZETTE WOODWORTH REESE (1856–1935)

11540 The truth does not vary because men forget or ignore or traduce it.
IRWIN EDMAN (1896–1954)

11541 The truth is not always what we want to hear.
JEWISH PROVERB

11542 The truth of God is only revealed to us by obedience.
OSWALD CHAMBERS (1874–1917)

11543 The truth would become more popular if it were not always stating ugly facts.
HENRY H. HASKINS

11544 The truth, however dreadful it is, is not so dreadful as uncertainty.
ANTON PAVLOVICH CHEKOV (1860–1904)

11545 The world is now too dangerous for anything but the truth; too small for anything but brotherhood.
ARTHUR POWELL DAVIES (1902–   )

11546 There are some truths that God will not make simple. The only thing God makes plain in the Bible is the way of salvation and sanctification.
OSWALD CHAMBERS (1874–1917)

11547 There is no power on earth more formidable than the truth.
MARGARET LEE RUNBECK

11548 There is nothing so powerful as truth—and often nothing so strange.
DANIEL WEBSTER (1782–1852)

11549 There is small chance of truth at the goal where there is not a childlike humility at the starting post.
SAMUEL TAYLOR COLERIDGE (1772–1834)

11550 Thus absolute truth is indestructible. Being indestructible, it is eternal. Being eternal, it is self-existent. Being self-existent, it is infinite. Being infinite, it is vast and deep. Being vast and deep, it is transcendental and intelligent.
CONFUCIUS (C. 551–479 B.C.)

11551 Time and truth are friends, although there are many moments hostile to truth.
JOSEPH JOUBERT (1754–1824)

11552 Time tries truth.
ENGLISH PROVERB

11553 Truth and oil always come to the surface.
SPANISH PROVERB

11554 Truth consists of having the same idea about something that God has.
JOSEPH JOUBERT (1754–1824)

11555 Truth does not blush.
TERTULLIAN (C. 160–AFTER 220)

11556 Truth exists; only falsehood has to be invented.
GEORGES BRAQUE (1882–1963)

11557 Truth has no responsibility to make us comfortable.
DAVID L. RUSSELL

11558 Truth has no special time of its own. It's hour is now—always.
ALBERT SCHWEITZER (1875–1965)

11559 Truth hath a quiet breast.
WILLIAM SHAKESPEARE (1564–1616)

11560 Truth is a divine thing, a friend more excellent than any human friend.
SAINT THOMAS AQUINAS (1225–1274)

11561 Truth is a glorious but hard mistress. She never consults, bargains, or compromises.
A. W. TOZER (1897–1963)

11562 Truth is a torch, but a terrific one; therefore we all try to grasp it with closed eyes, fearing to be blinded.
JOHANN WOLFGANG VON GOETHE (1749–1832)

11563 Truth is always the strongest argument.
SOPHOCLES (C. 496–406 B.C.)

11564 Truth is better than gold.
ARABIAN PROVERB

11565 Truth is heavy, so few men carry it.
JEWISH PROVERB

11566 Truth is incontrovertible. Panic may resent it; ignorance may deride it; malice may distort it; but there it is.
SIR WINSTON CHURCHILL (1874–1965)

11567 Truth is its own witness.
JEWISH PROVERB

11568 Truth is mightier than eloquence; the spirit stronger than genius; faith greater than learning.
MARTIN LUTHER (1483–1546)

11569 Truth is not discerned intellectually, it is discerned spiritually.
OSWALD CHAMBERS (1874–1917)

11570 Truth is often eclipsed but never extinguished.
LIVY (59 B.C.–A.D. 17)

11571 Truth is the cry of all, but the game of the few.
GEORGE BERKELEY (1685–1753)

11572 Truth lies in character. Christ did not simply speak the truth; he was Truth—truth through and through, for truth is a thing not of words but a life and being.
FREDERICK WILLIAM ROBERTSON (1816–1853)

11573 Truth may be blamed but shall never be shamed.
PROVERB

11574 Truth must necessarily be stranger than fiction; for fiction is the creation of the human mind and therefore congenial to it.
G. K. CHESTERTON (1874–1936)

11575 Truth needs no defense; it is beyond attack.
JAMES BOLEN

11576 Truth needs no flowers of speech.
ALEXANDER POPE (1688–1744)

11577 Truth on this side of the Pyrenees may be heresy on the other!
BLAISE PASCAL (1623–1662)

11578 Truth which is merely told is quick to be forgotten; truth which is discovered lasts a lifetime.
WILLIAM BARCLAY (1907–1978)

11579 Truth, crushed to earth, shall rise again;
Th' eternal years of God are hers;
But Error, wounded, writhes in pain
And dies among his worshipers.
WILLIAM CULLEN BRYANT (1794–1878)

11580 Truth, like surgery, may hurt but it cures.
HAN SUYIN

11581 Truths are not created, they exist.
JOSEPH JOUBERT (1754–1824)

11582 Truths turn into dogmas the moment they are disputed.
G. K. CHESTERTON (1874–1936)

11583 Unused truth becomes as useless as an unused muscle.
A. W. TOZER (1897–1963)

11584 We should not think that eternal truths depend upon the human understanding or on other existing things; they must depend on God alone, who as the supreme legislator, ordained them from all eternity.
RENÉ DESCARTES (1596–1650)

11585 What are the axiomatic truths upon which all human life may rest with confidence? They are not many:
Only God is great.
Only God is wise.
Apart from God, nothing matters.
Only what we do in God will remain to us at last.
Human sin is real.
With God there is forgiveness.
Only what God protects is safe.
A. W. TOZER (1897–1963)

11586 When two truths seem to directly oppose each other, we must not question either but remember there is a third—God—who reserves to himself the right to harmonize them.
MADAME ANNE SOPHIE SOYMANOV SWETCHINE (1782–1857)

11587 When you add to the truth, you subtract from it.
TALMUD

11588 When you tell the truth, you don't have to remember what you said.
JEWISH PROVERB

U

UNBELIEF

11589 Every man will have to decide for himself whether or not he can afford the terrible luxury of unbelief.
A. W. TOZER (1897–1963)

11590 God . . . has created us perfectly free to disbelieve in him as much as we choose. If we do disbelieve, then he and we must take the consequences in a world ruled by cause and effect.
DOROTHY L. SAYERS (1893–1957)

11591 In all unbelief there are these two things: a good opinion of one's self and a bad opinion of God.
HORATIUS BONAR (1808–1889)

11592 Incredulity robs us of many pleasures and gives us nothing in return.
JAMES RUSSELL LOWELL (1819–1891)

11593 None so blind as those who will not see.
MATTHEW HENRY (1662–1714)

11594 The opposite of joy is not sorrow. It is unbelief.
LESLIE D. WEATHERHEAD (1893–1976)

11595 Unbelief . . . makes the world a moral desert, where no divine footsteps are heard, where no angels ascend and descend, where no living hand adorns the fields, feeds the birds of heaven, or regulates events.
FRIEDRICH WILHELM KRUMMACHER (1796–1868)

11596 What greater rebellion, impiety, or insult to God can there be than not to believe his promises?
MARTIN LUTHER (1483–1546)

UNCERTAINTY

11597 A person who doubts himself is like a man who enlists in the ranks of his enemies and bears arms against himself. He makes his failure certain.
ALEXANDRE DUMAS (1802–1870)

11598 If the risks and potential dangers of sailing your ship in the vast oceans of uncertainty make you seasick, you'd better anchor yourself near the shallow shore of security.
CHARLES R. SWINDOLL (1934–   )

11599 If you doubt yourself, you stand on shaky ground.
HENRIK IBSEN (1828–1906)

11600 It is a miserable thing to live in suspense; it is the life of a spider.
JONATHAN SWIFT (1667–1745)

11601 It's useless to put your best foot forward—and then drag the other.
PROVERB

11602 Straddling an issue is like straddling the middle of the road. You are likely to be hit from both sides.
PROVERB

11603 To stand at the crossroads requires more strength than you possess.
HEINRICH HEINE (1797–1856)

11604 Uncertain ills torment us most.
LUCIUS ANNAEUS SENECA (C. 4 B.C.–A.D. 65)

11605 We are all impatient of uncertainty, either in opinion or in conduct; but if you are not quite sure what God wants you to do, you may be quite sure that he does not at present want you to do anything.
ALEXANDER MACLAREN (1826–1910)

UNDERSTANDING

11606 Because our understanding is earthbound . . . human to the core . . . limited . . . finite . . . we operate in a dimension totally unlike our Lord . . . who knows no such limitations. We see now. He sees forever.
CHARLES R. SWINDOLL (1934–)

11607 Don't try to reach God with your understanding; that is impossible. Reach him in love; that is possible.
CARLO CARRETTO (1910–)

11608 Everyone wants to understand painting. Why is there no attempt to understand the song of birds?
PABLO RUIZ Y PICASSO (1881–1973)

11609 If there is anything hidden from us as disciples today, it is because we are not in a fit state to understand it. As soon as we become fit in spiritual character, the thing is revealed, it is concealed at God's discretion until the life is developed sufficiently.
OSWALD CHAMBERS (1874–1917)

11610 It is a luxury to be understood.
RALPH WALDO EMERSON (1803–1882)

11611 It's taken me all my life to understand that it is not necessary to understand everything.
RENÉ-JULES-GUSTAVE COTY (1882–1962)

11612 Man is always inclined to be intolerant toward the thing, or person, he hasn't taken time to understand.
ROBERT R. BROWN

11613 No one can develop fully in this world and find a full life without feeling understood by at least one person.
PAUL TOURNIER (1898–1986)

11614 O God, help us not to despise or oppose what we do not understand.
WILLIAM PENN (1644–1718)

11615 Sometimes I think I understand everything, then I regain consciousness.
ASHLEIGH BRILLIANT

11616 The unexplained things in life are more than the explained. God seems careless as to whether men understand him or not; he scarcely vindicates his saints to men.
OSWALD CHAMBERS (1874–1917)

11617 To understand everything is to hate nothing.
ROMAIN ROLLAND (1866–1944)

11618 To understand is to complicate.
LUCIEN LEFEBVRE

11619 Understanding a person does not mean condoning; it only means that one does not accuse him as if one were God or a judge placed above him.
ERICH FROMM (1900–1980)

11620 We do not understand:
Joy . . . until we face sorrow
Faith . . . until it is tested
Peace . . . until faced with conflict
Trust . . . until we are betrayed
Love . . . until it is lost
Hope . . . until confronted with doubts.

UNITY

11621 All for one, one for all!
ALEXANDRE DUMAS (1802–1870)

11622 There can be no unity, no delight of
love, no harmony, no good in being,
where there is but one. Two at least
are needed for oneness.
GEORGE MACDONALD (1824–1905)

11623 Unity creates strength.
FRENCH PROVERB

11624 Weak things united become strong.
PROVERB

UNIVERSE

11625 A handful of sand is an anthology of
the universe.
DAVID MCCORD (1897–)

11626 A penny will hide the biggest star in
the universe if you hold it close
enough to your eye.
SAMUEL GRAFTON

11627 A world above man's head, to let him
see
How boundless might his soul's horizon be.
MATTHEW ARNOLD (1822–1888)

11628 Almighty Ruler of the all
Whose power extends to great and
small
Who guides the stars with steadfast
law,
Whose least creation fills with awe,
Oh, grant thy mercy and thy grace
To those who venture into space.
ROBERT HEINLEIN

11629 Everywhere I find the signature, the
autograph of God.
JOSEPH PARKER (1830–1902)

11630 I felt God's presence on the moon
more than I have ever felt it here on
earth.
JAMES B. IRWIN (1930–)

11631 If we consider boundless space or
boundless duration, we shrink into
nothing before it.
JOHN WESLEY (1703–1791)

11632 If you can be with God on earth, you
can be with God in space as well.
JAMES MCDIVITT (1929–)

11633 Man makes a great fuss about this
planet, which is only a ball-bearing in
the hub of the universe.
CHRISTOPHER DARLINGTON MORLEY
(1890–1957)

11634 Night has a thousand eyes.
JOHN LYLY (C. 1554–1606)

11635 Only God understands the universe.
GERMAN PROVERB

11636 Silently, one by one, in the infinite
meadows of heaven,
Blossomed the lovely stars, the forget-
me-nots of the angels.
HENRY WADSWORTH LONGFELLOW
(1807–1882)

11637 Stars are golden fruits upon a tree all
out of reach.
GEORGE ELIOT (1819–1880)

11638 Stars are the daisies that begem the
blue fields of the sky.
DAVID MACBETH MOIR (1798–1851)

11639 Stars: blessed candles of the night.
WILLIAM SHAKESPEARE (1564–1616)

11640 Stars: Flowers of the sky!
ERASMUS DARWIN (1731–1802)

11641 The created world is but a small parenthesis in eternity.
SIR THOMAS BROWNE (1605–1682)

11642 The exploration of outer space has a
bright future; it will never run out of
space to explore.

11643 The God I worship is too big for space
to contain.
JOHN HERSCHEL GLENN (1921–)

11644 The more we learn about the wonders
of our universe, the more clearly we
are going to perceive the hand of God.
FRANK BORMAN (1928–)

11645 The sun with one eye vieweth all the
world.
WILLIAM SHAKESPEARE (1564–1616)

11646 The universe is a thought of God.
JOHANN FRIEDRICH VON SCHILLER
(1759–1805)

11647 The universe is centered on neither the earth nor the sun. It is centered on God.
ALFRED NOYES (1880–1958)

11648 The universe is not hostile, nor yet is it friendly. It is simply indifferent.
JOHN HAYNES HOLMES (1879–1964)

11649 Then stars arise, and the night is holy.
HENRY WADSWORTH LONGFELLOW (1807–1882)

11650 There is beauty in space, and it is orderly. There is no weather, and there is regularity. It is predictable. . . . Everything in space obeys the laws of physics. If you know these laws and obey them, space will treat you kindly.
WERNHER VON BRAUN (1912–1977)

11651 Though I have looked everywhere I can find nothing lowly in the universe.
ARCHIE RANDOLPH AMMONS (1926–)

11652 To make God a momentary Creator who once and for all finished his work would be cold and barren. . . . We see the presence of divine power shining as much in the continuing state of the universe as in its inception.
JOHN CALVIN (1509–1564)

UNSELFISHNESS

11653 The least-used words by an unselfish person are *I, me, my,* and *mine.*
CHARLES R. SWINDOLL (1934–)

11654 Unselfishness is letting other people's lives alone, not interfering with them.
OSCAR WILDE (1854–1900)

V

VALUES

11655 All good things are cheap; all bad are very dear.
HENRY DAVID THOREAU (1817–1862)

11656 An infant is born with a clenched fist, but an old man dies with an open hand. Life has a way of prying loose our grasp on all that seems so important.

11657 Every man is worth just so much as the things are worth about which he busies himself.
MARCUS AURELIUS ANTONINUS (121–180)

11658 In the physical universe, energy does not perish but is transformed. In like manner, religious values are lifted into a higher case or degenerate into a lower one. When the nuns gave up their long habits, the girls put on maxicoats; when the rosary as a devotion was dropped, the hippies put beads around their necks; when mysticism evaporated into an irrelevant ideal, youths sought the ecstasy, not through the long haul of asceticism, but the short trip through pharmaceuticals; when seminaries, schools, and convents dropped discipline, which is an inner violence against our vices, the street mobs picked up violence but directed it against neighbor, race, and state. When the pulpits no longer resounded with the Name "above every name," the young began calling themselves "Jesus people."
ARCHBISHOP FULTON J. SHEEN (1895–1979)

11659 Learn to hold loosely all that is not eternal.
AGNES MAUDE ROYDEN (1876–1956)

11660 Never value anything as profitable to thyself which shall compel thee to break the promise, to lose thy self-respect, to hate any man, to suspect, to curse, to act the hypocrite, to desire anything which needs walls and curtains.
MARCUS AURELIUS ANTONINUS (121–180)

11661 No one who is a lover of money, a lover of pleasure, or a lover of glory is a lover of man.
EPICTETUS (C. 55–C. 135)

11662 Teach us that wealth is not elegance, that profusion is not magnificence, that splendor is not beauty.
BENJAMIN DISRAELI (1804–1881)

11663 The human value is not the ultimate, but only the penultimate value; the last, the highest value is God the Father. He alone is the cause and the measure of all things, cause and measure of all valuations, cause and measure of all love.
KARL ADAM

11664 The value of a thing sometimes lies not in what one attains with it, but in what one pays for it—what it costs us.
FRIEDRICH WILHELM NIETZSCHE (1844–1900)

11665 Things are only worth what you make them worth.
MOLIÈRE (1622–1673)

11666 Values that Christ has declared to be false are brought back into evangelical favor and promoted as the very life and substance of the Christian way. How eagerly do we seek the approval of this or that man of worldly reputation. How shamefully do we exploit the converted celebrity.
A. W. TOZER (1897–1963)

11667 We must accept the fact that God cares deeply about those in his family. Then why doesn't he prove his love? He does, but his values differ from ours. We value health; he values patience. We value comfort; he values peace. We value life without struggle; he values faith in the midst of struggle. Thus, though he loves us, he doesn't exempt us from the tragic heartaches of life.
ERWIN W. LUTZER (1941–)

11668 What you get free costs too much.
JEAN ANOUILH (1910–)

11669 What you value is what you miss, not what you have.
JORGE LUIS BORGES (1899–1986)

VICTORY

11670 The first step on the way to victory is to recognize the enemy.
CORRIE TEN BOOM (1892–1983)

11671 The smile of God is victory.
JOHN GREENLEAF WHITTIER (1807–1892)

11672 The triumphant Christian does not fight for victory; he celebrates a victory already won. The victorious life is Christ's business, not yours.
REGINALD WALLIS

11673 True triumphs are God's triumphs over us. His defeats of us are our real victories.
HENRY ALFORD (1810–1871)

VIOLENCE

11674 He who achieves power by violence does not truly become lord or master.
SAINT THOMAS AQUINAS (1225–1274)

11675 Returning violence for violence multiplies violence, adding deeper darkness to a night already devoid of stars.
MARTIN LUTHER KING, JR. (1929–1968)

11676 The violence done to us by others is often less painful than that which we do to ourselves.
FRANÇOIS, DUC DE LA ROCHEFOUCAULD (1613–1680)

11677 Violence defeats its own ends.
WILLIAM HAZLITT (1778–1830)

11678 Violence is a lie, for it goes against the truth of our faith, the truth of our humanity. Violence destroys what it claims to defend: the dignity, the life, the freedom of human beings. Violence is a crime against humanity for it destroys the very fabric of society.
POPE JOHN PAUL II (1920–)

VIRTUE

11679 A heart unspotted is not easily daunted.
WILLIAM SHAKESPEARE (1564–1616)

11680 Be virtuous and you will be eccentric.
MARK TWAIN (1835–1910)

11681 Be virtuous and you will be happy; but
you will be lonesome, sometimes.
EDGAR WILSON NYE (1850–1896)

11682 Birth counts for nothing if virtue is not
there.
MOLIÈRE (1622–1673)

11683 Blood is an inheritance; virtue an
acquisition.
MIGUEL DE CERVANTES (1547–1616)

11684 Commerce is of trivial import; love,
faith, truth of character, the aspiration
of man, these are sacred.
RALPH WALDO EMERSON (1803–1882)

11685 Do not despise others because they do
not possess the virtues you thought
they had; they may be pleasing to God
for other reasons which you cannot
discover.
SAINT JOHN OF THE CROSS (1542–1591)

11686 Give me simple laboring folk,
Who love their work,
Whose virtue is a song
To cheer God along.
HENRY DAVID THOREAU (1817–1862)

11687 God is each virtue's goal, its impulse
and its crown,
He is its only why, reward,
and sole renown.
ANGELUS SILESIUS (1624–1677)

11688 God wants to get us out of the love of
virtue and in love with the God of virtue—stripped of all possessions but
our knowledge of him.
OSWALD CHAMBERS (1874–1917)

11689 God will wither up every spring you
have. He will wither up your natural
virtues, he will break up confidence in
your natural powers, he will wither up
your confidence in brain and spirit
and body, until you learn by practical
experience that you have no right to
draw your life from any source other
than the tremendous reservoir of the
resurrection life of Jesus Christ.
OSWALD CHAMBERS (1874–1917)

11690 Here and there people flee from public
altercation into the sanctuary of private virtuousness. But anyone who
does this must shut his mouth and his
eyes to the injustice around him. What

he leaves undone will rob him of his
peace of mind.
DIETRICH BONHOEFFER (1906–1945)

11691 Love means to love that which is
unlovable, or it is no virtue at all; forgiving means to pardon that which is
unpardonable, or it is no virtue at all—
and to hope means hoping when
things are hopeless, or it is no virtue at
all.
G. K. CHESTERTON (1874–1936)

11692 Love virtue, she alone is free;
She can teach you how to climb
Higher than the spherey clime;
Or if virtue feeble were,
Heaven itself would stoop to her.
JOHN MILTON (1608–1674)

11693 Moral indignation . . . permits envy or
hate to be acted out under the guise of
virtue.
ERICH FROMM (1900–1980)

11694 Rags are royal raiment when worn for
virtue's sake.
BARTLEY T. CAMPBELL (1843–1888)

11695 Superior people are only those who let
it be discovered by others; the need to
make it evident forfeits the very virtue
they aspire to.
SYDNEY J. HARRIS (1917–1986)

11696 That peace is truly rich that passes all
understanding. Peace is rich, modesty
is rich, faith is rich, for to the faithful
the whole world is a possession. Simplicity is rich, for there are also the
riches of simplicity; for she scrutinizes
nothing, has no mean, no suspicious,
no deceitful thoughts, but pours herself forth with pure affection. Goodness too is rich, and if a man preserve
it, he is fed by the riches of the heavenly inheritance.
SAINT AMBROSE (C. 340–397)

11697 The attributes of a great lady may still
be found in the rule of the four S's: sincerity, simplicity, sympathy, and serenity.
EMILY POST ((1872–1960)

11698 The virtue of a man ought to be measured, not by his extraordinary exertions, but by his everyday conduct.
BLAISE PASCAL (1623–1662)

11699 There are seven deadly virtues: respectability, childishness, mental timidity, dullness, sentimentality, censoriousness, depression of spirits.
DOROTHY L. SAYERS (1893–1957)

11700 There is never an instant's truce between virtue and vice.
HENRY DAVID THOREAU (1817–1862)

11701 To cling to my natural virtues is quite sufficient to obscure the work of God in me.
OSWALD CHAMBERS (1874–1917)

11702 To many people virtue consists chiefly in repenting of faults, not in avoiding them.
GEORG CHRISTOPH LICHTENBERG (1742–1799)

11703 Virtue is a state of war, and to live in it we have always to combat with ourselves.
JEAN JACQUES ROUSSEAU (1712–1778)

11704 Virtue is bold and goodness never fearful.
WILLIAM SHAKESPEARE (1564–1616)

11705 Virtue is its own reward.
CLAUDIUS CLAUDIANUS (C. 370–C. 404)

11706 Virtue is like a rich stone—best plain set.
FRANCIS BACON (1561–1626)

11707 Virtue is like precious odors—most fragrant when they are incensed or crushed.
FRANCIS BACON (1561–1626)

11708 Virtue is not hereditary.
CHARLES R. SWINDOLL (1934–   )

11709 Virtue is not the absence of vices or the avoidance of moral dangers; virtue is a vivid and separate thing, like pain or a particular smell.
G. K. CHESTERTON (1874–1936)

11710 Virtue is so praiseworthy that wicked people practice it from self-interest.
LUC DE CLAPIERS, MARQUIS DE VAUVENARGUES (1715–1747)

11711 Virtue is the safest helmet.
—Motto of the original sixteenth-century ship *The Golden Hind* and that of Sir Christopher Hatton, the major shareholder in Francis Drake's venture to circumnavigate the world

11712 Virtue is to the soul what health is to the body.
FRANÇOIS, DUC DE LA ROCHEFOUCAULD (1613–1680)

11713 Virtue naked and bare can't endure before God,
With love it must be decked, that fair it may be thought.
ANGELUS SILESIUS (1624–1677)

11714 Virtue will have nought to do with ease. . . . It demands a rough and thorny path.
MICHEL EYQUEM DE MONTAIGNE (1533–1592)

11715 Virtue, though in rags, will keep me warm.
JOHN DRYDEN (1631–1700)

11716 Virtues, like essences, lose their fragrance when exposed.
WILLIAM SHENSTONE (1714–1763)

11717 We become what we do. One of the greatest mistakes we can make—and some of the smartest men who ever lived have made it—is to assume that we can do false or discreditable things and still "deep inside us" remain good people or the same people.
SYDNEY J. HARRIS (1917–1986)

11718 We know God will forgive us our sins; the question is, what will he think of our virtues?
PETER DEVRIES (C. 1910–   )

11719 We need greater virtues to bear good fortune than bad.
FRANÇOIS, DUC DE LA ROCHEFOUCAULD (1613–1680)

11720 What the world calls virtue, without Christ, is a name and a dream. The foundation of all human excellence must be laid deep in the blood of the Redeemer's cross and in the power of his resurrection.
FREDERICK WILLIAM ROBERTSON (1816–1853)

11721 Wisdom is knowing what to do next; virtue is doing it.
DAVID STARR JORDAN (1851–1931)

11722 You are a man, not God; you are human, not an angel. How can you expect to remain always in a constant

state of virtue when this was not possible even for an angel of heaven, nor for the first man in the Garden?
THOMAS À KEMPIS (C. 1380–1471)

VIRTUE/VICE

11723 He who is only kept from vice by the fear of punishment by no means embraces virtue.
BENEDICT SPINOZA (1632–1677)

11724 Vice is ignorance. Virtue is knowledge.
PLATO (C. 428–348 B.C.)

11725 Vice quickly creeps in; virtue is difficult to find. She requires rulers and guides. But vice can be acquired without a tutor.
LUCIUS ANNAEUS SENECA (C. 4 B.C.–A.D. 65)

11726 Virtue is health; vice is sickness.
PETRARCH (1304–1374)

VISION

11727 'Tis looking downward makes one dizzy.
ROBERT BROWNING (1812–1889)

11728 A blind man's world is bounded by the limits of his touch; an ignorant man's world by the limits of his knowledge; a great man's world by the limits of his vision.
E. PAUL HOVEY (1908–)

11729 A man with the vision of God is not devoted simply to a cause or a particular issue but to God himself.
OSWALD CHAMBERS (1874–1917)

11730 A vision without a task is a dream; a task without a vision is drudgery; a vision and a task is the hope of the world.

11731 Give us clear vision that we may know where to stand and what to stand for, because unless we stand for something, we shall fall for anything.
PETER MARSHALL (1902–1949)

11732 He who wants a great deal must not ask for a little.
ITALIAN PROVERB

11733 Only he who can see the invisible can do the impossible.
FRANK GAINES (1892–1977)

11734 Poor eyes limit your sight; poor vision limits your deeds.
FRANKLIN FIELD

11735 The Christians who have turned the world upside down have been men and women with a vision in their hearts and the Bible in their hands.
T. B. MASTON

11736 Vision encompasses vast vistas outside the realm of the predictable, the safe, the expected.
CHARLES R. SWINDOLL (1934–)

11737 Vision is the art of seeing things invisible.
JONATHAN SWIFT (1667–1745)

11738 Vision looks inward and becomes a duty. Vision looks outward and becomes aspiration. Vision looks upward and becomes faith.
STEPHEN SAMUEL WISE (1874–1949)

WAR

11739 "Peace upon earth!" was said. We sing it,
  And pay a million priests to bring it.
  After two thousands years of mass,
  We've got as far as poison gas.
  THOMAS HARDY (1840–1928)

11740 After a few minutes I saw something coming up the road along the river that looked like a parade of roast chickens. Some of them kept asking for "Water! Water!"
  They were all naked, and they were skinned. The skin of their hands had been torn away at the wrists. It was hanging from their fingertips just behind the nails, turned inside-out like a glove. In the dim light I thought I saw many other children lying all about the yard.
  —Concerning the 1945 Atom Bomb
  TAKASHI NAGAI

11741 As I watched, two things that looked like great big hideous lizards crawled in slowly, making croaking, groaning sounds. Others followed. I was paralyzed with horror for minutes. Then the light got a little stronger, and I could see they were human beings— skinned alive by fire or heat, their bodies all smashed where they had been thrown against something hard.
  —Concerning the 1945 Atom Bomb
  TAKASHI NAGAI

11742 Better an egg in peace than an ox in war.
  PROVERB

11743 But those wars also are just, without doubt, which are ordained by God himself, in whom is no iniquity, and who knows every man's merits.
  SAINT AUGUSTINE OF HIPPO (354–430)

11744 Can anything be more ridiculous than that a man should have the right to kill me because he lives on the other side of the water, and because his ruler has a quarrel with mine, though I have none with him?
  BLAISE PASCAL (1623–1662)

11745 Every gun that is made, every warship launched, every rocket fired, signifies in the final sense a theft from those who hunger and are not fed, those who are cold and are not clothed. This world in arms is not spending money

alone. It is spending the sweat of its
laborers, the genius of its scientists,
the houses of its children. This is not a
way of life. . . . Under the cloud of
war, it is humanity hanging itself on a
cross of iron.
DWIGHT D. EISENHOWER (1890–1969)

11746 Give me the money that has been spent
in war, and I will clothe every man,
woman, and child in an attire of which
kings and queens would be proud. I
will build a schoolhouse in every valley
over the whole earth. I will crown
every hillside with a place of worship
consecrated to the gospel of peace. I
will support in every pulpit an able
teacher of righteousness so that on
every Sabbath morning the chime on
one hill should answer to the chime on
another round the earth's wide circumference; and the voice of prayer and the
song of praise should ascend like an
universal holocaust to heaven.
CHARLES SUMNER (1811–1874)

11747 Good kings never make war, but for
the sake of peace.
PROVERB

11748 If Christian nations were nations of
Christians, there would be no wars.
SOAME JENYNS (1704–1787)

11749 If there is another war, there will be no
victors, only losers.
RICHARD M. NIXON (1913–)

11750 In front of us a curious figure was
standing, a little crouched, legs strad-
dled, arms held out from his sides. He
had no eyes and the whole of his body,
nearly all of which was visible through
tatters of burnt rags, was covered with
a hard black crust speckled with yellow pus. A Korean woman by his side
began to speak, and the interpreter
said: "He has to stand, cannot sit or
lie." He had to stand because he was
no longer covered with a skin, but
with a crust like crackling which
broke easily.
—Concerning the 1952 Napalm Bomb
RENE CUTFORTH

11751 In peace sons bury fathers, but war
violates the order of nature and
fathers bury sons.
HERODOTUS (C. 484–C. 425 B.C.)

11752 In war there is no such thing as victor
and vanquished. . . . There is only a
loser and that loser is mankind.
U THANT (1909–1974)

11753 It is forbidden to kill; therefore all
murderers are punished unless they
kill in large numbers and to the sound
of trumpets.
VOLTAIRE (1694–1778)

11754 Laws are silent amidst the clash of
arms.
CICERO (106–43 B.C.)

11755 Man's inhumanity to man
Makes countless thousands mourn.
ROBERT BURNS (1759–1796)

11756 O war! thou son of hell!
WILLIAM SHAKESPEARE (1564–1616)

11757 Older men declare war. But it is youth
who must fight and die. And it is
youth who must inherit the tribulation, the sorrow, and the triumphs
that are the aftermath of war.
HERBERT HOOVER (1874–1964)

11758 One murder makes a villain; millions a
hero.
BEILBY PORTEUS (1731–1808)

11759 One word can start a war.
JEWISH PROVERB

11760 The Bible nowhere prohibits war. In
the Old Testament we find war and
even conquest positively commanded,
and although war was raging in the
world in the time of Christ and his
apostles, still they said not a word of
its unlawfulness and immorality.
HENRY WAGER HALLECK (1815–1872)

11761 The church knows nothing of a sacred-
ness of war. The church that prays the
"Our Father" asks God only for peace.
DIETRICH BONHOEFFER (1906–1945)

11762 The most persistent sound that reverberates through men's history is the
beating of war drums.
ARTHUR KOESTLER (1905–1983)

11763 The tragedy of war is that it uses man's best to do man's worst.
HARRY EMERSON FOSDICK (1878–1969)

11764 The wars that rage within the world are a reflection of the wars that rage inside people.
LEIGHTON FORD

11765 The world started with wars, and it shall be destroyed by wars.
ARABIAN PROVERB

11766 There are no athiests in foxholes.
WILLIAM THOMAS CUMMINGS (1903–1944)

11767 War does not determine who is right—only who is left.

11768 War is an evil thing; but to submit to the dictation of other states is worse.... Freedom, if we hold fast to it, will ultimately restore our losses, but submission will mean permanent loss of all that we value.
THUCYDIDES (460–C. 401 B.C.)

11769 War is death's feast.
PROVERB

11770 War is kinder than a godless peace.
GEOFFREY ANKETELL STUDDERT-KENNEDY (1883–1929)

11771 War is the business of barbarians.
NAPOLEON BONAPARTE (1769–1821)

11772 War is the most ghastly experience that can come to any country. And always it is the people—not the handful of men in positions of power—who must pay the full price. The price in dollars and cents. The price in dismembered families. The price in heart agonies. The price in bodily suffering. The price in numbed minds. The price in precious human lives. The price in putting together the nation's pieces afterwards. Always it is the masses who pay.
ROBERT MARION LA FOLLETTE (1855–1925)

11773 War is the science of destruction.
JOHN STEVENS CABOT ABBOTT (1805–1877)

11774 War would end if the dead could return.
STANLEY BALDWIN (1867–1947)

11775 We (Christians in war) are called to the hardest of all tasks: to fight without hatred, to resist without bitterness, and in the end if God grant it so, to triumph without vindictiveness.
WILLIAM TEMPLE (1881–1944)

11776 We punish murderers and massacres among private persons. What do we do respecting wars, and the glorious crime of murdering whole nations? The love of conquest is a murderess. Conquerors are scourges not less harmful to humanity than floods and earthquakes.
LUCIUS ANNAEUS SENECA (C. 4 B.C.–A.D. 65)

11777 What a fine looking thing is war! Yet, dress it as we may, dress and feather it, daub it with gold, huzzah it, and sing swaggering songs about it, what is it but murder in uniform?
DOUGLAS WILLIAM JERROLD (1803–1857)

11778 When the rich make war, it's the poor who die.
JEAN PAUL SARTRE (1905–1980)

11779 Within me there is a force. It says that gentleness, which is not prepared to kill or be killed to destroy the evil that assails life, is not gentleness. It is weakness. It is the weakness of the merely well-meaning. It is the suspended goodness of the men of mere good will whose passivity in the face of evil first of all raises the question whether they are men. It is the permanent temptation of the Christian who, in the world of force, flinches from the Crucifixion which alone can give kindness and compassion force.
WHITTAKER CHAMBERS

11780 You can't say civilization isn't advancing; in every war, they kill you in a new way.
WILL ROGERS (1879–1935)

WAR/PEACE

11781 A few conquer by fighting, but more battles are won by submitting.
ELBERT GREEN HUBBARD (1856–1915)

11782 I intend to leave after my death a large fund for the promotion of the peace

idea, but I am skeptical as to its results. The savants will write excellent volumes. There will be laureates. But wars will continue just the same until the force of circumstances renders them impossible.
ALFRED BERNHARD NOBEL (1833–1896)

11783 Nations have found
Cohesion in war and dispersion in peace;
Wisdom in war and deception in peace;
Training in war and betrayal in peace.
YATES STERLING (1873–1942)

11784 The best soldier is not warlike; the best fighter is never angry; the best conqueror takes no part in war.
LAO-TSE (C. 604–C. 531 B.C.)

11785 We make war that we may live in peace.
ARISTOTLE (384–322 B.C.)

WEAKNESS

11786 God comes in where my helplessness begins.
OSWALD CHAMBERS (1874–1917)

11787 God wanted weakness—who so weak as I?
HANNAH HURNARD (1905–1990)

11788 Men's weaknesses are often necessary to the purposes of life.
MAURICE MAETERLINCK (1862–1949)

11789 My weakness—my helplessness—my sense of inferiority has turned out to be my greatest strength.
HAROLD RUSSELL

11790 Our weaknesses make us appreciate God's strength.
ERWIN W. LUTZER (1941–)

11791 Very few true disciples of the Lord Jesus are allowed always to appear sensible and correct. It is not likely that the Lord of love will let us bypass the way of weakness and foolishness altogether.
HANNAH HURNARD (1905–1990)

WEALTH

11792 A fool and his money are soon parted, but you never call him a fool till the money is gone.

11793 A golden bit does not make a better horse.
LATIN PROVERB

11794 A great fortune is a great slavery.
LUCIUS ANNAEUS SENECA (C. 4 B.C.–A.D. 65)

11795 A miser's money takes the place of wisdom.
DUTCH PROVERB

11796 A miser's wealth is the devil's.
ARABIAN PROVERB

11797 A miser: one who experiences a dollar's worth of frustration when he loses a dime.

11798 Ahab sold himself for a vineyard; Judas, a bag of silver; Achan, a wedge and a garment; Gehazi, silver and raiment. Are you for sale?
ORIN PHILIP GIFFORD (B. 1847)

11799 As riches grow, care follows, and a thirst for more and more.
HORACE (65–8 B.C.)

11800 Better rich in God than rich in gold.
PROVERB

11801 Building one's life on a foundation of gold is just like building a house on foundations of sand.
HENRIK IBSEN (1828–1906)

11802 Chains of gold are stronger than chains of iron.
PROVERB

11803 Curst greed of gold, what crimes thy tyrant power has caused!
VIRGIL (70–19 B.C.)

11804 Even asses know straw is better than gold.
HERODOTUS (C. 484–C. 425 B.C.)

11805 Every man serves a useful purpose: a miser, for example, makes a wonderful ancestor.

11806 Few people have the spiritual resources needed to be both wealthy and godly.
ERWIN W. LUTZER (1941–)

11807 Fortune does not change men; it
unmasks them.
MADAME NECKER (1766–1841)

11808 Fortune is shallow, misfortune deep.
Fortune dulls, misfortune whets.
JONAH ROSENFELD

11809 God has to take some people out of
this world in order to set their money
in circulation.

11810 Gold and riches, the chief causes of
war.
CORNELIUS TACITUS (C. 56–C. 120)

11811 Gold begets in brethren hate;
Gold in families debate;
Gold does friendship separate;
Gold does civil wars create.
ABRAHAM COWLEY (1618–1667)

11812 Gold is a living god.
PERCY BYSSHE SHELLEY (1792–1822)

11813 Gold is cold and lifeless and can't see
or hear,
And in the time of trouble it is powerless to cheer.
It has no ears to listen, no heart to understand,
It cannot bring you comfort or reach
out a helping hand.
HELEN STEINER RICE

11814 Gold opens every gate; e'en that of
hell.
MONANDER (C. 342–291 B.C.)

11815 Gold will be slave or master.
HORACE (65–8 B.C.)

11816 Gold! Gold! Gold! Gold! Bright and
yellow, hard and cold.
THOMAS HOOD (1799–1845)

11817 Gold? A transcient, shining trouble.
JAMES GRAINGER (C. 1721–1766)

11818 Great wealth and content seldom live
together.
SIR THOMAS FULLER (1608–1661)

11819 Great wealth implies great loss.
CHINESE PROVERB

11820 He has not acquired a fortune; the fortune has acquired him.
BION (FL. C. 100 B.C.)

11821 He is rich who owes nothing. He is
poor who has nothing but money.
PROVERB

11822 If money be not your servant, it will
be your master.
ITALIAN PROVERB

11823 If you want to make your money go as
far as possible, give it to foreign missions.

11824 If your riches are yours, why don't
you take them with you to the other
world?
BENJAMIN FRANKLIN (1706–1790)

11825 In all abundance there is lack.
HIPPOCRATES (C. 460–C. 377 B.C.)

11826 It is better to live rich than to die rich.
SAMUEL JOHNSON (1709–1784)

11827 It is miserable to have few things to
desire and many things to fear; and yet
that commonly is the case of kings.
FRANCIS BACON (1561–1626)

11828 It is much better to have your gold in
the hand than in the heart.
SIR THOMAS FULLER (1608–1661)

11829 It is not what we take up but what we
give up that makes us rich.
HENRY WARD BEECHER (1813–1887)

11830 It's hard for a rich man to enter the
kingdom of heaven, but easy for him
to get on the church board of trustees.

11831 John D. Rockefeller made his millions
in oil, but if a benevolent God had not
put the oil in the ground, and hadn't
endowed man with the sense to refine
it and market it, there would be no fortunes in oil.
BILLY GRAHAM (1918–   )

11832 Let us not envy some men their accumulated riches. Their burden would be
too heavy for us. We could not sacrifice as they do, health, quiet, honor,
and conscience, to obtain them. It is to
pay so dear for them that the bargain
is a loss.
JEAN DE LA BRUYÈRE (1645–1696)

11833 Little wealth, little care.
PROVERB

11834 Living in the lap of luxury isn't bad,
except that you never know when luxury is going to stand up.
PROVERB

11835 Man must govern, not serve, gold.
SIR THOMAS FULLER (1608–1661)
GERMAN PROVERB

11836 Men have a touchstone whereby to try
gold, but gold is the touchstone
whereby to try men.
SIR THOMAS FULLER (1608–1661)

11837 Misers are very kind people: they
amass wealth for those who wish their
death.
KING LESZCZYNSKI STANISLAW I
(1677–1766)

11838 Moderate riches will carry you; if you
have more, you must carry them.
PROVERB

11839 My riches consist not in the extent of
my possessions but in the fewness of
my wants.
JOSEPH BROTHERTON (1783–1857)

11840 No man can tell whether he is rich or
poor by turning to his ledger. It is the
heart that makes a man rich.
HENRY WARD BEECHER (1813–1887)

11841 No shah or president or king or general or scientist or pope; no banker or
merchant or cartel or oil company or
ayatollah holds the key to as much
power as she has. None is as rich. For
hers is the invincible weapon against
the evils of this earth: the caring heart.
And hers are the everlasting riches of
this life: the wealth of the compassionate spirit.
—On Mother Teresa
ROBERT FULGHUM

11842 O fortune, fortune! All men call thee
fickle.
WILLIAM SHAKESPEARE (1564–1616)

11843 O, cursed love of gold; when for thy
sake,
The fool throws up his interest in both
worlds,
First starved in this, then damn'd in
that to come.
JAMES BLAIR (1656–1743)

11844 Rank and riches are chains of gold,
but still chains.
GIOVANNI RUFFINI (1807–1881)

11845 Riches are the least worthy gifts which
God can give to man. What are they
to God's Word, to bodily gifts, such as

beauty and health, or to the gifts of
the mind, such as understanding, skill,
wisdom! Yet men toil for them day
and night and take no rest.
MARTIN LUTHER (1483–1546)

11846 Riches enlarge rather than satisfy appetites.
SIR THOMAS FULLER (1608–1661)

11847 Riches exclude only one inconvenience
and that is poverty.
SAMUEL JOHNSON (1709–1784)

11848 Riches have made more men covetous
than covetousness has made men rich.
PROVERB

11849 Riches have wings and grandeur is a
dream.
WILLIAM COWPER (1731–1800)

11850 Saint-seducing gold.
WILLIAM SHAKESPEARE (1564–1616)

11851 Satan now is wiser than of yore,
And tempts by making rich, not mak-
ing poor.
ALEXANDER POPE (1688–1744)

11852 Some have much, and some have more,
Some are rich, and some are poor,
Some have little, some have less,
Some have not a cent to bless;
Their empty pockets, yet possess
True riches in true happiness.
JOHN OXENHAM (1861–1941)

11853 Tell, priests, what is gold doing in a
holy place?
PERSIUS (34–62)

11854 The bad side of poverty is the fear that
it creates, but I would certainly think
that the unreality of life for the rich,
and ultimately the boredom of life for
them, is a worse misfortune.
MALCOLM MUGGERIDGE (1903–1990)

11855 The bread that you store up belongs to
the hungry; the cloak that lies in your
chest belongs to the naked; the gold
that you have hidden in the ground
belongs to the poor.
SAINT BASIL (C. 330–379)

11856 The golden age only comes to men
when they have forgotten gold.
G. K. CHESTERTON (1874–1936)

11857 The loss of wealth is loss of dirt,
As sages in all times assert;
The happy man's without a shirt.
JOHN HEYWOOD (C. 1497–C. 1580)

11858 The lust of gold, unfeeling and
remorseless!
The last corruption of degenerate man.
SAMUEL JOHNSON (1709–1784)

11859 The only thing wealth does for some
people is to make them worry about
losing it.
ANTOINE DE RIVAROL (1753–1801)

11860 The prosperous man is never sure that
he is loved for himself.
LUCAN (39–65)

11861 The rich must live more simply that
the poor may simply live.
CHARLES BIRCH

11862 The Scriptures first taught the futility
of riches. It took income tax to drive
the lesson home.

11863 There are a thousand ways to wealth
but only one way to heaven.
JOHN LOCKE (1632–1704)

11864 There are two ways of being rich. One
is to have all you want, the other is to
be satisfied with what you have.
PROVERB

11865 There is a burden of care in getting
riches; fear in keeping them; temptation in using them; guilt in abusing
them; sorrow in losing them; and a
burden of account at last to be given
concerning them.
MATTHEW HENRY (1662–1714)

11866 There is no fortune, only God.
SPANISH PROVERB

11867 There is nothing that makes men rich
and strong but that which they carry
inside of them. Wealth is of the heart,
not of the hand.
JOHN MILTON (1608–1674)

11868 Those who condemn wealth are those
who have none and see no chance of
getting it.
WILLIAM PENN PATRICK

11869 To be clever enough to get all that
money, one must be stupid enough to
want it.
G. K. CHESTERTON (1874–1936)

11870 To dispense wealth is the best way to
preserve it.
ISAAC BARROW (1630–1677)

11871 To have money is a fear; not to have
it, a grief.
PROVERB

11872 Treasures in heaven are accumulated
by our attitude to our treasures (or
lack of them) on earth.
ERWIN W. LUTZER (1941–)

11873 Wealth is a good servant, a very bad
mistress.
FRANCIS BACON (1561–1626)

11874 Wealth is like a viper that is harmless
if a man knows how to take hold of it;
but if he does not, it will twine round
his hand and bite him.
SAINT CLEMENT (30–100)

11875 Wealth is like seawater; the more we
drink, the thirstier we become; the
same is true of fame.
ARTHUR SCHOPENHAUER (1788–1860)

11876 Wealth is not his that has it, but his
that enjoys it.
ITALIAN PROVERB

11877 Wealth lightens not the heart and care
of man.
LATIN PROVERB

11878 When I wish I am rich, then I know I
am ill.
D. H. LAWRENCE (1885–1930)

11879 Wherever there is too much, something is lacking.
JEWISH PROVERB

WICKEDNESS

11880 A wicked man is his own hell.
ENGLISH PROVERB

11881 All wicked men are slaves.
CICERO (106–43 B.C.)

11882 Flee the wicked, even when they are
agreeable, instructive, and charming.
EUGÈNE DELACROIX (1798–1863)

11883 For never, never wicked man was wise.
HOMER (C. EIGHTH CENTURY B.C.)

11884 God permits the wicked, but not forever.
SIR THOMAS FULLER (1608–1661)

11885 He has blood like that of the bed bug.
ARABIAN PROVERB

11886 He is as restless as a hen wanting to
lay an egg.
ARABIAN PROVERB

11887 If man suddenly took to virtue, many
thousands would be reduced to starvation.
GEORG CHRISTOPH LICHTENBERG
(1742–1799)

11888 Keep five yards from a carriage, ten
yards from a horse, and a hundred
yards from an elephant; but the distance one should keep from a wicked
man cannot be measured.
INDIAN PROVERB

11889 No man ever became very wicked all
at once.
JUVENAL (C. 60–C. 127)

11890 No wickedness proceeds on any
grounds of reason.
LIVY (59 B.C.–A.D. 17)

11891 Some wicked people would be less dangerous had they no redeeming qualities.
FRANÇOIS, DUC DE LA ROCHEFOUCAULD
(1613–1680)

11892 The wicked flee when no man
pursueth—but they make better time
when the righteous are after them.
CHARLES HENRY PARKHURST (1842–1933)

11893 The wicked shun the light as the devil
shuns the cross.
DUTCH PROVERB

11894 What wicked men do should not disturb the good man's tranquility.
A. W. TOZER (1897–1963)

11895 Wickedness is always easier than virtue; it takes the shortcut to everything.
SAMUEL JOHNSON (1709–1784)

WISDOM

11896 A fool sees a man's clothes, a wise
man sees a man's spirit.
JEWISH PROVERB

11897 A short life with wisdom is better than
a long life without it.
MOSES BEN JACOB IBN EZRA (C. 1135)

11898 A single conversation across the table
with a wise man is worth a month's
study of books.
PROVERB

11899 A wise man cares not for what he cannot have.
GEORGE HERBERT (1593–1633)

11900 The art of being wise is the art of
knowing what to overlook.
WILLIAM JAMES

11901 A wise man lowers a ladder before he
jumps into a pit.
JEWISH PROVERB

11902 A wise man sees as much as he ought,
not as much as he can.
MICHEL EYQUEM DE MONTAIGNE
(1533–1592)

11903 Any man who understands his own
foolishness is already a little wise.
JEWISH PROVERB

11904 As for me, all I know is that I know
nothing.
SOCRATES (470–399 B.C.)

11905 Being in the right does not depend on
having a loud voice.
CHINESE PROVERB

11906 But wisdom, awful wisdom! which
        inspects,
Discerns, compares, weighs, separates,
        infers,
Seizes the right, and holds it to the last.
EDWARD YOUNG (1683–1765)

11907 Caution is the eldest child of wisdom.
VICTOR HUGO (1802–1885)

11908 Colors fade, temples crumble, empires
fall, but wise words endure.
EDWARD L. THORNDIKE (1874–1949)

11909 Consideration is the parent of wisdom.
PROVERB

11910 Consideration is the soil in which wisdom may be expected to grow.
RALPH WALDO EMERSON (1803–1882)

11911 Don't expect wisdom to come into your life like great chunks of rock on a conveyor belt. It isn't like that. It's not splashy and bold . . . nor is it dispensed like a prescription across a counter. Wisdom comes privately from God as a by-product of right decisions, godly reactions, and the application of spiritual principles to daily circumstances. Wisdom comes . . . not from trying to do great things for God . . . but more from being faithful to the small, obscure tasks few people ever see.
CHARLES R. SWINDOLL (1934–   )

11912 Every delay is hateful, but it gives wisdom.
PUBLILIUS SYRUS (FIRST CENTURY B.C.)

11913 Every scrap of a wise man's time is worth saving.
PROVERB

11914 From the errors of others a wise man corrects his own.
PUBLILIUS SYRUS (FIRST CENTURY B.C.)

11915 God grant me the serenity
To accept the things I cannot change,
The courage to change the things I can,
And the wisdom to know
One from the other.
REINHOLD NIEBUHR (1892–1971)

11916 God never meant that man should scale the heavens
By strides of human wisdom.
WILLIAM COWPER (1731–1800)

11917 He that thinks himself the happiest man really is so; but he that thinks himself the wisest is usually the greatest fool.
CHARLES CALEB COLTON (1780–1832)

11918 If your head is wax, don't walk in the sun.
BENJAMIN FRANKLIN (1706–1790)

11919 In our sleep, pain that cannot forget falls drop by drop upon the heart until, in our own despair, against our will, comes wisdom through the awful grace of God.
AESCHYLUS (C. 525–456 B.C.)

11920 In the midst of great joy do not promise to give anything; in the midst of great anger do not answer a letter.
CHINESE PROVERB

11921 It is better to envy wisdom than riches.
GREEK PROVERB

11922 It is characteristic of wisdom not to do desperate things.
HENRY DAVID THOREAU (1817–1862)

11923 It is never wise to be cocksure.
OSWALD CHAMBERS (1874–1917)

11924 It's easier to be wise for others than for ourselves.
FRANÇOIS, DUC DE LA ROCHEFOUCAULD (1613–1680)

11925 Job—How to suffer
Psalms—How to pray
Proverbs—How to act
Ecclesiastes—How to enjoy
Song of Solomon—How to love
OSWALD CHAMBERS (1874–1917)

11926 Knowledge comes, but wisdom lingers.
ALFRED, LORD TENNYSON (1809–1892)

11927 Knowledge is a process of piling up facts; wisdom lies in their simplification.
MARTIN H. FISCHER (1879–1962)

11928 Knowledge is horizontal. Wisdom is vertical—it comes down from above.
BILLY GRAHAM (1918–   )

11929 Knowledge leads us from the simple to the complex; wisdom leads us from the complex to the simple.

11930 Man is wise only while he searches for wisdom; if he thinks he has found it, he is a fool.
SOLOMON BEN GABIROL (C. 1020–1070)

11931 No man ever became wise by chance.
LUCIUS ANNAEUS SENECA (C. 4 B.C.–A.D. 65)

11932 Nothing that is worth knowing can be taught.
OSCAR WILDE (1854–1900)

11933 Now that I know I'm no wiser than anyone else, does this wisdom make me wiser?
HUGH PRATHER

11934 One pound of learning requires ten pounds of common sense to apply it.
PERSIAN PROVERB

11935 One's first step in wisdom is to question everything. And one's last is to come to terms with everything.
GEORG CHRISTOPH LICHTENBERG (1742–1799)

11936 Only a fool tests the depth of the water with both feet.
AFRICAN PROVERB

11937 Out of intense complexities intense simplicities emerge.
SIR WINSTON CHURCHILL (1874–1965)

11938 Reproof never does a wise man harm.
PROVERB

11939 Stature comes not with height but with depth.
BENJAMIN LICHTENBERG

11940 The art of being wise is the art of knowing what to overlook.
WILLIAM JAMES (1842–1910)

11941 The beginning of wisdom is to call things by their right names.
CHINESE PROVERB

11942 The doorstep to the temple of wisdom is a knowledge of our own ignorance.
CHARLES HADDON SPURGEON (1834–1892)

11943 The first step of wisdom is to know what is false.
LATIN PROVERB

11944 The heart of a wise man lies quiet like limpid water.
PROVERB

11945 The intellect of the wise is like glass; it admits the light of heaven and reflects it.
AUGUSTUS JOHN CUTHBERT HARE (1834–1903)

11946 The man who has understanding has everything.
JEWISH PROVERB

11947 The man who understands his foolishness is wise.
JEWISH PROVERB

11948 The one who knows most speaks least.
SPANISH PROVERB

11949 The road to wisdom?
Well, it's plain
And simple to express:
Err and err
And err again

But less
And less
And less.
PIET HEIN

11950 The wise man carries his possessions within him.
BIAS OF PRIENE (C. 570 B.C.)

11951 The wise man, even when he holds his tongue, says more than the fool when he speaks.
YIDDISH PROVERB

11952 There is no wisdom like frankness.
BENJAMIN DISRAELI (1804–1881)

11953 There is no wisdom like silence.
GERMAN PROVERB

11954 To go too far is as bad as to fall short.
CHINESE PROVERB

11955 To know one's ignorance is the best part of knowledge.
CHINESE PROVERB

11956 To seek wisdom in old age is like a mark in the sand; to seek wisdom in youth is like an inscription on stone.
SOLOMON BEN GABIROL (C. 1020–1070)

11957 Unlearn'd, he knew no schoolman's subtle art,
No language, but the language of the heart.
By nature honest, by experience wise.
ALEXANDER POPE (1688–1744)

11958 We can be knowledgeable with other men's knowledge, but we cannot be wise with other men's wisdom.
MICHEL EYQUEM DE MONTAIGNE (1533–1592)

11959 We hate delay, and yet it makes us wise.
PROVERB

11960 When clouds are seen, wise men put on their coats.
ITALIAN PROVERB

11961 Where the river is deepest, it makes the least noise.
ITALIAN PROVERB

11962 Wisdom and virtue are like the two wheels of a cart.
JAPANESE PROVERB

11963 Wisdom at proper times will forget.
LATIN PROVERB

11964 Wisdom comes by disillusionment.
GEORGE SANTAYANA (1863–1952)

11965 Wisdom comes by suffering.
AESCHYLUS (C. 525–456 B.C.)

11966 Wisdom does not enter into a malicious mind.
FRANÇOIS RABELAIS (C. 1483–1553)

11967 Wisdom does not inspect but behold. We must look a long time before we can see.
HENRY DAVID THOREAU (1817–1862)

11968 Wisdom is a good purchase though we pay dear for it.
PROVERB

11969 Wisdom is like a dawn that comes up slowly out of an unknown ocean.
EDWIN ARLINGTON ROBINSON (1869–1935)

11970 Wisdom is oftentimes nearer when we stoop than when we soar.
WILLIAM WORDSWORTH (1770–1850)

11971 Wisdom is seeing life from God's perspective.
BILL GOTHARD

11972 Wisdom is the combination of honesty and knowledge applied through experience.
DENIS WAITLEY

11973 Wisdom is the right use of knowledge. To know is not to be wise. Many men know a great deal, and are all the greater fools for it. To know how to use knowledge is to have wisdom.
CHARLES HADDON SPURGEON (1834–1892)

11974 Wisdom is the wealth of the wise.
PROVERB

11975 Wisdom is to the soul what health is to the body.
FRENCH PROVERB

11976 Wisdom outweighs any wealth.
SOPHOCLES (C. 496–406 B.C.)

11977 Wise men are not always silent, but they know when to be.
PROVERB

11978 Wise men change their minds, fools never.
ENGLISH PROVERB

11979 Wise men say nothing in dangerous times.
JOHN SELDEN (1584–1654)

WOMAN

11980 How are our churches beautified, our sick tended, our poor fed, our children taught and cared for and civilized? Do you think the masculine element goes for much in these things? No, Westray; women are the church's strong rock. As they were the last at the foot of the cross, so they have become the first at the altar.
MARY ELIZABETH BRADDON (1837–1915)

11981 The model of woman in tribal patriarchalism is the brood mare; in hedonistic naturalism, she is the bunny or plaything; in feminist ideology, she is the self-sufficient career woman; in romanticism, she is the fairy princess or maiden in distress waiting to be rescued; in biblical faith, she is the partner in ministry.
DONALD G. BLOESCH (1928–   )

11982 The woman was formed out of man— not out of his head to rule over him; not out of his feet to be trampled upon by him; but out of his side to be his equal, from beneath his arm to be protected, and from near his heart to be loved.
MATTHEW HENRY (1662–1714)

11983 What sir, would the people of the earth be without woman? They would be scarce, sir, mighty scarce.
MARK TWAIN (1835–1910)

11984 Whatever women do they must do twice as well as men to be thought half as good. Luckily, this is not difficult.
CHARLOTTE WHITTON (1896–1975)

WORDS

11985 Cold words freeze people, and hot words scorch them, and bitter words make them bitter, and wrathful words make them wrathful. Kind words . . .

soothe, and quiet, and comfort the hearer.
BLAISE PASCAL (1623–1662)

11986 Do not the most moving moments of our lives find us without words?
MARCEL MARCEAU (1923–)

11987 Good words are worth much and cost little.
GEORGE HERBERT (1593–1633)

11988 Kind words can be short and easy to speak but their echoes are truly endless.
MOTHER TERESA OF CALCUTTA (1910–)

11989 Little keys can open big locks. Simple words can express great thoughts.
WILLIAM ARTHUR WARD (1812–1882)

11990 No one means all he says, and yet very few say all they mean, for words are slippery and thought is sticky.
HENRY BROOKS ADAMS (1838–1918)

11991 Sometimes it seems that our many words are more an expression of our doubt than of our faith. It is as if we are not sure that God's Spirit can touch the hearts of people: we have to help him out and, with many words, convince others of his power. But it is precisely this wordy unbelief that quenches the fire.
HENRI J. M. NOUWEN

11992 The difference between the right word and the almost right word is the difference between lightning and the lightning bug.
MARK TWAIN (1835–1910)

11993 The greatest word is *God*. The deepest word is *soul*. The longest word is *eternity*. The swiftest word is *time*. The nearest word is *now*. The darkest word is *sin*. The meanest word is *hypocrisy*. The broadest word is *truth*. The strongest word is *right*. The tenderest word is *love*. The sweetest word is *home*. The dearest word is *mother*.
JAMES L. GORDON

11994 The most important words in our vocabulary are *yes* to God, and sometimes *no* to the requests that come from the world.
JOHN MICHAEL TALBOT

11995 The sweetest music isn't in oratorios, But in kind words.
RALPH WALDO EMERSON (1803–1882)

11996 To be articulate at certain times we are compelled to fall back upon "Oh!" or "O!"—a primitive exclamatory sound that is hardly a word at all.
A. W. TOZER (1897–1963)

11997 Words are born in the heart, not in the head.
OSWALD CHAMBERS (1874–1917)

11998 Words are instruments of music. An ignorant man uses them for jargon; but when a master touches them they have unexpected life and soul. Some words sound out like drums; some breathe memories sweet as flutes; some call like a clarinet; some show a charge like trumpets; some are sweet as children's talk; others rich as a mother's answering back.

11999 Words are loaded pistols.
JEAN PAUL SARTRE (1905–1980)

12000 Words are nails for fixing ideas.
H. GIORNALE

12001 Words are not just letters strung together. Words are the incarnation of emotions and the stimulators or emotion. A word can be a balm or a bomb. A positive word makes you feel good. A negative word leaves you feeling depressed and defeated. Words release energy. A single word can turn you on, or it can turn you off. A negative word can defuse your enthusiasm for a project. A positive word releases positive energy and becomes a creative force.
ROBERT HAROLD SCHULLER (1926–)

12002 Words are things, and a small drop of ink
Falling like dew upon a thought, produces
That which makes thousands, perhaps millions, think.
LORD GEORGE NOEL GORDON BYRON (1788–1824)

12003 Words can sting like anything. But silence breaks the heart.
PHYLLIS McGINLEY (1905–1977)

12004 Words—so innocent and powerless as they are, as standing in a dictionary, how potent for good and evil they become, in the hands of one who knows how to combine them!
NATHANIEL HAWTHORNE (1804–1864)

12005 Words. Do you fully understand their power? Can any of us really grasp the mighty force behind the things we say? Do we stop and think before we speak, considering the potency of the phrases we utter?
JONI EARECKSON TADA

WORK

12006 A task without a vision is drudgery; a vision without a task is a dream; a task with a vision is victory.

12007 God give me work
Till my life shall end
And life
Till my work is done.
WINIFRED HOLTBY (1898–1935)

12008 God respects me when I work, but he loves me when I sing.
SIR RABINDRANATH TAGORE (1861–1941)

12009 I like work; it fascinates me. I can sit and look at it for hours.
JEROME K. JEROME (1859–1927)

12010 If you would have your lamp burn, you must pour oil into it.
GERMAN PROVERB

12011 In order that people may be happy in their work, three things are needed: they must be fit for it; they must not do too much of it; and they must have a sense of success in it.
JOHN RUSKIN (1819–1900)

12012 It is better to wear out than to rust out.
BISHOP RICHARD CUMBERLAND (1631–1718)

12013 It is not only prayer that gives God glory but work. Smiting on an anvil, sawing a beam, whitewashing a wall, driving horses, sweeping, scouring, everything gives God glory if being in his grace you do it as your duty. To go to Communion worthily gives God great glory, but to take food in thankfulness and temperance gives him glory too. To lift up the hands in prayer gives God glory, but a man with a dungfork in his hand, a woman with a slop pail, gives him glory too. He is so great that all things give him glory if you mean they should.
GERARD MANLEY HOPKINS (1844–1889)

12014 It is our best work that God wants, not the dregs of our exhaustion. I think he must prefer quality to quantity.
GEORGE MACDONALD (1824–1905)

12015 Lord, turn the routines of work into celebrations of love.

12016 Lord, when thou seest that my work is done,
Let me not linger on,
With failing powers,
Amid the weary hours—
A workless worker in a world of work.
But, with a word,
Just bid me home,
And I will come
Right gladly—
Yea, right gladly
Will I come.
JOHN OXENHAM (1861–1941)

12017 Nothing is really work unless you would rather be doing something else.
SIR JAMES M. BARRIE (1860–1937)

12018 The best things are nearest: breath in your nostrils, light in your eyes, flowers at your feet, duties at your hand, the path of God just before you. Then do not grasp at the stars, but do life's plain, common work as it comes.
ROBERT LOUIS BALFOUR STEVENSON (1850–1894)

12019 The difficult we do immediately; the impossible takes a little longer.
—U.S. Army Services Forces slogan

12020 When love and skill work together, expect a masterpiece.
JOHN RUSKIN (1819–1900)

12021 When your work speaks for itself, don't interrupt.
HENRY J. KAISER (1882–1967)

12022 Work and play are an artificial pair of opposites because the best kind of play contains an element of work, and the

most productive kind of work must include something of the spirit of play.
SYDNEY J. HARRIS (1917–1986)

12023 Work as if you were to live a hundred years; pray as if you were to die tomorrow.
BENJAMIN FRANKLIN (1706–1790)

12024 Work is man's great function. He is nothing, he can do nothing, he can achieve nothing, fulfill nothing, without working. If you are poor—work. If you are rich—continue working. If you are burdened with unseemingly unfair responsibilities—work. If you are happy, keep right on working. Idleness gives room for doubt and fears. If disappointments come—work. If your health is threatened—work. When faith falters—work. When dreams are shattered and hope seems dead— work. Work as if your life were in peril. It really is. No matter what ails you—work. Work faithfully—work with faith. Work is the greatest remedy available for mental and physical afflictions.

12025 Work is not a curse, it is a blessing from God who calls man to rule the earth and transform it so that the divine work of creation may continue with man's intelligence and effort.
POPE JOHN PAUL II (1920–)

12026 Work is not primarily a thing one does to live, but the thing one lives to do. It is, or should be, the full expression of the worker's faculties, the thing in which he finds spiritual, mental, and bodily satisfaction, and the medium in which he offers himself to God.
DOROTHY L. SAYERS (1893–1957)

12027 Work is the greatest thing in the world so we should always save some of it for tomorrow.
DON HEROLD

12028 Work is the meat of life, pleasure the dessert.
B. C. FORBES

12029 Work, work, from early until late. In fact, I have so much to do that I shall spend the first three hours in prayer.
MARTIN LUTHER (1483–1546)

WORLD

12030 All the world is a hospital and everyone in it is a terminal patient.

12031 Far from turning us away from the world, Christ directs us to it. He awakens within us an altogether new concern for it.
PAUL TOURNIER (1898–1986)

12032 Farewell, vain world;
My soul bids you adieu;
My Savior taught me
To abandon you.
Your charms may gratify
A sensual mind,
But cannot please
A soul for God designed.
DAVID BRAINERD (1718–1747)

12033 I have not loved the world, nor the world me;
I have not flatter'd its rank breath, nor bow'd
To its idolatries a patient knee.
LORD GEORGE NOEL GORDON BYRON (1788–1824)

12034 If I walk with the world, I can't walk with God.
DWIGHT LYMAN MOODY (1837–1899)

12035 If you are in with God, you are at outs with this world.
GYPSY SMITH (B. 1860)

12036 It is so impossible for the world to exist without God that if God should forget it, it would immediately cease to be.
SØREN AABYE KIERKEGAARD (1813–1855)

12037 My habitual feeling is that the world is so extremely odd, and everything in it is so surprising. Why should there be green grass and liquid water, and why have I got hands and feet?
JOHN JAY CHAPMAN (1862–1933)

12038 The world embarrasses me, and I cannot dream
That this watch exists and has no watchmaker.
VOLTAIRE (1694–1778)

12039 The world is a beautiful book, but of little use to him who cannot read it.
CARLO GOLDONI (1707–1793)

12040 The world is a great stage on which God displays his many wonders.
SAINT FRANCIS OF SALES (1567–1622)

12041
The world is full of beauty,
     as other worlds above,
And if we did our duty,
     it might be as full of love.
GERALD MASSEY (1828–1907)

12042 The world is God's book, which he set man at first to read and every creature is a letter or syllable or word or sentence more or less, declaring the name and will of God.
RICHARD BAXTER (1615–1691)

12043 The world is God's nursery for his upper rooms.
GEORGE MACDONALD (1824–1905)

12044 The world is just the materializing of God's thoughts, for the world is a thought in God's eye. He made it first from a thought that came from his own mighty mind, and everything in the majestic temple he has made has a meaning.
CHARLES HADDON SPURGEON (1834–1892)

12045 The world is now too dangerous for anything but the truth, too small for anything but brotherhood.
ARTHUR POWELL DAVIES (1902–   )

12046 The world is too much with us; late and soon,
Getting and spending, we lay waste our powers.
WILLIAM WORDSWORTH (1770–1850)

12047 The world is wrong side up. It needs to be turned upside down in order to be right side up.
BILLY SUNDAY (1862–1935)

12048 The world's thy book; there I can read Thy power, wisdom, and thy love.
RICHARD BAXTER (1615–1691)

12049 This world . . . is still a miracle, Wonderful, inscrutable, magical, and more,
To whosoever will think it.
THOMAS CARLYLE (1795–1881)

WORLDLINESS

12050 If we are not nourished by the Bread from heaven, we will satiate ourselves with crumbs from the world.
ERWIN W. LUTZER (1941–   )

12051 The world is a net; the more we stir in it, the more we are entangled.
PROVERB

12052 The world is a sure teacher, but it requires a fat fee.
FINNISH PROVERB

12053 Worldliness is excluding God from our lives and, therefore, consciously or unconsciously accepting the values of a man-centered society.
ERWIN W. LUTZER (1941–   )

12054 Worldliness is not only doing what is forbidden but also wishing it were possible to do it. One of its distinctives is mental slavery to illegitimate pleasure. Worldliness twists values by rearranging their price tags.
ERWIN W. LUTZER (1941–   )

WORRY

12055 'Tain't worthwhile to wear a day all out before it comes.
SARAH ORNE JEWETT (1849–1909)

12056 A day of worry is more exhausting than a day of work.
SIR JOHN LUBBOCK (1834–1913)

12057 Ah, what is more blessed than to put cares away!
GAIUS VALERIUS CATULLUS (C. 84–C. 54 B.C.)

12058 Care admitted as a guest quickly turns to be master.
CHRISTIAN NESTELL BOVEE (1820–1904)

12059 Cares are more difficult to throw off than sorrows; the latter die with time; the former grow upon it.
JOHANN PAUL FRIEDRICH RICHTER (1763–1825)

12060 Don't tell me that worry doesn't do any good. I know better. The things I worry about don't happen.

12061 For one that big misfortunes slay, Ten die of little worries.
GEORGE ROBERT SIMS (1847–1922)

12062 Happy is the man who is too busy to worry by day, and too sleepy to worry at night.

12063 If only we would stop lamenting and look up. God is here. Christ is risen. The Spirit has been poured out from on high. All this we know as theological truth. It remains for us to turn it into joyous spiritual experience.
A. W. TOZER (1897–1963)

12064 If we bring into one day's thoughts the evil of many, certain and uncertain, what will be and what will never be, our load will be as intolerable as it is unreasonable.
JEREMY TAYLOR (1613–1667)

12065 It ain't no use putting up your umbrella till it rains.
ALICE CALDWELL RICE

12066 It is distrust of God to be troubled about what is to come; impatience against God to be troubled with what is present; and anger at God to be troubled for what is past.
SIMON PATRICK (1625–1707)

12067 Leave tomorrow's trouble to tomorrow's strength; tomorrow's work to tomorrow's time; tomorrow's trial to tomorrow's grace and to tomorrow's God.

12068 Life's too short for worrying. Yes, that's what worries me.

12069 Misfortunes hardest to bear are those which never happen.
JAMES RUSSELL LOWELL (1819–1891)

12070 No man ever sank under the burden of the day. It is when tomorrow's burden is added to the burden of today that the weight is more than a man can bear. Never load yourself so.
GEORGE MACDONALD (1824–1905)

12071 Not work, but worry makes us weary.
S. I. MCMILLEN

12072 One is given strength to bear what happens to one, but not the one hundred and one different things that might happen.
C. S. LEWIS (1898–1963)

12073 Only man clogs his happiness with care, destroying what is, with thoughts of what may be.
JOHN DRYDEN (1631–1700)

12074 Only one type of worry is correct: to worry because you worry too much.
JEWISH PROVERB

12075 Quick is the succession of human events; the cares of today are seldom the cares of tomorrow; and when we lie down at night, we may safely say to most of our troubles, "You have done your worst, and we shall meet no more."
WILLIAM COWPER (1731–1800)

12076 Seventy percent of all patients who come to physicians could cure themselves if they only got rid of their fears, worries, and bad eating habits.
O. F. GOBER

12077 So shaken as we are, so wan with care.
WILLIAM SHAKESPEARE (1564–1616)

12078 The essence of worry . . . is the absence of thought, a failure to think.
D. MARTYN LLOYD-JONES (1899–1981)

12079 There are people who are always anticipating trouble; they manage to enjoy many sorrows that never really happen to them.
JOSH BILLINGS (1818–1885)

12080 To carry care to bed is to sleep with a pack on your back.
THOMAS CHANDLER HALIBURTON (1796–1865)

12081 When worry is present, trust cannot crowd its way in.
BILLY GRAHAM (1918–   )

12082 Where care lodges, sleep will never lie.
WILLIAM SHAKESPEARE (1564–1616)

12083 Work won't kill, but worry will.
ENGLISH PROVERB

12084 Worms eat you when you're dead; worries eat you when you're alive.
JEWISH PROVERB

12085 Worry gives a small thing a big shadow.
SWEDISH PROVERB

12086 Worry is a species of myopia—near-sightedness.
E. STANLEY JONES (1884–1973)

12087 Worry is an indication that we think God cannot look after us.
OSWALD CHAMBERS (1874–1917)

12088 Worry is like a rocking chair. It gives you something to do but doesn't get you anywhere.
BERNARD MELTZER

12089 Worry never robs tomorrow of its sorrow, it only saps today of its strength.
ARCHIBALD JOSEPH CRONIN (1896–1981)

12090 Worry: the interest paid by those who borrow trouble.
GEORGE W. LYON

12091 Worry? Why worry? What can worry do?
It never keeps a trouble from overtaking you.
It gives you indigestion and sleepless hours at night
And fills with gloom the days, however fair and bright.
HELEN STEINER RICE

12092 Your ship is equal to the load of today; but when you are carrying yesterday's worry and tomorrow's anxiety, lighten up or you will sink.

WORSHIP

12093 A man can no more diminish God's glory by refusing to worship him than a lunatic can put out the sun by scribbling the word *darkness* on the walls of his cell.
C. S. LEWIS (1898–1963)

12094 And now the wants are told, that brought
Thy children to thy knee;
Here, lingering still, we ask for naught
But simply worship thee.
WILLIAM BRIGHT (1921–)

12095 Ay, call it holy ground,
The soil where first they trod!
They have left unstained what there they found—
Freedom to worship God.
FELICIA HEMANS (1793–1835)

12096 By making a lot of religious din we assure our faltering hearts that everything is well, and, conversely, we suspect silence and regard it as a proof that the meeting is "dead."
A. W. TOZER (1897–1963)

12097 First worship God.
He that forgets to pray
Bids not himself good-morrow
Or good-day.
THOMAS RANDOLPH (1523–1590)

12098 God is looking for worshipers. And if the religious elite are too proud or too busy to learn to worship him, he seeks the worship of those whose lives are trapped in moral ruin.
ERWIN W. LUTZER (1941–)

12099 God wants worshipers before workers; indeed the only acceptable workers are those who have learned the lost art of worship. . . . The very stones would praise him if the need arose and a thousand legions of angels would leap to do his will.
A. W. TOZER (1897–1963)

12100 He who knows God reverences him.
LUCIUS ANNAEUS SENECA (C. 4 B.C.–A.D. 65)

12101 How often Christians assume they have worshiped God simply because they have been in church! We are told that the church building is "God's house" (an inaccurate designation borrowed from the Old Testament temple) and conclude that worship must take place there! Not necessarily. God was not pleased with the worship at Jerusalem (the Holy City). Nor is he impressed with beautiful cathedrals.
ERWIN W. LUTZER (1941–)

12102 I lay my "whys"
before your cross
in worship kneeling,
my mind too numb
for thought,
my heart beyond
all feeling:
And worshiping,
realize that I

in knowing you
don't need a "why."
RUTH BELL GRAHAM

12103 In worship we meet the power of God
and stand in its strengthening.
NELS F. S. FERRÉ (1769–1821)

12104 If we haven't learned to be worshipers,
it doesn't really matter how well we
do anything else.
ERWIN W. LUTZER (1941–   )

12105 If worship does not change us, it has
not been worship. To stand before the
Holy One of eternity is to change.
Worship begins in holy expectancy; it
ends in holy obedience.
RICHARD J. FOSTER (1942–   )

12106 If you can leave your church on Sunday morning with no feeling of discomfort, of conviction, of brokenness, of
challenge, then for you the hour of
worship has not been as dangerous as
it should have been. The ease with
which we go on being Christian sentimentalists is one of our worst faults.
PAUL STROMBERG REES (1900–   )

12107 It is only when men begin to worship
that they begin to grow.
CALVIN COOLIDGE (1872–1933)

12108 Jesus, where'er thy people meet,
There they behold thy mercy seat;
Where'er they seek thee thou art
    found,
And every place is hallowed ground.
WILLIAM COWPER (1731–1800)

12109 Man cannot live all to this world. If
not religious, he will be superstitious.
If he worships not the true God, he
will have his idols.
THEODORE PARKER (1810–1860)

12110 Man is a religious being; the heart
instinctively seeks for a God. Whether
he worships on the banks of the Gan-
ges, prays with his face upturned to
the sun, kneels toward Mecca or,
regarding all space as a temple, com-
munes with the heavenly Father
according to the Christian creed, man
is essentially devout.
WILLIAM JENNINGS BRYAN (1860–1925)

12111 Many regular church attenders consistently focus their minds on sporting
events, business affairs, or matters of
personal interest as soon as the sermon begins. Many so-called worshipers can tell you what dress the pastor's
wife wore in the service, but cannot
recall the text of the sermon or the
application of the message to their
lives.
RICHARD OWEN ROBERTS (1931–   )

12112 More spiritual progress can be made
in one short moment of speechless
silence in the awesome presence of
God than in years of mere study.
A. W. TOZER (1897–1963)

12113 Prostrate before thy throne to lie,
And gaze and gaze on thee!
FREDERICK WILLIAM FABER (1814–1863)

12114 Silent worship seems to friends to be
their natural method. It is healing; it is
uniting; it cleanses, challenges,
stimulates. It helps us to get down to
those deeper currents of the soul that
are so often neglected in life's hurry
and bustle; it enables us to center
down into fellowship with the Eternal
and to hear the still small voice of God.
GERALD K. HIBBERT (1872–1957)

12115 The dearest idol I have known,
Whate'er that idol be,
Help me to tear it from its throne,
And worship only thee.
WILLIAM COWPER (1731–1800)

12116 The glory of God is a living man; and
the life of man consists in beholding
God.
SAINT IRENAEUS (C. 130–C. 200)

12117 The one essential condition of human
existence is that man should always be
able to bow down before something
infinitely great. The Infinite and the
Eternal are as essential for man as the
little planet on which he dwells.
FYODOR MIKHAYLOVICH DOSTOYEVSKI
(1821–1881)

12118 The philosopher aspires to explain
away all mysteries, to dissolve them
into light. Mystery on the other hand
is demanded and pursued by the reli-

gious instinct; mystery constitutes the essence of worship.
HENRI FRÉDÉRIC AMIEL (1821–1881)

12119 The worship of God is not a rule of safety—it is an adventure of the spirit.
ALFRED NORTH WHITEHEAD (1861–1947)

12120 There are delights that the heart may enjoy in the awesome presence of God that cannot find expression in language; they belong to the unutterable element in Christian experience. Not many enjoy them because not many know that they can. The whole concept of ineffable worship has been lost.
A. W. TOZER (1897–1963)

12121 There may be worship without words!
JAMES RUSSELL LOWELL (1819–1891)

12122 This is adoration: not a difficult religious exercise, but an attitude of the soul.
EVELYN UNDERHILL (1875–1941)

12123 Those who worship God merely from fear would worship the devil, too, if he appear.
SIR THOMAS FULLER (1608–1661)

12124 To worship is to quicken the conscience by the holiness of God, to feed the mind with the truth of God, to purge the imagination by the beauty of God, to open the heart to the love of God, to devote the will to the purpose of God.
ARCHBISHOP WILLIAM TEMPLE (1881–1944)

12125 Transfixed with thanks, folded in love, I cannot adore enough. I cannot speak.
MYRNA REID GRANT (1934–)

12126 We pay God honor and reverence, not for his sake (because he is of himself full of glory to which no creature can add anything), but for our own sake.
SAINT THOMAS AQUINAS (1225–1274)

12127 What comes from the Lord because it is impossible for humans to manufacture it? Wisdom. What comes from humans because it is impossible for the Lord to experience it? Worry. And what is it that brings wisdom and dispels worry? Worship.
CHARLES R. SWINDOLL (1934–)

12128 What was our Lord thinking about as he walked along the roads of Galilee, so often alone? What were his thoughts in times of repose, during the journeys by boat that he liked making with his disciples after a day's exhausting preaching? What occupied his mind among the hills where he liked to go alone, without even the disciples? The answer, we may think, is easy: he was thinking of men, of sinners and their salvation, and what he had to do to effect that salvation. But, surprising as it may seem to us, it wasn't with us that Jesus was concerned. The constant object of his meditation, the natural orientation of his heart and mind and soul, the food that constantly nourished him, was his Father.
LOUIS EVELY (1910–)

12129 Whatever is outward in worship must come as a direct result of what is inward—otherwise, it will be form without power.
HOWARD BRINTON

12130 Who worship God, shall find him.
Humble love,
And not proud reason, keeps the door of heaven;
Love finds admission, where proud science fails.
JOHN GREENLEAF WHITTIER (1807–1892)

12131 Without the worship of the heart, liturgical prayer becomes formal routine.
AELRED GRAHAM (1909–)

12132 For worship is a thirsty land crying out for rain,
It is a candle in the act of being kindled,
It is a drop in quest of the ocean, . . .
It is a voice in the night calling for help,
It is a soul standing in awe before the mystery of the universe, . . .
It is time flowing into eternity, . . .
[It is] a man climbing the altar stairs to God.
DWIGHT BRADLEY

12133 Worship is a way of living, a way of seeing the world in the light of God . . . to rise to a higher level of

existence, to see the world from the point of view of God.
ABRAHAM J. HESCHEL (1907–1972)

12134 Worship is giving to God the best he has given us.
OSWALD CHAMBERS (1874–1917)

12135 Worship is not a part of the Christian life; it is the Christian life.
GERALD VANN (1906–1963)

12136 Worship is pictured at its best in Isaiah when the young prophet became aware of the Father, aware of his own limitations, aware of the Father's directives, and aware of the task at hand.
DAVID JULIUS

12137 Worship is the highest and noblest act that any person can do. When men worship, God is satisfied! And when you worship, you are fulfilled! Think about this: why did Jesus Christ come? He came to make worshipers out of rebels. We who were once self-centered have to be completely changed so that we can shift our attention outside of ourselves and become able to worship him.
RAYMOND C. ORTLUND

12138 Worship is transcendent wonder.
THOMAS CARLYLE (1795–1881)

12139 Worship isn't listening to a sermon, appreciating the harmony of the choir, and joining in singing hymns! It isn't even prayer, for prayer can be the selfish expression of an unbroken spirit. Worship goes deeper. Since God is spirit, we fellowship with him with our spirit; that is, the immortal and invisible part of us meets with God, who is immortal and invisible.
ERWIN W. LUTZER (1941–)

12140 Worship means "to feel in the heart."
A. W. TOZER (1897–1963)

12141 Worship renews the spirit as sleep renews the body.
RICHARD CLARKE CABOT (1868–1939)

12142 Worship requires only a man and God.

WRITING

12143 All morning I worked on the proof of one of my poems, and I took out a comma; in the afternoon I put it back.
OSCAR WILDE (1854–1900)

12144 All who have been concerned in the day-by-day reporting of the game's progress—I mean the collection, presentation, and dissemination of what is called news—know better than anyone how slight, fragile, and fraudulent are the available sources. The bucket dropped into the well of truth is leaky indeed, and such water as it brings up, brackish and polluted.
MALCOLM MUGGERIDGE (1903–1990)

12145 Chaucer had talent, but he couldn't spell.
ARTEMUS WARD (1727–1800)

12146 God is not interested only in Christian writers as such. He is concerned with all kinds of writing. In the same way a sacred calling is not limited to ecclesiastical functions. The man who is weeding a field of turnips is also serving God.
C. S. LEWIS (1898–1963)

12147 If my stories are incomprehensible to Jews or Muslims or Taoists, then I have failed as a Christian writer. We do not draw people to Christ by loudly discrediting what they believe, by telling them how wrong they are and how right we are, but by showing them a light that is so lovely that they want with all their hearts to know the source of it.
MADELEINE L'ENGLE (1918–)

12148 In a very real sense, the writer writes in order to teach himself.
ALFRED KAZIN (1915–)

12149 It is my ambition to say in ten sentences what others say in a whole book.
FRIEDRICH WILHELM NIETZSCHE (1844–1900)

12150 Less is more.
ROBERT BROWNING (1812–1889)

12151 Let me make the newspapers, and I care not what is preached in the pulpit or what is enacted in Congress.
WENDELL PHILLIPS (1811–1884)

12152 Logic teaches that if an educated person knows how to use colons in writing, a semieducated person must know how to use semicolons.

12153 The making of indexes is what gives editors that haggard and querulous look.
SAXE COMMINS

12154 The most valuable of all talents is that of never using two words when one will do.
THOMAS JEFFERSON (1743–1826)

12155 The writer is a kind of evangelist, more subtle than Billy Graham, of course, but of the same stuff.
SHIRLEY ANN GRAU (1929–)

12156 There is a type of writing that causes people to commit crime—and that's the type of writing that's done every day in the newspapers. One story about a hijacker breeds a thousand. It's sensationalism. It's more the exposure than the quality of writing.
People know a work of fiction is make-believe. People don't commit murders after reading Agatha Christie. People do commit murder after reading about murder in the paper. Similar murders.
WILLIAM SEWARD BURROUGHS (1914–)

12157 When I am grappling with ideas which are radical enough to upset grown-ups, then I am likely to put these ideas into a story which will be marketed for children, because children understand what their parents have rejected and forgotten.
MADELEINE L'ENGLE (1918–)

12158 Writing a book or a manifesto is the nearest a man gets to having a baby.
JOHN R. W. STOTT (1921–)

12159 Writing is so difficult that I often feel that writers, having had their hell on earth, will escape all punishment hereafter.
JESSAMYN WEST (1907–)

YOUTH

12160 A youth is a person who is going to carry on what you have started. He will assume control of your cities, states, and nations. He is going to take over your churches, schools, and corporations. You may adopt all the policies you please, but how they are carried out depends on him. So it might be well to pay him some attention.

12161 Adolescence is a fascinating and crazy time of life.
JAMES C. DOBSON (1936–)

12162 Adolescents: those who are quickest to discern hypocrisy.
EUGENE E. BRUSSELL

12163 Don't laugh at a youth for his affectations. He is only trying on one face after another to find his own.
LOGAN PEARSALL SMITH (1865–1946)

12164 Heaven lies about us in our infancy! Shades of the prison-house begin to close
Upon the growing boy.
WILLIAM WORDSWORTH (1770–1850)

12165 I remember my youth and the feeling that will never come back any more— the feeling that I could last forever, outlast the sea, the earth, and all men.
JOSEPH CONRAD (1857–1924)

12166 If you refuse to be made straight when you are green, you will not be made straight when you are dry.
AFRICAN PROVERB

12167 If youth be a defect, it is one that we outgrow only too soon.
JAMES RUSSELL LOWELL (1819–1891)

12168 In early youth, as we contemplate our coming life, we are like children in a theater before the curtain is raised, sitting there in high spirits and eagerly waiting for the play to begin.
ARTHUR SCHOPENHAUER (1788–1860)

12169 In his youth, everybody believes that the world began to exist only when he was born, and that everything really exists only for his sake.
JOHANN WOLFGANG VON GOETHE
(1749–1832)

12170 In sorrow he learned this truth—
One may return to the place of his
birth,
He cannot go back to his youth.
JOHN BURROUGHS (1837–1921)

12171 No young man ever thinks he shall die.
WILLIAM HAZLITT (1778–1830)

12172 Since teenagers are too old to do the
things kids do and not old enough to
do things adults do, they do things
nobody else does.

12173 The destiny of any nation depends on
the opinions of its citizens under
twenty-five.
JOHANN WOLFGANG VON GOETHE
(1749–1832)

12174 The isms of youth are the wasms of
age.

12175 There is a feeling of eternity in youth.
WILLIAM HAZLITT (1778–1830)

12176 Who will give me back those days
when life had wings and flew just like
a skylark in the sky?
MARCELINE DESBORDES-VALMORE
(1786–1859)

12177 Young people do the impossible before
they find out it's impossible—that's
why God uses them so often.
LOREN CUNNINGHAM

12178 Young people need control and authority; and without it they are unhappy,
confused, frustrated, and miserable.
This is one of the psychological secrets
that Hitler and Mussolini used so effectively in gaining control of the youth
of Germany and Italy.
BILLY GRAHAM (1918–)

12179 Young people seem so cynical, precisely because they are so idealistic;
when they learn that a god has clay
feet, they do not merely demote him,
they designate him as the devil incarnate.
SYDNEY J. HARRIS (1917–1986)

12180 Young people will respond if the
challenge is tough enough and hard
enough. Youth wants a master and a
controller. Young people were built for
God, and without God as the center of
their lives they become frustrated and
confused, desperately grasping for and
searching for security.
BILLY GRAHAM (1918–)

12181 Youth have exalted notions because
they have not yet been humbled by life
or learned its necessary limitations. . . . They would always rather
do noble deeds than useful ones; their
lives are governed more by feeling
than by reasoning. . . . All their mistakes are in the direction of doing
things excessively and vehemently. . . .
They love too much, they hate too
much; they think they know everything; that is why they overdo everything.
ARISTOTLE (384–322 B.C.)

12182 Youth is happy because it has the
capacity to see beauty. Anyone who
keeps the ability to see beauty never
grows old.
FRANZ KAFKA (1883–1924)

12183 Youth is not properly definable by
age. It is a spirit of daring, creating,
asserting life, and openly relating to
the world.
MALCOLM BOYD (1923–)

12184 Youth is one thing that never returns.
JEWISH PROVERB

12185 Youth is wholly experimental.
ROBERT LOUIS BALFOUR STEVENSON
(1850–1894)

12186 Youth is youth and age is age, and we
have no business to require the head
of age on the shoulders of youth.
OSWALD CHAMBERS (1874–1917)

12187 Youth would be an ideal state if it
came a little later in life.
EARL ASQUITH (1852–1928)

12188 Youth, large, lusty, loving—youth, full
of grace, force, fascination, do you
know that old age may come after you
with equal grace, force, fascination?
WALT WHITMAN (1819–1892)

YOUTH/OLD AGE

12189 'Tis the defect of age to rail at the pleasures of youth.
SUSANNAH CENTLIVRE (C. 1667–1723)

12190 I was born in the wrong generation. When I was a young man, no one had any respect for youth. Now I am an old man and no one has any respect for age.
BERTRAND ARTHUR WILLIAM RUSSELL (1872–1970)

12191 In youth we learn; in age we understand.
MARIE EBNER-ESCHENBACH (1830–1916)

12192 Nothing so dates a man as to decry the younger generation.
ADLAI E. STEVENSON (1900–1965)

12193 Old age lives minutes slowly, hours quickly; childhood chews hours and swallows minutes.
MALCOLM DE CHAZAL

12194 The Hebrews regarded life as complete when it was full of days and riches and honor. Age was looked upon as a sign of favor. Whenever a nation becomes unspiritual, it reverses this order; the demand is not for old age but for youth. This reversal in the modern life of today is indicative of apostasy, not of advance.
OSWALD CHAMBERS (1874–1917)

12195 The young have aspirations that never come to pass; the old have reminiscences of what never happened.
H. H. MUNRO (1870–1916)

12196 When young, we run into difficulties; when old, difficulties run into us.
JOSH BILLINGS (1818–1885)

12197 Young men lose their lives by violence; old men by ripeness.
CICERO (106–43 B.C.)

12198 Youth has to do with spirit, not age. Men of seventy and eighty are often more youthful than the young.
HENRY MILLER (1891–1980)

12199 Youth is a blunder; manhood a struggle; old age a regret.
BENJAMIN DISRAELI (1804–1881)

12200 Youth looks forward, but age looks back.

INDEX OF AUTHORS

Anonymous quotes, proverbs, and folk sayings are not listed. Also, authors with more than 200 quotes have been omitted from this index.

ℬ

Bathurst, William H. *3768*

Battisti, O. A. *3853*

Baudelaire, Charles (1821–1867), *2640, 2692, 8982*

Bauer, Gerard (1888–1967), *1883*

Baxter, Richard (1615–1691), *4693, 4770, 5379, 5635, 6923, 7196, 9037, 10425, 11312, 12042, 12048*

Bayly, Joseph (1920–1986), *2259, 2827, 3070, 7181, 8820*

Beadle, E. R. (1812–1879), *2465*

Beale, Howard *11045*

Beam *1414*

Beaumarchais, Pierre Augustin Caron de (1732–1799), *6340*

Beaumont, Francis (1584–1616), *2907*

Beaumont, Joseph (1615–1699), *463*

Beck, Frederick *8836*

Becker, Edna *7715*

Becker, May Lamberton *8180*

Becque, Henry François (1837–1899), *3247*

Beecher, Henry Ward (1813–1887), *189, 228, 290, 470, 471, 624, 713, 801, 1009, 1288, 1437, 1636, 1721, 1816, 2187, 2507, 2511, 2529, 2714, 3046, 3314, 3345, 3437, 3899, 3902, 3973, 4081, 4223, 4225, 4289, 4563, 4641, 4895, 4998, 5140, 5258, 5284, 5507, 6027, 6101, 6112, 6302, 6565, 6719, 6738, 6739, 6893, 7185, 7516, 7536, 7857, 7859, 7982, 8004, 8422, 8551, 8739, 8828, 8856, 9099, 9712, 10000, 10618, 10642, 10666, 10732, 10773, 11013, 11078, 11207, 11440, 11455, 11829, 11840*

Beecher, Lyman (1775–1863), *1824*

Beerbohm, Sir Max (1872–1956), *3056*

Beethoven, Ludwig van (1770–1827), *2444, 7929*

Behrman, Samuel Nathaniel (1893–1973), *8133*

Belasco, David (1853–1931), *1981*

Belinski, Vissarion Grigorevich (1811–1848), *4594*

Bell, Alexander Graham (1847–1922), *8229*

Bell, Bernard Iddings (1886–1958), *4694, 7944*

Bell, Mary (1957–), *7882*

Bellarmine, Robert (1542–1621), *3349*

Belloc, Hilaire (1870–1953), *6212*

Bellow, Saul (1915–), *10891*

Ben Gabirol, Solomon (c. 1020–1070), *1835, 6099, 7354, 8701, 11930, 11956*

Ben Joseph, Rabbi Akiba (c. 40–135), *1953*

Ben-Gurion, David (1886–1973), *669*

Benét, Stephen Vincent (1898–1943), *6972*

Benham, Sir William Gurney (1859–1944), *1873, 7730, 11484*

Bennett, Alan *6976*

Bennett, Arnold (1867–1931), *11356*

Bennett, William *134*

Benson, Edward White (1829–1896), *5880*

Benson, Robert H. (1871–1914), *3055, 4272, 4741, 10255, 10700*

Bentham, Jeremy (1748–1832), *10410*

Beran, C. Raymond *4173*

Berdyaev, Nikolai Aleksandrovich (1874–1948), *2018, 3399, 4127, 4130, 4149*

Berenson, Bernard (1865–1959), *1747, 5601, 6950*

Bergson, Henri (1859–1941), *11257*

Bering, Frank *8144*

Berkeley, George (1685–1753), *11352, 11571*

Berkhof, Hendrik *2100, 6286*

Berkhof, Louis (1873–1957), *1387*

Bernanos, Georges (1888–1948), *3688, 5693, 8994*

Bernard, Dorothy *1919*

Bernard, Thomas D. (1750–1818), *10349*

Berry, Joseph F. (1856–), *2317*

Berston, Hyman Maxwell *1678*

Bethune, Mary McLeod (1875–1955), *11131*

Betterton, Thomas (c. 1635–1710), *9130*

Bias of Priene (c. 570 B.C.), *11950*

Bickmore, Lee (1908–), *7361*

Biederwolf, William Edward (1867–1939), *5648, 6046, 6349*

Bierce, Ambrose Gwinnett (1842–c.1914), *395, 2619, 6052, 9713*

Bilkey, James G. *9977*

Billings, Josh (1818–1885), *6083, 6726, 7259, 7816, 8509, 8993, 10008, 10327, 11074, 11098, 11456, 12079, 12196*

Bingen, Saint Hildegarde of (1098–1179), *3191, 4753*

Bion (fl. c. 100 B.C.), *5701, 11820*

Birch, Charles *11861*

Bisch, Louis E. *10892*

Bishop, Amish *1218*

Bismarck, Otto Eduard Leopold von (1815–1898), *2915*

Bisse, James *1348*

Blackfeet, Crowfoot of the (1821–1890), *2457, 7082*

Blackie, John Stuart (1809–1895), *77, 10534*

Blair, James (1656–1743), *11843*

Blake, William (1757–1827), *386, 596, 808, 813, 1554, 3179, 3482, 4145, 8506, 9185, 10402*

Blamires, Harry *7768, 11239*

Blanding, Don *9886*

Blanqui, Auguste (1805–1881), *5969*

Blau, Joel *11208*

Blessington, Marguerite Countess of (1789–1849), *5563*

Blinco, Joseph D. *5674*

Bloesch, Donald G. (1928–), *11981*

Blois, Louis de *4978*

Bloom, Archbishop Anthony (1914–), *4660, 10123*

Blount, Sir Thomas Pope (1649–1697), *3192*

Bloy, Léon Henri Marie (1846–1917), *6183, 6548, 10890*

Blue, Lionel *8754*

Blum, Léon (1872–1950), *11241*

Boardman, George Dana (1801–1831), *9163*

Bode, John E. *5418*

Boehme, Carlyle *4422*

Boethius, Anicius Manlius Severinus (c. 480–524), *4883, 5027*

Böhme, Jakob (1575–1624), *357, 2652, 4028, 4861, 6570, 7550, 9936*

Bohn, Henry George (1796–1884), *1711, 2677, 4354, 5921, 6002, 9298, 11258*

Boice, James Montgomery *874*

Bois, W. E. B. Du (1868–1963), *1487*

Bok, Derek *3012*

Bolen, James *11575*

Bolingbroke, Viscount Henry St. John (1678–1751), *5286, 6868*

Bolt, David *8762*

Bolton, Edmund (c.1575–c.1633), *6123*

Bolton, Samuel (1606–1654), *2372*

Bonaparte, Napoleon (1769–1821), *732, 2347, 4415, 5278, 5728, 6351, 6396, 7675, 10695, 10865, 11771*

Bonar, Horatius (1808–1889), *994, 5412, 5456, 7519, 8451, 10133, 11287, 11591*

Bonaventure, Saint (1221–1274), *7286*

Bonhoeffer, Dietrich (1906–1945), *84, 466, 1253, 1594, 2151, 4457, 4899, 4914, 5257, 7170, 7562, 8109, 10049, 10297, 10547, 10814, 10859, 11531, 11690, 11761*

Boniface, Saint (680–c.754), *1398*

Bonnell, John Sutherland *1420*

Boom, Betsie ten (1885–1944), *4980*

Boom, Corrie ten (1892–1983), *9, 587, 2805, 3515, 3658, 3678, 3679, 3713, 4020, 4620, 4776, 4917,*

5135, 5451, 5461, 5491, 8119, 8785, 8848, 8955, 9575, 9842, 9860, 9914, 11670

Booth, Catherine (1829–1890), *2435, 3748*

Booth, Evangeline Cory (1865–1950), *325, 6933*

Booth, William (1829–1912), *1724, 3342, 10975*

Boothe, Clare Luce (1903–1987), *5953*

Boreham, F. W. *2761, 9740, 10517*

Borges, Jorge Luis (1899–1986), *7681, 11669*

Borland, Hal (1900–1978), *239*

Borman, Frank (1928–), *11644*

Boros, Ladislaus *10246*

Bosley, Harold A. (1907–1975), *10857*

Bossuet, Jacques Bénigne (1627–1704), *8112*

Boston, Thomas (1676–1732), *3283, 3295, 5644*

Boswell, James (1740–1795), *5688*

Bouhours, Dominique (1628–1702), *7809*

Boulding, Kenneth *10795*

Bounds, Edward McKendree (1835–1913), *1436, 6776, 8768, 8889, 8903, 8914, 8930, 8940, 8969, 8976, 9015, 9160*

Bourdillon, Francis William (1852–1921), *7306*

Bovee, Christian Nestell (1820–1904), *1782, 2895, 4334, 7756, 10234, 10385, 12058*

Bowden, W. S. *8949*

Bowes, George Seaton (c. 1875), *6559*

Bowles, William Lisle (1762–1850), *4143*

Bowring, Sir John (1792–1872), *2133, 3865, 4592*

Boyd, Malcolm (1923–), *12183*

Boyd, Myron F. *11492*

Boyle, Robert (1627–1691), *668*

Braddon, Mary Elizabeth (1837–1915), *11980*

Bradford, Gamaliel (1863–1932), *7391*

Bradford, John (c. 1510–1555), *5234*

Bradley, Dwight *12132*

Bradley, Francis Herbert (1846–1924), *7394*

Bradley, Omar Nelson (1893–1981), *1705*

Bradley, Preston (1888–1983), *3596*

Bradshaw, Christopher William *1716*

Bradstreet, Anne (c. 1612–1672), *182*

Brainard, Mary Gardiner (c. 1860), *5419, 8079, 11471*

Brainerd, David (1718–1747), *12032*

Braley, Berton (1882–1966), *8230*

Brand, Paul *2132*

Brande, Dorothea *8533*

Brandeis, Louis D. (1856–1941), *445, 8072*

Braque, Georges (1882–1963), *3057, 6867, 11556*

Braun, Wernher von (1912–1977), *6090, 11650*

Braunstein, Richard (b. 1885), *7299*

Bray, Billy *2728*

Brecht, Bertolt (1898–1956), *3352, 3375, 4112*

Breland *967*

Brendan (c. 486–578), *1290*

Brevint, Daniel (1616–1695), *4965*

Bridges, Jerry *5753*

Bridges, Robert Seymour (1844–1930), *4234*

Briffault, Robert (1876–1948), *2525*

Bright, John (1811–1889), *2371, 770*

Bright, William (1921–), *12094*

Brightman, Edgar Sheffield (1884–1953), *5023*

Brilliant, Ashleigh *11615*

Brink, Frederick W. *1174*

Brinton, Howard *12129*

Briscoe, Stuart *401*

Bristol, Lee H. Jr., (1923–1979), *10949*

Brodie, J. F. *2030*

Brogan, Sir D. W. (1900–1974), *6706*

Brome, Alexander (1620–1666), *2694*

Bromfield, Louis (1896–1956), *701, 1101*

Brontë, Charlotte (1816–1855) *4251*

Brontë, Emily (1818–1848) *3765, 6875, 9232*

Brook, F. *4428*

Brooks, Phillips (1835–1893), *237, 551, 714, 723, 916, 929, 936, 1401, 1723, 2468, 2985, 3195, 3428, 3714, 4577, 5480, 6037, 6108, 6293, 6381, 6441, 6452, 6882, 7055, 7057, 8649, 8753, 8780, 8833, 8849, 8895, 10304, 10434, 10821*

Brooks, Thomas Benton (1608–1680), *1317, 3432, 4696, 5205, 11472*

Brooks, Van Wyck (1886–1963), *433*

Brotherton, Alice Williams *11175*

Brotherton, Joseph (1783–1857), *11839*

Broun, Heywood (1888–1939), *484, 4007, 5841*

Brower, Charles *10480*

Brown, A. Douglas *4892*

Brown, Hugh B. *7230*

Brown, Joe E. (1892–1973), *6532*

Brown, John (1715–1766), *2301, 3495, 7052, 10879*

Brown, Mary Elizabeth (1842–1917), *5420*

Brown, Robert R. *11612*

Brown, William Adams (1865–1943), *3774*

Browne, Borden P. *10922*

Browne, Matthew (1823–1882), *8010*

Browne, Sir Thomas (1605–1682), *605, 1706, 1968, 2070, 2405, 3173, 3284, 3802, 3977, 4502, 5454, 6023, 6585, 7021, 10492, 11641*

Browne, William (1591–1643), *9878*

Browning, Elizabeth Barrett (1806–1861), *6, 365, 1609, 1710, 1802, 1952, 2120, 2345, 2695, 3269, 4988, 5339, 5908, 8489, 9862, 10634, 10870*

Browning, Robert (1812–1889), *948, 1063, 1615, 2697, 2945, 3739, 4083, 4420, 4758, 4825, 5157, 5408, 5636, 6275, 6322, 6591, 6914, 7294, 7478, 7652, 7706, 8030, 8054, 8082, 8083, 8132, 8233, 9653, 9940, 9981, 10116, 11122, 11727, 12150*

Bruce, F. F. (1910–1990), *725*

Bruce, Michael *10597*

Brunner, Emil (1889–1966), *3361, 3835, 4738*

Brussell, Eugene E. *12162*

Bruyère, Jean de La (1645–1696), *4045, 6954, 7050, 10570, 11832*

Bryan, William Jennings (1860–1925), *702, 1991, 1992, 2719, 6095, 7939, 12110*

Bryant, Anita (1940–), *5594, 8335*

Bryant, William Cullen (1794–1878), *47, 983, 1966, 2203, 7449, 8036, 8078, 11579*

Buber, Martin (1878–1965), *4549, 4667*

Buchan, John (1875–1940), *474*

Büchner, George (1813–1837), *7403, 8277*

Buck, Pearl S. (1892–1973), *122, 7991, 9933*

Buckminster, J. S. *1082*

Buechner, Frederick (1926–), *2963, 4448*

Buffon, Georges-Louis Leclerc de (1707–1788), *4392, 8402*

Bulver, John (c. 1654), *7199*

Bulwer, Sir Henry (1801–1872), *4330*

Bulwer-Lytton, Edward George (1803–1873), *2471, 3146, 5054, 6696, 6718, 9571*

Bunyan, John (1628–1688), *278, 665, 875, 1278, 1804, 2325, 2366, 2455, 2590, 2881, 2969, 4348, 4364, 4524, 5016, 5212, 5660, 5912, 6001, 6121, 6393, 8442, 8844, 8915, 8974, 9601, 9803, 10157, 10313, 10344, 10376, 10663, 11089, 11095, 11102, 11522*

Burbank, Luther (1849–1926), *11228, 11230*

Burgess, Gelett (1866–1951), *9318*

Burghley, Baron William Cecil (1520–1598), *7464*

Burke, Billie *10223*

Burke, Edmund (1729–1797), *863, 1623, 2541, 2601, 2717, 3160, 3402, 4048, 8407, 10967, 11245*

Burket, Gail Brook *1927*

Burkholder, Esther York *4357*

Burnett, Ivy Compton (1884–1969), *9405*

Burns, James Drummond *2441*

Burns, Robert (1759–1796), *30, 921, 5885, 6666, 6958, 7007, 7537, 9928, 10038, 11159, 11755*

Burroughs, John (1837–1921), *5296, 8011, 8225, 9759, 11301, 12170*

Burroughs, William Seward (1914–), *12156*

Burrows, V. W. *8661*

Burton, Henry (1840–1930), *6640*

Burton, Robert (1577–1640), *241, 2376, 2548, 3154, 6247, 7279, 9252*

Busch, Wilhelm (1832–1908), *3917*

Bushnell, Horace (1802–1876), *683, 1419, 4077, 5156, 5324, 6791, 6888, 8219, 8306, 9216, 9562, 10205*

Butler, Bishop Joseph (1692–1752), *10025*

Butler, Nicholas Murray (1862–1947), *3827, 7041*

Butler, Samuel (1612–1680), *1557, 1674, 2747, 4235, 6966, 6967, 6971, 6974, 7585, 8085, 8702, 9179, 9238*

Butler, Samuel (1835–1902), *1996*

Butterfield, Herbert (1900–), *2159*

Buttrick, George Arthur (1892–1980), *4633, 4689, 7155, 10337, 10361*

Butts, Mary Frances (1836–1902), *11362*

Buxton, Charles (1823–1871), *1704, 2074*

Byrne, Frankie *9645*

Byrne, Robert *2334*

Byrnes, James Francis (1879–1972), *4239, 11502*

Byron, George Noel Gordon, Lord (1788–1824), *144, 618, 803, 1553, 1737, 5505, 6716, 7278, 7680, 9048, 9567, 9935, 10470, 10530, 10541, 10614, 11261, 12002, 12033*

C

C. S. Lewis (1898–1963), *2407*

Cabot, Richard Clarke (1868–1939), *12141*

Caedmon (d. c. 680), *2639*

Caesar, Augustus (63 B.C.–A.D. 14), *5578*

Calcagnini, Celio (1479–1551), *6926*

Calcutta, Mother Teresa of (1910–), *23, 1366, 5261, 5754, 6163, 6569, 7132, 8693, 8910, 10250, 10708, 10779, 11988*

Calkin, Ruth Harms (1918–), *897*

Call, Cadle *5357*

Calvin, John (1509–1564), *99, 363, 648, 799, 1458, 3048, 3088, 4833, 5946, 6115, 7437, 10020, 11652*

Camden, William (1551–1623), *390*

Campbell, Bartley T. (1843–1888), *11694*

Campbell, George (1719–1796), *2902*

Campbell, Jane Montgomery (1817–1879), *4596, 4625*

Campbell, Joseph (1881–1944), *8125*

Campbell, Thomas (1733–1795), *4946, 9709*

Campion, Thomas (1567–1620), *3948*

Campolo, Tony *4751, 5014, 6467*

Camus, Albert (1913–1960), *3552, 6312, 6866, 11264*

Camus, Jean Pierre (1584–1652), *372, 6334, 10701*

Canetti, Elias (1905–), *3278*

Canton, William *1120*

Cantor, Eddie (1892–1964), *1661, 7257, 10790*

Capon, Robert F. *4782*

Cardozo, Benjamin Nathan (1870–1938), *9685, 10697*

Carey, William (1761–1834), *10118*

Carlyle, Thomas (1795–1881), *851, 981, 1038, 1099, 1851, 1870, 2198, 2627, 3090, 3140, 3268, 3272, 3450, 3486, 3952, 4429, 4436, 5272, 5509, 5765,*

6405, 6764, 7013, 7381, 7409, 7440, 8052, 8194, 8683, 9671, 10178, 10263, 10265, 10649, 10754, 10835, 12049, 12138

Carman, Bliss (1861–1929), *8035*

Carmichael, Alexander *5375*

Carmichael, Amy (1867–1951), *4507, 4785, 5939, 7187, 7188, 7350, 7727, 8795, 9045, 10604*

Carnegie, Andrew (1835–1919), *2788*

Carnegie, Dale (1888–1955), *441, 2019, 2055, 4306, 9518, 10483*

Carnell, Edward John (1919–1967), *11044*

Carney, Julia A. Fletcher (1823–1908), *2503, 6659*

Carr, Emily (1871–1945), *7151*

Carr, Eugene Asa (1830–1910), *3993*

Carr, Jesse (1901–), *8703*

Carrel, Alexis (1873–1944), *7963, 8764, 8954, 9410*

Carretto, Carlo (1910–), *7554, 10067, 10565, 11607*

Carroll, Lewis (1833–1898), *8157*

Carroll, Paul Vincent (1900–1968), *3418*

Carruth, W. H. (1859–1924), *1988*

Carter, Jimmy (1924–), *876, 2837*

Carter, Sydney *9690*

Cartwright, Peter (1611–1643), *7264*

Carver, George Washington (c. 1864–1943), *8013*

Cary, Alice (1820–1871), *7150, 7315*

Cary, Joyce (1888–1957), *2307, 3983, 7428*

Cary, Phoebe (1824–1871), *7061*

Casals, Pablo (1876–1973), *1701, 3039, 3077*

Cash, Johnny (1932–), *11126*

Caspi, Joseph Ben Abba Mari (1280–1340), *9417*

Cassels, Louis (1922–1974), *642, 693, 1287, 1535, 1602, 4779, 5226, 5791, 6500, 7304, 8103, 8108, 8756, 8876, 9428, 9691, 9693, 9832*

Cassidy, Sheila (1937–), *10931*

Cather, Willa Sibert (1873–1947), *4261, 5984*

Catherwood, Mary H. (1847–1901), *7006*

Cato the Elder (234–149 B.C.), *369, 5164, 6905, 10476*

Catullus, Gaius Valerius (c. 84–c. 54 B.C.), *12057*

Caussade, Jean Pierre de (1675–1751), *3794, 4790, 9566*

Caussin, Nicholas (1583–1651), *1080, 9616*

Cavell, Edith (1865–1915), *2452*

Cecil, Richard (1748–1810), *1500, 5144, 8804, 9135, 9166, 9679*

Cecil, Robert (1563–1612), *3703, 3818*

Céline, Louis Ferdinand (1894–1961), *3520*

Centlivre, Susannah (c. 1667–1723), *12189*

Cerminara, Gina *7641*

Cervantes, Miguel de (1547–1616), *2781, 2848, 3264, 4807, 7894, 9138, 9376, 9610, 11342, 11683*

Chadwick, John White (1840–1904), *2319*

Chadwick, Samuel (1832–1917), *3182, 5806, 8805, 8985*

Chafer, Lewis Sperry (1871–1952), *5632*

Chagall, Marc (1887–1985), *2022*

Chalfant, Morris *2069*

Chalmers, Allan K. *2044*

Chalmers, Thomas (1780–1847), *8908*

Chamberlain, Will *452*

Chambers, Whittaker *11779*

Chamfort, Sébastien Roch Nicolas (1741–1794), *2561, 5303, 7002, 7399, 10523*

Chanel, Gabrielle Coco (1883–1971), *6192*

Channing, William Ellery (1780–1842), *736, 2624, 2715, 3252, 3350, 4291, 5297, 6170, 6172, 6201, 8490, 9092, 9962, 10654*

Chapin, Edwin Hubbel (1814–1880), *105, 1166, 2790, 3150, 4095, 5063, 5508, 5723, 8071, 10882*

Chaplin, Ralph (1887–1961), *426*

Chapman, George (c. 1559–1634), *3213, 3554*

Chapman, J. Wilbur (1859–1918), *5077, 7036*

5657, 5684, 5966, 6126, 6489, 6909, 7320, 7384, 7712, 8487, 8749, 9600, 9668, 10511, 10659, 10661

Dooley, Thomas *10125*

Dorr, Julia C. R. (1825–1913), *2292, 10481*

Dostoyevski, Fyodor Mikhaylovich (1821–1881), *583, 1027, 1718, 2691, 3989, 5501, 5707, 7101, 7945, 8769, 8918, 10331, 12117*

Doudney, Sarah (1843–1926), *2365*

Douglas, Helen Gahagan *7664*

Douglas, Norman (1868–1952), *4161, 7687, 9400*

Douglass, Fredrick Augustus Washington Bailey (1817–1895), *9312*

Dow, Lorenzo (1777–1834), *9576*

Dowty, A. A. (1873–), *9607*

Draper, Kenneth L. (1957–), *1136*

Draxe, Thomas (d. 1618), *2149*

Dreier, Thomas (1884–), *580, 598*

Droz, Gustave *42*

Drummond, Henry (1851–1897), *1163, 1332, 3887, 4893, 5849, 5852, 6240, 6376, 6379, 6665, 7348*

Drummond, John (1851–1897), *2816, 2930, 3315, 4233, 4948, 6494, 9286, 9415, 10676*

Drummond, William Hawthorden (1585–1649), *9375*

Drummond, William Henry (1854–1907), *6140, 9503*

Dryden, John (1631–1700), *1612, 2330, 3255, 3777, 4240, 6343, 6598, 7418, 7765, 7925, 10886, 10925, 11049, 11715, 12073*

Du Bos, Charles (1882–1939), *3054*

Duche, Rev. J. *9102*

Duffus, R. L. *90*

Dumas, Alexandre (1802–1870), *10516, 11597, 11621*

Dunbar, Paul Laurence ((1872–1906), *2418, 6204*

Duncan, J. (b. 1870), *6366*

Dunne, Irene (1904–), *4632*

Dunsany, Lord (1906–), *5970*

Durant, Will (1885–1981), *1865, 2083, 3000, 3024, 8588*

Duranty, Walter *7763*

Durrell, Lawrence (1912–), *5713*

Dwight, Timothy (1752–1817), *711, 1395*

Dyer, John (1699–1757), *9792*

Dylan, Bob (1941–), *10650*

E

East, John *4990*

Eastman, George (1854–1932), *10942*

Eastwood, John H. *11080*

Eberhart, Richard (1904–), *10939*

Ebner-Eschenbach, Marie (1830–1916), *310, 12191*

Eckhart, Meister (c. 1260–c.1327), *5, 148, 1542, 2612, 3986, 3995, 4408, 4452, 4486, 4488, 4499, 4533, 4562, 4564, 4621, 4801, 4923, 5356, 5967, 6137, 7477, 7543, 7773, 8791, 8839, 9982, 10060, 10084, 10258, 10360, 10601, 10617, 10664, 10671, 10699, 10885, 11316*

Edersheim, Alfred (1825–1889), *164, 769*

Edison, Thomas Alva (1847–1931), *2870, 2871, 4391, 6709*

Edman, Irwin (1896–1954), *11540*

Edman, Victor Raymond (1900–1967), *2818, 2885, 3705, 3762, 5803, 8962*

Edmeston, James (1791–1867), *5428*

Edwards, Jonathan (1703–1758), *109, 569, 4523, 4898, 5218, 6024*

Edwards, Robert C. *1068*

Edwards, Tryon (1809–1894), *1579, 2355, 2400, 2678, 3076, 5690, 5736, 7064, 7942, 8195, 9554, 9598, 9672, 9869, 11193*

Ehrlich, Paul (1854–1915), *6085*

Eifert, Lorenz *6473*

Einstein, Albert (1879–1955), *2005, 2775, 3362, 3376, 4930, 5282, 6333, 7130, 7365, 8452, 9527, 9867, 10785*

Eiphilus (320 B.C.), *8695*

Eisenhower, Dwight D. (1890–1969), *1582, 6799, 11745*

Elbert Green Hubbard (1856–1915), *8598, 10423*

Eldrige, Paul *1053*

Elijah de Vidas (Sixteenth Century), *9734, 10257*

Eliot, George (1819–1880), *107, 1814, 1837, 2420, 3231, 3506, 4105, 4441, 4874, 5132, 5597, 6284, 6595, 6599, 7149, 7748, 8496, 10386, 10502, 11637*

Eliot, T. S. (1888–1965), *313, 599, 2620, 4979, 8617, 9220*

Elliot, Elizabeth *11525*

Elliot, Jim (1927–1956), *1195, 1349, 1533, 3186*

Elliott, Charlotte (1789–1871), *716*

Ellis, George (1753–1815), *9876*

Ellis, Havelock (1859–1939), *3202, 4389, 5669, 6388, 7068, 9317, 9329, 11259*

Ellul, Jacques *8847, 8852*

Emans, Elaine *3836*

Emerson, Ralph Waldo (1803–1882), *301, 456, 535, 997, 1004, 1011, 1058, 1061, 1394, 1641, 1733, 1947, 1969, 1976, 1997, 2176, 2190, 2291, 2552, 2776, 2782, 3178, 3546, 3557, 3561, 3601, 3654, 3798, 3962, 3964, 3997, 4165, 4205, 4206, 4243, 4275, 4525, 5004, 5305, 5516, 5727, 5899, 6194, 6195, 6219, 6226, 6807, 6879, 7373, 7752, 8038, 8220, 8375, 8528, 8574, 8646, 8664, 8774, 9128, 9134, 9143, 9165, 9343, 9379, 9814, 9873, 10172, 10280, 10338, 10543, 10573, 10620, 10668, 10693, 10755, 10792, 10907, 10929, 11174, 11275, 11366, 11465, 11610, 11684, 11910, 11995*

Emmons, Nathanael (1745–1840), *5739*

Empedocles (c. 494–c. 430 B.C.), *4851*

English, Wilda *1364*

Engstrom, Ted W. (1916–), *161*

Epictetus (c. 55–c.135), *308, 507, 1780, 1793, 1800, 2735, 3979, 4139, 7545, 8745, 11661*

Epicurus (341–270 B.C.), *209, 2751, 7059, 9815*

Epp, Theodore Herman (1907–1985), *10849*

Erasmus, Desiderius (c. 1466–1536), *823, 1625, 3417, 6360, 8182*

Erskine, John (1509–1591), *317, 8198, 8337*

Erskine, Thomas (1750–1823), *9938*

Ertz, Susan *6100*

Esar, Evan *7095*

Etten, Henry Van *6985*

Etty, William (1787–1849), *2459*

Euripides (c. 484–406 B.C.), *2843, 4186, 4267, 5073, 6310, 6581, 7086, 8150, 9373, 11385*

Evans, Arthur Benoni (1781–1854), *3687*

Evans, Edith (1888–1976), *9931*

Evans, Richard L. *8635*

Evely, Louis (1910–), *603, 1173, 1312, 1978, 2092, 2116, 4900, 5395, 7329, 7512, 8864, 8916, 9695, 9937, 10439, 11423, 12128*

Everett, David *8657*

Everett, Edward (1794–1865), *1450*

Ezra, Moses Ben Jacob Ibn (c. 1135), *5602, 7147, 11897*

Ezra, Shirat Yisrael Moses Ibn (1055–1135), *11267*

F

Faber, Frederick William (1814–1863), *973, 1763, 2732, 2801, 3232, 3270, 4605, 4659, 4720, 4794, 4795, 4799, 4968, 4981, 5460, 5788, 6040, 6378, 6460, 6645, 6648, 6669, 7745, 8426, 10273, 10603, 11429, 12113*

Fadiman, Clifton (1904–), *1105*

Failing, George *8810*

Fairbairn, Andrew Martin (1838–1912), *1956, 7995*

Fairbanks, Charles B. *5160*

Farrar, Frederic William (1831–1903), *6997*

Farrell, Joseph *3497, 6689*

Farrell, Walter (1902–1951), *7144*

Faulkner, William Cuthbert (1897–1962), *455*

Feather, William (1889–), *5512, 5585, 6309, 9159, 11348*

Fechner, Gustav Theodore (1801–1887), *8967*

Feeney, Leonard (1898–1978), *7936*

Felix, Marcus M. *4665*

Felltham, Owen (c. 1602–1668), *2584, 3826, 4262*

Fénelon, François (1651–1715), *1964, 2110, 2331, 2395, 3634, 4134, 4322, 4639, 5452, 8453, 8521, 8800, 8813, 8830, 8968, 8970, 9042, 9144, 9497, 9835, 9919, 10014, 10329, 11395*

Ferber, Edna (1887–1968), *1386*

Feuerbach, Ludwig Andreas (1804–1872), *2688, 5060*

Fey, Imogene *815*

Ficke, Arthur Davison *9979*

Field, Franklin *11734*

Field, Henry Martyn (1822–1907), *920, 6921*

Fielding, Henry (1707–1754), *145, 5032, 7801, 9418*

Fields, W. C. (1880–1946), *6936*

Finney, Charles G. (1792–1875), *5202, 5797, 8961, 9118, 10097*

Firbank, Ronald (1886–1926), *3203*

Fischer, Martin H. (1879–1962), *11927*

Fisher, J. T. *531*

Fitzgerald, F. Scott (1896–1940), *2594*

Fitzhenry, R. I. *2424*

Flack, Roberta *7615*

Flavel, John (1627–1691), *742, 6039, 8218, 10033, 10655*

Flavel, John (c. 1627–1691), *5722*

Fleming, Peter (1907–1971), *8260*

Fletcher, Giles (1584–1623), *6391*

Fletcher, John (1579–1625), *2656, 2669, 10066, 10105*

Fletcher, Joseph *1242, 4494, 5233, 6612, 6812, 6816, 6820, 6827, 7166, 7244, 7274, 7307, 7312*

Flint, Annie Johnson (1862–1932), *5223, 5407, 7570, 10122*

Follette, Robert Marion La (1855–1925), *11772*

Fontaine, Charles (1515–1590), *9548*

Foote, Samuel (1720–1777), *1766*

Forbes, B. C. *1022, 2730, 5612, 9526, 12028*

Ford, Gerald R. (1913–), *5168*

Ford, Henry (1863–1947), *3110*

Ford, Leighton *3305, 5768, 11764*

Foreman, A.D. Jr., *6466*

Forster, E. M. (1879–1970), *9359*

Forsyth, P. T. (1848–1921), *117, 4144, 7396, 8942, 9292, 10167, 10220, 11109*

Fortunatus of Poitiers, Saint Venatius Honorius Clementianus (c.530–c.610), *2986*

Fosdick, Harry Emerson (1878–1969), *961, 1146, 1490, 1958, 2188, 2522, 2852, 3292, 3747, 3965, 4543, 5596, 6325, 6965, 7455, 7622, 8798, 8936, 9971, 10195, 11763*

Foster, George Burman (1858–1918), *4136*

Foster, John (1836–1917), *9246*

Foster, Richard J. (1942–), *121, 350, 1755, 1760, 1882, 2556, 2608, 3235, 6008, 6622, 6828, 8719, 8890, 8904, 9005, 9963, 10259, 10440, 10539, 10548, 12105*

Fowler, Gene (1890–1960), *10069*

Fowler, Lona M. *6428*

Fowles, John (1926–), *100, 8602, 10051*

Fox, George (1624–1691), *425, 6504*

France, Anatole (1844–1924), *853, 3282, 4324, 5678, 5973, 6081, 7025, 9181*

Frances, Juana *5975*

Francis, Brendan *3982, 10993*

Francis of Assisi, Saint (c. 1181–1226), *2219, 2321, 4090, 4455, 4971, 6520, 8403, 9086, 10876*

Francis of Sales, Saint (1567–1622), *415, 1815, 2333, 4000, 4845, 5068, 5427, 5907, 6041, 6087, 7121, 7352, 7710, 8392, 8414, 8790, 9082, 9162, 9857, 10027, 10462, 10705, 10710, 10752, 11056, 12040*

Frank, Anne (1929–1945), *8445*

Frankfurter, Felix (1882–1965), *5245*

Frankl, Viktor E. (1905–), *519, 3484, 10871*

Franklin, Benjamin (1706–1790), *69, 323, 333, 444, 550, 789, 1196, 1574, 1617, 1917, 2204, 2244, 2265, 2569, 2891, 3010, 3164, 3447, 3500, 3519, 3930, 4933, 4942, 5072, 5178, 5312, 5588, 5634, 5814, 5956, 5990, 6768, 6864, 6886, 7065, 7175, 7668, 7792, 7814, 8307, 8398, 8547, 8736, 9247, 9335, 9449, 9500, 9615, 9772, 9918, 10916, 11194, 11305, 11318, 11376, 11384, 11407, 11436, 11461, 11824, 11918, 12023*

Franklin, William Buel (1823–1903), *3921*

Frayn, Michael (1933–), *11291*

Freeman, Robert (1878–1940), *926, 1002, 2364*

Freud, Sigmund (1856–1939), *2946, 2968, 5868*

Friederich, Johann Paul (1763–1825), *8301*

Friswell *8690*

Frohman, Charles (1860–1915), *2458*

Fromm, Erich (1900–1980), *2970, 3079, 3824, 4370, 5024, 6199, 7143, 7194, 7853, 7858, 8718, 9485, 10575, 10726, 10743, 11307, 11619, 11693*

Frost, David (1939–), *11035*

Frost, Gerhard E. *2201, 3144, 3180, 11137, 11319*

Frost, Paul (1938–), *7596, 7683*

Frost, Robert (1874–1963), *2589, 3403, 5831, 9056*

Froude, James Anthony (1818–1894), *1017, 1071, 6481, 10574, 10630*

Fry, Christopher (1907–), *8618*

Fugal, Lavina Christensen *8309*

Fulghum, Robert *2023, 2208, 8577, 10002, 11841*

Fuller, Andrew (1754–1815), *1328*

Fuller, David Otis *1292*

Fuller, Margaret (1810–1850), *5813*

Fuller, R. Buckminster (1895–1983), *3029*

Fuller, Sir Thomas (1608–1661), *337, 662, 907, 1462, 1751, 1923, 1934, 1949, 2202, 2258, 2262, 2896, 3095, 3214, 3466, 3547, 3583, 3914, 3954, 4219, 4252, 4811, 5277, 5595, 5641, 5663, 5875, 6800, 7075, 8446, 9071, 9177, 9377, 9474, 9609, 9637, 9729, 10093, 10107, 10309, 10461, 10590, 11050, 11116, 11409, 11412, 11418, 11818, 11828, 11836, 11846, 11884, 12123*

Fuller, Thomas (1654–1734), *322, 486*

Furlong, Monica *24*

Furtado, Maria A. *10733*

G

Grenfell, Joyce (1910–1979), *2412*
Grenfell, Sir Wilfred Thomason (1865–1940), *747, 9025*
Greve, Fred *10834*
Grey, Lady Jane (1537–1554), *733*
Griffiths, Michael *3785*
Grimké, Angelina (1805–1879), *3230, 5197, 8824*
Grimshaw, William (1708–1763), *7717*
Griswold, Whitney *9995*
Grogan, Geoffrey *8114*
Grooms, Jordon *7781*
Groote, Gerard (1340–1384), *8523*
Gropius, Walter (1883–1969), *7770*
Grou, Jean Nicolas (1731–1803), *169, 2746, 5397,*
    8788, 9683, 9851, 10006
Grubb, Norman *4537, 9061*
Gruenberg, Simon *4595*
Guardini, Romano (1885–1968), *1975*
Guérin, Eugénie de (1805–1848), *9608*
Guest, Edgar Albert (1881–1959), *2792, 3435, 4217,*
    10098
Guinon, Albert *10552*
Guiteau, Charles J. (1841–1882), *2439*
Guiterman, Arthur (1871–1943), *11284*
Gurnall, William (1617–1679), *10409*
Gurney, Dorothy Frances (1858–1932), *8032*
Gustafson, Roy *9545*
Guthrie, Thomas (1803–1873), *280, 6030, 6925*
Guthrie, William (1620–1665), *4809*
Guyon, Madame Jeanne Marie de La Mothe
    (1648–1717), *1461, 2090, 2094, 2545, 2744, 4697,*
    4796, 4836, 4869, 5771, 7707, 8098, 8608, 8630,
    10254, 10272, 10864, 10974

$\mathcal{H}$

Hacohen, Johanan *4727*
Haddon, Walter (1516–1572), *7908*
Hageman, Samuel Miller *10256*
Hagen, Walter C. (1892–1969), *9530*
Haggai, Tom *3113*
Haldane, J. B. S. (1892–1964), *9407*
Haldeman, I. M. (1845–1933), *6404*
Hale, Edward Everett (1822–1909), *106, 1926, 2500,*
    8379, 10151, 11443
Haliburton, Thomas Chandler (1796–1865), *1089,*
    2238, 8342, 8614, 12080
Halifax, Marquis of (1633–1695), *1598, 3858, 7358*
Hall, Douglas John *4823*
Hall, John (1829–), *2771*
Hall, Joseph (1574–1656), *2663, 3996, 6901, 9612*
Hall, Robert (1764–1831), *8953*
Hall, Thomas (1610–1665), *2703*
Hallam, Arthur Henry (1811–1833), *8269*
Halleck, Fitz-Greene (1790–1867), *7972*
Halleck, Henry Wager (1815–1872), *11760*
Hallesby, Ole *8901*
Halsey, William Frederick, Jr. (1882–1959), *8668*
Halsted, Anna Roosevelt (1906–1975), *10303*
Halverson, Richard C. (1916–), *1480, 2713, 5388,*
    6427
Hamerton, Philip G. (1834–1894), *9388*
Hamilton, Alexander (1757–1804), *7416*
Hamilton, Charles Hamilton Aïdé (1826–1906), *8827*
Hamilton, Edith (1867–1963), *11217*
Hamilton, Eleanor *1570*
Hamilton, J. Wallace *1632*
Hamilton, James (1814–1867), *5065, 5848*
Hamilton, Robert Browning (1812–1889), *10596*

Hammarskjöld, Dag (1905–1961), *1026, 1365, 1912,*
    3549, 4021, 4024, 4538, 5066, 6931, 7011, 7125,
    7140, 7458, 7688, 7695, 7705, 8897, 9055, 9058,
    9481, 10811, 11143, 11326
Hammerstein, Oscar (1895–1960), *4421*
Hammill, Carrie Esther *4608*
Handel, George Frideric (1685–1759), *7896*
Hankey, Donald (1874–1917), *8436*
Hansel, Tim *10, 141, 499, 755, 1225, 1469, 1610, 1936,*
    2716, 2738, 3769, 5221, 5534, 5562, 5610, 6528,
    6530, 6539, 6556, 6727, 6729, 6918, 8264, 8265,
    10720, 11199, 11521
Hardy, Thomas (1840–1928), *10507, 11739*
Hare, August W. (1792–1834), *3857, 10284, 10477*
Hare, Augustus John Cuthbert (1834–1903), *5298,*
    11945
Hare, Augustus W. (1792–1834), *1144*
Harkness, Georgia (1891–1979), *7164, 9010*
Harper, John *5807*
Harries, Bishop Richard *10399*
Harris, E. T. *684*
Harris, Joel Chandler (1848–1908), *2482*
Harris, Sydney J. (1917–1986), *571, 579, 1048, 1128,*
    2178, 2510, 3019, 3026, 3030, 3031, 3089, 3168,
    3581, 3932, 4177, 4283, 5041, 5194, 5571, 5618,
    5873, 6175, 6323, 7232, 7233, 7415, 7626, 7632,
    7633, 7660, 7838, 7854, 8250, 8312, 8450, 8553,
    9353, 9355, 9486, 9730, 9941, 10227, 10718,
    10749, 11216, 11695, 11717, 12022, 12179
Harrison, Elisabeth *3142*
Harrison, Paul W. *4736*
Harrison, Thomas *7674*
Hart, Joseph *4787*
Hartman von Aue (c. 1170–c.1215), *10146*
Hartmann, Eduard von (1842–1906), *7957*
Hartog, Eva Den *10739*
Harvey, Paul (1918–), *9287*
Harvey, William (1578–1657), *6677*
Hasidic song, *4518*
Haskins, Henry H. *2863, 3028, 11543*
Haskins, Minnie Louise (1875–1957), *5417*
Hatch, Edwin (1835–1889), *5774*
Haukey, Donald (1874–1917), *4151*
Havergal, Frances Ridley (1836–1879), *3106, 8077,*
    8866, 10112, 10120
Havner, Vance *525, 1360, 1410, 2102, 4717, 5440,*
    5676, 6429, 9532, 9606, 10185, 10902
Hawthorne, Nathaniel (1804–1864), *1224, 1686, 2207,*
    2875, 3565, 3648, 5518, 9955, 12004
Hay, Will (1888–1949), *2284*
Hayakawa, S. I. *3611*
Haydn, Franz Joseph (1732–1809), *7931*
Hayne, Paul Hamilton (1830–1886), *6878*
Hays, Will *4953*
Hayward, Percy R. *2964*
Hazlitt, William (1778–1830), *242, 1827, 1871, 3410,*
    6066, 7413, 8716, 9184, 10035, 10283, 11224,
    11677, 12171, 12175
Head, David *5661*
Hebbel, Friedrich (1813–1863), *2807*
Heber, Reginald (1783–1826), *3266, 9895*
Hecht, Ben (1894–1964), *2397, 11334*
Hedges, Sid G. *9085, 9093, 9094, 9106*
Heidegger, Martin (1889–1976), *11235*
Heimsath, Charles H. (1894–), *1424*
Hein, Piet *11949*
Heine, Heinrich (1797–1856), *750, 1137, 2651, 3521,*
    3730, 4082, 4634, 7932, 11603
Heinlein, Robert *11628*

M

N

Nouwen, Henri J. M. *1513, 1546, 2223, 3080, 5590, 7954, 8413, 10003, 10162, 10211, 10253, 10514, 10531, 10540, 10545, 10551, 10558, 10561, 10562, 10901, 11991*
Novales (1772–1801), *1261*
Novatian, Antipope (d. 258), *4700*
Noyes, Alfred (1880–1958), *11647*
Nye, Edgar Wilson (1850–1896), *11681*
Nye, Harold *4366*
Nygard, Leigh *4565*

O

O'Connell, Daniel (1775–1847), *9180*
O'Connor, Flannery (1925–1964), *1438*
O'Malley, Austin (1858–1932), *9370, 10108, 10621*
O'Neill, Eugene Gladstone (1888–1953), *4654*
Obadiah, Mordecai (1810–1882), *746*
Ode, Chaldee *4748*
Odell, Jack *9809*
Ogilvie, Lloyd John (1930–   ), *944, 6987, 6999*
Oliver, Vic *7800*
Omar Khayyám (c. 1048–1122), *7031*
Orben, Robert *1571, 8565*
Orchard, William E. (1877–1955), *1405*
Orczy, Baroness Emmuska (1865–1947), *2667*
Origen (c. 185–c. 254), *5047*
Orione, Don (1872–1940), *2774*
Orr, James (1844–1913), *11226*
Ortlund, Raymond C. *12137*
Orwell, George (1903–1950), *591, 5540, 8710*
Osborn, Ronald E. *68, 2758*
Osler, Sir William (1849–1919), *6734, 8383, 10207*
Ostman, Virginia *1732*
Otto, Jean *2798*
Ouida (1839–1908), *4237*
Oursler, Fulton (1949–   ), *6128*
Ovid (43 B.C.–A.D. 17), *1086, 5330, 6839, 7476, 7534, 7920, 9686, 10319, 11354*
Owen, Franklin *4241*
Owen, George *5106*
Owen, John (1616–1683), *1496, 2858, 8812*
Oxenham, John (1861–1941), *911, 1155, 3847, 5413, 5434, 5448, 6109, 7218, 9072, 10163, 10489, 10679, 10964, 10969, 11852, 12016*

P

Packer, J. I. (1926–   ), *655, 687, 2887, 5550, 6125, 8256, 10239*
Page, Kirby (1890–1957), *4133, 4721, 6564*
Paget, Catesby (d. 1742), *4859*
Paine, Thomas (1737–1809), *40, 1036, 1628, 2447, 4581, 9621*
Paley, William (1743–1805), *7154*
Palladas (c. 400), *5952*
Palmer, Arnold (1929–   ), *8567*
Palmerston, Lord (1784–1865), *5121, 8199*
Paman, Clement (c. 1660), *6149*
Panin, Nikita Ivanovich (1718–1783), *1977, 4572, 7549*
Panton, D. M. *9749*
Papini, Giovanni (1923–   ), *6362*
Paquda, Bahya Ibn (1050–1120), *7726*
Paré, Ambroise (1517–1590), *5611*
Pare, Philip *9946*
Parker, Dorothy (1893–1967), *8003, 10943*

Parker, Joseph (1830–1902), *706, 4885, 5005, 11629*
Parker, Theodore (1810–1860), *1959, 2526, 2794, 9116, 9572, 9681, 10130, 12109*
Parkhurst, Charles Henry (1842–1933), *2039, 8503, 11355, 11892*
Parnell, Thomas (1679–1718), *2267*
Parr, Elnathan *3047*
Pascal, Blaise (1623–1662), *173, 270, 492, 572, 597, 951, 1298, 1329, 2504, 3201, 3285, 3559, 3724, 3814, 4553, 4677, 4722, 4762, 4771, 4905, 4908, 5101, 5191, 5301, 5384, 5502, 5520, 5560, 5766, 5996, 6238, 6461, 6580, 6707, 6771, 7084, 7117, 7180, 7406, 7439, 7479, 7508, 8022, 8576, 9101, 9133, 9367, 9421, 9614, 10013, 10076, 10127, 10404, 10660, 11231, 11268, 11577, 11698, 11744, 11985*
Pasteur, Louis (1822–1895), *8040*
Paterson, Sir Alec *9096*
Patman, Keith *1368, 2123*
Patmore, Coventry Kersey Dighton (1823–1896), *9775, 9783*
Paton, Alan Stewart (1903–   ), *3199, 3992*
Patrick, Saint (c. 389–c.461), *5400*
Patrick, Simon (1625–1707), *12066*
Patrick, William Penn *11868*
Paul VI, Pope (1897–1978), *8469, 9431*
Paul, Saint Vincent de (1581–1660), *8391, 8698*
Pavese, Cesare (1908–1950), *3480, 11272*
Pavlova, Anna (1882–1931), *10822*
Pavlovich, Anton Chekov (1860–1904), *11544*
Payson, Edward (1783–1827), *5230*
Peale, Norman Vincent (1898–   ), *1635, 3177, 3185, 3991, 5927, 6102, 6203, 7219, 8741, 8923, 9983, 10096, 10780*
Pearson, Carlton *2653*
Pearson, Roy M. (1914–   ), *5993*
Peattie, Donald Culross *5731*
Peck, M. Scott (1936–   ), *202, 2736, 3367, 3396, 5037, 7012, 7231, 8300, 9967*
Pedretti, Claire *5368*
Péguy, Charles (1873–1914), *2553*
Pelagius (c. 354–after 418), *230*
Penington, Isaac (1616–1679), *4629*
Penn, William (1644–1718), *199, 1037, 2796, 2853, 3291, 4137, 4774, 5010, 5994, 6348, 6899, 7319, 7483, 7651, 8096, 8408, 9095, 9374, 10459, 11059, 11397, 11614*
Pepys, Samuel (1633–1703), *8924*
Pericles (c. 495–429 B.C.), *11347*
Persius (34–62), *995, 11853*
Pestalozzi, Johann Heinrich (1746–1827), *5844, 8327*
Pestel, T. (1584–1659), *6129*
Peter, Laurence J. (1919–   ), *2999, 4213, 8585*
Peterson, Eugene *6824, 8738*
Petit-Senn, John *8613, 8636, 9213*
Petrarch (1304–1374), *3288, 7323, 8435, 11726*
Petronius, Gaius (d. c. 66), *8494*
Pettingill, William Leroy (1866–1950), *7502*
Phaedrus (c. 15 B.C.–A.D. 50), *5577*
Phelps, C. C. *11419*
Phelps, William Lyon (1865–1943), *753, 3898, 5567, 7026, 11002*
Phifer, Marjorie Maddox *6131*
Philemon (c. 363–c. 264 B.C.), *11014*
Philip II (382–336 B.C.), *2344*
Phillips, J. B. (1906–1982), *123, 159, 513, 532, 1133, 1168, 1188, 1232, 1234, 1430, 2234, 2431, 2737, 3290, 4458, 4468, 4479, 4683, 4701, 4739, 4788, 4803, 4864, 5046, 5645, 5777, 6110, 6127, 6144,*

S

Thomas, Bonnie Barrows *1512*

Thomas, Dylan Marlais (1914–1953), *8619, 9948*

Thomas, George *3233*

Thompson, Francis (1859–1907), *319, 473, 810, 2676, 6456*

Thompson, Joseph Parrish (1819–1879), *1177, 4414*

Thomson, Edward (1810–1870), *2725*

Thomson, James (1700–1748), *4711, 4960, 9883, 9897, 10962*

Thoreau, Henry David (1817–1862), *95, 116, 468, 540, 1476, 1761, 2610, 2966, 3405, 3795, 4255, 4329, 4424, 4526, 4575, 5185, 5887, 6048, 6784, 6902, 6903, 7001, 7203, 7214, 7813, 7921, 8012, 8042, 8629, 9877, 10007, 10266, 10281, 10537, 10549, 10572, 10657, 10665, 10827, 11290, 11526, 11655, 11686, 11700, 11922, 11967*

Thorndike, Edward L. (1874–1949), *11908*

Thornton, L. S. *4657*

Thorold, A. W. *11480*

Thucydides (460–c. 401 B.C.), *11768*

Thurber, James Grover (1894–1961), *268, 6688*

Tibullus, Albius (c. 55–c. 19 B.C.), *10488*

Tillich, Paul Johannes Oskar (1886–1965), *423, 2937, 3651, 3707, 4846, 6277, 6536, 7072, 7131, 7133, 7301, 7466, 9446, 9817, 9985, 10023, 10542, 10546, 10564, 10579*

Tillinghast *11320*

Tilton, Theodore (1835–1907), *974*

Tippett, Donald *10135*

Tittle, Ernest Fremont (1885–1949), *1192*

Toast, Old English *5009*

Tobey, Charles W. *7989*

Tocqueville, Alexis (1805–1859), *3244, 4928*

Toffler, Alvin (1928–   ), *10524*

Tolkien, J. R. R. (1892–1973), *8239*

Tolstoy, Leo (1828–1910), *625, 964, 984, 4124, 4517, 4542, 6927, 7472, 8705, 8722, 9925, 10858*

Tomlin, Lily (1939–   ), *6832, 9035*

Toplady, Augustus Montague (1740–1778), *2101, 2221, 4636*

Torrey, R. A. (1856–1928), *4789, 9017*

Torriano (c. 1666), *10149*

Tournier, Paul (1898–1986), *255, 256, 660, 694, 1165, 1241, 1567, 1647, 2054, 2959, 2988, 3321, 3365, 3582, 3693, 3702, 3726, 3904, 3980, 3990, 4160, 4277, 4615, 5385, 5392, 5423, 5441, 5474, 5477, 5981, 6086, 6813, 6851, 6896, 7327, 7366, 7383, 7398, 7405, 7630, 7699, 7713, 8110, 8569, 8779, 8883, 8887, 8906, 9351, 10784, 10912, 11296, 11613, 12031*

Tourville, Abbe Henri de (1842–1903), *4747, 4853*

Towne, C. H. *9887*

Towne, Charles Hansom *8014*

Townsend, Marchioness *10985*

Traherne, Thomas (c. 1637–1674), *1249, 6253, 11219*

Trapp, John *1826, 2841, 9537*

Traubel, Horace *4250*

Trench, Archbishop Richard Chenevix (1807–1886), *8867, 8933, 10377, 11168*

Trevelyan, George Macaulay (1876–1962), *1411, 2997*

Trollope, Anthony (1815–1882), *1939*

Trotter, I. Lilias *5748*

Trueblood, D. Elton (1900–   ), *4768, 7035, 8767, 9254*

Truman, Harry S (1884–1972), *902*

Tupper, Martin Farquhar (1810–1889), *1889, 3251, 8270*

Turgenev, Ivan Sergeyevich (1818–1883), *7268*

Turnbull, Bob (1775–1833), *10321*

Turner, Ted (1938–   ), *11027*

Tusser, Thomas (c. 1524–1580), *4043*

Twain, Mark (1835–1910), *675, 761, 802, 817, 860, 959, 1494, 1573, 1662, 1697, 1920, 1950, 1951, 1994, 2429, 2559, 2916, 3429, 3433, 3551, 3928, 4080, 4593, 5495, 5628, 5985, 5986, 6989, 7376, 7390, 7411, 7427, 8188, 8851, 9223, 9652, 10228, 10332, 10652, 11073, 11434, 11680, 11983, 11992*

Tyger, Frank *50, 7276*

Tyndale, William (c. 1494–1536), *3123, 5091*

Tyrrell, George (1861–1909), *4686*

$\mathcal{U}$

Ullanthorne, William Bernard (1806–1889), *1095, 5229, 6076*

Unamuno, Miguel de (1864–1936), *3776, 3793, 4802, 7484*

Underhill, Evelyn (1875–1941), *1228, 3491, 3844, 5219, 6113, 6566, 7263, 7956, 7969, 9923, 12122*

Unknowing, The Cloud of (1370), *2557, 4679, 7395*

Urquhart, Colin (1940–   ), *46, 524, 9321*

Ustinov, Peter (1921–   ), *3017, 8350*

$\mathcal{V}$

Valery, Paul (1871–1945), *1676, 1728, 5949, 11236, 11242*

Vanbrugh, Sir John (1664–1726), *11263*

Van der Rohe, Mes *4484*

Van Dyke, Henry (1852–1933), *559, 645, 1062, 1258, 1271, 1358, 1933, 2426, 4192, 5148, 5851, 6298, 7243, 8472, 9656, 9944, 10074, 10662, 11185, 11234, 11333*

Vanhorn, J. A. *11346*

Van Loon, Hendrick Willem (1882–1944), *3273, 9678*

Vann, Gerald (1906–1963), *3370, 9013, 12135*

Varley, Henry *2835*

Varnhagen, Rachel L. *7841*

Vaughan, Bill *9889*

Vaughan, Henry (1622–1695), *780, 3276, 4506, 7475, 8031, 11138*

Vauvenargues, Luc de Clapiers, Marquis de (1715–1747), *3063, 9506, 10285*

Vega, Lope de (1562–1635), *2403*

Venable, Charles L. *4731*

Venning, Ralph (c. 1621–1674), *10418*

Vermeil, Dick *2629*

Verploegh, Harry (1908–   ), *7893*

Vianney, Saint Jean Baptiste Marie (1786–1859), *2095, 4797, 4817, 5207, 11097*

Vichy-Chamrond, Marie de (1697–1780), *545*

Vigny, Alfred de (1797–1863), *10854*

Vincent, John Heyl (1832–1920), *7514, 10636*

Vinci, Leonardo da (1452–1519), *2224, 6765*

Viorst, Judith Stahl (1931–   ), *11507*

Virgil (70–19 B.C.)*2295, 3575, 3720, 8242, 8344, 11803*

Vivekananda (1863–1902), *10090*

Vogelweide, Walther von der (1170–1230), *9903*

Voltaire (1694–1778), *437, 1643, 4377, 8236, 9091, 11753, 12038*

#

Wagner, Richard (1813–1883), *6541*

Waitley, Denis *2048, 4226, 4296, 5528, 9520, 10179, 11972*

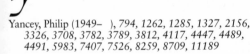

INDEX

A

ABANDON
All hope a, ye who enter here
5683
all to Christ 1536
get life out to sea in reckless a. to
God 9564
God could not possibly a. us 4617
labor, habit easy to a. 3109
others a. faults 3950
To attempt to a. bad habits in
own strength 11108
To be another I must a. that I am
9848
to take Jesus seriously was to a.
habits 6421

ABANDONED
God can do what he likes with
man a. to him 9557
hell, when men see themselves a.
by God 5698
Lord jealous over saint a. to him
8608
the Lord a. to God's blazing wrath
6383

ABANDONMENT
never considerations in real a.
9560
who thinks of serving God, says
prayers of a. 8840

ABANDONS
When man is self-seeking, he a.
love 7246

ABASHED
loftiest eloquence retreats
confused, a. 4750

ABATED
time has not a. forces of church
1419

ABDICATED
creative thinking a. to enemy 3027

self exists to be a. 9927

ABDICATION
by a. becomes more truly self 9927

ABEDNEGO
conduct of A. 5197

ABEL
was murdered 1211

ABHOR
fix thought more on God than on
sin you a. 10305
God doth a. neutralities 4920

ABIDE
a heart of faith that I may a. in
thee 7458
by the truth 11527
O thou who changest not, a. with
me 947
with me—fast falls eventide 2538

ABIDES
That there a. a peace of thine
8430

ABIDING
marketplace one of God's a. places
4866
Rest tranquilly in a. conviction
4747

ABILITIES
are like tax deductions 1
disillusionment with our own a.
10
leave your a. at the cross 10048
managerial a. not test of father's
leadership 3925
Remember your a. 9271
use them or we lose them 1

ABILITY
called to live beyond natural a.
1284
commandments given irrespective
of human a. 1526
declines 11326

depend on God for supernatural a.
1284
Endurance not just a. to bear
3149
Give me a. to see good things
8575
God does not ask about 3
God's a. to heal soul profound
10845
greatness is a. to develop greatness
in others 6804
Happiness a. to cope with conflict
5526
having a, refused to obey 10387
Holiness a. not to sin 5745
It is not my a. 9
Love not dependent on a. 7235
Maturity a. to be comfortable
with people not like us 7694
my response to God's a. 9
never known man of a. to be
ungrateful 5255
Never underestimate a. of humans
to get tangled up 5976
not to panic or lose perspective
3769
Peace is a. to cope with conflict
8458
problem in a. to hear 2931
puts only 25% of a. into work
2788
Self-control a. to keep cool 9961
success a. to help others 10815
Tact a. to describe others as they
see themselves 10989
to be at peace through activities of
the day 6828
to forget true greatness 4068
to keep mouth shut priceless 1876
to pace ourselves 6828
to rest, take time to enjoy beauty
6828
to say "no" greatest gift parent has
8326

to speak several languages asset 1876

what keeps a. to see beauty never grows old 12182

Whence a. to wish evil, refuse good 5051

ABLAZE

Christ, message set society a. 6375

God send us men with hearts a. 7986

Spirit-filled souls a. for God 3182

ABLE

anything Jesus did we should be a. to do 10138

don't seem to be a. to say my prayers 8887

Freedom does not mean a. to do whatever 4122

God a. to bring good out of evil and pain 5046

God a. to empower us 9199

God a. to enter human personality and change it 5777

God a. to fulfill all his designs 4521

God a. to work failures into his plans 3613

grace given that we may be a. to do good works 5209

heart made a. to receive uncreated light 4749

hoped to be a. to do without God 5395

important a. to tell we are converted 1903

in heaven a. to wipe tears, won't have to 11016

Love a. to undertake all things 7220

majority opinion of the least a. 5191

Never man bent a. to make others straight 3444

no one a. to strike terror into others 4001

problem not that God is not a. 4823

to be a. to do without is power 1818

to disagree without being disagreeable 1878

to discover own darkness 6004

to do something well 50

to encourage all who journey with us 9059

to explain suffering clearest indication never suffered 10918

to live peaceably with hard persons 5236

to love himself, a. to love others 9985

to make this water calm 9098

to say how much you love is to love little 7323

to smile at anything 6961

to thank Creator for way he made us 9993

well as I'm a. 6134

who has faith in himself a. to be faithful 9485

you must be very big to be a. to judge 4553

ABNORMAL

Shrinking from death a. 2255

ABODE

sun as bright as from rich man's a. 7001

ABOLISH

God did not a. evil 4931

Why did God a. the law 9755

would a. rose 8580

ABOLISHED

evangelicals who a. slave trade 5656

evil and suffering could be a. 4149

Jesus audaciously a. death 2322

ABOLISHES

Sometimes a nation a. God 4897

ABOMINABLE

satanic does not mean a. 9853

Slander that a. tittle-tattle 10470

ten thousand times more a. 4523

ABORTION

cannot treat human embryo as worthless 24

critics will ask 18

fighting a. by adoption 23

fruit is present in the seed 16

horror of a. 18

I can't get it out of my mind. 22

I do not believe in a. 19

It's haunting me. 22

legal a. rather than bury 19

no instrument to procure a. 21

please do not destroy 23

prefer to counsel a woman 19

stops a beating heart 15

to forbid birth is quicker murder 16

What if Mary and Joseph had decided to have 25

Where was the church 18

ABORTIVE

all that is a. in universe 4997

ABOUNDING

grace hope of mankind 5203

humility is the quiet valley, fertile and a. in life 6026

in wealth, yet miserable 249

sin terror of world 5203

ABOUNDS

Grace a. when genuine repentance 5210

ABOVE

all is God 4607

as long as you're looking down, can't see a. 9188

Be thou a guiding star a. me 5375

cannot doubt power comes from a. 4949

forgiving enemy sets you a. him 4073

God a, outside, beyond all measurement 4710

God a. all existing things 4609

God a. existence itself 4609

God a. in rank, station 4607

God is a, but not raised up 4848

God is a, presiding 4848

God is a. all things but not beyond reach 4612

God's actions outside, a. human sciences 5237

God's gifts on shelves one a. the other 6017

God's greatness a. our capacity, reach 4681

God's infinitude places him a. knowing 4702

great minds rise a. misfortune 5281

hand that gives is a. hand that takes 4375

Heaven is a. all, yet 4716

His experience of knowing is a. reason 5809

holy life is living a. the world 5736

keeping watch a. his own 5377

Light is a. us, color around us 7108

not against reason because a. it 7938

one who thought himself a. me 9251

soaring far a. all human thought 7970

Ten thousand suns which shine a. us nightly 4592

This a. all 6318

to reach heart must come from a. 7929

To write the love of God a. 4748

Unless within that which is a. 11108

was a. me until he had that thought 9251

Wisdom is vertical, it comes down from a. 11928

world a. man's head 11627

ABRAHAM

did not know the way 5372

God tested A. 11061

knew the Guide 5372

treated God with startling familiarity 7526

ABRAHAM'S

contemporaries could not understand him 10877

ABRAM'S

With God A. day and this day the same 4591

ABROAD

Awake, asleep, at home, a. 4876

thou wert within and I a. 4805

ABROGATE

not to a. obedience but to add to its spirit 6811

ABSALOM
vain about hair, hanged by hair 9190

ABSENCE
desert does not mean a. of men 10565
Happiness not a. of conflict 5526
joy in nature is a. of man 8035
of occupation is not rest 3085
Peace is not a. of war 8455
represents a. of self-love 6229
seldom solid home in a. of religious inspiration 5858
worry a. of thought 12078

ABSENT
always in the wrong 10471
dare not think God is a. 7556
When Jesus is a, all is hard 6512
where right thinking a. 4124

ABSENTEE
perfect job, hours of an a. 3121

ABSOLUTE
dangerous to set up impulse as a. guide 7836
God is holy with a. holiness 4658
God shows himself a. mystery 4738
I believe in God of a, unbounded love 4997
no a. knowledge 6706
rest is death 6771
Thou art a. safety from trouble 9052
truth belongs to God alone 11495
truth is indestructible 11550

ABSOLUTELY
no God anything less than a. glorious 4504
Real friends have great time doing a. nothing 4265
souls who give themselves a. to him 4790

ABSOLUTES
experience hardship, stress 953

ABSOLVED
Fully a. through these I am 4719

ABSORB
Bible like trying to mop ocean with sponge 748

ABSORBED
in God 9840
spirit a. in depths of divine ocean 7968

ABSORBING
pain most a. of human experience 8260

ABSTAINERS
Does church arrange services for Total A. from Usury 10086

ABSTAINS
from giving wordy evidence 1837

ABSTINENCE
Jesus finds few companions in a. 2828

ABSURD
dream is not a. 2968
specific requests to God ... a. 8821
things just which are unjust 11506
thought a. by what it seeks 11242
to argue men into believing 590
to call Christianity nonresistance 1206
to put God into a definition 7487
to question authority of God a. 4955
to say a man can't love one woman 7621

ABSURDITIES
forget as soon as you can 11366
no doubt crept in 8375

ABSURDITY
attraction of Christianity to me 1216
children understand better than wise 1216
cross revealed God in a. 6471
fools understand better than wise 1216
has champion to defend it 3256
illiterates understand better than wise 1216
meek, not arrogant, inherit earth 1216
poor, not rich, are blessed 1216
pure in heart, not strong in mind, see God 1216

ABUNDANCE
contemplate God's munificence in a. of earth 4581
God's mercy, not withholding a. from unthankful 4581
In all a. there is lack 11825
like want, ruins men 9335
Love, never an a. 7251
never generous with a. 4366
not necessity but a. produces greed 5318
providence of God about us in a. 8002
what we enjoy constitutes a. 8636

ABUNDANT
Christ offers a. life 7022
conversion, entrance into a. life 1900
Good, the more communicated, more a. grows 5062
more a. the ore 737

ABUSE
A beast does not know he is a beast 26
cruelty springs from weakness 27
feeds on tears 29
Give account if I a. it 11303
guilty of inhumanity when we a. 901
isn't softened by tears 29
makes countless thousands mourn 30
Men, making one another unhappy 31

owes its pleasures to another's pain 28

ABUSED
prisoners a. as children 32

ABUSES
have not shaken stability of church 1419

ABUSING
guilt in a. riches 11865

ABUSIVE
may see God as a. parent 4489

ABYSS
Bible an a. 734
like a little strip of pavement over an a. 7090
Man an a. 7403
O Conscience, into what a. of fears 1694
silence like gaping a. which can swallow up 10253
solitude without fellowship a. of despair 10547

ACCENT
a lie may be told by a. on a syllable 6859
on youth, stress on parents 8354

ACCENTUATE
the positive 8231

ACCEPT
a. uncertainties quietly 7435
afraid to a. what is given us 7072
authority of Jesus 524
bitter truth revealed to us 1719
Christ by impulse of mind, emotions 3333
Christ without knowing how it works 1893
Christ's cross as our cross 3335
Christ's enemies as our enemies 3335
Christ's friends as our friends 3335
Christ's future as our future 3335
Christ's life as our life 3335
Christ's rejection as our rejection 3335
Christ's ways as our ways 3335
crucifixion with Christ 10048
Divine humility will a. convert even on such terms 9829
easy to tell poor to a. poverty 8678
equally God's gifts 1461
even our incomplete knowledge of God 7435
Everything we a. undergoes change 966
everything, even problems, with joy 5261
God asks no man whether he will a. life 6893
God asks no one to a. life 1140
God can only a. my badness 5059
God cannot a. goodness from me 5059

God kind enough to a. little time I give back 11296

grace to a. things that cannot be changed 9060

help us a. ourselves, failures and all 9993

humility of God hard to a. 4683

if unwilling to a. righteous reign of God 8818

if you a. my decisions 39

if you can a. poverty as God's will for yourself 8678

it, life no longer difficult 7012

Jesus as Savior, a new life 876

judged by light refused to a. 6579

learning how to a. the impossible 7692

often refuse to a. idea 9516

old age calmly, wisely 8158

or reject God's initiative 585

our will subjected to God not easy to a. 5467

suffering as inseparable from love 7953

suffering graciously 10833

suffering, find peace 10833

the impossible 6961

Tomorrow lose opportunity to a. Christ 11404

will of God 7485

willingly whatever a loving Father sends 33

with faith, resignation his holy will 4688

Word of God, a. or reject 686

ACCEPT CHRIST
attitude likely wrong 3333

ACCEPTABLE
No man gives anything a. to God 10119

only a. workers those who worship 12099

ACCEPTANCE
before God is complete, secure 9992

Christ's words provoked a. or rejection 6377

church, indulge in community a. 952

conversion, not a. of creed 1909

first step to overcoming misfortune 154

God speaks to us of a. 4900

How could I know a. without rejection 1512

If the Giver gives you a hill, plough 35

level of joy proportional to level of a. 6556

live with a, learn to find love 1114

look unblinkingly at reality 33

of one's worth core of personality 9980

Silence is brother of a. 10264

when it is raining, let it rain 34

ACCEPTANCES
Contentment, result of a. 1807

ACCEPTED
all those in Christ a. equally 3236

because Jesus died 46

Christianity never a. on large scale 1188

not a. by God because 46

not because you deserve 46

not because you worked hard 46

Real joy is sorrow a, transformed 6557

ACCEPTING
Christ as Lord will bring heaven down 5681

Christians a. noisiest as best 5891

Emotional stability a. the inevitable 2563

joyfully a. conditions of earthly pilgrimage 9090

of God's dealings 7728

ourselves as we are 1712

Patience, a. difficult situation 8415

peace in a. master plan 8440

through a. circumstances, self is crucified 1473

ACCEPTS
At beginning God a. us in sinfulness 9832

Christian a. circumstances from God 3638

Difficulty is excuse history never a. 2718

evil without protesting is co-operating 3374

friend a. who you've become 4169

friend a. you today just the way you are 4172

Love a. people as they are 7207

nothing has nothing to return 9457

passively a. evil involved in it 3374

suffering perfects one who a. call of God 10920

trouble generally a. 11458

Unselfishness a. variety of types 9512

ACCESSIBLE
Never know how a. men are 3345

willing to make ideas a. 11007

ACCIDENT
atheist believes himself an a. 473

driver late for his a. 1738

have a, other driver's fault 3947

Man calls sin an a, God an abomination 4560

pleasure to have good action found out by a. 8607

popularity an a. 1010

You aren't an a. 10004

ACCIDENTAL
Nothing with God a. 1475

nothing with God can be a. 4927

ACCIDENTALLY
God is never found a. 4919

ACCIDENTS
apart from God, difficulties are a. 10598

form actuating motives of prayers 8788

Temptations not a. 11093

ACCLAIM
Jesus' a. lies in ridicule 6443

ACCOMMODATE
My soul is too small to a. you 9089

ACCOMMODATES
to win applause a. himself to others 1585

vain man a. himself to others 9189

ACCOMPANIED
faith a. by expectation 3809

with way of escape 11432

ACCOMPLICE
Conscience, my a. 1678

To ignore evil is to become a. 3411

ACCOMPLISH
Denying we can a. God's work is worst kind of pride 9199

desire more than I can a. 61

do less, but a. more 60

great deal of activity, but a. little 9017

insisting impossible because he cannot a. 7793

Jesus knew what he was to a. 4425

not by what we a. 53

Only Christ can a. goal within us 8113

perfect work God will a. 1468

to a. it perfectly 9062

to a. things striving for 4439

what violence fails to a. 4403

ACCOMPLISHED
When a. daily task, go to sleep in peace 11489

ACCOMPLISHES
better nobody who a. something 3856

man a. what he believes 613

Minstry that costs nothing a. nothing 10173

than somebody who a. nothing 3856

ACCOMPLISHMENT
airplane, atomic bomb, zipper 90

cross a. of salvation 3582

Holy Spirit, chief energizer 63

prune back activity not fruitful 60

Sitting on a tack often useful 88

something small in a big way 58

start by carrying small stones 59

try and find you can 95

ACCOMPLISHMENTS
Afflictions triggers a. 10834

contributions to children rank as greatest a. 8294

Great a. often attempted 3593
Great a. only occasionally reached 3593
no editorials praise mother's a. 7844
possibility of future exceeds a. of past 4329
Some men dream of worthy a. 89
Some men dream, others stay awake 89

ACCORD
Christian in full a. with psychology 9351

ACCOUNT
Give a. if I abuse it 11303
to be given for riches 11865
wealth laid up in heavenly banking a. 3751

ACCOUNTABILITY
need to answer only for yourself 74

ACCOUNTABLE
to others for injury 70

ACCOUNTABLENESS
awake to a. of the immortal soul 10654

ACCUMULATED
Treasures in heaven a. by attitude 11872

ACCUMULATES
if a man a. money 7800

ACCUMULATING
poverty, a. debts 4040

ACCURATE
response to temptation a. barometer of love for God 11079

ACCURATELY
Jesus tells us a. about life after death 2323
reporting a. what we see, are 6219

ACCURSED
thrice a. is indifference 6161

ACCUSATION
flies faster than defense 10453
no enemy can make an a. stick 4884

ACCUSE
didn't actually a. God 380
not Eve and Adam 763
understanding means one does not a. 11619
3079

ACCUSED
Christians a. of being morbid 9758
martyrs a. of efforts to find truth 11501
strengthen all persons unjustly a. 9104

ACCUSER
guilty conscience needs no a. 5473

Remorse to carry own a. within your breast 9573
wicked is his own a. 3996

ACCUSES
He who excuses himself a. himself 3475

ACCUSING
the times is excusing ourselves 1462

ACCUSTOM
yourself to thought that God loves you 4747

ACCUSTOMED
to relying on words to manage, control 10259
to wearing disguise 6067
we stand stripped of a. defenses 5238

ACHAN
sold himself for wedge, garment 11798

ACHE
Every heart has its own a. 10590
our teeth still a. 8253
shoulders a. with fatigue 11420
Shriveling hurt until sun grew forth from a. a leaf 5368

ACHES
Forget a. and pains 9270
won't have to worry about a, pains 2346

ACHIEVE
cherish just, lasting peace 5199
don't have time to a. understanding 7648
end of life not to a. pleasure 5554
fail greatly, a. greatly 87
Freedom means to a. all God wants 4122
inner health through forgiveness 4103
Love flowering of personality nothing else can a. 7268
Optimists a. improvement 8238
possessed to a. ends he vaguely understands 4399
power of God to a. our welfare 7093
prayed for strength that he might a. 8806
will never a. fulfillment unless God in control 9558
4309

ACHIEVED
Bible gives no encouragement perfection a. 9254
character a. through conflict 1632
environment in which maturity can be a. 4721
has a. success who has lived, laughed, loved 10781
Nothing great ever a. without enthusiasm 3178
only thing a. without effort is failure 2773

Peace can only be a. by understanding 8452
perfection of human expression a. 740
strength that God's will may be a. 4803
world a. brilliance without conscience 1705

ACHIEVEMENT
a bell doesn't ring on its own 75
before which a. vain 6494
chastenings carry soul to spiritual a. 2850
crown of a. is crown of thorns 10849
easy to overestimate the importance 84
Everyone wants high a. 4731
few want to pay price of a. 4731
Forgiveness highest a. 4077
Four steps to a. 80
greatest works done by the ones 91
have something difficult to do 77
man has leaped ahead in scientific a. 9872
Marriage is adventure, not an a. 7638
never walk back 82
no gathering the rose without thorns 94
not enough to aim, you must hit 83
Not in a. 3150
not possible without persistent work 85
not who soared to heights of a. 6175
Only those who dare to fail 87
Peace won by compromise a short-lived a. 8464
plan, prepare, proceed, pursue 80
roots of true a. lie in the will 92
Some men dream, others stay awake 89
successful marriage an a. 7598
the best that you can become 92
this one thing I do 81
To find God greatest human a. 7542
too often work is worshiped, not God 97
try and find you can 95
when the pressure within is stronger 78
worth doing at all, worth doing well 96

ACHIEVEMENTS
God doesn't demand our a. 8094
Humility recognizing God, others responsible for my a. 6011
promise of what man is going to be 7429

ACHIEVES
Patience a. more than force 8407
who a. power by violence 11674

ACHING
heard the cock crow thrice with an a. heart 9569
If I can ease one life the a. 6922
only one thing can satisfy a. abyss of heart 5359
redemption of Jesus can satisfy a. soul 6402

ACKNOWLEDGE
enemies without pretense 5890
faults to repair damage 3956
negative attitudes 503
to a. it truthfully 9062

ACKNOWLEDGED
God a. with one heart, voice by the American people 11176

ACKNOWLEDGING
greatness in a. good turn 5263

ACKNOWLEDGMENT
of divine power 479
than imperfect a. of his love 7171

ACORN
burst forth from prison walls 6095
creation of thousand forests in one a. 8664
thousand forests in one a. 1969
touch with divine power the buried a. 6095

ACORN-CUP
like unborn forests in a. 4769

ACORNS
hundred a. sown in silence by breeze 8052
Tall oaks from little a. grow 8657

ACQUAINT
thyself with God 4737

ACQUAINTANCE
begin with compliment 1572
stranger a friend whose a. you haven't made 9443

ACQUAINTANCES
If a man does not make new a. 4249
Money brings a, but not friends 7807
talk about pleasures to a. 4276

ACQUAINTED
how should avarice, happiness become a. 5312
with wickedness of our own heart 10306

ACQUIESCENCE
God does not ask for a. of indolence 4507
Peace springs from a. 8453
perpetual yes of universal a. 1645
spirituality that preaches a. 10698

ACQUIESCES
Unselfishness a. in variety of types 9512

ACQUIRE
cannot a. experience by experiments 3552
confidence in recourse to God 8796
enthusiasm 3189
skill to do difficult things easily 8406
when sense of self depends on what I can a. 10003
work to become, not to a. 3124

ACQUIRED
fortune has a. him 11820
has not a. a fortune 11820
nuisance knowledge a. by hard work 3014
second half of life habits a. during first half 5501
Strength of character may be a. at work 5849
very nature a. within families 3881
vice a. without a tutor 11725

ACQUIRES
Education a. higher grade of prejudices 2999

ACQUIRING
not a. habit of reading and study a mistake 7793

ACQUISITION
next best a. to good friends, good book 854
virtue an a. 11683

ACQUISITIVE
Man is a. 10068

ACT
A few dozen a. 100
able to a. in what they ought to do 2485
according to custom 1648
as if impossible to fail 8533
as if you love your neighbor 8055
Children a. like their parents 1109
Children will a. like their parents 8289
compiling anthology an a. of thanksgiving 9381
Do every a. as if last 556
dreams a. part learned in waking hours 2966
each party claims to a. in will of God 4972
Faith is an a. 3680
Faith is an a. of man 3690
Forgiveness not occasional a. 4078
Freedom, to a. rightly 4123
from honest motives 559
hear but do not a. 1414
human to think wisely, a. foolishly 5973
in the living present 4331
insist all look, talk, a. alike 6824
Let each man think himself an a. of God 4557
like a man of thought 11257

Nobody will know God is love unless you a. it 7281
Nothing more rare in man than own a. 1641
of injustice to the sheep 6283
of obedience better than 100 sermons 8109
of sin may pass 5489
Old age, play's last a. 8166
one a. of thanksgiving when things go wrong 11157
One kind a. will teach more love of God 6661
out excitement 3185
Proverbs—How to a. 11925
rather than delay 1138
Repentance an attitude rather than single a. 9588
Revenge in cold blood is devil's a. 9723
Revival sovereign a. of God 9746
right to a. way they decide 6193
salvation reduced to once-done a. 9816
So a. that your action might be made law 3453
Sow a, reap habit 1041
Sow thought, reap a. 1041
spirit in every thought, word, a. 10697
the honest man on the scaffolding 6295
think anew, a. anew 976
To a. in everything with highest motives 6913
Tomorrow the day when fools a. sensibly 11404
upon faith within our power 3721
way we a. behind the wheel 1331
way we a. praying in pew 1331
We know how God would a. if in our place 6151
what was God saying in this significant a. 6500
when a. uprightly 3457
When you must a, will open 5444
with as much energy 3816
with disregard for opinions of others 6291
Worship highest, noblest a. 12137

ACTED
and behold duty was joy 9663
If man has a. right 5032
looking like owl when a. like ass 6162

ACTING
Christ is God a. like God 6371
Love is just being there and a. 3835

ACTION
A few dozen act 100
and contemplation, not contradictory 1766
as exact in each a. as if success depended upon it 9041
balance between prayer, a. 4156
be very cautious 572

Christian a. defined as a. of God through a person 10122
Christian a. not of ourselves 104
Christian a. spirit of Christ 104
Christianity, not a. 1173
consequences of a. without thought 11278
conviction without a. worthless 3737
Determine plan of a. 555
Every a. has a keynote 6379
Every a. touches some chord 105
faith foundation, a. as stone laid 3826
faith sees a. of God 3794
fold not your a. 3718
for sake of one good a. 4074
generous a. own reward 4345
God considers not a, but spirit of a. 7861
God's a. masterpiece of partiality, love 4747
goodness is love in a. 7202 5065
greatest pleasure is good a. by stealth 8607
If God has you out of a. for awhile 5391
Justice is truth in a. 6613
keen spirit starts into instant a. 8224
lack of charity in a. murders faith 3829
least a. has consequences 572
Life in Christ string of a. verbs 1235
look at whom a. affects 572
Love an a, an activity 7231
Making peace requires a. 4094
measure by which a. to be judged 7307
must look beyond a. 572
Nothing more frightful than ignorance in a. 6084
relection without commitment paralysis of a. 1532
sends us back to contemplation 1766
senses see a. of the creatures 3794
shortage of effective Christian a. 111
So act that a. might be made law 3453
social a. mistaken for evangelism 3341
substituted reflex a. for revelation 5808
Talking easy, a. difficult 2537
than good a. which puffs up 3931
theology what you are when a. starts 11215
Think like a man of a. 11257
times demand a. 3339
Unite contemplation with a. 1766

ACTIONS

Attitudes determine a. 501
be right in ordinary a. 6295
cause evil not only by a. 3346
defend my a. or explain 39

determined by impulse to follow leader 6199
Do not wait to do good a. 623
don't always speak louder than words 1833
foolish a. require courage to confess 1603
God knows how to use disordered wishes, a. 4644
God's a. outside, above human sciences 5237
good name got by many a, lost by one 9611
hundred evil a. should be forgotten 4074
Incredible echoes mirror a. 1740
Jesus speaks of motives rather than a. 6450
Kind words and a. right 6647
love weighs a. in scales of his honor 6457
Man sees a, God motives 7866
never interpret a. in ill-sense 1080
not only by a. but by inaction 70
People consider a. 1067
Right a. best apologies for wrong a. 9598
some content not to do mean a. 110
subject thoughts, a. to the laws 7434
take their hues from the heart 103
Think not those faithful who praise a. 3955
turning disordered a. to our advantage 4644
value is extent inspired by God 7366
we judge others by their a. 6596
When we cling to a. as self-identification 10531
When we cling to results of our a. 10531

ACTIVE

Christians to be a, not passive 1271
confidence in Christ makes us a. 1611
desperately a. people a nuisance 126
God promised to be a. among men 5724
God, most a. and dynamic of all 4520
life begins, ends on earth 1764
Lord, I've been a. all my life 5661
nor has man right to a. life 9670
nor man right to be so immersed in a. life 7004
so a. in the service of Christ 117
to assimilate Christ a. faith 3801

ACTIVISM

philosophy of a. victims 130

ACTIVITIES

an overplus of Christian a. 127
at peace through a. of the day 6828
Beware a. instead of being 938

employment as sacred as Sunday a. 3104
for God are secondary 124
many useless, others ridiculous 115
nervous a. found in place of Christ 1230
prefer meaningless a. to being alone 10575
producing a. faster than faith 1449
soul's a. continue through eternity 6094
vocational a. develop qualities 5014
we do for God are secondary 8972
worthwhile a. become damaging when 7617

ACTIVITY

a cheap anesthetic 120
a human dynamo 118
Apart from God a. is 113
beware of barrenness 114
chances are prayer a. will fizzle out 7725
Christian's a. have root in gratitude 5240
deadens the pain of empty life 120
delusion sex is an a. 10227
do less, but accomplish more 60
Faith is an a. 3679
God a dynamic, pulsating a. 11425
God not in whirlwind of a. 10747
great deal of a. but accomplish little 9017
Holy Spirit, chief energizer of a. 63
hurt people when too busy 129
if relationship is faulty, a. cannot be satisfactory 10227
is a blessing 6753
itself proves nothing 112
lose contact with Lord of the work 115
Love an action, an a. 7231
not enough to be busy 116
Nothing more terrible than a. without insight 4429
Nothing so terrible as a. without thought 6084
passing whiff of insignificance 113
Prayer a supernatural a. 8916
prune back part of our a. 60
Purposeless a. phase of death 122
stable spirit not distracted by a. 4307
this alone constitutes living 130
wear people out 115
What are we busy about 116
which is not fruitful 60
whirl of religious a. 4410
Witnessing not a once-a-week a. 3344

ACTOR

Condemn the fault, not the a. 3936

dream theater where dreamer a.
2972

Samson, most popular a. 791

ACTORS
children become plausible a. 1105

ACTS
All God's a. consistent with
attributes 4579

count the a. you have done 107

desire my a. be according to his
will 5411

do not find vanishing a. amusing
2303

faith a. on supernatural facts 3807

Great thoughts become great a.
11223

hardest tasks are moral a. 7838

He most lives who a. best 1056

He who a. unjustly a. unjustly to
himself 6262

heroic a. of a great mind 6281

His little, nameless,
unremembered a. 6664
626

Little a. of kindness are silent
threads of gold 6997

notice how he a. when loses money
7802

of grace cannot be reversed 4626

of this life destiny of the next
7024

revelation record of God's a. in
time 9710

Silence the sequel to foolish a.
10266

through personal obedience God a.
5385

trouble a. different on people
11431

virtue measured by habitual a.
5502

ACUTE
kind of knowing which most a.
thinker cannot imitate 5809

most a. cannot obtain entire
knowledge of Bible 737

ADAM
And the old A. in me, rises up
8966

ate apple because forbidden 761

ate the apple 8253

created to be friend, companion
of God 758

got so much out of surgical
operation 759

has filled whole earth with pieces
760

introduced sin into world 757

knew nobody said it before 1994

Lord made A. from dust 1127

not to have dominion over himself
758

Originally one, he has fallen 760

second A. is greater than first A.
5031

should have been more adamant
756

still dream what A. dreamt 9309

switched from God's design 757

That A. was not Adamant 11113

to have dominion over all life 758

took rule over himself 757

would retort, "You gave it to me"
7659

ADAM AND EVE
Accuse not E. and A. 763

into the far wilderness 365

Think of squabbles A. must have
had 7659

ADAM'S
In A. fall, we sinned all 10323

ADAMANT
Adam should have been more a.
756

That Adam was not A. 11113

ADAPTS
reasonable man a. to world 980

unreasonable man a. world to
himself 980

wise man a. to circumstances
1463

ADD
are here to a. what we can to life
10207

could a. two hours to my working
day 9531

When a. to truth, you subtract
from it 11587

ADDED
all who told it a. something new
9757

do not believe God has a. to his
revelation 9711

Lord a. electricity to toddler 1127

ADDICT
Man created a God a. 7496

we must a. ourselves to prayer
8765

ADDICTION
a spiritual problem 134

Gluttons dig graves with teeth 132

Gluttony an emotional escape 133

on skid row 135

ADDICTS
are good actors and actresses 135

drug and alcohol a. in America
135

many attend churches regularly
135

ADDING
gossip makes mountain of molehill
by a. dirt 5114

ADDITION
God is without a. 4680

ADDRESS
Bible, letter from God with
personal a. 704

Flee temptation, don't leave a.
11055

ADDRESSED
God may only be a, not expressed
4667

gospel a. not to reason but faith
3796

ADDS
Friendship a. radiance to
prosperity 4228

Laughter a. richness to ordinary
days 6727

ADEQUATE
No eloquence a. to tell of beauty
10274

Only in quiet mind is a. perception
7718

ADHERANCE
greatness in steadfast a. to
promises made 5283

ADIEU
My soul bids you a. 12032

ADJUDGED
If God's justice a. by human
reckoning, not divine 4728

ADJUST
can a. sails 4056

our lives to God 1304

ADJUSTED
Certainly Jesus was poorly a. to
society 6196

ADJUSTER
Christ, the master a. 1906

ADJUSTING
process of a. public image 1882

ADJUSTMENT
Every new a. is crisis in self-esteem
9984

Peace is deliberate a. of life to will
of God 8460

ADJUSTMENTS
make necessary a. in light of own
ideals 3060

too impatient to make a. marriage
entails 7648

ADJUSTS
A, sustains, and agitates the whole
4711

realist a. the sails 8249

ADMINISTRATION
hope of nation not in justice of its
a. 5190

to conduct the affairs of this a.
6304

ADMINISTRATORS
angels a. of divine beneficence 363

ADMIRABLE
To be one's self more a. than
conformity 6216

ADMIRATION
who loves God has no need of a.
10877

ADMIRATIONS
governed by a. rather than disgusts 8472

ADMIRE
heroes of tragedy 10877
people suited to contemplative life 1759
Sainthood makes it possible to a. everybody 9778
simple men a. studies 2996
To a. is to have no wish to change 1590
to a. is to love with the mind 7326
To love is to a. with the heart 7326
we praise with enthusiasm only those who a. us 8726
Who and what we a. 10016

ADMIRED
Only baby a. for opening his mouth 5151

ADMIRERS
Great talents have some a. 7

ADMISSION
Love finds a. where proud science fails 12130

ADMIT
Authentic men aren't afraid to a. wrong 3916
Divine love can a. no rival 4929
if faults to a, how can he be perfect 3949
If too afraid to a. you are hurting 9211
most narrow-minded Christian must a. 5791
seek proof, a. doubt 3806
sign of strength to a. don't know answers 10748
to a. evil thoughts like setting up idol in temple 7759
you're wrong, you're right 9665

ADMITS
envies another a. own inferiority 3219
No man perfect unless a. faults 3949

ADMITTED
Care a. as guest turns to master 12058
once to his embrace 4737
until first a. was in trouble 11444

ADMONISHMENT
wind of God's a. may burst doors, windows 4775

ADMONITION
if conscience smite thee once 1686

ADOLESCENCE
Don't panic during storms of a. 8295
fascinating, crazy time of life 12161
inadequate memories who think a. happy 1101
not happy, carefree time 1101

ADOLESCENT
death of child, a. is born 2390

ADOLESCENTS
quickest to discern hypocrisy 12162

ADOPTED
talent only extemporaneous half-expression 6226

ADOPTION
fighting abortion by a. 23
God's decree ties knot of a. 4616

ADORATION
an attitude of the soul 12122
attributes of God helps express a. 4580
Breathless with a. 8980
crown studded with gems of sacrifice, a. 7073
highest form of prayer 8756
Idolatry not only a. of images 6071
living doxology for a. 1243
No prayer of a. higher than "I love you, God" 8876
not a religious exercise 12122
of God become occupation of soul 3987
woods upon their summits wave in a. 7997

ADORE
I cannot a. enough. I cannot speak 12125
May we a. thee for time and eternity 11424
rebellious deny as freely as devout a. 4129
This, this is the God we a. 4787
Wait the great teacher death, and God a. 5913
Yet I love thee and a. 9077

ADORED
Incessantly a. 4659
prostitutes, thieves a. Jesus 6412

ADORING
Light'ning their eyes to vision and a. 8454

ADULT
bigger world of a. life 1126

ADULTERY
Divorce, sacrament of a. 2923
invaded the church 2919
not just refrain from a, but from desiring 6444

ADULTS
are obsolete children 8478
childhood dies, corpses called a. 1135
value of marriage that children produce a. 7669

ADVANCE
discipline through which we a. 3252
Faith means believing in a. 3708

God will a. mile in blazing light 2962
in spiritual life has dangers 10700
spirituality desire to see others a. at his expense 10719
dare to be in a. of their time 11252
thought is always in a. 11264

ADVANCED
by those who suffered, world has a. 10858
who believes himself a. in spiritual life 10701

ADVANCEMENT
He that perseveres makes difficulty an a. 8542
hell, everyone concerned about own a. 5705

ADVANCES
alas, no a. in peace 8450
Humanity a. or retreats 5969
On from fact divine God a. 4906

ADVANCING
only a. in life whose heart is getting softer 6898
see only ebb of a. wave 5944

ADVANTAGE
do not rightly love God when love for a. 4801
If seek own a. 8839
looks for a. out of friendship 4245
never seek one's a. 5066
of congregational singing 1415
of crises, deadlocks 2043
of praising oneself 9238
responsible for how well we take a. of opportunities 9660
seek their own a. 10084
turning disordered actions to our a. 4644

ADVANTAGES
consecration is taking a. as trust funds 1721
Our many a. do us harm 9337
Silence has many a. 1866
will never set my heart on worldly a. 10875

ADVENT
arrival of light in our darkness 6119
celebrate a. of life 1369
coming of quiet joy 6119
hope day at hand when a. of God will appear 9909
proper that Christmas follow A. 1365

ADVENTURE
approach new person in spirit of a. 9468
Death an awfully big a. 2243
Death the great a. 2259
death, most beautiful a. in life 2458
goal of a. to which God commits is in heaven 5385
Hope is an a. 5918

gone when determined to
concentrate 6056

AFFECTATIONS
Don't laugh at youth's a. 12163

AFFECTED
entire ocean a. by pebble 6238
God not a. by our mutability 4587
put together have not a. life as
powerfully 6353

AFFECTION
Authentic men aren't afraid to
show a. 3916
Christian love not a vague feeling
of a. 7304
feel the breath of God's a. 7484
friend's a. greatest treasure 4181
gift great if given with a. 4352
home must be warmed by a. 5848
husband and wife one in a. 3868
not dead, the child of our a. 2392
palace without a. poor hovel 5816
property of friendship 4227
Selfishness enemy of all a. 10082
Simplicity pours herself forth with
pure a. 11696
when receive a, ask what right we
have to them 10842
which no unworthy a. may drag
downwards 9057

AFFECTIONATE
Love is not a. feeling 7242

AFFECTIONS
at home a. are trained 5849
in touch with people through our
a. 7428
must be bathed in new element
880
must be re-born 880
must be reconsecrated to Maker
880
soul's moanings are the a,
yearning for the Infinite 7516

AFFECTS
death a. outlook 2240
Evangelism a. the other fellow
9739
least action a. everything 572
look at whom action a. 572
revival a. me 9739
teacher a. eternity 2993

AFFINITIES
tidal pressure of a. 683

AFFIRM
cleavage between truths we a,
values we live by 6068

AFFIRMATION
bold, creative a. of self 4160
Faith is an a. 3680

AFFIRMATIVE
Latch on to the a. 8231

AFFIRMS
Recognition of individual a.
respect for human dignity 9952

AFFLICT
apprehensions that a. the
earth-bound 5781
purpose of darkness not to a.
2608

AFFLICTED
Men prefer prosperous error to a.
truth 3261
sin, all a. with the disease 10415
think of a. as grace 2565

AFFLICTION
able to drown out every earthly
voice 274
absolutely functional 10834
Beauty against a. 10844
blessing to those who do not
struggle 298
blessing to those who lie still 298
can be a treasure 10834
can stand a. better than prosperity
250
consoling in depths of a. 957
Count each a, whether light or
grave 5331
Count each a. God's messenger
160
deeply I feel for you in your a.
3076
faith takes bitterness from a. 3818
fire burns gold pure and clean 294
God has many sharp cutting
instruments 285
God's shepherd dog 275
greater merit to suffer a. patiently
234
irrelevant voices brought to silence
274
is to put him into in furnace of a.
8804
like the iron-smith 275
meet a. solemnly, slowly 296
meet a. with humility and faith
296
no a. can touch confidence 1613
out of a. grasp the splendor of
God's love 281
out of Jesus' a. came a new sense
of love 281
shapes as it smites 275
the blessing of a. 298
the highlands of a. 295
To added a. he addeth his mercy
5223
to draw us back to the fold 275
triggers accomplishments 10834
triggers greatest insights 10834
waves of misery will divide 296
When in the cellar of a. 300

AFFLICTIONS
deep, experimental, knowing,
profound 278
end in godly man's good 3996
evidences of God's love, grace to
bear a. 4778
God uses pain along with other a.
8256
godly knows a. come from a
loving God 3996

godly not afraid of a. 3996
make the heart more deep 278
makes heart able to hold, contain,
beat 278
makes the world too hot to hold
283
Poetry has soothed my a. 8616
shadow of God's wings 277

AFFLICTS
God ne'er a. us more than our
desert 286

AFFLUENCE
If live at same level of a. 10734

AFFLUENT
society euphemism for selfishness
10051

AFFORD
no life so meager greatest can a.
to despise it 7055
whether he can a. luxury of
unbelief 11589

AFFRIGHT
Let nothing a. thee 4588

AFIRE
every common bush a. with God
1710

AFLAME
even when thornbush a. with
glory of God 9064
In wonder-workings, or some
bush a. 8019

AFLOAT
cannot sink someone else's boat
and keep your own a. 10480

A-FLYING
old time is still a. 8214

AFRAID
all hell terribly a. of cross 2122
And I am not a. 7452
Authentic men aren't a. to show
affection 3916
be a. of the indifferent 6158
be a. only of standing still 5365
Be not a. of growing slowly 5365
Be not a. to pray, to pray is right
8768
can say, Of whom shall I be a.
3985
children a. to go to parents for
counsel 8311
devil not a. of Bible with dust 729
Do not be a. of defeat 2511
Do not be a. of enemies 6158
Do not be a. of friends 6158
Don't be a. to take big step 3650
godly a. of nothing 3996
godly not a. of afflictions 3996
godly not a. of God 3996
godly not a. of himself 3996
godly not a. of Satan 3996
I am a. of dying 2300
I fear God, yet am not a. of him
3977
I, a stranger and a. 3978

If a. of loneliness, don't marry 7128

If too a. to admit you are hurting 9211

Jesus wasn't a. to associate with anyone 4253

let me never be a. to pray for the impossible 9046

man of courage not a. of truth 6845

Man only animal of which I am a. 7410

man ought not to be a. of anything 3999

many stay walled up a. of being hurt 4290

more a. of my own heart 9929

neither a. to fail 10802

never be a. of anything 566

not a. of being lonely 7141

not a. to die, honey 2312

of free discussion 2904

of men who believe everything 586

Old age, men are a. of you 8149

Parents a. to put foot down 8323

Railing at life, yet a. of death 8163

secretly a. will miss the way 3758

see all, nor be a. 8132

Some thought brave a. to run 1934

to accept what is given us 7072

to care too much 4290

to do last hour of life 109

To fear and not to be a, paradox of faith 3788

to laugh in God's presence 6723

To man who is a. everything rustles 4002

to show each other who we really are 6057

to the very core of his being 3824

we would not have food for ourselves 10540

When know the Cross, no longer a. of truth 11531

Whenever I look inside myself, I am a. 9957

wicked a. of everything 3996

wicked a. of God's creatures 3996

wicked a. of God, he is enemy 3996

wicked a. of himself, his own executioner 3996

wicked a. of Satan, he is tormentor 3996

Without faith man becomes a. 3824

AFRESH

Fill us a. with hope 5939

whenever in need, God enlightens me a. 5426

With God you can always start a. 8080

AFTER

cannot get behind the a. of death 5459

God comes padding a. me like Hound of Heaven 4534

In eternity there is neither before or a. 11316

Life an event arrive a, depart before 6957

swallowed up in eternity before, a. 4905

swallowed up in the eternity before and a. 7084

the friendship of God 4181

AFTERNOON

do not know what to do on a rainy Sunday a. 6100

How softly runs the a. 9887

AFTERWARDS

only a. we see we had to go that way 5423

AGAIN

Christianity, land of beginning a. 1178

just thou, a. thou, always thou 4518

Love must be learned a. and a. 7265

Why wish for living past life a. 7091

AGAINST

a man convinced a. his will 9179

a tight place and everything goes a. you 236

bad to lean a. falling wall 3380

beating head a. wall 8553

carry on struggle a. evil 3414

Close ear a. him who opens mouth a. another 10447

conservatism of Jesus' times a. him 6452

contend a. giants of passion, pride 9233

deed that harms the poor done a. Christ 8698

Don't pay much attention to who is for, a. you 6260

dunces all in confederacy a. genius 4400

fight a. unbelief, despair 2590

for you today, a. you tomorrow 9521

form invincible host a. difficulty 10829

From hearts that shut a. them with a snap 8694

full knowledge of everything a. us 4884

fury of so many a. Christ proof he is not dead 6362

God cannot be for, a. same thing 4972

God harden me a. myself 2583

God has set a Saviour a. sin 5016

Guard a. grounding commitment on experiences 3550

He who does wrong does wrong a. himself 6262

himself that everybody sins 10325

If find revival not spoken a. 9745

If hug resentment a. anybody 9634

If tiniest grudge in mind a. anyone 9633

if we measure our lives a. eternity 7080

if you do not tell truth, power a. you 11510

invincible weapon a. evils of earth 11841

man who truly repents cries out a. his heart 9601

Men are not a. you 10069

men have perpetrated horrors a. one another 2667

nature fights a. thought of venturing forth 9930

not as ball a. wall to rebound 4222

not necessarily a. reason because above it 7938

nothing can ever come to pass a. our will 9835

O God, stand by me a. all the world 9109

our feelings 8104

our will, comes wisdom 11919

preferable to have world a. thee than Jesus offended 8525

Right is right, even if everyone a. it 1037

Right predominates, nothing prevails a. it 6621

shut door a. earthly noise 10554

sin a. neighbor is sin a. God 7164

soul can rise up a. odds 3621

stand at real height a. higher nature 6037

Strength from struggle a. obstacles 8850

than speak reckless word a. servant of Christ 5143

trying to live serene lives in houses divided a. themselves 6068

we react decisively a. those who take freedom from us 9463

When everything goes a. you 8568 2614

when God sees men rising up a. fellowmen 4895

who doubts bears arms a. himself 11597

Who lies for you will lie a. you 6862

AGE

always the same a. inside 315

arctic loneliness of a. 8165

best improve with a. 7419

best in four things 304

comes without effort 305

defect of a. to rail at pleasures of youth 12189

Forty old a. of youth 307

gives light to every a. 634

God hath not forgotten my a. 8140

How old do you think you'd be 309

important events in every a. 5725

In a. we understand 12191
310
is a quality of mind 8122
isms of youth the wasms of a.
12174
Life happier if born at a. eighty
6989
Live your life, forget your a. 8144
looked upon as sign of favor
12194
looks back 12200
Love makes those young whom a.
doth chill 7264
Morality comes with sad wisdom
of a. 7829
No a. can heap its outward years
on thee 4605
no business to require head of a.
on shoulders of youth 12186
not important unless cheese 8123
Now old man, no one has respect
for a. 12190
now old, no respect for a. 9647
Our a. is but the falling of a leaf
11287
Reading, joy not dulled by a. 858
serenity of a. takes the place of
riotous youth 7101
signs of approaching a. 314
thinks of nothing but health 5619
use fires of youth to drive engines
of a. 11323
ushering in new a, new dimension
of existence 5711
what toil can scarcely reach in an
a. 7223
Youth has to do with spirit, not a.
12198
Youth is youth, a. is a. 12186
Youth not definable by a. 12183

AGED
So is the beauty of an a. face 8125

AGENCIES
Almighty does make use of
human a. 4949
great event touched off by small a.
5720

AGENCY
Jesus didn't commit gospel to
advertising a. 2827

AGENT
If ever the devil had an a. 2447

AGES
cross, breadth to former,
following ages 2154
Hardening of heart a. people more
quickly 6159
principles are for the a. 1009
Rock of A, cleft for me 4636
seven a. of man 7037
through the a. divided over "Who
is Jesus" 6518
world lies down in sepulchre of a.
3266

AGING
With God no a. 11355

AGITATED
music calms the a. heart 7935

AGITATES
Adjusts, sustains, and a. the whole
4711

AGITATIONS
Music can calm a. of the soul
7914

AGNOSTIC'S
prayer: if there is a God 318

AGNOSTICISM
everlasting perhaps 319

AGONIZE
nor a. to find your will 8820

AGONY
Better in bitterest a. to lie 10969
Christ seeking justice for those in
a. 1277
Grief is the a. of an instant 5337
Man's unique a. as a species 7415
Then a. and toil a paradise become
2604

AGREE
Confession, to a. with God
regarding sin 1597
don't like to talk with people who
a. 1851
forgiveness beautiful idea 4104
Hearts may a. though heads differ
9461
If love does not a. with justice,
holiness 4755
If men would consider wherein
they a. 9465
in what they do than think 62
Many a. with God in principle,
not in practice 1336
The devil and me, we don't a.
2671
When you say you a. in principle
2915

AGREEABLE
a thousand thanks when things a.
11157
Flee the wicked, even when they
are a. 11882
Love can make any place a. 7210
most a. of companions is frank
person 4204
person agrees with me 9483

AGREED
Dependability, fulfilling what I a.
to do 2533
If Bible a. with science, would
soon be out of date 9865
owe knowledge not to those who
have a. 6710

AGREEMENT
because of silent a, betrayal and
murder exist 6158
with Christians rather than God
1281

AGREES
agreeable person a. with me 9483

book that a. with our views 11216
where his opinion a. with mine
8204

AGRICULTURE
less would not suffice for a. of
God 5332

AGRIPPA
failed to get grip on situation 786

AHAB
sold himself for a vineyard 11798

AHEAD
better things a. than behind 2293
fear, greed, lust, ambition look a.
8376
gentle come out a. 4402
If you no longer look a. 8122
insistence upon seeing a. natural
3758
man has leaped a. in scientific
achievement 9872
obedience to whatever lies a. 5370
power behind greater than task a.
7878
task a. never as great as Power
behind 3804
with Christ life and warmth of
day a. 7094
Without Christ life as twilight
with night a. 7094

AID
Bible understood only by
supernatural a. 708
give thanks to the Almighty, seek
his a. 5411
In trouble go not out of yourself
for a. 2734
my soul rejects the a. of language
8792
neither can kingdom rise without
his a. 4933
Suffering a. to faith 10896
vanity can give no hollow a.
10530

AIDED
things threatened to extinguish
have a. 730

AIDING
means of a. progress so feeble
5944

AIM
After sanctification difficult to
state a. in life 9830
at heaven and you get earth
thrown in 5630
at perfection in everything 3463
clear in principle and a. 4974
Fanaticism redoubling effort,
forgotten a. 3908
God's a. is production of saints
5757
God's a. looks like missing the
mark 347
If a. to be a servant will never be
frustrated 10160
Not enough to a., hit 83

AIMING

Not failure, but low a. is crime 3610
our only a. God's glory 4507
Peace, sure to miss if a. at directly 8459
Perception of ideas a. of education 3021
plans miscarry because no a. 4433
To follow one a. 10822
useless a. thwarts happiness 4411
When his work is done, his a. fulfilled 6803

AIMING
shooting without a. 1873

AIMLESS
Cain 10573
life, a. comet burning out in self-will 6937

AIMS
must be bathed in new element 880
must be re-born 880
must be reconsecrated to Maker 880
Selfishness a. at absolute uniformity 10079

AIN'T
people know so much that a. so 6083
trouble a. that people ignorant 6083
what we gonna be 9825
what we want to be 9825
what we was 9825

AIR
As on the a. 8878
Before tomorrow the a. may change 7895
Bible, recreating effect like fresh a. 697
breathe not stale a. 4976
breathing new a, finding it celestial a. 2399
Christianity, not idea in a. 1174
corruptions like the a. before the sun shines 9852
do not know how I am going to stay "in the a." 9908
full-blossomed trees filled a. with fragrance, joy 2977
God as present as the a. 4844
gospel like cool a. in heat of summer 5097
Love pressing round us like a. 4785
not sold by cubic foot 3838
shot arrow in a, it stuck 3194
Their fronded palms in a. 4763
troubles, can cure by perspiration, fresh a. 11455
With such a lot of nice fresh a. 8016

ALABASTER
Do not keep a. boxes 4223

ALACRITY
Atheists, false a. 476

ALARM
fear something different than a. 3983
loving any person better than Christ take a. 6925
marriage is the a. clock 7631
realizes God in midst, quiet in midst of a. 3972

ALARMED
though a, love is not confounded 7283
time to be a. is when things undisturbed 7040

ALARMING
to enter upon a strange, a. life 6421

ALARMS
I sink in life's a. 10973

ALAS
if my best Friend 4069
oh, love is dead 7159
our A. please devil 2661

ALBUMS
Our lives are a. written 7017

ALCHEMIST
divine A. can miraculously change 10628

ALCOHOL
drug and a. addicts in America 135
greatest criminal in history 331
turned men into brutes 331

ALCOHOLIC
always tight as a drum 324
never fit as a fiddle 324

ALECK
others think him a fool 450
smart a. knows everything 450

ALERT
nothing more wonderful than a, eager mind 7776

ALEXANDER THE GREAT
founded empires upon force 6351
Jesus conquered more millions than A. 6449
more evidence Jesus rose than A. died 9700

ALIBI
dictatorship not a. for conscience 1689
proof that you did do 3473

ALIENATES
difference of opinion a. little minds 11392

ALIENATION
Christ went to cross to avert 4781
church trapped by a. 1460
man pushes into self-chosen a. 4781
Punishment sharpens a. 2038

ALIENS
cannot forget true homeland 2975

ALIGHT
sit down quietly, happiness may a. upon you 5518

ALIGNING
Trinity with bone 6131

ALIKE
all men a. 921
And meet them all a. 9655
Are fingers of your hand all a. 6166
esteem more highly those who think a. 3032
God never made two people exactly a. 6191
insist all look, talk act a. 6824
We are all a. on the inside 5985
Where all think a. 11279

ALIVE
best proof Christ risen is he is still a. 9695
Bible is a. 712
bury problem a. 9291
Christ a. as Christians love one another 9695
emotions remain a. in subconscious 3061
flesh very much a. 9861
funny old world, man's lucky if gets out a. 6936
glory of God is man fully a. 4566
God is a. 8817
Keep effort a. 8546
loneliness by the sea personal, a. 7145
long past usual date of disintegration 8139
loved by mother means to be a. 7853
No church thrives unless differences a. 1411
sin remains a. because there is nothing for which it will die 11394
When life's a. in everything 9899
worries eat you when you're a. 12084

ALL
And having nothing, yet hath a. 9959
Be courteous to a. 4218
But 'tis enough that Christ knows a. 5635
can have it a. on the wire called Jesus Christ 6521
charity, to do a, a. that we can 7320
Christ Lord of a, or not Lord at a. 6437
comes to him who knows how to wait 8391
Each more precious than a. 6200
easier for me to give thee a. 7125
Faithfulness is a. 3845
for one, one for a. 11621
God will have a, or none 4920
good lives on, loves on, conquers a. 11129

gossip speaks ill of a. and a. of her 5113

Grasp a, lose a. 5314

have lost a. and found myself 9559

have propensity to grasp at forbidden fruit 11112

He who insists having a. will give up a. 5315

heart that finds joy in a. things 6524

If a. experience God same way 6169

in a. things, charity 7196

information is imperfect 6706

injury to one concern of a. 6603

insist a. look, talk, act alike 6824

is well, tho faith and form 3644

Jesus does it a, I do nothing 5426

Know a, you will pardon a. 4092

Lord wants a. of my life 9561

mankind of one Author 5966

men desire peace 8428

men would lead happy life 4227

My wisdom and my a. 5456

No man gives at all until he has given a. 10119

not complete if a. not given to God 5734

of life is a war 6874

passes, nothing lasts 11288

Please a, please none 1583

Soul lost, a. lost 9263

Truth is cry of a. 11571

truth to love, a. wrong to hate 7986

We a. find time to do what we want to do 11348

We are a. alike on the inside 5985

We are a. beggars, each in his own way 5986

When character is lost, a. is lost 1066

Who has God, has a. 4519

ALL-ABOUNDING
Fountain of life, a. grace 4836

ALL-CONSUMING
desire to be filled with Spirit must be a. 5772

ALLEGIANCE
to one set of principles, live by another 6068

ALLELUJAHS
In panegyric A. 8749

ALL-EMBRACING
Great little one! whose a. birth 6153

Spirit of God will enfold you in a love so a. 5776

ALLEVIATE
quickly find something else to a. thirst 7538

ALLIANCE
endurance show a. with God 3150

of error, truth obtain extensive circulation 3254

ALLIES
Neutral men are devil's a. 8071

ALL-IMPORTANT
speaking truth in love a. 9158

ALL-KNOWING
thou mighty River, a, all-seeing 7492

ALLOT
If you a. your day 11370

ALLOTS
God a. our work where he chooses 2831

ALLOTTED
brief instant of time a. to yourself 7063

By whose direction this place, time been a. 4905

ALLOW
as easy for God not to a. 4831

God does a. bad men to triumph 4957

God does a. sin 4957

God does a. the devil 4957

God does a. tyrants to rule 4957

God does not a. us to make the rules 7828

God would not a. evil to be 4831

life of Jesus to be manifested 4539

Spirit of God will not a. you to boast 5757

than we a. Christ to get into us 6502

to a. pain to corrode your spirit is to have chosen 8264

tragedies a. hearts to shrink until 5625

whatever God may a, soul should embrace 4978

ALLOWANCE
Set a. against loss 1776

ALLOWANCES
Unless a. for friend's foibles 4294

ALLOWED
Children like clocks must be a. to run 1108

he's a. me to go up to the mountain 4975

no room a. for mysticism pure and simple 7959

ALLOWING
too many rivals of God 9552

ALLOWS
circumstances to bludgeon him 3830

God a. man insolently to deny him 4673

God a. man to cut throat of his fellowmen 4673

God a. men to live without him 1142

God a. us to play the game 7828

God rarely a. soul to see blessing he is 6233

our judgment to mislead us 9851

our own schemes to fail 9851

supernatural love a. you to love enemy 7340

who a. the oppression shares the crime 5962

ALL-POWERFUL
attach feeble will to a. will 9835

If truth be mighty and God a. 4134

ALL-SEARCHING
O Thou, to whose a. sight 4140

ALL-SEEING
thou mighty River, all-knowing, a. 7492

ALL-WISE
no idea by which a. God perceives 4986

ALMIGHTY
appeared on earth as helpless human baby 6125

directly intervenes in human affairs 4949

does make use of human agencies 4949

does nothing without reason 4492 3781

give thanks to the A, seek his aid 5411

has his own purposes 4950

is working on a great scale 8419

Kept by A. power 4490

moment we forget he is A. 4830

needing to be fed, changed, taught to talk 6125

the A. finds a way of letting me know 5410

to a. power no more difficult to make one than the other 7940

unable to do more than lie, stare, wriggle, make noises 6125

Who is mightier than the A. 4955

will not be hustled by peevish impetuosity 8419

ALMS
money put to interest in other world 11359

never make poor 4350

ALMSHOUSE
sun reflected from windows of a. 7001

ALOFT
Bible, rising a. into mysteries of heaven 750

on sky and mountain wall 8047

ALONE
a denier of God 483

acted right, has done well, though a. 5032

And looks to that a. 3717

as if you a. had done the wrong 9672

Being a. and resting is Christlike 9533

Being a. and resting not selfish 9533

can dare to live a. 4286
can scale hardest peaks a. 1927
Christ's method of better world a.
  succeeds 6487
developed phobia of being a.
  10575
Do not believe you a. can be right
  8196
don't be a. in hurt 1516
easier to suffer with others than a.
  10859
emerging will never walk a. 10567
enter world a, leave it a. 10574
Every man must do two things a.
  2280
Faith does nothing a. 3660
faith never found a. 3809
For to be a. in silence 10256
Free of family, Jesus remained a.
  6508
God a. knows all the facts 7828
God a. knows secret of history
  4694
God's ideals, hopes, doings made
  known 10532
God's real greatness known to
  himself a. 4665
I a. am responsible for wrong I do
  9661
I cannot face it all a. 5413
I weep for what I'm like when a.
  10538
if longing heart finds living water,
  will be a. 10536
If never a. with God 7482
In God a. can man meet man
  9429
In solitude, when we are least a.
  10541
in the crowds feel frightfully a.
  7124
Inside myself place where I live all
  a. 9933
Is to be a. with God 10256
know we are not a. 10539
know why man a. laughs 6742
knowledge that we are never a.
  4863
known most certainly I was not a.
  8051
least lonely when most a. 10568
Leave scandal a. never touch it
  5154
Let him not in community beware
  of being a. 10547
Let him who cannot be a. beware
  of community 10547
liberty to know that God a.
  matters 4151
loneliness, pain of being a. 7131
Look right, left, I dwell a. 2587
Man a. can smile, laugh 6737
Man a. has capacity to walk, talk
  with God 7497
man hates to stand a. in opinions
  1639
man likes to go a. for walk 1639
Man shall enjoy God a. 9481

man with his God must strive
  10530
more a. while living than going,
  coming 7151
no feeling exists in that heart a.
  4019
None goes his way a. 919
One can endure sorrow a. 10607
people do not want to be a. with
  God 10536
People who cannot be a. worst
  company 10552
prefer trivial company to being a.
  10575
Self-respect comes when we are a.
  9995
Silence a. is great enough to hold
  10274
sit a. with conscience judgment
  enough 1707
solitude, glory of being a. 7131
strongest man is he who stands
  most a. 10759
teachings of Christ a. can solve
  difficulties 6487
than go a. in the light 5419
To be a. fate of all great minds
  10571
to sit a. with my conscience 1663
We live as we dream, a. 7079
what is hid with God made known
  10532
will not fear being a. 10539
will soon find himself a. 4249
You come into world a. 7151
you go out of world a. 7151

ALONENESS
need to leave prison of his a. 7143
of Jesus stands out most 6508
Practice art of a. 10553

ALOOF
Christ was not a. 6436
from curious eyes of reason 4743

ALOUD
friend with whom I may think a.
  4165

ALPHABET
accidental jumbling of a. 1989
of love avowals and consents
  7297

ALTAR
let your knee be a sacred a. 7847
Who sprinkles the a. he rears to
  thee 3369
women last at the cross, first at
  the a. 11980
Worship is man climbing a. stairs
  to God 12132

ALTER
Christ came to a. disposition 6424
God will a. in two seconds 238
home where man can a.
  arrangements 5842
no slander can a. man's character
  1060
People can a. attitudes 510

To repent is to a. way of looking
  at life 9605

ALTERATION
Time dressmaker specializing in a.
  11335

ALTERED
Revivals a. hearts of men 9752
When feelings conceited, ask to
  have a. 4013
When feelings cowardly, ask to
  have a. 4013
When feelings selfish, ask to have
  a. 4013
within zone of God's voice,
  profoundly a. 7540

ALTERING
Death power of a. desires 2240

ALTERNATION
condition of saint admits no a.
  4626

ALTERNATIVE
no significance to love with no a.
  1141
Old age isn't bad when consider a.
  8160
to eternal life is eternal
  punishment 3286
to wrath is neutrality 4999
to wrath of God not love 4999

ALTERNATIVES
right to create a. of choice 4155

ALTERS
God a. the inevitable 4937
God a. the mainspring 8570
God a. the things that matter
  9276
God a. things while we wait 8395
man who never a. opinion like
  standing water 9185
Repentance a. the entire life-style
  9589
Spirit of God a. my dominating
  desires 9276

ALTHOUGH
We love someone a. 7333

ALWAYS
able to discover own darkness
  6004
amid change, things we can a.
  count on 4643
Anything the devil does is a. done
  well 2640
Candor a. double-edged sword
  5869
cannot a. understand ways of God
  4688
Christ Jesus a. found among
  humble people 5992
Defeat school in which truth a.
  grows strong 2507
devil a. leaves stink behind him
  2670
do right 3429
Faith should a. be simple,
  unbending 7168

3839
Falsehood is a. first 6865
find God present 4845
finds time to attend his funeral
5589
found praying difficult 8821
God a. at hand 4621
God a. preserving beauty of his
order 4644
God doesn't a. smooth the path
4808
God has not a. answered my
prayers 8797
God is a. on time 4456
God is a. there first 7461
Grass a. greener in next lawn
2873
Great spirits have a. encountered
opposition 5282
Great works do not a. lie in our
way 5068
heart that loves is a. young 7302
hope I shall a. possess virtue
enough 5881
How haphazard God seems a.
4674
if decisions wrong, God will a.
check 5464
If have love, you a. have
something to give 7189
Just thou, again thou, a. thou
4518
laugh when you can 6716
Life with Christ not a. easy 6987
live for others 5066
live up a. to best, highest 3468
mistakes, a. another chance 3598
Morality a. higher than law 7831
never arrive, a. on the way 7035
once burnt mouth a. blows soup
3536
plenty of seats available in subway
7049
poorest man a. wanting more
2874
Promised Land a. lies on other
side of wilderness 5669
realize God had a. been speaking
5395
result a. in God's hands 4945
springtime in heart that loves God
4797
Successful marriage a. a triangle
7653
sufficient will a. sufficient means
7869
think last opinion right 8203
Those who wish to sing a. find a
song 5264
Tis a. morning somewhere 5902
traffic a. moves faster in next lane
2873
True love a. costly 7328
Truth a. the strongest argument
11563
Warmth a. stronger than force,
fury 4296
Weeds a. flourish 3417

While time lasts will a. be a future
4335
wicked a. outnumber the good
5182
wind of God a. blowing but must
hoist sail 5452
wrong way a. seems more
reasonable 5453

AM
Lord, teach me what I a. in thy
sight 9081
To be another than I a. must
abandon that I a. 9848

AMATEUR
hurry, impatience are marks of the
a. 6113
unless a. gardener 1727

AMAZED
at folk drinking gospel in 9544
more I study nature, more a. at
Creator 8040
to realize all packed into one day
8090

AMAZEMENT
Poetry language in which man
explores a. 8618

AMAZING
body, a. example of teamwork
846
church should be a. people 1392
Death a. power of altering desires
2240
wealth of the Bible 694

AMAZINGLY
all a. know their path 7945

AMBASSADOR
tongue a. of the heart 11416

AMBIGUITIES
life with all its tragedies, a. 3685

AMBIGUITY
obedient to God, no a. in you
10278

AMBIGUOUS
Words seem so a. 7934

AMBITION
before which every a. is folly 6494
can drive you into work 2862
cannot be everything 352
destroys its possessor 339
Discontent follows a. like shadow
2863
enemy to peace 8435
fling away a. 346
forgo a. when end is gained 3153
grand enemy of peace 342
greed for power 340
hindering the gospel 349
I had a, by which sin 5694
if doesn't try to get money, lacks a.
7800
if full of a. no room for Spirit of
God 5783
is ruthless 341
looks ahead 8376

never satisfied 345
Quotations tell of a. 9385
to become a foreman 343
wants infused into us by a. 2861
when goads of a. lifted 6842
work one's self to death 344

AMBITIONS
All a. lawful except 338
atheist, bedlam of a. 493
troubled with great a. 348
when personal a. are at stake
5467

AMBITIONS'
If your a. fires are dead 8122

AMBITIOUS
devil entangles a. with power
2677
man a. to lead disqualified as
leader 6794
too a. in my deed 1802

AMBITIOUSLY
who a. seek after world while
living 2344

AMEN
cannot say a. if 8818
Like the sound of a great A. 7919

AMENITIES
shallow a. of life ordained by God
7038

AMERICA
everyone can become taxpayer
7983
has more things than any other
nation 8624
impresses me about A. is parents
obey children 8357
land of opportunity 7983
more books on how to find
happiness 8624
no culture so obsessed with
immediacy 7990
television holding A. together
11043

AMERICAN
God acknowledged with one
heart, voice by the A. people
11176
missing in A. life 7990
pioneers endured hardships 3147

AMERICANS
millions are clever, fearless 1130
so tense impossible to put to sleep
with sermon 10096

AMERICA'S
future determined by home, school
5818

AMIABLE
life with our family more a. 7611
O a. lovely death 2269

AMISS
If the way be straight, cannot go a.
5471
Self-love lessens everything a. in
ourselves 10025

Self-love magnifies everything a.
in others 10025
Undo that which we have done a.
9054

AMMUNITIONS
Satan wastes no a. on those dead
in sins 9860

AMONG
secret a. three is everybody's secret
5115
so many, can God care 4834

AMOUNT
rewards depend on a. of
contributions we make 10179

AMPLE
one day will have a. explanation
7060

AMPUTEES
Our Father yet heals spirit of a.
5614

AMUSEMENTS
tell God that you prefer vilest a.
8830

AMUSING
do not find vanishing acts a. 2303
terribly a. how many different
climates of feelings 4014
to coquette with echo, but tiring
1851

ANALYSIS
of conscience has taken place of
childlike simplicity 6813

ANALYZE
Love does not a. its object 7214

ANALYZED
God doesn't care about being a.
4447
story of Jesus a. more than any
other in history 5729

ANANIAS
as he did in days of A, Sapphira
4717

ANATHEMAS
Conscience priest in its a. 1673

ANATOMY
study a, never be an atheist 1983

ANCESTOR
miser makes a wonderful a. 11805

ANCHOR
better a. near shallow shore of
security 11598
Better lose a. than whole ship
9555
Consistency, a. worth weighing
1749
hope is the Christian's a. 5638
steadfast as an a. 4204

ANCIENT
Beauty of a. days, yet ever new
4805
happy man confines himself
within a. limits 2875

heavens through thee fresh, strong
4598
O Beauty so a. and new 7473
people from a. times speak today
9385
reached *w* of *now n* is a. history
11291
Still stands the a. sacrifice 6036
than great men of a. and modern
times 6449

ANCIENT OF DAYS
except thou deign 47

ANDERSON
discrimination and Marian A. 161

ANESTHETIC
God doesn't use a. 890

ANEW
Springtime invites you to believe a.
9896

ANGEL
a spiritual creature 354
Be you our a. unawares 1396
by every man as he is born 366
God would never have created a.
5020
had the a. gone to the elite 6147
had the a. gone to the successful
6147
Had the a. gone to the theologians
6147
Himself, his Maker, and the a.
Death 4209
keeps time with applauding wings
463
Man not an a. whose reason
works perfectly 9417
My wife is an a. 7649
not possible for a. of heaven
11722
one to occupy a throne 3232
simple shepherds heard a. 1373
some a. and some God in man
5013
stands an a. by every man 366
the falling tears of an a. 365
the other to clean a road 3232
this a. unique 4993
Though a. on the outward side
2470
to guide through life 366
to struggle all night with the a.
9777
went to the shepherds 6147
without a body 354
you are human, not an a. 11722

ANGEL OF DEATH
abroad throughout the land 2371
hear the beating of his wings 2371

ANGEL'S
Kind words some a. song that lost
its way 6645
Than spheres, or a. praises be
8749

ANGELIC
host described in Scripture 359
love for sake of loving is a. 7325

Of elements and an a. sprite 7384

ANGELIC GLORY
Christians should never fail to
sense 360

ANGELS
are waiting for me 2445
are winds 359
ask nothing more to make them
satisfied 4995
At our repentance, a. rejoice 1285
bar entrance to Eden 359
bright still, though brightest fell
355
by that sin fell the a. 346
cannot preach the gospel 3296
Could not hear the a. sing 2217
desire of power in excess caused
a. to fall 3556
direct our ways 363
dispensers and administrators 363
don't sing to sheep 6147
dressed in white 359
earth to sun what man is to a. 364
eclipses demonic powers 360
even the a. help me 9066
evil tugging to make us animals,
not a. 3406
exercise a constant solicitude 363
flames of fire 359
Funeral among men, wedding
feast among a. 2205
gift of thought giving as a. give
11225
giving as the a. give 4189
guard you when you walk 356
Guardian a. God will lend thee
1123
had already drawn their swords
6418
heaven's spectators 2359
holiness, shares with a, redeemed
men 4658
Holy a. guard thy bed 361
humility makes men as a. 6020
joyful to attend 2221
listen for your songs 8725
love kept Jesus from calling a. to
his rescue 6418
man who lives on better terms
with a. 3899
messengers of God 359
might be asked to stay with us
5862
Music language spoken by a. 7907
not always gentle 359
not find themselves out of their
element 5862
of God upturned the sod 778
one of your a. is missing 7852
Painting enables us to see beauty
of a. 2015
pride changed a. into devils 6020
radiant power takes us by surprise
359
regard our safety 363
see only the light 357
send plagues upon Egyptians 359
send two a. to earth 3232

stars, the forget-me-nots of the a. 11636
such sight a. behold 4995
support us 2359
Thank God not a. 839
The a. fell 5694
the Messengers of God 358
thousand legions of a. would leap to do his will 12099
throng about saying "A man is born" 2408
training thee for part a. cannot sing 10600
turn the pages of our years 7017
Unbelief where no a. ascend, descend 11595
undertake our defense 363
When a. come, devils leave 367
where a. fear to tread 4060
where only God and his a. have charge 10486
wild and radiant power 359
with mighty battalions of a. 6503

ANGER
a virtue 4722
an expensive luxury 370
at God to be troubled for what is past 12066
believe in loving a. of God 4997
cannot speak against Christianity without a. 1185
continuance of a. is hatred 396
Do not that which would a. you 376
Don't fly into a rage 377
dying Jesus evidence of God's a. toward sin 6473
enemy to peace 8435
enters, wisdom departs 405
Even God attributes to himself a. 4722
expect rough sailing 382
Forgiveness saves expense of a. 4089
God feels a. 4491
greed and a, brother and sister of false self 10003
Hatred and a. powerless when met with kindness 6639
Heat not so hot a furnace 383
Hitting the ceiling worst way 384
Hot heads never solved anything 385
in a. do not answer a letter 11920
in heart, murder not far off 406
in right way not easy 373
in right way not within everybody's power 373
is a weed 371
is raging 389
kicks up a storm 382
like city without defenses 368
mere fleabites in comparison with pride 9240
natural reaction to critical word 10003
one letter short of danger 375
prepare for rough landing 377
quieted by gentle word 372

remedy for a. is delay 397
right for God to display a. against sin 4729
sacrifice of praise requires trading in a. 8724
seducer of thought 400
the dust is blown high 389
think of a. as sin 401
to hear truth about yourself, a. your neighbor 8058
trivial indulgence in a. 5021
voice of intelligence extinguished by a. 6331
When a. enters the mind 405
When a. in Cain's heart, murder not far off 10383
When a. was in Cain's heart 406
who shall put out the flame 389

ANGLE
genius sees world at different a. 4389

ANGLER
caught a fish so big 3424

ANGLO-SAXON
Jesus comes across as A, Protestant Republican 6467

ANGRY
Anybody can become a. 373
at the right time 373
be a. and sin not 381
Be not a. others not as you wish 993
become a. is easy 373
best fighter never a. 11784
best speech you will ever regret 395
count down before blasting off 407
don't get a. at person who displease 378
easier to swallow than eat a. words 388
for I had no shoes 387
for the right purpose 373
gentleness, soothing effect on those a. 4402
God is not a. but disciplines us 2844
God purely, perfectly a. with sin 401
I need not be a. with him 9579
I was a. with my foe 386
I was a. with my friend 386
in the right way 373
Kind words soften a. hearts of men 6645
live with hostility, learn to be a. 1114
man a. cannot be in right 394
man opens his mouth 369
man shuts his eyes 369
man within is a. 1706
never at what he can help 404
never at what he cannot help 404
not be a. with anything but sin 381

not just refrain from killing, but from being a. 6444
see the wounded and a. 7300
sometimes sinful not to be a. 401
take a lesson from technology 407
Thou art a, yet serene 4954
to the right degree 373
When a, I can write, pray and preach well 408
When a. my understanding is sharpened 408
who repents is a. with himself 9579
with God for creating world 481
with God for not existing 481
with the right person 373
would be far less a. feeling in world 9465

ANGUISH
could only raise my mind in a. to God 10931
God is a specialist when a. deep 10845
gospel like comfort in a. of conscience 5097
In all thy a. lay 6878
man to make his way best he can in a. 3495
no great a. on its heart 1441
nothing else but love 7329
occasions for a. often leave us calm 3056
on that wood in love, a. placed his Son 2173
to have a, still perform daily tasks 8423
Who see the world's great a. 426

ANIMAL
Man by origin is a herd a. 6199
man descended from inferior a. 1992
Man only a. of which I am afraid 7410
Man the only a. that blushes 7411
To get good is a. 5085

ANIMALS
evil tugging to make us a, not angels 3406
Human beings wild a. when born 7382
If human beings as wise as a. 5963
Men are the only a. 31
Men are very queer a. 7420
Noah rounded up all the a. 781

ANIMATED
men a. by love of Christ feel united 3081

ANIMATES
Christ a. all life, history 6369
Hope a. man to do his utmost 5917

ANIMOSITIES
in touch with people through our a. 7428

ANIMOSITY
cloaked in piety is a demon 9631

ANNIHILATED

must the soul lie almost a. 10649
Self is not to be a. 9942

ANNIVERSARIES

secret a. of the heart 7720

ANNOTATED

Bible, annotated by God's Spirit
706

ANNOUNCEMENT

gospel is an a. 5098

ANNOY

little things that a. us 9636

ANNOYANCE

of good example 3433

ANOTHER

Agape love profound concern for
a. 7158
allegiance to one set of principles,
live by a. 6068
appreciating what is noble, loving
in a. 4220
beside me sits a. 6398
Beware of discernment of a. 2804
bitter to look into happiness
through a. man's eyes 3220
catches flies 6205
climbs highest who helps a. up
3134
delusion that one person can
make a. happy 5549
do will of a. rather than thine own
8448
does good to a. does good to
himself 4362
enjoy life without comparing to a.
1787
giving a. privilege of sharing 4277
God has one plan, man a. 4563
God rejoices when one beggar
scratches a. 9454
greatest desire to please God,
serve one a. 6924
Humanity beautiful when
forgiving a. 4086
If any little lift ease burden of a.
910
If you love good in a. 564
in this life as in a. man's house
7077
likely to believe worst about a.
3412
Love greatest gift person can give
a. 7249
more power in silence than a. has
by words 3428
no human being can be
permanent source of happiness
to a. 9481
No man should become that of a.
6201
people who strengthen one a.
4241
pray for a, will be helped yourself
8838
thing to go through every day
glorifying God 7129
To be a. than I am 9848

We turn to meet a. year 8082

ANOTHER'S

can't get warm on a. fur coat 6782
forfeits own blood that spills a.
7881
highest privilege to share a. pain
4276
hold torch to light a. path 3145
Kindness in a. trouble 6657
Let it wipe a. tears 6640
No one knows what is taking
place in a. kingdom 6171
One man's music, a. noise 7918
seeks applause has happiness in a.
keeping 5892
Teach me to feel a. woe 1552
those who carry burden of a. sin
as their own 5029
to cast comforting shadow across
a. life 7714

ANSWER

best a. to misrepresentation 9677
bird doesn't sing because has a.
7883
can find no a, will find fear 4008
Christ gave no a, neither can you
10917
Christ's a. to legalism 6811
Church, do not have to a. back
1389
Clearly dost thou a, though all do
not clearly hear 5381
doesn't mean we've received final
a. 5439
Don't expect thousand-dollar a. to
ten-cent prayer 8783
fathomless a, the cross of Christ
9398
fool has a. on edge of tongue 4067
God does not always a. prayers as
we request 8882
Here is the a. to your puzzle 9922
His only a. was a blameless life
6356
If God were to a. dogs' prayers
8831
in anger do not a. a letter 11920
let miraculous deliverance from
furnace a. 5197
more glory to God when a. comes
9028
Never try to forecast way God is
going to a. prayer 8873
no a. when world's satire turned
on you 10917
not a. that enlightens but the
question 9365
not at home 8136
not every question deserves an a.
9364
Not to a, one kind of a. 1864
senators do not know whether to
a. present or not guilty 5198
some expect God's instant a. 693
Some expect thousand-dollar a. to
one-minute prayer 8963
Sometimes God delays a. to our
prayer 8924

Till every note and string shall a.
thine 7527
to prayer may let us in for more
than we ask 8850
To question knowing never can
full a. be found 7435
to suffer as a Christian is to have
no a. 10917
what dusty a. gets soul 946
Yes, Lord, my a. still shall be 1538
You a. only for yourself 74
You do not a. for others 74

ANSWERED

Faith a. No one was there 3968
God has not always a. my prayers
8797
his prayer is a. 9034
lived to thank God all my prayers
not a. 8823
never notice prayers are not a.
9019
not remotest expectation prayers
will be a. 8845
prayers never a. on golf course
8986
serious thing is that prayer may be
a. 8850
Slander a. best with silence 10464
triumphantly by the cabbage 8580
what crises would face you if your
prayers a. 8891

ANSWERING

God's way of a. the Christian's
prayer 8804

ANSWERS

be thankful God's a. are wiser
than your prayers 8861
better to ask some questions than
know all a. 6688
beyond your comprehension 39
Christian do not have all a. 1268
God always a. us in the deeps
8795
God never a. the why 167
Heaven where questions and a.
become one 5647
Holy Spirit expects us to take
seriously a. provided 5445
Life a test that has more questions
than a. 6953
questions to which I had a. not
important questions 9366
sign of strength to admit don't
know a. 10748
this I know God a. prayer 8825
to these questions 39
was a time when I had all the a.
9366

ANT

every insect and a. so amazingly
know their path 7945
God hears the footsteps of an a.
4697
is praised 112
its labor has begun 8039
None preaches better than a. 3447

What would a. do if had head of
bull 6221
witness to mystery of God 7945

ANTAGONISM
Holiness only manifested by a.
5740

ANTAGONIST
Heat not so hot a furnace for a.
383
Our a. is our helper 1623

ANTEDATES
Whose position a. that of the
Eternal 4955

ANTHEMS
Rise with its a. to holier sphere
10960

ANTHOLOGY
an a. says thank you 9381
compiling a. act of thanksgiving
9381
handful of sand a. of universe
11625

ANTI-CHRIST
Motives, forces behind racism
1488

ANTICIPATE
Do not a. trouble 3500
future with transcendental senses
4329
look into future and a. more
trouble 11450
only God could a. every situation
5438

ANTICIPATED
Hopelessness is a. defeat 5951

ANTICIPATES
hope a. promise 9322

ANTICIPATING
people who are always a. trouble
12079

ANTICIPATION
Conscience an a. of the opinion of
others 1675
If pleasures greatest in a. 8598
more delightful than realization
7160
trouble greatest in a. 8598
unexpected gives a. surprise 4318

ANTICLIMAX
life of Jesus Christ a. of failure
10813

ANTI-GOD
man's right to happiness a. 5553
Pride the complete a. state of mind
9240

ANTI-INTELLECTUAL
Faith not a. 3690

ANTI-INTELLECTUALISM
By our a. may be storing up
judgment of God 6679
danger of Christianity 3027

ANTISEPTIC
Faith is a. of the soul 3694

ANTISOCIAL
Grief a very a. state 5335

ANTITHEISTS
a whirl of contradictions 481
angry with God 481
maintain God did not exist 481

ANTITHESIS
self-loving spirit a. of real living
10053

ANTITHETICAL
history enriched by a. elements
5020

ANTONIO
could not make violins without A.
4441

ANTS
Cheerios: hula-hoops for a. 8650
If a. so busy, how attend picnics
9266
not enough to be busy; so are a.
116

ANVIL
always on the a. 228
Forge thy tongue on a. of truth
11503
God's a. stands 7875
hammer out convictions on a. of
relationships 5832
on the a. of everyday living 3863
When you are the a, bear 9655

ANXIETIES
success, a. engendered relentless
10817

ANXIETY
a channel into which all thoughts
are drained 410
a pain 411
a weakness 411
beginning of a. end of faith 424
beginning of faith, end of a. 424
cannot remove by arguing 423
desire that things happen as we
wish 414
diligent without a. 9041
does not empty tomorrow of its
sorrows 409
empties today of its strength 409
fear trickling through the mind
410
has its use 3961
interest paid on trouble 412
Make my heart sit down 419
Man's world, encompassed by a.
420
memorizing Scripture help in a.
747
nothing else but love 7329
Patience, waiting without a. 8414
restless a. not crosses from God
4322
sand in machinery of life 3731
scoured off by oil of mirth 6738

so many jobs to be done in a short
time 8424
stimulating us to seek 3961
thin stream of fear 410
Thou art jealous, without a. 4954
when hopes centered short of God
and his will 412
yesterday's worry and tomorrow's
a. 12092

ANXIOUS
always a. to know what is
expected 6810
become a. about what others say
6824
if too a. about each day's affairs
8818
or troubled, when with us is
prayer 8867
spare a. hearts a needless care
8098

ANXIOUSLY
memorize the script assigned to us
6824

ANYBODY
as good as a. if had equal chance
3228
earth too wonderful for a. to
realize 2974
God will never send a. to hell
5686

ANYONE
can build a house 5819
happier because you passed his
way 3136
Jesus wasn't afraid to associate
with a. 4253
Never hold a. by the button 1862
pushes you nearer to God is friend
4190
remember you spoke to him today
3136
save Jesus only in your cloud 2562
when a. is nothing 3604
who keeps ability to see beauty
never grows old 12182
who stops learning is old 2995
with heart of friendship 4216

ANYTHING
Be able to smile at a. 6961
course of true a. never runs smooth
2747
do not know one millionth of one
percent about a. 6709
In a. great, small, large, petty
never give in 8546
need others if we are to know a.
9513
Scarce a. about us is as it seems
9623
Thankful for a. 8775
that cramps my prayer life 7036
that dims my vision of Christ
7036
that makes Christian work
difficult 7036
that takes away my taste for Bible
study 7036

the devil does is always done well 2640

took God years to teach me to say "Lord a." 4892

we shall fall for a. 11731

You cannot be a. 352

You have capacity for a. 3039

ANYTHINGARIAN
he is an a. 9553

ANYTIME
What may be done at a. will be done at no time 9304

ANYWHERE
I will go a. provided forward 2628

with Christ a. 3822

Worry doesn't get you a. 12088

APART
from Christ, life broken pillar 1163

God cannot give happiness a. from himself 5510

holiest of all holidays in silence and a. 7720

hopelessly strive to invent happiness a. from God 5570

Jesus blew everything a. 4136

Love puts the sad in a. 7269

Man's love is of man's life a thing a. 7278

may just plain come a. 9532

must not tear close-shut leaves a. 5403

spirit not a thing a. 10697

With doctrine world taken a, put together 11213

APARTNESS
God made our a. from himself 6177

APATHETIC
Christians a. when loads to lift 3339

mourn the a. throng 426

APATHY
immediate neighbors of tolerance 11400

no transforming of a. into movement without emotion 3053

Where a. is master, all men slaves 427

APERTURE
Christ the a. through which God can be seen 6373

APHORISMS
only way to read book of a. 9387

APOLOGETIC
about gospel, never 5092

APOLOGIES
Right actions best a. for wrong actions 9598

APOLOGY
after doing wrong thing 428

saying right thing 428

APOSTASY
indicative of a. 12194

APOSTLES
Bible, congregation of a. 716

Children are God's a. 1107

No person more skeptical of resurrection than a. 9693

Saints, a, prophets, martyrs 6892

APOTHEGMS
form shortcut to much knowledge 9378

APOTHEOSIS
of cross, beatification of martyrdom 2118

of cross, death of death 2118

of cross, defeat of sin 2118

of cross, defiance of pain 2118

of cross, voluntary sacrifice 2118

APPALLING
number of half-done things 9300

Regret an a. waste of energy 9440 5486

silence of good people 6285

APPEAL
Being ceased to have a. 1753

Where is the greater one to whom God must a. 4955

APPEALING
being dead, an a. prospect 2300

Music weapon used to make perverse a. 7910

APPEAR
hope day at hand when advent of God will a. 9909

human soul, life will a. simple 10653

immense a. sins we have not committed 10316

make one that which we are, that which we a. to be 6296

make things a. what they are not 2465

Most fervent believer may a. paradoxical 8569

things a. little in comparison with eternal realities 4559

To judge wisely must know how things a. to unwise 6595

APPEARANCE
serious look, may be divine peace and joy 431

takes energy to maintain a. of greatness 433

APPEARANCES
Do not judge men by a. 431

APPEARS
as if God were unnatural 896

Happiness vanishes when envy a. 3218

man a. consummate ass 482

Prepare the way! A God, a God a. 6138

sun a. as setting but is rising 2350

teaching of Christ at first a. lukewarm 6486

tomb a. as prison, but is release for soul 2350

When a true genius a. in world 4400

world a. very little 4707

APPEASE
trying to a. dies in sadness 1581

APPENDAGE
belief in resurrection not a. to faith 9696

APPETITE
Envy never ceasing in a. 3211

Money brings food, but not a. 7807

more a. than dinners 10523

more dinners than a. 10523

puts educator inside so a. for learning persists 3031

Rules blunt a. for Christ 6819

APPETITES
Riches enlarge rather than satisfy a. 11846

When a. darkened 2565

APPLAUD
Beware when enemies a. 3158

APPLAUSE
harder to avoid censure than gain a. 2066

not tricked by desire for a. 836

seeks a. has happiness in another's keeping 5892

to win a. accommodates himself to others 1585

vain man wants to win a. 9189

APPLE
Adam ate a. because forbidden 761

Adam ate the a. 8253

Dear as the a. of thine eye 1395

is eaten, core sticks in throat 10385

Luther threw a. of discord 1625

rotten a. spoils his companions 9500

The a. pressed 11113

wasn't a. that started trouble 762

APPLES
bad tree does not yield good a. 986

APPLIED
Faith something to be a. 3679

APPLIES
Evangelism a. supernatural remedy 3304

soul never a. itself simply 10660

APPLY
Bible principles to society 2523

goodly a. rotten at the heart 5011

imagine God having to a. to higher body 4955

Measurements cannot a. to God 4710

ten pounds of common sense to a. learning 11934

test of universality 2494

APPLYING
shows Christ a. to us 3333

APPOINTED
Like pilgrims to th' a. place 2330
things move along an a. path 9173

APPOINTMENT
God will launch you to place of
his a. 5430
Have an a. with the Lord and
keep it 8785
people there by divine a. 3316
Unfaithfulness in keeping a.
dishonesty 2914

APPOINTS
ask to keep you ready to do as he
a. 10120
do with cheerful heart the work
God a. 10150

APPRECIATE
and accept fact everyone different
6180
destitute to fully a. grace of God
2605
God's point of view by long
discipline 2846
live with praise, learn to a. 1114
make us, O God, a. our privileges
9085
members of family for who they
are 6168
must a. failure to a. success 3637
the more grief better fitted to a. joy
5357
weaknesses make us a. God's
strength 11790

APPRECIATED
craving to be a. 440
deepest craving to be a. 3141
prayer only a. when spend time in
it 8865

APPRECIATING
what is noble, loving in another
4220

APPRECIATION
Brotherhood is a. 924
comes from the heart out 441
difference between a. and flattery
441
is a wonderful thing 437
is sincere 441
is universally admired 441
is unselfish 441
makes what is excellent in others
belong to us 437
Thank you for a warm hand 438
work out a. of redemption 11274

APPRECIATIVE
darkness makes a. of sight 824

APPREHENDED
Christ a. that thou mightest escape
6393

APPREHENSIONS
Atheists, false courage in a. 476

that afflict the earth-bound 5781

APPREHENSIVE
world always a. 10512

APPRENTICE
Begin as a mere a. 7352

APPRENTICES
we are all a. when we come to
death 2226

APPROACH
Christ not one of many ways to a.
God 6372
Christ the only way to a. God
6372
each man by right door 3345
Life happier if born at eighty,
gradually a. eighteen 6989
more natural to a. God in solitude
1445
must simplify our a. to God 7709
steady, unrelenting a. of him
whom I desired not to meet
9829

APPROACHES
God a, asks us to be his friends
4564
great men, finds they are men
5300
who blows own horn has
everyone dodging when he a.
9242

APPROACHING
in touch with a new a. life 7101
The rocks proclaim the a. Deity
6138

APPROPRIATE
Of all epithets to Christ, mild
seems least a. 6462
true, a. in all situations 957

APPROPRIATING
to receive Christ a. faith 3801

APPROVAL
accept Christ receive God's a.
3854
as God's a. of our way 5443
Christians have given a. to
self-assertive 5891
live with a. learn to like themselves
1114
not to pure in heart who see God
5891
Picking up quotations get chirp of
a. 9380
seek a. of man of worldly
reputation 11666
to publicity hunter who seeks
headlines 5891

APPROVE
If God doesn't a, fly doesn't move
4943

APPROVES
gleam brightly in pattern of life
God a. 6997

APPROVING
Speak a. cheering words 4223

APRIL
Every A. God rewrites Genesis
9885
showers bring May flowers 9884

APT
to want to interfere 10927
words power to asuage 3129

APTITUDE
darkness an a. for sensitivity 2612

ARABS
shall fold their tents like the A.
7887

ARBITRARY
Peace is not a. 8456
so a. are transient laws 10516

ARCH
rainbow, mild a. of promise 9392

ARCH'D
Heaven-gates not so highly a.
5649

ARCH-TRAITOR
myself, a. to myself 2583

ARCHANGEL'S
world to die amid blast of a.
trumpet 7886

ARCHENEMY
legalism, a. of church 6817

ARCHER
When a. misses mark 9680
who overshoots misses as well
6592

ARCHERS
found by One who had himself
been hurt by the a. 9798

ARCHITECT
God is a. man is contractor 4563
Integrity the a. 5848

ARCTIC
loneliness of age 8165

ARDENTLY
to desire a. all that is pleasing to
thee 9062

ARDUOUS
process of conversion long, a.
1897

ARE
afraid to show each other who we
really a. 6057
All that we a. comes from God
11135
All we possess qualified by what
we a. 8622
central stream of what we a.
indeed 7369
difference between what things a,
ought to be 7413
Flesh what we a. when left to own
devices 9926
friend knows you as you a. 4169
God interested only in what we a.
9539
God knows what you a. 1067

goodness inward thing we a. 5063
I love you for what you a. 4248
I will tell you what you a. 7296
if evaluate things as they really a. 8497
in small matters men as they a. 7391
make one that which we a, that which we appear to be 6296
Men become what they really a. 9741
Sickness shows us what we a. 6088
to tell another exactly what we a. 7428
treat men the way they a. will never improve them 5971
We a. because God is 3489
We know what we a, but know not what we may be 8672
We see things not as they a, but as we a. 8514
what they a. is what others want to be 6224
what we a. not, make us 9083
What we have to be is what we a. 1059
What you a, that you a. 1681
What you a. is God's gift to you 8560
What you a. thunders so loud 1061
what you a. will be yours forever 1062
Where you a, be all there 3186
You a. only what you a. when no one is looking 1068

ARGUE
absurd to a. men into believing 590
inner voice of God does not a. 4967
never a. with another 447
world can a. against Christianity as institution 1307

ARGUED
God may neither be demonstrated nor a. down 4678

ARGUES
voice of subconscious a. 4967

ARGUING
cannot remove anxiety by a. 423
no good in a. 44
Where desire to learn, much a. 6711
with the inevitable 44

ARGUMENT
Behind every a. ignorance 445
doesn't want explanation, wants a. 167
exchange of ignorance 2901
height of this great a. 7566
how many reasoned out of faith by a. 3742
less sound man's a, louder he talks 448

many hold no more water than puppy 446
meet a. with a. 2630
no a. against Christlike person 1307
people brought to faith in Christ not by a. 3759
Prayer not an a. with God 8925
Truth always the strongest a. 11563
with an east wind 44

ARGUMENTS
One example worth thousand a. 3450

ARIGHT
do not love a. 10084
never sought in vain that sought Lord a. 7537
So shall I walk a. 5412

ARISE
approach Bible, new world will a. 637
doubts, fear a. from dim perceptions 6713
stars a, and the night is holy 11649
To the dead he sayeth: A. 6497

ARISES
from image of God in nature of man 7531
yearning a. from image of God in nature of man 4744

ARISTOCRAT
Every person an a. 5967

ARITHMETIC
God's a. 4360
Persecution used in theology, not a. 8529
vice is false moral a. 10410

ARK
always along with the Flood 11432
By perseverance the snail reached the a. 8535
Dogma a. within which church floats safely 11187

ARM
Prayer moves the a. which moves the world 8950
There is an A. that never tires 4569
Thy a. directs lightnings through the sky 4827
Truth, limping along on time's a. 6865
woman formed from beneath a. to be protected 11982

ARMCHAIR
do not just sit down in an a. 3830

ARMED
Life like fly in room with boys a. with swat 6968
no government a. in power 5196

ARMIES
All a. that ever marched 6353
Christ did not conquer by a. 6389
in the march of God's a. 4712
Opinions stronger than a. 8199

ARMING
faith shines equal, a. me from fear 3765

ARMORED
Christ had no a. guards 6433

ARMOUR
is for the battle of prayer 8973
is to shield us while we pray 8973

ARMS
around each other's shoulders 2990
Christ nailed to cross with a. wide open 6393
Contemplation like sleep in a. of God 1756
Fallen man a rebel who must lay down his a. 9577
God will bear you in his a. 5907
Jesus without a. conquered millions 6449
Laws silent amidst clash of a. 11754
lie in God's a. and babble to him 5807
love of God, a. extended on cross 4781
Nor can we fall below a. of God 4774
round about, underneath are everlasting a. 422
Strength'ning their a. to warfare glad and grim 8454
The Infinite Goodness has such wide a. 4645

ARMY
than the whole a. of great men 6449

AROUND
Glorious the world of God a. us 10535
God is everywhere a. me 7968
not God's will we see before or a. us 5397

AROUSE
Lord appeared to a. us by his teaching 6477

AROUSES
knowledge of ourselves a. us to seek God 10020
legalism a. pride 6823

ARRANGED
Everything a. upon definite principles 4948
theology ideas of truth a. 11207
What if God a. things 577

ARRANGEMENTS
home where man can alter a. 5842
wishing to forestall God's a. 4322

ARRANGES
Great Director of music a. 7895
Praying a. life anew 8899

ARRAYED
Midst flaming worlds, in these a. 4719

ARREST
great thoughts a. the mind 11281
I'm under God's a. 5482

ARRESTED
for being Christian, evidence to convict 1292

ARRIVAL
of radiant light in our darkness 6119
should we not look forward to a. 2315

ARRIVALS
unexpected a. of pleasure 8612

ARRIVE
And to the end persisting safe a. 1664
flowering of person not state at which we a. 7699
Happiness not a state to a. at 5523
Life an event a. after, depart before 6957
never a, always on the way 7035

ARRIVED
hour of departure has a. 2378

ARRIVES
taken through difficulties and a. safely 2713
Tomorrow perfect when it a. 11403
Truth a. last 6865

ARROGANCE
built-in misery 451
compassion better than a. 6326
fear, replaced with gratitude, joy 1356
result will be a. in three-piece suit 7425

ARROGANT
a. usually most mistaken 458
Humility is sure, not a. 6012
if foresight of prosperity 4314
in wisdom of world a. stupidity 2809
meek, not a, inherit earth 1216
person hurts himself 451
person offends others 451

ARROW
as an a. to the mark to stick there 4222
God preparing you as his chosen a. 5430
shot a. in air, it stuck 3194
single a. easily broken 9442
than wound caused by a. 5119

ARROWS
Envy slays itself by own a. 3215

of sarcasm barbed with contempt 1771
pierce the body 374

ARSENAL
fear, a. is vast 3971

ART
And laughter oft is but an a. 6740
challenge basic assumptions of secular age 1998
cultivate fine a. of thanksgiving 11151
desire to know a. of living 10935
Develop a. of solitude 10553
fine a. of deception we call finesse 2483
Great is the a. of beginning 56
highest when used for God's glory 1995
if clash with God-made object, bad a. 2022
Jesus furnished themes for more works of a. 6449
Laughter is an a. 6727
Leadership, a. of getting someone else to do 6799
Life is an a. 6971
lost a. of century is meditation 7721
lost a. of worship 12099
more a. done with Crayolas 2023
Music is the a. of the prophets 7914
Music only a. of earth we take to heaven 7904
Music only a. of heaven given to earth 7904
Mysticism a. of union with reality 7956
Nature is a. of God Eternal 8025
of being wise is a. of knowing what to overlook 11940
of looking like owl when acted like ass 6162
only an imitation of nature 8043
point the world toward ultimate truth 1998
power of love will lead to master of the a. 7352
Practice a. of aloneness 10553
Procrastination is a. of keeping up with yesterday 9299
reach beyond the subculture 1998
shadow of divine perfection 1993
Teaching is an a. 11002
the a. of ending 56
To live remains an a. 7068
Vision a. of seeing things invisible 11737
when pursued for money 1996
where fantasy, earthly things metamorphosed into a. 7435
Yes, music is the prophet's a. 7935

ARTERIES
more quickly than hardening of the a. 6159

ARTFUL
suspicious parent makes a. child 8342

ARTICULATE
Gratitude one of least a. of emotions 5245
To be a. at certain times 11996

ARTIFICER
God, so great an a. in great things 4940

ARTIFICIAL
Day of Judgment to clear away a. virtues 1055

ARTIFICIALITY
Dignity never savors of a. 2761

ARTIST
God is a Master A. 10844

ARTIST'S
love of God persistent as a. love for work 4792

ARTS
Staying happily married should rank among the fine a. 7615

ASCENDED
into hell 5694

ASCENDS
mind a, beholds majesty of God 7971
while one a. the other descends 8884

ASCENSION
completion of Transfiguration 462
every angel keeps time with applauding wings 463
In his a, Christ a king 6410
our Lord entered heaven 459
placed Jesus Christ back in the glory 462

ASCENSION DAY
If upward you can soar 460
if you let God have his way 460

ASCERTAIN
Reason can a. profound difficulties 9420

ASCETIC
holy life not a. 5736

ASCETICISM
all very well if 465
black shadow of 467
favorite color, black 467
favorite hour, midnight 467
favorite music, a dirge 467
favorite text, deny yourself 467
favorite theme, tombstone 467
if no element of a. in our lives 466
mistake of 467
passion of giving up things 465
recognizable in life, not born again 465
spread over sky of Puritan Fathers 467

ASCRIBED

Election a. to God the Father
   3043
sanctification a. to God the Spirit
   3043

ASH

astonishing that I—dust, a, mud
   7489

ASHAMED

Holy Spirit will never let man be
   ashamed 1064
in land of naked, people a. of
   clothes 1638
need never be a. of our tears
   11023
never be a. to admit wrong 3249
of my lack of desire 9097

ASHES

jealousy extinguishes love as a.
   smother flame 6347

ASIDE

God deliberately stands a. 4891
jostled a. to make room for
   converted playboy 4410
stand a. and watch yourself go by
   10009

ASK

angels a. nothing more 4995
answer to prayer may let us in for
   more than we a. 8850
Authentic men aren't afraid to a.
   3916
better to a. some questions than
   know all answers 6688
better to a. way ten times 5424
can a. me to explain mystery of
   God 7939
courage to a. blessings of heaven
   1929
dared to a. of men what Christ
   asked 6419
do not a. for impossibilities 45
does not a. question remains fool
   forever 6683
Don't a. God for what you think
   is good 8781
Faith a gift but can a. for it 3674
Faith does not a. for lifting of
   darkness 3714
for courage that endures 1921
for guiding and strength of God
   4803
for strength to hold on 10931
for what you want as from a father
   4924
freedom to a. favor 4285
give audience to all who a. counsel
   5381
God does not a. about our ability
   3
God does not a. for acquiescence
   of indolence 4507
God for what he thinks is good
   for you 8781
God to keep you ready to do what
   he appoints 10120

God wants us to a. question of
   truth 10564
God will give what you a. or
   something better 2568
I do not a. to see distant scene
   5429
   2551
I do not a. to walk smooth paths
   1927
if any person whose happiness is
   more real to me than my own
   7184
If don't wish his good, you a. for
   your death 8067
let us a. what right we have 10842
Lord did not a. us to give up
   things 9974
love does not a. us to be doormats
   7337
Love will a. more than the law
   7273
make it possible for God to say
   yes to what we a. 8924
may a. as largely as we will 9028
mystery why people a. if empty
   seat occupied 8477
No one needed to a. if received
   Holy Ghost 5806
None can ever a. too much 9000
not for life free from grief 1921
not likely to a. amiss 8997
not that all troubles end 152
not where they go 5431
of him to be our friend 1510
of the devil, use magic 2618
only learn when a. questions 9363
reason we must a. God for things
   he intends to give 8990
Salvation is a gift you can a. for
   9808
shepherds didn't a. God if he
   knew what he was doing 6147
Some will never a. for information
   9236
sometimes a. that two and two
   not make four 9023
Sometimes withhold in mercy
   what we a. 8877
those coming back 269
to a. God to do things man can do
   is to waste prayers 10199
to take care before a. for strength
   8850
used to a. God to help me 4994
We a. God to come when he is
   already present 8843
What God sends better than what
   men a. for 4991
what we shall wish we had done
   2484
What you wish for your neighbor,
   a. for yourself 8067
Whatever love may a. of us 7337
When feeling conceited, a. to have
   altered 4013
When feelings cowardly, a. to
   have altered 4013
When feelings selfish, a. to have
   altered 4013

when you are outraged 45
who wants a great deal must not
   a. for little 11732

ASK'D

The ill, though a, deny 8979

ASKED

angels might be a. to stay with us
   5862
boy asked, "Have I ever seen a
   Christian" 3912
I a, my soul bethought of this
   4834
I a. God for all things so I could
   enjoy life 6906
Jesus a. if he might be let off the
   final sacrifice 6384
Jesus' standards a. more than any
   other 6444
not be a. what we have read 49
received nothing that he a. for
   8806
That which is often a. of God
   5443
Then I a. if I might help God 4994
who waits to be a. for help is
   unkind 10148
You a. for a loving God, you have
   one 4792

ASKER

legalist is a what a. 6820

ASKING

big things come a. to be done
   2534
ended up a. God to work through
   me 4994
even without our a. for them 8796
God for benefits 11166
God to conduct a major operation
   7155
God to do things he has already
   done 8843
no good a. God to make us happy
   our own way 7459
no good a. for simple religion
   9402
riches of heaven yours for a. 8662
Selfishness a. others to live as one
   wishes to live 10081
Some think God does not like
   constant a. 8964
Tis only God may be had for the a.
   9795
   2641
with my empty cup uncertain in a.
   4653

ASKS

a question is fool for five minutes
   6683
Christ never a. anyone to define
   position 6431
church a. God only for peace
   11761
communion with God that a. for
   nothing, yet everything 8997
God a. no man whether he will
   accept life 6893
God a. no one to accept life 1140

God a. nothing but pure heart,
single mind 7450

God a. us to cooperate with him
4507

God a. you do your best, not
Saint Teresa's best 9013

God approaches, a. us to be his
friends 4564

God does all before he a. us to do
anything 4536

God does before he a. 1519

Lord a. us to yield to him 2490

Lord never a. us to decide for him
2490

Love a. us to walk many miles
7273

man differs from animals, a.
questions 7398

man who loves God a. no favors
of God 4803

ASLEEP

Awake, a, at home, abroad 4876

God doesn't do work while we
are a. 890

when a. in world of his own 2965

ASPECT

know, praise some one a. of the
divine beauty 6169

ASPECTS

life can have but different a. 6985

ASPIRATION

and contentment, fast friends 471

do not make contentment and a.
quarrel 471

fruit of gospel 471

of man is sacred 11684

perfect in faith who come to God
without a. 3780

root, bud, bough desire to be more
471

to heart what spring is to earth
471

To see God, highest a. of man
7547

Vision looks outward, becomes a.
11738

ASPIRATIONS

Do not give up a. 1241

God will direct 1241

heavens as deep as a. high 468

place in God's hands a. 1241

Quotations tell of a. 9385

When right with God, he gives a.
9280

young have a. that never come to
pass 12195

ASPIRE

do not a. to comprehend God
10876

man may a. yet be content 471

to relieve suffering of others
10876

ASPIRES

Honor a. to death 2363

ASS

Jest with a, will flap in face with
tail 9477

looking like owl when acted like a.
6162

makes himself a. 4063

man appears consummate a. 482

went seeking for horns, lost ears
2872

ASSAIL'D

by scandal and the tongue of strife
6356

ASSAILED

greatness in speaking up for truth
when a. 5283

ASSASSINS

more likely we are all a. 912

ASSAULT

Every tempest an a. in siege of love
4775

response to a. reveal values by
which you live 6288

ASSAULTED

neighbor a. by exploitation 6163

ASSEMBLY-LINE

You aren't an a. product 10004

ASSENT

mentally to God's control 5467

Sin is then a. 10368

ASSENTS

lightly a. seldom keep word 1534

ASSERT

As sages in all times a. 11857

I may a. eternal Providence 7566

ASSERTING

youth a spirit of a. life 12183

ASSERTIVELY

not only model but a. reach out to
help 3901

ASSES

Even a. know straw is better than
gold 11804

ASSET

ability to speak several languages
a. 1876

ASSETS

claim to be citizen of heaven 7948

friend, one of life's greatest a.
4163

Humanity's most valuable a, the
nonconformists 9311

Remember your a. 9271

so-called negatives are a. 5357

ASSIGNED

anxiously memorize the script a.
6824

Each has sentry post a. by Lord
3088

if different lot a. you 8219

ASSIMILATE

to a. Christ active faith 3801

ASSIMILATED

when conscious obedience a. 7690

ASSISTANCE

With that a. I cannot fail 5179

Without a. of divine being cannot
succeed 5411

Without a. of that Divine Being
5179

ASSOCIATE

Jesus wasn't afraid to a. with
anyone 4253

Lord, make me worthy to a. with
thee 8786

When dove begins to a. with crows
9517

ASSOCIATES

more liable to catch vices than
virtues 9514

when one a. with vice 10326

ASS-STUBBORNNESS

Man a mixture of
horse-nervousness, a,
camel-malice 7420

ASSUME

Christians a. worshiped because
in church 12101

happy when not a. object of life is
happiness 5540

Often a. God unable to work
3613

ASSUMES

If God be what our faith a. 3774

science a. permanence, uniformity
of natural laws 9869

ASSUMPTIONS

no a. from public conduct 571

ASSURANCE

If a. is child of faith 6714

Pentecost, a. of heart 5806

to wait patiently 3744

ASSURANCES

uprooted from earth-born
securities and a. 7488

ASSURE

religious din a. everything is well
12096

ASTERISKS

in a. her webs are spread 6118

ASTEROID

hen who has laid egg cackles as if
laid a. 9223

ASTONISH

do right, surprise some, a. rest
3429

ASTONISHED

at how much the old man had
learned 3928

Bunyan's book a. whole world
1193

I am a. at being here rather than
there 4905

ASTONISHING
how little one feels poverty when
  one loves 7199
Man's conquest of nature a. 7414
that I—dust, ash, and mud 7489

ASTONISHMENT
reflect with a. on little
  competitions 2423

ASTOUNDED
Be a. God should have written to
  us 644

ASTRAY
Believe, even if men go a. 583
Faith in faith is faith a. 3667
in darkness soul avoids going a.
  2547
My heart may go a. 9091

ASTRONAUT
runs in circle, gets somewhere
  3086

ASTRONOMY
no more than symbolize
  emanation of God 4593

ASYLUM
Had there been a lunatic a. in
  Jerusalem 6388
prayer closet not an a. for
  worthless Christian 8976

ATHEISM
Few men so obstinate in a. 479
Knowledge of nature, a.
  incompatible 6696
number one cause, Christians 487
rather in lip than heart 475

ATHEIST
a zoo of lusts 493
alone in the universe 483
an orphaned heart 483
bedlam of ambitions 483
believes himself an accident 473
By night, half believes God 477
cannot find God 472
cannot guard faith too carefully
  493
could not affect God 491
dangers lie in wait 493
harem of fondled hatreds 493
has lost greatest of fathers 483
I am a, thank God 480
insist there is no God 484
like a six-year-old 485
man without support 474
moods in which Christianity
  terribly probable 1305
My name was legion 493
nobody to thank 488
nursery of fears 493
opposite of religious fanatic is not
  the fanatical a. 9549
Really, a young a. 493
sees man as helpless 3495
study anatomy, never be an a.
  1983
to make his way as best he can
  3495
were every man a. 491

worst moment 488

ATHEISTS
a whirl of contradictions 481
angry with God 481
dead for this life 490
haven't experienced God 485
hope for no other life 490
in fair weather 486
like children 476
maintain God did not exist 481
no a. in foxholes 489
put on alacrity 476
put on false courage 476
say we cannot rise again 492
What reasons have a. 492

ATHENIANS
When A. wanted society to give to
  them 4156

ATHENS
then A. ceased to be free 4155

ATHLETIC
Difficulty rocks into a. proportion
  2719

ATMOSPHERE
breathe fresh, exhilarating a. of
  eternity 4976
Cheerfulness, a. in which things
  thrive 1191
create a. of harmony 580
introduce another to Christ by a.
  of life 3306
of churches man-centered 1422
of formal denial of relevance of
  God 3036
renewing a, bringing in fresh
  salubrity 5848
we darken the a. in which we move
  4255
where you live and work 580

ATOM
Bomb, 1945 11740
Man an a. lost in endless vale of
  tears 10878
nor mountain greater miracle than
  an a. 7940
proof little things count 8663
smallest, when split becomes
  biggest 8648

ATOMIC
hunger more explosive than a.
  weaponry 8692
nation praying more awe-inspiring
  than explosion of a. bomb 8991

ATOMS
And the a. march in tune 1976
fortuitous concourse of a. 1989
How play with a. and fail to be
  touched by awe 9866
teaching of Christ splits to a.
  every notion 6486

ATONEMENT
animal sacrifices, cover sins 496
Calvary, puts away sin 496
Christ a Priest to make a. 6370

means "at-one-ment with God"
  498
means "to cover up," OT 496
means "to put away," NT 496
not delivered by believing a.
  sufficient 3753
saved by making a. my trust 3753

ATTACH
feeble will to all-powerful will
  9835
Real goodness does not a. itself to
  life 5079

ATTACHED
family first community to which a.
  3888
forgiveness, condition a. 4096

ATTACHES
services they render us a. people
  to us 5256

ATTACHMENT
nothing else but love 7329

ATTACK
enemy may launch a. otherwise
  impossible 5021
if a. personality, it can only defend
  itself 8312
If cause be good, a. of enemies
  will not injure 1823
Truth is beyond a. 11575
When spider would a. thee 11115

ATTACKED
Bible more frequently a. 726
dog barks when his master is a. 99
God's truth a., yet remain silent
  99
Though God be a. outcome never
  in doubt 4822

ATTAIN
highest point we can hope to a.
  4976
honesty, maturity equally hard to
  a. 5873
Light after light well us'd they
  shall a. 1664
to excellence in single pursuit
  3470
To something nobler we a. 3538
When shall I a. to this 11136

ATTAINABLE
standard infinitely higher more a.
  6812

ATTAINED
not a. by sudden flight 8566
we have not yet a. 2887

ATTAINMENT
For a. of divine knowledge 6681
happiness more a disposition than
  a. 5571
Spirit-filled life no goal difficult of
  a. 5803
Strenuousness open foe of a.
  10757
to be humble when praised rare a.
  6019

ATTAINS
No one a. success simply by what
   is required 2784
value not in what one a. 11664

ATTEMPT
Democracy a. to apply Bible
   principles 2523
great things for God 10118
legalism, God satisfied with a. to
   obey moral code 6814
let us not a. to distort 38
never test resources of God until
   a. impossible 3815
out of hopeless a. has come
   human history 5570
rather a. to do something great
   3595
than a. to do nothing and succeed
   3595
to a. to do is to waste efforts
   10199
to communicate vision to all
   others 6169
unless I can recall an earnest a. to
   serve the God who made me
   6919

ATTEMPTED
Great accomplishments often a.
   3593
Nothing a. if objections first
   overcome 2741

ATTEMPTING
less than others 1802
to compel others to believe, live as
   he does 7793
to find new ways of bettering
   things 9311

ATTEMPTS
at description futile 4995
God disappoints our a. to escape
   5395
In great a. glorious to fail 3600
Love a. what is above its strength
   7220
sins a. to fill voids 10295

ATTEND
always finds time to a. his funeral
   5589
If ants so busy, how a. picnics
   9266
Unnumber'd worlds a. 4672

ATTENTION
changed to shift a. outside
   ourselves 12137
difference is a. to detail 64
doing engages almost everyone's a.
   1753
Don't pay much a. to who is for,
   against you 6260
give a. to persons, matters
   external to ourselves 5550
glorifying God when no a. 1295
Lighthouses don't ring bells to call
   a. 6022
Lord's Prayer, fixing a. on a few
   great points 7154

never known person filled with
   Holy Spirit who drew a. to
   himself 6018
only with single-minded a. to
   Christ 10551
Pay a. to the Source 10180
pay a. to tree trunk in his own eye
   6590
Pay a. to your enemies 3169
perfect church, a. on God 1383
Profanity fixes a. on words rather
   than thoughts 9305
so concentrated no time to
   wonder how we look 6056
Tell me to who you pay a. 9273
thousand voices clamor for a.
   7447
Turn your a. to God 6271
We pay more a. when quoted than
   when we read 9388
well to pay youth a. 12160
When laughing a. focused 6746
when nobody is paying any a. to
   you 7129
would pay more a. to spiritual
   progress 10703

ATTENTIVE
Wisdom in minds a. to their own
   6690

ATTIC
worse than flooded basement is
   flooded a. 8581

ATTIR'D
with stars, we shall forever sit
   5679

ATTIRE
clad in acceptable a. 4025

ATTITUDE
Accept Christ a. likely wrong
   3333
adoration an a. of the soul 12122
Christian love [agape] an a. 7166
clover leaves sleeping in a. of
   worship 8000
corresponding inner a. of love,
   honesty 6811
determines disease or reward 509
difference is a. 516
Emotional stability an a. 2563
enter trials with a. of gratitude
   181
extreme a. a flight from the self
   9924
failure is an a. 3581
faith demands complete change of
   a. 3785
Father, we know not, don't tell us
   574
Forgiveness a permanent a. 4078
freedom to choose 519
God's will an a. 5406
Happiness depends on a. toward
   blessings 5513
Happiness matter of a. 5515
inward a. of man who loves God
   different 5046
is not such a. unbelief 8632

Joy is an a. 6528
living determined by a. 522
maintain reverent a. toward God's
   place, influence 3993
No matter what a. you have 183
of child certain God knows what
   he is about 9912
One's a. determines impact 201
pain of a new a. 520
place ourselves in a. to be helped
   9010
poor in spirit a. of dependence on
   God 6025
prayer is a life a. 8931
proper a. toward disobedience
   8332
Repentance an a. rather than
   single act 9588
right a. problems not failure 521
to crucifixion must be "We did it"
   2159
to treasures on earth 11872
whose a. toward me uncertain,
   hostile 7102
wrong a, not a success 521

ATTITUDES
a single decade to lay foundation
   of a. 8314
determine actions 501
determine good or bad 501
home, there we cultivate a. 5832
If not concentrated, affect many a.
   6056
make pleasant or painful 500
revivals altered social a. 9752
We're the ones that determine
   people's a. 11027
within our power 5538

ATTRACT
Kindness will always a. kindness
   6655
magnet that will a. true friends
   4282

ATTRACTION
holy life constant a. or perpetual
   reproof 5735
where only a. is God 1403

ATTRACTIVE
Nothing a. about gospel to
   natural man 5108
relaxed Christian more a. 9529
saint one who makes goodness a.
   9770
where evil is a. 3347

ATTRACTIVENESS
grace, winsome a. of God 5227
many avenues of a. to God 7532
of mass movement 10526

ATTRACTS
smile reaches out, a. 5504
when church different from world
   she a. 5096

ATTRIBUTE
Creativity, basic a. of God 1999
forgetting with God is divine a.
   4637

Love not a. of God, is God 4755

ATTRIBUTE OF GOD
Justice an a. 6628

ATTRIBUTES
all God's a. are holy 5749
All God's acts consistent with a.
4579
From God's other a. we learn
about his love 4750
God a. to himself jealousy, anger
4722
of a great lady 11697

ATTRIBUTES OF GOD
all harmonize and blend 4579
can only be received by faith 4584
explain each other 4583
glimpses the mind enjoys of
Godhead 4583
helps to express God's perfections
4580
helps to express our adoration
4580
highest science 4631
human ways of conceiving abyssal
All 4580
intelligible to us on surface 4584
loftiness speculation 4631
mightiest philosophy 4631
No a. contradicts any other 4579
suitable to our capacities 4580
transcend our comprehension
4584

ATTUNED
let Christ be note to which life a.
6379

AUDACITY
O unholy a. 230

AUDIBLE
God, voice too still, small to be
easily a. 4465

AUDIENCE
dream theater where dreamer a.
2972
large a. for strip-tease act 7360

AUDITOR
no reason why miner not
intellectual as a. 6332

AUGUST
put off until October chores in A.
9882

AUGUSTINE
who could be harmed if he knew
something about A. 5733

AUSPICIOUS
Oh spring to light, a. Babe, be
born 6143

AUSTERE
perseverance may be employed by
smallest of us 8557

AUTHENTIC
men aren't afraid to show affection
3916

AUTHENTICATOR
God the Holy Spirit a. of Holy
Scripture 655

AUTHOR
All mankind is of one A. 2216
devil, a. of confusion 2659
dream theater where dreamer a.
2972
expect A. will have something to
say to each of us 9911
God is music's a. not man 7891
God is the a, men the players
5639
God the Spirit a. of Holy Scripture
655
knows the play 9911
Life like a library owned by an a.
6965
No one graduates from Bible
study unless he meets a. 684
recognize in God the A. of our
goods 8796

AUTHORITARIANISM
dangerous 523
twists good into lust for power
9952
twists good into repressive control
9952

AUTHORITATIVE
knows in deep and a. way 5809

AUTHORITY
a biblical notion 9952
accept a. of Jesus 524
Christ Lion in a. 6425
Christ seated in place of a. 235
cross made clear a. is service 2166
Destiny is tyrant's a. for crime
2619
family first a. under which person
lives 3888
for humanizing society 10506
for restraining evil 10506
fumes of it invade the brain 8702
great in this world exercise a. 526
if saint tries to exercise a. 526
In theology predominance of a.
11191
intoxicates 8702
is God-ordained 523
make men giddy, proud, and vain
8702
Man forced to seek higher a. 7499
message seasoned with a. 3310
no good government without a.
5194
no stronger test of character than
a. 8721
obedience foundation of
subjection to God's a. 8355
obedience to parental a.
foundation of good citizenship
8355
of service correspond to life of
prayer 10192
Self-chosen a, an impertinence 526
Sin defiance to a. of God 10362

sin rebellion against divine a.
10390
solve problems by a. 11227
To discuss a. of God seems
meaningless 4955
to question a. of God absurd 4955
Young people need control, a.
12178

AUTOGRAPH
Everywhere I find the a. of God
11629
The awful a. of God 8015

AUTOMATA
world of a. hardly worth creating
4120

AUTOMATIC
Christian life never a. 1221

AUTOMATICALLY
what is old not a. obsolete 3660

AUTOSUGGESTION
substituted a. for conversion 5808

AUTUMN
bounty shines in a. unconfined
9883
In heaven it is always a. 5657

AUXILIARY
Praise the best a. to prayer 8735

AVAILABILITY
our ability or our inability, but
our a. 3

AVAILABLE
because holiness made a, God
requires it 4658
Discouraged people need a.
someone 3066
God's mercy a. in present situation
4815
God's resources a, endless 4458
plenty of seats a. in subway 7049

AVALANCHES
of Napoleon have melted away
730

AVARICE
a virtue 4722
and happiness never saw each
other 5312
Even God attributes to himself a.
4722

AVENUES
many a. of attractiveness to God
7532

AVERAGE
Christian a harmless enough thing
1318
person puts only 25 percent into
work 2788

AVERTS
One no a. seventy evils 3392

AVOCATIONS
earthly employment a. 3095

AVOID

avoidance of suffering means a.
  growth 10899
confession determination to a. sin
  1599
end of life not to a. pain 5554
if course wrong a. though lose life
  as consequence 6291
shame, do not seek glory 4406
  3850
the last minute rush 2768
To a. criticism do, say, be nothing
  2082
trouble, breathe through nose
  1884

AVOIDANCE

important thing is not a. of
  mistakes 8110
of suffering means avoid growth
  10899
Virtue is not a. of moral dangers
  11709

AVOIDED

two dangers to be a. in the church
  1400
When eyes to be a. 5480
  2468

AVOIDING

philosophy complicated method
  of a. important problems 8597
to many people virtue not a. faults
  11702

AVOIDS

Glory a. those who chase after it
  4407
Who escapes duty, a. gain 9681

AVOWALS

alphabet of love, a. and consents
  7297

AWAITS

God a. our desire 4639
patience quietly a. promise 9322

AWAKE

All men whilst a. in common
  world 2965
asleep, at home, abroad 4876
don't lie a. nights to succeed
  10828
God is a. 11489
in duties of our callings 9668
Some men dream, others stay a.
  89
stay a. and listen to sermon at
  church 10100
thank God that you live to lie a.
  10489
to sublime greatness of the soul
  10654
to succeed stay a. days 10828
truest life in dreams a. 2966
we are only half a. 8651
ye dead 9692
You a. us to delight in your praise
  7578

AWAKEN

in others, same attitude 518
religious awakening that does not
  a. sleeper to love 9737
single event can a. within a
  stranger unknown to us 6873

AWAKENED

Christ stirring to be a. 1757
Through sorrow sympathies are a.
  10640

AWAKENING

best a. of reverence is
  contemplation of works of God
  9734
Death the final a. 2273
religious a. that does not awaken
  sleeper to love 9737
to love again 5360

AWAKENS

Christ a. within us concern for
  world 12031
confident in Christ a. 1611

AWARE

Be a. rigidity imprisons 6809
become a. God is enough 4516
God makes a. of sinfulness 4660
God wants to make soul a. of him
  4562
heart is a. of God, not reason
  3750
Jesus has to be a. of his suffering
  10868
of stature, freedom and evil in man
  7494
Worship a. of Father's directives
  12136
Worship, a. of own limitations
  12136
Worship, a. of task at hand 12136
Worship, a. of the Father 12136

AWARENESS

give birth to new a. 10540
greater a. of dependent on God
  5226
of God presupposes his existence
  4606

AWAY

All we can hold is what we have
  given a. 4349
anything that takes a. my taste for
  Bible study 7036
as silently steal a. 7887
big print giveth, small print taketh
  a. 9328
But, how many were sorry when
  he passed a. 7423
can come to light to turn God a.
  from us 4884
Christ's words never pass a. 6523
comfort of having friend may be
  taken a. 4271
darkest day will have passed a.
  2575
do not most people drift a. 3742
don't open door to devil, he goes
  a. 2654
Don't stay a. from church because
  hypocrites 6050

Earth breaks up, time drops a.
  5636
Even this shall pass a. 974
evening beam smiles clouds a. 618
fish lies about man he got a. from
  3426
from distraction so you see God
  2556
giving a. what no longer belongs
  to him 4377
God a. down here, close up 8801
God gives, but he does not give a.
  4821
God never farther a. than the door
  4621
God sends no one a. empty 9200
Had borne my breath a. 2588
hope withers a. 7291
If God stayed a. as much as a
  hairbreadth 7477
kind word never thrown a. 6672
Life is changed, not taken a. 2343
Love doesn't start to multiply
  until give it a. 7238
Love isn't love until you give it a.
  7258
love must help child grow a. from
  mother 7858
Man born with face turned a.
  from God 9583
masks torn a, hollow smiles fade
  9741
more love you give a, the more
  comes back 7232
more money you give a, less you
  have 7232
Music washes a. dust of life 7912
neglects present moment, throws
  a. all he has 11300
no right to open door of prison
  and run a. 10941
not God a. off up yonder 8801
Riches fly a. 6455
Self-centeredness a movement a.
  from God 9946
Slip useless a. 2198
strange about Jesus is you can
  never get a. from him 6485
Take a. love and earth is a tomb
  7294
The poor too often turn a,
  unheard 8694
this, too, shall pass a. 957
Thy grief shall pass a. 6878
turn a. on grounds too
  well-dressed to be honest 10086
What day may bring day may
  take a. 2202
what more blessed than to put
  cares a. 12057
What sweetness left if take a.
  friendship 4299
who sings frightens a. ills 7894

AWE

Character gives a. to gray hairs
  997
How play with universe and fail
  to be touched with a. 9866
stand in a, call him Father 3921

starry heavens, moral law 1709
television dulls a. 11031
Whose least creation fills with a.
  11628
works of God, transparent
  greatness inspire a. 9734
Worship is a soul in a. before
  mystery of universe 12132

AWED
My heart a. within me when I
  think 1966

AWE-INSPIRING
Christ's words have same a.
  relevance 6359
nation praying more a. than
  explosion of atomic bomb 8991
wisdom, power so a. 4995

AWESOME
human intellect an a. work of God
  7776
Repentance process by which we
  see God as he is: a. 9594
silence in a. presence of God
  12112

AWESTRUCK
Do not be a. by other people
  9983

AWFUL
And a. purity 4659
Can ease my a. load 8451
climax of isolation on the cross
  6383
gracious, beautiful voice for
  which he listened 4965
hour when necessity of hiding
  comes 5480
Loud o'er my head, though a.
  thunders roll 4827
nothing more a. than conscious
  humility 6038
skunk puts on a. airs 1588
The soul itself its a. witness is
  3404
to live without prayer not merely
  an a. thing 8833
Trinity 11429
wisdom, a. wisdom 11906

AWKWARDNESS
custom of today, a. of tomorrow
  10516

AWOKE
and saw life was duty 9663
earth a. with first rush of sound
  11330

AX
who didn't have a. to grind 6147

AXE
Only when a. put to the tree
  10346

B

BAAL
serve God or fall down before B.
  4920

BABBLE
lie in God's arms and b. to him
  5807

BABE
A blessed b, infant full of power
  6123
Oh spring to light, auspicious B,
  be born 6143
When you'd lie, a b. again 1368

BABES
God discovers himself to b. 7709
Out of the mouths of b. 3882

BABY
Almighty appeared on earth as
  helpless b. 6125
an inestimable blessing 802
an inestimable bother 802
arms, legs appear God's
  afterthoughts 807
fresh fallen from God's home 804
fresh fallen to flower on earth 804
God's confidence in man 815
inside the womb 17
Only b. admired for opening his
  mouth 5151
rose with sweetest leaves yet folded
  803
send either one, if it can't be twins
  814
sweet new blossom of humanity
  804
Through the black space of death
  to b. life 6148
Unfathomed mystery 805
Unwritten history 805
What is man? A foolish b. 7440
wheels b. carriage call him Papa
  3921
writing book nearest a man gets
  to having a b. 12158

BABY'S
Men overlooked a b. birth 6458

BABYHOOD
of the Son of God a reality 6125

BABYLON
way to B. will never bring you to
  Jerusalem 10403

BABYLONIANS
have not learned to live together
  any better than the ancient B.
  9353

BACK
age looks b. 12200
can bring b. no past by longing
  8368
can never turn b. 9846
can't turn b. clock 8373
cannot be a front without a b.
  5357

carry care to bed, sleep with pack
  on b. 12080
do not come b. to thank him 6251
doesn't get slap on b. 2772
either lighten my burden or
  strengthen my b. 9071
feeling that will never come b.
  12165
Four things come not b. 8213
Goodness is love with burden on
  b. 5065
heaviest load man carries on b.
  4098
I never walk b. 82
I pray for stronger b. 929
Ignorance content with b. to truth
  3258
joy that comes b. to you 6561
Look forward and not b. 8379
Love bade me welcome, yet my
  soul drew b. 5481
Love if not reciprocated will flow
  b. 7241
must turn b. on one-half of world
  9151
no use going b. for lost
  opportunity 8226
of all is God 4607
There is no way out, no way b.
  5407
What people say behind b. is your
  standing in community 9628
wise to let God hold you b. 5422
with no looking b. to what might
  have been 4688

BACKBONE
Prayer is b. of revival 9743

BACKS
our own sins behind our b. 10348

BACKWARD
never a b. glance of regret 4281
To Christ everything looks
  forward, b. 5710

BACKWARDS
Life only understood b. 6941

BAD
an incredibly b. world 1293
And to make b. matters worse
  2589
are passionate, restless 5045
aren't such things as good, b.
  impulses 7839
as place of training world not so b.
  5535
Bible, deals with good and b. 721
called good when worse happens
  153
can't make good cloak out of b.
  cloth 1069
Christian thanks God when
  everything b. 3638
conscience embitters comforts
  1650
conscience is snake in heart 1651
dark night of soul not b. 2608
difference between good and b.
  5042

difference between good and b.
person 5041

don't like to open letter that has
b. news 10012

enemy will fill mind with b.
thoughts 7764

enough to know the past 4317

Feelings go b. when they make
themselves into false gods 4016

get b. wife, become a philosopher
7606

God does allow b. men to triumph
4957

good word costs no more than b.
3128

greater in possibility for good or b.
10015

He would take b, make good 967

holds the ladder, as b. as thief
2036

Hope is a b. supper 5915

If clash with God-made object, b.
art 2022

If lightning bolts in response to b.
doctrine 11189

Insults like b. coins 2918

Living in lap of luxury isn't b.
11834

man b. enough now 10898   .

man worse when pretends to be
saint 6045

Men come up to what is expected,
good or b. 3505

mistaking weakness for strength
10749

Most divorces are not b. marriages
2926

Murder isn't that b. 7882

My case is b, Lord, be my
advocate 5482

need greater virtues to bear good
fortune than b. 11719

never at unity with one another
5045

no company preferable to b. 4286

no such thing as b. weather 8005

nothing either good or b. 11255

Nothing in its place is b. 5036

Nothing so b. that good may not
come 2755

Old age isn't b. when consider
alternative 8160

opinion of God 11591

passions are b. masters 10225

past is starting point for better
things 9590

person loves things and uses
people 5041

pessimist, everything b. except
himself 8248

possible for b. men to become
good 9438

side of poverty is fear it creates
11854

sins of flesh least b. of all sins
10400

so much b. in the best of us 3953

Something of my old self, my old,
b. life 8966

survive all manner of b. treatment
4237

Talebearers as b. as talemakers
5158

than feast it with b. 4219

the day man becomes content
8649

thing of b. quality expensive
10291

thing to be satisfied spiritually
10704

things are very dear 11655

thoughts bear b. fruit 11223

To abandon b. habits in own
strength 11108

To go too far as b. as to fall short
11954

to lean against falling wall 3380

tree does not yield good apples
986

Wealth a very b. mistress 11873

What was good, b. changed places
984

When outlook b, try uplook 9030

When things are b, thou! Thou!
Thou! 4518

Whether black cat brings b. luck
8584

wouldn't have time to complain
about the b. 11150

BADE
Love b. me welcome; yet my soul
drew back 5481

BADGES
leave b. of schism behind 5671

BADLY
have lived b. on my own 9070

Impulse manages all things b.
5580

like men who sleep b. 5541

no faults in thing we want b.
11100

No wonder Cain turned out b.
8318

profit even from those who talk b.
7114

treating b. precious thing God has
made 9923

What's got b, goes b. 1743

BADNESS
God can only accept my b. 5059

BAFFLE
No difficulties can b. God 1468

BAFFLED
Better b. faith than no faith 3645

God not b. by what baffles us
4701

BAG
can be b. of grapes 9524

can choose to be b. of marbles
9524

BAGGAGE
take half the b, twice the money
6836

BAGS
Without thy presence, wealth b.
of cares 4877

BAIT
Better shun b. than struggle in
snare 11049

Do not bite at b. of pleasure
11051

first caught by the devil's b. 2696

BAKER
Be not b. if head butter 11048

BAKERY
Lord isn't running a b. 6755

BAKING
God expects us to do the b. 9657

BALANCE
between prayer, action 4160

Christ's prescriptions never out of
b. 6429

Happy is man who strikes b. justly
1240

Holy leisure refers to b. in life
6828

Humor is the pole that adds b.
6715

In celebration high, mighty regain
b. 3235

revival out of b. is revival out of
power 9738

Time, no one knows b. 11340

BALANCED
Christianity system of b.
obligations 1240

BALD
Experience comb nature gives
when b. 3518

BALDNESS
as if grief could be lessened by b.
5345

sign of approaching age 314

BALL
get him back his b. 1363

Hit the b. over the fence 3467

Keep your eye on the b. 3503

not as b. against wall to rebound
4222

BALL-AND-CHAIN
mentality keeps us from giving in
fresh, innovative ways 6825

BALL-BEARING
planet b. in hub of universe 11633

BALM
Come, blessed darkness, come
bring thy b. 10481

Gold no b. to wounded spirit
7798

Hope, b. and lifeblood of the soul
5933

of death releases 1332

Silence a b. to every chagrin
10266

to fester'd wounds 3129

word can be a b. or a bomb
12001

BALMY
We saw thee in thy b. nest 6152

BAMBOOZLED
to imagine Omniscience so easily b. 8750

BANANA
foot on earth is on a b. peel 6915

BAND
you'll never get to lead the b. 6797

BAND-AID
Psychotherapy will put b. on gash 5616

BANDAGES
God not about to hand out spiritual b. 1013

BANISH
And pleasures b. pain 5670
I will b. thee 1310
To bring a smile, to b. a tear 7423

BANK
Time deposit in b. of God 11340

BANKER
no b. holds key to as much power 11841

BANKERS
lend money 7826

BANKING
wealth laid up in heavenly b. account 3751

BANKRUPT
God has a plan for this b. world 4902
worst b. lost enthusiasm 3183

BANKRUPTCY
drink, plunged people into 325
No man rich to whom grave brings eternal b. 6101

BANNED
Bible—b, burned, beloved 726

BAPTISM
Christian is born 529
cross of Jesus Christ and his b. express same thing 9437
direction is indicated 529
If we seek b. of Holy Ghost 5784
more a promise than fact 529
new self emerges 529
of Holy Ghost does not make us wonder-workers 5790
of Holy Ghost does not mean great venture for God 5789
of Holy Ghost makes us witnesses to Jesus 5790
of Holy Ghost means we are a satisfaction to Jesus 5789
points back to work of God 528
points forward to life of faith 528
self is buried 529

BAPTISMAL
may go to hell with b. water on face 9537

BAPTIST
not a B. in heaven 5671

BAPTIZES
God b. us with Holy Ghost that he may be all in all 5784

BAPTIZING
Sorrow b. us with bitter tears 10616

BAR
himself, the prisoner at the b. 1684
no b. or wall in the soul 4525
When I have crossed the b. 2368

BARBARIANS
War is the business of b. 11771

BARBARIC
funeral, b. and miserable 2311

BARBED
arrows of sarcasm b. with contempt 1771

BARE
I saw a stable, low and very b. 6133

BARGAIN
I b. for nothing 9084
Life, the cheapest b. 6996

BARGAINS
man an animal that makes b. 7404
Truth never b. 11561

BARK
Don't judge tree by b. 432
our duty to b. in house of the Lord 9150

BARKS
honest man not worse because dog b. at him 5866

BARN-BARE
helpless on a b. floor 6142

BAROMETER
reponse to temptation b. of love for God 11079

BARREL
plenty of sound in an empty b. 9250

BARREN
bleak winter of sorrow, loneliness 968
Boredom, b, meaningless existence 865
life that holds only happiness 5537
Pleasure-seeking is a b. business 5550
To seek a b. wilderness 4118
Wise sayings often fall on b. ground 6672

BARRENNESS
beware of b. of busy life 114
Lord I crawled across the b. to you 4653

Treat fruitfulness, b. same way 1461

BARRICADE
themselves behind newspaper 3904

BARRIER
between you and truth 4801
false b. between secular, sacred 10720
Sin builds b. 1595
When church fails to break cultural b. 1456

BARRIERS
Between contrite heart and majesty of heaven no b. 8771
hope for breaking down b. 3325

BARROOM
Why not Gideon Bibles in b. 751

BARS
love of God b. way to hell 4781
my bones the b. of death 3482
we find security in iron b, solid walls 6825

BASE
God choose b, lowly, unknown 3861

BASED
civilization b. on foundation of murder 10513
misery because world b. on freedom 4149

BASEMENT
every church would need morgue in b. 4717
worse than flooded b. is flooded attic 8581

BASES
can take time going around b. 3467

BASIC
family b. unit of government 3888
family established society's b. values 3888
family, b. unit of human organization 3880
home, kind of school where life's b. lessons taught 5853
Hope draws power from b. goodness of mankind 5928
test of freedom 4142

BASIL THE GREAT
who could be harmed if he knew something about B. 5733

BASIS
all science rests on b. of faith 9869
building without a b. cannot stand 3826
Faith, b. on which we stand 3835
God's decree b. on which perseverance depends 4616
of fellowship to live in the open 4026
stand before God on b. of grace 1057

BASKED
He b. beneath the sun 6756

BASKET
If pray for bread and bring no b.
2947

BASS
first string musician touches is b.
10663

BAT'S
eyes for our own faults 3957

BATH
temporary but it does you good
9753

BATHE
Everybody ought to b. in mirth
6738

BATHROOM
sing in b. while brushing teeth
8168

BATTALIONS
sorrows come in b. 10646
with mighty b. of angels 6503

BATTER
my heart, three-person'd God
2840
not good that man b. at gate of
heaven 8854
through fires, floods to b. us into
shape 4570

BATTER'D
soul's dark cottage, b. and decay'd
7701

BATTERED
And b. with the shocks of doom
2599

BATTLE
armour is for the b. of prayer
8973
care for him who borne the b.
5199
Christ gives us power to go on
with b. 11451
Christ has not lost a b. yet 6367
Christ in you that fights the b.
6381
Christianity, a b. not dream 1167
Consistency, b. worth winning
1749
devil's b. is human heart 2691
Everyone fighting hard b. 6635
He moves into the b. wholly
weaponless 6124
How hard the b. goes, the day
how long 6256
I shall not fear the b. 5418
if refuse to stand for truth where
b. rages 3846
life a b. and a march 7087
many a b. fought world knows
nothing about 7061
means to fight hardest b. human
being can fight 6215
Prayer is the b. 8973
Prepare yourself for b. 9861

Strength to b. difficulties 1809
Temptation is a call to b. 11087
will be exhausted in b. of life
10159

BATTLE OF NEWBURY
prayer before B. 9076

BATTLEFIELD
faith is love on the b. 7202
prayer closet the b. of the church
8976

BATTLEGROUNDS
souls are b. for civil wars 6068

BATTLES
better to have lost some b. 10777
inner b. torn them between doubt,
faith 2959
more b. won by submitting 11781
soul where man's b. are fought
10672
who fight b. on their knees 8861

BE
All I could never b. 9981
best is yet to b. 8132
Christ came to make us what he
teaches we should b. 6403
desire children to become, we
must b. 5861
expectation of what man can b.
timorous 3507
face life as it is, not as we feel it
ought to b. 6939
For all that shall b, yes 9055
freedom to simply b. themselves
4285
friend helps us b. our best selves
4178
From Christ all come to b. 6475
God making us into what he
wants us to b. 6978
God tells us who he wants us to b.
6830
greatest thing you can do is to b.
10141
I love you for what you are going
to b. 4248
I'll b. what you want me to b.
5420
I'm not the thing I should b. 9928
If I try to b. like him 6188
If it's going to b, it's up to me
4423
In great matters men as they wish
to b. seen 7391
in power of each to b. an
individual 6209
Life is to b. 6980
life never will b. what ought to b.
6939
make one that which we are, that
which we appear to b. 6296
Most must be content to b. as
though not been 6023
nature to b. like person you live
with most 6235
never do, do with the Lord, but b,
b. 6313

Nor am I even the thing I could b.
9928
not, it will b. he 9556
only way to have friend is b. one
4205
Pray more, b. more, serve more
9016
that we may b. what we were not
7272
then bees are bees because they b.
6185
time in which to b. 6830
To b. another than I am 9848
to b. good is divine 5085
To b. like Christ our goal 8113
To b. one's self more admirable
than conformity 6216
to b. what no others are 6170
To b. with God, no need to be in
church 7541
To dream of person you would
like to b. 6217
To the still more wonderful is to b.
4313
treat men the way you want them
to b. 5971
Walk beside me, b. my friend
4224
way to b. nothing is do nothing
6778
what they are is what others want
to b. 6224
what things ought to b. 7413
What we have to b. is what we are
1059
What will b. will b. well 8243
who will b. like me 6188
Why is it so many want to b.
what they're not 6224

BEACH
dreamed he was walking along
the b. with the Lord 5437

BEACON
Modest doubt call'd b. of the wise
2951

BEAM
evening b. smiles clouds away 618
love should b. forth 7168

BEAMS
How far that little candle throws
his b. 2499

BEANS
Be the meal of b. and peas 5860

BEAR
a god whom we can easily b. 4846
boughs that b. most hang lowest
6029
burden of life no longer 2591
burdens of others 1080
Christianity teaches to b. burdens
931
evidences of God's love, grace to
b. afflictions 4778
grudge, like a b. with bad breath
coming out of hibernation 9639
Hate too great a burden to b.
7182

If home unbearable, maybe you're
the b. 5839
Injustice relatively easy to b. 6267
March, hanging around like polar
b. that's depressing 9889
May I be willing, Lord, to b. 2098
must have iron nails that scratches
b. 11062
Nor b. an easy load 1927
One can b. grief 5351
patiently the dryness of your mind
7123
patiently your exile 7123
reason polar b. wears fur coat
6213
the intolerable 6961
Those who commit injustice b.
greatest burden 6279
weight more than man can b.
4319
what we are unable to b. God
keeps secret 9708
Which I have borne and yet must
b. 2882
with all faults of man 3948

BEARABLE
Faith makes life b. 3685
Human beings b. when their
defenses down 892
Solitude b. only with God 10555

BEARING
what trouble you were b. 1545

BEARS
greatest b. heaviest burdens
cheerfully 5297
Life b. love's cross 7204
Stoic b. 6563

BEAST
and devil may be conquered 5013
conversion slaying of b. within
1900
cuddle self-pity, you'll have a b.
10034
does not know he is a b. 26
much b. and some devil in man
5013
no wild b. so ferocious as
Christians 11212
serpent subtlest b. of all the field
2700
that no b. would consider us tasty
8526
tongue a wild b. 11415

BEASTS
man, the most terrible of the b.
8066
most dangerous of tame b, a
flatterer 10472
most dangerous of wild b, a
slanderer 10472
three most intractable b. 10774
transform ourselves into b. 332

BEAT
can't b. the weather 9879
God will b. the time for us 7056
If b. devil in prayer can b. him
anywhere 8837

If devil can b. you in prayer, he
can b. you anywhere 8837

BEATEN
My father had never b. us 3983
power has not b. back church
1419
soul b. down can rise up 3621
stand upright when others b. down
1915
Unless b. within, bound to win
3627

BEATIFIC
something-or-other in sermons
5661

BEATING
head against wall 8553
Prophets, b. hearts of the Old
Testament 9333
To understand, feel b. of heart
3078

BEATITUDE
child of God visible b. 1243
God is my b. 7462

BEATITUDES
enriched moral existence 530
The Peoples B. 532
yeast of love into dough of human
greed 530

BEATS
Christ's teaching never b. about
the bush 6440
One b. the bush 6205
same heart b. in every human
breast 917

BEAUTIES
Unwrap hidden b. in ordinary day
2201

BEAUTIFIER
Love is a great b. 7227

BEAUTIFIERS
Cheerfulness, contentment great b.
1087

BEAUTIFUL
a field rested gives b. crop 6839
agree forgiveness b. idea 4104
awful, gracious, b. voice for
which he listened 4965
Better ugly truth than b. lie 11498
Bible grows more b. 699
death, most b. adventure in life
2458
easy to turn religious life into b.
memories 10165
Friendship without self-interest
rare, b. 4238
God makes b. something broken
885
Honesty a b. and refreshing
simplicity 5874
How b. the sight of thee must be
4659
Humanity b. when praying 4086
Laughter most b. and beneficial
therapy 6733
Love can make duty b. 7165

3087
luxury of believing all things b.
are what they seem 7972
most b. poems are filled with
despair 8621
most b. poetry born from womb
of silence 10269
Nothing more b. than cheerfulness
in an old face 8148
one source, God 538
one's inmost thoughts in another
11256
scarcely anything on earth more b.
than spirit-filled mind 7776
show is so grand, b, exciting 6092
Snow is b. when watching fellow
shovel 9904
teaching of Christ at first appears
b. 6486
That which is b. not always good
5080
that which is good always b. 5080
things b. beyond belief 5360
Time has way of insulting b. things
11328
To conquer one's self is the b.
10022
wise man tells woman mouth b.
when closed 2889
world a b. book 12039

BEAUTIFULLY
If man carries cross b. 5252
world b. serenaded at the start
7886

BEAUTY
a flower without perfume 536
a joy forever 534
against affliction 10844
All is b. 8030
And b. in a tear 9024
boughs drink in new b. 2508
Charity does work of b. upon
giver 1075
cup of blessing 535
devil entangles youth with b. 2677
Each moment of year has its own
b. 9873
Every sky has its b. 8005
Everything has its b, not everyone
sees it 8492
Exuberance is b. 3179
God always preserving b. of his
order 4644
God concerned with character,
not outward b. 1033
God is b. 4455
God leading world by vision of b.
4474
God maintains sun in bright,
ordered b. 4619
God's handwriting 535
Grant us a heart wide open to joy,
b. 9064
greed ruthlessly ready to crush b,
life 5327
if b. in character, harmony in home
8441

if righteousness in heart, b. in character 8441
immutability of God most perfect b. 977
in every fair face 535
in every fair flower 535
in every fair sky 535
in space 11650
In the face of the sun see God's b. 4858
In time must fade and b. lose 8172
Jesus Christ, b. within 6352
know, praise some one aspect of the divine b. 6169
Marriage less of b. than single life 7635
mind dwells on b. of world 11301
move b. from faces into hearts 8169
My b. are, my glorious dress 4719
nature, extravagant wealth of b. 8046
no cosmetic for b. like happiness 5563
No eloquence adequate to tell of b. 10274
no picture can express 539
no transient b. scorn 11375
not eye that sees b. of heaven 10656
O B. so ancient and new 7473
of ancient days, yet ever new 4805
of Bible poetry 701
of character learned at home 5849
of restoring b. is solved by redemption of soul 10668
of the home is order 5851
of thy peace 8431
Peace within makes b. without 8463
perception of b. a moral test 540
Photography records b. of earth, skies 2016
Sea of Galilee makes b. 10195
serene, silent b. of a holy life 5766
shall find God satisfying our sense of b. 3774
sickness blurred b, delivered from pride 1776
so full of b. was the concept of mother 7859
So is the b. of an aged face 8125
some are drawn to God through his b. 7532
Some no matter how old never lose b. 8169
soul that sees b. of heaven 10656
splendor is not b. 11662
stars giving b. to the world 9116
such seems your b. still 8179
take time to enjoy b. 6828
Thought shows b. within 11267
To marry woman for her b. 7661
to plough heart takes away natural b. 896
unaccompanied by virtue is 536
wayside sacrament 535
wherever glance falls God turns to b. 4463

who keeps ability to see b. never grows old 12182
will never pass into nothingness 534
Without whose vesting b. 7109
world is full of b. 12041
worship, to purge imagination by b. of God 12124
Your b. is in God 7689
Youth happy because capacity to see b. 12182

BECAUSE
We like someone b. 7333

BECKONING
Grace the b. nudge 5221

BECOME
an excited person 3185
aware God is enough 4516
cannot b. creative without solitude 10579
desire children to b, we must be 5861
Freedom means set free to b. what God wants 4122
friend accepts who you've b. 4169
Heaven where questions, answers b. one 5647
Let us b. like Christ 2121
No man should b. that of another 6201
tell man brave, help him b. so 3140
To b. like Christ only thing worth caring for 6494
We b. what we do 11717
what might not the heart of man b. 8655
work to b, not to acquire 3124

BECOMES
child b. largely what he is taught 5818
one's mouth what one b. 10687

BECOMING
a father easy enough 3917
Prayer is not getting but b. 8928
present gone in instant of b. 11389

BED
better go to b. supperless 4033
by going to b. for hour after luncheon 9531
carry care to b, sleep with pack on back 12080
Death put to b. with a shovel 2275
Death, no need to get out of b. 2241
dread the grave as little as my b. 2370
Everyone constructs own b. of nails 1729
faith has no b. to sleep upon 3760
Holy angels guard thy b. 361
If cannot rise from my b. 8135
If it's heads, I go to b. 3011
in sickness, Christ makes my b. 6498

Make thee a b, soft undefiled 1357
O b, delicious b. 10484
to ornament your manger b. 6118

BEDBUG
wicked, has blood like that of b. 11885

BEDRIDDEN
What will you do when disease makes b. 11151

BEDROCK
mystical experience b. of faith 7948

BEDROOM
sins of b. not the only ones 10399

BEDROOMS
Why put Gideon Bibles only in b. 751

BEE
busy b. teaches two lessons 3454
every ant and b. so amazingly know their path 7945
giant feels sting of b. 8700
witness to mystery of God 7945

BEEF
lest devil brings us b. 2703
too much find himself in stew 2068

BEEN
For all that has b, thanks 9055
Forever God must remain what he has forever b. 4821
friend knows where you've b. 4169
Love slays what we have b. 7272

BEES
like to see preacher act as if fighting b. 9141
Men must not turn into b. 9721
then b. are b. because they be 6185

BEETHOVEN
after becoming deaf 155
came and wiped away my tears 1817
Deafen, you have a Ludwig van B. 161
sweep streets as B. composed music 2777
you may become a B. 3039

BEETLE
in eyes of mother every b. a gazelle 7846

BEFORE
all is God 4607
an eternity behind, an eternity b. 7052
Be thou a bright flame b. me 5375
cannot get behind the b. of birth 5459
for endless eternities b. 4694
God can make the heart a garden 896
God created universe 4879

God never is b. his time 4477

I can say like a lightning flash 7070

In eternity neither b. or after 11316

Life an event arrive after, depart b. 6957

Life is half-spent b. we know what it is 6964

matter came into being 4694

me lies Dawn and the day 5471

not God's will we see b. or around us 5397

Nothing b, nothing behind 3767

Nothing said not said b. 10686

part of man knows which never knew b. 5809

part of man sees which never saw b. 5809

swallowed up in eternity b, after 4905

swallowed up in the eternity b. and after 7084

thee in humility 4021

there was an earth at all 4694

us a future all unknown 5376

we can be filled with the Spirit 5772

we were born, God was God 4527

what lies b. tiny compared with within us 1058

you borrow money from friend 4032

you can cure diseases of the body 6085

BEFOREHAND

Chance does nothing not prepared b. 4928

grace cannot be stockpiled b. 5226

Nothing so good as seems b. 3506

BEFRIENDED

had he b. those really in need 7423

BEG

Whatsoever we b. of God 2791

BEGAN

I followed him, new life b. 1147

BEGEM

Stars daisies that b. blue fields of sky 11638

BEGGAR

Be grateful to the b. 621

gives you chance to do good 621

God rejoices when one b. scratches another 9454

BEGGAR'S

Holding a b. child 7178

wealth 5932

BEGGARS

We are all b, each in his own way 5986

BEGIN

as a mere apprentice 7352

at bottom in everything except learning to swim 6021

by being humble 5997

Christian does not b. with human intellect 3783

glory comes from daring to b. 102

He who would climb ladder must b. at bottom 10782

In creating, the only hard thing's to b. 2007

journey of a thousand miles b. with single step 6871

learned how to b. again 542

lost world, b. to find ourselves 10549

Relying on God has to b. all over every day 7515

right that you should b. again every day 10705

Spring cleaning should b. with head, end with heart 5756

the work will be completed 48

till they b. to sweat in seeking them 9037

to be satisfied spiritually, b. to degenerate 9234

to discuss things that really matter 4029

To know man we must b. with God 4571

to see from God's perspective 11152

tomorrow serenely 8375

tragedy of life is we wait so long to b. it 7042

when b. to worship, b. to grow 12107

when tempted to b. with "If people would" 579

where we will, God there first 4835

wish to rise, b. by descending 6788

with certainties, end in doubts 950

with doubts, end in certainties 950

You b. a new life every morning 7091

youth eagerly waiting for play to b. 12168

BEGINNING

All revolutions from b. to end of world 4898

At b. God accepts us in sinfulness, selfishness 9832

at b. of every enterprise call upon God 8757

at b. of God's resources 897

Christianity, land of b. again 1178

confession of evil works b. of good works 5040

Death b. of life's procession down eternity 2245

Death is a new b. 2253

Doubt, b. not end, of wisdom 2934

end may be new b. 3632

every b. ends something 1728

Every b. is consequence 1728

Every end new b. 963

Evil sweet in the b. 3360

fear rather life will not have b. 2283

God at b, end of time simultaneously 11314

God self-existent, his love had no b. 4750

God's work from b. is revelation 4906

God, a radical b. of goodness 4698

Grace b. of glory in us 5216

grace of God had no b. 4656

human race playing at children's games from b. 5982

In eternity everything is just b. 3278

In my end is my b. 2318

In the b. love a flame 7236

In the very b. God loved his chosen creatures 4769

is half done 541

Knowledge of sin is b. of salvation 9815

Love destroying all memory of a b. 7229

man knows death is a b. 2343

Martyrdom is only the b. 7676

most important part 544

no better way to finish spiritual life than to be ever b. 10705

no end to God's b. 4602

of greatness is to be little 5293

of pride was in heaven 9218

of wisdom is to call things by right names 11941

only God knows b. of things 6705

rather fear life shall never have a b. 6891

reform thy world, b. with me 9103

revive the church, b. with me 9741

Self-complacency, pride b. of degeneration 9234

Sin sweet in the b. 10375

Some people tempted strongly at b. 11083

the art of b. 56

To have found God not an end, but a b. 7544

who believes advanced in spiritual life has not made b. 10701

will remain at b. of godly life 6708

With God no getting away from b. 11355

BEGINNINGS

And very small b. 7119

Satan content for us to make b. 9857

Through God turn endings into b. 3629

BEGINS

acquaintance that b. with compliment 1572

active life b, ends on earth 1764

as soon as existence mysterious,
  thought b. 11220
Bible b. with a garden 723
cannot tell where God b. 4602
Charity b. at home, should not
  end there 5822
Christian b. with what God has
  revealed 3783
devil's country b. where men eat
  men 4913
Education b. at home 3006
eternal life b. with faith 3652
God b. by stripping of all
  self-confidence 9851
God comes in where helplessness
  b. 11786
God's country b. where men love
  to serve their fellows 4913
Happiness b. in the head 5515
He who b. many things 57
Heaven b. where sin ends 5642
Knowledge b. with wondering
  6691
Life b. on other side of despair
  2597
martyr dies, his rule b. 7679
neurosis b. at home 3006
Nothing b. and nothing ends 810
Prayer b. by talking to God 8902
quality of life b. when confidence
  transferred to God 5645
theology b. and ends with Christ
  as Savior 11182
to care he does not cheat neighbor
  5004
When boasting ends, dignity b.
  2766
when God b. to deal with
  sanctified souls 9840
when new century b. 11329
When words leave off, music b.
  7932
whenever heart b. to burn with
  desire for God 4749
where God, the cause, b. 4525
where human will leaves, divine
  grace b. 5200
with a cry and ends with a groan
  7089
with one step 4435
With renunciation life b. 7092
Worship b. in holy expectancy
  12105
Youth b. when objects to parents
  having own way 3905
Youth b. when parents become
  retarded 3906

BEGS
God b. you leave future to him
  4319

BEGUN
birth, nothing but death b. 811
eternity will have just b. 3294
forces of evil have b. decisive
  offense 3400
friendship will not continue b. for
  an end 4222
If well thou hast b. 543

leaves as much to learn as if never
  b. 4702
Life, arrive after it has b. 6957
Our Father's full giving is only b.
  7570
Say rather that morn has just b.
  2418

BEHAVE
as receiving great guest 552
craves specific rules to know how
  to b. 6810
Jesus had things to say about how
  we should b. 6444
love you too much to let you b.
  like that 8332
the gospel 5107

BEHAVED
If b. like Christians, no pagans
  565

BEHAVING
as if you loved, you will come to
  love him 8055

BEHAVIOR
civil government boundaries for
  human b. 5177
decisions regarding 563
Determine, evaluate 555
divine b. modification 577
Environmental influences do not
  account for b. 558
evil is natural b. 11204
If theology doesn't change b.
  11190
imitate b. of winners 549
is mirror image 553
is something from within 558
not too bitter, not too sweet 557
religions with no influence on b.
  1232
shaped by mind of Christ 10562
Solitude shows way to let b. be
  shaped 10562
sturdy, upright in b. 836
what matters is b. 3051

BEHIND
an eternity b, an eternity before
  7052
And leaves our sphere b. 8078
And, departing, leave b. us 5288
  3441
be a kindly Shepherd b. me 5375
better things ahead than b. 2293
can spring be far b. 9874
cannot get b. the before of birth
  5459
casts shadow of our burden b. us
  5923
clouds is sun still shining 10582
do away with everything b. man
  4315
Don't walk b. me, I may not lead
  4224
Fill up that which our lives have
  left b. 9054
God never is b. 4477
grow young as I leave my me b.
  9920

heard your voice b. me telling me
  to return 9070
If you have left your dreams b.
  8122
In front a precipice, b. a wolf
  2733
Jesus Christ b. everything we see
  5716
joy may be a callous temperament
  10583
life's darkest clouds 10964
man has lagged b. morally 9872
many Christians have future b.
  them 4321
many Christians, glory b. them
  4321
minds speculate on what lies b.
  nature 4704
Nothing before, nothing b. 3767
power b. us greater than task
  ahead 7878
something is b. them: that is God
  4962
sorrow always sorrow 10583
task ahead never as great as
  Power b. 3804
the cloud the starlight lurks 5904
the dim unknown 5377
What lies b. us tiny compared
  with within us 1058
What people say b. back is your
  standing in community 9628
While prayers to heal her wrongs
  move slow b. 6269
Who can see b. and in chance God
  4961
who hides b. hypocrite smaller
  than hypocrite 6046

BEHOLD
Joy is to b. God in everything
  6550
Wisdom does not inspect but b.
  11967

BEHOLDEN
for two discoveries, b. to Jesus
  2308

BEHOLDING
Remorse is b. heaven and feeling
  hell 9574

BEING
A b. wholly here, wholly there
  4840
a father can be rough 3917
afraid to the very core of b. 3824
and doing one in God 4579
astonished at b. here rather than
  there 4905
before matter came into b. 4694
Beware activities, instead of b.
  938
Bible, quickens my total b. 722
ceased to have appeal 1753
deeper sorrow carves into your b.
  10626
do more good by b. good 3456
do you fill all things with whole b.
  4854

in loving anger of God 4997
in the sun even when it is not
  shining 3732
inclined to b. those we do not
  know 610
Is it so difficult to b. in God 615
is to b. in a God who is a demon
  6280
likely to b. worst about another
  3412
ludicrous for Christian to b. he is
  object of public worship 9217
man cannot b. until he knows
  Christ 611
Man prefers to b. what he prefers
  to be true 595
man who refuses to b. anything
  3710
natural man must know to b.
  3743
Never b. anything bad about
  anybody 5148
never really know how much you
  b. 616
no one can b. for me 594
no one can drive me to b. or
  disbelieve 594
not that we b. Jesus Christ can do
  things 589
not that we don't b. in God 10509
not the gospel you b, but yourself
  588
not understand that he may b.
  4910
nothing, not enough 602
only possibilities, not faith 605
people who influence you are
  people who b. in you 6240
possibilities, mere philosophy 605
power behind greater than task
  ahead 7878
praying because we b. we are right
  9021
Read not to b, take for granted
  856
reward of faith to see what we b.
  3701
righteous who b. themselves
  sinners 10404
saint makes it easy to b. in Jesus
  9771
Satan to exist for two reasons
  9854
seek not to understand that you
  may b. 609
sinners who b. themselves
  righteous 10404
Some preachers don't b. in revivals
  9750
spiritual man must b. to know
  3743
Springtime invites you to b. anew
  9896
sun has risen 1197
task ahead never as great as
  Power behind 3804
that evil dies 11129
that you may understand 609

they conquer who b. they can
  3720
Those who control what young
  people b. 8360
those who do not b. no
  explanation possible 608
though all Providence becomes
  pandemonium 584
To b. God made lower creatures
  for prey 6280
To b. greatly, necessary to doubt
  greatly 2958
To b. in God is to know rules will
  be fair 4508
To b. in heaven is not to run from
  life 5674
To b. on Christ is initial faith
  3801
to be a child b. in belief 1122
to be a child b. in love 1122
to be a child b. in loveliness 1122
to know what he ought to b. 9824
to the end 583
To those who b. no explanation
  necessary 608
too late b. in eternal punishment
  5700
unbelief is won't b. 2930
What I b. about God most
  important 614
what we b. their opinion of us is
  9486
when cease to b. in a personal
  deity 4538
while making us b. self-love is not
  there 10027
will b. in your Redeemer 3324
with a faith that kindles 3182
with certainty, begin with doubting
  606
would not b. in eternal life 5700
Write, say, think nothing you
  cannot b. to be true 9871

BELIEVED
by discrediting what they b.
  12147
Christ too truthful to be b. 6507
He who has not b. will not
  experience 3535
in God, life made sense 7011
in God, world had meaning 7011
liar isn't b. even when speaks truth
  6844
missed the glory of those who b.
  6464
Nothing so firmly b. as least
  known 6082
whatever they did, God ordained
  3113

BELIEVER
believes that he may understand
  4910
does not understand that he may
  believe 4910
Every b, God's miracle 1279
freed from death as curse 2372
God alone makes man b. 585

God gives b. new set of inner eyes
  8495
great thing to be a b. 589
Lord does not let b. have
  pleasures outside of himself
  8608
makes decisions on eternal values
  10707
mature b. a searching b. 7700
most fervent b. may appear
  paradoxical 8569
special to the God of the universe
  9999
whether a b. or not, loneliness is
  homesickness for God 7146

BELIEVER'S
In a b. ear 1507

BELIEVERS
church brotherhood of b. 916
for their faith 1328
Jesus divides into b, nonbelievers
  686
motivated by legalism 6810

BELIEVES
As man b, so he is 581
atheist b. himself an accident 473
believer b. that he may understand
  4910
By night, atheist half b. in God
  477
discovers someone else b. in him
  4275
Faith b. promise 9322
Faith b. the unbelievable 3713
friend b. in your future 4172
he is worthy of heaven 5668
lightly, has not much belief 2949
man accomplishes what he b. 613
man who b. everything is as far
  from God 3710
No man b. unless God inclines his
  heart 597
saint never b. circumstances
  haphazard 1324
Salvation is to him who b. 9810
sin that b. in nothing 11394
to one who b, life is victory 607
who b. himself advanced in
  spiritual life 10701
youth b. everything exists for his
  sake 12169

BELIEVING
absurd to argue men into b. 590
Beware of b. human soul simple
  10653
faith b. beyond sense, sight 3657
faith b. God will 3691
Faith b. in advance 3708
Faith b. that it will come true
  5927
Faith b. what will only make
  sense in reverse 3708
Faith b. where we cannot prove
  3682
Faith not b. God can 3691
faith not b. without evidence 3657

for salvation reduced to
  once-done act 9816
God must need him there 2792
God understands everything 7560
God's promises, arrives safely
  2713
he who dies b. 2228
impossible without thinking 617
like donkey b. crowds cheering
  him 9217
luxury of b. all things beautiful
  are what they seem 7972
man can walk over Niagara Falls
  3669
must do his own b. 2280
My warrant is the Word of God,
  naught else is worth b. 9813
People think thing's worth b. if
  hard 3773
reward a liar by b. nothing he says
  6863

BELL
doesn't ring on its own 75
Fear is kind of b. on approach of
  danger 3973
God comes to see us without a b.
  4525
if someone doesn't pull or push 75
Never send to know for whom the
  b. tolls 2339

BELLBOY
God not a cosmic b. 4543

BELLIGERENCE
Neutrality at times graver sin than
  b. 8072

BELLIGERENT
individual, full of hate, bitterness
  5594

BELLOWS
Ill words b. to slackening fire
  5145
Slanderers devil's b. to blow up
  contention 10469

BELLS
a rationalist, but liked ringing of
  church b. 9394
Character like b. which ring out
  sweet notes 6293
Lighthouses don't ring b. 6022
mortals ring b, fire off pistols
  11329
Sundays when the b. do chime
  10957

BELLY
Bridle the b. 9960
hates a long sermon 10107

BELONG
collectivities b. to the devil 6176
Faith and thought b. together 617
God does not b. to existing things
  4609
God's thoughts b. to world of
  spirit 10692
I don't b. here 6929
Infinitude can b. to but One 4703
to people who do things 93

BELONGED
Christ b. to his times 6359
things that b. to peace connected
  with Jesus 6420

BELONGING
Besides b. to eternity 6359
whatever we think of as b. to God
  holy 5749

BELONGS
Absolute truth b. to God alone
  11495
Bible falling apart b. 632
bread b. to me if everyone has
  share 625
bread you store up b. to the
  hungry 11855
Every soul b. to God. 4529
failure to put God where he b.
  7046
Faith b. to men in God 3698
friends, property of one b. to the
  other 4186
Joy arises from being where one b.
  1807
Reality b. to eternity 9404
Use everything as if it b. to God
  10740

BELOVED
Bible, banned, burned, b. 726
He gives his b. sleep 8120

BELOW
Be thou a smooth path b. me 5375
Doing injury puts you b. enemy
  4073
God is b, but not depressed 4848
Here b. all is incomprehensible
  6096
Nor can we fall b. arms of God
  4774
search for pearls must dive b.
  3255

BEND
Better to b. than break 4055
cannot b. ourselves to will of God
  4984
love should b. to every necessity
  7168
our conscience to our dealings
  1687
Your force, to break, blow, burn
  2840

BENDING
Lo, earth receives him from the b.
  skies 6138
stands erect by b. over the fallen
  10144
Why is God b. as he chooses 3042

BENDS
riper he grows, more lowly he b.
  head 6030

BENEATH
God is b, sustaining 4841
God's gifts on shelves one b. the
  other 6017
living b. our privileges 5778

shining qualities b. rough exterior
  5078
The rock b. 3767

BENEDICTION
he who seeks to serve two masters
  misses b. 1332
New Testament, greater b. 243

BENEFACTOR
reminded of the greater B. 4526
want everyone to be your b. 9448

BENEFICENCE
angels administrators of divine b.
  363

BENEFICIAL
Happiness b. for the body 5340
Laughter most b. therapy 6733

BENEFIT
fringe b. of Christian, sense of
  identity 1266
of trial consists in silence, patience
  2734
Thanksgiving invites God to
  bestow a second b. 11162
whatever devil does, God can use
  for Christian's b. 9858

BENEFITS
Grace inclines God to bestow b.
  upon undeserving 4652
gratitude secret desire of greater b.
  5262
great b. of our life, health 6255
greatest b. become greatest curse
  3895
Justification foundation that
  supports all b. 6633
must repudiate seeking God for b.
  4806
spend as much time thanking God
  for b. 11166
that Lord has done to me 7568
Write injuries in dust, b. in marble
  9523

BENEVOLENCE
God is fashioning to b. 4514
God is virtue of highest b. 4514
love of God not a senile b. 4792
Peace is a disposition for b. 8455
sin, self-seeking instead of b.
  10359

BENEVOLENT
so b. held umbrella over duck
  6641
The heart b. and kind 6666

BENIGHTED
walks under mid-day sun 1683

BENIGN
How gracious, how b. is solitude
  10578

BENT
As twig is b, tree inclines 8344
As twig is b, tree's inclined 2991
don't get b. out of shape because
  you wobble 6187
Never has man b. himself 3444

To be b. is to become straight
7071

will break bow if keep b. 9536

BEQUEATHED

by those who would part with
nothing 10078

BESETTING

mystery of myself solved by this b.
God 4889

BESIDE

me sits another 6398

us a friend well loved, known
5376

Walk b. me, be my friend 4224

BEST

All is b, though we oft doubt 4985

And all was for the b. 6914

answer to misrepresentation 9677

awakening of reverence is
contemplation of works of God
9734

Aye, with the b. of us 6932

be b. for thee and me 5415

belief that God knows what is b.
for us 9993

Bible b. formula for justice 701

books haven't been written 8230

Christ must have the b. chamber
6504

Christians accepting noisiest as b,
greatest 5891

Christians must be at their b.
1353

comfort in suffering and pain
10926

compliment to set free to make
own inquiries 6207

conqueror takes no part in war
11784

corruption of b. becomes the worst
10718

cure for empty day 2558

Day of all the week the b. 10953

death, b. of all things created
2231

difference between b. for God,
yourself 3469

dispense wealth is b. way to
preserve it 11870

doing well is wisest and b. 67

Experience the b. teacher 3526

faith develops b. when fog rolls in
3789

faith from conflict often b. 2935

fighter never angry 11784

foretaste of heaven 7198

friend helps us be our b. selves
4178

friend helps us put forth b. efforts
4178

friend makes me do my b. 4170

friend makes you at your b. 4192

friends should be "No problem"
type 4226

gain is to lose 4339

garments whitest will b. perceive
spots 6004

get b. out of man, go to b. in him
3471

get into habit of looking for b.
10780

give as love-gift b. I have 9762

God asks you do your b, not Saint
Teresa's b. 9013

God does b. work in difficult
circumstances 3769

God estimates us at our b. not our
worst 4650

God gives b, leave choice with him
1139

God knows b. what is b. 4640

God wants our b. work 941

God would give b, man will not
take 2571

God's gifts put man's b. dreams to
shame 4988

God's third way b. 1120

godly knows God his b. friend
3996

good example b. 3449

Good example b. sermon 3427

government b. which governs least
5187

Grace grows b. in winter 5215

He b. can part with life without a
sigh 10046

He most lives who acts b. 1056

He prayeth b. who loveth b. 7174
8807

He who knows himself b. 1711

Helplessness is your b. prayer
8901

Home b. security of civilization
5835

Home, spot of earth supremely b.
5834

hope for the b. 5911

Hope is grief's b. music 5921

if from life you take the b. 8122

If God does not know what is b.
who would 4552

if my b. Friend who laid down life
4069

if no birds sang except those who
sang b. 7926

in company, even with b,
wearisome 10572

In lonely solitude God delivers his
b. thoughts 10544

in silence worshiped b. 10249

Is well and b. 4746

is yet to be 8132

know how to prize friends 4286

Knowing God's own time b. 3800

knows himself b. esteems himself
least 6002

knows not b. emotions of the heart
5349

Lead thou the way, thou guidest b.
4977

legacies father can leave children
3924

little, nameless, unremembered
acts 626

live up always to b, highest 3468

Living well is b. revenge 9719

Lord, grant that my last hour be
my b. 2332

majority is b. way because visible
5191

man does not want the b. 2571

man to make his way b. he can
3495

Marriage infinitely rewarding at
its b. 7641

men improve with age 7419

Men of few words are b. 1860

mind functions b. when open
7770

mirror is an old friend 4200

mirror shows everyone his b.
friend 9998

mother challenges kids to do their
b. 7844

Music is God's b. gift to man
7904

My name is Death; the last b.
friend am I 2337

of healers is good cheer 5617

of men still sinners 3861

of us are poor wretches saved
from shipwreck 10386

of whom we speak least on earth
b. known in heaven 9616

one of God's b. gifts 4220

one who can serve b. seldom loses
10170

or worst in this life another matter
10789

Parents giving children nothing
but b. 8324

Past and to come seem b. 8382

people who related to God b.
7526

perfect means do b. with graces
God has given 9013

philosophy not b. expressed in
words 1148

play contains work 12022

pleases God must be b. 1563

portions of a good man's life 6664
626

Power will intoxicate the b. 8714

Practice b. of all instructors 3543

prayers often have more groans
than words 8974

profits most who serves b. 10143

proof of immortality in sharing
life of God 6105

race hasn't been run 8230

revenge is not to be like him who
did injury 9727

Right actions b. apologies for
wrong actions 9598

saints which God loves b. 9788

Scriptures teach b. way of living
742

secret b. kept by keeping secret
1614

servant does his work unseen
10191

Silence in times of suffering b.
10886

silent closet b. declares God's
reality 10554

simple, unassuming life b. for everyone 7365

Slander answered b. with silence 10464

so much bad in the b. of us 3953

soldier is not warlike 11784

Solitude often the b. society 10557

Solitude soul's b. friend 10559

some in whose company we are always at our b. 9503

Sorrow makes silence her b. orator 10619

stops in our nature drawn out 9503

stuck true to God will come out b. 10789

Suffering b. gift God has to give us 10894

teacher gets most out of pupil 3026

That which each can do b. none but his Maker can teach 6226

That's b. which God sends 7520

the b. that you can become 91

the will to become the b. 92

theology is divine life 11200

thing about future 4320

thing is to let it rain 34 1789

thing to give child, example 511

thing to give enemy, forgiveness 511

thing to give father, deference 511

thing to give friend, heart 511

thing to give men, charity 511

thing to give mother, conduct 511

thing to give opponent, tolerance 511

thing to give yourself, respect 511

things are nearest 829

things in life are free 3838

Though we love our own the b. 3900

time to relax is when you don't have time to relax 9534

to be with those in time 4252

to forget 4083

to rearrange prejudices 11228

to yourself when good to others 6673

useless to put b. foot forward, drag other 11601

war uses man's b. to do man's worst 11763

way for child to learn to fear God 8327

way to cheer yourself up 2559

way to keep from stepping on toes 11286

way to keep is to let go 4733

way to show gratitude to God 5261

way to understand wrath of God 4999

We love thee well, Jesus loves thee b. 2365

what are we like with those we know us b. 9845

while my b. hopes lie shattered 11470

who wear shoe know b. where pinches 8275

will do b. I can without fear, favor 7006

worked my b. 6591

Worship giving to God b. he has given us 12134

Worship pictured at its b. in Isaiah 12136

worst and b. are both inclined 5048

BESTIAL

unconscious not only b. 7772

what remains is b. 9622

BESTOW

The Lord will happiness on contrite hearts b. 5557

BESTOWS

He who b. his goods upon the poor 4364

BETHLEHEM

As seed sprouted Christ born in B. 5731

coming of Christ by way of B. manger 6145

cross already raised in B. 1365

Though Christ a thousand times in B. be born 878

would have done no better than people of B. 8061

BETRAY

Christ's spirit of love 2988

he to whom you b. another 629

indifferent do not kill or b. 6158

Jesus Christ by keeping mouth shut 628

know you will b. him 629

man endowed with liberty he may b. 3495

man may b. Christ by speaking too many words 628

mass movement, new freedom to b. 10526

Silence a friend who will never b. 10260

somebody else, also b. yourself 631

temptation to b. best we know 5283

worst friends can do is b. you 6158

BETRAYAL

and murder exist on earth 6158

nations have found b. in peace 11783

BETRAYED

Christ b. that thou mightest go free 6393

do not understand trust until b. 11620

BETRAYS

television b. us 11041

BETTER

a fall than not to climb 3585

Any truth b. than make-believe 5887

baffled faith than no faith 3645

be pruned to grow than cut to burn 2841

be sinner than hypocrite 6049

Big not necessarily b. 1386

blind in eye b. than blind in heart 8511

break engagement than marriage 7605

check to see if you're going downhill 6877

Cheerful man will do b. 1099

child cry than father 8284

children understand b. than venerable 1216

Christ's method of making b. world alone succeeds 6487

Christian b. foundation than stoicism 1563

cottage where merry, than palace where one weeps 5821

Count not thyself b. than others 9195

creates out of past something b. 8368

defeat first step to something b. 2517

delay b. than disaster 8389

devil b. served by exploiting virtues 2648

die, live, which is b. 2378

difficulties intended to make b. 2748

Don't expect neighbor to be b. than neighbor's neighbor 9450

dry dates and content 1778

egg in peace than ox in war 11742

Eloquent silence b. than eloquent speech 10244

enemy of good 3156

equipped to accomplish things 4439

Even asses know straw is b. than gold 11804

Every person has one thing can do b. than most 6175

exchange things of earth for b. things 9974

Experience makes a person b. or bitter 3528

experiencing is b. than hearing 3535

far b. to serve neighbor than have own way 9963

fare hard with good men 4219

feet slip than tongue 11408

fewer the words, b. the prayer 8978

fools understand b. than wise 1216

forbearance b. than intolerance 6326

gentleness is b. than cruelty 6326

get new things, b. things 3315

give one shilling than lend pound 4368

given infirmity that he might do b. things 8806

go to bed supperless than rise in debt 4033

go to heaven in rags than hell in embroidery 9262

God b. served in resisting temptation 11059

God found a b. way for woman 1120

God judged it b. to bring good out of evil 5018

God looks for b. men 7501 3318

God never takes unless gives b. 4630

God will give what you ask or something b. 2568

God's b. plan takes effort to grab 2607

golden bit does not make b. horse 11793

good heart b. than all heads in world 5054

good is b. than evil 6326

Good is not good where b. is expected 3466

good name b. than great riches 9610

grow neither b. nor worse 8180

half hang'd than ill wed 7604

hated for what you are than loved for what you are not 1025

have not learned to live together any b. than the ancient Babylonians 9353

Health b. than wealth 5609

heart yearns for something b. 470

hold tongue than them 1862

holy clumsiness b. than sinful eloquence 9121

how much b. this world is than hell 2592

hundred enemies outside house than one inside 5820

If a man can make b. church organs 2776

If I had known you b. 4653

if you accept decisions 39

illiterates understand b. than learned 1216

in bitterest agony to lie 10969

Knowledge given to lead us to b. service 6693

last in traffic than first in funeral 1943

like silent church b. than preaching 1394

little chiding than great heartbreak 8283

Little from God b. than great deal from men 4524

lose anchor than whole ship 9555

love of God makes b. men 7303

loving any book b. than Bible 6925

loving any pleasure b. than prayers 6925

make present b. than past 8377

Marriage does not make us b. 7633

May b. read the darkened soul 6583

Men look for b. methods 7501 3318

most handle demotion b. than promotion 9221

music thousand times b. than words 7934

nature understands her business b. 3196

never b. enjoy ourselves than when we enjoy God 7558

never trouble Trouble 11430

no b. and no worse than I 4255

no b. example of extremism than 3557

no b. way to finish spiritual life 10705

No nation b. than individuals 7987

no work b. than another 3123

nobody who accomplishes something 3856

None preaches b. than ant 3447

not b. person because praised 1067

not well-adjusted who makes world b. place 6196

nothing is b. in heaven than love 7283

obscurity b. than name 10875

often surprised people perform b. 2799

Old age can love God b. 7286

One act of obedience b. than 100 sermons 8109

ounce of help b. than pound of preaching 3146

Our Father knows our weaknesses b. than we do 9832

pain b. than pleasure 10875

Pain can either make b. or bitter 8265

poor and live, than rich and perish 8675

poor than wicked 8674

poverty b. than riches 10875

prayer, b. heart without words than words without heart 8844

preach b. sermon with life than lips 3462

quote others, the b. to express myself 9382

repentance is starting point for b. things 9590

reproach b. than honor 10875

resigns pleasures to enjoy others b. 1298

rich in God than rich in gold 11800

saying yes to something far b. 11110

serve devil for b. wages 2646

short life with wisdom b. than long life without it 11897

shun bait than struggle in snare 11049

silence b. than truth without charity 1831

silent than stupid 10243

smallest good deed b. than grandest intention 2505

smallest seed of faith b. 3795

still the work will thrive 8296

surprised by having them perform b. than hoped 9469

temptation leaves us b. or worse 11052

than any other creature can 6169

That shall be to you b. than light 5417

the more grief, b. fitted to appreciate joy 5357

the self-image, larger the capacity for loving 9997

things ahead than behind 2293

Tis b. to be lowly born 1772

to ask some questions than know all answers 6688

to ask way ten times 5424

to be content with poverty 10777

to be lied about than to lie 6852

to be lowly born 6016

to be uncertain ahd not promise 9327

to bend than break 4055

to dare mighty things 1922

to die of hunger 3979

to envy wisdom than riches 11921

to fail in cause that will succeed 3615

to fail in originality 2008

To find that b. way 9067

to have failed serving God 10777

to have gold in hand than heart 11828

to have little than nothing 7120

to have lost some battles 10777

to have loved and lost 7161

to have taken some risks and lost 10777

to keep friend from falling than help up 4191

to learn late than never 3015

to light one small candle than curse darkness 10164

to live rich than die rich 11826

to love God and die unknown 10777

To pray well b. half of study 9007

to remain silent 1836

to risk being considered indecisive 9327

to show up for work at sunset 8141

To someone may be b. than you think 4356

to suffer ill than do ill 10838

to wear out than rust out 6767 12012

to weep with wise men than laugh with fools 9475

to win glorious triumphs 1922
Truth b. than gold 11564
Two heads b. than one 403
Two heads not b. when soreheads 403
ugly face sometimes b. than real one 6057
ugly truth than beautiful lie 11498
understand b. nature of distinction 2989
understanding among people 3229
We are not the b. for our Christianity 8065
well done is b. than well said 69
What b. way could you choose 356
what God chooses b. 1800
What God sends b. than what ask for 4991
When from our b. selves we have been parted 10578
which is b, I can't say 814
who lives on b. terms with angels 3899
who never retract, love themselves b. than truth 8207
Who rises from prayer a b. man 9034
will have changed for the b. 8957
Wish for a b. light 727
wished to make them b. 7896
world b. off without ignorance, doubt 3778
world by making b. men 6487
world esteems as good, b. sheltered from temptation 5042
worshiper no b. morally than before 8845
would have done no b. than people of Bethlehem 8061
would know man b. if not anxious to resemble 1649
Year by year b. equipped 4439

BETTERING
attempting to find new ways of b. things 9311

BETTERS
always comparing themselves with their b. 6813

BETWEEN
cleavage b. truths, values 6068
contrite heart and majesty of heaven no barriers 8771
difference b. Christian love and values of world evident 6278
intelligent person has learned to "choose b." 6326
No church can stand b. God and man 7505
no distinction b. spiritual, material work 6985
One life, gleam of time b. two eternities 7013
secret b. two is secret of God 5115
Silences real conversations b. friends 4268

BEWARE
activities, instead of being 938
in prayer of limiting God 8772
Let him not in community b. of being alone 10547
Let him who cannot be alone b. of community 10547
lose substance by grasping at shadow 11499
my lord, of jealousy 6346
of a manipulator 7582
of allowing discernment of wrong 2804
of ambition 2862
of being in bondage to yourself, other people 5773
of believing human soul simple 10653
of desperate steps 2575
of doubt 2929
of emphasis on what prayer costs us 8773
of man who harbors vengeance 398
of man who is vindictive 398
of man who smoulders 398
of no man more than yourself 9921
of saying, "haven't time to pray" 9966
of sublime prayers and the lies they make us tell 8864
of succumbing to failure 3586
of the barrenness of busy life 114
of worshiping Jesus while you blaspheme 3646
that not from your own lax living 8363
the middle mind 5048
the opportunist 7583
when enemies applaud 3158

BEWILDER
us and prevent us from listening to God 8800

BEWILDERED
God not b. by what b. us 4701
When people b, become gullible 7978
where millions of b. infants 7530

BEWILDERMENTS
In Christ at peace in midst of b. 8470

BEYOND
Bible, to see b. 714
Cheerfulness costs nothing, yet is b. price 5612
conscious ego 2971
Faith reaches b. our five senses 3690
God above, outside, b. all measurement 4710
God in me, God without! B. compare! 4840
God is above all things but not b. reach 4612
God is b. our ken 4665

God is the b. in midst of life 4457
God's essence b. human thought 4670
God's promises b. wildest dreams 4458
his love and care 4763
Kind words, power b. natural causes 6645
look b. the action 572
love b. the world cannot be separated 7319
Love is fervent b. measure 7283
made one human being a little b. 6660
move b. superficialities of culture 1760
only the living, on earth and b. 2390
out there b. the eyes' horizon 6111
point where need signs to discern 5396
reaching b. boundaries of human efforts 10540
Reason's last step is recognition things b. it 9421
searching for something b. what world contains 7521
sewing on button b. them 5841
something b. what you have mastered 2758
source b. all reason 4538
that which is b. your strength 4747
There is ever a b. of mystery 4686
this vale of tears 5633
Truth is b. attack 11575
what you have already mastered 68
when pursued, always just b. grasp 5518
when we believe God b. all we can think 4685
Who pass into life b. 6109

BIAS
God's freedom from b. 6630
no business to limit God's revelations to b. of mind 11273

BIBLE
A bit of the Book in morning 633
a book now speaking 637
a congregation 716
a field of promises 716
a fire, flaming out meanings, truth 683
a living book 705
A loving Personality dominates 635
a matchless temple where I delight to be 668
a stream where elephant may swim 707
a stream where lamb may wade 707
a supernatural book 708
a well that has no bottom 678
accept or reject 686
all I want, there I find 716

all wisdom gathered up 710
Always a living Person present 635
always open 716
amazing wealth of the B. 694
an abyss 734
an ever-enlarging book 705
annotated by God's Spirit 706
anything that takes away my taste for B. study 7036
asserts spiritual values 701
assures peasant he is son of God 645
banned, burned, beloved 726
bedrock foundation of all literature 703
begins with garden, ends with city 723
Beware of saying "haven't time to read B." 9966
birth and death 750
blueprint of Master Architect 679
book of books, Biblia 750
book that makes you think 728
born in the East 645
bread for daily use 715
broke forth amidst general gloom 736
cannot obtain entire knowledge 737
cannot really be translated 669
cannot reconcile with human origin 736
centuries of experience has tested 646
chapter best which is longest 662
Children listen to its stories 645
Children listen with wonder, delight 645
Christians with vision in hearts, B. in hands 11735
cleanses my emotions 722
closed my B. and prayed for faith 3735
clothed in Oriental form, imagery 645
comes into the cottage 645
comes into the palace 645
comprehends man, his thoughts 703
constantly finding new treasures 665
constitution of Christianity 718
contains best formula for living 701
contains human weaknesses, strengths 701
contains more of my philosophy than libraries 695
contradictions caused by translations 679
critics claim fiction 679
critics claim forgery 679
critics claim unfulfilled promises 679
danger of forgetting B. reveals 4661
dead without illumination of Holy Spirit 752

deals with all the devil can do 696
deals with God, devil 721
deals with good, bad 721
deals with heaven, hell 721
deals with right, wrong 721
deals with salvation, damnation 721
deals with such grand themes 719
deals with terrors, upsets 696
Democracy attempt to apply B. principles to society 2523
devil not afraid of B. with dust 729
dictators executed those who read 726
dictators outlawed it 726
difficult book to study 694
difficult to get away from B. 653
difficult to support if faith in B. cease 5189
difficulties lie with critics 679
directs the conduct 737
divine descent 736
does not thrill 697
does not yield secrets to censorious 687
does not yield secrets to irreverent 687
doesn't promise loaves to the loafer 6774
dull, when I am dull 683
Education useless without B. 3003
encountered an actual Person 4491
enlightens my mind 722
enters land after land 645
essential for Holy Spirit to reveal 752
everybody's book 725
everything implied, anticipated 746
everything is in this book 750
exalts the body 840
find difficult because 749
finds its own everywhere 645
finds me at depth of my being 663
first morning business 681
first-hand story of goose-bump courage 1936
follows man like memory of mother 653
foundation of society, government rests on B. 5189
free gift inside 690
freedom from earthly mixtures 736
full meaning only in Hebrew 669
gallery of human portraits 703
Give the B. to the people 653
given for transformation 689
gives a light to every age 634
gives, but borrows none 634
glory without dimness 710
God the Father giver 655
God the Son theme 655
God the Spirit authenticator 655
God the Spirit author 655
God the Spirit interpreter 655
God walks in Holy Scriptures 643

God-active-in-history of whom B. speaks 5724
great and wide as the world 750
grows more beautiful 699
guide 688
has come from God 744
has feet 712
has hands 712
has lasted for thousands of years 664
has no meaning until we are born again 709
has said everything there is to be said 746
haunts like an old song 653
higher and wider than need 691
I will open the B. for you 7123
I've read the last page of the B. 4316
idea of sacrifice 9762
ideals so high best, noblest look upward 702
ideals within sight of weakest, lowliest 702
If B. agreed with science, would soon be out of date 9865
if we love Lord Jesus, we love B. 636
If you have a B. creed, it is well 2030
illustrates the ways of men 737
illustrates the work of God 737
impossible to explain how profound 734
impossible to explain how simple 734
impossible to govern world without B. 5181
In B, clouds connected with God 10598
in B. three distinctive meanings of grace 5227
In New Testament old laid open 674
In Old Testament new lies hidden 674
in perplexity opens B. at random 5441
incongruity with age of its birth 736
indicates sleep not meant only for body 10487
intellectuals attempt to discredit 726
intense light, darkness 672
is alive 712
is full of logic 3830
is God's chart to steer by 713
is inspired 663
is no twilight 672
is still best-seller worldwide 664
Joy great note all through B. 6547
joy in reading B. 733
judge that ends strife 710
keeps you from bottom of sea 713
key of knowledge to B. 743
knowledge worth more than college 640

laws in B. include treatment of earth 3200

learn about human nature 753

letter from God with personal address 704

light like body of heaven 679

light without darkness 710

like an old and revered teacher 653

like telescope 714

look through, see beyond 714

loving any book better than B. 6925

Magna Charta of poor, oppressed 700

majestic prose 676

make B. reading pleasure, not penance 662

make it your daily business 681

many divine qualities 687

many troubles you cannot cure by B. 11455

moon without its paleness 710

more deeply he works the mine 737

more frequently attacked than any book 726

more powerful than weapons 726

more widely read than any book 726

most human book 701

most thought-suggesting book 719

multiplies discoveries 683

my church 716

my confessional 716

my psalm of praise 716

my thanksgiving 716

natural view and B. view of man different 7429

never deals with domain of human minds 721

never failed to give light, strength 670

never had doubt about divine origin 664

never knew all there was in B. 665

new light continually beams 737

No one ever graduates from B. study 684

no other book equals 728

nobody ever outgrows 685

not as an arsenal for arms, weapons 668

not book for scholars only 725

not cake for special occasions 715

not possible to exhaust 678

not the same as any other book 749

not to be read at a distance 654

nourishes 697

Nowhere in B. does God claim grandchildren 9818

nowhere prohibits war 11760

obey in all you understand 681

of inestimable value 737

one controlling, guiding, unifying mind 652

one mind operative through ages 652

one of plainest statements in B. 4949

only place can find clear message 8023

only thing God makes plain in B. 11546

only thing that can combat devil 720

opened my B. and began to study 3735

original, unborrowed, solitary greatness 736

packed full of overwhelming riches 656

page torn out of human life 706

parables of life 645

part of the warp and woof of life 653

parts I understand bother me 675

passed through critical fires 646

perfect and pure 710

power of B. persists through years 654

principles of B. groundwork of human freedom 5965

produces humility and hope 738

profound source of literary stimulation 676

promise and fulfillment 750

proves God's word enduring 730

proves transient noblest monument 730

Psalms contains all that is found in B. 796

pure, unalloyed, perfect truth 710

quickens my total being 722

quote B. devil will run 720

read B. to know what people ought to do 666

read in relation to whole message 642

recreating effect, real as fresh air 697

redirects my will 722

reminds man of frailty, weakness 660

resolved to try B. as in courtroom 744

reveals depths faster than I can note 683

reveals intense, blazing holiness of God 4661

rising aloft into mysteries of heaven 750

rock upon which republic rests 5188

rooted in the abysmal depths of creation 750

runs after me 712

says devil exists 2650

science smilingly disposed of B. as guide 9870

sets man face to face with God 660

Shakespeare dependence obvious 673

Shakespeare leans upon the B. 673

shows how to reach harbour 713

shows how world progresses 723

shows where the harbour is 713

sin will keep you from 692

single line has consoled more than all books 639

smuggled into prison cells 726

soldiers carry into battle 726

some put B. on par with ouija board 693

some reduce to absurd kind of magic 693

sorry for men who do not read B. 661

source of heavenly knowledge 737

speaks in hundreds of languages 645

speaks to heart of man 645

Spirit of God makes B. a fire 683

star without a speck 710

study B. as I gather apples 667

such excellent medicine 717

sun without a blot 710

sunrise and sunset 750

supernatural book 744

taught me how to live, die 671

teaches best way of living 742

teaches most comfortable way of dying 742

teaches noblest way of suffering 742

teaches our greatness 738

teaches our nothingness 738

tells how we got here 735

tells the monarch he is a servant 645

tells what we are 735

tells what we are required to do 735

tells what we could never learn 735

tells who we are 735

tells why we are here 735

that's falling apart 632

the beauty of its poetry 701

The Book of books 727

the great mystery 693

the whole human drama 750

things desirable to men in B. 641

Though B. urges us on to perfection 9254

threats to extinguish have aided it 730

to absorb like mopping up ocean with sponge 748

too big for systems 703

transformed ruthless killers 726

treats us roughly 724

truth has endured flames 646

uncrushable certainty 696

understood only by supernatural aid 708

unique, uplifting, unfathomable 652

unsearchable 656

untainted by error 710

use like sword to drive temptation away 720

variety like scenes of nature 679

vastness like bottom of sea 679

vehicle to express thoughts that
overwhelm 698
vein of pure gold 710
verse of B. may be dangerous 642
walks the ways of all the world
645
walks with familiar feet 645
When I am really alive, B. opens
683
where wit and reason fail 710
whole compendium of human
experience 701
widens and deepens with years
685
will keep from sin 692
window in this prison-world 711
window to look into eternity 711
wise men ponder 645
without a particle of folly 710
world reads Christians more than
B. 575
worldy spirit shuts B. 683

BIBLES
Why put Gideon B. only in
bedrooms 751

BIBLICAL
authority a b. notion 9952
comes across not as b. Jesus 6467
in b. faith, woman is partner in
ministry 11981
new morality and b. morality part
7837
writers hold love served by
keeping commandments of God
7837

BIBLICALLY
church an organism 1385

BICYCLE
like going through car wash on b.
7023

BIDS
not himself good-day 12097

BIFOCALS
sign of approaching age 314

BIG
Angler caught fish so b. 3424
Don't be afraid to take b. step
3650
Don't think so b. others look small
1587
Faithfulness in little things, a b.
thing 3843
For one that b. misfortunes slay
12061
God I worship too b. for space to
contain 11643
government b. enough to give you
everything you want 5168
government b. enough to take
from you everything you have
5168
he who cannot do something b.
58
However b. whale may be 11071
If God is God, he's b. 4479
if interested in b. things 8139

must be very b. to be able to judge
4553
my boat is so small, your ocean so
b. 9110
need b. heart that wants will of
God 5442
never b. things that disturb 1472
No problem too b. for God 9288
not necessarily better 1386
Our God has a b. eraser 4635
print giveth, small print taketh
away 9328
should not be said by b. mouths
3461
so shall b. things come by and by
2534
something small in a b. way 58
thing he is about too b. for him
5592
world is b, its troubles still bigger
10520
Worry gives a small thing a b.
shadow 12085

BIGAMY
such hatred of divorce I prefer b.
2925

BIGGER
blotted finger makes b. blot 2906
Fear makes wolf b. 3969
higher the hill, b. the vista 3488
love grows b. the more you take
from it 7252
not happy unless b. sinners to
point to 10442
To a b. brighter room 2364
When it's b. than I am, so is God
10236
world is big, its troubles still b.
10520
world of adult life 1126

BIGGEST
atom smallest, when split becomes
b. 8648
blessing in your life 5792
mistake, doing nothing 7792
penny will hide b. star in universe
7795
test of all 8394

BIGOT
who will not reason is a b. 9415

BIGOTED
people most b. have no convictions
9186

BIGOTRY
no head and cannot think 9180
no heart and cannot feel 9180

BIGOTS
Without b. world would not
progress 9318

BILLOWS
look as if they would overwhelm
291
Son of God walks on b. 291
upheaves the b. in their mirth
4505

BILLS
ages of man: b. 7037
Cheer up, birds have b. 4034
sin, b. come in later 10421

BIN
mind not b. to store facts 3021

BIND
in thy love every nation and race
11424
No cord can b. so fast as love
7279
Self the only prison that can b. the
soul 9944
that freedom b. us dearer to
himself 6177
the hearts we have wounded 9054
to b. up nation's wounds 5199

BINDING
choices of time b. in eternity 1150

BINDS
as if torn asunder bond that b.
humanity to God 8967
Cut any cord but the one that b.
me to thy heart 9080
faith subtle chain that b. to infinite
2929
Grace b. with stronger cords than
duty 5211
Peace, wisp of straw that b. sheaf
of blessings 8465
Sunday clasp that b. together the
week 10956
that b. him to him who made his
freedom 6177
Which b. us to the infinite 3700

BIOFOCALS
I can manage 8146

BIOGRAPHY
Sermon on the Mount is Christ's b.
6482
theology must become b. 11199

BIRD
a little b. comes to this rock 3273
Among first things created 7886
be like a b. for a moment perched
11475
calmly clinging to his little twig
11478
doesn't sing because has answer
7883
Faith is b. that sings when dawn
still dark 3695
God builds nest of blind b. 4444
God gave a loaf to every b. 10030
God gives every b. its food 3091
God like sky to small b. 4544
had stamped her foot and cried
"Give me" 8878
He guides me and the b. 5408
how long before mountain
removed by b. 3295
leaving God to think for him
11478
Life's shadow of b. in flight 6993
of dawning singeth night long
1371

sings because has a song 7883

without caring for tomorrow's lodging 11478

BIRDS

Cheer up, b. have bills 4034

Collecting quotations similar to b. who pick up pebbles 9380

entangled by their feet 11409

God gives b. food, but they must fly 3093

if no b. sang except those who sang best 7926

Unbelief where no hand feeds b. 11595

Why no attempt to understand song of b. 11608

BIRTH

Bible, b. and death 750

border, nor breed, nor b. 915

cannot get behind the before of b. 5459

Christ, b. and death one continual act 6489

counts for nothing if virtue not there 11682

Death important as b. 2255

Deny the virgin b. of Christ and you paralyze redemption 6404

events in a man's life 7050

first work after new b. 4537

give b. to new awareness beyond human efforts 10540

God's confidence in man 815

Great little one! whose all-embracing b. 6153

greatest fact history records is b. of Christ 5710

He chose its day of b. 3227

In new b. God does three impossible things 9800

incongruity of Bible with age of b. 736

Into the dangerous world I leapt 808

Jesus calls these pains b. pains 10901

little boy of heavenly b. 1363

made us mortal 812

making ourselves ready for another b. 2225

man should be mourned at b. not death 2209

Men overlooked a baby's b. 6458

most outstanding record is date of b. of Jesus Christ 5726

My mother groaned, my father wept 808

no cure for b, death save enjoy the interval 7054

no human b. compare to supernatural b. 874

nothing but death begun 817

of new fellowship 1513

One lie gives b. to another 6856

One may return to place of b. 12170

Reason, logic have to do with time between b. and death 9419

Run, shepherds, run, solemnize his b. 6140

Send either one, if can't be twins 814

to forbid b. is quicker murder 16

was trouble for our mothers 11459

Wherein Savior's b. celebrated 1371

Why rejoice at b, grieve at funeral 2429

worth of a man as man, regardless of b. 7423

Yet Love still takes the risk of b. 6155

BIRTH PANG

of a new attitude 520

BIRTHDAY

day you fear the end is b. of your eternity 2225

BIRTHDAYS

No matter how the b. fly 8122

BIT

golden b. does not make better horse 11793

I am straying here for a b. 6929

BITE

brazen serpents reared where snakes b. 11432

more than hope lions will not b. 3787

rub wrong way will b. 9482

BITES

underneath a rivalry that b. 10527

vacationeer returns with mosquito b. 6841

BITING

instead of b. let's support 9498

BITTER

beating up thro' all the b. world 8911

But oft for our own the b. tone 3900

cynic reads b. lessons from past 2178

difficulties intended to make better, not b. 2748

Evil b. in the end 3360

Experience makes person better or b. 3528

first-tasting b. earth 6142

If God has made your cup b. 289

love of wealth makes b. men 7303

no quarrel so b. as religious quarrel 9360

Pain can either make better or b. 8265

Parents wonder why streams b. 8352

Patience is b, fruit sweet 8410

prayers b. irony if lip service 3320

Revivals and comfortable truths are b. enemies 9744

Sin b. in the end 10375

Sorrow baptizing us with b. tears 10616

to look into happiness through another's eyes 3220

vinegar truly tastes b. 2147

whether in itself sweet or b. 4978

who has not tasted the b. 10903

words make people b. 11985

BITTEREST

enemy could be your friend 3167

most virtuous men also b. 6821

preserve peace in midst of b. pain 8453

BITTERLY

Poverty makes people b. satirical 8690

We must not cry too b. 2425

BITTERNESS

as will blot out all hatred, b. 7170

belligerent individual, full of b. 5594

faith takes b. from affliction 3818

From b. of disease man learns 5605

Ills have no weight, tears no b. 7474

Love a mixture of honey, b. 7228

Many might have failed beneath b. of trial 4236

poison of b, paranoia 10034

respond to enemies with love, not b. 5890

smiles betray b. 10500

source of power stronger than b. 6491

to resist without b. 11775

Whether sweetness or b. 1461

Who planted seedling of b. 5051

you dispelled my b. 7579

BLACK

born b. in racial discrimination 161

danced on a Friday when sky turned b. 9690

devil paints himself b. 2687

don't want them to see my face is b. 3229

favorite color of asceticism 467

feathers white but heart grows b. 9517

hand and white hold each other 3237

shadow of asceticism 467

Through the b. space of death to baby life 6148

whitewashed crow shows b. again 2462

BLACKENS

others does not whiten himself 10451

BLACKNESS

Up the b. streaking 3800

BLADE

If b. of grass can grow in concrete walk 3736

BLAME

continue to b. ourselves is sin 5491

Democracy, people free to choose who will get b. 5173
Do not b. God for tiger 11140
do not b. life 505
does not Lord hear nations b, yet remain silent 4894
feel no one has right to b. us 6230
I know, through thee, the b. was mine 7480
man who is silent 2080
man who speaks too little 2080
man who speaks too much 2080
praise at morning, b. at night 8203
praise loudly, b. softly 8729
wants to b. finds sugar sour 2063
When we b. ourselves 6230
Why b. the brute creation 10361

BLAMED
Humility to be at rest when b. 6010
Truth may be b. but never shamed 11573

BLAMELESS
His only answer was a b. life 6356
If God has not made us b. 9837

BLAMING
his rashness 6599
old age b. the present 8186

BLANDISHMENTS
When b. of life are gone 10948

BLANK
Creation's blot, Creation's b. 4374
Without God life a b. 7098

BLASPHEME
worshiping Jesus while you b. him 3646

BLAST
draw upon God's power to hold up under b. 2742
God must b. out what he cannot bless 893
world to die amid b. of archangel's trumpet 7886

BLAZING
God will advance a mile in b. light 2962
intense, b. holiness of God 4661
meteor only a stone 4395
the Lord abandoned to God's b. wrath 6383

BLEAK
barren, b. winter of sorrow, loneliness 968
Pride is the mountain peak, sterile and b. 6026

BLED
Before lambs b. in Egypt 2123
Christ b. for Adam's helpless race 495
He b, and died, I have been transfused 2979
When Christ hung, b, died 7173

BLEED
I fall upon the thorns of life! I b! 6911
thorns have torn, I b. 1737

BLEEDING
In exposure of b. love on the cross 9741

BLEMISHES
Cover b. of friend 4183

BLEND
Attributes of God, all harmonize and b. 4579

BLENDING
can be bag of grapes, b. into one another's lives 9524

BLESS
all who worship thee 619
Give to thy servants skill to soothe, b. 9045
God must blast out what he cannot b. 893
instead of curse 7190
Is he sure to b. 6892
Much praying asking God to b. folks that are ill 8871
Normal day let me b. you before you depart 2197
Some have not a cent to b. 11852
the squire and his relations 3112
Thee in their orbits b. 4592
them that curse us 5001

BLESS'D
Never dejected while another's b. 3074

BLESSED
A b. babe, infant full of power 6123
are they who have gift of making friends 4220
conversion, b. defeat 1899
courtesy twice b. 1944
don't have to be flawless to be b. 5442
God to b, an ever-joyful guest 4548
is he who expects nothing 5905
is love 6161
less b. is hatred 6161
Man never is, but always to be b. 5913
Meekness that Christ pronounced b. 7728
O b. are the patient meek 6274
O what a b. thirst 9780
poor, nor rich, were b. 5001
remain eternally different 6169
the poor, not the rich 1216
those who see God in circumstances 1464
what more b. than put cares away 12057

BLESSEDNESS
beyond joy, sorrow 6536
Celibacy: Single b. 10222
God disciplines to condition for b. 2845

God is highest b. 4514
Learn b. of unoffended 7727
makes joy possible in ectasy, sorrow 6536
makes joy possible in happiness, unhappiness 6536
makes joy possible in pleasure, pain 6536
This is the b. of a saint 4626

BLESSES
God does and b. us 4575

BLESSETH
him that gives and him that takes 7744

BLESSING
Activity is a b. 6753
Adversity b. of the New Testament 243
baby, an inestimable b. 802
biggest b. in your life 5792
every misery I miss is a new b. 820
For every b. sent 11168
Fountain of good, all b. flows from thee 7456
gives b. to empty vessel 831
gives that hope to be thy b. now 5913
God not an eternal b. machine 5757
God rarely allows soul to see b. he is 6233
Gratitude to God makes b. taste of heaven 5248
greatest b. to know we are destitute 830
I don't know a b. when it comes my way 5587
if human being blind, deaf for few days 824
If seek b. through God, not seeking God 8839
know not if the b. sought will come 8825
Let us now a b. seek 10953
nor does any earthly b. appear to be wanting 7100
Not even b. but himself, my God 4428
of God as a protecting canopy, glory 5848
of the home is contentment 5851
Once it was the b. 6465
pray for b. upon daily rod 2858
Prosperity b. of the Old Testament 243
prove a b. since God wills it 169
receive b. often makes men unmindful 819
Sin causes cup of b. to spring a leak 10356
'Tis expectation makes b. dear 3496
uncertainty or b. 1461
what seems hindrance will prove b. 169
Work a b. from God 12025
Yet possessing every b. 5428

BLESSINGS

Among God's b. there is no one
  small 1820
As if thy b. had spare days 5265
Christian work crippled by b. of
  the past 10124
Conscience priest in its b. 1673
crosses are b. in disguise 288
Enjoy b. of this day 11365
every man has many 828
for man conscious of his own
  poverty 5299
for man hungry for goodness
  5299
for man sad for his own sins 5299
gently falling on thy head 361
God b. on those who need him
  821
God's b. steal into life noiselessly
  4641
Happiness doesn't depend on b.
  5513
Happy person must enjoy b. 818
Heavenly b. without number 361
hold on to past b, postpone new b.
  968
How many b. I enjoy 1810
humble man counts b. 6035
May we have joyful sense of our b.
  9092
neither self-proclaiming nor
  self-announcing 4641
of the Christian view 5299
Peace wisp of straw that binds
  sheaf of b. 8465
pray for b. on my friends, enemies
  4069
Prayer mother of a thousand b.
  8987
prayer opens to us God's b. 8846
Prayers go up, b. come down
  8956
Reflect on present b. 828
Remember b. from God, forget
  irritations 9270
Remember the day's b. 11158
Unwelcomed visitors bring b. 832
will bring larger b. 10074
will multiply capacity to enjoy b.
  5254
wouldn't have courage to ask b.
  of heaven 1929

BLEST

We saw thee; and we b. the sight
  6152

BLEW

And b. a breath into it 1982
Jesus b. everything apart 4136

BLIND

As b. man no idea of colors 4986
Be to her faults a little b. 7603
blessing if human being b. for few
  days 824
Christ never suggested turn b. eye
  to evil 9789
deaf husband, b. wife happy
  couple 7589

divine illumination would b. eyes
  4657
eye to trivial faults 9456
Eyes let me be to groping men and
  b. 10130
Faith b. to impossibilities 3683
Faith is b, except upward 3683
Father of Light! how b. is he 3369
Give me the b. obstinate eyes
  4530
God builds nest of b. bird 4444
God guides as though you were b.
  2565
Hatred is b. as well as love 5595
If a master be sometimes b. 2896
in eye better than b. in heart 8511
Kindness a language b. can see
  6650
kingdom of b, one-eyed man is
  king 823
Love b, marriage restores sight
  7629
Love b. to every interest but its
  Lord 6457
Love is b. 6344
man's world bounded by limits of
  touch 11728
None so b. as those who will not
  see 11593
not miserable to be b. 10861
one-eyed man among b. has full
  sight 8572
ostrich as b. to opportunity as
  disaster 8211
sell b. horse, praise feet 2466
shalt perceive thou wast b. before
  4737
Sit no longer b. Lord God 1487
sky not less blue because b. man
  does not see it 9409
so weak is man, so ignorant and b.
  8877
tears so b. our eyes cannot see
  mercies 10033
To b. men, Christ is sight 6391
To be b. is bad 6289
To weep, sigh because I'm b. 1810
unbelief is sure to err 5378
We know God as men born b.
  know fire 4690
will is strong b. man who carries
  918

BLINDED

drink, b. more eyes 325
must the soul lie b. 10649
Optimism is b. 8237
truth, try to grasp with closed
  eyes, fearing to be b. 11562

BLINDFOLD

Let him lead thee b. onwards
  5431

BLINDING

Through b. tears I see 7178

BLINDLY

Pass by trifling errors b. 4217

BLINDNESS

Man calls sin a blunder, God a b.
  4560
miserable to be incapable of
  enduring b. 10861
sin b. of the sense 10360
Thou shonest, didst dispel my b.
  4805
you sent my b. reeling 7473
your splendor drove out my b.
  1910

BLINDS

hatred b. us to virtues 5602
legalism, its poison b. our eyes
  6823
Love b. us to faults 5602
mind to claims of Jesus Christ
  10044
too much light b. us 3559
Truth, like light, b. 6866

BLINK

live less than time it takes to b. an
  eye 7080

BLISS

antedate the b. above 7911
by our sufferings we learn to
  praise our b. 10925
Earth has no higher b. 4799
  1763
grown great with b. 6140
highest b. in heaven 5667
No b. I seek, but to fulfill 8098
Oh the pain, the b. of dying 2404
Poetry makes you know your b.
  forever shared 8619
suppose I shall inherit eternal b.
  2419
way to b. lies not on beds of down
  2112
What future b. he gives not thee
  to know 5913

BLISTER

Jealousy a b. on the heels of
  friendship 6339

BLISTERS

Life is full of b. 192
Some people are like b. 6773

BLOCK

Rather let my head stoop to the b.
  7677

BLOCKAGE

repentance to clear the b. 10369

BLOCKING

Ridigity restrains creativity, b.
  progress 6818

BLOCKS

play with building b. of universe,
  and fail to be touched by awe
  9866
trying to spell God with wrong b.
  7530
wisdom to make stepping-stones
  out of stumbling b. 9073

BLOOD

advancing in life whose b. warmer 6898

church ceased to manufacture b. cells 3341

earth drowned in b. and tears 4902

Every person of royal b. 5967

flesh and b. so cheap 8682

forfeits own b. that spills another's 7881

God brought man here with heart's b. expense 4532

guilt washed out by b. of Christ 10419

Hope will wade through sea of b. 5912

Human b. all one color 907

is an inheritance 11683

Jesus, thy b. and righteousness 4719

of Christ grim, repulsive 2141

of Christ precious 2141

of Christians is fresh seed 7678

Revenge in cold b. is devil's act, deed 9723

shed does not rest 7880

that cause b. to flow like rivers 4895

that from Lord's beloved wounds flow 2142

Thy b. alone, O Lamb of God 8451

transfusion for courageous living 5804

wicked, b. like that of bed bug 11885

With the b. and tears of humanity 3369

Yet doth his b. nourish and warm my root 8254

BLOODLESS

pale, b, heartless thing 1487

BLOOM

lilies of the field whose b. is brief 2380

Love is the fairest b. in God's garden 7247

man makes deserts b, lakes die 3197

then b. of life is gone 5480

thoughts which have b. on them 4255

BLOOMS

Nothing grows, b. save by giving 4342

BLOSSOM

sweet new b. of humanity 804

under praise like flowers in sun 3144

BLOSSOMED

flower of Easter b. 2984

the lovely stars 11636

BLOT

Cleaning b. with blotted finger 2906

Creation's b, Creation's blank 4374

out all hatred, bitterness 7170

that thou mayst find no b. upon my shield 9088

BLOTS

God b. out his people's sins, not their names 4626

BLOW

b. thou winter wind 6249

break, b, burn, make me new 2840

Hope will endure many a b. 5912

isn't necessary to b. out other person's light 10457

Lighthouses b. no horns, only shine 5737

man can b. hot, cold with same breath 6054

me-first has power to b. our world to pieces 10087

Never b. your own horn 9222

Slander vice that strikes double b. 10463

windbag can b. one-minute experience into 3420

with breath of kindness b. rest away 4260

with one b. of hand 4951

with the self-same winds that b. 4432

BLOWING

wind of God b. but must hoist sail 5452

winds of God are b. 5810

BLOWN

by tempest of unbelievable power 7488

BLOWOUT

Collapse seldom b. 939

BLOWS

along comes devil and b. 10226

dust in others' eyes 10411

learn patience by taking life as it b. 8422

once burnt mouth always b. soup 3536

spirit, lamp world b. upon 10696

who b. own horn has everyone dodging when he approaches 9242

Wind b. it back again 596

BLUDGEON

allows circumstances to b. him 3830

BLUE

fields of the sky 11638

of heaven larger than the cloud 10634

BLUEBIRD

Happiness like b. of Maeterlinck 5519

BLUEPRINT

Bible, b. of Master Architect 679

BLUES

Anyone who sings b. has broken spirit 7888

are songs of despair 7890

Christian thanks God for "b." 3638

moody, sad and make you cry 7888

praising God takes away the b. 2564

BLUFF

worse tumble when fall over own b. 7587

BLUNDER

grief, the b. of a life 5337

Man calls sin a b., God a blindness 4560

Youth is a b. 12199 7097

BLUNDERED

failure b. not to cash in on experience 3580

BLUNDERS

forget as soon as you can 11366

no doubt crept in 8375

BLUNT

Rules b. appetite for Christ 6819

thick, hammered through 2135

BLURRED

nothing but b. memories 8353

BLURRY

look at Jesus to correct b. vision 4489

BLUSH

Truth does not b. 11555

BLUSHES

Man the only animal that b. 7411

BOARDROOM

sins of b. as much concern 10399

BOARDS

If a man has good b. to sell 2776

BOAST

my friend, the b. is poor 3174

Spirit of God will not allow you to b. 5776

BOASTING

When b. ends, dignity begins 2766

BOASTS

of his own knowledge proclaims ignorance 6682

of sin is a devil 10309

BOAT

can't sink someone else's end of b. 10480

Help your brother's b. across 905

Mine was the b. his the voice 1148

my b. is so small, your ocean so big 9110

My b. on the raging sea 6398

Noah brave to sail wooden b. with termites 1931

tugs on oars hasn't time to rock b. 10187
Two captains in one b. make it sink 6808

BOATS
One foot cannot stand on two b. 6058

BODIES
friend, single soul in two b. 4211
Friendship, two b, one soul 4298
Malignity of soul often dwells in diseased b. 5613
take excellent care of our b. 10680
treat b. as temple of Spirit 836
value b, minds so we never mar 836
we grow spiritually, even while b. waste away 8256
will be image of God 839

BODY
a chemical laboratory 842
a marvelous machine 842
a powerhouse 842
aches, pains of this poor physical b. 2346
amazing example of teamwork 846
angel without a b. 354
Arrows pierce the b. 374
As sight in b, so is reason in soul 9412
Before you can cure diseases of the b. 6085
Bible exalts b. 840
bound with chains, spirit never 4112
brain, b. machines to express personality 843
brain, pure mechanisms 843
bring into harmony with God 847
Christianity thoroughly approves of b. 1200
create through man alone 1960
create through man, woman 1960
create through woman alone 1960
create without either man or woman 1960
Every part needs the other 846
friction a warning 847
From the b. of one guilty deed 5476
full of secrets, marvels 842
God does not regulate for us 847
God does not suppress nor counteract 837
God has four ways to make 1960
God will wither up confidence in brain, spirit, b. 11689
God's creation 841
guilt made him sick in b. and mind 5485
Happiness beneficial for the b. 5340
Heaven is a city and a b. 6169
home is no home unless food for b. 5813

ingenious assembly of plumbing 833
is given to us in heaven 1200
last hour of b. but not of soul 2225
man more gregarious in mind than b. 1639
man's psychological makeup probably due to b. 1030
medium for disposition of Jesus Christ 838
mortality related to b. which dies 3482
most gracious gift God has given 837
Night to rest b. and the mind 8085
not a home, an inn 834
nothing but notes, b. without spirit 7929
old crumbling house losing its appeal 2394
pain of mind worse than pain of b. 8272
Part of his b, I transcend this flesh 4125
Revival inrush of Spirit into b. that threatens to become corpse 9749
silence to spirit what sleep is to b. 9374
simple, unassuming life best for b. 7365
sleep not meant only for recuperation of b. 10487
sleep, profound developments go on in b. 10486
soap for the b, tears for the soul 10644
soul without b, a ghost 5088
spirit, soul and b. are kept in harmony 6897
spiritual revelation in a physical b. 835
stands so broad, brawny 10649
temple of the Holy Ghost 838
through b. God's Spirit works 837
through b. Satan works 837
till soul and b. sever 9813
treat b. as servant of Jesus Christ 848
what a wonder it is 3039
when b. dies, real man will stand naked 1030
when neglected, God is insulted 841
Wisdom is to the soul what health is to the b. 11975
without soul, a corpse 5088

BODY'S
And made the b. health 5606

BOG
Each b, each rugged hill 8081

BOILING
all things everywhere are b. 9909

BOLD
and confident affirmation of self 4160
God speaks of plan unimaginably b. 4900
Humility is strong, not b. 6012
in determination to be b. become brazen 9502
In divine things no prudence not b. 2732
shall I stand in thy great day 4719
Virtue is b. 11704
wisdom is not splashy and b. 11911

BOLDLY
Speak b, speak truly 2669

BOLDNESS
has genius, power and magic 48

BOLT
If only one could b. the door 8136
Prayer b. of the night 8943

BOLTS
to ward off b. of divine wrath 4998

BOMB
Atom B. 1945 11740
do not fear explosive power of atom b. 3376
Napalm, 1952 11750
nation praying more awe-inspiring than explosion of atomic b. 8991
word can be a balm or a b. 12001

BONAPARTE
founded empires upon force 6351

BOND
as if torn asunder b. that binds humanity to God 8967
children common b. of care, love 3868
freer the man, the stronger the b. 6177
sorrow creates b. nothing seems able to break 10641

BONDAGE
Beware of being in b. to yourself, other people 5773
higher we go in social life, more b. 4159
is with world, not saints 4159
many people in b. to success 10776
Marriage offers extremes of happiness and b. 7641
worst kind of b. 4122
you shall be free from b. 7193

BONDMAN
If any a b, Christ is free 6391

BONDS
Grief knits in closer b. than happiness 5338
Oh, burst these b, and set it free 4140

BONE
aligning Trinity with b. 6131
defeat turns b. to flint 2511
Know your own b; gnaw, bury,
  unearth it 6902

BONES
good is oft interred with their b.
  5043
Lust like rot in the b. 7356
my b. the bars of death 3482
no dog exchanges b. with another
  7404
what turns b. into jelly 4551
When rattling b. together fly 6598

BOOBY-TRAPPED
world b. by devil 2701

BOOK
A bit of the B. in morning 633
Bible, supernatural b. 708
Bible most frequently attacked b.
  726
Bible most widely read b. 726
Bible not b. for scholars only 725
Bible not same as other b. 749
Bible, b. of books, Biblia 750
Bible, ever-enlarging b. 705
Bible, living b. 705
Bible, most human b. 701
Bible, most thought-suggesting b.
  719
Bible, the Book of b. 727
Bunyan's b. astonished whole
  world 1193
Christ wrote no b. yet words
  counsel everywhere 6394
every burned b. enlightens the
  world 8528
God has b. for people's tears
  11012
Gospel a b. surpassing all others
  732
Gospel not merely a b. 732
in the world as words in a b. 7076
Life is a great b. 6945
like garden in pocket 849
loving any b. better than Bible
  6925
next to good friends, is good b.
  854
read not one which thinks for you
  728
read one that makes you think
  728
real b. one that reads us 638
say in ten sentences what others
  say in b. 12149
Sin will keep you from b. 692
that agrees with our views 11216
under your head when dying 649
way to read b. of aphorisms 9387
world a beautiful b. 12039
world is God's b. 12042
world's thy b. 12048
Writing b. nearest man gets to
  having a baby 12158

BOOKENDS
Parents should work together as
  two b. 8322

BOOKS
America more b. on how to find
  happiness 8624
best b. haven't been written 8230
Bible, most human collection of b.
  701
conversation with wise worth
  month's study of b. 11898
for all the b. I want to read 11301
given for information 689
good for uneducated to read b. of
  quotations 9383
in library a few b. he wrote himself
  6965
in my library, people have lent me
  853
line in Bible consoled more than
  all b. 639
Lord needs neither b. nor teachers
  5426
magic perservation in b. 851
most important events never reach
  history b. 5725
Never lend b. 853
nobody ever returns 853
other b. to be swallowed 859
promise of resurrection not in b.
  alone 9694
reading b. like conversation with
  finest men 861
Some b. are to be tasted 859
some few to be chewed, digested
  859
who does not read good b. 860
who love good b. happiest people
  in world 5567

BOOTH
At the devil's b. are all things sold
  2641

BOOTS
always have one's b. on 2354
devil's b. don't creak 2693
while truth putting her b. on 6846

BORDER
nor breed, nor birth 915
Prayer serves as an edge, b. 8953

BORE
an intolerable b.—ourselves 9939
gives you twice as many details
  1829
nobody who isn't b. to somebody
  869
Recipe for being a b. 1866
shown world typical Christian as
  b. 867
talks to you about himself 5112
uses his mouth to talk while you
  yawn 1828
waking up always the same person
  870

BORED
Christ never b. a soul 867
eye b. by repetition 844
God's children b. with him 1403

people b. with their own selves
  871
when times demand action 3339
Why are so many Christians b.
  3339

BOREDOM
a form of criticism 2053
consciousness of meaningless
  existence 865
more drunkards than thirst 864
more gamblers than greed 864
of life for the rich is worse
  misfortune 11854
perhaps as many suicides as
  despair 864
when we lose contact with
  universe 866

BORES
give aspirin headache 1872
If God b. you, tell him he b. you
  8830
prefer comfortable vice to virtue
  that b. 3941
We all denounce b. 869

BORING
Somebody's b. me 9948
where goodness is b. 3347

BORN
All things b. through strife 1621
an angel by every man as he is
  born 366
are b. subjects 8115
as natural to die as to be b. 2320
As seed sprouted Christ b. in
  Bethlehem 5731
Before we were b, God was God
  4527
black in racial discrimination 161
Children b. from relationship
  secondary 10239
Christ the Lord is b. 6141
Christ was b. a martyr 6489
crying, live complaining, die
  disappointed 7075
death of child, adolescent is b.
  2390
Every moment one is b. 806
Everything b. of God no shadowy
  work 872
expected from supernaturally b.
  men 10206
from intimate depths of divine
  nature 5967
Gratitude b. in hearts that count
  mercies 5244
Happiness was b. a twin 5505
have so lived not b. in vain 7005
He who governed world before I
  was b. 10145
heavy price to pay for being b.
  3487
Human beings wild animals when
  b. 7382
I am not b. for one corner 908
If Christ's not b. in thee 878
If you are b. of God 7689

in dying we are b. to eternal life
9086

in hour of need faith b. within
3820

In presence of hope, faith is b.
5937

in wrong generation 12190

In youth world began to exist
when he was b. 12169

infant is b. with clenched fist
11656

Life a sentence to serve for being
b. 6952

Life happier if b. at age eighty
6989

Life is ever since man was b. 6963

living, new man b. from living
God 872

Man b. with face turned away
from God 9583

Man is b. broken 4654

misery to be b. 186

more difficult to be b. or rise 492

No man is b. wise 11342

not conscious of being b. 7050

not yet b. to tomorrow 11365

Oh spring to light, auspicious
Babe, be b. 6143

only one way to be b. 2393

Some are b. to endless night 813

Some are b. to sweet delight 813

The house where I was b. 2588

Thine I am, I was b. for thee 1538

'tis better to be lowly b. 6016
1772

to be hanged shall never be
drowned 9176

To live is to be slowly b. 6873

True prayer b. out of brokenness
9011

We are b. helpless 9513

we are b. in other's pain 810

We know God as men b. blind
know fire 4690

When God thought, the world
was b. 11244

When is the time for love to be b.
6155

Words b. in the heart, not head
11997

world's great Shepherd now is b.
6123

BORN AGAIN

a foundation fact 879

Bible no meaning until we are b.
709

fact to recognize is we must be b.
9801

nor man Christian till b. 875

not a command, but a fact 879

not natural men, we are b. 1346

we begin to see what Jesus sees
709

BORNE

Burdens become light when
cheerfully b. 1086

God sends nothing but can be b.
2546

Thou hast b. all for me 2098

When pain is to be b. 8280

Which I have b. and yet must bear
2882

BORROW

Before you b. money from friend
4032

Don't b. trouble 4035

Don't marry for money, can b.
cheaper 7612

may as well b. person's money as
time 2914

money, trouble will come 4035

use all the brains I have, and all I
can b. 6795

Worry interest paid by those who
b. trouble 12090

BORROWED

ideas from Socrates 2019

manger, tomb framed his earthly
life 6433

BORROWING

Who goeth a b. 4043

BORROWS

He who b. sells his freedom 4038

It gives, but b. none 634

BOSOM

almost worshiping the female b.
10238

BOSS

talked to God as one might talk to
a b. 7526

teenager waits impatiently to
become own b. 3867

BOT

And b. the ill with tears 7017

BOTH

chose b. fear and self-denial 467

Takes b. rain, sunshine to make
rainbow 2550

BOTHER

baby, an inestimable b. 802

Don't b. much about your feelings
4013

BOTHERED

most by flies 11056

BOTTLE

Be glad b. half full 11141

Don't be sorry if b. half empty
11141

Examine the contents, not the b.
6576

God has b. for people's tears
11012

grief up, never soften it 5343

BOTTOM

begin at b. in everything except
learning to swim 6021

cannot get to top by sitting on b.
6783

eternity a deep where we find no
b. 3283

He who would climb ladder must
begin at b. 10782

line is in heaven 5665

Me is always at the b. of sin 9916

Pride at the b. of all great mistakes
9228

tomorrow at b. of ladder 7062

BOTTOMLESS

God's love a vast, b, shoreless sea
4750

BOUGHS

drink in new beauty 2508

that bear most hang lowest 6029

BOUGHT

except to be b. and sold 3045

Love gives itself, is not b. 7222

BOUND

body b. with chains, spirit never
4112

Grace free, but you are b. to the
Giver 5211

Life a voyage that's homeward b.
6956

not b. to make the world go right
10150

when love b. to God, fear is done
3986

BOUNDARIES

civil government b. for human
behavior 5177

penetrate to b. of being 10564

reaching beyond b. of human
efforts 10540

BOUNDARY

His power no b. known unto men
7570

BOUNDARY-LINE

sharp b. yoke easy 1332

BOUNDLESS

But b. inconceivables 4676

grace of God, b. as infinitude
4656

How b. might soul's horizon be
11627

If consider b. space, shrink into
nothing 11631

love, b. treasures hidden within its
depths 7211

Marriage a b. adventure 7630

O God, your mercy a b. ocean
4816

Thine endless wisdom, b. power
4659

Who b. Spirit all 4711

BOUNDS

God b. 4709

God in his mercy made eternal b.
4813

God's greatness exceeds b. of
thought 4692

I break the b. 5471

love of God, no b. 4760

BOUNTIFUL

field rested gives b. crop 9686

BOUNTY
Faith has never outstripped b. of
  Lord 3664
shines in autumn unconfined 9883

BOW
Than these knees b. to any save
  God 7677
thy meek head to mortal pain
  2981
too tensely strung easily broken
  943
will break b. if keep bent 9536

BOW'D
nor b. to world's idolatries a
  patient knee 12033

BOWL
My life is like a broken b. 7003

BOX
at weekends get into another b.
  on wheels 5859
every night sit staring at another b.
  5859
in morning run off to another b.
  called office 5859
We give people b. in suburbs
  called a house 5859

BOXES
Do not keep alabaster b. 4223

BOY
asked question that pierced
  father's heart 3912
asked, "Daddy, have I ever seen a
  Christian" 3912
little b. of heavenly birth 1363
more joy in smile of a b. 814
prevented him from developing
  initiative 8337
Shades of the prison-house upon
  the growing b. 12164
Some folks pray for a b. 814
When a b. of fourteen 3928
When saved b. from making
  mistake 8337

BOY'S
small b. little freckled face 814

BOYS
God to whom little b. say their
  prayers 7855
Life like fly in room with b.
  armed with swatter 6968
tame b, can tame anything 7382

BRACE
If experiencing easy times, b.
  yourself 969

BRACES
wind b. up 8033

BRAGGED
never known person filled with
  Holy Spirit who b. about it
  6018

BRAHMS
kept falling asleep at piano 8565
took seven years to compose his
  Lullaby 8565

BRAIN
advancing in life whose b. quicker
  6898
body, machines to express
  personality 843
body, pure mechanisms 843
can store one million billion
  "bits" of information 7738
fumes of authority invade the b.
  8702
God will wither up confidence in
  b. 11689
heart has eyes b. knows nothing of
  8503
idle b. is devil's workshop 6754
next generation will have no b. at
  all 11028
rich furniture of the b. 3018
stir up b. to think God's line 1012
tongue inches from b, sounds
  miles away 1880
tongue into gear before gets b.
  a-going 11419

BRAINS
all have b, what we need is work
  7755
Don't insult God telling him he
  forgot to give you b. 7755
God looks at heart before b. 7378
handful of patience worth more
  than bushel of b. 8390
I use all I can borrow 259
Jazz people hear through feet
  instead of b. 7898
not b. that matter most 1027
owe it to God that we refuse rusty
  b. 11274
Shall we think with tiny b. we can
  unravel mysteries 7944
use not only all the b. I have, but
  all I can borrow 6795

BRANCHES
are of unmeasurable length 2907
thousand hacking at b. of evil
  3405

BRASS
Men's evil manners live in b. 9619

BRAVE
fray of duty that b. endure 3174
I would be b. to dare 1018
Intimidates the b, degrades the rest
  5479
live on 10948
Noah b. to sail wooden boat with
  termites 1931
Some thought b. afraid to run
  1934
Tell man he is b. 3140
When feelings are b. give thanks
  for them 3051

BRAVELY
Cheer the youth who's b. trying
  4217
in all things to serve thee b. 9088

BRAVERY
of God in trusting us 11479

BRAZEN
in determination to be bold
  become b. 9502

BREACH
sin a b. of nature 10360

BREAD
Bible, b. for daily use 715
broken b, poured out wine to
  feed, nourish 887
Brown b. and gospel good fare
  5090
cannot say give us this day our
  daily b. if 8818
cast b. upon waters while seasick
  4373
Christ b. for men's souls 6374
Christ is b. to feed his people
  6370
Christianity is b. for daily use
  1169
Don't loaf and depend on Lord
  for b. 6755
existence of hunger presupposes b.
  4606
for myself a material question 622
for neighbor a spiritual question
  621
God gives ingredients for daily b.
  9657
If any chance to hunger, Christ is
  b. 6391
if everyone has share 625
if no one starves while I eat 625
If not nourished by B. from heaven
  12050
If you pray for b. and bring no
  basket 2947
In Lord's Prayer first petition for b.
  7152
knows he is loved, content with
  piece of b. 7176
Love has to be made, like b. 7217
make us broken b, poured out
  wine as he chooses 9850
Never fall out with b. butter 3105
Night more nourishing than b,
  wine 2553
O God, that b. should be so dear
  8682
only belongs to me 625
something greater in vocation
  than b. 3107
upon waters more nourishing than
  pie in sky 10742
We thank thee for our daily b.
  11172
who gives us teeth will give us b.
  9349
you store up belongs to hungry
  11855

BREADTH
of cross to former, following ages
  2154
that is in God 5016

BREAK
bend your force to b, make me
  new 2840

Better to bend than b. 4055

Christian under trouble doesn't b. up 11452

down fortified walls of self-defenses 10043

I b. the bounds 5471

if not for hope heart would b. 5935

let God b. life from its moorings in some storm 9564

man can only b. himself against laws of God 7493

Man cannot b. the laws of God 7493

off the yoke and set me free 2583

people would b. God's windows 4480

Real doesn't often happen to people who b. easily 5886

sin, death, hell cannot b. God's decree 4616

tests of life make, not b. us 214

through superficiality to deeper life 2738

to b. one commandment is to b. the law 6812

whispers the o'erfraught heart, bids it b. 5333

will b. bow if keep it bent 9536

Your hammers b. 7875

BREAKDOWN

high crime rate traceable to b. in moral fiber 5858

nothing enviable or spiritual about a nervous b. 9533

BREAKFAST

Hope is a good b, bad supper 5915

BREAKING

God rescues us by b. us 882

God takes delight in b. up our programs 5401

If I can stop one heart from b. 6922

sinners improved by b. 898

Why is God b. as he chooses 3042

without b. any rules God has made 5046

BREAKS

Christian under trouble b. out 11452

Doubt hammer that b. windows 2936

Earth b. up, time drops away 5636

Holy Spirit b. the heart, makes it whole 5794

If link is broken, chain b. 2536

man votes, b. tie 1145

silence b. the heart 12003

BREAST

And thy b. will ne'er be lonely 4798

And trusting lean upon thy b. 4977

Hope springs eternal in the human b. 5913

How guilt, once harbor'd in the conscious b. 5479

Lay down thy head upon Savior's b. 2365

light within his own clear b. 1683

Music has charms to soothe savage b. 7901

Remorse to carry own accuser within your b. 9573

same heart in every human b. 917

Truth has a quiet b. 11559

BREASTPLATE

What stronger b. than a heart untainted 6320

BREATH

breathe a b. at a time 4885

Breathe on me, b. of God 5774

by turns we catch the fatal b. 2233

Crumbles in the b. of prayer 8789

Desire runs out of b. 2567

flowers to wither at northwind's b. 2324

Had borne my b. away 2588

I drew in b. and panted for thee 4805

Let man think life a b. of God 4557

man can blow hot, cold with same b. 6054

man has but an hour of b. 11519

mouth, ears, eyes 6120

night is given to take b, to pray 6947

Prayer the b. of the newborn soul 8938

Princes and lords but b. of kings 5885

returning, sweaty and out of b. to your fountain 9070

soul b. of God bestowed in heaven 10649

spirits stirred by b. of Holy Spirit 10490

spirituality a b. 5981

strings need only be swept by divine b. 7921 10665

Waiting to hush our latest b. 2219

with the b. of kindness blow rest away 4260

world b. of one eternal idea 4594

BREATHE

a breath at a time 4885

air we b. not sold by cubic foot 3838

broken out of time's hard shell to b. 4976

don't understand respiratory system, but I b. 3733

fresh, exhilarating atmosphere of eternity 4976

healthiest relationships b. 9494

in the atmosphere of the Incarnation 6378

knock, b, shine, seek to mend 2840

more 5604

Not where I b. but where I love 7282

on me, breath of God 5774

teach me to b. deeply in faith 3779

to b. the name 1763

To think the thought, to b. the name 4799

words b. memories sweet as flutes 11998

yearning to b. free 7985

BREATHED

God has b, they are dispersed 7874

BREATHES

not pretend to love everything that b. 5890

BREATHING

Closer is he than b. 4862

new air, finding it celestial air 2399

solemn pause, b. space of man 10960

When Lord does come, will be as natural as b. 9912

BREATHLESS

haste, b. for no reason 5577

men pursue pleasure with b. haste 8601

with adoration 8980

BREATHS

We live in thoughts, not b. 1056

BREATHTAKING

In Christ move into b. future 8364

BREECHES

If you loan your b. 4367

BREED

border, nor b, nor birth 915

Idle hours b. wandering thoughts 6760

BREEDS

extreme love, hatred b. satiety 3554

BREEZE

hundred acorns shown in silence by b. 8052

Known comfort in cool kiss of the b. 8051

thought of God gentle b. which bears us up 11249

BREEZY

sneezy, freezy 9876

BRETHREN

Gold begets in b. hate 11811

love should bend to every necessity of our b. 7168

love should bend to necessity of b. 3839

named b. for their love 1328

BRETON FISHERMAN'S

prayer for protection 9110

BREVITY

If we fully comprehended b. of life 6924

Interest comes garbed in b. 9149

BRIARS

of unbelief, selfishness and sin 7073

BRIBES

Death takes no b. 2265

BRICKS

must be cemented together 4020

wall with loose b. not good 4020

BRIDEGROOM

God, my b. in his ardent love 7951

spends money on new suit nobody notices 7588

BRIDGE

destroy b. by which God would come to you 9634

Faith builds b. across gulf of death 3655

Life b. of groans across stream of tears 2598

Life is a b. 6943

ruins b. over which he is to pass 4084

BRIDGE-MANIA

as intemperate as someone who gets drunk 9269

BRIDGEHEADS

smash b. of clever self-sufficiency 10043

BRIDGES

Men build b. 5841

People lonely, build walls instead of b. 7139

sign of approaching age 314

BRIDLE

for tongue necessary furniture 11405

the belly 9960

BRIEF

Life is b. 11287

life of the individual so b. 5944

lilies of the field whose bloom is b. 2380

pain is b. joy eternal 2383

the b. fleeting instant of time allotted 7063

BRIEFING

Don't forget his daily b. 1311

BRIEFLY

Body: an inn, only b. 834

folks we know b, quickly forget 4281

BRIGHT

Angels b. still 355

crystals of delight 10639

dawn of our eternal day 6152

Faith makes outlook b. 3705

He treasures up his b. designs 4941

keep yourself clean, b. 8573

3438

no eyestrain from looking on b. side 8240

Sin may open b. as morning 10377

sorrow touch'd by thee grows b. 10633

sun as b. as from rich man's abode 7001

BRIGHTEN

may b. as I draw near 8079

our inward light 4974

Serves but to b. all our future days 10879

smiles b. by spiritual vivacity 10500

which will b. to all eternity 6796

BRIGHTENING

cannot light another's path without b. our own 3145

hope, b. the darkened paths 5940

BRIGHTER

darker the night, b. stars shine 9323

Friendship adds b. radiance to prosperity 4228

the glitter, the more easily broken 9336

To a bigger, b. room 2364

BRIGHTEST

Angels, the b. fell 355

blazes of gladness kindled by unexpected sparks 8606

Candor b. gem of criticism 5870

He whose crown shines b. 6004

of all things, the sun has spots 3951

sun shines clearly in darkest day as in b. 4772

thunderbolt from darkest storm 220

BRIGHTLY

gleam b. in pattern of life God approves 6997

thousand worlds roll around us b. 4592

BRIGHTNESS

Dark things reach out toward b. 5906

good name keeps b. even in dark days 6292

in b, Christ is my sin 6498

Moses only saw b. of Lord 4874

BRILLIANCE

world achieve b. without conscience 1705

BRILLIANCY

success does not depend upon b. 8534

BRILLIANT

conversationalist talks to you about yourself 5112

exchange most b. wit 4204

BRIM

God fills me to the b. 4852

heart filled to b. with joy must be still 6559

BRIMMING

world is b. with happy thoughts 2020

BRING

And he will b. us through 5448

April showers b. May flowers 9884

do not b. old life up to higher plane 9839

every thought, imagination into captivity 1014

If b. into one day's thoughts evil of many 12064

law could not b. us righteousness 9755

Let us b. what is our own 4558

No evil example can b. joy to doer 5035

no season such delight can b. 9878

not what we b. with us 8

Nothing in my hand I b. 2101

sometimes fear to b. troubles to God 4789

Those to b. sunshine to others 6567

thy soul, interchange with mine 3065

To b. a smile, to banish a tear 7423

To b. them to his side 10122

Unwelcomed visitors b. blessings 832

What day may b. day may take away 2202

will b. larger blessings 10074

Will b. me hence 5469

BRINGS

death b. love's crown 7204

friend's love b. joy to heart 4382

God b. us to resigning ourselves 5395

God orders, b. into line 5175

Of Highest Wisdom b. about 4985

Worship b. wisdom 12127

BRINK

Men live on b. of mysteries 3654

BROADCASTING

think of nature as unlimited b. station 8013

BROADENING

immense b. of interest in God 9831

BROADEST

word is truth 11993

BROKE

need that b. me at thy feet 10969

you b. through my deafness 1910

BROKEN

Anyone who sings blues has b. spirit 7888

bow too tensely strung easily b. 943

bread, poured out wine to feed, nourish 887

brighter the glitter, the more easily b. 9336

Christ can do wonders with b. heart 10584

face filled with b. commandments 10315

fathom depth to extent heart is b. 900

fellowship of b. 1513

For they were b. by a nail 2162

God closest to b. hearts 1505

God makes useful something b. 885

habit too weak until too strong to be b. 5500

How else but through a b. heart 9794

If link is b. chain breaks 2536

In life-melody music is b. off by rests 7056

In love's service only b. hearts will do 895

In solitude can become b. 10540

In which the power of Satan b. is 6140

Let there be naught unfinished, b, marred 7519

make us b. bread, poured out wine as he chooses 9850

Man is born b. 4654

must be b. into life 899

My life is like a b. bowl 7003

out of time's hard shell to breathe 4976

reed of human support 3132

Reputation once b. may possibly be repaired 9612

single arrow easily b. 9442

soul is a b. field ploughed by pain 8262

string may be joined, knot will remain 9624

stumbling, b. cry can find its way to God 8849

through b. heart may Lord Christ enter 891

to will of God 4984

When outward strength is b. 3818

whose Word cannot be b. 9813

wounds shelter b. hearts 1443

BROKENHEARTED

God can make b. radiant, loving person 890

BROKENNESS

cut, cleanse, break so healing can take place 890

God plants where conviction brought b. 888

God uses circumstances 883

healing comes through b. 2519

If leave church with no b. 12106

is not revival 881

True prayer born out of b. 9011

vital, indispensable step toward revival 881

we object to fingers used to crush 883

when God uses someone we dislike 883

BROOD

Don't b. you're not a hen 2542

let your little b. be your congregation 7847

BROODS

gentleness of heaven b. o'er the sea 8980

BROOM

A new b. sweeps clean 251

BROOMS

If God willed, b. would shoot 4944

BROTH

not so much as taste of devil's b. 2703

BROTHER

bless you, he's my b. 926

Can a man love God ignoring need of b. 10052

Christ a B. to relieve 6370

digs pit for b. shall fall into himself 3373

faith is doubt's twin b. 2932

fold to thy heart thy b. 7284

God, my b. in his humanity 7951

I can't see my b. when he's walking past 5587

I want to be white man's b. 1485

If do justice to b. even though not like him 6609

is donkey, what are you 2065

Lord, b. in joy and pain 7506

my b, he's just like me inside 926

None ever yet his b. knew 6583

Silence is b. of acceptance 10264

BROTHER'S

Help your b. boat across 905

BROTHERHOOD

a divine command 902

Christian movements suggest b. 916

Help your brother's boat across 905

helping yourself by helping others 903

Human blood all one color 907

is giving appreciation 924

is giving dignity 924

is giving others your rights 924

live, think, suffer with men of your time 904

no b. without fatherhood of G. 920

proclaim b, harbor prejudice 6068

trying to build b. of man 4632

whole world my native land 908

world too small for anything but b. 11545

BROTHERLY

Without faith hard time being b. 925

BROTHERS

a destiny that makes us b. 919

can't spell b. without spelling others 9525

learn to live together as b. 923

must learn to live together as b. 5987

silly pretending we are all b. 912

To know all men b. 921

BROUGHT

by love, b. to God 3834

God b. man here with heart's blood 4532

he who has b. me so far 3712

Naked to earth was I b. 5952

Things do not happen, are b. about 4953

Who b. me hither 5469

within zone of God's voice 7540

BROW

hope, word God has written on b. 5947

Time has wrinkled my b. 11328

time writes no wrinkles on b. of eternity 3266

BROWS

how many knotted b. in marketplace 10507

If wrinkles must be written upon b. 8137

BRUISE

tests b. but build character 211

BRUISED

making peace requires getting b. 4094

BRUSH

old b. knows all the corners 251

BRUSH-SALESMAN

soul-winning may degenerate into b. 7867

BRUTALITY

more satisfaction out of b. than honesty 5884

BRUTALLY

People who are b. honest 5884

BRUTE

cuddle self-pity, you'll have a raging b. 10034

Why blame the b. creation 10361

BRUTES

alcohol, turned men into b. 331

BUBBLE

fame, an empty b. 3862

lasts a while and bursts 6927

Life is mostly froth and b. 6657

that b. is me 6927

BUBBLE-ORGANISM

in infinite spece is formed a b. 6927

BUBBLES
we buy with a whole soul's tasking
2641

BUCKET
dropped in well of truth leaky
indeed 12144
I'd have come running with a b.
4653

BUCKETS
Let down your b. where you are
9344
prayer, mercy like two b. in well
8884

BUCKLES
what b. the knees 4551

BUD
In every b, the coming day 8009

BUDDHISM
accepts gloom as fact 9551
without benefit of theology 3301

BUDDHIST
stand apart disillusioned 6563

BUDDHISTS
build wall between B. 2988

BUDGE
Ten Commandments will not b.
1687

BUDGET
record of how you spend more
than you earned 4030

BUDGETS
church concerned with b. 1409

BUFFALO
life is breath of a b. in winter
2457

BUILD
a little fence of trust 11362
Adversity can either destroy or b.
141
Anyone can b. a house 5819
can't b. on regret 9440
5486
cannot b. hopes on confusion,
misery, death 8445
could b. society of love out of
puppets 4133
God offers to help us b. cathedral
of love, praise 7684
how transient is monument men b.
730
I b. my faith on that 4758
if b. for love of God 10064
If b. to please ourselves 10064
If we would b. on sure foundation
4251
If world is cold, b. fires 4250
Men b. bridges 5841
People lonely, b. walls instead of
bridges 7139
rather than destroy 1138
so will world we b. around us
10694
Sunday foundation to b. six-story
week 10958

To b. a ship of truth 11519
trying to b. brotherhood of man
4632
up inspiration, excitement, joy
3185
wall between Buddhists, Jews
2988

BUILDERS
become house b. through building
houses 6620

BUILDING
church concerned with b.
programs 1409
Everything contributes to b. of
kingdom 4732
house on foundations of sand
7796
like b. house on sand 11801
Love compared to b. sandcastle
7233
missionaries as scaffolding around
rising b. 7780
Of the b. of life 4563
on the rock 10064
on the sand 10064
one's life on foundation of gold
7796
11801
play with b. blocks of universe
and fail to be touched by awe
9866
without basis cannot stand 3826

BUILDINGS
deeper than human b. reared
upon it 4783

BUILDS
an eternal now that b. something
better 8368
Character b. slowly 996
Faith b. bridge across gulf of death
3655
God b. nest of blind bird 4444
relationship on less than honesty
building on sand 9447
Sin b. barrier 1595

BUILT
a harbor, not what ships are b. for
76
all navies that ever were b. 6353
Character, evidence b. on right
foundation 1057
Glory b. on selfish principles is
shame, guilt 10054
In education, everything b. on
difficulty 1024
pretences b. up to hide emptiness
3395
The world was b. in order 1976
truth cannot be b. on swampy
ground of scepticism 11530
Young people were b. for God
12180

BUILT-IN
home is God's b. training facility
5854

BULBS
unless spent time as b. in the dark
5369

BULGES
sign of approaching age 314

BULL
What would ant do if had head of
b. 6221

BULL RING
not the same as to be in b. 3537

BULL'S-EYE
failure to hit b. never fault of
target 9680

BULLS
not the same to talk of b. 3537

BULLY
devil is a b. 2682
mass movement, new freedom to
b. 10526

BULWARKS
These are the b. of the state 7986

BUNDLE
Life a great b. of little things 6946
man wrapped up in himself makes
small b. 9918
not ten in a b. 9442

BUNDLES
Souls are not saved in b. 9814

BUNNY
Easter b. never rose again 2983

BUNYAN
book astonished whole world
1193
Lock him in a prison cell 161

BURDEN
bear b. of life no longer 2591
casts shadow of our b. behind us
5923
either lighten my b. or strengthen
my back 9071
Friendship lightens b. of adversity
4228
God gives shoulder to b. 928
Goodness is love with b. on back
5065
greatest b. we carry is self 9949
Hate too great a b. to bear 7182
If any little lift may ease b. of
another 910
loosed from off his shoulders
9803
Love feels no b. 7220
never bear b. of sin, doubt 937
No b. heavy when carried with
love 934
No man ever sank under b. of day
4319
of care in getting riches 11865
of life is from ourselves 5229
pleasures become his b. 7363
riches, b. too heavy for us 11832
Selfishness turns life into a b.
10083
shared lighter load 927

those who carry b. of another's sin 5029

Those who commit injustice bear greatest b. 6279

thought of God never a b. 11249

to damned God is b. in excess 4548

To friendship every b. light 4288

tomorrow's b. added is too much 935

when tomorrow's b. added to b. of today 4319

who lightens b. for anyone else 10175

will of God b. we carry or power which carries us 5451

without healing of spirit duties b. 8857

you must bear the b. 183

Yours the b. of wise guidance 8363

BURDENED
with the unbearable weight of ourselves 9917

BURDENS
bear b. of others 1080

bears heaviest b. cheerfully 5297

become light when cheerfully borne 1086

Christianity teaches to bear b. 931

days when b. weigh us down 9059

God wants us to roll b. on him 937

He giveth more grace when b. grow greater 5223

little emphasis on bearing b. 933

Marriages lies under more b. 7635

Money, time are heaviest b. 932

no one can escape life b. 931

not concerned enough to bear b. 933

people do not know b. exist 933

Pray not for lighter b. 8896

Relinquishment of b. begins 3987

some b. placed on us by God 937

Unselfishness turns b. into life 10083

What heavy b. from our bosoms take 8867

BURDENSOME
Cast aside thy b. cares 7708

BURGLAR
Quaker to b. 1550

BURIAL
After sixty years b. service personal 2213

Religion can offer man b. service 7022

stern sentence of the b. service 2213

BURIED
Died at thirty, b. at sixty 7041

In baptism, self is b. 529

my body and they thought I'd gone 9690

no disappointment if wills b. in will of God 4981

touch with divine power the b. acorn 6095

yesterday I was b. with Christ 2121

BURIES
God b. his workmen, carries on his work 2286

BURN
bend your force to b, make me new 2840

Better be pruned to grow than cut to b. 2841

candle where people dying in darkness 7779

God is the fuel our spirits designed to b. 7459

God knows how to b, then to gently cool 7951

Great men meteors designed to b. so earth lighted 5278

have one candle of life to b. 7779

Heat not so hot a furnace that you b. yourself 383

If you would have your lamp b. 12010

Never b. fingers to snuff another man's candle 10458

Spendthrifts b. money 7826

whenever heart begins to b. with desire for God 4749

BURNED
Bible—banned, b, beloved 726

but not consumed 7872

cancelled note, b. up 4081

every b. book enlightens the world 8528

Thou touchedst me, I b. for thy peace 4805

to know your peace 7473

BURNED OUT
replaced, forgotten, a lie 945

BURNING
all things everywhere are b. 9909

Behold! the b. bush still burns 7996

Hatred like b. down own house to get rid of rat 5596

Life the b. of the candle 6973

life, aimless comet b. out in self-will 6937

love is as a b. torch 7283

Thy love is like a b. fire 4795

we are like the b. bush 4874

BURNOUT
Work without love spells b. 944

BURNS
Behold! the burning bush still b. 7996

hate sin with fierceness that b. 3182

BURNT
child dreads the fire 3512

once b. his mouth always blows soup 3536

BURR
stick to Christ as b. to topcoat 2446

BURROWS
Jesus, digging mankind out of snug b. 6421

BURST
Jesus Christ b. from grave 1905

Now b. all our bell throats 8731

Oh, b. these bonds, and set it free 4140

to make acorn b. forth from its prison walls 6095

BURSTS
bubble lasts a while and b. 6927

Spring b. today 2982

BURY
counsel a woman rather than b. 19

do not b. emotions dead 3061

In peace sons b. fathers 11751

in which to b. faults of friends 4225

Let the dead past b. its dead 4331

not to b. hatchet 4079

the hatchet but leave handle out 9641

weakness of friend in silence 4183

You don't b. problem dead, you b. it alive 9291

BUS
three days late at b. station 4266

BUSH
Behold! the burning b. still burns 7996

Christ's teaching never beats about the b. 6440

every common b. afire with God 1710

In wonder-workings, or some b. aflame 8019

Moses never took heed what sort of b. 4874

One beats the b. 6205

thief doth fear each b. an officer 5488

we are like burning b. 4874

BUSINESS
Be about your Father's b. 9261

daily b. to obey Bible 681

does not differ from prayer 8471

drain away the b. with which we inevitably get involved 6830

equality a difficult b. 3247

forgive is God's b. 4082

get men, women to realize 3308

glory of God is the real b. of life 7027

God will forgive me, that's his b. 4634

how I am going to stay "in the air" no b. of mine 9908

Joy the serious b. of heaven 6549

keep nose out of people's b. 5152

love b. most, that is your god 7338

love one b. in which it pays to be
spendthrift 7252
Love's b. not to play favorites
7274
man's b. to do will of God 566
me first philosophy power to
blow b. to pieces 10087
men I have seen succeed went
about b. with a smile 10816
My b. is to think about God 9934
nature understands her b. better
3196
neighbor is man whom b. has
brought you into contact 8069
no b. receipt of value 5726
no b. to limit God's revelations
11273
no halfway b. with God 5038
not my b. to think about myself
9934
not to do something for church
1418
not to see what lies at a distance
9671
obedience would be mechanical b.
8091
of Christians to pray 8766
our shrines are our places of b.
6068
Pleasure-seeking is a barren b.
5550
put away thy toilsome b. 7708
Satan exists, I've done b. with him
9854
sciences, b. is to show the truth
9871
sick of world's b. 10578
sticking nose into other people's b.
5147
temptation is Satan's b. 11060
Think often on God in your b.
7723
to do something with church 1418
to do what lies closely at hand
9671
Trouble may demolish a man's b.
214
Use God to obtain success in b.
7517
victorious life is Christ's b. 11672
War is b. of barbarians 11771
When pleasure b. of life, ceases to
be pleasure 8614
when repressions of society and b.
are gone 6842
world cold, make it your b. to
build fires 4250

BUSY
barrenness of b. life 114
Be b, but not a busybody 5120
bee teaches two lessons 3454
Christian has b. hands 1260
Christians b. with mechanics 1301
clock passes time by keeping b.
2786
except when b, then needs an
hour of prayer 8790
Happy is man too b. to worry by
day 12062

haste, b. doing nothing 5577
He needed me, I was too b. 8685
hurt people by being too b. 129
If ants so b, how attend picnics
9266
If never alone with God, is not
because you are too b. 7482
If religious elite too b. 12098
Lord, I shall be very b. this day
9076
majority of us b. trying to place
ourselves 8395
not enough to be b. 4424
116
not get b. when nothing to do
2223
so b. . . . would not get through
the day 8816
So many are b. "using" God 7517
too b. providing for old age 119
too b. to pray 10211
too b. to pray, too b. to have
power 9017
until the b. world is hushed 9105
What are we b. about 4424
116
when you are very b. 7710

BUSYBODIES
Are we jabbering b. 10117

BUSYBODY
Be busy, but not a b. 5120

BUT
Lord, thy will be done without a b.
9082

BUTTER
Be not baker if head b. 11048
Never fall out with bread, b. 3105
something greater in vocation
than bread, b. 3107
that makes the temptation 11070

BUTTERFLY
Happiness is as a b. 5518
in chrysalis, death sets free the b.
2261
with human beings b. turns into
caterpillar 7392

BUTTON
Never hold anyone by the b. 1862
sewing on b. beyond them 5841

BUTTONS
don't cut off the b. 4367

BUTTRESS
If we need something to b. us
4768

BUY
All money made will never b.
back soul 10650
Bubbles we b. with whole soul's
tasking 2641
friend you b. won't be worth
what you pay 4176
Love only service money cannot b.
7253
Men whom the spoils of office
cannot b. 6299

Money can b. everything but
happiness 7810
Money not required to b.
necessity of the soul 7813
Money will b. dog, but not wag of
tail 7816
No man rich enough to b. back
past 1735

BUYS
Money b. everything except love
7806
pain b. intimacy with Christ
10906

BY-PRODUCT
fulfillment b. of love for God
4735
irritating characteristic b. of
respected quality 8571
Wisdom b. of right decisions
11911

BYPASS
not likely to b. way of weakness
11791

CABBAGE
answered triumphantly by c. 8580

CABIN
Roughing it: c. without television
6838

CABINET
During my many years in the c.
5094
let not one c. be locked up from
Christ 8092

CABLE
No c. can draw so forcibly 7279

CABLES
Habits cobwebs, then become c.
5497

CACKLES
hen who has laid egg c. as if laid
asteroid 9223

CAESAR
Christianity balanced between
God, C. 1240
empire of C. is gone 730
founded empires upon force 6351
Jesus conquered more millions
than C. 6449
more talked about in his time than
Jesus 6362
wear tinsel crown with pride of C.
2821

CAGE
Marriage is like a c. 7640

CAIN
chill, houseless, fatherless, aimless
C. 10573
first civilization founded by C.
10513

hears only the sound of his own
footsteps 10573
No wonder C. turned out badly
8318

CAIN'S
When anger in C. heart, murder
not far off 10383

CAJOLES
mother c. kids to do, be their best
7844

CAKE
Bible, not c. for special occasions
715
Christianity, not c. for special
occasions 1169
man without God like c. without
flour, milk 7446
turn c. for love of God 10208

CAKES
Since we have loaves, let us not
look for c. 1811

CALAMITIES
Satan tries to make us think c.
spring from God 9859

CALAMITY
finds his own c. light 177
He who sees the c. of other people
177
is virtue's opportunity 157
Job experienced c. because
righteous 2857
perfect glass to see and know
ourselves 156
productive of the greatest minds
220
test of integrity 158

CALCULATE
forces we cannot c. or cope with
5458

CALCULATION
God's principles not replaced in
favor of human c. 7828
without c, love 7348

CALCULATIONS
endless defeat of our c. 5395

CALEB
his body and rocking chair 764
peers were yawning, C. yearning
764

CALENDAR
Death keeps no c. 2262
With God no c. 11355

CALENDARS
successful would have looked at
their c. 6147

CALL
And death what men c. life 7086
at beginning of enterprise always
c. upon God 8757
comes to every one of us 7784
Discernment God's c. to
intercession 2805
does not come to chosen few 7784

God's c. comes to individuals
5385
God's c. founded on his decree
4626
God's c. not for impoverishment
but for enrichment 9351
Hail, Father! Whose creating c.
4672
his the c, mine the choice 11487
if too tired to c. for God to help
me 7478
need is the c, the c. is the presence
5781
Nothing makes one feel so strong
as c. for help 10177
of Christ always a promotion
10186
of Christ vs. men 3300
on God, but row away from the
rocks 8774
one clear c. for me 2368
suffering perfects one who accepts
c. of God 10920
Temptation is a c. to battle 11087
that shall never c. retreat 4715
to suffering requires faith, patience
10937
When they c. the roll in the Senate
5198

CALL'D
the devil and he came 2651

CALLED
are we c. people 1634
even if c. to give up wealth 4615
God has c. me to be faithful
10779
God has not c. me to be successful
10779
If a man is c. to be streetsweeper
2777
Many are c. but most frozen 3045
not c. to be successful with
ordinary standards 10823
not c. to live long on planet 1722
person c. to do missionary work
7784
to an everlasting preoccupation
with God 7551
to be God's transmitters 1340
to be holy at every cost 1722
to do the impossible 1284
to live beyond natural ability 1284
to love with special intensity
10937
What is this thing c. the world
3485
You c. me, Lord, you c. 7579

CALLEDST
Thou c, shoutedst, pierce my
deafness 4805

CALLING
Every c. is great 79
forth simple faith 164
God always c. on us to do the
impossible 10138
God's c. the shots 4939

sacred c. not limited to
ecclesiastical functions 12146
With your c. and crying 1910

CALLS
Christ's c. to detachment 9351
God c. each in secret to make
sacrifices 5385
God c. for volunteers to oppose
evil 3378
If God c. you to be a missionary
7781
Lord c. to himself 1308
Lord c. to no special work 1308
soul c. and is called 7967
When Christ c. a man 10049
When God c. a man 4626
When Master of earth c. shots,
things happen 3819

CALM
'Tis nothing to hold up head in c.
1915
able to make this water c. 9098
and heavenly frame 7507
and morning cannot be stayed
8444
Christ, great c. always there 6376
conversion c. of conviction to
unquiet mind 1900
Emotional peace and c. come after
doing God's will 8432
gentleness being c. surrounded by
heated atmosphere 4402
I can be c. and free from care
4869
Is a place of central c. 8429
me more 8430
Music can c. agitations of soul
7914
No storm can shake inmost c. 232
occasions for anguish often leave
us c. 3056
occasions for rapture often leave
us c. 3056
occasions for wrath often leave us
c. 3056
passing from stress to perfect c.
2399
set of soul decides, not the c. 4432
soul of all things 8430
Strength that wins is c. 10757
that fatal c. that precedes the
storm 10352
Time's glory is to c. contending
kings 11344
When we are restless, God
remains c. 4587

CALMEST
greatest is c. in storms 5297

CALMLY
accept old age c. 8158
bird c. clinging to his little twig
11478

CALMNESS
Of trust, strength, c. from above
9050
to remember or courage to forget
8827

CALMS
music c. the agitated heart 7935
troubled sea of lives 4863

CALM'ST
who c. the elemental war 9048

CALVARY
erected to divide men into two
  classes 2124
know nothing of C. love 7187
love Lord as much on C. as Mt.
  Tabor 2094
love represents C. 7297
magnitude of rebellion expressed
  by C. 10371
need for forgiveness answered at
  C. 7400
puts away sin 496
the eternal sword 2124
the place of decision 2124
through the clouds of C. 11129
to intercede for others 2175
to join band of intercessors 2175
to learn how to be forgiven 2175
to learn how to forgive others
  2175

CALYXES
Time will reveal c. of gold 5403

CAMARADERIE
superficial social c. 3337

CAME
God, planting the secret genes of
  God 6148
to love you late 7473
When he c, there was no light
  6510
Youth ideal state if c. later in life
  12187

CAMEL
Death a c. that lies down at every
  door 2242
never sees own hump 2075
No c. route is long with good
  company 4256
steals an egg would steal a c. 2912

CAMEL-MALICE
Man a mixture of
  horse-nervousness,
  ass-stubbornness, c. 7420

CAMP
Jesus is prophet of the losers' c.
  6447

CAMPAIGN
Christianity, c. of sabotage 1190

CAMPAIGNING
Prosperity good c. weather for
  devil 9338

CAN
always tell a real friend 4213
conquer who believe they c. 3798
decide to let Jesus make holy 5752
Do all the good you c. 5057
do something small in big way 58
Do what you c. 10128
dream you c. 48

Enjoy when you c. 3148
expectation of what man c. learn,
  do, be, low 3507
Faith not believing God c. 3691
God sends nothing but c. be borne
  2546
I ought, therefore I c. 9662
Man does what he c. 7495
only make most of today 3502
only the redeemed c. keep his
  commandments 4536
ours to offer what we c. 10166
Some things we c. count on 4643
stand what I know 6685
they conquer who believe they c.
  3720
try and find you c. 95
What I c. do, that I ought to do
  1926

CAN'T
be enthusiastic and unhappy at
  same time 3189
beat the weather 9879
build on regret 5486
comprehend: trust me 2414
cross chasm in two small jumps
  3650
do anything about length of life
  7095
doubt is c. believe 2930
drive straight on twisting lane
  4440
Experience one thing you c. get
  for nothing 3532
fanatic c. change mind 3907
get warm on another's fur coat
  6782
have a mountain without valleys
  10934
hold man down without staying
  down with him 10479
I c. do everything, but can do
  something 1926
If you c. face the music 6797
If you c. turn faith into vernacular
  3741
live a holy life 5752
make good cloak out of bad cloth
  1069
never say I c. 14
pump up faith out of your own
  heart 3828
take it with you 8640
teach people how wicked they are
  4773
Tis what I feel, but c. define 7245
Tis what I know, but c. express
  7245
trust God when you c. trace him
  3663
turn back clock 8373
What c. be cured must be endured
  3154
What c. be done by advice 3460
What you don't get, you c. lose
  8639
where devil c. go, he sends
  grandmother 2706
who says it c. be done 66

You c. reason with your heart
  5628

CANCELED
Yesterday is a c. check 11390

CANCELLED
Forgiveness like a c. note 4081

CANCELS
Death c. everything but truth
  2239
illusion that time c. sin 10419

CANCER
not c. but man himself greatest
  danger 7397
Pride is spiritual c. 9229
Sin is a c. 8467

CANCERS
Infidelity, marital conflict c. 3873

CANDIDATE
one less c. for misery 10979

CANDIDATES
for God's generous grace 5238

CANDLE
As a white c. in a holy place 8125
better to light c. than curse
  darkness 10164
burning c. of life in service of devil
  9576
Faith can put c. in darkest night
  3656
have one c. of life to burn 7779
Hope lights c, instead of cursing
  darkness 5928
How far that little c. throws his
  beams 2499
Life is not the c. 6973
loses nothing but lighting another
  c. 10113
Never burn fingers to snuff
  another man's c. 10458
not enough darkness to put out c.
  8241
of the Lord lighted by God 7430
spirit in man is c. of the Lord
  7430
spread light, be a c. 3455
teacher like c. which lights others
  11005
Unshared joy is unlighted c. 4295
Worship c. in act of being kindled
  12132

CANDLELIGHT
Choose neither wife or linen by c.
  7609

CANDLES
Some Christians like c. 1313
Stars blessed c. of night 11639

CANDOR
always double-edged sword 5869
brightest gem of criticism 5870
guileless c. of childhood 7709
indispensble requisite to salvation
  9793
may heal or may separate 5869

CANDY
wooed with striped c. 1403

CANNIBAL
Is it progress if c. uses fork 9313

CANNIBALS
missionary teaches c. to say grace 7777

more likely we are all c. 912

CANNOT
alter Christ's essential nature 1750

always understand ways of God 4688

as aliens c. forget true homeland 2975

atheist c. find God 472

be a front without a back 5357

be an up with a down 5357

be content with evangelism which 3337

be wise with other men's wisdom 11958

become creative without solitude 10579

build hopes on confusion, misery, death 8445

building without basis c. stand 3826

c. live, fight, conquer without prayer 9015

change yesterday 3502

choose our own work 5446

choose to be strong 6530

Christian c. live by philosophy 9703

church c. be content with social camaraderie 3337

confer on me fullness of life 5549

control evil tongues of others 5164

convey to others, can but use for ourselves 6178

crucify my old nature 9836

Death c. kill what never dies 7319 3291

delights that c. find expression in language 12120

depend on people 9521

devil c. harm us 2682

devil c. lord it over servants of God 2673

direct the wind 4056

do evil to others without doing to ourselves 3413

Do not let what you c. do interfere 8652

dream yourself into character 1071

Earth has no sorrow heaven c. heal 5637

Emotions c. be cut out of life 3052

enter kingdom of heaven head first 9426

Even God c. fill what is full 10708

Faith believing where we c. prove 3682

faith c. be proved 3724

faith that hasn't been tested c. be trusted 3640

Faith will lead you where you c. walk 3716

Faith, c. believe he is going to let me down 3712

find time for recreation, find time for illness 6835

find, creates means 2624

finite minds c. solve it 6277

fool all people all of the time 2480

frail mind of man c. explain reason 3781

get behind the before of birth 5459

get to top by sitting on bottom 6783

go back to his youth 12170

God c. accept goodness from me 5059

God c. be comprehended in human words 4682

God c. be fitted into a diagram 4851

God c. be for, against same thing at same time 4972

God c. be found by thought 4738

God c. believe for us 3721

God c. come in any way but his own way 4664

God c. control human beings 5983

God c. do our repenting for us 9578

God c. get humanity out of his mind 5983

God c. give happiness apart from himself 5510

God c. relinquish perfections 4821

God c. work in a vacuum 4824

God c. work with empty minds 4824

God c. work with prejudice 4824

God does what we c. do 8570

God is all you see, all you c. see 4692

God must condemn, blast out what he c. bless 893

God whose ways you c. understand 3684

God without whom one c. live 4542

God's to supply what we c. 10166

God, greatness c. be conceived 4700

good end c. sanctify evil means 5010

grace c. be stockpiled beforehand 5226

grace to accept things that c. be changed 9060

Happiness perfume c. pour on others 5516

happy without things we c. have 8635

have love apart from faith, hope 3837

He that is fallen c. help him that is down 2585

He who c. do something big 58

He who fears death c. enjoy life 3975

hear for what you are 560

Hears what one c. say 8515

holy man not one who c. sin 5762

Holy Spirit c. be located as guest in house 5796

house divided c. stand 1620

I c. adore enough. I c. speak 12125

I c. and I won't 1810

I c. do everything 106 2500

I c. face it all alone 5413

I c. judge motivation of another 4247

I c. row it myself 6398

I only know I c. drift 4763

If but the way be straight, c. go amiss 5471

If c. find God in your house 4856

If c. work or rise from my chair 8132

if c. work out will of God 4974

if followers of God, c. take initiative 5446

If God has work for me to do, I c. die 6921

If I c. do great things 10155

imitate being full of Holy Ghost 5805

immortal rapture that c. die 7952

Is this the end? I know it c. be 2319

kill time without injury to eternity 6784

know at what moment flash forth with life of God 7055

know future 4337

know what God is 4687

lazy man does not, will not, c. pray 6776

learn without pain 8276

life of Jesus c. be discussed in same way as any other man 6476

light another's path without brightening our own 3145

Love and Self c. stand together 9936

love beyond the world c. be separated 7319 3291

Love c. be inactive 7211

love c. compel 4126

love c. lie idle in soul of lover 7167

Love c. put up with fear, pain 3986

love fellow creature till you love God 7351

love good if do not hate evil 5050

Love only service power c. command 7253

love without giving 7350

luxuries of world c. satisfy lonely 7176

make others as you wish 993

make straight lines out of crooked lot 4885

make yourself as you wish 993

Man c. cover what God would reveal 9709

Man c. find God unless God reveals himself 4910

Man c. find joy anywhere but in God 6552

Man c. live all to this world 12109

Man c. seek God 4910

Man did not make, and c. mar peace 8430

man endowed with liberty he c. deny 3495

man who c. live his own life 6872

may be thought c. wisely be said 2898

Measurements c. apply to God 4710

men may despise grace of God, but c. extinguish it 4655

Men whom the spoils of office c. buy 6299

mind of man c. explain reason 4492

Misunderstanding c. thwart purposes of God 2740

most important c. be taught 3030

most rewarding often look like c. be done 8567

mystery a fact about which we c. know everything 7936

never failed c. be great 3594

no fool to gain what he c. lose 1195

no fool who gives what he c. keep 1195

no life so humble it c. reflect God's light 7055

nothing can happen which c. be turned into good 4803

O senseless man who c. make a worm 6073

One foot c. stand on two boats 6058

past c. be changed 8385 3623

Peace c. be kept by force 8452

People who c. be alone worst company 10552

Political reputation c. last forever 5079

pray as you would, pray as you can 9032

psychologize grace of God 5237

put off living until ready 11388

reach distant horizons 4544

Reason does not prove God c. exist 3776

reason your way to belief in God 9428

regard everyone as stranger 922

repent too soon 9609

Satan c. counterfeit peace of God 5396

Satan c. hurt godly 3996

satisfaction from other human beings they c. give 9496

say Lord's Prayer if 8818

see outer limits 4544

simultaneously will sin and repentance 5210

sin, death, hell c. break God's decree 4616

Since you c. do good to all 9673

speak of measure and God 4680

speak too freely, too trustfully to God 8968

statement once let loose c. be caught by four horses 5117

step twice into same river 985

stop alarming number of divorces 2928

stop near dissolution of family unit 2928

tell where God begins 4602

tendency to worry about things that c. be changed 7793

that we c. do our work on earth 6108

they that know themselves c. be proud 6039

things that count most c. be counted 7039

Time heals what reason c. 11332

train ourselves to be Christians 4984

trust c. crowd its way in 12081

turn any human being from destiny 2618

understand how in presence of Lord 4853

Understanding can wait, obedience c. 8114

Unless start with doubt c. have faith 2949

unscramble eggs 1744

ways of Providence c. be reasoned out 5450

we c. be supreme over ourselves 7552

Weak persons c. be sincere 10431

When God's goodness c. be seen 7750

When know philosphy, you know what you c. know 8594

when you c. stand, God will bear you in his arms 5907

Where devil c. put head, puts tail 2707

Where reason c. wade, faith may swim 3821

while government c. redeem world 5177

Who rides tiger c. dismount 11121

wise man cares not for what he c. have 11899 1775

without assistance of Divine Being c. succeed 5179

Without assistance of divine being I c. succeed 5411

Without God we c. 10221 7576

word rashly spoken c. be brought back 10681

Words c. express joy friend imparts 4269

Words c. speak for grief or ectasy 10274

world man c. understand 3495

yearning to know what c. be known 7531

You c. carve rotten wood 1070

You c. put same shoe on every foot 6225

You c. say you are friendless 4214

CANON

Lighthouses don't fire c. 6022

CANOPY

as a protecting c, the blessing of God 5848

CANTALOUPES

eyeballs as big as c. 11028

CANVAS

God the c. on which picture painted 4495

on which God paints truths 10844

CAPABILITIES

Cultivate your own c. 6168

CAPABLE

all c. of evil thoughts 11272

Everyone c. of familiar conversation with God 7541

heart c. of containing God's gift of himself 8910

heart c. of unlimited extension 5625

Love for Lord intensest of which human heart c. 7221

man technically c. of destroying world 9872

no government c. of contending 5196

of holding office or place of trust, profit 5183

only rarely of evil deeds 11272

People c. of recruiting themselves to evil 3396

Prayer highest energy of which the mind is c. 8900

science dragon c. of destroying world 9870

Whoever is c. of giving is rich 10743

CAPACITY

better the self-image, larger the c. for loving 9997

depth of c. for patience 8403

each individual shall have c. 4

Faith is c. to trust God 3696

for evil so pronounced in ourselves 3412

for reformation within 3596

God's greatness above our c, reach 4681

Man alone has c. to walk, talk with God 7497

Man's c. for justice 2528

memory c. of human mind
fabulous 7738

passes c. of finite mind 4989

potential c. of human heart 5625

skeptical about c. to express
existence 3488

to care gives life significance 3077

will multiply c. to enjoy blessings
5254

You have c. for anything 3039

Youth happy because c. to see
beauty 12182

CAPITAL
Golden Rule would reconcile c.
and labor 5005

If c. one gives 11360

CAPITALIST
if a man keeps money, he's a c.
7800

CAPRICE
In Christ no c. 1750

CAPTAIN
Christ a C. to defend his people
6370

CAPTAINS
and kings depart 6036

Two c. in one boat make it sink
6808

CAPTIVATED
Jesus c. his listeners 6444

not c. by any external thing 8611

CAPTIVE
conscience c. to word of God
1692

Make me a c, Lord 10973

CAPTIVE'S
Thou c. freedom, thou sick man's
health 5932

CAPTIVITY
bring thought, imagination into c.
1014

Jesus' c. is our freedom 6453

CAPTURE
inner stronghold of pride 10043

CAR
friend with noisy old c. disturbing
3223

friend with quiet new c. disturbing
3223

God doesn't start stalled c. 4782

life like going through c. wash on
bicycle 7023

When teenagers get c, want money
3903

When teenagers get money, want c.
3903

CARAVAN
halt of toil's exhausted c. 10960

CARCASSES
not a soul would recognize their
skinny c. 6853

CARDINALS
than the pope and all his c. 9929

CARDS
Murder no better than c. 10324

CARE
a little home where grief and c.
4921

A poor life this if, full of c. 6829

admitted as guest turns to master
12058

afraid to c. too much 4290

Alcohol does not drown 323

Among so many, can he c. 4834

And did God c. 8878

And weep away life of c. 2882

begins to c. he does not cheat
neighbor 5004

Beyond his love and c. 4763

burden of c. in getting riches
11865

capacity to c. gives life significance
3077

children common bond of c, love
3868

dollars will take c. of themselves
9674

don't be surprised if nobody
seems to c. 9211

Entirely to thy c. 7503

everlasting Father will take c. of
you tomorrow 415

feed me with a shepherd's c. 9350

Find me men on earth who c.
4118

for him who borne the battle 5199

for his widow and orphan 5199

God does not c. what good you
did 7862

God give me love, c, strength to
help 910

God takes c. of man 566

God's c. will carry you 1543

Grim c. scoured off by oil of mirth
6738

Guard it with c. 3847

how well we c. for others part of
meditation 7725

I can be calm and free from c.
4869

If any c. of mine make friend's the
fleeter 910

Little wealth, little c. 11833

man takes c. neighbor does not
cheat 5004

Marriage has more c. but less
danger 7635

must c. for the poor 8698

never give impression we c. when
in a hurry 7327

not what is preached in pulpit
12151

Only man clogs happiness with c.
12073

ought to take c. before ask for
strength 8850

public life will take c. of itself
6321

reads the prayer and lifts my c.
7478

Real friends don't c. if socks don't
match 4264

riches grow, c. follows 11799

save our souls from being steeped
in c. 9064

shall take c. of it when I am dead
10145

Sleep vanishes before house of c.
10488

so wan with c. 12077

spare anxious hearts a needless c.
8098

strength to bear our portion of the
weight of c. 8863

Take c. of the pennies 9674

take excellent c. of our bodies
10680

take no c. for tomorrow 411

Teach us to c, and not to c. 4979

Tend it with c. 3847

That we are ever overborne with c.
8867

The oxen knew him, had him in
their c. 6133

there are those who c. 1018

To carry c. to bed 12080

to live until chose to die 5530

To suppose God could not c. 9010

too busy to c. 129

Wealth lightens not c. of man
11877

when God should take c. of us,
we c. for ourselves 10425

Where c. lodges, sleep will never
lie 12082

who don't c. who gets the credit
10134

why take so little c. of your
children 8290

Without debt, without c. 4044

world full of c. 10639

world of c. without 5817

CARED
He c. as much 8878

if fruitful, c. not who did condemn
10157

CAREER
near the close of an unproductive
c. 8661

While coldly discussing a man's c.
6599

CAREFUL
be c. not to exceed feed limit 7020

Conceit is self-given, be c. 10994

for nothing, prayerful for
everything 8775

Most people are c. drivers 3947

We have c. thought for the
stranger 3900

CAREFULLY
Real doesn't often happen to
people who have to be c. kept
5886

Spin c, prayerfully 3117

CARELESS
Be c. in dress if you must 10652

confidence in Christ does not
make c. 1611

God seems c. as to whether men understand him 11616

if foresight of prosperity 4314

CARELESSNESS
requisite of good health calculated c. about oneself 5618

CARES
All here hae got their c. 1396

Cast aside thy burdensome c. 7708

everlasting Father who c. for you 415

feelings not what God c. about 4777

friend who c. faces powerlessness 3080

God does not promise protect from material c. 5385

God has communicated he c. 4779

Grace is love that c. 5220

grow with time 12059

If desires be endless, c. will be too 5317

in dusty atmosphere of little c. 1401

is great who c. nothing about honors 5285

Jesus' coming final, unanswerable proof God c. 6136

less troubled by c. on earth 5028

Light c. speak, great ones silent 10599

Man c. most for sexual intercourse 10228

more difficult to throw off than sorrows 12059

of today seldom c. of tomorrow 12075

One joy dispels a hundred c. 6555

that infest the day 7887

warrant for believing God c. 4779

wealth bags of c. 4877

what more blessed than to put c. away 12057

wise man c. not for what he cannot have 11899 1775

CAREY
arose to carry revelations to land far off 9740

Wesley in one generation, C. in next is inevitable 9740

CARICATURE
doctrines in excess a c. of truth 9122

CARICATURES
degenerate c. of human beings 3881

CARING
Discouraged people need c. someone 3066

more gentle and more c. 1545

Solitude molds into c. persons 10561

that transcends human inclinations 1541

To become like Christ only thing worth c. for 6494

without c. for tomorrow's lodging 11478

CARLYLE
When C. saw city, he philosophized 10522

CARNAL
refreshing vacation not c. 9533

CARPENTER
By a C. mankind was made 6360

only by that C. can mankind be remade 6360

CARRIAGE
The c. held but just ourselves 2230

wheels baby c. call him Papa 3921

CARRIED
it was then that I c. you 5437

Jesus gives truth c. on wings of love 6176

Jug never c. under coat for honest reason 2905

So when I'm c. in 1391

whole cross more easily c. than half 1332

CARRIER
small moment c. of God's gift 11319

CARRIES
bundles, call him Papa 3921

Each of us c. own life-form 6214

God c. your picture in wallet 4751

heaviest load man c. on back 4098

hope c. us on pleasantly to end of life 5934

If man c. cross beautifully 5252

They travel lightly whom God's grace c. 5235

will of God power which c. us 5451

wise man c. his possessions within him 11950

CARRY
burden of another's sin 5029

courageous step would c. through fear 3982

God's care will c. you 1543

Moderate riches will c. you 11838

one small head should c. all it knew 2994

own lantern, and you need not fear dark 6167

soldiers c. Bible into battle 726

takes little effort to watch man c. load 6160

Truth is heavy, few men c. it 11565

we c. our worst enemies within us 3157

With every cross comes strength to c. it 8108

CARRYING
away small stones 59

yesterday's worry, tomorrow's anxiety 12092

CARS
grow older become like old c. 8181

CART
Wisdom and virtue like two wheels of c. 11962

CARTEL
no c. holds key to as much power 11841

CARVE
cannot c. rotten wood 1070

CARVER
discrimination and a George Washington C. 161

CARVES
deeper sorrow c. into your being 10626

CARVING
Conservation is but c. 1838

CASE
Christ has never lost his c. 6415

My c. is bad, Lord, be my advocate 5482

CASES
no recipe for living that suits all c. 6214

CASH
Today is c. 11390

CASH REGISTER
Life is like a c. 71

CAST
bread upon waters while seasick 4373

in the fire the perished thing 7003

in utter helplessness c. all on Christ 6354

Love lets us c. off our false exteriors 7254

off everything not yourself 995

CASTIGATE
fault, not child 8312

CASTING
aside of veil after veil 4906

I my net was c. in the sea 1147

Man has the c. vote 9175

CASTLE
rich man at his c. 4501

CASTLES
carefully created c. washed away 2798

CASTS
God c. the die, not the dice 4930

CASUAL
Children not c. guests 1110

CAT
If man crossed with c. would improve man, deteriorate c. 7390

like c. on hot stove lid 3551

play with c, bear its scratches 11067

To a mouse, a c. is a lion 9528

Whether black c. brings bad luck 8584

CATARACTS
vision impaired by c. of sin 10436

CATASTROPHE
charisma without character c. 987

CATCH
can't c. wind in net 10723

cost devil little trouble to c. lazy man 6766

devil's snare does not c. unless 2696

easier to c. flies with honey than vinegar 6643

God is there to c. you 4627

more apt to c. vices than virtues 4286

must lose fly to c. trout 4343

some little glimpse of God's designs 4578

Trust knowing God will c. you 11486

try to c. it, loses its color 5519

CATCHES
another c. flies 6205

CATCHING
nothing in haste except c. fleas 5583

CATEGORIES
Man fits into no c. of thought 7405

CATERPILLAR
with human beings butterfly turns into c. 7392

CATHEDRAL
Christian religion like c. 1224

dim with age, where oft-repeated prayers arise 4921

easy to turn religious life into c. for memories 10165

faith is a grand c. 3648

God offers to help us build c. of love, praise 7684

I sought him in a great c. 4921

where oft-repeated prayers arise 4921

CATHEDRALS
God not impressed with beautiful c. 12101

CATHOLIC
God not interested in C. religion 9539

not a C. in heaven 5671

CATHOLICS
We are not C. 1343

CATS
Most people are like c. 9482

CATTLE
Slander cud eschewed by human c. 10470

CAUGHT
Angler c. a fish so big 3424

But c. no glimpse of him 4921

first c. by the devil's bait 2696

Is c. into his left 4628

Love like a friendship c. on fire 7236

No one can be c. in place he does not visit 5484

statement let loose cannot be c. 5117

that I might be free 6120

CAUSE
Charity sees the need, not the c. 7163

Christ never asks us to devote to c. 2836

Christianity, not devotion to c. 1176

Christians to c. change 961

combated by relentless forces 2630

Cut any cord but the one that binds me to thy c. 9080

God does not c. us to sin 10306

good c. will fear no judge 6602

greatest griefs are those we c. ourselves 5355

If c. be good 1823

in world ruled by c. and effect 11590

Is Christ thy advocate to plead thy c. 6415

man with vision of God not devoted simply to c. 11729

Nature an effect, whose c. is God 8024

never fail who die in a great c. 7680

not my c. but thine 9109

not the death makes the martyr 7675

of atheism, Christians 487

of freedom is c. of God 4143

of man's unhappiness 5560

only God knows c. of things 6705

strong in him whose c. is ours 10756

we believe to be just 3625

where God, the c, begins 4525

CAUSED
deepest emotion c. by trivial 3056

Happiness c. by things which happen 6529

trouble c. by people wanting to be important 9220

wound c. by words more painful 5119

CAUSES
God knows all c. 4881

Gold and riches, chief c. of war 11810

he who c. things to be 7944

thousand c. vie for support 7447

CAUTION
as much c. to tell truth as to conceal it 11514

eldest child of wisdom 11907

CAUTIOUS
In each action, be c. 572

of professing too much 586

CAVERN
God is in the c. of man's sin 10434

CEASE
And the shuttles c. to fly 10606

every change shall c. 3288

Facts do not c. to exist 3579

family lacking, c. to be a human nature 3881

friendship that can c. never real 4274

If God could forget it, world would instantly c. 4597

If these hands of mine c. from their clinging 7478

Never c. loving a person 3167

pray for friends though c. to be so 4069

since I soon must c. to live 9048

those who know pain may not c. 9045

Till all our strivings c. 8431

we c. to shape our lives by faith 3688

we die when lives c. to be illumined 4538

when c. to grow, you are old 8189

When good people c. vigilance, evil men prevail 7991

When men c. to be faithful to God 3849

When shall I c. to be my own 7961

when we c. to believe in a personal deity 4538

when we take initiative we c. to follow 5446

CEASED
after heart has c. to reach to human beings 7548

Athens c. to be free 4155

Being c. to have appeal 1753

church c. to manufacture blood cells 3341

ministry of church c. while quarrel over Prince of Peace 9361

since Christians have c. to think of other world 5656

to believe, c. desiring what I wished 984

CEASELESS
Love a c. effort to know, feel 7211

with c. praise his works behold 362

CEASES
charity proclaims deeds c. to be charity 1081

God never c. to speak to us 8800

to be controversy, c. interest 1827

to be friend never was good one 4244

When hand c. to scatter, heart c.
to pray 4385
When pleasure business of life, c.
to be pleasure 8614
where man c, God begins. 4525

CEASING
Envy never c. in appetite 3211
poetry of earth c. never 2976

CEILING
Grace refuses to put c. on concern
5233
Hitting the c. worst way 384

CELEBRATE
all eternity to c. our victories 3293
Yet if we c. let it be 6156

CELEBRATED
Wherein Savior's birth c. 1371

CELEBRATES
triumphant Christian c. victory
already won 11672

CELEBRATION
gigantic c. in unseen world 3326
high, mighty regain balance 3235
weak, lowly receive new stature
3235

CELEBRATIONS
Lord, turn routines of work into
c. of love 12015

CELEBRITIES
God not impressed with c. 3854

CELEBRITY
more than stimulation of c. status
9996
shamefully exploit converted c.
11666

CELESTIAL
breathing new air, finding it c. air
2399
Sleep is God's c. nurse 10486

CELIBACY
Single blessedness 10222

CELL
family, essential c. of society 3890

CEMENT
Suffering is the true c. of love
7293

CEMENTED
bricks must be c. together 4020

CEMETERY
Every man should keep fair-sized
c. 4225

CENSORIOUS
Bible does not yield secrets to c.
687

CENSORIOUSNESS
one of seven deadly virtues 11699

CENSURE
Encouragement after c, as sun
after shower 3130
harder to avoid c. than gain
applause 2066

No man can justly c. or condemn
6585
to escape c. do no foolish thing
2066

CENSURED
man sooner c. than exposed 1055

CENT
Some have not a c. to bless 11852

CENTENARIANS
old enough to know better 7607
seldom marry 7607

CENTER
God an infinite circle whose c. is
everywhere 4842
God's love c. of holiness 4661
little speck in c. of eternity but a
minute 7052
man cannot enter into deepest c.
of himself 7962
of God's will is safety 4980
of me is a terrible pain 7521
Our source, our c, our dwelling
place 4836
pass through that c. into God
7962
power lies at c. of life 10576
rationalist makes himself his own
c. 9396
rest there in God, c. of their souls
5644
Situation ethics puts people at c.
of concern 6820
without God as c. of lives young
people frustrated 12180

CENTERED
For most men world is c. in self
8436
Self is to be rightly c. in God 9942
universe is c. on God 11647
world c. in God is peace 8436

CENTERING
true c. of yourself in God 10159

CENTRAL
Christ great c. fact in world's
history 5710
cross is the great c. point 6424
God on side of poor c. to theology
8696
gradually giving c. place to God
7713
life revolves around Christ, its c.
sun 6937
Loneliness c. fact of human
existence 7137
stream of what we are indeed
7369

CENTURIES
From the c. that are gone 6497
Jesus leaps across the changing c.
6448
martyrs put to death through long
c. 1211
of experience have tested Bible
646
reading books conversation with
men of c. 861

through all c. of fearful fog 3974
To the c. that shall be 6497

CENTURY
lost art of c. is meditation 7721
when new c. begins 11329

CEREMONIAL
Christianity not a c. 1172
Religion merely c. can never satisfy
9546

CEREMONIES
mysticism not rites or c. 7947

CERTAIN
as c. of God as God is of himself
9800
attitude of child c. God knows
what he is about 9912
can be c. about God 11214
death of fear c. 3962
go through life never quite c. 3758
God got message through plain
and c. 7029
If one c. principles are right 6306
makes his failure c. 11597
no longer have to be treated c. way
9963
not c. everything is uncertain 951
Nothing c. except the past 8365
nothing c. in life 954
nothing c. in this world 7062
Nothing so c. as death 2341
only one corner c. of improving,
your own self 9953
only thing c. of is change 969
people c. about something false
3384
saint c. everything is all right 9785
that a faithful hand will take, sift
4260
Truth lies within a c. compass
6868
walk of disciple gloriously c. 2834
want not more certainty about
you, but to be more c. in you
7565

CERTAINTIES
begin with c, end in doubts 950
begin with doubts, end in c. 950
doubts will not avail against great
c. 5028
few c. in mortal experience 953
soul hot for c. in life 946

CERTAINTY
believe with c, begin with doubting
606
Bible, uncrushable c. 696
But c. 6463
God changes death to triumph
2373
God judging men with
unperplexed c. 4720
Guessing turns to c. when 949
imperturbable c. in contact with
God 955
of divine participation gives
courage 6277
want not more c. about you, but
to be more certain in you 7565

with c. crucifixion most famous
death 2137

CESSATION
to reap little of life but c. 6280

CHAFF
and grain together 4260
We were c, now wheat 1348

CHAFING
Rather than c. become still, wait
2556

CHAGRIN
Silence a balm to every c. 10266

CHAIN
all into one c. of justice, mercy,
truth 4904
as with an iron c. 8684
Every c. that spirits wear 8789
Faith is the subtle c. 3700
faith, subtle c. that binds to
infinite 2929
If link is broken, whole c. breaks
2536
In triumph wear Christlike c.
1299
love does not measure by
surveyor's c. 4789
no stronger than weakest link
10744
tongue, let loose difficult to c.
11415

CHAINS
body bound with c, spirit never
4112
do not hold a marriage together
7608
of gold stronger than c. of iron
11802
of habit too weak to be felt 5500
Rank and riches c. of gold 11844

CHAIR
If cannot work or rise from my c.
8135
talked to God as if he were sitting
in c. beside them 7526
While God Incarnate made a c.
6458
Worry like a rocking c. 12088

CHAIRS
If a man can make better c. 2776

CHALLENGE
art, c. basic assumptions of
secular age 1998
Give him a dream, you c. heart
3307
If leave church with no c. 12106
thank God he will use sin to c. you
11152
translation of belief into life-style
1225
Young people will respond if c.
tough enough 12180

CHALLENGES
Christian thinker c. prejudices
11239

great c. which ordinary men rise
to meet 8668
mother c. kids to do their best
7844
Motherhood full of c. 8313
Silent worship c. 12114

CHAMBER
A quiet c. kept for thee 1357
Christ must have the best c. 6504
give Christ key of every c. 8092
inner c. into which God only can
enter 7127
of sickness is chapel of devotion
6089

CHAMBERS
more lonely among men than in
our c. 10572

CHAMPION
absurdity has c. to defend it 3256

CHANCE
as good as anybody if equal c.
3228
beggar gives c. to do good 621
by no extraordinary c. put
together second time 6173
Could blind c. create symmetry
1958
death rids us of c. 2251
do not feel I am product of c.
11124
does nothing not prepared
beforehand 4928
foolish to think earth could come
by c. 1979
Man calls sin a c., God a choice
4560
mistakes, always another c. 3598
name for our ignorance 6078
no c, no gamble 1159
No man ever became wise by c.
11931
nothing left to c. 4904
Nothing that happens in world by
c. 4948
Once chosen, he's no c. 6463
pass awhile under category of c.
5454
prayer, c. to change your mood
8957
small c. of truth at the goal 11549
superhuman c. of mankind 4549
think there's no c. for you 8230
Triumphing over death, c. and
thee, O Time 5679
waits for c. never sure of dinner
8215
Who can see behind c. and in c.,
God 4961

CHANCES
are prayer activity will fizzle out
7725
Do not look forward to c. of life
in fear 5907
of blowing it porportional to 1892
Vice a miscalculation of c. 10410

CHANGE
all our wishing cannot c. things 38

allow hurts, trials to c. us 972
amid all the c. things we can
count on 4643
and decay all around I see 947
as schools c, theology must c.
11207
Before tomorrow the air may c.
7895
can c. thing that is wrong 3596
cannot c. yesterday 3502
cannot step twice into same river
985
capacity for c. within 3596
Christianity will c. world 1196
Christians to cause c. 961
Christians to endure c. 961
Christians to profit by c. 961
constant in happiness must often c.
4057
conversion c. of heart 1909
courage to c. things which should
be changed 9060
Death called c. 2372
death rids us of c. 2251
difficult times will c. soon 969
direction of life, desires different
984
do not c. to question mark 5468
Even this shall pass away 974
ever needful 981
every c. shall cease 3288
Everything changes but c. 965
Everything we accept undergoes c.
966
Evil minds c. good to own nature
5015
faith demands complete c. of
attitude 3785
fanatic can't c. mind 3907
fanatic won't c. subject 3907
Fashions in sin c. 10303
Fit for every c. and chance 974
foolish and dead never c. opinions
8206
fortune does not c. men 11807
Give man Christ, c. heart 3307
God able to enter human
personality and c. it 5777
God does not c. 4590
God's creative method is c. 4469
Grace urges us to c, grow 5221
handmaiden nature requires 959
He would not c. the ground 967
if unafraid of c. 8139
If worship does not c. us 12105
If you can't c. circumstances, c.
response 1469
In every c. he faithful will remain
1502
In God no c. possible 977
in men c. impossible to escape 977
is painful 981
It will c. soon 969
Lord, what a c. within us one
short hour 8867
man what he is, not what he used
to be 990
no c. soul is dead 1590
no death, only c. of worlds 2391

entered little into depths of Master's c. 6390

evidence built on right foundation 1057

exhibited, not made, in crisis 1002

Faith confidence in c. of God 3684

Faith reposes on c. of God 4443

faith trusts in c. of God 3842

family stamped c. upon child 1126

formed in stormy billows 1042

From man's face can read his c. 8494

gives awe to wrinkled skin, gray hairs 997

gives splendor to youth 997

God concerned with c, not outward beauty 1033

God does not supply c. 1014

God has program of c. development 1015

God more concerned about c. than comfort 1016

God sums up man's worth by c. 11238

good c. perform to fullest potential 1019

habit long continued 1003

hammer, forge yourself into c. 1071

home where c. molding carried on 5850

home, cultivate c. 5832

hope of nation in individual c. 5190

human being intended to have c. of his own 6170

human being intended to have own c. 1008

If beauty in the c, harmony in home 8441

In heaven stand in c. of Savior 1072

in saint means Christ manifested 998

inconsistent with c. of God 3712

inner switchboard of c. 1712

is a distant goal 1000

is consolidated thought 1012

keeps doors open 1034

knocked out, get up and face them 1024

laud c, but climb to top at any cost 6068

like bells which ring out sweet notes 6293

like tree, real thing 1001

Live thy creed 994

lizard on cushion will still seek leaves 989

lost when ideal sacrificed 999

man discloses own c. when describes anothers 981

man shows c. by laughter 982

man what he is, not what he used to be 990

man you honor, kind of man you are 1038

Marriage a perpetual test of c. 7637

Misfortune an occasion to demonstrate c. 195

mold, hammer, forge 1000

most enviable, the c. of an honest man 5881

mother interpreter of father's c. 8341

never meritorious before God 1057

never put c. in place of faith 1057

no shortcut 1000

no slander can alter man's c. 1060

no stronger test of man's c. than power, authority 8721

no weakness in our c. can come to light 4884

not brains that matter, but c. 1027

not good doing but God-likeness 1044

not obtained instantly 1000

off guard man reveals c. 1028

Only one thing endures, c. 1010

poor c, fail to play to potential 1019

Prayer is spiritual c. 8914

purpose of Christianity to produce c. 1229

reactions to choices 1000

repeating involuntarily the c. of those among whom we live 6243

reputation would not know c. if met on street 9618

revelation of God determined by c. 1050

righteousness in heart, beauty in the c. 8441

Satan uses problems to slander God's c. 9859

see men of contrary c. examine ourselves 1065

Sermon on the Mount outlines c. 513

Simplicity of c. result of profound thought 10283

smile, each having distinct c. 10500

Solitude improves our c. 10560

Sow c, reap destiny 1041

Sow habit, reap c. 1041

stand before neighbors on c. 1072

strength of c. 8

Strength of c. may be acquired at work 5849

submit to self-discipline 1000

Suffering can file rough edges off c. 10933

sum total of decisions 1000

sum total of deeds 1000

take care of c, reputation takes care of itself 1020

temptation c. development curriculum 11058

ten men will talk about c. of Jesus 2174

test a man's c, give him power 8706

test of man's c. is his tongue 11414

tests bruise but build c. 211

the taller we grew in Christian c. 6017

think about people, c. will take care of itself 1023

to judge c. by only one manifestation 1053

to the observer doth thy history unfold 1052

torn down with incredible swiftness 996

Tribulation: God's fastest road to c. 225

Trouble builds up c. 214

Truth lies in c. 11572

truth of c. is sacred 11684

until we fashion the c. 8924

very few care to listen to defense of c. 1055

virtues of c. vital to society's survival 3880

what God, angels know of us 1036

what man would do if never found out 1047

What we stand up for proves our c. 1060

what you are in dark 1005

what you are when no one is looking 1068

what you are will be yours forever 1062

what you really are 1035

when a man does things he likes to do, c. revealed 6842

When c. is lost, all is lost 1066

wish to know the c. of a love 7167

with trifles man reveals c. 1028

word of parent fibre woven into c. of child 8346

CHARACTERISTIC

irritating c. by-product of respected quality 8571

of Christ was submission to his Father 6414

of Jesus' praying 8890

of new birth 879

of spiritual life is unaging youth 10712

of wisdom not to do desperate things 11922

quiet life c. of great men 5274

CHARACTERISTICS

if transformed, will exhibit divine c. 1044

of God Almighty mirrored in Jesus 4493

Salvation the incoming into human nature of c. of God 9811

Sin has four c. 10359

CHARACTERIZE

As honesty, integrity c. our lives 5874

CHEATED

Every man takes care neighbor does not c. him 5004
He who cheats friend would c. God 2911
not saint on knees, c. in shop 1908
to c. of kinship with humanity 8334
who fails to pray does not c. God 8810

CHEATED

do not be c. out of today 5507
most c. who cheats himself 2909

CHEATER

That old bald c, Time 11315

CHEATING

finest c. done under guise of honesty 5888

CHEATS

He who c. friend would cheat God 2911
most cheated who c. himself 2909
We're all c. and liars, really 1839
who fails to pray c. himself 8810

CHECK

better c. to see if you're going downhill 6877
each c. to our desires 4578
if decisions wrong, God will always c. 5464
no signed c. valid 5726
Yesterday is a canceled c. 11390

CHECKLIST

love eclipsed as it turns into clipboard with c. 6823

CHECKS

decisions are God's will unless he c. 5464

CHEEFULNESS

keeps daylight in the mind 1092

CHEEK

like villain with smiling c. 5011

CHEEKS

Time will fade your rosy c. 11328

CHEER

best of healers is good c. 5617
best way to c. yourself up 2559
Give man dollar, c. heart 3307
Gold in trouble powerless to c. 11813
the youth who's bravely trying 4217
To c. God along 11686
To c. the soul when tired with human strife 7917
try to c. somebody else up 2559
up, birds have bills 4034
Up—only dentist down in mouth 2539
Was he ever ready with word or good c. 7423

CHEERFUL

company shortens miles 4221

do with c. heart the work God appoints 10150
God has given me a c. heart 7931
man better than sad 1099
men I have seen succeed always c. 10816
Not every heart that laughs is c. 10605

CHEERFULLY

Burdens become light when c. borne 1086
greatest bears heaviest burdens c. 5297

CHEERFULNESS

and contentment beautifiers, preservers 1087
atmosphere in which things thrive 1091
costs nothing, yet is beyond price 5612
enables us to work with fewer creaks, groans 1093
fills mind with serenity 1092
habit of looking at good side 1095
habit of the mind 1094
Health and c. mutually beget each other 5607
honor time with c. 11377
is health 1089
is no sin 1090
Keep your face to the sunshine 1098
lubricates inward machinery 1092
Nothing more beautiful than c. in an old face 8148
prayer for c. 9092
removes rust from mind 1093
result of strenuous discipline 1088
Wondrous is power of endurance 1099
Wondrous is strength of c. 1099

CHEERING

hope, c. the lonely way 5940
like donkey believing crowds c. him 9217
Speak approving, c. words 4223

CHEERIOS

hula-hoops for ants 8650

CHEESE

Age not important unless c. 8123
delicious, but way to it is risky 11103

CHEMICAL

body, a c. laboratory 842

CHERISH

all happy moments 5506
Character formed as we c. principles 1000
just, lasting peace 5199

CHERISHED

more rarely is excellence c. 3472
most c. possession is my faith 3761
on ruins of c. schemes 3631

CHERISHES

Hope c. no illusions 5928

CHERUBIM

described in Scripture 359
Like thrones of the c. 7927

CHESTERFIELD

swiped ideas from C. 2019

CHEW

more 5604
willing to swallow, too lazy to c. 6758

CHEWED

some few books to be c, digested 859

CHEWING

Meditation the soul's c. 7717

CHEWS

childhood c. hours, swallows minutes 12193

CHICANERY

different names for c. 4115

CHICKEN

get c. by hatching egg 8420

CHICKENS

Corn can't expect justice from c. 6605

CHIDE

friend in private 4182
Husbands in heaven whose wives c. not 7618
no heathen in world but myself 3942

CHIDING

Better little c. than great heartbreak 8283

CHIEF

event of life, a mind that startled us 7752
To be c. of people serve them 6806

CHILD

A little c. in a manger 6133
a loving God provident as a father's love for c. 4792
a sheer delight 1100
A silent c, I follow on 4977
Be content to be a c. 4629
be vigilant over c. 8282
be vigilant over c. in April of his understanding 8282
become like c. before Scriptures 650
becomes largely what he is taught 5818
believe in belief 1122
believe in love 1122
believe in loveliness 1122
best compliment to a c. 6207
best way for c. to learn to fear God 8327
Better c. cry than father 8284
burnt c. dreads fire 3512
castigate fault not c. 8312

character determines how c. fits into society 8346

death of c, adolescent is born 2390

decision to have c. momentous 8310

Difficult c. is unhappy 1125

discipline is for the c. 8331

do not destroy 23

Do not try to produce ideal c. 8293

elves can whisper in ear 1122

Ere a c. has reached to seven 8296

fairy godmother in soul 1122

faith is c. of knowledge 6714

family stamped character upon c. 1126

fifteen years teaching c. to be quiet 8336

freedom is justice's c. 6628

Give a little love to a c. 8297

give good example 511

great word to master 7000

His c. and he 6398

Holding a beggar's c. 7178

how c. handles hate determines Harvard or San Quentin 8281

I would lie down like a tired c. 2882

ideal c. would find no fitness in world 8293

identifies parents with God 8339

If assurance is c. of faith 6714

If c. tells lie, don't call him liar 8301

in womb not lawful to destroy 16

Know you to be a c. 1122

let me be Thy little c. 306

Level with c. by being honest 8349

lies, will find a severe parent 8362

like a c. walk with thee down all my days 9051

Look upon a little c. 1117

Lord, thy will be done in c. 9082

love must help c. grow away from mother 7858

Maturity allowing a c. space to grow up 7696

Mother spoils c, fattens serpent 8330

mother understands what c. does not say 7842

Music c. of prayer 7906

My c., better for you 38

never been another c. like you 3039

no other c. exactly like you 3039

no prayer life yourself useless to make c. say prayers 8348

Nobody spots phony quicker than a c. 8349

not dead, the c. of our affection 2392

Old age, a second c, by nature curs'd 8163

Old age, twice a c. 8167

parent who does not reach c. to obey is cruel 8355

religion of c. depends on what parents are, not what they say 8356

says nothing but heard by fire 3885

seeking to crush, flush, kill, spill 1100

sees parents living without self-discipline 8300

Set a c. to wondering, on road to understanding 6691

Sleep, my c, peace attend thee 1123

smallest c. can be converted 1896

spend three years teaching c. to walk 8336

spoiled c. never loves mother 1103

successful parents get behind eyes of c. 8329

suspicious parent makes artful c. 8342

sweater worn by c. when mother cold 3866

Take clay and dust, fashion a c. 4608

taught Sunday, remember Monday 1134

tells in streets what father, mother say at home 8340

the Christ c. stood at Mary's knee 6470

there'd have been no room for the c. 9414

to be a c. of God for eternity 5308

to have a thankless c. 1119

to withhold from c. world's sorrows 8334

Truth is c. of time 10448

turn lowness into liftiness 1122

turn mice into horses 1122

turn nothing into everything 1122

turn pumpkins into coaches 1122

utterly maddening 1100

wants man for father, not formula 3929

What will c. learn sooner than a song 7930

when c. three years old 8306

who fears noises becomes man who hates noises 4004

who said, "Could you be a daddy to me" 3920

word of parent fibre woven into character of c. 8346

CHILD OF GOD

no human birth compare to birth of c. 874

wonder that c. should have sad heart 1096

CHILD'S

great man who does not lose c. heart 5294

Let c. first lesson be obedience 8307

misery fills whole of his world 1101

mother eases a c. fear 7844

mother's heart is c. schoolroom 7857

naive is c. strength 7977

proper attitude toward c. disobedience 8332

suffering real, deep 1101

CHILDHOOD

chews hours, swallows minutes 12193

dies, corpses called adults 1135

earlier miniature world 1126

greatest benefit God has conferred 3895

guileless candor of c. 7709

Learning in c. like engraving on rock 8305

Life the c. of our immortality 6098

model of the greater world 1126

Old age is but a second c. 8156

shows the man 1124

when nightmares occur only during sleep 1106

CHILDISH

quest for power c. 3469

CHILDISHNESS

one of seven deadly virtues 11699

CHILDLIKE

analysis of conscience has taken place of c. simplicity 6813

Christ dealt with things in lordly, c. manner 6509

science measured against reality c. 9867

Thy lodging is in c. hearts 6040

where not a c. humility at starting post 11549

CHILDREN

act like their parents 1109

Adults are obsolete c. 8478

afraid to go to parents for counsel 8311

as they grow older, judge parents 1111

Authentic men aren't afraid to hug c. 3916

become plausible actors 1105

begin by loving parents 1111

best legacies father can leave c. 3924

better terms with angels than c. 3899

born from relationship secondary 10239

can get insanity from your c. 3874

common bond of care, love 3868

communicate Christianity to his c. 3927

contributions to c. rank as greatest accomplishments 8294

cut to core of issue 1116

deprived c. do nothing to get wants 1128

determined to face opposite direction 1113

don't fit "to do" list 8287

easier for father to have c. 3922

either c. of God or the devil 8075

expose life to the bone 1116
faith, trust are second nature 1116
fallacy that having c. makes a mother 7854
fear to go into the dark 476
Give me the c. 1117
God manifests himself in his c. 9707
God puts his c. in the fire 151
God's apostles 1107
God's c. of infinite value, eternally loved 6042
have more trouble solving parents' problems 3883
have not mastered deception 1116
humble only when we know we are God's c. 6042
if c. spend most formative period 3036
If gratitude due from c. to parent 5253
important to be real mother to c. 7856
impresses me about America is parents obey c. 8357
In praise of little c. 1120
instill foundation of values 1110
is to be kind to his other c. 6665
joy of parents in c. most holy joy of humanity 5844
lately come from God 1116
learn what they observe 1114
learning to yield to leadership of God 8338
like clocks, must be allowed to run 1108
like flowers in bouquet 1113
listen to Bible stories with wonder, delight 645
little need to deceive themselves 1132
live with acceptance, learn to find love 1114
live with approval, learn to like themselves 1114
live with criticism, learn to be judgmental 1114
live with encouragement, learn confidence 1114
live with fairness, learn justice 1114
live with friendship, learn to find love 1114
live with hostility, learn to fight 1114
live with praise, learn to appreciate 1114
live with ridicule, learn to be withdrawn 1114
live with security, learn faith 1114
live with shame, learn guilt 1114
live with tolerance, learn patience 1114
loaned temporarily 1110
love c. enough to discipline 8309
Men but c. of larger growth 7418
moments when c. will hate you 8281

more need of models than critics 8286
most divine are c. 1120
most priceless possession 1115
Mother name for God in hearts of c. 7848
natural mimics 1109
need praise more than bread, butter 8309
need to be talked to like grownups 8311
never failed to imitate elders 1112
never good at listening to elders 1112
never trouble where c. resemble parents 3898
no illegitimate c, only illegitimate parents 1131
no obstructions to faith 1116
not casual guests 1110
not entering into conversation with c. 3904
not to give his c. taste of his delights 9037
of all created things, loveliest are c. 1120
of the next generation 562
Old age is but older c. 8157
Only c. paused to stare 6458
Parents bones on which c. sharpen teeth 8350
Parents giving c. nothing but best 8324
Parents have little time for c. 8351
parents prevent c. learning lessons 8320
preach of love, hope, peace 1107
Raising c. not unlike long-distance race 3884
reactions to reading 852
saw many other c. lying all about the yard 11740
second half of lives ruined by c. 3892
sing to keep up courage 476
sometimes they forgive parents 1111
Sorrow makes us all c. again 10620
strip away our sophisticated pseudo-civilization 1116
talk with integrity 1105
teach c. in school what they are 3039
teaches c. responsibility provides fortune 3913
tendency to not allow c. to make mistakes 8320
than c. to have a real father 3922
to c. parents are heaven's lieutenants 5856
to shock parents 562
understand better than venerable 1216
understand what parents have rejected 12157
unrefined wisdom 1116
value of marriage that c. produce adults 7669

want parents more than junk we buy 8288
way parents obey their c. 3897
weed bouquet says it all 1102
what we desire c. to become, we must be 5861
when outgrow tender Shepherd, find heroes elsewhere 1133
When think c. are naive 8319
while little c. go hungry, I'll fight 3342
whistle to keep up courage 476
who step on parents toes 8323
whom the Father leadeth 5431
why take so little care of your c. 8290
will act like their parents 8289
will be gone so quickly 8353
without c. without newness, color 1104
Without family c. have no moral foundation 3877
Without family, c. moral illiterates 3877
woman under whose hands c. grow up strong, pure 5857
youth like c. in a theatre 12168

CHILDREN OF GOD
impossible for us to be c. naturally 9801

CHILDREN OF ISRAEL
longed for other meat 1813

CHILDREN'S
human race playing at c. games from beginning 5982
Parents have trouble solving c. problems 3883
teeth set on edge 8328
words sweet as c. talk 11998

CHILL
aimless Cain 10573
cynic can c. with single word 2176
Love makes those young whom age doth c. 7264

CHILLING
fear of holy enthusiasm 3184

CHIME
in with harmonies of creation 7921
Sundays when the bells do c. 10957
to c. in with harmonies of creation 10665

CHIMERA
What a c, then, is man 7439

CHIMES
cracked c. of courageous human spirit 7171

CHIMNEY
Who hangs himself in c. 11120

CHIMNEY-SWEEPERS
As c. come to dust 2290

CHIN
When in trouble, hold your c. up
11463

CHINA
can learn from philosophers of C.
2988

CHINESE
symbol for crisis identical to
opportunity 2048
through New Testament in C. 682

CHINKS
Lets in new light through c. time
hath made 7701

CHIPPEWA INDIAN
Voyager's Prayer 9098

CHISEL
God uses pain as c. for sculpting
our lives 8256

CHOICE
difficulty in life is c. 1152
fullness of life has to be my c.
5549
God calls sin a chance, God a c.
4550
God gave us free c. 1141
God gives best, leave c. with him
1139
God's side or human reasoning
1156
goes to hell by own c. 5686
happiness in worth, c. of friends
4293
have no c. but to be guilty 5493
his the call, mine the c. 1147
if no choice make no difficulty
1158
In darkness no c. 1144
is how you live life 1140
Jesus compelled individuals to
make a c. 6516
Laughter is a c. 6727
Life is not the c. 1140
never seems to question c. of
husband 7655
no freedom to determine end of c.
1149
no freedom to negotiate results of
c. 1159
Not mine, not mine, the c. 5456
not to make a c, a c. 1157
On the c. of friends 4198
right to create alternatives of c.
4155
taking away freedom of c. from
man 4133
This path is mine, I made the c.
5415
Though this test be not thy c.
11107
whether to accept life not the c.
6893
Why, rain's my c. 37
without c. man an instrument
4155
Without c. man not a man 4155

CHOICES
Character sum total of c. 1000
free c, God's foreordained decrees
1153
God does not make c. easier
11058
of time binding in eternity 1150
philosophy best expressed in c.
1148
refer to Scriptures for c. 650
ultimately our responsibility 1148

CHOIR
being educated for c. invisible
10600
human soul silent harp in God's c.
7921
stillness of nature louder than c.
of voices 8041
Worship isn't appreciating
harmony of the c. 12139

CHOKE
faults by gaining virtues 3959
God's Word with a yawn 11349
Tiny fly can c. a big man 8701

CHOKES
God squeezes but never c. 4464
suppressed grief c. within 5330

CHOOSE
a commitment to joy 499
a posture of grace 499
always to have less rather than
more 8448
an attitude of gratitude 499
As would have a daughter, so c. a
wife 7602
can be as wretched as you c.
10816
can c. to be bag of marbles 9524
can c. to be joyful 6530
can c. to live without God 1142
cannot c. our own work 5446
cannot c. to be strong 6530
Democracy, people free to c. who
will get blame 5173
disbelieve in God as we c. 11590
free to c. whether free 4152
Freedom is right to c. 4155
freedom to c. attitude 519
freedom to take course we c. 1149
fresh start any moment you c.
3598
God did not c. because worthy
3044
I c. the Christ 11129
I c. to believe 6091
I dare not c. my lot 5412
if c. to remain in situation where
tempted 8818
If I must c. between peace,
righteousness 6305
intelligent person has learned to
"c. between" 6326
Judge yourself by the friends you
c. 4194
life partly made by friends we c.
4254
may or may not as we c. 3721

must c. to forgive 4109
neither wife nor linen by
candlelight 7609
Of two evils, c. neither 3390
only when c. to praise for rough
spots 11152
out the path for me 5456
reasons which moved God to c.
order of universe 4989
Satan first of beings to c. evil 3370
stalled who c. not to be chosen
3045
thou for me, my God 5412
time when we must c. course to
follow 2491
to act rather than delay 1138
to be dominated by sin or
righteousness 10510
to build rather than destroy 1138
To c. what is difficult 3803
to forgive rather than curse 1138
to give rather than grasp 1138
to heal rather than wound 1138
to love rather than hate 1138
to persevere rather than quit 1138
to praise rather than gossip 1138
to pray rather than despair 1138
to smile rather than frown 1138
What better way could you c. 356
What God does not c. to give
4958
what life's color shall be 522
wife by ear rather than eye 7610

CHOOSES
big difference to fly which side he
c. 8076
Christian c. to be great in
presence of God 1259
God allots our work where he c.
2831
God c. base, lowly, unknown
3861
happy so long as c. to be happy
5538
make us broken bread, poured
out wine as he c. 9850
No man c. evil because evil 3386
seldom know why Lord c. whom
5894
take what God c. to send 5911
the right with invincible resolution
5297
what a sovereign God c. to do
through us 8094
what God c. better 1800
when God c. he will alter
circumstances 238
Why is God doing as he c. 3042

CHOOSING
by c. us God makes us worthy
3044
Christianity because mysteries
incomprehensible 1213
power of c. good, evil within reach
5047
putting minds together in shapes
of our own c. 8710

CHORAL
sudden pause in c. hymn of our lives 7056

CHORD
Every good deed touches c. that vibrates in heaven 6670

struck one c. of music like the sound of a great Amen 7919

will vibrate in eternity 105

CHORDS
In the cloud God is deepening thy c. 10600

tune and touch the c. till every note shall answer thine 7527

CHORE
Some people regard discipline as a c. 9975

CHORES
put off until October c. in August 9882

CHORUSES
sing c. for God's ears alone 8424

CHOSE
both fear and self-denial 467

care to live until c. to die 5530

He c. its day of birth 3227

never cared to live until I c. to die 2308

road with most rocks 467

the saddest, somberest colors 467

the ugliest coat 467

CHOSEN
Adversity depends on c. response 141

call does not come to a c. few 7784

cross end of path c. after counting cost 2103

God loved his c. creatures 4769

God preparing you as his c. arrow 5430

God's reply in some verse thus c. 5441

have c. the wrong day 10961

having thus c. our course 1918

Once c, he's no chance 6463

see Christ's c. saint 1299

stalled who choose not to be c. 3045

Suffering God gives only to c. friends 10894

to allow pain to corrode spirit is to have c. 8264

To let others dictate your future is to have c. 8264

transformed into image of Christ by circumstances is to have c. 8264

What God had c. was my defeat 2518

would have c. suffering ahead of anything 10872

CHRIST
a fathomless answer, the Cross of C. 9398

a granite stone 6517

A Man spoke as never man before 1147

a path if any be misled 6391

a realist 1154

a robe if any naked be 6391

a Savior 5208

accept C. receive God's approval 3854

accept C. without knowing how it works 1893

accepting C. as Lord will bring heaven down 5681

Ah C, that it were possible 2214

alive as Christians love one another 9695

all great purposes of God culminate in him 5710

all lines of history converge upon him 5710

All we want in C, we shall find in C. 6354

an example, showing us how to live 6410

And C. our Lord the way hath trod 2219

anything that dims my vision of C. 7036

Apart from C. life a broken pillar 1163

aperture through which God seen 6373

Art thou his client 6415

as God is fatherland where we are going 6364

as man is way by which we go 6364

As seed sprouted C. born in Bethlehem 5731

asks, Why does he give 10735

awakens within us concern for world 12031

became like us 2121

became man for us 2121

Because he lives, I can face tomorrow 2978

because he was once emptied 2979

become part of personality of C. 2822

behavior shaped by mind of C. 10562

belonged to his times 6359

best proof C. has risen is he is still alive 9695

bids him come and die 10049

birth, death but one continual act 6489

bled for Adam's helpless race 495

bled, and died, I have been transfused 2979

blood of C. grim, repulsive 2141

blood of C. precious 2141

bread for men's souls 6374

bread, wine, milk to feed his people 6370

brings his cross, presence 2120

brings us his ability 11

Brother to relieve 6370

But 'tis enough that C. knows all 5635

call of C. 3300

call of C. always a promotion 10186

calls to carry cross 3300

came into our condition 6121

came into valley, shadow of death 6121

came where we were, where we are 6121

can do wonders with broken heart 10584

can never go to heaven without C. 9792

cannot alter essential nature 1750

cannot have Christian principles without C. 1355

cannot live his life without 1270

Captain to defend 6370

carries forward work of administration 235

certainty 6463

characteristic was submission to his Father 6414

child stood at Mary's knee 6470

chose disciples who were poor 8698

Christianity, C. himself 1170

Christianity, devotion to C. 1176

Christianity, life with C. 1172

church to bring crucified C. to world 1405

claims to be more than man 6349

combines qualities of every race 6363

coming of C. by way of Bethlehem manger 6145

complaint that C. not religious enough 6416

conquer by love 6389

Conscience, true vicar of C. 1673

could not afford to be wrong 11509

Counselor to advise 6370

creative wave of love, sacrifice 6419

cross of C. an offense to world 6317

cross of C. is Christ's glory 2152

crucified by Fundamentalists 9541

deal only with surface find C. an offense 6422

deed that helps or harms poor, for or against C. 8698

degree to which life emblazon character of C. 5306

demanding everything 6419

deny the virgin birth of C. and you paralyze redemption 6404

desire C. for perpetual guest 8092

develop same character traits as exist in C. 6301

did not come only to teach us 6403

did not come to conquer by force 6389

did not die a martyr 2126

did not explain suffering 10880

did not limit concern to spiritual 1551

did not only come into our flesh 6121

did not simply speak truth 11572

died a common criminal 2126

directs us to the world 12031

disadvantage to life in C. 1211

disillusioned with C, didn't get high 3493

disposition a peculiar, subdued sadness 6390

either deceived mankind by fraud 6366

embodies, animates all life, history 6369

emptied himself of all but love 495

enduring everything 6419

enemies of C. are triumphant, they say 1443

enemy in prayer is lack of knowledge of what we are in C. 8815

enters world to heal its wounds 6487

eternally faithful 9521

ever at service of men 1754

Every day should make us more like C. 1347

Every step toward C. kills a doubt 2940

executed by a corrupt church 2171

executed by a fickle proletariat 2171

executed by a timid politician 2171

Father to provide 6370

Feed on C, then go live life 6381

feel so little need of C. 1350

first and also last 6475

Following C. is hard, rugged life 1282

For him to see me mended 2128

Foundation to support 6370

Fountain to cleanse 6370

From him all come to be 6475

fruits of the Spirit are the virtues of C. 10714

garment of righteousness 6370

gave love, service, himself 10731

gave me his policy 1906

gave no answer, neither can you 10917

get no deeper into C. 6502

give C. keys of your heart 8092

give him range of every room 8092

Give man C, change heart 3307

give reputation to C, gain it 9629

Give the earth to C. 1363

giver of grace 5208

gives us light 1144

gives us power to go on with battle 11451

glory by sacrifice 2152

God acting like God 6371

God has given us the mind of C. 6679

God impressed by only one man—C. 3854

goes behind law to disposition 1526

gospel of C. same forever 5103

grasp him and be led securely home 6517

great calm always there 6376

great central fact in world's history 5710

greatest contemplative ever lived 1754

greatest fact which history records is birth of C. 5710

guilt washed out by blood of C. 10419

had enemies, detractors 9448

hard to present C. before men 3222

hard to train for service of C. 466

has never lost his case 6415

has no hands but our hands 10122

has not lost a battle yet 6367

has turned our sunsets into dawns 6368

have no time for C. whose work it is 10117

have not understood the words of C. 10182

Have your heart right with C. 5529

he was deluded or divine 6366

Head to guide 6370

Health, wealth wean us of need for C. 5608

helps us by his weakness, suffering 4899

helps us not by virtue of his omnipotence 4899

highest love, the love of C. for men 6506

himself doth rule 2392

his coming meant war 6375

His life is C, his death is gain 1299

his limitless ways 11

his mystery 6369

his task and responsibility 123

his two fundamental rules for life 10053

history incomprehensible without C. 5709

holds the future 2978

Husband to protect 6370

I choose the C. 11129

I have a great C. for my need 6399

I have a great need for C. 6399

I must see him torn 2128

I want none beside him 6498

I will pray C. to cling to me 9022

identified with C. in crucifixion 2138

identified with C. in resurrection 2138

If any be a bondman, he is free 6391

If any be weak, how strong is he 6391

If any chance to hunger, he is bread 6391

If C. controlling personalities 1289

If C. did not speak truth in all matters 11509

If C. lives in us 1289

If C. not born in thee, soul forlorn 878

If could comprehend C, no greater than myself 6459

If I could hear C. praying for me 8832

If impossible for C. to triumph over death 9691

If love C. much, shall trust him much 11472

If you don't surrender to C. 10971

in Bethlehem be born 1374

in brightness, he is my sin 6498

In C. church has enough to feed world 6374

In C. move into breathtaking future 8364

In C. move into meaningful present 8364

In C. move out of past 8364

In C. no caprice 1750

In C. no changeableness 1750

In C. no east or west 911

In C. no south or north 911

In C. relaxed and at peace 8470

in darkness, he is my star 6498

in death he shall be death of death 6498

in him all comes to rest 6475

In his ascension, C. a king 6410

In his death, C. a sacrifice 6410

in his intercession, C. a high priest 6410

In his resurrection, C. a conqueror 6410

in his weakest hour 2127

In life he is my life 6498

in poverty, C. my riches 6498

in sickness, he makes my bed 6498

In the cross of C. I glory 2133

in tribulations made like unto C. 234

in utter helplessness, cast all on C. 6354

in you that fights the battle 6381

in you that helps the poor 6381

in you that lives your life 6381

in you that tells the truth 6381

in you that wins the crown 6381

infinite mercy, goodness 5208

inmost being where C. lives 10254

inner life sea of glass 6376

investigated, cancelled policy 1906

is a great Savior 9797

Is C. thy advocate 6415

is Lord of heaven and earth 232

is master, Scriptures servant 647

is no Moses, exactor, giver of laws 5208

is our true self 10551

is praying for me 8832

is risen, all earth's at play 2982

is the Christian's pilot 5638

is the head of this house 5823

Judas sold himself, not C. 775

judge our conduct by 563

Lamb in gentleness 6425

Lamb in meekness 6425

Lamb in patience 6425

leads me through no darker rooms 5379

leaving to C. matter of how happy he shall be 5543

left his Father's throne 495

less satisfied with superficial views of C. 6480

let C. be inward spring 6379

let C. be note to which life attuned 6379

let men spit upon him, crucify him 6503

Let us become like C. 2121

Life in C, string of action verbs 1235

life on its proper basic principles 159

life revolves around C, its central sun 6937

Life with C. an endless hope 5938

Life with C. never dull 6987

Life with C. not always easy 6987

lightness of life from grace of C. 5229

Lion in authority 6425

Lion in power, raising the dead 6425

live as though C. coming this afternoon 2837

lives among poor, oppressed 1277

living at heart of world 6369

lordly, childlike manner 6509

loses us until we find him 10839

love counts royalty but drudgery if cannot reign for C. 6457

love that C. commands not easy 7304

loving any person better than C. 6925

made commandments more difficult 1526

made himself servant of the poor 8698

made no promise 159

makes C. stand hat-in-hand awaiting verdict 3333

makes his disciples like himself 6411

May chance be no other man but C. 4355

Meekness that C. pronounced blessed 7728

men animated by love of C. feel united 3081

men never the same after listening to him 6377

message a fire that set society ablaze 6375

message revolutionizing 6377

met, willed, transformed suffering 10880

mind made incandescent by indwelling C. 7776

more involved in life's troubles when come to C. 11451

more you know about C. 6480

moves among pots and pans 5824

must despair to obtain grace of C. 5201

must do your work 1536

must have the best chamber 6504

must live in your family 1536

must live in your neighborhood 1536

nearer to C, more intensely missionary we become 7785

never a slave of the clock 123

never bored a soul 867

never gave anyone money 10731

never impressed by numbers 123

never in a hurry 123

no deeper into C. than 1345

no discovery of truth without committing to C. 6490

no greater opportunity to influence fellowman for C. 6278

No kingdom with as many civil wars 1215

no promise of immunity from pain 159

no right to draw life from other source than C. 11689

no rosy promises 1154

not an unknown country, C. is there 5659

not best of several ways to approach God 6372

not driven by crises 4425

not lonely, for C. is with you 5659

not on externals 513

not one of many ways to approach God 6372

not overoptimistic 1154

not perplexed by circumstances 1472

not visionary 1154

not your hold of C. that saves you 9802

of all epithets to C. mild seems least appropriate 6462

of the poor confronted me 8685

offers new life 7022

Once chosen, he's no chance 6463

Once rooted and grounded in C. 10141

Only C. can accomplish goal within us 8113

only know ourselves through C. 6461

only with single-minded attention to C. 10551

our task is to live personal communication with C. 3321

outwardly troubled 6376

pain buys intimacy with C. 10906

passed through world like flame 867

Peace rules day when C. rules mind 8462

people gathered to C. by love 6396

people have not yet understood command of C. 7349

people were drawn to C. 6396

performed greatest work 2127

Physician to heal 6370

Plato taught more science than C. 6362

pleasure without loss 6391

poise and quietness of C. 123

Praise is the saint reflecting C. 8734

Preach nothing up but the C. 9156

presence of C. brings us his power 11

Priest to make atonement 6370

Prince to rule 6370

promises joy and courage 159

promises love and confidence 159

Prophet to teach 6370

provided unity, not uniformity 1451

question no longer what we think of C. 4718

question will be what C. thinks of us 4718

religion put C. on the cross 9541

rich enough who is poor with C. 8676

Root to quicken 6370

Rules blunt appetite for C. 6819

saint has same spirit, judgment, will with C. 9766

science of C. only learned by the heart 5110

seeking justice for those in agony 1277

seems difficult to put on yoke of C. 2824

shared their poverty 8698

shows C. applying to us 3333

simplicity in C. rarely found 1230

sin was his errand 6505

so active in the service of C. 117

so easy to receive C. 5653

so free, so infinite his grace 495

society not community radiant with love of C. 10514

something C. wants to hurt to death 6407

sought a crown of thorns 2152

Spirit of C. is spirit of missions 7785

spirit of C. operating in our lives 104

spoke of dying to live 6359

spoke to those to whom no one spoke 6433

standing beside him, helping him to pray 8761

stick to C. as burr to topcoat 2446

stirring to be awakened 1757

stone rolled away not to permit C. to come out 9699

stooped when he conquered 2152

suffers watching our suffering 10839

sufficient for all his people 6370

Sun to enlighten 6370

teaching of C. at first appears lukewarm 6486

teaching of C. ripping, tearing torpedo 6486

teaching of C. splits to atoms every preconceived notion 6486

teachings of C. alone can solve difficulties 6487

than we allow C. to get into us 6502

the all of Christmas 1364

the express image of God 6355

The hands of C. 2162

the Life everlasting 6397

the Lion in majesty, rebuking winds, demons 6425

the Lord is born 6141

the master adjuster 1906

the only way to approach God 6372

the perfect representation of God 6355

the slumbering C. 1757

the Truth infallible 6397

the Way unchangeable 6397

theology begins, ends with C. as Savior 11182

they will never tear the living C. from my heart 7103

think every day of C. 8472

those luminous words of his 6419

Though C. a thousand times be born 878

'Tis a gift for C. his sake 5860

to accept crucifixion with C. 10048

to assimilate C. active faith 3801

To be like C. our goal 8113

to become like C. only thing worth caring for 6494

To believe on C. initial faith 3801

to blind men, sight 6391

To dead men, life is he 6391

To forsake C. for world 6495

to him everything looks forward, backward 5710

To love as C. loves a practical thing 7324

to receive C. appropriating faith 3801

to sick men, health 6391

to tear your name from this world 6496

to the needy, wealth 6391

to understand C. intelligent faith 3801

today people would make fun of C, 6405

today they would ask him to dinner 6405

told the world the truth about itself 11525

told us to be like doves 5631

told whole truth 1154

Tomorrow lose opportunity to accept C. 11404

too simple to be grasped 6507

too truthful to be believed 6507

too weak to cling to C. 9022

tore through temple like a mad man 6392

traitors to C. 3846

Treasure to enrich 6370

treasure without stealth 6391

true disciples of C. love most 7318

True have his promises been 6498

turned world's standards upside down 5001

unseen guest at every meal 5823

unseen listener to every conversation 5823

Unspeakably wise 6499

values which C. declared false 11666

want to be saved, insist C. do dying 2821

war raging in time of C. 11760

was apprehended 6393

was betrayed 6393

was born a martyr 6489

was condemned 6393

was killed 6393

was nailed to the cross 6393

was Truth 11572

was willing to suffer 9448

We do not draw people to C. by discrediting 12147

We have C. in our neighbor 8061

weakness deepens dependence on C. for strength 8256

wept and mourned 6393

what fits soul for C. 10676

When C. calls a man 10049

When C. came into my life 11130

When C, hung, bled, died 7173

When he came, there was no light 6510

When he left, there was no darkness 6510

when put on yoke of C. becomes easy 2824

when we take C. out of manger 6145

When you have C. you are rich 9521

who but God would have asked of men what he asked 6419

Who stumbles upon C. 6517

will be to us whole treasury of God 6354

will provide everything you need 9521

will rise on Easter day 2985

will turn earth into heaven 5529

will turn homes into temples 5529

will turn meals into sacraments 5529

will turn weekdays into Sundays 5529

will visit you often 5529

willed to be born poor 8698

wisely speechless 6499

with C. and nothing else can be happy 3761

with C. anywhere 3822

with C. life is dawn of morning with day ahead 7094

with C. light, warmth of full day ahead 7094

With every cross in obedience to C. comes strength 8108

without C. a hopeless end 5938

without C. and all else you'll never be happy 3761

Without C. life as twilight with dark night ahead 7094

Without C. not one step 3822

words provoked acceptance or rejection 6377

words simple, yet profound 6377

wore a crown of thorns 6393

wrestled with justice 6393

wrote no book, yet his words counsel everywhere 6394

You are beauty 6520

You are eternal life 6520

You are peace 6520

You are wisdom 6520

CHRIST JESUS

always found among humble people 5992

came to world clothed in humility 5992

must be found in C. not in some formula 7105

CHRIST-CENTERED

suffer when they disappoint others 10911

CHRISTENDOM

angel created for service of C. 354

CHRISTIAN

a controversialist 1825

a God-intoxicated man 1261

a harmless enough thing 1318

a moment—and a lifetime 1287

accepts circumstances from God 3638

action is action of God mediated through a person 10122

action is the spirit of Christ 104

action not of ourselves 104

admits wrong, declared right 1265

always in process of becoming 1250

am no more a C. than Pilate was 7099

an oak flourishing in winter 1249

an ordinary C. kneels to say his prayers 8761

an overplus of C. activities 127

anything that makes C. work difficult 7036

are you a fool 1272

arrested for being C, enough evidence 1291

begins with what God has revealed 3783

better foundation than stoicism 1563

better just after conversion 1347

both a pessimist and an optimist 8252

came to end of trying to be a C. 5792

can be like sack of marbles 1273

can be no C. life without prayer 8938

can elevate himself by meditation 7707

cannot be a C. anywhere 1288

cannot have C. principles without Christ 1355

cannot live by philosophy 9703

ceased to be commentator 1168

ceased to be spectator 1168

characters not passive but active 1271

Chastity a requisite of C. singleness 10236

child wearing harness of warrior 1318

consistent only to life of God in him 2025

crashing, ill-natured bore 867

criticized for not being C. enough 1342

daily process to be more like Christ 1269

death crowns a C. 1280

dies so he can live 1265

difference between C. love and values of world evident 6278

discerns cosmic conflict 1168

dissolution can do the C. no harm 2325

division high, deep between C. and world 1338

does not begin with human intellect 3783

does not sweep dirt under rugs 1263

does not understand God in terms of love 4494

ease with being C. sentimentalists 12106

empties himself to be full 1265

enhanced meaning in life 1168

entitled to God's kingdom 1267

Every believer, God's miracle 1279

Every C. needs half hour of prayer each day 8790

exults 6563

failed as C. writer 12147

faith founded upon fact of history 6144

Faith makes a C. 1280

father described what a C. was 3912

feels love for one he has never seen 1265

finds God in ordinary occurrences 1297

finds peace in accepting master plan 8440

forces ranged against him 1168

forsakes to have 1265

fringe benefit sense of identity 1266

given peace like none in world 1904

gives away to keep 1265

God loves him for what God is 1904

God pity the C. world gets best of 1330

goes down to get up 1265

Going to church doesn't make you a C. 1286

hand through which Christ helps 1248

happiest when he feels worst 1265

has God's honor at stake 1246

has obligation like no obligation in world 1904

has smile of God 1323

has succumbed to secularization 7768

has that which is impossible to world 10512

have a Friend thou canst never separate 1310

hears the inaudible 1265

heart through which Christ loves 1248

heightened personal responsibility 1168

here for God's design, not our own 139

How long does it take 1287

If C. nations Christians would be no wars 11748

if house not happier for your being a C. 3872

If man cannot be C. where he is 1288

If trying to be a C. 1291

If you do not love, do not know meaning of C. life 7191

is an odd number anyway 1265

is like ripening corn 6030

is more music when he prays 8749

is on the throne until on the cross 2821

is salt 1252

issue as C. is not to pretend we love everything 5890

Joy gigantic secret of the C. 6546

just as C. came up with the cross 9803

keyhole through which folks see God 1254

know, care about the questions 1268

knows that which passes knowledge 1265

learn knack of listening like C. instead of critic 10110

leaving behind parasitical concerns 1306

life a reproduction, not an imitation 1258

life hid with Christ in God 1310

life not meant for solitude 916

life not suited to solitude 916

life on feeling, gigantic collapse 1257

life proves a C. 1280

life that we call C. different from what we think 6918

like a child before the Scriptures 650

like a good watch 1260

living sermon 1247

love an affair of the will 4777

love links love of God and neighbor 7164

love not vague feeling of affection 7304

love [agape] an attitude 7166

love [agape] not feeling 7166

loved with love like no other in world 1904

loving dead men into life 1306

ludicrous for C. to believe he is object of public worship 9217

may give up things for special reasons 1217

means taking risks 1244

meditation that does not make a difference 7725

men at head of great movements are C. men 5094

mind has succumbed to secular drift 7768

mind through which Christ thinks 1248

mind, degree of weakness unmatched in C. history 7768

misplaced C. energy 111

misplaced C. money 111

moods in which whole thing looks improbable 1305

Morality does not make a C. 7830

more hand than tongue 1317

more life than lip 1317

more motion than notion 1317

more than an instantaneous conversion 1269

more work than word 1317

most dutiful servant of all 1255

most free of all 1255

most narrow-minded C. must admit 5791

must, as a C, turn away from it 7036

necessities form motives of prayers of ordinary C. 8788

needs no status symbols 1323

never forgets what God had done for him 5240

never in state of completion 1250

never know where a true C. may be 1341

never strong enough for today and tomorrow 417

No C. ever known to recant on deathbed 3764

no man can be a C. without morality 7830

No man ever repented of being a C. on death bed 2340

no understanding of a long-faced C. 6532

nor man C. until born again 875
not by ecclesiastical manipulation
   1256
not consistent to creeds 2025
not one man at church, another at
   home 1908
not one who withdraws 1251
not only temptation that tries the
   C. 10328
not saint on knees, cheat in shop
   1908
occupies some kind of pulpit 1245
on his knees sees more than
   philosopher on tiptoe 8975
one of the things a C. is meant to
   do 5629
one who has found right road
   1320
one who infiltrates 1251
ought to be a living doxology
   9856
out of question a C. government
   5182
partner of God 3327
pray that God would make C.
   taste so bad 8526
prayer closet base of supplies for
   the C. 8976
prayer closet not an asylum for
   worthless C. 8976
preaches some kind of sermon
   1245
prefer to be respectable, smooth
   1337
preserve society from corruption
   1252
proper study of C. is Godhead
   4631
question whether you really are a
   C. 3872
Recognize, O C. thy dignity 2763
refer to Scriptures for choices 650
refreshing to watch a new C. 1339
relaxed C. more attractive 9529
reproduction of life of Christ 1258
resigns some pleasure to enjoy
   others better 1298
response to assault reveal C.
   values by which you live 6288
richest when poorest 1265
salt of the earth 1271
seeking direction in Scriptures 650
seeking in Scripture effective
   remedy 650
seeking to bandage world's
   wounds 1306
sees falsity, illusions, limitations
   1168
sees illusions of humanist thinking
   1168
sees the invisible 1265
sets eternity against time 1259
shares the sufferings of God 1253
should act with disregard for
   opinions of others 6291
should not resemble a Christmas
   tree 1322
should resemble a fruit tree 1322
sick eaglet 1318

sin also tries the C. 10328
small part of battlefield his alone
   1168
sniffing wilted flowers 1318
some think C. sugar of earth 1315
spent pilgrim who has given up
   1318
strongest when weakest 1265
subject to everyone 1255
subject to none 1255
supernatural made natural 1044
supposed to love his neighbor
   7654
takes all of you, brains and all
   1193
talks to someone he cannot see
   1265
taller we grew in C. character
   6017
thanks God when everything goes
   good, bad 3638
thanks God whether he feels like
   it or not 3638
there is no longer a C. mind 7768
to cleanse, sweeten world 1271
to do wrong is to wound Friend
   1283
to get up, starts down 1294
to give justice 1207
to give new flavor to human
   existence 1271
to keep world from decay 1271
to model new heaven and earth
   1327
to share what one has 1207
to think as a C. greatest effort
   11270
too C. to enjoy sinning 10417
treasure is in heaven 1310
trials confirm a C. 1280
triumphant C. celebrates victory
   already won 11672
triumphant C. does not fight for
   victory 11672
truth of C. religion 5183
trying to be, sign you are not 1291
under trouble doesn't break up
   11452
understands love in terms of God
   4494
understands more than
   philosopher 1326
voice through which Christ speaks
   1248
walks with God, lives like Christ
   1015
wanting the unwanted 1306
wavering C. no respect from
   church, world 2771
whatever devil does to discourage
   a C. 9858
When a C. guards secret life with
   God 6321
when matched beside foolishness
   of the C. 10512
who flinches from the Crucifixion
   11779
who lives one-half inch from hell
   890

who squeaks when he walks 9529
who tugs on oars hasn't time to
   rock boat 10187
who whines when he talks 9529
will find his intelligence sharpened
   1193
will not neglect mercy, judgment
   1908
will not tithe mint, cummin 1908
window through which world sees
   God 3438
wits and wisdom taking Christ's
   place 127
work crippled by blessings,
   traditions of past 10124
work is worshiped, not God 97
worker must be sent 10188
world can no longer revolve
   around you 1306
world is my Father's house 1310
Worship is the C. life 12135
you'll have to revolve around the
   world 1306

CHRISTIAN EDUCATION
without C. we are rearing pagans
   8308

CHRISTIAN LIFE
is liberty 4160
no aim of our own 347

CHRISTIANITY
a battle, not dream 1167
a leak in your C. 6534
a relationship 1175
a resurrection religion 9689
absurd to call C. nonresistance
   1206
accepts gloom as fact 9551
admit, submit, commit, transmit
   1164
always a package deal 8108
an education 1193
an invitation to living 1168
ancient history or current events
   1204
bases religion on knowledge
   11226
believes that matter is good 1200
Bible, constitution of C. 718
body is given to us in heaven 1200
bread for daily use 1169
by it I see everything 1197
can't judge C. by comparing
   product 1316
cannot be moderately important
   1184
cannot speak against it without
   anger 1185
cannot speak for it without love
   1185
challenge is translation into
   lifestyle 1225
choose because mysteries
   incomprehensible 1213
Civil society renovated by
   teachings 1187
communicate C. to his children
   3927
condensed into four words 1164

Critics complain not good religion 1188

critics misunderstand nature 1188

danger of C. is anti-intellectualism 3027

definite, positive teaching 11226

Deity indwelling man 1189

demands high level of caring 1541

devil willing for person to profess, but not practice C. 2686

devotion to Christ 1176

dispels more mystery than it involves 1214

does contain doctrine 11226

does not make life easy 1229

does not remove load 931

does not teach doctrine of weakness 1165

enemy, all that makes it small, narrow 1233

Everything in C. that matters is 6176

family circle the supreme conductor of C. 5852

family, highest realization where C. prevails 3868

family, supreme conductor of C. 3887

feet on ground going God's way 1174

genuine C. has always vital throb of praise 6251

glimpse of a country 1181

God coming to men through Christ 1219

God focused himself in man 1232

great campaign of sabotage 1190

greatest attraction is absurdity 1216

greatest proof is practice 599

greatest proof not to logically analyze 599

has been found difficult, left untried 1220

has glorified marriage 1200

has not been tried and found wanting 1220

has taught function of suffering 10880

has taught true peace 10880

hold on to plough while wiping tears 1236

human race brought from death to life 1187

human race lifted to better things 1187

I believe in C. 1197

If C. has never disturbed us 1201

If C. small enough for understanding 1202

if false, of no importance 1184

if resurrection didn't happen C. gigantic fraud 9691

if true, of infinite importance 1184

In C. God not a static thing 11425

in C. we find the poem itself 1203

in full accord with psychology 9351

influence far from negligible 1188

introduced new spirit of government 5170

introduced no new forms of government 5170

is a failure, they say 1443

is an organism 1186

is Christ himself 1170

is God-directed strength 1165

is living every day with Christ 1180

is participation 1173

is resistance unto blood against sin 1206

is twilight in world 1214

isn't going to church 1180

king has landed in disguise 1190

land of beginning again 1178

life connected with Christ 1172

life of eternal quality 1188

like cathedral with dimly lighted windows 1224

like shining of silver 1227

love to God and man inseparably linked 1232

love worth more than intelligence 1183

made martyrdom sublime 1166

made sorrow triumphant 1166

makes us great enough for life 1229

man's text 1177

mistake to present as charming, popular 1198

moods as atheist in which C. looked probable 1305

more it is rubbed, brighter it grows 1227

more than a doctrine 1170

more than don'ts 1171

need not more C. but more Christians 1307

neither a creed nor ceremonial 1172

neither common sense or rationalism 533

neither comtemplation nor action 1173

never been accepted on large scale 1188

never promises to make independent 4116

no control over state of world 1188

no fault of C. that hypocrite sins 1208

no provision for privileged class 1234

not "This do," but "This happened" 1228

not a religion 1175

not an idea in the air 1174

not cake for special occasions 1169

not devotion to a cause 1176

not devotion to doctrine 1176

not devotion to work 1176

not much practical C. where 3899

not the obliteration of the old 6424

not to be judged by failure to reform world 1188

not to be judged by success 1188

offers power of God 1182

one of C. most serious evils 1414

only world religion that is evangelical 3301

opposed to corruptions of C. 1238

outside, no beauty 1224

people dislike C. 1205

persecution never fatal 1218

power of God in soul of man 1179

principles of primitive C. 1196

principles will change world 1196

promises to make free 4116

Prosperity often fatal 1218

purpose not to avoid difficulty 1229

purpose to produce character 1229

quit fiddling around fringes of C. 9691

real C. is hard 8108

religion of the open tomb 9688

remove resurrection, C. destroyed 9689

result a powerless C. 1239

resurrection lies at its heart 9689

revelation of true way of living 1188

revelation of way to know God 1188

revelation of way to live 1188

rightful king has landed 1190

seems at first about morality 1181

seems duties, rules, guilt, virtue 1181

sin an expulsion of C. 10360

Spirit-filled life not deluxe edition 1231

spread rapidly during first century 3302

strength different from natural strength 1165

system of balanced obligations 1240

teaches to bear burdens 931

test is wear, tear of daily life 1227

test of C. is what we do not give 4371

the transfiguration of the old 6424

thoroughly approves of the body 1200

too fond of sinning to enjoy C. 10417

unnatural for C. to be popular 1209

We are not the better for our C. 8065

wins victories over evil, self 1165

wish I could give to my family 1199

within a harmony of splendor 1223

without C. in world, night 1213

without C. we are rearing pagans
8308
world can argue against C. as
institution 1307
world rejects C. 1188
would not be large enough for our
needs 1202

CHRISTIAN'S
Christ is the C. pilot 5638
death is the C. harbor 5638
Faith is the C. foundation 5638
goal not power but justice 6623
God's way of answering the C.
prayer 8804
heaven is the C. country 5638
Heaven is the C. vocation 3095
hope is the C. anchor 5638
object of C. faith unseen reality
3831
place is in the world 1330
whatever devil does, God can use
for C. benefit 9858

CHRISTIANS
accepting noisiest as best 5891
accused of being morbid 9758
all things possible to C. 587
aren't perfect 4110
Arrogance, fear replaced with
gratitude, joy 1356
assume worshiped God because in
church 12101
Be united with other C. 4020
become C. instanteously by faith
in Christ 5738
blood of C. is fresh seed 7678
business of C. to pray 8766
cannot train ourselves to be C.
4984
Christ alive as C. love one another
9695
church not gallery of eminent C.
1437
church school for imperfect C.
1437
concern of devil is to keep C.
from praying 8985
deny God with life-style 487
despised, persecuted but care not
1293
difference between C. is in
contrast of their praying 8976
difficulty of C. stems from
unwillingness 1304
disillusionment with C. 1262
do not have all the answers 1268
don't work to go to heaven 1356
early C. looking for cleavage in
sky called Glory 9913
early C. not looking for cleft in
ground 9913
early C. so much in other world
5666
envy saints their joy 3224
envy sinners their pleasure 3224
equate popularity with excellence
5891
Evangelicals not the only C. 2987
excuse is division among C. 3477

expect pastor to perform spiritual
functions 1499
faith works fear of death out of C.
2375
found joy thousand times better
than pleasure 1293
generation of nervous C. 10576
greatest C. of all time 5733
greatest love poetry produced by
C. 1200
have fallen into habit of 5891
have given approval to
self-assertive 5891
have learned great secret 1293
have overcome world 1293
have shirked responsibilities 1499
hundreds of faultfinders among C.
2085
I am one of them 1293
If as much time praying as
grumbling 1561
If behaved like C, no pagans 565
If Christian nations C. would be
no war 11748
in common with non-Christians
3303
in war called to hardest of all tasks
11775
inconsistencies of C. the excuse
1334
kept from falling altogether 4623
know almost nothing about inner
life 1753
know God, do not love earth
3201
lack symmetry 1753
light of the world, but must turn
on switch 1354
like sack of grapes 1273
many C. are in trouble about the
future 6912
many C. have future behind them
4321
Many C. long for Rapture 9910
masters of their souls 1293
may not see eye to eye 1274
misplaced energy, money, C. 111
most C. are mediocre 1302
Most do not want Lord to be
inquisitive 1303
must see, hear for themselves
1275
need C. prepared to trust God
completely 11488
need more C. not more
Christianity 1307
never C. because just, honorable
1312
never see each other for last time
2401
no wild beast so ferocious as C.
11212
not defeated, simply disobedient
5753
not to mark time 1327
nothing to grumble about 1561
number one cause of atheism 487
ought to be flexing muscles 3339

physical organism through which
Christ acts 1352
process of surrender what C. call
repentance 9577
proclaim God with mouths 487
purpose to ascertain mind of Holy
Spirit 1351
quiet, holy 1293
responsible for disseminating
gospel 3302
Scriptures give four names to C.
1328
self-sins permitted, excused by
most C. 5776
should be in vanguard 1277
should never fail to sense angelic
glory 360
should walk arm in arm 1274
since C. have ceased to think of
other world 5656
so busy with mechanics 1301
Some C. like candles 1313
some C. like flashlight 1313
some C. like lasers 1313
some C. like searchlight 1313
Some C. refer with smug
satisfaction 10182
Some C. sure they will receive a
great reward 10182
some think themselves not capable
1312
staking reputations on church
attendance 1300
strength of the first C. 3292
strip of pleasures other C. enjoy
5776
than idly repeat clanderous darts
C. are hurling 5143
their lives seem so pale 2959
they too are C. 2987
to cause change 961
to endure change 961
to profit by change 961
types of 1313
usual problems common to men
1296
were chaff, now wheat 1348
were dross, now gold 1348
were harlots, now virgins 1348
were ravens, now sheep 1348
were strangers, now citizens 1348
were thistles, now lilies 1348
were thorns, now grapes 1348
What can't be cured can be
enjoyed 1335
What makes C. apathetic 3339
What makes C. shrug shoulders
3339
who did most for this world 5629
who have turned world upside
down 11735
who say they have never doubted
2959
Why are so many bored 3339
with vision in hearts, Bible in
hands 11735
work because they are going to
heaven 1356

world at its worst, C. must be at their best 1353

world reads us more than Bible 575

CHRISTLIKE

Being alone and resting is C. 9533

In triumph wear C. chain 1299

it is for sin to grieve 10334

jostled aside for converted playboy 4410

no convincing argument against C. person 1307

no matter how C. they are 5782

CHRISTMAS

a state of mind 1361

and Good Friday the same day 6489

began in heart of God 1359

benediction 1364

complete when reaches heart 1359

could Satan have devised system 1370

endless quill-driving 1367

every time you smile at your brother 1366

gifts of no use 1370

God's gift to man, man's gift to God 1360

graft plus bunkum 1370

holds all time together 1362

ill from overeating 1370

little boy of heavenly birth 1363

million C. mornings 1368

not a date 1361

proper that C. follow Advent 1365

ready to keep C. 1358

shepherds found their Lamb 1373

so hallow'd is the time 1371

sort of nightmare to me 1367

the all of C, Christ 1364

Tho' Christ a thousand times be born 1374

wise men found their Wisdom 1373

CHRISTMASTIME

compact not to write at C. 1367

CHRIST'S

accept C. cross as our cross 3335

accept C. enemies as our enemies 3335

accept C. friends as our friends 3335

accept C. future as our future 3335

accept C. life as our life 3335

accept C. rejection as our rejection 3335

accept C. ways as our ways 3335

answer to legalism 6811

Bearing wrong part of fellowship with C. sufferings 6257

believe C. existence, and history is explained 5728

betray C. spirit of love 2988

calls to detachment 9351

death made our value skyrocket 9989

definition of sin 10300

doubts dim perceptions of C. gospel 6713

examples are commandments 1517

Grace can justify us with C. righteousness 5212

life that transforms 1536

look that penetrates 1536

method of making better world alone succeeds 6487

nature of C. existence mysterious 5728

never get to the end of C. words 6523

no sin not included in C. death 10299

purpose of C. redeeming work 9438

reject C. existence, world inexplicable riddle 5728

see C. chosen saint 1299

sermon merely translated C. life into language 6482

Sermon on the Mount is C. biography 6482

teaching not intended to abrogate obedience 6811

till life finds pull of C. love 6937

victorious life is C. business 11672

When C. presence becomes guide 5396

When try to understand C. teaching with our heads 6515

words never pass away 6523

words pass into laws, doctrines 6523

words pass into proverbs 6523

words that carry weight 1536

CHRONIC

Satan is a c. grumbler 9856

CHRYSALIS

in the c. death sets free the butterfly 2261

CHURCH

a group of fishermen, the whole c. 1381

a rationalist, but liked ringing of c. bells 9394

abuses have not shaken stability 1419

After service speak with neighbor 1384

All are not saints that go to c. 9772

All here got fears, cares 1396

all members share common life 1445

all one great work 1447

Although c. and state stand separate 5169

And all the c. with his presence glowed 2638

angel created for service of c. 354

anxious to ingratiate itself with people 1442

as trapped as most non-Christians 1460

asks God only for peace 11761

avoid cold heart, hot head 1400

aware of no power, presence, reality 1399

be restored to New Testament splendor 10080

Be you our angel unawares 1396

become disciples, c. would be transformed 2819

Before service speak to God 1384

Bible, is my c. 716

boast his c. was live 115

both evangelism, social action 1426

brotherhood of believers 916

built not with motes from neighbor's eye 1402

built with beams out of one's eye 1402

business not to do something for c. 1418

can limit God's power 4829

cannot be content with social camaraderie 3337

cannot fail 1430

cannot increase God's power 4829

caught up in success mania 1409

ceased to manufacture blood cells 3341

charged with high calling 1412

chief trouble, you and I 1424

Christ executed by corrupt c. 2171

Christianity isn't going to c. 1180

Christians assume have worshiped because in c. 12101

closet and c. full of reverberations of God 4965

communities of loving defiance 1439

community of compassion 1414

complementing, helping by their differences 1445

concerned with budgets, building 1409

conclude worship must take place in c. 12101

conduit, conveying God's blessings 1440

confronts world 1428

could attend c. if day came some other time 10961

Creative men, women are in the c. 1998

creed of c. exciting, dramatic 1205

Dear as the apple of thine eye 1395

demon even if sits in c. praising the Creator 9631

devil talks glibly of c. and state 2651

different outlooks, education 1455

different view of c. 2987

differs in temperament 1445

disliked their hymns 1455

Divorce, adultery invaded the c. 2919

do not have to answer back 1389
do something with c. 1418
Does c. arrange services for Total
    Abstainers from Usury 10086
does not affect everyday life 1399
does not draw people in 1427
does not echo world 1428
does not lead the world 1428
doesn't attend because hypocrites
    do 1397
Dogma ark within which c. floats
    safely 11187
Don't hunt through c. for
    hypocrite 6053
Don't stay away from c. because
    hypocrites 6050
door locked in winter 1382
During service let God speak 1384
duty not to abandon 1398
dying of leukemia 3341
easy for rich to get on c. board
    11830
economic, racial differences
    surmounted 1492
enemy anxious to keep us from c.
    1190
even if c. swarms with faults 1458
every c. would need morgue in
    basement 4717
Everytime I pass a c. 1391
example of how differences dealt
    with 1492
exists for those outside it 1429
exists wherever Word of God is
    preached 1458
family established before the c.
    3871
for many c. irrelevant 1446
for many c. to be ignored 1446
for many, not worth criticizing
    1446
for proclamation of gospel 10506
force for good in world of evil
    1433
force for love in world of hatred
    1433
force for peace in world of
    violence 1433
founded as slap to other c. 7867
from the c. receive postulates of
    order 5169
future of c. depend on family
    3894
go actively seeking 1459
go out of the c. to be the c. 1444
God expects miraculous group
    1392
God hewing out the pillars 1401
Going to c. doesn't make you a
    Christian 1286
grace is God's energy within his c.
    5219
graven on thy hand 1395
guided by a bad spiritual
    philosophy 115
half dollar goes to c. more often
    11357
hard won progress 1430
has many tasks 3328

has only one mission 3328
Her walls before thee stand 1395
holiest moment of c. service 1444
home, kind of c. where God is
    honored 5853
hospital for sinners 1379
I like the silent c. 1394
I love thy c. 1395
If a man can make better c. organs
    2776
If after kirk ye bide a wee 1396
if every member like me 1454
If leave c. Sunday morning 12106
if souls not saved, something
    wrong 1404
imitate Christ's example 1378
In Christ c. has enough to feed
    world 6374
in conflict with values of society
    1385
in midst of hostile world 1392
in what strange quarries 1401
incubator to hatch converts 1393
inscription on c. door 1382
is a community 1385
is a movement 1385
is an organism 1385
Is c. ready to deal with financial
    immorality 10086
Is c. ready to found welfare
    societies 10086
is scared 1442
is to make society uncomfortable
    1427
is under orders 3329
isolated c. keeps evangelizing
    same people 1456
keep her on course 1398
knows nothing of a sacredness of
    war 11761
largely clubs of conformity 1439
lasted longer than any comparable
    institution 1431
legalism, archenemy of c. 6817
like a bank 1435
like most institutions of society
    1442
like salt, flavors, preserves 1427
like ship pounded by waves 1398
like yeast, unsettles mass around it
    1427
listening to secret wireless 1190
looking for better methods 1436
looks in pain at shortcomings
    1443
loss of intellectual morale in the c.
    7768
love one gift open to every
    member of the c. 7235
Many c. attenders focus minds on
    sporting events 12111
Many Christians staking
    reputations on c. 1300
many critics, no rivals 1432
may cry to God the c. be restored
    10080
measures to which c. driven by
    heresies 11186

member would do well to look in
    concordance 10185
members directing the c. 525
membership based on unworthy
    candidates 1425
ministry of c. ceased while quarrel
    over Prince of Peace 9361
more concerned with budgets
    1409
more emphasis on growth than
    repentance 1409
most effective when declares 3796
most universal body in world
    1277
Mrs. Chapman had her c. 1408
music only art fully accepted by c.
    1998
must be practicing members 1445
must not go to c. like empty basket
    1459
new order, new values 1385
no anguish, no music 1441
No c. can stand between God and
    man 7505
No c. thrives unless struggles 1411
not a home and foreign c. 1447
not a monument 1385
not a museum for saints 1379
not a refrigerator to preserve piety
    1393
not an orderly gathering 1385
not an organization 1385
not comfortable niche 1427
not either-or but both-and 1426
not fraternity of faith fans 1414
not gallery of eminent Christians
    1437
not one man at c. another at home
    1908
not part of community 1385
not reservoir 1440
not to retain God's blessings 1440
not united by natural affinities
    1445
Not, what was his c. 7423
note is supernatural note 1428
nothing can save c. whose root
    dried up 1380
often in sharp conflict 1385
one c. here, so I go to it 1447
only mission finally is to entertain
    itself 1456
open to criticism 1430
perfect c. service one unaware of
    1383
Persecution has not crushed c.
    1419
Power has not beaten back c.
    1419
prayer closet base of supplies for
    the c. 8976
prayer closet the battlefield of the
    c. 8976
primitive c. thought more about
    Second Coming than death
    9913
problem is indifference 1446
problem not hostility to c. 1446
prosperity not discipleship 2813

reconciliation not honest, effective 1492

Revival act of God upon c. 9746

revive the c, beginning with me 9741

says covetousness a deadly sin 10086

school for imperfect Christians 4137

sees structure or Savior 1416

sends people out 1427

shadowy unreality 1399

should be amazing people 1392

signboard 1417

so many degrees, so little temperature 1410

so much machinery, so little oil 1423

Some wish to live within sound of c. 7783

some would speak to ye 1396

song of c. would have no symphony 6169

Soulariums 1390

soundly rooted cannot be destroyed 1380

squeaks like threshing machine 1423

stay awake and listen to sermon at c. 10100

staying away from 317

suffer as much from c. as for it 1438

Suffering love, the cross, heart of c. 2139

take on three jobs at c. 9970

Television can turn parlor into a c. 11044

Theological beliefs get one into c. 601

Time has not abated forces of c. 1419

To be with God, no need to be in c. 7541

to bring crucified Christ to world 1405

To c. Pentecost brought light, power, joy 5806

to confront men with Jesus Christ 1412

trapped by material concerns and alienation 1460

two dangers to be recognized 1400

union is external 1387

unity is internal 1387

Unless we reshape institutional c. life 8696

until equality recognized 3230

use of laymen crippled c. impact 1499

want c. that will move the world 1452

wavering Christian no respect from c. 2771

We don't go to c, we are the c. 1444

went to c, not greatly depressed 1453

What can the poor c. do 3036

What would c. be like 1454

when c. fails to break cultural barrier 1456

When c. secure, too many freedoms 952

When c. transcends culture, can transform 1457

When different from world c. attracts 5096

When people sleep in c, preacher should wake up 9171

when secure, freedom to doubt 952

when secure, indulge in acceptance 952

when secure, major on minor issues 952

when speak to c. about Pentecost 5811

Where is c. Monday morning 1377

Where was the c. 18

wherever God's people are 1377

wooed with striped candy 1403

works of Holy Spirit not confined to institutional c. 5791

workshop, not dormitory 1434

worshiper in suspended mentation 1399

CHURCH-GOERS
like coals in fire 1388

CHURCHES
addicts attend c. regularly 135

Christ provided unity, not uniformity 1451

close because of sin 1421

drug treatment programs by c. effective 134

filled with actors and actresses 135

filled with people who live as if God were dead 1314

God not confined in c. 4866

gospel-driven 1407

liberty, last thing we have in many c. 5800

little emphasis on bearing burdens 933

man-centered, entertainment-oriented 1422

market-driven 1407

Satan splitting the body of Christ 392

Some c. train their ushers to smile 6062

Youth going to take over c. 12160

CHURCHIANITY
is an organization 1186

CHURCHLY
have too much c. institutionalism 9552

CHURCH'S
women are the c. strong rock 11980

CICERO
never read, Come unto me all ye that labour 930

read in C. sayings wise, beautiful 930

CINCH
Inch by inch life's a c. 6930

CIRCLE
family c. the supreme conductor of Christianity 5852

God an infinite c. 4842

sewing c, the Protestant confessional 5160

wheel is come full c. 1739

CIRCLES
Am I going in c. 5344

astronaut runs in c, gets somewhere 3086

Sins like c. in water 10383

CIRCLING
will I stay and taste encircling love 7970

Within thy c. power I stand 4876

CIRCULATE
Slander, who would not coin, c. without qualms 10465

CIRCULATION
alliance of error and truth extensive c. 3254

to set their money in c. 11809

CIRCUMFERENCE
God an infinite circle whose c. is nowhere 4842

CIRCUMSTANCES
allows c. to bludgeon him 3830

are the creatures of men 1474

assuming c. not controlled by God 11152

awaken our religion 8788

Blessed are those who see God in c. 1464

by c. brought into closer connection with you 9673

Christ not perplexed by c. 1472

Christian accepts c. from God 3638

deception that c. responsible for responses 1467

developed because of c. 1471

discover delight in somber c. 10639

do color life 522

Do not wait for extraordinary c. 623

Do not wait for extraordinary c. to do good 5058

freedom to choose attitude 519

God does best work in difficult c. 3769

God engineers our c. 8395

God keeps his word even when c. point to the opposite 9321

God uses c. to crush us 883

God uses every cloud that comes 188

happier c. free from difficult
complications 4974
If you can't change c, change
response 1469
independent of God, dependent
on c. 1480
learn to listen to God in c. 1477
learn to look on the bright c. 9092
mastery in c. is needed 1471
of great pressure and trial, much
strength 7486
of life indication of God's will
5444
saint never believes c. haphazard
1324
spiritual power independent of c.
4015
the awful c. of their being 892
through accepting c. self is
crucified 1473
transformed into image of Christ
by c. is to have chosen 8264
transforms c. into growth 1468
wars will continue until c. renders
impossible 11782
when God chooses he will alter c.
238
will mar happiness 6529
wise man adapts to c. 1463
Worship God in difficult c. 238

CIRCUMSTANTIAL
suggesting happiness is c. 5562

CIRCUS
Time is a c. 11334

CISTERNS
not c. made for hoarding 10729

CITADELS
Christ could have stormed c. 6503

CITIES
Youth will assume control of c.
12160

CITIZEN
assets claim to be c. of heaven
7948

CITIZENS
be conscientious in work as good
c. 10525
destiny of nation depends on c.
under 25 12173
mother teaches next generation of
c. 7844
obliged to pray if c. of God's
Kingdom 9015
We were strangers, now c. 1348

CITIZENSHIP
obedience to authority foundation
of c. 8355

CITY
Bible ends with holy c. 723
different ways of seeing the c.
10522
Great men like solitary towers in
c. of God 5280
Heaven is a c. and a body 6169
let it ring from every c. 4157

like a c. without defenses 368
of truth cannot be built on
swampy ground of scepticism
11530
out of crowded c, on to crowded
highway 9901
poet sees c. as silhouette against
sky 10522
shall kindle fire, light up entire c.
5751
spark will set whole c. on fire
10445
statistician sees c. as social unit
10522
When Carlyle saw c. he
philosophized 10522
When Jesus saw c, he wept 10522
When Wordsworth saw c, grew
lyrical 10522

CITY'S
To feel, amid the c. jar 8430

CIVIL
government boundaries for
human behavior 5177
souls are battlegrounds for c. wars
6068
to all 550

CIVILIZATION
based on foundation of murder
10513
compared with man is only a
moment 7389
dignity of individuals measure of c.
3894
family varies with c. 3868
first c. founded by Cain 10513
Home best security of c. 5835
our is likewise dying 6359
unhappy c. is always gregarious
10515
universities stamp c. with own
ideas 3040
varies with the family 3868
whole cockeyed c. series of
pricetags 10519

CIVILIZATIONS
rise and wane 4694

CIVILIZED
Bible contains formula for c.
justice 701
life vast, complicated system of
murder 10513

CLACKING
against each other 1273

CLAIM
God's better plan takes faith to c.
2607
of redemption of Jesus is that he
can satisfy aching soul 6402
right you c. for yourself 11282
sin c. to my right to myself 10389
So none may c. superior grade
3227

CLAIMED
by God, counterclaimed by Satan
4918

When c. Jesus just for himself
became easy 7105

CLAIMS
blinds mind to c. of Jesus Christ
10044
Christ c. to be more than a man
6349
devil seeks slaves, c. obedience
4912
each party c. to act in will of God
4972
God seeks comrades, c. love 4912
Gossip, no one c. to like 5133

CLAM
if c. could conceive of God 4909

CLAMOR
nature rose without c. 1956
Not in the c. of crowded street
10794
thousand voices c. for attention
7447

CLANG
nature rose with c. 1956

CLAPPING
trees c. their hands 8017

CLARIFIED
My intelligence is c. 7964

CLARINET
words call like a c. 11998

CLARITY
At edge of despair dawns c. 2574

CLASH
If c. with God-made object, bad
art 2022
Laws silent amidst c. of arms
11754
with own customs, privileges,
beliefs 4124

CLASHED
Nearly everyone c. with Jesus
6516

CLASHINGS
Is it strange there are c, collisions
4563

CLASP
black, white hold each other with
equal c. 3237
Faith prays him to c. hand closely
3714

CLASPS
soul c. and is closely embraced
7967

CLASS
no provision for privileged c. 1234
or teach a ragged c. 3845

CLASSES
Calvary erected to divide men into
two c. 2124
In God's sight only two c. of
people 3236
mankind divided into three c.
10504

CLASSIC
Leviticus 25 c. on rights of earth 3200

CLASSIFIED
Jesus would not let himself be c. 6508
theology ideas of truth c. 11207

CLASSROOM
Prayer not learned in a c. 8930

CLAY
history c. in which God works 5718
soul freed from c. 10675
Take c. and dust, fashion a child 4608
Unless c. be well pounded 8559

CLEAN
A new broom sweeps c. 251
angel to c. a road 3232
getting into hot water keeps you c. 11435
glove often hides dirty hand 2460
God takes notice of c, not full hands 9754
humble receives praise way c. window takes light 6033
keep yourself c, bright 8573
kept c. all day by integrity 9600
Sleep with c. hands 9600
Tears c. windows of the soul 11017
Tomorrow comes at midnight very c. 11403
Unless vessel c. what you pour turns sour 1054
washed c. at night by repentance 9600
whole street is c. 9664

CLEAN-LIVING
upright life based on self-realization 10044

CLEANER
country needs dirtier fingernails, c. minds 7775

CLEANING
blot with blotted finger 2906
Spring c. should begin with head, end with heart 5756

CLEANSE
Christ a Fountain to c. 6370

CLEANSER
Love, not law, is greatest c. 7275

CLEANSES
Bible c. my emotions 722
Silent worship c. 12114

CLEANSING
Grief should be c. 5331
prayer, tears shed bring c. 9039
Suffering a c. fire 10892

CLEAR
as the morning or the evening rose 4746
Bible only place can find c. message 8023

Give us c. vision 11731
happy religion is c. knowledge of Jesus Christ 6713
If you want to c. the stream 10322
in principle and aim 4974
law to make c. how much you must do 5233
Love has a c. eye 6457
Make it c. 10279
make their righteousness c. as light 9104
now with purpose, full and c. 8082
One day nearer when mysteries c. 5676
point of cross becomes c. 892
We sigh to c. our hearts 5627
with eye on God, strike note full, c. 7056

CLEARER
tears prepare for c. vision of God 11024

CLEAREST
able to explain suffering c. indication never suffered 10918

CLEARING
God's word for my c. 5400

CLEARLY
defined goals simplified decisions 4425
dost thou answer, though all do not c. hear 5381
easier to see c. into liar than man who tells truth 6866
Every victory of science reveals more c. divine design 9866
more c. we perceive hand of God 11644
Only eyes washed by tears see c. 2555
said at all, can be said c. 11222
sun shines as c. in darkest day as in brightest 4772
think without confusion c. 559
thought at all, can be thought c. 11222
to see c. reason needs light of heaven 9422
To see thee more c. 9043
To think c. without hurry or confusion 6913
understand some part of Bible c. 681

CLEARNESS
Bible's light like body of heaven in c. 680
insight not from c. of intellect 8504

CLEAVAGE
distressing c. between truths, values 6068
early Christians looking for c. in sky called Glory 9913

CLEAVE
O man c. close to God 2604

CLEFT
Rock of Ages, c. for me 4636

CLENCHED
how many c. fists would we see in marketplace 10507
infant is born with c. fist 11656
more power in open hand than c. fist 8720

CLERGY
ounce of mother worth pound of c. 7843
People expect c. to 1497
Some c. prepare their sermons 10104

CLERGYMEN
care not whether c. or laymen 9136
If c. defrocked 1732

CLEVER
And all c. people were good 909
enough to get money 11869
fearless, four years old 1130
If all good people were c. 909
makes man more c. devil 3005
smash bridgeheads of c. self-sufficiency 10043
The c. so rude to the good 909
The good are so harsh to the c. 909

CLICHES
mental activity mouthing of c. 11237
use c. so they won't have to think 8476

CLICKIN'
sets my heart a c. 9880

CLIENT
Art thou Christ's c. 6415

CLIFF
If fig tree grow in side of mountain c. 3736

CLIMATES
how many different c. of feelings 4014

CLIMAX
awful c. of isolation on the cross 6383

CLIMB
Better a fall than not to c. 3585
Ducks look funny trying to c. 6168
every mountain 4421
He who would c. ladder must begin at bottom 10782
higher the hill that you c. 3488
laud character but c. to top at any cost 6068
Life more than a c. 350
our heav'nly-guided soul shall c. 5679
To c. rock-strewn road 1927
until I c. over 2633
upward on the miseries of others 338

virtue can teach you how to c.
11692

who didn't have ladder to c. 6147

work to c. a mountain to pray
8860

CLIMBED
I c, and step by step, O Lord 5694

CLIMBER
Reason has never been a mountain
c. 3716

CLIMBERS
Hasty c. have sudden falls 6114

CLIMBING
Worship is man c. altar stairs to
God 12132

CLIMBS
high soul c. the high way 10679

highest who helps another up
3134

CLIME
My country is in every c. 4869

CLING
And c. to hope: this, too, shall
pass away 6878

foolish to c. to life 2299

in darkness we c. closely to thee
9053

new life not property to c. to
10545

People c. to possessions instead of
sharing 8632

pray Christ to c. to me 9022

Simply to thy cross I c. 2101

to natural virtues sufficient to
obscure work of God 11701

too weak to c. to Christ 9022

weaker, sadder ones 179

When c. to actions as
self-identification 10531

When we c. to results of our
actions 10531

with body, soul to temporality
1272

CLINGING
bird calmly c. to his little twig
11478

Christian work crippled by c. to
traditions of the past 10124

faith, like man hanging to boat
3797

If these hands of mine cease from
their c. 7478

While to that refuge c. 232

CLINGS
fragrance c. to hand that gives
roses 4344

human nature c. to man with such
persistance 5974

pain c. cruelly to us 8271

To one fixed trust my spirit c.
4642

CLIPBOARD
love eclipsed as turns into c. with
checklist 6823

CLIPPINGS
proud man counts newspaper c.
6035

CLIPS
Ridigity c. future's wings 6818

CLIQUES
Jesus, no intention to speak to c.
6451

CLOAK
can't make good c. out of bad
cloth 1069

in chest belongs to naked 11855

CLOAKED
Animosity c. in piety is a demon
9631

CLOCK
can't turn back c. 8373

futile as c. that will tick through
eternity 5718

Like the tickin' of a c. 9880

marriage is the alarm c. 7631

Quiet minds like c. in
thunderstorm 8466

Take a lesson from the c. 2786

When man happy does not hear c.
strike 5572

CLOCKS
Children, like c. must be allowed
to run 1108

good c. ticking out goodness
10337

in town wrong time 2803

CLOD
How marvelous that I, a filthy c.
8814

CLOG
My c. whatever road I go 2583

CLOGS
Only man c. happiness with care
12073

CLOSE
churches because sin 1421

doubt so c. to faith 7081

failures did not realize c. to success
3607

God so c. up that when you pray
8801

heartbreak so c. to happiness
7081

if hold penny c. enough to eye
7795

If you don't feel c. to God 4857

impulse to have c. contact with
other animals around him 6199

it is God away down here, c. up
8801

Live c. to Me 10706

no one can c. heaven or hell for me
594

O man, cleave c. to God 2604

sorrow so c. to joy 7081

though distant c. in spirit 4280

To find a friend c. one eye 4161

to keep a friend c. two eyes 4161

CLOSED
look so long at c. door do not see
one opened 5573

look so regretfully at c. door 8229

Year is c, record made 8082

CLOSELY
Faith prays him to clasp hand c.
3714

God puts his ear so c. down 8801

in darkness, doubt we cling c. to
thee 9053

to do what lies c. at hand 9671

CLOSELY KNIT
family should be a c. group 5853

CLOSER
Grief knits two hearts c. than
happiness 5338

is he than breathing 4862

O for a c. walk with God 7507

one gets to light, more
imperfections show 7522

to God, more one feels a sinner
10439

CLOSES
Hope opens doors, despair c. them
5928

Life c. in twilight, opens in dawn
11132

When one door c, another opens
8229

When one door of happiness c,
another opens 5573

CLOSE-SHUT
must not tear c. leaves apart 5403

CLOSEST
closet of prayer will become your
c. friend 9039

God c. to broken hearts 1505

Gossip can estrange c. friends
5127

times when Lord holding me c.
10853

CLOSET
and church full of reverberations
of God 4965

base of supplies for the Christian,
church 8976

is the battlefield of the church
8976

no skeleton can come out of
hidden c. 4884

not a nursery where none but
babes belong 8976

not an asylum for worthless
Christian 8976

Prayer learned in the c. 8930

scene of heroic, unearthly conflicts
8976

silent c. best declares God's reality
10554

will seek not the crowd but the c.
10567

CLOSETED
was c. in time 6357

CLOSING
clouds c. over him in darkness forever 6101

CLOTH
can't make good cloak out of bad c. 1069

CLOTHE
And c. myself with fruit 8254
God has all righteousness to c. you 4696

CLOTHED
God c. himself in vile man's flesh 6126
God c. himself with our lowliness 6130
lies should be c. 6869

CLOTHES
do not make the man 9626
Faith wears everyday c. 3715
fool sees a man's c. 11896
infant world, wrapped in swaddling c. of light 7886
Kindness love in work c. 6652
land of naked, people ashamed of c. 1638
problems opportunities in work c. 2726
Respect is love in plain c. 9645
Scandal treated as mud on c. 5154

CLOTHING
finest c. made is person's own skin 7427
Holiness has humility for its c. 5739

CLOUD
anyone save Jesus in your c. 2562
Behind the c. the starlight lurks 5904
blue of heaven larger than the c. 10634
dark, tremendous sea of c. 2945
Do not try to penetrate c. God brings 11485
Every c. has silver lining 2797
evil, that dark c. that hangs over creation 3350
feared as they entered the c. 2562
God in this c. in this darkness 2557
God saw through thick c. 4904
God uses every c. that comes 188
In every c. God brings 188
In the c. God is deepening thy chords 10600
Like a fiend hid in a c. 808
motives with smoke screen of excuses 3476
music in the twilight c. 7927
no rainbow without c. and storm 10636
Oft the c. which wraps present hour 10879
Serves to brighten future days 10879
to bring us nearer to God 188
when the c. of God's presence moved 10124

CLOUDED
by sense of guilt 4864
windows c. with human fancies 2936

CLOUDLESS
days are fine 2540

CLOUDS
apart from God, c. of difficulties accidents 10598
are lies, cannot last 11129
behind life's darkest c. 10964
behind the c, the Father's feet 1515
Behind the c. is sun still shining 10582
Beneath the billowy c. of June 9887
closing over him in darkness forever 6101
difference not in sun, but in c. 4772
Even though there are c. around 169
evening beam smiles c. away 618
giraffe only animal that can keep feet on ground, head in c. 9244
Hope like c, some pass by, others bring rain 5922
huge c. nothing more than dust on eyelashes 11442
In Bible, c. connected with God 10598
In eternity, mountains as transient as c. 3279
no c. would not need faith 10598
of doubt created 2931
one has music and the flying c. 10673
plan a tower that shall pierce c. 6788
through the c. of Calvary 11129
trailing c. and glory 809
When c. seen, wise put on coats 11960
will not know how to pray when c. roll in 8809

CLOUDY
bring thy sunshine into c. places 9106

CLOVER
folded quietly as though for prayer 8000
leaves sleeping in attitude of worship 8000

CLUE
Without God world a maze without a c. 4522

CLUMSINESS
holy c. better than sinful eloquence 9121

CLUTCH
through pain forced to c. thy hand 9053

CLUTTERS
Procrastination c. up our lives 9300

CO-OPERATING
accepts evil without protesting c. 3374

COACH
neglect God for rattling of a c. 7712

COACHES
turn pumpkins into c. 1122

COAL
Envy's a c. come hissing hot from hell 3216
no getting white flour out of c. sack 2475

COALS
Church-goers like c. in fire 1388
love becomes as c. deep-burning, unquenchable 7236

COARSE
Behind joy may be c. temperament 10583

COAT
can't get warm on another's fur c. 6782
jug never carried under c. for honest reason 2905
reason polar bear wears fur c. 6213
wears c. of mail that none can pierce 9986

COATS
chose ugliest one 467
When clouds seen, wise put on c. 11960

COAXED
habit must be c. down stairs 5495

COBWEBS
Habits c. at first 5497

COCK
crows, daybreak is from God 2199
heard the c. crow thrice with an aching heart 9569
Sad the home where hen crows, c. silent 5847

COCK-CROW
is coming 5672

COCKEYED
civilization series of pricetags 10519

COCKSURE
never wise to be c. 11923
stupid c, intelligent full of doubt 10518

COERCES
Lord never c. 8106

COERCIVENESS
Life is c. 11388

COEXIST
Compassion can never c. with judgment 10162

COFFIN
cynic smells flowers, looks for c. 2177
large enough for presidents 2235
living c. of dead soul 7760
own anything that won't fit c. 1801
room without door, skylight 2236
small enough for bums 2235

COGS
world a collection of c. 9501

COHERENCE
Good is a principle of c. 5023

COHERENTLY
When in pain difficult to pray c. 10931

COHESION
nations have found c. in war 11783

COINCIDE
whether or not they c. with your own 6207

COINS
Insults like bad c. 2918

COLD
All we can hold in our c. dead hands 4349
As heat opposed to c. 5205
cannot be c. without heat 5357
Conscience credit that belongs to c. feet 1665
Either be hot or c. 4920
extreme heat and c. kills 3554
frozen in corporate or collective c. 3045
Gold is c. 11813
If hope is c. 8122
If world is c, build fires 4250
In the c. God is molding thy expression 10600
job that was too c. last winter 9902
love grown c. can kindle again 3167
love of God not c. philanthropy 4792
man can blow hot, c. with same breath 6054
Men of c. passions have quick eyes 3565
must wait for God in the c. 5460
Pride is the c. mountain peak 6026
Revenge in c. blood is devil's act, deed 9723
shivers go up, down spines of cultured people 5811
sweater worn by child when mother c. 3866
warm hand on a c. morning 438
Water is c, dark, deep 5527
We'd all seem c, stiff 1396
When leave God's love, we grow dark, c. 9354
Whenever knowledge leaves us c. something wrong 6704

without inspiring is hammering on c. iron 11000
words freeze people 11985

COLDLY
While c. discussing a man's career 6599

COLLAPSE
Christian life on feeling headed for c. 1257
headed for gigantic c. 4011
seldom blowout 939
usually a slow leak 939

COLLAPSES
work evades facing truth of God 938

COLLAPSING
world more conducive to understanding truth 11491

COLLEAGUES
Jesus never clung to c. 6508

COLLECT
student used to write, now calls c. 3896

COLLECTING
quotations similar to birds who pick up pebbles 9380

COLLECTION
Bible most human c. of books 701
world a c. of cogs 9501

COLLECTIVE
frozen in corporate or c. cold 3045

COLLECTIVITIES
belong to the devil 6176
easily respond to devil's persuasion 6176

COLLEGE
knowledge of Bible worth more than c. 640
more tests to get in than out 3034
student used to write, now calls collect 3896

COLLIDED
My life c. with me 1906

COLLISION
faith that cannot survive c. with truth 3639

COLLISIONS
Is it strange there are c. 4563

COLONS
if educated knows how to use c. 12152

COLOR
choose what the c. shall be 522
Could blind chance create c. 1958
Human blood all one c. 907
if we have not c. in our eyes 7108
Laughter adds c. to ordinary days 6727
Light is above us, c. around us 7108
meet different c. to yourself 3234

music showing all changes of c. 7905
no matter what c, same nourishment 3243
of asceticisms, black 467
The c. of its face 3227
try to catch it, loses its c. 5519
world without children without c. 1104

COLOR-BLIND
truly wise are c. 8245

COLORED
world was painting 1981

COLORLESS
c. uniformity 6179

COLORS
As blind man has no idea of c. 4986
chose saddest, somberest 467
joy of heart c. face 6560
We weave with c. all our own 3289

COLOSSAL
Eternity, a stern c. image 3269

COMB
Experience c. nature gives to men when bald 3518
theologian with fine-toothed c. 5786

COMBAT
Bible can c. devil 720
with ourselves 11703

COMBATED
cause c. by relentless forces 2630

COMBINATIONS
God planned all perfect c. 7891

COMBINE
dependence on God's Spirit with own researches 6681

COMBINES
Christ c. qualities of every race 6363

COME
as we look back over way we have c. 5392
blessed darkness, c. bring thy balm 10481
death, the dawn has c. 2252
destroy bridge by which God would c. to you 9634
do not c. back to thank him 6251
drifting home with broken masts and sails 11470
feelings c. and go, God's love does not 4777
Four things c. not back 8213
gentle c. out ahead 4402
God cannot c. in any way but his own way 4664
God will not permit knowledge of things to c. 4314
Have you c. to the Red Sea place in life 5407

Hope, reaching out for something
to c. 3835

interpretation will c. as God
pleases 4885

Let wife make husband glad to c.
home 7627

Lord may not c. when you want
him 4500

No harm from him can c. to me
6916

Nothing shall be to c, and nothing
past 3288

Oppression, depression never c.
from Spirit of God 5773

out of strife, doubt, struggle 4577

Past and to c. seem best 8382

People c. to poverty two ways
4040

so shall big things c. 2534

Suffer me to c. to thee 1117

thoughts that c. worth more than
thought we seek 11250

time will c. when every change
shall cease 3288

Time will c. when I will make you
forget these painful moments
7123

Wait and God will c. 5460

We ask God to c. when he is
already present 8843

we c. from God who is our home
809

wheel is c. full circle 1739

will c. one day a touch from God
7060

You c. into world alone 7151

COMEDY

Life a c. for those who think 6954

to one who thinks, life is c. 607

COMES

a time when love can only weep
4781

All c. to him who knows how to
wait 8391

All glory c. from daring to begin
102

All that we are c. from God 11135

all we send into lives of others c.
back 1726

back into our own 919

cannot doubt power c. from above
4949

Comfort c. as a guest 7361

Everything great c. from neurotics
4390

Fame c. when thinking about
something else 3852

friend c. in when world has gone
out 4167

fulfillment c. as by-product of
love for God 4735

future c. one day at a time 4320

Go out and God c. in 9556

God c. and sits with you in
snowbank 4782

God c. padding after me like
Hound of Heaven 4534

God c. to see us without a bell
4525

God c. when we think he is
farthest off 4837

God c. without ringing doorbell
4838

God never c. to those who do not
wait 5460

God will help thee bear what c.
11362

God's order c. in the haphazard
5401

golden age only c. when men have
forgotten gold 11856

grace God provides c. only with
task 5226

Happiness a thing that c. and goes
5517

I don't know a blessing when it c.
my way 5587

If winter c. 9874

joy that c. back to you 6561

Knowledge c, wisdom lingers
11926
6692

Mischief c. from much opening of
mouth 10685

Morality c. with sad wisdom of
age 7829

more love you give away, the more
c. back 7232

mystery of grace never c. too late
5228

Old age c. from God 8151

Strength c. from struggle against
obstacles 8850

Sun's self c. in with him 4195

sweet joy c. through sorrow
10638

take witholding of honor that c.
from men quietly 5901

What God throws my way c. 5416

When God c., go with him slowly
5460

COMET

life, aimless c. burning out in
self-will 6937

COMFORT

After crises, c. 2042

All human c. vain, short 1501

behind the thunder, c. 229

best c. in suffering and pain 10926

closet of prayer will bring c. 9039

comes as a guest 7361

doctrine affords c. 3047

fear of God, source of c. 3993

God does not c. to make us
comfortable 1503

God gives c. in despair 2582

God more concerned about
character than c. 1016

God will disappoint as c. 4468

Gold cannot bring you c. 11813

gospel like c. in anguish of
conscience 5097

great thing to live without human,
divine c. 1508

in the cool kiss of the breeze 8051

In trouble may find c. 11439

Kind words smooth, quiet c.
11985

Learn to c. thyself 234

lingers to become a host 7361

made possible by Christ 1516

nation that thinks more of c. 7984

not difficult when we have God's
c. 1508

not quiet in minds, c. will do no
more 1804

of having friend may be taken
away 4271

Oh, the c, the inexpressible c.
4260

Only God can do that 3076

outward c. will do no more than
slipper on gouty foot 8442

people who love God for c. 4801

poems, repeat for c. in sleepless
nights 9381

Quotations c. 9385

reason dog such c. 1511

Sad soul, take c. nor forget 5942

salvation and c. unite 9812

sigh of distress from heart 1513

sit in silence 1513

stays to enslave 7361

Sweet spirit c. me 1514

that is unspeakable 229

things might have been worse
11439

those who weep by weeping 1506

to shed tears in grief 1513

too busy to drop note of c. 129

we value c, God values peace
11667

who love God for riches or c.
10084

yourself with God who nails to
cross 2091

COMFORTABLE

church largely c. clubs of
conformity 1439

church not c. niche 1427

feel c. take another look 2013

God does not comfort to make us
c. 1503

Maturity to be c. with people not
like us 7694

prefer c. vice to virtue that bores
3941

Revival and c. truths are bitter
enemies 9744

Scriptures teach most c. way of
dying 742

Truth has no responsibility to
make us c. 11557

COMFORTABLY

No leader ever did his work c.
5289

COMFORTED

And therefore I am c. 7952

Be c. thy grief shall pass away
6878

have not c. one another as Christ
conforts us 9087

COMFORTER
applied to Holy Spirit means
"with strength" 5804
Call C. by term you think best
5775
conveys indefinable sympathy
5775
Death, C. of him whom time
cannot console 2260
Holy C, ineffable motherhood of
God 5775
needs only to be summoned 5781

COMFORTERS
God comforts to make us c. 1503

COMFORTETH
Love c. like sunshine after rain
7212

COMFORTING
deep, c. sense things unseen are
eternal 3746
most c. fact imaginable 4779
most c. thoughts heart can
entertain 3719
to cast c. shadow across another's
life 7714

COMFORTLESS
God does not leave us c. 1504

COMFORTS
adversity not without c. and hopes
247
bad conscience embitters sweetest
c. 1650
God c. to make us comforters
1503
helpers fail, c. flee 2538
Jesus Christ, his c. refreshing 6352
one who has not suffered knows
nothing of 10914
Spirit of God convicts, c. 5773
still, small voice that c. 1515
vanish 7291
What though my c. die 232

COMING
advent, c. of quiet joy 6119
Christ, his c. meant war 6375
Cock-crow is c. 5672
If we saw all good things c. 4318
Jesus' c. final, unanswerable proof
God cares 6136
Many live in dread of what is c.
4318
more alone while living than
going, c. 7151
My love c. to you through
kindness of others 5271
of Christ by way of manger 6145
of Jesus into the world 6146

COMMA
took out c, in afternoon put it
back 12143

COMMAND
At your c. all resources of heaven,
earth are at my disposal 9066
belief that does not c. not real 612
born again, not a c. 879
Brotherhood, divine c. 902

If God gives c, he expects
obedience 11173
learned to obey will know how to
c. 6792
Love only service power cannot c.
7253
people have not yet understood c.
of Christ 7349
praying so positive, a direct,
authoritative c. 8890
Riches serve a wise man, c. a fool
7820
to repent goes unregarded 4726

COMMANDED
In Old Testament war c. 11760
Nature, to be c, must be obeyed
3198
Never think Jesus c. a trifle 8097

COMMANDING
In c. us to glorify him 4554

COMMANDMENT
eleventh c. shall not be found out
1529
to break one c. is to break the law
6812
to love fellowmen follows c. to
love God 3242

COMMANDMENTS
always humanly difficult 1521
can never be kept while 1525
Christ goes behind law to
disposition 1526
Christ made c. more difficult 1526
Christ's deeds, examples 1517
consummation was on Golgotha
281
designed to make us happy 1528
does not need duty 1525
does not need struggle 1525
easy when we obey 1521
face filled with broken c. 10315
given irrespective of human ability
1526
given with the inexorable
awfulness of Almighty God
1527
If do not keep c. 8106
in rhyme 1531
inclined to hunt for c. to obey
7690
little too severe 1523
love served by keeping c. of God
7837
man can break himself against c.
1524
man is overwhelmed 1525
may read aright his c. 10591
millions of laws to enforce 1518
needs power of life 1525
needs strength of love 1525
No man can break any of the c.
1524
not made to human nature 1521
only the redeemed can keep his c.
4536
Ten C. will not budge 1687

the Cross, their image and
fulfillment 281
weight of broken pieces 1525
When we begin to mature, we
obey c. unconsciously 7690

COMMANDMENTS, TEN
short and to the point 779

COMMANDS
Charity scope of God's c. 1076
Earnestness c. respect 2771
fulfill God's destiny in life 8111
God c. us to be filled with the
Spirit 5778
love that Christ c. not easy 7304
No man safely c. 7422
saint uses c. of Lord 8111

COMMEND
friend publicly 2855

COMMENDED
If fruitless, mattered not who c. me
10157

COMMENDS
Who errs, mends to God himself c.
3264

COMMENTARIES
on Scriptures, good examples best
3449
theologians would have consulted
c. 6147

COMMENTARY
of the times 5863

COMMERCE
cannot find joy in trade and c.
10527
of trivial import 11684

COMMISSIONED
Jesus c. disciples 2827

COMMIT
a major sin, all lesser sins follow
10301
faith, c. himself, life, hopes to God
3999
Jesus didn't c. gospel to
advertising agency 2827
joy, c. ourselves to God's way
6566
let us now c. Golden Rule to life
5007
life to God for hours of sleep
10486
Rather suffer an injustice than c.
one 6276
than repent of sins intend to c.
10327
Those who c. injustice bear
greatest burden 6279
to concrete plans for increasing
giving 10739
to Jesus' mission of liberating
oppressed 1439

COMMITAL
prove faith by c. to it 612

COMMITMENT
guard against grounding c. on experiences 3550
must be renewed 1535
must strengthen c. to families 3901
reflection without c. paralysis 1532
where self supersedes c. to others 3901
without reflection is fanaticism 1532

COMMITS
faith c. to obedience 3808
He who defends injury next to him who c. it 6261
Slander wounding both him that c. and him against whom committed 10463

COMMITTED
easier to repent of sins we have c. 10327
God needs minority fully c. 1192
how horrible sins look c. by someone else 10343
immense appear sins we have not c. 10316
Lord's Prayer c. to memory quickly 7153
Some sins we have c. 10384
the Golden Rule to memory 5007

COMMITTING
no discovery of truth without c. to Christ 6490

COMMON
All men whilst awake in c. world 2965
Christians, non-Christians in c. 3303
every c. bush afire with God 1710
Eyes that look are c. 8493
fear of death c. 2375
Freethinkers state of mind not c. 4124
gluttons have one thing in c. 131
God must love the c. man 4545
Hell where no one has anything in c. 5692
in earth's c. things he stands revealed 8019
most c. way to get ulcers 1566
not made from c. mold 6206
prosper as we do c. things in uncommon way 9344
smooth green grasses more c. still 10634
suffering a far stronger link than joy 5338
Thou know'st 'tis c. 2402
Thy fate is c. fate of all 10582
unsuccessful men with talent c. 8555

COMMON GROUND
between cross, reason is impossible 1239

COMMON SENSE
God's way contrary to c. 1294

not basis of Christianity 533
Pride eats the possibility of c. 9229
question of c. would abolish rose 8580
review past with c. 4329
shines with double lustre in humility 5994
ten pounds of c. to apply learning 11934

COMMON SPECIES
However wretched, still member of c. 906

COMMONEST
fallacy among women 7854

COMMONLY
is the case of kings 11827

COMMONPLACE
daily burden of a c. life 9683
discern God in humdrum c. 10721
God changes from c. to special 4487
the c. is full of wonder 6918

COMMONSENSE
decisions are God's will unless he checks 5464

COMMUNE
with own selves 3935

COMMUNICATE
attempt to c. vision to all others 6169
God does not c. things to us 4537
If work not going to c. 9147
meaning of Christianity to children 3927

COMMUNICATED
God has c. he cares 4779
Good, the more c, more abundant grows 5062

COMMUNICATION
God is looking for people who long for c. with him 8972
long for c. with God 124
Mass c. aid in evangelism 3317
task to live personal c. with Christ 3321

COMMUNION
God in still, small voice of c. 10747
heaven, uninterrupted c. with God 5644
Mysticism is c. with God 7955
scarce disturbed c. of higher life 1332
silent c. of closet best declares God's reality 10554
soul enriched by c. with God 10567
To go to C. gives God glory 12013
which I spent not in c. with God 6909
with God one thing, familiarity another 8777
with God that asks for nothing, yet everything 8997

COMMUNISM
an insidious ideology 9952

COMMUNITY
church not part of c. 1385
church, a whole new c. 1385
family, first c. to which person attached 3888
is good 9952
Let him not in c. beware of being alone 10547
Let him who cannot be alone beware of c. 10547
restoring sense of c. 3325
shall only resist disintegration of c. 6286
society not c. radiant with love of Christ 10514
What people say behind back is your standing in c. 9628

COMPANION
Adam, created to be c. of God 758
faith a gracious c. 3689
never found c. so companionable as solitude 10537
of truth is humility 11535
Patience the c. of wisdom 8412
peace is justice's c. 6628
world, a jolly, kind c. 515

COMPANIONABLE
never found companion so c. as solitude 10537

COMPANIONS
happiness is friendship of a few select c. 5568
If man does not keep pace with his c. 10827
Jesus finds many c. of table 2828
most agreeable of all c. 4204
rotten apple spoils his c. 9500
they, while their c. slept 8566

COMPANIONSHIP
but a step from c. to slavery 10326
he has unseen c. 10567

COMPANY
A crowd is not c. 7122
Cheerful c. shortens miles 4221
in c. wearisome, dissipating 10572
no c. preferable to bad 4286
No camel route is long with good c. 4256
People who cannot be alone worse c. 10552
prefer trivial c. to being alone 10575
we enjoy 10016
who love good c. happiest people in world 5567
With merry c. dreary way endured 4304

COMPARE
God in me, God without! Beyond c! 4840
no human birth c. to supernatural birth 874

no self-confidence c. with
confidence in Christ 1611
To what shall I c. this life of ours
7070

COMPARED
friend shadow c. with Jesus Christ
4201
hate c. to foot that destroys
sandcastle 7233
Love c. to building of sandcastle
7233
No revolution c. to words of Jesus
Christ 5721
Our knowledge, c. with God's, is
ignorance 6699
with what we ought to be 8651

COMPARES
wisdom, awful wisdom which c.
11906

COMPARING
always c. themselves with their
betters 6813
can't judge Christianity by c.
product 1316
enjoy life without c. to another
1787
Stop c. 6168

COMPARISON
achievements in c. with what we
owe 84
game sure way to poor self-image
6208
In c. with a loving human being
7195
little in c. with eternal realities
4559
must be hatred in c. to our love
for Jesus 7280
things little in c. with eternal
realities 3281
Words vague in c. with genuine
music 7934

COMPASS
Truth lies within a little, certain c.
6868
your own destruction 10024

COMPASSED
When c. about on every side 234

COMPASSION
better than arrogance 6326
can never coexist with judgment
10162
church community of c. 1414
dew of c. a tear 1553
for others who hurt 10610
God judging men with
undisturbed c. 4720
God will never dismiss c. 1547
God's c. flows out of his goodness
4724
Grief, helping you feel c. for others
5334
Hearin'is one thing, listenin'
another 1544
means justice 1542
prayer for c. 9065

requires inner disposition 1546
Through sorrow human c. kindled
10640

COMPASSIONATE
free to be c. 10162
how hard to be c. 1546
infirmities of others 1080
wealth of the c. spirit 11841

COMPATIBLE
joy c. with pain 6571
tragedy not c. with belief 591
with everything is meaningless
1578

COMPEL
acknowledgement of divine power
479
Attempting to c. others to believe
as he does 7793
love cannot c. 4126

COMPELLED
army of demons c. to obey Jesus
9858
God c. to conceal himself from
world 4657
if c. to take part, where is director
3485
Jesus c. individuals to decide 6516
not where man goes when c. to go
4147
Thy hand c. it, Master, thine 7480
to praise, even as logic screams
8724
you c. my deaf ears to hear you
7579

COMPENDIUM
Bible c. of human experience 701
Lord's Prayer c. of doctrine 7156

COMPENSATED
evil will be c. for by God 3385

COMPENSATION
God our c. for every sacrifice
4550

COMPENSATIONS
one who has not suffered knows
nothing of 10914

COMPETE
No job can c. with shaping a new
human being 8317
pressed to confirm or c. 1634

COMPETITION
dog is still c. for a husband 7611
of wise man is with himself 1630

COMPETITIVE
even missionary activity may
become c. 7867

COMPILING
anthology act of thanksgiving
9381

COMPLACENT
Christian thinker disturbs c.
11239

COMPLAIN
Critics c. Christianity not good
religion 1188
death, no right to c. 2307
discontented with ourselves, c.
about others 1567
do you dare c. 9448
grumble and c. 37
more you c, more to c. about 1559
should not c. of smoke 11120
to one who can help 1556
to whom to c. 3203
wouldn't have time to c. about the
bad 11150

COMPLAINED
wrong was his who wrongfully c.
1565

COMPLAINERS
greatest persecutors 1557

COMPLAINING
born crying, live c, die
disappointed 7075
God takes personally 1558
Instead of c. God has hidden
himself 4908
Man spends life c. of present 8380
might seem innocent 1558

COMPLAININGS
our c. please devil 2661
still our tongues of weak c. 9090

COMPLAINS
imperfection c. of what is
imperfect 8521
No great man c. of want of
opportunity 8220
only imperfection that c. of what
is imperfect 11395
pessimist c. about the wind 8249

COMPLAINT
decisions without c. 39
Lord, it is my chief c. 9077
Whither shall I turn with my c.
3485

COMPLAINTS
chief c. was Christ not religious
enough 6416
if expect perfection 2799
life a series of c. 9469

COMPLEMENT
Male, female c. of the other 3239

COMPLETE
Acceptance before God c. 9992
Are you c. in yourself 1450
Experience is never c. 3524
God made the c. instrument, the
human voice 7893
gospel a development more c. than
limits of nature 9351
Holy means c. 5734
more c. our sense of need 7524
not c. if all not given to God 5734
Satan content as long as we never
c. anything 9857
security where peace c. 3961

thy purpose, that we may become thy perfect image 7519

will have a c. explanation 7060

COMPLETED

continually successful yet never c. 6169

the work will be c. 48

COMPLETELY

God knows us c. 4884

solves problems c. 3784

COMPLETER

Christ is C. of unfinished people, work, times 6428

COMPLETING

virtue of deeds lies in c. 65

COMPLETION

Christian, never in state of c. 1250

heaven, find c. of all desires 5644

waits only the c. of present task 9658

COMPLEX

human being more c. than social sytem 10505

human soul, life too c. to touch 10653

Knowledge leads from simple to c. 11929

Love a c. emotion 7233

Man a c. being 3197

wisdom leads from c. to simple 11929

COMPLEXES

nasty things due to c. will fall off 1030

COMPLEXION

hues from the c. of the heart 103

COMPLEXITIES

Out of c. simplicities emerge 11937

COMPLEXITY

and mystery of a human being 4247

Humanity, two poles of simplicity, c. 7383

lost in maze of fine distinctions 7383

COMPLICATE

To understand is to c. 11618

COMPLICATED

civilized life c. system of murder 10513

If devil succeeds in making c. 10653

men insist on making life c. 6977

COMPLICATES

Love c. life of God as it c. every life 4823

COMPLICATIONS

happier circumstances free from difficult c. 4974

which you can hardly get to end of 9402

COMPLIMENT

a gift not to throw away 1570

acquaintance that begins with c. 1572

best c. to set free to make own inquiries 6207

can live two months on good c. 1573

Difficulties a c. of God 2714

God has paid intolerable c. of loving us 7186

God pays men c. 1142

happiness of life made up of heartfelt c. 5556

to treat person as exception to rules 1575

trusted greater c. than loved 1576

verbal sunshine 1571

Whenever friends c. about looking young 8185

COMPLIMENTS

when you don't know what to say 1577

COMPORTMENT

and activity have root in gratitude 5240

COMPOSE

How to c. your life 6902

COMPOSED

crowd is c. of individuals 6209

grand pieces played on earth c. in heaven 5639

Life must be c. by ear, feeling, instinct 6966

neurotics have c. our masterpieces 4390

COMPOSER

Holy Spirit is c. and conductor 5799

COMPOUND

Good and evil increase at c. interest 5021

COMPREHEND

can you c. how Christ could be both God and man 6459

can't c. trust God 2414

do not aspire to c. God 10876

finite can never c. infinite 4690

If I could c. Christ, he would be no greater than myself 6459

intellect can never c. spirit 10692

may know but not c. God 4693

No man fit to c. heavenly things 198

None can c. eternity but God 3283

Whom none can c. 4672

Whose utterance cannot c. 4962

yearning to c. the incomprehensible 7531

COMPREHENDED

God cannot be c. in human words 4682

God is no God at all 4662

If we fully c. brevity of life 6924

If work of God be c. by reason 3841

If works of God easily c. 9411

COMPREHENDING

Jehovah! c. all 4672

nearer to c. true nature of existence 3488

COMPREHENDS

Bible c. man, his thoughts 703

saint c. that all is well 10910

COMPREHENSIBLE

just another philosophy 1213

COMPREHENSION

attributes of God transcend c. 4584

far beyond your c. 39

COMPROMISE

human problems gray areas 1582

If c. with surrender 10972

makes good umbrella 1580

makes poor roof 1580

more devastating than misfortune 1584

often results in loss 1579

Peace won by c. a short-lived achievement 8464

sacrifice of one for another 1579

swift wind of c. devastating 1584

temporary expedient 1580

COMPROMISES

Truth never c. 11561

COMPROMISING

reform from uncompromising in c. age 1457

COMPULSION

God's c. is our liberation 4498

COMPULSIONS

can let c. melt away 10551

social c. of an unredeemed world 10003

COMPULSIVE

in c. self-seclusion toward our world 7072

love does not ask us to be c. pleasers 7337

COMPULSORY

Obedience to Jesus Christ not c. 8106

COMPUTABLE

Love superior to money on c. basis 7232

COMPUTER

hooked up to huge c. 4332

COMRADE

Hunger a suitable c. for work-shy 6759

COMRADES

God seeks c, claims love 4912

COMRADESHIP

give us sense of c. with heroes, saints of every age 9059

CONCEAL

as much caution to tell truth as to c. it 11514

Friendship ought never to c. what it thinks 4238

God compelled to c. himself from world 4657

Like cuttlefish we c. ourselves 4255

sadness under pretended gaiety 10587

unless greater hurt to c. 10459

CONCEALED

at God's discretion 11609

goodness a sort of vice 5056

infinity of God not c. but incomprehensible 4684

Men look for God, fancy him c. 8019

Noble deeds c. are esteemed 2504

to be right within where all c. 6295

until life developed sufficiently 11609

CONCEALMENT

keep clear of need of c. 5480

CONCEALS

He that c. his grief finds no remedy 5341

Night c. world, reveals universe 8083

CONCEIT

enemy tactic 1190

if full of c. no room for Spirit of God 5783

is self-given, be careful 10994

makes everyone sick 1586

my c. just began peeling off 1455

puffed up with c. 6704

weird disease 1586

CONCEITED

When feelings are c. ask to have them altered 3051

CONCEIVE

compare with all he can c, Nadir of Weakness 6698

could we c. of God's greatness 4700

if clam could c. of God 4909

unity of God which we can never c. 4580

CONCEIVED

God can neither be spoken nor c. 4580

God's greatness cannot be c. 4700

thought worth thinking c. in suffering 10835

world was poetry 1981

CONCEIVING

attributes of God are human ways of c. abyssal 4580

CONCENTRATE

mistake that we do not c. on present day 8381

CONCENTRATED

attention so c. no time to wonder how we look 6056

If not c. we affect many attitudes 6056

wretch c. all in self 10088

CONCENTRATES

Hate c. on thing hated 7262

CONCENTRATION

Punishment produces c. 2038

CONCEPT

of ineffable worship has been lost 12120

of spirituality varies among groups 10713

wrong c. of God leads to 4568

CONCEPTION

creation surpassed my c. 4603

deepest c. of meekness 7728

incorrect c. of ourselves, neighbor, God 8059

CONCERN

Agape love c. without desire to control 7158

Agape love profound c. for another 7158

all mankind's c. is charity 1079

Christ awakens c. for world 12031

Christ did not limit c. to spiritual 1551

Don't meddle with that which does not c. you 5122

God's main c. 10141

Grace refuses to put ceiling on c. 5233

injury to one c. of all 6603

Love universalizes its c. 7274

Maturity, c. for others outweighing c. for yourself 7693

more c. than destruction of millions 10035

sins of boardroom as much c. 10399

Situation ethics puts people at center of c. 6820

This is your major c. 6260

to know where history is going 5724

what happens when gospel preached 5105

CONCERNED

church c. with budgets, building 1409

God c. with all kinds of writing 12146

God is more c. about keeping us 5390

God more c. about character than comfort 1016

Jesus was, is c. with individual souls 6176

more c. about agreement with Christians than God 1281

need not be c. how high God's standard is 8518

not c. enough to bear burdens 933

our Lord c. for people 6519

should be c. about future 4333

singing groups c. about being inoffensive 5109

wasn't with us Jesus was c. 12128

whether I am on God's side 7471

CONCERNS

My future not one of my c. 5471

selfish, parasitical c. drain time, energy 1306

CONCERT

all strings in c. of his joy 4028

We are all strings in the c. of God's joy 6570

CONCISENESS

Lord's Prayer for c. without obscurity 7154

CONCLUDE

crimes committed because God wills 3349

human affairs not governed by God 3349

must c. God's ways are perfect 4443

worship must take place in church 12101

CONCLUDES

"dust to dust" c. her noblest song 7088

CONCLUSIONS

Don't jump to c. too quickly 8394

Jumping to c. seldom leads to happy landings 6582

to come to c. right for him 6207

CONCORDANCE

church members would do well to look in c. 10185

CONCRETE

If grass can grow in c. walk 3736

CONCUR

when c. with promptings of the Spirit 5444

CONCUSSION

beating head against wall likely to produce c. 8553

CONDEMN

Crafty men c. studies 2996

Do not c. your neighbor 6572

Don't c. the sinner 10432

futile to c. myself 3049

God must c, blast out what he cannot bless 893

God no faultfinder looking for things to c. 4650

if fruitful, cared not who did c. 10157

live with criticism, learn to c. 1114

Lord's concern to save and not c. 6519

No man can justly c. another 2070

No man can justly censure or c. 6585

ourselves to spiritual superficiality 6693

the fault, not the actor 3936

the wrong, yet the wrong pursue 10319

wealth who see no chance of getting it 11868

what they do not understand 2081

who c. wealth are those who have none 11868

CONDEMNATION
if conscience smite thee twice 1686

CONDEMNED
Christ c. that thou mightest be justified 6393

Christian c. for what he does not do 6594

man c. for continuing to do wrong 6586

man c. for not coming out of darkness 6586

man c. for not coming to the light 6586

Our inner life grows stronger when outwardly c. 6270

Though all my heart should feel c. 9813

though God has c. us 7186

CONDEMNING
examine oneself before c. others 2072

Sainthood delivers from c. 9778

CONDEMNS
who judges others c. himself 6578

world esteems as good, c. as bad 5042

CONDENSED
Christianity c. into four words 1164

theology c. into four words 11195

CONDESCENSION
Christ, c. of divinity 6441

CONDITION
Christ came into our c. 6121

difficulty inherent in human c. 8569

failure is not a c. 3581

Forgetting oneself first c. of love 7169

forgiveness, c. attached 4096

God disciplines to c. for usefulness 2845

highest possible c. of a man 4983

Ignorance necessary c. of life itself 6081

incapable of understanding one's c. 7126

joy a c. of the soul 6568

Life used to c. for eternity 6944

Lord's Prayer for suitableness to every c. 7154

Love is the law of our c. 6614

love, rather a c. of the heart and will 7304

no human c. which divine presence does not penetrate 6277

of saint admits no alternation 4626

Prosperity more than economic c. 9339

Reason can ascertain difficulties of our c. 9420

sees man in evolution from lesser to greater c. 9351

Self-knowledge is first c. of repentance 9599

CONDITIONING
things you read, c. your mind 862

CONDITIONS
Cross, the most extreme of all human c. 6277

friendship, c. of existence 4237

impossible for God to manifest himself under c. set up 8929

joyfully accepting c. of earthly pilgrimage 9090

unless meditation results in changing c. in world 7725

CONDONING
Understanding a person does not mean c. 11619

Understanding does not mean c. 3079

CONDUCIVE
collapsing world more c. to understanding truth 11491

CONDUCT
are all impatient of uncertainty in c. 11605

as unspoken sermon 554

asking God to c. a major operation 7155

Bible to direct c. 737

Devotion regulates all our c. 9731

give to mother 511

I make myself pure in c. 1012

if we judge our c. by Christ 563

inquisitive about c. or service 1303

is the only effective sermon 9132

Morality not only correct c. on outside 7832

no assumptions from public c. 571

no distinction in c. between small, great 567

reputation of thousand years determined by c. of one hour 9625

responsibility for human c. rests with "I" 579

to c. affairs of this administration 6304

toward enemy as if one day friend 3172

tune we call goodness or right c. 7839

virtue of man measured by everyday c. 11698

What was c. of Shadrach, Meshach, Abednego 5197

CONDUCTOR
family circle the supreme c. of Christianity 5852

family supreme c. of Christianity 3887

Holy Spirit is composer and c. 5799

CONFEDERACY
dunces all in c. against genius 4400

CONFER
cannot c. on me fullness of life 5549

CONFERRED
greatest benefits God has c. become curse 3895

CONFESS
devil delights tormenting when we c. Christ 2661

eyes c. secrets of the heart 3569

foolish actions require courage to c. 1603

Grace to c, forsake sin 1809

Should we all c. sins to one another 10353

The world c. its sin 4642

We c. our sins 9087

without confession his glory is inexplicable 4681

CONFESSED
Faith is refusing to feel guilty over c. sins 3672

fault c, new virtue 1592

CONFESSES
man who c. no longer alone with himself 1594

not own sins, but sins of neighbors 5160

realities have begun 1600

shams are over 1600

CONFESSING
Explaining is half-confessing 1598

leave the world c. 737

CONFESSION
brings to light unconscious darkness 1596

brings to light underdeveloped creativity 1596

confess without c. his glory is inexplicable 4681

discipline which God requires 1597

Gossip personal c. of malice or imbecility 5128

necessary for fellowship 1595

of evil works is beginning of good works 5040

open lives to healing 1602

painful, sometimes literally 1601

prayer of c. 9087

restores fellowship 1597

Revenge a c. of pain 9724

sin brought into light 1594

sometimes incredibly hard 1601
three things necessary 1599
to agree with God about sin 1597
two grave dangers 1604
word love is a semantic c. 7312

CONFESSIONAL
Bible, my c. 716
Protestant c, the sewing circle
5160

CONFESSOR
foolish sheep makes wolf his c.
9473

CONFESSORS
Bible, congregation of c. 716

CONFIDENCE
acquire c. in recourse to God 8796
before you give them your c. 4218
Birth God's c. in man 815
blossom when surrounded by c.
2054
Christ promises love and c. 159
cure for spiritual degeneration
1613
Difficulties, proof of God's c.
2714
Faith c. in character of God 3684
fear of God, spur to c. 3993
God will break up c. in your
natural powers 11689
God will wither up c. in brain,
spirit, body 11689
God's fastest road to c. 225
great c. in friend to tell your faults
3930
greater c. in friend to tell him his
faults 3930
Idolatry putting c. in riches, power
6071
in Christ awakens 1611
in Christ does not make lazy 1611
in Christ makes us do good 1611
in Christ, makes us live righteous
1611
in Christ, urges us on 1611
in natural world, self-reliance
1605
in spiritual world, God-reliance
1605
Joy c. God is in control 6544
keeping chin up 1607
Kindness in words creates c. 6649
learn to mistrust ourselves, put all
c. in God 9851
live with encouragement, learn c.
1114
maturity the quiet c. God is in
control 7697
mistrust of himself, greater c. in
God 10328
no tribulation, affliction can
touch c. 1613
Peace is c. 8455
plant of slow growth 1606
Psalms, firmness of man's c. 798
should supersede fear 6326
that God will not us cast aside
4005

Trustfulness based on c. in God
11487
what you have before you
understand situation 8361
when central c. transferred to God
5645
whether faith will not justify c.
3774
who has c. in himself will lead the
rest 6791
with joy to loving c. in God 4747

CONFIDENT
affirmation of self 4160
Hope c. search for a rewarding life
5918
stars shine, fearless and c. 4618

CONFIDENTLY
hope that all will yet be well 5179
trust reckons c. 3676

CONFINE
tongue, lest it c. you 11411

CONFINED
God not c. in churches 4866
No steam, gas drives anything
until c. 2852
works of Holy Spirit not c. to
institutional church 5791

CONFINEMENT
all sentenced to solitary c. 7148

CONFINES
happy man c. himself within limits
2875

CONFIRM
to strengthen, c. new, weak faith
3744

CONFIRMED
sin becomes c. 10287

CONFIRMING
Grief should be c. 5331

CONFLICT
a kind of cosmic c. 1168
antagonist is our helper 1623
between conscience, will 3367
between desire to stand out, need
to blend in 7415
bound to result 3752
cannot have crown without c.
1633
character achieved through c.
1632
Church often in c. 1385
do not understand peace until c.
11620
faith from c. often strongest, best
2935
Happiness ability to cope with c.
5526
harder the c. more glorious the
triumph 1628
Holiness is victory through c.
5743
human spirit to grow strong by c.
2715
in c. we find strength 9090
keep mouth shut 1627

Life without c. impossible 6988
main ingredient in God's
character development 1029
marital c. cancers that gnaw on
soul 3873
more intensified the c. 1629
neutrality in c. of world 4999
not many things so interesting
1631
Peace is ability to cope with c.
8458
Peace not absence of c. 8458
saints interest us when in c. with
devil 1631
with defeated foes 235

CONFLICTS
prayer closet scene of unearthly c.
8976
prayer restores minds after all c.
8857

CONFORM
my will to thine 9101
or by seeking to c. to cultural
mores 8520
pressed to c. or compete 1634
To be holy God does not c. to a
standard 5749

CONFORMING
do not think much of that 6048
outwardly, living own life inwardly
6048
unreservedly to that of God 9835

CONFORMIST
has to follow herd 1635
not a free man 1635

CONFORMITY
act according to custom 1648
Character lost when conformity
999
church largely clubs of c. 1439
crow tried to emulate partridge
1644
easy cowardice of surrender to c.
6216
holiness is c. to will of God 5758
land of naked people ashamed of
clothes 1638
most fundamental dishonesties of
all 1635
science reveals remarkable c. in all
things 9866
To be one's self more admirable
than c. 6216
To pray means to put our lives
into c. with God 8944

CONFOUNDED
though alarmed, love is not c.
7283

CONFOUNDS
Death c. 'em all 2384
idea of creation c. me 4603

CONFRONT
Character sum total of choices
that c. us 1000
think positively or c. life as it is
9401

CONFRONTATION
Character out of daily c. 1000
Only in c. does man become aware 7494

CONFRONTED
do not understand hope until c. with doubts 11620
except as he knows himself c. by God 7494
the Christ of the poor c. me 8685
with contempt powers of Jerusalem c. Jesus 6420

CONFRONTING
mercy c. human misery, guilt 5206

CONFRONTS
church c. world 1428
no major sin when his grace c. you 10405
no minor sin when his justice c. you 10405

CONFUSED
Give me the c. self 4530
God makes beautiful something c. 885
joy too great to be c. with happiness 6564
loftiest eloquence retreats. 4750
without control young people c. 12178
without God young people c. 12180

CONFUSING
redirecting our lives often c. 5449

CONFUSION
cannot build hopes on c. 8445
conversation more likely deliberate c. 1839
devil, author of c. 2659
dust raised by devil 2642
God turned life into inextricable c. 4885
ideas clear that have same degree of c. 8491
In midst of c. deep inner silence 10539
need not be overwhelmed with c. 4924
Photography records c. man has created 2016
productive of the greatest minds 220
think without c. clearly 559
through all the c. God got message through 7029
To think clearly without hurry or c. 6913
what happens when gospel preached 5105
without framework all is c. 3980

CONFUSIONS
In Christ at peace in midst of c. 8470

CONFUTE
Read not to contradict, c. 856

CONGENIAL
fiction c. to human mind 11574

CONGESTION
never any traffic c. on straight, narrow path 9819

CONGREGATION
Bible, a c. 716
each member of worshiping c. 5799
fewer requirements on c. 1499
let your little brood be your c. 7847
We confess our sins as a c. 9087

CONGREGATIONAL
advantage of c. singing 1415

CONGREGATIONS
filled with actors and actresses 135

CONGRESS
care not what is enacted in C. 12151
First Prayer in Congress 9102
is so strange 5171

CONGRUOUS
honest joy must be c. with tragedy 6571

CONJECTURES
Rumor pipe blown by c. 9756

CONNECTED
Christianity, life c. with Christ 1172
things that belonged to peace c. with Jesus 6420

CONNECTIONS
in everyone's life certain c. 5454

CONNECTS
God c. 4709

CONNEXION
Knowledge and wisdom oftimes no c. 6690

CONQUER
A few c. by fighting 11781
as we perceive, c. more glaring faults 10006
can c. who believe they can 3798
Christ did not c. by force 6389
Christ, c. by love 6389
God sends weapon to c. 3418
gospel cannot c. without prayer 9015
must c. the world or the world will c. you 7096
no power can c. Spirit of God 10751
Pain no evil unless it c. 8268
that they might learn to c. world 8805
they c. who believe they can 3720
To c. one's self is the beautiful 10022
withhold not courage by which we can c. 9090
You will c, never fear 8558

CONQUERED
beast and devil may be c. 5013
Christ stooped when he c. 2152
enemy c. only to God, not to us 3163
Jesus c. millions 6449
Loneliness c. only by those who can bear solitude 7133
look upon enemy of our souls as c. 3163
spirit always has c. the sword 10695

CONQUEROR
best c. takes no part in war 11784
In his resurrection, Christ a c. 6410
live a c, die a man 2353
who knows how to suffer c. of himself 10851

CONQUERS
Evil never c. 3366
good lives on, loves on, c. all 11129
grace alone c. sin 5231
is mighty who c. himself 9968

CONQUEST
Christ, glory as much in stooping as c. 2152
glory springs from silent c. of ourselves 4414
Man's c. of nature astonishing 7414

CONSCIENCE
a built-in feature 1698
A c. to the base and weak 10130
a Christian must walk a sterner light 1688
a monarch in its preemptoriness 1673
a priest in its blessings 1673
a prophet in its information 1673
a sacred sanctuary 1666
a thousand witnesses 1667
a three-pointed thing 1668
a walkie-talkie set 1669
an imperfect mental faculty 1699
analysis of c. has taken place of childlike simplicity 6813
anticipation of opinion of others 1675
arises from fear of God 3988
asks, Is it right 1679
bad c. embitters sweetest comforts 1650
Bad c. is snake in heart 1651
bad c. like muddy stream 1693
bend our c. to our dealings 1687
captive to the word of God 1692
Confession an examination of c. 1599
conflict between c, will 3367
content whose c. is pure 1681
cross readjusts man in c. to God 2172
dictatorship not alibi for c. 1689
disease of evil c. beyond physicians 1700

does right because of his own c. 1051

does tell us of God 8023

Even voice of c. undergoes mutation 1680

Fear is tax c. pays to guilt 3966

follow c. as a wheelbarrow 1691

from deep to deeper plung'd 1694

gets credit that belongs to cold feet 1665

God speaks in our c. 8257

God's presence in man 1670

good c. can sleep in mouth of cannon 1653

good c. continual feast 1654

good c. soft pillow 1655

gospel like comfort in anguish of c. 5097

guilty c. a hidden enemy 5472

guilty c. hell on earth 1656

guilty c. needs no accuser 5473

haunts the sinner, helps the preacher 1698

have one friend left, down inside of me 1685

if checks forego, Thou art his deadliest foe 1695

if he will thy friendly checks forego 1695

importance is eternal, like love 1701

in nothing which could not review with quiet c. 11312

is the God-relationship 1657

Little praying a salve for the c. 8889

Living with c. like driving with brakes on 1690

lose honor rather than c. 1658

man within is angry 1706

Man's most faithful friend 1695

Memory the registry of c. 7733

message of God fragmentary 8023

microbe of c. eats into the soul 1682

must be bathed in new element 880

must be re-born 880

must be reconsecrated to Maker 880

my accomplice 1678

My Umpire C. whom if they hear 1664

no evil intolerable but guilty c. 9092

O C, into what abyss of fears 1694

of godly, at peace 3996

only tyrant I accept is voice within 1703

punishes us as a judge 1677

pure c. like looking into clear stream 1693

quicken the c. by the holiness of God 12124

quiet c. sleeps in thunder 1659

reigns, does not govern 1676

scar on c. same as wound 1660

Sleep cannot silence c. 2970

sleeping pill will not replace clear c. 1661

smite thee once, an admonition 1686

smite thee twice, a condemnation 1686

some sins c. makes us run from 1698

takes the fun from 1698

throughly well-bred 1674

to sit alone with c. judgment enough 1707

to sit alone with my c. 1663

true vicar of Christ in soul 1673

trust in nothing man who has not c. 1708

two witnesses God, our own c. 4872

uneasy c. hair in mouth 1662

unravels if single stitch dropped 1704

voice that makes you feel smaller 1672

void of offense an inheritance for eternity 5079

warns us as a friend 1677

warns us someone may be looking 1671

we push c. in direction we want to go 1691

Whatever impairs tenderness of c. is sin 10424

where God alone is judge 1666

world achieved brilliance without c. 1705

CONSCIENCES

deadly opiate for c. of millions 4726

no notice of pain on others 1697

not afraid of tender c. 586

CONSCIENTIOUS

first stage of Christian life c. carefulness 1714

in our work as good citizens 10525

to be c. become overscrupulous 9502

CONSCIOUS

beyond c. ego 2971

blessings for man c. of his own poverty 5299

Christ either deceived by c. fraud, was deluded or divine 6366

emotion source of all becoming-c. 3053

fully c. we discover loneliness 9513

God is imparting life to be c. of him 4514

greatest fault to be c. of none 3952

holiest person most c. of sin 5761

How guilt, once harbour'd in the c. breast 5479

Jesus' sacrifice must be c. 10868

not c. intellectual process 1126

not c. of being born 7050

not even c. of where God puts us 7509

not when c. of faults most wicked 10329

nothing more awful than c. humility 6038

of an amazing simplicity of life 7509

Once c. we are more than we can fathom 10015

painfully c. of my need of grace 9097

peace for hours of sleep 10486

preach as if c. dying sinners 3338

soul long before c. ego 2971

when c. obedience assimilated 7690

when saint becomes c. of being saint 10722

CONSCIOUSLY

gain identity that Jesus had 9840

saint c. dependent on God 9768

saint never c. a saint 9768

CONSCIOUSNESS

As soon as c. is reached 3479

Boredom c. of barren existence 865

croons away our c. 10486

Experience suspended in chamber of c. 3524

hell, c. no longer able to love 5707

lose c. of own identity 9840

many on borders on c. 1714

most use small portion of c. 8659

mystic loses c. of creature distinctions 7966

Mysticism is the filling of the c. with content 7957

no doubt on horizon of c. 5402

of duty performed gives music at midnight 9675

of well-doing ample reward 5069

Suffering origin of c. 1718

then I regain c. 11615

theology, attempt to systematize c. of God 11209

torn by pain of grief 900

CONSECRATED

human emotion to be c. to God 6728

takes c. men to do great things 1723

what God can do in man fully c. to Christ 2835

CONSECRATION

Faithfulness is c. in overalls 3844

going out into world for God 1721

handing God a blank sheet 1720

mature life, unconscious c. 1714

narrow, lonely way to love 1722

not wrapping up in holy web 1721

taking advantages as trust funds 1721

using every power for God's glory 1721

CONSECRATIONS
reservations damnations of c. 1724

CONSENT
deriving just powers from c. of governed 3246
No one can make you feel inferior without your c. 6228
no way to kill righteousness but by own c. 11102
will not save us without our c. 9796

CONSENTS
alphabet of love avowals and c. 7297
How reluctantly the mind c. to reality 9400

CONSEQUENCE
Every beginning is c. 1728
Happiness is a c. 5522
if course wrong, avoid though lose life as c. 6291
of defying moral order 4721
of little c. whether pagan idolator or proud Pharisee 10041
only thing of c. is what we do 8117

CONSEQUENCES
Faith is doing right thing regardless of c. 3671
If clergymen defrocked 1732
If disbelieve must take c. 11590
least action has c. 572
need not worry about c. 6306
never violate laws of God without c. 10336
of action without thought 11278
overcoming c. of misfortune 154
sin seems worse in c. than intentions 10294
sorrow because of c. is remorse 9580
with ruinous c. to society 10503

CONSERVATISM
Jesus so long identified with c. 6452
of Jesus' times against him 6452

CONSERVATIVE
Jesus Christ was not a c. 6435
organization keeps us c. 2014
Reality always more c. than ideology 9406

CONSIDER
I will c. my earthly existence wasted 6919
If c. boundless space, shrink into nothing 11631
Read to weigh, c. 856
the nobility within thee 9982
When c. well-being of others 9520
When I c. my crosses, I shame myself 10928
When I c. short duration of my life 7084

CONSIDERATE
a c. God 4318

CONSIDERATION
parent of wisdom 11909
soil in which wisdom may grow 11910
thou standest where I am to shoot 1550

CONSIDERATIONS
never c. in real abandonment 9560

CONSIDERS
God c. not action, but spirit of action 7861

CONSIGNS
God c. offense to everlasting forgetfulness 4638
God c. offense to forgetfulness 4107

CONSIST
Love does not c. in gazing at each other 7215

CONSISTENCY
anchor worth weighing 1749
battle worth winning 1749
contrary to nature, life 1745
jewel worth wearing 1749
quality of stagnant mind 1746
requires ignorant today as year ago 1747
thou art a jewel 1748
thread worth weaving 1749

CONSISTENT
All God's acts c. with attributes 4579
completely c. people are dead 1745

CONSOLATION
expectancy of another life 6096
God visiting them for c. 4514
inexhaustible source of c. 9835
Jesus has many desirous of c. 2828
Many want c, few desire adversity 9268
of death, end of taxes 2352
wait with resignation return of c. 2883

CONSOLATIONS
Christ's words pass into c. 6523

CONSOLE
Death, Comforter of him whom time cannot c. 2260
If thou suffer injustice, c. thyself 6265
must c. the poor 8698
Never c. one who pines under My chastening 2851
not seek to be consoled, as to c. 9086

CONSOLED
Bible has c. more than all books 639
not seek to be c. as to console 9086

CONSOLES
eternity c. for shortness of life 3287
virtue c. even in pains 10412

CONSOLING
how c. in depths of affliction 957

CONSORTING
Jesus always c. with sinners 5791

CONSPIRING
All revolutions c. to that great event 4898

CONSTANCY
hope the c. of faith 5946

CONSTANT
holy life c. attraction or perpetual reproof 5735
in happiness must often change 4057
must keep friendships in c. repair 4249
not c. thought of sins 4660
process of adjusting public image 1882
What is God saying to me c. question 6086

CONSTANTLY
Husbands, wives should c. guard against overcommitment 7617
stars are c. shining 2560
talks so c. about God 484

CONSTITUTED
God has so c. us 4128

CONSTITUTES
freedom c. dignity of man 4149

CONSTITUTION
Bible, c. of Christianity 718
Death as necessary to c. as sleep 2244
inadequate for government of any other 5196
of State of North Carolina, 1836 5183
Our c. made for moral, religious people 5196

CONSTRAINED
When you see inclinations c. 2565

CONSTRAINT
grudge giving comes from c. 10736
man is c, nature is freedom 8012

CONSTRICTED
In man evil is c. 3377

CONSTRUCTS
Everyone c. own bed of nails 1727

CONSULTED
theologians would have c. commentaries 6147
Why was I not c. 3485

CONSULTS
Truth never c. 11561

CONSUME
greed, one object is to c. 5327

grief, strong to c. small troubles 5331

last ounce of energy 7617

no right to c. happiness without producing 5569

no right to c. wealth without producing 5569

think that his Fire will c. my soul 7951

CONSUMED
Burned but not c. 7872

CONSUMES
Envy c. the soul 3212
Love either c. or purifies 7248
Nothing c. more quickly than resentment 9638
serve with devotion that c. 3182

CONSUMING
love of God, c. fire himself 4792

CONSUMMATION
Death c. of union with God 2257

CONTACT
Boredom, when lose c. with universe 866
bringing mind into c. with divine revelation 5094
heroes, c. withers them 8516
imperturbable certainty c. with God 955
impulse to have close c. with other animals around him 6199
in c. with divine resources 1143
lose c. with the Lord of the work 115
man who has lost c. with God 7523
neighbor is man whom business has brought you into c. 8069
personal c. a movement that must be rediscovered 7630

CONTAGIOUS
Disease more c. than health 4286
Indifference to evil more c. than evil itself 3379
live Christ as to make it c. 3321

CONTAIN
deeper the sorrow, the more joy you can c. 10626
do heavens c. you 4854
God I worship too big for space to c. 11643
History too fragile to c. Jesus 5714
Nor could the scroll c. the whole 4748

CONTAINED
deep mysteries c. in Lord's Prayer 7156
I am in God 4852
Nobility grows out of c. emotion 3057
things desirable to men c. in Bible 641
Would in tiny sponge c. be 4839

CONTAINERS
We are the c. 4537

CONTAINING
heart capable of c. God's gift of himself 8910

CONTAMINATED
Christ never c. his inner kingdom 6501

CONTEMPLATE
God's munificence in abundance of earth 4581
God's power in immensity of creation 4581
God's wisdom in unchangeable order 4581
Learn less, c. more 1762
Painting to c. sovereignty of God 2015

CONTEMPLATED
Some sins we have c. 10384

CONTEMPLATES
to soul that c. greatness of God 4707

CONTEMPLATING
thoughts overwhelm when c. universe 698

CONTEMPLATION
a twenty-four-hour-a-day job 1755
and action, not contradictory 1766
best awakening of reverence is c. of works of God 9734
brings peace, rest, sweetness, delight 1758
Christianity, not c. 1173
death brings c. of Creator 2353
history of our Lord inexhaustible c. 6380
involves all of life 1755
like sleep in arms of God 1756
looking at God as an object 1173
No c. will humble more than thoughts of God 4745
No man right to lead life of c. 7004
of the Divinity improving to the mind 4745
recreating silences of c. 1760
strengthens for action 1766
to neglect c. of God 7004
true c. a theological grace 1765
Unite c. with action 1766

CONTEMPLATIVE
admire people suited to c. life 1759
Christ greatest c. 1754
life will continue into eternity 1764
life, Mary's part 1764

CONTEMPT
arrows of sarcasm barbed with c. 1771
death out of c. into glory 2325

difference which rouses c. of world 10917
God has never regarded us with c. 7186
has overcome c. for others 9985
Many can bear adversity, few c. 1768
obscurity and c. better than name 10875
Sin is the c. of God's love 10376
treat you with c. 175
with c, powers of Jerusalem confronted Jesus 6420

CONTEMPTIBLE
Love is c. in its own sight 7246
to me possessions c. 7365

CONTEND
against giants of passion, pride 9233

CONTENDERS
Male, female not c. for supremacy 3239

CONTENDING
no government capable of c. with human passions 5196

CONTENT
And range with humble lives in c. 6016
1772
are in danger of never knowing happiness 5565
Bad the day man becomes c. 8649
Be c. to be a child 4629
be c. to leave everything the way it is 5099
be c. with one pulsation at a time 4885
Better dry dates and c. 1778
better to be c. with poverty 10777
can't inhale gospel's fragrance and be c. 5099
cannot be c. with evangelism which 3337
church cannot be c. with social camaraderie 3337
God not c. to have us remain in sinfulness 9832
Great wealth, c. seldom live together 11818
Ignorance c. with back to truth 3258
Ignorance is c. to stand still 3258
in their own niceness 7827
is the philosopher's stone 1779
knows he is loved, c. with piece of bread 7176
Life a matter of c. 6970
man may aspire, yet be c. 471
Most must be c. to be as though not been 6023
my crown is call'd c. 1808
Mysticism is the filling of the consciousness with c. 7957
Nature makes me c. with this world 8012
never c. with our lot 11387
richest who is c. with least 1794

Satan c. as long as we never complete anything 9857

Satan c. for us to make beginnings 9857

so c. changed into mummy 1816

Some c. not to do mean actions 110

Sweet are thoughts that savour of c. 1812

This is the last of earth! I am c. 2453

to live or die 11468

to observe there is evil 3383

truly wise if c. 1820

Unbelief is c. with darkness 2930

until time to rise 471

What man c. with one crime 2041

Whatever comes, let's be c. withall 1821

who is c. can never be ruined 1797

whose conscience is pure 1681

with strength you've got 1777

with what happens 1800

with what we can and cannot understand 1820

work among Christ's little ones, c. 1802

CONTENTED

I will be 1810

living, nine requisites 1809

man enjoys scenery along detours 1773

man is never poor 1814

mind, continual feast 1774

need not lie nor flatter 1798

never be c. with what we are 1806

right to be c. with what we have 1806

CONTENTEDNESS

maintain perpetual c. 9092

CONTENTION

Golden Rule would reconcile political c. 5005

Religious c. is the devil's harvest 9548

Slanderers devil's bellows to blow up c. 10469

CONTENTIOUS

man will never lack words 9357

CONTENTMENT

affirmative, creative 1819

an inexhaustible treasure 1781

and aspiration, fast friends 471

blessing of the home is c. 5851

blueprint for 531

busied with c. God gives 1815

Cheerfulness, c. beautifiers, preservers 1087

contented with his lot 1816

do not make c. and aspiration quarrel 471

Faith on full stomach may be c. 3711

flying and resting, parts of c. 471

is not happiness 1782

Laughter the c. of God 6732

letting life flow through us 1807

not fulfillment of what you want 1783

not wealth but few wants 1780

occupied with God who gives us c. 1815

Pride eats the possibility of c. 9229

quiet mind richer than crown 1812

real, active virtue 1819

realization of how much you have 1783

realizing God has given everything I need 1784

result of acceptances, humilities 1807

Those who chase happiness run from c. 5566

with c. crowns the thought of worth 4505

CONTENTS

Examine the c, not the bottle 6576

CONTEST

He that perseveres makes every c. a victory 8542

history of world c. between God, Satan, fallen men 4916

outcome of c. not in doubt 4916

CONTESTANTS

Raising children c. must pace themselves 3884

CONTEXT

larger c. which makes life meaningful 10871

sense of c. missing in America 7990

CONTINENT

Every man a piece of the c. 10511

CONTINENTS

New c. of love, truth, might 2319

CONTINGENT

a relative and c. holiness God shares 4658

CONTINUAL

Christ, birth and death but one c. act 6489

contented mind, c. feast 1774

Damnation: c. dying 5684

feel joys so c. and great 6533

Jesus c. forgiveness of sin 10402

life of Christ a c. passion 6489

Sunday c. message of Easter 10955

CONTINUALLY

God works c. 6525

learn to think c. of God 11269

other waters c. flowing 985

shifting systems of false religion c. changing 5103

successful, yet never completed 6169

CONTINUANCE

of anger is hatred 396

of pride is on earth 9218

proof of immortality not in demonstrating c. of life 6105

CONTINUATION

heaven c. of quality of life 5645

CONTINUE

contemplative life will c. into eternity 1764

friendship will not c. begun for an end 4222

groaning toward perfection 9832

pray for though they c. enemies 4069

soul's activities c. through eternity 6094

to make ourselves guilty is sin 5491

CONTINUED

Character, habit long c. 1003

Unrepented sin is c. sin 9575

CONTINUES

Bible c. to be everybody's book 725

CONTINUING

divine power shining in c. state of universe 11652

God's creative method is c. search 4469

man condemned for c. to do wrong 6586

CONTINUITY

strengthens belief in c. of existence after death 6090

CONTINUOUS

eloquence is tedious 9133

God a c. unbroken is 4604

perseverance may be employed by smallest of us 8557

CONTRACT

A sea which can c. itself 5788

God made marriage indissoluble c. 2924

CONTRACTOR

God is architect, man is c. 4563

CONTRADICT

most important thoughts c. emotions 11236

Read not to c, confute 856

than I should c. myself 6294

we c. the Lord 230

CONTRADICTED

voice of intelligence c. by shame 6331

CONTRADICTION

what a c. is man 7439

CONTRADICTIONS

atheists, whirl of c. 481

faith belief in face of c. 3693

in Bible caused by translations 679

CONTRADICTORIES

beyond c. God mayst be seen 7950

CONTRADICTS
God never c. reason 9413
No attribute of God c. any other 4579

CONTRARY
consistency c. to nature, life 1745
Extremes, though c, have like effects 3554
God's way c. to common sense 1294
God's way c. to wisdom on earth 1294
Miracles c. to what we know about nature 8021
Miracles not c. to nature 8021
see men of c. character, examine ourselves 1065
that which is c. to his nature 4513
To be able to live with persons c. to us 5236
wisdom c. to world 3752

CONTRAST
between Christ's mode of gathering people 6396
difference between Christians is c. of their praying 8976
Jerusalem and Jesus! What a c! 6420

CONTRASTED
sinfulness evident when c. with holiness 10440

CONTRIBUTES
Everything c. to building of kingdom 4732

CONTRIBUTION
each generation makes own c. to understanding 9711

CONTRIBUTIONS
rewards depend on c. we make 10179
to children rank as greatest accomplishments 8294

CONTRITE
a humble and a c. heart 6036
Between c. heart and majesty of heaven, no barriers 8771
happiness on c. hearts bestow 5557
heart or no 5557
In solitude can become c. 10540

CONTROL
accustomed to relying on words to c. 10259
Agape love concern without desire to c. 7158
assent mentally to God's c. 5467
authoritarianism twists good into repressive c. 9952
cannot c. evil tongues of others 5164
Christianity, no c. over state of world 1188
Direct, c, suggest this day 9047
Fine dying man can himself c. 2336

gentleness includes having strength under c. 4402
God cannot c. human beings 5983
God will take c. 10259
God's either in full c. or off throne 4939
If we are silent, who will take c. 10259
Joy confidence God is in c. 6544
lost c. when picked up cross 2111
man who can't c. temper 368
Maturity is life under c. of God 7685
maturity the quiet confidence God is in c. 7697
My transport to c. 4795
never fulfillment unless God in c. 4309
none of man's institutions c. nature 8012
others do not c. us 10539
psychological secrets used to c. youth 12178
quelled by music's divine c. 7935
See how it feels to be in c. 4419
Spirit's c. will replace sin's c. 5802
subjected to God's c. not easy to accept 5467
To attempt to c. passion in own strength 11108
to take Jesus seriously was to c. instincts 6421
who c. what young people are taught 8360
will never achieve fulfillment unless God in c. 9558
will never let God take c. until we trust him 10259
Young people need c, authority 12178
yourself 375
Youth will assume c. of cities, states, nations 12160

CONTROLLED
assuming circumstances not c. by God 11152
by other power than my own will 4949
by Spirit means not c. by what happens on outside 9849
little praise for sexually c. single 10236

CONTROLLER
Youth wants master, c. 12180

CONTROLLING
all dangerous without God's c. hand 4956
Christ c. our personalities 1289
extraordinary c. people 3367
We try to escape life instead of c. it 7072

CONTROLS
Memory c. youth 7735

CONTROVERSIALIST
Cannot be a Christian without being a c. 1825

CONTROVERSIES
most savage c. about matters with no good evidence 8529

CONTROVERSY
ceases to be c, ceases to be interest 1827
No great advance without c. 1824
Volumes of angry c. about creeds 2033

CONVENIENCE
God will disappoint as c. 4468

CONVENIENT
future c. place for dreams 4324

CONVERGE
all lines of history c. upon Christ 5710

CONVERSATION
across table with wise worth month's study of books 11898
Christ unseen listener to every c. 5823
confusion rather than communication 1839
couldn't start c. if weather didn't change 7998
enriches the understanding 10533
Everyone capable of familiar c. with God 7541
expect to pass through death in c. with God 9025
happiness, friendship, and c. of select companions 5568
is but carving 1838
lacks depths, makes up in length 1849
men not entering into c. with wives, children 3904
mention Jesus, people want to stop c. 6518
more likely deliberate evasion 1839
one of greatest pleasures 1840
reading books like c. with finest men 861
secret of success in c. 1878
Silence great art of c. 1871
wants leisure 1840
who love good c. happiest people in world 5567

CONVERSATIONALIST
brilliant c. talks to you about yourself 5112

CONVERSATIONS
Jesus Christ, c. sweet 6352
Silences real c. between friends 4268
without weather, how to start c. 1841

CONVERSE
makes sharp the glittering wit 10534
May yet hold friendly c. with my God 8814
oratory of heart to c. with God 7541

with God refreshes, restores, renews minds 8857

CONVERSING
with greatest minds of the past 3027

CONVERSION
a change of heart 1909
a deep heart work 1895
better just after our c. 1347
calm of conviction 1900
Christian more than an instantaneous c. 1269
Christian partner of God in c. 3327
critics suspicious of c. not in refrigerator 3052
entrance into liberty 1900
forces of a soul at war with itself 1900
gigantic celebration in unseen world 3326
goes throughout man, mind, life 1895
may occur in an instant 1897
more abundant life 1900
not acceptance of creed 1909
people can tell you day, hour of c. 1314
process long, arduous 1897
slaying of beast within 1900
so profound theologians ponder depth 1896
so simple smallest child can be converted 1896
story of c. story of blessed defeat 1899
substituted autosuggestion for c. 5808
turn involves two things 1894
turning around 1898
without discipleship implied 2815

CONVERSIONS
many services but few c. 9017

CONVERT
knows God loves him for what God is 1904
most dejected, reluctant c. in all England 9829
not one man at church, another at home 1908
to c. rebellious will cost God crucifixion 2134
will accept c. even on such terms 9829

CONVERTED
If 10 percent holy, world c. before year's end 5750
jostled aside to make room for c. playboy 4410
Kindness has c. more sinners 6648
not necessary to tell where or how 1903
People who think once c. all happy 1309
shamefully exploit c. celebrity 11666
usually not too well c. 4410

CONVERTS
Buddhism c. without theology 3301
church incubator to hatch c. 1393
Hinduism doesn't try 3301
Islam c. by force 3301
Time c. knowledge into wisdom 11323

CONVEY
cannot c. to others, can but use for ourselves 6178
eyes c. the soul 3563
thy love to thy friends 4222

CONVICT
Arrested for being Christian, evidence to c. 1292
Nothing will c. like way we respond 3319

CONVICTED
of sin finds gospel attractive 5108

CONVICTION
Faith is inner c. overwhelmed by God 3681
God plants where c. brought brokenness 888
God promised to be active among men 5724
If leave church with no c. 12106
immortality a deep c. 6102
not open to c, not qualified for discussion 2903
not the road of mathematical c. 3793
of his own ignorance 737
overwhelming c. nowhere else to go 8822
Rest tranquilly in abiding c. 4747
that God has worked in past history 5724
what happens when gospel preached 5105
without action is worthless 3737

CONVICTIONS
Jesus lived great life c. 6448
Never for sake of peace deny c. 1912
never give in except to c. of honor 8548
people most bigoted have no c. 9186
strength of religious c. 7988
with family hammer out c. 5832

CONVICTS
Spirit of God c. and comforts 5773

CONVINCE
inner voice of God does not try to c. 4967
Nothing will c. like way we respond 3319
voice of subconscious tries to c. 4967
with many words c. of God's power 11991

CONVINCED
he deserves hell 5668

If God has spoken, why is universe not c. 4963
man c. against his will 9179
of the reality of their faith 7472
people open to Christian message 3310
soul is indestructible 6094

CONVINCING
experience of knowing is c. 5809
the longer I live the more c. proof 4942

CONVOY
vessels that sail without c. 2664

COOK
Govern family as c. fish 3868
should marry woman who would rather shop than c. 7656

COOL
At c. of day, with God I walk 7452
God knows how to burn, then to gently c. 7951
gospel like c. air in heat of summer 5097
Hot tempers c. friendships 9488
If interest in work of others c. 7187
One c. judgment worth thousand hasty councils 6587
Or c. one pain 6922
Self-control, keep c. while someone making it hot for you 9961

COOLS
Forgiveness c. sting 4075

COOPERATE
God asks us to c. with him 4507
wanting to c. with God's own purposes 4468

COOPERATION
body teamwork 846
God must have c. of his people 11269

COPE
forces we cannot calculate or c. with 5458
Happiness ability to c. with conflict 5526
If stable at heart can normally c. 2737
Integrity essential to c. with difficulties 6310
Peace is ability to c. with conflict 8458

COPPER
gold in house, looking for c. outside 5840

COPY
A c. Lord, of thine 5620
Do not try to c. other people 9983
no other models but themselves to c. 3451

CORD
Cut any c. but the one that binds me to thy heart 9080
No c. can draw so forcibly 7279
With thee, one full responsive vibrant c. 7928

CORDS
Grace binds with stronger c. than duty 5211

CORE
Acceptance of one's worth c. of personality 9980
afraid to the very c. of being 3824
apple is eaten, c. sticks in throat 10385
God probes the c, tests the root 7862
God strikes at c. of motivations 7863
To get at the c. of God at his greatest 7543

CORN
can't expect justice from chickens 6605
Christian like ripening c. 6030
If a man has good c. to sell 2776
shall have c. to sell, keep 3115

CORNER
playing religious games in one c. 10124
round the c. a new road or secret gate 8239
unexpected around the c. 4318

CORNERS
From the four c. of the sky 6598
old brush knows all the corners 251
windows bringing light on dark c. 3019

CORNERSTONE
before earth's c. was placed 2123
what seems misfit becomes c. 10901

CORONARY
nothing enviable about a c. breakdown 9533

CORPORATE
frozen in c. or collective cold 3045

CORPORATENESS
of mass movement 10526

CORPORATIONS
Youth going to take over c. 12160

CORPSE
body without soul, a c. 5088
drunken man a living c. 334
like cover of old book 2204
man without faith, a walking c. 3791
of the universe 483
Revival, inrush of Spirit into body that threatens to become c. 9749
will appear in new, more beautiful edition 2204

CORPSES
childhood dies, c. called adults 1135

CORRECT
a little 9489
By obedience led to c. errors 8110
easier to be critical than c. 2067
few disciples allowed to appear c. 11791
God calls for volunteers to c. evil 3378
gospel can c. everything needing correction 5094
If c. at every point 3846
laws God gives us, we would c. 10425
look at Jesus to c. blurry vision 4489
Morality c. thinking within 7832
Only one type of worry c. 12074
Repentance chance to c. what man left crooked 9596
what use is c. time 2803

CORRECTED
another world where wrongs are c. 5678
No one ever c. by a sarcasm 6645
to worry about things that cannot be c. 7793
wait upon God, shall be c. 5440

CORRECTION
as place of c. world not so bad 5535
does much 3130
gospel can correct everything needing c. 5094
more harm by example than good by c. 3914

CORRECTIONS
Disappointments c. of heaven 2796

CORRECTNESS
Martyrdom, intensity not c. of belief 1911

CORRECTS
From errors of others wise man c. his own 3257
never c. mistakes, never wiser tomorrow 8195

CORRESPOND
power of service c. to life of prayer 10192

CORRESPONDING
inner attitude of love, honesty 6811

CORRODE
to allow pain to c. your spirit is to have chosen 8264

CORRODING
anxieties engendered by success are c. 10817

CORRUPT
Christ executed by c. church 2171
majority let experience c. 3534

teach to esteem more highly those who think alike 3032
there sits a judge no king can c. 4716

CORRUPTED
justice, without being c. by process necessary 6623

CORRUPTIBLE
I go from c. to incorruptible crown 2304

CORRUPTION
Christians preserve society from c. 1252
Evil c. of substance 3357
indifference toward neighbor assaulted by c. 6163
is a tree whose branches are 2907
last c. of degenerate man 11858
of best becomes the worst 10718
one strand of faith amongst c. 3749

CORRUPTIONS
full of stains and c. 9852
like the air before the sun shines 9852
opposed to c. of Christianity 1238

CORRUPTS
Flattery c. receiver, giver 4048
rust c. iron, envy c. man 3207

COSMETIC
no c. for beauty like happiness 5563

COSMIC
dream opens into primeval c. night 2971
fight of c. proportions has started 3400
God not a c. bellboy 4543
Salvation is c. 9817
to remake history by c. creative event 5711

COSMOS
mysteries of him who made vast c. 7944
One may understand the c, never the ego 9352

COST
Any c. dear Lord, by any road 4428
cross path chosen after counting c. 2103
Five words c. Zacharias silence 11412
Forgiveness saves c. of hatred 4089
God everything to make it possible for us to pray 8773
Good words worth much, c. little 11987
happiness overlooked because doesn't c. anything 5542
laud character, but climb to top at any c. 6068
never c. disciple to follow Jesus 2823

sacrifice of praise will always c. something 8724

talk about c. when in love an insult 2823

that gives value 8563

to convert rebellious wills c. God crucifixion 2134

to give and not to count the c. 9113

what it may, this is my prayer 8818

will c. intense narrowing of interests 9831

COSTLY
Experience a c. school 3519

True love always c. 7328

COSTS
Beware of emphasis on what prayer c. us 8773

Cheerfulness c. nothing, yet is beyond price 5612

courtesy c. nothing, conveys much 1944

Death c. a life 2263

Discipleship c. everything we have 2832

Each ounce of dross c. its ounce of gold 2641

good word c. no more than bad 3128

If obedience c. your life, pay it 1722

Ministry that c. nothing accomplishes nothing 10173

Politeness goes far, c. nothing 1945

service that counts is service that c. 10196

smile c. nothing but creates much 10494

value in what it c. us 11664

What you get free c. too much 11668

COTTAGE
Better c. where merry than palace where one weeps 5821

Bible comes into c. 645

Death knocks at poor man's c. 2361

soul's dark c, batter'd and decay'd 7701

COUCH
Be first in field, last to c. 2769

wraps the drapery of his c. 2203

COUGH
We c. to clear our throats 5627

COUNCIL
Peace not made at c. tables 8457

COUNCILS
One cool judgment worth thousand hasty c. 6587

COUNSEL
children afraid to go to parents for c. 8311

Christ wrote no book yet words c. everywhere 6394

give audience to all who ask c. 5381

Give neither c. nor salt unless asked 258

in midday give c. 6928

not of him who makes you laugh 264

Prayer is to enter into God's c. 8909

prefer to c. a woman 19

Seek c. of him who makes you weep 264

COUNSELOR
Christ a C. to advise his people 6370

Despair an evil c. 2579

talked to God as one might talk to a c. 7526

COUNSELORS
Wait for wisest of c, time 11347

COUNSELS
God governed all things by c. of his will 4904

in heavenly places see God's c. 2809

keep in reserve God's deep c. 4322

COUNT
amid all change things we can c. on 4643

atom proof little things c. 8663

each affliction God's messenger 5331

Gratitude born in hearts that c. mercies 5244

I c. life just a stuff 6908

I c. that part of life lost 6909

if we want some things to c. 7714

it the greatest sin to prefer life to honor 6883

the acts you have done 107

Things that c. most in life 7039

things we can always c. on 4643

time by heartthrobs 1056

to give and not to c. the cost 9113

When rogue kisses you, c. your teeth 2478

you may c. that day well spent 107

COUNT DOWN
When angry, c. before blasting off 407

COUNTED
faster we c. our spoons 5899

usually things that cannot be c. 7039

COUNTENANCE
Flowers have an expression of c. 8004

no grace in solemn c. 1090

smiles soften c. by tenderness 10500

COUNTERACTED
sin must die right out, not be c. 9841

COUNTERCLAIMED
claimed by God, c. by Satan 4918

COUNTERFEIT
man can c. love, faith, hope 5989

Satan cannot c. peace of God 5396

Slander like c. money 10465

very difficult to c. humility 5989

COUNTLESS
grope and totter and make c. mistakes 9851

hear c. tongues 1368

times each day a mother does what no one else can do 7844

COUNTRY
as music is, so are people of c. 7889

Death not going to strange c. 2249

death, undiscover'd c. 2388

devil's c. begins where men eat men 4913

God's c. begins where men serve 4913

great deal of unmapped c. within us 8669

heaven is the Christian's c. 5638

heaven not an unknown c, Christ is there 5659

may be called upon to die for it 10525

My c. is in every clime 4869

My c. right or wrong like saying 7980

needs dirtier fingernails, cleaner minds 7775

ought to seek, work for good of c. 10525

strength of c. is strength of convictions 7988

things wrong with the c, total of things wrong with individuals 7989

warranted by laws of c. 4115

When good people in any c. 7991

COUNTS
Birth c. for nothing if virtue not there 11682

God who c. the tears 10877

humble man c. blessings 6035

isn't the fact you're hurt that c. 11446

may be other half that c. 2770

never needing to say is what c. 4268

proud man c. newspaper clippings 6035

Service that c. is service that costs 10196

what you learn after you know it all that c. 7691

COUPLE
deaf husband, blind wife happy c. 7589

married for trivial reasons 2922

COUPLED
obedience to law c. with love, honesty 6811

COURAGE
ask for c. that endures 1921
Atheists put on false c. 476
Bible, story of goose-bump c. 1936
brother! Do not stumble 5995
by bringing high c. of devout soul 4974
can support man in fear 1923
cannot answer for c. if never in danger 1930
certainty of divine participation gives c. 6277
charity is c. when misfortune falls 1085
children sing to keep up c. 476
children whistle to keep up c. 476
Christ promises joy and c. 159
eccentricity proportional to c. 1007
fear of God, spur to c. 3993
foolish actions require c. to confess 1603
Give me such c. I can scale 1927
God planted c. in soul 3973
Had bred but c, love, and valiant will 4921
Have c. to appear poor 8679
have c. to believe firmly 4747
Have plenty of c. 1924
have teeth fixed 1941
if show true selves suddenly would lose c. 10006
in your own 6657
is fear that has said its prayers 1919
is mastery of fear 1920
is resistance to fear 1920
Jesus wants to give c. 3316
joy, strength, c. are with thee 8867
Life's perils for our c. 6995
lost, much lost 9263
love gives c. to the cowardly 7260
man of c. not afraid of truth 6845
man without c, knife without edge 1917
Many would be cowards if enough c. 1949
Nature herself gives us c. 2338
not absence of fear 1920
Oftimes test of c. is to live rather than die 7009
One man with c. makes majority 1932
prayer will give fresh c. 8769
Problems create c. and wisdom 202
rarest sort of c. 42
ready to renew your life with c. 9896
Reconciliation demands c. 9431
Renew the c. that prevails 1933
requires more c. to suffer than die 10856
souls have lost their c. 9059
talent lost for want of c. 1916
test of c. when in minority 1938
Then your c. should appear 8558
to change things which should be changed 9060
to endure riddle of inequality 6277
to forget 8827
to love, c. to suffer 1939
whose c. never ceased 11175
Why not go out on limb 1940
withhold not c. by which we can conquer 9090
wouldn't have c. to ask blessings of heaven 826

COURAGEOUS
blood transfusion for c. living 5804
cracked chimes of c. human spirit 7171
pray for strength 1937
step carry us through fears 3982

COURAGEOUSLY
to accept bitter truth 1719

COURSE
cannot be tolerant of any other c. 9965
concern for c. of history not irrelevant 5724
determine future c. of nation 8360
fight deviation from c. Jesus set for us 9965
find this to be God's usual c. 9037
Forgiveness is required c. 4076
having thus chosen our c. 1918
If c. is right, take it because it is right 6291
if c. is wrong avoid though lose life as consequence 6291
of true anything never runs smooth 2747
sets c. for how we live in seen world 3812
shall not travel an uncharted c. 5945
time when we must choose c. to follow 2491
whole c. of our lives out of joint 7571

COURSES
no c. in peace 8450

COURT
Corn can't expect justice from c. of chickens 6605
Day of Judgment c. in perpetual session 6589
ever has about him a silent c. 1684

COURTEOUS
be as c. to man as to picture 1947
Be c. to all 4218
give man advantage of good light 1947

COURTESY
cheapest of pleasures 1944
costs nothing, conveys much 1944
gentleness, gracious c. 4402
key to success 10799
like mercy, twice blessed 1944
Nothing lost by c. 1944
pleases him who gives 1944
pleases him who receives 1944
with c. receive God's messenger 160
With c. receive him 5331

COURTROOM
resolved to try Bible as in c. 744

COURTS
Christ tore through the temple c. like a mad man 6392

COUSINS
Much speaking and lying are c. 6854

COVENANT
rainbow, God's glowing c. 9393

COVER
blemishes of friend 4183
Man cannot c. what God would reveal 9709

COVERAGE
where is c. our mothers rightfully deserve 7844

COVERED
with a crust like crackling which broke easily 11750

COVERS
Humility c. our good deeds 6005
veil which c. face of future 4330

COVET
easy to c. another man's success 10788
nothing that is your neighbor's 8472

COVETED
Old age, though despised, is c. 8164

COVETOUS
man ever in want 5324
man pines in plenty 5325
never c, yet exacting usury 4954
Riches have made more men c. 11848

COVETOUSNESS
church says c. a deadly sin 10086
does but lie in her cradle 10092
industrious with c. 9041
its daughter injustice 5313
its friend violence 5313
its mother unlawful desire 5313
sin may spell c. but is some form of "me" 9916
than c. has made men rich 11848
wants infused into us by c. 2861

COW
Some people see God as they see a c. 4801

COWARD
Give me the c. heart 4530
if I saw God's truth attacked, and remained silent 99

No c. soul is mine 3765
seeks release from pressure 1937
sneaks to death 10948
This c. with pathetic voice 2583
wicked is a c. 3996
You've been a c. in the fight 3174

COWARDICE
asks, Is it safe 1679
different names for c. 4115
easy c. of surrender to conformity 6216
Fear has use, c. none 1048
fear nothing except c. 8472
principles protection against c. 1951
Reconciliation is not c. 9431
surest protection against temptation 1950
Take patience too far, it's c. 8409
wonder if c. makes us give tips 1637

COWARDLY
devil c. 2678
goal of fear, to create c. souls 3971
love gives courage to the c. 7260
When feelings are c. ask to have them altered 3051

COWARDS
makes c. out of men 6282
Many would be c. if enough courage 1949
we are nation of social c. 1642

COWERED
disciples c. in darkness 2132

COWS
dairymaid can milk c. to glory of God 3082

CRABBY
even for those who tend to be c. and short-tempered 7304

CRACK
world will always keep eyes on spot where c. was 9612

CRACKED
chimes of courageous human spirit 7171
reputation easily c, never well mended 9615
When wall c, fall will be speedy 9257

CRACKLING
laughter of sin as c. of burning thorns 10393

CRADLE
And God in c. lies 6129
covetousness does but lie in her c. 10092
Greet in c. our Savior 1375
Satan rocks c. at devotions 2663

CRAFTSMAN
planned, gifted, positioned on earth by Master C. 10004

CRAFTY
men condemn studies 2996

CRAM
do you c. heavens to overflowing 4854

CRAMMED
Earth's c. with heaven 1710

CRAMP
God did not send his Son to c. our life-style 9558

CRAMPING
restrictions of hard work 6386

CRAMPS
anything that c. my prayer life 7036

CRANES
Sparrows should not dance with c. 9493

CRANKS
Old c. have practiced all their lives 5503
Without c. world would not progress 9318

CRASH
towers fall with heavier c. who higher soar 9216

CRASHED
a hammer c. in heaven 2123

CRAVE
misers c. money 7826
specific rules so can know precisely how to behave 6810

CRAVES
ear c. familiar 844
eye c. the novel 844
man who c. more is poor 2868
Who c. for ease, rest, joys 2583

CRAVING
deepest c. to be appreciated 3141
luxuries of world cannot satisfy c. of lonely 7176
Man's c. is for the spiritual 9546
more Spirit of God touches our spirit, greater our c. 5764
to be appreciated 440

CRAWLED
Lord I c. across the barrenness to you 4653

CRAWLING
How can we little c. creatures 4673

CRAYOLAS
more art done with c. 2023

CRAZE
generation characterized by c. for subjective 4017

CRAZY
love c. sayings in New Testament 1216
world where your message is c. tale 592
Youth a c. time of life 12161

CREAK
devil's boots don't c. 2693

CREAKS
Cheerfulness enables us to work with fewer c. 1093

CREAM
not well for man to pay c, live skim milk 8856

CREAM PUFF
sin treated like c. instead of rattlesnake 10345

CREATE
a God in our image 6467
Being Father made God want to c. 1978
cannot c. experience 3552
Could blind chance c. 1958
goal of fear, to c. cowardly, joyless souls 3971
God can c. something surpassingly good 219
if fail to c. harmony 580
image try to c. in minds of others 9950
image try to c. in my own mind 9950
No man can c. faith in himself 3766
philosophers c. God in their image 8590
Problems c. courage and wisdom 202
restless urge to c. 4643
right to c. alternatives of choice 4155
silence 10271
Six things requisite to c. happy home 5848
Thou didst c. the world—'twas thy proud mandate 4592

CREATED
Adam c. to be friend, companion of God 758
All c. things but crumbs from table of God 1955
All men c. equal 3246
among ends for which individual c. 6169
Among first things c. 7886
angel c. by God 354
Before God c. universe 4879
Clouds of doubt c. 2931
death, best of all things c. 2231
everything c. has need of God 4452
God c. free beings 3370
God c. man because 4535
God c. men to be holy 5757
God c. us free to disbelieve in him 11590
God would have c. me otherwise 6186
God would never have c. angel, man 5020
God would not have c. man to exist only for a day 6104

God would not have c. us without plan 5398

God's love can enfold whole c. world 4760

God's truth judges c. things out of love 4914

He who c. us without our help 9796

Hell c. for devil and his angels 5686

Man c. a God addict 7496

Man trampled by same forces he has c. 5975

never knowing happiness for which c. 5565

Of all c. things, loveliest are 1120

Origin can apply only to things c. 4613

response of c. personalities to Creating Personality, God 9543

soul c. in a place between time, eternity 10671

supernaturally c. for a supernatural work 10206

Thank God for having c. this world 5678

things originated somewhere at some time 4613

To ear of God everything he c. makes music 8743

Truths are not c, they exist 11581

try to be own masters as if c. ourselves 5570

When Jehovah c. world it was good 3205

Why else were individuals c. 6169

Without free will man not c. in image of God 4158

world a parenthesis in eternity 1968

You are I were c. for joy 6571

CREATES

cannot find, c. means 2624

eternal now c. something new, better 8368

God c. out of nothing, you say 9773

God sees scar, c. star 8278

Judgment c. distance 10162

Kindness in giving c. love 6649

Kindness in thinking c. profoundness 6649

Kindness in words c. confidence 6649

smile costs nothing but c. much 10494

sorrow c. bond nothing seems able to break 10641

Unity c. strength 11623

when listened to, c. us 1857

woman who c. home creator second only to God 5857

CREATING

angry with God for c. world 481

Hail, Father! Whose c. call 4672

idea of c. hand refers to God 11124

In c, the only hard thing's to begin 2007

kind, c. hand of our God 10487

Power more easily manifested in destroying than c. 8712

Selfishness aims at c. absolute uniformity 10079

wisdom which can enter men's suffering 10884

world of automata, hardly worth c. 4120

youth a spirit of c. life 12183

CREATION

a silent process 1956

a thousand forests in one acorn 1969

All c. God gives to humankind 3191

Arising from c. his praise, echo clear 8029

begin new c. for my life 2798

Bible, rooted in depths of c. 750

body is God's c. 841

can never be fathomed 1975

chime in with harmonies of c. 7921

confounds me, surpasses my conception 4603

contemplate God's power in immensity of c. 4581

continues into vast unknown 1975

essentially subjective 2972

evil, that dark cloud that hangs over c. 3350

Fiction, c. of human mind 11574

Genesis account brief 1972

glory of c, infinite diversity 1973

God created some for sheer fun 1961

God is all in all, he made us of himself 1962

God's c, overflowing of love, delight 1978

God's justice permits c. to punish 3191

human being, ingenious assembly of plumbing 833

involves limitation 4117

is God's work 4911

Lord came down to the lowest reach of c. 9437

Magnificient, his six days' work, a world 1967

more skill, design than works of man 1964

need Lord for c. of a home 5819

Nothing in all c. so like God as stillness 10258

Nothing supplied for God 1975

of thousand forests in one acorn 8664

Of thy c, finished, yet renewed 1966

profusions on profligacies with vigor 1971

Remind us not to waste, litter, pollute 9117

science strives unceasingly to penetrate 1975

show so grand, beautiful, exciting 6092

soul would take its place below the whole c. 7971

That was a great day 1982

the Father, work of c. 11426

the richness of your c. 9117

to chime in with harmonies of c. 10665

unlawful to teach theory that denies c. 1986

We are God's property by c. 7552

whole show is on fire 1971

Whose least c. fills with awe 11628

Why blame the brute c. 10361

CREATION'S

blot, C. blank 4374

loftiest symphony 12

CREATIVE

cannot become c. without solitude 10579

dialogue in which c. inspiration sought 4160

eternally c. and recreative love 10562

force fills heaven, earth 1997

God's c. method is change 4469

knew loneliness was when c. mood would work 7141

Listening a c. force 1857

Loving is c. 7277

men, women are in the church 1998

out of despair by c. effort of God 2613

positive word becomes c. force 12001

responsible for c. efforts 1712

thinking abdicated to enemy 3027

to remake history by cosmic c. event 5711

Without fantasy no c. work comes to birth 2024

CREATIVELY

don't want us free to express love c. in world 6824

CREATIVENESS

Joy of c. should be ours 2002

CREATIVITY

basic attribute of God 1999

Confession brings to light underdeveloped c. 1596

identical with God's uniqueness 1999

Intellectual sophistication can dry up c. 6325

is satisfaction for those who give 2018

kissed on forehead, high heels invented 2003

Rigidity restrains c, blocking progress 6818

underdeveloped c. of our deeper layers 1596

CREATOR

a being only a C. could put here 11124

able to thank C. for way he made us 9993

All I have seen teaches me to trust the C. 11465

death brings contemplation of C. 2353

demon even if sits in church praising the C. 9631

endowed by C. with certain unalienable rights 3246

everything perfect from hands of C. 3193

God is c. of minds to receive his fulness 4514

God is our C. 2002

God, omniscient C. 1520

God, uncreated C. 4595

ground came from C. 3199

I am as my C. made me 9987

into primordial night to make light 1980

listening to four-year-old talk 3918

men of same earth by same C. 3225

more I study nature, more amazed at C. 8040

of earth is owner 1970

that great event which C. has in view 4898

The great C. from his work return'd 1967

To make God a momentary C. 11652

trust C. for all I have not seen 11465

woman who creates home c. second only to God 5857

worth of an individual endowed by the C. 10001

CREATOR-CREATURE

Salvation is bringing back to normal the C. relation 9807

CREATORS

Therefore we are c. 2002

CREATURE

every c. declaring name, will of God 12042

only c. they would segregate is skunk 5963

CREATUREHOOD

God knows all c. and all creatures 4881

CREATURES

God draws us by his c. 7949

God has delegated power to his c. 4821

God has no need of his c. 4452

God in likeness of most defenseless of c. 6154

God knows all creaturehood and all c. 4881

How can we little, crawling c. 4673

of habit 5503

senses see action of the c. 3794

spiritual c. walk the earth 362

that worked like machines 4120

To believe God made lower c. for prey 6280

world in which c. do good or harm 4132

CREDENCE

to man's hope of life beyond the grave 5711

CREDIBLE

message needs c. messenger 987

To be c, we must be truthful 6319

CREDIT

Conscience gets c. that belongs to cold feet 1665

take no c. for generosity 4387

who don't care who gets the c. 10134

CREED

Christ never asks anyone to understand a c. 6431

Christianity, not a c. 1172

confesses three persons, one divine essence 11426

conversion not acceptance of c. 1909

Enough for faith or c. today 4118

fanaticism today, fashionable c. tomorrow 3911

filled out, inspired by Christian love 2030

good as far as it goes 2026

If you have a Bible c. it is well 2030

is road, street 2022

Jesus never asks us to devote to c. 2836

Live thy c. 994

Not, what was his c. 7423

note of greatness in your c. 3042

of church, interesting, exciting, dramatic 1205

only c. worth twopence 2031

out of own experience of Christ 2031

put c. into deed 1011

question to be asked, Is it true 2032

the whole of the good man's c. 2028

worthless if it doesn't take us to Christ 2026

would stifle me that shelters you 2027

CREEDS

Believe me, than in half the c. 2957

Christian not to be consistent to c. 2025

human hopes and human c. 2029

life of truth from death of c. 11504

Volumes of angry controversy 2033

CREEP

Events c. or fly as God pleases 4820

Vices c. in under name of virtues 10413

CREEPING

Give me the little c. treasons 4530

Soft drowsy hours c. 1123

sort of c. comes over skin 2637

CREEPS

slander flies as well as c. 10456

Vice quickly c. in 11725

CREMATORIA

sky still streaked with smoke of c. 3416

CRIED

aloud for Holy Spirit to deliver me 5781

and c, "Give me" 8878

don't let us forget we c. 6743

CRIES

And c. it shall be done 3717

false repentance, c. out against something else 9601

Like a weak infant c. 6129

man who truly repents c. out against his heart 9601

CRIME

allows oppression, shares the c. 1484

although with truth speakest evil that also is c. 11497

Destiny a tyrant's authority for c. 2619

germ in every man 2034

guilty is he who merely meditates a c. 5490

high c. rate traceable to disintegration of home 5858

holds the ladder as bad as thief 2036

inherent in human nature 2034

Not failure, but low aim is c. 3610

of murdering whole nations 11776

Popularity is c. when sought 3858

Poverty is not a c. 8688

profits by c. commits it 2037

Purposeless mother of c. 2039

Sin a c. against love 10355

sins as much who holds the bag 2035

So many shapes 2040

type of writing that causes c. 12156

Violence a c. against humanity 11678

What man content with one c. 2041

who allows the oppression shares the c. 5962

Whoever profits by the c. is guilty 5494

CRIMES

conclude c. committed because God wills 3349

gold, what c. thy tyrant power has
caused 11803
History little more than register of
c. 5719
My thoughts, my words, my c.
forgive 9048
Success consecrates the foulest c.
10803

CRIMINAL
alcohol, greatest c. in history 331
Christ died a common c. 2126
stuff that makes the c. makes the
saint 8667

CRIMINALS
Sainthood can find good in c.
9778

CRIMSON
will they remember c. 1368

CRIPPLE
him, you have a Sir Walter Scott
161

CRIPPLED
Christian work c. by blessings,
traditions of the past 10124

CRISES
Christ not driven by c. 4425
discover what you are 2044
force us to think 2043
God steps in to comfort, teach
2042
Great c. show how great our
resources are 8659
refine life 2044
what c. would face you tomorrow
if your prayers answered 8891
What we call c, God ignores
10721

CRISIS
Any idiot can face a c. 6876
Character exhibited, not made in
c. 1002
Chinese symbol for 2048
Every new adjustment c. in
self-esteem 9984
Growth depends on obedience in
c. 2046
hell reserved for those who in
moral c. maintain neutrality
8074
less likely to faint or fail in c.
5226
love demands toughness in c.
2045
most daring course often safest
2047
one thing to go through a c.
grandly 7129
opportunity riding dangerous wind
2048
way you endure more important
514
Wherever Jesus went he produced
a c. 6516

CRISIS-PRODUCING
Jesus, most c. individual 6516

CRITERION
insist upon Resurrection as c. of
orthodoxy 6604
meaningful experience c. for truth
3493

CRITIC
dream theater where dreamer c.
2972
Holy Ghost in true position of c.
2078
learn knack of listening like
Christian instead of c. 10110

CRITICAL
anger natural reaction to c. word
10003
attitude and saint impossible 2056
Bible has passed through c. fires
646
easier to be c. than correct 2067
What God reveals as c. moments
10721
what people think of Jesus
because of me is c. 9627
whether take things for granted or
with gratitude 5268

CRITICISM
A malignant deity 2050
advice conceals veiled c. 256
advice, if honest, is also c. 253
arouses resentment 2055
beef too much find himself in stew
2068
blame man who is silent 2080
blame man who speaks too little
2080
blame man who speaks too much
2080
Boredom a form of c. 2053
camel never sees own hump 2075
Candor brightest gem of c. 5870
cares neither for praise nor c.
1681
church open to c. 1430
claws like a cat 2050
Do not remove fly with hatchet
2058
do not run down God's people
576
Find grain of truth in c. 2059
Gossip leads to c. 5135
hurts sense of importance 2055
if isn't true, forget it 2071
if true mend your ways 2071
is dangerous 2055
is futile 2055
kills love 5135
live with c, learn to condemn
1114
looked only upon herself 2050
makes man justify himself 2055
most would rather be ruined by
praise than saved by c. 8741
nagging, form of continual c.
2069
pointing fingers, rarely hold out
hands 2073
puts man on defensive 2055

should be gentle enough to nourish
2057
sieve to needle: hole in head 2079
Silence sometimes severest c. 2074
stifling power of c. 2054
swallow grain of truth in c. 2059
To avoid c. do, say, be nothing
2082
will not lead soul to Christ 2085
wounds pride 2055

CRITICIZE
cannot c. New Testament 754
Do not fear when enemies c. you
3158
if painful to c. safe 2064
if pleasure, hold your tongue 2064
right to c. if heart to help 2060
right to c. must be earned 267
those who encourage more than c.
3142

CRITICIZED
And so it c. each flower 2052
for not being Christian enough
1342
God for men of color 1495
not more worthless if c. 1681
through fear of being c. people tell
lies 6851

CRITICIZES
another needs to be outstanding
2061
New Testament c. you 754
Rigidity c. future for not flying
6818

CRITICIZING
flatter own virtue by c. the sinful
5029
for many church not worth c.
1446
man who is forever c. wife's
judgment 7655

CRITICS
Children more need of models
than c. 8286
church has many c. 1432
claim Bible fiction 679
claim Bible forgery 679
claim Bible has unfilled promises
679
Discouraged people don't need c.
3066
misunderstand nature of
Christianity 1188
suspicious of conversion not in
refrigerator 3052

CRITICISM
most would rather by ruined by
praise than saved by c. 8741

CROOKED
cannot make straight lines out of
our c. lot 4885
law tells me how c. I am 5232
paths look straighter at end 2374
Repentance chance to correct
what man left c. 9596
stick will have c. shadow 988

CROP

field rested gives bountiful c. 9686
in one year c. to make up for ten 889

CROSS

a fathomless answer, the C. of Christ 9398
accept Christ's c. as our c. 3335
accomplishment of salvation 3582
all-absorbing interest 2111
already raised in Bethlehem 1365
arms stretch out to limitless reaches 2167
at the c. no racial barriers 1491
Bear patiently c. of grief, pain 1502
beatification of martyrdom 2118
believer's c. no longer suffering 2103
believer's c. social nonconformity 2103
beyond the c. manifestion of presence 2138
beyond the c. resurrection 2138
breadth, former, following ages 2154
can't c. chasm in two small jumps 3650
Carry the c. patiently 2088
Christ brings his c. his presence 2120
Christ calls to carry c. 3300
Christ nailed to c. with arms wide open 6393
Christian is on the throne until on the c. 2821
Comfort yourself with God who nails to c. 2091
common ground between c, reason is impossible 1239
crystallized point in history 2148
Daily my c. for thee 2098
death of death 2118
defeat of sin 2118
defiance of pain 2118
desire to carry his c. 10719
Desperately we call for c. our own size 2116
destroyed equation religion equals happiness 2151
destroyed formula that might is right 2166
devil shuns the c. 11893
difference between power, love 2156
end of path chosen after counting cost 2103
ere foot of Love will c. threshold 4775
Evangelism is c. in heart of God 3305
Every pious mood stripped off before c. 2160
everywhere in wait for you 2105
exposure of bleeding love on the c. 9741
few follow ignominy of c. 2828
few who bear his c. 9268

For the Lord only isolation on the c. 6383
forced to carry the c. 183
gave his heart that mine might be made new 2173
God gives us the c. 2090
God lets himself be pushed on c. 4899
God proved his love on the c. 7173
has disarmed powers 2100
he that has no c. deserves no crown 2112
health of soul 2096
height of virtue 2096
high above opinions of men 2157
hope lies in Man we put on c. 5941
hope of eternal life 2096
hurts us where vulnerable 2092
I lay my whys before your c. 12102
If c. suited us, no longer a c. 2092
If man carries c. beautifully 5252
If you carry the c. willingly 182
If you throw away 183
image and fulfillment of commandments 281
imparts to man power to do all God wants 2172
In the c. of Christ I glory 2133
in the end c. shall carry you 2088
is always ready 2105
is God's truth about us 11531
is health 2096
is heavenly sweetness 2096
is I crossed out 2104
is life 2096
is protection from enemies 2096
is real wood 2147
is rough, deadly, effective 2106
is strength of mind 2096
is the great central point 6424
it will carry you 183
Jesus came to resurrection through the c., not around it 5768
Jesus had joy, even under shadow of the c. 6538
Jesus has few bearers of c. 2828
Jesus, no evasion of the c. 8819
joy of the Spirit 2096
Just as Christian came up with the c. 9803
key to healing 2145
key to life 2145
key to peace 2145
legend, reality intersect 2150
length to heaven, earth 2154
Life bears love's c. 7204
little delighted with the c. 10312
Lord promised c. and scars 2102
lost control when picked up c. 2111
love meeting evil with good 2146
love meeting hate with love 2146
love of God, arms extended on c. 4781

love of the c. must swallow up personal grief 5356
made clear authority is service 2166
man always on c. cannot be happy 2087
man with c. no longer controls destiny 2111
man's self is greatest c. 9919
manger as uneasy as his c. 6489
meeting negatives with positives 2146
men ignore meaning of c. 2122
minus turned into a plus 2119
most extreme of all human conditions 6277
must flee it or die upon it 2117
never the right one 2116
No c. for us 2821
no c. no crown 199
no crown wearers who were not c. bearers 216
no escaping the c. 2113
not c. if destroyed only artificial 2109
not what God suddenly became 2163
nothing pleasant about it 2097
O show thy c. to me 2228
of Christ an offense to the world 6317
of Christ God's last, endless word 2153
of Christ is Christ's glory 2152
of Christian, an experience 2108
of Jesus Christ a revelation 2108
of Jesus Christ and his baptism express same thing 9437
of Jesus, only one of ten will talk about 2174
open house for universe 2155
orgasm has replaced c. as focus of longing 10233
Our c. and his 2135
our personal touch-point with Lord 10930
overwhelming interference 2111
pain involved in doing will of God 2107
passion of our Lord did not end on the c. 2164
perfection of holiness 2096
picture of death 2145
picture of suffering 2145
picture of violence 2145
poetical, almost pleasant 2097
point of c. is point of life 892
possible to be Christ's without c. 2815
presences man with divinity, the Holy Spirit 2172
present glory 2099
put to shame self-assertion of heroism 2166
radiant with glory of meek, gentle spirit 5252
raised at center of marketplace 2131

readjusts a man in conscience, heart to God 2172

reconciling heaven, earth together 2154

refuses the c, remains on throne 2821

religion put Christ on the c. 9541

results in meaningless c. 1239

resurrection follows 2087

revealed God in suffering 2143

revealed God in weakness 6471 2143

revealed goodness not enough 2144

sacrifice with imperishable dignity 2166

seems harmful 2116

seems humiliating 2116

seems intolerable 2116

seems mean 2116

shows how God could become man 2150

shows man become God 2150

Simply to thy. c. I cling 2101

social reality of representing Order to come 2103

sovereignty of Christ from c. new 2166

stands at heart of church 2139

strikes at root of tree 2158

supreme triumph of God 3582

symbol of God's nature 2167

symbol of his greatest suffering 10930

Take the c. he sends as it is 293

take up c. means take stand for Lord 2115

take up c. sounds hard 8108

teach me glory of my c. 2099

that comes our way never right one 2116

the c. gives us God 2090

the ladder to heaven 2149

the only power which can make us truthful 11531

the supreme failure 3582

through defeat of c. God glorified 2519

throw away one c, another may be heavier 183

to c. all opinions come for judgment 2157

to leave your plans at the c. 10048

to repair irreparable 2165

to resist one's c. is to make heavier 2114

tongue, have it nailed to c. 7190

voluntary sacrifice 2118

war is humanity hanging itself on c. of iron 11745

way of life 2146

what God always was, ever shall be 2163

When know the C. no longer afraid of truth 11531

when man on c. with Jesus Christ 2087

where c. preached disarming of powers 2100

where eternity merges with time 2148

where history, life intersect 2150

where time, eternity intersect 2150

whole c. more easily carried than half 1332

will cut into life where it hurts worst 2093

will defeat, bring selfish life to end 2093

will not spare reputation 2093

winepress of c, juice nourishes, strengthens 2095

With every c. comes strength to carry it 8108

women last at the c, first at the altar 11980

world's one, only remedy is c. 2169

CROSS-CARRYING
Christian a pessimist and optimist 8252

CROSSES
After c. and losses, men grow humbler, wiser 5990

blessings in disguise 288

E'en c. from his sovereign hand 288

greatest of all c. is self 2110

ladders that lead to heaven 162

my c. what are they in comparison to sufferings of Christ 10928

refuse those that hurt, refuse all c. 2092

restless anxiety not c. from God 4322

When I consider my c. I shame myself 10928

which he sends, sacrifices he demands 4688

which we make for ourselves 4322

CROSSING
Death is but c. the world 7319

hasn't time to stop at railroad c. 5589

street when light red 4094

CROSSROADS
are down here 1151

crucified at c. so cosmopolitan 2131

To stand at c. requires strength 1137

CROW
tried to emulate partridge's gait but forgot his own 1644

whitewashed c. shows black again 2462

CROWD
A c. is not company 7122

God speaks to the c. 5385

God thrusts us out of the c. 10564

great man in midst of c. keeps independence 6195

is composed of individuals 6209

Never follow c. if you want c. to follow you 6801

pleasant to not feel the c. 10529

ready to treat great men as lunatics 4393

saints always among unofficial c. 9786

She faced the c. and cried 9947

Until we c. it thence 3700

will seek not the c. but the closet 10567

Women and men in the c. meet, mingle 7150

CROWDED
Not in the clamor of c. street 10794

out of c. city, on to c. highway 9901

world c. with God 4871

CROWDS
in the midst of the c. feel frightfully alone 7124

Jesus, no intention to speak to c. 6451

like donkey believing c. cheering him 9217

love to pool their misery 10515

not going to heaven because I've preached to c. 5653

Our Adversary majors in c. 121

Silence isolates us from the c. 10515

CROWN
all making a c. out of daily lives 7073

cannot have c. without conflict 1633

Christ had no c. 6433

Christ in you that wins the c. 6381

Christ sought c. of thorns 2152

Christ wore c. of thorns that thou mightest wear c. of glory 6393

death brings love's c. 7204

either a c. of love or a thorny c. 7073

from corruptible to incorruptible c. 2304

God has all happiness to c. you 4696

God is each virtue's c. 11687

God tests that he may c. 11096

he that has no cross deserves no c. 2112

He whose c. shines brightest 6004

His hair was like a c. 6470

is in my heart, not on my head 1808

martyrs, when the joyful c. is given 7672

my c. is call'd content 1808

no c. wearers who were not cross bearers 216

no cross, no c. 199

of achievement is c. of thorns 10849

of all crowns was one of thorns 10613

of golden, divine love 7073

of the home is godliness 5851

Old age, c. of life 8166
Quiet mind richer than c. 1812
studded with gems of sacrifice,
adoration 7073
that seldom kings enjoy 1808
thorny c. filled with cruel briars
7073
until time comes to enjoy c. 5912
wear tinsel c. with pride of Caesar
2821

CROWNED

head that once was c. with thorns
is c. with glory now 9697
our utmost wish is c. 7451

CROWNS

crown of all c. was one of thorns
10613
It is the end that c. us 543
Men seek to get c. of gold 2152
suggest share God's splendor,
power, joy 5631
with contentment c. the thought
of worth 4505

CROWS

cock c. but daybreak is from God
2199
Sad the home where hen c, cock
silent 5847
When dove begins to associate
with c. 9517

CRUCIAL

more c. than what we know 6680
Whenever faced with c. decision
5467

CRUCIBLES

If a man can make better c. 2776

CRUCIFIED

As Plato foresaw, the Man was c.
11525
at crossroads so cosmopolitan
2131
at the town garbage heap 2131
Christ c. by Fundamentalists 9541
church to bring c. Christ to world
1405
definitive adjective to describe
Christian life 1161
invalidates success for standard
10814
Lord c. in culture, intellect of men
2125
Only c. preaching can give life
9160
preaching can come only from c.
man 9160
sin must be c. 9841
three marks of one who is c. 9846
where cynics talk smut 2131
where soldiers gamble 2131
where thieves curse 2131
world c. Jesus, couldn't stand him
2168

CRUCIFIXION

attitude must be, "We did it"
2159
God did not stop the c. 4931

identified with Christ in c. 2138
most famous death in history 2137
remembered with intensity,
concern 2137
to accept c. with Christ 10048
to convert rebellious will cost God
c. 2134
what c. must have done to human
hand 2132
who flinches from the C. 11779

CRUCIFY

cannot c. my old nature 9836
Christ let me spit upon him, c. him
6503
today people would not c. Christ
6405

CRUDE

Love makes a subtle man out of a
c. one 7260

CRUEL

contacts man has with man 1401
Discipline c. that it may be kind
2839
God at times seems c. 8631
God is too kind to do anything c.
4461
in his hands and feet, the c. scars
9798
pandemonium shouting God is c.
584
parent who does not teach child
to obey is c. 8355
Rebuke is c. in adversity 203
world tough in a thousand c. ways
1211
writhe under tyrannies of c. master
6280

CRUELEST

lies often told in silence 6858

CRUELLY

pain clings c. to us 8271

CRUELTY

a detested sport 28
feeds on tears 29
gentleness is better than c. 6326
isn't softened by tears 29
owes pleasure to another's pain 28
performing gross deeds of c. 4895
power likely coupled with c. 8705
springs from weakness 27
this c. too will end 8445

CRUMB

But just a c. to me 10030

CRUMBLES

Every chain c. in the breath of
prayer 8789
Time c. things 11324

CRUMBLING

in place of c. sand 7448

CRUMBS

created things c. from table of God
1955
will satiate ourselves with c. from
world 12050

CRUSH

greed ruthlessly ready to c. beauty,
life 5327
intimate with God, disloyalty of
friend will not c. 9470
we object to fingers God uses to c.
883

CRUSHED

by sense of powerlessness 5395
diffuse sweetness all around 150
easily c. and fragile 6651
if sarcasm clever enough 6645
In solitude can become c. 10540
on heel of one who c. it 4080
or trodden to the ground 150
Persecution has not c. church
1419
saint is hilarious when c. 2722
Self-esteem can be c. so easily
9994
Truth, c. to earth, shall rise again
11579
Virtue most fragrant when c.
11707
wine must be c. 2820

CRUSHERS

God uses circumstances 883
God uses someone we dislike 883
we object to fingers God uses 883

CRUSHES

That c. into dumb despair 8863
Whatever c. individuality is
dictatorship 6222

CRUSHING

delusion personal gain made by c.
others 7793

CRUTCHES

When all sins go upon c. 10092

CRY

all c. salt tears 11025
Authentic men aren't afraid to c.
3916
begins with a c. and ends with a
groan 7089
Better child c. than father 8284
blues moody, sad and make you c.
7888
easier to c. than change 975
For restful death I c. 2285
grandeur in c. from depths 10676
of desolation live, not recorded
2147
out of the depths must we c. 9020
Poetry makes you c. 8619
Still will I c, I trust in thee 11470
stumbling, broken c. can find its
way to God 8849
Truth c. of all 11571
We must not c. too bitterly 2425
why same thing makes us laugh, c.
10660
will to neither strive nor c. 8430
with no language but a c. 2576
You need not c. very loud 4878

CRYING

An infant c. in the night 2576

born c, live complaining, die disappointed 7075
my face was in his breast—c. 10853
With your calling and c. 1910

CRYSTAL
Thou wouldst behold c. dome above 4708

CRYSTALS
metallurgists build defects into c. 3932
of delight hidden in somber circumstances 10639

CUBIC FOOT
air not sold by c. 3838

CUBIT
Whosoever walks toward God one c. 7573

CUD
Slander c. eschewed by human cattle 10470

CUDDLE
self-pity as an infant 10034

CUES
Sensitivity, listening to c. kids give 8325

CULMINATE
all great purposes of God c. in Christ 5710

CULT
individualism ego c. of one 9952

CULTIVATE
fine art of thanksgiving 11151
habit of receptivity 4537
home, c. valuable things in life 5832
neither a sin nor shame to c. reason 9425
thankful spirit 11139
world is yours, now c. it 3195
your own capabilities 6168

CULTIVATES
Love c. 7216

CULTIVATING
lifetime c. knowledge of God 4702

CULTIVATION
own gift cumulative force of life's c. 6226

CULTURAL
or by seeking to conform to c. mores 8520
society has recreated Jesus in own c. image 6467
when church fails to break c. barrier 1456

CULTURALLY
sermons c. forbidden to talk back 10103

CULTURE
decadent, impersonalized c. 3325
Lord crucified in c. of men 2125

move beyond superficialities of c. 1760
no c. so obsessed with immediacy 7990
When church transcends can transform c. 1457
where self supersedes commitment 3901

CULTURED
cold shivers go up, down spines of c. people 5811

CUMULATIVE
own gift c. force of life's cultivation 6226

CUNNING
devil c. observer 4915
history but a contest between God and c. of Satan 4916
Though men spin c. schemes 4887

CUNNINGLY
I am a little world made c. 7384

CUP
A royal c. for him, my King 7003
dashed no c. from perjured lip 3174
Found in each poppy's c. of gold 7996
poison in c. of sorrow if we put it there 10637
Sin causes c. of blessing to spring a leak 10356
that c. of sin be drained to dregs 5423
with my empty c. uncertain in asking 4653

CURATIVE
Loving is c. 7277

CURATIVENESS
gentleness, winsomeness without c. 1315

CURB
Yet one there is can c. myself 2583

CURBED
sin must die right out, not be c. 9841

CURE
70 percent of patients could c. themselves 12076
Before you can c. diseases of the body 6085
best c. for empty day 2558
can c. troubles by perspiration, fresh air 11455
death is the c. for all diseases 2405
Death, Physician of him whom medicine cannot c. 2260
for fear is faith 3991
many troubles you cannot c. by Bible 11455
must c. diseases of the soul 6085
no c. for birth, death save enjoy the interval 7054
only c. for suffering is to face head on 10905

The only cheap and universal c. 5932

CURED
delusions that evils c. by legislation 5184
I treated him, God c. him 5611
of tendency to state a thing can't be done 90
What can't be c. must be endured 3154

CURER
Great Physician c. of ravages of sin 10436

CURES
Love c. people 7213
Truth may hurt but it c. 11580

CURIOSITY
if insatiable in intellectual c. 8139
kernel of forbidden fruit 11050
look forward to death with intense c. 2306
not ideal philosophical c. 5724
when sense of c. has withered 7829

CURIOUS
a c. wild pain 7521
God, aloof from c. eyes of reason 4743
great men have c. feeling 5291
Loneliness far from being a c. phenomenon 7137

CURRENT
Christianity, history or c. events 1204
God is the c. 7554
In matters of taste, swim with c. 6308
power is to let the c. pass through us 7554

CURSE
believer freed from death as c. 2372
benefits become c. if Christ not head 3895
better to light candle than c. darkness 10164
bless instead of c. 7190
bless them that c. us 5001
Choose to forgive, rather than c. 1138
crucified where thieves c. 2131
Suffering was c. from which man fled 10896
To c. is to pray to the devil 9306
Work is not a c. 12025

CURSED
and remains silent a partner of God 4894
love of gold 11843

CURSING
Hope lights candle instead of c. darkness 5928

CURST
greed of gold 11803

CURTAILED
he is c. who overflowed all skies, all years 6120

CURTAIN
draw c. before stains of friend 4183

may be rung down at any moment 9911

merciful God to lift c. on today 4318

CURVE
smile a c. to set things straight 10495

CUSHION
happy moments make fine c. for old age 5506

lizard on c. will still seek leaves 989

CUSTODY
in man evil is under c. as in prison 3377

CUSTOM
act according to c. 1648

of today awkwardness of tomorrow 10516

CUSTOMS
clash with own c. 4124

resurrection permeated our c. 9702

CUT
any cord but the one that binds me to thy heart 9080

Better pruned to grow than c. to burn 2841

by unrepented sin c. off sense of God 4864

Do not c. down tree that gives shade 5241

don't c. off the buttons 4367

God allows man to c. throat of his fellowmen 4673

Measure a thousand times, c. once 2783

Never c. what you can untie 8401

ourselves off from riches of God's grace 6693

CUT-AND-DRIED
Don't like to hear c. sermons 9141

CUTS
Evil is all that c. life to pieces 5024

sharp word c. deeper than weapon 2051

tongue not steel, yet c. 1881

CUTTLEFISH
Like c. we conceal ourselves 4255

CYCLE
those who follow in the never-ending c. 7372

CYCLONE
At the heart of the c. tearing the sky 8429

CYMBALS
harps in heaven, c. in hell 5703

CYNIC
actions either openly bad or secretly bad 2187

blind to light 2187

can chill, dishearten with single word 2176

human owl 2187

looks at life with magnifying glass 2179

man who knows price of everything 2189

Never be even a gentle c. 2185

never fails to see bad quality 2187

never let man become gloomy c. 1064

never sees good quality 2187

one who knows value of nothing 2189

opposite of religious fanatic is the gentle c. 9549

prematurely disappointed in future 2178

reads bitter lessons from past 2178

smells flowers, looks for coffin 2177

vigilant in darkness 2187

who cares not whether there is a God 9549

CYNICAL
Watch what people are c. about 2188

Young people seem so c. 12179

CYNICISM
freezes life 3747

hate c. a great deal 2183

nor does hope yield to c. 5928

perhaps c. and the devil same thing 2183

substitute for intelligence 2181

unpleasant way of saying truth 2180

CYNICS
crucified where c. talk smut 2131

D

DA VINCI, LEONARDO
not afraid of being lonely 7141

DABBLE
I do, not d. in 81

DAD
makes pal of you 3921

no other has quite so fine a father 3921

DADDY
Could you be a d. to me 3920

DAFFODILS
It's raining d. 8498

DAILY
all making a crown out of d. lives 7073

business to obey Bible 681

Character sum total of d. reactions 1000

Christianity, bread for d. use 1169

circumstances of d. life indication 5444

Don't forget his d. briefing 1311

evidence in d. life that Jesus is powerless 3646

God gives ingredients for d. bread 9657

how d. life is 7010

illuminated by radiance, renewed d. 4538

In Lord's Prayer first petition for d. bread 7152

key word to commitment 1535

Kind words toward those you d. meet 6647

Let the Father proportion out d. 4629

many a battle fought d. world knows nothing about 7061

my cross for thee 2098

opportunities open on road of d. duties 8217

power to have anguish, and still perform d. tasks 8423

prayer for d. life 9099

thank thee for d. tasks to do 11148

whose d. living is to d. die 10046

DAINTIES
If hate son, cram with d. 8303

DAIRYMAID
can milk cows to glory of God 3082

DAISIES
stars d. that begem blue fields of sky 11638

DALE
Hill and d. in slumber steeping 1123

DAMAGE
Acknowledge faults to repair d. 3956

endless d. to the life 465

in midst of enemies that mean d. 11078

mistakes won't irreparably d. lives 3616

DAMAGING
wisdom to keep silent when d. words spoken 6271

worthwhile activities become d. when 7617

DAMNATION
Bible, deals with salvation and d. 721

continual dying 5684

DAMNATIONS
our reservations are d. of consecrations 1724

DAMNED
devil predestines every man to be d. 9175

interview with Satan would alone have d. 6388

man is impenitent, then obstinate, then d. 10287

to the d. God is a burden in excess 4548

What do d. endure but despair 5706

DAMNS
No one d. like a theologian 9360

DANCE
all must join the d. 3180

eye can make heart d. for joy 3561

God a kind of d. 11425

gospel makes man d. for joy 5091

I am the d. and I still go on 9690

Lord of the D. said he 9690

notes d. and leap from my pen 7931

Sparrows should not d. with cranes 9493

Unless you lead me, Lord, I cannot d. 7970

DANCED
on a Friday when sky turned black 9690

DANCES
who lives in hope d. without a fiddle 5909

DANCING
Joy is peace d. 6542

DANDELIONS
are everywhere and don't need us 8577

gorgeous bloom, pretty as can be 239

If d. were rare, fragile 8577

thriving as only d. can 239

DANGER
acknowledgement of divine power 479

And the world's d. 6133

Anger one letter short of d. 375

Art thou in d? Still let reason sway 6878

As soon as d. past devotion vanishes 8788

As soon as there is life, there is d. 6879

cannot answer for courage if never in d. 1930

content in d. of never knowing happiness 5565

each extreme to equal d. tends 3558

Fear can keep man out of d. 1923

fear gong on approach of d. 3973

few say truth in spite of d. of losing touch 6199

God protects me against d. 4992

in d. of magic 5441

man himself is mankind's greatest d. 7397

Marriage has more care but less d. 7635

more d. of rusting out than wearing out 8177

no d. of eyestrain looking on bright side 8240

of being amateur providence 263

of Christianity is anti-intellectualism 3027

of evil lurking within 3382

of forgetting Bible reveals 4661

organization in d. of killing creativity 2014

Refuge from d. 6468

signals life is on wrong track 5466

That when in d. knows no fear 3768

to the service of God 425

when throws tongue into high gear 11419

wise man prays not for safety from d. 3997

DANGEROUS
all d. folk without God's controlling hand 4956

authoritarianism 523

Crisis opportunity riding d. wind 2048

Criticism is d. 2055

error more d, the more truth it contains 3250

Errors to be d. have truth mingled 3254

Growth may seem d. 5366

half-truth a d. thing 11492

idea that isn't d. hardly an idea 2013

Indifference to evil more d. than evil itself 3379

Into the d. world I leapt 808

Knowledge without integrity d. 3013

lie no sense unless truth d. 8362

life more d. than most of us think 6918

little learning, d. thing 2992

Money a d. master 7809

most d. of tame beasts, a flatterer 10472

most d. of wild beasts, a slanderer 10472

Nothing more d. than discontinued labor 3109

passions d. through their excess 10234

past d. used as hitching post 8367

raw power 523

single verse of Bible may be d. 642

society d. network of manipulation 10514

Some wicked people would be less d. 11891

Temptations d. in religious garb 11092

to take one impulse to follow 7836

tongue most d. of weapons 11417

when devil looks noble, he is most d. 2648

Wise men say nothing in d. times 11979

wolves more d. than flies 11056

world too d. for anything but the truth 11545

worship has not been as d. as should have been 12106

DANGERS
advance in spiritual life has d. 10700

are temptations that surprise 11078

atheist, d. lie in wait 493

in false emotionalism 3052

meet d. with prayer 2630

One of d. focusing on evil is lose bearings 5037

to be recognized in the church 1400

too little, too much 1604

DANIEL
God could have kept D. out of lion's den 165

heaven wasn't very far from D. 5651

lions didn't eat because grit, backbone 1046

vegetable diet 765

DARE
better to d. mighty things 1922

can d. to live alone 4286

endure is greater than to d. 3153

friend with whom you d. to be yourself 4173

I d. not choose my lot 5412

let us d. to do our duty 3755

Never d. to trifle 8097

not speak 426

not trifle with eternal future 4726

only in place of healing d. to show wounds 10551

there is much to d. 1018

Those who d. to fail 87

to be true 3937

DARES
to forgive injury 4095

DARING
All glory comes from d. to begin 102

Faith is d. to go farther than can see 3697

In crisis most d. course often safest 2047

Life either a d. adventure or nothing 6962

more d. the request, more glory to God 9028

to believe with or without feelings 3748

youth a spirit of d. life 12183

DARK
a terrible feeling, a leap in the d. 9937

as my path may seem to others 3649

Carry own lantern, and you need not fear d. 6167

Character what you are in d. 1005

Christ a window in d. dungeon of
   ego 6434
even though your way seems d.
   169
Everyone has a d. side 7376
Faith a terrific venture in the d.
   3668
Faith grows only in the d. 3663
Faith is bird that sings when dawn
   still d. 3695
Faith walking in d. with God
   3714
God's ways seem d. but soon or
   late 11299
good name keeps brightness even
   in d. days 6292
ground of the soul is d. 10664
he that hides d. soul, foul thoughts
   1683
Hope is faith holding out its
   hands in the d. 5920
However d. it be 5456
I don't want to go home in the d.
   2454
joy flows on through the d. 6529
Life can never be d. or futile 6940
life is stronger than d. 2985
Lord, it is d. 2600
Man's enemies d. forces within
   3165
must wait for God in the d. 5460
My soul is d. within 9048
Never doubt in d. 2885
night of soul always three in
   morning 2594
No problem ever as d. when you
   have a friend 4196
O God, thy world is d. 10878
often do not see stars until d.
   2560
Out of his d. I glow 4125
Recognize d. night for what it is
   2556
Sin will end d. as night 10377
Some days must be d. and dreary
   2549
soul's d. cottage, batter'd and
   decay'd 7701
than man keep straight line
   walking in d. 6614
thank thee that d, uncertain is our
   future 9053
The d. threads are as needful
   10606
The days were d. to me 5413
The night is d, I am far from home
   5429
things reach out toward brightness
   5906
this d. satanic earth 4902
though thy path be d. as night
   5995
Through this d. and stormy night
   3800
time as bulbs in d. totally ignored
   5338
unconscious is not only d. but
   also light 7772
uneasy world of family life 3886

Water is cold, d, deep 5527
What in me is d, illumine 7566
what looks d. in the distance 8079
What other dungeon so d. as one's
   own heart 9955
When d. enough men see stars
   10929
When leave God's love, we grow
   d. 9354
will relieve none in the d. 10037
windows bringing light on d.
   corners 3019
Without Christ life is as twilight
   with d. night ahead 7094
would rather walk with God in
   the d. 5419

DARKEN
our sight with foolish tears 10964
we d. the atmosphere in which we
   move 4255

DARKENED
God, a light that is never d. 4698
hope, brightening the d. paths
   5940
May better read the d. soul 6583
save our souls from being d. by
   passion 9064
When schoolroom d, see most
   10855
When you see appetites d. 2565
within your d. stable shed 6118

DARKER
Christ leads me through no d.
   rooms 5379
the night, brighter stars shine
   9323

DARKEST
behind life's d. clouds 10964
brightest thunderbolt from d.
   storm 220
day lived till tomorrow will have
   passed away 2575
E'en when my sky is d. 4490
Faith can put candle in d. night
   3656
God's d. threatenings 11432
hours have some intent 4885
look back on my d. periods 10853
providences have meaning 4885
sees in the d. night 8515
sun shines clearly in d. day as in
   brightest 4772
Time and hour runs through d.
   day 10585
word is sin 11993

DARKNESS
always able to discover own d.
   6004
And the voice through the d. heard
   7943
aptitude for sensitivity 2612
arrival of radiant light in our d.
   6119
as light opposed to d. 5205
Atheists, false courage in d. 476
better to light candle than curse d.
   10164

Bible light without d. 710
clouds closing over him in d.
   forever 6101
Come, blessed d, come bring thy
   balm 10481
Confession brings to light
   unconscious d. 1596
cynic vigilant in d. 2187
death raises from d. into light
   2250
death, through d. into light 2426
deepens, Lord with me abide
   2538
devil comes in hour of d. 2674
devils see only the d. 357
Faith does not ask for lifting of d.
   3714
falls from wings of night 8086
Go out into the d. 5417
God gives light in d. 2582
God guides you in d. 2565
God has set in my d. lamp of faith
   11144
God has set light against d. 5016
God hides himself in d. from the
   wise, prudent 7709
God in this cloud in this d. 2557
God is the light in my d. 4459
God, the light in my d. 6907
has its wonders 1788
hideth not from him, but glows
   4746
Hope lights candle instead of
   cursing d. 5928
in d, Christ is my star 6498
in d, doubt we cling closely to thee
   9053
In d. feels no doubt 3768
In d. no choice 1144
in d. soul avoids going astray
   2547
in d. soul gains virtues 2547
in God, a deep but dazzling d.
   4506
In the Bible, intense d. 672
in the d. you shall hear God's voice
   298
infinity, d. of the pure,
   unsearchable sea 4684
intellect lies in d. 7776
Into the d. of the night 303
is my point of view, my right to
   myself 7106
Jehovah takes his ministers into d.
   163
Light against d. 10844
Light in d, tempering sorrow 4758
little distracted with useless things
   2547
Lord, are you there in my d. 2600
lunatic put out sun by scribbling d.
   4442
makes appreciative of sight 824
man condemned for not coming
   out of d. 6586
more productive than light 2541
no transforming of d. into light
   without emotion 3053

not d. where you are going, for
   God is light 5659
not enough d. to put out candle
   8241
Out of the finite d. 2360
potential for vulnerability 2612
powers of d. paralyzed by prayer
   8988
Pray in the d. if there be no light
   8768
praying saint performs havoc
   among forces of d. 9014
purpose of d. not to punish or
   afflict 2608
purpose of d. to set free 2608
Receive every d. with both thy
   hands 7698
rich sensitivity which will make
   whole 2612
secure from empty, false joy 2547
secure from pride, presumption
   2547
shows us worlds of light 10633
some anomaly drops out of d.
   2790
souls has deeper d. than the nights
   7539
spiritual d. and dry spells 181
The d. shineth as the light 4140
Thou shoutedst, didst pierce my d.
   4805
to the intellect 4743
Turn d. into light 6647
unbelief is content with d. 2930
wait in d. as long as necessary
   2557
wait in quietness until light in d.
   3718
What though the d. gather 232
When Christ left, there was no d.
   6510
where people dying in d. 7779
where there is d, light 9086
whether light or d. 1461
which is above the intellect 1767
write his name in fire on the
   midnight d. 4712
you are living in land of d. 4969

DARLINGS
Mothers' d. make milksop heroes
   8315

DARTS
than idly repeat slanderous d.
   Christians are hurling 5143
With gentle force soliciting the d.
   9798

DASHED
no cup from perjured lip 3174

DATE
alive long past usual d. of
   disintegration 8139
Christmas not a d. 1361
eternally out of d. 3265
If Bible agreed with science, it
   would soon be out of d. 9865
most outstanding record is d. of
   birth of Jesus Christ 5726

DATED
God's promises sealed to us, but
   not d. 4470

DATES
Nothing so d. a man as to decry
   younger generation 12192

DAUGHTER
As would have a d, so choose a
   wife 7602
Covetousness has for d. injustice
   5313
good father will leave imprint on
   d. 3915

DAUNTED
by no difficulty is greatness 3153
heart unspotted not easily d.
   11679

DAVID
From D. learn to give thanks
   11145
he who has not wept in D. 5224
stay humble, like D. with sheep
   after anointed king 5391
swung. God made his point 766
treated God with startling
   familiarity 7526
When D. took his harp and played
   7935

DAWN
before me lies D. and the day
   5471
Bright d. of our eternal day 6152
death, the d. has come 2252
emerge lame but victorious at d.
   9777
Faith is bird that sings when d.
   still dark 3695
I greet the d, not setting sun 2418
Life closes in twilight, opens with
   d. 11132
O night more lovely than the d.
   2554
Promise of the d. 6141
Wisdom like d. that comes up
   slowly 11969
with Christ life is d. of morning
   7094

DAWNING
Another year is d. 8077
bird of d. singeth night long 1371
music in the d. morn 7927
old age, love you as d. of eternal
   day 8149
one day nearer the d. when fog
   will lift 5676
So here hath been d. 2198

DAWNS
At edge of despair d. clarity 2574
Christ has turned our sunsets into
   d. 6368
this day ne'er d. again 11363

DAY
a messenger of God 2195
a single d. of eternity 3273
abiding d. that has no night 229
add word a d. to vocabulary 1853

after d. spent in blessed toil 11287
All but God changing d. by d.
   4586
all he packed into one d. 8090
an epitome of the year 9877
And the d. but one 7306
Another blue d. 2198
another d. will begin next morning
   11132
another thing to go through every
   d. glorifying God 7129
As morning shows the d. 1124
At cool of d, with God I walk
   7452
at peace through activities of the d.
   6828
Bad the d. man becomes content
   8649
before me lies Dawn and the d.
   5471
best cure for empty d. 2558
Bold shall I stand in thy great d.
   4719
breaks but never falls 8084
Bright dawn of our eternal d.
   6152
by d, dear Lord 9043
By night and also d. he suffers still
   2164
By prostrate spirits d. and night
   4659
cannot say give us this d. our
   daily bread if 8818
cares that infest the d. 7887
Christ will rise on Easter d. 2985
Christmas and Good Friday the
   same d. 6489
Christmas d. that holds time
   together 1362
comes when he begins to care he
   does not cheat neighbor 5004
could add two hours to my
   working d. 9531
count that d. well spent 107
Countless times each d. 7844
death draws every d. nearer 4726
Direct, control, suggest this d.
   9047
dream of a d. that had never been
   8371
Each d. a little life 2193
Each d. comes bearing its gifts
   2192
Each d. is a wonderful gift 6524
each d. refilled 2979
Each d. so short, so few 7219
endless d. that is our Father God
   3772
Enjoy blessings of this d. 11365
enjoy bright d. 1683
everlasting Father will take care of
   you every d. 415
Every Christian needs half hour of
   prayer each d. 8790
Every d. a d. of reckoning 2194
every d. a new enjoyment of life
   8737
Every d. a new page 6901
Every d. feast of lanterns 3501

Every d. should be passed as if our last 6887

Every d. should make us more like Christ 1347

Every d. we are changing 962

every d. we are dying 962

Evil flourishes more in shadows than d. 3381

evils of d. bear patiently 11365

eyes grown weary of the garish d. 10481

Faith sees the d. 2939

Father made me learn Bible verses every d. 651

feelings one can go through in one d. 4014

Finish every d. and be done with it 8375

future comes one d. at a time 4320

give me faith to live from d. to d. 9072

given to God is a sacrament 2196

God does not die on the d. we cease to believe 4538

God does not love one d, hate another 4626

God gives me gift of 24 hours d. 11296

God would not have created man to exist only for a d. 6104

Happy is man too busy to worry by d. 12062

He chose its d. of birth 3227

heaven, rest not d. nor night 5644

help me live from d. to d. 9075

help us, this and every d. 9040

hemmed with prayer less likely to unravel 8841

his works behold d. and night 362

hope d. at hand when advent of God will appear 9909

hour of pain as long as d. of pleasure 149

How hard the battle goes, the d. how long 6256

How I have wasted half my d. 9049

I dream of a d. 3229

I miss a lot of good things d. by d. 5587

I shall emerge one d. 2945

If cannot find God in the d. duty 4856

if did not spend hours each d. in prayer 8816

If for one whole d. 8090

If I neglect prayer for a d. 8945

If you allot your d. 11370

important how we spend each d. 10733

In every bud, the coming d. 8009

In flows heaven, with its new d. 5636

In the d. when all men stand before God 4718

Infinite d. excludes the night 5670

introduce kingdom of heaven into our d. 4974

is a miniature eternity 2190

is all that is good, fair 8375

is done 8086

is lost on which one has not laughed 6744

is time no one wealthy enough to waste 2191

It runs through the nightland up to the d. 4313

joy flows in the night as well as the d. 6529

kept clean all d. by integrity 9600

Laughing 100 times a d. works the heart 6725

Leaving the world their d. 7475

let me be aware of the treasure you are 2197

Life but a d. at most 6958

Life lost d. by dragging d. 6972

life short d. in which sun hardly rises 7083

life, twinkle of star in God's eternal d. 7015

live a d. at a time 4885

Lived till tomorrow will have passed away 2575

Living each d. as if only d. 6999

Living one d. in Spirit worth more than thousand in flesh 5787

longest d. will have an end 10629

Lord, I shall be very busy this d. 9076

Love every d. 7219

mistake that we do not concentrate on present d. 8381

more sure than d. and night 4209

must follow as night the d. 6318

my own wisdom insufficient for the d. 8822

No man sank under burden of the d. 935

Nor brought too long a d. 2588

Nor feel unwanted at close of d. 8145

Not for a single d. 5434

not good that man batter d, night at heaven 8854

O Lord, support us all d. long 9105

of all the week the best 10953

of sorrow longer than month of joy 10580

of strange, almost curious peace 10120

of worry more exhausting than d. of work 12056

old age like the evening of a fine d. 8184

old age, love you as dawning of eternal d. 8149

One d. along that silent shore 1148

one d. at a time is enough 10120

One half in d, the other dipt in night 10673

Peace rules d. when Christ rules mind 8462

perfectly good d. coming tomorrow 5591

place all hours of d. at his disposal 10120

powerful King of D. 10962

Praying fills the grayest, gloomiest d. 8899

prays much by night, face fair by d. 8808

prefer to be king of the mountain for a d. 5308

Receive every d. as a resurrection from death 8737

refuse to sit quietly for a while each d. 9367

Relying on God has to begin all over every d. 7515

Repentance a natal d. when life begins 9591

right that you should begin again every d. 10705

seems long in coming 235

Seize the d. 8222

seize the pleasures of the present d. 8600

sight angels behold d, night forever 4995

something new every d. if you look 3509

soul shall shine a star of d. 10675

speed up d. when sing, Free at last 4157

still find each d. too short 11301

strength has failed ere the d. is half done 7570

Summer in winter. D. in night 6153

sun makes not the d, but thee 4502

sun shines as clearly in darkest d. as in brightest 4772

Tain't worthwhile to wear a d. all out 12055

Talk about question of the d. 5094

Thanksgiving never meant to be a single d. 11177

That was a great d. 1982

That woke it unto d. 4592

the d. of judgment 49

the shining hills of d. 287

The very light of d. 4195

They touch the shining hills of d. 11299

think every d. of Christ 8472

think every d. the last 7021

this d. ne'er dawns again 11363

this d. only is ours 11365

This d. with hopes and invitations 8375

This is that night—no, d. 6140

Though the fool waits, the d. does not 6780

three in the morning, d. after d. 2593

Time and hour runs through darkest d. 10585

to go forth to work till evening 6947

To hallow the end of d. 633

to live every d. as if it were our last
9120

To soar to endless d. 6923

to use strength given us 6947

Today, one d. nearer home 5676

Tomorrow is a new d. 8375
11366

Tomorrow must be longest d. of
week 9302

Tomorrow the d. lose opportunity
to accept Christ 11404

Tomorrow the d. on which loafers
work 11404

Tomorrow the d. when fools act
sensibly 11404

too dear to waste a moment on
yesterdays 8375

Unwrap beauties in ordinary d.
2201

we die on the d. 4538

well-spent d. brings happy sleep
2224

What d. may bring d. may take
away 2202

When all is done, say not my d. is
o'er 2418

Who can tell what a d. may bring
forth 9120

Who gives the d. 5434

will come one d. a touch from God
7060

will happen whether or not you
get up 2200

Will the day's journey take the
whole long d. 6885

with Christ life and warmth of d.
ahead 7094

With God Abram's d. and this d.
the same 4591

with hopes, invitations 11366

worlds of light we never saw by d.
10633

would attend church if d. came
some other time 10961

would not get through the d. 8816

You don't learn to praise in a d.
8747

you fear the end is birthday of
your eternity 2225

DAY OF JUDGMENT

concept of time makes us speak of
D. 6589

in reality a summary court in
perpetual session 6589

tell tragedies of weakness, failure
1055

that awful, merciless eulogy 1055

the real defense 1055

would clear away artifical virtues
1055

DAY'S

down to grave, shall have ended
d. work 11132

Forget the d. troubles 11158

From promise to deed a d. journey
9320

If bring into one d. thoughts evil
of many 12064

if too anxious about each d. affairs
8818

My soul is sick with every d.
report 6273

Remember the d. blessings 11158

Will the d. journey take the whole
long day 6885

DAYBREAK

cock crows but d. is from God
2199

DAY-BREAKING

For the full d. 3800

DAYDREAMING

dare not think God is d. 7556

DAYLIGHT

Cheerfulness keeps d. in the mind
1092

DAYS

activity these d. a cheap anesthetic
120

All d. journey toward death 2428

As if thy blessings had spare d.
5265

Beauty of ancient d, yet ever new
4805

blessing if blind, deaf for few d.
824

Cloudless d. are fine 2540

Fish, visitors smell in three d.
5956

For all your d. prepare 9655

frequent church language these d.
1406

good name keeps brightness even
in dark d. 6292

good old d. next generation will
hear about 11381

in d. of Ananias, Sapphira 4717

in d. of youth remembered God
8140

in his leaner and weaker d. 7564

Laughter adds richness to
ordinary d. 6727

like a child walk with thee down
all my d. 9051

Money brings d. of joy, but not
peace 7807

need d. of silence to recover from
futility of words 10556

no d. when God's fountain does
not flow 4647

no use to pray for old d. 8377

Nothing to discuss but glories of
d. past 4321

numbered the d. of genuine
happiness 7100

One of these d. is none of these d.
9298

Our d. are numbered 8098

Serves but to brighten all our
future d. 10879

Seven d. without prayer makes
one weak 8960

Some d. must be dark, deary 2549

Spring full of sweet d. and roses
9891

The d. were dark to me 5413

three d. late at bus station 4266

to succeed stay awake d. 10828

To untell the d, to redeem these
hours 9568

when burdens weigh us down
9059

Who has shared our morning d.
4208

Who will give me back d. when
life had wings 12176

worry fills with gloom the d.
12091

years teach much d. never knew
3546

DAY-TO-DAY

It's d. living that wears you out
6876

DAZZLES

Genius, that power that d. mortal
eyes 8539

DAZZLING

in God, a deep but d. darkness
4506

radiant hope 5940

DEAD

a weeping in world as though our
Lord were d. 2611

Alas, oh, love is d. 7159

All we can hold in our cold, d.
hands 4349

Anyone not coming to be a d. one
2222

Awake ye d. 9692

being d. an appealing prospect
2300

Christ Lion in power, raising the d.
6425

completely consistent people are d.
1745

do not bury emotions d. 3061

faults will drop off like d. leaves
3940

Few drop d. from overwork 3089

foolish and d. never change
opinions 8206

for this live 490

friends not d. but simply gone
before us 2327

fury against Christ proof he is not
d. 6362

God will not bring forth d. fruit
872

he rose from the d. 4931

home, they say, d. decorum,
routine 5842

I shall be more alive than now
2367

If faith without works is d. 3737

If your ambitions' fires are d.
8122

laid the d. man there 778

Let the d. past bury its d. 4331

life turns d. on our hands 4437

lives only for himself truly d. to
others 10059

living coffin of d. soul 7760

more evidence Jesus rose from d.
  than Julius Caesar lived 9700
Mourn not the d. 426
no change, soul is d. 1590
no d. people, only the living 2390
no right to whine when he is d.
  2317
not d. the child of our affection
  2392
O how small a portion of earth
  will hold us when d. 2344
over the d. united world has no
  power 2395
Over the happy d. 2425
poetry of earth never d. 2976
praise d. saints, persecute living
  ones 8530
root that produces nothing is d.
  3699
shall live, the living die 7925
shall take care of it when I am d.
  10145
She is not d. but gone unto that
  school 2392
so long as you refuse to die 10050
stopped d. by some reverse 5395
The devil to fetch the d. 2638
The man is d. 7442
three may keep secret if two are d.
  1617
To d. men, life is Christ 6391
To the d. he sayeth: Arise 6497
until friends are d. 4223
wailing of newborn mingled with
  dirge for the d. 7043
we are d. to yesterday 11365
When snake is d. venon d. 3419
when sure self is d. it turns up
  9943
year in a shroud of leaves d, is
  lying 11321

DEAD SEA
gets to keep 10195
has no outlet 10195
makes horror 10195

DEAD-AND-ALIVE
Christian no respect 2771

DEADEN
the pain of an empty life 120

DEAD-END
on d. street with man who denies
  God 7523

DEADLIEST
Myself, my d. foe 2583
trap of devil is religious 2701

DEADLINE
without giving God d. to remove it
  8415

DEADLOCKS
force us to think 2043

DEADLY
All the seven d. sins self-destroying
  10296
church says covetousness a d. sin
  10086
cross is d. 2106

Hatred is like fire, makes light
  rubbish d. 5597
Ignorance and power and pride a
  d. mixture 9212
life, aimless comet till halts d. way
  6937
Luxury more d. than any foe 7362
opiate for consciences of millions
  4726
Self is a d. thing 9936
Seven d. virtues 11699
spiritual pride, most d. form sin
  can take 9254
thought of solitude 10569

DEAF
Beethoven composed his deepest
  music 155
blessing if blind, d. for few days
  824
Faith d. to doubt 3683
give us sympathy for those who
  are d. 9094
Have d. ear for unkind remarks
  9456
husband, blind wife happy couple
  7589
If a servant be sometimes d. 2896
Kindness a language d. can hear
  6650
None so d. as those who will not
  hear 261
prayer for the d. 9094
you compelled my d. ears to hear
  you 7579

DEAFEN
you have a Ludwig van Beethoven
  161

DEAFENING
God, voice d. in its thunderousness
  4465

DEAFENS
Too much noise d. us 3559

DEAFNESS
charity is d. when scandal flows
  1085
My d. I endure 8146
you broke through my d. 1910

DEAL
Don't fight fact, d. with it 3576
not good for other party, isn't
  good for you 1022
only with surface, find Christ an
  offense 6422
with faults of others gently 3938

DEALING
with creatures of emotion 9518

DEALINGS
bend our conscience to our d.
  1687

DEALT
friendship should be d. with
  delicately 4237
If God d. with people today 4717

DEAR
as d. to God is peasant as prince
  3225
Tis expectation makes a blessing d.
  3496

DEARER
Friend is d. than light of heaven
  4269
home, d. sweeter spot than all the
  rest 5834
that freedom bind us d. to himself
  6177

DEAREST
friend on earth is mere shadow
  4201
The d. idol I have known 6074
things are swept from sight forever
  10645
word is mother 11993

DEARLY
How d. thou hast paid for me
  2136
Love thee more d. 9043

DEARTH
come to God in utter d. of feelings
  3780

DEATH
a camel that lies down at every
  door 2242
a fathomless answer, the Cross of
  Christ 9398
a favor to many 2274
a gift to some 2274
a mouse can bite him to d. 2859
a new beginning 2253
a punishment to some 2274
a voyage home 2249
absolute rest is d. 6771
All days journey toward d. 2428
All men equal in d. 3226
all the trumpets sounded 2366
an awfully big adventure 2243
an experience robbed of terror
  2234
And d. or life shall be the sweeter
  2229
And perish in our own 810
and taxes inevitable 2238
angels throng about saying "A
  man is born" 2408
are all apprentices 2226
as an experience it does not exist
  2234
As chimney-sweepers, come to
  dust 2290
as lover's pinch which hurts 2387
as necessary to the constitution as
  sleep 2244
Back into your kennel 2277
balm of d. releases 1332
be ready to depart when God calls
  2355
Be still prepared for d. 2229
Because I could not stop for d.
  2230
believer freed from d. as curse
  2372

Bible, birth and d. 750

Birth nothing but d. begun 811

breathing new air, finding it celestial air 2399

brings every human being to individuality 2353

brings love's crown 7204

but a piece of the world's order 2338

by God I will get through this d. 7674

called sleep, change, departing 2372

can desire d. 2407

can fear d. 2407

can ignore d. 2407

Can vengeance be pursued further than d. 9716

cancels everything but truth 2239

cannot break God's decree 4616

cannot build hopes on d. 8445

cannot get behind the after of d. 5459

cannot influence d. can influence style 2336

cannot kill what never dies 7319 3291

cannot laugh God out of your d. 2432

cannot say I have finished my life 2422

Christ came into the shadow of d. 6121

Christ saying, "You are coming to me" 2409

Christ's d. made our value skyrocket 9989

Christ, birth and d. one continual act 6489

clutches only that which he has given away 2416

Come lovely, soothing d. 2237

comes to young men 2349

Comforter of him whom time cannot console 2260

confounds 'em all 2384

consolation of d, end of taxes 2352

consummation of union with God 2257

costs a life 2263

coward sneaks to d. 10948

cross a picture of d. 2145

cross from one territory to another 2227

cross, d. of d. 2118

crowns a Christian 1280

crucifixion most famous d. 2137

day, night, to all, to each 2237

days travel toward d. 2215

Desire getting, doth but gain his d. 2567

difference between d. of Christian, non-Christian 2305

Dishonesty a scorpion that will sting itself to d. 2908

divinely entertaining 2272

Do not keep me waiting 2301

Down you mongrel, D. 2277

draws every day nearer 4726

drink, death-dealing waves 325

Each departed friend a magnet 2278

easier to suffer d. than spiritual suffering 10859

end of labor 2256

entrance is incontestable 2227

entry into rest 2256

Eternal life does not begin with d. 3652

eternal supreme evil 5033

event in a man's life 7050

evil is all that serves d. 5024

expect to pass through d. in conversation with God 9025

experience it but once 2226

experience of d. in some way necessary 10884

Faith builds bridge across gulf of d. 3655

faith works fear of d. out of Christians 2375

Fear not that life shall come to end 2283

fear of d. 3971

fear of d. common 2375

fear of d. worse than d. 2376

Fear preoccupies d. 2363

feeling invigorated, finding it immortality 2399

first requisite for immortality is d. 6107

flowering of life 2257

For restful d. I cry 2285

From d. of old the new proceeds 11504

from storm, stress to perfect calm 2399

funeral of sorrows, evils 2266

Give me d. or give me life 1538

God buries his workmen, carries on his work 2286

God changes d. to triumph 2373

God has gone through human experience of d. 6386

God knows all d. 4881

God's delightful way of giving life ›2246

God's finger touched him, he slept 2289

going among kith, kin 2249

going to our Father's house 2249

Good night! Good night! Good night! 2365

Good-bye proud world! I'm going home 2291

Grief flys to d. 2363

Grumbling, d. of love 1560

have boots on, ready to go 2354

He who fears d. cannot enjoy life 3975

Here's d, twitching my ear 2295

Himself, his Maker, and the angel D. 4209

His life is Christ, his d. is gain 1299

His maker kissed his soul away 2296

Honor aspires to d. 2363

How strange this fear of d. 2297

How wonderful is D. and his brother Sleep 2298

human race from back from d. by Christianity 1187

I go where no disturbance can have place 2304

I was my own d. 9070

If d. be terrible, the fault is thee 2314

If don't wish his good, you ask for your d. 8067

If impossible for Christ to triumph over d. 9691

if man would ever pass to God 2267

If this is d, it's sweet 2437

in chrysalis sets free butterfly 2261

in d. Christ shall be the d. of d. 6498

in d. extraordinary what takes place 10667

in flower, sets free perfume 2261

In his d. Christ a sacrifice, satisfying our sins 6410

In life, in d, thy lovely will 8098

in man sets free the soul 2261

intense contemplation of Creator 2353

intimate with God, d. of friend will not crush 9470

into company of faithful friends 2325

is a friend 2338

is but crossing the world 7319

is but sharp corner 2245

is not d. if raises into light 2250

is of very little importance 6912

is only a horizon 6097

is stepping on shore, finding it heaven 2399

is strong, life stronger 2985

is the Christian's harbor 5638

is the cure for all diseases 2405

is the godly man's wish 2372

Is this the end? I know it cannot be 2319

is wicked man's fear 2372

It is but D. who comes at last 2218

Jesus audaciously abolished d. 2322

Jesus Christ has abolished d. 2234

Jesus tells us accurately about life after d. 2323

Jesus' d. is our life 6453

keeps no calendar 2262

kind of looking forward to it 2312

knows d. not an end, but a beginning 2343

Liberator of him whom freedom cannot release 2260

Library where every book shall lie open 2216

Life a predicament that precedes d. 6951

life is perfected by d. 10870

life of truth from d. of creeds
11504
life or d. his mercy underlies 6916
life to d. to eternal living 5945
life well used brings happy d.
2224
lightsome, glorious 2272
Like a full-fed guest, depart to rest
2338
live in fear of d. is many times to
die 2403
Live, says he, for I am coming
2295
look forward to d. with reverent
curiosity 2306
Lord appeared to redeem us by
his d. 6477
Lord makes little of physical d.
2358
Lord makes much of moral d.
2358
Lord makes much of spiritual d.
2358
Lord sung the night went to his d.
7923
Lord will take care of your d.
2369
love offered in spite of d. 7239
Love pulls God into d. 7237
Love slights d. 2363
Make it a good experience 2333
man should be mourned at birth,
not d. 2209
martyrs put to d. by painful
methods 1211
may be free, but costs a life 2263
Men fear d. as children fear dark
2335
Men fear d. refuse to understand
2336
Men fear thought more than d.
11232
Mental slavery is mental d. 7760
miserable is he who fears d. 2357
misers amass wealth for those
who wish their d. 11837
moment of my d. most precious
2373
more universal than life 6884
most beautiful adventure in life
2458
most dreaded event 2232
moving from one home to another
2247
my bones the bars of d. 3482
my day's work will begin the next
morning 2422
name is D. the last best friend am I
2337
nature of d. taken away, name
changed 2372
nature telling you to slow down
2248
no cure for birth, d. save enjoy
interval 7054
no d, only change of worlds 2391
no d, what seems so is transition
2392

no longer needs our poor
protection 2392
No man ever repented of being
Christian on d. bed 2340
no matter what happens, there's
always d. 2347
no need to get out of bed 2241
no one wants to believe it 2279
no other d. aroused one
hundredth part of interest 2137
no sin not included in Christ's d.
10299
no trouble with visas 2227
no utterance for love or d. 10274
not afraid, but I don't want to be
there 2313
not extinguishing the light 2252
not going to strange country 2249
not greatest loss in life 2254
not journeying into unknown land
2249
not master of the house 2253
not on his payroll 2309
not the end 2253
nothing but a moment 2390
Nothing seems worse than d.
2342
Nothing so certain as d. 2341
nothing so uncertain as hour of d.
2341
notice that our lease has expired
2406
O amiable lovely d. 2269
O God, hear these my final words
9091
of child, adolescent is born 2390
Of course, I do not want to go
2346
of fear certain 3962
of Jesus goes underneath deepest
sin 2160
of Jesus not the d. of a martyr
6472
of Jesus only entrance into his life
2161
of Jesus was revelation of heart of
God 6472
Old age an island surrounded by
d. 8155
Old age more to be feared than d.
8159
Old men go to d. 2349
One can survive everything except
d. 2351
One who longs for d. is miserable
2357
only the porter at King's lodge
2253
opening of more subtle life 2261
opens unknown doors 2264
or be subject to law of d. 3756
Our ships shall sail upon another
sea 2319
out of contempt into glory 2325
out of troubles into rest 2325
pain is brief, joy eternal 2383
Pale D. with impartial step 2361
parents stand between us, d. 2424

passage out of prison into palace
2325
passing through dark entry 2272
People living deeply, no fear of d.
2362
Physician of him whom medicine
cannot cure 2260
picture Christ as coming to save
2409
power of altering what man
desires 2240
prayer on facing d. 9048
primitive church thought more
about Second Coming than d.
9913
profoundly affects outlook 2240
psychologically important as birth
2255
Purposeless activity a phase of d.
122
put to bed with a shovel 2275
question of justice may bring us d.
10564
Quotations tell of struggles with d.
9385
Railing at life, yet afraid of d.
8163
raises from darkness into light
2250
raises from sinfulness into holiness
2250
raises from weakness into strength
2250
ready at any time 2301
realizes nothing terrible in d. 7059
really great word to master, d.
7000
Reason, logic have to do with
time between birth, d. 9419
repentance means undergoing a
kind of d. 9577
representative already there 2227
resurrection of joy 2266
resurrection substituted fear of d.
for eternal life 9702
return from life to d. 2338
Revenge triumphs over d. 2363
reward of sin is d. 10395
rids us of chance, change 2251
rids us of doubt, fear 2251
rids us of space, time 2251
Salvation is moving from living d.
to deathless life 9809
serenely arriving, arriving 2237
shall go on a planned voyage 5945
Shall I think of d. as doom 2364
shall not travel an uncharted
course 5945
shall rise refreshed 2244
shrinking away robs life of
purpose 2255
shrinking away unhealthy,
abnormal 2255
Sin a d. of the soul 10360
sin cost God d. of his Son 1013
sin d. of good works 10360
sin d. of grace 10360
sin d. of virtue 10360
single d. is tragedy 2211

Sleep is so like d. 10492
So do our minutes hasten to their
    end 2329
sole equality on earth is d. 3245
some face proudly, some in abject
    terror 2336
Sooner or later, delicate d. 2237
space trips pale into insignificance
    2259
stand in d. together with those
    who grieve 2223
statistics on d. quite impressive
    2386
step from provisional to
    permanent 2390
strengthens belief in existence
    after d. 6090
stroke of d. as a lover's pinch
    2387
sudden d. sudden joy 2212
takes no bribes 2265
takes toll of all but truth 11519
taking hold of hand, finding it
    God's 2399
thank thee there will be d. 9053
the best of all things created 2231
the cause, not the d, makes the
    martyr 7675
the dawn has come 2252
the final awakening 2273
the gate of life 2270
the grand leveller 2258
the great adventure 2259
the great reconciler 2420
the grisly terror 2271
the last day arrives there 2428
There is no d. 6109
They bring it to you, free 2241
think of arriving 2409
think of life as beginning 2409
think of meeting 2409
this old crumbling house is losing
    appeal 2394
Thou hast all seasons for thine
    own, O D. 2324
thou shalt die 2356
thou, most kind and gentle d.
    2219
three things can do about d. 2407
through d. alone we become
    liberated 2231
through darkness into light 2426
Through the black space of d. to
    baby life 6148
through valley of d. on way to
    greatness 5289
time of your d. under God's
    supervision 2316
time to give life back 2307
time to rest 2284
to dust returneth, Was not spoken
    of soul 2328
to him only emigration 2415
Triumphing over d, chance and
    thee, O Time 5679
uncolored by hesitation 2299
undiscover'd country, no traveller
    returns 2388

Wait the great teacher d, and God
    adore 5913
waking and finding it home 2399
was my own d. 11515
way man dies more important
    than d. itself 2336
We must not cry too bitterly 2425
What a beautiful day! 2456
what so intricate, so entangling as
    d. 2220
what you are will be yours forever
    1062
What you possess will belong to
    someone else 1062
when belief becomes life or d. 616
when d. takes us by the hand
    2284
When rationalist points out d.
    9398
when soul shall emerge from
    sheath 2276
Where is thy sting 2389
where life and d. are one in the
    Lord 3649
who does not fear d, no fear of
    threats 2294
Who knows but d. what men call
    life 7086
Who knows but life be that which
    men call d. 7086
Whose portal we call d. 2392
will make us immortal 812
Wonderful, wonderful, this d.
    2459
world's an inn, d. the journey's end
    2330
Yield your torch to others as in a
    race 2338
you are tired, lie down, sleep 2284

DEATHBED
No Christian ever known to
    recant on d. 3764
one case of d. repentance recorded
    9602
repentance is blowing snuff in the
    face of heaven 9576
repentance is burning candle of
    life in service of the devil 9576

DEATH-BLOW
If love God, selfishness received d.
    10063

DEATHLESS
Salvation is moving from living
    death to d. life 9809

DEATH'S
but a path that must be trod 2267
slips through d. mesh 9805
truer name is Onward 2268
War is d. feast 11769
When d. approach is seen so
    terrible 2348

DEATHS
daily d. destroy power of final
    dying 2110
live longer by century of shrieking
    d. 6258
million d. a statistic 2211

DEBATE
devil well skill'd in d. 2651
Gold in families d. 11811
gospel neither discussion nor d.
    5098

DEBT
grace directed toward human d.
    5206
than rise in d. 4033
to imagination incalculable 2024
willing to go into d. for work of
    God 3297
Without d, without care 4044

DEBTS
poverty, accumulating d. 4040

DECADE
reminder of Resurrection at start
    of each new d. 8080
single d. to lay foundation of
    values 8314

DECADENT
impersonalized culture 3325

DECAY
All growth not toward God
    growing to d. 5363
Change, d. all around I see 947
Christians to keep world from d.
    1271
have not found solution for moral
    d. 2928
People in a hurry cannot d. 5584
senses d. 6455
Shall bid that world d. 4592

DECAY'D
soul's dark cottage, batter'd and d.
    7701

DECAYED
all that is d. in universe 4997

DECEIT
clean glove hides dirty hand 2460
fox preaches, look to geese 2479
Ill-gotten gains never prosper
    2467
kiss of enemy full of d. 2473
no white flour out of coal sack
    2475
sell blind horse praise feet 2466
to make things appear what they
    are not 2465
when rogue kisses you count your
    teeth 2478
whitewashed crow shows black
    again 2462
You k'n hide de fier 2482

DECEITFUL
hope exceedingly d. 5924
How d. hope may be 5934
Simplicity has no d. thoughts
    11696

DECEIVE
children little need to d. 1132
easiest person to d. is one's self
    2471
however we d. ourselves 3225
Or d. his heart, omniscient 4888

DECEIVED
Christ either d. mankind by fraud 6366
God is not d. by externals 9269
most d. that trust most in themselves 10040
the mother of mankind 9863
those we do not know never d. us 610

DECEIVES
prosperity d. adversity instructs 241
time d. us 11354

DECEIVING
experts at d. others, ourselves 2477

DECEMBER
that we might have roses in D. 7732

DECENCY
pretenses of d. 4115

DECENT
no synthetic replacement for d. home life 5858

DECEPTION
essence of lying in d, not words 6859
fine art of d. we call finesse 2483
nations have found d. in peace 11783

DECEPTIVE
lure of distant and difficult is d. 8225
presupposition 1467

DECIDE
all means permitted to fight evil 5012
can d. to let Jesus make holy 5752
in perfect delightful friendship with God 5464
Individuals as much right to act way they d. as we 6193
Jesus compelled individuals to d. 6516
Lord never asks us to d. for him 2490
Not to d. is to d. 2487
Once to every man, nation comes moment to d. 2489
People do not d. to be drunkards 11080
sin must die right out 9841

DECIDED
to stick with love 7182

DECIDES
set of a soul that d. goal 4432

DECIDETH
And every man d. 1155

DECIPHER
For mortals to d. yet 8049

DECISION
bring happiness or unhappiness 2494
Calvary, place of d. 2124

Forgiveness a d. of the will 4109
Love, d. to make your problem my problem 7240
Opinion helps us make d. without information 8198
that the Bible is a supernatural book 744
to have child momentous 8310
when to discard toothbrush 2492
Whenever faced with crucial d. 5467

DECISIONS
accept my d. without complaint 39
are God's will unless he checks 5464
believer makes d. on eternal values 10707
Character sum total of d. 1000
defined goals simplified his d. 4425
free to make wrong d. 2486
gray rather than black, white 1242
No one learns to make right d. without 2486
regarding behavior 563
relentless drift of events will make d. 2491
which of two d. to make 2494
Wisdom by-product of right d. 11911

DECISIVE
forces of evil have begun d. offensive 3400

DECISIVELY
we react d. against those who take freedom from us 9463

DECLARATION OF INDEPENDENCE
pursuit of happiness slipped in at last moment 5548

DECLARE
Who shall d. this good, that ill 4338

DECLARES
church most effective when she d. 3796
through mysteries God d. himself 10255

DECLINES
ability d. 11326

DECLUSIONS
one of the most persistent, widely believed d. 5549

DECORUM
home, they say, dead d. 5842

DECREASE
When you share grief, you d. it 5353

DECREE
God's call founded on his d. 4626
God's d. is immutable 4626

God's d. pillar on which perseverance depends 4616
God's d. ties knot of adoption 4616

DECREED
Heaven's eternal wisdom has d. 9462

DECREES
God's foreordained d. 1153

DECREPIT
among the d. is where Jesus went 2812

DECRY
Nothing so dates a man as to d. younger generation 12192

DEDICATE
your life to others 10125

DEDICATED
No life grows great until d. 2852

DEDICATION
power of service will correspond to d. to prayer 10192
will not be a sacrifice 10125

DEED
Because they his d. and word 2639
Do that kind d. you would leave 'till tomorrow 6671
each kindly d. a prayer 7284
Every d. for Christ away from discouragement 2940
every d. is registered and recorded 71
Every good d. touches chord that vibrates in heaven 6670
From promise to d. a day's journey 9320
From the body of one guilty d. 5476
good man makes no noise over good d. 2495
Honestly honest in every d. 2028
hopes to do d. without God's knowledge, errs 2501
In thought, d. 2287
is everything 4416
last d. done, last word said 8082
No d. that sets evil example can bring joy 5035
O God, let no d. be done that is not your d. 8748
of parent fibre woven into character of child 8346
one self-denying d., one word 107
put creed into d. 1011
Revenge in cold blood is devil's d. 9723
reward for good d. is to have done it 10194
smallest good d. better than intention 2505
so deep an impression as one d. 101
So shines good d. in naughty world 2499

thankless man never does thankful d. 11134

that helps or harms poor for or against Christ 8698

Till of heaven the d. appears 6640

to do the difficult d. 6599

worth of kind d. lies in love 2506

DEEDS

are fruits, words are leaves 2532

Bad the day man becomes content with d. he is doing 8649

capable only rarely of evil d. 11272

Character sum total of d. 1000

charity that proclaims good d. ceases to be charity 1081

Christ's d. are commandments 1517

Every syllable already written down in d. 6482

Fill the space with loving d. 11362

God values not your d. 7864

good d. with same zeal 108

Humility covers our good d. 6005

Little d. of kindness 2503

man of words and not of d. like garden of weeds 9319

Noble d. concealed are esteemed 2504

performing gross d. of cruelty 4895

poor vision limits d. 11734

repent not so much for evil d. of wicked people 6285

seedcorn of eternity 2496

sow gentle words, useful d. 1574

Sweetest things turn sourest by their d. 5039

thoughts are seeds of future d. 11244

to render d. of mercy 7747

virtue of d. is completing them 65

We live in d. not years 1056

Youth would rather do noble than useful d. 12181

DEEP

calleth unto d. 4744

comforting sense things unseen are eternal 3746

Conversion a d. work 1895

distress has humanized my soul 10830

Divinity so d. pride drowned in its infinity 4745

experience never peaceful 3514

For we are weak and need some d. revealing 9050

God has d. emotions 4491

God is a specialist when anguish d. 10845

God is the ocean d. 4852

God is too d. to explain himself 4461

Gratitude least articulate when d. 5245

grow so wide, d. nothing human is strange 10540

heavens as d. as aspirations high 468

Hope draws power from d. trust in God 5928

If roots are d. 6307

if we penetrate d. enough beneath surface 5716

in God a d. but dazzling darkness 4506

In midst of noise d. inner silence 10539

inspire me to send my roots d. 9111

is plowing of grief 5332

It matters not how d. intrenched the wrong 6256

joyful sharing replaces polite prattle 4029

keep in reserve God's d. counsels 4322

knows in d. and authoritative way 5809

knows where holes are d. 3541

love of God how d. and great 4776

mind of God so vast and d. 4675

Misfortune d. 11808

mysteries contained in the Lord's Prayer 7156

night given to drink d. at fountain of power 6947

Oh, the depths of the fathomless d. 7943

only God meets d. needs 4310

our total nature, mysterious and d. 7463

Plough d. while sluggards sleep 3115

relationship requires watchfulness, nourishment 9446

roots grow d. when winds strong 212

Silence is d. as eternity 10263

so d. an impression as one deed 101

so d. was the concept of mother 7859

Still waters run d. 10267

Thoughts too d. to be expressed 3059

truth being infinite is d. 11550

voice of a d. life within 3700

water is cold, dark, d. 5527

Where much light, shadow is d. 6712

will do d. inner work 10706

DEEP-BURNING

love becomes as coals, d. and unquenchable 7236

DEEPENED

faith that follows after grief 5360

DEEPENING

In the cloud God is d. thy chords 10600

DEEPENS

As knowledge increases, wonder d. 6678

darkness d, Lord, with me abide 2538

Scripture widens and d. 685

weakness d. dependence on Christ for strength 8256

DEEPER

A d. voice across the storm 3644

break through superficiality to d. life 2738

Far d. than man's deepest hate 4776

Feeling d. than all thought 10678

get no d. into Christ 6502

higher your structure, d. must be foundation 5997

Knowledge given to lead us to d. holiness 6693

Life will take on d. interest 3185

Light griefs can speak, d. ones dumb 5347

no d. into Christ than we allow 1345

rock of divine love d. down 4783

Sends down a d. root 2508

sharper word cuts d. than weapon 2051

Silent worship down to d. currents of the soul 12114

sorrow carves into your being 10626

soul has d. darkness than the nights 7539

Stillness an essential part of growing d. 7711

Stronger, d. roots less visible 7703

the sorrow, less tongue has to say 10627

Thought is d. than all speech 10678

truths reveal a life d. than known 11521

underdeveloped creativity of our d. layers 1596

we plunge, more we learn 7936

DEEPEST

become truly rich in d. sense 9520

cannot enter into d. center of himself unless 7962

capacity to care gives life d. significance 3077

conception of meekness 7728

craving to be appreciated 3141

death of Jesus goes underneath d. sin 2160

dream door in d. sanctum of soul 2971

Far deeper than man's d. hate 4776

Forgiveness man's d. need 4077

God can overflow d. demands 7463

God knows d. possibilities in me 4889

God present in d, most central part of soul 4868

holy life will produce d. impression 5737

life in fullest, d. sense possible 7969

loving in the d, most tragic sense 7186

must feel d. tenderness of God 4012

Pain d. thing in our nature 8269

reaches of mind not cared for enough 3027

sacrifice, one of the d. truths 9758

tenderness for others 4012

tree of d. root 8174

When river is d, makes least noise 2810

word is soul 11993

DEEPLY

designs of God's providence d. hidden 3349

doubt anyone's friend very d. 4283

highest love showed how d. he must suffer 6506

man suffers so d. had to invent laughter 6742

more d. he works the mine 737

People living d, no fear of death 2362

possible for bad men to become d. good 9438

What can wound more d. 4210

DEEP-ROOTED

lives in the desert, d. in God 2609

DEEPS

God always answers us in the d. 8795

God wants us into d. 3544

God's judgments as great d. 3349

DEER

Happiness like a young d. 5548

was a stricken d. that left the herd 9798

DEFEAT

But in ourselves are triumph, d. 10794

cross will d. selfish life 2093

cross, d. of sin 2118

Deliverance only by d. of old life 882

do not be afraid of d. 2511

don't invest much d. doesn't hurt 2629

endless d. of our calculations 5395

first step to something better 2517

formed heroid natures 2511

fresh stimulus 2509

God has gone through human experience of d. 6386

Hopelessness is anticipated d. 5951

in ourselves, triumph, d. 1031

is an orphan 2516

Jesus' victory lies in d. 6443

makes men invincible 2511

may serve as well as victory 2508

mosquitoes who d. us 2512

most significant witness was my d. 2518

never so near to victory 2511

no d. save from within 3627

not outward storms, stresses that d. 2737

not the giants who d. us 2512

nothing but education 2517

nothing can d. God 9983

Psalms, despair of man's d. 798

school in which truth grows strong 2507

should never be source of discouragement 2509

story of conversion, story of blessed d. 1899

through d. of cross God glorified 2519

turns bone to flint 2511

turns gristle to muscle 2511

twilight that knows not d. 1922

Victory comes through d. 2519

well if stopped using terms victory and d. 5753

which educates us 3601

DEFEATED

Christians not d, simply disobedient 5753

conflict with d. foes 235

gains most who is d. 2510

God is never d. 4822

negative word leaves you d. 12001

too often say d. by sin 5753

DEFEATING

can take away from life d. 3596

DEFEATS

God never d. himself by taking away choice 4133

God's d. of us are our victories 11673

mistaking weakness for strength 10749

Remember to forget d. 9270

some d. more triumphant than victories 2514

Violence d. its own ends 11677

DEFECT

Evil d. of substance 3357

If youth be a d. 12166

Man calls sin a d, God a disease 4560

of age to rail at pleasures of youth 12189

person's d. source of strength 3932

DEFECTS

Love overlooks d. 7266

love sometimes by reason of their d. 7332

make up for d. of others 1080

metallurgists build d. into crystals 3932

more quiet we become toward d. of others 8521

nature has d. to show she is only image of God 8022

repeating involuntarily the d. of those among whom we live 6243

DEFEND

ceases to d. himself 2087

Christ a Captain to d. his people 6370

devil pretends to d. truth 2689

Do not ask me to d. 39

every absurdity has champion to d. it 3256

Firm as fortress to d. right 1933

God has all power to d. you 4696

if attack personality, it can only d. itself 8312

the truth 11527

Violence destroys what it claims to d. 11678

DEFENDED

good must be doubted to be d. 2954

life not a possession to be d. 10545

sin is two sins when d. 10289

DEFENDING

man can't always be d. truth 11493

DEFENDS

He who d. injury next to him who commits it 6261

DEFENSE

accusation flies faster than d. 10453

angels understand our d. 363

of warmly held opinions 11216

Truth needs no d. 11575

very few care to listen to d. of character 1055

DEFENSELESS

God in likeness of most d. of creatures 6154

leaves one's old proud self d. 7488

DEFENSES

Human beings bearable when their d. are down 892

we stand stripped of d. 5238

DEFENSIVE

become possessive and d. 10531

criticism puts man on d. 2055

Work can be d. shield 3904

DEFER

let me not d. nor neglect it 10152

not d. or neglect kindness 6642

DEFERENCE

give to father 511

DEFIANCE

cross, d. of pain 2118

in open d. of Sermon on the Mount 5891

Sin d. to authority of God 10362

DEFINABLE

Youth not d. by age 12183

DEFINE
Christ never asks anyone to d. position 6431
Heaven hardly heaven if could d. 5648
if can d. God, am greater than God 7487
if can d. God, greater than God 9395
if we do not d. God 4691
Let one d. his terms, stick to definition 11193
Tis what I feel, but can't d. 7245
won't have anything to do with God because cannot d. him 9395

DEFINED
goals simplified his decisions 4425

DEFINITE
Everything arranged by d. principles 4948

DEFINITION
absurd to put God into a d. 7487
Christ's d. of sin 10300
God has no d. 4671
Let one define his terms, stick to d. 11193

DEFINITIONS
innumerable d. of God 4585
of God overwhelm, stun me 4585

DEFORMED
as I was, running after beauties thou hast made 4805

DEFORMITY
Sin is d. 10363

DEFROCKED
If clergyman d. 1732

DEFROSTING
Spring is winter d. 9893

DEFUSE
negative word can d. enthusiasm 12001

DEFY
I d. you to doubt Jesus 2961
man has power to d. God's wishes 4158

DEFYING
by d. purpose of God insulate ourselves 4864
consequence of d. moral order 4721

DEGENERATE
begin to be satisfied spiritually, begin to d. 9234
caricatures of human beings 3881
last corruption of d. man 11858
religious values lifted or d. 11658
saw good things coming would d. 4318
soul-winning may d. into brush-salesman 7867

DEGENERATES
Everything d. in hands of man 3193

DEGENERATION
Self-complacency and pride beginning of d. 9234

DEGRADED
from honor, freed from envy 1776

DEGRADES
He that despairs d. God 2584
Intimidates the brave, d. the rest 5479

DEGRADING
anxieties engendered by success are d. 10817
tendency to think of sex as d. 10235

DEGREE
feeling in some form or d. in every heart 4019
of fullness accords with intensity of desire 5772
pardon to d. we love 4106
to which life, work emblazon character of Christ 5306

DEGREES
absolute holiness that knows no d. 4658
church, so many d, so little temperature 1410
God will not look you over for d. 172
learning persists after pressure for d. has vanished 3031
no d. with God 4680

DEHUMANIZES
Evil is whatever d. 5014

DEITY
as a continued investigation of the D. 4742
Christianity, D. indwelling man 1189
inscribed on every heart 4833
mystic's spirit lost in abyss of D. 7966
Prosperity not a d. to be worshiped 9340
The rocks proclaim the approaching D. 6138
until d. square-knotted flesh 6131
when we cease to believe in a personal d. 4538

DEJECTED
most, reluctant convert in all England 9829
Never d. while another's bless'd 3074

DEJECTION
Preserve us from yielding to d. 9092

DELAY
better than disaster 8389
Choose to act, rather than d. 1138
Every d. is hateful, but gives wisdom 11912
greatest remedy for anger 397
in justice is injustice 6259

Though hope be weak or sick with long d. 8768
We hate d, yet it makes us wise 11959

DELAYED
Justice d. is justice denied 6611

DELAYS
God d, doesn't forget 4445
loses thanks who promises and d. 2535
Never think God's d. are denials 8402
Sometimes God d. answer to our prayer 8924

DELEGATED
God has d. power to his creatures 4821

DELEGATES
to United Nations not as important 11027

DELIBERATE
Faith d. confidence in character of God 3684
God takes d. time with us 2846
Peace is d. adjustment to will of God 8460
Sin is d. independence of God 10372
sinned out of d. rebellion 10387
with d. purpose, God visited this planet 6144

DELIBERATELY
God d. stands aside 4891
planned, gifted, positioned on earth by Master Craftsman 10004
set ourselves up to fall 10422

DELIBERATION
Marriage to be entered with d. 7641

DELICACIES
a thousand intellectual d. 2021

DELICACY
love a d. unknown in material substances 4789
pretenses of d. 4115

DELICATE
are most who seek help 3069

DELICATELY
friendship should be dealt with d. 4237

DELICIOUS
cheese d. but way to it is risky 11103
life more d. than most of us think 6918
Sunshine is d. 8033

DELIGHT
By d. we all quote 9379
Children listen to Bible with d. 645
devil takes d. in tormenting us 2661

discover d. hidden in irksome tasks 10639

discover d. hidden in somber circumstances 10639

from understanding to d. 7970

God feels d. 4491

God is my d. 7462

God takes d. in breaking up our programs 5401

God's creation, overflowing of d. 1978

happiness united to God and each other in d. 4120

life of freedom, liberty, d. 5464

Love like a lovely rose, the world's d. 7179

no d. of love where there is but one 11622

no life dreary when work d. 3106

no season such d. can bring 9878

problems are the d. of life 9286

Revenge pure d. of little minds 9725

should find d. in work 3127

Sin then d. 10368

Some are born to sweet d. 813

the pang that gives d. 5349

There is a land of pure d. 5670

What sweet d. quiet life affords 9375

You awake us to d. in your praise 7578

DELIGHTED
little d. with the cross 10312

DELIGHTFUL
Anticipation more d. than realization 7160

Death God's d. way of giving life 2246

decide in perfect, d. friendship with God 5464

God is so completely d. 7463

home joys most d. earth affords 5844

most d. saint chastened through sorrow 9781

Music one of most d. presents God has given 7914

sin becomes d. 10287

Unselfishness recognizes variety of types as d. 9512

DELIGHTS
are snares 4877

Few d. equal one we trust 4184

God d. in our temptations 11057

heart may enjoy in presence of God 12120

Jesus Christ d. to dwell within 6352

love d. in servitude as much as in honor 6457

Memory d. old age 7735

not to give his children taste of his d. 9037

Of all d. of this world 10228

that cannot find expression in language 12120

who d. in multitude of words 10245

DELIVER
cannot say d. us from evil if 8818

cried aloud for Holy Spirit to d. me 5781

Fear of God can d. from fear of man 3970

God d. us from rights 10842

God d. us from sullen saints 9774

me from fantasies 5781

me from lust of vindicating myself 9722

Prayer does not d. from situation 8927

should this not d. from griefs, fears 7545

DELIVERANCE
Faith for my d. not faith in God 3662

from fear advanced by prayer 8976

Holiness d. from standing still 5746

let miraculous d. from furnace answer 5197

must be found in Christ Jesus, not in some formula 7105

no hope of d. cure for degeneration 1613

only by defeat of old life 882

Thou alone art d. 9052

wise man prays for d. from fear 3997

DELIVERED
supernaturally d. 10206

whether visibly d. or not 3662

DELUDED
Christ was d. or divine 6366

man of correct insight among d. 2803

may be d. by supernatural forces 5458

DELUSION
Little praying a d. 8889

personal gain made by crushing others 7793

sex is an activity 10227

DELUSIONS
that evils cured by legislation 5184

that one person can make another happy 5549

world so rich in d. truth is priceless 11523

DEMAND
God does d. we keep moving 9832

God doesn't d. our achievements 8094

gospel not so much a d. as an offer 5100

human to d. justice 1207

more I d. love of others, less I deserve 9497

not d. more from you 55

not for old age but for youth 12194

Spirit of God will d. to be Lord of your life 5776

times d. action 3339

We d. proof of God 4689

DEMANDED
Mystery is d. by religious instinct 12118

DEMANDING
a God too d. 2959

all, deserving nothing 7440

Christ d. everything 6419

good is very d. 561

Growth is d. 5366

Self-admiration so d. little left over 1589

DEMANDS
A time like this d. 6299

Can there be love which does not make d. 7162

Christianity d. high level of caring 1541

crosses he sends, sacrifices he d. 4688

faith d. complete change of attitude 3785

God can overflow deepest d. 7463

God d. obedience 8094

God d. perfection from his creatures 8518

God d. so much only he can supply 4473

God's d. are so great 1194

immediate person makes d. in his prayer 8981

love d. toughness in crisis 2045

mercy, shows none 4084

misery because one person d. of another complete understanding 9455

more self is indulged, more it d. 10027

only God can supply what he d. 1194

prayer d. energy 6776

rationalist d. explanation of everything 9395

Satisfaction not felt by those who make d. 2018

Success d. strange sacrifices 10801

tolerance that marriage d. 7648

Virtue d. rough thorny path 11714

who does not know God d. 9496

DEMENTIA
Throughout history truth considered form of d. 5730

DEMERIT
grace directed toward human d. 5206

DEMOCRACY
assumes extraordinary possibilities 2522

attempt to apply Bible principles to society 2523

future of church and humanity d. on family 3894

Happiness doesn't d. on blessings 5513

made body's health d. upon the soul 5606

more we d. on God, more dependable we find he is 11481

must d. on God for ability 1284

On little things d. 7119

Rewards d. on contributions we make 10179

Salvation will d. on never looking back 9828

serpent beguiled Eve to d. on reason alone 9424

DEPENDABILITY

fulfilling what I agreed to do 2533

DEPENDABLE

more we depend on God, more d. we find he is 11481

DEPENDED

Pray as though everything d. on God 8892

Work as though everything d. on you 8892

DEPENDENCE

able to express my d. better on my knees 8759

Adam, instead of maintaining d. on God 757

combine d. of God's Spirit with own researches 6681

Extreme independence as destructive as total d. 7614

God made our d. 6177

God wants to teach us d. 8990

independent in proportion to d. on God 1647

Marriage, d. mutual 7642

more satisfactory is our d. on God 7524

poor in spirit attitude of d. on God 6025

weakness deepens d. on Christ for strength 8256

DEPENDENT

greater awareness of d. on God 5226

independent of God, d. on circumstances 1480

Love not d. on ability, popularity 7235

on God from hour to hour 5226

Repentance process by which we see ourselves as d. people 9594

saint consciously d. on God 9768

DEPENDING

on the mind of God 7753

DEPENDS

believe happiness d. on being more virtuous 6821

destiny of nation d. on citizens under 25 12173

each d. on the other 9501

future d. on priorities, purposes today 4325

Happiness d. on attitude toward blessings 5513

Happiness d. on what happens 6527

holiness d. on God's grace, our will 5754

How happy person is d. upon gratitude 5249

If happiness d. on what somebody says 5536

in world everything d. on taking initiative 5446

More d. on walk than talk 3443

on how we look at things 506

on relationship toward God 4957

on whether man or mouse 8584

Our good or evil name d. 4198

salvation d. more on God's love of us than our love of him 9806

upon this short time eternity d. 6894

when sense of self d. on what I can acquire 10003

When sense of self d. on what others say 10003

DEPOSIT

Time d. in bank of God 11340

DEPRAVITY

Man not left in valley of d. 10436

DEPRESSED

God is below, but not d. 4848

negative word leaves you d. 12001

went to church, not greatly d. 1453

DEPRESSING

hanging around like polar bear d. 9889

DEPRESSION

never come from Spirit of God 5773

of spirits one of seven deadly virtues 11699

refusing to yield to d. 2563

When laughing, d. stops 6746

DEPRIVATION

Evil means d. 3364

of God's recreating, loving peace 8697

DEPRIVE

ourselves of royal display of wisdom 4995

DEPRIVED

children do nothing to get wants 1128

of greater good Lord had designed 4901

Who will not grieve when d. of hope 2616

DEPTH

Bible greater d. than any other book 663

build up surging d. of joy 3185

can do something about life's width and d. 7095

conversation lacks d, makes up in length 1849

every step we rise nearer God increases d. we may fall 10700

faith must seek greater d. 3756

fathom d. of My heart to extent your heart is broken 900

finding our plumb line cannot sound its d. 4745

history of our Lord unfathomable d. 6380

Holy Ghost reveals d. of iniquity 10391

How happy person is depends upon d. of gratitude 5249

if desire d. to emerge 7714

knows about d, knows about God 7466

man can fall is height to which he can rise 8666

music in the d. of night 7927

of capacity for patience 8403

sermon seldom wearies people by its d. 10095

soul is the secret of d. 10669

Stature comes not with height but d. 11939

that is in God 5016

theologians ponder d. of conversion 1896

To weep is to make less d. of grief 5361

truth lies in the d. 3259

DEPTHS

as welcome as surest heaven 9930

At profoundest d. men talk not about God but with him 8767

Bible reveals d. 683

Bible rooted in d. of creation 750

born from intimate d. of divine nature 5967

consoling in d. of affliction 957

Faith instructs us in d. of God 3670

Gaiety often ripple over d. of despair 5508

God an utterable sigh in d. of the soul 4843

grandeur in cry from d. 10676

has entered little into d. of Master's character 6390

Heights of us, d. of us 6932

How shall I sound thy d. 7492

invaded to of one's being by God's presence 7488

like deep sea divers in twilight of d. 6110

love, boundless treasures hidden within its d. 7211

Most saints sank to d. of service 6175

of spirituality 125

Oh, the d. of the fathomless deep 7943

out of the d. must we cry 9020

powers in unconscious d. of man 1712

sense d. which are of God 10257

soul has greater d. than any sea 7539

spirit submerged in d. of divine ocean 7968

through shoreless d. 4712

trying to absorb d. of Bible 748

Who plumbs the d. of God 9791

Without silence cannot plumb d. of being 10246

DEPUTY
mother is God's d. on earth 7841

DERELICTS
world is full of educated d. 8555

DERIDE
ignorance may d. truth 11566

DERIVE
Laughter or tears, both d. from God 6736

DERIVED
right of God's sovereignty d. from omnipotence 4952

DERIVING
just powers from consent of governed 3246

DESCEND
In prayer we d. with mind into the heart 10562

Naked to earth I d. 5952

thou didst d. with noiseless tread 6150

to d. is to rise 9701

DESCENDED
man d. from inferior animal 1992

DESCENDING
to their level in vengeance 9730

wish to rise, begin by d. 6788

DESCENDS
meteor, when it d. to earth 4395

while one ascends, the other d. 8884

DESCRIBES
man discloses own character when d. another 981

DESCRIBING
dislocated both shoulders d. it 3424

DESCRIPTION
attempts at d. futile 4995

of what happens when gospel preached 5105

windbag, two-hour d. 3420

would but make love less 7245

DESERT
All sunshine makes the d. 2709

does not mean absence of men 10565

God does not d. those who serve him 4615

lives in the d. deep-rooted in God 2609

means presence of God 10565

of everyday hurry and strain 10247

pyramids sinking in d. sands 730

Unbelief makes world moral d. 11595

Without God life a d. 7098

DESERTS
man makes d. bloom, lakes die 3197

Men throw railroads across d. 5841

DESERVE
doing what we ought, d. no praise 3100

Emotion most d. reverence 3054

In doing what we ought d. no praise 2779

Kindness is loving people more than they d. 6653

more I demand love of others, less I d. that love 9497

no man so good would not d. hanging 7434

no praise, it is our duty 9666

where is coverage our mothers d. 7844

who d. the severest discipline 6533

worthier to d. than to possess honor 5893

DESERVED
No creature that d. redemption 5483

DESERVES
he that has no cross d. no crown 2112

man convinced he d. hell 5668

No one d. right to lead without 6802

DESERVEST
to serve thee as thou d. 9113

DESERVING
Demanding all, d. nothing 7440

DESIGN
Adam switched off from God's d. 757

All I d, or do, or say 9047

But to fulfill the vast d. 4338

Engineer of universe made me part of d. 4565

Every victory of science reveals more clearly divine d. 9866

God doesn't reveal his grand d. 4448

more skill, d. than works of man 1964

mosaic in d. of God's universe 4005

Not without d. does God write music of our lives 7056

Prayer means raised up into d. with God 8909

DESIGNED
deprived me of greater good Lord had d. 4901

God d. human machine to run on himself 7459

Great men meteors d. to burn so earth lighted 5278

Man d. to carry load of the moment 421

man magnificent ruin of what God d. 7429

soul for God d. 12032

universe seems d. by mathematician 1974

work d. for eternity only done by Spirit 10181

DESIGNS
catch some glimpse of God's d. 4578

God able to fulfill all his d. 4521

happiness God d. 4120

He treasures up his bright d. 4941

of God's providence hidden 3349

DESIRABLE
forbidden unspeakably d. 761

Sin presents itself as a most d. thing 10354

Theology teaches what ends are d. 11210

things d. to men in Bible 641

DESIRE
a god whose destruction we never d. 4846

a solitude we did not d. 10564

Agape love concern without d. to control 7158

All men d. peace 8428

all my works, according to his will 5411

ashamed of my lack of d. 9097

can d. death 2407

Charity, d. to be useful without recompense 1084

Christ for perpetual guest 8092

Covetousness has for mother unlawful d. 5313

degree of fullness accords with intensity of d. 5772

Faith does not d. 3659

few d. things that make for peace 8428

Fix thought more on the God you d. 10305

getting, doth but gain his death 2567

Glory, lovelier to d. than possess 4409

God awaits our d. 4639

God is prompting to d. him 4514

God's love disposes him to d. our welfare 4754

goodness of God to d. our welfare 7093

gratitude surest secret d. of greater benefits 5262

greatest d. to please God, serve one another 6924

himself, runs out of breath 2567

I d. only your love 4561

if d. depth to emerge 7714

if d. for God, God put it there
7461

in d. to be frank become rude
9502

love's insatiable d. 7211

man's d. to stand out 7415

Many want consolation, few d.
adversity 9268

miserable to have few things to d,
many to fear 11827

more than I can accomplish 61

no d. however trifling or vulgar
7536

No man should d. to be happy
who is not holy 5543

not tricked by d. for applause 836

nothing but God 9136

nothing but spirit of the Holy
Jesus 6385

of knowledge in excess caused
man to fall 3556

of love, joy, life, peace 9274

of power in excess caused angels
to fall 3556

of the soul, heaven 9274

only d. to do will of his Father
9280

Prayer is the soul's sincere d. 8948

refusal of praise a d. to be praised
twice 8723

sin goes to our inner d. 10300

so to conduct affairs of this
administration 6304

some great d. to do something
larger 8649

success, no end to escalation of d.
10817

Thou dost d. my worthless heart
7456

to be filled with Spirit must be
all-consuming 5772

to be holy rather than happy
10719

to d. ardently all that is pleasing
to thee 9062

to do away with suffering 1546

to find quick cure for suffering
1546

to flee from suffering 1546

to have heaven, hell ever in my eye
6910

to know art of living 10935

to know what he ought to d. 9824

torn between d. to think positively
or confront life 9401

true leader likely has no d. to lead
6785

unashamed effort to protract
physical d. 10229

voice of intelligence ignored by d.
6331

What but thyself canst thou d.
7456

what we d. children to become,
we must be 5861

whenever heart begins to burn
with d. for God 4749

Where d. to learn, many opinions
6711

who make this quest supreme d.
6494

will be for what you can ask in
God's name 10780

DESIRED

death, as lover's pinch, is d. 2387

pleasure, not pain 577

Some sins we have d. 10384

DESIRES

all d. have been reduced to one
9282

come to God in utter dearth of his
d. 3780

Death power of altering d. 2240

direction of life, d. different 984

Do not give up d. 1241

each check to our d. 4578

free rein to the d. of flesh 466

God d. but sincerity, transparency
7450

God knows all d. 4881

God makes clear what he d. 1149

God unable to grant heart's d. till
9282

God will direct 1241

greed flares up when d. frustrated
10003

he who d. nothing always free
1796

heaven, find satisfaction of all d.
5644

honors, not worthy of honor 9203

I had never known suddenly
comes on the horizon 9276

I pray for your d. that they may
be great 4248

If d. be endless, cares will be too
5317

If d. not met by God 7538

If hearts open, d. known 10507

increase with possessions 2869

mean and petty man's d. 7381

my d. are satisfied 7964

need heart that d. will of God
5442

our Lord saw people's d. 6519

place in God's hands d. 1241

precious things God finds in us
10666

right with God, he gives d. 9280

so impatient 5944

Spirit of God alters my
dominating d. 9276

To pray is conformity with what
God d. 8944

DESIRING

not just refrain from adultery, but
from d. 6444

DESIROUS

Be d. to do the will of another
rather than thine own 8448

not d. of looking into faults of
others 6597

DESOLATE

daily burden of a d. life 9683

However d. life's monody sounds
7895

made in image of God must know
him or be d. 7465

Where Christ is, none is d. 2120

DESOLATION

cry of d. live, not recorded 2147

In times of d. be patient 2883

Obedience to God will mean d.
8105

Receive every d. with both thy
hands 7698

DESPAIR

a frightful queerness 2578

About the world's d. 2589

agnosticism has done its withering
work 320

Alcohol does not drown 323

an evil counselor 2579

At edge of d. dawns a clarity 2574

Blues are songs of d. 7890

can become a kind of sanctuary
2581

Choose to pray, rather than d.
1138

church, deep in crushed d. 1401

damp of hell 2580

Devil now fiercer by d. 2643

Disappointment, parent of d.
2795

don't be too quick to d. 2593

doubles our strength 2577

forget valley of d. 9270

friend who cares silent in d. 3080

Gaiety often ripple over depths of
d. 5508

God gives comfort in d. 2582

God has gone through human
experience of d. 6386

hell, d. 5698

Hope opens doors, d. closes them
5928

ideal which leads to d. 6401

If determination fixed, do not d.
8544

if show our true selves suddenly
would d. 10006

impossible to d. who remembers
his Helper omnipotent 2595

in hell called d. 11394

In idleness perpetual d. 6764

in our own d. comes wisdom
11919

Jesus' life would drive us to d.
2161

Life begins on other side of d.
2597

Love can hope where reason
would d. 7209

most beautiful poems filled with d.
8621

music can make d. and madness
please 7911

must d. to obtain grace of Christ
5201

no way out, around or through
2578

only possible ending 8237

out of d. by creative effort of God
2613

preach people into d. 9838
Psalms, d. of man's defeat 798
repentance recorded of penitent
thief that none should d. 9602
so long will I fight against d. 2590
solitude without fellowship abyss
of d. 10547
Surrendering to d. man's favorite
pastime 2607
tells us difficulty insurmountable
5931
That crushes into dumb d. 8863
thinking will never get out of d.
2613
this is not the time to d. 2590
What do damned endure but d.
5706
when temptations drive us to d.
11057
Where Christ is, no room for d.
2120
where there is d, hope 9086
work on in d. 2601

DESPAIRING
if foresight of adversity 4314

DESPAIRS
He that d. degrades God 2584
He who d. wants love, faith 2586

DESPERATE
Beware of d. steps 2575
characteristic of wisdom not to do
d. things 11922
fear without love makes men d.
9736
in hour of d. need faith born
within 3820
Marriage is a d. thing 7636
people do d. things 8692
Why d. haste to succeed 10827

DESPERATELY
active people a nuisance 126
difficult to be honest with oneself
5880
in need of salvation 7827
we call for cross our own size
2116
without God young people d.
grasping for security 12180

DESPERATION
men lead lives of quiet d. 2610

DESPISE
Do not d. others 11685
God doth d. neutralities 4920
help us not to d, oppose what we
do not understand 9095
If I hate or d. any one man in
world 5599
may d. grace of God, but cannot
extinguish 4655
no life so meager greatest can
afford to d. it 7055
nothing except falsehood,
meanness 8472
people d. Christianity 1205
Resolved, never to d. 569
that which God loves 5599

DESPISED
and persecuted, but care not 1293
Humility is to be at rest when d.
6010
Old age, though d, is coveted
8164

DESPONDENCY
gives up perfection as unattainable
3463
God's designs infinitely wise 2545
Preserve us from d. 9092

DESSERT
pleasure the d. of life 12028

DESTESTED
Cruelty is a d. sport 28

DESTINATION
Life not a d. 11374

DESTINED
end of man is holiness 5757
thou art d. to greatness 9982
to be in God 3490

DESTINIES
awake to d. of the immortal soul
10654
Life, training for d. of eternity
6979
revivals altered d. of nations 9752

DESTINY
a fool's excuse for failure 2619
a tyrant's authority for crime 2619
acts of this life d. of the next 7024
And in the field of D. 2622
cannot turn human being from d.
2618
Christ makes human d. depend on
relationship to himself 6431
commands fulfill God's d. in life
8111
determined by us 1149
eternity, intimations of astounding
d. 1757
man with cross no longer controls
d. 2111
not determined for us 1149
of nation depends on citizens
under 25 12173
poorly read his origin and d. 7087
Sow character, reap d. 1041
that I may grow toward the stars
of my d. 9111
that makes us brothers 919
Think of d, how puny a part you
are 7063
waits in the hand of God 2620
will never change your d. 11190

DESTITUTE
blessing to know d. spiritually 830
fully appreciate grace of God
2605
Only those who see themselves d.
2605

DESTROY
Adversity can either d. or build
141
alcohol, d. the weak 331

bridge by which God would come
to you 9634
child in womb not lawful to d. 16
Choose to build, rather than d.
1138
daily deaths d. power of final
dying 2110
do not d. the child 23
evil they set out to d. 5012
explain a trial, d. its purpose 164
God's loving anger must devour
and d. 4997
Grace does not d. nature 5214
ground and man is destroyed
3199
hear ever-approaching thunder
which will d. us 8445
Intelligence must never d. faith
6327
murder when we d. people with
words 10683
one sin will d. a sinner 10344
qualities to success most likely to
d. 10819
rests not to d. melody 9684
safe way to d. enemy 3170
Waves need not always d. 2798
What does not d. makes stronger
231

DESTROYED
conquered but in this life never d.
5013
cross d. formula that might be right
2166
cross d. religion equals happiness
2151
destroy ground and man is d.
3199
remove resurrection, Christianity
d. 9689
sometimes will of God everything
d. 5423
world started with wars, shall be
d. by wars 11765

DESTROYER
suffering can also be a d. 10933

DESTROYING
evil consists in d. life 5044
God's method to preserve by d.
4556
Love d. all fear of an end 7229
Love d. all memory of a beginning
7229
man technically capable of d.
world 9872
Men think God is d. when tuning
290
Only man clogs happiness with
care, d. what is 12073
Power more easily manifested in
d. than creating 8712
science dragon capable of d. world
9870
Without d. me in process, how
could God reveal himself 2963

DESTROYS

Hate compared to foot that d. sandcastle 7233

Holy Spirit d. personal life 5795

one vicious or thoughtless kick d. 7233

Prosperity d. appreciation of the right 245

selfishness d. spiritual nature 10073

Sorrow d. differences of intellect 10620

the mighty, the humble spares 4505

Violence d. fabric of society 11678

Violence d. what it claims to defend 11678

DESTRUCTION

compass your own d. 10024

Job felt hand of d. 4556

lease pain of more concern than d. of millions 10035

Music glorifying d. 7910

War the science of d. 11773

Your d. is Satan's highest priority 9855

DESTRUCTIVE

dark night of soul not d. 2608

Extreme independence as d. as total dependence 7614

funerals d. to true memory 2311

life without a quiet center becomes d. 10531

power of evil unlimited if on earth alone 3377

Rest and motion equally d. 9685

television likely to prove most d. 11032

to act out negative attitudes 503

victories won over others 1165

What is d. is impatience, haste 6116

DETACHED

Sunday self and weekday self not good if d. 10949

DETACHMENT

Christ's calls to d. 9351

poor in spirit d. from earthly supports 6025

DETACHMENTS

Christ's d. inside toward God 6436

DETAIL

difference is attention to d. 64

Life is frittered away by d. 10281

DETAILS

bore gives twice as many d. 1829

Christ, oblivious of d. 6501

drown tales in d. 1867

God is in the d. 4484

DETECTS

law d. 5231

DETER

probability we shall fail should not d. 3625

DETERIORATE

improve man, d. cat 7390

DETERIORATING

according to schedule 8134

DETERMINATION

confession, d. to avoid sin 1599

difference between impossible, possible 2631

Fretfulness, a d. to get my own way 416

If d. fixed do not despair 8544

in d. to be bold become brazen 9502

Leaders ordinary people with extraordinary d. 6798

that we exist is God's free d. 3481

DETERMINE

Attitudes d. actions 501

future course for nation 8360

never to be idle 51

not freedom to d. end of choice 1149

plan of action 555

War does not d. who is right 11767

We're the ones that d. people's attitudes 11027

DETERMINED

actions d. by impulse to follow leader 6199

America's future d. by home, school 5818

combated by d. forces 2630

destiny d. by us 1149

destiny not d. for us 1149

living d. by attitude 522

living d. not by what happens 522

living d. not by what life brings 522

reputation of thousand years d. by conduct of one hour 9625

revelation of God d. by character 1050

so d. to get own way writes diary in advance 10772

DETERMINES

attitude d. disease or reward 509

Character d. revelation 2830

God alone d. morality 7828

how child fits into fabric of society 8346

One's attitude d. impact 201

over and above the required d. distinction 2784

set of sails d. where they go 4432

whether work sacred or secular 7865

DETERRENT

fear of God, d. to want 3993

DETHRONEMENT

No d. for us 2821

DETHRONES

Sin sovereign until sovereign grace d. it 10373

DETOUR

no d. to holiness 5768

DETOURS

contented man enjoys scenery along d. 1773

hard to understand d. God takes us 5423

Take d. as evidence on right route 2745

DETRACT

forget irritations that d. from happiness 9270

DETRACTORS

Christ had d. 9448

DETROYS

God never d. work of his own hands 7685

DEVASTATING

society by every mischief ingenuity can invent 4895

swift wind of compromise d. 1584

DEVASTATION

pains of hell d. of spirit 3482

Satan fails to speak of spiritual d. 2662

DEVELOP

art of solitude 10553

compliment d. into friendship 1572

faith seems to d. best when fog rolls in 3789

God able to test, d. faith 3744

God wants to d. same character traits as in Christ 6301

greatness is ability to d. greatness in others 6804

New habits take time to d. 8747

No one can d. fully 11613

powers of spiritual receptivity 7564

DEVELOPED

because of circumstances 1471

concealed until life d. sufficiently 11609

Holiness means life of Jesus d. in us 5748

inner, outer life harmoniously d. 1766

phobia of being alone 10575

DEVELOPING

faith gradual process 5738

prevented from d. initiative 8337

DEVELOPMENT

aid in d. of Christians 3317

evil hindering d. of life 5044

God has program of character d. 1015

God in no way hinders struggle for d. 4129

God is without d. 4680

God wills the d. of all men 9351

gospel a d. more complete than limits of nature 9351

meaning of earthly existence is d. of the soul 9342

Neglecting d. of mind 7793

silly question first intimation of new d. 6703

temptation character d. curriculum 11058

use leisure as means of mental d. 5567

DEVELOPMENTS

sleep, profound d. in spirit, soul, body 10486

DEVELOPS

God never d. one part of our being at expense of other 6897

grief d. powers of the mind 5340

DEVIATE

To d. is to sin 9965

DEVIATION

fight d. from course Jesus set for us 9965

DEVICE

The poor d. of man 7572

DEVICES

In solitude heart can take off protective d. 10540

DEVIL

a diplomatist 2651

a man in prime of life 2651

a man of the world 2651

a master strategist 2660

along comes d. and blows 10226

always leaves stink behind him 2670

always voting against man 1145

and me, we don't agree 2671

Anything the d. does always done well 2640

Ask of the d. use magic 2618

author of confusion 2659

beast and d. may be conquered 5013

begins advocacy of self-pity 10036

believe in d. for three reasons 2650

better served by exploiting our virtues 2648

Bible can combat d. 720

Bible deals with all that d. can do 696

Bible says he exists 2650

boasts of sin is a d. 10309

burning candle of life in service of d. 9576

call'd the d. and he came 2651

can cite Scripture for his purpose 2672

can keep us terrified of thinking 11218

can wrestle with but not overcome 2673

cannot harm us 2682

cannot lord it over servants of God 2673

categorically refuses to do will of God 4915

changes hunger for God into haste 7512

collectivities belong to the d. 6176

collectivities easily respond to devil's persuasion 6176

comes in hour of darkness 2674

concern of d. is to keep Christians from praying 8985

Confusion dust raised by d. 2642

cost d. little trouble to catch lazy man 6766

deadliest trap of d. is religious 2701

deals with God and d. 721

did grin, for his darling sin 9192

difficult to get rid of him 2657

do not have to let him in 2674

do not have to listen 2674

does not come along lines we understand 2702

does not tempt unbelievers, sinners 2675

doesn't believe in revivals 9750

doesn't know how to sing 2676

easy to bid d. be your guest 2657

either a lunatic or d. of hell 6350

either children of God or the d. 8075

entangles ambitious with power 2677

entangles learned with false doctrine 2677

entangles miser with gold 2677

entangles youth with beauty 2677

Everything d. does, God overreaches 2644

fears nothing from prayerless studies, work, religion 8985

fight d. with own weapons, overmatch 2647

flatterers meet, d. goes to dinner 4054

forever fogging minds with smokescreens 2660

Gainst the logic of the d. 2636

God does allow the d. 4957

God stronger than d. 1924

hard to dance with d. on your back 9690

has nothing to say about will of God 4915

has one good quality 2678

has power to suggest evil 2679

has three children 2680

hate cynicism worse than d. 2183

hates will of God 4915

hath power to assume pleasing shape 2681

Hell created for d. and his angels 5686

Hell highest reward d. can offer 5689

hide from temptestuous storms of d. 2652

hunger for God, d. rides it, spurs it on 7512

Hurry not of the d, is the d. 5579

hypocrites greatest dupes d. has 6055

idle person tempts d. to tempt him 11047

If beat d. in prayer, can beat him anywhere 8837

If d. can beat you in prayer, he can beat you anywhere 8837

If d. ever laughs, must be at hypocrites 6055

If d. knocked you out, get up 1024

If d. succeeds in making complicated 10653

If ever the d. had an agent 2447

If money your god, will plague like d. 7801

if you don't open door to d. he goes away 2654

Illusion dust d. throws in eyes of foolish 2655

In heaven he scorns to serve 2656

intriguer 4915

is a bully 2682

is a demogogue, sloganeer 6176

is handsome, charming man 2651

is making his pitch 2683

is not lame 2651

is not ugly 2651

is running from me 2653

is sincere, but sincerely wrong 10429

laughs at toil, mocks at wisdom 8985

laughs in his fist 2661

lest he bring us to eat of beef 2703

long spoon to eat with d. 2645

looks upon us as his property 11097

love would sweep away strongholds of d. 7349

loves man out of egotism 2688

loves to fish in troubled waters 1826

makes man more clever d. 3005

media provided d. with opportunity 2698

Men naturally tempted by the d. 6770

method to obscure himself behind object of worship 2699

mischief-maker 4915

much beast and some d. in man 5013

never sleeps 9861

no d. can hinder you from serving 10159

no mind to trade with d. 11065

no plan to retain this or that of the d. 9864

no power to compel against will 2679

not afraid of Bible with dust 729

not always at one door 2685

not running from the d. 2653

now fiercer by despair 2643

now in hell he reigns 2656

obliging 2651

only knows how to howl 2676

only the d. who praises himself 9214

paints himself black 2687

passions, impatiences please devil 2661

pequ'd such saintship to behold 2690

perhaps cynicism and d. same thing 2183

playing for sympathy 2648

Preach nothing down but the d. 9156

predestines every man to be damned 9175

presents us with magnificent set-up 2648

pretending to defend truth 11533

pretends to defend truth 2689

Prosperity good campaigning weather for d. 9338

quote Scriptures, d. will run 720

refuses to stand under God 4915

saints interest us when in conflict with d. 1631

scholars have recognized existence 2650

see his work everywhere 2650

seeks slaves, claims obedience 4912

serve d. for better wages 2646

Shame the d. 2669

shuns the cross 11893

sin fellowship with the d. 10360

sometimes speaks the truth 11532

Sometimes the d. is a gentleman 2668

songs, psalms sorely vex, grieve d. 2661

stands outside as cunning observer 4915

strongest, fiercest spirit in heaven 2643

takes delight in tormenting 2661

talks glibly of church and state 2651

tells lies about men 1060

Temptation is d. looking through keyhole 11088

tempts not least 9788

tempts that he may ruin 11096

tests us that we might stumble 171

than to have succeeded serving the d. 10777

that old stager 2697

though cowardly, safety for us 2678

through pride d. became the d. 9240

To curse is to pray to the d. 9306

to fetch the dead 2638

torments when we confess 2661

trembles when we pray 8985

tries to shake truth 11533

tugging to make us animals 3406

wanted to involve Jesus in exigencies of power 2704

we see him rose-colored 2687

well skill'd in debate 2651

whatever d. does God can use for Christian's benefit 9858

when close eyes to d. be sure not a wink 2705

when d. looks most noble he is most dangerous 2648

When God says today, d. says tomorrow 2493

when going in same direction as the d. 8762

when hearts are purest, comes and soils 2649

when I hear the d. quote Scriptures 2637

When we do ill, d. tempts us 11116

When we do nothing, we tempt d. 11116

where d. can't go, he sends grandmother 2706

Where d. cannot put head, puts tail 2707

Whispered insinuations rhetoric of the d. 10478

who leads downward, fiddles all the way 2697

whole world booby-trapped by d. 2701

will flee if we resist 2678

willing for person to profess but not practice Christianity 2686

With silence one irritates the d. 10276

with wonder his form I closely scan 2651

would worship d. if he appear 12123

wrestles with God 2691

young people designate god with clay feet as d. incarnate 12179

DEVILISH

devil's most d. when respectable 9862

purpose in pain, otherwise d. 8274

return evil for good d. 4102

to persist d. 7065

to remain in sin is d. 10408

DEVIL-POSSESSED

among the d. is where Jesus went 2812

DEVIL'S

At the d. booth are all things sold 2641

best ruse is to persuade he does not exist 2692

boots don't creak 2693

country begins where men eat men 4913

ever kind to his own 2694

field of battle is human heart 2691

first caught by the d. bait 2696

gossip's mouth is d. mailbag 5146

idle brain is d. workshop 6754

Idleness, the d. pillow 6762

miser's wealth is the d. 11796

most devilish when respectable 9862

Neutral men are d. allies 8071

not so much as taste the d. broth 2703

Nothing sets person out of d. reach as humility 6024

rejects God's truth in favor of d. impure philosophies 11512

Religious contention is the d. harvest 9548

Revenge in cold blood is d. act, deed 9723

sacrifice to God of d. leavings 8183

Self-righteousness the d. masterpiece 10039

Slanderers d. bellows 10469

snare does not catch unless 2696

Sour godliness is d. religion 2186

wrap yourself in God, escape the d. sight 2658

DEVILS

And them all the Lord transformed to d. 2639

impulse, into d. if set up as absolute guide 7836

Money and marriage make d. or saints 7805

pride changed angels into d. 6020

see only the darkness 357

suffering makes some people d. 10860

When angels come, d. leave 367

DEVISE

plan by which good people go to heaven 5632

DEVOTE

Christ asks us to d. ourselves to him 2836

Men d. themselves assiduously 31

rebellious deny as freely as d. adore 4129

will to purpose of God 12124

DEVOTED

immature are consciously d. to God 1714

Love is d. to God 7246

man with vision of God d. to God himself 11729

worship of himself: more d. a man is, the fewer proselytes 9249

DEVOTEDLY

Lord loves you d, individually 4747

DEVOTING

yourself singleheartedly to God 10703

DEVOTION

As soon as danger passes, d. vanishes 8788

chamber of sickness is chapel of d. 6089

Christianity, d. to Christ 1176

Christianity, not d. to a cause 1176

Christianity, not d. to doctrine 1176

Christianity, not d. to work 1176

Deep in my soul the still prayer of d. 8778

difference between d. to
  principles, person 2836
end of reliance of natural d. 5792
extends over every instant of life
  9731
habital, fixed, permanent 9731
hymns sung with d. 1455
not a thing that passes 9731
regulates all our conduct 9731
Service with d. that consumes
  3182

DEVOTIONS
get up at 4 A.M. every morning for
  d. 9970
Satan rocks cradle at d. 2663

DEVOUR
God's loving anger must d. and
  destroy 4997

DEVOURING
instead of d. let's support 9498

DEVOUT
as a d. investigation of the Deity
  4742
by bringing high courage of d. soul
  4974
Man is essentially d. 12110
Nobody can always have d.
  feelings 4777
pose gone when determine to
  concentrate 6056

DEVOUTLY
Pray d, hammer stoutly 8894

DEW
Falling like d. upon a thought
  12002
Is most precious d. he will on us
  bestow 2142
like flowers in sun, d. 3144
of compassion, a tear 1553
rose is sweetest wash'd with
  morning d. 7309

DEWDROP
before I can say like a d. 7070
Life a d. on lotus leaf 6959
Pleasure frail like a d. 8604

DEWDROPS
are God's thoughts in pearls 8048

DEWS
Drop thy still d. of quietness 8431

DIAGRAM
God cannot be fitted into a d.
  4851

DIALOGUE
in which creative inspiration
  sought 4160
Prayer is d. 8932
Prayer is love's tender d. 8926
to enter into d. with God 8779

DIAMOND
cut, brighter it sparkles 280
life facets of one d. reflecting light
  6985

DIAMOND DUST
heaven polishes jewels with d. 143

DIAMONDS
crown not deck'd with d. 1808
Many individuals like uncut d.
  8658

DIARY
Memory is the d. we carry with us
  7734
writes d. in advance 10772

DICE
God casts the die, not the d. 4930

DICTATE
To let others d. your future is to
  have chosen 8264

DICTATION
to submit to d. worse than war
  11768

DICTATORS
outlawed Bible 726

DICTATORSHIP
not an alibi for conscience 1689
Whatever crushes individuality is
  d. 6222

DICTIONARY
not words we have to look up in d.
  7000
only place where success before
  work 3118
Words innocent, powerless in a d.
  12004

DID
And how I do and d. 1855
are the d. and did-not of yesterday
  1734
do what you didn't do 3473
God does not care what good you
  d. 7862
They will say, "We d. this
  ourselves" 6803

DID-NOT
are the did and d. of yesterday
  1734

DIDN'T
did do what you d. do 3473

DIE
a thousand ways to d. 2393
a trouble to d. 186
all that lives must d. 2402
and you live in God 9556
as natural to d. as to be born 2320
as we shall wish when we come to
  d. 9120
before you d. 9833
Better to d. of hunger 3979
Better to live rich than d. rich
  11826
Better to love God and d.
  unknown 10777
Bible taught me how to d. 671
born crying, live complaining, d.
  disappointed 7075
By turns we catch the fatal breath
  and d. 2233
can't d. linked to permanent life
  of God 2431

care to live until chose to d. 5530
content to live or d. 11468
dead shall live, the living d. 7925
dead so long as you refuse to d.
  10050
Death, thou shalt d. 2356
desire to d. right rather than live
  wrong 10719
Every man knows he will d. 2279
God casts the d, not the dice 4930
God does not d. on the day 4538
God, an unwearied life that
  cannot d. 4698
great enough to d. for 7140
he bids him come and d. 10049
I d. hard but I am not afraid to go
  2436
I shall d. but that is all I shall do
  2309
I should like to slip out without
  fuss 2421
I to d, you to live 2378
If God has work for me to do, I
  cannot d. 6921
if I did not laugh I should d. 6747
if live in God and d. to own will
  10047
If want to d. happily, learn to live
  6926
if you would live happily, learn to
  d. 6926
immortal rapture that cannot d.
  7952
In lowly pomp ride on to d. 2981
Instruct me how to d. 9048
Let all live as they would d. 6938
Let me d. as the leaves d, gladly
  2326
live a conqueror, a king, d. a man
  2353
live in fear of death is many times
  to d. 2403
lives holiest life fittest far to d.
  2427
Lord Jesus, you died to help me d.
  2331
Lord, look out for me when I d.
  2333
Love neglected will soon wither, d.
  7230
man makes deserts bloom, lakes d.
  3197
many curl up, d. because of
  undersatisfaction 3089
Many learned men d. slaves 3018
may be called upon to d. for
  country 10525
may d. in hour of unwise word
  4237
millions of men would d. for Jesus
  Christ 6351
most grand to d. 2264
Most people would d. sooner than
  think 11233
must flee cross or d. upon it 2117
never cared to live until I chose to
  d. 2308
never fail who d. in a great cause
  7680

No young man ever thinks he shall d. 12171

nobody wants to d. 2282

nor let me d. before I have begun to live 8430

not afraid to d, honey 2312

Not, how did he d. 7423

Ofttimes test of courage is to live rather than d. 7009

One out of one people d. 2386

Our people drift and d. 9224

pray as if you were to d. tomorrow 12023

process never ends until we d. 1148

requires more courage to suffer than d. 10856

rich make war, poor who d. 11778

should d. of roar which is other side of silence 8496

sin must d. right out 9841

sin remains alive because there is nothing for which it will d. 11394

slander would starve and d. 10455

solitude should teach us how to d. 10530

something great enough to d. for 8897

Son cannot d. for whom the Father never elected 3043

Sorrows d. with time 12059

stormy old friends silent after they d. 2397

Ten d. of little worries 12061

than d. a slave to wealth 10777

think they will not have grace enough to d. by 6912

to be of service to others we have to d. to them 10162

To d. for a religion easier than to live it 7681

to d. is to live 9701

To d. to our neighbors 10162

We all d. sometime 7782

we d. on the day 4538

when I have seen God I shall never d. 2310

Whenever sounds of world d. out in soul 4968

who guide lives by integrity d. happy 6309

whose daily living is to daily d. 10046

will show you how to d. 9142

with all their music in them 8647

with hand on doorlatch they d. outside 3654

world to d. amid blast of archangel's trumpet 7886

You'll get pie in sky when you d. 5682

Young men may d, old men must 2433

Youth who must fight and d. 11757

DIED

And d. with nothing done 6756

at thirty, buried at sixty 7041

dying as Christ d. who d. to himself 6365

from suffocating luxury 10739

he bled, and d, I have been transfused 2979

If Jesus Christ is God and d. for me 9761

It simply d. of frost 7159

Jesus d. even for Judas 6469

Jesus d. for you 46

Lord Jesus, you d. to help me die 2331

On the soft bed of luxury, most kingdoms have d. 7364

To tell me how he d. 10122

Until he d. 4199

When Christ hung, bled, d. 7173

DIEHARD

to demonstrate to d. doubter he wasn't a ghost 9693

DIES

A good man never d. 2206

childhood d, corpses called adults 1135

Christian, d. to live 1265

Death cannot kill what never d. 7319

error, d. among his worshipers 11579

Every moment d. a man 806

Everyone d, but not everyone lives 6884

grave of one who d. for truth holy ground 11534

greatest loss what d. inside while we live 2254

he who d. believing 2228

Hope last thing that d. in man 5924

in pain 7050

Man who d. out of Christ 2381

martyr d, his rule begins 7679

mortality related to body which d. 3482

No man d. before his hour 2338

Nothing d. harder than theological difference 11198

old man d. with open hand 11656

safely through thy love 2228

seed d. into new life, so does man 2385

Slander, at every word a reputation d. 10468

tumult and shouting d. 6036

tyrant d, his rule ends 7679

way man d. more important than death itself 2336

What we have done for ourselves d. with us 10091

when body d, real man will stand naked 1030

When friend d, part of yourself d. 4300

when honor d. 7442

when man d, clutches only that which he has given away 2416

while pleasure laughs, it d. 8604

will all fall apart when he d. 63

Yet the light of a whole life d. 7306

DIET

more you put it off, more you put on 9294

DIFFER

business does not d. from prayer 8471

God's values d. from ours 11667

Grant us true judgment to distinguish things that d. 9063

Hearts may agree though heads d. 9461

not so much wherein they d. 9465

sacrifice may d. from person to person 5385

who d. concerning their faith 11212

DIFFERED

owe knowledge to those who have d. 6710

DIFFERENCE

between appreciation and flattery 441

between best to glory God, yourself 3469

between Christian love and values of world evident 6278

between Christians is contrast of their praying 8976

between death of Christian and non-Christian 2305

between devotion to principles, person 2836

between duty and love 7297

Between esteemed good, condemned as bad 5042

between failure, success 8227

between faith and works 3786

between go and let's go 9505

between good and great 64

between good person and bad person 5041

between heaven, hell 2305

between impossible, possible is determination 2631

between life as it is and ought to be 9408

between perseverance, obstinacy 10773

between physical, spiritual power 8715

between right because of conscience, presence of others 1051

between right word and almost right word 11992

between saying prayers and praying 8998

between true, false repentance 9601

between what happens when man says 3611

between what things are and
ought to be 7413
between worldliness, godliness is
renewed mind 7769
big d. to fly which side he chooses
8076
big d. whether positive or negative
516
character makes 1019
cross reveals d. between power,
love 2156
distance makes no d. 8832
doctrine of value if makes d. in
lives 11180
does not make d. if neighbor loves
you 8057
essential d. between you and the
world 10917
hardly any d. between doing, being
10561
is attention to detail 64
is attitude 516
is droll 8244
little d. in people 516
lose emphasis that what we do
makes a d. 7481
Love makes d. between execution,
martyrdom 7263
meditation that does not make a
d. short-circuited 7725
not in sun, but in clouds 4772
Nothing dies harder than
theological d. 11198
of opinion alienates little minds
11392
scholar sees, seer sees through
3021
Small numbers make no d. to God
10800
way through testings makes all
the d. 166
What d. does it make to you 74
which rouses contempt of the
world 10917

DIFFERENCES

between husband, wife 7670
church sample of d. surmounted
1492
complementing, helping by d.
1445
God rejoices in d. 1445
half the d. in theology would end
11193
Honest d. sign of progress 1624
light enables us to see d. 1144
No church thrives unless d. 1411
social d. have lost power to divide
6286
Sorrow destroys d. of intellect
10620

DIFFERENT

all men d. 921
blessed remain eternally d. 6169
completely d. people in heart,
spirit, mind 3766
concept of spirituality varies
among d. groups 10713

deaf live in silent world so remote,
d. 9094
direction of life, desires d. 984
disposition looks through same
eyes 8583
everyone d. and no one perfect
6180
Everyone is ignorant, only on d.
subjects 6079
Everyone's d. 7377
fear something d. than alarm 3983
For each, God has a d. response
7127
friends are all d. 4297
from image try to create in minds
of others 9950
genius sees world at d. angle 4389
God knows me is d. from God is
omniscient 11179
God never points out pathway d.
4969
good sermon helps in d. ways
10094
he may not say much but you feel
d. 6241
hears a d. drummer 10827
how many d. climates of feelings
4014
inward attitude of man who loves
God so d. 5046
life can have but d. aspects 6985
life in the Spirit a d. life 10715
life we call Christian d. from what
we think it is 6918
meet d. race, color to yourself
3234
mistake to think time of prayer d.
from any other time 8881
natural view and Bible view of
man d. 7429
Never think could do something if
d. lot 8219
only d. kinds of good weather
8033
people with d. outlooks, d.
education 1455
praise God for having made a d.
world 5678
race, d. colored roses 3234
saint totally d. motive 9783
see God, everything becomes d.
8583
sort of evidence required 3657
strength of Christianity d. from
natural strength 1165
than those who think d. 3032
To be irreplaceable must be d.
6192
trouble acts d. on people 11431
view of church, ministry 2987
ways of seeing the city 10522
when church d. from world 5096
When you pray, you begin to be d.
9033

DIFFERENTLY

God, loving all, should love each
d. 6169
music understood by thousands,
all who feel d. 7905

DIFFERS

because he d. in opinion 8193
Heavenly Father never d. from
himself 4590
Jesus d. from all other teachers
6442

DIFFICULT

acquire skill to do d. things easily
8406
After sanctification d. to state aim
in life 9830
All things are d. before easy 2710
always found praying d. 8821
anything that makes Christian
work d. 7036
Bible d. book to study 694
Cares more d. to throw off than
sorrows 12059
child is unhappy 1125
Christian faith found d, left
untried 1220
Christian thinking d. 11221
commandments always humanly
d. 1521
cross God sends of necessity d.
2092
easy becomes d. with reluctance
2756
equality a d. business 3247
God does best work in d.
circumstances 3769
habit d. to resume 3109
happier circumstances free from
d. complications 4974
Hope thinks nothing d. 5931
How widely Jesus known d. to
judge 6395
However d. life may be 8440
inherent in human condition 8569
Is it so d. to believe in God 615
Lash love upon equals d. 7348
learn to deal with d. 2712
Love d. to sustain 7233
lure of distant and d. is deceptive
8225
Marriage most d. of relationships
7641
more d. to be born or rise 492
more d. to come than return 492
most d. thing we manage is self
9949
most fervent believer may appear
d. 8569
nice people might be more d. to
save 7827
no more d. to make million
worlds than one 7940
not d. when we have God's
comfort 1508
not that which is d. to his power
4513
Nothing d. to those who have will
8549
nothing more d. than to think well
11219
Nothing so easy but d. when done
reluctantly 3181
old age one of most d. chapters in
living 8178

Once we know life is d. 7012
only first step that is d. 2749
only one thing as d. as
   unscrambling egg 5163
Patience, accepting d. situation
   8415
required that we love the d. 2712
sacrifice of praise d. thing to do
   8724
safeguarding freedom of spirit, no
   matter how d. 4127
satisfaction comes when we do
   something d. 2757
seems d. to put on yoke of Christ
   2824
something d. to do 77
something d. will do you good
   2758
Spirit-filled life no goal d. of
   attainment 5803
Staying married more d. 7615
Talking easy, action d. 2537
things excellent as d. as rare 3465
Think d, shall be d. 517
through d. times, hold steady 969
time passed in the d. never lost
   2712
times will change 969
to be honest with oneself 5880
to be humble if always successful
   3603
To choose what is d. 3803
to counterfeit humility 5989
to get away from Bible 653
To get money is d. 7823
to get rid of devil 2657
to keep money more d. 7823
To know God easiest, most d. in
   world 7546
to know oneself 10008
to speak the d. word, do the d.
   deed 6599
to spend money wisely most d.
   7823
to stand on pedestal, and wash
   feet of those below 8717
tongue let loose d. to chain 11415
understand it, life no longer d.
   7012
virtue d. to find 11725
walk of disciple gloriously d. 2834
we do immediately 12019
When in pain d. to pray coherently
   10931
When Jesus is present, nothing
   seems d. 6512
when times are d. 8403
When we say, it is d. 230
Worldly people imagine saints
   find it d. to live 4159
Worship God in d. circumstances
   238
Writing so d. feel writers will
   escape all punishment hereafter
   12159

DIFFICULTIES
apart from God clouds of d. are
   accidents 10598
are God's errands 2714

Faith not shelter against d. 3693
in d. are friendly forces 2712
Integrity essential to cope with d.
   6310
Life's d. break through
   superficiality 2738
ludicrously impossible to anyone
   but God 2722
Many men owe grandeur to d.
   2739
meant to rouse, not discourage
   2715
meet d. with prayer 2630
No d. can baffle God 1468
no d. no triumphs 2730
no uphill without a downhill 2754
of every shape and size 2713
of life intended to make better,
   not bitter 2748
Reason can ascertain profound d.
   9420
Reason cannot remove d. 9420
saint hilarious when crushed with
   d. 2722
see d. not looking at Jesus Christ
   2731
show what men are 2735
stone out of which God's houses
   are built 2732
Strength to battle d. and overcome
   1809
taken through d. and arrives safely
   2713
teachings of Christ can solve
   personal d. 6487
to prevent our solving d. of own
   being 5384
two ways to handle 2753
when old d. run into us 12196
When young we run into d. 12196
where willingness is great, d. not
   great 2634

DIFFICULTY
a harsh nurse 2719
a severe instructor 2717
and joy mutual friends 2716
daunted by no d. is greatness 3153
despair tells us d. insurmountable
   5921
enthusiasm robs endurance of d.
   3188
excuse history never accepts 2718
Faith mastering d. in strength of
   Lord 3678
greater d. more glory 209
greater the d, greater the glory
   4417
He that perseveres make d. an
   advancement 8542
I walk through the Lord's
   goodness almost with d. 4646
In education everything built on d.
   1024
In front a precipice, behind a wolf
   2733
in great d, much grace 7486
in life is choice 1152
in making a truly heartfelt prayer
   8858

nurse of greatness 2719
optimist sees opportunity in every
   d. 8251
pessimist sees d. in every
   opportunity 8251
piled high with d. 976
purpose of Christianity not to
   avoid d. 1229
roughly rocks into strength 2719
shall form invincible host against
   d. 10829
stems from unwillingness 1304
What is God saying through this d.
   6086
where no choice, make no d. 1158

DIFFIDENT
and apologetic about gospel, never
   5092

DIFFUSE
Aromatic plants d. their sweetness
   150
sun has gone to d. light elsewhere
   6094

DIGESTED
some few books to be chewed, d.
   859

DIGESTION
Good spirits make for good d.
   5612
nice things due to good d. will fall
   off 1030
Praying is good for your d. 8899

DIGESTIVE
do not understand d. system but I
   eat 3733

DIGGING
Jesus, d. mankind out of snug
   burrows 6421

DIGNIFIED
every person a d. essential human
   soul 901
inordinately anxious to appear d.
   2761

DIGNIFY
all our daily life 9099

DIGNITY
as much d. in tilling field as
   writing poem 2762
Brotherhood is giving d. 924
consists in deserving honors 2759
cross, sacrifice with imperishable
   d. 2166
Democracy founded on d. of all
   men 2521
does not consist in possessing
   honors 2759
easiest way to d. is humility 6031
Faith sustains d. 3666
firmament cannot compare to
   your d. as a human being 7370
freedom constitutes d. of man
   4149
gentleness causes others to retain
   d. 4402
God exalted in d. and honor 4607

hell, where everyone concerned about own d. 5705
is like perfume 2760
man's d. to stand upright 7395
natural d. has respect 2761
never savors of artificiality 2761
never struggles to be dignified 2761
never struts or poses 2761
of individuals measure of civilization 3894
Recognition of individual affirms respect for human d. 9952
Recognize, O Christian, thy d. 2763
takes rank lightly raises own d. 6003
therein lies d. and merit 11231
True d. abides with him alone who 2764
True d. never gained by place 2765
True d. never lost when honors withdrawn 2765
Violence destroys d. 11678
When boasting ends, d. begins 2766
Where is there d. unless honesty 2767

DIGS
a pit for his brother shall fall into himself 3373
who seeks revenge d. two graves 9717

DILAPIDATED
house he lives in sadly d. 8142

DILEMMA
Which of two decisions to make 2494

DILIGENCE
Avoid last minute rush 2768
Be first in the field 2769
Doing this by halves worthless 2770
Everything requires effort 2773
Few things impossible to d, skill 8538
Has risen to nobility 2792
I think and think for months 2775
Keep your heart with all d. 2780
leading rule is d. 2789
Make hay while sun shines 2781
Make the most of yourself 2782
removes mountains 8408
Take care of the minutes 2787

DILIGENT
how d. God has been with us 2778
If God is d. 2778
most d. cannot obtain entire knowledge of Bible 737
ought to be d. in duty to God 2778
without anxiety 9041

DILUTED
message of gospel often d. 5109

DIM
Behind the d. unknown 5377
Beyond our vision weak and d. 10204
doubts from d. perceptions of Christ's gospel 6713
The eye of faith is d. 5635
though the sky stays d. 4195
When the world is still and d. 7927

DIMENSION
operate in d. totally unlike our Lord 11606
ushering in new d. of existence 5711

DIMINISH
man can no more d. God's glory 4442
to grow in love is to d. fear 3986
Whenever relationships d. humanness there is evil 5014

DIMINISHING
when you try to make yourself more, you are d. yourself 9941

DIMLY
not to see what lies d. at a distance 9671

DIMS
anything that d. my vision of Christ 7036
Failure to obey d. spiritual understanding 8100

DIN
religious d. assure everything is well 12096

DINED
Christ d. with lowest members of society 6433

DINNER
flatterers meet, devil goes to d. 4054
to average man time to do with d. 11346
today people would ask Christ to d. 6405
waits for chance never sure of d. 8215

DINNERS
more appetite than d. 10523
more d. than appetite 10523

DIPLOMAS
God will not look for d. 172

DIPLOMATIST
devil a d. too 2651

DIPLOMATS
we are not d. but prophets 9169

DIRECT
angels d. our ways 363
cannot d. wind 4056
control, suggest this day 9047
God can d. evil to good end 3371
God has all wisdom to d. you 4696
God will d. aspirations 1241

God will d. desires 1241
God will d. emotions 1241
God will d. instincts 1241
God will d. intelligence 1241
God will d. judgment 1241
God will d. knowledge 1241
God will d. likes 1241
God will d. reason 1241
God's might to d. me 5400
sees d. personal message from God 5441
skillful d. opinion 8205
will come a d. touch from God 7060

DIRECTED
grace d. toward human debt, demerit 5206
supernaturally d. 10206
to combine dependence of God's Spirit with own researches 6681
we shall be d. 5440

DIRECTING
God is d. them to equity 4514

DIRECTION
begin new d. for life 2798
By whose d. have this time, place been allotted 4905
earth, theatre for God's d. 4902
error proceeds in wrong d. 3258
facing in only one d. 9846
God judges by d. 4713
God's thoughts flashing from every d. 8045
great thing is direction we are moving 1914
If all men pulled in one d. 6184
Love, looking together in the same d. 7215
never loses sense of d. 688
No nation made progress in downward d. 7834
not much use if not in right d. 5409
of life, desires became different 984
push conscience in d. we want to go 1691
Sin is turning in the wrong d. 10370
so many evidences of God's d. 4949
Spirit of God will take d. of your life away from you 5776
stand with face in what d. he will 9151
we are moving 4434
when going in same d. as the devil 8762

DIRECTIONS
heart capable of unlimited extension in all d. 5625

DIRECTIVES
Worship aware of Father's d. 12136

DIRECTLY
Almighty d. intervenes in human affairs 4949

DIRECTOR
Great D. of music arranges program perfectly new 7895

if compelled to take part, where is d. 3485

DIRECTORS
Principles are illuminators, not d. 6816

DIRECTS
Christ d. us to the world 12031

Thy arm d. those lightnings through the sky 4827

with the last he still d. the just 4812

DIRGE
favorite music of asceticism 467

in minor may suddenly be jubilant song of glee 7895

wailing of newborn mingled with d. for the dead 7043

DIRT
flings d. upon another 10452

gossip makes mountain of molehill by adding d. 5114

is matter in wrong place 5121

loss of wealth is loss of d. 11857

molehills become mountains when someone adds d. 10443

notice d. God is most present 3609

trying to remove d. with mud 402

DIRTIER
country needs d. fingernails, cleaner minds 7775

DIRTIES
himself more 10452

DIRTY
clean glove often hides d. hand 2460

Gossip smoke that comes from d. tobacco pipes 5132

if few drops of ocean d, ocean not d. 5988

water does not wash clean 2463

DISABILITIES
forget your d. 9271

DISADVANTAGE
of congregational singing 1415

DISADVANTAGES
to life in Christ 1211

DISAGREE
Falsehoods not only d. with truths 6849

In faith, hope world will d. 1079

without being disagreeable 1878

DISAGREEABLE
able to disagree without being d. 1878

as if God required d. things of us 6813

DISAGREES
Nobody listens, then everybody d. 5171

DISAPPEAR
facts will not d. 3577

DISAPPEARED
if within reach of predatory human hands 3202

sun, moon, stars would have d. long ago 3202

DISAPPEARING
present already d. 982

DISAPPEARS
Suffering d. 10890

The world recedes, it d. 2389

DISAPPOINT
Christ-centered suffer when they d. others 10911

God never known to d. 4468

God will d. man attempting to use him 4468

self-centered suffer when others d. 10911

DISAPPOINTED
born crying, live complaining, die d. 7075

cynic prematurely d. in future 2178

even when d. in ourselves 9992

expect nothing, never be d. 3499

expect peace in friendship, likely to be d. 9470

expects nothing, shall never be d. 5905

God sends a time of d. plans 7056

he shall never be d. 2793

Humility is never to be d. 6010

if you wish to be d. look to others 6408

still d, still young 8126

DISAPPOINTMENT
Every cloud silver lining 2797

life may bring d. 4803

often salt of life 2794

Out of every d. treasure 2800

parent of despair 2795

patient spirit against d. 10844

Receive every d. with both thy hands 7698

Silence welcome after s. 10266

source of power stronger than d. 6491

to set ourselves up for d. 9478

with God 1262

DISAPPOINTMENTS
Fortify our minds against d. 9092

if expect perfection 2799

life a series of d. 9469

love tokens from God 4804

no d. if wills buried in will of God 4981

no d. in the will of God 2801

trials, corrections of heaven 2796

DISAPPOINTS
God d. our plans 5395

Mercy imitates God, d. Satan 7741

DISAPPROVAL
independent of fear of d. 1647

DISARM
fate's severest rage d. 7911

poverty of its sharpest sting 8679

suffering enough to d. hostility 3161

DISARMED
cross has d. powers 2100

cross hurts where d. vulnerable 2092

DISASTER
delay better than d. 8389

Evil gains equivalent of d. 3356

faced in fellowship with Christ 215

not fear d. will follow freedom of thought 4134

One moment of patience may prevent d. 8405

ostrich as blind to opportunity as to d. 8211

separation from God ultimate d. 5697

to feel at home on earth 2975

ultimate d. to feel at home on earth 2382

DISASTERS
of shallowness 2856

Why does God bring d. 229

DISASTROUS
most d. purpose "pursuit of happiness" 5548

DISBELIEF
bit of healthy d. sometimes needful 2948

DISBELIEVE
God created us free to d. in him 11590

If d. must take consequences 11590

no one can drive me to believe or d. 594

DISBELIEVES
one who watches others suffering who d. in God 10936

DISCARD
Tough decision: when to d. toothbrush 2492

DISCERN
Adolescents quickest to d. hypocrisy 12162

Can I d. my way 5434

God beneath moonlight of Gethsemane 4856

God in humdrum commonplace 10721

God on grass of Eden 4856

If you d. God's love in happiness 5254

need signs to d. guiding hand 5396

rays of light, hope 3350

what we first d. but surface 6380

DISCERNABLE
Spiritual truth d. only to pure
heart 11529

DISCERNED
Truth is d. spiritually 11569
Truth not d. intellectually 11569

DISCERNING
God's eye for d. 5400

DISCERNMENT
Beware of d. of wrong 2803
God's call to intercession 2805
look into people as well as at them
2811
not faultfinding 2805

DISCERNS
wisdom, awful wisdom which d.
11906

DISCIPLE
comes to find learning, truth,
forgiveness 2818
deliberately gives himself to Jesus
Christ 2817
never cost d. to follow Jesus 2823
walk of d. difficult, certain 2834

DISCIPLES
become d. church would be
transformed 2819
become d. impact on society
staggering 2819
Christ makes his d. like himself
6411
cowered in the darkness 2132
drifted away 2132
few d. allowed to appear sensible
11791
Jesus commissioned d. 2827
named d. for their knowledge
1328
stone rolled away to enable d. to
go in 9699
stumbling block if so gifted they
won't trust God 2833
true d. of Christ love most 7318
Was it not opposition Jesus
promised to d. 10784

DISCIPLESHIP
and salvation, two different things
2817
Conversion without d. implied
2815
costs everything we have 2832
Jesus Christ will never plead 2826
means discipline 2818
not that we work for God 2831
opportunity is there "if" 2826
stormy weather in initial stages
2822
that God works through us 2831
wine must be crushed 2820

DISCIPLINE
All excellence involves d. 3464
and love not antithetical 8292
and love, one function of the other
8292
appreciate God's point of view by
long d. 2846

before too late 8309
cannot d. ourselves to be saints
4984
Cheerfulness result of strenuous d.
1088
Confession d. which God requires
1597
cruel that it may be kind 2839
Discipleship means d. 2818
Error is d. through which we
advance 3252
God does not d. to subdue 2845
grown up with too little d. 8335
if d. taken out of your life 9977
Laughter is a d. 6727
love children enough to d. 8309
love son, plenty of d. 8303
must d. ourselves to fight
deviation from course 9965
neither a shame nor sin to d.
reason 9425
No saint dare interfere in d.
10927
not something to the child, is
something for the child 8331
of being merciful to the merciless
7746
one thing to praise d, another to
submit 2848
proof of our sonship 2842
Sanctification d. nine out of ten
will have nothing to do with
9843
Some people regard d. as a chore
9975
Spirit of God will reserve right to
d. you 5776
stern d. pervades nature 2839
takes love, hard work to d. 8335
that we understand d. of God
7485
tools to solve life's problems 9967
who deserve the severest d. 6533

DISCIPLINED
haven't d. myself to read or pray
9966
in pursuit of the d. life 9970
Meditation is d. thought 7721
No life grows great until d. 2852
obedience of loyal subject 8818

DISCIPLINES
teach us, O Lord, the d. of
patience 8418

DISCLOSE
inner fears, temptation, joys 4029

DISCLOSES
his own character when describes
another 991

DISCOMFORT
If leave church with no d. 12106

DISCONNECTED
Christ d. fundamentally from life
6436
Christ was inwardly d. 6439

DISCONTENT
ass went seeking for horns, lost
ears 2872
first step in progress 2864
follows ambition like a shadow
2863
gets what it wants 2876
loses what it has 2876
man's d. his worst evil 2860
Restlessness, d. necessities of
progress 2870
root of d. is self-love 10027
source of trouble, progress 2865
that works 2876
that wrings its hands 2876
the winter of our d. 10581
two kinds of d. 2876

DISCONTENTED
never rich 1814
trying to be something they are not
1807
trying to do something they cannot
1807
with ourselves, complain about
others 1567

DISCONTINUED
Nothing more dangerous than d.
labor 3109

DISCORD
Luther threw apple of d. 1625
proven that d. undermine health
5612
song no longer a d. but a hymn
divine 7451
the frantic d. of sin 8743

DISCORDANCE
Onward, no d. in the roll 2268

DISCORDS
Faith makes d. harmonies of future
3704

DISCOURAGE
Difficulties not meant to d. 2715
forget frustrations that d. 9270
need not d. us if full of doubts
2949
whatever devil does to d, God can
use 9858

DISCOURAGED
emotions poison life 3050
having fallen likely to become d.
10328
nor d. by failures 10802
not be d. at the rests 7915
people don't need critics 3066
see only ebb of advancing wave,
are thus d. 5944
so d. felt he could not continue as
minister 2886

DISCOURAGEMENT
Defeat should never be source of
d. 2509
disenchanted egotism 2880
Every thought for Christ away
from d. 2940
when we insist on having our own
way 2879

yield to d. too much thought to past, future 2887

DISCOURAGEMENTS
What you call d. are God's opportunities 8219

DISCOURAGING
not be upset when d. things happen 2887

DISCOURSE
Read not to find talk, d. 856

DISCOURSES
Silence the sequel to dull d. 10266

DISCOVER
always able to d. own darkness 6004

better persuaded by reasons we d. 270

delight hidden in irksome tasks 10639

enemies first to d. your mistakes 3169

forgiveness, healing one 4072

fully conscious we d. loneliness 9513

give to God, d. God gives to you 4386

help d. will of God and do it 5373

I d. an arrant laziness 662

in crises d. what you are 2044

never d. full richness of your humanity 8634

one can often d. what cynics lack 2188

only to d. and to do 10150

Seek righteousness, d. you are happy 5551

surrender will, d. resources 10769

treasure of tranquility 10553

what enemy fears most 4010

DISCOVERABLE
God not d. by scientific means 4739

DISCOVERED
does not begin with what intellect has d. 3783

God's grace sufficient 2518

mind of God as d. in Word and works 4675

questions not important questions 9366

Superior people let it be d. by others 11695

thoughts waiting to be d. 2020

truth d. lasts a lifetime 11578

weed is plant whose virtues not yet d. 8646

DISCOVERER
No d. ever did work cheaply, easily 5289

DISCOVERIES
Bible multiplies d. 683

for these two d. am beholden to Jesus 5530

greatest of d. man can make 4866

no d. in peace 8450

DISCOVERS
God d. himself to babes 7709

Hope d. what can be done 5928

one d. true savor of life 6086

someone else believes in him 4275

Suffering, d. things never discovered before 10893

Time d. the truth 11325

DISCOVERY
Education progressive d. of ignorance 3000

never made mistake, never made d. 3630

no d. of truth without committing to Christ 6490

Through every rift of d. 2790

DISCREDIT
intellectuals attempt to d. Bible 726

DISCREDITING
not by d. what they believe 12147

wisdom of God 6189

DISCRETION
concealed at God's d. 11609

is leaving a few things unsaid 2892

is not seeing as much as you can 2894

learn to keep mouth shut 2897

must be tried in friendship 4227

putting two and two together, keeping mouth shut 2893

salt that preserves life 2895

DISCRIMINATION
and a George Washington Carver 161

society filled with racial d. 161

you have a Booker T. Washington 161

you have a Marian Anderson 161

DISCUSS
begin to d. things that really matter 4029

Never d. great things 10242

Nothing to d. but glories of days past 4321

To d. authority of Almighty God meaningless 4955

DISCUSSED
life of Jesus cannot be d. in same way as any other man 6476

DISCUSSING
While coldly d. a man's career 6599

DISCUSSION
afraid of free d. in love with own opinion 2904

apt to become worse than useless 4124

exchange of knowledge 2901

Free d. firmest friend to truth 2902

gospel neither a d. nor a debate 5098

is so limiting and distracting 10242

makes things grow smaller 10242

man has right to liberty of d. 2900

not open for conviction, not qualified for d. 2903

DISCUSSIONS
Jesus furnished themes for more d. 6449

DISEASE
a fathomless answer, the Cross of Christ 9398

all afflicted with the d. 10415

attitude determines d. 509

Conceit weird d. 1586

divorce remedy worse than d. 2927

doubt d. of this restless age 2935

Envy like a d. 3212

From bitterness of d. man learns 5605

God a specialist in the sin d. 10308

indifference toward neighbor assaulted by d. 6163

Life is a hereditary d. 6948

lifted out of d. by prayer 8764

Man calls sin a defect, God a d. 4550

melancholy is d. 1089

more contagious than health 4286

Old age an incurable d. 8154

Sin is d. 10363

Sin is not a d. 10371

What will you do when d. makes bedridden 11151

When rationalist points out d. 9398

Winter is a d. 9907

world has d. called man 7432

DISEASED
Malignity of soul often dwells in d. bodies 5613

present state of world d. 10271

whole of life d. 10271

DISEASES
Before you can cure d. of the body 6085

by examining the tongue philosophers find d. of mind 11410

death is cure for all d. 2405

Music expels d. 7900

must cure d. of the soul 6085

DISENCHANTED
Discouragement d. egotism 2880

DISENGAGEMENT
Divorce d. for trivial reasons 2922

DISENTHRALL
we must d. ourselves 976

DISGRACE
Poverty no d. to man 8687

DISGRACEFULLY
world d. managed 3203

DISGUISE
crosses are blessings in d. 288
Is oft but perseverance in d. 8539
remove the d. 10019
touching God in his distressing d.
 6569
wearing d. before others 6067

DISGUISED
dream d. fulfillment of suppressed
 wish 2968
Lies can be d. in gorgeous
 wrappings 6853
opportunities come d. as problems
 2752
opportunities d. as impossible
 situations 8228
Opportunities usually d. as hard
 work 8221
virtues are frequently vices d.
 6060

DISGUST
difference which rouses d. of the
 world 10917

DISGUSTS
be governed by admirations rather
 than d. 8472

DISH
All are fragments from his d. 5860

DISHEARTEN
cynic can d. with single word
 2176

DISHEARTENS
fear d. 3965

DISHONEST
in forty-one ways, I think it is
 2916
never tempted, doesn't know how
 d. he is 11098
way of praising ourselves 2083
Yes, even I am d. 2916

DISHONESTIES
Conformity most fundamental d.
 of all 1635

DISHONESTY
a scorpion that will sting itself to
 death 2908
Unfaithfulness in keeping
 appointment d. 2914
worse d. among champions of
 religious opinions 9540

DISHONORED
martyr cannot be d. 8528

DISHONORS
what does not honor wife d.
 himself 7616

DISILLUSIONED
Buddhist, Hindu stand apart d.
 6563
with Christ because didn't get high
 3493

DISILLUSIONMENT
the most important 10
Wisdom comes by d. 11964
with other Christians 1262

with our own abilities 10

DISINTEGRATION
alive long past usual date of d.
 8139
high crime rate traceable to d. of
 home 5858
shall only resist d. of community
 6286

DISLIKE
God uses someone we d. to crush
 us 883
If injure someone you d. 8055
if person whom you d. 5144
only time people d. gossip 5159
people d. Christianity 1205
to d. whosoever is evil in thy eyes
 9063

DISLIKED
for our qualities 5601

DISLIKING
will find yourself d. him more
 8055

DISLOCATED
both shoulders describing it 3424

DISLOYALTY
intimate with God, d. of friend
 will not crush 9470

DISMAY
unworthiness may d. thee 3047
when new thought appears 11237
With doubt and d. you are smitten
 8230

DISMAYED
not be d. at the rests 7056
will not be d. by isolation 10567

DISMOUNT
Who rides tiger cannot d. 11121

DISOBEDIENCE
and sin same thing 10302
Evangelistic inactivity is d. 3329
If God to remove possibility of d.
 8091
no sin but d. 10302
proper attitude toward d. 8332
should use terms obedience and d.
 5753

DISOBEDIENT
Christians not defeated, simply d.
 5753

DISOBEYING
do right in d. law of sovereign
 5197

DISORDER
prayer beginning of uprising
 against d. 9001
Self-centeredness a serious d. 9946

DISORDERED
God knows how to use d. wishes,
 actions 4644
turning d. actions to our
 advantage 4644
world is horribly d. 10521

DISORDERLY
live peaceably with d. persons
 5236

DISORDERS
greatest of d. is to think we are
 whole 10045

DISPEL
Thou didst d. my blindness 4805

DISPELLED
you d. my bitterness 7579

DISPELS
One joy d. a hundred cares 6555
Worship d. worry 12127

DISPENSATION
Suffering divine d. to sanctify us
 10896

DISPENSE
can God d. us from grief 5352
moved God to d. grace in certain
 manner 4989
wealth best way to preserve it
 11870

DISPENSER
become channel and d. of life
 7548

DISPERSED
God has breathed, they are d.
 7874

DISPERSION
nations have found d. in peace
 11783

DISPIRITED
When we are d. God still
 unalterable I Am 4587

DISPLACES
In our journalism, trivial d.
 momentous 7990

DISPLAY
can sense that kind of d. 6062
deprive ourselves of royal d. of
 wisdom 4995
perfection of friend 4183
right for God to d. anger against
 sin 4729

DISPLEASE
angry at person who d. you 378

DISPLEASED
at finding perfections 3945
When God is d. 401

DISPLEASING
what pleaseth man ofttimes d. to
 God 9195

DISPOSAL
all resources of heaven, earth are
 at my d. 9066
place all hours of day at his d.
 10120

DISPOSED
God d. all strongly, sweetly 4904
Science smilingly d. of Bible as
 guide 9870

DISPOSES
God's love d. him to desire our welfare 4754

DISPOSITION
body, medium for manifesting d. Jesus Christ 838

Character in saint d. of Christ 998

Christ came to alter d. 6424

Christ goes behind law to d. 1526

Compassion requires inner d. 1546

different d. looks through same eyes 8583

God alters d. 1012

God plants in us a new d. 8570

happiness more a d. than attainment 5571

Jesus can put into man d. that ruled his life 9436

Master's d. a peculiar, subdued sadness 6390

Peace is a d. for benevolence 8455

DISPUTE
among divines 11194

DISPUTED
life, every inch is d. 6947

Truths turn into dogmas moment they are d. 11582

DISPUTING
doing will of God leaves no time for d. his plans 4970

DISQUALIFIED
for membership in Kingdom of God 4133

man ambitious to lead d. as leader 6794

DISQUIET
can be God sowing seeds of faith 3722

ever lurking d. in half withheld 9683

sin d. of the heart 10360

DISQUIETED
by One responsible to no one 4614

by thought of One who does not account to us 4614

DISREGARD
act with d. for opinions of others 6291

good life enables us to d. evil tongues 5164

DISREPUTE
ways of man that may bring d. upon us 10564

DISRUPT
inner conflict that d. personality 2737

not stresses that d. personality 2737

DISSENTER
resigns from the herd, thinks for himself 6210

DISSIPATE
wait upon men, d. energies 10764

DISSIPATING
in company wearisome, d. 10572

DISSOLUTION
cannot stop near d. of family unit 2928

DISSOLVE
before grave all hopes d. 1163

DISTANCE
A few miles d. from rocky shore 6111

between Almighty God and helpless worn 3786

difference measured by d. between infinite, finite 3786

enemies to be kept at a d. 10531

God judges not by d. 4713

heaven without speaking d. 5677

is nothing 2749

judgment creates d. 10162

makes no difference 8832

not to see what lies dimly at a d. 9671

one should keep from wicked cannot be measured 11888

Sin is not a d. 10370

to God magnitude and d. have no meaning 4582

too great d. prevents us being able to see 3559

what looks dark in the d. 8079

DISTANT
cannot reach d. horizons 4544

Character d. goal 1000

happiness is d. goal to which no shortcut 7648

I do not ask to see d. scene 5429

lure of d. and difficult is deceptive 8225

more we pursue humility more d. it becomes 6008

No d. Lord have I 7506

self is more d. than any star 9352

though d. close in spirit 4280

DISTASTEFUL
greater a man more d. praise, flattery 5296

to man way which leads him to himself 1717

DISTASTES
Prosperity not without fears and d. 247

DISTEMPER
his d. was allayed 7935

DISTINCT
happy religion is d. knowledge of Jesus Christ 6713

You are d. 6206

DISTINCTION
Jesus teaches no d. of race, merit, rank 913

no d. between small and great 567

no d. between spiritual, material work 6985

over and above determines ultimate d. 2784

understand better nature of d. 2989

without d, love 7348

DISTINCTIONS
mystic loses consciousness of creature d. 7966

DISTINCTIVE
reading Bible, encountered a d. person 4491

DISTINCTLY
Vaguely at first, then more d. 7436

DISTINGUISH
between right, wrong burden-bearing 937

give us wisdom to d. one from the other 9060

Grant us true judgment to d. things that differ 9063

inability to d. needs from greeds 5321

unable to d. what is worth reading 2997

DISTINGUISHED
all other beings d. by shadow 4472

God d. by light 4472

regard employments equally d. 3232

DISTORT
malice may d. truth 11566

things into what they are not 38

DISTORTS
individualism d. joy of identify 9952

DISTRACT
do not d. yourself by looking forward 9650

speed to d. hunger for God 7512

DISTRACTED
Jesus not d. with trivia 4425

move through life in d. way 5590

stable spirit not d. by activity 4307

DISTRACTING
Discussion is so d. 10242

DISTRACTION
God drawning away from d. so you can see him 2556

God whispering, do not hear because of d. 4968

life causes as it rushes on 10273

receive as from the Lord 1461

which life causes as it rushes on 4968

DISTRESS
a deep d. has humanized my soul 10830

Discouraged don't need more piled-on d. 3066

every d. will have an explanation 7060

not hypocrisy to rejoice in d. 221

sigh of d. from heart 1513
symbolizes escape from d. of age
  9910
way you and I respond to d. 3319
will become day of prosperity
  7698

DISTRESS'D
mind quite vacant is mind d. 3085

DISTRESSED
mind vacant is mind d. 6752

DISTRESSES
In all d. Bible never failed 670

DISTRESSING
cleavage between truths, values
  6068
frightening and d. bit of reality
  9408
touching God in his d. disguise
  6569

DISTRUST
of God to be troubled about what
  is to come 12066
What loneliness more lonely than
  d. 7149

DISTURB
God comes to d. us 3722
Let nothing d. thee 4588
never big things that d. 1472
passions that d. the soul 7935
things that now d. events for
  gratitude 5252
trivial things d. us 1472
wants d. human life 2861
What isn't part of ourselves
  doesn't d. us 5600
What wicked do should not d.
  good man's tranquility 11894

DISTURBANCE
I go where no d. can have place
  2304

DISTURBED
If Christianity has never d. 1201

DISTURBING
friend with noisy old car 3223
friend with quiet new car 3223
hide for a time from d. thoughts
  7708
You know no d. voice 4969

DISTURBS
Christian thinker d. complacent
  11239

DITCH
get rid of ox or fill up d. 10951
If ox gets in d. every Sabbath
  10951
Jesus spoke about ox in d. on
  Sabbath 10951

DITCHWATER
Is d. dull 8020
teams with quiet fun 8020

DIVE
search for pearls must d. below
  3255

DIVER
relief of d. coming back to
  sunlight, familiar faces 6110

DIVERS
like deep sea d. in twilight of
  depths 6110

DIVERSIONS
Think often on God in your d.
  7723

DIVERSITY
glory of creation, infinite d. 1973
man, d. in unity 7374
man, picturesque piece of d. in
  unity 6173

DIVIDE
Calvary erected to d. men into
  two classes 2124
God cannot d. himself 11422
love, joy, peace multiply when d.
  with others 4360
Nothing hard if d. into small jobs
  3110
social differences have lost power
  to d. 6286
The swords of scorn d. 9224
unity of God, can neither conceive
  nor d. 4580

DIVIDED
house d. cannot stand 1620
houses d. against themselves 6068
Joys d. are increased 6551
Mankind d. into three classes
  10504
nor can spirits be d. 3291
Nor d. that love in same divine
  principle 7319
over the question, "Who is Jesus"
  6518
Protestantism d. into 200 groups
  1420
The world is d. into people 93

DIVIDES
Doctrine d, service unites 10129
forgetting what d. 9093
Friendship doubles joy, d. grief
  4229
Jesus d. into believers,
  non-believers 686
nature of gospel is that it d. 5102

DIVIDING
Friendship, d. and sharing
  adversity 4228
Jesus throws down d. prejudices
  913

DIVINE
acknowledgment of d. power 479
Alchemist can miraculously change
  10628
And full of love d. 5620
art shadow of d. perfection 1993
behavior modification 577
best theology is d. life 11200
Bible, many d. qualities 687
Bible, strong indication of d.
  descent 736

born from intimate depths of d.
  nature 5967
bringing mind into contact with d.
  revelation 5094
Brotherhood, d. command 902
certainty of d. participation gives
  courage 6277
Christ d. paradox of lion, lamb
  6425
Christ was deluded or d. 6366
crown of golden, d. love 7073
Deep within us, a d. center 1757
do not exist by d. necessity 3481
endurance of soul show d.
  grandeur 3150
Every moment pregnant with d.
  purpose 11293
Every victory of science reveals
  more clearly d. design 9866
explusion of sin 10717
For attainment of d. knowledge
  6681
forgetting with God is d. attribute
  4637
God's justice adjudged by human
  reckoning, not d. 4728
God, so forgiving, so d. 4673
Grace a self-existent principle
  inherent in d. nature 4652
great men see d. in every other
  man 6032
heroes, mixture of d. and human
  755
holy life regulated by d. truth
  5736
Human problems never greater
  than d. solutions 9285
human will leaves, d. grace begins
  5200
Humility is a d. veil 6005
hurry is not a d. thing 5581
illumination would blind eyes
  4657
in contact with d. resources 1143
In d. things no prudence not bold
  2732
In d. things there is never hurry
  5581
Jesus shed more light on things d.
  than philosophers 6449
King rules forever by dying 2166
know, praise some one aspect of
  the d. beauty 6169
Knowledge of d. escapes us
  through want of faith 3754
light in both is d. 8008
light in every human being 7561
likeness of d. love 10331
love can admit no rival 4929
Love is something so d. 7245
most d. are children 1120
must be loved to be known 4762
nature is perfection 8522
nearest to d. nature, nearest to
  perfection 8522
no human condition which d.
  presence does not penetrate
  6277

notion that d. guidance is dispensed 693

On and on from fact d. God advances 4906

on knees sign of helplessness apart from d. enablement 8759

people there by d. appointment 3316

power shining in continuing state of universe 11652

Prayer girds weakness with d. strength 8912

Prayer identifying oneself with the d. will 8922

quelled by music's d. control 7935

receives d. illumination 8505

rock of d. love deeper down 4783

selfishness, preventing transformation into d. love 10067

sin rebellion against d. authority 10390

so d. was the concept of mother 7859

Sorrow is d. 10613

soul, of origin d, God's glorious image 10675

souls acts no longer except by d. impulse 7707

spirit submerged in depths of d. ocean 7968

strings need only be swept by d. breath 7921

Suffering d. dispensation to sanctify us 10896

the d. work in us 3766

things must be loved to be known 7180

thoughts which alone can be d. 4255

to be good is d. 5085

to repent d. 7065

to stand when others beaten down d. 1915

to ward off bolts of d. wrath 4998

touch with d. power the buried acorn 6095

transformed exhibit d. characteristics 1044

Truth is a d. thing 11560

Unbelief where no d. footsteps heard 11595

waiting for us in the D. garage 8181

wisdom has given us prayer 8977

Without assistance of d. being cannot succeed 5411

years we spend on earth first scene in d. drama 6106

DIVINELY

death d. entertaining 2272

that freedom d. bind us dearer to himself 6177

DIVINES

dispute among d. 11194

DIVINITY

Christ, condescension of d. 6441

contemplation of the D. improving to the mind 4745

doubted d. of Scriptures 744

humanity poor were not for d. that stirs within us 5979

nature lectures of d. 3192

so deep our pride drowned in infinity 4745

so vast all thoughts lost in immensity 4745

Some men pray whole system of d. 8961

temptations have been my masters in d. 11076

That's all the d. I know 9138

DIVISION

Christ, message set society ablaze with d. 6375

excuse is d. among Christians 3477

high as heaven, deep as hell 1338

Love multiplies by d. 7252

DIVISON

Time has no d. to mark passage 11329

DIVORCE

an easy escape, many think 2921

creating an epidemic-like atmosphere 2919

disengagement for trivial reasons 2922

hash made of domestic straps 2920

invaded the church 2919

marriage demands d. from self-love 7596

remedy worse than disease 2927

sacrament of adultery 2923

such hatred of d. I prefer bigamy 2925

DIVORCED

Truth d. from experience 3548

Virtue d. from thankfulness is maimed 11154

DIVORCES

cannot stop alarming number of d. 2928

Most d. are not bad marriages 2926

Most d. poorly prepared marriages 2926

DIZZY

looking downward makes one d. 11727

DO

able to act in what they ought to d. 2485

acquire skill to d. difficult things easily 8406

All find time to d. what we want to d. 11348

All I d. founded on oneness with God 547

All I design or d, or say 9047

all the good you can 10126

And d. what thou wouldst d. 5774

And how I d. and did 1855

angels would leap to d. his will 12099

any good thing I can d. 6642

best thing one can d. 34

can d. nothing without grace of God 5207

Charity, to d. all, all that we can 7320

Christ can d. wonders with broken heart 10584

did d. what you didn't d. 3473

do not know what God is going to d. next 5463

duty to d. what thou wouldst not 9667

duty to leave undone that thou wouldst d. 9667

every act as if last 556

every moment d. little works excellently 5068

Every person has one thing he can d. better than most 6175

few words will d. 4302

free will not liberty to d. whatever one likes 4111

Freedom does not mean able to d. whatever I want 4122

get up and d. something 88

God able to empower us to d. whatever he calls us to d. 9199

God always calling on us to d. the impossible 10138

God can d. what he likes with man abandoned to him 9557

God can no more d. without us 4533

God does all before he asks us to d. anything 4536

God does not d. anything with us 10136

God does not tell us what he is going to d. 4932

God does not want us to d. extraordinary things 7118

God does what we cannot d. 8570

God hath no other thing to d. 4834

God loved world, d. likewise 7172

God who so much for you did d. will d. yet more 4476

God will d. deep inner work 10706

God will make it possible to d. it 5226

God will not d. what I can d. for myself 8803

good to your friend to keep him 9449

good you d. not lost 5083

Goodness not in things we d. 5063

great things as if they were little 10127

greatest a man can d. for his heavenly Father 6665

greatest miracle that can d. 5759

greatest thing you can d. is to be 10141

Happiness is liking what one has
to d. 5525

hardest work is to d. nothing
6775

have to light my part 7107

Hope animates a man to d. his
utmost 5917

I alone am responsible for wrong I
d. 9661

I can't d. everything, can d.
something 1926

Idolaltry trusting people to d.
what only God can d. 6072

If ever in doubt about what to d.
2484

If God has work for me to d. 6921

If God wants you to d. something
5226

If I cannot d. great things 10155

if things we d. are worth doing
5590

injuries we d. and those we suffer
9495

Isn't there anything to d. in heaven
5661

It isn't the thing you d. 2502

it yesterday 2768

Jesus does it all, I d. nothing 5426

law to make clear how much you
must d. 5233

leadership, art of getting someone
else to d. something 6799

learning how to d. without the
indispensable 7692

less what free to d, than free not
to d. 4142

less, but accomplish more 60

let God d. it 4567

Life is to d. 6980

Life, all you have to d. is 6961

little things as if they were great
7117

little things now 2534

man free to d. what he likes 4150

man free to d. what he ought
4150

more apt to agree in what they d.
62

more good by being good 3456

must first be made good before
we can d. good 5087

must let God d. all we can 10980

never d, d. with the Lord 6313

Never put off till tomorrow what
you can d. today 11372

Never think could d. something if
different lot 8219

no profit to learn well if neglect to
d. well 3016

Nobody else can d. the work 6204

not able to find time to d. things
you don't want to d. 9301

not know one millionth of one
percent about anything 6709

not let what cannot d. interfere
with what can d. 8652

not to d. wrong, never d. anything
1636

not what we d. that matters 8094

Nothing you can d. to make God
love you more 4786

nought to d. but mark and tell
10038

one thing I d., not dabble in fifty
81

Only he who can see invisible can
d. impossible 11733

only thing of consequence is what
we d. 8117

ordinary things extraordinarily
well 10137

other things only man can d.
10199

patience to d. simple things
perfectly 8406

People who d. things, people who
get credit 93

Perseverance can d. anything
genius can d. 8551

Prayer can d. anything God can d.
8902

right when offer faith, works to
God 3829

right, God's recompense to you
power to d. more right 9648

sacred obligation to find out and
d. it 6175

Satan finds mischief for idle hands
to d. 6772

show love in everything we d.
4767

sin you d. by two and two 10398

so much to d. shall spent three
hours in prayer 12029

Some things only God can d.
10199

something beyond what you
mastered 68

something he knows he was
meant and made to d. 8649

something small in a big way 58

spend efforts seeking to d. will of
God 5543

teenagers d. things nobody else
does 12172

teenagers not old enough to d.
things adults d. 12172

teenagers too old to d. things kids
d. 12172

than friends by what we d. 1888

That which each can d. best none
but his Maker can teach 6226

The Lord will d. through you
6313

The sins ye d. by two and two 73

the thing you fear 3962

the truth you know 9649

theme is Get more, know more, d.
more 9016

then we and ours will d. for you
5009

thou must d. it, thou alone 9109

to attempt to d. is to waste efforts
10199

to d. for you and yours 5009

to d. good is human 5085

To d. it as for thee 10183

to d. no significance except in "to
be" 3491

to d. what no other can d. 6170

to know what he ought to d. 9824

today what you want to postpone
till tomorrow 9295

today's duty 9650

Trust in God and d. the right 5995

two things to d. about the gospel
5107

watch that you d. what you
should d. 9912

way to be nothing is d. nothing
6778

We become what we d. 11717

We d. the works 10209

We have nothing to d. with the
outflow 6232

We say must d. all we can 10980

what a sovereign God chooses to
d. through us 8094

What I can d. that I ought to d.
1926

what I ought to d, I shall d. 1926

What we d. with leisure time
10016

what we d. with years we live
6933

What we love to d. we find time
to d. 9277

What would ant d. if had head of
bull 6221

what you can 10128

What you d. not want others to d.
to you 5008

what you love 6902

Whatever women d. must d. twice
as well 11984

when a man does what he likes to
d, character revealed 6842

when Almighty wants me to d.
5410

When d. ill, devil tempts 11116

When d. nothing, we tempt devil
11116

When speak of hell, everyday face
will d. 5680

when we can d. no more 2774

who d. not know what to d. on a
rainy Sunday afternoon 6100

who waits to d. good will never d.
anything 5071

Why worry? What can worry d.
12091

will to d. God's will 5447

Wisdom knowing what to d. next
11721

with cheerful heart the work God
appoints 10150

Worldliness wishing the forbidden
possible to d. 12054

Worry gives you something to d.
12088

Worship highest act person can d.
12137

worst enemies can d. is kill you
6158

worst friends can d. is betray you
6158

Young people d. impossible before find out impossible 12177

your duty, leave rest to heaven 9651

Youth would rather d. noble than useful deeds 12181

DOCTORS

would be called in when people were well 6880

DOCTRINE

affords comfort 3047

best way to understand d. of wrath of God 4999

Christianity not d. of weakness 1165

Christianity, not devotion to d. 1176

devil entangles learned with false d. 2677

divides, service unites 10129

has value if it makes a difference 11180

If teacher fascinates with his d. 11003

in response to bad d. 11189

Live to explain d. by life 3440

Lord's Prayer compendium of d. 7156

mystery is d. unilluminated 7937

nails your faith 11184

of man's right to happiness anti-God 5553

revelation is d. illuminated 7937

scarcely necessary to expound d. 565

that will not bear investigation 11181

True d. master key to world's problems 11213

With d. world taken apart, put together 11213

won't make you happy 11185

DOCTRINES

Christ's words pass into d. 6523

in excess a caricature of truth 9122

Jesus expounded no d. 6448

DOCUMENT

no issued d. legal 5726

DODGING

who blows own horn has everyone d. when he approaches 9242

DOER

No evil example can bring joy to d. 5035

DOERS

great d. of history men of faith 5723

Great talkers never great d. 1846

DOES

All God d. agrees with all God is 4579

God d. all before he asks us to do anything 4536

God d. and blesses us 4575

God d. well what he d. 4446

hazards in anything one d. 6779

he who d. good turn should never remember it 5070

He who d. what he should not 5478

He who d. wrong d. wrong against himself 6262

man who d. things makes many mistakes 7792

not what man d. that determines sacred or secular 7865

sinister intent taints all he d. 4164

when a man d. what he likes to do, character revealed 6842

who means well useless unless d. well 6335

witness is not to what Jesus d, but to what he is 5790

DOG

barks when his master is attacked 99

honest man not worse because d. barks at him 5866

If stop every time d. barks, road will never end 8543

is still competition for a husband 7611

love of God despotic as man's love for d. 4792

Money will buy d, but not wag of tail 7816

no d. exchanges bones with another 7404

reason d. has so many friends 9499

To his d, every man is Napoleon 9509

wags tail intead of tongue 9499

DOGMA

ark within which church floats safely 11187

emergency measures to which church driven 11186

is the drama 11201

world does not understand d. 7313

DOGMAS

Experience dulls edges of d. 3516

of quiet past inadequate 976

Truths turn into d. moment they are disputed 11582

DOGMATIC

Great saints have always been d. 11188

DOGMATISM

need return to gentle d. that smiles while stands firm on Word of God 11188

nothing so shallow as d. 456

DOG'S

if husbands imitated a few of d. virtues 7611

DOGS

Flatterers as wolves resemble d. 4047

hence constant popularity of d. 9509

lies with d, rises with fleas 11063

DOING

as much greatness in acknowledging good turn as d. it 5263

Bad the day man becomes content with deeds he is d. 8649

becomes natural overflow of being 78

Being and d. one in God 4579

biggest mistake, d. nothing 7792

Emotional peace and calm come after d. God's will 8432

engages almost everyone's attention 1753

free will power of d. what ought to be done 4111

God works in us the d. of the works 10209

greater hazards in d. nothing 6779

Happiness is not in d. what one likes 5525

hardly any difference between d, being 10561

Hell where everyone d. own thing 5691

In d. what we ought 9666

In d. what we ought deserve no praise 2779

injury puts you below enemy 4073

life lost which I spent not in d. good 6909

mistakes of youth d. things excessively 12181

Paradise where everyone d. God's thing 5691

rather be d. something else 3111

Rest satisfied with d. well 2785

shepherds didn't ask God if he knew what he was d. 6147

things by halves is worthless 2770

Thinking evil same as d. it 3409

want to be d. mighty things 9679

we learn by d. 3545

well wisest and best 67

what somebody else said couldn't be done 8645

when pressure within is stronger 78

When talk of man d. anything for God 10214

Why is God d. as he chooses 3042

will of God leaves no time for disputing his plans 4970

Worldliness not only d. what is forbidden 12054

Worth d. at all, worth d. well 96

your d. not God's 4319

DOINGS

alone God's d. made known 10532

DOLLAR

Give man a d, cheer heart 3307

DOLLARS
will take care of themselves 9674

DOME
Thou wouldst behold crystal d. above 4708

DOMESTIC
Divorce hash made of d. straps 2920

DOMESTICITY
worst notion that d. is dull 5842

DOMINANT
note in Jesus' life, faithfulness 3848
saints one d. note is Jesus Christ 9786

DOMINATE
gospel not made to d. world 5099
Love does not d. 7216

DOMINATED
choose to be d. by sin or righteousness 10510

DOMINATES
loving Personality d. Bible 635

DOMINATING
Christ, d. interest hid with God 6501
Spirit of God alters my d. desires 9276

DOMINATION
no rule but personal d. of the Holy Spirit 5785
society network of d. 10514

DOMINION
Adam not to have d. over himself 758
Adam to have d. over all life 758

DOMINIONS
God knows all thrones, d. 4881

DONE
And cries it shall be d. 3717
And died with nothing d. 6756
as if you alone had d. the wrong 9672
big things come asking to be d. 2534
can't be d. by advice, often d. by example 3460
Christian never forgets what God has d. for him 5240
Day is d. 8086
don't show up until work is d. 6773
Duty d. is soul's fireside 9653
Finish every day and be d. with it 8375
God not saving world; it is d. 3308
highest service may be d. in humblest surroundings 10190
Hope discovers what can be d. 5928
how much may be d. 51
Humility is to wonder at nothing d. to me 6010

instead of grumbling about what cannot be d. 5928
Lord, when thou seest my work is d. 12016
Make the evil we have d. work for good 9054
most rewarding look like cannot be d. 8567
My work is d, why wait 10942
Not one thing d. for God has been lost 10176
nothing d. that God is not absolute Master 4937
Nothing great d. without suffering 10875
people tried for what they have d. 6413
reward for good deed is to have d. it 10194
than to have d. nothing and succeeded 10777
that's crying to be d. 10201
the sin d. for things there's money in 7819
to ponder how Son of God would have d. it 10140
Undo that which we have d. amiss 9054
Well d. better than well said 3459
What mattered was Father's will d. 4425
What may be d. at anytime will be d. at no time 9304
what we have d. 49
what we have d. for others remains 10091
What we have d. for ourselves dies with us 10091
what you and yours have d. for us 5009
whatever one sees ought to be d. 4111
When all is d, say not my day is o'er 2418
When his work is d, his aim fulfilled 6803
When love is d. 7306
When my task is d, let me out 7006
who says it can't be d. 66
work designed for eternity only d. by Spirit 10181
work well d. never needs doing over 8579
wrongdoer not always one who has d. something 6157
You have d. what you could 11366

DONKEY
If brother is d, what are you 2065
like d. believing crowds cheering him 9217

DONKEYS
who will drive the d. 10215

DO-NOTHING
the d. God 7556

DON'T
be ferocious with yourself 9923
borrow trouble 4035
bother much about your feelings 4013
brood, you're not a hen 2542
condemn the sinner 10432
cut off the buttons 4367
dream of happiness in future 5507
fence smile in 5504
have to light all the world 7107
hear one, judge two 6606
hurry, d. worry 9530
I d. belong here 6929
if d. want to work 3098
if we d. give thanks in all things 11152
If you d. enjoy what you have now 5532
If you d. invest much 2629
insult God telling him he forgot to give you brains 7755
invent with your mouth 5165
Kind words d. wear out tongue 6646
lead me, I may not follow 4224
Lighthouses d. ring bells 6022
look back on happiness 5507
mess with Mr. In-Between 8231
need to be right all the time 3929
not that we d. believe in God 10509
play games with God 4879
Real friends d. care if socks d. match 4264
run around with Henny Pennys 4226
sell people short 8479
sell yourself short 10001
speak well of yourself 5996
stay away from church because hypocrites 6050
things I worry about d. happen 12060
try and be useful 10141
try to reach God with your understanding 11607
understand: trust me 2414
walk behind me, I may not lead 4224
want us free to express faith creatively 6824
what d. know that frightens me 6685
What you d. get, you can't lose 8639
When your work speaks for itself, d. interrupt 6043
worry about rumor, slander 6271
You d. stop laughing because grow old 6747

DON'TS
Christianity, more than d. 1171

DOOM
And battered with the shocks of d. 2599
ourselves to shadows, weakness, sterility 2821

Shall I think of death as d. 2364

DOOMED
are the hotheads 379

DOOR
approach each man by right d. 3345

Coffin, room without d. 2236

devil not always at one d. 2685

do not see d. opened for us 8229

dream d. in deepest sanctum of soul 2971

Eternity, shall ever lose the d. 3283

exceed in interest knock at d. 4259

Faith, key to fit d. of hope 3836

Fear knocked at the d. 3968

foolish to punish neighbor by fire when live next d. 9718

God never farther away than the d. 4621

God watches to see d. move from within 4775

he is my open d. 6357

His life is highest, holiest entering at lowliest d. 6132

His winds of storm drive through my d. 11468

Humble love keeps d. of heaven 12130

I lift my lamp beside the golden d. 7985

I've shut the d. on yesterday 11369

If each sweeps in front of his own d. 9664

If God shuts one d, he opens another 5421

If only one could bold the d. 8136

if you don't open d. to devil 2654

Jesus transformed death from slammed d. to open d. 2322

look so long at closed d. do not see one opened 5573

look so regretfully at closed d. 8229

love of neighbor is d. out of dungeon of self 8063

Man prisoner who has no right to open d. 10941

must be opened by willing hand 4775

neglect God for whining of a d. 7712

no one can shut d. God has opened 4937

nor open d. God has shut 4937

Nor will God force any d. to enter in 4775

Obedience is key that unlocks d. 8101

Obedience is key to every d. 8102

Often God has to shut d. in our face 5436

Satan's friendship reaches to prison d. 2665

see him waiting at the open d. 7085

shut d. against earthly noise 10554

slamming d. in face of God 5955

to profound spiritual experience 8101

Trouble knocked at d, hearing laugh hurried away 11461

what seems obstacle becomes a d. 10901

When God shuts d, he opens window 5462

When one d. closes, another opens 8229

When one d. of happiness closes, another opens 5573

years come to my d. 11320

yielding to temptation is opening d. 11088

DOORBELL
God comes without ringing d. 4838

DOORKEEPERS
two d. to house of prayer 8996

DOORLATCH
with hand on d. they die outside 3654

DOORMAT
though men treat me like a d. 10156

DOORMATS
love does not ask us to be d. 7337

DOORPOST
Perseverance rope that ties soul to d. of heaven 8554

DOORS
Death opens unknown d. 2264

ears, eyes, d, windows of soul 845

Hope opens d, despair closes them 5928

shut in your face 184

wind of God's admonishment may burst d. 4775

DOORSTEP
to wisdom is knowledge of own ignorance 11942

DOORWAY
love that leads to d. of friend 4278

Often d. to success is 3612

When we turn into heaven's d. 7085

DORMITORY
church not d. 1434

DOUBLE
Common sense shines with d. lustre in humility 5994

man would d. his troubles 2569

No one has d. in friendship 4297

Slander vice that strikes d. blow 10463

Tongue d. brings trouble 2913

DOUBLE-EDGED
Candor always d. sword 5869

DOUBLES
Despair d. our strength 2577

Friendship d. joy, divides grief 4229

DOUBT
All is best, though we oft d. 4985

beginning, not end, of wisdom 2934

believe everything or d. everything 2956

beware of d. 2929

cannot d. power comes from above 4949

casting d. on God's wisdom 9993

church enjoys freedom to d. 952

Clouds of d. created 2931

come out of the d. 4577

death rids us of d. 2251

disease of this restless age 2935

dreads to take a step 2939

Every step toward Christ kills a d. 2940

Faith deaf to d. 3683

faith is d. twin brother 2932

faith is forged through d. 3726

gets you an education 2942

God's permission means no d. 5402

God, takes nothing away 491

hammer that breaks windows, lets in light 2936

he or she is anyone's friend 4283

how could God reveal himself with no room for d. 2963

humility not d. of own power 6032

I defy you to d. Jesus 2961

I will not d. though all my ships at sea 11470

Idleness gives room for d. 12024

If d. yourself, on shaky ground 11599

If in d. ask what we shall wish we had done 2484

If you pray for bread and bring no basket 2947

in d. we cling closely to thee 9053

In darkness feels no d. 3768

inner battles torn them between d, faith 2959

intelligent full of d. 2955

is an element of faith 2937

is can't believe 2930

is honesty 2930

is looking for light 2930

is negative 6091

isn't the opposite of faith 2937

It were too strong I should d. thy love 4758

makes the mountain which faith moves 2938

many words expression of d. 11991

may be sign a man is thinking 2933

memorizing Scripture helps in d. 747

Modest d. is call'd beacon of wise 2951

never bear burden of sin, d. 937

Never d. in dark 2885

no room for d. no room for me
2963
not always sign a man is wrong
2933
outcome of contest not in d. 4916
questions, "Who believes" 2939
robbing life of glow, meaning
6091
seek proof, admit d. 3806
sees the darkest night 2939
sees the obstacles 2939
Shall I d. my Father's mercy 2364
so close to faith 7081
speak out, remove all d. 1836
stupid cocksure, intelligent full of
d. 10518
There lives more faith in honest d.
2957
Thought starts with d. 11266
To believe greatly, necessary to d.
greatly 2958
Truth divorced from experience in
d. 3548
ultimate outcome never in d. 4822
When in d, go home 11114
When in d. look at Jesus 4489
when there is d. wait 5402
where there is d, faith 9086
Why d. the human seed 2350
With d. and dismay you are
smitten 8230
without d. God will quickly
respond 7709
Your uttered ignorance and
morbid d. 3778

DOUBTED
Christians who say they have
never d. 2959
divinity of Scriptures 744
good must be d. to be defended
2954
never to have d. does not know
faith 3726

DOUBTER
to demonstrate to diehard d. he
wasn't a ghost 9693

DOUBTFUL
in d. things, liberty 7196
sense of tragedy compatible with
belief 591

DOUBTING
believe with certainty, begin with
d. 606
Stop d. 10780

DOUBTINGS
draws nigh to God through d. dim
2962

DOUBTS
beg Holy Spirit to fill us while
preventing him by our d. 8843
begin with certainties, end in d.
950
begin with d, end in certainties
950
dim perceptions of Christ's gospel
6713

do not understand hope until
confronted with d. 11620
feeds faith will starve d. to death
3727
If a man d. his way Satan ready to
help 2944
need not discourage us if full of d.
2949
sinister d. lurk in the shadow
3649
Unless start with d. cannot have
deep-rooted faith 2949
When mind d. feather sways it
2960
who d. bears arms against himself
11597
will not avail against certainties
5028

DOUGHNUT
optimist sees the d. 8244

DOVE
When d. begins to associate with
crows 9517

DOVE'S
Time as he passes has d. wing
11345

DOVES
When Christ told us to be like d.
5631

DOWN
as long as you're looking d. can't
see above 9188
as treasures on earth laid d. 9565
can fall d. by myself 9044
can't hold a man d. without
staying d. with him 10479
cannot be an up without a d. 5357
Christian to get up starts d. 1294
Christian, goes d. to get up 1265
Failure is not falling d. 3588
failure is staying d. 3598
failure not the falling d. 3598
God will reach d. all the way 7514
God's restrictions hold us d. 4309
God's restrictions not only hold us
d. 9558
God's way is always d. 1294
Grace can help us when we are d.
5212
He that is d. need fear no fall
6001
he who does not love would faint
and lie d. 7220
I look d, I feel giddy 7090
Look up, not d. 8379
man drags man d. or man lifts
man up 9522
murder when put people d. 10683
only time to look d. on neighbor
is when bending over to help
8064
Patience, to put up with people
you'd like to put d. 8411
Play it d, pray it up 2606
Prejudice being d. on something
you're not up on 9183

proud man always looking d. on
things, people 9188
saints frequently experienced up
and d. 2593
tendency of world is d. 7529
when a person d. in world 3146
Wisdom is vertical, comes d. from
above 11928
world a ladder for some to go up,
some d. 7047
you struck me d. 7579

DOWNCAST
dog comfort, doesn't ask why
1511
No one needs to be d. 10603

DOWNHEARTED
wish to be d, look to yourself
6408

DOWNHILL
better check to see if you're going
d. 6877
Every uphill has its d. 6890
no uphill without a d. 2754

DOWNS
Life a tumble-about thing of ups,
d. 6955

DOWNWARD
devil leads d, fiddles all the way
2697
looking d. makes one dizzy 11727
No nation made progress in d.
direction 7834

DOWNWARDS
heart which no unworthy
affection may drag d. 9057

DOXOLOGY
Christian ought to be a living d.
9856
living d. for adoration 1242
living d. for gratitude 1242

DRAG
heart which no unworthy
affection may d. downwards
9057
useless to put best foot forward,
d. other 11601

DRAGGING
Lost day by d. day 6972
Many troubles are God d. us
11440

DRAGON
science d. capable of destroying
world 9870

DRAGS
man d. man down, or man lifts
man up 9522

DRAIN
away the business with which we
inevitably get involved 6830
Would d. the ocean dry 4748
You'll never d. love dry 7257

DRAINED
that cup of sin be d. to dregs 5423

DRAINPIPE
sat down under the d. 4062

DRAMA
Bible, the whole human d. 750
Christian faith most exciting d.
11201
do not know when world d. will
end 9911
dogma is the d. 11201
essence of the d. Jesus lived 6384
God almost a kind of d. 11425
peopled world, divine eternal d.
1981
years we spend on earth first scene
in divine d. 6106

DRAMATIC
creed of church d. 1205

DRAMATICALLY
future has habit of d. becoming
present 4323

DRAPERY
Like one that wraps the d. of his
couch 2203

DRAUGHT
I took one d. of life 3483

DRAW
curtain before stains of friend
4183
Love must d. the soul on 7167
No cable can d. so forcibly as love
7279
who sought to d. attention to
himself 6018

DRAWING
God's hand d. me 7484

DRAWN
people were d. to Christ 6396

DRAWS
nigh to God through doubtings
dim 2962

DREAD
highest trees have most reason to
d. thunder 9241
hope vaguely, d. precisely 5949
How d. are thine eternal years
4659
in the end does not d. the future
8184
Many live in d. of what is coming
4318
mortal d. of failure 10776
the grave as little as my bed 2370
Why do we d. ordeal 11459

DREADFUL
Eternity, thou pleasing d. thought
3271
How d. so'er it be 1663
knowledge without integrity d.
3013
truth not so d. as uncertainty
11544

DREADFULLY
like other people 7441

DREADS
burnt child d. fire 3512
Doubt d. to take a step 2939

DREAM
a perfectly valid phenomenon
2968
cannot d. yourself into character
1071
Christianity, a battle not a d. 1167
disguised fulfillment of wish 2968
don't d. of happiness in future
5507
equilibrium between d. and reality
7435
Every d. full of significance 2968
Give man d, challenge heart 3307
grandeur is a d. 11849
hidden door in deepest sanctum of
soul 2971
I d. of a day 3229
If laborer to d. he was king 8576
In a d. I walked with God 4024
is not absurd 2968
is not meaningless 2968
is the theater 2972
king d. he was laborer 8576
Love is one long sweet d. 7631
Maturity, releasing a d. 7696
of a day that had never been 8371
of the vast untrod 2964
One night a man had a d. 5437
opens into primeval cosmic night
2971
reveals psychological structure
2968
Some men d. of worthy
accomplishments 89
still d. what Adam dreamt 9309
that says, "Strike out with me"
2964
'til you find your d. 4421
To d. of person you would like to
be 6217
To play, to d, to drift 6881
vision without a task a d. 11730
vision without task a d. 12006
We live as we d, alone 7079
What world calls virtue a name, a
d. 11720
When a d. enslaves a man 2964
you can, begin it 48

DREAMED
height of holiness we never d.
10391
people d. of a Golden Age 8371
slept and d. life was joy 9663
world never before seen or d. of
6419

DREAMLIKE
Love for Lord not d. thing 7221

DREAMS
About him, and lies down to
pleasant d. 2203
act part learned in waking hours
2966
are not hypocrites in our sleep
6066

future convenient place for d.
4324
God loves you with intimacy
which surpasses d. 4747
God's gifts put man's best d. to
shame 4988
God's promises beyond wildest d.
4458
If you have left your d. behind
8122
man's best d. to shame 6
Sabbath when d. rekindled 10959
Than this world d. of 8869
Today unlocks tomorrow's d.
11382
touchstones of our characters
2966
true interpreters of inclinations
2967
truest life in d. awake 2966
We are here in the land of d. 5672
What is pleasant belongs to d.
9399

DREAMT
still dream what Adam d. 9309

DREARY
Hope of the d. 6468
No life d. when work delight 3106
Old age is d. solitude 8152
Some days must be dark, d. 2549
when the road seems d, endless
9059
With merry company d. way
endured 4304

DREGS
that cup of sin be drained to d.
5423

DRESS
Be careless in d. if you must
10652
Girded for war, humility his
mighty d. 6124
My beauty are, my glorious d.
4719

DRESSED
World, you are beautifully d. 8010

DREW
He d. them forth, healed and bade
me live 9798
Love bade me welcome, yet my
soul d. back 5481

DRIES
God d. you with his sun 4466

DRIFT
do not most people d. away 3742
I only know I cannot d. 4763
Our people d. and die 9224
relentless d. of events will make
decision 2491
The rest d. to and fro 10679
To play, to dream, to d. 6881
without faith people d. into hate
societies 925

DRIFTING
Come d. home with broken masts and sails 11470

DRILLS
ages of man: d. 7037

DRINK
God wills we eat, d, be merry 8603
night given to d. deep at fountain of power 6947
O Jesus, d. of me 7003
sin may spell d. but is some form of "me" 9916
the d. takes the man 330
When d. from stream 11170

DRINKER
has a hole under his nose 322

DRINKING
crutches for lame ducks 326
rufuge of the weak 326
Shallow amenities, eating and d. ordained by God 7038

DRINKS
to drown his sorrow 335

DRIPPING
from iron nails 1368

DRIVE
can't d. straight on twisting lane 4440
the long d. won't seem so long 7085
who will d. the donkeys 10215

DRIVEN
Are we d. people 1634
Christ not d. by crises 4425
Jesus d. to life of silence, solitude, simplicity 6358
Not all people d. by same stick 7868
storms of life have d. us 178

DRIVER
way d. speeds through traffic 1738

DRIVERS
Most people are careful d. 3947

DRIVES
And d. away his fear 1507
Laughter d. winter from the face 6735
Love d. us on 7273
Man d, God holds reins 4947
One ship d. east, another west 4432

DROP
A mere d. suffices for me 4816
Faults will d. off like dead leaves 3940
I am a single d, how can it be 7469
In sleep, pain that cannot forget falls d. by d. 11919
One d. of water for my soul 7003
to your knees beside wide road 4608

DROPS
Earth breaks up, time d. away 5636
if few d. of ocean are dirty, ocean not dirty 5988
without getting a few d. on yourself 5516

DROSS
Each ounce of d. costs its ounce of gold 2641
left in the crucible 223
We were d, now gold 1348
When earthly treasure proves but d. 4338

DROVE
your splendor d. out my blindness 1910

DROWN
by staying in water 3636
don't d. by falling in water 3636
tales in details 1867
To d. the outcry of the heart 6740

DROWNED
born to be hanged shall never be d. 9176
Divinity so deep pride d. in infinity 4745
Earth d. in blood and tears 4902
voice of intelligence d. out by roar of fear 6331

DROWSY
present life, only a d. half-waking 5672
Soft d. hours creeping 1123

DRUDGERY
love counts royalty but d. if cannot reign for Christ 6457
task without a vision is d. 11730
work not necessary d. 3127

DRUG
and alcohol addicts in America 135
if d. use isn't a sin 134

DRUG ADDICTS
People do not decide to be d. 11080

DRUGGED
Jesus refuses to swallow d. drink 10868

DRUGS
Music glorifying d. 7910

DRUM
alcoholic tight as a d. 324

DRUMMER
hears a different d. 10827

DRUMS
let your thunders roll like d. 4712
thunder rolls like d. in march of God's armies 7997
words sound out like d. 11998

DRUNK
golf-mania as intemperate as someone who gets d. 9269
Human nature like d. peasant 5968
If a man get d. breaks his leg 1731
my mother, d. or sober 7980

DRUNKARD
a better sermon against that vice 336
while there is a d. left, I'll fight 3342

DRUNKARDS
Boredom, made more d. than thirst 864
People do not decide to be d. 11080

DRUNKEDNESS
mere fleabites in comparison with pride 9240

DRUNKENNESS
a living corpse 334
domestic evils 333
is premature old age 329
is temporary death 329
momentary cessation of unhappiness 328
negative happiness 328
temporary suicide 328
the ruin of a person 329
trying to put out a fire with oil 335
voluntary madness 327

DRY
Intellectual sophistication can d. up creativity 6325
spiritual darkness and d. spells 181
the eyes which we have flooded 9054
When you see inclinations d. 2565
Whenever knowledge becomes d. something wrong 6704
where renew your springs that never d. up 9933
will not be made straight when d. 12166
Would drain the ocean d. 4748
You'll never drain love d. 7257

DRYNESS
Bear patiently the d. of your mind 7123
In times of d. must be patient 2883

DUCK
If God made you a d. saint 6187
umbrella over d. in rain 6641

DUCKS
look funny trying to climb 6168

DUG
But iron d. from central gloom 2599

DULL
acquiescence of indolence 4507
Bible d. when I am d. 683
daily burden of a d. life 9683
Duty does not have to be d. 7165

fear figures you will settle for d.
  existence 3971
genius often d, inert in society
  4395
how little people know who think
  holiness is d. 5750
Is ditchwater d. 8020
Life with Christ never d. 6987
Sharp words d. respect 9488
sinners, sleep no more 9692
worst notion that domesticity is d.
  5842

DULLED
Reading, not d. by age 858

DULLNESS
Criticism's child 2050
one of seven deadly virtues 11699
think, talk, act yourself into d.
  3185

DULLS
Failure to obey d. spiritual
  understanding 8100
Fortune d. 11808
legalism d. our edge 6823

DUMB
Kindness a language d. can speak
  6650
Light griefs can speak, deeper
  ones d. 5347
No one will grieve because your
  lips are d. 3778
shall in eternity be d. 8727
That crushes into d. despair 8863
the Word stern-sentenced to be
  nine months d. 6142

DUNCES
all in confederacy against genius
  4400

DUNGEON
all serving life-sentence in d. of life
  7074
Christ a window in dark d. of ego
  6434
Himself is his d. 10061
love of neighbor is door out of d.
  of self 8063
sin d. of hell 10360
What other d. so dark as one's
  own heart 9955

DUNGFORK
man with d. gives God glory 1237

DUPED
correct insight among d. 2803

DUPES
hypocrites greatest d. devil has
  6055

DUPLICITY
Honesty, an absence of d. 5874

DURATION
heaven, happiness endless in d.
  5634
If consider boundless d, shrink
  into nothing 11631

When I consider the short d. of
  my life 7084

DUST
And "d. to d." concludes her
  noblest song 7088
As chimney-sweepers, come to d.
  2290
astonishing that I—d, ash, mud
  7489
Blows d. in others' eyes 10411
Confusion d. raised by devil 2642
devil not afraid of Bible with d.
  729
do not feel I am speck of d. in
  universe 11124
grains of d. carried away 3295
Guilty of d. and sin 5481
huge clouds nothing more than d.
  on eyelashes 11442
Illusion d. devil throws in eyes of
  foolish 2655
legions of Rome smouldering in d.
  730
Life is d. nature lends man for an
  hour 6960
Lord made Adam from d. 1127
Man nothing but d. 7445
Music washes away d. of life 7912
nothing rises quicker than d. 3857
plays with d, eyes full of d. 11066
Take clay and d, fashion a child
  4608
tears rain upon blinding d. of earth
  11023
thou art, to d. returneth 2328
To the vile d. from whence he
  sprung 10088
When God scooped up handful of
  d. 1982
Write injuries in d, benefits in
  marble 9523

DUSTY
what d. answer gets soul 946

DUTIES
at your hand 829
Christianity at first seems to be
  about d. 1181
Great trials preparation for great
  d. 2725
Greatness in performance of d.
  5283
in years of uneventful d. 10190
Keep us, Lord, so awake in d. of
  our callings 9668
Life made up not of d. 6656
Man should perform d. to
  fellowmen as to God 9669
need not new d, but new strength
  9554
On the d. of a friend 4217
opportunities open on road of
  daily d. 8217
To discharge d. of professor
  11007
without healing of spirit d. burden
  8857

DUTY
acted and behold d. was joy 9663
awoke and saw life was d. 9663
bound to thank and praise 4992
Character out of response to d.
  1000
charity is promptness when stern
  d. calls 1085
deserve no praise, it is our d. 9666
do d. wisely, leave issue to God
  5176
Do today's d. 9650
Do your d, leave rest to heaven
  9651
does not have to be dull 7165
  3087
doing what we ought, our d. 3100
done is soul's fireside 9653
enthusiasm makes pleasure of d.
  3188
first d. is to find its Master 4144
first d. of love is to listen 7301
giving comes from obligation
  10736
giving says, "I ought to" 10736
God laid upon man d. of being
  free 4127
God never imposes d. without
  giving time 9659
Grace binds with stronger cords
  than d. 5211
Gratitude d. which ought to be
  paid 5242
great thing expressed in single
  word 10277
holy life faithful in Christian d.
  5736
if did d. world might be full of
  love 12041
is ours, events are God's 9654
joy replaced by pursuit of d. 6813
just report for d. 8782
let us dare to do our d. 3755
Love can fill d. with life 7165
  3087
Love can make d. beautiful 7165
  3087
mingled in the fray of d. 3174
my d. is to my family first 3871
Neither usefulness nor d. God's
  purpose 197
not effort of d. 1525
of safeguarding freedom of spirit
  4127
ought to be diligent in d. to God
  2778
our d. to bark in house of the Lord
  9150
performed gives music at midnight
  9675
represents Sinai 7297
times when d. to stop praying and
  trust 9009
to cultivate reason a d. 9425
to do what thou wouldst not 9667
to leave undone that thou wouldst
  do 9667
To persevere in one's d. 9677

Vision looks inward, becomes d.
 11738
Who escapes d, avoids gain 9681
Who gives from sense of d. 11358
would not think d. small if you
 were great 9682

DUTY'S
Nature's and d. never at odds
 3813

DWARF
giant in your eyes may be d. in
 ours 8484

DWARFED
must the soul lie d. 10649

DWELL
friends impart favor where they d.
 4269
Jesus Christ, delights to d. within
 6352
Look right, left, I d. alone 2587
thou within it, tune and touch the
 chords 7527

DWELLING
friend, single soul d. in two bodies
 4211
Make it thy quiet d. place 7454
Our source, our center, our d.
 place 4836
Praise will transform humblest d.
 to a hallowed heaven 5846

DWELLING-PLACE
heart, the d. of God 8474

DWELLINGS
God has two d. 5621

DWELLS
God d. in eternity 11295
 4600
God far more d. in me 4839
He d. himself in me 7506
Malignity of soul often d. in
 diseased bodies 5613
time d. in God 4600
time d. with God 11295
Where pity d, the peace of God is
 there 7284

DYING
as Christ died who died to himself
 6365
Be near me, Lord, when d. 2228
Because d. we come to thee 9053
book under your head when d.
 649
cannot forgive my friends for d.
 2303
Christ spoke of d. to live 6359
church d. of leukemia 3341
civilization is d. 6359
daily deaths destroy power of
 final d. 2110
Damnation: continual d. 5684
divine King rules forever by d.
 2166
do not require d. grace to live by
 6912

Every day we are d. 962
Fine d. is a man's privilege 2336
I am afraid of d. 2300
I am not d. I am entering into life
 2440
in d. that we are born to eternal
 life 9086
Jesus evidence of God's anger
 toward sin 6473
leaves money 7826
Life is not lost by d. 6972
lives to live forever, never fears d.
 6899
man's d. more the survivor's affair
 2210
maybe d. 4094
Must do his own d. 2280
no d. by proxy 2396
Oh the pain, the bliss of d. 2404
pride of d. rich raises loudest
 laugh in hell 9246
Scriptures teach most comfortable
 way of d. 742
Thinking is like loving and d.
 11260
This world is land of d. 2400
Tomorrow will be d. 8214
want to be saved, insist Christ do
 d. 2821
when the d. hour comes, there
 will be d. grace 6912
With the d. sun 7306
world d. for want of good hearing
 9163
world d. not for want of good
 preaching 9163
world is the land of the d. 7064
wretch doubly d, shall go down to
 vile dust 10088
Yesterday I was d. with Christ
 2121

DYNAMIC
God a d. pulsating activity 11425
God most active and d. of all 4520
Healthy questions keep faith d.
 2949

DYNAMICS
into inner d. of human organism
 9353

E

EACH
As more of heav'n in e. we see
 4197
check to our desires 4578
day is a wonderful gift 6524
depends on the other 9501
failure of our hopes 4578
For e, God has a different response
 7127
For e. of us the time coming 3719
generation like a line, a phrase
 7076

God calls e. in secret to make
 sacrifices
 5385
God, loving all, should love e.
 differently 6169
in power of e. to be an individual
 6209
individual either a sinner or a saint
 5038
Living e. day as if only day 6999
man as he really is 7443
man as he sees himself 7443
man as the other person sees him
 7443
Man enters e. stage of life as
 novice 7002
more precious than all 6200
of us carries own life-form 6214
of us must think for himself
 11260
one of us is a mystery 6171
ordering of his providence 4578
That which e. can do best none
 but his Maker can teach 6226

EACH OTHER
honest with ourselves, honest with
 each e. 5871
Love does not consist in gazing at
 e. 7215

EAGER
Many e. to share in Jesus' table
 9268
nothing more wonderful than
 alert, e. mind 7776

EAGERLY
seek approval of man of worldly
 reputation 11666
youth e. waiting for play to begin
 12168

EAGLE
eye cannot see its height 4745
If you're an e. saint, stop
 expecting squirrel saints to soar
 6187

EAGLE'S
eye for faults of others 3957

EAGLES
don't flock 6789
don't swim 6168
Fly with the e. 4226
have to find them one at a time
 6789

EAR
Choose wife by e. rather than eye
 7610
Close e. against him who opens
 mouth against another 10447
Comes sweet with music to thy
 wearied e. 10960
craves the familiar 844
elves reach to whisper in e. 1122
Give every man thy e. 1843
God's e. for my hearing 5400
Gods puts his e. so closely down
 8801

Have deaf e. for unkind remarks
9456
He hath an e. to hear
9024
If wife is small, stoop down and
whisper in e. 7620
In a believer's e. 1507
In every e. it spread 9757
Keep your e. to the ground 3503
Life must be composed by e. 6966
My e. is pain'd 6273
Nor e. can hear 9567
not e. that hears sweetness of
music 10656
shocked by the unexpected 844
tends to be lazy 844
To e. of God everything makes
exquisite music 8743

EARLIER
happy family an e. heaven 3865

EARLY
Christians so much in other world
5666
God of the e. mornings 7539
in e. stages of Christian experience
7690
In e. years of Christian experience
3744
light arrives too e. in morning
11309
soul has further horizons than e.
mornings 7539
Work, work from e. until late
12029

EARN
work to e. enough money 3098
Workers e. money 7826

EARNED
managed to spend more than you
e. 4030

EARNEST
Life is real! Life is e! 2328
man in e. finds means 2624

EARNESTNESS
commands respect of mankind
2771
not everything 2626
pray with as much e. 3816

EARS
a shout about my e. 2980
aren't made to shut 1875
ass went seeking for horns, lost e.
2872
Breath, mouth, e, eyes 6120
doors and windows of soul 845
eyes more exact witnesses than e.
3567
God is hearable with e. of inner
man 4509
good teacher one whose e. get as
much exercise as mouth 10998
Heav'n opens on my e. 2389
If you your e. would save from
jeers 1855
inner e. to hear what he could not
hear before 8495

love has e. to hear sighs, sorrows
7335
Man given two e. 1858
sing hymns for God's e. alone
8424
They took away what should have
been my e. 1817
What should not be heard by little
e. 3461
while their e. can hear 4223
you compelled my deaf e. to hear
you 7579

EARTH
active life begins, ends on e. 1764
Adam filled e. with the pieces 760
Aim at heaven and you get e.
thrown in 5630
all God's e. is holy ground 7996
all resources of heaven, e. are at
my disposal 9066
Almighty appeared on e. as
helpless human baby 6125
as treasures on e. laid down 9565
aspiration to heart what spring is
to e. 471
awoke with first rush of song
11330
Before there was an e. at all 4694
betrayal and murder exist on e.
6158
blown asunder by nuclear
weapons 10503
breaks up, time drops away 5636
but school preparative 6109
by attitudes to treasures on e.
11872
can produce nothing unless
fertilized by sun 5207
cannot say in e. as it is in heaven if
8818
changes, but soul, God stand sure
948
Christ will turn e. into heaven
5529
Christ, Lord of heaven and e. 232
Christians know God, do not love
e. 3201
confronted with sacraments of
God 8050
continuance of pride is on e. 9218
Creator of e. is owner 1970
cross points to heaven and e,
reconciling them 2154
dearest friend on e. mere shadow
4201
disaster to feel at home on e. 2975
drowned in blood and tears 4902
Every morning sun rises to warm e.
8002
feeling I could outlast the e. 12165
fellowship of love throughout the
whole wide e. 911
felt God's presence on moon more
than on e. 11630
felt the wound 10314
Find me men on e. who care 4118
first-tasting bitter e. 6142
foot on e. is on a banana peel
6915

For if thy work on e. be sweet
5635
foretaste on e. of what heaven will
be like 7198
fragile, failing, imperfect e. 7601
ghastly hush descend upon e.
1852
Give the e. to Christ 1363
God feeds even the worm in the e.
9347
God has given man a short time
upon e. 6894
God knows all things in e. 4881
God still wants as theatre for his
grace 4902
God who rules this e. 3227
God's way contrary to wisdom on
e. 1294
grand pieces played on e.
composed in heaven 5639
Great men meteors so e. lighted
5278
grows into heaven 6378
handful of e. to make God's image
1952
happiest miser on e. saves every
friend 4203
has no higher bliss 4799
has no sorrow heaven cannot heal
10589
Has not the whole e. a voice 7997
He who does not praise God
while on e. 8727
Heaven in e, and God in man
6153
heaven upon e. to weary head
10484
hell upon e. found in melancholy
heart 2548
Holy Ghost intercession in us on e.
8859
home joys most delightful e.
affords 5844
Home, spot of e. supremely best
5834
I have one foot on e. 6915
I would have rid the e. of him
4199
If God lived on e. 4480
If you can be with God on e.
11632
Infinite written name on e. in
flowers 4705
is God's long-suffering 5650
is painted green 8016
Jews know God, love only e. 3201
laws in Bible include treatment of
e. 3201
left their mark on e. 5656
Leviticus 25 classic on rights of e.
3200
Lifts e. to heaven, stoops heaven
to e. 6153
Lo, e. receives him from the
bending skies 6138
look at e. from heaven's point of
view 10707
Love like a rose, joy of all the e.
7179

make one like it—seed of e. 4608

Make our e. an Eden like heaven above 2503

makes e. a garden 4280

man only once on this e. 6173

meek, not arrogant, inherit e. 1216

men of same e. by same Creator 3225

meteor, when it descends to e. 4395

mother is God's deputy on e. 7841

Music almost all we have of heaven on e. 7902

Music only art of e. we take to heaven 7904

Music only art of heaven given to e. 7904

must not be so lost in work of e. 6108

Naked to e. I descend 5952

Naked to e. was I brought 5952

No masses of e. can block God's vision 4883

no one in e. can shut door God has opened 4937

no power on e. more formidable than truth 11547

none who has enjoyed God's goodness on e. 6092

nothing is better on e. than love 7283

Now native to e. as I am 6120

Of thy renewed e. 9898

of whom we speak least on e. best known in heaven 9616

Of wrong and outrage with which e. is fill'd 6273

on e. or else in heaven, another year for thee 8077

on e. sowed his name in tender flowers 8037

On this hapless e. 6740

only the living, on e. and beyond 2390

pagans do not know God, love only e. 3201

planned, gifted, positioned on e. by Master Craftsman 10004

poetry of e. never dead 2976

power of evil unlimited if on e. alone 3377

presence of God's power on e. 4865

provides enough for every man's need 5326

Rains come to water e. 8002

recedes, heaven opens 2437

relationship to God fits you to live on e. 4555

Religion originates on e. 9545

remorse puts man in hell while on e. 9584

same Jesus in heaven as on e. 6466

scarcely anything on e. more beautiful than Spirit-filled mind 7776

Seeking to perpetuate one's name on e. 3860

send two angels to e. 3232

Sin, what hast thou done to this fair e. 10342

small portion of e. will hold us when dead 2344

sole equality on e. is death 3245

soul on e. never to be unfolded 10649

spiritual creatures walk the e. 362

summit of love on e. 10331

Sweeps the wide e, tramples o'er mankind 6269

Take away love and e. is a tomb 7294

takes real faith to live life of heaven on e. 3752

teardrop on e. summons King of heaven 11011

Than anywhere else on e. 8032

that we cannot do our work on e. 6108

the dead in the cool e. lie 426

The inn is full on the planet e. 6155

the last of e! I am content 2453

They live on e. 2287

Think of yourself as seed wintering in e. 5672

this dark, satanic e. 4902

This e. would be God's Paradise 6882

though they come from ends of e. 915

Till e. and sky stand presently at 915

to find his ball, the e. 1363

to the sun what man is to angels 364

Trumpets! Lightnings! The e. trembles 6150

two spirits abroad in e. 877

ultimate disaster to feel at home on e. 2382

universe centered on neither e. nor sun 11647

Were every stalk on e. a quill 4748

What joy the happy e. to greet 9898

What would Jehovah say now 3205

When love unnoticed came to e. 6458

When Master of e. calls shots, things happen 3819

Why stay we on e. except to grow 7706

with thousand voices praises God 2973

years we spend on e. first scene in divine drama 6106

you're too wonderful to realize 2974

EARTH-BORN

uprooted from e. securities and assurances 7488

EARTHBOUND

apprehensions that afflict the e. 5781

Because understanding is e. 11606

EARTHLIES

ill-taught if look for results only in e. 9014

EARTHLY

all this e. grossness quit 5679

employments avocations 3095

freedom of Bible from e. mixtures 736

God's plan doesn't always make e. sense 5399

highest e. enjoyments a shadow 733

I will consider my e. existence wasted 6919

if course wrong avoid though lose e. treasure 6291

if pursuits on e. things 8818

introduce kingdom of heaven into midst of e. day 4974

life in touch with a new infinite life 7101

meaning of e. existence is development of the soul 9342

no e. thing can ever satisfy 3277

nor does any e. blessing appear wanting 7100

old man nearing end of e. journey 8121

Our e. rulers falter 9224

poor in spirit detachment from e. supports 6025

shut door against e. noise 10554

When e. treasure proves but dross 4338

EARTH'S

Christ is risen, all e. at play 2982

crammed with heaven 1710

highest station ends in "Here he lies" 7088

in e. common things he stands revealed 8019

EARTHS

rise and wane 4694

EASE

Can e. my awful load 8451

Can e. this weight of sin 8451

If any lift may e. burden of another 910

If I can e. one life the aching 6922

nation that thinks more of e. 7984

Only heart without stain knows e. 1696

tell God you only feel at e. when far from him 8830

Virtue nought to do with e. 11714

Who craves for e. rest, joys 2583

who speaks truth always at e. 11537

with being sentimentalists 12106

world owes onward impulses to men ill at e. 2875

EASED
self-denying deed, word e. heart
107

EASES
Music e. grief's smarting wound
7913
Politeness e. jolts 1946

EASIER
A grass-blade's no e. to make than
an oak 2007
excellence not often gained on e.
terms 3470
for father to have children 3922
for me to give thee all 7125
Friendship is like money, e. made
than kept 4235
God does not make choices e.
11058
hope, an e. way to journey's end
5924
Life is e. than you think 6961
Nothing e. than not able to find
time 9301
People cry e. than change 975
to be critical than correct 2067
to be honest with other people
5880
to be wise for others than
ourselves 11924
to catch flies with honey than
vinegar 6643
to denature plutonium than evil
3362
To die for a religion e. than to live
it 7681
to get into enemy's toils than out
11119
to know God than own soul 1713
to know mankind than man
individually 7393
to look wise than talk wisely 1856
to love humanity as a whole 5972
to meet evil in open than
underground 3381
to perceive error than truth 3259
to repent of sins we have
committed 10327
to see clearly into liar than man
who tells truth 6866
to stay out than get out 11073
to suffer as public heroes than
apart 10859
to suffer physical death than
spiritual suffering 10859
to suffer with others than alone
10859
to swallow than eat angry words
388
to walk six miles to hear sermon
than 7716
to wear mask 6057
Wickedness always e. than virtue
11895

EASIEST
for e. positions God must give
grace 7486
happiest life not necessarily e.
2563

person to deceive is one's self
2471
Prayer e. and hardest of all things
8940
To know God e., most difficult in
world 7546
way to dignity is humility 6031

EASILY
a god which we can e. bear 4846
acquire skill to do difficult things
e. 8406
brighter the glitter, the more e.
broken 9336
collectivities e. respond to devil's
persuasion 6176
crushed and fragile 6651
error is e. seen 3259
get entangled and lose our soul
10514
God, voice too still to be e. audible
4465
heart unspotted not e. daunted
11679
If works of God e. comprehended
9411
No leader ever did work e. 5289
people more e. fall victims to great
lie 7974
Real doesn't often happen to
people who break e. 5886
reputation e. cracked, never well
mended 9615
Self-esteem can be crushed so e.
9994
single arrow e. broken 9442
taller we grew, more e. we could
reach 6017
things which come e. have no
significance 2757
two ways to slide e. through life
2956
We know God e. 4691
well-defined spiritual life most e.
lived 1332
whole cross more e. carried than
half 1332

EAST
Bible born in the E. 645
In Christ there is no e. or west 911
is e. and west is west 915
Of e. or west 4746
One ship drives e, another west
4432
Rejoicing in the e. 10962

EASTER
bunny never rose again 2983
Christ will rise on E. day 2985
flower of E. blossomed 2984
ground trembled, rock of tomb
tumbled 2984
Sunday continual message of E.
10955
trees filled air with joy 2977
Twas E. Sunday 2977
vital red of love poured out 2979
Welcome happy morning 2986

EASTERN
monarch charged wise men 957

EAST WIND
put on your overcoat 44

EASY
All things are difficult before e.
2710
Anytime the going seems e. 6877
as e. for God not to allow 4831
becomes difficult with reluctance
2756
Becoming a father e. enough 3917
choose difficult as if e. 3803
Christianity does not make life e.
1229
commandments e. when we obey
1521
cowardice of surrender to
conformity 6216
difficult when done reluctantly
3181
Divorce an e. escape, many think
2921
Do not pray for e. lives 8780
enough to be pleasant 10493
experiencing e. times, brace
yourself 969
Faith does not make things e.
3706
Faith not an e. virtue 3689
find yourself on e. road ought to
worry 2745
for rich to get on church board
11830
Getting married is e. 7615
God has no e. time of it to smash
self-sufficiency 10043
God will make this death e. for me
7674
God's control not e. to accept
5467
great things e. because of Christ's
omnipotence 10127
habit e. to abandon 3109
Hate e. to maintain for lifetime
7233
If e. to raise kids, never would
start with labor 8302
in solitude to live after own
opinions 6195
in strangely paradoxical way, also
e. 8108
Injustice relatively e. to bear 6267
just as e. to rejoice 37
Kind words e. to speak 11988
Lash love upon the poor e. 7348
less e. to uproot faults 3959
Life with Christ not always e.
6987
like God to make most vital thing
e. 3737
love makes all things e. 7345
love that Christ commands not e.
7304
Luxury makes a man so soft e. to
trouble him 7363
no cheap, e. miracles 1013

Nobody promises you a good or
e. time 2182
Nor bear an e. load 1927
not e. to be like Christ 8113
nothing e. about following Christ
1282
nothing more e. than to think
11219
obtain too e, value too lightly
8563
ride a man, sit e. and light 9471
road to hell e. to travel 5701
saint makes it e. to believe in Jesus
9771
sin becomes e. 10287
so e. practice of presence of God
4873
Spirit of God in sharp opposition
to e. ways of world 5776
Talking is e, action difficult 2537
Think e, shall be e. 517
to be nice to enemy from lack of
character 1026
to believe in God in our little
world 592
to bid devil be your guest 2657
to buy that kind of advice 9976
to covet another man's success
10788
to hand it over to God may not be
e. 10979
to hear music in waves 8034
to live after world's opinions 6195
to misunderstand what NT means
589
to overestimate importance of
achievements 84
to play musical instrument 7897
to receive Christ 5653
to tell poor to accept poverty as
God's will 8678
to turn religious life into beautiful
memories 10165
two things not e. to reconcile
7069
When claimed Jesus for himself
became e. 7105
when right, makes us e. to live
with 9119
Work is e. for those who like to
work 3126
yoke of Christ becomes e. 2824

EASYGOING
Christian more attractive 9529
Jesus' standards far from lax and
e. 6444

EAT
devil's country begins where men
e. men 4913
Do not e. garlic, smell of garlic
1006
do not understand digestive
system, but I e. 3733
for sixty years got enough to e.
10783
God wills we e, drink, be merry
8603
if no one starves while I e. 625

less 5604
long spoon to e. with devil 2645
rather play golf than e. 7656
Takers e. well 10198
to flea, mosquito human being
something good to e. 9219
we have meat and we can e.
11159
worries e. you when you're alive
12084

EATEN
apple is e, core sticks in throat
10385
lest you be e. up 557
sinful because not e. of Tree of Life
10416
sinful not because e. of Tree of
Knowledge 10416

EATING
all e, none of the work 3097
If you surpass me in e. 6190
on an empty stomach 131
ordained by God 7038
repentance much harder than e.
humble pie 9577
rid of fears, worries, bad e. habits
12076
something is e. us 133

EATS
Envy e. nothing but own heart
3209
Loneliness e. into the soul 7134

EAVESDROPPERS
never hear good of themselves
5123

EBB
we often see only e. of advancing
wave 5944

ECCENTRIC
Be virtuous and you will be e.
11680

ECCENTRICITIES
God knows e. of my being 4889

ECCENTRICITY
and character 1007
proportional to genius, vigor,
courage 1007

ECCENTRICS
Without e. world would not
progress 9318

ECCLESIASTES
How to enjoy 11925

ECCLESIASTICAL
in much of our e. routine 5786
sacred calling not limited to e.
functions 12146

ECHO
amusing to coquette with e, but
tiring 1851
Arising from creation, his e. clear
8029
Change wakes no e. in mute
eternity 973
church does not e. world 1428

Don't expect anything original
from e. 2000
Hope is an e. 5919
Joy e. of God's life within 6545
Remorse the e. of lost virtue 9571
spirituality an e. of God's voice
5981
We e. the song 1375

ECHOES
grow forever and forever 1032
In living e. of thy tone 8866
Incredible e. mirror actions 1740
Kind words, e. truly endless
11988
long ere e. waked the solitudes
4769
roll from soul to soul 1032
We are all more or less e. 6243
When oak is felled, forest e. with
its fall 8052

ECLIPSED
love e. as turns into clipboard
with checklist 6823
temptation to be like God e. view
of God 4419
Truth often e, never extinguished
11570

ECOLOGY
prayer for e. 9117

ECONOMIC
Church, sample of e. differences
surmounted 1492
claims to equality intensity
inequality 3242
Prosperity more than e. condition
9339

ECONOMY
save in one store, spend in another
4036

ECSTASIES
Whenever e. of God unfit us for
practical life 5466

ECSTASY
for mystics, pain an e. 8255
high e. of vision 2856
music most strongly suggests e.
5631
Words cannot speak for grief or e.
10274

ECUMENICAL
movement brings back memory
2990

ECUMENISTS
We are not e. 1343

EDEN
angels, bar entrance 359
Before the worm tore E. 2123
discern God on grass of E. 4856
Eve, with all fruits of E. blest
11053
Make our earth an E. like heaven
above 2503

EDGE

At e. of despair dawns clarity 2574

fool has answer on e. of tongue 4067

If it stands on e. I study 3011

legalism dulls our e. 6823

must not venture too near e. 11068

rough stone to sharpen e. 190

EDGES

Real doesn't often happen to people who have sharp e. 5886

EDIFICE

marriage an e. that must be rebuilt every day 7597

EDITORIALS

no e. praise mother's accomplishments 7844

EDITORS

indexes gives e. haggard look 12153

EDUCABLE

Meek means e. 7729

EDUCATE

in what nobody knew yesterday 3035

EDUCATED

act with intelligent thinking 3041

being e. for choir invisible 10600

hold pleasures under control 3041

honorable in all dealings 3041

if e. knows how to use colons 12152

not e, merely trained 3031

not overcome by misfortune 3041

not spoiled by success 3041

those who control circumstances 3041

those who meet occasions manfully 3041

those who treat good-naturedly things disagreeable 3041

well-placed quotation sign of e. person 9389

world is full of e. derelicts 8555

EDUCATES

defeat e. us 3601

EDUCATION

acquires higher grade of prejudices 2999

always something to overcome 1024

and scholarship enable man to put things well 2998

and scholarship will not give insight 2998

begins at home 3006

Christianity an e. 1193

church e. of imperfect Christians 4137

church, so many degrees 1410

Defeat nothing but e. 2517

doubt gets you an e. 2942

everything built on difficulty 1024

If you think e. is expensive, try ignorance 3012

is a social process 3001

is growth 3001

is life itself 3001

is lighting of a fire 3002

is to turn mirrors into windows 3019

knowledge of Bible worth more than e. 640

might have disinterred, brought to light 3038

more tests to get in than out 3034

most worthwhile form of e. 3031

no e. like adversity 218

no patience with piety alone 3025

not filling of pail 3002

not preparation for life 3001

people mistake e. for intelligence 8510

perception of ideas aim of e. 3021

prayer is an e. 8769

process not of stuffing people 3026

process of eliciting potentialities hidden 3026

process to begin to learn how to learn 3017

produced population able to read 2997

produced population unable to distinguish 2997

progressive discovery of ignorance 3000

teaches how little man knows 3004

teaches how much man has to learn 3004

'Tis e. forms the common mind 2991

to soul like sculpture to block of marble 3038

useless without Bible 3003

will not take place of perseverance 8555

without religion make man more clever devil 3005

EDUCATOR

most worthwhile education puts e. inside 3031

EFFACE

engrave something no time can e. 6796

repent for years to e. fault 4091

EFFECT

familiar phrase have their superficial e. 8845

in world ruled by cause and e. 11590

Lust's e. is tempest after sun 7357

recreating e. of Bible 697

where man, the e. ceases 4525

EFFECTIVE

church most e. when she declares 3796

churches as effective as medical programs 134

Conduct is the only e. sermon 9132

cross is e. 2106

drug treatment programs run by churches 134

mercy e. when justice has done its work 4730

most e. remedy in Scriptures 650

politics teaches what means are e. 11211

relaxed Christian more e. 9529

social gospel needs theology to make e. 5104

takes time to be an e. parent 8287

EFFECTIVELY

Nobody can be you as e. as you can 9983

psychological secrets used e. to control youth 12178

EFFECTS

Extremes, though contrary, have like e. 3554

Jesus produced e. beyond reach of orator or poet 6449

Laughter a tranquilizer with no side e. 6730

EFFECTUAL

Some of our shortest prayers most e. ones 8962

EFFECTUALLY

Nothing blinds mind more e. than self-realization 10044

EFFICACY

gospel possesses mysterious e. 732

Holy Spirit imparts e. to Word preached 5794

EFFICIENCY

enhanced by what we relinquish 53

prayer for e. 9041

EFFICIENTLY

Nobody can be you as e. as you can 6203

Parents should work as e. as two bookends 8322

EFFORT

Everything requires e. 2773

Fanaticism redoubling e, forgotten aim 3908

Gaze on honest e. kindly 4217

God is quick to mark e. to please 4810

God's better plan takes e. to grab 2607

in e. to be right may go wrong 9502

It is for us to make the e. 4945

Keep e. alive 8546

kingdom of God does not exist because of your e. 4734

Love a ceaseless e. to know, feel 7211

not e. of duty 1525

out of despair by creative e. of God 2613

put away all e. to impress 7709

takes little e. to watch man carry load 6160

to be watchful become suspicious 9502

to get the work of the Lord done 115

to prove no God 478

to reach for God 478

to think as a Christian greatest e. 11270

To think is an e. 11270

to think rightly a great e. 11270

unashamed e. to protract physical desire 10229

years of e. to tame young human beings 7382

EFFORTLESSLY
God knows e. 4881

EFFORTS
Direct e. to preparing youth for path 8291

friend helps us put forth best e. 4178

God sends a time of frustrated e. 7056

make incredible e. but win no victories 6813

plod along hoping e. will pay off 6810

reaching beyond boundaries of human e. 10540

spend e. seeking to know, do will of God 5543

to attempt to do some things is to waste e. 10199

we are worth more than results of our e. 10545

EGG
as restless as hen wanting to lay e. 11886

Better e. in peace than ox in war 11742

get chicken by hatching e. 8420

steals an e. would steal a camel 2912

EGG'S
no chick by falling from hen 875

EGGS
cannot unscramble e. 1744

sets my house on fire to roast his e. 10057

EGO
accept Christ at no loss to e. 3333

agrees with views, gratifying to e. 11216

beyond conscious e. 2971

Christ a window in dark dungeon of e. 6434

Don't get stuck inside your own e. 9196

in which we all languish 6434

individualism e. cult of one 9952

never understand the e. 9352

our own e. makes e. of others intolerable to us 9215

soul long before conscious e. 2971

will become a prison 9196

EGOS
Human beings bearable when e. are down 892

EGOTISM
devil loves man out of e. 2688

Discouragement disenchanted e. 2880

grace to abandon e. 1719

EGOTIST
sees only the frame of his own portrait 9213

self-importance makes mind shrink, head swell 9191

talks to you about himself 9445

EGYPT
Before lambs bled in E. 2123

can learn from text of ancient E. 2988

EGYPTIANS
angels send plagues upon 359

EIGHT
Fall seven times, stand up e. 3592

EIGHTEEN
Life happier if born at eighty, gradually approach e. 6989

EIGHTY
Life happier if born at age e. 6989

Men of e. often more youthful than the young 12198

old, whether at e. 2995

EINSTEIN
did not create mathematical order 1958

uncovered truth already there 1958

uneducable, you have an Albert E. 161

EITHER
children of God or the devil 8075

Jesus, e. the Son of God or a madman 6350

love or hate 8075

ELATED
Art thou e? Ah, be not too gay 6878

Never e. while one man's oppress'd 3074

ELDERLY
person is ten years older than you are 8124

ELDERS
Children never good at listening to e. 1112

ELECT
are whosoever will 3046

Christian worker must not e. to go 10188

ELECTED
Son cannot die for whom Father never e. 3043

ELECTION
as to e. God is salvation 4514

ascribed to God the Father 3043

depends not on unworthiness 3047

depends upon will of God 3047

the university of e, predestination 11192

ELECTRIC
more like an e. fan 118

ELECTRICITY
like wave of e. going through me 5797

Lord added e. to toddler 1127

ELECTRONIC
soon living in e. village 4332

ELECTRONS
How play with e. and fail to be touched by awe 9866

ELECTS
God e. us not because handsome 3048

ELEGANCE
wealth is not e. 11662

ELEMENT
if no e. of asceticism in our lives 466

Silence e. in which great things fashion themselves 10265

wants e. it should live in 3826

ELEMENTS
history enriched by antithetical e. 5020

Of e. and an angelic sprite 7384

ELEPHANT
Bible, stream where e. may swim 707

not greater miracle than mite 7940

ELEVATE
Every Christian can e. himself by meditation 7707

time with the Master will e. thinking 8865

ELEVATES
Faith e. the soul 3666

ELEVATING
wisdom, power so e. 4995

ELEVATION
hope of nation in e. of character 5190

ELICIT
Grief can e. fortitude, patience 10640

ELICITING
Education process of e. potentialities 3026

ELIJAH
bear burden no longer, do as E. did 2591

ELIJAH'S
heaven not so far E. prayer not heard 5651

ELIMINATE
the negative 8231

would almost rather e. happiness 10898

ELIMINATED
Supposing you e. suffering 10898

ELITE
had the angel gone to the e. 6147
If religious e. too proud 12098
would have looked to see if anyone watching 6147

ELOQUENCE
Continuous e. is tedious 9133
holy clumsiness better than sinful e. 9121
is only air, noise to God 9002
is vehement simplicity 9135
Jesus without e. of school spoke words beyond reach of orator 6449
Kindness converted more sinners than e. 6648
loftiest e. retreats confused, abashed 4750
Love gives e. to the mute 7260
must consist in the man 9168
No e. adequate to tell to beauty 10274
not in speech 9168
not saying all that could be said 9167
power to translate truth into intelligible language 9134
safest e. is silence 4681
saying all that should be said 9167
Truth mightier than e. 11568
Well-timed silence more e. than speech 1889

ELOQUENT
are quiet trees 8014
silence better than e. speech 10244
Silence more e. than words 1870
the green listening sod 8014

ELOQUENTLY
Tears speak more e. than ten thousand tongues 11018

ELUDES
familiar e. us in life 6933

ELVES
reach to whisper in ear 1122

EMANATION
astrology, symbolize e. of God 4593

EMBALM'D
love is loveliest when e. in tears 7309

EMBARRASSES
world e. me 12038

EMBARRASSING
I find praise very e. 10784

EMBITTERS
bad conscience e. sweetest comforts 1650

EMBLAZON
character of Christ 5306

EMBLEM
of eternal rest 10953

EMBODIES
Christ e. all life, history 6369

EMBRACE
Admitted once to his e. 4737
whatever God may allow, soul should e. 4978

EMBRACED
foul things it has e. 8182

EMBRACES
by no means e. virtue 11723
God e. all history 10562
Trinity mystery faith e. 11428

EMBRACING
God is without, e. 4848

EMBROIDERY
Better go to heaven in rags than hell in e. 9262

EMBRYO
cannot treat as cheap and worthless 24

EMERGE
I shall e. one day 2945
if desire depth to e. 7714
Out of complexities simplicities e. 11937
shall e. from our necessary imprisonment 6110

EMERGED
Out of suffering e. strongest souls 10882

EMERGENCIES
Great e. show us how great our resources are 8659

EMERGENCY
Dogma e. measures to which church driven 11186

EMERGES
In baptism, new self e. 529

EMERGING
in grief, one keeps e. from a phase 5344
will never walk alone 10567

EMIGRATION
death was to him only e. 2415

EMOTION
chief source of all becoming-conscious 3053
dealing with creatures of e. 9518
forgiveness is not an e. 11173
Forgiveness not an e. 4109
God is a God of e. 4454
Hate a simple e. 7233
human e. to be consecrated to God 6728
Joy not a capricious e. 6568
Laughter and weeping, intensest forms of human e. 6728
little wave of e. enough for many 4471
Love difficult to sustain because complex e. 7233

may vary in religious experience 3052
no transforming without e. 3053
Nobility grows out of contained e. 3057
one of the words that most deserve reverence 3054
Thankfulness is not an e. 11173

EMOTIONAL
Erotic and philia love are e. 7166
Gluttony an e. escape 133
peace and calm come after doing God's will 8432
stability an attitude 2563
Tact is e. intelligence 10987

EMOTIONALISM
dangers in false e. 3052

EMOTIONALLY
loaded words have temporary effect 8845
Meek means e. stable 7729
minds e. speculate on unknowable 4704

EMOTIONS
accept Christ by impulse of e. 3333
alive in subconscious minds to hurt, trouble 3061
allow e. to arise to be identified 3060
Bible, cleanses my e. 722
by repressing e. we become holier-than-thou 3050
by starving e. become rigid 3050
cannot be cut out of life 3052
deepest e. caused by trivial 3056
discouraged e. poison life 3050
do not bury e. dead 3061
Do not pretend to e. you do not feel 8770
encouraged, e. perfume life 3050
experience of e. part of human condition 3058
Faith purifies e. 3666
few e. so satisfying 11253
God has deep e. 4491
God will direct e. 1241
Gratitude one of least articulate e. 5245
inheritance of every man 3058
knows not best e. of the heart 5349
many people solve problems by e. 11227
most important thoughts contradict e. 11236
people are windows reflecting e. 3019
place in God's hands e. 1241
remain alive in subconscious 3061
should be servants 3055
should not be masters 3055
should not be tyrants 3055
tell us things we never knew about ourselves 3062
when allowed illuminate inner selves 3062

Words incarnation of e. 12001

EMPATHY
become the wounded person 3071
help him at least with a sigh 3072
Humanness is realization of e.
    toward others 5014
Lord had deep e. with people
    6519
needs of others felt as their own
    3081
never ask wounded person how
    he feels 3071
Said wise man to one in sorrow
    3076
share pain with gentle hand 3080
to hurt where people hurt 3070
your pain in my heart 3068

EMPHASIS
church more e. on growth than
    repentance 1409
Jesus offends because e. on unseen
    life 6450
lose e. that what we do makes a
    difference 7481
Most churches, little e. on bearing
    burdens 933
society inordinate e. on feeling
    good 4017

EMPHASIZE
If fail to e. we can glorify God
    7481
the essentials 10279

EMPHASIZED
Money e. in Scripture 7811

EMPHATIC
Sin is e. independence of God
    10372

EMPIRE
Jesus Christ founded his e. upon
    love 6351
of Caesar is gone 730

EMPIRES
Alexander, Caesar, Charlemagne
    founded e. 6351
Skepticism has not founded e.
    5723

EMPLOYER
mistake is failure with human
    material 3120

EMPLOYMENT
as sacred as Sunday activities
    3104
difficult to resume 3109
habit easy to abandon 3109
Holiness has good of others as its
    e. 5739
is pure 3104

EMPLOYMENTS
earthly e. avocations 3095
regard e. equally distinguished,
    happy 3232

EMPLOYS
God e. several translators 2216

EMPOWER
God able to e. us to do whatever
    he calls us to do 9199

EMPOWERED
with invincible faith 3736

EMPOWERS
faith e. 3965

EMPRESS
Theology should be e. 11210

EMPTIED
As purse is e. heart is filled 4351
as water willing to flow into e.
    channel 4785
because he was once e. 2979

EMPTIES
If man e. purse in head 3010

EMPTINESS
All the e. and silence 2217
evil is e. 3370
God can take our e. fill it up with
    what he wants 6830
honors of this world are but e.
    5898
How could I know fullness
    without e. 1512
Loneliness is inner e. 10548
Materialism organized e. of spirit
    8633
neuroses of e. 4437
pretences built up to hide e. 3395

EMPTY
best cure for e. day 2558
coming out with e. hands 4426
deaden the pain of e. life 120
delights in multitude of words is
    e. within 10245
Don't be sorry bottle half e. 11141
experience silence as e. 10253
fame, an e. bubble 3862
God cannot work with e. minds
    4824
God sends no one away e. 9200
Heaven would be e. 4088
life turns e. 4437
Lord gives blessing to e. vessel 831
man like that turns out e. 8196
No one can worship God on e.
    stomach 7152
Outside noisy, inside e. 4064
plenty of sound in an e. barrel
    9250
pockets, have more love than ever
    7252
so full of himself is quite e. 9202
souls tend to extreme opinion
    8191
struggle between proud mind, e.
    purse 8679
To be e. is to be full 7071
unless able to e. himself 7962
vessel makes greatest sound 4066
When e. yourself, God Almighty
    rushes in 9956
with my e. cup 4653
world is so e. 4280

EMULATE
crow tried to e. partridge's gait
    1644
If testimony makes anyone wish to
    e. me 11125

EMULATION
No work noble or good of e. 2009

ENABLE
Education e. man to put things
    well 2998
love and confidence in God e. 159
me to manage affairs of life 9041
stone rolled away to e. disciples to
    go in 9699
to e. him to put other foot higher
    9316

ENABLED
Prayer e. to move ourselves God's
    way 8925

ENABLEMENT
on knees sign of helplessness apart
    from divine e. 8759

ENABLES
Experience e. you to recognize
    mistake 3517
God's sovereignty e. him to secure
    our welfare 4754
good life e. us to disregard evil
    tongues 5164
light e. us to see differences 1144
Prayer e. man to master situation
    8927

ENABLING
us to look on to mercy of eternity
    6384
us to look out from time, our
    prison 6384

ENACTED
care not what is e. in Congress
    12151

ENAMORMENT
Evil people e. with will 3367

ENCHANTING
please so much by your sorrow as
    by e. smile 10587
Trust not too much to e. face
    3575

ENCIRCLE
so do we e. God 7451

ENCIRCLING
and taste e. love 7970
Lead, kindly Light, amid the e.
    gloom 5429

ENCLOSED
God is within, but not e. 4848

ENCOMPASSES
Vision e. vast vistas 11736

ENCOUNTER
in life e. hurts, trials 970

ENCOUNTERED
Bible, e. an actual Person 4491
Great spirits always e. opposition
    5282

mind that startled us 7752

ENCOURAGE
may be able to e. all who journey
  with us 9059
Remember friends who e. 9270
those who e. more than criticize
  3142
will not e. us to mistake inns for
  home 7014

ENCOURAGED
emotions perfume life 3050
Some sins we have e. 10384
wish to be e, look upon Jesus
  Christ 6408

ENCOURAGEMENT
after censure as sun after shower
  3130
Bible gives no e. perfection
  achieved 9254
Correction does much, e. more
  3130
Discouraged people need e. 3066
is oxygen to soul 3133
live with e, learn confidence 1114
people fail for lack of e. 3138
too busy to drop note of e. 129

ENCOURAGES
faith e. 3965
who does not forbid sin, e. it
  10310

END
All revolutions from beginning to
  e. of world 4898
all suffering comes to an e. 10885
And to the e. persisting, safe arrive
  1664
becoming in the e. a treacherous
  man 7836
begin with certainties, e. in doubts
  950
begin with doubts, e. in certainties
  950
Believe to the e. 583
Charity begins at home, should
  not e. there 5822
crooked paths look straighter at e.
  2374
Death e. of labor 2256
Death is not the e. 2253
do not know when world drama
  will e. 9911
Doubt, beginning not e. of wisdom
  2934
Every e. new beginning 963
Evil bitter in the e. 3360
Fear not that life shall come to e.
  2283
free man does not fear to go to e.
  of thought 4145
friendship will not continue begun
  for an e. 4222
God at beginning, e. of time
  simultaneously 11314
God can direct evil to good e.
  3371
God guiding all to wise, holy e.
  5389

God incarnate is e. of fear 3972
God is final e. 4514
God pays at the e. 1730
God, love can have no e. 4750
good e. cannot sanctify evil means
  5010
grace of God can have no e. 4656
half the differences in theology
  would e. 11193
Happiness can never be an e. in
  itself 5517
Holiness has honor of God as its e.
  5739
Holiness not the e. of progress
  5746
Holiness, not happiness, e. of man
  5517
hope an easier way to journey's e.
  5924
hope carries us on pleasantly to e.
  of life 5934
human race will play games till
  the e. 5982
I wonder how I am ever to walk
  to the e. 7090
I'll fight to the very e. 3342
If stop every time dog barks, road
  will never e. 8543
In his e. does not lament the past
  8184
In my e. is my beginning 2318
in the e. cross shall carry you
  2088
In the e. good will triumph 5073
is birthday of your eternity 2225
Is this the e. 2319
It is the e. that crowns us 543
leave the e. with God 5415
longest day will have an e. 10629
Lord, I'm at the e. of resources
  897
Love destroying all fear of an e.
  7229
Love's e. sweetens all its means
  6457
man knows death not an e. 2343
Martyrdom does not e. something
  7676
may really be new beginning 3632
mysteries which you can hardly
  get to e. of 9402
nearer I approach the e. 11132
neither knows measure nor e.
  4787
never get to the e. of Christ's
  words 6523
no e. to God's beginning 4602
not freedom to determine e. of
  choice 1149
not yet come to e. of themselves
  10977
of life is not to be happy 5554
of life to do will of God 5554
of man is holiness 5757
of marrying when e. of living
  7667
of pride is in hell 9218
of reliance on natural devotion
  5792

of trying to be a Christian 5792
old man nearing e. of earthly
  journey 8121
Only Christian revelation gives e,
  means of life 9703
only God knows e. of things 6705
optimist sees light at e. of tunnel
  8250
others tempted strongly at e.
  11083
Peace does not mean e. of striving
  8454
present only thing that has no e.
  11378
pretense, hollow show that must
  come to an e. 8679
Sacred page not the e. 741
seeing how naked the e. 5952
Sin bitter in the e. 10375
Sin will e. dark as night 10377
small beginnings have oft a
  mighty e. 7119
So do our minutes hasten to their
  e. 2329
something great, in the e. out of
  sorrow 2667
Spring cleaning should begin with
  head, e. with heart 5756
Strength to the e. 6468
success, no e. to escalation of
  desire 10817
That shall lack a timely e. 1510
The passion of our Lord did not e.
  on the cross 2164
this cruelty will e. 8445
Through thorny ways leads to
  joyful e. 1502
Till my life shall e. 12007
To hallow the e. of day 633
To have found God not an e, but
  a beginning 7544
When at the e. of your rope 4627
when troubles e, life e. too 152
When we reach the e. of our
  hoarded resources 7570
When you get to e. of rope 2615
will e. in vanity 9467
With God no approaching toward
  e. 11355
without Christ a hopeless e. 5938
world's an inn, death the journey's
  e. 2330
Yes, to the very e. 6885

ENDANGER
if troubles large enough to e.
  welfare 4789

ENDANGERS
storm within that e, not storm
  without 3997

ENDEAVOR
what we desire children to
  become, must e. to be before
  them 5861
will e. to live as he prays 8812

ENDED
Life, depart from before e. 6957
song is e, melody lingers 7924

up asking God to work through me 4994

ENDING
despair only possible e. 8237
My life is e, I know that well 7101
the art of e. 56

ENDINGS
Through God turn e. into beginnings 3629

ENDLESS
a e. road, a hopeless maze 8638
Christmas, e. quill-driving 1367
coming from e. day that is our Father God 3772
cross, God's last, e. word 2153
damage to the life 465
defeat of our calculations 5395
eternities before 4694
God's resources available, e. 4458
great voices uttering e. love 4708
grope way through e. traffic jams 5859
heaven, happiness e. in duration 5634
How e. is volume God has written of world 6901
If desires be e. cares will be too 5317
Kind words, echoes truly e. 11988
Life with Christ an e. hope 5938
like a great ring of pure, e. light 3276
quest for truth 4643
riches of limitless time, e. years 3274
Some are born to e. night 813
Thine e. wisdom, boundless power 4659
To soar to e. day 6923
when the road seems dreary, e. 9059

ENDLESSLY
fascinated by new channels of thought 9468
great men are e. merciful 6032
Love can wait and worship e. 7353

ENDOWED
by Creator with certain unalienable rights 3246
Glory e. on many who did not pursue 4407
God e. us with sense, reason, intellect 6324
Man e. with liberty he cannot deny 3495
man e. with liberty he may betray 3495
Only man is e. with shame 9570
with a soul and a will to be saved 9425
with power of retreating from reality 3370
worth of an individual e. by the Creator 10001

ENDS
active life begins, e. on earth 1764

among e. for which individual created 6169
Bible e. with holy city 723
cannot tell where God e. 4602
Earth's highest station e. in "Here he lies" 7088
every beginning e. something 1728
forgive e. quarrel 4085
God will use you to further his e. 10141
Heaven begins where sin e. 5642
life begins with a cry, e. with a groan 7089
merits no thanks who does kindness for own e. 10056
Nothing begins, nothing e. 810
Prayer e. by listening to God 8902
process never e. until we die 1148
theology begins and e. with Christ as Savior 11182
Theology teaches what e. are desirable 11210
tragedy of life not that it e. so soon 7042
tyrant dies, his rule e. 7679
Violence defeats its own e. 11677
When boasting e. dignity begins 2766
Worship e. in holy obedience 12105

ENDURANCE
Cheerfulness, wondrous power of e. 1099
enthusiasm robs e. of difficulty 3188
greatness in patient e. 5283
in e. of human soul divine grandeur 3150
Meek e. without resistance 7728
not just ability to bear hard thing 3149
Patient e. perfection of charity 3152
turn e. into glory 3149
When we have exhausted our store of e. 7570

ENDURE
Christians to e. change 961
courage to e. riddle of inequality 6277
few are willing to e. anything for Jesus 2828
fray of duty that brave e. 3174
Hope will e. many a blow 5912
If knew everything, could not e. existence 6081
is greater than to dare 3153
Jazz will e. as long as people hear through feet 7898
learning how to e. the insupportable 7692
Lord cannot e. that any who love him be worried 3986
Man can e. suffering if purpose 10871
My deafness I e. 8146
Of all ills that men e. 5932
One can e. sorrow alone 10607

Over all shall love e. 4936
ready to suffer wounds, e. pain 9088
Virtue naked and bare can't e. before God 11713
way you e. more important 514
What do damned e. but despair 5706
when you must 3148
wise words e. 11908
wisest saints e. rather than escape pain 10847

ENDURED
pioneers e. hardships 3147
What can't be cured must be e. 3154
With merry company dreary way e. 4304
world says, What can't be cured must be e. 1335

ENDURES
ask for courage that e. 1921
Only one thing e, character 1010

ENDURING
Christ e. everything 6419
how e. word God has spoken 730
into the soil of life's e. values 9111
long-suffering is love e. 7202
Love when nourished becomes sturdy, e. 7230
miserable to be incapable of e. blindness 10861
Nothing great done without e. 3151
only e. substance is within 10654
realities are love, service 10829

ENEMIES
accept Christ's e. as our e. 3335
acknowledge e. without pretense 5890
Better hundred e. outside house than one inside 5820
Beware when e. applaud 3158
carry our worst e. within us 3157
Christ had e. 9448
death out of crowd of e. 2325
Do not be afraid of e. 6158
Do not fear when e. criticize you 3158
evil has two e, good and itself 5022
find suffering enough to disarm hostility 3161
first to discover your mistakes 3169
Five great e. to peace 8435
has hard time finding e. 4216
If cause be good, attack of e. will not injure 1823
If want e, excel others 9472
if you live in sin, are among God's e. 10427
impossible for us to love our e. 9801
in midst of e. that mean damage 11078
Love your e, they tell faults 3164

Lust and reason are e. 7354
make e. by what we say 1888
of Christ are triumphant, they say 1443
Pay attention to your e. 3169
pray for blessings on my e. 4069
pray for though they continue e. 4069
protection from e. in the cross 2096
read secret history of e. 3161
real e. make us feel so good 3168
respect taking stand 1913
respond to e. with love, not hate, bitterness 5890
Revival and comfortable truths are bitter e. 9744
should love our e. 5001
sinners, who are God's e, can go to heaven 5632
Surrounding you are e. that never rest 9861
tend to look at fellow human beings as e. 10531
think seldom of your e. 8472
to be kept at a distance 10531
two e. potential friends 3171
we carry our worst e. with us 9921
We make our friends, e. 8066
who doubts enlists in ranks of his e. 11597
who walk with God would not grieve e. 3166
will believe evil regardless 11502
wise man more use from e. than fool from friends 9444
worst e. can do is kill you 6158
would not fear a million e. 8832
You have no e, you say 3174

ENEMY

all that makes Christianity narrow 1233
Ambition grand e. of peace 342
An e. could send 10674
anxious to keep us from church 1190
Better is e. of good 3156
bitterest e. could be friend 3167
come and smite again thine e. 9045
conduct toward e. as if to be friend 3172
conquered only to God, not to us 3163
creative thinking abdicated to e. 3027
destroy e, make him your friend 3170
discover what e. fears most 4010
Do good to your e. to gain him 9449
Doing injury puts you below e. 4073
easy to be nice to e. from lack of character 1026
every man his greatest e. 3173
first step to victory to recognize e. 11670

forgiving e. sets you above him 4073
give forgiveness 511
God has set himself against power of e. 5016
God is e. of wicked 3996
Good has but one e, the evil 5022
greatest e. of truth is prejudice 11535
guilty conscience a hidden e. 5472
happiness an e. to pomp and noise 5568
I am a great e. to flies 2649
in prayer is lack of knowledge of what we are in Christ 8815
kiss of e. full of deceit 2473
look upon e. of our souls as conquered 3163
Man's chief e. own unruly nature 3165
may launch attack otherwise impossible 5021
may see God as e. 4489
my e. may become my friend 3162
my friend may become my e. 3162
never wise to underestimate e. 3163
no e. can make an accusation stick 4884
observing means e. uses to frighten 4010
Prosperity greatest e. man can have 9341
reactions to e. hurt more than e. 3175
revenging e. makes you even with him 4073
Selfishness e. of all affection 10082
supernatural love allows you to love e. 7340
Tact making point without making e. 10990
taking revenge, man even with e. 9715
there you are, an e. to God 10427
to get rid of e. turn him into friend 9484
to none 550
who feeds wolf strengthens his e. 11064
who has one e. shall meet him everywhere 9459
will fill mind with bad thoughts 7764
wine, an e. 337

ENEMY'S

easier to get into e. toils than out 11119

ENERGIES

democracy releases e. 2527
selfish, parasitical concerns drain e. 1306
They that wait upon men dissipate e. 10764
Time converts e. into experience 11323

ENERGIZED

so e. by the Spirit of God 8793

ENERGIZER

Holy Spirit, chief e. 63

ENERGY

act with as much e. 3816
And unremitting E, pervades 4711
consume last ounce of e. 7617
does not perish but is transformed 11658
expended trying to be like everyone else 1642
for work advanced by prayer 8976
Grace is e. as real as e. of electricity 5217
Grace is God's e. at work 5219
hope teaches to work with e. 3834
misplaced Christian e. 111
No e. will take place of thought 11234
of life does not fail for those who give 2018
only 25 percent of e. into work 2788
positive word releases positive e. 12001
prayer demands e. 6776
Prayer highest e. of which the mind is capable 8900
Prayer source of e. 8954
Regret an appalling waste of e. 9440
Sin is e. in the wrong channel 10364
takes e. to maintain appearance of greatness 433
Thought changes knowledge into e. 11265
Words release e. 12001

ENFOLD

God's love can e. whole created world 4760

ENFORCES

Lord never e. "thou shalts" 8106

ENFRANCHISING

shall find God e. life 3774

ENGAGE

Only e., then the mind grows 48

ENGAGED

in muchness and manyness 121

ENGAGEMENT

Better break e. than the marriage 7605

ENGAGES

doing e. almost everyone's attention 1753
faith e. profoundest problems 3784

ENGINEER

of universe made me part of design 4565
sit still and trust the e. 5461

ENGINEERS
God e. our circumstances 8395
God e. personal visit to his own
world 6127

ENGLAND
most dejected, reluctant convert in
all E. 9829

ENGRAVE
something no time can efface
6796

ENGRAVED
quotations when e. upon memory
give good thoughts 9383

ENGRAVING
Learning in childhood like e. on
rock 8305

ENGULFED
in infinite immensity of spaces
4905
in the infinite immensity 7084

ENHANCED
Efficiency is e. 53

ENHANCES
Falsehood, twilight that e. every
object 6866
Good e. life 5024

ENIGMAS
God knows all e. 4881
most people prefer to be thought e.
10985

ENJOY
Agape love is concern without
desire to e. process 7158
and e. bright day 1683
at same time e. peace of mind
4001
blessings of this day 11365
company we e. 10016
crown that seldom kings e. 1808
didn't stop to e. happiness 5585
Ecclesiastes—How to e. 11925
Epicurean seeks to e. 6563
Freedom means to e. all God
wants 4122
given life that he might e. all things
8806
God gave me life so I could e. all
things 6906
God is inviting us to e. him 4554
happy person must e. blessings
818
He who fears death cannot e. life
3975
how little some e. 3221
How many blessings I e. 1810
I asked God for all things so I
could e. life 6906
If person does not e. worship
5654
If you don't e. what you have now
5532
Man shall e. God alone 9481
many sorrows that never happen
11456

multiply capacity to e. blessings
5254
neither e. much nor suffer much
1922
never better e. ourselves than
when we e. God 7558
no cure for birth, death save e. the
interval 7054
Not what we have, but what we e.
8636
pleasures which other Christians e.
5776
prayed for all things that he might
e. life 8806
snatch, seize, e. every moment
11372
special freedom friends e. 4285
take time to e. beauty 6828
the fugitive hour 11373
too Christian to e. sinning 10417
too fond of sinning to e.
Christianity 10417
too young now, I will e. life 4886
until time comes to e. crown 5912
when you can 3148
your own life 1787

ENJOYED
Christians say, What can't be
cured can be e. 1335
home, where simple pleasures e.
5853
none who has e. God's goodness
on earth 6092
To be e. must be interrupted 443

ENJOYING
hinders himself from e. what he
has 5316
Love is trusting God even when
not e. his sweetness 7246

ENJOYMENT
every day a new e. of life 8737
happiness is e. of one's self 5568
Heaven perfectly ordered e. of
God 5646
heaven, full e. of God 5644
Hell is e. of your own way forever
5695
never let what we can't have spoil
e. of things we do have 8635
of existence is entwined 3479
Recreation not highest kind of e.
6837

ENJOYMENTS
highest earthly e. a shadow 733
Poetry has multiplied my e. 8616

ENJOYS
contented man e. scenery along
detours 1773
Gossip what everybody e. 5133
not because saint e. being wormy
9784
reputation of being most
remarkable person he knows
9197
sin that e. nothing 11394
Unselfishness e. variety of types
9512

Wealth is his that e. it 11876

ENKINDLING
God is e. with zeal 4514

ENLARGE
God will e. your heart 5427
Nothing will so e. the intellect
4742
Riches e. rather than satisfy
appetites 11846
thou my soul 10658

ENLARGEMENT
rumors, all who heard it made e.
too 9757

ENLARGES
Prayer e. our horizon, person
8906
Prayer e. the heart 8910

ENLARGING
God e. minds to receive him 4514
powers of thinking 3027
shall find God e. life 3774

ENLIGHTEN
Christ a Sun to e. 6370

ENLIGHTENED
Lord revels in mind renewed, e.
by grace 7776

ENLIGHTENS
Bible e. my mind 722
every burned book e. the world
8528
God e. me afresh 5426
not answer that e. but the question
9365

ENLISTED
if you live in sin, under Satan's
standard and e. there 10427

ENNOBLING
wisdom, power so e. 4995

ENORMITY
creation, ever-increasing e. 1975
infinity walled in a womb until
the next e. 6142

ENORMOUS
little wrong to others 4097
the e. leisure of God 4570

ENOUGH
But 'tis e. that Christ knows all
5635
Christ is e. 9521
for faith or creed today 4118
God is e. 4516
He who wants little has e. 1799
It is e. 2591
little wave of emotion e. for many
4471
one step e. for me 5429
Would be judgment e. for me
1663

ENRICH
Christ a Treasure to e. 6370
God has all grace to e. you 4696
neurotics suffered to e. world
4390

ENRICHED
Beatitudes e. moral existence 530
history e. by antithetical 5020
soul e. by communion with God 10567

ENRICHES
Conversation e. the understanding 10533
Robs me of that which not e. him 10449

ENRICHING
Faith, e. life in here and now 6091

ENRICHMENT
God's call not for impoverishment but for e. 9351

ENSLAVE
Comfort stays to e. 7361
Impossible to e. Bible-reading people 677

ENSLAVED
All spirits e. which serve evil 3348

ENSLAVES
When a dream e. a man 2964

ENSNARE
alcohol, e. the innocent 331

ENTANGLE
extends web to e. thee 11115

ENTANGLED
Birds e. by their feet 11409
easily get e. and lose our soul 10514
men e. by their tongues 11409
more we stir in world, more we are e. 12051

ENTANGLEMENTS
resist temptation to chase after social e. 5615

ENTANGLING
what so intricate, so e. as death 2220

ENTER
All hope abandon, ye who e. here 5683
cannot e. kingdom of heaven head first 9426
enlarge my soul that thou mayst e. in 10658
Gossips set on fire all houses they e. 5137
inner chamber into which God only can e. 7127
into paradise with right key 5641
May the Lord Christ e. in 9794
mysteries and harmonies men never e. 3654
Nor will God force any door to e. in 4775
Our part is to e. kingdom 4734
plan as if expect to e. hereafter tomorrow 6099
prayer, e. through our heart into heart of God 10562
they that e. Heaven-gates 5649

through broken heart may Lord Christ e. 891
upon a strange, alarming life 6421
will never e. blessed place 5668
world alone, leave it alone 10574

ENTERED
love has truly e. my life 7184
success is e. through failure 3612
They feared as they e. the cloud 2562

ENTERING
His life is highest, holiest e. at lowliest door 6132
If cannot find God ever e. afresh 4856
jewel mine 4426

ENTERPRISE
at beginning of every e. call upon God 8757
of Lord on earth 1381

ENTERPRISES
God the silent partner in great e. 4460

ENTERS
Christ e. world to heal its wounds 6487
Evil e. like a needle 3355
Man e. each stage of life as novice 7002
When anger e. the mind 405

ENTERTAIN
mission of church to e. itself 1456
Quotations e. 9385

ENTERTAINED
Television e. by people wouldn't have in home 11035

ENTERTAINING
are sought after 4410
death divinely e. 2272
sorry if only e. them 7896

ENTERTAINMENT
Go slowly to e. of thy friends 4242
No e. so cheap as reading 855

ENTERTAINS
Who practices hospitality e. God 5961

ENTHRALL
Orchids can e. 1102

ENTHUSIASM
element of success 3188
Every great movement triumph of e. 3178
fear of holy e. 3184
light that leads 3188
makes ordinary people extraordinary 3177
makes pleasure of duty 3188
negative word can defuse e. 12001
Nothing great ever achieved without e. 3178
praise with e. only those who admire us 8726
robs endurance of difficulty 3188

strength that lifts on, up 3188
succeed if unlimited e. 3176
worst bankrupt lost e. 3183

ENTHUSIAST
Opposition inflames e. 1626
Opposition never converts e. 1626

ENTHUSIASTIC
can't be e. and unhappy at same time 3189
No person e. about work 3108

ENTIRE
ocean affected by pebble 6238

ENTIRETY
perfections of Jesus Christ made your e. 9847

ENTOMB
The walls of gold e. us 9224

ENTRANCE
death of Jesus only e. into his life 2161

ENTRENCHED
deceptive presupposition 1467

ENTRUSTED
God e. his reputation to ordinary people 1285

ENTRY
Death e. into rest 2256

ENTWINED
consciousness reached existence e. with pain 3479

ENVIABLE
most e. of titles 5881
nothing e. about a nervous breakdown 9533

ENVIES
another, admits inferiority 3219
Take off all your e. 10787

ENVIOUS
person great when not e. of rival's success 3206

ENVIRONMENT
forbidden e. comes to be as if it were not 1332
in which maturity can be achieved 4721
of home must teach what to read 8333
shot arrow in air, it stuck 3194

ENVIRONMENTAL
influences will not account for behavior 558

ENVY
better to e. wisdom than riches 11921
child of devil 2680
consumes the soul 3212
corrupts man 3207
degraded from honor, freed from e. 1776
Don't e. man who has everything 3208

eats nothing but its own heart 3209
endless self torment 3211
enemy to peace 8435
gnaws its own foot in effort to escape 3211
green sickness 3217
Happiness vanishes when e. appears 3218
hell, where everyone lives deadly passions of e. 5705
impotent 10296
is a kind of praise 3210
is impotent 3211
knows no gratification 3211
lasts longer than happiness we e. 3222
Let us not e. accumulated riches 11832
like a disease 3212
like fly that dwells on sores 3213
looks through a microscope 7259
Moral indignation permits e. under guise of virtue 11693
never ceasing in appetite 3211
numbed with fear 3211
saints their joy 3224
Satan's truth judges out of e. 4914
shoots at others 3214
sinners their pleasure 3224
slays itself by own arrows 3215
Stirred up with e. and revenge 9863
ugliness of trapped rat 10296 3211
wants infused into us by e. 2861
would not be much e. in world 3221
wounds herself 3214

ENVYING
love would sweep away e. 7349
without e. his labors 10788

ENVY'S
a coal come hissing hot from hell 3216

EPHREM
who could be harmed if he knew something about E. 5733

EPICS
salvation more important than e. 3332

EPICURE
Live while you live, the E. would say 8600

EPICUREAN
seeks to enjoy 6563

EPISCOPALIAN
not an E. in heaven 5671

EPITHETS
Of all e. to Christ, mild seems least appropriate 6462

EPITOME
day an e. of the year 9877

EQUABLE
Grief should be e. 5331

EQUAL
all men created e. 3246
All men e. in death 3226
as good as anybody if had e. chance 3228
black, white hold each other with e. clasp 3237
faith shines e, arming me from fear 3765
Few delights e. one we trust 4184
God renders e. small and great 4727
Lord's Prayer without e. or rival 7154
Marriage, independence e. 7642
men are by nature e. 3225
No gift to mother can e. her gift 7850
no happiness e. to heart that understands 9504
Only as children of God are we e. 3242
only in love unequal made e. 3238
Pray for powers e. to your task 8780
ship is e. to load of today 12092
where woman e. with the man 3868
woman formed out of man's side to be his e. 11982
yet each with own station, role 3239

EQUALITY
all other claims to e. intensify inequality 3242
only want e. with superiors 3247
passion for e. produces uniformity 3244
sole e. on earth is death 3245
such a difficult business 3247
until e. embodied in practice 3230
until e. recognized 3230

EQUALLY
Accept e. God's gifts 1461
all e. responsible for world 9678
all those in Christ accepted e. 3236
God does not show himself e. to all 8929
honesty, maturity e. hard to attain 5873
regard employments e. distinguished 3232
Rest and motion e. destructive 9685

EQUALS
for whom we do least 7348
God e. all 4709
Lash love upon e, difficult 7348
Life minus love e. zero 7206
No other book e. Bible 728

EQUATE
Christians e. popularity with excellence 5891

EQUILIBRIUM
between dream, reality 7435

EQUIPPED
Year by year better e. 4439

EQUITY
God is directing to e. 4514
hope of nation not in e. of executive 5190

EQUIVOCATION
lie may be told by e. 6859

ERASE
Good works never e. guilt 5061

ERASER
Our God has a big e. 4635
when e. wears out ahead of pencil 3263

ERECT
houses of worship but our shrines are places of business 6068
Injustice suave, e. and unconfined 6269
stands e. by bending over the fallen 10144

ERNESTNESS
obsessed with method not the Master 2626
often subtle form of self-idolatry 2626

EROTIC
and philia love are emotional 7166

ERR
Blind unbelief is sure to e. 5378
nature of man to e. 3260
To e. is human 7065 3263
Too wise to e. 4990

ERRAND
Sin was Christ's e. 6505

ERRANDS
Difficulties are God's e. 2714

ERRED
If ever I have e. 9091

ERROR
a hardy plant 3251
as important as truth 3253
Bible untainted by any e. 710
easier to perceive e. than truth 3259
evolution staggering from one e. to another 1987
few observations, much reasoning leads to e. 9410
follows false light 3258
is always talkative 3256
is discipline 3252
is easily seen 3259
is immense 6868
is more presumptuous 3258
lies on the surface 3259
Man calls sin e, God an enmity 4560
more dangerous, the more truth it contains 3250
only fool perseveres in e. 3260
proceeds in wrong direction 3258

ERRORS

to think can understand mysteries 11203

wounded, writhes in pain 11579

ERRORS

both e. are impious 3349

By obedience led to correct e. 8110

From e. of others, wise man corrects his own 3257

from e. wise learn wisdom for future 7794

learn more from man's e. than his virtues 3262

like straws, upon surface flows 3255

Pass by trifling e. blindly 4217

to be dangerous have truth mingled 3254

Whatever e. I have committed 11278

ERRS

hopes to do deed without God's knowledge e. 2501

Who e. and mends, to God himself commends 3264

ERUPTED

great party has e. 3326

ESCALATION

no end to e. of desire 10817

ESCAPE

cannot e. cross 2105

change impossible to e. 977

Christ apprehended that thou mightest e. 6393

Divorce an easy e, many think 2921

Gluttony an emotional e. 133

God disappoints our attempts to e. 5395

God's revelation of e. 11432

Life burdens no one can e. 931

loneliness an e. from an inescapable God 7144

Many long for Rapture to e. from distress of age 9910

no way to e. evil 3383

not that they might e. the world 8805

the judgment to e. 9828

trying to e. from intolerable bore—ourselves 9939

we try to e. life instead of controlling it 7072

Who can e. eye of God, all seeing 4888

who marry to e. unhappy home 7660

wisest saints endure rather than e. pain 10847

wrap yourself in God, e. the devil's sight 2658

ESCAPES

Knowledge of divine e. us through want of faith 3754

Who e. duty, avoids gain 9681

ESCAPING

no e. the cross 2113

ESCAPISM

not form of e. or wishful thinking 5629

ESCHEWED

Slander cud e. by human cattle 10470

ESCORT

And e. thee quick to heav'n 2221

ESSENCE

God's e. beyond all thought 4670

God's e. hidden to human reason 4670

God's e. incomprehensible 4670

godliness genuine e. of the Lord 5771

Holiness has love for its e. 5739

Independence e. of sin 6414

Love in its e. is spiritual fire 7224

of faith is casting oneself on the promise 3753

of generosity is self-sacrifice 4365

of hell separation from God 5697

of idolatry, thoughts about God unworthy of him 6075

of lying is in deception, not words 6859

of perfect friendship 4272

of true holiness is conformity to will of God 5758

ESSENE

Jesus not an E. 6508

ESSENTIAL

every person a dignified, e, human soul 901

extrovert isn't e. to evangelism 3299

faith an e. guide 3689

family e. cell of society 3890

for Holy Spirit to reveal truth 752

Freethinkers e. for right thinking 4124

Half an hour's listening e. 7710

Infinite as e. for man as planet 12117

Integrity e. to cope with difficulties 6310

Obedience to Jesus Christ e. 8106

one e. condition of human existence 12117

Stillness an e. part of growing deeper 7711

teachings of Jesus revolutionary 6474

that we slow down at times 7714

what is e. invisible to the eye 5622

ESSENTIALLY

true faith e. reasonable 3842

ESSENTIALS

Emphasize the e. 10279

Renewal and restoration are e. 9533

strip down to e. 7709

ESTABLISH

government not tool to e. Kingdom of God 5177

using the law to e. righteousness 6810

ESTABLISHED

family e. before the church 3871

legal residence in heaven 5673

Skepticism has not e. principles 5723

Wherever God rules, kingdom of God e. 4736

ESTABLISHES

family e. society's most basic values 3888

ESTATE

And ordered their e. 4501

ESTEEM

everything is to e. nothing 5900

more highly those who think alike 3032

Raised voices lower e. 9488

to e. that which is most precious unto thee 9063

ESTEEMED

Noble deeds concealed are most e. 2504

weak, not strong, to be e. 5001

ESTEEMS

knows himself best, e. himself least 1711

ESTIMATE

Humility to make right e. of one's self 6014

ESTRANGE

Gossip can e. closest friends 5127

ESTRANGED

stranger to oneself, e. from others too 9519

ETERNAL

All that is not e. is out of date 3265

alternative to e. life is e. punishment 3286

as essential for man as planet 12117

As they draw near to their e. home 7701

because God e. his love can have no end 4750

believer makes decisions of e. values 10707

Bright dawn of our e. day 6152

But an e. now shall ever last 3288

Calvary, the e. sword 2124

Christianity, life of e. quality 1188

continual looking forward to e. world 5629

dare not trifle with e. future 4726

death e. supreme evil 5033

Emblem of e. rest 10953

Faith bids e. truth be fact 3680

God in his mercy made e. bounds 4813

God is light e. 4514

God not an e. blessing machine 5757

God, responsibility for our e. happiness 5511

grace of God is e. 4656

hanging on of an uncompleted task 9297

Hark, Hark, wise e. Word 6129

Heaven's e. wisdom has decreed 9462

hold loosely all that is not e. 3280

hope of e. life in the cross 2096

Hope springs e. in the human breast 5913

How dread are thine e. years 4659

I may assert e. Providence 7566

I suppose I shall inherit e. bliss 2419

idea of e. rest frightens me 5661

in comparison with e. realities 4559

in dying we are born to e. life 9086

in God men of faith find e. permanence 4589

In God's faithfulness lies e. security 4620

Learn to hold loosely all not e. 11659

Life e. is supreme good 5033

Life is e. 6097

life to death to e. living 5945

life, twinkle of star in God's e. day 7015

march of e. harmony 2268

movements of the e. mind 4990

No man rich to whom grave brings e. bankruptcy 6101

old age, love you as dawning of e. day 8149

only an e. now that builds 8368

Only e. values give meaning to temporal ones 11311

pain is brief, joy e. 2383

perpetual must be written on e. shores 3860

personality something for e. life 6183

raised to sweetness of e. life 4749

realized man is a e. stranger on this planet 7436

responsibility for our e. happiness 3758

resurrection substituted fear of death for e. life 9702

silence of these infinite spaces terrifies me 7084

soul in heaven's e. sphere 10675

spring is in my heart 8187

The e. eye that sees the whole 6583

things little in comparison with e. realities 3281

things unseen are e. 3746

To high e. gain 4338

too late believe in e. punishment 5700

transfers love from things temporal to things e. 9278

truth being indestructible is e. 11550

truth mysteriously suggests itself 7949

truths do not depend upon human understanding 11584

what we have done for others is e. 10091

Where except in present can e. be met 11353

Who fathoms the e. thought 7572

Whose position antedates that of the E. 4955

world breath thought of one e. idea 4594

years lie in God's heart 3274

ETERNAL LIFE

begins with faith 3652

does not begin with death 3652

ETERNALLY

All that is not eternal is e. out of date 3265

blessed remain e. different 6169

Christ e. faithful 9521

creative and recreative love 10562

God's children e. loved 6042

immortality related to spirit which lives e. 3482

One short sleep past, we wake e. 2356

To help—he lives e. 2206

ETERNITIES

for endless e. before 4694

gleam of time between two e. 7013

Read the e. 1476

ETERNITY

a deep where we find no bottom 3283

a labyrinth 3283

a single day of e. 3273

all e. to celebrate our victories 3293

an e. behind, an e. before 7052

And vast e. 4676

as if you could kill time without injuring e. 11290

Because e. 6357

Besides belonging to e. 6359

Bible, window to look into e. 711

breathe fresh, exhilarating atmosphere of e. 4976

bringest receding waves of e. nearer 7916

but beginning 3295

But e. is in it 11303

calling us home unto itself 1757

cannot extricate ourselves 3283

cannot kill time without injury to e. 6784

Change nursery of e. 960

Change wakes no echo in mute eternity 973

choices of time binding in e. 1150

chord that will vibrate in e. 105

Christian sets e. against time 1259

conscience void of offense inheritance for e. 5079

consoles for shortness of life 3287

contemplative life will continue into e. 1764

created world parenthesis in e. 1968

cross, where e. merges with time 2148

cross, where time, e. intersect 2150

day you fear end is birthday of your e. 2225

Death beginning of procession down e. 2245

deeds seedcorn of e. 2496

divine drama that extends into e. 6106

everything is just beginning 3278

everything present in one fresh-springing now 11316

feeling of e. in youth 12175

futile as clock that will tick through e. 5718

God abides in tranquil e. 8437

God dwells in e. 11295

God fills e. with one now 4601

God is motionless, timeless, changeless e. 4601

God ordained truth from all e. 11584

God's e, man's mortality 2288

grave threshold of e. 2377

has no gray hairs 3266

Heaven not where men sleep out e. 5644

if we measure our lives against e. 7080

image with blind eyes, grand dim lips that murmur God-God-God 3269

in e. human ideals fall short 1163

in e. mountains as transient as clouds 3279

In every rose, e. 8009

in gates of e. black, white hold each other 3237

incapacitated to conceive e. 4603

is an ocean 3283

is at our hearts 1757

is silent 10576

is the ocean, time the wave 3267

is to leave e. for a moment 6495

Jesus, peace for time and e. 6420

Life used to condition for e. 6944

Life, training for destinies of e. 6979

longest word is e. 11993

looks grander, kinder if 3268

Love a symbol of e. 7229

May we adore thee for time and e. 11424

mercy of e. our liberty 6384

neither before or after 11316

neither time nor space 11316

no vision of e, never get hold of time 3272

not long enough to learn all God is 3270

not long enough to praise God 3270

Older than e, now he is new 6120

Passing through nature to e. 2402

prefer to be child of God for e. 5308

pressing upon time-worn lives 1757

Reality belongs to e. 9404

Repentance golden key that opens palace of e. 9593

saw e. the other night 3276

seed stirring to life 1757

shall always be with God 3270

shall ever lose the door 3283

shall in e. be dumb 8727

shut in a span 6153

Silence is deep as e. 10263

sin e. of hell 10360

so set e. within my heart 3277

soul created in a place between time, e. 10671

soul with highest powers touches e. 10671

soul's activities continue through e. 6094

souls which we have for e. 10680

stands fronting God 3269

stern colossal image 3269

swallowed up in the e. before and after 7084

takes all time, e. to know God 4483

teacher affects e. 2993

The lesson of thy own e. 1966

those we hope to be with in e. 4252

Thou art thine own e. 4605

thou pleasing, dreadful thought 3271

thoughts wander through e. 7381

Time is e. 11333

Time must be servant of e. 11311

time plunges into e. 11293

time writes no wrinkles on brow of e. 3266

time, e. to experience God's thought 11229

Tomorrow may be down drain of e. 11385

upon this short time e. depends 6894

voice of e. cannot drown 274

voyage through time to e. 3689

warming with intimations of destiny 1757

we shall never see the shore 3283

what we need to know takes all time and e. 3513

Whatever befalls was preordained from e. 2623

which will brighten to all e. 6796

will have just begun 3294

work designed for e. only done by Spirit 10181

world is vestibule of e. 6670

Worship is time flowing into e. 12132

You trust e. 1272

ETERNITY-JUDGMENTS

spirituality, desire to make e. 10719

ETHEREAL

Love for Lord not e, dreamlike thing 7221

Music most e. language of passion 7905

ETHIC

of Jesus, no intention to speak to crowds 6451

ETHICAL

Jesus, radical personalization of e. problems 6451

world of nuclear giants, e. infants 1705

ETHICS

nature lectures of e. 3192

ETHNIC

radical simplicity of gospel's e. 1242

EUCLID

did not create mathematical order 1958

uncovered truth already there 1958

EULOGY

that awful, merciless e. 1055

EUNUCHS

sterile, unfruitful e. 130

EUPHEMISM

Affluent society e. for selfishness 10051

Good Book most remarkable e. 731

EUROPE

avalanches Napoleon hurled on E. 730

no place like home except E. 2877

EUTYCHUS

fell asleep during Paul's sermon 767

EVADE

may ignore, but can nowhere e. God 4871

EVALUATE

If you can e. things as they really are, you are wise 8497

things not as people report them to be 8497

EVALUATES

God e. intentions 1067

EVALUATING

to stop e. neighbors 10162

EVANGEL

shout to e. they bring 1375

EVANGELICAL

danger of e. Christianity is anti-intellectualism 3027

false values brought into e. favor 11666

Who among e. scholars is quoted as source 3040

EVANGELICALS

not the only Christians 2987

We are not e. 1343

who abolished slave trade 5656

Who among e. can stand up to great scholars 3040

EVANGELISM

affects the other fellow 9739

applies supernatural remedy 3304

approach by right door 3345

becomes a life-style 3313

beyond that stadium scene 3326

both uptight about e. 3303

cannot be content with e. which 3337

cross in heart of God 3305

extrovert isn't essential to e. 3299

frontline e. 3325

layman has opportunities for e. 3330

Mass communication aid in e. 3317

not a project 3313

taking the gospel to people 3325

When social action mistaken for e. 3341

which does not lead to converts 3337

will find e. happening naturally 3313

EVANGELIST

writer a kind of e. 12155

EVANGELISTIC

inactivity is disobedience 3329

EVANGELIZATION

prayers for e. irony if lip service 3320

what can e. even at most inspired do 3036

EVANGELIZING

isolated church keeps e. same people 1456

EVAPORATE

kindness causes misunderstanding to e. 6668

EVASION

conversation more likely deliberate e. 1839

Jesus, no e. of the cross 8819

prayer is not e. 8819

EVE

Accuse not E. and Adam 763

cries out against the serpent 9601

serpent enticed E. away from faith 9424

serpent beguiled E. to depend on reason alone 9424

snake invited E. to take a seat 4419

swallowed the hook 4419

temptation to be like God eclipsed her view of God 4419

When E. upon the first of men
11113
with all fruits of Eden blest 11053
would say, "You ate the apple"
7659

EVEN
get e. with someone is becoming
e. with them 9730
revenging enemy makes you e.
with him 4073
taking revenge, man e. with enemy
9715

EVENING
A bit of the Book in e. 633
beam smiles clouds away 618
Clear as the morning or the e. rose
4746
each e. passes judgment 11364
go forth to work till e. 6947
God lights the e. star 4596
in e. prayer shuts us up under
God's protection 8846
in the e. pray 6928
morning and e. are spring and fall
9877
of well-spent life brings lamps
with it 8171
old age like the e. of a fine day
8184
says prayers in e. captain posting
his sentries 8980

EVENING STAR
Sunset and e. 2368

EVENT
All revolutions conspiring to that
great e. 4898
chief e. of life 7752
coming of Jesus most stupendous
e. in history 6146
God leads us from e. to e. 5392
Life an e. arrive after, depart
before 6957
remake history by cosmic, creative
e. 5711
single e. can awaken within a
stranger totally unknown 6873
unless bears reference to this great
historic e. 5726
which Creator, Governor of world
has in view 4898

EVEN-TEMPERED
People who are born e. 9777

EVENTIDE
fast falls the e. 2538

EVENTS
awaken our religion 8788
Christianity, history or current e.
1204
creep or fly exactly as God pleases
4820
drift of e. will make the decision
2491
Duty is ours, e. are God's 9654
God speaks unceasingly through
e. of life 5395

Great e. on little things depend
7119
greatest e. not noisiest 10268
importance of e. by how recently
happened 7990
Many great e. touched off by
small agencies 5720
most important e. never reach
history books 5725
of life chafe our tempter 8857
Quick is succession of human e.
12075
resigned to leave all e. to thee
9041
things that now disturb e. for
gratitude 5252
three e. in man's life 7050
Time to us succession of e. 11314
Unbelief where no hand regulates
e. 11595

EVER-APPROACHING
hear e. thunder which will destroy
us 8445

EVER-ENLARGING
Bible e. book 705

EVER-JOYFUL
God to the blessed an e. guest
4548

EVER-PRESENT
God an e. Spirit 5389

EVERLASTING
called to an e. preoccupation with
God 7551
Christ offers e. life 7022
Christ the Life e. 6397
dimmed with grief no e. hills I see
2587
Friendship usually treated as
tough, e. 4237
God consigns offense to e.
forgetfulness 4638
God the e. portion of his people
4847
God's love is e. 4786
hint of the e. in vastness of sea
3290
ideas of truth not e. 11207
joys are like the e. hills 7569
O e. Lord 4659
round about, underneath are e.
arms 422
Sick of this e. change 973
splendors 8483
the e. perhaps 319
the individual is e. 7389
Truth is e. 11207
When God pardons, e.
forgetfulness 4107

EVERY
another thing to go through e. day
glorifying God 7129
Christ offers e. man new life 7022
day a new page 6901
day cannot be feast of lanterns
3501
day should be passed as if our last
6887

day we are changing 962
day we are dying 962
deity inscribed on e. heart 4833
delay is hateful, but gives wisdom
11912
devil predestines e. man to be
damned 9175
divine light in e. human being
7561
end new beginning 963
experience God gives preparation
for future 3515
feeling exists in e. heart 4019
first duty of e. soul is to find its
Master 4144
gift given great if given with
affection 4352
Give e. man thy ear 1843
God gives to e. man virtue 5387
God predestines e. man to be
saved 9175
happiest miser saves e. friend
4203
heart has its own ache 10590
heart is joy 9897
Hold sacred e. experience 6900
human being is my neighbor 8056
in e. man a loneliness 7127
Lord's goodness surrounds us at e.
moment 4646
Lord's Prayer for suitableness to e.
condition 7154
Love e. day 7219
love has its own force 7167
love one gift open to e. member of
the church 7235
man a part of the main 4026
man a piece of the continent
10511
man carries kingdom within 6171
man has rainy corner 2543
man his greatest enemy 3173
man his own executioner 3173
man is a miniature world 6487
man is a volume 6172
man knows he will die 2279
man lives by faith 3653
man must do two things alone
2280
man serves useful purpose 11805
man should keep fair-sized
cemetery 4225
man takes care neighbor does not
cheat him 5004
man unique being 6173
man's life a plan of God 6888
man's life lies within present 8374
mile is two in winter 2544
moment dies a man 806
moment of this life a miracle 6889
moment one is born 806
night sit staring at another box
5859
person a dignified, essential
human soul 9451
person an aristocrat 5967
person born from intimate depths
of divine nature 5967
possession a trust 8626

same heart in e. human breast 916
sick person faced with meaning of things 6086
sky has its beauty 8005
solution of a problem is a new problem 9284
soul belongs to God 4529
step toward Christ kills a doubt 2940
tempest an assault in siege of love 4775
To friendship e. burden light 4288
uphill has its downhill 6890
With e. man God has a secret 7127

EVERYBODY
able to know what e. else thinks 4332
equal failing to trust e, nobody 11473
formula for failure try to please e. 3619
friend to e, nobody same thing 4215
Gossip what e. enjoys 5133
is ignorant, only on different subjects 6079
man is slave of e. 7375
Nobody listens, then e. disagrees 5171
ought to bathe in mirth 6738
praises e, praises nobody 8728
Sainthood makes it possible to admire e. 9778
speak all the good I know of e. 5072
To love e. sincerely 6913
wants to go to heaven 2282

EVERYBODY'S
Bible intended to be e. book 725
secret among three is e. secret 5115
When I see someone who is e. friend 4283

EVERYDAY
bring to e. living high wisdom of God 3752
desert of e. hurry and strain 10247
Faith wears e. clothes 3715
giving central place to God in e. lives 7713
glorifying God 1295
Music washes away dust of e. life 7912
on the anvil of e. living 3863
virtue of man measured by e. conduct 11698
When speak of hell, e. face will do 5680

EVERYONE
can become taxpayer 7983
cannot regard e. as stranger 922
capable of conversation with God 7541
Christian, subject to e. 1255
Conceit makes e. sick 1586
constructs own bed of nails 1729

dies, but not e. lives 6884
different and no one perfect 6180
else is They 454
Everything has its beauty, not e. sees it 8492
excels in something 2
faces two fateful possibilities 8129
future something e. reaches 4327
Greatness within reach of e. 5283
Hell where e. doing own thing 5691
if wish to make e. same 6189
impossible to satisfy e. 9476
is a moon, has a dark side 7376
knows how to say good-bye 9452
mirror shows e. his best friend 9998
must learn, no one can teach 7068
neighbor is e. that needs help 913
Paradise where e. doing God's thing 5691
Pity home where e. the head 5845
Right is right, even if e. against it 1037
shall have liberty 2529
Seek to be inferior to e. 8448
should have a goal 4422
simple, unassuming life best for e. 7365
so you want e. to be your friend 9448
thinks of changing world 964
time to be right is when e. else is wrong 6805
used to tell troubles to e. I knew 2727
wants God 4731
wants high achievement 4731
wants kingdom of God 4731
who has one enemy shall meet him everywhere 9459
wrong is wrong, even if e. for it 1037
you meet fighting hard battle 6635
you meet is your mirror 9441

EVERYONE'S
different 7377
doing engages almost e. attention 1753
failure in e. sight but God's 5993
in e. life certain turns 5454

EVERYTHING
a thought of Infinite God 1959
accept e, even problems, with joy 5261
afraid of men who believe e. 586
Aim at perfection in e. 3463
arranged by definite principles 4948
begin at bottom in e. except learning to swim 6021
belief that man can do e. untenable 3415
believe e. or doubt e. 2956
believe that God will do e. for man untenable 3415
believing God understands e. 7560

Bible has said e. there is to be said 746
Bible, e. is in this book 750
born of God no shadowy work 872
but soul of man is a passing shadow 10654
can have e. on the wire called Jesus Christ 6521
can't do e, can do something 1926
capacity for e. 4
Cast off e. that is not yourself 995
changes but change 965
Christ demanding e. 6419
Christ enduring e. 6419
Christ will provide e. you need 9521
Christ, God's e. for man's total need 6427
compatible with e. meaningless 1578
Contentment, realizing God has given me e. 1784
contributes to building of kingdom 4732
cost God e. to make it possible for us to pray 8773
created has need of God 4452
cynic knows price of e. 2189
Death cancels e. but truth 2239
deed is e. 4416
degenerates in hands of man 3193
devil does, God overreaches 2644
directed to one purpose 1465
Discipleship costs e. we have 2832
do away with e. behind man 4315
Don't envy man who has e. 3208
Earnestness not e. 2626
else is worthless 7195
esteem e, esteem nothing 5900
evil is revenge 3351
faith develops best when e. fuzzes over 3789
Faith does e. through God 3660
fear of e. new 3980
filthy who has filthy hands 3352
first step in wisdom is to question e. 11935
For God e. that will happen has already happened 11314
God be with you in e. you do 6260
God must do e. for us 2097
God strips of e. 4790
God, when we have him, we have e. 4806
gospel can correct e. needing correction 5094
government big enough to give you e. you want 5168
great comes from neurotics 4390
has been thought of before 2001
has its beauty, not everyone sees it 8492
has its wonders 1788
Holy Spirit invades e. 5796
Holy Spirit will put e. right 894
I cannot do e. 106

I have been e. and e. is nothing 2442
I have is yours 9066
If knew e, could not endure existence 6081
If we knew e. said about us 9466
if you do not fear God, you fear e. else 3994
If you don't get e. you want 822
in Christianity that matters is 6176
In eternity e. is just beginning 3278
In eternity e. present in one fresh-springing now 11316
in life undergoes change 966
in space obeys laws of physics 11650
in world e. depends on taking initiative 5446
in world surprising 12037
intellectual world stale if we knew e. 9286
is a luxury 3480
is a miracle 7940
is under God's supervision 2316
Jesus blew e. apart 4136
Jesus Christ, absolute mastery over e. 2170
Joy is to behold God in e. 6550
key to e. is patience 8420
last step is to come to terms with e. 11935
Lord, thy will be done in e. 9082
love e. in life, even to be sad 10595
love in e. we say, do 4767
Love makes e. lovely 7262
Love, in life, e. 7276
man is slave of e. 7375
man who believes e. as far from God 3710
man who has understanding has e. 11946
man with e, ulcer too 3208
may be necessary to lose e. 4340
may be said to be a mystery 7940
may extract honey from e. 5575
mission e, personal life nothing 9279
Mistrust the man who finds e. evil 3555
Mistrust the man who finds e. good 3555
Mistrust the man who is indifferent to e. 3555
moments when e. goes well 3998
Money buys e. except love, personality 7806
Money can buy e. but happiness 7810
mystery a fact about which we cannot know e. 7936
not necessary to understand e. 11611
not young enough to know e. 6684
One can survive e. except death 2351

One man does not see e. 262
only when e. hopeless, hope a strength 5903
optimist thought e. good except the pessimist 8248
perfect from hands of Creator 3193
pessimist thought e. bad except himself 8248
Poverty wants much; greed e. 5322
Pray as though e. depended on God 8892
prayer, gives me strength for e. 8794
prayerful for e. 8775
public forgive e. except genius 4397
religious din assure e. is well 12096
repeats 5344
requires effort 2773
saint receives e. as God's goodness 9790
saint wills e. God wills 9790
See e, overlook a great deal 9489
see God, e. becomes different 8583
sees God in e. 5202
sees God sees e. else 8487
Sixty years ago I knew e. 3024
Sometimes I think I understand e. 11615
sometimes will of God e. destroyed 5423
Take e. as from hand of God 2744
Take glory in God who gives you e. 9272
that happens can help 1466
things mean nothing, God means e. 1325
those who expect e. from God 3816
those who expect e. from themselves 3816
though we succeed in e. else 6944
to a solitary and an exile friends are e. 4261
To act in e. with highest motives 6913
To believe e. is too much 602
To Christ e. looks forward, backward 5710
To ear of God e. he created makes music 8743
To man who is afraid, e. rustles 4002
To understand e. is to hate nothing 11617
tongue can undo e. you do 1833
turn nothing into e. 1122
understand e. I need to understand 6493
Use e. as if it belongs to God 10740
ways that lead to e. 7869
we must release grip on e. 972
We study e. but ourselves 9353
What God requires 4574

When e. goes against you 8568 2614
When e. goes dead wrong 10493
When have e, see God in e. 11490
When life's alive in e. 9899
when young sure of e. 956
who fears not God needs to fear e. else 9732
who has hope has e. 5910
who knows e. has lot to learn 9205
who knows how to be poor, knows e. 8677
wicked afraid of e. 3996
Work as though e. depended on you 8892
you gain, lose something else 8574
you missed, gained something else 8574
your point of view is e. 8517
youth believes e. exists for his sake 12169
youth overdo e. 12181
youth think they know e. 12181

EVERYWHERE
all things e. are boiling, burning, groaning 9909
Can special love be e. 4834
Christ wrote no book yet words counsel e. 6394
cross is e. in wait for you 2105
dandelions are e. and don't need us 8577
Feelings are e, be gentle 4401
God an infinite circle whose center is e. 4842
God is e. around me 7968
God walks e. incognito 4871
good listener popular e. 7111
I find the signature of God 11629
Jesus Christ is e. 5716
Lord, thy will be done e. 9082
man leaves some kind of mark 6231
optimist sees green light e. 8245
see devil's work e. 2650
There are nettles e. 10634
they spread e. 2907
thou who art e. 4867
Though God be e. present 4868

EVIDENCE
abstains from giving wordy e. 1837
Character e. built on right foundation 1057
controversies about matters with no good e. 8529
different sort of e. required 3657
dying Jesus e. of God's anger toward sin 6473
enough e. to convict you 1292
faith needs neither e. or research 3810
faith not believing without e. 3657
faking e. in trials 7836
in daily life that Jesus is powerless 3646

In natural matters faith follows e. 3743

judgment of God e. of love of God 4721

more e. Jesus rose than Julius Caesar lived 9700

Neutrality e. of weakness 8072

noise e. of weakness, not strength 10576

of growth in grace 5202

road hazards e. on right route 2745

To think we have humility, e. we don't 6008

try e. for and against Bible 744

without leaving worthy e. of your passage 11292

EVIDENCES

e. of God's direction 4949

of God's grace to bear afflictions 4778

EVIDENT

difference between Christian love, values of world e. 6278

need to make e. forfeits virtue 11695

sinfulness e. when contrasted with holiness 10440

EVIL

accepts e. without protesting is co-operating 3374

all capable of e. thoughts 11272

all means permitted to fight e. 5012

All spirits enslaved which serve e. 3348

although with truth speakest e, that also is crime 11497

aren't many really e. people 10070

As the e. spirit fled from Saul 7935

authority for restraining e. 10506

aware of stature, freedom, and e. in man 7494

believe half the e. they say of others 7973

believe that e. dies 11129

bitter in the end 3360

can but serve the right 4936

can feel pressure of e. forces 3400

can never be undone 3354

can only be purged, redeemed 3354

cannot be e. as it wills 3377

cannot control e. tongues of others 5164

cannot do e. to others without doing to ourselves 3413

cannot love good if do not hate e. 5050

cannot say deliver us from e. if 8818

capable only rarely of e. deeds 11272

capacity for e. so pronounced in ourselves 3412

carry on struggle against e. 3414

cause e. to others by inaction 70

Christ never suggested turn blind eye to e. 9789

Christianity wins victories over e. 1165

church force for good in world of e. 1433

confession of e. works beginning of good works 5040

consists in destroying life 5044

content to observe there is e. 3383

corruption of what has substance 3357

could be abolished 4149

cross, love meeting e. with good 2146

cuts life to pieces 5024

danger of e. lurking within 3382

death eternal supreme e. 5033

Despair an e. counselor 2579

devil has power to suggest e. 2679

do e, deny e, and call it good 5029

doing life injury 5044

easier to denature plutonium than e. 3362

easier to meet e. in open than underground 3381

enemies will believe e. regardless 11502

enters like a needle 3355

Everything e. is revenge 3351

examine tendency to e. habits 3935

existence of e. proof of God's existence 3399

existence of e. reveals God in his truth 3398

exorcism of e. an uncertain affair 3365

experience of e. in some way necessary 10884

fear explosive power of e. in human heart 3376

flourishes more in shadows than day 3381

focusing on e. you can lose your bearings 5037

follow good or e. path 1137

for the good or e. side 2489

for which we punish others 3397

forces of e. have begun decisive offensive 3400

forces of e. in opposition to will of God 8762

Free will makes e. possible 4120

From seeming e. worketh good to me 11470

future will hold both good, e. 5052

gains equivalent of disaster 3356

gentleness not prepared to destroy e. not gentleness 11779

God able to bring good out of e. 5046

God calls for volunteers to oppose e. 3378

God can direct e. to good end 3371

God did not abolish e. 4931

God guards me from e. 4992

God has set good against e. 5016

God has temporarily permitted e. to exist 3378

God knew of good which could come of e. 5020

God knows all e. 4881

God never permit e. if could not bring good 3372

God transformed e. 4931

God would not permit e. if good did not come of it 5017

God's irreconcilable hostility to e. 4999

God, better to bring good out of e. 5018

Good and e. increase at compound interest 5021

good becomes indistinguishable from e. 5012

good end cannot sanctify e. means 5010

Good has but one enemy, the e. 5022

good is better than e. 6326

greater the e, greater opportunity for good 3401

greatest e. today is lack of love 6163

has no substance of its own 3357

has two enemies, good and itself 5022

he that is e. a slave, though a king 4131

hindering development of life 5044

How exhausting it is to be e. 3375

hundred e. actions should be forgotten 4074

If bring into one day's thoughts e. of many 12064

If e. did not make dwelling in man 3377

If we saw all e. things 4318

if world had refrained from e. 5031

in face of e. three kinds of souls 5029

In man e. is constricted 3377

in man e. is under custody as in prison 3377

Indifference more insidious than e. itself 3379

is a principle of fragmentariness 5023

is all that serves death 5024

is emptiness 3370

is here? That's work to do 3358

is non-being 3370

is privation 3370

is ready for anything 3359

is the Satan that laughs at logic 5023

is whatever dehumanizes 5014

know good through e. 5030

lies in the spirit 3407

Life is wrestling with principle of e. 6947

Life neither good nor e. 5034

life scene of good and e. 5034

Look for good in people, not e. 5077

make out of e. a more noble good 5031

Make the e. we have done work for good 9054

makes for separateness 5025

man does bad deeds 108

man meddles with things they become e. 5019

man mistakes e. for happiness, good 3386

man's discontent his worst e. 2860

Many puzzled about origin of e. 3383

may cause e. not only by actions 3346

means deprivation 3364

means failure 3364

means substraction 3364

Men's e. manners live in brass 9619

method of e. one to obscure himself behind object of worship 2699

minds change good to own nature 5015

Mistrust the man who finds everything e. 3555

must go somewhere 3365

mystery of e. isn't as great 5037

narrows life 5024

natural behavior 11204

never conquers 3366

never feel God will cast e. out of world 3415

Never tell e. of a man 5149

No e. done can harm ultimately 3385

No e. example can bring joy 5035

no e. that does not offer inducements 11101

no e. thing success 10796

No great principle ever triumphed but through e. 5030

no immanent logic in e. 5023

No man chooses e. because e. 3386

no way to escape it 3383

Nonresistence to e. is way of promoting it 3388

nor must we do e. that good may come 5010

not only going to think no e. 7190

not problem of physics, but ethics 3362

not responsible for e. thoughts 11110

not so much an obstacle to faith 3399

not solved by multiplication 3387

nothing e. in matter itself 3407

Of e. grain, no good seed 3389

often triumphs 3366

Oh, what a sign it is of e. life 2348

One does e. enough when one does nothing good 3393

Only thing necessary for triumph of e. 3402

Our good or e. name depends 4198

our phenomenal failure to deal with e. 2159

paid high price to find that e. is e. 3416

Pain no e. unless it conquer 8268

passively accepts e. involved in it 3374

penalty of e. harvest not God's punishment 4721

People capable of recruiting themselves to e. 3396

People do not need Satan to recruit to e. 3396

people enamorment with own will 3367

people extraordinarily willful, controlling 3367

person may cause e. by inaction 3346

Pleasure greatest e. or greatest good 8605

pleasures Christians enjoy, to you refined e. 5776

power of choosing good, e. within reach 5047

power of e. unlimited if on earth alone 3377

powers of e. overcome them 11080

prayer means whereby we become strong to meet e. 8977

psychology must insist on reality of e. 3382

psychology must reject that e. insignificant 3382

Quotations tell of e. 9385

rash hand in e. hour 10314

repay with good 1191

repent not so much for e. deeds of wicked people 6285

responsibility to prevent e. thoughts from settling 11110

return e. for good devilish 4102

return good for e. godlike 4102

root of mystery 3353

Satan first of beings to choose e. 3370

Satan is at work through e. 5014

Say not in e. doing, "No one sees" 3404

secure from temptations to e. 9777

see e. in others, not in themselves 5029

See not e. in others 2808

snake stood up for e. in the Garden 3403

soul producing holy witness 5011

spreads like an oak tree 3355

stifles life 5024

Suffering, change e. into good 10891

sweet in beginning 3360

task of overcoming e. never hopeless 3378

Teach us that no e. is intolerable 9092

that dark cloud that hangs over creation 3350

that men do lives after them 5043

that which God does not will 3361

the e. in our own thinking, feeling 3397

They that know no e. suspect none 3408

Thinking e. same as doing it 3409

thoughts like setting up idol in temple 7759

thoughts quelled by music's divine control 7935

thousand hacking at branches of e. 3405

To a good man nothing that happens is e. 5049

to dislike whatsoever is e. in thy eyes 9063

To good man nothing is e. 1479

To ignore e. is to become accomplice 3411

to mourn for sin because e. 9581

to overcome e. 9088

tolerated poisons whole system 3368

tugging to make us animals, not angels 3406

unchecked grows 3368

unconscious not just e, also source of good 7772

utmost e. is pride 9240

vast e. of the world 2140

War is an e. thing 11768

Were it not good that e. things exist 4831

When God sends e. 3418

When good people cease vigilance, e. men prevail 7991

Whence ability to wish e, refuse good 5051

Whenever relationships diminish humanness there is e. 5014

where e. is full of charm 3347

who helps to peretrate e. 3374

will be compensated for by God 3385

words how potent for good, e. 12004

wrestling with e. hand to hand, foot to foot 6947

wrought by want of thought, heart 3363

EVIL-HEARING

When listeners refrain from e. 10477

EVILS

death, funeral of e. 2266

delusions that e. cured by legislation 5184

fight vigorously e. of the world 6619

greatest of e. not to be tempted 11097

if a God, whence come e. 5027

invincible weapon against e. of earth 11841

of day bear patiently 11365
Of two e, choose neither 3390
Of two e, pass up first, turn down
   other 3391
old age, more and greater e. than
   the first 8163
One no averts seventy e. 3392
One of Christianity's most serious
   e. 1414
seeing that e. go unpunished 3349
To great e. we submit 3410

EVIL-SPEAKING
When will talkers refrain from e.
   10477

EVOKES
punishment e. resentment 9355

EVOLUTION
bastard theory of e. 1985
man in e. from lesser to greater
   condition 9351
pure jackass nonsense 1985
Some call it e, others God 1987
staggering from one error to the
   other 1987

EVOLUTIONISTS
know everything except link is
   missing 1990

EXACT
eyes more e. witnesses than ears
   3567
in each action 9041
Life not an e. science 6971

EXACTER
Christ is no e. 5208

EXACTING
love of God e. as love between
   sexes 4792

EXACTLY
Events creep or fly e. as God
   pleases 4820
God never made two people e.
   alike 6191
No two human beings make e.
   same journey 5978

EXAGGERATE
To e. weakens what we say 3425

EXAGGERATED
sensitiveness an expression of
   inferiority 6227

EXAGGERATION
offshoot of lying 3421
truth that has lost temper 11500

EXAGGERATOR
Jealousy the great e. 6341

EXAGGERATORS
Love, hatred natural e. 3423

EXALT
God has said he will e. you in due
   time 11297
If I e. sanctification 9838

EXALTATION
Christ, e. of humanity 6441

EXALTED
firmament cannot compare to
   your e. dignity as human being
   7370
God e. in dignity, honor 4607
Joy is love e. 7202
man most e. of all God's works
   7395
where woman e. equal with the
   man 3868
Youth have e. notions 12181

EXALTING
God at work e. the poor 6630

EXALTS
Bible e. body 840
Music e. each joy 7900
Whatever man e. more than God
   is idolatry 6076

EXAMINATION
Could God pass e. in theology
   11183

EXAMINATIONS
no e. in peace 8450

EXAMINE
how happy those are who possess
   3498
it prudently 9062
not him who speaks 1842
oneself before condemning others
   2072
see men of contrary character, e.
   ourselves 1065
tendency to evil habits 3935
the contents, not the bottle 6576
what is said 1841

EXAMINED
If you e. hundred people who lost
   faith 3742

EXAMINING
tongue philosophers find diseases
   of mind 11410
tongue physicians find diseases of
   body 11410

EXAMPLE
a lesson men can read 3430
annoyance of good e. 3433
body, amazing e. of teamwork
   846
Christ an e, showing us how to
   live 6410
give to child 511
good e, improving two 3436
Good e. best sermon 3427
good e. tallest preaching 546
Lord appeared to kindle us by his
   e. 6477
more harm by e. than good by
   correction 3914
most powerful rhetoric 3432
No evil e. can bring joy 5035
Nothing so infectious as e. 3448
often done by e. 3460
One e. worth thousand arguments
   3450
only thing in influencing others
   3431

serve as horrible e. 3446
so insignifcant e. can do no harm
   3445
unctuous piety poor e. of
   spirituality 10707

EXAMPLES
Christ's e. are commandments
   1517
good e. best commentaries 3449

EXCEED
be careful not to e. feed limit 7020
in interest knock at door 4259
man's reach should e. grasp 4420
results will e. anything he may
   have hoped 7564

EXCEEDS
God far e. all words we can
   express 10249
God's greatness e. bounds of
   thought 4692
possibility of future e.
   accomplishments of past 4329

EXCEL
If want enemies, e. others 9472
if want friends, let others e. you
   9472

EXCELLENCE
All e. involves discipline 3464
attain e. single pursuit 3470
Christians equate popularity with
   e. 5891
foundation of human e. 11720
more rarely is e. cherished 3472
not often gained on easier terms
   3470
over and above that determines
   greatness 2784
quest for e. maturity 3469
True e. rarely found 3472
value of good works not based on
   e. 10115

EXCELLENT
All things e. are as difficult as rare
   3465
Bible, such e. medicine 717
take e. care of our bodies 10680
to have a giant's strength 8707
Truth, friend more e. than human
   friend 11560

EXCELLENTLY
every moment do little works e.
   5068
observed, say I 8204

EXCELS
Everyone e. in something 2
the rose with all its thorns e. them
   both 7179

EXCEPT
begin at bottom in everything e.
   learning to swim 6021

EXCEPTION
How glorious, painful to be an e.
   6182
If silent, an e. to the universe 7997

EXCESS
desire of knowledge in e. caused man to fall 3556
desire of power in e. caused angels to fall 3556
doctrines in e. a caricature of truth 9122
Evil e. of substance 3357
God to damned burden in e. 4548
in charity is no e. 3556
not the drinking, but the e. 321
passions dangerous through e. 10234
What may look like e. of self-love 6229

EXCESSIVELY
youth doing things e. and vehemently 12181

EXCHANGE
doubt anyone who has tasted joy would e. for pleasure 6540
gladly e. greatest genius 4204
God will give goodness of Jesus in e. 5059
most brilliant wit 4204
profoundest thinker 4204
progress e. of one nuisance for another 9317
things of earth for better things 9974

EXCHANGED
polite prattle e. on Sunday morning 4029

EXCHANGES
cruel slave driver for kind, gentle Master 10976

EXCITED
not too e. about being glorified 2232

EXCITEMENT
Think, talk, act, e. 3185

EXCITING
Christian faith most e. drama 11201
creed of church, e. 1205
don't invest much, winning not e. 2629
life more e. than most of us think 6918
Music weapon used to make perverse seem e. 7910
pleasures not the sort that look e. 5274
show is so grand, beautiful, e. 6092

EXCLAMATION
when question marks straighten into e. points 5676

EXCLUDE
Riches e. only one inconvenience 11847

EXCLUDED
God is outside all things, but not e. 4612
God is without, but not e. 4848

many e. by gospel 5093
to include the e. 7838

EXCLUDES
God e. none 4809
Infinite day e. the night 5670

EXCLUDING
Worldliness is e. God from our lives 12053

EXCUSE
Destiny a fool's e. for failure 2619
Difficulty e. history never accepts 2718
Doth make fault worse by e. 3934
failings of friend 4183
for not becoming Christians 3477
inconsistencies of Christians the e. 1334
is lie guarded 3474
is worse than lie 3474
Love pleads no e. of impossibility 7220
often for e. we say things impossible 7869
passive patience e. to do nothing 6619
Some people e. faults 3950
weaknesses of others 1080
work e. for not entering into conversation 3904
world glad of e. not to listen to gospel 1334

EXCUSED
self-sins e. by most Christians 5776

EXCUSES
cloud motives with smoke screen of e. 3476
heart unwilling will find thousand e. 7871
himself accuses himself 3475
may often make e. for another 3478
never make e. for yourself 3478
to know people study e. 2807

EXCUSING
Accusing the times is e. ourselves 1462
Ofttimes e. of a fault 3934

EXECUTE
journeymen cannot e. work of prayer 8914

EXECUTED
dictators e. those who read Bible 726

EXECUTES
Plans and performs, resolves and e. 8224

EXECUTION
Jesus offered us an e. 1210
Love makes difference between e. and martyrdom 7263

EXECUTIONER
every man his own e. 3173
Revenge proves its own e. 9726

wicked is his own e. 3996

EXECUTIONERS
of Christ, bloody, dusty, sweaty, sordid business 2171

EXECUTIVE
hope of nation not in wisdom of e. 5190
income of e. 3121

EXEMPT
adventurous life not e. from fear 3990
God doesn't e. from heartaches of life 11667

EXEMPTION
Holiness not e. from conflict 5743
peace not e. from suffering 8453

EXERCISE
being entirely honest with oneself a good e. 5868
do not find time for e. will find time for illness 9535
for stoics, pain an e. 8255
To e. spiritual ministry means to take time 7327
Today need e. after work 3114

EXERCISING
Laughing works heart as much as e. 6725

EXERT
Hope in the Lord, but e. yourself 5914

EXHALING
Prayer is e. spirit of man 8920

EXHAUST
not possible to e. Scriptures 678

EXHAUSTED
because we try to do God's work our way 940
Christ's words still not e. 6523
Faith possibility when human possibilities 3698
halt of toil's e. caravan 10960
impossible to get e. in God's work 940
When we have e. our store of endurance 7570
will be e. in battle of life 10159

EXHAUSTING
day of worry more e. than day of work 12056
it is to be evil 3375
most e. in life is being insincere 6063
Nothing so e. as indecision 2488

EXHAUSTION
God wants not dregs of e. 941

EXHIBITED
Character e, not made, in crisis 1002
Christ e. divine paradox of lion, lamb 6425

EXHIBITION

Humility e. of spirit of Jesus Christ 6013

EXHILARATED

My mind is e. 7964

EXHILARATING

atmosphere of eternity 4976
dedication will be an e. experience 10125
snow is e. 8033

EXILE

Bear patiently your e. 7123
supported me through years of e. 7102
to an e. friends are everything 4261

EXIST

believe Satan to e. for two reasons 9854
betrayal and murder e. on earth 6158
Can the world e. 45
devil's ruse to persuade he does not e. 2692
Facts do not cease to e. because ignored 3579
God and man e. for each other 4531
God did not e. 481
God has temporarily permitted evil to e. 3377
God would not be less if we did not e. 3481
God would not have created man to e. only for a day 6104
great majority of men e, do not live 7028
impossible for world to e. without God 4597
In youth world began to e. when he was born 12169
is God's free determination 3481
kingdom of God does not e. because of your effort 4734
life not make sense if God did not e. 3336
nothing can e. without God 4854
people do not know another's burdens e. 933
Were it not good that evil things e. 4831

EXISTED

We e. before foundation of world 3490

EXISTENCE

as soon as e. mysterious, thought begins 11220
Beatitudes enriched moral e. 530
believe Christ's e. and history is explained 5728
Boredom, barren, meaningless e. 865
By faith we know his e. 3814
consciousness reached, e. entwined with pain 3479
denies e. of God 482

fear figures you will settle for dull e. 3971
friendship, conditions of e. 4237
genius no success in explaining e. 3486
God above e. itself 4609
God does not take responsibility for e. of rebellious 5175
God lets rebellious deny his e. 4129
God's mind in infinity, eternity of its e. 4675
I loathe e. 3485
I stick my finger into e. 3485
I will consider my earthly e. wasted 6919
If knew everything, could not endure e. 6081
if miss joy, miss reason for e. 6571
Loneliness central fact of human e. 7137
longing for God presupposes his e. 4606
man can only find meaning for e. outside himself 3484
meaning of earthly e. is development of the soul 9342
mystery of our e. 4549
nature of Christ's e. mysterious 5728
nearer to comprehending e. 3488
of evil proof of God's e. 3399
of evil reveals God in his truth 3398
of fiddle presupposes music 4606
of hunger presupposes e. of bread 4606
one essential condition of human e. 12117
Precisely an e. 3483
reject Christ's e. world inexplicable riddle 5728
scholars have recognized devil's e. 2650
secret of e, best foretaste of heaven 7198
skeptical about capacity to express e. 3488
smells of nothing 3485
strengthens belief in e. after death 6090
'Tis woman's whole e. 7278
ushering in new dimension of e. 5711
world by e. proclaims God 1953
Worship higher level of e. 12133

EXISTENTIALISM

defined as stature of man 3494
facts considered irrelevant 3493
meaningful experience as criterion for truth 3493

EXISTING

God above all e. things 4609
Without hypocrisy no e. power can hold its own 8722

EXISTS

Bible says devil e. 2650

cannot dream watch e. and has no watchmaker 12038
Every soul e. by God's pleasure 4529
God e. in himself, above himself 4610
God e. more truly than imagined 4611
kingdom of God e. because God reigns 4734
Later never e. 9293
no feeling that e. in that heart alone 4019
Reason does not prove God e. 3776
self e. to be abdicted 9927
Thou art safety from every trouble that e. 9052
Truth e. 6867
Truths are not created, they e. 11581
youth believes everything e. for his sake 12169

EXORCISM

of evil an uncertain affair 3365

EXPAND

listened to, makes us e. 1857
thank thee our souls may e. upward to thee 10247

EXPANION

heaven e. of quality of life 5645

EXPECT

a masterpiece 12020
Author will have something to say 9911
can e. to pay the piper 4051
can we e. another to keep our secret 5141
Corn can't e. justice from chickens 6605
Don't e. thousand-dollar answer to ten-cent prayer 8783
Don't e. your neighbor to be better than neighbor's neighbor 9450
foolish to e. others to keep secret 1618
God does not e. faith without reason 3840
God does not e. us to become saints overnight 9832
God does not e. us to imitate Jesus Christ 4539
great things from God 10118
How can you e. God to speak 8813
How can you e. to remain in state of virtue 11722
Humility is to e. nothing 6010
If e. perfection from people 9469
If e. to find peace in friendship 9470
led people to e. something not possible 7601
little 5561
Live as if you e. to live forever 6099

marvellous things to happen 3830

Men e. too much, do too little 3504

must not e. friend to be above humanity 4237

none have right to e. gratitude 5242

People e. clergy to 1497

people e. him to roll up his sleeves 6290

perfection, life disappointment 2799

plan as if e. to enter hereafter tomorrow 6099

plants thorns must never e. to gather roses 10454

secret of power, to e. great things from God 3790

Some e. thousand-dollar answer to one-minute prayer 8963

Spirit of God will e. unquestioning obedience 5776

tendency to say, God won't e. me to . . . but he will 10978

those who e. everything from God 3816

those who e. everything from themselves 3816

to find three wonders in heaven 5655

to pass though life but once 6642

to pass through death in conversation with God 9025

to pass through this world but once 10152

EXPECTANCY

consolation is e. of another life 6096

Hope means e. when otherwise hopeless 5929

life full of spontaneous e. 5463

Worship begins in holy e. 12105

EXPECTATION

faith accompanied by e. 3809

not remotest e. prayers will be answered 8845

nothing else but love 7329

of man remarkably low, timorous 3507

Patience the mother of e. 8413

'Tis e. makes blessing dear 3496

EXPECTATIONS

doubt when e. meets God's silence 2931

dwell on e. oblivious to situation 3510

pitch e. low 9469 2799

EXPECTED

anxious to know what is e. of them 6810

Father e. a good deal of God 380

Good is not good where better is e. 3466

I am someone who was e. 11124

Men come up to what is e. 3505

Swift fly the years, and rise th' e. morn 6143

true gift, nothing e. in return 4384

victory in service to be e. 10206

Vision outside realm of e. 11736

EXPECTING

stop e. squirrel saints to soar 6187

too much too fast 6116

EXPECTS

Blessed is he who e. nothing 5905

God e. life of Jesus to be manifested 4539

God e. only what he has supplied 4810

God e. us to be participants in life 10135

God e. us to do the baking 9657

Holy Spirit e. us to take answers provided 5445

If God gives command, he e. obedience 11173

man gets wiser, e. less 3497

optimist e. wind to change 8249

poor man e. no change for worse 8695

probably gets more than e. 3497

EXPEDIENCY

asks, Is it politic 1679

EXPEDIENT

Compromise temporary e. 1580

Paul's case not politically e. 786

EXPEDIENTS

are for the hour 1009

EXPELS

Music e. diseases 7900

EXPENSE

desire to see others advance at his e. 10719

Forgiveness saves e. of anger 4089

EXPENSES

Marriage quadruples our e. 7634

EXPENSIVE

Anger e. luxury 370

If education e, try ignorance 3012

Nothing so e. as glory 4406

Quality workmanship not e. 3116

thing of bad quality e. 10291

EXPERIENCE

a costly school 3519

a kind of huge spider web 3524

always the best teacher 3526

an e, cross of Christian 2108

an immense sensibility 3524

Bible dull, when I am dull 683

blow one-minute e. into 3420

by e. we learn wisdom 3530

By nature honest, by e. wise 11957

cannot acquire e. by experiments 3552

cannot afford to forget any e. 3549

cannot create e. 3552

Centuries of e. have tested Bible 646

comb nature gives to men when bald 3518

dark night of soul e. to be welcomed 2608

dedication of life to others an exhilarating e. 10125

Deep e. never peaceful 3514

difference between e. of Christians is contrast of praying 8976

Don't judge until you have been through his e. 6575

door to profound spiritual e. 8101

dulls edges of our dogmas 3516

Emotion may vary in religious e. 3052

enables you to recognize mistake 3517

endlessly fascinated by new e. 9468

Every e. God gives preparation for future 3515

extract of suffering 3529

failure not to cash in on e. 3580

feeling led without knowing it 5392

Few men worthy of e. 3534

gateway to the One whom we trust 3525

generation craze for subjective e. 4017

get out of e. only wisdom 3551

gives test first, lessons afterwards 3522

God gives something to rely upon others do not e. 6178

God has gone through whole of human e. 6386

God uses e. 10306

God will not allow lack of e. to 3340

God's way of answering prayer for more e. 8804

good school but high fees 3521

Happiness is the spiritual e. 5528

hard teacher 3522

Hold sacred every e. 6900

If all e. God same way 6169

In early stages of Christian e. 7690

In early years of Christian e. 3744

In first e. of sanctification 9840

inner harmony by pondering e. of others 7687

is a dim lamp 3520

is a jewel 3523

is never complete 3524

is never limited 3524

is what you do with what happens 3527

Jesus speaks to the living e. of all time 6448

jolt of pain with sin 577

know from e. kingdom of heaven within us 5426

knowledge from e. outweighs hearsay 3535

lamp only lights one who bears it 3520

learn by e. how wicked 4773

majority let e. corrupt 3534
Make death a good e. 2333
makes a person better or bitter 3528
meaningful e. as criterion for truth 3493
moment's insight sometimes worth life's e. 8486
more e. of God's goodness 3744
mother of truth 3530
must be tested, verified by Word of God 3550
mystical e. bedrock of faith 7948
name people give to mistakes 3531
need e. of giving 4359
Never for sake of peace deny e. 1912
never the ground of our trust 3525
not a question of our e. 8
not always kindest of teachers 3526
not what happens to you 3527
of emotions part of human condition 3058
of evil, sickness, death necessary 10884
of knowing above reason 5809
often purchased at infinite rate 3523
one thing you can't get for nothing 3532
One thorn of e. worth wilderness of warning 3540
optimist is guy who has never had much e. 8232
pain, a solitary e. 8260
pain, most absorbing human e. 8260
personal e. never norm for other people 8883
producing activities faster than e. 1449
proverb a short sentence based on long e. 9376
Quotations tell of e. with love, joy 9385
silence as empty, hollow 10253
some learn no other way 3519
some type of mystical e. 4015
something you give yourself 10996
Time converts energies into e. 11323
time, eternity to e. God's thought 11229
to live modestly a richer e. 9758
Truth divorced from e. in doubt 3548
turn theological truth into e. 12063
unutterable element in Christian e. 12120
War the most ghastly e. 11772
weakest saint can e. power 9563
what you get when you didn't get what you wanted 3533

who control what young people e. 8360
will e. hardship, stress 953
Wisdom is knowledge applied through e. 11972
Worry impossible for the Lord to e. 12127

EXPERIENCED
atheists haven't e. God 485
few waves of glory e. 3184
God's mercy can be e. 7750
good the human race has e. was trouble for somebody 11459
He who has not e. will not understand 3535
Nothing becomes real until e. 3539
saints e. joy and sorrow 2593

EXPERIENCES
cease to be horrible e. 181
God, not reason 4771
guard against grounding commitment on e. 3550
insights of saint stem from e. as sinner 9776
joy not tied to fluctuating e. 6568
need spiritual power independent of e. 4015
on quicksands of fluctuating e. 3550
One of the saddest e. 8661
snare of e. 3544

EXPERIENCING
difficult times, hold steady 969
easy times, brace yourself 969
healed of suffering only by e. it 10921
is better than hearing 3535

EXPERIMENT
home place where man can make e. 5842

EXPERIMENTAL
Youth wholly e. 12185

EXPERIMENTS
cannot acquire experience by e. 3552

EXPERTS
at deceiving others, ourselves 2477

EXPIRED
great Landlord notice lease has e. 2406

EXPLAIN
can ask to e. mystery of God 7939
defend my actions or to e. 39
For God to e. a trial 164
God is too deep to e. himself 4461
Gospels do not e. the resurrection 9696
impossible to e. how profound Bible is 734
impossible to e. how simple Bible is 734
Jesus did not e. away suffering 10867

Live to e. doctrine by life 3440
mind of man cannot e. reason 4492
when you can e. mystery of watermelon 7939

EXPLAINABLE
only e. in relation to Christ 6515

EXPLAINED
believe Christ's existence and history is e. 5728
unexplained things in life more than e. 11616

EXPLAINING
genius no success in e. existence 3486
is half confessing 1598
Photography major force in e. man to man 2016

EXPLAINS
resurrection e. the Gospels 9696
when church declares rather than e. 3796

EXPLANATION
do not believe, no e. possible 608
doesn't want e., wants argument 167
has e. man without Spirit of God never has 7753
rationalist demands e. of everything 9395
Reason, logic no e. before birth, after death 9419
To those who believe, no e. necessary 608
will have a complete e. 7060

EXPLANATIONS
false e. for true reasons 3476

EXPLODED
Jesus Christ e. in my heart 1905

EXPLOIT
immortals whom we e. 8483
shamefully e. converted celebrity 11666

EXPLOITATION
indifference toward neighbor assaulted by e. 6163

EXPLOITING
devil better served by e. our virtues 2648

EXPLORATION
of outer space bright future 11642

EXPLORE
may so e. what unites that world become one family 9093
will never run out of space to e. 11642

EXPLORES
Poetry language in which man e. amazement 8618

EXPLOSION
salvation, an e. on the inside 9827

EXPLOSIVE
fear e. power of evil in human
    heart 3376
hunger more e. than atomic
    weaponry 8692
I do not fear e. power of atom
    bomb 3376

EXPOSE
To pray is to e. the mind to God
    9006

EXPOSED
Man would sooner be
    misunderstood than e. 1055
Revival means e. for what we are
    9741
Virtues lose fragrance when e.
    11716

EXPOSURE
of bleeding love on the cross 9741

EXPOUND
to e. a passage, live in it 9148

EXPOUNDED
Jesus e. no doctrines 6448
story of Jesus e. more than any
    other in history 5729

EXPRESS
attributes of God helps to e.
    adoration 4580
Bible, vehicle to e. thoughts that
    overwhelm 698
brain, body, machines to e.
    personality 843
don't want us free to e. faith
    creatively 6824
God far exceeds all words we can
    e. 10249
gratitude to them and to Me 5271
imagery attempt to e. inexpressible
    5631
love we e. part of greater love
    10545
no other way to e. richness of
    God, meagreness of men 9784
no statement can e. God 4700
quote others, the better to e.
    myself 9382
Simple words e. great thoughts
    11989
skeptical about capacity to e.
    existence 3488
'Tis what I know, but can't e.
    7245
Words cannot e. joy friend imparts
    4269

EXPRESSED
God may only be addressed, not e.
    4667
God more truly imagined than e.
    4611
healed of grief only when we e. it
    5362
Lord's Prayer e. in a few words
    7156
magnitude of rebellion e. by
    Calvary 10371

many great things e. in single
    words 10277
philosophy not best e. in words
    1148
Thoughts too deep to be e. 3059

EXPRESSES
faith e. itself by ability to be still
    3769

EXPRESSING
nearest to e. inexpressible 7884

EXPRESSION
delights that cannot find e. in
    language 12120
Exaggerated sensitiveness an e. of
    inferiority 6227
failure pioneer in new forms of e.
    3602
Faith grows by e. 3771
Flowers have e. of countenance
    8004
In the cold God is molding thy e.
    10600
is the most important 434
perfection of human e. achieved
    740
prayer can be selfish e. 12139

EXPULSION
sin e. of Christianity 10360
sin, a matter of divine e. 10717

EXQUISITELY
Selfishness never so e. selfish as on
    its knees 10080

EXTEMPORANEOUS
adopted talent only e.
    half-expression 6226

EXTENDED
love of God, arms e. on cross
    4781

EXTENDS
divine drama that e. into eternity
    6106

EXTENSION
gospel invades everything that
    opposes e. 732
heart capable of unlimited e. 5625

EXTENSIVE
error and truth e. circulation 3254

EXTENT
fathom depth to e. heart is broken
    900
Life not a matter of e. 6970
of our own ingratitude 6250

EXTERIOR
Many have shining qualities
    beneath rough e. 8658
shining qualities beneath rough e.
    5078

EXTERIORS
Love lets us cast of false e. 7254

EXTERNAL
church union e. 1387
liberation of e. influences 4160

not being captivated by e. thing
    8611
obedience to moral law coupled
    with attitude 6811
pressed into leadership by e.
    situation 6785

EXTERNALLY
simplicity that seems to be a
    haphazard life e. 7509

EXTERNALS
God is not deceived by e. 9269

EXTINCT
race resembling e. homo sapiens
    3881

EXTINGUISH
may despise grace of God, but
    cannot e. it 4655
threatened to e. Bible 730

EXTINGUISHED
false lights are e. 5103
Truth often eclipsed, never e.
    11570
voice of intelligence e. by anger
    6331

EXTINGUISHES
jealousy e. love as ashes smother
    flame 6347

EXTINGUISHING
Death not e. the light 2252

EXTOL
Him first, last, midst, without end
    8733
self-control and practice
    self-indulgence 6068

EXTOLS
father in praising son e. himself
    3926

EXTRACT
may e. honey from everything
    5575

EXTRAORDINARILY
God wants us to do ordinary
    things e. well 7118
willful, controlling people 3367

EXTRAORDINARY
by no e. chance put together
    second time 6173
Democracy assumes e. possibilities
    in ordinary people 2522
Do not wait for e. circumstances
    5058
Enthusiasm makes ordinary
    people e. 3177
God does not need people to do e.
    things 10137
God does not want us to do e.
    things 7118
how things fall off like autumn
    leaves 5785
in death e. what takes place 10667
Leaders ordinary people with e.
    determination 6798
mystery of human goodness 5037

No machine can do work of one
e. man 8660
origin of goodness so e. 11204
Revival is always e. 9747
Revival whereby God works in e.
power 9746
virtue measured not by e. exertions
11698

EXTRAVAGANCES
universe deals in e. 1971

EXTRAVAGANT
nature, e. wealth of beauty 8046

EXTREME
attitude a flight from the self 9924
Cross, the most e. of all human
conditions 6277
empty souls tend to e. opinion
8191
fear can neither fight nor fly 3963
heat and cold kills 3554
independence as destructive as
total dependence 7614
love, hatred breeds satiety 3554
Thus each e. to equal danger tends
3558

EXTREMELY
Many people e. happy but
worthless 5539

EXTREMES
are in gutters 1582
Marriage offers e. of happiness,
bondage 7641
though contrary, have like effects
3554

EXTREMISM
no better example of e. than 3557
the haughtiness of humility 3557

EXTREMITY
Man's e. is God's opportunity
8218

EXTRICATE
cannot e. ourselves from eternity
3283

EXTROVERT
isn't essential to evangelism 3299

EXUBERANCE
is beauty 3179
Pentecost, e. of joy 5806

EXULTATION
Nor the shouts of e. 2217

EXULTS
Christian e. 6563

EYE
a lie may be told by glance of the
e. 6859
And guard me with a watchful e.
9350
believer can look tomorrow
square in the e. 9999
blind e. to trivial faults 9456
blind in e. better than blind in
heart 8511
bored by repetition 844

can insult like hissing, kicking
3561
can make heart dance for joy
3561
can threaten like loaded gun 3561
Choose wife by ear rather than e.
7610
Christ never suggested turn blind
e. to evil 9789
craves the novel 844
Dear as the apple of thine e. 1395
deep inner work veiled to e. of
man 10706
desire to have heaven, hell ever in
my e. 6910
eagle e. cannot see its height 4745
Eagle's e. for faults of others 3957
Everything for the e. these days
11028
first thing God's e. nam'd not good
7136
for e, tooth for tooth 7331
God's e. for discerning 5400
God's e. over every place 4834
Happiness the harvest of a quiet e.
9370
if hold penny close enough to e.
7795
Keep your e. on the ball 3503
live less than time it takes to blink
an e. 7080
Love has a clear e. 6457
Mind should be e. to see with
3021
need e. single to God's glory 5442
not e. that sees beauty of heaven
10656
not with motes from neighbor's e.
1402
Obedience is the e. of the spirit
8100
Reason our intellectual e. 9422
Self-love a mote in every man's e.
10026
splinter within your e. between
you and Lord 6590
sun with one e. vieweth world
11645
tends to be impatient 844
The e. of faith is dim 5635
The eternal e. that sees the whole
6583
The upward glancing of an e.
8939
To find a friend close one e. 4161
tree trunk in his own e. 6590
what is essential is invisible to the
e. 5622
when first your e. I ey'd 8179
Who can escape e. of God all
seeing 4888
With e. on God, strike next note
full, clear 7056
would have no rainbow had e. no
tears 10631

EYEBALLS
as big as cantaloupes 11028

EYELASHES
huge clouds nothing more than
dust on e. 11442

EYELIDS
sleep, no more wilt weigh my e.
down 10485
Though e. get heavy 11420

EYES
All our finite e. could tell us 2217
always throwing dust in
someone's e. 7445
And in he came with e. of flame
2638
are what one is 10687
bat's e. for our own faults 3957
bitter to look into happiness
through another's e. 3220
Blows dust in others' e. 10411
Breath, mouth, ears, e. 6120
Christ cannot live his life without
our e. 1270
confess secrets of heart 3569
convey the soul 3563
created with two e. 3562
different disposition looks
through same e. 8583
divine illumination would blind e.
4657
doors and windows of soul 845
Dry the e. which we have flooded
9054
Eternity image with blind e. 3269
fear figures you will take e. off
peaks 3971
fixed e. on reality judged insane
5730
four see more than two 257
Genius, that power that dazzles
mortal e. 8539
giant in your e. may be dwarf in
ours 8484
Give me the blind, obstinate e.
4530
God gives new set of inner e. 8495
God is seeable with e. of inner
man 4509
God washes e. with tears 10591
grown weary of the garish day
10481
have great power 3563
heart has e. brain knows nothing
of 8503
Heav'n opens on my e. 2389
how many red e. in marketplace
10507
Humility hides our good deeds
from our e. 6005
if we have not light, color in our e.
7108
Illusion dust devil throws in e. of
foolish 2655
in e. of mother every beetle a
gazelle 7846
in e. of others only a thing which
stands in the way 8506
In people's e. I read malice, vice
3571

inward e. meet all-seeing e. of God 3737

jealous man's horns hang in his e. 6337

keep e. half shut after marriage 7624

keep e. of heart on Savior 10551

Keep e. wide open before marriage 7624

legalism, its poison blinds our e. 6823

let me be to groping men and blind 10130

life with e. shut kind of insanity 11234

lift e. to hills to see God, angels 2359

light in e. 829

Light'ning their e. to vision and adoring 8454

like sun which seems to our e. to set in night 6094

love has e. to see misery, want 7335

may have good e. yet see nothing 8502

Men of cold passions have quick e. 3565

more exact witnesses than ears 3567

night has a thousand e. 7306

no matter how good e. and feet 2565

Obstacles frightening when e. off goal 4430

of love see not one but two persons 7300

One's e. are what one is 3566

Only e. washed by tears see clearly 2555

Open e, world full of God 4861

Other men's sins before our e. 10348

plays with dust, e. full of dust 11066

see today with e. of tomorrow 11380

shut e. to future God hides from us 4322

shut mouth and e. to injustice around him 11690

sight of you good for sore e. 4207

successful parents get behind e. of child 8329

sufficient vision left to lift e. unto hills 10436

tears so blind our e. cannot see mercies 10033

tell what the heart means 3568

that look are common 8493

that see are rare 8493

These e, new faith receiving 2398

They took away what should have been my e. 1817

things of Spirit take shape before inner e. 8488

to keep a friend close two e. 4161

to see what he could not see before 8495

too wise to let you pull wool over his e. 3921

truth, try to grasp with closed e, fearing to be blinded 11562

turn our e. to skies full of promise 9059

two e. to see twice as much as they say 3564

untold novelties for him who has e. to see 8507

What you don't see with your e. 5165

When close e. to devil be sure not a wink 2705

When e. to be avoided 5480 2468

When heart is full, e. overflow 5269

world will always keep e. on spot where crack was 9612

worse is it to have e. and not see 6289

years to efface fault in e. of men 4091

Yet mine e. the watch do keep 1514

EYES'
out there beyond the e. horizon 6111

EYESTRAIN
no danger of e. from looking on bright side 8240

FABRIC
how shabby f. of history is 5714

need for prayer in f. of family life 3875

FABRICATED
by social compulsions of unredeemed world 10003

Self-respect cannot be f. out of public relations 9995

FABULOUS
memory capacity of human mind f. 7738

FACADE
less exhausting to become what you want to be 1048

FACE
a friend to f. it with you 4196

Any idiot can f. a crisis 6876

at least put a smile on your f. 9999

Because he lives I can f. tomorrow 2978

charms that sages have seen in thy f. 10550

Christian has open f. 1260

don't want them to see my f. black, white 3229

doors have shut in your f. 184

filled with broken commandments 10315

From man's f. can read his character 8494

frowning f. repels 5504

God has f. very like their mother's 7855

God redeemed human race when we were spitting in his f. 9434

Honesty looking painful truths in the f. 5876

I cannot f. it all alone 5413

I couldn't see the Lord's f. 10853

if we took every word at f. value 9466

If you can't f. the music 6797

in f. of overwhelming impulse 4111

in his Son, Jesus, God unveils his very f. 9706

in tragedy f. to f. with things never gave heed to 10667

it—'tis God's gift 6881

Jest with ass, will flap in f. with tail 9477

joy of heart colors f. 6560

Keep your f. to the sunshine 1098

Laughter drives winter from the f. 6735

life as is, not as we feel it ought to be 6939

Man born with f. turned away from God 9583

meaning on the f. of the high hills 4962

mirror of the mind 3569

my f. was in his breast—crying 10853

no problem can't f. if Jesus to strengthen 11126

Nothing more beautiful than cheerfulness in an old f. 8148

Often God has to shut door in our f. 5436

Photography records feelings on human f. 2016

pleasant f. silent recommendation 3570

portrait of the mind 435

Prayer enables man to f. situation 8927

prays much by night, f. fair by day 8808

Sin clasped so close cannot see ugly f. 10377

Sinning is turning from God's f. 10382

slamming door in f. of God 5955

So is the beauty of an aged f. 8125

stand with f. in what direction he will 9151

strong men stand f. to f. 915

The color of its f. 3227

The one who wears my f. 9947

Thy blessed f. to see 5635

Trust not too much to enchanting f. 3575

trying on one f. after another to find his own 12163

turn his f. toward the future 4315

ugly f. sometimes better than real one 6057

veil which covers f. of future 4330

voice is second f. 1883

what crises would f. you if your prayers answered 8891

What griefs in silence of your f. 1545

When speak of heaven, let f. light up 5680

When speak of hell, everyday f. will do 5680

with merry, wise f. 4195

world, reflection of man's f. 436

FACED

I f. a future all unknown 5413

Whenever f. with crucial decision 5467

with a mountain, I will not quit 2633

with opportunities disguised as impossible situations 8228

FACES

Be Lord of naked f. 6296

knowledge of God will result in falling on our f. 6705

move beauty from f. into hearts 8169

Old age puts more wrinkles in minds than on f. 8162

relief of diver coming back to familiar f. 6110

we see, hearts we know not 2464

when f. facts of life as they are 8237

world full of f. 8995

FACE-TO-FACE

Once f. with Word of God 686

until he meets author f. 684

FACETS

life f. of one diamond reflecting light 6985

FACILITY

home is God's built-in training f. 5854

FACING

frightened at f. ourselves 10575

God judges man by way he is f. 4713

in only one direction 9846

FACT

appreciate and accept f. everyone different 6180

At first laying down, as f. fundamental 4927

born again, a foundation f. 879

Christian faith founded upon f. of history 6144

Don't fight f, deal with it 3576

Faith bids eternal truth be f. 3680

greatest f. which history records 5710

hang on to f. Jesus Christ is true 589

isn't the f. you're hurt that counts 11446

key f. about God 4779

Loneliness central f. of human existence 7137

Men who are unhappy proud of the f. 5541

most comforting f. imaginable 4779

mystery a is f. about which we cannot know everything 7936

On from f. divine God advances 4906

only two religions accept gloom as f. 9551

presence of God a f. of life 4864

remains God is with us 4864

resurrection f. of history 9702

time does nothing to f. of sin 10419

to recognize is we must be born again 9801

where hypothesis, f. meet 7435

FACTORY

as much need of saint in f. as in monastery 9765

unconscious like vast subterranean f. 7767

FACTS

are stubborn things 3578

considered irrelevant 3493

do not cease to exist because ignored 3579

God alone knows all the f. 7828

God has all the f. on his side 8456

great world of f. 592

Knowledge process of piling up f. 11927

mind should not be bin to store f. 3021

Peace must be based on f. 8456

so obsessed with f. lost touch with truth 7990

true fact acts on supernatural f. 3807

truth more popular if not ugly f. 11543

We cannot make f. 38

when faces f. of life as they are 8237

will not disappear 3577

FACULTIES

When f. incapacitated 2565

FACULTY

Faith higher f. than reason 3675

FADE

In time must f. and beauty lose 8172

Like them we f. away 2380

masks torn away, hollow smiles f. 9741

Time will f. your cheeks 11328

FADES

Youth f. 7860

FADS

decisions not on passing f. of society 10707

FAIL

act as if impossible to f. 8533

better to f. in cause that will succeed 3615

better to f. in originality 2008

Bible where wit, reason f. 710

energy of life does not f. for those who give 2018

family, where greatest can f. 3886

glory in rising every time you f. 3620

God allows our schemes to f. 9851

if f. to create harmony 580

If f. to emphasize we can glorify God 7481

If God you f. to see 4926

In great attempts glorious to f. 3600

less likely to f. in crisis 5226

men f. through lack of purpose 4427

never f. who die in a great cause 7680

not marriage but people that f. 7622

People f. 9521

people f. for lack of encouragement 3138

probability we f. should not deter 3625

rather do something great and f. 3595

Success to those neither afraid to f. nor discouraged 10802

Temptation not meant to make us f. 11061

tend to f. at our strong point 10759

than succeed in cause that will f. 3615

Those who dare to f. 87

When other helpers f. 2538

With that assistance cannot f. 5411

FAILED

better to have f. when serving God 10777

Bible has never f. to give light, strength 670

Children never f. to imitate elders 1112

have f. as Christian writer 12147

have f. three times 3611

Many might have f. beneath trial 4236

miserably, first to see God's formula 3628

never f. cannot be great 3594

schemes of world reconstruction have f. 6487

strength has f. ere the day is half done 7570

The sunrise never f. us yet 5942

to fight for right, justice, goodness 1689

Where I have f. to meet thy thought 7480

FAILING
equal f. to trust everybody, nobody 11473
excuse f. of friend 4183
glory not in never f. 3620
something not possible on this f. earth 7601
strength, patience are f. him 6599
With f. powers 12016

FAILINGS
In solitude become broken by our f. 10540
See f. in yourself 2808

FAILS
as inward life f. 1761
believe the hand which never f. 11470
Excels in something in which another f. 2
giver never f. to receive 9763
God never f. to grant light 5397
Love finds admission where proud science f. 12130
Nothing f. like success 10795
perseverance rarely f. in its purpose 8557
person who succeeds not one who never f. 3624
Satan f. to speak of remorse of immorality 2662
The steady faith that never f. 1933
What to do when prosperity f. 11151
what violence f. to accomplish 4403
when church f. to break cultural barrier 1456
who f. to pray cheats himself 8810

FAILURE
am a f. 3611
Being humble involves willingness to be reckoned f. 5993
Better a fall than not to climb 3585
better to win though checkered by f. 1922
Beware of succumbing to f. 3586
Christianity is a f, they say 1443
Christianity, not to be judged by f. 1188
cross, the supreme f. 3582
Day of Judgment to tell tragedies of f. 1055
Destiny a fool's excuse for f. 2619
difference between success and f. 8227
each f. of our hopes 4578
Evil means f. 3364
fear of f. 3971
formula for f, try please everybody 3619
God chastises with f. to humble us 3603
God's remedy for f. 10812
have nothing to do with what men call f. 10824
his life has been a f. 8629
holds back fearing f. 3624

hopeful man sees success where others see f. 5943
How could I know forgiveness without f. 1512
in everyone's sight but God's 5993
invitation to recourse to God 3587
is not falling down 3588
is not the falling down 3598
is not worst thing in world 3589
is remaining down when fallen 3588
is someone who has given up trying 3581
is the pioneer in new lands 3602
is the staying down 3598
isn't fatal 3590
Jesus Christ's life an absolute f. 3605
learn only from f. 10795
learn wisdom from f. 3630
life may bring f. 4803
life of Jesus Christ anticlimax of f. 10813
life will have been a f. 6944
make f. stepping-stone to success 3586
makes his f. certain 11597
man who instructed thousands felt a f. 2886
Man's f. to conquer human nature tragic 7414
may consider himself f. 3596
measure judged success or f. is love 7307
mistake of employer f. with human material 3120
mortal dread of f. 10776
moves on in spite of f. 3624
must appreciate f. to appreciate success 3637
not a condition, but an attitude 3581
not able to cash in on experience 3580
Not f. but low aim is crime 3610
not someone who has tried, failed 3581
Nothing good is f. 10796
of rationalism 4495
Often success is entered through f. 3612
only thing achieve without effort is f. 2773
our phenomenal f. to deal with evil 2159
pioneers in new undertakings 3602
pioneers new forms of expression 3602
plan that would anticipate every f. 5438
prayer about f. 3615
Problems distinguish success and f. 202
real always checked with f. 9498
right attitude, not a f. 521
Rigidity threatened by risk, f. 6818

Show me satisfied man, I will show you f. 2871
Sin pays in f. 10379
soul faced by f. can rise up 3621
Success is f. turned inside out 10806
success or f. in hands of God 10776
succumbing to f. as inevitable 3586
takes only one to make marriage a f. 7623
teaches success 3591
to hit bull's-eye never fault of target 9680
to obey dulls spiritual understanding 8100
to put God where he belongs 7046
tragedy of life is f. to use talent 10997
true test of greatness 3594
Whatever f. I have known 11278
When success turns head faces f. 10826
within God's purpose, no longer f. 3582
without first persevering through f. 6802
worry f. to think 12078

FAILURES
did not realize close to success 3607
feel genuine sorrow at their f. 9963
finding f. were successes 3631
God able to work f. into his plans 3613
nine out of ten things were f. 10825
nor discouraged by f. 10802
not making plans, feel we are f. 130
prepare for triumphs 3593
Show a man his f. without Jesus 7425
temporary tests to prepare us 3593
to understand many f. 10594
will help us accept ourselves, f. and all 9993

FAINT
he who does not love would f, lie down 7220
less likely to f. in crisis 5226
No fear lest he should swerve or f. 1299
not, fight on 6256
That my love is weak and f. 9077

FAINTEST
God can hear your f. whisper 8801

FAINT-HEARTED
no lullaby for the f. 5804

FAINTLY
heard your voice only f. because of uproar of restless 9070

FAIR

All rules will be f. with God 604
discussion firmest friend to truth 2902
No matter how f. the sun shines 5544
To believe in God is to know rules will be f. 4508

FAIRER

Hope for f. times in future 10586

FAIREST

and sweetest rose 8172
Love is the f. bloom in God's garden 7247
rule by majority f. 5194

FAIRNESS

live with f, learn justice 1114

FAIR-SIZED

Every man should keep f. cemetery 4225

FAIRY

child has f. godmother in soul 1122
No f. takes, nor witch hath power 1371

FAITH

a gift, but you can ask for it 3674
a gracious companion 3689
A man can counterfeit f. 5989
a refusal to panic 3677
a strong power 3678
a terrific venture in the dark 3668
accept with f. his holy will 4688
act upon f. within our power 3721
acts on supernatural facts 3807
All is well, tho f. and form 3644
all science rests on basis of f. 9869
alone gave life meaning 7472
an act 3680
an act of man that reaches beyond limits 3690
an affirmation 3680
an essential guide 3689
and hope triumphant say 2985
and love spasmodic in best minds 3654
and obedience in same bundle 8089
and reason, not in opposition 3842
and sight, in opposition 3842
and thought belong together 617
answered. No one was there 3968
answers I 2939
antiseptic of the soul 3694
basis on which we stand 3835
beginning of anxiety, end of f. 424
beginning of f. end of anxiety 424
beholds feeble light 3800
belief in face of contradictions 3693
belief in resurrection not appendage to f. 9696
believe only possibilities, not f. 605
Believe with a f. that kindles 3182
believes promise 9322

believes the unbelievable 3713
believing beyond sense, sight 3657
believing in advance 3708
believing that it will come true 5927
believing what will only make sense in reverse 3708
believing where we cannot prove 3682
belongs to men in God 3698
best which exerciseth f. in God 7698
Better baffled f. than no f. 3645
bird that sings when dawn still dark 3695
blind to impossibilities 3683
brings power 3748
brought to f. in Christ by exposure to f. 3759
builds bridge across gulf of death 3655
By f. led beyond reason 3834
By f. led to knowledge of God 3834
By f. led to knowledge of ourselves 3834
By f. we know his existence 3814
call to suffering requires f. 10937
can do nothing without f. 3827
can do very little with f. 3827
Can f. that does nothing be sincere 3647
can put a candle in darkest night 3656
can survive all odds 3736
can't pump up f. out of your own heart 3828
cannot be forced 3686
cannot be proved 3724
cannot believe he is going to let me down 3712
cannot have love apart from f. and hope 3837
capacity to trust God 3696
cease to shape our lives by f. 3688
Christian f. a revolutionary f. 3785
Christian f. engages profoundest problems 3784
Christian f. founded upon fact of history 6144
Christian f. most exciting drama 11201
Christian f. staggered imagination of man 11201
church not fraternity of f. fans 1414
clinging, like man hanging to boat 3797
commits to obedience 3808
convinced of the reality of their f. 7472
cure for fear is f. 3991
dedication to duty and destiny under God 770
deepened f. that follows grief 5360
developing f. gradual process 5738

develops best when everything fuzzes over 3789
develops best when God stays silent 3789
develops best when the fog rolls in 3789
did not seem to come 3735
difference between f. and works 3786
do not understand f. until tested 11620
do not want merely to possess f. 3734
do right when offer f. and works to God 3829
Doctrine nails your f. 11184
does everything under, by, through God 3660
does not ask for lifting of darkness 3714
does not struggle 3658
does not wish, hope, desire 3659
does nothing alone 3660
don't keep f. with God, won't keep with man 3799
don't understand or don't believe f. 3741
don't want us free to express f. creatively 6824
Doubt is an element of f. 2937
Doubt is not opposite of f. 2937
Doubt makes the mountain which f. moves 2938
doubt so close to f. 7081
draws poison from every grief 3661
draws sting out of trouble 3818
elevates the soul 3666
empowered with invincible f. 3736
empowers 3965
encourages 3965
Enough for f. or creed today 4118
enough to make God real 1809
enriching life in here and now 6091
eternal life begins with f. 3652
Every man lives by f. 3653
evil not so much an obstacle to f. 3399
examined hundred people who lost f. 3742
expresses itself by ability to be still 3769
eye of f. is dim 5635
feeds his f. will starve his doubts 3727
finds food in famine 3703
finds table in wilderness 3703
Fold the arms of your f. 3718
for deliverance is not f. in God 3662
from conflict often strongest, best 2935
gets supernatural results 3807
give me f. to leave it all to thee 9072
give me f. to live from day to day 9072

Give us a heart of f. 9058
gives profound understanding 7383
gives simplicity of heart 7383
God able to test, develop f. 3744
God always receptive to f. 4590
God does it 3786
God does not expect f. without reason 3840
God is perceived intuitively 3750
God set in my darkness lamp of f. 11144
God values f. in midst of struggle 11667
God's better plan takes f. to claim 2607
gospel addressed not to reason but f. 3796
grammar school of f. 11192
great doers of history men of f. 5723
Great f. perseveres in God's silences 3725
great f. will bring heaven to your soul 3757
greater than learning 11568
grows by expression 3771
grows only in the dark 3663
has been growing ever since 3735
has never outstripped bounty of Lord 3664
has no bed to sleep upon 3760
He who despairs wants love and f. 2586
heals 3965
Healthy questions keep f. dynamic 2949
heart of f. that I may abide in thee 7458
heroic adventure that is f. 2959
higher faculty than reason 3675
Holy Spirit working in, through people who do not profess f. 5791
Hope is f. holding out its hands in the dark 5920
hope the constancy of f. 5946
hope, love, three torches that blend 2586
how many reasoned out of f. by argument 3742
Human misery too great without f. 3730
I build my f. on that 4758
I prayed for f. 3735
I will never have f. in riches, rank, power 10875
If assurance is child of f. 6714
If can be verified, we don't need f. 3740
if f. in Bible should cease 5189
if f. is gaze of heart at God 3737
If f. without works is dead 3737
If God be what our f. assumes 3774
If no clouds would not need f. 10598
If you can't turn f. into vernacular 3741

If you have f. in God, or man, or self 3778
illuminates the way 3649
important in life is obedience of f. 8110
in biblical f, woman is partner in ministry 11981
In f, hope world will disagree 1079
in f. is f. astray 3667
in hour of need f. born within 3820
in meaning of our pain, striving 4005
In natural matters f. follows evidence 3743
In old age f. most marvelous possession 8138
In presence of hope, f. is born 5937
in revolution of f. proud put underneath 3785
in that f. let us dare to do our duty 3755
In this f. I rest secure 4936
in trustworthiness of God 4005
in worthwhileness of life 4005
inner battles between doubt, f. 2959
inner conviction overwhelmed by God 3681
instructs us in depths of God 3670
Intelligence must follow 6327
is a gift of God 3721
is a grand cathedral 3648
is a light 3772
is a reasoning trust 3676
is an activity 3679
is believing God will 3691
is blind, except upward 3683
is casting oneself on the promise 3753
is child of knowledge 6714
is Christian's foundation 5638
is concerned with revealed data 3670
is confidence in character of God 3684
is daring to go farther than can see 3697
is deaf to doubt 3683
is dedication of personality 770
is doing right regardless of consequences 3671
is doubt's twin brother 2932
is essentially thinking 3830
is fire in heart 582
is forged through doubt 3726
is free 3838
is God holding on to you 3692
Is it possible to become free without f. 3745
is key to fit door of hope 3836
is knowing God will turn ultimate effect to good 3671
is like love, cannot be forced 3686
is love on the battlefield 7202
is not anti-intellectual 3690
is not believing God can 3691

is one thing, feeling another 8104
is positive 6091
is rich 11696
is sacred 11684
is taking God at his Word 3687
is the foundation 3826
is the root 3837
is the root of works 3699
is the subtle chain 3700
is to believe what we do not see 3701
is to trust God when you can't trace him 3663
kind of f. God values 3789
Knowledge given to lead us to greater f. 6693
Knowledge of divine escapes us through want of f. 3754
knowledge that transcends intellect 3673
knows God is light that can show the way 3702
knows it can never penetrate mysteries of God 3702
knows itself weak and uncertain 3702
lack of charity in action murders f. 3829
lack of f. will go in two seconds 3828
larger the God we know, the larger our f. 3790
laughs at shaking of spear 3703
lends holiness to commonest state 3666
lends nobility to life 3666
Let us have f. that right makes might 3755
lets God do it all 3658
liberates 3965
lies on the other side of reason 3685
Life's temptations for our f. 6995
light in Christmas 1364
like a lily, lifted high and white 7179
like believing man can walk on tightrope pushing wheelbarrow 3669
limits of reason make f. necessity 3840
listens only to God 3683
Little f. will bring soul to heaven 3757
live with security, learn f. 1114
lives by f. not judged on the law 6812
loses f. loses all 3729
lost f. what has he left 3728
loves, knows the one who is leading 3709
makes a Christian 1280
makes all things possible 7345
makes discords harmonies of future 3704
makes future glorious 3705
makes inlook favorable 3705
makes life bearable 3685
makes outlook bright 3705

makes serviceable 3965
makes things possible, not easy
3706
makes uplook good 3705
man of little f. does not think
3830
man perfect in f. who can come to
God 3780
man without f. a walking corpse
3791
man's weakness leaning on God's
strength 3775
mastering difficulty in strength of
Lord 3678
may pass for falsehood 10762
means grasped by power greater
than we are 3707
means I will stick to my belief
3662
means not worrying 3805
meet affliction with f. 296
mighty f, the promise sees 3717
miracles do not foster deep f.
3782
moment we turn in f. to God 3758
most cherished possession is my f.
3761
must be more than pious hope
3787
must be prepared to be martyr,
fool 3642
must be tried in friendship 4227
must include mysteries 11203
must never think of f. as purely
mystical 3830
must not lose f. in humanity 5988
must seek greater depth 3756
My f. has omnipotency 3760
mystical experience bedrock of f.
7948
need not shout my f. 8014
needs neither evidence nor
research 3810
neglect prayer, lose fire of f. 8945
never found alone 3809
never knows where it is being led
3709
never means gullibility 3710
never our merit God looks at, but
f. 3749
never put character in place of f.
1057
never to doubt does not know f.
3726
No man can create f. in himself
3766
no merit if reason provided proof
3841
no room for passivity in Christian
f. 1235
not a sense, sight, reason 3687
not a thing one loses 3688
not all f. pleases God 3823
not an easy virtue 3689
not an integrated personality 770
not believing without evidence
3657
not holding on to God 3692
not laying by of questions 770

not optional 2288
not shelter against difficulties
3693
not to be shaken won through
blood, tears 2949
O for a f. that will not shrink
3768
Obedience leads to f. 8103
object of f. unseen reality 3831
obtain proof render f. superfluous
3806
oil in machinery of life 3731
on full stomach may be
contentment 3711
one of the easiest things possible
3737
one strand of f. amongst
corruption 3749
only f. can do it 3661
paradox of f. 3788
Patience, like f, removes mountains
8408
peace that belongs to suffering
miracle of f. 10907
perfect f. would lift above fear
3643
Perfection in f. ingredient of prayer
8914
poetry to life 3666
possibility when human
possibilities exhausted 3698
Prayer the product of f. 8914
prays God to clasp hand more
closely 3714
precedes understanding, does not
follow 3743
precious thing God finds in us
10666
principal part of f, patience 3792
producing activities faster than f.
1449
professing f. in Jesus while you
blaspheme him 3646
prove f. by committal to it 612
proves herself in ordinary
situations 3715
purifies the emotions 3666
Put your f. to test of life 3774
quenches fire of every pain 3661
reaches beyond our five senses
3690
reason ought to follow, not
precede, f. 9411
Reason saw not till f. sprung the
light 3777
receives 3659
receives the impossible 3713
refusing to feel guilty over
confessed sins 3672
rejoices in its God 3965
releases life 3747
reposes on character of God 4443
requires we rise above law of
moral gravitation 3752
respect f. but doubt gets you
education 2942
resting, like man within boat 3797
restlessness can be God sowing
seeds of f. 3722

rests on the promises 3818
resurrection is the Christian f.
9696
reward of f. to see what we believe
3701
riddling the f. of yesterday 2953
salvation comes by f. 4015
say the yes of f. 1306
Scholarship should follow f. 3022
Science sometimes said to be
opposed to f. 9869
second nature to children 1116
Security never friend of f. 952
sees action of God 3794
sees the day 2939
sees the invisible 3713
sees the way 2939
Self-sufficiency instead of f. 10359
separate f. and works wrong 3829
serpent beguiled Eve away from f.
in God 9424
sets life free 3747
shines equal, arming me from fear
3765
should always be simple,
unbending 7168
show want of f. in God by false
wisdom 4322
simple f. and implicit obedience
164
Skepticism prepares way for f. of
tomorrow 2953
smallest seed of f. better 3795
soars on high 2939
solves problems by pointing to
Lamb of God 3784
something to be applied 3679
spiritual, strong searchlight 3649
stands above human system 3670
start with doubt for deep-rooted
faith 2949
steady f. that never fails 1933
steps of f. 3767
storms makes f. grow broad 1803
Strong minds, great hearts, true f,
ready hands 6299
struggling f. like man in deep
water 3797
subtle chain that binds to infinite
2929
Suffering aid to f. 10896
Surrender to this power is f. 3707
sustains human dignity 3666
takes bitterness from affliction
3818
takes real f. to live life of heaven
on earth 3752
takes sting from every loss 3661
Talk f. 3778
teach me to breathe deeply in f.
3779
temptation step in progress of f.
11093
that cannot survive collision with
truth not worth regrets 3639
that God will use us as piece of
mosaic 4005
that hasn't been tested can't be
trusted 3640

that men commit life, hopes to God 3999

that will shut the mouths of lions 3787

thaws life out 3747

There lives more f. in honest doubt 2957

These eyes, new f. receiving 2228

things not seen 3833

thought f. would strike me like lightning 3735

three kinds of faith 3797

Through f. unseen world takes shape 3812

till f. shall come 3778

To accept crucifixion requires absolute venture of f. 10048

to assimilate Christ active f. 3801

To believe on Christ initial f. 3801

to believe task ahead never as great as Power behind 3804

to choose difficult as easy is f. 3803

to pseudo f. nothing but God terrifying thought 3719

to real f. most comforting thought 3719

to receive Christ appropriating f. 3801

to strengthen, confirm new, weak f. 3744

To test stuff of rough-hewn f. 2964

to think can understand mysteries makes mockery of f. 11203

to understand Christ intelligent f. 3801

tread hidden paths of grace in f. 5397

trial of f. precious 3751

Trinity mystery f. embraces 11428

true f. essentially reasonable 3842

trusts in character, promises of God 3842

try to speak of great or little f. 4710

trying to live maximum life on minimum f. 3770

unbeliever can no longer refuse reality of our f. 10938

Understanding, reward of f. 609

until knowledge must take in f. 4578

Violence goes against truth of our f. 11678

Vision looks upward, becomes f. 11738

want f. that possesses me 3734

want to keep f, must share it 3771

We live by f, but f. is not the slave 3813

We master fear through f. 4005

wears everyday clothes 3715

When f. ends, God's begins 302

when f. in future becomes knowledge of past 7435

When f. is lost 7442

when f. is present God works through anyone 3723

when f. is starved 3828

when hungry, genuine 3711

when live on a f. basis 10780

When Lord leads someone to great f. 9029

Where reason cannot wade, f. may swim 3821

where there is doubt, f. 9086

Where there is f. there is love 4517

whether f. will not justify confidence 3774

who differ concerning their f. 11212

Who has ever seen f. 615

who has f. in himself able to be faithful 9485

who walks by f. accepts circumstances 3638

whole trouble with man of little f. 3830

will lead where you cannot walk 3716

will survive storm better than oak 3702

wise, sane Christian f. 3999

with thee in f. 4021

Without f, society of indifferent 925

without f. impossible to please God 3823

without f. in fatherhood of God 925

Without f. man becomes afraid 3824

Without f. man becomes sterile, hopeless 3824

Without f. people drift into hate societies 925

without thankfulness lacks strength, fortitude 11154

Workless f. God never regards 3825

works fear of death out of Christians 2375

Works without f. like fish without water 3826

FAITHFUL

Believe, even if only one f. 583

certain that a f. hand will take, sift 4260

Christ eternally f. 9521

Faithfully, f. to every trust 2028

friend an image of God 4162

friend, one of life's greatest assets 4162

God has called me to be f. 10779

God will sustain if remain f. 5385

Greatness lies in f. performance 5283

he who is f. is lord of cities 3845

holy life f. in Christian duty 5736

In every change he f. will remain 1502

Love is f. 7246

not f. to God, not f. to each other 3849

Our f. unchangeable friend 4787

slow in making promise most likely f. in performance 9325

stay f. 5391

Think not those f. who praise thy words 3955

those who kindly reprove thy faults 3955

to the f. whole world is a possession 11696

When men cease to be f. to God 3849

who has faith in himself able to be f. 9485

Wisdom comes from being f. to small tasks 11911

FAITHFULLY

help me f. to journey along my road 9074

home where processes of character molding are f. carried on 5850

in all things to serve thee f. 9088

Live f. by bit of light you have 8103

FAITHFULNESS

dominant note in Jesus' life 3848

God's immutability presuppose f. 4583

In God's f. lies eternal security 4620

in little things a big thing 3843

is all 3845

is consecration in overalls 3844

Money brings servants, but not f. 7807

the more experience of God's f. we have 3744

FAITHLESS

work God never rewards 3825

FAITHS

old f. light their candles all about 11539

FAKE

forgers f. money 7826

FAKING

evidence in trials 7836

FALL

Another thing to f. 11046

Better a f. than not to climb 3585

can f. down by myself 9044

cannot jump from summer to winter without a f. 9875

depth man can f. is height to which he can rise 8666

desire of knowledge in excess caused man to f. 3556

desire of power in excess caused angels to f. 3556

digs pit for brother shall f. into himself 3373

every step nearer God increases depth we may f. 10700

He that is down need fear no f. 6001

Hold me so firmly I cannot f. 7478

FALLACY

how lowsoever it be we f. 4774

I f. upon the thorns of life! I bleed! 6911

In Adam's f, we sinned all 10323

Into each life some rain must f. 2549

is soon over 9879

Leaves have their time to f. 2324

lets him f. in the niche ordained to f. 5387

mighty disaster theologians call the F. 4744

morning and evening are spring and f. 9877

Never f. out with bread, butter 3105

Nor can we f. below arms of God 4774

on the seeming void, and find 3767

our shadow selves, our influence, may f. 6242

Pride mounts the wall to hurry to that fatal f. 9231

seven times, stand up eight 3592

sin when deliberately set ourselves up to f. 10422

sparrow cannot f. without notice 4933

stumble may prevent f. 3583

Success, getting up more times than you f. 10804

They f. and perish 8363

To f. into sin is human 10408

To go too far as bad as to f. short 11954

towers f. with heavier crash which higher soar 9216

We cannot f. out of his safety 4618

we shall f. for anything 11731

When wall cracked, f. will be speedy 9257

Whether we stumble or f. 3634

who would not f. off precipice 11068

worse tumble when f. over own bluff 7587

FALLACY

attends proposals to "test efficacy of prayer" 8750

belief youth happiest time of life a f. 7026

that having children makes a mother 7854

FALLEN

Failure is remaining down when f. 3588

have f. likely to become discouraged 10328

He that is f. cannot help him that is down 2585

I have f, Lord 10318

law of mutation belongs to f. world 4589

Make kindling out of f. tree 3606

man not simply an imperfect creature 9577

man rebel who must lay down his arms 9577

Originally one, Adam has f. 760

prince of Pharaohs is f. 730

stands erect by bending over the f. 10144

FALLING

all things everywhere are f. 9909

bad to lean against f. wall 3380

better to keep friend from f. than help up 4191

chanting, sky is f. 4226

Christians kept from f. altogether 4623

Failure is not f. down 3588

failure not the f. down 3598

honors of this world are but peril of f. 5898

Keeping from f. better than helping up 260

leaves of life keep f. one by one 7031

My life is in the f. leaf 2587

not f. that is the worst 10318

not kept altogether from f. 4623

You don't drown by f. in water 3636

FALLS

as he who f. short 6592

Hasty climbers have sudden f. 6114

He that f. into sin is a man 10309

If sky f, hold up your hands 8834

No amount of f. will undo us 3609

Who f. for love of God 4791 3635

Whoever f. from God's right hand 4628

FALSE

Atheist put on f. courage 476

barrier between secular, sacred 10720

devil entangles learned with f. doctrine 2677

edge of security 1610

error follows f. light 3258

explanations for true reasons 3476

Fanaticism f. fire of overheated mind 3909

Feelings go bad when they make themselves into f. gods 4016

first step of wisdom is to know what is f. 11943

freedom, man free to do what he likes 4150

greed and anger, brother and sister of a f. 10003

Guilt by judgment of men f. guilt 5477

if f. Christianity of no importance 1184

if gamble on truth and proves f. 3724

lights extinguished 5103

Love lets us cast off f. exteriors 7254

ninety-nine times conclusion f. 2775

people certain about something f. 3384

repentance cries out against something else 9601

report spreads where recantation never reaches 10453

shifting systems of f. religion 5103

show want of faith in God by f. wisdom 4322

than a f. friend 4210

Thou canst not then be f. to any man 6318

to God, never true to man 7464

values brought into evangelical favor 11666

values that Christ declared f. are brought into evangelical favor 11666

vice is f. moral arithmetic 10410

With good or ill, with f. or true 7017

FALSEHOOD

child of devil 2680

despise nothing except f. and meanness 8472

faith may pass for f. 10762

has to be invented 6867

In the strife of truth and f. 2489

is always first 6865

Jesus is all truth, no f. 6498

tells f. about life 7601

To unmask f. and bring truth to light 11344

twilight that enhances every object 6866

FALSEHOODS

usually quarrel among themselves 6849

FALSITY

Christian sees f. 1168

FALTER

Our earthly rulers f. 9224

FAME

an empty bubble 3862

comes when thinking about something else 3852

do all you can without thought of f. 10818

is a fickle food 3851

is like seawater 11875

is vapor 1010

like flame, harmless until start inhaling 3853

more we drink, thirstier we become 11875

Rather than f, give me truth 11526

Success is neither f, wealth or power 10807

What tho' we wade in wealth, or soar in f. 7088

when goads of f. lifted 6842

FAMILIAR

ear craves f. 844

eludes us in life 6934

Everyone capable of f. conversation with God 7541

May on f. terms be with highest God 7489

phrase have their superficial effect 8845

relief of diver coming back to f. faces 6110

Vices f. we pardon 10414

with few 550

FAMILIARITY

Abraham treated God with startling f. 7526

Communion with God one thing, f. another 8777

FAMILIES

found least gratitude from f. 5250

Gold in f. debate 11811

Suffering can pull f. together 10933

Suffering can rip f. apart 10933

very nature acquired within f. 3881

We must strengthen commitment to f. 3901

FAMILY

appreciate member of f. for who they are 6168

basic unit of government 3888

cannot stop near dissolution of f. unit 2928

children, an occasional animal, common cold 3864

Christ must live in your f. 1536

circle the supreme conductor of Christianity 5852

Civilization varies with the f. 3868

dark, uneasy world of f. life 3886

established before the church 3871

establishes society's basic values 3888

first and essential cell of society 3890

first authority under which person lives 3888

first community to which person attached 3888

first school of human instruction 3880

for propagation of life 10506

Free of f, Jesus remained alone 6508

future of church and humanity depend on f. 3894

God working out f. likeness to his Son in us 5793

God's grace turns out f. likeness 4651

Govern small f. as cook small fish 3868

happy f. an earlier heaven 3865

high crime rate traceable to disintegration of f. life 5858

highest realization of f. found where Christianity prevails 3868

idea of perfect f. 3868

In God's f. one body of people: servants 10161

lacking, cease to be a human nature 3881

life with our f. more amiable 7611

measure of greatness of nation 3894

monogamous, indissoluble 3890

my duty is to my f. first 3871

need for prayer in fabric of f. life 3875

never trouble in f. where children resemble parents 3898

no other structure can replace f. 3877

Nobody's f. can hang out sign 3878

Nothing stops f. quarrel more quickly 3879

Ordained by God as basic human organization 3880

place where principles are hammered, honed 3863

should be a closely knit group 5853

stamped its character upon child 1126

substituted social control for f. worship 5808

traditions identify f. as unique 3876

trivial irritations of f. life 6386

twisting, warping innocent f. members 3873

unless I can recall a loving f. 6919

varies with civilization 3868

what can f, even at purest and noblest, do 3036

whose father is in heaven 5001

wish I could give Christianity to my f. 1199

with f. hammer out convictions 5832

Within the f. he's made 3227

Without f. children have no moral foundation 3877

Without f. children moral illiterates 3877

world one f. in love, forbearance, common joy 9093

you come from isn't as important as 3889

you're going to have 3889

FAMINE

faith finds food in f. 3703

FAMOUS

By success do not mean you become f. 10780

crucifixion most f. death 2137

FAN

more like an electric f. 118

seemed to f. me like immense wings 5797

FANATIC

one who can't change his mind 3907

opposite of religous f. is the gentle cynic 9549

wound that never healed 3910

FANATICISM

Commitment without reflection 1532

false fire of overheated mind 3909

redoubling effort, forgetting aim 3908

today, fashionable creed tomorrow 3911

FANS

no f. in hell 5704

FANTASIES

deliver me from f. 5781

FANTASTIC

Nothing in fiction so f. as Incarnation 6125

Reality more f. than we can imagine 9407

FANTASY

and earthly things metamorphosed into art 7435

back in the kingdom of f. 3347

Journalism, news is f. 9404

those who turned away from f. judged insane 5730

without f. no creative work comes to birth 2024

FAR

can spring be f. behind 9874

go singing as f. as we go 7899

God both f. away, near at hand 4465

God f. exceeds all words we can express 10249

he who has brought me so f. 3712

heaven not so f. as some imagine 5651

How f. that little candle throws his beams 2499

how f. we have progressed since yesterday 9832

However f. you go 5409

Knowledge and wisdom, f. from being one 6690

may say you are f. from hating God 10427

night is dark, I am f. from home 5429

possibility of future f. exceeds past 4329

Reach up as f. as you can 7514

Things held me f. from thee 4805

those who are f. will come 9480

To go too f. as bad as to fall short 11954

travel wide and f. to scout, see, search 4926

truth works f. and lives long 11516

We talk about heaven being so f. away 5677

We've got as f. as poison gas 11739

Where sheep, wolves never f. away 8531

FARCE
Little praying a f. 8889

FARCICAL
pietism that preaches from villas to slums about mansions 6065

FARE
Better f. hard with good men 4219
Brown bread and gospel good f. 5090
Money can pay f. to every place but heaven 7810

FAREWELL
I bid you an affectionate f. 5179
Memorial service: f. for someone already left 2324
vain world 12032

FARMER
love is to the heart what summer is to the f. 7339

FARTHER
Faith daring soul to go f. than can see 3697
God never f. away than door 4621
man knows himself from perfection, nearer to it 8523

FARTHEST
God comes when we think he is f. off 4837

FASCINATED
endlessly f. by new thought 9468

FASCINATES
Work f. me 12009

FASCINATING
Adolescence a f. time of life 12161

FASCINATION
Man calls sin a f, God a fatality 4560
old age equal grace, force, f. 12188
youth full of grace, force, f. 12188

FASHION
Honesty a fine jewel, much out of f. 5875
of today, outrage of tomorrow 10516
Take clay and dust, f. a child 4608

FASHIONABLE
fanaticism today, f. creed tomorrow 3911

FASHIONED
shaped and f. by what we love 7330

FASHIONING
God is f. to benevolence 4514

FASHIONS
in sin change 10303

FAST
come he slow or come he f. 2218
expecting too much too f. 6116
falls the eventide 2538
I am going too f. 5587

Lord, I am coming as f. as I can 2450
money thou canst go out so f. 4039
No cord can bind so f. as love with a thread 7279
The world is moving so f. 66
Trouble rides a f. horse 11462

FAST-ACTING
For f. relief, try slowing down 6832

FASTER
accusation flies f. than defense 10453
if patient, can wait much f. 8400
producing activities f. than faith 1449
tempo of life growing f. 3896
we counted our spoons 5899

FASTING
few will join Jesus in f. 9268

FASTS
greatest saint not he who f. most 9790

FATAL
By turns we catch the f. breath 2233
Failure isn't f. 3590
Pride mounts the wall to hurry to that f. fall 9231
Repentance not a f. day 9591
Sin f. in all languages 10367

FATE
like the winds of sea are ways of f. 4432
Thy f. is common f. of all 10582
To be alone f. of all great minds 10571

FATE'S
severest rage disarm 7911

FATHER
beautiful image of a f. 3918
Becoming a f. easy enough 3917
being a f. can be rough 3917
best legacies f. can leave children 3924
Better child cry than f. 8284
cannot say F. if 8818
characteristic of Christ was submission to his F. 6414
child wants man for f, not formula 3929
Children whom the F. leadeth 5431
Christ a F. to provide 6370
described what a Christian was 3912
easier for f. to have children 3922
expected a good deal of God 380
family whose f. is in heaven 5001
give deference 511
good f. will leave imprint on daughter 3915
greatest a man can do for his heavenly F. 6665
if f. onion, mother garlic 8298

If our God our F. be 5428
If wealthy, prominent, stand in awe 3921
in praising son extols himself 3926
Let the F. proportion out 4629
lifts men up to their F. in heaven 5844
Lord, thy will be done in f. 9082
made me learn so many Bible verses 651
My f. was a Methodist 8316
my f. wept 808
My God, by his nature, my F. above 7951
never lost temper with us 3983
object of Jesus' meditation was his F. 12128
of Light! 3369
One f. worth more than hundred schoolmasters 3923
Our F. refreshes us on the journey 7014
Our F. yet heals spirit of amputees 5614
Redeemer and Spirit of grace 11424
religion of child depends on what mother, f. are 8356
same everlasting F. 415
should treat son as guest 3891
so fine a f. call him Dad 3921
son should treat f. as host 3891
than children to have real f. 3922
the Lord forsaken by the F. 6383
times when love to f. must be hatred 7280
To have God for our f. 7545
was so ignorant 3928
what f, mother say at home 8340
whatever a loving F. sends 33
whipped son for swearing, swore himself 3914
who seeks the F. more than anything he can give 8997
who teaches responsibility provides fortune 3913
with humility, talk to God as to your F. 4924

FATHERHOOD
greatest benefit God has conferred 3895
no brotherhood without f. of God 920
without f. of God 4632
without faith in f. of God 925

FATHERING
is marathon, not sprint 3919

FATHERLAND
Christ as God is f. where we are going 6364

FATHERLESS
chill, houseless, f. Cain 10573

FATHER'S
acid test of f. leadership 3925
boy asked question that pierced f. heart 3912

Christ left F. throne 495
Death going to F. house 2249
home is test of f. leadership 3925
love of God provident as f. love 4792
most important responsibility 3927
mother interpreter of f. character 8341
Our F. full giving is only begun 7570
Thy joy to do the F. will 10133
whole world is my F. house 1310

FATHERS
eat sour grapes 8328
In peace sons bury f. 11751
lost greatest of f. 483
our f. called it Sunday 10952
To support us was trouble for our f. 11459
Victory finds a hundred f. 2516

FATHOM
cannot f. yet seeking to know satisfying 5450
depth to extent heart is broken 900
Once conscious we are more than we can f. 10015
Other things we may f. 4678
Trinity mystery reason cannot f. 11428
You f. the depth of My heart 900

FATHOMED
creation, can never be f. 1975

FATHOMLESS
answer, the Cross of Christ 9398
Oh, the depths of the f. deep 7943

FATHOMS
Who f. the eternal thought 7572

FATIGUE
scarcely sensible of f. 3090
shoulders ache with f. 11420
Thinking is greatest f. in world 11263

FATIGUING
most f. to seem other than you are 1048
Nothing so f. as an uncompleted task 9297

FATUOUS
these f. ineffectual yesterdays 8370

FAUCETS
Time heals, except leaky f. 11331

FAULT
by lie grow two 3937
can be reformed 8312
castigate f. not child 8312
Condemn the f. not the actor 3936
confessed, new virtue 1592
Doth make f. worse by excuse 3934
failure to hit bull's-eye never f. of target 9680

gives way to f. for year or two 3935
greatest f. to be conscious of none 3952
have accident, other driver's f. 3947
If death be terrible, the f. is thee 2314
laws God gives us we find f. with 10425
looks for f. within himself 9680
needs lie most 3937
no f. of Christianity that hypocrite sins 1208
no f. of our own unable to sense God 4864
ofttimes excusing of a f. 3934
repent for years to efface f. 4091
takes deep root 3935
To find f. with the rest of us 3953
To hide the f. I see 1552
when you publish another's secret f. 5167
which humbles of more use 3931

FAULTFINDER
bad memory who never remembers good 2049
God is no f. 4650
good memory who always remembers bad 2049
sharp eye for faults, blind eye for virtues 2076
will find faults even in Paradise 6903

FAULTFINDERS
hundreds of f. among Christians 2085

FAULTFINDING
Discernment not f. 2805

FAULTLESS
Christ never suggested pretend people f. 9789
He who is f. is lifeless 8519
seeks f. friend is friendless 4245

FAULTS
Acknowledge f. to repair damage 3956
against whom I know most f. 3942
as we perceive and conquer the more glaring f. 10006
bat's eyes for our own f. 3957
Be to her f. a little blind 7603
Bear with all f. of man 3948
blind eye to trivial f. 9456
by self-examination to know our own 10014
choke f. by gaining virtues 3959
confidence in friend to tell your f. 3930
Deal with f. of others gently 3938
denouncing people's vice, f. 1162
Do not think of f. of others 3939
Do not think of your f. 3940
eagle's eye for f. of others 3957
ease of sentimentalists one of worst f. 12106

enemies tell you your f. 3164
even if church swarms with f. 1458
faithful those who kindly reprove thy f. 3955
faultfinder sharp eye for f. 2076
Faultfinder will find f. even in Paradise 6903
Forget others' f. by remembering your own 5999
greater confidence to tell friend his f. 3930
if f. to admit, how can he be perfect 3949
if f. written on forehead 3943
If feel you have no f. 3946
If had no f. of our own 3944
If pleased at finding f. 3945
in which to bury f. of friends 4225
less easy to uproot f. 3959
like grain of sand beside mountain of mercies 4817
Looking at neighbor's f. gives incorrect conception 8059
Love blinds us to f. 5602
more pardonable than methods to hide 3933
neighbors' f. and folly 10038
no f. in thing we want badly 11100
No man perfect unless admits f. 3949
not desirous of looking to f. of others 6597
not for f. we are disliked 5601
not take pleasure in noticing f. of others 3944
not when conscious of f. most wicked 10329
of others like headlights 2077
of others seem more glaring 2077
others abandon f. 3950
see nothing but f. who look for nothing else 3954
Some people excuse f. 3950
such a great man I have forgotten his f. 5286
tender to f. of others 10014
think still less of other's f. 3940
to many virtue consists in repenting of f. 11702
When soul laid down f. at feet of God 9608
will drop off like dead leaves 3940
With all thy f, I love thee still 7346

FAULTY
if relationship f, activity cannot be satisfactory 10227
Think of what is f. in yourself 3939

FAVOR
Age looked upon as sign of f. 12194
death a f. to many 2274
false values brought into evangelical f. 11666
freedom to ask f. 4285

friends impart f. to places where
    they dwell 4269
God looks with f. at pure hands
    6300
God's principles not replaced in f.
    of human calculation 7828
Measure not God's f. by your
    feeling 4772
will do best I can without fear, f.
    7006

FAVORABLE
Faith makes inlook f. 3705

FAVORED
one person is f. 39

FAVORING
good consists in f. life 5044

FAVORITE
color of asceticisms, black 467
hour of asceticisms, midnight 467
Little silent victories over f.
    temptations 6997
March homeowner's f. 9888
music of asceticisms, a dirge 467
place of God in heart of man 4496
Surrendering to despair man's f.
    pastime 2607
text of asceticism, "deny yourself"
    467
theme of asceticisms, tombstone
    467

FAVORITES
does not mean God has f. 8929
Love's business not to play f. 7274

FAVORS
man who loves God asks no f. of
    God 4803

FEAR
Absolved from sin and f. 4719
adventurous life not exempt from
    f. 3990
And drives away his f. 1507
Anxiety a thin stream of f. 410
Anxiety, f. trickling through the
    mind 410
Arrogance, f. replaced with
    gratitude, joy 1356
arsenal is vast 3971
bad side of poverty is f. it creates
    11854
Be sundered in the night of f. 3644
Because he lives all f. is gone 2978
bell or gong on approach of
    danger 3973
can f. death 2407
can find no answer, will find f.
    4008
can keep man out of danger 1923
can rattle you to take eyes off
    peaks 3971
Carry own lantern, and you need
    not f. dark 6167
children f. to go into dark 476
chose both f. and self-denial 467
confidence should supersede f.
    6326

courage can support man in f.
    1923
Courage is f. that has said its
    prayers 1919
courage is mastery of f. 1920
courage is not absence of f. 1920
courage is resistence to f. 1920
courageous step would carry
    through f. 3982
cringing in f. of true individuality
    1642
cure for f. is faith 3991
death is wicked man's f. 2372
death of f. certain 3962
death rids us of f. 2251
deliverance from f, advanced by
    prayer 8976
Depart without f. out of this world
    2338
disheartens 3965
Do not f. when enemies criticize
    you 3158
Do not look forward to changes
    in f. 5907
Do the thing you f. 3962
doesn't want journey to mountain
    3971
Envy numbed with f. 10296
    3211
explosive power of evil in human
    heart 3376
Extreme f. can neither fight nor fly
    3963
faith shines equal, arming me
    from f. 3765
faith works f. of death out of
    Christians 2375
free man does not f. thought 4145
freezes life 3747
gives framework of habits 3980
go forward without f. 1918
goal to create cowardly, joyless
    souls 3971
God because goodness and truth
    3983
God incarnate is end of f. 3972
God will not allow f. to 3340
good cause will f. no judge 6602
greatness of God rouses f. within
    us 3788
has use, cowardice none 1948
He that is down need f. no fall
    6001
Hope a more gentle name for f.
    5916
How strange this f. of death 2297
I do not f. explosive power of
    atom bomb 3376
I f. God, yet am not afraid of him
    3977
I shall not f. the battle 5418
if I f. what my neighbors may say
    or do 8818
if you do not f. God, you f.
    everything else 3994
imbue men with just f. of God
    6796
imprisons 3965
in keeping riches 11865

independent of f. of social
    judgment 1647
is gong on approach of danger
    3973
is love's gateway 3986
is painful 3986
is sand in machinery of life 3967
is tax conscience pays to guilt
    3966
keep respectful f. of God 3993
knocked at the door 3968
leads love at first 3986
less 5604
life shall never have a beginning
    6891
live in f. of death is many times to
    die 2403
look forward without f. to
    appointed hour 2225
looks ahead 8376
Love cannot put up with f. 3986
Love destroying all f. of an end
    7229
love our Maker without f. of pain
    4807
love without f. makes men remiss
    9736
loved to be feared, f. to be loved
    4000
makes useless 3965
makes wolf bigger than he is 3969
man threatens while quakes for f.
    3981
man to make his way best he can
    in f. 3495
Maturity, not to hide one's
    strength out of f. 7695
meet future without f. 8378
Men f. death as children f. dark
    2335
Men f. death refuse to understand
    2336
Men f. thought 11232
Mercy for them that f. and sin not
    7742
miserable to have many things to f.
    11827
modus operandi to manipulate
    with mysterious 3971
mother eases a child's f. 7844
need not f. disaster will follow
    thought 4134
need not f. God's will 5405
Neither do we f. being with others
    10539
Never f. shadows 2602
new step what people f. most 3989
No f. lest he should swerve or faint
    1299
no f. wind will uproot tree 6307
no foe with thee at hand to bless
    7474
No one need f. to listen 4966
not f. disaster will follow freedom
    of thought 4134
not that life shall come to end
    2283
nothing but sin 9136
nothing except cowardice 8472

of being thought narrow 836
of death common 2375
of death worse than death 2376
of death, failure, God, tomorrow
3971
of everything new 3980
of God a healthy ingredient 3993
of God can deliver from f. of man
3970
of God to be united with love of
God 9736
of God, deterrent to want 3993
of God, insurance against loss
3993
of God, source of comfort,
understanding 3993
of God, spur to confidence 3993
of God, spur to courage 3993
of handicaps dropped away 11131
of holy enthusiasm 3184
of sinning killed spontaneity 6813
One does not f. God because
terrible 3983
paralyzes 3965
People gathered to us by f. 6396
People living deeply, no f. of death
2362
people weighed down by
obsessive f. 5474
perfect faith would lift above f.
3643
power which can resist f. is love
3992
preoccupies death 2363
puts hopelessness at heart of life
3965
rather that life not have beginning
2283
refusing to yield to f. 2563
resurrection substituted f. of death
for eternal life 9702
right f. is f. of losing God 3995
Shame arises from f. of men 3988
sickens 3965
so that you be free from pain and
f. 3979
something different than alarm
3983
sometimes f. to bring troubles to
God 4789
soul's signal for rallying 3973
springs from ignorance 3964
steel our hearts against all f. 9090
sure way to take f. out of living
3993
that man who fears not God 9453
That when in danger knows no f.
3768
thief doth f. each bush an officer
5488
through f. of being criticized
people tell lies 6851
Time too swift for those who f.
11333
To be feared is to f. 4001
To f. and not to be afraid, the
paradox of faith 3788
to grow in love is to diminish f.
3986

To have money a f. 11871
to taunt with unknown 3971
voice of intelligence drowned out
by roar of f. 6331
We f. something before we hate it
4004
We master f. through faith 4005
what people see in us 1882
Whatever you f. most you will
serve 4006
When I am with God my f. is gone
7569
When in f. difficult to pray
coherently 10931
when love bound to God, f. is
done away 3986
when you f. God, you f. nothing
else 3994
where angels f. to tread 4060
who does not f. death, no f. of
threats 2294
who fears God need f. nothing else
9732
who fears not God needs to f.
everything else 9732
Who lives in f, never a free man
4009
who worship God from f. 12123
why do we f. trouble 11459
Why dost thou f. thy last day
2428
why f. to tread pathway to future
home 6875
Wicked men obey from f. 5053
will do best I can without f, favor
7006
will not f. being alone 10539
wise man prays for deliverance
from f. 3997
without love makes men desperate
9736
would not f. a million enemies
8832

FEARED
Death not to be f. 2338
loved to be f, fear to be loved
4000
man to be f. who fears not God
7426
Nothing in life is to be f. 3984
Old age more to be f. than death
8159
They f. as they entered the cloud
2562
To be f. is to fear 4001
tongue more f. than sword 10474
When questions to be f. 5480

FEARFUL
Goodness is never f. 11704
in f. narrow-mindedness 10540
Lord's Prayer most f. prayer in the
world 8828
silence has become a f. thing
10253
through all centuries of f. fog
3974
With the f. strain on me night, day
6747

FEARING
holds back f. failure 3624
Man spends life f. for future 8380
thing about f. God is you fear
nothing else 3994
truth, try to grasp with closed
eyes, f. to be blinded 11562
without f. to understand 4124

FEARLESS
clever, f, four years old 1130
greatest most f. under menace
5297
stars shine f. and confident 4618

FEARS
a thousand ghostly f. 5476
adventurous go forward in spite
of f. 3990
adventurous life lived in full
knowledge of f. 3990
All here hae got their f. 1396
And heated hot with burning f.
2599
arise from dim perceptions of
Christ's gospel 6713
atheist, nursery of f. 493
child who f. noises becomes man
who hates noises 4004
disclose inner f, temptation, joys
4029
discover what enemy f. most 4010
give up f. and face our true nature
10551
He who f. death cannot enjoy life
3975
He who f. to suffer, suffers from f.
3976
heart numbed too much for
hopes, f. 2587
Hope enough to remove anxious f.
1809
Idleness gives room for f. 12024
lives to live forever, never f. dying
6899
man to be feared who f. not God
7426
Many f. are tissue-paper thin 3982
miserable is he who f. death 2357
O Conscience, into what abyss of
f. 1694
people think with hopes, f. rather
than minds 7763
proportion out what f. he sees fit
4629
Prosperity not without many f.
247
Relinquishment of f. begins where
3987
rid of f, worries, bad eating habits
12076
should this not deliver us from f.
7545
Take off all your f. 10787
Tommy's tears and Mary's f. 4003
Tomorrow holds no f. for me
11369
veil God's love at times with
faithless f. 10964

we perform according to our f. 5950

who bathes in worldly joys swims in world of f. 8615

who f. God need fear nothing else 9732

who f. not God needs to fear everything else 9732

FEAST

contented mind, continual f. 1774

Every day cannot be f. of lanterns 3501

Every meal shared in love a f. 5825

gather to the f. 11175

good conscience continual f. 1654

spreads a common f. for all that lives 9883

than f. with bad men 4219

thankful spirit a perpetual f. 11139

thankless feeder, his f. a robbery 11138

War is death's f. 11769

FEATHER

by f. goose is plucked 11054

Out Satan must go, every hair and f. 9864

When mind doubts f. sways it 2960

FEATHERBED

Are yoy laying a f. for me 10836

FEATHERS

nothing rises quicker than f. 3857

Squirrels don't have f. 6168

white but heart grows black 9517

FED

But it is f. and watered 4625

there are people to be f. 10165

FEE

world requires fat f. 12052

FEEBLE

attach f. will to all-powerful will 9835

Faith beholds f. light 3800

Great souls have wills, f. ones wishes 8541

if virtue f. were 11692

means of aiding progress so f. 5944

tremble before opinion 8205

FEEBLENESS

in spite of our f. and sin 4768

FEEBLEST

Christian has that which is impossible to world 10512

prayer of f. saint a terror to Satan 8988

FEED

And f. me with a shepherd's care 9350

be careful not to exceed f. limit 7020

God is the food our spirits designed to f. on 7459

Guard, guide, keep, f. us 5428

In Christ church has enough to f. world 6374

messiahs aren't found sleeping in a f. trough 6147

mind with truth of God 12124

must be a time to f. on truth 11493

on Christ then go live life 6381

Sleep and I shall f. you 3094

we must f. mosquitoes 1733

will show you a way to f. thousands 10205

FEEDING OF 5,000

William daily reenacts f. 1136

FEEDS

God f. even the worm in the earth 9347

his faith will starve his doubts 3727

mind grows by what it f. on 11246

The meat it f. on 6346

wolf, strengthens his enemy 11064

FEEL

and not f. the crowd 10529

Before we can f. tenderness for others 4012

believe in love even when do not f. it 3732

Bigotry has no heart and cannot f. 9180

can f. the sufferings of millions 8445

comfortable, take another look 2013

disaster to f. at home on earth 2975

doesn't f. you've done a permanent job 4213

Don't pray when you f. like it 8785

face life as it is, not as we f. it ought to be 6939

for others—in your pocket 4037

genuine sorrow at their failures 9963

given weakness that he might f. need of God 8806

gratitude we f. for what we take 5267

great man who makes man f. small 5304

Great men never f. great 7380

Grief, helping you f. compassion for others 5334

he may not say much but you f. different 6241

Holy Spirit makes soul tender, or it would never f. 5794

I f. the guilt within 4642

I look down, I f. giddy 7090

If f. you have no faults 3946

If you don't f. close to God 4857

in the fire f. God's heart warming 4858

in the midst of the crowds f. frightfully alone 7124

Judge from own feelings how God must f. 4895

larger gratitude we f. for what we give 5267

learn to give thanks even if don't f. thankful 11173

Life a tragedy for those who f. 6954

Love a ceaseless effort to know, f. 7211

Music understood by thousands, all who f. differently 7905

must f. tenderness of God 4012

never f. God will cast evil out of world 3415

No one can make you f. inferior without your consent 6228

no one has right to blame us 6230

Nor f. unwanted at close of day 8145

Nothing makes one f. so strong as call for help 10177

Obedience means marching f. like it or not 8104

Of what we say we f. 7369

pain we f. known to God 4804

positive word makes you f. good 12001

poverty of soul measured by how little it can f. 10677

power to f. with others give 8430

praise God even when we do not f. like it 2564

real enemies make us f. so good 3168

really great man makes every man f. great 5304

shall f. what he would not 5478

Small men never f. small 7380

Sorrow, helping you f. more compassion 10610

Suddenly I f. myself transformed, changed 7964

Teach me to f. another's woe 1552

tell God that you only f. at ease far from him 8830

'Tis what I f, but can't define 7245

To f, amid the city's jar 8430

ultimate disaster to f. at home on earth 2382

weaker we f, harder we lean on God 10761

weaker we f, the harder we lean 8256

wealth of soul measured by how much it can f. 10677

what did it f. like to be out of heaven 6456

When you f. all is lost 3633

Worship means "to f. in the heart" 12140

FEELING

a terrible f, a leap in the dark 9937

best compliment is f. free to make own inquiries 6207

Christian life based on f. headed for 1257

Christian love not a vague f. of
affection 7304
Christian love [agape] not a f.
7166
deeper than all thought 10678
Every time you pray, new f. and
new meaning 8769
Faith is one thing, f. another 8104
God has mysteriously guided us
5392
God knows all f. 4881
great men have curious f. 5291
Happiness is a f. 6528
I could last forever 12165
If leave church with no f. of
discomfort 12106
in some form or degree in every
heart 4019
inordinate emphasis on f. good
4017
Laughing f. good, showing it in
one spot 6726
led without knowing it 5392
life based on f. headed for collapse
4011
Life must be composed by f. 6966
Love not a f. 7231
Love not affectionate f. 7242
love of God no mere sentimental f.
4780
Measure not God's love by your f.
4772
miserable f. that useless to strive
anymore 4507
music showing all changes of f.
7905
my heart beyond all f. 12102
negative word leaves you f.
depressed 12001
no f. however trifling, vulgar 7536
no f. that exists in that heart alone
4019
of being uncared for greatest
poverty 7132
of eternity in youth 12175
of f. safe with a person 4260
often described as fear 3983
Once it was the f. 6465
philanthropy to save ourselves
uncomfortable f. 10071
Prayer is listening, seeing, f. 8923
Prayer means raised up into f.
with God 8909
Remorse is beholding heaven and
f. hell 9574
Respect oscillations of f. 4018
that will never come back 12165
the evil in our own f. 3397
will of God never leads to
miserable f. 4507
without f. understood by at least
one person 11613
would be far less angry f. in world
9465
youth governed more by f. than
reasoning 12181

FEELINGS
a wiser than you made them 4018

are all holy when God's hand on
reins 4016
are everywhere, be gentle 4401
are your life and your nature 4018
Authentic men aren't afraid to
release f. 3916
climates of f. one can go through
in one day 4014
come and go, God's love does not
4777
come to God in utter dearth of f.
3780
come, go, are deceiving 9813
daring to believe with or without f.
3748
Don't bother much about your f.
4013
expresses f, dialogue of truth
begins 8779
fellowship without solitude void
of words, f. 10547
freedom to show true f. 4285
go bad when they make
themselves into false gods 4016
guilt f. which made him sick 5485
Heed not your f. 3718
Judge from own f. how God must
feel 4895
Many times go against our f. 8104
need spiritual power independent
of f. 4015
No natural f. are high, low, holy,
unholy 4016
not responsible for my f. 3049
not what God cares about 4777
only a thing that happens to you
3051
Photography records f. on human
face 2016
precious thing God finds in us
10666
responsible for what I do with f.
3049
salvation apart from f. 4015
Sensitivity, tuning in to f. 8325
value is extent inspired by God
7366
We live in f, not figures 1056
When f. conceited, selfish,
cowardly, ask to have altered
4013
When f. humble, loving, brave,
give thanks 4013

FEELS
closer to God, more one f. a sinner
10439
generous heart f. others' ill 3063
God f. delight, frustration, anger
4491
He most lives who f. noblest 1056
how little one f. poverty when one
loves 7199
Love f. no burden 7220
no longer have to wonder how
God f. 4489
None f. true love of God till 4773
See how it f. to be in control 4419
See how it f. to have a name 4419
See how it f. to have power 4419

souls f. as though it had wings
9608
thanks God whether f. like it or
not 3638
to know someone who thinks, f.
with us 4280
To one who f, life is tragedy 607

FEES
Experience good school but high f.
3521

FEET
And felt the swiftly passing f. of
men 11330
And palms before my f. 2980
Better f. slip than tongue 11408
Bible has f. 712
Christianity, f. going God's way
1174
Conscience, credit that belongs to
cold f. 1665
difficult to stand on pedestal,
wash f. of those below 8717
firm based on granite 7448
flowers at your f. 829
futile to get mad for size of f.
3049
God a lantern to my f. 5394
He has no f. but our f. 10122
Home f. may leave, not hearts
5833
If swept off f, time to get on knees
8836
in his hands and f. the cruel scars
9798
Keep thou my f. 5429
2551
Let me be hands and f. 10130
love has f. to hasten to poor, needy
7335
met a man who had no f. 387
nearer than hands and f. 4862
no matter how good eyes, f. 2565
people hear jazz through f. 7898
Satan looks up between his f.
9940
sell blind horse, praise f. 2466
sleeps at God's f. 4847
stop long enough to let f. catch up
with mouth 9331
there are f. to be washed 10165
Though my f. are set in silent ways
6917
When heart right, f. swift 10213
When the will is ready, f. light
7870
Whichever way God turns my f, I
go 5416
why have I got hands and f.
12037

FELIX
walked fence like cat 786

FELL
The angels f. 5694

FELLOW
all f. passengers on same planet
9678

FELLOW BEINGS

cannot love f. creature till you
love God 7351
Evangelism affects the other f.
9739

FELLOW BEINGS

who do not love f. live unfruitful
lives 7321

FELLOWMAN

no greater opportunity to
influence f. for Christ 6278

FELLOWMEN

God allows man to cut throat of
his f. 4673
If going to live for service of f.
10159
if motive is love for f. 10159
ignoring needs of f. 8818
imbue men with love of f. 6796
love f. sincerely 559
Man should perform duties to f.
as to God 9669
to my f, a heart of love 5626
to obtain possible, man turns to f.
7490
when God sees men rising up
against f. 4895
will meet with ingratitude from
your f. 10159

FELLOWS

God's country begins where men
serve their f. 4913

FELLOWSHIP

birth of new f. 1513
Confession necessary for f. 1595
Confession restores f. 1597
environment in which maturity of
f. achieved 4721
Human f. can go to great lengths
4023
limited to ranks of perdictable
personalities 4025
of the broken 1513
one great f. of love 911
only basis is to live out in open
4026
sin f. with the devil 10360
solitude without f. abyss of despair
10547
stupid that f. limited to acceptable
attire 4025
until satisfied with f. with God
4311
What happens when God grants
gift of f. 4029
with God can go to all lengths
4023
with self-denying, suffering Savior
7698
without solitude void of words,
feelings 10547
Worship f. with God 12139

FELT

chains of habit too weak to be f.
5500
God's presence on moon more
than on earth 11630
Lust f. even by fleas and lice 7355

Where love reigns, joy of heaven f.
7342

FEMALE

almost worshiping the f. bosom
10238
Male and f. not contenders for
supremacy 3239
Small-folded in a warm dim f.
space 6142

FENCE

Build a little f. of trust 11362
Don't f. smile in 5504
Hit the ball over the f. 3467
than friends by being on f. 1913

FEROCIOUS

Don't be f. with yourself 9923
no wild beast so f. as Christians
11212

FERTILE

humility the quiet valley, f. and
abounding in life 6026
seeking f. regions where toil lighter
4974

FERTILITY

in the soil, life in the seeds 8002

FERTILIZE

Tears showers that f. world 10625

FERTILIZED

earth can produce nothing unless
f. by sun 5207

FERVENT

Love is f. beyond measure 7283

FERVENTLY

pray 576

FESTER

Lilies that f. smell worse than
weeds 5039
where troubles f. 3019

FESTIVAL

how or low at f. of God 3235

FESTUS

found Paul irritating as festering
sore 786

FEVER

The weariness, the f, and the fret
7044
until the f. of life is over 9105

FEW

A f. conquer by fighting 11781
A f. individuals can stand isolation
6199
A f. people think, many think they
think 8476
be intimate with f. 4218
call does not come to a chosen f.
7784
delights equal one whom we trust
4184
desire things that make for peace
8428
disciples allowed to appear
sensible 11791
Each day so short, so f. 7219

finishes but f. 57
Give f. men thy voice 1843
have spiritual resources to be both
wealthy and godly 11806
How many people stop because f.
say Go 3135
let those f. be well tried 4218
little years we spend on earth only
first scene 6106
Lord's Prayer expressed in a f.
words 7156
manage to combine simplicity,
complexity 7383
Many see, f. understand 8501
many services but f. conversions
9017
Many want consolation, f. desire
adversity 9268
marvel that Christ performed so f.
miracles 6503
men are worthy of experience
3534
men know how to praise 7586
Men of f. words are best 1860
men so obstinate in atheism 479
minds wear out, more rust out
7756
miserable to have f. things to
desire, many to fear 11827
much machinery but f. results
9017
neighborliness important on
frontier because so f. 8068
observations and much reasoning
leads to error 9410
of us go way the Son of God went
10165
people know how to be old 8130
people wish to be led 10160
proverb much matter decocted
into f. words 9377
so well-controlled f. waves of glory
3184
some f. books to be chewed,
digested 859
Spirit-filled life no mystery
revealed to select f. 5803
strain muscles to carry off a prize
7018
Strength the lot of a f. privileged
men 8557
Tennis one of f. pastimes where
love means nothing 7297
things impossible to diligence, skill
8538
Truth game of the f. 11571
Truth is heavy, f. men carry it
11565
truth where f. are willing to search
3259
very f. can think good thoughts
11272
very f. original thinkers in world
11254
very f. say all they mean 11990
want kingdom of God first 4731
want to pay price of achievement
4731
want to put God first 4731

who bear his cross 9268
will join Jesus in fasting 9268
words will do 4302

FEWER
the words, the better the prayer
8978

FEWNESS
riches in f. of my wants 11839

FIBRE
and the f. of your soul 2964

FICKLE
Fame is a f. food 3851
Love is not f. 7246
multitude is a f. master 10517
O fortune. All men call thee f.
11842
popularity is f. 6455

FICTION
creation of human mind,
congenial to it 11574
critics claim Bible f. 679
Nothing in f. so fantastic as
Incarnation 6125
People know f. makebelieve
12156
Truth must necessarily be stranger
than f. 11574

FIDDLE
existence of f. presupposes music
4606
older the f, sweeter the tune 8173
what lives in hope dances without
a f. 5909

FIDDLES
devil leads downard, f. all the way
2697

FIDDLING
quit f. around fringes of
Christianity 9691

FIELD
a f. rested gives beautiful crop
6839
a little f. well tilled 5814
And in the f. of destiny 3289
as much dignity in tilling f. as
writing poem 2762
Be first in f. last to couch 2769
dignity in tilling f. as writing poem
3240
He paints the lily of the f. 4761
lilies of the f. whose bloom is brief
2380
Love plays the f. 7274
Make of our hearts a f. 8730
rested gives bountiful crop 9686

FIELDS
blue f. of the sky 11638
We plough the f. and scatter 4625

FIEND
Like a f. hid in a cloud 808
Temptation f. at my elbow 11090

FIEND-LIKE
sin, f. it is to dwell therein 10334

FIENDS
either make us f. or saints 4957

FIER
hide de f, what do wid smoke
2482

FIERCE
One far f. hour, and sweet 2980

FIERCELY
human stories repeating as f. as if
had never happened before
5984

FIERCENESS
hate sin with f. that burns 3182

FIERCER
Devil now f. by despair 2643

FIERCEST
Devil, f. spirit that fought in
heaven 2643
iron most strongly united by f.
flame 4273
Music the f. grief can charm 7911

FIERY
let miraculous answer from f.
furnace answer 5197
Like a f. furnace red 2638
with a flick of her f. tail 9870

FIFTEEN
years teaching child to be quiet
8336

FIFTY
youth of old age 307

FIG
If f. tree grow in mountain cliff
3736

FIGHT
And makes us stand in every f.
1933
dandelions all weekend 239
decide all means permitted to f.
evil 5012
Don't f. fact, deal with it 3576
end that crowns, not the f. 543
Extreme fear can neither f. nor fly
3963
failed to f. for right, justice,
goodness 1689
Faint not, f. on 6256
for planet not vague matter of
future 3400
God loves those who don't give in
without f. 2959
God's creatures f. against wicked
3996
gospel cannot f. without prayer
9015
hardest battle human being can f.
6215
I f. with God 4855
I'll f. to the very end 3342
if not prepared to f. in spiritual
realm 8818
Jesus invited us to a f. 1210
Life is a hard f. 6947
live with hostility, learn to f. 1114

man's f. with himself worth
something 1063
must discipline ourselves to f.
deviation from course 9965
must f. against wrong, injustice,
evil 1689
of cosmic proportions for our
planet has started 3400
Only through inner trans-
formation we gain strength to f.
evils of world 6619
so long will I f. against unbelief,
despair 2590
the devil with own weapons,
overmatch 2647
'Tis man's to f. 10775
to f. and not to heed the wounds
9113
to f. without hatred 11775
To live is to f, suffer, love 7066
to the f. with temptation I owe my
force 11075
triumphant Christian does not f.
for victory 11672
We gird us for the coming f.
10756
when f. begins within himself
9940
while children go hungry, I'll f.
3342
while lost girl on streets, I'll f.
3342
while men go to prison, I'll f.
3342
while one dark soul without God,
I'll f. 3342
While some weep, I'll f. 3342
while there is a drunkard left, I'll f.
3342
who f. battles on their knees 8865
with your own sin 10304
You've been a coward in the f.
3174
Youth who must f. and die 11757

FIGHTER
best f. never angry 11784

FIGHTING
A few conquer by f. 11781
abortion by adoption 23
cannot overcome without f. 1633
Everyone you meet f. hard battle
6635
Gossip worse than f. 5134
Rather than f. become still, wait
2556

FIGHTS
Christ in you that f. the battle
6381
God himself f. for soul 2734
nature f. against venturing forth
9930
Vainly strives, and f, and frets
7440

FIGURES
God's f. written by finger of
sunlight 4454
We live in feelings, not f. 1056

FILE
owe more to the f. than anything
else 10855

FILL
as though God unwilling to f. us
4785
beg Holy Spirit to f. us while
preventing him by our doubts
8843
can f. tiny span of life with
meaning 7080
Could we with ink the ocean f.
4748
do you f. all things with whole
being 4854
Even God cannot f. what is full
10708
lives with sweetness 4223
Love can f. duty with life 7165
me with life anew 5774
praying for God to f. him when
full already with something else
5783
the little space I f. 7084
4905
To find his place and f. it 10821
us afresh with hope 5939
well storehouse of soul's delight
11375

FILLED
As purse is emptied, heart f. 4351
Heart f. to brim with joy must be
still 6559
if not f. living beneath our
privileges 5778
must free ourselves to be f. by God
10708
never known person f. with Holy
Spirit who bragged about it
6018
the night shall be f. with music
7887
vessel that grows as f. will never
be full 10699

FILLING
God is within, f. 4848
Instead of f. vacuum, money
makes one 7814
the world he lies in a manger 6122

FILLS
God f. 4709
God f. his work 4860
God f. me to the brim 4852
Who f. world's unempty'd
granaries 11138

FILM
waiting for the church to find
room for f. 1998

FILTHY
Everything f. who has f. hands
3352
How marvelous that I, a f. clod
8814

FINAL
death the f. awakening 2273

God does not promise f. victory in
this life 5385
Grace the f. word 5221
Jesus' coming f. unanswerable
proof God cares 6136
O God, hear these my f. words
9091
of universe, God is f. end 4514
Salvation is f. 9817
soul where man's f. battles are
fought 10672
truth belongs to heaven, not world
8596

FINANCIAL
Is church ready to deal with f.
immorality 10086

FIND
a pass though 2633
All f. time to do what we want to
do 11348
All we want in Christ, we shall f.
in Christ 6354
always f. God present 4845
atheist cannot f. God 472
attempting to f. new ways of
bettering things 9311
Bible difficult 749
Bible, all I want, there I f. 716
can f. no answer, will f. fear 4008
can f. some needful job crying to
be done 10201
can only help him f. it himself
11010
can seek and f. God 4509
cannot f. God unless God reveals
himself 4910
cannot f. time for recreation, f.
time for illness 6835
Christ loses us until we f. him
10839
deal only with surface f. Christ an
offense 6422
do not f. time for exercise will f.
time for illness 9535
do not need to go somewhere to f.
God 4870
do not want to agonize to f. your
will 8820
Everywhere I f. the signature of
God 11629
Fall on the seeming void, and f.
3767
Faultfinder will f. faults even in
Paradise 6903
Finding God is letting God f. us
7455
first duty of soul is to f. its Master
4144
flower upon inmost side 6583
Follow the river, f. the sea 5382
freedom when we f. God 4153
God in problems already solved
7562
God in what we know 7562
God's reply to problem 5441
greatest wonder to f. myself in
heaven 5655

have to f. eagles one at a time
6789
he killed it only to f. nothing 5328
heart willing will f. thousand ways
7871
heaven, f. completion of all desires
5644
hunts for flowers will f. flowers
5140
I do not f. God hard to live with
4478
if cannot f. creates means 2624
If cannot f. God in house 4856
If we want little, shall f. little 6354
If we want much, shall f. much
6354
If you f. yourself so loaded 4319
if you pursue happiness you will
never f. it 5558
impossible to f. God through
intellectual processes alone
6328
in and with God all loves 7334
loves weeds may f. weeds 5140
Man can only f. meaning outside
himself 3484
Man cannot f. true essential joy
6552
man returns home to f. what he
needs 5815
man trying to f. something which
will make him happy 5570
me the men on earth who care
4118
Most of us f. what we search for
5077
must not f. our own way 5446
No one can f. a full life 11613
not forced to take wings to f. God
4924
Not till we have lost world do we
f. ourselves 10549
nothing lowly in the universe
11651
On every side I f. thy hand 4876
one self-denying deed 107
only way can f. ourselves is in
sorrow 10643
paid high price to f. that evil is evil
3416
people who need you 2558
rationalism tries to f. God in world
4495
Seek for happiness, you will never
f. it 5551
take things as we f. them 38
thief cannot f. policeman 472
Those who wish to sing always f.
a song 5264
To f. a friend close one eye 4161
To f. God greatest human
achievement 7542
To f. his place and fill it 10821
To f. point where hypothesis, fact
meet 7435
To f. that better way 9067
virtue difficult to f. 11725
wakes to f. God there 4847
way to fundamental joy 10915

we f. security in iron bars, solid walls 6825

we sip reluctantly at truth we f. harsh 6870

What we love to do we f. time to do 9277

When you f. a hurt and heal it, you f. a need and fill it 10216

world quite intolerable 5535

FINDEST
thou f, yet didst never lose 4954

FINDING
displeased at f. perfections 3945

following, keeping, struggling 6892

God is letting God find us 7455

God, no need to seek peace 8433

has hard time f. enemies 4216

If pleased at f. faults 3945

our plumb line cannot sound its depth 4745

self comes through losing self 2519

some talk about f. God—as if he could get lost 7518

something great enough to die for 8897

something to live for 8897

spur you into f. something to live for 7140

Success in marriage more than f. right person 7652

FINDS
Almighty f. a way of letting me know 5410

always f. time to attend his funeral 5589

And whom he f. young, keeps young still 7264

fight devil with own weapons, f. him overmatch 2647

if longing heart f. living water will be alone 10536

Man f. God through truth 11518

man in earnest f. means 2624

man who f. truth lights torch 11536

Mistrust the man who f. everything good 3555

Satan f. mischief for idle hands to do 6772

the most precious things God f. in us 10666

theology f. the truth 11524

thought great by what it f. 11242

till life f. pull of Christ's love 6937

who f. gospel attractive 5108

who f. peace in his home 5827

FINESSE
fine art of deception we call f. 2483

FINEST
cheating done under guise of honesty 5888

FINGER
blotted f. makes bigger blot 2906

Don't point f. 3131

God's f. touched him, he slept 2289

History story written by f. of God 5712

I stick my f. into existence 3485

least pain in our little f. 10035

like man who uses only little f. 8659

of God never leaves identical fingerprints 4497

of God never leaves same fingerprint 6211

of God on a man's shoulder 7314

of scorn at another 1769

Revival is God's f. pointed right at me 9748

see f. of God in weather 4961

FINGERNAILS
country needs dirtier f, cleaner minds 7775

grow with inconvenient speed 279

grow, except the broken one 279

FINGERPRINT
finger of God never leaves same f. 6211

FINGERPRINTS
finger of God never leaves identical f. 4497

FINGERS
Are f. of your hand alike 6166

God's f. mold loveliness 537

God's figures written by f. of sunlight 4454

have not measured f. with God 4337

life flowing like water through f. 8381

Never burn f. to snuff another man's candle 10458

of God touch your life when 4202

pointing f, rarely hold out hands 2073

three f. of scorn at your own self 1769

Time slides through f. 11343

wandered idly over the noisy keys 7919

FINISH
every day and be done with it 8375

no better way to f. spiritual life 10705

strive on to f. work we are in 5199

FINISHED
God isn't f. with me yet 8417

Of thy creation, f, yet renewed 1966

That's a lie 945

FINISHES
begins many, f. few 57

FINITE
All our f. eyes could tell us 2217

although f. minds cannot solve it 6277

can never comprehend infinite 4690

cannot be reasoned out by f. mind 5450

Out of the f. darkness 2360

passes capacity of f. mind 4989

Prayer link between f. man, infinite God 8944

truly known as no f. men can know us 4768

understanding f. 11606

FIRE
angels, flames of f. 359

burns gold pure and clean 294

burnt child dreads f. 3512

Cast in the f. the perished thing 7003

child says nothing but heard by f. 3885

Christ, message a f. that set society ablaze 6375

Church-goers like coals in f. 1388

Education lighting of a f. 3002

Faith quenches f. of every pain 3661

Fanaticism false f. of overheated mind 3909

foolish to punish neighbor by f. when live next door 9718

gives gold a shining color 294

Gossips set on f. all houses they enter 5137

Hatred is like f, makes light rubbish deadly 5597

have too many irons in the f. 9552

he who sets f. to the suns 4951

hide de fier, what do wid smoke 2482

Holiness a f. whose warmth pervades universe 5741

I sit beside my lonely f. 8827

Ill words bellows to slackening f. 5145

in f. on the midnight darkness 4712

in the f. feel God's heart warming 4858

is self-evident 5806

let lightning write his name in f. 4712

let us warm ourselves 43

Lighthouses don't f. canon 6022

Love is spiritual f. 7224

Love is the f. of life 7248

Love like a friendship caught on f. 7236

love of God, consuming f. himself 4792

Love perfected in f. of God 3182

Man is f, woman tow 10226

martyrs, coronation robes glittering with f. 10882

must pass through the f. 7687

of suffering will bring gold of godliness 10864

owe more to f. and hammer than anything else 10855

passions are like f. 10234

put out a f. with oil 335

quenched by water 372

revival like prairie f. 9752

sets my house on f. to roast his eggs 10057

shall kindle f, light up entire city 5751

spark will set whole city on f. 10445

Straw should make no pact with f. 11085

Suffering a cleansing f. 10892

the f. is the love of God 7553

the house is on f. 43

Thy love is like a burning f. 4795

We know God as men born blind know f. 4690

when the f. of God's presence moved 10124

Where there's smoke there's f. 11118

FIRED

Life f. at us point blank 11388

FIREFLY

life, the flash of a f. in the night 2457

FIRES

Bible has passed through f. 646

forced to test beliefs in f. 612

If world is cold, build f. 4250

through f. to batter into shape 4570

FIRESIDE

Duty done is soul's f. 9653

FIRM

as a fortress to defend the right 1933

Feet f. based on granite 7448

need gentle dogmatism that smiles while f. on Word of God 11188

Three f. friends 4209

FIRMAMENT

cannot compare to your exalted dignity as human being 7370

FIRMER

If only I may grow f. 7688

FIRMEST

friendships formed in adversity 4273

FIRMLY

have courage to believe f. 4747

Hold me so f. I cannot fall 7478

Nothing so f. believed as least known 6082

FIRMNESS

hope I shall always possess f, virtue enough 5881

Psalms, f. of man's confidence 798

with f. in the right 5199

FIRST

Among f. things created 7886

be f. to give friendship sign 9479

Be not f. by whom new are tried 958

Begin where we will, God there f. 4835

By his f. work God gave me to myself 4528

Christ f. and also last 6475

Christ served others f. 6433

Christ, by f. work gave me to myself 6361

civilization founded by Cain 10513

Discontent f. step in progress 2864

duty of love is to listen 7301

duty of soul is to find its Master 4144

failed miserably often f. to see God's formula 3628

Falsehood is always f. 6865

family, f. and essential cell of human society 3890

family, f. authority under which person lives 3888

family, f. community to which person attached 3888

few want to put God f. 4731

Forgetting oneself f. condition of love 7169

God f. 9264

God f. in sequential order 4607

God f. put urge within us 4573

God is always there f. 7461

good should show itself f. in own household 5838

half of our lives ruined by parents 3892

hundred years the hardest 6992

If at f. you don't succeed 8558 3597

In f. experience of sanctification 9840

in field, last to couch 2769

In Lord's Prayer f. petition for bread 7152

Integrity f. step to greatness 6311

Jesus proclaims f. will be last 6447

keep peace within yourself 8434

last of life, for which the f. was made 8132

Lay f. foundation of humility 6788

Let child's f. lesson be obedience 8307

Lord doesn't want f. place in my life 9561

love-energy f. to God, then to other people 10053

must f. be made good before we can do good 5087

must f. be made just 5087

nod, smile, speak, forgive f. 9479

not laughed at that laughs at himself f. 6000

only f. step that is difficult 2749

part of life parents learn to stand you 3893

requisite for immortality is death 6107

second Adam is greater than f. Adam 5031

Self-knowledge is f. condition of repentance 9599

shall be last 10182

silly question f. intimation of new development 6703

stages of spiritual life 1714

step in wisdom is to question everything 11935

step is hardest 545

step of wisdom is to know what is false 11943

step to victory is to recognize enemy 11670

string musician touches is bass 10663

temptation was promise of learning and knowledge 6701

test of truly great man 6032

thing God's eye nam'd not good 7136

thing in morning she sharpens tongue 5125

thing Jesus promises is suffering 10901

thing that goes when you begin to think is your theology 11240

think f. about foundations of humility 5997

time life made sense 7011

when men f. saw their God 6154

When we seek f. kingdom of God 4735

without f. persevering through pain, heartache, failure 6802

women last at the cross, f. at the altar 11980

work after new birth 4537

world owes you nothing, it was here f. 9652

worship God 12097

years we spend on earth f. scene in divine drama 6106

FIRSTHAND

either know God f. or do not know him 7460

FIRST-RATE

mind only happy when thinking 11248

FIRST-TASTING

bitter earth 6142

FISH

And I like a little f. in thy great waters 7492

and visitors smell in three days 5956

Angler caught f. so big 3424

Give a man a f, he eats for a day 11001

Govern family as cook f. 3868

Have we flesh or have we f. 5860

Jonah down in mouth when f. swallowed 774

maybe f. goes home and lies 3426

Teach a man to f, eats for rest of life 11001

Works without faith like f. without water 3826

FISHERMAN'S
Tyre rock for f. nets 730

FISHERMEN
the whole church of God 1381

FISHES
Love is like five loaves, two f. 7238
with your five loaves and two f. 10205

FIST
a weed bouquet in chubby f. 1102
God lets rebellious shake their f. 4129
infant is born with clenched f. 11656
more power in open hand than clenched f. 8720

FISTS
how many clenched f. in marketplace 10507

FIT
alcoholic never f. as a fiddle 324
aren't f. to clean those boots 1455
God can f. heroes into their places 9174
God can make pieces of world's puzzle f. 4735
God in wherever able to help us 5467
it for the sky 10114
must be f. for work 12011 3101
No image but image of God can f. soul 10659
responsibility to keep f. to manifest Jesus 1014
when God does not see f. to grant us sunlight 5393

FITNESS
ideal child would find no f. in world 8293

FITS
a lie is the handle that f. them all 6857
Every shoe f. not every foot 6174
relationship to God f. you to live 4555
shoe that f. one person pinches another 6214
what f. soul for Christ 10676

FITTED
for us and our spiritual state 4578
God cannot be f. into a diagram 4851
more grief better f. to appreciate joy 5357

FITTEST
How, if to be f, can thoughts remain the same 981
lives holiest life f. far to die 2427

FITTING
God is f. to be worthy of him 4514

FIVE
asks a question is fool for f. minutes 6683
Faith reaches beyond our f. senses 3690
great enemies to peace 8435
If child learns before he's f. 8296
minutes thinking about God 7491
things observe with care 1855
words cost Zacharias silence 11412

FIX
thought more on the God you desire 10305

FIXED
Devotion is something f. 9731
The f. pains of hell 4813
To one f. trust my spirit clings 4642
what is from God f. as nail in sure place 4524
who f. their eyes on reality judged insane 5730

FIZZLE
chances are prayer activity will f. out 7725

FLAME
And in he came with eyes of f. 2638
Be thou a bright f. before me 5375
Christ passed through world like f. 867
Fame, like f. harmless until start inhaling 3853
In the beginning love a f. 7236
iron most strongly united by fiercest f. 4273
jealousy extinguishes love as ashes smother f. 6347
love a f. still only light, flickering 7236
love as a lively f. 7283
spirit an inward f. 10696
stars f. out in pomp of light 7927
To my God, a heart of f. 5626
who shall put out the f. 389
will not corrode or blacken gold 294

FLAME-FLOWERED
June 9886

FLAMING
Midst f. worlds 4719

FLAP
Jest with ass, will f. in face with tail 9477

FLARES
greed f. up when desires frustrated 10003

FLASH
And vivid lightings f. from pole to pole 4827
before I can say like a lightning f. 7070
Goodness does not f. 5067

Life, the f. of a firefly in the night 2457

FLASHED
every stone f. like a ruby 6423
long ere light f. through sky 4769

FLASHEDST
Thou f, shonest, dispel my blindness 4805

FLASHLIGHT
sort of believers look right through you 1313

FLAT
How f. seem all uses of this world 2603
where goodness is f, boring 3347

FLATLANDS
fear figures you will settle for existence on f. 3971

FLATTER
contented need not f. 1798
Many men know how to f. 7586
Men seldom f. without purpose 4051
own virtue by criticizing sinful 5029

FLATTER'D
have not f. its rank breath 12033

FLATTERED
himself on being a man without prejudices 9181

FLATTERER
doesn't value himself or others 4045
most dangerous of tame beasts, a f. 10472
sweet as salt in your mouth 4050
tells you your opinion, not his own 4046

FLATTERERS
look like friends 4047
meet, devil goes to dinner 4054
solitude hath no f. 10530

FLATTERS
swallow any lie that f. us 6870

FLATTERY
As long as matters hopeful, hope is mere f. 5903
comes from the teeth out 441
corrupts receiver, giver 4048
difference between appreciation and f. 441
greater a man more distasteful f. is to him 5296
Imitation sincerest form of f. 2006
is insincere 441
is poison 4053
is selfish 441
is universally condemned 441
its poison intoxicates 4053
mouth that praises, hand that kills 4049
they who listen to such music 4051

FLAVORS
church, like salt, f. 1427

FLAWLESS
don't have to be f. to be blessed 5442

FLAX
Get spindle ready, God will send f. 9346
God gives f. to spin 3092

FLEA
to f. human being something good to eat 9219

FLEABITES
anger mere f. in comparison with pride 9240

FLEAS
if f. are f. because they flee 6185
lies with dogs, rises with f. 11063
Lust felt even by f. and lice 7355
nothing in haste except catching f. 5583

FLED
As the evil spirit f. from Saul 7935
He f. from the rain 4062
present f. ere we could touch it 11389
Suffering was curse from which man f. 10896

FLEE
devil will f. if we resist 2678
for a little while thy occupations 7708
helpers fail, comforts f. 2538
into sanctuary of private virtuousness 11690
into the silence of solitude 2591
must f. cross or die upon it 2117
temptation, don't leave address 11055
the wicked, even when they are charming 11882
When you from Sodom f. 9828
wicked f. when no man pursueth 11892

FLEETER
If any care may make a friend's the f. 910

FLEETING
as the mystical experience is 7948
brief f. instant of time allotted 7063
Nothing more f. than years 11354

FLESH
and blood so cheap 8682
And laid his f. to rest 2296
Christ did not only come into our f. 6121
Christ release from servitude of the f. 6434
Christianity balanced between f, spirit 1240
free rein to the f. 466
God clothed himself in vile man's f. 6126
Have we f, or have we fish 5860

If knocked out, get up 1024
impossible in the f. to be like Christ 8113
in lowly raiments of human f. 6371
is the self-life 9926
love, two souls and one f. 4298
my f. is a prison 3482
No man free who is slave to f. 4138
one day in Spirit worth more than thousand in f. 5787
Part of his body, I transcend this f. 4125
saved to manifest Son of God in f. 1014
sins of f. least bad of all sins 10400
unperfected human nature 9926
until Deity square-knotted f. 6131
very much alive 9861
what we are when left to our devices 9926

FLESHLY
life filled with f. struggles 1276

FLEW
life f. like skylark in sky 12176

FLEXIBLE
stay f. 5391

FLEXING
Christians ought to be f. muscles 3339

FLICK
with a f. of her fiery tail 9870

FLICKERING
love a flame, still only light, f. 7236
Original sin malice ever f. within 10347

FLIES
A lover f. 7283
accusation f. faster than defense 10453
another catches f. 6205
bothered most by f. 11056
easier to catch f. with honey than vinegar 6643
I am a great enemy to f. 2649
If f. are f. because they fly 6185
keep mouth shut, f. won't get in 1854
No wonder time f. 11310
On the wings of time, grief f. away 5350
Sadness f. away on wings of time 10609 ·
slander f. as well as creeps 10456
Why didn't Noah swat those two f. 785
wolves more dangerous than f. 11056

FLIGHT
And in my f. 7475
extreme attitude a f. from the self 9924
Life's shadow of bird in f. 6993

Prayer is not f. 8927
Time has no f. 11330
Unmeasured by the f. of years 5633

FLINGS
dirt upon another 10452
Slander f. stones at itself 10461

FLINT
defeat turns bone to f. 2511

FLIPPER
shaking f. of trained seal 6062

FLOCK
Eagles don't f. 6789

FLOOD
Ark always along with the F. 11432
The f. may bear me far 2368
tossed by storm and f. 4642

FLOODED
worse than f. basement is f. attic 8581

FLOODS
through f, to batter us into shape 4570

FLOOR
Grace refuses to put f. on concern 5233
helpless on a barn-bare f. 6142

FLORIDA
no place like home except F. 2877

FLOUR
Back of the loaf is the snowy f. 9345
man without God like cake without f, milk 7446
no getting white f. out of coal sack 2475

FLOURISH
Weeds always f. 3417

FLOURISHES
Error f. in every soil 3251
Evil f. more in shadows than day 3381
Friendship f. at fountain of forgiveness 4229
reason sin f. 10345
Virtue f. in misfortune 226

FLOW
as water willing to f. into emptied channel 4785
blood to f. like rivers throughout globe 4895
Errors, like straw, upon surface f. 3255
God with his Godhead f. 9951
Let tears f. of their own accord 5346
Love if not reciprocated will f. back 7241
no days when God's fountain does not f. 4647
oil must from you, Jesus, f. 3323
out of us will f. rivers that will bless 6232

restore the f. of the Holy Spirit 10369

FLOWER
And so it criticized each f. 2052
find f. upon inmost side 6583
Forgiveness fragrance f. leaves 4080
God paints the wayside f. 4596
handsomest f. not sweetest 2472
Happiness shared is the f. 5514
If cannot find God in opening f. 4856
impress of its Maker 3192
In f. death sets free the perfume 2261
Life the f. of which love is the honey 7205
love, the perfect f. 3837
man is but a f. 6991
of Easter blossomed 2984
of sweetest smell is shy, lowly 6028
Self-esteem a fragile f. 9994
this same f. that smiles today 8214
waiting to come up f. in Gardener's time 5672

FLOWERING
Death f. of life 2257
Love produces f. of the personality 7268
of person is movement from incompleteness 7699

FLOWERS
And all the f. looked up at him 6470
And f. to wither at northwind's breath 2324
April showers bring May f. 9884
are heaven's masterpieces 8003
As if f. no longer grew in fields 8602
at your feet 829
blossom under praise like f. in sun 3144
children like f. in bouquet 1113
cynic smells f, looks for coffin 2177
God held my life and your life like f. in his hand 6895
God scatters countless f. around us 7993
God sees sweet f. growing 8673
have expression of countenance 8004
He who hunts for f. will find f. 5140
If he so loves the little f. 4761
Infinite written name on earth in tender f. 4705
love brings to harvest loveliest f. of the soul 7339
nice to get f. still smell fragrance 3137
on earth sowed his name in tender f. 8037
others plain, honest, upright 8004
road to glory not strewn with f. 4418

some smile, sad, pensive, diffident 8004
Spring season that says it with f. 9890
Spring unlocks the f. 9895
Stars f. of the sky 11640
stop and smell the f. 9530
Trees, f, grass grow in silence 10250
What sunshine is to f. 6745
While grass, f, stars spell out his name 8019
Wild f. on distant hills 8498

FLOWETH
That God, the whole ocean, f. into me 7469

FLOWING
can be bag of grapes, f. into one another's lives 9524
God, a fountain always f. 4698
life f. like water through fingers 8381
Love, forever f. free 6409
tears f. not inconsistent with peace, harmony 5346

FLOWN
The years have f. 179

FLOWS
Fountain of good, all blessing f. 7456
God's compassion f. out of his goodness 4724
In f. heaven, with its new day 5636
joy of God f. through people who influence us 6239
When life f. along like a song 10493

FLUCTUATING
joy not tied to f. experiences 6568
quicksand of f. experiences 3550

FLUSH
laugh out loud, helps f. out nervous system 6724

FLUTES
words breathe memories sweet as f. 11998

FLY
big difference to f. which side he chooses 8076
discipline sets me free to f. 9975
Do not remove f. with hatchet 2058
Envy like f. that dwells on sores 3213
Events creep or f. as God pleases 4820
Extreme fear can neither fight nor f. 3963
God gives birds food, but they must f. 3093
If God doesn't approve, f. doesn't move 4943
Life like f. in room with boys armed with swatter 6968
must lose f. to catch trout 4343

neglect God for noise of a f. 7712
Rabbits don't f. 6168
Riches f. away 6455
Swift f. the years, and rise th' expected morn 6143
tiny f. can choke a big man 8701
When rattling bones together f. 6598
with the eagles 4226
Yet 'tis thy voice, My God, that bids them f. 4827

FLYING
and resting, parts of contentment 471
Rigidity criticizes future for not f. 6818
rumors gather'd as they roll'd 9757

FLYS
Grief f. to death 2363

FOCUS
as we begin to f. on God 8488
on larger-than-life goals 9970
orgasm has replaced cross as f. of longing 10233
reflection of God badly out of f. 4579
revival to f. people upon Divine Leader 9751

FOCUSED
No life grows great until f. 2852
When laughing, attention f. 6746

FOCUSING
on evil you can lose your bearings 5037

FODDER'S
in the shock 9880

FOE
fear no f. with thee at hand to bless 7474
I would be friend of f, friendless 1018
Luxury more deadly than any f. 7362
Myself, my deadliest f. 2583
Strenuousness open f. of attainment 10757
Tho' pressed by every f. 3768
to God ne'er true friend to man 4164

FOES
If you have none 3174
Must have made some f. 3174
valleys filled with f. 2359

FOG
faith develops best when f. rolls in 3789
mist in pulpit, f. in pew 9123
one day nearer the dawning when f. will lift 5676
through all centuries of fearful f. 3974
try to understand Christ's teaching with heads, get into f. 6515

FOIBLES
unless allowances for friend's f. 4294

FOLK
Give me simple laboring f. 11686
We are all dangerous f. 4956

FOLKS
hand f. over to God's mercy 4105
never understand f. they hate 5593
we know briefly, quickly forget 4281

FOLLIES
History little more than f. of mankind 5719

FOLLOW
A silent child, I f. on 4977
actions determined by impulse to f. leader 6199
dangerous to take one impulse to f. 7836
Do not f. where path may lead 6787
Don't lead me, I may not f. 4224
every rainbow 4421
faith precedes understanding, does not f. 3743
good or evil path 1137
impossible for us to f. God naturally 9801
Intelligence must f. faith 6327
me, I am the way, truth, life 6382
must f, as night the day 6318
need not fear disaster will f. freedom of thought 4134
never cost disciple to f. Jesus 2823
Never f. crowd if you want crowd to f. you 6801
Reason ought to f, not precede, faith 9411
Scholarship should f. faith 3022
so long as we f. his leading 5397
the river, find the sea 5382
thee more nearly 9043
time when we must choose course to f. 2491
To f. one aim 10822
To the living: F. me 6497
when take initiative, cease to f. 5446

FOLLOWED
Every spiritual movement f. by missionary movement 9740
I f. him, new life began 1147

FOLLOWERS
if f. of God, cannot take initiative 5446
Jesus promised f. "The Strengthener" would be with them 5804

FOLLOWING
Christ is hard, rugged life 1282
Finding, f, keeping, struggling 6892

FOLLOWS
After one vice, greater f. 10293

error f. false light 3258
riches grow, care f. 11799

FOLLY
before which ambition is f. 6494
Bible without a particle of f. 710
Give me the vain lust, and the f. 4530
nought to do but mark and tell your neighbors' faults and f. 10038
Wisdom, but f. 4877

FOND
None so f. of secrets as those who do not keep them 5150
Some people f. of ill-luck 11449
too f. of our own will 9679
too f. of sinning to enjoy Christianity 10417
Why are we so f. of life 7089

FOOD
afraid we would not have f. for ourselves 10540
Christ rarely gave f. 10731
faith finds f. in famine 3703
Fame is a fickle f. 3851
gluttons don't eat on empty stomach 131
God gives every bird its f. 3091
God is the f. our spirits designed to feed on 7459
home is no home unless f. for mind, body 5813
Money brings f, but not appetite 7807
Mother is f. 7853
to take f. in thankfulness gives God glory 12013
What to one man is f. 6220

FOOL
alcohol, make wise man a f. 331
and money soon parted 11792
Any f. can govern with stick in hand 6786
asks a question is f. for five minutes 6683
can f. all people some of the time 2480
can f. some people all the time 2480
cannot f. all people all of the time 2480
does not ask question remains f. forever 6683
faith must be prepared to be f. 3642
has answer on edge of tongue 4067
if thinks he has found wisdom, is a f. 11930
never call him a f. till money gone 11792
no f. to gain what he cannot lose 1195
no f. who gives what he cannot keep 1195
none but f. persist in mistake 3584

Only a f. tests depth of water with both feet 11936
only f. perseveres in error 3260
others think smart aleck a f. 450
people call him a f. who never got anything 7800
refrain from calling someone a f. 6444
Riches serve a wise man, command a f. 7820
says more than the f. when he speaks 11951
sees a man's clothes 11896
silent and be thought a f. 1836
Spirit of God will never make man f. 1064
tears because didn't live thousand years ago 2430
tears because won't be alive thousand years from now 2430
than f. friends 3155
thinks himself wisest, usually greatest f. 11917
though a f. rule, is in slavery 4113
Though the f. waits, the day does not 6780
throws up his interest in both worlds 11843
wanders, wise travels 4058
when you've made a f. of yourself 4213
who cannot reason is a f. 9415
wise man more use from enemies than f. from friends 9444
You f. me once, shame on you 2481
You f. me twice, shame on me 2481

FOOLED
intellect always f. by the heart 6330

FOOLISH
and dead never change opinions 8206
As we get old, more f. and wiser 8127
deny opinion 8205
great man's f. sayings pass for wise ones 5273
if give up trying to pray 9013
Illusion dust devil throws in eyes of f. 2655
Jealousy is f. child of pride 6340
Let me be to the f, mind 10130
man tells woman to stop talking 2889
not denyin' women are f. 3231
sheep makes wolf his confessor 9473
Silence is f. if we are wise 1869
Silence is wise if we are f. 1869
Silence the sequel to f. acts 10266
things of God, wiser 1294
to cling to life 2299
to escape censure do no f. thing 2066
to expect others to keep secret 1618

to live without prayer a f. thing
8833

to punish neighbor by fire when
live next door 9718

to tear one's hair in grief 5345

to think heaven, earth could come
by chance 1979

What is man? A f. baby 7440

FOOLISHLY
great men are f. merciful 6032

human to think wisely, act f. 5973

think we have come to end of the
theme 7056

FOOLISHNESS
not likely to bypass way of f.
11791

when matched beside f. of the
Christian 10512

who understands his f. is wise
11947

FOOL'S
Destiny a f. excuse for failure
2619

FOOLS
better to weep with wise than
laugh with f. 9475

For I also had my hour 2980

Jesus proclaims f. are the wise
6447

Many men know a great deal, are
greater f. for it 11973

none but f. would keep 7019

or perish together as f. 5987
923

Pheasants f. if invite hawk to
dinner 11081

Poems made by f. like me 2017

rush in 4060

smart person isn't smart until get
along with f. 6323

Tomorrow the day when F. act
sensibly 11404

understand better than wise 1216

Wise men change their minds, f.
never 11978

FOOT
Every shoe fits not every f. 6174

handsome shoe often pinches f.
2461

inferior of any man whose rights I
trample under f. 11283

Misfortunes depart on f. 196

on earth is on a banana peel 6915

One f. cannot stand on two boats
6058

one f. in heaven and one f. on
earth 6915

Only baby admired for putting f.
in mouth 5151

Parents afraid to put f. down 8323

Sin is fleet of f. outrunning
everything 10374

slip of f. may be recovered 10444

slip of f. you may recover 11407

than slipper on gouty f. 8442

to hold f. long enough to put
other higher 9316

useless to put best f. forward,
drag other 11601

wrestling with evil, f. to f. 6947

You cannot put same shoe on
every f. 6225

FOOTBALL
players, difference character makes
1019

FOOTNOTES
Human life but a series of f. 6904

FOOTPATH
guideposts on the f. to peace 8472

FOOTPRINTS
man leaves f. when walks through
life 6231

on the sands of time 5288

some you can see, others invisible
6231

two sets of f. in the sand 5437

FOOTSTEPS
Cain who hears only the sound of
his own f. 10573

God hears the f. of an ant 4697

Goodness is love following his f.
5065

The unambiguous f. of God 4482

Unbelief where no divine f. heard
11595

FOR
God cannot be f, against same
thing 4972

FORBEARANCE
better than intolerance 6326

that world may become one
family in f. 9093

FORBID
birth is quicker murder 16

who does not f. sin, encourages it
10310

FORBIDDEN
Adam ate apple because f. 761

by something outside myself to let
my life go 10940

charm about the f. 761

Curiosity kernel of f. fruit 11050

environment comes to be as if
were not 1332

murder is f. 16

propensity to grasp at f. fruit
11112

Sermons culturally f. to talk back
10103

Things f. have secret charm 11104

Worldliness not only doing what is
f. 12054

Worldliness wishing the f. possible
to do 12054

FORCE
bend your f. to break, blow, burn
2840

Christ did not conquer by f. 6389

church f. for good in world of evil
1433

church f. for love in world of
hatred 1433

church, f. for peace in world of
violence 1433

Crises f. us to think 2043

Democracy not sanction of f. 2521

difficulties f. us to break through
superficiality 2738

Every love has its own f. 7167

founded empires upon f. 6351

Great men see spiritual stronger
than material f. 10693

Listening a creative f. 1857

Love the subtlest f. in world 7255

mighty f. behind things we say
12005

Nor will God f. any door to enter
in 4775

of prayer greater than
man-controlled powers 8991

old age equal grace, f, fascination
12188

overcomes but half his foe 527

own gift cummulative f. of life's
cultivation 6226

Patience achieves more than f.
8407

Peace cannot be kept by f. 8452

positive word becomes creative f.
12001

to the fight with temptation I owe
my f. 11075

Warmth stronger than f. 4296

Who overcomes by f. 527

With gentle f. soliciting the darts
9798

youth full of grace, f, fascination
12188

FORCED
against your will 183

Faith like love cannot be f. 3686

God sends time of f. leisure 7056

into position of leadership 6785

Man f. to seek higher authority
7499

not f. to take wings to find God
4924

Safety, peace only after f. to knees
882

tells a lie, f. to invent twenty more
6850

through pain f. to clutch thy hand
9053

to carry the cross 183

to test beliefs in fires 612

world f. to be good, happy 4149

FORCES
behind racism, anti-Christ 1488

combated by mighty, determined,
relentless f. 2630

deluded by supernatural f. 5458

God f. no one 4126

God never f. man 4130

love f. its way upwards 7283

Man trampled by same f. he has
created 5975

Man's chief enemy dark f. within
3165

of evil have begun decisive
offensive 3400

so many f. at work in, about us
  5458
two great f. at work in world
  today 4917
we cannot calculate or cope with
  5458

FORCIBLY
No cable can draw so f. as love
  with a thread 7279

FORD
every stream 4421

FORECAST
Never try to f. way God is going
  to answer prayer 8873

FOREFATHERS
succeeded because goal glory to
  God 3113

FOREHEAD
if faults written on f. 3943
kissed on f, high heels invented
  2003

FOREIGN
not a f. church 1447

FOREKNOWLEDGE
God's f. does not necessitate him
  4882

FOREORDAINED
free choices, God's f. decrees 1153

FORESAW
As Plato f., the Man was crucified
  11525
whose future wickedness he f.
  5020

FORESIGHT
if man had f. of prosperity 4314

FOREST
plenty of room in the f. 6168
The f. smiles 9897
When oak felled, f. echoes with its
  fall 8052

FORESTALL
wishing to f. God's arrangements
  4322

FORESTS
a thousand f. in one acorn 1969
creation of thousand f. in one
  acorn 8664
like unborn f. in acorn-cup 4769

FORETASTE
best f. of heaven 7198

FOREVER
Attir'd with stars, we shall f. sit
  5679
cannot say f. if 8818
clouds closing over him in
  darkness f. 6101
divine King rules f. by dying 2166
does not ask question remains
  fool f. 6683
Each of the redeemed shall f. know
  6169
echoes grow f. and f. 1032
exorcism of evil f. uncertain 3365

feeling that I could last f. 12165
God is f. seeking to manifest
  himself to us 7513
God must remain what he has f.
  been 4821
God permits the wicked, but not f.
  11884
good name is f. 9617
gospel of Christ same f. 5103
Grace free, but you are bound f.
  to the Giver 5211
Hell is enjoyment of your own
  way f. 5695
his Word shall stand f. 9813
Immortal Love, f. full, f. flowing
  free 6409
Injustice never rules f. 6268
life f. revolves around Christ 6937
Live as if you expect to live f.
  6099
lives a slave to others 6872
lives to live f, never fears dying
  6899
My open door to f. 6357
Night and storm look as if they
  would last f. 8444
No reward offered, gone f. 11306
Political reputation cannot last
  5079
Seems it strange thou shouldst live
  f. 6103
shared, f. whole 6409
Soft is the music that would
  charm f. 6028
spirit in once-born f. opposed to
  Spirit of twice-born 877
such sight angels behold f. 4995
Today, tonight and f. 5375
true friend is f. a friend 4180
wants another life which will last
  f. 3282
We see now. Lord sees f. 11606
what you are will be yours f. 1062
Would sink f. thro' the vast
  profound 4708

FORFEIT
Three-fourths of ourselves to be
  like other people 6218

FORFEITED
No man prosperous whose
  immortality f. 6101

FORFEITS
need to make evident f. virtue
  11695
own blood that spills another's
  7881

FORGE
always in the f. 228
hammer, f. yourself into character
  1071
mold, hammer, f. character 1000
thy tongue on anvil of truth
  11503

FORGED
Faith is f. through doubt 3726

FORGERS
fake money 7826

FORGERY
critics claim Bible f. 679

FORGET
ability to f. true greatness 4068
about impressing 10279
aches and pains 9270
after short act of gratitude, we f.
  God 8788
as aliens cannot f. true homeland
  2975
Best to f. 4083
blunders as soon as you can
  11366
can forgive but cannot f. 9712
cannot afford to f. experience
  3549
courage to f. 8827
disabilities 9271
Don't f. his daily briefing 1311
don't let us f. we cried 6743
folks we know briefly, quickly f.
  4281
Forgiveness not I will forgive, not
  f. 4079
frustrations that discourage 9270
God delays, doesn't f. 4445
God is a specialist 3613
God is willing to f. 4633
good you do not lost, though you
  f. it 5083
Great pains cause us to f. small
  ones 2724
happiest when we f. our precious
  selves 9245
he that receives should never f.
  4363
I would be giving, f. gift 1018
If God f. world, would cease to be
  4597
If I f, yet God remembers 7478
in prosperity we f. God 250
In sleep, pain that cannot f. falls
  drop by drop 11919
injuries, never f. kindnesses 6638
irritations that detract from
  happiness 9270
kindest those who forgive and f.
  6667
liabilities 9271
limitations 9271
Live your life, f. your age 8144
losses, setbacks, defeats 9270
may f. thee, but do not thou f. me
  9076
moment we f. he is Almighty 4830
negatives that needle you 9270
No man has right to f. service due
  his neighbor 9670
Nothing fixes thing so intensely in
  memory as wish to f. 7736
O, if I could, what grief should I f.
  5342
other's faults by remembering
  your own 5999
princes among us f. themselves,
  serve mankind 10193

Sad soul, take comfort nor f. 5942
say they will forgive but can't f.
9641
seeming restrictions 9271
sorrows 9271
the day's troubles 11158
the pain by which they purchased
heaven 7672
the worries in your head 240
tight shoes make you f. other
troubles 8509
To f. a wrong is mild revenge
9729
truth does not vary because men f.
it 11540
unforgiving spirit refuses to f.
9640
valley of despair 9270
weaknesses 9271
who receives good turn should
never f. 5070
will make you f. these painful
moments 7123
will remember well time you
forgive and f. 7737
Wisdom at proper times will f.
11963
yourself and think of those around
11284

FORGETFULNESS
God consigns offense to
everlasting f. 4638
steep my sense in f. 10485
When God pardons, everlasting f.
4107

FORGET-ME-NOTS
of the angels 11636

FORGETS
Christian never f. what God had
done for him 5240
generous man f. what he gives
4346
God's forgiveness f. 4637
He that f. to pray 12097
suffering in love 10877
to live 7050

FORGETTING
oneself first condition of love
7169
oneself not refinement of love
7169
what divides 9093
with God is divine attribute 4637

FORGIVE
as I also f. the nonsense of those
who think they talk sense 9056
Calvary to learn how to f. others
2175
can f, but cannot forget 9712
cannot f. my friends for dying
2303
cannot say f. us our trepasses if
8818
dares to f. injury 4095
first 9479
Forgiveness not I will f. not forget
4079

God will f, but man will hop
around 1731
God will f. me 4082
God will f. me, that's his business
4634
Good to f. 4083
Holy Spirit, power to f. sins
11426
If God not willing to f. 4088
impossible for us to f. 9801
kindest those who f. and forget
6667
man must learn to f. himself 9979
me for what I have been 9100
most, most forgiven 4101
must f. ourselves 4087
must f. whoever has wronged you
4109
my nonsense 9056
My thoughts, my words, my
crimes f. 9048
Public f. everything except genius
4397
rather than curse 1138
say they will f. but can't forget
9641
sometimes children f. parents
1111
When f. do change future 4108
When f. you in no way change
past 4108
will remember well time you f.
and forget 7737

FORGIVEN
Calvary to learn how to be f. 2175
Christians aren't perfect, just f.
4110
forgive most, most f. 4101
have not f. one another 9087
injury sooner f. than insult 4070

FORGIVENESS
a decision of the will 4109
a permanent attitude 4078
a required course 4076
achieve inner health through f.
4103
agree f. beautiful idea 4104
and healing one 4072
beautiful when praying for f. 4086
cools sting 4075
disciple comes with sin to find f.
2818
fragrance flower leaves 4080
Friendship flourishes at fountain
of f. 4229
give to enemy 511
God's f. forgets 4637
highest achievement 4077
How could I know f. without
failure 1512
is a funny thing 4075
is not an emotion 11173
Jesus continual f. of sin 10402
like a cancelled note 4081
living Jesus proof of God's f. 6473
man's deepest need 4077
need for f. answered at Calvary
7400

not an emotion 4109
not an occasional act 4078
not I will forgive, not forget 4079
not only others, also ourselves
4103
practice f. 4072
prayer for f. has condition
attached 4096
saves cost of hatred 4089
saves expense of anger 4089
voice of f. louder 4100
warms heart 4075
without f. becomes prison 4093

FORGIVERS
happy marriage union of two f.
7593

FORGIVES
ends quarrel 4085
If God f. us 4087
Love ever gives, f, outlives 7218
more man knows, more he f. 4099

FORGIVING
enemy sets you above him 4073
God, so f, so divine 4673
Humanity beautiful when f.
another 4086
means to pardon that which is
unpardonable 11691
Solitude molds into f. persons
10561
to the poor in spirit, God is f.
4649

FORGOES
soul never so strong as when f.
revenge 4095

FORGOTTEN
children understand what parents
have f. 12157
Fanaticism redoubling effort, f.
aim 3908
God hath not f. my age 8140
golden age only comes when men
have f. gold 11856
hundred evil actions should be f.
4074
in the whirl of religious activity
4410
Many have f. value of traditions
3876
no f. skeleton can come tumbling
out 4884
People have f. Satan 1309
such a great man I have f. his
faults 5286
Truth merely told quick to be f.
11578
You've been replaced, f. That's a
lie 945

FORK
Is it progress if cannibal uses f.
9313

FORLORN
Christ not born in thee, soul f.
878
thy soul is f. 1374

FORM
Our own heart f. true honor 5896

FORMAL
does not need to be f. prayer 8849
Without worship liturgical prayer becomes f. routine 12131

FORMATION
Relevance of God to f. of mind 3036

FORMED
Character f. as we learn, submit 1000
character f. in stormy billows 1042
firmest friendships f. in adversity 4273
He who f. our frame 5606
is f. a bubble-organism 6927
until Son of God is f. in us 9821
world was sculpture 1981

FORMER
Satan; his f. name heard no more in heaven 2665

FORMIDABLE
no power more f. than truth 11547

FORMING
training mind, f. habits of young 3037

FORMLESS
as mystical experience is 7948

FORMULA
Bible contains f. for justice 701
child wants man for father, not f. 3929
cross destroyed f. that might is right 2166
for failure, try please everybody 3619
found in Christ Jesus, not in some f. 7105
God's f. for success 3628
no f. to teach maturity 7705
tries to crowd God's fullness into f. 11208
which expresses law of nature 8001

FORSAKE
Grace to confess, f. sin 1809
To f. Christ for world 6495
To f. sin leave it without thought of returning 10409

FORSAKEN
the Lord f. by the Father 6383

FORSAKES
Christian, f. to have 1265

FORTH
love should beam f. on every side 7168

FORTIFIED
break down f. walls of self-defenses 10043

FORTIFY
our minds against disappointments 9092

FORTITUDE
Christian f. better foundation than stoicism 1563
Faith without thankfulness lacks f. 11154
Grief can elicit f. 10640
I pray for strength, f. 1927
with f. can bear suffering of other folks 10862

FORTRESS
Firm as a f. to defend the right 1933

FORTRESSES
Without f. no new power can arise 8722

FORTUNATELY
God more tolerant 4897

FORTUNE
can be great in good f. 5310
does not change men 11807
dulls 11808
father who teaches responsibility provides f. 3913
great f. a great slavery 11794
has acquired him 11820
has not acquired a f. 11820
I'd trade my f. for one happy marriage 7619
is shallow 11808
lost, nothing lost 9263
need greater virtues to bear good f. than bad 11719
No f, only God 11866
O f. All men call thee fickle 11842
Quiet minds go in f. or misfortune at own pace 8466
unmasks men 11807

FORTUNES
would be no f. in oil 11831

FORTUNE-TELLER
foretells bright future 7581

FORTY
old age of youth 307

FORWARD
adventurous life go f. in spite of fears 3990
continual looking f. to eternal world 5629
death, kind of looking f. to it 2312
Do not look f. 415
do not weaken yourself by looking f. 9650
go f. without fear 1918
going f. toward something great 4248
Hope is a going f. 5918
I will go anywhere, provided f. 2628
Look f. and not back 8379
look f. to death with intense curiosity 2306
should we not look f. to the arrival 2315
To Christ everything looks f, backward 5710
to lead us f. one by one 6178
Youth looks f. 12200

FORWARDS
Life must be lived f. 6941

FOSTER-CHILDREN
Difficulty roughly rocks f. into strength 2719

FOUGHT
Devil strongest spirit that f. in heaven 2643
many a battle f. world knows nothing about 7061
soul where man's battles are f. 10672

FOUL
He that hides dark soul, f. thoughts 1683
things it has embraced 8182

FOULEST
Success consecrates the f. crimes 10803

FOUND
by One who had himself been hurt by the archers 9798
faith never f. alone 3809
God cannot be f. by thought 4738
had they not f. a friend 4236
happiness never f. till we stop looking for it 5550
have lost all and f. myself 9559
I sought and f. him there 4921
in each poppy's cup of gold 7996
in register of God, not man 6023
least gratitude from greatest services 5250
Lost time never f. again 11305
messiahs aren't f. wrapped in rags 6147
miss happiness not because never f. it 5585
more joy in sorrow 10593
No one could ever have f. God 6137
peace f. by man in depths of own heart 8474
Pleasure seldom f. where sought 8606
Since I have f. today 11369
Tell me with whom thou art f. 4270
To have f. God not an end, but a beginning 7544
True excellence rarely f. 3472

FOUNDATION
Bible, bedrock f. of literature 703
born again, a f. fact 879
Building one's life on f. of gold 7796
Character, evidence built on right f. 1057
Christ a F. to support 6370

Christian, better f. than stoicism
1563
existed before f. of world 3490
Faith is the Christian's f. 5638
faith is the f. 3826
granted single decade to lay f. of
values 8314
high structures require solid f.
5991
higher your structure, deeper must
be f. 5997
Jesus f. of my whole life 11126
Justification f. that supports all
benefits 6633
Lay first f. of humility 6788
Lord's Day f. to build six-story
week 10958
obedience f. of subjection to
God's authority 8355
of human excellence 11720
of society, rests on Bible 5189
sure f. in friendship 4251
Without family, children have no
moral f. 3877
world based on f. of murder
10513

FOUNDATIONS
Christian thinker questions f.
about him 11239
think first about f. of humility
5997
would shake world to its f. 6496

FOUNDED
Christian faith f. upon fact of
history 6144
first civilization f. by Cain 10513
God's call f. on his decree 4626
Jesus Christ f. his empire upon
love 6351
neurotics have f. religions 4390
Opinions if f. in truth will prevail
8199
Skepticism has not f. empires
5723

FOUNTAIN
Christ a F. to cleanse 6370
Friendship flourishes at f. of
forgiveness 4229
God, a f. always flowing 4698
joy an unceasing f. bubbling up in
heart 6529
night given to drink deep at f. of
power 6947
no days when God's f. does not
flow 4647
of good, all blessing flows 7456
of life, all-abounding grace 4836
Parents have poisoned f. 8352
returning, sweaty and out of
breath, to your f. 9070

FOUNTAINS
Large streams from little f. flow
8657
Like f. of sweet waters in the sea
8911
quenched thirst at other f. 7500

FOUR
clever, fearless, f. years old 1130
No man ever more than f. steps
from God 9585
Sin has f. characteristics 10359
sometimes ask that two and two
not make f. 9023
steps to achievement 80
theology condensed into f. words
11195
things are property of friendship
4227
things come not back 8213
things go together 10248
things man must learn 559
things must be tried in friendship
4227
things to learn in life 6913

FOURTEEN
When I was a boy of f. 3928

FOUR-YEAR-OLD
Creator patiently listening to f.
talk 3918

FOX
preaches, look to your geese 2479
should not be on jury at goose's
trial 9177

FOXHOLES
no atheists in f. 489

FRAGILE
are most who seek help 3069
easily crushed and f. 6651
History too f. to contain Jesus
5714
pottery gets f. sitting in sun 2540
Self-esteem a f. flower 9994
something not possible on this f.
earth 7601

FRAGILITY
we are mortal men full of f. 7437

FRAGMENTARINESS
evil, principle of f. 5023

FRAGMENTS
All are f. from his dish 5860

FRAGRANCE
clings to hand that gives roses
4344
flowers while still smell f. 3137
Forgiveness f. flower leaves 4080
Friends like f. of orchids 4185
full-blossomed trees filled air with
f. 2977
gospel, can't inhale its f. and be
content 5099
How sweet f. if father onion,
mother garlic 8298
not progress when womanhood
lost its f. 7834
Thou didst send forth thy f. 4805
Virtues lose f. when exposed
11716

FRAGRANT
Virtue f. when incensed or crushed
227

FRAIL
Adversities do not make man f.
140
mind of man cannot explain
reason 4492
On a f. branch when he sings
11475
Pleasure f. like a dewdrop 8604
Seem very f. 2162

FRAILTY
as we through f. multiply
transgressions 5212

FRAME
A calm and heavenly f. 7507
He who formed our f. 5606

FRAMEWORK
without which all is confusion
3980

FRANATIC
one who won't change subject
3907

FRANCIS OF ASSISI
spent 75 percent of his time in
prayer 8793

FRANK
in desire to be f. become rude
9502
most agreeable is simple, f. person
4204
talk good soap for hearts 5864

FRANKLIN, BENJAMIN
not afraid of being lonely 7141

FRANKNESS
no wisdom like f. 11952

FRANTIC
discord of sin 8743
generation of f. Christians 10576
makes world pause in f, headlong
pursuits 10938

FRANTICALLY
not f. trying to make ourselves
good 7560

FRAUD
Christ either deceived mankind by
f. 6366
If resurrection didn't happen,
Christianity a gigantic f. 9691

FRAUDULENT
pietism preaches from villas to
slums about mansions 6065

FRAY
He who has mingled in the f. 3174

FREE
And then I shall be f. 10973
at last, f. at last 4119
become f. to be compassionate
10162
best compliment to set f. to make
own inquiries 6207
best things in life are f. 3838
Bible, f. gift inside 690
Break off the yoke and set me f.
2583

calm and f. from care 4869
caught that I might be f. 6120
Christ betrayed that thou mightest
 go f. 6393
Christian should act with
 disregard for opinions of others
 6291
Christian, most f. of all 1255
Christianity promises to make f.
 4116
conformist not a f. man 1635
Death may be f. 2263
Death sets f. the soul 2261
Democracy, f. to choose who will
 get blame 5173
desires nothing, always f. 1796
discipline sets me f. to fly 9975
discussion firmest friend to truth
 2902
does more than required, f. man
 3096
don't want us f. to express faith
 creatively 6824
exist, God's f. determination 3481
faith is f. 3838
faith sets life f. 3747
Father, set me f. in the glory of thy
 will 9052
for happiness must be f. 4120
Freedom means set f. to become
 what God wants 4122
friend, f. to be silly with 4177
from bondage 7193
God created f. beings 3370
God created us f. to disbelieve in
 him 11590
God gave us f. choice 1141
God laid upon man duty of being
 f. 4127
grace 495
Grace f, but you are bound to the
 Giver 5211
harmful to think prayer
 something to do during a f. hour
 10211
He that is good is f. though a slave
 4131
hope is f. 3838
I knew I was f. 4136
If any be a bondman, Christ is f.
 6391
In submission f. to value other
 people 9963
Is it possible to become f. without
 faith 3745
it was the f. who flocked to Jesus
 6452
Keep heart f. from hate 5561
less what f. to do than f. not to do
 4142
life f. from suffering 6506
love f. from pain 6506
Love is f. 3838
Love most f. when offered 7239
Love virtue, she alone is f. 11692
Love, forever flowing f. 6409
man f. to do what he likes 4150
man f. to do what he ought 4150
man f. to love God 566

man f. to love neighbor 566
man is he who does not fear
 thought 4145
Man's f. will, God's sovereign will
 1149
may be secure, but not f. 6824
must be f. willingness on our part
 4128
must f. ourselves to be filled by
 God 10708
No man f. who is not master of
 himself 4139
No man f. who is slave to flesh
 4138
obey, be f. 8115
Oh, burst these bonds, and set it f.
 4140
One's thoughts are f. 4112
only f. when Son sets us f. 4152
people who do not want us to be
 f. before God 6824
person f. even within prison 4112
purpose of darkness to set f. 2608
quiet mind f. from ties 7773
rein to the flesh 466
Salvation is f. 2832
so that you be f. from pain 3979
some never f. outside prison 4112
then Athens ceased to be f. 4155
to choose whether will be made f.
 4152
to make wrong decisions 2486
water f. for the taking 3838
What is freedom of most f. 4123
What we think about when f. to
 think 11277
What you get f. costs too much
 11668
where man goes when f. to go
 4147
Who lives in fear, never a f. man
 4009
yearning to breathe f. 7985

FREED
believer f. from death as curse
 2372
degraded from honor, f. from envy
 1776
soul f. from clay 10675

FREEDOM
aware of stature, f, and evil in men
 7494
basic test of f. 4142
begin to experience f. 10551
can never lose 4112
cause of f, cause of God 4143
church enjoys f. to doubt 952
church, f. to indulge in acceptance
 952
constitutes dignity of man 4149
Creation seems like pure f. 4117
Death Liberator whom f. cannot
 release 2260
does not mean able to do
 whatever I want 4122
false f, man free to do what he
 likes 4150

filling mind with God's thoughts
 4121
find f. when we find God 4153
fine word when rightly understood
 4123
first duty is to find, not f, but
 Master 4144
from the church fundamental
 postulates of f. 5169
given up intellectual f. 7760
glory of the gospel is its f. 5095
God never sets limit to man's f.
 4130
God's f. from bias 6630
God's service is perfect f. 4126
great thing expressed in single
 word 10277
He who borrows sells his f. 4038
Heresy, another word for f. of
 thought 6181
Holiness not f. from temptation
 5744
Human f. a precious thing 9463
in mass movement find f. to
 betray without shame 10526
is justice's child 6628
is right to chose 4155
Jesus' captivity is our f. 6453
less what free to do than free not
 to do 4142
life of f, liberty, delight 5464
likeness to God resides in f. 4149
lose f. when we lose God 4153
Love is true f. 7254
man in evolution from limited to
 greater f. 9351
Maturity, letting a friend have f.
 to be and do 7696
misery because world based on f.
 4149
Money buys everything except f.
 7806
must want spiritual f. 1013
nation that thinks more of ease
 than f. will soon lose its f. 7984
nature is f. 8012
need not fear disaster will follow
 f. of thought 4134
no f. to negotiate results 1159
no such thing as f. in world 4159
not f. to determine end of choice
 1149
of Bible from earthly mixtures 736
of speech, potent weapon 4154
only perfect f. is serving God 4148
principles of Bible groundwork of
 human f. 5965
publishing with utmost f. 4115
Rebellion seems like f. 4117
reject specialness, lose f. 1635
safeguarding f. of spirit 4127
set free to become what God
 wants 4122
Silence is f. to let justification rest
 with God 6622
something spiritual 4112
special f. friends enjoy 4285
Suffering raises us to f. 10888

support individual f. as we serve one another 9498

taking away f. of choice from man 4133

that binds him to him who made his f. 6177

that f. should bind us dearer to himself 6177

There lies f. indeed 4111

they wished for f. from responsibility 4155

Thou captive's f, thou sick man's health 5932

to achieve all God wants 4122

to acknowledge negative attitudes 503

to act rightly 4123

to ask favor 4285

to be themselves 4285

to choose attitude 519

to choose side 1159

to enjoy all God wants 4122

to give up our rights for good of others 9963

to share innermost thoughts 4285

to show true feelings 4285

to take course we choose 1149

to worship God 4114

true f, man free to do what he ought 4150

Violence destroys f. of human beings 11678

we react decisively against those who take f. from us 9463

What f. would you have 4123

What is f. of most free 4123

When we let f. ring 4157

will ultimately restore losses 11768

with f. of speech, responsibility 4154

FREEDOMS

church secure, too many f. 952

my f. grow, find wings 4125

two f. 4150

FREELY

cannot speak too f. to God 8968

grow in wisdom, pardon more f. 4071

happiness is f. united to God 4120

rebellious deny as f. as devout adore 4129

FREENESS

with what f. all his merits shall be bestowed 6393

FREER

the f. the man, the stronger the bond 6177

FREES

grease of gusto f. gears of generosity 4347

FREETHINKERS

those willing to use minds without prejudice 4124

FREEWAY

Wait on Lord in prayer as you sit on f. 8424

FREE WILL

If God thinks war worth paying for f. 4132

makes evil possible 4120

makes goodness possible 4120

makes joy possible 4120

man has power to defy God's wishes 4158

not liberty to do whatever one likes 4111

only thing that makes love possible 4120

power of doing what ought to be done 4111

Without f. man not in image of God 4158

FREEZE

Cold words f. people 11985

cynicism and fear f. life 3747

FREQUENT

Jesus Christ, his visits f. 6352

ornaments of house are friends who f. it 4206

sin becomes f. 10287

FREQUENTLY

program f. used word in church language 1406

saints f. experienced up, down, joy, sorrow 2593

virtues are f. vices disguised 6060

FRESH

Defeat f. stimulus 2509

exhilarating atmosphere of eternity 4976

gospel like f. air 5097

keeps us from giving in f. innovative ways to others 6825

legalism, lynching of f. thinking 6817

start any moment you choose 3598

FRESHNESS

uniqueness that gives f. to a relationship 6197

FRESH-SPRINGING

In eternity everything present in one f. now 11316

FRET

mind that is cumbered, will f. 425

Nor do I f. about ignorance of future life 6092

people f. over nuclear weapons 10503

The weariness, the fever, and the f. 7044

FRETFUL

without healing of spirit we become f. 8857

FRETFULNESS

a determination to get my own way 416

FRETS

his hour upon the stage 6994

Vainly strives, and fights, and f. 7440

FRETTED

Humility is never to be f. 6010

FRICTION

with body a warning 847

FRIDAY

danced on a F. when sky turned black 9690

FRIEND

a guide when you're searching 4174

a push when you've stopped 4174

a smile when you're sad 4174

a song when you're glad 4174

a word when you're lonely 4174

accepts who you've become 4169

accepts you today just the way you are 4172

Adam created to be f. of God 758

as one unloads one's heart to a dear f. 8970

Ask of him to be our f. 1510

Be a f. You don't need glory 4217

Before you borrow money from f. 4032

believes in your future 4172

Beside us a f. well loved, known 5376

best compliment to a f. 6207

best mirror is an old f. 4200

better to keep f. from falling than help up 4191

bitterest enemy could be your f. 3167

bury weakness in silence 4183

can always tell a real f. 4213

can hardly make f. in year 4305

can lose f. in hour 4305

can never replace f. 4297

ceases to be f, never was good one 4244

Chide f. in private 4182

closet of prayer will become your closest f. 9039

comes in when world has gone out 4167

comfort of having f. may be taken away 4271

commend f. publicly 2855

conduct toward enemy as if one day f. 3172

Conscience warns us as a f. 1677

Conscience, man's most faithful f. 1695

Cover blemishes of f. 4183

Covetousness has for f, violence 5313

dearest f. on earth mere shadow 4201

Death is a f. 2338

destroy enemy, make him your f. 3170

display his perfection 4183

Do good to your f. to keep him 9449

draw curtains before stains 4183

Each departed f. a magnet 2278

excuse failings of f. 4183

faithful f. an image of God 4162

faithful f. one of life's greatest assets 4163

foe to God, ne'er true f. to man 4164

Free discussion firmest f. to truth 2902

From morn to night, my f. 6885

from whom thou canst never separate 1310

gently invites you to grow 4169

gift of loving thought into heart of f. 4189

give your heart 511

God is the f. of silence 10250

godly knows God his best f. 3996

good man is his own f. 5082

great confidence in f. to tell your faults 3930

greater confidence in f. to tell him his faults 3930

greatest f. of truth is time 11535

had they not found a f. 4236

happiest miser saves every f. 4203

He who cheats f. would cheat God 2911

helps us be our best selves 4178

helps us put forth best efforts 4178

helps us think noblest thoughts 4178

Hold true f. with both hands 4188

I would be f. of foe, friendless 1018

If can't help f. with money 3072

If God my f, cannot be wretched 7476

if my best F. who laid down life 4069

If you treat f. shabbily while he lives 2317

in loneliness thou art more surely our f. 9053

intimate with God, disloyalty of f. will not crush 9470

is dearer than light of heaven 4269

kindest man will put his heel on his greatest f. 10527

knows all about you, likes you just the same 4168

knows you as you are 4169

loses f. loses more 3729

love that leads to doorway of f. 4278

makes me do my best 4170

mark of f. makes you wish to be at your best 4192

Maturity, letting a f. have freedom to be and do 7696

mirror shows everyone his best f. 9998

must not expect f. to be above humanity 4237

my enemy may become my f. 3162

my f. may become my enemy 3162

My f. peers in on me 4195

My name is Death; last best f. am I 2337

Myself, my hollowest f. 2583

never known until man have need 4166

never omiting making a f. 9491

No man is useless while he has f. 4257

No problem as dark when you have a f. 4196

On the duties of a f. 4217

one f. left down inside of me 1685

one who warns you 4171

only way to have f. is be one 4205

Our faithful, unchangeable f. 4787

person with whom I may think aloud 4165

praise f. in public 4182

proclaim virtues on housetop 4183

pushes you nearer to God 4190

remembers you in his prayers 4179

Reprove f. privately 2855

reveals himself utterly to the other 4272

Security never f. of faith 952

shall have at least one f. left 6304

She is but half a wife who is not a f. 7651

Silence a f. who will never betray 10260

single soul dwelling in two bodies 4211

so you want everyone to be your f. 9448

Solitude soul's best f. 10559

someone free to be silly with 4177

stillest tongue, truest f. 1879

stranger a f. whose acquaintance you haven't made 9443

takes a long time to grow an old f. 4193

than a false f. 4210

That f. is God 5376

That f. of mine 4199

that f. shall be down inside of me 6304

That which I love in my f. 4233

the soul unto itself an imperial f. 10674

There is no f. like an old f. 4208

thy best, thy heavenly F. 1502

to everybody, nobody same thing 4215

To find a f. close one eye 4161

to get rid of enemy turn him into f. 9484

to keep a f. close two eyes 4161

to one 550

true f. is forever a f. 4180

trusts you with secrets 4179

truth, f. more excellent than human f. 11560

understands where you've been 4169

understands your past 4172

Walk beside me, be my f. 4224

warms you by his presence 4179

What influences me in my f. is spirit 4233

What is God saying through this f. 6086

When f. dies 4300

When someone is everybody's f. 4283

when you touch a f. 4202

who cares faces powerlessness 3080

who cares silent in despair 3080

who has thousand friends has not a f. to spare 9459

who seeks faultless f. is friendless 4246

who was f. could again be f. 3167

will joyfully sing with you 4175

will silently walk beside you 4175

wine, first a f. 337

with noisy old car disturbing 3223

with quiet new car disturbing 3223

with whom you dare to be yourself 4173

Words cannot express joy f. imparts 4269

you buy won't be worth what you pay 4176

FRIEND'S

affection greatest treasure 4181

If any care may make a f. the fleeter 910

love brings joy to heart 4382

To a f. house road never long 4287

unless allowances for f. foibles 4294

FRIENDLESS

cannot say you are f. 4214

I would be friend of foe, f. 1018

who seeks faultless friend is f. 4246

FRIENDLINESS

stronger than force, fury 4296

FRIENDLY

in difficulties are f. forces 2712

lie in unexpected f. word 3143

man only animal on f. terms with victims 7585

May yet hold f. converse with my God 8814

One f. sign 4199

Philosophy, science not always f. toward God 8592

To the frightened, God is f. 4649

universe not f. 11648

voice of God, a f. voice 4966

FRIENDS

accept Christ's f. as our f. 3335

add word a day, f. will wonder 1853
are all different 4297
best f. should be "No problem" type 4226
best know how to prize f. 4286
Blessed are they who have gift of making f. 4220
can make more f. in two months 4306
cannot forgive my f. for dying 2303
contentment and aspiration 471
Convey thy love to thy f. 4222
day too short for all the f. I want to see 11301
deaf cannot hear voices of dearest f. 9094
Difficulty and joy mutual f. 2716
Do not be afraid of f. 6158
enemies f. who don't know each other 3171
enemies more respect than f. by being on fence 1913
Flatterers look like f. 4047
Go slowly to entertainment of thy f. 4242
God asks us to be his f. 4564
God intends us all to be f. 4243
good are f. to one another 5045
Gossip estrange closest f. 5127
Great talents have few f. 7
happiness in worth, choice of f. 4293
happiness not in multitiude of f. 4293
he that wrongs his f. 1684
I have called you f. 4214
if want f, let others excel you 9472
impart favor to places where they dwell 4269
in which to bury faults of f. 4225
Jesus does not tell us to pretend. f. 5890
Judge yourself by the f. you choose 4194
knew everything said would remain f. with no one 9466
life partly made by f. we choose 4254
Love's business not to find f. 7274
magnet that will attract true f. 4282
may go to heaven without f. 9792
Money brings acquaintances, but not f. 7807
move toward f. who listen 1857
moving toward world of throwaway f. 10524
must love f. for their sake 4251
My life, my f, my soul I leave 7503
next to good f. is good book 854
no wilderness like life without f. 4284
Old f. will lovelier be 4197
On the choice of f. 4198

ornaments of house are f. who frequent it 4206
performance must keep f. 4262
Plenty, as well as want, can sep'rate f. 3558
pray for though they cease to be f. 4069
prefer own f. who share life-style 5957
Promises may get f. 4262
property of one belongs to the other 4186
prosperity full of f. 4267
Real f. don't care if socks don't match 4264
Real f. have great time doing nothing 4265
Real f. know you have good reason 4266
real f. reserve nothing 4186
reason dog has so many f. 9499
remember f. who encourage 9270
Silences real conversations between f. 4268
Sorrow shown only to f. 10615
speak with words sweet, strong 4185
special freedom f. enjoy 4285
stormy old f. silent after they die 2397
Suffering God gives only to chosen f. 10894
Take glory neither in money nor f. 9272
talk about troubles to f. 4276
than f. by what we do 1888
than f. with whom we share gifts of life 10531
than fool from f. 3155
Then there are f. who sail together 4281
think often of your f. 8472
Thou wilt have no f. 1310
Three firm f. 4209
Time and truth are f. 11551
to a solitary f. are everything 4261
True f. no solitary joy, sorrow 4291
until f. are dead 4223
We make our f, enemies 8066
Wear a smile, have f. 10502
When God is weaning a soul from f. 10036
Whenever f. compliment about looking young 8185
Where there are f, there is wealth 4301
Wherever you are, f. make your world 4212
who has many f, has none 4187
who has thousand f. has not a friend to spare 9459
who understand each other 4185
who want f. least 4286
will be swept away 3719
will not believe ill of you 11502
winning f. meant most 4303
wise man more use from enemies than fool from f. 9444

wise man seeks f. with qualities he himself lacks 4279
With f. even poverty pleasant 4269
worst f. can do is betray you 6158

FRIENDSHIP
adds brighter radiance to prosperity 4228
Anyone with heart full of f. 4216
be first to give f. sign 9479
compliment sure to develop into f. 1572
doubles joy, divides grief 4229
essence of perfect f. 4272
flourishes at fountain of forgiveness 4229
Four things are property of f. 4227
Four things must be tried in f. 4227
glory of f. spiritual inspiration 4275
Gold does f. separate 11811
happiness is f. of select companions 5568
highest sign of f. 4277
If expect to find peace in f. 9470
independent of matter, space, time 4233
is a plant, not a roadside thistle 4237
is a sheltering tree 4232
is a simple story 4217
is a spiritual thing 4233
is in loving rather than being loved 4234
is like money, easier made than kept 4235
is treason 4877
Jealousy a blister on the heels of f. 6339
know f. with God 8327
leaves of f. fall 7860
lightens adversity by dividing, sharing it 4228
live with f, learn to find love 1114
looks for advantage out of f. 4245
Love is f. set to music 7234
Love like a f. caught on fire 7236
may die in an hour of unwise word 4237
must undergo, withstand shocks of adversity 4218
No one has double in f. 4297
not mature enough to enter into f. 4247
of itself, a holy tie 4240
one of the sweetest joys of life 4236
Only solitary men know full joys of f. 4261
ought never to conceal what it thinks 4238
painful truth through loving words is f. 4289
perfect, delightful f. with God 5464
plant which must often be watered 4231

Real f. shown in trouble 4267
removes ornament of f. who takes
    away respect 9642
Robbing life of f. 4299
Satan's f. reaches to prison door
    2665
should be dealt with delicately
    4237
So necessary is our f. to God 4564
strips f. of nobility 4245
sure foundation in f. 4251
that can cease never real 4274
through f. we love places, seasons
    4269
To f. every burden light 4288
True f. is plant of slow growth
    4218
true f. is still rarer 4263
True f. like sound health 4292
two bodies, one soul 4298
usually treated as tough,
    everlasting thing 4237
What sweetness left if take away f.
    4299
will not continue that is begun for
    an end 4222
with God means nature of God in
    man 7457
without self-interest rare, beautiful
    4238

FRIENDSHIPS
firmest f. formed in adversity
    4273
form among people who
    strengthen 4241
Hot tempers cool f. 9488
must keep f. in constant repair
    4249

FRIGHTEN
observing means enemy uses to f.
    4010
Try praising wife even if it does f.
    her 7662

FRIGHTENED
at facing ourselves 10575
I am f. and astonished at being
    here 4905
Man f. that he loses himself by
    giving himself 9937
never f. a Puritan 4965
never f. at a sunset 2297
People no longer sinful, only f.
    10350
Quiet minds cannot be perplexed
    or f. 8466
To the f, God is friendly 4649
when everything goes well, don't
    be f. 3998

FRIGHTENING
and distressing bit of reality 9408
Obstacles f. when eyes off goal
    4430
part that makes an idea an idea
    2013

FRIGHTENS
eternal silence of these infinite
    spaces f. me 7084

idea of eternal rest f. me 5661
what don't know that f. me 6685
who sings f. away ills 7894

FRIGHTFUL
Despair a f. queerness 2578
is solitude of soul without God
    10573
Nothing more f. than ignorance in
    action 6084

FRIGHTFULLY
in the crowds feel f. alone 7124

FRINGES
quit fiddling around f. of
    Christianity 9691

FRITTERED
Life is f. away by detail 10281

FROG
in well knows nothing of great
    ocean 8665

FROGS
Some go in jumps like spiritual f.
    10716

FROM
where you come f. not important
    4438

FRONDED
Their f. palms in air 4763

FRONT
cannot be a f. without a back
    5357
In f. a precipice, behind a wolf
    2733

FRONTIER
neighborliness important on f.
    because so few 8068

FROST
It simply died of f. 7159
What God will, no f. can kill 4959
When the f. is on the punkin 9880

FROTH
Life is mostly f. and bubble 6657

FROWN
Choose to smile, rather than f.
    1138
less and laugh more 9281
life, f. at it, it frowns back 6949

FROWNING
face repels 5504

FROWNS
greatest man is most fearless
    under f. 5297

FROZEN
in corporate or collective cold
    3045
Many are called but most f. 3045
spiritual lives have been f. 10369

FRUGAL
Life is dust f. nature lends man for
    an hour 6960
When axe is put to tree, f. of sin
    wither 10346

FRUIT
always present in seed 16
And clothe myself with f. 8254
bad thoughts bear bad f. 11223
Curiosity kernel of forbidden f.
    11050
Forth reaching to the f. 10314
God does not grade the f. 7862
God does not view the f. 7864
God is aiding to yield f. 4514
God will not bring forth dead f.
    872
Good thoughts bear good f.
    11223
Grief has tears for its f. 11014
I not only taste the f. 72
Judge a tree from its f. not leaves
    6581
of gospel, aspiration 471
out on limb 1940
Patience is bitter, f. sweet 8410
propensity to grasp at forbidden f.
    11112
self turns up to poison f. of our
    lives 9943
Sorrow is a f. 10611
than the largest f. of happiness
    3795
what f. would spring from such
    seed 1737
when axe is put to tree, f. of sin
    wither 10346

FRUITFUL
activity which is not f. 60
If f, cared not who did condemn
    10157
If f. mattered not who
    commended me 10157

FRUITFULNESS
Treat f, barrenness same way 1461

FRUITION
prospects more pleasing than f.
    3508

FRUITLESS
My search was f. still 4921

FRUITS
Deeds are f, words are leaves 2532
Eve, with all f. of Eden blest
    11053
Humanness is realization of f. of
    Spirit 5014
of the Spirit are virtues of Christ
    10714
Stars golden f. all out of reach
    11637

FRUSTRATE
Kids can f, irritate parents 8304

FRUSTRATED
A God who is f. 4579
God sends a time of f. efforts
    7056
greed flares up when desires f.
    10003
If you aim to be a servant, will
    never be f. 10160

If you wish to be leader, will be f. 10160

Satan must be most f. personality in universe 9858

without control young people f. 12178

without God young people f. 12180

FRUSTRATES
The Lord f. our plans 351

FRUSTRATION
consciousness reached, existence entwined with f. 3479

God feels f. 4491

God's grace sufficient 2518

miser, dollar's worth of f. when loses dime 11797

When f. of helplessness seemed greatest 2518

FRUSTRATIONS
forget f. that discourage 9270

Motherhood full of f. 8313

thorny, sour, crabbed f. of old age 8176

Watch f. melt into praise 8424

FUEL
God is the f. our spirits designed to burn 7459

We are the f. 7553

FULFILL
better uncertain than to promise and not f. 9327

commands f. God's destiny in life 8111

God above to f. all his designs 4521

responsible for how well we f. responsibilities 9660

simple it will be his precepts to f. 10047

that we f. purpose of God 7485

to f. the vast design 4338

work should f. itself to glory of God 3127

FULFILLED
f. by gifts of the Holy Ghost 4749

Love can never say, "I have f. my obligations" 7273

When his work is done, his aim f. 6803

When you worship, you are f. 12137

wish that will of God be f. in thee 8448

FULFILLMENT
Bible, promise and f. 750

by-product of love for God 4735 4308

Contentment not f. of what you want 1783

doubt deep, lasting f. 10062

dream a disguised f. of wish 2968

Solitude is inner f. 10548

Where f, there is joy 6536

Will it give me f. 5467

will never achieve f. unless God in control 9558

FULFILLS
God f. himself many ways 978

Jesus f. all procedures of the prophecies 6443

FULL
Anyone with heart f. of friendship 4216

Be glad bottle half f. 11141

Even God cannot fill what is f. 10708

except those who are f. of themselves 9200

God looks with favor at pure, not f. hands 6300

God takes notice of clean, not f. hands 9754

half-full of myself, no way f. of God 9932

heaven, f. enjoyment of God 5644

Immortal Love, forever f. 6409

Jesus is f, infinitely f. 6498

Life's a pudding f. of plums 6990

Live out life in its f. meaning 6998

makes for total life lived at f. potential 6999

my heart may go astray, but it is f. of thee 9091

No one can find a f. life 11613

of himself is quite empty 9202

strike at sin of which world is f. 10304

the commonplace is f. of wonder 6918

The inn is f. on the planet earth 6155

To be empty is to be f. 7071

vessel that grows as filled will never be f. 10699

wheel is come f. circle 1739

When heart f, eyes overflow 5269

When heart f, lips silent 5270

with eye on God, strike note f, clear 7056

world f. of God 4861

FULLER
nothing is f. or better in heaven than love 7283

FULLEST
life in f. deepest sense possible 7969

FULLNESS
cannot confer on me f. of life 5549

creator of minds to receive his f. 4514

degree of f. accords with intensity of desire 5772

How could I know f. without emptiness 1512

no want thy f. knows 7456

FULLY
conscious, we discover loneliness 9513

If we f. comprehended brevity of life 6924

No one can develop f. 11613

only enough life to pursue one object f. 9260

To live f, use things and love people 9510

FUMES
authority, f. of it invade the brain 8702

FUN
ditchwater teems with quiet f. 8020

lot a nerve to make f. of ostrich 4007

Love puts the f. in together 7269

repentance is no f. at all 9577

today people would make f. of Christ 6405

trouble starts out like f. 11448

FUNCTION
Minds only f. when open 7762

Work is man's great f. 12024

FUNCTIONAL
Affliction absolutely f. 10834

FUNCTIONS
sacred calling not limited to ecclesiastical f. 12146

universe f. best when God's laws obeyed 1520

FUNDAMENTAL
Conformity most f. dishonesties of all 1635

from church f. postulates of order 5169

idea of good 5044

To philosopher, time one of the f. quantities 11346

two f. rules for life 10053

FUNDAMENTALISTS
Christ crucified by F. 9541

We are not f. 1343

FUNDAMENTALLY
Christ disconnected f. from life 6436

no distinction between spiritual, material work 6985

FUNDS
for promotion of peace 11782

FUNERAL
always finds time to attend his f. 5589

among men, wedding feast among angels 2205

Death, f. of sorrows, evils 2266

Why rejoice at birth, grieve at f. 817

FUNERALS
are barbaric, miserable 2311

destructive to true memory 2311

FUNNY
Ducks look f. trying to climb 6168

Forgiveness is f. thing 4075

he'd look f. in woolen one 6213

Life was a f. thing that happened 6986

old world, man's lucky if gets out alive 6936

thing how trouble acts different 11431

thing, this human nature 5974

FUR

can't get warm on another's f. coat 6782

reason polar bear wears f. coat 6213

FURBISHED

Lies can be f. in gorgeous wrappings 6853

FURNACE

As God puts his children in the f., he will be in f. with them 151

heat not so hot a f. 383

Hebrew children out of the f. 165

let deliverance from f. answer 5197

Like a fiery f. red 2638

purest ore produced from hottest f. 220

some things only learned in fiery f. 3662

to put him into f. of affliction 8804

FURNITURE

bridle for tongue necessary f. 11405

FURTHERANCE

of spiritual life during sleep 10487

FURY

Christ release from f. of the will 6434

of so many proof Christ is not dead 6362

Warmth stronger than force, f. 4296

FUSS

death, slip out without f. 2421

doesn't want anyone to make f. over him 9201

Man makes great f. about this planet 11633

FUTILE

attempts at description f. 4995

Criticism is f. 2055

Life can never be dark or f. 6940

Looking for Jesus in history f. 5718

more f. men become in their thinking 11538

Nothing so f. as indecision 2488

to condemn myself 3049

to get mad for size of feet 3049

to pretend prayer indispensable 8852

FUTILITY

need silence to recover from f. of words 10556

Satan fails to speak of f. of immorality 2662

FUTURE

accept Christ's f. as our f. 3335

America's f. determined by home, school 5818

anticipate f. with transcendental senses 4329

as present expectation 8387

because worried about f. 8632

Before us a f. all unknown 5376

blueprints of my f. residence 2394

cannot know f. 4337

comes one day at a time 4320

convenient place for dreams 4324

cynic prematurely disappointed in f. 2178

dare not trifle with eternal f. 4726

depends on priorities, purposes today 4325

determine f. course of nation 8360

discouragement when too much thought to f. 2887

don't dream of happiness in f. 5507

Every experience preparation for f. 3515

Every saint has a past, every sinner a f. 8653

exploration of outer space bright f. 11642

Faith makes discords harmonies of f. 3704

Faith makes f. glorious 3705

fight for planet not vague matter of f. 3400

fortune-teller foretells bright f. 7581

friend believes in your f. 4172

from mistakes wise learn wisdom for f. 7794

Go forth to meet shadowy f. 8378

God at past, f. unaffected by either 11350

has habit of becoming the present 4323

Hope for fairer times in f. 10586

hope teaches to leave f. with God 3834

I faced a f. all unknown 5413

I know he holds the f. 2978

I know not what the f. hath 6916

I know of the f. judgment 1663

I know your f. 4764

In Christ move into breathtaking f. 8364

in man who holds job 3122

in the end does not dread the f. 8184

intolerable to know the f. 4317

is not yet ours 4322

is still in your power 8385

is uncertain 8374

isn't what it used to be 4327

leave f. to God 935

life yet unlived 4325

look into f. anticipate more trouble 11450

look into f. until collapse from exhaustion 11350

Man spends life fearing for f. 8380

many Christians already have f. behind them 4321

Many Christians are in trouble about the f. 6912

may never be 8384

meet f. without fear 8378

My f. is not one of my concerns 5471

no f. in any job 3122

Nor do I fret about ignorance of f. life 6092

of church and humanity depend on family life 3894

opportunity yet unmet 4325

path yet untraveled 4325

pauses for short while before becoming the past 8386

possibility of f. exceeds accomplishments of past 4329

present is period when f. pauses 8386

purchased by present 4326

restless anxiety as to f. 4322

Right actions for f. best apologies 9598

Rigidity criticizes f. for not flying 6818

Serves but to brighten all our f. days 10879

should all be concerned about f. 4333

shut eyes to f. God hides from us 4322

something everyone reaches 4327

still remains 4334

Thank God for unknown f. 4318

thank thee that dark, uncertain is our f. 9053

the f. his mercy shall clear 8079

The f. is thy gift 9072

thoughts are seeds of f. deeds 11244

thy love has hung 'twixt it and me 9072

To let others dictate your f. is to have chosen 8264

to make brighter f. for herself 7581

Trust f. to his providence 5457

Trust no f. howe'er pleasant 4331

turn his face toward the f. 4315

veil of f. woven by hand of mercy 4330

What f. bliss he gives not thee to know 5913

when faith in f. becomes knowledge of past 7435

When forgive do change f. 4108

While times lasts will always be a f. 5052

whose f. wickedness he foresaw 5020

why fear to tread pathway to f. home 6875

will hold both good and evil 4335

will spend rest of lives there 4333

with God, no past and no f. 11322

FUTURE'S
Rigidity clips f. wings 6818

FUZZES
faith develops best when
everything f. over 3789

G

GADGETS
slaves to g, power, security 9016

GAIETY
conceal sadness under pretended g.
10587
most profound joy has more
gravity than g. 6562
often ripple over despair 5508

GAIN
best g. is to lose 4339
consciously g. identity that Jesus
had 9840
delusion personal g. made by
crushing others 7793
Do good to your enemy to g. him
9449
everything you g, lose something
else 8574
getting, doth but g. his death 2567
give reputation to Christ, g. it
9629
greatest g. ready to be yours 3633
greed of g. has no time or limit
5327
His life is Christ, his death is g.
1299
If any idea how much inward
peace you would g. 10703
If you g. you g. all 3724
loss as well as g. in growth 5366
no fool to g. what he cannot lose
1195
No g. satisfies greedy mind 5319
no g. without pain 8273
no worldly g. without loss 1776
no worldly loss without g. 1776
Not, what did he g. 7423
right nothing but g. 1151
the gentle g. 4402
To g. that which is worth having
4340
To high, eternal g. 4338
To renounce all is to g. all 9701
When seeming g. but turns to loss
4338
Who escapes duty, avoids g. 9681

GAINED
excellence not often g. on easier
terms 3470
forgo ambition when end is g.
3153
God says, "Much can be g." 2800
have g. something else 8574
Humility never g. by seeking 6008
was anything real ever g. without
sacrifice 4341
What Protestantism has g. by its
simplicity 6827

GAINING
choke faults by g. virtues 3959

GAINS
Evil g. equivalent of disaster 3356
God, never in need, yet rejoicing
in g. 4954
Ill-gotten g. never prosper 2467
losses will seem like g. 5776
most who is defeated 2510

GAINST
the logic of the devil 2636

GALE
Patience is riding out the g. 8422

GALES
'tis the set of the sails, not the g.
4432

GALL
no g. no glory 199

GALLERY
Bible, great gallery of portraits
703

GALLING
O Life! Thou art a g. load 7007

GAMBLE
crucified where soldiers g. 2131
no chance, no g. 1159
what harm if g. on faith 3724

GAMBLERS
Boredom made more g. than greed
864
lose money 7826

GAME
comparison g. sure way to poor
self-image 6208
God allows us to play the g. 7828
Truth g. of the few 11571
We play the g, God keeps the score
6069

GAMES
Don't play g. with God 4879
Honesty, an absence of political g.
5874
human race playing at children's
g. from beginning 5982
playing religious g. in one corner
10124
wooed with religious g. 1403

GANGRENE
Selfishness is a g. 8467

GAPINGS
how many g. would we see in
marketplace 10507

GARAGE
waiting for us in the Divine g.
8181

GARBAGE
crucified at town g. heap 2131

GARDEN
before God can make heart a g.
896
Bible begins with g. 723
book like g. in pocket 849

God Almighty first planted a g.
8007
God, a g. of life 4698
Love is the fairest bloom in God's
g. 7247
makes earth a g. 4280
man of words and not deeds like
g. of weeds 9319
nearer God's heart in a g. 8032
purest of human pleasures 8007
sin of the G. was sin of power
8719
snake stood up for evil in G. 3403

GARDEN OF EDEN
pair on ground started trouble
762
wasn't apple that started trouble
762

GARDEN OF PARADISE
man hid from God 316

GARDENER
Man is his own g. 11223
unless amateur g. 1727

GARDENER'S
waiting to come up flower in G.
time 5672

GARDENERS
September month g. put off until
October 9882

GARDEN'S
My g. grateful shade 7452

GARLIC
do not eat g, will not smell of g.
1006

GARMENT
Christ is a g. of righteousness
6370
wore vice like a g. 10320

GARMENTS
He whose g. are whitest 6004

GAS
No g. drives anything until
confined 2852
We've got as far as poison g.
11739

GASH
Psychotheraphy will put Band-Aid
on g. 5616

GATE
A new road, or a secret g. 8239
Death the g. of life 2270
Gold opens every g. 11814
poor man at his g. 4501
who stood at the g. of the year
5417

GATES
of eternity black, white hold each
other 3237

GATEWAY
Experience g. to One whom we
trust 3525
fear is love's g. 3986

GATHER
to the feast 11175
ye rosebuds while ye may 8214

GATHERING
church not a g. 1385

GATHERS
hand that gives, g. 4376

GAVE
By his first work God g. me to myself 4528
by his next work God g. himself to me 4528
Christ g. love, service, himself 10731
Christ never g. anyone money 10731
God g. himself away 6137
God g. me life so I could enjoy all things 6906
God g. us life, liberty at same time 4146
God g. us memories 7732
God never g. man a thing to do 10140
God will not judge on what we g. 7797
honor reward for what he g. 5895
Jesus g. such insights we have not yet grasped significance 6196
life to every race 3227
she only g. 4379
The more he g, the more he had 4348
What I g, I have 4383
when God g. himself 4528

GAWD
Even bein' G. ain't bed of roses 4890

GAZE
And g. and g. on thee 12113
if all I have to do is g. and g. 5661
faith is g. of heart at God 3737
on honest effort kindly 4217
raising of inward eyes to meet eyes of God 3737
Sin is turning our g. in the wrong direction 10370

GAZED
still they g, still the wonder grew 2994

GAZELLE
In eyes of mother every beetle a g. 7846

GAZING
Love does not consist in g. at each other 7215

GEAR
danger when throw tongue into high g. 11419

GEARS
grease of gusto frees g. of generosity 4347

GEESE
When fox preaches, look to g. 2479

GEHAZI
sold himself for silver, raiment 11798

GEM
Candor brightest g. of candor 5870
not polished without rubbing 136

GEMS
crown studded with g. of sacrifice, adoration 7073
impregnates barren rock with priceless g. 1902
those who seek for g. 206

GENERAL
good g. knows when victory impossible 8485
good g. sees way to victory 8485
no g. holds key to as much power 11841

GENERATION
a pre-peace g. 9914
born in wrong g. 12190
characterized by craze for subjective 4017
Each g. like a line, a phrase 7076
each g. makes own contribution to understanding 9711
good old days next g. will hear about 11381
Life is for one g. 9617
mother teaches next g. of citizens 7844
not a post-war g. 9914
Nothing so dates a man as to decry younger g. 12192
of nervous, almost frantic Christians 10576
Wesley in one g, a Carey in next is inevitable 9740

GENERATIONS
of intellectuals discredit Bible 726

GENEROSITY
giving more than you can 4353
God loves you with a g. 4747
grease of gusto frees gears of g. 4347
is self-sacrifice 4365
Reconciliation demands g. 9431
take no credit for g. 4387
test of g, not how much you give 4378
test of g. how much you have left 4378
wonder if cowardice or g. makes us give tips 1637

GENEROUS
action is own reward 4345
Brotherhood not only a g. impulse 902
candidates for God's g. grace 5238
do not have to be rich to be g. 4388
God, his plan improbably g. 4900

heart feels others' ill 3063
If God is God, he's g. 4479
if not g. with meager income 4366
impossible to be just if not g. 6610
man forgets what he gives 4346
man remembers what he receives 4346
not brains that matter, but g. qualities 1027
Spirit of God will make man g. 1064
will never be g. with abundance 4366

GENES
Came God, planting the secret g. of God 6148
How play with g. and fail to be touched by awe 9866

GENESIS
account of creation brief 1972
account of creation prologue to human drama 1972
Every April God rewrites G. 9885
more truth in G. than quantum theory 745
third chapter, most important in Bible 743

GENIUS
99 percent perspiration 4391
Adversity reveals g. 147
Boldness has g. 48
Could it be g. is haunted by the Speaking Voice 4399
dunces all in confederacy against him 4400
eccentricity proportional to g. 1007
gladly exchange greatest g. 4204
Holy Spirit is stronger than g. 4396
is great patience 4392
must put up with inconvenience of g. 4394
never travels on well-worn paths 4393
no great g. without mixture of madness 4398
no success in explaining existence 3486
of a nation discovered in its proverbs 9386
often dull, inert in society 4395
one percent inspiration 4391
Patience is g. 8402
Perseverance can do anything g. can do 8551
power that dazzles mortal eyes 8539
prosperity conceals g. 147
public forgive everything except g. 4397
sees world at different angle 4389
Solitude is the school of g. 10533
spirit stronger than g. 11568
When a true g. appears in world 4400
will not take place of perseverance 8555

world spending g. of its scientists
11745

GENIUSES
world wants g. just like other
people 4394

GENTLE
Angels, not always g. 359
Anger quieted by g. word 372
at home g. life reaches us 5849
Bible transformed killers into g.
saints 726
Criticism should be g. enough to
nourish 2057
cross radiant with glory of g. spirit
5252
Feelings are everywhere, be g.
4401
Hope a more g. name for fear
5916
Instead of losing, the g. gain 4402
Jesus, meek and mild 1117
listen to the g. movement of the
Holy Spirit 10257
Love makes all hard hearts g.
7261
more g. and more caring 1545
more g. we become toward defects
of others 8521
more perfect we are, more g. we
are 11395
nothing so g. as strength 10752
response to g. moving of Holy
Spirit 5396
Solitude molds into g. persons
10561
to reap praise sow g. words,
useful deeds 1574
to the weak, God is g. 4649
touch, stronger than force, fury
4296

GENTLEMAN
Mr. Money is a powerful g. 7817
Sometimes the devil is a g. 2668

GENTLENESS
calm in heated atmosphere 4402
causes others to retain self-esteem
4402
Christ Lamb in g. 6425
emitting soothing effect 4402
God's g. to refresh you 4858
is better than cruelty 6326
is love in society 7202
not prepared to destroy evil not g.
11779
Nothing so strong as g. 10752
Nothing stronger than g. 4404
of heaven broods o'er the sea
8980
Patience and g. is power 8708
possessing gracious courtesy 4402
possessing tact 4402
Power can do by g. 4403
strength under control 4402
we think of g. as weakness 4402
without curativeness 1315

GENTLEST
Christ, g. of Saviors 6430

GENTLY
Deal with faults of others as g. as
with your own 3938
friend g. invites you to grow 4169
God works powerfully but g.
4814
Govern small family very g. 3868
treat men g, they will show
themselves great 6807

GENUINE
Faith when hungry, g. 3711
gift of g. Christian fellowship
4029

GEOCENTRIC
limitations of humanist g. thinking
1168

GERMANY
psychological secrets to control
youth of G. 12178

GET
all the gold goose could give 5328
best out of man, go to best in him
3471
can g. life for nothing 6996
cannot g. to top by sitting on
bottom 6783
even with someone is becoming
even with them 9730
Experience what you g. when you
didn't g. what you wanted 3533
happiness is wanting what you g.
5552
If insist on your own way, will g. it
5695
If you don't g. everything you
want 822
make a living by what we g. 4381
Man finds it hard to g. what he
wants 2571
new things, better things 3315
nice to g. flowers 3137
one thing can never g. enough of
is love 7308
ready for the worst 5911
spindle ready, God will send flax
9346
theme is g. more, know more, do
more 9016
to add what we can, not to g.
what we can 10207
To g. good is animal 5085
To g. money is difficult 7823
To g. to heaven, turn right, keep
straight 5675
We g. no deeper into Christ 6502
We g. what we give 1740
What you don't g, you can't lose
8639
What you g. free costs too much
11668
you'll never g. to lead the band
6797

GET UP
Stumblers who g. rare 3618

GETHSEMANE
God beneath moonlight of G.
4856

joy of finding you there 1512
You have brought me to G. 1512

GETS
discontent that works g. what it
wants 2876
never thinks he g. as much as he
deserves 5258
Politics , who g. what, when, why
5186
reward of labor not what he g.
3119
Temper g. people into trouble
9237

GETTING
burden of care in g. riches 11865
doth but gain his death 2567
leadership art of g. someone else
to do something 6799
Love is not g, but giving 7243
married is easy 7615
Prayer is not g. 8928
Success is g. what you want 5552
What am I g. out of this 10062
without g. a few drops on yourself
5516

GHASTLY
War the most g. experience 11772

GHETTOS
Love is needed in the g. 7251

GHOST
like a passionate love for a g.
7521
soul without body, a g. 5088
to demonstrate to diehard doubter
he wasn't a g. 9693

GHOSTLY
a thousand g. fears 5476

GHOSTS
words stand by like impotent pale
g. 10274

GIANT
feels sting of bee 8700
in your eyes may be dwarf in ours
8484
tyrannous to use strength like a g.
8707

GIANT'S
excellent to have a g. strength
8707

GIANTS
contend against g. of passion,
pride 9233
not the g. who defeat us 2512
world of nuclear g, ethical infants
1705

GIDDY
authority, make men g, proud and
vain 8702
I look down, I feel g. 7090

GIDEON BIBLES
Why put G. only in bedrooms 751

GIFT
ability to say no greatest g. parent
has 8326

Bible, free g. inside 690
Blessed who have g. of making friends 4220
Body most gracious g. God has given 837
Christ gave greatest g, himself 10731
compliment a g. not to throw away 1570
death a g. to some 2274
Each day is a wonderful g. 6524
Face it—'tis God's g. 6881
Faith is a g, but can ask for it 3674
Faith is a g. of God 3721
For g. or grace, surpassing this 2345
God gives me g. of 24 hours day 11296
gospel is g. of God 9545
great if given with affection 4352
heart capable of containing God's g. of himself 8910
I would be giving, forget g. 1018
Laughter is a g. 6727
life a g. to be shared 10545
look upon life as g. from God 2307
Love g. that grows bigger more you take from it 7252
Love greatest g. person can give another 7249
Love is a g. from God 7226
Love is the g. of oneself 7225
love one g. open to every member of the church 7235
man who maintains only he has g. to speak 8196
Music is God's best g. to man 7904
new life a g. to be received 10545
No g. to mother can equal her g. to you 7850
of genuine Christian fellowship 4029
of love is offering one's most honest self 7337
of loving thought into heart of friend 4189
of silence 10247
of thought giving as angels give 11225
own g. cumulative force of life's cultivation 6226
personal g, self-commitment 4277
Prayer is a rare g. 8914
remember g. of life 9270
Salvation is a g. you can ask for 9808
small moment carrier of God's g. 11319
successful marriage not a g. 7598
Suffering best g. God has to give us 10894
Tears best g. of God to suffering man 11020
Thanks to God for unspeakable g. 1372
The future is thy g. 9072

thick skin g. from God 2625
Time a precious g. of God 11337
to overwhelm us with g. of himself 4639
To see ourselves as others see us a g. 8513
true g, nothing expected in return 4384
What you are is God's g. to you 8560
What you make of yourself your g. to God 8560
Whate'er the g. may be 10210
will unearth the g. of serenity 10553
wise lover values not g. of lover 7157

GIFTED
planned, g, positioned on earth by Master Craftsman 10004
see the good and g. 7300
some so g. they won't trust God 2833

GIFTS
Accept equally God's g. 1461
according to the taker 5
arranged by infinite wisdom 12
billion or so g. 1370
Each day comes bearing g. 2192
fulfilled by g. of the Holy Ghost 4749
God's g. are meted out 5
God's g. on shelves one above the other 6017
God's g. put man's best dreams to shame 4988
God's g. so infinite do not see them 7993
God's g. sometimes become very good for us 10708
lest God make incomes match g. 4369
Love higher than other g. in value 7235
music among the g. God has sent 7935
obtain the most precious g. by waiting 8425
Once his g. I wanted 6465
one of God's best g. 4220
rather than g. God is offered 6334
Religious work done without g. of the Spirit 10181
Rich g. prove poor when givers unkind 4372
Riches least worthy g. God can give 11845
These are g. from God 12
to be used for God's glory 10708
To thank thee for these g. of thine 11136
whether we seek God or his g. 4800
who am not sensible of these g. 6253

GIGANTIC
celebration in unseen world 3326
headed for g. collapse 4011

if resurrection didn't happen Christianity a g. fraud 9691
Joy g. secret of the Christian 6546

GILDED-OVER
civilized life more or less g. system of murder 10513

GIMME
gimme-gimme 10075

GIMMICKS
without using g. God brings suffering 10844

GIRAFFE
only animal that can keep feet on ground while head in clouds 9244

GIRDED
for war, humility his mighty dress 6124

GIRL
bring more bliss to old home place 814
curls and cheeks of little g. 814
little g. who hears music for first time 7922
some pray for a golden-haired g. 814
while lost g. on streets, I'll fight 3342

GIRLS
Golden lads and g. all must 2290

GIVE
a little love to a child 8297
a man a dollar, cheer heart 3307
a man a fish, eats for a day 11001
all their living, have given much 10738
all unable to g. possesses you 10724
All you are unable to g. possesses you 8623
and cried, "G. me" 8878
and spend, God will send 4354
as love-gift the best I have 9762
As we g, we live 10725
attention to persons, matters external to ourselves 5550
be first to g. friendship sign 9479
before you g. them your confidence 4218
better g. one shilling than lend pound 4368
but little when g. possessions 10219
But what did he g. 7423
can g. without loving 7350
Christ asks, Why does he g. 10735
Christian to g. justice 1207
demands satisfaction from other human beings they cannot g. 9496
deny yourself that you may g. 4387
Didst thou g. me this inescapable loneliness 7125
Don't bother to g. God instructions 8782

easier for me to g. thee all 7125

energy of life does not fail for those who g. 2018

every man thy ear 1843

experience something you g. yourself 10996

few men thy voice 1843

foolish if g. up trying to pray 9013

For I have none to g. 4796

freedom to g. up our rights for good of others 9963

generosity, not how much you g. 4378

gift of thought giving as angels g. 11225

giving as the angels g. 4189

God above all wants to g. you himself 9272

God cannot g. happiness apart from himself 5510

God does not g. power to imitate him 9834

God doesn't merely have or g. love 7244

God finds it hard to g. 2571

God g. me love, care, strength to help 910

God g. me work 12007

God g. us men 6299

God gives, but he does not g. away 4821

God thanks for having revealed so much 4908

God wants to g. new values 7863

God will g. me goodness of Jesus 5059

God will g. what you ask or something better 2568

God will g. you strength 55

God would g. best, man will not take 2571

God, not the world, can g. peace 8456

government big enough to g. everything 5168

Great Spirit, g. to me 5640

having all will g. up all 5315

He who gives to me teaches me to g. 3434

him but rope enough 4061

I will not g. a woman 21

If g, yourself by halves, cannot find full rest 9683

If God should g. my soul all he ever made 7477

If have love, you always have something to g. 7189

in greater measure than we g. 1740

In joy do not promise to g. anything 11920

in midday g. counsel 6928

Instead of telling people to g. up things 3315

joy you g. to others 6561

larger gratitude we feel for what we g. 5267

Let us g. according to our incomes 4369

Lord did not ask us to g. up things 9974

love away, have more than ever 7252

Love cures both who g. love and who receive 7213

Love doesn't start to multiply until g. it away 7238

Love greatest gift person can g. another 7249

Love has power to g. in a moment 7223

Love is what we g. 7290 9646

Love isn't love until you g. it away 7258

love's prerogative, to g, and g, and g. 7218

make a life by what we g. 4381

make money go far, g. to foreign missions 11823

man Christ, change heart 3307

man dream, challenge heart 3307

man religion without reminding of his filth 7425

me a light that I may tread 5417

me a person who says 81

me a pure heart that I may see thee 7458

me ability to see good things 8575

me an unconquered heart 9057

me an upright heart 9057

me faith to live from day to day 9072

me power to live for mankind 10130

me simple laboring folk 11686

me such love for God and men 7170

me the confused self 4530

me the coward heart 4530

me the greedy heart 4530

me the little creeping treasons 4530

me the money spent in war 11746

me the proud heart 4530

me the ready hand rather than ready tongue 2497

me the shallow heart 4530

me the spiritless refusals 4530

me the vain lust, the folly 4530

me wisdom to make stepping-stones out of stumbling blocks 9073

me your tired, your poor 7985

me, O Lord, a steadfast heart 9057

meet man who has no smile, g. him yours 10496

Men g. advice, God gives guidance 5433

more love you g. away, the more comes back 7232

more money you g. away, less you have 7232

much 5561

much without sacrifice, given little 10738

my heart 1376

myself to thee to lead me anywhere 9084

never g. enough love 7308

never g. impression we care when in a hurry 7327

never g. up 236

never g. up hope for him 3167

never more like God than when we g. 4380

never tire of pleasures we g. 8613

Nobody needs smile as much as those who have none to g. 10498

Not how much we g. 4371

not to g. him anything back 5323

not to g. his children taste of his delights 9037

Of thy goodness, g. us 619

one thing more—a grateful heart 5265

others a piece of heart, not mind 10132

ourselves up to ownership of Jesus 8090

pauper can g. like a prince 4388

possessions, g. little 1725

power to feel with others g. 8430

quotations when engraved upon memory g. good thoughts 9383

rather than grasp 1138

Rather than love, g. me truth 11526

reputation to Christ, gain it 9629

resources to g. to those who could never g. in return 5957

right you claim for yourself 11282

safe rule is to g. more than we can spare 10734

Satisfaction felt by those who g. 2018

Sea of Galilee gets to g. 10195

So much God would g. 8662

Some will take all God has to g. us 5323

sorrow words 5333

strength to bear suffering 5907

Suffering best gift God has to g. us 10894

Sympathy never wasted except when g. to yourself 10981

thanks to the Almighty, seek his aid 5411

the blind, obstinate eyes 4530

The Giver makes you g. 5211

them grace to pray for such as do them wrong 9104

themselves absolutely to God 4790

things that disturb will be events to g. gratitude 5252

till the Master stops giving to you 10728

to child, example 511

to enemy, forgiveness 511

to father, deference 511

to friend, your heart 511

to g. and not to count the cost 9113

to God each moment as it flies 8600

to God, discover God gives to you 4386

To love is to g. one's time 7327

to men, charity 511

to mother, conduct 511

to opponent, tolerance 511

to thy servants skill to soothe, bless 9045

to tired and ill g. quietness 9045

to yourself, respect 511

Today I g. to God 1539

two hands, other to g. with 10729

unless able to g. to people in selfless love 7962

unless ready to g. myself to his service 8818

unto all, lest he whom thou deny'st 4355

up measuring value with yardstick of others 10162

up our right to ourselves 465

us a heart of faith 9058

us a heart of love 9058

us a humble heart 9058

us a pure heart 9058

us clear vision 11731

us courage to change things which should be changed 9060

us sense of comradeship with heroes, saints of every age 9059

us the man who sings at his work 3090

us wisdom to distinguish one from the other 9060

Use God to g. us safety 7517

We g. thee but thine own 10210

We get what we g. 1740

We owe God every honor in our power to g. 4529

What can I g. him 1376

What God does not choose to g. 4958

What reward shall I g. the Lord 7568

what we do not g. 4371

what we g. up makes us rich 624

what we have not, g. us 9083

What you g. to humanity you get back 10742

what you have 4356

what you must g. up 4431

When Athenians wanted society to g. to them 4155

when g. yourself you truly g. 10219

When I g, I g. myself 10121

who seeks the Father more than anything he can g. 8997

Who will g. me back days when life had wings 12176

world asks, How much does he g. 10735

would not g. one moment of heaven 5652

yourself up with joy to confidence in God 4747

yourself, truly g. 1725

GIVEN

account to be g. for riches 11865

afraid to accept what is g. us 7072

All we can hold is what we have g. away 4349

Bible g. for our transformation 689

Christians have g. approval to self-assertive 5891

Contentment, realizing God has g. me everything 1784

day to use strength g. us 6947

dies, clutches only that which he has g. away 2416

gift g. great if g. with affection 4352

God has g. man a short time upon earth 6894

God has g. me a cheerful heart 7931

God has g. us the mind of Christ 6679

God has g. us two hands 10729

grace g. that we may do good works 5209

healing words not our own but are g. to us 10545

If do not use mind God has g. us 6693

infirmity that he might do better things 8806

intellect g. to be used for God's glory 10708

Knowledge g. to lead us to worship, faith 6693

life is g. us so we may grow in love 6907

life that he might enjoy all things 8806

Man g. one tongue 1858

Man g. two ears 1858

martyrs, when the joyful crown is g. 7672

more soul wants, more it is g. 10699

most potent weapon God has g. man 4154

Music only art of heaven g. to earth 7904

night is g. to take breath, to pray 6947

No man gives at all unless he has g. all 10119

No man gives until first g. himself in love, sacrifice 10119

not complete if all not g. to God 5734

poverty that he might be wise 8806

Signs are g. us 5439

So much has been g. to me 5259

take lowest place, highest will be g. 5991

Thank you for all you have g. me 11161

Thou hast g. so much to me 5265

'Tis heaven alone that is g. away 9795

'Twas not g. for thee alone 6640

up right for people to return our love 9963

use for passions stuff g. for happiness 4359

vinegar with teaspoon, honey with ladle 2728

weakness that he might feel need of God 8806

What he hath g. 2287

wish God had not g. me what I prayed for 8879

world g. to man in trust 3195

Worship giving to God best he has g. us 12134

GIVER

Charity does work of grace upon g. 1075

Christ g. of grace 5208

Flattery corrupts receiver, g. 4048

God the Father g. of Holy Scripture 655

Grace free, but you are bound to the G. 5211

If the G. gives you a hill 35

makes you give 5211

never fails to receive 9763

Now the G. own 6465

wise lover values love of the g. 7157

GIVERS

Rich gifts poor when g. unkind 4372

sleep well 10198

GIVES

a field rested g. beautiful crop 6839

All of creation God g. to humankind 3191

All that God g. remains his own 4821

beggar g. chance to do good 621

Bible g. no encouragement perfection achieved 9254

blesseth him that g. and him that takes 7744

By this glance God g. himself to me 7953

certainty of divine participation g. courage 6277

Character g. awe to gray hairs 997

Character g. splendor to youth 997

Christ g. us light 1144

Christ g. us power to go on with battle 11451

Christian, g. to keep 1265

courtesy pleases him who g. 1944

Do not cut down tree that g. shade 5241

duty performed g. music at midnight 9675

Every delay is hateful, but g. wisdom 11912

Experience comb nature g. when bald 3518

Fear g. framework of habits 3951

field rested g. bountiful crop 9686

fragrance clings to hand that g. roses 4344

generous man forgets what he g. 4346

give to God, discover God g. to you 4386

God g, but he does not give away 4821

God g. best, leave choice with him 1139

God g. birds food, but they must fly 3093

God g. comfort in despair 2582

God g. every bird its food 3091

God g. light in darkness 2582

God g. me gift of 24 hours day 11296

God g. new set of inner eyes 8495

God g. no linen, but flax to spin 3092

God g. self-knowledge gradually 10006

God g. shoulder to burden 928

God g. something to rely upon others do not experience 6178

God g. something which takes place of all, love 4790

God g. the nuts but does not crack them 9348

God g. to every man virtue 5387

God g. us ability to work in his kingdom 4648

God g. us his very self 9834

God g. us the cross 2090

God g. us the ingredients 9657

God g. us will to will 11505

God g. without weight his mercy 4451

God g. wrath by weight 4451

God g. you and me lumber of our lives 7684

God is love, he g. himself 7244

God never g. strength for tomorrow 2722

God never takes unless g. better 4630

God only g. strength for the moment 2722

God only g. time to us moment by moment 11337

God only g. us light as we need for present 5397

Good when he g. supremely good 288

Grace is love that g. 5222

greatest saint not he who g. most 9790

guidance noiselessly 5426

hand that g. gathers 4376

hand that g. is above hand that takes 4375

He g. his beloved sleep 8120

He that g. should never remember 4363

He who g. to me teaches me to give 3434

He who g. what he would throw away 4365

If capital one g. 11360

If the Giver g. you a hill 35

important is what one g. 11360

Incredulity g. nothing in return 11592

It g. but borrows none 634

Jesus g. truth carried on wings of love 6176

Love ever g, forgives, outlives 7218

Love g. courage to the cowardly 7260

Love g. eloquence to the mute 7260

Love g. itself, is not bought 7222

man imagines he will lose if he g. 1537

Men give advice, God g. guidance 5433

no fool who g. what he cannot keep 1195

No man g. anything acceptable to God until 10119

No man g. at all until he has given all 10119

not only prayer that g. God glory 12013

nothing but worthless gold 11358

One lie g. birth to another 6856

quantity of money one g. 11360

rich, he who g. much 4370

Take glory in God who g. you everything 9272

Talent something God g. you 10996

that hope to be thy blessing now 5913

the cross g. us God 2090

'Tis God g. skill 4441

twice who g. quickly 4361

unexpected g. anticipation, surprise 4318

uniqueness that g. freshness, vitality to a relationship 6197

What future bliss he g. not thee to know 5913

What God g, and what we take 5860

When human strength g. way 4569

while love lives, it g. 7218

Who g. from sense of duty 11358

Who g. its lustre to an insect's wing 4482

who g. most light to world 6004

Who g. the day 5434

who g. to be seen 10037

Who g. to poor, lends to God 627

who g. us teeth will give us bread 9349

Who much receives, but nothing g. 4374

work g. God glory 12013

worry g. indigestion 12091

worry g. sleepless hours 12091

GIVETH

big print g, small print taketh away 9328

He g, and g, and g. again 7570

He g. his beloved sleep 2345

He g. more grace when burdens grow greater 5223

GIVE UP

Stumblers who g. dime a dozen 3618

GIVING

another privilege of sharing 4277

as God gives 6569

as the angels give 4189

Asceticism, passion of g. up 465

away what no longer belongs to him 4377

Brotherhood is g. appreciation 924

Brotherhood is g. dignity 924

Brotherhood is g. others your rights 924

cannot love without g. 7350

commit to concrete plans for g. 10739

Death God's way of g. life 2246

duty g. comes from obligation 10736

duty g. says, I ought to 10736

Generosity, g. more than you can 4353

gift of thought g. as angels give 11225

give till the Master stops g. to you 10728

God, ever g, yet has not less 4699

grudge g. comes from constraint 10736

grudge g. says, I hate to 10736

happy spirit takes grind out of g. 4347

highest form of potency 10726

I would be g. forget gift 1018

in g. that we receive 9086

is living, the angel said 10728

is thermometer of love 4358

is Yours 7575

joy if in right spirit 4357

keeps us from g. in fresh, innovative ways to others 6825

Kindness in g. creates love 6649

Love is not getting, but g. 7243

Man frightened that he loses himself by g. himself 9937

need experience of g. 4359

Nothing grows, blooms save by g. 4342

Our Father's full g. is only begun 7570

ourselves to the utmost 2774

Parents g. children nothing but best 8324

probably g. away too little 10734

secret of healthy life 10727

Self-discipline never means g. up anything 9974

Thanksgiving first thanks, then g. 11178

three kinds of g. 10736

we've missed purpose of g. 10738

When talk of man g. anything to God 10214

GIZZARD
Whoever is capable of g. is rich
10743
Worship is g. to God best he has
given us 12134

GIZZARD
Politics g. of society 5185

GLAD
Be g. bottle half full 11141
be g. of life 8472
friend, a song when you're g.
4174
gospel signifies g. tydings 5091
If life be long I will be g. 6923
Let wife make husband g. to come
home 7627
Light of the g. 6468
newborn life how g. 9898
only too g. to hand ourselves over
to God 10015
Strength'ning their arms to
warfare g. and grim 8454
takes two to be g. 10607
tidings send afar 6141
when great man reassures us of
humanity 5307
will scarcely hear g. sound of
Gospel 5224

GLADDENING
not much time for g. hearts 6658

GLADDENS
Love the wine that g. heart of man
7256

GLADLY
Let me die g. 2326
work for good of country g, as
unto God 10525

GLADNESS
brightest blazes of g. kindled by
unexpected sparks 8606
in nature can be glad with an
entire g. 8012
tried to give g. for a space 1545

GLAMOR
Old streets a g. hold 8143

GLAMOROUS
Music weapon used to make
perverse seem g. 7910

GLANCE
a lie may be told by g. of the eye
6859
By this g. God gives himself to me
7953
never a backward g. of regret
4281
one g. most kind 107
wherever God's g. falls he turns to
beauty 4463

GLASS
intellect of wise like g. 11945
more intense light is, less you see g.
6033
perfect g. to see and know
ourselves 156
That Time could turn up his swift
sandy g. 9568

GLEAM
brightly in pattern of life God
approves 6997
One life, g. of time between two
eternities 7013

GLEE
turned into jubilant song of g.
7895

GLIB
When too g. in prayer 9031

GLIDES
Winged time g. on 11354

GLIMMER
No man happy whose path but g.
of light 6101

GLIMPSE
But caught no g. of him 4921
catch some g. of God's designs
4578
of next three feet of road more
important 5371

GLISTENING
garment of truth 5714

GLITTER
brighter the g, the more easily
broken 9336

GLITTERING
Converse makes sharp the g. wit
10534

GLITTERS
All not gold that g. 430

GLOBE
blood to flow like rivers
throughout g. 4895

GLOOM
All were wrapt in g. 7109
And if in g. I see thee not 4977
Bible burst forth amidst g. 736
But iron dug from central g. 2599
Lead, kindly Light amid the,
encircling g. 5429
only two religions accept g. as fact
9551
Was the sadness and the g. 2217
Will pierce the g. 2945
worry fills with g. the days 12091

GLOOMIEST
Praying fills the grayest, g. day
8899

GLOOMY
holy life not g. 5736
Music is moonlight to g. night of
life 7909
never let man become g. cynic
1064

GLORIES
I see heaven's g. shine 3765
Nothing to discuss but g. of days
past 4321

GLORIFIED
God's work isn't finished until we
are g. 2232

not too excited about being g.
2232
through defeat of cross God g.
2519
today I am g. with Christ 2121

GLORIFIETH
glory of the Garden g. every one
10201

GLORIFY
A God to g. 10114
difference between g. God,
yourself 3469
If fail to emphasize we can g. God
7481
In commanding us to g. him 4554

GLORIFYING
another thing to go through every
day g. God 7129
everyday g. God 1295
God when no witness, limelight,
attention 1295
means of g. God, salvation of souls
7027

GLORIOUS
death lightsome and g. 2272
Faith makes future g. 3705
God intrudes in g, myriad ways
7556
God's promises g. 4458
harder the conflict, more g. the
triumph 1628
hours even in a poorhouse 7001
How g. it is to be an exception
6182
In great attempts g. to fail 3600
Life a g. opportunity 6944
more g. the world of God within
us 10535
My beauty are, my g. dress 4719
no God anything less than
absolutely g. 4504
the world of God around us
10535
willingness, fearful, g. power 4128

GLORY
A g. gilds the sacred page 634
A g. never sung 8047
actually pursuing own g. 10076
All g. comes from daring to begin
102
as a protecting canopy, g. the
blessing of God 5848
Avoid shame, do not seek g. 4406
avoids those who chase after it
4407
Be a friend. You don't need g.
4217
Bible, g. without dimness 710
built on selfish principles is
shame, guilt 10054
came to my life 7105
cannot say thine is the g. if 8818
Christ crown of thorns that thou
mightest wear crown of g. 6393
Christ seeks g. by sacrifice of
himself 2152
cross of Christ is Christ's g. 2152

cross radiant with g. of meek, gentle spirit 5252

cross, a present g. 2099

dairymaid can milk cows to g. of God 3082

death out of contempt into eternal g. 2325

Defeat may serve to let the g. out 2508

Do rays of loftier g. round thee play 6878

early Christians looking for cleavage in sky called G. 9913

Father, set me free in the g. of thy will 9052

For the g. of the Garden 10201

forefathers goal was g. to God 3113

God of himself full of g. 12126

God, lone in g. 11429

Grace beginning of g. in us 5216

Grace is but g. begun 5218

greater the difficulty, greater the g. 4417

greater the difficulty, more g. 209

head that once was crowned with thorns, crowned with g. now 9697

his g. is inexplicable 4681

if I am seeking my own g. first 8818

in g. we shall know his nature 3814

in rising every time you fail 3620

In thy sole g. may unite 9047

intellect given to be used for God's g. 10708

is endowed on many who did not pursue 4407

Is not speech a g. 6253

is perfected grace 4408

is suffering and then g. 10863

Jesus Christ, g. within 6352

Jesus' g. lies in obscurity 6443

Jesus, anything but g. 2813

love sees things in light of his g. 6457

Lovelier to desire than possess 4409

lucky who can obliterate pursuit of g. 4411

man can no more diminish God's g. 4442

Man seeks to win g. by sacrifice of others 2152

man with dungfork gives God g. 1237

Man, the g. of the world 7417

many Christians, g. behind them 4321

mirror in which g. of God reflected 10339

missed the g. of those who heard, saw, believed 6464

more daring the request, more g. to God 9028

more g. to God when answer comes 9028

mother does not have much g. 7856

naught 4416

need eye single to God's g. 5442

no gall, no g. 199

No one who is lover of g. is lover of man 11661

not only prayer that gives God g. 12013

Nothing so expensive as g. 4406 3850

nothing, smoke, shadow, pain 4412

of creation, infinite diversity 1973

of friendship spiritual inspiration 4275

of God is man fully alive 4566

of God is the real business of life 7027

of spring how sweet 9898

of the gospel is its freedom 5095

of the home is hospitality 5851

of the star, sun 6108

of the stars 4643

or never behold g. in the highest 9020

our only aim God's g. 4507

path of humility is path to g. 6034

People imagine pursuing g. of God 10076

prayer changes us, therein lies its g. 8855

prayer gives God g. 1237

presence of God's g. is in heaven 4865

price, g. of mortal's life 7035

resurrection g. derived from no other source 9702

revival to give g. to a great Savior 9751

road to g. not strewn with flowers 4418

Sad as g. itself 4415

saints have their g. 5301

Saints in g. perfect made 2221

so well-controlled few waves of g. 3184

solitude, g. of being alone 7131

springs from silent conquest of ourselves 4414

standing without, no g. 3648

Success for g. of God or your own 10811

Take g. in God who gives you everything 9272

Take g. neither in money nor friends 9272

teach me g. of my cross 2099

Temptation g. of manhood 11061

the g. and poetry of God 4704

thornbush aflame with g. of God 9064

Time's g. is to calm contending kings 11344

turn hard thing into g. 3149

turned back on the g. 6488

useless aim which thwarts happiness 4411

What will thy g. be 5635

which thou canst not see 4708

who has enjoyed God's g. on earth 6092

woman with slop pail gives God g. 1237

work gives God g. 12013

work to g. of God 3127

GLORY'S

Popularity g. small change 3859

GLOVE

clean g. often hides dirty hand 2460

like a rubber g. 6131

GLOW

Doubt robbing life of g, meaning 6091

Out of his dark I g. 4125

we g. when God stirs us 7534

GLOWED

And all the church with his presence g. 2638

GLOWING

Rainbow, God's g. covenant 9393

GLOWS

darkness hideth not from him, but g. 4746

Goodness g. 5067

love with a love that g. 3182

GLUE

grace of God is g. 4654

GLUTTON

Christ's life so social called a g. 6436

GLUTTONS

dig their graves with teeth 132

don't believe in eating on empty stomach 131

have one thing in common 131

GLUTTONY

an emotional escape 133

sign that something is eating us 133

GNASHING

hell, g. of teeth 5698

GNAW

cancers that g. on the soul 3873

GO

a road that we must g. 8081

afterwards we see we had to g. that way 5423

another thing to g. through every day glorifying God 7129

Ask not where they g. 5431

best way to keep is to let g. 4733

convinced deserves to g. to hell 5668

difference between g. and let's g. 9505

do not need to g. somewhere to find God 4870

feelings come and g, God's love does not 4777

forth to meet shadowy future 8378

forward without fear 1918

get best out of man, g. to best in him 3471

God loved world, g. and do likewise 7172

How many people stop because few say G. 3135

However far you g. 5409

I will g. anywhere, provided forward 2628

I'll g. where you want me to g, dear Lord 5420

labor on, spend and be spent 10133

must not elect to g. 10188

one thing to g. through a crisis grandly 7129

out and God comes in 9556

put your creed into deed 1011

searching all the way 7475

send me where thou wilt, only g. with me 9080

shall g. on planned voyage 5945

singing as far as we g. 7899

slowly to entertainment of thy friends 4242

So I securely g. 5434

than g. alone in the light 5419

time stays, we g. 11327

To g. too far as bad as to fall short 11954

When God comes g. with him slowly 5460

When in doubt, g. home 11114

where no path, leave trail 6787

Wherever I g—only thou 4518

Wherever we g, find God present 4845

Wherever you g, g. with whole heart 3187

whichever way God turns my feet, I g. 5416

With God, g. over the sea 5470

world a ladder for some to g. up, some down 7047

You don't g. witnessing 3344

you g. out of world alone 7151

GOADS

when g. of money, fame, and ambition are lifted 6842

GOAL

And the grave is not its g. 2328

Character, distant g. 1000

Christian's g. not power but justice 6623

Everyone should have a g. 4422

forefathers g. was glory to God 3113

God is each virtue's g. 11687

God's g. not to pamper physically 1016

God's g. to perfect spiritually 1016

greatness in unyielding loyalty to g. 5283

happiness is distant g. to which no shortcut 7648

Life without g. like 4426

My g. is God himself 4428

not joy nor peace 4428

not material wealth 3113

Obstacles frightening when eyes off g. 4430

of adventure to which God commits 5385

of fear, to create cowardly, joyless souls 3971

Only Christ can accomplish g. within us 8113

set of a soul that decides g. 4432

small chance of truth at g. 11549

Spirit-filled life no g. difficult of attainment 5803

To be like Christ our g. 8113

When g. goes, meaning goes 4437

when God goes, g. goes 4437

willing to exchange piece of life 4422

GOALS

clearly defined g. simplified decisions 4425

focus eyes on larger-than-life g. 9970

God alone sets all the g. 7828

GOD

A being wholly here, wholly there 4840

a continuous, unbroken is 4604

a deep but dazzling darkness 4506

a dynamic, pulsating activity 11425

a fountain always flowing 4698

a G. too demanding 2959

a G. who suffers 4788

a garden of life 4698

a god from we do not hide 4846

a god whom we can easily bear 4846

a god whom we do not hate in moments 4846

a god whose destruction we never desire 4846

a kind of dance 11425

a leveler who renders equal small, great 4727

a life 11425

a light that is never darkened 4698

a loving confidence in G. 4747

A man without G. 7446

a present help or not much help at all 4701

a radical beginning of goodness 4698

a robber in the sight of G. 10060

a seminary of wisdom 4698

a specialist in the sin disease 10308

abides in tranquil eternity 8437

able to bring good out of evil and pain 5046

able to empower us to do whatever he calls us to do 9199

able to fulfill his designs 4521

able to test, develop faith 3744

able to work failures into his plans 3613

able, willing to enter human personality, change it 5777

above all existing things 4609

above all wants to give you himself 9272

above but not raised up 4848

above existence itself 4609

above in rank, station 4607

above, all measurement 4710

above, presiding 4848

Absolute truth belongs to G. alone 11495

absorbed in G. 9840

absurd to put G. into a definition 7487

accept even our incomplete knowledge of G. 7435

Acceptance before G. is complete, secure 9992

accepted G. as part of my life 5594

Acquaint thyself with G. 4737

acquire confidence in recourse to G. 8796

action of G. mediated through a person 10122

activities we do for G. are secondary 8972

Adam, created friend, companion of G. 758

adjust lives to G. 1304

adoration, worship of G. become occupation 3987

afflictions from a loving G. 3996

afflicts less than grace can suffer 286

After crises G. steps in 2042

after short act of gratitude, we forget G. 8788

After the friendship of G. 4181

Ah! for a vision of G. 7448

aiding to yield fruit 4514

All but G. changing day by day 4586

All G. does agrees with all G. is 4579

all great purposes of G. culminate in Christ 5710

All growth not toward G. is decay 5363

all long for heaven where G. is 6569

All of creation G. gives to humankind 3191

all rules will be fair 604

All service ranks the same with G. 10116

all sorts of notions about G. 4489

All that G. gives remains his own 4821

All that we are comes from G. 11135

all you see, all you cannot see 4692

allots our work where he chooses 2831

allowing too many rivals of G. 9552

allows man insolently to deny him 4673

allows man to cut throat of his fellowmen 4673

allows men to live without him 1142

allows us to play the game 7828

Almighty first planted a garden 8007

almost a kind of drama 11425

alone beholds the end of what is sown 10204

alone knows all the facts 7828

alone knows how to lead his children 169

alone knows meaning of mystery called time 4694

alone knows secret of history 4694

alone makes man believer 585

alone man with his G. must strive 10530

alone may enter as judge 1666

alone suffices 4588

alone what is hid with G. made known 10532

alone with silence, along with G. 10256

aloof from curious eyes of reason 4743

already had you in mind 4879

alters our disposition 1012

alters the inevitable 4937

alters the mainspring 8570

alters the things that matter 9276

alters things while we wait 8395

always answers us in the deeps 8795

always at hand 4621

always calling on us to do impossible 10138

always find G. present 4845

always man who is reconciled to G. 9430

always receptive to misery, need 4590

always springtime in heart that loves G. 4797

always to be found unchanged 4867

Among so many, can he care 4834

an atheist, thank G. 480

an ever-joyful guest 4548

an ever-present Spirit 5389

An honest man's the noblest work of G. 5885

an infinite circle 4842

an unwearied life that cannot die 4698

an utterable sigh, planted in the soul 4843

And did G. care 8878

And G. in cradle lies 6129

And justify the ways of G. to men 7566

And let the face of G. shine through 10670

and love synonymous 4755

and man exist for each other 4531

and people, two things that mattered 3331

angel created by G. 354

angels, messengers of G. 359

angels, the messengers of G. 358

anger at G. to be troubled for what is past 12066

another thing to go through every day glorifying G. 7129

Apart from G. activity is 113

appears as if G. were unnatural 896

appointed storms 191

arrayed all gloriously 7952

art angry, yet serene 4954

art jealous without anxiety 4954

as dear to G. is peasant as prince 3225

as G. gives us to see right 5199

as if G. required disagreeable things of us 6813

as if one were G. or judge placed above him 11619

As made him know his G. by night 780

as our last and feeblest resource 178

as present as the air 4844

as retire to rest, give soul and G. time together 10486

as to election, G. is salvation 4514

as to himself, G. hath knowledge 4514

as we begin to focus on G. 8488

as you recognize Me as your source 7548

Aside from G. nothing self-caused 4613

ask for guiding and strength of G. 4803

Ask G. for what he thinks is good for you 8781

asking G. to conduct a major operation 7155

asks no man whether he will accept life 6893

asks no one to accept life 1140

asks nothing but pure heart, single mind 7450

asks us to be his friends 4564

asks us to cooperate 4507

asks you do your best, not Saint Teresa's best 9013

assume G. unable to work 3613

assuming circumstances not controlled by G. 11152

astrology, no more than symbolize emanation of G. 4593

at beginning, end of time simultaneously 11314

At beginning, G. accepts us in sinfulness 9832

At cool of day, with G. I wal∴ 7452

at once within, without his works 4692

at past, future unaffected by either 11350

At profoundest depths men talk not about G. but with him 8767

at times seems cruel 8631

At whose throne would G. kneel 4955

at work in history casting down the rich 6630

atheist cannot find G. 472

atheist could not affect G. 491

atheist half believes in G. 477

atheists haven't experienced G. 485

Attempt great things for G. 10118

attitude of child, certain G. knows what he is about 9912

attitude of man who loves G. different 5046

attributes of G. transcend comprehension 4584

attributes to himself 4722

author of human weakness 230

awaits our desire to overwhelm us with himself 4639

aware G. is enough 4516

back of all, above all, before all 4607

bad opinion of G. 11591

baptizes us with Holy Ghost that he may be all in all 5784

Batter my heart, three-person'd G. 2840

Be astounded G. should have written 644

Be natural before G. 8770

be ready to depart when G. calls 2355

be thank'd for those, and these 5860

bear witness to mystery of G. 7945

became man 6125

because of silence mysteries of G. known to saints 10252

becomes partner of God 4894

before all 4607

before G. can feel at home within us 7450

before G. can make the heart a garden 896

Before G. created universe 4879

Before service speak to G. 1384

Before we were born, G. was G. 4527

before works can please G. 5087

begin by loving G. 4802

Begin where we will, G. there first 4835

begs you leave future to him 4319

being and doing are one 4579

being happy with G. means 6569

being One, fills eternity with one now 4601

being self-sufficient, G. cannot relinquish perfections 4821

being with G. for all twenty-four hours 6569

belief that G. knows what is best for us 9993

belief that G. will do everything for man untenable 3415

believe G. can do miraculous one thing 3669

believe in G, there will be wonderful surprises 4508

believe in G. adds nothing to perfections 491

believe in G. even when he is silent 3732

believe in loving anger of G. 4997

believed in G, life made sense 7011

believed in G, world had meaning 7011

believed whatever they did G. ordained 3113

believer special to the G. of the universe 9999

Believing G. must need him there 2792

believing G. understands everything 7560

below but not depressed 4848

benefits G. has conferred become curse 3895

best awakening of reverence is contemplation of works of G. 9734

best proof of immortality in sharing life of G. 6105

best way for child to learn to fear G. 8327

best way to show gratitude to G. 5261

best way to understand wrath of G. 4999

bestows many things out of liberality 8796

Better rich in G. than rich in gold 11800

better served in resisting temptation 11059

better to have failed when serving G. 10777

Better to love G. and die unknown 10777

between ourselves and troubles 41

Between the soul and G. 8926

Beware in prayer of limiting G. 8772

beyond contradictories thou mayst be seen 7950

Bible comes from G. 744

Bible illustrates the work of G. 737

Bible, deals with G. and devil 721

Bible, letter from G. with personal address 704

blessing from G. to know we are destitute 830

blessing of G. as a protecting canopy 5848

blessing those who need him 821

blots out his people's sins, not their names 4626

both far away, near at hand 4465

bravery of G. in trusting us 11479

breadth, length, depths and height of grace in himself 5016

bring our own, G. will supply the rest 4558

bring to everyday living wisdom of G. 3752

brings dark contrast of suffering into your life . 10844

brings problems so we can mature 2844

brings spirit into harmony with G. 8093

brings us through victoriously 165

brings us to resigning ourselves 5395

brought man here with heart's blood expense 4532

builds nest of blind bird 4444

buries his workmen, carries on his work 2286

By anti-intellectualism may be storing up judgment of G. 6679

by choosing us G. makes us worthy 3044

by defying purpose of G. insulate ourselves 4864

by devoting yourself singleheartedly to G. 10703

by failure to put G. where he belongs 7046

By faith led to knowledge of G. 3834

By his first work, G. gave me to myself 4528

by justifying us G. makes us worthy 6631

by love soul unites to G. 7967

by love, brought to G. 3834

by obedience we understand teaching of G. 8095

by permissive government G. lines up his purpose 5175

by practicing mercy resemble G. 7740

by the next work G. gave himself to me 4528

By this glance G. gives himself to me 7953

Call on G, but row away from the rocks 8774

called to an everlasting preoccupation with G. 7551

calls adversity opportunity 233

calls each in secret to make sacrifices 5385

calls for volunteers to oppose, correct evil 3378

calls our loved ones 2287

calls us to life we cannot live 1284

Came G, planting the secret genes of G. 6148

came to show us how to live 6128

Can a man love G. ignoring need of brother 10052

can at any rate be grateful to G. 6251

can be certain about G. 11214

can be with G. in space 11632

can do little things for G. 10208

can do nothing 8

can do nothing until limit of possible 8642

can do tremendous things through people 10134

can do what he likes with man abandoned to him 9557

can fit heroes into their places 9174

can G. dispense us from grief 5352

can give us in one year crop to make up for ten 889

can hear your faintest whisper 8801

can make brokenhearted radiant, loving person 890

can make world's puzzle fit together 4308

can make you anything you want to be 10970

can meet, overflow deepest demands 7463

can neither be demonstrated nor argued down 4678

can neither be spoken nor conceived 4580

can no more do without us 4533

can only accept my badness 5059

can only be known through manifestation 4738

can see repentance coming a great way off 9582

can take our emptiness, fill it up with what he wants 6830

can't make wine if we object 883

cannot accept goodness from me 5059

cannot be comprehended in human words 4682

cannot be fitted into a diagram 4851

cannot be for, against same thing at same time 4972

cannot be found by thought 4738

cannot be used as stop-gap 7562

cannot believe for us 3721

cannot come in any way but his own way 4664

cannot control human beings 5983

cannot divide himself 11422

cannot do our repenting for us 9578

cannot get humanity out of his mind 5983

cannot give us happiness apart from himself 5510

cannot laugh G. out of your death 2432

cannot love fellow creature till you love G. 7351

cannot love his neighbor unless he loves G. 7287

cannot make us walk 1143

cannot reason your way to belief in G. 9428

cannot speak too freely to G. 8968

cannot thrust human beings aside 5983

cannot work in a vacuum 4824

cannot work with empty minds 4824

cannot work with prejudice 4824

canvas on which G. paints truths 10844

carries your picture in wallet 4751

casts the die, not the dice 4930

cause of freedom, cause of G. 4143

center is everywhere 4842

certainty in contact with G. 955

Change finds no likeness to itself in thee 973

changes death to triumph 2373

changes from commonplace to special 4487

Changes, surprises, and G. made it all 8054

changest thy works, thy purpose unchanged 4954

character never meritorious before G. 1057

characteristics of G. mirrored in Jesus 4493

charge G. of all knowledge with ignorance 230

chastises with failure to humble 3603

child identifies parents with G. 8339

chooses base, lowly, unknown 3861

Christ aperture through which G. seen 6373

Christ as G. fatherland where we are going 6364

Christ is G. acting like G. 6371

Christ revealing what G. is like 6426

Christ reveals a G. who stands in thick of whole thing 6432

Christ the express image of G. 6355

Christ the only way to approach G. 6372

Christ the perfect representation of G. 6355

Christ will be whole treasure of G. 6354

Christ's detachments inside toward G. 6436

Christian accepts circumstances from G. 3638

Christian love links love of G. and neighbor 7164

Christian never forgets what G. has done for him 5240

Christian thanks G. when everything good, bad 3638

Christian understands love in terms of G. 4494

Christian, partner of G. 3327

Christianity balanced between G, neighbor 1240

Christianity, power of G. in soul of man 1179

Christianity, way to know G. 1188

circumference is nowhere 4842

claimed by G, counterclaimed by Satan 4918

cling to natural virtues sufficient to obscure work of G. 11701

closer to G, more one feels a sinner 10439

closest to broken hearts 1505

closet and church reverberations of G. 4965

clothed himself in vile man's flesh 6126

clothed himself with our lowliness 6130

comes and sits with you in snowbank 4782

comes in where helplessness begins 11786

comes not only to give us peace but to disturb us 3722

comes padding after me like Hound of Heaven 4534

comes to see us without a bell 4525

comes when we think he is farthest off 4837

comes wisdom through the awful grace of G. 11919

comes without ringing doorbell 4838

comforts to make us comforters 1503

commands us to be filled with the Spirit 5778

communion with G. that asks for nothing, yet everything 8997

compelled to conceal himself from world 4657

comprehended G. is no G. at all 4662

concerned about keeping us in his will 5390

concerned with all kinds of writing 12146

concerned with character, not outward beauty 1033

conclude crimes committed because G. wills 3349

Confession, discipline G. requires 1597

Confession, to agree with G. regarding sin 1597

confidence G. will not cast aside 4005

conforming unreservedly to that of G. 9835

conscience arises from fear of G. 3988

Consecration is handing G. blank sheet 1720

considers not actions, but spirit of action 7861

consigns offense to everlasting forgetfulness 4638

contained I am in him 4852

Contemplation like sleep in arms of G. 1756

content to be found in register of G, not man 6023

converse with G. refreshes, restores, renews 8857

cost G. everything to make it possible for us to pray 8773

Could G. pass examination in theology 11183

could have kept Daniel out of the lions' den 165

could have kept Hebrews out of the furnace 165

could have kept Paul and Silas out of jail 165

could not be good if he were not just 4724

could not possibly abandon us 4617

could only raise my mind in anguish to G. 10931

create a G. in our image 6467

created free beings 3370

created life as a manifold thing 6985

created man because 4535

created men to be holy 5757

creates out of nothing 884

Creativity basic attribute of G. 1999

cross revealed G. in weakness 6471

cross shows how G. could become man 2150

cross the supreme triumph of G. 3582

cross, not what G. suddenly became 2163

cross, what G. always was 2163

cross, what G. ever shall be 2163

cynic who cares not whether there is a G. 9549

dairymaid can milk cows to glory of G. 3082

dare not think G. is absent, daydreaming 7556

David swung. G. made his point 766

daybreak is from G. 2199

dead-end street with man who denies G. 7523

deals with unconscious 10486

Death consummation of union with G. 2257

death of Jesus was revelation of heart of G. 6472

delays, doesn't forget 4445

deliberately stands aside 4891

delights in our temptations 11057

deliver us from rights 10842

deliver us from sullen saints 9774

demands our obedience 8094

demands perfection from his creatures 8518

demands so much only he can supply his demands 4473

denier of G. 483

denies existence of G. 482

deny G. opportunity of working through weakness 10407

deny G. with life-style 487

depend on G. for supernatural ability 1284

dependent on G. from hour to hour 5226

depending on the mind of G. 7753

desert means presence of G. 10565

designed human machine to run on himself 7459

desire nothing but G. 9136

desires but sincerity, transparency 7450

despise that which G. loves 5599

destined to be in G. 3490

Destiny waits in the hand of G. 2620

destitute to fully appreciate grace of G. 2605

destroy bridge by which G. would come to you 9634

devil refuses to stand under G. 4915

devil will limit work of G. 11218

devil wrestles with G. 2691

devote will to purpose of G. 12124

did not abolish evil 4931

did not choose us because worthy 3044

did not stop the crucifixion 4931

did not write solo parts for very many of us 10135

didn't actually accuse G. 380

die and you live in G. 9556

difference between glory G, yourself 3469

Difficulties, compliment of G. 2714

disappoints our plans 5395

discern G. in humdrum commonplace 10721

discovers himself to babes 7709

discrediting wisdom of G. 6189

distinguished by light 4472

distrust of G. troubled about what is to come 12066

do duty wisely, leave issue to G. 5176

do not aspire to comprehend 10876

Do not blame G. for tiger 11140

do not find G. hard to live with 4478

do not have to give him information 9010

do not know what G. is going to do next 5463

do not need to go somewhere to find G. 4870

Do not try to imagine G. 4663

Do not try to penetrate cloud G. brings 11485

do right when offer faith, works to G. 3829

do with cheerful heart the work G. appoints 10150

does all before he asks us to do anything 4536

does allow bad men to triumph 4957

does allow sin 4957

does allow the devil 4957

does allow tyrants to rule 4957

does best work in difficult circumstances 3769

does demand we keep moving 9832

does not account to us for his being 4614

does not accuse as if one were G. 3079

Does not all nature praise G. 7997

does not allow us to make the rules 7828

does not always answer our prayers as we request 8882

does not ask about our ability 3

does not ask for dull, weak, sleepy acquiescence 4507

does not belong to existing things 4609

does not care what good you did 7862

does not cause us to sin 10306

does not change mind about anything 4590

does not comfort to make us comfortable 1503

does not communicate things to us 4537

does not desert those who serve him 4615

does not die when we cease to believe 4538

does not do anything with us 10136

does not expect faith without reason 3840

does not expect us to become saints overnight 9832

does not expect us to imitate Jesus Christ 4539

does not fill with Holy Spirit those who believe 5779

does not give power to imitate him 9834

does not go their road 5460

does not heed, goes on stretching 139

does not hurry 2846

does not intend all to be rich 4243

does not justify us because worthy 6631

does not keep immune from trouble 2721

does not keep office hours 4590

does not leave us comfortless 1504

does not live in isolation 11423

does not love one day, hate another 4626

does not maintain neutrality in struggle for justice 6630

does not make choices easier 11058

does not make our character 1012

does not make sorrow grow on limbs too weak 10611

does not mean G. has favorites 8929

does not need majority to work wonders 1192

does not need our money 4359

does not need people to do extraordinary things 10137

does not offer a way out of testings 166

does not pay weekly 1730

does not play hide-and-seek 5386

does not promise final victory in this life 5385

does not promise he will protect from trials 5385

does not promise success 5385

does not regard past sins 10311

does not regulate body for us 847

does not require 4

does not show himself equally to all 8929

does not take responsibility for existence of rebellious 5175

does not tell us what he is going to do 4932

does not throw food into nest 3091

does not want us to do extraordinary things 7118

does not weary of mankind 4896

does not wish us to remember what he is willing to forget 4633

does speak 8835

does well what he does 4446

does what he will 7495

does what we cannot do 8570

doesn't always smooth the path 4808

doesn't care about being analyzed 4447

doesn't demand our achievements 8094

doesn't do his work while we sleep 890

doesn't exempt from heartaches 11667

doesn't merely have or give love 7244

doesn't reveal his grand design 4448

doesn't start stalled car 4782

doesn't use an anesthetic 890

doesn't want our success 8094

Don't ask G. for what you think is good 8781

Don't bother to give G. instructions 8782

Don't insult G. telling him he forgot to give you brains 7755

don't like to hear G. called "you" 8777

Don't play games with G. 4879

Don't try to reach G. with your understanding 11607

doubtful tragedy compatible with belief in G. 591

drawing you away from distraction 2556

draws us in three ways 7949

draws us into relationship with him 5395

dries you with his sun 4466

dwells in eternity 11295

each ordering of his providence fitted for us 4578

Earth with thousand voices praises G. 2973

earth, confronted with sacraments of G. 8050

easier to know G. than own soul 1713

easy for G. not to allow 4831

easy for G. to do what he will 4831

easy to believe in G. in our little world 592

effort to prove no G. 478

effort to reach for G. 478

either children of G. or the devil 8075

either permits or brings about himself 4828

eloquence is only air, noise to G. 9002

embraces all history 10562

employs several translators 2216

end is knowing G. himself 741

ended up asking G. to work through me 4994

endless day that is our Father G. 3772

endowed us with sense, reason, intellect 6324

endurance show alliance with G. 3150

enemy conquered only to G, not to us 3163

enemy of wicked 3996

engineers our circumstances 8395

enkindling minds with zeal 4514

enlarging to receive him 4514

enter through our heart into heart of G. 10562

entrusted his reputation to ordinary people 1285

essence of hell, separation from G. 5697

estimates us at our best, not our worst 4650

eternal truths depend on G. alone 11584

eternity not long enough to learn all G. is 3270

Eternity not long enough to praise G. 3270

Eternity stands fronting G. 3269

evaluates intentions 1067

Evangelism cross in heart of G. 3305

Even bein' Gawd ain't bed of roses 4890

Even G. cannot fill what is full 10708

Events creep or fly as G. pleases 4820

ever giving, yet has not less 4699

Every April G. rewrites Genesis 9885

every common bush afire with G. 1710

Every day a messenger of G. 2195

Every experience G. gives preparation 3515

Every man's life a plan of G. 6888

Every soul belongs to G. 4529

every step we rise nearer G. increases depth we may fall 10700

Everyone capable of familiar conversation with G. 7541

Everyone wants G. 4731

Everything a thought of infinite G. 1959

Everything born of G. no shadowy work 872

everything created has need of G. 4452

Everything devil does, G. overreaches 2644

everywhere can hear 8029

Everywhere I find the signature of G. 11629

Evil that which G. does not will 3361

evil will be compensated for by G. 3385

exalted in dignity, honor 4607

except as he knows himself confronted by G. 7494

excludes none 4809

existence of evil reveals G. in his truth 3398

exists in himself, of himself 4610

exists more truly than imagined 4611

expect everything from G. 3816

expect great things from G. 10118

expect to pass through death in conversation with G. 9025

expects church to prove miraculous 1392

expects life of Jesus to be manifested 4539

expects only what he has supplied 4810

expects us to be participants 10135

fact remains God is with us 4864

failure invitation to recourse to G. 3587

Faith believing G. will 3691

Faith belongs to men in G. 3698

Faith confidence in character of G. 3684

faith develops best when G. stays silent 3789

Faith does everything through G. 3660

faith in deliverance not faith in G. 3662

faith in trustworthiness of G. 4005

Faith inner conviction overwhelmed by G. 3681

Faith instructs us in depths of G. 3670

Faith is G. holding on to you 3692

faith is G. perceived intuitively 3750

Faith is taking G. at his Word 3687

faith lets G. do it all 3658

Faith listens only to G. 3683

Faith not believing G. can 3691

Faith not you holding on to G. 3692

faith rejoices in its G. 3965

Faith reposes on character of G. 4443

faith sees action of G. 3794

faith trusts in character, promises of G. 3842

Faith walking in dark with G. 3714

faithful friend image of G. 4162

Faithless work G. never rewards 3825

false that G. torn between justice, mercy 4579

false to G. never true to man 7464

far exceeds all words we can express 10249

far more dwells in me 4839

fashioned time and space 6128

fashioning minds to benevolence 4514

Father expected a good deal of G. 380

faults grain of sand beside mountain of mercies of G. 4817

favorite place of G. in heart of man 4496

fear of G, deterrent to want 3993

fear of G, insurance against loss 3993

fear of G, source of comfort, understanding 3993

fear of G, spur to courage, confidence 3993

Fear of G. a healthy ingredient 3993

Fear of G. can deliver from fear of man 3970

fear of G. to be united with love of G. 9736

fears G, fears nothing else 8487

feed mind with truth of G. 12124

feeds even the worm in the earth 9347

feeling G. has mysteriously guided us 5392

feelings not what G. cares about 4777

feels delight, frustration, anger 4491

feels pulse, prescribes medicine 4449

Fellowship with G. can go to all lengths 4023

few want to put G. first 4731

fills every root and seed 8049

fills me to the brim 4852

fills, bounds, connects, equals all 4709

find freedom when we find G. 4153

find G. in ordinary occurrences 1297

find G. in problems already solved 7562

find in and with G. all loves 7334

Finding G, no need to seek peace 8433

Finding G. is letting G. find us 7455

finds it hard to give 2571

finger of G. never leaves same fingerprint 6211

finger of G. on a man's shoulder 7314

fingers of G. touch your life 4202

first 9264

first in sequential order 4607

first made man 1120

first put urge within us to pursue him 4573

First worship G. 12097

fitting minds to be worthy of him 4514

five minutes thinking about G. 7491

Fix thought more on the G. you desire 10305

flash forth with life of G. 7055

flings Job hundred riddles 772

foe to G. ne'er true friend to man 4164

foolish things of G. wiser 1294

For each, G. has a different response 7127

For G, who loveth all his works 5904

for G. everything that will happen has already happened 11314

For G. time does not pass, it remains 3274

For G. to explain a trial 164

For the dear G. who loveth us 7174

forces no one 4126

forefathers goal was glory to G. 3113

forever asking G. to do things he has already done 8843

forever presenting new aspect of himself 603

forgetting with G. is divine attribute 4637

forgive is his business 4082

formal denial of relevance of G. 3036

frame in which picture set 4495

Freedom means to achieve all G. wants 4122

Freedom means to enjoy all G. wants 4122

Freedom to worship G. 4114

Friendship with G. means nature of G. in man 7457

frightful is solitude of soul without G. 10573

From thee, great G. we spring 5383

fulfillment by-product of love for G. 4735

fulfills himself many ways 978

G. does not conform to a standard 5749

G. must remain what he has forever been 4821

gave a loaf to every bird 10030

gave himself away 6137

gave me back myself 4528

gave me life so I could enjoy all things 6906

gave the primrose its rough leaves 4618

gave us free choice 1141

gave us life, liberty at same time 4146

gave us memories 7732

get life out to sea in reckless abandon to G. 9564

Get spindle ready, G. will send flax 9346

get to grips with living G. 7485

gifts from G. 12

Give and spend, G. will send 4354

Give G. thanks for having revealed so much 4908

give me love, care, strength to help 910

Give me such love for G. and men 7170

give me work 12007

give to G, discover G. gives to you 4386

give to G. each moment as it flies 8600

give us men 6299

given weakness that he might feel need of G. 8806

giver of Holy Scriptures 655

gives ability to work in his kingdom 4648

gives best, leave choice with him 1139

gives birds food, but they must fly 3093

Gives comfort in despair 2582

gives every bird its food 3091

gives freedom to acknowledge attitudes 503

gives his wrath by weight 4451

Gives light in darkness 2582

gives me gift of 24 hours a day 11296

gives new set of inner eyes 8495

gives no linen, but flax to spin 3092

gives self-knowledge gradually 10006

gives shoulder to burden 928

gives something to rely upon others do not experience 6178

gives something which takes place of all, love 4790

gives the nuts but does not crack them 9348

gives to every man virtue 5387

gives us his grace and Spirit 837

gives us his very self 9834

gives us life of his Son 1014

gives us the cross 2090

gives us the ingredients 9657

gives us unbroken peace 8438

gives us will to will 11505

gives you and me lumber of our lives 7684

gives, but he does not give away 4821

giveth his mercy without measure 4811

gleam brightly in pattern of life G. approves 6997

Glorious the world of G. around us 10535

glory of G. is man fully alive 4566

glory of G. is the real business of life 7027

go from nature's G. down to nature 8034

Go out and G. comes in 9556

goal to perfect us 1016

God's gifts sometimes become very g. for us 10708

God's justice incomprehensible 4728

God's manifestations are innumerable 4585

God's problem is that G. loves 4823

godly man's best friend 3996

Gold a living g. 11812

Good when he gives, supremely good 288

goodness a loan, G. the owner 5055

Goodness is like praise to G. 5064

goodness of G. to desire our welfare 7093

gospel is gift of G. 9545

gospel what G. has done for men 9545

gospel, offer of new life to man by grace of G. 5100

governed all things by counsels of his will 4904

Government originated as ordinance of G. 5177

governs in the affairs of men 4933

governs the world 5176

governs through men 8099

grace G. provides comes only with task 5226

Grace inclines G. to bestow benefits upon undeserving 4652

Grace is the good pleasure of G. 4652

grace means mercy and love of G. 5227

grace of G. can have no end 4656

grace of G. had no beginning 4656

grace of G. is glue 4654

grace of G. is infinite, eternal 4656

grace, strength of G. to overcome 5227

grace, winsome attractiveness of G. 5227

gradually giving central place to G. 7713

grant they read the good with smiles 7017

Gratitude to G. makes blessing taste of heaven 5248

Great as is the power of G. 4824

Great men like solitary towers in city of G. 5280

great of the world are those who loved G. more 5295

greater than all language 4700

greater than mind itself 4700

greatest desire to please G, serve one another 6924

greatest miracle that G. can do 5759

greatest moments are when G. got message through to you 7029

greatest word is G. 11993

greatness cannot be conceived 4700

greatness of G. rouses fear within 3788

ground on which soul stands 1713

Guardian angels G. will lend thee 1123

guards me from all evil 4992

guides to a place you know not 2565

guides you in darkness 2565

had an only Son, a missionary 7778

Had I not gotten to know G. 5594

had one Son without sin 10843

half-full of myself, no way full of G. 9932

hand it over to G. may not be easy 10979

hangs stars in awful hollows of space 4618

happiness G. designs 4120

happiness is united to G. 4120

Happiness union of ourselves with G. 5520

hard to understand detours G. takes us 5423

harden me against myself 2583

has a big eraser 4635

has all goodness to supply you 4696

has all grace to enrich you 4696

has all happiness to crown you 4696

has all mercy to pardon you 4696

has all power to defend you 4696

has all righteousness to clothe you 4696

has all the facts on his side 8456

has all wisdom to direct you 4696

has already made peace 494

has already suffered it 10601

has been in our place 6151

has bottle, book for people's tears 11012

has breathed, they are dispersed 7874

has brought us on our way 10953

has called me to be faithful 10779

has charged himself with responsibility 5511 3758

has communicated he cares 4779

has constituted us thinking beings 6679

has created us free to disbelieve in him 11590

has deep emotions 4491

has delegated power to his creatures 4821

has face very like their mother's 7855

has given man one tongue, two ears 7112

has given man short time here upon earth 6894

has given me everything 1784

has given us the mind of Christ 6679

has gone through whole of human experience 6386

has his own stairway into heart 4540

has led, will lead, is leading 5388

has lived all our tomorrows, yesterdays 4600

has many sharp cutting instruments 285

has never had a majority 1192

has never needed us 4527

has never regarded us with contempt 7186

has never surrendered iota of power 4821

has never turned away searcher 2941

has no before or after 4601

has no definition 4671

has no easy time to smash self-sufficiency 10043

has no grandchildren 7460

has no need of his creatures 4452

has no need of marionettes 1142

has no stones to throw 4453

has not always answered my prayers 8797

has not called me to be successful 10779

has nothing to say to self-righteous 10307

has one plan, man another 4563

has ordained three institutions for society 10506

has other work for you 9658

has plan for this bankrupt world 4902

has preoccupied rarest human spirits 7547

has profound interest in man's being good 5060

has program of character development 1015

has said he will exalt you in due time 11297

has set a Savior against sin 5016

has set himself against power of enemy 5016

has so constituted us 4128

has taken world upon his heart 10922

has taken you up into his purposes 9830

has to plough the heart 896

has to take some people out of this world 11809

has two dwellings 5621

has worked in past history 5724

hate something G. cannot hate 5599

hates our temptations 11057

hates those who praise themselves 9198

hath no other thing to do 4834

hath not forgotten my age 8140

Have G. to be his guide 6001

have never heard God speak 5426

have never thanked G. for thorn 2099

have not a G. off in sky 7557

have not measured fingers with G. 4337

Have some time for yourself and G. 9265

he disbelieves in G. 10936

He has no word that gives a hint of G. 10274

He is a considerate G. 4318

He loses nothing who loses not G. 4475

He that despairs degrades G. 2584

He that obeys G, trusts G. 8089

he that serves G. for money 2646

He who cheats friend would cheat G. 2911

he who loves G. has no need of admiration 10877

healthy self-image is seeing yourself as G. sees you 9978

hears God in every sound 4847

hears no sweeter music 7171

hears the footsteps of an ant 4697

hears what they are saying 4886

heart aware of G. not reason 3750

heart experiences G, not reason 4771

heart instinctively seeks for a G. 12110

heart not yet sure of its G. 6723

heart of G. is so much on us 4770

heart of good man sanctuary of G. 5084

heart right when wills what G. wills 2566

Heart within and G. o'erhead 4331

heart, the dwelling-place of G. 8474

Heaven in earth, and G. in man 6153

Heaven perfectly ordered enjoyment of G. 5646

heaven, enjoyment and communion with G. 5644

heaven, rest there in G. 5644

held my life and your life like flowers in his hand 6895

hell, when men abandoned by G. 5698

Helplessness calls from your heart to the heart of G. 8901

helps us view world from new perspective 4735

hewing out pillars for his temple 1401

hides in thick darkness from wise 7709

hides nothing 4906

high or low at festival of G. 3235

highest blessedness 4514

highest standard G. has is himself 4567

highest value is G. 11663

hills are mute, yet how they speak of G. 8014

him, not them, whom G. made in his image 6200

himself fights for soul 2734

himself is the reason why 7574

himself is your peace 8433

himself will beat the time for us 7056

his endless defeat of our calculations 5395

His godhead is your sap 7689

His greatness exceeds bounds of thought 4692

His heart profoundly kind 4477

his purpose is in sight 139

His substance is indivisible 4610

His wisdom is sublime 4477

history contest between G, Satan, fallen men 4916

History story written by finger of G. 5712

history, clay in which G. works 5718

Holds G. 6149

holds us responsible for what we could have 8654

holds us responsible for what we might be 8654

Holiness has honor of G. as its end 5739

Holy Comforter represents ineffable motherhood of G. 5775

Holy is the way G. is 5749

Holy Spirit turns life into thoroughfare for G. 5795

Home, each lives for the other, all live for G. 5837

home, kind of church where G. is honored 5853

honoring G. out there 1377

hope day at hand when advent of G. will appear 9909

Hope draws power from deep trust in G. 5928

hope teaches to leave future with G. 3834

hope teaches trust in G. 3834

hope word G. has written on brow 5947

hopelessly strive to invent happiness apart from G. 5570

How can we measure the greatness of G. 4673

How can you expect G. to speak 8813

how could G. reveal himself with no room for doubt 2963

How endless is volume G. has written of world 6901

how enduring word G. has spoken 730

How haphazard G. seems 4674

How long G. waits for us to learn lesson 7056

How many have you made homesick for G. 3309

How often we look upon G. 178

How shall we rest in G. 9683

hugs you 4753

human emotion to be consecrated to G. 6728

humility of G. hard thing to accept 4683

Humility recognizing G, others responsible for my achievements 6011

I am as rich as G. 7470

I am never without G. 4855

I am the vase of G. 4852

I asked G. for all things so I could enjoy life 6906

I believe G. has made me 4992

I believe in G. of absolute, unbounded love 4997

I don't believe in a vindictive G. 9354

I fear G, yet am not afraid of him 3977

I fight with G. 4855

I found G. wasn't there 2589

I have need of nothing 4561

I know G. is within me 5426

I know that G. is good 4642

I love, my G, but with no love of mine 4796

I make up with G. 4855

I quarrel with G. 4855

I shall not live 'til I see G. 2310

I sought him in a great cathedral 4921

I treated him, G. cured him 5611

I turned to speak to G. 2589

I want what G. wants 4971

I worship too big for space to contain 11643

I would rather walk with G. in the dark 5419

idea of creating hand refers to G. 11124

Idolaters put what G. has done in place of himself 6077

idolatry thoughts about G. unworthy of him 6075

Idolatry trusting people to do for me what only G. can do 6072

If a G. whence come evils 5027

If absolutely obedient to G. 10278

If all experience G. same way 6169

If all things are possible with G. 587

if believe G. is perfect 4443

if build for love of G. 10064

If but to G. we turn 1510

if can define G, am greater than G. 7487

if cannot work out will of G. 4974

if decisions wrong G. will check 5464

if desire for G, G. put it there 7461

If desires not met by G. 7538

If do not use mind G. has given us 6693

If fail to emphasize we can glorify G. 7481

If faith gaze of heart at G. 3737

If G. be what our faith assumes 3774

If G. bores you, tell him he bores you 8830

If G. calls to be a missionary 7781

If G. consistently sent out lightning bolts 11189

If G. dealt with people today 4717

if G. deny gracious presence, fall into sin 4865

if G. deny merciful presence, fall into hell 4865

If G. deny powerful presence, fall into nothing 4865

If G. does not know what is best, who would 4552

If G. doesn't approve, fly doesn't move 4943

if G. forget world, would cease to be 4597

If G. forgives us 4087

If G. gives command, he expects obedience 11173

if G. had not put oil in ground 11831

If G. had wanted me otherwise 6186

If G. has let you suffer 10856

If G. has made your cup sweet 289

If G. has not sanctified us 9837

If G. has work for me to do 6921

If G. is anything, he must be joy 6532

If G. is diligent 2778

If G. is G, he's big, generous, magnificent 4479

If G. kind of God-active-in-history 5724

if G. lets him lie ill 9782

If G. lived on earth 4480

If G. loved you as you love him 4765

If G. made you a duck saint 6187

If G. maintains sun, planets 4619

if G. makes you run 5427

If G. my friend, cannot be wretched 7476
If G. not willing to forgive 4088
if G. observes mathematics 4454
if G. of love, he is more than kindness 7186
If G. should give my soul all he ever made 7477
If G. shuts one door, he opens another 5421
If G. stayed away as much as a hairbreadth 7477
If G. thinks war worth paying for free will 4132
If G. to remove possiblity of disobedience 8091
If G. to send two angels to earth 3232
if G. took away all your Christian work 97
If G. wants you to do something 5226
If G. were to answer dogs' prayers 8831
If G. willed, brooms would shoot 4944
If G. you fail to see 4926
if grudge, spiritual penetration into knowledge of G. stops 9633
If he has spoken, why is universe not convinced 4963
If heart right with G. 8056
If I forget, yet G. remembers 7478
if intimate with G, disloyalty of friend will not crush 9470
If Jesus Christ is G. and died for me 9761
if leans on G. becomes powerful 10766
if listen for voice of G, learn of him 4964
If literally G. is love 4766
if live in G. and die to own will 10047
If love G, selfishness received death-blow 10063
if mainspring of service is love for G. 10159
If man is made for G. 7479
If man is man and G. is G. 8833
If man too little for G. to speak to him 4553
if man would ever pass to G. 2267
If men thanked G. for good things 11150
If not governed by G, ruled by tyrants 7483
if not sure what G. wants you to do 11605
if one realized that G. heard 4886
If our G. our Father be 5428
If takes sin to show G. in true colors 11072
if there is a G. save my soul 318
If there should be [a G.], what will become of me 2447
If truth be mighty and G. all-powerful 4134

if want to know what G. is like 4493
If we can understand mind of G. 4135
if we do not define G. 4691
If we knew how to listen to G. 8835
If we miss seeing G. in his works 4995
If we seek G. for our own good, profit 4923
If work for G. because brings me good opinion 10158
If work of G. be comprehended by reason 3841
If works of G. easily comprehended 9411
If worships not G, will have idols 12109
If you are born of G. 7689
If you can be with G. on earth 11632
if you do not fear G, you fear everything 3994
If you don't feel close to G. 4857
If you have faith in G, or man, or self 3778
If you make money your g. 7801
if you succeed, tell me there's no G. 4608
If you want to know about G. 8840
illuminating for knowledge 4514
image of G. in nature of man 7531
image timid, gentle, vulnerable—a lamb 2143
imagine G. having to apply to higher body 4955
imagine G. having to request permission 4955
imbue men with just fear of G. 6796
immense broadening of interest in G. 9831
immersed in the silence of G. 10240
immutability of G. most perfect beauty 977
imparting to minds life to be conscious of him 4514
impatience against G. to be troubled with present 12066
impossible for G. to manifest himself under conditions set up 8929
impossible for us to follow G. naturally 9801
impossible for world to exist without G. 4597
impossible to find G. through intellectual processes alone 6328
impossible to govern world without G. 5181
impressed by only one man—Christ 3854
impulse of love is voice of G. within 4278

in all things 4845
in Bible one who suffers 10908
In Bible, clouds connected with G. 10598
In Christianity G. not a static thing 11425
in circumstances of life 1464
in days of youth remembered G. 8140
in death extraordinary what takes place in heart toward G. 10667
in every place 4845
in forgiveness of G, he also forgets 4637
In G. alone can man meet man 9429
In G. history and prophecy are one 4604
In G. no change possible 977
In guidance when G. shows us a sign 5439
in him men of faith find eternal permanence 4589
in his mercy made 4813
in his Son, Jesus, G. unveils his face 4906
in likeness of most defenseless of creatures 6154
In lonely solitude G. delivers his best thoughts 10544
In lovely nature see the G. of love 8006
in me, G. without! Beyond compare! 4840
in no ways hinders struggle for development 4129
in one short hour learn more from G. 4964
in order that G. may make us great servants 5784
In prayer sees life as G. sees it 8917
in prosperity we forget G. 250
in silence G. is known 10255
In silence he is heard 10249
in silence worshiped best 10249
in still, small voice of communion 10747
In that moment, G. stopped me 10940
In the cloud G. is deepening thy chords 10600
In the cold G. is molding thy expression 10600
in the fire feel his heart warming 4858
In the great quiet of G. 7569
In the humanity of Jesus, G. speaking our language 6135
In the night G. is preparing thy song 10600
In the rain G. is sweetening thy melody 10600
In the valley G. is tuning thy voice 10600
in the water his gentleness to refresh you 4858
in way other than predetermined by G. 11082

in whom we trust keeps us 11474
in with G, at outs with world 12035
In worship we meet power of G. 12103
in you G. will green 7689
Incarnate in flesh and blood 835
incarnate is end of fear 3972
incomprehensible, inaccessible to man's understanding 4728
inconceivable goodness 4580
inconsistent with character of G. 3712
incorrect conception of ourselves, neighbor, G. 8059
indivisibly one 4503
inevitableness of G. 1149
inexhaustibly various 4503
infinite, immense 4665
infinity of G. unfathomable 4684
influence from person rightly related to G. incalculable 6241
inheritance we receive from G. limitless 4694
inner chamber into which G. only can enter 7127
inner voice of G. does not argue 4967
innumerable definitions of G. 4585
insight that relates us to G. 8504
insist there is no G. 484
Instead of complaining G. has hidden himself 4908
instinct in our souls that turns us to G. 7535
instructs, guides me 5426
insulted when body neglected 841
intellect an awesome work of G. 7776
intends us all to be friends 4243
intense, blazing holiness of G. 4661
interested only in what we are 9539
interpretation will come when, as G. pleases 4885
intrudes in glorious, myriad ways 7556
invaded by G. 1936
invented mothers 7845
invoked or not, G. will be present 4875
inward stirring and touching of G. 5764
is a G. of emotion 4454
is a G. of order 4948
is a Master Artist 10844
is a Specialist 885
is a specialist when anguish deep 10845
is a theology in itself 4503
is a tranquil Being 8437
is above all things, but not beyond reach 4612
is above, presiding 4841
is aiming at something 139
is alive 8817
is all we need 7472

is always on time 4456
is always previous 7461
is architect, man is contractor 4563
is at home, we are strangers 4562
is at work through the good 5014
is awake 11489
is beauty 4455
is beneath, sustaining 4841
is beyond our ken 4665
is directing all 169
is doing things all the time 126
is dreadfully provoked 4523
is each virtue's goal 11687
is enough for saints 5301
is eternal, his love can have no end 4750
is eternity 4601
is ever ready 4562
is everywhere around me 7968
is G, not man 9010
Is G. all-wise 4885
Is G. not merciful 10841
Is G. not omnipotent 10841
Is G. unable to prevent suffering 10841
is good 4936
is guiding all that happens to a wise, holy end 5389
is hearable 4509
is hewing out the pillars 237
is himself in us 4537
is himself not surrounded 4850
is his own interpreter 5338
is holy 169
is holy with absolute holiness 4658
is holy, his love is spotless purity 4750
is immense, his love is vast 4750
is immutable 4589
is in me 7968
is in me as sun is in the fragrance of a flower 6907
is in the cavern of man's sin 10434
is in the details 4484
is in, we are out 4562
is inescapable 4846
is infinite, his love has no limit 4750
is inviting us to enjoy him 4554
Is it so difficult to believe in G. 615
is knowable 4509
is lavish in every degree 8046
is liberty to know that G. alone matters 4151
is looking for people who long for communication with him 8972
is looking for worshipers 12098
is love, he gives himself 7244
Is man a g. or worm 3494
is measureless 4710
is my being, me, strength, beautitude, good, delight 7462
is my strength and song 4490
is nearer to us than we think 4878
is never defeated 4822
is never found accidentally

is never in a hurry 4456
is never in a panic 4937
is no faultfinder 4650
is not a foolish speculator 9989
is not confined in churches 4866
is not deceived by externals 9269
is not greater for our being 3481
is not incomprehensible to our love 4679
is not merely in the sunshine 10434
is not saving the world 3308
is not subject to time 11298
is not the G. of yesterday 10124
is omnipotent will 4514
is omniscient Creator 1520
is on the side of the poor 6604
is our Creator 2002
is outside all 4848
is outside all things, but not excluded 4612
is outside of me 7968
is peace 8444
is perfect love, wisdom 9799
is preparing his heroes 9174
is preparing you as his chosen arrow 5430
is quick to mark effort to please 4810
is seeable 4509
is self-existent, love had no beginning 4750
is shaping us for higher things 228
is so completely delightful 7463
is so vastly wonderful 7463
is that standard 5749
is the author, men the players 5639
is the beyond in midst of life 4457
is the current 7554
is the everlasting portion of his people 4847
is the friend of silence 10250
is the fuel our spirits designed to burn 7459
is the G. of promise 9321
is the G. of today 10124
is the great reality 4458
is the light in my darkness 4459
is the most unique being 4993
is the ocean deep 4852
is the organist 7892
is the physician 10415
is the poet of the world 4474
is the voice in my silence 4459
is there to catch you 4627
is there to meet repentance 9582
is to believe in a G. who is a demon 6280
is too deep to explain himself 4461
is too kind to do anything cruel 4461
is too wise to make a mistake 4461
is touchable 4509
is Unity 11429
is unthinkable if we are innocent 5493

is very patient 4892
is waiting for me 2451
is what he is in himself 491
is where he was 4849
is whispering to us incessantly
10273
is with the sinner wherever he can
be 10434
is with those who persevere 8540
is within all things, but not
included 4612
is within, filling 4841
is without growth, addition,
development 4680
is without regard to any other 491
is working on a great scale 8419
is your Keeper 5907
is, all is well 4935
isn't finished with me yet 8417
It is for G. to think about me
9934
it is G. away down here, close up
8801
Jesus Christ, life of G. 497
Jesus is G. spelling himself out in
language man can understand
6445
Jesus is G. with skin on 6446
Jesus' coming final unanswerable
proof G. cares 6136
Jesus, a man acting like G. 6514
Jesus, G. acting like himself in man
6514
Job feels rod, blesses G. 771
Job flings G. one riddle 772
Joy confidence G. is in control
6544
joy deeply rooted in life of G.
6568
Joy is to behold G. in everything
6550
Joy most infallible sign of presence
of G. 6548
joy of G. flows through people
who influence us 6239
Joy the wine that G. is ever
pouring 8454
Judge from own feelings how G.
must feel 4895
judged it better to bring good out
of evil 5018
judges a man by way he is facing
4713
judges by direction 4713
judges not by distance 4713
judging men with perfect
knowledge 4720
judging men with undisturbed
compassion 4720
judging men with unperplexed
certainty 4720
judgment of G. evidence of love of
G. 4721
judgment of G. not proof of his
wrath 4721
judgment of G. reaping that
comes from sowing 4721
Keep not thou silent O G. 1487

keep respectful fear of G. in lives
3993
keeps his word, even when seems
impossible 9321
keeps open house for universe
2155
keeps the score 7559
key fact about G. 4779
kind enough to accept little time I
give back 11296
kind of faith G. values 3789
kind, creating hand of our G.
10487
kingdom of G. a paradox 2519
kingdom of G. exists because G.
reigns 4734
knew us before we knew him
4884
know G. that thou mayst love
him, be like him 10010
know there is a G. without
knowing what he is 3814
Know thyself that thou mayst
know G. 10010
knowing G. gradual process 5738
knowledge of ourselves arouses us
to seek G. 10020
knows best rules 1520
knows best what is best 4640
knows deepest possibilities in me
4889
knows eccentricities of my being
4889
knows how to burn, then to
gently cool 7951
knows how to use disordered
wishes, actions 4644
knows instantly, effortlessly 4881
knows me is different from God is
omniscient 11179
knows us completely 4884
knows us through and through
4578
knows what he's about 5391
knows what you are 1067
knows who shall lose or win 4887
knows, I'm not the thing I should
be 9928
knows, not I, the reason why
11468
laid upon man duty of being free
4127
Laughter a sacred sound to G.
6729
Laughter or tears, both derive
from G. 6736
Laughter the contentment of G.
6732
lay before G. what is in us 8853
leading world by vision of truth
4474
leads us step by step 5392
learn to love G. and man by loving
7352
learn to think continually of G.
11269
learning to yield to leadership of
G. 8338
leave future to G. 935

leave it to G. 36
leave thread to G. 3117
Leave to thy G. to order, provide
1502
Leave tomorrow's trial to
tomorrow's G. 12067
leaves as much to learn as if never
begun 4702
leaving G. to think for him 11478
less theorizing you do about G.
4499
less would not suffice for
agriculture of G. 5332
lest G. make incomes match gifts
4369
let each man think himself an act
of G. 4557
Let each man think his mind a
thought of G. 4557
Let each man think life a breath
of G. 4557
let G. have his way 460
let G. lift life by great tide 9564
Let G. put you on his wheel and
whirl 2849
let G. speak to you 1384
let me handle the matter 184
Let me know myself O G, that I
may know thee 9068
let us trust his skill 224
lets himself be misrepresented
4891
lets himself be pushed on to the
cross 4899
lets himself be slandered 4891
lets rebellious deny his existence
4129
lets rebellious shake their fist 4129
life of man consists in beholding
G. 12116
Life, G. making us into what he
wants us to be 6978
lifeless g. of logic 3793
lifetime cultivating knowledge of
G. 4702
lifts his heart to G. with his hands
8811
light eternal 4514
lightness of life from love of G.
5229
lights the evening star 4596
like G. to make most vital thing
easy 3737
like sky to small bird 4544
likeness to G. resides in freedom
4149
likes help when helping people
10139
little by little tames us 5395
Little from G. better than great
deal from men 4524
Live near to G. 4559
3281
live with G. to solve problems
9292
lived to thank G. all my prayers
not answered 8823
lives in his spoken words 654

living, new man born from living G. 872

logical mind our own grotesque G. 4689

Lone in grandeur, lone in glory 11429

loneliness a homesickness for G. 7146

loneliness an escape from an inescapable G. 7144

longing for G. presupposes his existence 4606

Look at it as G. looks at it 2742

look at life as G. sees it 4732

look upon life as gift from G. 2307

looking for better men 1436

looks at heart before brains 7378

looks at intention of heart 6334

looks for better men 7501

looks totally indifferent 8394

looks with favor at pure hands 6300

Lord was G. Incarnate 9437

lose freedom when we lose G. 4153

love and confidence in G. 159

Love complicates love of G. 4823

love excels 11427

love for G. tested 4800

love G, you will love neighbor 8057

Love is a gift from G. 7226

Love is like a magnet, pulls me into G. 7237

Love not attribute, is G. 4755

love of G, how deep and great 4776

love of G, no bounds 4760

love of G. makes better men 7303

love of G. prompts 98

Love perfected in fire of G. 3182

love served by keeping commandments of G. 7837

Love thy G. and love him only 4798

love, facet of essential nature of G. 4760

love-energy first to G, then to other people 10053

loved his chosen creatures 4769

loved world, do likewise 7172

loves convert for what G. is 1904

loves each as if only one 4756

loves life; he invented it 6896

loves me when I sing 12008

loves those who don't give in without fight 2959

loves us, not for anything we are, but for what he is 6634

loves, wanted object to love 4535

loving all infinitely, should love each differently 6169

loving any house better than house of G. 6925

made and loveth all 7174

made contentment and aspiration fast friends 471

made in image of G. must know him or be desolate 7465

made marriage an indissoluble contract 2924

made moon as well as sun 5393

made our apartness from himself 6177

made our dependence 6177

made our individuality 6177

made rich by man's necessity 4541

made so many of the common man 4545

made the perfect, complete instrument 7893

made time, man made haste 5576

made us hear and understand 7891

made us in his image, likeness 2002

made women to match the men 3231

magnitude and distance have no meaning 4582

maintained G. did not exist 481

make man as certain of G. as G. is of himself 9800

make sin, misery out of everything G. sends 10816

makes a promise 9322

makes a sudden pause in choral hymn of lives 7056

makes all things good 5019

makes beautiful something confused 885

makes clear what he desires 1149

makes it impossible to lose our way 5397

makes our next door neighbor 8066

makes pure in heart 1012

makes saints out of sinners 9773

makes shoes upside down 4668

makes the glow worm and star 8008

makes useful something broken 885

Man alone has capacity to walk, talk with G. 7497

Man born with face turned away from G. 9583

Man calls it a blunder, G. a blindness 4560

Man calls it a chance, G. a choice 4560

Man calls it a defect, G. a disease 4560

Man calls it a fascination, God a fatality 4560

Man calls it a liberty, G. lawlessness 4560

Man calls it a luxury, G. a leprosy 4560

Man calls it a mistake, G. madness 4560

Man calls it a trifle, G. a tragedy 4560

Man calls it an accident, G. an abomination 4560

Man calls it an error, G. an enmity 4560

Man calls it an infirmity, G. an iniquity 4560

Man calls it weakness, G. willfullness 4560

Man cannot break the laws of G. 7493

man cannot cover what G. would reveal 9709

Man cannot find G. unless G. reveals himself 4910

Man cannot find joy anywhere but in G. 6552

Man cannot seek G. 4910

Man created a G. addict 7496

Man drives, G. holds reins 4947

Man finds G. through truth 11518

man free to love G. 566

Man groping for G, hoping to hide from him 7402

man himself when most possessed by G. 5200

man magnificent ruin of what G. designed 7429

Man makes plans, G. changes them 5432

Man rides, G. holds the reins 7498

man said, let us make G. in our image 4547

Man sees actions, G. motives 7866

Man shall enjoy G. alone 9481

Man should perform duties to fellowmen as to G. 9669

man sold G. for thirty pence 4532

Man the great inscrutable mystery of G. 7409

man to be feared who fears not G. 7426

man to work out in world will of G. 3195

man weeding turnips also serving G. 12146

man who has lost contact with G. 7523

man who loves G. asks no favors of G. 4803

man who loves G. in unassailable position 4803

man who stuck true to G. will come out best 10789

man with vision of G. devoted to G. himself 11729

man would have lost likeness to G. 4149

man's business to do will of G. 566

Man, wrap yourself in G. 2658

manifests himself in his children 9707

Many agree with G. in principle, not practice 1336

many avenues of attractivenss to G. 7532

many helpers, see G. in all your helpers 11490

many surprises 604

Many troubles are G. dragging us 11440

matrix of our personality 7557

Maturity is life under control of G. 7685

maturity, quiet confidence G. is in control 10709

may cry to G. the church be restored 10080

May on familiar terms be with the highest G. 7489

may only be addressed, not expressed 4667

may say far from hating G. 10427

may seem to overact his part 286

may send tempest about house 4775

May yet hold friendly converse with my G. 8814

may yet make something of him 3604

may, though no fault of our own,be unable to sense G, 4864

means of glorifying G, salvation of souls 7027

means to guide our steps by moonlight 5393

measurements can never embrace G. 4680

Measurements cannot apply to G. 4710

meets G. at every turn 4847

meets needs in striking ways 3744

meets us on level where we operate 5439

Men cut themselves off from G. 4437

Men give advice, G. gives guidance 5433

Men look for G, fancy him concealed 8019

men may despise grace of G, but cannot extinguish 4655

Men must be governed by G. 4137

men unmindful of what they owe G. 819

Men who walk with G. would not grieve enemies 3166

merciful G. to lift curtain on today 4318

Mercy imitates G, disappoints Satan 7741

mere simplicity before G. 10278

mind ascends, beholds majesty of G. 7971

mind of G. as discovered in Word and works 4675

mind of G. so vast, deep 4675

Mind the world less and G. more 2443

mind too limited to understand G. 4665

mirror in which glory of G. reflected 10339

Mirth offered sparkling with life to G. 6739

mistrust of himself, greater confidence in G. 10328

Misunderstanding cannot thwart purposes of G. 2740

molds history to his purposes 5718

moment we turn in faith to G. 3758

moral law reflection of G. nature 1520

more clearly we perceive hand of G. 11644

more concerned about character than comfort 1016

more daring the request, more glory to G. 9028

more glorious world of G. within us 10535

more interested in G. than in work for him 10141

more man denies himself, more obtain from G. 9562

more natural to approach G. in solitude 1445

more real to me than any thought, thing, person 7098

more satisfactory is our dependence on G. 7524

more truly imagined than expressed 4611

more we depend on G, more dependable we find he is 11481

most active and dynamic of all 4520

most beneficial therapy G. granted humanity 6733

most potent weapon G. has given man 4154

most precious things G. finds in us 10666

Mother name for G. in hearts of children 7848

mourn for sin because offensive to G. 9581

much greater is our G. than our greatest need 7468

music among the gifts G. has sent 7935

Music one of most delightful presents G. has given 7914

must condemn, blast out what he cannot bless 893

must do everything for us 2097

must feel deepest tenderness of G. 4012

must free ourselves to be filled by G. 10708

must go to G. simply for himself 8958

must let G. do all we can 10980

must love the common man 4545

must renounce other loves for love of G. 7334

must see G. today 11391

must simplify our approach to G. 7709

must speed to my G. before all things 7951

must wait for G. 5460

My business is to think about G. 9934

My goal is G. himself 4428

my hope, stay, guide, lantern 5394

my individual responsibility to G. 7525

My soul lives on G. 7953

my whole being is from my most sweet G. 5051

mystery of myself solved by this besetting G. 4889

mystic too full of G. to speak to world 7965

mysticism attempt to draw near to G. 7947

Mysticism is communion with G. 7955

name of G. may be written upon that soul 10475

Nature an effect, whose cause is G. 8024

nature defects to show only image of G. 8022

Nature has perfections to show image of G. 8022

nature hymn of praise to G. 8002

Nature is art of G. 8025

nature of G. to make something out of nothing 3604

Nature shows something worthy of a G. 8026

Naught but G. can satisfy the soul 7504

ne'er afflicts more than our desert 286

Near, so very near to G. 4859

nearer than own soul 1713

nearest thing to G. is human soul 10651

needs and wants our love 4527

needs minority fully committed 1192

needs no one 3723

needs people who do ordinary things extraordinarily well 10137

neglect G. for noise of a fly 7712

never answers the why 167

never better enjoy ourselves than when we enjoy G. 7558

never built a Christian strong enough for today and tomorrow 417

never ceases to speak to us 8800

never changes 4588

never comes to those who do not wait 5460

never contradicts reason 9413

never defeats himself by taking away freedom of choice 4133

never destroys work of his own hands 7685

never develops one part of our being at expense of other 6897

never does anything hysterical 9912

never doubt what G. told you in light 2885

never fails to grant light 5397

never farther away than the door 4621

never feel G. will cast evil out of world 3415

never forces man 4130

never gave man a thing to do 10140

never gives strength for tomorrow 2722

never imposes duty without giving time 9659

never in a hurry 4570

never in need, yet rejoicing in gains 4954

never is before his time 4477

never is behind 4477

Never is G. said to be reconciled to man 9430

never known to disappoint 4468

never leaves 4621

never made two people exactly alike 6191

never meant that man should scale the heavens 11916

never more like G. than when we give 4380

never our merit G. looks at but faith 3749

never permit evil if could not bring good 3372

never points out pathway different from one you planned 4969

never produces hysterics 9912

never promised to keep us from trouble 215

never promised to keep us out of hard places 165

never put anyone in place too small to grow 4987

Never question where G. has put period 3763

never see until we see G. 8583

never sets limit to man's freedom 4130

never stands up for saints 1060

never takes unless gives better 4630

never tempts any man 11060

never test resources of G. until attempt impossible 3815

Never try to forecast way G. is going to answer prayer 8873

never vindicates himself 4891

never violate laws of G. without consequences 10336

No attribute of G. contradicts any other 4579

no brotherhood without fatherhood of G. 920

No contemplation will humble more than thoughts of G. 4745

no degrees with G. 4680

No difficulties can baffle G. 1468

no disappointments in will of G. 2801

no end but to perfect our graces 280

no fortune, only G. 11866

No G, no world 4485

no G. less than absolutely glorious 4504

no good government without G. 5194

no grades of perfection with G. 3236

no halfway business with G. 5038

no helpers, see all your helpers in G. 11490

no idea by which G. perceives things 4986

No image but image of G. can fit soul 10658

no lifeless, powerless work 872

no longer have to wonder how G. feels 4489

no longer have to wonder what G. is like 4489

No man believes unless G. inclines his heart 597

No man comes to himself without meeting G. 1907

No man ever more than four steps from G. 9584

No man gives anything acceptable to G. 10119

No masses of earth can block G. vision 4883

No one can know G. who has not first known himself 7543

no one can return more in response to our love 7533

No one can worship G. on empty stomach 7152

No one could ever have found G. 6137

no one in earth can shut door G. has opened 4937

no one more worthy of our love 7533

no other time than now with G. 11322

no packages of spiritual victory sent special delivery 1013

no parts, single in unitary being 4610

No person who shall deny being of G. 5183

No problem too big for G. 9288

no room for G. in man full of himself 10089

no royal road to becoming worker for G. 9564

no separation unless we make it ourselves 7557

no situation too much for G. 168

no statement can express him 4700

no was or will be 4604

no weakness can turn G. away from us 4884

no work better than another to please G. 3123

Nobody can judge men but G. 4720

noise, passion prevent us from listening to him 8800

None feels true love of G. till 4773

None of our talents significant to G. 4527

Nor can we fall below arms of G. 4774

nor open door G. has shut 4937

Nor will G. force any door to enter in 4775

not a cosmic bellboy 4543

not a supernatural interferer 4847

not about to hand out spiritual bandages 1013

not accepted by G. 46

not affected by our mutability 4587

not all faith pleases G. 3823

not baffled by what baffles us 4701

not be G. if he could not be known 4740

not bewildered by what bewilders us 4701

not complete if all not given to G. 5734

not content to have us remain in sinfulness 9832

not darkness for G. is light 5659

not demonstrable by scientific means 4739

not discoverable by scientific means 4739

not eternal blessing machine 5757

Not even blessing, but himself, my G. 4428

not even G. could build society of love out of puppets 4133

not fond of slackers 1193

not forced to take wings to find G. 4924

not G. away off up yonder 8801

not greater if you reverence him 9732

not his will that we should see before or around us 5397

not impressed with beautiful cathedrals 12101

not impressed with celebrities 3854

not in whirlwind of activity 10747

not interested in organized religion 9539

not interested in sermons 1414

not interested only in Christian writers 12146

not less great in small things 4940

not necessarily opposed to G. 5467

not one life not so near to G. 7057

Not one thing done for G. has been lost 10176

not only prayer that gives G. glory 12013

not pleased with worship at Jerusalem 12101

not presume to separate what G. has united 6681

not seeking G. at all 8839

not that we are at work for G. 5793

not that we don't believe in G. 10509

not the world, can give peace 8456

not tucked away in far corner of universe 7556

Not without design does G. write music of our lives 7915

nothing but his hand that holds you 4523

nothing can defeat G. 9983

nothing can exist without you 4854

nothing can happen save that which G. wills 9835

nothing done that G. is not absolute Master 4937

Nothing small if G. is in it 10800

Nothing small in the service of G. 7121

Nothing so like G. as stillness 10258

nothing that I with G. do not share 7470

Nothing void of G, he fills his work 4860

Nothing with G. can be accidental 4927

Nothing you can do to make G. love you more 4786

notice dirt G. is most present 3609

nowhere else to go 178

Nowhere in Bible does G. claim grandchildren 9818

O for a closer walk with G. 7507

O G, your mercy a boundless ocean 4816

O G. of hope 5939

O man, cleave close to G. 2604

O world, as G. has made it 8030

Obedience to G. will mean desolation 8105

obey because you loved G. 577

object of Jesus' meditation was his Father 12128

Observe G. in his works 8031

obtain a higher, more reverent view of G. 4720

of all mercy a G. unjust 4723

of followers of G, cannot take initiative 5446

of G. before you 829

of himself full of glory 12126

of the early mornings 7539

of the late-at-nights 7539

of the mountain peaks 7539

of the sea 7539

of universe, he is final end 4514

offers a better plan 2607

offers a way through testings 166

offers tough love 7686

Often G. has to shut a door in our face 5436

often uses tools upon those he loves 285

oftens visits us 4546

Oh the joy of life with, in and for G. 6554

Old age can love G. better 7286

Old age comes from G. 8151

old age leads on to G. 8151

On any shore, since G. is there 4869

On from fact divine G. advances 4906

on the side of poor, oppressed 8696

One does not fear G. because terrible 3983

One kind act will teach more love of G. 6661

one more insult to G. 6275

one of your listeners 1891

one thing to know how G. thinks 5425

Only a G. who knows all things 5438

only being who can afford to be misunderstood 4891

only being who loves perfectly 7316

Only G. can devise plan 5632

only G. can make a tree 2017

only G. can supply what he demands 1194

only G. may be had for the asking 2641

only G. meets deep needs 4310

Only G. permanently interesting 4678

Only G. understands universe 11635

only gives strength for the moment 2722

only gives time to us moment by moment 11337

only gives us light we need for present 5397

Only he who knows G. truly moral 7835

only in G. fully understand what you are 8634

only perfect freedom is serving G. 4148

only send what is for your good 8578

only thing he would change was me 967

Only to sit and think of G. 4799 1763

only too glad to hand ourselves over to G. 10015

only when knelt before G. can we stand before men 8880

Open eyes, world full of G. 4861

or G. brings it about himself 4828

ordered their estate 4501

orders, brings into line 5175

ordinary day given to G. a sacrament 2196

ought to be diligent in duty to G. 2778

our best work that G. wants 941

our changes do not affect G. 4587

Our lives are what we think about G. 7016

Our nature hungers for G. 7512

Our pursuit of G. is successful 7513

out of despair by creative effort of G. 2613

out of soul G. coins unspeakable riches 10666

out of the power of G. 425

outside circle of our knowledge 4614

Outside of G. nothing but nothing 4488

outtops thought 4678

over all things 4848

owe it to G. that we refuse rusty brains 11274

packs our life with surprises 5463

paid intolerable compliment of loving us 7186

paints the wayside flower 4596

pandemonium shouting G. is cruel 584

pass through center of himself into G. 7962

passes through thicket of world 4463

path to pleasure is pleasing G. 8609

Path, motive, guide, original, and end 5383

patiently G. works to teach 7056

pays at the end 1730

pays men compliment 1142

peace comes from the love of G. 8469

peace in his will 4979

penny-in-the-slot manner, insult to G. 693

people do not want to be alone with G. 10536

People imagine pursuing glory of G. 10076

people who related to G. best 7526

perfect church service, attention on G. 1383

perfect oneness with G. 547

permits us to be perplexed 8396

permits wicked, but not forever 11884

persecuting G. 2084

perseveres in speaking in his own language 4900

personality written, signed by G. 6183

pervades us as the sunbeam 9852

philosophers create God in their image 8590

Philosophy, science not always friendly toward G. 8592

pity the Christian the world gets best of 1330

pity the ship when the sea gets in 1330

place where thou art found unveiled 7950

plan of G, responsibility is God's 4803

planned all perfect combinations 7891

plans personal visit to his own world 6127

planted fear in soul 3973

plants in us new disposition 8570

plants where conviction brought brokenness 888

plants where soil watered with tears 888

plead for G. to speak when he has spoken, is speaking 8843

pleased to make everyone different, no one perfect 6180

pleasing to G. for other reasons 11685

pool wherein serene light of G. can be mirrored 8437

poor in spirit attitude of dependence on G. 6025

possibilities limited only by omnipotence of G. 8940

possiblity a hint from G. 8641

power of G. to achieve our welfare 7093

Power passing mine, immeasurable G. 4825

praise G. even when we do not feel like it 2564

praise G. in loneliness 583

Praising G. takes away blues 2564

pray as though everything depended on G. 8892

Pray to G. in the storm, but keep rowing 8898

Pray, G, keep us simple 10282

Prayer a sacrifice to G. 8915

Prayer avenue G. uses to transform us 9005

Prayer begins by talking to G. 8902

Prayer can do anything G. can do 8902

Prayer does not change G. 8907

Prayer does not mean bring G. down 8909

prayer ends by listening to him 8902

prayer gives G. glory 1237

Prayer is a greater work for G. 8908

Prayer is a ladder on which thoughts mount to G. 8913

Prayer is inhaling spirit of G. 8920

Prayer is to wait till one hears G. speak 8935

Prayer link between man and G. 8944

Prayer means I am raised up into G. 8909

Prayer not an argument with G. 8925

Prayer not to persuade G. to move our way 8925

Prayer rope that pulls G, man together 8947

prayer simply being in the presence of G. 8958

prayer tapping infinite resources of G. 8991

prayer voice of man to G. 9704

praying for G. to fill him when full already with something else 5783

praying to G. to give victory 9021

pre-existed in sight of G. 3490

predestines every man to be saved 9175

prefer quality to quantity 941

prefer to be child of G. for eternity 5308

Prepare the way! A G, a G. appears 6138

presence of G. a fact of life 4864

present in deepest, most central part of soul 4868

probes the core, tests the root 7862

problem is an opportunity to prove G. 9283

proclaim G. with mouths 487

promised to be active among men 5724

promises a safe landing 170

promises not a calm passage 170

promises only that he will be with them 5385

prompting minds to desire him 4514

prophet knows what G. is trying to say 9332

proportions the frequency and weight 224

protects me against danger 4992

proved his love on the cross 7173 2129

providence of G. about us in abundance 8002

provides me with all I need 4992

pure light of G. pierces a man 9741

purely, perfectly angry with sin 401

purge imagination by beauty of G. 12124

pushes you nearer to G. 4190

put your hand into the hand of G. 5417

puts his children in the fire 151

puts his ear so closely down 8801

puts questions to man 7398

puts right all that was wrong 837

puts tape around heart, not head 4576

puts us in contact with divine resources 1143

puts us in situations that are too much 168

quick to overlook imperfections 4810

quicken the conscience by the holiness of G. 12124

Race prejudice, denial of G. 1490

raised up Jesus to shatter history 5711

rarely allows soul to see blessing he is 6233

rationalism tries to find G. in world 4495

rationalist does not go to G. 9396

rationalist implies G. must come to him 9396

Reach G. in love 11607

reached by way of love, suffering 4802

realize G. had always been speaking 5395

realizes G. in midst, quiet in midst of alarm 3972

Reason does not prove G. exists 3776

reason must ask G. for things he intends to give 8990

receivest what thou findest, yet never lose 4954

receivest, that thou mayst owe 4954

recognize in G. the Author of our goods 8796

redeemed human race when we were spitting in his face 9434

redeems before he enjoins 4536

referring to his time not yours 11297

regenerates us 1143

rejoices when one beggar scratches another 9454

relationship to G. fits you to live 4555

relationship to G. only simple thing 10653

relationship to G. that of a child 188

relationship with G. marked with stamp of own temperament 8883

Religion is man's quest for G. 9545

Religion what man tries to do for God 9545

Religion without guilt tries to make G. big pal 5487

Religions are man's search for G. 9547

rely upon G. 13

Relying on G. has to begin all over every day 7515

Relying on G. to begin over again every day 11476

Remember blessings from G. 9270

remember G. is listening while you tell it 5148

removes what would pervert 7685

repentance is grieved because sinned against G. 9580

Repentance process by which we see G. as he is 9594

repentest, yet grievest not 4954

required that we love G. 8821

rescues us by breaking us 882

rescues us by wiping out resistence 882

reserves right to harmonize truths 11586

Resignation is putting G. 41

Resistance to tyrants is obedience to G. 5964

respects me when I work 12008

response of created to Creating Personality, G. 9543

response to temptation barometer of love for G. 11079

responsible to no one 4614

rest for a little time in G. 7708

restless anxiety, not crosses from G. 4322

restlessness can be G. sowing seeds of faith 3722

reveals himself 4448

reveals himself to thoughtful seeker 4907

reveals that which is our profit to know 9708

revelation of G. determined by character 1050

revelation secret whispering of G. in ear of a soul 9705

revelation voice of G. to man 9704

revival is G. revealing himself 9745

Revival sovereign act of G. 9746

rewards us for working in his kingdom 4648

Riches least worthy gifts G. can give 11845

richness of G, meagreness of men 9784

right fear is fear of losing G. 3995

right for G. to display anger against sin 4729

right with G, he gives desires, aspirations 9280

right with G. has often meant in trouble with men 9507

runs toward him twain 7573

sacrifice to G. of devil's leavings 8183

safest eloquence concerning G. is silence 4681

saint always thankful to G. 9790

saint consciously dependent on G. 9768

saint has heart ready to praise G. 9790

saint knit into shape by G. 9767

saint wills everything G. wills 9790

saints which G. loves best 9788

salvages the individual 886

Salvation the incoming into human nature of characteristics of G. 9811

sanctification is himself in me 9843

Sanctification not something our Lord does in me 9843

sat in silence 2130

Satan cannot counterfeit peace of G. 5396

Satan tries to make us think wrongs spring from G. 9859

satanically-managed man has no need of G. 9853

saved and sanctified for G. 9850

saw through thick cloud 4904

say millions never think of G. 7561

saying to world, "I love you" 7173

saying yes to G. means no to things that offend his holiness 5755

says "Much can be gained" 2800

says, stop depending on human resources 184

scarcely vindicates his saints to men 11616

scatters countless flowers around us 7993

search for G. is surrender to his search for us 7455

searching observations about G. 155

secret between two is secret of G. 5115

secret of power is to know G. 3790

secret thought not hidden from G. 4578

see all in G. 11490

see G, everything becomes different 8583

see ourselves more as G. sees us 4578

seed of G. stirred 2984

Seeing G, Job forgets all he wanted to say 773

Seeing G. means understanding 7547

seek nothing else but pleasing G. 4922

seeking man 643

seeks comrades, claims love 4912

seeks honor that comes from G. only 5901

seeks worship of those trapped in moral ruin 12098

seems careless as to whether men understand him 11616

sees G. incomprehensible, infinite 7971

sees G. sees everything else 8487

sees scar, creates star 8278

sees something good in suffering 10856

sees sweet flowers growing 8673

Self is to be rightly centered in G. 9942

Self the veil that hides G. from us 9945

Self-centeredness a movement away from G. 9946

self-existent, self-dependent, self-sufficient 4614

Self-knowledge critically important in pursuit of G. 10019

Self-knowledge grows out of self-confrontation with G. 10018

send us men with hearts ablaze 7986

sends no one away empty 9200

sends nothing but can be borne 2546

sends ten thousand truths 6565

sends time of forced leisure 7056

sends us on stony paths 180

sense depths which are of G. 10257

sense of sin in proportion to nearness to G. 10349

servant of G. has good master 1329

set free to become what G. wants 4122

shallow amenities of life ordained by G. 7038

shepherds didn't ask G. if he knew what he was doing 6147

should find G. in what we know 7562

should preach above all presence of G. 4873

shouts in our pains 8257

show want of faith in G. by false wisdom 4322

shows himself to be absolute mystery 4738

shut eyes to future G. hides from us 4322

shut out all thoughts save that of G. 7708

sides with poor because of their vulnerability 6630

sighings are sighings for G. 7516

silence in awesome presence of G. 12112

silence in the presence of G. 7707

Silence is freedom to let justification rest with G. 6622

Silence will illuminate you in G. 10245

Silence will unite you to G. 10245

silence, how fully pleasing to G. 10252

Silent worship enables us to hear voice of G. 12114

Simply wait upon G. 5440

Sin a departure from G. 10365

Sin defiance to authority of G. 10362

Sin is independence of G. 10372

Sin is red-handed rebellion against G. 10371

Sin rebellion against rule of G. 10366

sin that shocks G. 10397

sin willful refusal to obey G. 10387

sin, two witnesses our own selves and G. 10418

sinfulness evident contrasted with holiness of G. 10440

single tear suffices with G. 4091

Small numbers make no difference to G. 10800

smart when he made man 7379

smile of G. is victory 11671

snail's progress toward G. 8630

so forgiving, so divine 4673

So G. loves me 7178

so great all things give him glory 1237

So lonely 'twas that G. himself 7142

So many are busy "using" G. 7517

so much for you did do 4476

So much G. would give 8662

So necessary is our friendship to G. 4564

so powerful can direct evil to good end 3371

so young, so strong, so sure of G. 1609

Solitude bearable only with G. 10555

some angel and some G. in man 5013

some are drawn to G. through his beauty 7532

Some call it evolution, others G. 1987

some only hear G. in public worship 1477

Some people for seeing G. as they see a cow 10084

some say G. too good to be true 4504

some talk about finding G.—as if he could get lost 7518

Some things only G. can do 10199

Some think G. does not like constant asking 8964

some truths G. will not make simple 11546

Some will take all G. has to give us 5323

someone far beyond us 603

something is behind them: that is G. 4962

Sometimes a nation abolishes G. 4897

sometimes fear to bring troubles to G. 4789

Sometimes G. delays answers to our prayer 8924

sometimes puts springs in wagon 4808

sometimes strikes more than flesh can bear 286

sometimes withhold in mercy what we ask 8877

sought only for heart of G. 2652

soul a never ending sigh after G. 7528

soul and G. stand sure 948

soul breath of G. bestowed in heaven 10649

soul enriched by communion with G. 10567

soul for G. designed 12032

soul would instantly rush toward G. 8630

source of the beautiful 538

sovereign G. wants to be loved for himself 4806

spares us because he is good 4724

speaks in language we do not know 4900

speaks in language we do not want to learn 4900

speaks in our conscience 8257

speaks of acceptance, sacrifice, renunciation 4900

speaks to the crowd 5385

speaks to us if we will tune in 8013

speaks unceasingly through events of life 5395

specific requests to G. unseemly 8821

spend as much time thanking G. for benefits 11166

Spirit of G. hunts our spirit 5764

Spirit-filled souls ablaze for G. 3182

spiritual health proportional to love for G. 4793

spiritual revelation in physical body 835

spoke a book 654

springs of love are in G, not in us 4784

spurs us to the pursuit 4573

squeezes but never chokes 4464

stand before G. on basis of grace 1057

stand still, listen to speech of G. 4965

standeth G. within the shadow 5377

stands ready to take over management of our lives 5511

still I can pray, so that G. can hear 9025

stones would praise G. if need arose 12099

stooped to work by, in his children 4467

stoops o'er his head 9940

strengthening for virtue 4514

stretches and strains us 139

strikes at core of motivations 7863

stripped of all possessions but knowledge of G. 11688

strips of everything 4790

stronger than devil 1924

Study sciences before G. 9871

studying thought of G. 1959

substitute love for G. 4766

Success for glory of G. or your own 10811

Success is seeking, knowing, loving G. 10807

success or failure in hands of G. 10776

Suffering best gift G. has to give us 10894

suffering G. only one who does not mock us 10908

suffering of man also the suffering of G. 10912

suffering perfects one who accepts call of G. 10920

sums up man's worth by character 11238

Sun of G. smiling 5810

supreme legislator 11584

Surely thou, too, art not white 1487

surrendered own plans to greater plan of G. 4803

surrounded still with G. 4876

surrounding all things 4850

take care not to make intellect our g. 6333

Take everything as from hand of G. 2744

Take glory in G. who gives you everything 9272

take what G. chooses to send 5911

Take, O G, thy power and reign 2981

takes all time, eternity to know G. 4483

takes care of man 566

takes complaining personally 1558

takes deliberate time with us 2846

takes life's pieces 8438

takes notice of clean, not full hands 9754

takes weak and makes them strong 10745

takes, keeps initiative 585

Talent something G. gives you 10996

talk about G, nobody gets upset 6518

talked to G. as if he were sitting in chair beside them 7526

talked to G. as one might talk to a counselor 7526

talked with G. this morning 8817

talking to G. for men greater still 8969

Talking to men for G. great thing 8969

talks so constantly about G. 484

teacher sent from G. clears way to Jesus 11003

Tears best gift of G. to suffering man 11020

tears prepare for clearer vision of G. 11024

tell G. you only feel at ease far from him 8830

tell G. you prefer vilest amusements 8830

tells us who he wants us to be 6830

tempering for wisdom 4514

temporarily permitted evil to exist 3378

temptation shows work G. has to do 11086

temptation to be like G. eclipsed view of G. 4419

temptation, to induce us to substitute for G. 11099

temptation, to obscure G. 11099

Temptations that find us leaning on G. 11094

terror of G. is other side of his love 4775

tested Abraham 11061

tests that he may crown 11096
tests us that we might stand 171
Than these knees bow to any save G. 7677
Thank G. Almighty, I'm free at last 4119
Thank G. don't have to be flawless to be blessed 5442
thank G. for beauty 535
thank G. for having created this world 5678
thank G. for how he will use sin 11152
Thank G. for my handicaps 11147
thank G. for not having given tiger wings 11140
Thank G. for the way he made you 6206
Thank G. for unknown future 4318
Thank G. we will not be angels 839
Thank G. when you get up you have something to do 11159
thank him for his prescription 224
thanked G. for roses 2099
Thankfulness response of gratitude to G. 11173
thanks G. as much as he were sound and well 9782
Thanks to G. for unspeakable gift 1372
Thanksgiving invites G. to bestow second benefit 11162
That friend is G. 5376
That G, the whole ocean, floweth into me 7469
that G. be with you in everything you do 6260
that G. marked out for you 6204
that we understand discipline of G. 7485
That which is often asked of G. 5443
That's best which G. sends 7520
The awful autograph of G. 8015
the canvas on which picture painted 4495
the do-nothing G. 7556
the fire is the love of G. 7553
the food our spirits designed to feed on 7459
the glory and poetry of G. 4704
the inexorable awfulness of Almighty G. 1527
the infinite weight of G. 1657
the Judge, sovereignly declared me pardoned 3672
The larger the G. we know, the larger our faith 3790
the Light in my darkness 6907
The more men suppress the truth of G. 11538
The most resembles G. 6666
the silent partner in great enterprises 4460
The unambiguous footsteps of the G. 4482
the universal intelligence 4692

the very life of our lives 7557
the Voice in my silence 6907
Then alone do we know G. truly 4685
Then I asked if I might help G. 4994
then you are wise and G. is your teacher 8497
theology science of mind applied to G. 11207
Theology, attempt to systematize G. 11209
There but for the grace of G. 5234
There is a G. within us 7534
there you are, an enemy to G. 10427
They should have known Jesus was G. 6492
they that know G. will be humble 6039
thick skin gift from G. 2625
things mean nothing, G. means everything 1325
think G. turned life into inextricable confusion 4885
Think how good G. is 4648
this I know G. answers prayer 8825
this world two hundred times more real than G. 7491
This, I was worth to G. 9981
This, this is the G. we adore 4787
thornbush aflame with glory of G. 9064
Thou are love! I build my faith on that 4758
thou art an image of G. 9982
thou art the G. of these, be my G. 7539
Thou art thine own eternity 4605
Thou lovest without passion 4954
Though G. be everywhere present 4868
Though G. be opposed, outcome never in doubt 4822
though G. has condemned us 7186
though G. has often rebuked us 7186
though we know not goodness of G. 4578
thought of G. never a burden 11249
thoughts go into the memory of G. 11280
three persons in one essence 11423
three things I thank G. for 11144
three things only G. knows 6705
through defeat of cross G. glorified 2519
Through G. turn endings into beginnings 3629
through handicaps found my G. 11147
through mysteries G. declares himself 10255
through pain we enter into G. 8277

through personal obedience G. acts 5385
thrusts us out of the crowd 10564
till know something of what G. is 7438
Time a precious gift of G. 11337
Time deposit in bank of G. 11340
time dwells in G. 4600
Time is nothing to G. 11338
time so precious G. deals it out second by second 11293
Timeless, spaceless, single, lonely 11429
times when G. asks silence, patience, tears 10635
tipped scales in favor of hope 2130
'Tis G. gives skill 4441
'Tis only G. may be had for the asking 9795
to all who love G, trials are love tokens 4804
to ask G. to do is to waste prayers 10199
To be with G, no need to be in church 7541
To believe G. made lower creatures for prey 6280
To believe in G. is to know rules will be fair 4508
To cheer G. along 11686
To discuss authority of G. seems meaningless 4955
To do his work G. must have cooperation 11269
to ear of G. everything makes exquisite music 8743
to enter into dialogue with G. 8779
to explain mystery of G. 7939
To fall in love with G. greatest of all romances 7542
To find G. greatest human achievement 7542
To G, no great, no small 4709
To G. no high, no low 4709
To G. we use simplest, shortest words 9002
To get at core of G. at his greatest 7543
to glorify 10114
To have found G. not an end, but a beginning 7544
To have G. for our mother, father, guardian 7545
to have perfect love we must have nature of G. 7316
to imagine G. unsure, frustrated, unstable 4579
To know G. easiest, most difficult in world 7546
To know man we must begin with G. 4571
To know nature is to know there must be a G. 6696
To know reasons which have moved G. 4989
to know soul seek G. 1713

To make G. a momentary Creator 11652

to man doth speak in solitude 10534

To meet G. a terrifying adventure 4551

To my G, a heart of flame 5626

to neglect contemplation of G. 7004

to obey G. is perfect liberty 8115

to place upon G. human limitations 9010

To pray is to expose the mind to G. 9006

To pray means to put our lives into conformity with G. 8944

to question authority of G. absurd 4955

to read his mind, think his thoughts 7766

To reconcile man with man and not with G. 9432

to reserve right of instructing us 5384

to ruin a man for service of G. 6407

To see G. highest aspiration of man 7547

To seek G. greatest of all adventures 7542

to soul that contemplates greatness of G. 4707

to the damned, is a burden in excess 4548

To the frightened, G. is friendly 4649

to the poor in spirit, G. is forgiving 4649

to the stranger, G. is hospitable 4649

to the weak, G. is gentle 4649

to thee we tend 5383

To trust in G. unhesitatingly 6913

to want what G. wants 5425

to whom little boys say their prayers 7855

To whom would G. go for permission 4955

To write the love of G. above 4748

took him years to teach me "Lord, anything" 4892

torn asunder bond that binds humanity to G. 8967

touches G. with sorrow or joy 7057

touching G. in his distressing disguise 6569

transcends reason 9413

transformed evil 4931

treasures up his bright designs 4941

treated G. like a person 7526

treated G. with startling familiarity 7526

treating badly precious thing G. has made 9923

treats sinner as if good man 6634

triangle of love between ourselves, G, other people 7198

trinity of the mind is the image of G. 7771

trouble is we won't let G. help us 11454

trouble only time people think of G. 11441

troubles must seem so small to G. 4789

true joy of man's life in relationship to G. 9467

true knowledge of G. will result in wonder 6704

True understanding of G. comes 7548

trust G, heaven securely 559

Trust G. for great things 10205

trust G. when you can't trace him 3663

Trust G. where you cannot trace him 11485

trust G. while not able to make sense of everything 3696

Trust G: see all, nor be afraid 8132

Trust in G. and do the right 5995

Trust knowing G. will catch you 11486

Trust past to mercy of G. 5457

trust reckons upon trustworthiness of G. 3676

Trustfulness based on confidence in G. 11487

trusting us a risky thing to do 11479

trusts G, obeys G. 8089

Truth having same idea G. has 11554

trying to find something other than G. 5570

trying to get a message through 184

trying to spell G. with the wrong blocks 7530

turn cake for love of G. 10208

turn from limitations to G. who has none 3274

Turn your attention to G. 6271

turns everything into ruin 896

turns from wrath, never from love 4757

turns well-examined, prove to be hand of G. 5454

Two men please G. 4572

two reasons for loving G. 7533

two witnesses: G, and our own conscience 4872

unable to grant us heart's desires till 9282

uncreated Creator 4595

under all things 4848

underestimates what G. can do 766

understood only through his self-revelation 4738

undertakes special protection of man 3999

union between Father and Son a person 11425

universe is a thought of G. 11646

universe is centered on G. 11647

universe under reign of G. 1285

unless G. himself teaches 4910

unless I can recall an earnest attempt to serve the G. who made me 6919

Unless we love G. cannot love neighbor 1240

unlimited power of G, limited power of Satan 4917

until learned to be satisfied with G. 7447

Until satisfied with fellowship with G. 4311

up to G. to make man good as he is 4567

up to me to let G. do it 4567

Up to the light where G. himself appears 8454

Use everything as if it belongs to G. 10740

Use G. to get a job 7517

used my powerlessness 2518

used to ask G. to help me 4994

uses chronic pain, weakness 8256

uses circumstances to crush us 883

uses every cloud which comes 188

uses experience 10306

uses our sins to remind us of weakness 10306

uses someone we dislike to crush us 883

uses struggles to give housecleaning 1013

uses struggles to make dependent 1013

uses struggles to reorganize priorities 1013

vague, tenuous hope G. too kind to punish 4726

value of good works based on love of G. 10115

values not your deeds 7864

very angry with G. 481

Virtue naked and bare can't endure before G. 11713

virtue of highest benevolence 4514

vision of holiness of G. 4660

voice of G. a friendly voice 4966

voice of G. just speaks 4967

vouchsafes to speak to us one by one 6178

Wait the great teacher death, and G. adore 5913

waiting for us to recognize him 8843

Waiting upon G. not idleness 7724

Waiting upon G. work which beats all work 7724

wake at three, live an hour with G. 8794

wakes to find him there 4847

walks among pots and pipkins 5826

walks everywhere incognito 4871

walks in Holy Scriptures 643
walks with us as of old 7996
want to lobby for G. 3311
wanted weakness, who so weak as I 11787
wanted world to have music at the start 7886
wants no wallflowers 3180
wants not dregs of exhaustion 941
wants same character in us as exist in Christ 6301
wants to be loved 4447
wants to bring us beyond point 5396
wants to come to his world through man 4549
wants to make soul aware of him 4562
wants to rebuild minds, give new values 7863
wants to teach us dependence 8990
wants to teach us our need for himself 8990
wants us 8094
wants us in love with G. of virtue 11688
wants us into deeps 3544
wants us living sermons 1414
wants us out of love of virtue 11688
wants us to ask question of truth 10564
wants us to break through ordinary ways of man 10564
wants us to do ordinary things extraordinarily well 7118
wants us to give up our right 465
wants us to grow, not grovel 1608
wants us to know when we have him, we have everything 4806
wants us to overcome, not be overwhelmed 1608
wants us to roll burdens on him 937
wants us to soar, not sink 1608
wants us to unlearn something 188
wants us victors, not victims 1608
wants worshipers before workers 12099
warrant for believing that G. cares 4779
wars just which are ordained by G. 11743
washes eyes by tears 11013
washes eyes with tears 10591
watches to see door move from within 4775
way from G. to human heart is 3334
way to trouble G. is not to come at all 8964
We are because G. is 3489
we are to love as G. does 7316
We are valuable because G. loves us 4752
We ask G. to come when he is already present 8843

we can do nothing without grace of G. 5207
we can ignore, but nowhere evade G. 4871
we can know that G. is 4687
We can seek G. and find him 4509
we cannot always understand ways of G. 4688
we cannot know what G. is 4687
we cannot psychologize grace of G. 5237
we cannot speak of measure and G. 4680
we cannot tell where G. begins or ends 4602
we come from G. who is our home 809
We demand proof of G. 4689
We do not seek G, G. seeks us 4624
we fit G. in wherever he is able to help 5467
we glow when he stirs us 7534
We have as much of G. as we actually want 5772
We know G. as men born blind know fire 4690
We know G. easily 4691
we know G. through Jesus Christ 10013
We know how G. would act if in our place 6151
We must repudiate seeking G. for benefits 4806
we need not wonder whether God in receptive mood 4590
we never let him take control until we trust him 10259
We owe G. every honor in our power to give 4529
We pay G. honor for our own sake 12126
We play the game, G. keeps the score 6069
We please G. most by 7560
we say hard things about him 229
we see G. all around us 8048
we shall have only G. 3719
we value health, G. values patience 11667
We were bondslaves to Satan, now heirs of G. 1348
weak and powerless in the world 4899
weak, mental reflection of G, badly out of focus 4579
weaker we feel, harder we lean on G. 10761
Were the works of G. readily understandable 4510
Were there no G. 11167
wets you with his rain 4466
What does G. require 4574
What else can I do but sing hymns to G. 8745
what G. chooses better 1800
What G. does not choose to give 4958
What G. does, he does well 4996

What G. gives, and what we take 5860
what G. has revealed to me 956
What G. is in himself is our hope 4587
what G. is willing to forget 4633
What G. may do on world scale 7564
What G. reveals as critical moments 10721
What G. sends better than what ask for 4991
What G. throws my way comes 5416
What G. will, no frost can kill 4959
what God knows is well and best 4746
What happens when G. grants fellowship 4029
what he is we know little 4690
What I believe about G. most important 614
What idea of G. without the sky 4512
What if G. arranged things 577
what is from G. fixed as nail in sure place 4524
what is greater still, pulls G. into death 7237
What is impossible to G. 4513
what is prompting him to pray is G. 8761
What is reason for saying G. does not heed us 7567
What kind of habitation pleases G. 7450
what pleaseth man ofttimes displeasing to G. 9195
what sovereign G. chooses to do through us 8094
what was G. saying in this significant act 6500
what we are unable to bear G. keeps secret 9708
What we call crises, G. ignores 10721
What will G. think of our virtues 11718
what will satisfy if G. himself will not 7508
What would G. have done 25
What you make of yourself your gift to G. 8560
What, but G. Inspiring G. 4711
Whate'er we leave to G, G. does 4575
whatever devil does, G. can use for Christian's benefit 9858
whatever G. allow, soul should embrace 4978
Whatever G. asks of you 55
Whatever G. is, love is 4755
whatever G. may will, soul should will 4978
Whatever man seeks more than G. is idolatry 6076
Whatever obscures sense of G. is sin 10424

whatever we think of as belonging to G. holy 5749

whatever you love most is your g. 7338

whatever you suffer G. has suffered first 10885

Whatsoever we beg of G. 2791

when all men stand before G. 4718

When all thy mercies, O my G. 4819

When angry, is perfectly angry 401

when believe G. beyond all we can think 4685

when confidence transferred to G. 5645

when faith is present, G. works through anyone 3723

when G. begins to deal with sanctified souls 9840

When G. calls a man, he does not repent of it 4626

When G. comes go with him slowly 5460

When G. conceived world 1981

when G. does not see fit to grant us sunlight 5393

when G. goes, goal goes 4437

When G. inclines the heart to pray 9024

When G. is displeased 401

When G. is putting saints through millstones 10927

When G. is seeking a person 3340

When G. is weaning a soul 10036

when G. knows we meant to do his w. 4810

when G. leads in higher path of sanctification 9851

when G. lets loose a thinker 11217

When G. makes presence felt through us 4874

When G. measures men in next world 6112

When G. our strength, it is strength 10767

When G. pardons 4638

when G. quickens his pace, quicken yours 5460

When G. says today, devil says tomorrow 2493

When G. scooped up handful of dust 1982

when G. sees men rising up against fellowmen 4895

When G. sends evil 3418

when G. sets the soul in tune for himself 10663

When G. should guide us, we guide ourselves 10425

When G. shuts a door, he opens window 5462

When G. slackens, slacken at once 5460

When G. sorts out 37

when G. talks to us, we're schizophrenic 9035

When G. thought of mother 7859

when G. thought, the world was born 11244

When have everything, see G. in everything 11490

When have nothing but G. 11490

when I have seen G. I shall never die 2310

When I think upon my G. 7931

When in prayer clasp your hands, G. opens his 9026

When it's bigger than I am, so is G. 10236

when love bound to G, fear is done 3986

When man reasons, G. laughs 9427

When man repents, he is turned toward G. 9583

when man wishes impossible, he remembers G. 7490

when men first saw their G. 6154

When men worship, G. is satisfied 12137

when mind not in vision of G. 4989

when mind of man, Spirit of G. meet 949

When minds filled with G. 10932

When none but G. is near 8939

When our requests honor G. 9028

When rightly related to G. 5463

When soul laid down faults at feet of G. 9608

When talk of man doing anything for G. 10214

when universe lay in mind of G. 4769

When we are obedient, G. guides our steps and stops 8119

When we are restless, G. remains serene 4587

When we have nothing left but G. 4516

when we shall have nothing but G. 3719

when we think about G, most important thing about us 7563

When we turn to G. our souls have rest 7451

when you cannot stand, G. will bear you in his arms 5907

When you empty yourself, G. rushes in 9956

when you fear G. you fear nothing else 3994

When you walk with G, you get where he's going 5465

when young people learn a g. has clay feet 12179

whence comes good if no G. 5027

whenever heart begins to burn with desire for G. 4749

whenever in need, G. enlightens me afresh 5426

Whenever visions of G. unfit us for practical life 5466

where G, the cause, begins 4525

Where G. has put a period 5468

where is G, not? 4832

Where is the greater one to whom G. must appeal 4955

Where need is highest, G. is nighest 4515

where only attraction is G. 1403

where only G. and his angels have charge 10486

Where pity dwells, the peace of G. is there 7284

Where there is G, there is no need 4517

Where there is peace, G. is 8475

Where there is peace, there is G. 4517

Wherever G. rules human heart as King 4736

wherever his glance falls he turns all to beauty 4463

whether we seek G. or his gifts 4800

which I spent not in communion with G. 6909

Which is better, only G. knows 2378

Whichever way G. turns my feet, I go 5416

While G. Incarnate made a chair 6458

whispers to us in our pleasures 8257

who art everywhere 4867

Who can deceive his heart, onmniscient 4888

Who can escape eye of G. all seeing 4888

Who can see behind and in chance G. 4961

Who can see finger of G. in weather 4961

who cares for you today 415

who counts the tears 10877

who does not know G. demands satisfaction from human beings 9496

who does not praise G. while on earth 8727

who fails to pray does not cheat G. 8810

Who falls for love of G. 4791 3635

who fears G. need fear nothing else 9732

who fears not G. needs to fear everything else 9732

Who gives to poor, lends to G. 627

Who has G, has all 4519

who has G. not, has less than nothing 4519

Who has G. wants nothing 4588

who hath ought that is not thine 4954

who knows about depth knows about G. 7466

who knows G. reverences him 12100

who love G. for riches or comfort 10084

who needs no one 4467
who offers to G. second place,
    offers no place 7467
Who plumbs the depth of G. 9791
Who practices hospitality
    entertains G. 5961
who rules this earth 3227
who seek for goods before they
    seek for G. 8638
who sees in secret 10877
who serves G. has a good master
    10149
who truly loves, will chastise well
    2847
who worship G. from fear 12123
Who worship G. shall find him
    12130
whose ways you cannot
    understand 3684
Whosoever walks toward G. one
    cubit 7573
Why and how is G. to be loved
    7574
Why did G. abolish the law 9755
Why does G. bring disasters 1515
Why doesn't G. do something
    10922
Why is G. at work in me 3042
why must G. be a noun 4520
why must G. be neglected 7723
Why not a verb 4520
Why should we question him
    4640
Why when we talk to G, we're
    praying 9035
wicked afraid of G. 3996
widens the space 1156
will advance a mile in blazing light
    2962
will all that G. wills 9835
will be in the furnace 151
will be our compensation for
    every sacrifice 4550
will beat the time for us 9684
will come one day a touch from G.
    7060
will direct aspirations 1241
will direct desires 1241
will direct emotions 1241
will direct instincts 1241
will direct intelligence 1241
will direct judgment 1241
will direct knowledge 1241
will direct likes 1241
will direct reason 1241
    1241
will disappoint man attempting to
    use him 4468
Will do yet more 4476
will find thee work 10142
will forgive but man will hop
    around 1731
will forgive me, that's his business
    4634
Will G. unroll the pattern 10606
will give me goodness of Lord
    Jesus in exchange 5059
will give what you ask or
    something better 2568

will give you unfailing strength
    415
will have all, or none 4920
will have last word, will be good
    4938
will help thee bear what comes
    11362
will hold us responsible 9660
will hold us responsible for
    knowledge we have 6679
will incline us to repent 9578
will judge on basis of what we
    kept 7797
will lauch you to that place of his
    appointment 5430
will listen as you walk 8874
will look after the outflow 10180
will look after the universe 2780
will look you over for scars 172
will make it possible to do it 5226
will make us broken bread 887
will make us poured out wine 887
will make you specialist in that
    truth 11528
will never achieve fulfillment
    unless G. in control 9558
will never dismiss compassion
    1547
will never plant seed on hard spirit
    888
will never send anybody to hell
    5686
will not be hustled by peevish
    impetuosity 8419
will not bring forth dead fruit 872
will not demand 55
will not do what I can do for
    myself 8803
will not look you over for medals
    172
will not permit knowledge of
    things to come 4314
will of G. never leads to miserable
    feeling 4507
will provide strong shoes 180
will put tape about their heart
    6112
will reach down all the way 7514
will roar all about us 10554
will sustain if remain faithful 5385
will take care of you tomorrow
    415
will take nine steps toward us, but
    not the tenth 9578
will treat us without pity 2089
will use us as piece of mosaic 4005
will use you to further his ends
    10141
will wither up every spring you
    have 11689
wills a rich harmony 6179
wills man should be good, happy
    5060
wills the development of all men
    9351
wills us to tread hidden paths
    5397
wills we eat, drink, be merry 8603

wind of G. always blowing but
    must hoist sail 5452
window through which world sees
    G. 3438
winds of G. are blowing 5810
Wisdom comes privately from G.
    11911
wisdom of G. to plan our welfare
    7093
wise man in storm prays to G.
    3997
wise man trusts wisdom of G, not
    his own wits 5459
wise to let G. hold you back 5422
wish G. had not given me what I
    prayed for 8879
wishes each of us to work hard
    2774
with deliberate purpose, G. visited
    this planet 6144
With every man G. has a secret
    7127
with eye on G, strike note full,
    clear 7056
With G, go over the sea 5470
With G. Abram's day and this day
    the same 4591
With G. no calendar 11355
With G. you can always start
    afresh 8080
with his Godhead flow 9951
with humility, talk to G. as to
    your Father 4924
With knowledge of G. comes love
    7347
with one glance of his intelligence,
    G. sees all 4883
with patience leading world 4474
with so much love as G. embraces
    the soul 7958
within but not enclosed 4848
within, filling 4848
without but not excluded 4848
without doubt G. will quickly
    respond 7709
Without faith impossible to please
    G. 3823
Without faith in Fatherhood of G.
    925
without fatherhood of G. 4632
Without free will man not in
    image of G. 4158
without G, go not over the
    threshold 5470
without G. in this life, without G.
    in next 1142
Without G. we cannot 7576
Without G. world maze without
    clue 4522
without G. young people
    frustrated 12180
without giving G. deadline 8415
without need to understand why
    G. does what he does 7697
without us G. will not 7576
Without us, G. will not 10221
without whom one cannot live
    4542
without, embracing 4848

woman who creates home creator
  second only to G. 5857
won't have anything to do with G.
  because cannot define him 9395
work gives G. glory 12013
work is worshiped, not G. 97
work out what G. has worked in
  1012
work to glory of G. 3127
working out family likeness to his
  Son in us 5793
Workless faith G. never regards
  3825
works continually 6525
works his sovereign will 4941
works in us the doing of the works
  10209
works powerfully, but gently,
  gradually 4814
world by existence proclaims G.
  1953
world centered in G. is peace 8436
world charged with grandeur of G.
  8044
world crowded with G. 4871
world has yet to see what G. can
  do 2835
world stage on which G. displays
  wonders 12040
world takes notion of G. from
  Christians 575
world thought of one eternal G.
  4594
Worldliness is excluding G. from
  our lives 12053
worried and not knowing G. 7888
Worry indication G. cannot look
  after us 12087
Worship fellowship with G. 12139
Worship G. in difficult
  circumstances 238
Worship giving to G. best he has
  given us 12134
Worship is man climbing altar
  stairs to G. 12132
worship of G. an adventure of the
  spirit 12119
Worship requires only a man and
  G. 12142
Worship to see world from point
  of view of G. 12133
worshiper is no nearer to G. than
  before 8845
worth to G. in public is what I am
  in private 6315
would give best, man will not take
  2571
would have created me otherwise
  6186
would never invest in worthless
  property 9989
would not be G. if fully known to
  us 4740
would not be less if we did not
  exist 3481
would not change ground
  whereon I stood 967
would not have created man to
  exist only for a day 6104

would not have created us
  without plan 5398
would not part waters of sea 967
would not permit evil if good did
  not come of it 5017
would not take bad, make good
  967
wrath of G. is pure 401
wrong concept of G. leads to
  wrong concept of sin 4568
yearning arises from image of G.
  in man 4744
yield room for some little time to
  G. 7708
You are a man, not G. 11722
you are greater if you serve G.
  9732
you are slamming door in face of
  G. 5955
You may know but not
  comprehend G. 4693
Young people were built for G.
  12180
Young people, why G. uses them
  so often 12177
Your G. is too small 7580
zeal for G. rather than zeal of G.
  7502

GOD-APPOINTED
Each problem a G. instructor
  2720

GODDESS
Science, sweet talking g. 9870

GOD-DIRECTED
Christianity, G. strength 1165

GOD-GIVEN
how did he play his G. part 7423
individuality, uniqueness 1635
Talent is G, be thankful 10994
try G. method for revivals 9743

GODLY
afflictions end in g. man's good
  3996
afraid of nothing 3996
Death is g. man's wish 2372
few have spiritual resources to be
  both wealthy and g. 11806
knows God his best friend 3996
live by g. priorities 3901
No man poor who has had g.
  mother 7851
not afraid of afflictions 3996
not afraid of God 3996
not afraid of himself 3996
not afraid of Satan 3996
not self-willed determination 547
response to obstacles kicks
  crutches from skeptic 10938
will remain at beginning of a g. life
  6708
Wisdom by-product of g. reaction
  11911

GODHEAD
attributes of God glimpses mind
  enjoys of G. 4583
highest science is study of G. 4631
His g. is your sap 7689

GODLESS
War is kinder than a g. peace
  11770

GODLIKE
it is all sin to leave 10334
To return good for evil g. 4102

GODLINESS
crown of the home is g. 5851
difference between worldiness, g.
  is renewed mind 7769
exercise himself unto g. 7564
fire of suffering will bring gold of
  g. 10864
genuine essence of the Lord 5771
Hospitality test for g. 5957
is no longer valued 4410
Sour g. is devil's religion 2186

GOD-LOVING
Repentance is G. 9592

GOD-MADE
I hold G. object up to picture
  2022
if clash with G. object, bad art
  2022

GODMOTHER
child has fairy g. in soul 1122

GOD-ORDAINED
Authority is G. 523

GOD-REGARDING
Repentance is G. 9592

GOD-RELIANCE
Confidence in spiritual world
  1605

GOD'S
a wideness in G. mercy 7745
ability that counts 9
ability to heal soul profound
  10845
Accept equally G. gifts 1461
acceptance of G. dealings 7728
action masterpiece of partiality,
  love 4747
actions outside, above human
  sciences 5237
acts consistent with attributes
  4579
Adam switched off from G. design
  757
admitting G. presence 5395
affliction, G. messenger 160
Afflictions shadow of G. wings
  277
afraid to laugh in G. presence
  6723
aim is production of saints 5757
aim is the message of the gospel
  197
all dangerous without G.
  controlling hand 4956
all G. attributes are holy 5749
all G. earth is holy ground 7996
All G. great works are silent 1956
All our winters are G. 10581
All that man bears for G. sake 148
Almighty hand 4625

almighty Spirit 14

alone G. ideals, hopes, doings made known 10532

am concerned that I am on G. side 7471

And seen G. hand thro a lifetime 6914

anvil stands 7875

appreciate G. point of view by long discipline 2846

approval of our way 5443

are all strings in the concert of G. joy 6570

Are G. great pictures hung 8047

arithmetic 4360

as near to G. secret as anyone can get 10592

assent mentally to G. control 5467

be still, G. plan is wrought 9556

be thankful G. answers are wiser than your prayers 8861

Beauty is G. handwriting 535

become channels of G. universal love 4768

begin to see from G. perspective 11152

being he owes to no one 4610

Bible, G. chart to steer by 713

birth, G. confidence in man 815

blessings steal into life noiselessly 4641

body is G. creation 841

bring us to point of recognizing his will 5395

call comes to individuals 5385

call founded on his decree 4626

call not for impoverishment, but for enrichment 9351

called to be G. transmitters 1340

calling the shots 4939

candidates for G. generous grace 5238

care will carry you 1543

casting doubt on G. wisdom 9993

catch some glimpse of G. designs 4578

center of G. will is safety 4980

Charity, scope of G. commands 1076

Children are G. apostles 1107

children bored with him 1403

children of infinite value, eternally loved 6042

Christ's life failure from every standpoint but G. 3605

Christ, G. everything for man's total need 6427

Christian has G. honor at stake 1246

church can limit G. power 4829

church cannot increase G. power 4829

church wherever G. people are 1377

combine dependence on G. Spirit with own researches 6681

commands fulfill G. destiny 8111

compassion flows out of his goodness 4724

compulsion is our liberation 4498

concealed at G. discretion 11609

Conflict in G. character development 1029

Conscience G. presence in man 1670

contemplate G. munificence in abundance of earth 4581

contemplate G. power in immensity of creation 4581

contemplate G. wisdom in unchangeable order 4581

country begins where men serve 4913

coward if G. truth is attacked, yet remain silent 99

creation is G. work 4911

creative method is change 4469

creative method is continuing search 4469

creative method is movement 4469

creative method is ongoing inquiry 4469

Cross is G. truth about us 11531

cut ourselves off from riches of G. grace 6693

darkest threatenings 11432

Death G. way of giving life 2246

decree basis on which perseverance depends 4616

decree is immutable 4626

decree ties knot of adoption 4616

defeats of us are our victories 11673

demands are so great 1194

demonstrate G. love, listen to people 7115

Denying we can accomplish G. work is worse kind of pride 9199

designs infinitely wise 2545

designs of G. providence hidden 3349

designs, not our own 139

dewdrops G. thoughts in pearls 8048

difficulties are G. errands 2714

difficulties proof of G. confidence 2714

Discernment G. call to intercession 2805

do not run down G. people 576

Do right, G. recompense to you power to do more right 9648

Duty is ours, events are G. 9654

dying Jesus evidence of G. anger toward sin 6473

ear for my hearing 5400

earth is G. long-suffering 5650

either in full control or off throne 4939

Eternal years lie in G. heart 3274

eternity, man's mortality 2288

Every believer, G. miracle 1279

Every soul exists by G. pleasure 4529

evidence of G. love, is grace to bear afflictions 4778

evidences of G. direction 4949

exist G. free determination 3481

existence of evil proof of G. existence 3399

expect to find G. instant answer 693

eye for discerning 5400

eye over every place 4834

Face it—'tis G. gift 6881

failed miserably often first to see G. formula 3628

failure in everyone's sight but G. 5993

faith is weakness leaning on G. strength 3775

fearful symmetry which is G. language 5718

feelings all holy when G. hands on reins 4016

feelings come and go, G. love does not 4777

felt G. presence on moon more than on earth 11630

find this to be G. usual course 9037

finger touched him, he slept 2289

fingers mould loveliness 537

first thing G. eye nam'd not good 7136

foreknowledge does not necessitate him 4882

forgiveness forgets 4637

formula for success 3628

free choices, G. foreordained decrees 1153

Freedom filling mind with G. thoughts 4121

freedom from bias 6630

From G. other attributes we learn about his love 4750

gifts are meted out 5

gifts on shelves one above the other 6017

gifts put man's best dreams to shame 4988

gifts so infinite do not see them 7993

gospel is G. search for man 9547

Government, G. response to nature of people 5177

grace G. goodness directed toward debt, demerit 5206

grace sufficient 2518

grace turns out family likeness to Christ 4651

great faith perseveres in G. silences 3725

great judgment seat 915

greatness above our capacity, reach 4681

groves were G. first temples 8036

guidance not mysterious 5370

hand folks over to G. mercy 4105

handful of earth to make G. image 1952

happiness and joy from G. standpoint 5531

heart capable of containing G. gift of himself 8910

heaven is G. love 5650

heavenly plan doesn't always make earthly sense 5399

hell is G. justice 5650

holiness depends on G. grace and our will to be holy 5754

home is G. built-in training facility 5854

hopes to do deed without G. knowledge errs 2501

human soul is G. treasury 10666

human soul silent harp in G. choir 7921

humble only when we know we are G. children 6042

I just want to do G. will 4975

I press G. lamp 2945

I'll trust in G. unchanging Word till soul and body sever 9813

I'm under G. arrest 5482

if live in sin, among G. enemies 10427

if shipwreck, will be in wide sea of G. love 9930

If this is G. world 3233

If we would think G. thoughts 11269

If you discern G. love in happiness 5254

In G. faithfulness lies eternal security 4620

In G. family one body of people: servants 10161

In G. sight, only two classes of people 3236

in heavenly places see G. counsels 2809

in his heaven 8233

In his will is our peace 4973

In the face of the sun see G. beauty 4858

In the hollow of G. palm 8429

in the march of G. armies 4712

infinitude places him above knowing 4702

intellect given to be used for G. glory 10708

interfering with G. working within us 10977

investment in us so great 4617

irreconcilable hostility to evil 4999

is G. world still 3194

is your doing not G. 4319

Joy echo of G. life within 6545

joy, commit ourselves to G. way 6566

judgment, G. not man's 6591

judgments are of another sort 9195

judgments as great deeps 3349

justice permits creation to punish humanity 3191

justice stands forever 4726

justice, love are one 4725

keep in reserve treasures of G. deep counsels 4322

Knowing G. own time best 3800

last, endless word 2153

Laughter is G. hand on troubled world 6731

law reflects G. holiness 1530

left the past in G. keeping 8079

lie in G. arms and babble to him 5807

life in us 1044

life is G. life 6998

life under G. leadership 4160

life, twinkle of star in G. eternal day 7015

light is G. point of view 7106

living Jesus proof of G. love, forgiveness 6473

love can enfold created world 4760

love center of holiness 4661

love disposes him to desire our welfare 4754

love for sinners wonderful 4893

love is always shining 10964

love is measureless 4760

Love is the fairest bloom in G. garden 7247

love makes sense when seen as personal 4782

love personal, not mechanical 4782

love proclaimed with each sunrise 4759

love safer subject than our love for him 4777

love something he is 4760

love unconditional, impartial, perfect 4786

main concern 10141

maintain reverent attitutude toward G. place 3993

man can no more diminish G. glory 4442

man has power to defy G. wishes 4158

Man is G. risk 7407

man most exalted of all G. works 7395

Man's extremity is G. opportunity 8218

Man's free will, G. sovereign will 1149

marketplace one of G. abiding places 4866

Measure not G. love by your feeling 4772

mercies ever in their maturity 5657

mercy available in present situation 4815

mercy can be experienced 7750

mercy is G. goodness confronting misery, guilt 5206

messenger sent down to thee 5331

method to preserve by destroying 4556

might to direct me 5400

mill grinds slow but sure 6607

Mirth is G. medicine 6738

more experience of G. goodness we have 3744

mother is G. deputy on earth 7841

mountains are G. thoughts upheaved 8048

Music is G. best gift to man 7904

my response to G. ability 9

mystery is G, the promise is yours 11485

nearer G. heart in a garden 8032

need eye single to G. glory 5442

need not be concerned how high G. standard is 8518

neither usefulness or duty G. purpose 197

never interfere with G. dealings 1549

never missed the runway 3974

Never think G. delays are denials 8402

no business to limit G. revelations 11273

no days when G. fountain does not flow 4647

no end to G. beginning 4602

no life so humble it cannot reflect G. light 7055

no vacuum into which G. deep water may rise 9938

none who has enjoyed G. goodness on earth 6092

not specimens in G. showroom 9850

Nothing that is G. obtainable by money 7818

Nowhere G. principles to be replaced in favor of human calculation 7828

obedience foundation of subjection to G. authority 8355

oceans are G. thoughts imbedded 8048

one eye to see G. greatness 3562

one of G. best gifts 4220

One on G. side is a majority 7510

only see a little of G. loving 6111

order comes in the haphazard 5401

Our knowledge, compared with G, is ignorance 6699

our only aim G. glory 4507

Our prayer, G. mercy like two buckets in well 8884

out of options, ready for G. surprises 2596

outward imperfections G. priorities 1033

own truth 4804

pain thread in pattern of G. weaving 10915

Paradise where everyone doing G. thing 5691

path is up 7529

patience with ill-natured saints mystery 4893

penalty of evil harvest not G. punishment 4721

people would break G. windows 4480

permission means no shadow of doubt 5402

perpetual flow of grace 7553

place in G. hands aspirations 1241
place in G. hands desires 1241
place in G. hands emotions 1241
place in G. hands instincts 1241
place in G. hands intelligence 1241
place in G. hands judgment 1241
place in G. hands knowledge 1241
place in G. hands likes 1241
place in G. hands reason 1241
plan, like lilies, unfold 5403
poverty, deprivation of G. peace 8697
power is irresistible 8886
power to protect me 5400
Prayer enabled to move ourselves G. way 8925
Prayer G. psychotherapy for his children 8921
Prayer is not overcoming G. reluctance 8933
Prayer is putting oneself under G. influence 8936
Prayer is to carry out G. purpose fully 8909
Prayer is to enter into G. counsel 8909
prayer key that shuts us up under G. protection 8846
prayer opens to us G. mercies, blessings 8846
prayers track down which G. power can come 8886
presence of G. grace with his people 4865
presence of G. justice in hell 4865
presence of G. power on earth 4865
presence of God's glory is in heaven 4865
problem is that God loves 4823
problem not in G. silence 2931
problem not that God not able 4823
promises are obligations he imposes upon himself 9324
promises beyond wildest dreams 4458
promises like the stars 9323
promises real, glorious 4458
promises sealed to us, but not dated 4470
providence upsets your timetable 11370
putting pressure back into G. hand 11466
Rainbow, G. glowing covenant 9393
Reason's voice and G. 3813
rejects G. truth in favor of devil's impure philosophies 11512
remedy for failure 10812
reply to new problem 5441
required that we fall in with G. purposes 8821
resources are mine, for he is mine 7486
resources available, endless 4458
restrictions not only hold us down but up 9558

restrictions show our need 1522
result always in G. hands 4945
Revelation is G. word 4911
revelation of escape 11432
revelation record of G. acts in time 9710
Revival is G. finger pointed right at me 9748
rivers are G. thoughts in motion 8048
running the show 4939
saint receives everything as G. goodness 9790
salvation depends on G. love of us than our love of him 9806
Satan uses problems to slander G. character 9859
service is perfect freedom 4126
side winning side 1159
silent closet best declares G. reality 10554
sin not breaking G. law so much as breaking G. heart 10355
sing hymns for G. ears alone 8424
Sinning is turning from G. face 10382
Sleep is G. celestial nurse 10486
small moment carrier of G. gift 11319
So let it be in G. own might 10756
soul silent harp in G. choir 10665
soul, G. glorious image 10675
sound of your goings and G. goings the same 8093
sovereignty derived from omnipotence 4952
sovereignty enables him to secure our welfare 4754
spirituality an echo of G. voice 5981
Spring G. way of saying hello 9892
stick in hand not G. way 6786
strange misunderstanding of G. ways 9840
streets are sacred, because G. presence is there 4866
strength worth more than world 10768
struggling to supplement G. providence with our own 4322
symbol of G. nature is cross 2167
take G. program, can have G. power 4826
takes delight in breaking up our programs 5401
taking hold of a hand, finding it G. 2399
Temptation is G. magnifying glass 11086
the Lord abandoned to G. blazing wrath 6383
They travel lightly whom G. grace carries 5235
things placed in G. hands I still possess 8628
This earth would be G. Paradise 6882

those who accept Christ receive G. approval 3854
thought G. purpose to make me full of happiness, joy 5531
thoughts are man's home 1790
thoughts belong to world of spirit 10692
thoughts flashing from every direction 8045
through our bodily lives G. Spirit works 837
thrill at G. willingness 4135
time of your death under G. supervision 2316
time, eternity to experience G. thought 11229
To repent is G. point of view instead of one's own 9605
to supply what we cannot 10166
treasure like infinite ocean 4471
trial is G. alchemy 223
Trouble often lever in G. hands 11460
troubles large enough to touch G. love 4789
True triumphs are G. triumphs over us 11673
truth judges created things out of love 4914
turn mountain into gold mine with G. help 2633
universe one of G. thoughts 11251
values differ from ours 11667
voice deafening in its thunderousness 4465
voice in response to mine 8932
voice too still, small to be easily audible 4465
warped view of G. values 3861
way always down 1294
way becomes plain when start walking 5404
way contrary to common sense 1294
way contrary to wisdom on earth 1294
way of answering Christian's prayer 8804
way often insignificant and unobstrusive 4664
way to the top in G. kingdom 10161
ways are perfect 4443
ways seem dark, but soon or late 11299
ways touch the shining hills of day 287
We are G. property 7552
We are obliged to pray if citizens of G. Kingdom 9015
We impoverish G. ministry to us 4830
we put on foot on G. side 1156
weaknesses make us appreciate G. strength 11790
what must G. mind be in all its undisclosed resources 4675
What you are is G. gift to you 8560

What you call obstacles are G. opportunities 8219

When G. goodness cannot be seen 7750

When G. people repent will have a song 9606

When G. will to plague a man 2859

When leave G. love, we grow dark, cold 9354

when the cloud of G. presence moved 10124

When we take to ourselves place that is G. 7571

Whoever falls from G. right hand 4628

wind of G. admonishment may burst doors 4775

wisdom in dailyness of living 1803

wisdom seeing life from G. perspective 11971

wise and good were all G. ways 4904

wisest saints endure rather than escape pain 10847

wishing to forestall G. arrangements 4322

within G. purpose, no failure 3582

within zone of G. voice, profoundly altered 7540

word for my clearing 5400

work from beginning is revelation 4906

works unique 4993

world a thought in G. eye 12044

world is G. book 12042

world is G. nursery 12043

world, balanced, calm, in order 420

wrath toward you burns like fire 4523

GOD'S WILL

all things happen because of, with, in G. 10926

circumstances indication of G. 5444

doing G. may not lead to popularity 10778

easy to tell poor to accept poverty as G. 8678

Emotional peace and calm come after doing G. 8432

hard against our stubbornness 10771

highest way of doing G. 8416

if you can accept poverty as G. for yourself 8678

need not fear G. 5405

not an itinerary but an attitude 5406

only way to know is to will to do G. 5447

pain contrary to G. absolutely but not relatively 8258

prayers of abandonment to G. 8840

when G. is done we grumble 8791

you are G. 5464

GOD'S WORD

can choke G. with a yawn 11349

highest function of mind is to listen to G. 7766

is a seed 9137

joy in reading G. 733

when home is ruled according to G. 5862

GOD'S WORK

exhausted when try to do G. our own way 940

impossible to get exhausted in G. 940

GOD, THE FATHER

giver of Holy Scriptures 655

power excels 11427

work of creation 11426

GOD, THE SON

theme of Holy Scriptures 655

wisdom excels 11427

work of redemption 11426

GOD, THE SPIRIT

authenticator of Holy Scripture 655

author of Holy Scripture 655

interpreter of Holy Scripture 655

love excels 11427

power to forgive sins 11426

GODS

Feelings go bad when they make themselves into false g. 4016

voice of parents is voice of g. to children 5856

We actually have too many g. 9552

yet makes g. by dozens 6073

GODWARD

prayer a wish turned G. 8753

GOES

Happiness a thing that comes and g. 5517

not where man g. when compelled to go 4147

Time g, you say 11327

Time g. by 11326

What's got badly, g. badly 1743

When goal g, meaning g. 4437

when God g, goal g. 4437

When meaning g, value g. 4437

where he g. when free to go 4147

GOING

Anytime the g. seems easy 6877

better check to see if you're g. downhill 6877

Christ as God is fatherland where we are g. 6364

concern to know where history is g. 5724

do not know what God is g. to do next 5463

He lived a life of g.-to-do 6756

Hope is a g. forward 5918

I love you yet more for what you are g. to be 4248

If it's g. to be, it's up to me 4423

important where you are g. 4438

more alone while living than g, coming 7151

When you walk with God, you get where he's g. 5465

Without the way no g. 6382

You are g. forward toward something great 4248

GOINGS

sound of your g. and God's g. the same 8093

GOLD

a living god 11812

All not g. that glitters 430

and riches, chief causes of war 11810

begets in brethren hate 11811

Better rich in God than rich in g. 11800

better to have g. in hand than heart 11828

Bible, a vein of pure g. 710

Bright and yellow, hard and cold 11816

Building one's life on foundation of g. 7796

cannot bring you comfort 11813

cannot reach out helping hand 11813

Chains of g. stronger than chains of iron 11802

character enriched with g. 223

Christian made of pure g. 1260

cursed love of g. 11843

Curst greed of g. 11803

devil entangles miser with g. 2677

does civil wars create 11811

does friendship separate 11811

Each ounce of dross costs its ounce of g. 2641

Even asses know straw is better than g. 11804

fire burns g. pure and clean 294

fire of suffering will bring g. of godliness 10864

flame will not corrode or blacken g. 294

Found in each poppy's cup of g. 7996

give nothing but worthless g. 11358

God impregnates barren rock with g. 1902

golden age only comes when men have forgotten g. 11856

has no ears to listen 11813

has no heart to understand 11813

hidden in ground belongs to poor 11855

in families debate 11811

in house, looking for copper outside 5840

in trouble powerless to cheer
11813

is cold, lifeless, can't see or hear
11813

is touchstone to try men 11836

lust of g, unfeeling and remorseless
11858

Man must govern, not serve, g.
11835

Men have touchstone to try g.
11836

Men seek to get crowns of g.
2152

morning hour has g. in its hand
11318

no balm to wounded spirit 7798

O love, thou triumphest even over
g. 7285

of real service 9759

opens every gate, e'en that of hell
11814

Rank and riches chains of g.
11844

saint-seducing g. 11850

silent threads of g. when woven
together 6997

slave or master 11815

suggest timelessness of heaven
5631

The walls of g. entomb us 9224

Time will reveal calyxes of g.
5403

to get all the g. the goose could
give 5328

transient, shining trouble 11817

Truth better than g. 11564

We were dross, now g. 1348

what crimes thy tyrant power has
caused 11803

what is g. doing in a holy place
11853

GOLD MINE

stay and turn the mountain into g.
2633

GOLDEN

bit does not make better horse
11793

crown of g, divine love 7073

Speech is silver, silence g. 1874

GOLDEN AGE

only comes when men have
forgotten gold 11856

people dreamed of a G. 8371

GOLDEN RULE

committed G. to memory 5007

let us now commit G. to life 5007

would reconcile capital, labor
5005

would reconcile political
contention 5005

would reconcile selfishness, greed
5005

GOLF

prayers never answered on g.
course 8986

.would rather play g. than eat
7656

GOLF-MANIA

as intemperate as someone who
gets drunk 9269

GOLGOTHA

consummation of commandments
on G. 281

Jesus took road that would end
on G. 6384

manger situated on G. 1365

GOLIATH

nobody roots for 452

such a thing never entered my
head 768

underestimates God, rocks in head
766

GONE

Because he lives all fear is g. 2978

children will be g. so quickly
8353

empire of Caesar g. 730

friend comes in when world has g.
out 4167

From the centuries that are g.
6497

Had I g. my own way 5594

No reward offered, g. forever
11306

present g. in instant of becoming
11389

then bloom of life is g. 5480

to diffuse light elsewhere 6094

weight and strain are g. 7486

when repressions of society and
business are g. 6842

GONG

fear g. on approach of danger
3973

GONNA

ain't what we g. be 9825

GOOD

A g. man never dies 2206

afflictions end in godly man's g.
3996

All g. things are cheap 11655

all g. things are yours 5604

And all clever people were g. 909

and evil increase at compound
interest 5021

and ill together 7045

and wise lead quiet lives 9373

annoyance of g. example 3433

any g. thing I can do 6642

appalling silence of g. people 6285

aren't such things as g. and bad
impulses 7839

as g. as anybody if had equal
chance 3228

Ask God for what he thinks is g.
for you 8781

authoritarianism twists g. into lust
for power 9952

Bad is called g. when worse
happens 153

bad tree does not yield g. apples
986

bath temporary but it does you g.
9753

be a g. master 3099

becomes indistinguishable from
evil 5012

beggar gives chance to do g. 621

believe half the g. people tell us of
ourselves 7973

best portions of a g. man's life
6664
626

best to yourself when g. to others
6673

Better fare hard with g. men 4219

Better is enemy of g. 3156

better sheltered from temptation
5042

Bible, deals with g. and bad 721

Brown bread and gospel g. fare
5090

can be great when in g. fortune
5310

cannot love g. if we do not hate
evil 5050

cause will fear no judge 6602

ceases to be friend, never was g.
one 4244

Charity enough to see g. in
neighbor 1809

Cheerfulness, habit of looking at
g. side 1095

Christian thanks God when
everything g. 3638

church force for g. in world of evil
1433

Community is g. 9952

confession of evil works beginning
of g. works 5040

consists in favoring life 5044

consists in preserving life 5044

cross, love meeting evil with g.
2146

day is all that is g, fair 8375

death may be height of g. luck
2342

difference between g. and bad
5042

difference between g. and great 64

difference between g. person and
bad person 5041

Do all the g. you can 10126
5057

do evil, deny evil, call it g. 5029

do g. to them that hate us 5001

Do g. to your friend to keep him
9449

Do more g. by being g. 3456

Do not consider painful what is g.
2843

Do not wait for extraordinary
circumstances to do g. 5058

Do not wait to do g. actions 623

does g. to another does g. to
himself 4362

does g. to another, does g. to
himself 5069

Don't ask God for what you think
is g. 8781

Eavesdroppers never hear g. of themselves 5123

end cannot sanctify evil means 5010

enhances life 5024

Every g. thought touches chord that vibrates in heaven 6670

evil has two enemies, the g. and itself 5022

Evil minds change g. to own nature 5015

Evil repay with g. 1191

example best 3449

example is best sermon 3427

example, tallest preaching 546

Experience g. school but high fees 3521

Faith makes uplook g. 3705

first thing God's eye nam'd not g. 7136

Follow g. or evil path 1137

for g. men to do nothing 3402

For sake of one g. action 4074

for the g. or evil side 2489

for uneducated to read quotations 9383

Fountain of g, all blessing flows 7456

frank talk g. soap for hearts 5864

freedom to give up our rights for g. of others 9963

from mistakes g. learn wisdom for future 7794

From seeming evil worketh g. to me 11470

fundamental idea of g. 5044

future will hold both g, evil 4335

God able to bring g. out of evil and pain 5046

God allows trial for greater g. 2883

God can direct evil to g. end 3371

God could not be g. if not just 4724

God does not care what g. you did 7862

God grant they read the g. with smiles 7017

God has lively, profound interest in man's being g. 5060

God has set g. against evil 5016

God he knew of g. which could come of evil 5020

God is at work through the g. 5014

God is g, and God is light 4936

God is my g. 7462

God judged it better to bring g. out of evil 5018

God knows all g. 4881

God makes all things g. 5019

God never permit evil if could not bring g. 3372

God sees something g. in suffering 10856

God spares us because he is g. 4724

God treats sinner as if g. man 6634

God will have last word, will be g. 4938

God wills that man should be g. 5060

God would not permit evil if g. did not come of it 5017

God, too g. to be unkind 4990

goodness, not greatness, will do you g. 5074

gospel is g. news 9545

gospel signifies g. tydings 5091

Grace is the g. pleasure of God 4652

greater in possibility for g. or bad than we know 10015

greater the evil, greater opportunity for g. 3401

greatest pleasure is g. action by stealth 8607

greatness in acknowledging g. turn 5263

has but one enemy, the evil 5022

has not made a g. beginning 10701

He that is g. is free though a slave 4131

He would take bad, make g. 967

heart better than all heads in world 5054

heart of g. man sanctuary of God 5084

heaven not reward for being g. boy 5645

Hell paved with g. intentions 5688

Holiness has g. of others as its employment 5739

Hope is a g. breakfast, bad supper 5915

Hope looks for the g. in people 5928

human race has experienced was trouble for somebody 11459

Humility covers our g. deeds 6005

husband makes g. wife 7590

I have always tried to be g. 561

I know that God is g. 4642

I laugh and shout for life is g. 6917

I think not of the great, but of the g. 6245

If all g. people were clever 909

If any g. in you 5838

if don't wish his g, you ask for your death 8067

If love g. in another 564

If men thanked God for g. things 11150

If there be g. in what I wrought 7480

If try to improve by g. example 3436

If we saw all g. things coming 4318

If we seek God for our own g. 4923

If work for God because it brings me g. opinion 10158

if you would have g. servants 3099

In his g. time 5408

in judgment of g. we can make mistakes 5086

In the end g. will triumph 5073

in wanting to bring life to highest value 5044

injures g. men who spare wicked 6608

is all that serves life 5024

is better than evil 6326

is not g. where better is expected 3466

is oft interred with their bones 5043

is principle of totality 5023

is reverence for life 5024

kings never make war but for peace 11747

knowing God will turn ultimate effect to g. 3671

leader prepared to deny himself much 6793

Learn luxury of doing g. 5076

Let a g. man do g. deeds 108

Let no man be sorry he has done g. 5032

life enables us to disregard evil tongues 5164

Life eternal is supreme g. 5033

life is the scene of g. and evil 5034

life lost which I spent not in doing g. 6909

listener popular everywhere 7111

little, nameless, unremembered acts 626

lives on, loves on, conquers all 11129

Look for g. in people not evil 5077

look, honor, rejoice in, imitate what is g. 3940

Lord not merely a g. man 9437

love is steady wish for loved person's g. 7242

love Maker without hope of g. 4807

love what we think is g. 5086

love you want other person's g. 7197

Make death a g. experience 2333

Make the evil we have done work for g. 9054

makes for unity 5025

makes hearts pure, g. 5844

man is his own friend 5082

man makes no noise over g. deed 2495

man mistakes evil for the g. he seeks 3386

man must know g. through evil 5030

man too g. for world, no g. for his wife 7594

Men come up to what is expected, g. or bad 3505

Men have never been, are not, never will be g. 7421

men obey from love 5053

men pay for not being interested in politics 5193

miss a lot of g. things day by day 5587

Mistrust the man who finds everything g. 3555

Money a g. servant 7809

more communicated, more abundant grows 5062

more harm by example than g. by correction 3914

Most people are g. 10070

must be doubted to be defended 2954

must first be made g. before do g. 5087

name better than great riches 9610

name got by many actions, lost by one 9611

name is forever 9617

name keeps brightness even in dark days 6292

need greater virtues to bear g. fortune than bad 11719

next to g. friends, g. book 854

night where in g. rise and wicked sink 10878

No camel route is long with g. company 4256

no g. asking God to make us happy our own way 7459

no g. government without God 5194

no g. in arguing 44

no g. in being where there is but one 11622

No man g. enough to be trusted with unlimited power 8714

no man so g. would not deserve hanging 7434

no matter how g. eyes, feet 2565

No work, noble or g. of emulation 2009

Nobody promises g. time 2182

none going to heaven because g. 5653

nor must we do evil that g. may come 5010

not enough to do g. 5075

not frantically trying to make ourselves g. 7560

not g. advertisement for way of God 5474

not g. for other party, isn't g. for you 1022

not so g. as I thought 8879

nothing can happen which cannot be turned into g. 4803

Nothing can make man great but being g. 5290

nothing either g. or bad 11255

Nothing g. is failure 10796

Nothing is often g. thing to say 1865

Nothing out of place is g. 5036

Nothing so bad that g. may not come 2755

Nothing so g. as seems beforehand 3506

O Will, that willest g. alone 4977

Occupy mind with g. thoughts 7764

Of a g. leader, who talks little 6803

Of evil grain, no g. seed 3389

old days next generation will hear about 11381

One does evil enough when one does nothing g. 3393

One must do g. in right way 5075

only different kinds of g. weather 8033

only send what is for your g. 8578

opinion in g. men is knowledge in making 6711

opinion of one's self 11591

optimist thought everything g. except the pessimist 8248

ought to seek, work for g. of country 10525

Our g. or evil name depends 4198

out of evil a more noble g. 5031

passions are g. servants 10225

Perfect and right and pure and g. 5620

person loves people, uses things 5041

plan by which g. people go to heaven 5632

plan of mine would have deprived me of g. the Lord had designed 4901

Pleasure greatest evil or greatest g. 8605

positive word makes you feel g. 12001

possible for bad men to become g. 9438

power of choosing g, evil within reach 5047

Praying is g. for your digestion 8899

quotations when engraved upon memory give g. thoughts 9383

real enemies make us feel so g. 3168

Real friends know you have g. reason 4266

Religion is g. views 9545

retentive memory g. thing 4068

return evil for g. devilish 4102

return g. for evil godlike 4102

return g. for g. human 4102

Sainthood can find g. in criminals 9778

scare worth more than g. advice 3960

see all things g. 8578

See g. in the other 2808

see g. things in unexpected places 8575

See not g. in yourself 2808

see the g. and gifted 7300

sight of you g. for sore eyes 4207

sin death of g. works 10360

Since you cannot do g. to all 9673

smallest g. deed better than grandest intention 2505

so much g. in the worst of us 3953

So shines g. deed in naughty world 2499

society an inordinate emphasis on feeling g. 4017

some say God too g. to be true 4504

something difficult will do you g. 2758

something g. must come out of sorrow 2667

speak all the g. I know of everybody 5072

spirits make for g. digestion 5612

spread money around, does a world of g. 7812

Suffering, change evil into g. 10891

suffering, profound potential for g. 10933

Sunday self and weekday self not g. if detached 10949

takes a great man to make a g. listener 7113

than g. action which puffs up 3931

that people sometimes misunderstand us 6270

that we have sorrows and adversities 187

That which is beautiful not always g. 5080

that which is g. always beautiful 5080

The clever so rude to the g. 909

The g, are like one another 5045

The g. are so harsh to the clever 909

The g. have no need of an advocate 5081

The people have poor opinion of us even when intentions g. 6270

the whole of the g. man's creed 2028

Think of how g. God is 4648

think of what is g. in others 3939

thoughts bear g. fruit 11223

To a g. man nothing that happens is evil 5049

to be g, very demanding 561

to be g. is divine 5085

to do g. is human 5085

to endure contradictions 187

to flea, mosquito human being something g. to eat 9219

to forgive 4083

To g. man nothing is evil 1479

To get g. is animal 5085

To strive with one's self is the g. 10022

toil until g. accomplished 1809

unask'd in mercy grant 8979

unconscious is also source of highest g. 7772

unfairly judged when we do g. 187

up to God to make man as g. as
   he is 4567
upright life based on
   self-realization 10044
use ordinary situations to do g.
   623
very few can think g. thoughts
   11272
wall with loose bricks not g. 4020
we always love what is g. 5086
Wealth a g. servant 11873
Were it not g. that evil should exist
   4831
what matters is not how long, but
   how g. 6935
What was g, bad changed places
   984
What wicked do should not
   disturb g. man's tranquility
   11894
When g. and ill so interwine 4338
When g. people cease vigilance,
   evil men prevail 7991
when God gives, supremely g. 288
When Jesus is present, all is g.
   6512
When things are g.—thou 4518
Whence ability to wish evil, refuse
   g. 5051
whence comes g, if no God 5027
who are so g. yourself 10038
who does g. turn should never
   remember 5070
who receives g. turn should never
   forget 5070
who serves God has a g. master
   10149
Who shall declare this g, that ill
   4338
who waits to do great deal of g.
   5071
whose g. opinion I wish to have
   10158
wicked always outnumber the g.
   5182
wife makes a g. husband 7592
will got by many actions, lost by
   one 9611
Wisdom a g. purchase though we
   pay dear for it 11968
wise and g. were all God's ways
   4904
With g. or ill, with false or true
   7017
word costs no more than bad one
   3128
words how potent for g, evil
   12004
words worth much, cost little
   11987
works never erase guilt 5061
world forced to be g, happy 4149
world in which creatures do g. or
   harm 4132
would be g. clock ticking out
   goodness 10337
yet unenjoyed impairs enjoyment
   of g. 2869

you do is not lost, though you
   forget 5083

GOOD BOOK
most remarkable euphemism 731

GOOD FRIDAY
Christmas and G. the same day
   6489

GOOD MORNING
God, I love you 9061

GOOD SENSE
travels on well-worn paths 4393

GOOD WILL
cannot add to peace and g. 580

GOOD-BYE
Everyone knows how to say g.
   9452
It hurt that he didn't say g. 2208
proud world! I'm going home
   2291

GOOD-DAY
Bids not himself g. 12097

GOODLY
apple rotten at the heart 5011

GOOD-MORROW
Bids not himself g. 12097

GOOD-NATURED
Fat people generally g. 399

GOODNESS
All our g. a loan; God the owner
   5055
blessing for man hungry for g.
   5299
Christ infinite, g. 5208
Concealed g. a sort of vice 5056
cross revealed g. not enough 2144
does not attach itself merely to
   this life 5079
does not flash 5067
extraordinary mystery of human g.
   5037
fear God because g. and truth
   3983
For everything thy g. sends 11174
Free will makes g. possible 4120
glows 5067
God cannot accept g. from me
   5059
God has all g. to supply you 4696
God leading world by vision of g.
   4474
God will give me g. of Lord Jesus
   5059
God's compassion flows out of his
   g. 4724
God's g. encourages us not to be
   afraid of him 3788
God, a radical beginning of g.
   4698
grace, God's g. directed toward
   debt, demerit 5206
greatness is tied to g. 5276
Hope draws power from basic g.
   of mankind 5928

hungry for g. he does not possess
   5299
I walk through the Lord's g.
   almost with difficulty 4646
in inward thing we are 5063
Infinite G. has wide arms 4645
Infinite G. takes whatever turns to
   it 4645
is like praise to God 5064
is love following his footsteps
   5065
is love in action 7202
is love with burden on back 5065
is love with hand to plow 5065
is rich 11696
is silent 5719
is uneventful 5067
joy bound up with g. 6568
Lord's g. surrounds us at every
   moment 4646
mercy God's g. confronting
   misery, guilt 5206
more experience of God's g. we
   have 3744
need for g. answered at Pentecost
   7400
never fearful 11704
No man progressed to g. but
   through mistakes 5030
none who has enjoyed God's g. on
   earth 6092
not greatness, will do you good
   5074
not in outward things we do 5063
not tied to greatness 5276
of God, preserving beauty of his
   order 4644
of God to desire our welfare 7093
Of thy g. give us 619
origin of g. so extraordinary
   11204
power not likely coupled with g.
   8705
saint one who makes g. attractive
   9770
saint receives everything as God's
   g. 9790
smiles announce g. 10500
so simple 5066
Son no more thought of his own g.
   6484
though we know not g. of God
   4578
thy g. both satisfied and made me
   thirsty 9097
tune we call g. or right conduct
   7839
When God's g. cannot be seen
   7750
where g. is flat, boring 3347
without g, no happiness 5060
without justice is not g. 4724
would be good clocks ticking out
   g. 10337

GOODS
recognize in God the Author of
   our g. 8796
who bestows his g. upon the poor
   4364

who seek for g, before they seek for God 8638

who withholds g. from his neighbor 10060

GOOSE

Feather by feather g. is plucked 11054

to get all the gold the g. could give 5328

GOOSE'S

fox should not be on jury at g. trial 9177

GORGEOUS

Lies can be disguised in g. wrappings 6853

GOSPEL

a living being 732

a living power 732

a mysterious efficacy 732

addressed not to reason, but faith 3796

amazed at folk drinking g. in 9544

Angels cannot preach the g. 3296

anything less partial g. 1426

apologetic about g. never 5092

behave it 5107

believe it 5107

Brown bread and g. good fare 5090

can, will correct everything 5094

cannot live, fight, conquer without prayer 9015

Christians responsible for disseminating g. 3301

church for proclamation of g. 10506

could only reveal itself in simplest of garments 5089

development more complete than limits of nature 9351

devil wanted to neutralize g. of love 2704

doubts, dim perceptions of Christ's g. 6713

fruit of g, aspiration 471

glory of the g. is its freedom 5095

God speaks in his g. 8835

God's aim is message of g. 197

good, merry, glad, joyful tydings 5091

grain of sand that upsets world's machinery 5099

hindering the spread of the g. 349

If you believe what you like 588

invades everything that opposes extension 732

is an announcement 5098

is gift of God 9545

is God's search for man 9547

is good news 9545

is Savior God seeking lost men 9545

is simply irresistible 5101

Jesus came that there might be a g. to preach 5111

justice brightest emanation from the g. 6628

learn nothing of g. except by feeling its truths 5110

like fresh, mild, cool air in heat of summer 5097

makes man sing, dance, leap for joy 5091

many excluded by g. 5093

message of g. often diluted 5109

nature of g. is that it divides 5102

neither a discussion nor a debate 5098

No one excluded from g. 5093

not made to dominate world 5099

not so much a demand as an offer 5100

not the g. you believe, but yourself 588

Nothing attractive about g. to natural man 5108

of Christ is same forever 5103

of Jesus Christ nothing if not g. of growth 9351

offer of new life to man by grace of God 5100

one can't inhale its fragrance and be content 5099

one question, that is the g. 5094

only man who finds g. attractive 5108

originated in heaven 9545

personal g. like soul without body 5088

possesses secret virtue 732

social g. like body without soul 5088

songs are songs of hope 7890

strangest truth of g. is redemption comes through suffering 9439

to govern with g. 5182

two things to do about g. 5107

warmth which penetrates the heart 732

warmth which soothes the heart 732

what God has done for men 9545

what happens when g. preached 5105

when prepared for popular consumption 5109

will scarcely hear glad sound of 5224

work, crowded out g. of Christ 130

world glad of excuse not to listen to g. 1334

world has many religions, one g. 5106

GOSPEL-DRIVEN

What happened to g. churches 1407

GOSPELS

do not explain the resurrection 9696

people who have never troubled seriously to study four G. 6417

resurrection explains the G. 9696

GOSSIP

Choose to praise, rather than g. 1138

estrange closest friends 5127

Hating g. ourselves, grateful to those who do it well 5138

is nature's telephone 5130

lack of worthy theme 5131

leads to criticism 5135

like mud thrown against clean wall 5129

makes mountain out of molehill by adding dirt 5114

may not stick but leaves mark 5129

no one claims to like 5133

people dislike g. when g. about them 5159

personal confession of malice 5128

proves nothing but bad taste 5132

selling parrot to town g. 1039

smoke that comes from dirty tobacco pipes 5132

social sewage 5136

speaks ill of all and all of her 5113

talks to you about others 5112

what everybody enjoys 5133

worse than fighting 5134

GOSSIP'S

mouth is devil's mailbag 5146

GOSSIPS

set on fire all houses they enter 5137

to you will g. about you 5139

GOT

Life is what you've g. 6983

What's g. badly, goes badly 1743

GOUTY

than slipper on g. foot 8442

GOVERN

a small family as cook small fish 3868

Any fool can g. with stick in hand 6786

impossible to rightly g. world without God 5181

Man must g, not serve, gold 11835

to g. with gospel 5182

GOVERNED

be g. by your admirations 8472

by men worse than themselves 5193

conclude human affairs not g. by God 3349

deriving just powers from consent of g. 3246

God g. all things by his will 4904

He who g. world before I was born 10145

If not g. by God, ruled by tyrants 7483

Men must be g. by God 4137

youth g. more by feeling than reasoning 12181

GOVERNMENT

best which governs least 5187
big enough to give you everything 5168
big enough to take everything 5168
by permissive g. God lines up his purpose 5175
cannot be tool to establish Kingdom of God 5177
cannot redeem world 5177
Christianity balanced between God, Caesar 1240
Christianity introduced new spirit of g. 5170
civil g. boundaries for human behavior 5177
Democracy form of g. where you can say what you think 5172
Democracy worst form of g. 2525
family, basic unit of g. 3888
foundation of g. rests on Bible 5189
God's response to nature of people 5177
hope of nation not in g. 5190
impersonal hand of g. 8062
no g. capable of contending 5196
no good g. without authority 5194
no good g. without God 5194
no good g. without justice 5194
no good g. without law, order 5194
originated as ordinance of God 5177
our constitution inadequate for g. of any other 5196
out of the question Christian g. even over one land 5182
perpetual irony of g. 5194
who shall introduce principles of Christianity 5178

GOVERNMENTS

instituted among men 3246
Love is needed in the g. 7251

GOVERNS

God g. in affairs of men 4933
God g. the world 5176
God g. through men 8099
government best which g. least 5187
Order g. the world 2659
rule that g. my life is this 7036

GRAB

God's better plan takes effort to g. 2607

GRACE

a divine energy 5217
a g. of kind listening 6669
a g. of kind speaking 6669
abounding g. hope of mankind 5203
abounds when genuine repentance 5210
Acts of g. cannot be reversed 4626
afflicts less than g. can suffer 286

alone conquers sin 5231
beginning of glory in us 5216
binds with stronger cords than duty 5211
can do nothing without g. of God 5207
can heal us when wounded 5212
can help us when down 5212
can justify us with Christ's righteousness 5212
can multiply pardons 5212
can pardon our ungodliness 5212
can put Spirit of Christ within us 5212
candidates for God's generous g. 5238
cannot be stockpiled beforehand 5226
cannot psychologize g. of God 5237
central invitation to life 5221
Charity does work of g. upon giver 1075
Christ giver of g. 5208
Come, Lord, when g. has made me meet 5635
comes into the soul as sun into world 5213
comes wisdom through the awful g. of God 11919
contemplation a theological g. 1765
cut ourselves off from riches of God's g. 6693
destitute appreciate g. of God 3614
directed toward human debt, demerit 5206
do not require dying g. to live by 6912
does not destroy nature 5214
earth, theatre for God's g. and direction 4902
energy as real as energy of electricity 5217
enough to confess, forsake sin 1809
evidence of God's love, is g. to bear afflictions 4778
evidence of growth in g. 5202
Father! replenish with thy g. 7454
for easiest positions God must give g. 7486
For gift or g, surpassing this 2345
Fountain of life, all-abounding g. 4836
free and infinite 495
free, but you are bound forever to the Giver 5211
Give them g. to pray for such as do them wrong 9104
give us g. to labor for 9676
given that we may to do good works 5209
gives us power to pull it off 5221
Glory is perfected g. 4408
God gives us g. 837
God has all g. to enrich you 4696

God provides comes only with task 5226
God uses struggle to make dependent on g. 1013
God's g. sufficient 2518
God's g. turns out family likeness to Christ 4651
God's perpetual flow of g. 7553
gospel, offer of new life to man by g. of God 5100
grows best in winter 5215
growth of g. like polishing of metals 5230
Happiness is living every minute with g. 5528
He giveth more g. when burdens grow greater 5223
his g. and power are such 9000
his g. has no measure 7570
holiness depends on God's g, our will to be holy 5754
Humility necessary prerequisite for g. 6007
If I am right, thy g. impart 9067
important that we have g. enough to live by 6912
In confession we open lives to g. 1602
in great difficulty, much g. 7486
inclines God to bestow benefits 4652
inherent in the divine nature 4652
is but glory begun 5218
is God himself 5219
is God's energy at work within his church 5219
is love that cares, stoops, rescues 5220
is the beckoning nudge 5221
is the final word 5221
is the good pleasure of God 4652
its use to sinful men 4652
Jesus is to be all g, no wrath 6498
knows little what g. is 5224
Leave tomorrow's trial to tomorrow's g. 12067
lightness of life from g. of Christ 5229
live by assurance of g. 5204
Lord revels in mind renewed, enlightened by g. 7776
love that gives 5222
love that loves unlovable 5222
makes you gracious 5211
may be some work of g. there 10475
Measure growth in g. by sensitiveness to sin 10335
men may despise g. of God, but cannot extinguish 4654
mercy and love of God 5227
moved God to dispense g. in certain manner 4989
must despair to obtain g. of Christ 5201
mystery of g, it never comes too late 5228
no g. in solemn countenance 1090

no major sin when his g. confronts you 10405

not a mere thought of Almighty 5217

not mere sentiment 5217

not necessarily lost his g. 2883

O for g. to love thee more 9077

of God can have no end 4656

of God had no beginning 4656

of God is glue 4654

of God is infinite, eternal 4656

of God sufficient 1504

of God, boundless as infinitude 4656

old age equal g, force, fascination 12188

Only in context of g. can we face sin 10551

opposed to sin 5205

overwhelming, undeserved mercy 5221

painfully conscious of my need of g. 9097

perfects nature 5214

presence of God's g. with his people 4865

refuses to put ceiling on concern 5233

refuses to put floor on concern 5233

sin a death of g. 10360

Sin sovereign until sovereign g. dethrones it 10373

stand before God on basis of g. 1057

straightens me out 5232

strength of God to overcome 5227

that is in God 5016

There but for the g. of God 5234

They travel lightly whom God's g. carries 5235

think of affliction as g. 2565

think they will not have g. enough to die by 6912

three meanings of g. 5227

to abandon egotism 1719

to abandon inertia 1719

to accept bitter truth 1719

to accept things that cannot be changed 9060

to live peaceably with contrary is g. 5236

to submit to demands of the Spirit 1719

tread hidden paths of g. in faith 5397

urges us to change, grow 5221

What but thy g. can foil tempter's power 5225

When humiliated, g. is on the way 6007

when the dying hour comes, there will be dying g. 6912

where human will leaves, divine g. begins 5200

who has given me g. to work 10208

winsome attractiveness of God 5227

youth full of g, force, fascination 12188

GRACEFULLY

learn to say no g. 5615

GRACES

no end but to perfect g. 280

GRACIOUS

awful, g, beautiful voice for which he listened 4965

faith a g. companion 3689

Grace makes you g. 5211

How g, how benign is solitude 10578

if God deny g. presence, fall into sin 4865

So hallow'd so g. is the time 1371

GRACIOUSLY

Accept suffering g. 10833

GRADE

God does not g. the fruit 7862

So none may claim superior g. 3227

GRADES

learning persists after pressure for g. vanished 3031

no g. of perfection with God 3236

GRADUAL

developing faith g. process 5738

knowing God g. process 5738

safest road to hell is g. 5702

GRADUALLY

giving central place to God 7713

God gives self-knowledge g. 10006

God works powerfully, but gently, g. 4814

grief passes g. into quiet, tender joy 7101

Life happier if born at eighty, g. approach eighteen 6989

GRADUATES

in heaven's highest school of art 8914

No one ever g. from Bible study 684

GRAIN

chaff and g. together 4260

faults like g. of sand beside mountain of mercies 4817

gospel g. of sand that upsets world's machinery 5099

Life sifting like g. from bag 8381

Of evil g, no good seed 3389

We could not have the golden g. 11172

when swallowing her g. 11142

GRAINS

Little g. of sand 6659

of dust carried away 3295

GRAMMAR

no g. for language of inner life 7705

school of faith, repentance 11192

GRANARIES

Who fills world's unempty'd g. 11138

GRAND

Death, the g. leveller 2258

God doesn't reveal his g. design 4448

show is so g, beautiful, exciting 6092

GRANDCHILDREN

God has no g. 7460

Nowhere in Bible does God claim g. 9818

too many g. of Christ 9818

GRANDER

Eternity looks g, kinder if 3268

GRANDEUR

endurance of soul show divine g. 3150

God, lone in g. 11429

in cry from depths 10676

in order to invest us with his g. 6130

is a dream 11849

Many men owe g. to difficulties 2739

world charged with g. of God 8044

GRANDFATHERS

our g. called it the Sabbath 10952

GRANDLY

one thing to go through a crisis g. 7129

GRANDMOTHER

where devil can't go, he sends g. 2706

GRANITE

Feet firm based on g. 7448

Quarry the g. rock with razors 9233

who is a g. stone 6517

GRANT

God never fails to g. light 5397

Lord, g. that I may desire more 61

The good unask'd in mercy g. 8979

us a heart wide open to joy, beauty 9064

when God does not see fit to g. us sunlight 5393

GRANTED

healthy to question things taken for g. 2950

so often take providence of God for g. 8002

we take for g. speech, music, sounds 9094

whether take for g. or with gratitude 5268

GRAPES

fathers eat sour g. 8328

made to be bruised, used 9524

We were thorns, now g. 1348

yield and cling 9524

GRASP

all, lose all 5314
Choose to give, rather than g.
1138
Happiness when pursued, just
beyond g. 5518
him and be led securely home
6517
Life way of prying loose g. 11656
man's reach should exceed g. 4420
present has melted in our g. 11389
propensity to g. at forbidden fruit
11112
truth, try to g. with closed eyes,
fearing to be blinded 11562

GRASPED

Christ too simple to be g. 6507
Faith means g. by power greater
than we are 3707
Jesus gave such insights we have
not yet g. significance 6196

GRASPING

God's hand g. me 7484
without God young people g. for
security 12180

GRASS

always greener in next lawn 2873
blade of g. witness to mystery of
God 7945
grows above all graves 2292
If blade of g. can grow in concrete
walk 3736
like hearing g. grow 8496
the wonderful g. upon your breast
8010
Trees, flowers, g. grow in silence
10250
While g, flowers, stars spell out
his name 8019
why green g. and liquid water
12037

GRASS-BLADE'S

A g. no easier to make than an oak
2007

GRASSES

smooth green g. more common still
10634

GRATEFUL

Be g. God drawing you away
from distraction 2556
Be g. to the beggar 621
can at any rate be g. to God 6251
Give one thing more—a g. heart
5265
Hating gossip ourselves, g. to
those who do it well 5138
hearts and no one to thank 11167
My garden's g. shade 7452
proud man seldom g. 5258
Some people are g. for the roses
6254
There's more and more to be g. for
11163
thought to heaven the most
perfect prayer 8755

GRATIFICATION

Envy knows no g. 10296
3211

GRATIFICATIONS

world can no longer evolve
around your g. 1306

GRATIFIED

would often be sorry if wishes g.
2573

GRATITUDE

activity have root in g. 5240
after short act of g. we forget God
8788
Arrogance, fear replaced with g.
1356
best way to show g. to God 5261
born in hearts that count mercies
5244
disciple gives himself to Jesus in g.
2817
due to our Father in heaven 5253
duty which ought to be paid 5242
enter trials with g. 181
events that now disturb events for
g. 5252
for what we give 5267
for what we take 5267
found least g. from greatest
services 5250
Happiness is living every minute
with g. 5528
How happy person is depends
upon g. 5249
If g. due from children to parent
5253
is heart's memory 5246
learn to express g. to them and to
Me 5271
living doxology for g. 1243
looks to the past 8376
none have right to expect 5242
of most is desire of greater benefits
5262
one of least articulate of emotions
5245
only with g. life becomes rich
5257
seasoning for all seasons 5243
sign of noble souls 5247
soul o'erfraught with g. 8792
Swift g. is sweetest 5260
Thankfulness is an intelligent
response of g. 11173
to God makes blessing taste of
heaven 5248
Two kinds of g. 5267
whether take for granted or with
g. 5268

GRAVE

a thoroughfare 2422
a veil over reunion of paradise
2350
affliction, whether light or g. 160
And the g. is not its goal 2328
As g. grows nearer, and theology
growing simple 11182
before g. all hopes dissolve 1163

By an unfaltering trust, approach
thy g. 2203
closes in twilight to open in dawn
2422
Count each affliction, whether
light or g. 5331
down to g, shall have ended day's
work 11132
dread the g. as little as my bed
2370
early Christians not looking for g.
9913
go to g. saying, "A man is dead"
2408
hopes of life beyond the g. 5711
Jesus Christ burst from g. 1905
Jesus only one who has returned
from g. 2323
No man rich to whom g. brings
eternal bankruptcy 6101
no repentance in the g. 9603
not a blind alley 2422
of one who dies for truth holy
ground 11534
on the way to the g. 6986
One small g. is what he gets 7440
passeth from life to his rest in the
g. 9225
preaches short, pithy sermon 2207
There lies a lonely g. 778
thoughts, thoughts lasting to the
end 5331
threshold of eternity 2377
Where is thy victory 2389

GRAVEL

pleasure, more g. than pearls 8599
Politics full of gut and g. 5185

GRAVEN

And g. on thy hand 1395

GRAVES

drink, dug more d. 325
Gluttons dig g. with teeth 132
Grass grows at last above all g.
2292
who seeks revenge digs two g.
9717

GRAVITATION

faith requires we rise above law of
moral g. 3752

GRAVITY

most profound joy has more g.
than gaiety 6562

GRAY

Character gives awe to g. hairs
997
Eternity has no g. hairs 3266
skies seem g, threatening 9059

GRAYEST

Praying fills the g, gloomiest day
8899

GREASE

of gusto frees gears of generosity
4347
the one that gets the g. 8564

GREAT

accomplishments only
occasionally reached 3593

All g. men make mistakes 7787

All g. things are simple 10277

All God's g. works are silent 1956

All men at head of g. movements
are Christian 5094

All revolutions conspiring to that
g. event 4898

All things both g. and small 7174
8807

Almighty working on a g. scale
8419

and small suffer same mishaps
173

Are levell'd. Death confounds 'em
all 2384

Attempt g. things for God 10118

atttributes of a g. lady 11697

Be silent about g. things 10242

Behave as receiving g. guest 552

benefits of our life, health 6255

Bible contains nearly all the g.
stories 701

Bible g. and wide as world 750

Bible g. gallery of portraits 703

can be g. when in good fortune
5310

can do small things in g. way
10155

challenges which ordinary men
rise to 8668

Christ is a g. Savior 9797

Christian chooses to be g. in
God's presence 1259

confidence in friend to tell him
your faults 3930

crises show us how g. our
resources are 8659

cross is the g. central point 6424

crowd treat g. men as lunatics
4393

Death the g. adventure 2259

difference between good and g. 64

Do g. things as if they were little
10127

Do little things as if they were g.
7117

Do you wish to be g. 5997

doers of history men of faith 5723

does not take g. men 1723

doesn't matter how g. the pressure
185

Don't be so humble. You're not
that g. 5998

doubts will not avail against g.
certainties 5028

enough to die for 7140

events on little things depend
7119

events touched off by small
agencies 5720

Every calling is g. 79

Every g. movement triumph of
enthusiasm 3178

Everything g. comes from
neurotics 4390

Everything g. grows in silence
10246

expect g. things from God 10118

faith perseveres in God's silences
3725

faith will bring heaven to your
soul 3757

find no loss g. 1776

first test of truly g. man 6032

For every g. temptation many
small ones 11056

fortune a g. slavery 11794

Genius only g. patience 4391

gift is g. if given with affection
4352

glad when g. man reassures us of
his humanity 5307

God became Incarnate in flesh
835

God does not intend all to be g.
4243

God is the g. reality 4458

God not less g. in small things
4940

God rarely allows soul to see g.
blessing he is 6233

God renders equal small, and g.
4727

God so g. all things give him glory
1237

God takes g. delight in breaking
up our programs 5401

God the silent partner in g.
enterprises 4460

God's demands are so g. 1194

God's investment in us so g. 4617

God's judgments as g. deeps 3349

God, so g. an artificer in g. things
4940

good name better than g. riches
9610

Greek picture of a g. man 5299

grown g. with bliss 6140

guileless mind g. treasure, 5865

haste makes g. waste 5588

Hate too g. a burden to bear 7182

heights of g. men reached and kept
8566

Here lived a g. streetsweeper 2777

heroic acts of a g. mind 6281

Home where g. are small and
small are g. 5829

hopes make g. men 5277

house, field, wife g. riches 5814

How g. a God we need 7468

Human misery too g. without faith
3730

I am a g. sinner 9797

I have a g. Christ for my need
6399

I have a g. need for Christ 6399

I pray for your desires that they
may be g. 4248

I think not of the g, but of the
good 6245

If I cannot do g. things 10155

In anything g. never give in 8548

In g. attempts glorious to fail
3600

In g. matters men show
themselves as they wish to be
seen 7391

In heaven, all will be g. 5658

in order that God may make us g.
servants 5784

In the g. quiet of God 7569

In things g. or small 5456

is the art of beginning 56

is the power of God 4824

Jealousy the g. exaggerator 6341

joy too g. to be confused with
happiness 6564

joys, like griefs, are silent 6526

Let g. things grow inside you
10242

Life a g. bundle of little things
6946

Life is a g. book 6945

life's g. joys 50

Light cares speak, g. ones silent
10599

like a g. ring of pure, endless light
3276

little one! whose all-embracing
birth 6153

Little strokes fell g. oaks 8547

Lives of g. men all remind us 5288

Loneliness g. price to pay for
independence 7135

Lord's Prayer for attention upon a
few g. points 7154

Lord's Prayer, many and g.
mysteries 7156

Love is a g. beautifier 7227

love of God how deep and g. 4776

majority of men exist, do not live
7028

man in midst of crowd keeps
independence 6195

man is he who does not lose
child's heart 5294

Man makes g. fuss about this
planet 11633

man shows greatness by way he
treats little men 5272

Man thinks he amounts to a g.
deal 9219

man who makes man feel small
5304

man's foolish sayings pass for wise
ones 5273

man's world bounded by limits of
his vision 11728

many g. things expressed in single
words 10277

men endlessly, foolishly, incredible
merciful 6032

men have curious feeling 5291

men meteors designed to burn so
earth lighted 5278

men never feel g. 7380

men never know they are g. 5279

men see divine in every other man
6032

men see spiritual stronger than
material force 10693

men stand like solitary towers
5280

men think heroes of tragedy g. 10877

minds have purposes 5281

minds rise about misfortune 5281 193

minds talk about ideas 1845

moment of our lives 9841

more one approaches g. men, more one finds they are men 5300

Most of world's g. souls have been lonely 7138

mystery of evil isn't as g. as goodness 5037

mystery of human life 7101

natural view is man g. being in the making 7429

Neither g. poverty nor riches will hear reason 9418

Never discuss g. things 10242

never failed cannot be g. 3594

no distinction between small, g. 567

no g. genius without madness 4398

No g. man complains of want of opportunity 8220

No g. mind ever ungrateful 6251

No g. principle ever triumphed but through evil 5030

no g. thing to be humble when brought low 6019

No life grows g. until disciplined 2852

No matter how g. sorrow may be 10601

No people became g. by lowering standards 7834

no people ever g. which did not pass through valley 5289

no sacrifice can be too g. 9761

not g. enough for our need 9538

not so g. a struggle with my vices 6115

Nothing can make man g. but being good 5290

Nothing g. done without enduring 3151

Nothing g. done without suffering 10875

Nothing g. ever achieved with enthusiasm 3178

Of the g. miracle that still goes on 1966

of world those who loved God more 5295

one g. fellowship of love 911

opportunity is where you are 8225

overlook a g. deal 9489

pains cause us to forget small ones 2724

people more easily fall victims to a g. lie than to small one 7974

person g. when not envious of rival's success 3206

Prosperity is a g. teacher 242

quiet life characteristic of g. men 5274

quiet, holy people learned g. secret 1293

rather attempt to do something g. 3595

Real friends have g. time doing nothing 4265

really g. man makes every man feel g. 5304

responsibility and guilt as g. and personal 9672

saints have always been dogmatic 11188

saints have often been g. sinners 9775

secret of power, expect g. things from God 3790

serve a g. man, will know what sorrow is 5292

Silence alone is g. enough to hold 10274

Silence element in which g. things fashion themselves 10265

Silence g. art of conversation 1871

Simple love can do g. things 6708

Simple words express g. thoughts 11989

small leak will sink g. ship 5116

small troubles shall seem g. 11433

something g. must come out of sorrow 2667

souls have wills, feeble ones wishes 8541

souls suffer in silence 10848

spirits always encountered opposition 5282

Strong minds, g. hearts, true faith, ready hands 6299

such a g. man I have forgotten his faults 5286

sufferers do world's work 10849

takes a g. man to make a good listener 7113

takes consecrated men to do g. things 1723

talents have some admirers 7

talkers never g. doers 1846

Talking to men for God g. thing 8969

task ahead never as g. as Power behind 3804

temptations the most harmless 11078

than g. thing in prospect 7116

That was a g. day 1982

The g. Creator from his work return'd 1967

thing is what direction we are moving 4434

thing to be a believer 589

thing to live without human, divine comfort 1508

things often leave us calm 3056

thought g. by what it finds 11242

thoughts become g. acts 11223

thoughts of God, crystallized in words 835

thoughts, grave thoughts, thoughts lasting to the end 5331

To be alone fate of all g. minds 10571

To be g. is to be misunderstood 5305

to be humble when praised g. attainment 6019

to be simple is to be g. 10280

To g. evils we submit 3410

To God no g, no small 4709

to see physical pluck 8545

to think rightly a g. effort 11270

tranquillity who cares neither for praise or criticism 1681

treat him as any other g. man 9201

treat men gently, they will show themselves 6807

tree of being 1450

trials preparation for g. duties 2725

troubled with g. ambitions 348

troubles shall seem small 11433

Trust God for g. things 10205

two g. forces at work in world today 4917

use of life 10189

Wait the g. teacher death, and God adore 5913

we try to speak of g. or little faith 4710

wealth implies g. loss 11819

wealth, content seldom live together 11818

When g. oak is straining in wind 2508

when greatly pursued 79

When Lord leads someone to g. faith 9029

When prodigals return, g. things are done 9607

Where willingness is g. difficulties not g. 2634

Who can mistake g. thoughts 11281

who cares nothing about high honors 5285

who considers himself small 5285

who has g. power should use it lightly 8704

who realizes his own smallness becomes spiritually g. 5309

Who see the world's g. anguish 426

who wants a g. deal must not ask for little 11732

Whose love is as g. as his power 4787

Whose power extends to g. and small 11628

Whosoever would be g. is small 5309

wisdom to keep silent when damaging words spoken 6271

with g. freedom of speech, responsibility 4154

words to master are short 7000

works do not always lie in our way 5068

works performed by perseverance 8544

world g. in resources 10512

world of facts 592

world's g. men not commonly g. scholars 5302

would not think duty small if you were g. 9682

You are going forward toward something g. 4248

GREAT DIVIDE

Transfiguration was G. in life of Lord 6488

GREAT PHYSICIAN

curer of ravages of sin 10436

GREATER

a man, more distasteful flattery is 5296

adversity is a g. teacher 242

After once vice, g. follows 10293

confidence in friend to tell him his faults 3930

faith g. than learning 11568

Faith means grasped by power g. than we are 3707

faith must seek g. depth 3756

God allows trial for g. good 2883

God is g. than all language 4700

God is g. than mind itself 4700

God is not g. for our being 3481

God not g. if you reverence him 9732

gratitude secret desire of g. benefits 5262

hazards in doing nothing 6779

He giveth more grace when burdens grow g. 5223

how much g. is our God than our greatest need 7468

Human problems never g. than divine solutions 9285

I am g. than the stars 7385

if can define God, am g. than God 7487

if can define God, g. than God 9395

if comprehend Christ, no g. than myself 6459

in g. measure than we give 1740

in possibility for good or bad than we know 10015

is the art of ending 56

Knowledge given to lead us to g. faith 6693

Life will take on g. meaning 3185

love we express part of g. love 10545

man g. than universe 1984

man in evolution from lesser to g. condition 9351

merit to suffer affliction patiently 234

mistrust of himself, g. confidence in God 10328

need g. virtues to bear good fortune than bad 11719

New Testament, g. benediction 243

no g. opportunity to influence fellowman for Christ 6278

no g. position than a mother 7856

no one thing g. miracle than another 7940

One g. than my heart whose Word cannot be broken 9813

our awareness dependent on God 5226

power behind g. than task ahead 7878

power of perseverance grows g. with time 8557

prayed for wealth that he might do g. things 8806

prayer g. than man-controlled powers 8991

Prayer is a g. work for God 8908

second Adam is g. than first Adam 5031

sees something g. in vocation than bread 3107

soul has g. depths than any sea 7539

Spirit's power g. than power of sin 5802

surrendered own plans to g. plan of God 4803

the difficulty, g. the glory 4417

the evil, g. opportunity for good 3401

The g. the difficulty 209

to endure is g. than to dare 3153

to see moral pluck 8545

trusted g. compliment than loved 1576

What g. rebellion than not to believe God's promises 11596

What g. work than training mind 3037

what is g. still, pulls God into death 7237

Where is the g. one to whom God must appeal 4955

Words cannot make you g. 1681

you are g. if you serve God 9732

GREATEST

alcohol, g. criminal in history 331

are least in own opinion 5991

as much a part of human race as the g. 9988

bears heaviest burdens cheerfully 5297

benefits God has conferred become curse 3895

Bible unquestionably g. of books 701

blessing to know we are destitute 830

burden we carry is self 9949

Christ gave g. gift, himself 10731

Christ performed g. work 2127

Christ, g. contemplative 1754

Christians accepting noisiest as best, g. 5891

Christians of all time 5733

Complainers g. persecutors 1557

contributions to children rank as g. accomplishments 8294

conversing with g. minds of past 3027

Count it g. sin to prefer life to honor 6883

cross symbol of his g. suffering 10930

danger of Christianity is anti-intellectualism 3027

death not g. loss in life 2254

discoveries man can make 4866

empty vessel makes g. sound 4066

enemy of truth is prejudice 11535

events not noisiest 10268

events our stillest hours 10268

evidence of God's love, is grace to bear afflictions 4778

evil today is lack of love 6163

excuse for not becoming Christians 3477

family, where g. can fail 3886

fault to be conscious of none 3952

feeling of being uncared for g. poverty 7132

found least gratitude from g. services 5250

friend of truth is time 11535

friend's affection g. treasure 4181

friend, one of life's g. assets 4163

gain ready to be yours 3633

gladly exchange g. genius 4204

griefs are those we cause ourselves 5355

happiness is knowing you do not require happiness 5555

how much greater is our God than our g. need 7468

ideas born from womb of silence 10269

If pleasures g. in anticipation 8598

If poll taken to name six g. men in world 9988

in later stages, g. love of life appears 8174

is calmest in storms 5297

is most unfaltering 5297

loss what dies inside while we live 2254

Love g. gift person can give another 7249

Love, not law, is g. cleanser 7275

man himself is mankind's g. danger 7397

man his g. enemy 3173

Man is the g. miracle, g. problem 7408

Man the g. marvel in the universe 7497

man's self is g. cross 9919

men are simplest 10284 5298

miracle that God can do 5759

moments when God got message through to you 7029

most fearless under menace 5297

most momentous fact which history records 5710

Motherhood g. privilege of life 7849

need not more Christianity, but more Christians 1307

no life so meager g. can afford to despise it 7055

number of letters 1761

of evils not to be tempted 11097

one of world's g. tragedies 5625

path is open to least of travelers 7235

Pleasure g. evil or g. good 8605

pleasure is good action by stealth 8607

poverty, loneliness 7132

pretences built up to hide emptiness 3395

proof of Christianity is practice 599

Prosperity g. enemy man can have 9341

reaches of mind not cared for enough 3027

reliance on truth, virtue, God 5297

sermon ever preached 10102

slave of g. slave who serves himself 10055

than g. of things without meaning 7030

thing a man can do for his heavenly Father 6665

thing you can do is to be 10141

thinks himself wisest, usually g. fool 11917

Those who commit injustice bear g. burden 6279

To fall in love with God g. of all romances 7542

To find God g. human achievement 7542

To get at core of God at his g. 7543

to see spiritual pluck 8545

To seek God g. of all adventures 7542

to think as a Christian g. effort 11270

truths are simplest 10284 5298

weakness my g. strength 11789

When frustration of helplessness g. 2518

who chooses right with invincible resolution 5297

who resists temptations within, without 5297

wonder to find myself in heaven 5655

word is God 11993

works done by individuals 91

GREAT-GRANDFATHERS

our g. called it the holy Sabbath 10952

GREATLY

dare to fail g., achieve g. 87

To believe g, necessary to doubt g. 2958

GREATNESS

ability to forget is true g. 4068

and immensity of the blueness 4544

awake to sublime g. of the soul 10654

beginning of g. is to be little 5293

Bible teaches us our g. 738

daunted by no difficulty 3153

Difficulty nurse of g. 2719

Failure test of g. 3594

family measure of g. of nation 3894

God's g. above our capacity and reach 4681

God's g. exceeds bounds of thought 4692

God's real g. known to himself alone 4665

God, g. cannot be conceived 4700

Goodness not tied to g. 5276

goodness, not g, will do you good 5074

How can we measure g. of God 4673

in adherence to promises made 5283

in patient endurance 5283

in resistance to temptation to betray 5283

in speaking up for truth 5283

in unyielding loyalty to a goal 5283

increase of g. to be less 5293

Integrity first step to g. 6311

is matter of quality 5283

is this a g. apt to make a show 5297

is tied to goodness 5276

is unconscious 5275

lies in faithful performance 5283

lies in right use of strength 5284

lies not in being strong 5284

melancholy that stems from g. of mind 5303

No man progressed to g. but through mistakes 5030

not a matter of size 5283

not in men but through men 5291

note of g. in your creed 3042

Nothing more simple than g. 10280

of God rouses fear within 3788

of man's power is his surrender 10975

of mind in acknowledging good turn 5263

one eye to see God's g. 3562

original, unborrowed, solitary g. of Bible 736

over and above required determines g. 2784

perfection of g. to be nothing 5293

rough road that leads to g. 8287

shows g. by way he treats little men 5272

small acts of kindness 5283

soul that contemplates g. of God 4707

takes energy to maintain appearance of g. 433

thou art destined to g. 9982

through valley of death on way to g. 5289

to forgo ambition when end is gained 3153

to go through intrigue spotless 3153

to keep heart when all have lost it 3153

to tire out hostile fortune 3153

true g. is ability to develop g. in others 6804

true g. measured by 5306

will show how small g. is 6037

within reach of everyone 5283

works of God, transcendent g. inspire awe 9734

Ye storms howl out his g. 4712

GREATS

if take pride in g. of world 3861

GREED

abundance produces g. 5318

Ambition g. for power 340

and anger, brother and sister of false self 10003

And by g. and pride the sky is torn 6155

Curst g. of gold 11803

disease of the soul 6085

enemy to peace 8435

flares up when desires frustrated 10003

Golden Rule would reconcile selfishness, g. 5005

has pity neither for nature or human beings 5327

Its one object is to produce, consume 5327

looks ahead 8376

mere fleabites in comparison with pride 9240

molding beauty and life into money 5327

No work noble or good of g. 2009

not for every man's g. 5326

not sufficiency in world for man's g. 3204

not willing to listen, form of g. 1885

of gain has no time or limit 5327

Poverty wants much; g. everything 5322

ruthlessly ready to crush beauty and life 5327

talking, a form of g. 1885

unlively dough of human g. 530

GREEDS

inability to distinguish needs from g. 5321

GREEDY

Give me the g. heart 4530

No gain satisfies g. mind 5319

O g. men, what will satisfy if God himself will not 7508

Some people g. even when they
pray 8963

GREEK
can learn from G. philosophers
2988
no farther on road to peace than
ancient G. city-states 8450
picture of a great man 5299

GREEN
As long as you're g, you're
growing 5364
If refuse to be made straight when
g. 12166
in you God will g. 7689
man who studies revenge keeps
own wounds g. 9714
optimist sees g. light everywhere
8245
smooth, g. grasses more common
still 10634

GREENER
Grass always g. in next lawn 2873

GREEN-EY'D
monster which doth mock 6346

GREENNESS
radiant g. after rain 5360

GREET
I g. the dawn, not a setting sun
2418
in cradle our Savior 1375
What joy the happy earth to g.
9898

GREETED
when g. by man smiling because
trained 6062

GREETERS
Some churches train their g. to
smile 6062

GREETING
if smile, life returns g. 6949
No g. like his welcome 4208

GREGARIOUS
unhappy civilization is always g.
10515

GREW
by silence the saints g. 10252
more I told troubles, more
troubles g. 2727
rumor, on every tongue it g. 9757
still they gazed, still the wonder g.
2994
taller we g, more easily we could
reach 6017

GRIEF
a little home where g. and care
4921
a very antisocial state 5335
as if g. could be lessened by
baldness 5345
ask not for life free from g. 1921
attitude determines g. 509
Bear patiently cross of g. 1502
Beside you in your g. 1509
can be your servant 5334

can God dispense us from g. 5352
can purge us of pettiness,
selfishness 10640
conceals g, finds no remedy 5341
consciousness torn by pain of g.
900
Deep is the plowing of g. 5332
deepened faith that follows g.
5360
develops powers of the mind 5340
dimmed with g. no everlasting
hills I see 2587
Do not rejoice at my g. 10588
elicit from us fortitude, patience
10640
Even thy cup of g. to share 2098
Faith draws poison from every g.
3661
flys to death 2363
foolish to tear one's hair in g.
5345
Friendship doubles joy, divides g.
4229
has tears for its fruit 11014
healed of g. only when we express
it 5362
helping you feel compassion for
others 5334
If cannot find God in the secret g.
4856
If you bottle g. up, you'll never
soften it 5343
In g, nothing "stays put" 5344
is itself a medicine 5336
is the blunder of a life 5337
is the indulgence of g. 5337
Joy is g. remade again 6543
knits two hearts closer than
happiness can 5338
love of the cross must swallow up
g. 5356
may be joy misunderstood 5339
merely shadows to the unseen g.
5348
Music allays each g. 7900
Music as seasonable in g. as joy
7903
Music the fiercest g. can charm
7911
My g. lies all within 5348
no g. which time does not lessen,
soften 5358
not to have money, a g. 11871
O, if I could, what g. should I
forget 5342
old g. passes into quiet, tender joy
7101
On the wings of time g. flies away
5350
One can bear g. 5351
one keeps emerging from a phase
5344
Only the soul that knows the
mighty g. 2508
Only when g. finds work done
5352
poverty, 'tis full of g. and pain
8684
Quotations tell of g. 9385

shall pass away 6878
should be like joy, majestic
equable, sedate 5331
straining to sweetness of peace
2120
Strong to consume small troubles
5331
suppressed g. chokes, seethes 5330
suppressed g. multiplying its
strength 5330
Than perked up in a glistering g.
1772
that does not speak 5333
the agony of an instant 5337
the more g. inflicted 5357
Time a physician that heals every
g. 11336
To lie down in time of g. 8423
To weep is to make less depth of g.
5361
weight of world's g. 1064
when mine old, yours new 10588
when you share g, you decrease it
5353
will pass away 10586
With courtesy receive him 5331
Words cannot speak for g. or
ecstasy 10274

GRIEF'S
Hope is g. best music 5921
Music eases g. smarting wound
7913

GRIEFS
Great joys, like g, are silent 6526
greatest g. are those we cause
ourselves 5355
Light g. can speak, deeper ones
dumb 5347
Marriage halves our g. 7634
should this not deliver us from g.
7545
What g. in silence of your face
1545

GRIEVANCE
hell where everyone has g. 5705

GRIEVE
at funeral, not person involved
817
Christ-like it is for sin to g. 10334
Men who walk with God would
not g. enemies 3166
No one will g. because your lips
are dumb 3778
Our songs, psalms g. devil 2661
stand in death together with those
who g. 2223
Time too long for those who g.
11333
Who will not g. when deprived of
hope 2616
Why rejoice at birth, g. at funeral
817
wise man does not g. for what he
has not 1793

GRIEVED
repentance is g. because sinned
against God 9580

GRIEVES
at sin is a saint 10309

GRIEVEST
Thou repentest, yet g. not 4954

GRIEVING
vanity of g. for those we must follow 2423

GRIM
blood of Christ g. subject 2141
Strength'ning their arms to warfare glad and g. 8454

GRIME
to be a mother grit and g. 7856

GRIMMER
is men reduced to subhuman state 10503

GRIND
happy spirit takes g. out of giving 4347
who didn't have ax to g. 6147

GRINDS
God's mill g. slow but sure 6607

GRINS
how many broad g. in marketplace 10507

GRIP
Many seize self with so tight a g. 8630
release g. on everything 972

GRIPS
any greater need than get to g. with living God 7485

GRISTLE
defeat turns g. to muscle 2511

GRIT
lions didn't eat Daniel because g. 1046
to be a mother g. and grime 7856

GROAN
begins with a cry, ends with a g. 7089
I hear with g. and travail-cries 4642
To him there's music in a g. 9024
where men sit, hear each other g. 7044

GROANING
all things everywhere are g. 9909
continue g. toward perfection 9832

GROANS
best prayers often have more g. than words 8974
Cheerfulness enables us to work with fewer g. 1093
Life bridge of g. across stream of tears 2598

GROPE
and totter and make countless mistakes 9851
way through endless traffic jams 5859

GROPES
low soul g. the low 10679

GROPING
Eyes let me be to g. men and blind 10130
Man g. for God and hoping to hide from him 7402

GROSS
deeds of cruelty 4895

GROSSNESS
Then all this earthly g. quit 5679

GROTESQUE
logical mind would be our own g. God 4689

GROUCH
looks weaned on pickle 1555

GROUND
all God's earth is holy g. 7996
Ay, call it holy g. 4114
came from the Creator 3199
Christianity, feet on g. going God's way 1174
crushed or trodden to the g. 150
destroy g. and man is destroyed 3199
early Christians not looking for cleft in g. 9913
Experience never the g. of our trust 3525
Faith, g. on which we stand 3835
grave of one who dies for truth holy g. 11534
He would not change the g. 967
If doubt yourself, on shaky g. 11599
is holy 3199
Keep your ear to the g. 3503
keeps, guards, cares for men 3199
Life is the training g. 6978
not falling that is worst, but staying on the g. 10318
of the soul is dark 10664
Pride the g. in which all other sins grow 9230
trembled, rock of tomb tumbled 2984
truth cannot be built on swampy g. of scepticism 11530
where sorrow, there is holy g. 10648
Wise sayings often fall on barren g. 6672

GROUNDED
Once rooted and g. in Christ 10141

GROUNDING
Guard against g. commitment on experiences 3550

GROUNDS
What parched g. refresh as with a shower 8867

GROUNDWORK
principles of Bible g. of human freedom 5965

GROUP
family should be a closely knit g. 5853

GROUPS
concept of spirituality varies among g. 10713
Jesus popular in some g. 3493

GROUSE
in monotony we g. 10643

GROVEL
God wants us to grow, not g. 1608

GROVES
were God's first temples 8036

GROW
After losses, g. humbler, wiser 5990
as we g. older become like old cars 8181
Better pruned to g. than cut to burn 2841
Cares g. with time 12059
Consideration soil in which wisdom may g. 11910
Discussion makes things g. smaller 10242
echoes g. forever and forever 1032
even when they will not g. legs 5614
fault by lie g. two 3937
friend gently invites you to g. 4169
God never put anyone in place too small to g. 4987
God wants us to g. not grovel 1608
Grace urges us to g. 5221
happier as we g. older 7026
harder we lean, stronger we g. 10761
He giveth more grace when burdens g. greater 5223
I only I may g. 7688
If fig tree g. in side of mountain cliff 3736
If grass can g. in concrete walk 3736
If spiritual life does not g. where we are 10702
in wisdom, pardon more freely 4071
Let great things g. inside you 10242
life is given us so we may g. in love 6907
like hearing grass g. 8496
love must help child g. away from mother 7858
lovely, growing old 8143
Maturity, allowing a child space to g. up 7696
more like ourselves 8180
my freedoms g, find wings 4125
neither better or worse 8180
old along with me 8132
one is to g. older, the other not 8129

only when begin to worship, begin to g. 12107

People in a hurry cannot g. 5584

Pride the ground in which all other sins g. 9230

riches g, care follows 11799

seed in furrow to g. shrank instead 5338

so wide, deep nothing human is strange 10540

souls may quietly g. 10247

spirit should not g. old 8137

Spiritually, we never g. old 10712

strong by conflict 2715

takes a long time to g. an old friend 4193

Tall oaks from little acorns g. 8657

teenager waits impatiently to g. up 3867

tend to g. cooler rather than warmer 1347

that I may g. toward the stars of my destiny 9111

the more quickly we g. 7678

Till our steps g. slow 8120

'Tis sweet to g. old 8120

to be more and more like Christ 1269

to g. in love is to diminish fear 3986

Trees g. in silence 10250

under praise we open, reach, g. 3144

Unless something beyond mastered, never g. 2758

Unless you try, you will never g. 68

we g. spiritually, even while bodies waste away 8256

What seed ever went into earth which did not g. 2350

What we love we shall g. to resemble 7336

when cease to g, you are old 8189

When leave God's love, we g. dark, cold 9354

Why stay we on earth except to g. 7706

woman under whose hands children g. up strong, pure 5857

You are the one who must g. up 6931

You don't g. old 8189

You don't stop laughing because you g. old 6748

you g. old because you stop laughing 6748

young as I leave my me behind 9920

GROWING

All growth not toward God is g. to decay 5363

As long as you're green, you're g. 5364

Be not afraid of g. slowly 5365

faith has been g. ever since 3735

friends think he is g. old 8185

God sees sweet flowers g. 8673

grow lovely, g. old 8143

Hear our prayer for those g. old 8145

No man loves life as he who's g. old 8147

not g. taller, but stooping lower 6017

Shades of the prison-house upon the g. boy 12164

soul that is g. in holiness 10568

Stillness an essential part of g. deeper 7711

tempo of life g. faster 3896

GROWN

great with bliss 6140

only people who have g. hopeless 5953

Strength must be g. 8850

GROWN-UPS

Unlike g, children little need to deceive 1132

GROWS

As grave g. nearer, theology growing simple 11182

As love g. older, hearts mature 7236

Bible g. more beautiful 699

Defeat school in which truth g. strong 2507

Earth g. into heaven 6378

Everything true, great g. in silence 10246

Evil unchecked g. 3368

Faith g. by expression 3771

Faith g. only in the dark 3663

feathers white but heart g. black 9517

Good, the more communicated, more abundant g. 5062

Grace g. best in winter 5215

humble mind is soil of which thanks g. 5258

keeps ability to see beauty never g. old 12182

Kindness sunshine in which virtue g. 6654

love g. bigger more you take from it 7252

mind g. by what it feeds on 11246

more soul receives, more it g. 10699

No life g. great until disciplined 2852

Nobility g. out of contained emotion 3057

Nothing g, blooms save by giving 4342

Our inner life g. stronger when outwardly condemned 6270

out of tune and needs a hand divine 7527

power of perseverance g. with time 8557

riper he g, more lowly he bends head 6030

Self-knowledge g. out of self-confrontation with God 10018

sharp tongue g. keener with use 11406

soul wakes and g. 9940

Strength g. out of weakness 10755

time g. meaner, more hostile 3268

vessel that g. as filled will never be full 10699

GROWTH

All g. not toward God is growing to decay 5363

any person whose g. as real as my own 7184

avoid suffering means avoid g. 10899

began when I discovered 9366

best tests of g. occur in mainstream of life 1319

church more emphasis on g. than repentance 1409

Confidence, plant of slow g. 1606

depends on obedience in crisis 2046

Education is g. 3001

evidence of g. in grace 5202

God is without g. 4680

gospel of Christ nothing if not gospel of g. 9351

Harebells, sweet lilies show a thornless g. 7179

is demanding 5366

lest you become obstacle to spiritual g. 2851

loss as well as gain in g. 5366

make adjustments in light of hopes for g. 3060

may seem dangerous 5366

Measure g. in grace by sensitiveness to sin 10335

Men but children of larger g. 7418

of grace like polishing of metals 5230

transformed hindrances into g. 1468

True friendship is plant of slow g. 4218

GRUDGE

giving comes from constraint 10736

giving says, I hate to 10736

if continue to harbor g. against anyone 8818

If tiniest g. in mind against anyone 9633

like a bear with bad breath coming out of hibernation 9639

Resentment becomes a black, furry, growling g. 9639

GRUDGES

heaviest load pack of g. 4098

GRUMBLE

human nature to g. in morning 439

no use to g. and complain 37

nothing to g. about 1561

others g. at the thorns 6254

when God's will is done we g. 8791

GRUMBLER
Satan is a chronic g. 9856

GRUMBLING
as much time praying as g. 1561
because roses have thorns 1564
death of love 1560
instead of g. about what cannot
  be done 5928

GRUMBLINGS
if expect perfection 2799
life a series of g. 9469

GUARANTEE
Neglect of prayer g. not victors
  8872

GUARANTEES
Obedience to revealed truth g.
  guidance 5435

GUARD
against grounding commitment on
  experience 3550
Angels g. you when you walk 356
Holy angels g. thy bed 351
it with care 3847
me with a watchful eye 9350
us, guide, keep, feed us 5428
when off g. man reveals character
  1028

GUARDED
excuse is lie g. 3474
Love is g. in all the senses 7246

GUARDIAN
angels God will lend thee 1123
To have God for our g. 7545

GUARDS
Christ had no armored g. 6433
God g. me from evil 4992
Poor men need no g. 8686
secret life with God 6321
Who g. his post 2792

GUESSING
turns to certainty when 949

GUEST
behave as receiving great g. 552
Care admitted as g. turns to master
  12058
Christ unseen g. at every meal
  5823
Comfort comes as a g. 7361
desire Christ for perpetual g. 8092
easy to bid devil be your g. 2657
father should treat son as g. 3891
God to blessed is an ever-joyful g.
  4548
his feast a very robbery, himself
  no g. 11138
Like a full-fed g. depart to rest
  2338
more quickly than unexpected g.
  3879
smiles for the sometime g. 3900

GUESTS
Children not casual g. 1110

GUIDANCE
becomes almost unconscious
  response 5396
gives g. noiselessly 5426
God's g. not mysterious 5370
if refuse to take g. of Jesus Christ
  5458
In g. when God shows us a sign
  5439
in matters unrevealed 5435
in Scriptures 650
Men give advice, God gives g.
  5433
must God not give me much g.
  7486
not dispensed in penny-in-the-slot
  manner 693
not g. you want as much as a
  guide 5380
Obedience to revealed truth
  guarantees g. 5435
prayer for g. 9047
theology supplies, certainty of
  escaping self-delusion 7946
Yours the burden of wise g. 8363

GUIDE
Abraham knew the G. 5372
an angel to g. him 366
Be thou my g, my strength 5456
Bible, To g. in the night 727
by thy spirit, g. us 619
Christ a Head to g. 6370
Christ alone qualified to g. into
  unknown 2323
dangerous to take one impulse as
  g. 7836
faith an essential g. 3689
friend, a g. when you're searching
  4174
God means to g. our steps by
  moonlight 5393
God shall be my g. 5394
Guard, g, keep, feed us 5428
Have God to be his g. 6001
If thou wilt be my g. 5418
in order to g. our souls 5426
lives by integrity will die happy
  even though poor 6309
no other g. I seek 5469
not guidance you want as much as
  a g. 5380
place within them as a g. 1664
Scholarship should not g. faith
  3022
Science smilingly disposed of Bible
  as g. 9870
There's a star to g. the humble
  5995
use Bible as g. 688
When Christ's presence becomes g.
  5396
When God should g. us, we g.
  ourselves 10425
who canst g. the wandering star
  9048

GUIDED
feeling God has mysteriously g. us
  5392

have g. missiles, misguided men
  9868

GUIDEPOST
past is valuable as a g. 8367

GUIDEPOSTS
on the footpath to peace 8472

GUIDES
At every moment God g. me 5426
God g. as though you were blind
  2565
God g. in darkness 2565
God g. to place you know not
  2565
He g. me and the bird 5408
not brains but that which
  g.—character, ideas 1027
thought of God light which g.
  11249
Virtue requires g. 11725
When obedient God g. our steps,
  stops 8119
Who g. the stars with steadfast law
  11628

GUIDEST
Lead thou the way, thou g. best
  4977

GUIDING
Be thou a g. star above me 5375
does ask for g. and strength of
  God 4803
God g. all that happens to wise,
  holy end 5389
O g. night 2554
where need signs to discern g.
  hand 5396

GUILE
infernal serpent whose g. stirred
  up envy, revenge 9863

GUILELESS
mind great treasure, worth any
  price 5865

GUILT
absolved from g. and shame 4719
as great and personal 9672
can be more tragic than problem
  2921
Christianity at first seems to be
  about g. 1181
clouded by sense of g. 4864
Discouraged people don't need g.
  3066
Fear is tax conscience pays to g.
  3966
Glory built on selfish principles is
  g. 10054
Good works never erase g. 5061
How g, once harbour'd in the
  conscious breast 5479
I feel the g. within 4642
in abusing riches 11865
Jesus' g. is our innocence 6453
judgment of men false g. 5477
mercy confronting human g. 5206
Religion without g. tries to make
  God big pal 5487

time does nothing to g. of sin
10419
to relieve a patient of g. 5485
washed out by blood of Christ
10419
washed out by repentance 10419
washed out not by time 10419
yet g. remains 5489

GUILTY
conscience a hidden enemy 5472
conscience hell on earth 1656
conscience needs no accuser 5473
continue to make ourselves g. is
sin 5491
Every g. person his own hangman
5475
Faith is refusing to feel g. over
confessed sins 3672
From the body of one g. deed
5476
have no choice but to be g. 5493
is he who merely meditates a crime
5490
live with shame, learn to be g.
1114
no evil intolerable but g.
conscience 9092
No self-respecting wolf g. of our
wars 10361
of dust and sin 5481
of inhumanity when we snub or
abuse 901
of slander never can repair 10453
purpose of being g. is to bring us
to Jesus 5491
Suspicion always haunts the g.
mind 5488
where should I hide g. head 4069
whether to answer present or not
g. 5198
who has g. secret is lonely 1702
Whoever profits by the crime is g.
5494

GUISE
finest cheating done under g. of
honesty 5888
Moral indignation permits hate
under g. of virtue 11693
Passed by a man in workman's g.
6458
Will come in just the g. I thought
8825

GUITAR
wife is not a g. 7599

GULF
Faith builds bridge across g. of
death 3655

GULLIBILITY
Faith never means g. 3710

GULLIBLE
When people bewildered, become
g. 7978

GUM
Prayer not holy chewing g. 8754

GUN
Every g. that is made 11745

eye can threaten like loaded g.
3561

GUSTO
grease of g. frees gears of
generosity 4347

GUT
Politics full of g. 5185

GUTS
takes g. to leave ruts 1928

GUTTER
result will be found in roadside g.
7425

GYMNASIUM
Prayer, g. of the soul 8941

ℋ

HABIT
cannot be tossed out window
5495
Character h. long continued 1003
Cheerfulness, h. of looking at
good side 1095
Cheerfulness, h. of the mind 1094
Christians have fallen into h. of
5891
creatures of h. 5503
cultivate h. of receptivity 4537
discontinued labor, h. lost 3109
easy to abandon 3109
future has h. of becoming the
present 4323
get into h. of looking for best
10780
mistake, not acquiring h. of
reading, study 7793
must be coaxed down stairs 5495
shirt made of iron 5496
Sow act, reap h. 1041
Sow h, reap character 1041

HABITATION
What kind of h. pleases God 7450

HABITS
chains of h. too weak to be felt
5500
cobwebs, then become cables
5497
examine reasons for evil h. 3935
New h. take time to develop 8747
not tricked into bad h. 836
Prayer draws us out of limits
within which h. confine us
8906
second half of life made up of h.
acquired 5501
servants that regulate sleep, work,
thought 5498
To attempt to abandon bad h. in
own strength 11108
to take Jesus seriously was to
abandon h. 6421
training minds, forming h. of
young 3037

HABITUAL
Devotion is something h. 9731
sin becomes h. 10287
virtue measured by h. acts 5502

HACKING
thousand h. at branches of evil
3405

HAD
What I spent, I h. 4383

HAIR
Absalom vain about h, hanged by
h. 9190
foolish to tear one's h. in grief
5345
His h. was like a crown 6470
Out Satan must go, every h. and
feather 9864
rainbow is ribbon nature puts on
after washing h. 9391

HAIRBREADTH
If God stayed away as much as a
h. 7477

HAIRLINE
between truth and superstition
10968

HAIRS
Character gives awe to gray h.
997
Eternity has no gray h. 3266

HALF
ever lurking disquiet in h. withheld
9683
hears but h. who hears one party
only 9182
If man could have h. his wishes
2569
may be other h. that counts 2770
our doubts, fear arise from dim
perceptions 6713
truth is a whole lie 6843
whole cross more easily carried
than h. 1332
Youth shows but h. 8132

HALF DOLLAR
goes to church more often 11357

HALF-BAKED
sermon causes spiritual indigestion
10108

HALF-DONE
appalling number of h. things
9300

HALF-EXPRESSION
adopted talent only
extemporaneous h. 6226

HALF-FULL
If h. of myself 9932

HALF-SPENT
Life is h. before we know what it
is 6964

HALF-TRUTH
a dangerous thing 11492

HALFWAY
ill-luck, some run h. to meet it 11449

no h. business with God 5038

HALLOWED
And every place is h. ground 12108

cannot say h. be thy name if 8818

Praise will transform humblest dwelling to a h. heaven 5846

So h. so gracious is the time 1371

HALLWAY
success entered through h. of failure 3612

HALO
Hypocrisy, prejudice with a h. 6052

HALTER
Mention not h. in house of him that was hanged 11285

HALTS
life, aimless comet till h. deadly way 6937

HALVES
Doing things by h. is worthless 2770

give yourself by h, cannot find full rest 9683

HAMLET
let it ring from every h. 4157

not his world, that is wrong 7396

HAMMER
a h. crashed in heaven 2123

and forge yourself character 1071

away ye hostile hands 7875

Doubt is h. that breaks the windows 2936

mold, h. forge character 1000

owe more to fire and h. than anything else 10855

Pray devoutly, h. stoutly 8894

When you are the h, strike 9655

with family h. out convictions 5832

HAMMERED
Blunt, thick, h. through 2135

family, where principles are h, honed 3863

HAMMERING
without inspiring is h. on cold iron 11000

HAMPER
Charities should h. us 10734

HAND
all dangerous without God's controlling h. 4956

And graven on thy h. 1395

And let me take your h. 1509

And seen God's h. thro a lifetime 6914

Any fool can govern with stick in h. 6786

Are fingers of your h. all alike 6166

Be simple, take our Lord's h. 5374

believe the h. which never fails 11470

better to have gold in h. than heart 11828

black h. and white hold each other 3237

ceases to scatter, heart ceases to pray 4385

certain that a faithful h. will take, sift 4260

Christian more h. than tongue 1317

Christian, h. through which Christ helps 1248

Christmas every time you offer your h. 1366

clean glove often hides dirty h. 2460

destruction, preservation, all one h. 4556

door must be opened by willing h. 4775

duties at your h. 829

Faith prays him to clasp h. closely 3714

Father, let me hold thy h. 9051

feel God's invisible and tangible h. 7484

Feelings all holy when God's h. on rein 4016

Flattery, h. that kills 4049

folks over to God's mercy 4105

fragrance clings to h. that gives roses 4344

Give me the ready h. rather than ready tongue 2497

God always at h. 4621

God held my life and your life like flowers in his h. 6895

God, a h. which supports us 11249

Gold cannot reach out a helping h. 11813

Goodness is love with h. to plow 5065

government can never replace helping h. of neighbor 8062

Grows out of tune and needs a h. divine 7527

His h. upheaves the billows 4505

hold anyone by the h. 1862

hold out helping h. 3131

hope, things not in h. 3833

impersonal h. of government 8062

it over to God may not be easy 10979

Laughter is God's h. on troubled world 6731

Lead me by thine own h. 5456

Let not right h. know what left is doing 10169

little thing in h. worth more 7116

more clearly we perceive h. of God 11644

more power in open h. than clenched fist 8720

morning hour has gold in its h. 11318

My times are in thy h. 7503

not a h. so weak and white 10201

nothing but his h. that holds you 4523

Nothing in my h. I bring 2101

old man dies with open h. 11656

On every side I find thy h. 4876

on the doorlatch they die outside 3654

Our times are in his h. 8132

over too glad to h. ourselves over to God 10015

pain, loving touch of God's h. 4804

put your h. into the h. of God 5417

putting pressure back into God's h. 11466

rash h. in evil hour 10314

stretching h. to save falling man 1554

Take everything as from h. of God 2744

taking hold of a h, finding it God's 2399

that gives is above h. that takes 4375

that gives, gathers 4376

The just h. is precious ointment 6624

through pain forced to clutch thy h. 9053

Thy h. compelled it, Master, thine 7480

to do what lies closely at h. 9671

Unbelief where no h. regulates events 11595

Unto my h. cling 179

veil of future woven by h. of mercy 4330

wealth is of the heart, not the h. 11867

well-examined prove h. of God 5454

what crucifixion must have done to human h. 2132

where need signs to discern guiding h. 5396

Whoever falls from God's right h. 4628

with my h. in thine just go thy way 9072

with one blow of h. 4951

With one h. he put 6070

workman's h. hath toiled 47

wrestling with evil, h. to h. 6947

HANDFUL
of earth to make God's image 1952

of sand anthology of universe 11625

HANDICAP
One's attitude toward h. determines impact 201

strength often as great a h. as weakness 10750

HANDICAPPED
prayer for the h. 9085

HANDICAPS
my fear of h. dropped away
11131
thank God for my h. 11147
through h. found myself, work,
God 11147

HANDLE
a lie is the h. that fits them all
6857
bury the hatchet but leave h. out
9641
most h. sudden demotion better
than sizable promotion 9221
that you and I cannot h. 4622
To h. others, use your heart 9508
To h. yourself, use your head 9508

HANDMAID
Truth is justice's h. 6628

HANDMAIDEN
Change h. nature requires 959

HANDS
All we can hold in our cold dead
h. 4349
Bible has h. 712
Christ has no h. but our h. 10122
Christian has busy h. 1260
Christians with vision in hearts,
Bible in h. 11735
coming out with empty h. 4426
disappeared if within predatory
human h. 3202
everything degenerates in h. of
man 3193
Everything filthy who has filthy h.
3352
Everything perfect from h. of
Creator 3193
father believed in laying on of h.
8316
God has given us two h. 10729
God looks with favor at pure h.
6300
God takes notice of clean, not full
h. 9754
God touchable with h. of the
inner man 4509
Hammer away ye hostile h. 7875
have sunbeams in them 6531
hold fast 2162
Hold true friend with both h.
4188
Hope is faith holding out its h. in
the dark 5920
If sky falls, hold up your h. 8834
If these h. of mine cease from
their clinging 7478
in his h. and feet the cruel scars
9798
join h. and sing, Free at last 4157
joins h. with heaven 9805
Let me be h. and feet 10130
life turns dead on our h. 4437
life, once key to meaning in our h.
6940
lifts his heart to God with his h.
8811

love ever stands with open h.
7218
love has h. to help others 7335
made with mouths only, no h.
3097
moment we put h. on it, melts
away 11288
nearer than h. and feet 4862
noblest service comes from unseen
h. 10191
one to receive, other to give 10729
open my h. to accept willingly 33
our h. reach always upward 7575
pointing fingers, rarely hold out h.
2073
Prayer cannot be seized by
untrained h. 8914
Receive every disappointment
with both thy h. 7698
result always in God's h. 4945
Revival, God intervenes to lift
situation out of human h. 9746
Satan finds mischief for idle h. to
do 6772
shaking h. with a northeast storm
6531
skill but not without men's h.
4441
Sleep with clean h. 9600
Strong minds, great hearts, true
faith, ready h. 6299
The h. of Christ 2162
things in my h, have lost them all
8628
things placed in God's h. I still
possess 8628
To clasp h. in prayer beginning of
uprising against disorder 9001
Tomorrow puts itself in our h.
11403
Trouble often lever in God's h.
11460
trying to hold water in h. 5519
We have in our h. most potent
weapon 4154
When in prayer you clasp your h.
9026
which are too small 6931
why have I got h. and feet 12037
With thoughtless and impatient h.
6117
woman under whose h. children
grow up strong, pure 5857
yet the h. divine hold me 7478

HANDSHAKE
first h. greatest of all 816
is always soft 1645

HANDSOME
devil really a h. man 2651
God elects us not because we are
h. 3048
is not what is h. 1792
is what pleases 1792

HANDSOMELY
sin pays h. 10421

HANDSOMEST
flower not sweetest 2472

HANG
boughs that bear most h. lowest
6029
Nobody's family can h. out sign
3878
rope enough, he'll h. himself 4061
tie a knot and h. on 2615
Voices are saying, "Let it all h.
out" 9976

HANGED
Absalom vain about hair, h. by
hair 9190
Better half h. than ill wed 7604
born to be h. shall never be
drowned 9176
Mention not halter in house of
him that was h. 11285

HANGING
war is humanity h. itself on cross
of iron 11745
would not deserve h. ten times
7434

HANGMAN
Every guilty person his own h.
5475

HANGS
thereby h. a tale 11302
Wo h. himself in chimney 11120

HANGUPS
If h. called sin by Lord 10321

HAPHAZARD
Blessed those who see God in h.
1464
God's order comes in the h. 5401
How h. God seems, not
sometimes but always 4674
saint never believes circumstances
h. 1324
seems a h. life externally 7509

HAPLESS
On this h. earth 6740

HAPPEN
all things h. because of, with, in
God's will 10926
day will h. whether or not you get
up 2200
Do not look forward to what may
h. 415
Do not worry about what may
never h. 3500
enjoy many sorrows that never h.
11456
expect marvellous things to h.
3830
For God everything that will h.
has already happened 11314
God either permits it to h. 4828
Happiness caused by things which
h. 6529
Let not that h. which I wish 9069
Misfortunes hardest to bear never
h. 12069
nothing can h. save that which
God wills 9835
nothing can h. which cannot be
turned into good 4803

nothing is going to h. to me 4622
Real doesn't h. all at once 5886
something of real importance can h. 4132
Things do not h. in world, they are brought about 4953
Things I worry about don't h. 12060
When Master of earth calls shots, things h. 3819

HAPPENED
acceptance of what has h. first step 154
at the lowest, saddest times in his life 5437
have known many troubles, most never h. 11434
human stories repeating as if never h. before 5984
importance of events by how recently h. 7990
Life was a funny thing that h. 6986
nothing which h. in this world important 5666
question about miracle not how it h, but why 6500

HAPPENING
controlled by what is h. on inside 9849
evangelism h. naturally 3313

HAPPENS
Bad called good when worse h. 153
content with what h. 1800
description of what h. when gospel preached 5105
difference between what h. when man says 3611
Everything that h. can help 1466
Experience not what h. to you 3527
Experience what you do with what h. 3527
Feelings are only a thing that h. to you 3051
God guiding all that h. to wise, holy end 5389
Happiness depends on what h. 6527
how I react to what h. 508
Life is what h. while making other plans 6982
no matter what h. there's always death 2347
not controlled by what h. on outside 9849
not what h. to me 508
Nothing h. that is not significant 1716
Nothing h. unless Omnipotent wills it 4828
Nothing that h. in world h. by chance 4948
Plant love and watch what h. 7289
Real is a thing that h. to you 5886

To a good man nothing that h. is evil 5049
to light upon passages which meets need 5441
What h. when God grants fellowship 4029
whatever h. Jesus Christ is true 589

HAPPIER
anyone h. because you passed his way 3136
circumstances free from complications 4974
grow h. as we grow older 7026
how can you be h. with more 5532
if house not h. for your being a Christian 3872
Life h. if born at age eighty 6989
made one human being a little h. 6660
Marriage cannot make anyone h. 7632
Prescription for h, healthier life 5615
rise h. than a king 10208

HAPPIEST
belief youth h. time of life a fallacy 7026
Christian h. when he feels worst 1265
He is h, be he king or peasant 5827
life not necessarily easiest 2563
miser saves every friend 4203
person thinks most interesting thoughts 7026
thinks himself h. man, really is so 11917
use leisure, h. people in world 5567
when we forget our precious selves 9245

HAPPILY
if live h, learn to die 6926
lived h. ever after, tragic sentence in literature 7601
Staying h. married should rank among the fine arts 7615
want to die h, learn to live 6926

HAPPINESS
ability to cope with conflict 5526
all equally responsible for h. of world 9678
always just beyond our reach 5518
America more books on how to find h. 8624
an enemy to pomp and noise 5568
and intelligence rarely found in same person 5512
and joy from God's standpoint 5531
any person whose h. as real as my own 7184
as a butterfly 5518

As we value h. let us not forget it 8635
Avarice and h. never saw each other 5312
barren life that holds only h. 5537
begins in the head 5515
being freely, voluntarily united to God 4120
believe h. depends on being more virtuous 6821
beneficial for the body 5340
bitter to look into h. through another's eyes 3220
can never be an end in itself 5517
caused by things which happen 6529
circumstances will mar h. 6529
comes from root word, happening 5562
constant in h, must often change 4057
content with themselves in danger of never knowing h. 5565
Contentment is not h. 1782
cross destroyed religion equals h. 2151
depends on attitude toward blessings 5513
depends on what happens 6527
destined end of man not h. 5757
distant goal to which no shortcut 7648
Do not speak of own h. to someone unhappy 3067
doesn't depend on blessings 5513
don't dream of h. in future 5507
Don't look back on h. 5507
enjoyment of one's self 5568
envy last longer than h. of those we envy 3222
for this must be free 4120
forget irritations that detract from h. 9270
friendship, conversation of select companions 5568
gave up pursuing h. 5530
God cannot give h. apart from himself 5510
God designs 4120
God has all h. to crown you 4696
God, responsibility for our eternal h. 5511
greatest h. is knowing you do not require h. 5555
Grief knits two hearts closer than h. can 5338
having what you want 5524
heaven, h. endless in duration 5634
heaven, h. infinite in degree 5634
held is the seed 5514
holiness, not h, end of man 5517
hopelessly strive to invent h. apart from God 5570
If h. depends on what somebody says 5536
if pursue h. you will never find it 5558

if sit down quietly, may alight
    upon you 5518
If think of world as place for h.
    5535
If you discern God's love in h.
    5254
in doing what one likes 5525
in place of righteousness, will
    never get it 5564
in worth, choice of friends 4293
is a consequence 5522
is a feeling 6528
is liking what one has to do 5525
is of retired nature 5568
is perfume cannot pour on others
    5516
is united to God and each other
    4120
is wanting what you get 5552
joy is reverse of h. 6538
joy too great to be confused with
    superficial h. 6564
kinship of heart to heart 5538
life, liberty and pursuit of h. 3246
light on the water 5527
like a sunbeam 174
like a young deer 5548
like bluebird of Maeterlinck 5519
like trying to hold water in hands
    5519
lives in sin and looks for h. 10313
living with love, grace, gratitude
    5528
man mistakes evil for h. 3386
man's right to h. anti-God 5553
manner of traveling 5523
Marriage offers extremes of h.
    and bondage 7641
matter of attitude 5515
Men happy only when object of
    life not h. 5540
miss h. because didn't stop to
    enjoy 5585
Money can buy everything but h.
    7810
more you squeeze, more it runs
    away 5519
most disastrous purpose is
    "pursuit of h." 5548
neither within or without us 5520
never found till we stop looking
    for it 5550
never knew joy until gave up
    pursuing h. 2308
nice, subtle h. of reading 858
no cosmetic for beauty like h.
    5563
no h. equal to heart that
    understands 9504
no human being can be
    permanent source of h. to
    another 9481
No one truly knows h. who has
    not suffered 5545
no right to consume h. without
    producing it 5569
not a question of not having
    problems 5521
not a reward 5522

not level of prosperity 5538
not state to arrive at 5523
not the absence of conflict 5526
not there but here 11374
not tomorrow, but today 11374
nothing in money's nature to
    produce h. 7814
numbered the days of genuine h.
    7100
of life made up of minute fractions
    5556
Only man clogs h. with care
    12073
overlooked because doesn't cost
    anything 5542
pain confers h. 8260
people mistake wealth for h. 8510
pursuit of h. most ridiculous
    phrase 5558
pursuit of happiness slipped into
    Declaration of Independence
    5548
responsibility for our eternal h.
    3758
result of what happens of an
    agreeable sort 6538
search for h. source of
    unhappiness 5559
Seek for h. and you will never find
    it 5551
seeks applause has h. in another's
    keeping 5892
shared the flower 5514
small change of human h. 3143
success and h. lie in you 10829
Suffering strange initiation into h.
    10896
suggesting h. is circumstantial
    5562
sure to miss if aim at directly 8459
than largest fruit of h. 3795
the harvest of a quiet eye 9370
the least shadow intercepts 174
The Lord will h. on contrite
    hearts bestow 5557
thing that comes and goes 5517
Those who chase h. run from
    contentment 5566
thought God's purpose to make
    me full of h, joy 5531
to essay an incredible h. 6421
True riches in true h. 11852
try to catch it, loses color 5519
union of ourselves with God 5520
use for passions stuff given for h.
    4359
useless aim which thwarts h. 4411
vanishes when envy appears 3218
visible beatitude for h. 1243
wanting what you have 5524
was born a twin 5505
way to h. 5561
way we look at the world 5538
what we call h. more a disposition
    than attainment 5571
When one door of h. closes
    another opens 5573
Where your heart is, there is your
    h. 5574

who does not bring ingredients
    for h. into marriage 7632
without goodness, no h. 5060
world in which heartbreak so
    close to h. 7081
would almost rather eliminate h.
    10898
would decision bring the world h.
    2494

HAPPY

all men would lead h. life 4227
are those who suffer with God
    2091
Be virtuous and you will be h.
    11681
being h. with God means 6569
Cherish all h. moments 5506
Christian ideal not to be h. but
    holy 5767
commandments designed to make
    us h. 1528
deaf husband, blind wife h. couple
    7589
delusion that one person can
    make another h. 5549
desire to be holy rather than h.
    10719
Doctrine won't make you h.
    11185
don't think self-realization will
    make you h. 9196
drowsily wishes you h. in your
    own way 4792
end of life is not to be h. 5554
examine how h. those are who
    possess it 3498
family an earlier heaven 3865
God wills that man should be h.
    5060
guide lives by integrity die h. even
    though poor 6309
Help to make earth h. like the
    heaven above 6659
hours with h. prospects in view
    pleasing 3508
How h. person is depends upon
    gratitude 5249
If don't have heartache, how do
    you know when h. 5533
If h. at heart can normally cope
    2737
if h. in small ways 8139
if move ten inches to be h, never
    will be 5534
in work three things needed 3101
is man too busy to worry by day
    12062
is man who strikes balance justly
    1240
Jumping to conclusions seldom
    leads to h. landings 6582
learning to be h. without things
    we cannot have 8635
leaving to Christ how h. he shall
    be 5543
Make h. those who are near 9480
man confines himself within
    ancient limits 2875

man h. so long as he chooses to be h. 5538

man trying to find something which will make him h. 5570

man's without a shirt 11857

Many people h, but worthless to society 5539

marriage union of two forgivers 7593

Men only h. when object of life not happiness 5540

Money never made a man h, nor will it 7814

must not cry too bitterly over the h. dead 2425

no good asking God to make us h. our own way 7459

No man h. whose path but glimmer of light 6101

No man should desire to be h. who is not holy 5543

No one more h. than poor man 8695

not h. unless bigger sinners to point to 10442

O what a h. hunger 9780

O what a h. soul am I 1810

obey, be h. 8115

old age most h. time of life 8149

person must enjoy blessings 818

prayed for riches that he might be h. 8806

regard employments equally h. 3232

Resolve to keep h. 10829

root of a h. religion 6713

Seek righteousness, discover you are h. 5551

Six things requisite to create h. home 5848

Spirit of God will make man h. 1064

spirit takes grind out of giving 4347

struggling against adversity, yet h. 249

think once converted all h. 1309

three things needed to be h. in work 12011

to go with shepherds to see Lord in manger 8061

truly h. who are seeking to be righteous 5564

we try to tell how h. we are 3184

Welcome h. morning 2986

were but little h. if I could say how much 6558

What joy the h. earth to greet 9898

When man is h. does not hear clock strike 5572

why is man h. only in God 7479

with Christ and nothing else you can be h. 3761

without Christ and all else never be h. 3761

world forced to be good, h. 4149

world is brimming with h. thoughts 2020

Youth h. because capacity to see beauty 12182

HARBOR

A ship in a h. is safe 76

Bible, shows how to reach h. 713

Bible, shows where h. is 713

death is the Christian's h. 5638

Man has no h. 11373

not what ships are built for 76

proclaim brotherhood and h. prejudice 6068

When a man does not know what h. 4433

HARBOUR'D

How guilt, once h. in the conscious breast 5479

HARD

ability to bear h. thing 3149

because his sacrifice is a h. one 6599

Behind joy may be h. temperament 10583

Better fare h. with good men 4219

broken out of time's h. shell to breathe 4976

can choose to be bag of marbles, h. 9524

confession sometimes incredibly h. 1601

cramping restrictions of h. work 6386

deny yourself sounds h. 8108

do not shun and call life h. names 6903

Everyone fighting h. battle 6635

Experience a h. teacher 3522

Following Christ, h. rugged life 1282

for rich to enter heaven 11830

God finds it h. to give 2571

God go with us through h. places 165

God will never plant seed on h. spirit 888

God's will is h. against our stubbornness 10771

has h. time finding enemies 4216

honest, maturity equally h. to attain 5873

How h. the battle goes, the day how long 6256

humility of God h. to accept, believe 4683

I do not find God h. to live with 4478

In creating, the only h. thing's to begin 2007

Kind words soften h. hearts of men 6645

Life is a h. fight 6947

Love makes all h. hearts gentle 7261

Love's as h. as nails 2135

Man finds it h. to get what he wants 2571

no promise to keep us out of h. places 165

Nothing h. if divide into small jobs 3110

Opportunities usually disguised as h. work 8221

patience is h, I tell you it is h. 11464

Real Christianity is h. 8108

so h. it is impossible 3222

takes h. work to discipline 8335

test of what is real 9399

thing's worth believing if h. 3773

to believe, h. to obey 593

to present Christ before men 3222

to see one's self 10007

to train for service of Christ 466

to understand detours God takes us 5423

Truth a h. mistress 11561

We have h. work to do 6881

When Jesus is absent, all is h. 6512

When we say it is h. 230

Yard by yard life is h. 6930

you overpowered my h. heart 7579

Young people will respond if challenge h. enough 12180

HARDEN

God h. me against myself 2583

Suffering can further h. you 10933

HARDENING

of heart ages people more quickly than h. of the arteries 6159

HARDENS

Punishment h, numbs 2038

HARDER

nothing h. than softness of indifference 6165

repentance much h. than eating humble pie 9577

the conflict, more glorious the triumph 1628

to see today when looking at tomorrow 11371

to wait often h. than to work 8418

weaker we feel, h. we lean on God 10761

weaker we feel, the h. we lean 8256

HARDEST

first hundred years the h. 6992

First step is h. 545

is to exercise patience in the street 8423

lessons to learn 9941

means to fight h. battle human being can fight 6215

Misfortunes h. to bear never happen 12069

Prayer h. of all things 8940

task to think 11275

The h. peaks alone 1927

three h. tasks in world 7838

work is to do nothing 6775

HARDNOSED
toddler, h. opponent of law, order 1129

HARDSHIP
power to continue under h. 8423
will experience h, stress 953

HARDSHIPS
pioneers endured h. 3147

HARDY
Error a h. plant 3251

HAREBELL
Hope like a h, trembling from its birth 7179

HAREM
one good wife a spiritual h. 7663

HARLOTS
We were h, now virgins 1348

HARM
devil cannot h. us 2682
dissolution can do the Christian no h. 2325
example can do no h. 3445
greater their power to h. 210
I would do thee no h. 1550
Judas cried "all hail," he meant all h. 630
Love truth though it do h. 11517
more h. by example than good by correction 3914
No evil done can h. ultimately 3385
No h. from him can come to me 6916
nothing I never said ever did me h. 10682
Our many advantages do us h. 9337
Reproof never does a wise man h. 11938
what h. if gamble on faith 3724
world in which creatures do good or h. 4132

HARMFUL
cross we bear seems h. 2116

HARMLESS
Fame, like flame, h. until inhaling 3853
great temptations the most h. 11078

HARMONIES
Faith makes discords h. of future 3704
God laid the keynote of all h. 7891
Men live on brink of h. 3654
to chime in with h. of creation 7921

HARMONIOUS
Heaven h. enjoyment of God 5646

HARMONIOUSLY
inner, outer life h. developed 1766

HARMONIZE
Attributes of God h. and blend 4579

God reserves right to h. truths 11586

HARMONY
And march of eternal h. 2268
at variance not likely to be in h. 5045
bring our wills into h. with his 9799
brings spirit into h. with God 8093
create atmosphere of h. 580
ever attained inner h. by pondering experience of others 7687
God wills a rich h. 6179
if beauty in character, will be h. in the home 8441
If h. in the home 8441
learn to bring body into h. with God 847
more a person is in h. with himself 8505
no h. where there is but one 11622
of history enriched by antithetical elements 5020
of unspeakable splendors 3648
sounds which Holy Spirit weaves together in heavenly h. 5799
spirit, soul and body are kept in h. 6897
tears not inconsistent with inward h. 5346
Tune me, O Lord, into one h. 7928
where you live and work 580

HARMS
deed that h. the poor done against Christ 8698

HARNESSED
No horse gets anywhere until h. 2852

HARP
become h. players through playing h. 6620
human soul silent h. in God's choir 7921
soul silent h. in God's choir 10665
The soul alone, like a neglected h. 7527
When David took his h. and played 7935

HARPING
instead of h. on worst in people 5928

HARPOON
tiny h. can rob of life 11071

HARPS
in heaven, cymbals in hell 5703

HARSH
Difficulty a h. nurse 2719
O h. old age 8150
perseverance may be employed by smallest of us 8557
The good are so h. to the clever 909

we sip reluctantly at truth we find h. 6870
words pierce the soul 374

HARSHLY
Don't judge anyone h. until 6575

HARVEST
evil h. is not God's punishment 4721
Happiness the h. of a quiet eye 9370
love brings to h. loveliest flowers of the soul 7339
Religious contention is the devil's h. 9548
time is hid with God 10204

HARVEST'S
And thanks unto the h. Lord 11175

HAS
more a man h, more he wants 7814
Who h. God, h. all 4519
Who h. him not, h. less than nothing 4519

HASH
Divorce h. made of domestic straps 2920

HASTE
breathless for no reason 5577
busy doing nothing 5577
devil changes hunger for God into h. 7512
God made time, man made h. 5576
great h. makes great waste 5588
Make h. slowly 5582
Make h. to be kind 6658
Men pursue pleasure with breathless h. 8601
Nothing should be done in h. except catching fleas 5583
Rashness and h. make all things insecure 5586
Too great h. to repay obligation 5266
What is destructive is h. 6116
Why desperate h. to succeed 10827
with breathless h. hurry past happiness 8601

HASTEN
love has feet to h. to poor, needy 7335
slowly 5578
So do our minutes h. to their end 2329

HASTY
climbers have sudden falls 6114
One cool judgment worth thousand h. councils 6587

HATCHET
bury the h. but leave handle out 9641
Do not remove fly with h. 2058
not to bury h. 4079

HATE

a god whom we do not h. in moments 4846

a simple emotion 7233

All truth to love, all wrong to h. 7986

cannot be love without h. 5357

cannot love good if do not h. evil 5050

Choose to love, rather than h. 1138

Christ, still people who love or h. him 6362

compared to foot that destroys sandcastle 7233

concentrates on thing hated 7262

cross, love meeting h. with love 2146

do good to them that h. us 5001

do injustice, come to h. him 6609

easy to maintain for lifetime 7233

either love or h. 8075

Far deeper than man's deepest h. 4776

Folks never understand folks they h. 5593

full of h. and bitterness 5594

God does not love one day, h. another 4626

Gold begets in brethren h. 11811

grudge giving says, I h. to 10736

hatred sinks us below those we h. 5603

Hell is where all h. one another 5692

how child handles h. determines Harvard or San Quentin 8281

I h. him, and he hates me 2671

if h. son, cram with dainties 8303

If I h. or despise any one man in world 5599

If you h, you h. something that is part of yourself 5600

imperfections, but love them 1080

in hell most perfect h. 5685

is the tree 371

Keep heart free from h. 5561

less 5604

love is superior to h. 6326

mass movement, new freedom to h. 10526

moments when children will h. you 8281

Moral indignation permits h. under guise of virtue 11693

needs no instruction 7265

proud h. pride—in others 9247

respond to enemies with love, not h. 5890

sin with fierceness that burns 3182

the lie though it please you 11517

to be a kicker 8564

to return love for h. 7838

To understand everything is to h. nothing 11617

too great a burden to bear 7182

voice of intelligence hissed away by h. 6331

waits only to be provoked 7265

We fear something before we h. it 4004

We h. delay, yet it makes us wise 11959

Without faith people drift into h. societies 925

worst sin is not to h, but be indifferent 6164

young people say parents h. them 8335

youth h. too much 12181

HATED

better h. for what you are 1025

Hate concentrates on thing h. 7262

not for faults we are h. 5601

religious who h. Jesus' guts 6412

world h. crucified Jesus 2168

HATEFUL

a h. injustice 6258

Every delay is h, but gives wisdom 11912

old age, how h. is your reign 8150

HATES

belly h. a long sermon 10107

child who fears noises becomes man who h. noises 4004

devil h. will of God 4915

God h. our temptations 11057

God h. those who praise themselves 9198

man h. to stand alone in opinion 1639

sin that h. nothing 11394

HATING

gossip ourselves, grateful to those who do it well 5138

may say far from h. God 10427

HATRED

and anger powerless when met with kindness 6639

as will blot out all h, bitterness 7170

blinds us to virtues 5602

church is love in world buried with h. 1433

continuance of anger is h. 396

difference which rouses h. of the world 10917

Forgiveness saves cost of h. 4089

indifference neither love nor h. 6161

is blind as well as love 5595

is like fire, makes light rubbish deadly 5597

is self-punishment 5598

less blessed is h. 6161

like burning down own house to get rid of rat 5596

Love and h. natural exaggerators 3423

may bring h. upon us 10564

Satan's truth judges out of h. 4914

sinks us below those we hate 5603

such h. of divorce I prefer bigamy 2925

times when love to father, mother must be h. 7280

to fight without h. 11775

to teach us about h. of sin 10306

Where there is h, give love 9086

HATREDS

atheist, harem of h. 493

Most have no real h. 6161

HAUGHTINESS

extremism, h. of humility 3557

HAUGHTY

In vain our h. reason swells 4676

HAUNTED

by the Speaking Voice 4399

in knowledge most h. with inevitable limitation 6689

HAUNTING

It's h. me 22

thoughts proceed 5476

HAUNTS

Bible h. like old song 653

Suspicion always h. the guilty mind 5488

HAVE

Happiness is wanting what you h. 5524

Many a h. and have-not 1734

Think on what you h. 11164

to h. no significance except in "to be" 3491

What I gave, I h. 4383

what we h. not, give us 9083

HAVE-NOT

Many a have and h. 1734

HAVEN

storms driven us into desired h. 178

HAVING

form of h. and not h. 9446

In solitude discover being more important than h. 10545

To gain that which is worth h. 4340

HAVOC

praying saint performs h. among forces of darkness 9014

HAWK

Pheasants fools if invite h. to dinner 11081

HAY

Make h. while sun shines 2781

HAZARDOUSLY

satisfactions which may be h. little 4248

HAZARDS

greater h. in doing nothing 6779

in anything one does 6779

road h. evidence on right route 2745

HE

His child and h. 6398

I have one passion only, it is h. 6400

HEAD

All men at h. of great movements are Christian men 5094

always bobbing in perpetual yes 1645

Be not baker if h. butter 11048

beating h. against wall 8553

benefits become curse if Christ not h. 3895

Blessings gently falling on thy h. 361

Bow thy meek h. to mortal pain 2981

cannot enter kingdom of heaven h. first 9426

Christ a H. to guide 6370

Christ is h. of this house 5823

crown is in my heart, not on my h. 1808

Even hen lifteth her h. toward heaven 11142

giraffe only animal that can keep feet on ground, h. in clouds 9244

God made six holes in h. 7379

God puts tape around heart, not h. 4576

God stoops o'er his h. 9940

God will put tape about heart, not h. 6112

good sermon is one that goes over his h. 10106

Happiness begins in the h. 5515

heaven upon earth to weary h. 10484

Hope sets the h, heart to work 5917

I'll let my h. be just in sight 10501

If h. wax, don't walk in sun 11918

If man empties purse in h. 3010

Lay down thy h. upon Savior's breast 2365

Loud o'er my h, though awful thunders roll 4827

most obscure believer can hold h. high 9999

no business to require h. of age on shoulders of youth 12186

not a h. so thick 10201

on us for same reason pin has 10992

one small h. should carry all it knew 2994

Pity home where everyone the h. 5845

Rather let my h. stoop to the block 7677

riper he grows, more lowly he bends h. 6030

self-importance makes mind shrink, h. swell 9191

some sciences may be learned by h. 5110

Splinters help you forget worries in your h. 240

Spring cleaning should begin with h, end with heart 5756

that once was crowned with thorns 9697

'Tis nothing to hold up h. in calm 1915

To handle yourself, use your h. 9508

To lay his h. upon the Savior's breast 11476

What would ant do if had h. of bull 6221

Where devil cannot put h, puts tail 2707

Winter is on my h. 8187

With joy shall I lift up my h. 4719

Words born in the heart, not h. 11997

world above man's h. 11627

HEADLINES

approval to publicity hunter who seeks h. 5891

HEADS

amazed never scratching h. for questions 9544

good heart better than all h. in world 5054

Hearts may agree though h. differ 9461

If it's h. I go to bed 3011

in success we lose our h. 10643

Knowledge dwells in h. replete with thoughts of men 6690

Swelled h. shrink influence 9488

Two h. better than one 403

Two h. not better when soreheads 403

when the trees bow down their h. 8053

When try to understand Christ's teaching with our h. 6515

HEAL

always to h. and never hurt 6519

Candor may h. or separate 5869

Christ a Physician to h. his people 6370

Christ enters world to h. its wounds 6487

Earth has no sorrow heaven cannot h. 5637

find a hurt and h. it 10216

God's ability to h. soul profound 10845

Grace can h. us when wounded 5212

prayed for Lord to h. me 5610

rather than wound 1138

To h. the blows of sound 10241

too many wounds to h. 10211

What wound did ever h. but by degrees 8399

While prayers to h. her wrongs move slow behind 6269

HEALED

fanatic a wound that never h. 3910

He drew them forth, h. and bade me live 9798

Lord h. me of need to be h. 5610

of grief only when we express it to the full 5362

of suffering only by experiencing it 10921

once spirit is h, legs done without 5614

unforgiving spirit refuses to be h. 9640

HEALERS

best of h. is good cheer 5617

HEALING

comes through brokenness 2519

cross key to h. 2145

cut, cleanse, break so h. can take place 890

for h. men's lives must be changed within 5616

forgiveness and h. are one 4072

In confession we open lives to h. 1602

in old trees 8143

Once I sought for h. 6465

only in place of h. dare to show wounds 10551

pleasure contains no h. for soul 8610

power of time 4643

Salvation is h. 9817

Silent worship is h. 12114

Solitude a fount of h. 10556

without h. of spirit duties burdens 8857

words not our own 10545

HEALS

faith h. 3965

Faith means grasped by power that h. us 3707

It h. his wounds 1507

Our Father yet h. spirit of amputees 5614

Silence, how thoroughly it h. 10252

Time a physician that h. every grief 11336

Time h. all things 11331

Time h. what reason cannot 11332

wound h, but scar remains 10446

HEALTH

achieve inner h. through forgiveness 4103

age thinks of nothing but h. 5619

and cheerfulness mutually beget each other 5607

and wealth wean us of need for Christ 5608

better than wealth 5609

Cheerfulness is h. 1089

destined end of man not h. 5757

Disease more contagious than h. 4286

enough to make work pleasure 1809

for the great benefits of our h. 6255

Give h. or give infirmity 1538

If thankfulness springs up through h. 11151

in the cross 2096

made the body's h. 5606

may go to heaven without h. 9792

Money brings medicine, but not h. 7807

nasty things due to bad h. will fall off 1030

Pain teaches luxury of h. 8270

proven that worry undermine h. 5612

requisite of good h. calculated carelessness about oneself 5618

single verse may be dangerous to spiritual h. 642

spiritual h. proportional to love for God 4793

sweetness of h. 5605

terms for salvation designate h. 9817

Those obsessed with h. not healthy 5618

thou sick man's h. 5932

To be enjoyed, h. must be interrupted 443

to sick men, Christ is h. 6391

True friendship like sound h. 4292

Virtue is h. 11726

we value h, God values patience 11667

When h. is lost, something is lost 1066

who has h. has hope 5910

will be swept away 3719

Wisdom is the soul what h. is to the body 11975

world, omnipotent surgery before expect h. 10521

Youth thinks nothing of h. 5619

HEALTHIER

Prescription for happier, h. life 5615

HEALTHIEST

relationships breathe 9494

HEALTHY

fear of God, a h. ingredient 3993

Giving is secret of h. life 10727

holy is h.—completely h. 5765

Honest differences h. sign of progress 1624

isms convert h. ideas into ideologies 9952

old word for holy also means h. 5765

self-image is seeing yourself as God sees you 9978

Those obsessed with health not h. 5618

to hang questions on things taken for granted 2950

HEALTHY-MINDED

Optimism h. but blinded 8237

HEAR

all do not clearly h. 5381

but do not act 1414

cannot h. for what you are 560

cannot h. what you say to the contrary 1061

deaf cannot h. voices of dearest friends 9094

deaf, those who will not h. 261

does not Lord h. nations blame 4894

Don't h. one, judge two 6606

Don't like to h. cut-and-dried sermons 9141

easier to walk six miles to h. sermon 7716

easy to h. music in waves 8034

Eavesdroppers never h. good of themselves 5123

ever-approaching thunder which will destroy us 8445

God can h. your faintest whisper 8801

God everywhere can h. 8029

God made us h. and understand 7891

good old days next generation will h. about 11381

He hath an ear to h. 9024

humble heart that I may h. thee 7458

I h. his voice among the trees 7452

I h. with groan and travail-cries 4642

I shall h. in heaven 2444

I'd rather see a sermon than h. one any day 3435

If I could h. Christ praying for me 8832

if people unwilling to h. you 1862

inner ears to h. what he could not h. before 8495

Kindness a language deaf can h. 6650

love has ears to h. sighs and sorrows 7335

may h. twice as much as we speak 7112

mouth keeps silent to h. heart speak 10270

music which thou canst not h. 4708

My Umpire Conscience whom if they h. 1664

Neither great poverty nor riches will h. reason 9418

Nor ear can h. 9567

O God, h. these my final words 9091

our prayer for those growing old 8145

people h. jazz through feet 7898

plainer I h. immortal symphonies of world to come 11132

Prayer is not to h. oneself speak 8935

problem in ability to h. 2931

rarely h. man suffering who says 10936

same prayers repeated each Sunday 8845

should quietly h. both sides 6618

Silent worship enables us to h. voice of God 12114

Some only h. God in public worship 1477

still I can pray so that God can h. 9025

terrible to h. such things 5155

than h. one any day 10098

That we may h. thee 9058

to h. truth about yourself, anger your neighbor 8058

Tomorrow h. the lazy people say 9303

truth not always what we want to h. 11541

we h. these whisperings of God 4968

Well roars the storm to those that h. 3644

When happy does not h. clock strike 5572

When I can neither see, h, nor speak 9025

when I h. the devil quote Scripture 2637

where men sit, h. each other groan 7044

while their ears can h. 4223

will scarcely h. glad sound of gospel 5224

you compelled my deaf ears to h. you 7579

HEARABLE

God is h. 4509

HEARD

And the voice through the darkness h. 7943

child says nothing but h. by fire 3885

eased the heart of him who h. 107

has not h. from himself 1761

have never h. God speak 5426

have to do without things parents never h. of 8582

I h. without the night wind moan 5413

if never h. mountains singing 8017

if one realized that God h. 4886

In silence he is h. 10249

mistake for thought repetition of what they h. 11237

only faintly because of uproar of restless 9070

Only judge when you have h. all 6588

Our thoughts are h. in heaven 11155

Pilate had never h. of Jesus 6395

rumors, all who h. it made enlargement too 9757

Scarce any tale was sooner h. than told 9757

That will be h. in heaven 8694

the cock crow thrice with an aching heart 9569

The less he spoke the more he h.
1832
trumpet shall be h. on high 7925
What should not be h. by little
ears 3461
when one h. Old Age was coming
8136
your voice behind me telling me
to return 9070

HEARING
experiencing is better than h. 3535
God's ear for my h. 5400
Is not h. a treasure 6253
is one thing, listen' another 1544
like h. grass grow 8496
world dying for want of good h.
9163

HEARS
a different drummer 10827
but half who h. one party only
9182
Cain who h. only the sound of his
own footsteps 10573
Christian, h. the inaudible 1265
God h. no sweeter music 7171
God h. the footsteps of an ant
4697
God h. what they are saying 4886
God in every sound 4847
himself cursed and remains silent
is partner of God 4894
Let him step to music he h. 10827
little girl who h. music for first
time 7922
not ear that h. sweetness of music
10656
Prayer is to wait till one h. God
speak 8935
prayer is when person praying is
one who h. 8980
soul that h. sweetness of music
10656
Speak to him, thou, for he h. 4862
what one cannot say 8515

HEARSAY
knowledge from experience
outweighs h. 3535

HEART
A contrite h. or no 5557
a humble and a contrite h. 6036
able to receive uncreated light
4749
Abortion stops a beating h. 15
aching abyss of human h. 5359
Afflictions make the h. more deep
278
always springtime in h. that loves
God 4797
an orphaned h. 483
Anyone with h. of friendship 4216
approval not to pure in h. who see
God 5891
As purse is emptied, h. filled 4351
Atheism rather in lip than h. 475
awed within me when I think
1966
Bad conscience is snake in h. 1651

Batter my h, three-person'd God
2840
before God can make h. a garden
896
begins to burn with desire for God
4749
best cure for longing h. 2558
better to have gold in hand than h.
11828
Bible speaks to h. of man 645
blind in eye better than blind in h.
8511
boy asked question that pierced
father's h. 3912
But, had he a h. 7423
By hope kept young of h. 3834
can't pump up faith out of your
own h. 3828
capable of almost unlimited
extension in 5625
change sorrowing h. of lead
10628
Christ can do wonders with
broken h. 10584
Christ cannot live his life without
our h. 1270
Christian, h. through which
Christ loves 1248
completely different people in h.
3766
Conversion a h. work 1895
conversion change of h. 1909
conversion, going to be tug at h.
3052
cross, h. of church 2139
crown is in my h, not on my head
1808
Cut any cord but the one that
binds me to thy h. 9080
death of Jesus was revelation of h.
of God 6472
devil's field of battle is human h.
2691
Do not cheat thy h. 10586
do with cheerful h. the work God
appoints 10150
doors shut, take h. 184
Empathy is your pain in my h.
3068
enter through our h. into h. of
God 10562
Envy eats nothing but own h.
3209
eternal spring is in my h. 8187
Evangelism is cross in h. of God
3305
even for people blessed with
warmth of h. 7304
ever is to return to its repose 8444
Every h. has its own ache 10590
every h. is joy 9897
evidence of thankful h. 5202
Evil wrought by want of h. 3363
experiences God, not reason 4771
eye can make h. dance for joy
3561
eyes confess secrets of the h. 3569
eyes tell what the h. means 3568
faith gives simplicity of h. 7383

fathom depths to extent h. is
broken 900
favorite place of God in h. of man
4496
fear explosive power of evil in
human h. 3376
feather white but h. grows black
9517
feeling in some form or degree in
every h. 4019
filled to brim with joy must be still
6559
fold to thy h. thy brother 7284
For the h. that finds joy 6524
Forgiveness warms h. 4075
friend's love brings joy to h. 4382
from very h. of the shadows 1443
generous h. feels others' ill 3063
gift of loving thought into h. of
friend 4189
give Christ keys of your h. 8092
Give man Christ, change h. 3307
Give man dollar, cheer h. 3307
Give man dream, challenge h.
3307
Give me a pure h. that I may see
thee 7458
Give me an unconquered h. 9057
Give me an upright h. 9057
Give me the coward h. 4530
Give me the greedy h. 4530
Give me the proud h. 4530
Give me the shallow h. 4530
Give me, O Lord, a steadfast h.
9057
Give my h. 1376
Give one thing more—a grateful h.
5265
Give others a piece of your h, not
mind 10132
give to friend 511
Give us a h. of faith 9058
Give us a h. of love 9058
Give us a humble h. 9058
Give us a pure h. 9058
God asks nothing but pure h.
7450
God dwelling in a meek, thankful
h. 5621
God has his own stairway into h.
4540
God has taken the world upon his
h. 10922
God has to plough the h. 896
God looks at h. before brains
7378
God looks at intention of h. 6334
God makes pure in h. 1012
God puts tape around h. not head
4576
God rules human h. as King 4736
God will enlarge your h. 5427
God will put tape about their
heart, not head 6112
God, h. profoundly kind 4477
good h. better than all heads in
world 5054
goodly apple rotten at the h. 5011

gospel penetrates, soothes the h. 732

Grant us a h. wide open to joy, beauty 9064

great man who does not lose child's h. 5294

grief bids h. break 5333

hand ceases to scatter, h. ceases to pray 4385

happiness is kinship of h. to h. 5538

Hardening of h. ages people more quickly 6159

has eyes brain knows nothing of 8503

has its moments of longing 470

has its own laws 5628

Have your h. right with Christ 5529

heard the cock crow twice with an aching h. 9569

Helplessness calls from your h. to the h. of God 8901

Holding a beggar's child against my h. 7178

Holy Spirit breaks the h, makes it whole 5794

Hope sets the head, h. to work 5917

How else but through a broken h. 9794

Humility is perfect quietness of h. 6010

I carry a major light in my h. 3649

If faith gaze of the h. at God 3737

If h. right with God 8056

If I am wrong, O teach my h. 9067

If I can stop one h. from breaking 6922

if longing h. finds living water, will be alone 10536

if not for hope h. would break 5935

If righteousness in the h. 8441

If your h. is troubled 418

in death extraordinary what takes place in h. toward God 10667

in every h. a spark of heavenly fire 244

In every pang that rends the h. 10597

in every thought renewed 5620

In lowliness of h. 2764

in my h. stable 6134

In prayer we descend with mind into the h. 10562

In solitude h. can take off protective devices 10540

in the fire feel God's h. warming 4858

insight arises from purity of h. 8504

instinctively seeks for a God 12110

intellect always fooled by the h. 6330

is aware of God, not reason 3750

is restless until it rests in you 7578

Jesus Christ exploded in my h. 1905

Jesus instructs the h. 6442

joy of h. colors face 6560

keep eyes of h. on Savior 10551

Keep h. free from hate 5561

Keep your h. with all diligence 2780

knows not best emotions of the h. 5349

Laughing 100 times a day works the h. 6725

Lend me a h. replete with thankfulness 11156

let wrinkles not be written upon the h. 8137

lifts his h. to God with his hands 8811

Lord Jesus, make my h. sit down 419

Lord's Prayer slowly learnt by h. 7153

Lord, behold my h. 8792

Love for Lord intensest of which human h. capable 7221

love in your h, always something to give 7189

love is to the h. what summer is to the farmer 7339

Love puts the joy in a h. 7269

Love the wine that gladdens h. of man 7256

Love will soften, purify the h. 7241

love, a condition of the h. and will 7304

man who truly repents cries out against his h. 9601

mind has a thousand eyes, the h. but one 7306

more afraid of my own h. 9929

mother's h. is child's schoolroom 7857

mouth keeps silent to hear h. speak 10270

music calms the agitated h. 7935

my chastened h, a sacrifice complete 10969

my h. beyond all feeling 12102

My h. may go astray 9091

My h. within me like a stone 2587

My Spirit searches the h. 72

no charity, worse kind of h. trouble 1077

no great anguish on its h. 1441

no happiness equal to h. that understands 9504

No language, but the language of the h. 11957

No sky is heavy if h. be light 6553

nor yet a h. so sick 10201

not a question of intellect but of purity of h. 11529

Not every h. that laughs is cheerful 10605

not yet sure of its God 6723

Nothing impossible to willing h. 10797

O Lord! my h. is sick 973

O, it sets my h. a clickin' 9880

of G. so much on us 4770

of good man is sanctuary of God 5084

of wise man lies quiet like limpid water 11944

oft times wakes when we sleep 2969

One greater than my h. whose Word cannot be broken 9813

only advancing in life whose h. is getting softer 6898

Only h. that hurts has right to joy 6571

Only the h. without stain knows ease 1696

only with h. one can see rightly 5622

Or deceive his h, omniscient 4888

Our own h. form true honor 5896

overpowered my hard h. 7579

peace found by man in depths of own h. 8474

Pentecost, assurance of h. 5806

poor h. that never rejoices 6535

potential capacity of human h. 5625

Prayer enlarges the h. 8910

Prayer requires more the h. than tongue 8952

prayer, better h. without words than words without h. 8844

quiet my h. with throbs of another h. 6258

raised to sweetness of eternal life 4749

right when wills what God wills 2566

saint has h. ready to praise God 9790

same h. beats in every human breast 917

science of Christ only learned by the h. 5110

Search thine own h. 3452

Search, prove my h, it pants for Thee 4140

secret anniversaries of the h. 7720

secret of own h. you can never know 5624

secret working of the h. 4749

sense of deity inscribed on every h. 4833

Sighs are natural language of the h. 5623

silence breaks the h. 12003

sin disquiet of the h. 10360

sin is breaking God's h. 10355

Sincerity an openness of h. 10428

Skepticism has not changed world's h. 5723

smiles, kindness win, preserve the h. 6656

so set eternity within my h. 3277

Solitude a state of mind, h. 10548

soothe the wayward h. by sorrow rent 7917

Sorrows stretch out spaces in h. for joy 10623

Spiritual truth discernable only to pure h. 11529

Spring cleaning should begin with head, end with h. 5756

stretch out spaces in h. for joy 2508

sunshine to the h. 4743

Sympathy is your pain in my h. 10982

tastes the joys of heaven 4749

teach me to silence my own h. 10257

Tell God all that is in your h. 8970

that desires, wants will of God 5442

that eased the h. of him who heard 107

that loves is always young 7302

that makes rich 11840

the complexion of the h. 103

the dwelling-place of God 8474

The h. benevolent and kind 6666

This longing h. of mine 7454

Thou dost desire my worthless h. 7456

Though all my h. should feel condemned 9813

thumps about things which intellect scorns 5628

To drown the outcry of the h. 6740

To handle others, use your h. 9508

to keep h. when all have lost it, is greatness 3153

To love is to admire with the h. 7326

to my fellowmen, a h. of love 5626

To my God, a h. of flame 5626

to myself, a h. of steel 5626

To understand, feel beating of h. 3078

tongue ambassador of the h. 11416

Tongues is a h. language 5807

transcends all visible things 4749

troubles touch God's h. of love 4789

unspotted not easily daunted 11679

unwilling h. will find thousand excuses 7871

Wake for shame, my sluggish h. 8671

walking around outside body 8310

way from God to human h. is through human h. 3334

wealth is of the h, not the hand 11867

Wealth lightens not h, care of man 11877

What h. did think, tongue would click 1890

What is to reach h. must come from above 7929

what might not the h. of man become 8655

What other corner so dark as one's own h. 9955

what quakes the h. 4551

What stronger breastplate than a h. untainted 6320

when acquainted with wickedness of own h. 10306

When full, lips silent 5270

When God inclines the h. to pray 9024

When h. is full, eyes overflow 5269

When h. right, feet swift 10213

when Spirit illuminates the h. 5809

Where least h, most tongue 5166

Where room in h, room in house 5960

Where your h. is, there is your happiness 5574

Where your treasure is, there is your h. 5574

Wherever you go, go with whole h. 3187

whose pulse may be thy praise 5265

will never tear the living Christ from my h. 7103

willing h. will find thousand ways 7871

With tranquil h. to do my simple part 9072

within and God o'erhead 4331

Within my h, that it may be 1357

Within my narrow h. 5788

woman formed from near h. to be loved 11982

wonder that child of God should have sad h. 1096

Words born in the h, not head 11997

Worship means "to feel in the h." 12140

worshiping h. needs no proof 600

yearning for something better, nobler, holier 470

You can't reason with your h. 5628

You fathom the depth of My own h. 900

HEARTACHE
If don't have h, how do you know when happy 5533

Which gives you a bit of h. 2502

without first persevering through h. 6802

HEARTACHES
God doesn't exempt from h. of life 11667

HEARTBEAT
hearing squirrel's h. 8496

HEARTBREAK
Better little chiding than great h. 8283

language of h. learned in suffering 10902

so close to happiness 7081

HEART-DEEP
Plant love h. in a person's life 7289

HEARTFELT
difficulty in making a truly h. prayer 8858

happiness of life made up of h. compliment 5556

HEARTLESS
pale, bloodless, h. thing 1487

That we should ever weak or h. be 8867

HEART'S
anything that tells h. need can find its way to God 8849

God brought man here with h. blood expense 4532

Gratitude is h. memory 5246

pumps through my own h. core 2979

yearning for love 4643

HEARTS
are lonely 9059

Bind the h. we have wounded 9054

Christians with vision in h, Bible in hands 11735

drink, broken more h. 325

Eternity is at our h. 1757

Faces we see, h. we know not 2464

frank talk good soap for h. 5864

go forward with manly h. 1918

God closest to broken h. 1505

God send us men with h. ablaze 7986

Gratitude born in h. that count mercies 5244

Grief knits two h. closer than happiness can 5338

He is sifting out the h. of men 4715

his joy to enter sorrowful h. 10603

Home feet may leave, not h. 5833

home joys make h. pure, good 5844

if h. open, desires known 10507

improved by breaking, h. of sinners 898

In love's service only broken h. will do 895

Jesus' joy to enter sorrowful h. 6460

Knit h. with unslipping knot 7625

Love is needed in individual h. 7251

Love makes all hard h. gentle 7261

Make of our h. a field 8730

may agree though heads differ 9461

Mother name for God in h. of children 7848

move beauty from faces into h. 8169

opened in pure transparency 5667

our h. are restless until they rest in you 4312

Peace made in h. of men 8457

Prophets the beating h. of the Old Testament 9333

revivals altered h. of men 9752

right temperature at home maintained by warm h. 5855

right that h. should be on God 4770

steel our h. against all fear 9090

storm rages but our h. are at rest 8470

Strong minds, great h, true faith, ready hands 6299

that shut against them with a snap 8694

Thy lodging is in childlike h. 6040

tragedies allow h. to shrink 5625

tune our h. to brave music 9059

We sigh to clear our h. 5627

When h. are blest or striken 10274

Where h. are true, few words will do 4302

while their h. can be thrilled 4223

HEARTTHROBS

count time by h. 1056

HEAT

As h. opposed to cold 5205

cannot be cold without h. 5357

extreme h. and cold kills 3554

gospel like cool air in h. of summer 5097

not so hot a furnace 383

supply light not h. 6587

HEATED

And h. hot with burning fears 2599

the mind grows h. 48

HEATHEN

chide no h. in world but myself 3942

Yes, you'd know him for h. 926

HEAVEN

a city and a body 6169

a hammer crashed in h. 2123

accepting Christ as Lord will bring h. down to yourself 5681

admits light of h. and reflects it 11945

Aim at h. and you get earth thrown in 5630

All h. waiting to help 5373

all long for h. where God is 6569

all resource of h, earth are at my disposal 9066

all will be great 5658

an interracial neighborhood 1486

As truly in his h. 2287

assets claim to be citizen of h. 7948

At his ascension, Lord entered h. 459

beginning of pride was in h. 9218

begins where sin ends 5642

best foretaste of h. 7198

Better go to h. in rags than hell in embroidery 9262

Between humble heart and majesty of h. no barriers 8771

Bible deals with h. and hell 721

Bible's light like body of h. 680

Bible, rising aloft into mysteries of h. 750

blowing snuff in the face of h. 9576

blue of h. larger than the cloud 10634

body is given to us in h. 1200

both h. and hell in this world 7078

bottom line is in h. 5665

can never go to h. without Christ 9792

cannot say in earth as it is in h. if 8818

cannot say who art in h. if 8818

Christ will turn earth into h. 5529

Christ, Lord of h. and earth 232

Christians work because they are going to h. 1356

cross ladder to h. 2149

cross, length to h. and earth 2154

cross, reconciling h. earth together 2154

Crosses are ladders to h. 162

crown wearers in h. 216

depths as welcome as surest h. 9930

desire of the soul, h. 9274

desire to have h. and hell ever in my eye 6910

Devil strongest spirit that fought in h. 2643

difference between h. and hell 2305

Disappointments corrections of h. 2796

Do your duty, leave rest to h. 9651

Earth grows into h. 6378

Earth has no sorrow h. cannot heal 5637

Earth recedes, h. opens 2437

Earth's crammed with h. 1710

enjoyment of God 5646

enjoyment of one another in God 5646

established legal residence in h. 5673

Even hen lifteth her head toward h. 11142

even the least is a great thing 5658

Every good deed touches chord that vibrates in h. 6670

Everybody wants to go to h. 2282

expect to find three wonders 5655

expect to meet some had not thought to see there 5655

expect to miss some I had expected 5655

find completion of all desires 5644

Forget the pain by which they purchased h. 7672

friend is dearer than light of h. 4269

full enjoyment of God 5644

gentleness of h. broods o'er the sea 8980

get to h. by accepting Christ as Savior 5681

goal to which God commits is in h. 5385

God dwelling in h. 5621

God has set a h. against hell 5016

God knows all h. 4881

God's in his h. 8233

going to h. because Christ died on cross 5653

Gold suggest timelessness of h. 5631

gospel originated in h. 9545

grand pieces played on earth composed in h. 5639

grateful thought to h. the most perfect prayer 8755

grateful thought toward h. a prayer 5239

Gratitude to God makes blessing taste of h. 5248

great faith will bring h. to your soul 3757

greatest wonder to find myself there 5655

happiness endless in duration 5634

happiness infinite in degree 5634

happy family an earlier h. 3865

hard for rich to enter h. 11830

hardly h. if could define 5648

harps in h, cymbals in hell 5703

have it in our power to be in h. right now 6569

Hell was our inheritance, now h. our possession 1348

highest bliss in h. 5667

Humble love keeps door of h. 12130

Husbands in h. whose wives chide not 7618

I am my own h. and hell 7386

I have one foot in h. 6915

I shall hear in h. 2444

idea of eternal rest frightens me 5661

If not allowed to laugh in h. 6721

If not nourished by Bread from h. 12050

in earth, and God in man 6153

In flows h, with its new day 5636

in h. able to wipe tears, won't have to 11016

In h. he scorns to serve 2656

in h. most perfect charity 5685

In h. stand in character of Savior 1072

infinite meadows of h. 11636

interested in cross 2122

is above all yet 4716

is always autumn 5657

is God's love 5650

is not a resting place 5644

is our home, the world our inn 7077

is place prepared for those prepared 5643

is the Christian's country 5638

is the Christian's vocation 3095

is won today 2986

Isn't there anything to do in h. 5661

itself would stoop to virtue 11692

Jesus Christ intercession for us in h. 8859

Jesus is the joy of h. 6460 10603

Jesus makes h. wherever he is 6378

joins hands with h. 9805

joy of h. improvement of spirit 3482

joy the serenity of h. 2580

Joy the serious business of h. 6549

leave badges of schism behind 5671

left mark because occupied with h. 5656

lies about us in our infancy 12164

Lifts earth to h, stoops h. to earth 6153

lifts men up to their Father in h. 5844

light and truth and love of h. 10756

Little faith will bring soul to h. 3757

live a holy life, then go see 5660

Lord keeps door open for humanity 459

loving any indulgence better than hope of h. 6925

Make our earth an Eden like h. above 2503

man who believes he is worthy of h. 5668

Marriage is h. or hell 7639

may go to h. without health, riches 9792

Men full of the Spirit look right into h. 5651

mercy droppeth as the gentle rain from h. 7744

mind can make h. of hell 512

mind can make hell of h. 512

miserable if have to gaze and gaze 5661

Money can pay fare to every place but h. 7810

mount to h. on ruins of cherished schemes 3631

Music almost all we have of h. on earth 7902

Music only art of earth we take to h. 7904

music only art of h. given to earth 7904

must not be so full of hope of h. 6108

ne'er helps man who will not help himself 2498

neither a place nor a time 7947

no h. with a little of hell in it 9864

No man can resolve himself into h. 5662

No man ever scared into h. 5663

no one can go to hell or h. for me 594

no one can open or close h. or hell 594

no one in h. can shut door God has opened 4937

not a reward for being good boy 5645

not eye that sees beauty of h. 10656

not going to h. because I've preached to crowds 5653

not good that man batter at gate of h. 8854

not inspired by hope of h. 6108

not proud reason keeps door of h. 12130

not so far as some imagine 5651

not so large as yours 5640

nothing is better in h. than love 7283

of whom we speak least on earth best known in h. 9616

Oh, surely melody from h. was sent 7917

on earth or else in h, another year for thee 8077

only one way to h. 11863

Or what's a h. for 4420

Our thoughts are heard in h. 11155

Out of h. and just like me 6456

overwhelmed by advantages of new home 2394

Perseverance rope that ties soul to h. 8554

plan by which good people go to h. 5632

plan whereby sinners can go to h. 5632

polishes jewels with diamond dust 143

Praise will transform humblest dwelling to hallowed h. 5846

Prayer is battering h. with storms of prayer 8919

prayers, from h. they came 9012

preaches from villas to slums about mansions in h. 6065

presence of God's glory in h. 4865

primitive church thought more about Second Coming than h. 9913

quality of life 5645

rare fabric of h. and earth 1979

Reach h. at last 2162

Remorse is beholding h. and feeling hell 9574

Repentance change of nature befitting h. 9597

rest there in God 5644

revolts against h. 2959

same Jesus in h. as on earth 6466

Satan, his name heard no more in h. 2666

sex, man has left it out of his h. 10228

should we not look forward to the arrival 2315

since Christians have ceased to think of h. 5656

soul that sees beauty of h. 10656

stepping on shore, finding it h. 2399

takes real faith to live life of h. on earth 3752

tastes the joys of h. 4749

Teach him all the way to h. 8296

That will be heard in h. 8694

There's no marrying in h, that's why its h. 7658

think they must storm h. with loud outcries 8787

This man and I must go to h. 1278

through tears have the sorrowful seen gates of h. 10882

Till of h. the deed appears 6640

'Tis h. alone that is given away 9795

To believe in h. is not to run from life 5674

To get to h, turn right, keep straight 5675

to see clearly reason needs light of h. 9422

toil, weariness no place there 5644

Treasures in h. accumulated by attitude 11872

Treasures in h. laid up only 9565

Trouble often lever to raise us to h. 11460

trust God, h. securely 559

truth belongs to h. not world 8596

uninterrupted communion with God 5644

upon earth to weary head 10484

Use God to provide h. at last 7517

voice rises to h. when you praise 8725

we ourselves do not look up toward h. 7567

We talk about h. being so far away 5677

were not h, if we knew what it were 3496

When you speak of h, let face light up 5680

Where love reigns, joy of h. felt 7342

where questions, answers become one 5647

where wrongs of the world are corrected 5678

Why live beggarly when riches of h. are yours 8662

within speaking distance 5677

work is rest, recreation 5644

worshiper no surer of h. than before 8845

would be empty 4088

would be out of place in h. 5654
would not give one moment of h. for all the world 5652
yearnings are homesickness for h. 7516

HEAVEN-GATES
not so highly arch'd 5649

HEAVENLY
A calm and h. frame 7507
Bible source of h. knowledge 737
Christ came to lift us to h. places 6402
from the h. throng 1375
God's h. plan doesn't always make earthly sense 5399
greatest a man can do for his h. Father 6665
Humility, from which all h. virtues shoot 6015
Jesus has many lovers of h. kingdom 2828
life joyous with h. song 11144
Lord's Prayer compendium of h. doctrine 7156
Philosophy a longing after h. wisdom 8593
sounds which Holy Spirit weaves together in h. harmony 5799
speak of h. fire 244
sweetness in the cross 2096
wealth laid up in h. banking account 3751

HEAVEN'S
angels h. spectators 2359
eternal wisdom has decreed 9462
Flowers are h. masterpieces 8003
graduates in h. highest school of art 8914
I see h. glories shine 3765
look at earth from h. point of view 10707
Man h. masterpiece 1965
rainbow h. promise in technicolor 9390
soul in h. eternal sphere 10675
to children parents are h. lieutenants 5856
to give success 10775
When we turn into h. doorway 7085

HEAVENS
ancient h. through thee fresh, strong 4598
as deep as aspirations high 468
do the h. contain you 4854
God never meant that man should scale the h. 11916
Infinite has written name on h. in shining stars 4705
Infinite sowed his name in h. in stars 8037
Open, ye h. your living doors 1967
starry h. above me 1709
yet if I look up into the h. 8445

HEAVIER
another cross may be h. 183

to resist one's cross is to make h. 2114
towers fall with h. crash who higher soar 9216

HEAVIEST
Everyone thinks his sack h. 10029
greatest bears h. burdens cheerfully 5297
load pack of grudges 4098
Money, time are h. burdens 932

HEAVILY
Leaning too h. on another person 9478

HEAV'N
And escort thee quick to h. 2221
As more of h. in each we see 4197
opens on my eyes, my ears 2389

HEAV'NLY-GUIDED
When once our h. soul shall climb 5679

HEAV'NS
And were the h. of parchment made 4748

HEAVY
No burden h. carried with love 934
No sky is h. if heart be light 6553
On long journey even straw is h. 8550
One's life h. price to pay 3487
riches, burden too h. for us 11832
sanctification not a h. yoke 9842
Though eyelids get h. 11420
Truth is h, few men carry it 11565
What h. burdens from our bosoms take 8867

HEBREW
only in H. full meaning of Bible 669

HEDGE
Love neighbor, but don't pull down h. 8060

HEDGEHOG
irritable person like h. rolled up wrong way 9630
Some think have to look like h. to be pious 6822

HEED
in tragedy face to face with things never gave h. to 10667
take h. add no offense of our own 6317
we ourselves do not h. God 7567
What is reason for saying God does not h. us 7567

HEEDLESS
that we pass h, unseeing 9064

HEEL
kindest man will put h. on greatest friend 10527

HEELS
High h. invented by somebody kissed on forehead 2003

Jealousy a blister on the h. of friendship 6339

HEIGHT
depth man can fall is h. to which he can rise 8666
eagle eye cannot see its h. 4745
Holy Ghost reveals h. of holiness 10391
Lust, at its h, does not know shame 7358
on wings of mysticism can spirit soar to full h. 7963
stand at real h. against higher nature 6037
Stature comes not with h. but depth 11939

HEIGHTS
not who soared to h. of achievement 6175
of great men reached and kept 8566
of us, depths of us 6932
rough road that leads to h. of greatness 8287

HEIRS
receive money 7826

HELD
Happiness h. is the seed 5514

HELL
all h. terribly afraid of cross 2122
all hate one another 5692
Ascended into h. 5694
Better go to heaven in rags than h. in embroidery 9262
Bible deals with heaven, h. 721
both heaven and h. in this world 7078
cannot break God's decree 4616
Christian who lives one-half inch from h. 890
created for devil and his angels 5686
desire to have heaven, h. ever in my eye 6910
Despair damp of h. 2580
difference between heaven, h. 2305
either a lunatic or devil of h. 6350
end of pride is in h. 9218
Envy's a coal come hissing hot from h. 3216
everyone perpetually concerned about own dignity 5705
full of the ungrateful 5687
gnashing of teeth, despair 5698
God has set a heaven against h. 5016
God knows all h. 4881
God that holds you over the pit of h. 4523
God will never send anybody to h. 5686
Gold opens every gate, e'en that of h. 11814
guilty conscience h. on earth 1656
harps in heaven, cymbals in h. 5703

highest reward devil can offer 5689

how much better this world is than h. 2592

I am my own heaven and h. 7386

if God deny merciful presence, fall into h. 4865

if leave Jesus Christ out, toboggan slide to h. 9172

in h. called despair 11394

in h. most perfect hate 5685

is enjoyment of your own way forever 5695

is God's justice 5650

is truth seen too late 5690

It is h. to be alone 2447

Jealousy the injured lover's h. 6342

love of God bars way to h. 4781

madame, is to love no longer 5693

man convinced he deserves h. 5668

man goes to h. by own choice 5686

Marriage is heaven or h. 7639

may go to h. with baptismal water on face 9537

mind can make h. of heaven 512

mind can make heaven of h. 512

no fans in h. 5704

no heaven with a little of h. in it 9864

no longer able to love 5707

no one can go to h. or heaven for me 594

no one can open or close heaven or h. 594

not question of saved from h. 1014

now in h. he reigns 2656

O war, thou son of h. 11756

our inheritance, heaven our possession 1348

pains of h. ignorance, lust 3482

paved with good intentions 5688

prayer ineffectual 5700

presence of God's justice in h. 4865

pride of dying rich raises loudest laugh in h. 9246

principle of h. "I am my own" 5699

punishment without penitence 5700

Remorse is beholding heaven and feeling h. 9574

remorse puts man in h. while on earth 9584

road to h. easy to travel 5701

safest road to h. is gradual 5702

self-realization way you will end in your own h. 9196

separation from God 5697

sin a banquet of h. 10360

sin a dungeon of h. 10360

sin an eternity of h. 10360

society, politer name of h. 1135

Teeth will be provided 5696

The fixed pains of h. 4813

Thought looks into pit of h. 11232

thousand paths lead to h. 5664

to mourn for sin because it exposes us to h. 9581

today is vanquished 2986

tortures of that inward h. 9567

upon earth found in melancholy heart 2548

weeping useless 5700

when men see themselves abandoned by God 5698

When speak of h, everyday face will do 5680

where everyone doing own thing 5691

where everyone has a grievance 5705

where everyone lives deadly passions 5705

where no one has anything in common 5692

who has not rest at home in world's h. 5828

wicked man is his own h. 11880

wish to run rescue mission within yard of h. 7783

HELLISH

It were a h. wrong 6258

HELLO

Spring God's way of saying h. 9892

HELMET

Virtue is the safest h. 11711

HELP

All heaven waiting to h. 5373

as source of life and h. 7548

assertively reach out to h. others 3901

better to keep friend from falling than h. up 4191

can only h. him find it himself 11010

Charity, helping man to h. himself 1073

Complain to one who can h. 1556

even the angels h. me 9066

Everything can h. me in Christian life 1466

fit God in wherever able to h. 5467

For we have no h. but thee 5428

Fragile, delicate are most who seek h. 3069

give me strength to h. my toiling brother 910

God a present h. or not much h. at all 4701

God likes h. when helping people 10139

God will h. thee bear what comes 11362

Grace can h. us when down 5212

He that is fallen cannot h. him that is down 2585

He who created us without our h. 9796

him at least with a sigh 3072

If can't h. with money 3072

if I am too tired to call for him to h. me 7478

loneliness knowledge that human beings incapable of bringing h. 7126

Lord Jesus, you died to h. me die 2331

Lord, h. me to remember 4622

love has hands to h. others 7335

me faithfully to journey along my road 9074

me get up 9044

me live from day to day 9075

me never to judge another 9065

me to tear it from thy throne 6074

memorizing of Scripture h. in doubt 747

neighbor is everyone that needs h. 913

Nothing makes one feel so strong as call for h. 10177

of the helpless, O abide with me 2538

only time to look down on neighbor is when bending over to h. 8064

Or h. one fainting robin 6922

right to criticize if heart to h. 2060

Shut out past except that which will h. tomorrows 8383

success ability to h. others 10815

tell man brave, h. him become so 3140

the poor 8698

the world go around 9114

Then I asked if I might h. God 4994

to make earth happy like the heaven above 6659

to think we are whole and need no h. 10045

trouble is we won't let God h. us 11454

truest h, call out man's best strength 936

turn mountain into gold mine with God's h. 2633

us accept ourselves, failures and all 9993

us not to despise, oppose what we do not understand 9095

us this and every day 9040

us to be masters of ourselves 9096

used to ask God to h. me 4994

Wherever our life touches yours, h. or hinder 9522

who waits to be asked for h. 10148

with h. of spading, fertilizing 9884

Worship voice in night calling for h. 12132

wrong attitude, h. not success 521

your brother's boat across 905

HELPED

me to understand failures, ruins 10594

place ourselves in attitude to be h. 9010

pray for another, will be h. yourself 8838

HELPER

impossible to despair who remembers his H. omnipotent 2595

HELPERS

many h, see God in all your h. 11490

no h, see all your h. in God 11490

When other h. fail 2538

HELPFUL

contemplation, action mutually h. 1766

Love enough to be h. 1809

HELPING

as God helps 6569

Brotherhood: h. yourself by h. others 903

Charity, h. man to help himself 1072

each other through joy, strife 4281

God likes help when h. people 10139

Gold cannot reach out a h. hand 11813

government can never replace h. hand of neighbor 8062

Grief, h. you feel compassion for others 5334

hold out h. hand 3131

Sorrow, h. you feel more compassion 10610

HELPLESS

Adam's h. race 495

Almighty appeared on earth as h. baby 6125

atheist who sees man h. 3495

difference between Almighty God and h. worm 3786

Has there ever been more h. image 2132

help of the h. O abide with me 2538

Human beings bearable when h, humbled 892

Man is no h. invalid 10436

naked, piping loud 808

on a barn-bare floor 6142

Only he who is h. can truly pray 8901

to remain silence makes us feel h. 10259

utterly h. as he has made us 4673

We are born h. 9513

Without prayer, would be h. 8794

HELPLESSNESS

calls from your heart to the heart of God 8901

God comes in where h. begins 11786

God's grace sufficient 2518

greater effect than uttered pleas 8901

in utter h. cast all on Christ 6354

is your best prayer 8901

my greatest strength 11789

Prayer and h. inseparable 8901

sign of h. apart from divine enablement 8759

When frustration of h. seemed greatest 2518

HELPS

Christ h. us by his weakness, suffering 4899

Christ in you that h. the poor 6381

Christian, hand through which Christ h. 1248

climbs highest who h. another up 3134

deed that h. poor done for Christ 8698

friend h. us be our best selves 4178

friend h. us put forth best efforts 4178

friend h. us think noblest thoughts 4178

God h. us view world from new perspective 4735

good sermon h. in different ways 10094

Heaven ne'er h. man who will not help himself 2498

naive h. one go through life smoothly 7976

smile a curve that h. to set things straight 10495

who h. in saving others 10146

who h. to perpetrate evil 3374

HEN

as restless as h. wanting to lay egg 11886

Don't brood, you're not h. 2542

egg's no chick by falling from h. 875

Even h. lifteth head toward heaven 11142

Sad the home where h. crows, cock silent 5847

who has laid egg cackles as if laid asteroid 9223

HENNY PENNYS

Don't run around with H. 4226

HERALD

Silence is perfectest h. of joy 6558

HERD

a stricken deer that left the h. 9798

conformist has to follow h. 1635

dissenter resigns from the h, thinks for himself 6210

Man by origin is a h. animal 6199

HERE

astonished at being h. rather than there 4905

happiness not there but h. 11374

no reason why h. rather than there 4905

HEREAFTER

plan as if expect to enter h. tomorrow 6099

satisfy aching soul, not h. only but here and now 6402

HEREDITARY

Insanity is h. 3874

Life is a h. disease 6948

Virtue is not h. 11708

HERESIES

measures to which church driven by h. 11186

HERESY

another word for freedom of thought 6181

Truth this side of Pyrenees may be h. on the other 11577

HERETICS

Without h. world would not progress 9318

HERITAGE

Lord of himself, h. of woe 9935

HERO

education might have brought to light 3038

murder, millions make a h. 11758

No h. ever did work cheaply, easily 5289

potential h. in every man—and potential skunk 8670

than to love world and be a h. 10777

HEROES

children outgrow Shepherd, find h. elsewhere 1133

contact withers them 8516

easier to suffer as public h. 10859

give us comradeship with h, saints of every age 9059

God can fit h. into their places 9174

God is preparing his h. 9174

men think h. of tragedy great 10877

mixture of divine, human 755

mixture of majestic, ordinary 755

Mothers' darlings make milksop h. 8315

of Bible 755

true h. of the human race 6199

Worship your h. from afar 8516

HEROIC

acts of great mind 6281

defeat formed h. natures 2511

prayer closet scene of h. and unearthly conflicts 8976

HEROISM

cross put to shame self-assertion of h. 2166

Reconciliation sometimes demands h. 9431

HESITATION
death uncolored by h. 2299

HIBERNATION
grudge like a bear with bad breath
   coming out of h. 9639

HID
alone what is h. with God made
   known 10532
God h. knot so low we cannot
   reach 5384
harvest time is h. with God 10204
These things keep mildly h. 1855

HIDDEN
As yet your shaft h. in his quiver
   5430
because not in fit state to
   understand 11609
designs of God's providence
   deeply h. 3349
discover delight h. in irksome tasks
   10639
Education, eliciting potentialities
   h. 3026
God wills us to tread h. paths
   5397
God's essence h. to human reason
   4670
guilty conscience a h. enemy 5472
honesty, no h. meanings 5874
Instead of complaining that God
   has h. himself 4908
love, boundless treasures h. within
   its depths 7211
no skeleton can come out of h.
   closet 4884
power of service will correspond
   to h. life of prayer 10192
secret throught not h. from God
   4578
shows subtler, more h.
   imperfections 10006
Sin, most of its power h. 10357
Thirty years of Lord's life h. 8112
Unwrap h. beauties in ordinary
   day 2201

HIDE
a god from whom we do not h.
   4846
faults more pardonable than
   methods to h. them 3933
for a time from disturbing
   thoughts 7708
God knows thoughts you try to h.
   4764
Let me h. myself in thee 4636
Man groping for God and hoping
   to h. from him 7402
Maturity, not to h. one's strength
   out of fear 7695
O what may man within him h.
   2470
penny will h. biggest star in
   universe 7795
pretences built up to h. emptiness
   3395
therein to h. from storms of devil
   2652

To h. the fault I see 1552
where should I h. guilty head
   4069

HIDE-AND-SEEK
God does not play h. 5386

HIDES
behind hypocrite smaller than
   hypocrite 6046
God h. in thick darkness from wise
   7709
God h. nothing 9706
he that h. dark soul, foul thoughts
   1683
Humility h. our good deeds from
   our eyes 6005
man h. within himself 316
man imagines he will keep if he h.
   1537
Self the opaque veil that h. God
   9945
shut eyes to future God h. from us
   4322
truth of a man is what he h. 7431

HIDETH
darkness h. not from him, but
   glows 4746

HIDING
awful hour when first necessity of
   h. comes 2468
awful hour when necessity of h.
   comes 5480
places will be swept away 3719

HIGH
A h. way and a low 1155
As soon as h. consciousness is
   reached 3479
Bible so h. best look upward 702
courage of a devout soul 4974
Everyone wants h. achievement
   4731
God hid knot so h. so we cannot
   reach. 5384
God made them h. or lowly 4501
heavens as deep as aspirations h.
   468
if we imbue men with h. principles
   6796
In celebration h, mighty regain
   balance 3235
most obscure believer can hold
   head h. 9999
need not be concerned how h.
   God's standard is 8518
No man will rise h. who jeers at
   sacred things 9735
No natural feelings h. in
   themselves 4016
paid h. price to find that evil is evil
   3416
soul climbs the h. way 10679
structures require solid foundation
   5991
To God no h, no low 4709
To h. eternal gain 4338
Who can be h. or low at festival
   of God 3235

HIGH PRIEST
Bible, there is H. ever waiting 716
In his intercession, Christ a h.
   6410

HIGHER
blessings waiting on h. level 968
do not bring old life up to h. plane
   9839
Earth has no h. bliss 4799
   1763
Faith h. faculty than reason 3675
For h. ministry 6109
God shaping us for h. things 228
imagine God having to apply to h.
   body 4955
judged by standard h, more
   attainable 6812
Knowledge given to lead us to h.
   worship 6693
Love h. than other gifts in value
   7235
Man forced to seek h. authority
   7499
Morality always h. than law 7831
No prayer of adoration h. than "I
   love you, God" 8876
nothing is h. than love 7283
Prayer getting a h. look 8917
religious values into h. or lower
   case 11658
Scripture far h. and wider 691
setting up ourselves as h. tribunal
   4087
soul has h. peaks than any
   mountain 7539
stand at real height against h.
   nature 6037
the hill that you climb 3488
thinking in its h. forms a kind of
   poetry 11259
to enable him to put other foot h.
   9316
towers fall with heavier crash
   which h. soar 9216
view of God 4720
we go in social life, more bondage
   there is 4159
when God leads in h. path of
   sanctification 9851
Who is h. than the Highest 4955
Worship h. level of existence
   12133
your structure, deeper must be
   foundation 5997

HIGHEST
Adoration is h. form of prayer
   8756
bliss in heaven 5667
charity is charity toward
   uncharitable 1082
climbs h. who helps another up
   3134
Earth's h. station ends in "Here he
   lies" 7088
family, h. realization where
   Christianity prevails 3868
Forgiveness h. achievement 4077

function of mind is to listen to God's Word 7766

Giving h. form of potency 10726

God is h. blessedness 4514

God is virtue of h. benevolence 4514

good wanting to bring life to h. value 5044

goodness of God to desire our h. welfare 7093

Hell h. reward devil can offer 5689

His life is h, holiest entering at lowliest door 6132

Holy Spirit lifts personality to h. use 5798

live up always to best, h. 3468

love, the love of Christ for men 6506

Next to theology I give music h. place 7914

part of soul stands above time 11316

Patient waiting often h. way of doing God's will 8416

point we can hope to attain 4976

possible condition of a man 4983

Prayer h. energy of which the mind is capable 8900

privilege to share another's pain 4276

Recreation not h. kind of enjoyment 6837

reward for labor what it does for him 3119

reward what man becomes 1045

science is study of Godhead 4631

service prepared for in humblest surroundings 10190

shall never behold glory in the h. 9020

sign of friendship 4277

soul with h. powers touches eternity 10671

standard God has is himself 4567

take lowest place, h. will be given 5991

To act in everything with h. motives 6913

To see God h. aspiration of man 7547

trees have most reason to dread thunder 9241

value is God 11663

Where need is h, God is nighest 4515

Who is higher than the h. 4955

Worship h, noblest act 12137

Your destruction is Satan's h. priority 9855

HIGHLY

Men think h. who rise rapidly 3857

HIGHWAY

A wonderful way is the King's H. 4313

out of crowded city, on to crowded h. 9901

HILARIOUS

saint is h. when crushed 2722

HILL

and dale in slumber steeping 1123

Each bog, each rugged h. 8081

higher the h. that you climb 3488

I sought him then atop a lonely h. 4921

plough, don't level it 35

HILLS

A God, a God! the vocal h. reply 6138

a meaning on the face of the high h. 4962

are mute, yet how they speak of God 8014

dimmed with grief no everlasting h. I see 2587

joys are like the everlasting h. 7569

They touch the shining h. of day 11299

Wild flowers on distant h. 8498

HILT

Live to the h. every situation 3186

HIM

not them, whom God made in his image 6200

HIMSELF

able to love h, able to love others 9985

Adam not to have dominion over h. 758

against h. that everybody sins 10325

Ah, how unjust to nature and h. 3190

as to h, God hath knowledge 4514

at rest within h. 4307

Bids not h. good-day 12097

blackens others does not whiten h. 10451

bore talks to you about h. 5112

By this glance God gives h. to me 7953

Christ gave greatest gift, h. 10731

Christ, by next work gave h. to me 6361

dirties h. more 10452

dissenter resigns from herd, thinks for h. 6210

each man as he sees h. 7443

Each of us must think for h. 11260

falls in love with h. will have no rivals 7175

genuinely great who considers h. small 5285

God exists in h. and of h. 4610

God is h. in us 4537

God's promises are obligations he imposes upon h. 9324

God's real greatness known to h. alone 4665

godly not afraid of h. 3996

good leader prepared to deny h. much 6793

good to another, good to h. 4362

has not heard from h. 1761

he h. is very well 8142

he'll hang h. 4061

highest standard God has is h. 4567

hinders h. from enjoying what he has 5316

his Maker, and the angel Death 4209

how in presence of Lord could think about h. 4853

in library a few books he wrote h. 6965

is his dungeon 10061

is mighty who conquers h. 9968

is not laughed at, who laughs at h. first 6000

knows h. best esteems h. least 6002

knows h. best, esteems h. least 1711

Let each man think h. an act of God 4557

Let him that would move world, move h. 3439

live for h, small troubles seem great 11433

lives only for h. truly dead to others 10059

looks for fault within h. 9680

Lord of h, heritage of woe 9935

Lord of h, though not of lands 9959

makes h. an ass 4063

Man can only find meaning outside h. 3484

man h. when most possessed by God 5200

man has power to bring misery on h. 4158

man morally incapable of restraining h. 9872

Man primarily interested in h. 10068

man who does not love God, in love with h. 4803

mistrust of h, greater confidence in God 10328

more a person is in harmony with h. 8505

more man denies h, more obtain from God 9562

No man comes to h. without meeting God 1907

No man free who is not master of h. 4139

No one can know God who has not first known h. 7543

no one thinks of changing h. 964

no room for God in man full of h. 10089

none more lonely than man who loves only h. 7147

one must first get into core of h. 7543

one who thought h. above me 9251

only the devil who praises h. 9214

pessimist thought everything bad
    except h. 8248
praises h. spatters h. 9204
rationalist makes h. his own center
    9396
slave of greatest slave who serves
    h. 10055
so full of h. is quite empty 9202
thinks h. happiest man, really is so
    11917
thinks h. wisest, usually greatest
    fool 11917
thinks of h, says prayers of
    petition 8840
unless able to empty h. 7962
unless able to give h. to people in
    selfless love 7962
until first given h. in love, sacrifice
    10119
way which leads to h. 1717
When fight begins within h. 6322
    9940
when God gave h. 4528
who does not honor wife
    dishonors h. 7616
who doubts bears arms against h.
    11597
who fails to pray cheats h. 8810
who has confidence in h. will lead
    the rest 6791
who has faith in h. able to be
    faithful 9485
who helps in saving others saves h.
    10146
who repents is angry with h. 9579
who respects h. is safe from others
    9986
who thinks too much of h. thinks
    too little of others 9243

HINDER
no devil can h. you from serving
    10159
time with God by remembering
    other things to do 11349
Wherever our life touches yours,
    help or h. 9522

HINDERING
evil h. development of life 5044
the spread of the gospel 349

HINDERS
God in no way h. struggle for
    development 4129
himself from enjoying what he has
    5316

HINDRANCE
to spiritual progress 3758
what seems h. becomes a way
    10901
what seems h. will prove a blessing
    169

HINDRANCES
are God's opportunities 8219
transforms h. into growth 1468

HINDU
stand apart disillusioned 6563

HINDUISM
doesn't try 3301

HINT
He has no word that gives a h. of
    God 10274
of the everlasting in the sea 3290
possibility a h. from God 8641

HIP
You've hit no traitor on the h.
    3174

HISSED
voice of intelligence h. away by
    hate 6331

HISSING
Envy's a coal come h. hot from
    hell 3216
eye can insult like h. 3561

HISTORIAN
prophet in reverse 5708

HISTORIC
unless bears reference to great h.
    event 5726

HISTORIES
Man writes h. 5719
Sin writes h. 10380

HISTORY
alcohol, greatest criminal in h.
    331
all lines of h. converge upon Christ
    5710
Baby: Unwritten h. 805
believe Christ's existence and h. is
    explained 5728
Bible most frequently attacked in
    h. 726
Bible most widely read in h. 726
Bible shows how world progresses
    723
by the time we've reached *w* of
    now, n ancient h. 11291
Christ embodies all h. 6369
Christ great central fact in world's
    h. 5710
Christian faith founded upon fact
    of h. 6144
Christian mind has weakness
    unmatched in Christian h. 7768
Christianity, ancient h. or current
    events 1204
clay in which God works 5718
coming of Jesus most stupendous
    event in h. 6146
concern for course of h. not
    irrelevant 5724
concern to know where h. is going
    5724
conviction that God has worked
    in h. 5724
cross, crystallized point in h. 2148
cross, where h. and life intersect
    2150
crucifixion most famous death in
    h. 2137
Difficulty excuse h. never accepts
    2718

Dogma is ark within which
    church floats down h. 11187
endless repetition of wrong way
    of living 5713
enriched by antithetical elements
    5020
fearful symmetry which is God's
    language 5718
God alone knows secret of h.
    4694
God at work in h. casting down
    the rich 6630
God embraces all h. 10562
God molds h. to his purposes
    5718
God raised up Jesus to shatter h.
    5711
God's often violent intrusions into
    h. 9710
great doers of h. men of faith
    5723
greatest, most momentous fact
    which h. records 5710
how shabby fabric of h. is 5714
If read secret h. of enemies 3161
immersion in h. of thought, spirit
    3027
In God h. and prophecy are one
    4604
incomprehensible without Christ
    5709
Jesus changes our h. 10901
Jesus Christ is Lord of h. 5716
Jesus Christ, God Incarnate,
    manifested at one point of h.
    5717
little more than register of
    misfortunes 5719
Looking for Jesus in h. futile 5718
man trying to find something
    which will make him happy
    5570
men who make h. 1712
most important events never reach
    h. books 5725
most persistent sound through h.
    is war drums 11762
most revolutionary statement in h.
    7305
name of Jesus plowed into h. of
    world 5727
of our Lord unfathomable depth
    6380
of pride in three chapters 9218
of thought absurd by what it seeks
    11242
of world a contest between God,
    Satan, fallen men 4916
out of hopeless attempt has come
    human h. 5570
Providence put together present
    beautiful h. 5722
read h, Christians who did most
    for this world 5629
record of not keeping
    commandments 1527
resurrection fact of h. 9702
shows how unprofitable pride is
    9218

story of Jesus told more than any other in h. 5729

story written by finger of God 5712

teaches mistakes we are going to make 5715

teaches us to hope 5944

theologians throughout h. ponder conversion 1896

thoughtful mind sees h. of nation 7982

Throughout h. truth considered form of dementia 5730

to remake h. by cosmic, creative event 5711

too fragile, indeterminate a structure to contain Jesus 5714

total redirection of h. 5720

we live in moment of h. 982

What a terrific moment in h. 6154

HIT

failure to h. bull's-eye never fault of target 9680

likely to be h. from both sides 11602

the ball over the fence 3467

The two h. it off as they should 909

You've h. no traitor on the hip 3174

HITCHING POST

past dangerous used as h. 8367

HITHER

Who brought me h. 5469

HITLER

psychological secrets H. used 12178

HOARD

Don't h. talent 10993

HOARDED

When we reach the end of our h. resources 7570

HOARDING

not cisterns made for h. 10729

HOBBIES

resist temptation to chase after h. 5615

HOG

get the h. out of the spring 10322

HOIST

wind of God blowing but must h. sail 5452

HOLD

A broken bowl that cannot h. 7003

All we can h. in our cold dead hands 4349

better h. tongue than them 1862

can't h. a man down without staying down with him 10479

Christ's h. of you that saves you 9802

God's restrictions h. us up, down 4309

it seems you could not h. on a minute longer 2614

loosely all that is not eternal 3280

most obscure believer can h. head high 9999

Never h. anyone by the button 1862

no vision of eternity, never get h. of time 3272

Normal day, let me h. you while I may 2197

not your h. of Christ that saves you 9802

on to plough while wiping tears 1236

on, fast, out 8402

out helping hand 3131

sacred every experience 6900

seems you could not h. on minute longer 8568

some God-made object up to picture 2022

things that h. in slippery world 4643

through difficult times, h. steady 969

'Tis nothing to h. up head in calm 1915

Tomb, thou shalt no h. him longer 2985

torch to light another's path 3145

true friend with both hands 4188

wise to let God h. you back 5422

yet the hands divine h. me 7478

HOLDING

a beggar's child 7178

Faith is God h. on to you 3692

Faith not merely you h. on to God 3692

letter of truth 9826

times when Lord h. me closest 10853

HOLDS

Do not look upon the vessel, but upon what it h. 6297

God 6149

Man drives, God h. reins 4947

Man rides, God h. the reins 7498

nothing but his hand that h. you 4523

Seizes the right, h. it to the last 11906

soul h. and is held 7967

HOLE

pessimist sees the h. 8244

HOLES

knows where h. are deep 3541

HOLIDAY

George Washington born on national h. 7981

HOLIDAYS

holiest of all h. in silence and apart 7720

HOLIER

heart yearns for something h. 470

man is, less understood by men of world 5760

Rise with its anthems to h. sphere 10960

HOLIER-THAN-THOU

repressing emotions we become h. 3050

HOLIEST

His life is highest, h. entering at lowliest door 6132

Jesus h. man who ever lived 6412

lives h. life fittest far to die 2427

moment of the church 1444

of all holidays in silence and apart 7720

person most conscious of sin 5761

souls ever lived pessimistic 8586

Trinity, perfect in Unity 11424

HOLINESS

a fire whose warmth pervades universe 5741

a relative and contingent h. God shares 4658

ability not to sin 5745

Christ, perfect, spotless h. of his manhood 6488

death raises from sinfulness into h. 2250

deliverance from standing still 5746

destined end of man is h. 5757

difference between h. of Christians is contrast of praying 8976

Faith lends h. to life 3666

God holy with absolute h. 4658

God leads in paths of h. 169

God requires h. 4658

God shares h. by imputation, impartation 4658

God's love center of h. 4661

great by partaking of God's h. 5290

has good of others as its employment 5739

has honor of God as its end 5739

has humility for its clothing 5739

has love for its essence 5739

height of h. we never dreamed 10391

how little people know who think h. is dull 5750

If 10 percent holy, world converted before year's end 5750

If love does not agree with h. 4755

intense, blazing h. of God 4661

inwrought by Holy Spirit 5742

is conformity to nature, will of God 5758

is irresistible 5750

is only manifested by antagonism 5740

is victory through conflict 5743

Knowledge given to lead us to deeper h. 6693

law reflects God's h. 1530

Lord showing his h. through you 9847

lost interest in h. 10698

means life of Jesus developed in us 5748

means more than sweeping away sin 5748

must be found in Christ Jesus, not in some formula 7105

no detour to h. 5768

not exemption from conflict 5743

not freedom from temptation 5744

not happiness is the end of man 5517

not inability to sin 5745

not the end of progress 5746

perfection of h. in the cross 2096

power to overcome temptation 5744

Prayer the product of h. 8914

progress in h. depends of God's grace, our will 5754

quicken the conscience by the h. of God 12124

Revival is God revealing himself in h. 9745

sinfulness evident contrasted with h. of God 10440

soul that is growing in h. 10568

test of sanctification is not our about h. 9845

the symmetry of the soul 5747

vision of h. of God 4660

which God shares with angels, redeemed men 4658

yes to God means no to things that offend his h. 5755

HOLLOW

experience silence as h. 10253

In the h. of God's palm 8429

masks torn away, h. smiles fade 9741

vanity can give no h. aid 10530

HOLLOWEST

myself, my h. friend, my deadliest foe 2583

HOLLYWOOD

has not recognized what tingles spine 4551

HOLY

all God's attributes are h. 5749

all God's earth is h. ground 7996

As a white candle in a h. place 8125

Ay, call it h. ground 4114

Bible ends with h. city 723

both the natural and the h. are the same 9821

called upon to be h. 1722

can decide to let Jesus make h. 5752

can't live a h. life 5752

Christ came to make men h. 6424

clumsiness better than sinful eloquence 9121

Deep within us, a h. place 1757

desire to be h. rather than happy 10719

evil soul producing h. witness 5011

fear of h. enthusiasm 3184

Feelings all h. when God's hand on rein 4016

Friendship, of itself a h. tie 4240

God created men to be h. 5757

God guiding all that happens to wise, h. end 5389

God h. with absolute holiness 4658

God is h, his love spotless purity 4750

God only is h. 169

grave of one who dies for truth h. ground 11534

great grandfathers called it the h. Sabbath 10952

ground is h. 3199

healthy—completely healthy 5765

heart filled with h. joy must be still 6559

heaven, live h. life, then go see 5660

holiness depends on God's grace, our will to be h. 5754

if I am not h. 8818

If ten lead h. life 5751

impossible for us to be h. 9801

is the way God is 5749

joy of parents in children most h. joy of humanity 5844

life attraction or reproof 5735

life faithful in Christian duty 5736

life is a voice 5735

life is living above world 5736

life not ascetic, gloomy, solitary life 5736

life regulated by divine truth 5736

life speaks when tongue silent 5735

life will produce deepest impression 5737

make man put him back into unholy world 5759

man most humble you can meet 5763

man not one who cannot sin 5762

man one who will not sin 5762

No man should desire to be happy who is not h. 5543

No natural feelings h. in themselves 4016

not more h. if praised 1681

old word for h. also means healthy 5765

people learn way to be made h. 9838

people learned great secret 1293

pretense of being h. until stand in light 9741

put man into unholy world, keep him h. in it 5757

Religion what sinful man tries to do for h. God 9545

Repentance process by which we see God as he is: h. 9594

same root word as *wholly,* means complete 5734

serene, silent beauty of a h. life 5766

Sex a very h. subject 10230

So pious and so h. 10038

stars arise, and the night is h. 11649

takes time to be h. 5738

Things h. revealed only to men who are h. 5769

thought h. men unapproachable 3331

time is quiet 8980

To be h. God does not conform to standard 5749

true Christian ideal not to be happy but h. 5767

union through pain seemed more h. 8269

what is gold doing in a h. place 11853

where sorrow, there is h. ground 10648

with infinite, incomprehensible purity 5749

Worship begins in h. expectancy 12105

Worship ends in h. obedience 12105

HOLY GHOST

able to show wrong without wounding 2078

baptism of H. does not make us wonder-workers 5790

baptism of H. does not mean put into great venture for God 5789

baptism of H. makes us witnesses to Jesus 5790

baptism of H. means we are a satisfaction to Jesus 5789

body is temple of H. 838

cannot imitate being full of H. 5805

Come, H, for moved by thee 648

destroys personal life 5795

fulfilled by gifts of the H. 4749

God baptizes us with H. that he may be all in all 5784

If h. indwelling a man or woman 5782

intercession in us on earth 8859

No one needed to ask if received H. 5806

reveals depths of iniquity 10391

reveals height of holiness 10391

true position of critic 2078

Unlock the truth, thyself the key 648

Unseal the sacred book 648

HOLY GRAIL

Behold! the H. is found 7996

HOLY OF HOLIES

Man's mind is the H. 7759

HOLY SCRIPTURES

God walks in H. 643

tell us how we got here 735

tell us what we are 735

tell us what we are required to do 735

tell us who we are 735

tell us why we are here 735

tell what we could never learn 735

HOLY SPIRIT

activity which is not fruitful in the H. 60

beg H. to fill us while preventing him by our doubts 8843

breaks heart, makes it whole 5794

by inward pressure of H. 6785

cannot be located as guest in house 5796

Christ came to plant in men the H. 6424

Christians ascertain mind of H. 1351

composer and conductor 5799

cried aloud for H. to deliver me 5781

cross presences man with H. 2172

descended in manner that seemed to go through me 5797

do not recognize need of H. for thinking 11243

does not obliterate man's personality 5798

essential for H. to reveal truth 752

expects us to take seriously answers provided 5445

guidance response to moving of H. 5396

If H. is scrutinizing you 894

if not chief energizer of activity 63

imparts efficacy to Word preached 5794

impossible except by power of H. 3222

intellect in darkness until illuminated by H. 7776

invades everything 5796

is stronger than genius 4396

Let H. searchlight go straight down 894

lifts personality to highest use 5798

listen to the gentle movement of the H. 10257

Love is the H. working in us 7244

makes man generous 1064

makes soul tender 5794

makes us one with God 498

may make sad with world's grief 1064

more H. reigns, more intensified the conflict 1629

never known person filled with H. who bragged about it 6018

no rule but personal domination of the H. 5785

not directing churches 525

quickens soul or it would lie dead 5794

recognize necessity of H. for living 11243

restore the flow of the H. 10369

so little oil of H. 1423

sounds which H. weaves together in heavenly harmony 5799

spirits stirred by H. go forward even in sleep 10490

Spirituality means "H. at work" 10711

taught by H. seer rather than scholar 3021

to find H. recognizably present with power 5786

turns life into thoroughfare for God 5795

unites us with God 498

When by the reception of the H. 4889

will make man happy 1064

will make man warmhearted, responsive 1064

will make past as though it had never been 894

will never let man be ashamed 1064

will never let man become gloomy cynic 1064

will never make fool of man 1064

will never make man silly 1064

will put everything right 894

willing to come as pauper, receive H. 5792

without illumination of H. 752

working in, through people who do not profess faith in Christ 5791

works of H. not confined to institutional church 5791

works of the H. unpredictable 5791

HOMAGE

Hypocrisy h. vice pays to virtue 6051

No h. like his praise 4208

HOME

a little h. where grief and care 4921

America's future determined by h, school 5818

Answer, not at h. 8136

As they draw near to their eternal h. 7701

at h. affections are trained 5849

at h. gentle life reaches us 5849

at h. true heaven life reaches us 5849

Awake, asleep, at h, abroad 4876

beauty of character learned at h. 5849

beauty of the h. is order 5851

before God can feel at h. within us 7450

best security of civilization 5835

blessing of the h. is contentment 5851

Body an inn, not a h. 834

but far from h. today 1363

can make experiment 5842

Charity begins at h, should not end there 5822

Christian h. is the Master's workshop 5850

come drifting h. with broken masts and sails 11470

come from God who is our h. 809

crown of the h. is godliness 5851

cultivate valuable things in life 5832

dearer, sweeter spot than all the rest 5834

Death a voyage h. 2249

Death moving from one h. to another 2247

disaster to feel at h. on earth 2975

each lives for the other, all live for God 5837

Education begins at h. 3006

feet may leave, not hearts 5833

glory of the h. is hospitality 5851

God is at h, we are strangers 4562

God's built-in training facility 5854

Good-bye proud world! I'm going h. 2291

grasp him and be led securely h. 6517

great word to master, h. 7000

greatest benefit God has conferred 3895

has not rest at h. in world's hell 5828

heaven is our h, the world our inn 7077

high crime rate traceable to disintegration of h. 5858

I am far from h. 2551

I don't want to go h. in the dark 2454

If beauty in character, will be harmony in the h. 8441

If harmony in the h, order in nation 8441

If we really think h. is elsewhere 2315

If your h. unbearable, maybe you're the bear 5839

indulge in a whim 5842

Inside h, they say, dead decorum, routine 5842

into loveliness, satisfaction of our true h. 6110

is no h. unless food, fire for mind, body 5813

is test of father's leadership 3925

is where life makes up its mind 5832

joys most delightful earth affords 5844

kind of church where God is honored 5853

kind of school where life's basic lessons taught 5853

Let wife make husband glad to come h. 7627

Let your h. be your parish 7847

Life is not our h. 6978

loved by mother means to be at h. 7853

man returns h. to find what he needs 5815

maybe fish goes h. and lies 3426

most of the time we are not at h. 4546

must be lighted up with cheerfulness 5848

must be warmed by affection 5848

must teach what to believe 8333

must teach what to read 8333

need Lord for creation of a h. 5819

neurosis begins at h. 3006

no place like h. except Florida, Mexico, Europe 2877

no synthetic replacement for decent h. life 5858

not a h. church 1447

not one man at church, another at h. 1908

not the one tame place in world of adventure 5842

not where you live, but where they understand you 5830

of the stranger 6468

only place of liberty 5842

outside h. is adventure, variety 5842

Pity h. where everyone the head 5845

quit life as an inn, not a h. 7005

Religion and h. life are supplementary 5858

right temperature at h. maintained by warm hearts 5855

Sad the h. where hen crows, cock silent 5847

seldom solid h. in absence of religious inspiration 5858

should be self-contained shelter of security 5853

Six things requisite to create happy h. 5848

spot of earth supremely best 5834

strength of a nation 5836

sweetest word is h. 11993

The night is dark, I am far from h. 5429

think life is a "wandering to find h." 2315

Thou leadest h. the child of God 2219

Thy h. is with the humble, Lord 6040

to be right in our own h. 6295

to know God is in us is to be at h. 1790

Today, one day nearer h. than ever before 5676

ultimate disaster to feel at h. on earth 2382

used to write h. for money, now calls collect 3896

waking and finding it h. 2399

what father, mother say at h. 8340

When h. is ruled according to God's Word 5862

When in doubt, go h. 11114

when you go there, they have to take you in 5831

where a man can alter arrangements suddenly 5842

where great are small, small are great 5829

where processes of character molding are carried on 5850

where wholesome recreation, simple pleasures enjoyed 5853

who finds peace in his h. 5827

who loves not to rest at h. 7422

who marry to escape unhappy h. 7660

who never stir from h. read only a page 6945

why fear to tread pathway to future h. 6875

wild place in world of rules and set tasks 5842

will not encourage us to mistake inns for h. 7014

woman who creates h. creator second only to God 5857

HOMELAND

as aliens cannot forget true h. 2975

HOMELESS

Send the h, tempest-tossed to me 7985

HOMEOWNER'S

March h. favorite 9888

HOMES

A myriad h, a myriad ways 4834

alcohol, made millions of h. unhappy 331

Christ will turn h. into temples 5529

future of church, humanity depend on family life in h. 3894

Love is needed in the h. 7251

HOMESICK

How many people have you made h. for God 3309

HOMESICKNESS

loneliness a h. for God 7146

yearnings are h. for heaven 7516

HOMEWARD

Life a voyage that's h. bound 6956

HONED

family, where principles are hammered, h. 3863

HONEST

act from h. motives purely 559

advice, if h. also criticism 253

By nature h, by experience wise 11957

differences sign of progress 1624

difficult to be h. with oneself 5880

Gaze on h. effort kindly 4217

Honestly h. in every deed 2028

I keep six h. serving men 6686

joy must be congruous with tragedy 6571

jug never carried under coat for h. reason 2905

Level with child by being h. 8349

love is offering one's most h. self 7337

man hardly knows whether he is h. 145

man not worse because dog barks at him 5866

man's the noblest work of God 5885

may act h. man on the scaffolding 6295

most enviable, the character of an h. man 5881

much easier to be h. with other people 5880

not fit tenant for mind of h. man 11181

People who are brutally h. 5884

repentance, thief becomes h. 9604

spirit not distracted by activity 4307

than h. man thinks of his honesty 6484

There lives more faith in h. doubt 2957

To be h. as this world goes 5867

to be h. is to be one man picked out of a thousand 5867

turn away on grounds too well-dressed to be h. 10086

with ourselves, h. with each other 5871

with yourself a good exercise 5868

HONESTIES

Little h. silent threads of gold 6997

HONESTLY

When h. consider well-being of others 9520

HONESTY

absence of hypocrisy 5874

absence of political games 5874

absence of verbal superficiality 5874

and maturity equally hard to attain 5873

beautiful and refreshing simplicity 5874

builds relationship on less than h. 9447

Doubt is h. 2930

fine jewel, much out of fashion 5875

finest cheating done under guise of h. 5888

first chapter of book of wisdom 5879

He has but one word 5872

looking painful truths in the face 5876

more h. man has, less air of saint 5889

more satisfaction out of brutality than h. 5884

no hidden meanings 5874

no need to manipulate others 5874

no ulterior motives 5874

obedience to law coupled with love, h. 6811

often in the wrong 5877

praised, but left to shiver 5878

principle of 1712

than honest man thinks of his h. 6484

unwillingness to lie to others 5873

Where is there dignity unless h. 2767

Wisdom is h. and knowledge applied through experience 11972

word h. now preceded by old-fashioned 5863

yesterday you got on my nerves 5882

HONEY

dip arrow's point in h. 271

easier to catch flies with h. than vinegar 6643

Licking h. from a thorn 6963

Life the flower of which love is the h. 7205

Lord has given h. with ladle 2728

Lord has given me both vinegar and h. 2728

Love a mixture of h, bitterness 7228

may extract h. from everything 5575

scab is a scab even if smear h. on it 10288

Temptations if overcome a nest of h. 11095

HONEYED

Treachery lurks in h. words 4052

HONOR

aspires to death 2363

being what Jesus was and is 4413

Christian has God's h. at stake 1246

degraded from h, freed from envy 1776

desire to see h. of God advanced 10719

desires honors, not worthy of h. 9203

except to convictions of h, good sense 8548

Give h. or give obloquy 1538

God exalted in h. 4607

great thing expressed in single word 10277

greatest sin to prefer life to h. 6883

Holiness has h. of God as its end 5739

husband and wife one in h. 3868

lose h. rather than conscience 1658

lost, more lost 9263

louder he talked of his h. 5899

love delights in servitude as much as in h. 6457

love weighs actions in scales of his h. 6457

man you h, kind of man you are 1038

Men who have h; men who will not lie 6299

Next to theology I give music highest h. 7914

Our own heart form true h. 5896

reproach better than h. 10875

reward for what he gave 5895

seeks h. that comes from God only 5901

to cultivate reason an h. 9425

We owe God every h. in our power to give 4529

We pay God h. for our own sake 12126

what is good, strong 3940

when h. dies 7442

When our requests h. God 9028

who does not h. wife dishonors himself 7616

will take withholding of h. from men quietly 5901

worthier to preserve than possess h. 5893

HONORED

home, kind of church where God is h. 5853

No person ever h. for what he received 5895

sovereign God wants to be h. for himself 4806

thou art h. above all creatures 9982

HONORING

God out there 1377

HONORS

desires h, not worthy of honor 9203

Dignity consists in deserving h. 2759

Dignity does not consist in possessing h. 2759

given out later 2102

great who cares nothing about h. 5285

immortal h. or everlasting splendors 8483

may go to heaven without h. 9792

of this world are puff, emptiness, peril 5898

True dignity never lost when h. withdrawn 2765

Whatever man h. more than God is idolatry 6076

when receive h. ask what right 10842

HOOFMARKS

see h. going in, none coming out 11119

HOOK

Eve swallowed the h. 4419

HOOKED

up to huge computer 4332

HOPE

A man can counterfeit h. 5989

a more gentle name for fear 5916

a vigorous principle 5917

abounding grace h. of mankind 5203

All h. abandon, ye who enter here 5683

an easier, more pleasant way to journey's end 5924

And cling to h. this, too, shall pass away 6878

animates man to do his utmost 5917

answering prayer for more h. 8804

anticipates promise 9322

As long as hopeful, h. is mere flattery 5903

balm, lifeblood of the soul 5933

bears up mind under sufferings 5930

Bible produces animating h. 738

brightening the darkened paths 5940

By h. kept young of heart 3834

cannot have love apart from faith, h. 3837

carries us on pleasantly to end of life 5934

cheering the lonely way 5940

cherishes no illusions 5928

confident search for a rewarding life 5918

day at hand when advent of God will appear 9909

dazzling, radiant h. 5940

discern rays of h. 3350

discovers what can be done 5928

Do not h. for that not yet come 1786

do not understand h. until confronted with doubts 11620

draws its power from deep trust in God 5928

draws power from basic goodness of mankind 5928

enough to remove anxious fears 1809

evils cured by legislation is delusion 5184

exceedingly deceitful 5924

Faith does not h. 3659

faith must be more than pious h. 3787

faith, h. love, three torches which blend 2586

Faith, h. triumphant say 2985

Faith, key to fit door of h. 3836

fill us afresh with h. 5939

for breaking down barriers 3325

for fairer times in future 10586

for no other life 490

for nothing but spirit of the Holy Jesus 6385

for the best 5911

for tomorrow 11304

force and worth 981

gives poverty of spirit 3834

gives that h. to be thy blessing now 5913

God does not weary of mankind 4896

God planted h. in soul 3973

God shall be my h. 5394

God tipped scales in favor of h. 2130

gospel songs are songs of h. 7890

great thing expressed in single word 10277

great word to master, h. 7000

h. that all will yet be well 5179

Has left his h. with all 5904

has thick skin 5912

highest point we can h. to attain 4976

history teaches us to h. 5944

How deceitful h. may be 5934

humbly then 5913

If h. is cold 8122

if not for h. heart would break 5935

if this world were all man, would lose all h. 8012

In a patient h. I rest 3800

In faith, h. world will disagree 1079

In kingdom of h. there is no winter 5936

In presence of h, faith is born 5937

in the Lord, but exert yourself 5914

is a going forward 5918

is a good breakfast, bad supper 5915

is an adventure 5918

is an echo 5919

is as unreasonable as it is indispensable 5903

is faith holding out its hands in the dark 5920

is free 3838

is grief's best music 5921

is like the sun 5923

is the Christian's anchor 5638

is the stem 3837

keep house open to h. 8345

last thing that dies in man 5924

lies in Man we put on cross 5941

lies not in man we put on moon 5941

Life with Christ an endless h. 5938

lights a candle 5928

like a harebell, trembling from its birth 7179

like clouds, some pass by, others bring rain 5922

lives in h. dances without a fiddle 5909

look to changes with h. 5907

look with h. toward tomorrow 3502

looks for the good in people 5928

Love can h. where reason would despair 7209

Love puts the h. in tomorrow 7269

loving any indulgence better than h. of heaven 6925

major weapon against suicide 5925

makes mind rejoice in sufferings 5930

makes soul exercise patience 5912

means expectancy when otherwise hopeless 5929

means hoping when things are hopeless 11691

more 5604

more h. for sinner than self-conceited saint 5948

mother whispers word of h. 7844

must not be so full of h. of heaven 6108

never give up h. for him 3167

no h. of deliverance cure for degeneration 1613

nor does h. yield to cynicism 5928

O God of h. 5939

of eternal life in the cross 2096

of good use traveling through life 5924

of nation in character of people 5190

of nation not in government 5190

of nation not in justice 5190

of nation not in wisdom of executive 5190

of the dreary 6468

only h. for world 5094

only when everything hopeless h. a strength 5903

opens door where despair closes them 5928

ought to love our Maker without h. of good 4807

physician of every misery 5926

Pray if thou canst with h, but ever pray 8768

precious thing God finds in us 10666

Psalms, rapture of man's h. 798

reaching out for something to come 3835

regards problems as opportunities 5928

renew life with h, courage 9896

resurrection h. derived from no other source 9702

resurrection of Jesus Christ our h. 5945

Sabbath when h. reborn 10959

saves from solicitude 3834

sets the head, heart to work 5917

Spirit of God inspires h. 5800

springs eternal in the human breast 5913

sustaining power of h. 4643

teaches to leave future to God 3834

teaches to trust in God 3834

teaches to work with all energy 3834

that not inspired by h. of heaven 6108

the constancy of faith 5946

the only cheap, universal cure 5932

things not in hand 3833

thinks nothing difficult 5931

those we h. to be with in eternity 4252

thou beggar's wealth 5932

thou captive's freedom 5932

thou lover's victory 5932

thou sick man's health 5932

Though h. be weak or sick with long delay 8768

ties itself yonder, yonder 5919

Tribulation: God's fastest road to h. 225

vague, tenuous h. God too kind to punish 4726

vaguely but dread precisely 5949

vision and task is h. of world 11730

What change thou bringest to hopeless 5940

What God is in himself is our h. 4587

When h. ends, God's begins 302

where there is despair, h. 9086

who has h. has everything 5910

who has health has h. 5910

Who will not grieve when deprived of h. 2616

will endure all things of right kind 5912

will endure many a blow 5912

will put on patience as a vestment 5912

will wade through sea of blood 5912

wishing for a thing to come true 5927

withers away 7291

without thankfulness lacking in perception 11154

word God has written on brow of every man 5947

HOPED

received all that he h. for 8806

results will exceed anything he may have h. 7564

surprised by having them perform better than you had h. 9469

to be able to do without God 5395

HOPEFUL

As long as matters h, hope is mere flattery 5903

man sees success where others see failure 5943

men I have seen succeed always h. 10816

world h. in prospects 10512

HOPELESS

alcohol, changed men into h. parasites 331

an endless road, a h. maze 8638

Hope means expectancy when otherwise h. 5929

hope means hoping when things are h. 11691

no h. situations 5953

only people who have grown h. about them 5953

only when everything h, hope a strength 5903

out of h. attempt has come human history 5570

task of overcoming evil never h. 3378

What change thou bringest to h. 5940

when you say situation h. 5955

without Christ a h. end 5938

Without faith man becomes h. 3824

HOPELESSLY
strive to invent happiness apart from God 5570

HOPELESSNESS
fear puts h. at heart of life 3965

is anticipated defeat 5951

HOPES
adversity not without comforts and h. 247

alone God's h. made known 10532

before grave all h. dissolve 1163

cannot build h. on confusion, misery, death 8445

each failure of our h. 4578

Great h. make great men 5277

heart numbed too much for h, fears 2587

Human h. and human creeds 2029

Lord lets us see wreck of h. 351

make adjustments in light of h. for growth 3060

people think with h, fears rather than minds 7763

This day with h. and invitations 8375

to give credence to h. beyond grave 5711

Tomorrow h. we've learnt from yesterday 11403

we promise according to our h. 5950

while my best h. lie shattered 11470

HOPING
hope means h. when things are hopeless 11691

Love is h. in God 7246

my willing and h. are optimistic 8247

HOPPY
croppy, droppy 9876

HORIZON
death is only a h. 6097

God's permission means no doubt on h. 5402

How boundless might soul's h. be 11627

nothing save limit of sight 6097

out there beyond the eyes' h. 6111

Prayer enlarges our h. 8906

squalls surge across everyone's h. 191

HORIZONS
cannot reach distant h. 4544

soul has further h. than early mornings 7539

HORIZONTAL
Knowledge is h. 11928

HORN
Never blow your own h. 9222

who blows own h. has everyone dodging when he approaches 9242

HORNS
ass went seeking for h, lost ears 2872

jealous man's h. hang in his eyes 6337

Lighthouses blow no h, only shine 5737

HORRIBLE
cease to be h. experiences 181

how h. sins look committed by someone else 10343

serve as h. example 3446

HORRIFIED
by dreadfulness of own sin 10297

HORROR
Dead Sea makes h. 10195

miserable when old age looks back with h. 8182

of abortion 18

of pious types 5791

paralyzed with h. for minutes 11741

HORRORS
And h. hast thou driv'n me 1694

men have perpetrated h. against one another 2667

HORSE
golden bit does not make better h. 11793

No h. gets anywhere until harnessed 2852

ride a h, sit close and tight 9471

sell a blind h, praise the feet 2466

Trouble rides a fast h. 11462

HORSE-NERVOUSNESS
Men a mixture of h, ass-stubborness, camel-malice 7420

HORSES
turn mice into h. 1122

HOSPITABLE
to the stranger, God is h. 4649

HOSPITAL
All the world is a h. 12030

church h. for sinners 1379

HOSPITALITY
glory of the home is h. 5851

one form of worship 5958

test for godliness 5957

Unwelcomed vistors bring blessings 832

Who practices h. entertains God 5961

HOSPITALS
Love is needed in the h. 7251

HOST
Comfort lingers to become a h. 7361

love of God not care of h. for guests 4792

son should treat father as h. 3891

HOSTILE
Hammer away ye h. hands 7875

many moments h. to truth 11551

person lives in a h. world 9441

time grows meaner, more h. 3268

universe is not h. 11648

whose attitude toward me uncertain, h. 7102

HOSTILITY
kindness causes h. to evaporate 6668

live with h, learn to be angry, fight 1114

problem not h. to church 1446

suffering enough to disarm all h. 3161

HOT
And heated h. with burning fears 2599

believe in getting into h. water 11435

Either be h. or cold 4920

Envy's a coal come hissing h. from hell 3216

heads never solved anything 385

in h. water, teakettle sings 205

man can blow h, cold with same breath 6054

Self-control, keep cool while someone making it h. for you 9961

soul h. for certainties 946

summer's too h. 9879

tempers cool friendships 9488

too h. to do job that was too cold last winter 9902

trouble like h. weather 11431

words scorch people 11985

HOTHEADS
Doomed are the h. 379

right temperature at home not maintained by h. 5855

HOUND OF HEAVEN
God comes padding after me like H. 4534

HOUR
awful h. when necessity of hiding comes 5480

can lose friend in h. 4305

dependent on God from h. to h. 5226

enjoy the fugitive h. 11373

except when busy, then needs h.
8790

Expedients are for h. 1009

favorite h. of asceticism, midnight
467

For I also had my h. 2980

from h. to h, we rot and rot
11302

from h. to h. we ripe and ripe
11302

God never gives strength for h.
2722

going to bed for h. after luncheon
9531

harmful to think prayer
something to do during free h.
10211

Has but an h. of breath 11519

hot stove for minute seems like h.
9527

I need thy presence every passing
h. 5225

If knew everything, could not
endure existence for single h.
6081

in h. of need faith born within
3820

in one short h. learn more from
God 4964

last h. of body, but not of soul
2225

last h. of my life 109

Life is dust nature lends man for
an h. 6960

look forward without fear to
appointed h. 2225

Lord, grant that my last h. be my
best 2332

Lord, what a change within us
one short h. 8867

may die in h. of unwise word
4237

morning h. has gold in its hand
11318

my h. from three to four each
morning 8794

nothing so uncertain as h. of death
2341

of departure has arrived 2378

of pain long as day of pleasure
149

Oft the cloud which wraps
present h. 10879

One far fierce h, and sweet 2980

One h. of justice worth hundred
of prayer 6617

one short h. to win victories 3293

Pray one h. before going to war
7650

pretty girl for h. seems like minute
9527

rash hand in evil h. 10314

rate of sixty minutes an h. 4327

reputation of thousand years
determined by conduct of one h.
9625

Safe in temptation's h. 4490

struts, frets his h. upon the stage
6994

than spend quarter h. meditating
7716

Time and the h. runs through
darkest day 10585

Truth, its h. is now, always 11558

wake at three, live an h. with God
8794

when busy a full h. is needed 7710

when faith in future becomes
knowledge of past 7435

when the dying h. comes, there
will be dying grace 6912

Why all this toil for triumphs of
an h. 7088

worrying on our knees is not
prayer 9009

HOUR'S

Half an h. listening essential 7710

HOURS

being with God for all
twenty-four h. 6569

can sit and look at work for h.
12009

childhood chews h, swallows
minutes 12193

Christianity, living 24 h. with
Christ 1180

could add two h. to my working
day 9531

darkest h. have some intent 4885

God does not keep office h. 4590

God gives me gift of 24 h. day
11296

greatest events our stillest h.
10268

have no time to sport away the h.
11287

Idle h. breed wandering thoughts
6760

if did not spend h. each day in
prayer 8816

in dreams act part learned in
waking h. 2966

invest few extra h. in quiet
reverence 9906

Lost, two golden h. 11306

obliging alike at all h. 4204

of absentee, perfect job 3121

Old age lives minutes slowly, h.
quickly 12193

place all h. of day at his disposal
10120

Pray three h. before getting
married 7650

Pray two h. before going to sea
7650

Soft drowsy h. creeping 1123

spend sixteen h. daily thinking
about world 7491

To ruinate proud buildings with
thy h. 11344

To untell the days, to redeem
these h. 9568

will take care of themselves 2787

with happy prospects in view
pleasing 3508

Within one of his h. 4521

HOUSE

A little h. well filled 5814

all her h. and land 4379

Anyone can build a h. 5819

become h. builders through
building houses 6620

Better hundred enemies outside h.
than one inside 5820

box in suburbs called a h. 5859

broad, hard-beaten road to h.
2776

Christ is head of this h. 5823

Death going to Father's h. 2249

divided cannot stand 1620

God may send tempest about h.
4775

good laugh sunshine in h. 5812

Hatred like burning down own h.
to get rid of rat 5596

he lives in sadly dilapidated 8142

in this world as in another man's
h. 7077

keep h. open to hope 8345

like building h. on foundations of
sand 7796

loving any h. better than h. of God
6925

Many who have gold in h.
looking for copper outside
5840

not happier for your being a
Christian 3872

on a rock 189

on the sand 189

ornaments of h. are friends who
frequent it 4206

sets my h. on fire to roast his eggs
10057

Since the h. is on fire 43

The h. where I was born 2588

To a friend's h. road never long
4287

When h. doth sigh, weep 1514

where room in heart, room in h.
5960

HOUSE OF PRAYER

Go thou and seek the H. 8006

HOUSEHOLD

should show itself first in own h.
5838

HOUSELESS

simless Cain 10573

HOUSES

erect h. of worship, but our
shrines are our place of business
6068

Gossips set on fire all h. they enter
5137

many h, life a failure 8629

trying to live serene lives in h.
divided against themselves 6068

HOUSETOP

proclaim virtues of friend on h.
4183

HOUSEWORK

From h. to heights of prayer 6113

HOVEL
palace without affection a poor h.
5816

HOW
And h. and when and where 1855
And H. and Where and Who 6686
learned to obey will know h. to
command 6792
man flung without h. or why into
world 3495
Politics, h. who gets what, when,
why 5186
question about miracle, not h. it
happened but why 6500
Why and h. is God to be loved
7574
without limit is h. God is to be
loved 7574

HOWL
devil only knows how to h. 2676
goes with wolves learns to h. 9458
Ye storms h. out his greatness
4712

HUB
like trying to make wheel without
h. 4632
planet ball-bearing in h. of
universe 11633

HUES
actions take their h. from the heart
103

HUG
Authentic men aren't afraid to h.
children 3916
If you h. resentment against
anybody 9634

HUGS
God h. you 4753

HULA-HOOPS
Cheerios, h. for ants 8650

HUMAN
aching abyss of h. heart 5338
Almighty does make use of h.
agencies 4949
Almighty intervenes in h. affairs
4949
as much a part of h. race as
greatest 9988
beings must be known to be loved
4762
Beware of believing h. life simple
10653
Bible contains all h. weaknesses,
strengths 701
Bible page torn out of volume of
h. life 706
Bible treats us as h. life, roughly
724
Bible, compendium of h.
experience 701
Bible, gallery of h. portraits 703
Bible, most h. book 701
Bible, never deals with domains of
h. minds 721
Bible, the whole h. drama 750
blood all one color 907

broken reed of h. support 3132
By strides of h. wisdom 11916
cannot reconcile Bible with h.
origin 736
cannot treat h. embryo as cheap
24
changing conditions that cause h.
suffering 7725
cheer the soul tired with h. strife
7917
civil government boundaries for h.
behavior 5177
comfort vain, short 1501
commandments not made to h.
nature 1521
compassion kindled 10640
conclude h. affairs not governed
by God 3349
cracked chimes of courageous h.
spirit 7171
Cross, the most extreme of all h.
conditions 6277
deepest principle in h. nature 3141
devil's field of battle is h. heart
2691
difficulty inherent in h. condition
8569
disappeared if within predatory h.
hands 3202
easily comprehended by h. reason
9411
emotion to be consecrated to God
6728
emotions part of h. condition
3058
extraordinary mystery of h.
goodness 5037
failure with h. material 3120
faith no merit where h. reason
provides proof 3665
Faith stands above h. system 3670
Faith sustains h. dignity 3666
family, basic unit of h.
organization 3880
family, first school of h. instruction
3880
fear power of evil in h. heart 3376
Flesh is Bible's word for
unperfected h. nature 9926
foundation of h. excellence 11720
freedom precious thing 9463
funny thing, this h. nature 5974
God cannot be comprehended in
h. words 4682
God designed h. machine to run
on himself 7459
God has gone through whole of h.
experience 6386
God has preoccupied rarest h.
spirits 7547
God negates h. ordering of life
5395
God's actions above h. sciences
5237
God's principles not replaced in
favor of h. calculation 7828
God, author of h. weakness 230
good h. race has experienced was
trouble for somebody 11459

grace directed toward h. debt,
demerit 5206
great mystery of h. life 7101
grow so wide, deep nothing h. is
strange 10540
Have their hopes in h. needs 2029
Heroes, mixture of divine, h. 755
Hope springs eternal in the h.
breast 5913
hopes and h. creeds 2029
If h. beings as wise as animals
5963
If we try to find lasting joy in h.
relationship 9467
If your h. plan and calculation
184
improvement from within outward
1017
in eternity h. ideals fall short 1163
in lowly raiments of h. flesh 6371
In spiritual matters, h. reasoning
not in order 9416
in the endurance of h. soul 3150
intellect can never comprehend
spirit 10692
intellect, an awesome work of God
7776
into inner dynamics of h. organism
9353
Jesus shed more light on things h.
than philosophers 6449
Laughter and weeping, intensest
forms of h. emotion 6728
learn about h. nature 753
life but a series of footnotes 6904
life resembles iron 6905
logic strives in vain 2636
Loneliness central fact of h.
existence 7137
Lord understood h. predicament
6519
Love for Lord intensest of which
h. heart capable 7221
majesty of h. suffering 10854
make h. life tolerable in world
4999
mercy is God's goodness
confronting h. misery 5206
mind like an umbrella 7770
mind, uneasiness about Uncreated
4614
Mirth wine of h. life 6739
nature like drunk peasant 5968
nature sticking nose into other
people's business 5147
Never does h. soul appear so
strong 4095
no feeling in h. heart that exists in
that heart alone 4019
no government capable of
contending with h. passions
5196
no h. birth compare to
supernatural birth 874
no h. condition which divine
presence does not penetrate
6277
No one can resign from h. race
5977

No two h. beings make same journey in life 6202

None of our h. talents are significant to God 4527

not h. repression of sin 10717

not to have had pain is not to have been h. 8263

O sad estate of h. wretchedness 8877

one essential condition of h. existence 12117

One half the h. race 8863

only two or three h. stories 5984

our understanding is h. to the core 11606

out of hopeless attempt has come h. history 5570

passing judgment on all h. life 24

perfection of h. expression achieved 740

personality written, signed by God 6183

politics based on premise society must be changed 10528

potential capacity of h. heart 5625

Prayer girds h. weakness with divine strength 8912

principles of Bible groundwork of h. freedom 5965

problems gray areas 1582

problems never greater than divine solutions 9285

props have been knocked out 184

Psalms, songs of h. soul 797

reaching beyond boundaries of h. efforts 10540

recognize no rights but h. rights 3230

redemption of Jesus can satisfy aching of h. soul 6402

responsibility for h. conduct rests with "I" 579

return good for good h. 4102

Revival, God intervenes to lift situation out of h. hands 9746

safety for h. race to follow Bible 744

salvation of h. souls the real business of life 7027

Salvation the incoming into h. nature of characteristics of God 9811

same heart beats in every h. breast 917

Self indestructible by h. means 9943

selfishness means stopping at h. limits 10067

Slander cud eschewed by h. cattle 10470

small change of h. happiness 3143

soul can rise up against odds 3621

soul is God's treasury 10666

soul is a silent harp in God's choir 7921

soul so mysterious 10667

soul, life too complex to touch 10653

spirit to grow strong by conflict 2715

stop depending on inadequate h. resources 184

stories go on repeating themselves 5984

such mature insights into h. nature 6196

that stands over me the h. insect 4526

things must be known to be loved 7180

thinks he's a h. dynamo 118

to demand justice 1207

to do good is h. 5085

To err is h. 7065

To fall into sin is h. 10408

To find God greatest h. achievement 7542

to keep what one has 1207

To love for the sake of being loved is h. 7325

to think wisely, act foolishly 5973

Tolerance respect for another because he is h. 11399

true heroes of the h. race 6199

Truth friend more excellent than h. friend 11560

value only the penultimate value 11663

voice, the perfect instrument 7893

wants which disturb h. life 2861

way from God to h. heart is through h. heart 3334

ways of conceiving abyssal All 4580

Were works of God understandable by h. reason 4510

When h. strength gives way 4569

where h. will leaves, divine grace begins 5200

Wherever God rules h. heart as King 4736

Why doubt the h. seed 2350

windows clouded with h. fancies 2936

Without God h. reliance is vain 5411

you are h, not an angel 11722

HUMAN BEING

blessing if h. blind, deaf for few days 824

cannot turn h. from destiny 2618

complexity, mystery of a h. 4247

death brings h. to individuality 2353

Democracy releases energies of every h. 2527

divine light in every h. 7561

Don't brood, a h. not hen 2542

every h. is my neighbor 8056

In comparison with loving h. 7195

ingenious assembly of plumbing 833

intended to have own character 1008

more complex than social system 10505

no h. can be permanent source of happiness to another 9481

recognize Jesus Christ in every h. 914

relationship to another h. requires nourishment 9446

to flea, mosquito h. something good to eat 9219

To live through sorrow with another h. 10641

HUMAN BEINGS

bearable when defenses are down 892

bearable when helpless, humbled 892

cease to reach to h. as source of life, help 7548

degenerate caricatures of h. 3881

demands satisfaction from other h. they cannot give 9496

God cannot control h. 5983

God cannot simply thrust h. aside 5983

like nothing else in nature 5983

loneliness knowledge that h. incapable of bringing help 7126

Never underestimate ability of h. to get tangled up 5976

No two h. make same journey in life 5978

pain of fellow h. 10540

skinned alive by fire or heat 11741

tend to look at fellow h. as enemies 10531

wild animals when born 7382

with h. butterfly turns into caterpillar 7392

years of patience to tame young h. 7382

HUMAN EXISTENCE

Christians to give new flavor to h. 1271

HUMAN NATURE

cannot meet Christ's demands 1223

clings to man with such persistance 5974

craving to be appreciated 440

Crime is inherent in h. 2034

Jesus Christ never trusted h. 2184

Man's failure to conquer h. tragic 7414

to grumble in the morning 439

HUMAN RACE

God redeemed h. when we were spitting in his face 9434

imagination of h. poured out like river 2023

lifted up by Christianity 1187

playing at children's games from the beginning 5982

HUMANIST

limitations of h. geocentric thinking 1168

HUMANITARIAN
not satisfied by religion merely h.
9546

HUMANITY
A sweet new blossom of h. 804
advances or retreats 5969
automobile travelling without
  lights at terrific speed 5970
beautiful garden of h. 3234
beautiful when praying 4086
begin to lose our h. 7481
but one race, h. 1482
Christ, exaltation of h. 6441
creation to punish h. 3191
easier to love h. as a whole 5972
faking evidence for the sake of h.
  7836
future of church and h. depend on
  family life 3894
glad when great man reassures us
  of his h. 5307
God cannot get h. out of his mind
  5983
God, my Brother in his h. 7951
If love Jesus Christ will serve h.
  10156
In the h. of Jesus, God speaking
  our language 6135
is an ocean 5988
joy of parents in children most
  holy joy of h. 5844
law of h. that man know good
  through evil 5030
life of h. is so long 5944
Lord keeps door open for h. 459
message of God to h. 5089
might think love of h. safe 7836
moralist sees city as microcosm of
  h. 10522
most beneficial therapy God
  granted h. 6733
must not expect friend to be
  above h. 4237
must not lose faith in h. 5988
my rightful place in the procession
  of h. 9074
never discover full richness of
  your h. 8634
never stands still 5969
poor were not for divinity that
  stirs within us 5979
prayer relates own needs to needs
  of h. 8917
smiles are to h. 6745
to cheat of kinship with h. 8334
torn asunder bond that binds h. to
  God 8967
two poles of simplicity, complexity
  7383
Violence a crime against h. 11678
Violence goes against truth of our
  h. 11678
war is h. hanging itself on cross of
  iron 11745
What you give to h. you get back
  10742
With the blood, tears of h. 3369

HUMANITY'S
most valuable assets, the
  nonconformists 9311

HUMANIZE
tender tears that h. the soul 5349

HUMANIZED
a deep distress has h. my soul
  10830

HUMANIZING
authority for h. society 10506

HUMANKIND
All of creation God gives to h.
  3191

HUMANLY
to live separated life h. impossible
  10717
To put sin out of life h. impossible
  10717

HUMANNESS
is realization of love 5014
Whenever relationships diminish
  h. there is evil 5014

HUMANS
Wisdom impossible for h. to
  manufacture 12127

HUMBLE
adversities help us to be h. 187
and a contrite heart 6036
And range with h. lives in content
  6016
and self-forgetting we must be
  5092
begin by being h. 5997
Between h. heart and majesty of
  heaven, no barriers 8771
Christ Jesus always found among
  h. people 5992
confirmed pride when you think
  you are h. 9259
Destroys the mighty, the h. spares
  4505
difficult to be h. if always
  successful 3603
Don't be so h. you're not that
  great 5998
enough to bow before mystery of
  human being 4247
Give us a h. heart 9058
God chastises with failure to h. us
  3603
He that is h. ever shall 6001
heart that I may hear thee 7458
holy man most h. you can meet
  5763
humility makes no pretence of
  being h. 6041
I would be h. for I know my
  weakness 1018
instrument in hands of heavenly
  Father 5411
involves willingness to be
  reckoned failure 5993
Love is h. 7246
man counts blessings 6035
man or woman depending on God
  has explanation 7753

mind is soil of which thanks grows
  5258
No contemplation will h. more
  than thoughts of God 4745
no great thing to be h. when
  brought low 6019
no life so h. it cannot reflect God's
  light 7055
Only h. have resources to give of
  themselves 5957
only when we know we are God's
  children 6042
person changed humiliation into
  humility 6007
pie, never tasty 429
receives praise the way clean
  window takes light of sun 6033
repentance much harder than
  eating h. pie 9577
repentance, proud becomes h.
  9604
spiritually h. who know what
  peace is 8447
stay h. 5391
There's a star to guide the h. 5995
They that know God will be h.
  6039
Thy home is with the h, Lord
  6040
way to be h. is not to stoop 6037
When feelings are h. give thanks
  3051
When feelings h. give thanks 4013
when praised a rare attainment
  6019
when soul becomes h. 7971
wisdom is h. that he knows no
  more 6695

HUMBLED
another thing to be h. 9581
Human beings bearable when
  helpless, h. 892
value of being h. 6007
Youth not yet h. by life 12181

HUMBLER
After crosses, losses, men grow h.
  and wiser 5990

HUMBLES
fault which h. of more use 3931

HUMBLEST
Christian has that which is
  impossible to world 10512
family, where h. succeed 3886
highest service prepared for in h.
  surroundings 10190
Praise will transform h. dwelling
  to a hallowed heaven 5846

HUMBLY
Hope h. then 5913

HUMDRUM
discern God in h. commonplace
  10721
However h. life may be 8440

HUMILIATED
When h, grace is on the way 6007

HUMILIATING
cross God sends of necessity h. 2092
cross we bear seems h. 2116

HUMILIATION
God has gone through human experience of h. 6386
humble person changed h. into humility 6007
Nothing great done without h. 10875

HUMILITIES
Contentment, result of h. 1807

HUMILITY
at peace when all around is trouble 6010
Before thee in h. 4021
Bible produces h. 738
Christ Jesus came to world clothed in h. 5992
Common sense shines with double lustre when set in h. 5994
companion of truth is h. 11535
covers our good deeds 6005
Denying we can accomplish God's work not h. 9199
depth of capacity for h. 8403
easiest way to dignity is h. 6031
exhibition of the spirit of Jesus Christ 6013
extremism, haughtiness of h. 3557
failure to keep us in state of h. 3603
from which all heavenly virtues shoot 6015
Girded for war, h. his mighty dress 6124
God desires but h. 7450
Holiness has h. for its clothing 5739
humble person changed humiliation into h. 6007
is a divine veil 6005
is a most strange thing 6006
is never to be irritated, disappointed 6010
is nothing but truth 6009
is path to glory 6034
is quiet, not speechless 6012
is strong, not bold 6012
is sure, not arrogant 6012
is the quiet valley, abounding in life 6026
is to be at rest when blamed, despised 6010
is to be at rest when nobody praises 6010
is to expect nothing 6010
is to have no trouble 6010
is to wonder at nothing 6010
key to success 10799
Lay first foundation of h. 6788
learn how to view others with h. 10306
makes men as angels 6020
makes no pretence of being humble 6041
meet affliction with h. 296

more we pursue h. more distant it becomes 6008
more worthy, more h. will be seen 5991
necessary prerequisite for grace 6007
never gained by seeking 6008
never so proud as when striking attitude of h. 9187
not doubt of own power 6032
nothing more awful than conscious h. 6038
Nothing sets person out of devil's reach as h. 6024
of God is a hard thing to accept 4683
perfect quietness of heart 6010
Perfection in h. ingredient of prayer 8914
pride that apes h. 9192
proud in h, proud they are not proud 9252
recognizing God and others responsible for my achievements 6011
scarcely ever utters words of h. 6041
self-righteousness instead of h. 10359
test of great man is his h. 6032
that low, sweet root 6015
think first about foundations of h. 5997
think you have h, you have lost it 6006
to make right estimate of one's self 6014
To think we have h. evidence we don't 6008
Too much h. is pride 9255
touchstone of saintliness 6013
treat information with h. 6706
very difficult to counterfeit h. 5989
where not a childlike h. at starting post 11549
with h. talk to God as to your Father 4924
word thanksgiving prompts h. 11153

HUMOR
makes all things tolerable 6719
pole that adds balance 6715
Quotations tell of h. 9385
sunshine of the mind 6718

HUMORLESS
By starving emotions we become h. 3050

HUMOROUS
life more h. than most of us think 6918
white man's notion he is less savage 1494

HUNDRED
Better h. enemies outside house than one inside 5820

evil actions should be forgotten 4074
first h. years the hardest 6992
injures one, threatens a h. 10450
One act of obedience better than h. sermons 8109
One father worth more than h. schoolmasters 3923
One joy dispels a h. cares 6555
Victory finds a h. fathers 2516

HUNDREDS
do not often do much 91
of tiny threads sew people together 7608
prayed h. of times for Lord to heal me 5610

HUNDREDTH
time I am right 2775

HUNG
When Christ h, bled, died 7173

HUNGER
a suitable comrade for work-shy 6759
better to die of h. 3979
devil changes h. for God into haste 7512
for God, devil rides it, spurs it on 7512
I perish with h. 10676
I tasted, it made me h. and thirst 7473
If any chance to h, Christ is bread 6391
more explosive than atomic weaponry 8692
O what a happy h. 9780
presupposes existence of bread 4606
soul's h. for prayer 4643
speed is to distract h. for God 7512
theft from those who h. 11745
threat to stability of world is h. 8692

HUNGERING
begin by h. for God 4802

HUNGERS
Our nature h. for God 7512

HUNGRY
blessings for man h. for goodness 5299
bread you store up belongs to h. 11855
Faith when h, genuine 3711
touching of God makes us h, yearning 5764
when h. came to Christ 10731
while children go h, I'll fight 3342

HUNT
Don't h. through church for a hypocrite 6053

HUNTED
Self-repect cannot be h. 9995

HUNTER
approval to publicity h. who seeks
headlines 5891

HUNTS
He who h. for flowers will find
flowers 5140
Spirit of God h. our spirit 5764

HUNTSMAN
Jesus like some moral h. 6421

HURLED
whose vigor h. 6139

HURLY-BURLY
learn patience by going into h.
world 8422

HURRICANE
in the h. you shall see God's form
298

HURRY
desert of everyday h. and strain
10247
Don't h, don't worry 9530
God does not h. 2846
God is never in a h. 4456
God whispering, do not hear
because of h. 4968
impatience marks of the amateur
6113
In divine things there is never h.
5581
is not a divine thing 5581
Jesus never in a h. 4425
life causes as it rushes on 10273
neglected in life's h. and bustle
12114
never give impression we care
when in a h. 7327
not of the devil, is the devil 5579
Our Adversary majors in h. 121
People in a h. cannot think, grow,
decay 5584
To think clearly without h. or
confusion 6913
Whoever is in a h, thing he is
about too big for him 5592
why people today are in such a h.
7512
with breathless haste, h. past
happiness 8601

HURRYING
parted by the h. world 10578
What's use of h. when 5591

HURT
always to heal and never h. 6519
charity is patience when
neighbor's h. 1085
Charity is silence when words
would h. 1085
children of God, persecuting God
2084
don't be alone in h. 1516
don't invest much, defeat doesn't
h. 2629
emotions in subconscious minds
to h. us 3061
found by One who had himself
been h. by the archers 9798

God will not h. godly 3996
Grief, helping you feel
compassion for others who h.
5334
he is wealthy who can lose
without h. 8637
If never h. by statement of Jesus
6407
isn't the fact your're h. that counts
11446
It h. that he didn't say good-bye
2208
many stay walled up afraid of
being h. 4290
more compassion for others who
h. 10610
Never report what may h. another
10459
people by being too busy 129
power of love makes them h.
10897
reactions to enemy h. more than
enemy 3175
Satan cannot h. godly 3996
Shriveling h. until sun drew forth
from the ache a leaf 5368
something Christ wants to h. to
death 6407
things that h. instruct 10916
To speak kindly does not h. tongue
11421
topsoils of h. are shoved away
8468
Truth may h. but it cures 11580
unless greater h. to conceal 10459
When Real, you don't mind being
h. 5886
When you find a h. and heal it
10216

HURTING
h. ourselves more 2084
Holy Ghost able to show wrong
without h. 2078
If too afraid to admit you are h.
9211

HURTS
allow to change us 970
anyway you grasp it, it h. 10330
arrogant person h. himself 451
cross h. where disarmed,
vulnerable 2092
death, as lover's pinch which h.
2387
He h. himself, not you 6287
in life h, trials 970
it is justice that h. 6267
mistaking weakness for strength
10749
Only heart that h. has right to joy
6571
our Lord saw people's h. 6519
to leave yourself at the cross h.
10048
way you and I respond to h. 3319

HUSBAND
and wife one in honor, influence,
affection 3868
Christ a H. to protect 6370

deaf h, blind wife happy couple
7589
dog is still competition for a h.
7611
good h. makes a good wife 7590
good wife makes a good h. 7592
ideal wife has an ideal h. 7600
let h. make wife sorry to see him
leave 7627
never seems to question choice of
h. 7655

HUSBANDS
and wives should constantly
guard against overcommitment
7617
if h. imitated a few of dog's virtues
7611
in heaven whose wives chide not
7618
wives try to tell h. of troubles
3904

HUSH
ghastly h. descend upon earth
1852

HUSHED
are the stars, whose power never
spent 8014
until the busy world is h. 9105

HUSTLED
Almighty not h. by peevish
impetuosity 8419

HUT
meanest h. with love a palace for
the soul 5816

HYMN
Each smile a h. 7284
nature h. of praise to God 8001
song no longer a discord but a h.
divine 7451
sudden pause in choral h. of our
lives 7056

HYMNS
I disliked their h. 1455
sing h, choruses for God's ears
alone 8424
test of sanctification not singing
pious h. 9845
What else can I do but sing h. to
God 8745
Worship isn't singing h. 12139

HYPOCHONDRIACS
more talk out of a minor pain
3422

HYPOCRISY
Adolescents quickest to discern h.
12162
different names for h. 4115
homage vice pays to virtue 6051
Honesty, an absence of h. 5874
meanest word is h. 11993
not h. to rejoice in distress 221
prejudice with a halo 6052
Without h. no new power can
arise 8722

HYPOCRITE
Better be sinner than h. 6049
no fault of Christianity that h. sins
1208
who hides behind h. smaller than
h. 6046

HYPOCRITES
always room for one more 6050
doesn't attend because h. do 1397
Don't stay away from church
because there are h. 6050
greatest dupes devil has 6055
If devil ever laughs, must be a h.
6055
in church, lodge, at home 6053
make the number one less 6053
more likely we are all h. 912
We are not h. in our sleep 6066

HYPOCRITICAL
to pretend, phoney and h. 5890

HYPOTHESIS
To find point where h. and fact
meet 7435

HYSTERICAL
God never does anything h. 9912

HYSTERICS
God never produces h. 9912

I

I
Myself and I, and mine and my
1855
responsibility for human conduct
rests with I 579

ICE
Sin like i. in our pipes 10369
sun makes i. melt 6668

IDEA
As blind man no i. of colors 4986
Bible i. of sacrifice 9762
Christianity, not i. in air 1174
forgiveness beautiful i. 4104
fundamental i. of good 5044
more useful than an i. 88
not slave, not master i. of
democracy 2520
of a God perfect as they could
imagine 4504
of the infinite torments me 3275
often refuse to accept i. 9516
shock part that makes an i. an i.
2013
that isn't dangerous hardly worth
calling i. 2013
that our will subjected to God's
control not easy to accept 5467
Truth, having same i. God has
11554
What i. of God without the sky
4512
Who has ever seen an i. 615
willing to pursue i. wherever it
may lead 11007

world breath of one eternal i.
4594

IDEAL
Character lost when i. sacrificed
999
child would find no fitness in
world 8293
Do not try to produce i. child
8293
method of time management
11466
not to be happy, but holy 5767
vowed never to marry until found
i. woman 7665
which leads to despair 6401
wife has an i. husband 7600
woman was waiting for i. man
7665
Youth i. state if came later in life
12187

IDEALISTIC
Young people cynical because i.
12179

IDEALS
alone God's i. made known 10532
Bible holds i. for weakest, noblest
702
in eternity human i. fall short
1163
love you for your i. 4248
make adjustments in light of our i.
3060

IDEAS
clear that have same degree of
confusion 8491
Darkness more productive of i.
2541
do not make i. of contentment
and aspiration quarrel 471
Great minds talk about i. 1845
greatest i. born from womb of
silence 10269
I borrowed i. from Socrates 2019
I stand for are not mine 2019
I stole i. from Jesus 2019
I swiped i. from Chesterfield 2019
Instead of substituting new i. 9743
isms convert health i. into
ideologies 9952
legalism, lynching of new i. 6817
not brains that matter, but
progressive i. 1027
of contentment and aspiration fast
friends 471
of truth not everlasting 11207
Perception of i. rather than storing
3021
theology i. of truth classified,
arranged 11207
universities stamp civilization
with own i. 3040
When grappling with i. radical
enough 12157
willing to make i. accessible
11007
Words nails for fixing i. 12000

IDENTICAL
finger of God never leaves i.
fingerprints 4497
if all returned God i. worship
6169

IDENTIFIED
allow emotions to rise to be i.
3060
Lord came down from the mount
to be i. with sin 6488
with Christ in crucifixion 2138
with Christ in resurrection 2138

IDENTIFY
in suffering i. with Jesus 10930
joy when we i. our own thoughts
11253
traditions i. family as unique 3876
with others who fight battles on
their knees 8865

IDENTIFYING
Prayer i. oneself with the divine
will 8922

IDENTITY
consciousness gain i. Jesus had
9840
fringe benefit of Christian, sense
of i. 1266
individualism distorts joy of i.
9952
lose consciousness of own i. 9840
lose our nature i. 9840

IDEOLOGIES
isms convert healthy ideas into i.
9952

IDEOLOGY
communism an insidious i. 9952
into vacuum some kind of i. 8351

IDIOT
Any i. can face a crisis 6876

IDLE
bee teaches not to be i. 3454
brain is devil's workshop 6754
determine never to be i. 51
hours breed wandering thoughts
6760
Life is not as i. ore 2599
love cannot lie i. in soul of lover
7167
love makes the i. quick and sharp
7260
man tempts devil 6770
not i. philosophical curiosity 5724
person tempts devil to tempt him
11047
Satan finds mischief for i. hands
to do 6772
tongue of i. person never i. 6777
unconscious is never i. 7767

IDLENESS
a sort of suicide 6761
devil's pillow 6762
gives room for doubt, fears 12024
is such a thing as sacred i. 7722
pains of hell i. 3482

perpetual despair 6764
Waiting upon God not i. 7724

IDLY
man who i. sits and thinks 11244
my fingers wandered i. over the
noisy keys 7919
repeat slanderous darts 5143

IDOL
evil thoughts like setting up i. in
temple 7759
The dearest i. I have known 6074

IDOLATOR
of little consequence whether
pagan i. or Pharisee 10041
put what God has done in place
of himself 6077

IDOLATRIES
nor bow'd to world's i. a patient
knee 12033

IDOLATRY
not only adoration of images 6071
putting confidence in riches, power
6071
thoughts about God that are
unworthy of him 6075
trust in own righteousness 6071
trusting people to do what only
God can do 6072
whatever man honors more than
God is i. 6076

IDOLS
If worships not God, will have i.
12109
We are naturally our own i. 10425

IF
cannot say Lord's Prayer i. 8818
consider boundless space 11631
Jesus talked about discipleship
with an "i." 2826
Lord, thy will be done without an
i. 9082
not sure what God wants you to
do 11605
the Lord God stop you 425
the Lord God take your goods
425
we saw all evil things 4318
we saw all good things coming
4318

IGNATIUS OF ANTIOCH
who could be harmed if he knew
something about I. 5733

IGNOMINY
better than honor 10875

IGNORANCE
and power and pride a deadly
mixture 9212
argument exchange of i. 2901
Behind every argument, i. 445
boasts of own knowledge
proclaims i. 6682
Chance is a name for our i. 6078
charge God of all knowledge with
i. 230
content with back to truth 3258

conviction of his own i. 737
Criticism's father, husband 2050
disciple comes with i. to find
learning 2818
disease of the soul 6085
Education progressive discovery
of i. 3000
Fear springs from i. 3964
has brought theology to sorry
plight 11196
has no light 3258
If you think education is
expensive, try i. 3012
is content to stand still 3258
may deride truth 11566
mystery another name for i. 7942
necessary condition of life itself
6081
Nor do I fret about i. of future life
6092
Nothing more frightful than i. in
action 6084
Our knowledge, compared with
God's, is i. 6699
pains of hell i, lust 3482
Prejudice the child of i. 9184
Silence will deliver you from i.
10245
To know one's i. best part of
knowledge 11955
truth has more virtue than i. 6326
Vice is i. 11724
voice of intelligence silenced by i.
6331
wisdom is knowledge of our own
i. 11942
wisdom must sometimes refuse
what i. may ask 8971
Your uttered i. and morbid doubt
3778

IGNORANT
Consistency as i. today as year ago
1747
Everybody is i, only on different
subjects 6079
father was so i. 3928
man or woman depending on God
has explanation 7753
man's world bounded by limits of
knowledge 11728
never met man so i. couldn't learn
from him 6080
so weak is man, so i. and blind
8877
spaces of which I am i. and which
knows me not 4905
trouble ain't that people i. 6083
uses words for jargon 11998

IGNORE
can i. death 2407
equally prominent biblical
teaching 6604
God, refuse to obey him 1014
may i. but can nowhere evade God
4871
men more or less i. meaning of
cross 2122

To i. evil is to become accomplice
3411
truth does not vary because men i.
it 11540

IGNORED
All men i. in me 9981
Facts do not cease to exist because
i. 3579
for many, church to be i. 1446
if love of God i. 4781
spent time as bulbs in dark totally
i. 5369
voice of intelligence i. by desire
6331

IGNORES
every other religion i. gloom as
fact 9551
What we call crises, God i. 10721

IGNORING
by i. central biblical teaching 6604
Can a man love God i. need of
brother 10052
needs of fellowmen 8818

ILL
Better to suffer i. than do i. 10838
blot the i. with tears 7017
friends will not believe i. of you
11502
generous heart feels others' i.
3063
good and i. together 7045
gossip speaks i. of all and all of her
5113
I will speak i. of no man 5072
If God lets him lie l. 9782
it i. behooves any of us 3953
must not take it i. 4063
Of one i, come many 1736
Speak i. of others, praising
ourselves 2083
The i. though ask'd, deny 8979
to tired and i. give quietness 9045
weary and i. at ease 7919
When good and i. so intertwine
4338
When we do i, devil tempts us
11116
Who shall declare this good, that i.
4338
wish I am rich, then know I am i.
11878
With good or i, with false or true
7017
words bellows to slacking fire
5145

ILL WILL
Love can take insults without i.
7207

ILLEGAL
legal abortion rather than i. 19

ILLEGITIMATE
concern for course of history not i.
5724
no i. children, only i. parents 1131
Worldliness mental slavery to i.
pleasure 12054

ILL-GOTTEN
gains never prosper 2467

ILL-HEALTH
life may bring i. 4803

ILLIMITABLE
i. void of space 4712

ILLITERATES
moral i. whose only law is self
3877
understand better than learned
1216

ILL-LUCK
Some people fond of i. 11449
some run halfway to meet it
11449

ILL-MANNERS
Criticism's child 2050

ILL-NATURED
God's patience with i. saints
mystery 4893
Hating i. gossip ourselves 5138

ILLNESS
as though no need to pray except
in i. 8788
cannot find time for recreation,
find time for i. 6835
do not find time for exercise will
find time for i. 9535
Old age an i. in itself 8153
take unhappy times bit by bit, like
an i. 5354
the doctor to whom we pay most
heed 8261

ILLOGICAL
most fervent believer may appear i.
8569

ILLS
ages of man: i. 7037
have no weight, tears no bitterness
7474
irreparable, murmur ungrateful
1563
love the panacea for i. of world
7203
Of all i. that men endure 5932
remediless, murmur in vain 1563
Uncertain i. torment most 11604
who sings frightens away i. 7894

ILL-SENSE
never interpret actions in i. 1080

ILL-TAUGHT
if look for results only in earthlies
9014

ILLUMINATE
Silence will i. you in God 10245
when emotions i. inner selves 3062

ILLUMINATED
by Scriptures 650
intellect in darkness until i. by
Holy Spirit 7776
revelation doctrine viewed on i.
side 7937

ILLUMINATES
when Spirit i. the heart 5809

ILLUMINATING
God is i. for knowledge 4514

ILLUMINATION
divine i. would blind eyes 4657
Pentecost, i. of mind 5806
receives divine i. 8505
sacrifice source of i. 9758
Without i. of Holy Spirit 752

ILLUMINATORS
Principles are i, not directors 6816

ILLUMINE
What in me is dark, i. 7566

ILLUMINED
by steady radiance, renewed daily
4538
when our lives cease to be i. 4538

ILLUMINES
faith i. the way 3649
the glow that i. 268

ILLUSION
dust devil throws in eyes of foolish
2655
that mere time cancels sin 10419

ILLUSIONS
Christian sees i. 1168
Hope cherishes no i. 5928

ILLUSTRATED
proverb no proverb until life has i.
it 3539
story of Jesus i. more than any
other in history 5729

ILLUSTRATION
man's life, i. of Christianity 1177

IMAGE
arises from i. of God in nature of
man 7531
beautiful i. of a father 3918
Behavior is mirror i. 553
bodies will be i. of God 839
Christ the express i. of God 6355
constant process of adjusting
public i. 1882
create a God in our i. 6467
cross, seen in i. of a lamb 6471
different from i. try to create in
minds of others 9950
Eternity, a stern, colossal i. 3269
faithful friend i. of God 4162
found in Scriptures of truth 1645
God i. of vulnerable lamb 2143
God made us in his i. 2002
handful of earth to make God's i.
1952
made in i. of God must know him
or be desolate 7465
man said, Let us make God in our
i. 4547
nature has defects to show she is
only i. of God 8022
Nature has perfections to show i.
of God 8022

No i. but i. of God can fit soul
10659
of God in nature of man 4744
of myself I try to create 9950
popular i. of man of God 1645
see soul with i. of God 1278
society has recreated Jesus in own
cultural i. 6467
soul, God's glorious i. 10675
that we may become thy perfect i.
7519
thou art an i. of God 9982
trinity of the mind is the i. of God
7771
whom God made in his i. 6200
Without free will man not in i. of
God 4158

IMAGERY
Bible clothed in Oriental i. 645
scriptural i. attempt to express
inexpressible 5631

IMAGES
Idolatry not only adoration of i.
6071

IMAGINABLE
most comforting fact i. 4779

IMAGINARY
Most troubles i. 11442
you will have an i. God 4663

IMAGINATION
Beatitudes enriched beyond i. 530
bring thought, i. into captivity
1014
Christian faith staggered i. of man
11201
debt to i. incalculable 2024
Memory the cabinet of i. 7733
more important than knowledge
2005
of human race poured out like
river 2023
purge i. by beauty of God 12124
real life phantom of one's i. 2750
Sin a strong i. 10368

IMAGINATIVE
understanding and love 9094

IMAGINE
children of next generation 562
Do not try to i. God 4663
God having to apply to higher
body 4955
God having to request permission
4955
heaven not so far as some i. 5651
idea of a God perfect as they
could i. 4504
People i. pursuing glory of God
10076
Reality more fantastic than we can
i. 9407
to i. a God who is unsure,
frustrated, unstable 4579
Worldly people i. saints find it
difficult to live 4159

IMAGINED
God exists more truly than i. 4611

God more truly i. than expressed 4611

IMBALANCE
most of our miseries, misfortunes 1240

IMBEDDED
oceans are God's thoughts i. 8048

IMBUE
if we i. men with high principles 6796

IMITATE
behavior of winners 549
cannot i. being full of Holy Ghost 5805
Children never failed to i. elders 1112
God does not expect us to i. Jesus Christ 4539
God does not give power to i. him 9834
Insist on yourself, never i. 6194
kind of knowing which most acute thinker cannot i. 5809
Some shoppers i. General Custer 4041
what is good, strong 3940

IMITATED
if husbands i. a few of dog's virtues 7611

IMITATES
Mercy i. God, disappoints Satan 7741

IMITATION
art only an i. of nature 8043
sincerest form of flattery 2006
than to succeed in i. 2008

IMITATIONS
one kind of love, a thousand i. 7317

IMMANENT
no i. logic in evil 5023

IMMATURE
consciously serving, devoted to God 1714
love says, "I love you because need you" 7194
People no longer sinful, only i. 10350

IMMATURITY
science at odds with religion, token of i. 9866

IMMEASURABLE
corpse of the universe 483
Power passing mine, i. God 4825
quality i. though quantity insignificant 7080

IMMEDIACY
no culture so obsessed with i. 7990

IMMEDIATE
knowing is i. 5809
person makes demands in his prayer 8981

IMMEDIATELY
difficult we do i. 12019

IMMENSE
appear sins we have not committed 10316
because God i. his love is vast 4750
Error is i. 6868
seemed to fan me like i. wings 5797
work of progress so i. 5944

IMMENSITY
Christ aperture through which i. of God seen 6373
contemplate God's power in i. of creation 4581
Divinity, so vast all thoughts lost in i. 4745
engulfed in infinite i. of spaces 4905
engulfed in the infinite i. 7084
greatness and i. of the blueness 4544

IMMERSED
Christ's outward life i. in world 6439
in the silence of God 10240
nor man right to be so i. in active life 7004

IMMERSION
in history of thought, spirit 3027

IMMORAL
satanic does not mean i. 9853

IMMORALITY
as church does with sexual i. 10086
Is church ready to deal with financial i. 10086
Satan fails to speak of remorse of i. 2662

IMMORTAL
awake to greatness of i. soul 10654
death will make us i. 812
have lost the i. part of myself 9622
honors or everlasting splendors 8483
if we work upon men's i. minds 6796
know i. lines that are nothing but sobs 8621
love is i. 6097
Love, forever full 6409
plainer I hear i. symphonies of world to come 11132
rapture that cannot die 7952
Where saints i. reign 5670

IMMORTALITY
a deep conviction or instinct 6102
best proof of i. in sharing life of God 6105
carriage held just ourselves and i. 2230
do not understand i. 6091

feeling invigorated, finding it i. 2399
first requisite for i. is death 6107
Life the childhood of our i. 6098
man was made for i. 6104
Millions long for i. 6100
Money buys everything except i. 7806
No man prosperous whose i. forfeited 6101
not a demonstration or proposition 6102
Only you can prove i. to yourself 6102

IMMORTALS
whom we joke, work with 8483
whom we marry, snub, exploit 8483

IMMOVABLE
those that are i. 10504

IMMUNE
God does not keep i. from trouble 2721

IMMUNITY
no i. from pain and sorrow 159

IMMUTABILITY
God's i. presuppose faithfulness 4583
of God most perfect beauty 977

IMMUTABLE
God is i. 4589
God's decree is i. 4626

IMPACT
become disciples, i. on society staggering 2819
if desire i. to be made 7714

IMPAIRED
vision i. by cataracts of sin 10436

IMPAIRS
something yet unenjoyed i. enjoyment 2869
Whatever i. tenderness of conscience is sin 10424

IMPART
absolute holiness God cannot i. 4658

IMPARTATION
God shares holiness by imputation, i. 4658

IMPARTIAL
God's love is i. 4786
Pale Death, with i. step 2361

IMPARTS
Spirit of God i. love 5800

IMPASSE
life has been brought to an i. 3485

IMPATIENCE
against God to be troubled with present 12066
hurry and i. marks of the amateur 6113
not so great a struggle with vices as with i. 6115

One moment of i. may ruin a life 8405

What is destructive is i. 6116

IMPATIENCES
our i. please devil 2661

IMPATIENT
are all i. of uncertainty 11605

eye tends to be i. 844

our desires so i. 5944

philosophy i. with anything that refuses account of itself 8592

science, i. with anything that refuses account of itself 8592

too i. to make adjustments marriage entails 7648

With thoughtless and i. hands 6117

without healing of spirit we become i. 8857

IMPATIENTLY
teenager waits i. to grow up 3867

IMPEDES
us in our natural outlook and ways 9821

IMPENETRABLE
conversion, an i. mystery 1902

IMPENITENT
man is i, then obstinate, then damned 10287

IMPERFECT
All information is i. 6706

Fallen man not simply an i. creature 9577

imperfection complains of what is i. 8521

not possible on this i. earth 7601

only imperfection that complains of what is i. 11395

ringing in i. acknowledgement of his love 7171

treating badly precious if i. thing 9923

IMPERFECTION
complains of what is imperfect 8521

only i. that complains of what is imperfect 11395

real always checked with i. 9498

IMPERFECTIONS
closer one gets to light, more i. show 7522

God quick to overlook i. 4810

hate their i. but love themselves 1080

outward reminder of God's priorities 1033

perfection to bear with i. of others 7682

shows subtler, more hidden i. 10006

with all our i. 7560

IMPERISHABLE
cross, sacrifice with i. dignity 2166

IMPERSONAL
hand of government 8062

IMPERSONALIZED
decadent, i. culture 3325

IMPERTINENCE
Self-chosen authority 526

IMPERTURBABLE
certainty in contact with God 955

IMPETUOSITY
Almighty not hustled by peevish i. 8419

success does not depend upon i. 8534

IMPIETY
not to believe God's promises 11596

IMPIOUS
both errors are i. 3349

IMPLIED
Everything is i. in Bible 746

IMPLIES
rationalist i. God must come to him 9396

IMPLY
Seniority in kingdom of God does not i. superiority 5897

IMPORTANCE
beliefs of little i. unless rich life 598

Criticism hurts sense of i. 2055

death is of very little i. 6912

easy to overestimate the i. of achievements 84

if false, Christianity of no i. 1184

if true, Christianity of infinite i. 1184

Lord's Prayer for i. of its petition 7154

not so much for i. of our works 7288

of events by how recently happened 7990

of i. to learn more every year 3017

something of real i. can happen 4132

IMPORTANT
able to tell we are converted 1903

Age not i. unless cheese 8123

beginning most i. part of work 544

Christianity cannot be moderately i. 1184

death psychologically i. as birth 2255

Delegates to United Nation not as i. 11027

discovered questions not i. 9366

everything is i. 572

expression is most i. 434

father's most i. responsibility 3927

glimpse of next three feet more i. 5371

have not placed reading before praying because more i. 8824

how to begin again 542

how we spend each day 10733

i. moments in lives 5392

if time more i. than soul 7327

Imagination more i. than knowledge 2005

In solitude discover being more i. than having 10545

is what one gives 11360

is where you are going 4438

isn't as i. as family you're going to have 3889

live life for something more i. than life 7034

more i. that we have grace enough to live by 6912

most i. cannot be taught 3030

most i. events never reach history books 5725

most i. occupation for woman 7856

most i. part no one sees 1049

most i. thing about us 7563

most i. thing in life 7034

most i. thought I ever had 7525

most i. thoughts contradict our emotions 11236

most i. words in vocabulary 11994

neighborliness i. on frontier because so few 8068

neighborliness more i. now because so many 8068

not where man goes when compelled 4147

Nothing really i. in life 972

nothing which happened in this world i. 5666

one of the most i. things 10

Prayer most i. thing in my life 8945

prepared messenger more i. than prepared message 9129

prying loose grasp on all that seems i. 11656

salvation more i. than 3332

Self-knowledge critically i. in pursuit of God 10019

Speaking the truth i. 9158

the individual incomparably more i. 7389

thing is not avoidance of mistakes 8110

thing is obedience of faith 8110

trouble in world caused by people wanting to be i. 9220

way man dies more i. than death itself 2336

What I believe about God most i. 614

What is i. is not where you come from 4438

What people think of me becoming less i. 9627

where man goes when free to go 4147

you are as i. as next person, no more i. 3248

you are more i. than you think 10001

IMPOSED
liberation from trammels i. by
external influences 4160

IMPOSES
God never i. duty without giving
time 9659
God's promises are obligations he
i. upon himself 9324

IMPOSSIBILITIES
do not ask for i. 45
Faith blind to i. 3683
Laughs at i. 3717

IMPOSSIBILITY
Christian life stamped with i.
1223
Love pleads no excuse of i. 7220

IMPOSSIBLE
Accept the i. 6961
act as if i. to fail 8533
believing i. without thinking 617
called to do i. 1284
change i. to escape 977
Christian has that which is i. to
world 10512
common ground between cross,
man's reason 1239
complete understanding
absolutely i. 9455
Contrary to his nature is i. to God
4513
difference between i. and possible
determination 2631
enemy may launch attack
otherwise i. 5021
even to put them to sleep with
sermon 10096
Every noble work at first i. 8536
except by power of Holy Spirit
3222
Faith receives the i. 3713
Faith says, to let me down is i.
3712
Few things i. to diligence, skill
8538
for God to manifest himself under
conditions set up 8929
for us to be children of God
naturally 9801
for world to exist without God
4597
God always calling on us to do
the i. 10138
God keeps his word, even when
seems i. 9321
God makes it i. to lose our way
5397
good general knows when victory
i. 8485
If i. for Christ to triumph over
death 9691
In natural matters faith i. without
evidence 3743
In new birth God does three i.
things 9800
in the flesh to be like Christ 8113
Insisting i. because he cannot
accomplish it 7793

learning how to accept the i. 7692
let me never be afraid to pray for
the i. 9046
Life without conflict i. 6988
love Christ commands not i. 7304
Make possible for me which is i.
by nature 8643
money and sex, i. to be truthful
ever 11494
natural world, i. to be made over
873
never test resources of God until
attempt i. 3815
Nothing i. to willing heart 10797
Nothing is i. 7869
   8644
often for excuse we say things i.
7869
Only he who can see invisible can
do i. 11733
only when man wishes i. that he
remembers God 7490
opportunities disguised as i.
situations 8228
takes a little longer 12019
temptation, neutrality i. 11052
to be both sinner and saint 5038
to be holy 9801
to be just if not generous 6610
to be neutral 5038
to be pure 9801
to despair who remembers Helper
omnipotent 2595
to enslave Bible-reading people
677
to explain how profound Bible is
734
to explain how simple Bible is 734
to find God through intellectual
processes alone 6328
to follow God naturally 9801
to forgive 9801
to get exhausted in God's work
940
to live in inmost being without
loving silence 10254
to live separated life humanly i.
10717
to love our enemies 9801
To put sin out of life humanly i.
10717
to reach God with understanding
11607
to rightly govern world without
God 5181
to satisfy everyone 9476
to say where human will leaves,
divine grace begins 5200
Wisdom i. for humans to
manufacture 12127
Without faith i. to please God
3823
Worry i. for the Lord to experience
12127
Young people do i. before find out
i. 12177

IMPOTENT
A few dozen act, millions stand i.
100
Envy is i. 10296
words stand by like i. pale ghosts
10274

IMPOVERISH
We i. God's ministry to us 4830

IMPOVERISHMENT
God's call not for i. but for
enrichment 9351
is in us, not in God 4830

IMPREGNATES
how God i. barren rock with gold
1902

IMPRESS
put away all effort to i. 7709

IMPRESSED
God i. by only one man—Christ
3854
God not i. with celebrities 3854

IMPRESSES
me about America is way parents
obey children 8357
thing that i. me about North .
America 3897

IMPRESSING
Forget about i. 10279

IMPRESSION
holy life will produce deepest i.
5737
like wave of electricity going
through me 5797
never give i. we care when in a
hurry 7327
so deep an i. as one deed 101

IMPRESSIVE
statistics on death quite i. 2386

IMPRINT
good father will leave i. on
daughter 3915

IMPRISONMENT
From his i. my freedoms grow
4125
God used my powerlessness 2518
shall emerge from our necessary i.
6110

IMPRISONS
Be aware rigidity i. 6809
fear i. 3965

IMPROBABLE
moods in which Christianity looks
i. 1305

IMPROVE
best i. with age 7419
defects i. strength 3932
If try to i. by good example 3436
If try to i. without good example
3436
man, deteriorate cat 7390
My part is to i. the present
moment 10145

People seldom i. when no model 3451

treat men the way they are, will never i. them 5971

Wisely i. the present 8378

without good example won't i. anybody 3436

IMPROVED
Emotional stability improving that which can be i. 2563

sinners i. by breaking 898

IMPROVEMENT
Fall man imperfect creature who needs i. 9577

Human i. from within outward 1017

joy of heaven i. of spirit 3482

not to neglect i. of talents 9041

Optimists achieve i. 8238

Optimists do not wait for i. 8238

IMPROVES
Solitude i. our character 10560

IMPROVING
contemplation of the Divinity i. to the mind 4745

good example, i. two 3436

only one corner certain of i, your own self 9953

IMPRUDENCE
Criticism's child 2050

IMPUDENCE
outraged by somebody's i. 45

IMPUDENT
exist without i. people 45

IMPULSE
actions determined by i. to follow leader 6199

dangerous to set up one i. as guide 7836

God is each virtue's i. 11687

Hope the major weapon against suicide i. 5925

in face of otherwise overwhelming i. 4111

manages all things badly 5580

of love is voice of God within 4278

Prayer not an occasional i. 8931

soul acts no longer except by divine i. 7707

spirituality an i. 5981

to accept Christ by i. 3333

IMPULSES
aren't such things as good, bad i. 7839

to take Jesus seriously was to control i. 6421

IMPURE
thoughts will not stand against pure words 5028

IMPUTATION
God shares holiness by i. 4658

IN
Go out and God comes i. 9556

God is i, we are out 4562

God is i. me 7968

see behind and i. chance God 4961

what is i. us, not what ought to be i. us 8853

INABILITY
God does not ask 3

Holiness not i. to sin 5745

our ability or our i. 3

to distinguish needs from greeds 5321

INACCESSIBLE
God i. to man's understanding 4728

INACTION
may cause evil by i. 3346

not only by actions but by i. 70

saps vigor of the mind 6765

INACTIVE
Love cannot be i. 7211

INACTIVITY
Evangelistic i. is disobedience 3329

INADEQUATE
dogmas of quiet past i. 976

our constitution i. for government of any other 5196

Stop depending on i. human resources 184

INARTICULATE
soul's i. moanings are affections for the Infinite 7516

INAUDIBLE
Christian hears the i. 1265

noiseless foot of time 11317

IN-BETWEEN
Don't mess with Mr. I. 8231

on the misty flats 10679

INCALCULABLE
debt to imagination i. 2024

influence from person rightly related to God i. 6241

INCANDESCENT
mind made i. by indwelling Christ 7776

INCAPABLE
loneliness knowledge that human beings i. of bringing help 7126

man morally i. of restraining himself 9872

miserable to be i. of enduring blindness 10861

misfortune to be i. of solitude 10570

of mean thought or feeling 110

of understanding one's condition 7126

purity i. of being other than it is 5749

INCAPACITATED
to conceive idea of eternity 4603

When your faculties i. 2565

INCAPACITY
my own i. to recover 6459

INCARNATE
God i. is end of fear 3972

While God I. made a chair 6458

INCARNATION
difficult to understand 11203

faith must include mystery of the i. 11203

for us an element of mystery 11203

God understands the i. 11203

live, breathe in the atmosphere of e I. 6378

not unintelligible 11203

Nothing in fiction so fantastic as I. 6125

INCESSANTLY
adored 4659

God is whispering to us i. 10273

INCH
by i. life's a cinch 6930

every square i, claimed by God 4918

Life, every i. is disputed 6947

We march, but have not progressed an i. 9309

INCLINATION
Man's i. to injustice makes democracy necessary 2528

INCLINATIONS
dreams true interpreters of i. 2967

think according to i. 1648

When i. dry, constrained 2565

INCLINE
God will i. us to repent 9578

more mind will i. toward solitude 10566

INCLINED
Man i. to be intolerant 11612

to believe those we do not know 610

INCLINES
Grace i. God to bestow benefits 4652

When God i. the heart to pray 9024

INCLUDE
to i. the excluded 7838

INCLUDED
God is within all things, but not i. 4612

Lord's Prayer, every prayer i. 7156

INCOGNITO
God walks everywhere i. 4871

INCOHERENCE
evil is a principle of i. 5023

INCOME
even if called to give up i. 4615

If give part of i, is not righteousness 11360

If not generous with meager i. 4366

of executive, perfect job 3121

INCOME TAX
took i. to drive lesson home
11862

INCOMES
lest God make i. match our gifts
4369

INCOMING
of totally new point of view 9827

INCOMPARABLE
God's unspeakable gift 1372

INCOMPARABLY
the individual i. more important
7389

INCOMPATIBILITY
sexual i. in marriage 10227

INCOMPATIBLE
Knowledge of nature and atheism
i. 6696

INCOMPLETE
accept even our i. knowledge of
God 7435

INCOMPLETENESS
flowering of person is movement
that results from perpetual i.
7699

INCOMPREHENSIBLE
God i. to man's understanding
4728
God not i. to our love 4679
God's essence i. 4670
God's justice i. 4728
Here below all is i. 6096
history i. without Christ 5709
holy with infinite, i. purity 5749
If stories i. to Jews, Muslims,
Taoists 12147
infinity of God not concealed, but
i. 4684
majesty of God i. 7971
mysteries of Christianity i. 1213
Only to our intellect is God i.
4679
soul sees God i, infinite 7971
suffering i. to all others 10873
yearning to comprehend the i.
7531

INCOMPREHENSIBLY
God's love an i. vast sea 4750

INCONCEIVABLES
boundless i. 4676

INCONGRUITY
of Bible with age of birth 736

INCONSISTENCIES
of Christians the excuse 1334

INCONSISTENT
Science sometimes said to be i.
with faith 9869
tears not i. with peace, harmony
5346
to let me down is i. with character
of God 3712

unjust to nature, himself is i. man
3190

INCONSPICUOUS
However i. life may be 8440

INCONTROVERTIBLE
Truth is i. 11566

INCONVENIENCE
just a little, temporary i. 4226
must put up with i. of genius 4394
no i. to way of life 3333
Riches exclude only one i. 11847

INCONVENIENT
most i. to know oneself 10008
no moral precept not i. 7840
poverty is confoundedly i. 8687

INCORRECT
conception of ourselves, neighbor,
God 8059

INCORRUPTIBLE
from corruptible to i. crown 2304

INCREASE
church cannot i. God's power
4829
desires i. with possessions 2869
Good and evil i. at compound
interest 5021
He sendeth more strength when
labors i. 5223
of greatness is to be less 5293
rich i. money 7826
when you share joy, you i. it 5353

INCREASED
Joys divided are i. 6551
love of life i. with years 8174

INCREASES
As knowledge i, wonder deepens
6678
Reputation i. 11326

INCREASING
life span of woman constantly i.
312
more to life than i. speed 7053

INCREASINGLY
Through faith unseen world i.
takes shape 3812

INCREDIBLE
Character torn down with i.
swiftness 996
make i. efforts but win no victories
6813
quarrels inevitable at the time, i.
afterwards 9359
to essay an i. happiness 6421

INCREDIBLY
great men are i. merciful 6032

INCREDULITY
gives nothing in return 11592
robs of pleasures 11592

INCURABLE
Old age an i. disease 8154

INDECISION
not to make a choice, a choice
1157
Nothing so exhausting as i. 2488

INDECISIVE
better to risk being considered i.
9327

INDEPENDENCE
essence of sin 6414
Extreme i. as destructive as total
dependence 7614
great man in midst of crowd
keeps i. 6195
is not strength 6414
is unrealized weakness 6414
Loneliness great price to pay for i.
7135
Marriage relation in which i. is
equal 7642
no i. in our Lord 6414
Sin is i. of God 10372
When lose individual i. 10526

INDEPENDENT
can choose to be bag of marbles, i,
9524
Christianity never promises to
make i. 4116
Friendship i. of matter, space, time
4233
in proportion to dependence on
God 1647
love must help child become fully
i. 7858
of God, dependent on
circumstances 1480

INDESCRIBABLE
God's unspeakable gift 1372

INDESTRUCTIBLE
absolute truth is i. 11550
convinced soul is i. 6094
Self i. by human means 9943

INDETERMINABLE
form which cannot be superseded
by any other 6214

INDETERMINATE
History too i. a structure to
contain Jesus 5714

INDEX
Speech i. of the mind 10690

INDEXES
gives editors haggard look 12153

INDIA
can learn from sages of I. 2988

INDICATION
circumstances i. of God's will
5444
Worry i. God cannot look after us
12087

INDICATIVE
of apostasy 12194
of our walk with God 1331

INDIFFERENCE
neither love nor hatred 6161

nothing harder than softness of i. 6165

problem is i. to church 1446

terrible i. toward one's neighbor 6163

thrice accursed is i. 6161

to evil more insidious than evil itself 3379

Tolerance another word for i. 11401

when Lord comes matter of i. 9912

INDIFFERENT
be afraid of the i. 6158

do not kill or betray 6158

God looks totally i. 8394

Mistrust the man who is i. to everything 3555

noisy world where people are i. 592

universe simply i. 11648

Whatever is i. is wrong 1242

Without faith, society of i. 925

worst sin is not to hate, but be i. 6164

INDIGESTION
half-baked sermon causes spiritual i. 10108

worry gives i. 12091

INDIGNATION
Moral i. permits hate under guise of virtue 11693

INDISPENSABLE
Absolute candor i. requisite to salvation 9793

Brokenness, i. step toward revival 881

Do without the i. 6961

futile to pretend prayer i. 8852

hope is as unreasonable as i. 5903

Knowledge i. to Christian life, service 6693

learning how to do without the i. 7692

no i. man 7433

So long as loved by others, we are i. 7292

INDISSOLUBLE
family, monogamous and i. 3890

God made marriage an i. contract 2924

INDISTINGUISHABLE
their good becomes i. from evil 5012

INDIVIDUAL
among ends for which i. created 6169

belligerent i, full of hate, bitterness 5594

each i. a sinner or a saint 5038

each i. shall have capacity 4

Everything in Christianity that matters is from i. to i. 6176

God salvages the i. 886

hope of nation in i. character of its people 5190

in power of each to be an i. 6209

is everlasting 7389

Jesus was, is concerned with i. souls 6176

life of the i. so brief 5944

Love is needed in i. hearts 7251

no one is prevented from being an i. 6209

nothing completely, merely i. 1450

one i. on a small planet 7387

Recognition of i. affirms respect for human dignity 9952

Recognition of i. affirms uniqueness of each person 9952

responsibility to God 7525

satanically managed man is i. 10044

Seek not every quality in one i. 9490

Suffering always i. 10889

support i. freedom as we serve one another 9498

the i. incomparably more important 7389

When we lose our i. independence 10526

worth of an i. endowed by the Creator 10001

worth of an i. not ascribed by law 10001

INDIVIDUALISM
distorts joy of identity 9952

ego cult of one 9952

In our rough-and-rugged i. 4402

INDIVIDUALISTS
nation of i, one American myth 1642

INDIVIDUALITY
cringing in fear of true i. 1642

death brings human being to i. 2353

God made our i. 6177

human voice gives i. 7893

is something altogether sacred 6183

lose nightmare of separate i. 2822

No man should part with own i. 6201

water down i, we lose freedom 1635

Whatever crushes i. is dictatorship 6222

written and signed by God 6183

INDIVIDUALLY
easier to know mankind than man i. 7393

Lord loves devotedly, i. 4747

INDIVIDUALS
A few i. can stand isolation 6199

are the power and the might 91

as much right to act way they decide as we 6193

crowd is composed of i. 6209

dignity of i. measure of civilization 3894

God's call comes to i. 5385

Jesus compelled i. to decide 6516

Many i. have shining qualities beneath rough exterior 8658

No nation better than i. 7987

nothing wrong with being i. 9952

things wrong with country total of things wrong with i. 7989

Why i. created but that God should love each differently 6169

Winning world to Christ means winning i. 3343

INDIVISIBLE
God, substance is i. 4610

INDIVISIBLY
God, i. one 4503

INDOCTRINATE
when I transfer beliefs, I i. 11009

INDOLENCE
God does not ask for acquiescence of 4507

INDUCE
temptation, i. us to substitute for God 11099

INDUCEMENTS
no evil that does not offer i. 11101

INDULGE
home where man can i. in a whim 5842

INDULGED
more self is i, more it demands 10027

INDULGENCE
i. of grief 5337

loving any i. better than hope of heaven 6925

through i. in own vices 10503

trivial i. in lust or anger 5021

INDUSTRIOUS
without covetousness 9041

INDUSTRY
must be the ventilator 5848

Success depends upon i. 10805

INDWELLING
Christianity, deity i. man 1189

If Holy Ghost i. a man or woman 5782

INEFFABLE
concept of i. worship has been lost 12120

majesty of God, i. 7971

motherhood of God 5775

INEFFECTIVE
ceased to think of other world become i. in this 5656

Self can turn a pure prayer into an i. one 10080

INEFFECTUAL
factuous, i. yesterdays 8370

hell, prayer i. 5700

INEFFICIENCY
didn't actually accuse God of i. 380

INEFFICIENT
take folks as i. creatures they are 2799
taking folks as i. creatures 9469

INEQUALITY
courage to endure riddle of i. 6277
other claims to equality intensify i. 3242

INERT
genius often dull, i. in society 4395

INERTIA
grace to abandon i. 1719

INESCAPABLE
Didst thou give me this i. loneliness 7125
God is i. 4846
loneliness an escape from an i. God 7144
Only that which is i. is God 4846

INESTIMABLE
Bible, of i. value 737
God's unspeakable gift 1372

INEVITABLE
arguing with the i. 44
Death, taxes i. 2238
Emotional stability accepting i. 2563
God alters the i. 4937
in knowledge most haunted with i. limitation 6689
Pain i. for all 8266
Quarrels i. at the time, incredible afterwards 9359
struggles of life 4768
succumbing to failure as i. 3586
that God's justice incomprehensible 4728
Wesley in one generation, Carey in next is i. 9740

INEVITABLENESS
of God, not law 1149

INEXHAUSTIBLE
Contentment, an i. treasure 1781
history of our Lord i. matter for contemplation 6380
Man an i. mystery 7405
source of peace, consolation 9835

INEXHAUSTIBLY
God, i. various 4503

INEXORABLE
love of God i. as love between sexes 4792
loving in the deepest, most i. sense 7186
What jailer so i. as one's self 9955

INEXORABLY
pulled down into quicksand of smugness 3168

INEXPLICABLE
God's glory is i. 4681
reject Christ's existence world i. riddle 5728
see God in i. circumstances 1464

INEXPRESSIBLE
God's unspeakable gift 1372
nearest to expressing i. is music 7884
Oh, the comfort, the i. comfort 4260
symbolical attempt to express i. 5631

INEXTRICABLE
God turned life into i. confusion 4885

INFALLIBLE
Christ the Truth i. 6397
circumstances of life i. indication 5444
Joy most i. sign of presence of God 6548
theologian never i. 11197

INFANCY
Heaven lies about us in our i. 12164

INFANT
An i. crying in the night 2576
blessed babe, i. full of power 6123
born with clenched fist 11656
cuddle, nurse self-pity as an i. 10034
first handshake, clasp of i. 816
Like a weak i. cries 6129
wailing of newborn i. mingled with dirge for the dead 7043
world, wrapped in swaddling clothes of light 7886

INFANTS
trying to spell God with the wrong blocks 7530

INFECTIOUS
Nothing so i. as example 3448

INFERIOR
No one can make you feel i. without your consent 6228
of any man whose rights I trample under foot 11283
Seek to be i. to everyone 8448

INFERIORITY
envies another admits own i. 3219
Exaggerated sensitiveness an expression of i. 6227
my greatest strength 11789
my sense of i. dropped away 11131

INFERIORITY COMPLEX
substituted i. for sin 5808

INFERIORS
Treat i. as you would be treated 5006

INFERS
wisdom, awful wisdom which i. 11906

INFEST
cares that i. the day 7887

INFIDELITY
cancers that gnaw on the soul 3873
swept by flood of French i. 8347

INFILTRATES
Christian, one who i. 1251

INFINITE
all that concerns our Lord i. 6380
as essential for man as planet 12117
bear through the i. remote the name of God 4712
Christ i. mercy, goodness 5208
day excludes the night 5670
distance between i. and finite 3786
earthly life in touch with a new i. life 7101
endurance show alliance with i. God 3150
engulfed in i. immensity of spaces 4905
eternal silence of these i. spaces frightens me 7084
Everything a thought of i. God 1959
faith subtle chain that binds to i. 2929
finite can never comprehend i. 4690
glory of creation, i. diversity 1973
God an i. circle 4842
God is i, his love has no limit 4750
God with his i. sensibility 4895
God's children of i. value 6042
God's gifts so i. do not see them 7993
God's love is i. 4786
God's treasure like i. ocean 4471
Goodness takes whatever turns to it 4645
grace 495
grace of God is i, eternal 4656
has written name on earth in flowers 4705
has written name on the heavens in stars 4705
heaven, happiness i. in degree 5634
holy with i, incomprehensible purity 5749
idea of the i. torments me 3275
If I want the I. to be reflected in me 7715
if true, Christianity of i. importance 1184
In i. time, matter, space 6927
Into the i. light 2360
justice must be i. love 4725
man's spirit stretches outward to i. 7381
meadows of heaven 11636
only a God who has i. wisdom 5438
out of his i. riches in Jesus 7570

Prayer link between finite man, i. God 8944

prayer tapping i. resources of God 8991

Reason's last step is recognition i. number of things beyond it 9421

remarkable conformity from infinitesimal to i. 9866

soul sees God imcomprehensible, i. 7971

soul's moanings are the affections, yearning for the I. 7516

sowed his name in heavens in stars 8037

sowed his name on earth in flowers 8037

take i. wisdom of God 3758

The i. Goodness has such wide arms 4645

there alone man finds rest 7381

truth being self-existent is i. 11550

unique, no modifiers 4706

Which binds us to the i. 3700

INFINITELY

All we know i. less than remains unknown 6677

God, loving all i. 6169

greater in possibility for good or bad 10015

playing it well matters i. 9911

INFINITESIMAL

remarkable conformity from i. to infinite 9866

INFINITUDE

Before i. we stand silent 4706

can belong to but One 4703

God's i. places him above knowing 4702

grace of God, boundless as i. 4656

INFINITY

darkness of the pure, unsearchable sea 4684

Divinity, so deep our pride drowned in i. 4745

futile as yardstick that will measure i. 5718

if the spaces of i. 4708

music most strongly suggests i. 5631

of God not mysterious, only unfathomable 4684

philosopher, a particle pontificating on i. 8588

walled in a womb until the next enormity 6142

INFIRMITIES

compassionate i. of others 1080

INFIRMITY

Give health or give i. 1538

given i. that he might do better things 8806

Man calls sin an i, God an iniquity 4560

INFLAMES

Opposition i. enthusiast 1626

INFLICTED

the more grief i. upon you 5357

INFLUENCE

cannot i. death but can i. style of departure 2336

Christianity, i. far from negligible 1188

from person rightly related to God incalculable 6241

husband and wife one in i. 3868

maintain reverent attitude toward God's i. 3993

most powerful i. in world 5766

negative or positive, never neutral 6248

no greater opportunity to i. fellowman for Christ 6278

our shadow selves, our i, may fall 6242

people who i. stood unconsciously for right 6239

people who i. us like stars, lilies 6239

people who i. you are people who believe in you 6240

Prayer is putting oneself under God's i. 8936

religions with no i. of man's behavior 1232

Struggle with oneself means by which we i. 3414

Swelled heads shrink i. 9488

teacher can never tell where i. stops 2993

teacher defends against personal i. 11006

INFLUENCED

When I think of those who have i. my life most 6245

INFLUENCES

liberation from external i. 4160

What i. me in my friend is spirit 4233

INFLUENCING

Example main thing in i. others 3431

INFORM

No talebearer can i. on us 4884

Quotations i. 9385

INFORMATION

All i. is imperfect 6706

books for i, Bible for transformation 689

brain can store one million billion "bits" of i. 7738

Conscience prophet in its i. 1673

do not have to give God i. 9010

one hole for i. to come out, six holes in head for i. to go in 7379

Opinion helps us make decision without i. 8198

treat i. with humility 6706

will never ask for i, implies they do not know 9236

INFORMING

Prayer not just i. God of our needs 8929

INGRATITUDE

As man's i. 6249

Charity may meet with i. 1075

daughter of pride 6252

form of weakness 5255

no i. can hinder you from serving 10159

pardon my i, pity my dullness 6253

surprise will be the extent of our own i. 6250

Thank for i. 1191

the unfailing mark of a narrow soul 6251

Too great haste a kind of i. 5266

will meet with i. from your fellowmen 10159

INGREDIENT

Conflict main i. in character development 1029

fear of God, a healthy i. 3993

Love one i. of which world never tires 7251

INGREDIENTS

God gives i. for daily bread 9657

who does not bring i. for happiness into marriage 7632

INHABITANTS

Proclaim liberty through all i. 4141

INHALE

gospel, can't i. its fragrance and be content 5099

INHALING

Fame, like flame, harmless until i. 3853

Prayer is i. spirit of God 8920

INHERIT

I suppose I shall i. eternal bliss 2419

meek, not arrogant, i. earth 1216

Youth must i. aftermath of war 11757

INHERITANCE

Blood is an i. 11683

conscience void of offense i. for eternity 5079

emotions i. of every man 3058

Hell was our i. 1348

we receive from God limitless 4694

INHUMANITY

guilty of i. when we snub or abuse 901

makes countless thousands mourn 30

Man's i. to man 30

INIQUITY

a fathomless answer, the Cross of Christ 9398

depth of i. that makes us shudder 10391

Man calls sin an infirmity, God an i. 4560

practice all pleasant forms of i. 4726

When rationalist points out i. 9398

INITIAL
To believe on Christ i. faith 3801

INITIATION
Suffering strange i. into happiness 10896

INITIATIVE
accept or reject God's i. 585

God takes, keeps i. 585

if followers of God, cannot take i. 5446

in world everything depends on taking i. 5446

of saint toward knowing Jesus Christ 1324

of saint, not toward self-realization 1324

prevented from developing i. 8337

when take i. cease to follow 5446

INITITATED
into wisdom 10010

INJURE
If i. someone you dislike 8055

What power does anyone have to i. you with words 6287

INJURED
finer person i. by adversity 7683

He who i. you either stronger or weaker 6263

Jealousy, the i. lover's hell 6341

weak person is i. by prosperity 7683

INJURES
He i. good men who spare wicked 6608

one, threatens a hundred 10450

INJURIES
Forget i, never forget kindnesses 6638

Men more prone to revenge i. 9720

we do and those we suffer 9495

Write i. in dust, benefits in marble 9523

INJURING
As if you could kill time without i. eternity 11290

INJURIOUS
to mourn for sin because i. to ourselves 9581

INJURY
accountable to others for i. 70

best revenge is not to be like him who did i. 9727

cannot kill time without i. to eternity 6784

dares to forgive i. 4095

Doing i. puts you below enemy 4073

evil consists in doing life i. 5044

He who defends i. next to him who commits it 6261

sooner forgiven than insult 4070

to one, concern of all 6603

where there is i, pardon 9086

INJUSTICE
a selfish, hateful, violent i. 6258

act of i. to the sheep 6283

anywhere is a threat to justice everywhere 6266

Christ died to save us, not from i, but from being unjust 6365

Covetousness has for daughter, i. 5313

Delay in justice is i. 6259

do i. because do not love him our brother 6609

greater i. among champions of religious opinions 9540

If not for i, men would not know justice 6264

If thou suffer i, console thyself 6265

love offered in spite of i. 7239

Man's inclination to i. makes democracy necessary 2528

moral dimension of sin i. 10394

never rules forever 6268

Rather suffer an i. than commit one 6276

relatively easy to bear 6267

shall only resist social i. 6286

shut mouth and eyes to i. around him 11690

social dimension of sin i. 10394

suave, erect, unconfined 6269

Those who commit i. bear greatest burden 6279

true unhappiness is in doing i. 6265

will have an explanation 7060

INK
a small drop of i. 12002

Could we with i. the ocean fill 4748

INLOOK
Faith makes i. favorable 3705

INMOST
find flower upon i. side 6583

impossible to live in i. being without loving silence 10254

one's i. thoughts in another 11256

Thy sacred i. shrine 7454

INN
Heaven is our home, the world our i. 7077

quit life as an i, not a home 7005

The i. is full on the planet earth 6155

world's an i, death the journey's end 2330

INNER
achieve i. health through forgiveness 4103

capture i. stronghold of pride 10043

chamber into which God only can enter 7127

Christ never contaminated his i. kingdom 6501

corresponding i. attitude of love 6811

disclose i. fears, temptation, deepest joys 4029

ears to hear what he could not hear before 8495

giving central place to God, not only in our i. selves 7713

God gives new set of i. eyes 8495

God hearable with ears of i. man 4509

God knowable with mind of i. man 4509

God seeable with eyes of i. man 4509

God touchable with hands of i. man 4509

In midst of noise deep i. silence 10539

into i. dynamics of human organism 9353

know almost nothing about i. life 1753

life of Christ sea of glass 6376

Loneliness is i. emptiness 10548

man who has no i. life 7033

nature of sin 10387

no grammar for language of i. life 7705

no torment like i. torment of unforgiving spirit 9640

Only through i. transformation strength to fight 6619

Our i. life grows stronger when outwardly condemned 6270

Outside show poor substitute for i. worth 6061

see i. man, his real self 6842

sharing i. thought 4277

sin goes to i. desire 10300

Solitude is i. fulfillment 10548

things of Spirit take shape before i. eyes 8488

voice of God does not argue 4967

ways of awakening i. reverence in man 9734

when emotions illuminate i. selves 3062

will do deep i. work veiled to eye of man 10706

INNERMOST
freedom to share i. thoughts 4285

INNOCENCE
Jesus' guilt is our i. 6453

of morning 4643

INNOCENT
Complaining might seem i. 1558

God is unthinkable if we are i. 5493

In the case of some sins we are i. 10384

twisting, warping i. family members 3873

Words i. in a dictionary 12003

INNOVATIVE
keeps us from giving in i. ways to
others 6825
legalism, lynching of i. programs
6817

INNS
Our Father refreshes us with
pleasant i. 7014

INNUMERABLE
definitions of God 4585
manifestations of God i. 4585
possess all things, and more i.
5575

INOFFENSIVE
singing groups concerned about
being i. 5109

INORDINATE
society i. emphasis on feeling good
4017

INORDINATELY
anxious to appear dignified walks
on stilts 2761

INPOURING
more receptive to his i. 4499

INQUIRIES
best compliment to set free to
make own i. 6207

INQUIRY
God's creative method is ongoing
i. 4469

INQUISITIVE
Christians do not want Lord to be
i. 1303
Shun the i. 5156

INRUSH
Revival i. of Spirit into body that
threatens to become corpse
9749

INSANE
those who fixed eyes on reality
judged i. 5730

INSANITY
can get i. from your children 3874
is hereditary 3874
life with eyes shut a kind of i.
11234

INSATIABLE
love, its i. desire 7211

INSATISABLE
if i. in intellectual curiosity 8139

INSCRIBED
a sense of deity i. on every heart
4833

INSCRIPTION
over church door 1382
to seek wisdom in youth like i. on
stone 11956

INSCRUTABLE
God's essence i. 4670
world is wonderful, i, magical
12049

INSECT
every i. so amazingly know their
path 7945
particle of i. impress of its Maker
3192
stands over me, the human i. 4526
witness to mystery of God 7945

INSECT'S
Who gives its luster to an i. wing
1963
Who gives its lustre to an i. wing
4482

INSECURE
futile to condemn myself for
feeling i. 3049
Rashness, haste make all things i.
5586

INSENSITIVITY
For the Lord only wooden i. 6383

INSEPARABLE
Joy and sorrow i. 10626
Prayer and helplessness i. 8901
suffering, accept as i. from love
7953

INSIDE
Better hundred enemies outside
house than one i. 5820
cannot shut out what is i. 464
Christ's insulation on the i. 6501
controlled by what is happening
on i. 9849
have an awful lot of people i. me
9931
he's just like me i. 926
home, they say, dead decorum,
routine 5842
Let great things grow i. you 10242
Most of us do not like to look i.
ourselves 10012
myself place where I live all alone
9933
Outside noisy, i. empty 4064
salvation, an explosion on the i.
9827
solitary confinement i. our own
skins 7148
We are all alike on the i. 5985
Whenever I look i. myself, I am
afraid 9957

INSIDIOUS
communism an i. ideology 9952
Indifference more i. than evil itself
3379

INSIGHT
activity without i. 4429
arises from purity of heart 8504
comes from pureheartedness 2998
correct i. among duped, deluded
2803
Education, scholarship unable to
give i. 2998
find at center of my pain amazing
i. 8279
miracles associated with i. Jesus
wanted to give 6500

moment's i. sometimes worth life's
experience 8486
not from clearness of intellect
8504
that relates us to God 8504

INSIGHTS
Affliction triggers greatest i.
10834
Jesus gave such i. we have not yet
grasped significance 6196
Jesus gave such mature i. into
human nature 6196
of saint stem from experiences as
sinner 9776

INSIGNIFICANCE
activity, passing whiff of i. 113
death, space trips pale into i. 2259

INSIGNIFICANT
God's way often i. and
unobstrusive 4664
murder when treat people as i.
10683
No man so i. 3445
psychology must reject that evil i.
3382
quality immeasurable though
quantity i. 7080
sin, however i, covers mirror with
smoke 10339

INSINCERE
most exhausting in life is being i.
6063

INSINUATES
Self-love i. itself into everything
10027

INSINUATIONS
Whispered i. rhetoric of the devil
10478

INSIST
all look, talk, act alike 6824
discouragement when we i. on our
own way 2879
men i. on making life complicated
6977
on your own way, will get it 5695
on yourself, never imitate 6194

INSISTENCE
lost through puritanical i. on
moral rules 6827
upon seeing ahead natural 3758

INSISTING
impossible because he cannot
accomplish it 7793

INSISTS
He who i. having all will give up
all 5315
upon new ways of bettering things
9311

INSOLENCE
is pride when mask pulled off
2917

INSOLENTLY
God allows man i. to deny him
4673

INSPECT
Wisdom does not i. but behold 11967

INSPECTS
wisdom, awful wisdom which i. 11906

INSPIRATION
build up i. 3185
dialogue in which creative i. sought 4160
Genius, one percent i. 4391
received put into practice 4160
seldom solid home in absence of religious i. 5858

INSPIRE
me to send my roots deep 9111
Quotations i. 9385
with thy love, i. us 619
works of God, transcendent greatness i. awe 9734

INSPIRED
Creed i. by Christian love 2030
by gifts of the Holy Ghost 4749
I know Bible is i. 663
that not i. by hope of heaven 6108

INSPIRES
Spirit of God i. hope 5800

INSPIRING
to teach without i. is hammering on cold iron 11000
What, but God? I. God! 4711

INSTALLMENT
We sin on the i. plan 10421

INSTANCES
controlled by other power 4949

INSTANT
brief fleeting i. of time allotted 7063
Conversion may occur in an i. 1897
expect to find God's i. answer 693
Grief is the agony of an i. 5337
Starts into i. action 8224

INSTANTANEOUSLY
become Christians i. by faith in Christ 5738

INSTANTLY
Character not obtained i. 1000
God knows i. 4881
response to assault i. reveal values by which you live 6288

INSTINCT
a native, elemental, homing i. 7535
immortality an i. 6102
in our souls that turns us to God 7535
Life must be composed by i. 6966
moral law isn't any one i. 7839
Mystery is demanded by religious i. 12118
something queer about the sex i. among us 7360

INSTINCTIVE
actions determined by i. impulse to follow 6199

INSTINCTIVELY
heart i. seeks for a God 12110
regard seen world as real world 3812

INSTINCTS
Do not give up i. 1241
God will direct 1241
to take Jesus seriously was to control i. 6421

INSTITUTED
governments i. among men 3246

INSTITUTION
church lasted longer than comparable i. 1431
Marriage is an i. 7643

INSTITUTIONAL
works of Holy Spirit not confined to i. church 5791

INSTITUTIONALISM
have too much churchly i. 9552

INSTITUTIONS
God had ordained three i. for society 10506
Jesus, no intention to speak to i. 6451
none of man's i. control nature 8012
seek to make i. of power just 6623
We are going to meet unmerciful i. 7746

INSTRUCT
me how to die 9048
things that hurt i. 10916

INSTRUCTED
man who i. thousands felt a failure 2886

INSTRUCTING
God to reserve right of i. us 5384

INSTRUCTION
family, first school of human i. 3880
Hate needs no i. 7265

INSTRUCTIONS
Don't bother to give God i. 8782

INSTRUCTIVE
Flee the wicked, even when they are i. 11882

INSTRUCTOR
Difficulty a severe i. 2717
Each problem a God-appointed i. 2720

INSTRUCTORS
Practice best of all i. 3543

INSTRUCTS
At every moment God i. me 5426
Faith i. us in depths of God 3670
Jesus i. the heart 6442
prosperity deceives, adversity i. 241

INSTRUMENT
easy to play musical i. 7897
God made the perfect i. 7893
humble i. in hands of heavenly Father 5411
Life like learning i. as one goes on 6967
no i. to procure abortion 21
Prosperity an i. to be used 9340
we are his i. 7892
will play by itself 7897
without choice man an i. 4155

INSTRUMENTS
like orchestra in which all i. played same note 6169
Words i. of music 11998
wrong i. being used for job 4739

INSUFFICIENT
my own wisdom i. for the day 8822

INSULATE
ourselves from God's presence 4864

INSULT
Don't i. God telling him he forgot to give you brains 7755
eye can i. like hissing, kicking 3561
injury sooner forgiven than i. 4070
not to believe God's promises 11596
one more i. to God 6275
penny-in-the-slot manner, i. to God 693
talk about cost when in love an i. 2823

INSULTED
when body neglected, God is i. 841

INSULTING
Time has way of i. beautiful things 11328

INSULTS
are like bad coins 2918
love can take i. without ill will 7207

INSUPPORTABLE
learning how to endure the i. 7692

INSURANCE
fear of God, i. against loss 3993
Justice is i. on our lives 8096

INSURMOUNTABLE
despair tells us difficulty i. 5931

INTEGRATED
truths reveal a life more i. than known 11521

INTEGRITY
Calamity, test of i. 158
children talk with i. 1105
essential to cope with life's difficulties 6310
first step to true greatness 6311

guide lives by i, will die happy, even though poor 6309
Jesus Christ teaching supernormal i. 6314
kept clean all day by i. 9600
knowledge without i. dangerous 3013
mother interpreter of father's i. 8341
needs no rules 6312
no need to manipulate others 5874
personal i. key to success 10799
stand true to i. of Jesus Christ 8545
Success depends upon i. 10805
test of joy's i. 6571
the architect 5848
without knowledge, weak 3013

INTELLECT
always fooled by the heart 6330
an awesome work of God 7776
can give no explanation before birth or after death 9419
can never comprehend spirit 10692
Christian does not begin with human i. 3783
Christian thinking puts i. second 11238
darkness above the i. 1767
Darkness to the i. 4743
Faith knowledge that transcends i. 3673
God endowed us with i. 6324
heart thumps about things i. scorns 5628
in darkness until illuminated by Holy Spirit 7776
insight not from clearness of i. 8504
Lord crucified in i. of men 2125
man's thoughts belong to world of i. 10692
must be bathed in new element 880
must be re-born 880
must be reconsecrated to Maker 880
not a question of i. but of purity of heart 11529
Nothing will so enlarge the i. 4742
of wise like glass 11945
Only to our i. is God incomprehensible 4679
powerful muscles, but no personality 6333
relationship of life, not of i. 6515
Sorrow destroys differences of i. 10620
Spiritual truth not discernable to i. 11529
take care not to make i. our god 6333
to be used for God's glory 10708
to do with time between birth, death 9419
while spirit can embrace i. 10692

INTELLECTUAL
a thousand i. delicacies 2021
attempt to systematize God 11209
claims to equality intensity inequality 3242
if insatiable in i. curiosity 8139
impossible to find God through i. processes alone 6328
loss of i. morale in the church 7768
Love for Lord not i. thing 7221
no reason why miner not i. as poet 6332
not conscious, i. process 1126
Reason our i. eye 9422
saints need no i. greatness 5301
sophistication can dry up creativity 6325
want most rigorous i. training 3025
who has given up his i. freedom 7760
world stale, unprofitable if we knew everything 9286

INTELLECTUALLY
Most live i. in restricted circle 8659
Truth not discerned i. 11569

INTELLECTUALS
attempt to discredit Bible 726
remain socially powerless, suspect 6323

INTELLIGENCE
Christian will find i. sharpened 1193
Cynicism, substitute for i. 2181
God the universal i. 4692
God will direct 1241
Happiness and i. rarely found in same person 5512
insects know path, though have not i. 7945
is clarified 7964
Joy holy fire that keeps i. aglow 10829
love worth more than i. 1183
must follow, never precede faith 6327
of those who put man in same circle as hyena 1991
one glance of God's i. he sees all 4883
people mistake education for i. 8510
reminded of the greater i. 4526
Success depends upon i. 10805
Tact is emotional i. 10987
voice of i. soft and weak 6331

INTELLIGENT
full of doubt 2955
God must have i. cooperation 11269
no matter how i. or well-educated 752
person has learned to "choose between" 6326

stupid cocksure, i. full of doubt 10518
Thankfulness is an i. response of gratitude 11173
to understand Christ i. faith 3801
truth being vast and deep is i. 11550

INTELLIGIBLE
Eloquence power to translate truth into i. language 9134

INTELLIGIBLY
mystic too full of God to speak i. to world 7965

INTEMPERATE
golf-mania as i. as someone who gets drunk 9269

INTEND
God does not i. us all to be rich 4243
than repent of sins i. to commit 10327

INTENDED
difficulties i. to make better, not bitter 2748
human being i. to have character of his own 6170
human being i. to have own character 1008

INTENDS
God i. us all to be friends 4243

INTENSE
blazing holiness of God 4661
death brings i. contemplation of Creator 2353
let him makes our lives i. 2829
look forward to death with i. curiosity 2306
more i. light is, less you see glass 6033
Out of i. complexities i. simplicities emerge 11937
requires i. love on mother's side 7858
will cost i. narrowing of interests on earth 9831

INTENSELY
man never so i. himself as when possessed by God 5200
nearer to Christ, more i. missionary we become 7785

INTENSEST
Laughter and weeping, i. forms of human emotion 6728
Love for Lord i. love 7221

INTENSIFIED
more i. becomes the conflict 1629

INTENSIFIES
Marriage i. what is already there 7633

INTENSITY
called to love with special i. 10937
crucifixion remember with i. 2137
degree of fullness accords with i. of desire 5772

live Christ with i. 3321
Martyrdom, i. not correctness of
   belief 1911
Pentecost, i. of love 5806

INTENT
darkest hours in life have i. 4885
Love is not i. on vanities 7246
not needful we know i. 4885
Some sinister i. taints all he does
   4164

INTENTION
God looks at i. of heart 6334
I cannot judge i. of another 4247
must be tried in friendship 4227
no i. of carrying it out in practice
   2915
Satan, ultimate i. is to ruin you
   9855
smallest good deed better than
   grandest i. 2505

INTENTIONS
God evaluates i. 1067
Hell paved with good i. 5688
poor opinion of us even when i.
   good 6270
sin seems worse in consequences
   than i. 10294
what matters is i. 3051

INTERCEDE
Calvary, to i. on others' behalf
   2175

INTERCESSION
Discernment God's call to i. 2805
Holy Ghost i. in us on earth 8859
In his i, Christ a high priest 6410
Jesus Christ i. for us in heaven
   8859
saints carry on i. for all men 8859
who thinks of neighbor says
   prayers of i. 8840

INTERCESSOR
like live wire between power of
   God and men 8760
one in vital contact with God and
   man 8760

INTERCESSORS
Calvary to join band of i. 2175

INTERCHANGE
Bring thy soul and i. with mine
   3065

INTEREST
alms money put to i. in other
   world 11359
becomes throbbing with i. 6086
ceases to be controversy, ceases to
   be i. 1827
Christ, dominating i. hid with God
   6501
comes garbed in brevity 9149
exceed in i. knock at door 4259
God, profound i. in man's being
   good 5060
Good and evil increase at
   compound i. 5021
If i. in work of others cool 7187

immense broadening of i. in God
   9831
Life will take on deeper i. 3185
Love blind to every i. but its Lord
   6457
Love has a social i. 7274
nothing else but love 7329
saints i. us when in conflict with
   devil 1631
Worry i. paid by those who
   borrow trouble 12090

INTERESTED
by becoming i. in other people
   4306
by trying to get other people i. in
   you 4306
God i. only in what we are 9539
God not i. in organized religion
   9539
if i. in big things 8139
in others when they are i. in us
   9515
Man primarily i. in himself 10068
more i. in God than in work for
   him 10141

INTERESTING
conflict, not many things so i.
   1631
Creed of church, i. 1205
happiest person thinks most i.
   thoughts 7026
Man more i. than men 6200
Only God is permanently i. 4678
To make message i. to world 5109
world, it's an i. place 6929

INTERESTS
if i. on earthly things 8818
will cost intense narrowing of i.
   9831

INTERFERE
Do not let what you cannot do i.
   8652
must not i. in people's lives 263
Never i. with God's dealings 1549
No saint dare i. in discipline
   10927

INTERFERENCE
cross an overwhelming i. 2111

INTERFERER
God not a supernatural i. 4847

INTERFERES
sin that i. with nothing 11394

INTERFERING
Unselfishness not i. with people's
   lives 11654
with God's order for others 263
with God's working within us
   10977

INTERMISSION
Make life a mission, not i. 10171

INTERNAL
church unity i. 1387
result of i. surgery 8583
serpent, whose guile stirred up
   envy, revenge 9863

INTERPRET
never i. actions in ill-sense 1080
Scholars can i. the past 9334
takes prophets to i. the present
   9334

INTERPRETATION
will come when, as God pleases
   4885

INTERPRETER
God is his own i. 5378
God the Spirit, i. of Holy Scripture
   655
Mother i. of father's character
   8341
Spirit sole seer, i. 4911

INTERPRETERS
Dreams true i. of inclinations
   2967

INTERRACIAL
heaven, an i. neighborhood 1486

INTERRED
good is oft i. with bones 5043

INTERRUPT
When your work speaks for itself,
   don't i. 6043

INTERRUPTED
by someone doing it 66
To be enjoyed, sleep, health, and
   wealth must be i. 433

INTERRUPTION
free from i. 8794

INTERRUPTIONS
people not i. to schedule 3316
precisely one's real life 2750
unpleasant things not i. 2750

INTERTWINE
When good, ill so i. 4338

INTERVAL
no cure for birth, death save enjoy
   the i. 7054

INTERVENES
Almighty directly i. in human
   affairs 4949
Revival God i. to lift situation out
   of human hands 9746

INTERVIEW
with Satan would alone have
   damned 6388

INTIMACY
God loves you with i. which
   surpasses dreams 4747
Now—i. closer still, he dwells
   himself in men 7506
pain buys i. with Christ 10906

INTIMATE
born from i. depths of divine
   nature 5967
dream, door in most i. sanctum of
   soul 2971
his words are i. on many myriad
   tongues 6394
if i. with God, disloyalty of friend
   will not crush 9470

Marriage most i. of relationships
7641
mystical is i. quality of spiritual
life 7954
with few 4218

INTIMATION
silly question first i. of new
development 6703

INTIMIDATED
Be not i. by any terrors 4115

INTIMIDATES
the brave, degrades the rest 5479

INTIMIDATION
God will not allow i. to 3340

INTOLERABLE
an i. bore—ourselves 9939
Bear the i. 6961
cross we bear seems i. 2116
find world quite i. 5535
God has paid i. compliment of
loving us 7186
load will be as i. as it is
unreasonable 12064
man i. if never suffered 10898
our own ego makes ego of others
i. to us 9215
Teach us that no evil is i. 9092
to know the future 4317

INTOLERANCE
disease of the soul 6085
forbearance better than i. 6326
shown in support of tolerance
11393

INTOLERANT
learned toleration from i. 5251
Man inclined to be i. 11612

INTOXICATE
Power will i. the best 8714

INTOXICATES
Authority i. 8702
flattery, poison i. us 4053

INTOXICATION
Reading, selfish, serene, lifelong i.
858

INTRACTABLE
three most i. beasts 10774

INTRENCHED
It matters not how deep i. the
wrong 6256

INTRICATE
what so i, so entangling as death
2220

INTRICATED
poor, i. soul 10661

INTRIGUER
devil i. 4915

INTRIGUES
Joy i. 6819

INTRIGUING
where evil is i. 3347

INTRODUCE
can i. another to Jesus Christ 3306

into public affairs Christianity
1196
kingdom of heaven into midst of
earthly day 4974

INTRODUCED
Christianity i. new spirit of
government 5170

INTRODUCES
Adversity i. a man to himself 142

INTRUDE
do not like strangers to i. upon
private lives 5957
Scholarship should not i. upon
faith 3022

INTRUDES
God i. in glorious, myriad ways
7556

INTRUSIONS
God's often violent i. into human
history 9710

INTUITIVELY
faith is God perceived i. 3750
more he understands i. 8505

INVADED
God has i. our lives with purpose
6156
ordinary people i. by living God
1936
to depths of one's being by God's
presence 7488

INVADES
gospel i. everything 732
Holy Spirit i. everything 5796

INVALID
Every i. is a physician 10840
Man is no hopeless i. 10436

INVALIDATES
Crucified i. success for standard
10814

INVENT
hopelessly strive to i. happiness
apart from God 5570
I i. nothing. I rediscover 2004
man suffers to deeply had to i.
laughter 6742
tells a lie, forced to i. twenty more
6850
what you don't see, don't i. 5165

INVENTED
Falsehood has to be i. 6867
11556
God i. mothers 7845
God loves life; he i. it 6896

INVEST
few extra hours in quiet reverence
9906
God would never i. in worthless
property 9989
I will i. my life 6920
If you don't i. much 2629
in order to i. us with his grandeur
6130

INVESTIGATION
continued i. of the Deity 4742
doctrine that will not bear i. not
fit tenant 11181
ought to follow, not precede, faith
9411

INVESTMENT
God's i. in us so great 4617
Kids long-term i. 1121
Married life will require all-out i.
7647
unless I can recall a consistent i. in
people 6919

INVIGORATED
feeling i, finding it immortality
2399

INVINCIBLE
defeat makes men i. 2511
empowered with i. faith 3736
greatest who chooses right with i.
resolution 5297
shall form i. host against difficulty
10829

INVISIBLE
being educated for choir i. 10600
Christian, sees the i. 1265
Faith sees the i. 3713
feel God's i. and tangible hand
drawing me 7484
footprints, some you can see,
others i. 6231
God knows all things i. 4881
God washes eyes by tears until
behold i. land 11013
Only he who can see i. can do
impossible 11733
Poetry makes i. appear 8620
real things are i. 615
root of Christian life, belief in i.
3831
Vision seeing things i. 11737
what is essential i. to the eye 5622

INVITATION
Christianity, an i. to living 1168
Failure i. to recourse to God 3587
Grace central i. to life 5221
Sorrows visitors that come
without i. 10622

INVITATIONS
This day with hopes and i. 8375

INVITE
Pheasants fools if i. hawk to
dinner 11081

INVITED
suicide like going where you
haven't been i. 10939
to a fight 1210
to an execution 1210
to pilgrimage 1210

INVITES
friend gently i. you to grow 4169
Springtime i. you to try out its
splendor 9896
Thanksgiving i. God to bestow
second benefit 11162

INVITING
God is i. us to enjoy him 4554
trouble, it generally accepts 11458

INVOKED
Whether i. or not, God will be
present 4875

INVOLUNTARILY
repeating i. the character of those
among whom we live 6243

INVOLUNTARY
how can voluntary act of
self-surrender be i. 9799

INVOLVE
sacrifices which always i. risk
5385

INVOLVED
drain away business with which
we get i. 6830
life more i. than most of us think
6918
more i. in life's troubles when
come to Christ 11451
process i. in redirecting our lives
painful 5449
who passively accepts evil i. in it
3374

INVOLVES
All excellence i. discipline 3464
Contemplation i. all of life 1755
Creation i. limitation 4117
Rebellion i. limitation 4117

INWARD
as i. life fails 1761
attitude of man who loves God
different 5046
brighten our i. light 4974
by i. pressure of Holy Spirit 6785
concur with i. promptings of the
Spirit 5444
goodness consists in i. thing we are
5063
If any idea how much i. peace you
would gain 10703
If possess i. solitude 10539
let Christ be i. spring 6379
outward worship result of what is
i. 12129
Quotations tell of i. thoughts
9385
spirit an i. flame 10696
stirring, touching of God 5764
thou shalt have i. liberty 4922
tortures of that i. hell 9567
Vision looks i, becomes duty
11738
Who in the silent hour of i.
thought 2764

INWARDLY
Christ was i. disconnected 6439
conforming outwardly, living own
life i. 6048
experience of knowing is i.
satisfying 5809
grasped something i. with
embracement of love 7964
more simple person is i. 8505

IOTA
God has never surrendered i. of
his power 4821

IRKSOME
discover delight hidden in i. tasks
10639

IRON
But i. dug from central gloom
2599
Habit is shirt made of i. 5496
Human life resembles i. 6905
most strongly united by fiercest
flame 4273
must have i. nails that scratches
bear 11062
nails are real i. 2147
rust corrupts i, envy corrupts man
3207
rusts from disuse 6765
to teach without inspiring is
hammering on cold i. 11000
war is humanity hanging itself on
cross of i. 11745
we are not made of i. 7437
we find security in i. bars and
solid walls 6825

IRONS
have too many i. in the fire 9552

IRONY
perpetual i. of government 5194
prayers bitter i. if lip service 3320
that Christ not religious enough
6416

IRRATIONAL
nothing so i. as rationalism 9397

IRRECONCILABLE
God's i. hostility to evil 4999

IRRECOVERABLE
overwhelming, i. loss, his soul
2381

IRRELEVANT
concern for course of history not i.
5724
Facts considered i. 3493
for many, church i. 1446

IRREPARABLE
If ills i, murmur ungrateful 1563
No ruins so i. as reputation 9619
purpose of cross to repair i. 2165
things in life i. 7051

IRREPARABLY
mistakes won't i. damage lives
3616

IRREPLACEABLE
To be i. must be different 6192

IRRESISTIBLE
God's power is i. 8886
gospel is simply i. 5101
holiness is i. 5750
purpose of Christ's life 6439
Sin does not appear to be i. 10357

IRRESISTIBLY
power of perseverance grows i.
greater with time 8557

IRREVERANCE
indication of weakness 9735

IRREVERENT
Bible does not yield secrets to i.
687
never i. to ponder how Son of
God would have done it 6387

IRREVOCABLE
Nor deem the i. past 3538

IRRITABLE
Never become i. while waiting
8400
person like hedgehog rolled up
wrong way 9630
without healing of spirit we
become i. 8857

IRRITANT
ultimately produces the pearl 204

IRRITATE
Kids can frustrate, i. parents 8304

IRRITATED
Humility is never to be i. 6010

IRRITATES
With silence one i. the devil 10276

IRRITATING
characteristic by-product of
respected quality 8571
nothing more i. than a Savior
when not ready to be saved
9819

IRRITATION
precious jewel conceived through i.
10883

IRRITATIONS
forget i. that detract from
happiness 9270
from trivial i. of family life 6386

IS
each man as he really i. 7443
eyes are what one i. 10687
From man's mouth can tell what
he i. 5126
From the wonderful was, by the
wonderful i. 4313
God a continuous, unbroken i.
4604
God i, all is well 4935
God i. where he was 4849
Man never i, but always to be
blessed 5913
not what Jesus does, but what he i.
5790
rich or poor according to what he
i. 6302
We are because God i. 3489
what i, i. well 8243
Where there is peace, God i. 8475

ISAIAH
he who has not wondered in I.
5224
treated God with startling
familiarity 7526
Worship pictured at its best in I.
12136

ISLAM
converts by force 3301

ISLAND
No man is an i. 10511
Old age an i. surrounded by death 8155
The larger the i. of knowledge 6702

ISLANDS
I know not where his i. lift 4763
New i. yet shall break upon our sight 2319

ISMS
convert healthy ideas into ideologies 9952
of youth the wasms of age 12174
problem is with "ism" 9952

ISOLATE
question of truth that may i. us from most men 10564

ISOLATED
by misfortune 5395
church keeps evangelizing same people 1456
we're all i. in our minds 7428

ISOLATES
pain i. 9812
Silence i. us from the crowds 10515

ISOLATION
A few individuals can stand i. 6199
For the Lord only i. on the cross 6383
God does not live in i. 11423
Savior chose i. 1516
soul enriched by God will not be dismayed by i. 10567

ISSUE
as Christian is not to pretend we love everything 5890
do duty wisely, leave i. to God 5176
man with vision of God not devoted simply to i. 11729
no room to question final i. 235
Self-acceptance a spiritual i. 9993
Straddling an i. like straddling middle of road 11602

ISSUES
church, major on minor i. 952

ISTHMUS
while I stand on this i. of life 6910

ITALY
psychological secrets to control youth of I. 12178

ITCHINESS
silence creates i. 10253

ITINERARY
God's will not an i. 5406

J

JABBERING
Are we j. busybodies 10117

JACOB
disabled, learned to use other weapons 769
learned other weapons than wrestling 769

JAILER
What j. so inexorable as one's self 9955

JAMES
could pray for days 8858
skin of knees hard as camel's 8858

JAMS
grope way through endless traffic j. 5859

JAR
To feel, amid the city's j. 8430

JARGON
ignorant uses words for j. 11998
thousand who talk j. about Christ 3306

JASMINE
walls of j, trumpet-creeper 4454

JAUNDICE
Jealousy, j. of the soul 6343

JAZZ
people hear it through their feet 7898

JEALOUS
Lord j. over saint abandoned to him 8608
love of God j. as love between sexes 4792
man's horns hang in his eyes 6337
Spirit of God will be j. over you for good 5776
Thou art j. without anxiety 4954
torment to themselves 6348
troublesome to others 6348

JEALOUSIES
Rumor pipe blown by j. 9756
Take off all your j. 10787

JEALOUSY
a blister on the heels of friendship 6339
a virtue 4722
beware, my lord, of j. 6346
Even God attributes to himself j. 4722
extinguishes love as ashes smother flame 6347
foolish child of pride 6340
green-ey'd monster which doth mock 6346
jaundice of the soul 6343
more self-love than love 6338
not love that produces j. 7200
sees too much 6344
selfishness produces j. 7200
Some say j. is love, I deny it 6347

the great exaggerator 6341
the injured lover's hell 6342
thou magnifier of trifles 6345

JEERS
If you your ears would save from j. 1855
no man will rise high who j. at sacred things 9735

JEHOVAH
comprehending all 4672
sharpens and prepares 163
takes his ministers into darkness 163
What would J. say now 3205
when J. created world, it was good 3205

JEHOVAH'S
Safe in J. keeping 4490

JELLY
what turns bones into j. 4551

JEREMIAH
doubtful if he knew peace 770
man of peace, not a J. 770
no integrated personality 770
treated God with startling familiarity 7526

JERUSALEM
and Jesus! What a contrast! 6420
God not pleased with worship at J. 12101
Had there been lunatic asylum in J. 6388
like doney carrying Jesus into J. believing crowds cheering him 9217
way to Babylon will never bring you to J. 10403
with contempt powers of J. confronted Jesus 6420

JEST
Man, the j. of the world 7417
with an ass, will flap in face with tail 9477

JESTS
He j. at scars that never felt a wound 10850

JESUS
A man who said things J. said 6350
accept authority of J. 524
accept J. as Savior, a new life 876
Ah! dearest J. Holy Child 1357
all desire to rejoice with J. 2828
all making a crown for J. out of daily lives 7073
alone is true to us 6455
aloneness stands out most 6508
always returned to his ultimate prayer 6384
anyone save J. only in your cloud 2562
anything but glory 2813
anything J. did we should be able to do 10138

army of demons compelled to obey J. 9858

audaciously abolished death 2322

baptism of Holy Ghost makes us witnesses to J. 5790

baptism of Holy Ghost means we are a satisfaction to J. 5789

Because J. was not wanted 6358

becomes two-edged sword 686

Beware of worshiping J. while you blaspheme 3646

blew everything apart 4136

Caesar more talked about than J. 6362

calls these pains birth pains 10901

came that there might be a gospel to preach 5111

came to fill suffering with his presence 10867

came to resurrection through, not around the cross 5768

can decide to let J. make holy 5752

cannot be discussed in same way as any other man 6476

captivated his listeners 6444

Certainly J. was poorly adjusted to society 6196

changes our history 10901

characteristic of J. praying 8890

claim of redemption of J. can satisfy aching soul 6402

comes across as Anglo-Saxon, Protestant Republican 6467

comes across not as biblical J. 6467

coming of J. into the world 6146

commissioned disciples 2827

compelled individuals to decide 6516

complete summary of all J. taught 10102

conquered more millions than Alexander 6449

consciously gain identity J. had 9840

conservatism of his times against him 6452

consorting with sinners 5791

continual forgiveness of sin 10402

cuts right down middle 686

death goes underneath the deepest sin 2160

death of J. not the death of a martyr 6472

death of J. was revelation of heart of God 6472

death only entrance into his life 2161

Democracy child of J. teachings 2523

departed that he might return 461

departed, and behold, he is here 461

devil wanted to involve J. in exigencies of power 2704

devil wanted to neutralize gospel of love 2704

did not attain perfection by rules, regulations 8520

did not explain away suffering 10867

died even for Judas 6469

died for you 46

differs from all other teachers 6442

digging mankind out of snug burrows 6421

divided over the question, Who is J. 6518

dividing into believers and nonbelievers 686

does it all, I do nothing 5426

does not tell us to pretend friends 5890

dominant note was faithfulness 3848

dying J. evidence of God's anger toward sin 6473

easily ignorable 2813

either the Son of God or a madman 6350

essence of the drama he lived 6384

evidence in daily life that J. is powerless 3646

expounded no doctrines 6448

face-to-face model of social relations 6451

few follow J. to drinking of cup 2828

few will join J. in fasting 9268

few willing to endure for J. 2828

fight deviation from course J. set for us 9965

finds few companions of abstinence 2828

finds many companions of his table 2828

first thing J. promises is suffering 10901

for these two discoveries am beholden to J. 5530

for thirty years, obscure 2813

for two discoveries, beholden to J. 2308

foundation of my whole life 11126

Free of family, J. remained alone 6508

fulfills all procedures of prophecies 6443

furnished themes for sermons, orations, discussions 6449

furnished themes for works of art, songs of praise 6449

gave such insights we have not yet grasped significance 6196

Gentle J, meek and mild 1117

give ourselves up to ownership of J. 8090

gives truth carried on wings of love 6176

God acting like himself in man 6514

God expects life of J. to be manifested 4539

God raised up J. 5711

God will give me goodness of J. 5059

Had I lived in the time of J. 6464

had joy even under shadow of the cross 6538

had things to say about how we should behave 6444

has few bearers of his cross 2828

has few desirous of tribulation 2828

has many desirous of consolation 2828

has many lovers of heavenly kingdom 2828

has to be aware of his suffering 10868

hatred in comparison to our love for J. 7280

his acclaim lies in ridicule 6443

his glory lies in obscurity 6443

his joy to enter sorrowful hearts 10603

his victory lies in defeat 6443

History too fragile to contain J. 5714

holiest man who ever lived 6412

Holiness means life of J. developed in us 5748

honor, being what J. was and is 4413

How sweet the name of J. sounds 1507

How widely J. known difficult to judge 6395

I defy you to doubt him 2961

I stole ideas from J. 2019

if J. leaves them, they complain 2828

If never hurt by statement of J. 6407

imparts inward taste for truth 6442

In his Son, J, God unveils his face 4906

in his Son, J, God unveils his very face 9706

in name of lowly J. 1370

in suffering identify with J. 10930

In the humanity of J, God speaking our language 6135

instructs the heart 6442

invited us not to frolic 1210

invited us not to picnic 1210

invited us to a fight 1210

invited us to pilgrimage 1210

is all truth, no falsehood 6498

is full, infinitely full 6498

is God with skin on 6446

is risen, he shall the world restore 9692

is the joy of heaven 6460

is to me all grace, no wrath 6498

Jerusalem and J! What contrast! 6420

knew what he was to accomplish 4425

knows we must come apart and rest 9532

leaps across the changing centuries 6448

Let J. be loved for himself 6454

life of silence, solitude, simplicity 6358

life would drive us to despair 2161

like donkey carrying J. into Jerusalem believing crowds cheering him 9217

like some moral huntsman 6421

Little J. was thou shy 6456

lived great life convictions 6448

living J. proof of God's love, forgiveness 6473

look at J. to correct blurry vision 4489

Looking for J. in history futile 5718

loudest in protest no such person as J. 6417

love kept J. from calling angels to his rescue 6418

makes heaven wherever he is 6378

man acting like God 6514

many follow J. to breaking of bread 2828

many love J. so long as no adversities 2828

many praise, bless when consolations 2828

many reverence his miracles 2828

many who love his heavenly kingdom 9268

mention J. people want to stop conversation 6518

miracles associated with lesson J. trying to teach 6500

miracles of J. ordinary works of his Father 6479

mission everything, personal life nothing 9279

mission, liberating oppressed 1439

more evidence J. lived than Alexander the Great died 9700

name of J. plowed into history of world 5727

Nearly everyone clashed with J. 6516

never clung to his colleagues 6508

never cost disciple to follow J. 2823

never in a hurry 4425

Never think J. commanded a trifle 8097

nights in prayer 8860

no evasion of the cross 8819

no intention to speak to crowds 6451

No one could have a more sensitive love than J. 7280

no problem can't face if J. to strengthen 11126

Nobody knows but J. 11445

not an Essene, not a Pharisee 6508

not distracted with trivia 4425

not slogans carried on thrust of power 6176

not what J. does, but what he is 5790

O J, drink of me 7003

O J. quicken me 2587

obeying his orders 8090

object of his meditation was his Father 12128

offends because emphasis on unseen life 6450

offered us an execution 1210

offered us not an excursion 1210

one-fifth of all J. had to say was about money 7804

only in suffering will we know J. 10930

Only J. worldwide remembrance 1369

out of his infinite riches in J. 7570

pain, how J. responded 8259

Peace for time and eternity 6420

perfect because never made a move without his Father 8520

Pilate had never heard of J. 6395

popular in some groups because 3493

prefer J. to Amos or Caiaphas 7099

preferable world against thee than J. offended 8525

proclaims first will be last 6447

proclaims fools are the wise 6447

proclaims weak are the strong 6447

produced effects beyond reach of orator, poet 6449

promised followers "The Strengthener" would be with them 5804

prophet of the losers' not the victors' camp 6447

prostitutes, thieves who adored him 6412

pulls each person from behind his mask 9741

radical personalization of ethical problems 6451

redefines meaning of love 7201

refuses to swallow drugged drink 10868

religious who hated J. guts 6412

restless, progressive people flocked to him 6452

retired to deserted places to pray 8860

saint makes it easy to believe in J. 9771

same J. in heaven as on earth 6466

sanctified for God to do with us as he did with J. 9850

saved for God to do with us as he did with J. 9850

says its murder when destroy with words 10683

says must let God do all we can 10980

shed more light than philosophers, scholars combined 6449

Show a man his failures without J. 7425

society has recreated J. in own cultural image 6467

something in J. rebuked world 2168

speaks as one who knew what was in man 6448

speaks of motives rather than actions 6450

speaks to living experience of all time 6448

spelling himself out in language man can understand 6445

spoke about ox in ditch on Sabbath 10951

spoke to the unchanging needs of men 6448

spoke words never spoken before or since 6449

standards asked more than any other ever has 6444

standards far from lax and easygoing 6444

story of J. told more than any other in history 5729

strange about J. is you can never get away from him 6485

talked a great deal about money 7804

talked about sparrows and lilies 6451

talked to fishermen, peasants, outcasts 6451

teaches no distinction of race, merit, rank 913

teaches universal love 913

theme of his life 6384

They should have known J. was God 6492

things that belonged to peace connected with J. 6420

throws down dividing prejudices 913

thy blood and righteousness 4719

to take him seriously 6421

took road that would end on Golgotha 6384

transformed death from door that slammed to one that opened 2322

tried for who he was 6413

wants us to see their needs 3316

was a radical 6452

was a simple rural figure 6451

was a solitary man 6508

Was it not opposition J. promised to disciples 10784

was, is concerned with individual souls 6176

wasn't afraid to associate with anyone 4253

wasn't with us J. was concerned 12128

what people think of J. because of me is critical 9627

When claimed J. for himself became easy 7105

When J. comes, shadows depart 7879

When J. is absent, all is hard 6512

When J. is present nothing seems difficult 6512

When J. is present, all is good 6512

When J. saw city, he wept 10522

When life rosy may slide by knowing about J. 10930

Wherever J. went he produced a crisis 6516

with contempt powers of Jerusalem confronted J. 6420

without writing a line set more pens in motion 6449

work was in marketplace 3331

world couldn't stand him 2168

would not let himself be classified 6508

JESUS'

captivity is our freedom 6453

coming final, unaswerable proof God cares 6136

death is our life 6453

guilt is our innocence 6453

Let all be loved for J. sake 6454

Many eager to share J. table 9268

patience should have proved he was God 6492

power of persuasion so overwhelming 5485

promise is valid 5781

JESUS CHRIST

a borrowed manger, tomb 6433

a window in the tiny dark dungeon of ego 6434

absolute mastery over everything 2170

alone qualified to guide into unknown 2323

always speaks from source of things 6422

an amazing sanity 2170

as powerfully as this one solitary life 6353

Ascension placed J. back in the glory 462

asks, "Who am I to you" 6431

benefits become curse if J. not head 3895

betray J. by keeping mouth shut 628

blinds mind to claims of J. 10044

body, medium for manifesting J. 838

burst from the grave 1905

By his first work he gave me to myself 6361

by next he gave himself to me 6361

came into my prison cell 6423

came to alter disposition 6424

came to do what no human being can do 6424

came to lift us up to heavenly places 6402

came to make men holy 6424

came to make men new creatures 6424

came to make us what he teaches we should be 6403

came to make worshipers out of rebels 12137

came to plant in men the Holy Spirit 6424

came to redeem men 6424

can have it all on the wire called J. 6521

Character, disposition of J. manifested 998

characteristics of God mirrored in J. 4493

Christianity, living with J. 1180

Completer of unfinished people, work, times 6428

condescension of divinity 6441

contrary to common sense 533

cross of J. and his baptism express same thing 9437

deal with surface find him an offense 6422

delights to dwell within 6352

detachments were inside toward God 6436

did not come to teach men to be holy 6424

did not cut himself off from society 6436

did things apparently unreligious 6501

didn't commit gospel to advertising agency 2827

dined with lowest members of society 6433

disconnected fundamentally from life 6436

divine paradox of lion, lamb 6425

divine Physician, Pharmacist 6429

dominating interest was hid with God 6501

exaltation of humanity 6441

exploded in my heart 1905

founded his empire upon love 6351

friend shadow compared with J. 4201

fury against J. proof he is not dead 6362

gave me back myself that I had lost 6361

glory and beauty come from within 6352

God does not expect us to imitate J. 4539

God Incarnate manifested at one point of history 5717

God's everything for man's total need 6427

God's grace turns out family likeness to J. 4651

gospel of J. nothing if not gospel of growth 9351

Grace can put Spirit of J. within us 5212

had no servants or armored guards 6433

had no throne, crown 6433

had twofold personality 6426

hang on to fact that J. is true 589

has no tenderness toward 6407

his comforts refreshing 6352

his conversations sweet 6352

his life oblivious of details 6501

his prescriptions never out of balance 6429

human destiny depends on a relationship to him 6431

Humility exhibition of spirit of J. 6013

if I lift up J. 9838

If J. is God and died for me 9761

If J. only a teacher 6403

if J. should come, we would kneel 6406

if leave J. out, toboggan slide to hell 9172

If love J. will serve humanity 10156

if refuse to take guidance of J. 5458

In J. nothing secular and sacred 6411

insulation on the inside 6501

intercession for us in heaven 8859

introduce another to J. by way he lives 3306

inwardly disconnected 6439

is behind everything 5716

is being dethroned 127

is everywhere 5716

is Lord of history 5716

is unique 9741

Keep J. in your hearts 914

kingdom on the inside 6501

know J, belief spontaneous, natural 611

let men take his strength from him 2170

letting in a light 6434

life of God poured out 497

life of J. anticlimax of failure 10813

life so social called a winebibber 6436

live most with J. 6235

lived in another world 6436

Lord of all or not Lord at all 6437

makes us real, not merely sincere 9403

man cannot believe until he knows J. 611

man may betray J. by speaking 628

most outstanding record is date of birth of J. 5726

never asks anyone to define position 6431

never asks anyone to understand a creed 6431

never asks us to devote ourselves to cause, creed 2836

never contaminated his inner kingdom 6501

never insists on being Master 8106

never suggested pretend people faultless 9789

never suggested turn blind eye to evil 9789

never trusted human nature 2184

no panic 2170

No revolution compared to words of J. 5721

not a solitary man 464

not blood of martyr 497

not one man for another 497

Obedience to J. essential 8106

Obedience to J. not compulsory 8106

offering a way of release 6434

One whom, alas, we know so little 6522

only one who has returned from grave 2323

opens mouth so wide embraces all heaven, earth 6511

outward life immersed in world 6439

peace passing all understanding 6352

perfections of J. made your entirety 9847

providing a vista 6434

purpose was to do will of his Father 6439

recognize J. face in every human being 914

Redemption means J. can put into man disposition that ruled his life 9436

release from fury of the will 6434

release from servitude of the flesh 6434

resurrection of J. our hope 5945

reveals a God who stands in thick of whole thing 6432

saints one dominant note is J. 9786

Satan tried J. becoming King of world 11082

see difficulties, not looking at J. 2731

served others first 6433

Son of God revealing what God is like 6426

Son of Man revealing what man is to be like 6426

source of power 6491

spiritual world, J. makes possible 873

sternest, gentlest of Saviors 6430

still people who love or hate him 6362

talked about discipleship with an "if" 2826

taught men not to sit in judgment 9789

teaching has no meaning unless enter his life 6424

teaching supernormal integrity 6314

then J. was no saint 9789

thousand who talk jargon about J. 3306

to know God, study J. 4493

to redeem the world 497

today people would not crucify him 6405

touched the untouchable 6433

tremendous reservoir of resurrection life of J. 11689

unique incarnation of truth 2988

visits within are frequent 6352

was among the ordinary things of life 6436

was not a conservative 6435

was not a recluse 6436

was not aloof 6436

we know God through J. 10013

we only know ourselves through J. 10013

well-defined knowledge of J. 6713

when J. utters a word 6511

will never strong-arm his way into your life 6438

wire will never snap 6521

wish to be encouraged, look upon J. 6408

wits and wisdom taking his place 127

would have been shut up in asylum 6388

JESUS CHRIST'S

life an absolute failure 3605

teaching never beats about the bush 6440

JEWEL

Consistency, j. worth wearing 1749

Consistency, thou art a j. 1748

Experience is a j. 3523

Honesty a fine j, much out of fashion 5875

Is not sight a j. 6253

life like entering a j. mine 4426

precious j. conceived through irritation 10883

will know when lost a j. 6004

JEWELS

heaven polishes j. with diamond dust 143

mind will shine with accumulation of j. 3023

JEWS

build wall between J. 2988

If stories incomprehensible to J. 12147

know God, love only earth 3201

JOB

a self-portrait of the person 54

can find some needful j. 10201

comforted with conundrums 772

description of perfect j. 3121

devil longed to tempt like J. of old 2690

doesn't feel you've done a permanent j. 4213

experienced calamity because righteous 2857

feels rod, blesses God 771

felt hand of destruction 4556

felt hand of preservation 4556

flings God one riddle 772

future is in man who holds j. 3122

God flings J. hundred riddles 772

How to suffer 11925

no future in j. 3122

No j. can compete with shaping new human being 8317

parent to work yourself out of j. 8343

pastor needs patience of J. 9125

Seeing God, J. forgets all he wanted to say 773

streetsweeper who did j. well 2777

too hot to do j. that was too cold last winter 9902

Use God to get a j. 7517

wrong instruments being used for j. 4739

JOBS

Nothing hard if divide into small j. 3110

take on three j. at church 9970

JOCKEYING

most go through life j. for position 3758

JOHN

Like the beloved J. 11476

will rest little in J. 5224

JOHN CHRYSOSTOM

who could be harmed if he knew something about J. 5733

JOHN QUINCY ADAMS

will have to move out before long 8142

JOHN THE BAPTIST

Sorrow is our J. 10616

JOIN

all must j. the dance 3180

hands and sing, Free at last 4157

JOINED

broken string may be j, knot will remain 9624

JOINS

hands with heaven 9805

JOINT

whole course of our lives out of j. 7571

JOKE

immortals whom we j. with 8483

JOLT

of pain with sin 577

JOLTS

Politeness eases j. 1946

JONAH

felt down in the mouth 774

JORDAN'S

On this side J. wave 778

JOSEPH

if Mary and J. had decided 25

sold into slavery 1211

JOSTLED

aside to make room for converted playboy 4410

JOURNALISM

is pure fantasy 9404

trivial replaces momentous 7990

JOURNEY

All days j. toward death 2428

encourage souls who j. with us 9059

fear doesn't want j. to mountain 3971

From promise to deed a day's j. 9320

help me faithfully to j. along my road 9074

Life is a j. 11374

No two human beings make same j. in life 5978

of a thousand miles 4435

of a thousand miles begins with single step 6871

old man nearing end of earthly j. 8121

On long j. even straw is heavy 8550

Our Father refreshes us on the j. with pleasant inns 7014

thus to j. on 11476

toward hope 5923

what man's j. is about 7435

Will the day's j. take the whole long day 6885

JOURNEYING

Death not a j. into unknown land 2249

JOURNEYMEN

cannot execute work of prayer 8914

JOURNEY'S

hope, an easier way to j. end 5924

world's an inn, death the j. end 2330

JOURNEYS

no one j. so far afield 4867

JOY

a Christian word, thing 6538

a secret spring 6529

accept everything, even problems, with j. 5261

acted and behold duty was j. 9663

Advent, coming of quiet j. 6119

against sorrow 10844

all strings in concert of his j. 4028

All who j. would win must share it 5505

an unceasing fountain 6529

and sorrow inseparable 10626

Arrogance and fear replaced with j. 1356

Behind j. may be callous temperament 10583

blessedness beyond j. 6536

bound up with love, goodness 6568

build up surging depth of j. 3185

cannot find j. in civilized life 10527

Change nursery of j. 960

Christ promises j. and courage 159

Christians envy saints their j. 3224

Christians, talk of j. of sacrificing 9758

confidence God is in control 6544

day of sorrow longer than month of j. 10580

deeper the sorrow, the more j. you can contain 10626

deeply rooted in life of God 6568

desire of love, j. 9274

Difficulty and j. mutual friends 2716

disquiet sadness 4877

do not understand j. until face sorrow 11620

does not depend on what happens 6527

does not mean drying of tears 8454

doubt anyone who has tasted j. would exchange for pleasure 6540

echo of God's life within 6545

every heart is j. 9897

eye can make heart dance for j. 3561

find way to fundamental j. 10915

flows in night as well as day 6529

flows right on through trouble 6529

flows though persecution, opposition 6529

For the heart that finds j. 6524

found more j. in sorrow 10593

Free will makes j. possible 4120

friend's love brings j. to heart 4382

Friendship doubles j. 4229

full-blossomed trees filled air with j. 2977

gigantic secret of the Christian 6546

Give yourself up with j. to loving confidence in God 4747

Giving j. if we do in right spirit 4357

goal not j. nor peace 4428

gospel makes man sing for j. 5091

Grant us a heart wide open to j, beauty 9064

great note all through Bible 6547

great word to master, j. 7000

Grief may be j. misunderstood 5339

grief passes into quiet, tender j. 7101

Grief should be like j. 5331

happiness and j. from God's standpoint 5531

has springs deep down inside 6538

heart filled to brim with j. must be still 6559

Helping each other through j. and strife 4281

his j. to enter sorrowful hearts 10603

hold on to past j, postpone blessings 968

holy fire that keeps purpose warm 10829

honest j. must be congruous with tragedy 6571

Humanness is realization of ecstactic j. 5014

if any idea j. you would bring to others 10703

If God is anything, he must be j. 6532

If no j. in your religion 6534

If try to find lasting j. in human relationship 9467

in darkness secure from empty, false j. 2547

in j. a warm, positive effluence of love 6537

In j. do not promise to give anything 11920

in j. one does not only feel secure 6537

in nature is absence of man 8035

in reading God's Word 733

in small things, in all things 6524

individualism distorts j. of identity 9952

intrigues 6819

is a positive thing 6537

is an attitude, posture, position, place 6528

is an option 1516

is grief remade again 6543

is in us 6541

is j. compatible with pain 6571

is j. that comes back to you 6561

is love exalted 7202

is never in our power 6540

is not in things 6541

is peace dancing 6542

is sorrow inside out 6543

is to behold God in everything 6550

it is j. unspeakable 7964

Jesus had j. even under shadow of the cross 6538

Jesus is the j. of heaven 6460 10603

Jesus' j. to enter sorrowful hearts 6460

keeps intelligence aglow 10829

level of j. proportional to level of acceptance 6556

like subterranean spring waters whole life 6568

Lord gives his people perpetual j. 6529

Lord, brother in j. and pain 7506

Love like a rose, j. of all the earth 7179

Love puts the j. in a heart 7269

love, j, peace multiply when divide with others 4360

magnified when shared 6539

Man cannot find j. anywhere but in God 6552

miss j. miss reason for existence 6571

Money brings days of j, but not peace 7807

more in sorrow than you could find in j. 10593

most infallible sign of presence of God 6548

most profound j. more gravity than gaiety 6562

Music as seasonable in grief as j. 7903

Music exalts each j. 7900

never knew j. until gave up happiness 2308

never knew what j. was until 5530

No evil example can bring j. to doer 5035

no happiness equal to j. of finding heart that understands 9504

no longer strive for our own way 6566

not a capricious emotion 6568

not a thing of moods 6568

of creativeness should be ours 2002

of finding you already there 1512

of God flows through people who influence us 6239

of heart colors face 6560

Of j. or sorrow 11362

of life arises from being where one belongs 1807

of parents in children most holy j. of humanity 5844

of the sad 6468

of the Spirit in the cross 2096

Oh the j. of life with, in and for God 6554

Oh what a j. it is 4799 1763

on through the dark 6529

One j. dispels a hundred cares 6555

Only heart that hurts has right to j. 6571

opposite of j. is unbelief 11594

opposite of j. not sorrow 11594

pain is brief, j. eternal 2383

peace is j. at rest 6542

Pentecost, exuberance of j. 5806

people so empty of j. 6531

property of friendship 4227

Psalm 23 filled world with melodious j. 801

Quotations tell of j. 9385

reached me like a solemn j. 4758

Reading, j. not dulled by age 858

Real j. is sorrow accepted, transformed 6557

rejoice with j. that radiates 3182

replaced by pursuit of duty 6813

reverse of happiness 6538

sacrifice a great j. 9758

saints experienced of j. and sorrow 2593

secret of j. to commit ourselves to God's way 6566

serenity of heaven 2580

sheer j. of wanting to get up 9114

Silence is perfectest herald of j. 6558

slept and dreamed life was j. 9663

soil watered with tears of repentance, j. 888

Sorrow more alert to open door than grandson J. 8996

sorrow so close to j. 7081

Sorrows come to stretch out spaces for j. 2508

Sorrows remembered sweeten present j. 10624

Sorrows stretch out spaces in heart for j. 10623

state, condition of the soul 6568

strength, courage are with thee 8867

sudden death, sudden j. 2212

suffering a far stronger link than j. 5338

suffering will become quiet j. 10932

survives through pain, sorrow 6568

sweet j. comes through sorrow 10638

Temper thy j, this, too, shall pass away 6878

that belongs to suffering miracle of faith 10907

that world may become one family in common j. 9093

the more grief better fitted to appreciate j. 5357

the serious business of heaven 6549

the wine that God is ever pouring 8454

thing of beauty, a j. forever 534

thought God's purpose to make me full of j. 5531

thousand times better than pleasure 1293

Thy j. to do the Father's will 10133

To the church, Pentecost brought j. 5806

too great, grand to be confused with happiness 6564

touches God with sorrow or j. 7057

True friends no solitary j. 4291

true j. of man's life in relationship to God 9467

Unshared j. is unlighted candle 4295

visible beatitude for j. 1242

We are all strings in the concert of God's j. 6570

what is j. of heaven but improvement of spirit 3482

What is the j. about 3400

What j. the happy earth to greet 9898

When I think upon my God, my heart so full of j. 7931

when recognize My love coming to you 5271

when we identify our own thoughts 11253

when you share j, you increase it 5353

Where j, there is fulfillment 6536

where j. abides 3649

Where love reigns, j. of heaven felt 7342

where there is sadness, j. 9086

who find great j. on their knees 8865

With j. shall I lift up my head 4719

You and I were created for j. 6571

you give to others comes back to you 6561

JOY'S

test of j. integrity 6571

JOYFUL

can choose to be j. 6530

deep j. sharing replaces polite prattle 4029

gospel signifies j. tydings 5091

kneel in j. silence 4750

let your j. heart praise 8737

life full of spontaneous j. uncertainty 5463

Love is j. 7246

martyrs, when the j. crown is given 7672

May we have j. sense of our blessings 9092

sanctification a j. liberation 9842

Through thorny ways leads to j. end 1502

JOYFULLY

accepting conditions of earthly pilgrimage 9090

friend will j. sing with you 4175

in all things to serve thee j. 9088

JOYLESS

goal of fear to create j. souls 3971

JOYOUS

resting place of my spirit 7961

turn theological truth into j. experience 12063

JOYS

a thousand j. he would pour into you at once 6525

are like the everlasting hills 7569

death resurrection of j. 2266

disclose inner fears, temptation, deepest j. 4029

divided are increased 6551

empathy, j. of others felt as their own 3081

feel j. so continual and great 6533

for all j, riches of the world 5652

found in what is real 9399

Friendship one of the sweetest j. of life 4236

Great j, like griefs, are silent 6526

home j. most delightful earth affords 5844

life with its sudden, startling j. 3685

life's great j. 50

Marriage doubles our j. 7634

Marriage fuller of sorrow and j. 7635

Only solitary men know full j. of friendship 4261

Remember your j. 9271

silence teaches j. of sound 824

tastes the j. of heaven 4749

What though my j. die 232

which long to be ours 6565

Who bathes in worldly j. swims in world of fears 8615

Who craves for ease, rest, j. 2583

JUBILANT

turned into j. song of glee 7895

JUDAS

cried "all hail" whereas he meant all harm 630

Jesus died even for J. 6469

kiss'd his master 630

sold himself for a bag of silver 11798

sold himself, not Christ 775

JUDGE

a tree from its fruit, not leaves 6581

As children grow older they j. parents 1111

as if one were God or j. placed above him 11619

Bible j. that ends strife 710

can't j. Christianity by comparing product 1316

conduct by Christ 563

Conscience punishes us as a j. 1677

Do not give up faculty to j. 1241

Do not j. a man until you know whole story 6573

Do not j. by appearances 431

does not accuse as if one were j. 3079

Don't hear one, j. two 6606

Don't j. a tree by bark 432

Don't j. any man until walked in his moccasins 6574

Don't j. until been through his experience 6575

Forbear to j. for we are sinners all 6577

from own feelings how God must feel 4895

God will direct faculty to j. 1241

God will j. on basis of what we kept 7797

God, the J, sovereignly declared pardoned 3672

good cause will fear no j. 6602

help me never to j. another 9065

How widely Jesus known difficult to j. 6395

I cannot j. intention, motivation of another 4247

less tempted to j. others 10306

Most j. men only by success 6584

Never to j. rashly 1080

Nobody can j. men but God 4720

Only j. when you have heard all 6588

ourselves by our motives 6596

resolved as j. to try Bible as in courtroom 744

there sits a j. no king can corrupt 4716

to j. character by only one manifestation 1053

To j. wisely, must know how things appear to unwise 6595

we j. others by their actions 6596

where God alone may enter as j. 1666

wise j. opinion 8205

you must be very big to be able to j. 4553

yourself by friends you choose 4194

JUDGED

am not j. by light I have 6579

by standard higher, more attainable 6812

Christianity, not to be j. by success, failure 1188

God j. it better to bring good out of evil 5018

If you j. him by the hide 926

lives by faith and love not j. on the law 6812

measure by which action to be j. 7307

service j. by how much of me is in it 10119

service not j. by how much done 10119

unfairly j. when we do good 187

JUDGES

did not resolve Paul's case 786

God j. by direction 4713

God j. man by way he is facing 4713

God j. not by distance 4713

God's truth j. created things out of love 4914

Man j. from a partial view 6583

more one j, less one loves 6593

Satan's truth j. out of envy, hatred 4914

who j. others condemns himself 6578

JUDGING

from number of things going to do then 9302

God j. men with perfect knowledge 4720

God j. men with undisturbed compassion 4720

God j. men with unperplexed certainty 4720

like j. sea by jugful of water 1053

Sainthood delivers from j. others 9778

stop j. neighbors 10162

struggle against evil by j. ourselves 3414

struggle against evil not by j. others 3414

JUDGMENT

before his j. seat 4715

By our anti-intellectualism may be storing up j. of God 6679

Compassion can never coexist with j. 10162

creates distance 10162

each evening passes j. 11364

God allows our j. to mislead us 9851

God's great j. seat 915

God's, not man's 6591

Grant us true j. to distinguish things that differ 9063

Guilt suggested by j. of men 5477

I know of the future j. 1663

If love does not agree with j. 4755

implacable light of j. 1719

in j. of good we can make mistakes 5086

independent of fear of social j. 1647

inner support by j. of God 5477

Jesus Christ taught not to sit in j. 9789

looking down his nose 1217

man forever criticizing wife's j. 7655

of God evidence of love of God 4721

of God is reaping that comes from sowing 4721

of God not proof of his wrath 4721

one cool j. worth thousand hasty councils 6587

passing j. on all human life 24

plead them against me in j. 4069

saint has same j. with Christ 9766

sincere convert will not neglect j. 1908

sit alone with conscience j. enough 1707

the day of j. 49

the j. to escape 9828

to cross all opinions come for j. 2157

We bring God to j. 229

worked my best subject to ultimate j. 6591

Would be j. enough for me 1663

JUDGMENTAL

live with criticism, learn to be j. 1114

JUDGMENTS

God's j. are of another sort 9195

God's j. as great deeps 3349

let j. be provisional 571

not ultimate 571

JUDICIAL

temptation to make relation to God j. 9816

JUG
never carried under coat for honest reason 2905

JULIUS CAESAR
more evidence Jesus rose than J. lived 9700

JULY
when mothers realize why teachers need vacations 9900

JUMP
don't throw away ticket and j. off 5461
from worship to waiting to work 10716
on to one side or the other 1156

JUMPS
can't cross chasm in two small j. 3650
Some go in j. like spiritual frogs 10716

JUNE
Beneath the billowy clouds of J. 9887
Flame-flowered, yellow-petalled J. 9886
may be had by the poorest comer 2641

JUNGLE
we do not live under law of j. 7331

JURY
ever about him silent court and j. 1684
fox should not be on j. at goose's trial 9177

JUST
achieve, cherish j. lasting peace 5199
become j. by doing things j. 6620
cause we believe to be j. 3625
God could not be good if not j. 4724
hand is precious ointment 6624
imbue men with j. fear of God 6796
impossible to be j. if not generous 6610
Is God j. 10841
must first be made j. 5087
Righteously righteous, justly j. 2028
says some lies are j. 11506
says some sins are j. 11506
seek to make institutions of power j. 6623
slips upon snow unjust doesn't clear away 9905
sun shine upon j. and unjust 4129
things j. which are unjust 11506
thou, again thou, always thou 4518
wars j. which are ordained by God 11743
with the last he still directs the j. 4812

JUSTICE
an attribute of God 6628
Bible contains formula for j. 701
brightest emanation from the gospel 6628
Christ seeking j. 1277
Christ wrestled with j. 6393
Christian to give j. 1207
Christian's goal not power but j. 6623
Corn can't expect j. from chickens 6605
Delay in j. is injustice 6259
delayed is j. denied 6611
Democracy only form of social order consistent with j. 2525
false that God torn between j, mercy 4579
fundamental postulates of j. 5169
God does not maintain neutrality in j. 6630
God's j, love are one 4725
God's j. incomprehensible 4728
God's j. permits creation to punish humanity 3191
God's j. stands forever 4726
goodness without j. is not goodness 4724
great thing expressed in single word 10277
greatest saint not he who is eminent for j. 9790
Hell is God's j. 5650
hope of nation not in j. of administration 5190
human to demand j. 1207
if j, mercy prevail in own common life 6286
If love does not agree with j. 4755
If not for injustice, men would not know j. 6264
If we do j, will come to love him 6609
If you leave out j. 7836
Infinite j. must be infinite love 4725
Injustice anywhere is a threat to j. everywhere 6266
is compassion 1542
is insurance on our lives 8096
is love working out problems 6612
is truth in action 6613
it is j. that hurts 6267
live with fairness, learn j. 1114
love asks us to walk many miles not demanded by j. 7273
Man's capacity for j. makes democracy possible 2528
mercy not effective until j. has done 4730
must be more than j. 6614
no good government without j. 5194
no minor sin when his j. confronts you 10405
one connected chain of j, mercy, truth 4904

One hour of j. worth a hundred of prayer 6617
Opinions if founded in j. will prevail 8199
Peace is j. 8455
pearl of j. found in heart of mercy 6625
prayer for j. 9104, 9109
presence of God's j. in hell 4865
punishment works with sense of j. 9355
question of j. that may bring suffering, death 10564
righteousness of Christmas 1364
Sin is the dare of God's j. 10376
stubborn struggle for j. 4643
There's a kindness in his j. 7745
will not be satisfied until j. rolls down like waters 6629
without love can no more render j. 6614

JUSTICE'S
Truth is j. handmaid 6628

JUSTIFICATION
foundation that supports all benefits 6633
means "just-as-if-I-never-sinned" 6632
Silence is freedom to let our j. rest with God 6622

JUSTIFIED
Christ condemned that thou mightest be j. 6393
glad to be called, j. 2232

JUSTIFY
And j. the ways of God to men 7566
criticism makes man j. himself 2055
God does not j. us because worthy 6631
Grace can j. us with Christ's righteousness 5212
if wrong, sanction of mankind will not j. 5032
whether faith will not j. confidence 3774

JUSTIFYING
by j. us God makes us worthy 6631

JUSTLY
Happy is man who strikes balance j. 1240
No man can j. censure or condemn another 6585

JUVENILES
high crime rate among j. 5858

K

KANGAROO
creation for sheer fun 1961

KEEL
world would k. over 6184

KEEP

A charge to k. I have 10114
ability to k. mouth shut priceless 1876
ask to k. you ready to do as he appoints 10120
best way to k. from stepping on toes 11286
best way to k. is to let go 4733
better to k. friend from falling than help up 4191
but k. a tidy soul 10652
cannot expect another to k. secret 5141
Christian, gives away to k. 1265
Dead Sea gets to k. 10195
Do good to your friend to k. him 9449
Do not k. alabaster boxes 4223
don't k. faith with God, won't k. with man 3799
ear to the ground 3503
Every man should k. fair-sized cemetery 4225
eye on the ball 3503
Guard, guide, k. feed us 5428
heart free from hate 5561
henceforth k. within this line 1802
human to k. what one has 1207
I k. six honest serving men 6686
if in life you k. the zest 8122
If we do not k. commandments 8106
If you your lips would k. from slips 1855
in reserve treasures of God's deep counsels 4322
in the sunlight 3500
leaves of life k. falling one by one 7031
Legalists k. law to merit award 6815
life, none but fools would k. 7019
main thing is to k. the main thing the main thing 9275
man imagines he will k. if he hides 1537
mind free from worry 5561
must k. friendships in constant repair 4249
no fool who gives what he cannot k. 1533
None so fond of secrets as those who do not mean to k. them 5150
not a custom to k. money to look at 7803
only the redeemed can k. God's commandments 4536
performance must k. friends 4262
Pray, God, k. us simple 10282
praying, but be thankful God's answers are wiser 8861
put man into unholy world, k. him holy in it 5759
respectful fear of God in lives 3993
secret is wisdom 1618
shall have corn to sell, k. 3115

shoulder to the wheel 3503
task in solitude to k. mind on Savior 10551
thou my feet 5429
three may k. secret if two dead 1617
to k. a friend, close two eyes 4161
to k. money more difficult 7823
Tomorrow I k. for God 1539
us from going too far 10992
want to k. faith, must share it 3771
what is worth keeping 4260
will break bow if k. bent 9536
within own little sphere 4885
your face to the sunshine 1098
yourself clean and bright 3438, 8573

KEEPER

God is your K. 5907

KEEPETH

Where he hath put and k. you 4834

KEEPING

fear in k. riches 11865
Finding, following, k, struggling 6892
God more concerned about k. us 5390
keep what is worth k. 4260
Love alone his watch is k. 1123
Safe in Jehovah's k. 4490
Unfaithfulness in k. appointment dishonesty 2914
watch above his own 5377
who seeks applause has happiness in another's k. 5892

KEEPS

And whom he finds young, k. young still 7264
ball-and-chain mentality k. us from giving 6825
God in whom we trust k. us 11474
God k. his word even when seems impossible 9321
God k. the score 7559
good name k. brightness even in dark days 6292
great man in midst of crowd k. independence 6195
if k. money, he's a capitalist 7800
not our trust that k. us 11474
Pride k. them in trouble 9237
We play the game, God k. the score 6069

KEN

God is beyond our k. 4665

KEPT

by Almighty power 4490
Christians not k. altogether from falling 4623
Friendship is like money, easier made than k. 4235
God will judge on basis of what we k. 7797
him a living soul 8911

I know thee, thou hast k. my path 4758
Real doesn't often happen to people who have to be carefully k. 5886
secret best k. by keeping secret 1614
What I k, I lost 4383

KERNEL

Meditation is the k. 7726
Money can buy the husk, but not the k. 7807

KEY

And thrown the k. away 11369
doctrine master k. to world's problems 11213
enter into paradise with right k. 5641
fact about God 4779
Faith, k. to fit door of hope 3836
life, once k. to meaning in our hands 6940
Obedience is k. that unlocks door 8101
Obedience is k. to every door 8102
of every chamber 8092
Prayer k. of the morning 8943
prayer k. that opens to us God's mercies, blessings 8846
prayer k. that shuts us up under God's protection 8846
Repentance is k. that opens any lock 9586
sings own praise usually off k. 9206
to everything is patience 8420
touch right k. at right time 7897
we are all looking for the k. 6976

KEYHOLE

Christian, k. through which folks see God 1254
Temptation is devil looking through k. 11088

KEYNOTE

Every action has a k. 6379
God laid the k. of all harmonies 7891
rests not to change k. 9684

KEYS

give Christ k. of your heart 8092
Little k. open big locks 11989

KICK

in teeth may be best 138
one vicious or thoughtless k. destroys 7233
Tact is pat on back when feel like k. in pants 10988
the whine out ruthlessly 10032

KICKER

hate to be a k. 8564

KICKING

eye can insult like k. 3561

KICKS

up a storm 382

KIDS

a long-term investment 1121
can frustrate, irritate parents 8304
if easy to raise k, never would start with labor 8302
mother challenges k. to do their best 7844
not a short-term loan 1121
rewards of raising k. 8304
teenagers too old to do things k. do 12172

KILL

Death cannot k. what never dies 7319
does not know what to do with time except k. it 11307
in every war they k. you a new way 11780
indifferent do not k. or betray 6158
Men whom the lust of office does not k. 6299
no way to k. righteousness but by own consent 11102
punished unless k. in large numbers 11753
right to k. because his ruler has quarrel with mine 11744
so many trying to k. time 11310
themselves in stinging others 9721
They will k. me if they please 7103
tongue can k. man six feet high 5161
You cannot k. time without injury to eternity 6784
What God will, no frost can k. 4959
Work won't k, worry will 12083
worst enemies can do is k. you 6158

KILLED

alcohol, k. more men than wars 331
Christ k. that thou mightest live 6393
fear of sinning k. spontaneity 6813
it only to find nothing 5328
Saints usually k. by their own people 9779

KILLERS

Bible transformed k. into saints 726

KILLING

not just refrain from k. but from being angry 6444
repentance means k. part of yourself 9577

KILLS

Criticism k. love 5135
Every step toward Christ k. a doubt 2940
extreme heat and cold k. 3554
Flattery, hand that k. 4049
He who k. time k. opportunities 6757

Pride k. thanksgiving 6027

KIND

a grace of k. listening 6669
a grace of k. speaking 6669
Be k, everyone is fighting hard battle 6635
Be to her virtues very k. 7603
devil's ever k. to his own 2694
discipline cruel that it may be k. 2839
Do that k. deed you would leave 'till tomorrow 6671
ever remember when regretted having said k. word 6636
God is too k. to do anything cruel 4461
God, heart profoundly k. 4477
happiness of life made up of a k. look 5556
hope God too k. to punish the ungodly 4726
is to be k. to his other children 6665
Make haste to be k. 6658
Meek means k. 7729
Misers very k. people 11837
never sorry you were k. 6674
O be the New as k. 8078
one glance most k. 107
One k. act will teach more love of God 6661
One k. word can warm three winter months 6662
Speak that k. word to sweeten a sorrow 6671
Speak your k. words soon 6663
sweetest music in k. words 11995
The heart benevolent and k. 6666
word never thrown away 6672
words and actions right 6647
words don't wear out tongue 6646
words music of the world 6645
words short, easy to speak 11988
words smooth, quiet, comfort 11985
words toward those you daily meet 6647
words, echoes truly endless 11988
world so k. you leave with regret 2293
worth of k. deed lies in the love 2506

KINDER

Eternity looks grander, k. if 3268
War is k. than a godless peace 11770

KINDERGARTEN

world kind of spiritual k. 7530

KINDEST

are those who forgive and forget 6667
Experience not always k. of teachers 3526
man will put heel on his greatest friend 10527

KINDLE

fire, light up entire city 5751
if world seems cold, k. fires to warm it 5959
Lord appeared to k. us by his example 6477
love grown cold can k. again 3167

KINDLED

brightest blazes of gladness k. by unexpected sparks 8606
Through sorrow human compassion k. 10640
Worship candle in act of being k. 12132

KINDLES

Believe with a faith that k. 3182

KINDLING

Make k. out of fallen tree 3606

KINDLY

each k. deed a prayer 7284
faithful those who k. reprove thy faults 3955
Gaze on honest effort k. 4217
If obey laws, space will treat you k. 11650
Lead k. Light 2551
Lead, k. Light, amid encircling gloom 5429
Shepherd behind me 5375
To speak k. does not hurt tongue 11421
Treat temptations k, they will return 11091

KINDNESS

a language blind can see 6650
a language deaf can hear 6650
a language dumb can speak 6650
acts of k. and love 626
any k. that I can show 6642
causes misunderstanding to evaporate 6668
Greatness lies in small acts of k. 5283
has converted more sinners 6648
Hatred, anger powerless when met with k. 6639
Have you had a k. shown 6640
If God is love, he is more than k. 7186
in another's trouble 6657
in giving creates love 6649
in his justice 7745
in thinking creates profoundness 6649
in words creates confidence 6649
is love in work clothes 6652
learned k. from unkind 5251
like a rose 6650
Little acts of k. silent threads of gold 6997
Little deeds of k. 2503
loving people more than they deserve 6653
meet denunciations with k. 2630
merits no thanks who does k. for own ends 10056

My love coming to you through k.
  of others 5271
never omitting opportunity of k.
  9491
Of k. and love 6664
part of the k. of God 4643
sunshine in which virtue grows
  6654
to k. we make promises, pain we
  obey 8261
will always attract k. 6655
win, preserve the heart 6656
with breath of k. blow rest away
  4260

KINDNESSES
Forget injuries, never forget k.
  6638
than to requite k. 9720

KINDS
In face of evil three k. of souls
  5029
many k. of smiles 10500
two k. of people 5455

KING
A royal cup for him, my K. 7003
Christianity, k. has landed in
  disguise 1190
divine K. rules forever by dying
  2166
don't stoop to be a k. 7781
dream he was laborer 8576
greet in cradle Savior, K. 1375
He is happiest, be he k. or peasant
  5827
he that is evil a slave, though a k.
  4131
I shall see the K. 5676
If laborer to dream he was k.
  8576
In his ascension, Christ a k. 6410
In kingdom of blind, one-eyed
  man is k. 823
like David with sheep after
  anointed k. 5391
live a k, die a man 2353
no k. holds key to as much power
  11841
prefer to be k. of the mountain for
  a day 5308
remain k. within kingdom of
  Mansoul 2821
rise happier than a k. 10208
Satan tried Jesus Christ becoming
  K. of world 11082
there sits a judge no k. can corrupt
  4716
Thou art coming to a K. 9000
Wherever God rules human heart
  as K. 4736
Whether k. or subject 10527

KING OF HEAVEN
teardrop on earth summons K.
  11011

KING'S
A wonderful way is the K.
  Highway 4313

KINGDOM
cannot say thine is the k. if 8818
cannot say thy k. come if 8818
Christ never contaminated his
  inner k. 6501
Christ, k. on the inside 6501
Christians entitled to God's k.
  1267
Every man carries k. within 6171
God gives us ability to work in his
  k. 4648
God rewards us for working in his
  k. 4648
In k. of hope there is no winter
  5936
in the k. of fantasy 3347
into k. acting, not saying Lord,
  Lord 1349
inward invisible k. that causes
  saint to sing through sorrow
  5775
Jesus has many lovers of heavenly
  k. 2828
Jesus has many who love his
  heavenly k. 9268
Love rules k. without sword 7270
neither can k. rise without his aid
  4933
No k. with as many wars as k. of
  Christ 1215
No one knows what is taking
  place in another's k. 6171
of blind, one-eyed man is king
  823
of God a paradox 2519
of Jesus, king is servant 526
Our part is to enter k. 4734
politics of K. people must be
  changed to change society
  10528
remain king within k. of Mansoul
  2821
until k. of this world is k. of our
  Lord 6939
way to the top in God's k. 10161

KINGDOM OF GOD
disqualified for membership in k.
  4133
does not exist because of your
  effort 4734
Everyone wants k. 4731
everything contributes to building
  of k. 4732
exists because God reigns 4734
few want k. first 4731
government not tool to establish
  K. 5177
In k. surest way to lose is to
  protect 4733
kingdom of God wherever God
  rules, there k. established 4736
Seniority in k. does not imply
  superiority 5897
When we seek first k. 4735

KINGDOM OF HEAVEN
better to show up for work in k.
  at sunset 8141
cannot enter k. head first 9426

introduce k. into midst of earthly
  day 4974
know from experience k. within us
  5426
Theological beliefs do not get one
  into K. 601

KINGDOMS
On the soft bed of luxury, most k.
  have died 7364
rise and wane 4694

KINGLIKE
art thou? This, too, shall pass
  away 6878

KINGS
all k. that ever reigned 6353
captains and k. depart 6036
commonly is case of k. 11827
crown that seldom k. enjoy 1808
Death knocks at palaces of k.
  2361
Good k. never make war but for
  peace 11747
Princes and lords but breath of k.
  5885
Time's glory is to calm contending
  k. 11344

KINSHIP
happiness is k. of heart to heart
  5538
to cheat child of k. with humanity
  8334

KISS
of enemy full of deceit 2473
when you pray, more a whisper
  than a k. 8801

KISSES
When rogue k. you, count your
  teeth 2478

KITCHEN
in k. as great tranquility as upon
  knees 8471

KNACK
Tact k. of making point without
  making enemy 10990

KNEE
let your k. be a sacred altar 7847
The Christ child stood at Mary's k.
  6470

KNEEL
At whose throne would God k.
  4955
before you leap 8862
Humility is to shut the door, k. in
  secret 6010
if Christ should come we would k.
  6406
in joyful silence 4750
knees shaking, k. on them 8842
mother used to make me k. by her
  side 8347
That even when I k. to pray 9075
We k, how weak! 8867
You stand tall when you k. to pray
  9038

KNEELING
awaiting his verdict on us 3333
Father, in thy mysterious presence k. 9050
in worship k. 12102

KNEELS
an ordinary Christian k. to say his prayers 8761

KNEES
able to express my dependence better on my k. 8759
Christian on his k. sees more than philospher on tiptoe 8975
Don't let your sorrow come higher than your k. 8784
driven many times to my k. 8822
Drop to your k. beside wide road 4608
hour worrying on our k. is not prayer 9009
If swept off feet, time to get on k. 8836
in kitchen as great tranquility as upon k. 8471
man is powerful on his k. 8785
moments when the soul is on its k. 8776
Must go upon their k. 5649
not saint on k, cheat in shop 1908
on k. sign of helplessness apart from divine enablement 8759
Safety, peace only after forced to k. 882
Selfishness never so selfish as on its k. 10080
shaking, kneel on them 8842
Than these k. bow to any save God 7677
The weakest saint upon his k. 8959
what buckles the k. 4551
When life knocks you to your k. 9027
who fight battles on their k. 8865
who find great joy on their k. 8865

KNELT
only when k. before God can we stand before men 8880

KNEW
Abraham k. the Guide 5372
educate in what nobody k. yesterday 3035
emotions tell us things we never k. 3062
God k. of good which could come of evil 5020
God k. us before we k. him 4884
Heaven were not heaven if we k. what it were 3496
I k. I was free 4136
I never k. the worth of him 4199
If I k. myself, I'd run away 10011
If k. everything, could not endure existence 6081
if only k. worth of suffering 10872

If we k. everything said about us 9466
If we k. how to listen to God 8835
intellectual world stale if we k. everything 9286
Jesus k. what he was to accomplish 4425
loneliness when creative mood would work 7141
never k. how to worship until k. how to love 7185
None ever yet his brother k. 6583
one small head should carry all it k. 2994
Sixty years ago I k. everything 3024
Solomon k. how little he k. 795
They taught me all I k. 6686
years teach much which days never k. 3546

KNIFE
man without courage, k. without edge 1917

KNIGHT'S PRAYER
Inscribed in Chester Cathedral 9088

KNIT
hearts with unslipping knot 7625

KNITS
Grief k. two hearts closer than happiness can 5338

KNIVES
If a man can make better k. 2776

KNOCK
As yet but k, breathe, shine, mend 2840
Don't k. the weather 7998
exceed in interest k. at door 4259
themselves and their world upside down 8850

KNOCKED
Fear k. at the door 3968

KNOCKS
When life k. you to your knees 9027

KNOT
broken string may be joined, k. will remain 9624
God hid k. so low we cannot reach 5384
God's decree ties k. of adoption 4616
in de plank will show through whitewash 2469
Knit hearts with unslipping k. 7625
tie a k. and hang on 2615

KNOTS
Let Lord untie k. 2802

KNOTTED
how many k. brows in marketplace 10507

KNOW
A voice in the wind I do not k. 4962
able to k. what everybody else thinks 4332
Abraham did not k. the way 5372
all amazingly k. their path 7945
all I k. is that I k. nothing 11904
All we k. infinitely less than remains unknown 6677
all, you will pardon all 4092
Almighty finds a way of letting me k. 5410
almost nothing about inner life 1753
always k. our proper stations 3112
amazed how much young people k. about sex 10222
anxious to k. what is expected of them 6810
bad enough to k. the past 4317
before you k. how little you k. 6700
Behold my needs which I k. not myself 9042
best k. how to prize friends most 4286
best why man alone laughs 6742
better to ask some questions than k. all answers 6688
blessing to k. destitute spiritually 830
But this I surely k. 5434
By faith we k. his existence 3814
by self-examination to k. our own faults 10014
came to k. God is all we need 7472
can k. him who knows heart's secret 5624
can never k. who or what we are 7438
can stand what I k. 6685
cannot fathom yet seeking to k. satisfying 5450
cannot k. at what moment flash forth with life of God 7055
cannot k. what God is 4687
Christianity, way to k. God 1188
crucial what we do not want to k. 6680
desire to k. art of living 10935
difficult to k. oneself 10008
Do not judge a man until you k. whole story 6573
do not k. a man until we k. his leisure 6842
do not k. how I am going to stay "in the air" 9908
do not k. how soon may be too late 9609
do not k. nation until we k. pleasures 6842
do not k. one millionth of one percent about anything 6709
do not k. what God is going to do next 5463
do not k. what I was playing 7919

do not k. what to do on a rainy
Sunday afternoon 6100

do not k. when world drama will
end 9911

Do the truth you k. 9649

Do you k. what you are 3039

does not k. how to stay quietly in
his room 5560

does not k. what to do with time
he gains 11307

doesn't k. how dishonest he is
11098

don't k. ourselves well enough to
tell another 7428

Each of the redeemed shall forever
k. 6169

easier to k. God than own soul
1713

easier to k. mankind than man
individually 7393

either k. God firsthand or do not
k. him 7460

enemies friends who don't k. each
other 3171

Even asses k. straw is better than
gold 11804

Faces we see, hearts we k. not
2464

Few people k. how to be old 8130

first step of wisdom is to k. what
is false 11943

folks we k. briefly, quickly forget
4281

friendship with God 8327

from experience kingdom of
heaven within us 5426

God reveals that which is our
profit to k. 9708

God that thou mayst love him, be
like him 10010

God wants us to k. when we have
him, we have everything 4806

Great men never k. they are great
5279

how little people k. who think
holiness dull 5750

how sublime a thing it is 10869

how to listen 7114

humble only when we k. we are
God's children 6042

I do not believe. I k. 11123

I don't k. a blessing when it comes
my way 5587

I k. God is within me 5426

I k. he loves me well 4761

I k. my weakness 1018

I k. not what the future hath 6916

I k. not where his islands lift 4763

I k. that God is good 4642

I k. thee, thou hast kept my path
4758

I k. through thee, the blame was
mine 7480

I only k. I cannot drift 4763

If God does not k. what is best,
who would 4552

If k. laws space will treat you
kindly 11650

If not for injustice, men would not
k. justice 6264

If souls can suffer and I hardly k. it
7188

If think you k. it all, haven't been
listening 9210

If want to k. what a man is like
7802

if want to k. what God is like
4493

if you do not k. it for certainty
5149

If you do not love, do not k.
meaning of Christian life 7191

if you k. how to read him 6172

If you k. you will love 10807

If you want to k. about God 8840

in glory we shall k. his nature
3814

intolerable to k. the future 4317

Is this the end? I k. it cannot be
2319

known as no finite men can k. us
4768

law of humanity that man k. good
through evil 5030

learned to obey will k. how to
command 6792

Let me k. myself, O God, that I
may k. thee 9068

Let not right hand k. what left is
doing 10169

liberty to k. God alone matters
4151

Life is half-spent before we k.
what it is 6964

light so lovely will want to k.
source 12147

live up to best, highest you k.
3468

Lord God, you k. each bog 8081

Love a ceaseless effort to k, feel
7211

Love needs not to k. 5431

Lust, at its height, does not k.
shame 7358

made in image of God must k.
him or be desolate 7465

man a volume if you k. how to
read him 8490

Man does not k. himself truly
7494

Many men k. a great deal, are
greater fools for it 11973

may k. there is a God without
knowing what he is 3814

Men who didn't k. enough to tell
God 6147

Miracles contrary to what we k.
about nature 8021

more crucial than what we k.
6680

more men suppress the truth of
God which they k. 11538

more we learn, more we realize
how little we k. 3029

more you k. about Christ 6480

most inconvenient to k. oneself
10008

must live with people to k. their
problems 9292

My life is ending, I k. that well
7101

mystery is a fact about which we
cannot k. everything 7936

natural man must k. to believe
3743

need others if we are to k.
anything 9513

never k. how accessible men are
3345

never k. how much you believe
616

never k. how soon will be too late
6663

never k. love of parent until
become parents 3902

never k. when luxury going to
stand up 11834

Never send to k. for whom the
bell tolls 2339

never will world k. all it owes to
neurotics 4390

No one can k. God who has not
first known himself 7543

Nobody will k. "God is love"
unless you act it 7281

not by what methods rare 8825

not gotten to k. God 5594

not if the blessing sought 8825

not needful we k. intent 4885

not possible to k. God that we
may love him 4802

not young enough to k. everything
6684

nothing of Calvary love 7187

nothing of men's, women's rights
3230

now I k. nothing 3024

Now that I k. I'm no wiser than
anyone 11933

once we k. life is difficult 7012

Only in suffering will we k. Jesus
10930

only k. ourselves through Christ
6461

Only solitary men k. full joys of
friendship 4261

only way to k. is to will to do
God's will 5447

Real friends k. you have good
reason 4266

reputation would not k. character
if met on street 9618

secret of own heart you can never
k. 5624

secret of power is to k. God 3790

see him walk, k. his thoughts
8494

seldom k. why Lord chooses
whom 5894

serve a great man, will k. what
sorrow is 5292

should find God in what we k.
7562

should spend efforts seeking to k,
do will of God 5543

so much that ain't so 6083

something of what God is 7438

spiritual man must believe to k. 3743

spiritually humble who k. what peace is 8447

Strange how much you've got to k. 6700

Strange that I did not k. him then 4199

suddenly understand I k. nothing 6493

takes all time, eternity to k. God 4483

Tell me how much you k. of sufferings 7295

that we may k. where to stand 11731

the more we k. the more we wonder 4686

the One of whom, alas, we k. so little 6522

the resources of God 7485

theme is Get more, k. more, do more 9016

Then alone do we k. God truly 4685

They that k. God will be humble 6039

They that k. no evil will suspect none 3408

they that k. themselves cannot be proud 6039

this I k. God answers prayer 8825

Those who would k. much 6708

though we k. not goodness of God 4578

thyself that thou mayest k. God 10010

time, if no one asks, I k. 11351

time, if I want to explain it, I do not k. 11351

'Tis what I k, but can't express 7245

To believe in God is to k. rules will be fair 4508

To judge wisely must k. how things appear to unwise 6595

To k. all men brothers 921

To k. God easiest, most difficult in world 7546

to k. how God thinks 5425

To k. how to grow old 8178

To k. is not to be wise 11973

To k. man we must begin with God 4571

To k. nature is to k. there must be a God 6696

To k. one's ignorance best part of knowledge 11955

To k. one's self is the true 10022

to k. people study excuses 2807

To k. reasons which have moved God 4989

to k. someone who thinks, feels with us 4280

to k. soul seek God 1713

to k. that which is worth knowing 9063

To k. the road ahead 269

to k. what he ought to believe 9824

to k. what he ought to desire 9824

to k. what he ought to do 9824

true disciples of Christ not who k. most 7318

true value of time 11372

truly see and k. ourselves 156

venturing forth we k. not where 9930

want to k. anything, Bible is where you go 703

we are not alone 10539

we can k. that God is 4687

We do not k. the play 9911

We k. God as men born blind k. fire 4690

We k. God easily 4691

we k. God through Jesus Christ 10013

We k. how God would act if in our place 6151

We k. we sin 10442

we only k. ourselves through Jesus Christ 10013

We shall never k, never find out 4704

weren't for obstacles never k. what we want 2729

what are we like with those who k. us best 9845

what don't k. that frightens me 6685

What future bliss he gives not thee to k. 5913

what God is we k. little 4690

what some people must k. tomorrow 3035

what we are, but k. not what we may be 8672

what we k. not, teach us 9083

What we need to k. takes all time, eternity 3513

what you learn after you k. it all that counts 7691

When a man does not k. what harbor 4433

When k. philosophy, you k. what you cannot k. 8594

When we k. the Cross, no longer afraid of truth 11531

where history is going 5724

who does not k. God demands satisfaction from human beings 9496

who has not suffered, what does he k. 10832

who suffers much will k. much 10852

who wear shoe k. best where pinches 8275

will never ask for information, implies they do not k. 9236

will not k. how to pray when clouds roll in 8809

will not save me to k. Christ is Savior 3753

Wise men not always silent, but k. when to be 11977

wish I am rich, then k. I am ill 11878

wish to k. the character of a love 7167

won't k. until accepted 1893

would k. man better if 1649

yearning to k. what cannot be known 7531

Yes, you'd k. him for heathen 926

You k. no disturbing voice 4969

You may k. but not comprehend God 4693

you what it is to be a child 1122

you're getting old when 8190

your own bone; gnaw, bury, unearth it 6902

youth think they k. everything 12181

KNOW-IT-ALL

solution in the hollow of his head 449

the solution to every problem 449

KNOW-IT-ALLS

two k. always disagee 453

KNOWABLE

God is k. 4509

KNOWEST

Speak less than thou k. 2899

thou k. the whole truth 9104

KNOWING

art of k. what to overlook 11900

being wise is k. what to overlook 11940

end is k. God himself 741

experience feeling led without k. it 5392

Faith is k. God will turn effect to good 3671

God gradual process 5738

God's infinitude places him above k. 4702

greatest happiness is k. you do not require happiness 5555

he has wings 11475

Initiative of saint toward k. Jesus Christ 1324

is above reason 5809

is convincing 5809

is immediate 5809

is inwardly satisfying 5809

loving before k. God 4802

man flung without k. how or why into world 3495

may know there is a God without k. what he is 3814

men sigh on, not k. what the soul wants 7516

Nothing worth k. can be taught 11932

One half of k. what you want 4431

question k. never can full answer be found 7435

Success is k. God 10807

to know that which is worth k. 9063

Trust k. God will catch you 11486
what you must give up 4431
When life rosy may slide by k.
  about Jesus 10930
when to say nothing 7626
which most acute thinker cannot
  imitate 5809
who withholds goods k. neighbor
  to be in need 10060
Wisdom k. what to do next 11721
Without the truth no k. 6382
worried and not k. God 7888

KNOWLEDGE
about sublime worth more than
  trivialities 6676
accept even our incomplete k. of
  God 7435
and wisdom, far from being one
  6690
Apothegms form shortcut to
  much k. 9378
As k. increases, wonder deepens
  6678
as to himself, God hath k. 4514
begins with wondering 6691
Bible source of heavenly k. 737
boasts of own k. proclaims
  ignorance 6682
By faith led to k. of God 3834
By faith led to k. of ourselves
  3834
by suffering entereth 10870
can be knowledgeable with other
  men's k. 11958
cannot obtain entire k. of Bible
  737
charge God of all k. with
  ignorance 230
Christian knows that which
  passes k. 1265
come to religion through k. of
  limitations of science 9866
comes, wisdom lingers 6692
  11926
desire of k. in excess caused man
  to fall 3556
Discussion exchange of k. 2901
divine life rather than k. 11200
Do not give up k. 1241
dwells in heads replete with
  thoughts of men 6690
enemy in prayer is lack of k. of
  what we are in Christ 8815
everything means of k. of Jesus
  Christ 1324
experience outweighs k. from
  hearsay 3535
faith is child of k. 6714
Faith k. that transcends intellect
  3673
first temptation was promise of
  learning and k. 6701
For attainment of divine k. 6681
full k. of everything against us
  4884
given to lead us to worship, faith,
  holiness, service 6693
given us to be used 6693
God is illuminating for k. 4514

God judging men with perfect k.
  4720
God outside circle of our k. 4614
God will direct 1241
God will hold us responsible for
  k. we have 6679
God will not allow lack of k. to
  3340
God will not permit k. of things
  to come 4314
hopes to do deed without God's k.
  errs 2501
if grudge, spiritual penetration
  into k. of God stops 9633
ignorant man's world bounded by
  limits of k. 11728
Imagination more important than
  k. 2005
in k. most haunted with inevitable
  limitation 6689
indispensable to Christian life,
  service 6693
Integrity without k. weak 3013
is horizontal 11928
is power 6694
is proud has learned so much
  6695
larger the island of k. 6702
leads from simple to complex
  11929
life lived in full k. of fears 3990
lifetime cultivating k. of God 4702
loneliness k. human beings
  incapable of bringing help 7126
My k. is pessimistic 8247
My k. of that life is small 5635
no absolute k. 6706
not a question of our k. 8
nuisance that k. only acquired by
  hard work 3014
of Bible worth more than college
  640
of Christ the Lord dawns upon
  the soul 7971
of divine escapes us through want
  of faith 3754
of nature, atheism incompatible
  6696
of ourselves arouses us to seek
  God 10020
of Scripture no obstacle to sin
  10392
of sin is beginning of salvation
  9815
opinion in good men is k. in the
  making 6711
our k. compared with God's, is
  ignorance 6699
owe k. to those who have differed
  6710
pain root of k. 3353
pope and peasant know more
  between them 266
Prayer not a shortcut to k. 8924
process of piling up facts 11927
Simple love, with even little k.
  6708
Sorrow is k. 10614

stripped of all possessions but k.
  of God 11688
strong or weak depending on k. of
  God 1321
such is my k. of own incapacity
  6459
thanks God has vouchsafed me k.
  of his works 11144
that something remains unenjoyed
  impairs 2869
that we are never alone 4863
Thought changes k. into energy
  11265
Time converts k. into wisdom
  11323
to k. we make promises, pain we
  obey 8261
To know one's ignorance best part
  of k. 11955
too long, short distance obscures
  k. 3559
true k. of God will result in sheer
  wonder 6704
unnecessary display of k. is
  weakness 6694
until we accumulate k. 8924
until we come to k. must take in
  faith 4578
Virtue is k. 11724
well-defined k. of Jesus Christ
  6713
when faith in future becomes k. of
  past 7435
When I transfer k. I teach 11009
Whenever k. dry something wrong
  6704
Wisdom is honesty, k. applied
  through experience 11972
wisdom is k. of our own ignorance
  11942
Wisdom is right use of k. 11973
With k. of God comes love 7347
without integrity dangerous 3013

KNOWLEDGEABLE
can be k. with other men's
  knowledge 11958

KNOWN
Alone God's ideals, hopes, doings
  made k. 10532
alone what is hid with God made
  k. 10532
And safer than a k. way 5417
Beside us a friend well loved, k.
  5376
desires I had never k. suddenly
  comes on the horizon 9276
divine things must be loved to be
  k. 4762
friend never k. until man have
  need 4166
God can only be k. through
  manifestation 4738
God never k. to disappoint 4468
God not God if could not be k. at
  all 4740
God not God if fully k. to us 4740
God's real greatness k. to himself
  alone 4665

have k. many troubles, most never happened 11434
How widely Jesus k. difficult to judge 6395
Human beings must be k. to be loved 4762
If hearts open, desires k. 10507
If I had k. trouble you were bearing 1545
If I had k. you better 4653
in silence God is k. 10255 4741
Lives for the meanest mortal k. 10085
most certainly I was not alone 8051
mysteries of God k. to saints 10252
never k. man of ability to be ungrateful 5255
No Christian ever k. to recant on deathbed 3764
No one can know God who has not first k. himself 7543
Nothing so firmly believed as least k. 6082
of whom we speak least on earth best k. in heaven 9616
pain we feel is k. to God 4804
permit real selves to be k. 10019
should have k. what fruit 1737
strange to be k. universally, yet be so lonely 7130
The dearest idol I have k. 6074
They should have k. Jesus was God 6492
truly k. as no finite men can know us 4768
value seldom k. until lost 4292
world would have k. little progress 9311
yearning to know what cannot be k. 7531

KNOWS
All comes to him who k. how to wait 8391
Author k. the play 9911
belief that God k. what is best for us 9993
But 'tis enough that Christ k. all 5635
Christian k. more than philosopher 1326
comforts one who has not suffered k. nothing of 10914
Education teaches us how little man k. 3004
enjoys reputation of being most remarkable person he k. 9197
Every man k. he is unique being 6173
Every man k. he will die 2279
Everyone k. how to say good-bye 9452
Faith k. itself weak, uncertain 3702
Faith k. the one who is leading 3709

Faith never k. where it is being led 3709
farther man k. himself from perfection, nearer to it 8523
friend k. all about you, likes you just the same 4168
friend k. you as you are 4169
frog in well k. nothing of ocean 8665
God alone k. all the facts 7828
God alone k. secret of history 4694
God k, I'm not the thing I should be 9928
God k, not I, the reason why 11467
God k. and what he k. 4746
God k. best what is best 4640
God k. deepest possibilities in me 4889
God k. eccentricities of my being 4889
God k. how to burn, then to gently cool 7951
God k. how to use disordered wishes, actions 4644
God k. instantly, effortlessly 4881
"God k. me" is different from "God is omniscient" 11179
God k. me, precious possession 11179
God k. us completely 4884
God k. us through and through 4577
God k. what he's about 5391
God k. what you are 1067
God k. who shall lose or win 4887
God who k. the need 10877
godly k. God his best friend 3996
good general k. when victory impossible 8485
good listener after awhile k. something 7111
he is loved, content with piece of bread 7176
he who has travelled k. where holes are deep 3541
He who k. himself best 1711
heart has eyes brain k. nothing of 8503
himself best esteems himself least 6002
himself confronted by God 7494
in deep and authoritative way 5809
little what grace is 5224
Lord k. no limitations 11606
Love often k. no limits 7283
man k. death not an end but a beginning 2343
Man k. more than he understands 6697
Man k. nothing without being taught 7412
many a battle fought world k. nothing about 7061
more man k, more he forgives 4099
no man truly k. another 6585

No one k. sorrows of another 10602
No one k. what is taking place in another's kingdom 6171
No one really k. what he looks like 7444
No one truly k. happiness who has not suffered 5545
Nobody k. the trouble I've seen 11445
not the best emotions of the heart 5349
not victory nor defeat 1922
O sacred sorrow, he who k. not thee 5349
one who k. most speaks least 11948
Only a God who k. all things 5438
Only he who k. God is truly moral 7835
Only the soul that k. mighty grief 2508
Only the wearer k. where shoe pinches 3542
part of man k. which never knew before 5809
prepare for what no one k. yet 3035
prophet k. his times 9332
river touches places of which source k. nothing 6232
saint k. not why he suffers 10910
smart aleck k. everything 450
something he k. he was meant and made to do 8649
The Pilot k. the unknown seas 5448
three things only God k. 6705
truth but keeps silent 2910
what he k. needs no reasoned proof 5809
when God k. we meant to do his will 4810
When one k. oneself well 6597
Which is better only God k. 2378
who k about depth k. about God 7466
Who k. but life be that which men call death 7086
who k. everything has lot to learn 9205
who k. God reverences him 12100
who k. how to be poor k. everything 8677
who k. how to suffer will enjoy peace 10851
Who neither k. measure nor end 4787
who serves him because he k. him 4572
wisdom is humble that he k. no more 6695

KOINONIA
not frilly fellowship 4022
unconditional sharing of lives 4022

KOREAN
woman began to speak 11750

L

LABEL
is all one note 6212

LABELLING
his opinions 6599

LABOR
Death end of l. 2256
enthusiasm lifts struggles of l.
3188
give us grace to l. for 9676
Go l. on, spend and be spent
10133
Golden Rule would reconcile
capital and l. 5005
Just a little l. spend 4217
Nothing more dangerous than
discontinued l. 3109
powerful medicine 3103
refreshment from repose 3102
reward is not what he gets for it
3119
reward is what it does for him
3119
The ant its l. has begun 8039
to l. and not to ask for reward
9113
Why should I l. for nought 5952
without envying his l. 10788
yoke device to make hard l. light
2816

LABORATORY
body, a chemical l. 842

LABORER
If l. to dream he was king 8576
king to dream he was l. 8576

LABORING
Give me simple l. folk 11686

LABORS
He sendeth more strength when l.
increase 5223
love thinks nothing of l. 7283
who l. as he prays 8811

LABOR-SAVING
Prayer not a l. device 8803

LABYRINTH
Eternity a l. 3283

LABYRINTHICAL
Riddling, perplexed, l. soul 10661

LACK
ashamed of my l. of desire for God
9097
attitude to treasures or l. of them
11872
Gossip l. of worthy theme 5131
greatest evil is l. of love 6163
In all abundance there is l. 11825
more men fail through l. of
purpose than l. of talent 3608

of charity in action murders faith
3829
of faith will go in two seconds
3828
people fail for l. of encouragement
3138
sin against neighbor through l. of
love is sin against God 7164
That shall l. a timely end 1510
Think not on what you l. 11164
worst hardship l. of sunglasses
3147

LACKING
where power predominates, love
is l. 7343
Wherever too much, something l.
11879

LACKS
conversation l. depth, makes up in
length 1849
if doesn't try to get money, l.
ambition 7800
wise man seeks friend with
qualities he himself l. 4279

LADDER
cross the l. to heaven 2149
He who would climb l. must
begin at bottom 10782
not leaning against right wall 353
Prayer is a l. on which thoughts
mount to God 8913
rung of l. never meant to rest upon
9316
tomorrow at bottom of l. 7062
We make l. of our vices 10420
who didn't have l. to climb 6147
world a l. for some to go up, some
down 7047

LADDERS
Around our pillows, golden l. rise
358
Crosses are l. to heaven 162

LADS
Golden l. and girls all must 2290

LADY
attributes of a great l. 11697
Being powerful like being a l.
8703

LAGGED
man has l. behind morally 9872

LAID
as treasures on earth l. down 9565
faith foundation, action as stone l.
3826

LAKE
Great Spirit! Thou hast made this
l. 9098
if, like the l. that has the boon
7715

LAKES
man makes deserts bloom, l. die
3197

LAMB
Bible stream where l. may wade
707
Christ divine paradox of lion, l.
6425
Christ L. in gentleness 6425
Christ L. in meekness 6425
Christ L. in patience 6425
cross, seen in image of a l. 6471
I would bring a l. 1376
many a sheep and l. by wolf is rent
8363
shepherds found their L. 1373
That leads me to the L. 7507

LAMB OF GOD
solves problems by pointing to L.
3784

LAMBS
Before l. bled in Egypt 2123

LAME
devil is not l. 2651
emerge l. but victorious at dawn
9777
will carries l. man who can see
918

LAMENT
our part missing 7056
our voices must be silent 7056

LAMENTING
stop l. and look up 12063

LAMP
death only putting out l. 2252
Experience is a dim l. 3520
I lift my l. beside the golden door
7985
I press God's l. 2945
If you would have your l. burn
12010
should first my l. spread light
3323
spirit l. world blows upon 10696

LAMPS
evening of well-spent life brings l.
with it 8171
like l. nobody sees until tunnel
comes 10914

LAND
Bible enters l. after l. 645
Christianity, l. of beginning again
1178
Death not journey into unknown l.
2249
invisible l. where tears shall come
no more 11013
living in l. of slavery, darkness
4969
Make the mighty ocean and the
pleasant l. 6659
next world is l. of the living 7064
of naked, people ashamed of
clothes 1638
than in l. flooded with light 7779
The good seed on the l. 4625
There is a l. of pure delight 5670
There lies the l. of song 10535
there lies the poet's native l. 10535

Two mites, two drops (yet all her house, l.) 4379

We are here in the l. of dreams 5672

whole world is my native l. 908

world is the l. of the dying 7064

Worship thirsty l. crying out for rain 12132

LANDED

when I saw where the pieces l. 4136

LANDLOCKED

by the mighty disaster 4744

LANDLORD

great L. will give notice lease has expired 2406

LANDS

failure pioneer in new l. 3602

LANDSCAPE

belongs to man who looks at it 8038

LANDSCAPES

As l. their variety from light 103

LANE

can't drive straight on twisting l. 4440

traffic moves faster in next l. 2873

LANGUAGE

among people whose l. I could not understand 7102

delights that cannot find expression in l. 12120

Eloquence power to translate truth into intelligible l. 9134

fearful symmetry which is God's l. 5718

God is greater than all l. 4700

God perseveres in speaking in his own l. 4900

God speaks in l. we do not want to learn 4900

In the humanity of Jesus, God speaking our l. 6135

Jesus spelling himself out in l. man can understand 6445

Kindness a l. blind can see 6650

Kindness a l. deaf can hear 6650

Kindness a l. dumb can speak 6650

Linguist, make mistakes in more than one l. 7782

Music l. spoken by angels 7907

Music purest l. of passion 7905

My soul rejects the aid of l. 8792

no grammar for l. of inner life 7705

No l, but the l. of the heart 11957

No one can say prayers poor when using l. of love 8875

of heartbreak learned in suffering 10902

only sufficient l. is l. of Scripture 10888

people smile in same l. 548

Poetry l. in which man explores amazement 8618

resigning ourselves to listening to God's l. 5395

resurrection permeated our l. 9702

sermon merely translated Christ's life into l. 6482

Sighs are natural l. of the heart 5623

silence is the soul's l. 8902

speaks a l. of silent power 6651

Tongues is a heart l. 5807

universal l. of soul 10676

with no l. but a cry 2576

LANGUAGES

ability to speak several l. asset 1876

Bible speaks in hundreds of l. 645

Sin fatal in all l. 10367

thousand l, smile speaks them all 10499

LANGUISH

ego in which we all l. 6434

LANTERN

Carry own l, and you need not fear dark 6167

God shall be a l. to my feet 5394

LANTERNS

Every day feast of l. 3501

LARGE

A heaven not so l. as yours 5640

But l. enough for me 5640

Christianity never accepted on l. scale 1188

Christianity would not be l. enough for needs 1202

enough for a wish, l. enough for a prayer 8763

In anything l. never give in 8548

Is your place a l. place 3847

speak of l. or meager talents 4710

streams from little fountains flow 8657

troubles l. enough to endanger welfare 4789

troubles l. enough to touch God's love 4789

Youth, l, lusty, loving 12188

LARGER

better the self-image, l. the capacity for loving 9997

gratitude we feel for what we give 5267

life becomes l. 9827

Men but children of l. growth 7418

some great desire to do something l. 8649

the island of knowledge 6702

The l. the God we know, the l. our faith 3790

LARGER-THAN-LIFE

focus on l. goals 9970

LARGEST

than l. fruit of happiness 3795

LARK

is up to greet the sun 8039

LASER-TYPES

of Christians, cut through tomfoolery 1313

LAST

always think l. opinion right 8203

Be first in field, l. to couch 2769

But an eternal now shall ever l. 3288

Christ first and also l. 6475

clouds are lies, cannot l. 11129

cross, God's l. endless word 2153

deed done, l. word said 8082

Do every act as if l. 556

don't think marriage built on sex can l. 10229

Every day should be passed as if our l. 6887

feeling that I could l. forever 12165

Free at l, free at l. 4119

God will have l. word, will be good 4938

goes well, it won't l. 3998

Hope l. thing that dies in man 5924

I've read the l. page of the Bible 4316

Jesus proclaims first will be l. 6447

live every day as if it were our l. 9120

Lord, grant that my l. hour be my best 2332

never see each other for l. time 2401

Night and storm look as if they would l. forever 8444

of life, for which the first was made 8132

Old age, play's l. act 8166

part of life you learn to stand parents 3893

Political reputation cannot l. forever 5079

Reason's l. step is recognition things beyond it 9421

Seizes the right, holds it to the l. 11906

Self l. 9264

shall be first 10182

step is to come to terms with everything 11935

That man may l. but never lives 4374

think every day the l. 7021

This is the l. of earth! I am content 2453

to lay old aside 958

Truth arrives l. 6865

What is before our nose we see l. 6933

women l. at the cross, first at the altar 11980

words of Noah Webster 2379

world going to have music at the l. 7886

LASTED

church l. longer than comparable
institution 1431

LASTING

achieve, cherish just, l. peace 5199
no pleasure so l. as reading 855
only l. treasure is spiritual 4148

LASTS

All passes, nothing l. 11288
bubble l. a while and bursts 6927
He who laughs, l. 6717
truth discovered l. a lifetime
11578
While time l. will always be a
future 5052

LATCH

on to the affirmative 8231

LATE

better to learn l. than never 3015
discipline before too l. 8309
do not know how soon may be
too l. 9609
for his accident 1738
God of the l.-at-nights 7539
God's ways seem dark but soon or
l. 11299
Hell is truth seen too l. 5690
I came to love you l. 7473
mystery of grace, it never comes
too l. 5228
never know how soon will be too
l. 6663
three days l. at bus station 4266
too l. believe in eternal punishment
5700
Too l. loved I thee 4805
Work, work from early until l.
12029

LATER

never exists 9293
sin, bills come in l. 10421
Youth ideal state if came l. in life
12187

LAUD

character but climb to top at any
cost 6068

LAUGH

afraid to l. in God's presence 6723
all see 10647
Always l. when you can 6716
Among those who l, do not weep
3064
Among those who weep, do not l.
3064
and shout for life is good 6917
at trouble 504
at, with world 515
better to weep with wise than l.
with fools 9475
cannot l. God out of your death
2432
Christ wept that thou mightest l.
6393
Don't l. at youth's affectations
12163
Frown less and l. more 9281

good l. sunshine in house 5812
I would look up, l. 1018
if I did not l. I should die 6747
If not allowed to l. in heaven 6721
If you don't learn to l. at trouble
6720
just as sacred to l. as to pray 6722
Lord, teach us to l. again 6743
Man alone can smile, l. 6737
man appears for a little while to l.
7372
One l. = 3 Tbsp. Oat Bran 6741
out loud 6724
Poetry makes you l. 8619
pride of dying rich raises loudest l.
in hell 9246
Trouble knocked at door, hearing
l. hurried away 11461
What we l. at 10016
why same thing makes us l, cry
10660
won't have anything to l. at when
old 6720
would all l. at lack of originality
10353

LAUGHED

day is lost on which one has not l.
6744
God must have l. with satisfaction
7859
has achieved success who has l.
often 10781
not l. at, laughs at himself first
6000

LAUGHING

100 times a day works the heart
6725
feeling good, showing it in one
spot 6726
to paint the l. soil 9895
When l. attention focused 6746
You don't stop l. because you
grow old 6748
you grow old because you stop l.
6748

LAUGHS

at impossibilities 3717
evil is the Satan that l. at logic
5023
Faith l. at shaking of spear 3703
He who l, lasts 6717
If devil ever l, must be at
hypocrites 6055
know why man alone l. 6742
Man only animal that l. and weeps
7413
Not every heart that l. is cheerful
10605
not laughed at, l. at himself first
6000
Pleasure, while it l. it dies 8604
shows character by what he l. at
982
When man reasons, God l. 9427

LAUGHTER

a sacred sound to God 6729

adds richness to ordinary days
6727
and weeping, intensest forms of
human emotion 6728
Behind l. may be callous
temperament 10583
bubbles on lip 431
contentment of God 6732
God's hand on troubled world
6731
is cheap medicine 6716
is music of life 6734
man suffers so deeply had to
invent l. 6742
most beneficial therapy 6733
of sin as crackling of burning
thorns 10393
oft is but an art 6740
often mantles over sadness 431
or tears, both derive from God
6736
sun that drives winter from the
face 6735
tranquilizer with no side effects
6730

LAUNCH

God will l. you to place of his
appointment 5430

LAVISH

God is l. in every degree 8046

LAW

a plumbline 1530
action might safely be made l. for
world 3453
Christ goes behind l. to disposition
1526
could not bring righteousness
9755
could not bring what we need
9755
detects 5231
faith requires we rise above l. of
moral gravitation 3752
God knows all l. and every l. 4881
He who has not suffered under
the L. 5224
He who makes l. his standard
6812
Legalists keep l. for self-glory
6815
lives by faith, and love not judged
on the l. 6812
Love is the l. of our condition
6614
Love will ask more than l. could
ever require 7273
Love, not l, is greatest cleanser
7275
majority opinion will become l.
4332
moral illiterates whose only l. is
self 3877
moral l. isn't any one instinct 7839
moral l. makes a kind of tune
7839
moral l. within me 1709
Morality always higher than l.
7831

motive, purpose behind l. 5233
no good government with l, order 5194
not to abrogate obedience of moral l. 6811
obedience to l. coupled with love, honesty 6811
of humanity that man know good through evil 5030
of mutation belongs to fallen world 4589
or be subject to l. of death 3756
powerless 9755
reflects God's holiness 1530
result, not inevitableness of l. 1149
right in disobeying l. of sovereign 5197
sin not breaking God's l. 10355
standards reflected God's righteousness 9755
tells me how crooked I am 5232
to break one commandment is to break the l. 6812
to make clear how much you must do 5233
toddler, opponent of l, order 1129
'twas searching for thy l. 9091
using the l. to establish righteousness 6810
we do not live under l. of jungle 7331
We have a new l. 7331
Why did God abolish the l. 9755
worth of an individual not ascribed by l. 10001

LAWFUL
All ambitions l. except 338
child in womb not l. to destroy 16
Love thinks all things l. 7220
Theology teaches what means are l. 11210

LAWGIVER
Moses, a great l. 779

LAWLESSNESS
Man calls sin a liberty, God a l. 4550

LAWN
Grass always greener in next l. 2873

LAWN MOWER
not yet time to get out l. 9888

LAWS
and order made prominent 5192
Christ is no giver of l. 5208
Christ's words pass into l. 6523
heart has its own l. 5628
if we had making of l, would have made them otherwise 10425
in Bible include treatment of earth 3200
man can only break himself against l. of God 7493
Man cannot break the l. of God 7493
millions of l. to enforce commandments 1518

moral l. reflection of God's nature 1520
never violate l. of God without consequences 10336
nonbeliever lives by faith in natural l. 3653
science assumes permanence, uniformity of natural l. 9869
silent amidst clash of arms 11754
so arbitrary are transient l. 10516
space obeys l. of physics 11650
to submit thoughts, actions to the l. 7434
universe functions best when God's l. obeyed 1520
warranted by l. of country 4115
which God gives us, we find fault with 10425

LAWSUIT
go into as pig, come out as sausage 9713

LAWYER
Moses, no ordinary l. 779
resolved as l. to try Bible as in courtroom 744

LAX
Beware that not from own l. living 8363
Jesus' standards far from l. and easygoing 6444

LAY
can l. it on thick in right places 9238
first foundation of humility 6788
last to l. old aside 958
on me what thou wilt, only sustain me 9080
to l. down one's power for others in need 7435
To l. his head upon the Savior's breast 11476

LAYMAN
has opportunities minister will never have 3330
use of l. crippled church impact 1499

LAYMEN
care not whether clergymen or l. 9136

LAZINESS
enemy tactic 1190
gives up perfection as unattainable 3463
I discover an arrant l. 662
Pride and l. keys of poverty 8691
resting before you get tired 6769
travels so slowly poverty soon overtakes 6768
wears you out 6753

LAZY
confidence in Christ does not make l. 1611
cost devil little trouble to catch l. man 6766
ear tends to be l. 844
Hear the l. people say 9303

man does not, will not, cannot pray 6776
man workshop for Satan 6749
Prayer not a l. substitute for work 8924
sheep thinks its wool heavy 6750
willing to swallow, too l. to chew 6758

LEAD
a true life 4974
All men would l. happy life 4227
ambitious to l. disqualified as leader 6794
change sorrowing heart of l. 10628
church does not l. world 1428
Do not follow where path may l. 6787
Doing God's will may not l. to profits 10778
Don't l. me, I may not follow 4224
Don't walk behind me, I may not l. 4224
Faith will l. you where you cannot walk 3716
God alone knows how to l. 169
God will l. 5388
good and wise l. quiet lives 9373
I give myself to thee to l. me anywhere 9084
If ten l. holy life 5751
kindly Light, amid encircling gloom 5429
Knowledge given to l. us to worship, faith 6693
Let him l. thee blindfold onwards 5431
me by thine own hand 5456
men l. lives of quiet desperation 2610
No man right to l. life of contemplation 7004
No one deserves right to l. without 6802
power of love will l. to master of the art 7352
secretly dreaming I be the one to l. her 10080
thou me on 5429
thou the way, thou guidest best 4977
thousand paths l. to hell 5664
'Tis his to l. me there 4428
To l. men in his way 10122
to living Truth of whom can learn anything 11004
true leader likely has no desire to l. 6785
Unless you l. me, Lord 7970
us forward one by one 6178
us, heavenly Father, l. us 5428
ways that l. to everything 7869
who has confidence in himself will l. the rest 6791
you all in the dance, said he 9690
you'll never get to l. the band 6797

LEADER

actions determined by impulse to follow l. 6199
ambitious to lead disqualified as l. 6794
as parent establish yourself as l. 8343
good l. prepared to deny himself much 6793
If wish to be l. will be frustrated 10160
No l. ever did work cheaply, easily 5289
Of a good l, who talks little 6803
true l. likely has no desire to lead 6785

LEADERS

ordinary people with extraordinary determination 6798

LEADERSHIP

acid test of father's l. 3925
art of getting someone else to do something 6799
forced into position of l. 6785
home is test of father's l. 3925
is service to others 8717
learning to yield to l. of God 8338
life under God's l. 4160
power can separate from true nature of Christian l. 8717
They will say, "We did this ourselves" 6803
While yielding to parental l. 8338
Without human l. revivals have altered men 9752

LEADETH

Children whom the Father l. 5431

LEADING

Faith loves, knows the one who is l. 3709
God is l. 5388
God with patience l. world 4474
God's hand l. me 7484
so long as we follow God's l. 5397

LEADS

Christ l. me through no darker rooms 5379
devil l. downward, fiddles all the way 2697
enthusiasm light that l. 3188
fear l. love at first 3986
few observations and much reasoning l. to error 9410
God l. us step by step 5392
Gossip l. to criticism 5135
impulse of love that l. to doorway of friend 4278
Obedience l. to faith 8103
old age l. on to God 8151
One path l. to Paradise 5664
road that l. us to living God 3793
rough road that l. to greatness 8287
See where love l. 7167
That l. me to the Lamb 7507
way which l. to himself 1717

when God l. in higher path of sanctification 9851
will of God never l. to miserable feeling 4507
wrong concept of God l. to 4568

LEAF

As doth a l. 2380
fall of l. teaches 2355
Life dewdrop on lotus l. 6959
My life is in the falling l. 2587
Our age is but the falling of a l. 11287
promise of resurrection in every l. in springtime 9694
sun drew forth from ache a l. 5368
unbelief trembles at shaking of l. 3703

LEAK

Collapse usually slow l. 939
in your Christianity 6534
Sin causes cup of blessing to spring a l. 10356
small l. will sink great ship 5116

LEAKY

bucket dropped in well of truth l. indeed 12144
sure to find him l. 5156
Time heals, except l. faucets 11331

LEAN

able to l. on one another 1300
And trusting l. upon thy breast 4977
Bad to l. against falling wall 3380
harder we l, stronger we grow 10761
l. upon thy love unknown 4977
weaker we feel, harder we l. 8256

LEANING

faith is weakness l. on God's strength 3775
Prayer is weakness l. on omnipotence 8949
Temptations that find us l. on God 11094
too heavily on another person 9478

LEANS

if man l. on God, he becomes powerful 10766

LEAP

gospel makes man l. for joy 5091
Kneel before you l. 8862
notes dance and l. from my pen 7931
Would you have me l. and spring 7970

LEAPED

man has l. ahead in scientific achievement 9872

LEAPS

Jesus l. across the changing centuries 6448

LEAPT

from my throat like sobbing 10021

LEARN

always ready to l. 3008
as much to l. as if never begun 4702
Be it ours to l. the tune 7056
begins to l. how to l. 3017
best way for child to l. to fear God 8327
better to l. late than never 3015
by experience how wicked 4773
by experience we l. wisdom 3530
by our sufferings we l. to praise our bliss 10925
can l. from Greek philosophers 2988
cannot l. without pain 8276
Children l. what they observe 1114
deeper we plunge, more we l. 7936
Education teaches how much man has to l. 3004
Eternity not long enough to l. all God is 3270
everyone must l, no one can teach 7068
expectation of what man can l. timorous 3507
Experience, some l. no other way 3519
first part of life parents l. to stand you 3893
Four things man must l. 559
four things to l. in life 6913
From David l. to give thanks 11145
from errors wise l. wisdom for future 7794
from mean man how not to live 3159
from some we have much to l. 2987
from those who reject you 175
from those who treat you with contempt 175
from yesterday 11304
God speaks in language we do not want to l. 4900
hardest lessons to l. 9941
How long God waits for us to l. lesson 7056
how to view others with humility 10306
if live happily, l. to die 6926
If you don't l. to laugh at trouble 6720
in one short hour, l. more from God 4964
In youth we l. 12191
knack of listening like Christian instead of critic 10110
last part of life you l. to stand parents 3893
lead to living Truth of whom can l. anything 11004
less, contemplate more 1762
lessons well in obscurity 5430

listen for voice of God, l. of him 4964
luxury of doing good 5076
man must l. to forgive himself 9979
Men l. to pray as they l. to love 8914
more about human nature in NY 753
more by five minutes' obedience 8116
more from man's errors than his virtues 3262
more we l. about wonders of universe 11644
more we l. more we realize how little we know 3029
most important to l. cannot be taught 3030
must l. from life how to suffer it 10923
Never l. anything talking 9363
never met man so ignorant couldn't l. from him 6080
Normal day, let me l. from you 2197
nothing of gospel except by feeling its truths 5110
of birds, and springs, and flowers 8671
of importance to l. more every year 3017
Oh, that one could l. to l. in time 3020
only from failure 10795
only l. when ask questions 9363
ours to l. the time 7915
patience by going into hurly-burly world 8422
patience by taking life as it blows 8422
perplexed that we may l. patience 8396
prayer means whereby l. to do without good things of earth 8977
prosper as we l. to do common in uncommon way 9344
real mistake one from which we l. nothing 3622
Scriptures tell us what we could never l. 735
seventy years to l. to keep mouth shut 2897
shall l. truth you need to know 9649
Suffering only way some can l. 10897
that no situation is too much 168
that they might l. to conquer world 8805
the blessedness of the unoffended 7727
to bring body into harmony with God 847
to deal with difficulties 2712
to express gratitude to them and to Me 5271

to give thanks even if don't feel thankful 11173
to hold loosely all not eternal 11659
to hold loosely all that is not eternal 3280
to hold thy tongue 11412
to laugh at trouble 504
to listen to God in circumstances 1477
to live for others 4282
to live together as brothers 5987 923
to look on bright circumstances 9092
To lose is to l. 2515
to love God and man by loving 7352
to mistrust ourselves and put confidence in him 9851
to say no gracefully 5615
to speak by speaking 7352
To teach is to l. twice 11008
to teach without inspiring to l. is hammering on cold iron 11000
to think continually of God 11269
to use things and love people 9510
too busy to l. to worship 12098
too old to l, probably always too old to l. 3028
truth of God 7485
two years to l. to talk 2897
want to die happily, l. to live 6926
way to be made holy 9838
we l. by doing 3545
What will child l. sooner than a song 7930
what you l. after you know it all that counts 7691
when young people l. a god has clay feet 12179
Where much desire to l, many opinions 6711
who knows everything has lot to l. 9205
wisdom from failure more than success 3630
wisest mind something yet to l. 3033
You don't l. to praise in a day 8747

LEARNED
astonished at how much the old man had l. 3928
beauty of character l. at home 5849
cannot obtain entire knowledge of Bible 737
Christians have l. to equate popularity with excellence 5891
devil entangles l. with false doctrine 2677
have not l. to live together 9353
how to begin again 542
If haven't l. to be worshipers 12104
if l. men not well pleased 9170
illiterates understand better than l. 1216

in dreams act part l. in waking hours 2966
In sorrow he l. this truth 12170
intelligent person has l. to "choose between" 6326
kindness from unkind 5251
Knowledge is proud has l. so much 6695
language of heartbreak l. in suffering 10902
Love must be l. again and again 7265
Many l. men live, die slaves 3018
no profit to have l. well if neglect to do well 3016
not yet l. what Christianity is 1201
oh, the things I l. from Sorrow 10596
Prayer l. in the closet 8930
question whether l. except through rod 10855
quiet, holy people l. great secret 1293
science of Christ only l. by heart 5110
silence from talkative 5251
some sciences may be l. by head 5110
some things only l. in fiery furnace 3662
This l. I from the shadow of a tree 6242
to have seen thee is to have l. all things 7960
to obey will know how to command 6792
to overcome self-contempt 9985
toleration from intolerant 5251
until l. to be satisfied with God 7447
who have l. lost art of worship 12099
Youth not yet l. limitations 12181

LEARNER
Call him a slow l. 161

LEARNING
anyone who stops l. is old 2995
appetite for l. persists 3031
begin at bottom in everything except l. to swim 6021
disciple comes with ignorance to find l. 2818
faith greater than l. 11568
first temptation was promise of l. and knowledge 6701
God's wisdom for l. 5400
how to accept the impossible 7692
how to do without the indispensable 7692
how to endure the insupportable 7692
I am still l. 3009
in childhood like engraving on rock 8305
Kindness converted more sinners than l. 6648

less ready if l. God's appointment 10112

Life like l. instrument as one goes on 6967

little l. dangerous thing 2992

Living is l. meaning of words 7000

may go to heaven without l. 9792

One pound of l. requires 11934

parents prevent children l. lessons 8320

speak according to l. 1648

still l. at Thy knee 306

to be happy without things we cannot have 8635

without l, Jesus shed more light than scholars 6449

LEARNS

as much dignity in tilling field as writing poem 3240

family first authority under which person l. to live 3888

He who goes with wolves l. to howl 9458

If he l. before he's five 8296

In suffering one l. to pray best 10857

man l. sweetness of health 5605

No one l. to make right decisions without 2486

who is defeated l. most 2510

LEARNT

Lord's Prayer slowly l. by heart 7153

Tomorrow hopes we've l. from yesterday 11403

LEASE

great Landlord will give notice l. has expired 2406

LEAST

devil tempts not l. 9788

government best which governs l. 5187

gratitude from greatest services 5250

Gratitude one of l. articulate of emotions 5245

greatest are l. in own opinion 5991

greatest path is open to l. of travelers 7235

In heaven, even the l. a great thing 5658

In solitude, when we are l. alone 10541

knows himself best, esteems himself l. 1711

lonely when most alone 10568

majority, the opinion of the l. able 5191

may pray l. when say most 9018

may pray most when say l. 9018

movement affects all nature 572

Nothing so firmly believed as l. known 6082

of things with meaning worth more 7030

of whom we speak l. on earth best known in heaven 9616

one who knows most speaks l. 11948

Riches l. worthy gifts God can give 11845

richest who is content with l. 1794

talk most who have l. to say 1834

those who want friends l. 4286

When river is deepest, makes l. noise 2810

Where l. heart, most tongue 5166

who knows himself best esteems himself l. 6002

LEAST-USED

words by unselfish person 11653

LEAVE

a treasure for a trifle 6495

all for Lord to order 9930

And, departing, l. behind us 5288

be content to l. everything way it is 5099

best legacies father can l. children 3924

bury the hatchet but l. handle out 9641

do duty wisely, l. issue to God 5176

duty to l. undone that thou wouldst do 9667

dying l. money 7826

enter world alone, l. it alone 10574

eternity for a moment 6495

future to God 4319

give me faith to l. it all to thee 9072

Go where no path, l. trail 6787

good father will l. imprint on daughter 3915

grow young as I l. my me behind 9920

Home feet may l. but not hearts 5833

hope teaches to l. future with God 3834

It's the thing you l. undone 2502

let husband make wife sorry to see him l. 7627

My life, my friends, my soul I l. 7503

need to l. prison of his aloneness 7143

reality for a shadow 6495

scandal alone, never touch it 5154

sin without thought of returning 10409

some things unsaid 10279

takes guts to l. ruts 1928

the end with me 5415

thread to God 3117

tomorrow's trouble to tomorrow's strength 12067

Whate'er we l. to God 4575

When l. God's love, we grow dark, cold 9354

world so kind you l. with regret 2293

your plans at the cross 10048

LEAVES

And l. our sphere behind 8078

Deeds are fruits, words are l. 2532

devil always l. stink behind him 2670

doing will of God l. no time for disputing his plans 4970

everywhere man l. some kind of mark 6231

faults will drop off like dead l. 3940

finger of God never l. identical fingerprints 4497

Forgiveness fragrance flower l. 4080

God never l. 4621

Gossip may not stick but l. mark 5129

has never raked l. 8579

have their time to fall 2324

Holiness more than sweeping away old l. of sin 5748

Judge a tree from its fruit, not l. 6581

Let me die as the l. die, gladly 2326

lizard on cushion seek l. 989

lured me, now l. me here 3485

man l. footprints when walks through life 6231

Man sees but withered l. 8673

man who l. money to charity in will 4377

men as generation of l. 7368

must not tear close-shut l. apart 5403

of friendship fall 7860

of life keep falling one by one 7031

Whenever knowledge l. us cold something wrong 6704

year in a shroud of l. dead, is lying 11321

LEAVING

the world their d. 7475

LEAVINGS

sacrifice to God of devil's l. 8183

LECTURE

had to prepare l. on Christian view of poverty 8685

suffering person doesn't need a l. 10887

LECTURES

nature l. of ethics, divinity 3192

LED

By faith l. not against, but beyond reason 3834

By obedience l. to correct errors 8110

experience feeling l. without knowing it 5392

Faith never knows where it is being l. 3709

few people wish to be l. 10160

God has l. 5388

grasp him and be l. securely home 6517

Men l. more by patterns than precepts 3442

people to expect something not possible 7601

LEFT

a stricken deer that l. the herd 9798

brings but loss 1150

Christ l. Father's throne 495

Is caught into his l. 4628

Let not right hand know what l. is doing 10169

light that then shone never l. me 7472

look at what you have l. 825

Lord's Prayer nothing l. out 7156

Man not l. in valley of depravity 10436

nothing l. to chance 4904

test of generosity, how much you have l. 4378

Thank you for all you have l. me 11161

They have l. unstained 4114

War determines who is l. 11767

What sweetness l. if take away friendship 4299

When he l, there was no darkness 6510

When we have nothing l. but God 4516

who has lost faith, what l. to live on 3728

LEG

A lie stands on one l, truth on two 6864

hop around on one l. 1731

One l. in stocks, or two 11447

When you break your l, be thankful it isn't neck 11169

LEGACIES

best l. father can leave children 3924

LEGAL

established l. residence in heaven 5673

no issued document l. 5726

rights before the throne 8815

LEGALISM

archenemy of church 6817

arouses pride 6823

belief God satisfied with attempt to obey moral code 6814

Believers motivated by l. always anxious 6810

Christ's answer to l. 6811

dulls our edge 6823

is self-righteousness 6814

its poison blinds our eyes 6823

Let l. have enough rope, lynching of new ideas 6817

love asks us to walk many miles not demanded by l. 7273

Rigidity trademark of l. 6817

spreads paralyzing venom 6823

LEGALIST

is a what asker 6820

LEGALISTS

keep law for self-glory 6815

keep law to merit reward 6815

using law to establish righteousness 6810

LEGEND

cross, where l. and reality intersect 2150

If such a l. why am I so lonely 10786

Of text and l. 3813

LEGIONS

of Rome smouldering 730

LEGISLATION

that evils cured by l. 5184

LEGISLATOR

God, the supreme l. 11584

LEGISLATORS

pass laws to enforce commandments 1518

LEGS

not a pair of l. so thin 10201

once spirit is healed, l. can be done without 5614

LEISURE

conversation wants l. 1840

do not know a man until we know his l. 6842

God sends time of forced l. 7056

Holy l. refers to sense of balance in life 6828

is the mother of philosophy 6834

losing l, may be losing soul 6833

the enormous l. of God 4570

use l. as mental development 5567

use l. happiest people in world 5567

What we do with l. time 10016

LEND

Bankers l. money 7826

better give one shilling than l. pound 4368

Guardian angels God will l. thee 1123

me a heart replete with thankfulness 11156

Never l. books 853

LENDS

Life is dust nature l. man for an hour 6960

Who gives to poor, l. to God 627

LENGTH

can't do anything about l. of life 7095

conversation lacks depth, makes up in l. 1849

sermon wearies people by its l. 10095

that is in God 5016

LENGTHS

Fellowship with God can go to all l. 4023

LEOPARD

To spare the ravening l. 6283

LEPERS

adored Jesus 6412

LEPROSY

Man calls sin a luxury, God a l. 4550

LESS

All we know infinitely l. than remains unknown 6677

Blessed is love; l. blessed is hatred 6161

Choose to have l. rather than more 8448

deeper the sorrow, l. tongue has to say 10627

Description would but make it l. 7245

do l. but accomplish more 50

Eat l. 5604

far l. angry feeling in world 9465

Fear l. 5604

Frown l. and laugh more 9281

God ever giving, yet has not l. 4699

God not l. great in small things 4940

God would not be l. if we did not exist 3481

Hate l. 5604

holier man is, l. understood by world 5760

increase of greatness to be l. 5293

Is it l. strange thou shouldst live at all 6103

is more 4484

Learn l, contemplate more 1762

Let religion be l. a theory, more a love affair 9542

live l. than time it takes to blink an eye 7080

man gets wiser, expects l. 3497

Mind the world l. and God more 2443

more honesty man has, l. air of saint 5889

more I demand love of others, l. I deserve 9497

more intense light is, l. you see glass 6033

more money you give away, l. you have 7232

Nothing you can do to make God love you l. 4786

one does not love place l. for having suffered in it 5843

Preach l. and practice more 9281

pride, taking l. than you need 4353

Ride l. and walk more 9281

road will be l. tedious 7899

satisfied with superficial views of Christ 6480

Some have little, some have l. 11852

Speak l. than thou knowest 2899

time, no one receives more or l. 11356

To weep is to make l. depth of grief 5361
What people think of me becoming l. important 9627
Whine l. 5604
Who has God not, has l. than nothing 4519
will of God, nothing l. 7876
Worry l. and work more 9281

LESSEN
no grief which time does not l. 5358

LESSENS
self-love l. everything amiss in ourselves 10025

LESSER
man in evolution from l. to greater condition 9351

LESSON
Example l. all men can read 3430
from the mosquito 8223
How long God waits for us to learn l. 7056
Let child's first l. be obedience 8307
miracles associated with l. Jesus trying to teach 6500
receiving music l. from thy Father 10600
Take a l. from the clock 2786
Take l. from tea 2743
taught far outweighs the pain 10586
The l. of thy own eternity 1966
'Tis a l. you should heed 8558
When angry, take l. from technology 407

LESSONS
Busy bee teaches two l. 3454
Experience gives test first, l. afterward 3522
fall of leaf teaches 2355
from those who reject you 175
hardest l. to learn 9941
home, kind of school where life's basic l. taught 5853
Learn l. well in obscurity 5430
parents prevent children learning l. 8320

LET
best way to keep is to l. go 4733
wise to l. God hold you back 5422

LETS
God l. himself be pushed on to the cross 4899

LETTER
Bible l. from God with personal address 704
don't like to open l. that has bad news 10012
holding l. of truth 9826
in anger do not answer a l. 11920

LETTERS
greatest number of l. 1761

LEUKEMIA
church dying of l. 3341

LEVEL
God meets us on l. where we operate 5439
of joy porportional to l. of acceptance 6556

LEVELER
Death the grand l. 2258
God a l. who renders equal small and great 4727

LEVER
Trouble often l. to raise us to heaven 11460

LEVITICUS 25
great classic on rights of earth 3200

LEWD
repentance, the l. becomes pure 9604

LIABILITIES
forget your l. 9271

LIAR
best reward a l. by believing nothing he says 6863
easier to see clearly into l. than who tells truth 6866
If child tells lie, don't call him l. 8301
isn't believed even when speaks truth 6844
No man good enough memory to make successful l. 6855
punishment of a l. 6861
repentance, l. becomes truthful 9604

LIARS
more likely we are all l. 912
We're all cheats and l, really 1839

LIBERALITY
God bestows many things out of l. 8796

LIBERATED
through death alone we become l. 2231

LIBERATES
faith l. 3965

LIBERATING
Jesus' mission, l. oppressed 1439

LIBERATION
from trammels imposed by external influences 4156
God's compulsion is our l. 5000
sanctification a joyful l. 9842

LIBERATOR
Death, L. whom freedom cannot release 2260

LIBERTY
Christian life is l. 4160
conversion entrance into larger l. 1900
democratic idea, every one shall have l. 2529

For simple l. to pray 4118
free will not l. to do whatever one likes 4111
God gave us l. 4146
home is the only place of l. 5842
If man lost his l. 4133
in doubtful things, l. 7196
last thing we have in many churches 5800
life of freedom, l, delight 5464
life, l, and pursuit of happiness 3246
love of l. is love of others 8716
Man calls sin a l, God lawlessness 4560
man endowed with l. he may betray 3495
Man has right to l. of discussion 2900
mercy of eternity, our l. 6384
now will I teach thee the way of inward l. 8448
Proclaim l. throughout all inhabitants 4141
Spirit of God gives l. 5800
tell secrets, resign l. 1619
thou shalt have inward l. 4922
to know God alone matters l. 4151
to obey God is perfect l. 8115
to toss spiritual head and say "No" 2826
wheedled out of l. 4115
Which is more than l. 7745
wise man, though slave, at l. 4113

LIBERTY BELL
inscription on L. 4141

LIBRARY
books in my l. people have lent me 853
Life like a l. owned by an author 6965
where every book shall lie open 2216

LICE
Lust felt even by fleas and l. 7355

LICENSE
too much l. tempts chastity 3554

LICKING
Life, l. honey from a thorn 6963

LIE
better to be lied about than to l. 6852
Better ugly truth than beautiful l. 11498
contented, need not l. 1798
excuse is a l. guarded 3474
excuse worse than a l. 3474
fault by l. grow two 3937
fault needs a l. most 3937
Great works do not always l. in our way 5068
half truth is a whole l. 6843
hate the l. though it please you 11517
Honesty, unwillingness to l. to others 5873

I could l. down like a tired child
2882

in God's arms and babble to him
5807

is handle that fits them all 6857

is refuge of weakness 6845

mass movement, new freedom to l.
10526

maturity unwillingness to l. to
oneself 5873

may be told by attaching peculiar
significance to a sentence 6859

may be told by silence 6859

Men who have honor; men who
will not l. 6299

might get lunch, but not supper
2476

no sense unless truth dangerous
8362

Nothing can need a l. 3937

One l. gives birth to another 6856

people more easily fall victims to a
great l. than to small one 7974

rope of a l. is short 6860

stands on one leg, truth on two
6864

swallow any l. that flatters us
6870

tells a l, forced to invent twenty
more 6850

thank God that you live to l.
awake 10489

travels around world 6846

Violence is a l. 11678

Who lies for you will l. against you
6862

You've been replaced, forgotten.
That's a l. 945

LIED

better to be l. about than to lie
6852

LIES

All l. are not told, some are lived
6847

And God in cradle l. 6129

before me l. Dawn and the day
5471

Beware of sublime prayers and the
l. they make us tell 8864

can be disguised in gorgeous
wrappings 6853

child l, will find a severe parent
8362

clouds are l, cannot last 11129

cruelest l. often told in silence
6858

devil tells l. about men 1060

Filling the world he l. in a manger
6122

I see the wrong that round me l.
4642

keeps silent like him who tells l.
2910

maybe fish goes home and l. 3426

Our business to do what l. closely
at hand 9671

power l. at center of life 10576

Quiet he l. 6139

says some l. are just 11506

should be clothed 6869

speculate on what l. behind nature
4704

Television l. about what world is
like 11041

There l. freedom indeed 4111

There l. the land of song 10535

there l. the poet's native land
10535

through fear of being criticized,
people tell l. 6851

Who l. for you will lie against you
6862

LIEUTENANTS

to children parents are heaven's l.
5856

LIFE

a battle and a march 7087

a comedy for those who think
6954

a dewdrop on the lotus leaf 6959

a funny thing that happened 6986

a gift to be shared 10545

a glorious opportunity 6944

a great bundle of little things 6946

a lot like tennis 10170

a matter of content 6970

A poor l. this if, full of care 6829

a predicament that precedes death
6951

a royal cup for him, my King
7003

a sentence to serve for being born
6952

A span of l. is nothing 7080

a test that has more questions
than answers 6953

a tragedy for those who feel 6954

a tumble-about thing of ups,
downs 6955

a vast, obscure unfinished
masterpiece 6904

a voyage that's homeward bound
6956

accept Christ's l. as our l. 3335

accept Jesus as Savior, new l. 876

accepted God as part of my l.
5594

accepting circumstances in l. 1473

active l. begins, ends on earth
1764

acts of this l. destiny of the next
7024

Adolescence a fascinating time of l.
12161

advance in spiritual l. has dangers
10700

adventurous 6918

adventurous l. not exempt from
fear 3990

afraid if last hour of my l. 109

After sanctification difficult to
state aim in l. 9830

aimless comet burning out in
self-will 6937

all men would lead happy l. 4227

All of l. is a war 6874

All one's l. is music 7885

all serving life-sentence in
dungeon of l. 7074

all that l. is love 5633

All you have to do is 6961

alternative to eternal l. is eternal
punishment 3286

always urgent 11388

an amazing simplicity of l. 7509

an event at which arrive after,
depart before 6957

And death or l. shall be the
sweeter 2229

And death what men call l. 7086

And every l. a l. like yours 6882

And l. till my work is done 12007

And weep away l. of care 2882

angel to guide through l. 366

Apart from Christ, l. a broken
pillar 1163

are here to add what we can to l.
10207

as a bow and arrow in hands of
archer 139

as inward l. fails 1761

As soon as there is l, there is
danger 6879

as source of l, help 7548

as we voyage along through l.
4432

as we walk tightrope of l. 6715

ask not for l. free from grief 1921

Assured alone that l. or death
6916

at home gentle l. reaches us 5849

attain excellence, spend l. single
pursuit 3470

Attitude determines impact on l.
201

attitude you bring to l. 522

awoke and saw l. was duty 9663

Bad the day man becomes content
with l. he is living 8649

barren l. that holds only happiness
5537

be glad of l. 8472

Be such a man, live such a l. 6882

Be thou the rainbow to the storm
of l. 618

bear burden of l. no longer 2591

bears love's cross 7204

become channel and dispenser of l.
7548

becomes larger 9827

begin a new l. every morning 7091

begin new creation for l. 2798

begins on other side of despair
2597

belief youth happiest time of l. a
fallacy 7026

beliefs of little importance unless
rich l. 598

believed in God, l. made sense
7011

best or worst in this l. another
matter 10789

best portions of a good man's l.
6664

best proof of immortality in sharing l. of God 6105

best theology is divine l. 11200

best things in l. are free 3838

beware of barrenness 114

Beware of believing human l. simple 10653

Bible page torn out of volume of human l. 706

Bible treats us as human l. does, roughly 724

Bible, parables of l. 645

Bible, warp and woof of l. 653

bigger world of adult l. 1126

biggest blessing in your l. 5792

bloom of l. is gone 5480

boredom of l. for the rich is worse misfortune 11854

break through superficiality to deeper l. 2738

bridge of groans across stream of tears 2598

bring l. under God's sovereign will 4734

Building one's l. on foundation of gold 7796

built in power of endless l. 2093

burden of l. is from ourselves 5229

burning candle of l. in service of devil 9576

burning of the candle 6973

but a day at most 6958

call forth its riches 505

came from death to l, return from l. to death 2338

can be no Christian l. without prayer 8938

can change thing that is wrong in his l. 3596

can do something about width and depth 7095

can fill tiny span of l. with meaning 7080

can get it for nothing 6986

can have but different aspects 6985

can never be dark or futile 6940

can take away from l. thing defeating it 3596

can you say my l. not a success 10783

can't do anything about length of l. 7095

can't live a holy l. 5752

cannot confer on me fullness of l. 5549

cannot find joy in civilized l. 10527

capacity to care gives l. significance 3077

certain must lose l. 954

Change nursery of l. 960

cheapest bargain 6996

chief event of l. 7752

childhood of our immortality 6098

choice is how you live l. 1140

choose the color 522

choose to praise for rough spots in l. 11152

Christ among the ordinary things of l. 6436

Christ animates all l. 6369

Christ in you that lives your l. 6381

Christ offers new l. 7022

Christ re-establishing l. 159

Christ the L. everlasting 6397

Christ will never strong-arm his way into your l. 6438

Christ's l. outwardly troubled 6376

Christ's l. so social called winebibber 6436

Christ's l. that transforms 1536

Christ's outward l. immersed in world 6439

Christ's teaching no meaning unless enter his l. 6424

Christian l, a reproduction 1258

Christian l. a social life 916

Christian l. a way through l. 1222

Christian l. can't be done without miracle 1223

Christian l. never automatic 1221

Christian l. not a way out 1222

Christian l. not meant for solitude 916

Christian l. not suited for solitude 916

Christian l. stamped with impossibility 1223

Christian more l. than lip 1317

Christianity does not make l. easy 1229

Christianity makes us great enough for l. 1229

Christianity, l. connected with Christ 1172

Christianity, l. of eternal quality 1188

Christianity, test is wear, tear of daily l. 1227

Christianity, way to live l. 1188

Circumstances color l. 522

circumstances of l. indication of God's will 5444

civilized l. vast, complicated system of murder 10513

closes in twilight, opens with dawn 11132

Collapse in l. seldom blowout 939

commands fulfill God's destiny in saint's l. 8111

Complaining about l. 1558

concealed until l. developed sufficiently 11609

conforming outwardly, living own l. inwardly 6048

conquered but in this l. never destroyed 5013

Consistency contrary to l. 1745

consists not in the space, but the use 2338

consolation is expectancy of another l. 6096

Contemplation involves all of l. 1755

contemplative l. will continue into eternity 1764

Contentment, letting l. flow through us 1807

Conversion goes throughout entire l. 1895

conversion, entrance into abundant l. 1900

Crises refine l. 2044

cross, a way of l. 2146

cross, key to l. 2145

cross, where history, l. intersect 2150

Crucified, definitive adjective for Christian life 1161

cynic looks at l. with magnifying glass 2179

cynicism, fear freeze l. 3747

danger signals l. is on wrong track 5466

dangerous 6918

dark, uneasy world of family l. 3886

darkest hours in l. have intent 4885

dead for this l. 490

Death costs a l. 2263

Death flowering of l. 2257

Death God's way of giving l. 2246

Death is strong, l. stronger 2985

Death more universal than l. 6884

Death not greatest loss in l. 2254

death of Jesus only entrance into his l. 2161

Death opening of more subtle l. 2261

Death, the gate of l. 2270

Dedicate your l. to others 10125

delicious 6918

Deliverance only by defeat of old l. 882

desire of l, peace 9274

did not want my l. 10940

difference between l. as it is and ought to be 9408

difference in quality of one's outer l. 7725

difficulties of l. to make better, not bitter 2748

difficulty in l. is choice 1152

direction of l, desires different 984

disadvantage to l. in Christ 1211

disappointment if expect perfection 2799

Disappointment often salt of l. 2794

discouraged emotions poison l. 3050

distraction which l. causes as it rushes on 4968

Do every act in l. as if last 556

do not blame l. 505

do not bring old l. up to higher plane 9839

Do not look forward to change of l. in fear 5907

gospel, offer of new l. to man by grace of God 5100

Grace, central invitation to l. 5221

great mystery of human l. 7101

great word to master, l. 7000

greatest moments of your l. 7029

greatest sin to prefer l. to honor 6883

Greatness in performance of duties l. places upon us 5283

greatness is degree to which one's l, 5306

greed ruthlessly ready to crush l. 5327

grief, the blunder of a l. 5337

guards secret l. with God 6321

half spent before we know what it is 6964

hand over mainspring of l. to God 837

happier if born at eighty, gradually approach eighteen 6989

happiest l. not necessarily easiest 2563

happiness of l. made up of minute fractions 5556

hard crushes of l. 1273

has a way of prying loose our grasp 11656

has anything to fear from l. 3108

has been brought to an impasse 3485

has burdens no one can escape 931

has taught me to think 6942

has taught me we are disliked for our qualities 5601

have but one candle of l. to burn 7779

have not affected the l. of man as powerfully 6353

Have you come to the Red Sea place in l. 5407

He best can part with l. without a sigh 10046

He lived a l. of going-to-do 6756

He who fears death cannot enjoy l. 3975

heaven expansion of quality of l. 5645

here and now 11388

high crime rate traceable to disintegration of family l. 5858

higher we go in social l, more bondage 4159

his l. has been a failure 8629

His l. is Christ, his death is gain 1299

His l. is highest, holiest entering at lowliest door 6132

his l. that now pumps 2979

His only answer was a blameless l. 6356

holy l. attraction or reproof 5735

holy l. faithful in Christian duty 5736

holy l. is a voice 5735

holy l. is living above the world 5736

holy l. not ascetic, gloomy, or solitary 5736

holy l. regulated by divine truth 5736

holy l. speaks when tongue silent 5735

holy l. will produce deepest impression 5737

Holy leisure refers to balance in l. 6828

Holy Spirit destroys personal l. 5795

Holy Spirit turns l. into thoroughfare for God 5795

Home is where l. makes up its mind 5832

home, cultivate valuable things in l. 5832

hope carries us on pleasantly to end of l. 5934

Hope confident search for a rewarding l. 5918

hope for no other l. 490

hope of eternal l. in the cross 2096

hope of good use while traveling through l. 5924

hopes of l. beyond the grave 5711

how daily l. is 7010

How to compose your l. 6902

how to look at l. as God sees it 4732

However humdrum l. may be 8440

However mean your l. is, meet it and live it 6903

However painful l. may be 8440

Human l. but a series of footnotes 6904

Human l. resembles iron 6905

Human race brought from death to l. 1187

humility the valley, abounding in l. 6026

humorous 6918

I asked God for all things so I could enjoy l. 6906

I count l. just a stuff 6908

I count that part of l. lost 6909

I fall upon the thorns of l! I bleed! 6911

I followed him, new l. began 1147

I laugh and shout for l. is good 6917

I took one draught of l. 3483

I will invest my l. 6920

I will not just live my l. 6920

I will not just spend my l. 6920

If cannot find God in the procession of l. 4856

if cannot relate l. to larger context 10871

if course wrong, avoid though lose l. as consequence 6291

if from l. you take the best 8122

If had keen vision of all that is ordinary in l. 8496

If I can ease one l. the aching 6922

If I can put thought of sunset in l. 1097

If I do lose thee 7019

if in l. you keep the zest 8122

if justice, mercy prevail in own common l. 6286

If l. be long I will be glad 6923

if l. seems poor 505

If little love of mine make l. sweeter 910

If obedience costs l, pay it 1722

if pressure taken out of your l. 9977

if smile, it returns greeting 6949

If spiritual l. does not grow where we are 10702

If ten lead holy l. 5751

If we fully comprehended brevity of l. 6924

If you do not love, do not know meaning of Christian l. 7191

Ignorance necessary condition of l. itself 6081

immersed in active l. 7004

important in l. is obedience of faith 8110

important thing in l. 542

in Christ, string of action verbs 1235

in dying we are born to eternal l. 9086

2321

in everyone's l. connections, twists, turns 5454

in fullest deepest sense possible 7969

In l, in death, thy lovely will 8098

In l. he is my l. 6498

In prayer relates own l. to l. of humanity 8917

In prayer sees l. as God sees it 8917

in pursuit of the disciplined l. 9970

in solving problems, l. has meaning 2736

in the cross 2096

in the great symphony of l. 10135

In the morning of l, work 6928

in the seeds 8002

in the Spirit a different l. 10715

in this l. as in another man's house 7077

inevitable struggles of l. 4768

infinitely more subtle 6918

inner chamber of peculiar l. 7127

inner, outer l. harmoniously developed 1766

inside our own skins, for l. 7148

interruptions real l. 2750

Into each l. some rain must fall 2549

involved 6918

irresistible purpose of Christ's l. 6439

is "wandering to find home" 2315

is a bridge 6943

is a great book 6945

is a hard fight 6947

is a hereditary disease 6948
is a journey 11374
is a mess most of the time 6984
is a mirror 6949
is a one-way street 6950
is a struggle 6947
is an art 6971
is brief 11287
is changed, not taken away 2343
is coerciveness 11388
is dust nature lends man for an
  hour 6960
is easier than you think 6961
is eternal 6097
is for one generation 9617
is frittered away by detail 10281
is given us so we may grow in love
  6907
is God's l. 6998
Is l. so wretched 6931
Is l. worth living 6932
is like a cash register 71
is like music 6966
is made up of little things 6656
is made up of sobs, sniffles, smiles
  6969
is mostly froth and bubble 6657
is not as idle ore 2599
is not doing a sum 6975
is not lost by dying 6972
is not our home 6978
is not so bad as you are 6903
is not the choice 1140
is painting a picture 6975
is partly what we make it 4254
is perfected by death 10870
is rather like a tin of sardines
  6976
is real! L. is earnest 2328
is really simple 6977
is registered and recorded 71
is short 6658
is short and full of blisters 192
is the preparation 6978
is the soul's nursery 6979
is the test of us 6932
is the training ground 6978
is to be, do, do without, depart
  6980
is very simple 7692
is warfare 6981
is what you've got 6983
is worth the living 2978
is wrestling with evil 6947
isn't logical, sensible, orderly 6984
isn't what you want 6983
Jesus Christ's l. an absolute failure
  3605
Jesus Christ, l. of God 497
Jesus driven to l. of silence,
  solitude, simplicity 6358
Jesus offends because emphasis on
  unseen l. 6450
Jesus tells us accurately about l.
  after death 2323
Jesus' death is our l. 6453
Jesus' l. would drive us to despair
  2161

Jesus, foundation of my whole l.
  11126
Joy echo of God's l. within 6545
Joy of l. arises from being where
  one belongs 1807
joy waters whole l. 6568
joyous with heavenly song 11144
judgment on all human l. 24
know almost nothing about inner
  l. 1753
know belief when it becomes l. or
  death 616
Knowledge indispensable to
  Christian l. 6693
Lamenting sore his sinful l. 7743
last of l, for which the first was
  made 8132
last part of l. you learn to stand
  parents 3893
Laughter is music of l. 6734
lead a true l. 4974
learn patience by taking l. as it
  blows 8422
least of things with meaning
  worth more in l. 7030
leaves of l. keep falling one by one
  7031
let Christ be note to which l.
  attuned 6379
Let each man think his l. a breath
  of God 4557
let God break l. from its moorings
  in some storm 9564
let God lift l. by great tide 9564
let us now commit Golden Rule to
  l. 5007
liberty, and the pursuit of
  happiness 3246
Licking honey from a thorn 6963
lightness of l. from grace of
  Christ, love of God 5229
like a library owned by an author
  6965
like fly in room with boys armed
  with swatter 6968
like going through car wash in
  bicycle 7023
like learning violin as one plays in
  public 6967
like needlework 8388
live l. for something more
  important than l. 7034
Live out l. in its full meaning 6998
live such a l. 551
Live to explain doctrine by l. 3440
Live your l, forget your age 8144
lived in full knowledge of fears
  3990
lived without forgiveness 4093
lives holiest l. fittest far to die
  2427
look upon l. as gift from God
  2307
looks poorest when you are richest
  6903
Lord doesn't want first place in
  my l. 9561
Lord wants all of my l. 9561

Lord, I've been active all my l.
  5661
Lord, make my l. a window 9079
lost in thousand, small, uncaring
  ways 6972
lost minute by minute 6972
Love can fill duty with l. 7165
  3087
Love complicates every l. 4823
Love complicates l. of God 4823
love everything in l, even to be sad
  10595
love has truly entered my l. 7184
Love is the fire of l. 7248
love of l. increased with years
  8174
Love your l, poor as it is 7001
Love, in l. everything 7276
lowest times in his l. 5437
magnificent 6918
Make l. a mission, not
  intermission 10171
makes for total l. lived at full
  potential 6999
making of music often slow
  process in l. 7915
Man does not know what to do
  with l. 3282
Man enters each stage of l. as
  novice 7002
man has only enough l. to pursue
  one object fully 9260
man in prime of l. is the devil
  2651
man leaves footprints when walks
  through l. 6231
Man spends l. complaining of
  present 8380
Man spends l. fearing for future
  8380
Man spends l. reasoning on past
  8380
man who cannot resolve to live
  his own l. 6872
man who has no inner l. 7033
man's l, illustration of Christianity
  1177
Man's love is of man's l. a thing
  apart 7278
Man's speech is like his l. 10684
mature l. unconscious consecration
  1714
Maturity is l. under control of God
  7685
may flash forth with l. of God
  7055
may hear a man say, l. is not
  worth living 6880
May I not be my l. 9070
Meet and remould it, till it be
  7003
memorizing Scripture help in l.
  747
Men happy only when object of l.
  not happiness 5540
men insist on making it
  complicated 6977
minus love equals zero 7206

Mirth offered sparkling with l. to God 6739

Mirth wine of human l. 6739

missing in American l. 7990

mission everything, personal l. nothing 9279

more than a climb to top 350

more to l. than increasing speed 7053

most exhausting in l. is being insincere 6063

most important in l. cannot be taught 3030

most important thing in l. 7034

mother's gift to you, l. 7850

Motherhood greatest privilege of l. 7849

move through l. in distracted way 5590

Music is moonlight in gloomy night of l. 7909

Music washes away dust of l. 7912

must be broken into l. 899

must be composed by ear, feeling, instinct 6966

must be lived forwards 6941

must be sacramental 6985

must learn from l. how to suffer it 10923

My l, my friends, my soul I leave 7503

My l. as his 9805

My l. collided with me 1906

My l. is ending, I know that well 7101

My l. is in the falling leaf 2587

My l. is like a broken bowl 7003

My l. is one great suffering 10873

mystic, to participate here and now in that real l. 7969

Mystical, intimate quality of the spiritual l. 7954

naive helps one go through l. smoothly 7976

neither good nor evil 5034

never will be what ought to be 6939

new l. we bring forth gift to be received 10545

newborn l. how glad 9898

no better way to finish spiritual l. 10705

no grammar for language of inner l. 7705

no inconvenience to way of l. 3333

No l. dreary when work delight 3106

No l. great until disciplined 2852

no l. so humble it cannot reflect God's light 7055

no l. so meager greatest can afford to despise it 7055

No man has right to a l. of contemplation 9670

No man loves l. as he who's growing old 8147

No one can find a full l. 11613

no right to draw l. from other source than Christ 11689

no synthetic replacement for decent home l. 5858

No two human beings make same journey in l. 5978

no wilderness like l. without friends 4284

noise l. causes as it rushes on 10273

none but fools would keep 7019

Nor do I fret about ignorance of future l. 6092

nor has man right to active l. 9670

not a destination 11374

not a matter of extent 6970

not a possession to be defended 10545

not an exact science 6971

not one l. not so near to God 7057

not storms, stresses of l. that defeat 2737

not the wick or the candle, but the burning 6973

not what happens to you 522

nothing certain in l. 954

Nothing in l. is to be feared, only understood 3984

Nothing really important in l. 972

nothing swifter in l. than voice of rumor 5142

nothing terrible in l. for man who realizes 7059

nothing, smoke, shadow, pain 4412

O L! thou art a galling load 7007

O Lord that lends me l. 11156

of civilization compared with man only a moment 7389

of contemplation 7004

of freedom, liberty, delight 5464

of humanity is so long 5944

of Jesus cannot be discussed in same way as any other man 6476

of Jesus Christ anticlimax of failure 10813

Of kindness and love 626

of man consists in beholding God 12116

Of the building of l. 4563

of the individual so brief 5944

of the L. to be 3289

of truth from death of creeds 11504

Oh the joy of l. with, in and for God 6554

Oh, what a sign it is of evil l. 2348

Old age blessed time of l. 8149

old age most happy time of l. 8149

Old age, crown of l. 8166

once key to meaning in our hands 6940

once we know l. is difficult 7012

One l, gleam of time between two eternities 7013

one long process of getting tired 6974

One moment of impatience may ruin a l. 8405

one solitary l. 6353

one stitch at a time taken patiently 8388

one who loves l. 4204

one who understands use of l. 4204

One's l. heavy price to pay 3487

only advancing in l. whose heart is getting softer 6898

Only Christian revelation gives end, means of l. 9703

Only crucified preaching can give l. 9160

only understood backwards 6941

option to choose 499

Our inner l. grows stronger when outwardly condemned 6270

pain of an empty l. 120

pain, the sharper the more evidence of l. 8267

partly made by friends we choose 4254

passes 6455

passeth from l. to his rest in the grave 9225

Peace is adjustment of l. to will of God 8460

Peace not absence of conflict from l. 8458

personality something for eternal l. 6183

Plant love heart-deep in a person's l. 7289

pleasure the dessert of l. 12028

point of cross is point of l. 892

power lies at center of l. 10576

power of service correspond to l. of prayer 10192

powerful 6918

prayed for all things that he might enjoy l. 8806

prayer for daily l. 9099

prayer is a l. attitude 8931

Prayer preserves l. from unravelling 8953

Prayer the pulse of l. 8946

Praying arranges l. anew 8899

preach better sermon with l. than lips 3462

Prescription for happier, healthier l. 5615

presence of God a fact of l. 4864

present l, only a drowsy half-waking 5672

price and glory of a mortal's l. 7035

problems are the delight of l. 9286

proof of immortality not in demonstrating continuance of l. 6105

prosper as we do common things in l. in uncommon way 9344

proverb is no proverb until l. has illustrated it 3539

proves a Christian 1280

public l. will take care of itself
6321
pure in heart who understood
what l. was about 5001
Put your faith to test of l. 3774
quality immeasurable though
quantity insignificant 7080
quality of l. begins when
confidence transferred to God
5645
quiet l. characteristic of great men
5274
quit l. as an inn, not a home 7005
Quotations tell of struggles with l.
9385
Railing at l, yet afraid of death
8163
raised to sweetness of eternal l.
4749
rather fear l. shall never have a
beginning 6891
ready to renew your l. with hope,
courage 9896
Real l. seems to have no plots
9405
real masterpiece of l. 3107
Reason thus with l. 7019
Recipe for a long l. 7020
Reckon not upon a long l. 7021
reduced to possessions 8634
relationship of l, not of intellect
6515
Religion and home l. are
supplementary 5858
remember gift of l. 9270
repentance a natal day when new
l. begins 9591
Repentance to fill that which is
wanting in one's l. 9596
repents, leaves his old l. 9583
resembles Olympic Games 7018
resurrection brought l. to light
9702
resurrection substituted fear of
death for eternal l. 9702
Reward in l. depend on
contributions we make 10179
Robbing l. of friendship 4299
rule that governs my l. is this 7036
runs quick through unresting race
973
runs quick through varied range
973
runs tediously quick 973
rust of l. scoured off by oil of
mirth 6738
sacredness upon every part of our
l. 9099
saint never thinks of l. as secular
and sacred 1324
Salvation is moving from living
death to deathless l. 9809
Sanctification means l. of
discipline 9843
sanctified l. often misunderstood
2856
Satan uses problems of l. to
slander God's character 9859
scene of good and evil 5034

second half of l. habits acquired
5501
see God in circumstances of l.
1464
seed dies into new l, so does man
2385
seems a haphazard l. externally
7509
seldom solid home l. in absence of
religious inspiration 5858
Self toughest plant in garden of l.
9943
Selfishness turns l. into a burden
10083
serene, silent beauty of a holy l.
5766
shadow which loses itself in the
sunset 2457
shadows of l. caused by standing
in one's own sunshine 2552
shallow amenities of l. ordained
by God 7038
short day in which sun hardly rises
7083
short l. with wisdom better than
long l. without it 11897
should all like l. free from
suffering 6506
Shrinking from death robs l. of
purpose 2255
sifting like grain from bag 8381
Silence a rich pause in music of l.
10262
simple, unassuming l. best for
everyone 7365
simplifies itself 11153
sins against this l. who slights the
next 6093
slept and dreamed l. was joy 9663
slow, painful process in this l.
7056
sniffles predominating 6969
society will pay any price to
prolong l. 2232
soften down the rugged road of l.
7917
Sojourn in every place as if spend
l. there 9491
Solitude makes l. worth living
10556
some of us are going to come to l.
9822
Something of my old self, my old,
bad l. 8966
soul hot for certainties in l. 946
Spirit of God will take direction
of l. away from you 5776
Spirit-filled l. no goal difficult of
attainment 5803
Spirit-filled l. no mystery revealed
to select few 5803
spiritual l. is unaging youth 10712
spiritual process lasts all through l.
10006
spontaneous joyful uncertainty,
expectancy 5463
storms of l. have driven us 178
stronger than dark, light, wrong,
right 2985

suburb of the l. elysian 2392
Take care of your l. 2369
Take everything in l. as from hand
of God 2744
take for granted or with gratitude
5268
Take my l. I draw no protective
line 2331
take on new zest, interest, meaning
3185
taken l. on the sad side 10594
takes faith to live l. of heaven on
earth 3752
tells falsehood about l. 7601
tempo of l. growing faster 3896
tests of growth in mainstream of l.
1319
tests of l. make, not break us 214
thanks have another l. to look
forward to 11144
that lifts him into l. 5387
the breath of a buffalo in winter
2457
the flash of a firefly in the night
2457
the last hour of my l. 569
their l. becomes a ministry 10561
then human l. will appear simple
10653
There is a l. above 5633
things in l. irreparable 7051
things that count most in l. 7039
think God turned l. into
inextricable confusion 4885
three events in man's l. 7050
Through the black space of death
to baby l. 6148
till l. finds pull of Christ's love
6937
Till my l. shall end 12007
time to be alarmed in l. 7040
time, that's the stuff l. is made of
6886
tiny harpoon can rob of l. 11071
tissue of the L. to be 3289
To believe in heaven is to run
toward l. 5674
To dead men, l. is Christ 6391
to death to eternal living 5945
to enter upon a strange, alarming
l. 6421
to live separated l. humanly
impossible 10717
to lose what makes l. worth living
6883
to one who believes, l. is victory
607
to one who feels, l. is tragedy 607
to one who thinks, l. is comedy
607
To put sin out of l. humanly
impossible 10717
to reap little of l. but cessation
6280
To repent is to alter way of
looking at l. 9605
To what shall I compare this l. of
ours 7070

Today I am brought to l. with
Christ 2121

too young now, I will enjoy l.
4886

torn between desire to think
positively or confront l. as it is
9401

tragedy of l. is failure to use talent
10997

tragedy of l. is we wait so long to
begin it 7042

training place for destinies of
eternity 6979

tremendous reservoir of
resurrection l. of Christ 11689

trivial irritations of family l. 6386

troubles of l. come because refuse
to sit quietly 9367

true joy of man's l. in relationship
to God 9467

True prayer a way of l. 8954

truest l. in dreams awake 2966

trust, obey substance of
Spirit-filled l. 5803

truth not words, but a l. and being
11572

truths reveal a l. deeper than
known 11521

truths upon which human l. may
rest 11585

trying to live maximum l. on
minimum faith 3770

turn sin-battered l. toward Great
Physician 10436

turns dead on our hands 4437

turns empty, inane, meaningless
4437

twinkle of star in God's eternal day
7015

two fundamental rules for l.
10053

two ways to slide easily through l.
2956

ultrabusy schedule not mark of
productive l. 9533

under God's leadership 4160

understand it, l. no longer difficult
7012

unexamined not worth living
7032

unexplained things in l. more than
explained 11616

unknown puts adventure into l.
4318

unless doctrine translated into l.
11185

Unselfishness turns burdens into l.
10083

until the fever of l. is over 9105

used to condition us for eternity
6944

victorious l. is Christ's business
11672

Violence destroys l. 11678

voice of a deep l. within 3700

wants another l. which will last
forever 3282

wants disturb human l. 2861

way out of the testings of l. 166

we call Christian different from
what we think 6918

we make a l. by what we give
4381

we try to escape l. instead of
controlling it 7072

We value l. without struggle
11667

weaknesses necessary to purposes
of l. 11788

web of l. is of a mingled yarn
7045

well used brings happy death
2224

well-defined spiritual l. most easily
lived 1332

what happens while making other
plans 6982

what one calls real l. is phantom
2750

What sweet delight quiet l. affords
9375

What sweetness left in l. if take
away friendship 4299

When blandishments of l. are gone
10948

When Christ came into my l.
11130

when faces facts of l. as they are
8237

When I consider short duration of
l. 4905

When I consider the short
duration of my l. 7084

When I think of those who have
influenced my l. most 6245

When l. flows along like a song
10493

When l. isn't the way you like
1822

When l. knocks you to your knees
9027

When l. rosy may slide by
knowing about Jesus 10930

When l. snarled up 2802

When people serving, l. no longer
meaningless 10212

When pleasure business of l,
ceases to be pleasure 8614

when troubles end, l. ends too 152

When you don't use l, rust
consumes it 6905

When you use it, it wears out
6905

Whenever visions of God unfit us
for practical l. 5466

where l. and death are one in the
Lord 3649

where mystery of l. appears 10564

Wherever our l. touches yours,
help or hinder 9522

wherever your l. touches ours,
make us stronger or weaker
9522

while I stand on this isthmus of l.
6910

who believes himself far advanced
in spiritual l. 10701

who in this mortal l. would see
303

Who knows but l. be that which
men call death 7086

Who pass into l. beyond 6109

Who will give me back days when
l. had wings 12176

whole course of l. upset 7046

whole l. series of disappointments
9469

whole of l. diseased 10271

Why are we so fond of l. 7089

Why is l. so tragic 7090

Why wish for living past l. again
7091

will be exhausted in battle of l.
10159

will encounter hurts, trials 970

Will make this l. of ours most
sweet 6647

will never wish for prizes of l.
10875

will not be able to change 970

will remain at beginning of godly l.
6708

Wisdom seeing l. from God's
perspective 11971

with all its tragedies, ambiguities
3685

with Christ an endless hope 5938

with Christ l. is dawn of morning
7094

with Christ never dull 6987

with Christ not always easy 6987

with eyes shut a kind of insanity
11234

with gratitude l. becomes rich
5257

with its sudden, startling joys
3685

with l. as with a play 6935

with our family might be more
amiable 7611

With renunciation l. begins 7092

without a quiet center becomes
destructive 10531

Without Christ l. as twilight with
night ahead 7094

without conflict impossible 6988

without goal is like entering a
jewel mine 4426

Without God in this l, without
him in next 1142

Without God l. a blank, desert,
shoreless, trackless waste 7098

without possible postponement
11388

without purpose 4437

without thankfulness devoid of
love 11154

Without the l. there is no living
6382

Witnessing a quality of l. 3344

work a way of l. 3127

Work is the meat of l. 12028

worry, anxiety sand in machinery
of l. 3731

Worship is the Christian l. 12135

would like to live long l. 4975

would not believe in eternal l. 5700
Yard by yard l. is hard 6930
Yet the light of a whole l. dies 7306
You must take it 6893
youth a spirit of asserting l. 12183
Youth ideal state if came later in l. 12187
Youth not yet humbled by l. 12181

LIFEBLOOD
Hope, balm and l. of the soul 5933

LIFE-FORM
Each of us carries own l. 6214

LIFELESS
God of logic 3793
God, no l. powerless work 872
Gold is l. 11813
He who is faultless is l. 8519

LIFELONG
Reading, selfish, serene, l. intoxication 858

LIFE-MELODY
In our l. music is broken off by rests 7056

LIFE'S
a pudding full of plums 6990
a short summer 6991
a tough proposition 6992
As l. shadows longer creep 8120
behind l. darkest clouds 10964
beyond our l. horizon 6111
but a walking shadow, a poor player 6994
days into the soil of l. enduring values 9111
difficulties break through superficiality 2738
Discipline tools to solve l. problems 9967
do l. plain, common work as it comes 12018
Faith proves herself in l. situations 3715
friend, one of l. greatest assets 4163
God takes l. pieces 8438
home kind of school where l. basic lessons taught 5853
However desolate l. monody sounds 7895
I sink in l. alarms 10973
Inch by inch l. a cinch 6930
moment's insight sometimes worth l. experience 8486
more involved in l. troubles when come to Christ 11451
mysteries for our worship 6995
neglected in l. hurry and bustle 12114
one of l. great joys 50
opportunities open on road of daily duties 8217
own gift cumulative force of l. cultivation 6226

perils for our courage 6995
shadow of bird in flight 6993
sorrows for our trust 6995
temptations for our faith 6995
too short for worrying 12068
When l. alive in everything 9899

LIFE-SENTENCE
all serving l. in dungeon of life 7074

LIFE-STYLE
challenge is translation into l. 1225
deny God with l. 487
evangelism a l. 3313
God did not send his Son to cramp our l. 9558
prefer own friends who share l. 5957
Repentance alters the entire l. 9589

LIFETIME
And seen God's hand thro a l. 6914
body, have only for a l. 10680
cultivating knowledge of God 4702
Hate easy to maintain for l. 7233
in l. brain can store one million billion "bits" of information 7738
Marriage is for a l. 7641
Staying happily married for a l. among the fine arts 7615
to become a Christian 1287
truth discovered lasts a l. 11578
word out of season may mar a l. 2890

LIFT
And loads to l. 6881
Christ came to l. us to heavenly places 6402
I know not where his islands l. 4763
I would look up, l. 1018
If any little l. may ease burden of another 910
if l. up Jesus Christ 9838
let God l. life by great tide 9564
my lamp beside the golden door 7985
one day nearer the dawning when fog will l. 5676
With joy shall I l. up my head 4719

LIFTED
great load of responsibility from Almighty 9915
human race l. up by Christianity 1187
religious values l. or degenerate 11658

LIFTINESS
turn lowness into l. 1122

LIFTING
Faith does not ask for l. of darkness 3714

men who are l. world upward 3142
Prayer way of l. ourselves 8917
rises by l. others 10144

LIFTS
earth to heaven, stoops heaven to earth 6153
his heart to God with his hands 8811
Holy Spirit l. personality to highest use 5798
man drags man down, or man l. man up 9522
men up to their Father in heaven 5844
reads the prayer and l. my care 7478
soul l. and is lifted up 7967

LIGHT
A l. to shine upon the road 7507
abscond into his l. 2658
affliction, whether l. or grave 160
after l. well us'd they shall attain 1664
against darkness 10844
am not judged by l. I have 6579
An infant crying for the l. 2576
and truth and love of heaven 10756
Angels see only the l. 357
arrival of radiant l. in our darkness 6119
As landscapes their variety from l. 103
better to l. candle than curse darkness 10164
Bible l. without darkness 710
Bible never failed to give l. 670
Bible's l. like body of heaven 680
brighten our inward l. 4974
Burdens become l. when cheerfully borne 1086
cares speak, great ones silent 10599
Christ gives us l. 1144
Christ letting in a l. 6434
closer one gets to l, more imperfections show 7522
Confession brings to l. unknown 1596
Could blind chance create l. 1958
Count each affliction, whether l. or grave 5331
cynic blind to l. 2187
Darkness more productive than l. 2541
darkness shows us worlds of l. 10633
Death not extinguishing l. 2252
death raises from darkness into l. 2250
death, through darkness into l. 2426
discern rays of l, hope 3350
divine l. in every human being 7561
do have to l. my part 7107
don't have to l. all the world 7107

Doubt is looking for l. 2930
enables us to see differences 1144
enthusiasm l. that leads 3188
error follows false l. 3258
Every l. casts a shadow 255
Faith beholds feeble l. 3800
Faith is a l. 3772
Faith, like l, should be unbending 7168
Faith, like l. simple, unbending 3839
few are windows bringing l. 3019
finds his own calamity l. 177
Flood the path with l. 9059
For each new morning with its l. 11174
for me in darkness, tempering sorrow 4758
For the true l. 7475
friend is dearer than l. of heaven 4269
Give me a l. that I may tread 5417
gives l. to every age 634
glow that illumines, glare that obscures 268
God distinguished by l. 4472
God gives l. in darkness 2582
God has set l. against darkness 5016
God is good, and God is l. 4936
God is l. eternal 4514
God is the l. in my darkness 4459
God makes l. and sweet 148
God never fails to grant l. 5397
God only gives us l. we need for present 5397
God will advance a mile in blazing l. 2962
God, a l. that is never darkened 4698
God, the l. in my darkness 6907
griefs can speak, deeper ones dumb 5347
Happiness l. on the water 5527
he has already shed 5445
He that has l. within his breast 1683
He who gives most l. to world 6004
I am bound to live by l. I have 6303
I carry a magic l. in my heart 3649
If the l. is red or yellow 5422
if we have not l. and color in our eyes 7108
Ignorance has no l. 3258
In Bible, intense light 672
in both is divine 8008
in eyes 829
infant world, wrapped in swaddling clothes of l. 7886
Into the infinite l. 2360
is above us, color around us 7108
is God's point of view 7106
isn't necessary to blow out other person's l. 10457
Jesus shed more l. than philosophers, scholars 6449

judged by l. refused to accept 6579
Lead, kindly L, amid encircling gloom 5429
Lets in new l. through chinks that time has made 7701
life is stronger than l. 2985
life, facets of one diamond reflecting l. 6985
like a great ring of pure, endless l. 3276
Live faithfully by bit of l. you now have 8103
long ere l. flashed through sky 4769
love a flame, still only l, and flickering 7236
love sees things in l. of his glory 6457
make my life a window for your l. to shine through 9079
make their righteousness clear as l. 9104
makes no noise 1956
man condemned for not coming to the l. 6586
more intense l. is, less you see glass 6033
Most people object to speed of l. 11309
Nature's resplendent robe 7109
need not new l. but new sight 9554
never doubt what God told you in l. 2885
new l. continually beams from Bible 737
New Testament, a strong l. 739
no darkness into l. without emotion 3053
no life so humble it cannot reflect God's l. 7055
No man happy whose path but glimmer of l. 6101
No Niagara turned into l. until tunneled 2852
No sky is heavy if heart be l. 6553
no sound to the ear 1956
not darkness for God is l. 5659
not enough darkness to put out l. of candle 8241
of the glad 6468
Oh spring to l, auspicious Babe, be born 6143
opposed to darkness 5205
optimist sees green l. everywhere 8245
optimist sees l. at end of tunnel 8250
optimist sees l. where there is none 8246
others receive l. temptation 11083
pessimist sees only red l. 8245
pessimist tries to put l. out 8246
Pray in the darkness if there be no l. 8768
prayer for l.—for strength to bear 8863

pretense of being holy until stand in l. 9741
proportion out what l. he sees fit 4629
pure l. of God pierces a man 9741
realist sees tunnel and l. 8250
Reason saw not till faith sprung the l. 3777
receives praise the way clean window takes l. 6033
resurrection brought life, mortality to l. 9702
ride a man, sit easy and l. 9471
saint is one l. shines through 9769
shadows mean there's a l. shining somewhere 2602
shall kindle fire, l. up entire city 5751
should lamp spread l. 3323
so lovely will want to know source 12147
Solitude like l, mightiest of agencies 10563
stars flame out in pomp of l. 7927
Study sciences in l. of truth 9871
sun gone to diffuse l. elsewhere 6094
supply l. not heat 6587
than go alone in the l. 5419
than in land flooded with l. 7779
that is beyond all l. 303
That shall be to you better than l. 5417
that then shone never left me 7472
The darkness shineth as the l. 4140
The very l. of day 4195
though passes through pollution, not polluted 7110
thought of God l. which guides 11249
To friendship every burden l. 4288
to make l. with a word 1980
to see clearly reason needs l. of heaven 9422
To the church, Pentecost brought l. 5806
too much l. blinds us 3559
Touched by a l. that hath no name 8047
true l. ever shines 5103
Truth, like l, blinds 6866
Turn darkness into l. 6647
Two ways of spreading l. 3455
unconscious is not only dark but also l. 7772
Up to l. where God himself appears 8454
wait in quietness until l. in darkness 3718
We rejoice in the l. 1375
We saw thee by thine own sweet l. 6152
When Christ came, there was no l. 6510
When speak of heaven, let face l. up 5680
When will ready, feet l. 7870
where there is darkness, l. 9086

Where there is much l, shadow is
   deep 6712
whether l. or darkness 1461
wicked shun the l. 11893
Wise Nicodemus saw such l. 780
Wish for a better l. 727
with Christ, l. and warmth of full
   day ahead 7094
with rays of glowing l. 8899
Yet the l. of the bright world dies
   7306

LIGHTED
Great men meteors designed to
   burn so earth l. 5278
home must be l. up with
   cheerfulness 5848
with living splendors 4708

LIGHTEN
either l. my burden or strengthen
   my back 9071
up or you will sink 12092
your load by lightening his 8689

LIGHTENS
Friendship l. adversity 4228
love's object l. its toil 6457
Wealth l. not heart, care of man
   11877
who l. burden for anyone else
   10175

LIGHTER
burden shared l. load 927
I do not pray for l. load 929
Pray not for l. burdens 8896

LIGHTHOUSES
blow no horns, only shine 5737
don't ring bells 6022

LIGHTING
candle loses nothing by l. another
   10113
candle of the Lord l. men to God
   7430
Education l. of a fire 3002

LIGHTINGS
And vivid l. flash from pole to pole
   4827

LIGHTLY
assents seldom keep word 1534
obtain too easy, value too l. 8563
takes rank l. raises own dignity
   6003
They travel l. whom God's grace
   carries 5235
who has great power, should use
   it l. 8704

LIGHTNESS
of life from grace of Christ, love
   of God 5229

LIGHT'NING
their eyes to vision and adoring
   8454

LIGHTNING
before I can say like a l. flash
   7070

behind the l, day with no night
   1515
bolts in response to bad doctrine
   11189
difference between l. and l. bug
   11992
Does not the l. write God's name
   in fire 7997
let l. write his name in fire 4712
Many like religion as sort of l. rod
   4998
must wait for God in the l. 5460
thought faith would strike me like
   l. 3735

LIGHTNING'S
saw the l. gleaming rod 8015

LIGHTNINGS
Thy arm directs those l. through
   the sky 4827
Trumpets! the earth trembles 6150

LIGHTS
false l. extinguished 5103
God l. the evening star 4596
Hope l. a candle, instead of
   cursing darkness 5928
man who finds truth l. torch
   11536
of a thousand stars do not make
   one moon 6198
teacher like candle which l. others
   11005
Turn up the l. 2454

LIKE
Christ makes his disciples l.
   himself 6411
Christ revealing what man is to be
   l. 6426
Christ, Son of God revealing what
   God is l. 6426
do not always l. being taught
   3008
don't l. to hear God called "you"
   8777
dreadfully l. other people 7441
easy for those who l. to work
   3126
forfeit ourselves to be l. other
   people 6218
good are l. one another 5045
Gossip, no one claims to l. 5133
I l. work 12009
If do justice to brother even
   though you do not l. him 6609
If I try to be l. him 6188
if want to know what God is l.
   4493
know God that thou mayst be l.
   him 10010
life the way it is 1822
live with approval, learn to l.
   themselves 1114
natural to be l. person you live
   with most 6235
Nothing so l. God as stillness
   4486
Out of heaven and just l. me 6456

people we don't particularly l.
   7304
produces l. 5211
selfish do not l. needy strangers to
   intrude 5957
should all l. life free from suffering
   6506
sunrises, Mondays, new seasons
   8080
temptation to be l. God eclipsed
   view of God 4419
To be l. Christ our goal 8113
To dream of person you would l.
   to be 6217
To understand the world and to l.
   it 7069
We l. someone because 7333
We may say what we l. 4957
what are we l. where no one sees
   us 9845
what are we l. with those who
   know us best 9845
who will be l. me 6188
will be people we do not l. that do
   not l. us 5890

LIKENED
you to those I saw you with 9464

LIKENESS
God in l. of most defenseless of
   creatures 6154
God made us in his l. 2002
God working our family l. to his
   Son in us 5793
God's grace turns out family l. to
   Christ 4651
man would have lost l. to God
   4149
of divine love 10331

LIKES
free will not liberty to do
   whatever one l. 4111
friend knows all about you, l. you
   just the same 4168
God l. help when helping people
   10139
God will direct 1241
Happiness is not in doing what
   one l. 5525
man free to do what he l. 4150
man l. to go alone for walk 1639
No one l. skunk 1588
on account of your l. 3577
when a man does what he l. to do,
   character revealed 6842

LIKEWISE
God loved world, do l. 7172

LIKING
For truth-teller world has little l.
   11501
Happiness is l. what one has to do
   5525

LILIES
can never be l. unless spend time
   as bulbs 5369
God's plan, like l, unfold 5403
Jesus talked about sparrows and l.
   6451

of the field whose bloom is brief 2380

show a thornless growth 7179

that fester smell worse than weeds 5039

We were thistles, now l. 1348

LILY

Faith like a l, lifted high and white 7179

He paints the l. of the field 4761

Perfumes each l. bell 4761

LIMB

go out on l. 1940

LIMELIGHT

glorifying God when no l. 1295

LIMIT

be careful not to exceed feed l. 7020

Christ did not l. concern to spiritual 1551

church can l. God's power 4829

devil will l. work of God 11218

God can do nothing until l. of possible 8642

God is infinite, his love has no l. 4750

God never sets l. to man's freedom 4130

greed of gain no time or l. 5327

His love has no l. 7570

horizon nothing save l. of our sight 6097

Lord, thy will be done without a l. 9082

no business to l. God's revelations 11273

without l. is how God is to be loved 7574

LIMITATION

knowledge most haunted with inevitable l. 6689

Lord knows no l. 11606

Rebellion involves l. 4117

LIMITATIONS

Christian sees l. 1168

come to religion through l. of science 9866

Creation involves l. 4117

forget your l. 9271

help us accept ourselves, l. and all 9993

of humanist geocentric thinking 1168

Philosophy science of l. of human mind 8594

to place upon God human l. 9010

to release men from l. 4135

turn from l. to God who has none 3274

Worship aware of l. 12136

Youth not yet learned l. 12181

LIMITED

Experience is never l. 3524

fellowship l. to predictable personalities 4025

man in evolution from l. to greater freedom 9351

Our mind too l. to understand God 4665

power of Satan 4917

tragedy is not being l. to one talent 10997

understanding l. 11606

LIMITING

Beware in prayer of l. God 8772

Discussion is so l. 10242

way God can touch us 10720

LIMITLESS

cross, arms stretch out to l. reaches 2167

inheritance we receive from God l. 4694

resources in his l. ways 11

riches of l. time, endless years 3274

LIMITS

cannot see outer l. 4544

gospel a development more complete than l. of nature 9351

great man's world bounded by l. of vision 11728

happy man confines himself with l. 2875

Love often knows no l. 7283

Love seeks not l. but outlets 7271

of reason make faith necessity 3840

Patience has its l. 8409

poor vision l. deeds 11734

Prayer draws us out of narrow l. 8906

selfishness means stopping at human l. 10067

LIMPING

Truth, l. along on time's arm 6865

LIMPS

virtue divorced from thankfulness l. 11154

LINCOLN

Memorial Speech, 1963 4157

not afraid of being lonely 7141

poverty and Abraham L. 161

LINE

Each generation like a l, a phrase 7076

God orders, brings into l. 5175

LINEN

God gives no l, but flax to spin 3092

LINES

cannot make straight l. out of crooked 4885

God l. up his purpose 5175

LINGER

Let me not l. on 12016

We would not l. on the lower slope 5939

LINGERS

Comfort l. to become a host 7361

Knowledge comes, wisdom l. 6692

song is ended, melody l. 7924

LINGUIST

make mistakes in more than one language 7782

LINING

Every cloud has silver l. 2797

LINK

a golden l. into chain of order 2790

If l. is broken, chain breaks 2536

Prayer l. between finite man, infinite God 8944

suffering, a stronger l. than joy 5338

LINKS

Christian love l. love of God and neighbor 7164

LION

Christ divine paradox of l, lamb 6425

Christ L. in authority 6425

Christ L. in majesty, rebuking winds, demons 6425

Christ L. in power, raising the dead 6425

No one objects to March coming in like l. 9889

Temptations as l. that roared upon Samson 11095

To a mouse, a cat is a l. 9528

LIONS

didn't eat Daniel because grit, backbone 1046

faith that will shut mouths of l. 3787

LIP

Atheism rather in l. than heart 475

Christian more life than l. 1317

dashed no cup from perjured l. 3174

light laughter that bubbles on l. 431

only give l. service 3320

LIPS

grand dim l. murmur, "God-God-God" 3269

If you your l. would keep from slips 1855

Mother name for God in l. of children 7848

No one will grieve because your l. are dumb 3778

preach better sermon with life than l. 3462

When heart full, l. silent 5270

LIQUID

waves and waves of l. love 5797

LIQUIDATING

God l. him, raising him to new life 886

LIQUIDATION
world was in l. 784

LIST
Children don't fit "to do" l. 8287
Christianity, more than l. of don'ts 1171
deeper than l. of sins on membership card 10300
do not want to keep a prayer l. 8820

LISTEN
demonstrate God's love, l. to people 7115
do not have to l. to devil 2674
first duty of love is to l. 7301
for voice of God and learn of him 4964
God will l. as you walk 8874
Gold has no ears to l. 11813
highest function of mind is to l. to God's Word 7766
If we know how to l. to God 8835
Know how to l. 7114
learn to l. to God in circumstances 1477
move toward friends who l. 1857
No one need fear to l. 4966
not willing to l, a form of greed 1885
stand still, l. to speech of God 4965
stay awake and l. to sermon 10100
takes time to l. 8287
to the gentle movement of the Holy Spirit 10257
to the truth 11527
too busy to l. 129
twice as much as speaks 1858
very few care to l. to defense of character 1055
who loves to l. 7422
world glad of excuse not to l. to gospel 1334

LISTENED
I l. quiet and still 5415
to, creates, makes us unfold, expand 1857
voice for which he l. 4965

LISTENER
Christ unseen l. to every conversation 5823
good l. popular everywhere 7111
suffering person needs a l. 10887
takes a great man to make a good l. 7113

LISTENERS
Jesus captivated his l. 6444
When l. refrain from evil-hearing 10477
When speak, God one of your l. 1891

LISTENIN'
Hearin' is one thing, l. is another 1544

LISTENING
a creative force 1857
a grace of kind l. 6669
a magnetic, strange thing 1857
Children never good at l. to elders 1112
Creator patiently l. to four-year-old 3918
Half an hour's l. essential 7710
If think you know it all, haven't been l. 9210
learn knack of l. like Christian instead of critic 10110
Men never the same after l. to Christ 6377
noise of world prevent us from l. to God 8800
Prayer ends by l. to God 8902
Prayer is l, seeing, feeling 8923
prayer is l. 8751
remember God is l. while you tell it 5148
resigning ourselves to l. to God's language 5395
Sensitivity, l. to cues 8325
silence, l, prayer, truth go together 10248
sin of sermon l. 1414

LISTENS
Faith l. only to God 3683
He who l, reaps 1848
Nobody l, then everybody disagrees 5171
with interest to person who knows nothing 1942

LISTLESS
if foresight of adversity 4314

LITERAL
repressing emotions become l. 3050

LITERALLY
People who take symbols l. 5631

LITERARY
belongs to l. circle, call him Papa 3921

LITERATURE
Bible, bedrock foundation of all l. 703
memory is private l. 7731
most tragic sentence in l. 7601
resurrection permeated our l. 9702
suppress l. that getting on in world chief object in life 10086

LITTER
Remind us not to l. your creation 9117

LITTLE
a good leader, who talks l. 6803
able to say how much you love is to love l. 7323
acts of kindness, silent threads of gold 6997
atom proof l. things count 8663
before you know how l. you know 6700

beginning of greatness is to be l. 5293
Better to have l. than nothing 7120
can do l. things for God 10208
can do very l. with faith 3827
correct a l. 9489
cost devil l. trouble to catch lazy man 6766
deeds of kindness, words of love 2503
delighted with the cross 10312
difference of opinion alienates l. minds 11392
Do great things as if they were l. 10127
Do l. things as if they were great 7117
Do l. things now 2534
doubts will not avail against certainties 5028
dread the grave as l. as my bed 2370
drops of water 6659
Education teaches how l. man knows 3004
enormous the l. wrong you did 4097
entered l. into depths of Master's character 6390
every moment we may do l. works excellently 5068
Expect l. 5561
faith will bring soul to heaven 3757
Faithfulness in l. things, big thing 3843
few l. years on earth only first scene 6106
from God better than great deal from men 4524
give but l. when give possessions 10219
Give me the l. creeping treasons 4530
give much without sacrifice, given l. 10738
God kind enough to accept l. time I give back 11296
Good words worth much, cost l. 11987
grains of sand 6659
great deal of activity, but accomplish l. 9017
Great events on l. things depend 7119
Great l. one! whose all-embracing birth 6153
He who wants l. has enough 1799
His l, nameless, unremembered acts 6664
honesties, silent threads of gold 6997
How can we l. crawling creatures 4673
how l. one feels poverty when one loves 7199
how l. some enjoy 3221

If man too l. for God to speak to him 4553

If we want l, shall find l. 6354

in comparison with eternal realities 4559

just a l, temporary inconvenience 4226

Just a l. labor spend 4217

keep within own l. sphere 4885

keys open big locks 11989

Large streams from l. fountains flow 8657

Life a great bundle of l. things 6946

Life is made up of l. things 6656

life like a l. strip of pavement over an abyss 7090

like man who uses only l. finger 8659

Lord makes l. of physical death 2358

Lord, I am thanking thee for l. things 11148

many observations, l. reasoning leads to truth 9410

Men expect too much, do too l. 3504

minds tamed, subdued by misfortune 5281

more we learn, more we realize how l. we know 3029

not satisfied with l. 1805

not the man who has too l. who is poor 2868

of l. consequence whether idolator or Pharisee 10041

Old age needs so l. 8161

Old age needs that l. so much 8161

One life, l. gleam of time between two eternities 7013

One of whom, alas, we know so l. 6522

Only see a l. of God's loving 6111

Parents have l. time for children 8351

perhaps l. praying worse than no praying 8889

poverty of soul measured by how l. it can feel 10677

praying kind of make-believe 8889

probably giving away too l. 10734

provided for from within needs l. from without 5780

Revenge delight of l. minds 9725

room for l. beside ourselves 5625

satisfactions which may be hazardously l. 4248

self-denials, silent threads of gold 6997

shows greatness by way he treats l. men 5272

Simple love with even l. knowledge 6708

So much God would give, so l. received 8662

Some have l, some have less 11852

space I fill and can see 7084

speak of great or l. faith 4710

speck in center of life but a minute 7052

strokes fell great oaks 8547

takes l. effort to watch man carry load 6160

Tall oaks from l. acorns grow 8657

Ten die of l. worries 12061

the l. space I fill 4905

thing in hand worth more 7116

things that annoy us 9636

things that matter most 9267

Those who would love l. 6708

To have l. is to possess 7071

trouble praying when in l. trouble 8870

trust the morrow as l. as possible 8222

Truth lies within a l, certain compass 6868

victories over temptations, silent threads of gold 6997

wave of emotion enough for many 4471

We only see a l. of the ocean 6111

we resent l. provocations 3410

wealth, l. care 11833

what God is we know l. 4690

What should not be heard by l. ears 3461

Who does not thank for l. 11171

who thinks too much of himself thinks too l. of others 9243

who wants a great deal must not ask for l. 11732

with what l. understanding world is ruled 5174

words of sympathy, silent threads of gold 6997

world appears very l. 4707

world would have known l. progress 9311

LITURGICAL

prayer becomes formal routine 12131

LIVE

a conqueror, die a man 2353

a day at a time 4885

a king, die a man 2353

a pain to l. 186

allegiance to one set of principles, l. by another 6068

always l. for others 5066

as if you expect to l. forever 6099

as though Christ coming this afternoon 2837

As we give, we l. 10725

Attempting to compel others to l. as he does 7793

basis of fellowship to l. in the open 4026

Be such a man, l. such a life 6882

Better poor and l, than rich and perish 8675

Better to l. rich than die rich 11826

Bible contains formula by which people can l. 701

born crying, l. complaining, die disappointed 7075

brave l. on 10948

But, how did he l. 7423

by assurance of grace 5204

by godly priorities 3901

called to l. beyond natural ability 1284

can dare to l. alone 4286

can't l. a holy life 5752

care to l. until chose to die 5530

Cause us to l. at present 9120

Choice is how you l. life 1140

Christ an example, showing us how to l. 6410

Christ died that we might l. as he lives 6365

Christ killed that thou mightest l. 6393

Christ spoke of dying to l. 6359

Christian cannot l. by philosophy 9703

Christian, dies to l. 1265

Christianity, way to l. life 1188

cleavage between truths we affirm, values we l. by 6068

close to Me 10706

content to l. or die 11468

create harmony, love where you l. 580

dead shall l, the living die 7925

desire to die right rather than l. wrong 10719

die and you l. in God 9556

do not love fellow beings l. unfruitful lives 7321

do not require dying grace to l. by 6912

does not believe who does not l. 1751

easy in solitude to l. after own opinions 6195

easy to l. after world's opinions 6195

faith to l. life of heaven on earth 3752

faithfully by light you now have 8103

family first authority under which person l. 3888

finding something to l. for 7140

foolish to punish neighbor by fire when l. next door 9718

For by thy love I l. 4796

for himself, small troubles seem great 11433

for others, great troubles seem small 11433

for today 11304

forgets to l. 7050

give me faith to l. from day to day 9072

Give me power to l. for mankind 10130

God allows men to l. without him 1142

God came to show us how to l. 6128

God does not l. in isolation 11423

God without whom one cannot l. 4542

gospel cannot l. without prayer 9015

great majority of men exist, do not l. 7028

Great wealth, content seldom l. together 11818

greatest loss what dies inside while we l. 2254

have not learned to l. together 9353

He drew them forth, healed and bade me l. 9798

heart of faith, that we may l. thee 9058

help me l. from day to day 9075

Home not where you l. but where they understand you 5830

Home, each lives for the other, all l. for God 5837

I am bound to l. by light I have 6303

I do not find God hard to l. with 4478

I shall not l. 'till I see God 2310

I shall not l. in vain 6922

I to die, you to l. 2378

I will not just l. my life 6920

If going to l. for service of fellowmen 10159

If l. at same level of affluence 10734

if l. happily, learn to die 6926

if l. in God and die to own will 10047

if l. in sin, are among God's enemies 10427

important that we have grace enough to l. by 6912

impossible to l. in inmost being without loving silence 10254

in a moment of history 982

in fear of death is many times to die 2403

in gray twilight 1922

in neutral world a nightmare 4999

in pleasure when l. to thee 8600

in the atmosphere of the Incarnation 6378

Inside myself place where I l. all alone 9933

Is it less strange thou shouldst l. at all 6103

learn from mean man how not to l. 3159

learn to l. for others 4282

learn to l. together as brothers 923

less than time it takes to blink an eye 7080

Let all l. as they would die 6938

life for something more important than life 7034

lives to l. forever, never fears dying 6899

longer by century of shrieking deaths 6258

longer I l, more convincing proof 4942

lost faith, what left to l. on 3728

make war that we may l. in peace 11785

Man cannot l. all to this world 12109

Many l. in dread of what is coming 4318

Many learned men l. slaves 3018

Men l. on brink of mysteries 3654

men who l. with degree of serenity 5204

Men's evil manners l. in brass 9619

might as well l. 10943

must l. with people to know their problems 9292

must learn to l. together as brothers 5987

must watch how we l. 5818

natural to be like person you l. with most 6235

near to God 4559

never cared to l. until I choose to die 2308

no longer l. the good news 6824

None can l. in love without suffering 7246

Nor can spirits be divided that l. in same divine principle 7319

nor let me die before I have begun to l. 8430

not called to l. long on planet 1722

not how many years we l. 6933

not well for man to pray cream, l. skim milk 8856

O Lord, let me not l. to be useless 7008

Oftimes test of courage is to l. rather than die 7009

out life in full meaning 6998

People expect clergy to l. on food of canary 1497

people l. in things they possess 8631

pray only as well as we l. 8885

relationship to God fits you to l. 4555

repeating involuntarily the character of those among whom we l. 6243

Resolved, to l. with all might 569

response to assault reveal values by which you l. 6288

rich must l. more simply that poor may simply l. 11861

says he, for I'm coming 2295

Seems it strange thou shouldst l. forever 6103

self-centered people l. in unpleasant surroundings 10077

Selfishness asking others to l. as one wishes to l. 10081

Selfishness not living as one wishes to l. 10081

sets course for how we l. in seen world 3812

simply 5561

since I soon must cease to l. 9048

So l. not mind selling parrot to gossip 1039

So l. that your principles might safely be made law 6237

Some wish to l. within sound of church 7783

something to l. for 8897

Still, thank him that you l. 10489

such a life 551

Teach me to l. that I may dread 2370

than l. in plenty and be troubled 3979

thank Thee that I l. 7048

therefore l. most with Jesus Christ 6235

they l. in one another still 7319

They l. on earth 2287

They only truly l. 6109

think, suffer with your time 904

thinking has not taught me to l. 6942

Those who l. in the Lord 2401

thy creed 994

to a ripe old age 119

To be able to l. peaceably with hard persons 5236

To die for a religion easier than to l. it 7681

to die is to l. 9701

to explain doctrine by life 3440

to expound a passage, l. in it 9148

to l. every day as if it were our last 9120

To l. fully use things, love people 9510

To l. is to be slowly born 6873

To l. is to fight, suffer, love 7066

To l. long, necessary to l. slowly 7067

to l. modestly richer experience 9758

To l. more nearly as we pray 9040

To l. remains an art 7068

to l. separated life humanly impossible 10717

To l. through stress, sorrow with another 10641

To l. with thorn uncomplainingly 8256

to l. without prayer a foolish thing 8833

to the hilt every situation 3186

trying to l. maximum life on minimum faith 3770

trying to l. serene lives in houses divided against themselves 6068

up always to best, highest 3468

upon our daily rations 3112

want to die happily, learn to l. 6926

we do not l. under law of jungle 7331

We l. as we dream, alone 7079

We l. by faith; but faith not slave 3813

We l. in deeds, not years 1056

We l. in feelings, not figures 1056

We l. in thoughts, not breaths 1056

When repress things you don't want to l. with 9291

when right, make us easy to l. with 9119

When shall nothing but thyself l. in me 7961

where I love, I l. 7282

While we l, let us l. to him 7104

while you l. the Epicure would say 8600

who cannot resolve to l. his own life 6872

Why l. beggarly when riches of heaven are yours 8662

will endeavor to l. as he prays 8812

with God to solve problems 9292

Work as if you were to l. a hundred years 12023

Work not a thing one does to l. 12026

world in which creatures do good or harm 4132

Worldly people imagine saints find it difficult to l. 4159

would like to l. a long life 4975

your life, forget your age 8144

LIVED

a life of going-to-do 6756

All lives are not told, some are l. 6847

Christ l. in another world 6436

darkest day l. till tomorrow will have passed away 2575

essence of the drama Jesus l. 6384

God has l. all our tomorrows, yesterdays 4600

Had I l. in the time of Jesus 6464

happily ever after, most tragic sentence in literature 7601

has achieved success who has l. well 10781

have l. badly on my own 9070 11515

have so l. not born in vain 7005

I have l, sir, a long time 4942

I have l. and seen God's hand 6914

If God l. on earth 4480

Jesus l. great life convictions 6448

life l. in full knowledge of fears 3990

Life l. without forgiveness 4093

Life must be l. forwards 6941

Lord l. to give standard for our lives 568

makes for total life l. at full potential 6999

Nor do I regret I have l. 7005

not in one world but in two 3292

Theology must be l. in midst of life's mess 6984

to thank God all my prayers not answered 8823

Who could stand to see whole week before l. 4336

world seeing truth l. through us 3317

LIVELY

God has l. interest in man's being good 5060

LIVES

a mimicry 1640

adjust our l. to God 1304

all that l. must die 2402

All we send into l. of others 919

all we send into l. of others comes back 1726

And let our ordered l. confess 8431

And range with humble l. in content 6016
1772

As honesty, integrity characterize our l. 5874

Because he l. all fear is gone 2978

Because he l. I can face tomorrow 2978

by faith and love not judged on the law 6812

calms troubled sea of our l. 4863

can be bag of grapes, flowing into one another's l. 9524

cease to shape our l. by faith 3688

Christ in you that l. your life 6381

Christ operating in our l. 104

dead-end street with man who denies God 7523

do not like strangers to intrude upon 5957

Do not pray for easy l. 8780

doctrine of value if makes difference in l. 11180

drink, blasted more l. 325

eternity, pressing upon time-worn l. 1757

Every action of our l. touches some chord 105

Every man l. by faith 3653

every person God puts in our l. 3515

everyone dies, but not everyone l. 6884

evil that men do l. after them 5043

Fill l. with sweetness 4223

Fill up that which our l. have left behind 9054

first half of our l. ruined by parents 3892

For a cap and bells our l. we pay 9795

for healing l. must be changed within 5616

Forever l. a slave to others 6872

giving central place to God in practical, everyday l. 7713

God gives you and me lumber of our l. 7684

God ready to take over management of our l. 5511

God seeks worship of those whose l. in moral ruin 12098

God stands ready to take management of our l. 3758

God the very life of our l. 7557

God uses pain as chisel for sculpting our l. 8256

God writes the music of our l. 7056

good and wise lead quiet l. 9373

good l. on, loves on, conquers all 11129

great moment of our l. 9841

guide l. by integrity die happy though poor 6309

has invaded our l. with purpose 6156

have no music in them 9059

He most l. who acts best 1056

He most l. who feels noblest 1056

He most l. who thinks most 1056

He walks with God, he l. like Christ 1015

Home, each l. for the other, all live for God 5837

hostile person l. in a hostile world 9441

house he l. in sadly dilapidated 8142

however small visible measure of our l. 6232

If Christ l. in us 1289

If I had ten thousand l. 7674

if no element of asceticism in l. 466

if our l. were radiant 565

if we measure our l. against eternity 7080

If you treat friend shabbily while he l. 2317

immortality related to spirit which l. eternally 3482

in hope dances without a fiddle 5909

in the desert, deep-rooted in God 2609

inmost being where Christ l. 10254

introduce to Jesus Christ by way he l. 3306

Justice is insurance on our l. 8096

keep respectful fear of God in l. 3993

koinonia, unconditional sharing of l. 4022

leave marks on l. we touch 1289

let him make our l. narrow, intense 2829

Lord, normal standard for our l. 568

loving person l. in a loving world 9441

making a crown out of daily l. 7073

Man l. by mending 4654

man who l. on better terms with angels 3899

Man who l. that span is something 7080

men lead l. of quiet desperation 2610

mistakes won't irreparable damage l. 3616

moving moments of our l. find us without words 11986

My soul l. on God 7953

Not many l, only one have we 11287

Not without design does God write music of our l. 7915

of great men all remind us 5288 3441

of youth governed more by feeling than reasoning 12181

Old age l. minutes slowly, hours quickly 12193

Old cranks, saints have practiced all their l. 5503

Old men lose l. by ripeness 12197

only for himself truly dead to others 10059

Our l. are albums written through 7017

Our l. are what we think about God 7016

owe grandeur of their l. to difficulties 2739

People can alter l. 510

person who l. right 3428

poetry and glory of our l. 4704

prayers only as powerful as our l. 8885

preaches well who l. well 9138

Procrastination clutters up our l. 9300

reconsider important moments in l. 5392

redirecting our l. painful 5449

second half of our l. ruined by children 3892

self turns up to poison fruit of our l. 9943

shaped by those who love us 6236

sin that l. for nothing 11394

soul not where it l. but where it loves 7310

spend l. pleasing ourselves 5467

spend our l. conjugating three verbs 3491

Spirit of God puts words of Jesus into our personal l. 5801

Spiritual l. have been frozen 10369

spreads a common feast for all that l. 9883

sudden pause in choral hymn of our l. 7056

That man may last, but never l. 4374

To help—he l. eternally 2206

To pray means to put our l. into conformity with God 8944

To struggle in our l. 10407

truth works far and l. long 11516

trying to live serene l. in houses divided against themselves 6068

Unselfishness letting people's l. alone 11654

We can make our l. sublime 5288 3441

we shape l, ourselves 1148

What we do with our l. outwardly 7725

when our l. cease to be illumined 4538

when survey progress of our l. 5392

while it l, it gives 7218

who do not love fellow beings live unfruitful l. 7321

who l. for self alone l. for the meanest mortal known 10085

Who l. in fear never a free man 4009

who l. in sin and looks for happiness 10313

who l. to live forever, never fears dying 6899

whole course of our l. out of joint 7571

will spend rest of l. in future 4333

without God as center of l. young people frustrated 12180

Work is the thing one l. to do 12026

Worldliness is excluding God from our l. 12053

Young men lose l. by violence 12197

LIVETH

The Lord my Savior l. 232

LIVING

Act—act in the l. present 4331

Bad the day man becomes content with life he is l. 8649

beneath our privileges 5778

Beware that not from own lax l. 8363

Bible, l. book 705

blood transfusion for courageous l. 5804

bring to everyday l. high wisdom of God 3752

cannot put off l. 11388

Christian ought to be a l. doxology 9856

Christianity, true way of l. 1188

coffin of dead soul 7760

conforming outwardly, l. own life inwardly 6048

Contented l, nine requisites 1809

dead shall live, the l. die 7925

desire to know art of l. 10935

determined by attitude 522

determined not by what happens 522

determined not by what life brings 522

Don't go around saying world owes you l. 9652

each day as if our only day 6999

end of marrying when end of l. 7667

for sake of l. to lose what makes life worth l. 6883

forced to test beliefs in fires of l. 612

give all their l, have given much 10738

giving is l, the angel said 10728

glory of God is a l. man 12116

God in likeness of most defenseless of l. creatures 6154

God's wisdom in dailyness of l. 1803

gospel, a l. power, being 732

Happiness l. every minute with love, grace, gratitude 5528

History endless repetition of wrong way of l. 5713

holy life is l. above the world 5736

if longing heart finds l. water, will be alone 10536

in a whirl of contradictions 481

In l. echoes of thy tone 8866

in land of slavery, darkness 4969

in lap of luxury isn't bad 11834

in obedience to whatever lies ahead 5370

in our selfishness means 10067

invitation to true l. 1168

is learning meaning of words 7000

Is life worth l. 6932

it's day-to-day l. that wears you out 6876

Jesus proof of God's love, forgiveness 6473

Kept him a l. soul 8911

life is worth the l. 2978

life to death to eternal l. 5945

life unexamined not worth l. 7032

Lighted with l. splendors 4708

like majority of pople 9758

like so many atheists 481

make a l. by what we get 4381

may hear a man say, Life is not worth l. 6880

more alone while l. than going, coming 7151

new man born from l. God 872

next world is land of the l. 7064

no recipe for l. that suits all cases 6214

not l. up to belief 418

old age difficult chapter in art of l. 8178

on the anvil of everyday l. 3863

one day in the Spirit worth more than thousand in flesh 5787

only the l, on earth and beyond 2390

People l. deeply, no fear of death 2362

praise dead saints, persecute l. ones 8530

Prayer from a l. source within the will 8911

recognize necessity of Holy Spirit for l. 11243

Salvation is moving from l. death to deathless life 9809

Scriptures teach best way of l. 742

self-loving spirit antithesis of real l. 10053

Selfishness is not l. as one wishes to live 10081

shall forfeit fair renown 10088

Solitude makes life worth l. 10556

soon l. in electronic village 4332

streams of l. water flowing 5810

sure way to take fear out of l. 3993

thank thee that I am l. 11149

The road that leads us to l. God 3793

they will never tear the l. Christ from my heart 7103

this alone constitutes l. 130

To the l: Follow me 6497

today ready to spend in l. 11390

well is best revenge 9719

who ambitiously seek after world while l. 2344

whose daily l. to daily die 10046

Why wish for l. past life again 7091

Without the life no l. 6382

Worship a way of l. 12133

LIVING ROOM
let your l. be a sanctuary 7847

LIZARD
on cushion still seek leaves 989

LIZARDS
looked like great big hideous l. 11741

LOAD
burden shared lighter l. 927

Can ease my awful l. 8451

Can roll the strangling l. from me 2583

Christianity does not remove l. 931

heaviest l. pack of grudges 4098

I do not pray for lighter l. 929

lifted great l. of responsibility from Almighty 9915

lighten your l. by lightening his 8689

Man, designed to carry the l. of the moment 421

Never l. yourself so 4319

Nor bear an easy l. 1927

O Life! Thou art a galling l. 7007

takes little effort to watch man carry l. 6160

will be as intolerable as it is unreasonable 12064

LOADS
And l. to lift 6881

LOAF
Back of the l. is the snowy flour 9345

Don't l. away time 6755

God gave a l. to every bird 10030

LOAFER
Bible doesn't promise loaves to the l. 6774

LOAFERS
Tomorrow day on which l. work 11404

LOAN
All our goodness a l, God the owner 5055

If you l. your breeches 4367

Kids not short-term l. 1121

LOANED
Children l. temporarily 1110

LOATHE
I l. existence 3485

LOAVES
Bible doesn't promise l. to the loafer 6774

Love is like five l, two fishes 7238

Since we have l, let us not look for cakes 1811

with five l. and two fishes 10205

LOBBY
want to l. for God 3311

LOCKED
church door l. in winter 1382

let not one cabinet be l. up from Christ 8092

LOCOMOTIVE
Like mighty l. God's power is irresistible 8886

LODGES
Where care l, sleep will never lie 12082

LODGING
If nobody took slander in and gave l. 10455

Thy l. is in childlike hearts 6040

without caring for tomorrow's l. 11478

LOFTIER
Do rays of l. glory around thee play 6878

LOFTIEST
on l. throne still sitting on own rump 9248

LOFTINESS
eloquence retreats confused, abashed 4750

speculation is study of the Godhead 4631

LOFTY
pine that by the storm is oftener tossed 9216

trees have most reason to dread thunder 9241

LOGIC
Bible is full of l. 3830

can give no explanation before birth or after death 9419

compelled to praise, even as l. screams 8724

evil is the Satan that laughs at l. 5023

Gainst the l. of the devil 2636

Human l. strives in vain 2636

lifeless god of logic 3793

no immanent l. in evil 5023

not dealing with creatures of l. 9518

sacrifice of praise requires trading in human l. 8724

screams God has no idea what he's doing 8724

to do with time between birth, death 9419

LOGICAL
free choices, foreordained decrees 1153

Life isn't l. 6984

mind would be our own grotesque God 4689

LONELINESS
a homesickness for God 7146

a stimulating l. 7145

an escape from an inescapable God 7144

anything that tells heart's l. can find its way to God 8849

arctic l. of age 8165

barren, bleak winter of l. 968

by the sea personal, alive 7145

can be more tragic than problem 2921

central fact of human existence 7137

conquered only by those who can bear solitude 7133

Didst thou give me this inescapable l. 7125

discipline of sanctified life, l. 2856

eats into the soul 7134

far from being a rare, curious phenomenon 7137

first thing God's eye nam'd not good 7136

fully conscious we discover l. 9513

great price to pay for independence 7135

greatest poverty 7132

How could I know togetherness without l. 1512

If afraid of l, don't marry 7128

in every man a l. 7127

in l. thou art more surely our friend 9053

is inner emptiness 10548

Jehovah takes his ministers into l. 163

Jesus wants us to see their l. 3316

knew l. was when creative mood would work 7141

knowledge that human beings incapable of bringing help 7126

pain of being alone 7131

praise God in l. 583

Pray that l. spur you into 7040

Satan fails to speak of l. of immorality 2662

thank thee there will be l. 9053

What l. more lonely than distrust 7149

When marriage solution for l. it rarely satisfies 7666

LONELY
consecration is l. way to love 1722
Doubt, pain too l. to know faith 2932
friend, a word when you're l. 4174
hearts are l. 9059
hope, cheering the l. way 5940
I sit beside my l. fire 8827
If such a legend, why am I so l. 10786
In l. solitude God delivers his best thoughts 10544
least l. when most alone 10568
luxuries of world cannot satisfy l. 7176
more l. among men than in our chambers 10572
Most of world's great souls have been l. 7138
none more l. than man who loves only himself 7147
not afraid of being l. 7141
not l. for Christ is with you 5659
People l, build walls instead of bridges 7139
So l. 'twas that God himself 7142
sought him then atop a l. hill 4921
strange to be known universally, yet be so l. 7130
thy breast will ne'er be l. 4798
What loneliness more l. than distrust 7149
who has guilty secret is l. man 1702

LONESOME
Be virtuous and you will be l. sometimes 11681

LONG
always l. for peace 8564
As l. as ever you can 10126
day seems l. in coming 235
drive won't seem so l. 7085
for nothing but spirit of the Holy Jesus 6385
hour of pain as l. as day of pleasure 149
How hard the battle goes, the day how l. 6256
How l. God waits for us to learn the lesson 7056
I have lived, sir, a l. time 4942
If life be l. I will be glad 6923
In politics week very l. time 5180
life of humanity is so l. 5944
Life one l. process of getting tired 6974
little speck of life however l, but a minute 7052
Many Christians l. for the Rapture 9910
Millions l. for immortality 6100
miracles like many still l. for 3782
must look a l. time before we can see 11967
must wait for God l. 5460

No camel route is l. with good company 4256
On l. journey, even straw is heavy 8550
proverb a short sentence based on l. experience 9376
Real takes a l. time 5886
Recipe for a l. life 7020
Reckon not upon a l. life 7021
Safe though the night be l. 4490
short life with wisdom better than l. life without it 11897
takes a l. time to grow an old friend 4193
That I may l. obey 6923
Time too l. for those who grieve 11333
To a friend's house road never l. 4287
to be filled with longing 9097
To live l, necessary to live slowly 7067
too l. or short a distance obscures knowledge 3559
truth works far and lives l. 11516
We all l. for heaven where God is 6569
what matters is not how l, but how good 6935
would like to live l. life 4975

LONG-DISTANCE
Raising children not unlike l. race 3884

LONGER
day of sorrow l. than month of joy 10580
envy last l. than happiness of those we envy 3222
I live, more convincing proof 4942
I live, more mind dwells on beauty of world 11301
impossible takes a little l. 12019
Some people stay l. in hour than others in week 9492
the l. the shore line of wonder 6702
Tomb, thou shalt not hold him l. 2985

LONGEST
day will have an end 10629
Tomorrow must be l. day of week 9302
word is eternity 11993

LONGEVITY
has its place 4975

LONG-FACED
no understanding of a l. Christian 6532

LONGING
begin by l. for God 4802
best cure for l. heart 2558
can bring back no past by l. 8368
for God presupposes his existence 4606
heart has moments of l. 470
if l. heart finds living water, will be alone 10536

long to be filled with l. 9097
orgasm has replaced cross as focus of l. 10233
Philosophy a l. after heavenly wisdom 8593
This l. heart of mine 7454

LONGINGS
Jesus wants us to see their l. 3316
leave your l. at the cross 10048

LONG-LIVED
Slanders not l. 10448

LONGS
One who l. for death miserable 2357
soul l. to return to its source 4744
stands upon the shore, l. to cross over 7916

LONG-SUFFERING
develop faith by teaching l. 3744
earth is God's l. 5650
hope makes soul exercise l. 5912
is love enduring 7202
Love is l. 7246

LONG-TERM
Kids l. investment 1121

LONGUS
tonus is mono, tempus is l. 9140

LOOK
at it as God looks at it 2742
at Jesus to correct blurry vision 4489
at life as God sees it 4732
at what you have left 825
back on my darkest periods 10853
back over way we have come 5392
beyond the action 572
bitter to l. into happiness through another's eyes 3220
can l. backward in time until past vanishes 11350
can sit and l. at work for hours 12009
Christ's l. that penetrates 1536
crooked paths l. straighter at end 2374
Do not l. forward to changes in fear 5907
Do not l. upon the vessel, but upon what it holds 6297
Don't l. back on happiness 5507
don't l. down upon wealthy 3228
easier to l. wise than talk wisely 1856
Eyes that l. are common 8493
fear, greed, lust, ambition l. ahead 8376
feel comfortable, take another l. 2013
for good, not evil 5077
for strength in people, not weakness 5077
for the Lord's choicest wines 300
for what is good, strong 3940
forward and not back 8379

forward to death with intense curiosity 2306

from heaven's point of view 10707

happiness, way we l. at the world 5538

how horrible sins l. committed by someone else 10343

I l. down, I feel giddy 7090

I never really l. for anything 5416

I would l. up 1018

If you no longer l. ahead 8122

ill-taught if l. for results only in earthlies 9014

in, see Christ's chosen saint 1299

insist all l, talk, act alike 6824

into future until collapse from exhaustion 11350

into people as well as at them 2811

learn to l. on bright circumstances 9092

Men full of the Spirit l. right into heaven 5651

Men l. for better methods 7501

Men l. for God, fancy him concealed 8019

Most of us do not like to l. inside ourselves 10012

must l. a long time before we can see 11967

need l. to no other 7548

Never l. at what you lost 825

no time to wonder how we l. 6056

not a custom to keep money to l. at 7803

not mournfully into past 8378

only time to l. down on neighbor is when bending over to help 8064

out and not in 8379

Prayer getting a higher l. 8917

real things l. simple, but they're not 9402

see faults who l. for nothing else 3954

seek solitude, l. within 4924

serious l. may be divine peace and joy 431

should we not l. forward to the arrival 2315

so long and regretfully upon closed door 8229

so long at closed door do not see one opened 5573

so long will I wait or l. for mercy 2590

some l. at the show to see how and why 7018

Some think have to l. like hedgehog to be pious 6822

something new every day if you l. 3509

stop lamenting and l. up 12063

tend to l. at fellow human beings as enemies 10531

the way you l. at problems 507

to changes with full hope 5907

to ensure it is revival 9745

tomorrow square in the eye 9999

up, God will beat the time for us 9684

up, not down 8379

upon a little child 1117

upon life as gift from God 2307

upon world as my parish 3312

want to do what is necessary to l. respectable 6810

we l. upon enemy of our souls as conquered 3163

we ourselves do not l. up toward heaven 7567

What does love l. like 7335

What may l. like excess of self-love 6229

Whenever I l. inside myself, I am afraid 9957

wish to be disappointed, l. to others 6408

wish to be downhearted, l. to yourself 6408

wish to be encouraged, l. upon Jesus Christ 6408

with hope toward tomorrow 3502

yet if I l. up into the heavens 8445

LOOKED

elite would have l. to see if anyone watching 6147

have l. everywhere, find nothing lowly in universe 11651

I've l. over 4975

successful would have l. at calendars 6147

LOOKING

as long as you're l. down, can't see above 9188

at neighbor's faults gives incorrect conception 8059

at wound of sin will never save anyone 9804

Cheerfulness, habit of l. at good side 1095

church l. for better methods 1436

Conscience warns us someone may be l. 1671

continual l. forward to eternal world 5629

death, kind of l. forward to it 2312

do not weaken yourself by l. forward 9650

downward makes one dizzy 11727

early Christians l. for cleavage in sky called Glory 9913

early Christians not l. for cleft in ground 9913

for Jesus in history futile 5718

for the key 6976

get into habit of l. for best 10780

God is l. for people who long for communication with him 8972

God is l. for worshipers 12098

God l. for better men 1436

happiness never found till we stop l. for it 5550

harder to see today when l. at tomorrow 11371

Honesty l. painful truths in the face 5876

in the wrong place 7105

like owl when acted like ass 6162

Love, l. together in the same direction 7215

Many who have gold in house, l. for copper outside 5840

no danger of eyestrain from l. on bright side 8240

no l. back to what might have been 4688

proud man always l. down on things, people 9188

Salvation will depend on never l. back 9828

Temptation is devil l. through keyhole 11088

To repent is to alter way of l. at life 9605

up chanting, sky is falling 4226

Whenever friends compliment about l. young 8185

You are what you are when no one is l. 1068

LOOKING GLASS

world is a l. 436

LOOKS

age l. back 12200

And l. to that alone 3717

different disposition l. through same eyes 8583

envy l. through a microscope 7259

for advantage out of friendship 4245

for fault within himself 9680

God l. at heart before brains 7378

God l. at intention of heart 6334

God l. for better men 7501

God l. totally indifferent 8394

God l. with favor at pure hands 6300

Gratitude l. to the past 8376

grouch l. weaned on pickle 1555

Hope l. for the good in people 5928

landscape belongs to man who l. at it 8038

lives in sin and l. for happiness 10313

Love l. through a telescope 7259

love l. to the present 8376

miserable when old age l. back with horror 8182

No one really knows what he l. like 7444

pessimist l. both ways crossing one-way street 8585

To Christ everything l. forward, backward 5710

Vision l. inward, becomes duty 11738

Vision l. outward, becomes aspiration 11738

Vision l. upward, becomes faith 11738

Youth l. forward 12200

LOOM
Not until each l. is silent 10606

LOOPHOLES
'Tis pleasant, through l. of retreat 10529

LOOSE
Life has a way of prying l. our grasp 11656
like some monster l. in your beautiful world 7473
statement let l. cannot be caught 5117
tongue let l. difficult to chain 11415
tongues stretch truth 9488
wall with l. bricks not good 4020

LOOSELY
Learn to hold l. all not eternal 11659
What we l. call happiness more a disposition 5571

LOOSEN
up, smile 5504

LORD
A copy of thine 5620
accepting Christ as L. will bring heaven down to yourself 5681
added electricity to toddler 1127
All our L. succeeded in doing 1381
always voting for man 1145
And them all the L. transformed to devils 2639
are you there in my darkness 2600
arouse us by his teaching 6477
asks us to yield to him 2490
At his ascension, L. entered heaven 459
Be L. of naked faces 6296
calls to himself 1308
calls to no special work 1308
cannot endure any who love him be worried 3986
cares for the love with which works are done 7288
Christ L. of all or not L. at all 6437
Christ, L. of heaven and earth 232
concerned for people 6519
cross, our personal touch-point with the L. 10930
deep empathy with people 6519
did not ask us to give up things 9974
does not care so much for importance of our works 7288
does not L. hear nations blame him 4894
does not let believer have pleasures outside of himself 8608
does not tell us we are w. 8106
does not truly become l. or master 11674
Faith mastering difficulty in strength of L. 3678

finally healed me of need to be healed 5610
frustrates our plans 351
gives blessing to empty vessel 831
gives his people perpetual joy 6529
godliness genuine essence of the L. 5771
grant that I may desire more 61
grant that my last hour be my best 2332
happy to go with shepherds to see L. in manger 8061
has little good to say of unilluminated mind 7776
his concern always to uplift 6519
Hope in the L, but exert yourself 5914
I crawled across the barrenness to you 4653
I'm at the end of my resources 897
if hangups called sin by L. 10321
If I only had three years to serve the L. 6687
If the L. should ask me to choose 814
In form of servant is the L. 6129
is always going to be on time 4500
isn't running a bakery 6755
jealous over saint abandoned to him 8608
keeps door open for humanity 459
kindle us by his example 6477
knows no limitations 11606
leave all for L. to order 9930
leaves his prayers unanswered 9029
lets some people get into trouble 11441
lets us see the wreck of hopes 351
life and death one in the L. 3649
lived to give normal standard for life 568
look out for me when I die 2333
Love blind to every interest but its L. 6457
Love for L. not ethereal, dreamlike thing 7221
made Adam from dust 1127
may not come when you want him 4500
Moses only saw brightness of L. 4874
need L. for creation of a home 5819
needs neither books or teachers 5426
never asks us to decide for him 2490
never coerces 8106
never do, do with the L. but be, be 6313
never enforces "thou shalts" 8106
never outstripped bounty of L. 3664
never sought in vain that sought L. aright 7537

no independence in our L. 6414
Now it is the L. 6465
O L, let me not live to be useless 7008
O L. my heart is sick 973
of himself, heritage of woe 9935
of himself, though not of lands 9959
of the Dance, said he 9690
of this world also L. of every other 6092
once blessing, now it is the L. 827
Only he who can say, L. is strength 3985
prayed for L. to heal me 5610
presence of L. is revealing 9741
promised cross, scars 2102
promises us himself 10758
quiet waiting before the L. 8957
redeem us by his death 6477
renew us by his resurrection 6477
revels in mind renewed, enlightened by grace 7776
seldom know why L. chooses whom 5894
shatters our purposes 351
showing love, purity, holiness through you 9847
speak to me that I may speak 8866
spirit in man is candle of the L. 7430
Surrender not only what the L. does to you 10974
teach us to laugh again 6743
The L. is on thy side 1502
The L. my pasture shall prepare 9350
The L. my Savior liveth 232
the L. of the work 115
The L. will happiness on contrite hearts bestow 5557
The L. won't say 1391
times when L. holding me closest 10853
took God years to teach me to say "L. anything" 4892
understood human predicament 6519
wait upon L, renew strength 10764
wants all of my life 9561
was not a martyr 9437
was stretched on hard, painful tree 10836
we tangle up the plans the L. hath wrought 6117
weeping in world as though our L. were dead 2611
what a change within us one short hour 8867
What reward shall I give the L. 7568
When L. leads someone to great faith 9029
When you work for the L. 10217
whispers, not your work but you 351
will take care of your death 2369

Worry impossible for the L. to experience 12127

LORD CHRIST
May the L. enter in 9794
through broken heart may L. enter 891

LORD JESUS
for L. only isolation on the cross 6383
for the L. no fellowship in suffering 6383
forsaken by the Father 6383
if we love L. we shall love Bible 636
make my heart sit down 419
only wooden insensitivity of disciples 6383
you died to help me die 2331

LORD JESUS CHRIST
make time to realize center of power is L. 11349
what a wonderful being the L. is 5782

LORD'S
Be simple, take our L. hand 5374
blood from L. beloved wounds flow 2142
gathered myrrh from L. persecutions 10913
goodness surrounds us at every moment 4646
loving any table better than L. Table 6925
owe more to the fire than anything else in L. workshop 10855
sovereign right to demote, promote 5894
Thirty years of L. life hidden 8112
your L. limitless love 378

LORDS
Princes and l. but breath of kings 5885

LORD'S DAY
firm foundation to build six-story week 10958

LORD'S PRAYER
a revolutionary petition 8828
cannot say L. if 8818
committed to memory quickly 7153
compendium of heavenly doctrine 7156
conciseness without obscurity 7154
deep mysteries contained in L. 7156
every petition and prayer included 7156
first petition is for daily bread 7152
fixing attention upon a few great points 7154
for importance of its petition 7154
for sufficiency 7154
for weight of its petition 7154

has condition attached 4096
is without equal or rival 7154
many and great mysteries 7156
most fearful prayer in the world 8828
mother taught me to repeat L. 8347
mysteries expressed in a few words 7156
no such thing as getting through it 8828
nothing left out 7156
rich in spiritual power 7156
slowly learnt by heart 7153
succession of solemn thought 7154
suitableness to every condition 7154
used to think L. a short prayer 8828
we plead in the L. "Thy will be done" 8791

LORDSHIP
only thinkable relationship is full L. of God 4529

LOSE
begin to l. our humanity 7481
best gain is to l. 4339
Better l. anchor than whole ship 9555
Beware l. substance by grasping at shadow 11499
Boredom, when we l. contact with universe 866
But we l. not wholly 2287
can l. friend in hour 4305
can never l. freedom 4112
certain must l. life 954
consciousness of own identity 9840
Don't l. heart in process 2849
easily get entangled and l. our soul 10514
focusing on evil you can l. your bearings 5037
For everything you gain, l. something else 8574
for sake of living to l. what makes life worth living 6883
freedom when we l. God 4153
gamblers l. money 7826
God knows who shall l. or win 4887
God makes it impossible to l. our way 5397
Grasp all, l. all 5314
great man does not l. child's heart 5294
Having nothing, nothing can he l. 8627
if course wrong, avoid though l. life as consequence 6291
if l. money, can still offer thanks 11151
if neglect prayer should l. fire of faith 8945
if we flinch or rebel 214
if you l, you l. nothing 3724

imitate winners when you l. 549
In time must fade and beauty l. 8172
life, if I do l. thee 7019
man imagines he will l. if he gives 1537
may be necessary to l. everything 4340
memory of past trials 7964
must l. fly to catch trout 4343
must not l. faith in humanity 5988
must suffer if I l. it 11303
nation that thinks more of ease will l. freedom, ease, and comfort too 7984
nightmare of separate individuality 2822
no fool to gain what he cannot l. 1195
Old men l. lives by ripeness 12197
our natural identity 9840
People l. weight by keeping mouths shut 9972
Resolved, never to l. one moment 569
Some no matter how old never l. beauty 8169
surest way to l. is to protect 4733
Talent, use it or l. it 10995
thou findest, yet didst never l. 4954
To l. is to learn 2515
Tomorrow l. opportunity to accept Christ 11404
try to polish reputation, l. it 9629
wealthy who can l. all he has 8637
wealthy who can l. without hurt or pain 8637
What you don't get, you can't l. 8639
When l. individual independence 10526
Young men l. lives by violence 12197

LOSER
In war l. is mankind 11752

LOSERS
If another war, no victors only l. 11749

LOSERS'
Jesus prophet of the l. camp 6447

LOSES
candle l. nothing by lighting another 10113
Christ l. us until we find him 10839
discontent that doesn't work l. what it has 2876
faith l. all 3729
Faith not a thing one l. 3688
friend l. more 3729
He l. nothing who l. not God 4475
Man frightened that he l. himself by giving himself 9937
money l. much 3729

one who can serve best seldom l. 10170

take notice how he acts when l. money 7802

thanks who promises, delays 2535

LOSING

finding self comes through l. self 2519

in spite of danger of l. touch 6199

Instead of l, the gentle gain 4402

leisure, may be l. soul 6833

right fear is fear of l. God 3995

sorrow in l. riches 11865

wealth makes people worry about l. it 11859

LOSS

as well as gain in growth 5366

Christ pleasure without l. 6391

Death not greatest l. in life 2254

existence entwined with l. 3479

Faith takes sting from every l. 3661

fear of God, insurance against l. 3993

find no l. great 1776

Great wealth implies great l. 11819

greatest l. what dies inside while we live 2254

life may bring l. 4803

no worldly gain without l. 1776

no worldly l. without gain 1776

of intellectual morale in church 7768

of wealth is l. of dirt 11857

one overwhelming, irrecoverable l. 2381

pull left brings but l. 1151

resist l, postpone blessings 968

Set allowance against l. 1776

submission will mean l. of all we value 11768

When seeming gain but turns to l. 4338

LOSSES

After l. men grow humbler, wiser 5990

Freedom will ultimately restore l. 11768

Remember to forget l. 9270

will seem like gains 5776

LOST

All my requests l. in one 8088

all the rest 11053

art of century is meditation 7721

ass went seeking for horns, l. ears 2872

better to have l. some battles 10777

Better to have loved and l. 7161

better to have taken some risks and l. 10777

Character l. when ideal sacrificed 999

Charity is never l. 1075

Christ gave me back myself that I had l. 6361

Christ has never l. his case 6415

Christ has not l. a battle yet 6367

concept of ineffable worship has been l. 12120

Courage l, much l. 9263

day is l. on which one has not laughed 6744

discontinued labor, habit l. 3109

Divinity, so vast all thoughts l. in immensity 4745

do not understand love until it is l. 11620

faith, what has he left 3728

Fortune l, nothing l. 9263

God gave me back myself that I had l. 4528

good name got by many actions, l. by one 9611

good not l. though you forget 5083

greatest of fathers 483

has l. through rigidity 6827

have l. all and found myself 9559

have l. the immortal part of myself 9622

held things in hand, l. them all 8628

Honor l, more l. 9263

I count that part of life l. 6909

If man l. his liberty 4133

If soul be l, man is l. 10655

In quarreling truth always l. 9358

Life is not l. by dying 6972

Life is l. minute by minute 6972

Love is never l. 7241

man who has l. contact with God 7523

man would have l. likeness to God 4149

may be sorry you won or l. 6674

must not be so l. in work of earth 6108

Never look at what you l. 825

no use going back for l. opportunity 8226

Not one thing done for God has been l. 10176

Not till we have l. world do we find ourselves 10549

O I have l. my reputation 9622

Remorse the echo of l. virtue 9571

Satan whispers, "All is l." 2800

sixty diamond minutes 11306

so obsessed with facts l. touch with truth 7990

social differences have l. power to divide 6286

some talk about finding God—as if he could get l. 7518

Soul l, all l. 9263

souls have l. their courage 9059

talent l. for want of courage 1916

That all was l. 10314

That which one sacrifices never l. 9764

think you have humility, you have l. it 6006

time never found again 11305

time passed in the difficult never l. 2712

Transported with the view, I'm l. 4819

two golden hours 11306

value seldom known until l. 4292

way to love is to realize it might be l. 7311

wealth, l. trouble 1776

What I kept, I l. 4383

When a man has l. his shirt 6290

When all else is l. 4334

When character is l, all is l. 1066

When faith is l. 7442

When health is l, something is l. 1066

When wealth is l, nothing is l. 1066

When you feel all is l. 3633

who have learned l. art of worship 12099

will know when l. a jewel 6004

worst bankrupt is l. enthusiasm 3183

yesterday, somewhere between sunrise, sunset 11306

LOT

cannot make straight lines out of crooked l. 4885

I dare not choose my l. 5412

if different l. 8219

LOT'S WIFE

A sight more strange 776

Ah foolish woman 776

LOTUS

Life a dewdrop on l. leaf 6959

LOUD

Being in right does not depend on l. voice 11905

can choose to be bag of marbles, l. 9524

Helpless, naked, piping l. 808

Laugh out l. 6724

o'er my head, though awful thunders roll 4827

think l. outcries or prayers are of no avail 8787

voice of sin is l. 4100

what you are thunders so l. 1061

You need not cry very l. 4878

LOUDER

Actions don't always speak l. than words 1833

he talked of his honor 5899

less sound man's argument, l. he talks 448

stillness of nature l. than choir of voices 8041

voice of forgiveness l. 4100

LOUDEST

in protest no such person as Jesus 6417

pride of dying rich raises l. laugh in hell 9246

worst screeches l. 1561

LOUDLY

praise l, blame softly 8729

LOVABLE

If you would be loved, love and
be l. 7192

LOVE

a ceaseless effort to know, feel
7211

a complex emotion 7233

A man can counterfeit l. 5989

a man even in his sin 10331

a mirror to reflect your l. to all I
meet 9079

a mixture of honey, bitterness
7228

a positive emotion 7233

A rose can say I l. you 1102

a symbol of eternity 7229

able to l. himself, able to l. others
9985

able to say how much you l. is to
l. little 7323

able to undertake all things 7220

absurd a man can't l. one woman
all the time 7621

accepts people as they are 7207

act as if you l. your neighbor 8055

acting 3835

acts of kindness and l. 626

Agape l. concern without desire to
control 7158

Agape l. profound concern for
another 7158

Alas, oh, l. is dead 7159

all that life is l. 5633

All truth to l, all wrong to hate
7986

alone his watch is keeping 1123

alphabet of l. avowals and
consents 7297

alternative to wrath of God not l.
4999

an action, an activity 7231

an attitude 7166

And full of l. divine 5620

and hatred natural exaggerators
3423

and Self cannot stand together
9936

and taste encircling l. 7970

and tenderness sealed up 4223

and wrath obverse and reverse of
same thing 4999

answering prayer for more l. 8804

Anticipation more delightful in l.
7160

as a lively flame, burning torch
7283

as Christ loves a practical thing
7324

as for l. with which works are
done 7288

As l. grows older, our hearts
mature 7236

as l. with single thread 7279

asks us to walk many miles not
demanded by legalism 7273

attempts what is above its strength
7220

attributes to the Holy Ghost
works in which l. excels 11427

awakening to l. again 5360

bade me welcome; yet my soul
drew back 5481

be swift to l. 6658

Beatitudes, yeast of l. 530

become channels of God's
universal l. 4768

becomes as coals, deep-burning,
unquenchable 7236

Begin as a mere apprentice 7352

behaving as if you l, you will
come to l. him 8055

believe in l. even when I do not
feel it 3732

bend to necessity of brethren 3839

betray Christ's spirit of l. 2988

Better to l. God and die unknown
10777

Beyond his l. and care 4763

beyond the world cannot be
separated 7319

Bind in thy l. every nation and race
11424

Blessed is l. 6161

blind to every interest but its Lord
6457

blinds us to faults 5602

blossoming when surrounded by l.
2054

both the ones who give l. and the
ones who receive 7213

boundless treasures hidden within
its depths 7211

brings to harvest loveliest flowers
of the soul 7339

build society of l. out of puppets
4133

But for those who l. 11333

by l. brought to God 3834

by l. soul unites to God 7967

by thy l. I live 4796

called to l. with special intensity
10937

Can a man l. God ignoring need
of brother 10052

can fill duty with life 7165

can hope where reason would
despair 7209

can make any place agreeable
7210

can make duty beautiful 7165

can never get enough of 7308

can never say, "I have done
enough" 7273

can see only one thing 6457

Can special l. be everywhere 4834

can take insults without ill will
7207

Can there be l. which does not
make demands 7162

can wait and worship endlessly
7353

cannot be inactive 7211

cannot be l. without hate 5357

cannot compel 4126

cannot have l. apart from faith,
hope 3837

cannot l. fellow creature till you l.
God 7351

cannot l. good if do not hate evil
5050

cannot l. his neighbor unless he
loves God 7287

cannot l. without giving 7350

cannot lie idle in soul of lover
7167

cannot put up with fear, pain
3986

cannot speak for Christianity
without l. 1185

capable of uniting living beings
7208

causes suffering 7329

Cease to resist, l. takes possession
4785

children common bond of l. 3868

children enough to discipline 8309

Christ alive as Christians l. one
another 9695

Christ commands not easy 7304

Christ conquer by l. 6389

Christ gave them l. 10731

Christ promises l. and confidence
159

Christ, creative wave of l. 6419

Christ, still people who l. or hate
him 6362

Christian feels l. for one he has
never seen 1265

Christian l. an affair of the will
4777

Christian l. links l. of God and
neighbor 7164

Christian l. not a vague feeling of
affection 7304

Christian l. [agape] an attitude
7166

Christian l. [agape] not feeling
7166

Christian supposed to l. his
neighbor 7654

Christian understands l. in terms
of God 4494

Christmas when you l. 1366

church community of l. 1414

church force for l. in world of
hatred 1433

comes a time when l. can only
weep 4781

comforteth like sunshine after rain
7212

commandments need strength of l.
1525

compared to building tall
sandcastle 7233

complicates every life 4823

complicates life of God 4823

Consecration narrow, lonely way
to l. 1722

Convey thy l. to thy friends 4222

counts royalty but drudgery if
cannot reign for Christ 6457

courage to l, courage to suffer
1939

creed inspired by Christian l. 2030
Criticism kills l. 5135
cross reveals difference between power, l. 2156
cross, l. meeting hate with l. 2146
cultivates 7216
cures people 7213
cursed l. of gold 11843
decision to make your problem my problem 7240
delicacy unknown in material substances 4789
delights in servitude as much as in honor 6457
demands toughness in crisis 2045
demonstrate God's l, listen to people 7115
Description would but make it less 7245
desire of l, joy 9274
destroying all fear of an end 7229
destroying memory of a beginning 7229
devil wanted to neutralize gospel of l. 2704
Dies safely through thy l. 2228
difference between Christian l. and values of world evident 6278
difference between execution and martyrdom 7263
Discipline and l. not antithetical 8292
Discipline and one function of the other 8292
Divine l. can admit no rival 4929
do injustice because do not l. him 6609
do justice, will come to l. him 6609
do little works with great l. 5068
do not l. aright 10084
do not rightly l. God when l. for advantage 4801
do not understand l. until it is lost 11620
Do what you l. 6902
does not analyze its object 7214
does not consist in gazing at each other 7215
does not dominate 7216
does not measure by merchant's scales 4789
doesn't just sit there, like a stone 7217
doesn't start to multiply until you give it away 7238
Dost thou l. life 6886
draws me into God 7237
drives us on 7273
droops 7860
easier to l. humanity as a whole 5972
eclipsed as turns into clipboard with checklist 6823
either a crown of l. or a thorny crown 7073
either consumes or purifies 7248
either l. or hate 8075

enduring realities are l. and service 10829
enough to be useful, helpful 1809
ere foot of L. will cross threshold 4775
Erotic and philia l. are emotional 7166
essential to evangelism 3299
eternally creative and recreative l. 10562
ever gives, forgives, outlives 7218
ever stands with open hands 7218
every day 7219
Every l. has its own force 7167
Every meal shared in l. a feast 5825
everybody sincerely 6913
everything in life, even to be sad 10595
extreme l, hatred breeds satiety 3554
eyes of l. see not one but two persons 7300
facet of essential nature of God 4760
Faith and l. spasmodic in best minds 3654
faith is l. on the battlefield 7202
Faith like l. cannot be forced 3686
faith, hope, l, three torches that blend 2586
falls in l. with himself will have no rivals 7175
fear leads l. at first 3986
fear of God to be united with l. of God 9736
fear without l. makes men desperate 9736
feelings come and go, God's l. does not 4777
feels no burden 7220
fellowmen sincerely 559
finds admission where proud science fails 12130
first duty of l. is to listen 7301
For I have none to give 4796
for Lord intensest, most vital l. 7221
for Lord not ethereal dreamlike thing 7221
for neighbor means l. for any man in need 7201
for sake of being loved is human 7325
for sake of loving is angelic 7325
forces its way upwards 7283
forgets suffering in l. 10877
Forgetting oneself first condition of l. 7169
Forgetting oneself not refinement of l. 7169
Free will makes l. possible 4120
friend's l. brings joy to heart 4382
from your l. to understanding 7970
Frontline l. 3325
fulfillment comes as by-product of l. for God 4735
gentleness is l. in society 7202

Give a little l. to a child 8297
give it away, tomorrow have more than ever 7252
Give me such l. for God and men 7170
Give us a heart of l. 9058
given up right for them to return our l. 9963
gives courage to the cowardly 7260
gives eloquence to the mute 7260
gives itself, is not bought 7222
Giving is thermometer of l. 4358
God alone cause, measure of all l. 11663
God always receptive to l. 4590
God and l. synonymous 4755
God desires but l. 7450
God does not l. one day, hate another 4626
God doesn't merely have or give l. 7244
God give me l, care, strength to help 910
God gives something which takes place of all, l. 4790
God is eternal, his l. can have no end 4750
God is holy, his l. is spotless purity 4750
God is infinite, his l. has no limit 4750
God is l, he gives himself 7244
God is perfect l. 9799
God is self-existent, his l. had no beginning 4750
God loves, wanted object to l. 4535
God loving all, should l. each different 6169
God must l. the common man 4545
God needs and wants our l. 4527
God not incomprehensible to our l. 4679
God offers to help us build cathedral of l. 7684
God offers tough l. 7686
God proved his l. on the cross 7173
God reached by way of l. 4802
God saying to world "I l. you" 7173
God seeks comrades, claims l. 4912
God turns from wrath, never from l. 4757
God wants us in l. with God of virtue 11688
God wants us out of l. of virtue 11688
God! Thou are l. 4758
God's action masterpiece of l. 4747
God's country begins where men l. to serve 4913
God's creation, overflowing of l. 1978
God's fastest road to l. 225

is fervent beyond measure 7283
is free 3838
is friendship set to music 7234
is guarded in all the senses 7246
is humble 7246
is immortal 6097
is joyful 7246
is just being there 3835
is like a magnet 7237
is like five loaves, two fishes 7238
is long-suffering 7246
is loveliest when embalm'd in tears 7309
is mean, contemptible in its own sight 7246
is medicine for sickness of world 7250
is nails 2135
is never lost 7241
is never self-seeking 7246
is no respecter of persons 7274
is not a state 7630
is not fickle 7246
is not getting, but giving 7243
is not intent on vanities 7246
is not sentimental 7246
is not the work of the Holy Spirit 7244
is obedient to superiors 7246
is offering one's most honest self 7337
is patient 7246
is pleasant 7246
is prudent 7246
is pure 7246
is quiet 7246
is restless 7273
is sacred 11684
is sober 7246
is something so divine 7245
is spiritual fire 7224
is steadfast 7246
is steady wish for loved person's good 7242
is strong 7246
is submissive 7246
is superior to hate 6326
is swift 7246
is tender 7246
is the fairest bloom in God's garden 7247
is the fire of life 7248
is the gift of oneself 7225
is the Holy Spirit working in us 7244
is the law of our condition 6614
is to admire with the heart 7326
is to give one's time 7327
is true freedom 7254
is trusting in God even when not enjoying his sweetness 7246
is upright 7246
is vigorous 7246
is watchful 7246
is what we give 7290
isn't l. until give it away 7258
isn't like a reservoir 7257
It were too strange I should doubt thy l. 4758

its end sweetens all its means 6457
its insatiable desire 7211
its object lightens its toil 6457
its object removes its weariness 6457
jealousy extinguishes l. as ashes smother flame 6347
Jesus Christ founded his empire upon l. 6351
Jesus gives truth carried on wings of l. 6176
Jesus has many who l. his heavenly kingdom 9268
Jesus redefines meaning of l. 7201
Jesus teaches universal l. 913
joy bound up with l. and goodness 6568
Joy is l. exalted 7202
joy, peace multiply when divide with others 4360
judgment of God evidence of l. of God 4721
Justice is l. working out problems 6612
kept Jesus from calling angels to his rescue 6418
Kindness in giving creates l. 6649
Kindness l. in work clothes 6652
know God that thou mayst l. him 10010
know nothing of Calvary l. 7187
Lash it upon the rich, who often need it most 7348
Lash l. upon equals, difficult 7348
Lash l. upon the poor, easy 7348
learn to l. God and man by loving 7352
Let l. be purified, rest will follow 7203
Let religion be more a l. affair 9542
let us l. our occupations 3112
lets us be our real selves 7254
lets us cast off false exteriors 7254
life is given us so we may grow in l. 6907
Life minus l. equals zero 7206
Life the flower of which l. is the honey 7205
Life without thankfulness devoid of l. 11154
light and truth and l. of heaven 10756
lightness of life from l. of God 5229
like a friendship caught on fire 7236
like a lovely rose; the world's delight 7179
like a natural spring 7257
like a passionate l. for a ghost 7521
like a rose, joy of all the earth 7179
likeness of divine l. 10331
little words of l. 2503
live with acceptance, learn to find l. 1114

lives shaped by those who l. us 6236
living Jesus proof of God's l. 6473
long-suffering is l. enduring 7202
longer and farther it flows 7257
looking together in the same direction 7215
looks through a telescope 7259
looks to the present 8376
Lord cannot endure any who l. him be worried 3986
Lord showing his l. through you 9847
Lord, turn routines of work into celebrations of l. 12015
makes a subtle man out of a crude one 7260
makes all hard hearts gentle 7261
makes all things easy 7345
makes everything lovely 7262
makes the idle quick and sharp 7260
makes those young whom age doth chill 7264
man free to l. God 566
man free to l. neighbor 566
man who does not l. God, in l. with himself 4803
Man's l. is of man's life a thing apart 7278
Marriage supported by strengths of l. 7635
Mature l. says "I need you because l. you" 7194
meanest hut with l. palace for the soul 5816
means to l. that which is unlovable 11691
measure by which to be judged right or wrong is l. 7307
measure by which to be judged success or failure is l. 7307
Measure not God's l. by your feeling 4772
meekness is l. in school 7202
men animated by l. of Christ feel united 3081
Men learn to pray as they learn to l. 8914
mind can remember, understand, l. its maker 7771
Money buys everything except l. 7806
money, nobody who did not l. it 5320
more 5604
more I demand l. of others, less I deserve that l. 9497
more l. you give away, the more comes back 7232
most free when offered 7239
Mother is l. 7853
mother's secret l. outlives them all 7860
multiplies by division 7252
Music is l. itself 7905
must be learned again and again 7265
must draw the soul on 7167

must help child become fully
  independent 7858
must help child grow away from
  mother 7858
must l. friends for their sake 4251
must renounce other loves for l. of
  God 7334
nature because a retreat from man
  8012
needed in homes, hospitals, hearts
  7251
needed in the ghettos and
  governments 7251
needed in the marketplace and
  mansions 7251
needs not to know 5431
neglected will soon wither and die
  7230
never an abundance 7251
never knew how to worship until
  knew how to l. 7185
never know l. of parent until
  become parents 3902
Never l. unless you can bear with
  faults 3948
New continents of l. 2319
new moralists think l. defined by
  human beings 7837
No burden heavy carried with l.
  934
no delight of l. where there is but
  one 11622
No one can l. neighbor on empty
  stomach 7152
No one can say prayers poor
  when using language of l. 8875
No one had more sensitive l. than
  Jesus 7280
no power like l. 3836
no significance to l. with no
  alternative 1141
no true l. without suffering 6506
no utterance for l. or death 10274
Nobody will know "God is l."
  unless you act it 7281
None can live in l. without
  suffering 7246
None feels true l. of God till 4773
Nor can spirits be divided that l.
  in same divine principle 7319
Normal day, let me l. you 2197
not a feeling 7231
not affectionate feeling 7242
not attribute of God, l. is God
  4755
not because of intense l. for the
  Lord 9910
not dependent on ability,
  popularity 7235
not l. that produces jealousy 7200
not law, is greatest cleanser 7275
not possible to know God that we
  may l. him 4802
not seek to be loved as to l. 9086
not to pretend we l. everything
  5890
Nothing fuller or better in heaven
  than l. 7283

nothing fuller or better on earth
  than l. 7283
nothing is higher than l. 7283
nothing is stronger than l. 7283
Nothing is sweeter than l. 7283
nothing is wider than love 7283
nothing makes us l. a man so
  much as praying for him 8998
nothing more pleasant than l.
  7283
nothing so loyal as l. 7315
Nothing you can do to make God
  l. you more 4786
Nurture l. with a smile and prayer
  7289
O for grace to l. thee more 9077
obedience to law coupled with l.
  and honesty 6811
of God exacting as l. between
  sexes 4792
of God makes better men 7303
of God persistent as artist's l. for
  work 4792
of God provident as father's l.
  4792
of God, how deep and great 4776
of God, no bounds 4760
Of kindness and l. 6664
of liberty is l. of others 8716
of life increased with years 8174
of neighbor door out of dungeon
  of self 8063
of power is l. of ourselves 8716
of the cross must swallow up grief
  5356
Of their great voices uttering
  endless l. 4708
of wealth makes bitter men 7303
often knows no limits 7283
often rejoices 7283
Old age can l. God better 7286
old age, l. you as dawning of
  eternal day 8149
on that wood in l, anguish placed
  his Son 2173
one does not l. place less for
  having suffered in it 5843
one gift open to every member of
  the church 7235
one great fellowship of l. 911
one ingredient of which world
  never tires 7251
One kind act will teach more l. of
  God 6661
one kind of l, a thousand
  imitations 7317
one long sweet dream 7631
one thing we never give enough is
  l. 7308
one's most honest self-disclosure
  7337
only in l. unequal made equal
  3238
only service money cannot buy
  7253
only service power cannot
  command 7253
ought to l. our Maker for his own
  sake 4807

Our l. for God tested 4800
Over all shall l. endure 4936
overlooks defects 7266
pardon to degree we l. 4106
passes securely through all 7283
pays to be an absolute spendthrift
  7252
peace comes from the l. of God
  8469
peace expresses itself in l. for men
  8469
peace is l. in repose 7202
Pentecost, intensity of l. 5806
people gathered to Christ by l.
  6396
people have not yet understood
  command 7349
people mistake sex for l. 8510
people, not things 7267
perfected in fire of God 3182
Plant l. and watch what happens
  7289
Plant l. heart-deep in a person's life
  7289
plays the field 7274
pleads no excuse of impossibility
  7220
possible to forget to l. Christ 117
Power can do everything but
  control l. 8709
power of l. makes them hurt
  10897
power of l. will lead to master of
  the art 7352
power which can resist fear is l.
  3992
pressing round us like air 4785
price is always l. 9759
Pride eats the possibility of l. 9229
problem regarding content of l.
  7837
produces flowering of personality
  7268
property of friendship 4227
pulse with vital red of l. 2979
pure l. the panacea for ills of
  world 7203
puts the fun in together 7269
puts the hope in tomorrow 7269
puts the joy in a heart 7269
puts the sad in apart 7269
Quotations tell of l. 9385
Rare as is true l. 4263
rather than hate 1138
Rather than l, give me truth
  11526
Reach God in l. 11607
real l. want other person's good
  7197
recognize My l. coming to you
  5271
religious awakening that does not
  awaken sleeper to l. 9737
remains to me, I can pray 8135
represents Calvary 7297
required that we l. God 8821
required that we l. the difficult
  2712

requires intense l. on mother's side 7858

resistless in thy might 7285

Respect is l. in plain clothes 9645

respond to enemies with l. 5890

respond with l. when unmistakably wronged 6278

response to temptation barometer of l. for God 11079

Revival and l. of comfortable truths bitter enemies 9744

romantic l. you want the other person 7197

rules kingdom without sword 7270

salvation depends more on God's l. of us than our l. of him 9806

Satan cannot counterfeit l. of God 5396

secure in thy l, strength 9051

seeks not limits but outlets 7271

sees things in light of his glory 6457

selfishness, preventing transformation into divine l. 10067

served by keeping commandments of God 7837

shaped and fashioned by what we l. 7330

should all like l. free from pain 6506

should beam forth on every side 7168

should bend to necessity of brethren 7168

should l. our enemies 5001

show l. in everything we say, do 4767

Simple l. can do great things 6708

Sin a crime against l. 10355

sin against neighbor through lack of l. sin against God 7164

Sin is the contempt of God's l. 10376

slays what we have been 7272

slights death 2363

So long as we l, we serve 7292

so shall I spring into your l. 7970

society not community radiant with l. of Christ 10514

Some people l. God as they l. their cow 4801

Some say jealousy is l, I deny it 6347

sometimes by reason of their defects 7332

son, plenty of discipline 8303

Song of Solomon—How to l. 11925

soul of peace is l. 8469

speaking truth in l. all-important 9158

Spirit of God imparts l. 5800

Spirit of God will enfold in l. so vast 5776

spiritual health proportional to l. for God 4793

springs of l. are in God, not in us 4784

stays with us 7291

strips 7329

stronger, deeper, clearer l. becomes 7257

substitute l. for God 4766

subtlest force in world 7255

such as world had never before seen 6419

suffering accept as inseparable from l. 7953

Suffering l, heart of church 2139

suffering must become l. 966

Suffering the true cement of l. 7293

suffers as the voice sings 7953

summit of l. on earth 10331

superior to money 7232

supernatural l. allows you to l. enemy 7340

Take away l. and earth is a tomb 7294

takes l. to discipline 8335

talk about cost when in l. an insult 2823

tears have carried me to your l. 1512

Tell me whom you l. 7296

temperance is l. in training 7202

temptation to l. money inexplicably powerful 7811

tenderest word is l. 11993

Tennis few pastimes where l. means nothing 7297

terror of God is other side of his l. 4775

than to l. one's neighbor 5972

than to l. world and be a hero 10777

That as I l. the tiny, piteous thing 7178

That I may l. what thou dost l. 5774

That my l. is weak and faint 9077

that we radiate the l. of God 7485

That which I l. in my friend 4233

that world may become one family in l. 9093

the fire is the l. of God 7553

the majesty of human suffering 10854

The one is mercy, the next is l. 4812

the perfect flower 3837

the truth 11527

thee more dearly 9043

think l. of humanity safe 7836

thinks all things lawful 7220

thinks all things possible 7220

thinks nothing of labors 7283

thinks nothing of trouble 7220

Those who tease you l. you 7322

Those who would l. little 6708

Thou of uncreated l. 5788

though alarmed is not confounded 7283

though pressed, is not straitened 7283

Though wearied is not tired 7283

Thought we l. our own the best 3900

through friendship we l. places, seasons 4269

thy God and l. him only 4798

thy l. has hung 'twixt it and me 9072

Thy l. is like a burning fire 4795

thy neighbor, even when plays trombone 11396

till life finds pull of Christ's l. 6937

times when l. to father, mother must be hatred 7280

'Tis what I feel, but can't define 7245

'Tis what I know, but can't express 7245

to admire is to l. with the mind 7326

to be a child believe in l. 1122

To fall in l. with God greatest of all romances 7542

to grow in l. is to diminish fear 3986

to have perfect l. we must have nature of God 7316

to l. that which is worth loving 9063

To live is to fight, suffer, l. 7066

to my fellowmen, a heart of l. 5626

to obtain and hold power, must l. it 8705

to return l. for hate 7838

to the heart what summer is to the farmer's year 7339

To worship rightly is to l. each other 7284

To write the l. of God above 4748

too busy for assurance of l. 129

tough l. that turns us into stronger persons 7686

transfers l. from things temporal to things eternal 9278

Transfixed with thanks, folded in l. 12125

triangle of l. between ourselves, God, other people 7198

triumphest even over gold 7285

troubles large enough to touch God's l. 4789

true disciples of Christ l. most 7318

True l. always costly 7328

Trust present to his l. 5457

truth though it do harm 11517

turn cake for l. of God 10208

two souls and one flesh 4298

Two vanities can never l. one another 9256

universalizes its concern 7274

unless able to give to people in selfless l. 7962

Unless we l. God, cannot l. neighbor 1240

until first given himself in l. 10119

Unto thy praise, all l. and melody 7928

use things and l. people 9510

value of good works based on l. of God 10115

virtue, she alone is free 11692

warmth of Christmas 1364

warrants things to take effect 7220

waves and waves of liquid l. 5797

way to l. is realize it might be lost 7311

We always l. what is good 5086

we are to l. as God does 7316

we can express part of a greater l. 10545

We don't l. qualities, we l. a person 7332

We l. someone although 7333

We l. thee well, Jesus loves thee best 2365

weighs actions in scales of his honor 6457

What does l. look like 7335

what is greater still, it pulls God into death 7237

What we l. to do we find time to do 9277

What we l. we shall grow to resemble 7336

Whatever God is, l. is 4755

Whatever l. may ask of us 7337

Whatever you l. most is your god 7338

When a man is self-seeking, he abandons l. 7246

When is the time for l. to be born 6155

When l, skill work together 12020

when l. bound to God, fear is done away 3986

When l. ends, God's begins 302

When l. is done 7306

When l. unnoticed came to earth 6458

When leave God's l, we grow dark, cold 9354

when properly nourished becomes sturdy, enduring 7230

When we l, it is Christ loving through us 1270

where I l, I live 7281

Where l. is not, can be no pleasures 7341

Where l. reigns, joy of heaven felt 7342

Where l. rules, no will to power 7343

Where marriage without l. will be l. without marriage 7668

Where no l, put l. in and you will draw out l. 7343

Where power predominates, l. is lacking 7343

Where there is faith, there is l. 4517

Where there is hatred, give l. 9086

Where there is l. there is peace 4517

which knoweth not how to seek self 7960

while it lives, it gives 7218

while l. may come suddenly 7648

who do not l. fellow beings live unfruitful lives 7321

who do not l. God, trials a nuisance 4804

who does not l. would faint, lie down 7220

Who falls for l. of God 3635

Who has ever seen l. 615

who l. God for riches or comfort 10084

who l. God, trials are l. tokens from him 4804

who lives by faith, and l. not judged on the law 6812

who never retract l. themselves better than truth 8207

whom he finds young, keeps young still 7264

Whom none can l. whom none can thank 4374

Whom you would change, you must first l. 6246

Whose l. is as great as his power 4787

wife should be deepest l. 7654

will ask more than law require 7273

will never drain it dry 7257

will soften, purify the heart 7241

wine that gladdens heart of man 7256

wipes out all sense of time 7229

wise lover values l. of the giver 7157

wish to know the character of a l. 7167

with a l. that glows 3182

With all thy faults, I l. thee still 7346

With knowledge of God comes l. 7347

With l. virtue must be decked 11713

with so much l. as God embraces the soul 7958

with thy l, inspire us 619

without calculation, l. 7348

without distinction, l. 7348

without fear makes men remiss 9736

without l. can no more render justice 6614

without procrastination, l. 7348

word l. is a semantic confession 7312

word l. is a swampy one 7312

Work without l. spells burnout 944

world of l. shut in 5817

world understands l. and sympathy 7313

world will never outgrow need for l. 7251

worth more than intelligence 1183

worth of kind deed lies in l. 2506

would change whole aspect of world 7349

would sweep away envying, strife 7349

would sweep away prisons 7349

would sweep away strongholds of the devil 7349

Yet I l. thee and adore 9077

Yet L. still takes the risk of birth 6155

you because you're mine 4764

you for what you are 4248

you for your ideals 4248

you more today than yesterday 5882

you not because you're perfect 7183

you not so much for your realities 4248

you yet more for what you are going to be 4248

your enemies, they tell faults 3164

your life, poor as it is 7001

your Lord's limitless l. 378

your neighbor, but don't pull down hedge 8060

yourself in such a way 10024

youth l. too much 12181

LOVE OF GOD

arms extended on cross 4781

bars way to hell 4781

if l. ignored, rejected, refused 4781

is redemptive power 4780

no need to plead l. shall fill heart 4785

not a senile benevolence 4792

persistent as artist's love for his work 4792

provident, venerable as father's love 4792

that made the worlds 4792

the consuming life himself 4792

the great spirit so lightly involved 4792

LOVED

behaving as if you l. someone 8055

better hated for what you are than l. for what you are not 1025

Better to have l. and lost 7161

by mother means to be alive 7853

convert l. with love like no other 1904

divine must be l. to be known 4762

divine things must be l. to be known 7180

Friendship is in loving rather than being l. 4234

God l. world, do likewise 7172

God wants to be l. 4447

God's children eternally l. 6042

great of world those who l. God more 5295

has achieved success who has l. much 10781

have not l. one another 9087

have not l. world nor the world me 12033

Human beings must be known to be l. 4762

Human things must be known to be l. 7180

I will tell you how much you have l. them 7295

If God l. you as you love him 4765

If would be l, love and be lovable 7192

knows he is l, content with piece of bread 7176

Let all be l. for Jesus' sake 6454

Let Jesus be l. for himself 6454

love is steady wish for l. person's good 7242

no surprise more magical than surprise of being l. 7314

not seek to be l. as to love 9086

prosperous man never sure l. for himself 11860

So long as l. by others, we are indispensable 7292

sovereign God wants to be l. for himself 4806

than not to have l. at all 7161

The souls we l. 2214

to be feared, fear to be l. 4000

to be trusted greater compliment than l. 1576

To love for the sake of being l. is human 7325

Too late I l. thee 4805

Why and how is God to be l. 7574

woman formed from near heart to be l. 11982

LOVE-ENERGY

first to God, then to other people 10053

LOVE-GIFT

give as l. best I have 9762

LOVELIER

Glory, l. to desire than possess 4409

Old friends, old scenes will l. be 4197

LOVELIEST

love brings to harvest l. flowers of the soul 7339

love is l. when embalm'd in tears 7309

Of all created things, l. are children 1120

LOVELINESS

God's fingers mould into l. 537

increases 534

into l, satisfaction of our true home 6110

look on l. of world 10592

to be a child believe in l. 1122

LOVELY

Let me grow l, growing old 8143

Love makes everything l. 7262

O amiable l. death 2269

O night more l. than the dawn 2554

The world is very l. 7048

LOVER

A l. flies, runs, rejoices 7283

love cannot lie idle in soul of l. 7167

No one who is l. of money is l. of man 11661

talked to God as one might talk to a l. 7526

wise l. values love of the giver 7157

wise l. values not gift of l. 7157

LOVER'S

Jealousy the injured l. hell 6342

stroke of death as l. pinch 2387

Thou l. victory 5932

LOVERS

Jesus has l. of heavenly kingdom 2828

LOVE'S

as hard as nails 2135

business not to "fall for one-and-only" 7274

business not to find friends 7274

business not to play favorites 7274

death brings l. crown 7204

fear is l. gateway 3986

In l. service only broken hearts will do 895

Life bears l. cross 7204

Prayer is l. tender dialogue 8926

prerogative, to give, and give, and give 7218

LOVES

always springtime in heart that l. God 4797

attitude of man who l. God different 5046

bad person l. things and uses people 5041

be certain that our Lord l. you 4747

cannot love his neighbor unless he l. God 7287

Christian, heart through which Christ l. 1248

despise that which God l. 5599

devil too l. man 2688

does not make difference if neighbor l. you 8057

Faith l. the one who is leading 3709

find in and with God all l. 7334

God l. each as if only one 4756

God l. life; he invented it 6896

God l. me when I sing 12008

God l. those who don't give in without a fight 2959

God l. us, not for anything we are, but for what he is 6634

God l. wanted object to love 4535

God's problem is that God l. 4823

God, who truly l. will chastise well 2847

good lives on, l. on, conquers all 11129

good person l. people, uses things 5041

Grace l. the unlovely, unlovable 5222

he who l. God has no need of admiration 10877

he who l. weeds may find weeds 5140

heart that l. is always young 7302

how little one feels poverty when one l. 7199

I know he l. me well 4761

If he so l. the little flowers 4761

Lord l. you, devotedly, individually 4747

more man l, more he suffers 10904

more one judges, less one l. 6593

Most have no real l. 6161

mother l. next generation of citizens 7844

must renounce other l. for love of God 7334

No man l. life as he who's growing old 8147

none more lonely than man who l. only himself 7147

one who l. life 4204

only one being who l. perfectly 7316

saints which God l. best 9788

So God l. me 7178

soul l. and is loved in return 7967

soul not where it lives, but where it l. 7310

spoiled child never l. mother 1103

To love as Christ l. a practical thing 7324

valuable because God l. us 4752

who l. God asks no favors of God 4803

who l. God in unassailable position 4803

who l. not to rest at home 7422

who l. something mentions it often 7177

LOVEST

Thou l, without passion 4954

LOVETH

For God, who l. all his works 5904

For the dear God who l. us 7174

He made and l. all 7174

He prayeth best who l. best 7174

LOVING

a power as well as a process 7277

anger of God 4997

appreciating what is noble, l. in another 4220

as God loves 6569

begin by l. God 4802

better the self-image, larger the capacity for l. 9997

can give without l. 7350

Children begin by l. parents 1111

confidence in God 4747

find yourself l. any pleasure better than prayers 6925

Friendship is in l. rather than being loved 4234

gift of l. thought into heart of friend 4189

God can make brokenhearted radiant, l. person 890

God has paid intolerable compliment of l. us 7186

God, l. all, should love each differently 6169

Grace, God's l. energy at work 5219

impossible to live in inmost being without l. silence 10254

In comparison with l. human being 7195

in the deepest, most tragic sense 7186

is creative 7277

is curative 7277

Kindness l. people more than they deserve 6653

learn to love God and man by l. 7352

love for sake of l. is angelic 7325

Never cease l. a person 3167

no wish to see you l. anyone 10024

Only see a little of God's l. 6111

pain l. touch of God's hand 4804

painful truth through l. words 4289

person lives in a l. world 9441

Personality dominates Bible 635

poverty, deprivation of God's l. peace 8697

prayer consists of l. 8893

results in more l. relationships 7725

Success is l. God 10807

Thinking is like l. and dying 11260

thinks of l. God, says prayers of abandonment 8840

to love that which is worth l. 9063

two reasons for l. God 7533

When feelings are l. give thanks for them 3051

When feelings l, give thanks 4013

You asked for a l. God; you have one 4792

Youth large, lusty, l. 12188

LOVINGLY

God l. drawing you from distraction 2556

home where character molding l. carried on 5850

turning disordered actions to our advantage 4644

LOW

A high way and a l. 1155

expectation of man remarkably l. 3507

God hid knot so l. we cannot reach 5384

He that is l. need fear no pride 6001

I saw a stable, l. and very bare 6133

No feelings high or l. in themselves 4016

no great thing to be humble when brought l. 6019

pitch expectations l. 9469

soul gropes the l. 10679

To God no high, no l. 4709

what is l. raise and support 7566

When we are l. God still unalterable I Am 4587

Who can be high or l. at festival of God 3235

LOWER

not growing taller, but stooping l. 6017

not progress when moral tone l. 7834

Raised voices l. esteem 9488

religious values into higher or l. case 11658

Thinking in l. grades comparable to money 11259

To believe God made l. creature for prey 6280

We would not linger on the l. slope 5939

LOWERING

No people became great by l. standards 7834

LOWEST

boughs that bear most hang l. 6029

Christ dined with l. members of society 6433

happened at the l. times in his life 5437

Seek always the lowest place 8448

take l. place, highest will be given 5991

LOWLAND

grace to follow thee up from this misty l. 9097

LOWLIEST

Bible within sight of l. 702

His life his highest, holiest entering at l. door 6132

LOWLINESS

cross revealed God in l. 6471

God clothed himself with our l. 6130

In l. of heart 2764

the other eye to see man's l. 3562

LOWLY

Although but l. toil it be 2792

find nothing l. in the universe 11651

flower of sweetest smell is shy, l. 6028

God chooses base, l, unknown 3861

God made them, high or l. 4501

In celebration l. receive new stature 3235

In l. pomp, ride on to die 2981

in l. raiments of human flesh 6371

riper he grows, more l. he bends head 6030

'tis better to be l. born 6016 1772

LOWNESS

turn l. into liftiness 1122

LOWSOEVER

how l. it be we fall 4774

LOYAL

ask that thou wilt keep us l. 9115

disciplined obedience of l. subject 8818

nothing so l. as love 7315

LOYALTY

greatness in unyielding l. to a goal 5283

LUBRICATES

Cheerfulness l. inward machinery 1093

LUCK

death may be height of good l. 2342

Whether black cat brings bad l. 8584

LUCKY

funny old world, man's l. if gets out alive 6936

may be l. or unlucky 4803

who can obliterate pursuit of glory 4411

LUDICROUS

for Christian to believe he is object of public worship 9217

LUKEWARM

teaching of Christ at first appears l. 6486

LULLABY

no l. for the fainthearted 5804

LUMBER

God gives you and me l. of our lives 7684

LUMINOUS

words of Christ 6419

LUNACY

television advertising about right 11030

LUNATIC

either a l. or devil of hell 6350

Had there been a l. asylum in Jerusalem 6388

put out sun by scribbling darkness 4442

LUNATICS

crowd treat great men as l. 4393

LUNCH

lie might get l. but not supper 2476

LURE
of distant, difficult deceptive 8225

LURED
me, now leaves me here 3485

LURK
sinister doubts l. in the shadow
  3649

LURKING
ever l. disquiet in half withheld
  9683

LURKS
Behind the cloud the starlight l.
  5904
Treachery l. in honeyed words
  4052

LUST
and reason are enemies 7354
at its height does not know shame
  7358
authoritarianism twists good into
  l. for power 9952
deliver me from l. of vindicating
  myself 9722
felt even by fleas and lice 7355
for power rooted in weakness
  8718
Give me the vain l, the folly 4530
is frozen 2153
like rot in the bones 7356
looks ahead 8376
Men whom the l. of office does
  not kill 6299
of gold, unfeeling and remorseless
  11858
pains of hell ignorance, l. 3482
Rule l. 9960
says, "I must have it at once"
  7353
sin may spell l. but is some form
  of "me" 9916
trivial indulgence in l. or anger
  5021

LUST'S
effect is tempest after sun 7357

LUSTER
Common sense shines with double
  l. in humility 5994
rough treatment gives souls l. 280
saints have their l. 5301
Who gives its l. to an insect's wing
  1963

LUSTS
atheist, zoo of l. 493

LUSTY
Youth large, l, loving 12188

LUTHER
threw apple of discord into world
  1625

LUXURIES
of world cannot satisfy lonely
  7176
Renewal and restoration not l.
  9533

LUXURY
a l. to be understood 11610
a nice master, hard to be pleased
  7363
all died from suffocating l. 10739
being in the world 3480
Every l. must be paid for 3480
Everything is a l. 3480
in self-reproach 6230
Learn l. of doing good 5076
Living in lap of l. isn't bad 11834
makes man so soft hard to please
  him 7363
Man calls sin a l, God a leprosy
  4560
miserable even amidst l. 10871
more deadly than any foe 7362
never know when l. going to
  stand up 11834
On the soft bed of l. most
  kingdoms have died 7364
Pain teaches l. of health 8270
Prayer is a l. 10211
terrible l. of unbelief 11589
to me l. contemptible 7365

LYING
All sin a kind of l. 6848
essence of l. is in deception, not
  words 6859
Exaggeration offshoot of l. 3421
Much speaking and l. are cousins
  6854
Pride nothing but l. 6009
The safety of the world was l.
  there 6133
Without l. no new power can arise
  8722

LYNCHING
Let legalism have enough rope, l.
  of new ideas 6817

LYRICAL
When Wordsworth saw city, he
  grew l. 10522

M

MACHINE
body, a marvelous m. 842
God not an eternal blessing m. for
  men 5757
No m. can do work of one
  extraordinary man 8660

MACHINERY
Fear is sand in m. of life 3967
gospel, grain of sand that upsets
  world's m. 5099
much m. but few results 9017

MACHINES
brain, body m. to express
  personality 843
creatures that worked like m.
  4120

MAD
A man there was, they called him
  m. 4348

Christ tore through the temple
  like a m. man 6392
futile to get m. at myself for size
  of feet 3049
get m. clear through 399
I am not m, I would to heaven I
  were 5342

MADDENING
Yet, in the m. maze of things 4642

MADE
Changes, surprises, and God m. it
  all 8054
Engineer of universe m. me part
  of design 4565
Friendship easier m. than kept
  4235
God m. and loveth all 7174
God m. moon as well as sun 5393
God m. our individuality 6177
God m. the perfect instrument,
  human voice 7893
God m. them, high or lowly 4501
God m. us out of himself 1962
God never m. two people exactly
  alike 6191
He who m. us also remade us
  1901
I am as my Creator m. me 9987
I believe God has m. me 4992
If man is m. for God 7479
In a world I never m. 3978
Love has to be m, like bread 7217
man a perfect whole 5606
man was m. for immortality 6104
not m. from common mold 6206
praise God for having m. another,
  quite different world 5678
Real isn't how you are m. said the
  Skin Horse 5886
Thank God for the way he m. you
  6206
way will be m. through oceans,
  rivers, wastes, rocks 5444
year is closed, record m. 8082
you have m. us for yourself 7578

MADMAN
either the Son of God or a m.
  6350

MADNESS
for sheep to talk peace with wolf
  8446
mirth but pleasing m. 4877
no great genius without mixture
  of m. 4398
O blind m. 230
Theology m. gone systematic
  11208

MAETERLINCK
Happiness like bluebird of M.
  5519

MAGIC
an absurd kind of m. 693
Ask of the devil, use m. 2618
genius, power and m. 48
I carry a m. light in my heart 3649
in danger of m. 5441
perservation in books 851

Thinking is the m. of the mind
11261

MAGICAL
no surprise more m. than surprise
of being loved 7314
world is wonderful, inscrutable, m.
12049

MAGNA CHARTA
Bible, m. of poor, oppressed 700

MAGNET
Each departed friend a m. 2278
Love is like a m, pulls me into God
7237
that will attract true friends 4282

MAGNETIC
Listening a m. strange thing 1857

MAGNIFICENCE
Christ aperture through which m.
of God seen 6373
profusion is not m. 11662

MAGNIFICENT
his six days' work, a world 1967
If God is God, he's m. 4479
life more m. than most of us think
6918
Music one of most m. presents
God has given 7914
mystery of evil isn't as great or m.
5037
sex is m. 10235

MAGNIFIED
Joy m. when shared 6539

MAGNIFIER
Jealousy, thou m. of trifles 6345

MAGNIFIES
Self-love m. everything amiss in
others 10025
weak mind m. trifling things 7754

MAGNIFY
nothing will so m. the soul of man
4742

MAGNIFYING
cynic looks at life with m. glass
2179
Temptation is God's m. glass
11086

MAGNITUDE
of rebellion expressed by Calvary
10371
to God m. and distance have no
meaning 4582

MAILBAG
gossip's mouth is devil's m. 5146

MAIMED
virtue divorced from thankfulness
m. 11154

MAIN
Every man a part of the m. 10511
thing is to keep the m. thing the
m. thing 9275

MAINSPRING
God alters the m. 8570

hand over m. of life to God 837
if m. of service is love for God
10159

MAINSTREAM
best tests of growth occur in m. of
life 1319

MAINTAIN
Hate easy to m. for lifetime 7233
perpetual contentedness 9092
post when others have quitted
1915
what I consider most enviable of
titles 5881

MAINTAINED
God did not exist 481
right temperature at home m. by
warm hearts 5855

MAINTAINS
If God m. sun, planets 4619
only he has gift to speak 8196
only he has power to reason
correctly 8196

MAINTENANCE
man responsible for marriage m.
7613

MAJESTIC
Grief should be m. 5331
heroes mixture of m. and ordinary
755
like the sun 634
Repentance process by which we
see God as he is: m. 9594

MAJESTY
Christ the Lion in m, rebuking
winds, demons 6425
mind ascends, beholds m. of God
7971
of God, ineffable,
incomprehensible 7971
of human suffering 10854
Remember m. of the mountains
9270
Ride on! Ride on in m. 2981

MAJOR
asking God to conduct a m.
operation 7155
hope the m. weapon against
suicide 5925
no m. sin when his grace
confronts you 10405
than others out of m. operation
3422
This is your m. concern 6260

MAJORITIES
mean nothing 782

MAJORITY
best way because visible 5191
busy trying to place ourselves
8395
God does not need m. to work
wonders 1192
God has never had a m. 1192
great m. of men exist, do not live
7027
let experience corrupt 3534

living like m. of people 9758
One man with courage makes m.
1932
One on God's side is a m. 7510
opinion of the least able 5191
opinion will become law 4332
rule by m. fairest 5194
strength to make itself obeyed
5191
test of tolerance when in m. 1938
third-rate mind happy thinking
with m. 11248

MAKE
a life by what we give 4381
a living by what we get 4381
can decide to let Jesus m. holy
5752
can hardly m. friend in year 4305
can m. more friends in two months
4306
can only m. most of today 3502
Christ came to m. men holy 6424
Christ came to m. us what he
teaches we should be 6403
could not m. violins without
Antonio 4441
crosses which we m. for ourselves
4322
God can m. pieces of world's
puzzle fit 4735
God can m. you anything you
want to be 10970
God may yet m. something of him
3604
God, m. everyone different, no
one perfect 6180
Great hopes m. great men 5277
haste m. all things insecure 5586
I m. up with God 4855
If a man does not m. new
acquaintances 4248
if wish to m. everyone same 6189
It is for us to m. the effort 4945
kindling out of fallen tree. 3606
lest God m. incomes match gifts
4369
Life is partly what we m. it 4254
man holy, put him back into
unholy world 5759
man said, Let us m. God in our
image 4547
man who could m. one rose 7993
me what thou wouldst have me
9084
Morality does not m. a Christian
7830
nature of God to m. something
out of nothing 3604
not bound to m. the world go right
10150
not frantically trying to m.
ourselves good 7560
Nothing can m. man great but
being good 5290
Nothing you can do to m. God
love you more 4786
Now m. one like it—seed of earth
4608

O senseless man who cannot m. a
  worm 6073
one that which we are, that which
  we appear to be 6296
only God can m. a tree 2017
Or a trouble is what you m. it
  11446
spheres God brings us into meant
  to m. us something 7702
takes a great man to m. a good
  listener 7113
tests of life m. not break us 214
the mighty ocean and the pleasant
  land 6659
up to God to m. man good as he is
  4567
We cannot m. facts 38
We did not m. ourselves 7552
We m. our friends, enemies 8066
what we are not, m. us 9083
What you m. of yourself your gift
  to God 8560
When try to m. yourself more, you
  are diminishing yourself 9941
Wherever you are, friends m. your
  world 4212
Will m. them old before their years
  4003
wise man will m. more
  opportunities than he finds
  8210

MAKE-BELIEVE
Any truth better than m. 5887
If I can't pray, I will not m. 9036
Little praying a kind of m. 8889
where there is no m. 6295

MAKER
Himself, his M. and the angel
  Death 4209
His m. kissed his soul away 2296
love M. without hope of good
  4807
ought to love our M. for his own
  sake 4807
rationalist his own center, not his
  M. 9396
ready to meet my M. 2302
That which each can do best none
  but his M. can teach 6226
Whether my M. prepared for me
  another matter 2302

MAKER'S
to spread her M. praise abroad
  8026

MAKES
Christ m. his disciples like himself
  6411
Converse m. sharp the glittering
  wit 10534
earth a garden 4280
empty vessel m. greatest sound
  4066
enemies a person m. by taking
  stand 1913
faith m. all things possible 7345
Faith m. discords harmonies of
  future 3704

fallacy that having children m. a
  mother 7854
Fear m. wolf bigger 3969
for total life lived at full potential
  6999
friend m. me do my best 4170
God m. all things good 5019
God m. it impossible to lose our
  way 5397
God m. our next door neighbor
  8066
God m. promise, faith believes it
  9322
God m. shoes upside down 4668
God m. the glow worm and star
  8008
gossip m. mountain of molehill by
  adding dirt 5114
Gratitude to God m. blessing taste
  of heaven 5248
great man m. man feel small 5304
himself an ass 4063
If God m. you run 5427
its very unhappiness sublime
  10676
Jesus Christ m. us real, not merely
  sincere 9403
Love m. a subtle man out of a
  crude one 7260
Love m. all hard hearts gentle
  7261
love m. all things easy 7345
love m. the idle quick and sharp
  7260
love of God m. better men 7303
love of wealth m. bitter men 7303
Man m. plans, God changes them
  5432
not well-adjusted who m. world
  better place 6196
Peace within m. beauty without
  8463
really great man m. every man feel
  great 5304
revenging enemy m. you even
  with him 4073
stuff that m. criminal m. saint
  8667
Sun m. not the day, but thee 4502
why same thing m. us laugh, cry
  10660

MAKING
all m. a crown out of daily lives
  7073
if had m. of laws, would have
  made them otherwise 10425
natural view is man great being in
  the m. 7429
of music in a rest 7056
of music often slow, painful
  process 7056
opinion in good men is
  knowledge in the m. 6711
peace requires action 4094
while we are m. other plans 6982

MALE
and female not contenders for
  supremacy 3239

MALICE
Gossip personal confession of m.
  5128
has a strong memory 9637
In people's eyes I read m, vice
  3571
may distort truth 11566
never spoke well 390
Original sin m. ever flickering
  within 10347
With m. toward none 5199

MALICIOUS
Wisdom does not enter a m. mind
  11966

MALIGNANT
criticism m. deity 2050
Satan in most m. mood 1370

MALIGNITY
of soul often dwells in diseased
  bodies 5613

MAN
a chaos 7439
a complex being 3197
a contradiction 7439
a foolish baby 7440
a little world made cunningly
  7384
A m, sir, must keep friendships
  4249
A M. spoke as never m. before
  1147
A m. there was, they called him
  mad 4348
A m. who said things Jesus said
  6350
A m. without God 7446
a marvelously picturesque piece
  7374
a monster 7439
a novelty 7439
a peculiar, puzzling paradox 7402
A pigmy standing on crest of
  planet 7381
a prodigy 7439
a religious being 12110
a stranger and sojourner 187
a super-age-savage 10068
a thinking reed 7406
a unique being 7374
absurd a m. can't love one woman
  all the time 7621
accomplishes what he believes 613
acquisitive 10068
act like a m. of thought 11257
Adam, only m. who knew nobody
  said it before 1994
Adversities do not make m. frail
  140
Adversities show what sort of m.
  140
Adversity introduces a m. to
  himself 142
Adversity makes a m. wise, not
  rich 146
all m. can see, at Zenith of Power
  6698

All that m. bears for God's sake 148

alone can smile, laugh 6737

alone has capacity to walk, talk with God 7497

alone m. with his God must strive 10530

always m. who is reconciled to God 9430

always throwing dust in someone's eyes 7445

ambitious to lead disqualified as leader 6794

an abyss 7403

an animal that makes bargains 7404

an atom lost in endless vale of tears 10878

an eternal stranger on this planet 7436

an inexhaustible mystery 7405

an upstanding human being 10436

And every m. a scribe by trade 4748

And every m. decideth 1155

angry cannot be in right 394

angry m. shuts his eyes 369

Any m. may make mistake 3584

Any m. may play his part in mummery 6295

appears as consummate ass 482

appears for a little while 7372

are, or were, or could be as this m. 10432

arises from image of God in nature of m. 7531

As blind m. no idea of colors 4986

As m. believes 581

as m. speaks, so is he 10689

As Plato foresaw, the M. was crucified 11525

asks if any way out 7398

Atheism rather in lip than heart of m. 475

atheist sees m. helpless 3495

attitude of m. who loves God different 5046

bad m. worse when pretends to be saint 6045

Be such a m, and live such a life 6882

Be such a m. 551

Bear with all faults of m. 3948

becoming in the end a treacherous m. 7836

before which every ambition of m. is folly 6494

belief God will do everything for m. untenable as belief m. can do everything for himself 3415

Beware of no m. more than yourself 3157

Bible comprehends m, his thoughts 703

Bible sets m. face to face with God 660

Bible speaks to heart of m. 645

Birth, God's confidence in m. 815

blind m. carries lame m. who can see 918

born with face turned away from God 9583

bush still burns for m, whichever way he turns 7996

by origin is herd animal 6199

calls sin a blunder, God a blindness 4560

calls sin a chance, God a choice 4560

calls sin a defect, God a disease 4560

calls sin a fascination, God a fatality 4560

calls sin a liberty, God lawlessness 4560

calls sin a luxury, God a leprosy 4560

calls sin a mistake, God madness 4560

calls sin a trifle, God a tragedy 4560

calls sin a weakness, God wilfulness 4560

calls sin an accident, God an abomination 4560

calls sin an error, God an enmity 4560

calls sin an infirmity, God an iniquity 4560

Can a m. love God ignoring need of brother 10052

can always be defending truth 11493

can be saint in factory, monastery 9765

can blow hot, cold with same breath 6054

can counterfeit love, faith, hope 5989

can endure suffering if a purpose 10871

can fill tiny span of life with meaning 7080

can no more diminish God's glory 4442

can only break himself against laws of God 7493

can only find meaning outside himself 3484

can succeed if unlimited enthusiasm 3176

can't hold a m. down without staying down with him 10479

cannot be the m. I should be without quietness 7711

cannot believe until he knows Christ 611

cannot break the laws of God 7493

cannot cover what God would reveal 9709

cannot enter into deepest center of himself 7962

cannot find God unless God reveals himself 4910

cannot find joy anywhere but in God 6552

cannot live all to this world 12109

cannot seek God 4910

cannot shut out 464

cares most for sexual intercourse 10228

certainty about m. in contact with God 955

Charity, helping m. to help himself 1073

child wants m. for father, not formula 3929

child who fears noises becomes m. who hates noises 4004

Childhood shows the m. 1124

Christ as m. is way by which we go 6364

Christ claims to be more than a m. 6349

Christ offers every m. new life 7022

Christ revealing what m. is to be like 6426

Christ tore through temple like a mad m. 6392

Christian faith staggered imagination of m. 11201

Christianity, power of God in soul of m. 1179

Clothes do not make the m. 9626

condemned for continuing to do wrong 6586

confronted by God 7494

Conscience God's presence in m. 1670

conscious of his responsibility 7398

conscious of his weakness 7398

contented m. enjoys scenery along detours 1773

contentious m. will never lack words 9357

Conversion goes throughout m. 1895

convicted of sin 5108

convinced against his will 9179

convinced he deserves hell 5668

corruption of degenerate m. 11858

cost devil little trouble to catch lazy m. 6766

covetous m. ever in want 5324

created a God addict 7496

created with two eyes 3562

cross shows how God could become m. 2150

cross shows m. could become God 2150

Death alters what m. desires 2240

Demanding all, deserving nothing 7440

Democracy, free to choose m. who will get blame 5173

denies existence of God 482

depends on whether m. or mouse 8584

depth m. can fall is height to which he can rise 8666

descended from inferior animal 1992

designed to carry the load of the moment 421

desire of knowledge in excess caused m. to fall 3556

destined end of m. is holiness 5757

devil predestines every m. to be damned 9175

devil too loves m. 2688

devil voting against m. 1145

did not make, and cannot mar 8430

dies, clutches only that which he has given away 2416

differs from animals, asks questions 7398

discloses own character when describes another 991

Discontent first step in progress of m. 2864

distance one should keep from wicked m. cannot be measured 11888

distasteful way which leads to himself 1717

diversity in unity 7374

do away with everything behind m. 4315

Do not judge a m. until you know whole story 6573

do not know a m. until we know his leisure 6842

do not understand m. 7394

does not know himself truly 7494

does not know what to do with life 3282

does what he can 7495

don't care how much m. may consider himself a failure 3596

Don't envy m. who has everything 3208

Don't judge any m. until walked in his moccasins 6574

don't keep faith with God, won't keep with m. 3799

Doubt may be sign m. is thinking 2933

Doubt not always sign m. is wrong 2933

drags m. down, or m. lifts m. up 9522

drives, God holds reins 4947

each m. as he really is 7443

each m. as he sees himself 7443

each m. as the other person sees him 7443

Each morning puts m. on trial 11364

earth to sun what m. is to angels 364

easier to know mankind than m. individually 7393

Education enable m. to put things well 2998

Education teaches us how little m. knows 3004

Education teaches us how much m. has to learn 3004

eloquence must consist in the m. 9168

emotions inheritance of every m. 3058

endowed with liberty he cannot deny 3495

endowed with liberty he may betray 3495

enjoys reputation of being most remarkable person he knows 9197

enters each stage of life as novice 7002

envy corrupts m. 3207

Even mean m. has value 3159

every m. a part of the main 4026

Every m. a piece of the continent 10511

Every m. a volume if you know how to read him 8490

Every m. carries kingdom within 6171

every m. has many blessings 828

Every m. has rainy corner 2543

Every m. his greatest enemy 3173

Every m. I meet my superior in some way 7373

Every m. is a miniature world 6487

Every m. is a volume 6172

Every m. knows he will die 2279

Every m. lives by faith 3653

Every m. must do two things alone 2280

every m. piece of the continent 4026

Every m. serves useful purpose 11805

Every m. should keep fair-sized cemetery 4225

Every m. unique being 6173

Every moment dies a m. 806

Everything but soul of m. passing shadow 10654

everything degenerates in hands of m. 3193

everywhere he passes, m. leaves some kind of mark 6231

expectation remarkably low, timorous 3507

Faith believing a m. can walk over Niagara Falls 3669

Faith is an act of m. 3690

Fallen m. not simply an imperfect creature 9577

falls into sin is a m. 10309

false to God, never true to m. 7464

far-reaching spirit stretches to the infinite 7381

favorite place of God is in heart of m. 4496

Fear of God can deliver from fear of m. 3970

finds God through truth 11518

finds it hard to get what he wants 2571

first test of great m. 6032

fish lies about size of m. 3426

fits into no categories of thought 7405

flung without knowing why, how into a world 3495

foe to God ne'er true friend to m. 4164

fool wanders, wise m. travels 4058

foolish m. tells woman to stop talking 2889

For m. sound in body, serene of mind 8005

For never, never wicked m. was wise 11883

forced to seek higher authority 7499

forever criticizing wife's judgment 7655

Four things m. must learn 559

frail mind of m. cannot explain reason 4492

free m. is he who does not fear thought 4145

free to do what he likes 4150

free to do what he ought 4150

free to love God 566

free to love neighbor 566

freedom constitutes dignity of m. 4149

friend never known until m. have need 4166

Friendship with God means nature of God in m. 7457

frightened that he loses himself by giving himself 9937

From errors of others wise m. corrects his own 3257

future in m. who holds job 3122

generous m. forgets what he gives 4346

gets up to speak and says nothing 5171

gets wiser, expects less 3497

Give a m. a dollar, cheer heart 3307

Give a m. a fish, eats for a day 11001

Give every m. thy ear 1843

Give m. Christ, change heart 3307

Give m. dream, challenge heart 3307

Give m. religion without reminding of his filth 7425

given one tongue 1858

glad when great m. reassures us of his humanity 5307

glory of God is a living m. 12116

glory of God is m. fully alive 4566

glory, jest, riddle of world 7417

God allows m. insolently to deny him 4673

God allows m. to cut throat of his fellowmen 4673

God alone makes m. believer 585

God and m. exist for each other 4531

God asks no m. whether he will accept life 6893

God became m. 6125

God brought m. here with heart's blood expense 4532

God can do what he likes with m. abandoned to him 9557

God first made m. 1120

God gives to every m. virtue 5387

God has given m. a short time upon earth 6894

God has one plan, m. another 4563

God impressed by only one m, Christ 3854

God is architect, m. is contractor 4563

God is music's author, not m. 7891

God judges m. by way he is facing 4713

God laid upon m. duty of being free 4127

God made time, m. made haste 5576

God must love the common m. 4545

God never forces m. 4130

God never meant that m. should scale the heavens 11916

God never tempts any m. 11060

God predestines every m. to be saved 9175

God puts questions to m. 7398

God smart when he made m. 7379

God takes care of m. 566

God to m. doth speak in solitude 10534

God undertakes special protection of m. 3999

God wants to come to his world through m. 4549

God will disappoint m. attempting to use him 4468

God will not permit m. to have 4314

God wills that m. be good 5060

God would give best, m. will not take 2571

God would never have created m. 5020

God would not have created m. to exist only for a day 6104

goes to hell by own choice 5686

good m. is his own friend 5082

good m. makes no noise over good deed 2495

gospel is God's search for m. 9547

gospel, new life to m. by grace of God 5100

great m. does not lose child's heart 5294

great m. in midst of crowd keeps independence 6195

great m. makes every m. feel small 5304

Great m. shows greatness by way he treats little men 5272

greater a m, more distasteful praise is to him 5296

greater than the stars 7385

greater than universe 1984

greatest a m. can do for his heavenly Father 6665

greatest is m. who chooses right with resolution 5297

greatest marvel in the universe 7497

greatest of discoveries m. can make 4866

groping for God and hoping to hide from him 7402

grows old and dies 3266

grows tired standing still 6751

Happy is m. too busy to worry by day 12062

happy m. confines himself within limits 2875

happy so long as he chooses to be happy 5538

hardly knows whether he is honest 145

hardness of God softer than softness of m. 4498

Has any m. attained to inner harmony 7687

has been given two ears 1858

has lagged behind morally 9872

has leaped ahead in scientific achievement 9872

has no harbor 11373

has power to bring misery on himself, others 4158

has power to defy God's wishes 4158

has right to liberty of discussion 2900

has the casting vote 9175

has two great spiritual needs 7400

hates to stand alone in opinion 1639

heart of good m. sanctuary of God 5084

heart of wise m. lies quiet like limpid water 11944

heart that makes a m. rich 11840

Heaven in earth, and God in m. 6153

Heaven ne'er helps m. who will not help himself 2498

heaven's masterpiece 1965

heaviest load m. carries on back 4098

hid from God in garden 316

hides within himself 316

highest possible condition of m. 4983

himself is mankind's greatest danger 7397

himself when most possessed by God 5200

his own executioner 3173

holier m. is, less understood by men of world 5760

Holiness, not happiness end of m. 5517

holy m. most humble you can meet 5763

holy m. not one who cannot sin 5762

holy m. one who will not sin 5762

honest m. not worse because dog barks at him 5866

Hope animates a m. to do his utmost 5917

Hope last thing that dies in m. 5924

hope lies in M. we put on cross 5941

hope lies not in m. we put on moon 5941

hope, word God has written on brow of every m. 5947

hopeful m. sees success where others see failure 5943

human nature clings to m. with such persistance 5974

humble m. counts blessings 6035

humble m. receives praise way clean window takes light 6033

I can assure you, a wicked creature 10333

I said to the m. who stood at the gate 5417

I will speak ill of no m. 5072

I'm a self-made m. you know 9915

ideal woman waiting for ideal m. 7665

idle m. tempts the devil 6770

If a m. has good corn to sell 2776

If a m. is called to be a streetsweeper 2777

If ever a m. becomes proud 9209

if every m. were such as you 6882

If evil did not make dwelling in m. 3377

If I hate or despise any one m. in world 5599

If m. carries cross beautifully 5252

if m. could have half his wishes, double his troubles 2569

If m. crossed with cat 7390

If m. does not keep pace with his companions 10827

If m. does not make new acquaintances 4248

If m. empties purse in head 3010

if m. had foresight of prosperity 4314

If m. has acted right 5032

If m. in pew trained to think 9146

If m. is m. and God is God 8833

If m. is made for God 7479

If m. lost his liberty 4133

If m. runs after money, he's money-mad 7800

If m. suddenly took to virtue 11887

If m. too little for God to speak to him 4553

If soul be lost, m. is lost 10655

if this world were all m, would lose all hope 8012

If want to know what a m. is like 7802

If you have faith in God, or m. or self 3778

ignorant m. uses words for jargon 11998

imagines he will keep if he hides 1537

imagines he will lose if he gives 1537

improve m, deteriorate cat 7390

in constant flux 977

in earnest finds means 2624

in every m. a loneliness 7127

in evolution from lesser to greater condition 9351

In God alone can m. meet m. 9429

in knowledge m. most haunted with limitation 6689

In m. evil is constricted 3377

in same class with wolf, skunk 1991

in sleep m. cannot silence conscience 2970

inclined to be intolerant 11612

inferior of any m. whose rights I trample 11283

Infinite as essential for m. as planet 12117

inhumanity to m. makes thousands mourn 30

intolerable if never suffered 10898

is a constant puzzle 7401

is born broken 4654

is but a flower 6991

is but a reed 7406

is constraint. nature is freedom 8012

is essentially devout 12110

is fire, woman tow 10226

is first startled by sin 10287

is free to act 1984

is God's risk 7407

Is he a god or a worm 3494

is his own gardener 11223

is impenitent, then obstinate, then damned 10287

is made for thinking 11231

is no helpless invalid 10436

is not an angel whose reason works perfectly 9417

is powerful on his knees 8785

is the greatest miracle, problem 7408

is what he is, not what used to be 990

Jesus can put into m. disposition that ruled his life 9436

Jesus Christ not a solitary m. 464

Jesus spelling himself out in language m. can understand 6445

Jesus spoke to the unchanging needs of m. 6448

Jesus was a solitary m. 6508

Jesus, a m. acting like God 6514

Jesus, God acting like himself in m. 6514

joined in praise until he fell 8743

joy in nature is absence of m. 8035

judges from a partial view 6583

kindest m. will put heel on greatest friend 10527

know good through evil 5030

know why m. alone laughs 6742

knows death not an end but a beginning 2343

knows he exists 1984

knows more than he understands 6697

laid the dead m. there 778

lazy m. does not, will not, cannot pray 6776

lazy m. is workshop for Satan 6749

learn from mean m. how not to live 3159

learn to love God and m. by loving 7352

led more by patterns than precepts 3442

Let a good m. do good deeds 108

Let each m. himself an act of God 4557

Let each m. think his life a breath of God 4557

Let each m. think his mind a thought of God 4557

Let no m. be sorry he has done good 5032

Life a sentence m. has to serve for being born 6952

Life is dust nature lends m. for an hour 6960

Life is ever since m. was born 6963

life of civilization compared with m. only a moment 7389

life of Jesus cannot be discussed in same way as any other m. 6476

life of m. a broken pillar 1163

life of m. consists in beholding God 12116

like m. who uses only little finger 8659

like that turns out empty 8196

like the bridge 421

likes to go alone for walk 1639

Live a conqueror, die a m. 2353

live a king, die a m. 2353

lives by mending 4654

living, new m. born from living God 872

Lord always voting for m. 1145

Lord not merely a good m. 9437

Love a m. even in his sin 10331

love for neighbor means love for any m. in need 7201

Love makes a subtle m. out of a crude one 7260

love nature because retreat from m. 8012

Love the wine that gladdens heart of m. 7256

Luxury makes a m. so soft hard to please him 7363

Made m. a perfect whole 5606

magnificent ruin of what God designed 7429

make m. all over again 9800

make m. as certain of God as God is of himself 9800

make m. holy, put back into unholy world 5759

makes deserts bloom, lakes die 3197

makes great fuss about planet 11633

makes m. more clever devil 3005

makes me wish for another world 8012

makes plans, God changes them 5432

mark of m. how he treats person of no possible use 573

may act honest m. on the scaffolding 6295

may aspire, yet be content 471

may betray Jesus Christ by speaking 628

may go to hell with baptismal water on face 9537

Mean and petty his wants, desires 7381

meddles, they become evil 5019

meet m. who has no smile, give him yours 10496

met a m. who had no feet 387

mind of m, God meet 949

mind of m. cannot explain reason 3781

Mistrust the m. who finds everything evil 3555

Mistrust the m. who finds everything good 3555

Mistrust the man indifferent to everything 3555

molded shape of m. 1982

Money never made a m. happy, nor will it 7814

morally incapable of restraining himself 9872

more a m. has, more he wants 7814

more gregarious in mind than body 1639

more honesty m. has, less air of saint 5889

more interesting than men 6200

more m. denies himself, more obtain from God 9562

more m. knows, more he forgives 4099

more m. loves, more he suffers 10904

more powerful than matter 1474

more skill, design than works of m. 1964

mosquito preceded m. in divine order of creation 9209

most exalted of all God's works 7395

most potent weapon God has given m. 4154

much beast and some devil in m. 5013

Music is God's best gift to m. 7904

must despair to obtain grace of Christ 5201

must do first in his mind 578

must govern, not serve, gold 11835

must learn to forgive himself 9979

must never be afraid 566

mute before elemental truth 10274

mystery of Christ's existence meets wants of m. 5728

natural m. must know to believe 3743

natural view is m. great being in the making 7429

natural view, Bible view of m. different 7429

nature of m. to err 3260

nearer a m. gets to being a beast 26

nearer to weary soul of m. 7916

need of m. is to overcome his separateness 7143

need of man is to leave prison of aloneness 7143

neighbor is m. next to you at the moment 8069

neighbor is m. who needs you 8070

neighbor is m. whom business has brought you into contact 8069

Never has m. bent himself 3444

Never is God said to be reconciled to m. 9430

never is, but always to be blessed 5913

never known m. of real ability to be ungrateful 5255

never met m. so ignorant couldn't learn from him 6080

never so proud as when striking attitude of humility 9187

Never tell a m. you can read him 10985

Never tell evil of a m. 5149

no brotherhood of m. without fatherhood of God 920

No great m. complains of want of opportunity 8220

no indispensable m. 7433

No m. became very wicked all at once 11889

No m. can create faith in himself 3766

No m. can justly censure or condemn 6585

No m. can resolve himself into heaven 5662

No m. chooses evil because evil 3386

No m. comes to himself without meeting God 1907

No m. ever became wise by chance 11931

No m. ever got out of trouble 11444

No m. ever more than four steps from God 9585

No m. ever sank under burden of day 4319

No m. ever scared into heaven 5663

No m. fit to comprehend 198

No m. free who is slave to flesh 4138

No m. gives anything acceptable to God 10119

No m. gives at all until he has given all 10119

no m. got so much out of surgical operation as Adam 759

No m. happy whose path but glimmer of light 6101

No m. has good enough memory to lie 6855

No m. has right to lead life of contemplation 7004

No m. is an island 10511

No m. is born wise 11342

No m. is fit who hath not resigned 198

No m. is free who is not master of himself 4139

No m. is perfect unless admits faults 3949

No m. is prosperous whose immortality forfeited 6101

No m. is useless while he has friend 4257

No m. loves life as he who's growing old 8147

No m. need stay way he is 1146

No m. poor who has had godly mother 7851

No m. progressed to greatness but through mistakes 5030

No m. rich enough to buy back past 1735

No m. rich to whom grave brings eternal bankruptcy 6101

No m. safely travels, talks, rules, commands 7422

No m. should desire to be happy who is not holy 5543

No m. should part with own individuality 6201

no m. so good would not deserve hanging 7434

No m. so insignificant 3445

No m. to be trusted with unlimited power 8714

no m. truly knows another 6585

No m. will rise high who jeers at sacred things 9735

No machine can do work of one extraordinary m. 8660

no matter what a m. does 63

No one who is lover of money is lover of m. 11661

no room for God in m. full of himself 10089

No young m. ever thinks he shall die 12171

none more lonely than m. who loves only himself 7147

none more wonderful than m. 7424

nor has m. right to active life 9670

nor is m. a mule whose reason works not at all 9417

nor m. Christian till born again 875

nor m. made perfect without trials 136

nor m. right to be so immersed in active life 7004

not Bible, needed correcting 679

not complete in spiritual stature if all not given to God 5734

not fit tenant for mind of honest m. 11181

not good that m. batter at gate of heaven 8854

not left in valley of total depravity 10436

not possible for first m. in Garden 11722

not what m. does that determines sacred or secular 7865

not where m. goes when compelled 4147

Nothing attractive about gospel to natural m. 5108

nothing but dust 7445

Nothing can make m. great but being good 5290

Nothing consumes a m. more quickly than resentment 9638

Nothing seems worse to m. than his death 2342

Nothing so dates a m. as to decry younger generation 12192

nothing terrible for m. who realizes 7059

nothing will so magnify the soul of m. 4742

Now old m, no one has repect for age 12190

O m. cleave close to God 2604

O what may m. within him hide 2470

Obedience not servitude of m. to m. 8099

Of all God's creatures, m. alone is poor 8683

of courage not afraid of truth 6845

Of elements and an angelic sprite 7384

of little faith does not think 3830

of the earth, yet thoughts with stars 7381

of words and not deeds like garden of weeds 9319

off guard m. reveals character 1028

old m. dies with open hand 11656

old m. nearing end of earthly journey 8121

on dead-end street with m. who denies God 7523

Once believed could make own pleasure 8602

One m. does not see everything 262

One more wrong to m. 6275

One night a m. had a dream 5437

One small grave is what he gets 7440

only animal of which I am afraid 7410

only animal on friendly terms with victims 7585

only animal that knows difference between what they are and ought to be 7413

only animal that laughs and weeps 7413

Only m. clogs happiness with care 12073

Only m. endowed with shame 9570

only once on this earth 6173

only when m. wishes the impossible, he remembers God 7490

other things only m. can do 10199

overwhelmed with commandments 1525

part of m. knows which never knew before 5809

part of m. sees which never saw before 5809

Passed by a m. in workman's guise 6458

peace found by m. in depths of own heart 8474

pervasive sinfulness of m. evident 10440

Pharisee m. who prays publicly, preys privately 6047

Photography force in explaining m. to m. 2016

picturesque piece of diversity in unity 6173

poor in spirit 1325

poor m. at his gate 4501

poorest m. always wanting more 2874

potential hero in every m.—and potential skunk 8670

Poverty no disgrace to m. 8687

powers in unconscious depths of m. 1712

Prayer is exhaling spirit of m. 8920

Prayer link between finite m, infinite God 8944

Prayer rope that pulls God, m. together 8947

prayer voice of m. to God 9704

prays for strength without much thought 8850

predatory 10068

prefers to believe what he prefers to be true 595

present is all of which m. is master 8384

pretense harasses a ruined m. 8679

primarily interested in himself 10068

prisoner who has no right to open door 10941

probably gets more than expects 3497

progress depends on unreasonable m. 980

Prosperity greatest enemy m. can have 9341

prosperous m. never sure loved for himself 11860

proud m. always looking down on things, people 9188

proud m. counts newspaper clippings 6035

proud m. seldom grateful m. 5258

Psalms, music of the heart of m. 798

Psalms: mirror in which m. sees his soul 800

pure love of God pierces a m. 9741

pushes into self-chosen alienation 4781

race of m. unfinished pyramid 1163

rarely hear m. suffering who says he disbelieves in God 10936

rational m. without Spirit of God 7753

real m. is maze of a million notes 6212

really great m. makes every m. feel great 5304

reasonable m. adapts to world 980

reasoning, rather than reasonable, animal 7416

redemption brings m. back into tune with praise 8743

Religion can offer m. burial service 7022

Religion what m. tries to do for God 9545

Religion without guilt tries to make God big pal of m. 5487

remorse puts m. in hell while on earth 9584

Repentance chance to correct what m. left crooked 9596

Reproof never does a wise m. harm 11938

returns home to find what he needs 5815

revelation voice of God to m. 9704

rich m. at his castle 4501

ride a m, sit easy and light 9471

rides, God holds the reins 7498

ridiculous that a m. have right to kill me 11744

Sad is the m. who has nothing but money 7821

said, Let us make God in our image 4547

Sarcasm weapon of weak m. 1770

satanically-managed m. has no need of God 9853

satanically-managed m. self-governed 9853

see him walk, know his thoughts 8494

see inner m, his real self 6842

seed dies into new life, so does m. 2385

seeks to win glory by sacrifice of others 2152

sees actions, God motives 7866

sees but withered leaves 8673

serve a great m, will know what sorrow is 5292

seven ages of m. 7037

shall commune with creatures to his profit 9481

should be mourned at birth, not death 2209

should ever stand in need of m. 9462

should perform duties to fellowmen as to God 9669

should take all things as if prayed for them 10926

Show a m. his failures without Jesus 7425

shows character by laughter 982

six mistakes of m. 7793

sky not less blue because blind m. does not see it 9409

slave of everything, everybody 7375

so weak is m, so ignorant and blind 8877

sold God for thirty pence 4532

solemn pause, breathing space of m. 10960

some angel and some God in m. 5013

sooner misunderstood than exposed 1055

soul of m. like the rolling world 10673

soul weakened by virus of pride 10436

spends life complaining of present 8380

spends life fearing for future 8380

spends life reasoning on past 8380

spirit in m. is candle of the Lord 7430

spiritual m. must believe to know 3743

Spring makes everything young except m. 9894

stands an angel by every m. 366

Stature of m. 3494

strong m. must have something difficult 77

strongest m. is he who stands, most alone 10759

subject to storm and tempests 282

Success ratio between what a m. is and might be 10808

such a great m. I have forgotten his faults 5286

suffering of m. also the suffering of God 10912

Suffering was curse from which
m. fled 10896

suffers so deeply had to invent
laughter 6742

take unholy m. out of unholy
world 5759

takes a great m. to make a good
listener 7113

takes care neighbor does not cheat
him 5004

takes little effort to watch m.
carry load 6160

taking away freedom of choice
from m. 4133

taking revenge, m. even with
enemy 9715

Teach a m. to fish, eats for rest of
life 11001

technically capable of destroying
world 9872

Tell m. he is brave 3140

than learn from m. in thousand
years 4964

than m. keep straight line walking
in dark 6614

thankless m. never does thankful
deed 11134

That m. may last, but never lives
4374

the freer the m, the stronger the
bond 6177

the germ is in every m. 2034

the great inscrutable mystery of
God 7409

The m. is dead 7442

the m. takes the drink 330

the m. who says can't 66

the miracle of miracles 7409

the most terrible of the beasts
8066

the only animal that blushes 7411

the only animal that knows
nothing without being taught
7412

The poor device of m. 7572

the small print of m. soul 739

Think like a m. of action 11257

thinks he amounts to a great deal
9219

thinks he loses time 11307

thinks himself happiest m, really
is so 11917

this m. unique 4993

threatens while he quakes for fear
3981

Tiny fly can choke a big m. 8701

'Tis not for m. to trifle 11287

To a good m. nothing that
happens is evil 5049

to average m. time to do with
dinner 11346

to be feared who fears not God
7426

to be found in register of God, not
m. 6023

to be honest is to be one m.
picked out of a thousand 5867

to build brotherhood of m. 4632

To every m. there openeth 10679

to get best out of m. go to best in
him 3471

To his dog, every m. is Napoleon
9509

To know m. we must begin with
God 4571

to m. of pseudo faith nothing but
God terrifying thought 3719

To m. who is afraid everything
rustles 4002

to make his way best he can 3495

To make no mistakes not in
power of m. 7794

to obtain possible, m. turns to
fellowmen 7490

To reconcile m. with m. and not
with God is to reconcile no one
9432

to ruin a m. for service of God
6407

To see God, highest aspiration of
m. 7547

to work out in world will of God
3195

tongue can kill m. six feet high
5161

too good for world is no good for
his wife 7594

too old to learn probably always
too old 3028

trampled by same forces he has
created 5975

travels world in search of what he
needs 5815

treat him as any other great m.
9201

tries to make best of both worlds
1332

Trust in nothing m. who has not
conscience 1708

truth of a m. is what he hides
7431

trying to find something which
will make him happy 5570

unreasonable m. adapts world to
himself 980

until m. is nothing 884

up to God to make m. good as he
is 4567

vain m. accommodates himself to
others 9189

vain m. can never be utterly
ruthless 9189

vain m. wants to win applause
9189

Vainly strives, fights, frets 7440

veiled to eye of m. 10706

virtue of m. measured by everyday
conduct 11698

vision impaired by cataracts of sin
10436

votes, breaks tie 1145

walking chemical factory 7367

was made for immortality 6104

way a m. dies more important
than death 2336

ways of awakening inner
reverence in m. 9734

Wealth lightens not heart of m.
11877

weeding turnips is also serving
God 12146

weight more than m. can bear
4319

what a chimera, then, is m. 7439

what God can do in m. fully
consecrated to Christ 2835

What m. content with one crime
2041

What m. has written m. may read
8049

what might not the heart of m.
become 8655

what pleaseth m. ofttimes
displeasing to God 9195

What to one m. is food 6220

whatever m. honors more than
God is i. 6076

When a dream enslaves a m. 2964

when a m. does what he likes to
do, character revealed 6842

When a m. has lost his shirt 6290

When a m. has no strength 10766

when a m. is self-seeking, he
abandons love 7246

When Christ calls a m. 10049

When God calls a m. 4626

When God measures a m. 4576

when greeted by m. smiling
because trained 6062

When m. does not know what
harbor 4433

When m. is happy does not hear
clock strike 5572

When m. reasons, God laughs
9427

When Spirit of God comes into a
m. 7786

When talk of m. doing anything
for God 10214

When you see an old m. amiable,
mild 8184

When young m. no one had
respect for youth 12190

where an ordinary m. is saying his
prayers 8761

where m, the effect ceases 4525

Where m. can find no answer, will
find fear 4008

where m. goes when free to go
4147

where woman equal with the m.
3868

While m. rests on own merits
10041

who beef too much, find himself
in stew 2068

who believes everything is far
from God 3710

who believes he is worthy of
heaven 5668

who blows own horn has
everyone dodging when
approaches 9242

who can't control temper 368

who cannot make a worm, yet
makes gods by dozens 6073

who cannot resolve to live his own life 6872

who could make one rose 7993

who craves more is poor 2868

who delights in multitude of words 10245

who dies out of Christ 2381

who does not love God, in love with himself 4803

who does not read has no advantage over m. who cannot 860

who does things makes many mistakes 7792

who finds gospel attractive 5108

who finds truth lights torch 11536

who flares up 398

who harbors vengeance 398

who has faith must be prepared to be martyr, fool 3642

who has given up intellectual freedom 7760

who has guilty secret is lonely m. 1702

who has lost contact with God 7523

who has never been tempted 11098

who has no inner life 7033

who has not suffered, what does he know 10832

who has understanding has everything 11946

who hasn't time to stop at railroad crossing 5589

who hides behind hypocrite smaller than hypocrite 6046

who idly sits and thinks 11244

who is vindictive 398

who leaves money to charity 4377

who lives for self alone 10085

Who lives in fear, never a free m. 4009

who lives on better terms with angels 3899

who lives that span is something 7080

who loses his temper 398

who loves God asks no favors of God 4803

who loves God in unassailable position 4803

who loves his wife 636

who never alters opinion like standing water 9185

who refuses to believe anything 3710

Who rises from prayer a better m. 9034

who smoulders 398

who speaks truth always at ease 11537

who stuck true to God will come out best 10789

who studies revenge keeps wounds green 9714

who thinks he is righteous is not righteous 9254

who thinks must be pessimistic 8587

who thinks too much of himself thinks too little of others 9243

who truly repents cries out against his heart 9601

who understands his foolishness is wise 11947

who would rather play golf than eat 7656

whole trouble with m. of little faith 3830

Why comes temptation but for m. to meet 11122

wicked m. is his own hell 11880

will the Father leave neglected the soul of m. 6095

wise m, even when he holds his tongue says more 11951

wise m, though slave, at liberty 4113

wise m. adapts to circumstances 1463

wise m. cares not for what he cannot have 11899

wise m. carries his possessions within him 11950

wise m. does not grieve for what he has not 1793

wise m. gets more use from enemies 3155

wise m. in storm prays to God 3997

wise m. more use from enemies than fool from friends 9444

wise m. prays for deliverance from fear 3997

wise m. prays not for safety from danger 3997

wise m. rejoices for what he has 1793

wise m. seeks friend with qualities he himself lacks 4279

Wise m. sees a man's spirit 11896

wise m. sees as much as he ought 11902

wise m. tells woman mouth beautiful when closed 2889

wise m. trusts wisdom of God 5459

wise m. will make more opportunities than he finds 8210

wise only while he searches for wisdom 11930

with dungfork gives God glory 1237

With every m. God has a secret 7127

with everything, ulcer too 3208

with his burning soul 11519

with trifles m. reveals character 1028

with vision of God devoted to God himself 11729

Without choice m. not a m. 4155

without courage, knife without edge 1917

Without faith m. becomes sterile, hopeless 3824

without faith, walking corpse 3791

Without free will m. not in image of God 4158

without prayer like tree without roots 8752

without purpose like ship without rudder 4436

world given to m. in trust 3195

world has disease called m. 7432

world m. cannot understand 3495

Worship is m. climbing altar stairs to God 12132

Worship requires only a m. and God 12142

worst bankrupt is m. who has lost enthusiasm 3183

worth as much as 11657

worth measured by objects pursued 469

worth of a m. as m. regardless of birth 7423

worthwhile is the one who will smile 10493

would blind eyes of moral m. 4657

would have lost likeness to God 4149

would have married the wrong m. 8797

would not rob a m. of his problems 9286

wrap yourself in God 2658

wrapped up makes small package 1591

writes histories 5719

yearning arises from image of God in m. 4744

yet no m. can be a Christian without morality 7830

You are a m, not God 11722

you honor, kind of m. you are 1038

you need to beware of 398

MAN OF GOD
popular image of 1645

MAN OF NAZARETH
carries forth work of administration 235

seated in place of authority 235

MAN OF SORROWS
had a part 10597

most perfect being called M. 10630

most perfect being who trod soil of planet 6481

MANAGE
accustomed to relying on words to m. 10259

enable me to m. affairs of life 9041

most difficult thing we m. is self 9949

MANAGED
world disgracefully m. 3203

MANAGEMENT
God ready to take over m. of our
lives 5511
God stands ready to take m. of
our lives 3758
ideal method of time m. 11466

MANAGERIAL
abilities not test of father's
leadership 3925

MANAGES
Impulse m. all things badly 5580

MAN-CENTERED
Worldliness accepting values of m.
society 12053

MAN-CONTROLLED
prayer greater than m. powers
8991

MANDATE
world thy proud m. 4592

MANGER
A little child in a m. 6133
as uneasy as his cross 6489
borrowed m, tomb framed his
earthly life 6433
coming of Christ by way of m.
strange, stunning 6145
Filling the world he lies in a m.
6122
happy to go with shepherds to see
Lord in m. 8061
situated on Golgotha 1365
to ornament your m. bed 6118
when we take Christ out of m.
6145

MANHOOD
a riper thing 311
a struggle 7097

MANIA
church caught up in success m.
1409

MANIFEST
God forever seeking to m. himself
to us 7513
impossible for God to m. himself
under conditions set up 8929
responsibility to m. Jesus 1014
saved to m. Son of God in flesh
1014
to m. himself to us one by one
6178

MANIFESTATION
God only known through m. 4738
Our lives a m. of what we think
about God 7016
seen by others, not by us 9707
to judge character by only one m.
1053

MANIFESTATIONS
of God innumerable 4585

MANIFESTED
Character in saint Christ m. 998
God expects life of Jesus to be m.
4539

Holiness only m. by antagonism
5740

MANIFESTING
Body medium for m. Jesus Christ
838

MANIFESTS
God m. himself in his children
9707

MANIFOLD
God created life as a m. thing
6985

MANIPULATE
fear m. with mysterious 3971
honesty, integrity no need to m.
others 5874

MANIPULATION
Christian, not by ecclesiastical m.
1256
society network of m. 10514
tongue powerful weapon of m.
1882

MANIPULATOR
shakes hand one minute, pulls leg
the next 7582

MANKIND
abounding grace hope of m. 5203
All m. is of one Author 2216
All m. is one volume 2216
And ride m. 9343
By a Carpenter m. was made 6360
Christ either deceived m. by fraud
6366
Christ has done more to
regenerate m. 6483
easier to know m. than man
individually 7393
Earnestness commands respect of
m. 2771
Give me power to live for m.
10130
Hope draws power from basic
goodness of m. 5928
hope that God does not weary of
m. 4896
if wrong, sanction of m. will not
justify 5032
In war loser is m. 11752
Jesus, digging m. out of snug
burrows 6421
Night is sabbath of m. 8085
only by that Carpenter can m. be
remade 6360
Our true nationality is m. 5980
princes among us forget
themselves, serve m. 10193
reflect with sorrow on
competitions 2423
serpent deceived the mother of m.
9863
superhuman chance of m. 4549
Sweeps the wide earth, tramples
o'er m. 6269
those that are immovable,
moveable, move 10504
world is God's epistle to m. 8045

would know better if not anxious
to resemble 1649

MANKIND'S
all m. concern is charity 1079
man himself is m. greatest danger
7397

MAN-LIKE
it is to fall into sin 10334

MAN-MADE
millenium 9870
Religion is m. 9545

MAN-MAID
Life full of troubles, most m. 7628

MANNER
Happiness a m. of traveling 5523

MANNERS
in spite of attempt to teach good
m. 1109
Men's evil m. live in brass 9619
once vices, now m. 3958

MAN'S
A m. worth something 9940
An honest m. the noblest work of
God 5885
As m. ingratitude 6249
best portions of a good m. life
6664
broad world of m. voyage 3689
business to do will of God 566
capacity for justice makes
democracy possible 2528
chief enemy own unruly nature
3165
Christ, God's everything for m.
total need 6427
conquest of nature astonishing
7414
Conscience, m. most faithful friend
1695
craving is for the spiritual 9546
desire to stand out 7415
dignity to stand upright 7395
discontent his worst evil 2860
Every m. life a plan of God 6888
Every m. life lies within present
8374
Every scrap of wise m. time worth
saving 11913
extraordinary capacity for success
10819
extremity is God's opportunity
8218
eyes have great power 3563
failure to conquer human nature
tragic 7414
faith is m. weakness leaning on
God's strength 3775
Far deeper than m. deepest hate
4776
fight with himself worth
something 1063
finger of God on a m. shoulder
7314
Forgiveness m. deepest need 4077
free will, God's sovereign will
1149

From m. face can read his character 8494

from m. mouth can tell what he is 5126

funny old world, m. lucky if gets out alive 6936

God clothed himself in vile m. flesh 6126

God has interest in m. being good 5060

God incomprehensible, inaccessible to m. understanding 4728

God is in the cavern of m. sin 10434

God looks at m. heart before brains 7378

God made rich by m. necessity 4541

God never sets limit to m. freedom 4130

God sums up m. worth by his character 11238

God's eternity, m. mortality 2288

God's gifts put m. best dreams to shame 4988

great m. foolish sayings pass for wise ones 5273

great m. world bounded by limits of vision 11728

greatness of a m. power is his surrender 10975

happy m. without a shirt 11857

heart right when wills what God wills 2566

highest function of m. mind is to listen to God's Word 7766

Holy Spirit dos not obliterate a m. personality 5798

home are God's thoughts 1790

I want to be white m. brother 1485

in this world as in another m. house 7077

inclination to injustice makes democracy necessary 2528

inhumanity makes thousands mourn 30

jealous m. horns hang in his eyes 6337

judgment, God's not m. 6591

learn more from m. errors than his virtues 3262

less sound m. argument, louder he talks 448

life, illustration of Christianity 1177

love is of m. life a thing apart 7278

make m. past as though it had never been 9800

Many a m. reputation would not know character 9618

mind is the Holy of Holies 7759

naive m. weakness, child's strength 7977

need to blend in 7415

neighbor is everyone that needs help 913

no slander can alter m. character 1060

no way to kill m. righteousness but by consent 11102

nothing certain in m. life 954

One m. music, another's noise 7918

One m. word is no m. word 6618

psychological makeup probably due to body 1030

reach should exceed grasp 4420

Religion is m. quest for God 9545

right to happiness anti-God 5553

Righteousness should be m. pursuit 5001

sap m. strength: worry, travel, sin 10406

second half of m. life habits acquired 5501

self his greatest cross 9919

Self-knowledge grows out of m. self-confrontation with God 10018

Self-love a mote in every m. eye 10026

sorrows will not let me sleep 1548

soul where m. battles are fought 10672

speech is like his life 10684

spiritual health proportional to love for God 4793

strength of m. virtues measured by habitual acts 5502

sun as bright as from rich m. abode 7001

Surrendering to despair m. favorite pastime 2607

test a m. character, give him power 8706

test of m. character is his tongue 11414

text, Christianity 1177

the other eye to see m. lowliness 3562

the whole of the good m. creed 2028

thou sick m. health 5932

thoughts belong to world of intellect 10692

three events in m. life 7050

'Tis m. to fight 10775

to hold m. foot long enough 9316

true joy of m. life in relationship to God 9467

unique agony as a species 7415

value in likeness to God 7366

war uses m. best to do m. worst 11763

what m. journey is about 7435

What wicked do should not disturb good m. tranquility 11894

when m. central confidence transferred to God 5645

When success turns m. head he faces failure 10826

While coldly discussing a m. career 6599

Why does one m. yawning make another yawn 6247

Work is m. great function 12024

world above m. head 11627

world has become nervous 420

world, encompassed by anxiety 420

world, reflection of m. face 436

MANSION

Narrow is the m. of my soul 10658

MANSIONS

Love is needed in the m. 7251

preaches from villas to slums about m. in heaven 6065

MANSOUL

remain king within kingdom of M. 2821

MANUFACTURE

church ceases to m. blood cells 3341

MANURE

Money is like m. 7812

MANY

a man threatens while quakes for fear 3981

Among so m. can he care 4834

are called but most frozen 3045

avenues of attractiveness to God 7532

But, how m. were sorry when he passed away 7423

Christians already have future behind them 4321

church has m. tasks 3328

eager to share in Jesus' table 9268

excluded by gospel 5093

fears are tissue-paper thin 3982

Glory endowed on m. who did not pursue 4407

God fulfills himself m. ways 978

God made so m. of the common man 4545

good name got by m. actions, lost by one 9611

great things expressed in single words 10277

have forgotten value of traditions 3876

have shining qualities beneath rough exterior 8658

helpers, see God in all your helpers 11490

If bring into one day's thoughts evil of m. 12064

Jesus has m. who love his heavenly kingdom 9268

kinds of smiles 10500

little wave of emotion enough for m. 4471

men know how to flatter 7586

might have failed beneath trial 4236

miracles like m. still long for 3782

miserable to have m. things to fear 11827

moments hostile to truth 11551

neighborliness more important now because so m. 8068

not how m. years we live 6933

observations, little reasoning leads to truth 9410

Of one ill, come m. 1736

Our m. advantages do us harm 9337

people think they think 8476

puzzled about origin of evil 3383

religions, but one gospel 9547

see, few understand 8501

So m. men, so m. opinions 8202

stay walled up afraid of being hurt 4290

want consolation, few desire adversity 9268

Where much desire to learn, m. opinions 6711

who has m. friends, has none 4187

world has m. religions, one gospel 5106

MAR
Man did not make, and cannot m. 8430

MARATHON
Fathering is a m, not a sprint 3919

Married life is a m. 7646

MARBLE
education to soul like sculpture to block of m. 3038

If we work upon m, it will perish 6796

Write injuries in dust, benefits in m. 9523

MARBLES
can choose to be bag of m. 9524

Christians can be like sack of m. 1273

made to be counted, kept 9524

scar and clank 9524

MARCH
And the atoms m. in tune 1976

homeowner's favorite 9888

in the m. of God's armies 4712

life a battle and a m. 7087

No one objects to M. coming in like a lion 9889

of providence is so slow 5944

of that eternal harmony 2268

of the human mind is slow 11245

thunder rolls like drums in m. of God's armies 7997

We m, but have not progressed an inch 9309

MARCHED
All armies that ever m. 6353

MARCHING
Obedience means m. feel like it or not 8104

MARIONETTES
God has no need of m. 1142

MARITAL
conflict cancers that gnaw on the soul 3873

MARK
as an arrow to the m. to stick there 4222

everywhere he passes, man leaves some kind of m. 6231

God is quick to m. effort to please 4810

Gossip may not stick but leaves m. 5129

ingratitude the unfailing m. of a narrow soul 6251

left their m. on earth 5656

of friend makes you at your best 4192

MARKED
he who has m. off forbidden ground finds yoke easy 1332

work that God m. out for you 6204

MARKET
is sacred as well as sanctuary 5770

The m. price, they said 3483

MARKET-DRIVEN
churches 1407

MARKETPLACE
cross raised at center of m. 2131

Jesus' work was in m. 3331

Love is needed in the m. 7251

one of God's abiding places 4866

ought to be a sanctuary 4866

MARKS
hurry, impatience m. of the amateur 6113

MARRED
Let there be naught unfinished, broken, m. 7519

MARRIAGE
a movement, a boundless adventure 7630

a perpetual test of character 7637

an edifice that must be rebuilt every day 7597

an institution, but not a reform school 7643

Better break the engagement than the m. 7605

burdens are delightful 7635

cannot make anyone happier 7632

Chains do not hold a m. together 7608

Christianity has glorified m. 1200

demands divorce from self-love 7596

dependence mutual 7642

does not make us better 7633

does not make us worse 7633

don't think m. built on sex can last 10229

doubles our joys 7634

family grounded on m. freely contracted 3890

fuller of sorrows, joys than single life 7635

God made m. an indissoluble contract 2924

good m. not where perfection reigns 7591

good m. overlooks "unresolvables" 7591

halves our griefs 7634

happy m. union of two forgivers 7593

has less beauty than single life 7635

has less danger than single life 7635

has more care than single life 7635

has more safety than single life 7635

independence equal 7642

Infinitely rewarding at its best 7641

intensifies what is already there 7633

is a desperate thing 7636

is adventure, not an achievement 7638

is for a lifetime 7641

is heaven or hell 7639

is like a cage 7640

is more merry and sad than single life 7635

is not for a moment 7641

is supported by strengths of love 7635

is the alarm clock 7631

keep eyes half shut after m. 7624

keep eyes wide open before m. 7624

Knowing when to say nothing, 90 percent of m. 7626

lies under more burdens 7635

like long trip in tiny rowboat 7595

Love blind, m. restores sight 7629

man responsible for maintenance 7613

me first philosphy power to blow m. to pieces 10087

Money and m. make devils or saints 7805

most intimate and difficult of relationships 7641

no perfect m, no perfect people 7657

not a state 7630

not m. but people that fail 7622

not to be leaped into 7641

obligation reciprocal 7642

offers extremes of happiness, bondage 7641

paper torn up at whim 2924

quadruples our expenses 7634

requires long, serious preparation 7641

resembles a pair of shears 7644

sexual incompatibility in m. 10227

solution for loneliness rarely satisfies 7666

Success in m. is being the right person 7652

Success in m. more than finding
right person 7652
Successful m. always a triangle
7653
successful m. an achievement
7598
successful m. not a gift 7598
take two to make m. a success
7623
takes only one to make m. a
failure 7623
to be entered with deliberation
7641
tolerance that m. demands 7648
too impatient to make
adjustments m. entails 7648
trade my fortune for one happy m.
7619
unspeakably oppressive at its
worst 7641
value of m. not that adults
produce children 7669
value of m. that children produce
adults 7669
When m. works nothing can take
its place 7664
Where m. without love will be
love without m. 7667
who does not bring ingredients
for happiness into m. 7632
will require all-out investment
7647
with peace is world's paradise
7645
with strife is life's purgatory 7645
world has made m. scrap of paper
2924

MARRIAGES
Most divorces not bad m. 2926
Most divorces poorly prepared m.
2926
moving toward world of
throwaway m. 10524

MARRIED
couple m. for trivial reasons 2922
Getting m. is easy 7615
life is a marathon 7646
life offers no panacea 7647
Octembruary, best month to get m.
9881
Pray three hours before getting m.
7650
Staying happily m. should rank
among the fine arts 7615
Staying m. more difficult 7615
waits to become his own boss,
then gets m. 3867
would have m. the wrong man
8797

MARRY
Centenarians seldom m, old
enough to know better 7607
Don't m. for money, can borrow
cheaper 7612
golfer should m. woman who
would rather shop than cook
7656

If afraid of loneliness, don't m.
7128
immortals whom we m. 8483
To m. woman for her beauty 7661
vowed never to m. until found
ideal woman 7665
who m. to escape unhappy home
7660

MARRYING
end of m. when end of living 7667
There's no m. in heaven, that's
why its heaven 7658

MARTYR
cannot be dishonored 8528
Christ did not die a m. 2126
Christ was born a m. 6489
death of Jesus not the death of a
m. 6472
dies, his rule begins 7679
faith must be prepared to be m.
3642
Jesus Christ, not blood of m. 497
Lord was not a m. 9437
the cause, not the death, makes
the m. 7675

MARTYRDOM
Christianity made m. sublime
1166
cross, beatification of m. 2118
does not end something 7676
intensity, not correctness of belief
1911
is only the beginning 7676
Love makes difference between
execution, m. 7263

MARTYR'S
only John escapes a m. grace 2825

MARTYRS
accused of efforts to find truth
11501
Bible, congregation of m. 716
others die m. 6489
Painting enables us to see
constancy of m. 2015
put on coronation robes glittering
with fire 10882
put to death by painful methods
1211
put to death down the long
centuries 1211
Saints, apostles, prophets, m.
6892
when the joyful crown is given
7672

MARVEL
Man the greatest m. in the
universe 7497
not that he performed miracles
6503
Of m. or surprise 6916
that he performed so few miracles
6503
You are a m. 3039

MARVELOUS
expect m. things to happen 3830
How m. that I, a filthy clod 8814

In old age faith most m. possession
8138

MARY
Had M. been filled with reason
9414
if M. and Joseph decided 25

MARY'S
contemplative life M. part 1764
The Christ child stood at M. knee
6470
Tommy's tears and M. fears 4003

MASK
easier to wear m. 6057
Insolence pride when m. pulled off
2917
Jesus pulls each person from
behind m. 9741
Pain wears no m. 10583
When m. of self-righteousness
torn from us 5238

MASKS
torn away, hollow smiles fade
9741

MASS
After two thousand years of m.
11739
attractiveness of m. movement
10526
communication aid in evangelism
3317
in corporateness of m. movement,
new freedom 10526
of men lead lives of quiet
desperation 2610

MASSES
of people fall victims to great lie
7974
prevents himself by becoming one
of the m. 6209
Your huddled m, yearning to
breathe free 7985

MASS-PRODUCED
You weren't m. 10004

MASTER
adversary a m. strategist 2660
As I would not be slave, I would
not be m. 2520
as the M. shall the servant be
10604
be a good m. 3099
Care admitted as guest turns to m.
12058
Christian finds peace in accepting
m. plan 8440
Death not m. of the house 2253
does not truly become lord or m.
11674
dog barks when his m. is attacked
99
either m. or slave 7096
first duty of soul is to find its M.
4144
give till the M. stops giving to you
10728
Gold slave or m. 11815
great word to m, short 7000

If a m. be sometimes blind 2896
It is the way the M. went 10133
Jesus Christ never insists on being M. 8106
Judas kiss'd his M. 630
Luxury a nice m, hard to be pleased 7363
Money a dangerous m. 7809
money will be your m. 11822
multitude is a fickle m. 10517
No man free who is no m. of himself 4139
nothing done God is not M. 4937
over self advanced by prayer 8976
power of love will lead to m. of the art 7352
Prayer enables man to m. situation 8927
present is all of which man is m. 8384
servant of God has good M. 1329
temptation for man to meet and m. 11122
time with the M. will elevate thinking 8865
to grow old m. work of wisdom 8178
We m. fear through faith 4005
What wilt thou, M, have of me 1538
when M. of earth calls shots, things happen 3819
where apathy is the m, all men slaves 427
who serves God has a good M. 10149
word remains unspoken, you are m. 1835
Youth wants m, controller 12180

MASTER ARCHITECT
Bible, blueprint of M. 679

MASTERED
beyond what you have m. 68 2758

MASTERING
Faith m. difficulty in strength of Lord 3678

MASTERPIECE
God's action m. of partiality, love 4747
life, a vast, obscure unfinished m. 6904
Man heaven's m. 1965
real m. of life 3107
Self-righteousness the devil's m. 10039
When love, skill work together expect a m. 12020

MASTERPIECES
Flowers are heaven's m. 8003
neurotics have composed our m. 4390

MASTER'S
Christian home is the M. workshop 5850

MASTERS
Emotions should not be m. 3055
help us to be m. of ourselves 9096
of their souls 1293
passions are bad m. 10225
try to be own m. as if created ourselves 5570
We cannot be our own m. 7552
who seeks to serve two m. misses benediction 1332

MASTERY
Jesus Christ, absolute m. over everything 2170

MATCH
God made women to m. the men 3231
Real friends don't care if socks don't m. 4264

MATCHED
beside foolishness and weakness of the Christian 10512

MATE
You'll never see perfection in your m. 7671

MATERIAL
Bread for myself m. question 622
God does not promise he will protect from m. cares 5385
Great men see spiritual stronger than m. force 10693
love a delicacy unknown in m. substances 4789
no distinction between spiritual, m. work 6985

MATERIALISM
organized emptiness of spirit 8633

MATERIALISTIC
concerns never sufficient 8634
unjust, m. status quo 8696

MATHEMATICAL
not the road of m. conviction 3793

MATHEMATICIAN
universe seems designed by pure m. 1974

MATHEMATICIANS
great m. uncovered truth already there 1958

MATHEMATICS
if God observes m. 4454
set to music 4454

MATRIX
God the m. of our personality 7557

MATTER
before m. came into being 4694
begin to discuss things that m. 4029
Dirt is m. in wrong place 5121
doesn't m. how great the pressure 185
Friendship independent of m, space, time 4233
God alters the things that m. 9276

God knows all m. 4881
In infinite time, m, space 6927
Let God handle the m. 184
Life a m. of content 6970
Little things that m. most 9267
man more powerful than m 1474
not brains that m. most 1027
nothing evil in m. itself 3407
Nothing the M. Here 3878
of life and death 616
Peace is when time doesn't m. as it passes by 8461

MATTERED
two things m, God and people 3331
what m. was Father's will done 4425

MATTERS
And to make bad m. worse 2589
Everything in Christianity that m. from individual to individual 6176
God knows all m. 4881
guarantees guidance in m. unrevealed 5435
In great m. men show themselves as they wish to be seen 7391
In natural m. faith follows evidence 3743
in small m. men as they are 7391
In spiritual m, human reasoning not in order 9416
liberty to know God alone m. 4151
not what happens that m. 508
not what we do that m. 8094
What m. is intentions, behavior 3051
what m. is not how long, but how good 6935

MATTHEW
will rejoice little in M. 5224

MATURE
As love grows older, hearts m. 7236
begin to m, obey commandments unconsciously 7690
believer a searching believer 7700
God disciplines us so we can m. spiritually 2844
Jesus gave world such m. insights 6196
life unconscious consecration 1714
love says "I need you because love you" 7194
not m. enough to enter into friendship unless 4247
Who is m. enough for offspring before offspring arrive 7669

MATUREST
stage, God does his will unconsciously 7690

MATURING
larger process of m. than we can see 10884

MATURITY
allowing a child space to grow up 7696
concern for others outweighing concern for yourself 7693
environment in which m. can be achieved 4721
God's mercies ever in their m. 5657
honesty and m. equally hard to attain 5873
is life under control of God 7685
letting a friend have freedom to be and do 7696
no formula to teach m. 7705
no shortcuts to m. 5738
not to hide one's strength out of fear 7695
product of process is m. 1105
quest for excellence m. 3469
quiet confidence God is in control 7697
releasing a dream 7696
Spiritual m. confidence God is in control 10709
to be comfortable with people not like us 7694
unwillingness to lie to oneself 5873
without need to understand why God does what he does 7697

MAXIM
Graved a m. true, wise 974

MAXIMS
are illuminators, not directors 6816
miserable in measuring each other by own moral m. 6826

MAXIMUM
trying to live m. life on minimum faith 3770

MAY
April showers bring M. flowers 9884
He that will not when he m. 8216
In every snow, the promised M. 8009

MAZE
an endless road, a hopeless m. 8638
real man is m. of a million notes 6212
Without God world m. without clue 4522
Yet, in the maddening m. of things 4642

ME
always at the bottom of sin 9916
God is my m. 7462
grow young as I leave my m. behind 9920
least used word by unselfish person 11653
only thing he would change was m. 967
sin may spell pride but is some form of "m." 9916

that bubble is m. 6927
yourself and m. 9958

ME FIRST
philosophy of "m." 10087

MEADOWS
infinite m. of heaven 11636

MEAGER
no life so m. greatest can afford to despise it 7055
not generous with m. income 4366
We try to speak of large or m. talents 4710

MEAGERNESS
richness of God, m. of men 9784

MEAL
Be the m. of beans and peas 5860
Christ unseen guest at every m. 5823
Every m. shared in love a feast 5825

MEALS
Christ will turn m. into sacraments 5529

MEAN
among the m. is where Jesus went 2812
and petty man's desires 7381
cross we bear seems m. 2116
Even m. man has value 3159
However m. your life is, meet it and live it 6903
If I am m, God will appear m. 1050
learn from m. man how not to live 3159
Love is m. in its own sight 7246
Nobody will know what you m. by "God is love" 7281
Simplicity has no m. thoughts 11696
'Tis because I am m, thy ways look m. 1050
When we are m, God still unalterable I Am 4587

MEANER
time grows m, more hostile 3268

MEANEST
hut with love a palace for the soul 5816
Lives for the m. mortal known 10085
word is hypocrisy 11993

MEANING
before his teaching has any m. 6401
believed in God, world had m. 7011
can fill tiny span of life with m. 7080
Christ's teaching no m. unless enter his life 6424
darkest providences have m. 4885
Doubt, robbing life of glow, m. 6091

enhanced m. in life 1168
Every time you pray new feeling and m. 8769
faith alone gave life m. 7472
faith in m. of pain and striving 4005
give up measuring m. with yardstick of others 10162
God alone knows m. of mystery called time 4694
Good is a principle of m. 5023
If you do not love, do not know m. of Christian life 7191
Jesus redefines m. of love 7201
least of things with m. worth more 7030
Life will take on greater m. 3185
life, once key to m. in our hands 6940
Live out life in its full m. 6998
Living is learning m. of words 7000
Man can endure suffering if m. 10871
Man can only find m. outside himself 3484
Nothing in world without m. 4903
of earthly existence is development of the soul 9342
on the face of the high hills 4962
Only eternal values give m. to temporal ones 11311
prayer gives solitude real m. 10562
promises that point to real m. 9351
sick person faced with m. of things 6086
solving problems that life has m. 2736
than greatest of things without m. 7030
unfolds, strangeness vanishes 6145
When goal goes, m. goes 4437
When m. goes, value goes 4437

MEANINGFUL
experience criterion for truth 3493
In Christ move into m. present 8364
larger context which makes life m. 10871

MEANINGLESS
Boredom, barren, m. existence 865
compatible with everything 1578
dream is not m. 2968
life turns m. 4437
prefer m. activites to being alone 10575
To discuss authority of God seems m. 4955
When people serving, life no longer m. 10212

MEANINGS
Honesty, no hidden m. 5874
in Bible three m. of grace 5227

MEANLY
Resolved, never to think m. 569

MEANNESS
despise nothing except falsehood, m. 8472

MEANS
By all the m. you can 10126
decide all m. permitted to fight evil 5012
good end cannot sanctify evil m. 5010
if sufficient will, always sufficient m. 7869
Love's end sweetens all its m. 6457
of aiding progess so feeble 5944
of glorifying God, salvation of souls 7027
who m. well useless unless does well 6335

MEANT
How come he thought I m. it 11507
When God knows we m. to do his will 4810
winning friends m. most 4303

MEASURE
a thousand times, cut once 2783
by which action to be judged 7307
cannot speak of m. and God 4680
dignity of individuals m. of civilization 3894
family m. of greatness of nation 3894
futile as yardstick that will m. infinity 5718
God giveth his mercy without m. 4811
growth in grace by sensitiveness to sin 10335
his grace has no m. 7570
How can we m. the greatness of God 4673
however small visible m. of our lives 6232
if we m. our lives against eternity 7080
importance of events by recently happened 7990
love does not m. by merchant's scales 4789
Love is fervent beyond m. 7283
merits to m. the worth of a man 7423
nor m. words 4260
not God's love by your feeling 4772
Who neither knows m. nor end 4787

MEASURED
distance one should keep from wicked cannot be m. 11888
have not m. fingers with God 4337
power that m, weighed, spanned world 4592
True greatness m. by 5306

virtues m. by habitual acts 5502
worth of man m. by objects pursued 469

MEASURELESS
God is m. 4710
God's love is m. 4760

MEASUREMENT
God above, outside, beyond all m. 4710

MEASUREMENTS
cannot apply to God 4710
Our concepts of m. can never embrace God 4680

MEASURES
When God m. a man 4576
When God m. men in next world 6112

MEASURING
give up m. value with yardstick of others 10162
miserable m. each other by own moral maxims 6826

MEAT
we have m. and we can eat 11159
Work is the m. of life 12028

MECHANICAL
God's love personal, not m. 4782
obedience would be m. business 8091

MECHANICS
of religion 1301

MEDALS
God will not look for m. 172
Lord promised cross not m. 2102

MEDDLE
Don't m. with that which does not concern you 5122
snob has little time to m. with you 455

MEDDLES
man m. they become evil 5019

MEDIA
provided devil with opportunity 2698

MEDICINE
Bible, such excellent m. 717
Death, Physician of him whom m. cannot cure 2260
gigantic strides in m. 2928
God feels pulse, prescribes m. 4449
Grief is itself a m. 5336
Labor powerful m. 3103
laugh, it is cheap m. 6716
Love is m. for sickness of world 7250
Mirth is God's m. 6738
Money brings m. but not health 7807
Music m. of troubled mind 7908
refusing to accept m. 1276
Words are like m. 272

MEDICINES
Trials are m. we need 224

MEDIOCRE
Great spirits always opposition from m. minds 5282
minds talk about things 1845
most Christians are m. 1302

MEDIOCRITY
uniformity produces m. 3244

MEDITATE
open at random, close book, m. 9387

MEDITATES
guilty is he who merely m. a crime 5490

MEDITATING
easier to walk six miles than spend quarter hour m. 7716

MEDITATION
Every Christian can elevate himself by m. 7707
is disciplined thought 7721
is the kernel 7726
is the soul's chewing 7717
lost art of century is m. 7721
object of Jesus' m. was his Father 12128
refreshes, restores, renews minds 8857
silence in the presence of God 7707
souls acts no longer except by divine impulse 7707
that does not make a difference short-circuited 7725
unless results in richer relationships 7725

MEEK
answer lies in the word itself 7729
approval not to m. but self-assertive 5891
Bow thy m. head to mortal pain 2981
cross radiant with glory of m gentle spirit 5252
Gentle Jesus, m. and mild 1117
in a m, thankful heart 5621
means educable 7729
means emotionally stable 7729
means kind 7729
means mighty 7729
not arrogant, inherit earth 1216
O blessed are the patient m. 6274

MEEKLY
must wait for God m. 5460

MEEKNESS
Christ, Lamb in m. 6425
deepest conception of m. 7728
is love in school 7202
is not weakness 7730
that Christ pronounced blessed 7728

MEET

a man who enjoys reputation of being most remarkable person he knows 9197

a man who has no smile, give him yours 10496

a mirror to reflect your love to all I m. 9079

different race, color to yourself 3234

Everyone you m. fighting hard battle 6635

Everyone you m. is your mirror 9441

flatterers m, devil goes to dinner 4054

for a moment, sail out of sight 4281

Go forth to m. shadowy future 8378

God can m. and overflow deepest demands 7463

great challenges which ordinary men rise to 8668

heaven, expect to m. some had not thought to see 5655

If only one could refuse to m. his Old Age 8136

ill-luck, some run halfway to m. it 11449

Jesus, where'er thy people m. 12108

Kind words toward those you daily m. 6647

never twain shall m. 915

People m. superficial needs 4310

ready to m. my Maker 2302

Spirit with Spirit can m. 4862

steady, unrelenting approach of him whom I desired not to m. 9829

temptation for man to m. and master 11122

To find point where hypothesis, fact m. 7435

To m. God a terrifying adventure 4551

We turn to m. another year 8082

when mind of man, God m. 949

Whenever two people m. 7443

who has one enemy shall m. him everywhere 9459

Women and men in the crowd m, mingle 7150

MEETING

No man comes to himself without m. God 1907

MEETS

God at every turn 4847

God m. us on level where we operate 5439

happens to light upon passage which m. need 5441

mystery of Christ's existence m. wants of man 5728

MEGAPHONE

Pain, God's m. to rouse a deaf world 8257

MELANCHOLY

hell on earth found in m. heart 2548

is disease 1089

lifted out of m. by prayer 8764

proven that m. undermine health 5612

that stems from greatness of mind 5303

MELLOWNESS

change heart of lead into golden m. 10628

MELODY

Could blind chance create m. 1958

In the rain God is sweetening thy m. 10600

Oh, surely m. from heaven was sent 7917

rests not to destroy m. 9684

song is ended, m. lingers 7924

Unto thy praise, all love and m. 7928

MELT

and remould my life, till it be 7003

sun makes ice m. 6668

MELTED

avalanches Napoleon hurled m. away 730

present has m. in our grasp 11389

MELTS

away like smoke 11288

MEMBER

if every m. like me 1454

love, gift open to every m. of the church 7235

without choice man a m. 4155

MEMBERS

Christ dined with lowest m. of society 6433

worthy m. of family whose father is in heaven 5001

MEMBERSHIP

deeper than list of sins on m. card 10300

disqualified for m. in Kingdom of God 4133

MEMORIAL

service: farewell party for someone already left 2324

MEMORIES

easy to turn religious life into beautiful m. 10165

God gave us m. that we might have roses in December 7732

home, cultivate m. 5832

nothing but blurred m. 8353

words breathe m. sweet as flutes 11998

MEMORIZE

anxiously m. the script assigned 6824

not only verses, but chapters 9970

MEMORIZING

of Scripture help in doubt 747

MEMORY

alone remains 8082

Bible like m. of mother 653

cabinet of imagination 7733

capacity of human mind fabulous 7738

controls youth 7735

council chamber of thought 7733

delights old age 7735

diary we carry with us 7734

ecumenical movement brings back m. 2990

faultfinder, person with good or bad m. 2049

funerals destructive to true m. 2311

Gratitude is heart's m. 5246

is private literature 7731

its force and worth 981

Lord's Prayer committed to m. quickly 7153

lose m. of past trials 7964

Love destroying all m. of a beginning 7229

Malice has a strong m. 9637

mitigates adversity 7735

No man has good enough m. to lie 6855

Nothing fixes thing so intensely in m. as wish to forget 7736

of child, "Could you be a daddy to me" 3920

Pithy sentences force truth upon our m. 9384

quotations when engraved upon m. give good thoughts 9383

registry of conscience 7733

remains of joy, griefs, gains 8082

retentive m. good thing 4068

tempers prosperity 7735

thoughts go into the m. of God 11280

treasury of reason 7733

With light of m. 11375

MEN

absurd to argue m. into believing 590

Abundance, like want, ruins m. 9335

afraid of m. who believe everything 586

After losses, m. grow humbler, wiser 5990

Alcohol, killed more m. than wars 331

alcohol, turned m. into brutes 331

All great m. make mistakes 7787

all m. alike 921

All m. at head of great movements are Christian m. 5094

all m. created equal 3246

All m. desire peace 8428

all m. different 921

All m. equal in death 3226

all m. have some misfortunes 828

All m. ignored in me 9981

All m. whilst awake in common world 2965

All m. would lead happy life 4227

All wicked m. are slaves 11881

And death what m. call life 7086

And felt the swiftly passing feet of m. 11330

And justify the ways of God to m. 7566

and nations sink or soar 10510

animals devoted to making one another unhappy 31

animated by love of Christ feel united 3081

are by nature equal 3225

are like wine 7419

are merely for themselves 10069

are not against you 10069

are so possessed by themselves 9938

are very queer animals 7420

as generation of leaves 7368

At profoundest depths m. talk not about God but with him 8767

Authentic m. aren't afraid to show affection 3916

become what they really are 9741

Believe, even if all m. go astray 583

best improve with age 7419

best of m. still sinners 3861

Better fare hard with good m. 4219

better to weep with wise m. than laugh with fools 9475

better world by making better m. 6487

Bible, illustrate ways of m. 737

born with two eyes, one tongue 3564

break through ordinary ways of m. 10564

build bridges 5841

but children of larger growth 7418

by themselves are priced 775

called Christ a glutton, winebibber 6436

Calvary erected to divide m. into two classes 2124

Christ came to make m. holy 6424

Christ came to redeem m. 6424

Christ ever at service of m. 1754

Christianity promises to make m. free 4116

come up to what is expected 3505

Converse with m. makes sharp the glittering wit 10534

Crafty m. condemn studies 2996

crowd treat great m. as lunatics 4393

cut themselves off from root of being, God 4437

dared to ask of m. what Christ asked 6419

death comes to young m. 2349

defeat makes m. invincible 2511

Democracy founded on dignity of all m. 2521

desert does not mean absence of m. 10565

devil tells lies about m. 1060

devil's country begins where m. eat m. 4913

Difficulties show what m. are 2735

Do not judge m. by appearances 431

does not take great m. 1723

entangled by their tongues 11409

evil that m. do lives after them 5043

Example a lesson all m. can read 3430

expect too much, do too little 3504

Experience, comb nature gives m. when bald 3518

Eyes let me be to groping m. and blind 10130

fail through lack of purpose 4427 3608

Faith belongs to m. in God 3698

fear death as children fear dark 2335

fear death refuse to understand 2336

fear thought 11232

fear without love makes m. desperate 9736

feeling I could outlast all m. 12165

few m. know how to praise 7586

Few m. so obstinate in atheism 479

Few m. worthy of experience 3534

Find me m. on earth who care 4118

for good m. to do nothing 3402

For most m. world is centered in self 8436

for troubles wrought of m, patience is hard 11464

Fortune does not change m. 11807

Fortune unmasks m. 11807

from supernaturally born m. 10206

full of fragility 7437

full of the Spirit look right into heaven 5651

give advice, God gives guidance 5433

give charity 511

Give few m. thy voice 1843

Give me such love for God and m. 7170

God allows m. to live without him 1142

God created m. to be holy 5757

God does allow bad m. to triumph 4957

God give us m. 6299

God governs in affairs of m. 4933

God governs through m. 8099

God is the author, m. the players 5639

God judging m. with perfect knowledge 4720

God judging m. with undisturbed compassion 4720

God judging m. with unperplexed certainty 4720

God looking for better m. 1436

God looks for better m. 7501

God made women to match the m. 3231

God not an eternal blessing machine for m. 5757

God pays m. compliment 1142

God promised to be active among m. 5724

God scarcely vindicates his saints to m. 11616

God seems careless whether m. understand him 11616

God send us m. with hearts ablaze 7986

God wills the development of all m. 9351

God's country begins where m. love to serve 4913

gold is touchstone to try m. 11836

golden age only comes when m. have forgotten gold 11856

good m. obey from love 5053

gospel is Savior God seeking lost m. 9545

gospel what God has done for m. 9545

governed by m. worse than themselves 5193

governments instituted among m. 3246

gratitude of m. to Father in heaven 5253

gratitude of most m. is secret desire of greater benefits 5262

great challenges ordinary m. meet 8668

great doers of history always m. of faith 5723

Great hopes make great m. 5277

great m. have curious feeling 5291

great m. incredibly merciful 6032

Great m. meteors designed to burn so earth lighted 5278

Great m. never feel great 7380

Great m. never know they are great 5279

great m. not commonly great scholars 5302

great m. see divine in every other man 6032

Great m. see spiritual stronger than material force 10693

Great m. stand like solitary towers 5280

great majority of m. exist, do not live 7028

greatest truths are simplest, so are greatest m. 5298

grimmer is that m. be reduced to subhuman state 10503

ground keeps, guards, cares for m. 3199

Guilt by judgment of m. false guilt 5477

have guided missiles, misguided m. 9868

have never been, are not, never will be good 7421

have perpetrated horrors against one another 2667

have touchstone to try gold 11836

he injures good m. who spare wicked 6608

He is sifting out the hearts of m. 4715

Heaven not where m. sleep out eternity 5644

heights of great m. reached and kept 8566

hell, when m. abandoned by God 5698

highest love, the love of Christ for m. 6506

history contest between God, Satan, fallen m. 4916

holiness shares with angels, redeemed m. 4658

how transient is noblest monument m. build 730

humility makes m. as angels 6020

I have seen succeed 10816

I keep six honest serving m. 6686

If all m. pulled in one direction 6184

if m. ride him 4063

If m. thanked God for good things 11150

If m. would consider wherein they agree 9465

If not for injustice, m. would not know justice 6264

If poll taken to name six greatest m. in world 9988

if we imbue m. with high principles 6796

immutability of God, mutability of m. 977

In great matters m. as they wish to be seen 7391

in m. change impossible to escape 977

in small matters m. as they are 7391

In the day when all m. stand before God 4718

independent of disapproval of m. 1647

insist on making life complicated 6977

Jesus offends m. because emphasis on unseen life 6450

Knowledge dwells in heads replete with thoughts of m. 6690

learn to pray as they learn to love 8914

lifts m. up to their Father in heaven 5844

like m. who sleep badly 5541

little from God better than great deal from m. 4524

live on brink of mysteries 3654

Lives of great m. all remind us 5288

look for better methods 7501

look for God, fancy him concealed 8019

love of God makes better m. 7303

love of wealth makes bitter m. 7303

love without fear makes m. remiss 9736

m. most sure and arrogant, usually most mistaken 458

make m. giddy, proud, and vain 8702

makes cowards out of m. 6282

Man more interesting than m. 6200

Many m. know how to flatter 7586

Many m. owe grandeur to difficulties 2739

mass of m. lead lives of quiet desperation 2610

may despise grace of God, but cannot extinguish it 4655

millions of m. would die for Jesus Christ 6351

more apt to agree in do than think 62

more lonely among m. than in our chambers 10572

more m. suppress truth, more futile in thinking 11538

more one approaches great m, more one finds they are m. 5300

more or less ignore meaning of cross 2122

more prone to revenge injuries than requite kindnesses 9720

Most judge m. only by success 6584

most positive m. are most naive 7975

most virtuous m. also bitterest, unhappy 6821

must be governed by God 4137

must not turn into bees 9721

naturally tempted by the devil 6770

Nature gave m. two ends 10793

Nearly all m. can stand adversity 8706

Neutral m. are devil's allies 8071

Never know how accessible m. are 3345

never the same after listening to Christ 6377

never violate laws of God without consequences 10336

no great m, only great challenges 8668

Nobody can judge m. but God 4720

O greedy m, what will satisfy if God himself will not 7508

of 70 and 80 often more youthful than the young 12198

Of all ills that m. endure 5932

of cold passions have quick eyes 3565

of few words are best 1860

of genius often dull, inert in society 4395

of same earth by same Creator 3225

Old m. go to death 2349

Old m. lose lives by ripeness 12197

Older m. declare war 11757

only happy when object of life not happiness 5540

Only solitary m. know full joys of friendship 4261

only when m. begin to worship, begin to grow 12107

Only when we have knelt before God can we stand before m. 8880

opinion in good m. is knowledge in the making 6711

overlooked a baby's birth 6458

pay for not being interested in politics 5193

peace expresses itself in love for m. 8469

Peace made in hearts of m. 8457

Poor m. need no guards 8686

possible for bad m. to become good 9438

Practical m. know where they are 8482

Pray to be stronger m. 8780

prayed for power that he might have the praise of m. 8806

prefer prosperous error to afflicted truth 3261

pursue pleasure with breathless haste 8601

quiet life characteristic of great m. 5274

raise question whether m. are significant 7481

reading books conversation with finest m. 861

resemble deserted palaces 1715

revivals altered hearts of m. 9752

Riches have made more m. covetous 11848

richness of God, meagreness of m. 9784

right with God has often meant in trouble with m. 9507

saints carry on intercession for all m. 8859

see m. of worth, become like them 1065

seek crowns of gold 2152

seldom flatter without purpose 4051

Shame arises from fear of m. 3988

should put an enemy in their mouths 332

showing unto m. of truth after truth 4906

shows greatness by way he treats little m. 5272

sigh on, not knowing what the soul wants 7516

simple m. admire studies 2996

Small m. never feel small 7380

So many m, so many opinions 8202

Some m. dream of worthy accomplishments 89

some turn to vinegar 7419

Sorrow makes m. sincere 10618

sorry for m. who do not read Bible 661

speak of yoke of Christ as slavery 2816

spiritual power uses m. 8715

Strength the lot of a few privileged m. 8557

Stronger by weakness 7701

struggling against adversity, yet happy 249

stumble over pebbles, never over mountains 2513

takes consecrated m. to do great things 1723

talking to God for m. greater still 8969

Talking to m. for God great thing 8969

than great m. of ancient and modern times 6449

things desirable to m. in Bible 641

Things holy revealed only to m. who are holy 5769

think God is destroying when tuning 290

think heroes of tragedy great 10877

think highly of those who rise rapidly 3857

Though m. spin cunning schemes 4887

throw railroads across deserts 5841

To blind m, Christ is sight 6391

To dead m, life is Christ 6391

To know all m. brothers 921

To m. he was a stranger 6133

to release m. from limitations 4135

to sick m, Christ is health 6391

treat m. the way they are, will never improve them 5971

treat m. the way you want them to be 5971

treat them gently, they will show themselves great 6807

truly known as no finite m. can know us 4768

Trust m. and they will be true to you 6807

truth does not vary because m. ignore 11540

Truth is heavy, few m. carry it 11565

two kinds of m. 10404

Two m. please God 4572

two strong m. stand face to face 915

unsuccessful m. with talent common 8555

use physical power 8715

wait upon m, dissipate energies 10764

we are not natural m. 1346

We know God as m. born blind know fire 4690

What God sends better than what m. ask 4991

What is from m. is uncertain 4524

What wicked m. do should not disturb good man's tranquility 11894

When clouds seen, wise m. put on coats 11960

When dark enough m. see stars 10929

When God measures m. in the next world 6112

when God sees m. rising up against fellowmen 4895

When good people cease vigilance, evil m. prevail 7991

When m. cease to be faithful to God 3849

when m. first saw their God 6154

When m. grow virtuous in old age 3183

When m. worship, God is satisfied 12137

when we see m. of contrary character 1065

where apathy master, all m. slaves 427

where m. sit and hear each other groan 7044

while m. go to prison, I'll fight 3342

who are lifting world upward 3142

who are unhappy proud of the fact 5541

who could not sin would not be m. 10337

who didn't know enough to tell God 6147

who have honor; m. who will not lie 6299

Who knows but life be that which m. call death 7086

who live with degree of serenity 5204

who possess opinions and a will 6299

who walk with God would not grieve enemies 3166

whom the lust of office does not kill 6299

whom the spoils of office cannot buy 6299

Wicked m. obey from fear 5053

wild animals when born 7382

will take withholding of honor from m. quietly 5901

Wise m. change their minds, fools never 11978

Wise m. not always silent, but know when to be 11977

Wise m. say nothing in dangerous times 11979

wise m. use studies 2996

wish to be saved from mischief of vices 10338

Women and m. in the crowd meet, mingle 7150

years to efface fault in eyes of m. 4091

Young m. lose lives by violence 12197

Young m. may die, old m. must 2433

MENACE

greatest most fearless under m. 5297

MEND

another thought can m. 11276

seek to m. 2840

MENDED

For him to see me m. 2128

reputation easily cracked, never well m. 9615

MENDING

Man lives by m. 4654

MENDS

Who errs and m, to God himself commends 3264

MEN'S

evil manners live in brass 9619

for healing m. lives must be changed within 5616

if we work upon m. immortal minds 6796

know nothing of m. rights 3230

Other m. sins before our eyes 10348

own heart, not m. opinions, form true honor 5896

weaknesses necessary to purposes of life 11788

MENTAL

activity mouthing of cliches 11237

God gives us m. ability to work in his kingdom 4648

slavery is m. death 7760

use leisure as means of m. development 5567

Worldliness m. slavery to illegitimate pleasure 12054

MENTALITY

ball-and-chain m. keeps us from giving 6825

MENTALLY

assent m. to God's control 5467

MENTION

not halter in house of him that was hanged 11285

MENTIONS

who loves something m. it often 7177

MERCHANT'S

love does not measure by m. scales 4789

MERCIES
faults like grain of sand beside mountain of m. of God 4817
God's m. ever in their maturity 5657
Gratitude born in hearts that count m. 5244
prayer opens to us God's m. 8846
tears so blind our eyes cannot see m. 10033
When all thy m. O my God 4819

MERCIFUL
discipline of being m. to the merciless 7746
God is to lift curtain on today 4318
great men are incredibly m. 6032
if God deny m. presence, fall into hell 4865
Is God not m. 10841
so m. held umbrella over duck 6641

MERCILESS
discipline of being merciful to the m. 7746

MERCY
a wideness in God's m. 7745
by practicing m. resemble God 7740
Christ infinite m, goodness 5208
comes down from heaven to earth 7740
confronting human misery, guilt 5206
demands m, shows none 4084
Every misery I miss a new m. 7739
false that God torn between justice, m. 4579
for them that fear and sin not 7742
Fountain of m! Whose prevailing eye 8792
God gives without weight his m. 4451
God has all m. to pardon you 4696
God in his m. made 4813
God of all m. a God unjust 4723
God's m. available in present situation 4815
God's m. can be experienced 7750
grace overwhelming, undeserved m. 5221
grace, the m. and love of God 5227
great thing expressed in single word 10277
hand folks over to God's m. 4105
His m. underlies 6916
if justice, m, prevail in own common life 6286
imitates God, disappoints Satan 7741
in thy m. receive us 619
like m. courtesy twice blessed 1944
Lord, let thy m. come 7743
may repent wrong choice 1159

money does not have me at its m. 11151
not effective until justice done 4730
not for them that sin and fear not 7742
not withholding abundance from unthankful 4581
O God, your m. is a boundless ocean 4816
one connected chain of justice, m, truth 4904
Open thy gate of m. gracious God 292
Our prayer, God's m. like two buckets in well 8884
pearl of justice found in heart of m. 6625
quality of m. is not strain'd 7744
Shall I doubt my Father's m. 2364
Sin is the rape of God's m. 10376
sincere convert will not neglect m. 1908
so long will I wait or look for m. 2590
Sometimes withhold in m. what we ask 8877
That m. I to others show 1552
That m. show to me 1552
the future his m. shall clear 8079
The good unask'd in m. grant 8979
the m. of eternity, our liberty 6384
The one is m, the next is love 4812
There they behold thy m. seat 12108
To added afflictions he addeth his m. 5223
to render deeds of m. 7747
Trust past to m. of God 5457
veil of future woven by hand of m. 4330
We do pray for m. 7747
We were children of wrath, now sons of m. 1348
yoke instrument of m. 2816

MERE
A m. drop suffices for me 4816

MERIT
Faith has no m. where reason provides proof 3665
faith no m. if reason provided proof 3841
greater m. in affliction than good works 234
greater m. to suffer affliction patiently 234
Jesus teaches no distinction of race, m, rank 913
Legalists keep law to m. reward 6815
never our m. God looks at but faith 3749
no m. where no trial 10762
therein lies dignity and m. 11231

MERITORIOUS
character never m. before God 1057

MERITS
God knows every man's m. 11743
Idolatry trust in one's own m. 6071
no thanks who does kindness for own ends 10056
to measure the worth of a man 7423
While man rests on his own m. 10041
with what freeness all his m. shall be bestowed 6393

MERRY
Better cottage where one m, than palace where one weeps 5821
God wills we eat, drink, be m. 8603
gospel signifies m. tydings 5091
Marriage more m. and more sad 7635
that's why I am so m. 4971
With m. company, dreary way endured 4304
with m. wise face 4195

MESH
slips through death's m. 9805

MESHACH
What was conduct of M. 5197

MESS
Don't m. with Mr. In-Between 8231
Life is a m. most of the time 6984
Theology must be lived in midst of life's m. 6984

MESSAGE
an ultimatum 9169
believers can scarcely find biblical m. 5109
Christ's m. revolutionizing 6377
Christ, m. set society ablaze 6375
convinced people open to Christian m. 3310
credible m. needs credible messenger 987
God's aim is m. of the gospel 197
greatest moments are when God got m. through to you 7029
m. of God to humanity 5089
not a compromise 9169
of gospel often diluted 5109
prepared messenger more important than prepared m. 9129
read Bible in relation to whole m. 642
sees direct personal m. from God 5441
world where m. a crazy tale 592

MESSENGER
affliction, God's m. 160
credible m. needs credible m. 987
Every day a m. of God 2195
God's m. sent down to thee 5331

prepared m. more important than
   prepared message 9129

MESSENGERS
angels, m. of God 359
angels, the m. of God 358

MESSIAHS
aren't found wrapped in rags 6147

MET
I am a part of all that I have m.
   6234
If desires not m. by God 7538
never m. man so ignorant couldn't
   learn from him 6080
reputation would not know
   character if m. on street 9618

METALLURGISTS
build defects into crystals 3932

METALS
growth of grace like polishing of
   m. 5230

METAMORPHOSED
where fantasy and earthly things
   m. into art 7435

METAPHYSICS
For philosophers, pain a problem
   of m. 8255

METED
God's gifts are m. out 5

METEOR
blazing m. only a stone 4395

METEORS
Great men m. designed to burn so
   earth lighted 5278

METHOD
Christ's m. of making better
   world alone succeeds 6487
Earnestness obsessed with m. not
   the Master 2626
God's creative m. is change 4469
God's m. to preserve by destroying
   4556
ideal m. of time management
   11466
of evil one to obscure himself
   behind object of worship 2699
try God-given m. for revivals 9743

METHODIST
father was a M. 8316

METHODS
church looking for better m. 1436
faults more pardonable than m. to
   hide them 3933
found in place of Christ 1230
know not by what m. rare 8825
Men look for better m. 7501
   3318
world manifold in m. 10512

METHUSELAH
lived without a bathtub 777

MEXICO
no place like home except M.
   2877

MICE
turn m. into horses 1122

MICHELANGELO
sweep streets as M. painted 2777
you may become a M. 3039

MICROBES
not m, but man himself greatest
   danger 7397

MICROSCOPE
Envy looks through a m. 7259
to find reasons 1420
weak mind like m. 7754

MIDDAY
Benighted walks under m. sun
   1683
in m. give counsel 6928

MIDDLE
both tug, he's left in the m. 9940
But, O, beware the m. mind 5048
like straddling m. of road 11602
no m. territory 5038

MIDDLE AGES
great men who built up M. 5656

MIDNIGHT
duty performed gives music at m.
   9675
favorite hour of asceticism 467
in fire on the m. darkness 4712
Tomorrow comes at m. very clean
   11403

MIDST
God is the beyond in m. of life
   4457
great man in m. of crowd keeps
   independence 6195
in the m. of sorrow 3818
in the m. of the crowds feel
   frightfully alone 7124
of noise a deep inner silence
   10539
realizes God in m. quiet in m. of
   alarm 3972
Safe in m. of perils 4490
Theology must be lived in m. of
   life's mess 6984

MIGHT
cross destroyed formula that m. is
   right 2166
God's m. to direct me 5400
Let us have faith that right makes
   m. 3755
never prays 10042
New continents of m. 2319
O love, resistless in thy m. 7285
So let it be in God's own m.
   10756
That all my powers with all their
   m. 9047

MIGHT-HAVE-BEENS
poor M. 8370

MIGHTIER
oil can m. than the sword 10991
Truth m. than eloquence 11568

Who is m. than the Almighty
   4955

MIGHTIEST
philosophy, study of Godhead
   4631

MIGHTY
A few rich treasures from his m.
   store 6111
as dear to God is peasant as m.
   prince 3225
better to dare m. things 1922
combated by m. forces 2630
Destroys the m, the humble spares
   4505
Girded for war, humility his m.
   dress 6124
Have oft a m. end 7119
If truth be m. and God
   all-powerful 4134
In celebration high, m. regain
   balance 3235
is m. who conquers himself 9968
Meek means m. 7729
Only the soul that knows m. grief
   2508
Spirit of God will enfold you in a
   love so m. 5776
the M, after submission to a
   woman's pains 6142
want to be doing m. things 9679
with m. battalions of angels 6503

MILD
Gentle Jesus, meek and m. 1117
gospel like m. air in heat of
   summer 5097
Of all epithets to Christ, m. seems
   least appropriate 6462

MILDEST
God in likeness of m. of all living
   creatures 6154

MILE
Every m. is two in winter 2544
God will advance a m. in blazing
   light 2962
walked a m. with Pleasure 10596
walked a m. with Sorrow 10596

MILES
A few m. distance from rocky
   shore 6111
Cheerful company shortens m.
   4221
journey of a thousand m. begins
   with single step 6871
Love asks us to walk many m.
   7273
outlook may be m. different from
   yours 6168

MILESTONES
road to hell without m. 5702

MILK
Christ is m. to feed his people
   6370
dairymaid can m. cows to glory of
   God 3082
man without God like cake
   without flour, m. 7446

not well for man to pray cream, live skim m. 8856

MILKMAID
no reason why m. not as intellectual as poet 6332

MILKSOPS
likeness to Jesus Christ, not m. 4651

MILL
back of the flour the m. 9345
God's m. grinds slow but sure 6607

MILLENNIUM
man-made m. 9870

MILLION
Beneath a m. m. trees 1368
man is maze of a m. notes 6212
no more difficult to make m. worlds than one 7940
would not fear a m. enemies 8832

MILLIONS
can feel the sufferings of m. 8445
deadly opiate for consciences of m. 4726
few dozen act while m. stand impotent 100
Jesus conquered more m. than 6449
long for immortality 6100
murder, m. make a hero 11758
of Americans, clever and fearless 1130
of bewildered infants trying to spell God with wrong blocks 7530
of men would die for Jesus Christ 6351
of spiritual creatures walk earth 362
pain in finger more concern than destruction of m. 10035
stumble over sheer simplicity 5653
we say m. never think of God 7561
Words make thousands, perhaps m, think 12002

MILLSTONES
When God is putting saints through m. 10927

MILTON'S PARADISE
But I remembered M. 1817

MIMICRY
lives a m. 1640

MIMICS
Children are natural m. 1109

MIND
accept Christ by impulse of m. 3333
Age is a quality of m. 8122
an eye to see with 3021
And to the foolish, m. 10130
anger enters m, wisdom departs 405

Anxiety, fear trickling through the m. 410
Are all the movements of the eternal m. 4990
ascends, beholds majesty of God 7971
at same time enjoy peace of m. 4001
Bear patiently the dryness of your m. 7123
behavior shaped by m. of Christ 10562
Belief is truth held in m. 582
Bible enlightens my m. 722
bringing m. into contact with divine revelation 5094
But, O, beware the middle m. 5048
can make a heaven of hell 512
can make a hell of heaven 512
can remember, understand, love its maker 7771
can't get it out of my m. 22
cannot be reasoned out by finite m. 5450
Cheerfulness fills m. with serenity 1092
Cheerfulness keeps daylight in the m. 1092
Cheerfulness removes rust from m. 1093
Cheerfulness, habit of the m. 1094
Christian m. has succumbed to secular drift 7768
Christmas a state of m. 1361
completely different people in m. 3766
Consistency quality of stagnant m. 1746
contemplation of the Divinity improving to the m. 4745
contented m, continual feast 1774
conversion calm of conviction to unquiet m. 1900
Conversion goes throughout m. 1895
could only raise my m. in anguish to God 10931
depending on the m. of God 7753
difference between worldliness, godliness is renewed m. 7769
egotist, self-importance makes m. shrink, head swell 9191
encountered m. that startled us 7752
enemy will fill with bad thoughts 7764
Enter inner chamber of thy m. 7708
examining tongue philosophers find diseases of m. 11410
face the mirror of the m. 3569
face, portrait of the m. 435
fanatic can't change m. 3907
Fanaticism false fire of overheated m. 3909
fear rings m. into quick life 3973
feed m. with truth of God 12124

fiction creation of human m, congenial to it 11574
first-rate m. only happy when thinking 11248
Fortify our m. against disappointments 9092
frail m. of man cannot explain reason 4492
Freedom filling m. with God's thoughts 4121
Freethinkers state of m. not common 4124
functions best when open 7770
Give others a piece of your heart, not m. 10132
glimpses m. enjoys of Godhead 4583
God already had you in m. 4879
God cannot get humanity out of his m. 5983
God does not change m. 4590
God has given us the m. of Christ 6679
God is greater than m. itself 4700
God knowable with the m. of inner man 4509
God knows all m, every m. 4881
God would not created without plan in m. 5398
God's m. in infinity, eternity of existence 4675
great thoughts shake the m. 11281
greatness of m. in acknowledging good turn 5263
grief develops powers of the m. 5340
grows by what it feeds on 11246
guileless m. great treasure, worth any price 5865
guilt feelings made him sick in m. 5485
has a thousand eyes 7306
heroic acts of a great m. 6281
highest function of m. is to listen to God's Word 7766
home is no home unless food, fire for m, body 5813
Home is where life makes up its m. 5832
Hope not only bears up m. under sufferings 5930
how I miss my m. 8146
How reluctantly m. consents to reality 9400
human m. like an umbrella 7770
humble m. is soil of which thanks grows 5258
Humor is sunshine of the m. 6718
If do not use m. God has given us 6693
if saint lets his m. alone 7757
If tiniest grudge in your m. against anyone 9633
If we can understand m. of God 4135
In prayer we descend with m. into the heart 10562
inaction saps vigor of the m. 6765
is exhilarated 7964

is its own place 512
It's haunting me 22
Keep m. free from worry 5561
Let each man think his m. a
    thought of God 4557
lifted into love of God 4749
live in plenty, be troubled in m.
    3979
logical m. would be our own
    grotesque God 4689
longer I love, more m. dwells on
    beauty of world 11301
Lord has little good to say of
    unilluminated m. 7776
Lord revels in m. renewed,
    enlightened by grace 7776
love Lord with all thy m. 11221
made incandescent by indwelling
    Christ 7776
man more gregarious in m. than
    body 1639
man must do first in his m. 578
Man's m. is the Holy of Holies
    7759
march of the human m. is slow
    11245
melancholy that stems from
    greatness of m. 5303
memory capacity of human m.
    fabulous 7738
Merely having open m. is nothing
    7761
more powerful and original a m.
    10566
Music medicine of troubled m.
    7908
narrow m, wide mouth go together
    4059
Neglecting development of m.
    mistake 7793
Night to rest body and the m.
    8085
no business to limit God's
    revelations to bias of m. 11273
No contemplation humble m.
    more than thoughts of God
    4745
No gain satisfies greedy m. 5319
No great m. ever ungrateful 6251
no longer a Christian m. 7768
no m. to trade with devil 11065
No sleep tranquil unless m. at rest
    8449
no thoughts enter my m. that are
    not your thoughts 8748
not cared for enough 3027
not fit tenant for m. of honest man
    11181
not his will that we neglect the m.
    7758
Nothing blinds m. more
    effectually than self-realization
    10044
nothing more wonderful than
    alert, eager m. 7776
Occupy m. with good thoughts
    7764
of God as discovered in Word and
    works 4675

of God so vast and deep 4675
Only in quiet m. is adequate
    perception 7718
opening m. to shut on something
    solid 7761
Our m. too limited to understand
    God 4665
own m., then rely upon God 13
pain of m. worse than pain of
    body 8272
Painting raises m. beyond stars
    2015
passes capacity of finite m. 4989
Peace is a state of m. 8455
Peace rules day when Christ rules
    m. 8462
Pentecost, illumination of m. 5806
Philosophy science of limitations
    of human m. 8594
Possession pampers the m. 242
power pent up in unconscious m.
    1712
prayer for freedom of m. 9041
Prayer the highest energy of which
    the m. is capable 8900
Pride the complete anti-God state
    of m. 9240
privation trains and strengthens
    242
profoundest problems human m.
    can entertain 3784
Prosperity a state of m. 9339
pure in heart, not strong in m, see
    God 1216
quiet m. one that nothing worries
    7773
Quiet m. richer than crown 1812
quite vacant is m. distress'd 3085
relevance of God to formation of
    m. 3036
Rule your m. or it will rule you
    6329
scarcely anything on earth more
    beautiful than Spirit-filled m.
    7776
second-rate m. happy thinking
    with minority 11248
should not be bin to store facts
    3021
simple life best for the m. 7365
Solitude a state of m, heart 10548
Songs spring forth weblike from
    m. at peace 7920
Speech index of the m. 10690
strength of m. in the cross 2096
struggle between proud m, empty
    purse 8679
Superstition poison of the m.
    10966
Suspicion always haunts the guilty
    m. 5488
task in solitude to keep m. on
    Savior 10551
that is cumbered, will fret 425
that sees God in everything 5202
the m. grows heated 48
the present 935
things you read condition m. 862

Thinking is the magic of the m.
    11261
third-rate m. happy thinking with
    majority 11248
thoughtful m. sees the nation itself
    7982
through which Christ thinks 1248
'Tis education forms the common
    m. 2991
to admire is to love with the m.
    7326
To pray is to expose the m. to God
    9006
to read God's m, to think his
    thoughts 7766
To the quiet m. all things possible
    7773
too numb for thought 12102
trinity of the m. 7771
True silence is rest of m. 9374
tumors of troubled m. 3129
Two things fill m. 1709
unbelieving m. not convinced by
    proof 600
uneasiness about the Uncreated
    4614
unless made up m. to resist 4966
unoccupied it cannot be 7764
Untilled m. will bring thistles,
    thorns 7774
Use God to give us peace of m.
    7517
Use your own m. 13
vacant is m. distressed 6752
value bodies, m. so that we never
    mar them 836
want perfection of the m. 3025
weak m. cannot receive great
    things 7754
weak m. like a microscope 7754
weak m. magnifies trifling things
    7754
what must God's m. be in
    undisclosed resources 4675
When m. doubts, feather sways it
    2960
when m. not in vision of God
    4989
when m. of man, God meet 949
when this great universe lay in m.
    of God 4769
will become rubbish head for
    Satan 7757
will shine with accumulation of
    jewels 3023
Wisdom does not enter a
    malicious m. 11966
wisest m. something yet to learn
    3033
worst is that which persecutes the
    m. 7765

MIND-READING
Tact a kind of m. 10986

MINDS
are like parachutes 7762
Bible never deals with domains of
    human m. 721

confusion produces greatest m. 220

conversing with greatest m. of the past 3027

country needs dirtier fingernails, cleaner m. 7775

difference of opinion alienates little m. 11392

emotionally speculate on unknowable 4704

emotions in subconscious m. to hurt, trouble 3061

Evil m. change good to own nature 5015

Faith and love spasmodic in best m. 3654

Few m. wear out, more rust out 7756

finite m. cannot solve it 6277

fogging up our m. with smokescreens 2660

God cannot work with empty m. 4824

God is creator of m. to receive his fullness 4514

God wants to rebuild m, give new values 7863

Great m. have purposes 5281

Great m. rise above misfortune 5281

Great m. talk about ideas 1845

If bring m. back again to God 7713

If we have not quiet in our m. 1804

if we work upon men's immortal m. 6796

left mark because m. occupied with heaven 5656

Little m. tamed, subdued by misfortune 5281

mediocre m. talk about things 1845

Old age puts more wrinkles in m. than on faces 8162

only function when open 7762

opposition from mediocre m. 5282

people think with hopes, fears rather than m. 7763

prayer refreshes, restores, renews m. 8857

putting m. together in shapes of our own choosing 8710

Quiet m. cannot be perplexed or frightened 8466

Revenge delight of little m. 9725

small m. talk about people 1845

Strong m, great hearts, true faith, ready hands 6299

Superstition religion of feeble m. 10967

tearing human m. to pieces 8710

To be alone fate of all great m. 10571

we're all isolated in our m. 7428

well for people who think to change their m. 11228

What comes into m. when we think about God 7563

When m. filled with God 10932

willing to use m. without prejudice 4124

Wisdom in m. attentive to their own 6690

Wise men change their m, fools never 11978

MIND-SET

basic m. "What am I getting out of this" 10062

MINE

God's resources are m, for he is m. 7486

I and m. causes whole misery 10090

least used word by unselfish person 11653

Life like entering jewel m. 4426

love you because you're m. 4764

more deeply he works the m. 737

Myself and I, and m. and my 1855

Not m, not m. the choice 5456

plan of m. would have proved my ruin 4901

That friend of m. 4199

This path is m, not thine 5415

Thy way, not m, O Lord 5456

'Twas his will, it is m. 7520

two tiny words taken from them, m. and thine 4227

MINER

no reason why m. not as intellectual as poet 6332

MINGLE

Women and men in the crowd meet, m. 7150

MINGLED

Errors to be dangerous have truth m. 3254

good and evil, world made to m. pattern 4335

He who has m. in the fray 3174

wailing of newborn m. with dirge for the dead 7043

web of life of a m. yarn 7045

world is made to m. pattern 5052

MINGLING

can be bag of grapes, m. 9524

MINIATURE

childhood, earlier m. world 1126

Every man is a m. world 6487

MINIMIZE

must never m. suffering of another 10924

MINIMUM

trying to live maximum life on m. faith 3770

MINISTER

can do nothing other than m. 10561

expected to execute duties well 1499

felt he could not continue as m. 2886

God will m. to you in secret 10706

layman opportunities m. will never have 3330

lives behind stained glass curtain 3330

the more competent the better 1499

what m. is on his knees that he is 1496

MINISTERED

to by God through the saints 126

MINISTERS

ignorance on part of m. 11196

mother m. to next generation of citizens 7844

world looks at m. out of pulpit 1500

MINISTRY

For higher m. 6109

in biblical faith, woman is partner in m. 11981

most sacred, exacting, humbling vocation 9153

no greater m. than a mother 7856

of church ceased while quarrel over Prince of Peace 9361

spiritual m. means to take time 7327

temptation of separating m. from spirituality 10211

that costs nothing accomplishes nothing 10173

their life becomes a m. 10561

those who hold different view of m. 2987

We impoverish God's m. to us 4830

MINOR

dirge in m. may suddenly be turned into glee 7895

more talk out of m. pain 3422

no m. sin when his justice confronts you 10405

MINORITIES

almost always in right 5194

MINORITY

Every new opinion a m. of one 8194

God needs m. fully committed 1192

second-rate mind happy thinking with m. 11248

test of courage when in m. 1938

MINUS

cross, a m. turned into a plus 2119

Life m. love equals zero 7206

MINUTE

Avoid the last m. rush 2768

can grasp the m. you want to 4079

could not hold on m. longer 236

every m. of time valuable 11289

Happiness living every m. with love 5528

happiness of life made up of m. fractions 5556

hot stove for m. seems like hour 9527

In the vast and the m. we see 1963

Just a tiny little m. 11303

Life lost m. by m. 6972

life, little speck in center but a m. 7052

One m. of patience, ten years of peace 8404

pretty girl for hour seems like m. 9527

seems could not hold on a m. longer 2614

Seize this very m. 48

MINUTENESS
creation, ever-decreasing m. 1975

MINUTES
asks a question is fool for five m. 6683

childhood chews hours, swallows m. 12193

five m. thinking about God 7491

Lost, sixty diamond m. 11306

Old age lives m. slowly, hours quickly 12193

So do our m. hasten to their end 2329

Take care of the m. 2787

takes fifteen m. to read greatest sermon ever preached 10102

MIRACLE
Christian life can't be without m. 1223

elephant not greater m. than mite 7940

Every believer, God's m. 1279

Every moment of this life a m. 6889

everything is a m. 7940

greatest m. that God can do 5759

Jesus performing quickly the slow m. in vineyards 6513

Man is the greatest m. 7408

Man the m. of miracles 7409

never a greater m. than myself 7388

no cheap, easy m. 1013

no one thing greater m. 7940

nor mountain greater m. than an atom 7940

of God at work in human souls 5717

question about m. not how it happened but why 6500

the great m. that still goes on 1966

world is still a m. 12049

MIRACLES
associated with lesson Jesus trying to teach 6500

contrary to what we know about nature 8021

do not foster deep faith 3782

dramatic, show-stopping m. 3782

Many reverence Jesus' m. 2828

marvel that Christ performed so few m. 6503

nature requires change to do m. 959

not contrary to nature 8021

of Jesus small, swift that we might take them in 6479

of Jesus were ordinary works of his Father 6479

MIRACULOUS
believe God can do m. one thing 3669

God's willingness to do m. another 3669

let m. deliverance from furnace answer 5197

MIRAGE
Don't pour away water because of m. 2806

MIRROR
be m. that reflects light 3455

Behavior is m. image 553

best m. is an old friend 4200

Everyone you meet is your m. 9441

face m. of the mind 3569

in which glory of God reflected 10339

Life is a m. 6949

Only in quiet waters things m. undistorted 7718

Psalms: m. in which man sees his soul 800

shows everyone his best friend 9998

sin covers m. with smoke 10339

soul is like a m. 10339

Speech a m. of the soul 10689

Thought serves as a m. 11267

to reflect your love to all I meet 9079

world is a looking glass 436

MIRRORED
characteristics of God m. in Jesus 4493

pool wherein serene light of God can be m. 8437

MIRRORS
education to turn m. into windows 3019

in spite of all the m. in world 7444

Most people are m. 3019

MIRTH
but pleasing madness 4877

Everybody ought to bathe in it 6738

honor time with m. 11377

is God's medicine 6738

offered sparkling with life to God 6739

rust of life scoured off by oil of m. 6738

small sincerity of m. 6740

upheaves the billows in their m. 4505

wine of human life 6739

MISCALCULATION
Vice a m. of chances 10410

MISCARRIED
human plan and calculation m. 184

MISCARRY
plans m. because no aim 4433

MISCHIEF
comes from much opening of mouth 10685

devastating society by every m. ingenuity can invent 4895

Satan finds m. for idle hands to do 6772

wish to be saved from m. of vices, but not vices 10338

MISCHIEF-MAKER
devil the m. 4915

MISER
devil entangles m. with gold 2677

dollar's worth of frustration when loses dime 11797

Don't dole talent out like m. 10993

ever in want 5311

happiest m. saves every friend 4203

makes a wonderful ancestor 11805

what he has is of no more use than what he has not 5329

MISERABLE
abounding in wealth, yet m. 249

even amidst luxury 10871

feeling that useless to strive anymore 4507

funerals barbaric, m. 2311

in measuring each other by own moral maxims 6826

more m. is he who fears death 2357

nice people as desperately in need as a m. world 7827

not m. to be blind 10861

One who longs for death is m. 2357

shall be thoroughly m. in heaven 5661

to be incapable of enduring blindness 10861

to be m. think about what people think of you 10816

to be m. think about yourself 10816

to have few things to desire, many to fear 11827

to live in suspense 11600

when old age looks back with horror 8182

will of God never leads to m. feeling 4507

without control young people m. 12178

MISERABLY
failed m, first to see God's formula
3628

MISERIES
climb upward on the m. of others
338
Satan tries to make us think m.
spring from God 9859
to imbalance are due most m.
1240

MISER'S
money takes place of wisdom
11795
wealth is the devil's 11796

MISERS
amass wealth for those who wish
their death 11837
crave money 7826
very kind people 11837

MISERY
Arrogance, built-in m. 451
Art thou in m. brother 6878
because world based on freedom
4149
cannot build hopes on m. 8445
child's m. fills whole of his world
1101
crowds love to pool their m.
10515
Every m. I miss a new mercy 7739
God always receptive to m. 4590
Half the m. in the world comes
9455
Hope the physician of every m.
5926
Human m. too great without faith
3730
I and mine causes whole m. 10090
I miss is a new blessing 820
is optional 8266
It is m. to be born 186
love has eyes to see m. and want
7335
make sin, m. out of everything
God sends 10816
man has power to bring m. on
himself, others 4158
mercy confronting human m.
5206
one less candidate for m. 10979
see no way out of the world's m.
7099
That m. might be stayed 4813
vast neurotic m. of world 4437
will seem sweet 10833
world centered in self 8436

MISFIT
what seems m. becomes
cornerstone 10901

MISFORTUNE
an occasion to demonstrate
character 196
boredom of life for the rich is
worse m. 11854
charity is courage when m. falls
1085

compromise more devastating
than m. 1584
deep 11808
first step to overcoming m. 154
great minds rise above m. 5281
isolated by m. 5395
Little minds tamed, subdued by m.
5281
only in m. can you be sublime
5310
Quiet minds go on in m. at own
private pace 8466
Quotations tell of m. 9385
sudden jolt of m. 1584
tamed and subdued by m. 193
to be incapable of solitude 10570
To mourn adversity multiples m.
221
Virtue flourishes in m. 226
whets 11808

MISFORTUNES
all men have some 828
come on wings 196
depart on foot 196
For one that big m. slay 12061
hardest to bear never happen
12069
History, register of m. of mankind
5719
longer we dwell, greater their
power 210
quickly to their m. 4242
Reflect not on your past m. 828
to imbalance are due most m.
1240

MISGUIDED
have guided missiles, m. men 9868

MISHAPS
Great and small suffer same m.
173

MISJUDGMENT
meet m. with patience 2630

MISLEAD
God allows our judgment to m. us
9851
not tricked by advertisements that
m. 836

MISLED
Christ path if any be m. 6391

MISPLACED
zeal is zeal for God rather than
zeal of God 7502

MISREPRESENTATION
best answer to m. 9677

MISREPRESENTED
God lets himself be m. 4891

MISS
Every misery I m. is a new blessing
820
heaven, expect to m. some I had
expected 5655
how I m. my mind 8146
I m. a lot of good things day by
day 5587

if we m. joy, we m. reason for
existence 6571
If we m. seeing God in his works
4995
Peace, sure to m. if aim at directly
8459
People m. happiness because
didn't stop to enjoy it 5585
To thank thee for the things I m.
11136
you value what you m, not what
you have 11669

MISSED
For everything you have m, have
gained something 8574
God's never m. the runway 3974
purpose of giving 10738
respect coming and going 9647
the glory of those who believed
6464

MISSES
archer who overshoots m. as well
6592
When archer m. mark 9680

MISSILES
have guided m, misguided men
9868

MISSING
in American life 7990
lament our part m. 7056
one of your angels is m. 7852

MISSION
church has only one m. 3328
everything, personal life nothing
9279
Make life a m, not intermission
10171
only m. of church is to entertain
1456
wish to run rescue m. within yard
of hell 7783

MISSIONARIES
scaffolding around a rising
building 7780

MISSIONARY
even m. activity may become
competitive 7867
Every spiritual movement
followed by m. movement 9740
God had an only Son, a m. 7778
If God calls you to be a m. 7781
more intensely m. we become
7785
person called to do m. work 7784
teaches canibals to say grace 7777

MISSIONS
make money go far, give to foreign
m. 11823
Spirit of Christ is spirit of m. 7785

MISSPENDING
time kind of self-homicide 11308

MIST
in pulpit, fog in pew 9123

MISTAKE

Any man may make m. 3584
biggest m, doing nothing 7792
Experience enables you to
    recognize m. 3517
God is too wise to make a m.
    4461
Man calls sin a m, God madness
    4560
Never m. remorse for repentance
    9584
never made m. never made
    discovery 3630
of asceticism 467
of employer failure with human
    material 3120
only real m. one from which we
    learn nothing 3622
people m. education for
    intelligence 8510
save boy from making m. 8337
that we do not concentrate upon
    present day 8381
to present Christianity as
    charming, popular 1198
to think time of prayer different
    from any other time 8881
Vice a m. in estimating value
    10410
Who can m. great thoughts 11281
will not encourage us to m. inns
    for home 7014

MISTAKEN

a thousand times 956
arrogant, usually most m. 458
He that speaks much, much m.
    1847
testimony, not a witness to Jesus
    11125
When social action m. for
    evangelism 3341

MISTAKES

All great men make m. 7787
always another chance 3598
always right who suspects he
    makes m. 7791
assume God unable to work in
    our m. 3613
enemies first to discover m. 3169
Experience name people give to m.
    3531
from m. wise learn wisdom for
    future 7794
grope and totter and make
    countless m. 9851
History teaches m. we are going
    to make 5715
important thing is not avoidance
    of m. 8110
in judgment of good we can make
    m. 5086
Linguist can make m. in more
    than one language 7782
man m. evil for happiness, good
    3386
man who does things makes many
    m. 7792
never corrects his m. 8195

No man progressed to greatness
    but through m. 5030
of youth doing things excessively
    12181
Pride at the bottom of all great m.
    9228
six m. of man 7793
sneering at his m. 6599
suppose m. published every day
    like those of ball player 7789
tendency to not allow children to
    make m. 8320
To make no m. not in power of
    man 7794
won't irreparably damage lives
    3616

MISTAKING

weakness for strength defeats
    10749

MISTRESS

Truth a hard m. 11561
Wealth a very bad m. 11873

MISTRUST

kindness causes m. to evaporate
    6668
learn to m. ourselves, put all
    confidence in him 9851
of himself, greater confidence in
    God 10328
source of power stronger than
    ingrained m. 6491
the man who finds everything evil
    3555
the man who finds everything
    good 3555
the man who is indifferent to
    everything 3555

MISTY

in-between on the m. flats 10679

MISUNDERSTAND

easy to m. what NT means 589
good that people sometimes m. us
    6270

MISUNDERSTANDABLE

Words seem so easily m. 7934

MISUNDERSTANDING

cannot thwart purposes of God
    2740
kindness causes m. to evaporate
    6668
strange m. of God's ways 9840

MISUNDERSTOOD

among the m. is where Jesus went
    2812
God only being who can afford to
    be m. 4891
Grief may be joy m. 5339
Man would sooner be m. than
    exposed 1055
philosophy of activism m. 130
sanctified life often m. 2856
To be great is to be m. 5305

MISUSED

If privilege m. creation to punish
    humanity 3191

MITE

elephant not greater miracle than
    a m. 7940
what a m. of it is yours 7063

MITES

Two m, two drops (yet all her
    house, land) 4379

MITIGATES

Memory m. adversity 7735

MIXED

multitudes within precincts of
    religion 5776

MIXTURE

Ignorance and power and pride a
    deadly m. 9212
Love a m. of honey, bitterness
    7228
Men a m. 7420
no great genius without m. of
    madness 4398

MOAB

In vale in land of M. 778

MOAN

I heard without the night wind m.
    5413
Psalms, m. of man's penitence 798
That is not paid with m. 810

MOANING

may there be no m. at the bar
    2368

MOANINGS

soul's m. are the affections,
    yearning for the Infinite 7516

MOCCASINS

Don't judge any man until walked
    in his m. 6574
until I have walked in his m. 9065

MOCK

green-ey'd monster which doth m.
    6346
on, m. on, Voltaire, Rousseau 596
on; 'tis all in vain 596
suffering God only one who does
    not m. us 10908

MOCKERY

evil is a principle of m. 5023
makes m. of faith 11203

MODEL

childhood m. of greater world
    1126
not only m. but assertively reach
    out to help 3901
seldom improve when no other m.
    but themselves 3451
strengthen commitment to m.
    strong families 3901

MODELS

Children more need of m. than
    critics 8286

MODERATE

riches will carry you 11838

MODERATELY
Christianity cannot be m.
  important 1184

MODERN
than great men of ancient and m.
  times 6449

MODESTLY
to live m. a richer experience 9758

MODESTY
is rich 11696

MODIFICATION
divine behavior m. 577

MODIFIERS
infinite can have no m. 4706

MODUS OPERANDI
of fear 3971

MOLD
hammer, forge character 1000
not made from common m. 6206

MOLDING
home where character m. carried
  on 5850
In the cold God is m. thy
  expression 10600
No job can compete with m. new
  human being 8317

MOLDS
God m. history to his purposes
  5718

MOLEHILL
gossip makes mountain of m. by
  adding dirt 5114

MOLEHILLS
become mountains when someone
  adds a little dirt 10443
climb over m. way to get ulcers
  1566

MOMENT
a picture never seen before 9873
a picture which shall never been
  seen again 9873
a tiny m. at a time 11339
At every m. God instructs, guides
  me 5426
at precise m. God will reach for
  you 5430
comes a m. when death takes us
  by the hand 2284
curtain may be rung down at any
  m. 9911
day too dear to waste a m. on
  yesterdays 8375
Death nothing but a m. 2390
do not know from m. to m. what
  is coming 4704
Each m. of year has its own beauty
  9873
emotion passing with the m.
  enough for many 4471
Every m. dies a man 806
Every m. of this life is a miracle
  6889
Every m. one is born 806

Every m. pregnant with divine
  purpose 11293
every m. we may do little works
  excellently 5068
fresh start any m. you choose
  3598
give to God each m. as it flies
  8600
God can fit heroes into their
  places in a m. 9174
God only gives strength for m.
  2722
God only gives time to us m. by m.
  11337
God only gives us light for present
  m. 5397
great m. of our lives 9841
holiest m. of church service 1444
If you discern God's love in m. of
  happiness 5254
is to leave eternity for a m. 6495
life of civilization compared with
  man only a m. 7389
life, cannot know at what m. may
  flash forth with life of God
  7055
live in a m. of history 982
Lord's goodness surrounds us at
  every m. 4646
Love has power to give in a m.
  7223
Man, designed to carry load of
  the m. 421
Marriage is not for a m. 7641
meet for a m, sail out of sight
  4281
more spiritual progress in one
  short m. of silence 12112
must not be permitted to slip
  away unappreciated 11319
My part is to improve the present
  m. 10145
neighbor is man next to you at the
  m. 8069
of my death most precious of life
  2373
Once to every man, nation comes
  m. to decide 2489
One m. of impatience may ruin a
  life 8405
One m. of patience may prevent
  disaster 8405
passed is no longer 8384
Resolved, never to lose one m.
  569
small m. carrier of God's gift
  11319
snatch, seize, enjoy every m.
  11372
to be happy with God at this very
  m. 6569
to become a Christian 1287
we forget he is Almighty 4830
we put hands on it, melts away
  11288
we turn in faith to God 3758
What a terrific m. in history 6154
who neglects present m. 11300
worst m. for atheist 488

would not give one m. of heaven
  5652

MOMENTARY
No man happy whose path but m.
  glimmer of light 6101
To make God a m. Creator 11652

MOMENTOUS
decision to have child m. 8310
greatest, most m. fact which
  history records 5710
trivial displaces m. 7990

MOMENT'S
insight sometimes worth life's
  experience 8486
Resolve upon a m. notice 6872

MOMENTS
a god whom we do not hate in m.
  4846
Cherish all happy m. 5506
Do not most moving m. find us
  without words 11986
greatest m. are when God got
  message through to you 7029
many m. hostile to truth 11551
of longing 470
of yearning for something better,
  nobler, holier 470
reconsider important m. in lives
  5392
remaining few m. in the day 7617
Self-respect comes in quiet m.
  9995
when everything goes well 3998
when the soul is on its knees 8776
will make you forget these painful
  m. 7123

MONARCH
Bible tells m. he is servant 645
Conscience m. in its
  preemptoriness 1673
Eastern m. charged wise men 957

MONASTERY
as much need of saint in factory
  as in m. 9765

MONDAY
child taught Sunday, remember M.
  1134

MONDAYS
I like sunrises, M, new seasons
  8080

MONEY
a good servant, but a dangerous
  master 7809
adds no more to wise than clothes
  to beautiful 7815
All m. made will never buy back
  soul 10650
alms m. put to interest in other
  world 11359
and marriage make devils or saints
  7805
and time are heaviest burdens 932
are slaves who are unhappy from
  lack of m. 8681

Before you borrow m. from friend 4032

borrow m, trouble will come 4035

bridegroom spends m. on new suit nobody notices 7588

brings acquaintances but not friends 7807

brings food, but not appetite 7807

brings joy, but not peace 7807

brings medicine, but not health 7807

brings servants, but not faithfulness 7807

buys everything except love 7806

can buy the husk, but not kernel 7807

can buy you everything but happiness 7810

can pay fare to every place but heaven 7810

Charity, m. put to interest in other world 1074

Christ never gave anyone m. 10731

clever enough to get m. 11869

does not have me at its mercy 11151

Don't marry for m, can borrow cheaper 7612

emphasized in Scripture 7811

fool and m. soon parted 11792

Friendship is like m, easier made than kept 4235

from cramping restrictions of lack of m. 6386

Give me the m. spent in war 11746

God does not need our m. 4359

greed molding beauty and life into m. 5327

hole that m. runs into 322

How we use our m. 10016

I could use it 7826

I get rid of m. as quickly as possible 7824

If can't help friend with m. 3072

if I lose it, can still offer thanks 11151

If m. be not your servant 11822

If man runs after m, he's money-mad 7800

If want to make m. go as far as possible 11823

If you make m. your god 7801

impossible to be truthful ever 11494

Instead of filling vacuum, m. makes one 7814

is all God's 10737

is like manure 7812

is poor who has nothing but m. 11821

Jesus talked a great deal about m. 7804

Jesus without m. conquered more millions 6449

leaves m. to charity in will 4377

loses m. loses much 3729

Love only service m. cannot buy 7253

Love superior to m. 7232

may as well borrow person's m. as time 2914

miser's m. takes place of wisdom 11795

misers crave m. 7826

misplaced Christian m. 111

more m. you give away, less you have 7232

Mr. M. is a powerful gentleman 7817

much m, life a failure 8629

never call him a fool until m. gone 11792

never made a man happy, nor will it 7814

never yet made anyone rich 7808

No one who is lover of m, is lover of man 11661

no portion of m. that is our m. 10737

not a custom to keep m. to look at 7803

not required to buy one necessity of the soul 7813

not to have m, a grief 11871

Nothing that is God's obtainable by m. 7818

O, m. m. m. 4039

one-fifth of all Jesus had to say was about m. 7804

penny will hide biggest star 7795

pile it up, stinks to high heaven 7812

powerless to purchase 10906

quantity of m. one gives of little importance 11360

Rather than m, give me truth 11526

Righteousness, not m. should be man's pursuit 5001

Sad is the man who has nothing but m. 7821

serves God for m. 2646

Slander like counterfeit m. 10465

spread it around, does world of good 7812

stupid enough to want m. 11869

swore solemnly that nobody who did not love it should have it 5320

Take glory neither in m. nor friends 9272

take half the baggage, twice the m. 6836

take notice how he acts when loses m. 7802

temptation to love m. inexplicably powerful 7811

the sin done for things there's m. in 7819

Thinking in lower grades comparable to m. 11259

thou canst go out so fast 4039

thou comest in so slowly 4039

To get m. is difficult 7823

To have m. a fear 11871

to keep m. more difficult 7823

to set their m. in circulation 11809

to spend m. wisely most difficult 7823

used to write home for m. now calls collect 3896

when art pursued for m. 1996

when goads of m. lifted 6842

When m. speaks, truth is silent 7825

When teenagers get car, want m. 3903

When teenagers get m, want car 3903

will be your master 11822

will buy dog, but not wag of tail 7816

will plague you like the devil 7801

work not making m. 3127

work to earn enough m. 3098

MONEY-MAD

If man runs after money, he's m. 7800

MONO

tonus is m, tempus is longus 9140

MONODY

However desolate life's m. sounds 7895

MONOGAMOUS

family, m. and indissoluble 3890

MONOLOGUE

Prayer is not m. 8932

Prayer not artful m. 8926

MONOTONY

in m. we grouse 10643

think, talk, act yourself into m. 3185

MONSTER

cuddle self-pity, you'll have a m. 10034

green-ey'd m. which doth mock 6346

like some m. loose in your beautiful world 7473

never a greater m. than myself 7388

What a m. is man 7439

MONSTROUS

all that is decayed, m, abortive in universe 4997

MONTH

day of sorrow longer than m. of joy 10580

MONTHS

I think and think for m. 2775

One kind word can warm three winter m. 6662

MONUMENT

church not a m. 1385

how transient is noblest m. 730

MOOD

need not wonder whether God in receptive m. 4590

people mirrors reflecting m. 3019
prayer will give God chance to
    change your m. 8957
Satan in most malignant m. 1370

MOODS
as atheist in which Christianity
    looked probable 1305
in which Christianity looks
    improbable 1305
Joy not a thing of m. 6568

MOODY
blues make you m, sad, and make
    you cry 7888

MOODY, D. L.
have more trouble with M. than
    any other man 9969

MOON
Bible m. without paleness 710
Death adventure beside which m.
    landings pale 2259
disappeared if within reach of
    human hands 3202
Everyone is a m, has a dark side
    7376
felt God's presence on m. more
    than on earth 11630
God made m. as well as sun 5393
have put men on m. 2928
He slept beneath the m. 6756
hope lies not in man we put on m.
    5941
Lights of a thousand stars do not
    make one m. 6198
Of cradling the little m. 7715
stars, m, sun how they move in
    silence 10250

MOONLIGHT
God means to guide our steps by
    m. 5393
Music is m. in gloomy night of life
    7909

MOONLIGHTING
today ten hours a day is called m.
    3083

MOONS
Don't judge until walked two m.
    in his moccasins 6574

MOOR
the vessel with a thread of silk
    9233

MOORINGS
let God break life from its m. in
    some storm 9564

MORAL
Beatitudes enriched m. existence
    530
consequence of defying m. order
    4721
dimension of sin is injustice 10394
furtherance of spiritual, m. life
    during sleep 10487
God seeks worship of those
    trapped in m. ruin 12098
greater to see m. pluck 8545
hardest tasks are m. acts 7838

have not found solution for m.
    decay 2928
hell reserved for those who in m.
    crisis maintain neutrality 8074
high crime rate traceable to
    breakdown in m. fiber 5858
illiterates whose only law is self
    3877
indignation permits hate under
    guise of virtue 11693
Jesus like some m. huntsman 6421
law isn't any one instinct 7839
law makes a kind of tune 7839
laws reflection of God's nature
    1520
Lord makes much of m. death
    2358
miserable in measuring each other
    by own m. maxims 6826
no m. precept not inconvenient
    7840
not progress when m. tone lower
    7834
not to abrogate obedience to m.
    law 6811
obedience to m. law coupled with
    attitude 6811
Only he who knows God truly m.
    7835
Our constitution made for m.
    people 5196
perception of beauty, a m. test 540
puritanical insistence on m. rules
    6827
rise above law of m. gravitation
    3752
satanically managed man is m.
    10044
Unbelief makes world m. desert
    11595
vice is false m. arithmetic 10410
Virtue is not avoidance of m.
    dangers 11709
Without family, children no m.
    foundation 3877

MORALE
loss of intellectual m. in the church
    7768

MORALIST
sees city as microcosm of
    humanity 10522

MORALISTS
new m. love defined by human
    beings 7837
new m. love tailored to meet
    situation 7837

MORALITY
always higher than law 7831
Christianity at first seems to be
    about m. 1181
comes with sad wisdom of age
    7829
does not make a Christian 7830
God alone determines m. 7828
human passions unbridled by m.
    5196
is correct thinking within 7832

Music used to ridicule m. 7910
new m. and biblical m. part 7837
no man can be a Christian
    without m. 7830
not only correct conduct on
    outside 7832
without religion is a tree without
    roots 7833

MORALLY
man has lagged behind m. 9872
man m. incapable of restraining
    himself 9872
Most live m. in restricted circle
    8659
worshiper no better m. than before
    8845

MORBID
Christians accused of being m.
    9758
Your uttered ignorance and m.
    doubt 3778

MORE
a man has, m. he wants 7814
alone while living than going,
    coming 7151
America has m. things than any
    other nation 8624
Anticipation m. delightful than
    realization 7160
apt to catch vices than virtues
    4286
As m. of heav'n in each we see
    4197
Beware of no man m. than
    yourself 9921
breathe m. 5604
chew m. 5604
Choose to have less rather than m.
    8448
clearly we perceive hand of God
    11644
closer to God, m. one feels a sinner
    10439
deeper we plunge, m. we learn
    7936
depends on walk than talk 3443
desire m. than I can accomplish
    61
do less, but accomplish m. 60
do m. good by being good 3456
Each m. precious than all 6200
Fix thought m. on the God you
    desire 10305
flings dirt upon another dirties
    himself m. 10452
Frown less and laugh m. 9281
Generosity, giving m. than you can
    4353
Give one thing m.—a grateful
    heart 5265
God will do yet m. 4476
Good, the m. communicated, m.
    abundant grows 5062
great of world those who loved
    God m. 5295
greater a man, m. distasteful
    flattery is to him 5296

grow in wisdom, pardon m. freely 4071

harm by example than good by correction 3914

have repented speech than silence 1861

honesty man has, less air of saint 5889

Hope m. 5604

how can you be happier with m. 5532

hypocrites, always room for one m. 6050

I demand love of others, less I deserve 9497

I love you m. for what you are going to be 4248

I told troubles, m. my troubles grew 2727

Imagination m. important than knowledge 2005

importance to learn m. every year 3017

in one short hour, learn m. from God 4964

intense light is, less you see glass 6033

Jesus' standards asked m. than any other ever has 6444

Justice must be m. than justice 6614

Learn less, contemplate m. 1762

learn m. by five minutes' obedience 8116

Less is m. 4484

Let religion be m. a love affair 9542

little thing in hand worth m. 7116

love grows bigger the m. you take from it 7252

love m. 5604

Love will ask m. than law could ever require 7273

love you give away, the m. comes back 7232

man denies himself, m. obtain from God 9562

man knows, m. he forgives 4099

man loves, m. he suffers 10904

men suppress truth of God, m. futile in thinking 11538

Mind the world less and God m. 2443

money you give away, less you have 7232

Never say m. than necessary 1863

Nothing you can do to make God love you m. 4786

O for grace to love thee m. 9077

Once conscious we are m. than we can fathom 10015

one approaches great men, m. one finds they are men 5300

one judges, less one loves 6593

poorest man always wanting m. than he has 2874

power in open hand than clenched fist 8720

Pray m, be m, serve m. 9016

Preach less and practice m. 9281

probably gets m. than expects 3497

progress in silence than in years of study 12112

riches grow and a thirst for m. and m. 11799

Ride less and walk m. 9281

seeks m. than he needs 5316

self is indulged, the m. it demands 10027

Shall have as much again, ask ten times m. 4364

Some have much, some have m. 11852

soul receives, m. it grows 10699

soul wants, m. it receives 10699

story of Jesus told m. than any other in history 5729

sure than day and night 4209

the m. grief inflicted upon you 5357

The m. he gave, the m. he had 4348

the m. laws, and order are made prominent 5192

The m. thou thine own self 9951

the m. we know the m. we wonder 4686

The m. you mow us down 7678

theme is Get m, know m, do m, 9016

There's m.—there's m. 6111

There's m. and m. to be grateful for 11163

thoughts that come to us worth m. 11250

time, no one receives m. or less 11356

to life than increasing speed 7053

we depend on God, m. dependable we find he is 11481

we learn about wonders of universe 11644

we learn, m. we realize how little we know 3029

we pursue humility more distant it becomes 6008

When try to make yourself m, you are diminishing yourself 9941

will of God, nothing m, nothing less 7876

Worry less and work m. 9281

worthy they are, m. humility will be seen 5991

you know about Christ 6480

you pray, the m. will be revealed 8865

MORGUE

every church would need m. in basement 4717

MORN

Came peeping in at m. 2588

From m. to night, my friend 6885

music in the dawning m. 7927

Swift fly the years, and rise th' expected m. 6143

To wake the m, sentinel the night 11344

MORNING

A bit of the Book in m. 633

and evening are spring and fall 9877

another day will begin next m. 11132

arrives too early in m. 11309

As m. shows the day 1124

calm and m. cannot be stayed 8444

Clear as the m. or the evening rose 4746

day's work will begin the next m. 2422

Death, rise refreshed in m. 2244

Determine action in m. 555

Each m. puts man on trial 11364

First thing in m. she sharpens tongue 5125

For each new m. with its light 11174

From three to four each m. 8794

Grace comes into soul as m. sun into world 5213

hour has gold in its hand 11318

human nature to grumble in m. 439

in dark night of soul always three in m. 2594

In m. prayer key that opens treasures of God's mercies 8846

in m. run off to another box called office 5859

In the m. of life, work 6928

innocence of m. 4643

Make it the first m. business 681

no time for Christ in the m. 10117

polite prattle exchanged Sunday m. 4029

praise at m, blame at night 8203

Prayer key of the m. 8943

rose is sweetest wash'd with m. dew 7309

Sin may open bright as m. 10377

talked with God this m. 8817

Thank God every m. when you get up 11159

'Tis always m. somewhere 5902

Welcome happy m. 2986

Who has shared our m. days 4208

with Christ life is dawn of m. 7094

You begin a new life every m. 7091

MORNINGS

God of the early m. 7539

million Christmas m. 1368

On how many m. have I, like Peter 9569

soul has further horizons than early m. 7539

MOROSENESS

scoured off by oil of mirth 6738

MORROW

trust the m. as little as possible 8222

MORTAL

birth made us m. 812
Bow thy meek head to m. pain 2981
dread of failure 10776
few certainties in m. experience 953
have never met a mere m. 8483
Lives for the meanest m. known 10085
m. men full of fragility 7437
Quit, oh quit, this m. frame 2404
So here in the roar of m. things 8429
why should the spirit of m. be proud 9225

MORTALITY

eternity, m. persuade us faith not option 2288
God's eternity, man's m. 2288
resurrection brought m. to light 9702
wrapped in m. 3482

MORTAL'S

price, glory of m. life 7035

MORTALS

For m. to decipher 8049
ring bells, fire off pistols 11329
why should m. fear to tread pathway to future home 6875

MOSAIC

in design of God's universe 4005

MOSES

a great lawgiver 779
Christ is no M, exacter, giver of laws 5208
he who has not trembled in M. 5224
Like M. once 4921
never took heed what sort of bush 4874
no ordinary lawyer 779
only saw brightness of Lord 4874
treated God with startling familiarity 7526

MOSQUITO

ant praised, m. swatted 112
doesn't get slap on back until 2772
makes an opening 8223
never waits for an opening 8223
preceded man in divine order of creation 9209
Take a lesson from the m. 8223
to m. human being something good to eat 9219
vacationeer returns with m. bites 6841

MOSQUITOES

we must feed m. 1733
who defeat us 2512

MOST

agreeable of all companions 4204
beautiful poetry born from womb of silence 10269
bothered m. by flies 11056
boughs that bear m. hang lowest 6029
can only make m. of today 3502
Christians who did m. for this world 5629
comforting fact imaginable 4779
exhausting thing in life is being insincere 6063
father's m. important responsibility 3927
forgive m, m. forgiven 4101
gains m. who is defeated 2510
He who gives m. light to world 6004
important occupation for woman 7856
important thing in life 7034
important words in vocabulary 11994
knowledge m. haunted with inevitable limitation 6689
least lonely when m. alone 10568
Life but a day at m. 6958
Life is a mess m. of the time 6984
Little things that matter m. 9267
Make m. of yourself 2781
Many are called but m. frozen 3045
may pray least when say m. 9018
may pray m. when say least 9018
moment of my death m. precious 2373
must be content to be as though not been 6023
new step what people fear m. 3989
of the time we are not at home 4546
of world's great souls have been lonely 7138
one who knows m. speaks least 11948
people are good 10070
people are other people 1640
people brought to faith by exposure 3759
perfection in m. things unattainable 3463
positive men are m. naive 7975
powerful influence in world 5766
profits m. who serves best 10143
profound thoughts born from womb of silence 10269
satanic type of pride 6038
seeking to know m. satisfying thing in world 5450
suffers m. who is m. selfish 10058
talk m. who have least to say 1834
The m. resembles God 6666
therefore live m. with Jesus Christ 6235
things that count m. in life 7039
tragic sentence in literature 7601

true disciples of Christ love m. 7318
Uncertain ills torment m. 11604
valuable of all talents 12154
What we think about m. 10016
What we want m. 10016
what will surprise us m. 6250
Whatever you fear m. you will serve 4006
Whatever you love m. is your god 7338
When I think of those who have influenced my life m. 6245
When schoolroom darkened, see m. 10855
who is defeated learns m. 2510
winning friends meant m. 4303

MOTE

Self-love a m. in every man's eye 10026

MOTES

not with m. from neighbor's eye 1402

MOTHER

all-enveloping, protective, nourishing power 7853
Bible like memory of mother 653
cajoles kids to do their best 7844
can become wedge that keeps apart 8341
can help bond together in love 8341
challenges kids to do their best 7844
dearest word is m. 11993
does what no one else can do as well 7844
eases a child's fear 7844
Experience is m. of truth 3530
fallacy that having children makes a m. 7854
give conduct to make her proud 511
I call her M. 7852
if father onion, m. garlic 8298
important to be real m. to children 7856
in eyes of m. every beetle a gazelle 7846
interpreter of father's character 8341
is earth 7853
is food 7853
is God's deputy on earth 7841
is love 7853
is warmth 7853
Leisure is the m. of philosophy 6834
like saying my m, drunk or sober 7980
Lord, thy will be done in m. 9082
love must help child grow away from m. 7858
loved by m. means to be alive 7853
loved by m. means to be at home 7853

loved by m. means to be rooted
7853
loves next generation of citizens
7844
ministers to next generation of
citizens 7844
My m. groaned 808
name for God in hearts of children
7848
No gift to m. can equal her gift to
you 7850
no greater position than a m.
7856
No man poor who has had godly
m. 7851
nurtures next generation of
citizens 7844
ounce of m. worth pound of clergy
7843
Patience the m. of expectation
8413
Progress the m. of problems 9313
Purposeless m. of crime 2039
religion of child depends on what
m, father are 8356
serpent deceived the m. of
mankind 9863
so full of soul, power, beauty 7859
so rich, deep, divine 7859
spoiled child never loves m. 1103
spoils child, fattens serpent 8330
sweater worn by child when m.
cold 3866
taught me to repeat Lord's Prayer
8347
teaches next generation of citizens
7844
times when love to m. must be
hatred 7280
To have God for our m. 7545
understands what child does not
say 7842
used to make me kneel by her side
8347
what father, m. say at home 8340
When God thought of m. 7859
whispers word of hope 7844
wipes away a tear 7844

MOTHER TERESA
difference between welfare and
Missionaries of Charity 1212
on M. of India 11841

MOTHER-CHILD
relationship paradoxical, tragic
7858

MOTHERHOOD
full of frustrations, challenges
8313
greatest benefit God has conferred
3895
greatest privilege of life 7849
Holy Comforter represents
ineffable m. of God 5775

MOTHER'S
God has face very like their m.
7855
heart is child's schoolroom 7857

requires intense love on m. side
7858
secret love outlives them all 7860
words rich as m. answering back
11998

MOTHERS
birth was trouble for our m.
11459
God invented m. 7845
July when m. realize why teachers
need vacations 9900
where is coverage our m.
rightfully deserve 7844
World poverty is a hundred
million m. weeping 8699

MOTHERS'
darlings make milksop heroes
8315

MOTION
Christian more m. than notion
1317
God knows all m. 4881
Rest and m. equally destructive
9685
rivers are God's thoughts in m.
8048

MOTIONLESS
God is m. eternity 4601

MOTIVATED
Believers who are m. by legalism
6810

MOTIVATION
I cannot judge m. of another 4247

MOTIVATIONS
God strikes at core of m. 7863
sin goes to m. 10300

MOTIVE
and purpose behind law 5233
God 5383
if m. is love for fellowmen 10159
saint totally different m. 9783

MOTIVES
act from honest m. purely 559
behind racism, anti-Christ 1488
cloud m. with smoke screen of
excuses 3476
emulation or greed, m. spiritually
the same 2009
honesty, no ulterior m. 5874
Jesus speaks of m. rather than
actions 6450
judge ourselves by our m. 6596
Man sees actions, God m. 7866
necessities form m. of prayers of
ordinary Christians 8788
To act in everything with highest
m. 6913

MOULD
God's fingers m. into loveliness
537

MOULDING
Why is God m. me just as he
chooses 3042

MOUND
What a towering m. of sin 3492

MOUNT
Lord came down from M. to be
identified with sin 6488
to heaven on ruins of cherished
schemes 3631

MOUNT TABOR
love Lord as much on Calvary as
M. 2094

MOUNTAIN
Aloft on sky and m. wall 8047
can sit on a m. but not a tack
9636
can't have a m. without valleys
10934
Climb every m. 4421
Doubt makes m. which faith
moves 2938
faced with a m. I will not quit
2633
faults like grain of sand beside m.
of mercies of God 4817
fear doesn't want journey to m.
3971
God of the m. peaks 7539
gossip makes m. of molehill by
adding dirt 5114
He who moves a m. 59
he's allowed me to go up to the m.
4975
If fig tree grow in side of m. cliff
3736
nor m. greater miracle than an
atom 7940
O'er m, or plain, or sea 5420
prefer to be king of the m. for a
day 5308
Pride is the cold m. peak 6026
Reason has never been a m.
climber 3716
should be removed by bird 3295
soul has higher peaks than any m.
7539
turn the m. into gold mine 2633
work to climb a m. to pray 8860

MOUNTAIN-CLIMBING
get ulcers m. over molehills 1566

MOUNTAINEERS
Make us thy m. 5939

MOUNTAINS
are God's thoughts upheaved
8048
before the m. were brought forth
4769
By our prayers, m. are moved
1285
Do not m. praise God 7997
if never heard m. singing 8017
In eternity, m. as transient as
clouds 3279
Men never stumble over m. 2513
molehills become m. when
someone adds little dirt 10443
must scale m. if view plain 8562
Patience, diligence removes m.
8408

Remember majesty of the m. 9270

MOUNTAINTOP
when on the the m. 4175

MOURN
inhumanity makes thousands m. 30
not the dead 426
one thing to m. for sin because exposes us to hell 9581
the apathetic throng 426
the cowed and meek 426
To m. adversity multiples misfortune 221
to m. for sin because evil 9581
Who see and dare not speak 426

MOURNED
Christ m. that thou mightest rejoice 6393
man should be m. at birth, not death 2209

MOURNER
approval not to m. but to self-assured 5891

MOURNFULLY
Look not m. into past 8378

MOUSE
a m. can bite him to death 2859
depends on whether man or m. 8584
said to m, "cheese on cat's whiskers" 11103
To a m, a cat is a lion 9528

MOUTH
ability to keep m. shut priceless 1876
betray Jesus Christ by keeping m. shut 628
bore uses m. to talk while you yawn 1828
Breath, m, ears, eyes 6120
Cheer up—only dentist down in m. 2539
Christ cannot live his life without our m. 1270
Christ opens m. so wide embraces all heaven, earth 6511
Close ear against him who opens m. against another 10447
Discretion is keeping your m. shut 2893
don't invent with your m. 5165
Flattery, m. that praises 4049
From his sweet silence my m. sings 4125
from man's m. can tell what he is 5126
good teacher whose ears get as much exercise as m. 10998
gossip's m. is devil's mailbag 5146
hold chin up, will keep m. shut 11463
If keep m. shut, flies won't get in 1854
is made to shut 1875
keep m. shut 1627

keeps silent to hear heart speak 10270
keeps the m. shut 1884
let space become one m. for song 4712
Make me the m. for such as cannot speak 10130
Mischief comes from much opening of m. 10685
narrow mind, wide m. go together 4059
once burnt his m. always blows soup 3536
one's m. is what one becomes 3566
one's m. what one becomes 10687
Only baby admired for opening m. 5151
seventy years to learn to keep m. shut 2897
shut m. and eyes to injustice around him 11690
stop long enough to let feet catch up with m. 9331
sweet as salt in your m. 4050
time you spend with m. open 1892
Wide is our m. 7575
wise man tells woman m. beautiful when closed 2889
Z is keeping your m. shut 10785

MOUTHING
mental activity m. of cliches 11237

MOUTHS
faith that will shut m. of lions 3787
made with m. only, no hands 3097
Out of the m. of babes 3882
People lose weight by keeping m. shut 9972
proclaim God with m. 487
should not be said by big m. 3461

MOVE
Adams will have to m. out before long 8142
beyond superficialities of culture 1760
darken the atmosphere in which we m. 4255
God hath two wings, which he doth ever m. 4812
God watches to see door m. from within 4775
healthiest relationships breathe—m. out and then m. back together 9494
If God doesn't approve, fly doesn't m. 4943
If m. ten inches to be happy, never will be 5534
In Christ m. into breathtaking future 8364
In Christ m. into meaningful present 8364
In Christ m. out of past 8364

Jesus never made a m. without his Father 8520
Let him that would m. world m. himself 3439
Things m. along an appointed path 9173
those that m. 10504
through life in distracted way 5590
toward friends who listen 1857
want church that will m. the world 1452
While prayers to heal her wrongs m. slow behind 6269

MOVEABLE
those that are m. 10504

MOVED
By our prayers, mountains are m. 1285
if don't feel close to God, who m? 4857
To know reasons which have m. God 4989

MOVEMENT
attractiveness of mass m. 10526
church is a m. 1385
Every great m. triumph of enthusiasm 3178
Every spiritual m. followed by missionary m. 9740
flowering of person m. from incompleteness 7699
God's creative method is m. 4469
in corporateness of mass m, new freedom 10526
least m. affects all nature 572
listen to the gentle m. of the Holy Spirit 10257
Love is a m. 7630
Marriage a m, a boundless adventure 7630
no transforming apathy into m. without emotion 3053
Our nature lies in m. 6771
Personal contact a m. that must be rediscovered 7630
Self-centeredness a m. away from God 9946
spirituality a m. 5981

MOVEMENTS
All men at head of great m. are Christian men 5094
Christian m. suggest brotherhood 916
of the eternal mind 4990
repeating involuntarily the m. of those among whom we live 6243

MOVES
He m. into the battle wholly weaponless 6124
He who m. a mountain 59
not to pretend we love everything that m. 5890
one who m. on in spite of failure 3624

Prayer m. the arm which m. the world 8950

toy world which m. when pull strings 4132

traffic m. faster in next lane 2873

MOVIES

wooed with religious m. 1403

MOVING

all things everywhere are m. 9909

Death m. from one home to another 2247

direction we are m. 4424

God does demand we keep m. 9832

great thing is direction we are m. 1914

response to gentle m. of Holy Spirit 5396

Salvation is m. from living death to deathless life 9809

The world is m. so fast 66

Time always packing up and m. 11334

toward world of throwaway products, friends, marriages 10524

MOW

The more you m. us down 7678

MUCH

able to say how m. you love is to love little 7323

Contentment, realization of how m. you have 1783

Courage lost, m. lost 9263

Education teaches us how m. man has to learn 3004

expecting too m. too fast 6116

few observations and m. reasoning leads to error 9410

give all their living, have given m. 10738

give God thanks for having revealed so m. 4908

Give m. 5561

give m. without sacrifice, given little 10738

God so m. for you did do 4476

good leader prepared to deny himself m. 6793

Good words worth m, cost little 11987

have so m. feel little need of Christ 1350

have too m. of too m. 9552

He that speaks m, m. mistaken 1847

heart of God so m. on us 4770

If love Christ m, shall trust him m. 11472

If we want m, shall find m. 6354

if you think too m. of yourself, other people won't 9253

little trouble praying when in m. trouble 8870

Men expect too m, do too little 3504

Mischief comes from m. opening of mouth 10685

no situation too m. for God 168

Not how m. we give 4371

not satisfied with m. 1805

Not who has m. is rich, but who gives m. 4370

Old age needs that little so m. 8161

one who has too m. to say 10272

Poverty wants m; greed, everything 5322

prays m. by night, face fair by day 8808

proverb m. matter decocted into few words 9377

situations too m. for us 168

So m. God would give 8662

So m. has been given to me 5259

Some have m, some have more 11852

speaking and lying are cousins 6854

Strange how m. you've got to know 6700

test of generosity, how m. you have left 4378

test of generosity, not how m. you give 4378

that may be thought cannot wisely be said 2898

they know so m. that ain't so 6083

Those who would know m. 6708

Thou hast given so m. to me 5265

Too m. humility is pride 9255

Too m. rest is rust 6781

trouble praying when in little trouble 8870

want m. always m. in need 2878

We have as m. of God as we actually want 5772

Where m. desire to learn, many opinions 6711

Where m. light, shadow is deep 6712

Wherever too m, something lacking 11879

who does not thank for little, will not thank for m. 11171

Who m. receives, but nothing gives 4374

who promises too m. means nothing 9326

who suffers m. will know m. 10852

who thinks too m. of himself thinks too little of others 9243

world is too m. with us 12046

years teach m. days never knew 3546

youth hate too m. 12181

youth love too m. 12181

MUD

astonishing that I—dust, ash, m. 7489

Gossip like m. thrown against clean wall 5129

Scandal should be treated as m. on clothes 5154

Sorrow, like rain, makes roses and m. 10621

trying to remove dirt with m. 402

MUDDIED

vision which is m. 6931

MUDDY

very m. and tattered children 3609

MUFFLED

I wait the m. oar 6916

MUHAMMAD

Jesus conquered more millions than M. 6449

MULE

nor man a m. whose reason works not at all 9417

MULLED

story of Jesus m. over more than any other in history 5729

MULTIPLES

Love m. by division 7252

violence for violence m. violence 11675

MULTIPLICATION

evil not solved by m. 3387

fanaticism today, trite as m. table week after 3911

MULTIPLIED

Poetry has m. my enjoyments 8616

To m. trials, his m. peace 5223

MULTIPLIES

Bible m. discoveries 683

To mourn adversity m. misfortune 221

MULTIPLY

as we through frailty m. transgressions 5212

Grace can m. pardons 5212

Love doesn't start to m. until give it away 7238

love, joy, peace m. when divide with others 4360

will m. thousandfold capacity to enjoy blessings 5254 4293

MULTITUDE

happiness not in m. of friends 10517

is a fickle master 10517

Sin with the m. 9672

MUMMERY

Any man may play his part in the m. 6295

MUMMY

so content changed into mummy 1816

MUMPS

theological problems are the soul's m. 11202

MUNDANE

work sacred as parson's 3113

MUNIFICENCE

contemplate God's m. in abundance of earth 4581

MURDER

betrayal and m. exist on earth 6158

civilized life complicated system of m. 10513

forbid birth is quicker m. 16

I helped m. somebody 22

is once for all forbidden 16

isn't that bad 7882

mass movement, new freedom to m. 10526

millions make a hero 11758

no better than cards 10324

One m. makes a villain 11758

People commit m. after reading about m. 12156

Slander is a kind of m. 10462

Suicide worse form of m. 10945

what is war but m. in uniform 11777

When anger in Cain's heart, m. not far off 10383

When angry, m. not far off 406

when put people down 10683

when treat people as insignificant 10683

when we destroy people with words 10683

world based on foundation of m. 10513

MURDERERS

People do not decide to be m. 11080

punish m. among private persons 11776

punished unless kill in large numbers 11753

MURDERING

crime of m. whole nations 11776

MURDERS

lack of charity in action m. faith 3829

Without m. no new power can arise 8722

MURMUR

if ills irreparable, m. ungrateful 1563

if ills remediless, m. in vain 1563

MURMURING

denying wisdom of God 1569

Meek endurance, obedience without m. 7728

MURMURS

For m. or lament 11168

MUSCLE

defeat turns gristle to m. 2511

Unused truth as useless as unused m. 11583

MUSCLES

a few strain m. to carry off a prize 7018

Christians ought to be flexing m. 3339

intellect has powerful m, but no personality 6333

MUSEUM

church, not m. for saints 1379

MUSHROOMS

No rain, no m. 4485

MUSIC

after silence, m. nearest to inexpressible 7884

All one's life is m. 7885

all possible changes of color, feeling 7905

allays each grief 7900

almost all we have of heaven on earth 7902

Along the Psalmist's m. deep 2345

art of the prophets 7914

as m. is, so are people of country 7889

as seasonable in grief as joy 7903

as world had me at start, it will have m. at the last 7886

calms the agitate heart 7935

can calm agitations of the soul 7914

can make despair please 7911

can soften pain 7911

Change nursery of m. 960

child of prayer 7906

Christian is more m. when he prays 8749

Comes sweet with m. to thy wearied ear 10960

die with all their m. in them 8647

duty performed gives m. at midnight 9675

eases grief's smarting wound 7913

easy to hear m. in waves 8034

enjoy m. but have no idea of cost 2021

evil thoughts quelled by its divine control 7935

exalts each joy 7900

existence of fiddle presupposes m. 4606

Expels diseases 7900

fate's severest rage disarm 7911

favorite m. of asceticism, a dirge 467

fiercest grief can charm 7911

fills soul 7934

find a m. in our souls never felt before 9503

glorifying drugs, sexual promiscuity 7910

God hears no sweeter m. 7171

God is its author, not man 7891

God wanted world to have m. 7886

God writes the m. of our lives 7056

Great Director of m. arranges program perfectly new 7895

has charms to soothe savage breast 7901

Hope is grief's best m 5921

human voices gives you m. 7893

If you can't face the m. 6797

in the dawning morn 7927

in the depth of night 7927

in the twilight cloud 7927

is God's best gift to man 7904

is love itself 7905

is moonlight in gloomy night of life 7909

is the prophet's art 7935

Kind words m. of the world 6645

language spoken by angels 7907

Laughter is m. of life 6734

Let him step to m. which he hears 10827

Life is like m. 6966

little girl who hears m. for first time 7922

lives have no m. in them 9059

Love is friendship set to m. 7234

making of m. in a rest 7056

making of m. often slow, painful process 7056

Mathematics set to m. 4454

medicine of troubled mind 7908

most strongly suggests ecstasy, infinity 5631

next to theology I give m. highest place 7914

night shall be filled with m. 7887

no great m. on its lips 1441

No m. but the making of m. in a rest 9687

not ear that hears sweetness of m. 10656

Not without design does God write m. of our lives 7056

of the spheres made of sighs and sobs 10878

one has m. and the flying cloud 10673

One man's m, another's noise 7918

one of the most magnificent presents God has given 7914

only art fully accepted by church 1998

only art of earth we take to heaven 7904

only art of heaven given to earth 7904

passions quelled by its divine control 7935

Psalms, m. of heart of man 798

purest language of passion 7905

receiving m. lesson from thy Father 10600

shall untune the sky 7925

Silence a rich pause in m. of life 10262

Soft is the m. that would charm forever 6028

softens every pain 7900

struck one chord of m. 7919

Subdues rage of poison and plague 7900

sweetest m. in kind words 11995

sweetest m. isn't in oratorios 11995

temptations quelled by its divine control 7935

the soul that hears the sweetness of m. 10656

they who listen to such m. 4051

thou bringest eternity nearer 7916

thousand times better than words 7934

To ear of God everything he created makes m. 8743

To him there's m. in a groan 9024

tune our hearts to brave m. 9059

understood by thousands 7905

used to ridicule religion, morality 7910

washes away dust of life 7912

we take for granted speech, m, sounds 9094

weapon used to make perverse seem glamorous 7910

When words leave off, m. begins 7932

which thou canst not hear 4708

while marches to m. 3090

who love good m. happiest people in world 5567

woods with m. ring 8039

words in comparison with genuine m. 7934

Words instruments of m. 11998

MUSICAL
easy to play m. instrument 7897

MUSICIAN
first string m. touches is bass 10663

How does the m. read the rest 7056

MUSING
If cannot find God in the night m. 4856

MUSLIM
submits 6563

MUSLIMS
build wall between M. 2988

If stories incomprehensible to M. 12147

MUSSOLINI
psychological secrets M. used 12178

MUST
choose to forgive 4109

Endure when you m. 3148

Love m. be learned again and again 7265

put up with inconvenience of genius 4394

repudiate seeking God for benefits 4806

MUTABILITY
God not affected by our m. 4587

immutability of God, m. of men 977

MUTATION
Even voice of conscience undergoes m. 1680

law of m. belongs to fallen world 4589

MUTE
hills are m, yet how they speak of God 8014

Love gives eloquence to the m. 7260

man m. before elemental truth 10274

MUTTERING
God does not look down toward earth 7567

MUTUAL
Marriage, dependence m. 7642

MUTUALLY
Health, cheerfulness m. beget each other 5607

MY
least used word by unselfish person 11653

Myself and I, and mine and m. 1855

MYOPIA
Worry a species of m. 12086

MYRIAD
A m. homes, a m. ways 4834

God intrudes in m. ways 7556

his words are intimate on many m. tongues 6394

MYRRH
gathered m. from among Lord's persecution 10913

represents suffering 10913

MYSELF
and I, and mine and my 1855

arch-traitor to m. 2583

Behold my needs which I know not m. 9042

By his first work God gave me to m. 4528

can fall down by m. 9044

chide no heathen in world but m. 3942

Christ by first work gave me to m. 6361

Darkness is my point of view, my right to m. 7106

God gave me back 4528

God will not do what I can do for m. 8803

have had all I can take of m. 8133

have lost all and found m. 9559

have lost the immortal part of m. 9622

If half-full of m. 9932

If I knew m, I'd run away 10011

image of m. I try to create 9950

in order that I may love m. 9950

Inside m. place where I live all alone 9933

Let me know m. O God, that I may know thee 9068

mystery of m. solved by this besetting God 4889

never a greater miracle or monster than m. 7388

not my business to think about m. 9934

quote others, the better to express m. 9382

right to m. sin that shocks God 10397

sin claim to my right to m. 10389

Suddenly I feel m. transformed, changed 7964

than I should be at odds with m. and contradict m. 6294

through handicaps found m. 11147

to m, a heart of steel 5626

When I give, I give m. 10121

Whenever I look inside m, I am afraid 9957

MYSTERIES
agnosticism, m. remain 320

Bible, rising aloft into m. of heaven 750

deep m. contained in the Lord's Prayer 7156

error to think can understand m. 11203

Faith can never penetrate m. of God 3702

faith must include m. 11203

God knows all m. 4881

Life's m. for our worship 6995

Men live on brink of m. 3654

of Christianity incomprehensible 1213

of God known to saints 10252

philosopher aspires to explain m. 12118

Shall we think with tiny brains we can unravel m. 7944

through m. God declares himself 10255

when m. clear 5676

which you can hardly get to end of 9402

MYSTERIOUS
as soon as existence m. thought begins 11220

fear manipulate with m. 3971

free choices, foreordained decrees 1153

God's guidance not m. 5370

gospel possesses m. efficacy 732

human soul so m. 10667

infinity of God not m, only unfathomable 4684

nature of Christ's existence m. 5728

our total nature, m. and deep 7463

We are so m. in personality 5458

MYSTERIOUSLY
eternal truth m. suggests itself 7949

feeling God has m. guided us 5392

MYSTERY
angel to guide through m. 366

another name for ignorance 7942
Baby, unfathomed m. 805
bear witness to m. of God 7945
Christ, his total m. 6369
Christianity dispels more m. 1214
complexity and m. of a human
  being 4247
constitutes essence of worship
  12118
conversion, an impenetrable m.
  1902
doctrine unilluminated 7937
Each one of us is a m. 6171
everything may be said to be a m.
  7940
evil root of m. 3353
extraordinary m. of human
  goodness 5037
fact about which we cannot know
  everything 7936
God alone knows meaning of m.
  called time 4694
God shows himself absolute m.
  4738
God's patience with ill-natured
  saints m. 4893
great m. of human life 7101
is demanded by religious instinct
  12118
is God's; the promise is yours
  11485
Man an inexhaustible m. 7405
Man the great inscrutable m. of
  God 7409
of Christ's existence meets wants
  of man 5728
of evil isn't as great 5037
of grace, never comes too late
  5228
of myself solved by this besetting
  God 4889
of the Bible 738
of the ordinary 6918
Seeing God means seeing into m.
  of things 7547
Spirit-filled life no m. revealed to
  select few 5803
the m. of our existence 4549
Theology attempt to understand
  the m. 11206
There is ever a beyond of m. 4686
to explain m. of God 7939
Trinity, m. faith embraces 11428
Trinity, m. reason cannot fathom
  11428
when you can explain m. of
  watermelon 7939
where m. of life appears 10564
why people ask if empty seat
  occupied 8477
Worship, is a soul in awe before
  m. of universe 12132

MYSTIC
for m. important theology should
  flourish 7946
loses consciousness of creature
  distinctions 7966
to participate here and now in
  that real life 7969

too full of God to speak
  intelligibly to world 7965

MYSTICAL
experience bedrock of faith 7948
experience formless, vague,
  fleeting 7948
experience soul acting as unity
  7948
greatest paradoxes of m. life 7962
intimate quality of spiritual life
  7954
means real 7954
must never think of faith as purely
  m. 3830
some type of m. experience 4015

MYSTICISM
art of union with reality 7956
attempt to draw near to God 7947
filling consciousness with content
  7957
hard word for "Kingdom of
  Heaven within" 7947
is communion with God 7955
no room allowed for m. pure and
  simple 7959
on wings of m. can spirit soar to
  full height 7963

MYSTIC'S
spirit lost in abyss of Deity 7966

MYSTICS
for m, pain an ectasy 8255

MYTHS
nation of rugged individualists
  1642

𝒩

NADIR OF WEAKNESS
all that man can conceive, N.
  6698

NAGGING
form of continual criticism 2069

NAIL
they were broken, by a n. 2162
what is from God fixed as n. in
  sure place 4524

NAILED
take tongue, have it n. to cross
  7190
to my poor planet 6120

NAILS
are real iron 2147
dripping from iron n. 1368
Love's as hard as n. 2135
Pithy sentences like sharp n. 9384
were driven 2123
Words n. for fixing ideas 12000

NAIVE
helps one go through life smoothly
  7976
is man's weakness, child's strength
  7977

most positive men are most n.
  7975
risk as much in n. as in suspicious
  7979
When think children are n. 8319

NAKED
Be Lord of n. faces 6296
Christ a robe, if any n. be 6391
cloak in chest belongs to n. 11855
Helpless, n, piping loud 808
in land of n. people ashamed of
  clothes 1638
Lord, I am now a n. soul 7952
seeing how n. the end 5952
to earth I descend 5952
to earth was I brought 5952
Truth may walk around n. 6869

NAKEDNESS
Not in utter n. 809

NAME
blank sheet with n. signed at
  bottom 1720
cannot say hallowed be thy n. if
  8818
Chance n. for our ignorance 6078
chanting your n. 1368
Christ, to tear your n. from this
  world 6496
Death's truer n. is Onward 2268
Experience n. people give to
  mistakes 3531
good n. better than great riches
  9610
good n. got by many actions, lost
  by one 9611
good n. is forever 9617
good n. keeps brightness even in
  dark days 6292
He that filches from me my good
  n. 10449
Hope a more gentle n. for fear
  5916
How sweet the n. of Jesus sounds
  1507
in n. of lowly Jesus 1370
Infinite sowed his n. in heavens in
  stars 8037
Infinite sowed his n. on earth in
  flowers 8037
Infinite written n. on heavens in
  stars 4705
let lightning write his n. in fire
  4712
Mother n. for God in hearts of
  children 7848
Need is our n. 7575
obscurity, contempt better than n.
  10875
of God may be written upon that
  soul 10475
of Jesus plowed into history of
  world 5727
Our good or evil n. depends 4198
Satan, his n. heard no more in
  heaven 2666
secret of a new n. 7127
See how it feels to have a n. 4419

Seeking to perpetuate one's n. on
  earth 3860
society, politer n. of hell 1135
through infinite remote the n.
  4712
to breathe the n. 1763
To think the thought, to breathe
  the n. 4799
What world calls virtue a n, a
  dream 11720
While grass, flowers, stars spell
  out his n. 8019

NAMELESS
His little, n, unremembered acts
  6664
Little n. acts of kindness 6997
little, n, unremembered acts 626

NAMES
beginning of wisdom is to call
  things by right n. 11941
do not shun and call life hard n.
  6903
for Christians: saints, believers,
  brethren, disciples 1328
God blots out his people's sins,
  not their n. 4626
Their n. are What and Why and
  When 6686

NAPALM
Bomb, 1952 11750

NAPOLEON
avalanches of N. melted away 730
Jesus conquered more millions
  than N. 6449
To his dog, every man is N. 9509

NARROW
agrees with our views, makes us
  n. and rigid 11216
Consecration n. lonely way to love
  1722
enemy of Christianity, all that
  makes it n. 1233
every other seal too n. for soul
  10659
fear of being thought n. 836
ingratitude the unfailing mark of
  a n. soul 6251
is the mansion of my soul 10658
let him make our lives n. 2829
mind, wide mouth go together
  4059
never any traffic congestion on
  straight, n. path 9819
Prayer draws us out of n. limits
  8906
Within my n. heart 5788

NARROWING
sanctification will cost intense n.
  of interests 9831

NARROW-MINDED
most n. Christian must admit
  5791

NARROW-MINDEDNESS
in fearful n. 10540

NARROWS
Evil is all that n. life 5024

NASTY
reply to a n. remark 402
things due to complexes will fall
  off 1030

NATAL
Repentance a n. day when new
  life begins 9591

NATION
America more things than any
  other n. 8624
Bind in thy love every n. and race
  11424
destiny of n. depends on citizens
  under 25 12173
determine future course of n. 8360
Discontent first step in progress of
  n. 2864
do not know n. until we know
  pleasures 6842
family measure of greatness of n.
  3894
harmony in home, will be order in
  the n. 8441
Home strength of a n. 5836
hope of n. in character of its
  people 5190
hope of n. not in government
  5190
hope of n. not in its administration
  5190
hope of n. not in wisdom of
  executive 5190
If order in the n, peace in world
  8441
needs changing 1333
No n. better than individuals 7987
No n. made progress in
  downward direction 7834
Should any civilized n. give right
  to kill 20
Sometimes a n. abolishes God
  4897
spectacle of a n. praying 8991
that thinks more of ease, comfort
  7984
thoughtful mind sees n. itself 7982
we are n. of social cowards 1642
Whenever n. becomes unspiritual
  12194
wit of a n. discovered in its
  proverbs 9386

NATIONAL
George Washington born on n.
  holiday 7981

NATIONALITY
Jesus throws down dividing
  prejudices of n. 913
Our true n. is mankind 5980

NATION'S
to bind up n. wounds 5199

NATIONS
betrayal in peace 11783
cohesion in war 11783

crime of murdering whole n.
  11776
deception in peace 11783
dispersion in peace 11783
does not Lord hear n. blame, yet
  4894
If Christian n. were Christians,
  there would be no war 11748
Men and n. sink or soar 10510
peace among ourselves, and with
  all n. 5199
revival altered destinies of n. 9752
These are the patriots n. need
  7986
training in war 11783
wisdom in war 11783
Youth will assume control of n.
  12160

NATIVE
Now n. to earth as I am 6120
there lies the poet's n. land 10535

NATURAL
and the holy are the same 9821
as n. to die as be born 2320
Be n. before God 8770
blessed with n. warmth of heart
  7304
Children are n. mimics 1109
Confidence in n. world,
  self-reliance 1605
end of reliance on n. devotion
  5792
impedes us in our n. outlook and
  ways 9821
In n. matter faith follows evidence
  3743
in n. world everything depends on
  taking initiative 5446
insistence upon seeing ahead n.
  3758
love like a n. spring 7257
Love, hatred n. exaggerators 3423
man must know to believe 3743
nonbeliever lives by faith in n.
  laws 3653
not n. to be like Christ 8113
Nothing attractive about gospel to
  n. man 5108
sanctification, lose our n. identity
  9840
science assumes permanence,
  uniformity of n. laws 9869
Sighs are n. language of the heart
  5623
some find more n. to approach
  God in solitude 1445
strength of Christianity different
  from n. strength 1165
to be like person you live with
  most 6235
view and Bible view of man
  different 7429
we are not n. men 1346
When Lord does come, will be as
  n. as breathing 9912
world, impossible to be made over
  873

NATURALLY

evangelism happening n. 3313
impossible for us to be children of
    God n. 9801
impossible for us to follow God n.
    9801
our own idols 10425

NATURE

a different kind of right prevails
    8012
Ah, how unjust to n. and himself
    3190
art of God Eternal 8025
art only an imitation of n. 8043
balm of death numbing lower n.
    1332
best stops in our n. drawn out
    9503
Bible's variety like scenes of n. 680
born from intimate depths of
    divine n. 5967
By n. honest, by experience wise
    11957
can be glad with entire gladness
    8012
cannot crucify my old n. 9836
cannot jump from winter to
    summer 9875
Change is handmaiden n. requires
    959
comprehending true n. of existence
    3488
Consistency contrary to n. 1745
Does not all n. praise God 7997
Every victory of science reveals
    more clearly divine design in n.
    9866
Evil minds change good to own n.
    5015
Experience comb n. gives when
    bald 3518
extravagant wealth of beauty
    8046
Feelings are your life and n. 4018
fights against venturing forth
    9930
formula which expresses law of n.
    8001
gave men two ends 10793
give up fears, face our true n.
    10551
go from nature's God down to n.
    8034
Grace does not destroy n, it
    perfects it 5214
greed has pity neither for n. or
    human beings 5327
happiness of a retired n. 5568
has defects to show she is only
    image of God 8022
has perfections to show image of
    God 8022
holiness is conformity to n. of God
    5758
hymn of praise to God 8001
in glory we shall know his n. 3814
in her laws tells of God 8023
In lovely n. see the God of love
    8006

inner n. of sin 10387
is freedom 8012
joy in n. is absence of man 8035
Knowledge of n. and atheism
    incompatible 6696
least movement affects all n. 572
lectures of ethics or divinity 3192
Life is dust n. lends man for an
    hour 6960
locked in her clasp 8027
love n. because a retreat from man
    8012
Make possible for me which is
    impossible by n. 8643
makes me content with this world
    8012
Man's conquest of n. astonishing
    7414
men are by n. equal 3225
message of God not too clear
    8023
minds speculate on what lies
    behind n. 4704
Miracles contrary to what we
    know about n. 8021
Miracles not contrary to n. 8021
more I study n, more amazed at
    Creator 8040
My God, by his n. my Father
    above 7951
name for effect whose cause is
    God 8024
none of man's institutions control
    her 8012
Observe God in his works 8031
of Christ's existence mysterious
    5728
of God to make something out of
    nothing 3604
of gospel is that it divides 5102
of man to err 3260
Old age, a second child, by n.
    curs'd 8163
Our n. hungers for God 7512
Our n. lies in movement 6771
our total n, mysterious and deep
    7463
passing through n. to eternity
    2402
permit n. to have her way 3196
powerless to come closer to her
    8027
powerless to leave her 8027
rainbow is ribbon n. puts on after
    washing hair 9391
reliability of n. 4643
Repentance change of n. befitting
    heaven 9597
root, bud, and bough desire to be
    more 471
rose without clang, clamor 1956
selfishness destroys spiritual n.
    10073
shows something worthy of a God
    8026
sighing through all her works
    10314
sin a breach of n. 10360

stand at real height against higher
    n. 6037
stern discipline pervades n. 2839
stillness of n. louder than choir of
    voices 8041
surrounded by her 8027
symbol of God's n. is cross 2167
takes us up into whirl of her dance
    8027
tells us nothing of love, grace of
    God 8023
that which is contrary to his n.
    4513
think of n. as unlimited
    broadcasting station 8013
tip from n. 1875
to be commanded, must be obeyed
    3198
to have perfect love we must have
    n. of God 7316
To know n. is to know must be a
    God 6696
very n. acquired within families
    3881
war violates order of n. 11751
with open volume stands 8026
yearning arises from image of
    God in n. of man 7531
    4744
Your n. must be bathed in new
    element 880
Your whole n. must be re-born
    880
Your whole n. must be
    reconsecrated to Maker 880

NATURE'S

and duty's never at odds 3813
Death n. way to slow down 2248
Gossip is n. telephone 5130
Light! N. resplendent robe 7109
soft nurse 10485
Tired n. sweet restorer, balmy sleep
    10491

NATURES

What must our n. be like 7450

NAUGHTY

So shines good deed in n. world
    2499

NAUSEA

of being the thing I was 10021

NAVIES

all n. that ever were built 6353

NEAR

God both far away, n. at hand
    4465
I am as n. as he 4859
Live n. to God 4559
Make happy those who are n.
    9480
mysticism attempt to draw n. to
    God 7947
not one life not so n. to God 7057
O be thou n. to me 5413
so very n. to God 4859
to God's secret as anyone can get
    10592
When none but God is n. 8939

NEARER

As grave grows n, theology growing simple 11182
bringest receding waves of eternity n. 7916
death draws every day n. 4726
every step n. God increases depth we may fall 10700
God is n. to us than we think 4878
God n. than own soul 1713
God's heart in a garden 8032
I approach the end 11132
I cannot be 4859
one day n. home than ever before 5676
pushes you n. to God 4190
than hands and feet 4862
to comprehending existence 3488
we get to Christ, more intensely missionary we become 7785
Wisdom oftentimes n. when stoop than soar 6044
worshiper is not n. to God than before 8845

NEAREST

best things are n. 829
music n. to expressing inexpressible 7884
thing to God is human soul 10651
to divine nature, n. to perfection 8522
word is now 11993

NEARLY

Follow thee more n. 9043

NEARNESS

sense of sin in proportion to n. to God 10349

NEAR-SIGHTEDNESS

Worry a species of n. 12086

NEBO'S

By N. lonely mountain 778

NECESSARILY

not n. against reason because above it 7938
not n. well-adjusted who makes world better place 6196
Truth must n. be stranger than fiction 11574
What is new not n. needed 3660

NECESSARY

bridle for tongue n. furniture 11405
Confession n. for fellowship 1595
Death as n. as sleep 2244
Humility n. prerequisite for grace 6007
Ignorance n. condition of life itself 6081
In n. things, unity 7196
inclination to injustice makes democracy n. 2528
isn't n. to blow out other person's light 10457
make n. adjustments in light of ideals 3060

Make yourself n. to somebody 10172
may be n. to lose everything 4340
more repairs are n. 8181
Never say more than n. 1863
never tell unless absolutely n. 5148
not n. to tell where or how converted 1903
not n. to understand everything 11611
Only humble have n. resources to give of themselves 5957
Only thing n. for triumph of evil 3402
shall emerge from our n. imprisonment 6110
So n. is our friendship to God 4564
so n. practice of presence of God 4873
Three things n. for salvation 9824
To believe greatly, n. to doubt greatly 2958
To live long, n. to live slowly 7067
To those who believe, no explanation n. 608
trials n. preparation for great duties 2725
understanding of redemption not n. to salvation 9433
want to do what is n. to look respectable 6810
weaknesses n. to purposes of life 11788
work not a n. drudgery 3127
Youth not yet learned n. limitations 12181

NECESSITATE

God's foreknowledge does not n. him 4882

NECESSITIES

form motives of prayers of ordinary Christian 8788
Restless, discontent n. of progress 2870

NECESSITY

awful hour when first n. of hiding comes 5480
By n. we all quote 9379
God made rich by man's n. 4541
limits of reason make faith n. 3840
love should bend to n. of brethren 3839
Money not required to buy one n. of the soul 7813
Not n. but abundance produces greed 5318
of n. will be much arguing 6711
Precisely their n. 10501
recognize n. of Holy Spirit for living 11243
to cultivate reason a n. 9425
we do not exist by divine n. 3481

NECK

take him by scruff of his n. 4315

When break leg, be thankful isn't n. 11169

NEED

a superhuman Savior 6459
all n. God-appointed storms 191
any greater n. than get to grips with living God 7485
anything that tells heart's n. can find its way to God 8849
as desperately in n. of salvation 7827
as though no n. to pray except in illness, sorrow 8788
Be a friend. You don't n. glory 4217
Believing God must n. him there 2792
big heart that desires will of God 5442
came to know God is all we n. 7472
Can a man love God ignoring n. of brother 10052
Carry own lantern, and you n. not fear dark 6167
Charity sees the n, not the cause 7163
Children little n. to deceive 1132
Children more n. of models than critics 8286
children n. to be talked to like grown-ups 8311
Christ will provide everything you n. 9521
Christ, God's everything for man's total n. 6427
Christians prepared to trust God completely 11488
Death, no n. to get out of bed 2241
devil distracts hunger for God 7512
do not n. to go somewhere to find God 4870
do not recognize n. of Holy Spirit for thinking 11243
don't n. to be right all the time 3929
earth provides enough for every n. 5326
everything created has n. of God 4452
eye single to God's glory 5442
find a n. and fill it 10216
find people who n. you 2558
Finding God, no n. to seek peace 8433
For we are weak and n. some deep revealing 9050
Forgiveness man's deepest n. 4077
friend never known until man have n. 4166
given weakness that he might feel n. of God 8806
God always receptive to n. 4590
God does not n. our money 4359
God has given me everything I n. 1784

God has no n. of his creatures 4452

God has no n. of marionettes 1142

God only gives us light we n. for present 5397

God provides me with all I n. 4992

God wants to teach us our n. for himself 8990

God who knows the n. 10877

God's blessings on those who n. him 821

God's restrictions show our n. 1522

greater is our God than our greatest n. 7468

greater virtues to bear good fortune than bad 11719

greatest n. more true Christians 1307

had he befriended those really in n. 7423

happens to light upon passage which meets n. 5441

have so much feel little n. of Christ 1350

Health, wealth wean us of n. for Christ 5581

honesty and integrity, no n. to manipulate 5874

I have a great Christ for my n. 6399

I have a great n. for Christ 6399

I have n. of nothing 4561

I n. not be angry with him 9579

I n. thy presence every passing hour 5225

I n. your yes 1536

If no clouds would not n. faith 10598

If we n. something to buttress us 4768

Immature love says, "I love you because I n. you" 7194

impossible to overstate n. for prayer 3875

in hour of n. faith born within 3820

is our name 7575

is the call, call is the presence 5781

Lash love upon the rich, who often n. it most 7348

law could not bring what we n. 9755

look to no other 7548

Lord for creation of a home 5819

Lord healed me of n. to be healed 5610

love for neighbor means love for any man in n. 7201

man should ever stand in n. of man 9462

man's n. to blend in 7415

Mature love says, "I n. you because I love you" 7194

might not n. me, yet they might 10501

more complete our sense of n. 7524

never in n, yet rejoicing in gains 4954

No man n. stay way he is 1146

no n. that others weep for him 10877

no n. to plead love of God 4785

not be overwhelmed with confusion 4924

not fear disaster will follow freedom of thought 4134

not great enough for our n. 9538

not shout my faith 8014

Nothing can n. a lie 3937

of man to leave prison of his aloneness 7143

of man to overcome separateness 7143

One alone can supply our n. 6455

others if we are to know anything 9513

painfully conscious of my n. of grace 9097

People do not n. Satan to recruit to evil 3396

People used to n. rest after work 3114

pride, taking less than you n. 4353

saints n. no intellectual greatness 5301

satanically-managed man has no n. of God 9853

Scripture, higher, wider than n. 691

shall never n. wish for a better light 727

silence to recover from futility of words 10556

spiritual power independent of feelings 4015

stones would praise God if n. arose 12099

sufficiency in world for man's n. 3204

that broke me at thy feet 10969

The good have no n. of an advocate 5081

through prayer to place ourselves in attitude to be helped 9010

To be with God, no n. to be in church 7541

to lay down one's power for others in n. 7435

to make evident forfeits virtue 11695

to stop long enough to let feet catch up with mouth 9331

to stop talking about prayer and pray 8825

Today n. exercise after work 3114

understand everything I n. to understand 6493

want much always much in n. 2878

What we n. to know takes all time, eternity 3513

whenever in n. God enlightens me afresh 5426

Where n. is highest, God is nighest 4515

where n. signs to discern guiding hand 5396

Where there is God, there is no n. 4517

who loves God has no n. of admiration 10877

who sees n. and waits to be asked for help 10148

who think no n. of others become unreasonable 9506

who withholds goods knowing neighbor to be in n. 10060

without n. to understand why God does what he does 7697

world will never outgrow n. for love 7251

would still n. redemption 9435

You and I n. experience of giving 4359

Young people n. control, authority 12178

NEEDED

few have resources n. to be both wealthy and godly 11806

God has never n. us 4527

He n. me, I was too busy 8685

incapable of bringing help n. 7126

Love n. in marketplace, mansions 7251

mastery in circumstances 1471

No one n. to ask if received Holy Ghost 5806

three things n. to be happy in work 12011

Two are n. for oneness 11622

What is new not necessarily n. 3660

When busy, a full hour is n. 7710

NEEDFUL

bit of healthful disbelief sometimes n. 2948

can find some n. job 10201

Change, ever n. 981

not n. we know intent 4885

The dark threads are as n. 10606

NEEDING

gospel can correct everything n. correction 5094

NEEDLE

Evil enters like a n. 3355

forget negatives that n. you 9270

sieve to n, hole in head 2079

NEEDLESS

spare anxious hearts a n. care 8098

NEEDLEWORK

Life like n. 8388

NEEDS

Behold my n. which I know not myself 9042

body, every part n. other 846

Christianity would not be large enough for n. 1202

country n. dirtier fingernails, cleaner minds 7775

faith n. neither evidence or research 3810

God meets n. in striking ways 3744

God n. and wants our love 4527

God n. no one 3723

God n. people who do ordinary things extraordinarily well 10137

God who n. no one 4467

Have their root in human n. 2029

if no room for others and their n. 8818

ignoring n. of fellowmen 8818

In prayer relates own n. to n. of humanity 8917

inability to distinguish n. from greeds 5321

Jesus wants us to see their n. 3316

Lord n. neither books nor teachers 5426

Lord saw people's n. 6519

Love n. not to know 5431

Man has two great spiritual n. 7400

man returns home to find what he n. 5815

man travels world in search of what he n. 5815

neighbor is everyone that n. help 913

neighbor is man who n. you 8070

Nobody n. smile as much as those who have none to give 10498

Old age n. so little 8161

Old age n. that little so much 8161

only God meets deep n. 4310

People meet superficial n. 4310

Prayer not just informing God of our n. 8929

provided for from within n. little from without 5780

seeks more than he n. 5316

social gospel n. theology to make effective 5104

suffering person n. a listener 10887

theology n. social gospel to vitalize it 5104

too busy to notice people's n. 129

too many n. to attend to 10211

Wealth enough to support n. 1809

what he knows n. no reasoned proof 5809

world can no longer evolve around your n. 1306

NEEDY

break to the n. sweet charity's bread 10728

frequently rich wealthy because neglected to aid n. 6630

love has feet to hasten to n. 7335

Repentance process by which we see ourselves as n. people 9594

selfish do not like n. strangers 5957

to the n, Christ is wealth 6391

NEGATES

God n. human ordering of life 5395

NEGATIVE

Doubt is n. 6091

Eliminate the n. 8231

influence n. or positive, never neutral 6248

word can defuse enthusiasm 12001

word leaves you depressed 12001

NEGATIVES

cross, meeting n. with positives 2146

forget n. that needle you 9270

if n. called sin by Lord 10321

so-called n. are assets 5357

NEGLECT

God for noise of a fly 7712

If I n. prayer for a day 8945

let me not defer or n. kindness 10152

no profit to learn well if n. to do well 3016

not his will that we n. the mind 7758

not to n. improvement of talents 9041

not to n. my family 3871

of prayer guarantee not victors 8872

sincere convert will not n. mercy, judgment 1908

to n. contemplation of God 7004

NEGLECTED

beautiful things it has n. 8182

frequently rich wealthy because n. to aid needy 6630

in life's hurry and bustle 12114

leave n. the soul of man 6095

Love n. will soon wither, die 7230

to remember I n. him 4069

why must God be n. 7723

NEGLECTING

development of mind 7793

NEGLECTS

present moment, throws away all he has 11300

NEGLIGENCE

Or by n. in chastening 8363

NEGLIGENT

confidence in Christ does not make n. 1611

Under a shepherd soft and n. 8363

NEGLIGIBLE

Christianity, influence far from n. 1188

NEGOTIATE

no freedom to n. results of choice 1159

NEIGHBOR

act as if you love your n. 8055

After service speak to n. 1384

begins to care he does not cheat n. 5004

cannot love his n. unless he loves God 7287

Charity enough to see good in n. 1809

Christian love links love of God and n. 7164

Christian supposed to love his n. 7654

Christianity balanced between God, n. 1240

Do not condemn your n. 6572

Do not that to thy n. 5003

does not make difference if n. loves you 8057

Don't expect n. to be better than your neighbor's n. 9450

every human being is my n. 8056

Every man takes care n. does not cheat him 5004

far better to serve n. than have own way 9963

foolish to punish n. by fire when live next door 9718

God makes our next door n. 8066

government can never replace helping hand of n. 8062

Grace refuses to put ceiling on concern for n. 5233

if n. is worse for our Christianity 8065

incorrect conception of ourselves, n, God 8059

is everyone that needs help 913

is man next to you at the moment 8069

is man who needs you 8070

let n. see what Christ has done for you 3314

lives by roadside assaulted by exploitation 6163

love for n. means love for any man in need 7201

love God, will love your n. 8057

Love n. but don't pull down hedge 8060

love of n. is door out of dungeon of self 8063

Love thy n, even when plays trombone 11396

man free to love n. 566

man whom business has brought you into contact 8069

meaning of love for n. 7201

No one can love n. on empty stomach 7152

No one rich enough to do without n. 4258

only time to look down on n. is when bending over to help 8064

seek profit of thy n. 4922

seldom weigh n. in same balance 1752

sin against n. through lack of love is sin against God 7164

terrible indifference toward one's n. 6163

than to love one's n. 5972
thinks of his n, says prayers of
  intercession 8840
to forget service due to n. 7004
to hear truth about yourself,
  anger your n. 8058
Unless we love God, cannot love n.
  1240
We have Christ in our n. 8061
What you wish for your n, ask for
  yourself 8067
who withholds goods from his n.
  10060
wife is nearest n. 7654

NEIGHBORHOOD
Christ must live in your n. 1536
heaven, an interracial n. 1486

NEIGHBORLINESS
important on frontier because so
  few 8068
more important now because
  neighbors so many 8068

NEIGHBOR'S
Avoid suspicion when walking
  through n. melon patch 9613
charity is patience when n. hurt
  1085
looking at n. faults gives incorrect
  conception 8059
not with motes from n. eye 1402

NEIGHBORS
a good sermon hits one of his n.
  10106
better terms with angels than n.
  3899
if I fear what my n. may say or do
  8818
sewing circle confesses sins of n.
  5160
stand before n. on character 1072
To die to our n. 10162

NEIGHBORS'
faults and folly 10038

NERVE
a lot of n. to make fun of ostrich
  4007

NERVES
Yesterday, you really got on my n.
  5882

NERVOUS
generation of n, almost frantic,
  Christians 10576
laugh out loud, helps flush n.
  system 6724
Man's world has become n. 420
nothing enviable or spiritual
  about a n. breakdown 9533

NERVOUSNESS
silence creates n. 10253

NEST
God builds n. of blind bird 4444
God does not throw food into n.
  3091
We saw thee in thy balmy n. 6152

NET
While I my n. was casting 1147
world is a n. 12051

NETS
Tyre rock for fisherman's n. 730

NETTLES
There are n. everywhere 10634

NETWORK
society n. of domination,
  manipulation 10514

NEUROSES
of emptiness 4437

NEUROSIS
begins at home 3006
Education, like n, begins at home
  3006

NEUROTIC
vast n. misery of world 4437

NEUROTICS
Everything great comes from n.
  4390
have composed our masterpieces
  4390
have founded religions 4390
never will world know all it owes
  to them 4390
suffered to enrich world 4390

NEUTRAL
impossible to be n. 5038
influence negative or positive,
  never n. 6248
men are devil's allies 8071
no n. ground in universe 4918
no such thing as being n. 8075
to live in n. world nightmare 4999
To remain n. where God criticized
  1495

NEUTRALITIES
God doth despise n. 4920

NEUTRALITY
alternative to wrath is n. 4999
at times graver sin than
  belligerence 8072
evidence of weakness 8073
God does not maintain n. in justice
  6630
hell reserved for those who in
  moral crisis maintain n. 8074
in conflict of world 4999
maintain n. by saying two sides to
  every question 8076
temptation, n. impossible 11052
twilight is torn away ruthlessly
  8075
want at least n. to Jesus Christ
  3025

NEVER
a kind word n. thrown away 6672
according to our scheming,
  planning 5401
Alms n. make poor 4350
an instant's truce between virtue,
  vice 11700
apologetic about gospel, n. 5092

arrive, always on the way 7035
at random 4948
Avarice and happiness n. saw each
  other 5312
bad n. at unity with one another
  5045
bear burden of sin, doubt 937
become irritable while waiting
  8400
believe anything bad about
  anybody 5148
Better n. trouble Trouble 11430
better to learn late than n. 3015
big things that disturb, but trivial
  9635
blow your own horn 9222
body can be bound with chains,
  spirit n. 4112
can n. replace friend 4297
can n. turn back 9846
cease loving a person 3167
changes opinions, n. wiser
  tomorrow 8195
Christ has n. lost his case 6415
Christ will n. strong-arm his way
  into your life 6438
Christ's words n. pass away 6523
Christianity n. promises to make
  independent 4116
content with our lot 11387
corrects mistakes, n. wiser
  tomorrow 8195
course of true anything n. runs
  smooth 2747
cut what you can untie 8401
deny own experience, convictions
  1912
devil n. sleeps 9861
Difficulty excuse history n. accepts
  2718
do anything so secretly 4872
doubt in dark 2885
Easter bunny n. rose again 2983
Eavesdroppers n. hear good of
  themselves 5123
Evil can n. be undone 3354
expect nothing, n. be disappointed
  3499
faith n. found alone 3809
Faith n. knows where it is being
  led 3709
Faith n. means gullibility 3710
Faithless work God n. rewards
  3825
fall out with bread, butter 3105
false report spreads where
  recantation n. reaches 10453
false to God, n. true to man 7464
fear shadows 2602
feel God will cast evil out of world
  3415
feeling that will n. come back
  12165
finger of God n. leaves same
  fingerprint 6211
finite can n. comprehend infinite
  4690
follow crowd if you want crowd
  to follow you 6801

For n, n. wicked man was wise 11883

forget kindnesses 6638

friend n. known until man have need 4166

Friendship ought n. to conceal what it thinks 4238

future may n. be 8384

genius n. travels on well-worn paths 4393

get to the end of Christ's words 6523

give impression we care when in a hurry 7327

give in except to convictions of honor 8548

give up 236

give up then 8568

God has n. needed us 4527

God is n. defeated 4822

God is n. found accidentally 4919

God is n. in a hurry 4456

God is n. in a panic 4937

God n. ceases to speak to us 8800

God n. comes to those who do not wait 5460

God n. contradicts reason 9413

God n. defeats himself by taking away freedom of choice 4133

God n. does anything hysterical 9912

God n. fails to grant light 5397

God n. farther away than door 4621

God n. forces man 4130

God n. gives strength for tomorrow 2722

God n. is before his time 4477

God n. is behind 4477

God n. known to disappoint 4468

God n. leaves 4621

God n. made two people exactly alike 6191

God n. sets limit to man's freedom 4130

God n. takes unless gives better 4630

God n. tempts any man 11060

God n. vindicates himself 4891

God squeezes but n. chokes 4464

God turns from wrath, n. from love 4757

God's n. missed the runway 3974

Good works n. erase guilt 5061

Goodness is n. fearful 11704

Great men n. feel great 7380

Great men n. know they are great 5279

happiness n. found till we stop looking for it 5550

has man who has bent himself able to 3444

have known many troubles, most n. happened 11434

He that gives should n. remember 4363

he that receives should n. forget 4363

help me n. to judge another 9065

hold anyone by button 1862

Human problems n. greater than divine solutions 9285

Humanity n. stands still 5969

Humility n. gained by seeking 6008

I am n. without God 4855

I n. knew the worth of him 4199

If you bottle grief up, you'll n. soften it 5343

In divine things there is n. hurry 5581

in need, yet rejoicing in gains 4954

influence negative or positive, n. neutral 6248

Insist on yourself, n. imitate 6194

intellect can n. comprehend spirit 10692

Jug n. carried under coat for honest reason 2905

knew how to worship until knew how to love 7185

know how accessible men are 3345

know how soon will be too late 6663

know love of parent until become parents 3902

known man of ability to be ungrateful 5255

Later n. exists 9293

learn anything talking 9363

lend books 853

life n. will be what ought to be 6939

load yourself so 4319

look at what you lost 825

Lord n. asks us to decide for him 2490

Lord n. coerces 8106

Lord n. enforces "Thou shalts" 8106

Lost time n. found again 11305

Love is n. lost 7241

love unless you can bear with faults 3948

Love, n. an abundance 7251

makes biggest mistake, doing nothing 7792

man must n. be afraid 566

Man n. is, but always to be blessed 5913

Materialistic concerns n. sufficient 8634

Men n. the same after listening to Christ 6377

met man so ignorant couldn't learn from him 6080

Money n. made a man happy, nor will it 7814

more like Christ than when we give 4380

most important events n. reach history books 5725

mystery of grace, it n. comes too late 5228

Nature's and duty's n. at odds 3813

Nothing I n. said ever did me harm 10682

Oppression, depression n. come from Spirit of God 5773

Our concepts of measurements can n. embrace God 4680

put off till tomorrow what you can do today 11372

put question mark where God has put period 3763

reputation easily cracked, n. well mended 9615

Resolved, n. to despise 569

Resolved, n. to lose one moment 569

Resolved, n. to revenge 569

ride on wave that went out yesterday 8372

ripe till made so by suffering 10642

Salvation will depend on n. looking back 9828

say more than necessary 1863

secret of own heart you can n. know 5624

Security n. friend of faith 952

see until we see God 8583

seek one's advantage 5066

send to know for whom the bell tolls 2339

so strong as when forgoes revenge 4095

somehow, 'tis seldom or n. 909

sorry you were kind 6674

soul n. applies itself simply 10660

Souls to souls can n. teach 10678

tell evil of a man 5149

tell unless absolutely necessary 5148

test resources of God until attempt impossible 3815

That man may last, but n. lives 4374

That purrs and n. shows a tooth 5048

The sunrise n. failed us yet 5942

There is an Arm that n. tires 4569

they will n, n. tear living Christ from my heart 7103

thing so real it n. can be told 10274

think could do something if different lot 8219

think God's delays are denials 8402

think Jesus commanded a trifle 8097

thinking can n. produce optimism 8587

thinks he gets as much as he deserves 5258

To a friend's house road n. long 4287

Truth n. consults, bargains, compromises 11561

Truth often eclipsed, n. extinguished 11570

Two vanities can n. love one another 9256

ultimate outcome n. in doubt
4822
underestimate ability to get
tangled up 5976
value anything as profitable
11660
we are n. alone 4863
we say millions n. think of God
7561
We shall n. know, n. find out
4704
Who lives in fear, n. a free man
4009
who n. retract, love themselves
better than truth 8207
who n. stirs from home read only
a page 6945
will n. achieve fulfillment unless
God in control 4309
will n. be wiser tomorrow than
today 8195
will n. have faith in riches, rank
10875
will of God n. leads to miserable
feeling 4507
wise men change their minds,
fools n. 11978
wise to be cocksure 11923
wise to underestimate enemy 3163
With n. a backward glance 4281
without Christ you'll n. be happy
3761
work well done n. needs doing
over 8579
Workless faith God n. regards
3825
world n. before seen or dreamed of
6419
world will n. outgrow need for
love 7251
Worry n. robs tomorrow of sorrow
12089
you'll n. get to lead the band 6797
Youth one thing that n. returns
12184

NEVER-EBBING
A n. sea 6409

NEVER-ENDING
soul a n. sigh after God 7528
who follow in the n. cycle 7372

NEW
accept Jesus as Savior, n. life 876
approach n. person in spirit of
adventure 9468
As our case n, think anew, act
anew 976
attempting to find n. ways of
bettering things 9311
Be not first by whom n. are tried
958
Beauty of ancient days, yet ever n.
4805
bend your force to break, make
me n. 2840
By bearing old wrongs provoke n.
ones 9632
Christ came to make men n.
creatures 6424

Christ offers n. life 7022
Christianity introduced n. spirit of
government 5170
continents of love, truth, might
2319
creates out of past something n.
8368
Death is n. beginning 2253
earthly life in touch with a n.
infinite life 7101
end may be n. beginning 3632
endlessly fascinated by n. thought
9468
Every a n. page 6901
Every end n. beginning 963
Every misery I miss a n. mercy
7739
Every n. adjustment crisis in
self-esteem 9984
Every n. opinion a minority of one
8194
Every solution of a problem is a n.
problem 9284
Every time you pray n. feeling and
n. meaning 8769
failure pioneer in n. undertakings
3602
fear of everything n. 3980
first work after n. birth 4537
For each n. morning with its light
11174
From death of old the n. proceeds
11504
give birth to n. awareness 10540
God helps us view world from n.
perspective 4735
God plants in us a n. disposition
8570
God wants to give n. values 7863
God, forever presenting n. aspect
of himself 603
gospel, offer of n. life to man by
grace of God 5100
Great Director of music arranges
a program perfectly n. 7895
grief, when mine old, yours n.
10588
hold on to past, postpone n.
blessings 968
I followed him, n. life began 1147
If a man does not make n.
acquaintances 4249
In flows heaven, with its n. day
5636
In n. birth God does three
impossible things 9800
increased possession loads us with
n. weariness 8625
Instead of substituting n. ideas
9743
islands yet shall break upon our
sight 2319
legalism, lynching of n. ideas 6817
life not property to cling to 10545
life we bring forth gift to be
received 10545
living, n. man born from living
God 872

Love has to be remade, made n.
7217
morality and biblical morality part
7837
need not n. light in religion 9554
need not n. paths in religion 9554
never a thunderstorm to announce
n. year 11329
O be the N. as kind 8078
O Beauty so ancient and n. 7473
old order yielding place to n. 978
Old truths always n. to us 11522
Older than eternity, now he is n.
6120
repentance natal day when n. life
begins 9591
Repentance opportunity of a n.
start 9596
round the corner, n. road, or a
secret gate 8239
rumor, all who told it added
something n. 9757
secret of a n. name 7127
seed dies into n. life, so does man
2385
silly question first intimation of n.
development 6703
something n. every day if you look
3509
step what people fear most 3989
throw stones at those showing n.
road 1643
To shake off old ordeal, get ready
for n. 7435
Tomorrow is a n. day 8375
totally n. point of view 9827
understanding of my truth 7123
understanding of their oneness
9093
ushering in n. age, n. dimension of
existence 5711
vices we rebuke 10414
We have a n. law 7331
What is n. not necessarily needed
3660
when n. thought appears, dismay
and resentment 11237
You begin a n. life every morning
7091

NEW TESTAMENT
according to N. such people
legalists 6810
adversity blessing of the N. 243
cannot criticize N. 754
carries the greater benediction 243
church be restored to N. splendor
10080
clearer revelation of God's favor
243
criticizes you 754
does not envisage solitary religion
1445
easy to misunderstand what N.
means 589
holds up strong light 739
knows little what grace is in N.
5224
love crazy sayings in N. 1216
preacher has to be surgical 9124

read small print of man's soul 739
through N. in Chinese 682

NEW TESTAMENT'S
terrifying phrase 9832

NEW YEAR
and a road that we must go 8081

NEW YORK
learn more by reading Bible than
living in N. 753

NEWBORN
life how glad 9898
Prayer the breath of the n. soul
8938
wailing of n. infant mingled with
dirge for the dead 7043

NEWNESS
God salvages, raising to n. of life
886
world without children, without n.
1104

NEWS
collection, presentation,
dissemination of n. 12144
don't like to open letter that has
bad n. 10012
gospel is good n. 9545
is fantasy 9404
Reality has no n. value 9404
slight, fragile, fraudulent are the
available sources 12144

NEWSPAPER
barricade themselves behind n.
3904
Not, what did the sketch in the n.
say 7423
proud man counts n. clippings
6035
read n. to know what people are
doing 666

NEWSPAPERS
Let me make the n. 12151

NEWTON
did not create mathematical order
1958
uncovered truth already there
1958

NEXT
neighbor is man n. to you at the
moment 8069
to good friends is good book 854
world is land of the living 7064

NIAGARA
No N. turned into light until
tunneled 2852

NIAGARA FALLS
believing man can walk over N.
3669

NICE
easy to be n. to enemy from lack
of character 1026
things due to good digestion will
fall off 1030
to get flowers while still smell
fragrance 3137

world of n. people might be more
difficult to save 7827
world, it's a very n. place 6929

NICENESS
content in their own n. 7827

NICER
The world would be n. than ever
909

NICE-SOUNDING
smoke screen of n. excuses 3476

NICHE
church not comfortable n. 1427
God lets him fall in n. ordained to
fill 2617
lets him fall in the n. ordained to
fall 5387

NICODEMUS
As made him know his God by
night 780
Wise N. saw such light 780

NIGHEST
Where need is highest, God is n.
4515

NIGHT
abiding day that has no n. 229
An infant crying in the n. 2576
and storm look as if they would
last forever 8444
As made him know his God by n.
780
Be sundered in the n. of fear 3644
Bible to guide in n. 727
bird of dawning singeth n. long
1371
But now, I often wish the n. 2588
By n. and also day he suffers still
2164
by n. atheist half believes God 477
By prostrate spirits day and n.
4659
comes down through the n. 1375
conceals world, reveals universe
8083
dark n. of soul always three in
morning 2594
darker the n, brighter stars shine
9323
darkness falls from wings of n.
8086
descending into primordial n.
1980
Doubt sees the darkest n. 2939
dream opens into primeval cosmic
n. 2971
every n. sit staring at another box
5859
Faith can put candle in darkest n.
3656
falls but never breaks 8084
For rest and shelter of the n.
11174
From morn to n, my friend 6885
given to drink deep at fountain of
power 6947
has a thousand eyes 7306
11634

heaven, rest not day nor n. 5644
his works behold day and n. 362
I heard without the n. wind moan
5413
If cannot find God in the n.
musing 4856
In the n. God is preparing thy song
10600
in world without Christianity
1214
Infinite day excludes the n. 5670
Into the darkness of the n. 303
is given us to take breath, to pray
6947
is sabbath of mankind 8085
is the winter 9877
joy flows in the n. as well as the
day 6529
life is the flash of a firefly in the n.
7082
life, the flash of a firefly in the n.
2457
like sun which seems to set in n.
6094
more nourishing than bread, wine
2553
more sure than day and n. 4209
music in the depth of n. 7927
Music is moonlight in gloomy n.
of life 7909
must follow, as n. the day 6318
no time for Christ at n. 10117
not good that man batter day, n.
at heaven 8854
O guiding n. 2554
O n. more lovely than the dawn
2554
One n. a man had a dream 5437
praise at morning, blame at n.
8203
Prayer bolt of the n. 8943
Praying gives peaceful sleep at n.
8899
prays much by n, face fair by day
8808
Recognize dark n. for what it is
2556
Safe though the n. be long 4490
saw eternity the other n. 3276
sees in the darkest n. 8515
shall be filled with music 7887
Shallow natures tremble for a n.
after sin 10352
Sin will end dark as n. 10377
Sleep, all through the n. 1123
Some are born to endless n. 813
Songs in the n. God giveth 232
stars arise, and the n. is holy
11649
Stars blessed candles of n. 11639
such sight angels behold day, n.
forever 4995
Summer in winter. Day in n. 6153
The n. is dark, I am far from home
5429
the other dipt in n. 10673
This is that n.—no, day 6140
those who pass like ships in n.
4281

though thy path be dark as n. 5995

Through this dark and stormy n. 3800

to rest body and the mind 8085

to struggle all n. with the angel 9777

To wake the morn, sentinel the n. 11344

Tomorrow may be n. 11375

too sleepy to worry at n. 12062

washed clean at n. by repentance 9600

Were toiling upward in the n. 8566

wherein the good rise, wicked sink 10878

Without Christ life as twilight with n. ahead 7094

worry gives sleepless hours at n. 12091

Worship voice in n. calling for help 12132

NIGHTLAND
It runs through the n. up to the day 4313

NIGHTLY
Ten thousand suns which shine above us n. 4592

NIGHTMARE
lose n. of separate individuality 2822

to live in neutral world n. 4999

NIGHTMARES
Childhood, when n. occur only during sleep 1106

Today locks out yesterday's n. 11382

NIGHTS
are wholesome, no planets strike 1371

don't lie awake n. to succeed 10828

God of the late-at-n. 7539

of pleasure are short 10340

poems, repeat for comfort in sleepless n. 9381

see Jesus spending n. in prayer 8860

soul has deeper darkness than the n. 7539

NINE
God will take n. steps toward us, but not the tenth 9578

NINETY-NINE
times conclusion false 2775

NO
Ability to say n. greatest gift parent has 8326

absolute knowledge 6706

atheists in foxholes 489

brotherhood without fatherhood of God 920

cannot say n. to temptation 11110

company preferable to bad 4286

fortune, only God 11866

gain without pain 8273

God, n. world 4485

good asking for simple religion 9402

great men in this world 8668

helpers, see all your helpers in God 11490

human being can be permanent source of happiness to another 9481

indispensable man 7433

learn to say n. gracefully 5615

machine can do work of one extraordinary man 8660

man became very wicked all at once 11889

man can create faith in himself 3766

man ever sank under burden of day 4319

man is an island 10511

man is born wise 11342

man is useless while he has friend 4257

man poor who has had godly mother 7851

man should part with own individuality 6201

middle territory 5038

moral precept not inconvenient 7840

most important words, n. to world 11994

nation better than individuals 7987

One n. averts seventy evils 3392

panic in trust 11482

perfect marriage, n. perfect people 7657

perhaps little praying worse than n. praying 8889

person ever honored for what he received 5895

power more formidable than truth 11547

problem too big for God 9288

rain, n. mushrooms 4485

room for God in man full of himself 10089

struggle, n. progress 9312

such thing as being neutral 8075

There is n. friend like an old friend 4208

To make n. mistakes not in power of man 7794

use going back for lost opportunity 8226

use to pray for the old days 8377

way to kill righteousness but by own consent 11102

Were there n. God 11167

Where n. love, put love in, you will draw out love 7343

Where there is God, there is n. need 4517

who offers to God second place, offers n. place 7467

yes to God means n. to things that offend his holiness 5755

You think there's n. chance for you 8230

NO ONE
able to strike terror into others 4001

can bar road to truth 11520

can be caught in place he does not visit 5484

can believe for me 594

can develop fully 11613

can drive me to believe or disbelieve 594

can go to hell or heaven for me 594

can know God who has not first known himself 7543

can love neighbor on empty stomach 7152

can make masterpiece of life 3107

can make you feel inferior without your consent 6228

can open or close heaven or hell 594

can resign from human race 5977

can worship God on empty stomach 7152

Christ spoke to those to whom n. spoke 6433

could ever have found God 6137

damns like a theologian 9360

deserves right to lead without perservering 6802

ever attains success by what is required 2784

ever corrected by a sarcasm 6645

ever graduates from Bible study 684

everyone must learn, n. can teach 7068

excluded from gospel 5093

feel n. has right to blame us 6230

God asks n. to accept life 1140

God forces n. 4126

God needs n. 3723

God sends n. away empty 9200

God who needs n. 4467

God's being he owes to n. 4610

Gossip, n. claims to like 5133

had more sensitive love than Jesus 7280

has double in friendship 4297

is prevented from being an individual 6209

is useless in this world 10175

knows sorrows of another 10602

knows what is taking place in another's kingdom 6171

learns to make right decisions without 2486

Let n. say we are worthless 9989

Life burdens n. can escape 931

likes skunk 1588

means all he says 11990

need be downcast 6460

need fear to listen 4966

needed to ask if received Holy Ghost 5806

needs to be downcast 10603

Now old man, n. has respect for age 12190
perfect 6180
really knows what he looks like 7444
Say not in evil doing, "N. sees" 3404
suspects his pain except thee 10877
thinks of changing himself 964
Time, n. knows balance 11340
time, n. receives more or less 11356
truly knows happiness who has not suffered 5545
understands me 6171
weep, n. sees 10647
When young man n. had respect for youth 12190
who is lover of money is lover of man 11661
will grieve because your lips are dumb 3778
with grateful hearts and n. to thank 11167
would remain friends with n. 9466

NO PROBLEM
best friends should be n. type 4226

NOAH
best financier in Bible 784
brave to sail wooden boat with termites 1931
floated his stock 784
knew enough to get out of rain 782
only had two worms 783
rounded up all the animals 781
Why didn't N. swat those two flies 785

NOBILITY
Consider the n. within thee 9982
Faith lends n. to life 3666
grows out of contained emotion 3057
Has risen to n. 2792
Reconciliation demands n. 9431
strips friendship of n. 4245

NOBLE
appreciating what is n. in another 4220
deeds concealed are esteemed 2504
Every n. work at first impossible 8536
Every person n. 5967
Gratitude sign of n. souls 5247
How to use thy n. powers 8671
No work n. or good of emulation 2009
when devil looks most n, is most dangerous 2648
Youth would rather do n. than useful deeds 12181

NOBLER
heart yearns for something n. 470

To something n. we attain 3538

NOBLEST
An honest man's the n. work of God 5885
And "dust to dust" concludes her n. song 7088
friend helps us think n. thoughts 4178
function of mind is to listen to God's Word 7766
He most lives who feels n. 1056
how transient is n. monument 730
Scriptures teach n. way of suffering 742
service comes from unseen hands 10191
Worship highest, n. act 12137

NOBODY
better n. who accomplishes something 3856
can always have devout feelings 4777
can be you as effectively as you can 9983
can judge men but God 4720
don't be surprised if n. seems to care 9211
educate in what n. knew yesterday 3035
else can do the work 6204
equal failing to trust everybody, n. 11473
ever outgrows Scripture 685
friend to everybody, n. same thing 4215
If n. took slander in and gave lodging 10455
knows the trouble I've seen 11445
listens, then everybody disagrees 5171
money swore that n. who did not love it 5320
needs smile as much as those who have none to give 10498
praises everybody, praises n. 8728
spots phony quicker than a child 8349
studies peace 8450
teenagers do things n. else does 12172
to thank 488
wants to die 2282
when n. is paying any attention to you 7129
who isn't a bore to somebody 869
will know "God is love" unless you act it 7281

NOBODY'S
family can hang out sign 3878

NOBODY-BUT-MYSELF
To be n. in world doing best to make you everybody else 6215

NOD
first 9479

NOISE
Criticism's child 2050

eloquence is only air, n. to God 9002
God whispering, do not hear because of n. 4968
good man makes no n. over good deed 2495
happiness an enemy to pomp and n. 5568
In midst of n. deep inner silence 10539
life causes as it rushes on 10273
Light makes no n. 1956
neglect God for n. of a fly 7712
of the world without 8800
One man's music, another's n. 7918
our Adversary majors in n. 121
proves nothing 9223
shut door against earthly n. 10554
so much n. with rapid reflections 8813
speed and n. evidence of weakness 10576
Too much n. deafens us 3559
very n. of the siege will drown still small voice 8854
When river is deepest, makes least n. 2810

NOISELESS
inaudible, n. foot of time 11317
thou didst descend with n. tread 6150

NOISELESSLY
gives guidance n. 5426
God's blessings steal into life n. 4641

NOISES
child who fears n. becomes man who hates n. 4004
nature rose without n. that distract 1956

NOISIEST
Christians accepting n. as best, greatest 5891
greatest events not n. 10268

NOISY
are sought after 4410
Outside n, inside empty 4064
Over the n. keys 7919
time is n. 10576
world where people are indifferent 592

NONBEING
evil is n. 3370

NONBELIEVER
lives by faith in natural laws 3653

NONELIEVERS
Jesus divides into believers, n. 686

NONCHALANCE
art of looking like owl when acted like ass 6162

NONCONFORMIST
never yields to passive patience 6619
to deny self is to become n. 1646

NONCONFORMISTS
Humanity's most valuable assets 9311

NONCONFORMITY
believer's cross price of social n. 2103

NONE
as rich 11841
but fools would keep 7019
can comprehend eternity 3283
can live in love without suffering 7246
demands mercy, shows n. 4084
feels true love of God till 4773
For I have n. to give 4796
God excludes n. 4809
God will have all, or n. 4920
goes his way alone 919
greatest fault is to be conscious of n. 3952
have right to expect gratitude 5242
It gives, but borrows n. 634
may claim superior grade 3227
of our human talents are significant to God 4527
One of these days is n. of these days 9298
optimist sees light where there is n. 8246
Please all, please n. 1583
preaches better than ant 3447
so fond of secrets as those who do not mean to keep them 5150
who has many friends, has n. 4187
Whom n. can love, whom n. can thank 4374

NONELECT
are whosoever won't 3046

NONRESISTANCE
to evil is way of promoting it 3388

NONSENSE
as I also forgive the n. of those who think they talk sense 9056
evolution, pure jackass n. 1985
Forgive me my n. 9056
to say suffering makes saints 10860

NOON
is the summer 9877

NORM
by which thought or action to be judged 7307
personal experience never n. for other people 8883

NORMAL
praising God restores us to n. 2564
Salvation is bringing back to n. Creator-creature relation 9807

NORTH
In Christ no south or n. 911

NORTH AMERICA
thing that impresses me about N. 3897

NORTH CAROLINA
constitution of state of N, 1836 5183

NORTHWIND'S
And flowers to wither at n. breath 2324

NOSE
human nature sticking n. into other people's business 5147
keep n. out of other people's business 5152
man's tongue has broken his n. 1859
What is before our n. we see last 6933

NOT
Ask n. where they go 5431
by seeking fertile regions where toil lighter 4974
Christian condemned for what he does n. do 6594
Do n. follow where path may lead 6787
even God could build society of love out of puppets 4133
every heart that laughs is cheerful 10605
every question deserves an answer 9364
Forgiveness n. an occasional act 4078
Forgiveness n. I will forgive but n. forget 4079
future is n. yet ours 4322
God values n. your deeds 7864
God would n. have created man to exist only for a day 6104
good that man batter day, night at gate of heaven 8854
hypocrites in our sleep 6066
I love thee so, I know n. how 4795
lazy man does n, will n, cannot pray 6776
less what free to do, than free n. to do 4142
my business to think about myself 9934
one life not so near to God 7057
punished for our sins, but by them 9356
well for man to pray cream, live skim milk 8856
well-adjusted who makes world better place 6196
what a man does 7865
what we have, but what we enjoy 8636
Who has him n, has less than nothing 4519
will n. when he may shall n. when he will 8216
Without Christ n. one step 3822
without us God will n. 7576

NOTE
Forgiveness like a cancelled n. 4081
Joy great n. all through Bible 6547
label is all one n. 6212
let Christ be n. to which life attuned 6379
like orchestra in which all played same n. 6169
strike the next n. full and clear 9684
strikes the n. and tune of our strings 7550
Till every n. and string shall answer thine 7527
with eye on God, strike n. full, clear 7056

NOTES
dance, leap from my pen 7931
if touches n. rightly and in time 7885
man is maze of a million n. 6212
nothing but n, body without spirit 7929

NOTHIN'
I had the world, it was n. 3855

NOTHING
A span of life is n. 7080
accepts n. has n. to return 9457
age thinks of n. but health 5619
all I know is that I know n. 11904
All passes, n. lasts 11288
Almighty does n. without reason 4492
And having n, yet hath all 9959
ant says n, preaches better 3447
As earth can produce n. unless fertilized by sun 5207
attempted if objections first overcome 2741
attractive about gospel to natural man 5108
before, n. behind 3767
begins, and n. ends 810
believe n. not enough 602
bequeathed by those who would part with n. 10078
Better to have little than n. 7120
biggest mistake, doing n. 7792
Birth counts for n. if virtue not there 11682
Blessed is he who expects n. 5905 2793
but blurred memories 8353
but his hand that holds you 4523
but notes, body without spirit 7929
can come out of sack but what is in it 6316
can defeat God 9983
can do n. without faith 3827
can do n. without grace of God 5207
can ever come to pass against our will 9835
can exist without God 4854
Can faith that does n. be sincere 3647

can happen save that which God wills 9835

can happen which cannot be turned into good 4803

can make man truly great but being truly good 5290

can need a lie 3937

can take place of perseverance 8555

Careful for n. 8775

causes more trouble than tongue 11413

certain except the past 8365

certain in this world 7062

Chance does n. not prepared beforehand 4928

Cheerfulness costs n, yet is beyond price 5612

communion with God that asks for n, yet everything 8997

completely, merely individual 1450

confused self you can do n. with 4530

consumes more quickly than resentment 9638

courtesy costs n, conveys much 1944

cynic knows value of n. 2189

Defeat n. but education 2517

Demanding all, deserving n. 7440

deprived children do n. to get wants 1128

desire n. but God 9136

desire n. but spirit of the Holy Jesus 6385

Desires n. always free 1796

devil has n. to say about will of God 4915

died with n. done 6756

dies harder than theological difference 11198

difficult to those who have will 8549

distance is n. 2749

easier than not able to find time 9301

esteem everything, esteem n. 5900

ever becomes real until experienced 3539

ever lost by courtesy 1944

evil enough when one does n. good 3393

existence smells of n. 3485

Experience one thing you can't get for n. 3532

Faith does n. alone 3660

fears God fears n. else 8487

fixes thing so intensely in memory as wish to forget 7736

for good men to do n. 3402

Fortune lost, n. lost 9263

found that is not unique 4993

frog in well knows n. of ocean 8665

gets up to speak and says n. 5171

God can do n. until limit of possible 8642

God creates out of n. 884

God creates out of n. you say 9773

God has n. to say to self-righteous 10307

God hides n. 9706 4906

God sends n. but can be borne 2546

godly afraid of n. 3996

gospel of Christ n. if not gospel of growth 9351

great done without enduring 3151

great done without suffering 10875

greater hazards in doing n. 6779

grows, blooms save by giving 4342

happens that is not significant 1716

happens unless Omnipotent wills it 4828

hard if divide into small jobs 3110

harder than softness of indifference 6165

hardest work is to do n. 6775

haste, busy doing n. 5577

Having n, n. can he lose 8627

having n. to say 1837

he killed it only to find n. 5328

He loses n. who loses not God 4475

heart has eyes brain knows n. of 8503

Humility is to expect n. 6010

Humility n. but truth 6009

I bargain for n. 9084

I have been everything, and everything is n. 2442

I have need of n. 4561

I invent n. I rediscover 2004

I never said ever did me harm 10682

If consider boundless space, shrink into n. 11631

If God deny powerful presence, fall into n. 4865

If God you fail to see, you have n. observed 4926

If I will n. of my own 4977

impossible to willing heart 10797

In Christ n. secular and sacred 6411

In grief, n. "stays put" 5344

in its place is bad 5036

in life is to be feared 3984

in money's nature to produce happiness 7814

in my hand I bring 2101

in world without meaning 4903

Incredulity gives n. in return 11592

is going to happen that you and I cannot handle 4622

is impossible 7869

is often good thing to say 1865

is ordinary if you know how to use 2010

is poor who has n. but money 11821

is rich who owes n. 11821

is so certain as death 2341

is sweeter than love 7283

is void of God, he fills his work 4860

is without voice 8029

is work unless 12017

Jesus does it all, I do n. 5426

know n. of Calvary love 7187

know n. of men's, women's rights 3230

Knowing when to say n. is 50 percent of tact 7626

learn n. of gospel except by feeling its truths 5110

left to chance 4904

Life either a daring adventure or n. 6962

Life, can get it for n. 6996

Lord's Prayer n. left out 7156

Love thinks n. of trouble 7220

Love, in tennis, n. 7276

makes one feel so strong as a call for help 10177

Man knows n. without being taught 7412

Man n. but dust 7445

many a battle fought world knows n. about 7061

may have good eyes, yet see n. 8502

merely having open mind is n. 7761

Ministry that costs n. accomplishes n. 10173

mission everything, personal life n. 9279

more awful than conscious humility 6038

more beautiful than cheerfulness in old face 8148

more fleeting than years 11354

more frightful than ignorance in action 6084

more simple than greatness 10280

more terrible than activity without insight 4429

more wonderful than alert, eager mind 7776

nature of God to make something out of n. 3604

no n. to make anything 1962

Noise proves n. 9223

now I know n. 3024

one who has n. to say keeps silent 10272

out of place is good 5036

Outside of God, n. but n. 4488

passive patience excuse to do n. 6619

perfection of greatness to be n. 5293

permanent except change 7058

presented to soul is simple 10660

Pride n. but lying 6009

Real friends have great time doing n. 4265

real friends reserve n. 4186

real mistake one from which we learn n. 3622

realize n. is secular in world 4732

realizes n. terrible in death 7059

really important in life 972

recedes like success 10798

received n. that he asked for 8806

Right predominates, n. prevails against it 6621

rises quicker than dust, straw, feathers 3857

root that produces n. is dead 3699

Sad is the man who has n. but money 7821

said not said before 10686

Sanctification a discipline nine out of ten will have n. to do with 9844

see n. but faults who look for n. else 3954

seek n. else but the pleasing of God 4922

seems worse to man than his death 2342

sets person out of devil's reach as humility 6024

shall be to come, and n. past 3288

should be done in haste 5583

Simplicity scrutinizes n. 11696

sin that believes in n. 11394

sin that interferes with n. 11394

slave of greatest slave who serves n. but himself 10055

small if God is in it 10800

small in the service of God 7121

smile costs n. but creates much 10494

smites n. so sharp, nor smelleth so sour 5492

so bad that good may not come 2755

so dates a man as to decry younger generation 12192

so distasteful as himself 1717

so easy but becomes difficult with reluctance 2756

so exhausting as indecision 2488

so expensive as glory 4406

so firmly believed as least known 6082

so gentle as strength 10752

so good as seems beforehand 3506

so infectious as example 3448

so irrational as rationalism 9397

so like God as stillness 10258

so loyal as love 7315

so powerful as truth 11548

so strong as gentleness 10752

so terrible as activity without thought 6084

so uncertain as hour of death 2341

stronger than gentleness 4404

suddenly understand I know n. 6493

swifter in life than voice of rumor 5142

Tennis few pastimes where love means n. 7297

terrible for man who realizes n. terrible in death 7059

than attempt to do n. and succeed 3595

than somebody who accomplishes n. 3856

that happens in world by chance 4948

that I with God do not share 7470

that is God's obtainable by money 7818

the Matter Here 3878

things mean n, God means everything 1325

though you get it for n. 10291

time does n. to guilt of sin 10419

Time is n. to God 11338

'Tis n. to hold up head in calm 1915

To a good man n. that happens is evil 5049

To avoid criticism do, say, be n. 2082

to discuss but glories of days past 4321

to grumble about 1561

to have done n. and succeeded 10777

to see when he looks back 4315

To understand everything is to hate n. 11617

true gift, n, is expected in return 4384

trust in n. man who has not conscience 1708

turn n. into everything 1122

until man is n. 884

way to be n. is do n. 6778

We have n. to do with the outflow 6232

when anyone is n. 3604

When do n, we tempt devil 11116

When have n. but God 11490

When Jesus is present, n. seems difficult 6512

When n. to say, say n. 10691

When shall n. but thyself live in me 7961

When we have n. left but God 4516

when we shall have n. but God 3719

When wealth is lost, n. is lost 1066

when you fear God, you fear n. else 3994

which happened in this world important 5666

who fears God need fear n. else 9732

Who has God wants n. 4588

Who has him not, has less than n. 4519

Who much receives, but n. gives 4374

who promises too much means n. 9326

will convince like way we respond 3319

will ever be attempted 86

will make us so charitable 10014

will of God, n. more, n. less 7876

Wise men say n. in dangerous times 11979

with Christ and n. else can be happy 3761

with God can be accidental 4927

without purpose a n. 4436

world n. to rely upon 10512

world owes you n, it was here first 9652

worth knowing can be taught 11932

Write, say, think n. cannot believe to be true 9871

you can do to make God love you more 4786

Youth thinks n. of health 5619

NOTHINGNESS

Bible teaches us our n. 738

no original n. for refuge 1962

retreating from reality into n. 3370

NOTICE

God takes n. of clean, not full hands 9754

never n. prayers not answered 9019

Resolve upon a moment's n. 6872

sparrow cannot fall without n. 4933

take n. how he acts when loses money 7802

NOTICED

saints always among crowd not n. 9786

NOTORIOUS

Christians accepting most n. as best, greatest 5891

NOUN

Why must God be a n. 4520

NOURISH

growth without destroying roots 2057

Yet doth his blood n. and warm my root 8254

NOURISHED

If not n. by Bread from heaven 12050

Love when n. becomes sturdy, enduring 7230

NOURISHES

in winepress of cross juice n. 2095

The Bible n. 697

NOURISHING

Bread upon waters more n. than pie in sky 10742

Night, more n. than bread, wine 2553

NOURISHMENT

deep relationship requires n. 9446

no matter what color same amount of n. 3243

silence is n. 9374

NOVEL

eye craves n. 844
waiting for church to find room
for n. 1998

NOVELTIES

world is full of untold n. 8507

NOVELTY

What a n. is man 7439

NOVICE

Man enters each stage of life as n.
7002

NOW

have it in our power to be in
heaven right n. 6569
In eternity everything present in
one fresh-springing n. 11316
nearest word is n. 11993
no other time than n. with God
11322
only an eternal n. that builds 8368
Truth, it's hour is n. 11558
watchword of the wise 11361
We see n. Lord sees forever 11606
why n. rather than then 4905

NOWHERE

God an infinite circle whose
circumference is n. 4842
is to walk into n. 4982

NUCLEAR

people fret over n. weapons 10503
world of n. gaints, ethical infants
1705

NUDGE

Grace the beckoning n. 5221

NUISANCE

Christian thinker is a n. 11239
exchange of one n. for another n.
9317
human race playing games n. for
people who grow up 5982
that knowledge only acquired by
hard work 3014
To all who do not love God, trials
a n. 4804

NUMB

my mind too n. for thought 12102

NUMBED

Heart n. too much for hopes, fears
2587

NUMBER

'Tis thine to n. out our days 8098
value of good works not based on
n. 10115

NUMBERED

the days of genuine happiness
7100

NUMBERLESS

are the world's wonders 7424

NUMBERS

Small n. make no difference to
God 10800

NUMBNESS

dreamy n. creeps upon worshiper
1399

NUMBS

Punishment n. 2038

NURSE

Difficulty n. of greatness 2719
Nature's soft n. 10485
self-pity as an infant 10034
Sleep is God's celestial n. 10486

NURSERY

Change n. of music, joy, life,
eternity 960
Life is the soul's n. 6979
prayer closet not a n. where none
but babes belong 8976
world is God's n. for his upper
rooms 12043

NURTURE

love with a smile and a prayer
7289

NURTURED

Talent n. in solitude 1042

NURTURES

mother n. next generation of
citizens 7844

NUTS

God gives the n. but does not
crack them 9348

O

OAK

A grass-blade's no easier to make
than an o. 2007
to soften rocks or bend knotted o.
7901
When o. felled, forest echoes with
its fall 8052
When the great o. is straining
2508

OAKS

Little strokes fell great o. 8547
Tall o. from little acorns grow
8657

OAR

I wait the muffled o. 6916

OARS

tugs on o. hasn't time to rock boat
10187

OAT BRAN

One laugh = 3 Tbsp. O. 6741

OBEDIENCE

behind o. onmipotent power 1521
By o. led step by step to correct
errors 8110
by o. we understand teaching of
God 8095
devil seeks slaves, claims o. 4912
discipled o. of loyal subject 8818
essential to evangelism 3299
Faith and o. in same bundle 8089
faith commits to o. 3808

foundation of subjection to God's
authority 8355
God demands o. 8094
Growth depends on o. in crisis
2046
if costs your life, pay it 1722
If God gives command, he expects
o. 11173
important in life is o. of faith
8110
is eye of the spirit 8100
is key that unlocks door 8101
is premium we pay 8096
is submission to will of God 8099
key to every door 8102
leads to faith 8103
learn more by five minutes' o.
8116
Let child's first lesson be o. 8307
means marching feel like it or not
8104
meek o. without resistance 7728
not servitude of man to man 8099
not to abrogate o. but to add to
its spirit 6811
nothing to do with result of o.
10824
One act of o. better than 100
sermons 8109
rather should use terms o. and
disobedience 5753
Resistance to tyrants is o. to God
5964
simple faith and implicit o. 164
Spirit of God will expect
unquestioning o. 5776
through personal o. God acts
5385
to authority is foundation of
citizenship 8355
to God will mean desolation 8105
to Jesus Christ essential 8106
to Jesus Christ not compulsory
8106
to law coupled with love, honesty
6811
to rejoice in distress 221
to revealed truth guarantees
guidance 5435
truth of God only revealed to us
by o. 11542
Understanding can wait, o. cannot
8114
when conscious o. assimilated
7690
will of God, o. to whatever lies
ahead 5370
With every cross in o. to Christ
8108
Worship ends in holy o. 12105
would be mechanical business
8091
would be no value in o. 8091

OBEDIENT

God stooped to work by, in his o.
children 4467
If absolutely o. to God 10278
Love is o. to superiors 7246

When o. God guides our steps, stops 8119

OBEY

army of demons compelled to o. Jesus 9858

because desire pleasure 577

because you loved God 577

begin to mature, o. commandments unconsciously 7690

better expressed by word "use" 8111

daily business to o. Bible 681

Failure to o. dulls spiritual understanding 8100

good men o. from love 5053

having ability, refused to o. 10387

If o. laws space will treat you kindly 11650

If you love, you will o. 10807

ignore God, refuse to o. him 1014

impresses me about America is parents o. children 8357

inclined to hunt for commandments to o. 7690

learned to o. will know how to command 6792

legalism, God satisfied with attempt to o. moral code 6814

made weak that he might o. 8806

not those who desire, but those who o. 5779

pain we o. 8261

parent who does not teach child to o. is cruel 8355

pros and cons means refuse to o. 8117

shall be free, safe, happy 8115

sin willful refusal to o. God 10387

so hard to believe, so hard to o. 593

sounds hard 8108

That I may long o. 6923

to o. God is perfect liberty 8115

trust and o. substance of Spirit-filled life 5803

want to o. 8820

way parents o. their children 3897

who loves to o. 7422

Wicked men o. from fear 5053

will mean to follow 1277

OBEYED

majority has strength to make itself o. 5191

Nature, to be commanded, must be o. 3198

Theological truth useless until o. 11205

universe functions best when God's laws o. 1520

OBEYING

Jesus' orders 8090

Success is o. God 10807

OBEYS

God, trusts God 8089

space o. laws of physics 11650

OBJECT

Contemplation is looking at God as an o. 1173

Falsehood, twilight that enhances every o. 6866

God can't make wine if we o. 883

God loves, wanted o. to love 4535

I hold God-made o. up to picture 2022

Love does not analyze its o. 7214

love's o. lightens its toil 6457

Most people o. to speed of light 11309

of faith, unseen reality 3831

of temptation 11099

to suffering, be ill at ease 10833

We o. to fingers God uses 883

OBJECTIONS

if all o. must first be overcome 86

Nothing attempted if o. first overcome 2741

Nothing will be attempted if o. 86

OBJECTS

No one o. to March coming in like lion 9889

Obligation is to persons, not o. 6820

worth of man measured by o. pursued 469

Youth begins when o. to parents having own way 3905

OBLIGATION

convert has o. like no o. in world 1904

duty giving comes from o. 10736

Grace binds with stronger cords than o. 5211

is to persons, not to objects 6820

look upon ourselves as under no o. 6255

Marriage, o. reciprocal 7642

sacred o. to find out and do it 6175

Too great haste to repay o. 5266

OBLIGATIONS

Christianity system of balanced o. 1240

God's promises are o. he imposes upon himself 9324

Love can never say, "I have fulfilled my o." 7273

OBLIGED

to pray if citizens of God's Kingdom 9015

OBLIGING

alike at all hours 4204

devil o. 2651

OBLITERATE

Holy Spirit does not o. man's personality 5798

lucky who can o. pursuit of glory 4411

OBLITERATION

Christianity not the o. of the old 6424

OBLIVIOUS

Christ, o. of details 6501

to requirements of situation 3510

OBLOQUY

Give honor or give o. 1538

OBNOXIOUS

prefer o. company to being alone 10575

OBSCURE

cling to natural virtue sufficient to o. work of God 11701

In o. offices the Son of God grew 10190

life, a vast, o. unfinished masterpiece 6904

method of evil one to o. himself behind object of worship 2699

most o. believer can hold head high 9999

object of temptation, to o. God 11099

OBSCURES

glare that o. 268

too long, short distance o. knowledge 3559

Whatever o. sense of God is sin 10424

OBSCURITY

better than name 10875

Jesus' glory lies in o. 6443

Learn lessons well in o. 5430

Lord's Prayer for conciseness without o. 7154

OBSERVATIONS

few o. and much reasoning leads to error 9410

many o, little reasoning leads to truth 9410

OBSERVE

Children learn what they o. 1114

content to o. there is evil 3383

Five things o. with care 1855

God in his works 8031

sin, two witnesses present to o. 10418

OBSERVED

excellently o, say I 8204

If God you fail to see, you have nothing o. 4926

OBSERVER

devil cunning o. 4915

OBSERVES

If God o. mathematics 4454

OBSERVING

means enemy uses to frighten 4010

world o. way we undergo trials 3319

OBSESSED

Earnestness o. with method not the Master 2626

no culture so o. with immediacy 7990

so o. with facts lost touch with truth 7990

Those o. with health not healthy 5618

OBSESSIVE

people weighed down by o. fear 5474

OBSOLETE

Adults are o. children 8478

what is old not automatically o. 3660

OBSTACLE

evil not so much o. to faith 3399

knowledge of Scripture no o. to sin 10392

lest you become o. to spiritual growth 2851

often unrecognized opportunity 2711

what seems o. becomes a door 10901

OBSTACLES

are God's opportunities 8219

Doubt sees the o. 2939

frightening when eyes off goal 4430

godly reponse to o. kicks crutches from skeptic 10938

if weren't for o. never know what we want 2729

in pathway of weak 10754

Strength from struggle against o. 8850

Success is o. overcome trying to succeed 10809

OBSTINACY

difference between perseverance and o. 10773

unbelief is o. 2930

OBSTINATE

few men so o. in atheism 479

Give me the blind, o. eyes 4530

Jesus so long identified with conservatism of o. sort 6452

man does not hold opinions 8192

man is impenitent, then o, then damned 10287

opinions hold o. man 8192

OBSTRUCTS

Christian thinker o. pragmatists 11239

OBTAIN

more man denies himself, more o. from God 9562

must despair to o. grace of Christ 5201

proof render faith superfluous 3806

the most precious gifts by waiting for them 8425

to o. and hold power, must love it 8705

too easy, value too lightly 8563

OBTAINABLE

Nothing that is God's o. by money 7818

OBVERSE

love, wrath o. and reverse of same thing 4999

OBVIOUS

overlooked more o. things 9970

OCCASION

Misfortune is o. to demonstrate character 195

piled high with difficulty 976

Seizes the prompt o. 8224

Sleep only o. man cannot silence conscience 2970

we must rise with o. 976

Winter ideal o. to slow down 9906

OCCASIONAL

Forgiveness not o. act 4078

OCCASIONS

Bible not cake for special o. 715

Christianity not cake for special o. 1169

OCCUPATION

Absence of o. not rest 6752 3085

adoration, worship become o. 3987

most important o. for woman 7856

Witnessing not a spare-time o. 3344

OCCUPATIONS

Flee for a little while thy o. 7708

let us love our o. 3112

OCCUPIED

left mark because o. with heaven 5656

plenty of other people o. with affairs of world 9261

OCCUPY

mind with good thoughts 7764

OCCUR

best tests of growth o. in mainstream of life 1319

Conversion may o. in an instant 1897

OCEAN

Could we with ink the o. fill 4748

entire o. affected by pebble 6238

Eternity is an o. 3283

Eternity is the o, time the wave 3267

frog in well knows nothing of great o. 8665

God is the o. deep 4852

God's treasure like infinite o. 4471

great o. of truth lay all undiscovered before me 11508

if few drops of o. are dirty, ocean not dirty 5988

Make the mighty o. and the pleasant land 6659

my boat is so small, your o. so big 9110

O God, your mercy a boundless o. 4816

On o. or on shore 6916

pond is an o. to a tadpole 8517

spirit submerged in depths of divine o. 7968

that God, the whole o, floweth into me 7469

We only see a little of the o. 6111

wide flowing o. 5788

Wisdom like dawn that comes up slowly out of unknown o. 11969

Worship is a drop in quest of the o. 12132

Would drain the o. dry 4748

OCEANS

are God's thoughts imbedded 8036

way will be made through o. 5444

OCTEMBRUARY

best month to get married 9881

OCTOBER

put off until O. chores in August 9882

ODD

real Christian o. number 1265

world so extremely o. 12037

ODDS

All things are at o. 11217

faith can survive all o. 3736

Nature's and duty's never at o. 3813

rather that world be at o. with me 6294

science seemed at o. with religion 9866

soul can rise up against o. 3621

than I should be at o. with myself 6294

OFF

single word can turn you on, o. 12001

OFFEND

arrogant person o. others 451

yes to God means no to things that o. his holiness 5755

OFFENDED

preferable world against thee than Jesus o. 8525

OFFENDS

Jesus o. because emphasis on unseen life 6450

OFFENSE

conscience void of o. inheritance for eternity 5079

conscience, void of o, inheritance for eternity 1652

cross of Christ an o. to the world 6317

deal only with surface find Christ an o. 6422

God consigns o. to everlasting forgetfulness 4638

God consigns o. to forgetfulness 4107

mistake to present Christianity with no o. 1198

poor sermon that gives no o. 10101

take heed add no o. of our own 6317

OFFENSIVE

forces of evil have begun decisive o. 3400

to mourn for sin because o. to God 9581

OFFER

do right when o. faith, works to God 3829

God does not o. us a way out of testings 166

gospel not so much a demand as an o. 5100

gospel, o. of new life to man by grace of God 5100

Hell highest reward devil can o. 5689

no evil that does not o. inducements 11101

ours to o. what we can 10166

Religion can o. man burial service 7022

Vices tempt by rewards they o. 11101

OFFERED

insults, cannot help being o. but need not take 2918

love o. in spite of suffering, injustice, death 7239

rather than gifts he is o. 6334

OFFERING

bring o. even then 583

OFFERS

Christ o. new life 7022

God o. a way through testings 166

God o. to help us build cathedral of love, praise 7684

God o. tough love 7686

No matter how many pleasures Satan o. you 9855

who o. to God second place, o. no place 7467

OFFICE

in morning run off to another box called o. 5859

Men whom the lust of o. does not kill 6299

Men whom the spoils of o. cannot buy 6299

responsibility of o. boy 3121

OFFICER

thief doth fear each bush an o. 5488

OFFICES

Jesus, no intention to speak to o. 6451

OFFSHOOT

Exaggeration o. of lying 3421

OFFSPRING

Who is mature enough for o. before o. arrive 7669

OFT

But o. for our own the bitter tone 3900

OFTEN

as o. as ever you can 5057

assume God unable to work 3613

can't be done by advice o. done by example 3460

constant in happiness must o. change 4057

for excuse we say things impossible 7869

Friendship plant which must o. be watered 4231

God o. visits us 4546

God's way o. insignificant and unobstrusive 4664

Great accomplishments o. attempted 3593

loves something, mentions it o. 7177

making of music o. slow, painful process 7056

message of gospel o. diluted 5109

Real doesn't o. happen to people who break easily 5886

redirecting our lives o. painful 5449

success entered through failure 3612

The poor too o. turn away, unheard 8694

Truth o. eclipsed, never extinguished 11570

Young people, why God uses them so o. 12177

OFTTIMES

excusing of a fault 3934

OH

compelled to fall back upon O. 11996

OIL

can mightier than the sword 10991

faith o. in machinery of life 3731

If God had not put o. in ground 11831

made his millions in o. 11831

must pour o. into it 12010

must then from you, dearest Jesus, flow 3323

no o. company holds key to as much power 11841

rust of life scoured off by o. of mirth 6738

so little o. of Holy Spirit 1423

Truth and o. always come to the surface 11553

would be no fortunes in o. 11831

OINTMENT

just hand is precious o. 6624

OLD

a healing in o. trees 8143

anyone who stops learning is o. 2995

best mirror is an o. friend 4200

By bearing o. wrongs provoke new ones 9632

can be young and o. at same time 11323

cannot crucify my o. nature 9836

Christianity not the obliteration of the o. 6424

Christianity the transfiguration of the o. 6424

comes to be an o. one 2222

cranks, saints have practiced all their lives 5503

Deliverance only by defeat of o. life 882

do not bring o. life up to higher plane 9839

Few people know how to be o. 8130

friends, o. scenes will lovelier be 4197

From death of o. the new proceeds 11504

grief passes into quiet, tender joy 7101

grief, when mine o, yours new 10588

grow lovely, growing o. 8143

Grow o. along with me 8132

Hear our prayer for those growing o. 8145

keeps ability to see beauty never grows o. 12182

know you're getting o. when 8190

last to lay o. aside 958

man dies with open hand 11656

man nearing end of earthly journey 8121

men go to death 2349

men lose lives by ripeness 12197

more foolish and wiser 8127

need new strength to walk o. paths 9554

Next to the very young, very o. most selfish 10072

No man loves life as he who's growing o. 8147

Nothing more beautiful than cheerfulness in an o. face 8148

now o, no respect for age 9647

Now o. man, no one has respect for age 12190

One thing about getting o. 8168

repents, leaves his o. life 9583

Some no matter how o. never lose beauty 8169

spirit should not grow o. 8137

Spiritually, we never grow o. 10712

streets a glamor hold 8143

take a long time to grow an o. friend 4193

teenagers not o. enough to do things adults do 12172

teenagers too o. to do things kids
    do 12172
The o. order changeth 978
Then you are o. 8122
There is no friend like an o. friend
    4208
things will drop off 3315
think he is growing o. 8185
Tis sweet to grow o. 8120
To know how to grow o. 8178
To me you can never be o. 8179
to shake off o. ordeal, get ready
    for the new 7435
too o. to learn probably always
    too o. 3028
truths always new to us 11522
what is o. not automatically
    obsolete 3660
When all sins are o. in us 10092
when cease to grow, you are o.
    8189
When o. difficulties run into us
    12196
When you see an o. man amiable,
    mild 8184
whether at twenty or eighty 2995
Will make them o. before their
    years 4003
won't have anything to laugh at
    when o. 6720
You are not o. 8122
You don't grow o. 8189
You don't stop laughing because
    you grow o. 6748
you grow o. because you stop
    laughing 6748
Young men may die, o. men must
    2433

OLD AGE
a regret 12199
    7097
a second child, by nature curs'd
    8163
accept it calmly, wisely 8158
an illness in itself 8153
an incurable disease 8154
an island surrounded by death
    8155
arctic loneliness of age 8165
blaming the present 8186
blessed time of life 8149
brighter, calmer, more serene 311
can love God better than a doctor
    of theology can 7286
comes from God 8151
crown of life 8166
demand not for o. but for youth
    12194
Description of o. 8121
desirous to live to o. 308
difficult chapter in art of living
    8178
equal grace, force, fascination
    12188
fifty youth of o. 307
grow more like ourselves 8180
grow older like old cars 8181
happy moments make cushion for
    o. 5506

how hateful is your reign 8150
In o. faith marvelous possession
    8138
is but a second childhood 8156
is but older children 8157
is coveted 8164
is dreary solitude 8152
isn't bad when consider alternative
    8160
leads on to God 8151
like plane flying through storm
    8158
like the evening of a fine day 8184
live to a ripe o. 119
lives minutes slowly, hours quickly
    12193
love you as dawning of eternal day
    8149
Memory delights o. 7735
Men are afraid of you 8149
miserable when o. looks back
    with horror 8182
more to be feared than death 8159
most happy time of life 8149
needs so little 8161
needs that little so much 8161
O harsh o. 8150
old authors best to read 304
old friends best to trust 304
Old men lose lives by ripeness
    12197
old wine best to drink 304
old wood best to burn 304
Once abroad, nothing you can do
    8158
play's last act 8166
praising times past 8186
productivity in o. 8128
puts more wrinkles in minds than
    on faces 8162
reminiscences of what never
    happened 12195
sees last day hanging over its head
    8182
sing in bathroom while brushing
    teeth 8168
sins of youth paid for in o. 10401
stop feeling oats, start feeling corns
    8175
thorny, sour, crabbed frustrations
    of o. 8176
tired at beginning of action 313
To seek wisdom in o. like mark on
    sand 11956
twice a child 8167
unlovely personality a
    continuation 8176
Weak, sickly, full of pains 8163
weakness in which strength
    perfected 8170
When men grow virtuous in o.
    3183
When old difficulties run into us
    12196
when one heard o. was coming
    8136
With more and greater evils than
    the first 8163

OLD TESTAMENT
has not felt sin in O. 5224
If we read O. prophets 5423
In O. war commanded 11760
Prophets the beating hearts of the
    O. 9333
Prosperity blessing of the O. 243

OLDER
As children grow o. they judge
    parents 1111
As love grows o, hearts mature
    7236
Elderly person is ten years o. than
    you 8124
grow o. become like old cars 8181
Old age is but o. children 8157
than eternity, now he is new 6120
the fiddle, sweeter the tune 8173
two possibilities, one to grow o,
    the other not 8129
we grow happier as we grow o.
    7026

OLD-FASHIONED
honesty not preceded by o. 5863

OLYMPIC GAMES
life resembles O. 7018

OMITTED
never o. opportunity of kindness
    9491
rests not to be o. 9684

OMNIPOTENCE
Christ helps us not by virtue of his
    o. 4899
great things easy because of
    Christ's o. 10127
possibilities limited only by o. of
    God 8940
Prayer is weakness leaning on o.
    8949
right of God's sovereignty derived
    from o. 4952

OMNIPOTENCY
My faith has o. 3760

OMNIPOTENT
Forever G. must remain the Lord
    God o. 4821
God is o. will 4514
God would not allow evil to be
    4831
impossible to despair who
    remembers Helper o. 2595
Is God not o. 10841
Nothing happens unless O. wills it
    4828
power behind obedience 1521
public opinion almost o. 8200
world must come under o. surgery
    10521

OMNISCIENCE
to imagine O. so easily
    bamboozled 8750

OMNISCIENT
God is o, a mere theological
    statement 11179

God knows me is different from
God is o. 11179
God o. Creator 1520
if o. all would be plain 7942
Of an o. will 4338
Or deceive his heart, o. 4888

ON
single word can turn you o, off
12001

ONCE
expect to pass through life but o.
6642
Measure a thousand times, cut o.
2783
than take wrong road o. 5424
to every man, nation comes
moment to decide 2489
You fool me o, shame on you
2481

ONCE-A-WEEK
Witnessing not a o. activity 3344

ONCE-BORN
spirit in o. opposed to Spirit of
twice-born 877

ONCE-DONE
salvation reduced to o. act 9816

ONE
A lie stands on o. leg, truth on two
6864
a thousand forests in o. acorn
1969
act of obedience better than 100
sermons 8109
act of thanksgiving when things
go wrong 11157
After o. vice, greater follows
10293
all desires have been reduced to o.
9282
All for o, o. for all 11621
All mankind of o. Author 5966
All my requests lost in o. 8088
all packed into o. day 8090
alone is true to us 6455
And the day but o. 7306
attain excellence in o. single
pursuit 3470
beats the bush 6205
begins with o. step 4435
best thing o. can do 34
Better hundred enemies outside
house than o. inside 5820
but o. question, that is the gospel
5094
can bear grief 5351
can endure sorrow alone 10607
can remain alive long past usual
date of disintegration 8139
case of death-bed repentance
recorded 9602
church has only o. mission 3328
connected chain of justice, mercy,
truth 4904
cool judgment worth thousand
hasty councils 6587
creation of thousand forests in o.
acorn 8664

crop in o. year that makes up for
ten 889
day at a time is enough 10120
do not know o. millionth of o.
percent 6709
Don't hear o, judge two 6606
drop of water for my soul 7003
essential condition of human
existence 12117
Eve, rather than leave that o.
unknown 11053
Every moment o. is born 806
Every new opinion a minority of o.
8194
example worth thousand
arguments 3450
eyes of love see not o. but two
persons 7300
facing in only o. direction 9846
father worth more than hundred
schoolmasters 3923
feelings one can go through in o.
day 4014
find eagles o. at a time 6789
flesh experience an expression
10239
foot cannot stand on two boats
6058
foot on earth 6915
For o. that big misfortunes slay
12061
For sake of o. good action 4074
forgiveness, healing o. 4072
friend, o. of life's greatest assets
4163
friendly sign 4199
Friendship o. of the sweetest joys
of life 4236
Friendship, two bodies and o. soul
4298
future comes o. day at a time
4320
Genius, o. percent inspiration
4391
Give o. thing more—a grateful
heart 5265
God acknowledged with o. heart,
voice by American people
11176
God loves each as if only o. 4756
God vouchsafes to speak to us o.
by o. 6178
God's justice, love are o. 4725
God, indivisibly o. 4503
Good has but o. enemy, the evil
5022
good name got by many actions,
lost by o. 9611
has o. enemy shall meet him
everywhere 9459
hears but half who hears o. party
only 9182
Heaven when questions, answers
become o. 5647
honest o. man picked out of a
thousand 5867
how little o. feels poverty when o.
loves 7199
I am only o, but I am o. 1926

I have o. foot in heaven 6915
I have o. passion only, it is he
6400
If all men pulled in o. direction
6184
If bring into o. day's thoughts evil
of many 12064
If I can stop o. heart from
breaking 6922
In eternity everything present in o.
fresh-springing now 11316
In God history, prophecy are o.
4604
individual on a small planet 7387
individualism ego cult of o. 9952
Infinitude can belong to but O.
4703
injures o, threatens a hundred
10450
injury to o, concern of all 6603
joy dispels a hundred cares 6555
kind act will teach more love of
God 6661
kind of love, a thousand imitations
7317
kind word can warm three winter
months 6662
Knowledge and wisdom, far from
being o. 6690
label is all o. note 6212
laugh = 3 Tbsp Oat Bran 6741
leaves of life keep falling o. by o.
7031
leg in stocks, or two 11447
lie gives birth to another 6856
life facets of o. diamond reflecting
light 6985
Life is for o. generation 9617
Life o. stitch at a time taken
patiently 8388
life, gleam of time between two
eternities 7013
Love can see only o. thing 6457
love o. business pays to be
spendthrift 7252
Love o. gift open to every member
of the church 7235
Love o. gift that grows bigger
7252
Love o. ingredient of which world
never tires 7251
Love o. treasure that multiples by
division 7252
love, two souls and o. flesh 4298
make o. that which we are, that
which we appear to be 6296
man's music, another's noise 7918
man's word is no man's word
6618
many religions, but o. gospel 9547
may return to place of birth
12170
minute of patience, ten years of
peace 8404
moment of impatience may ruin a
life 8405
moment of patience may prevent
disaster 8405

Money not required to buy o. necessity of the soul 7813

More spiritual progress in o. short moment of silence 12112

murder makes a villain 11758

Never attempt to bear more than o. kind of trouble at once 11443

never using two words when o. will do 12154

No machine can do work of o. extraordinary man 8660

no unity where there is but o. 11622

Not many lives, only o. have we 11287

not o. life not so near to God 7057

Not o. thing done for God has been lost 10176

o. day nearer home 5676

of God's best gifts 4220

Of o. ill come many 1736

of these days is none of these days 9298

of world's greatest tragedies 5625

on God's side is a majority 7510

only enough life to pursue o. object fully 9260

only o. being who loves perfectly 7316

only o. corner of universe certain of improving 9953

only o. thing can satisfy aching abyss of human heart 5359

Only o. type of worry correct 12074

only o. way to be born 2393

only o. way to heaven 11863

only o. who understands 6171

out of o. people die 2386

passions dangerous only in o. way 10234

path leads to Paradise 5664

pound of learning requires 11934

Pray o. hour before going to war 7650

radiating influence from o. person incalculable 6241

reputation of thousand years determined by conduct of o. hour 9625

Seek not every quality in o. individual 9490

sin will destroy a sinner 10344

sins, must pay for o. by o. 10398

small word "to be" 3492

societal problems solved o. person at a time 3901

solitary life 6353

step enough for me 5429

striking thing about following 5446

takes only o. to make marriage a failure 7623

that world may become o. family 9093

The o. who wears my face 9947

thing can never get enough of is love 7308

thing to go through a crisis grandly 7129

thing we never give enough is love 7308

thing, not fifty things 81

thorn of experience worth wilderness of warning 3540

to break o. commandment is to break the law 6812

To find a friend close o. eye 4161

To follow o. aim 10822

To o. fixed trust my spirit clings 4642

to o. striking at the root 3405

today worth two tomorrows 11376

trouble with trouble 11448

Tune me, O Lord, into o. harmony 7928

Two captains in o. boat make it sink 6808

two in o. 7952

When o. door closes, another opens 8229

When o. knows oneself well 6597

who thought himself above me 9251

will come o. day a touch from God 7060

with o. blow of hand 4951

With o. hand he put 6070

Within o. of his hours 4521

Without Christ not o. step 3822

without o. single original thought 11237

word can start a war 11759

world has many religions, o. gospel 5106

world's o, only remedy is cross 2169

would not give o. moment of heaven 5652

year of self-surrender 10074

You are the o. who must grow up 6931

your goings and God's goings are o. 8093

Youth o. thing that never returns 12184

ONE-AND-ONLY

Love's business not the "fall" for o. 7274

ONE-EYED

man among blind has full sight 8572

ONE-FIFTH

of all Jesus had to say was about money 7804

ONE HALF

of knowing what you want 4431

ONE-MINUTE

blow o. experience into 3420

ONENESS

new understanding of their o. 9093

prayer for o. 9093

Two are needed for o. 11622

ONE'S

always have o. boots on 2354

good opinion of o. self 11591

happiness is enjoyment of o. self 5568

life heavy price to pay 3487

love is offering o. most honest self 7337

never seek o. advantage 5066

originality being o. self 6219

power of going out of o. self 4220

than to love o. neighbor 5972

thoughts are free 4112

To be o. self more admirable than conformity 6216

To love is to give o. time 7327

To repent is God's point of view instead of o. own 9605

What jailer so inexorable as o. self 9955

ONESELF

advantage of praising o. 9238

difficult to be honest with o. 5880

difficult to know o. 10008

entirely honest with o. a good exercise 5868

Forgetting o. first condition of love 7169

Forgetting o. not refinement of love 7169

Love is the gift of o. 7225

maturity, unwillingness to lie to o. 5873

most inconvenient to know o. 10008

Prayer is putting o. under God's influence 8936

Reconciliation an overcoming of o. 9431

right to create for o. alternatives of choice 4155

stranger to o, estranged from others too 9519

ONE-WAY

Life is a o. street 6950

pessimist looks both ways crossing o. street 8585

ONGOING

God's creative method is o. inquiry 4469

Repentance an o. process 9589

resurrection is an o. thing 9698

ONLY

acceptable workers those who worship 12099

an eternal now that builds 8368

become like Christ o. thing worth caring for 6494

Believe, even if o. one faithful 583

But o. how did you take it 11446

by that Carpenter can mankind be remade 6360

Christ can accomplish goal within us 8113

cure for suffering is to face head on 10905

death of Jesus o. entrance into his life 2161

desire to do will of his Father 9280

enduring substance is within 10654

Example o. thing in influencing others 3431

falsehood has to be invented 6867

free when Son sets us free 4152

God can devise plan 5632

God expects o. what he has supplied 4810

God is permanently interesting 4678

God loves each as if o. one 4756

God meets deep needs 4310

God understands universe 11635

God would not have created man to exist o. for a day 6104

great challenges which ordinary men rise to meet 8668

he who can see invisible can do impossible 11733

His o. answer was a blameless life 6356

humble o. when we know we are God's children 6042

I am o. one 106

I desire o. your love 4561

I have one passion o, it is he 6400

Idolatry trusting people to do for me what o. God can do 6072

If I o. had three years to serve the Lord 6687

in God fully understand what you are 8634

inner chamber into which God o. can enter 7127

inner health o. through forgiveness 4103

lasting treasure is spiritual 4148

lives o. for himself truly dead to others 10059

Living each day as if o. day 6999

Love can see o. one thing 6457

Love is the o. true freedom 7254

Love o. service money cannot buy 7253

Love thy God and love him o. 4798

man clogs happiness with care 12073

man who finds gospel attractive 5108

no fortune, o. God 11866

one being who loves perfectly 7316

one type of worry correct 12074

one who can see value of being humbled that is righteous 6007

one who understands 6171

path to pleasure is pleasing God 8609

perfect freedom is serving God 4148

science of Christ o. learned by heart 5110

see a little of God's loving 6111

Solitude bearable o. with God 10555

sought o. for the heart of God 2652

suffering God o. one who does not mock us 10908

Suffering o. way some can learn 10897

the redeemed can keep his commandments 4536

thing can do on shoestring is trip 4031

thing God makes plain in Bible 11546

this day o. this ours 11365

Those o. who make quest supreme desire 6494

to sit and think of God 4799

two or thee human stories 5984

warrant for believing God cares 4779

way to have friend is be one 4205

way to know is to will to do God's will 5447

we o. know ourselves through Jesus Christ 10013

when begin to worship, begin to grow 12107

when choose to praise for rough spots 11152

when man wishes impossible, he remembers God 7490

Wherever I go, o. thou 4518

with gratitude that life becomes rich 5257

world's one, o. remedy is cross 2169

Worship requires o. a man and God 12142

years on earth o. first scene in divine drama 6106

you can prove immortality to yourself 6102

ONWARD

men who are lifting world o. 3142

world owes o. impulses to men ill at ease 2875

ONWARDS

Let him lead thee blindfold o. 5431

OPEN

at random, close book, meditate 9387

Christ nailed to cross with arms wide o. 6393

Christianity is a religion of the o. tomb 9688

convinced people o. to Christian message 3310

easier to meet evil in o. than underground 3381

eyes, world full of God 4861

Grant us a heart wide o. to joy, beauty 9064

greatest path is o. to least of travelers 7235

having o. mind is nothing 7761

he is my o. door 6357

I will o. the Bible for you 7123

If hearts o, desires known 10507

if you don't o. door to devil 2654

Keep eyes wide o. before marriage 7624

Love ever stands with o. hands 7218

mind functions best when o. 7770

Minds only function when o. 7762

more power in o. hand than clenched fist 8720

no one can o. or close heaven or hell 594

no right to o. door of prison and run away 10941

nor o. door God has shut 4937

o. door through which God wants us to go 5436

old man dies with o. hand 11656

temptations the most harmless 11078

under praise we o, reach, grow 3144

When you must act, will o. 5444

ye heavens, your living doors 1967

OPENED

door must be o. by willing hand 4775

Hearts o. in pure transparency 5667

look so long at closed door do not see one o. 5573

no one in earth can shut door God has o. 4937

OPENETH

To every man there o. 10679

To every soul there o. 1155

OPENING

Death o. of more subtle life 2261

Mischief comes from much o. of mouth 10685

mosquito never waits for an o. 8223

No o. could I see 5413

object of o. mind is to shut it on something solid 7761

Only baby admired for o. mouth 5151

shall find God o. up an enlarging life 3774

OPENNESS

is to wholeness as secrets to sickness 5883

Sincerity an o. of heart 10428

who builds relationship on less than o. 9447

OPENS

Bible at random 5441

Gold o. every gate 11814

Hope o. doors, despair closes them 5928

If God shuts one door, he o. another 5421

Life closes in twilight, o. in dawn 11132

When God shuts door, he o. window 5462

When I am really alive, Bible o. 683

When in prayer clasp your hands, God o. his 9026

When one door closes, another o. 8229

When one door of happiness closes, another o. 5573

OPERATE

God meets us on level where we o. 5439

in dimension totally unlike our Lord 11606

OPERATION

asking God to conduct a major o. 7155

than others out of major o. 3422

OPIATE

deadly o. for consciences of millions 4726

OPINION

always think last o. right 8203

are all impatient of uncertainty in o. 11605

bad o. of God 11591

because he differs in o. 8193

Conscience anticipation of o. of others 1675

Criticism's sister 2050

difference of o. alienates little minds 11392

empty souls tend to extreme o. 8191

Every new o. a minority of one 8194

feeble tremble before o. 8205

flatterer tells you your o. 4046

foolish deny o. 8205

good o. of one's self 11591

greatest are least in own o. 5991

have poor o. of us even when intentions good 6270

helps us make decision without information 8198

If work for God because brings me good o. 10158

in good men is knowledge in making 6711

Is of the same o. still 9179

majority o. of the least able 5191

majority o. will become law 4332

man who never alters o. like standing water 9185

more in love with own o. 2904

Private o. is weak 8200

public o. almost omnipotent 8200

Refusing to have an o. a way of having one 8201

right to stupid o. 447

skillful direct o. 8205

what we believe their o. of us is 9486

where his o. agrees with mine 8204

whose good o. I wish to have 10158

wise judge o. 8205

Your o. of others apt to be their o. of you 9526

OPINIONS

cross high above o. of men 2157

defense of our warmly held o. 11216

destiny of nation depends on o. of citizens under 25 12173

easy in solitude to live after own o. 6195

easy in world to live after world's o. 6195

foolish and dead never change o. 8206

hold obstinate man 8192

if founded in truth will prevail 8199

labelling his o. 6599

lends weight to one's own o. 9389

man hates to stand alone in o. 1639

Men who possess o. and a will 6299

never changes his o, never wiser tomorrow 8195

obstinate man does not hold o. 8192

Our o. of others depends 9486

own heart, not men's o, form true honor 5896

Satan ready to help to new o. 2944

should act with disregard for o. of others 6291

So many men, so many o. 8202

Speak according to o. 1648

stronger than armies 8199

thoughts are someone else's o. 1640

to cross all o. come for judgment 2157

Where much desire to learn, many o. 6711

worse dishonesty among champions of religious o. 9540

OPPONENT

give tolerance 511

toddler o. of law, order 1129

OPPORTUNIST

has no use for people he cannot use 7583

OPPORTUNITIES

come disguised as problems 2752

disguised as hard work 8221

disguised as impossible situations 8228

He who kills time kills o. 6757

Hope regards problems as o. 5928

layman has o. minister will never have 3330

Life's o. open on road of daily duties 8217

most people don't recognize o. 8221

obstacles are God's o. 8219

problems o. in work clothes 2726

responsible for how well we take advantage of o. 9660

to train ourselves to wait on the Lord 8421

wise man will make more o. than he finds 8210

OPPORTUNITY

America still land of o. 7983

appears to make out of evil more noble good 5031

Calamity is virtue's o. 157

Chinese symbol for 2048

Crisis o. riding dangerous wind 2048

deny God o. of working through weakness 10407

for discipleship is there "if" 2826

future o. yet unmet 4325

God calls adversity o. 233

great o. is where you are 8225

greater the evil, greater the o. for good 3401

Life a glorious o. 6944

Man's extremity is God's o. 8218

media provided devil with o. 2698

never omiting o. of kindness 9491

No great man complains of want of o. 8220

no greater o. to influence fellowmen for Christ 6278

no use going back for lost o. 8226

obstacles often unrecognized o. 2711

optimist sees o. in every difficulty 8251

ostrich as blind to o. as to disaster 8211

pessimist sees difficulty in every o. 8251

problem is an o. to prove God 9283

Repentance o. of a new start 9596

Suffering o. for change of heart 10901

Suffering o. to change evil into good 10891

To recognize o. is difference between failure, success 8227

Tomorrow lose o. to accept Christ 11404

OPPOSE

God calls for volunteers to o. evil 3378

help us not to despise, o. what we do not understand 9095

help us not to o. what we do not understand 11397

rather that world should o. me 6294

When two truths seem to directly o. 11586

OPPOSED
grace is o. to sin 5205
not necessarily o. to God 5467
Science sometimes said to be o. to faith 9869
spirit in once-born o. to Spirit of twice-born 877
Though God be o. outcome never in doubt 4822
why is man o. to God 7479

OPPOSES
gospel invades everything that o. extension 732

OPPOSITE
of joy is unbelief 11594
of joy not sorrow 11594
of religious fanatic is the gentle cynic 9549
when circumstances point to the o. 9321

OPPOSITES
Pleasure and pain are o. 5353
Work and play, artificial pair of o. 12022

OPPOSITION
faith and reason not set in o. 3842
Faith and sight set in o. 3842
forces of evil in o. to will of God 8762
Great spirits always encountered . o. 5282
inflames enthusiast 1626
joy flows all through o. 6529
never converts enthusiast 1636
Spirit of God in sharp o. to easy ways of world 5776
Was it not o. Jesus promised to disciples 10784

OPPRESS
us with weight of the tomb 2611

OPPRESS'D
Never elated while one man's o. 3074

OPPRESSED
Bible, Magna Charta of o. 700
Christ lives among the o. 1277
frequently rich wealthy because o. poor 6630
God is on the side of the o. 6604
God is on the side of the poor, o. 8696
Jesus' mission, liberating o. 1439
they've sought way to relieve themselves 7888

OPPRESSES
Spirit of God never o. 5773

OPPRESSION
allows o, shares the crime 1484
allows the o. shares the crime 5962
every o. will have an explanation 7060
never come from Spirit of God 5773

OPPRESSIVE
Marriage unspeakably o. at its worst 7641
without high pretensions to o. greatness 4204

OPTIMISM
blueprint for 531
healthy-minded, but blinded 8237
maintaining everything right when wrong 8236
thinking can never produce o. 8587

OPTIMIST
Christian both a pessimist and an o. 8252
expects wind to change 8249
has never had much experience 8232
not much use being anything else 8234
sees green light everywhere 8245
sees light at end of tunnel 8250
sees light where none 8246
sees opportunity in every difficulty 8251
sees the doughnut 8244
thought everything good except the pessimist 8248
Twixt the o. and the pessimist 8244

OPTIMISTIC
my willing and hoping are o. 8247

OPTIMISTS
achieve improvement 8238
do not wait for improvement 8238

OPTION
Joy is an o. 1516
to choose attitude of gratitude 499
to choose commitment to joy 499
to choose posture of grace 499

OPTIONAL
eternity, mortality persuade us faith not o. 2288
misery is o. 8266

OPTIONS
out of o. ready for God's surprises 2596

ORATIONS
furnished themes for more o. 6449

ORATOR
produced effects beyond o. or poet 6449
Sorrow makes silence her best o. 10619

ORATORIOS
sweetest music isn't in o. 11995

ORATORY
of heart to converse with God 7541
Trying to settle problem with o. 9290

ORBITS
Thee in their o. bless 4592

ORCHESTRA
like o. in which all played same note 6169
Never blow own horn unless in an o. 9222

ORCHIDS
can enthrall 1102
friends like fragrance of o. 4185

ORDAINED
by God as basic unit of human organization 3880
foolish to cling to life when God o. otherwise 2299
forefathers believed whatever they did God o. 3113
God has o. three institutions for society 10506
God lets him fall in niche o. to fill 2617
God o. truth from all eternity 11584
lets him fall in the niche o. to fall 5387
shallow amenities of life o. by God 7038
that in conflict we find strength 9090
wars just which are o. by God 11743

ORDEAL
great o. of meeting me 2302
To shake off old o, get ready for the new 7435
Why do we dread o. 11459

ORDER
a golden link into chain of o. 2790
beauty of the home is o. 5851
By whose o. have this place, time been allotted 4905
concerned only with o. 10698
consequence of defying moral o. 4721
contemplate God's wisdom in unchangeable o. 4581
discipline a kind of o. that sets me free to fly 9975
fundamental postulates of o. 5169
God always preserving beauty of his o. 4644
God first in sequential o. 4607
God is a God of o. 4948
God's o. comes in the haphazard 5401
governs the world 2659
If harmony in home, will be o. in the nation 8441
If o. in the nation, peach in world 8441
In spiritual matters, human reasoning not in o. 9416
leave all for Lord to o. 9930
Leave to thy God to o. 1502
moved God to choose o. of universe 4989
no good government without o. 5194

O Lord, o. what I shall be 9100
old o. changeth 978
political o. cannot be renewed
  without theological virtues
  5169
the more laws and o. made
  prominent 5192
The world was built in o. 1976
toddler, opponent of law, o. 1129
war violates o. of nature 11751

ORDERED
And let our o. lives confess 8431
And o. their estate 4501
Heaven perfectly o. enjoyment of
  God 5646
maintains sun in bright o. beauty
  4619

ORDERING
each o. of his providence 4578
God negates human o. of life 5395

ORDERLY
Life isn't o. 6984
space is o. 11650

ORDERS
church under o. 3329
God o, brings into line 5175
we are still giving some o. 10977

ORDINANCE
Government originated as o. of
  God 5177

ORDINARY
be right in o. actions 6295
break through o. ways of men
  10564
Christ was among the o. things of
  life 6436
Christian knows more than
  philosopher 1326
day given to God a sacrament
  2196
Democracy assumes extraordinary
  possibilities in o. people 2522
Enthusiasm makes o. people
  extraordinary 3177
Faith proves herself in o. situations
  3715
God entrusted his reputation to o.
  people 1285
God needs people who do o.
  things 10137
God wants us to do o. things
  extraordinarily well 7118
great challenges which o. men rise
  to meet 8668
Heroes, mixture of majestic, o.
  755
if had keen vision of all that is o.
  in life 8496
Jesus Christ not teaching o.
  integrity 6314
Laughter adds richness to o. days
  6727
Leaders o. people with
  extraordinary determination
  6798
miracles of Jesus o. works of his
  Father 6479

must not think ourselves o. people
  1346
mystery of the o. 6918
no o. people 8483
not called to be successful with o.
  standards 10823
Nothing is o. if you know how to
  use 2010
people are restoring universe to its
  place 1285
people invaded by living God
  1936
Unwrap hidden beauties in o. day
  2201
use o. situations 5058
use o. situations to do good 623
what God can do with o. 766
where an o. man is saying his
  prayers 8761

ORE
Life not as idle o. 2599
purest o. produced from hottest
  furnace 220
richer and more abundant he finds
  o. 737

ORGAN
Seated one day at the o. 7919

ORGANISM
Christianity an o. 1186
Christians physical o. through
  which Christ acts 1352
church is an o. 1385
into inner dynamics of human o.
  9353

ORGANIST
God is the o. 7892

ORGANIZATION
church not an o. 1385
Churchianity, an o. 1186
family, basic unit of human o.
  3880
in danger of killed originality
  2014
keeps us conservative 2014
makes our hands feeble 2014
Without o. revivals have altered
  men 9752

ORGANIZATIONS
found in place of Christ 1230
going to meet unmerciful o. 7746

ORGANIZED
Materialism o. emptiness of spirit
  8633

ORGANS
If a man can make better church o.
  2776

ORGASM
has replaced cross as focus of
  longing 10233

ORIENTAL
Bible clothed in O. form 645

ORIENTATION
of Jesus' heart, mind, soul was his
  Father 12128

ORIGIN
can apply only to things created
  4613
cannot reconcile Bible with
  human o. 736
Man by o. is a herd animal 6199
Many puzzled about o. of evil
  3383
never had doubt about divine o.
  of Bible 664
poorly read his o. and destiny
  7087
Suffering o. of consciousness 1718
the soul senses its o. 4744

ORIGINAL
Don't expect anything o. from
  echo 2000
God 5383
If you want to be o. 6191
Less than 15 percent do o.
  thinking 11230
more powerful and o. a mind
  10566
unborrowed, solitary greatness of
  Bible 736
very few o. thinkers in world
  11254
without one single o. thought
  11237

ORIGINALITY
being one's self 6219
better to fail in o. 2008
not saying what no one has said
  2011
organization in danger of killing o.
  2014
reporting accurately what we see,
  are 6219
saying what you think 2011
too often undetected plagiarism
  2012
would all laugh at lack of o.
  10353

ORIGINALLY
don't want us free to express faith
  o, creatively 6824

ORIGINATED
created things o. somewhere 4613
gospel o. in heaven 9545
Government o. as ordinance of
  God 5177

ORIGINATES
Religion o. on earth 9545

ORION
sought by him who made Pleiades
  and O. 4768

ORNAMENT
to o. your manger bed 6118

ORNAMENTS
of our house are friends who
  frequent it 4206

ORPHAN
care for his widow and o. 5199
defeat an o. 2516

ORPHANED
denier of God 483

ORTHODOXY
insist on Resurrection as criterion of o. 6604

OSCILLATIONS
Respect o. of feeling 4018

OSTENTATION
charity that proclaims good deeds is only o. 1081

OSTRICH
as blind to opportunity as to disaster 8211
lot of nerve to make fun of o. 4007

OTHER
afraid to show each o. who we really are 6057
all o. beings distinguished by shadow 4472
And with the o. took a shilling out 6070
dreadfully like o. people 7441
each man as the o. person sees him 7443
Evangelism affects the o. fellow 9739
God without regard to any o. 491
Helping each o. through joy, strife 4281
Home, each lives for the o, all live for God 5837
if you think too much of yourself, o. people won't 9253
Life is what happens while making o. plans 6982
love-energy first to God, then to o. people 10053
men's sins are before our eyes 10348
Most people are o. people 1640
much easier to be honest with o. people 5880
not good for o. party, isn't good for you 1022
own heart, not o. men's opinions, form true honor 5896
real love you want o. person's good 7197
romantic love you want the o. person 7197
side pray, too, for victory 9021
terror of God is o. side of his love 4775
to do what no o. can do 6170
where men sit, hear each o. groan 7044

OTHER'S
Forget o. faults by remembering your own 5999
think still less of o. faults 3940

OTHERS
able to love himself, able to love o. 9985
All we send into lives of o. 919

All we send into lives of o. comes back 1726
always live for o. 5066
aspire to relieve suffering of o. 10876
assertively reach out to help o. 3901
Attempting to compel o. to believe as he does 7793
Be not angry o. not as you wish 993
become anxious about what o. say 6824
believe half the evil they say of o. 7973
best to yourself when good to o. 6673
bids o. think of his vices 9207
blackens o. does not whiten himself 10451
Brotherhood is giving o. your rights 924
Brotherhood: helping yourself by helping o. 903
can't spell brothers without spelling o. 9525
cannot convey to o, can but use for ourselves 6178
cannot do evil to o. without doing to ourselves 3413
cannot make o. as you wish them 254
Christ served o. first 6433
Christ-centered suffer when they disappoint o. 10911
Count not thyself better than o. 9195
Deal with faults of o. gently 3938
Dedicate your life to o. 10125
deepest tenderness for o. 4012
delusion personal gain made by crushing o. 7793
desire to see o. advance at his expense 10719
destructive victories won over o. 1165
different from image try to create in minds of o. 9950
discontented, complain about o. 1567
do not control us 10539
Do not despise o. 11685
do not do to o. 5008
Do not think of faults of o. 3939
eagle's eye for faults of o. 3957
easier to be wise for o. than ourselves 11924
easier to suffer with o. than alone 10859
Envy shoots at o. 3214
evil for which we punish o. 3397
expect o. to keep secret foolish 1618
experts at deceiving o. 2477
faults of o. seem more glaring 2077
feed, nourish o. 887
Feel for o. in your pocket 4037
Forever lives a slave to o. 6872

forgiveness not only of o, also ourselves 4103
freedom to give up our rights for good of o. 9963
From errors of o, wise man corrects his own 3257
Give o. a piece of your heart, not mind 10132
give up measuring value with yardstick of o. 10162
God gives something to rely upon o. do not experience 6178
God wants o. to look at our lives 1015
gossip talks to you about o. 5112
greatness is ability to develop greatness in o. 6804
Grief, helping you feel compassion for o. 5334
Happiness perfume cannot pour on o. 5516
has overcome contempt for o. 9985
Have deaf ear for unkind remarks about o. 9456
have done evil 5032
Holiness has good of o. as its employment 5739
Honesty unwillingness to lie to o. 5873
how well we care for o. 7725
Humility recognizing God, o. responsible for my achievements 6011
identify with o. who fight battles on their knees 8865
if any idea joy you would bring to o. 10703
If interest in work of o. cool 7187
if no room for o. and their needs 8818
If want enemies, excel o. 9472
if want friends, let o. excel you 9472
in eyes of o. a thing in the way 8506
inner harmony by pondering experience of o. 7687
interested in o. when they are interested in us 9515
is strong who conquers o. 9968
joy you give to o. 6561
keeps us from giving in innovative ways to o. 6825
kill themselves in stinging o. 9721
learn how to view o. with humility 10306
learn to live for o. 4282
lives only for himself truly dead to o. 10059
love has hands to help o. 7335
love of liberty is love of o. 8716
love, causes us to seek welfare of o. 7304
love, joy, peace multiply when divide with o. 4360
magnifies everything amiss in o. 10025

maintain post when o. have
quitted 1915

man has power to bring misery on
o. 4158

Man seeks to win glory by
sacrifice of o. 2152

Maturity, concern for o.
outweighing concern for
yourself 7693

may often make excuses for o.
3478

may view results 10706

more compassion for o. who hurt
10610

more I demand love of o, less I
deserve 9497

more quiet we become toward
defects of o. 11395

My love coming to you through
kindness of o. 5271

My prayer shall be for o. 9075

need o. if we are to know anything
9513

Neither do we fear being with o.
10539

Never man bent himself able to
make o. straight 3444

no need to manipulate o. 5874

no one able to strike terror into o.
4001

not desirous of looking into faults
of o. 6597

not pleasure in noticing faults of o.
3944

Our opinions of o. depends 9486

own ego makes ego of o.
intolerable 9215

perfection to bear with
imperfections of o. 7682

power to feel with o. give 8430

proud hate pride—in o. 9247

quote o, the better to express
myself 9382

reform o. unconsciously when act
uprightly 3457

regard as enormous wrong to o.
4097

rises by lifting o. 10144

second 9264

see evil in o, not in themselves
5029

See not evil in o. 2808

self-centered suffer when o.
disappoint 10911

Selfishness asking o. to live as one
wishes to live 10081

should act with disregard for
opinions of o. 6291

So long as loved by o, we are
indispensable 7292

Solitude makes us tender toward
o. 10560

Some people stay longer in hour
than o. in week 9492

stand upright when o. beaten
down 1915

stranger to oneself, estranged
from o. too 9519

struggle against evil not by
judging o. 3414

success ability to help o. 10815

sunshine to o, sunshine to their
own 10965

Superior people let it be
discovered by o. 11695

teacher like candle which lights o.
11005

tears shed for o. sign of strength
11026

tender to faults of o. 10014

That mercy I to o. show 1552

that we may be servants of o.
9096

think of what is good in o. 3939

Those who bring sunshine to o.
6567

Through sorrow can enter
suffering of o. 10640

to be of service to o. we have to
die to them 10162

to be what no o. are 6170

To handle o, use your heart 9508

to lay down one's power for o. in
need 7435

to see o. as they see themselves
8513

To see ourselves as o. see us a gift
8513

we judge o. by their actions 6596

wearing disguise before o. 6067

What paineth thee in o. 3452

what they are is what o. want to
be 6224

what we have done for o. remains
10091

What you do not want o. to do
5008

When consider well-being of o.
9520

When sense of self depends on
what o. say 10003

where self supersedes commitment
to o. 3901

who has faith in himself able to be
faithful to o. 9485

who helps in saving o. 10146

who loved God more than o. 5295

who respects himself is safe from
o. 9986

who think no need of o. become
unreasonable 9506

who thinks too much of himself
thinks too little of o. 9243

who will live for o. 11433

wish to be disappointed, look to o.
6408

won't have to count on o. 9521

working for o. with same zeal
3125

Your opinion of o. apt to be their
opinion of you 9526

OTHERS'

Blow dust in o. eyes 10411

generous heart feels o. ill 3063

OTHERWISE

If God had wanted me o. he
would have created me o. 6186

Some wise, some o. 4065

OUGHT

Compared with what we o. to be
8651

duty giving says, I o. to 10736

Friendship o. never to conceal
what it thinks 4238

I o, therefore I can 9662

In doing what we o. deserve no
praise 3100

man free to do what he o. 4150

not what o. to be in us 8853

Say what you have to say, not
what you o. 5887

to love our Maker for his own
sake 4807

to seek, work for good of country
10525

to take care before ask for strength
8850

What I o. to do, I shall do 1926

what things o. to be 7413

what you o. to do for people 1023

whatever one sees o. to be done
4111

who prays as he o. 8812

wise man sees as much as he o.
11902

OUIJA BOARD

puts Bible on par with o. 693

OUNCE

of help better than pound of
preaching 3146

of performance worth more than
pound of preachment 9131

Oh, trouble's a ton, or trouble's
an o. 11446

OUR

cannot say o. if 8818

OURS

Be it o. to learn the tune 7056

Duty is o, events are God's 9654

future is not yet o. 4322

then we and o. will do for you
5008

to offer what we can 10166

To what can I compare this life of
o. 7070

When we and o. have it in our
power 5009

OURSELVES

ability to pace o. 6828

Accusing the times is excusing o.
1462

afraid we would not have food for
o. 10540

an intolerable bore—o. 9939

believe half the good people tell us
of o. 7973

between o. and troubles 41

burden of life is from o. 5229

burdened with the unbearable
weight of o. 9917

But in o. are triumph, defeat 10794

By faith led to knowledge of o. 3834

cannot be supreme over o. 7552

cannot do evil to others without doing to o. 3413

capacity for evil so pronounced in o. 3412

changed to shift attention outside o. 12137

Christ died to save us from o. 6365

condemn o. to spiritual superficiality 6693

crosses which we make for o. 4322

cut o. off from riches of God's grace 6693

deliberately set o. up to fall 10422

disaster to feel o. at home on earth 2975

discontented with o, complain about others 1567

don't know o. well enough to tell another 7428

draw back from sacrifice of o. 3320

easier to be wise for others than o. 11924

emotions tell us about o. 3062

experts at deceiving o. 2477

find o. left in barren, bleak winter 968

forfeit o. to be like other people 6218

forgiveness not only of others, also o. 4103

frightened at facing o. 10575

give o. up to ownership of Jesus 8090

give up our right to o. 465

glory springs from silent conquest of o. 4414

God, no separation unless we make it o. 7557

greatest griefs are those we cause o. 5355

Happiness union of o. with God 5520

help us accept o, failures and all 9993

help us to be masters of o. 9096

holiest of all holidays kept by o. 7720

honest with o, honest with each other 5871

however we deceive o. 3225

If build to please o. 10064

In o. triumph, defeat 1031

incorrect conception of o, neighbor, God 8059

insulate o. from God's presence 4864

judge o. by our motives 6596

keeps from from giving o. in fresh ways to others 6825

knowledge of o. arouses us to seek God 10020

learn to mistrust o, put all confidence in God 9851

less painful than violence we do to o. 11676

let us warm o. 43

Like cuttlefish we conceal o. 4255

love of power is love of o. 8716

majority busy trying to place o. 8395

mold, hammer, forge o. character 1000

Most of us do not like to look inside o. 10012

must discipline o. to fight deviation from course 9965

must forgive o. 4087

must free o. to be filled by God 10708

need others if we are to know o. 9513

never better enjoy o. than when we enjoy God 7558

not frantically trying to make o. good 7560

Not till we have lost world do we find o. 10549

only too glad to hand o. over to God 10015

only way can find o. is in sorrow 10643

philanthropy to save o. uncomfortable feeling 10071

Prayer enabled to move o. God's way 8925

Prayer way of lifting o. 8917

Repentance process by which we see o. as we are 9594

see men of contrary character, examine o. 1065

see o. more as God sees us 4578

seek solitude, look within o. 4924

seldom weigh neighbor as o. 1752

Self-love lessens everything amiss in o. 10025

setting up o. as higher tribunal 4087

show no mercy o. 4105

Solitude makes us tougher toward o. 10560

spend lives pleasing o. 5467

struggle against evil by judging o. 3414

They will say, "We did this o." 6803

to live in virtue combat with o. 11703

To see o. as others see us a gift 8513

to set o. up for disappointment 9478

triangle of love between o, God, other people 7198

truly see and know o. 156

unable to recognize o. 6067

we did not make o. 7552

We must disenthrall o. 976

We must not think of o. as ordinary people 1346

we o. do not look up toward h. 7567

we o. must will the truth 11505

we only know o. through Christ 6461

we only know o. through Jesus Christ 10013

we punish o. 9354

we shape lives, o. 1148

We study everything but o. 9353

What isn't part of o. doesn't disturb us 5600

what we have done for o. dies with us 10091

when disappointed in o. 9992

When God should guide us, we guide o. 10425

When we blame o. 6230

when we o. do not heed God 7567

When we take to o. place that is God's 7571

Why should we do o. this wrong 8867

OUT

And with the other took a shilling o. 6070

Bear to wear o. than rust o. 12012

easier to stay o. than get o. 11073

friend comes in when world has gone o. 4167

Go o. and God comes in 9556

God has to take some people o. of this world 11809

God is in, we are o. 4562

Nothing o. of place is good 5036

of his dark I glow 4125

Satan must go, every hair and feather 9864

There is no way o, no way back 5407

To walk o. of his will 4982

When my task is done, let me o. 7006

world is o. of joint 10521

world of strife shut o. 5817

you go o. of world alone 7151

OUTCOME

of contest not in doubt 4916

Real spirituality has an o. 1404

Though God be opposed, o. never in doubt 4822

OUTCRY

To drown the o. of the heart 6740

OUTER

cannot see o. limits 4544

exploration of o. space bright future 11642

quality of one's o. life 7725

OUTFLOW

God will look after the o. 10180

We have nothing to do with the o. 6232

OUTGROW

children o. Shepherd, find heroes elsewhere 1133

world will never o. need for love
7251
youth defect we o. too soon
12166

OUTGROWS
Nobody ever o. Scriptures 685

OUTLAST
feeling I could o. sea, earth, all
men 12165

OUTLASTS
spend life for something that o. it
10189

OUTLAWED
dictators o. Bible 726

OUTLET
Dead Sea has no o. 10195
Sea of Galilee has o. 10195

OUTLETS
Love seeks not limits but o. 7271

OUTLIVES
Love ever gives, forgives, o. 7218
mother's secret love o. them all
7860

OUTLOOK
death affects o. 2240
Faith makes o. bright 3705
impedes us in our natural o. and
ways 9821
Spirit of God gives worldwide o.
7786
though o. or style may be different
6168
When o. bad, try uplook 9030

OUTNUMBER
wicked always o. the good 5182

OUTRAGE
fashion of today, o. of tomorrow
10516
Of wrong and o. with which earth
is fill'd 6273

OUTRAGED
by somebody's impudence 45
do not ask for impossibilities 45
When you are o. 45

OUTRUN
scientific power has o. spiritual
power 9868

OUTRUNNING
Sin is fleet of foot o. everything
10374

OUTS
in with God, at o. with world
12035

OUTSIDE
Better hundred enemies o. house
than one inside 5820
God above, o, beyond all
measurement 4710
God is o. all 4848
God is o. all things, but not
excluded 4612
God is o. of me 7968

God's actions o. above human
sciences 5237
home is adventure, variety 5842
love o. that would be inside 4775
Many who have gold in house
looking for copper o. 5840
Morality not only correct conduct
on o. 7832
noisy, inside empty 4064
not controlled by what happens
on o. 9849
of God, nothing but nothing 4488
show is poor substitute for inner
worth 6061
What is o. yourself does not
convey much worth 9626
You were within me and I was o.
7473

OUTSTRIPPED
Faith has never o. bounty of Lord
3664

OUTTOPS
God o. thought 4678

OUTWARD
And find, to o. sense denied 6583
Christ's o. life immersed in world
6439
comfort will do no more than
slipper on gouty foot 8442
Goodness not in o. things we do
5063
Human improvement from within
o. 1017
Peace does not dwell in o. things
8453
Though angel on the o. side 2470
Vision looks o, becomes aspiration
11738
Whatever is o. in worship 12129
When o. strength is broken 3818

OUTWARDLY
Christ's life o. troubled 6376
conforming o, living own life
inwardly 6048
Our inner life grows stronger
when o. condemned 6270
What we do with our lives o.
7725

OUTWEIGHING
sense concern for others o.
concern for yourself 7693

OUTWEIGHS
lesson taught far o. the pain
10586
Wisdom o. any wealth 11976

OVER
God is o. all things 4848
passing o. revenge is superior
9715

OVERACT
God may seem to o. his part 286

OVERALLS
Faithfulness is consecration in o.
3844

OVERCOAT
put on your o. 44

OVERCOME
by half his foe 527
cannot o. without fighting 1633
devil can wrestle with but not o.
2673
God wants us to o, not be
overwhelmed 1608
grace, strength of God to o. 5227
has learned to o. self-contempt
9985
has o. contempt for others 9985
Holiness power to o. temptation
5744
if all objections must first be o. 86
In education always something to
o. 1024
need to o. separateness 7143
Nothing attempted if objections
first o. 2741
powers of evil o. them 11080
Strength to battle difficulties and
o. 1809
Success obstacles o. trying to
succeed 10809
Temptations if o. a nest of honey
11095
Thou shall not be o. 176
to o. evil 9088
valiant will to o. 4643

OVERCOMES
Who o. by force 527

OVERCOMING
Acceptance first step to o. 154
evil never hopeless 3378
Prayer is not o. God's reluctance
8933
Reconciliation an o. of oneself
9431

OVERCOMMITMENT
Husbands, wives should
constantly guard against o.
7617

OVERCONFIDENCE
sticking neck out 1607

OVERDO
youth o. everything 12181

OVERFLOW
doing becomes natural o. of being
78
God can o. deepest demands 7463
into what do you o. 4854
When heart is full, eyes o. 5269

OVERFLOWED
he is curtailed who o. all skies, all
years 6120

OVERFLOWING
do you cram heavens to o. 4854

OVERHEATED
Fanaticism false fire of o. mind
3909

OVERLOOK
a great deal 9489

art of knowing what to o. 11900

being wise is knowing what to o. 11940

God quick to o. imperfections 4810

unjust reproach with a generous neglect 6281

OVERLOOKED

happiness o. because doesn't cost anything 5542

Men o. a baby's birth 6458

more immediate, obvious things 9970

OVERLOOKS

good marriage o. "unresolvables" 7591

Love o. defects 7266

OVERMATCH

fight devil with own weapons, finds him o. 2647

OVERNIGHT

God does not expect us to become saints o. 9832

takes 20 years to be o. success 10790

OVEROPTIMISTIC

Christ, not o. 1154

OVERPOWERED

you o. my hard heart 7579

OVERRATED

Perseverance most o. of traits 8553

OVERREACHES

Everything devil does, God o. 2644

OVERSCRUPULOUS

to be conscientious become o. 9502

OVERSHOOTS

archer who o. misses as well 6592

OVERSTATE

impossible to o. need for prayer 3875

OVERTAKES

Laziness travels so slowly poverty soon o. him 6768

sin, o. us by surprise 10422

OVERTAKING

worry never keeps trouble from o. you 12091

OVERTAXED

don't swell with pride, may look o. 9258

OVERWHELM

Bible, vehicle to express thoughts that o. 698

billows which o. 291

innumerable definitions of God o. me 4585

to o. us with gift of himself 4639

OVERWHELMED

Faith inner conviction o. by God 3681

God wants us to overcome, not be o. 1608

man o. with commandments 1525

need not be o. with confusion 4924

soul o. can rise up 3621

OVERWHELMING

and irrecoverable loss, his soul 2381

conviction nowhere else to go 8822

God's Book packed full of o. riches 656

Jesus' power of persuasion so o. 5485

will come one day a complete, o. explanation 7060

OVERWORK

Few drop dead from o. 3089

OWE

it to God that we refuse rusty brains 11274

knowledge to those who have differed 6710

Many men o. grandeur to difficulties 2739

more to fire and hammer 10855

Respect is what we o. 7290

Thou receiveth, that thou mayst o. 4954

to make men unmindful of what they o. God 819

We o. God every honor in our power to give 4529

OWES

Don't go around saying world o. you living 9652

God's being he o. to no one 4610

is rich who o. nothing 11821

never will world know all it o. to neurotics 4390

world o. onward impulses to men ill at ease 2875

world o. you nothing, it was here first 9652

OWL

looking like o. when acted like ass 6162

OWN

All that God gives remains his o. 4821

always able to discover o. darkness 6004

anything that won't fit coffin 1801

But oft for our o. the bitter tone 3900

cannot light another's path without brightening our o. 3145

Carry o. lantern, and you need not fear dark 6167

combine dependence on God's Spirit with o. researches 6681

comes back into our o. 919

Commune with o. selves 3935

conforming outwardly, living o. life inwardly 6048

Cultivate your o. capabilities 6168

easy in solitude to live after o. opinions 6195

ego makes ego of others intolerable 9215

fight devil with o. weapons, overmatch 2647

Forget others' faults by remembering your o. 5999

gift cumulative force of life's cultivation 6226

God allows our o. schemes to fail 9851

God cannot come in any way but his o. way 4664

greatest are least in o. opinion 5991

have lived badly on my o. 9070 11515

healing words not our o. 10545

Hell is enjoyment of your o. way forever 5695

Hell where everyone doing o. thing 5691

human being intended to have character of his o. 6170

humility not doubt of o. power 6032

If I will nothing of my o. 4977

insist on your o. way, will get it 5695

keeping watch above his o. 5377

Let us bring what is our o. 4558

man who cannot resolve to live his o. life 6872

merits no thanks who does kindness for o. ends 10056

more afraid of my o. heart 9929

must not find our o. way 5446

Never blow your o. horn 9222

no longer has any plans of his o. 9846

Nothing more rare than o. act 1641

Our o. heart form true honor 5896

prefer o. friends who share life-style 5957

principle of hell, "I am my o." 5699

sin, two witnesses our o. selves and God 10418

surrendered o. plans to greater plan of God 4803

takes rank lightly raises o. dignity 6003

Though we love our o. the best 3900

trying on one face after another to find his o. 12163

We are all beggars, each in his o. way 5986

We are not our o. 7552

What other corner so dark as one's o. heart 9955

when asleep in world of his o.
2965
When shall I cease to be my o.
7961
Wisdom in minds attentive to
their o. 6690

OWNED
Life like a library o. by an author
6965

OWNER
All our goodness a loan, God the
o. 5055
Creator of earth is o. 1970

OWNERSHIP
give ourselves up to o. of Jesus
8090

OX
Better egg in peace than o. in war
11742
get rid of o. or fill up ditch 10951
If o. gets in ditch every Sabbath
10951
Jesus spoke about o. in ditch on
Sabbath 10951

OXEN
The o. knew him, had him in their
care 6133

OXYGEN
Encouragement o. to soul 3133

OYSTER
Rejection sand in o. 204
skill of science not able to make o.
1979

OYSTERS
never wounded, fit only for stew
10883
Some o. never wounded 206

𝒫

PACE
ability to p. ourselves 6828
contestants must learn to p.
themselves 3884
If man does not keep p. with his
companions 10827
Quiet minds go at own private p.
8466
resolve to slow your p. 5615
When God quickens his p, be sure
before you quicken yours 5460

PACK
carry care to bed, sleep with p. on
back 12080
heaviest load p. of grudges 4098

PACKAGE
Christianity a p. deal 8108

PACKS
God p. our life with surprises
5463

PACT
Straw should make no p. with fire
11085

PADDING
God comes p. after me like
Hound of Heaven 4534

PAGAN
religions doctrinal element at
minimum 11226

PAGANS
do not know God, love only earth
3201
If behaved like Christians, no p.
565
without Christianity rearing p.
8308

PAGE
Bible p. torn out of volume of
human life 706
Every day a new p. 6901
I've read the last p. of the Bible
4316
who never stir from home read
only a p. 6945

PAGES
The p. of our years 7017

PAID
Every luxury must be p. for 3480
Every sin already p. for 10299
Gratitude duty which ought to be
p. 5242
high price to find evil is evil 3416
How dearly thou hast p. for me
2136
I'll tell you what I p. 3483
sins of youth p. for in old age
10401
That is not p. with moan 810
Worry interest p. by those who
borrow trouble 12090

PAIL
Education not filling p. 3002

PAIN
a curious wild p. 7521
a little human sympathy helps
more than much courage 8280
a p. to live 186
allow p. to corrode your spirit is
to have chosen 8264
Although today he prunes my
twigs with p. 8254
and perish is our own 810
And pleasures banish p. 5670
appropriate "spiritual" response
8259
aspire to relieve p. of others
10876
Bear patiently cross of p. 1502
best comfort in suffering and p.
10926
better than pleasure 10875
birth pang of a new attitude 520
blessedness makes joy possible in
p. 6536
Bow thy meek head to mortal p.
2981
Brother in joy and p. 7506
buys intimacy with Christ 10906

can either make better or bitter
8265
cannot learn without p. 8276
cannot really remember it 8260
church looks in p. at shortcomings
1443
Clings cruelly to us 8271
confers real happiness 8260
consciousness torn by p. of grief
900
contrary to God's will, absolutely
but not relatively 8258
cross is p. involved in doing will
of God 2107
cross, defiance of p. 2118
deepest thing in our nature 8269
dies in p. 7050
do not aspire to understand p.
10876
Doubt is p. too lonely to know
faith 2932
Empathy is your p. in my heart
3068
end of life not to avoid p. 5554
Error, wounded, writhes in p.
11579
every p. will have an explanation
7060
existence entwined with p. 3479
faith in meaning of our p. 4005
Faith quenches fire of every p.
3661
find at center of my p. amazing
insight 8279
for mystics, p. a ecstasy 8255
For philosophers, p. problem of
metaphysics 8255
for religious, p. a travail to be
borne 8255
for stoics, p. an exercise 8255
Forget the p. by which they
purchased heaven 7672
God able to bring good out of p.
5046
God has gone through human
experience of p. 6386
God uses chronic p. 8256
great word to master, p. 7000
hell, p. of punishment without
penitence 5700
highest privilege to share another's
p. 4276
hour of p. long as day of pleasure
149
how Jesus responded 8259
in our little finger 10035
In sleep, p. that cannot forget falls
drop by drop 11919
In solitude become crushed by p.
of fellow human beings 10540
inevitable for all 8266
is brief, joy eternal 2383
is life 8267
is solitary 8260
isolates 9812
jolt of p. with sin 577
joy compatible with p. 6571
joy survives through p. 6568

PALACE

Better cottage when one merry than p. where one weeps 5821
Bible comes into p. 645
death passage out of prison into p. 2325
meanest hut with love a p. for the soul 5816
without affection a poor hovel 5816

PALACES

as princes' p. they that enter there 5649
Death knocks at p. of kings 2361
men resemble deserted p. 1715

PALATABLE

To make message p. to world 5109

PALE

bloodless, heartless thing 1487

PALM

In the hollow of God's p. 8429
No pain, no p. 199
Their fronded p. in air 4763

PALMS

And p. before my feet 2980

PAMPER

God's goal not to p. physically 1016

PAMPERS

Possession p. the mind 242

PANACEA

Married life offers no p. 7647
pure love the p. for ills of world 7203
think divorce a p. find remedy worse 2927

PANDEMONIUM

Believe though all Providence becomes a p. 584

PANG

In every p. that rends the heart 10597
that gives delight 5349

PANIC

Don't p. during storms of adolescence 8295
Faith a refusal to p. 3677
faith ability not to p. 3769
God is never in a p. 4937
Jesus Christ, no p. 2170
may resent truth 11566
no p. in trust 11482
saints not overcome by p. 126

PANS

Christ moves among pots and p. 5824

PANTED

I drew in breath and p. for thee 4805

PANTS

Search, prove my heart, it p. for Thee 4140

PAPA

belongs to literary circle 3921
wheels baby carriage, carries bundles 3921

PAPER

world has made marriage scrap of p. 2924

PARACHUTES

Minds are like p. 7762

PARADISE

agony and toil a p. become 2604
As in p. God seeking man 643
As in p. God walks in Holy Scriptures 643
earth be God's p. 551
enter into p. with right key 5640
Faultfinder will find faults even in P. 6903
grave a veil over p. 2350
Marriage with peace is world's p. 7645
one path leads to P. 5664
This earth would be God's P. 6882
where everyone doing God's thing 5691

PARADOX

Christ divine p. of lion, lamb 6425
comes into all religious thought 4682
human being precious, squandered 2343
kingdom of God a p. 2519
Man a peculiar, puzzling p. 7402
of punishment 9355

PARADOXES

greatest p. of mystical life 7962

PARADOXICAL

in strangely p. way cross is easy 8108
most fervent believer may appear p. 8569
mother-child relationship p. 7858

PARALYZE

Deny the virgin birth and you p. redemption 6404

PARALYZED

if we saw all evil things 4318
powers of darkness p. by prayer 8988
with horror for minutes 11741

PARALYZES

fear p. 3965

PARALYZING

break through p. boundaries 1513
cross God sends of necessity p. 2092
legalism spreads p. venom 6823

PARANOIA

poison of bitterness, p. 10034

PARASITES

on the body of society 130

PARCHED

What p. grounds refresh as with a shower 8867

PARCHMENT

And were the heav'ns of p. made 4748

PARDON

cheaper to p. than resent 4089
forgiving means to p. that which is unpardonable 11691
God has all mercy to p. you 4696
Grace can p. our ungodliness 5212
grow in wisdom, p. more freely 4071
Know all, you will p. all 4092
my ingratitude, pity my dullness 6253
to degree we love 4106
Vices familiar we p. 10414
where there is injury, p. 9086

PARDONABLE

faults more p. than methods to hide them 3933

PARDONED

God, the Judge, sovereignly declared p. 3672
in pardoning that we are p. 9086

PARDONING

in p. that we are pardoned 9086

PARDONS

Grace can multiply p. 5212
When God p, everlasting forgetfulness 4107
When God p. 4638

PARENT

ability to say "no" greatest gift p. has 8326
at some time father of unreturned prodigal 8345
child lies, will find a severe p. 8362
clasp of infant around finger of p. 816
establish yourself as leader 8343
If gratitude due from children to p. 5253
may see God as abusive p. 4489
never know love of p. until become parents 3902
Pride the p. from which all other sins come 9230
suspicious p. makes artful child 8342
takes time to be an effective p. 8287
talked to God as one might talk to a p. 7526
who does not teach child to obey is cruel 8355
word of p. fibre woven into character of child 8346
work yourself out of job 8343

PARENT'S

children have trouble solving p. problems 3883

PARENTAL

obedience to p. authority is foundation of citizenship 8355

While yielding to p. leadership 8338

PARENTHESIS
created world p. in eternity 1968

PARENTING
Don't let p. years get away 8294
modeled after relationship between God and man 8299

PARENTS
accent on youth, stress on p. 8354
afraid to put foot down 8323
As children grow older, they judge p. 1111
bones on which children sharpen teeth 8350
can afford to give allowances 8321
child identifies p. with God 8339
child sees p. living without self-discipline 8300
Children act like their p. 1109
children afraid to go to p. for counsel 8311
Children begin by loving p. 1111
children to shock p. 562
children understand what p. have rejected 12157
Children want p. more than junk we buy 8288
Children will act like their p. 8289
first half of our lives ruined by p. 3892
first part of life p. learn to stand you 3893
fringe benefits break them 8321
future of church and humanity depend on p. 3894
giving children nothing but best 8324
have children step on their toes 8323
have little time for children 8351
have poisoned fountain 8352
have trouble solving children's problems 3883
illegitimate p. 1131
impresses me about America is p. obey children 8357
joy of p. in children most holy joy of humanity 5844
jump forward to bail children out 8320
Kids can frustrate p. 8304
last part of life you learn to stand p. 3893
most do without things p. never heard of 8582
never trouble where children resemble p. 3898
prevent children learning lessons 8320
should work together as two bookends 8322
Slow down, p. 8353
sometimes children forgive p. 1111
successful p. get behind eyes of child 8329

to children p. are heaven's lieutenants 5856 8358
voice of p. is voice of gods to children 8358
way p. obey their children 3897
what tangled web do p. weave 8319
wind up with nothing but worst 8324
wonder why streams bitter 8352
young people say p. hate them 8335
Youth begins when objects to p. having own way 3905
Youth begins when p. become retarded 3906

PARISH
Let your home be your p. 7847
look upon world as my p. 3312

PARLIAMENTS
all p. that ever sat 6353

PARROT
live so not mind selling p. to gossip 1039

PARSON'S
mundane work sacred as p. 3113

PART
as much a p. of human race as the greatest 9988
Christian finds peace in playing his p. in master plan 8440
do have to light my p. 7107
each of us has played 9911
God never develops one p. of our being at expense of other 6897
He would not p. waters of sea 967
how did he play his God-given p. 7423
I am a p. of all that I have met 6234
I count that p. of life lost 6909
I want to be p. of it 9061
I would do my p. 1376
if compelled to take p, where is director 3485
If you hate, you hate something that is p. of yourself 5600
lament our p. missing in the music 7056
Man of Sorrows had a p. 10597
My p. is to improve the present moment 10145
new morality and biblical morality p. 7837
No man should p. with own individuality 6201
of his body, I transcend this flesh 4125
Our p. is to enter kingdom 4734
Our p. to bring life under God's sovereign will 4734
think of destiny, how puny a p. you are 7063
training thee for p. angels cannot sing 10600

What isn't p. of ourselves doesn't disturb us 5600
who would p. with nothing 10078
with him when he goes wrong 6303
With tranquil heart to do my simple p. 9072
Worship not p. of Christian life 12135

PARTED
fool and money soon p. 11792
When from our better selves we have been p. 10578

PARTIAL
Man judges from a p. view 6583

PARTIALITY
God's action masterpiece of p. and love 4747

PARTICIPANTS
God expects us to be p. 10135
marriage paper torn up at whim of p. 2924

PARTICIPATE
in God, go to the cross 1173
mystic to p. here and now in that real life 7969

PARTICIPATION
certainty of divine p. gives courage 6277
Christianity is p. 1173

PARTICLE
philosopher a p. pontificating on infinity 8588

PARTING
is here 2412

PARTLY
Life is p. what we make it 4254
life p. made by friends we choose 4254

PARTNER
Christian p. of God 3327
God the silent p. in great enterprises 4460
hears himself cursed and remains silent is p. of God 4894
in biblical faith, woman is p. in ministry 11981

PARTRIDGE
crow tried to emulate p. gait 1644

PARTS
All revolutions various p. of same scheme 4898
God did not write solo p. 10135
God has no p, single in unitary being 4610
in symphony none can take but thee 10600

PARTY
each p. claims to act in will of God 4972
great p. has erupted 3326
hears but half who hears one p. only 9182

not good for other p, isn't good
for you 1022
worrying about trash p. will make
7670
You're planning the next p. 7670

PASCAL
searching observations about G.
155

PASS
act of sin may p. 5489
awhile under category of chance
5454
by trifling errors blindly 4217
Christ's words p. into proverbs
6523
Even this shall p. away 974
expect to p. through life but once
6642
find a p. through 2633
For God, time does not p, it
remains 3274
great man's foolish sayings p. for
wise ones 5273
Grief will p. away 10586
Hope like clouds, some p. by,
others bring rain 5922
no people ever great which did
not p. through valley 5289
ruins bridge over which he is to p.
4084
this, too, shall p. away 957
thorns p, roses remain 10710
those who p. like ships in night
4281
through that center into God 7962
Thy grief shall p. away 6878
unless able to p. out of himself
7962
we p. heedless, unseeing 9064
Who p. into life beyond 6109

PASSAGE
happens to light upon p. which
meets need 5441
Time has no division to mark p.
11329
to expound a p. live in it 9148
Wait thy p. through the shade
2221
without leaving worthy evidence
of your p. 11292

PASSED
anyone happier because you p. his
way 3136
But, how many were sorry when
he p. away 7423
by a man in workman's guise
6458
darkest day will have p. away
2575
Every day should be p. as if our
last 6887
moment p. is no longer 8384

PASSENGERS
all fellow p. on same planet 9677

PASSES
All p, nothing lasts 11288
capacity of finite mind 4989

Devotion not a thing that p. 9731
everywhere man p. he leaves some
kind of mark 6231
God p. through thicket of world
4463
grief p. into quiet, tender joy 7101
Life p. 6455
Light, though p. through
pollution, not polluted 7110
love p. securely through all 7283
Peace is when time doesn't matter
as it p. by 8461

PASSETH
from life to his rest in the grave
9225

PASSING
All things are p. 4588
Everything but soul p. shadow
10654
If cannot find God p. by 4856
Little p. words of sympathy 6997
Power p. mine, immeasurable God
4825
through nature to eternity 2402

PASSION
content against giants of p, pride
9233
I have one p. only, it is he 6400
Music purest language of p. 7905
of giving up things 465
save our souls from being
darkened by p. 9064
The p. of our Lord did not end on
the cross 2164
Thou lovest, without p. 4954
To attempt to control p. in own
strength 11108
when young, p. marvelous thing
10229

PASSIONATE
bad are p. and restless 5045
Love for Lord most p. love 7221

PASSIONS
a quotation 1640
are like fire 10234
dangerous through excess 10234
good servants, bad masters 10225
hell where everyone lives deadly p.
5705
human p. unbridled by morality
5196
Men of cold p. have quick eyes
3565
must be bathed in new element
880
must be re-born 880
must be reconsecrated to Maker
880
our p. please devil 2661
quelled by music's divine control
7935
tumult of our p. within 8800
use for p. stuff given for happiness
4359
useful in a thousand ways 10234

PASSIVE
patience excuse to do nothing
6619

PASSIVELY
he who accepts evil is involved in
it 3374

PASSIVITY
no room for p. in Christian faith
1235

PASSWORD
only p. is prayer 8771

PAST
and to come seem best 8382
anger at God to be troubled for
what is p. 12066
as present memory 8387
As soon as danger p. devotion
vanishes 8788
back into p. rake up all troubles
ever had 11450
bad enough to know the p. 4317
bad p. is starting point for better
things 9590
best apologies for wrong actions
in p. 9598
can bring back no p. by longing
8368
can look backward in time until
p. vanishes 11350
cannot be changed 8385
3623
conversing with greatest minds of
p. 3027
creates out of p. something new,
better 8368
cynic reads bitter lessons from p.
2178
dangerous used as hitching post
8367
discouragement when too much
thought to p. 2887
does not lament the p. 8184
dogmas of quiet p. inadequate 976
Every saint has a p, every sinner a
future 8653
friend understands your p. 4172
future pauses for short while
before becoming the p. 8386
God at p, future unaffected by
either 11350
God does not regard p. sins 10311
Gratitude looks to the p. 8376
Holy Spirit will make p. as though
it had never been 894
I've left the p. in God's keeping
8079
In Christ move out of p. 8364
is spent and done with 8374
Let the dead p. bury its dead 4331
Look not mournfully into p. 8378
make present better than p. 8377
Man spends life reasoning on p.
8380
No man rich enough to buy back
p. 1735
Nor deem the irrevocable p. 3538

Nothing certain except the p. 8365

Nothing shall be to come, and nothing p. 3288

Nothing to discuss but glories of days p. 4321

old age praising times p. 8186

possibility of future exceeds accomplishments of p. 4329

Prayer draws us out of limits within which p. confine us 8906

prayer for the p. 9054

response to p. can be changed 3623

review p. with common sense 4329

Scholars can interpret the p. 9334

Shut out p. except that which will help tomorrows 8383

The good Old Year is with the p. 8078

to abash us and expose our p. 4884

to make man's p. as though it had never been 9800

Trust p. to mercy of God 5457

valuable as a guidepost 8367

when faith in future becomes knowledge of p. 7435

When you forgive you in no way change p. 4108

Why wish for living p. life again 7091

with God, no p. and no future 11322

PASTIME
despair man's favorite p. 2607

PASTIMES
Tennis few p. where love means nothing 7297

PASTOR
agility of a greyhound 9161

as many lives as a cat 9161

cast-iron stomach 9125

energy of a father 9144

exuberant affection of a mother 9144

guided by bad spiritual philosophy 115

heart of a lion 9161

industry of an ant 9161

patience of a donkey 9161

patience of Job 9125

skin of a hippopotamus 9161

strength of Samson 9125

tact of a diplomat 9125

wisdom of an elephant 9161

wisdom of Solomon 9125

zeal of a friend 9144

PASTORS
if refrain from saying anything that might be misunderstood 9145

will end by never saying anything worth hearing 9145

PASTURE
The Lord my p. shall prepare 9350

PASTURES
we want green p. 229

PAT
Tact p. on back when feel like kick in pants 10988

PATH
Adversity first p. to truth 144

all amazingly know their p. 7945

Be thou a smooth p. below me 5375

Before us a p. untrod 5376

Choose out the p. for me 5456

Christ p. if any be misled 6391

cross end of p. chosen after counting cost 2103

Dark as my p. may seem to others 3649

Death's a p. that must be trod 2267

Direct efforts to preparing youth for p. 8291

Do not follow where p. may lead 6787

Flood the p. with light 9059

follow good or evil p. 1137

future is p. yet untraveled 4325

Go where no p, leave trail 6787

God doesn't always smooth the p. 4808

God's p. is up 7529

greatest p. is open to least of travelers 7235

hold torch to light another's p. 3145

never any traffic congestion on straight, narrow p. 9819

No man happy whose p. but glimmer of light 6101

of God before you 829

of humility is p. to glory 6034

One p. leads to Paradise 5664

only p. to pleasure is pleasing God 8609

things move along an appointed p. 9173

This p. is mine, not thine 5415

thou hast kept my p. 4758

though thy p. be dark as night 5995

Virtue demands rough thorny p. 11714

when God leads in higher p. of sanctification 9851

PATHETIC
This coward with p. voice 2583

PATHOS
Psalms, p. of man's sorrow 798

PATHS
crooked p. look straighter at end 2374

genius never travels on well-worn p. 4393

God sends us on stony p. 180

God wills us to tread hidden p. 5397

hope, brightening the darkened p. 5940

I do not ask to walk smooth p. 1927

need new strength to walk old p. 9554

need not new p. in religion 9554

thousand p. lead to hell 5664

walk on well-trodden p. throw stones 1643

PATHWAY
God never points out p. different? 4969

Nor wander from the p. 5418

why fear to tread p. to future home 6875

PATIENCE
ability to put up with people you'd like to put down 8411

accepting difficult situation 8415

achieves more than force 8407

and gentleness is power 8708

answering prayer for more p. 8804

because strength and p. are failing him 6599

benefit of trial consists in p. 2734

call to suffering requires p. 10937

charity is p. when neighbor's hurt 1085

Christ a Lamb in p. 6425

companion of wisdom 8412

Dear God, grant me p. 8393

depth of capacity for p. 8403

discipline of sanctified life, p. 2856

enough to toil until good accomplished 1809

gains all things 4588

Genius only great p. 4391

God with p. leading world 4474

God's p. with ill-natured saints mystery 4893

Grief can elicit p. 10640

handful of p. worth more than bushel of brains 8390

hardest to exercise p. in the street 8423

has its limits 8409

have no p. with reason alone 3025

Have p! All things difficult before easy 8397

have p, can have what he wills 8398

Have p, slanders not long-lived 10448

hope makes soul exercise p. 5912

Hope will put on p. as a vestment 5912

How poor they that have not p. 8399

is bitter, fruit is sweet 8410

is genius 8402

is hard, I tell you it is hard 11464

is riding out the gale 8422

Jesus' p. should have proved he was God 6492

key to everything is p. 8420
learn p. by going into hurly-burly world 8422
learn p. by taking life as it blows 8422
meet misjudgment with p. 2630
mother of expectation 8413
must be tried in friendship 4227
no p. with piety alone 3025
no such thing as preaching p. into people 8422
nonconformist never yields to passive p. 6619
not giving God deadline 8415
One minute of p, ten years of peace 8404
One moment of p. may prevent disaster 8405
passive p. excuse to do nothing 6619
perplexed that we may learn p. 8396
pray for p. to bear troubles 2091
prayer for p. 8418
price is always p. 9759
principal part of faith, p. 3792
quietly awaits promise 9322
removes mountains 8408
sermon so long have to practice p. 8422
Sin is the jeer of God's p. 10376
Take p. too far, it's cowardice 8409
teach us disciplines of p. 8418
times when God asks nothing except p. 10635
to do simple things perfectly 8406
Tribulation: God's fastest road to p. 225
waiting without anxiety 8414
we value health, God values p. 11667
With time and p. mulberry leaf becomes satin 8561
years of p. to tame young human beings 7382

PATIENT
Be p. with everyone, above all yourself 8392
endurance perfection of charity 3152
everyone a terminal p. 12030
God is very p. 4892
greatness in p. endurance 5283
how p. God has been with us 2778
if p, can wait much faster 8400
In a p. hope I rest 3800
In desolation must be p. 2883
in doubts 950
live with tolerance, learn to be p. 1114
Love is p. 7246
O blessed are the p. meek 6274
Please be p. 8417
spirit against pain, disappointment 10844
to relieve a p. of guilt 5485

waiting often highest way of doing God's will 8416

PATIENTLY
assurance to wait p. 3744
Bear p. cross of grief, pain 1502
Bear p. the dryness of your mind 7123
Bear p. your exile 7123
Carry the cross p. 2088
Creator p. listening to four-year-old 3918
evils of day bear p. 11365
God works to teach 7056
Life one stitch at a time taken p. 8388
merit to suffer affliction p. 234
seed p. wintering in earth 5672

PATIENTS
70% of p. could cure themselves 12076

PATRIOTISM
is not enough 2452
Music used to ridicule p. 7910

PATRIOTS
These are the p. nations need 7986

PATTERN
For the p. which he planned 10606
Give children p. they can see clearly 8289
gleam brightly in p. of life God approves 6997
good and evil, world made to mingle p. 4335
Will God unroll the p. 10606
world is made to mingled p. 5052

PATTERNS
Man led more by p. than precepts 3442

PAUL
case not politically expedient 786
case not resolved by judges 786
God could have kept P. and Silas out of jail 165
medical analysis of vision 787
was beheaded 1211

PAUL'S
preaching ended in either a riot or revival 9155

PAUPER
can give like a prince 4388
willing to come as p, receive Holy Spirit 5792

PAUSE
makes world p. in frantic, headlong pursuits 10938
Silence a rich p. in music of life 10262
solemn p, breathing space of man 10960
sudden p. in choral hymn of lives 7056

PAUSES
present is period when future p. 8386

PAVED
Hell p. with good intentions 5688

PAVEMENT
Life like a little strip of p. over an abyss 7090

PAY
any price to say "All will be saved" 9799
attention to the Source 10180
attention to your enemies 3169
can expect to p. the piper 4051
few want to p. price of achievement 4731
For a cap and bells our lives we p. 9795 2641
friend you buy won't be worth what you p. 4176
God does not p. weekly 1730
heavy price to p. for being born 3487
Loneliness great price to p. for independence 7135
man believes must p. for pleasure 8602
may not be so hot 10217
Money can p. fare to every place but heaven 7810
more attention to spiritual progress 10703
must p. for, one by one 73
obedience is premium we p. 8096
one must p. the price 9759
plod along hoping efforts will p. off 6810
sins, must p. for one by one 10398
to p. attention to tree trunk in his own eye 6590
Wisdom good purchase through we p. dear for it 11968

PAYING
If God thinks war worth p. for free will 4132
poverty, p. debts off 4040
when nobody is p. attention to you 7129

PAYROLL
Death, I am not on his p. 2309

PAYS
Fear is tax conscience p. to guilt 3966
God p. at the end 1730
God p. men compliment 1142
Hypocrisy homage vice p. to virtue 6051
love p. to be absolute spendthrift 7252
sin p. handsomely, relentlessly 10421
Sin p. in remorse, regret, failure 10379
value in what one p. 11664

PEACE

ability to be at p. through activities of the day 6828

Accept suffering, find p. 10833

achieve and cherish a just, lasting p. 5199

advancing in life whose spirit entering into living p. 6898

All men desire p. 8428

all we have to do is enter into it 8427

always long for p. 8564

Ambition, grand enemy of p. 342

among ourselves and with all nations 5199

and tranquility will return again 8445

at same time enjoy p. of mind 4001

beauty of thy p. 8431

Better egg in p. than ox in war 11742

can bring p. to others 8434

Can give me p. within 8451

can only be achieved by understanding 8452

cannot add to p, good will if 580

cannot be kept by force 8452

Christian finds p. in accepting master plan 8440

Christianity has taught true p. 10880

church asks God only for p. 11761

church, force for p. in world of hatred 1433

Come near, that even so they may have p. 9045

comes from the love of God 8469

conscience of godly at p. 3996

conscious p. for the hours of sleep 10486

convert given p. like none in world 1904

cross key to p. 2145

day of strange, almost curious p. 10120

deliberate adjustment of life to will of God 8460

deprivation of God's recreating, loving p. 8697

desire of life, p. 9274

do not understand p. until conflict 11620

does not dwell in outward things 8453

does not mean end of striving 8454

dwells within the soul 8453

Emotional p. and calm come after doing God's will 8432

enter into it 494

expresses itself in love for men 8469

few desire things that make for p. 8428

Finding God, no need to seek p. 8433

First keep p. within yourself 8434

Five great enemies to p. 8435

found p. among the silver trees 8051

funds for promotion of p. 11782

Give p. profound or daily strife 1538

go to sleep in p. 11489

goal not joy nor p. 4428

God cannot give p. apart from himself 5510

God comes to us to give p. 3722

God gives us unbroken p. 8438

God has not left p. for us to do 8427

God himself is your p. 8433

God is p. 8444

God, not the world, can give p. 8456

Good kings never make war but for p. 11747

guideposts on the footpath to p. 8472

has already been done 8427 494

Humanness is realization of inner p. 5014

Humility is the quiet valley, p. lives there 6026

Humility to be at p. when all around is trouble 6010

I burned to know your p. 7473

If any idea has much inward p. you would gain 10703

If expect to find p. in friendship 9470

If I must choose between p, righteousness 6305

In Christ relaxed and at p. 8470

In God's will is our p. 4973

In p. sons bury fathers 11751

in so doing find our p. 6566

in thee in p. 4021

inexhaustible source of p, consolation 9835

is a disposition for benevolence 8455

is a state of mind 8455

is a virtue 8455

is ability to cope with conflict 8458

is confidence 8455

is joy at rest 6542

is justice 8455

is justice's companion 6628

is love in repose 7202

is not absence of war 8455

is not arbitrary 8456

Is not prayer precisely p. 8847

is rich 11696

is when time doesn't matter as it passes by 8461

Jesus Christ, his p. passing all understanding 6352

Jesus, P. for time and eternity 6420

Joy is p. dancing 6542

love, joy, p. multiply when divide with others 4360

made in hearts of men 8457

madness for sheep to talk p. with wolf 8446

make me an instrument of thy p. 9086

make war that we may live in p. 11785

Making p. requires action 4094

man of p, not a Jeremiah 770

many people are trying to make p. 8427

Marriage with p. is world's paradise 7645

may preserve if will firm, submissive 8453

may preserve in midst of bitterest pain 8453

Money brings days of joy, but not p. 7807

must be based upon definite facts 8456

nations have found betrayal in p. 11783

nations have found deception in p. 11783

nations have found dispersion in p. 11783

never for sake of p. deny convictions 1912

no course, no examinations in p. 8450

no discoveries, no advances in p. 8450

no farther on road to p. than ancient Greek city-states 8450

Nobody studies p. 8450

not absence of conflict 8458

not an exemption from suffering 8453

not for us to do 494

not made at council tables 8457

not made by treaties 8457

now will I teach thee the way of p. 8448

One minute of patience, ten years of p. 8404

only after forced to knees 882

others drawn to God's p. 7532

Our p. in his will 4979

people trying to make p. 494

power that comes to souls arriving 8454

prayer for p. 8473

Prayer provides p. 8951

quick revolving wheel shall rest in p. 3288

radiate the p. of God 7485

rhythm of our wills with Jesus' love-will 8467

rules day when Christ rules mind 8462

Satan cannot counterfeit p. of God 5396

security where p. complete, unassailable 3961

self turns up to trouble our p. 9943

Sleep, my child, p. attend thee 1123

Songs spring forth weblike from
   mind at p. 7920
soul of p. is love 8469
Sowing seeds of p. like sowing
   beans 8468
speaks p. to our souls 4863
spiritually humble who know
   what p. is 8447
springs from acquiescence 8453
straining grief to sweetness of p.
   2120
Success for p. of mankind or your
   own 10811
sure to miss if we aim at directly
   8459
tears not inconsistent with inward
   p. 5346
that belongs to suffering miracle
   of faith 10907
That there abides a p. of thine
   8430
that we may sleep in p. 9668
things that belonged to p.
   connected with Jesus 6420
Thou touchedst me, I burned for
   thy p. 4805
to be able to sleep in the storm
   8470
To multiplied trials, his multiplied
   p. 5223
True p. found by man in depths of
   own heart 8474
unattainable by those ignorant of
   sorrow 2120
Use God to give us p. of mind
   7517
War is kinder than a godless p.
   11770
war must end in p. 11129
we value comfort, God values p.
   11667
What he leaves undone will rob
   him of p. of mind 11690
Where pity dwells, the p. of God
   is there 7284
Where there is love, there is p.
   4517
Where there is p, God is 8475
Where there is p. there is God
   4517
which comes only from the Father
   422
which the world cannot give 422
which the world cannot take away
   422
who finds p. in his home 5827
Who has not sought p. in a song
   7933
who knows how to suffer will
   enjoy p. 10851
will be p. in the world 8441
wisp of straw that binds sheaf of
   blessings 8465
within makes beauty without
   8463
won by compromise short-lived
   achievement 8464
world centered in God is p. 8436
world you have not p. 10512

PEACEABLY
To be able to live p. with hard
   persons 5236

PEACE-AT-ANY-PRICE
love does not ask us to be p.
   persons 7337

PEACE-DESTROYING
Flows through life with p. power
   10645

PEACEFUL
and positive way we respond to
   hurts 3319
Deep experience never p. 3514
gentleness, p. when surrounded by
   heated atmosphere 4402
Praying gives p. sleep at night
   8899

PEACEMAKER
Silence a great p. 10261

PEAK
Pride is the cold mountain p. 6026

PEAKS
fear figures you will take eyes off
   p. 3971
The hardest p. alone 1927

PEARL
Rejection ultimately produces the
   p. 204
sown a tear will come up a p.
   11012

PEARLS
are product of pain 10883
dewdrops are God's thoughts in p.
   8048
pleasure, more gravel than p. 8599
search for p. must dive below
   3255

PEAS
Be the meal of beans and p. 5860

PEASANT
as dear to God is p. as mighty
   prince 3225
Bible assures p. he is son of God
   645
He is happiest, be he king or p.
   5827
Human nature like drunk p. 5968
pope and p. know more between
   them 266

PEBBLE
entire ocean affected by p. 6238

PEBBLES
Collecting quotations similar to
   birds who pick up p. 9380
Men stumble over p. 2513
troubles are as p. on the road
   7569

PECULIAR
inner chamber of p. life 7127
Master's disposition a p. sadness
   6390
Self-love medium of p. kind 10025

PECULIARITIES
reassures of humanity by
   possessing a few p. 5307

PEDANTRY
Criticism's child 2050

PEDDLING
spiritual soothing syrup 8108

PEDESTAL
difficult to stand on p, wash feet
   of those below 8717

PEEL
foot on earth is on a banana p.
   6915

PEEP
at such a world 10529

PEEPING
Came p. in at morn 2588

PEERS
My friend p. in on me 4195

PEN
notes dance and leap from my p.
   7931

PENALTY
for not being interested in politics
   5193
of evil harvest not God's
   punishment 4721
Temptation not p. 11061

PENCE
man sold God for thirty p. 4532

PENCIL
when eraser wears out ahead of p.
   3263

PENETRATE
Do not try to p. cloud God brings
   11485
Faith can never p. mysteries of
   God 3702
if we p. deep enough beneath
   surface 5716
no human condition which divine
   presence does not p. 6277
to boundaries of being 10564

PENETRATES
Christ's look that p. 1536
gospel p. and soothes heart 732

PENETRATION
if grudge, spiritual p. into
   knowledge of God stops 9633

PENITENCE
anything that tells heart's p. can
   find its way to God 8849
hell, punishment with fruit of p.
   5700
looking up to God's loveliness
   9586
not looking on our badness 9586
Psalms, moan of man's p. 798

PENITENT
repentance recorded of p. thief
   that none should despair 9602

PENNIES
Take care of the p. 9674

PENNY
in the urn of poverty 6070
will hide biggest star in universe 7795

PENNY-IN-THE-SLOT
guidance not dispensed in p. manner 693

PENT
dark forces p. up within 3165

PENTECOST
assurance of heart 5806
exuberance of joy 5806
fullness of power 5806
illumination of mind 5806
intensity of love 5806
need for goodness answered at P. 7400
To the church, P. brought light, power, joy 5806
when speak to church about P. 5811

PENULTIMATE
human value only the p. value 11663

PEOPLE
A few p. think 8476
abstraction for "I and thou" 579
All p. smile in same language 548
always anticipating trouble 11456
an awful lot of selfish p. 10070
And all clever p. were good 909
appalling silence of good p. 6285
are strange 8481
Are we driven or called p. 1634
aren't many really evil p. 10070
as music is, so are p. of country 7889
as variable as the wind 9521
bad person loves things and uses p. 5041
because p. live in things they possess 8631
become house builders though building houses 6620
becoming interested in other p. 4306
believe half the good p. tell us of ourselves 7973
Bible contains formula by which p. can live 701
bitter words make p. bitter 11985
bored primarily with their own selves 871
broken, jaded and twisted 126
brought to Christ by exposure to faith 3759
call him a fool who never got anything 7800
can alter attitudes 510
can alter their lives 510
can fool all p. some of the time 2480
can tell you day, hour of conversion 1314

can't teach p. how wicked they are 4773
cannot believe creed of church exciting 1205
cannot find time for recreation, find time for illness 6835
cannot fool all p. all of the time 2480
capable of recruiting themselves to evil 3396
change and fail 9521
Christ Jesus always found among humble p. 5992
Christ never suggested pretend p. faultless 9789
Christ sufficient for all his p. 6370
Christ, Completer of unfinished p. 6428
Christ, still p. who love or hate him 6362
church does not draw p. in 1427
church sends p. out 1427
church should be amazing p. 1392
church wherever God's p. are 1377
cling to possessions instead of sharing 8632
cold shivers go up, down spines of cultured p. 5811
Cold words freeze p. 11985
cold, precise, perfect p. 1636
come to poverty two ways 4040
commit murder after reading about murder 12156
complete consistent p. are dead 1745
consider actions 1067
convinced p. open to Christian message 3310
cry easier than change 975
dealing with creatures of emotion 9518
Democracy assumes extraordinary possibilities in ordinary p. 2522
Democracy, p. free to choose who will get blame 5173
demonstrate God's love, listen to p. 7115
Desperate p. do desperate things 8692
desperately active p. nuisance 126
different p. in heart, spirit, mind 3766
Discouraged p. don't need guilt 3066
Do not be awestruck by other p. 9983
do not decide to be drunkards 11080
do not know burdens exist 933
do not most p. drift away 3742
do not need Satan to recruit them to evil 3396
do not run down God's p. 576
Do not try to copy other p. 9983
do not want to be alone with God 10536
do right, surprise some p. 3429

Do you wish p. to think well of you 5996
Doctors would be called in when p. were well 6880
don't like to talk with p. who agree 1851
don't recognize opportunities 8221
Don't sell p. short 8479
dreadfully like other p. 7441
dream of better understanding among p. 3229
dreamed of a Golden Age 8371
Education not process of stuffing p. 3026
Enthusiasm makes ordinary p. extraordinary 3177
even for p. blessed with warmth of heart 7304
even p. who have done us wrong 7304
everyone else is They 454
Evil p. kind of enamorment with own will 3367
examined hundred p. who lost faith 3742
exist with impudent p. 45
expect clergy to 1497
expect him to roll up his sleeves 6290
expect perfection from p. 2799
Experience name p. give to mistakes 3531
extraordinary willful, controlling p. 3367
fail for lack of encouragement 3138
fat p. good-natured 399
fear what p. see in us 1882
feeling certain about something false 3384
few p. have resources to be both wealthy and godly 11806
Few p. know how to be old 8130
few p. wish to be led 10160
find p. who need you 2558
find sincerity in very few p. 10428
flee into sanctuary of private virtuousness 11690
forfeit ourselves to be like other p. 6218
fret over nuclear weapons 10503
Friendships form among p. who strengthen 4241
gathered to Christ by love 6396
gathered to us by fear 6396
Give the Bible to the p. 653
givers and takers 10198
God acknowledged with one heart, voice by American p. 11176
God and p, two things that mattered 3331
God can do nothing with p. 8
God can do tremendous things through p. 10134
God does not need p. to do extraordinary things 10137

God entrusted reputation to ordinary p. 1285

God has to take some p. out of this world 11809

God is looking for p. who long for communication with him 8972

God likes help when helping p. 10139

God must have cooperation of his p. 11269

God needs p. who do ordinary things extraordinarily well 10137

God never made two p. exactly alike 6191

good person loves p, uses things 5041

good that p. sometimes misunderstand us 6270

Government, God's response to nature of p. 5177

grumbling because roses have thorns 1564

Hardening of heart ages p. more quickly 6159

have an awful lot of p. inside me 9931

have been made meaner by suffering 10920

have forgotten Satan 1309

have not yet understood command of Christ 7349

he who sees the calamity of p. 177

Hear the lazy p. say 9303

Holy Spirit working in, through p. who do not profess faith 5791

Hope looks for the good in p. 5928

hope of nation in character of its p. 5190

hot words scorch p. 11985

how little p. know who think holiness is dull 5750

How many p. have you made homesick for God 3309

How many p. stop because so few say "Go" 3135

human race playing games nuisance for p. who grow up 5982

hundreds of tiny threads sew p. together 7608

Idolatry trusting p. to do what only God can do 6072

If all good p. were clever 909

if expect perfection from p. 9469

If God dealt with p. today 4717

if p. showed their souls 10507

if p. unwilling to hear you 1862

if you think too much of yourself, other p. won't 9253

imagine pursuing glory of God 10076

impossible to enslave Bible-reading p. 677

in a hurry cannot think, grow, decay 5584

In God's family one body of p. 10161

In God's sight only two classes of p. 3236

In order that p. be happy in work 12011

In submission free to value other p. 9963

in touch with p. through our affections 7428

including p. we don't particularly like 7304

instead of harping on worst in p. 5928

Instead of telling p. to give up things 3315

Jesus, where'er thy p. meet 12108

keep p. from jumping down throat 1627

Kindness loving p. more than they deserve 6653

land of naked, p. ashamed of clothes 1637

Leaders ordinary p. with extraordinary determination 6798

learn way to be made holy 9838

led p. to expect something not possible 7601

like us are We 454

living deeply, no fear of death 2362

living like majority of p. 9758

lonely, build walls instead of bridges 7139

Look for strength in p, not weakness 5077

Look into p. as well as at them 2811

Lord gives his p. perpetual joy 6529

Lord had deep empathy with p. 6519

Lord lets some p. get into trouble 11441

lose weight by keeping mouths shut 9972

Love accepts p. as they are 7207

Love cures p. 7213

Love p, not things 7267

love-energy first to God, then to other p. 10053

many p. are trying to make peace 8427

Many p. happy, but worthless to society 5539

many p. in bondage to success 10776

many p. never think for themselves 11227

many p. think they think 8476

many p. trying to make peace 494

Maturity to be comfortable with p. not like us 7694

meet superficial needs 4310

mention Jesus, p. want to stop conversation 6518

miss happiness because didn't stop to enjoy it 5585

mistake education for intelligence 8510

mistake sex for love 8510

mistake wealth for happiness 8510

more easily fall victims to a great lie 7974

More p. would live to old age 119

most bigoted have no convictions 9186

most have some sort of religion 317

Most p. are careful drivers 3947

Most p. are good 10070

Most p. are like cats 9482

Most p. are mirrors 3019

most p. are other p. 1640

Most p. judge men only by success 6584

Most p. live in restricted circle of potential being 8659

Most p. object to speed of light 11309

most p. prefer to be thought enigmas 10985

Most p. would die sooner than think 11233

much easier to be honest with other p. 5880

murder when put p. down 10683

murder when treat p. as insignificant 10683

murder when we destroy p. with words 10683

must be changed to change society 10528

must live with p. to know their problems 9292

mystery why p. ask if empty seat occupied 8477

new step what p. fear most 3989

no dead p, only the living 2390

no longer sinful 10350

no ordinary p. 8483

No p. became great by lowering standards 7834

no p. ever great which did not pass through valley 5289

no perfect marriage, no perfect p. 7657

no such thing as preaching patience into p. 8422

no unimportant p. 3233

no uninteresting things, only uninterested p. 868

noisy world where p. are indifferent 592

Not all p. driven by same stick 7868

not interruptions to schedule 3316

not marriage but p. that fail 7622

of God to model new heaven, new earth 1327

of Jesus' day thought holy men unapproachable 3331

One out of one p. die 2386

only thing wealth does for some p. 11859

only time p. dislike gossip 5159

opportunist has no use for p. he cannot use 7583

ordinary p. invaded by living God 1936

ordinary p. restoring universe 1285

other p. tempted strongly at end 11083

Our constitution made for moral, religious p. 5196

our Lord concerned for p. 6519

Our p. drift and die 9224

Patience, to put up with p. you'd like to put down 8411

personal experience never norm for other p. 8883

pigs got clean, p. dirty 8500

plan by which good p. go to heaven 5632

plenty of other p. occupied with affairs of world 9261

pointing fingers, rarely hold out hands 2073

Poverty makes p. satirical 8690

Proud p. breed sorrows for themselves 9232

Prayer changes p. and p. change things 8905

preach p. into despair 9838

presence of God's grace with his p. 4865

pricetags for p. to read each other by 10519

problem is why some p. do not suffer 10909

progress resulted from p. who took unpopular positions 9308

prophet knows what God is trying to say to p. 9332

proud man always looking down on p. 9188

quiet, holy p. learned great secret 1293

read Bible to know what p. ought to do 666

read newspaper to know what p. are doing 666

Real doesn't often happen to p. who break easily 5886

remarkable thing about way p. talk about God 4886

repent not so much for evil deeds of wicked p. 6285

revival to focus p. upon Divine Leader 9751

safer to tell p. to seek kingdom of God 3315

Saints usually killed by their own p. 9779

say hard to present Christ before men 3222

see talents in unexpected p. 8575

seldom improve when no model 3451

self-centered p. live in unpleasant surroundings 10077

sermon helps p. in different ways 10094

services they render us attaches p. to us 5256

Situation ethics puts p. at center of concern 6820

six p. present 7443

small minds talk about p. 1845

society must be changed to change p. 10528

Some p. are content not to do mean actions 110

Some p. are grateful for the roses 6254

Some p. are like blisters 6773

Some p. excuse faults 3950

some p. expect God's instant answer 693

Some p. fond of ill-luck 11449

Some p. for seeing God as they see a cow 10084

some p. never lose beauty 8169

Some p. regard discipline as a chore 9975

Some p. see God as they see a cow 4801

some p. stab fingers at a verse 693

Some p. stay longer in hour than others in week 9492

Some p. strengthen society 1040

Some p. talk about finding God—as if he could get lost 7518

some p. tempted strongly at beginning 11083

some such bores they give aspirin headache 1872

some think not capable to be Christian 1312

some try to reduce Bible to magic 693

Some wicked p. would be less dangerous 11891

staying away from church 317

Successful p. apply God's remedy for failure 10812

such p. are legalists 6810

summer p. out of crowded city on to crowded highway 9901

Superior p. let it be discovered by others 11695

surprised p. perform better than hoped 2799

Temper gets p. into trouble 9237

tempted to begin, "If people would" 579

That other p. don't 1810

there are p. to be fed 10165

there by divine appointment 3316

there will be p. we do not like, do not like us 5890

think about what to do for p. 1023

think once converted all happy 1309

think they are thinking when rearranging prejudices 9178

think thing's worth believing if hard 3773

think with hopes, fears rather than minds 7763

through fear of being criticized, p. tell lies 6851

To all the p. you can 10126 5057

To be chief of p. serve them 6806

to emerge lame but victorious at dawn 9777

to know p. study excuses 2807

to many p. virtue in repenting of faults 11702

Today p. need exercise after work 3114

today p. would make fun of Christ 6405

today p. would not crucify Christ 6405

Tombstones of some p. should read 7041

Tomorrow p. lose opportunity to accept Christ 11404

too busy providing for old age 119

too many p. to respond to 10211

torture for most p. to think 11230

tough times never last, p. do 222

triangle of love between ourselves, God, other p. 7198

tried for what they have done 6413

trouble ain't that p. ignorant 6083

trouble in world caused by p. wanting to be important 9220

trouble only time p. think of God 11441

trying to get other p. interested in you 4306

two kinds of p. 5455

two kinds of p. keep silent 10272

unless able to give to p. in selfless love 7962

unless I can recall a consistent investment in p. 6919

unmerciful good, bad p. 7746

use cliches so they won't have to think 8476

use leisure, happiest p. in world 5567

use things and love p. 9510

used to need rest after work 3114

very little difference in p. 516

want back of church 8481

want center of attention 8481

want front of bus 8481

war, always the p. who pay full price 11772

wars within world reflection of wars inside p. 11764

Watch what p. are cynical about 2188

We do not draw p. to Christ by discrediting 12147

We give p. box in suburbs called a house 5859

we hurt p. by being too busy 129

We must not think ourselves ordinary p. 1346

we say millions of p. never think of God 7561

wear our p. out 115

weighed down by obsessive fear 5474

well for p. who think to change minds 11228

were drawn to Christ 6396

What other p. think of me becoming less important 9627

What p. say behind back is your standing in community 9628

What p. say you cannot do, you can 95

what some p. must know tomorrow 3035

What they think of Jesus because of me is critical 9627

What would p. of earth be without woman 11983

When God's p. repent, will have a song 9606

When good p. cease vigilance, evil men prevail 7991

When p. bewildered, become gullible 7978

When p. serving, life no longer meaningless 10212

When p. sleep in church, preacher should wake up 9171

Whenever two p. meet 7443

who are always anticipating trouble 12079

who are born even-tempered 9777

who are brutally honest 5884

who cannot be alone worst company 10552

who do not want us to be free before God 6824

who do things, p. who get credit 93

who fly into a rage 391

who have grown hopeless 5953

who have never needed to struggle all night with the angel 9777

who have never seriously studied four Gospels 6417

who have no secrets do not weigh their words 8970

who influence stood unconsciously for right 6239

who influence you are p. who believe in you 6240

who live as if God were dead 1314

who love God for wealth 4801

who related to God best 7526

who take symbols literally 5631

who tell me there is no God 485

who utter so many prayers 5474

who would not coin slander, circulate without qualms 10465

whose language I could not understand 7102

why p. are in such a hurry 7512

will look at anything rather than each other 11034

wise if evaluate things not as p. report them 8497

wish p. to think well of you 9614

Without faith p. drift into hate societies 925

witness not stirring p. up 3336

world of nice p. difficult to save 7827

world wants geniuses just like other p. 4394

Worldly p. imagine saints find it difficult to live 4159

would break God's windows 4480

wrathful words make p. wrathful 11985

PEOPLED
world with living beings 1981

PEOPLE'S
denouncing p. vices, faults 1162

God blots out his p. sins, not their names 4626

God has bottle for p. tears 11012

human nature sticking nose into other p. business 5147

In p. eyes I read malice, vice 3571

Unselfishness letting other p. lives alone 11654

PERCEIVE
as we p, conquer more glaring faults 10006

easier to p. error than truth 3259

more clearly we p. hand of God 11644

shalt p. that thou wast blind before 4737

To p. is to suffer 8512

will best p. spots upon them 6004

PERCEIVED
faith is God p. intuitively 3750

PERCEIVES
no idea by which God p. things 4986

PERCENT
Genius 99 p. perspiration 4391

Genius one p. inspiration 4391

PERCEPTION
Hope without thankfulness lacking in p. 11154

of beauty, a moral test 540

of ideas rather than storing 3021

Only in quiet mind is adequate p. 7718

PERCEPTIONS
doubts dim p. of Christ's gospel 6713

PERFECT
and right and pure and good 5620

because you're so p. for me 7183

Bible p, pure 710

Bible pure, unalloyed, p. truth 710

Christ the p. representation of God 6355

Christians aren't p. 4110

church service 1383

description of p. job 3121

essence of p. friendship 4272

Everything p. from hands of Creator 3193

faith would lift above fear 3643

God is p. love, wisdom 9799

God judging men with p. knowledge 4720

God made the p. instrument 7893

God planned all p. combinations 7891

God's goal to p. spiritually 1016

God's love is p. 4786

God's service is p. freedom 4126

grateful thought to heaven the most p. prayer 8755

Herein truly is p. love 4749

Holiest Trinity, p. in Unity 11424

Humility is p. quietness 6010

idea of a God p. as they could imagine 4504

idea of p. family 3868

if believe God is p. 4443

if faults to admit, how can he be p. 3949

immutability of God most p. beauty 977

in heaven most p. charity 5685

in hell most p. hate 5685

Jesus p. because never made a move without his Father 8520

love is the p. flower 3837

love you not because you're p. 7183

Made man a p. whole 5606

man p. in faith who can come to God 3780

means to do your best with graces God has given 9013

more p. we are, more gentle we are 11395

most p. being who trod planet called Man of Sorrows 6481

must conclude God's ways are p. 4443

No man p. unless admits faults 3949

no one p. 6180

no p. marriage, no p. people 7657

nor man made p. without trials 136

nothing p. in this world 2085

only p. freedom is serving God 4148

passing from stress to p. calm 2399

prayer, unaware he is praying 8888

Sex is never p. 10232

Strength made p. in weakness 8170

than imperfect acknowledgment of his p. love 7171

that we may become thy p. image 7519

to have p. love we must have nature of God 7316

to obey God is p. liberty 8115

Tomorrow p. when it arrives 11403

work God will accomplish 1468

PERFECTED
Glory is p. grace 4408

in wisdom 10010

life is p. by death 10870

Love p. in fire of God 3182

PERFECTION
Aim at p. in everything 3463
art shadow of divine p. 1993
Bible gives no encouragement p. achieved 9254
continue groaning toward p. 9832
display p. of friend 4183
divine nature is p. 8522
expect p, life is disappointment 2799
farther man knows himself from p, nearer to it 8523
God demands p. from his creatures 8518
God himself must supply p. 8518
good marriage not where p. reigns 7591
if expect p. from people 9469
in most things unattainable 3463
in simplicity, humility, faith ingredients of prayer 8914
Jesus did not attain p. by rules, regulations 8520
loving God with heart, mind, soul, strength 8524
nearest to divine nature, nearest to p. 8522
no grades of p. with God 3236
of greatness to be nothing 5293
of holiness in the cross 2096
of human expression achieved 740
Patient endurance p. of charity 3152
Though Bible urges us on to p. 9254
Thy will at once thy p. and mine 9052
to bear with imperfections of others 7682
want p. of the mind 3025
You'll never see p. in your mate 7671

PERFECTIONS
displeased at finding p. 3945
God cannot relinquish p. 4821
Nature has p. to show image of God 8022
of Jesus Christ made your entirety 9847

PERFECTLY
Heaven p. ordered enjoyment of God 5646
Man not an angel whose reason works p. 9417
only one being who loves p. 7316
patience to do simple things p. 8406
to accomplish it p. 9062

PERFECTS
Grace p. nature 5214
not right to say all suffering p. 10920
suffering p. one who accepts call of God 10920

PERFORM
according to our fears 5950

Be slow to promise, quick to p. 2531
Man should p. duties to fellowmen as to God 9669
strength to have anguish, still p. daily tasks 8423
surprised by having them p. better than hoped 9469

PERFORMANCE
acre of p. worth world of promise 2530
Greatness lies in p. of duties 5283
ounce of p. worth more than pound of preachment 9131
slow in making promise most likely faithful in p. 9325
that must nurse, keep friends 4262

PERFORMED
duty p. gives music at midnight 9675
God values how deeds are p. 7864
least gratitude in which p. greatest services 5250
marvel not that Christ p. miracles 6503
marvel that Christ p. so few miracles 6503
supernaturally prepared to be supernaturally p. 10206

PERFORMING
gross deeds of cruelty 4895

PERFORMS
Plans and p, resolves and executes 8224

PERFUME
Dignity like p. 2760
encouraged emotions p. life 3050
flattery, p. intoxicates 4053
Happiness is p. cannot pour on others 5516
In flower, death sets free the p. 2261

PERFUMES
each lily bell 4761

PERIL
honors of this world are but p. of falling 5898
produces steadfastness 952

PERILS
awake to p. of the immortal soul 10654
Life's p. for our courage 6995
of spirituality 10718
Safe in midst of p. 4490

PERIOD
Never question where God has put p. 3763
Where God has put a p. 5468

PERISH
And p. in our own 810
Better poor and live, than rich and p. 8675
energy does not p. but is transformed 11658
How could it p. thus 7159

If we work upon marble, it will p. 6796
Men and nations survive or p. 10510
or p. together as fools 923
They fall and p. 8363

PERISHED
Cast in the fire the p. thing 7003

PERISHES
solitude without fellowship p. in despair 10547

PERJURED
dashed no cup from p. lip 3174

PERKED
Than to be p. up in a glistering grief 6016

PERMANENCE
in God men of faith find eternal p. 4589
science assumes p. and uniformity of natural laws 9869

PERMANENT
can't die, linked to p. life of God 2431
Cheerfulness, p. habit of mind 1094
Devotion is something p. 9731
doesn't feel you've done a p. job 4213
failures prepare for p. triumphs 3593
Forgiveness a p. attitude 4078
no human being can be p. source of happiness to another 9481
nothing p. except change 7058
surrendered own plans to p. plan of God 4803

PERMANENTLY
Only God is p. interesting 4678

PERMEATED
resurrection p. our customs, literature, language 9702

PERMISSIBLE
popular misdeed does not make it p. 3387

PERMISSION
God's p. means no doubt 5402
imagine God having to request p. 4955
To whom would God go for p. 4955

PERMISSIVE
by p. government God lines up with his purpose 5175

PERMIT
God never p. evil if could not bring good 3372
God will not p. knowledge of things to come 4314
God would not p. evil if good did not come of it 5017
nature to have her way 3196
real selves to be known 10019

reasons which moved God to p. sin 4989

stone rolled away not to p. Christ to come out 9699

PERMITS

God either p. it to happen 4828

God p. us to be perplexed 8396

God p. wicked, but not forever 11884

God's justice p. creation to punish humanity 3191

Moral indignation p. hate under guise of virtue 11693

PERMITTED

decided all means p. to fight evil 5012

divine Surgeon must be p. to use scalpel 890

God temporarily p. evil to exist 3378

self-sins p. by most Christians 5776

sin repeated seems p. 10290

PERPETRATE

who helps to p. evil 3374

PERPETUAL

Cheerfulness fills minds with p. serenity 1092

Day of Judgment court in p. session 6589

desire Christ for p. guest 8092

holy life attraction or p. reproof 5735

In idleness p. despair 6764

In silence, round me—the p. work 1966

irony of government 5194

Lord gives his people p. joy 6529

maintain p. contentedness 9092

must be written on eternal shores 3860

preserved in state of p. puerility 5584

thankful spirit a p. feast 11139

the tide is God's p. flow of grace 7553

yes of universal acquiescence 1645

PERPETUALLY

angels ask nothing more to make them p. satisfied 4995

PERPETUATE

Seeking to p. one's name on earth 3860

PERPLEXED

Christ not p. by circumstances 1472

God permits us to be p. 8396

Quiet minds cannot be p. or frightened 8466

Riddling, p. labyrinthical soul 10661

that we may learn patience 8396

To have plenty is to be p. 7071

PERPLEXITIES

godly response to p. kicks crutches from skeptic 10938

In all p. Bible never failed 670

In Christ at peace in midst of p. 8470

PERPLEXITY

every p. will have an explanation 7060

if God places me in great p. 7486

in moment of p. opens Bible at random 5441

PERSECUTE

praise dead saints, p. living ones 8530

when p. children of God, persecuting God 2084

PERSECUTED

despised, p. but care not 1293

probability truth on p. side 8532

PERSECUTES

worst is that which p. the mind 7765

PERSECUTION

gathered myrrh from Lord's p. 10913

has not crushed the church 1419

joy flows all through p. 6529

never fatal to Christianity 1218

pray that God would make every Christian taste so bad 8526

used in theology, not arithmetic 8529

Was it not p. Jesus promised to disciples 10784

will separate wheat from tares 8527

PERSECUTORS

Complainers greatest p. 1557

PERSERVATION

magic p. in books 851

PERSEVERANCE

By p. the snail reached the ark 8535

can do anything genius can do 8551

difference between p. and obstinacy 10773

God's decree basis on which p. depends 4616

Great works performed by p. 8544

if unaccompanied by talent 8553

Is oft but p. in disguise 8539

may be employed by smallest of us 8557

more prevailing than violence 8552

most overrated of traits 8553

Nothing can take place of p. 8555

power grows greater with time 8557

rarely fails in its purpose 8557

rope that ties soul to heaven 8554

PERSEVERE

at perfection in everything 3463

Cheerful man will p. longer 1099

God is with those who p. 8540

if you will p, you will conquer 8558

rather than quit 1138

To p. in one's duty 9677

PERSEVERES

God p. in speaking in his own language 4900

Great faith p. in God's silences 3725

He that p. makes difficulty an advancement 8542

He that p. makes every contest a victory 8542

only fool p. in error 3260

PERSEVERING

without first p. through pain, heartache, failure 6802

PERSIA

Once in P. reigned a king 974

PERSIST

to p. devilish 7065

PERSISTANCE

human nature clings to man with such p. 5974

PERSISTENT

love of God, p. as artist's love for work 4792

most p. sound the beating of war drums 11762

No great achievement possible without 85

PERSISTENTLY

Character in saint Christ p. manifested 998

proceed positively, pursue p. 80

purposefully, prayerfully, positively, p. 80

PERSISTING

And to the end p. safe arrive 1664

PERSISTS

appetite for learning p. 3031

PERSON

accountable to others for injury 70

action of God mediated through a p. 10122

an agreeable p. agrees with me 9483

any p. whose growth as real as my own 7184

approach new p. in spirit of adventure 9468

as important as next p, no more important 3248

average p. puts only 25% into work 2788

bad p. loves things and uses people 5041

become an excited p. 3185

called to do missionary work 7784

can never go to heaven without Christ 9792

delusion that one p. can make another happy 5549

difference between good p. and bad p. 5041

doesn't attend church because hypocrites do 1397

down in world, ounce of help better 3146

easiest p. to deceive is one's self 2471

Elderly p. is ten years older 8124

enemies a p. makes by taking a stand 1913

enjoys reputation of being most remarkable p. he knows 9197

Every guilty p. his own hangman 5475

every p, is a letter, syllable, word, sentence 12042

every p. a dignified, essential human soul 901

Every p. an aristocrat 5967

Every p. born from intimate depths of divine nature 5967

every p. declaring name, will of God 12042

Every p. God puts in our lives 3515

Every p. has one thing he can do better than most 6175

Every p. noble 5967

Every p. of royal blood 5967

Experience makes a p. better or bitter 3528

failure is p. not able to cash in on experience 3580

family first authority under which p. lives 3888

family first community to which p. attached 3888

finer p. injured by adversity 7683

finest p. injured by neither prosperity or adversity 7683

flowering of p. is movement from incompleteness 7699

flowering of p. not state at which we arrive 7699

For in the p. of his Son 4859

free even within prison walls 4112

friend, p. with whom I may think aloud 4165

Give me a p. who says, one thing I do 81

God can make brokenhearted radiant, loving p. 890

God more real to me than any p. 7098

good p. loves people, uses things 5041

happiest p. is p. who thinks most interesting thoughts 7026

Happiness, intelligence rarely found in same p. 5512

holiest p. most conscious of sin 5761

hostile p. lives in a hostile world 9441

How happy p. is depends upon gratitude 5249

how he treats p. of no possible use 573

humble p. changed humiliation into humility 6007

idle p. tempts devil to tempt him 11047

If p. does not enjoy worship 5654

If p. whom you dislike 5144

if treat p. as he is, will stay as he is 8656

If try to improve p. by good example 3436

immediate p. makes demands in his prayer 8981

influence from p. rightly related to God incalculable 6241

intelligent p. learned to "choose between" 6326

intolerant toward p. hasn't taken time to understand 11612

irritable p. like hedgehog rolled up wrong way 9630

is to waste p. you are 6217

Jesus pulls each p. from behind his mask 9741

Leaning too heavily on another p. 9478

least-used words by unselfish p. 11653

liberation of p. from external influences 4160

Love greatest gift p. can give another 7249

loving any p. better than Christ 6925

loving p. lives in a loving world 9441

may cause evil by his inaction 70

may cause evil by inaction 3346

may go to heaven without health, riches 9792

misery because p. demands of another complete understanding 9455

more p. in harmony with himself 8505

more simple p. is inwardly 8505

most agreeable is simple, frank p. 4204

natural to be like p. you live with most 6235

Never cease loving a p. 3167

never met p. without possibilities 3596

No p. absolutely unnecessary 3446

No p. enthusiastic about work 3108

No p. ever honored for what he received 5895

No p. more skeptical of resurrection than apostles 9693

No p. who shall deny being of God 5183

not better p. because praised 1067

not worse p. if somebody denigrates 1067

nothing more precious than human p. 2343

Nothing sets p. out of devil's reach as humility 6024

of feeling safe with a p. 4260

Prayer enlarges our p. 8906

prayer is when p. praying is one who hears 8980

reading Bible, encountered a p. unique, distinctive, colorful 4491

Recognition of individual affirms uniqueness of each p. 9952

romantic love you want the other p. 7197

sacrifices differ from p. to p. 5385

saint does everything any other p. does 9783

self-portrait of the p. 54

shoe that fits one p. pinches another 6214

sick p. faced with meaning of things 6086

smart p. isn't smart until he knows how to get along with fools 6323

societal problems solved one p. at a time 3901

Success in marriage is being right p. 7652

suffering p. doesn't need a lecture 10887

to be happy a p. must enjoy blessings 818

To dream of p. you would like to be 6217

To move from one sort of p. to another is repentance 9604

Tolerance respect for p. because he is human 11399

tongue of idle p. never idle 6777

transfers love from things temporal to things eternal 9278

treated God like a p. 7526

truly great when not envious of rival's success 3206

understanding a p. does not mean condoning 11619

We don't love qualities, we love a p. 7332

weak p. is injured by prosperity 7683

well-placed quotation sign of educated p. 9389

What a bore waking up the same p. 870

When God is seeking a p. 3340

When p. renewed from day to day 9278

When you say p. is hopeless 5955

who asks why doesn't want an explanation 167

who asks why wants an argument 167

who doubts bears arms against himself 11597

who lives right 3428

who succeeds moves on in spite of failure 3624

who thinks he's a human dynamo 117

why one p. is favored 39

will never be p. you can be if 9977

Worship highest act p. can do
  12137

PERSONAL
After sixty burial service p. 2213
Bible letter from God with p.
  address 704
contact a movement that must be
  rediscovered 7630
delusion that p. gain made by
  crushing others 7793
fear gives p. life stability 3980
God plans p. visit to his own
  world 6127
God's love makes sense seen as p.
  4782
Gossip p. confession of malice
  5128
Holy Spirit destroys p. life 5795
loneliness by the sea p, alive 7145
love of the cross must swallow up
  p. grief 5356
mission everything, p. life nothing
  9279
our task is to live p.
  communication with Christ
  3321
purely p. gospel like soul without
  body 5088
sees direct p. message from God
  5441
Sin with multitude, responsibility
  as great and p. 9672
Spirit of God puts words of Jesus
  in our p. lives 5801
teacher defends against p.
  influence 11006
teachings of Christ can solve p.
  difficulties 6487
temptation to make relation to
  God judicial instead of p. 9816
through p. obedience God acts
  5385
when p. ambitions are at stake
  5467
when we cease to believe in a p.
  deity 4538
will come a p. touch from God
  7060

PERSONALISTIC
situationists are p. 6820

PERSONALITIES
Christ controlling our p. 1289
God knows all p. 4881
narrow ranks of predictable p.
  4025
split spiritual p. 6068

PERSONALITY
Acceptance of one's worth core of
  p. 9980
attack p, can only defend itself
  8312
become part of p. of Christ 2822
brain, body, are machines to
  express p. 843
destroy concept of p. in God 4766
endlessly fascinated by new p.
  9468

God able to enter human p. and
  change it 5777
God the matrix of our p. 7557
has power to open doors 1034
Holy Spirit does not obliterate a
  man's p. 5798
Holy Spirit lifts p. to highest use
  5798
human voice gives p. 7893
inner conflicts disrupt p. 2737
intellect has powerful muscles, but
  no p. 6333
is something altogether sacred
  6183
Jesus Christ, a twofold p. 6426
Love produces flowering of the p.
  7268
Money buys everything except p.
  7806
mother interpreter of father's p.
  8341
mysterious in p. 5458
person's defect also strength for p.
  3932
saint knit into shape by ruling p.
  of God 9767
Satan must be most frustrated p.
  in universe 9858
unlovely p. a continuation 8176
what you seem to be 1035
willing to let your p. be taken over
  5776
written and signed by God 6183

PERSONALIZATION
Jesus, radical p. of ethical
  problems 6451

PERSONALLY
God takes complaining p. 1558

PERSON'S
defect also strength for personality
  3932
finest clothing made is p. own skin
  7427
love is steady wish for loved p.
  good 7242
may as well borrow p. money as
  time 2914
Plant love heart-deep in a p. life
  7289
real love want other p. good 7197

PERSONS
eyes of love see not one but two p.
  7300
love does not ask us to be
  peace-at-any-price p. 7337
Love is no respecter of p. 7274
Obligation is to p, not objects
  6820
Solitude molds into caring p.
  10561
Some p. think look like hedgehog
  to be pious 6822
To be able to live peaceably with
  hard p. 5236
tough love that turns us into
  stronger p. 7686
Weak p. cannot be sincere 10431

PERSPECTIVE
begin to see from God's p. 11152
faith expresses itelf by ability not
  to lose p. 3769
God helps us view world from
  new p. 4735
good marriage when p. overlooks
  unresolvables 7591
Wisdom seeing life from God's p.
  11971

PERSPIRATION
Genius, 99 percent p. 4391
troubles, can cure by p, fresh air
  11455

PERSUADE
devil's ruse is to p. he does not
  exist 2692
Prayer not to p. God to move our
  way 8925

PERSUADED
better p. by own reasons 270

PERSUASION
collectivities easily respond to
  devil's p. 6176
Jesus' power of p. so
  overwhelming 5485

PERSUASIVE
To be p. we must be believable
  6319

PERVADE
none of man's institutions p.
  nature 8012

PERVADES
And unremitting Energy, p. 4711
God p. us as the sunbeam 9852
Holiness a fire whose warmth p.
  universe 5741

PERVASIVE
sinfulness of man evident 10440

PERVERSE
Music weapon used to make p.
  seem glamorous 7910
To be able to live peaceably with
  p. persons 5236

PERVERSION
Evil p. of substance 3357
of the will turned aside from thee
  10317

PERVERT
God removes what would p. 7685

PESSIMIST
Christ a p. and an optimist 8252
complains about the wind 8249
looks both ways crossing one-way
  street 8585
optimist, everything good except
  the p. 8248
sees difficulty in every opportunity
  8251
sees only red light 8245
sees only the tunnel 8250
sees the hole 8244
thought everything bad except
  himself 8248

tries to put light out 8246
Twixt the optimist and the p. 8244

PESSIMISTIC
holiest souls p. 8586
man who thinks must be p. 8587
My knowledge is p. 8247

PESSIMISTS
attempted to revel in suffering 10880

PETER
more a sandpile than a rock 3617
On how many mornings have I, like P. 9569

PETITION
for forgiveness has condition attached 4096
In Lord's Prayer first p. for bread 7152
Lord's Prayer a revolutionary p. 8828
Lord's Prayer every p. included 7156
Lord's Prayer for importance of its p. 7154
who thinks of himself, says prayers of p. 8840

PETITIONS
large p. with thee bring 9000

PETTINESS
Grief can purge us of p. 10640

PETTY
In anything p. never give in 8548
Mean and p. man's wants, desires 7381

PEW
mist in pulpit, fog in p. 9123

PHANTOM
real life p. of one's imagination 2750

PHARAOHS
prince of P. is fallen 730

PHARISEE
a little P. in all of us 6825
Jesus not a P. 6508
of little consequence whether idolator or proud P. 10041
prays publicly, preys privately 6047

PHARMACIST
Christ the divine P. 6429

PHASE
activity may be a p. of death 122
in grief one keeps emerging from a p. 5344

PHEASANTS
fools if invite hawk to dinner 11081

PHENOMENON
dream a perfectly valid p. 2968
Loneliness far from being a rare, curious p. 7137

PHILANTHROPY
love of God not cold p. 4792
to save ourselves uncomfortable feeling 10071

PHILIA
Erotic and p. love are emotional 7166

PHILOSOPHER
a particle pontificating on infinity 8588
a problem for every solution 8589
aspires to explain mysteries 12118
Christian on his knees sees more than p. on tiptoe 8975
education might have brought to light 3038
get bad wife, become a p. 7606
To p. time one of the fundamental quantities 11346

PHILOSOPHERS
books petty compared with Gospels 659
can learn from p. of China 2988
create God in their image 8590
For p, pain problem of metaphysics 8255
more light than p. and scholars combined 6449
so highly educated 8591
take simplest, turn into unintelligible 8591
voluntarily sought adversity 241

PHILOSOPHICAL
not ideal p. curiosity 5724

PHILOSOPHIES
rejects God's truth in favor of devil's impure p. 11512

PHILOSOPHIZED
When Carlyle saw city, he p. 10522

PHILOSOPHY
a longing after heavenly wisdom 8593
all our p. penetrated hardly an inch 9353
believe only possibilities, mere p. 605
best expressed in choices 1148
Bible contains more of my p. 695
Christian cannot live by p. 9703
complicated method of avoiding important problems 8597
dedicated to accounting for things 8592
guided by bad spiritual p. 115
half the differences in p. would end 11193
if comprehensible, just another p. 1213
impatient with anything that refuses account of itself 8592
In p. predominance of reason 11191
ingenious treatise of p. 1989
Leisure is the mother of p. 6834

mightiest p, study of attributes of Godhead 4631
not always friendly toward God 8592
not best expressed in words 1148
of "me first" 10087
of today, existentialism 3493
piecemeal, provisional like science 8596
science of limitations of human mind 8594
science that considers truth 8595
seeks the truth 11524
soak in p. 11196
theology's servant 11210
victims of p. of activism 130
when know p, you know what you cannot know 8594

PHOBIA
developed p. of being alone 10575

PHONY
Nobody spots p. quicker than a child 8349
Remind religious p. splinter between you and Lord 6590
to pretend we love everything, p. and hypocritical 5890

PHOTOGRAPHY
major force in explaining man to man 2016
records beauty of earth, skies 2016
records gamut of feelings 2016
records wealth, confusion man has created 2016

PHRASE
Each generation like a line, a p. 7076
familiar p. have their superficial effect 8845
pursuit of happiness most ridiculous p. 5558

PHYSICAL
aches, pains of this poor p. body 2346
Christians, p. organism through which Christ acts 1351
God gives us p. ability to work in his kingdom 4648
great thing to see p. pluck 8545
Lord makes little of p. death 2358
men use p. power 8715
unashamed effort to protract p. desire 10229

PHYSICALLY
God's goal not to pamper p. 1016
Most live p. in restricted circle 8659

PHYSICIAN
Christ a P. to heal his people 6370
Christ, the divine P. 6429
Death, P. of him whom medicine cannot cure 2260
Every invalid is a p. 10840
God had an only Son, a p. 7778
God is the p. 10415

Hope the p. of every misery 5926

No man good p. who has never been sick 3075

PHYSICS

space obeys laws of p. 11650

PICK

up a stone to turn in your hand 4608

PICKED

to be honest is to be one man p. out of a thousand 5867

PICKLE

grouch looks weaned on p. 1555

PICNICS

If ants so busy, how attend p. 9266

PICTURE

God carries your p. in wallet 4751

God the canvas on which p. painted 4495

Life is painting a p. 6975

no p. can express beauty 539

which was never seen before 9873

PICTURED

Worship p. at its best in Isaiah 12136

PICTURES

Are God's great p. hung 8047

who love good p. happiest people in world 5567

why paint p. that make sense 8508

PICTURESQUE

man a marvelously p. piece 7374

man p. piece of diversity in unity 6173

PIE

humble p, never tasty 429

more nourishing than p. in sky 10742

repentance much harder than eating humble p. 9577

You'll get p. in sky when die 5682

PIECE

Every man a p. of the continent 10511

Give others a p. of your heart 10132

PIECEMEAL

Philosophy p, provisional like science 8596

PIECES

Adam has filled earth with p. 760

Christ wonders with broken heart if given p. 10584

Evil is all that cuts life to p. 5024

God can make p. of world's puzzle fit together 4308

when I saw where the p. landed 4136

PIERCE

Arrows p. the body 374

coat of mail that none can p. 9986

plan a tower that shall p. clouds 6788

splendor, soon or late, will p. the gloom 2945

Thou shoutedst and didst p. my darkness 4805

PIERCED

boy asked question that p. father's heart 3912

PIERCES

pure love of God p. a man 9741

PIETISM

fraudulent p. that preaches from villas to slums about mansions 6065

PIETY

Animosity cloaked in p. is a demon 9631

church not refrigerator to preserve p. 1393

no patience with p. alone 3025

unctuous p. poor example of spirituality 10707

PIG

lawsuit is machine go into as p, come out as sausage 9713

PIGEONS

prayers like carrier p. 9012

PIGMY

man a p. standing on crest of planet 7381

PIGS

If a man has good p. to sell 2776

PILATE

am no more a Christian than P. was 7099

had never heard of Jesus 6395

PILE

money up, stinks to high heaven 7812

rear the p. 47

PILGRIM

As the p. entered in 2217

toast the sturdy P. band 11175

PILGRIMAGE

Jesus invited us to p. 1210

joyfully accepting conditions of p. 9090

no rest stops, no plateaus 9832

spend a lifetime walking it 9832

PILGRIMS

Like p. to th' appointed place 2330

PILLAR

God's decree p. on which perseverance depends 4616

PILLARS

God hewing out p. for his temple 1401

PILLOW

good conscience soft p. 1655

Hov'ring, round thy p. bend 2221

Idleness, the devil's p. 6762

takes more than soft p. 10482

PILLOWS

Around our p. golden ladders rise 358

PILLS

ages of man: p. 7037

PILOT

Christ is the Christian's p. 5638

good p. best tried in storm 137

I hope to see my P. face to face 2368

knows the unknown seas 5448

PILOTS

skilful p. gain reputation from storms 209

PIN

head on us for same reason p. has 10992

PINCH

Charities should p. us 10734

PINCHES

handsome shoe often p. foot 2461

shoe that fits one person p. another 6214

Those who wear shoe know best where it p. 8275

PINE

I p. for one to whom I can speak my thoughts 4255

lofty p. that by the storm is oftener tossed 9216

PINES

Never console one who p. under My chastening 2851

PINIONS

with trembling p. soar 5913

PINK

Vacation: getting into p. by going into red 6840

PINNACLE

of spiritual life is trust 11480

of spiritual life not happy joy 11480

PIONEER

failure p. in new undertakings 3602

PIONEERS

American p. endured hardships 3147

PIOUS

Every p. mood stripped off before cross 2160

faith must be more than p. hope 3787

pose gone when determine to concentrate 6056

So p. and so holy 10038

Some think have to look like hedgehog to be p. 6822

teaching of Christ at first appears p. 6486

to horror of p. types 5791

PIPE
His Spirit sounds each p. 7892
Rumor p. blown by jealousies 9756

PIPER
can expect to pay the p. 4051

PIPES
Gossip smoke that comes from dirty tobacco p. 5132
Sin like ice in our p. 10369

PIPKINS
God walks among pots and p. 5826

PISTOLS
Words are loaded p. 11999

PIT
digs p. for brother shall fall into himself 3373

PITCH
expectations low 9469

PITCHER
no p. can be made 8559

PITEOUS
That as I love the tiny, p. thing 7178

PITHY
sentences force truth upon our memory 9384
sentences like sharp nails 9384

PITIES
Oh what a thousand p. 11113

PITY
God did not save men out of p. 5757
God must smile in great p. 7944
God p. the Christian the world gets best of 1330
God p. the ship when the sea gets in 1330
God will treat us without p. 2089
greed has p. neither for nature or human beings 5327
him who's sadly sighing 4217
home where everyone the head 5845
my simplicity 1117
Where p. dwells, the peace of God is there 7284

PIVOT
jeweled p. on which lives must turn 901

PLACE
a tight p. and everything goes against you 236
all hours of day at his disposal 10120
And every p. is hallowed ground 12108
And God's eye over every p. 4834
and purpose of sex 10239
and time tide will turn 2614
As a white candle in a holy p. 8125

By whose direction this p. been allotted 4905
Christian's p. is in the world 1330
Dirt is matter in wrong p. 5121
favorite p. of God is in heart of man 4496
For tho' from out our bourne of P. 2368
future convenient p. for dreams 4324
giving central p. to God 7713
God gives something which takes p. of all, love 4790
God guides to place you know not 2565
God has been in our p. 6151
God is in every p. 4845
God never put anyone in p. too small to grow 4987
God will launch you to p. of his appointment 5430
Great supplicants sought secret p. of Most High 8805
had been looking in the wrong p. 7105
Have you come to the Red Sea p. in life? 5407
Heaven is p. prepared for those prepared 5643
Heaven neither a p. nor a time 7947
holding my rightful p. in the procession of humanity 9074
home not the one tame p. in world of adventure 5842
home wild p. in world of rules, set tasks 5842
I have a p. where my spirit sings 8429
in its time and p. recreation as proper as prayer 6837
In just that very p. of his 4834
Inside myself p. where live all alone 9933
Is a p. of central calm 8429
Is your p. a large p. 3847
Is your p. a small p. 3847
Joy is a p. 6528
joyous resting p. of my spirit 7961
Life is the p. where God begins his work 6978
Life's training p. for eternity 6979
Like pilgrims to th' appointed p. 2330
Lord doesn't want first p. in my life 9561
Love can make any p. agreeable 7210
maintain reverent attitude toward God's p. 3993
majority busy trying to p. ourselves 8395
Make it thy quiet dwelling p. 7454
mind is its own p. 512
Money can pay fare to every p. but heaven 7810
Never wait for fitter p. to talk to God 8874

Next to theology I give music highest p. 7914
no greater p. of ministry than a mother 7856
No one can be caught in p. he does not visit 5484
no p. like home except Florida 2877
No snowflake ever falls in wrong p. 8028
not well-adjusted who makes world better p. 6196
Nothing in its p. is bad 5036
Nothing out of p. is good 5036
one does not love p. less for having suffered in it 5843
One may return to p. of birth 12170
only in p. of healing dare to show wounds 10551
Our source, our center, our dwelling p. 4836
pleasure in one p. today, vain to seek it there tomorrow 8612
secret p, the land of tears 11015
Seek lowest p. 8448
Sojourn in every p. as if spend life there 9491
soul created in a p. between time, eternity 10671
soul would take its p. below creation 7971
take lowest p, highest will be given 5991
this not the p. of despair 2590
To find his p. and fill it 10821
To me remains not p. nor time 4869
try putting yourself in their p. 3073
We know how God would act if in our p. 6151
Whate'er your p. not yours alone, but his 3847
When we take to ourselves p. that is God's 7571
When you get into a tight p. 2614
who offers to God second p, offers no p. 7467
will be restless with p. in world 4311
within them as a guide 1664
world, a very nice p, an interesting p. 6929

PLACED
whatever p. in God's hands, still possess 8628
why has God p. us there 4974

PLACES
bring thy sunshine into cloudy p. 9106
can lay it on thick in right p. 9238
does not matter where God p. me 7486
false religion continually changing p. 5103
friends impart favor to p. where they dwell 4269

God can fit heroes into their p.
9174

In all the p. you can 10126

in p. where only God and his
angels have charge 10486

marketplace one of God's abiding
p. 4866

Repair the p. we have wasted
9054

see good things in unexpected p.
8575

Self-respect comes in quiet p. 9995

through friendship we love p.
4269

PLACID
People born p. 9777

PLAGIARISM
undetected, frequently unconscious
2012

PLAGUE
If money your god, will p. like
devil 7801

Music subdues rage of poison and
the p. 7900

When God's will to p. a man 2859

PLAGUES
angels send p. upon Egyptians 359

PLAIN
And he will make it p. 5378

God got message through p. and
certain 7029

God's way becomes p. when start
walking 5404

if omniscient all would be p. 7942

must scale mountain if view p.
8562

O'er mountain, or p, or sea 5420

only thing God makes p. in Bible
11546

PLAINER
I hear immortal symphonies of
world to come 11132

PLAINEST
one of p. statements in Bible 4949

PLAN
a tower that shall pierce clouds
6788

as if expect to enter hereafter
tomorrow 6099

be still, God's p. is wrought 9556

by which good people go to
heaven 5632

Christian finds peace in accepting
master p. 8440

Every man's life a p. of God 6888

God has a p. for this bankrupt
world 4902

God has one p. man another 4563

God speaks to us of p. vast in scale
4900

God's heavenly p. doesn't always
make sense 5399

God's p, like lilies, unfold 5403

human p. and calculation 184

no p. to retain this or that of the
devil 9864

of God, the responsibility is God's
4803

of mine would have proved my
ruin 4901

prepare, proceed, pursue 80

purposefully, prepare prayerfully
80

surrendered own plans to greater
p. of God 4803

Temptation part of a p. 11093

that would anticipate every
situation 5438

We sin on the installment p.
10421

whereby sinners can go to heaven
5632

Who talks of scheme and p. 7572

wisdom of God to p. our welfare
7093

would have deprived me of good
Lord had designed 4901

PLANET
all fellow passengers on same p.
9677

ball-bearing in hub of universe
11633

fight for our p. has started 3400

Infinite as essential for man as p.
12117

man a pigmy standing on crest of
p. 7381

man an eternal stranger on this p.
7436

Man makes great fuss about this p.
11633

nailed to my poor p. 6120

not called to live long on p. 1722

one individual on a small p. 7387

The inn is full on the p. earth
6155

with deliberate purpose, God
visited this p. 6144

would sparkle like Christmas tree
11189

PLANETS
If God maintains sun, p. 4619

nights wholesome, no p. strike
1371

PLANNED
For the pattern which he p. 10606

gifted, positioned on earth by
Master Craftsman 10004

God p. all perfect combinations
7891

pathway different from one you p.
4969

shall go on p. voyage 5945

Who saith, "A whole I p." 8132

PLANNING
most go through life p. a little
3758

never according to our p. 5401

well is wiser 67

You're p. the next party 7670

PLANS
as prop for man's own p, God will
disappoint 4468

commit to concrete p. for
increasing giving 10739

doing will of God leaves no time
for disputing his p. 4970

God able to work failures into his
p. 3613

God disappoints our p. 5395

God p. personal visit to his own
world 6127

God sends time of disappointed p.
7056

Life is what happens while
making other p. 6982

Man makes p, God changes them
5432

miscarry because no aim 4433

no longer has any p. of his own
9846

performs, resolves and executes
8224

surrendered own p. to greater
plan of God 4803

to leave your p. at the cross 10048

we tangle up the p. the Lord hath
wrought 6117

PLANT
Error a hardy p. 3251

fibre of p. impress of its Maker
3192

Friendship p. which must often be
watered 4231

friendship, p. not roadside thistle
4237

God will never p. seed on hard
spirit 888

Like roots of a p. faith must seek
greater depth 3756

love heart-deep in person's life
7289

Love is a tender p. 7230

True friendship is p. of slow
growth 4218

where conviction has brought
brokenness 888

PLANTED
God an utterable sigh, p. in the
soul 4843

God p. fear in soul 3973

thorns reap'd of tree p. 1737

Who p. seedling of bitterness 5051

PLANTING
Came God, planting the secret genes of
God 6148

PLANTS
Aromatic p. diffuse their
sweetness when crushed 150

no spicy fragrance while they grow
150

thorns must never expect to
gather roses 10454

PLATE
Upon a shifting p. 3851

PLATEAUS
no p. on pilgrimage 9832

PLATITUDE

As long as as matters hopeful, hope mere p. 5903

PLATO

As P. foresaw, the Man was crucified 11525

never read, "Come unto me all ye that labour" 930

read in P. sayings wise, beautiful 930

taught more science than Christ 6362

PLAUDITS

Not in shouts and p. of the throng 10794

PLAY

Author knows the p. 9911

best p. contains work 12022

Christ is risen, all earth's at p. 2982

Don't p. games with God 4879

God allows us to p. the game 7828

God does not p. hide-and-seek 5386

how did he p. his God-given part 7423

it down, pray it up 2606

Love's business not to p. favorites 7274

man appears for a little while to p. 7372

productive work must include p. 12022

still find some little part of p. 8145

those who p. with building blocks of universe 9866

To p, to dream, to drift 6881

waiting for church to find room for the p. 1998

We do not know the p. 9911

We p. the game, God keeps the score 6069

with cat, bear scratches 11067

with life as with a p. 6935

Work and p, artificial pair of opposites 12022

youth eagerly waiting for p. to begin 12168

PLAYBOY

if a man spends money, he's a p. 7800

jostled aside to make room for converted p. 4410

PLAYED

grand pieces p. on earth composed in heaven 5639

like orchestra in which all p. same note 6169

part each of us has p. 9911

PLAYER

Life's but a poor p. 6994

PLAYERS

God is the author, men the p. 5639

PLAYING

human race p. at children's games from the beginning 5982

it well matters infinitely 9911

Life like p. violin solo in public 6967

religious games in one corner 10124

Without p. with fantasy no creative work 2024

PLAY'S

Old age, p. last act 8166

PLAYS

God also p. upon this string 10663

Love p. the field 7274

who love good p. happiest people in world 5567

with dust, eyes full of dust 11066

PLEAD

does not expect us to p. for things already denied 5445

for God to speak when he has spoken, is speaking 8843

Is Christ thy advocate to p. thy cause 6415

them against me in judgment 4069

PLEADS

Love p. no excuse of impossibility 7220

PLEASANT

easy enough to be p. 10493

face a silent recommendation 3570

forms of iniquity 4726

hope, an easier, more p. way to journey's end 5924

hours even in a poorhouse 7001

Love is p. 7246

nothing is more p. than love 7283

refreshed us on the journey with p. inns 7014

spring would not be so p. 182

'Tis p. through loopholes of retreat 10529

Trust no future howe'er p. 4331

weakness that comes after pain 5360

What is p. belongs to dreams 9399

With friends even poverty is p. 4269

PLEASANTLY

hope carries us on p. to end of life 5934

PLEASE

all, p. none 1583

as much by sorrow as by smile 10587

before works can p. God 5087

formula for failure try to p. everybody 3619

God is quick to mark effort to p. 4810

greatest desire to p. God, serve one another 6924

hate the lie though it p. you 11517

If build to p. ourselves 10064

Luxury makes a man so soft hard to p. him 7363

make despair and madness p. 7911

no work better than another to p. God 3123

try to p. appease, dies in sadness 1581

Two men p. God 4572

unreasonable for preacher to p. all 9151

We p. God most by 7560

Without faith impossible to p. God 3823

PLEASED

if learned men not well p. 9170

If p. at finding faults 3945

Luxury a nice master, hard to be p. 7363

PLEASERS

love does not ask us to be compulsive p. 7337

PLEASES

courtesy p. him who gives, receives 1944

Events creep or fly as God p. 4820

Handsome is what p. 1792

interpretation will come as God p. 4885

not all faith p. God 3823

What kind of habitation p. God 7450

PLEASETH

Nor thankful when it p. me 5265

to praise that which p. thee most 9063

what p. man ofttimes displeasing to God 9195

PLEASING

desire ardently all that is p. to thee 9062

devil hath power to assume p. shape 2681

Eternity, thou p. dreadful thought 3271

hours with prospects more p. than fruition 3508

mirth but p. madness 4877

path to pleasure is p. God 8609

seek nothing else but p. of God 4922

silence, how fully p. to God 10252

sin becomes p. 10287

spend lives p. ourselves 5467

to God for other reasons 11685

PLEASURE

and pain are opposites 5353

cannot lay a trap for it 8612

Christ p. without loss 6391

Christians envy sinners their p. 3224

contains no healing for soul 8610

dessert of life 12028

Do not bite at bait of p. 11051

doing nothing that gives them p. 6813

doubt anyone who has tasted joy would exchange for p. 6540

end of life not to achieve p. 5554

enthusiasm makes p. of duty 3188

Every soul exists by God's p. 4529

frail like a dewdrop 8604

Grace is the good p. of God 4652

greatest evil or greatest good 8605

greatest p. is good action by stealth 8607

Health enough to make work p. 1809

hour of pain long as day of p. 149

I read Gospel every day with same p. 732

if full of p. no room for Spirit of God 5783

in criticism, hold your tongue 2064

Joy never in our power, p. is 6540

Joy, thousand times better than p. 1293

kindled by unexpected sparks 8606

let no p. pass untasted 11375

live in p. when I live to thee 8600

love p. most, that is your god 7338

man believes he must pay for p. 8602

man once believed could make own p. 8602

Men pursue p. with breathless haste 8601

more gravel than pearls 8599

Nights of p. are short 10340

No one who is lover of p. is lover of man 11661

no p. comparable to 8611

no p. so lasting as reading 855

not found in what is real 9399

not p. in noticing faults of others 3944

nothing, smoke, shadow, pain 4412

obey God because desired p. 577

of pride like p. of scratching 9245

oft a visitant 8271

one place today, vain to seek it there tomorrow 8612

pain better than p. 10875

Pain, unlike p, wears no mask 10583

path to p. is pleasing God 8609

resigns p. to enjoy others better 1298

Righteousness, not p. should be man's pursuit 5001

seldom found where sought 8606

small pains will seem like p. 5776

surprising arrivals, departures 8612

taught to ask, will it give me p. 5467

tickle of p. with virtue 577

unexpected arrivals, departures 8612

walked a mile with p. 10596

When p. business of life, ceases to be p. 8614

Where your p. is, there is your treasure 5574

while it laughs it dies 8604

who does not love God, in love with p. 4803

Worldliness mental slavery to illegitimate p. 12054

you desire p, not pain 577

PLEASURE'S

but pain 4877 5550

PLEASURES

become his burden 7363

conversation one of greatest p. 1840

courtesy cheapest of p. 1944

defect of age to rail at p. of youth 12189

do not know nation until we know its p. 6842

garden, purest of human p. 8007

God whispers to us in our p. 8257

heaven, p. banish pain 5670

home where simple p. enjoyed 5853

If p. greatest in anticipation 8598

Incredulity robs of p. 11592

Lord does not let believer have p. outside of himself 8608

mistake in estimating value of p. 10410

never tire of p. we give 8613

No matter how many p. Satan offers you 9855

not sort that look exciting 5274

of world's p. tired 10578

other Christians enjoy, to you refined evil 5776

owes its p. to another's pain 28

resist temptation to chase after p. 5615

seize the p. of the present day 8600

Spirit of God may strip you of borderline p. 5776

talk about p. to acquaintances 4276

tire of p. we take 8613

Vice stings even in p. 10412

Where love is not, can be no p. 7341

worst p. are purely spiritual 10400

PLEASURE-SEEKING

is a barren business

PLEIADES

sought by him who made the P. and Orion 4768

PLENTY

as well as want, can sep'rate friends 3558

covetous man pines in p. 5325

of room in the forest 6168

of seats in available subway 7049

than live in p. and be troubled 3979

To have p. is to be perplexed 7071

PLIGHT

ignorance has brought theology to sorry p. 11196

PLINY

I will banish thee 1310

I will drive thee away from men 1310

I will slay thee 1310

I will take away thy treasures 1310

PLOD

along hoping efforts will pay off 6810

PLOTS

Real life seems to have no p. 9405

PLOUGH

deep while sluggard sleep 3115

God has to p. the heart 896

hold on to p. while wiping tears 1236

We p. the fields and scatter 4625

will take away natural beauty 896

PLOW

Goodness is love with hand to p. 5065

PLOWED

name of Jesus p. into history of world 5727

PLOWING

Deep is p. of grief 5332

PLOWMAN

no reason why p. not as intellectual as poet 6332

PLUCKED

Feather by feather goose is p. 11054

PLUMB LINE

finding our p. cannot sound its depth 4745

law p. to show us we are crooked 1530

PLUMBING

Human being, ingenious assembly of p. 833

PLUMBS

Who p. the depth of God 9791

PLUMS

Life's a pudding full of p. 6990

PLUNGE

deeper we p, more we learn 7936

PLURALITY

God knows all p. and all pluralities 4881

PLUS

cross a minus turned into a p. 2119

PLUTONIUM

easier to denature p. than evil 3362

POCKET
book like garden in p. 849
Feel for others in your p. 4037

POCKETS
love, can empty p. and have more than ever 7252
shroud has no p. 8640

POEM
as much dignity in tilling field as writing p. 2762
find p. itself in Christianity 1203
In science, read only notes to p. 1203

POEMS
made by fools like me 2017
most beautiful p. are filled with despair 8621
repeat for comfort in sleepless nights 9381
worked on proof of one of my p. 12143

POET
God is the p. of world 4474
Jesus produced effects beyond orator or p. 6449
no reason why miner not as intellectual as p. 6332
not p. enough 505
sees city as silhouette against sky 10522

POETRY
beauty of Bible p. 701
bliss, suffering forever shared 8619
conceived world was p. 1981
Faith lends p. to life 3666
glory and p. of God 4704
greatest love p. produced by Christians 1200
has endeared solitude 8616
has multiplied my enjoyments 8616
has soothed my affictions 8616
language in which man explores amazement 8618
makes invisible appear 8620
makes you know you are alone in unknown world 8619
makes you laugh, cry, prickle, be silent 8619
makes you want to do this, that, nothing 8619
makes your toenails twinkle 8619
making truth more real 8617
most beautiful p. born from womb of silence 10269
not as assertion of truth 8617
of earth is never dead 2976
thinking in its higher forms a kind of p. 11259
tree is full of p. 8042

POET'S
there lies the p. native land 10535

POINT
cross is the great central p. 6424
Don't p. finger 3131

God judges not by p. man has reached 4713
highest p. we can hope to attain 4976
promises that p. to real meaning 9351

POINT OF VIEW
appreciate God's p. by long discipline 2846
look from heaven's p. 10707
To repent is God's p. instead of one's own 9605

POINTED
Revival is God's finger p. right at me 9748

POINTING
solves problems by p. to Lamb of God 3784

POINTS
God never p. pathway different 4969
Lord's Prayer for attention upon a few great p. 7154
Real goodness p. to another world 5079

POISE
and quietness of Christ 123
Prayer provides p. 8951

POISON
discouraged emotions p. life 3050
Faith draws p. from every grief 3661
flattery is p. 4053
in sorrow if we put it there 10637
legalism, p. blinds our eyes 6823
Music subdues rate of p. 7900
of bitterness, paranoia 10034
self turns up to p. fruit of our lives 9943
smallest revenge will p. soul 9728
to another is rank p. 6220
We've got as far as p. gas 11739

POISON IVY
vacationeer returns with p. 6841

POISONED
drink, p. scourge 325
Parents have p. fountain 8352

POISONS
Evil tolerated p. whole system 3368

POLE
Humor is the p. that adds balance 6715
lightings flash from p. to p. 4827

POLICEMAN
may see God as p. 4489
thief cannot find p. 472

POLICIES
how carried out depends on youth 12160

POLISH
try to p. reputation, lose it 9629

POLISHED
not p. without rubbing 136

POLISHING
growth of grace like p. of metals 5230

POLITE
man listens to person who knows nothing 1942
prattle exchanged on Sunday morning 4029
Reading, p, unpunished vice 858

POLITENESS
eases jolts 1946
goes far, costs nothing 1945
like air cushion 1946
pretenses of p. 4115

POLITIC
Expediency asks, Is it p. 1679

POLITICAL
Golden Rule would reconcile p. contention 5005
Honesty, an absence of p. games 5874
order cannot be renewed without theological virtues 5169
reputation cannot last forever 5079

POLITICALLY
Paul's case not p. expedient 786

POLITICIAN
Christ executed by a timid p. 2171

POLITICS
gizzard of society, full of gut, gravel 5185
human p, society must be changed 10528
In p. a week is a very long time 5180
me first philosophy power to blow p. to pieces 10087
of Kingdom, people must be changed 10528
penalty men pay for not being interested in p. 5193
science of how who gets what, when, why 5186
teaches what means are effective 11211

POLL
If p. taken to name six greatest men in world 9988

POLLUTE
Remind us not to p. your creation 9117

POLLUTED
and landlocked by the mighty disaster 4744
Light, though passes through pollution, not p. 7110
Protestants will not be p. if 5733

POLLUTION
Light, though passes through p. not polluted 7110

POLTROONS
more likely we are all p. 912

POLYGAMY
Variability of woman obviates p. 7663

POMP
happiness an enemy to p. and noise 5568
In lowly p. ride on to die 2981
stars flame out in p. of light 7927

POND
is an ocean to a tadpole 8517

PONDER
how Son of God would have done it 10140

PONDERED
theologians p. meaning of conversion 1896

PONDERING
inner harmony by p. experience of others 7687

POOL
wherein serene light of God can be mirrored 8437

POOR
A p. life this if, full of care 6829
Alms never make p. 4350
among the p. is where Jesus went 2812
And makes me p. indeed 10449
Are levell'd. Death confounds 'em all 2384
as I am? 1376
Better p. and live, than rich and perish 8675
Better p. than wicked 8674
Bible, Magna Charta of p. 700
blame yourself 505
Christ chose disciples who were p. 8698
Christ in you that helps the p. 6381
Christ lives among the p. 1277
Christ made himself servant of the p. 8698
Christ willed to be born p. 8698
come to us in many forms 8693
comparison game way to p. self-image 6208
contented man is never p. 1814
dear to God is p. peasant as mighty prince 3225
Death knocks at p. man's cottage 2361
deed that helps or harms p, for or against Christ 8698
do not blame life 505
easy to tell p. to accept poverty 8678
frequently rich wealthy because oppressed p. 6630
Give me your tired, your p. 7985
God at work exalting the p. 6630
God is on the side of the p, oppressed 8696

God sides with p. because of vulnerability 6630
gold hidden in ground belongs to p. 11855
guide lives by integrity die happy even though p. 6309
Have courage to appear p. 8679
heart that never rejoices 6535
How p. they that have not patience 8399
If life seems p. 505
intricated soul 10661
is p. who has nothing but money 11821
Lash love upon the p, easy 7348
Life's but a p. player 6994
love has feet to hasten to p. 7335
Love your life, p. as it is 7001
man at his gate 4501
man in evolution from p. to truer wealth 9351
man who craves more is p. 2868
men need no guards 8686
Might-Have-Beens 8370
must care, console, help, support the p. 8698
my friend, the boast is p. 3174
nailed to my p. planet 6120
No man p. who has had godly mother 7851
No one can say prayers p. when using language of love 8875
No one more happy than p. man 8695
not rich were blessed 5001
not rich, are blessed 1216
Of all God's creatures, man alone is p. 8683
Outside show p. substitute for inner worth 6061
palace without affection is a p. hovel 5816
people have p. opinion of us even when intentions good 6270
rich enough who is p. with Christ 8676
Rich gifts p. when givers unkind 4372
rich make war, p. who die 11778
rich or p. according to what he is 6302
Satan tempts by making rich not p. 2690
Self-centeredness result of a p. self-image 6229
she no longer needs our p. protection 2392
Some are rich, and some are p. 11852
that p. may simply live 11861
the Christ of the p. confronted me 8685
to the p. in spirit, God is forgiving 4649
too often turn away, unheard 8694
unctuous piety p. example of spirituality 10707
vision limits deeds 11734

were not for divinity that stirs within us 5979
when p. came to Christ 10731
when we turn our backs on the p. 8693
who bestows his goods upon the p. 4364
Who gives to p, lends to God 627
who knows how to be p, knows everything 8677
without Christianity 1199
wretches saved from shipwreck 10386

POOR IN SPIRIT
attitude of dependence on God 6025
detachment from earthly supports 6025
God means everything 1325
things mean nothing 1325

POOREST
Christian richest when p. 1265
June may be had by the p. comer 2641
Life is p. when you are richest 6903
man always wanting more than he has 2874
within possibility for p. 3737

POORHOUSE
glorious hours even in a p. 7001

POORLY
Jesus was p. adjusted to society 6196

POP
in shirt sleeves at ball game 3921

POPE
and peasant know more between them 266
no p. holds key to as much power 11841
than the p. and all his cardinals 9929

POPPY'S
Found in each p. cup of gold 7996

POPULAR
good listener p. everywhere 7111
image of man of God 1645
Jesus p. in some groups 3493
misdeed does not make it permissible 3387
mistake to present Christianity as p. 1198
Prayer not a p. gift 8914
truth more p. if not ugly facts 11543
unnatural for Christianity to be p. 1209
Vanity asks, Is it p. 1679

POPULARITY
an accident 1010
Character lost when ideal sacrificed to p. 999
Christians equate p. with excellence 5891

Doing God's will may not lead to
p. 10778
glory's small change 3859
hence constant p. of dogs 9509
is a crime when sought 3858
is fickle 6455
Love not dependent on p. 7235
only a virtue where 3858

POPULATION
Education produced p. able to
read 2997
Education produced p. unable to
distinguish 2997

PORT
we too shall come into p. 6398

PORTER
Death p. at King's lodge 2253

PORTION
Our p. of the weight of care 8863

PORTIONS
best p. of a good man's life 6664
626

PORTRAIT
egotist sees only the frame of his
own p. 9213
face, p. of the mind 435

PORTRAITS
Bible gallery of human p. 703

POSES
Dignity never p. 2761

POSITION
Christ never asks anyone to define
p. 6431
forced into p. of leadership 6785
Joy is a p. 6528
man who loves God in
unassailable p. 4803
most go through life jockeying for
p. 3758
no greater p. than a mother 7856
Success not p. one has reached
10809
who does not love God, in love
with his p. 4803
Whose p. antedates that of the
Eternal 4955
you're in p. to pray 9027

POSITIONED
planned, gifted, p. on earth by
Master Craftsman 10004

POSITIONS
for easiest p. God must give grace
7486
Idolatry trusting p. to do what
only God can do 6072
progress resulted from people
who took unpopular p. 9308

POSITIVE
Accentuate the p. 8231
Faith is p. 6091
influence negative or p, never
neutral 6248
Joy is a p. thing 6537
men are most naive 7975

praying was so p. 8890
way we respond to hurts 3319
word becomes creative force
12001
word makes you feel good 12001
word releases p. energy 12001

POSITIVELY
proceed p., pursue persistently 80
purposefully, prayerfully, p.,
persistently 80
torn between desire to think p. or
confront life as it is 9401

POSITIVES
cross, meeting negatives with p.
2146

POSSESS
all things, and more innumerable
5575
All we p. qualified by what we are
8622
because people live in things they
p. 8631
do not want merely to p. faith
3734
examine how happy those are
who p. it 3498
Glory, lovelier to desire than p.
4409
hope I shall always p. virtue
enough 5881
how little some enjoy things they
p. 3221
hungry for goodness he does not p.
5299
If p. inward solitude 10539
Men who p. opinions and a will
6299
things placed in God's hands, still
p. 8628
To have little is to p. 7071
what we p. not our own 7552
What you p. will belong to
someone else 1062
worthier to preserve than p. honor
5892

POSSESSED
man himself when most p. by God
5200
Men are so p. by themselves 9938
to achieve ends he vaguely
understands 4399

POSSESSES
All you are unable to give p. you
8623
religion p. the truth 11524
want faith that p. me 3734

POSSESSING
For thy sure p. 11379
reassures of humanity by p. a few
peculiarities 5307
that, I still possess the whole 1817
Yet p. every blessing 5428

POSSESSION
Cease to resist, love takes p. 4785
Children, our most priceless p.
1115

Every p. a trust 8626
give p. give little 1725
God knows me, a precious p.
11179
Hell was our inheritance, now
heaven our p. 1348
In old age faith most marvelous p.
8138
increased p. loads us with new
weariness 8625
life not a p. to be defended 10545
makes not rich 8637
My most cherished p. is my faith
3761
pampers the mind 242
to the faithful world is a p. 11696

POSSESSIONS
be satisfied with your p. 8472
desires increase with p. 2869
give but little when give p. 10219
Idolatry trusting p. to do what
only God can do 6072
if loaded down with material p.
8630
leave your p. at the cross 10048
life reduced to p. 8634
people cling to p. instead of
sharing 8632
riches not in my p. 11839
stripped of all p. but knowledge
of God 11688
time, most precious of p. 11356
to me these have always been
contemptible 7365
wise man carries his p. within him
11950

POSSESSIVE
become p. and defensive 10531

POSSESSOR
Ambition destroys its p. 339

POSSIBILITIES
believe only p. not faith 605
Faith possibility when human p.
exhausted 3698
God knows deepest p. in me 4889
never met a person without p.
3596
only p. mere philosophy 605
Prayer, results lie outside human p.
8940
Remember your p. 9271
saint is creature of vast p. 9767
two p, one to grow old, the other
not 8129

POSSIBILITY
a hint from God 8641
Faith p. when human possibilities
exhausted 3698
greater in p. for good or bad than
we can know 10015
of future exceeds
accomplishments of past 4329
within p. for weakest, poorest
3737

POSSIBLE
all things p. to Christians 587
Chastity is p. 10236

cost God everything to make it p. for us to pray 8773

difference between impossible, p. determination 2631

do not believe, no explanation p. 608

faith makes all things p. 7345

Faith makes things p. 3706

for bad men to become good 9438

Free will makes evil p. 4120

Free will makes love, goodness, joy possible 4120

God can do nothing until limit of p. 8642

God will make it p. for you to do it 5226

highest p. condition of a man 4983

If all things are p. with God 587

In God no change p. 977

Is it p. to become free without faith 3745

life in fullest deepest sense p. 7969

Love thinks all things p. 7220

make it p. for God to say yes 8924

Make p. for me which is impossible by nature 8643

Man's capacity for justice makes democracy p. 2528

not p. for angel of heaven 11722

not p. for first man in Garden 11722

not p. on this imperfect earth 7601

not p. to know God that we may love him 4802

Sainthood makes it p. to admire everybody 9778

to forget to love Christ 117

to make p. a resurrection 5423

to obtain p, man turns to fellowmen 7490

to reach God in love 11607

To the quiet mind all things p. 7773

Worldliness wishing the forbidden p. to do 12054

POSSIBLILITY

Pride eats the p. of love, contentment 9229

POSSIBLITIES

Democracy assumes extraordinary p. in ordinary people 2522

POSSIBLITY

If God to remove p. of disobedience 8091

POST

maintain p. when others have quitted 1915

POST OFFICE

we go more desperately to p. 1761

POSTHUMOUS

charities essence of selfishness 10078

POSTPONE

Do today what you want to p. till tomorrow 9295

hold on to past, p. new blessings 968

POSTPONEMENT

Life without possible p. 11388

POSTURE

Joy is a p. 6528

POST-WAR

not a p. generation 9914

POTENCY

Giving is highest form of p. 10726

of prayer 8987

POTENT

most p. weapon God has given man 4154

Words—how p. for good, evil, in hands of one who knows how to combine 12004

POTENTIAL

capacity of human heart 5625

darkness p. for vulnerability 2612

enemies p. friends 3171

good character, fullest p. 1019

hero in every man—and p. skunk 8670

makes for life lived at full p. 6999

Most people live in restricted cirle of p. 8659

poor character, fail to play up to p. 1019

suffering, profound p. for good 10933

POTENTIALITIES

Education process of eliciting p. hidden 3026

Remember your p. 9271

POTHOLES

Take p. as evidence on right route 2745

POTS

Christ moves among p. and pans 5824

God walks among p. and pipkins 5826

POTTERY

gets fragile sitting in sun 2540

POUND

better give one shilling than lend p. 4368

ounce of help better than p. of preaching 3146

ounce of performance worth more than p. of preachment 9131

POUNDED

Unless clay be well p. 8559

POUR

a thousand joys he would p. into you at once 6525

Happiness perfume cannot p. on others 5516

Unless vessel clean, what you p. turns sour 1054

POURED

vital red of love p. out 2979

POURING

Joy the wine that God is ever p. 8454

POVERTY

A penny in the urn of p. 6070

accumulating debts, paying them off 4040

bad side of p. is fear it creates 11854

Bear your neighbor's p. 8689

better than riches 10875

better to be content with p. 10777

blessings for man conscious of his own p. 5299

Christ shared their p. 8698

confoundedly inconvenient 8687

disarm p. of its sharpest sting 8679

easy to tell poor to accept p. 8678

feeling of being uncared for greatest p. 7132

given p. that he might be wise 8806

have mistaken the nature of p. 8697

hope gives p. of spirit 3834

how little one feels p. when one loves 7199

if you can accept p. as God's will for yourself 8678

in p. Christ is my riches 6498

In p. of solitude all riches present 10542

indifference toward neighbor assaulted by p. 6163

is a weary thing 8684

is not a crime 8688

keepest down the soul of man 8684

Laziness travels so slowly p. soon overtakes him 6768

lecture on Christian view of p. 8685

loneliness, greatest p. 7132

makes people satirical 8690

Neither great p. nor riches will hear reason 9418

no disgrace to man 8687

not p. so much as pretense 8679

of soul measured by how little it can feel 10677

of the soul 8697

People come to p. two ways 4040

Pride and laziness keys of p. 8691

Riches exclude only p. 11847

share some of their p. 8678

the load of some 8689

wants much; greed everything 5322

With friends even p. is pleasant 4269

World p. is a hundred million mothers weeping 8699

you have an Abraham Lincoln 161

POVERTY-STRIKEN
and starvation-ridden world
10051

POWER
act upon faith within our p. 3721
Ambition greed for p. 340
angels, wild and radiant p. 359
Apt words p. to asuage 3129
attitudes within our p. 5538
attributes to the Father works in
which p. excels 11427
authoritarianism twists good into
lust for p. 9952
because of silence p. of God dwelt
in saints 10252
behind us greater than task ahead
7878
blessed babe, infant full of p. 6123
blown by tempest of unbelievable
p. 7488
by thy p. protect us 619
can do by gentleness 4403
can do everything but control love
8709
can separate from true nature of
Christian leadership 8717
cannot doubt p. comes from above
4949
cannot say thine is the p. if 8818
center of p. is Lord 11349
Cheerfulness, wondrous p. of
endurance 1099
Christ brings us his p. 11
Christ gives us p. to go on with
battle 11451
Christ Lion in p, raising the dead
6425
Christian's goal not p. but justice
6623
Christianity offers p. of God 1182
Christianity, p. of God in soul of
man 1179
church can limit God's p. 4829
church cannot increase God's p.
4829
commandments need p. of life
1525
compel acknowledgment of divine
p. 479
consecration is using every p. for
God 1721
contemplate God's p. in creation
4581
controlled by other p. than my
own will 4949
cross imparts p. to do all God
wants 2172
cross reveals difference between p,
love 2156
Cross the only p. which can make
us truthful 11531
Death amazing p. of altering
desires 2240
deprive ourselves of royal display
of p. 4995
desire of p. in excess caused
angels to fall 3556
devil entangles ambitious with p.
2677

devil has p. to suggest evil 2679
devil hath p. to assume pleasing
shape 2681
devil loves man to extend his p.
2688
devil no p. to compel against will
2679
devil wanted to involve Jesus in
exigencies of p. 2704
difference between physical,
spiritual p. 8715
divine p. shining in continuing
state of universe 11652
do not fear explosive p. of atom
bomb 3376
Do right, God's recompense to
you p. to do more right 9648
Do you fully understand p. of
words 12005
draw upon God's p. to hold up
2742
endowed with p. of retreating
from reality 3370
every p. for God's glory 1721
Faith brings p. 3748
Faith is a strong p. 3678
Faith means grasped by p. greater
than we are 3707
fear explosive p. of evil in human
heart 3376
free will p. of doing what ought to
be done 4111
future is still in your p. 8385
Genius, that p. that dazzles mortal
eyes 8539
genius, p. and magic 48
Give me p. to live for mankind
10130
God does not give p. to imitate
him 9834
God has all p. to defend you 4696
God has delegated p. to his
creatures 4821
God has never surrendered iota of
his p. 4821
God has set himself against p. of
enemy 5016
God's p. is irresistible 8886
God's p. to protect me 5400
gold, what crimes thy tyrant p.
has caused 11803
Gospel a living p. 732
Grace gives us p. to pull it off
5221
Grant me, O God, the p. to see
8009
Great as is the p. of God 4824
greater their p. to harm 210
greatness of a man's p. is his
surrender 10975
has more p. in silence 3428
has not beaten church back 1419
have it in our p. to be in heaven
right now 6569
healing of time 4643
his grace and p. are such 9000
His p. no boundary known unto
men 7570

holds key to as much p. as
Mother Teresa 11841
Holiness p. to overcome
temptation 5744
Hope draws p. from deep trust in
God 5928
humility not doubt of own p.
6032
Hushed are the stars, whose p.
never spent 8014
Idolatry putting confidence in p.
6071
if not tell truth, p. against you
11510
If you have no p. 36
Ignorance, p. and pride a deadly
mixture 9212
impossible except by p. of Holy
Spirit 3222
impossible not that which is
difficult to his p. 4513
in p. of each to be an individual
6209
In which the p. of Satan broken is
6140
In worship we meet p. of God
12103
is like saltwater 8711
is self-evident 5806
is to let the current pass through
us 7554
Jesus' p. of persuasion so
overwhelming 5485
Jesus, no intention to speak to p.
6451
Joy is never in our p. 6540
Kept by Almighty p. 4490
Kind words p. beyond natural
causes 6645
kindness speaks a language of
silent p. 6651
Knowledge is p. 6694
Let not thy will roar when p. can
but whisper 6800
lies at center of life 10576
likely coupled with pride, cruelty
8705
Lord's Prayer rich in spiritual p.
7156
Love has p. to give in a moment
7223
love of God redemptive p. 4780
love of p. is love of ourselves 8716
Love only service p. cannot
command 7253
Loving a p. as well as a process
7277
lust for p. rooted in weakness
8718
man has p. to bring misery on
himself, others 4158
man has p. to defy God's wishes
4158
Man's eyes have great p. 3563
men use physical p. 8715
more easily manifested in
destroying than creating 8712
more p. in open hand than
clenched fist 8720

never have faith in p. 10875
night given to drink deep at fountain of p. 6947
no government armed in p. 5196
no greater p. than a mother 7856
No man to be trusted with unlimited p. 8714
No Niagara turned into p. until tunneled 2852
no p. can conquer Spirit of God 10751
no p. like love 3836
no p. more formidable than truth 11547
no stronger test of character than p. 8721
no witch hath p. to charm 1371
not likely coupled with goodness 8705
of choosing good, evil within reach 5047
of evil unlimited if on earth alone 3377
of God to achieve our welfare 7093
of going out of one's self 4220
of love will lead to master of the art 7352
of perseverance grows with time 8557
of service correspond to life of prayer 10192
of silence 10252
omnipotent p. behind obedience 1521
only p. resist p. of fear is p. of love 3992
others attracted by God's p. 7532
out of the p. of God 425
over the dead world has no p. 2395
passing mine, immeasurable God 4825
Patience and gentleness is p. 8708
Peace p. that comes to souls arriving 8454
pent up in unconscious mind 1712
Pentecost brought fullness of p. 5806
Personality p. to open doors 1034
prayed for p. that he might have praise of men 8806
Prayer is p. 8927
Prayer provides p. 8951
prayers track down which God's p. can come 8886
presence of God's p. on earth 4865
proportion out what p. he sees fit 4629
putting minds together in shapes of our own choosing 8710
quest for p. childish 3469
raw p. dangerous 523
Revival is God revealing himself in p. 9745
revival out of balance is revival out of p. 9738

Revival whereby God works in extraordinary p. 9746
Righteousness, not p. should be man's pursuit 5001
saints have their p. 5301
same p. that measured, weighed, spanned world 4592
scientific p. has outrun spiritual p. 9868
secret of p. is to know God 3790
See how it feels to have p. 4419
seek to make institutions of p. just 6623
Sin is the slight of God's p. 10376
sin of the Garden was sin of p. 8719
sin weakening of p. 10360
Sin, most of its p. hidden 10357
slaves to gadgets, p, security 9016
so full of p. was the concept of mother 7859
social differences have lost p. to divide 6286
source of p. stronger than disappointment 6491
Spirit's p. greater than p. of sin 5802
spiritual p. uses men 8715
stifling p. of criticism 2054
substituted spirit of the wheels for p. of Spirit 5808
Success is neither fame, wealth or p. 10807
Surrender to this p. is faith 3707
sustaining p. of hope 4643
take God's program, can have God's p. 4826
Take, O God, thy p. and reign 2981
task ahead never as great as P. behind 3804
tell truth, infinite p. supporting you 11510
test a man's character, give him p. 8706
that brought Christ from dead operative in Christians 9698
that shakes, turns, transforms, heals us 3707
that we realize the p. of God 7485
Thine endless wisdom, boundless p. 4659
to almighty p. no more difficult 7940
to be able to do without is p. 1818
to blow our world to pieces 10087
to continue under hardship 8423
to feel with others 8430
to find Holy Spirit present with p. 5786
to go forth armed with thy p. 9088
to lay down one's p. for others in need 7435
To make no mistakes not in p. of man 7794
to obtain and hold p, must love it 8705

to touch with divine p. the buried acorn 6095
to work under stress 8423
too busy to pray, too busy to have p. 9017
transfiguring p. of prayer 8995
transform from negative to positive 1712
unlimited p. of God, limited p. of Satan 4917
We owe God every honor in our p. to give 4529
We rise, how full of p. 8867
weakest saint can experience p. 9563
What but thy grace can foil tempter's p. 5225
What p. does anyone have to injure you with words 6287
when I lay down the reins of p. 6304
When we and ours have it in our p. 5009
Where love rules, no will to p. 7343
where p. predominates, love is lacking 7343
who achieves p. by violence 11674
who has great p. should use it lightly 8704
who maintains only he has p. to reason correctly 8196
Whose love is as great as his p. 4787
whose p. extends to great and small 11628
will intoxicate the best 8714
Will is p. 2635
will of God p. which carries us 5451
willingness, fearful and glorious p. 4128
Within thy circling p. I stand 4876
Without hypocrisy no existing p. can hold its own 8722
Without hypocrisy no new p. can arise 8722
worshiper aware of no p. 1399

POWERFUL

Being p. like being a lady 8703
Bible more p. than weapons 726
By success do not mean you may become p. 10780
Example most p. rhetoric 3432
God does not intend all to be p. 4243
God so p. can direct evil to good end 3371
If God deny p. presence, fall into nothing 4865
if have to tell people you are, you ain't 8703
if leans on God becomes p. 10766
intellect has p. muscles, but no personality 6333
Labor p. medicine 3103
life more p. than most of us think 6918
man is p. on his knees 8785

man more p. than matter 1474
more p. and original a mind 10566
most p. influence in world 5766
Mr. Money is a p. gentleman 7817
nothing so p. as truth 11548
Prayer the most p. of all things 8940
prayers only as p. as our lives 8885
Self can turn p. prayer into weak one 10080
temptation to love money inexplicably p. 7811
tongue p. weapon of manipulation 1882

POWERFULLY
as p. as this one solitary life 6353
God works p. but gently, gradually 4814

POWERLESS
evidence in daily life that Jesus is p. 3646
God, no lifeless, p. work 872
God, p. in the world 4899
Gold in trouble p. to cheer 11813
Hatred, anger p. when met with kindness 6639
intellectuals remain socially p. 6323
law as system replaced because p. 9755
money p. to purchase 10906
Words p. in a dictionary 12004

POWERLESSNESS
crushed by sense of p. 5395
friend who cares faces p. 3080
God used my p. for his purpose 2518

POWERS
completely different people in all our p. 3766
cross has disarmed P. 2100
deriving just p. from consent of governed 3246
develop p. of spiritual receptivity 7564
Do not pray for tasks equal to your p. 8780
God will break up confidence in your natural p. 11689
Grief can elicit p. of fortitude, patience 10640
grief develops p. of the mind 5340
How to use thy noble p. 8671
Immense hidden p. lurk in unconscious 1712
of darkness paralyzed by prayer 8988
of evil overcome them 11080
Pray for p. equal to your task 8780
prayer greater than man-controlled p. 8991
That all my p. with all their might 9047

under pressure responsible for great creative efforts 1712
we lay waste our p. 12046

PRACTICAL
doctrine p. value if makes difference 11180
giving central place to God in p. everyday lives 7713
men know where they are 8482
not much p. Christianity where 3899
To love as Christ loves a p. thing 7324
Whenever visions of God unfit us for p. life 5466

PRACTICE
all pleasant forms of iniquity 4726
art of aloneness 10553
best of all instructors 3543
devil not willing for person to p. Christianity 2686
extol self-control, and p. self-indulgence 6068
forgiveness 4072
forgiveness beautiful until we have to p. 4104
inspiration received put into p. 4160
Many agree with God in principle, not p. 1336
no intention of carrying it out in p. 2915
Preach less and p. more 9281
spend lives pleasing ourselves 5467
until equality embodied in p. 3230

PRACTICED
Old cranks, saints have p. all their lives 5503

PRACTICES
Who p. hospitality entertains God 5961

PRACTICING
by p. mercy resemble God 7740

PRAGMATISTS
Christian thinker obstructs p. 11239

PRAISE
Another year of p. 8077
Arising from creation, his p. 8029
at morning, blame at night 8203
awaken us to delight in your p. 8742
best auxiliary to prayer 8735
Bible, my psalm of p. 716
blossom under p. like flowers in sun 3144
by our sufferings we learn to p. our bliss 10925
children for important things 8309
children need more than bread, butter 8309
compelled to p. even as logic screams 8724

dead saints, persecute living ones 8530
deserve no p, it is our duty 9666
devil delights in tormenting when we p. Christ 2661
Do not mountains p. God 7997
Does not all nature p. God 7997
Does not thunder p. God as it rolls 7997
doing what we ought, deserve no p. 3100
don't learn to p. in a day 8747
duty bound to thank and p. 4992
Envy kind of p. 3210
Eternity not long enough to p. God 3270
fetus of p. grows deep in my spirit 8738
few men know how to p. 7586
find p. embarrassing 10784
friend in public 4182
genuine Christianity has always vital throb of p. 6251
God even when we do not feel like it 2564
God for having made another, quite different world 5678
God hates those who p. themselves 9198
God in loneliness 583
God offers to help us build cathedral of p. 7684
Good preaching leads people to p. Savior 10097
Goodness is like p. to God 5064
Great sermons lead people to p. preacher 10097
greater a man more distasteful p. is to him 5296
He who does not p. God while on earth 8727
humble receives p. way clean window takes light of sun 6033
In doing what we ought deserve no p. 2779
In p. of little children 1120
In wonder, love and p. 4819
is more than singing 8734
is the saint reflecting life of Christ 8734
Jesus furnished themes for more songs of p. 6449
know and p. some one aspect of divine beauty 6169
let your joyful heart p. 8737
little p. for sexually controlled single 10236
live with p, learn to appreciate 1114
loudly, blame softly 8729
man joined in p. until he fell 8743
meanest p. speaks well, qualifies with a "but" 8739
most would rather be ruined by p. than saved by criticism 8741
My great Redeemer's p. 8732
nature hymn of p. to God 8001
no editorials p. mother's accomplishments 7844

No homage like his p. 4208
one thing to p. discipline, another to submit 2848
only when choose to p. for rough spots 11152
ours to give them to thy p. 8098
prayed for power that he might have the p. of men 8806
rather than gossip 1138
reap p, sow seeds 1574
rebellious deny as freely as devout p. 4129
redemption brings man back into tune with p. 8743
refusal of p. a desire to be praised twice 8723
sacrifice of p. will always cost something 8724
saint has heart ready to p. God 9790
stones would p. God if need arose 12099
such a heart whose pulse may be thy p. 5265
sweetest of all sounds is p. 8740
Think not those faithful who p. thy words 3955
to p. that which pleaseth thee most 9063
to raise your p. 8730
To spread her Maker's p. abroad 8026
to the undeserving is satire 8736
tranquillity is his who cares not for p. 1791
under p. we open, reach, grow 3144
Unto thy p, all love and melody 7928
voice rises to heaven when you p. 8725
Watch frustrations melt into p. 8424
Who can say more than this rich p. 6223
who sings own p. usually off key 9206
will transform humblest dwelling to hallowed heaven 5846
with ceaseless p. his works behold 362
with enthusiasm only those who admire us 8726
You awake us to delight in your p. 7578

PRAISED

Honesty p, but left to shiver 5878
not better person because p. 1067
Not more holy if p. 1681
refusal of praise a desire to be p. twice 8723
to be humble when p. great attainment 6019
would have p. you more had you p. me less 7584

PRAISES

Earth with thousand voices p. God 2973

everybody, p. nobody 8728
Flattery, mouth that p. 4049
himself spatters himself 9204
Humility is to be at rest when nobody p. 6010
only the devil who p. himself 9214
sings p. through tears 10628
Than spheres, or angel's p. be 8749

PRAISEWORTHY

Virtue so p. wicked practice it 11710

PRAISING

advantage of p. oneself 9238
demon even if sits in church p. Creator 9631
father in p. son extols himself 3926
God restores us to normal 2564
God takes away the blues 2564
old age p. times past 8186
speak ill of others, way of p. ourselves 2083
Try p. wife even if it does frighten her 7662

PRATTLE

polite p. exchanged on Sunday morning 4029
prayer not p, is warfare 8871

PRAY

And if for any wish thou dare not p. 8768
And will not let me p. 8966
armour is to shield us while we p. 8973
as if you were to die tomorrow 12023
as though everything depended on God 8892
as though no need to p. except in illness, sorrow 8788
as you can 9032
Be not afraid to p, to p. is right 8768
best to read weather forecast before p. for rain 8851
best way for child to learn to p. 8327
Beware of saying, "I haven't time to p." 9966
business of Christians to p. 8766
Christ standing beside him helping him to p. 8761
Christ to cling to me 9022
cost God everything to make it possible for us to p. 8773
courageous p. for strength 1937
Devil trembles when we p. 8985
devoutly, hammer stoutly 8894
Do not p. for easy lives 8780
Don't p. when you feel like it 8785
don't want to keep a prayer list but to p. 8820
Each time I p, I fervently plea 8786

Every time you p, new feeling and new meaning 8769
except we p. to God de profundis 9020
fervently 576
foolish if give up trying to p. 9013
for another, will be helped yourself 8838
for blessing upon daily rod 2858
for blessings on my friends, enemies 4069
for calmness to remember 8827
for courage to forget 8827
for powers equal to your task 8780
For simple liberty to p. 4118
for strength, patience 2091
for stronger backs 8896
for them that use us 5001
for wisdom yet 8827
Give them grace to p. for such as do them wrong 9104
God so close that when you p. 8801
God, keep us simple 10282
hand ceases to scatter, heart ceases to p. 4385
He that forgets to p. 12097
I do not p. for lighter load 929
I don't p. you be delivered from troubles 2091
I p. for strength, fortitude 1927
I p. for stronger back 929
If I can't p, I will not make-believe 9036
if thou canst with hope, but ever p. 8768
If you p. for bread and bring no basket 2947
ill-taught if look for results in earthlies when we p. 9014
in nothing you might not p. for blessing of God 11312
In suffering one learns to p. best 10857
in the darkness if there be no light 8768
in the evening p. 6928
is a terribly serious thing to p. 8850
Jesus retired to deserted places to p. 8860
just as sacred to laugh as to p. 6722
lazy man does not, will not, cannot p. 6776
let me never be afraid to p. for the impossible 9046
Lord, teach us how to p. 9108
love remains to me, I can p. 8135
Make a rule and p. to God 6660
may p. least when say most 9018
may p. most when say least 9018
Men learn to p. as they learn to love 8914
Might never p. 10042
more you p, the more will be revealed 8865
more, be more, serve more 9016

need to stop talking about prayer and p. 8825

night is given to take breath, to p. 6947

no use to p. for old days 8377

not for crutches, but for wings 8895

not for lighter burdens 8896

not well for man to p. cream, live skim milk 8856

obliged to p. if citizens of God's Kingdom 9015

Of thee three things I p. 9043

one hour before going to war 7650

only as well as we live 8885

Only he who is helpless can truly p. 8901

other side p, too, for victory 9021

Play it down, p. it up 2606

Psalms—How to p. 11925

rather than despair 1138

Some men p. whole system of divinity 8961

Some people greedy even when they p. 8963

sometimes ask when we p. that two and two not make four 9023

still I can p. so that God can hear 9025

That even when I kneel to p. 9075

that your loneliness may spur you 8897

Then p. to God to cast that wish away 8768

Those things we p. for 9676

three hours before getting married 7650

till everybody wishes they would stop 8961

time to p. is not when in tight spot 8993

to be stronger men 8780

To curse is to p. to the devil 9306

to God in the storm, but keep rowing 8898

To live more nearly as we p. 9040

To p. "in Jesus' name" 9004

to p. aright must understand what we are praying for 8824

To p. is to change 9005

To p. is to expose the mind to God 9006

To p. means to put our lives into conformity with God 8944

To p. when one ought to be working 9008

To work is to p. 7877

too busy to p, too busy to have power 9017

too busy to p. 10211

two hours before going to sea 7650

We do not p. to change God's will 9799

We do p. for mercy 7747

We p. for what we want 6251

well is better half of study 9007

what is prompting him to p. is God 8761

When angry, I can p. well 408

When cannot p. as you would 9032

When God inclines the heart to p. 9024

when I p, my heart is in my prayer 9036

When in pain difficult to p. coherently 10931

When you p, things remain the same 9033

When you p, you begin to be different 9033

who does not p. when sun shines 8809

who fails to p. cheats himself 8810

Why p? What can praying do 8899

will not know how to p. when clouds roll in 8809

will p. unanswerable prayers 3415

will they p. 1368

wish to p. a prayer in itself 8994

with as much earnestness 3816

work to climb a mountain to p. 8860

You stand tall when you kneel to p. 9038

you're in position to p. 9027

PRAYED

for all things that he might enjoy life 8806

for Lord to heal me 5610

for power that he might have praise of men 8806

for riches that he might be happy 8806

for strength that he might achieve 8806

for wealth that he might do greater things 8806

his tone was loud and angry 380

I p. for faith 3735

knew will of God before they p. 8890

like a dissatisfied guest 380

Of course I p. 8878

take all things as if p. for them 10926

wish God had not given me what I p. for 8879

PRAYER

a life attitude 8931

a mine never exhausted 8987

a sacrifice to God 8915

a scourge to Satan 8915

a shield to the soul 8915

a supernatural activity 8916

a treasure undiminished 8987

a way of being with God 8847

a way of lifting ourselves 8917

a wish turned Godward 8753

about alcohol 332

about failure 3615

about gossip 5146

about heaven 5661

about reading Bible 662

Adoration highest form of p. 8756

All Christian virtues locked up in word p. 8758

all spiritual results advanced by p. 8976

an all-efficient panoply 8987

an exercise to move ourselves God's way 8925

and helplessness inseparable 8901

answer to p. may let us in for more than we ask 8850

Anxious or troubled, when with us is p. 8867

anything that cramps my p. life 7036

armour is for the battle of p. 8973

as simple as child making wants known to parents 8937

at first he thought p. was talking 8751

avenue God uses to transform us 9005

backbone of revival 9743

balance between p, action 4160

battering heaven with storms of p. 8919

before Battle of Newbury 9076

before study 9062

beginning of uprising against disorder of world 9001

begins by talking to God 8902

better heart without words than words without heart 8844

Beware in p. of limiting God 8772

Beware of emphasis on what p. costs us 8773

bolt of the night 8943

breath of the newborn soul 8938

Breton fisherman's p. for protection 9110

business does not differ from prayer 8471

can be no Christian life without it 8938

can be selfish expression 12139

can do anything God can do 8903

cannot be seized by untrained hands 8914

catapults us onto frontier of spiritual life 8904

chances are p. activity will fizzle out 7725

changes him who prays 8907

changes people and people change things 8905

changes us, therein lies its glory, purpose 8855

Chippewa Indian Voyager's P. 9098

closet of p, more you visit, more you will return 9039

closet of p. will become your closest friend 9039

closet of p. will bring comfort 9039

clover folded quietly as if for p. 8000

cost what it may, this is my p.
8818
Crumbles in the breath of p. 8789
day hemmed with p. less likely to
unravel 8841
Deep in my soul the still. p. of
devotion 8778
deliverance from fear advanced by
p. 8976
demands energy 6776
difficulty in making a truly
heartfelt p. 8858
discipline of sanctified life, p.
2856
do not have to speak in religious
language 8770
do not want to keep a p. list, want
to pray 8820
does not change God 8907
does not deliver from situation
8927
does not enable us to do greater
work for God 8908
does not mean I bring God down
8909
does not need to be formal p.
8849
doesn't consist of thinking, but of
loving 8893
doesn't pull God down to us 8947
Don't expect a thousand-dollar
answer to a ten-cent p. 8783
doth teach us all to render deeds
of mercy 7747
draws us out of narrow limits
8906
each kindly deed a p. 7284
easiest, hardest of all things 8940
enables man to master situation
8927
ends by listening to God 8902
enemy in p. lack of knowledge of
what we are in Christ 8815
energy for work advanced by p.
8976
enlarges our horizon, person 8906
enlarges the heart 8910
Every Christian needs half hour of
p. each day 8790
fallacy to "test efficacy of p."
8750
fewer the words, the better the p.
8978
First P. in Congress 9102
for a son 8285
for body and mind 836
for cheerfulness 9092
for civil rights 1487
for compassion 9065
for courage 9090
for daily life 9099
for ecology 9117
for efficiency 9041
for faith 3779
for freedom of mind 9041
for guidance 9047
for help 4622
for justice 9104
for oneness in world 9093

for oneness with God 8748
for patience 8418
for peace 422
for rain 9118
for safety 9098
for serenity 9060
for the deaf 9094
for the handicapped 9085
for the past 9054
for those growing old 8145
for those in pain 9045
for those in space 11628
for three things 9043
for tolerance 9095
for tranquility 9111
1758
for transparency 6296
for understanding 9065
for unity 9093
Francis of Assisi spent 75 percent
of his time in p. 8793
from a living source within the will
8911
From housework to heights of p.
6113
futile to pretend p. indispensable
8852
getting a higher look 8917
girds human weakness with divine
strength 8912
gives God glory 1237
gives solitude real meaning 10562
God reads the p. unspoken in my
heart 7478
God will listen as you walk 8874
God's pychotherapy for his
children 8921
God's voice in response to mine
8932
God's way of answering the
Christian's p. 8804
gospel cannot live, fight, conquer
without p. 9015
grateful thought to heaven most
perfect p. 8755
greater than man-controlled
powers 8991
gymnasium of the soul 8941
harmful to think p. something to
do during a free hour 10211
heaven unruffled by storm 8987
hell, p. ineffectual 5700
Helplessness is your best p. 8901
highest energy of which the mind
is capable 8900
highest use to which speech can
be put 8942
his p. is answered 9034
hour worrying on our knees is not
p. 9009
I would only breathe a p. 1509
identifying oneself with the divine
will 8922
If beat devil in p, can beat him
anywhere 8837
If devil can beat you in p, can beat
you anywhere 8837
if did not spend hours each day in
p. 8816

if no p. life, useless to make child
say prayers 8348
immediate person makes demands
in his p. 8981
impossible to overstate need for p.
3875
In p. one relates his life to life of
humanity 8917
In p. one sees life as God sees it
8917
In p. we descend with mind into
the heart 10562
In voiceless p. 10969
is a greater work for God 8908
is a ladder on which thoughts
mount to God 8913
is a luxury 10211
is a rare gift 8914
is a sort of understanding 8748
is an education 8769
is becoming 8928
is dialogue 8932
is exhaling spirit of man 8920
is inhaling spirit of God 8920
is laying hold of God's highest
willingness 8933
is listening 8751
is listening, seeing, feeling 8923
is love's tender dialogue 8926
is more than words 8923
is not evasion 8819
is not flight 8927
is not getting 8928
is not monologue 8932
is not overcoming God's reluctance
8933
Is not p. peace, silence, strength
8847
is not to hear oneself speak 8935
is power 8927
is putting oneself under God's
influence 8936
is spiritual character 8914
is the battle 8973
is the burden of a sigh 8939
is the product of faith 8914
is the product of holiness 8914
is the soul's sincere desire 8948
is to arrive at silence and continue
being silent 8935
is to wait till one hears God speak
8935
is voice of man to God 9704
is weakness leaning on
omnipotence 8949
is when person praying is one
who hears 8980
its chief ingredients 8914
Jesus always returned to his
ultimate p. 6384
Jesus wrote no book, yet his
words and p. 6394
journeymen cannot execute work
of p. 8914
key of the morning 8943
Knight's P. inscribed in Chester
Cathedral 9088
large enough for a wish, large
enough for a p. 8763

learned in the closet 8930
leave my p. to him alone 8825
Let one unceasing, earnest p. 8863
lifted out of disease by p. 8764
lifted out of melancholy by p. 8764
limited only by omnipotence of God 8940
link between man and God 8944
Lord's Prayer every p. included 7156
Lord's Prayer most fearful p. in world 8828
Lord, hear our p. for those growing old 8145
Loving, like p, is a power as well as process 7277
Make sickness itself a p. 6087
man gets along very well without it 8852
man without p. like tree without roots 8752
mastery over self advanced by p. 8976
means I am raised up into God 8909
means whereby we become strong to meet evil 8977
means whereby we learn to do without good things of earth 8977
meet difficulties, dangers with p. 2630
mistake to think time of p. different from any other time 8881
More things wrought by p. 8869
most blessed result would be 8983
most important thing in my life 8945
mother of a thousand blessings 8987
moves the arm which moves the world 8950
Music child of p. 7906
must go to God simply for himself 8958
My p. shall be for others 9075
need for p. in fabric of family life 3875
need to stop talking about p. and pray 8825
neglect of p. guarantee not victors 8872
Never try to forecast way God is going to answer p. 8873
No p. of adoration higher than "I love you, God" 8876
not a labor-saving device 8803
not a lazy substitute for work 8924
not a popular, ready gift 8914
not a shortcut to skill, knowledge 8924
not an argument with God 8925
not an occasional impulse 8931
not artful monologue 8926
not as means whereby to obtain good things of earth 8977

not holy chewing gum 8754
not just informing God of our needs 8929
not learned in a classroom 8930
not means whereby we escape evil 8977
not only p. that gives God glory 12013
not prattle, is warfare 8871
not something we do at specific time 8934
not that p. changes God 8855
not the fruit of natural talents 8914
not to persuade God to move our way 8925
not what disciple says in public p. 2830
Nurture love with a smile and a p. 7289
of acceptance for cross 2099
of agnostic 318
of benediction 619
620
of commitment 9084
of confession 9087
of feeblest saint a terror to Satan 8988
of selfishness 10075
of St. Francis of Assisi 9086
of surrender 9084
of thanks 9053
of thanks for eternity 3277
of thanks for life 11149
of thanks for little things 11148
of thanks for silence 10247
of thanks for tears 1512
of thanksgiving 11174
of the saints 8840
on facing death 9048
on the scaffold 2450
One hour of justice worth hundred of p. 6617
only appreciated when spend time in it 8865
only password is p. 8771
opens to us God's mercies, blessings 8846
Our p. and God's mercy like two buckets in well 8884
Perfect p, unaware he is praying 8888
power of service correspond to life of p. 10192
powers of darkness paralyzed by p. 8988
Praise the best auxiliary to p. 8735
preceding all prayers 8989
provides power, poise, peace, purpose 8951
pulls us up to God 8947
recreation as proper as p. 6837
refreshes, restores, renews minds 8857
Remember privilege of p. 9270
renunciation of one's own will 8922

requires more of heart than tongue 8952
results lie outside human possibilities 8940
rope that pulls God, man together 8947
Satan tries to keep minds fussy till cannot think in p. 8988
see Jesus spending nights in p. 8860
Self can turn powerful p. into weak one 10080
serious thing is that p. may be answered 8850
serves as an edge, border 8953
Service and p. can never be separated 10211
Seven days without p. makes one weak 8960
shuts us up under God's protection 8846
silence, listening, p, truth go together 10248
simplest and sublimest 8940
simply being in presence of God 8958
Sioux Indian p. 9065
sky unobscured by clouds 8987
so much to do shall spend three hours in p. 12029
Some expect thousand-dollar answer to one-minute p. 8963
Some men spin out a long p. 8961
Some people preach, other exhort 8961
something we do all the time 8934
Sometimes God delays answer to our p. 8924
Sorrow more alert to open door than Joy 8996
soul's hunger for p. 4643
source of energy 8954
Speak as naturally, as easily as to a friend 8770
steering wheel or spare tire 8848
substituted psychology for p. 5808
Take p. out of the world 8967
Talk to him in p. of all your wants 8968
tapping infinite resources of God 8991
tears shed there bring cleansing 9039
Tell him whatever is on your mind 8770
temptation of separating service from p. 10211
the fountain 8987
The path of p. thyself hast trod 9108
the potency of p. 8987
the pulse of life 8946
the root 8987
this I consider to be p. 8829
this I know God answers p. 8825
through p. to place ourselves in attitude to be helped 9010

saint performs havoc among forces of darkness 9014
sin to work when one ought to be p. 9008
so positive 8890
spectacle of a nation p. 8991
to God to give victory 9021
to keep us plugging along 8871
to stop p. and trust 9009
Why when we talk to God, we're p. 9035

PRAYS
Christian is more music when he p. 8749
Faith p. him to clasp hand closely 3714
for strength without much thought 8850
greatest saint not he who p. most 9790
much by night, face fair by day 8808
Pharisee p. publicly, preys privately 6047
Prayer changes him who p. 8907
who labors as he p. 8811
who p. as he ought 8812
will endeavor to live as he p. 8812
wise man in storm p. to God 3997
wise man p. for deliverance from fear 3997
wise man p. not for safety from danger 3997 3490

PREACH
Angels cannot p. the gospel 3296
better sermon with life than lips 3462
can p. sociology, psychology, or other ology 9172
devil delights in tormenting when we p. Christ 2661
Jesus came that there might be a gospel to p. 5111
less and practice more 9281
nothing down but the devil 9156
nothing up but Christ 9156
only you and I can p. 3296
people into despair 9838
practice of presence of God 4873
Sermon on the Mount took only eighteen minutes to p. 9154
to love those to whom we p. another thing 9166
To love to p. one thing 9166
we p. as if men conscious dying sinners 3338
When angry, I can p. well 408
When I p. I regard neither doctors nor magistrates 9170
whether you p. in Westminster Abbey 3845

PREACHED
care not what is p. in pulpit 12151
description of what happens when gospel p. 5105
greatest sermon ever p. 10102
Holy Spirit imparts efficacy to Word p. 5794

not going to heaven because I've p. to crowds 5653
sermon p. as exhibition of talent 7867
where cross p. disarming of powers 2100

PREACHER
a live coal to kindle church 9128
a shepherd 9127
a soldier 9127
agility of a greyhound 9161
as many lives as a cat 9161
be able to bite, fight 9127
cast-iron stomach 9125
energy of a father 9144
exuberant affection of a mother 9144
Great sermons lead people to praise p. 10097
heart of a lion 9161
industry of an ant 9161
leads men from what they want to what they need 9126
life-giving p. man of God 9160
like to see p. act as if fighting bees 9141
Live while you live the sacred p. cries 8600
must defend 9127
must have teeth in his mouth 9127
must nourish 9127
must teach 9127
never a word from his soul 9165
New Testament p. has to be surgical 9124
patience of a donkey 9161
patience of Job 9125
preached from his ears and memory 9165
skin of a hippopotamus 9161
strength of Samson 9125
tact of a diplomat 9125
test of p. "I will do something" 9162
test of p. not "What a lovely sermon" 9162
unreasonable for p. to please all 9151
Were I a p. 4873
When people sleep in church, p. should wake up 9171
wisdom of an elephant 9161
wisdom of Solomon 9125
zeal of a friend 9144

PREACHERS
Some p. don't believe in revivals 9750
speak of things real as if imaginary 9130
who desire nothing but God 9136
who fear nothing but sin 9136

PREACHES
Christian p. some kind of sermon 1245
from villas to slums about mansions 6065
None p. better than ant 3447

not what disciple p. from pulpit 2830
well who lives well 9138
When fox p, look to geese 2479

PREACHING
Crucified p. can come only from crucified man 9160
good example, tallest p. 546
Good p. leads people to praise Savior 10097
like silent church better than p. 1394
no such thing as p. patience into people 8422
Only crucified p. can give life 9160
ounce of help better than pound of p. 3146
Paul's p. ended in either a riot or revival 9155
strengthened by p. 1444
thirty minutes to raise the dead 9157
world dying not for want of good p. 9163

PREACHMENT
ounce of performance worth more than pound of p. 9131

PRECEDE
Intelligence must never p. faith 6327
reason ought to follow, not p, faith 9411

PRECEDED
mosquito p. man in divine order of creation 9209
word *honesty* now p. by *old-fashioned* 5863

PRECEDES
faith p. understanding, does not follow 3743
Life a predicament that p. death 6951

PRECEPT
no moral p. not inconvenient 7840

PRECEPTS
Man led more by patterns than p. 3442
simple it will be his p. to fulfill 10047

PRECIOUS
blood of Christ p. 2141
Each more p. than all 6200
God knows me, a p. possession 11179
God's unspeakable gift 1372
Human freedom p. thing 9463
Is most p. dew he will on us bestow 2142
moment of my death most p. 2373
most p. things God finds in us 10666
nothing more p. than person 2343
Sorrow like p. treasure 10615
Suffering too p. to be shared 10895

time so p. God deals it out second by second 11293

to esteem that which is most p. unto thee 9063

treating badly p. thing God has made 9923

trial of faith p. 3751

Virtue like p. odors 11707

PRECIOUSNESS
Gold suggest p. of heaven 5631

PRECIPICE
In front a p, behind a wolf 2733

who would not fall off p. 11068

PRECISE
at p. moment God will reach for you 5430

PRECISELY
an existence 3483

crave specific rules to know p. how to behave 6810

hope vaguely, dread p. 5949

PRECONCEIVED
teaching of Christ splits to atoms every p. notion 6486

PREDATORY
disappeared if within reach of p. human hands 3202

Man is p. 10068

PREDESTINATION
university of election and p. 11192

PREDESTINES
devil p. every man to be damned 9175

God p. every man to be saved 9175

PREDETERMINED
in way other than p. by God 11082

PREDICAMENT
Life a p. that precedes death 6951

Lord understood the human p. 6519

PREDICTABLE
narrow ranks of p. personalities 4025

space is p. 11650

Vision outside realm of p. 11736

PREDOMINATES
Right p, nothing prevails against it 6621

Where power p, love is lacking 7343

PREDOMINATING
Life, sniffles p. 6969

PREEMPTORINESS
Conscience monarch in its p. 1673

PREEXISTED
in the sight of God

PREFER
comfortable vice to virtue that bores 3941

greatest sin to p. life to honor 6883

Jesus to Amos or Caiaphas 7099

may not p. world in which sorrow so close to joy 7081

Men p. prosperous error to afflicted truth 3261

own friends who share life-style 5957

tell God you p. vilest amusements 8830

to be king of mountain or child of God? 5308

trivial company to being alone 10575

PREFERABLE
no company p. to bad 4286

to have world against thee than Jesus offended 8525

PREFERENCES
Refusing to set aside trivial p. 7793

PREFERS
Man p. to believe what he p. to be true 595

PREFIGURED
am someone p. 11124

PREJUDICE
being down on something you're not up on 9183

disease of the soul 6085

God cannot work with p. 4824

greatest enemy of truth is p. 11535

Hypocrisy, p. with a halo 6052

proclaim brotherhood, and harbor p. 6068

Race p. denial of God 1490

the child of ignorance 9184

this pretension itself a p. 9181

willing to use minds without p. 4124

PREJUDICES
best to rearrange p. 11228

Christian thinker challenges p. 11239

creatures bustling with p. 9518

Education, higher grade of p. 2998

flattered himself on being a man without p. 9181

Jesus throws down dividing p. 913

people think they are thinking when rearranging p. 9178

PREMISE
human politics based on p. society must be changed 10528

PREMIUM
obedience is p. we pay 8096

PREOCCUPATION
called to an everlasting p. of God 7551

PREOCCUPIED
God has p. rarest human spirits 7547

with what we are saved from 9826

PREOCCUPIES
Fear p. death 2363

PREORDAINED
Whatever befalls was p. from eternity 2623

PREPARATION
Education not p. for life 3001

Every experience p. for future 3515

Great trials p. for great duties 2725

Life is the p. 6978

Marriage requires long, serious p. 7641

PREPARATIVE
see earth but school p. 6109

PREPARE
failures tests to p. us 3593

For all your days p. 9655

for what no one knows yet 3035

Jehovah, sharpen and p. 163

plan, proceed, pursue 80

prayerfully, proceed positively 80

Some clergy p. sermons, others p. themselves 10104

The Lord my pasture shall p. 9350

the way! A God, a God appears 6138

yourself for battle 9861

PREPARED
am someone p. 11124

can change any time he is p. 3596

Chance does nothing not p. beforehand 4928

faith must be p. to be martyr, fool 3642

for a rough landing 373

for what sanctification will do 9831

good leader p. to deny himself much 6793

Heaven is place p. for those p. for it 5643

highest service may be p. for in humblest surroundings 10190

if not p. to fight in spiritual realm 8818

messenger more important than p. message 9129

supernaturally p. to be supernaturally performed 10206

Whether my Maker p. for me another matter 2302

PREPARES
Skepticism p. way for faith 2953

PREPARING
God is p. his heroes 9174

God p. you as his chosen arrow 5430

In the night God is p. thy song 10600

would spend two years studying, p. 6687

PRE-PEACE
a p. generation 9914

PREREQUISITE
far-reaching reformation of church p. 1439

Humility necessary p. for grace 6007

PREROGATIVE
this is love's p, to give, and give, and give 7218

PRESBYTERIAN
not a P. in heaven 5671

PRESCRIBES
God feels pulse, p. medicine 4449

PRESCRIPTION
for happier, healthier life 5615

PRESCRIPTIONS
Christ's p. never out of balance 6429

PRESENCE
admitting God's p. 5395

All men equal in p. of death 3226

And all the church with his p. glowed 2638

another year of proving thy p. all the days 8077

call is the p. 5781

Christ brings his p. 2120

Conscience God's p. in man 1670

desert means p. of God 10565

dirt sign of God's p. 3609

Father, in my mysterious p. kneeling 9050

felt God's p. on moon more than on earth 11630

Few delights equal p. of one we trust 4184

friend warms by his p. 4179

God, the sky his p. snares 4505

His p. shall my wants supply 9350

how in p. of Lord anyone could think about himself 4853

I need thy p. every passing hour 5225

if God deny gracious p, we fall into sin 4865

if God deny merciful p, we fall into hell 4865

If he deny powerful p, we fall into nothing 4865

In p. of hope, faith is born 5937

invaded to depths of one's being by God's p. 7488

Jesus came to fill suffering with his p. 10867

Joy most infallible sign of p. of God 6548

life and death one in p. of the Lord 3649

may ignore but can nowhere evade p. of God 4871

may insulate ourselves from God's p. 4864

no human condition which divine p. does not penetrate 6277

of Christ brings us his power 11

of God a fact of life 4864

of God's glory is in heaven 4865

of God's grace with his people 4865

of God's justice in hell 4865

of God's power on earth 4865

of Lord is revealing 9741

of two witnesses: God and our conscience 4872

prayer simply being in the p. of God 8958

preach practice of p. of God 4873

silence in awesome p. of God 12112

streets sacred, God's p. there 4866

what a change one hour spent in thy p. will make 8867

When Christ's p. becomes guide 5396

When God makes p. felt through us 4874

when the cloud of God's p. moved 10124

Without thy p, wealth are bags of cares 4877

worshiper aware of no p. 1399

PRESENT
Act—act in the living p. 4331

already disappearing 982

always find God p. 4845

as we experience it 8387

Cause us to live at p. 9120

dogmas of past inadequate to p. 976

Every man's life lies within p. 8374

Faith makes discords of p. the harmonies of future 3704

fled ere we could touch it 11389

future as p. expectation 8387

future has habit of suddenly becoming 4323

future purchased by p. 4326

God a p. help or not much help at all 4701

God as p. as the air 4844

God gives us light we need for p. 5397

God p. in deepest, most central part of soul 4868

God's mercy available in p. situation 4815

gone in instant of becoming 11389

has melted in our grasp 11389

impatience against God to be troubled with p. 12066

In Christ move into meaningful p. 8364

In eternity everything p. in one fresh-springing now 11316

In poverty of solitude, all riches p. 10542

invoked or not, God will be p. 4875

is all of which man is master 8384

is period when future pauses 8386

love looks to the p. 8376

make p. better than past 8377

Man spends life complaining of p. 8380

mind the p. 935

mistake that we do not concentrate on p. day 8381

My part is to improve the p. moment 10145

notice dirt God is most p. 3609

Oft the cloud which wraps the p. hour 10879

old age blaming the p. 8186

only thing that has no end 11378

past as p. memory 8387

seize the pleasures of the p. day 8600

seldom the p. that is unbearable 5354

sin, two witnesses p. to observe 10418

Sorrows remembered sweeten p. joy 10624

takes prophets to interpret the p. 9334

the p, the p. is all thou hast 11379

things p. seem worst 8382

Though God be everywhere p. 4868

Time a threefold p. 8387

to find Holy Spirit p. with power 5786

Trust p. to his love 5457

waits only the completion of p. task 9658

We ask God to come when he is already p. 8843

when faith is p. God works through anyone 3723

When Jesus is p, all is good 6512

When worry is p. 12081

Whenever two people meet really six people p. 7443

Where except in p. can eternal be met 11353

Where is it, this p. 11389

whether to answer p. or not guilty 5198

who neglects p. moment 11300

Wisely improve the p. 8378

worst time is always the p. 11387

PRESERVATION
God has ordained state for p. of life 10506

Job felt hand of p. too 4556

of epics and tragedies in world 3332

PRESERVE
dispense wealth best way to p. it 11870

God's method to p. by destroying 4556

peace in midst of bitterest pain 8453

smiles, kindness win, p. the heart 6656

Thou dost p. the stars from wrong 4598

us from despondency 9092

PRESERVED
in state of perpetual puerility 5584
To yield is to be p. whole 7071

PRESERVERS
Cheerfulness, contentment famous
p. of looks 1087

PRESERVES
church, like salt, p. 1427
Prayer p. life from unravelling
8953

PRESERVING
God always p. beauty of his order
4644
good consists in p. life 5044

PRESIDENT
no p. holds key to as much power
11841
of today postage stamp tomorrow
979

PRESIDING
God is above, p. 4841

PRESS
of external situation 6785

PRESSED
Tho' p. by every foe 3768
though p. love is not straitened
7283
to conform or compete 1634

PRESSING
Love p. round us like air 4785

PRESSURE
by inward p. of the Holy Spirit
6785
can feel p. of evil forces 3400
circumstances of great p, trial,
much strength 7486
coward seeks release from p. 1937
doesn't matter how great the p.
185
if p. taken out of your life 9977
learning persists after p. for grades
3031
matters where the p. lies 185
matters whether p. comes between
you and God 185
presses you nearer God's heart
185
putting p. back into God's hand
11466
responsible for great creative
efforts 1712
stronger than the p. without 78
when p. within is stronger 78

PRESUME
not p. to separate what God has
united 6681
only one death-bed repentance
recorded that none should p.
9602

PRESUMPTUOUS
error is more p. 3258

PRESUPPOSES
longing for God p. his existence
4606

PRETENCE
humility makes no p. of being
humble 6041

PRETENCES
built up not to hide evil but
emptiness 3395

PRETEND
Christ never suggest p. people
faultless 9789
Do not p. to emotions you do not
feel 8770
futile to p. prayer indispensable
8852
not to p. we love everything 5890
phony and hypocritical 5890

PRETENDED
conceal sadness under p. gaiety
10587

PRETENDING
devil p. to defend truth 11533
silly p. we are all brothers 912

PRETENDS
bad man worse when p. to be saint
6045
devil p. to defend truth 2689

PRETENSE
acknowledge enemies without p.
5890
harasses a ruined man 8679
not poverty so much as p. 8679
of being holy until stand in light
9741

PRETENSES
of politeness, delicacy, decency
4115

PRETENSION
this p. itself a prejudice 9181

PRETENSIONS
without high p. to oppressive
greatness 4204

PREVAIL
if justice, mercy p. in own
common life 6286
no power to p. 36
Opinions if founded in truth will
p. 8199
When good people cease
vigilance, evil men p. 7991

PREVAILING
Perseverance more p. than violence
8552

PREVAILS
I believe the will of God p. 5411
Renew the courage that p. 1933
Right predominates, nothing p.
against it 6621

PREVENT
Is God unable to p. suffering
10841
noise p. us from listening to God
8800
One moment of patience may p.
disaster 8405

parents p. children learning lessons
8320
responsibility is to p. evil thoughts
from settling 11110
stumble may p. a fall 3583
that person from finding him
3340
to p. our solving difficulties of
own being 5384

PREVENTED
from developing initiative 8337
no one is p. from being an
individual 6209

PREVENTING
beg Holy Spirit to fill us while p.
him by our doubts 8843
selfishness, p. transformation into
divine love 10067

PREVENTS
himself by becoming one of the
masses 6209
Silence p. being suffocated by
world 10562

PREVIOUS
God is always p. 7461

PREY
To believe God made lower
creatures for p. 6280

PREYS
Pharisee prays publicly, p.
privately 6047

PRICE
and glory of mortal's life 7035
at p. of repudiation evil could be
abolished 4149
Cheerfulness costs nothing, yet is
beyond p. 5612
cynic knows p. of everything 2189
few want to pay p. of achievement
4731
guileless mind worth any p. 5865
Loneliness great p. to pay for
independence 7135
No p. is set on lavish summer
2641
one must pay the p. 9759
One's life heavy p. to pay 3487
paid high p. to find that evil is evil
3416
The market p, they said 3483
war in universe p. worth paying
4132
war, always the people who pay
full p. 11772
would pay any p. to say "All will
be saved" 9799

PRICELESS
ability to keep mouth shut p. 1876
Children, p. possession 1115
mosaic in design of God's universe
4005
Quality workmanship p. 3116
Stumblers who get up p. 3618
world so rich in delusions truth is
p. 11523

PRICETAGS
for people to read each other by
10519

PRICKED
no gathering the rose without
being p. 94

PRICKLES
tormenting himself with own p.
9630

PRIDE
a form of selfishness 9227
And by greed and p. the sky is torn
6155
and laziness keys of poverty 8691
and weakness are Siamese twins
9226
at the bottom of all great mistakes
9228
beginning of p. was in heaven
9218
But take away our p. 9224
capture inner stronghold of p.
10043
changed angels into devils 6020
Charity that proclaims deeds is p.
1081
chastening in hour of p. 957
child of devil 2680
church, out of humiliated p. 1401
complete anti-God state of mind
9240
confirmed p. when you think you
are humble 9259
content against giants of passion,
p. 9233
continuance of p. is on earth 9218
core of p. is self-rejection 9239
creatures motivated by p. 9518
Criticism wounds man's p. 2055
Criticism's mother 2050
Denying we can accomplish God's
work is worse kind of p. 9199
Divinity, so deep p. drowned in
infinity 4745
don't swell with p, may look
overtaxed 9258
eats the possibility of love,
contentment 9240
end of p. is in hell 9218
enemy to peace 8435
essential vice is p. 9240
he that is low need fear no p.
2881
He that is low, no p. 6001
history of p. in three chapters
9218
history shows how unprofitable p.
is 9218
If full of p. no room for Spirit of
God 5783
if take p. in greats of world 3861
Ignorance and power and p. a
deadly mixture 9212
in darkness secure from p. 2547
Ingratitude daughter of p. 6252
Insolence p. when mask pulled off
2917
is spiritual cancer 9229

is taking less than you need 4353
is the cold mountain peak 6026
Jealousy is foolish child of p. 6340
keeps them in trouble 9237
leads to every other vice 9240
legalism arouses p. 6823
most satanic type of p. 6038
mounts the wall to hurry to that
fatal fall 9231
nothing but lying 6009
of dying rich raises loudest laugh
in hell 9246
Once, in my p. 4199
person who thinks he's a human
dynamo 118
pleasure of p. like pleasure of
scratching 9245
power likely coupled with p,
cruelty 8705
proud hate p.—in others 9247
sacrifice of praise requires trading
in p. 8724
shield us from vainglory 187
sickness delivered thee from p.
1776
sin may spell p. but is some form
of "me" 9916
sin that shocks God 10397
slays thanksgiving 5258
smiles betray p. 10500
soul weakened by virus of p.
10294
spiritual p, most deadly form sin
can take 9254
spiritual p. beginning of
degeneration 9234
that apes humility 9192
the ground in which all other sins
grow 9230
the parent from which all other
sins come 9230
through p. devil became the devil
9240
Too much humility is p. 9255
treat him as any other great man
9201
unseasonable, unfitting 9231
wants infused into us by p. 2861
wear tinsel crown with p. of
Caesar 2821

PRIEST
Christ a P. to make atonement
6370
Conscience p. in its blessings 1673
No p. can stand between God and
man 7505

PRIMARILY
likeness to God p. resides in
freedom 4149

PRIME
devil man in p. of life 2651

PRIMEVAL
dream opens into p. cosmic night
2971

PRIMITIVE
science measured against reality p.
9867

PRIMROSE
God gave p. its rough leaves 4618

PRINCE
Christ a P. to rule 6370
dear to God is peasant as p. 3225
pauper can give like a p. 4388
When you are a p, and I am a p.
10215

PRINCE OF PEACE
ministry of church ceased while
quarrel over P. 9361

PRINCES
among us forget themselves, serve
mankind 10193
and lords but breath of kings
5885

PRINCES'
palaces; they that enter there 5649

PRINCIPAL
part of faith, patience 3792
until p. of equality is recognized
3230

PRINCIPLE
Adversity is trial of p. 145
clear in p. and aim 4974
deepest p. in human nature 3141
evil is a p. of fragmentariness
5023
Good is p. of totality 5023
Grace a p. inherent in divine
nature 4652
Hope is a vigorous p. 5917
In matters of p. stand like rock
6308
Life is wrestling with p. of evil
6947
Many agree with God in p, not
practice 1336
No great p. ever triumphed but
through evil 5030
of hell is, "I am my own" 5699
So act that p. of action 3453
When you say you agree in p.
2915

PRINCIPLES
allegiance to one set of p. and live
by another 6068
are for the ages 1009
are illuminators, not directors
6816
cannot have Christian p. without
Christ 1355
Character formed as we cherish p.
1000
Democracy attempt to apply Bible
p. to society 2523
Everything arranged by definite p.
4948
family, where p. are hammered,
honed 3863
Glory built on selfish p. is shame,
guilt 10054
If one certain p. are right 6306
if we imbue men with high p.
6796
life on proper basic p. 159

Nowhere in Scripture are God's p.
replaced 7828
of Bible groundwork of human
freedom 5965
of Christianity will change world
1196
protection against cowardice 1951
Skepticism has not established p.
5723
thoughtful mind sees p. of nation
7982
Wisdom, application of spiritual p.
11911
without p. of Christ rearing
pagans 8308

PRINT
big p. giveth, small p. taketh away
9328
read small p. of man's soul 739

PRIORITIES
future depends on p. today 4325
live by godly p. 3901
live by same p. Jesus had 3313
outward imperfections reminder
of God's p. 1033

PRIORITY
Your destruction is Satan's highest
p. 9855

PRISON
Bible smuggled into p. cells 726
death passage out of p. into palace
2325
ego will become a p. 9196
Jesus Christ came into my p. cell
6423
look out from time, our p. 6384
my flesh is a p. 3482
need to leave p. of his aloneness
7143
no right to open door of p. and
run away 10941
person free even within p. walls
4112
Satan's friendship reaches to p.
door 2665
Self the only p. that can bind soul
9944
some never free outside p. 4112
to make acorn burst forth from its
p. walls 6095
tomb appears as p, but is release
for soul 2350
while men go to p, I'll fight 3342
without forgiveness becomes p.
4093

PRISON HOUSE
Shades of the p. begin to close
12164
world not a p. but a kindergarten
7530

PRISONER
himself, the p. at the bar 1684
Man p. who has no right to open
door 10941

PRISONERS
abused as children 32

slaves to p. of security 9016
PRISON-WORLD
Bible, window in this p. 711
PRISONS
love would sweep away p. 7349
PRIVATE
Chide friend in p. 4182
do not like strangers to intrude
upon p. lives 5957
memory is p. literature 7731
opinion is weak 8200
worth to God in public is what I
am in p. 6315

PRIVATELY
Pharisee prays publicly, preys p.
6047
Reprove friend p. 2855
Wisdom comes p. from God
11911

PRIVATION
evil is p. 3370

PRIVILEGE
Fine dying is a man's p. 2336
giving another p. of sharing 4277
highest p. to share another's pain
4276
misused, creation to punish
humanity 3191
Motherhood greatest p. of life
7849
sex an enormous p. 10235
Why wish for the p. of living life
again 7091

PRIVILEGED
no provision for p. class in
Christianity 1234
Strength the lot of a few p. men
8557

PRIVILEGES
clash with own p. 4124
not filled living beneath our p.
5778
same p. in God's world they have
9988
to appreciate our p. 9085

PRIZE
a few strain muscles to carry off a
p. 7018
best know how to p. friends 4286

PRIZES
never wish for p. of life 10875

PROBABILITY
that we fail in struggle should not
deter 3625
truth on persecuted side 8532

PROBES
God p. the core, tests the root
7862

PROBLEM
an opportunity to prove God
9283
Each p. a God-appointed
instructor 2720

Every solution of a p. is a new p.
9284
God's p. is that God loves 4823
God's p. not that God not able
4823
guilt more tragic than p. 2921
If happiness depends on
somebody, you have p. 5536
in ability to hear 2931
is shipwrecked soul in world 7396
is to think of it again 2001
Love decision to make your p. my
p. 7240
Man is the greatest p. 7408
no p. can't face if Jesus to
strengthen 11126
No p. ever as dark when you have
a friend 4196
No p. too big for God 9288
not hostility to church 1446
not in God's silence 2931
not why some people suffer 10909
of evil not solved by multiplication
3387
of meaning of things 6086
of restoring beauty is redemption
of soul 10668
philosopher, p. for every solution
8589
regarding content of love 7837
right to kill another to solve p. 20
Trying to settle p. with oratory
9290
why some people do not suffer
10909
with "ism" 9952
you bury p. alive 9291

PROBLEMS
accept everything, even p, with joy
5261
are the cutting edge 202
are the delight of life 9286
because of p. we grow 202
children more trouble solving
parent's p. 3883
Christians, usual p. common to
men 1296
create courage and wisdom 202
Discipline tools to solve life's p.
9967
doctrine key to world's p. 11213
faith solves p. by pointing to lamb
of God 3784
find God in p. already solved
7562
God brings p. so we can mature
2844
Happiness not a question of not
having p. 5521
Hope regards p. as opportunities
5928
how you look at them 507
human p. gray areas 1582
Human p. never greater than
divine solutions 9285
in meeting, solving p. life has
meaning 2736
It isn't your p. 507

Jesus talked about p. money causes man 7804

Justice is love working out p. 6612

live with God to solve p. 9292

memorizing Scripture help in p. of life 747

must live with people to know their p. 9292

opportunities come disguised as p. 2752

opportunities in work clothes 2726

Parents have trouble solving children's p. 3883

philosophy complicated method of avoiding important p. 8597

profoundest p. human mind can entertain 3784

Progress the mother of p. 9314

right attitude, not a failure 521

Satan uses p. of life to slander God's character 9859

societal p. solved one person at a time 3901

solve p. by emotions, authority 11227

teachings of Christ can solve world's p. 6487

that are bothering you 507

theological p. are the soul's mumps 11202

would not rob a man of his p. 9286

PROCEED

from one guilty deed haunting thoughts p. 5476

plan, prepare, pursue 80

positively, pursue persistently 80

PROCEEDS

error p. in wrong direction 3258

No wickedness p. on reason 11890

PROCESS

Agape love concern without desire to enjoy p. 7158

Christian always in p. of becoming 1250

constant p. of adjusting public image 1882

Creation a silent p. 1956

deep inner work, p. will be secret 10706

Democracy p. where people choose man who will get blame 5173

developing faith gradual p. 5738

Don't lose heart in p. 2849

Education a social p. 3001

in p. of solving problems life has meaning 2736

involved in redirecting our lives painful 5449

knowing God gradual p. 5738

Knowledge p. of piling up facts 11927

larger p. of maturing than can see 10884

Life one long p. of getting tired 6974

Loving, a power as well as a p. 7277

making of music often slow p. in life 7915

never ends until we die 1148

not conscious, intellectual p. 1126

of conversion long, arduous 1897

product of p. is maturity 1105

Repentance an ongoing p. 9589

spiritual p. lasts all through life 10006

without being corrupted by p. necessary 6623

PROCESSES

home where p. of character molding carried on 5850

PROCESSION

Death beginning of p. down eternity 2245

If cannot find God in the p. of life 4856

my rightful place in the great p. of humanity 9074

PROCLAIM

brotherhood and harbor prejudice 6068

liberty throughout all inhabitants 4141

The rocks p. th' approaching Deity 6138

thy righteousness 4592

virtues of friend on housetop 4183

PROCLAIMED

God's love p. with each sunrise 4759

PROCLAIMING

will not have to go up, down earth p. love 4767

PROCLAIMS

boasts of own knowledge p. ignorance 6682

world by existence p. God 1953

PROCLAMATION

church for p. of the gospel 10506

Sunday continual p. of message of Easter 10955

Thanksgiving p. 1863

PROCLIVITY

By p. we all quote 9379

PROCRASTINATION

art of keeping up with yesterday 9299

clutters up our lives 9300

thief of time 9300

without p, love 7348

PROCREATION

Sex for p. marvelous thing 10229

PRODIGAL

at some time father of unreturned p. 8345

PRODIGAL SON

could still be saved 3167

PRODIGALS

When p. return, great things are done 9607

PRODIGY

what a p. is man 7439

PRODUCE

could p. same effect by saying, sins be forgiven 5485

earth can p. nothing unless fertilized by sun 5207

greed, its one object is to p, consume 5327

holy life will p. deepest impression 5737

nothing in money's nature to p. happiness 7814

thinking can never p. optimism 8587

PRODUCED

Education p. population able to read 2997

Education p. population unable to distinguish 2997

effects beyond reach of orator or poet 6449

PRODUCES

God never p. hysterics 9912

Like p. like 5211

Love p. flowering of personality 7268

not love that p. jealousy 7200

not necessity but abundance p. greed 5318

peril p. steadfastness 952

Rejection p. the pearl 204

root that p. nothing is dead 3699

PRODUCING

activities faster than faith 1449

evil soul p. holy witness 5011

no right to consume happiness without p. it 5569

than to consume wealth without p. it 5569

PRODUCT

Self-centeredness p. of pain 6229

You aren't an assembly-line p. 10004

PRODUCTION

God's aim is p. of saints 5757

of epics and tragedies in world 3332

PRODUCTIVE

Darkness more p. than light 2541

ultrabusy schedule not mark of p. life 9533

work must include play 12022

PRODUCTIVITY

in old age 8128

Music used to ridicule p. 7910

PRODUCTS

moving toward world of throwaway p. 10524

PROFANITY
fixes attention on words rather than thoughts 9305

PROFESS
devil willing for person to p. Christianity 2686

PROFESSING
Beware of p. faith in Jesus while you blaspheme him 3646

PROFESSIONAL
reputation cannot last forever 5079

PROFESSOR
To discharge duties of p. 11007

PROFIT
Christians to p. by change 961
even from those who talk badly 7114
God reveals that which is our p. to know 9708
If we seek God for our own p. 4923
Man shall commune with creatures to his p. 9481
no p. to learn well if neglect to do well 3016
others bring trinkets to sell for a p. 7018
seek p. of thy neighbor 4922
taught to ask, will it give me p. 5467

PROFITABLE
Never value anything as p. 11660

PROFITS
by crime commits it 2037
Doing God's will may not lead to p. 10778
most who serves best 10143
Whoever p. by crime is guilty 5494

PROFOUND
Agape love p. concern for another 7158
Christ's words simple yet p. 6377
Conversion so p. theologians ponder 1896
faith gives p. understanding 7383
God has p. interest in man's being good 5060
God's ability to heal soul p. 10845
impossible to explain how p. Bible is 734
most p. joy has more gravity than gaiety 6562
most p. thoughts born from womb of silence 10269
Obedience unlocks door to p. spiritual experience 8101
Simplicity result of p. thought 10283
where evil is p. 3347
Would sink forever thro' the vast p. 4708

PROFOUNDEST
At p. depths men talk not about God but with him 8767
exchange p. thinker for 4204
faith engages p. problems 3784

PROFOUNDLY
God, heart p. kind 4477
within zone of God's voice, p. altered 7540

PROFOUNDNESS
Kindness in thinking creates p. 6649

PROFUSION
is not magnificence 11662

PROGESSIVE
not brains that matter, but p. ideas 1027

PROGRAM
frequent church language 1406
God has p. of character development 1015
Great Director of music arranges a p. perfectly new 7895
take God's p, have God's power 4826

PROGRAMS
drug treatment p. run by churches 134
found in place of Christ 1230
God takes delight in breaking up our p. 5401
legalism, lynching of innovative p. 6817

PROGRESS
Another year of p. 8077
church has made hard won p. 1430
depends on unreasonable man 980
differences sign of p. 1624
Discontent first step in p. 2864
Discontent source of p. 2865
Every step of p. world has made 7673
exchange of one nuisance for another nuisance 9317
hindrance to spiritual p. 3758
Holiness not the end of p. 5746
in holiness depends on God's grace, our will 5754
Is it p. if cannibal uses fork 9313
means of aiding p. so feeble 5944
More p. in silence than in year of study 12112
mother of problems 9314
No nation made p. in downward direction 7834
no struggle, no p. 9312
not p. when moral tone lower 7834
not p. when purity not as sweet 7834
of spiritual things 5751
pay more attention to spiritual p. 10703
Restlessness, discontent necessities of p. 2870

resulted from people who took unpopular positions 9308
Rigidity restrains creativity, blocking p. 6818
signposts along the way all marked p. 5970
snail's p. toward God 8630
Were it not for nonconformists, world would have known little p. 9311
when survey whole p. of our lives 5392
Without heretics world would not p. 9318
work of p. so immense 5944

PROGRESSED
how far we have p. since yesterday 9832
No man p. to greatness but through mistakes 5030
We march, but have not p. an inch 9309

PROGRESSES
Bible shows how world p. 723

PROGRESSIVE
Education p. discovery of ignorance 3000
it was the p. people who flocked to Jesus 6452

PROJECT
evangelism not a p. 3313
negative word can defuse enthusiasm for p. 12001

PROLETARIAT
Christ executed by fickle p. 2171

PROMINENT
doctrine of value if p. in our thoughts 11180
If p. call him Father 3921
the more laws are order are made p. 5192

PROMISCUITY
Music glorifying sexual p. 7910

PROMISE
acre of performance worth world of p. 2530
baptism signifies p. 529
Be slow to p, quick to perform 2531
better to be uncertain and not p. 9327
Bible doesn't p. loaves to the loafer 6774
Bible, p. and fulfillment 750
Christ made no p. 159
Faith believes p. 9322
faith is casting oneself on the p. 3753
Faith, mighty faith, the p. sees 3717
first temptation was p. of learning and knowledge 6701
From p. to deed a day's journey 9320
God does not p. final victory in this life 5385

God does not p. he will protect
from trials 5385

God does not p. success 5385

God is the God of p. 9321

God makes a p. 9322

hope anticipates p. 9322

In joy do not p. to give anything
11920

Jesus' p. is valid 5781

mystery is God's, p. is yours
11485

of the dawn 6141

patience quietly awaits p. 9322

rainbow is heaven's p. in
technicolor 9390

Rainbow, mild arch of p. 9392

slow in making p. most likely
faithful in performance 9325

than to p. and not fulfill 9327

we p. according to our hopes
5950

where skies are full of p. 9059

PROMISED

God p. to be active among men
5724

God p. to go with us 165

Jesus p. followers "The
Strengthener" would be with
them 5804

Lord p. cross, scars 2102

Was it not persecution Jesus p. to
disciples 10784

PROMISED LAND

always lies on other side of
wilderness 5669

I've seen the P. 4975

wilderness today, P. tomorrow
1935

PROMISES

Bible, field of p. 716

Christ, no rosy p. 1154

Christianity never p. to make
independent 4116

Christianity p. to make free 4116

faith rests on the p. 3818

faith trusts in p. of God 3842

first thing Jesus p. is suffering
10901

God p. only that he will be with
them 5385

God's p. are obligations he
imposes upon himself 9324

God's p. beyond wildest dreams
4458

God's p. like the stars 9323

God's p. real, glorious 4458

God's p. sealed to us, but not
dated 4470

greatness in adherence to p. made
5283

Lord p. us himself 10758

loses thanks who p. and delays
2535

may get friends 4262

Nobody p. a good or easy time
2182

that point to real meaning 9351

to kindness, knowledge we make
p. only 8261

too much means nothing 9326

True have his p. been 6498

What greater rebellion than not to
believe God's p. 11596

PROMISSORY

tomorrow is a p. note 11390

PROMOTE

Lord's sovereign right to demote,
p. 5894

PROMOTING

Nonresistence to evil is way of p. it
3388

PROMOTION

call of Christ always a p. 10186

funds for p. of peace 11782

most handle demotion better than
p. 9221

PROMPT

Seizes the p. occasion 8224

PROMPTING

God is p. to desire him 4514

PROMPTINGS

when concur with p. of Spirit,
Word of God 5444

PROMPTNESS

charity is p. when duty calls 1085

PRONE

Men more p. to revenge injuries
9720

PRONOUNCED

capacity for evil so p. in ourselves
3412

Meekness that Christ p. blessed
7728

PROOF

alibi p. that you did do 3473

atom p. little things count 8663

best p. Christ risen is he is still
alive 9695

best p. of immortality in sharing
life of God 6105

convincing p. of this truth 4942

Discipline p. of sonship 2842

existence of evil p. of God's
existence 3399

faith no merit if reason provided p.
3841

fury against Christ p. he is not
dead 6362

greatest p. of Christianity is
practice 599

Jesus' coming final, unanswerable
p. God cares 6136

living Jesus p. of God's love,
forgiveness 6473

Martyrdom, p. of intensity 1911

obtain p, render faith superfluous
3806

seek p, admit doubt 3806

unbelieving mind not convinced
by p. 600

We demand p. of God 4689

what he knows needs no reasoned
p. 5809

worshiping heart needs no p. 600

PROP

God will disappoint as p. 4468

PROPAGANDA

witness not p. 3336

PROPAGATION

family for p. of life 10506

PROPELLED

by winds of our times 1634

PROPENSITY

to grasp at forbidden fruit 11112

PROPER

always know our p. stations 3112

recreation as p. as prayer 6837

PROPERTY

consider scholarship not as p.
11007

devil looks upon us as his p.
11097

Four things are p. of friendship
4227

friends, p. of one belongs to the
other 4186

God would never invest in
worthless p. 9989

new life not p. to cling to 10545

We are God's p. 7552

PROPHECIES

Jesus fulfills all the procedures of
the p. 6443

PROPHECY

In God history and p. are one
4604

PROPHET

Christ a P. to teach 6370

Conscience p. in its information
1673

historian a p. in reverse 5708

Jesus p. of the losers' camp 6447

knows his times 9332

knows what God is trying to say
to people 9332

No p. ever did work cheaply, easily
5289

PROPHETIC

tints tomorrow with p. ray 618

PROPHET'S

Yes, music is the p. art 7935

PROPHETS

beating hearts of the Old
Testament 9333

Bible, congregation of p. 716

experienced up, down, joy, sorrow
2593

If we read Old Testament p. 5423

Music is the art of the p. 7914

Saints, apostles, p, martyrs 6892

takes p. to interpret the present
9334

we are not diplomats but p. 9169

wrote and spoke 648

PROPORTION
Difficulty rocks into athletic p. 2719

Let the Father p. out daily 4629

sense of sin in p. to nearness to God 10349

PROPORTIONAL
level of joy p. to level of acceptance 6556

spiritual health p. to love for God 4793

PROPORTIONS
fight of cosmic p. has started 3400

PROPOSITION
immortality not a p. 6102

Life's a tough p. 6992

PROPS
human p. have been knocked out 184

Solomon depended more on p. 794

spend time serving as religious p. 1300

PROSPECT
being dead, an appealing p. 2300

frightened at the p. of facing ourselves 10575

than great thing in p. 7116

PROSPECTS
hours with happy p. in view pleasing 3508

world hopeful in p. 10512

PROSPER
as we do common things in uncommon way 9344

Ill-gotten gains never p. 2467

No race can p. until 3240

PROSPERING
meaning of earthly existence not in p. 9342

PROSPERITY
a state of mind 9339

an instrument to be used 9340

blessing of the Old Testament 243

can stand affliction better than p. 250

church p. not discipleship 2813

conceals genius 147

destroys appreciation of right 245

finest injured by neither p. or adversity 7683

Friendship adds brighter radiance to p. 4228

full of friends 4267

good campaigning weather for devil 9338

greatest enemy man can have 9341

hath killed his ten thousands 241

heavenly fire lies dormant in p. 244

if man had foresight of p. 4314

If thankfulness arises through p. 11151

in p. we forget God 250

is a great teacher 242

is happily miserable 241

Memory tempers p. 7735

more than economic condition 9339

not a deity to be worshiped 9340

not p. that makes happiness 5538

not without many fears 247

often fatal to Christianity 1218

the broad daylight of p. 244

trial will become day of p. 7698

weak person is injured by p. 7683

What to do when p. fails 11151

would not be so welcome 182

PROSPEROUS
man never sure loved for himself 11860

Men prefer p. error to afflicted truth 3261

No man p. whose immortality forfeited 6101

PROSTITUTES
adored Jesus 6412

People do not decide to be p. 11080

PROSTRATE
before thy throne to lie 12113

By p. spirits day and night 4659

PROTECT
by thy power, p. us 619

Christ a Husband to p. 6370

God does not promise he will p. from trials 5385

God's power to p. me 5400

In kingdom of God surest way to lose is to p. 4733

me, my Lord, my boat is so small 9110

who didn't have reputation to p. 6147

PROTECTED
we shall be p. 5440

woman formed from beneath arm to be p. 11982

PROTECTING
as a p. canopy, the blessing of God 5848

PROTECTION
from enemies in the cross 2096

God undertakes special p. of man 3999

prayer key that shuts us up under God's p. 8846

she no longer needs our poor p. 2392

PROTECTIVE
In solitude heart can take off p. devices 10540

Take my life. I draw no p. line 2331

PROTECTS
God p. me against danger 4992

PROTEST
loudest in p. no such person as Jesus 6417

To sin by silence when should p. 6282

PROTESTANT
confessional, the sewing circle 5160

God not interested in P. religion 9539

Jesus comes across as P. Republican 6467

not a P. in heaven 5671

PROTESTANTISM
divided into 200 groups 1420

What P. has gained by its simplicity 6827

PROTESTANTS
We are not P. 1343

will not be polluted if 5733

PROTESTING
He who accepts evil without p. is cooperating 3374

PROUD
authority, make men giddy, p. and vain 8702

Be not p. of good works 9195

Be not p. of race, face, place, grace 9193

door guarded by p. spirit of Reason 7950

Give me the p. heart 4530

hate pride—in others 9247

If ever a man becomes p. 9209

if religious elite too p. 12098

If too p. to admit you are hurting 9211

in humility, p. they are not p. 9252

Knowledge is p. has learned so much 6695

leaves one's old p. self defenseless 7488

Love finds admission where p. science fails 12130

man always looking down on things, people 9188

man counts newspaper clippings 6035

man seldom grateful 5258

Men who are unhappy p. of the fact 5541

never so p. as when striking attitude of humility 9187

not p. reason keeps door of heaven 12130

people breed sorrows for themselves 9232

put themselves underneath 3785

repentance, p. becomes humble 9604

satanically managed man is p. 10044

struggle between p. mind, empty purse 8679

they that know themselves cannot be p. 6039

Unhappy are they who are p. 379

Why should the spirit of mortal be p. 9225

world thy p. mandate 4592

PROUDLY
some face death p, valiantly 2336

PROVE
effort to p. no God 478
Faith believing where we cannot p.
    3682
faith by commital to it 612
if we could p. God 4689
Only you can p. immortality to
    yourself 6102
problem is an opportunity to p.
    God 9283
Reason does not p. God exists
    3776
Search, p. my heart, it pants for
    Thee 4140
well-examined, p. hand of God
    5454

PROVED
faith cannot be p. 3724
God p. his love on the cross 7173
    2129
Jesus' patience should have p. he
    was God 6492

PROVEN
scientifically p. worry undermine
    health 5612

PROVERB
is no p. till life has illustrated it
    3539
much matter decocted into few
    words 9377
short sentence based on long
    experience 9376

PROVERBS
Christ's words pass into p. 6523
How to act 11925
wit of a nation discovered in its p.
    9386

PROVES
Bible p. how transient is noblest
    monument 730
Faith p. herself in ordinary
    situations 3715
Gossip p. nothing but bad taste
    5132
if gamble on its truth and p. false
    3724
Noise p. nothing 9223
When earthly treasure p. but dross
    4338

PROVIDE
Christ a Father to p. 6370
Christ will p. everything you need
    9521
God will p. strong shoes 180
Leave to thy God to p. 1502

PROVIDED
from within needs little from
    without 5780
hell, teeth will be p. 5696
Holy Spirit expects us to take
    seriously answers p. 5445

media p. devil with opportunity
    2698

PROVIDENCE
danger of amateur p. 263
designs of God's p. deeply hidden
    3349
each ordering of his p. 4578
God's p. upsets your timetable
    11370
hand of divine p. takes over 2774
I may assert eternal P. 7566
like a curious piece of arras 5722
march of p. is so slow 5944
of God about us in abundance
    8002
put together present beautiful
    history 5722
struggling to supplement God's p.
    with our own p. 4322
Trust future to his p. 5457
ways of P. cannot be reasoned out
    5450

PROVIDENCES
darkest p. have meaning 4885

PROVIDENT
love of God p. as father's love for
    child 4792

PROVIDENTIAL
Never interfere with God's p.
    dealings 1549

PROVIDES
earth p. enough for every man's
    need 5326
father who teaches responsibility
    p. fortune 3913
God p. me with all I need 4992
grace God p. comes only with task
    5226

PROVIDING
Christ p. a vista 6434
too busy p. for old age 119

PROVISIONAL
let judgments be p. 571
Philosophy piecemeal, p. like
    science 8596

PROVOCATIONS
we resent little p. 3410

PROVOKE
By bearing old wrongs p. new ones
    9632

PROVOKED
Christ's words p. acceptance or
    rejection 6377
God is dreadfully p. 4523
Hate waits only to be p. 7265

PROXIMITY
too much of p. prevents being
    able to see 3559

PROXY
no dying by p. 2396

PRUDENCE
In divine things no p. which is not
    bold 2732

PRUDENT
God hides in darkness from the p.
    7709
Love is p. 7246

PRUDENTLY
to examine it p. 9062

PRUNE
back part of our activity 60

PRUNED
Better p. to grow than cut to burn
    2841

PRUNES
Although today he p. my twigs
    with pain 8254

PRYING
Life way of p. loose grasp 11656

PSALM 23
has filled the world with joy 801
nightingale of the psalms 801
singing shyly out of obscurity 801

PSALMIST'S
Along the P. music deep 2345

PSALMS
a "Little Bible" 796
anatomy of the soul 799
book of P. sown with seeds of
    thanksgiving 11145
contains all that is found in Bible
    796
contains despair of man's defeat
    798
contains firmness of man's
    confidence 798
contains lyrical burst of man's
    tenderness 798
contains moan of man's penitence
    798
contains music of heart of man
    798
contains pathos of man's sorrow
    798
contains rapture of man's hope
    798
contains triumph of man's victory
    798
How to pray 11925
mirror in which man sees his soul
    800
perfection of human expression
    740
songs of the human soul 797
timeless, universal 797
vex, grief the devil 2661

PSEUDO
to p. faith nothing but God
    terrifying thought 3719

PSEUO BELIEF
belief that does not command, p.
    612

PSYCHIATRISTS
require many sessions 5485

PSYCHOLOGICAL
Every dream reveals p. structure
    2968

godly response kicks p. crutches from skeptic 10938

man's p. makeup probably due to body 1030

secrets Hitler, Mussolini used 12178

true contemplation not a p. trick 1765

PSYCHOLOGICALLY
Death p. as important as birth 2255

PSYCHOLOGIZE
cannot p. grace of God 5237

PSYCHOLOGY
all our p. penetrated hardly an inch 9353

Christianity in full accord with p. 9351

must insist on reality of evil 3382

reject that evil is insignificant 3382

soak in p. 11196

substituted p. for prayer 5808

PSYCHOTHERAPY
Prayer God's p. for his children 8921

will put Band-Aid on gash 5616

PUBLIC
easier to suffer as p. heroes 10859

forgive everything except genius 4397

introduce into p. affairs, Christianity 1198

Life like playing violin in p. 6967

life will take care of itself 6321

no assumptions from p. conduct 571

opinion almost omnipotent 8200

praise friend in p. 4182

wonderfully tolerant 4397

worth to God in p. is what I am in private 6315

PUBLIC RELATIONS
not test of father's leadership 3925

Self-respect cannot be fabricated out of p. 9995

PUBLICITY
approval to p. hunter who seeks headlines 5891

not tricked by p. 836

to me p. contemptible 7365

PUBLICLY
commend friend p. 2855

Pharisee prays p, preys privately 6047

PUBLISH
when you p. another's secret fault 5167

PUBLISHED
mistakes p. every day like those of ball player 7789

PUBLISHING
with utmost freedom 4115

PUDDING
Life's a p. full of plums 6990

PUERILITY
preserved in state of perpetual p. 5584

PUFF
honors of this world are but p. 5898

PUFFED
up with conceit 6704

PUFFS
than good action which p. up 3931

PULL
till life finds p. of Christ's love 6937

toy world which moves when p. strings 4132

PULLED
down into quicksand of smugness 3168

If all men p. in one direction 6184

PULLS
Love is like a magnet, p. me into God 7237

what is greater still, p. God into death 7237

Who p. or steers with me 6398

PULPIT
care not what is preached in p. 12151

Christian occupies some kind of p. 1245

mist in p, fog in pew 9123

not what disciple preaches from p. 2830

PULSATING
God a dynamic, p. activity 11425

PULSE
But such a heart whose p. may be thy praise 5265

God feels p, prescribes medicine 4449

Prayer the p. of life 8946

spirit-arteries p. with red of love 2979

PUMP
can't p. up faith out of your own heart 3828

PUMPKINS
turn p. into coaches 1122

PUNCH
will versus will, p. versus p. 1622

PUNISH
creation to p. humanity 3191

evil for which we p. others 3397

foolish to p. neighbor by fire when live next door 9718

hope God too kind to p. ungodly 4726

murderers among private persons 11776

purpose of darkness not to p. 2608

we p. ourselves 9354

PUNISHED
not p. for our sins, but by them 9356

unless kill in large numbers 11753

PUNISHES
Conscience p. us as judge 1677

don't believe in a God who p. to get even with sinners 9354

PUNISHMENT
alternative to eternal life is eternal p. 3286

death a p. to some 2274

evokes resentment, vow of retaliation 9355

hardens, numbs 2038

hell, pain of p. without penitence 5700

paradox of p. 9355

penalty of evil harvest not God's p. 4721

produces concentration 2038

seeds of p. sown at time commit sin 10396

self-inflicted p. 9354

sharpens consciousness of alienation 2038

strengthens resistance 2038

This is the p. of a liar 6861

too late believe in eternal p. 5700

vice is its own p. 10298

who is kept from vice by p. 11723

works with sense of justice 9355

PUNISHMENTS
Without p. no new power can arise 8722

PUNKIN
When the frost is on the p. 9880

PUNY
think of destiny, how p. a part you are 7063

PUPIL
best teacher gets most out of p. 3026

best teacher not one who crams into p. 3026

Today is yesterday's p. 11384 3547

PUPILS
to teach without inspiring p. to learn 11000

PUPPETS
build society of love out of p. 4133

slaves to p. of power 9016

PURCHASE
money powerless to p. 10906

wisdom good p. though we pay dear for it 11968

PURCHASED
future p. by present 4326

Self-respect cannot be p. 9995

PURE

approval not to p. in heart who see God 5891
Bible p, unalloyed, perfect truth 710
Bible perfect, p. 710
content whose conscience is p. 1681
Creation seems like p. freedom 4117
employment is p. 3104
Give us a p. heart 9058
God asks nothing but p. heart 7450
God looks with favor at p. hands 6300
God makes p. in heart 1012
heart that I may see thee 7458
Hearts opened in p. transparency 5667
home joys makes hearts p, good 5844
I make myself p. in conduct 1012
I would be p. 1018
If your love p, simple, well-ordered 7193
impossible for us to be p. 9801
Impure thoughts will not stand against p. words 5028
in heart who understood what life was about 5001
in heart, not sophisticated and worldly 5001
in heart, not strong in mind, see God 1216
infinity, darkness of the p. unsearchable sea 4684
light of God pierces a man 9741
like a great ring of p. endless light 3276
Love is p. 7246
love the panacea for ills of world 7203
Perfect and right and p. and good 5620
repentance, lewd becomes p. 9604
Self can turn p. prayer into an ineffective one 10080
spirit not distracted by activity 4307
Spiritual truth discernable only to p. heart 11529
There is a land of p. delight 5670
woman under whose hands children grow up strong, p. 5857
wrath of God is p. 401

PURELY

act from honest motives p. 559

PUREST

garden, p. of human pleasures 8007
Music p. language of passion 7905
should lamp p. rays bestow 3323
when hearts are p. devil soils 2649

PURGATORY

Marriage with strife is life's p. 7645

PURGE

Grief can p. us of pettiness, selfishness 10640
imagination by beauty of God 12124

PURGED

Evil can only be p, redeemed 3354

PURIFICATION

Suffering p. of soul 10896

PURIFIED

Let love be p, rest will follow 7203
When soul is p. and serene 7971

PURIFIES

Faith p. emotions 3666
Love either consumes or p. 7248

PURIFY

Love will soften, p. the heart 7241

PURITAN

never frightened a P. 4965

PURITAN FATHERS

black shadow of asceticism 467
chose fear and self-denial 467
chose rocky roads 467
chose somberest colors 467
chose ugliest coat 467
favorite color, black 467
favorite hour, midnight 467
favorite music, a dirge 467
favorite text, deny yourself 467
favorite theme, tombstone 467

PURITANICAL

lost through p. insistence on moral rules 6827

PURITY

And awful p. 4659
God's love spotless p. 4750
holy with infinite, incomprehensible p. 5749
hope of nation not in p. of administration 5190
If love does not agree with p. 4755
incapable of being other than it is 5749
insight arises from p. of heart 8504
Lord showing his p. through you 9847
must be found in Christ Jesus, not in some formula 7105
not a question of intellect but of p. of heart 11529
not progress when p. not as sweet 7834
Painting enables us to see p. of the virgins 2015
radiance of Christmas 1364
stagnant water loses its p. 6765

PURPOSE

an upright heart which no unworthy p. may tempt aside 9057
angry for the right p. 373
behind law 5233
by defying p. of God insulate ourselves 4864
by permissive government God lines up with his p. 5175
Complete thy p, that we may become 7519
devil can cite Scripture for his p. 2672
devote will to p. of God 12124
Every man serves useful p. 11805
Every moment pregnant with divine p. 11293
Everything directed to one p. 1465
excellence involves tenacity of p. 3464
explain a trial, destroy its p. 164
God used my powerlessness for his p. 2518
God's p. in the cloud to simplify our belief 188
has invaded our lives with p. 6156
in pain, otherwise devilish 8274
irresistible p. of Christ's life 6439
Joy holy fire that keeps p. warm 10829
life without p. 4437
Man can endure suffering if p. 10871
man without p. like ship without rudder 4436
men fail through lack of p. 4427 3608
Men seldom flatter without p. 4051
most disastrous p. is "pursuit of happiness" 5548
Neither usefulness nor duty God's p. 197
of being guilty is to bring us to Jesus 5491
of Christ's redeeming work 9438
of cross to repair irreparable 2165
of darkness not to punish or afflict 2608
of darkness to set free 2608
of education to turn mirrors into windows 3019
of revival 9751
perseverance rarely fails in its p. 8557
place and p. of sex 10239
prayer changes us, therein lies its p. 8855
Prayer is to carry out God's p. fully 8909
Prayer provides p. 8951
Shrinking from death robs life of p. 2255
sin that finds p. in nothing 11394
that we fulfill the p. of God 7485
Thou changest thy works, p. unchanged 4954

thought God's p. to make me full of happiness, joy 5531

we're missed p. of giving 10738

with deliberate p, God visited this planet 6144

with p. full and clear, turn to meet another year 8082

within God's p, no failure 3582

without a p. waif, a nothing, a no man 4436

PURPOSEFULLY
Plan p., prepare prayerfully 80

prayerfully, positively, persistently 80

PURPOSELESS
activity a phase of death 122

PURPOSELESSNESS
mother of crime 2039

PURPOSELY
He who p. cheats friend would cheat God 2911

PURPOSES
all great p. of God culminate in Christ 5710

Almighty has his own p. 4950

future depends on p. today 4325

God has taken you up into his p. 9830

God molds history to his p. 5718

Great minds have p. 5281

Misunderstanding cannot thwart p. of God 2740

Prayer does not mean bring God down to my p. 8909

Prayer link between man and infinite p. of God 8944

required that we fall in with God's p. 8821

The Lord shatters our p. 351

wanting to cooperate with God's own p. 4468

weaknesses necessary to p. of life 11788

PURR
rub them right way will p. 9482

PURRS
That p. and never shows a tooth 5048

PURSE
As p. is emptied, heart filled 4351

If man empties p. in head 3010

struggle between proud mind, empty p. 8679

PURSUE
Adam and Eve p. their way 365

Condemn the wrong, yet the wrong p. 10319

Glory endowed on many who did not p. 4407

if you p. happiness you will never find it 5558

Men p. pleasure with breathless haste 8601

more we p. humility more distant it becomes 6008

only enough life to p. one object fully 9260

plan, prepare, proceed, p. 80

We p. God because 4573

PURSUED
Can vengeance be p. further than death 9716

great when greatly p. 79

Happiness when p. always beyond grasp 5518

Mystery is p. by religious instinct 12118

PURSUES
worth measured by objects he p. 469

PURSUING
gave up p. happiness 5530

own glory 10076

people imagine p. glory of God 10076

PURSUIT
excellence one single p. 3470

God spurs us to the p. 4573

joy replaced by p. of duty 6813

lucky who can obliterate p. of glory 4411

of God is successful 7513

of happiness most ridiculous phrase 5558

of the disciplined life 9970

Righteousness, not power, should be p. 5001

Self-knowledge important in p. of God 10019

PURSUITS
if p. on earthly things 8818

makes world pause in frantic, headlong p. 10938

PUSH
friend, a p. when you've stopped 4174

PUSHED
God lets himself be p. on to the cross 4899

PUSHES
man p. into self-chosen alienation 4781

Self-love p. itself into everything 10027

you nearer to God 4190

PUT
failure to p. God where he belongs 7046

God never p. anyone in place too small to grow 4987

Patience, to p. up with people you'd like to p. down 8411

Where he hath p. and keepeth you 4834

Where no love, p. love in 7343

Who has p. me here 4905

PUTS
Doing injury p. you below enemy 4073

PUZZLE
God can make pieces of world's p. fit 4735

Here's the answer to your p. 9922

Man is a constant p. 7401

working on a p, pure and simple 9922

PUZZLED
Many p. about origin of evil 3383

PYRAMID
race of man, unfinished p. 1163

PYRAMIDS
sinking in desert sands 730

PYRENEES
Truth this side of P. may be heresy on the other 11577

PYTHAGORAS
used to say life resembles Olympic Games 7018

Q

QUAKER
not a Q. in heaven 5671

to burglar 1550

QUAKES
man threatens while q. for fear 3981

what q. the heart 4551

QUALIFIED
Christ alone q. to guide into unknown 2323

not open to conviction, not q. for discussion 2903

QUALITIES
Bible, many divine q. 687

Christ combines q. of every race 6363

had they no redeeming q. 11891

led to success also most likely to destroy 10819

Life has taught me we are disliked for our q. 5601

Many have shining q. beneath rough exterior 8658

that are key to success 10799

Three q. vital to success 10820

We don't love q, we love a person 7332

Whenever relationships develop q. 5014

wise man seeks friend with q. he himself lacks 4279

QUALITY
Age is a q. of mind 8122

Christianity, life of eternal q. 1188

Consistency q. of stagnant mind 1746

devil has one good q. 2678

difference in q. of one's outer life 7725

God must prefer q. to quantity 941

Greatness a matter of q. 5283

heaven expansion of q. of life 5645

immeasurable though quantity insignificant 7080

more exposure than q. of writing 12156

mystical is intimate q. of the spiritual life 7954

of life begins when confidence transferred to God 5645

of mercy is not strain'd 7744

often irritating characteristic by-product of respected q. 8571

ratio between quantity and q. 4283

rewards depend on q. of contributions we make 10179

Seek not every q. in one individual 9490

thing of bad q. expensive 10291

Witnessing a q. of life 3344

workmanship not expensive 3116

workmanship priceless 3116

QUALMS
who would not circulate slander without q. 10465

QUANTITY
God must prefer quality to q. 941

of money one gives of little importance 11360

quality immeasurable though q. insignificant 7080

ratio between q. and quality 4283

QUANTUM THEORY
more truth in Genesis than q. 745

QUARREL
do not make contentment and aspiration q. 471

Falsehoods usually q. among themselves 6849

forgive ends q. 4085

I q. with God 4855

ministry of church ceased while we q. over Prince of Peace 9361

no q. so bitter as a religious q. 9360

Nothing stops family q. more quickly 3879

right to kill because his ruler has q. with mine 11744

QUARRELING
In q. truth always lost 9358

QUARRELS
inevitable at the time, incredible afterwards 9359

weapons of the weak 9362

QUARRELSOME
wants make us q. with others 2861

QUARRY
the granite rock with razors 9233

QUARTER
still a few things for a q. 4042

QUEERNESS
Despair a frightful q. 2578

QUELLED
by music's divine control 7935

QUENCHED
fire q. by water 372

have q. thirst at other fountains 7500

Thirst must be q. 7538

QUENCHES
Faith q. fire of every pain 3661

wordy unbelief that q. the fire 11991

QUEST
endless q. for truth 4643

for excellence maturity 3469

for power childish 3469

Religion is man's q. for God 9545

Those only who make q. supreme desire 6494

Worship is a drop in q. of the ocean 12132

QUESTION
about miracle is not how it happened but why 6500

all q. marks straighten into exclamation points 5676

asks a q. is fool for five minutes 6683

boy asked q. that pierced father's heart 3912

Bread for myself material q. 622

bread for neighbor spiritual q. 622

but one q. that is the gospel 5094

divided over the q. "Who is Jesus" 6518

do not change to q. mark 5468

does not ask q. remains fool forever 6683

first step in wisdom is to q. everything 11935

God wants us to ask q. of truth 10564

healthy to hang q. on things taken for granted 2950

Never put q. mark where God has put period 3763

never seems to q. choice of husband 7655

no longer what we think of Christ 4718

no room to q. final issue 235

not a q. of growing taller, but of stooping lower 6017

not a q. of intellect but of purity of heart 11529

not a q. of our equipment 8

not answer that enlightens, but the q. 9365

not every q. deserves an answer 9364

not q. of saved from hell 1014

not what a man can find fault with 442

not what a man can scorn 442

of common sense 8580

of our poverty 8

of truth that can be asked only in solitude 10564

out of the q. a Christian government 5182

raise q. whether men are significant 7481

significant q. what Christ thinks of us 4718

silly q. first intimation of new development 6703

Talk about q. of the day 5094

to be asked about creed, Is it true 2032

To q. authority of God absurd 4955

To q. knowing never can full answer be found 7435

two sides to every q. 8076

what a man can love, value, appreciate 442

What are we busy about 116

What is God saying to me constant q. 6086

When it is a q. of God's almighty Spirit 14

whether learned except through the rod 10855

whether we seek God or his gifts 4800

whether you really are a Christian 3872

Why should we then q. God 4640

QUESTIONABLE
whether have really heard Jesus speak 6407

QUESTIONS
amazed never scratching heads for q. 9544

better to ask some q. than know all answers 6688

Christian thinker q. foundations about him 11239

Christians care about q. 1268

discovered q. not important q. 9366

go far beyond comprehension 39

God has never turned away q. 2941

God puts q. to man 7398

Healthy q. keep faith dynamic 2949

Heaven where q. and answers become one 5647

Life a test that has more q. than answers 6953

man differs from animals, asks q. 7398

only learn when ask q. 9363

When q. to be feared 5480

QUICK
Be slow to promise, q. to perform 2531

don't be too q. to despair 2593

God is q. to mark effort to please 4810

God q. to overlook imperfections 4810

is succession of human events
12075
life runs tediously q. 973
love makes the idle q. and sharp
7260
Men of cold passions have q. eyes
3565
not q. to be like Christ 8113
Truth merely told q. to be
forgotten 11578

QUICKEN
Christ a Root to q. 6370
O Jesus, q. me 2587
the conscience by holiness of God
12124

QUICKENS
When God q. his pace 5460

QUICKER
advancing in life whose brain q.
6898
Nobody spots phony q. than a
child 8349
nothing rises q. than dust 3857

QUICKEST
Adolescents q. to discern hypocrisy
12162

QUICKLY
Care admitted as guest q. turns to
master 12058
children will be gone so q. 8353
Don't jump to conclusions too q.
8394
folks we know briefly, then q.
forget 4281
get rid of money as q. as possible
7824
gives twice who gives q. 4361
Hardening of heart ages people
more q. 6159
Jesus performing q. the slow
miracle occurring in vineyards
6513
Lord's Prayer committed to
memory q. 7153
Man thinks he loses when he does
not do things q. 11307
Nothing consumes more q. than
resentment 9638
Nothing stops family quarrel more
q. 3879
Old age lives minutes slowly,
hours q. 12193
the more q. we grow 7678
to their misfortunes 4242
understanding never comes q.
7648
Vice q. creeps in 11725
without doubt God will q. respond
7709

QUICKSAND
of smugness and self-satisfaction
3168

QUICKSANDS
on q. of fluctuating experiences
3550

QUIET
Advent, coming of q. joy 6119
conscience sleeps in thunder 1659
fifteen years teaching child to be q.
8336
good and wise lead q. lives 9373
grief passes into q, tender joy
7101
Happiness the harvest of a q. eye
9370
he lies 6139
heart of wise man lies q. like
limpid water 11944
holy people learned great secret
1293
holy time is q. 8980
Humility is q. 6012
humility is the q. valley fertile and
abounding in life 6026
I listened—q. and still 5415
If have no q. in minds 8442
If we have not q. in our minds
1804
In the great q. of God 7569
invest few extra hours in q.
reverence 9906
Kind words smooth, q. comfort
11985
life characteristic of great men
5274
life without a q. center becomes
destructive 10531
Love is q. 7246
Make it thy q. dwelling place
7454
men lead lives of q. desperation
2610
mind is richer than crown 1812
mind one that nothing worries
7773
minds cannot be perplexed or
frightened 8466
minds go at own private pace
8466
minds like clock in thunderstorm
8466
more perfect we are the more q.
we become toward defects of
others 8521
more q. we become toward defects
of others 11395
my heart with throbs of another
heart 6258
Never for sake of q. deny
convictions 1912
Only in q. mind is adequate
perception 7718
Only in q. waters things mirror
themselves undistorted 7718
realizes God in midst, q. in midst
of alarm 3972
Self-respect comes in q. moments
9995
spiritual maturity, q. confidence
God is in control 10709
suffering will become q. joy 10932
Through q. waters, stormy
weather 4281

to be q. under adverse fortune
implies great strength 8423
to q. mind all things possible 7773
Truth has a q. breast 11559
waiting upon the Lord 8957
What sweet delight q. life affords
9375

QUIETED
Anger q. by gentle word 372

QUIETER
If only I may grow q. 7688

QUIETLY
does not know how to stay q. in
his room 5560
patience q. awaits promise 9322
should q. hear both sides 6618
sit down q, happiness may alight
upon you 5518
troubles come because we refuse
to sit q. 9367
walk on uninterruptedly and very
q. 5427
who q. suffer wrong 6274
will take withholding of honor q.
5901
with deliberate purpose, God
visited planet 6144

QUIETNESS
Drop thy still dews of q. 8431
Humility is perfect q. of heart
6010
in q. and turning within 7725
Lord, to the tired and ill give q.
9045
of the stars seemed to reproach me
4618
poise and q. of Christ 123
wait in q. until light in darkness
3718
without times of q. 7711

QUILL
Were every stalk on earth a q.
4748

QUINTESSENCE
God's love q. of spotless purity
4750

QUIT
all this earthly grossness q. 5679
Choose to persevere, rather than q.
1138
faced with a mountain I will not q.
2633
fiddling around fringes of
Christianity 9691
life as an inn, not a home 7005
oh q. this mortal frame 2404
Repentance to be sorry enough to
q. 9595
trying to use Lord for our ends
1226

QUITTED
maintain post when others have q.
1915

QUIVER
As yet your shaft hidden in his q.
5430

QUOTATION
passions a q. 1640
well-placed q. sign of educated
person 9389

QUOTATIONS
Collecting q. similar to birds who
pick up pebbles 9380
good for uneducated to read q.
9383
people from ancient times speak
today 9385
Picking up q. get chirp of approval
9380
tell of inward thoughts, aspirations
9385
tell of struggle with life, death
9385
when engraved upon memory give
good thoughts 9383
Writers love q. 9389

QUOTE
By necessity, proclivity, delight we
all q. 9379
others, the better to express myself
9382
Scriptures, devil will run 720

QUOTED
pay more attention when q. than
when we read 9388

R

RABBIT
stop expecting r. saints to build
same nests you do 6187

RABBITS
don't fly 6168

RACE
Adam's helpless r. 495
as much a part of human r. as the
greatest 9988
best r. hasn't been run 8230
Bind in thy love every nation and r.
11424
but one r.—humanity 1482
Christ combines qualities of every
r. 6363
different colored roses 3234
Gave life to every r. 3227
is not always to the swift 9111
life runs quick through unresting r.
973
meet different r. to yourself 3234
no matter what color require
same nourishment 3243
No one can resign from human r.
5977
No r. can prosper until 3240
One half the human r. 8863
Raising children not unlike
long-distance r. 3884

resembling extinct homo sapiens
3881
true heroes of the human r. 6199
without distinction of r, merit,
rank 913
Yield torch to others as in r. 2338

RACE DISCRIMINATION
at the cross, no racial barriers
1491
didn't occur to birds to leave 1493
humorous that white man less
savage 1494
Skin color does not matter to God
1491
standing together against r. 1489
Surely thou, too, art not white
1487

RACIAL
at the cross, no racial barriers
1491
church, r. differences surmounted
1492
society filled with r. discrimination
161

RACISM
assertion God made creative
mistake 1483
denying man made in divine image
1488
Motives, forces behind r.
anti-Christ 1488

RADIANCE
Friendship adds brighter r. to
prosperity 4228
illuminated by steady r. renewed
daily 4538

RADIANT
arrival of r. light in our darkness
6119
cross r. with glory of meek, gentle
spirit 5252
Dazzling r. hope 5940
God can make brokenhearted r,
loving person 890
greenness after rain 5360
if our lives were r. 565
society not community r. with
love of Christ 10514

RADIATE
that we r. the peace, love of God
7485

RADIATES
rejoice with joy that r. 3182

RADIATING
influence from one person is
incalculable 6241

RADICAL
God, a r. beginning of goodness
4698
grappling with ideas r. enough to
upset grownups 12157
Jesus was a r. 6452
Jesus, r. personalization of ethical
problems 6451
simplicity of gospel's ethnic 1242

RADICALLY
possible for bad men to become r.
good 9438

RAGE
always make a bad landing 391
Don't fly into a r. 377
fate's severest r. disarm 7911
Music subdues r. of poison and
the plague 7900
People who fly into a r. 391
prepared for rough landing 377

RAGES
if refuse to stand for truth where
battle r. 3846
Safe when the tempest r. 4490

RAGGED
whether you teach r. class 3845

RAGING
cuddle self-pity, you'll have a r.
brute 10034
My boat on the r. sea 6398

RAGS
Better go to heaven in r. than hell
in embroidery 9262
messiahs aren't found wrapped in
r. 6147
royal raiment when worn for
virtue's sake 11694
Virtue, though in r, will keep
warm 11715

RAILING
at life, and yet afraid of death
8163

RAILROAD
man who hasn't time to stop at r.
crossing 5589

RAILROADS
Men throw r. across deserts 5841

RAIMENT
In new, bright r. clad 9898

RAIN
adversity often as the r. of spring
174
best to read weather forecasts
before pray for r. 8851
does not feel the r. 40
droppeth as the gentle r. from
heaven 7744
God sends r. 37
God wets you with his r. 4466
He fled from the r. 4062
Hope like clouds, some pass by,
others bring r. 5922
In the r. God is sweetening thy
melody 10600
Into each life some r. must fall
2549
is refreshing 8033
It's not raining r. to me 8498
Lord, send us r. 9118
Love comforteth like sunshine
after r. 7212
No r, no mushrooms 4485
Noah knew enough to get out of r.
782

prayer for r. 9118

praying for r. with tub wrong side up 8868

radiant greenness after r. 5360

takes both r, sunshine to make rainbow 2550

tears r. upon blinding dust of earth 11023

umbrella over duck in r. 6641

when it's raining, let it r. 1789

Without thy sunshine and thy r. 11172

RAINBOW

Be thou the r. to the storm of life 618

Follow every r. 4421

God's glowing covenant 9393

heaven's promise in technicolor 9390

Mild arch of promise 9392

no b. without cloud and storm 10636

ribbon nature puts on after washing hair 9391

soul would have no r. had eye no tears 10631

takes both rain, sunshine to make r. 2550

RAINBOWS

Of r. smiling down at me 8009

RAINED

so hard pigs got clean, people dirty 8500

RAINING

It's not r. rain to me 8498

It's r. daffodils 8498

when it is r, let it rain 34

RAIN'S

Why, r. my choice 37

RAINS

ain't no use putting up umbrella till it r. 12065

come to water earth 8002

RAINY

do not know what to do on a r. Sunday afternoon 6100

Every man has r. corner 2543

Spring is too r. 9879

RAISE

could only r. my mind in anguish to God 10931

If easy to r. kids, never would start with labor 8302

to r. your praise 8730

what is low r. and support 7566

RAISED

God is above, but not r. up 4848

God r. up Jesus 5711

Prayer means I am r. up into God 8909

to sweetness of eternal life 4749

voices lower esteem 9488

RAISES

Suffering r. us to freedom 10888

who takes rank lightly r. own dignity 6003

RAISING

children not unlike long-distance race 3884

Christ Lion in power, r. the dead 6425

God liquidating, then r. to new life 886

Grief should be r. 5331

of inward eyes to meet all-seeing eyes of God 3737

RAKED

has never r. leaves 8579

RALLYING

fear is soul's signal for r. 3973

RANDOM

in perplexity opens Bible at r. 5441

never arranged at r, 4948

open at r, close book, meditate 9387

RANK

and riches chains of gold 11844

God above in r. and station 4607

never have faith in r. 10875

than to take r. with poor spirits 1922

who takes r. lightly raises own dignity 6003

without distinction of race, merit, r. 913

RANKS

All service r. same with God 10116

RAPIDLY

Men think highly of those who rise r. 3857

RAPTURE

immortal r. that cannot die 7952

Many Christians long for the R. 9910

occasions for r. often leave us calm 3056

Psalms, r. of man's hope 798

RARE

All things excellent as difficult as r. 3465

as is true love 4263

Christian thinking r. 11221

eyes that see are r. 8493

Friendship without self-interest r, beautiful 4238

If dandelions were r, fragile 8577

know not by what methods r. 8825

Loneliness far from being a r. phenomenon 7137

Nothing more r. than own act 1641

Prayer is a r. gift 8914

Stumblers who get up r. 3618

to be humble when praised r. attainment 6019

True spirituality as r. as true bestiality 10718

RARELY

capable only r. of evil deeds 11272

God r. allows soul to see blessing he is 6233

Happiness, intelligence r. found in same person 5512

hear man suffering who says 10936

more r. is excellence cherished 3472

perseverance r. fails in its purpose 8557

True excellence r. found 3472

When marriage a solution for loneliness r. satisfies 7666

RARER

true friendship is still r. 4263

RAREST

God has preoccupied r. human spirits 7547

sort of courage 42

RASH

hand in evil hour 10314

RASHLY

Never to judge r. 1080

word r. spoken cannot be brought back 10681

RASHNESS

and haste make all things insecure 5586

blaming his r. 6599

RAT

Envy ugliness of trapped r. 3211

Hatred like burning down own house to get rid of r. 5596

RATHER

than love, give me truth 11526

RATIO

between quantity and quality 4283

Success r. between what a man is and might be 10808

RATIONAL

God has explanation r. man without Spirit of God never has 7753

not the road of r. conviction 3793

RATIONALISM

not basis of Christianity 533

nothing so irrational as r. 9397

tries to find God in picture of world 4495

RATIONALIST

a r, but liked ringing of church bells 9394

demands explanation of everything 9395

implies God must come to him 9396

makes himself his own center 9396

says, "How does God answer
  that" 9398
When r. points out sin, disease,
  death 9398

RATIONALITIES
God would be within compass of
  our r. 4689

RATIONALIZATION
false explanations for true reasons
  3476
reigned supreme 2919

RATIONS
Live upon our daily r. 3112

RATTLE
fear figures if he can r. you enough
  3971

RATTLESNAKE
sin treated like cream puff instead
  of r. 10345

RATTLING
neglect God for r. of a coach 7712
When r. bones together fly 6598

RAVENS
We were r, now sheep 1348

RAY
tints tomorrow with prophetic r.
  618

RAYS
should lamp purest r. bestow 3223

RAZORS
Quarry the granite rock with r.
  9233

REACH
assertively r. out to help others
  3901
cannot r. distant horizons 4544
ceased to r. to human beings as
  source of help 7548
courage to r. out 3316
Dark things r. out toward
  brightness 5906
disappeared if within r. of
  predatory hands 3202
Don't try to r. God with your
  understanding 11607
effort to r. for God 478
God hid knot so low we cannot r.
  5384
God in love 11607
God is above all things, but not
  beyond r. 4612
God will r. down all the way 7514
God will r. for you 5430
God's greatness above our r. 4681
Greatness within r. of everyone
  5283
heaven at last 2162
How shall I r. thy shores 7492
However high we r. 345
most important events never r.
  history books 5725
Nothing sets person out of devil's
  r. as humility 6024
our hands r. always upward 7575

power of choosing good, evil
  within r. 5047
should exceed grasp 4420
Stars golden fruits all out of r.
  11637
taller we grew, more easily we
  could r. 6017
the heart must come from above
  7929
under praise we open, r, grow
  3144
up as far as you can 7514
what toil can scarcely r. in an age
  7223
When we r. the end of our
  hoarded resources 7570

REACHED
As soon as consciousness is r.
  3479
God judges not by point man has
  r. 4713
God r. by way of love, suffering
  4802
Great accomplishments only
  occasionally r. 3593
heights of great men r. and kept
  8566
me like a solemn joy 4758
Success not position one has r.
  10809

REACHES
at home gentle life r. us 5849
Faith r. beyond our five senses
  3690
false report spreads where
  recantation never r. 10453
future something everyone r. 4327
Satan's friendship r. to prison door
  2665
smile r. out, attracts 5504

REACHING
beyond boundaries of human
  efforts 10540
Hope, r. out for something to
  come 3835

REACT
it's how I r. 508
to situations as Christ did 6301
we r. decisively against those who
  take freedom from us 9463

REACTION
anger natural r. to critical word
  10003
of world is to get rid of him 6127
surrender your r. to what the Lord
  does 10974

REACTIONS
Character sum total of r. 1000
to enemy hurt you more than
  enemy 3175
Wisdom by-product of godly r.
  11911

READ
Bible in relation to whole message
  642
Bible more widely r. 726

Children don't r. to find identity
  852
dictators executed those who r.
  Bible 726
Example a lesson all men can r.
  3430
From man's face can r. his
  character 8494
God grant they r. the good with
  smiles 7017
good for uneducated to r.
  quotations 9383
home must teach what to r. 8333
How does the musician r. the rest
  7056
I never omit to r. Gospel 732
I r. Gospel every day with same
  pleasure 732
I've r. the last page of the Bible
  4316
if could r. secret history of enemies
  3161
If we r. Old Testament prophets
  5423
In people's eyes I r. malice, vice
  3571
in Plato, Cicero sayings wise,
  beautiful 930
man a volume if you know how
  to r. him 8490
May better r. the darkened soul
  6583
nature can r. lectures of ethics,
  divinity 3192
not asked what we have r. 49
not the times 1476
not to believe and take for granted
  856
not to contradict, confute 856
not to find talk, discourse 856
pay more attention when quoted
  than when we r. 9388
pricetags for people to r. each
  other by 10519
real book not one that we r. 638
small print of man's soul 739
the Bible 690
the eternities 1476
things you r. condition mind 862
to weigh, consider 856
Tombstones of some people
  should r. 7041
way to r. book of aphorisms 9387
weather forecasts before pray for
  rain 8851
what man has written man may r.
  8049
who never stir from home r. only
  a page 6945
without reflecting like eating
  without digesting 863
world of little use who cannot r. it
  12039

READERS
diamonds, rare and valuable who
  profit 857
divided into four classes 857
Sandglasses, retain nothing 857
Sponges, absorb 857

Stainbags, retain dregs 857

READILY

Were the works of God r.
understandable 4510

READING

Give time to r. of Bible 697

have not placed r. before praying
because more important 8824

joy in r. God's Word 733

joy not dulled by age 858

like a conversation with finest men
861

make r. of your Word a pleasure
661

mistake not acquiring habit of r,
study 7793

nice, subtle happiness of r. 858

No entertainment so cheap as r.
855

no pleasure so lasting as r. 855

People commit murder after r.
about murder 12156

polite, unpunished vice 858

selfish, serene, lifelong intoxication
858

unable to distinguish what is
worth r. 2997

READS

real book one that r. us 638

the prayer unspoken in my heart
7478

READY

always r. to learn 3008

be r. to depart when God calls
2355

boots on, r. to go 2354

can change any time he is r. 3596

cannot put off living until r. 11388

Evil is r. for anything 3359

get r. for the worst 5911

Get spindle r, God will send flax
9346

Give me the r. hand rather than r.
tongue 2497

God is ever r, we are so unready
4562

God stands r. to take over
management of our lives 3758

Have thy tools r. 10142

I am r. at any time 2301

not r. today will not be r.
tomorrow 9296

out of options r. for God's
surprises 2596

Prayer not a r. gift 8914

Satan r. to help to new opinions
2944

Strong minds, great hearts, true
faith, r. hands 6299

to meet my Maker 2302

Was he ever r. with word or good
cheer 7423

When will is r, feet light 7870

REAL

a thing that happens to you 5886

always checked with failure,
imperfection 9498

any person whose growth as r. as
my own 7184

belief that does not command not
r. 612

can always tell a r. friend 4213

Christianity is hard 8108

dim perceptions of r. nature of
gospel 6713

doesn't happen all at once 5886

doesn't often happen to people
who break easily 5886

For a mighty grasp of the r. 7448

friends don't care if socks don't
match 4264

friends have great time doing
nothing 4265

friends know you have good
reason 4266

friendship shown in trouble 4267

friendship that can cease never r.
4274

glory of God is the r. business of
life 7027

glory springs from silent conquest
of ourselves 4414

God more r. to me than any
thought, thing, person 7098

God's promises r, glorious 4458

goodness does not attach itself
merely to this life 5079

growth began when discovered
9366

important to be r. mother to
children 7856

In Christ, it was all r. 6411

inner man, his r. self 6842

interruptions r. life 2750

isn't how you are made 5886

Jesus Christ makes us r, not
merely sincere 9403

joy is sorrow accepted,
transformed 6557

Life is r! Life is earnest 2328

life seems to have no plots 9405

Love lets us be our r. selves 7254

love want other person's good
7197

man is maze of a million notes
6212

May it be the r. I who speaks 8989

Most have no r. hatreds 6161

Most have no r. loves 6161

most r. shadowy unreality 1399

mystic, to participate here and
now in that r. life 7969

Mystical means r. 7954

Nothing becomes r. until
experienced 3539

once you are r, you can't be ugly
5886

permit r. selves to be known
10019

Poetry making truth more r. 8617

prayer gives solitude r. meaning
10562

regard seen world as r. world
3812

self-loving spirit antithesis of r.
living 10053

Silences r. conversations between
friends 4268

spirituality has outcome 1404

stand at r. height against higher
nature 6037

takes a long time 5886

test of what is r. 9399

than children to have r. father
3922

thing so r. it never can be told
10274

things are invisible spiritual
realities 615

things aren't simple 9402

this world two hundred times
more r. than God 7491

ugly face sometimes better than r.
one 6057

union through pain seemed more
r, holy 8269

unseen world takes shape as r.
world 3812

up into the r. world, the r. waking
5672

was anything r. ever gained
without sacrifice 4341

When R. you don't mind being
hurt 5886

REALIST

adjusts the sails 8249

Christ, a r. 1154

sees tunnel and light 8250

REALITIES

confesses, r. have begun 1600

enduring r. are love, service 10829

faith believing in r. beyond sense,
sight 3657

little in comparison with eternal r.
4559

real things are invisible spiritual r.
615

things little in comparison with
eternal r. 3281

REALITY

always more conservative than
ideology 9406

babyhood of the Son of God a r.
6125

beginning to think tube is r. 11045

belongs to eternity 9404

convinced of the r. of their faith
7472

cross social r. of representing
Order to come 2103

cross, where legend, r. intersect
2150

equilibrium between dream, r.
7435

friend who cares faces r. of
powerlessness 3080

frightening and distressing bit of r.
9408

God is the great r. 4458

has no news value 9404

How reluctantly mind consents to
r. 9400

in r. soul, life too complex to touch
10653

is not God at all and has no r.
4846

is to leave r. for a shadow 6495

look unblinkingly at the r. 33

more fantastic than we can image
9407

more fantastic than we think 9407

Mysticism art of union with r.
7956

object of faith, unseen r. 3831

Reality always more conservative
than r. 9406

retreating from r. into nothingness
3370

science measured against r. is
primitive and childlike 9867

silent closet best declares God's r.
10554

substituted relativity for r. 5808

those who fixed eyes on r. judged
insane 5730

To deny r. of sin 10407

unbeliever can no longer refuse r.
of our faith 10938

Without silence fall short of r.
10246

worshiper aware of no r. 1399

REALIZATION

Anticipation more delightful than
r. 7160

Contentment, r. of how much you
have 1783

Humanness is r. of love 5014

REALIZE

earth, you're too wonderful to r.
2974

failure to r. dealing with human
material 3120

failures did not r. close to success
3607

God had always been speaking
5395

how wicked we are 4773

I cannot judge intention of another
4247

more we learn, more we r. how
little we know 3029

nothing is secular in world 4732

societal problems solved one
person at a time 3901

the power of God 7485

way to love is r. it might be lost
7311

REALIZED

if one r. that God heard 4886

man is an eternal stranger on
planet 7436

REALIZES

God in midst, quiet in midst of
alarm 3972

his smallness, becomes spiritually
great 5309

Love ceaseless effort to r.
boundless treasures 7211

soul hardly ever r. it 7146

who r. nothing terrible in death
7059

REALIZING

Contentment, r. God has given me
everything 1784

REALLY

afraid to show each other who we
r. are 6057

great man makes every man feel
great 5304

great words to master are short
7000

REALM

if not prepared to fight in spiritual
r. 8818

Vision outside r. of predictable
11736

REAP

as ye sow, so shall ye r. 1727

praise, sow seeds 1574

Sow act, r. habit 1041

Sow character, r. destiny 1041

Sow habit, r. character 1041

Sow thought, r. act 1041

We r. as we have sown 3289
2622

REAP'D

thorns r. of tree planted 1737

REAPING

judgment of God r. that comes
from sowing 4721

REAPS

He who listens, r. 1848

REARED

brazen serpent r. where snakes bite
11432

REARING

without Christianity r. pagans
8308

REARRANGE

best to r. prejudices 11228

REARRANGING

people think they are thinking
when r. prejudices 9178

REASON

Almighty does nothing without r.
3781

And explain the r. why 10606

As sight in body, so is r. in soul
9412

Bible, where wit and r. fail 710

By faith led not against, but
beyond r. 3834

can ascertain difficulties 9420

can give no explanation before
birth or after death 9419

cannot r. your way to belief in God
9428

cannot remove difficulties 9420

common ground between cross, r.
impossible 1239

Do not give up r. 1241

does not prove God exists 3776

dog has so many friends 9499

door guarded by proud spirit of R.
7950

easily comprehended by human r.
9411

endowed with r. to be sharpened
9425

Faith higher faculty than r. 3675

Faith is not r. 3687

Faith lies on the other side of r.
3685

faith no merit if r. provided proof
3841

faith, r. not in opposition 3842

God does not expect faith without
r. 3840

God endowed us with r. 6324

God himself is the r. why 7574

God is r. unchangeable 4514

God knows, not I, the r. why
11468

God never contradicts r. 9413

God not reached by r. 4802

God transcends r. 9413

God will direct r. 1241

God's essence hidden to human r.
4670

gospel addressed not to r. but faith
3796

Had Mary been filled with r. 9414

has never been a mountain climber
3716

haste, breathless for no r. 5577

have no patience with r. alone
3025

head on us for same r. pin has
10992

heart aware of God not r. 3750

heart which experiences God, not
r. 4771

highest trees have most·r. to dread
thunder 9241

If work of God be comprehended
by r. 3841

impaired 1239

In philosophy predominance of r.
11191

In vain our haughty r. swells 4676

infinitely aloof from curious eyes
of r. 4743

knowing is above r. 5809

limits of r. make faith necessity
3840

Love can hope where r. would
despair 7209

Lust and r. are enemies 7354

Man not an angel whose r. works
perfectly 9417

many are troubled 10977

Memory the treasury of r. 7733

mind of man cannot explain r.
4492

miss joy, miss r. for existence 6571

More fail for lack of
encouragement than any other r.
3138

neither a shame or sin to cultivate
r. 9425

neither does r. prove God cannot
exist 3776

Neither great poverty nor riches
will hear r. 9418

no r. why here rather than there 4905

no r. why miner not an as intellectual as poet 6332

No wickedness proceeds on r. 11890

nor is man a mule whose r. works not at all 9417

not necessarily against r. because above it 7938

not proud r. keeps door of heaven 12130

ought to follow, not precede, faith 9411

our intellectual eye 9422

polar bear wears fur coat 6213

Real friends know you have good r. 4266

saw not till faith sprung the light 3777

serpent beguiled Eve to depend on r. alone 9424

source beyond all r. 4538

Still let r. sway 6878

thus with life 7019

Time heals what r. cannot 11332

to do with time between birth, death 9419

to see clearly needs light of heaven 9422

Trinity mystery r. cannot fathom 11428

we must ask God for things he intends to give 8990

Were works of God understandable by human r. 4510

What is r. for saying God does not heed us 7567

Whatever weakens r. is sin 10424

Where r. cannot wade, faith may swim 3821

who cannot r. is a fool 9415

who dares not r. is a slave 9415

who maintains only he has power to r. correctly 8196

who will not r. is a bigot 9415

You can't r. with your heart 5628

REASONABLE

Man a reasoning, rather than r, animal 7416

man adapts to world 980

that God's justice also incomprehensible 4728

true faith essentially r. 3842

when devil looks most r, is most dangerous 2648

wrong way always seems more r. 5453

REASONABLENESS

Grant us r. in our dealings with each other 9106

REASONED

how many r. out of faith by argument 3742

ways of Providence cannot be r. out 5450

what he knows needs no r. proof 5809

REASONING

Faith is a r. trust 3676

few observations and much r. leads to error 9410

In spiritual matters, human r. not in order 9416

Man a r. rather than reasonable animal 7416

Man spends life r. on past 8380

many observations, little r. leads to truth 9410

one foot on God's side, one on human r. 1156

youth governed more by feeling than r. 12181

REASON'S

last step is recognition things beyond it 9421

voice and God's 3813

REASONS

believe in devil for three r. 2650

believe Satan to exist for two r. 9854

couple married for trivial r. 2922

Divorce disengagement for trivial r. 2922

examine r. to evil habits 3935

false explanations for true r. 3476

persuaded by r. we discover ourselves 270

pleasing to God for other r. 11685

To know r. which have moved God 4989

two r. for loving God 7533

When man r, God laughs 9427

REASSURES

glad when great man r. us of his humanity 5307

REBEL

fallen men a r. who must lay down his arms 9577

right to seek and r. 4135

REBELLION

involves limitation 4117

magnitude of r. expressed by Calvary 10371

Meek endurance, obedience without r. 7728

not to believe God's promises 11596

one's feelings of r. 8779

religious dimension of sin r. against God 10394

Sin is red-handed r. against God 10371

sin r. against divine authority 10390

Sin r. against rule of God 10366

sinned out of deliberate r. 10387

REBELLIOUS

God does not take responsibility for existence of r. 5175

God lets r. deny his existence 4129

God lets r. shake their fist 4129

to convert r. will cost God crucifixion 2134

REBELS

Jesus Christ came to make worshipers out of r. 12137

REBORN

Sabbath when hope r. 10959

Your whole nature must be r. 880

REBOUND

not ball against wall to r. 4222

REBUILD

God wants to r. minds, give new values 7863

REBUILT

marriage an edifice that must be r. every day 7597

REBUKE

cruel in adversity 203

new vices we r. 10414

thank God he will use sin to r. you 11152

REBUKED

something in Jesus r. world 2168

though God has often r. us 7186

REBUKES

ought not to have more salt than sugar 2854

REBUKING

Christ Lion in majesty r. winds, demons 6425

RECALL

unless I can r. a loving family 6919

RECANT

No Christian ever known to r. on deathbed 3764

RECANTATION

false report spreads where r. never reaches 10453

RECAPTURE

cannot r. relationship to another human being 9446

RECEDES

Nothing r. like success 10798

The world r, it disappears 2389

RECEIPT

no business r. of value 5726

RECEIVE

both the ones who give love, and the ones who r. 7213

does not r. inner support by judgment of God 5477

from church we r. postulates of order 5169

giver never fails to r. 9763

God is creator of minds to r. his fullness 4514

God is enlarging to r. him 4514

heart made able to r. uncreated light 4749

High Priest waiting to r. me 716

In celebration weak, lowly r. new stature 3235

in giving that we r. 9086
in thy mercy, r. us 619
inheritance we r. from God
   limitless 4694
joy when recognize My love
   coming to you 5271
so easy to r. Christ 5653
to r. Christ appropriating faith
   3801
two hands, one to r. 10729
willing to come as pauper, r. Holy
   Spirit 5792
with courtesy r. God's messenger
   160

RECEIVED
all that he hoped for 8806
inspiration r. put into practice
   4160
No one needed to ask if r. Holy
   Ghost 5806
No person ever honored for what
   he r. 5895
nothing that he asked for 8806
So much God would give, so little
   is r. 8662

RECEIVER
Flattery corrupts r, giver 4048

RECEIVES
courtesy pleases him who r. 1944
faith r. 3659
Faith r. the impossible 3713
generous man remembers what he
   r. 4346
he that r. should never forget 4363
he who r. good turn should never
   forget it 5070
humble r. praise way clean
   window takes light 6033
Lo, earth r. him from the bending
   skies 6138
more soul r, more it grows 10699
saint r. everything as God's
   goodness 9790
Who much r. but nothing gives
   4374

RECEIVEST
Thou r. again what thou findest
   4954
Thou r. over and above 4954
Thou r. that thou mayst owe 4954

RECEIVING
gratitude, secret desire of r. greater
   benefits 5262

RECENTLY
importance of events by how r.
   happened 7990

RECEPTION
When by the r. of the Holy Spirit
   4889

RECEPTIVE
God always r. to misery, need
   4590
more r. to his inpouring 4499
need not wonder whether God in
   r. mood 4590

RECEPTIVITY
cultivate habit of r. 4537
develop powers of spiritual r.
   7564

RECIPE
for a long life 7020
for being a bore 1867
no r. for living that suits all cases
   6214

RECIPROCAL
Marriage, obligation r. 7642

RECIPROCATED
Love if not r. will flow back 7241

RECITE
anxiously memorize, r. script
   assigned 6824

RECKLESS
Gaiety often r. ripple over depths
   of despair 5508
get life out to sea in r. abandon to
   God 9564
than speak r. word against servant
   of Christ 5143

RECKON
not upon a long life 7021

RECKONING
Every day a day of r. 2194

RECLUSE
Christ was not a r. 6436

RECOGIZING
God's will 5395

RECOGNITION
of individual affirms respect for
   human dignity 9952
of individual affirms uniqueness
   of each person 9952
pain thread in God's weaving
   10915
Reason's last step is r. things
   beyond it 9421

RECOGNIZE
as you r. Me as your source 7548
dark night for what it is 2556
Experience enables you to r.
   mistake 3517
face of Jesus Christ in every
   human being 914
fact to r. is we must be born again
   9801
first step to victory to r. enemy
   11670
flattery is poison 4053
God waiting for us to r. him 8843
I r. power passing mine 4825
in God the Author of our goods
   8796
joy when r. My love coming to you
   5271
lies, not a soul would r. their
   skinny carcasses 6853
most people don't r. opportunities
   8221
necessity of Holy Spirit for living
   11243

no rights but human rights 3230
O Christian, thy dignity 2763
only sovereign I r. 4951
opportunity difference between
   failure, success 8227
unable to r. ourselves 6067

RECOGNIZED
Hollywood has not r. what tingles
   spine 4551
scholars have r. devil's existence
   2650
two dangers to be r. in the church
   1400
until equality is r. 3230

RECOGNIZING
Humility r. God, others
   responsible for my achievements
   6011

RECOMMENDATION
pleasant face a silent r. 3570
Self-praise is no r. 9235

RECOMPENSE
charity to be useful without r.
   1084
Do right, God's r. to you power to
   do more right 9648

RECONCILE
cannot r. Bible with human origin
   736
Golden Rule would r. political
   contention 5005
Golden Rule would r. selfishness,
   greed 5005
To r. man with man and not with
   God is to r. no one 9432
two things not easy to r. 7069
yourself to wait in darkness 2557

RECONCILED
always man who is r. to God 9430
Never is God said to be r. to man
   9430
two spirits can never be r. 877

RECONCILER
death, the great r. 2420

RECONCILIATION
ascribed to Jesus Christ 3043
demands courage 9431
demands generosity 9431
demands nobility 9431
not weakness or cowardice 9431
overcoming of oneself rather than
   adversary 9431
preaching standard of r. not her
   own 1492
repentance is the r. 9582
sometimes demands heroism 9431

RECONCILING
cross, r. heaven, earth together
   2154
In confession we open lives to r.
   1602

RECONSIDER
important moments in lives 5392

RECONSTRUCTION
schemes of world r. have failed 6487

RECORD
budget r. of how you spend more than earned 4030
found in register of God, not r. of man 6023
if make r. true 559
most outstanding is date of birth of Jesus Christ 5726
Revelation r. of God's acts in time 9710
simple r. of three short years 6483
Year is closed, r. made 8082

RECORDED
every thought, deed is registered and r. 71
one case of death-bed repentance r. 9602

RECORDS
greatest, most momentous fact which history r. 5710

RECOURSE
acquire confident in r. to God 8796
Failure invitation to r. to God 3587

RECOVER
my own incapacity to r. 6459
need silence to r. from futility of words 10556
slip of foot may r. 11407

RECOVERED
slip of foot may be r. 10444
slip of tongue perhaps never r. 10444

RECOVERY
should take place in churches 134

RECREATED
society has r. Jesus in own cultural image 6467

RECREATES
Sleep r. 10487

RECREATING
effect of Bible 697
poverty, deprivation of God's r, loving peace 8697
silences of contemplation 1760

RECREATION
as proper as prayer 6837
cannot find time for r, find time for illness 6835
erect houses of worship but our shrines are our places of r. 6068
heaven, work is continual r. 5644
home where wholesome r. enjoyed 5853
not highest kind of enjoyment 6837

RECREATIVE
eternally creative and r. love 10562

RECRUIT
People do not need Satan to r. to evil 3396

RECRUITING
People capable of r. themselves to evil 3396

RECUPERATION
sleep not meant only for r. of body 10487

RED
If the light is r. or yellow 5422
Like a fiery furnace r. 2638
My sin is r. 5482
pessimist sees only r. light 8245
Vacation: getting into pink by going into r. 6840

RED SEA
Have you come to the R. place in life 5407

REDEEM
Christ came to r. men 6424
Jesus Christ, to r. world 497
Lord appeared to r. us by his death 6477
To untell the days, to r. these hours 9568
While government cannot r. world 5177

REDEEMED
Each of the r. shall forever know 6169
Evil can only be purged, r. 3354
God r. human race when we were spitting in his face 9434
holiness shares with angels, r. men 4658
only the r. can keep his commandments 4536
Show me that you are r. 3324
Spirit will never sanctify whom Son has not r. 3043

REDEEMER
Father, R. and Spirit of grace 11424
will believe in your R. 3324

REDEEMING
purpose of Christ's r. work 9438

REDEEMS
God r. before he enjoins 4536

REDEFINES
Jesus r. meaning of love 7201

REDEMPTION
brings man back into tune with praise 8743
claim of r. of Jesus can satisfy aching soul 6402
Deny the virgin birth and you paralyze r. 6404
hope of nation in r. of character 5190
means Jesus can put into man disposition that ruled his life 9436
No creature that deserved r. 5483

problem of restoring beauty is r. of soul 10668
strangest truth is r. comes through suffering 9439
the Son, work of r. 11426
understanding of r. not necessary to salvation 9433
We are God's property by r. 7552
work out appreciation of r. 11274
would still need r. 9435

REDEMPTIVE
love of God r. power 4780
theology teaches mercy not effective until justice done 4730
Unearned suffering is r. 10919

REDIRECTING
process involved in r. our lives painful 5449

REDIRECTION
total r. of history 5720

REDIRECTS
Bible r. my will 722

REDISCOVER
I invent nothing. I r. 2004

REDISCOVERED
Personal contact a movement that must be r. 7630

REDOUBLING
Fanaticism r. effort, forgotten aim 3908

REDUCED
all desires have been r. to one 9282
life r. to possessions 8634

REDWOOD
What a story a r. stump could tell 5731

REED
broken r. of human support 3132
like r. faith will survive storm 3702

REELING
and staggering through life 11450
you sent my blindness r. 7473

REFER
to Scriptures for choices 650

REFERENCE
unless bears r. to this great historic event 5726

REFILLED
each day r. 2979

REFINE
Crises r. life 2044

REFINED
Poetry has r. my enjoyments 8616

REFINEMENT
Forgetting oneself is not r. of love 7169
neglecting r. of the mind 7793

REFLECT
a mirror to r. your love to all I meet 9079

no life so humble it cannot r.
  God's light 7055
on present blessings 828
with sorrow on competitions 2423

REFLECTED
If I want the Infinite r.
  undisturbed in me 7715
mirror in which glory of God r.
  10339

REFLECTING
life, facets of one diamond r. light
  6985
people mirrors reflecting mood
  3019
Praise is the saint r. Christ 8734
read without r. like eating without
  digesting 863

REFLECTION
different on lake, swamp 8929
wars within world r. of wars
  inside people 11764
weak, mental r. of God badly out
  of focus 4579
without commitment, paralysis
  1532
world, r. of man's face 436

REFLECTIONS
making so much noise with rapid
  r. 8813

REFLECTS
admits light of heaven and r. it
  11945
be mirror that r. light 3455
law r. God's holiness 1530
Our sociology r. our theology
  9487

REFLEX
substituted r. action for revelation
  5808

REFORM
Christianity not to be judged by
  success or failure to r. world
  1188
Marriage not a r. school 7643
not from state but from
  communities 1457
others unconsciously when act
  uprightly 3457
thy world, beginning with me
  9103
uncompromising in compromising
  age 1457

REFORMATION
capacity for r. within 3596
far-reaching r. of church is
  prerequisite 1439
permanent r. of the world 3230

REFORMATORY
by repressing emotions we become
  r. 3050

REFORMED
fault can be r. 8312

REFRAIN
not just r. from adultery, but from
  desiring 6444
not just r. from killing, but from
  being angry 6444
When listeners r. from evil-hearing
  10477
When will talkers r. from
  evil-speaking 10477

REFRAINED
if world had r. from evil 5031

REFRESH
God's gentleness to r. you 4858
What parched grounds r. as with a
  shower 8867

REFRESHED
Death, we shall rise r. 2244
wake from sermon r. 10094

REFRESHES
prayer r, restores, renews mind
  8857
us on the journey with pleasant
  inns 7014

REFRESHING
Honesty, a beautiful and r.
  simplicity 5874
Jesus Christ, comforts r. 6352
rain is r. 8033
to watch a new Christian 1339
without r. of spirit duties burdens
  8857

REFRESHMENT
Labor r. from repose 3102
silence is r. 9374
uncertain in asking any small
  drop of r. 4653

REFRESHMENTS
wooed with religious r. 1403

REFRIGERATOR
critics suspicious of conversion
  not in r. 3052

REFUGE
Discouraged people need a r. 3066
from danger 6468
Lie is r. of weakness 6845
no original nothingness for r. 1962
saved by making atonement my r.
  3753
Silence the universal r. 10266
While to that r. clinging 232

REFUSAL
Faith a r. to panic 3677
of praise a desire to be praised
  twice 8723
sin willful r. to obey God 10387

REFUSALS
Give me the spiritless r. 4530
to adapt to a God too demanding
  2959

REFUSE
dead so long as you r. to die
  10050
I will not r. to do something I can
  do 2500

If one could only r. to meet Old
  Age 8136
If r. to be made straight when
  green 12166
if r. to take guidance of Jesus
  Christ 5458
ignore God, r. to obey him 1014
lives shaped by those who r. us
  6236
Men fear death because they r. to
  understand 2336
often r. to accept idea 9516
owe it to God that we r. rusty
  brains 11274
pros and cons means r. to obey
  8117
Stand still, r. to retreat 2742
those that hurt us, we r. all crosses
  2092
to stand for truth 3846
troubles come because we r. to sit
  quietly 9367
unbeliever can no longer r. reality
  of our faith 10938
Whence ability to wish evil, r.
  good 5051
will not r. to do something I can
  do 106
wisdom must sometimes r. what
  ignorance may ask 8971
wretched r. of your teeming shore
  7985

REFUSED
as unkind as if had r. 10148
if love of God r. 4781
judged by light r. to accept 6579

REFUSES
devil categorically r. to do will of
  God 4915
devil r. to stand under God 4915
Grace r. to put ceiling on concern
  5233
man who r. to believe anything
  3710
nonconformist r. to be satisfied
  with things as they are 9311
the cross, remains on throne 2821
unforgiving spirit r. to be soothed,
  healed 9640

REFUSING
Faith is r. to feel guilty over
  confessed sin 3672
to have opinion a way of having
  one 8201
to set aside trivial preferences
  7793
to worship God 4442
to yield to depression, fear 2563

REGAIN
In celebration high, mighty r.
  balance 3235
then I r. consciousness 11615

REGARD
as enormous the little wrong to
  others 4097
cannot r. everyone as stranger 922
God without r. to any other 491

instinctively r. seen world as real
world 3812

REGARDS
Workless faith God never r. 3825

REGENERATE
has done more to r. and soften
mankind 6483

REGENERATES
God r. us 1143

REGENERATION
We are God's property by r. 7552
world without children, without r.
1104

REGIONS
not by seeking fertile r. where toil
lighter 4974
out of self, into unknown r. 9930

REGISTER
History little more than r. of
misfortunes 5719
sin, two witness present to r.
10418
to be found in r. of God, not man
6023

REGISTERED
every thought, deed is r. and
recorded 71

REGRET
an appalling waste of energy 9440
5486
best speech you will ever r. 395
can't build on it 9440
deepest r. not more time for Bible
study 682
do not r. what is past 1786
never a backward glance of r.
4281
never our tenderness that we r.
2420
Nor do I r. I have lived 7005
Old age a r. 12199
only good for wallowing in 9440
5486
our severity 2420
Sin pays in r. 10379
world so kind you leave with r.
2293

REGRETFULLY
look so r. at closed door 8229

REGRETS
faith that cannot survive collision
not worth r. 3639

REGRETTED
ever remember when r. having
said kind word 6636

REGULARITY
in space 11650
unfailing r. of the seasons 4643

REGULATE
God does not r. body for us 847
Habits servants that r. 5498

REGULATED
holy life r. by divine truth 5736

REGULATES
Devotion r. all our conduct 9731
Unbelief where no hand r. events
11595

REGULATIONS
Jesus did not attain perfection by
rules, r. 8520

REHEARSED
in dreams act part r. in waking
hours 2966

REIGN
if unwilling to accept righteous r.
of God 8818
love counts royalty but drudgery
if cannot r. for Christ 6457
old age, how hateful is your r.
8150
Take, O God, thy power and r.
2981
universe under the r. of God 1285
Where saints immortal r. 5670

REIGNED
all kings that ever r. 6353
Rationalization r. supreme 2919

REIGNS
Conscience r. 1676
good marriage not where
perfection r. 7591
kingdom of God exists because
God r. 4734
now in hell he r. 2656
Sorrow r. on thrones of universe
10613
Where love r, joy of heaven felt
7342

REIN
free r. to the flesh 466
which way to pull the r. 1151

REINS
Feelings all holy when God's hand
on r. 4016
Man rides, God holds the r. 7498

REJECT
accept or r. God's initiative 585
Christ's existence, world
inexplicable riddle 5728
if you r. what you don't like 588
learn from those who r. you 175
when we r. our specialness 1635
Word of God, accept or r. 686

REJECTED
children understand what parents
have r. 12157
if love of God r. 4781

REJECTION
accept Christ's r. as our r. 3335
Christ's words provoked
acceptance or r. 6377
How could I know acceptance
without r. 1512
produces the pearl 204
the sand in the oyster 204

REJECTS
God's truth in favor of devil's
impure philosophies 11512
my soul r. the aid of language
8792
world r. Christianity 1188

REJOICE
at birth, not person involved 817
At our repentance, angels r. 1285
Christ mourned that thou
mightest r. 6393
different race, r. among them 3234
Do not r. at my grief 10588
easy to r. 37
in what is good, strong 3940
It is his, therefore r. 11107
Jesus has many who r. with him
2828
makes mind r. in sufferings 5930
not hypocrisy to r. in distress 221
That they are never sated makes
all the saints r. 9780
Time too short for those who r.
11333
We r. in the light 1375
we sin by disobeying apostolic
injunction to r. 8744
Why r. at birth, grieve at funeral
817
will r. little in Matthew 5224
with joy that radiates 3182
with their successes 9963

REJOICES
A lover r. 7283
faith r. in its God 3965
God r. in differences 1445
God r. when one beggar scratches
another 9454
poor heart that never r. 6535
wise man r. for what he has 1793

REJOICING
in the east 10962
never in need, yet r. in gains 4954

REKINDLED
Sabbath when dreams r. 10959

RELATED
people who r. to God best 7526
When rightly r. to God 5463

RELATES
insight that r. us to God 8504
prayer r. life to life of humanity
8917

RELATING
youth a spirit of r. to the world
12183

RELATIONS
God knows all r. 4881

RELATIONSHIP
builds r. on less than honesty
building on sand 9447
cannot find joy anywhere but in r.
to God 6552
Children born from r. secondary
10239

Christ makes human destiny depend on r. to himself 6431

Christianity, a r. 1175

deep r. requires watchfulness, nourishment 9446

depends on r. toward God 4957

God draws us into r. with him 5395

if r. faulty, activity cannot be satisfactory 10227

If try to find lasting joy in human r. 9467

independence as destructive to r. as dependence 7614

live in things they possess instead of r. to God 8631

mother-child r. paradoxical, tragic 7858

of life, not of intellect 6515

Once we come into simple r. with God 7509

parenting modeled after r. between God and man 8299

sex primarily a r. 10227

taken up with r. to God 2822

to God fits you to live 4555

to God only simple thing 10653

to God that of a child 188

true joy of man's life in r. to God 9467

uniqueness that gives freshness, vitality to a r. 6197

with God marked with own temperament 8883

RELATIONSHIPS

hammer out convictions on anvil of r. 5832

healthiest r. breathe 9494

Marriage most difficult of r. 7641

Marriage most intimate of r. 7641

unless meditation results in richer, more loving r. 7725

Whenever personal r. develop qualities 5014

Whenever r. diminish humanness there is evil 5014

RELATIVITY

substituted r. for reality 5808

that's r. 9527

RELAX

best time to r. is when you don't have time to r. 9534

don't succeed, r. 3597

RELAXED

Christian more attractive 9529

In Christ r. and at peace 8470

RELEASE

Christ offering a way of r. 6434

coward seeks r. from pressure 1937

to r. men from limitations 4135

tomb is r. for soul 2350

we must r. grip on everything 972

Words r. energy 12001

RELEASES

balm of death r. 1332

faith r. life 3747

positive word r. positive energy 12001

RELENTLESS

anxieties engendered by success 10817

combated by r. forces 2630

drift of events make decision 2491

RELENTLESSLY

sin pays r. 10421

RELEVANCE

Christ's words have same r. 6359

formal denial of r. of God 3036

RELEVANT

To make message r. to world 5109

RELIABILITY

of nature 4643

RELIANCE

end of r. on natural devotion 5792

greatest whose r. on truth most unfaltering 5297

Without him human r. is vain 5411

RELIEF

For fast-acting r, try slowing down 6832

of diver coming back to sunlight, familiar faces 6110

Tears bring r. 1509

RELIEVE

aspire to r. suffering of others 10876

Christ a Brother to r. 6370

to r. a patient of guilt 5485

will r. none in the dark 10037

RELIGION

and home life are supplementary 5858

beats me 9544

can offer man burial service 7022

Christianity a resurrection r. 9689

Christianity is a r. of the open tomb 9688

Christianity not a r. 1175

Christianity only world r. that is evangelical 3301

cross destroyed r. equals happiness 2151

Education without r. 3005

Events, circumstances awaken our r. 8788

false r. continually changing places 5103

God not interested in organized r. 9539

have too much r. 9552

his r. is an Anythingarian 9553

human passions unbridled by morality, r. 5196

humans trying to work way to God 1219

If no joy in your r. 6534

if r. has no room for others and their needs 8818

is good views 9545

is man's quest for God 9545

is man-made 9545

Jesus' r. so long identified with conservatism 6452

Let r. be more a theory, more a love affair 9542

Many like r. as sort of lightning rod 4998

mechanics of r. 1301

merely ritual and ceremonial can never satisfy 9546

mixed multitudes within precincts of r. 5776

Morality without r. is tree without roots 7833

most have some sort of r. 317

Music used to ridicule r. 7910

need in r. new sight, strength 9554

need not new duties in r. 9554

need not new light 9554

need not new paths 9554

New Testament does not envisage solitary r. 1445

no good asking for simple r. 9402

No person shall deny truth of Christian r. 5183

of child depends on what parents are, not what they say 8356

originates on earth 9545

posesses the truth 11524

put Christ on the cross 9541

response of created personalities to God 9543

root of a happy r. 6713

science seemed at odds with r. 9866

scientists come to r. through limitations of science 9866

Sex the substitute r. 10231

shifting system of false r. 5103

small enough for our understanding 9538

Sour godliness is devil's r. 2186

Theology science of r. 11209

To die for a r. easier than to live it 7681

true r. is built upon the Rock 9550

what man tries to do for God 9545

without guilt tries to make God big pal of man 5487

without reminding hin of his filth 7425

RELIGIONS

are man's search for God 9547

concerned with worship of a god 1232

many r, but one gospel 9547

neurotics have founded r. 4390

no influence on man's behavior 1232

pagan r. doctrinal element at minumum 11226

two r. accept gloom as fact 9551

world has many r, one gospel 5106

RELIGIOUS

awakening that does not awaken sleeper to love 9737

beyond superficialities of r. culture 1760

boundary-line sharp, deep about r. life 1332

complaint that Christ not r. enough 6416

contention is the devil's harvest 9548

deadliest trap of devil is r. 2701

dimension of sin is rebellion against God 10394

din assure everything is well 12096

easy to turn r. life into beautiful memories 10165

Emotion may vary in r. experience 3052

escape r. stultification 1275

for the r, pain a travail to be borne 8255

greater injustice among champions of r. opinions 9540

hated Jesus' guts 6412

If not r, man will be superstitious 12109

If r. elite too proud 12098

Man a r. being 12110

movies, games, refreshments 1403

Mystery is demanded by r. instinct 12118

new world will arise from r. mists 637

no quarrel so bitter as r. quarrel 9360

opposite of r. fanatic is the gentle cynic 9549

Our constitution made for moral, r. people 5196

paradox comes into all r. thought 4682

persons knit into unity 1413

playing r. games in one corner 10124

pose gone when determine to concentrate 6056

Remind r. phony splinter is between you and Lord 6590

sects willing to be pushed around 1337

seldom solid home in absence of r. inspiration 5858

spend time serving as r. props 1300

strength of r. convictions 7988

Temptations dangerous in r. garb 11092

tone have their temporary effect 8845

values into higher or lower case 11658

Whenever r. life develop qualities 5014

whirl of r. activity 4410

work done without gifts of the Spirit 10181

RELINQUISH

God cannot r. perfections 4821

more often by what we r. 53

RELINQUISHMENT

of burdens, fears begins where 3987

RELUCTANCE

easy become difficult with r. 2756

Prayer is not overcoming God's r. 8933

RELUCTANT

most dejected, r. convert in all England 9829

RELUCTANTLY

How r. mind consents to reality 9400

Nothing so easy but difficult when done r. 3181

we sip r. at truth we find harsh 6870

RELY

Don't r. on human support 3132

God gives something to r. upon others do not experience 6178

mind, then r. upon God 13

world nothing to r. upon 10512

RELYING

accustomed to r. on words to manage, control 10259

on God has to begin over again every day 11477

REMADE

He who made us also r. us 1901

Love has to be r, made new 7217

only by that Carpenter can mankind be r. 6360

REMAIN

at beginning of godly life 6708

blessed r. eternally different 6169

cannot r. creative without solitude 10579

does not Lord hear nations blame, yet r. silent 4894

Forever God must r. what he has forever been 4821

God will sustain if r. faithful 5385

How can you expect to r. in state of virtue 11722

thorns pass, roses r. 10710

to r. in sin is devilish 10408

voice of a deep life within that will r. 3700

would r. friends with no one 9466

REMAINS

All that God gives r. his own 4821

For God, time r. 3274

future still r. 4334

having suffered r. always with us 10890

hears himself cursed and r. silent becomes partner of God 4894

love r. to me, I can pray 8135

memory alone r. 8082

refuses the cross, r. on throne 2821

To me r. not place nor time 4869

what r. is bestial 9622

what we have done for others r. 10091

wound heals, but scar r. 10446

yet guilt r. 5489

REMAKE

God raised up Jesus to r. history 5711

REMARK

Reply to a nasty r. 402

REMARKABLE

enjoys reputation of being most r. person he knows 9197

Good Book most r. euphemism 731

science reveals r. conformity in all things 9866

thing about fearing God is you fear nothing else 3994

thing about George Washington 7981

thing about way people talk about God 4886

with what fortitude bear suffering of others 10862

REMARKS

Have deaf ear for unkind r. 9456

man who r. it goes without saying 1877

REMEDILESS

ills r, murmur in vain 1563

REMEDY

Evangelism supernatural r. for world 3304

for anger is delay 397

God's r. for failure 10812

He that conceals his grief finds no r. 5341

most effective r. in Scriptures 650

must look at the r. 9804

state not r. for sin, but means to restrain 5177

think divorce panacea find r. worse 2927

world's one, only r. is cross 2169

REMEMBER

anyone r. you spoke to him today 3136

blessings from God 9270

child taught Sunday, r. Monday 1134

ever r. regretted having said kind word 6636

For calmness to r. 8827

friends who encourage 9270

gift of life 9270

God does not wish us to r. 4633

God is listening while you tell it 5148

he has a right to opinion 447

He that gives should never r. 4363

he who does good turn should never r. 5070

I r, I r. 2588

I r. my youth 12165

Lord, help me to r. 4622

majesty of the mountains 9270

mind can r, understand, love its maker 7771

present conflict is with defeated
foes 235
privilege of prayer 9270
the day's blessings 11158
the spring 11170
the teakettle sings 205
the way of the saints 234
to forget losses, setbacks, defeats
9270
well time you forgive and forget
7737
were to r. all instances in which
neglected him 4069
When tell truth, don't have to r.
what you said 11588
who your ruler is 1311
your abilities 9271
your assets 9271
your doing not God's 4319
your joys 9271
your possibilities 9271
your potentialities 9271
your strengths 9271
your triumphs, victories 9270

REMEMBERED
I strayed, yet I r. you 9070
in days of youth r. God 8140
Sorrows r. sweeten present joy
10624

REMEMBERING
Forget others' faults by r. your
own 5999

REMEMBERS
faultfinder always r. bad 2049
faultfinder never r. good 2049
friend r. you in his prayers 4179
generous man r. what he receives
4346
If I forget, yet God r. 7478
impossible to despair who r.
Helper is omnipotent 2595
when man wishes impossible, he r.
God 7490

REMEMBRANCE
Only Jesus worldwide r. 1369

REMIND
God uses our sins to r. us of
weakness 10306
Lives of great men all r. us 5288
3441
Lord, r. us gossip's mouth is devil's
mailbag 5146
religious phony splinter is
between you and Lord 6590
us not to waste, litter, pollute
9117
yourself God is with you 9983

REMINDED
of the greater Benefactor 4526

REMINDER
of Resurrection at start of each
new year 8080
outward imperfections r. of God's
priorities 1033

REMINISCENCES
old have r. of what never happened
12195

REMISS
love without fear makes men r.
9736

REMNANTS
twelve baskets full of r. 1136

REMORSE
beholding heaven, feeling hell
9574
Never mistake r. for repentance
9584
new freedom to betray without r.
10526
puts man in hell while on earth
9584
Repentance more than r. for sins
9597
Satan fails to speak of r. of
immorality 2662
Sin pays in r. 10379
sorrow because of circumstances
is r. 9580
the echo of lost virtue 9571
the pain of sin 9572
to carry own accuser within your
breast 9573

REMORSELESS
lust of gold, unfeeling and r.
11858

REMOTE
deaf live in silent world so r,
different 9094
through the infinite r. the name of
God 4712

REMOTEST
not r. expectation prayers will be
answered 8845

REMOULD
Melt and r. it, till it be 7003

REMOVE
Christianity does not r. load 931
Do not r. a fly with hatchet 2058
If God to r. possibility of
disobedience 8091
Patience and diligence r. mountains
8408
Reason cannot r. difficulties 9420
resurrection, Christianity
destroyed 9689
the disguise 10019
without giving God deadline to r.
it 8415

REMOVED
mountain r. by bird 3295

REMOVES
Cheerfulness r. rust from mind
1093
God r. what would pervert 7685
ornament of friendship who takes
away respect 9642

RENDER
obtain proof r. faith superfluous
3806
services they r. us attaches people
to us 5256

RENDERS
God a leveler who r. equal small
and great 4727

RENDING
the veil 2097

RENDS
In every pang that r. the heart
10597

RENEW
let us r. our trust in God 1918
Lord appeared to r. us by his
resurrection 6477
place where r. your springs that
never dry up 9933
the courage that prevails 1933

RENEWAL
and restoration are essentials 9533
and restoration not luxuries 9533

RENEWED
A heart in every thought r. 5620
commitment must be r. 1535
difference between worldliness,
godliness is r. mind 7769
illuminated by steady radiance, r.
daily 4538
Lord revels in mind r, enlightened
by grace 7776
Of thy creation, finished, yet r.
1966
Of thy r. earth 9898
political order cannot be r.
without theological virtues
5169
To be worn out is to be r. 7071
When person r. from day to day
9278

RENEWS
prayer r. minds 8857
same Lord who r. trees ready to r.
your life 9896
Worship r. the spirit 12141

RENOUNCE
must r. other loves for love of God
7334
To r. all is to gain all 9701

RENOVATED
society r. by Christianity 1187

RENOWN
God is virtue's r. 11687

RENUNCIATION
God speaks to us of r. 4900
hear God's call to r. 9351
Prayer the studied r. of one's own
will 8922
With r. life begins 7092

REPAIR
Acknowledge faults to r. damage
3956
cross to r. irreparable 2165

guilty of slander never can r. 10453

must keep friendships in constant r. 4249

the places we have wasted 9054

REPAIRED
Reputation once broken may possibly be r. 9612

REPAIRS
grow older, more replacements necessary 8181

REPAY
Evil r. with good 1191

Too great haste to r. obligation 5266

REPEAT
idly r. slanderous darts 5143

REPEATED
hear same prayers r. each Sunday 8845

sin r. seems permitted 10290

Vice r. like wand'ring wind 10411

REPEATING
human stories go on r. themselves 5984

involuntarily character of those among whom we live 6243

REPEATS
Everything r. 5344

REPELS
frowning face r. 5504

REPENT
cannot r. too soon 9609

command to r. goes unregarded 4726

easier to r. of sins committed than sins intend to commit 10327

for appalling silence of the good people 6285

for years with men 4091

God does not r. of it 4626

God will incline us to r. 9578

is God's point of view instead of one's own 9605

not so much for evil deeds of wicked people 6285

to r. divine 7065

To r. is to alter way of looking at life 9605

REPENTANCE
affects the whole man 9589

alters the entire life-style 9589

an attitude rather than single act 9588

an ongoing process 9589

At our r. angels rejoice 1285

cannot simultaneously will sin and r. 5210

chance to correct what man left crooked 9596

change of nature befitting heaven 9597

Death-bed r. is blowing snuff in face of heaven 9576

Death-bed r. is burning candle of life in service of the devil 9576

difference between true, false r. 9601

false r. cries out against something else 9601

from one sort of person to another is r. 9604

God can see r. coming a great way off 9582

God is there to meet r. 9582

golden key that opens palace of eternity 9593

Grace abounds when genuine r. 5210

grammar school of r. 11192

guilt washed out by r. 10419

is God-loving 9592

is God-regarding 9592

is grieved because sinned against God 9580

is no fun at all 9577

is not self-loathing 9592

is the reconciliation 9582

key that opens any lock 9587

means killing part of yourself 9577

means unlearning self-conceit, self-will 9577

minor note of r. 8743

more emphasis on growth than r. 1409

much harder than eating humble pie 9577

natal day when new life begins 9591

Never mistake remorse for r. 9584

no r. in the grave 9603

not fatal day when tears are shed 9591

not self-regarding 9592

one case of death-bed r. recorded 9602

opportunity of a new start 9596

process by which we see God as he is 9594

process by which we see ourselves as we are 9594

process of surrender what Christians call r. 9577

Self-knowledge is first condition of r. 9599

soil watered with tears of r, joy 888

something more than remorse for sin 9597

Sorrow preaching r. 10616

sorry enough to quit 9595

starting point for better things 9590

Suicide leaves no opportunity for r. 10945

to clear the blockage 10369

to fill that which is wanting in one's life 9596

true r. cries out against his heart 9601

undergoing a kind of death 9577

washed clean at night by r. 9600

REPENTANT
one must be forever r. 9589

REPENTED
More have r. speech than silence 1861

No man ever r. of being a Christian on death bed 2340

spend time in nothing you know must be r. of 11312

REPENTENCE
see ourselves as sinful, needy, dependent people 9594

REPENTEST
Thou r, yet grievest not 4954

REPENTING
God cannot do our r. for us 9578

to many virtue consists in r. of faults 11702

REPENTS
man who truly r. cries out against his heart 9601

When man r. is turned toward God 9583

who r. is angry with himself 9579

REPETITION
eye bored by r. 844

History endless r. of wrong way of living 5713

mistake for thought r. of what they heard 11237

REPLACE
can never r. friend 4297

government can never r. helping hand of neighbor 8062

No other structure can r. family 3877

Spirit's control will r. sin's control 5802

REPLACED
joy r. by pursuit of duty 6813

law as system r. because powerless 9755

Nowhere in Scripture are God's principles r. 7828

You've been r, forgotten. That's a lie 945

REPLACEMENT
no synthetic r. for decent home life 5858

REPLACEMENTS
grow older, more repairs necessary 8181

REPLACES
joyful sharing r. polite prattle 4029

REPLENISH
Father! r. with thy grace 7454

REPLY
A God, a God! the vocal hills r. 6138

To r. to a nasty remark 402

REPLYING
To forbear r. to an unjust reproach 6281

REPORT
false r. spreads where recantation never reaches 10453
My soul is sick with every day's r. 6273
Never r. what may hurt another 10459
wise evaluate things not as people r. them 8497

REPORTING
originality is r. accurately what we see, are 6219

REPOSE
heart ever is to return to its r. 8444
Labor refreshment from r. 3102
peace is love in r. 7202

REPOSES
Faith r. on character of God 4443

REPRESENT
thoughts which r. me truly 4255

REPRESENTATION
Christ the perfect r. of God 6355

REPRESENTING
in world Order to come 2103

REPRESENTS
duty r. Sinai 7297
love r. Calvary 7297

REPRESS
when r. things you don't want to live with 9291

REPRESSING
emotions become holier-than-thou 3050

REPRESSION
not human r. of sin 10717

REPRESSIONS
when r. of society and business are gone 6842

REPRESSIVE
authoritarianism twists good into r. control 9952

REPROACH
better than honor 10875
death out of r. into glory 2325
quietness of the stars seemed to r. me 4618
To forbear replying to an unjust r. 6281

REPROOF
holy life attraction or r. 5735
never does a wise man harm 11938

REPROVE
faithful those who kindly r. thy faults 3955
friend privately 2855

REPUBLIC
Bible rock upon which r. rests 5188

REPUBLICAN
Jesus comes across as Protestant R. 6467

REPUDIATE
our own wisdom 3758
We must r. seeking God for benefits 4806

REPUDIATION
at price of r. evil could be abolished 4149

REPULSIVE
blood of Christ r. subject 2141
with human beings butterfly turns into r. caterpillar 7392

REPUTATION
cross will not spare r. 2093
eagerly seek approval of man of worldly r. 11666
easily cracked, never well mended 9615
enjoys r. of being most remarkable person he knows 9197
give r. to Christ, gain it 9629
God entrusted his r. to ordinary people 1285
holiest souls r. for being pessimistic 8586
increases 11326
like tree shadow 1001
no ruins so irreparable as r. 9619
O I have lost my r. 9622
of thousand years determined by conduct of one hour 9625
once broken may possibly be repaired 9612
Political r. cannot last forever 5079
professional r. cannot last forever 5079
skillful pilots gain r. from storms 209
Slander, at every word a r. dies 10468
stand up for r, sign it needs standing up for 1060
take care of character, r. takes care of itself 1020
try to polish r, lose it 9629
what folks think you are 1035
what men, women think of us 1036
who didn't have r. to protect 6147
will never have faith in r. 10875
would not know character if met on street 9618

REPUTATIONS
staking r. on church attendance 1300

REPUTE
no r. for yourself 5167

REQUEST
God does not always answer prayers as we r. 8882

imagine God having to r. permission 4955
more daring the r, more glory to God 9028
ruined at our own r. 8877

REQUESTS
All my r. lost in one 8088
specific r. to God unseemly 8821
When our r. honor God 9028

REQUIRE
Discipline tools we r. to solve life's problems 9967
do not r. dying grace to live by 6912
God does not r. 4
greatest happiness is knowing you do not r. happiness 5555
high structures r. solid foundation 5991
Love will ask more than law could ever r. 7273
no business to r. head of age on shoulders of youth 12186
Psychiatrists r. many sessions 5485
What does God r. 4574

REQUIRED
as if God r. disagreeable things of us 6813
difference sort of evidence r. 3657
does more than r, free man 3096
does only what is r, a slave 3096
excellence over and above r. determines distinction 2784
Forgiveness is r. course 4076
Money not r. to buy necessity of the soul 7813
No one attains success by what is r. 2784
that we fall in with God's purposes 8821
that we love God 8821
that we love the difficult 2712

REQUIRES
because holiness made available, God r. it 4658
call to suffering r. faith 10937
Change is handmaiden nature r. 959
Confession, discipline God r. 1597
crucifixion r. absolute venture of faith 10048
deep relationship r. watchfulness, nourishment 9446
faith r. we rise above law of moral gravitation 3752
intense love on mother's side 7858
Making peace r. action 4094
Prayer r. more of heart than tongue 8952
To stand at crossroads r. strength 1137
Virtue r. rulers, guides 11725
Worship r. only a man and God 12142

REQUISITE
Absolute candor indispensable r. to salvation 9793

Chastity a r. of Christian singleness 10236

first r. for immortality is death 6107

of good health calculated carelessness about oneself 5618

other intelligence, skill, power r. in spiritual matters 9416

Six things r. to create happy home 5848

REQUISITES
nine r. for contented living 1809

REQUITE
than to r. kindnesses 9688

RESCUE
love kept Jesus from calling angels to his r. 6418

wish to run a r. mission within yard of hell 7783

RESCUES
God r. us by breaking us 882

God r. us by wiping out resistence 882

Grace is love that r. 5220

RESCUING
as God rescues 6569

RESEARCH
faith needs neither evidence or r. 3810

pour billions into r. of every kind 9353

RESEARCHES
combine dependence on God's Spirit with own r. 6681

RESEMBLE
by practicing mercy r. God 7740

Flatterers as wolves r. dogs 4047

Men r. deserted palaces 1715

never trouble where children r. parents 3898

What we love we shall grow to r. 7336

would know man better if not anxious to r. 1649

RESEMBLES
Human life r. iron 6905

The most r. God 6666

RESENT
cheaper to pardon than r. 4089

Panic may r. truth 11566

promised him I never would r. it 11507

we r. little provocations 3410

RESENTMENT
becomes a black, furry, growling grudge 9639

Criticism arouses r. 2055

hell state where everyone lives r. 5705

If hug r. against anybody 9634

Nothing consumes more quickly than r. 9638

punishment evokes r. 9355

when new thought appears, r. 11237

RESERVATIONS
damnations of consecrations 1724

RESERVE
God to r. right of instructing 5384

keep in r. treasures of God's deep counsels 4322

Lord, thy will be done without a r. 9082

real friends r. nothing 4186

Spirit of God will r. right to test you 5776

RESERVES
flings aside r. 4272

RESERVOIR
Love isn't like a r. 7257

tremendous r. of resurrection life of Christ 11689

RESIDENCE
established legal r. in heaven 5673

RESIDES
likeness to God r. in freedom 4149

RESIGN
No one can r. from human race 5977

tell secrets, r. liberty 1619

RESIGNATION
accept with faith and r. his holy will 4688

benefit of trial in r. 2734

putting God between our troubles 41

rarest sort of courage 42

state best which exerciseth r. to God 7698

wait with r. consolation 2883

with r. can bear suffering of other folks 10862

RESIGNED
himself to failure 3581

to leave all events to thee 9041

RESIGNING
God brings us to r. ourselves 5395

ourselves to listening to God's language 5395

RESIGNS
dissenter r. from the herd, thinks for himself 6210

pleasures to enjoy others better 1298

RESIST
Cease to r, love takes possession 4785

devil will flee if we r. 2678

loss and change, postpone blessings 968

power which can r. fear is love 3992

shall only r. social injustice 6286

temptation to chase after pleasures 5615

To attempt to r. temptation in own strength 11108

to r. one's cross is to make heavier 2114

unless made up mind to r. 4966

without bitterness 11775

RESISTANCE
Christianity is r. against sin 1206

God draws us without r. when will subdued 7949

God rescues us by wiping out r. 882

greatness in r. to temptation to betray 5283

Meek endurance, obedience without r. 7728

not suffering but r. to it 2746

Punishment strengthens r. 2038

to tyrants is obedience to God 5964

RESISTED
Though God be r. outcome never in doubt 4822

RESISTING
God better served in r. temptation 11059

RESISTLESS
O love, r. in thy might 7285

RESISTS
greatest r. sorest temptations 5297

RESOLUTION
greatest chooses right with invincible r. 5297

RESOLVE
man who cannot r. to live his own life 6872

No man can r. himself into heaven 5662

to keep happy 10829

to slow your pace 5615

upon a moment's notice 6872

RESOLVED
I am r. that in this world 1810

RESOLVES
Plans and performs, r. and executes 8224

RESOURCE
last and feeblest r. 178

RESOURCES
ability to use our limited r. 11

all r. of heaven and earth are at my disposal 9066

few have spiritual r. to be both wealthy and godly 11806

God's r. are mine, for he is mine 7486

God's r. available, endless 4458

Great crises show how great our r. are 8659

in contact with divine r. 1143

inadequate human r. 184

Lord, I'm at end of r. 897

most use small portion of soul's r. 8659

need r. of Holy Spirit for thinking 11243

never test r. of God until attempt
  impossible 3815
only the humble have r. to give of
  themselves 5957
prayer tapping infinite r. of God
  8991
surrender will, discover r. 10769
that we know the r. of God 7485
those who have r. within
  themselves 4286
what must God's mind be in
  undisclosed r. 4675
When we reach the end of our
  hoarded r. 7570
world great in r. 10512

RESPECT
Earnestness commands r. 2771
enemies r. taking stand 1913
give to yourself 511
is intended to operate on a
  two-way street 9644
is love in plain clothes 9645
is what we owe 7290
missed it coming and going 9647
no r. for youth when I was young
  9647
Now old man, no one has r. for
  age 12190
now old, no r. for age 9647
oscillations of feeling 4018
Recognition of individual affirms
  r. for human dignity 9952
removes ornament of friendship
  who takes away r. 9642
Sharp words dull r. 9488
Tolerance r. for another because
  he is human 11399
want to be respected, must r.
  yourself 9642
wavering Christian no r. 2771
Whatever you supremely r, you
  will serve 4006
When young man no one had r.
  for youth 12190

RESPECTABILITY
one of seven deadly virtues 11699

RESPECTABLE
Christian ranks prefer to be r,
  smooth 1337
devil's most devilish when r. 9862
  2695
selfishness 10073
want to do what is necessary to
  look r. 6810

RESPECTED
irritating characteristic by-product
  of r. quality 8571

RESPECTER
Love is no r. of persons 7274

RESPECTFUL
keep r. fear of God in lives 3993

RESPECTS
God r. me when I work 12008
who r. himself is safe from others
  9986

RESPIRATORY
don't understand r. system but I
  breathe 3733

RESPLENDENT
Light! Nature's r. robe 7109

RESPOND
can't change circumstances,
  change way you r. 1469
Children will r. like their parents
  8289
collectivities easily r. to devil's
  persuasion 6176
to enemies with love, not hate,
  bitterness 5890
too many people to r. to 10211
way we r. to hurts, distress 3319
with love when unmistakably
  wronged 6278
without doubt God will quickly r.
  7709
Young people will r. if challenge
  tough enough 12180

RESPONSE
Adversity depends on chosen r.
  141
Character out of r. to duty 1000
For each, God has a different r.
  7127
God's voice in r. to mine 8932
godly r. to obstacles kicks crutches
  from skeptic 10938
Government, God's r. to nature of
  people 5177
guidance becomes unconscious r.
  5396
not spontaneous r. to suffering
  1546
Thankfulness is an intelligent r. of
  gratitude 11173
to assault reveal values by which
  you live 6288
to bad doctrine 11189
to God's ability that counts 9
to past can be changed 3623
to temptation accurate barometer
  11079

RESPONSES
deceptive people responsible for r.
  1467

RESPONSIBILITIES
responsible for how well we fulfill
  r. 9660

RESPONSIBILITY
as great and personal as if you
  alone had done wrong 9672
choices ultimately our r. 1148
father who teaches r. provides
  fortune 3913
father's most important r. 3927
fit to manifest Jesus 1014
for human conduct rests with "I"
  579
for our eternal happiness 3758
freedom they wished for was
  freedom from r. 4155
God accepted r. for sin 2140

God does not take r. for existence
  of rebellious 5175
God has charged himself with r.
  5511
heightened personal r. 1168
is to prevent evil thoughts from
  settling 11110
lifted great load of r. from
  Almighty 9915
my individual r. to God 7525
of office boy, perfect job 3121
plan of God, r. is God's 4803
Truth has no r. to make us
  comfortable 11557

RESPONSIBLE
all equally r. for world 9678
Christians r. for disseminating
  gospel 3301
deceptive people r. for responses
  1467
disquieted by One r. to no one
  4614
for great creative efforts 1712
for way we pilot ourselves 1481
for what I do with my feelings
  3049
for what we could have 8654
for what we might be 8654
generous heart feels others' ill as if
  r. 3063
God will hold us r. 9660
God will hold us r. for knowledge
  we have 6679
Humility recognizing God, others
  r. for my achievements 6011
I alone am r. for wrong I do 9661
man r. for marriage maintenance
  7613
no suicide for which society not r.
  10947
not for what we are 8654
not for what we have 8654
not r. for evil thoughts 11110
not r. for my feelings 3049

RESPONSIVE
Holy Spirit will make man r. 1064
With thee, one full r. vibrant chord
  7928

REST
ability to r, take time to enjoy
  beauty 6828
Absence of occupation not r. 6752
absolute r. is death 6771
And laid his flesh to r. 2296
and motion equally destructive
  9685
As retire to r, give soul and God
  time together 10486
at r. within himself 4307
Blood shed does not r. 7880
confidence in himself will lead the
  r. 6791
Death entry into r. 2256
death out of troubles into r. 2325
death, time to r. 2284
Emblem of eternal r. 10953
for a little time in God 7708

For r. and shelter of the night
11174

give yourself by halves, cannot
find full r. 9683

has not r. at home is in world's hell
5828

heaven, r. there in God 5644

heaven, work is their r. 5644

Home, dearer, sweeter spot than
all the r. 5834

How does the musician read the r.
7056

How shall we r. in God 9683

Humility, at r. when robody
praises me 6010

idea of eternal r. frightens me
5661

If I r, I rust 6763

In a patient hope I r. 3800

in Christ all comes to r. 6475

In this faith I r. secure 4936

Jesus knows we must come apart
and r. 9532

Lost all the r. 11053

Made flesh for me, he cannot r.
7506

making of music in it 7056

night to r. body and the mind
8085

no r. stops on pilgrimage 9832

No sleep tranquil unless mind at r.
8449

O endless sense of r. 11476

of the weary 6468

our hearts are restless until they r.
in you 4312

passeth from life to his r. in the
grave 9225

peace is joy at r. 6542

People used to need r. after work
3114

quick revolving wheel shall r. in
peace 3288

rung of ladder never meant to r.
upon 9316

saints absolutely at r. 126

satisfied with doing well 2785

Sleep on, beloved, sleep, take thy r.
2365

souls may r. and quietly grow,
expand 10247

storm rages but our hearts are at r.
8470

Surrounding you are enemies that
never r. 9861

Take r, a field rested gives
beautiful crop 6839

Take r. 9686

that thou mightest have r. 6393

The r. drift to and fro 10679

The simple are thy r. 6040

to toil and not to seek for r. 9113

Too much r. is rust 6781

tranquilly in abiding conviction
4747

True silence is r. of mind 9374

Who craves for ease and r. and
joys 2583

who loves not to r. at home 7422

will r. little in John 5224

will spend r. of lives in future
4333

RESTED

a field r. gives beautiful crop 6839

field r. gives bountiful crop 9686

RESTFUL

For r. death I cry 2285

RESTING

Being alone and r. not selfish 9533

faith, like man within boat 3797

flying and r, parts of contentment
471

Heaven not a r. place 5644

joyous r. place of my spirit 7961

Laziness, r. before you get tired
6769

RESTLESS

anxiety not crosses from God
4322

as hen wanting to lay egg 11886

bad passionate and r. 5045

doubt disease of this r. age 2935

heard only faintly because of
uproar of r. 11515

heart is r. until it rests in you 7578

it was the r. people who flocked to
Jesus 6452

Love is r. 7273

our hearts are r. until they rest in
you 4312

uproar of the r. 9070

urge to create 4643

When we are r. God remains
serene 4587

will be r. with place in world 4311

with our place in the world 7447

world always r. 10512

RESTLESSNESS

and discontent necessities of
progress 2870

can be God sowing seeds of faith
3722

Suffering clears away r. 10892

RESTORATION

Renewal and r. are essential 9533

Renewal and r. not luxuries 9533

RESTORE

Jesus is risen, he shall the world r.
9692

the flow of the Holy Spirit 10369

RESTORED

may cry to God the church be r. to
New Testament splendor 10080

Sabbath when self-worth r. 10959

RESTORER

Tired nature's sweet r, sleep 10491

RESTORES

Confession r. fellowship 1597

Love blind, marriage r. sight 7629

praising God r. to normal 2564

prayer r. minds 8857

RESTORING

In confession we open lives to r.
grace 1602

problem of r. beauty is
redemption of soul 10668

sense of community 3325

RESTRAIN

state not remedy for sin, but
means to r. 5177

RESTRAINING

man morally incapable of r. himself
9872

RESTRAINS

Rigidity r. creativity, blocking
progress 6818

RESTRICT

we react decisively against those
who r. freedom 9463

RESTRICTED

Most people live in r. circle 8659

RESTRICTIONS

cramping r. of hard work 6386

difficult to live with r, 4159

forget your seeming r. 9271

God's r. hold us up 9558

God's r. hold us up, down 4309

God's r. show our need 1522

RESTS

Bible rock upon which republic r.
5188

faith r. on the promises 3818

foundation of society, government
r. on Bible 5189

heart is restless until it r. in you
7578

In life-melody music is broken off
by r. 7056

not be dismayed at the r. 7056

not to be omitted 9684

not to be slurred over 9684

not to change keynote 9684

not to destroy melody 9684

ours to not be discouraged at the r.
7915

RESULT

always in God's hands 4945

Cheerfulness, r. of discipline 1088

nothing to do with r. of obedience
10824

of choice inevitableness of God
1149

of internal surgery 8583

outward in worship r. of what is
inward 12129

Self-centeredness not the r. of
self-love 6229

Simplicity r. of profound thought
10283

true knowledge of God r. in sheer
wonder 6704

will be arrogance in three-piece
suit 7425

will be found in roadside gutter
7425

RESULTS

ill-taught if look for r. only in earthlies 9014

much machinery but few r. 9017

Others may view r. 10706

true faith gets supernatural r. 3807

unless meditation r. in richer relationships 7725

When we cling to r. of our actions 10531

will exceed anything he may have hoped 7564

worth more than r. of our efforts 10545

RESUME

habit difficult to r. 3109

RESURRECTION

a fact of history 9702

belief in R. not appendage to faith 9696

brought life, immortality to light 9702

Christianity a r. religion 9689

death r. of joys 2266

difficult to understand 11203

Either it happened or it didn't 9691

explains the Gospels 9696

faith must include mystery of the r. 11203

glory derived from no other source 9702

God understands the R. 11203

Gospels do not explain the R. 9696

hope derived from no other source 9702

identified with Christ in r. 2138

In his r, Christ a conqueror 6410

insist upon R. as criterion of orthodoxy 6604

is an ongoing thing 9698

is the Christian faith 9696

Jesus came to r. through, not around the cross 5768

look forward to latest R. model 8181

Lord appeared to renew us by his r. 6477

man on cross r. follows 2087

No person more skeptical of r. than apostles 9693

not completion of Transfiguration 462

not unintelligible 11203

of Jesus Christ our hope 5945

permeated our customs 9702

permeated our language 9702

permeated our literature 9702

personality something for the r. 6183

promise of r. in every leaf in springtime 9694

promise of r. not in books alone 9694

Receive every day as a r. from death 8737

reminder of R. at start of each new year 8080

Remove r, Christianity destroyed 9689

substituted fear of death for eternal life 9702

to make possible a r. 5423

tremendous reservoir of r. life of Christ 11689

Without sacrifice no r. 4342

RETAIN

no plan to r. this or that of the devil 9864

RETALIATION

punishment evokes vow of r. 9355

RETARDED

Youth begins when parents become r. 3906

RETENTIVE

memory good thing 4068

RETIRED

happiness of a r. nature 5568

RETIREMENT

can't beat r. plan 10217

RETRACT

never r, love themselves better than truth 8207

RETREAT

love nature because r. from man 8012

Stand still, refuse to r. 2742

that shall never call r. 4715

'Tis pleasant through loopholes of r. 10529

RETREATED

than to have r. from the war 10777

RETREATING

endowed with power of r. from reality 3370

RETREATS

Humanity advances or r. 5969

loftiest eloquence r. confused, abashed 4750

RETURN

accepts nothing has nothing to r. 9457

closet of prayer, more you visit more you will r. 9039

evil for good devilish 4102

God, no one can r. more in response to our love 7533

good for evil godlike 4102

good for good human 4102

heard your voice behind me telling me to r. 9070

heart ever is to r. to its repose 8444

One may r. to place of birth 12170

peace and tranquility will r. again 8445

to gentle dogmatism that smiles while stands stubborn 11188

to r. love for hate 7838

true gift, nothing is expected in r. 4384

When prodigals r, great things are done 9607

RETURNING

To forsake sin leave it without thought of r. 10409

RETURNS

life, if smile, it r. greeting 6949

man r. home to find what he needs 5815

Youth one thing that never r. 12184

REVEAL

essential for Holy Spirit to r. truth 752

God doesn't r. his grand design 4448

gospel could only r. itself in simplest of garments 5089

how could God r. himself with no room for doubt 2963

Man cannot cover what God would r. 9709

response to assault r. values by which you live 6288

Time will r. calyxes of gold 5403

truths r. a life deeper than known 11521

REVEALED

accept bitter truth r. to us 1719

Christian begins with what God has r. 3783

cross r. God in weakness 6471 2143

cross r. goodness not enough 2144

Faith is concerned with r. data 3670

give God thanks for having r. so much 4908

in earth's common things God stands r. 8019

more you pray, the more will be r. 8865

Obedience to r. truth guarantees guidance 5435

Spirit-filled life no mystery r. to select few 5803

Things holy r. only to men who are holy 5769

truth of God only r. to us by obedience 11542

what God has r. to me 956

when man does what he likes, character r. 6842

REVEALING

Christ r. what man is to be like 6426

Christ, Son of God r. what God is like 6426

For we are weak and need some deep r. 9050

presence of Lord is r. 9741

Revival is God r. himself 9745

REVEALS

Adversity r. genius 147

Bible r. depths 683

Bible r. intense, blazing holiness of God 4661

Christ r. a God who stands in thick of whole thing 6432

danger of forgetting Bible r. 4661

Every dream r. psychological structure 2968

Every victory of science r. more clearly divine design 9866

existence of evil r. God in his truth 3398

friend r. himself to the other 4272

God r. himself 4448

God r. himself to thoughtful seeker 4907

God r. that which is our profit to know 9708

God r. who he is 4932

Man cannot find God unless God r. himself 4910

man off guard r. character 1028

Night conceals world, r. universe 8083

What God r. as critical moments 10721

with trifles man r. character 1028

REVELATION

a r. cross of Jesus Christ 2108

bringing mind into contact with divine r. 5094

casting aside of veil after veil 9706

Character determines r. 2830

Christianity, r. of true way of living, the of way to know God 1188

Christianity, r. of way to live life 1188

death of Jesus was r. of heart of God 6472

doctrine illuminated 7937

each generation makes own contribution to understanding 9711

God's often violent intrusions into history 9710

God's r. of escape 11432

God's work from beginning is r. 4906

in his Son, Jesus God unveils his very face 9706

is God's word 4911

New Testament clearer r. 243

of God to me determined by character 1050

of truth secret whispering of God in ear of soul 9705

only Christian r. gives end, means of life 9703

records of God's acts in time 9710

showing men truth after truth 9706

substituted reflex action for r. 5808

Suffering is a r. 10893

voice of God to man 9704

What's point of r. if we can figure out 1213

REVELATION, BOOK OF

perfection of human expression 740

REVELATIONS

God located spiritual r. in physical body 835

no business to limit God's r. to bias of mind 11273

REVELS

Lord r. in mind renewed, enlightened by grace 7776

REVENGE

a confession of pain 9724

best r. is not to be like him who did injury 9727

Everything evil is r. 3351

in cold blood is devil's act, deed 9723

Living well is best r. 9719

man who studies r. keeps own wounds green 9714

Men more prone to r. injuries 9688

passing over r, is superior to enemy 9715

proves its own executioner 9726

pure delight of little minds 9725

Resolved, never to r. 569

smallest r. will poison soul 9728

soul never so strong as when forgoes r. 4095

Stirred up with envy and r. 9863

taking r, man even with enemy 9715

To forget a wrong is mild r. 9729

triumphs over death 2363

who seeks r. digs two graves 9717

REVENGEFUL

futile to condemn myself for feeling r. 3049

REVENGING

enemy makes you even with him 4073

REVERBERATES

every suppressed word r. 8528

REVERBERATIONS

closet and church full of r. of God 4965

REVERE

they his deed and word would not r. 2639

who can still r. himself 2764

REVERENCE

best awakening of r. is contemplation of works of God 9734

emotion one of the words that most deserve r. 3054

God not greater if you r. him 9732

Good is r. for life 5024

invest few extra hours in quiet r. 9906

Many r. Jesus' miracles 2828

sign of strength 9735

We pay God r. for our own sake 12126

REVERENCES

who knows God r. him 12100

REVERENT

look forward to death with r. curiosity 2306

maintain r. attitude toward God's place 3993

more r. view of God 4720

REVERSE

Faith believing what will only make sense in r. 3708

historian a prophet in r. 5708

Joy is r. of happiness 6538

love, wrath r. of same thing 4999

stopped dead by some r. 5395

REVERSED

Acts of grace cannot be r. 4626

REVIEW

past with common sense 4329

REVIVAL

a sovereign act of God 9746

affects me 9739

and comfortable truths are bitter enemies 9744

Brokenness is not r. 881

Brokenness, vital step toward r. 881

completely out of human hands 9746

exposed for what we are 9741

extraordinary power 9746

God revealing himself in holiness, power 9745

God's finger pointed right at me 9748

If we find r. not spoken against 9745

inrush of Spirit into body that threatens to become corpse 9749

is always extraordinary 9747

like prairie fire ignited by lightning 9752

look to ensure it is r. 9745

out of balance is r. out of power 9738

Paul's preaching ended in riot or r. 9155

Prayer is backbone of r. 9743

tell me r. is only temporary 9753

to focus eyes of people upon Divine leader 9751

to give glory to a great Savior 9751

to make God famous 9751

REVIVALS

have altered destinies of nations 9752

have altered hearts of men 9752

have altered social attitudes 9752

only hear God in the thunder of r. 1477

Some preachers don't believe in r. 9750

try God-given method for r. 9743

REVIVE
the church, beginning with me
9741

REVOLTS
against heaven 2959

REVOLUTION
Music glorifying r. 7910
No r. compared to words of Jesus
Christ 5721

REVOLUTIONARY
Christian faith a r. faith 3785
essential teachings of Jesus r. 6474
Lord's Prayer a r. petition 8828
most r. statement in history 7305

REVOLUTIONIZED
semiconductor r. technology 3932

REVOLUTIONIZING
Christ's message r. 6377

REVOLUTIONS
all conspiring to that great event
4898
All r. from beginning to end of
world 4898
All r. various parts of same scheme
4898

REVOLVES
life r. around Christ, its central sun
6937

REWARD
attitude determines r. 509
best r. a liar by believing nothing
he says 6863
consciousness of well-doing ample
r. 5069
for good deed is to have done it
10194
generous action own r. 4345
God is virtue's r. 11687
Happiness not a r. 5522
Heaven not a r. for being good boy
5645
Hell highest r. devil can offer 5689
highest r. what man becomes 1045
honor r. for what he gave 5895
Legalists keep law to merit r. 6815
No r. offered, gone forever 11306
of faith to see what we believe
3701
of labor is what it does for him
3119
of labor not what he gets for it
3119
of sin is death 10395
Some sure they will receive a great
r. 10182
to labor and not to ask for r. 9113
Understanding, r. of faith 609
virtue is its own r. 10298
11705
What r. shall I give the Lord 7568

REWARDED
Those who seek are r. 4469
we shall be r. 5440

REWARDING
Hope is a confident search for a r.
life 5918
Marriage infinitely r. at its best
7641
most r. often look like cannot be
done 8567

REWARDS
depend on quality of
contributions we make 10179
Faithless work God never r. 3825
God r. us for working in his
kingdom 4648
of raising kids 8304
Vices tempt by r. they offer 11101

REWRITES
Every April God r. Genesis 9885

RHETORIC
Example most powerful r. 3432
Whispered insinuations r. of the
devil 10478

RHYTHM
Could blind chance create r. 1958

RIBBON
rainbow is r. nature puts on after
washing hair 9391

RICH
A few r. treasures from his mighty
store 6111
Adversity makes a man wise, not r.
146
Are levell'd. Death confounds 'em
all 2384
Better poor and live, than r. and
perish 8675
Better r. in God than r. in gold
11800
Better to live r. than die r. 11826
boredom for the r. is worse
misfortune 11854
By success do not mean you may
become r. 10780
discontented never r. 1814
do not have to be r. to be generous
4388
easy for r. to get on church board
11830
enough who is poor with Christ ·
8676
frequently r. wealthy because
oppressed poor 6630
gifts prove poor when givers
unkind 4372
God at work in history casting
down the r. 6630
God does not intend all to be r.
4243
God made r. by man's necessity
4541
Goodness is r. 11696
hard for r. to enter heaven 11830
heart that makes r. 11840
I am as r. as God 7470
increase money 7826
is r. who owes nothing 11821
Lash love upon the r, who often
need it most 7348

Lord's Prayer r. in spiritual power
7156
make war, poor who die 11778
man at his castle 4501
Money never yet made anyone r.
7808
must live more simply 11861
No man r. enough to buy back
past 1735
No man r. to whom grave brings
eternal bankruptcy 6101
No one r. enough to do without
neighbor 4258
None is as r. 11841
Not he who has much is r. 4370
not r. only under dominion of
things 8681
only with gratitude life becomes r.
5257
or poor according to what he is
6302
Peace, modesty, faith is r. 11696
poor, not r, are blessed 1216
poor, not r. were blessed 5001
Possession makes not r. 8637
pride of dying r. raises loudest
laugh in hell 9246
Satan tempts by making r. 2690
Simplicity is r. 11696
so r. was concept of mother 7859
Some are r, and some are poor
11852
sun as bright as from r. man's
abode 7001
truly r. in deepest sense 9520
two ways of being r. 11864
Untilled mind, however r. 7774
Virtue like a r. stone 11706
what we give up makes us r. 624
When wish I am r. 11878
When you have Christ, you are r.
9521
Whoever is capable of giving is r.
10743
with Christianity 1199
words r. as mother's answering
back 11998
world so r. in delusions truth is
priceless 11523

RICHER
he finds the ore 737
Quiet mind r. than crown 1812
Time leaves us r. 11323
to live modestly a r. experience
9758
unless meditation results in r.
relationships 7725

RICHES
account to be given for r. 11865
better to envy wisdom than r.
11921
burden of care in getting r. 11865
burden too heavy for us 11832
call forth life's r. 505
cut ourselves off from r. of God's
grace 6693
enlarge rather than satisfy
appetites 11846

everlasting r. of this life 11841
exclude only one inconvenience 11847
fear in keeping r. 11865
fly away 6455
for all joys, r. of the world 5652
God's Book packed full of r. 656
Gold and r, chief causes of war 11810
good name better than great r. 9610
grow, care follows 11799
guilt in abusing r. 11865
have made more men covetous 11848
have wings 11849
house, field, wife great r. 5814
Idolatry putting confidence in r. 6071
If your r. are yours 11824
in fewness of my wants 11839
in poverty Christ is my r. 6498
In poverty of solitude, all r. present 10542
least worthy gifts God can give 11845
Let us not envy accumulated r. 11832
may go to heaven without r. 9792
men toil for them day and night 11845
Moderate r. will carry you 11838
Neither great poverty nor r. will hear reason 9418
never have faith in r. 10875
not extent of my possessions 11839
of limitless time, endless years 3274
out of his infinite r. in Jesus 7570
out of soul God coins unspeakable r. 10666
poverty better than r. 10875
prayed for r. that he might be happy 8806
Rank and r. chains of gold 11844
Scriptures first taught futility of r. 11862
Sea of Gailee gathers in r, pours them out to fertilize 10195
serve a wise man, command a fool 7820
sorrow in losing r. 11865
take wings 1010
temptation in using riches 11865
To have what we want is r. 1818
True r. in true happiness 11852
who love God for r. or comfort 10084
Why live beggarly when r. of heaven are yours 8662

RICHEST

Christian, r. when poorest 1265
Life is poorest when you are r. 6903
who is content with least 1794

RICHNESS

Laughter adds r. to ordinary days 6727
never discover full r. of your humanity 8634
of God, meagerness of men 9784
of your creation 9117

RID

difficult to get rid of devil 2657
get r. of ox or fill up ditch 10951
Hatred like burning down own house to get r. of rat 5596
I would have r. the earth of him 4199
of fears, worries, bad eating habits 12076
reaction of world is to get r. of him 6127
to get r. of enemy turn him into friend 9484

RIDDLE

courage to endure r. of inequality 6277
Man, the r. of the world 7417
Oh, the r. and secret of things 7943
reject Christ's existence world inexplicable r. 5728

RIDDLING

perplexed, labyrinthical soul 10661

RIDE

a horse, sit close and tight 9471
a man, sit easy and light 9471
and r. mankind 9343
can never r. on wave that went out yesterday 8372
if men r. him 4063
less and walk more 9281
on! R. on in majesty 2981

RIDES

Man r, God holds the reins 7498
Who r. tiger cannot dismount 11121

RIDICULE

Jesus' acclaim lies in r. 6443
live with r, learn to be withdrawn 1114
Music used to r. religion, morality 7910

RIDICULOUS

actions require courage to confess 1603
pursuit of happiness most r. phrase 5558
that a man have right to kill me 11744
time-consuming activities plain r. 115

RIGHT

actions best apologies for wrong actions 9598
admit you're wrong, you're r. 9665
All's r. with the world 8233

always r. who suspects he makes mistakes 7791
always think last opinion r. 8203
angry cannot be in r. 394
as God gives us to see r. 5199
Be not afraid to pray, to pray is r. 8768
be r. in our own home 6295
beginning of wisdom is to call things by r. names 11941
Being in the r. does not depend on loud voice 11905
believe we are r. 9021
Bible deals with r. and wrong 721
can lay it on thick in r. places 9238
Character, evidence built on r. foundation 1057
Christian, admits wrong to be r. 1265
Conscience asks, Is it r. 1679
cross destroyed formula that might is r. 2166
cross that comes our way never r. one 2116
darkness is my point of view, my r. to myself 7106
death, no r. to complain 2307
difference between r. because of conscience, presence of others 1051
difference between r. word and almost r. word 11992
distinguish between r, wrong burden-bearing 937
Do not believe you alone can be r. 8196
Do r, God's recompense to you power to do more r. 9648
do r. in disobeying law of sovereign 5197
do r. when offer faith, works to God 3829
do small things in r. spirit 9679
don't need to be r. all the time 3929
enter into paradise with r. key 5641
Evil can but serve the r. 4936
Faith is doing r. thing 3671
fear is fear of losing God 3995
feel no one has r. to blame us 6230
Firm as fortress to defend r. 1933
Flee from saying, "I was in the r." 10842
for God to display anger against sin 4729
Freedom is r. to choose 4155
Freethinkers essential for r. thinking 4124
Give the r. you claim for yourself 11282
give up our r. to ourselves 465
given up r. to return our love 9963
Giving a joy if we do in r. spirit 4357
God puts r. all that was wrong 837

God reserves r. to harmonize truths 11586

God to reserve r. of instructing 5384

greatest who chooses r. 5297

Greatness lies in r. use of strength 5284

Have your heart r. with Christ 5529

Holy Spirit will put everything r. 894

Humility to make r. estimate of one's self 6014

hundredth time I am r. 2775

I see the r. 10319

If course is r, take it because it is r. 6291

If heart r. with God 8056

If I am r, thy grace impart 9067

If man has acted r, he has done well 5032

If one certain his principles are r. 6306

If r. at every point 3846

if treat shabbily, no r. to whine when he is dead 2317

in effort to be r. may go wrong 9502

Individuals as much r. to act way they decide as we 6193

is r. even if everyone against it 1037

it will all come r. 8445

It's going to turn out all r. 4316

Let not your r. hand know what left is doing 10169

let us ask what r. we have 10842

Let us have faith that r. makes might 3755

life stronger than r. 2985

Lord's sovereign r. to demote, promote 5894

man has r. to liberty of discussion 2900

Man prisoner who has no r. to open door 10941

man's heart r. when wills what God wills 2566

man's r. to happiness anti-God 5553

measure by which judged r. or wrong is love 7307

minorities almost always in r. 5194

must stand with anybody that stands r. 6303

My country r. or wrong like saying 7980

never turned wrong to r. 3174

No man has r. to a life of contemplation 9670

No one deserves r. to lead without 6802

No one learns to make r. decisions 2486

no r. for me to suffer this 10842

no r. to consume happiness without producing it 5569

no r. to draw life from other source than Christ 11689

no r. to open door of prison and run away 10941

no wind is the r. wind 4433

none have r. to expect gratitude 5242

nor has man r. to active life 9670

not bound to make the world go r. 10150

not leaning against r. wall 353

not much use if not in r. direction 5409

not r. to say all suffering perfects 10920

nothing but gain 1150

of God's sovereignty derived from omnipotence 4952

One must do good in r. way 5075

one who has found r. road 1320

Only heart that hurts has r. to joy 6571

Optimism maintaining everything r. when wrong 8236

people who influence stood unconsciously for r. thing 6239

Perfect and r. and pure and good 5620

person who lives r, and is r. 3428

predominates, nothing prevails against it 6621

road hazards evidence on r. route 2745

rub them r. way will purr 9482

Seizes the r, holds it to the last 11906

sin claim to my r. to myself 10389

Sometimes have worst of it for doing r. 4555

Spirit of God will reserve r. to test you 5776

Still in the r. to stay 9067

stops when it injures or kills 20

strongest word is r. 11993

Success in marriage is being r. person 7652

temperature at home maintained by warm hearts 5855

that hearts should be on God 4770

that which is r. 9069

that you should begin again every day 10705

time to be r. is when everyone else is wrong 6805

to be contented with what we have 1806

to be r. within where all concealed 6295

to come to conclusions r. for him 6207

to create alternatives of choice 4155

to criticize if heart to help 2060

to criticize must be earned 267

to free speech 20

To get to heaven, turn r, keep straight 5675

to his own stupid opinion 447

to kill because his ruler has quarrel with mine 11744

to myself sin that shocks God 10397

to r. wrong 9088

to seek and rebel 4135

touch r. key at r. time 7897

Trust in God and do the r. 5995

unafraid whether r. or wrong 6216

War does not determine who is r. 11767

When heart r, feet swift 10213

when r, make us easy to live with 9119

Whoever falls from God's r. hand 4628

Wisdom by-product of r. decisions 11911

Wisdom is r. use of knowledge 11973

with firmness in the r. 5199

with God has often meant in trouble with men 9507

with God, he gives desires, aspirations 9280

RIGHTEOUS

he who waits to be r. will never enter 10402

humbled, completely r. 6007

Job experienced calamity because r. 2857

Righteously r. and justly just 2028

sinners who believe themselves r. 10404

truly happy who are seeking to be r. 5564

who believe themselves sinners 10404

who thinks he is r. is not r. 9254

RIGHTEOUSNESS

choose to be dominated by sin or r. 10510

Christ, a garment of r. 6370

God has all r. to clothe you 4696

Grace can justify us with Christ's r. 5212

happiness in place of r, will never get it 5564

I choose r. 6305

Idolatry is trust in own r. 6071

If give part of income, is not r. 11360

If I must choose between peace, r. 6305

If r. in the heart 8441

Jesus, thy blood and r. 4719

law could not bring us r. 9755

like a mighty stream 6629

make their r. clear as light 9104

no way to kill r. but by own consent 11102

not power should be man's pursuit 5001

Proclaim thy r. 4592

Seek r. and you will discover you are happy 5551

standards of law reflected God's r. 9755

to teach us about r. 10306

using the law to establish r. 6810

When we seek first r. 4735

RIGHTFUL

holding my r. place in the procession of humanity 9074

RIGHTFULLY

where is coverage our mothers r. deserve 7844

RIGHTLY

do not r. love God when love for advantage 4801

Freedom, fine word when r. understood 4123

Freedom, to act r. 4123

if touches notes r. and in time 7885

impossible to r. govern world without God 5181

influence from person r. related to God incalculable 6241

only with the heart one can see r. 5622

to think r. a great effort 11270

To worship r. is to love each other 7284

When r. related to God 5463

RIGHTS

Brotherhood is giving others your r. 924

endowed by Creator with certain unalienable r. 3246

freedom to give up our r. for good of others 9963

God deliver us from r. 10842

inferior of any man whose r. I trample under foot 11283

know nothing of men's, women's r. 3230

legal r. before the throne 8815

Leviticus 25 classic on r. of earth 3200

recognize no r. but human r. 3230

to secure these r. governments instituted 3246

RIGID

agrees with our views makes us narrow and r. 11216

brother who squeaks, whines 9529

starving emotions we become r. 3050

RIGIDITY

Be aware r. imprisons 6809

clips future's wings 6818

criticizes future for not flying 6818

Protestantism has lost through r. 6827

restrains creativity, blocking progress 6818

Threatened by risk and failure 6818

trademark of legalism 6817

RIGOR

too violent r. tempts chastity 3554

RIGOROUS

want most r. intellectual training 3025

RING

A bell doesn't r. on its own 75

let it r. from every village 4157

Lighthouses don't r. bells 6022

like a great r. of pure, endless light 3276

When we let freedom r. 4157

Who upon his signet r. 974

RINGING

God comes without r. doorbell 4838

in imperfect acknowledgment of his perfect love 7171

world to die amid r. blast of archangel's trumpet 7886

RIOT

Paul's preaching ended in r. or revival 9155

RIOTOUS

serenity of age takes the place of r. youth 7101

RIPE

As soon as you're r, you start to rot 5364

from hour to hour, we r. and r. 11302

never r. till made so by suffering 10642

RIPENESS

Old men lose lives by r. 12197

RIPENING

Christian like r. corn 6030

powers of thinking 3027

RIPENS

Time r. all things 11342

RIPER

he grows, more lowly he bends head 6030

RIPPING

teaching of Christ a r. tearing torpedo 6486

RIPPLE

Gaiety often r. over depths of despair 5508

RISE

content until time to r. 471

Death, we shall r. refreshed 2244

depth man can fall is height to which he can r. 8666

Dost thou wish to r. 6788

every step we r. nearer God 10700

fall for love of God shall r. a star 3635

great challenges ordinary men r. to meet 8668

great minds r. above misfortune 5281

happier than a king 10208

I soar and r. 7475

If cannot work or r. from my chair 8132

If Shakespeare should come we would r. 6406

Men think highly of those who r. rapidly 3857

more difficult to be born or r. 492

neither can kingdom r. without his aid 4933

No man will r. high who jeers at sacred things 9735

no vacuum into which God's deep water may r. 9938

our sins r. up to slay us 10423

shall r. a star 4791

solar systems r. and wane 4694

some r. from sermon strengthened 10094

soul beaten down can r. up 3621

Swift fly the years, and r. th' expected morn 6143

than r. in debt 4033

That I may r, stand, o'erthrow me 2840

to descend is to r. 9701

Today I r. with Christ 2121

Truth, crushed to earth, shall r. again 11579

up, I shall r. with you 3094

we must r. with the occasion 976

We r, how full of power 8867

RISEN

best proof Christ r. is he is still alive 9695

Christ is r, all earth's at play 2982

Has r. to nobility 2792

Jesus is r, he shall the world restore 9692

RISES

And the old Adam in me, r. up 8966

by lifting others 10144

lies with dogs, r. with fleas 11063

life short day in which sun hardly r. 7083

nothing r. quicker than dust 3857

soul r. above itself, becomes spirit 7948

Unheard by the world, r. silent to thee 8778

Who r. from prayer a better man 9034

RISING

Bible, r. aloft into mysteries of heaven 750

glory in r. every time you fail 3620

If, r. on its wrecks, at last 3538

must only think of r. again 3634

My r. soul surveys 4819

of sap from within 4156

sun appears setting but is r. 2350

when God sees men r. up against fellowmen 4895

RISK

as much in naive as suspicious 7979

better to r. being considered
  indecisive 9327
God's willingness to do miraculous
  3669
Man is God's r. 7407
of taking God's place 255
Rigidity threatened by r. and
  failure 6818
sacrifices which always involve r.
  5385
Yet Love still takes the r. of birth
  6155

RISKS
Being Christian means taking r.
  1244
better to have taken some r. and
  lost 10777

RISKY
cheese delicious but way to it is r.
  11103
God trusting us a r. thing to do
  11479

RITES
mysticism not r. or ceremonies
  7947

RITUAL
Religion that is merely r. can
  never satisfy 9546

RIVAL
Divine love can admit no r. 4929
Lord's Prayer without equal or r.
  7154

RIVALRY
underneath a r. that stings, bites
  10527

RIVAL'S
person great when not envious of
  r. success 3206

RIVALS
allowing too many r. of God 9552
church has no r. 1432
falls in love with himself will have
  no r. 7175

RIVER
cannot step twice into same r. 985
Follow the r, find the sea 5382
Lord, thou mighty R,
  all-knowing, all-seeing 7492
touches places of which source
  knows nothing 6232
When r. is deepest, makes least
  noise 2810

RIVERS
are God's thoughts in motion
  8048
blood to flow like r. throughout
  globe 4895
out of us will flow the r. that will
  bless 6232
way will be made through r. 5444

ROAD
A light to shine upon the r. 7507
Along a rough, a weary r. 7007
an endless r, a hopeless maze 8638

angel to clean a r. 3232
around the corner, a new r, or a
  secret gate 8239
At any cost, dear Lord, by any r.
  4428
broad, hard-beaten r. to house
  2776
Christian one who has found right
  r. 1320
Does the r. wind uphill all the way
  6885
Drop to your knees beside wide r.
  4608
find yourself on easy r. ought to
  worry 2745
glimpse of next three feet of r.
  more important 5371
God does not go their r. 5460
hazards evidence on right route
  2745
help me faithfully to journey
  along my r. 9074
If stop every time dog barks, r.
  will never end 8543
Jesus took r. that would end on
  Golgotha 6384
like straddling middle of r. 11602
My clog whatever r. I go 2583
no r. back to yesterday 7051
no royal r. to becoming worker
  for God 9564
Only he who has travelled r.
  knows where holes are deep
  3541
rough r. that leads to greatness
  8287
safest r. to hell is gradual 5702
seeking adventure on the high r.
  9088
Set a child to wondering, on r. to
  understanding 6691
soften down the rugged r. of life
  7917
than take wrong r. once 5424
that leads us to the living God
  3793
that we must go 8081
throw stones at those showing
  new r. 1643
To a friend's house r. never long
  4287
To climb rock-strewn r. 1927
to glory not strewn with flowers
  4418
to hell easy to travel 5701
To know the r. ahead 269
to wisdom 11949
troubles are as pebbles on the r.
  7569
when the r. seems dreary, endless
  9059
will be less tedious 7899

ROADS
chose most thorns and cutting
  rocks 467

ROADSIDE
If cannot find God upon the r.
  4856

result will be found in r. gutter
  7425

ROAR
God will r. all about us 10554
Let not thy will r. when power can
  but whisper 6800
So here in the r. of mortal things
  8429
which is other side of silence 8496

ROARS
Well r. the storm to those that hear
  3644

ROAST
sets my house on fire to r. his eggs
  10057

ROB
What he leaves undone will r. him
  of peace of mind 11690
would not r. a man of his problems
  9286

ROBBER
in the sight of God 10060

ROBBERS
seize money 7826
the more thieves, r. there will be
  5192

ROBBERY
his feast a very r, himself no guest
  11138

ROBBING
Doubt, r. life of glow, meaning
  6091
life of friendship like r. world of
  sun 4299

ROBE
Christ r. if any naked be 6391
Light! Nature's resplendent r.
  7109

ROBIN
Or help one fainting r. 6922
what will the r. do then 4803

ROBOTS
build society of love out of r.

ROBS
enthusiasm r. endurance of
  difficulty 3188
Incredulity r. of pleasures 11592
me of that which not enriches him
  10449
Worry never r. tomorrow of
  sorrow 12089

ROCK
a little bird comes to r. 3273
Bible r. upon which republic rests
  5188
building on the r. 10064
God impregnates barren r. with
  gold 1902
ground trembled, r. of tomb
  tumbled 2984
In matters of principle, stand like r.
  6308
Learning in childhood like
  engraving on r. 8305

of Ages, cleft for me 4636
of divine love deeper down 4783
Quarry the granite r. with razors 9233
sea changes because of r. 572
Simon Peter more a sandpile than a r. 3617
The r. beneath 3767
To hew the r. 47
true religion is built upon the R. 9550
tugs on oars hasn't time to r. boat 10187
Tyre r. for fisherman's nets 730
women are the church's strong r. 11980
world no r. under feet 10512

ROCKS
anyone who underestimates God has r. in head 766
Call on God, but row away from the r. 8774
chose road with cutting r. 467
Even among these r. 4979
soften r. or bend knotted oak 7901
The r. proclaim th' approaching Deity 6138
way will be made through r. 5444
we are not like r. 7437

ROCK-STREWN
To climb r. road 1927

ROCKY
A few miles distance from r. shore 6111

ROD
Job feels r, blesses God 771
Many like religion as sort of lightning r. 4998
question whether learned except through r. 10855

ROGUE
When r. kisses you, count your teeth 2478

ROLE
equal, yet each with own r. 3239

ROLL
A thousand worlds which r. around us brightly 4592
let your thunders r. like drums 4712
Loud o'er my head, though awful thunders r. 4827
people expect him to r. up his sleeves 6290
When they call the r. in the Senate 5198

ROLLED
stone r. away not to permit Christ to come out 9699
stone r. away to enable disciples to go in 9699

ROLLING
And wheels his throne upon the r. worlds 4482

can send worlds r. in space 4951

ROLLS
until justice r. down like waters 6629

ROMANCES
To fall in love with God greatest of all r. 7542

ROMANTIC
love you want the other person 7197

ROME
legions of R. smouldering 730

ROOM
A deeper voice across the r. 3644
allow hearts to shrink until r. for little beside ourselves 5625
does not know how to stay quietly in his r. 5560
give Christ range of every r. 8092
hypocrites, always r. for one more 6050
Life like fly in r. with boys armed with swatter 6968
no r. for doubt, no r. for me 2963
no r. for God in man full of himself 10089
no r. for the Spirit of God 5783
plenty of r. in the forest 6168
there'd have been no r. for the child 9414
To a bigger, brighter r. 2364
Where r. in heart, r. in house 5960
willing as light willing to flood r. 4785

ROOMS
Christ leads me through no darker r. 5379
world God's nursery for his upper r. 12043

ROOSEVELT
infantile paralysis and Franklin R. 161

ROOT
activity have r. in gratitude 5240
Christ a R. to quicken 6370
church whose r. is dried up 1380
cross strikes at r. of tree 2158
Faith is the r. 3837
Faith r. of works 3699
fault takes deep r. 3935
God fills every r. and seed 8049
God probes the core, tests the r. 7862
Have their r. in human needs 2029
Humility, that low, sweet r. 6015
Men cut themselves off from r. of being, God 4437
of a happy religion 6713
of Christian life, belief in invisible 3831
of discontent is self-love 10027
of innumerable tragedies 9446
sends down a deeper r. 2508
Sorrow r. of all virtue 10617
that produces nothing is dead 3699

to one striking at the r. 3405

ROOTED
Bible r. in depths of creation 750
joy deeply r. in life of God 6568
loved by mother means to be r. 7853
Once r. and grounded in Christ 10141
soundly r. church 1380

ROOTLESS
nothing can bring life to r. tree 1380

ROOTS
grow deep when winds strong 212
If r. are deep 6307
inspire me to send my r. deep 9111
Like r. of a plant, faith must seek greater depth 3756
man without prayer like tree without r. 8752
Nobody r. for Goliath 452
of true achievement lie in the will 92
Stronger, deeper r. less visible 7703

ROPE
Give him r. enough 4061
Let legalism have enough r, lynching of new ideas 6817
of a lie is short 6860
Perseverance r. that ties soul to heaven 8554
Prayer r. that pulls God, man together 8947
When at end of your r. 4627
When you get to end of r. 2615

ROSE
A man who could make one r. 7993
A r. can say I love you 1102
Clear as the morning or the evening r. 4746
Easter bunny never r. again 2983
fairest and sweetest r. 8172
he r. from the dead 4931
In every r, eternity 8009
is sweetest wash'd with morning dew 7309
Kindness like a r. 6651
Love like a lovely r, the world's delight 7179
Love like a r, joy of all the earth 7179
More evidence Jesus r. than Alexander the Great died 9700
no gathering the r. 94
Spiritual r. bushes 10710
with all its sweetest leaves yet folded 803
with all its thorns excels them both 7179
would abolish r. 8580

ROSEBUDS
Gather ye r. while ye may 8214

ROSE-COLORED
we see devil r. 2687

ROSES
Even bein' Gawd ain't bed of r. 4890

fragrance clings to hand that gives r. 4344

God gave us memories that we might have r. in December 7732

grumbling because r. have thorns 1564

plants thorns must never expect to gather r. 10454

Some people are grateful for the r. 6254

Sorrow, like rain, makes r. and mud 10621

Spring full of sweet days and r. 9891

thanked God for r. 2099

thankful thorns have r. 1564

thorns pass, r. remain 10710

You see r, he sees thorns 7670

ROSY
When life r. may slide by knowing about Jesus 10930

ROT
As soon as you're ripe, you start to r. 5364

from hour to hour, we r. and r. 11302

Lust like r. in the bones 7356

ROTTEN
apple spoils his companions 9500

cannot carve r. wood 1070

goodly apple r. at the heart 5011

ROUGH
Along a r, a weary road 7007

being a father can be r. 3917

cross is r. 2106

Many have shining qualities beneath r. exterior 8658 5078

only when choose to praise for r. spots 11152

road that leads to heights of greatness 8287

takes a r. stone to sharpen 190

test of what is real 9399

Virtue demands r. thorny path 11714

ROUGHING
it: cabin without television 6838

ROUGHLY
Bible treats us r. 724

ROUSE
Difficulties meant to r. 2715

pain, God's megaphone to r. a deaf world 8257

ROUSES
greatness of God r. fear within us 3788

ROUSSEAU
Mock on, mock on 596

ROUTE
No camel r. is long with good company 4256

road hazards evidence on right r. 2745

ROUTINE
in much of our ecclesiastical r. 5786

Inside home, they say, dead decorum, r. 5842

ROUTINES
Lord, turn r. of work into celebrations of love 12015

ROW
I cannot r. it myself 6398

ROWBOAT
marriage like long trip in tiny r. 7595

ROWING
Pray to God in the storm, but keep r. 8898

ROYAL
A r. cup for him, my King 7003

deprive ourselves of r. display of wisdom 4995

Every person of r. blood 5967

no r. road to becoming worker for God 9564

Rags r. raiment when worn for virtue's sake 11694

ROYALTY
as good as anybody if had equal chance 3228

I don't look down upon r. 3228

love counts r. but drudgery if cannot reign for Christ 6457

RUB
them right way will purr 9482

wrong way will bite, scratch 9482

RUBBER
like a r. glove 6131

RUBBING
gem not polished without r. 136

RUBBISH
Hatred is like fire, makes light r. deadly 5597

mind will become r. heap for Satan 7757

RUBY
every stone flashed like a r. 6423

RUDDER
man without purpose like ship without r. 4436

tongue r. of our ship 11418

RUDE
in desire to be frank become r. 9502

The clever so r. to the good 909

RUGGED
Each bog, each r. hill 8081

soften down the r. road of life 7917

RUIN
devil tempts that he may r. 11096

God seeks worship of those trapped in moral r. 12098

God turns everything into r. 896

man magnificent r. of what God designed 7429

One moment of impatience may r. a life 8405

plan of mine would have proved my r. 4901

Satan, ultimate intention is to r. you 9855

soul faced by r. can rise up 3621

to r. a man for service of God 6407

when God foretells Sodom's r. 11432

RUINATE
proud buildings with thy hours 11344

RUINED
alcohol, r. millions 331

at our own request 8877

first half of lives r. by parents 3892

most would rather be r. by praise than saved by criticism 8741

pretense harasses r. man 8679

second half of lives r. by children 3892

who is content can never be r. 1797

RUINOUS
consequences to society 10503

RUINS
Abundance, like want, r. men 9335

bridge over which he is to pass 4084

helped me to understand many r. 10594

mount to heaven on r. of cherished schemes 3631

No r. so irreparable as reputation 9619

RULE
Adam took r. over himself 757

by majority fairest 5194

came here to serve, not to r. 10218

Christ a Prince to r. 6370

Christ himself doth r. 2392

God does allow tyrants to r. 4957

leading r. is diligence 2789

Life must be composed not by r. 6966

lust 9960

Make a r. and pray to God 6660

martyr dies, his r. begins 7679

no r. but personal domination of the Holy Spirit 5785

of the four S's 11697

safe r. is to give more than we can spare 10734

Sin rebellion against r. of God 10366

that governs my life is this 7036

though a fool r, is in slavery 4113

tyrant dies, his r. ends 7679

when God should be our Sovereign, we r. ourselves 10425

your mind, or it will r. you 6329

RULED

If not governed by God, r. by tyrants 7483

in world r. by cause and effect 11590

or r. by tyrants 4137

When home is r. according to God's Word 5862

with what little understanding world is r. 5174

RULER

Almighty R. of the all 11628

Remember who your r. is 1311

right to kill because his r. has quarrel with mine 11744

Speech is a mighty r. 10688

RULERS

Our earthly r. falter 9224

RULES

are illuminators, not directors 6816

blunt appetite for Christ 6819

Christianity at first seems to be about r. 1181

crave specific r. to know how to behave 6810

divine king r. forever by dying 2166

for self discovery 10016

for sex are tremendously strict 10235

God does not allow us to make the r. 7828

God not interested in r. 7863

God who r. this earth 3227

home wild place in world of r, set tasks 5842

in God, all r. are fair 604

Injustice never r. forever 6268

Integrity needs no r. 6311

Jesus did not attain perfection by r, regulations 8520

Love r. kingdom without sword 7270

No man safely r. but he who loves to be subject 7422

Peace r. day when Christ r. mind 8462

puritanical insistence on moral r. 6827

To believe in God is to know r. will be fair 4508

two fundamental r. for life 10053

Where love r, no will to power 7343

Wherever God r. human heart as King 4736

Whose r. would you use 2019

without breaking any r. God has made 5046

RULING

saint knit into shape by r. personality of God 9767

RUMOR

a great traveler 5153

Don't worry about r, slander 6271

going around the shop 9822

nothing swifter in life than voice of r. 5142

pipe blown by surmises, jealousies, conjectures 9756

unspreading a r. difficult 5163

RUMORS

flying r. gather'd as they roll'd 9757

RUN

best race hasn't been r. 8230

Children, like clocks, must be allowed to r. 1108

course of true anything never does r. smooth 2747

Don't r. around with Henny Pennys 4226

if God makes you r. 5427

If I knew myself, I'd r. away 10011

ill-luck, some r. halfway to meet it 11449

in morning r. off to another box called office 5859

shepherds r, solemnize his birth 6140

Some thought brave afraid to r. 1934

Those who chase happiness r. from contentment 5566

To believe in heaven is to r. toward life 5674

we try to r. away 181

RUNG

of ladder never meant to rest upon 9316

RUNNING

devil is r. from me 2653

God's r. the show 4939

I'd have come r. with a bucket 4653

not r. from the devil 2653

RUNS

A lover r. 7283

Bible r. after me 712

Desire r. out of breath 2567

God r. toward him twain 7573

If man r. after money, he's money-mad 7800

It r. through the nightland up to the day 4313

RUNWAY

God's never missed the r. 3974

RURAL

all urban and r. sounds 4259

Jesus was a simple r. figure 6451

RUSH

And the r. of winnowing wings 7943

Avoid the last minute r. 2768

Fools r. in 4060

RUSHED

about wildly searching for you 7473

RUSHES

distraction life causes as it r. on 4968

noise life causes as it r. on 10273

time r. on 11373

When you empty yourself, God r. in 9956

RUST

better to wear out than r. out 6767

Cheerfulness removes r. from mind 1093

corrupts iron, envy corrupts man 3207

Few minds wear out, more r. out 7756

If I rest, I r. 6763

of life scoured off by oil of mirth 6738

Sunday clears away r. of the week 10954

Too much rest is r. 6781

When you don't use life, r. consumes it 6905

RUSTING

more danger of r. out than wearing out 8177

RUSTLES

To man who is afraid everything r. 4002

RUSTY

owe it to God that we refuse r. brains 11274

RUTHLESS

Ambition is r. 341

Bible transformed r. killers into saints 726

vain man can never be utterly r. 9189

vain man never utterly r. 1585

RUTHLESSLY

greed r. ready to crush beauty and life 5327

kick the whine out r. 10032

twilight is torn away r. 8075

RUTS

Take r. as evidence on right route 2745

takes guts to leave r. 1928

S

SABBATH

dreams rekindled 10959

fifty-two springs in every year 10950

grandfathers called it the S. 10952

great-grandfathers called it the holy S. 10952

hope reborn 10959
if ox gets in ditch every S. 10951
Jesus spoke about ox in ditch on S.
　10951
Night is s. of mankind 8085
self-worth restored 10959

SABOTAGE
Christianity, campaign of s. 1190

SACK
Everyone thinks his s. heaviest
　10029
Nothing can come out of s. but
　what is in it 6316

SACRAMENT
consider scholarship a s. 11007
Divorce, s. of adultery 2923
strengthened by s. 1444

SACRAMENTAL
Life must be s. 6985

SACRAMENTS
Christ will turn meals into s. 5529
earth, confronted with s. of God
　8050

SACRED
A glory gilds the s. page 634
calling not limited to ecclesiastical
　functions 12146
Conscience is a s. sanctuary 1666
employment is s. as Sunday
　activities 3104
false barrier between secular and s.
　10720
Hold s. every experience 6900
Human personality and
　individuality s, 6183
In Christ nothing secular and s.
　6411
Is made more s. by adversity 4240
is such a thing as s. idleness 7722
just as s. to laugh as to pray 6722
Laughter a s. sound to God 6729
let your knee be a s. altar 7847
love, faith, character, these are s.
　11684
market is s. as well as the
　sanctuary 5770
mundane work s. as parson's 3113
No man will rise high who jeers at
　s. things 9735
O s. sorrow, he who knows not
　thee 5349
obligation to find out and do it
　6175
saint never thinks of life as
　secular, s. 1324
Sorrow is a s. thing 10612
streets s, God's presence there
　4866
Suffering s. trial sent by eternal
　love 10896
that determines work s. or secular
　7865
thoughts which alone can be s.
　4255
Thy s. inmost shrine 7454

SACREDNESS
church knows nothing of a s. of
　war 11761
upon every part of our life 9099

SACRIFICAL
Sincere self-forgetting s. service
　9996

SACRIFICE
a great joy 9758
because his s. is a hard one 6599
Bible idea of s. 9762
Christ a s. satisfying our sins 6410
Christ seeks glory by s. of himself
　2152
compromise, s. of one for another
　1579
cross, s. with imperishable dignity
　2166
cross, voluntary s. 2118
crown studded with gems of s.
　and adoration 7073
deepest truths of Christian religion
　9758
draw back from s. of ourselves
　3320
far from being source of sadness
　9758
give much without s, given little
　10738
God our compensation for every s.
　4550
God speaks to us of s. 4900
I never made a s. 9760
Jesus asked if he might be let off
　the final s. 6384
Jesus' s. must be conscious 10868
Man seeks to win glory by s. of
　others 2152
my chastened heart, a s. complete
　10969
no matter how much s. 4127
no s. can be too great 9761
of praise will always cost
　something 8724
ought not to talk of s. 9760
Prayer a s. to God 8915
preempted by success,
　self-fulfillment 1409
satisfaction comes when s.
　involved 2757
source of illumination 9758
Still stands the ancient s. 6036
such as world had never before
　seen 6419
to God of devil's leavings 8183
until first given himself in s.
　10119
was anything real ever gained
　without s. 4341
Without s. no resurrection 4342
Your dedication will not be a s.
　10125

SACRIFICES
crosses he sends, s. he demands
　4688
God calls each in secret to make s.
　5385
Life made up not of great s. 6656

Satisfaction felt by those who
　make s. 2018
Success demands strange s. 10801
That which one s. never lost 9764
though it requires unexpected s.
　2533
which always involve risk 5385

SACRIFICING
when talk of joy of s. 9758

SAD
as glory itself 4415
Authentic men aren't afraid to cry
　when s. 3916
Be still, s. heart 10582
blessings for man s. for his own
　sins 5299
blues moody, s. and make you cry
　7888
friend, a smile when you're s.
　4174
If short—yet why should I be s.
　6923
is the man who has nothing but
　money 7821
Joy of the s. 6468
love everything in life, even to be s.
　10595
Love puts the s. in apart 7269
Marriage more merry and more s.
　7635
Morality comes with s. wisdom of
　age 7829
soul, take comfort nor forget 5942
Spirit of God may make man s.
　with world's grief 1064
taken life on the s. side 10594
wonder that child of God should
　have s. heart 1096

SADDEST
chose s. and somberest color 467
happened at the s. times in his life
　5437
One of the s. experiences 8661
sweetest songs tell of s. thought
　10608

SADDLE
Lift into s. on one side 5968
Things are in the s. 9343

SADDUCEE
because brings me good opinion, I
　am a S. 10158

SADLY
Pity him who's s. sighing 4217
Poverty makes people s. satirical
　8690

SADNESS
conceal s. under pretended gaiety
　10587
flies away on wings of time 10609
joy, disquiet, s. 4877
laughter often mantles over s. 431
Master's disposition a subdued s.
　6390
sacrifice far from being source of s.
　9758
trying to please everyone 1581

Was the s. and the gloom 2217
where there is s, joy 9086

SAFE

A ship in a harbor is s. 76
And to the end persisting s. arrive 1664
Cowardice asks, Is it s. 1679
God promises a s. landing 170
in Jehovah's keeping 4490
in midst of perils 4490
in temptation's hour 4490
obey, be s. 8115
of feeling s. with a person 4260
secret's s. 'twixt you, me, gatepost 1615
think love of humanity s. but it isn't 7836
though the night be long 4490
Vision vistas outside realm of the s. 11736
way to destroy enemy 3170
when the tempest rages 4490
who respects himself is s. from others 9986

SAFEGUARDING

s. freedom of spirit 4127

SAFELY

action might s. be made law for world 3453
Dies s, through thy love 2398
Dogma ark in which church floats down s. 11187
into the Unknown 5417
through another week 10953
Until we have s. passed over 9098

SAFER

And s. than a known way 5417
God's love for us s. subject than our love 4777
to tell people to seek kingdom of God 3315

SAFEST

eloquence is silence 4681
In crisis most daring course often s. 2047
road to hell is gradual 5702
Virtue is the s. helmet 11711

SAFETY

and peace only after forced to knees 882
angels regard our s. 363
cannot fall out of his s. 4618
center of God's will is s. 4980
for human race to follow teachings of Bible 744
Marriage has more of s. than single life 7635
prayer for s. 9098
The s. of the world was lying there 6133
Thou are absolute s. from trouble 9052
Use God to give us s. 7517
walks in justice's steps 6628
wise man prays not for s. from danger 3997

worship of God is not a rule of s. 12119

SAGES

As s. in all times assert 11857
can learn from s. of India 2988
That s. have seen in thy face 10550

SAID

A man who s. things Jesus s. 6350
at all, can be s. clearly 11222
Bible has s. everything there is to be s. 746
ever remember when regretted having s. kind word 6636
Examine what is s. 1842
If nobody ever s. anything 1852
If we knew everything s. about us 9466
last deed done, last word s. 8082
Man s. Let us make God in our image 4547
Much that may be thought cannot wisely be s. 2898
not everything thought can be s. 11222
Nothing I never s. ever did me harm 10682
Nothing s. not s. before 10686
should not be s. by big mouths 3461
the home where hen crows, cock silent 5847
Well done better than well s. 69 3459
When tell truth, don't have to remember what you s. 11588
words we shouldn't have s. 3882

SAIL

In which his soul may s. 11519
meet for a moment, s. out of sight 4281
Our ships shall s. upon another sea 2319
Satan watches for vessels that s. without convoy 2664
Then there are friends who s. together 4281
wind of God blowing but must hoist s. 5452

SAILING

experiencing smooth s, brace yourself 969

SAILS

can adjust s. 4056
realist adjust the s. 8249
'tis the set of the s, not the gales 4432

SAINT

always thankful to God 9790
As a s. in heaven unshod 10256
as much need of s. in factory as in monastery 9765
bad man worse when pretends to be s. 6045
certain everything is all right 9785
Character in s. Christ manifested 998

chastened through great sorrows 9781
comprehends that all is well 10910
condition admits no alternation 4626
consciously dependent on God 9768
creature of vast possibilities 9767
deems it the same 9782
does everything any other person does 9783
does not call himself a worm 9784
each individual either a sinner or a s. 5038
education might have brought to light 3038
Every s. has a past, every sinner a future 8653
greatest s. not he who is eminent for justice 9790
greatest s. not he who prays, fasts, gives most 9790
grieves at sin is a s. 10309
has same spirit, judgment, will with Christ 9766
heart always ready to praise God 9790
here for God's designs 139
If God made you a duck s. 6187
if s. lets his mind alone, soon a rubbish heep 7757
If you're an eagle s. stop expecting squirrel s. to soar 6187
impossible to be both sinner and s. 5038
impossible to develop if critical 2056
insights of s. stem from experiences as sinner 9776
is ever young 9785
is hilarious when crushed 2722
is one light shines through 9769
knit into shape by God 9767
knows not why he suffers 10910
lives by faith in God 3653
Lord jealous over s. abandoned to him 8608
makes it easy to believe in Jesus 9771
more honesty man has, less air of s. 5889
more hope for sinner than self-conceited s. 5948
never believes circumstances haphazard 1324
never consciously a s. 9768
never thinks of life as secular and sacred 1324
No s. dare interfere in discipline 10927
No s. ever did work cheaply, easily 5289
not s. on knees, cheat in shop 1908
old s. in elastic-side boots 1455
one who makes goodness attractive 9770

only with totally different motive 9783

Praise is the s. reflecting Christ 8734

prayer of feeblest s. a terror to Satan 8988

praying s. performs havoc among forces of darkness 9014

receives everything as God's goodness 9790

see Christ's chosen s. 1299

stuff that makes criminal makes s. 8667

The weakest s. upon his knees 8959

then Jesus Christ was no s. 9789

This is the blessedness of a s. 4626

uses commands of the Lord 8111

weakest s. can experience power 9563

when s. becomes conscious of being s. 10722

Who is greatest s. in world 9790

wills everything that God wills 9790

SAINT TERESA
God asks you do your best, not S. best 9013

SAINTHOOD
can find good in criminals 9778

delivers from condemning 9778

delivers from judging others 9778

makes it possible to admire everybody 9778

SAINTLINESS
Humility is touchstone of s. 6013

If this really is Christian s. 9789

SAINT'S
life in the hands of God 139

SAINTS
absolutely at rest 126

All are not s. that go to church 9772

always among the unofficial crowd 9786

apostles, prophets, martyrs 6892

because of silence mysteries of God known to s. 10252

Bible transformed killers into s. 726

bondage is with world, not s. 4159

by silence the s. grew 10252

cannot discipline ourselves to be s. 4984

carry on intercession for all men 8859

Christians envy s. their joy 3224

church not museum for s. 1379

comradeship with heroes, s. of every age 9059

do not exercise authority 526

dominant note is Jesus Christ 9786

either make us fiends or s. 4957

experienced up, down, joy, sorrow 2593

God deliver us from sullen s. 9774

God does not expect us to become s. overnight 9832

God is enough for them 5301

God makes s. out of sinners 9773

God never stands up for s. 1060

God scarcely vindicates his s. to men 11616

God's aim is production of s. 5757

God's patience with ill-natured s. mystery 4893

Great s. have always been dogmatic 11188

Great s. have often been great sinners 9775

have their power 5301

in glory perfect made 2221

interest us when in conflict with devil 1631

makes s. aware of sinfulness 4660

Money and marriage make devils or s. 7805

must be amused, not amazed 1422

name s. for their holiness 1328

need no worldly or intellectual greatness 5301

never become great s. 9777

nonsense to say suffering makes s. 10860

not overcome by panic 126

not who soared to heights of achievement 6175

old s. practiced all their lives 5503

one with God 126

Painting enables us to see humility of s. 2015

praise dead s, persecute living ones 8530

prayer of the s. 8840

stop expecting rabbit s. to build same nests you do 6187

tears of s. more sweet by far 9787

That they are never sated makes all the s. rejoice 9780

through the s. God is doing things 126

usually killed by their own people 9779

When God is putting s. through millstones 10927

Where s. immortal reign 5670

which God loves best 9788

who sank to depths of service 6175

wisest s. endure rather than escape pain 10847

Worldly people imagine s. find it difficult to live 4159

SAINT-SEDUCING
gold 11850

SAINTSHIP
devil piqu'd such s. to behold 2690

SALE
Are you for s. 11798

Self-respect is never for s. 9995

SALT
church like s. flavors, preserves 1427

Disappointment often s. of life 2794

Rebukes not to have more s. than sugar 2854

sweet as s. in your mouth 4050

SALTWATER
Power is like s. 8711

SALUTARY
moved God to dispense s. grace 4989

SALVAGES
God s. the individual 886

SALVATION
Absolute candor indispensable requisite to s. 9793

And brings s. down 8950

and comfort unite 9812

apart from feelings 4015

as to election, God is s. 4514

Bible deals with s. and damnation 721

bringing back to normal the Creator-creature relation 9807

comes by faith 4015

cross accomplishment of s. 3582

depends more on God's love of us than our love of him 9806

Discipleship, s. two different things 2817

discussed as though conditions for membership 2033

incoming into human nature of characteristics that belong to God 9811

is a gift you can ask for 9808

is cosmic 9817

is final 9817

is free 2832

is healing 9817

is moving from living death to deathless life 9809

is to him who believes 9810

is worth working for 9810

knowledge of sin is beginning of s. 9815

more important than preservation of epics 3332

nice people just as desperately in need of s. 7827

of human souls the real business of life 7027

only thing God makes plain in Bible 11546

reduced to once-done act 9816

terms for s. designate health 9817

Three things necessary for s. 9824

understanding of redemption not necessary to s. 9433

want s. of the soul 3025

will depend on never looking back 9828

wrong concept of s. 4568

SALVE

Little praying a s. for the conscience 8889

SAME

all fellow passengers on s. planet 9677

All revolutions various parts of s. scheme 4898

All service ranks the s. with God 10116

can't be enthusiastic, unhappy at s. time 3189

Christ's words have s. relevance 6359

Christmas and Good Friday the s. day 6489

cross of Jesus Christ and his baptism express s. thing 9437

finger of God never leaves s. fingerprint 6211

five fingers not all the s. 7377

friend to everybody, nobody, s. thing 4215

God cannot be for, against s. thing at s. time 4972

God gave us life, liberty at s. time 4146

gospel of Christ s. forever 5103

Happiness and intelligence rarely found in s. person 5512

have s. privileges in God's world 9988

hear s. prayers repeated each Sunday 8845

heart beats in every human breast 917

If all experience God s. way 6169

if wish to make everyone s. 6189

injuries we do, suffer seldom weighed in s. scales 9495

Is of the s. opinion still 9179

Jesus in heaven as on earth 6466

life of Jesus cannot be discussed in s. way as any other man 6476

like orchestra in which all instruments played s. note 6169

Love, looking together in the s. direction 7215

love, wrath reverse of s. thing 4999

man can blow hot, cold with s. breath 6054

Men never the s. after listening to Christ 6377

natural and the holy are the s. 9821

No two human beings make s. journey in life 5978 6202

Not all people driven by s. stick 7868

One leg in stocks, or two, all the s. 11447

people smile in s. language 548

power that brought Christ back from dead 9698

saint deems it the s. 9782

Truth having s. idea God has 11554

What a bore waking up the s. person 870

When you pray, things remain the s. 9033

why s. thing makes us laugh, cry 10660

With God Abram's day and this day the s. 4591

You cannot put s. shoe on every foot 6225

your goings and God's goings the s. 8093

zeal as if yourself 3125

SAMSON

brought the house down 791

did what Tarzan couldn't do 790

most popular actor 791

nothing worse than homemade haircut 793

pastor needs strength of S. 9125

ripped lion's head open 790

strong body, weak head 789

Temptations as lion that roared upon S. 11095

weakness was showing off his s. 792

SANCTIFICATION

a joyful liberation 9842

After s. difficult to state aim in life 9830

Are we prepared for what s. will do 9831

ascribed to God the Spirit 3043

discipline nine out of ten will have nothing to do with 9843

found in Christ Jesus, not in some formula 7105

If I exact s. 9838

In first experience of s. 9840

is himself in me 9843

not a heavy yoke 9842

not something Lord does in me 9843

only thing God makes plain in Bible 11546

test of s. not singing pious hymns 9845

test of s. not talk about holiness 9845

test of s. what are we like where no one sees us 9845

to love and help others, even though feel weak 8256

when God leads in higher path of s. 9851

SANCTIFIED

for God to do with us as he did with Jesus 9850

How does will become s. 9835

If God has not s. us 9837

life often misunderstood 2856

saved and s. for God 9850

when God begins to deal with s. souls 9840

SANCTIFY

good end cannot s. evil means 5010

Spirit will never s. whom Father hath not elected 3043

Spirit will never s. whom Son has not redeemed 3043

Suffering divine dispensation to s. 10896

what I am 9100

SANCTION

if wrong, s. of mankind will not justify 5032

SANCTUARY

a holy web in the s. 1721

Conscience is a sacred s. 1666

Despair can become a kind of s. 2581

flee into s. of private virtuousness 11690

heart of good man s. of God 5084

Let your living room be a s. 7847

market is sacred as well as the s. 5770

marketplace ought to be s. 4866

SANCTUM

dream door in deepest s. of soul 2971

SAND

all the universe in a grain of s. 1957

building on s. 9447

faults like s. beside mountain of mercies 4817

Fear is s. in machinery of life 3967

gospel, grain of s. that upsets world's machinery 5099

handful of s. anthology of universe 11625

in place of crumbling s. 7448

like building house on foundations of s. 7796

like writing on s. by seashore 3860

little grains of s. 6659

To seek wisdom in old age like mark on s. 11956

two sets of footprints in the s. 5437

understand grain of s, understand everything 1957

worry, anxiety s. in machinery of life 3731

You throw s. against the wind 596

SANDBANK

not to settle on s. of selfishness 9930

SANDCASTLE

Hate compared to foot that destroys s. 7233

Love compared to building of s. 7233

SANDPILE

Simon Peter more a s. than a rock 3617

SANDS

Footprints on the s. of time 5288 3441

pyramids sinking in desert s. 730

SANE
enough to bow before mystery of human being 4247

SANG
if no birds s. except those who s. best 7926

SANGUINE
it was the s. people who flocked to Jesus 6452

SANITY
an amazing s. about Jesus 2170

SANK
Most saints s. to depths of service 6175

No man ever s. under burden of day 4319

SAP
His godhead is your s. 7689

rising of s. from within 4160

strength: worry, travel, sin 10406

SAPPHIRA
as he did in days of Ananias, S. 4717

SAPS
inaction s. vigor of the mind 6765

Worry only s. today of its strength 12089

SARCASM
arrows of s. barbed with contempt 1771

crushed if s. clever enough 6645

No one ever corrected by a s. 6645

smiles betray s. 10500

to tear flesh from bone 1770

weapon of the weak 1770

SARDINES
Life is rather like a tin of s. 6976

SARTE
brand is atheist who sees man helpless 3495

SAT
down under the drainpipe 4062

SATAN
believe S. to exist for two reasons 9854

cannot counterfeit peace of God 5396

cannot hurt godly 3996

claimed by God, counterclaimed by S. 4918

content as long as we never complete anything 9857

content for us to make beginnings 9857

could S. have devised Christmas 1370

evil is the S. that laughs at logic 5023

exists because Bible says so 9854

exists, I've done business with him 9854

fails to speak of remorse of immorality 2662

finds mischief for idle hands to do 6772

first of beings to choose evil 3370

his army of demons compelled to obey Jesus 9858

his name heard no more in heaven 2666

history contest between God, S, fallen men 4916

If it takes sin to show S. in true colors 11072

In which the power of S. broken is 6140

interview with S. would alone have damned 6388

is a chronic grumbler 9856

is at work through evil 5014

keeps minds fussy till we cannot think in prayer 8988

lazy man is workshop for S. 6749

limited power of S. 4917

looks up between his feet 9940

Mercy imitates God, disappoints S. 7741

mind will become rubbish heap for S. 7757

must be most frustrated personality in universe 9858

No matter how many pleasures S. offers you 9855

now is wiser than of yore 2690

Out S. must go, every hair and feather 9864

People do not need S. to recruit to evil 3396

People have forgotten S. 1309

Prayer a scourge to S. 8915

prayer of saint a terror to S. 8988

ready to help to new opinions 2944

rocks the cradle at devotions 2663

through our bodily lives S. works 837

tormentor of wicked 3996

trembles when he sees 8959

tried Jesus Christ becoming King of world 11082

tries to make us think wrongs spring from God 9859

ultimate intention is to ruin 9855

uses problems of life to slander God's character 9859

wastes no ammunitions on those in sins 9860

watches for vessels that sail without convoy 2664

were bondslaves to S. now heirs of God 1348

whispers, "All is lost" 2800

Your destruction is his highest priority 9855

SATANIC
does not mean abominable 9853

does not mean immoral 9853

most s. type of pride 6038

this dark s. earth 4902

SATANICALLY-MANAGED
man absolutely self-governed 9853

man has no need of God 9853

SATAN'S
cunning cannot take simplicity by surprise 10278

friendship reaches to prison door 2665

most successful maneuver 392

temptation is S. business 11060

truth judges out of envy, hatred 4914

under S. standard and enlisted there 10427

SATED
That they are never s. makes all the saints rejoice 9780

SATIATE
will s. ourselves with crumbs from world 12050

SATIETY
extreme love, hatred breeds s. 3554

Silence welcome after s. 10266

SATIRE
no answer when world's s. turned on you 10917

Praise to the undeserving is s. 8736

SATIRICAL
Poverty makes people s. 8690

SATISFACTION
baptism of Holy Ghost means we are a s. to Jesus 5789

comes when we do something difficult 2757

demands s. from other human beings they cannot give 9496

felt by those who give, make sacrifices 2018

God must have laughed with s. 7859

heaven, find s. of all desires 5644

into loveliness, s. of our true home 6110

more s. out of brutality than honesty 5884

not felt by those who take, make demands 2018

Some Christians refer with smug s. to service 10182

SATISFACTIONS
may be hazardously little 4248

SATISFACTORY
if relationship is faulty, activity cannot be s. 10227

more s. is our dependence on God 7524

SATISFIED
angels ask nothing more to make them s. 4995

bad thing to be s. spiritually 10704

be s. with what you have 11864

be s. with your posssessions 8472

begin to be s. spiritually, begin to degenerate 9234

conformist refuses to be s. with things as they are 9311

endowed with reason to be s. 9425

less s. with superfical views of Christ 6480

My desires are s. 7964

neither is s. without the other 4531

not s. with little, not s. with much 1805

Show me s. man, I will show you failure 2871

since he is s, so am I 9987

thy goodness both s. and made me thirsty 9097

to meet together 1404

until learned to be s. with God 7447

well paid that is well s. 1795

When men worship, God is s. 12137

will not be s. until justice rolls down like waters 6629

SATISFIES

If money s. one want 7814

No gain s. greedy mind 5319

service s. my self-esteem more than status 9996

When marriage a solution for loneliness rarely s. 7666

SATISFY

impossible to s. everyone 9476

luxuries of world cannot s. lonely 7176

Naught but God can s. the soul 7504

no earthly thing can ever s. me 3277

only one being can s. aching heart 5359

redemption of Jesus can s. aching soul 6402

Religion that is merely ritual can never s. 9546

Riches enlarge rather than s. appetites 11846

what will s. if God himself will not 7508

SATISFYING

Cheerfulness, s. result of discipline 1088

few emotions so s. 11253

knowing is inwardly s. 5809

shall find God s. our sense of beauty 3774

to turn from limitations to God who has none 3274

SAUL

as the evil spirit fled from S. 7935

SAVAGE

Music has charms to soothe s. breast 7901

SAVE

A never-dying soul to s. 10114

Economy, s. in one store, spend in another 4036

If you your ears would s. from jeers 1855

Looking at wound of sin will never s. 9804

nice people might be more difficult to s. 7827

our souls from being steeped in care 9064

philanthropy to s. ourselves uncomfortable feeling 10071

stretching hand to s. falling man 1554

thrifty s. money 7826

to s. and not condemn 6519

will not s. to know Christ is Savior 3753

will not s. us without our consent 9796

will s. to trust Christ to be Savior 3753

SAVED

and sanctified for God 9850

by making atonement my trust 3753

endowed with a soul and a will to be s. 9425

for God to do with us as he did with Jesus 9850

God predestines every man to be s. 9175

if souls not s. something wrong 1404

not question of s. from hell 1014

nothing more irritating than Savior when not ready to be s. 9819

poor wretches s. from shipwreck 10386

preoccupied with what we are s. from 9826

Prodigal Son could still be s. 3167

rather than what we are s. to 9826

something has been s. from wreck 11072

Souls are not s. in bundles 9814

to manifest Son of God in mortal flesh 1014

want to be s, insist Christ do dying 2821

wish to be s. from mischief of vices but not vices 10338

would pay any price to say "All will be s." 9799

SAVES

Christ's hold of you that s. you 9802

Forgiveness s. expense of anger 4089

happiest miser s. every friend 4203

hope s. from solicitude 3834

who helps in saving others s. himself as well 10146

SAVING

Every scrap of wise man's time worth s. 11913

who helps in s. others 10146

SAVIOR

Christ is a great S. 9797

fellowship with self-denying, suffering S, 7698

God has set a S. against sin 5016

Good preaching leads people to praise S. 10097

greet in cradle our S. 1375

in heaven stand in character of S. 1072

need a superhuman S. 6459

nothing more irritating than S. when not ready to be saved 9819

O my S, make me see 2136

revival to give glory to a great S. 9751

task in solitude to keep mind on S. 10551

The Lord my S. liveth 232

theology begins, ends with Christ as S. 11182

will get to heaven by accepting Christ as S. 5681

SAVIOR GOD

gospel is S. seeking lost men 9545

SAVIOR'S

Lay down thy head upon S. breast 2365

To lay his head upon the S. breast 11476

Wherein our S. birth is celebrated 1371

SAVOR

one discovers true s. of life 6086

SAW

Avarice and happiness never s. each other 5312

awoke and s. life was duty 9663

God s. through thick cloud 4904

I s. a stable, low and very bare 6133

If we s. all evil things 4318

If we s. all good things coming 4318

likened you to those I s. you with 9464

more he s. the less he spoke 1832

Moses only s. brightness of Lord 4874

part of man sees which never s. before 5809

Reason s. not till faith sprung the light 3777

We s. thee in thy balmy nest 6152

when I s. where the pieces landed 4136

when men first s. their God 6154

worlds of light we never s. by day 10633

SAY

able to s. how much you love is to love little 7323

All I design, or do, or s. 9047
anxious about what others s. 6824
Below the surface-stream of what we s. we feel 7369
cannot hear what you s. 560
cannot s. Lord's Prayer if 8818
cannot s. one thing and mean another 9036
cannot s. what we will do 5446
cannot s. you are friendless 4214
Chatterbox talks while thinking of something to s. 1830
Compliment when you don't know what to s. 1577
deeper the sorrow, less tongue has to s. 10627
Democracy, can s. what you think 5172
devil has nothing to s. about will of God 4915
don't seem to be able to s. my prayers 8887
Everyone knows how to s. good-bye 9452
expect Author will have something to s. 9911
For all she had to s. 10596
freedom of speech, responsibility for what we s. 4154
having nothing to s. 1837
he may not s. much, but you feel different 6241
Hear the lazy people s. 9303
Hears what one cannot s. 8515
How many people stop because so few s. "Go" 3135
I s. just what I think 9036
I'll s. what you want me to s, dear Lord 5420
if things we s. are worth saying 5590
in ten sentences what others s. in book 12149
Jesus had things to s. about how we should behave 6444
Knowing when to s. nothing 7626
learn to s. no gracefully 5615
Let no one s. we are worthless 9989
make enemies by what we s. 1888
may pray least when s. most 9018
may pray most when s. least 9018
may s, "Life is not worth living" 6880
may s. far from hating God 10427
mighty force behind things we s. 12005
mother understands what child does not s. 7842
never needing to s. is what counts 4268
Never s. more than necessary 1863
not in evil doing, "No one sees" 3404
not right to s. all suffering perfects 10920
not true, s. it not 1021
Not, what did the sketch in the newspaper s. 7423

Nothing is often good thing to s. 1865
nothing you cannot believe to be true 9871
often for excuse we s. things impossible 7869
safely s. to most troubles, "We shall meet no more" 12075
see twice as much as they s. 3564
sigh can s. more than many words 8887
some s. God too good to be true 4504
talk most who have least to s. 1834
they will forgive but can't forget 9641
They will s. "We did this ourselves" 6803
those who s. "Thy will be done" 5455
To exaggerate weakens what we s. 3425
to s, "I was wrong" 7838
took God years to teach me to s. "Lord anything" 4892
very few s. all they mean 11990
we s. millions never think of God 7561
We s. must do all we can 10980
were but little happy if I could s. how much 6558
What Christ had to s. too simple to be grasped 6507
what father, mother s. at home 8340
What people s. behind back is your standing in community 9628
what you have to s, not what you ought 5887
When nothing to s, s. nothing 10691
When sense of self depends on what others s. 10003
when you s. situation hopeless 5955
Who can s. more than this rich praise 6223
who has nothing to s. keeps silent 10272
who has too much to s. keeps silent 10272
will show love in everything we s. 4767
Wise men s. nothing in dangerous times 11979

SAYING
Apology is s. right thing 428
could produce same effect by s, sins be forgiven 5485
Cynicism unpleasant way of s. truth 2180
Don't go around s. world owes you a living 9652
God hears what they are s. 4886
God s. to world, "I love you" 7173

goes without s, says it anyway 1877
My country, right or wrong like s. 7980
Nobody will know what you mean by s. "God is love" 7281
Not the s, but the never needing to say 4268
Originality not in s. what no one has said 2011
Originality, s. exactly what you think 2011
rather than s. something 9307
two sides to every question 8076
Voices are s, "Let it all hang out" 9976
What is reason for s. God does not heed us 7567
yes to God means s. no to things that offend his holiness 5755

SAYINGS
great man's foolish s. pass for wise ones 5273
in Plato and Cicero wise, beautiful 930
Wise s. often fall on barren ground 6672

SAYS
ant s. nothing, preaches better 3447
best reward a liar by believing nothing he s. 6863
child s. nothing but heard by fire 3885
church s. covetousness a deadly sin 10086
difference between what happens when man s. 3611
goes without saying, s. it anyway 1877
If happiness depends on what somebody s. 5536
Immature love s. "I love you because need you" 7194
man gets up to speak and s. nothing 5171
Mature love s. "I need you because love you" 7194
No one means all he s. 11990
rarely hear man suffering who s. 10936
Spring season that s. it with flowers 9890
those to whom God s, "Have it your way" 5455
When God s. today, devil s. tomorrow 2493
who s. it can't be done 66

SCAB
is a s. even if smear honey on it 10288

SCAFFOLD
from s. to s. from stake to stake 7673

SCAFFOLDING
may act honest man on the s. 6295

missionaries as s. around rising building 7780

SCALE
Almighty working on a great s. 8419
Christianity never accepted on large s. 1188
Give me such courage I can s. 1927
must s. mountains if view plain 8562

SCALES
love does not measure by merchant's s. 4789
seldom weighed in same s. 9495

SCALPEL
divine Surgeon must be permitted to use s. 890

SCAN
And s. his work in vain 5378

SCANDAL
Assail'd by s. and the tongue of strife 6356
charity is deafness when s. flows 1085
Leave s. alone, never touch it 5154
should be treated as mud on clothes 5154

SCANNED
though I s. the skies 4921

SCAR
God sees s, creates star 8278
No wound, no s. 10604
on conscience same as wound 1660
wound heals, but s. remains 10446

SCARCE
anything about us is as it seems 9623
God himself so seemed there to be 7142
sir, mighty s. 11983

SCARE
good s. worth more than advice 3960

SCARED
futile to condemn myself for feeling s. 3049
No man ever s. into heaven 5663

SCARS
God will look for s. 172
in his hands and feet the cruel s. 9798
jests at s. that never felt a wound 10850
Lord promised cross, s. 2102
most massive characters seamed with s. 10882
Turn s. into stars 299

SCATTER
hand ceases to s, heart ceases to pray 4385

We plough the fields and s. 4625

SCENE
do not ask to see distant s. 2551
dream theater where dreamer s. 2972
I do not ask to see distant s. 5429
Life, s. of good and evil 5034
years we spend on earth first s. in divine drama 6106

SCENERY
contented man enjoys s. along detours 1773

SCENES
Bible's variety like s. of nature 680
old s. will lovelier be 4197

SCEPTIC
If one a s. 2946

SCEPTICAL
well to be s. about one's scepticism 2946

SCEPTICISM
truth cannot be built on s. 11530

SCHEDULE
deteriorating according to s. 8134
people not interruptions to s. 3316
ultrabusy s. not mark of productive life 9533

SCHEME
All revolutions various parts of same s. 4898
in Bible for treatment of earth 3200
Who talks of s. and plan 7572

SCHEMES
God allows our own s. to fail 9851
of world reconstruction have failed 6487
on ruins of cherished s. 3631
though men spin cunning s. 4887

SCHEMING
never according to our s. 5401

SCHISM
leave badges of s. behind 5671

SCHIZOPHRENIC
when God talks to us we're s. 9035

SCHOLAR
sees, seer sees through 3021
taught by Holy Spirit, seer rather than s. 3021

SCHOLARS
Bible, not book for s. only 725
can interpret the past 9334
great men not commonly great s. 5302
have recognized devil's existence 2650
Jesus shed more light than philosophers and s. combined 6449

Who among evangelical s. is quoted as source 3040
Who among evangelicals can stand up to great s. 3040

SCHOLARSHIP
a sacrament 11007
enable man to put things well 2998
should follow faith 3022
should not guide or intrude upon faith 3022
will never give insight 2998

SCHOOL
America's future determined by home, s. 5818
church, s. for imperfect Christians 1437
Defeat s. in which truth grows strong 2507
Experience a costly s. 3519
Experience good s. but high fees 3521
family, first s. of human instruction 3880
graduates in heaven's highest s. of art 8914
grammar s. of faith, repentance 11192
home kind of s. where life's basic lessons taught 5853
is sorrow 10600
Marriage not a reform s. 7643
meekness is love in s. 7202
see earth but s. preparative 6109
she is not dead but gone unto that s. 2392
Solitude is the s. of genius 10533
teach children in s. what they are 3039

SCHOOLMASTERS
One father worth more than hundred s. 3923

SCHOOLROOM
Learn lessons well in s. of obscurity 5430
mother's heart is child's s. 7857
When s. darkened, see most 10855

SCHOOLS
as s. change, theology must change 11207
language of heartbreak not learned in s. of men 10902
prepare in s. for what no one knows yet 3035
Youth going to take over s. 12160

SCHOOLTEACHER
no reason why miner not as intellectual as s. 6332

SCHOOLTEACHERS
July when mothers realize why s. need vacations 9900

SCIENCE
all s. rests on basis of faith 9869
assumes permanence, uniformity of natural laws 9869
capable of destroying world 9870

come to religion through
limitations of s. 9866
dedicated to accounting for things
8592
Everything s. has taught me 6090
highest s. is study of attributes of
Godhead 4631
If Bible agreed with s. would soon
be out of date 9865
impatient with anything that
refuses account of itself 8592
is bound to change 9865
Life not an exact s. 6971
Love finds admission where proud
s. fails 12130
measured against reality is
primitive, childlike 9867
not always friendly toward God
8592
of Christ only learned by heart
5110
Philosophy piecemeal, provisional
like s. 8596
Philosophy s. of limitations of
human mind 8594
Philosophy, s. that considers truth
8595
Plato taught more s. than Christ
6362
Politics s. of how who gets what,
when, why 5186
reveals more clearly divine design
in nature 9866
reveals remarkable conformity in
all things 9866
seemed at odds with religion 9866
skill of s. not able to make oyster
1979
smilingly disposed of Bible 9870
sometimes said to be opposed to
faith 9869
strives unceasingly to penetrate
creation 1975
sweet talking goddess 9870
turned out to be a dragon 9870
we read notes to a poem 1203
without s. Jesus shed more light
than scholars 6449

SCIENCES
business is to show the truth 9871
God's actions above human s.
5237
may be learned by head 5110
Study s. in light of truth 9871

SCIENTIFIC
enthusiasm lifts struggles of s.
pursuits 3188
God not discoverable by s. means
4739
man has leaped ahead in s.
achievement 9872
power has outrun spiritual power
9868

SCIENTIFICALLY
proved that worry undermine
health 5612

SCIENTIST
no s. holds key to as much power
11841

SCIENTISTS
come to religion through
limitations of science 9866
world spending genius of its s.
11745

SCOFFERS
I fear I should have been among
the s. 6464

SCOPE
Charity, s. of God's commands
1076

SCORCH
hot words s. people 11985

SCORE
God keeps the s. 7559
We play the game, God keeps the
s. 6069

SCORN
finger of s. at another 1769
no transient beauty s. 11375
The swords of s. divide 9224
three fingers of s. at your own self
1769

SCORNS
heart thumps about things
intellect s. 5628
In heaven devil s. to serve 2656

SCORPION
Dishonesty a s. that will sting
itself to death 2908

SCOTT
Cripple him, and you have a Sir
Walter S. 161

SCOURED
rust of life s. off by oil of mirth
6738

SCOURGE
drink, poisoned s. 325
Prayer a s. to Satan 8915

SCOUT
You travel wide and far to s, see,
search 4926

SCOWL
wear a s, have wrinkles 10502

SCRATCH
a fanatic, find wound that never
healed 3910
rub wrong way will s. 9482

SCRATCHES
God rejoices when one beggar s.
another 9454
must have iron nails that s. bear
11062
play with cat, bear its s. 11067

SCRATCHING
amazed never s. heads for
questions 9544
pleasure of pride like pleasure of s.
9245

SCREECHES
worst s. loudest 1562

SCRIBE
And every man a s. by trade 4748

SCRIPT
anxiously memorize the s. assigned
6824

SCRIPTURAL
imagery symbolic attempt to
express inexpressible 5631

SCRIPTURE
angelic host described in S. 359
devil can cite S. for his purpose
2672
Faith, sight in opposition in S.
3842
focused on S. for period of time
7721
God on side of poor is central in S.
8696
higher, wider than need 691
knowledge of S. no obstacle to sin
10392
matchless temple where I delight
to be 668
Money emphasized in S. 7811
No truths simple especially those
of S. 11521
not an arsenal for arms, weapons
668
Nowhere in S. are God's
principles replaced 7828
only sufficient language is
language of S. 10888
when I hear the devil quote S.
2637

SCRIPTURES
become like child before S. 650
Christ is master, S. servant 647
commentaries on S, good example
best 3449
essential for Holy Spirit to reveal
S. 752
first taught futility of riches 11862
give four names to Christians
1328
memorizing S. help in doubt 747
need for guidance 650
Nobody ever outgrows S. 685
not possible to exhaust the mind
of S. 678
Quote s. devil will run 720
refer to always 650
remedy against weaknesses 650
resolved to try S. as in courtroom
744
Seek in S. effective remedy 650
teach us best way of living 742
teach us most comfortable way of
dying 742
teach us noblest way of suffering
742
the more he studied the S. 737
time when I doubted divinity of S.
744
use S. like sword 720
use to drive temptation away 720

SCROLL
Nor could the s. contain the whole
   4748

SCRUFF
take him by s. of his neck 4315

SCRUTINIZES
Simplicity s. nothing 11696

SCRUTINIZING
If Holy Spirit is s. you 894

SCULPTING
God uses pain as chisel for s. our
   lives 8256

SCULPTOR'S
world is a great s. shop 9822

SCULPTURE
Education to soul like s. to block
   of marble 3038
formed world was s. 1981

SEA
A never-ebbing s. 6409
And so beside the silent s. 6916
Bible's vastness like bottom of s.
   680
calms troubled s. of lives 4863
changes because of rock 572
feeling I could outlast the s. 12165
Follow the river, find the s. 5382
get life out to s. in reckless
   abandon to God 9564
God far more dwells in me than if
   entire s. 4839
God of the s. 7539
God pity the ship when the s. gets
   in 1330
God's love a vast, bottomless,
   shoreless s. 4750
hint of the everlasting in the s.
   3290
Hope will wade through s. of
   blood 5912
I my net was casting in s. 1147
I will not doubt, though all my
   ships at s. 11470
If cannot find God upon margin
   of s. 4856
if shipwreck, will be in wide s. of
   God's love 9930
is subject to storm and tempests
   282
Like fountains of sweet waters in
   the s. 8911
Like the wideness of the s. 7745
Like the winds of the s. are ways
   of fate 4432
loneliness by the s. personal, alive
   7145
My boat on the raging s. 6398
O'er mountain, or plain, or s.
   5420
O'er the world's tempestuous s.
   5428
Our ships shall sail upon another
   s. 2319
ships place is in the s. 1330
soul has greater depths than any s.
   7539

Two hours before going to s. 7650
When I put out to s. 2368
which can contract itself 5788
With God, go over the s. 5470
would not part waters of s. 967

SEA OF GALILEE
gathers in riches, pours them out
   to fertilize 10195
gets to give 10195
has outlet 10195
makes beauty 10195

SEAL
every other s. too narrow for soul
   10659
shaking flipper of trained s. 6062

SEALED
God's promises s. to us, but not
   dated 4470

SEANCE
Television nightly s. 11039

SEARCH
do not obtain the most precious
   gifts by going in s. of them
   8425
for God is surrender to his s. for us
   7455
for happiness chief sources of
   unhappiness 5559
for pearls must dive below 3255
God's creative method is
   continuing s. 4469
gospel is God's s. for man 9547
great thoughts s. the mind 11281
Hope is a confident s. for a
   rewarding life 5918
man travels world in s. of what he
   needs 5815
Most of us find what we s. for
   5077
my heart, it pants for Thee 4140
My s. was fruitless still 4921
Religions are man's s. for God
   9547
thine own heart 3452
truth where few are willing to s.
   3259
You travel wide and far to scout,
   see, s. 4926

SEARCHED
there I s. for thee 4805

SEARCHER
God never turned away questions
   of s. 2941

SEARCHES
Man wise only while he s. for
   wisdom 11930
My Spirit s. the deep things of the
   heart 72

SEARCHING
for something beyond that the
   world contains 7521
friend, a guide when you're s.
   4174
Go s. all the way 7465
mature believer a s. believer 7700

rushed about wildly s. for you
   7473
twas s. for thy law 9091
without God young people s. for
   security 12180

SEARCHLIGHT
Christians lead others out of
   darkness 1313
faith, the spiritual strong s. 3649
Let Holy Spirit's s. go straight
   down 894

SEAS
The Pilot knows the unknown s.
   5448

SEASHORE
like writing on sand by s. 3860

SEASICK
cast bread upon waters while s.
   4373
If uncertainty makes you s. 11598

SEASON
ever 'gainst that s. comes 1371
no s. such delight can bring 9878
Spring s. that says it with flowers
   9890
word out of s. may mar a lifetime
   2890

SEASONABLE
Music as s. in grief as joy 7903

SEASONING
Gratitude s. for all seasons 5243

SEASONS
Gratitude seasoning for all s. 5243
I like sunrises, Mondays, new s.
   8080
Thou hast all s. for thine own, O
   Death 2324
through friendship we love places,
   s. 4269
unfailing regularity of the s. 4643

SEAT
God's great Judgment s. 915
mystery why people ask if empty
   s. occupied 8477

SEATED
one day at the organ 7919

SEATS
plenty of s. available in subway
   7049

SEAWATER
Wealth is like s. 11875

SECOND
Adam is greater than first Adam
   5031
by no extraordinary chance put
   together s. time 6173
Christian thinking puts intellect s.
   11238
every square inch, every split s.
   4918
half of lives ruined by children
   3892
half of man's life 5501
Old age is but a s. childhood 8156

Others s. 9264

time so precious God deals it out
s. by s. 11293

who offers to God s. place, offers
no place 7467

woman who creates home creator
s. only to God 5857

SECOND COMING

only way to wait for S. 9912

primitive church thought more
about S. than death 9913

teaches us 9911

when a matter of indifference
9912

will be a natural as breathing
9912

SECONDARY

activities we do for God are s.
8972

Children born from relationship s.
10239

SECOND-RATE

mind happy thinking with
minority 11248

SECRET

among three is everybody's s. 5115

anniversaries of the heart 7720

as near to God's s. as anyone can
get 10592

best kept by keeping s. 1614

between two is s. of God 5115

Came God, planting the s. genes
of God 6148

can know him who knows heart's
s. 5624

Church, s. wireless from friends
1190

deep inner work, process will be s.
10706

expect others to keep is foolish
1618

Giving is s. of healthy life 10727

God alone knows s. of history
4694

God calls each in s. to make
sacrifices 5385

God has his own s. stairway into
heart 4540

God knows every unuttered s.
4881

God who sees in s. 10877

God will minister to you in s.
10706

gospel possesses a s. virtue 732

gratitude s. desire of greater
benefits 5262

Great supplicants sought s. place
of Most High 8805

guards s. life with God 6321

How can we expect another to
keep our s. 5141

Humility is to shut the door, kneel
in s. 6010

If cannot find God in the s. grief
4856

If read s. history of enemies 3161

joy a s. spring world can't see
6529

Joy gigantic s. of the Christian
6546

keep s. is wisdom 1618

keeping s. like trying to smuggle
daylight past rooster 1616

mother's s. love outlives them all
7860

of a new name 7127

of existence, best foretaste of
heaven 7198

of own heart you can never know
5624

of power is to know God 3790

of success 10818

of success in conversation 1878

Oh, the riddle and s. of things
7943

one aim, s. of success 10822

place, the land of tears 11015

quiet, holy people learned great s.
1293

relevation s. whispering of God in
ear of a soul 9705

round the corner, a new road, or a
s. gate 8239

sin goes to s. thoughts 10300

soul is s. of depth 10669

Things forbidden have s. charm
11104

thought not hidden from God
4578

Three may keep if two are dead
1617

what we are unable to bear God
keeps s. 9708

when you publish another's s. fault
5167

who has guilty s. is lonely 1702

With every man God has a s. 7127

working of the heart 4749

SECRETLY

dreaming I be the one to lead her
10080

never do anything so s. 4872

SECRET'S

safe 'twixt you, me, gatepost 1615

SECRETS

Bible does not yield s. to irreverent
687

eyes confess s. of the heart 3569

friend trusts you with s. 4179

None so fond of s. as those who
do not mean to keep them 5150

Openness is to wholeness as s. are
to sickness 5883

People who have no s. do not
weigh their words 8970

psychological s. Hitler, Mussolini
used 12178

tell s, resign liberty 1619

SECTIONS

two s. to society 10523

SECULAR

art, challenge assumptions of s.
age 1998

false barrier between s. and sacred
10720

In Christ nothing s. and sacred
6411

realize nothing is s. in world 4732

saint never thinks of life as s,
sacred 1324

that determines work sacred or s.
7865

SECULARIZATION

as thinking being Christian has
succumbed to s. 7768

SECURE

Acceptance before God s. 9992

church s, too many freedoms 952

God's sovereignty enables him to
s. our welfare 4754

in joy one does not only feel s.
6537

In this faith I rest s. 4936

in thy love and strength 9051

may be s. but not free 6824

to s. these rights 3246

SECURELY

grasp him and be led s. home
6517

love passes s. through all 7283

So I s. go 5434

trust God, heaven s. 559

SECURITIES

uprooted from earth-born s. and
assurances 7488

SECURITY

better anchor near shallow shore
of s. 11598

false edge of s. 1610

Home best s. of civilization 5835

home should be self-contained
shelter of s. 5853

if based on something that can be
taken away 1610

In God's faithfulness lies eternal s.
4620

live with s, learn faith 1114

never friend of faith 952

property of friendship 4227

slaves to gadgets, power, s. 9016

we find s. in iron bars, solid walls
6825

where peace complete,
unassailable 3961

Will it give me s. 5467

without God young people
searching for s. 12180

SEDATE

Grief should be s. 5331

SEDUCER

of thought 400

SEE

a glory which thou canst not s.
4708

all in God 11490

all nor be afraid 8132

all things good 8578

Although I cannot s. 1810

Angels s. only light 357

approval not to pure in heart who
s. God 5891

as God gives us to s. right 5199

as long as you're looking down,
can't s. above 9188

As more of heav'n in each we s.
4197

better check to s. if you're going
downhill 6877

by Christianity I s. everything
1197

cannot s. outer limits 4544

Change, decay all around I s. 947

Christian, keyhole through which
folks s. God 1254

couldn't s. his face 10853

desire to s. everything from God's
viewpoint 10719

Devils s. only darkness 357

difficulties, not looking at Jesus
Christ 2731

dimmed with grief no everlasting
hills I s. 2587

do not s. door opened for us 8229

do not s. God at all 4489

don't want them to s. face black,
white 3229

easier to s. clearly into liar than
man who tells truth 6866

everything 9489

evil in others, but not in
themselves 5029

eyes of love s. not one but two
persons 7300

Eyes that s. are rare 8493

eyes to s. what he could not s.
before 8495

Faces we s, hearts we know not
2464

failings in yourself 2808

Faith daring soul to go farther
than can s. 3697

Faith is to believe what we do not
s. 3701

fear what people s. in us 1882

footprints, some you can s, others
invisible 6231

Four eyes s. more than two 257

from God's perspective 11152

God comes to s. us without a bell
4525

God comes to s. without ringing
doorbell 4838

God drawing away from
distraction so you can s. him
2556

God rarely allows soul to s.
blessing he is 6233

God waiting at the open door
7085

God watches to s. door move
from within 4775

God's gifts so infinite do not s.
them 7993

God, all you s, all you cannot s.
4692

God, everything becomes different
8583

good in the other 2808

good things in unexpected places
8575

good you s. in another 564

Grant me, O God, the power to s.
8009

great men s. divine in every other
man 6032

Great men s. spiritual stronger
than material 10693

hard to s. one's self 10007

harder to s. today when looking
at tomorrow 11371

him walk, know his thoughts
8494

hoofmarks going in, none coming
out 11119

hopeful man sees success where
others s. failure 5943

how it feels to be in control 4419

how it feels to have a name 4419

how it feels to have power 4419

how many sighings would we s. in
marketplace 10507

I can't s. my brother when he's
walking past 5587

I do not ask to s. distant scene
5429
2551

I s. and nothing more 5471

I s. heaven's glories shine 3765

I s. not a step before me 8079

I s. the right 10319

I s. the wrong that round me lies
4642

I shall not live 'till I s. God 2310

I shall s. the King 5676

I'd rather s. a sermon 10098
3435

If God you fail to s, you have
nothing observed 4926

if in gloom I s. thee not 4977

if man compare with all he can s.
is at Zenith of Power 6698

if you can s. the significance 1716

In all things thee to s. 10183

in heavenly places s. God's
counsels 2809

in larger process of maturing than
can s. 10884

In the face of the sun s. God's
beauty 4858

In the vast and the minute we s.
1963

In the vast, and in the minute, we
s. 4482

Jesus wants us to s. loneliness
3316

Jesus wants us to s. longings 3316

Jesus wants us to s. needs 3316

joy a secret spring world can't s.
6529

Kindness a language blind can s.
6650

laugh, all s. 10647

Let neighbor s. what Christ has
done for you 3314

light enables us to s. differences
1144

Look in, s. Christ's chosen saint
1299

look so long at closed door do not
s. one opened 5573

looking to things you cannot s.
9650

Love can s. only one thing 6457

love has eyes to s. misery and want
7335

many helpers, s. God in all your
helpers 11490

Many s, few understand 8501

may have good eyes, yet s. nothing
8502

mind should be eye to s. with
3021

more intense light is, less you s.
glass 6033

must look a long time before we
can s. 11967

must s. God today 11391

never s. each other for last time
2401

never s. until we s. God 8583

no helpers, s. all your helpers in
God 11490

No opening could I s. 5413

no way out of the world's misery
7099

None so blind as those who will
not s. 11593

not evil in others 2808

not God's will we s. before or
around us 5397

not good in yourself 2808

not to s. what lies at a distance
9671

nothing but faults who look for
nothing else 3954

nothing to s. when he looks back
4315

O my Savior, make me s. 2136

Obstacles things you s. when eyes
off goal 4430

often do not s. stars until dark
2560

One man does not s. everything
262

one who can s. value of being
humbled 6007

only afterwards we s. we had to
go that way 5423

Only eyes washed by tears s.
clearly 2555

Only he who can s. invisible can
do impossible 11733

Only s. a little of God's loving
6111

Only those who s. themselves
destitute 2605
3614

only with the heart one can s.
rightly 5622

originality is reporting accurately
what we s. 6219

others as they s. themselves 8513

ourselves more as God sees us
4578

proximity prevents us from being able to s. 3559

pure heart that I may s. thee 7458

pure in heart, not strong in mind, s. God 1216

Repentance process by which we s. God as he is 9594

Repentance process by which we s. ourselves as we are 9594

reward of faith to s. what we believe 3701

senses s. the action of the creatures 3794

should s. twice as much as say 3564

sky not less blue because blind man does not s. it 9409

Some people for seeing God as they s. a cow 10084

sunshine where others s. shadows, storm 5943

Tact to describe others as they s. themselves 10989

talents in unexpected people 8575

Teach me in all things thee to s. 9112

tears so blind our eyes cannot s. mercies 10033

That we may s. thee 9058

That which I love in my friend, not that which I s. 4233

the little space I fill and even can s. 7084

things not as they are, but as we are 8514

this earth but school preparative 6109

Thought can s. too far ahead 11264

Through blinding tears I s. 7178

Thy blessed face to s. 5635

To hide the fault I s. 1552

to s. clearly reason needs light of heaven 9422

To s. God highest aspiration of man 7547

To s. ourselves as others s. us a gift 8513

To s. thee more clearly 9043

To think is to s. 11271

today with eyes of tomorrow 11380

truly s. and know ourselves 156

want them to s. my soul 3229

we often s. only ebb of advancing wave 5944

We only s. a little of the ocean 6111

we s. devil rose-colored 2687

We s. now. Lord sees forever 11606

What is before our nose, we s. last 6933

What you don't s. with your eyes 5165

When dark enough men s. stars 10929

when God does not s. fit to grant us sunlight 5393

When have everything, s. God in everything 11490

When I can neither s, hear, speak 9025

When schoolroom darkened, s. most 10855

where it leads 7167

Who can s. finger of God in weather 4961

Who could stand to s. whole week before lived 4336

who keeps ability to s. beauty never grows old 12182

Who of us can s, behind and in chance, God 4961

Who s. the world's great anguish and its wrong 426

will carries lame man who can s. 918

will s. God someday 11391

window through which you s. world 8573

world above man's head to let him s. 11627

world being turned into wilderness 8445

world has yet to s. what God can do 2835

worse is it to have eyes and not s. 6289

Worship to s. world from God's point of view 12133

You travel wide and far to scout, s, search 4926

Youth happy because capacity to s. beauty 12182

SEEABLE

God is s. 4509

SEED

as s. sprouted Christ born in Bethlehem 5731

dies into new life, so does man 2385

Eternity, s. stirring to life 1757

fruit is present 16

God fills every root and s. 8049

God plants s. where conviction brought brokenness 888

God will never plant s. on hard spirit 888

God's Word is a s. 9137

Happiness held is the s. 5514

If cannot find God in bursting s. 4856

Now make one like it—s. of earth 4608

Of evil grain, no good s. 3389

of God stirred, shoved, sprouted 2984

placed in furrow to grow shrank 5368

smallest s. of faith better 3795

the blood of Christians is fresh s. 7678

The good s. on the land 4625

Thine is the s. time 10204

Think of yourself as s. wintering in earth 5672

This supercilious s. 2052

what fruit would spring from such s. 1737

What s. ever went into earth which did not grow 2350

Why doubt the human s. 2350

SEEDCORN

deeds s. of eternity 2496

SEEDLING

who planted s. of bitterness 5051

SEEDS

life in the s. 8002

of punishment sown at time we commit sin 10396

SEEING

different ways of s. the city 10522

Discretion is not s. as much as you can 2894

God means s. into mystery of things 7547

God means understanding 7547

healthy self-image is s. yourself as God sees you 9978

how naked the end 5952

If we miss s. God in his works 4995

insistence upon s. ahead natural 3758

Prayer is listening, s, feeling. 8923

that evils go unpunished 3349

Vision s. things invisible 11737

Who can escape eye of God, all s. 4888

Wisdom s. life from God's perspective 11971

Worship s. world in light of God 12133

worship without s. 4322

SEEK

Anxiety stimulating to s. 3961

Avoid shame, do not s. glory 4406 3850

believer does not s. to understand that he may believe 4910

counsel of him who makes you weep 264

eagerly s. approval of man of worldly reputation 11666

faith must s. greater depth 3756

Finding God, no need to s. peace 8433

for happiness, you will never find it 5551

Fragile, delicate are most who s. help 3069

give thanks to the Almighty, s. his aid 5411

go to church to actively s. 1459

God and find him 4509

If s. own advantage 8839

If we s. baptism of Holy Ghost 5784

If we s. God for our own good, profit 4923

If you s. you will know 10807

knowledge of ourselves arouses us to s. God 10020

Let us now a blessing s. 10953
lizard on cushion s. leaves 989
love which knoweth not how to s.
  self 7960
love, causes us to s. welfare of
  others 7304
lowest place 8448
Man cannot s. God 4910
Man forced to s. higher authority
  7499
Men s. to get crowns of gold 2152
my soul flies through wounds to s.
  thee 292
never s. one's advantage 5066
No bliss I s, but to fulfill 8098
no other guide I s. 5469
not every quality in one individual
  9490
not so much s. to be consoled as
  to console 9086
not to understand 609
nothing else but pleasing of God
  4922
ought to s, work for good of
  country 10525
profit of thy neighbor 4922
proof, admit doubt 3806
right to s. and rebel 4135
righteousness, discover you are
  happy 5551
solitude, look within ourselves
  4924
the truth 11527
their own advantage 10084
Those who s. are rewarded 4469
thoughts that come worth more
  than thoughts we s. 11250
to be inferior to everyone 8448
to know soul s. God 1713
to make institutions of power just
  6623
To s. a barren wilderness 4118
To s. God greatest of all
  adventures 7542
To s. wisdom in old age like mark
  in sand 11956
to s. wisdom in youth like
  inscription on stone 11956
to toil and not to s. for rest 9113
We do not s. God, God seeks us
  4624
when s. to be serious become
  somber 9502
When we s. first kingdom of God
  4735
Where'er they s. thee thou art
  found 12108
whether we s. God or his gifts
  4800
who ambitiously s. after whole
  world 2344
who s. for goods before they s. for
  God 8638
will s. not the crowd but the closet
  10567

SEEKER

God unveils himself to thoughtful
  s. 4907
Situationist is a who s. 6820

SEEKING

adventure on the high road 9088
And later, s. in the skies 6458
ass went s. for horns, lost ears
  2872
cannot fathom yet s. to know
  satisfying 5450
God forever s. to manifest himself
  to us 7513
gospel is Savior God s. lost men
  9545
happy who are s. to be righteous
  5564
Humility never gained by s. 6008
if I am s. my own glory first 8818
In s. truth, get both sides of story
  11511
not by s. fertile regions where toil
  lighter 4974
not s. God at all 8839
reason many still s. 10977
Success is s. God 10807
till they begin to sweat in s. them
  9037
to know, do will of God 5543
to perpetuate one's name on earth
  3860
We must repudiate s. God for
  benefits 4806
When God is s. a person 3340

SEEKS

approval to publicity hunter who
  s. headlines 5891
Christ s. glory by sacrifice of
  himself 2152
coward s. release from pressure
  1937
devil s. slaves, claims obedience
  4912
faultless friend is friendless 4246
God s. comrades, claims love
  4912
God s. worship of those trapped
  in moral ruin 12098
heart instinctively s. for a God
  12110
honor that comes from God only
  5901
Love s. not limits but outlets 7271
Man s. to win glory by sacrifice of
  others 2152
more than he needs 5316
only for applause has happiness in
  another's keeping 5892
Philosophy s. the truth 11524
soul s. and is sought 7967
thought absurd by what it s.
  11242
We do not seek God, God s. us
  4624
Whatever man s. more than God
  is idolatry 6076
who s. him because he knows him
  not 4572
who s. revenge digs two graves
  9717
who s. the Father more than
  anything he can give 8997

wise man s. friend with qualities
  he himself lacks 4279

SEEM

luxury of believing all things are
  what they s. 7972
Past and to come s. best 8382
things present s. worst 8382
Things seldom what they s. 8510

SEEMEST

Be what thou s. 994

SEEMING

Fall on the s. void, and find 3767

SEEMLY

not s. do it not 1021

SEEMS

Creation s. like pure freedom
  4117
Nothing so good as s. beforehand
  3506
Rebellion s. like freedom 4117
Scarce anything about us is as it s.
  9623

SEEN

a picture which was never s. before
  9873
All I have s. teaches me to trust
  the Creator 11465
And s. God's hand thro a lifetime
  6914
Christ aperture through which
  God s. 6373
error is easily s. 3259
faith, things not s. 3833
God's love makes sense s. as
  personal 4782
Hell is truth s. too late 5690
I've s. the Promised Land 4975
in revelation things which could
  not be s. 9711
manifestation s. by others, not by
  us 9707
Nobody knows the trouble I've s.
  11445
regard s. world as real world 3812
sets course for how we live in s.
  world 3812
That sages have s. in thy face
  10550
things s. are temporal 3746
to have s. thee is to have learned
  all things 7960
trees clapping their hands 8017
When God's goodness cannot be s.
  7750
when I have s. God I shall never
  die 2310
who gives to be s. 10037
Who has s. the wind 8053
world never before s. or dreamed
  of 6419

SEER

scholar sees, s. sees through 3021
Spirit, sole s, interpreter 4911
taught by Holy Spirit, s. rather
  than scholar 3021

SEES

atheist who s. man helpless 3495

Charity s. the need, not the cause 7163

Christian on his knees s. more than philosopher on tiptoe 8975

direct personal message from God 5441

each man as he s. himself 7443

each man as the other person s. him 7443

egotist s. only the frame of his own portrait 9213

Everything has its beauty, not everyone s. it 8492

faith s. action of God 3794

Faith s. the invisible 3713

Faith, mighty faith, the promise s. 3717

fool s. a man's clothes 11896

genius s. world at different angle 4389

God s. all that has been, is, is to come 4883

God s. everything else 8487

God s. scar, creates star 8278

God s. something good in suffering 10856

God s. sweet flowers growing 8673

good general s. way to victory 8485

healthy self-image is seeing yourself as God s. you 9978

hopeful man s. success where others see failure 5943

how to look at life as God s. it 4732

In prayer s. life as God s. it 8917

in the darkest night 8515

Jealousy s. too much 6344

like lamps nobody s. until tunnel comes 10914

love s. things in light of his glory 6457

man in evolution from lesser to greater condition 9351

Man s. actions, God motives 7866

Man s. but withered leaves 8673

most important part no one s. 1049

not eye that s. beauty of heaven 10656

One s. "What a great church" 1416

One s. "What a great Savior" 1416

only he who s. takes off his shoes 1710

optimist s. green light everywhere 8245

optimist s. light at end of tunnel 8250

optimist s. light where there is none 8246

optimist s. opportunity in every difficulty 8251

optimist s. the doughnut 8244

part of the man s. which never saw before 5809

pessimist s. difficulty in every opportunity 8251

pessimist s. only red light 8245

pessimist s. only the tunnel 8250

pessimist s. the hole 8244

realist s. tunnel and light 8250

saint s. everything as knowledge of Christ 1324

Satan trembles when he s. 8959

Say not in evil doing, "No one s." 3404

scholar s, seer s. through 3021

soul that s. beauty of heaven 10656

state of mind that s. God in everything 5202

The eternal eye that s. the whole 6583

thoughtful mind s. nation itself 7982

We see now. Lord s. forever 11606

weep, no one s. 10647

what are we like where no one s. us 9845

whatever one s. ought to be done 4111

when God s. men rising up against fellowmen 4895

who s. need and waits to be asked for help 10148

window through which world s. God 3438

wise man s. a man's spirit 11896

SEETHES

suppressed grief chokes, s. within 5330

SEGREGATE

only creature they would s. is skunk 5963

SEIZE

robbers s. money 7826

self with so tight a grip 8630

snatch, s. enjoy every moment 11372

the day 8222

the pleasures of the present day 8600

this very minute 48

SEIZES

the prompt occasion 8224

the right, holds it to the last 11906

SELDOM

cares of today s. cares of tomorrow 12075

Great wealth, content s. live together 11818

know why Lord chooses whom 5894

lightly assents s. keep word 1534

Men s. flatter without purpose 4051

People s. improve when no model 3451

Pleasure s. found where sought 8606

proud man s. grateful 5258

solid home in absence of religious inspiration 5858

somehow, 'tis s. or never 909

the present that is unbearable 5354

Things s. what they seem 8510

value s. known until lost 4292

weigh neighbor in same balance 1752

weighed in same scales 9495

SELECT

Spirit filled life no mystery revealed to s. few 5803

SELF

bold, creative affirmation of s. 4160

by abdication becomes more truly s. 9927

can turn powerful prayer into weak one 10080

Christ is our true s. 10551

Christianity wins victories over s. 1165

culture where s. supersedes commitment 3901

easiest person to deceive is one's own s. 2471

exists to be abdicated 9927

extreme attitude a flight from the s. 9924

finding s. comes through losing s. 2519

For most men world is centered in s. 8436

Give me the confused s. 4530

God gives us his very s. 9834

good opinion of one's s. 11591

greatest burden we carry is s. 9949

greatest of all crosses 2110

greed and anger, brother and sister of false s. 10003

happiness is enjoyment of one's s. 5568

hard to see one's s. 10007

have within me the great pope, s. 9929

Humility to make right estimate of one's s. 6014

If you have faith in God, or man, or s. 3778

In baptism, new s. emerges 529

In baptism, s. is buried 529

indestructible by human means 9943

is a deadly thing 9936

is not to be annihilated 9942

is to be rightly centered in God 9942

last 9264

leaves one's old proud s. defenseless 7488

Love and S. cannot stand together 9936

Love hates s. 9936

love is offering one's most honest s. 7337

love of neighbor is door out of dungeon of s. 8063

love which knoweth not how to seek s. 7960

man who lives for s. alone 10085

man's s. his greatest cross 9919

mastery over s. advanced by prayer 8976

moral illiterates whose only law is s. 3877

more distant than any star 9352

more s. is indulged, more it demands 10027

more thine own s. 9951

most difficult thing we manage is s. 9949

one of the toughest plants 9943

only one corner certain of improving, your own s. 9953

only prison that can bind the soul 9944

opaque veil that hides God 9945

originality being one's s. 6219

out of s, into unknown regions 9930

power of going out of one's s. 4220

Prayer transcending s. 8917

see inner man, his real s. 6842

seize s. with so tight a grip 8630

Something of my old s, my old, bad life 8966

Sun's s. comes in with him 4195

Sunday s. and weekday s. not good if detached 10949

Tears shed for s. tears of weakness 11026

that which we call I 9936

To be one's s. more admirable than conformity 6216

To conquer one's s. is the beautiful 10022

to deny s. is to become nonconformist 1646

To know one's s. is the true 10022

To strive with one's s. is the good 10022

to thine own s. be true 6318

turns up to poison fruit of our lives 9943

turns up to trouble our peace 9943

What jailer so inexorable as one's s. 9955

when sense of s. depends on what I can acquire 10003

When sense of s. depends on what others say 10003

when sure s. is dead, it turns up 9943

wretch concentrated all in s. 10088

wrong concept of s. 4568

SELF DISCOVERY
rules for s. 10016

SELF-ACCEPTANCE
a spiritual issue 9993

SELF-ADMIRATION
so demanding little left over 1589

SELF-ANNOUNCING
God's blessing neither self-proclaiming nor s. 4641

SELF-APPROVAL
itch of self-regard shall want pleasure of s. 9245

SELF-ASSERTION
cross put to shame s. of heroism 2166

SELF-ASSERTIVE
are sought after 4410

SELF-ASSURED
approval not to mourner, but to s. 5891

SELF-AUTHENTICATING
voice of God s. 4967

SELF-AWARENESS
Humanness is realization of s. 5014

SELF-CAUSED
Aside from God, nothing s. 4613

SELF-CENTERED
people live in unpleasant surroundings 10077

suffer when others disappoint 10911

SELF-CENTEREDNESS
a movement away from God 9946

not result of self-love 6229

product of pain 6229

result of a poor self-image 6229

serious form of disorder 9946

SELF-CHOSEN
man pushes into s. alienation 4781

SELF-COMMITMENT
personal gift, s. 4277

SELF-COMPLACENCY
beginning of degeneration 9234

SELF-CONCEIT
repentance means unlearning s. 9577

SELF-CONCEITED
more hope for sinner than s. saint 5948

SELF-CONFIDENCE
God begins by stripping of all s. 9851

no s. compares with confidence in Christ 1611

SELF-CONFRONTATION
Self-knowledge grows out of s. with God 10018

SELF-CONTAINED
home should a s. shelter of security 5853

SELF-CONTEMPT
who has learned to overcome s. 9985

SELF-CONTROL
extol s. and practice self-indulgence 6068

keep cool while someone making it hot for you 9961

SELF-CONVICTED
more hope for s. sinner 5948

SELF-CRITICISM
Suicide severest form of s. 10944

SELF-DEFENSES
break down fortified walls of s. 10043

SELF-DELUSION
theology certainty of escaping s. 7946

SELF-DENIAL
chose both fear and s. 467

great virtues bear imprint of s. 9962

hear God's call to s. 9351

SELF-DENIALS
Little s, silent threads of gold 6997

SELF-DENYING
one s. deed, one word 107

SELF-DEPENDENT
disquieted by One who is s. 4614

SELF-DESTROYING
All the seven deadly sins s. 10296

SELF-DISCIPLINE
Character formed as we submit to s. 1000

child sees parent living without s. 8300

never means giving up anything 9974

SELF-DISCLOSURE
love, one's most honest s. 7337

SELF-ESTEEM
a fragile flower 9994

can be crushed so easily 9994

Every new adjustment crisis in s. 9984

Gentleness, causes others to retain s. 4402

service satisfies my s. more than status 9996

SELF-EVIDENT
Fire is s. 5806

power is s. 5806

SELF-EXAMINATION
to know our own faults 10014

SELF-EXISTENT
because God s. his love had no beginning 4750

disquieted by One who is s. 4614

God is s. 4613

Grace a s. principle 4652

If God s. must also be
  self-sufficient 4583
truth being eternal is s. 11550

SELF-FORGETFUL
In such a s. way 9075

SELF-FORGETTING
Humble and s. we must be always
  5092
Sincere s, sacrifical service 9996

SELF-FULFILLMENT
service preempted by s. 1409

SELF-GIVEN
Conceit is s, be careful 10994

SELF-GLORY
Legalists keep law for s. 6815

SELF-GOVERNED
satanically-managed man
  absolutely s. 9853

SELF-HELP
Christianity takes for granted
  absence of s. 1182

SELF-HOMICIDE
Misspending time kind of s.
  11308

SELF-IDENTIFICATION
When cling to actions as s. 10531

SELF-IDOLATRY
Earnestness often subtle form of s.
  2626

SELF-IMAGE
better the s, larger the capacity for
  loving 9997
comparison game way to poor s.
  6208
healthy s. seeing yourself as God
  sees you 9978
Self-centeredness result of a poor s.
  6229

SELF-IMPORTANCE
hell, where everyone lives s. 5705
makes mind shrink, head swell
  9191

SELF-INDULGENCE
extol self-control and practice s.
  6068

SELF-INFATUATION
solitude without fellowship abyss
  of s. 10547

SELF-INFLICTED
punishment 9354

SELF-INTEREST
Friendship without s. rare,
  beautiful 4238
slaughtered 2153
wicked practice virtue from s.
  11710

SELFISH
among the s. is where Jesus went
  2812
an awful lot of s. people 10070
Being alone and resting not s.
  9533

cross will defeat, bring s. life to
  end 2093
do not like needy strangers 5957
futile to condemn myself for
  feeling s. 3049
Glory built on s. principles is
  shame, guilt 10054
injustice 6258
Next to the very young, very old
  most s. 10072
parasitical concerns drain time,
  energies 1306
prayer can be s. expression 12139
Reading, s, serene, lifelong
  intoxication 858
Selfishness never so s. as on its
  knees 10080
suffers most who is most s. 10058
When feelings are s. ask to have
  them altered 3051
When we are s, God still
  unalterable I Am 4587

SELFISHNESS
Affluent society euphemism for s.
  10051
aims at absolute uniformity 10079
At beginning, God accepts us in
  all our s. 9832
enemy of all affection 10082
gimme-gimme-gimme 10075
Golden Rule would reconcile s.
  and greed 5005
Grief can purge us of s. 10640
If love God, s. will have received
  death-blow 10063
is a gangrene 8467
is asking others to live as one
  wishes to live 10081
is not living as one wishes to live
  10081
never so selfish as on its knees
  10080
Posthumous charities essence of s.
  10078
preventing transformation into
  divine love 10067
Pride a form of s. 9227
produces jealousy 7200
respectable s. 10073
stopping at human limits 10067
take care not to settle on
  sandbank of s. 9930
Take off all your s. 10787
than fourscore years of s. 10074
thorny crown filled with briars of
  s. 7073
turns life into a burden 10083

SELF-KNOWLEDGE
first condition of repentance 9599
God gives s. gradually 10006
grows out of self-confrontation
  with God 10018
important in pursuit of God
  10019

SELFLESS
unless able to give to people in s.
  love 7962

SELF-LIFE
Flesh is the s. 9926

SELF-LOATHING
Repentance is not s. 9592

SELF-LOVE
a mote in every man's eye 10026
excess of s. represents absence of s.
  6229
In jealousy more s. than love 6338
making us believe s. is not there
  10027
marriage demands divorce from s.
  7596
medium of peculiar kind 10025
pushes itself into everything
  10027
root of discontent is s. 10027
Self-centeredness not the result of
  s. 6229

SELF-LOVING
spirit antithesis of real living
  10053

SELF-MADE
I'm a s. man, you know 9915

SELF-PITY
cuddle, nurse s. as an infant
  10034
devil begins advocacy of s. 10036

SELF-PORTRAIT
Every job is a s. 54

SELF-PRAISE
is no recommendation 9235

SELF-PROCLAIMING
God's blessings neither s. nor
  self-announcing 4641

SELF-PUNISHMENT
Hatred is s. 5598

SELF-REALIZATION
don't think s. will make you happy
  9196
Nothing blinds mind more
  effectually than s. 10044
sin that shocks God 10397

SELF-REARED
not s. after fashion of Tarzan 3881

SELF-REGARD
itch of s. shall want pleasure of
  self-approval 9245

SELF-REGARDING
Repentance not s. 9592
spirit antithesis of real living
  10053

SELF-REJECTION
core of pride is s. 9239

SELF-RELIANCE
confidence in natural world 1605

SELF-REPROACH
luxury in s. 6230

SELF-RESPECT
cannot be fabricated out of public
  relations 9995
cannot be hunted 9995

cannot be purchased 9995
comes in quiet moments 9995
comes when we are alone 9995
is never for sale 9995
truest s. is not to think of yourself 10000

SELF-REVELATION
God understood only through his s. 4738

SELF-RIGHTEOUS
God has nothing to say to s. 10307
Solitude molds s. into caring persons 10561

SELF-RIGHTEOUSNESS
instead of humility 10359
Legalism is s. 6814
the devil's masterpiece 10039
When mask of s. torn from us 5238

SELF-SACRIFICE
essence of generosity is s. 4365
hear God's call to s. 9351
never entirely unselfish 9763
price is always s. 9759

SELF-SATISFACTION
quicksand of smugness, s. 3168

SELF-SECLUSION
compulsive s. toward our world 7072

SELF-SEEKING
if full of s. no room for Spirit of God 5783
instead of benevolence 10359
Love is never s. 7246
quiet mind free from s. 7773
spirit antithesis of real living 10053
When a man is s, he abandons love 7246

SELF-SINS
permitted, excused by most Christians 5776
Spirit of God will not tolerate s. 5776

SELF-SUFFICIENCY
God has no easy time of it to smash s. 10043
instead of faith 10359

SELF-SUFFICIENT
being s. God cannot relinquish his perfections 4821
disquieted by one who is s. 4614
If God is self-existent must also be s. 4583
Yet is as thou art 7456

SELF-SURRENDER
how can voluntary act of s. be involuntary 9799
One year of s. 10074

SELF-TORMENT
Envy endless s. 10296

SELF-WILL
instead of submission 10359

life, aimless comet burning out in s. 6937
Repentance means unlearning s. 9577
should be so completely poured out of soul 4978
sin may spell s. but is some form of "me" 9916

SELF-WORTH
Sabbath when s. restored 10959

SELL
a blind horse, praise feet 2466
Don't s. yourself short 10001
If a man has good corn to s. 2776
shall have corn to s, keep 3115

SELLS
He who borrows s. his freedom 4038

SELVES
Commune with own s. 3935
friend helps us be our best s. 4178
giving central place to God not only in our inner s. 7713
happiest when we forget our precious s. 9245
if show our true s. suddenly would despair 10006
Love lets us be our real s. 7254
our shadow s, our influence, may fall 6242
people bored primarily with own s. 871
permit real s. to be known 10019
sin, two witnesses our own s. and God 10418
When from our better s. we have been parted 10578

SEMANTIC
word love is a s. confession 7312

SEMICOLONS
semieducated must know how to use s. 12152

SEMICONDUCTOR
revolutionized technology 3932

SEMIHUMAN
unconscious not only s. 7772

SEMINARY
God, a s. of wisdom 4698

SENATE
When they call the roll in the S. 5198

SENATORS
do not know whether to answer present or not guilty 5198

SEND
All we s. into lives of others comes back 1726
Get spindle ready, God will s. flax 9346
Give and spend, God will s. 4354
Glad tiding s. afar 6141
God may s. tempest about house 4775

God s. us men with hearts ablaze 7986
God will never s. anybody to hell 5686
me where thou wilt, only go with me 9080
only s. what is for your good 8578
s. worlds rolling in space 4951
take what God chooses to s. 5911
the homeless, tempest-tossed to me 7985

SENDETH
He s. more strength when labors increase 5223

SENDS
church s. people out 1427
crosses which he s, sacrifices he demands 4688
God s. no one away empty 9200
God s. nothing but can be borne 2546
God s. ten thousand truths 6565
God s. time of forced leisure 7056
make sin, misery out of everything God s. 10816
That's best which God s. 7520
What God s. better than what ask for 4991
whatever a loving Father s. 33

SENILE
love of God not a s. benevolence 4792

SENIORITY
in kingdom of God does not imply superiority 5897

SENSE
And find, to outward s. denied 6583
believed in God, life made s. 7011
depths which are of God 10257
except to convictions of honor, good s. 8548
faith believing beyond s, sight 3657
Faith believing what will only make s. in reverse 3708
Faith is not a s. 3687
God endowed us with s. 6324
God's love makes s. seen as personal 4782
God's plan doesn't always make earthly s. 5399
Love wipes out all s. of time 7229
more complete our s. of need 7524
of sin in proportion to nearness to God 10349
the nonsense of those who think they talk s. 9056
when s. of curiosity has withered 7829
world doesn't make s. 8508

SENSELESS
Blessed those who see God in s. circumstances 1464
O s. man who cannot make a worm 6073

SENSES
anticipate future with
    transcendental s. 4329
decay 6455
Faith reaches beyond our five s.
    3690
Love is guarded in all the s. 7246
see the action of the creatures
    3794
soul s. its origin 4744

SENSIBILITY
Experience an immense s. 3524
God, with his infinite s. 4895

SENSIBLE
few disciples allowed to appear s.
    11791
Life isn't s. 6984
who am not s. of these gifts 6253

SENSIBLY
Tomorrow the day when fools act
    s. 11404

SENSITIVE
No one had more s. love than Jesus
    7280

SENSITIVENESS
Exaggerated s. an expression of
    inferiority 6227
Measure growth in grace by s. to
    sin 10335
    5367

SENSITIVITY
darkness an aptitude for s. 2612
listening to cues kids give 8325
tuning in to thoughts, feelings
    8325

SENT
Christian worker must be s.
    10188
Oh, surely melody from heaven
    was s. 7917

SENTENCE
Life a s. to serve for being born
    6952
most tragic s. in literature 7601
proverb a short s. based on long
    experience 9376

SENTENCED
all s. to solitary confinement 7148

SENTENCES
Pithy s. force truth upon our
    memory 9384
Pithy s. like sharp nails 9384
say in ten s. what others say in
    book 12149

SENTIMENT
Grace not mere s. 5217

SENTIMENTAL
Love is not s. 7246
love of God no mere s. feeling
    4780
Love superior to money on s. plane
    7232
To love as Christ loves not a s.
    thing 7324

SENTIMENTALISTS
ease with being Christian s. 12106

SENTIMENTALITY
one of seven deadly virtues 11699

SENTRY
Each has s. post assigned by Lord
    ·3088

SEP'RATE
Plenty, as well as want, can s.
    friends 3558

SEPARATE
Although church and state stand s.
    5169
Candor may heal or s. 5869
die out 1388
faith, works wrong 3829
Friend from whom thou canst
    never s. 1310
Gold does friendship s. 11811
not presume to s. what God has
    united 6681
power can s. from true nature of
    Christian leadership 8717

SEPARATED
love beyond the world cannot be s.
    7319
Service and prayer can never be s.
    10211
to live s. life humanly impossible
    10717

SEPARATENESS
evil makes for s. 5025
need to overcome s. 7143

SEPARATES
Sin s. 9812
wisdom, awful wisdom which s.
    11906

SEPARATING
temptation of s. ministry from
    spirituality 10211
temptation of s. service from
    prayer 10211

SEPARATION
God, no s. unless we make it
    ourselves 7557
hell, s. from God 5697

SEPENT
beguiled Eve by enticing away
    from faith 9424

SEPTEMBER
put off until October chores in
    August 9882

SEPULCHER
No man built that s. 778
till it came to the mouth of the s.
    9803

SEPULCHRE
world lies down in s. of ages 3266

SEQUEL
Silence the s. to dull discourses
    10266

SEQUENTIAL
God first in s. order 4607

SERAPHIC
With sound s. ring 2389

SERAPHIM
described in Scripture 359

SERAPHS
man who lives on better terms
    with angels, s. 3899

SERENADED
world beautifully s. at the start
    7886

SERENE
pool wherein s. light of God can
    be mirrored 8437
Reading, selfish, s, lifelong
    intoxication 858
silent beauty of holy life 5766
Thou art angry, yet s. 4954
trying to live s. lives in houses
    divided against themselves 6068
When soul is purified and s. 7971
When we are restless, God
    remains s. 4587

SERENELY
begin tomorrow s. 8375

SERENITY
attribute of a great lady 11697
Cheerfulness fills mind with s.
    1092
joy the s. of heaven 2580
men who live with degree of s.
    5204
mild s. of age takes the place of
    riotous youth 7101
prayer for s. 9060
to accept with s. things that
    cannot be changed 9060
unearth gift of s. 10553

SERIOUS
friend, not so much free to be s.
    with 4177
is a terribly s. thing to pray 8850
Joy the s. business of heaven 6549
Self-centeredness a s. disorder
    9946
thing that prayer may be answered
    8850
When we seek to be s. become
    somber 9502

SERIOUSLY
Holy Spirits expects us to take s.
    answers provided 5445
to take Jesus s. was to enter a
    strange life 6421

SERMON
a grave preaches a short, pithy s.
    2207
belly hates a long s. 10107
best s. by minister who has s. to
    preach 9159
Christian preaches some kind of s.
    1245
Christian, living s. 1247
Conduct is the only effective s.
    9132
Conduct, unspoken s. 554

drunkard a better s. 336

easier to walk six miles to hear s. 7716

Good example best s. 3427

good s. helps people in different ways 10094

good s. hits one of his neighbors 10106

good s. one that goes over his head 10106

greatest s. ever preached 10102

half-baked s. causes spiritual indigestion 10108

I'd rather see a s. than hear one any day 3435

impossible even to put them to sleep with s. 10096

learn knack of listening like a Christian instead of critic 10110

no s. of value without three Rs 9152

poor s. that gives no offense 10101

preach better s. with life than lips 3462

preached as exhibition of talent 7867

sin of s. listening 1414

so long have to practice patience 8422

Sometimes greatest s. is silence 10887

stay awake and listen to s. at church 10100

wearies people by its length 10095

world's shortest s. is traffic light 10109

Worship isn't listening to a s. 12139

worshipers cannot recall text of s. 12111

SERMON ON THE MOUNT

answer to restless, fruitless yearning 531

blueprint for contentment 531

blueprint for human life 531

blueprint for mental health 531

Christians in open defiance of S. 5891

cuts across differences 513

cuts across variations in capacity 513

is Christ's biography 6482

merely translated Christ's life into language 6482

not on externals 513

outlines character 513

took only eighteen minutes to preach 9154

vital internal attitudes 513

SERMONS

as try to get simple truth o' most s. 10099

beatific something-or-other in s. 5661

before he has heard too many s. 1339

culturally forbidden to talk back 10103

Don't like to hear cut-and-dried s. 9141

God not interested in s. 1414

God wants living s. 1414

Great s. lead people to praise preacher 10097

Jesus furnished themes for more s. 6449

kind act will teach more than a thousand s. 6661

One act of obedience better than 100 s. 8109

Some clergy prepare their s. 10104

SERPENT

beguiled Eve to depend on reason alone 9424

brazen s. reared where snakes bite 11432

cries out, as Eve, against s. or something else 9601

infernal s. whose guile stirred up envy, revenge 9863

mother spoils child, fattens s. 8330

Step not on sleeping s. 11084

subtlest beast of all the field 2700

SERPENT'S

How sharper than s. tooth 1119

SERVANT

as the Master shall the s. be 10604

best s. does his work unseen 10191

Christian, most dutiful s. of all 1255

diligent, honest, good 3084

Grief can be your s. 5334

highest reward devil can offer for being s. 5689

I am your s. 9066

If a s. be sometimes deaf 2896

If aim to be a s. will never be frustrated 10160

if money be not your s. 11822

In form of s. is the Lord 6129

Money a good s. 7809

must sing at work like bird in wood 3084

of God has good master 1329

Should not the s. tread it still 10133

Sorrow can be your s. 10610

than speak reckless word against s. of Christ 5143

Time must be s. of eternity 11311

treat body as s. of Jesus Christ 848

Wealth a good s. 11873

SERVANTS

better terms with angels than s. 3899

Emotions should be s. 3055

Give to thy s. skill to soothe, bless 9045

Habits are s. that regulate 5498

if you would have good s. 3099

In God's family one body of people: s. 10161

in order that God may make us great s. 5784

Jesus had no bevy of s. 6433

Money brings s, but not faithfulness 7807

passions are good s. 10225

that we may be s. of others 9096

SERVE

a great man, will know what sorrow is 5292

also s. who only stand and wait 10202

came here to s. not to rule 10218

columns it takes to list "s." references 10185

Defeat may s. as well as victory 2508

defect may s. as strength for personality 3932

Evil can but s. the right 4936

far better to s. neighbor than have own way 9963

God does not desert those who s. him 4615

God's country begins where men love to s. 4913

greatest desire to please God, s. one another 6924

heart of love that I may s. thee 7458

If I only had three years to s. the Lord 6687

If love Jesus Christ will s. humanity 10156

in all things to s. thee bravely 9088

In heaven devil scorns to s. 2656

Life a sentence to s. for being born 6952

Man must govern, not s, gold 11835

one can always s. as horrible example 3446

Pray more, be more, s. more 9016

princes among us forget themselves, s. mankind 10193

Riches s. a wise man, command a fool 7820

seeks to s. two masters misses benediction 1332

So long as we love, we s. 7292

support individual freedom as we s. one another 9498

that I s. him with cheerful spirit 7931

That we may s. thee 9058

To be chief of people s. them 6806

to s. thee as thou deservest 9113

unless I can recall an earnest attempt to s. the God who made me 6919

Whatever you fear most, you will s. 4006

whatever you supremely respect, you will s. 4006

who can s. best seldom loses 10170

will s. devil for better wages 2646
with devotion that consumes 3182
you are greater if you s. God 9732

SERVED
Christ s. others first 6433

SERVES
but to brighten all our future days 10879
evil is all that s. death 5024
God for money, will serve devil for better wages 2646
Good is all that s. life 5024
him with heart because he knows him 4572
profits most who s. best 10143
slave of greatest slave who s. himself 10055
who s. God has a good master 10149

SERVICE
All s. ranks same with God 10116
and prayer can never be separated 10211
angel created for s. 354
begin new s. for kingdom 2798
burning candle of life in s. of devil 9576
Charity may be of no s. 1075
Christ gave them s. 10731
Christ, at s. of men 1754
church community of s. 1414
cross made clear authority is s. 2166
Dear child, this s. will 5415
do with light feet, heart set free 4561
Doctrine divides, s. unites 10129
enduring realities are love and s. 10829
forget in own case s. due to neighbor 7004
God's s. is perfect freedom 4126
gold of real s. 9759
hard to train for s. of Christ 466
have not given ourselves in s. 9087
highest s. prepared for in humblest surroundings 10190
If going to live for s. of fellowmen 10159
if mainspring of s. is love for God 10159
In love's s. only broken hearts will do 895
inquisitive about conduct or s. 1303
Jehovah sharpens and prepares for s. 163
judged by how much of me is in it 10119
Knowledge given to lead us to better s. 6693
Knowledge indispensable to Christian s. 6693
leadership is s. to others 8717
Love only s. power cannot command 7253

Most saints sank to depths of s. 6175
No man has right to forget s. due neighbor 9670
noblest s. comes from unseen hands 10191
not judged by how much done 10119
Nothing small in the s. of God 7121
only give lip s. 3320
power of s. correspond to life of prayer 10192
preempted by success, self-fulfillment 1409
Religion can offer man burial s. 7022
satisfies my self-esteem more than status 9996
Sincere self-forgetting, sacrificial s. 9996
so active in the s. of Christ 117
temptation of separating s. from prayer 10211
that counts is s. that costs 10196
to be of s. to others we have to die to them 10162
to ruin a man for s. of God 6407
unless ready to give myself to his s. 8818
victory in s. to be expected 10206
whatever s. may follow 4561

SERVICEABLE
faith makes s. 3965
not satisfied by religion merely s. to mankind 9546

SERVICES
Does church arrange s. for Total Abstainers from Usury 10086
found least gratitude from greatest s. 5250
many s. but few conversions 9017
they render us attaches people to us 5256

SERVILE
fear without love makes men s. 9736

SERVING
all s. life-sentence in dungeon of life 7074
as God serves 6569
better to have failed when s. God 10777
I keep six honest s. men 6686
immature, consciously s. God 1714
man weeding turnips also s. God 12146
no devil can hinder you from s. 10159
only perfect freedom is s. God 4148
Talk to him in prayer of all your weariness in s. him 8968
than to have succeeded s. the devil 10777

thinks of s. God, prays prayers of abandonment 8840
When people s. life no longer meaningless 10212
you are s. me more than I am s. you 9066

SERVITUDE
Christ release from s. of the flesh 6434
love delights in s. as much as in honor 6457
Obedience not s. of man to man 8099

SESSION
Day of Judgment court in perpetual s. 6589

SESSIONS
Psychiatrists require many s. 5485

SET
Christ, message s. society ablaze 6375
free to become what God wants 4122
Gossips s. on fire all houses they enter 5137
He s. you there 3847
Love is friendship s. to music 7234
of a soul that decides goal 4432
Oh, burst these bonds, and s. it free 4140
ourselves as God's interpreters 4885
Still sun must set 5544
Though my feet are s. in silent ways 6917
'tis the s. of the sails, not the gales 4432

SET-UP
magnificent s, devil's method of working 2648

SETBACKS
Remember to forget s. 9270

SETS
forgiving enemy s. you above him 4073
God alone s. all the goals 7828
Hope s. the head, heart to work 5917
only free when Son s. us free 4152
when God s. the soul in tune for himself 10663

SETTING
At s. of the sun 2502
I greet the dawn and not s. sun 2418
sun appears s. but is rising 2350
sun as bright as from rich man's abode 7001
up ourselves as higher tribunal 4087

SETTLE
fear figures you will s. for dull existence 3971

Trying to s. problem with oratory 9290

SETTLING
responsibility is to prevent evil thoughts from s. 11110

SEVEN
ages of man 7037
All the s. deadly sins self-destroying 10296
days without prayer makes one weak 8960
deadly virtues 11699
Ere a child has reached to s. 8296
Fall s. times, stand up eight 3592

SEVENTY
Men of s. often more youthful than the young 12198
One no averts s. evils 3392
years to learn to keep mouth shut 2897

SEVER
I'll trust in God's unchanging Word till soul and body s. 9813

SEVERE
child lies, will find a s. parent 8362
Commandments too s. 1523
Difficulty a s. instructor 2717
rules for sex are s. 10235

SEVEREST
fate's s. rage disarm 7911
Silence sometimes s. criticism 2074
Suicide s. form of self-criticism 10944

SEVERITY
God's justice, utter s. 4726
that we regret 2420

SEW
hundreds of tiny threads s. people together 7608

SEWAGE
Gossip, social s. 5136

SEWING
circle, the Protestant confessional 5160
on button beyond them 5841

SEX
a very holy subject 10230
amazed how much young people know about s. 10222
an enormous privilege 10235
delusion s. is an activity 10227
don't think marriage built on s. can last 10229
for procreation marvelous thing 10229
impossible to be truthful 11494
is magnificent 10235
is never perfect 10232
man has left it out of his heaven 10228
people mistake s. for love 8510
place and purpose of s. 10239

primarily a relationship 10227
rules are severe 10235
rules are tremendously strict 10235
something queer about the s. instinct among us 7360
substitute religion 10231
tendency to think of s. as degrading 10235
thrills come at beginning 10224
thrills do not last 10224

SEXES
love of God, exacting as love between s. 4792

SEXUAL
as she does with s. immorality 10086
claims to equality intensify inequality 3242
incompatibility in marriage 10227
Man cares most for s. intercourse 10228
Music glorifying s. promiscuity 7910

SEXUALLY
little praise for s. controlled single 10236

SHADE
Do not cut down tree that gives s. 5241
My garden's grateful s. 7452

SHADOW
Afflictions s. of God's wings 277
all other beings distinguished by s. 4472
Beware lose substance by grasping at s. 11499
black s. of asceticism 467
casts s. of our burden behind us 5923
Christ came into s. of death 6121
crooked stick will have crooked s. 988
dearest friend on earth mere s. 4201
Discontent follows ambition like a s. 2863
Everything but soul of man a passing s. 10654
face to sunshine, cannot see s. 1098
God's permission means no s. of doubt 5402
highest earthly enjoyments a s. 733
least s. intercepts happiness 174
Life's but a walking s. 6994
Life's s. of bird in flight 6993
life, s. which loses itself in the sunset 2457
our s. selves, our influence, may fall 6242
Reputation like tree s. 1001
sinister doubts lurk in the s. 3649
standeth God within the s. 5377
This learned I from the s. of a tree 6242

to leave reality for a shadow 6495
Where much light, s. is deep 6712
Worry gives a small thing a big s. 12085

SHADOWS
As life's s. longer creep 8120
doom ourselves to s. 2821
Evil flourishes more in s. than day 3381
from the s. appears majestic Jesus 1443
leaden s. that descend on us 2611
Let truth not s. within me speak 11515
mean there's a light shining somewhere 2602
merely s. to the unseen grief 5348
Most s. of life caused by one's sunshine 2552
Never fear s. 2602
not the s. within me 9070
of life caused when stand in own sunshine 10792
sees sunshine where others see s. 5943
When Jesus comes, s. depart 7879
your shaft hidden in the s. 5430

SHADOWY
Everything born of God no s. work 872
Go forth to meet s. future 8378

SHADRACH
What was conduct of S. 5197

SHAFT
As yet your s. hidden in his quiver 5430

SHAH
no s. holds key to as much power 11841

SHAKE
Defeat may serve to s. the soul 2508
devil tries to s. truth 11533
God lets rebellious s. their fist 4129
great thoughts s. the mind 11281
house to its foundations 4775
No storm can s. inmost calm 232
to s. off old ordeal, get ready for the new 7435
world to its foundations 6496

SHAKEN
abuses have not s. church 1419
faith not to be s. won through blood, tears 2949
So s. as we are, so wan with care 12077

SHAKES
grasped by power that s. us 3707

SHAKESPEARE, WILLIAM
Bible woven in withe the very texture 673
dependence on Bible obvious 673
If Bible lost, language preserved in S. 673

If S. should come we would rise 6406

leans upon the Bible 673

sweep streets as S. wrote poetry 2777

To take Bible out of S. leave deep wound 673

you may become a S. 3039

not afraid of being lonely 7141

SHAKING
flipper of trained seal 6062

knees s, kneel on them 8842

SHAKY
If doubt yourself, on s. ground 11599

SHALL
not when he will 8216

SHALLOW
amenities of life ordained by God 7038

better anchor near s. shore of security 11598

every other seal too s. for soul 10659

Fortune is s. 11808

Give me the s. heart 4530

natures tremble for a night after their sin 10352

nothing so s. as dogmatism 456

sign of a s. nature 6251

Speech is s. as time 10263

SHALLOWNESS
disasters of s. 2856

SHALLOWS
never in the s. of our soul 8795

SHAME
absolved from guilt and s. 4719

arises from fear of men 3988

Avoid s, do not seek glory 4406 3850

best dreams to s. 6

cross put to s. self-assertion of heroism 2166

death out of s. into glory 2325

Glory built on selfish principles is s. 10054

God's gifts put man's best dreams to s. 4988

live with s, learn to feel guilty 1114

Lust, at its height, does not know s. 7358

neither a s. nor sin to cultivate reason 9425

new freedom to betray without s. 10526

nor smelleth so sour as s. 5492

Only man is endowed with s. 9570

the devil 2669

voice of intelligence contradicted by s. 6331

Wake for s, my sluggish heart 8671

You fool me once, s. on you 2481

You fool me twice, s. on me 2481

SHAMED
Truth may be blamed but never s. 11573

SHAMEFULLY
exploit converted celebrity 11666

SHAMS
confesses, s. are over 1600

SHAPE
cease to s. our lives by faith 3688

don't get bent out of s. because wobble 6187

saint knit into s. by God 9767

Through faith unseen world takes s. 3812

through fire, floods to batter us into s. 4570

To s. and use 2599

we s. lives, ourselves 1148

SHAPED
and fashioned by what we love 7330

lives s. by those who love us 6236

Solitude shows way to let behavior be s. 10562

SHAPES
Affliction s. as it smites 275

SHAPING
God is s. us for higher things 228

SHARE
All who joy would win must s. it 5505

Christian to s. what one has 1207

freedom to s. innermost thoughts 4285

friends with whom we s. gifts of life 10531

grief, decrease it 5353

highest privilege to s. another's pain 4276

joy, you it 5353

Many eager to s. Jesus' table 9268

nothing that I with God do not s. 7470

people miss s. of happiness 5585

prefer own friends who s. life-style 5957

some of their poverty 8678

those who s. firm belief in Christianity 2987

want to keep faith, must s. it 3771

world's sorrow 10592

SHARED
burden s. lighter load 927

Every meal s. in love a feast 5825

Forever s, forever whole 6409

Happiness s.is the flower 5514

Joy magnified when s. 6539

life a gift to be s. 10545

Suffering too precious to be s. 10895

Who has s. our morning days 4208

SHARES
who allows the oppression s. the crime 5962

SHARING
best proof of immortality in s. life of God 6105

channels made for s. 10729

Friendship lightens adversity by s. it 4228

giving another privilege of s. 4277

joyful s. replaces polite prattle 4029

koinonia, unconditional s. of lives 4022

people cling to possessions instead of s. 8632

SHARP
Converse makes s. the glittering wit 10534

Death but a s. corner 2245

love makes the idle quick and s. 7260

Real doesn't often happen to people who have s. edges 5886

smites nothing so s, nor smelleth so sour 5492

straws almost as s. as thorns after 6489

tongue grows keener with use 11406

word cuts deeper than weapon 2051

words dull respect 9488

words make more wounds 393

SHARPEN
takes a rough stone to s. 190

unknown something to s. our souls on 4318

SHARPENED
Christian will find intelligence s. 1193

endowed with a reason to be s. 9425

SHARPENING
powers of thinking 3027

SHARPENS
First thing in morning she s. tongue 5125

He that wrestles with us s. our skill 1623

Jehovah s. and prepares 163

SHARPER
How s. than serpent's tooth 1119

pain, the s. the more evidence of life 8267

Slander, edge s. than sword 10467

SHARPEST
disarm poverty of its s. sting 8679

SHATTER
God raised up Jesus to s. history 5711

SHATTERED
while my best hopes lie s. 11470

who stumbles upon Christ, lies s. 6517

SHATTERING
God rescues us by s. strength 882

SHEARS
Marriage resembles a pair of s. 7644

SHED
A s. that's thatched 6149
Blood s. does not rest 7880
light he has already s. 5445
within your darkened stable s. 6118

SHEEP
act of injustice to the s. 6283
angels don't sing to s. 6147
foolish s. makes wolf his confessor 9473
lazy s. thinks its wool heavy 6750
like David with s. after anointed king 5391
madness for s. to talk peace with wolf 8446
many a s. and lamb by wolf is rent 8363
We were ravens, now s. 1348
Where s, wolves never far away 8531

SHELF
push back upon the s. of silence 3778

SHELL
broken out of time's hard s. to breathe 4976
Words are but the s. 7726

SHELTER
Faith not s. against difficulties 3693
For rest and s. of the night 11174
greater in vocation than s. 3107
home should be a self-contained s. of security 5853

SHELTERED
good better s. from temptation 5042

SHELTERING
Friendship is a s. tree 4232

SHELTERS
Creed would stifle me that s. you 2027

SHELVES
God's gifts on s. one above the other 6017

SHEPHERD
be a kindly S. behind me 5375
children outgrow S, find heroes elsewhere 1133
If I were a s. 1376
Under a s. soft and negligent 8363
world's great S. now is born 6123

SHEPHERD'S
And feed me with a s. care 9350

SHEPHERDS
didn't ask God if he knew what he was doing 6147
found their Lamb 1373
happy to go with s. to see Lord in manger 8061

Run, s. run, solemnize his birth 6140
So the angels went to the s. 6147

SHIELD
armour is to s. us while we pray 8973
Prayer a s. to the soul 8915
that thou mayst find no blot upon my s. 9088
will either s. from suffering 5907
Work can be defensive s. 3904

SHIFTING
systems of false religion 5103
Upon a s. plate 3851

SHILLING
And with the other took a s. out 6070
better give one s. than lend pound 4368

SHINE
A light to s. upon the road 7507
And let the face of God s. through 10670
darker the night, brighter stars s. 9323
for your light to s. through 9079
I see heaven's glories s. 3765
knock, breathe, s, seek to mend 2840
Lighthouses blow no horns, only s. 5737
Lighthouses just s. on 6022
out, O Blessed Star 6141
soul shall s. a star of day 10675
stars s. fearless and confident 4618
sun s. upon just, unjust 4129
Ten thousand suns which s. above us nightly 4592
to let your own light s. 10457
were it to s. in full strength 4657

SHINES
Common sense s. with double lustre in humility 5994
corruptions like the air before the sun s. 9852
faith s. equal, arming me from fear 3765
He whose crown s. brightest 6004
Make hay while sun s. 2781
No matter how fair the sun s. 5544
saint is one light s. through 9769
So s. good deed in naughty world 2499
sun s. clearly in darkest day as in brightest 4772
true light ever s. 5103
who does not pray when sun s. 8809

SHINETH
The darkness s. as the light 4140

SHINING
Behind the clouds is sun still s. 10582

believe in the sun even when it is not s. 3732
God's love is always s. 10964
Has the sun ever stopped his s. 10964
Infinite written name on heavens in s. stars 4705
Lighthouses don't call attention to their s. 6022
Many have s. qualities beneath rough exterior 8658 5078
shadows mean there's a light s. somewhere 2602
stars are constantly s. 2560
Your s. and splendor drove out my blindness 1910

SHIP
a harbor, not what s. are built for 76
A s. in a harbor is safe 76
attempting to check by spider's thread progress of s. 11108
Better lose anchor than whole s. 9555
came about like a well-handled s. 11130
God pity the s. when the sea gets in 1330
is equal to the load of today 12092
man without purpose like s. without rudder 4436
One s. drives east, another west 4432
small leak will sink great s. 5116
To build a s. of truth 11519
tongue rudder of our s. 11418

SHIP'S
place is in the sea 1330

SHIPS
I will not doubt, though all my s. at sea 11470
Our s. shall sail upon another sea 2319
those who pass like s. in night 4281

SHIPWRECK
if make s. will be in wide sea of God's love 9930
poor wretches saved from s. 10386

SHIPWRECKED
problem is s. soul 7396

SHIRT
Habit s. made of iron 5496
happy man's without a s. 11857
sleeves at ball game, call him Pop 3921
When a man has lost his s. 6290

SHIVER
Honesty praised but left to s. 5878

SHIVERS
go up, down spines of cultured people 5811

SHOCK
part makes an idea an idea 2013

SHOCKED
ear s. by unexpected 844

SHOCKS
And battered with the s. of doom 2599
friendship must withstand s. of adversity 4218
sin that s. God 10397

SHOE
Avoid suspicion, don't tie your s. 9613
Every s. fits not every foot 6174
handsome s. often pinches foot 2461
Only the wearer knows where s. pinches 3542
that fits one person pinches another 6214
who wear s. know best where pinches 8275
You cannot put same s. on every foot 6225

SHOES
angry, for I had no s. 387
God makes s. upside down 4668
God will provide strong s. 180
put yourself in his s. 11286
tight s. make you forget other troubles 8509

SHOESTRING
only thing can do on a s. is trip 4031

SHONE
light that then s. never left me 7472

SHONEST
Thou s, didst dispel my blindness 4805

SHOOT
If God willed, brooms would s. 4944
thou standest where I am about to s. 1550

SHOOTING
without aiming 1873

SHOOTS
Envy s. at others 3214

SHOP
golfer should marry woman who would rather s. than cook 7656
rumor going around the s. 9822

SHOPPERS
Some s. imitate General Custer 4041

SHORE
A few miles distance from rocky s. 6111
as the waves make toward pebbled s. 2329
Eternity, we shall never see the s. 3283
keep coming back to s. 3544

lo, your own has reached s. 905
longer the s. line of wonder 6702
On any s. since God is there 4869
On ocean or on s. 6916
One day along that silent s. 1147
See, they throng the blissful s. 2221
stands upon the s, longs to cross over 7916
Time has no s. 11373
wretched refuse of your teeming s. 7985

SHORELESS
God's love a vast, bottomless, s. sea 4750
let unnavigated ether, through s. depths 4712
Without God life a s. trackless waste 7098

SHORES
How shall I reach thy s. 7492
perpetual must be written on eternal s. 3860

SHORT
Each day so s, so few 7219
God has given man a s. time upon earth 6894
great word to master, short 7000
he who falls s. 6592
human comfort s. 1501
If s.—yet why should I be sad 6923
in eternity human ideals fall s. 1163
Kind words s, easy to speak 11988
Life is s. 6658
Life is s. and full of blisters 192
life s. day in which sun hardly rises 7083
life with wisdom better than long life without it 11897
Life's a s. summer 6991
Life's too s. for worrying 12068
Nights of pleasure are s. 10340
One s. sleep past 2356
only here for s. visit 9530
proverb a s. sentence based on long experience 9376
rope of a lie is s. 6860
still find each day too s. 11301
Time too s. for those who rejoice 11333
To go too far as bad as to fall s. 11954
too long or too s. distance obscures knowledge 3559
upon this s. time eternity depends 6894
When I consider the s. duration of my life 7084

SHORTAGE
at centers of national influence 111
energy, money, Christians 111
of effective Christian action 111

SHORT-CIRCUITED
Meditation that does not make a difference s. 7725

SHORTCOMINGS
church looks in pain at s. 1443

SHORTCUT
Apothegms form s. to much knowledge 9378
happiness distant goal to which no s. 7648
no s. to character 1000
Prayer not a s. to skill 8924
Wickedness takes s. to everything 11895

SHORTCUTS
no s. to maturity 5738

SHORTENS
Cheerful company s. miles 4221

SHORTEST
Some of our s. prayers most effectual ones 8962
world's s. sermon is traffic light 10109

SHORT-LIVED
Peace won by compromise s. 8464

SHORTNESS
eternity consoles for s. of life 3287

SHORTSIGHTED
too s. to see what God is aiming at 347

SHORT-TEMPERED
even for those who tend to be s. 7304

SHORT-TERM
Kids not s. loan 1121

SHOT
arrow in air, it stuck 3194

SHOTS
God's calling the s. 4939
When Master of earth calls s, things happen 3819

SHOULD
I'm not the thing I s. be 9928

SHOULDER
finger of God on a man's s. 7314
God gives s. to burden 928
Keep your s. to the wheel 3503

SHOULDERS
ache with fatigue 11420
arms around each other's s. 2990
dislocated both s. describing it 3424
his burden loosed from off his s. 9803
no business to require head of age on s. of youth 12186
What makes Christians shrug s. 3339

SHOUT
a s. about my ears 2980
Ay! we s. to the evangel 1375
I laugh and s. for life is good 6917

need not s. my faith 8014

SHOUTEDST
Thou s. and didst pierce my deafness 4805

SHOUTING
tumult and s. dies 6036

SHOUTS
God s. in our pains 8257
Nor the s. of exultation 2217
Not in s. and plaudits of the throng 10794
Not in s. of throng 1031

SHOVED
seed of God stirred, s, sprouted 2984

SHOVEL
death put to bed with a s. 2275
Snow is beautiful when watching fellow s. 9904

SHOW
a man his failures without Jesus 7425
Adversities s. what sort of man he is 140
afraid to s. each other who we really are 6057
any kindness I can s. 6642
don't s. up until work is done 6773
freedom to s. true feelings 4285
God came to s. us how to live 6128
God's running the s. 4939
good should s. itself first in own household 5838
hollow s. that must come to an end 8679
I did not even s. him then 4199
is this a greatness apt to make a s. 5297
me you are redeemed 3324
none ourselves 4105
Outside s. poor substitute for inner worth 6061
sciences, business is to s. the truth 9871
so grand, beautiful, exciting 6092
some look at the s. to see how and why 7018
That mercy I to others s. 1552
treat men gently, they will s. themselves great 6807
want of faith in God by false wisdom 4322
will s. how small your greatness is 6037
Will s. the way 5434
you a way to feed thousands 10205

SHOW OFF
Many a solo sung to s. 7867
Spirit of God will not allow you to s. 5776

SHOWER
as sun after s. 3130

back of the mill is the wheat and the s. 9345
What parched grounds refresh as with a s. 8867

SHOWERS
April s. bring May flowers 9884
Tears s. that fertilize the world 10625
Through s. the sunbeams fall 5904

SHOWERY
flowery, bowery 9876

SHOWING
Christ an example, s. us how to live 6410
Laughing feeling good, s. it in one spot 6726
unto men of truth after truth 4906

SHOWN
Real friendship s. in trouble 4267

SHOWROOM
not specimens in God's s. 9850

SHOWS
demands mercy, s. none 4084
God s. himself absolute mystery 4738
great man s. greatness by way he treats little men 5272
himself for what he really is 4272
In guidance when God s. us a sign 5439
man s. character by laughter 982
mirror s. everyone his best friend 9998
Sickness s. us what we are 6088
That purrs and never s. a tooth 5048
thing he is about too big for him 5592

SHRANK
seed placed in furrow to grow s. instead 5368

SHREWDNESS
Love not dependent on s. 7235

SHRIEKING
live longer by century of s. deaths 6258

SHRINE
Thy sacred inmost s. 7454

SHRINES
erect houses of worship but our s. are places of business 6068

SHRINK
hearts s. until room for little beside ourselves 5625
If consider boundless space, s. into nothing 11631
O for a faith that will not s. 3768
self-importance makes mind s, head swell 9191
Swelled heads s. influence 9488
tragedies allow hearts to s. until 5625

SHRINKING
away from death unhealthy 2255

SHRIVEL
we let our souls s. 10680

SHRIVELING
hurt until sun drew forth a leaf 5368

SHRIVELLED
souls 10247

SHROUD
has no pockets 8640

SHRUG
What makes Christians s. shoulders 3339

SHUDDER
depths of iniquity that makes us s. 10391

SHUN
Better s. bait than struggle in snare 11049
do not s. and call life hard names 6903
not the struggle 6881
the inquisitive 5156
wicked s. the light as devil the cross 11893

SHUNS
devil s. the cross 11893

SHUT
ability to keep mouth s. priceless 1876
betray Jesus Christ by keeping mouth s. 628
door against earthly noise 10554
ears aren't made to s. 1875
Eternity s. in a span 6153
eyes to future God hides from us 4322
faith will s. mouths of lions 3787
From hearts that s. against them with a snap 8694
hold chin up, will keep mouth s. 11463
I've s. the door on yesterday 11369
keep eyes half s. after marriage 7624
keep mouth s, flies won't get in 1854
keeps the mouth s. 1884
mouth and eyes to injustice 11690
mouth is made to s. 1875
no one in earth can s. door God has opened 4937
nor open door God has s. 4937
Often God has to s. a door in our face 5436
opening mind to s. it on something solid 7761
out all thoughts save that of God 7708
since thou hast s. me up in this world 7006
world of love s. in 5817
world of strife s. out 5817

SHUTS

If God s. one door, he opens
  another 5421
When God s. door, he opens
  window 5462
worldly spirit s. Bible 683

SHUTTLES

And the s. cease to fly 10606

SHY

flower of sweetest smell is s. and
  lowly 6028
Little Jesus, was thou s. 6456
living with ridicule, learn to be s.
  1114

SICK

Conceit makes everyone s. 1586
guilt feelings which made him s.
  5485
My soul is s. with every day's
  report 6273
No man good physician who has
  never been s. 3075
nor yet a heart so s. 10201
O Lord! my heart is s. 973
of this everlasting change 973
of world's business 10578
People no longer sinful, only s.
  10350
person faced with meaning of
  things 6086
thou s. man's health 5932
Though hope be weak or s. with
  long delay 8768
to s. men, Christ is health 6391
yourself and me, am s. of both
  9958

SICKENS

fear s. 3965

SICKNESS

blurred beauty, delivered from
  pride 1776
chamber of s. is chapel of devotion
  6089
Envy green s. 3217
experience of s. in some way
  necessary 10884
God does not promise he will
  protect from s. 5385
God sends time of s. 7056
in s, Christ makes my bed 6498
Love is medicine for s. of world
  7250
Make s. itself a prayer 6087
Openness is to wholeness as
  secrets are to s. 5883
pains grow sharp and s. rages
  8174
shows us what we are 6088
vice is s. 11726

SIDE

am concerned that I am on God's
  s. 7471
big difference to fly which s. he
  chooses 8076
find flower upon inmost s. 6583
God's s. or s. of human reasoning
  1156

God's s. winning s. 1159
If thou art by my s. 5418
love should beam forth on every s.
  7168
no danger of eyestrain from
  looking on bright s. 8240
On every s. I find thy hand 4876
One on God's s. is a majority
  7509
The Lord is on thy s. 1502
We are on winning s. 1924
woman formed out of s. to be
  equal 11982

SIDELINED

If God has you s. 5391

SIDES

God s. with poor because of
  vulnerability 6630
In seeking truth, get both s. of
  story 11511
likely to be hit from both s. 11602
Love pressing on all s. like air
  4785
should quietly hear both s. 6618
two s. to every question 8076

SIDON

scarcely left wreck behind 730

SIEGE

Every tempest an assault in s. of
  love 4775
very noise of the s. will drown still
  small voice 8854

SIEVE

sifted them with coarse s. 1741
to needle: hole in your head 2079

SIFT

certain that a faithful hand will s.
  4260

SIFTED

them with coarse sieve 1741

SIFTING

He is s. out the hearts of men
  4715
life s. like grain from bag 8381

SIGH

can find its way to God 8849
can say more than many words
  8887
God an unutterable s. in the soul
  4843
He best can part with life without
  a s. 10046
help him at least with s. 3072
men s. on, not knowing what the
  soul wants 7516
Prayer is the burden of a s. 8939
soul is a never ending s. after God
  7528
To weep, s. because I'm blind
  1810
truest prayer sometimes a s. 8887
When the house doth s. and weep
  1514

SIGHING

nature s. through all her works
  10314
Pity him who's sadly s. 4217

SIGHINGS

are s. for God 7516
how many s. would we see in
  marketplace 10507

SIGHS

love has ears to hear s. and
  sorrows 7335
music of the spheres is made of s.
  and sobs 10878
natural language of the heart 5623
Not all my prayers nor s. nor tears
  8451

SIGHT

Bible within s. of weakest, noblest
  702
darkness makes appreciative of s.
  824
Faith and s. in opposition 3842
Faith is not s. 3687
faith means believing beyond s.
  3657
horizon nothing save limit of our
  s. 6097
I'll let my head be just in s. 10501
in body, so is reason in soul 9412
Is not s. a jewel 6253
Love blind, marriage restores s.
  7629
meet for a moment, sail out of s.
  4281
need new s. in religion 9554
New islands yet shall break upon
  our s. 2319
O Thou, to whose all-searching s.
  4140
of you good for sore eyes 4207
one-eyed man among blind has
  full s. 8572
Such s. angels behold 4995
The s. of thee must be 4659
To blind men, Christ is s. 6391
We saw thee; and we blest the s.
  6152
Welcome, all wonders in one s.
  6153

SIGN

be first to give friendship s. 9479
Doubt may be s. a man is thinking
  2933
Doubt not always s. man is wrong
  2933
Gratitude s. of noble souls 5247
highest s. of friendship 4277
In guidance when God shows us a
  s. 5439
Joy most infallible s. of presence
  of God 6548
means we're on the way 5439
Nobody's family can hang out s.
  3878
of a shallow nature 6251
Oh, what a s. it is of evil life 2348
One friendly s. 4199

trying to be Christian, s. you are
   not 1291
We s. to clear our hearts 5627

SIGNAL
fear, soul's s. for rallying 3973

SIGNALS
danger s. life is on wrong track
   5466

SIGNATURE
Everywhere I find the s. of God
   11629

SIGNED
personality written, s. by God
   6183

SIGNIFICANCE
capacity to care gives life s. 3077
Every dream full of s. 2968
if you can see the s. 1716
Jesus gave world such insights
   have not yet grasped s. 6196
no s. to love with no alternative
   1141
things which come easily have no
   s. 2757
want, have, do, no s. except in "to
   be" 3491

SIGNIFICANT
made s. mark on his world 8793
most s. witness was my defeat
   2518
None of our human talents are s.
   to God 4527
Nothing happens that is not s.
   1716
question what Christ thinks of us
   4718
raise question whether men are s.
   7481
that program, programming occur
   frequently 1406

SIGNPOSTS
along the way all marked Progress
   5970
road to hell without s. 5702

SIGNS
are given us because 5439
four s. of approaching age 314
where need s. to discern guiding
   hand 5396

SILAS
God could have kept Paul and S.
   out of jail 165

SILENCE
a friend who will never betray
   10260
a great peacemaker 10261
a lie may be told by s. 6859
a rich pause in music of life 10262
a sound through s. 365
After s. nearest to expressing
   inexpressible is music 7884
All the emptiness and s. 2217
alone is great enough to hold
   10274
appalling s. of good people 6285

as welcome after satiety as
   disappointment 10266
balm to every chagrin 10266
because of s. mysteries of God
   known to saints 10252
because of s. power of God dwelt
   in saints 10252
before which we kneel in joyful s.
   4750
benefit of trial consists in s. 2734
better than truth without charity
   1831
breaks the heart 12003
brother of acceptance 10264
bury weakness of friend in s. 4183
by s. the saints grew 10252
Charity is s. when words would
   hurt 1085
Create s. 10271
creates itchiness 10253
creates nervousness 10253
cruelest lies often told in s. 6858
doubt when expectations meet
   God's s. 2931
element in which great things
   fashion themselves 10265
Eloquent s. better than eloquent
   speech 10244
eternal s. of these infinite spaces
   terrifies me 7084
Everything great grows in s.
   10246
experience s. as empty, hollow
   10253
Five words cost Zacharias forty
   weeks' s. 11412
flee into the s. of solitude 2591
For to be alone in s. 10256
From his sweet s. my mouth sings
   4125
gift of s. 10247
God is the friend of s. 10250
God is the voice in my s. 4459
God sat in s. 2130
God, the Voice in my s. 6907
Great souls suffer in s. 10848
greatest ideas born from womb of
   s. 10269
hardly ever complete s. in our soul
   10273
has become a fearful thing 10253
has its wonders 1788
has many advantages 1866
holiest of all holidays in s. and
   apart 7720
how fully pleasing to God 10252
how thoroughly it heals 10252
hundred acorns sown in s. by
   breeze 8052
if love truth, be lover of s. 10245
immersed in the s. of God 10240
impossible to live in inmost being
   without loving s. 10254
In midst of noise deep inner s.
   10539
in presence of God 7707
In s, round me—the perpetual
   work 1966
in s. God is known 10255

4741
In s. he is heard 10249
In s. the Son of God grew 10190
in s. worshiped best 10249
in suffering is best 10886
intimately related to trust 10259
into absolute s. of thoughts, words
   1767
is deep as eternity 10263
is foolish if we are wise 1869
is freedom to let justication rest
   with God 6622
Is not prayer precisely s. 8847
is nourishment 9374
is refreshment 9374
is the soul's language 8902
isolates us from crowds 10515
Jesus driven to a life of s. 6358
Keep us from unkind s. 9106
learned s. from talkative 5251
like a poultice comes 10241
like gaping abyss which can
   swallow up 10253
listening, prayer, truth go together
   10248
lives right has more power in s.
   3428
more eloquent than words 1870
More have repented speech than s.
   1861
More progress in s. than in years
   of study 12112
need s. to recover from futility of
   words 10556
no wisdom like s. 11953
Now a blessed s. flows over us
   7952
O sinner, stop 763
one great art of conversation 1871
perfectest herald of joy 6558
power of s. 10252
prayer gives s. real meaning 10562
Prayer is to arrive at s, continue
   being silent 8935
Prayer of thanks for s. 10247
prevents being suffocated by world
   10562
problem not in God's s. 2931
push back upon the shelf of s.
   3778
rich, warm, generous 10247
roar which is other side of s. 8496
safest eloquence is s. 4681
sequel to dull discourses 10266
sit in s. with fellowman 1513
Slander answered best with s.
   10464
sleep cannot s. conscience 2970
Sometimes greatest sermon is s.
   10887
sometimes severest criticism 2074
Sorrow makes s. her best orator
   10619
Speech is silver, s. golden 1874
stars, moon, sun, how they move
   in s. 10250
teach me to s. my own heart
   10257
teaches joys of sound 824

teaches us to speak Word of God 10562

That swells with s. in the tortured soul 5348

the other s. and the wakeful stars 10673

the universal refuge 10266

times when God asks nothing except s. 10635

to deaf all is s. 9094

To sin by s. when should protest 6627
6282

to spirit what sleep is to body 9374

Trees grow in s. 10250

tried to formulate private prayer in s. 8762

True s. is rest of mind 9374

we suspect s, regard it as proof meeting is dead 12096

Well-timed s. eloquence 1889

What griefs in s. of your face 1545

who does not understand your s. 10251

will deliver you from ignorance 10245

will illuminate you in God 10245

will unite you to God himself 10245

With s. one irritates the devil 10276

Without s. cannot plumb depths of being 10246

Without s. fall short of reality 10246

SILENCED

voice of intelligence s. by ignorance 6331

SILENCES

Great faith perseveres in God's s. 3725

heard Word of God can bear s. 658

make real conversations between friends 4268

recreating s. of contemplation 1760

SILENT

A s. child, I follow on 4977

All God's great works are s. 1956

All in me is s. 10240

And so beside the s. sea 6916

Be s. about great things 10242

because of s. agreement, betrayal and murder exist 6158

Before infinitude we stand s. 4706

believe in God even when he is s. 3732

Better s. than stupid 10243

Better to remain s. 1836

Christ the s. listener to every conversation 5823

blame man who is s. 2080

communion of closet best declares God's reality 10554

Creation a s. process 1956

deaf live in s. world so remote, different 9094

do not be slow only, but s, very s. for he is God 5460

does not Lord hear nations blame, yet remain s. 4894

Eternity is s. 10576

faith develops best when God is s. 3789

friend who cares s. in despair 3080

glory springs from s. conquest of ourselves 4414

God the s. partner in great enterprises 4460

Goodness is s. 5719
10380

Great joys, like griefs, are s. 6526

hears himself cursed and remains s. becomes partner of God 4894

holy life speaks when tongue s. 5735

human soul s. harp in God's choir 7921

I like the s. church 1394

If I saw God's truth attacked, yet remain s. 99

If s, an exception to the universe 7997

If someone doesn't pull, a bell will remain s. 75

If we are s. who will take control 10259

Keep not thou s. O God! 1487

knows truth but keeps s. 2910

lament our voices must be s. 7056

Laws s. amidst clash of arms 11754

Light cares speak, great ones s. 10599

Little s. victories over favorite temptations 6997

mouth keeps s. to hear heart speak 10270

Not until each loom is s. 10606

pleasant face a s. recommendation 3570

Poetry makes you be s. 8619

power of perseverance grows with time 8557

Sad the home where hen crows, cock s. 5847

serene, s. beauty of a holy life 5766

shall I, can I, s. be 7997

soul s. harp in God's quire 10665

speaks a language of s. power 6651

Though my feet are set in s. ways 6917

threads of gold when woven together 6997

Three s. things 10275

To persevere and be s. best answer 9677

to remain s. makes us feel helpless 10259

two kinds of people keep s. 10272

Unheard by the world, rises s. to thee 8778

weakness to be s. when proper to speak 1887

weakness to speak when proper to be s. 1887

When heart full, lips s. 5270

When money speaks, truth is s. 7825

Who, in the s. hour of inward thought 2764

wisdom to keep s. when damaging words spoken 6271

Wise men not always s, but know when to be 11977

woods would be very s. if 7926

worship is healing 12114

SILENTLY

cares that infest the day s. steal away 7887

friend will s. walk with you 4175

home where character molding s. carried on 5850

one by one, in the infinite meadows of heaven 11636

SILHOUETTE

poet sees city as s. against sky 10522

SILK

moor the vessel with a thread of s. 9233

SILLY

friend, free to be s. with 4177

question first intimation of new development 6703

Spirit of God will never make man s. 1064

to pretend we are all brothers 912

SILVER

A spider spins her s. 6118

Christianity like shining of s. 1227

Every cloud has s. lining 2797

Judas sold himself for s. 11798

Speech is s. silence golden 1874

SIMILAR

Collecting quotations s. to birds who pick up pebbles 9380

SIMON PETER

more a sandpile than a rock 3617

SIMPLE

All great things are s. 10277

As grave grows nearer, my theology growing s. 11182

Be s, take our Lord's hand 5374

Beware of believing human soul s. 10653

Christ's words s. yet profound 6377

Christ, too s. to be grasped 6507

Conversion so s. child can be converted 1896

Faith should always be s, unbending 7168

For s. liberty to pray 4118

Friendship is a s. story 4217

Give me s. laboring folk 11686

God is quick to mark every s.
  effort to please 4810
Goodness so s. 5066
Hate a s. emotion 7233
home where s. pleasures enjoyed
  5853
human soul, and life will appear s.
  10653
If your love pure, is, s, well-ordered
  7193
impossible to explain how s. Bible
  is 734
it will be his precepts to fulfill
  10047
Knowledge leads from s. to
  complex 11929
Life is really s. 6977
Life is very s. 7692
love can do great things 6708
Make it s. 10279
men admire studies 2996
more s. person is inwardly 8505
most agreeable is s, frank person
  4204
My way is very s. 7953
no good asking for s. religion
  9402
No truths are s. 11521
Nothing more s. than greatness
  10280
Nothing presented to soul is s.
  10660
Once we come into s. relationship
  with God 7509
patience to do s. things perfectly
  8406
Pray, God, keep us s. 10282
Prayer as s. as child making wants
  known to parents 8937
real things aren't s. 9402
record of three short years 6483
relationship to God only s. thing
  10653
some truths God will not make s.
  11546
The s. are thy rest 6040
to be s. is to be great 10280
unassuming life best for everyone
  7365
way out of trouble never as s. as
  way in 11453
wisdom leads from complex to s.
  11929
words express great thoughts
  11989

SIMPLER
If only I may grow s. 7688

SIMPLEST
gospel could only reveal itself in s.
  of garments 5089
greatest truths are s, so are
  greatest men 5298
Philosophers take s, turn into
  unintelligible 8591
Prayer s. of all things 8940
To God we use s, shortest words
  9002

SIMPLICITIES
Out of complexities s. emerge
  11937

SIMPLICITY
an amazing s. of life 7509
analysis of conscience has taken
  place of childlike s. 6813
attribute of a great lady 11697
Eloquence is vehement s. 9135
faith gives s. of heart 7383
has no suspicious, deceitful
  thoughts 11696
Honesty a beautiful and
  refreshing s. 5874
Humanity, two poles of s. and
  complexity 7383
in Christ rarely found among us
  1230
is rich 11696
Jesus driven to a life of s. 6358
mere s. before God 10278
millions stumble over sheer s.
  5653
of gospel's ethnic 1242
Perfection in s, chief ingredient of
  prayer 8914
Pity my s. 1117
pure affection 11696
result of profound thought 10283
Satan's cunning cannot take by
  surprise 10278
scrutinizes nothing 11696
sees only one side 7383
temptation cannot take by surprise
  10278
What Protestantism has gained by
  its s. 6827
Within s. lies the sublime 10286

SIMPLIFICATION
wisdom lies in s. 11927

SIMPLIFIED
defined goals s. decisions 4425
Let the thing be s. 10279

SIMPLIFIES
Life s. itself 11153

SIMPLIFY
must s. our approach to God 7709

SIMPLY
But s. worship thee 12094
if thou wilt s. trust 5415
Live s. 5561
rich must live more s. that poor
  may s. live 11861
solves problems completely, s.
  3784
soul never applies itself s. 10660
thought too weak to be expressed
  s. 10285
wait upon God 5440

SIMULTANEOUSLY
cannot s. will sin and repentance
  5210
God at beginning, end of time s.
  11314

SIN
a breach of nature 10360

a crime against love 10355
a departure from God 10365
a fathomless answer, the Cross of
  Christ 9398
a man is first startled by s. 10287
a strong imagination 10368
aberration of the spirit 10360
Abounding s. terror of world
  5203
absolved from s. and fear 4719
act of s. may pass 5489
Adam introduced s. into world
  757
against neighbor through lack of
  love s. against God 7164
all afflicted with the disease 10415
All s. a kind of lying 6848
an affair of the will 10361
anyway you grasp it, it hurts
  10330
assent 10368
banquet of hell 10360
be angry and s. not 381
because we are sinners 10441
becomes confirmed 10287
becomes delightful 10287
becomes easy 10287
becomes frequent 10287
becomes habitual 10287
becomes pleasing 10287
bills come in later 10421
bitter in the end 10375
blindness of the sense 10360
boasts of s. is a devil 10309
book will keep you from s. 692
breaking God's heart 10355
builds barrier 1595
by disobeying apostolic injunction
  to rejoice 8744
by that s. fell the angels 346
by unrepented s. cut off sense of
  God 4864
Can ease this weight of s. 8451
cannot break God's decree 4616
cannot simultaneously will s. and
  repentance 5210
causes cup of blessing to spring a
  leak 10356
Cheerfulness is no s. 1090
choose to be dominated by s. or
  righteousness 10510
Christ's definition of s. 10300
Christ-like it is for s. to grieve
  10334
Christianity is resistance against s.
  1206
churches close because s. 1421
clasped so close cannot see ugly
  face 10377
Commit a major s, all lesser sins
  follow 10301
confession determination to avoid
  s. 1599
Confession to agree with God
  regarding s. 1597
contempt of God's love 10376
continue to make ourselves guilty
  is s. 5491
cost God death of his Son 1013

covers mirror with smoke 10339
covetousness a deadly s. 10086
cross, defeat of s. 2118
cumulative effect to edge man
    away from the light 10324
dare of God's justice 10376
darkest word is s. 11993
death of good works 10360
death of grace 10360
death of Jesus goes underneath
    deepest s. 2160
death of the soul 10360
death of virtue 10360
defiance to authority of God
    10362
deliberately set ourselves up to fall
    10422
delight 10368
devil did grin, for his darling s.
    9192
disciple comes with s. to find
    forgiveness 2818
Disobedience and s. same thing
    10302
disquiet of the heart 10360
divine explusion of s. 10717
does fruit of s. wither 10346
does not appear to be irresistible
    10357
dungeon of hell 10360
dying Jesus evidence of God's
    anger toward s. 6473
energy in the wrong channel
    10364
enough, soon unconscious of s.
    10358
eternity of hell 10360
Every s. already paid for 10299
expulsion of Christianity 10360
falls into s. is a man 10309
Fashions in s. change 10303
fatal in all languages 10367
fear nothing but s. 9136
fellowship with the devil 10360
Fight with your own s. 10304
first a simple suggestion 10368
frantic discord of s. 8743
God a specialist in the s. disease
    10308
God accepted responsibility for s.
    2140
God does allow s. 4957
God does not cause us to s. 10306
God had one Son without s.
    10843
God has set a Savior against s.
    5016
God is in the cavern of man's s.
    10434
God purely, perfectly angry with s.
    401
God-like it is all s. to leave 10334
goes to inner desire 10300
goes to motivations 10300
goes to secret thoughts 10300
grace alone conquers s. 5231
Grace enough to confess, forsake
    s. 1809
grace opposed to s. 5205

Great Physician curer of ravages
    of s. 10436
greatest s. to prefer life to honor
    6883
grieves at s. is a saint 10309
Guilty of dust and s. 5481
has four characteristics 10359
has many tools 6857
hate s. with fierceness that burns
    3182
Heaven begins where s. ends 5642
holds the ladder as bad as thief
    2036
holiest person most conscious of s.
    5761
Holiness ability not to s. 5745
Holiness more than sweeping
    away s. 5748
Holiness not inability to s. 5745
holy man not one who cannot s.
    5762
holy man one who will not s.
    5762
horrified by dreadfulness of own s.
    10297
I am thirsty for s. 10435
I had ambition, by which s. 5694
I, root of s. 10381
if God deny presence, we fall into
    s. 4865
If God not willing to forgive s.
    4088
If hangups called s. by Lord
    10321
If it takes s. to show God, Satan
    in true colors 11072
if live in s, are among God's
    enemies 10427
illusion that time cancels s. 10419
in brightness, Christ is my s. 6498
in spite of our feebleness and s.
    4768
Independence essence of s. 6414
inner nature of s. 10387
is a cancer 8467
is deformity 10363
is disease 10363
is fleet of foot outrunning
    everything 10374
is here 11287
is strong 10374
is two sins when defended 10289
is weakness 10363
is wrong being 10372
jeer of God's patience 10376
Jesus continual forgiveness of s.
    10402
jolt of pain with s. 577
Knowledge of s. is beginning of
    salvation 9815
knowledge of Scripture no
    obstacle to s. 10392
Laughter of s. as crackling of
    burning thorns 10393
like ice in our pipes 10369
lives in s. and looks for happiness
    10313
Looking at wound of s. will never
    save 9804

Lord came down from the Mount
    to be identified with s. 6488
Love a man even in his s. 10331
make s. and misery out of
    everything God sends 10816
Man calls s. a blunder, God a
    blindness 4560
Man calls s. a chance, God a
    choice 4560
Man calls s. a defect, God a
    disease 4560
Man calls s. a fascination, God a
    fatality 4560
Man calls s. a liberty, God
    lawlessness 4560
Man calls s. a luxury, God a
    leprosy 4560
Man calls s. a mistake, God
    madness 4560
Man calls s. a trifle, God a tragedy
    4560
Man calls s. a weakness, God
    wilfulness 4560
Man calls s. an accident, God an
    abomination 4560
Man calls s. an error, God an
    enmity 4560
Man calls s. an infirmity, God an
    iniquity 4560
Man-like it is to fall into s. 10334
may open bright as morning
    10378
may spell pride but is some form
    of "me" 9916
Me always at the bottom of s.
    9916
Measure growth in grace by
    sensitiveness to s. 10335
    5367
Men who could not s. would not
    be men 10337
Mercy for them that fear and s.
    not 7742
Mercy not for them that s. and
    fear not 7742
moral dimension of s. injustice
    10394
moved God to permit s. 4989
must be crucified 9841
must die right out 9841
must not be counteracted 9841
must not be curbed 9841
must not be suppressed 9841
my claim to my right to myself
    10389
My s. is red 5482
neither a shame nor s. to cultivate
    reason 9425
Neutrality at times graver s. than
    belligerence 8072
never bear burden of s, doubt 937
no major s. when his grace
    confronts you 10405
no minor s. when his justice
    confronts you 10405
no s. but disobedience 10302
no s. can hinder you from serving
    10159
No s. is small 10341

no s. not included in Christ's death 10299

not a distance 10370

not be angry with anything but s. 381

not breaking God's law 10355

not disease 10371

not enough to once feel sorrow over s. 9589

not human repression of s. 10717

not sinners because we s. 10441

not weakness 10371

not wrong doing 10372

of sermon listening 1414

of the Garden was s. of power 8719

on the installment plan 10421

one s. will destroy a sinner 10344

one thing to mourn for s. because exposes us to hell 9581

Only in context of grace can we face s. 10551

Original s. malice ever flickering within 10347

overtakes us by surprise 10422

pays handsomely, relentlessly 10421

pays in remorse, regret, failure 10379

plan that would anticipate every s. 5438

power is hidden 10357

pray when ought to be working as much a s. 9008

Prayerlessness is a s. 8954

presents itself as a most desirable thing 10354

rape of God's mercy 10376

reason s. flourishes 10345

rebellion against divine authority 10390

rebellion against rule of God 10366

red-handed rebellion against God 10371

religious dimension of s. rebellion against God 10394

remains alive, because there is nothing for which it will die 11394

Remorse the pain of s. 9572

repeated seems permitted 10290

reward of s. is death 10395

right for God to display anger against s. 4729

Rub out first, last letters and you have I 10381

saps strength 10406

seeds of punishment sown at time commit s. 10396

seems worse in consequences than intentions 10294

self-righteousness instead of humility 10359

self-seeking instead of benevolence 10359

self-sufficiency instead of faith 10359

self-will instead of submission 10359

sense of s. in proportion to nearness to God 10349

separates 9812

Shallow natures tremble for a night after s. 10352

single s. makes a hole 1704

slight of God's power 10376

So many shapes of crime 2040

social dimension of s. injustice 10394

sorrow of the spirit 10360

sovereign until sovereign grace dethrones it 10373

Spirit's power greater than power of s. 5802

spiritual lives have been frozen 10369

spiritual pride, most deadly form s. can take 9254

state not remedy for s, but means to restrain 5177

strike at the s. of which the world is full 10304

substituted inferiority complex for s. 5808

sweet in the beginning 10375

Temptation is not a s. 11087

thank God for how he will use s. 11152

that believes in nothing 11394

that cup of s. be drained to dregs 5423

that enjoys nothing 11394

that finds purpose in nothing 11394

that hates nothing 11394

that interferes with nothing 11394

that lives for nothing 11394

that s. has cast away 1363

that shocks God 10397

the s. done for things there's money in 7819

the s. you abhor 10305

The world confess its s. 4642

think of anger as s. 401

thorny crown filled with briars of s. 7073

those who carry another's s. as their own 5029

times does nothing to guilt of s. 10419

To deny reality of s. 10407

To deviate is to s. 9965

To fall into s. is human 10408

To forsake s. leave it without thought of returning 10409

to mourn for s. because evil 9581

To put s. out of life humanly impossible 10717

to remain in s. is devilish 10408

To s. by silence when should protest 6282
6627

to teach us about hatred of s. 10306

too often say defeated by s. 5753

towering mound of s. rises from "to be" 3492

treated like cream puff instead of rattlesnake 10345

tries the Christian 10328

turning in wrong direction 10370

two kinds of s. 10422

two witnesses present to observe 10418

Unrepented s. is continued s. 9575

use s. to teach, rebuke, challenge 11152

vision impaired by cataracts of s. 10436

voice of s. is loud 4100

was Christ's errand 6505

We know we s. 10442

weakening of power 10360

what hast thou done to this fair earth 10342

Whatever impairs tenderness of conscience 10424

Whatever obscures sense of God 10424

Whatever takes relish off spiritual things 10424

Whatever weakens your reason 10424

When rationalist points out s. 9398

who does not forbid s, encourages it 10310

who has not felt s. in Old Testament 5224

who is convicted of s.. 5108

Who swims in s. shall sink in sorrow 10426

whole massed s. of the race 9437

will end dark as night 10378

will keep you from this book 692

willful refusal to obey God 10387

with the multitude 9672

worst s. is not to hate, but be indifferent 6164

writes histories 10380

wrong concept of s. 4568

you do by two and two 10398

SIN-BATTERED
turn s. life toward Great Physician 10436

SIN'S
Spirit's control will replace s. control 5802

SINAI
duty represents S. 7297

SINCERE
Can faith that does nothing be s. 3647

devil is s, but sincerely wrong 10429

Jesus Christ makes us real, not merely s. 9403

Sorrow makes men s. 10618

Weak persons cannot be s. 10431

SINCERELY
love fellowmen s. 559

To love everybody s. 6913

SINCEREST
Imitation s. form of flattery 2006

SINCERITY
attribute of a great lady 11697
find it in very few people 10428
God desires but s. 7450
is openness of heart 10428
key to success 10799
repair by s. damage done by faults 3956

SINFUL
among the s. is where Jesus went 2812
because not eaten of Tree of Life 10416
holy clumsiness better than s. eloquence 9121
Lamenting sore his s. life 7743
lives with tragedy not necessarily more s. 2857
not because eaten of Tree of Knowledge 10416
People no longer s. 10350
Religion what s. man tries to do for holy God 9545
Repentance process by which we see ourselves as s. people 9594
sometimes s. not to be angry 401
who flatter own virtue by criticizing s. 5029

SINFULNESS
At beginning God accepts us in all our s. 9832
death raises from s. into holiness 2250
evident when contrasted with holiness of God 10440
from s. to new life long, arduous 1897
God not content to have us remain in s. 9832
makes saints aware of s. 4660
such is my sense of s. 6459

SING
Alas for those who never s. 8647
angels don't s. to sheep 6147
at work like bird in wood 3084
bird doesn't s. because has answer 7883
children s. to keep up courage 476
Could not hear the angels s. 2217
devil doesn't know how to s. 2676
friend will joyfully s. with you 4175
God loves me when I s. 12008
gospel makes man s. for joy 5091
hymns, choruses for God's ears alone 8424
in bathroom while brushing teeth 8168
invisible kingdom that causes saint to s. through sorrow 5775
join hands and s, Free at last 4157
O for a thousand tongues to s. 8732
shall never s, "Gloria in excelsis" 9020

Those who wish to s. always find a song 5264
training thee for part angels cannot s. 10600
Wake, and gladly s. thy part 8671
What else can I do, but s. hymns to God 8745
while we s, he smiles his last 8078
Yet straws can s. 6149

SINGETH
bird of dawning s. night long 1371

SINGING
advantage of congregational s. 1415
go s. as far as we go 7899
groups so concerned about being inoffensive 5109
How can I keep from s. 232
If never heard mountains s. 8017
Praise is more than s. 8734
test of sanctification not s. pious hymns 9845
Worship isn't s. hymns 12139

SINGLE
arrow easily broken 9442
as love with s. thread 7279
Celibacy: S. blessedness 10222
conversation with wise worth month's study of books 11898
courageous step would carry through fear 3982
event can awaken within a stranger unknown to us 6873
excellence one s. pursuit 3470
friend, s. soul in two bodies 4211
God asks nothing but s. mind 7450
God has no parts, s. in unitary being 4610
I am a s. drop, how can it be 7469
journey of a thousand miles begins with s. step 6871
little praise for sexually controlled s. 10236
many great things expressed in s. words 10277
may die in hour of s. unwise word 4237
music though true in only a s. instance 7905
need eye s. to God's glory 5442
Not for a s. day 5434
sorrows come not s. spies 10646
tear suffices with God 4091
word can turn you on, off 12001
Yet with itself every soul standeth s. 7150

SINGLEHEARTEDLY
devoting yourself s. to God 10703

SINGLE-MINDED
only with s. attention to Christ 10551

SINGLENESS
Chastity a requisite of Christian s. 10236

SINGS
Anyone who s. blues has broken spirit 7888
bird s. because he has a song 7883
every angel as he s. 463
Faith is bird that s. when dawn still dark 3695
From his sweet silence my mouth s. 4125
Give us the man who s. at his work 3090
I have a place where my spirit s. 8429
Love suffers as the voice s. 7953
On a frail branch when he s. 11475
own praise usually off key 9206
praises through tears 10628
Remember the teakettle s. 205
who s. frightens away ills 7894

SINISTER
doubts lurk in the shadow 3649
Some s. intent taints all he does 4164

SINK
cannot s. someone else's end of boat 10480
God wants us to soar, not s. 1608
in life's alarms 10973
lighten up or you will s. 12092
Men and nations s. or soar 10510
small leak will s. great ship 5116
Two captains in one boat make it s. 6808
Who swims in sin shall s. in sorrow 10426
Would s. forever thro' the vast profound 4708

SINKING
all things everywhere are s. 9909
pyramids s. in desert sands 730

SINNED
In Adam's fall, we s. all 10323
out of deliberate rebellion 10387
repentance is grieved because s. against God 9580

SINNER
Better be s. than hypocrite 6049
closer to God, more one feels a s. 10439
conscience haunts the s. 1698
Don't condemn the s. 10432
each individual either a s. or a saint 5038
Every saint has a past, every s. a future 8653
God is with the s. wherever he can be 10434
God treats s. as if good man 6634
God's justice stands forever against s. 4726
I am a great s. 9797
impossible to be both s. and saint 5038
insight of saint stem from experiences as s. 9776

more hope for self-convicted s.
5948
one sin will destroy a s. 10344
Silence, O s. stop 763
sins don't make me a s. 10437

SINNERS
are having good time 3338
best of men still s. 3861
Christians envy s. their pleasure
3224
church, hospital for s. 1379
devil does not tempt s. 2675
don't have to be supersaints, just
thirsty s. 1344
dull s, sleep no more 9692
Forebear to judge for we are s. all
6577
God makes saints out of s. 9773
God's love for s. wonderful 4893
Great saints have often been great
s. 9775
hearts of s. improved by breaking
898
Jesus always consorting with s.
5791
Kindness has converted more s.
6648
not happy unless bigger s. to point
to 10442
not s. because we sin 10441
plan whereby s. can go to heaven
5632
preach as if conscious they were
dying s. 3338
righteous who believe themselves
s. 10404
Than all the songs of s. are 9787
Under the first s. ever trust 4812
we sin because we are s. 10441
who believe themselves righteous
10404
who punishes to get even with s.
9354

SINNING
fear of s. killed spontaneity 6813
is nothing but turning from God's
face 10382
too Christian to enjoy s. 10417
too fond of s. to enjoy Christianity
10417

SINS
against himself everybody s.
10325
against this life who slights the
next 6093
All the seven deadly s.
self-destroying 10296
as much who holds the bag 2035
assume God unable to work in
our s. 3613
attempts to fill voids 10295
blessings for man sad for his own
s. 5299
Christ a sacrifice, satisfying our s.
6410
Commit a major sin, all lesser s.
follow 10301

confesses not own s, but s. of
neighbors 5160
confesses s, no longer alone 1594
could produce same effect by
saying, s. be forgiven 5485
deeper than list of s. on
membership card 10300
does not matter how small s. are
10324
don't make me a sinner 10437
easier to repent of s. committed
than s. intend to commit 10327
evidence a sinner 10437
Faith is refusing to feel guilty over
confessed s. 3672
God blots out his people's s, not
their names 4626
God does not regard past s. 10311
God uses our s. to remind us of
weakness 10306
Holy Spirit, power to forgive s.
11426
how horrible s. look committed
by someone else 10343
immense appear s. we have not
committed 10316
In solitude become broken by our
s. 10540
innocent only because we did not
succeed 10384
like circles in water 10383
must pay for, one by one 73
no fault of Christianity that
hypocrite s. 1208
no longer horrified by s. of a
brother 10297
not constant thought of s. 4660
not punished for our s, but by
them 9356
of bedroom not only ones 10399
of boardroom as much concern
10399
of flesh least bad of all s. 10400
of youth paid for in old age 10401
Other men's s. before our eyes
10348
our own behind our backs 10348
our s. rise up to slay us 10423
Pride the ground in which all
other s. grow 9230
Pride the parent from which all
other s. come 9230
Repentance more than remorse for
s. 9597
Satan wastes no ammunitions on
those dead in s. 9860
says some s. are just 11506
Should we all confess s. to one
another 10353
sin is two s. when defended 10289
Some s. we have committed 10384
Some we have contemplated
10384
Some we have desired 10384
Some we have encouraged 10384
We confess our s. 9087
When all s. are old in us 10092
ye do by two and two 73

SIOUX INDIAN
prayer 9065

SIP
reluctantly at truth we find harsh
6870

SIR
A man, s. must keep friendships
4249

SISSY
nothing s. about following Christ
1282

SIT
alone with conscience judgment
enough 1707
Among those who s, do not stand
3064
Among those who stand, do not s.
3064
Attir'd with stars, we shall forever
s. 5679
can s. on a mountain but not a
tack 9636
do not just s. down in an armchair
3830
down quietly, happiness may
alight upon you 5518
every night s. staring at another
box 5859
I s. beside my lonely fire 8827
If you s. down at set of sun 107
in radius of friends who listen
1857
Love doesn't just s. there 7217
May s. i' the center 1683
Only to s. and think of God 4799
1763
rest s. around it 1710
ride a man, s. easy and light 9471
still and trust the engineer 5461
Teach us to s. still 4979
to s. alone with my conscience
1663
troubles come because we refuse
to s. quietly 9367
two ends, one to s. on 10793
where men s. and hear each other
groan 7044

SITS
But beside me s. another 6398
demon even if s. in church
praising Creator 9631
God s. with you in snowbank
4782
man who idly s. and thinks 11244
there s. a judge no king can
corrupt 4716

SITTING
cannot get to top by s. on bottom
6783
on a tack is often useful 88
trouble is people always s. on them
7049

SITUATION
change s. or yourself 2753
Confidence what you have before
you understand s. 8361

God can create something good 219

God's mercy available in present s. 4815

if choose to remain in s. where tempted 8818

Live to the hilt every s. 3186

may not change 8957

new moralists think love tailored to meet s. 7837

no s. so chaotic 219

no s. too much for God 168

oblivious to requirement òf s. 3510

Patience, accepting difficult s. 8415

plan that would anticipate every s. 5438

Prayer does not deliver from s. 8927

Prayer enables man to master s. 8927

press of the external s. 6785

Revival, God intervenes to lift s. out of human hands 9746

when you say a s. hopeless 5955

SITUATION ETHICS
puts people at center of concern, not things 6820

SITUATIONIST
is a who seeker 6820

SITUATIONISTS
are personalistic 6820

SITUATIONS
do color life 522

Faith proves herself in ordinary s. 3715

God puts us in s. that are too much 168

no hopeless s. 5953

opportunities disguised as impossible s. 8228

react to s. as Christ did 6301

true, appropriate in all s. 957

Try to use ordinary s. 5058

use ordinary s. to do good 623

SIX
essential qualities key to success 10799

I keep s. honest serving men 6686

mistakes of man 7793

really s. people present 7443

things requisite to create happy home 5848

SIXTEEN
if s. hours daily thinking about world 7491

SIXTY
Died at thirty, buried at s. 7041

years ago I knew everything 3024

SIZABLE
most handle sudden demotion better than s. promotion 9221

SIZE
cannot speak of s. and God 4680

fish lies about s. of man 3426

Greatness not a matter of s. 5283

SKELETON
no forgotten s. can come tumbling out 4884

SKEPTIC
godly response kicks crutches from s. 10938

SKEPTICAL
about capacity to express existence 3488

No person more s. of resurrection than apostles 9693

SKEPTICISM
first step toward truth 2952

has not changed world's heart 5723

has not established principles 5723

has not founded empires 5723

prepares way for faith 2953

SKETCH
Not, what did the s. in the newspaper say 7423

SKIES
angels, up and down the s. 358

but though I scanned the s. 4921

he is curtailed who overflowed all s, all years 6120

I soar and rise up to the s. 7475

Lo, earth receives him from the bending s. 6138

seem grey, threatening 9059

turn our eyes to where s. are full of promise 9059

SKILL
acquire s. to do difficult things easily 8406

Few things impossible to diligence, s. 8538

Give to thy servants s. to soothe, bless 9045

He that wrestles with us sharpens our s. 1623

more s, design than works of man 1964

of science not able to make oyster 1979

Prayer not a shortcut to s. 8924

'Tis God gives s. 4441

When love, s. work together 12020

SKILLED
devil well s. in debate 2651

SKILLFUL
direct opinion 8205

SKILLS
social s. not test of father's leadership 3925

SKIN
Character gives awe to wrinkled s. 997

finest clothing made is person's own s. 7427

He stretched s. over spirit 6131

Hope has thick s. 5912

Jesus is God with s. on 6446

sort of creeping comes over s. 2637

thick s. gift from God 2625

vice now stuck to my s. 10320

SKINS
inside our own s, for life 7148

SKUNK
causing a stampede 781

No one likes s. 1588

only creature they would segregate is s. 5963

potential hero in every man—and potential s. 8670

SKY
Aloft on s. and mountain wall 8047

And by greed and pride the s. is torn 6155

And fit it for the s. 10114

At the heart of the cyclone tearing the s. 8429

chanting, s. is falling 4226

danced on a Friday when s. turned black 9690

E'en when my s. is darkest 4490

early Christians looking for cleavage in s. called Glory 9913

Every s. has its beauty 8005

From the four corners of the s. 6598

God like s. to small bird 4544

God, the s. his presence snares 4505

have not a God off in s. 7557

I'm glad the s. is painted blue 8016

If s. falls, hold up your hands 8834

life flew like skylark in s. 12176

long ere light flashed through s. 4769

music shall untune the s. 7925

No s. is heavy if heart be light 6553

not less blue because blind man does not see it 9409

Reach forth and write upon the s. 8015

soul can split the s. in two 10670

Stars daisies that begem blue fields of s. 11638

Stars flowers of the s. 11640

still streaked with smoke of crematoria 3416

Though stretch'd from s. to s. 4748

though the s. stays dim 4195

Thy arm directs those lightnings through the s. 4827

Til earth, s. stand presently 915

What idea of God without the s. 4512

You'll get pie in s. when you die 5682

SKYLARK
life flew like s. in sky 12176

SKYLIGHT
Coffin, room without s. 2236

SKYROCKET
Christ's death made our value s. 9989

SLACKENS
When God s., s. at once 5460

SLACKERS
God not fond of s. 1193

SLAMMING
door in face of God 5955

SLANDER
abominable tittle-tattle 10470
answered best with silence 10464
at every word a reputation dies 10468
cud eschewed by human cattle 10470
Don't worry about rumor, s. 6271
edge sharper than sword 10467
flies as well as creeps 10456
flings stones at itself 10461
guilty of s. never can repair 10453
If nobody took s. in and gave lodging 10455
If s. be a snake, is a winged one 10456
is a kind of murder 10462
like counterfeit money 10465
no s. can alter man's character 1060
Satan uses problems to s. God's character 9859
slays three persons 10466
vice that strikes double blow 10463
would starve and die 10455
wounding him that commits, him against whom committed 10463

SLANDERED
God lets himself be s. 4891

SLANDERER
most dangerous of wild beasts, a s. 10472

SLANDERERS
devil's bellows to blow up contention 10469

SLANDEROUS
idly repeat s. darts 5143

SLANDERS
not long-lived 10448

SLAP
church founded as s. to other church 7867

SLAVE
As I would not be s. I would not be master 2520
die a s. to wealth 10777
does only what is required, a s. 3096

evangelicals who abolished s. trade 5656
faith is not the s. 3813
Forever lives a s. to others 6872
Gold s. or master 11815
he that is evil a s. though king 4131
He that is good is free though a s. 4131
is a s. to his surroundings 7033
man is s. of everything, everybody 7375
must be either master or s. 7096
No man free who is s. to flesh 4138
of greatest s. who serves himself 10055
utter word, you are s. 1835
who dares not reason is a s. 9415
wise man, though s, at liberty 4113

SLAVERY
a step from companionship to s. 10326
few years ago ten hours a day called s. 3083
great fortune a great s. 11794
living in land of s. 4969
men speak of yoke of Christ as s. 2816
Mental s. is mental death 7760
though a fool rule, is in s. 4113
Worldliness mental s. to illegitimate pleasure 12054

SLAVES
All wicked men are s. 11881
devil seeks s, claims obedience 4912
to gadgets, power, security 9016
to the spirit of this world 3018
where apathy is master, all men s. 427
who are unhappy from lack of money 8681

SLAY
For one that big misfortunes s. 12061
our sins rise up to s. us 10423

SLAYS
Envy s. itself by own arrows 3215
Love s. what we have been 7272
Pride s. thanksgiving 5258
Slander s. three persons 10466

SLEEP
and I shall feed you 3094
cannot silence conscience 2970
carry care to bed, s. with pack on back 12080
Childhood when nightmares occur only during s. 1106
commit life to God for hours of s. 10486
Contemplation like s. in arms of God 1756
dare not trust it without my prayers 10492
Death as necessary as s. 2244

death called s. 2372
death, you are tired, lie down, s. 2285
dull sinners, s. no more 9692
faith has no bed to s. upon 3760
furtherance of spiritual life during s. 10487
Givers s. well 10198
go to s. in peace 11489
God's celestial nurse 10486
good conscience can s. in mouth of cannon 1653
Habits servants that regulate your s. 5498
He gives his beloved s. 8120
He giveth his beloved s. 2345
heart oft times wakes when we s. 2969
Heaven not where men s. out eternity 5644
How wonderful is Death and his brother S. 2298
I helped murder, I can't s. 22
If only could s. away winter time 9903
impossible to put to s. with sermon 10096
In s. pain that cannot forget falls drop by drop 11919
is so like death 10492
like men who s. badly 5541
Man's sorrows will not let me s. 1548
my child, peace attend thee 1123
Nature's soft nurse 10485
No s. tranquil unless mind at rest 8449
not hypocrites in our s. 6066
not meant only for recuperation of body 10487
O s, gentle s. 10485
on, beloved, s. take thy rest 2365
One short s. past 2356
Peace is to be able to s. in the storm 8470
Plough deep while sluggards s. 3115
Praying gives peaceful s. at night 8899
profound developments in spirit, soul, body 10486
recreates 10487
Satan rocks cradle when s. at devotions 2663
silence to spirit what s. is to body 9374
spirits stirred by Holy Spirit go forward even in s. 10490
takes more than soft pillow to insure sound s. 10482
Thank God for s. 10489
that we may s. in peace 9668
Tired nature's sweet restorer, balmy s. 10491
To be enjoyed, s. must be interrupted 443
truth happens not infrequently in morning s. 7949

vanishes before house of care 10488

well-spent day brings happy s. 2224

When people s. in church, preacher should wake up 9171

when we wake, and when we s. 362

when you cannot s. 10489

Where care lodges, s. will never lie 12082

with clean hands 9600

world is drowned in s. 1514

worry that gets you, not loss of s. 10483

you'll s. better that night 10100

SLEEPER
religious awakening that does not awaken s. to love 9737

SLEEPING
clover leaves s. in attitude of worship 8000

I surpass you in s. 6190

messiahs aren't found s. in feed trough 6147

pill will never take place of clear conscience 1661

SLEEPLESS
poems, repeat for comfort in s. nights 9381

worry gives s. hours 12091

SLEEPS
at God's feet 4847

devil never s. 9861

quiet conscience s. in thunder 1659

SLEEPY
acquiescence of indolence 4507

too s. to worry at night 12062

SLEEVES
people expect him to roll up his s. 6290

SLEPT
and dreamed life was joy 9663

God's finger touched him, he s. 2289

He s. beneath the moon 6756

they, while their companions s. 8566

SLIGHTS
Love s. death 2363

sins against this life who s. the next 6093

SLIP
death, s. out without fuss 2421

useless away 2198

SLIPPER
than s. on gouty foot 8442

SLIPPERY
things that hold in s. world 4643

words are s. 11990

SLIPS
If you your lips would keep from s. 1855

---

just s. upon snow unjust doesn't clear away 9905

through death's mesh 9805

SLOGANEER
devil is a demogogue and s. 6176

SLOGANS
not s. carried on thrust of power 6176

SLOP PAIL
woman with s. gives God glory 1237

SLOPE
We would not linger on the lower s. 5939

SLOW
Be s. to promise, quick to perform 2531

come he s. or come he fast 2218

Confidence plant of s. growth 1606

do not be s. only, but silent, very silent for he is God 5460

down, parents 8353

essential that we s. down at times 7714

God's mill grinds s. but sure 6607

I'm a s. walker 82

in coming to be like Christ 8113

in making promise most likely faithful in performance 9325

making of music often s, painful process 7056

march of providence is so s. 5944

march of the human mind is s. 11245

me down, Lord 5587 9111

redirecting our lives often s. 5449

resolve to s. your pace 5615

Till our steps grow s. 8120

Time too s. for those who wait 11333

True friendship is plant of s. growth 4218

While prayers to heal her wrongs move s. behind 6269

Winter ideal occasion to s. down 9906

SLOWING
For fast-acting relief, try s. down 6832

SLOWLY
Be not afraid of growing s. 5365

Character builds s. 996

Go s. to entertainment of thy friends 4242

Hasten s. 5578

Laziness travels so s. poverty soon overtakes him 6768

Let thy soul walk s. in thee 10256

Lord's Prayer s. learnt by heart 7153

Make haste s. 5582

money thou comest in so s. 4039

Old age lives minutes s, hours quickly 12193

---

pulled down into quicksand of smugness 3168

To live is to be s. born 6873

To live long, necessary to live s. 7067

When God comes go with him s. 5460

Wisdom like dawn that comes up s. 11969

SLUGGARDS
Plough deep while s. sleep 3115

SLUGGISH
Wake for shame, my s. heart 8671

SLUMBER
Hill, dale in s. steeping 1123

lie still and s. 361

SLUMS
preaches from villas to s. about mansions in heaven 6065

SLURRED
rests not to be s. over 9684

SMALL
All things both great and s. 7174 8807

Among God's blessings there is no one s. 1821

And very s. beginnings 7119

Are levell'd. Death confounds 'em all 2384

big print giveth, s. print taketh away 9328

can do s. things in great way 10155

can't cross chasm in two s. jumps 3650

chance of truth at goal 11549

do s. things in right spirit 9679

does not matter how s. sins are 10324

Don't think so big, others look s. 1587

drops of water hollow out a stone 8556

For every great temptation many s. ones 11056

genuinely great who considers himself s. 5285

gift given, though s, great if given with affection 4352

God a leveler who renders equal s. and great 4727

God never put anyone in place too s. to grow 4987

God not less great in s. things 4940

God, voice too s. to be easily audible 4465

Great and s. suffer same mishaps 173

great events touched off by s. agencies 5720

Great pains cause us to forget s. ones 2724

grief, strong to consume s. troubles 5331

heart that finds joy in s. things 6524

Home where great are s. and s.
are great 5829

however s. visible measure of our
lives 6232

If Christianity s. enough for
understanding 1202

if happy in s. ways 8139

If wife s, stoop down and whisper
in ear 7620

In anything s. never give in 8548

in s. matters men show themselves
as they are 7391

In things great or s. 5456

is great man who makes man feel
s. 5304

Is your place a s. place 3847

just so s. as I 6456

leak will sink great ship 5116

Life lost in thousand, s. uncaring
ways 6972

live for himself, s. troubles shall
seem great 11433

live for others, great troubles shall
seen s. 11433

men never feel s. 7380

minds talk about people 1845

miracles of Jesus s. that we might
take them in 6479

moment carrier of God's gift
11319

most use s. portion of
consciousness 8659

my boat is so s, your ocean so big
9110

My knowledge of that life is s.
5635

My soul is too s. to accommodate
you 9089

no distinction between s. and great
567

no foes, s. is the work you have
done 3174

No sin is s. 10341

Nothing hard if divide into s. jobs
3110

Nothing s. if God is in it 10800

numbers make no difference to
God 10800

O how s. a portion of earth will
hold us 2344

one s. word "to be" 3492

people more easily fall victims to a
great lie than to s. one 7974

Popularity glory's s. change 3859

religion s. enough for our
understanding 9538

smile as s. as mine might be 10501

something s. in a big way 58

through the years using only a s.
part of himself 8661

To God no great, no s. 4709

troubles must seem so s. to God
4789

whose power extends to great and
s. 11628

Whosoever would be great is s.
5309

will show how s. greatness is 6037

world too s. for anything but
brotherhood 11545

Worry gives a s. thing a big
shadow 12085

would not think duty s. if you
were great 9682

Your God is too s. 7580

your hands which are too s. 6931

SMALLER

Discussion makes things grow s.
10242

not to stoop until s. than yourself
6037

who hides behind hypocrite is s,
than hypocrite 6046

SMALLEST

atom s, split becomes biggest 8648

deed better than grandest intention
2505

perseverance may be employed by
s. of us 8557

revenge will poison soul 9728

seed of faith better 3795

SMALL-FOLDED

in a warm dim female space 6142

SMALLNESS

who realizes his s. becomes
spiritually great 5309

SMART

God s. when he made man 7379

person isn't s. until he knows how
to get along with fools 6323

SMARTING

Music eases grief's s. wound 7913

SMASH

God has no easy time of it to s.
self-sufficiency 10043

SMELL

Do not eat garlic, s. garlic 1006

Fish, visitors s. in three days 5956

flower of sweetest s. is shy, lowly
6028

flowers while still s. fragrance
3137

Lilies that fester s. worse than
weeds 5039

stop and s. the flowers 9530

SMELLETH

so sour as shame 5492

SMELLS

cynic s. flowers, looks for coffin
2177

existence s. of nothing 3485

SMILE

a curve to set things straight
10495

as small as mine might be 10501

at least put a s. on your face 9999

Be able to s. at anything 6961

Christmas when you s. 1366

costs nothing but creates much
10494

Don't fence it in 5504

Each s. a hymn 7284

first 9479

friend, a s. when you're sad 4174

Give him the s. he lacks 378

God must s. in great pity 7944

happiness of life made up of a s.
5556

if you s. life returns greeting 6949

In solitude we will have to s.
10540

Man alone can s. and laugh 6737

Man worthwhile is the one who
will s. 10493

meet man who has no s, give him
yours 10496

men I have seen succeed went
about business with a s. 10816

Nobody needs s. as much as those
who have none to give 10498

Nurture love with a s. and a
prayer 7289

of God is victory 11671

One may s. and s. and be a villain
6059

people s. in same language 548

please as much by sorrow as by s.
10587

rather than frown 1138

reaches out, attracts 5504

Some churches train their ushers
to s. 6062

thousand languages, s. speaks
them all 10499

To bring a s, to banish a tear 7423

upon the finished task to s. 47

Wear a s, have friends 10502

with s. of God needs no status
symbols 1323

SMILES

announce goodness, sweetness
10500

are to humanity 6745

betray sarcasm, bitterness, pride
10500

brighten by spiritual vivacity
10500

each having distinct character
10500

evening beam s. clouds away 618

for the sometime guest 3900

God grant they read the good
with s. 7017

If s. or tears be there 2206

Life must be composed by sobs,
sniffles, s. 6969

Many kinds of s. 10500

masks torn away, hollow s. fade
9741

Most s. started by another smile
10497

publications full of prescribed s.
3400

soften countenance by tenderness
10500

The forest s. 9897

this same flower that s. today
8214

while we sing, he s. his last 8078

win, preserve the heart 6656

Wrinkles should indicate where s. have been 8188

SMILING
like villain with s. cheek 5011
Of rainbows s. down at me 8009
Sun of God is s. 5810
when greeted by man s. because trained 6062

SMITES
nothing so sharp, nor smelleth so sour 5492

SMOKE
Gossip s. that comes from dirty tobacco pipes 5132
hide de fier, what do wid s. 2482
melts away like s, gone forever 11288
should not complain of s. 11120
sin covers mirror with s. 10339
sky still steaked with s. of crematoria 3416
Where there's s. there's fire 11118

SMOKE SCREEN
cloud motives with s. of excuses 3476

SMOKER
Gossip proves nothing but bad taste of s. 5132

SMOKESCREENS
fogging up our minds with s. 2660

SMOOTH
Be thou a s. path below me 5375
course of true anything never runs s. 2747
experiencing s. sailing, brace yourself 969
God doesn't always s. the path 4808
green grasses more common still 10634
I do not ask to walk s. paths 1927
Kind words s, quiet, comfort 11985

SMOOTHLY
naive helps one go through life s. 7976

SMOTHER
jealousy extinguishes love as ashes s. flame 6347

SMOULDERING
legions of Rome s. 730

SMUGNESS
quicksand of s. and self-satisfaction 3168

SMUT
crucified where cynics talk s. 2131

SNAIL
By perseverance the s. reached the ark 8535

SNAIL'S
progress toward God 8630

SNAKE
Bad conscience is s. in heart 1651

If slander be a s. is a winged one 10456
invited Eve to take a seat 4419
pulled back the curtain to the throne room 4419
stood up for evil 3403
When s. is dead, venom dead 3419

SNAKES
brazen serpent reared where s. bite 11432

SNAP
hearts that shut against them with a s. 8694
To s. like vixens at the truth 5048
wire will never s. 6521

SNARE
Better shun bait than struggle in s. 11049
devil's s. does not catch unless 2696
of experiences 3544

SNARES
delights are s. 4877
God, the sky his presence s. 4505

SNARLED
When life s. up 2802

SNATCH
seize, enjoy every moment 11372

SNEAKS
coward s. to death 10948

SNEER
Never help out a s. 2185

SNIFFLES
Life is made up of sobs, s, smiles 6969
Life, s. predominating 6969

SNOB
has litle time to meddle with you 455
spends so much time being a s. 455
word belongs to sourgrape vocabulary 457

SNOBBERY
Intellectual s. enemy tactic 1190

SNOBS
I like s. 455

SNOW
falls alike upon just, unjust 9905
In every s, the promised May 8009
In spring no one thinks of s. 1470
is beautiful when watching other fellow shovel 9904
is exhilarating 8033
just slips upon s. unjust doesn't clear away 9905
whiter white than s. 1368

SNOWBANK
God sits with you in s. 4782

SNOWFLAKE
No s. ever falls in wrong place 8028

SNOWSHOVEL
time to put away s. 9888

SNOWY
flowy, blowy 9876

SNUB
guilty of inhumanity when we s. or abuse 901
immortals whom we s. 8483

SNUFF
blowing s. in the face of heaven 9576

SNUG
Jesus, digging mankind out of s. burrows 6421

SOAK
and s. and s. continually in one great truth 11528
in philosophy, psychology 11196

SOAP
for the body, tears for the soul 10644
frank talk good s. for hearts 5864

SOAR
God wants us to s, not sink 1608
I s. and rise 7475
If upward you can s. 460
Men and nations sink or s. 10510
on wings of mysticism can spirit s. to full height 7963
stop expecting squirrel saints to s. 6187
to endless day 6923
towers fall with heavier crash which higher s. 9216
What tho' we wade in wealth or s. in fame 7088
Wisdom oftentimes nearer when stoop than s. 6044

SOARED
not who s. to heights of achievement 6175

SOARING
far above all human thought 7970

SOBBING
leapt from my throat like s. 10021

SOBER
like saying my mother, drunk or s. 7980
Love is s. 7246

SOBERLY
Poverty makes people s. satirical 8690

SOBS
know immortal lines that are nothing but s. 8621
Life is made up of s, sniffles, smiles 6969
music of the spheres is made of sighs, s. 10878

SOCIABLE
to many 550

SOCIAL
believer's cross price of s. nonconformity 2103

Christ's life so s. called a winebibber 6436

Christian life s. life 916

claims to equality intensify inequality 3242

compulsions of an unredeemed world 10003

differences have lost power to divide 6286

dimension of sin is injustice 10394

Education a s. process 3001

face-to-face model of s. relations 6451

fear gives s. life stability 3980

Gossip, s. sewage 5136

higher we go in s. life, more bondage 4159

human being more complex than s. system 10505

independent of s. judgment 1647

Love has a s. interest 7274

nation of s. cowards 1642

purely s. gospel like body without soul 5088

resist temptation to chase after s. entanglements 5615

revivals altered s. attitudes of millions 9752

shall only resist s. injustice if justice prevail 6286

skills not test of father's leadership 3925

statistician sees city as s. unit 10522

substituted s. control for family worship 5808

superficial s. camaraderie 3337

When s. action mistaken for evangelism 3341

SOCIAL GOSPEL
needs theology to make effective 5104

theology needs s. to vitalize it 5104

SOCIALLY
I don't look down upon the s. elect 3228

intellectuals remain s. powerless 6323

SOCIETAL
problems solved one person at a time 3901

SOCIETIES
Is church ready to found welfare s. 10086

Without faith people drift into hate s. 925

SOCIETY
acceptance of right to happiness tells a lot about s. 5553

Affluent s. euphemism for selfishness 10051

an inordinate emphasis on feeling good 4017

authority for humanizing s. 10506

become disciples, impact on s. staggering 2819

build s. of love out of puppets 4133

can easily get entangled 10514

can easily lose our soul 10514

character determines how child fits into s. 8346

Christ did not cut himself off from s. 6436

Christ dined with lowest members of s. 6433

Christ, message set s. ablaze 6375

Christians preserve s. from corruption 1252

church in conflict with values of s. 1385

church is to make s. uncomfortable 1427

dangerous network of domination, manipulation 10514

Democracy attempt to apply Bible principles to s. 2523

devastating s. by every mischief ingenuity can invent 4895

eccentricity in s. proportional to genius 1007

family, essential cell of s. 3890

family, state, church 10506

filled with racial discrimination 161

foundation of s, government rests on Bible 5189

genius often dull, inert in s. 4395

gentleness is love in s. 7202

God has ordained three institutions for s. 10506

human politics, s. must be changed to change people 10528

In this chatty s. 10253

Jesus was poorly adjusted to s. 6196

Many people happy but worthless to s. 5539

needs changing 1333

No revolution in s. can be compared 5721

no suicide for which s. not responsible 10947

not community radiant with love of Christ 10514

parasites on the body of s. 130

passing fads of s. 10707

politer name of hell 1135

Politics gizzard of s, full of gut, gravel 5185

politics of the Kingdom, people must be changed to change s. 10528

recreated Jesus in our own cultural image 6467

renovated by Christianity 1187

ruinous consequences to s. 10503

Solitude often the best s. 10557

Some people strengthen s. 1040

the horror of abortion 18

two sections to s. 10523

Violence destroys fabric of s. 11678

When Athenians wanted s. to give to them 4155

when repressions of s. and business are gone 6842

where was the church 18

will one day look back 18

will pay any price to prolong life 2232

Without faith, s. of indifferent 925

Worldliness accepting values of man-centered s. 12053

SOCIETY'S
family establishes s. basic values 3888

virtues of character vital to s. survival 3880

SOCIOLOGY
All our s. penetrated hardly an inch 9353

reflects our theology 9487

SOCKS
Real friends don't care if s. don't match 4264

SOCRATES
I borrowed ideas from S. 2019

SOD
angels of God upturned the s. 778

eloquent the green listening s. 8014

SODOM
they pitch tent toward S. 11080

When you from S. flee 9828

SODOM'S
when God foretells S. ruin 11432

SOFT
can be bag of grapes, s. 9524

drowsy hours creeping 1123

is the music that would charm forever 6028

Luxury makes a man so s. hard to please him 7363

On the s. bed of luxury most kingdoms have died 7364

think of gentleness as being s. 4402

Under a shepherd s. and negligent 8363

voice of intelligence s. and weak 6331

SOFTEN
down the rugged road of life 7917

has done more to s. mankind 6483

If you bottle grief up, you'll never s. it 5343

Kind words s. angry hearts of men 6645

Love will s, purify the heart 7241

Music can s. pain 7911

no grief which time does not lessen, s. 5358

To s. rocks or bend knotted oak
7901

SOFTENED
you s. my bitterness 7579

SOFTENS
Music s. every pain 7900

SOFTER
only advancing in life whose heart
is getting s. 6898

SOFTLY
How s. runs the afternoon 9887
praise loudly, blame s. 8729

SOFTNESS
hardness of God kinder than s. of
man 4498
nothing harder than s. of
indifference 6165

SOIL
Error flourishes in every s. 3251
fertility in the s. 8002
humble mind is s. of which thanks
grows 5258
into the s. of life's enduring values
9111
The s. where first they trod 4114
to paint the laughing s. 9895

SOILS
when hearts are purest, devil s.
2649

SOJOURN
in every place as if spend life there
9491

SOLACE
gospel like s. in anguish of
conscience 5097

SOLAR SYSTEMS
rise and wane 4694

SOLD
Ahab s. himself for a vineyard
11798
air not s. by cubic foot 3838
except to be bought and s. 3045
man s. God for thirty pence 4532

SOLDIER
best s. is not warlike 11784
Well spoke that s. 9022

SOLDIERS
believe Bible more powerful than
weapons 726
Best s. are not warlike 4404
best s. out of affliction 295
carry Bible into battle 726
crucified where s. gamble 2131

SOLEMN
Lord's Prayer for succession of s.
thought 7154
no grace in s. countenance 1090
reached me like a s. joy 4758

SOLEMNIZE
Run, shepherds, run, s. his birth
6140

SOLEMNLY
meet affliction s. 296

SOLICITING
With gentle force s. the darts 9798

SOLICITUDE
angels exercise a constant s. 363
hope saves from s. 3834

SOLID
high structures require s.
foundation 5991
opening mind to shut it on
something s. 7761
seldom s. home in absence of
religious inspiration 5858
we find security in iron bars, s.
walls 6825

SOLITARY
all sentenced to s. confinement
7148
Great men stand like s. towers
5280
holy life not s. life 5736
Jesus was a s. man 6508
New Testament does not envisage
s. religion 1445
one s. life 6353
Only s. men know full joys of
friendship 4261
original, unborrowed, s. greatness
of Bible 736
pain, a s. experience 8260
to a s. friends are everything 4261
True friends no s. joy, sorrow
4291

SOLITUDE
a fount of healing 10556
a state of mind, heart 10548
bearable only with God 10555
cannot remain creative without s.
10579
Christian life not meant or suited
for s. 916
deadly thought of s. 10569
Discover art of s. 10553
easy in s. to live after own
opinions 6195
emerging will never walk alone
10567
fellowship without s. void of
words, feelings 10547
flee into the silence of s. 2591
frightful is s. of soul without God
10573
furnace of transformation 10558
glory of being alone 7131
God to man doth speak in s.
10534
hath no flatterers 10530
How gracious, how benign is s.
10578
If possess inward s. 10539
improves our character 10560
in his s. perhaps shedding hot tears
6599
In lonely s. God delivers his best
thoughts 10544

in midst of crowd keeps
independence of s. 6195
In poverty of s. all riches present
10542
In s. can become contrite,
crushed, broken 10540
In s. discover life a gift to be
shared 10545
In s. discover life not a possession
to be defended 10545
In s. discover we are worth more
than results of our efforts
10545
In s. grow so wide, deep nothing
human is strange 10540
In s. heart can take off protective
devices 10540
In s. we discover being more
important than having 10545
In s. we will have to smile 10540
In s. when we are least alone
10541
into a s. we did not desire 10564
is inner fulfillment 10548
is the school of genius 10533
Jesus driven to a life of s. 6358
like light, mightiest of agencies
10563
Loneliness conquered only by
those who can bear s. 7133
makes life worth living 10556
makes us tender toward others
10560
makes us tougher toward ourselves
10560
misfortune to be incapable of s.
10570
molds into caring persons 10561
more natural to approach God in
s. 1445
more powerful a mind, more it
will incline toward s. 10566
never found companion so
companionable as s. 10537
O s, where are the charms 10550
often the best society 10557
Old age is dreary s. 8152
Poetry has endeared s. 8616
prayer gives s. real meaning 10562
question of truth asked only in s.
10564
seek s, look within ourselves 4924
should teach us how to die 10530
shows way to let behavior be
shaped 10562
silent as light 10563
soul enriched by communion with
God will welcome s. 10567
soul's best friend 10559
Talent nurtured in s. 1042
task in s. to keep mind on Savior
10551
unseen companionship 10567
vital to success 10820
without fellowship abyss of
despair 10547

SOLITUDES
long ere echoes waked the s. 4769

SOLO
God did not write s. parts 10135
Life like playing violin s. 6967
Many a s. sung to show off 7867

SOLOMON
depended more on props around
him 794
famous for his wisdom 795
knew how little he knew 795
pastor needs wisdom of S. 9125
perfection of human expression
740
wanted power and status 794

SOLUTION
Every s. of a problem is a new
problem 9284
have not found s. for moral decay
2928
in the hollow of his head 449
necessary work to arrive at s.
9009
philosopher, a problem for every s.
8589
to every problem 449
When marriage a s. for loneliness
rarely satisfies 7666

SOLUTIONS
Human problems never greater
than divine s. 9285

SOLVE
Discipline tools to s. life's
problems 9967
finite minds cannot s. riddle of
inequality 6277
live with God to s. problems 9292
many people s. problems by
emotions, authority 11227
teachings of Christ can s. world's
problems 6487

SOLVED
evil not s. by multiplication 3387
find God in problems already s.
7562
mystery of myself s. by this
besetting God 4889
societal problems s. one person at
a time 3901

SOLVES
problems completely and simply
3784

SOLVING
children more trouble s. parent's
problems 3883
Parents have trouble s. children's
problems 3883
to prevent our s. difficulties of
own being 5384

SOMBER
discover delight in s. circumstances
10639
When we seek to be serious
become s. 9502

SOMBEREST
chose saddest and s. color 467

SOME
are born to endless night 813
are born to sweet delight 813
are wise, otherwise 4065
can fool all people s. of the time
2480
can fool s. people all the time
2480
have much, s. have more 11852
never free outside prison 4112
say God too good to be true 4504
world a ladder for s. to go up, s.
down 7047

SOMEBODY
nobody who isn't bore to s. 869
than s. who accomplishes nothing
3856
try to cheer s. else up 2559

SOMEDAY
You say will see God s. 11391

SOMEONE
always s. worse off than yourself
217
am s. expected, prepared,
prefigured 11124
discovers s. else believes in him
4275
If s. doesn't pull or push 75
If you were s. else, could you
stand yourself 9990
to know s. who thinks, feels with
us 4280
To s. may be better than you think
4356
We like s. because 7333
We love s. although 7333
What s. else becomes, or says, or
does 74
when I see s. who is everybody's
friend 4283

SOMETHING
A man's worth s. 9940
better nobody who accomplishes s.
3856
can only find meaning in s.
outside himself 3484
can't do everything, can do s.
1926
Freedom s. spiritual 4112
God gives s. which takes place of
all, love 4790
God in his wisdom means to
make s. of us 2887
God may yet make s. of him 3604
good listener after awhile knows s.
7111
has been saved from wreck 11072
he knows he was meant and made
to do 8649
Hope, reaching out for s. to come
3835
I can do s. 4530
I will not refuse to do s. I can do
2500
If have love, you always have s. to
give 7189
in Jesus rebuked world 2168

is behind them: that is God 4962
live life for s. more important than
life 7034
man who lives that span is s. 7080
nature of God to make s. out of
nothing 3604
new every day if you look for it
3509
rather attempt to do s. great 3595
rather than saying s. 9307
still I can do s. 106
unless we stand for s. 11731
we engrave s. no time can efface
6796
When I swear, I am being s. 9307
When wealth is lost, s. is lost 1066
who loves s. mentions it often
7177

SOMETIMES
best gain is to lose 4339
God s. puts springs in wagon
4808
How haphazard God seems s.
4674
you will have worst of it for doing
right 4555

SOMEWHERE
Evil must go s. 3365

SON
father in praising s. extols himself
3926
father should treat s. as guest
3891
father whipped s. for swearing,
swore himself 3914
For in the person of his S. 4859
if hate s, cram with dainties 8303
if love son, plenty of discipline
8303
no more thought of his own
goodness 6484
only free when S. sets us free 4152
should treat father as host 3891

SON OF GOD
babyhood of the S. a reality 6125
Christ, S. revealing what God is
like 6426
either the S. or a madman 6350
ponder how S. would have done it
10140
saved to manifest S. in flesh 1014
the way the S. went 10165
until S. is formed in us 9821
Wherever the S. goes 5810

SON OF MAN
Christ, S. revealing what man is to
be like 6426

SONG
a bird sings because he has a s.
7883
And "dust to dust" concludes her
noblest s. 7088
Bible haunts like old s. 653
friend, a s. when you're glad 4174
God is my strength and s. 4490
In the night God is preparing thy s.
10600

is ended, the melody lingers 7924
Kind words some angel's s. that
    lost its way 6645
let space become one mouth for s.
    4712
no longer a discord, but a hymn
    divine 7451
There lies the land of s. 10535
Those who wish to sing always
    find a s. 5264
Tomorrow comes the s. 6256
turned into jubilant s. of glee 7895
We echo the s. 1375
What will child learn sooner than
    a s. 7930
When God's people repent, will
    have a s. 9606
When life flows along like a s.
    10493
Who has not sought peace in a s.
    7933
Whose virtue is a s. 11686
Why no attempt to understand s.
    of birds 11608

SONG OF SOLOMON
How to love 11925

SONG OF SONGS
perfection of human expression
    740

SONGS
Angels listen for your s. 8725
Blues are s. of despair 7890
can scarcely find biblical message
    in s. 5109
gospel s. are s. of hope 7890
in the night God giveth 232
in wild whisperings of winds 8034
Jesus furnished themes for more s.
    of praise 6449
Our s. vex, grieve the devil 2661
Psalms, s. of human soul 797
spring forth weblike from mind at
    peace 7920
sweetest s. tell of saddest thought
    10608
Than all the s. of sinners are 9787

SONS
In peace s. bury fathers 11751

SONSHIP
Discipline proof of s. 2842

SOON
As s. as there is life, there is danger
    6879
cannot repent too s. 9609
do not know how s. may be too
    late 9609
God's ways seem dark but s. or
    late 11299
It will change s. 969
Laziness travels so slowly poverty
    s. overtakes him 6768
never know how s. will be too late
    6663
Speak your kind words s. 6663
tragedy of life not that it ends so s.
    7042

SOONER
injury s. forgiven than insult 4070

SOOTHE
Give to thy servants skill to s, bless
    9045
Music has charms to s. savage
    breast 7901
the wayward heart by sorrow rent
    7917

SOOTHED
unforgiving spirit refuses to be s.
    9640

SOOTHES
gospel warmth that s. the heart
    732
It s. his sorrows 1507

SOOTHING
gentleness, s. effect on those angry
    4402
peddling spiritual s. syrup 8108

SOPHISTICATED
pure in heart, not s. and worldly
    5001

SOPHISTICATION
Intellectual s. can dry up creativity
    6325

SORE
sight of you good for s. eyes 4207

SORES
Envy like fly that dwells on s.
    3213

SORROW
And wear a golden s. 6016
    1772
as though no need to pray except
    in s. 8788
baptizing us with bitter tears
    10616
because of circumstances is
    remorse 9580
Behind s. always s. 10583
blessedness beyond s. 6536
blessedness makes joy possible in
    s. 6536
can be your servant 10610
Christianity made s. triumphant
    1166
Confession, examination of s.
    1599
day of s. longer than month of joy
    10580
deeper that s. carves into your
    being 10626
deeper the s, less tongue has to say
    10627
destroys all differences of intellect
    10620
do not understand joy until face s.
    11620
Don't let your s. come higher than
    your knees 8784
drinks to drown his s. 335
Earth has no s. heaven cannot heal
    5637
enough to disarm hostility 3161

found more joy in s. 10593
genuine s. at their failures 9963
Give s. words 5333
God does not make s. grow on
    limbs too weak 10611
I have known s. such as yours
    1509
in losing riches 11865
In s. he learned this truth 12170
in s. sympathy of God grow sure
    1504
in the midst of s. 3818
invisible kingdom that causes
    saint to sing through s. 5775
is a fruit 10611
is a sacred thing 10612
is divine 10613
is knowledge 10614
is our John the Baptist 10616
Joy against s. 10844
Joy and s. inseparable 10626
Joy is s. inside out 6543
joy survives through s. 6568
left in barren, bleak winter of s.
    968
Light in darkness, tempering s.
    4758
like precious treasure 10615
like rain, makes roses and mud
    10621
makes men sincere 10618
makes silence her best orator
    10619
makes us all children again 10620
memorizing Scripture help in s.
    747
more alert to open door than
    grandson Joy 8996
need not come in vain 10586
never s. of heart 1510
no immunity from pain and s. 159
No matter how great s. may be
    10601
not enough to once feel s. over sin
    9589
Of joy or s. 11362
One can endure s. alone 10607
only way can find ourselves is in s.
    10643
opposite of joy not s. 11594
peace attainable by those ignorant
    of s. 2120
please as much by s. as by smile
    10587
poison in s. if we put it there
    10637
preaching repentance 10616
Psalms, pathos of man's s. 798
Real joy is s. accepted,
    transformed 6557
reflect with s. on competitions
    2423
reigns on thrones of universe
    10613
root of all virtue 10617
Said wise man to one in s. 3076
saints experienced joy and s. 2593
school is s. 10600

serve a great man, will know what
  s. is 5292
share world's s. 10592
shown only to friends 10615
sin s. of the spirit 10360
something great must come out of
  s. 2667
soothe the wayward heart by s.
  rent 7917
Speak that kind word to sweeten
  a s. 6671
sweet joy comes through s. 10638
the winter of our s. 10581
Through s. can enter into
  suffering of others 10640
To live through s. with another
  10641
touch'd by thee grows bright
  10633
touches God with s. or joy 7057
True friends no solitary joy, s.
  4291
walked a mile with S. 10596
What is reason for saying in s.
  God does not need 7567
When S. walked with me 10596
When some great s. like a mighty
  river 10645
where s, there is holy ground
  10648
Who swims in sin shall sink in s.
  10426
world full of s. 10639
world in which s. so close to joy
  7081
Worry never robs tomorrow of s.
  12089

SORROWFUL
his joy to enter s. hearts 10603
Jesus' joy to enter s. hearts 6460
through tears have s. seen gates of
  heaven 10882

SORROWING
change s. heart of lead into golden
  mellowness 10628
God only one who does not mock
  us 10908
Goeth a s. 4043

SORROWS
Anxiety does not empty tomorrow
  of s. 409
Cares more difficult to throw off
  than s. 12059
come in battalions 10646
come not single spies 10646
come to stretch out spaces 2508
death, funeral of s. 2266
die with time 12059
enjoy many s. that never happen
  11456
    12079
forget your s. 9271
good that we have s. 187
how many s. crowd 8369
It soothes his s. 1507
Life's s. for our trust 6995
love has ears to hear sighs and s.
  7335

love tokens from God 4804
Man's s. will not let me sleep 1548
Marriage fuller of s. and joys
  7635
No one knows s. of another
  10602
Proud people breed s. for
  themselves 9232
remembered sweeten present joy
  10624
saint chastened through great s.
  9781
stretch out spaces in heart for joy
  10623
to withhold from child world's s.
  8334
visitors that come without
  invitation 10622

SORROW-STRIKEN
Of the s. room 2217

SORRY
But, how many were s. when he
  passed away 7423
Don't be s. if bottle half empty
  11141
felt s. for myself because I had no
  shoes 10031
for men who do not read Bible
  661
if only entertaining them 7896
let husband make wife s. to see
  him leave 7627
Let no man be s. he has done good
  5032
may be s. you spoke 6674
may be s. you stayed or went
  6674
may be s. you won or lost 6674
never s. you were kind 6674
often be s. if wishes gratified 2573
perhaps s. so much was spent
  6674
Repentance to be s. enough to quit
  9595
too proud to say, I'm s. 379

SOUGHT
and found him there 4921
by him who made Pleiades and
  Orion 4768
dialogue in which creative
  inspiration s. 4160
entertaining are s. after 4410
God in a great cathedral 4921
Great supplicants s. secret place of
  Most High 8805
him then atop lonely hill 4921
never s. in vain that s. Lord aright
  7537
Once I s. for healing 6465
only for the heart of God 2652
Pleasure, seldom found where s.
  · 8606
Popularity is crime when s. 3858
way of trying to relieve themselves
  7888
Who has not s. peace in a song
  7933

SOUL
a deep distress has humanized my
  s. 10830
a never ending sigh after God
  7528
A never-dying s. to save 10114
acting as unity with all its faculties
  7948
activities continue through eternity
  6094
acts no longer except by divine
  impulse 7707
Add you your s. unto prayers
  1396
adoration an attitude of the s.
  12122
All money made will never buy
  back s. 10650
amazing inner sanctuary of s.
  1757
an imperial friend 10674
and God stand sure 948
And the fibre of your s. 2964
as retire to rest, give s. and God
  time together 10486
As sight in body, so is reason in s.
  9412
awake to sublime greatness of the
  s. 10654
Be still, my s. 1502
Between the s. and God 8926
Beware of believing human s.
  simple 10653
body without s, a corpse 5088
breath of God bestowed in heaven
  10649
Bring thy s. interchange with mine
  3065
by love s. unites to God 7967
Calm s. of all things 8430
can split sky in two 10670
cancers that gnaw on the s. 3873
chastenings carry s. to spiritual
  achievement 2850
child has fairy godmother in s.
  1122
Christ not born in thee, s. forlorn
  878
Christianity, power of God in s. of
  man 1179
Conscience, vicar of Christ in s.
  1673
Conversion s. at war with itself
  1900
convinced s. is indestructible 6094
created in place between time,
  eternity 10671
Death sets free the s. 2261
death when s. shall emerge from
  sheath 2276
Deep in my s. the still prayer of
  devotion 8778
deepest word is s. 11993
Defeat may serve to shake the s.
  2508
Depend upon the s. 5606
desire of the s, heaven 9274
Dispose our s. for tranquility 1758

dream door in deepest sanctum of s. 2971

ears, eyes doors, windows of s. 845

easier to know God than own s. 1713

easily get entangled and lose our s. 10514

Echoes roll from s. to s. 1032

Encouragement oxygen to s. 3133

endowed with s. and will to be saved 9425

enlarge thou my s. 10658

enriched by communion with God 10567

Envy consumes the s. 3212

every other seal too narrow, too shallow for s. 10659

Every s. belongs to God 4529

Everything but s. of man a passing shadow 10654

evil s. producing holy witness 5011

exalted with grand, glorious aims 7381

exalted with immortal longings 7381

eyes convey the s. 3563

Faith daring s. to go farther than can see 3697

Faith elevates the s. 3666

Faith is antiseptic of s. 3694

first duty of s. is to find its Master 4144

for God designed 12032

freed from clay 10675

friend, single s. in two bodies 4211

Friendship, two bodies and one s. 4298

frightful is solitude of s. without God 10573

God an unutterable sigh planted in the s. 4843

God deals with unconscious life of s. 10486

God draws us by voice in s. 7949

God ground on which s. stands 1713

God himself fights for s. 2734

God nearer than own s. 1713

God planted fear in s. 3973

God present in deepest, most central part of s. 4868

God wants to make s. aware of him 4562

God's ability to heal s. profound 10845

God's glorious image 10675

Grace comes into s. as sun into world 5213

great faith will bring heaven to your s. 3757

ground of the s. is dark 10664

growing in holiness 10568

hardly ever complete silence in our s. 10273

hardly ever realizes it 7146

harsh words pierce the s. 374

has deeper darkness than nights 7539

has further horizons than early mornings 7539

has greater depths than any sea 7539

has higher peaks than any mountain 7539

He that hides dark s, foul thoughts 1683

He would not let them take away my s. 1817

high courage of devout s. 4974

high s. climbs the high way 10679

highest part of s. stands above time 11316

His maker kissed his s. away 2296

Holiness the symmetry of the s. 5747

Holy Spirit makes s.tender 5794

hope makes the s. exercise patience 5912

Hope, balm and lifeblood of the s. 5933

human s. and life will appear simple 10653

human s. can rise up against odds 3621

human s. is God's treasury 10666

human s. silent harp in God's choir 10665

human s. so mysterious 10667

human s. too complex to touch 10653

I am now a naked soul 7952

I asked, my s. bethought of this 4834

I'll trust in God's unchanging Word till s. and body sever 9813

If God should give my s. all he ever made 7477

if I have a s. 318

if our time more important than s. 7327

If s. be lost, man is lost 10655

in dark night of s. always three in morning 2594

in darkness s. gains virtues 2547

in endurance of human s. 3150

in heaven's eternal sphere 10675

in overwhelming, irrecoverable loss, his s. 2381

In which his s. may sail 11519

ingratitude the unfailing mark of a narrow s. 6251

is a broken field ploughed by pain 8262

is a dark ploughed field 8262

is like a mirror 10339

is like the rolling world 10673

is not where it lives but where it loves 7310

is secret of unfathomable depth 10669

Jealousy jaundice of the s. 6343

joy a state, condition of the s. 6568

keep a tidy s. 10652

Kept him a living s. 8911

knowledge of Christ dawns upon the s. 7971

last hour of body, but not of s. 2225

leave neglected the s. of man 6095

Let thy s. walk slowly in thee 10256

Little faith will bring s. to heaven 3757

living coffin of dead s. 7760

Loneliness eats into the s. 7134

long before conscious ego 2971

longs to return to its source 4744

losing leisure, may be losing s. 6833

lost, all lost 9263

Love bade me welcome, yet my s. drew back 5481

love brings to harvest flowers of the s. 7339

love cannot lie idle in s. of lover 7167

Love must draw the s. on 7167

loves and is loved in return 7967

low s. gropes the low 10679

Malignity of s. often dwells in diseased bodies 5613

Man with his burning s. 11519

May better read the darkened s. 6583

meanest hut with love palace for the s. 5816

meaning of earthly existence is development of the s. 9342

men sigh on, not knowing what the s. wants 7516

microbe of conscience which eats into s. 1682

moments which the s. is on its knees 8776

Money not required to buy one necessity of the s. 7813

more it receives, more it grows 10699

more it wants, more is given 10699

music bringest eternity nearer to weary s. of man 7916

Music can calm agitations of the s. 7914

music fills s. 7934

Music washes from s. dust of life 7912

must cure diseases of the s. 6085

must s. lie blinded, dwarfed 10649

My life, my friends, my s. I leave 7503

My rising s. surveys 4819

My s. bids you adieu 12032

my s. flies through these wounds 292

my s. is colorless 3229

My s. is dark within 9048

My s. is sick with every day's report 6273

My s. is too small to accommodate you 9089

My s. lives on God 7953

name of God may be written upon that s. 10475

Narrow is the mansion of my s. 10658

Naught but God can satisfy the s. 7504

nearest thing to God is human s. 10651

never applies itself simply 10660

never in the shallows of our s. 8795

never so strong as when forgoes revenge 4095

no bar or wall in the s. 4525

no change, s. is dead 1590

No coward s. is mine 3765

No image but image of God can fit s. 10659

Nothing presented to s. is simple 10660

nothing will so magnify the s. of man 4742

o'erfraught with gratitude 8792

odds world can throw against tortured s. 3736

of origin divine 10675

of peace is love 8469

on earth never to be unfolded 10649

One drop of water for my s. 7003

One half in day, the other dipt in night 10673

Only the s. that knows mighty grief 2508

out of s. God coins unspeakable riches 10666

passions that disturb the s. 7935

Peace dwells within the s. 8453

Perseverance rope that ties s. to heaven 8554

pleasure contains no healing for s. 8610

poor, intricated s. 10661

poverty of s. measured by how little it can feel 10677

poverty of the s. 8697

Prayer a shield to the s. 8915

Prayer the breath of the newborn s. 8938

Prayer, gymnasium of the s. 8941

problem is shipwrecked s. 7396

problem of restoring beauty is redemption of s. 10668

Psalms anatomy of the s. 799

Psalms, songs of human s. 797

Psalms: mirror in which man sees his s. 800

read small print of man's s. 739

redemption of Jesus can satisfy the aching s. 6402

Riddling, perplexed, labyrinthical s. 10661

rises above itself, becomes spirit 7948

Sad s, take comfort nor forget 5942

salvation of s. more important than 3332

see a s. with image of God 1278

Self the only prison that can bind the s. 9944

Self-will completely poured out of s. 4978

senses its origin 4744

set of a s. that decides goal 4432

shall shine a star of day 10675

Silent worship down to deeper currents of s. 12114

sin a death of the s. 10360

sleep, profound developments in s. 10486

smallest revenge will poison s. 9728

so full of s. was the concept of mother 7859

soap for the body, tears for the s. 10644

Speech a mirror of the s. 10689

spirit, s. and body are kept in harmony 6897

such as human s. could believe in 4504

Suffering purification of s. 10896

Tears clean windows of the s. 11017

tender tears that humanize the s. 5349

that hears sweetness of music 10656

That swells with silence in the tortured s. 5348

the most agonizing spy 10674

The s. alone, like a neglected harp 7527

The s. itself its awful witness 3404

the s. we clothe in earthly form, action 1757

think that his Fire will consume my s. 7951

Thinking is talking of the s. with itself 11262

thy s. is still forlorn 1374

tinged with color of its thoughts 11247

To cheer the s. when tired with human strife 7917

To every s. there openeth 1155

to know s. seek God 1713

to s. that contemplates greatness of God 4707

tomb is release for s. 2350

unbelief starves the s. 3703

universal language of s. 10676

Virtue to s. what health is to body 11712

voice which melts the s. 8813

wakes and grows 9940

want salvation of the s. 3025

want them to see my s. 3229

Was not spoken of the s. 2328

way of suffering is witness s. bears to itself 10866

weakened by virus of pride 10436

wealth of s. measured by how much it can feel 10677

what dusty answer gets s. 946

what fits s. for Christ 10676

whatever God may allow, s. should embrace 4978

whatever God may will, s. should will 4978

When God is weaning a s. 10036

when God leads s. in higher path of sanctification 9851

When God sets the s. in tune for himself 10663

when not forever beating at doors of his s. 8649

When once our heav'nly-guided s. shall climb 5679

when s. becomes humble 7971

When s. is purified and serene 7971

When s. laid down faults at feet of God 9608

Whenever sounds of world die out in s. 4968

where man's battles are fought 10672

Which way his s. shall go 1155

while one dark s. without God, I'll fight 3342

Wisdom is to the s. what health is to the body 11975

with highest power touches eternity 10671

with lower powers touches time 10671

with so much love as God embraces the s. 7958

Within my very s. 4795

without body, a ghost 5088

worship occupation of s. 3987

Worship s. in awe before mystery of universe 12132

would have no rainbow had eye no tears 10631

would instantly rush toward God 8630

would take its place below creation 7971

Yet with itself every s. standeth single 7150

SOUL'S

Bubbles we buy with whole s. tasking 2641

Duty done is s. fireside 9653

fear, s. signal for rallying 3973

Fill well storehouse of s. delight 11375

How boundless might s. horizon be 11627

hunger for prayer 4643

inarticulate moanings are the affections for the Infinite 7516

Life is the s. nursery 6979

Meditation the s. chewing 7717

Prayer is the s. sincere desire 8948

silence is the s. language 8902

Solitude s. best friend 10559

theological problems are the s. mumps 11202

To try the s. strength on 6908

SOUL-WINNING
may degenerate into
brush-salesman 7867

SOULS
are not saved in bundles 9814
battlegrounds for civil wars 6068
Borne inward into s. afar 2345
conversing with greatest s. of the
past 3027
dark cottage, batter'd and decay'd
7701
empty s. tend to extreme opinion
8191
find a music in our s. never felt
before 9503
goal of fear, to create joyless s.
3971
Grace God's energy at work
within our s. 5219
Gratitude sign of noble s. 5247
Great s. have wills, feeble ones
wishes 8541
have lost their courage 9059
holiest s. pessimistic 8586
if people showed their s. 10507
If s. can suffer and I hardly know
it 7188
In face of evil three kinds of s.
5029
in order to guide our s. 5426
in winepress of cross 2095
instinct in our s. that turns us to
God 7535
Jesus was, is concerned with
individual s. 6176
let our s. shrivel 10680
love, two s. and one flesh 4298
masters of s. 1293
may be able to encourage s. who
journey with us 9059
may rest, quietly grow, expand
10247
Most of world's great s. have been
lonely 7138
Out of suffering emerged
strongest s. 10882
rest there in God, center of their s.
5644
rough treatment gives s. luster 280
save our s. from being steeped in
care 9064
speaks peace to our s. 4863
Spirit-filled s. are ablaze for God
3182
stunted, shrivelled, starved 10247
Take from our s. the strain and
stress 8431
The s. we loved 2214
the salvation of human s. the real
business of life 7027
to s. can never teach 10678
tried and ripened 237
unknown something to sharpen s.
on 4318
we look upon enemy of our s. as
conquered 3163
when God begins to deal with
sanctified s. 9840

who give themselves absolutely to
him 4790

SOUND
Cain who hears only the s. of his
own footsteps 10573
earth awoke with first rush of s.
11330
empty vessel makes greatest s.
4066
finding our plumb line cannot s.
its depth 4745
hears God in every s. 4847
How shall I s. thy depths 7492
Laughter a sacred s. to God 6729
less s. a man's argument, louder
he talks 448
Light no s. to the ear 1956
Like the s. of a great Amen 7919
most persistent s. the beating of
war drums 11762
of your goings and God's goings
the same 8093
plenty of s. in an empty barrel
9250
silence teaches joys of s. 824
through the silence 365
Time, of a silken s. 11345
To heal the blows of s. 10241
whenever s. of world die out in
soul 4968
will scarcely hear glad s. of Gospel
5224
With s. seraphic ring 2389
words s. out like drums 11998

SOUNDED
He has s. forth the trumpet 4715

SOUNDETH
And that voice still s. on 6497

SOUNDS
all urban and rural s. 4259
His Spirit s. each pipe 7892
How sweet the name of Jesus s.
1507
However desolate life's monody s.
to you 7895
Not many s. in life 4259
sweetest of all s. is praise 8740
tongue inches from brain, s. miles
away 1880
we take for granted speech, music,
s. 9094
Whenever s. of world die out
10273
which Holy Spirit weaves together
in heavenly harmony 5799

SOUP
once burnt mouth always blows s.
3536

SOUR
fathers eat s. grapes 8328
godliness is devil's religion 2186
nor smelleth so s. as shame 5492
Things sweet prove s. 11105
Unless vessel clean, what you
pour turns s. 1054
wants to blame finds sugar s.
2063

SOURCE
as you recognize me as your s.
7548
beyond all reason 4538
Bible s. of heavenly knowledge
737
Christ speaks from s. of things
6422
Defeat should never be s. of
discouragement 2509
defect may be s. of strength 3932
Discontent, s. of trouble, progress
2865
emotion s. of all
becoming-conscious 3053
human beings as s. of life, help
7548
inexhaustible s. of peace,
consolation 9835
light so lovely will want to know s.
12147
no human being can be
permanent s. of happiness to
another 9481
no right to draw life from other s.
than Christ 11689
of power stronger than
disappointment 6491
Our s, our center, our dwelling
place 4836
Pay attention to the S. 10180
Prayer from a living s. within the
will 8911
resurrection hope derived from no
other s. 9702
river touches places of which s.
knows nothing 6232
sacrifice far from being s. of
sadness 9758
sacrifice s. of illumination 9758
soul longs to return to its s. 4744
unconscious is s. of highest good
7772

SOURCES
search for happiness one of chief
s. of unhappiness 5559

SOUREST
Sweetest things turn s. by their
deeds 5039

SOURS
trouble s. milk 11431

SOUTH
In Christ no s. or north 911

SOVEREIGN
And works his s. will 4941
God wants to be loved for himself
4806
Lord's s. right to demote, promote
5894
Man's free will, God's s. will 1149
only s. I recognize 4951
Our part to bring life under God's
s. will 4734
Revival s. act of God 9746
right in disobeying law of s. 5197
Sin s. until s. grace dethrones it
10373

what a s. God chooses to do through us 8094

When God should be our S, we rule ourselves 10425

SOVEREIGNTY

God's s. derived from omnipotence 4952

God's s. enables him to secure our welfare 4754

if unwilling to give up own s. 8818

SOW

act, reap habit 1041

As ye s, so shall ye reap 1727

character, reap destiny 1041

gentle words, useful deeds 1574

habit, reap character 1041

thought, reap act 1041

SOWING

judgment of God reaping that comes from s. 4721

restlessness can be God s. faith 3722

seeds of peace like s. beans 8468

SOWN

God alone beholds the end of what is s. 10204

seeds of punishment s. at time commit sin 10396

We reap as we have s. 2622

SOWS

He who speaks, s. 1848

SPACE

beauty in s. 11650

can be with God in s. as well 11632

can send worlds rolling in s. 4951

death adventure beside which s. trips pale 2259

exploration of outer s. bright future 11642

Friendship independent of matter, s. time 4233

God hangs us in awful hollows of s. 4618

God I worship too big for s. to contain 11643

God knows all s. 4881

God widens the s. 1156

If consider boundless s, shrink into nothing 11631

If know and obey laws, s. will treat you kindly 11650

In eternity neither time nor s. 11316

In infinite time, matter, s. 6927

is orderly 11650

is predictable 11650

is regularity 11650

let s. become one mouth for song 4712

no weather 11650

obeys laws of physics 11650

Prayer for those in s. 11628

Small-folded in a warm dim female s. 6142

solemn pause, breathing s. of man 10960

symbolize emanation of God 4593

the illimitable void of s. 4712

the little s. I fill and even can see 7084

Through s. universe swallows me up 11268

Through the black s. of death to baby life 6148

To those who venture into s. 11628

widest thing in universe not s. 5625

will never run out of s. to explore 11642

SPACES

engulfed in infinite immensity of s. 4905

eternal silence of these infinite s. terrifies me 7084

of Infinity 4708

of which I am ignorant and which knows me not 4905

Sorrows come to stretch out s. for joy 2508

SPADING

with help of s, fertilizing 9884

SPAN

can fill tiny s. of life with meaning 7080

Eternity shut in a s. 6153

of life is nothing 7080

SPANNED

same power that measured, weighed, s. world 4592

SPARE

He injures good men who s. wicked 6608

if he is stronger, s. yourself 6263

If weaker, s. him 6263

not the stroke! Do with us as thou wilt 7519

safe rule is to give more than we can s. 10734

To s. the ravening leopard 6283

who has thousand friends has not a friend to s. 9459

SPARES

Destroys the mighty, the humble s. 4505

God s. us because he is good 4724

SPARE-TIME

Witnessing not a s. occupation 3344

SPARK

of heavenly fire 244

will set whole city on fire 10445

SPARKLE

planet would s. like Christmas tree 11189

SPARKLING

Mirth offered s. with life to God 6739

SPARROW

cannot fall without his notice 4933

Lord has arms wrapped around big, fat s. 2312

SPARROW'S

who canst mark the s. fall 9048

SPARROWS

Jesus talked about s. and lilies 6451

should not dance with cranes 9493

SPASMODIC

Faith and love s. in best minds 3654

SPATTERS

praises himself s. himself 9204

SPEAK

ability to s. several languages asset 1876

according to learning, opinions 1648

Actions don't always s. louder than words 1833

After service s. to neighbor 1384

all the good I know of everybody 5072

And dare not s. 426

approving, cheering words 4223

Before service s. to God 1384

Bible s. in hundreds of languages 645

boldly, s. truly 2669

cannot s. against Christianity without anger 1185

cannot s. for Christianity without love 1185

cannot s. of measure and God 4680

cannot s. too freely, too trustfully to God 8968

Christ did not simply s. truth 11572

Do not s. of own happiness to one unhappy 3067

Do we stop, think before we s. 12005

Don't s. well of yourself 5996 9614

During service let God s. 1384 first 9479

friends s. with words sweet, strong 4185

God does s. 8835

God never ceases to s. to us 8800

God to man doth s. in solitude 10534

God vouchsafes to s. to us one by one 6178

grief that does not s. whispers 5333

have never heard God s. 5426

healing words we s. not our own 10545

hear conscience s. in sleep 2970

hills are mute, yet how they s. of God 8014

How can you expect God to s. 8813

I cannot adore enough. I cannot s. 12125

I turned to s. to God 2589

I will s. ill of no man 5072

If Christ did not s. truth in all matters 11509

If man too little for God to s. to him 4553

ill of others, praising ourselves 2083

Kind words short, easy to s. 11988

Kindness a language dumb can s. 6650

learn to s. by speaking 7352

less than thou knowest 2899

Let truth not shadows with me s. 11515

Let truth s. to me 9070

Light cares s, great ones silent 10599

Light griefs can s, deeper ones dumb 5347

Lord, s. to me that I may s. 8866

Make me the mouth for such as cannot s. 10130

man gets up to s. and says nothing 5171

men s. of yoke of Christ as slavery 2816

mouth keeps silent to hear heart s. 10270

mystic too full of God to s. to world 7965

nor s. with double tongue 1011

not to s. wrong, never s. 1636

of whom we s. least on earth best known in heaven 9616

Of whom you s. to whom you s. 1855

plead for God to s. when he has spoken, and is speaking 8843

Prayer is not to hear oneself s. 8935

Prayer is to wait till one hears God s. 8935

questionable whether really heard Jesus s. 6407

Quotations, people from ancient times s. today 9385

Silence teaches us to s. Word of God 10562

some would like to s. to ye 1396

Tears s. more eloquently than ten thousand tongues 11018

tenderly 576

than s. reckless word against servant of Christ 5143

than to s. out, remove all doubt 1836

that kind word to sweeten a sorrow 6671

Think today, s. tomorrow 11258

to him, thou, for he hears 4862

to me, not of me 5157

To s. kindly does not hurt tongue 11421

To s. painful truth 4289

to s. the difficult word, do the difficult deed 6599

to whom I can s. my first thoughts 4255

We try to s. of great or little faith 4710

weakness to be silent when proper to s. 1887

weakness to s. when proper to be silent 1887

When I can neither see, hear, nor s. 9025

When s. God one of listeners 1891

when s. of hell, everyday face will do 5680

when s. to church about Pentecost 5811

When you s. of heaven, let face light up 5680

who maintains only he has gift to s. 8196

Words cannot s. for grief or ecstasy 10274

your kind words soon 6663

SPEAKER

Slander slays s, spoken to, spoken of 10466

SPEAKING

a grace of kind s. 6669

betray by s. too many words 628

Bible, a book which is now s. 637

Deep within us, a s. voice 1757

eyes, without s. confess secrets of the heart 3569

God perseveres in s. in his own language 4900

greatness in s. up for truth 5283

heaven within s. distance 5677

In the humanity of Jesus, God s. our language 6135

man may betray Jesus Christ by s. 628

Much s. and lying are cousins 6854

never omitting s. true word 9491

plead for God to speak when he has spoken, is s. 8843

realize God had always been s. 5395

the truth important 9158

truth in love all-important 9158

without thinking 1873

SPEAKING VOICE

haunted by the S. 4399

SPEAKS

a language of silent power 6651

as man s, so is he 10689

Bible s. to me 712

Bible s. to us of Lord Jesus 636

blame man who s. too little 2080

blame man who s. too much 2080

Christ s. from source of things 6422

Christian, voice through which Christ s. 1248

devil sometimes s. the truth 11532

examine not him who s. 1842

God s. if we will tune in 8013

God s. in language we do not want to learn 4900

God s. in our conscience 8257

God s. to the crowd 5385

God s. unceasingly through events of life 5395

gossip s. ill of all and all of her 5113

He that s. much, much mistaken 1847

He who s. sows 1848

holy life s. when tongue silent 5735

Jesus s. not as a first-century theologian 6448

Jesus s. of motives rather than actions 6450

Jesus s. to living experience of all time 6448

liar isn't believed even when s. truth 6844

listen twice as much as s. 1858

May it be the real I who s. 8989

meanest praise s. well, qualifies with a "but" 8739

one who knows most s. least 11948

peace to our souls 4863

stillness of nature s. louder than choir of voices 8041

thousand languages, smile s. them all 10499

voice of God just s. 4967

When money s, truth is silent 7825

When your work s. for itself, don't interrupt 12021

who s. truth always at ease 11537

with stars 9805

SPEAR

Faith laughs at shaking of s. 3703

SPECIAL

believer s. to the God of the universe 9999

called to love with s. intensity 10937

Can s. love be everywhere 4834

freedom friends enjoy 4285

God changes from commonplace to s. 4487

God undertakes s. protection of man 3999

Lord calls to no s. work 1308

You are s. 6206

SPECIALIST

God a s. in the sin disease 10308

God is a S. 885

God is a s. when anguish deep 10845

God will make you a s. in that truth 11528

SPECIALISTS

Bible, not book for s. only 725

SPECIALNESS

When we reject our s. 1635

SPECIFIC
crave s. rules to know how to behave 6810
God would not created us without s. plan 5398

SPECIMENS
not s. in God's showroom 9850

SPECK
life, little s. in center but a minute 7052
universe swallows me up like a s. 11268

SPECTACLE
of a nation praying 8991

SPECTATORS
angels heaven's s. 2359

SPECULATE
minds emotionally s. on unknowable 4704

SPECULATION
loftiness s. study of attributes of Godhead 4631

SPECULATOR
God is not a foolish s. 9989

SPEECH
a mirror of the soul 10689
best s. you will ever regret 395
Eloquent silence better than eloquent s. 10244
freedom of s, potent weapon 4154
index of the mind 10690
is a mighty ruler 10688
Is not s. a glory 6253
is shallow as time 10263
is silver, silence golden 1874
Lincoln Memorial S. 1963 4157
listen to s. of God 4965
Man's s. is like his life 10684
More have repented s. than silence 1861
Prayer highest use to which s. can be put 8942
right to free s. 20
Thought is deeper than all s. 10678
Truth needs no flowers of s. 11576
we take for granted s, music, sounds 9094
Well-timed silence more eloquence than s. 1889
with freedom of s, responsibility 4154

SPEECHLESS
Christ, wisely s. 6499
Humility is quiet, not s. 6012

SPEED
and noise evidences of weakness 10576
is to distract hunger for God 7512
more to life than increasing its s. 9111
more to life than increasing s. 7053

Most people object to s. of light 11309
must s. to my God before all things 7951
'tis we who s. along 11330
up day when sing, Free at last 4157

SPEEDS
driver s. through traffic 1738

SPEEDY
when wall cracked, fall will be s. 9257

SPELL
Chaucer had talent but couldn't s. 12145
Sin may s. pride but is some form of "me" 9916
trying to s. God with wrong blocks 7530
While grass, flowers, stars s. out his name 8019

SPELLING
Jesus s. himself out in language man can understand 6445

SPEND
Give and s, God will send 4354
Go labor on, s. and be spent 10133
I will not just s. my life 6920
important how we s. each day 10733
Just a little labor s. 4217
lives pleasing ourselves 5467
managed to s. more than you earned 4030
save in one store, s. in another 4036
sixteen hours daily thinking about world 7491
talent lavishly 10993
to s. money wisely most difficult 7823
will s. rest of lives in future 4333
Women s. money 7826
would s. two years studying, preparing 6687
years we s. on earth only first scene 6106
your time 11312

SPENDS
if a man s. money, he's a playboy 7800

SPENDTHRIFT
love pays to be an absolute s. 7252
What a s. of his tongue 5124

SPENDTHRIFTS
burn money 7826

SPENT
count that day well s. 107
Give me the money s. in war 11746
Go labor on, spend and be s. 10133

life lost s. not in communion with God 6909
past is s, done with 8374
perhaps, sorry so much was s. 6674
what a change one hour s. in thy presence will make 8867
What I s, I had 4383

SPEW
God doth despise, abhor, s. out neutralities 4920

SPHERE
And leaves our s. behind 8078
keep within own little s. 4885
Never think could do something if different s. 8219
No trembler in world's storm-troubled s. 3765
Rise with its anthems to holier s. 10960

SPHERES
than s, or angel's praises be 8749

SPIDER
A s. spins her silver 6118
Experience a kind of huge s. web 3524
suspense, life of s. 11600
When s. would attack thee 11115

SPIDER'S
attempting to check by s. thread progress of ship 11108

SPIES
sorrows come not single s. 10646

SPILLS
ages of man: s. 7037
forfeits own blood that s. another's 7881

SPIN
carefully, prayerfully 3117
God gives flax to s. 3092
Though men s. cunning schemes 4887

SPINDLE
Get s. ready, God will send flax 9346

SPINE
Hollywood has not recognized what tingles s. 4551

SPINELESS
think of gentleness as s. 4402

SPINES
shivers go up, down s. of cultured people 5811

SPINS
A spider s. her silver 6118

SPIRAL
dare I hope I am on a s. 5344

SPIRIT
advancing in life whose s. entering into living peace 6898
always has conquered the sword 10695

Anyone who sings blues has broken s. 7888

As the evil s. fled from Saul 7935

body bound with chains, s. never 4112

brings your s. into harmony with God 8093

by thy s. guide us 619

can embrace intellect 10692

Christianity balanced between flesh, s. 1240

Christianity introduced new s. of government 5170

completely different people in s. 3766

concur with promptings of the S. 5444

controlled by S. means not controlled by outside 9849

cracked chimes of courageous human s. 7171

cross radiant with glory of meek, gentle s. 5252

Devil strongest s. that fought in heaven 2643

do small things in right s. 9679

Evil lies in the s. 3407

examines the roots 72

Father, Redeemer and S. of grace 11424

fruit, not push, drive, climb 350

fruits of the S. are virtues of Christ 10714

Giving is a joy if you do in right s. 4357

God an ever-present S. 5389

God considers not action but s. of action 7861

God gives us his S. 837

God knows all s, and all spirits 4881

God will wither up confidence in s. 11689

God's almighty S. 14

God's thoughts belong to world of s. 10692

Gold no balm to wounded s. 7798

Grace can put S. of Jesus Christ within us 5212

Grace free, but you are bound to s. of Giver 5211

happy s. takes grind out of giving 4347

He stretched skin over s. 6131

His S. sounds each pipe 7892

hope gives poverty of s. 3834

Humanness is realization of fruits of S. 5014

Humility exhibition of s. of Jesus Christ 6013

I have a place where my s. sings 8429

If s. within withers 10694

in an inward flame 10696

in every thought, word, act 10697

in man is candle of the Lord 7430

in once-born opposed to S. of twice-born 877

intellect can never comprehend s. 10692

joy of heaven improvement of s. 3482

joy of the S. in the cross 2096

joyous resting place of my s. 7961

lamp world blows on but never puts out 10696

life in the S. a different life 10715

man's far-reaching s. stretches to infinite 7381

Materialism organized emptiness of s. 8633

Men full of the S. look right into heaven 5651

My S. searches the deep things of the heart 72

mystic's s. lost in abyss of Deity 7966

no s. dare stir abroad 1371

not a thing apart 10697

not to abrogate obedience but to add to its s. 6811

nothing but notes, body without s. 7929

Obedience is the eye of the s. 8100

of a nation discovered in its proverbs 9386

of Christ is s. of missions 7785

of Christ operating in our lives 104

of God hunts our spirit 5764

on wings of mysticism can s. soar 7963

once s. is healed 5614

one day in S. worth more than thousand in flesh 5787

Our Father yet heals s. of amputees 5614

pains of hell devastation of s. 3482

Prayer is exhaling s. of man 8920

Prayer is inhaling s. of God 8920

Religious work done without gifts of the S. 10181

Revival inrush of S. into body that threatens to become corpse 9749

safeguarding freedom of s. no matter how difficult 4127

saint has same s. with Christ 9766

should not grow old 8137

silence to s. what sleep is to body 9374

sin sorrow of the s. 10360

sleep, profound developments in s. 10486

So must thy s. become a tranquil pool 8437

sole seer, interpreter 4911

soul and body are kept in harmony 6897

soul rises above itself, becomes s. 7948

stronger than genius 11568

submerged, absorbed in depths of divine ocean 7968

submit to demands of the S. 1719

substituted spirit of the wheels for power of S. 5808

Sweet s. comfort me 1514

tests the soundness of the tree 72

things of S. take shape before inner eyes 8488

though distant, close in s. 4280

To one fixed trust my s. clings 4642

to the poor in s. God is forgiving 4649

wealth of the compassionate s. 11841

What influences me in my friend is s. 4233

when S. illuminates heart 5809

Who boundless S. all 4711

Why should the s. of mortal be proud 9225

wise man sees a man's s. 11896

with S. can meet 4862

without healing of s. duties burdens 8857

work designed for eternity only done by S. 10181

worship an adventure of the s. 12119

Worship renews the s. 12141

youth a s. of daring 12183

Youth has to do with s. not age 12198

SPIRIT OF GOD

alters my dominating desires 9276

convicts, comforts 5773

explanation rational man without S. never has 7753

gives liberty 5800

gives worldwide outlook 7786

has habit of taking words of Jesus out of Scriptural setting 5801

imparts love 5800

in sharp opposition to easy ways of world 5776

inspires hope 5800

makes Bible a fire 683

may strip you of borderline pleasures 5776

never oppresses 5773

next to might of S. 5766

Oppression, depression never come from S. 5773

putting words of Jesus into setting of personal lives 5801

When S. comes into man 7786

will be jealous over you for good 5776

will demand to be Lord of your life 5776

will enfold you in love so vast, mighty 5776

will expect unquestioning obedience 5776

will not allow you to boast, show off 5776

will not tolerate self-sins 5776

will reserve right to test, discipline, chasten you 5776

will take direction of your life away from you 5776

SPIRIT-ARTERIES
pulse with vital red of love 2979

SPIRIT-FILLED
life no goal difficult of attainment 5803

life no mystery revealed to select few 5803

life not deluxe edition of Christianity 1231

scarcely anything on earth more beautiful than S. mind 7776

souls ablaze for God 3182

trust, obey substance of S. life 5803

SPIRITLESS
Give me the s. refusals 4530

SPIRIT'S
control will replace sins' control 5802

power greater than power of sin 5802

SPIRITS
By prostrate s. day and night 4659

Every chain that s. wear 8789

God has preoccupied rarest human s. 7547

God is the fuel our s. designed to burn 7459

God knows all spirit, and all s. 4881

Good s. make for good digestion 5612

Great s. always encountered opposition 5282

nor can s. be divided 3291

Nor can s. be divided that love in same divine principle 7319

stirred by Holy Spirit go forward even in sleep 10490

two s. abroad in earth 877

SPIRITUAL
a s. body to do with as I please 2346

advance in s. life has dangers 10700

angel, s. creature 354

Bible asserts s. values 701

Bible, human experience in s. world 701

bread for neighbor s. question 622

church unity 1387

condemn ourselves to s. superficiality 6693

Confidence in s. world, God-reliance 1605

darkness and dry spells 181

develop powers of s. receptivity 7564

door to profound s. experience 8101

easier to suffer death than s. suffering 10859

Every s. movement followed by missionary movement 9740

Failure to obey dulls s. understanding 8100

few have s. resources to be both wealthy and godly 11806

first stages of s. life 1714

fitted for us and our s. state 4578

Freedom something s. 4112

Friendship is a s. thing 4233

furtherance of s. life during sleep 10487

God gives us s. ability 4648

God not about to hand out s. bandages 1013

Great men see s. stronger than material force 10693

greatest to see s. pluck 8545

guided by bad s. philosophy 115

half-baked sermon causes s. indigestion 10108

Happiness is the s. experience 5528

health proportional to love for God 4793
1264

hindrance to s. progress 3758

if grudge, s. penetration into knowledge of God stops 9633

if not prepared to fight in s. realm 8818

If s. life does not grow where we are 10702

in jumps like s. frogs 10716

In s. matters, human reasoning not in order 9416

lest you become obstacles to s. growth 2851

life is unaging youth 10712

lives have been frozen 10369

Lord makes much of s. death 2358

Lord's Prayer rich in s. power 7156

Love is s. fire 7224

Man has two great s. needs 7400

man must believe to know 3743

Man's craving is for the s. 9546

maturity the quiet confidence God is in control 7697

ministry means to take time 7327

More s. progress in one short moment of silence 12112

must want s. freedom 1013

Mystical is intimate quality of the s. life 7954

no better way to finish s. life 10705

no distinction between s, material work 6985

no packages of s. victory sent special delivery 1013

no time left for s. part 1301

not complete in s. stature if all not given to God 5734

nothing s. about a nervous breakdown 9533

nothing s. about brain, body 843

one good wife a s. harem 7663

only lasting treasure is s. 4148

Only through s. transformation strength to fight 6619

pay more attention to s. progress 10703

peddling s. soothing syrup 8108

power uses men 8715

Prayer catapults us onto the frontier of s. life 8902

Prayer is s. character 8914

Pride is s. cancer 9229

pride, most deadly form sin can take 9254

process lasts all through life 10006

progress of s. things 5751

real things are s. 615

refreshing vacation is s. 9533

rose bushes 10710

saint never believes circumstances haphazard 1324

scientific power has outrun s. power 9868

Self-acceptance a s. issue 9993

selfishness destroys s. nature 10073

smiles brighten by their s. vivacity 10500

split s. personalities 6068

strengthens belief in s. existence after death 6090

surgery more painful than physical surgery 890

truth discernable only to pure heart 11529

truth of Bible has endured flames 646

turn theological truth into s. experience 12063

unconscious not only demonic but 7772

verse in Bible may be dangerous to s. health 642

Whatever takes relish off s. things is sin 10424

who believes himself far advanced in s. life 10701

wisdom, application of s. principles 11911

world, Jesus Christ makes possible 873

worshiper aware of no s. reality 1399

worst pleasures purely s. 10400

SPIRITUALITY
a breath, a movement, an impulse 5981

an echo of God's voice 5981

concept of s. varies among different groups 10713

concerned only with order 10698

does not depend upon changing 125

doing for God what we do for ourselves 125

means "Holy Spirit at work" 10711

perils of s. 10718

Real s. has an outcome 1404

that preaches acquiescence 10698

True s. 10719

true s. rare as true bestiality 10718

unctuous piety poor example of s. 10707

what becomes of your s. 11370

which has lost interest in holiness 10698

SPIRITUALLY

bad thing to be satisfied s. 10704

because of problems we grow s. 202

begin to be satisfied s, begin to degenerate 9234

blessing to know destitute s. 830

God's goal to perfect s. 1016

harder we lean, stronger we grow s. 8256

humble who know what peace is 8447

must s. renounce other loves for love of God 7334

temptation of separating ministry from s. 10211

Truth is discerned s. 11569

we never grow old 10712

who realizes his smallness becomes s. great 5309

SPIRITUALLY MINDED

look from heaven's point of view 10707

makes decisions on eternal values 10707

SPIT

And s. on it, molded shape of man 1982

Christ let men s. upon him, crucify him 6503

SPITE

unlively dough of human s. 530

Where, in s. of all you can do 5407

SPITTING

God redeemd human race when we were s. in his face 9434

SPLASHED

before sun or stars in s. heavens 4694

SPLASHY

wisdom is not s. and bold 11911

SPLENDOR

Character gives s. to youth 997

church be restored to New Testament s. 10080

is not beauty 11662

Springtime invites you to try out its s. 9896

you wrapped me in your s. 7473

Your shining and s. drove out my blindness 1910

SPLENDORS

everlasting s. 8483

harmony of unspeakable s. 3648

Lighted with living s. 4708

SPLINTER

Remind religious phony s. between you and Lord 6590

SPLINTERS

You need a few s. in your thumb 240

SPLIT

spiritual personalities 6068

SPLITS

teaching of Christ s. to atoms every notion 6486

SPOILED

child never loves mother 1103

SPOILS

Men whom the s. of office cannot buy 6299

Mother s. child, fattens serpent 8330

rotten apple s. his companions 9500

SPOKE

anyone remember you s. to him today 3136

Christ s. of dying to live 6359

Christ s. to those to whom no one s. 6433

Jesus s. to unchanging needs of man 6448

Jesus s. words of life never spoken before 6449

Malice never s. well 390

man who s. as never man before 1147

may be sorry you s. 6674

The less he s. the more he heard 1832

The more he saw the less he s. 1832

SPOKEN

how enduring word God has s. 730

If God has s, why is universe not convinced 4963

Music language s. by angels 7907

not how well we have s, but how well we have lived 6600

plead for God to speak when he has already s, is speaking 8843

Slander slays speaker, s. to, s. of 10466

Was not s. of the soul 2328

wisdom to keep silent when damaging words s. to you 6271

word rashly s. cannot be brought back 10681

SPONGE

Would in tiny s. contained be 4839

SPONTANEITY

fear of sinning killed s. 6813

SPONTANEOUS

know Jesus Christ, belief s. 611

life full of s. joyful uncertainty, expectancy 5463

SPOON

long s. to eat with devil 2645

SPOONS

faster we counted our s. 5899

SPORTS

love s, most, that is your god 7338

SPOT

Home, dearer, sweeter s. than all the rest 5834

Home, s. of earth supremely best 5834

SPOTLESS

go through intrigue s. is greatness 3153

God's love s. purity 4750

SPOTS

brightest of all, the sun has s. 3951

will best perceive s. upon them 6004

SPREAD

in asterisks her webs are s. 6118

poison of bitterness, paranoia 10034

rumor in every ear it s. 9757

should first my lamp s. light 3323

SPREADING

two ways of s. light 3455

SPREADS

a common feast for all that lives 9883

Evil s. like an oak tree 3355

false report s. where recantation never reaches 10453

legalism s. paralyzing venom 6823

SPRING

aspiration to heart what s. is to earth 471

bursts today 2982

can s. be far behind 9874

cannot jump from winter to summer without a s. 9875

cleaning should begin with head, end with heart 5756

eternal s. is in my heart 8187

From thee, great God, we s. 5383

full of sweet days and roses 9891

get the hog out of the s. 10322

glory of s. how sweet 9898

God will wither up every s. you have 11689

God's way of saying hello 9892

In s. no one thinks of snow 1470

is too rainy 9879

is winter defrosting 9893

joy a secret s. world can't see 6529

Joy like a subterranean s. waters whole life 6568

let Christ be inward s. 6379

love like a natural s. 7257

makes everything young except man 9894

morning and evening are s. and fall 9877

no time like s. 9899

of joy, never runs dry, no matter what happens 6538

Oh s. to light, auspicious Babe, be born 6143

remember the s. 11170

season that says it with flowers 9890

so shall I s. into your love 7970

Songs s. forth weblike from mind at peace 7920

unlocks the flowers 9895

would not be so pleasant 182

SPRINGS
God sometimes puts s. in wagon 4808

Hope s. eternal in the human breast 5913

Joy has s. deep down inside 6538

of love are in God, not in us 4784

renew your s. that never dry up 9933

Sabbath, fifty-two s. in every year 10950

SPRINGTIME
always s. in heart that loves God 4797

invites you to believe anew 9896

invites you to try out its splendor 9896

promise of resurrection in every leaf in s. 9694

SPRINKLES
Who s. the altar he rears to thee 3369

SPRINT
Fathering is a marathon, not a s. 3919

SPROUTED
As seed s. Christ born in Bethlehem 5731

seed of God stirred, shoved, s. 2984

SPRUNG
Reason saw not till faith s. the light 3777

SPUR
fear of God, s. to courage 3993

Pray that loneliness s. you into 7140

SPY
Or the most agonizing s. 10674

SQUABBLES
Think of s. Adam and Eve must have had 7659

SQUALLS
surge across everyone's horizons 191

SQUANDER
do not s. time 6886

SQUANDERED
nothing more s. than human being 2343

SQUARE-KNOTTED
until deity s. flesh 6131

SQUEAKING
wheel that does the s. 8564

SQUEAKS
Christian who s. when he walks 9529

SQUEEZES
God s. but never chokes 4464

SQUIRE
Bless the s. and his relations 3112

SQUIRREL
stop expecting s. saints to soar 6187

SQUIRREL'S
hearing s. heartbeat 8496

SQUIRRELS
don't have feathers 6168

STABILITY
abuses have not shaken s. of church 1419

Emotional s. an attitude 2563

fear gives life s. 3980

threat to s. of world is hunger 8692

STABLE
I saw a s, low and very bare 6133

If s. at heart can normally cope 2737

in my heart s. 6134

Meek means emotional s. 7729

spirit not distracted by activity 4307

within your darkened s. shed 6118

STADIUM
beyond that s. scene 3326

STAGE
Man enters each s. of life as novice 7002

struts, frets his hour upon the s. 6994

world, s. on which God displays many wonders 12040

STAGE MANAGER
dream theater where dreamer is s. 2972

STAGER
devil, that old s. 2697

STAGES
first s. of spiritual life 1714

In early s. of Christian experience 7690

STAGGERED
Christian faith s. imagination of man 11201

STAGGERING
become disciples, impact on society s. 2819

reeling and s. through life 11450

STAGNANT
Consistency quality of s. mind 1746

stick to theological point of view become s. 11240

water loses its purity 6765

STAIN
Only heart without s. knows ease 1696

STAINS
draw curtain before s. of friend 4183

full of s. and corruptions 9852

STAIRS
habit must be coaxed down s. 5495

STAIRWAY
God has his own s. into heart 4540

STAKE
progress has been from scaffold to scaffold, from s. to s. 7673

STALE
breathe not s. air 4976

How s. seem all uses of this world 2603

intellectual world s. if we knew everything 9286

STALK
Were every s. on earth a quill 4748

STALLED
God doesn't start s. car 4782

who choose not to be chosen 3045

STAMP
president today, postage s. tomorrow 979

STAMPED
family s. character upon child 1126

STAND
also serve who only s. and wait 10202

Among those who s. do not sit 3064

Among those who sit, do not s. 3064

And makes us s. in every fight 1933

aside and watch yourself go by 10009

at real height against higher nature 6037

before God on basis of grace 1057

Before infinitude we s. silent 4706

before neighbors on character 1072

Bold shall I s. in thy great day 4719

building without basis cannot s. 3826

devil refuses to s. under God 4915

difficult to s. on pedestal, wash feet of those below 8717

enemies respect taking s. 1913

Faith, basis on which we s. 3835

Fall seven times, s. up eight 3592

first part of life parents learn to s. you 3893

God tests us that we might s. 171
Great men s. like solitary towers 5280
great thing not where we s. 1914
He has to s, cannot sit or lie 11750
he who has taken his s. finds yoke easy 1332
Here I s. I can do no other 1925
his word shall s. forever 9813
house divided cannot s. 1620
I can s. what I know 6685
ideas I s. for are not mine 2019
If doubt yourself, you s. on shaky ground 11599
if refuse to s. for truth 3846
If you were someone else, could you s. yourself 9990
Ignorance is content to s. still 3258
In heaven s. in character of Savior 1072
In matters of principle s. like rock 6308
last part of life you learn to s. parents 3893
Love and Self cannot s. together 9936
man's dignity to s. upright 7395
millions s. impotent 100
must s. with anybody that stands right 6303
never know when luxury going to s. up 11834
not so much where we s. 4434
O God, s. by me against all the world 9109
One foot cannot s. on two boats 6058
Only when knelt before God can we s. before men 8880
pretense of being holy until s. in light 9741
shadows caused when we s. in our own sunshine 10792
soul, God s. sure 948
square where you are 8377
still, listen to speech of God 4965
still, refuse to retreat 2742
that I may rise, s, o'erthrow me 2840
that we may know what to s. for 11731
that we may know where to s. 11731
To s. at crossroads requires strength 1137
true to integrity of Jesus Christ 8545
two strong men s. face to face 915
Two things s. like stone 6657
unless we s. for something 11731
upright when others beaten down 1915
we have no time to s. and stare 6829
we s. stripped of accustomed defenses 5238

What we s. up for proves our character 1060
when all men s. before God 4718
when you cannot s. God will bear you in his arms 5907
Wherever I s, only thou 4518
while I s. on this isthmus of life 6910
Who could s. to see whole week before lived 4336
Why s. we here trembling 1554
with face in what direction he will 9151
Within thy circling power I s. 4876
worship, s. in its strengthening 12103
You s. tall when you kneel to pray 9038

STANDARD
God is that s. 5749
He who makes the law his s. 6812
highest s. God has is himself 4567
judged by s. higher, more attainable 6812
Lord, s. for our lives 568
need not be concerned how high God's s. is 8518
To be holy God does not conform to a s. 5749
under Satan's s. and enlisted there 10427

STANDARDS
Christ turned world's s. upside down 5001
Jesus' s. asked more than any other ever has 6444
Jesus' s. far from lax and easy-going 6444
No people became great by lowering s. 7834
not called to be successful with ordinary s. 10823
of law reflected God's righteousness 9755

STANDETH
God within the shadow 5377
Yet with itself every soul s. single 7150

STANDING
be afraid only of s. still 5365
Holiness deliverance from s. still 5746
man grows tired s. still 6751
man who never alters his opinion like s. water 9185
never stubbed toe s. still 3599

STANDPOINT
Christ's life failure from every s. but God's 3605
happiness and joy from God's s. 5531

STANDS
A lie s. on one leg, truth on two 6864
Christ reveals a God who s. in thick of whole thing 6432

erect by bending over the fallen 10144
God deliberately s. aside 4891
God s. ready to take over management of our lives 5511
God's anvil s. 7875
God's justice s. forever 4726
Humanity never s. still 5969
If it s. on edge, I study 3011
Love ever s. with open hands 7218
man s. upon the shore and longs to cross over 7916
over me the human insect 4526
Still s. the ancient sacrifice 6036
strongest man is he who s. most alone 10759

STAR
Be thou a guiding s. above me 5375
Bible, s. without a speck 710
falls for love of God shall rise a s. 3635
glory of the s. 6108
God lights the evening s. 4596
God makes the glow worm and s. 8008
God sees scar, creates s. 8278
in darkness, Christ is my s. 6498
life, twinkle of s. in God's eternal day 7015
penny will hide biggest s. in universe 7795
self more distant than any s. 9352
shall rise a s. 4791
Shine out, O Blessed S. 6141
soul shall shine a s. of day 10675
There's a s. to guide the humble 5995
who canst guide the wandering s. 9048

STARE
Only children paused to s. 6458
we have no time to stand and s. 6829

STARING
every night sit s. at another box 5859

STARLIGHT
Behind the cloud the s. lurks 5904

STARS
And all the s. looked down 6470
are constantly shining 2560
arise, and the night is holy 11649
Attir'd with s, we shall forever sit 5679
before sun or s. in splashed heavens 4694
blessed candles of night 11639
blossomed the lovely s. 11636
daisies that begem blue fields of sky 11638
disappeared if within reach of human hands 3202
flame out in pomp of light 7927
flowers of the sky 11640
giving beauty to the world 9116

glory of the s. 4643
God's promises like the s. 9323
golden fruits all out of reach 11637
Hushed are the s, whose power never spent 8014
Infinite sowed his name in heavens in s. 8037
Lights of a thousand s. do not make one moon 6198
magnificence but a little sparklet 9116
man greater than the s. 7385
man of earth, but thoughts with s. 7381
moon, sun, how they move in silence 10250
often do not see s. until dark 2560
quietness of the s. seemed to reproach me 4618
raiment of darkness 9116
shine on brightly 365
shine, fearless and confident 4618
silence and the wakeful s. 10673
speaks with s. 9805
the forget-me-nots of the angels 11636
Thou dost preserve the s. from wrong 4598
Turn scars into s. 299
When dark enough men see s. 10929
While grass, flowers, s. spell out his name 8019
Who guides the s. with steadfast law 11628

START
God doesn't s. stalled car 4782
Repentance opportunity of a new s. 9596
With God you can always s. afresh 8080
world had music at the s. 7886

STARTED
fight for our planet has s. 3400
fight of cosmic proportions has s. 3400

STARTING
repentence is s. point for better things 9590
where not a childlike humility at s. post 11549

STARTLED
a man is first s. by sin 10287
encountered mind that s. us 7752

STARTLING
life with its sudden, s. joys 3685

STARTS
by carrying away small stones 59
keen spirit s. into instant action 8224
trouble s. out like fun 11448

STARVATION
not s. but man himself greatest danger 7397

thousands would be reduced to s. 11887

STARVATION-RIDDEN
world 10051

STARVE
feeds faith, s. doubts to death 3727
slander would s. and die 10455

STARVED
souls 10247
when faith is s. 3828

STARVES
if no one s. while I eat 625
unbelief s. the soul 3703

STARVING
emotions we become rigid 3050

STATE
Although church and s. stand separate 5169
devil talks glibly of church and s. 2651
for preservation of life 10506
Happiness not a s. to arrive at 5523
joy a s. of the soul 6568
let it ring from every s. 4157
Love is not a s. 7630
not remedy for sin, but means to restrain 5177
Peace is a s. of mind 8455
preserved in s. of perpetual puerility 5584
These are the bulwarks of the s. 7986
Youth ideal s. if came later in life 12187

STATEMENT
God is omniscient, a theological s. 11179
God, no s. can express him 4700
If never hurt by s. of Jesus 6407
most revolutionary s. in history 7305
once let loose cannot be caught 5117

STATEMENTS
one of plainest s. in Bible 4949
paradox comes into all religious s. 4682

STATES
Youth will assume control of s. 12160

STATESMEN
Destiny waits not in the hands of s. 2620

STATIC
In Christianity God not a s. thing 11425

STATION
Earth's highest s. ends in "Here he lies" 7088
God above in rank, s. 4607
Not, what was his s. 7423
three days late at bus s. 4266

STATIONARY
so long as circumstances s, wait 5444

STATIONS
always know our proper s. 3112

STATISTICAL
reference to great historic event 5726

STATISTICIAN
sees city as social unit 10522

STATISTICS
on death quite impressive 2386

STATUES
We are the s. 9822

STATURE
become aware of s, freedom and evil in him 7494
comes not with height but depth 11939
In celebration weak, lowly receive new s. 3235
not complete in spiritual s. if all not given to God 5734

STATUS
service satisfies self-esteem more than celebrity s. 9996
with smile of God needs no s. symbols 1323

STATUS QUO
unjust, materialistic s. 8696

STAY
angels might be asked to s. with us 5862
do not know how I am going to s. "in the air" 9908
Don't s. away from church because hypocrites 6050
easier to s. out than get out 11073
God shall be my s. 5394
No man need s. way he is 1146
or s. and turn mountain into gold mine 2633
Some people s. longer in hour than others in week 9492
Still in the right to s. 9067
Why s. we on earth except to grow 7706

STAYED
If God s. away as much as a hairbreadeth 7477
may be sorry you s. or went 6674

STAYING
can't hold a man down without s. down with him 10479
drown by s. in water 3636
failure is the s. down 3598
happily married should rank among the fine arts 7615
married more difficult 7615
not falling down that is worst, but s. on the ground 10318

STAYS
Comfort s. to enslave 7361
Love s. with us 7291

though the sky s. dim 4195
time s, we go 11327

STEADFAST
as an anchor 4204
Give me, O Lord, a s. heart 9057
greatness in s. adherence to
   promises made 5283
Love is s. 7246

STEADFASTNESS
peril produces s. 952

STEADY
Cheefulness fills mind with s.
   serenity 1092
illuminated by s. radiance,
   renewed daily 4538
through difficult times, hold s.
   969

STEAL
an egg will s. a camel 2912
cares that infest the day silently s.
   away 7887
God's blessings s. into life
   noiselessly 4641
We taught him to s. 3458

STEALING
will continue s. 1687

STEALTH
Christ treasure without s. 6391
greatest pleasure is good action by
   s. 8607

STEAM
No s. drives anything until
   confined 2852

STEEL
our hearts against all fear 9090
to myself, a heart of s. 5626
tongue not s, yet cuts 1881

STEEPED
save our souls from being s. in care
   9064

STEER
Bible God's chart to s. by 713

STEERING WHEEL
prayer, s. or spare tire 8848

STEERS
Who pulls or s. with me 6398

STEM
hope is the s. 3837

STEMS
melancholy that s. from greatness
   of mind 5303

STEP
a s. from companionship to slavery
   10326
Acceptance is first s. 154
begins with one s. 4435
By obedience led s. by s. to correct
   errors 8110
cannot s. twice into same river
   985
courageous s. would carry
   through fear 3982

death, s. from provisional to
   permanent 2390
defeat first s. to something better
   2517
Discontent first s. in progress
   2864
Don't be afraid to take big s. 3650
Doubt dreads to take s. 2939
every s. nearer God increases
   depth we may fall 10700
Every s. of progress world has
   made 7673
Every s. toward Christ kills a
   doubt 2940
first s. in wisdom is to question
   everything 11935
First s. is hardest 545
first s. of wisdom is to know what
   is false 11943
first s. to victory to recognize
   enemy 11670
God leads us s. by s. 5392
habit coaxed down stairs s. at a
   time 5495
have children who s. on their toes
   8323
I climbed, and s. by s. O Lord
   5694
I see not a s. before me 8079
Integrity first s. to greatness 6311
journey of a thousand miles
   begins with single s. 6871
last s. is to come to terms with
   everything 11935
Let him s. to music which he hears
   10827
new s. what people fear most 3989
not on sleeping serpent 11084
one s. enough for me 5429
   2551
one s. through doubtings dim
   2962
only first s. that is difficult 2749
Pale Death, with impartial s. 2361
Reason's last s. is recognition
   things beyond it 9421
temptation a s. in progress of faith
   11093
Without Christ not one s. 3822

STEPHEN
stoned to death 1211

STEPPING
best way to keep from s. on toes
   11286
o'er the threshold 2364

STEPPING-STONE
Into a s. 1927
make failure s. to success 3586

STEPPING-STONES
obstacles become s. in pathway of
   strong 10754
View stumbling blocks as s. 2048
wisdom to make s. out of
   stumbling blocks 9073

STEPS
Beware of desperate s. 2575
Four s. to achievement 80

God means to guide our s. by
   moonlight 5393
God will take nine s. toward us,
   but not the tenth 9578
humor adds balance to our s. 6715
No man ever more than four s.
   from God 9585
safety walks in justice's s. 6628
The s. of faith 3767
Till our s. grow slow 8120
When obedient, God guides our s.
   8119

STEREOTYPED
By starving emotions we become s.
   3050

STERILE
Pride is the mountain peak, s. and
   bleak 6026
Without faith man becomes s,
   hopeless 3824

STERILITY
doom ourselves to spiritual s.
   2821

STERN
Eternity, s. colossal image 3269
God won't be so s. to expect me
   to give up that 10978

STERNEST
Christ, s. of Saviors 6430

STERN-SENTENCED
the Word s. to be nine months
   dumb 6142

STEW
beef too much find himself in s.
   2068
fit only for s. 206
oysters never wounded fit only for
   s. 10883

STEWARD ~~STEWARDSHIP 10724–~~
~~10743~~
You are God's s. 10740

STICK
Any fool can govern with s. in
   hand 6786
as an arrow to the mark to s. there
   4222
crooked s. will have crooked
   shadow 988
Faith means I will s. to my belief
   3662
Gossip may not s. but leaves mark
   5129
have decided to s. with love 7182
I s. my finger into existence 3485
Not all people driven by same s.
   7868

STICKING
nose into other people's business
   5147

STICKY
thought is s. 11990

STIFLE
creed would s. me that shelters you
   2027

STIFLES
Evil s. life 5024

STIFLING
power of criticism 2954

STILL
be afraid only of standing s. 5365
be s, God's plan is wrought 9556
Be s. my soul 1502
behind the thunder, s. small voice 1515
faith ability to be s. 3769
God, voice too s. to be easily audible 4465
heart filled to brim with joy must be s. 6559
Holiness deliverance from standing s. 5746
Humanity never stands s. 5969
I listened—quiet and s. 5415
I must be s. 7715
Ignorance is content to stand s. 3258
man grows tired standing s. 6751
never stubbed toe, standing s. 3599
Rather than fighting become s. 2556
sit s. and trust the engineer 5461
stand s, listen to speech of God 4965
Stand s, refuse to retreat 2742
Teach us to sit s. 4979
waters run deep 10267
When the world is s. and dim 7927

STILLEST
greatest events our s. hours 10268
tongue, truest friend 1879

STILLNESS
an essential part of growing deeper 7711
Nothing so like God as s. 10258 4486
of nature louder than choir of voices 8041

STILTS
no use mounting on s. 9248
walks on s. to seem bigger 2761

STIMULATES
Silent worship s. 12114

STIMULATING
a s. loneliness 7145
Anxiety s. us to seek security 3961

STIMULATION
more than s. of celebrity status 9996

STIMULATORS
Words s. or emotion 12001

STIMULUS
Defeat fresh s. 2509

STING
disarm poverty of its sharpest s. 8679

Dishonesty a scorpion that will s. itself to death 2908
faith draws s. out of trouble 3818
Faith takes s. from every loss 3661
Forgiveness cools s. 4075
giant feels s. of bee 8700
O death! Where is thy s. 2389
Words can s. 12003

STINGING
kill themselves in s. others 9721

STINGS
underneath a rivalry that s. 10527
Vice s. even in pleasures 10412

STINK
devil always leaves s. behind him 2670

STINKS
pile money up, s. to high heaven 7812

STIR
who never s. from home read only a page 6945

STIRRED
seed of God s, shoved, sprouted 2984
spirits s. by Holy Spirit go forward even in sleep 10490

STIRRING
inward s. and touching of God 5764

STIRS
humanity poor were not for divinity that s. within us 5979
we glow when God s. us 7534

STOCKPILED
grace cannot be s. beforehand 5226

STOIC
bears 6563

STOICAL
some are s. but feeling will be there 3052

STOICISM
better foundation than s. 1563

STOICS
declaring suffering good in itself 10880
for s. pain an exercise 8255
tried denying reality of suffering 10880

STOLE
ideas from Jesus 2019

STOMACH
eating on an empty s. 131
Faith on full s. may be contentment 3711
No one can worship God on empty s. 7152

STONE
action as s. laid 3826
blazing meteor only a s. 4395
every s. flashed like a ruby 6423

Love doesn't sit there like a s. 7217
My heart within me like a s. 2587
pick up a s. to turn in your hand 4608
rolled away not to permit Christ to come out 9699
rolled away to enable disciples to go in 9699
Small drops of water hollow out a s. 8556
this s. unique 4993
to seek wisdom in youth like inscription on s. 11956
Two things stand like s. 6657
Virtue like a rich s. 11706
who is a granite s. 6517

STONES
carrying away small s. 59
God has no s. to throw 4453
Slander flings s. at itself 10461
those who walk on well-trodden paths throw s. 1643
throw s. at those showing new road 1643
would praise God if need arose 12099

STONY
God sends us on s. paths 180

STOOD
ground whereon I s. 967
I said to the man who s. at the gate 5417
people who influence s. unconsciously for right 6239
snake s. up for evil 3403

STOOP
don't s. to be a king 7781
Heaven itself would s. to virtue 11692
If wife small, s. down and whisper in ear 7620
Rather let my head s. to the block 7677
way to be humble is not to s. 6037
Wisdom oftentimes nearer when s. than soar 6044

STOOPED
Christ s. when he conquered 2152
God s. to work by, in his children 4467

STOOPING
not growing taller, but s. lower 6017

STOOPS
God s. o'er his head 9940
Grace is love that s. 5220
Lifts earth to heaven, s. heaven to earth 6153

STOP
and smell the flowers 9530
cannot s. alarming number of divorces 2928
comparing 6168
God did not s. the crucifixion 4931

happiness never found till we s. looking 5550

How many people s. because so few say "Go" 3135

If I can s. one heart from breaking 6922

If s. every time dog barks, road will never end 8543

lamenting and look up 12063

long enough to let feet catch up with mouth 9331

mention Jesus people want to s. conversation 6518

people miss happiness because didn't s. to enjoy it 5585

When God checks, s. at once 5464

who hasn't time to s. at railroad crossing 5589

You don't s. laughing because grow old 6748

you grow old because you s. laughing 6748

STOP-GAP

God cannot be used as s. 7562

STOPPED

dead by some reverse 5395

friend, a push when you've s. 4174

He kindly s. for me 2230

In that moment, God s. me 10940

STOPPING

selfishness means s. at human limits 10067

STOPS

anyone who s. learning is old 2995

if grudge, spiritual penetration into knowledge of God s. 9633

no rest s. on pilgrimage 9832

Nothing s. family quarrel more quickly 3879

teacher can never tell where influence s. 2993

trial only s. when it is useless 5352

When laughing depression and stress s. 6746

When obedient, God guides our s. 8119

STORE

A few rich treasures from his mighty store 6111

mind should not be bin to s. facts 3021

save in one s, spend in another 4036

STOREHOUSE

Fill well s. of soul's delight 11375

STORIES

Bible contains nearly all the great s. 701

human s. go on repeating themselves 5984

If s. incomprehensible to Jews, Muslims, Taoists 12147

only two or three human s. 5984

STORING

By our anti-intellectualism may be s. up judgment of God 6679

Perception rather than s. of ideas 3021

STORM

And tossed by s. and flood 4642

Be thou the rainbow to the s. of life 618

brightest thunderbolt elicited from darkest s. 220

faith will survive s. better than oak 3702

fatal calm that precedes the s. 10352

good pilot best tried in s. 137

His winds of s. drive through my door 11468

In every s. the legacy 8009

in its very nature is transient 8444

kicks up a s. 382

let God break life's moorings in some s. 9564

lofty pine that by the s. is oftener tossed 9216

man subject to s. and tempests 282

Night and s. look as if they would last forever 8444

no rainbow without cloud and s. 10636

No s. can shake inmost calm 232

Old age like plane flying through s. 8158

passing from s. to perfect calm 2399

Peace is to be able to sleep in the s. 8470

Pray to God in the s, but keep rowing 8898

rages but our hearts are at rest 8470

sea is subject to s. and tempests 282

sees sunshine where others see shadows, s. 5943

shaking hands with a northeast s. 6531

think they must s. heaven with loud outcries 8787

Well roars the s. to those that hear 3644

wise man in s. prays to God 3997

within that endangers, not s. without 3997

STORMED

Christ could have s. citadels 6503

STORMS

finding God's way in suddenness of s. 1803

greatest is calmest in s. 5297

hide from temptestuous s. of devil 2652

life filled with God-appointed s. 191

make oaks take deeper root 207

not outward s. that defeat 2737

pilots gain reputation from s. 209

Prayer is battering heaven with s. of prayer 8919

S. make oaks take deeper root 207

Ye s. howl out his greatness 4712

STORM-TROUBLED

No trembler in world's s. sphere 3765

STORMY

character formed in s. billows 1042

Through quiet waters, s. weather 4281

Through this dark and s. night 3800

weather in initial stages of discipleship 2822

STORY

Do not judge a man until you know whole s. 6573

Friendship is a simple s. 4217

History, s. written by finger of God 5712

In seeking truth, get both sides of s. 11511

of conversion, s. of blessed defeat 1899

of Jesus told more than any other in history 5729

What a s. a redwood stump could tell 5731

STOVE

cat sits down on hot s. lid 3551

STRADDLING

an issue like s. middle of road 11602

STRADIVARI'S

could not make Antonio S. violins 4441

STRAIGHT

can't drive s. on twisting lane 4440

cannot make s. lines out of crooked lot 4885

If but the way be s. cannot go amiss 5471

If refuse to be made s. when green 12166

never able to make others s. 3444

never any traffic congestion on s, narrow path 9819

smile a curve to set things s. 10495

than man keep s. line walking in dark 6614

To be bent is to become s. 7071

To get to heaven, turn right, keep s. 5675

will not be made s. when dry 12166

STRAIGHTEN

when question marks s. into exclamation points 5676

STRAIGHTENS

Grace s. me out 5232

STRAIGHTER
crooked paths look s. at end 2374

STRAIN
a few s. muscles to carry off a prize 7018

desert of everyday hurry and s. 10247

Take from our souls the s. and stress 8431

weight and s. are all gone 7486

With the fearful s. on me 6747

STRAITENED
though pressed, love is not s. 7283

STRAITS
proportion out what s. he sees fit 4629

STRAND
one s. of faith amongst corruption 3749

STRANGE
about Jesus is you can never get away from him 6485

church, in what s. quarries 1401

coming of Christ by way of manger s, stunning 6145

Congress is so s. 5171

death not going to s. country 2249

enter upon a s, alarming life 6421

Every moment of this s. life a miracle 6889

grow so wide, deep nothing human is s. 10540

holiest souls pessimistic 8586

how much got to know before know how little 6700

How s. this fear of death 2297

However s. life's monody sounds 7895

Humility is a most s. thing 6006

Is it less s. thou shouldst live at all 6103

Is it s. there are clashings, collisions 4563

It were too s. I should doubt thy love 4758

Listening a magnetic, s. thing 1857

misunderstanding of God's ways 9840

often nothing so s. as truth 11548

One gets some very s. surprises 7561

People are s. 8481

Seems it s. thou shouldst live forever 6103

Success demands s. sacrifices 10801

Suffering s. initiation into happiness 10896

that I did not know him then 4199

to be known universally, yet be so lonely 7130

ungrateful to these teachers 5251

STRANGELY
With cryptic words, too s. set 8049

STRANGENESS
meaning unfolds and s. vanished 6145

STRANGER
cannot regard everyone as s. 922

friend whose acquaintance you haven't made 9443

Home of the s. 6468

I, a s. and afraid 3978

In this world I am a s. 6929

Is s. here than you 1396

man an eternal s. on this planet 7436

single event can awaken within s. unknown to us 6873

To men he was a s. 6133

to oneself, estranged from others too. 9519

to the s. God is hospitable 4649

Truth must necessarily be s. than fiction 11574

We have careful thought for the s. 3900

STRANGERS
God is at home, we are s. 4562

selfish do not like needy s. to intrude 5957

We were s, now citizens 1348

STRANGEST
truth of gospel is redemption comes through suffering 9439

STRANGLING
Can roll the s. load from me 2583

STRAPS
Divorce hash made of domestic s. 2920

STRATEGIST
adversary a master s. 2660

STRAW
Even asses know s. is better than gold 11804

nothing rises quicker than s. 3857

On long journey even s. is heavy 8550

Peace wisp of s. that binds sheaf of blessings 8465

should make no pact with fire 11085

STRAWS
almost as sharp as thorns 6489

Errors, like s. upon surface flow 3255

Yet s. can sing 6149

STRAY
God brings problems so we will not s. 2844

STRAYED
yet I remembered you 9070

STRAYING
I am s. here for a bit 6929

STREAKED
sky still s. with smoke of crematoria 3416

STREAKING
Up the blackness s. 3800

STREAM
Bible s. where elephant may swim 707

Bible s. where lamb may wade 707

ford every s. 4421

If you want to clear the s. 10322

Life bridge of groans across s. of tears 2598

righteousness like a mighty s. 6629

The central s. of what we are indeed 7369

When you drink from the s. 11170

STREAMS
Large s. from little fountains flow 8657

of living water flowing 5810

Parents wonder why s. bitter 8352

STREET
crossing s. when light red 4094

hardest to exercise patience in the s. 8423

Life is a one-way s. 6950

Not in the clamor of the crowded s. 10794

on dead-end s. with man who denies God 7523

pessimist looks both ways crossing one-way s. 8585

reputation would not know character if met on s. 9618

Respect is intended to operate on a two-way s. 9644

whole s. is clean 9664

STREETS
child tells in s. 8340

Old s. a glamor hold 8143

sacred, God's presence there 4866

sweep s. as Michelangelo painted 2777

while lost girl on s, I'll fight 3342

STREETSWEEPER
If a man is called to be a s. 2777

STRENGTH
Anxiety empties today of s. 409

As for that which is beyond your s. 4747

ask for s. to hold on 10931

Be content with s. you've got 1777

Be thou my guide, my s. 5456

because s. and patience are failing him 6599

Bible contains all human weaknesses, s. 701

Bible never failed to give s. 670

Christianity, God-directed s. 1165

Comforter as applied to Holy Spirit means "with us." 5804

commandments need s. of love 1525

courageous pray for s. 1937

day to use s. given us 6947

death raises from weakness into s. 2250

defects improve s. 3932

Despair doubles our s. 2577

difference between s. of Christians is contrast of praying 8976

Difficulty rocks into s. 2719

does ask for guiding, s. of God 4803

enthusiasm s. that lifts 3188

everlasting Father will give you unfailing s. 415

excellent to have a giant's s. 8707 10753

fact is, we have too much s. 10768

faith is weakness leaning on God's s. 3775

Faith mastering difficulty in s. of Lord 3678

Faith without thankfulness lacks s. 11154

from struggle against obstacles 8850

gentleness, s. under control 4402

get s. today to meet tomorrow 4318

God against s. of enemy 5016

God give me love, care, s, to help 910

God gives s. to do 55

God is my s. 7462

God is my s. and song 4490

God never gives s. for tomorrow 2722

God only gives s. for the moment 2722

God rescues us by shattering s. 882

God's s. worth more than world 10768

God's Spirit gives the tone its s. 7892

grace, s. of God to overcome 5227

Great works performed not by s. 8544

Greatness lies in right use of s. 5284

grows out of weakness 10755

has failed ere the day is half done 7570

He sendeth more s. when labors increase 5223

Home s. of a nation 5836

I pray for s, fortitude 1927

in circumstances of great trial, much s. 7486

in trial divine s. is found 2734

Independence is not s. 6414

Is not prayer precisely s. 8847

Jesus Christ let men take s. from him 2170

joy, s, courage are with thee 8867

Leave tomorrow's trouble to tomorrow's s. 12067

Look for s. in people, not weakness 5077

Lord is s. 3985

Love attempts what is above its s. 7220

lust for power not rooted in s. 8718

made perfect in weakness 8170

majority s. to make itself obeyed 5191

Maturity, not to hide one's s. out of fear 7695

mistaking weakness for s. defeats 10749

must be grown 8850

naive is child's s. 7977

need new s. to walk old paths 9554

noise evidence of weakness not s. 10576

nothing so gentle as s. 10752

O s. of the world 10512

of character may be acquired at work 5849

of cheerfulness 1099

of Christianity different from natural s. 1165

of country is s. of religious convictions 7988

of mind in the cross 2096

of the first Christians 3292

Of trust, s, calmness from above 9050

of virtue measured by habitual acts 5502

often as great a handicap as weakness 10750

One is given s. to bear what happens 200

Only through inner transformation s. to fight 6619

only when everything hopeless, hope a s. 5903

ordained that in conflict we find s. 9090

ought to take care before ask for s. 8850

our s. of character 8

person's defect serves as s. for personality 3932

pray for s. to bear troubles 2091

prayer for light—for s. to bear 8863

prayer for s. that he might achieve 8806

Prayer girds weakness with divine s. 8912

prayer, gives me s. for everything 8794

prays for s. without much thought 8850

real s. when tea into hot water 2743

Reverence sign of s. 9735

sap s: worry, travel, sin 10406

secure in thy love and s. 9051

sign of s. to admit don't know answers 10748

Strengthen me by sympathizing with s. 3139

tears shed for others sign of s. 11026

Temptation has become my s. 11075

that wins is calm 10757

the lot of a few privileged men 8557

thing to watch is our s. 10760

To attempt to abandon bad habits in own s. 11108

to battle difficulties 1809

to bear suffering 5907

To control passion in own s. 11108

To resist temptation in own s. 11108

To stand at crossroads requires s. 1137

to the end 6468

To try the soul's s. on 6908

truest help to call out afflicted man's best s. 936

tyrannous to use it like a giant 8707

Unguarded s. is double weakness 10765

Unity creates s. 11623

until we have time to build up s. 8924

wait upon Lord, renew s. 10764

weakness deepens dependence on Christ for s. 8256

weakness my greatest s. 11789

Weakness or s. add to my life 1538

weaknesses make us appreciate God's s. 11790

were it to shine in full s. 4657

when face adversity, they give me s. 10913

When God our s. is s. indeed 10767

When human s. gives way 4569

When man has no s. 10766

When outward s. is broken 3818

when s. is our own, it is weakness 10767

whether weakness or s. 1461

With every cross comes s. to carry it 8108

Worry only saps today of its s. 12089

STRENGTH'NING

their arms to warfare glad and grim 8454

STRENGTHEN

all persons unjustly accused 9104

Contemplation s. for action 1766

either lighten my burden or s. my back 9071

me by sympathizing with strength 3139

must s. commitment to families 3901

no problem can't face if Jesus to s. 11126

people who s. one another 4241

Some people s. society 1040

to s. and confirm new, weak faith 3744

STRENGTHENED

by preaching, sacrament 1444

some rise from sermon s. 10094

STRENGTHENER
Jesus promised followers "The S."
would be with them 5804

STRENGTHENING
God is s. for virtue 4514
worship, stand in its s. 12103

STRENGTHENS
belief in spiritual existence after
death 6090
feeds wolf, s. his enemy 11064
He that wrestles with us s. nerves
1623
in winepress of cross juice s. 2095
privation trains and s. the mind
242
Punishment s. resistance 2038
Religion and home life s. the other
5858

STRENGTHS
Marriage supported by s. of love
7635
Remember your s. 9271

STRENUOUS
Cheerfulness, result of s. discipline
1088
life with its eyes shut a kind of
wild insanity 11234

STRENUOUSNESS
open foe of attainment 10757

STRESS
accent on youth, s. on parents
8354
passing from s. to perfect calm
2399
power to work under s. 8423
Take from our souls the strain and
s. 8431
To live through s. with another
10641
When laughing s. stops 6746
will experience hardship, s. 953

STRESSES
not outward s. that defeat 2737

STRETCH
cross, arms s. out to limitless
reaches 2167
if world all man I could not s.
myself 8012
Loose tongues s. truth 9488
Sorrows s. out spaces in heart for
joy 10623

STRETCH'D
Though s. from sky to sky 4748

STRETCHED
hand of divine providence s. out
2774
He s. skin over spirit 6131
Lord was s. on hard, painful tree
10836

STRETCHING
hand to save falling man 1554

STRICT
rules for sex tremendously s.
10235

STRIDES
gigantic s. in medicine 2928

STRIFE
All things born through s. 1621
Assail'd by scandal and the
tongue of s. 6356
Bible, judge that ends s. 710
cheer the soul tired with human s.
7917
Christ, message set society ablaze
with s. 6375
come out of the s. 4577
Give peace profound or daily s.
1538
Helping each other through s.
4281
In the s. of truth and falsehood
2489
love would sweep away s. 7349
Marriage with s. is life's purgatory
7645
set of soul decides, not the s. 4432
world of s. shut out 5817

STRIKE
at the sin of which the world is full
10304
no one able to s. terror into others
4001
out or part with God 2964
the next note full, clear 9684
thought faith would s. me like
lightning 3735
When man is happy does not hear
clock s. 5572
When you are the hammer, s.
9655
with eye on God, s. note full, clear
7056

STRIKES
God s. at core of motivations 7863
Slander vice that s. double blow
10463

STRIKING
God meets needs in s. ways 3744
That which is s. not always good
5080
to one s. at the root 3405

STRING
broken s. may be joined, knot will
remain 9624
Till every note and s. shall answer
thine 7527
Time like well-greased s. 11343

STRINGS
all s. in concert of his joy 4028
in the concert of God's joy 7550
need only be swept by divine
breath 7921
10665
toy world which moves when pull
s. 4132

STRIP
down to essentials 7709

life like a little s. of pavement over
an abyss 7090
Spirit of God may s. you of
borderline pleasures 5776

STRIPPED
Every pious mood s. off before
cross 2160
of all possessions but knowledge
of God 11688
we stand s. of accustomed defenses
5238

STRIPPING
God begins by s. of all
self-confidence 9851

STRIPS
friendship of nobility 4245
God s. of everything 4790
love s. 7329

STRIP-TEASE
large audience for s. act 7360

STRIVE
alone man with his God must s.
10530
hopelessly s. to invent happiness
apart from God 5570
laud character but s. to climb to
top at any cost 6068
miserable feeling that useless to s.
4507
on to finish work we are in 5199
To s. with one's self is the good
10022
will to neither s. nor cry 8430

STRIVES
Human logic s. in vain 2636
Vainly s. and fights, and frets
7440

STRIVING
equipped to accomplish things s.
for 4439
faith in meaning of our s. 4005
keep on s. until I climb over 2633
Peace does not mean end of s.
8454
what are we actually s. for 4439

STRIVINGS
Till all our s. cease 8431

STROKE
of death as lover's pinch 2387
Spare not the s! Do with us as
thou wilt 7519

STRONG
A s. man must have something
difficult 77
alcohol, weaken the s. 331
ancient heavens through thee
fresh, s. 4598
And, s. in him whose cause is ours
10756
Be s! We are not here to play 6881
Be s. 6256
cannot choose to be s. 6530
Death is s, life stronger 2985
Defeat school in which truth
grows s. 2507

Faith is a s. power 3678

found myself as s. as forty years ago 7104

Friends speak with words sweet, s. 4185

God asks for something s. 4507

God takes the weak and makes them s. 10745

God will provide s. shoes 180

Greatness lies not in being s. 5284

grief, s. to consume small troubles 5331

habit too weak until too s. to be broken 5500

human spirit to grow s. by conflict 2715

Humility is s. 6012

I would be s. to suffer 1018

If any be but weak, how s. is Christ 6391

is s. who conquers others 9968

Jesus proclaims weak are the s. 6447

look, honor, rejoice in, imitate what is s. 3940

Love is s. 7246

Malice has a s. memory 9637

minds, great hearts, true faith, ready hands 6299

must strengthen commitment to s. families 3901

Nothing makes one feel so s. as a call for help 10177

Nothing so s. as gentleness 10752

obstacles become stepping-stones in pathway of s. 10754

prayer means whereby we become s. to meet evil 8977

roots grow deep when winds s. 212

Sin a s. imagination 10368

Sin is s. 10374

so young, so s, so sure of God 1609

soul never so s. as when forgoes revenge 4095

tend to fail at our s. point 10760

that we are not always s. 8867

thoughts too s. to be suppressed 3059

To suffer and be s. 10869

two s. men stand face to face 915

weak depending on knowledge of God 1321

Weak things united become s. 11624

weak, not s. to be esteemed 5001

will is s. blind man who carries 918

woman under whose hand children grow up s, pure 5857

STRONG-ARM

Christ will never s. his way into your life 6438

STRONGER

and deeper roots less visible 7702

become s. only when become weaker 10769

by weakness, wiser men become 7701

chain no s. than weakest link 10744

Chains of gold s. than chains of iron 11802

Death is strong, life s. 2985

God s. than devil 1924

Grace binds with s. cords than duty 5211

Great men see spiritual s. than material force 10693

harder we lean, s. we grow 10761

harder we lean, s. we grow spiritually 8256

He who injured you either s. or weaker 6263

Holy Spirit is s. than genius 4396

I pray for s. back 929

If he is s, spare yourself 6263

life s. than dark, light, wrong, right 2985

Nothing is s. than love 7283

Nothing s. than gentleness 4404

Opinions s. than armies 8199

Our inner life grows s. when outwardly condemned 6270

Pray for s. backs 8896

Pray to be s. men 8780

spirit s. than genius 11568

suffering a far s. link than joy 5338

Temptation emerge s. 11061

the freer the man, the s. the bond 6177

tough love that turns us into s. persons 7686

Warmth s. than force, fury 4296

What does not destroy makes s. 231

What s. breastplate than a heart untainted 6320

you make us s. or weaker 9522

STRONGEST

Christian, s. when weakest 1265

Devil, s. spirit that fought in heaven 2643

faith from conflict often s. 2935

man is he who stands most alone 10759

Out of suffering emerged s. souls 10882

Truth always the s. argument 11563

word is right 11993

STRONGHOLD

capture inner s. of pride 10043

STRONGHOLDS

love would sweep away s. of the devil 7349

STRONGLY

God disposed all s, sweetly 4904

iron most s. united by fiercest flame 4273

others tempted s. at end 11083

Some people tempted s. at beginning 11083

STRUCK

one chord of music 7919

you s. me down 7579

STRUCTURE

higher your s, deeper must be foundation 5997

No other s. can replace family 3877

STRUCTURES

high s. require solid foundation 5991

STRUGGLE

all night with the angel 9777

Better shun bait than s. in snare 11049

between proud mind, empty purse 8679

carry on s. against evil 3414

come out of the s. 4577

commandments do not need s. 1525

Faith does not s. 3658

God does not maintain neutrality in s. for justice 6630

God in no way hinders s. for development 4129

God values faith in midst of s. 11667

in our lives 10407

Life is a s. 6947

Manhood a s. 12199 7097

no s, no progress 9312

not so great a s. with my vices 6115

probability fail in s. should not deter 3625

Quotations tell of s. with life, death 9385

Shun not the s. 6881

Strength from s. against obstacles 8850

stubborn s. for justice 4643

We value life without s. 11667

When good people cease their s. 7991

with oneself means by which we influence 3414

STRUGGLES

Dignity never s. to be dignified 2761

enthusiasm lifts s. of pursuits 3188

God brings s. so we can mature 2844

God uses s. to give housecleaning 1013

God uses s. to make dependent 1013

God uses s. to reorganize priorities 1013

inevitable s. of life 4768

life filled with fleshly s. 1276

no church thrives unless s. 1411

STRUGGLING

against adversity, yet happy 249

faith brings power, not s. 3748

faith, like man in deep water 3797
Finding, following, keeping, s.
  6892
to supplement God's providence
  with our own 4322

STRUNG
bow too tensely s. easily broken
  943

STRUTS
and frets his hour upon the stage
  6994
Dignity never s. 2761

STUBBED
never s. toe, standing still 3599

STUBBORN
dogmatism that smiles while
  stands s. 11188
Facts s. things 3578
struggle for justice 4643

STUBBORNNESS
God's will hard against our s.
  10771

STUCK
man who s. true to God will come
  out best 10789
shot arrow in air, it s. 3194
vices now s. to my skin 10320

STUDENT
college s. used to write, now calls
  collect 3896
most diligent s. cannot obtain
  entire knowledge of Bible 737

STUDIED
the more he s. the Scriptures 737

STUDIES
Crafty men condemn s. 2996
man who s. revenge keeps own
  wounds green 9714
Nobody s. peace 8450
simple men admire s. 2996
wise men use s. 2996

STUDY
anatomy, never be an atheist 1983
anything that takes away my taste
  for Bible s. 7036
conversation with wise worth
  month's s. of books 11898
highest science is s. of Godhead
  4631
If it stands on edge, I s. 3011
learn more by obedience than s.
  8116
long, serious, profound s. 744
mistake not acquiring habit of s.
  7793
more I s. nature, more amazed at
  Creator 8040
more progress in silence than in
  years of s. 12112
never troubled seriously to s. four
  Gospels 6417
No one ever graduates from Bible
  s. 684
opened my Bible and began to s.
  3735

prayer before s. 9062
regret not more time for Bible s.
  682
sciences in light of truth 9871
the poise and quietness of Christ
  123
to know God, s. Jesus Christ 4493
to know people s. excuses 2807
To pray well better half of s. 9007
We s. everything but ourselves
  9353

STUDYING
the thought of Infinite God 1959
would spent two years s, preparing
  6687

STUFF
I count life just a s. 6908
that makes criminal makes saint
  8667
time, that's the s. life is made of
  6886
use for passions s. given for
  happiness 4359

STUMBLE
Courage, brother! Do not s. 5995
devil tests us that we might s. 171
may prevent a fall 3583
millions s. over sheer simplicity
  5653
on wonder upon wonder 1290
over pebbles, never over mountains
  2513
Whether we s. or fall 3634

STUMBLERS
who get up rare 3618
who give up dime a dozen 3618

STUMBLES
Who s. upon Christ 6517

STUMBLING
And transform every s. block
  1927
block, if people so gifted won't
  trust God 2833
broken cry can find its way to God
  8849
wisdom to make stepping-stones
  out of s. blocks 9073

STUMBLING BLOCKS
view s. as stepping-stones 2048

STUMP
What a story a redwood s. could
  tell 5731

STUN
innumerable definitions of God s.
  me 4585

STUNG
bee teaches not to get s. 3454

STUNNING
coming of Christ by way of
  manger strange, s. 6145

STUNS
too much of truth s. us 3559

STUNTED
souls 10247

STUPEFIED
must the soul lie s. 10649

STUPENDOUS
coming of Jesus into world most s.
  event in history 6146

STUPID
Better silent than s. 10243
cocksure, intelligent full of doubt
  10518
enough to want money 11869
right to own s. opinion 447
that fellowship limited to
  acceptable attire 4025

STUPIDITY
God's counsels in wisdom of
  world s. 2809

STURDY
be s. and upright in thinking 836
Love when nourished becomes s,
  enduring 7230

STYLE
cannot influence death but can
  influence s. 2336
Cultivate your own s. 6168
though outlook or s. may be
  different 6168

SUAVE
Injustice s. 6269

SUBCONSCIOUS
emotions in s. minds to hurt,
  trouble 3061
emotions remain alive in s. 3061
voice of s. argues 4967

SUBDUE
doesn't s, make you feel abject
  7145
God does not discipline to s. 2845

SUBDUED
God draws us when will s. 7949
Little minds s. by misfortune 5281
Master's disposition a s. sadness
  6390

SUBDUES
Music s. rage of poison and the
  plague 7900

SUBHUMAN
grimmer is men reduced to s. state
  10503

SUBJECT
disciplined obedience of loyal s.
  8818
Divinity, s. so vast all thoughts
  lost in immensity 4745
fanatic won't change s. 3907
God's love for us safer s. than our
  love 4777
He was s. unto them 8112
No man safely rules but he who
  loves to be s. 7422
or be s. to law of death 3756
soul never applies itself simply to
  any s. 10660
Whether king or s. 10527

SUBJECTED
idea that our will s. to God's control 5467

SUBJECTION
obedience foundation of s. to God's authority 8355

SUBJECTIVE
generation characterized by craze for s. 4017
whole creation essentially s. 2972

SUBJECTS
Everybody is ignorant, only on different s. 6079
We are born s. 8115
When s. that must not be touched 2468
which must not be touched 5480

SUBLIME
awake to s. greatness of the soul 10654
Beware of s. prayers and the lies they make us tell 8864
Christianity made martyrdom s. 1166
Darkness more productive of s. ideas than light 2541
God, wisdom is s. 4477
Know how s. a thing it is 10869
knowledge about s. worth more than trivialities 6676
makes its very unhappiness s. 10676
only in misfortune can you be s. 5310
We can make our lives s. 5288 3441
Within simplicity lies the s. 10286

SUBLIMEST
Prayer the s. of all things 8940

SUBMERGED
spirit s. in depths of divine ocean 7968

SUBMISSION
Carry the cross with s. 2088
characteristic of Christ was s. to his Father 6414
complete s. on our part 4529
In s. free to value other people 9963
Obedience is s. to will of God 8099
sin, self-will instead of s. 10359
the Mighty, after s. to a woman's pains 6142
will mean loss of all we value 11768

SUBMISSIVE
Love is s. 7246
preserve peace if will firm, s. 8453

SUBMIT
Character formed as we s. to self-discipline 1000
one thing to praise discipline, another to s. 2848
to demands of the Spirit 1719

To great evils we s. 3410
to s. thoughts, actions to the laws 7434
to s. to dictation worse than war 11768

SUBMITS
Muslim s. 6563

SUBMITTING
more battles won by s. 11781

SUBSCRIBE
afraid of men who s. to everything 586

SUBSTANCE
Beware lose s. by grasping at shadow 11499
evil corruption of s. 3357
Evil no s. of its own 3357
God, s. is indivisible 4610
only enduring s. is within 10654
trust, obey s. of Spirit-filled life 5803

SUBSTANCES
love a delicacy unknown in material s. 4789

SUBSTITUTE
Cynicism s. for intelligence 2181
false explanations for true reasons 3476
love for God 4766
Mass communication cannot be s. 3317
Outside show poor s. for inner worth 6061
Prayer not a lazy s. for work 8924
temptation to induce us to s. for God 11099

SUBSTITUTED
autosuggestion for conversion 5808
inferiority complex for sin 5808
psychology for prayer 5808
reflex action for revelation 5808
relativity for reality 5808
social control for family worship 5808
spirit of the wheels for power of the Spirit 5808

SUBSTITUTING
Instead of s. new ideas 9743

SUBTLE
analysis of conscience has taken place of childlike simplicity 6813
Faith is the s. chain 3700
life infinitely more s. than most of us think 6918
Love makes a s. man out of a crude one 7260

SUBTLER
more hidden imperfections 10006

SUBTLEST
Love the s. force in world 7255
serpent, s. beast of all the field 2700

SUBTLETY
God against s. of every enemy 5016
serpent beguiled Eve through s. 9424

SUBTRACT
When add to truth, you s. from it 11587

SUBTRACTION
Evil means s. 3364

SUBURBS
box in s. called a house 5859

SUBWAY
plenty of seats available in s. 7049

SUCCEED
better to fail in cause that will s. 3615
don't have to lie awake nights to s. 10828
don't s, relax 3597
family, where humblest s. 3886
I am not bound to s. 6303
If at first you don't s. 8558
if unlimited enthusiasm 3176
if you s, tell me no God 4608
men I have seen s. cheerful, hopeful 10816
sins, innocent only because did not s. 10384
success measured by obstacles overcome trying to s. 10809
than attempt to do nothing and s. 3595
than s. in cause that will fail 3615
than to s. in imitation 2008
though we s. in everything else 6944
to s. stay awake days 10828
Why desperate haste to s. 10827
without assistance of Divine Being cannot s. 5179 5411

SUCCEEDED
All our Lord s. in doing 1381
better to have failed serving God than to have s. serving the devil 10777
better to have taken risks than to have done nothing and s. 10777
forefathers s. because goal was glory to God 3113
sorry if only s. in entertaining 7896

SUCCEEDS
Christ's method of better world alone s. 6487
If devil s. in making complicated 10653
person who s. not one who holds back 3624

SUCCESS
a sort of suicide 10810
ability to help others 10815
and happiness lie in you 10829
anxieties engendered by s. are relentless 10817

must never minimize s. of another 10924

My life is one great s. 10873

myrrh represents s. 10913

never one without s. 10843

never ripe till made so by s. 10642

never violate laws of God without s. consequences 10336

No saint dare interfere in s. of another 10927

no true love without s. 6506

None can live in love without s. 7246

nonsense to say s. makes saints 10860

not right to say all s. perfects 10920

Nothing great done without s. 10875

object to s, be ill at ease 10833

of man also s. of God 10912

One discovers things never discovered before 10893

one who watches others s. who says he disbelieves in God 10936

only cure for s. is to face head on 10905

Only in s. will we know Jesus 10930

only sufficient language is language of Scripture 10888

only way some can learn 10897

opportunity for change of heart 10901

opportunity to change evil into good 10891

origin of consciousness 1718

Out of s. emerged strongest souls 10882

oysters never wounded fit only for stew 10883

peace not exemption from s. 8453

peace that belongs to s. miracle of faith 10907

perfects one who accepts call of God 10920

person doesn't need a lecture 10887

person needs a listener 10887

Pessimists attempted to revel in s. 10880

Poetry s. is forever shared 8619

preempted by success, self-fulfillment 1409

produces fork in the road 8264

profound potential for good 10933

purification of soul 10896

question of justice that may bring us s. 10564

raises us to freedom 10888

rarely hear man s. who says he disbelieves in God 10936

sacred trial sent by eternal love 10896

safeguarding freedom of spirit, no matter how much s. 4127

Scriptures teach noblest way of s. 742

Silence in times of s. best 10886

spontaneous response to s. 1546

Stoics declaring s. good in itself 10880

Stoics tried game denying reality 10880

strange initiation into happiness 10896

strangest truth is redemption comes through s. 9439

sublimest purpose of wisdom, love 3350

Supposing you eliminated s. 10898

Tears best gift of God to s. man 11020

the true cement of love 7293

thought conceived in s. 10835

Through sorrow can enter s. of others 10640

to explain s. clearest indication never suffered 10918

to save us not from s. 6365

too precious to be shared 10895

Unearned s. is redemptive 10919

union through s. more real, holy 8269

unknown, incomprehensible to all others 10873

unless meditation results in changing human s. 7725

was curse from which man fled 10896

way of s. witness soul bears to itself 10866

Whatsoever may be s. 10112

will become sweetness, quiet joy 10932

will either shield from or give strength to beat s. 5907

Wisdom comes by s. 11965

with fortitude bear s. of other folks 10862

would all like life free from s. 6506

SUFFERINGS

Bearing wrong part of fellowship with Christ's s. 6257

by our s. learn to praise our bliss 10925

can feel the s. of millions 8445

Christian shares s. of God 1253

empathy, s. of others felt as their own 3081

Hope bears up the mind under s. 5930

Hope makes mind rejoice in s. 5930

Tell me how much you know of s. 7295

SUFFERS

All the world s. 6533

By night and also day he s. still 2164

Christ s. watching our suffering 10839

God in Bible one who s. 10908

Love s. as the voice sings 7953

man s. so deeply had to invent laughter 6742

more man loves, more he s. 10904

most who is most selfish 10058

saint knows now why he s. 10910

we have a God who s. 4788

who s. much will know much 10852

SUFFICE

less would not s. for agriculture of God 5332

nothing will s. except blessing of God 5848

SUFFICES

A mere drop s. for me 4816

God alone s. 4588

single tear s. with God 4091

SUFFICIENCY

in world for man's need 3204

Lord's Prayer for s. 7154

not s. in world for man's greed 3204

SUFFICIENT

Christ s. for all his people 6370

cling to natural virtues s. to obscure work of God 11701

God's grace s. 2518

grace of God s. 1504

if s. will should always have s means 7869

Materialistic concerns never s. 8634

only s. language is language of Scripture 10888

SUFFOCATED

Silence prevents being s. by world 10562

SUFFOCATING

all died from s. luxury 10739

SUGAR

of the earth 1315

Rebukes not to have more salt than s. 2854

wants to blame finds s. sour 2063

SUGGEST

Direct, control, s. this day 9047

SUGGESTION

Sin first a simple s. 10368

SUICIDE

came over me that s. was wrong 10940

drink, driven to s. 325

Hope major weapon against s. 5925

Idleness a sort of s. 6761

leaves no opportunity for repentance 10945

like going where you haven't been invited 10939

no s. for which society not responsible 10947

severest form of self-criticism 10944

Success, a sort of s. 10810
to desert from world's garrison 10946
worst form of murder 10945

SUICIDES
Boredom, perhaps as many s. as despair 864

SUITABLENESS
Lord's Prayer for s. to every condition 7154

SUITS
no recipe for living that s. all cases 6214

SULKING
Meek endurance, obedience without s. 7728

SULLEN
God deliver us from s. saints 9774

SUMMARY
complete s. of all Jesus taught 10102

SUMMER
gospel like cool air in heat of s. 5097
in winter. Day in night 6153
Life's a short s. 6991
love is to the heart what s. is to the farmer 7339
No price set on lavish s. 2641
No s. then shall glow, nor winter freeze 3288
noon is the s. 9877
out of crowded city, onto crowded highway 9901
too hot to do job that was too cold last winter 9902
Until it woke one s. hour 2052
Winter cannot jump from winter to s. 9875

SUMMER'S
too hot 9879

SUMMIT
of love on earth 10331

SUMMITS
woods upon their s. wave in adoration 7997

SUMMONED
the Comforter needs only to be s. 5781

SUN
And the s. and the Father's will 9345
appears setting, but is rising 2350
As earth can produce nothing unless fertilized by s. 5207
as s. after shower 3130
At the setting of the s. 2502
before s. or stars in splashed heavens 4694
Behind the clouds is s. still shining 10582
believe in the s. even when it is not shining 3732

Benighted walks under mid-day s. 1683
Bible, s. without a blot 710
blossom under praise like flowers in s. 3144
Brightest of all, the s. has spots 3951
Christ a S. to enlighten 6370
corruptions like the air before the s. shines 9852
difference not in s. but in clouds 4772
disappeared if within reach of human hands 3202
discovers filth under white snow 2474
earth to s. what man is to angels 364
Every morning s. rises to warm earth 8002
glory of the s. 6108
God dries you with his s. 4466
God made moon as well as s. 5393
Grace comes into soul as s. into world 5213
Has s. ever stopped his shining 10964
He basked beneath the s. 6756
Hope is like the s. 5923
humble man receives praise way clean window takes light of s. 6033
I believe the s. has risen 1197
I greet the dawn, and not setting s. 2418
If God maintains s, planets 4619
If head wax, don't walk in s. 11918
In the face of the s. see God's beauty 4858
Laughter the s. that drives winter from the face 6735
life revolves around Christ, its central s. 6937
life short day in which s. hardly rises 7083
like robbing world of s. 4299
like s. which seems to set in night 6094
lunatic put out s. by scribbling darkness 4442
Lust's effect is tempest after s. 7357
Majestic like the s. 634
Make hay while s. shines 2781
makes ice melt 6668
makes not the day, but thee 4502
No matter how fair the s. shines 5544
of God is smiling 5810
pottery gets fragile sitting in s. 2540
really gone to diffuse light elsewhere 6094
setting s. as bright as from rich man's abode 7001
shine upon just, unjust 4129
shines clearly in darkest day as in brightest 4772

Shriveling hurt until s. drew forth a leaf 5368
sit down at set of s. 107
stars, moon, s. how they move in silence 10250
The lark is up to greet the s. 8039
The little window where the s. 2588
this s. unique 4993
universe centered on neither earth nor s. 11647
who does not pray when s. shines 8809
with one eye vieweth the world 11645
With the dying s. 7306

SUN'S
self comes in with him 4195

SUNBEAM
God pervades us as the s. 9852

SUNBEAMS
hands have s. in them 6531
Through showers the s. fall 5904

SUNBURN
vacationeer returns with s. 6841

SUNDAY
child taught S, remember Monday 1134
Christianity isn't going to church S. 1180
clears away rust of the week 10954
continual message of Easter 10955
employment as sacred as S. activities 3104
golden clasp that binds together the week 10956
hear same prayers repeated each S. 8845
If leave church S. morning 12106
must be S, everybody's telling the truth 11513
not know what to do on a rainy S. afternoon 6100
our fathers called it S. 10952
polite prattle exchanged S. morning 4029
self and weekday self not good if detached 10949

SUNDAYS
Christ, turn weekdays into S. 5529
'Tis angel's music 10957
when the bells do chime 10957

SUNDERED
Be s. in the night of fear 3644

SUNG
A glory never s. 8047
Lord s. the night went to his death 7923
Many a solo s. to show off 7867

SUNGLASSES
worst hardship lack of s. 3147

SUNLIGHT
figures written by fingers of s.
4454
Keep in the s. 3500
relief of diver coming back to s,
familiar faces 6110
when God does not see fit to
grant us s. 5393

SUNRISE
Bible, s. and sunset 750
God's love proclaimed with each s.
4759
Lost somewhere between s. and
sunset 11306
never failed us yet 5942

SUNRISES
I like s, Mondays, new seasons
8080

SUNS
he who sets fire to the s. 4951
Ten thousand s. which shine
above us nightly 4592

SUNSET
and evening star 2368
better to show up for work at s.
8141
Bible, sunrise and s. 750
If I can put one thought of rosy s.
1097
life, shadow which loses itself in s.
2457
Lost somewhere between sunrise
and s. 11306
never frightened at a s. 2297
times smell of s. 10508

SUNSETS
Christ has turned our s. into
dawns 6368

SUNSHINE
All s. makes the desert 2709
bring s. to others, bring s. to their
own 10965
bring thy s. into cloudy places
9106
compliment verbal s. 1571
glance fell like s. where it went
107
God is not merely in the s. 10434
good laugh is s. in a house 5812
Humor is s. of the mind 6718
is delicious 8033
Keep your face to the s. 1098
Kindness s. in which virtue grows
6654
Love comforteth like s. after rain
7212
shadows caused when we stand in
our own s. 10792
Spread the s. of your Lord 378
standing in one's own s. 2552
takes both rain, s. to make
rainbow 2550
Those who bring s. to others 6567
to the heart 4743
What s. is to flowers 6745
where others see shadows, storm
5943

Without thy s. and thy rain 11172

SUPER-AGE-SAVAGE
Man still a s. 10068

SUPERCILIOUS
This s. seed 2052

SUPERFICIAL
familiar phrase have s. effect 8845
less satisfied with s. views of Christ
6480
People meet s. needs 4310
social camaraderie 3337

SUPERFICIALITIES
beyond s. of culture 1760

SUPERFICIALITY
condemn ourselves to spiritual s.
6693
difficulties force us to break
through s. 2738
Honesty, an absence of verbal s.
5874

SUPERFLUOUS
obtain proof render faith s. 3806

SUPERHUMAN
chance of mankind 4549
need a s. Savior 6459
unconscious not only semihuman
but s. 7772

SUPERIOR
Every man I meet my s. in some
way 7373
love is s. to hate 6326
Love s. to money 7232
passing over revenge is s. to enemy
9715
people let it be discovered by
others 11695
So none may claim s. grade 3227

SUPERIORITY
Seniority in kingdom of God does
not imply s. 5897

SUPERIORS
Love is obedient to s. 7246
only want equality with s. 3247

SUPERNATURAL
Bible is s. book 744
Bible understood only by s. aid
708
Bible, s. book 708
depend on God for s. ability 1284
Evangelism s. remedy for world
3304
faith acts on s. facts, gets s. results
3807
God not a s. interferer 4847
love allows you to love enemy
7340
may be deluded by s. forces 5458
no human birth compare to s.
birth 874
Prayer a s. activity 8916
supernaturally created for a s.
work 10206
to be like Christ 8113

SUPERNATURALLY
created for a supernatural work
10206
delivered, sustained, directed
10206
prepared and s. performed 10206
Victory expected from s. born men
10206

SUPERNORMAL
Jesus Christ teaching s. integrity
6314

SUPERSAINTS
don't have to be s, just thirsty
sinners 1344

SUPERSEDE
confidence should s. fear 6326

SUPERSEDED
indeterminable form which
cannot be s. 6214

SUPERSEDES
where self s. commitment 3901

SUPERSTITION
disciple comes with s. to find truth
2818
hairline between truth and s.
10968
poison of the mind 10966
religion of feeble minds 10967

SUPERSTITIOUS
If not religious, man will be s.
12109

SUPERVISION
time of your death under God's s.
2316

SUPPER
Hope is a bad s. 5915
lie might get lunch but not s. 2476

SUPPERLESS
Better go to bed s. 4033

SUPPLEMENT
struggling to s. God's providence
4322

SUPPLEMENTARY
Religion and home life are s. 5858

SUPPLICANTS
sought secret place of Most High
8805

SUPPLIED
God expects only what he has s.
4810
we shall be s. 5440

SUPPLIES
prayer closet base of s. for the
Christian 8976

SUPPLY
God demands so much only he
can s. 4473
God has all goodness to s. you
4696
God will s. the rest 4558
God's to s. what we cannot 10166

His presence shall my wants s.
9350
light not heat 6587
One alone can s. our need 6455
only God can s. what he demands
1194

SUPPORT
angels s. us 2359
atheist without s. 474
broken reed of human s. 3132
Christ a Foundation to s. 6370
difficult to s. if faith in Bible cease
5189
if does not receive inner s. by
judgment of God 5477
individual freedom as we serve
one another 9498
must s. the poor 8698
O Lord, s. us all day long 9105
thousand voices vie for s. 7447
To s. us was trouble for our fathers
11459
what is low raise and s. 7566

SUPPORTED
me through years of exile 7102

SUPPORTING
tell truth, have infinite power s.
you 11510

SUPPORTS
Justification foundation that s. all
benefits 6633
poor in spirit, detachment from
earthly s. 6025

SUPPRESS
literature that getting on in world
chief object in life 10086
The more men s. truth of God
11538
When s. things you don't want to
live with 9291

SUPPRESSED
dream, disguised fulfillment of s.
wish 2968
every s. word reverberates
through earth 8528
grief chokes, seethes 5330
sin must die right out, not be s.
9841
thoughts too strong to be s. 3059

SUPREMACY
male, female not contenders for s.
3239

SUPREME
cross s. triumph of God 3582
cross the s. failure 3582
death eternal s. evil 5033
family circle the s. conductor of
Christianity 5852
Life eternal is s. good 5033
soul where man's s. battles are
fought 10672
Those only who make this quest s.
desire 6494
we cannot be s. over ourselves
7552

SUPREMELY
Good when he gives, s. good 288
Home, spot of earth s. best 5834

SURE
foundation in friendship 4251
God's mill grinds slow but s. 6607
heart not yet s. of its God 6723
Humility is s, not arrogant 6012
more s. than day and night 4209
most s. and arrogant, usually most
mistaken 458
only s. of today 5507
so young, so strong, so s. of God
1609
soul, God stand s. 948
way to destroy enemy 3170
way to take fear out of living
3993
when young, s. of everything 956

SUREST
way to lose is to protect 4733

SURFACE
attributes of God intelligible on s.
4584
deal only with s. find Christ an
offense 6422
error lies on the s. 3259
Errors, like straws, upon s. flow
3255
if we penetrate deep enough
beneath s. 5716
Truth and oil always come to the
s. 11553
what we first discern but s. 6380

SURFACE-STREAM
Below the s, shallow and light
7369

SURGEON
divine S. must be permitted to use
scalpel 890

SURGERY
result of internal s. 8583
spiritual s. more painful than
physical s. 890
world must come under
omnipotent s. 10521

SURGICAL
New Testament preacher has to be
s. 9124

SURMISES
Rumor pipe blown by s. 9756

SURPASS
I s. you in sleeping 6190
If you s. me in eating 6190

SURPASSED
God loves you with intimacy
which s. dreams 4747

SURPASSES
creation s. my conception 4603

SURPASSING
For gift or grace, s. this 2345

SURPRISE
dangers are temptations that s.
11078

do right, s. some people 3429
no s. more magical than s. of
being loved 7314
Of marvel or s. 6916
sin, overtakes us by s. 10422
temptation cannot take simplicity
by s. 10278
unexpected gives anticipation s.
4318
What will s. us most 6250

SURPRISED
don't be s. if nobody seems to care
9211
frequently s. having them perform
better than hoped 9469
hardly s. children outgrow
Shepherd 1133
people perform better than hoped
2799

SURPRISES
believe in God, there will be
wonderful s. 4508
Changes, s, and God made it all
8054
God packs our life with s. 5463
lie ahead 10182
many s. with God 604
One gets some very strange s.
7561
out of options, ready for God's s.
2596

SURPRISING
arrivals, departures of pleasure
8612
everything in world s. 12037

SURRENDER
easy cowardice of s. to conformity
6216
greatness of a man's power is his s.
10975
If compromise with s. 10972
If you don't s. to Christ 10971
not only what the Lord does to
you 10974
prayer of s. 9084
process of s. what Christians call
repentance 9577
search for God is s. to his search
for us 7455
to this power is faith 3707
will to God, discover resources
10769
you s. to chaos 10971
your reaction to what the Lord
does 10974

SURRENDERED
God has never s. iota of his power
4821
Holiness because we have s. 5742
own plans to greater plan of God
4803

SURRENDERING
to despair man's favorite pastime
2607

SURRENDERS
who s. to Christ exchanges cruel
slave driver for kind, gentle
Master 10976

SURROUNDED
God is himself not s. 4850
I am s. still with God 4876

SURROUNDING
you are enemies that never rest
9861

SURROUNDINGS
highest service prepared for in
humblest s. 10190
self-centered people live in
unpleasant s. 10077
who has no inner life is a slave to
his s. 7033

SURROUNDS
Lord's goodness s. us at every
moment 4646

SURVEY
when s. whole progress of our lives
5392

SURVEYOR'S
love does not measure by s. chain
4789

SURVEYS
My rising soul s. 4819

SURVIVAL
character vital to society's s. 3880

SURVIVE
all manner of bad treatment 4237
faith can s. all odds 3736
faith that cannot s. collision with
truth 3639
far more than s. 159
like reed, faith will s. storm 3702
Men and nations s. or perish
10510
One can s. everything except death
2351

SURVIVES
joy s. through pain, sorrow 6568
Word of God still s. 730

SURVIVOR'S
man's dying more s. affair 2210

SUSPECT
intellectuals remain socially s.
6323
They that know no evil s. none
3408
we s. silence, regard it as proof
meeting is dead 12096

SUSPECTS
always right who s. he makes
mistakes 7791
no one s. his pain except thee
10877

SUSPENDERS
at ball game, call him Pop 3921

SUSPENSE
life of spider 11600
miserable to live in s. 11600

SUSPICION
always haunts guilty mind 5488
Avoid s. when walking through
neighbor's melon patch 9613

SUSPICIOUS
critics s. of conversion not in
refrigerator 3052
in effort to be watchful become s.
9502
parent makes artful child 8342
risk as much in naive as s. 7979
Simplicity has no s. thoughts
11696

SUSTAIN
God will s. if remain faithful 5385
lay on me what thou wilt, only s.
me 9080
Love difficult to s. 7233

SUSTAINED
supernaturally s. 10206

SUSTAINING
God is beneath, s. 4841
power of hope 4643

SUSTAINS
Adjusts, s, and agitates the whole
4711
Faith s. human dignity 3666
woman who creates, s. home
creator second only to God
5857

SVITHJOD
in the land of S. 3273

SWADDLING
infant world, wrapped in s.
clothes of light 7886

SWAGGER
Spirit of God will not allow you
to s. 5776

SWALLOW
any lie that flatters us 6870
love of the cross must s. up
personal grief 5356
silence like gaping abyss which
can s. up 10253
willing to s, too lazy to chew 6758

SWALLOWED
Eve s. the hook 4419
other books to be s. 859
up in the eternity before and after
7084

SWALLOWING
when s. her grain 11142

SWALLOWS
childhood chews hours, s. minutes
12193
universe s. me up like a speck
11268

SWAMPY
truth cannot be built on s. ground
of scepticism 11530
word love is a s. one 7312

SWATTER
Life like fly in room with boys
armed with s. 6968

SWAY
that to and fro did s. against a wall
6242

SWAYS
When mind doubts, feather s. it
2960

SWEAR
When I s. I am being something
9307

SWEARING
father whipped son for s, swore
himself 3914

SWEAT
till they begin to s. in seeking them
9037

SWEATER
worn by child when mother cold
3866

SWEATY
returning, s. and out of breath
9070

SWEEP
streets as Michelangelo painted
2777

SWEEPS
A new broom s. clean 251
If each s. in front of his own door
9664
the wide earth, tramples o'er
mankind 6269

SWEET
are thoughts that savour of
content 1812
are uses of adversity 208
as salt in your mouth 4050
Evil s. in beginning 3360
For if thy world on earth be s.
5635
Friends speak with words s, strong
4185
From his s. silence my mouth sings
4125
glory of spring how s. 9898
God makes light and s. 148
How s. the name of Jesus sounds
1507
Humility, that low, s. root 6015
Jesus Christ, conversations s. 6352
joy comes through sorrow 10638
misery will seem s. 10833
One far fierce hour, and s. 2980
Patience is bitter, fruit s. 8410
Sin s. in the beginning 10375
Some are born to s. delight 813
spirit comfort me 1514
Spring full of s. days and roses
9891
tears of saints more s. by far 9787
Things s. prove sour 11105
'Tis s. to grow old 8120
We saw thee by thine own s. light
6152

What s. delight quiet life affords
9375
whether in itself s. or bitter 4978
who has not tasted the bitter does
not know what s. is 10903
Will make this life of ours most s.
6647
words breathe memories s. as
flutes 11998
words s. as children's talk 11998

SWEETEN
Sorrows remembered s. present joy
10624
Speak that kind word to s. a
sorrow 6671

SWEETENED
you s. my bitterness 7579

SWEETENING
In the rain God is s. thy melody
10600

SWEETENS
Love's end s. all its means 6457
trouble s. apples 11431

SWEETER
And death or life shall be the s.
2229
God hears no s. music 7171
Home, dearer, s. spot than all the
rest 5834
If any love of mine make life s.
910
Nothing is s. than love 7283
older the fiddle, s. the tune 8173
tough love that turns us into s.
persons 7686

SWEETEST
bad conscience embitters s.
comforts 1650
fairest and s. rose 8172
flower of s. smell is shy, lowly
6028
Friendship one of the s. joys of life
4236
handsomest flower not s. 2472
music in kind words 11995
of all sounds is praise 8740
rose is s. wash'd with morning dew
7309
songs tell of saddest thought
10608
Swift gratitude is s. 5260
things turn sourest by their deeds
5039
word is home 11993

SWEETLY
God disposed all strongly, s. 4904

SWEETNESS
diffuse their s. all around 150
Fill lives with s. 4223
heavenly s. in the cross 2096
Love is trusting in God even when
not enjoying his s. 7246
raised to s. of eternal life 4749
smiles announce s. 10500
soul that hears s. of music 10656

suffering will become full of s.
10932
What s. left if take away friendship
4299
Whether s. or bitterness 1461

SWEETS
you say this world seems drained
of s. 5575

SWELL
don't s. with pride, may look
overtaxed 9258
Its waves no further s. 4813
self-importance makes mind
shrink, head s. 9191

SWELLED
heads shrink influence 9488

SWELLS
That s. with silence in tortured
soul 5348

SWEPT
Health, wealth, friends will be s.
away 3719
If s. off feet, time to get on knees
8836

SWERVE
No fear lest he should s. or faint
1299

SWIFT
be s. to love 6658
fly the years, and rise th' expected
morn 6143
gratitude is sweetest 5260
Love is s. 7246
miracles of Jesus s. that we might
take them in 6479
race is not always to the s. 9111
Time is too s. for those who fear
11333
Time, unsoil'd and s. 11345
When heart right, feet s. 10213

SWIFTER
nothing s. in life than voice of
rumor 5142

SWIFTEST
word is time 11993

SWIFTLY
And felt the s. passing feet of men
11330

SWIFTNESS
Character torn down with
incredible s. 996

SWIM
begin at bottom in everything
except learning to s. 6021
Eagles don't s. 6168
In matters of taste, s. with current
6308
Where reason cannot wade, faith
may s. 3821

SWIMMING
upstream 4094

SWIMS
Who s. in sin shall sink in sorrow
10426

SWIPED
ideas from Chesterfield 2019

SWORD
Calvary, the eternal s. 2124
Candor always double-edged s.
5869
Jesus becomes two-edged s. 686
Love rules kingdom without s.
7270
oil can mightier than the s. 10991
Slander, edge sharper than s.
10467
spirit always has conquered the s.
10695
tongue more feared than s. 10474
use Scriptures like s. 720

SWORDS
angels had already drawn their s.
6418
The s. of scorn divide 9224

SWORE
father whipped son for swearing,
s. himself 3914

SYLLABLE
a lie may be told by accent on a s.
6859
Every s. already written down in
deeds 6482

SYMBOL
cross, s. of his greatest suffering
10930
Love a s. of eternity 7229
of God's nature is cross 2167

SYMBOLICAL
attempt to express inexpressible
5631

SYMBOLIZE
astronomy no more than s.
emanation of God 4593

SYMBOLIZES
long for Rapture, s. escape from
distress of age 9910

SYMBOLS
People who take s. literally 5631

SYMMETRY
Christians lack s. 1753
Could blind chance create s. 1958
fearful s. which is God's language
5718
Holiness the s. of the soul 5747

SYMPATHIES
in touch with people through our
s. 7428
Through sorrow s. are awakened
10640

SYMPATHIZING
Strengthen me by s. with strength
3139

SYMPATHY
attribute of a great lady 11697

devil playing for s. 2648
give us s. for those who are deaf
 9094
is your pain in my heart 10982
Little words of s. silent threads of
 gold 6997
never wasted except when give to
 yourself 10981
the Comforter, word conveys
 indefinable s. 5775
world understands love and s.
 7313

SYMPHONIES
plainer I hear immortal s. of world
 to come 11132

SYMPHONY
creation's loftiest s. 12
in the great s. of life 10135
parts in s. none can take but thee
 10600

SYNETHETIC
no s. replacement for decent home
 life 5858

SYNONYMOUS
God and love s. 4755

SYRUP
peddling spiritual soothing s. 8108

SYSTEM
civilized life complicated s. of
 murder 10513
Faith stands above human s. 3670
tries to crowd God's fullness into s.
 11208

SYSTEMATIC
Theology madness gone s. 11208

SYSTEMATIZE
intellectual attempt to s. God
 11209

SYSTEMS
Bible, too big for s. 703
shifting s. of false religion 5103

T

TABLE
complications which you can
 hardly get to end of 9402
faith finds t. in wilderness 3703
looks simple 9402
loving any t. better than Lord's T.
 6925
Many eager to share Jesus' t. 9268

TACK
can sit on a mountain but not a t.
 9636
Sitting on a t. is often useful 88

TACT
a kind of mind reading 10986
gentleness, possessing t. 4402
is emotional intelligence 10987
knack of making point without
 making enemy 10990

Knowing when to say nothing, 50
 percent of tact 7626
pat on back when feel like kick in
 pants 10988
to describe others as they see
 themselves 10989

TADPOLE
pond is an ocean to a t. 8517

TAIL
dog wags t. instead of tongue
 9499
Jest with ass, will flap in face with
 t. 9477
Where devil cannot put head, puts
 t. 2707
with a flick of her fiery t. 9870

TAILS
If it's t, I stay up 3011

TAINTS
Some sinister intent t. all he does
 4164

TAKE
But only how did you t. it 11446
can't t. it with you 8640
God does not choose to give, you
 cannot t. 4958
God's program, have God's power
 4826
government big enough to t.
 everything 5168
gratitude we feel for what we t.
 5267
Holy Spirit expects us to t.
 seriously answers provided
 5445
Home when you go there, they
 have to t. you in 5831
If course is right, t. it because it is
 right 6291
if followers of God, cannot t.
 initiative 5446
love grows bigger the more you t.
 from it 7252
lowest place, highest will be given
 5991
Music only art of earth we t. to
 heaven 7904
Some will t. all God has to give us
 5323
than t. wrong road once 5424
time for all things 5588
what God chooses to send 5911
What God gives, and what we t.
 5860
will t. witholding of honor quietly
 5901

TAKEN
comfort of having friend may be t.
 away 4271
Thank you for all you have t.
 from me 11161

TAKERS
eat well 10198

TAKES
a great man to make a good
 listener 7113

a long time to grow an old friend
 4193
all time and eternity to know God
 4483
anything that t. away my taste for
 Bible study 7036
blesseth him that gives and him
 that t. 7744
Cease to resist, love t. possession
 4785
God gives something which t.
 place of all, love 4790
God never t. unless gives better
 4630
hand that gives above hand that t.
 4375
two to be glad 5351

TAKETH
big print giveth, small print t.
 away 9328

TAKING
pride, t. less than you need 4353

TALE
Scarce any t. was sooner heard
 than told 9757
thereby hangs a t. 11302
world where message is crazy t.
 592

TALEBEARER
No t. can inform on us 4884

TALEBEARERS
as bad as talemakers 5158
set on fire all houses they enter
 5137

TALEMAKERS
Talebearers as bad as t. 5158

TALENT
adopted t. only extemporaneous
 half-expression 6226
Chaucer had t. but couldn't spell
 12145
Don't dole out like miser 10993
Don't hoard it 10993
have t, use in every way possible
 10993
is God-given, be thankful 10994
is like an arm or a leg 10995
is lost for want of courage 1916
more fail through lack of purpose
 than t. 3608
nurtured in solitude 1042
Perseverance if unaccompanied by
 t. 8553
sermon preached as exhibition of t.
 7867
something God gives you 10996
Spend lavishly 10993
than through lack of t. 4427
tragedy is failure to use t. 10997
tragedy not being limited to one t.
 10997
unsuccessful men with t. common
 8555
use it or lose it 10995
will not take the place of
 perseverance 8555

TALENTS
have some admirers, but few
friends 7
most valuable of all t. 12154
None of our human t. are
significant to God 4527
not to neglect improvement of t.
9041
Prayer not natural t. 8914
see t. in unexpected people 8575
We try to speak of large or meager
t. 4710

TALES
drown t. in details 1867

TALK
about cost when in love an insult
2823
about God, nobody gets upset
6518
about pleasures to acquaintances
4276
about question of the day 5094
about troubles to friends 4276
At profoundest depths men t. not
about God but with him 8767
bore uses mouth to t. while you
yawn 1828
Children will t. like their parents
8289
don't like to t. with people who
agree 1851
easier to look wise than t. wisely
1856
excitement 3185
faith 3778
frank t. good soap for hearts 5864
Great minds t. about ideas 1845
insist all look, t, act alike 6824
leave others to t. of you 2785
madness for sheep to t. peace with
wolf 8446
Man alone has capacity to walk,
t. with God 7497
mediocre minds t. about things
1845
More depends on walk than t.
3443
more t. out of minor pain 3422
much and arrive nowhere 1886
nonsense of those who think they
t. sense 9056
not the same to t. of bulls 3537
ought not to t. of sacrifice 9760
Read not to find t. and discourse
856
small minds t. about people 1845
Some t. about finding God—as if
he could get lost 7518
spend three years teaching child to
t. 8336
test of sanctification not t. about
holiness 9845
they t. most who have least to say
1834
thousand who t. jargon about
Christ 3306
to him in prayer of all your wants
8968

to straighten out understanding
1882
To t. about the rest of us 5162
5162
too busy when someone needs to t.
129
two years to learn to t. 2897
way people t. about God 4886
We t. about heaven being so far
away 5677
when t. of joy of sacrificing 9758
When t. of man doing anything
for God 10214
Why when we t. to God, we're
praying 9035
will profit even from those who t.
badly 7114
with humility t. to God as to your
Father 4924
words sweet as children's t. 11998

TALKATIVE
error is always t. 3256
learned silence from t. 5251

TALKED
But I had t. with God when young
1817
Caesar more t. about than Jesus
6362
children need to be t. to like
grownups 8311
Jesus t. a great deal about money
7804
Jesus t. about discipleship with an
"if" 2826
louder he t. of his honor 5899
to God as if he were sitting in
chair beside them 7526
to God as one might talk to a
counselor 7526
with God this morning 8817

TALKERS
Great t. never great doers 1846
When will t. refrain from
evil-speaking 10477

TALKING
at first he thought prayer was t.
8751
foolish man tells a woman to stop
t. 2889
is a form of greed 1885
is easy, action difficult 2537
need to stop t. about prayer and
pray 8825
Never learn anything t. 9363
often torment for me 10556
ordained by God 7038
People lose weight not by t. about
it 9972
Prayer begins by t. to God 8902
theology what you are when t.
stops 11215
Thinking is t. of the soul with itself
11262
to God for men greater still 8969
to men for God great thing 8969
unless he knew what he was t.
about 1852

TALKS
bore t. to you about himself 5112
brilliant conversationalist t. to
you about yourself 5112
Christian who whines when he t.
9529
devil t. glibly of church and state
2651
egoist t. to you about himself
9445
gossip t. to you about others 5112
less sound man's argument, louder
he t. 448
No man safely t. but he who loves
to listen 7422
Of a good leader, who t. little
6803
so constantly about God 484
so much tongue was sunburned
1868
when God t. to us we're
schizophrenic 9035
Who t. of scheme and plan 7572

TALL
oaks from little acorns grow 8657
You stand t. when you kneel to
pray 9038

TALLER
not growing t, but stooping lower
6017
the t. we grew, more easily we
could reach 6017

TAME
can t. boys, can t. anything 7382
home not the one t. place in world
of adventure 5842
most dangerous of t. beasts, a
flatterer 10472
years of patience to t. young
human beings 7382

TAMED
Little minds t. by misfortune 5281

TAMES
God little by little t. us 5395

TANGIBLE
feel God's invisible and t. hand
7484

TANGLE
we t. up the plans the Lord hath
wrought 6117

TANGLED
Never underestimate ability of
humans to get t. up 5976
what t. web do parents weave
8319

TANTALUS
like T. up to chin in water, yet
thirsty 5325

TAOISTS
If stories incomprehensible to T.
12147

TAPE
God will put t. about their heart
6112

TAPESTRY
compose the master t. 12

TARGET
failure to hit bull's-eye never fault of t. 9680

TARZAN
not self-reared after fashion of T. 3881

TASK
ahead never as great as the Power behind 3804

before me greater than that rested upon Washington 5179

grace God provides comes only with t. 5226

hardest t. to think 11275

in solitude to keep mind on Savior 10551

is to live our communication with Christ 3321

Nothing so fatiguing as unfinished t. 9297

of overcoming evil never hopeless 3378

power behind greater than t. ahead 7878

Pray for powers equal to your t. 8780

thank thee for daily t. to do 11148

upon the finished t. to smile 47

vision and t. is hope of world 11730

vision without t. a dream 12006

waits only the completion of present t. 9658

When accomplished daily t, go to sleep in peace 11489

When my t. is done, let me out 7006

with vision is victory 12006

without vision a drudgery 12006

Worship, aware of t. at hand 12136

would not give t. without time to do it 4425

TASKS
church has many t. 3328

discover delight hidden in irksome t. 10639

Do not pray for t. equal to your powers 8780

home, wild place in world of rules, set t. 5842

strength to have anguish, still perform daily t. 8423

three hardest t. in world 7838

Wisdom comes by being faithful to small t. 11911

TASTE
anything that takes away my t. for Bible study 7036

God gives t. that lifts into life 2617

God gives to every man t. 5387

Gossip proves nothing but bad t. of smoker 5132

Gratitude to God makes blessing t. of heaven 5248

If thou wouldst t. his works 4737

In matters of t, swim with current 6308

not so much as t. of devil's broth 2703

Things sweet to t. prove sour 11105

yearning to touch, t. the unapproachable 4744

TASTED
It, it made me hunger and thirst 7473

Some books to be t. 859

TASTES
the joys of heaven 4749

TASTY
Humble pie, never t. 429

that no beast would consider us t. 8526

TATTERED
muddy and t. children 3609

TAUGHT
child becomes largely what he is t. 5818

child t. Sunday, remember Monday 1134

Christianity t. love worth more than intelligence 1183

complete summary of all Jesus t. 10102

do not always like being t. 3008

Everything science has t. me 6090

home, kind of school where life's basic lessons t. 5853

Jesus Christ t. not to sit in judgment 9789

lesson t. far outweighs the pain 10586

Life has t. me to think 6942

Life has t. me we are disliked for our qualities 5601

Man knows nothing without being t. 7412

most important cannot be t. 3030

mother t. me to repeat Lord's Prayer 8347

Nothing worth knowing can be t. 11932

Plato t. more science than Christ 6362

They t. me all I knew 6686

thinking has not t. me to live 6942

We t. him to steal 3458

What unto themselves was t. 10678

who control what young people are t. 8360

TAUNT
fear, t. with unknown 3971

TAX
Fear is t. conscience pays to guilt 3966

TAX DEDUCTIONS
Abilities are like t. 1

TAXES
consolation of death, end of t. 2352

Death, t. inevitable 2238

take money 7826

TAXPAYER
Everyone can become t. 7983

TEA
Take lesson from t. 2743

TEACH
a man to fish, eats for rest of life 11001

After crises, God steps in to t. 2042

can't t. people how wicked they are 4773

cannot t. a man anything 11010

Christ a Prophet to t. 6370

Christ did not come only to t. us 6403

Christ did not come to t. men to be holy 6424

Christianity does not t. doctrine of weakness 1165

everyone must learn, no one can t. 7068

God wants to t. us dependence 8990

him all the way to heaven 8296

home must t. what to believe 8333

home must t. what to read 8333

If I am wrong, O t. my heart 9067

in spite of every attempt to t. manners 1109

Lord, t. me what I am in thy sight 9081

Lord, t. us how to pray 9108

Lord, t. us to laugh again 6743

love to t. as painter loves to paint 11002

me in all things thee to see 9112

me to breathe deeply in faith 3779

me to feel another's woe 1552

me to live 2370

me to silence my own heart 10257

me, My God and King 10183

miracles associated with lessons Jesus trying to t. 6500

must watch what we t. 5818

no formula to t. maturity 7705

not meant to t. us, but to make us something 7702

now will I t. thee the way of peace 8448

One kind act will t. more than a thousand sermons 6661

our children in school what they are 3039

parent who does not t. child to obey is cruel 8355

patiently God works to t. 7056

Scriptures t. best way of living 742

Scriptures t. most comfortable way of dying 742

Scriptures t. noblest way of suffering 742

silence would teach joys of sound 824

solitude should t. us how to die 10530

Souls to souls can never t. 10678

Tears t. us wisdom 11019

thank God he will use sin to t. you 11152

That which each can do best none but his Maker can t. 6226

the truth 11527

to esteem more highly those who think alike 3032

To t. is to learn twice 11008

to t. without inspiring is hammering on cold iron 11000

took God years to t. me to say "Lord anything" 4892

us about hatred of sin 10306

us about righteousness 10306

us all to render deeds of mercy 7747

us disciples of patience 8418

us that no evil is intolerable 9092

us to care and not to care 4979

us to sit still 4979

us wealth is not elegance 11662

virtue can t. you how to climb 11692

what we know not, t. us 9083

When I transfer knowledge I t. 11009

whether you t. ragged class 3845

writer writes to t. himself 12148

years t. much days never knew 3546

TEACHER

adversity is a greater t. 242

affects eternity 2993

attempting to teach without inspiring desire to learn 11000

best t. gets most out of pupil 3026

best t. not one who crams most into pupil 3026

Bible like old and revered t. 653

defends against own personal influence 11006

Experience a hard t. 3522

good t. one whose ears get as much exercise as mouth 10998

He, the t. of teachers 5426

If Jesus Christ only a t. 6403

If t. fascinates with his doctrine 11003

like candle which lights others 11005

No t. should make men think as he thinks 11004

Prosperity is a great t. 242

sent from God clears way to Jesus 11003

then you are wise and God is your t. 8497

Wait the great t. death, and God adore 5913

Were I a t. should advise world 4873

world a sure t. 12052

TEACHERS

Experience not always kindest of t. 3526

Jesus differs from all other t. 6442

Lord needs neither books nor t. 5426

teacher of t. gives guidance noiselessly 5426

ungrateful to these t. 5251

When God is weaning a soul from t. 10036

TEACHES

All I have seen t. me to trust the Creator 11465

Bible t. us our greatness 738

Bible t. us our nothingness 738

Busy bee t. two lessons 3454

Christ came to make us what he t. we should be 6403

Christianity t. to bear burdens 931

Education t. us how little man knows 3004

Failure t. success 3591

father who t. responsibility provides fortune 3913

He who gives t. me to give 3434

History t. mistakes we are going to make 5715

history t. us to hope 5944

hope t. trust in God 3834

Jesus t. universal love 913

mother t. next generation of citizens 7844

Pain t. luxury of health 8270

politics t. what means are effective 11211

Silence t. us to speak the Word of God 10562

Theology t. what ends are desirable 11210

Theology t. what means are lawful 11211

unless God himself t. him 4910

TEACHING

before his t. has any meaning 6401

by obedience we understand t. of God 8095

Christ's t. never beats about the bush 6440

Christ's t. no meaning until enter his life 6424

Christ's t. not intended to abrogate obedience 6811

develop faith by t. long-suffering 3744

fifteen years t. child to be quiet 8336

his t. never came from God 11003

is an art 11002

Jesus Christ t. supernormal integrity 6314

Lord appeared to arouse us by his t. 6477

of Christ at first appears beautiful 6486

of Christ ripping, tearing torpedo 6486

of Christ splits to atoms every preconceived notion 6486

reliable, steady light bulbs 1313

spend three years t. child to walk, talk 8336

When try to understand Christ's t. with heads 6515

TEACHINGS

Democracy child of Jesus' t. 2523

foundation of society rests on t. of Bible 5189

of Christ alone can solve difficulties 6487

of Jesus revolutionary 6474

TEAKETTLE

Remember the t. sings 205

TEAMWORK

body, amazing example of t. 846

TEAR

And beauty in a t. 9024

Christ, to t. your name from this world 6496

concern always to uplift, never to t. down 6519

dew of compassion, a t. 1553

every t. will have an explanation 7060

foolish to t. one's hair in grief 5345

Help me to t. it from thy throne 6074

mother wipes away t. 7844

must not t. close-shut leaves apart 5403

single t. suffices with God 4091

sown a t. will come up a pearl 11012

The falling of a t. 8939

they will never t. the living Christ from my heart 7103

To bring a smile, to banish a t. 7423

TEARDROP

on earth summons King of heaven 11011

TEARING

At the heart of the cyclone t. the sky 8429

human minds to pieces 8710

teaching of Christ ripping, t. torpedo 6486

TEARS

all cry salt t. 11025

And blot the ill with t. 7017

And dipt in baths of hissing t. 2599

as result of t, new life begins 9591

because he didn't live thousand years ago 2430

because he isn't alive thousand years from now 2430

best gift of God to suffering man 11020

Beyond this vale of t. 5633

bring relief 1509

clean windows of the soul 11017

Cruelty feeds on them 29
Cruelty isn't softened by t. 29
darken our sight with foolish t. 10964
earth drowned in blood and t. 4902
faith not to be shaken won through t. 2949
God has bottle for people's t. 11012
God plants where watered by t. of repentance 888
God washes eyes by t. 11013
God washes eyes with t. 10591
God who counts the t. 10877
Grief has t. for its fruit 11014
have carried me to your love 1512
hold on to plough while wiping t. 1236
I have no wit, no words, no t. 2587
If smiles or t. be there 2206
Ills have no weight, t. no bitterness 7474
in heaven able to wipe t, won't have to 11016
in his solitude perhaps shedding hot t. 6599
Joy does not mean drying of t. 8454
Laughter or t. both derive from God 6736
Let it wipe another's t. 6640
Let t. flow of their own accord 5346
Life bridge of groans across stream of t. 2598
love is loveliest when embalm'd in t. 7309
Man an atom lost in endless vale of t. 10878
need never be ashamed of our t. 11023
Not all my prayers nor sighs nor t. 8451
of saints more sweet by far 9787
oil of lamp Lord makes us carry 10881
Only eyes washed by t. see clearly 2555
prayer, t. shed there bring cleansing 9039
prepare for clearer vision of God 11024
rain upon blinding dust of earth 11023
secret place, the land of t. 11015
shed for others sign of strength 11026
shed for self t. of weakness 11026
shed t. in grief 1513
should be thankful for our t. 11024
showers that ferilize the world 10625
sings praises through t. 10628
so blind our eyes cannot see mercies 10033

soap for the body, t. for the soul 10644
Sorrow baptizing us with bitter t. 10616
soul would have no rainbow had eye no t. 10631
speak more eloquently than ten thousand tongues 11018
teach us wisdom 11019
Thank you, Father, for these t. 1512
the falling t. of an angel 365
Those tender t. that humanize the soul 5349
Through blinding t. I see 7178
through t. have sorrowful seen gates of heaven 10882
times when God asks nothing except t. 10635
Tommy's t. and Mary's fears 4003
tree which moves some to t. 8506
valleys filled with t. 2359
Where t. are hung on every tree 11021
where t. shall come no more 11013
With the blood, t. of humanity 3369

TEASE
Those who t. you love you 7322

TECHNICALLY
man t. capable of destroying world 9872

TECHNICOLOR
rainbow is heaven's promise in t. 9390

TECHNOLOGY
semiconductor revolutionized t. 3932
When angry, take lesson from t. 407

TEDIOUS
Continuous eloquence is t. 9133
road will be less t. 7899

TEDIOUSLY
life runs t. quick 973

TEENAGER
waits impatiently to grow up 3867

TEENAGERS
do things nobody else does 12172
not old enough to do things adults do 12172
too old to do things kids do 12172
When t. get car, want money 3903
When t. get money, want car 3903

TEETH
children's t. set on edge 8328
Gluttons dig graves with t. 132
have t. fixed to test courage 1941
hell, gnashing of t. 5698
hell, t. will be provided 5696
kick in t. may be best 138
our t. still ache 8253

Parents bones on which children sharpen t. 8350
sing in bathroom while brushing t. 8168
When rogue kisses you, count your t. 2478
who gives us t. will give us bread 9349

TELEPHONE
Gossip is nature's t. 5130

TELESCOPE
Bible, like a t. 714
Love looks through a t. 7259

TELEVISION
a mobile nation 11043
another kind of car 11043
automated day dreaming 11037
beginning to think tube is reality 11045
betrays us 11041
bland leading the bland 11033
can turn every parlor into a church 11044
chewing gum for eyes 11036
dulls wonder and awe 11031
entertained by people wouldn't have in home 11035
grinds down to spiritual dust 11032
human lunacy, t. course 11028
impoverishes life 11031
insinuates false values 11031
lies about what world is like 11041
likely to prove most destructive 11032
nightly seance 11039
nothing wrong that not watching won't cure 11042
polluting us 11041
radio with eyestrain 11040
relies on tricks 11038
Roughing it: cabin without t. 6838
thing holding America together 11043

TELL
as much caution to t. truth as to conceal it 11514
can always t. a real friend 4213
cannot t. where God begins 4602
Don't t. me worry doesn't do any good 12060
easy to t. poor to accept poverty as God's will 8678
Eyes t. what the heart means 3568
Father, please don't t. us 574
From man's mouth can t. what he is 5126
God all that is in your heart 8970
God does not t. us what he is going to do 4932
great confidence to t. friend your faults 3930
greater confidence to t. friend his faults 3930
I will t. thee who thou art 4270

If have to t. people you are, you
ain't 8703
if you succeed, t. me there's no
God 4608
Jesus does not t. us to pretend
friends 5890
Love your enemies, they t. faults
3164
made him swear he'd always t. me
nothing but the truth 11507
me how much you know of
sufferings 7295
me to who you pay attention 9273
me whom you love 7296
me with whom thou art found
4270
Never t. evil of a man 5149
never t. unless absolutely necessary
5148
No eloquence adequate to t. of
beauty 10274
nor tongue can t. 9567
nought to do but mark and t.
10038
remember God is listening while
you t. it 5148
secrets, resign liberty 1619
than merely t. the way 10098
3435
That t. of saddest thought 10608
through fear of being criticized,
people t. lies 6851
to t. another exactly what we are
7428
To t. men how he died 10122
truth, have infinite power
supporting you 11510
used to t. troubles to everyone I
knew 2727
What a story a redwood stump
could t. 5731
When t. truth, don't have to
remember what you said 11588
Why should I t. it 5149
will t. you who you are 9273

TELLS
a lie, forced to invent twenty more
6850
child t. in streets 8340
Christ in you that t. the truth
6381
despair t. us difficulty
insurmountable 5931
easier to see clearly into liar than
who t. truth 6866
God quietly t. us who we are 6830
God t. us who he wants us to be
6830

TEMPER
events of life chafe our t. 8857
Exaggeration truth that has lost t.
11500
father never lost t. with us 3983
gets people into trouble 9237
God gives t. that lifts into life
2617
God gives to every man t. 5387
like city without defenses 368

loses t. quickest, finds it quickest
398
man who can't control t. 368
the tongue 9960

TEMPERAMENT
Behind joy may be callous t.
10583
relationship with God marked
with own t. 8883
Sermon on the Mount cuts across
t. 513
uncolored by t. 8237

TEMPERANCE
greatest saint not he who is
eminent for t. 9790
is love in training 7202

TEMPERATURE
church, so little t. 1410
right t. at home maintained by
warm hearts 5855

TEMPERING
God is t. for wisdom 4514
Light in darkness, t. sorrow 4758

TEMPERS
Hot t. cool friendships 9488
Memory t. prosperity 7735

TEMPEST
blown by t. of unbelievable power
7488
Every t. an assault in siege of love
4775
God may send t. about house
4775
Lust's effect is t. after sun 7357
Safe when the t. rages 4490

TEMPEST-TOSSED
Send the homeless, t. to me 7985

TEMPESTS
gain reputation from storms and t.
209
hear God in fury of t. 8034

TEMPESTUOUS
O'er the world's t. sea 5428

TEMPLE
body is t. of the Holy Ghost 838
Christ tore through the t. courts
like a mad man 6392
evil thoughts like setting up idol
in t. 7759
hewing out pillars for his t. 237

TEMPLES
Christ will turn homes into t.
5529
groves were God's first t. 8036

TEMPO
of life growing faster 3896

TEMPORAL
Gratitude to God makes t.
blessing taste of heaven 5248
Only eternal values give meaning
to t. ones 11311
things seen are t. 3746
transfers love from things t. to
things eternal 9278

TEMPORALITY
cling with body, soul to t. 1272

TEMPORARILY
Children loaned t. 1110
God t. permitted evil to exist 3378
lose your sense of well-being 2593

TEMPORARY
Compromise t. expedient 1580
emotionally loaded words have
their t. effect 8845
Failures t. tests to prepare us 3593
just a little t. inconvenience 4226
tell me revival is only t. 9753

TEMPT
devil does not t. sinners 2675
devil longed to t. him 2690
idle person tempts devil to t. him
11047
no unworthy purpose may t. aside
9057
Vices t. by rewards they offer
11101
When we do nothing, we t. devil
11116

TEMPTATION
butter that makes the t. 11070
cannot say lead us not into t. if
8818
cannot say no to t. 11111
cannot take simplicity by surprise
10278
character development curriculum
11058
Character out of t. 1000
devil looking through keyhole
11088
disclose fears, t, joys 4029
emerge stronger 11061
fiend at my elbow 11090
first t. was promise of learning,
knowledge 6701
Flee t, don't leave forwarding
address 11055
For every great t. many small ones
11056
for man to meet and master
11122
glory of manhood 11061
God better served in resisting t.
11059
good better sheltered from t. 5042
greatness in resistance to t. to
betray 5283
has become my strength 11075
Holiness not freedom from t.
5744
Holiness power to overcome t.
5744
If takes t. to show God, Satan in
true colors 11072
in using riches 11865
is a call to battle 11087
is God's magnifying glass 11086
is not a sin 11087
leaves us better or worse 11052
master and make crouch beneath
his foot 11122

neutrality impossible 11052
not meant to make us fail 11061
not only t. that tries the Christian 10328
not penalty of manhood 11061
object of t. 11099
of separating ministry from spiritually 10211
of separating service from prayer 10211
part of a plan 11093
provokes me to look upward 11089
receive as from the Lord 1461
Receive every t. with both thy hands 7698
resist t. to chase after pleasures 5615
response to t. accurate barometer 11079
Scriptures, use to drive t. away 720
secure from t. to evil 9777
shows work God has to do in our lives 11086
step in progress of faith 11093
sublimest purpose of wisdom, love 3350
to be like God eclipsed her view of God 4419
to fight with t. I owe my force 11075
to love money inexplicably powerful 7811
to make relation to God judicial 9816
to obscure God 11099
To resist t. in own strength 11108
to substitute something else for God 11099
Why comes t. but for man to meet 11122
yielding is opening door, inviting in 11088

TEMPTATION'S
Safe in t. hour 4490

TEMPTATIONS
are like tramps 11091
as lion that roared upon Samson 11095
dangerous in religious garb 11092
dangers are t. that surprise 11078
enter t. with gratitude 181
God delights in our t. 11057
God hates our t. 11057
great t. the most harmless 11078
greatest resists sorest t. 5297
have been my masters in divinity 11076
if overcome a nest of honey 11095
less troubled by t. on earth 5028
Life's t. for our faith 6995
like winds that firmly root tree 11094
Little victories over t, silent threads of gold 6997
my t. what are they in comparison to sufferings of Christ 10928

not accidents 11093
others receive light t. 11083
quelled by music's divine control 7935
surest protection is cowardice 1950
that find us leaning on God 11094
treat t. kindly, they will return 11091
When I consider my t. I shame myself 10928
when t. drive us to despair 11057
when t. drive us to prayer 11057

TEMPTED
art thou? In all thine anguish lay 6878
greatest of evils not to be t. 11097
if choose to remain in situation where t. 8818
If ever t. to give up 8565
man who has never been t. 11098
Men naturally t. by the devil 6770
others t. strongly at end 11083
Some people t. strongly at beginning 11083
'Tis one thing to be t. 11046
to begin, "If people would" 579

TEMPTER'S
What but thy grace can foil the t. power 5225

TEMPTESTUOUS
storms of devil 2652

TEMPTS
devil t. not least 9788
devil t. that he may ruin 11096
God never t. any man 11060
idle man t. the devil 6770
Satan t. by making rich 2690
too much license t. chastity 3554
too violent rigor t. chastity 3554
When we do ill, devil t. us 11116

TEMPUS
tonus is mono, t. is longus 9140

TEN
better to ask way t. times 5424
crop in one year that makes up for t. 889
die of little worries 12061
Elderly person is t. years older 8124
If t. lead holy life 5751
One minute of patience, t. years of peace 8404
pounds of common sense to apply it 11934
Shall have as much again, and t. times more 4364

TEN COMMANDMENTS
best formula for justice 701

TEN THOUSAND
God sends t. truths 6565
room for t. times t. worlds beside 4760
suns which shine above us nightly 4592

times t. times t. years have passed 3294

TENACITY
All excellence involves t. 3464
hold the line with t. of tackle for football team 5615

TENANT
not fit t. for mind of honest man 11181

TENANTS
We are but t. 2406

TEND
it with care 3847
to grow cooler rather than warmer 1347
to look at fellow human beings as enemies 10531

TENDENCY
examine t. to evil habits 3935
of world is down 7529
to not allow children to make mistakes 8320
to think of sex as degrading 10235
to worry about things that cannot be changed 7793

TENDER
God with t. patience leading world 4474
grief passes into quiet, t. joy 7101
Holy Spirit makes soul t. 5794
Love is a t. plant 7230
Love is t. 7246
Nothing will make us so t. 10014
Solitude makes us t. toward others 10560

TENDEREST
word is love 11993

TENDERLY
friendship should be dealt with t. 4237

TENDERNESS
Christ has no t. toward anything that is going to ruin a man 6407
deepest t. for others 4012
God loves you with t. 4747
love and t. sealed up 4223
must feel deepest t. of God 4012
never t. we regret 2420
nothing else but love 7329
Psalms, lyrical burst of man's t. 798
smiles soften countenance by t. 10500
Whatever impairs t. of conscience is sin 10424

TENNIS
few pastimes where love means nothing 7297
Life a lot like t. 10170
Love, in t, nothing 7276

TENSE
Americans so t. impossible to put to sleep with sermon 10096

TENSELY
bow too t. strung easily broken 943

TENSION
if t. taken out of your life 9977

TENT
they pitch t. toward Sodom 11080

TENTATIVE
about theology 11214

TENTH
God will take nine steps, but not the t. 9578

TENTS
shall fold their t. like the Arabs 7887

TENUOUS
hope God too kind to punish 4726

TERESA OF AVILA
who could be harmed if he knew something about T. 5733

TERMINAL
everyone a t. patient 12030

TERMINOLOGY
may not use all our t. 2987

TERMITES
Noah brave to sail wooden boat with t. 1931

TERMS
bargain for nothing, make no t. 9084
Let one define his t, stick to definition 11193
May on familiar t. be with highest God 7489
rather should use t. obedience, disobedience 5753
well to stop using t. victory, defeat 5753
will accept convert even on such t. 9829

TERRIBLE
excuse worse, more t. than lie 3474
If death be t, the fault is thee 2314
indifference toward one's neighbor 6163
luxury of unbelief 11589
man, the most t. of the beasts 8066
Nothing more t. than activity without insight 4429
Nothing so t. as activity without thought 6084
nothing t. for man who realizes nothing t. in death 7059
One does not fear God because he is t. 3983
the center of me is a t. pain 7521
to hear such things 5155

When death's approach is seen so t. 2348

TERRIFIED
one thing to be t. 9581

TERRIFIES
eternal silence of infinite spaces t. me 3285

TERRIFYING
New Testament's t. phrase 9832
To meet God a t. adventure 4551
to pseudo faith nothing but God t. thought 3719

TERRITORY
no middle t. 5038

TERROR
Abounding sin t. of world 5203
Death grisly t. 2271
death, an experience robbed of t. 2234
no one able to strike t. into others 4001
of God is other side of his love 4775
prayer of saint a t. to Satan 8988
some face death in abject t. 2336

TERRORS
Be not intimidated by any t. 4115
Bible deals with t. 696

TEST
a man's character, give him power 8706
acid t. of father's leadership 3925
Apply t. of universality 2494
basic t. of freedom 4142
biggest t. of all 8394
Calamity, t. of integrity 158
Experience gives t. first, lessons afterwards 3522
Failure true t. of greatness 3594
first t. of truly great man 6032
God able to t. and develop faith 3744
God-made object, a kind of final t. 2022
home is t. of father's leadership 3925
Hospitality t. for godliness 5957
I t. the soundess of the tree 72
Life a t. that has more questions than answers 6953
Life is the t. of us 6932
never t. resources of God until attempt impossible 3815
no stronger t. of man's character 8721
not the shape of the tree, but the heart 72
not untrained to stand the t. 8546
of courage when in minority 1938
of joy's integrity 6571
of man's character is his tongue 11414
of sanctification what are we like with those who know us best 9845

of tolerance when in majority 1938
of what is real 9399
Ofttimes t. of courage to live, rather than die 7009
Put faith to t. of life 3774
Spirit of God will reserve right to t. you 5776
Though this t. be not thy choice 11107
To t. stuff of rough-hewn faith 2964

TESTED
by whether we seek God or his gifts 4800
Centuries of experience have t. Bible 646
do not understand faith until t. 11620
experience must be t. by Word of God 3550
faith that hasn't been t. cannot be trusted 3640
God t. Abraham 11061
Our love for God t. 4800

TESTIMONY
If t. makes anyone wish to emulate me 11125
mistaken t, not a witness to Jesus 11125

TESTINGS
a way out of the t. of life 166

TESTS
bruise but build character 211
devil t. us that we might stumble 171
Failures t. to prepare us 3593
God probes the core, t. the root 7862
God t. that he may crown 11096
God t. us that we might stand 171
more t. to get in than out 3034
of growth in mainstream of life 1319
of life make, not break us 214
relentless, incessant, persistent, continual 211

TEXT
favorite t. of asceticism, deny yourself 467
man's t, Christianity 1177
Of t. and legend 3813

TEXTURE
Laughter adds t. to ordinary days 6727

THANK
able to t. Creator for way he made us 9993
atheist, nobody to t. 488
do not come back to t. him 6251
duty bound to t. and praise 4992
Father, in heaven, we t. thee 11174
for ingratitude 1191
God Almighty, I'm free at last 4119

God don't have to be flawless to be blessed 5442
God for beauty 535
God for having created this world 5678
God for how he will use sin 11152
God for my handicaps 11147
God for not having given tiger wings 11140
God for sleep 10489
God for the unknown future 4318
God for the way he made you 6206
God we are not angels 839
God when you get up you have something to do 11159
I am an atheist, t. God 480
lived to t. God all my prayers not answered 8823
Still, t. him that you live 10489
thee for daily task to do 11148
thee for our daily bread 11172
thee for the things I miss 11136
thee for these gifts of thine 11136
thee that dark, uncertain is our future 9053
thee that I am living 11149
thee that I live 7048
thee that there will be pain 9053
thee there shall be death 9053
thee there will be loneliness 9053
three things I t. God for 11144
Who does not t. for little will not t. for much 11171
Whom none can love, whom none can t. 4374
with grateful hearts and no one to t. 11167
you for all you have given me 11161

THANK'D
God be t. for those, and these 5860

THANKED
Agape love concern without desire to be t. 7158
And so the Lord be t. 11159
God for roses 2099
have never t. God for thorn 2099
If men t. God for good things 11150
When thou hast t. thy God 11168

THANKFUL
atheist t, nobody to thank 488
be t. God's answers are wiser than your prayers 8861
can be t. to a friend 6255
Cultivate the t. spirit 11139
evidence of t. heart 5202
for anything 8775
502
in a meek, t. heart 5621
learn to give thanks even if don't feel t. 11173
Love is t. to God 7246
Nor t. when it pleaseth me 5265
saint always t. to God 9790
should be t. for our tears 11024

Talent is God-given, be t. 10994
thankless man never does t. deed 11134
that thorns have roses 1564
When break leg, be t. isn't neck 11169

THANKFULNESS
an intelligent response of gratitude to God 11173
Faith without t. lacks strength, fortitude 11154
Hope without t. lacking in perception 11154
If t. arises through prosperity 11151
If t. springs up through health 11151
is not an emotion 11173
Lend me a heart replete with t. 11156
life without t. devoid of love 11154
to take food in t. gives God glory 12013
virtue divorced from t. maimed 11154

THANKING
spend as much time t. God for benefits 11166
thee for little things 11148

THANKLESS
feeder is a thief 11138
man never does a thankful deed 11134
to have a t. child 1119
unjust to nature, himself is t. man 3190

THANKS
a thousand t. when things agreeable 11157
Accept my thoughts for t; I have no words 8792
and ever t. 11146
And t. unto the harvest's Lord 11175
Christian t. God when everything good, bad 3638
Christian t. God whether he feels like it or not 3638
For all that has been, t. 9055
for knowledge of his works 11144
for unspeakable gift 1372
From David learn to give t. 11145
give God t. for having revealed so much 4908
give t. even if don't feel thankful 11173
give t. for Someone to thank 11136
give t. to the Almighty, seek his aid 5411
have another life to look forward to 11144
humble mind is soil of which t. grows 5258
if lose money, can still offer t. 11151

If we don't give t, living in unbelief 11152
loses t. who promises, delays 2535
merits no t. who does kindness for own ends 10056
saint t. God as much as he were sound and well 9782
Thanksgiving first t, then giving 11178
that God set in my darkness lamp of faith 11144
Three things for which t. are due 11165
Transfixed with t, folded in love 12125
When feelings brave, give t. 4013
When feelings humble, give t. 4013
When feelings loving, give t. 4013

THANKSGIVING
an open heart into love of God 10736
Bible, my t. 716
comes from a full heart 10736
compiling anthology act of t. 9381
cultivate fine art of t. 11151
First t. Day 11175
first thanks, then giving 11178
invites God to bestow a second benefit 11162
never meant to be a single day 11177
One act of t. when things go wrong 11157
prayer of t. 11174
Pride kills t. 6027
proclamation, 1863 11176
Psalms sown with seeds of t. 11145
says, I want to 10736
word t. prompts humility 11153

THANK YOU
an anthology says t. 9381
for the sheer joy of wanting to get up 9114

THATCHED
A shed that's t. 6149

THAWS
faith t. life out 3747

THEATER
youth like children in a t. 12168

THEATRE
earth, t. for his grace and direction 4902

THEFT
from those who hunger 11745

THEM
him, not t, whom God made in his image 6200

THEME
favorite t. of asceticism, tombstone 467
Get more, know more, do more 9016

God the Son t. of Holy Scripture 655

Gossip lack of worthy t. 5131

of Jesus' life 6384

THEMES

Bible deals with such grand t. 719

Jesus furnished t. for more sermons 6449

THEMSELVES

70% of patients could cure t. 12076

always comparing t. with their betters 6813

bad never at unity with t. 5045

children little need to deceive t. 1132

do not know what to do with t. on a Sunday afternoon 6100

Eavesdroppers never hear good of t. 5123

except those who are full of t. 9200

freedom to simply be t. 4285

God hates those who praise t. 9198

knock t. and their world upside down 8850

Men are merely for t. 10069

Men are so possessed by t. 9938

never retract, love t. better than truth 8207

no other model but t. to copy 3451

People capable of recruiting t. to evil 3396

Proud people breed sorrows for t. 9232

see evil in others, not in t. 5029

seek only t. and their own advantage 10084

they that know t. cannot be proud 6039

What unto t. was taught 10678

THEN

why now rather than t. 4905

THEOLOGIAN

attempt to state things 11197

Jesus speaks not as a first-century t. 6448

never infallible 11197

No one damns like a t. 9360

would take t. with fine-toothed comb 5786

THEOLOGIANS

always bothering about origin of e. 11204

Conversion so profound t. ponder 1896

Had the angel gone to the t. 6147

would have consulted commentaries 6147

THEOLOGICAL

beliefs do not get one into Kingdom 601

beliefs get one into church 601

God is omniscient, a t. statement 11179

Nothing dies harder than t. difference 11198

political order cannot be renewed without t. virtues 5169

problems are the soul's mumps 11202

stick to t. point of view become stagnant 11240

True contemplation, t. grace 1765

truth useless until obeyed 11205

turn t. truth into experience 12063

THEOLOGY

As grave grows nearer, my t. growing simple 11182

as schools change, t. must change 11207

attempt to understand the mystery 11206

begins, ends with Christ as Savior 11182

best t. is divine life 11200

condensed into four words 11195

Could God pass examination in t. 11183

crowd God's fullness into formula 11208

finds the truth 11524

for mystic important t. should flourish 7946

God on side of poor central to t. 8696

God, a t. in itself 4503

goes when begin to think is t. 11240

half the difference in t. would end 11193

has been profoundly unorthodox 6604

have too much t. we don't understand 9552

ideas of truth classified, arranged 11207

If t. doesn't change behavior 11190

ignorance has brought t. to sorry plight 11196

In t. predominance of authority 11191

intellectual attempt to systematize God 11209

madness gone systematic 11208

must be lived in midst of life's mess 6984

must become biography 11199

mystic's certainty of escaping self-delusion 7946

needs social gospel to vitalize it 5104

next to t. I give music highest place 7914

Old age can love God better than doctor of t. 7286

Our sociology reflects our t. 9487

Persecution used in t, not arithmetic 8529

philosophy merely her servant 11210

Redemptive t, mercy not effective until justice done 4730

science of mind applied to God 11207

science of religion 11209

should be empress 11210

social gospel needs t. to make effective 5104

teaches what ends are desirable 11211

teaches what means are lawful 11210

tentative about t. 11214

Unless we reshape t. 8696

what you are when action starts 11215

what you are when talking stops 11215

world does not understand t. 7313

THEORIZING

less t. you do about God 4499

THEORY

bastard t. of evolution 1985

Let religion be less a t. 9542

THERAPY

after all other t. had failed 8764

Laughter most beneficial t. 6733

THERE

astonished at being here rather than t. 4905

happiness not t. but here 11374

no reason why here rather than t. 4905

THERE WAS

how many sorrows crowd into these two brief words 8369

THERMOMETER

Giving, t. of love 4358

THEY

everyone else is T. 454

THICK

Blunt, t. hammered through 2135

can lay it on t. in right places 9238

Christ reveals a God who stands in t. of whole thing 6432

God saw through t. cloud 4904

Hope has t. skin 5912

skin gift from God 2625

THICKET

a t. we are in 7936

God passes through t. of world 4463

THIEF

cannot find policeman 472

doth fear each bush an officer 5488

holds the ladder as bad as t. 2036

Procrastination is t. of time 9300

repentance recorded of penitent t. that none should despair 9602

repentance, t. becomes honest 9604

thankless feeder is a t. 11138

THIEVES

adored Jesus 6412
crucified where t. curse 2131
People do not decide to be t.
  11080
the more t, robbers there will be
  5192

THIN

Many fears are tissue-paper t.
  3982

THINE

This path is mine, not t. 5415
two tiny words taken from them,
  mine and t. 4227
who hath ought that is not t. 4954

THING

bad t. to be satisfied spiritually
  10704
Do the t. you fear 3962
feelings only a t. that happens to
  you 4013
Forgiveness is funny t. 4075
God cannot be for, against same t.
  4972
God created life as a manifold t.
  6985
God more real to me than any t.
  7098
God never gave man a t. to do
  10140
greatest t. a man can do for his
  heavenly Father 6665
greatest t. you can do is to be
  10141
Happiness a t. that comes and goes
  5517
I do lose a t. none but fools would
  keep 7019
I'm not the t. I should be 9928
It isn't the t. you do 2502
Let the t. be simplified 10279
Life a tumble-about t. of ups,
  downs 6955
Life was a funny t. that happened
  6986
little t. in hand worth more 7116
main t. is to keep the main t. the
  main t. 9275
Man's love is of man's life a t.
  apart 7278
most important t. in life 7034
nausea of being the t. I was 10021
nearest t. to God is human soul
  10651
no earthly t. can ever satisfy me
  3277
no one t. greater miracle 7940
no such t. as bad weather 8005
no such t. as being neutral 8075
Nor am I even the t. I could be
  9928
Not one t. done for God has been
  lost 10176
of bad quality expensive 10291
Only one t. endures, character
  1010
only t. he would change was me
  967

Philosophers take simplest t. 8591
Real is a t. that happens to you
  5886
relationship to God only simple t.
  10653
so real it never can be told 10274
spirit not a t. apart 10697
This one t. I do, not fifty t. 81
To become like Christ only t.
  worth caring for 6494
Truth is a divine t. 11560
value of t. is what it costs us
  11664
What a fine looking t. is war
  11777
What is this t. called the world
  3485
Who is it that has lured me into
  the t. 3485
why same t. makes us laugh, cry
  10660
without choice man a t. 4155
Youth one t. that never returns
  12184

THINGS

All good t. are cheap 11655
all good t. are yours 5604
All great t. are simple 10277
All t. are at odds 11217
All t. are difficult before easy
  2710
All t. born through strife 1621
All t. both great and small 7174
all t. desirable to men in Bible 641
all t. everywhere are boiling,
  burning, groaning 9909
all t. happen because of, with, and
  in God's will 10926
America has more t. than any
  other nation 8624
amid all change t. we can count on
  4643
appalling number of half-done t.
  9300
appear little in comparison with
  eternal realities 4559
are in the saddle 9343
as if God required disagreeable t.
  of us 6813
atom proof little t. count 8663
Attempt great t. for God 10118
attempting to find new ways of
  bettering t. 9311
bad person loves t. and uses people
  5041
bad t. are very dear 11655
Be silent about great t. 10242
beautiful beyond belief 5360
beginning of wisdom is to call t.
  by right names 11941
begins many t. finishes few 57
best t. are nearest 829
best t. in life are free 3838
Calm soul of all t. 8430
can do little t. for God 10208
can do small t. in great way 10155
Cheerfulness, looking at good side
  of t. 1095

Christ speaks from source of t.
  6422
Dark t. reach out toward
  brightness 5906
dearest t. are swept from sight
  forever 10645
divine t. must be loved to be
  known 7180
Do great t. as if they were little
  10127
Do little t. as if they were great
  7117
Do little t. now 2534
do not happen in world, are
  brought about 4953
do small t. in right spirit 9679
Doing t. by halves is worthless
  2770
expect great t. from God 10118
faith makes all t. possible 7345
Faithfulness in little t, a big thing
  3843
few desire t. that make for peace
  8428
Few t. impossible to diligence, skill
  8538
Five t. observe with care 1855
forbidden have secret charm
  11104
Four t. are property of friendship
  4227
Four t. come not back 8213
Four t. go together 10248
Four t. must be tried in friendship
  4227
four t. to learn in life 6913
get new t, better t. 3315
give us courage to change t. which
  should be changed 9060
give us grace to accept t. that
  cannot be changed 9060
given infirmity that he might do
  better t. 8806
given life that he might enjoy all t.
  8806
God alone cause, measure of all t.
  11663
God alters the t. that matter 9276
God bestows many t. out of
  liberality 8796
God does not communicate t. to us
  4537
God does not want us to do
  extraordinary t. 7118
God gave me life so I could enjoy
  all t. 6906
God in all t. 4845
God knows all t. visible, invisible
  4881
God needs people who do
  ordinary t. 10137
God surrounding all t. 4850
God wants us to do ordinary t.
  extraordinarily well 7118
God who causes t. to be 7944
God will not permit knowledge of
  t. to come 4314
good person loves people, uses t.
  5041

held in hands, lost them all 8628

held me far from thee 4805

holy revealed only to men who are holy 5769

how little some enjoy great t. 3221

how we look at t. 506

Human t. must be known to be loved 7180

I asked God for all t. so I could enjoy life 6906

I miss a lot of good t. day by day 5587

I worry about don't happen 12060

If I cannot do great t. 10155

if interested in big t. 8139

If men thanked God for good t. 11150

If t. go on as they have 562

if want some t. to count 7714

Impulse manages all t. badly 5580

in all t, charity 7196

In all t. thee to see 10183

in doubtful t, liberty 7196

in earth's common t. God stands revealed 8019

in life which are irreparable 7051

In necessary t, unity 7196

In t. great or small 5456

in tragedy face to face with t. never gave heed to 10667

Instead of telling people to give up t. 3315

Joy is not in t. 6541

judging from number of t. going to do 9302

learn to do without good t. of earth 8977

learning to be happy without t. we cannot have 8635

least of t. with meaning worth more 7030

Leave some t. unsaid 10279

Life a great bundle of little t. 6946

Life is made up of little t. 6656

little t. that annoy us 9636

Little t. that matter most 9267

Love able to undertake all t. 7220

love makes all t. easy 7345

Love people, not t. 7267

Love thinks all t. lawful 7220

Love thinks all t. possible 7220

luxury of believing all t. beautiful are what they seem 7972

man who does t. makes many mistakes 7792

many great t. expressed in single words 10277

mean nothing, God means everything 1325

mediocre minds talk about t. 1845

miserable to have few t. to desire, many t. to fear 11827

more t. to complain about 1559

More t. wrought by prayer 8869

most do without t. parents never heard of 8582

most important t. cannot be taught 3030

most precious t. God finds in us 10666

move along an appointed path 9173

must speed to my God before all t. 7951

never big t. that disturb 1472

never let t. we can't have spoil enjoyment of t. we do have 8635

no uninteresting t, only uninterested p. 868

not able to find time to do t. you don't want to do 9301

not rich man under dominion of t. 8681

Of all created t, loveliest are children 1120

Of thee three t. I pray 9043

often for excuse we say t. impossible 7869

Oh, the riddle and secret of t. 7943

old t. will drop off 3315

On little t. depend 7119

one of the t. a Christian is meant to do 5629

Only a God who knows all t. 5438

only God knows beginning of t. 6705

only God knows cause of t. 6705

only God knows end of t. 6705

only worth what you make them worth 11665

other t. only man can do 10199

overlooked more obvious t. 9970

people live in t. they possess 8631

prayed for all t. that he might enjoy life 8806

prayed for wealth that he might do greater t. 8806

Prayer changes people and people change t. 8905

Praying really changes t. 8899

present seem worst 8382

prosper as we do common t. in uncommon way 9344

proud man always looking down on t. 9188

real t. are invisible spiritual realities 615

real t. aren't simple 9402

reason must ask God for t. he intends to give 8990

Reason's last step is recognition t. beyond it 9421

science reveals conformity in all t. 9866

see all t. good 8578

see good t. in unexpected places 8575

see t. not as they are, but as we are 8514

Seeing God means seeing into mystery of t. 7547

seldom what they seem 8510

Silence element in which great t. fashion themselves 10265

Simple love can do great t. 6708

Situation ethics puts people at center, not t. 6820

Six t. requisite to create happy home 5848

So shall big t. come by and by 2534

Some t. only God can do 10199

sweet prove sour 11105

Sweetest t. turn sourest by their deeds 5039

take all t. as if prayed for them 10926

take t. as we find them 38

Teach me in all t. thee to see 9112

teenagers do t. nobody else does 12172

teenagers not old enough to do t. adults do 12172

teenagers too old to do t. kids do 12172

tendency to worry about t. that cannot be changed 7793

than greatest of t. without meaning 7030

thanking thee for little t. 11148

that belonged to peace connected with Jesus 6420

that clash with own beliefs 4124

that count most in life 7039

that hold in slippery world 4643

that hurt, instruct 10916

that mattered, God and people 3331

that now disturb events for gratitude 5252

the sin done for t. there's money in 7819

Those t. we pray for 9676

Three silent t. 10275

Three t. for which thanks are due 11165

three t. I thank God for 11144

Three t. only God knows 6705

Three t. sap man's strength 10406

Time crumbles t. 11324

Time ripens all t. 11342

time to be alarmed is when t. undisturbed 7040

To thank thee for the t. I miss 11136

To the quiet mind all t. possible 7773

To undo t. done, to call back yesterday 9568

transfers love from t. temporal to t. eternal 9278

trivial t. disturb us 1472

Trust God for great t. 10205

two t. not easy to reconcile 7069

Two t. stand like stone 6657

two t. that make devils or saints 7805

two t. to do about the gospel 5107

unexplained t. in life more than explained 11616

unless in thee, were not at all
4805
use t. and love people 9510
usually t. that cannot be counted
7039
Vision seeing t. invisible 11737
we can count on 4643
we have to learn before we can do
3545
we may fathom 4678
Weak t. united become strong
11624
What if God arranged t. so that
577
what t. are, and what they ought
to be 7413
When repress t. you don't want to
live with 9291
When you pray, t. remain the same
9033
where fantasy and earthly t.
metamorphosed into art 7435
whether take t. for granted or
with gratitude 5268
which come easily have no
significance 2757
who refuses to be satisfied with t.
as they are 9311
Yet in the maddening maze of t.
4642
you possess all t, and more
innumerable 5575

THINK

A few people t. 8476
about what to do for other people
1023
according to inclinations 1648
always t. last opinion right 8203
anew, act anew 976
bids others t. of his vices 9207
Bigotry has no head and cannot t.
9180
Children will t. like their parents
8289
confirmed pride when you t. you
are humble 9259
continually of God 11269
Crises force us to t. 2043
dare not t. God is absent,
daydreaming 7556
Democracy, can say what you t.
even if you don't t. 5172
difficult, shall be difficult 517
Do not t. of faults of others 3939
Do not t. of your faults 3940
Do we stop, t. before we speak
12005
Do you wish people to t. well of
you 5996
Don't t. so big others look small
1587
Each of us must t. for himself
11260
easy, shall be easy 517
esteem more highly those who t.
alike 3032
every day of Christ 8472
every day the last 7021
excitement 3185

first about foundations of humility
5997
first thing that goes when you
begin to t. is your theology
11240
for those who do not t. 11228
Forget yourself and t. of those
around 11284
friend helps us t. noblest thoughts
4178
friend, person with whom I may t.
aloud 4165
God comes when we t. he is
farthest off 4837
God has turned life into
inextricable confusion 4885
God is nearer to us than we t.
4878
God's love safer to t. about than
our love 4777
greatest torture for most is to t.
11230
hardest task to t. 11275
have not time to t. about God
4886
heart awed within me when I t.
1966
how little people know who t.
holiness dull 5750
human to t. wisely, act foolishly
5973
I t. and t. for months 2775
I t. not of the great, but of the
good 6245
if man in pew trained to t. 9146
If t. you know it all, haven't been
listening 9210
if things we t. are worth thinking
5590
If wish to be miserable, t. about
yourself 10818
If would t. God's thoughts 11269
if you t. too much of yourself,
other people won't 9253
It is for God to t. about me 9934
Just what I t, nothing more or less
9036
leaving God to t. for him 11478
Let each man t. himself an act of
God 4557
Let each man t. his life a breath of
God 4557
Let each man t. his mind a
thought of God 4557
Life a comedy for those who t.
6954
Life has taught me to t. 6942
Life is easier than you t. 6961
life that we call Christian different
from what we t. 6918
like a man of action 11257
live, t, suffer with your time 904
love of humanity safe, but it isn't
7836
love what we t. is good 5086
man of little faith does not t. 3830
many people t. they t. 8476
Men t. highly of those who rise
rapidly 3857

mistake to t. time of prayer
different from any other time
8881
Most people would die sooner
than t. 11233
must not t. ourselves ordinary
people 1346
must only t. of rising again 3634
My business is to t. about God
9934
never once to t. for themselves
11227
Never t. could do something if
different lot 8219
Never t. God's delays are denials
8402
Never t. Jesus commanded a trifle
8097
never t. of faith as purely mystical
3830
No man can t. clearly when fists
clenched 400
No teacher should make men t. as
he thinks 11004
not my business to t. about myself
9934
not on what you lack 11164
not only going to t. no evil 7190
not those faithful who praise thy
words 3955
nothing more difficult than to t.
well 11219
nothing more easy than to t.
11219
nothing you cannot believe to be
true 9871
of destiny, how puny a part you
are 7063
of how good God is 4648
of the totality of all being 7063
of things you don't want 822
of what is faulty in yourself 3939
of what is good in others 3939
of yourself as "he" instead of "I"
10009
of yourself as seed wintering in
earth 5672
often of your friends 8472
often on God, by day, by night
7723
Only to sit and t. of God 4799
1763
Our lives are what we t. about
God 7016
People in a hurry cannot t. 5584
People t. they are thinking when
rearranging prejudices 9178
People t. thing's worth believing if
hard 3773
people t. with hopes, fears rather
than mind 7763
problem is to t. of it again 2001
question no longer what we t. of
Christ 4718
read book that makes you t. 728
Reality more fantastic than we t.
9407
Resolved, never to t. meanly 569

Satan tries to make us t. wrongs
spring from God 9859
seldom of your enemies 8472
Shall I t. of death as doom 2364
since Christians have ceased to t.
of other world 5656
Some t. have to look like
hedgehog to be pious 6822
still less of other's faults 3940
tendency to t. of sex as degrading
10235
than those who t. differently 3032
that his Fire will consume my soul
7951
the nonsense of those who t. they
talk sense 9056
to read God's mind, to t. his
thoughts 7766
To someone may be better than
you t. 4356
to t. as a Christian greatest effort
11270
To t. clearly without hurry or
confusion 6913
To t. is an effort 11270
To t. is to see 11271
to t. rightly a great effort 11270
To t. the thought, to breathe the
name 4799
to t. we are whole and need no
help 10045
To t. we have humility evidence
we don't 6008
today, speak tomorrow 11258
torn between desire to t. positively
or confront life as it is 9401
trouble only time people t. of God
11441
truest self-respect is not to t. of
yourself 10000
two ends, one to t. with 10793
use cliches so they won't have to t.
8476
very few can t. good thoughts
11272
we say millions never t. of God
7561
we t. of gentleness as weakness
4402
well for people who t. to change
minds 11228
What comes into our minds when
we t. about God 7563
What heart did t, tongue would
click 1890
What must God t. of us 9021
what people t. of Jesus because of
me is critical 9627
What people t. of me becoming
less important 9627
What thought can t. 11276
What we t. about most 10016
What we t. about when free to t.
11277
When I t. of those who have
influenced my life 6245
When I t. upon my God 7931
When t. children are naive 8319

when we believe God beyond all
we can t. 4685
Where all t. alike 11279
who t. no need of others become
unreasonable 9506
wilt thou let it slip useless away
2198
wish people to t. well of you 9614
with our tiny brains unravel
mysteries 7944
without confusion clearly 559
Words make thousands, perhaps
millions, t. 12002
worry is failure to t. 12078
would not t. duty small if you
were great 9682
you are more important than you
t. 10001
you have humility, you have lost it
6006
youth t. they know everything
12181

THINKER
Christian t. challenges prejudices
11239
Christian t. disturbs complacent
11239
Christian t. is a nuisance 11239
Christian t. obstructs pragmatists
11239
Christian t. questions foundations
about him 11239
exchange profoundest t. 4204
I wish I were a deep t. 870
kind of knowing which most
acute t. cannot imitate 5809
when God lets loose a t. 11217

THINKERS
few original t. in world 11254
know wither we are going 8482

THINKING
as t. being the Christian has
succumbed to secularization
7768
Bad the day man becomes content
with thoughts he is t. 8649
be sturdy, upright in t. 836
believing impossible without t.
617
But t. makes it so 11255
can never produce optimism 8587
Christian t. puts intellect second
11238
Christian t. rare, difficult 11221
creative t. abdicated to enemy
3027
devil can keep us terrified of t.
11218
do not recognize need of Holy
Spirit for t. 11243
Doubt may be sign man is t. 2933
enlarging powers of t. 3027
evil same as doing it 3409
faith is essentially t. 3830
Fame comes when t. about
something else 3852
first-rate mind only happy when t.
11248

Freethinkers essential for right t.
4124
God has constituted us t. beings
6679
has not taught me to live 6942
if five minutes t. about God 7491
in higher forms a kind of poetry
11259
in lower grades comparable to
money 11259
is greatest fatigue in world 11263
is like loving and dying 11260
is magic of the mind 11261
Kindness in t. creates
profoundness 6649
legalism, lynching of fresh t. 6817
less than 15 percent do original t.
11230
limitations of humanist geocentric
t. 1168
Man is a t. reed 7406
Man is made for t. 11231
mode of t. 3040
Morality correct t. within 7832
more futile become in their t.
11538
not form of escapism or wishful t.
5629
people think they are t. when
rearranging prejudices 9178
prayer doesn't consist of t. 8893
same substance as evil in our own
t. 3397
second-rate mind happy t. with
minority 11248
shall find God unifying our t.
3774
sixteen hours daily t. about world
7491
Speaking without t. 1873
talking of the soul with itself
11262
third-rate mind happy t. with
majority 11248
time with the Master will elevate t.
8865
to believe, doubt everything, save
us from t. 2956
well is wise 67
will never get out of despair 2613

THINKS
able to know what everybody else
t. 4332
Age t. of nothing but health 5619
average man never t. 11237
Christian mind through which
Christ t. 1248
dissenter resigns from herd, t. for
himself 6210
Everyone t. his sack heaviest
10029
Everyone t. of changing world 964
Friendship ought never to conceal
what it t. 4238
happiest person t. most interesting
thoughts 7026
He most lives who t. most 1056
himself happiest man, really is so
11917

himself wisest, usually greatest fool 11917

Hope t. nothing difficult 5931

In spring no one t. of snow 1470

Love t. all things lawful 7220

Love t. all things possible 7220

Love t. nothing of trouble 7220

Man t. he amounts to a great deal 9219

man who idly sits and t. 11244

man who t. must be pessimistic 8587

never t. he gets as much as he deserves 5258

no one t. of changing himself 964

No young man ever t. he shall die 12171

of himself, says prayers of petition 8840

of his neighbor, says prayers of intercession 8840

of serving God, says prayers of abandonment 8840

one thing to know how God t. 5425

read not book that t. for you 728

saint never t. of life as secular and sacred 1324

significant question what Christ t. of us 4718

to know someone who t, feels with us 4280

To one who t, life is comedy 607

too much of his virtues 9207

who t. he is righteous is not righteous 9254

who t. too much of himself t. too little of others 9243

Youth t. nothing of health 5619

THIRD

God's t. way best 1120

THIRD-RATE

mind happy thinking with majority 11248

THIRST

have quenched t. at other fountains 7500

I tasted, still I hunger and t. 4805

must be quenched 7538

O what a blessed t. 9780

quickly find something else to alleviate t. 7538

riches grow and a t. for more and more 11799

to be made more thirsty 9097

THIRSTY

I am t. for sin 10435

like Tantalus up to chin in water, yet t. 5325

Many not t. for God 7500

thirst to be made more t. 9097

thy goodness both satisfied and made me t. 9097

Worship t. land crying out for rain 12132

THIRTY

Died at t, buried at sixty 7041

man sold God for t. pence 4532

years of Lord's life hidden 8112

THISTLE

friendship is a plant, not roadside t. 4237

THISTLES

Untilled ground, mind will bring t. 7774

We were t, now lilies 1348

THOMAS AQUINAS

said of his theology, "reminds me of straw" 8983

who could be harmed if he knew something about T. 5733

THORN

Life is licking honey from a t. 6963

never thanked God for t. 2099

of experience worth wilderness of warning 3540

teach me value of my t. 2099

To live with t. uncomplainingly 8256

THORNBUSH

aflame with glory of God 9064

THORNLESS

Harebells, sweet lilies show a t. growth 7179

THORNS

chose road with most t. 467

Christ sought crown of t. 2152

Christ wore crown of t. 6393

crown of achievement is crown of t. 10849

crown of all crowns one of t. 10613

grumbling because roses have t. 1564

head that once was crowned with t. 9697

I fall upon the t. of life! I bleed! 6911

laughter of sin as crackling of burning t. 10393

no gathering the rose without t. 94

no t. no throne 199

others grumble at the t. 6254

pass, roses remain 10710

plants t. must never expect to gather roses 10454

reap'd, of tree I planted 1737

rose with all its t. excels 7179

straws almost as sharp as t. after 6489

thankful t. have roses 1564

Untilled ground, mind will bring t. 7774

We were t, now grapes 1348

You see roses, he sees t. 7670

THORNY

either a crown of love or a t. crown 7073

Through t. ways leads to joyful end 1502

Virtue demands rough t. path 11714

THOROUGHFARE

Holy Spirit turns life into t. for God 5795

tomb a t. 2422

THOU

Be t. the rainbow to storm of life 618

Just t, again t, always t. 4518

THOUGH

we know not goodness of God 4578

THOUGHT

A heart in every t. renewed 5620

absurd by what it seeks 11242

Accustom yourself to t. God loves you 4747

act like a man of t. 11257

another t. can mend 11276

as soon as existence mysterious, t. begins 11220

at all, can be t. clearly 11222

bring t, imagination into captivity 1014

can see too far ahead 11264

careless to well-tried wisdom of the ages 11232

changes knowledge into energy 11265

Character is consolidated t. 1012

Charity, useful without t. of recompense 1084

consequences of action without t. 11278

creation, t. by God 1975

deadly t. of solitude 10569

destructive, terrible 11232

discouragement when too much t. to past, future 2887

endlessly fascinated by new t. 9468

Eternity, thou pleasing, dreadful t. 3271

Every good t. touches chord that vibrates in heaven 6670

Every t. for Christ away from discouragement 2940

every t. is registered and recorded 71

Everything has been t. of before 2001

Everything is a t. of Infinite God 1959

Evil wrought by want of t. 3363

Faith and t. belong together 617

Falling like dew upon a t. 12002

fearless t. in advance of their time 11252

Feeling deeper than all t. 10678

Fix t. more on the God you desire 10305

free man does not fear t. 4145

gift of loving t. into heart of friend 4189

gift of t. giving as angels give 11225

Freedom filling mind with God's t. 4121

freedom to share innermost t. 4285

friend helps us think noblest t. 4178

go into memory of God 11280

God knows all t. 4881

God's t. belong to world of spirit 10692

God's t. flashing from every direction 8045

Good t. bear good fruit 11223

Great t, grave t, t. lasting to the end 5331

Great t. become great acts 11223

happiest person thinks most interesting t. 7026

haunting t. proceed 5476

having neither to weigh t. nor words 4260

He that hides foul t. 1683

hide for a time from disturbing t. 7708

How, if t. to be fittest, continue the same 981

I know your t. 4764

Idle hours breed wandering t. 6760

idolatry t. about God unworthy of him 6075

If bring into one day's t. evil of many 12064

If we would think God's t. 11269

Impure t. will not stand against pure words 5028

In lonely solitude God delivers his best t. 10544

joy when we identify our own t. 11253

Knowledge in heads replete with t. of men 6690

man of earth, but t. with stars 7381

man's t. belong to world of intellect 10692

most important t. contradict emotions 11236

most profound t. born from womb of silence 10269

mountains are God's t. upheaved 8048

My t, my words, my crimes forgive 9048

no better and no worse than I 4255

No contemplation will humble more than t. of God 4745

no t. enter my mind that are not your t. 8748

not responsible for evil t. 11110

Occupy mind with good t. 7764

oceans God's t. imbedded 8048

Of all the t. of God 2345

of God, crystallized in words 835

one's inmost t. in another 11256

One's t. are free 4112

Our t. are heard in heaven 11155

Prayer does not bring bring God down to my t. 8909

Prayer is a ladder on which t. mount to God 8913

precious thing God finds in us 10666

Profanity fixes attention on words rather than t. 9305

Quotations tell of inward t. 9385

quotations when engraved upon memory give good t. 9383

rivers God's t. in motion 8048

see him walk, know his t. 8494

Sensitivity, tuning in to t. 8325

shelf of silence all your t. 3778

shut out all t. save that of God 7708

silence of t, words 1767

Simple words express great t. 11989

Simplicity has no deceitful t. 11696

sin goes to secret t. 10300

soul tinged with color of its t. 11247

sweep the heavens 7381

Sweet are t. that savour of content 1812

that come worth more than t. we seek 11250

to read God's mind, to think his t. 7766

to submit t, actions to the law 7434

to whom I can speak my t. 4255

too deep to be expressed 3059

transmit God's t. to others 1340

universe one of God's t. 11251

value is extent inspired by God 7366

very few can think good t. 11272

waiting to be discovered 2020

wander through eternity 7381

We live in t, not breaths 1056

which alone can be sacred or divine 4255

which have bloom on them 4255

which represent me truly 4255

Who can mistake great t. 11281

world is brimming with happy t. 2020

writing my t. in prose, verse 11132

you try persistently to hide 4764

THOUSAND

causes vie for support 7447

Conscience is a t. witnesses 1667

creation of t. forests in one acorn 8664

Earth with t. voices praises God 2973

forests in one acorn 1969

ghostly fears 5476

hacking at branches of evil 3405

heart willing will find t. ways 7871

journey of a t. miles begins with single step 6871

joy t. times better than pleasure 1293

joys he would pour into you at once 6525

kind act will teach more than a t. sermons 6661

languages, smile speaks them all 10499

legions of angels would leap to do his will 12099

Life lost in t, small, uncaring ways 6972

Lights of a t. stars do not make one moon 6198

Measure a t. times, cut once 2783

mistaken a t. times 956

O for a t. tongues to sing 8732

Oh what a t. pities 11113

One cool judgment worth t. hasty councils 6587

one day in Spirit worth more than t. in flesh 5787

One example worth t. arguments 3450

one kind of love, a t. imitations 7317

Passions useful in a t. ways 10234

paths lead to hell 5664

Prayer mother of a t. blessings 8987

reputation of t. years determined by conduct of one hour 9625

t. worlds which roll around us brightly 4592

than learn from man in t. years 4964

The night has a t. eyes 7306

Though Christ a t. times in Bethlehem be born 878

to be honest is to be one picked out of a t. 5867

voices clamor for attention 7447

ways to die 2393

ways to wealth 11863

who has t. friends has not a friend to spare 9459

who talk jargon about Christ 3306

words will not leave so deep an impression 101

worth a t. thanks when things agreeable 11157

THOUSANDFOLD

will multiply t. capacity to enjoy blessings 5254

THOUSANDS

even if lasted for t. and t. of years 5652

music understood by t. of men 7905

prayed hundred, if not t. of times 5610

will show you a way to feed t. 10205

Words make t. perhaps millions, think 12002

would be reduced to starvation 11887

THREAD
as love with single t. 7279
Consistency, t. worth weaving
  1749
leave t. to God 3117
moor the vessel with a t. of silk
  9233
pain t. in pattern of God's weaving
  10915

THREADS
dark t. are as needful 10606
hundreds of tiny t. sew people
  together 7608
silent t. of gold when woven
  together 6997

THREAT
Injustice anywhere is a t. to justice
  everywhere 6266
to stability of world is hunger
  8692

THREATEN
eye can t. like loaded gun 3561

THREATENED
Rigidity t. by risk, failure 6818
things t. to extinguish Bible 730

THREATENING
skies seem grey, t. 9059

THREATENINGS
God's darkest t. 11432

THREATENS
injures one, t. a hundred 10450
man t. while quakes for fear 3981

THREATS
who does not fear death, no fear
  of t. 2294

THREE
days late at bus station 4266
events in man's life 7050
faith must include t. mysteries
  11203
firm friends 4209
Fish, visitors smell in t. days 5956
God draws us in t. ways 7949
God has ordained t. institutions
  for society 10506
hardest tasks in world 7838
history of pride in t. chapters
  9218
If I only had t. years to serve the
  Lord 6687
In Bible t. meanings of grace 5227
In face of evil t. kinds of souls
  5029
In new birth God does t.
  impossible things 9800
kinds of giving 10736
kinds of trouble 11457
mankind divided into t. classes
  10504
marks of one who is crucified
  9846
most intractable beasts 10774
Of thee t. things I pray 9043
only two or t. human stories 5984

pray t. hours before getting
  married 7650
qualities vital to success 10820
secret among t. is everybody's
  secret 5115
silent things 10275
simple record of t. short years
  6483
Slander slays t. persons 10466
Some people bear t. kinds of
  trouble 11443
spend t. years teaching child to
  walk 8336
Success depends upon t. I's 10805
things can do about death 2407
things for which thanks are due
  11165
things I thank God for every day
  11144
things necessary for salvation
  9824
things needed to be happy in work
  12011
things only God knows 6705
things sap man's strength 10406
years old, have done more than
  half 8306
Yet sublimely T. 11429

THREEFOLD
Time a t. present 8387

THREE-FOURTHS
forfeit t. of ourselves to be like
  other people 6218

THRESHOLD
ere foot of Love will cross t. 4775
grave t. of eternity 2377
Or the stepping o'er the t. 2364
without God, not over the t. 5470

THRICE
accursed is indifference 6161
heard the cock crow t. with an
  aching heart 9569

THRIFTY
save money 7826

THRILL
at God's willnessness 4135
The Bible does not t. 697

THRILLED
while their hearts can be t. 4223
you will be t. by new
  understanding of my truth 7123

THRILLING
hours even in a poorhouse 7001

THRILLS
ages of man: t. 7037
sex, t. come at the beginning
  10224

THRIVE
Cheerfulness atmosphere in which
  things t. 1091

THRIVES
no church t. unless struggles 1411

THRIVING
as only dandelions can 239

THROAT
apple is eaten, core sticks in t.
  10385
God allows man to cut t. of his
  fellowmen 4673
leapt from my t. like sobbing
  10021

THROATS
Now burst, all our bell t. 8731
We cough to clear our t. 5627

THROB
genuine Christianity has always
  vital t. of praise 6251

THROBBING
becomes t. with interest 6086

THROBS
quiet my heart with t. of another
  heart 6258

THRONE
an angel to occupy a t. 3232
And wheels his t. upon the rolling
  worlds 4482
And wheels his t. upon the
  whirling worlds 1963
At whose t. would God kneel
  4955
Christ had no t. 6433
Christ left Father's t. 495
Christian on t. until puts himself
  on cross 2821
from the heavenly t. 1375
God's either in full control or off t.
  4939
Help me to tear it from thy t.
  6074
legal rights before the t. 8815
no thorns, no t. 199
on loftiest t. still sitting on own
  rump 9248
Prostrate before thy t. to lie 12113
refuses the cross, remains on t.
  2821

THRONES
God knows all t. and dominions
  4881
Like t. of the cherubim 7927
Sorrow reigns on t. of universe
  10613

THRONG
Not in shouts, plaudits of t. 1031

THROUGH
And he will bring us t. 5448
greatness not in them but t. them
  5291
There is no other way but t. 5407
when t. changing, you're t. 971

THROW
can t. love away, have more than
  ever 7252
don't t. away ticket and jump off
  5461
God does not t. food into nest
  3091
God has no stones to t. 4453

He who gives what he would t.
  away 4365
You t. sand against the wind 596

THROWAWAY
moving toward world of t.
  products, friends, marriages
  10524

THROWING
man always t. dust in someone's
  eyes 7445

THROWN
a kind word never t. away 6672
Gossip like mud t. against clean
  wall 5129

THROWS
away all he has 11300
Illusion dust devil t. in eyes of
  foolish 2655
What God t. my way comes 5416

THRUST
God cannot simply t. human
  beings aside 5983

THRUSTS
God t. us out of the crowd 10564

THUMB
You need a few splinters in your t.
  240

THUMPS
heart t. about things intellect
  scorns 5628

THUNDER
behind the t, still, small voice
  1515
cannot hear for t. of what you are
  560
Does not t. praise God as it rolls
  7997
hear every-approaching t. which
  will destroy us 8445
hear God in rolling of t. 8034
highest trees have most reason to
  dread t. 9241
must wait for God in the t. 5460
quiet conscience sleeps in t. 1659
rolls like drums in march of God
  of armies 7997
Take not thy t. from us 9224

THUNDERBOLT
brightest t. elicited from darkest
  storm 220

THUNDERCLOUDS
Why does God bring t. 229

THUNDEROUSNESS
God, voice deafening in its t. 4465

THUNDERS
let your t. roll like drums 4712
Loud o'er my head, though awful
  t. roll 4827
What you are t. so loud 1061

THUNDERSTORM
never a t. to announce beginning
  of new year 11329
Quiet minds like clock in t. 8466

THWART
Misunderstanding cannot t.
  purposes of God 2740

THWARTS
useless aim which t. happiness
  4411

THY KINGDOM COME
prayer, T. asking God to conduct
  a major operation 7155

THYSELF
Count not t. better than others
  9195
Know t. that thou mayest know
  God 10010
more thine own self out of t. dost
  throw 9951

TICKET
don't throw away t. and jump off
  5461

TICKIN'
Like the t. of a clock 9880

TICKLE
of pleasure with virtue 577

TIDE
is God's perpetual flow of grace
  7553
let God lift life by a great t. 9564
place and time t. will turn 8568
  2614
the t. will turn 236

TIDINESS
the upholsterer of a happy home
  5848

TIDINGS
Glad t. send afar 6141

TIDY
keep a t. soul 10652

TIE
a knot and hang on 2615
Friendship a holy t. 4240

TIED
Goodness not t. to greatness 5276
greatness is t. to goodness 5276

TIES
God's decree t. knot of adoption
  4616
hope t. itself yonder, yonder 5919
Perseverance rope that t. soul to
  heaven 8554

TIGER
Do not blame God for t. 11140
thank God for not having given t.
  wings 11140
Who rides t. cannot dismount
  11121

TIGHT
place and everything goes against
  you 236
When into a t. place 8568

TIGHTROPE
as we walk t. of life 6715

on t. while pushing wheelbarrow
  3669

TILLING
as much dignity in t. field as
  writing poem 3240

TIME
a physician that heals every grief
  11336
a precious gift of God 11337
A t. like this demands 6299
a threefold present 8387
a tiny moment at a t. 11339
All find t. to do what we want to
  do 11348
always finds t. to attend his
  funeral 5589
always packing up and moving
  11334
and eternity to experience God's
  thought 11229
and hour runs through darkest day
  10585
and truth are friends 11551
as he passes has dove's wing
  11345
As if you could kill t. without
  injuring eternity 11290
as much t. praying as grumbling
  1561
as retire to rest, give soul and God
  t. together 10486
attention so consecrated no t. to
  wonder how we look 6056
be content with one pulsation at a
  t. 4885
belief youth happiest t. of life a
  fallacy 7026
best t. to relax is when you don't
  have t. to relax 9534
best to be with those in t. 4252
Beware of saying, "haven't t. to
  pray" 9966
breathe a breath at a t. 4885
brief fleeting instant of t. allotted
  7063
By whose direction this t. been
  allotted 4905
Caesar more talked about in his t.
  than Jesus 6362
can be young and old at same t.
  11323
can fool all people some of the t.
  2480
can fool some people all the t.
  2480
can look back in t. until past
  vanishes 11350
can never be lilies unless spend t.
  as bulbs 5369
can take t. going around bases
  3467
can't be enthusiastic, unhappy at
  same t. 3189
cannot find t. for recreation, find
  t. for illness 6835
cannot fool all people all of the t.
  2480

cannot kill t. without injury to eternity 6784

Cares grow with t. 12059

carries us with it 11373

cheerful man will do more in same t. 1099

Choices of t. binding in eternity 1150

Christian sets eternity against t. 1259

Christians not to mark t. 1327

Christmas holds all t. together 1362

clock passes t. by keeping busy 2786

clocks in town wrong t. 2803

comes a t. when love can only weep 4781

coming to give life back 2307

coming when bodies image of God 839

concept of t. makes us speak of Day of Judgment 6589

converts energies into experience 11323

converts knowledge into wisdom 11323

count t. by heartthrobs 1056

cross, where eternity merges with t. 2148

crumbles things 11324

day is t. no one wealthy enough to waste 2191

death rids us of t. 2251

Death, Comforter of him whom t. cannot console 2260

death, t. to rest 2284

deceives us 11354

deposit in bank of God 11340

discovers the truth 11325

do not find t. for exercise will find t. for illness 9535

do not squander t. 6886

do not take t. to wonder if 5590

Do not walk through t. without 11292

does not know what to do with t, except kill it 11307

does nothing to fact or guilt of sin 10419

doing will of God leaves no t. for disputing his plans 4970

don't have t. to achieve understanding 7648

Don't loaf away t. 6755

dwells in God 4600

Earth breaks up, t. drops away 5636

engrave something no t. can efface 6796

Eternity is the ocean, t. the wave 3267

eternity was closeted in t. 6357

ever remember t. regretted having said kind word 6636

every minute of t. valuable 11289

Every scrap of wise man's t. worth saving 11913

fact remains God with us all the t. 4864

fearless thought in advance of their t. 11252

Footprints on the sands of t. 5288 3441

For each of us the t. is coming 3719

for first t. life made sense 7011

For God t. does not pass, it remains 3274

For tho' from out our bourne of T. 2368

Friendship independent of t. 4233

Give t. to reading of Bible 697

glory in rising every t. you fail 3620

God alone knows meaning of mystery called t. 4694

God at beginning, end of t. simultaneously 11314

God cannot be for, against same thing at same t. 4972

God gave us life, liberty at same t. 4146

God has given man a short t. upon earth 6894

God is always on t. 4456

God is not subject to t. 11298

God kind enough to accept little t. I give back 11296

God knows all t. 4881

God made t, man made haste 5576

God never imposes duty without giving t. to do it 9659

God never is before his t. 4477

God only gives it to us moment by moment 11337

God referring to his t. not yours 11297

God sends t. of forced leisure 7056

God takes deliberate t. with us 2846

God will beat the t. for us 7056 9684

God will exalt you in due t. 11297

goes by 11326

goes, you say 11327

Gratitude born in hearts that take t. to count mercies 5244

greatest Christians of all t. 5733

greatest friend of truth is t. 11535

greed of gain no t. or limit 5309

grows meaner, more hostile 3268

guilt washed out not by t. but by repentance 10419

Had I lived in the t. of Jesus 6464

harvest t. is hid with God 10204

has hard t. finding enemies 4216

has no divisions to mark passage 11329

has no flight 11330

has no shore 11373

has not abated church 1419

has way of insulting beautiful things 11328

has wrinkled my brow 11328

have no t. for Christ whose work it is 10117

have no t. to sport away the hours 11287

have no t. to stand and stare 6829

have not t. to think about God 4886

Have some t. for yourself and God 9265

haven't the t. to take t. 128

He who kills t. kills opportunities 6757

healing power of t. 4643

heals all things 11331

heals what reason cannot 11332

Heaven neither a place nor a t. 7947

highest part of soul stands above t. 11316

hinder t. with God by remembering other things to do 11349

holy t. is quiet 8980

honor him with mirth 11377

hundredth t. I am right 2775

I am ready at any t. 2301

I have lived, sir, a long t. 4942

ideal method of t. management 11466

If no one asks, I know 11351

If swept off feet, t. to get on knees 8836

if t. more important than soul 7327

if touches notes rightly and in t. 7885

if want to explain, I do not know 11351

illusion that t. cancels sin 10419

In eternity neither t. nor space 11316

In his good t. 5408

In infinite t, matter, space 6927

in its t. and place recreation as proper as prayer 6837

In politics week a very long t. 5180

in small amount of t. 8793

In t. must fade and beauty lose 8172

In t. we must release grip 972

in which God quietly tells us who we are 6830

in which to be 6830

inaudible, noiseless foot of t. 11317

is 11333

is a circus 11334

is a dressmaker specializing in alteration 11335

is all God's 10737

is eternity 11333

is noisy 10576

is nothing to God 11338

It is but for a t. 2945

Jesus speaks to living experience of all t. 6448

Jesus, peace for t. and eternity 6420

Truth has no special t. of its own 11558

Truth is child of t. 10448

tugs on oars hasn't t. to rock boat 10187

Unsoil'd and swift 11345

unstealable 11356

until t. comes to enjoy crown 5912

upon this short t. eternity depends 6894

voyage through t. to eternity 3689

Wait for wisest of counselors, t. 11347

waiting to come up flower in Gardener's t. 5672

was a t. when I had all the answers 9366

What may be done at anytime will be done at no t. 9304

What t. is it 6671

what use is correct t. 2803

What we do with leisure t. 10016

What we love to do we find t. to do 9277

When is the t. for love to be born 6155

when we must choose course to follow 2491

Whenever attempt to frame idea of t. 11352

where t, eternity intersect 2150

Whereto the world beats t. 2268

While t. lasts will always be a future 5052
     4335

will come when every change shall cease 3288

will come when I will make you forget these painful moments 7123

will fade your cheeks 11328

will reveal calyxes of gold 5403

willing to take one world at a t. 6092

Winged t. glides on 11354

With t. and patience mulberry leaf becomes satin 8561

with the Master will elevate thinking 8865

world guided by clocks that show wrong t. 2803

Worship is t. flowing into eternity 12132

worst t. is always the present 11387

would not give task without t. to do it 4425

writes no wrinkles on brow of eternity 3266

yield room for some little t. to God 7708

you spend with mouth open 1892

TIME-CONSUMING

many t. activities useless 115

TIMELESS

God is t. eternity 4601

Psalms, t. and universal 797

TIMELESSNESS

Gold suggest t. of heaven 5631

TIMELY

That shall lack a t. end 1510

TIME'S

broken out of t. hard shell to breathe 4976

glory is to calm contending kings 11344

truth, limping along on t. arm 6865

TIMES

Accusing the t. is excusing ourselves 1462

All truth not to be told at all t. 11496

As sages in all t. assert 11857

At all the t. you can 10126

better to ask way ten t. 5424

cannot be man I should be without t. of quietness 7711

Christ belonged to his t. 6359

Christ, Completer of unfinished t. 6428

commentary of the t. 5863

conservatism of Jesus' t. against him 6452

demand action 3339

difficult t, hold steady 969

essential that we slow down at t. 7714

experiencing easy t, brace yourself 969

Fall seven t, stand up eight 3592

God has preoccupied human spirits at all t. 7547

happened at the lowest t. in his life 5437

Hope for fairer t. in future 10586

In t. like these, recall there have always been t. like these 9287

In t. of dryness must be patient 2883

Measure a thousand t, cut once 2783

missed many t. before 3593

mistaken a thousand t. 956

My t. are in thy hand 7503

Our t. are in his hand 8132

prayer restores minds at all t. 8857

propelled by winds of our t. 1634

prophet knows his t. 9332

Read not the t. 1476

reflecting mood, emotions of t. 3019

Silence in t. of suffering best 10886

smell of sunset 10508

take unhappy t. bit by bit, hour by hour 5354

than great men of ancient and modern t. 6449

These are trying t. 8582

To be articulate at certain t. 11996

Tough t. never last 222

true, appropriate at all t. 957

when God asks nothing except silence, patience, tears 10635

when Lord holding me closest 10853

when love to father, mother must be hatred 7280

when t. are troubled, difficult 8403

Wise men say nothing in dangerous t. 11979

TIMETABLE

God's providence upsets your t. 11370

TIME-WORN

eternity, pressing upon t. lives 1757

TIMIDITY

mental t. one of seven deadly virtues 11699

TIMOROUS

expectation of man remarkably t. 3507

TIN

Life is rather like a t. of sardines 6976

TINGLES

Hollywood has not recognized what t. spine 4551

TINIEST

If t. grudge in mind against anyone 9633

TINSEL

wear t. crown with pride of Caesar 2821

TINTS

tomorrow with prophetic ray 618

TINY

fill t. span of life with meaning 7080

fly can choke a big man 8701

harpoon can rob of life 11071

That as I love the t, piteous thing 7178

TIP

from nature 1875

TIPTOE

Christian on his knees sees more than philosopher on t. 8975

TIRE

never t. of pleasures we give 8613

of pleasures we take 8613

prayer, steering wheel or spare t. 8848

TIRED

death, you are t, lie down, sleep 2284

Give me your t, your poor 7985

if I am too t. to call for God to help me 7478

Laziness, resting before you get t. 6769

lie down like a t. child 2882

Life one long process of getting t.
  6974
Lord, to the t. and ill give
  quietness 9045
man grows t. standing still 6751
nature's sweet restorer, balmy sleep
  10491
of world's pleasures 10578
old t. at beginning of action 313
Though wearied love is not t.
  7283
To cheer the soul when t. with
  human strife 7917
young feel t. at end of action 313

TIRES
coquette with echo, soon t. 1851
Love one ingredient of which
  world never t. 7251
There is an Arm that never t. 4569

TISSUE
of the Life to be 2622

TISSUE-PAPER
Many fears are t. thin 3982

TISSUES
of life to be 3289

TITHE
will not t. mint, cummin 1908

TITTLE-TATTLE
Slander abominable t. 10470

TOBACCO
Gossip smoke that comes from
  dirty t. pipes 5132

TODAY
A shed that's thatched 6149
admit wrong, wiser t. than
  yesterday 3249
Although t. he prunes my twigs
  with pain 8254
Anxiety empties t. of strength 409
anyone remember you spoke to
  him t. 3136
brought to life with Christ 2121
call it the weekend 10952
can only make most of t. 3502
cares of t. seldom cares of
  tomorrow 12075
Consistency as ignorant t. as year
  ago 1747
custom of t. awkwardness of
  tomorrow 10516
do not be cheated out of t. 5507
Do t. what you want to postpone
  till tomorrow 9295
Enough for faith or creed t. 4118
everlasting Father who cares for
  you t. 415
fanaticism t, fashionable creed
  tomorrow 3911
for you t, against you tomorrow
  9521
friend accepts you t. just the way
  you are 4172
get strength t. to meet tomorrow
  4318
give to God 1539
glorified with Christ 2121

God, what are you up to, t. 9061
happiness not tomorrow but t.
  11374
harder to see t. when looking at
  tomorrow 11371
have and have-not of t. 1734
Heaven is won t. 2986
Hell t. is vanquished 2986
If God dealt with people t. 4717
if we all did as well t. 3511
in the wrong, wiser t. than
  yesterday 1593
is cash 11390
is not yesterday 981
is the God of t. 10124
key that locks out yesterday's
  nightmares 11382
key that unlocks tomorrow's
  dreams 11382
Live for t. 11304
Live full t. 11375
love you more t. than yesterday
  5882
merciful God to lift curtain on t.
  4318
must see God t. 11391
Never put off till tomorrow what
  can do t. 11372
not ready t. will not be ready
  tomorrow 9296
nothing is going to happen t. 4622
one day nearer home 5676
One t. worth two tomorrows
  11376
only sure of t. 5507
people need exercise after work
  3114
people would make fun of Christ
  6405
people would not crucify Christ
  6405
pleasure in one place t. 8612
president of t. postage stamp
  tomorrow 979
ready to spend in living 11390
rise with Christ 2121
see t. with eyes of tomorrow
  11380
ship is equal to the load of t.
  12092
Since I have found t. 11369
special block of time 11382
Spring bursts t. 2982
the tomorrow you worried about
  yesterday 11383
Think t, speak tomorrow 11258
through difficult times t, hold
  steady 969
Today's t. 11385
Tomorrow, tomorrow, not t. 9303
tonight and forever 5375
two great forces at work in world
  t. 4917
we are on top 7062
what you can do t. 2789
When God says t, devil says
  tomorrow 2493
when tomorrow's burden added to
  t. 4319

wilderness t, Promised Land
  tomorrow 1935
will never be wiser tomorrow than
  t. 8195
worry about tomorrow, be
  unhappy t. 11402
Worry only saps t. of its strength
  12089

TODAY'S
Do t. duty 9650
today 11385

TODDLER
hardnosed opponent of law, order
  1129
Lord added electricity 1127

TOE
never stubbed t, standing still
  3599

TOES
best way to keep from stepping on
  t. 11286
have children who step on their t.
  8323

TOGETHER
bricks must be cemented t. 4020
by no extrordinary chance put t.
  second time 6173
Faith and thought belong t. 617
Four things go t. 10248
God can make pieces of puzzle fit
  t. 4308
good and ill t. 7045
have not learned to live t. 9353
keep flame aglow 1388
learn to live t. as brothers 923
Love and Self cannot stand t.
  9936
Love puts the fun in t. 7269
Love, looking t. in the same
  direction 7215
must learn to live t. as brothers
  5987
narrow mind, wide mouth go t.
  4059
Parents should work t. as two
  bookends 8322
Real friends have great time doing
  nothing t. 4265
silent threads of gold when woven
  t. 6997
Then there are friends who sail t.
  4281
When love, skill work t. 12020
With doctrine world taken apart,
  put t. 11213

TOGETHERNESS
How could I know t. without
  loneliness 1512

TOIL
Although but lowly t. it be 2792
Day after day spent in blessed t.
  11287
heaven, t. and weariness no place
  there 5644
highest reward for man's t, what
  he becomes 1045

love's object lightens its t. 6457
men t. for riches day and night 11845
not by seeking fertile regions where t. lighter 4974
Patience enough to t. until good accomplished 1809
Then agony and t. a paradise become 2604
to t. and not to seek for rest 9113
vital to success 10820
what t. can scarcely reach in an age 7223
Why all this t. for triumphs of an hour 7088

TOILED
hand hath t. in vain 47
in vain 47
to hew the rock 47

TOILING
Were t. upward in the night 8566

TOIL'S
halt of t. exhausted caravan 10960

TOILSOME
put away thy t. business 7708

TOKEN
ability to forget true t. of greatness 4068

TOLD
a lie may be t. by silence 6859
All lies are not t, some are lived 6847
All truth not to be t. at all times 11496
more I t. troubles, more troubles grew 2727
now the wants are t. 12094
rumor, all who t. it added something new 9757
Scarce any tale was sooner heard than t. 9757
story of Jesus t. more than any other in history 5729
thing so real it never can be t. 10274
Truth merely t. is quick to be forgotten 11578

TOLERABLE
Humor makes all things t. 6719
makes human life t. in world 4999

TOLERANCE
a tremendous virtue 11400
another word for indifference 11401
give to opponent 511
immediate neighbors are apathy, weakness 11400
In world called t. 11394
intolerance shown in support of t. 11393
live with t, learn to be patient 1114
prayer for t. 9095
respect for another because he is human 11399

test of t. when in majority 1938
that marriage demands 7648

TOLERANT
Be entirely t. 1137
cannot be t. of any other course 9965
fortunately God more t. 4897
Public wonderfully t. 4397
To understand all makes one t. 11398

TOLERATE
Spirit of God will not t. self-sins 5776

TOLERATED
Evil t. poisons whole system 3368

TOLERATION
learned t. from intolerant 5251

TOLLS
Never send to know for whom the bell t. 2339

TOMB
a thoroughfare 2422
appears as prison 2350
borrowed manger, t. framed his earthly life 6433
Christianity is a religion of the open t. 9688
closes in twilight to open in dawn 2422
is release for soul 2350
not a blind alley 2422
oppress us with weight of the t. 2611
rock of t. tumbled 2984
Take away love and earth is a t. 7294
thou shalt not hold him longer 2985

TOMBS
pyramids raised to be t. sinking 730

TOMBSTONE
favorite theme of asceticism 467

TOMBSTONES
of some people should read 7041

TOMMY'S
tears and Mary's fears 4003

TOMORROW
Anxiety does not empty t. of sorrow 409
at bottom of ladder 7062
Because he lives I can face t. 2978
Before t. the air may change 7895
begin t. well, serenely 8375
cares of today seldom cares of t. 12075
comes at midnight very clean 11403
comes the song 6256
custom of today, awkwardness of t. 10516
darkest day lived till t. will have passed away 2575
day on which loafers work 11404

day people lose opportunity to accept Christ 11404
day when fools act sensibly 11404
Do not look forward to t. 415
Do that kind deed you would leave 'till t. 6671
Do today what you want to postpone till t. 9295
everlasting Father will take care of you t. 415
fanaticism today, fashionable creed t. 3911
fear of t. 3971
for you today, against you t. 9521
get strength today to meet t. 4318
give love away, t. have more than ever 7252
God never gives strength for t. 2722
happiness not t. but today 11374
harder to see today when looking at t. 11371
holds no fears for me 11369
Hope for t. 11304
hopes we've learned from yesterday 11403
I keep for God 1539
I shall put forth buds again 8254
is a new day 8375
11366
is a promissory note 11390
look t. square in the eye 9999
look with hope toward t. 3502
Love puts the hope in t. 7269
may be down drain of eternity 11385
may be night 11375
must be longest day of week 9302
never changes opinions, never wiser t. 8195
never corrects mistakes, never wiser t. 8195
Never mind about t. 10120
Never put off till t. what can do today 11372
never put off until t. 2789
not ready today, will not be ready t. 9296
not yet born to t. 11365
perfect when it arrives 11403
perfectly good day coming t. 5591
plan as if expect to enter hereafter t. 6099
pray as if you were to die t. 12023
president today, postage stamp t. 979
puts itself in our hands 11403
save some work for t. 12027
see today with eyes of t. 11380
Skepticism prepares way for faith of t. 2953
t, not today 9303
take no care for t. 411
Think today, speak t. 11258
tints t. with prophetic ray 618
Today the t. you worried about yesterday 11383
what some people must know t. 3035

TOMORROW'S

When God says today, devil says t. 2493

wilderness today, Promised Land t. 1935

will be dying 8214

worry about t, be unhappy today 11402

Worry never robs t. of sorrow 12089

TOMORROW'S

Leave t. trouble to t. strength 12067

Today unlocks t. dreams 11382

when t. burden added to today 4319

without caring for t. lodging 11478

yesterday's worry and t. anxiety 12092

TOMORROWS

God has already lived our t. 11295

One today worth two t. 11376

shut out past except that which will help t. 8383

TON

Oh, trouble's a t, or trouble's an ounce 11446

TONE

and gives the t. its strength 7892

because t. of voice unsympathetic 9516

But oft for our own the bitter t. 3900

In living echoes of thy t. 8866

of Master's disposition a peculiar sadness 6390

religious t. have their temporary effect 8845

TONGUE

a wild beast 11415

ambassador of the heart 11416

Assail'd by scandal and the t. of strife 6356

Better feet slip than t. 11408

better hold t. than them 1862

breaketh bone, though itself have none 10473

bridle for t. necessary furniture 11405

but three inches long 5161

can be dangerous weapon 5118

can kill man six feet high 5161

can undo everything you do 1833

Christian more hand than t. 1317

Confine t, lest it confine you 11411

danger when throws t. into high gear 11419

deeper the sorrow, less t. has to say 10627

dog wags tail instead of t. 9499

double brings trouble 2913

examining t. philosophers find diseases of mind 11410

examining t. physicians find diseases of body 11410

First thing in morning she sharpens t. 5125

fool has answer on edge of t. 4067

Forge thy t. on anvil of truth 11503

Give me ready hand rather than ready t. 2497

holy life speaks when t. silent 5735

inches from brain, sounds miles away 1880

Kind words don't wear out t. 6646

Learn to hold thy t. 11412

Man given one t. 1858

man's t. has broken his nose 1859

more feared than sword 10474

most dangerous of weapons 11417

nor speak with double t. 1011

nor t. can tell 9567

not steel, yet cuts 1881

Nothing causes more trouble than t. 11413

O boy, hold thy t. 1866

of idle person never idle 6777

pleasure in criticism, hold your t. 2064

powerful weapon of manipulation 1882

Prayer requires more of heart than t. 8952

registers no weariness 11420

rudder of our ship 11418

rumor, on every t. it grew 9757

sharp t. grows keener with use 11406

slip of t. never get over 11407

slip of t. perhaps never recovered 10444

so long can seal envelope in mailbox 1850

stillest t, truest friend 1879

struck dumb the t. of the child 8967

take t, have it nailed to cross 7190

talks so much t. was sunburned 1868

Temper the t. 9960

test of man's character is his t. 11414

They took away what should have been my t. 1817

To speak kindly does not hurt t. 11421

Toll, every clapper t. 8731

What a spendthrift of his t. 5124

What heart did think, t. would click 1890

Where least heart, most t. 5166

wise man even when he holds his t. says more 11951

TONGUES

cannot control evil t. of others 5164

He has no t. but our t. 10122

hear countless t. chanting 1368

his words are intimate on myriad t. 6394

is a heart language 5807

Loose t. stretch truth 9488

men entangled by their t. 11409

O for a thousand t. to sing 8732

still our t. of weak complainings 9090

TONGUE-TIED

have sat t, crying out to be given utterance 5781

TONIGHT

Today, t. and forever 5375

TONUS

is mono, tempus is longus 9140

TOO

Men expect t. much, do t. little 3504

TOOK

And with the other t. a shilling out 6070

I t. one draught of life 3483

TOOL

government t. to establish Kingdom of God 5177

TOOLS

Discipline t. to solve life's problems 9967

Have thy t. ready 10142

Sin has many t. 6857

TOOTH

eye for eye, t. for t. 7331

How sharper than serpent's t. 1119

That purrs and never shows a t. 5048

TOOTHBRUSH

Tough decision, when to discard t. 2492

TOP

cannot get to t. by sitting on bottom 6783

in some revolutions those underneath get on t. 3785

laud character, but climb to t. at any cost 6068

today we are on t. 7062

way to the t. in God's kingdom 10161

TOPICS

You have but two t. 9958

TOPPLES

over he t. on other side 5968

TORCH

hold t. to light another's path 3145

love is as a burning t. 7283

man who finds truth lights t. 11536

Truth is a t. 11562

Yield t. to others as in race 2338

TORE

Before the worm t. Eden 2123

TORMENT

Envy endless self t. 3211

jealous t. to themselves 6348

no t. like inner t. of unforgiving
   spirit 9640
Talking often t. for me 10556
Uncertain ills t. most 11604

TORMENTING
devil takes delight in t. us 2661
himself with own prickles 9630

TORMENTOR
Satan is t. of wicked 3996

TORMENTS
idea of the infinite t. me 3275

TORN
And by greed and pride the sky is
   t. 6155
as if t. bond that binds humanity
   to God 8967
between desire to think positively
   or confront life 9401
Character t. down with incredible
   swiftness 996
forgiveness cancelled note t. in two
   4081
I must see him t. 2128
marriage paper to be t. up at whim
   2924
masks t. away, hollow smiles fade
   9741
thorns have t. me 1737
twilight is t. away ruthlessly 8075
When mask of self-righteousness
   t. from us 5238

TORPEDO
teaching of Christ ripping, tearing
   t. 6486

TORTURE
greatest t. for most is to think
   11230
mass movement, new freedom to t.
   10526
yoke not instrument of t. 2816

TORTURED
odds world can throw against t.
   soul 3736
That swells with silence in the t.
   soul 5348

TORTURES
of that inward hell 9567

TOSSED
by storm and flood 4642
habit cannot be t. out window
   5495
lofty pine that by the storm is
   oftener t. 9216

TOTAL
Christ, God's everything for man's
   t. need 6427
Extreme independence as
   destructive as t. dependence
   7614
makes for t. life lived at full
   potential 6999

TOTALITY
Good is a principle of t. 5023
Think of the t. of all being 7063

TOTALLY
single event can awaken within
   stranger t. unknown 6873

TOTTER
grope and t. and make countless
   mistakes 9851

TOUCH
blind man's world bounded by
   limits of t. 11728
earthly life in t. with a new
   infinite life 7101
few certainties that t. all 953
fingers of God t. your life 4202
gentle t, stronger than force, fury
   4296
human soul, life too complex to t.
   10653
in spite of danger of loving t. 6199
in t. with people through
   affections 7428
leave marks on lives we t. 1289
Leave scandal alone, never t. it
   5154
limiting way God can t. us 10720
pain loving t. of God's hand 4804
present fled ere we could t. it
   11389
right key at right time 7897
They t. the shining hills of day
   11299
troubles large enough to t. God's
   love 4789
tune and t. the chords 7527
when you t. a friend 4202
will come one day a t. from God
   7060
with divine power the buried
   acorn 6095
yearning to t. and taste
   unapproachable 4744

TOUCH-POINT
cross our personal t. with the Lord
   10930

TOUCHABLE
God is t. 4509

TOUCHED
Christ t. the untouchable 6433
day coming tomorrow that hasn't
   been t. 5591
day t. by God a sacrament 2196
God's finger t. him, he slept 2289
How play with universe and fail
   to be t. with awe 9866
When subjects which must not be
   t. 5480
you t. me, I burned to know your
   peace 7473

TOUCHEDST
Thou t. me, I burned for thy peace
   4805

TOUCHES
Every good deed t. chord that
   vibrates in heaven 6670
God with sorrow or joy 7057
if t. notes right and in time 7885
our lives t. some chord 105

river t. places of which source
   knows nothing 6232
Wherever our life t. yours, help or
   hinder 9522
wherever your life t. ours, make
   us stronger or weaker 9522

TOUCHING
God in his distressing disguise
   6569
inward stirring and t. of God
   5764

TOUCHSTONE
gold is the t. to try men 11836
Humility is t. of saintliness 6013
Men have t. to try gold 11836

TOUCHSTONES
Dreams t. of our characters 2966

TOUGH
Friendship usually treated as t.
   thing 4237
God offers t. love 7686
Life's a t. proposition 6992
times never last, people do 221
world t. in a thousand ways 1211
Young people will respond if
   challenge t. enough 12180

TOUGHER
Solitude makes us t. toward
   ourselves 10560

TOUGHEST
Self one of the t. plants 9943

TOUGHNESS
love demands t. in crisis 2045

TOW
Man is fire, woman t. 10226

TOWARD
Dark things reach out t. brightness
   5906
God runs t. him twain 7573
going forward t. something great
   4248
look with hope t. tomorrow 3502
To believe in heaven is to run t. life
   5674
When man repents is turned t.
   God 9583
Whosoever walks t. God one cubit
   7573

TOWER
plan a t. that shall pierce clouds
   6788

TOWERING
o'er the wrecks of time 2133
What a t. mound of sin 3492

TOWERS
fall with heavier crash who higher
   soar 9216
Great men stand like solitary t.
   5280

TOY
world which moves when pull
   strings 4132

TRACE
trust God when you can't t. him
3663

TRACEABLE
high crime rate t. to disintegration
of home 5858

TRACK
danger signals life is on wrong t.
5466
prayers t. down which God's
power can come 8886

TRACKLESS
Without God life a shoreless, t.
waste 7098

TRADE
And every man a scribe by t. 4748
cannot find joy in t. and commerce
10527
my fortune for one happy
marriage 7619
no mind to t. with devil 11065

TRADEMARK
Rigidity t. of legalism 6817

TRADESMEN
if time more important than a
soul, we are but t. 7327

TRADITIONS
Christian work crippled by t. of
the past 10124
identify family as unique, different
3876
many have forgotten value of t.
3876

TRADUCE
truth does not vary because men t.
it 11540

TRAFFIC
driver speeds through t. 1738
grope way through endless t. jams
5859
moves faster in next lane 2873
never any t. congestion on
straight, narrow path 9819

TRAGEDIES
allow hearts to shrink until room
for little beside ourselves 5625
Day of Judgment to tell t. of
weakness, failure 1055
getting what one wants 2570
life with all its t, ambiguities 3685
not getting what one wants 2570
one of world's greatest t. 5625
root of innumerable t. 9446

TRAGEDY
existence entwined with t. 3479
genius sees different angle, there is
his t. 4389
honest joy must be congruous
with t. 6571
in t. face to face with things never
gave heed to 10667
is failure to use talent 10997
Life a t. for those who feel 6954

lives with t. not necessarily more
sinful 2857
men think heroes of t. great 10877
of life is we wait so long to begin it
7042
of trying to live maximum life on
minimum faith 3770
of war 11763
to discover ladder of success
against wrong wall 10777
To one who feels, life is t. 607
tragedy not compatible with belief
591

TRAGIC
God doesn't exempt from t.
heartaches 11667
guilt more t. than problem 2921
loving in the deepest, most t. sense
7186
Man's failure to conquer human
nature t. 7414
most t. sentence in literature 7601
mother-child relationship
paradoxical, t. 7858
waste of truth 3758
Why is life so t. 7090

TRAGICALLY
ball-and-chain mentality keeps us
from giving ourselves 6825

TRAIL
Go where no path, leave t. 6787

TRAILING
clouds of glory 809

TRAIN
cannot t. ourselves to be Christians
4984
hard to t. for service of Christ 466
opportunities to t. ourselves to
wait on the Lord 8421
Some churches t. their ushers to
smile 6062
When t. goes through tunnel 5461

TRAINED
at home affections are t. 5849
not educated, merely t. 3031
shaking flipper of t. seal 6062

TRAINING
home is God's built-in t. facility
5854
Life is t. for destinies of eternity
6979
Life is the t. ground 6978
temperance is love in t. 7202
thee for part angels cannot sing
10600
What greater work than t. mind
3037
world as place of t. not so bad
5535

TRAINS
privation t. and strengthens the
mind 242

TRAITOR
You've hit no t. on the hip 3174

TRAITORS
more likely we are all t. 912
to Christ 3846

TRAITS
Perseverance most overrated of t.
8553

TRAMMELS
liberation from t. imposed by
external influences 4160

TRAMPLE
inferior of any man whose rights I
t. under foot 11283
not on any, may be work of grace
there 10475

TRAMPLED
Man t. by same forces he has
created 5975

TRAMPLES
Sweeps the wide earth, t. o'er
mankind 6269

TRANQUIL
God abides in t. eternity 8437
God is a t. Being 8437
No sleep t. unless mind at rest
8449
So must thy spirit become a t. pool
8437
With t. heart to do my simple part
9072

TRANQUILITY ·
discover treasure of t. 10553
Dispose our soul for t. 1758
in kitchen as great t. as upon knees
8471
is his who cares for neither praise
nor blame 1791
peace and t. will return again
8445
prayer for t. 9111
What wicked do should not
disturb good man's t. 11894

TRANQUILIZER
Laughter a t. with no side effects
6730

TRANQUILLY
Rest t. in abiding conviction 4747

TRANSCEND
Part of his body, I t. this flesh
4125

TRANSCENDENT
works of God, t. greatness inspire
awe 9734
Worship is t. wonder 12138

TRANSCENDENTAL
anticipate future with t. senses
4329
truth being vast and deep is t.
11550

TRANSCENDING
Prayer t. self 8917

TRANSCENDS
caring that t. human inclinations
1541

Faith knowledge that t. intellect 3673
God t. reason 9413
heart t. all visible things 4749

TRANSFERRED
when confidence t. to God 5645

TRANSFERS
love from things temporal to things eternal 9278

TRANSFIGURATION
Ascension, completion of T. 462
Christianity the t. of the old 6424
Great Divide in life of Lord 6488

TRANSFIGURING
power of prayer 8995

TRANSFORM
And t. every stumbling block 1927
ourselves into beasts 332
Praise will t. humblest dwelling to a hallowed heaven 5846
Prayer avenue God uses to t. us 9005

TRANSFORMATION
Bible given for our t. 689
Only through inner t. gain strength to fight 6619
selfishness, preventing t. into divine love 10067
Solitude furnace of t. 10558

TRANSFORMED
and them all the Lord t. to devils 2639
become disciples, church would be t. 2819
Bible t. ruthless killers into gentle saints 726
Christ t. suffering 10880
Christianity t. old spirit of government 5170
energy does not perish but is t. 11658
God t. evil 4931
If t, exhibit divine characteristics 1044
into image of Christ by circumstances is to have chosen 8264
Real joy is sorrow accepted, t. 6557
Suddenly I feel myself t. 7964

TRANSFORMING
no t. of darkness into light without emotion 3053

TRANSFORMS
Christ's life that t. 1536
Faith means grasped by power that t. us 3707

TRANSFUSED
bled, and died, I have been t. 2979

TRANSFUSION
blood t. for courageous living 5804

TRANSGRESSIONS
as we through frailty multiply t. 5212

TRANSIENT
Bible proves how t. is noblest monument 730
In eternity, mountains as t. as clouds 3279
no t. beauty scorn 11375
so arbitrary are t. laws 10516
storm in its very nature is t. 8444

TRANSITION
no death, what seems so is t. 2392

TRANSLATED
Bible cannot really be t. 669
sermon merely t. Christ's life into language 6482
unless doctrine t. into life 11185

TRANSLATIONS
contradictions in Bible caused by t. 679

TRANSLATORS
God employs several t. 2216

TRANSMITTERS
called to be God's t. 1340

TRANSPARENCY
God desires but t. 7450
Hearts opened in pure t. 5667
Prayer for t. 6296

TRANSPARENT
we are not t. 4255

TRANSPLANT
God does not need to t. us 1468

TRANSPORT
My t. to control 4795

TRANSPORTED
with the view, I'm lost 4819

TRAP
cannot lay t. for pleasure 8612
deadliest t. of devil is religious 2701

TRAPPED
church t. by material concerns 1460
God seeks worship of those t. in moral ruin 12098

TRASH
worries about all the t. in the world 7670

TRAVAIL
for the religious, pain a t. to be borne 8255

TRAVAIL-CRIES
I hear with groan and t. 4642

TRAVEL
And so we t. on 5415
Let it t. down the years 6640
lightly whom God's grace carries 5235
road to hell easy to t. 5701
saps strength 10406

shall not t. an uncharted course 5945
wide and far to scout, see, search 4926

TRAVELER
Rumor a great t. 5152

TRAVELERS
death, no t. returns 2388
greatest path is open to least of t. 7235

TRAVELING
Happiness a manner of t. 5523
hope is of good use while t. through life 5924

TRAVELLED
Only he who has t. road knows where holes are deep 3541

TRAVELS
a lie t. around world 6846
fool wanders, wise t. 4058
genius never t. on well-worn paths 4393
Laziness t. so slowly poverty soon overtakes him 6768
man t. world in search of what he needs 5815
No man safely t. 7422

TREACHEROUS
becoming in the end a t. man 7836

TREACHERY
lurks in honeyed words 4052

TREAD
as I t. on another year 8079
Give me a light that I may t. 5417
God wills us to t. hidden paths 5397
Should not the servant t. it still 10133
thou didst descend with noiseless t. 6150
where angels fear to t. 4060
why fear to t. pathway to future home 6875

TREASON
Friendship is t. 4877

TREASONS
Give me the little creeping t. 4530

TREASURE
Affliction can be a t. 10834
Christ a T. to enrich 6370
Christ t. without stealth 6391
Contentment an inexhaustible t. 1781
discover t. of tranquility 10553
friend's affection greatest t. 4181
God's t. like infinite ocean 4471
guileless mind great t, worth any price 5865
if course wrong, avoid though lose earthly t. 6291
Is not hearing a t. 6253
is to leave t. for a trifle 6495

TREASURES

Love one t. that multiplies by division 7252
my t. is in heaven 1310
Normal day, be aware of t. you are 2197
only lasting t. is spiritual 4148
out of every disappointment t. 2800
Sorrow like precious t. 10615
When earthly t. proves but dross 4338
Where your pleasure is, there is your t. 5574
Where your t. is, there is your heart 5574

TREASURES

A few rich t. from his mighty store 6111
He t. up his bright designs 4941
I will take away thy t. 1310
in heaven accumulated by our attitude 11872
in heaven laid up only as t. on earth laid down 9565
keep in reserve t. of God's deep counsels 4322
love, boundless t. hidden within its depths 7211
prayer opens to us t. of God's mercies 8846

TREASURY

Christ will be whole t. of God 6354
human soul is God's t. 10666

TREAT

bodies as temple of Spirit 836
crowd t. great men as lunatics 4393
father should t. son as guest 3891
God will t. us without pity 2089
him as any other great man 9201
him as he ought to be 8656
If obey laws, space will t. you kindly 11650
If t. person as he is, will stay as he is 8656
If you t. friend shabbily 2317
inferiors as you would be treated 5006
information with humility 6706
men gently and they will show themselves great 6807
men the way they are, will never improve them 5971
men the way you want them to be 5971
murder when t. people as insignificant 10683
son should t. father as host 3891
temptations kindly, they will return 11091
though men t. me like doormat 10156

TREATED

Friendship usually t. as tough, everlasting 4237
God like a person 7526

God with startling familiarity 7526
I t. him, God cured him 5611
no longer have to be t. certain way 9963

TREATIES

Peace not made by t. 8457

TREATING

badly precious thing God has made 9923

TREATMENT

laws in Bible include t. of earth 3200
programs run by churches effective 134
survive all manner of bad t. 4237

TREATS

Bible t. us roughly 724
God t. sinner as if good man 6634
how he t. person of no possible use 573
shows greatness by way t. little men 5272

TREE

As twig is bent, t. inclines 8344
bad t. does not yield good apples 986
Character like t. real thing 1001
Christian should resemble fruit t. 1322
Corruption is a t. whose branches 2907
cross strikes at root of t. 2158
Do not cut down t. that gives shade 5241
Don't judge t. by bark 432
Evil spreads like oak t. 3355
Friendship is a sheltering t. 4232
great t. of being 1450
Hate is the t. 371
If fig t. grow in side of mountain cliff 3736
In autumn I feed you 8018
In spring I delight you 8018
In summer I cool you 8018
In winter I warm you 8018
is full of poetry 8042
Judge a t. from its fruit, not leaves 6581
Lord was stretched on hard, painful t. 10836
Make kindling out of fallen t. 3606
man without prayer like t. without roots 8752
no fear wind will uproot t. 6307
nothing can bring life to rootless t. 1380
of deepest root is found 8174
only God can make a t. 2017
Only when axe put to the t. 10346
Stars golden fruits upon a t. out of reach 11637
Temptations like winds that firmly root t. 11094
test the soundness of the t. 72

This learned I from the shadow of a t. 6242
thorns reap'd of t. planted 1737
trunk in his own eye 6590
Where tears are hung on every t. 11021
which moves some to tears 8506

TREE OF KNOWLEDGE

sinful not because eaten of T. 10416

TREE OF LIFE

sinful because not eaten of T. 10416

TREE'S

as twig is bent, t. inclined 2991

TREES

a healing in old t. 8143
Beneath a million million t. 1368
clapping their hands 8017
eloquent are quiet t. 8014
flowers, grass grow in silence 10250
found peace among the silver t. 8051
full-blossomed t. filled air with joy 2977
highest t. have most reason to dread thunder 9241
I hear his voice among the t. 7452
when the t. bow down their heads 8053

TREMBLE

feeble t. before opinion 8205
Shallow natures t. for a night after sin 10352

TREMBLED

ground t, rock of tomb tumbled 2984
he who has not t. in Moses 5224

TREMBLER

No t. in world's storm-troubled sphere 3765

TREMBLES

Devil t. when we pray 8985
Satan t. when he sees 8959
Trumpets! Lightnings! The earth t. 6150
unbelief t. at shaking of leaf 3703

TREMBLING

Hope like a harebell, t. from its birth 7179
man to make his way best he can in t. 3495
Why stand we here t. 1554
with t. pinions soar 5913

TREMENDOUS

furtherance of spiritual life during sleep 10487
God can do t. things through people 10134
owe grandeur to t. difficulties 2739
reservoir of resurrection life of Christ 11689

TRESPASSES

cannot say forgive us our t. if 8818

TRIAL

Adversity is t. of principle 145

character enriched with gold 223

Each morning puts man on t. 11364

For God to explain a t. 164

fox should not be on jury at goose's t. 9177

God allows t. for greater good 2883

good pilot best tried in storm 137

in circumstances of great t, much strength 7486

in t. divine strength found 2734

is God's alchemy 223

Jesus tried for who he was 6413

Leave tomorrow's t. to tomorrow's grace 12067

Many might have failed beneath t. 4236

no merit where no t. 10762

of faith precious 3751

only stops when it is useless 5352

people tried for what they have done 6413

proves one thing weak, another strong 189

Suffering sacred t. sent by eternal love 10896

will become day of prosperity 7698

TRIALS

allow to change us 970

chief pang of most t. is our resistence 2746

confirm a Christian 1280

Disappointments t. of heaven 2796

enter t. with gratitude 181

find yourself faking evidence 7836

God does not promise he will protect from t. 5385

God promises only he will be with them in t. 5385

God proportions the frequency and weight 224

Great t. preparation for great duties 2725

I lose memory of past t. 7964

in life, hurts and t. 970

love tokens from God 4804

medicines because we need them 224

nor man made perfect without t. 136

not able to change 970

prayer restores minds under all t. 8857

shaping us for higher things 228

to all who do not love God, t. a nuisance 4804

To multiplied t, his multiplied peace 5223

way we handle t. makes world pause 10938

world observing way we undergo t. 3319

TRIANGLE

of love between ourselves, God, other people 7198

Successful marriage always a t. 7653

TRIBULATION

God's fastest road to patience 225

Jesus has few desirous of t. 2828

no t. can touch confidence 1613

patience, character, hope, confidence, love 225

which no t. can wear out 9057

TRIBULATIONS

in this made like unto Christ Jesus 234

my t. what are they in comparison to sufferings of Christ 10928

on every side with t. 234

the way of the saints 234

through t. passed to kingdom of heaven 234

When I consider my t. I shame myself 10928

TRIBUNAL

setting up ourselves as higher t. 4087

TRICKS

without using blatant t. God brings suffering 10844

TRIED

And t. give you gladness 1545

Be not first by whom new are t. 958

four things must be t. in friendship 4227

Jesus t. for who he was 6413

let few be well t. 4218

people t. for what they have done 6413

souls t. and ripened 237

TRIES

not only temptation that t. the Christian 10328

rationalism t. to find God in picture of world 4495

sin also t. the Christian 10328

Time t. truth 11552

TRIFLE

dare not t. with eternal future 4726

is to leave treasure for a t. 6495

Man calls sin a t. God a tragedy 4560

Never dare to t. 8097

Never think Jesus commanded a t. 8097

'Tis not for man to t. 11287

TRIFLES

Jealousy, thou magnifier of t. 6345

with t. man reveals character 1028

TRIFLING

no feeling, however t. 7536

no thought however t. 7536

no yearning, however t. 7536

Pass by t. errors blindly 4217

regard as t. great wrong to you 4097

weak mind magnifies t. things 7754

TRIGGERS

Affliction t. greatest insights 10834

TRILEMMA

no getting out of this t. 6366

TRINITY

act in harmonious unity 11422

aligning T. with bone 6131

an element of mystery 11203

Awful T. 11429

difficult to understand 11203

faith must include mystery of t. 11203

God understands the t. 11203

Holiest T, perfect in Unity 11424

mystery my faith embraces 11428

mystery my reason cannot fathom 11428

not unintelligible 11203

of the mind is the image of God 7771

three persons in one essence 11423

three persons, one divine essence 11426

Yet sublimely Three 11429

TRIP

marriage like long t. in tiny rowboat 7595

only thing can do on a shoestring is t. 4031

TRITE

fanaticism today, t. as multiplication table week after 3911

TRIUMPH

And so be pedestaled in t. 11122

But in ourselves are t, defeat 10794

cross is the supreme t. of God 3582

every great movement t. of enthusiasm 3178

God changes death to t. 2373

God does allow bad men to t. 4957

harder the conflict, more glorious the t. 1628

human soul beaten down can t. 3621

If impossible for Christ to t. over death 9691

in ourselves t, defeat 1031

In t. wear his Christlike chain 1299

In the end good will t. 5073

Only thing necessary for t. of evil 3402

Psalms, t. of man's victory 798

to t. without vindictiveness 11775

TRIUMPHANT

Christian celebrates victory already won 11672

Christian does not fight for victory 11672

Christianity made sorrow t. 1166

collapsing world more conducive to truth than t. world 11491

enemies of Christ are t, they say 1443

Faith and hope t. say 2985

some defeats more t. than victories 2514

TRIUMPHANTLY

be answered t. by the cabbage 8580

TRIUMPHED

No great principle ever t. but through evil 5030

TRIUMPHEST

O love, thou t. even over gold 7285

TRIUMPHING

over death and chance and thee, O Time 5679

TRIUMPHS

better to win glorious t. 1922

Evil often t. 3366

failures prepare for t. 3593

most significant witness not t. but defeat 2518

no difficulties, no t. 2730

remember your t. 9270

Revenge t. over death 2363

True t. are God's t. over us 11673

Why all this toil for t. of an hour 7088

TRIVIA

Jesus not distracted with t. 4425

TRIVIAL

blind eye to t. faults 9456

Commerce of t. import 11684

couple married for t. reasons 2922

deepest emotions caused by t. 3056

displaces momentous 7990

Divorce disengagement for t. reasons 2922

indulgence in lust or anger 5021

irritations of family life 6386

never big things that disturb, but t. 9635

prefer t. company to being alone 10575

Refusing to set aside t. preferences 7793

things disturb us 1471

TRIVIALITIES

knowledge about sublime worth more than t. 6676

TRIVIALITY

Suffering clears away t. 10892

TROD

Death's a path that must be t. 2267

The soil where first they t. 4114

TRODDEN

crushed or t. to the ground 150

TROMBONE

Love thy neighbor, even when he plays t. 11396

TROUBLE

a t. to die 186

acts different on people 11431

ain't that people ignorant 6083

all they have had, have now, expect to have 11443

Anxiety, interest paid on t. 412

Better never t. T. 11430

birth was t. for our mothers 11459

borrow money, t. will come 4035

children more t. solving parent's problems 3883

Christian under t. doesn't break up 11452

cost devil little t. to catch lazy man 6766

deep spiritual t. 3335

demolish business, build character 214

Discontent source of t. 2865

Do not anticipate t. 3500

Don't borrow t. 4035

emotions in subconscious minds to t. us 3061

faith draws sting out of t. 3818

generally accepts 11458

God does not keep immune from t. 2721

God never promised to keep us from t. 215

Gold a transcient, shining t. 11817

Gold in t. powerless to cheer 11813

good human race has experienced was t. for somebody 11459

greatest in anticipation 8598

have more t. with D.L. Moody than any other man 9969

Humility is to have no t. 6010

Humility to be at peace when all around is t. 6010

I will be with him in t. 215

If you don't learn to laugh at t. 6720

In t. may find comfort 11439

in t. presence of God grow sure 1504

in world caused by people wanting to be important 9220

is people always sitting on them 7049

it t. go not out of yourself for aid 2734

Jehovah takes his ministers into t. 163

joy flows on through t. 6529

Kindness in another's t. 6657

knocked at door, hearing laugh hurried away 11461

language of heartbreak learned in crucible of t. 10902

laugh at t. 504

Leave tomorrow's t. to tomorrow's strength 12067

like hot weather 11431

little t. praying when in much t. 8870

look into future and anticipate more t. 11450

Lord lets some people get into t. 11441

lost wealth, lost t. 1776

Love thinks nothing of t. 7220

Luxury makes a man so soft easy to t. him 7363

Many Christians are in t. about the future 6912

money, others, yourself 11457

much t. praying when in little t. 8870

Never attempt more than one t. at once 11443

never t. where children resemble parents 3898

no charity, worse kind of heart t. 1077

No man ever got out of t. 11444

Nobody knows the t. I've seen 11445

Nothing causes more t. than tongue 11413

of church, you and I 1424

often lever to raise us to heaven 11460

One t. with t. 11448

only time people think of God 11441

Or a t. is what you make it 11446

pair on ground started trouble 762

Parents have t. solving children's problems 3883

people who are always anticipating t. 12079

Real friendship shown in t. 4267

Receive every t. with both thy hands 7698

rides a fast horse 11462

right with God has often meant in t. with men 9507

self turns up to t. our peace 9943

Some people bear three kinds 11443

sours milk, sweetens apples 11431

starts out like fun 11448

Temper gets people into t. 9237

Thou art safety from every t. 9052

To avoid t. breathe through nose 1884

To support us was t. for our fathers 11459

Tongue double brings t. 2913

unless first admitted was in t. 11444

Until T. troubles you 11430

wasn't apple that started t. 762

way out of t. never as simple as way in 11453

way to t. God is not to come at all 8964

What is God saying through this t. 6086

what t. you were bearing 1545

When in t, hold your chin up 11463

whole t. is we won't let God help us 11454

whole t. with man of little faith 3830

why do we fear it 11459

with growing old is 8175

with world is 10518

Worry interest paid by those who borrow t. 12090

worry never keeps t. from overtaking you 12091

TROUBLE'S

Oh, t. a ton, or t. an ounce 11446

TROUBLED

anger at God to be t. for what is past 12066

Anxious or t. when with us is prayer 8867

calms t. sea of lives 4863

Christ's life outwardly t. 6376

devil loves to fish in t. waters 1826

distrust of God to be t. about what is to come 12066

do not allow hearts to be t. 188

If your heart is t. 418

impatience against God to be t. with present 12066

Laughter is God's hand on t. world 6731

Music medicine of t. mind 7908

reason many are t. 10977

than live in plenty and be t. 3979

tumors of t. mind 3129

when times are t. 8403

with great ambitions 348

TROUBLES

are as pebbles on the road 7569

ask not that all t. end 152

back into past, rake up all t. ever had 11450

can cure by perspiration, fresh air 11455

come because we refuse to sit quietly 9367

death, out of sea of t. into haven of rest 2325

for t. wrought of men, patience is hard 11464

Forget the day's t. 11158

grief, strong to consume small t. 5331

have known many t, most never happened 11434

I don't pray delivered from t. 2091

if man have half his wishes, double his t. 2569

if t. large enough to endanger welfare 4789

large enough to touch God's love 4789

let God proportion out what t. he sees fit 4629

Life full of t, most man-maid 7628

live for himself, small t. shall seem great 11433

live for others, great t. shall seem small 11433

love tokens from God 4804

Many t. are God dragging us 11440

many t. you cannot cure by Bible 11455

more I told t. more t. grew 2727

more involved in life's t. when come to Christ 11451

Most t. imaginary 11442

must seem so small to God 4789

pray for strength, patience to bear t. 2091

putting God between ourselves and t. 41

safely say to most t. "We shall meet no more" 12075

seem as if they will never pass away 8444

sometimes fear to bring t. to God 4789

talk about t. to friends 4276

Talk to him in prayer of all your t. 8968

tight shoes make you forget other t. 8509

used to tell t. to everyone I knew 2727

when t. end, life ends too 152

wives try to tell husbands of t. 3904

world is big, its t. still bigger 10520

TROUBLESOME

during most t. times in my life 5437

free from t. people 4974

jealous are t. to others 6348

life more t. than most of us think 6918

TROUBLING

God's instant answer to t. 693

TROUGH

messiahs aren't found sleeping in feed t. 6147

TROUT

must lose fly to catch t. 4343

TRUCE

never an instant's t. between virtue, vice 11700

TRUE

ability to forget t. greatness 4068

and appropriate at all times 957

Be t. to God, yourself and watch 1549

believe what he prefers to be t. 595

Christ is our t. self 10551

comprehending t. nature of existence 3488

course of t. anything never runs smooth 2747

Dare to be t. 3937

disciples of Christ love most 7318

doctrine key to world's problems 11213

Dreams t. interpreters of inclinations 2967

Everything t. grows in silence 10246

excellence rarely found 3472

Failure t. test of greatness 3594

faith accompanied by expectation 3809

faith acts on supernatural facts 3807

Faith believing that it will come t. 5927

faith commits to obedience 3808

faith essentially reasonable 3842

faith needs neither evidence nor research 3810

faith never found alone 3809

false explanations for t. reasons 3476

false to God, never t. to man 7464

foe to God ne'er t. friend to man 4164

For the t. light go searching all the way 7475

freedom, man free to do what he ought 4150

friend is forever a friend 4180

friends no solitary joy, sorrow 4291

friendship is plant of slow growth 4218

friendship is still rarer 4263

friendship like sound health 4292

gift, nothing expected in return 4384

give up fears, face our t. nature 10551

greatness is ability to develop greatness in others 6804

greatness measured by 5306

happiness in worth, choice of friends 4293

have his promises been 6498

heroes of human race 6199

Hold t. friend with both hands 4188

Hope wishing for a thing to come t. 5927

I am bound to be t. 6303

I would be t. 1018

if not true, say it not 1021

If t, Christianity of infinite importance 1184

If takes sin to show God, Satan in t. colors 11072

If we have t. love of God 4767

into loveliness of our t. home 6110

invitation to t. living 1168

joy of man's life in relationship to God 9467

knowledge of God result in sheer wonder 6704

lead a t. life 4974
leader likely has no desire to lead 6785
light ever shines 5103
love always costly 7328
love can never say, "I have done enough" 7273
Love is t. freedom 7254
magnet that will attract t. friends 4282
Man cannot find t. essential joy 6552
man who stuck t. to God will come out best 10789
Music though t. in only a single instance 7905
never omitting speaking t. word 9491
no t. love without suffering 6506
no vision of eternity, never get t. hold of time 3272
One alone is t. to us 6455
Our own heart form t. honor 5896
Our t. nationality is mankind 5980
peace found in depths of own heart 8474
power can separate from t. nature of Christian leadership 8717
question to be asked about creed, "Is it t." 2032
Rare as is t. love 4263
religion is built upon the Rock 9550
riches in t. happiness 11852
Selfishness enemy of all t. affection 10082
silence is rest of mind 9374
some say God too good to be t. 4504
spirituality manifests itself in 10719
spirituality rare as t. bestiality 10718
stand t. to integrity of Jesus Christ 8545
Strong minds, great hearts, t. faith, ready hands 6299
Suffering the t. cement of love 7293
To know one's self is the t. 10022
to thine own self be t. 6318
triumphs are God's triumphs over us 11673
Trust men and they will be t. to you 6807
understanding of God comes after ceased to reach out to human beings 7548
unless know it to be t. 5148
Where hearts are t. 4302
With good or ill, with false or t. 7017
worth of man measured by objects pursued 469
Write, say, think nothing you cannot believe to be t. 9871

TRUER
Death's t. name is Onward 2268
light is, less you see glass 6033
man in evolution from poor to t. wealth 9351

TRUEST
life in dreams awake 2966
prayer sometimes a sigh 8887
self-respect is not to think of self 10000
stillest tongue, t. friend 1879

TRULY
Speak boldly, speak t. 2669

TRUMPET
He has sounded forth the t. 4715
shall be heard on high 7925
world to die amid blast of archangel's t. 7886

TRUMPET-CREEPER
walls of jasmine, and t. 4454

TRUMPETS
all the t. sounded on the other side 2366
Lightnings! the earth trembles 6150
punished unless kill to the sound of t. 11753
words charge like t. 11998

TRUNK
tree t. in his own eye 6590

TRUST
At, O Lord, from thee 10210
All I have seen teaches me to t. the Creator 11465
and obey is substance of Spirit-filled life 5803
begets truth 11484
Build a little fence of t. 11362
By an unfaltering t, approach thy grave 2203
cannot crowd its way in 12081
do not understand t. until betrayed 11620
equal failing to t. everybody, nobody 11473
Every possession a t. 8626
Experience gateway to One whom we t. 3525
Experience never ground of our t. 3525
Faith is a reasoning t. 3676
Faithfully faithful to every t. 2028
Few delights equal one we t. 4184
future to his providence 5457
God for great things 10205
God in whom we t. keeps us 11474
God when you can't trace him 3663
God where you cannot trace him 11485
God while not able to make sense of everything 3696
God, heaven securely 559
God: see all, nor be afraid 8132

Hope draws power from deep t. in God 5928
hope teaches t. in God 3834
Idolatry t. in own righteousness 6071
If love Christ much, shall t. him much 11472
If thou wilt simply t. 5415
in God and do the right 5995
in God's unchanging Word till soul and body sever 9813
in nothing man who has not conscience 1708
involves letting go 11486
knowing God will catch you 11486
let us renew our t. in God 1918
Life's sorrows for our t. 6995
like getting in the wheelbarrow 3669
Lord Jesus, make my heart sit down 419
may not put t. in worldly thing 187
men and they will be true to you 6807
most deceived that t. the most in themselves 10040
need Christians prepared to t. God completely 11488
no future, howe'er pleasant 4331
no panic in t. 11482
not our t. that keeps us 11474
not too much to enchanting face 3575
O holy t. 11476
Of t, strength, calmness from above 9050
Our part is to t. 2097
past to mercy of God 5457
pinnacle of spiritual life is absolute t. 11480
present to God's love 5457
putting pressure back into God's hand 11466
reckons thoughtfully, confidently 3676
reckons upon trustworthiness of God 3676
saved by making atonement my t. 3753
second nature to children 1116
Silence intimately related to t. 10259
sit still and t. the engineer 5461
some so gifted they won't t. God 2833
someone else willing to t. him 4275
Still will I cry, I t. in thee 11470
the morrow as little as possible 8222
there are those who t. me 1018
To one fixed t. my spirit clings 4642
to stop praying and t. 9009
To t. in God unhesitatingly 6913
Under the first sinners ever t. 4812

when you don't understand t. me
2414
will never let God take control
until we t. him 10259
world given to man in t. 3195
You t. eternity 1272

TRUSTED
faith that hasn't been tested
cannot be t. 3640
greater compliment than loved
1576
Jesus Christ never t. human nature
2184
No man to be t. with unlimited
power 8714

TRUSTFULLY
cannot speak too t. to God 8968

TRUSTFULNESS
based on confidence in God
11487

TRUSTING
And t. lean upon thy breast 4977
bravery of God in t. us 11479
God t. us a risky thing to do
11479
God's wisdom in dailyness of
living 1803
Idolatry t. people to do what only
God can do 6072
Love is t. in God 7246

TRUSTS
faith t. in character, promises of
God 3842
friend t. you with secrets 4179
God, obeys God 8089
wise man t. wisdom of God 5459

TRUSTWORTHINESS
faith in t. of God 4005
trust reckons upon t. of God 3676

TRUSTWORTHY
Science smilingly disposed of Bible
as t. guide 9870

TRUTH
A few say the t. 6199
A lie stands on one leg, t. on two
6864
Abide by the t. 11527
Absolute t. belongs to God alone
11495
absolute t. is indestructible 11550
Adversity first path to t. 144
All t. not to be told at all times
11496
All t. to love, all wrong to hate
7986
although with t. speakest evil, that
also is crime 11497
always the strongest argument
11563
and oil always come to the surface
11553
any greater need than that we
learn t. of God 7485
Any t. better than make-believe
5887
arrives last 6865

art, point world toward ultimate t.
1998
as much caution to tell t. as to
conceal it 11514
as try to get simple t. o' most
sermons 10099
barrier between you and t. 4801
being eternal, is self-existent
11550
Being indestructible, is eternal
11550
being infinite, is vast, deep 11550
being self-existent, is infinite
11550
being vast and deep, is intelligent
11550
belief in Christmas 1364
Belief is t. held in mind 582
better than gold 11564
Better ugly t. than beautiful lie
11498
Bible pure, unalloyed, perfect t.
710
Bible, flaming out glorious, t. 683
broadest word is t. 11993
bucket dropped in well of t. leaky
indeed 12144
burly T. comes by and puts them
out 11539
chew, swallow grain of t. 2059
Christ did not simply speak t.
11572
Christ in you that tells the t. 6381
Christ the T. infallible 6397
Christ told whole t. 1154
Christ told world t. about itself
11525
Christ was T. 11572
city of t. cannot be built on
swampy ground 11530
Clearly dost thou answer 5381
collapsing world more conducive
to understanding t. 11491
companion of t. is humility 11535
courageously accept bitter t. 1719
Cross is God's t. about us 11531
crushed to earth, shall rise again
11579
Cynicism unpleasant way of
saying t. 2180
Death cancels everything but t.
2239
death takes toll of all but t. 11519
Defeat school in which t. grows
strong 2507
defend the t. 11527
devil pretends to defend t. 2689
devil sometimes speaks the t.
11532
devil tries to shake t. 11533
2689
disciple comes with superstition to
find t. 2818
discovered lasts a lifetime 11578
divorced from experience 3548
Do the t. you know 9649
doctrines in excess a caricature of
t. 9122
does not blush 11555

does not vary because men ignore
11540
easier to perceive error than t.
3259
easier to see clearly into liar than
who tells t. 6866
Eloquence power to translate t.
into intelligible language 9134
endless quest for t. 4643
endorsed by actual experience
1168
ere long shall appear to vindicate
10448
Error as important as t. 3253
error more dangerous, more t. it
contains 3250
Errors to be dangerous have t.
mingled 3254
essential for Holy Spirit to reveal t.
752
eternal t. mysteriously suggests
itself 7949
ever-renewed, gleaming, glistening
garment of t. 5714
Exaggeration t. that has lost
temper 11500
existence of evil reveals God in his
t. 3398
exists 6867
Experience mother of t. 3530
expresses feeling, dialogue of t.
begins 8779
Faith bids eternal t. be fact 3680
faith that cannot survive collision
with t. 3639
far more t. in Genesis than
quantum theory 745
feed mind with t. of God 12124
final t. belongs to heaven, not
world 8596
Find grain of t. in criticism 2059
Forge thy tongue on anvil of t.
11503
Free discussion firmest friend to t.
2902
friend more excellent than human
friend 11560
game of the few 11571
give audience to all who ask
counsel 5381
glorious but hard mistress 11561
God leading world by vision of t.
4474
God ordained t. from all eternity
11584
God wants us to ask question of t.
10564
God will make you a specialist in
that t. 11528
God's own t. 4804
God's t. attacked, yet would
remain silent 99
God's t. judges out of love 4914
grave of one who dies for t. holy
ground 11534
great ocean of t. lay all
undiscovered 11508
greatest enemy of t. is prejudice
11535

greatest friend of t. is time 11535

greatest whose reliance on t. most unfaltering 5297

greatness in speaking up for t. 5283

hairline between t. and superstition 10968

half t. is a whole lie 6843

has more virtue than ignorance 6326

has no responsibility to make us comfortable 11557

has no special time of its own 11558

hath a quiet breast 11559

having same idea God has 11554

he who knows t. but keeps silent 2910

Hell is t. seen too late 5690

holding letter of t. 9826

holy life regulated by divine t. 5736

Humility nothing but t. 6009

ideas of t. not everlasting 11207

If Christ did not speak t. in all matters 11509

if gamble on its t. and proves false 3724

if love t, be lover of silence 10245

if not tell t, power against you 11510

if refuse to stand for t. 3846

If t. be mighty and God all-powerful 4134

Ignorance content with back to t. 3258

ignorance may deride t. 11566

In quarreling t. always lost 9358

In seeking t, get both sides of story 11511

In sorrow he learned this t. 12170

in the cry of all 11571

In the strife of t. and falsehood 2489

is a divine thing 11560

is a torch 11562

is beyond attack 11575

is child of time 10448

is discerned spiritually 11569

is everlasting 11207

is heavy, few men carry it 11565

is home only place of liberty 5842

is incontrovertible 11566

is its own witness 11567

is justice's handmaid 6628

It's hour is now, always 11558

Jesus gives t. carried on wings of love 6176

Jesus imparts inward taste for t. 6442

Jesus is all t, no falsehood 6498

Justice is t. in action 6613

lead to living T. of whom can learn anything 11004

Let t. not shadows within me speak 11515

Let t. speak to me 9070

liar isn't believed even when speaks t. 6844

lie no sense unless t. dangerous 8362

lies in character 11572

lies in the depth 3259

life of t. from death of creeds 11504

light and t. and love of heaven 10756

like light, blinds 6866

limping along on time's arm 6865

Listen to the t. 11527

Loose tongues stretch t. 9488

Love t. though it do harm 11517

made him swear he'd always tell me nothing but the t. 11507

malice may distort t. 11566

man can't always be defending t. 11493

Man finds God through t. 11518

man mute before elemental t. 10274

man of courage not afraid of t. 6845

man who finds t. lights torch 11536

many moments hostile to t. 11551

many observations, little reasoning leads to t. 9410

martyrs accused of efforts to find t. 11501

mathematicians uncovered t. 1958

may be blamed but never shamed 11573

may hurt but it cures 11580

may walk around naked 6869

meaningful experience criterion for t. 3493

Men prefer prosperous error to afflicted t. 3261

merely told is quick to be forgotten 11578

mightier than eloquence 11568

more convincing proof of this t. 4942

more in love with own opinion than t. 2904

more popular if not ugly facts 11543

must be a time to feed on t. 11493

must be Sunday, everybody's telling the t. 11513

needs no defense 11575

needs no flowers of speech 11576

never consults, bargains, compromises 11561

New continents of t. 2319

new understanding of my t. 7123

no discovery of t. without committing to Christ 6490

No one can bar road to t. 11520

no power more formidable than t. 11547

not always what we want to hear 11541

not discerned intellectually 11569

not so dreadful as uncertainty 11544

not words but a life and being 11572

Nothing in fiction so fantastic as t. of Incarnation 6125

nothing so powerful as t. 11548

nothing so strange as t. 11548

Obedience to revealed t. guarantees guidance 5435

of a man is what he hides 7431

of Bible has endured flames 646

of Christian religion 5183

of God only revealed to us by obedience 11542

often eclipsed, never extinguished 11570

one connected chain of justice, mercy, t. 4904

One t. to heart: this, too, shall pass away 6878

Opinions if founded in t. will prevail 8199

Panic may resent t. 11566

Philosophy seeks the t. 11524

Philosophy, science that considers t. 8595

Pity sentences force t. upon our memory 9384

Poetry making t. more real 8617

Poetry not an assertion of t. 8617

probability t. on persecuted side 8532

question of t. that may isolate us from most men 10564

Rather than love, give me t. 11526

religion possesses the t. 11524

revelation a showing to men of t. after t. 9706

revelation of t. secret whispering of God in soul 9705

Satan's t. judges out of envy, hatred 4914

sciences, business is to show the t. 9871

Seek the t. 11527

shall learn t. you need to know 9649

showing unto men of t. after t. 4906

silence better than t. without charity 1831

silence, listening, prayer, t. go together 10248

sip reluctantly at t. we find harsh 6870

Skepticism first step toward t. 2952

small chance of t. at goal 11549

so obsessed with facts lost touch with t. 7990

Soak continually in one great t. 11528

speaking t. in love all-important 9158

Speaking the t. important 9158

Spiritual t. discernable only to pure heart 11529

stranger than fiction 11574

strangest t. is redemption comes through suffering 9439

Study sciences in light of t. 9871

Teach the t. 11527

tell t, have infinite power supporting you 11510

The more men suppress t. of God 11538

The safe appeal of T. to Time 11299

Theological t. useless until obeyed 11205

theology finds the t. 11524

theology ideas of t. classified, arranged 11207

this side of Pyrenees may be heresy on the other 11577

thou knoweth the whole t. 9104

Throughout history t. considered form of dementia 5730

Time and t. are friends 11551

Time discovers the t. 11325

Time tries t. 11552

to advance cause ready to accept death 11520

To build a ship of t. 11519

to hear t. about yourself, anger your neighbor 8058

To snap like vixens at the t. 5048

To speak painful t. 4289

To unmask falsehood, bring t. to light 11344

too much t. stuns us 3559

tragic waste of t. 3758

Trust begets t. 11484

try to grasp with closed eyes, fearing to be blinded 11562

turn theological t. into experience 12063

Unlock the t. 648

Unused t. as useless as unused muscle 11583

vast and deep, is transcendental 11550

Violence goes against t. of our faith 11678

we ourselves must will the t. 11505

When add to t. you subtract from it 11587

When know the Cross, no longer afraid of t. 11531

When money speaks, t. is silent 7825

when rejects God's t. in favor of devil's impure philosophies 11512

When tell t, don't have to remember what you said 11588

when you shoot an arrow of t. 271

where few are willing to search 3259

while t. putting her boots on 6846

who never retract, love themselves better than t. 8207

who speaks t. always at ease 11537

within a little, certain compass 6868

Without the t. no knowing 6382

works far and lives long 11516

world seeing t. lived through us 3317

world so rich in delusions t. is priceless 11523

world too dangerous for anything but the t. 11545

TRUTH-TELLER

always unpopular 11501

For t. world has little liking 11501

TRUTHFUL

Christ too t. to be believed 6507

Cross only power which can make us t. 11531

money and sex, impossible to be t. 11494

repentance, liar becomes t. 9604

To be credible, we must be t. 6319

TRUTHFULLY

to acknowledge it t. 9062

TRUTHS

are not created, they exist 11581

canvas on which God paints t. 10844

cleavage between t. we affirm, values we live by 6068

eternal t. depend on God alone 11584

eternal t. do not depend upon human understanding 11584

Falsehoods not only disagree with t. 6849

God reserves right to harmonize t. 11586

God sends ten thousand t. 6565

greatest t. are simplest 10284 5298

hold t. to be self-evident 3246

Honesty looking painful t. in the face 5876

learn nothing of gospel except by feeling its t. 5110

No t. are simple 11521

Old t. always new to us 11522

reveal a life deeper than known 11521

Revival and comfortable t. are bitter enemies 9744

sacrifice one of the deepest t. 9758

some t. God will not make simple 11546

thoughtful mind sees t. of nations 7982

turn into dogmas moment they are disputed 11582

upon which human life may rest 11585

When two t. seem to directly oppose 11586

TRY

and find you can 95

being yourself 6191

Do not t. to imagine God 4663

Do not t. to produce ideal child 8293

Don't t. and be useful 10141

formula for failure, t. to please everybody 3619

God-given method for revivals 9743

If I t. to be like him 6188

something beyond what you have mastered 68

t. again 8558

to be own masters as if created ourselves 5570

To t. the soul's strength on 6908

we t. to escape life instead of controlling it 7072

we t. to speak of great or little faith 4710

When we t. to understand Christ's teaching 6515

when you t. to make yourself more, you are diminishing yourself 9941

worst is not to t. 3589

TRYING

came to end of t. to be a Christian 5792

Cheer the youth who's bravely t. 4217

Ducks look funny t. to climb 6168

like t. to make wheel without hub 4632

majority busy t. to place ourselves 8395

man t. to find something which will make him happy 5570

many people are t. to make peace 8427

not frantically t. to make ourselves good 7560

These are t. times 8582

to be Christian, sign you are not 1291

to hold water in hands 5519

to live serene lives in houses divided against themselves 6068

to settle problem with oratory 9290

TUG

both t, he's left in the middle 9940

conversion, going to be t. at heart 3052

TUGGING

evil t. to make us animals, not angels 3406

TUGS

on oars hasn't time to rock boat 10187

TUMBLE

worse t. when fall over own bluff 7587

TUMBLE-ABOUT

Life a t. thing of ups, downs 6955

TUMBLED

rock of tomb t. 2984

TUMORS

of a troubled mind 3129

TUMULT

of our passions within 8800

t. and shouting dies 6036

TUMULTUOUS
world always t. 10512

TUNE
And the atoms march in t. 1976
and touch the chords 7527
Be it ours to learn the t. 7056
God speaks if we will t. in 8013
Grows out of t. and needs a hand
  divine 7527
me, O Lord, into one harmony
  7928
older the fiddle, sweeter the t.
  8173
our hearts to brave music 9059
redemption brings man back into
  t. with praise 8743
strikes the note and t. of our
  strings 7550
we call goodness or right conduct
  7839
When God sets the soul in t. for
  himself 10663

TUNING
In the valley God is t. thy voice
  10600

TUNNEL
like lamps nobody sees till t. comes
  10914
optimist sees light at end of t.
  8250
pessimist sees only the t. 8250
realist sees t. and light 8250
When train goes through t. 5461
will t. underneath 2633

TUNNELED
No Niagara turned into power
  until t. 2852

TURN
away on grounds too well-dressed
  to be honest 10086
can never t. back 9846
Christ never suggest t. blind eye to
  evil 9789
darkness into light 6647
Faith is knowing God will t. effect
  to good 3671
hard thing into glory 3149
his face toward the future 4315
involves two things 1894
It's going to t. out all right 4316
Lord t. routines of work into
  celebrations of love 12015
meets God at every t. 4847
must t. back on one-half of world
  9151
must, as a Christian t. away from
  it 7036
our eyes to where skies are full of
  promise 9059
place and time tide will t. 8568
  2614
Self can t. powerful prayer into
  weak one 10080
single word can t. you on, off
  12001
stay and t. mountain into gold
  mine 2633

Sweetest things t. sourest by their
  deeds 5039
theological truth into experience
  12063
Through God t. endings into
  beginnings 3629
To get to heaven, t. right, keep
  straight 5675
We t. to meet another year 8082
weak, sin-battered life toward
  Great Physician 10436
When we t. to God our souls have
  rest 7451
your attention to God 6271

TURNCOAT
wine is a t. 337

TURNED
back on the glory 6488
Christ has t. our sunsets into
  dawns 6368
Christ t. world's standards upside
  down 5001
Christians who have t. world
  upside down 11735
dirge in minor suddenly t. into
  song of glee 7895
never t. wrong to right 3174
nothing can happen which cannot
  be t. into good 4803
think God t. life into inextricable
  confusion 4885
When man repents is t. toward
  God 9583

TURNING
Conversion, t. around 1898
disordered actions to our
  advantage 4644
Sinning is t. from God's face
  10382
terminus a quo, t. from something
  1894
terminus ad quem, t. toward
  something 1894

TURNIPS
man weeding t. also serving God
  12146

TURNS
bush still burns for man,
  whichever way he t. 7996
Faith means grasped by power
  that t. us 3707
God t. from wrath, never from
  love 4757
Guessing t. to certainty when 949
in everyone's life certain t. 5454
instinct in our souls that t. us to
  God 7535
Life t. dead on our hands 4437
Selfishness t. life into a burden
  10083
to obtain possible, man t. to
  fellowmen 7490
Unselfishness t. burdens into life
  10083
what t. bones into jelly 4551
When seeming gain but t. to loss
  4338

wherever glance falls God t. to
  beauty 4463
whichever way God t. my feet, I go
  5416

TUTOR
vice acquired without a t. 11725

TWAIN
God runs toward him t. 7573
never t. shall meet 915

TWENTY-FIVE
destiny of nation depends on
  citizens under t. 12173

TWENTY-FOUR
being with God for all t. hours
  6569

TWENTY-ONE
When I got to be t. 3928

TWICE
cannot step t. into same river 985
gives t. who gives quickly 4361
You fool me t, shame on me 2481

TWIG
As t. is bent, tree inclines 8344
As t. is bent, tree's inclined 2991

TWILIGHT
Falsehood, t. that enhances every
  object 6866
In the Bible, no t. 672
in world with Christianity 1214
is torn away ruthlessly 8075
Life closes in t, opens with dawn
  11132
like deep sea divers in t. of depths
  6110
live in gray t. 1922
music in the t. cloud 7927
that knows not victory, defeat
  1922
tomb closes in t. to open in dawn
  2422
Without Christ life as t. with dark
  night ahead 7094

TWIN
faith is doubt's t. brother 2932
Happiness was born a t. 5505

TWINING
through veins 6131

TWINKLE
life, t. of star in God's eternal day
  7015

TWINS
Pride and weakness are Siamese t.
  9226
Send either one, if can't be t. 814

TWISTING
and warping innocent family
  members 3873
can't drive straight on t. lane 4440

TWISTS
authoritarianism t. good into lust
  for power 9952
in everyone's life certain t. 5454

TWO

A lie stands on one leg, truth on t. 6864

are needed for oneness 11622

believe Satan to exist for t. reasons 9854

Busy bee teaches t. lessons 3454

captains in one boat make it sink 6808

could add t. hours to my working day 9531

Don't hear one, judge t. 6606

Every mile is t. in winter 2544

evil has t. enemies, good and itself 5022

eyes of love see not one but t. persons 7300

fateful possibilities 8129

freedoms 4150

friend is single soul in t. bodies 4211

Friendship, t. bodies and one soul 4298

fundamental rules for life 10053

God hath t. wings, which he doth ever move 4812

God never made t. people exactly alike 6191

good example, improving t. 3436

great forces at work in world today 4917

he who seeks to serve t. masters 1332

if only t. tiny words taken from them 4227

In all unbelief there are t. things 11591

In God's sight only t. classes of people 3236

Into these t. brief words 8369

kinds of gratitude 5267

kinds of men 10404

kinds of people 5455

kinds of people keep silent 10272

Laughter, weeping are t. intensest forms of human emotion 6728

love t. souls and one flesh 4298

men please God 4572

mites, t. drops (yet all her house, land) 4379

No t. human beings make same journey in life 5978 6202

Of t. evils, choose neither 3390

Of t. evils, pass up first, turn down other 3391

One foot cannot stand on t. boats 6058

One life, gleam of time between t. eternities 7013

One today worth t. tomorrows 11376

only t. or three human stories 5984

only t. religions accept gloom as fact 9551

People come to poverty t. ways 4040

pray t. hours before going to sea 7650

reasons for loving God 7533

secret between t. is secret of God 5115

sections to society 10523

sides to every question 8076

sin is t. sins when defended 10289

sin you do by t. and t. 10398

sometimes ask that t. and t. not make four 9023

takes t. to be glad 10607 5351

takes t. to make marriage a success 7623

things not easy to reconcile 7069

things stand like stone 6657

things that make devils or saints 7805

things that mattered 3331

things to do about the gospel 5107

to keep a friend close t. eyes 4161

vanities can never love one another 9256

ways of being rich 11864

ways of spreading light 3455

ways to handle difficulties 2753

we are t. in one 7952

We sin t. kinds of sin 10422

When t. truths seem to directly oppose 11586

Whenever t. people meet 7443

would spend t. years studying, preparing 6687

years to learn to talk 2897

You have but t. topics 9958

TWO-FACEDNESS

will meet with t. 10159

TWOFOLD

Jesus Christ had a t. personality 6426

TWO-WAY

Respect is intended to operate on a t. street 9644

TYPE

best friends should be "No problem" t. 4226

most satanic t. of pride 6038

TYPICAL

Christian, a bore 867

TYRANNIES

Of all the t. on humankind 7765

writhe under t. of cruel master 6280

TYRANNOUS

to use strength like a giant 8707

TYRANT

dies, his rule ends 7679

gold, what crimes thy t. power has caused 11803

only t. I accept is voice within 1703

TYRANT'S

Destiny a t. authority for crime 2619

TYRANTS

Emotions should not be t. 3055

God does allow t. to rule 4957

If not governed by God, ruled by t. 7483

or ruled by t. 4137

Resistance to t. is obedience to God 5964

TYRE

rock for fisherman's nets 730

U

UGLIEST

chose u. coat 467

UGLINESS

Envy u. of trapped rat 3211

Thought show u. within 11267

UGLY

Better u. truth than beautiful lie 11498

devil is not u. 2651

face sometimes better than real one 6057

once you are real, you can't be u. 5886

pretences not to hide the u, but emptiness 3395

Sin clasped so close cannot see u. face 10377

through u. defeat of cross God glorified 2519

truth more popular if not u. facts 11543

ULCER

man with everything, u. too 3208

ULCERS

many ways to get u. 1566

ULTERIOR

honesty, no u. motives 5874

ULTIMATE

disaster to feel at home on earth 2382

human value not the u. 11663

Jesus always returned to his u. prayer 6384

judgments not u. 571

separation from God u. disaster 5697

Though God be opposed, u. outcome never in doubt 4822

ULTIMATELY

event which Creator has u. in view 4898

No evil done can harm u. 3385

ULTRABUSY

schedule not mark of productive life 9533

UMBRELLA
ain't no use putting up u. till it
   rains 12065
human mind like u. 7770
over duck in rain 6641

UMPIRE
My U. Conscience whom if they
   hear 1664

UNABLE
All u. to give possesses you 10724
All you are u. to give possesses you
   8623
Almighty u. to do more than lie,
   stare, wriggle 6125
God u. to grant heart's desires till
   9282
Is God u. to prevent suffering
   10841
no fault of our own u. to sense
   God 4864
often assume God u. to work
   3613
to distinguish what is worth
   reading 2997
to recognize ourselves 6067
what we are u. to bear God keeps
   secret 9708

UNAFFECTED
can choose to be bag of marbles,
   u. by others 9524

UNAFRAID
I walk u. 3649
if u. of change 8139
whether right or wrong 6216

UNAGING
spiritual life is u. youth 10712

UNALIENABLE
endowed by Creator with certain
   u. rights 3246

UNALLOYED
Bible, pure, u, perfect truth 710

UNAMBIGUOUS
The u. footsteps of the God 4482
   1963

UNANSWERABLE
Jesus' coming final, u. proof God
   cares 6136
will pray u. prayers 3415

UNANSWERED
Lord leaves his prayers u. 9029

UNAPPRECIATED
moment must not be permitted to
   slip away u. 11319

UNAPPROACHABLE
thought holy men u. 3331
to touch and taste the u. 7531
yearning to touch the u. 4744

UNASHAMED
effort to protract physical desire
   10229

UNASK'D
The good u. in mercy grant 8979

UNASSAILABLE
man who loves God in u. position
   4803
security where peace u. 3961

UNASSUMING
simple, u. life best for everyone
   7365

UNATTAINABLE
perfection in most things u. 3463

UNAWARE
perfect church service, one we are
   almost u. of 1383
perfect prayer, u. he is praying
   8888

UNBEARABLE
burdened with the u. weight of
   ourselves 9917
If home u, maybe you're the bear
   5839
redirecting our lives seems u. 5449
seldom the present that is u. 5354
soul can rise up against u. odds
   3621

UNBELIEF
Beware of limiting God by u.
   8772
Blind u. is sure to err 5378
God cannot do because of u. 8843
If don't give thanks, living in u.
   11152
In all u. there are two things
   11591
is content with darkness 2930
is not such attitude u. 8632
is obstinacy 2930
is won't believe 2930
makes world a moral desert 11595
opposite of joy is u. 11594
result of u. trying to live
   maximum life on minimum faith
   3770
so long will I fight against u. 2590
starves the soul 3703
terrible luxury of u. 11589
thorny crown filled with briars of
   u. 7073
trembles at shaking of leaf 3703
wordy u. that quenches the fire
   11991

UNBELIEVABLE
blown by tempest of u. power
   7488
deny God with life-style 487
Faith believes the u. 3713

UNBELIEVER
can no longer refuse reality of our
   faith 10938

UNBELIEVERS
devil does not tempt u. 2675

UNBELIEVING
mind not convinced by proof 600
world 487
world observing way we undergo
   trials 3319

UNBENDING
Faith should always be simple, u.
   7168
Faith should always be u. 3839

UNBORN
like u. forests in acorn-cup 4769

UNBORROWED
original, u, solitary greatness 736

UNBOUNDED
I believe in God of u. love 4997

UNBRIDLED
human passions u. by morality,
   religion 5196

UNBROKEN
God a continuous, u. is 4604
God will never plant seed on u.
   spirit 888

UNCARED
feeling of being u. for greatest
   poverty 7132

UNCARING
God not u. 7556
Life lost in thousand, small u.
   ways 6972

UNCEASINGLY
God speaks u. through events of
   life 5395

UNCERTAIN
better to be u. and not promise
   9327
Exorcism of evil u. affair 3365
Faith knows itself u. 3702
future is u. 8374
ills torment most 11604
in asking any small drop of
   refreshment 4653
not certain everything is u. 951
Nothing so u. as hour of death
   2341
thank thee that dark, u. is our
   future 9053
What is from men is u. 4524
whose attitude toward me u,
   hostile 7102

UNCERTAINTIES
to accept u. quietly 7435

UNCERTAINTY
are all impatient of u. 11605
If u. makes you seasick 11598
life full of spontaneous joyful u.
   5463
man to make his way best he can
   in u. 3495
receive as from the Lord 1461
The everlasting perhaps 319
truth not so dreadful as u. 11544

UNCHANGEABLE
beg you, do not be u. 8196
Christ the Way u. 6397
contemplate God's wisdom in u.
   order 4581
God is reason u. 4514
Our faithful, u. friend 4787

UNCHANGED
God always to be found u. 4867
not possible to remain u. 8264
thy purpose unchanged 4954

UNCHANGING
I'll trust in God's u. Word till soul
and body sever 9813
if God is u, he could not be
unfaithful 4583
Jesus spoke to the u. needs of man
6448

UNCHARITABLENESS
would be far less u. in world 9465

UNCHARTED
shall not travel an u. course 5945

UNCHASTITY
mere fleabites in comparison with
pride 9240

UNCHECKED
Evil u. grows 3368
Rest and motion, unrelieved and
u. equally destructive 9685

UNCOLORED
by temperament 8237

UNCOMFORTABLE
church is to make society u. 1427
philanthropy to save ourselves u.
feeling 10071

UNCOMMON
prosper as we do common things
in u. way 9344

UNCOMPLAININGLY
To live with thorn u. 8256

UNCOMPLETED
Nothing so fatiguing as u. task
9297

UNCOMPROMISING
reform from u. in compromising
age 1457

UNCONDITIONAL
God's love is u. 4786
koinonia, u. sharing of lives 4022

UNCONFINED
bounty shines in autumn u. 9883
Injustice u. 6269

UNCONQUERED
Give me an u. heart 9057

UNCONSCIOUS
bestial, semihuman, demonic 7772
Confession brings to light u.
darkness 1596
God deals with u. 10486
greatness is u. 5275
guidance becomes u. response
5396
in the classical sense, divine 7772
intricate machinery that is never
idle 7767
like vast subterranean factory
7767
mature life, u. consecration 1714
not just evil by nature 7772
not only dark, also light 7772

powers in u. depths of man 1712
Sin enough, soon u. of sin 10358
source of highest good 7772
superhuman, spiritual 7772
they dream of a day that had
never been 8371
work goes on day and night 7767

UNCONSCIOUSLY
begin to mature, obey
commandments u. 7690
believe happiness depends on
being more virtuous 6821
God does his will for the most
part u. to us 7690
people who influence stood u. for
right thing 6239
reform others u. when act upright
3457

UNCOVERED
mathematicians u. truth 1958

UNCREATED
God, u. Creator 4595
heart made able to receive u. light
4749
Thou of u. love 5788
understandable uneasiness about
the U. 4614

UNCUT
like u. diamonds, qualities beneath
5078

UNDEFILED
Make thee a bed, soft, u. 1357

UNDER
God is u. all things 4848
I'm u. God's arrest 5482

UNDERESTIMATE
how hard to be compassionate
1546
Never u. ability of humans to get
tangled up 5976
never wise to u. enemy 3163

UNDERESTIMATES
Anyone who u. what God can do
766

UNDERGO
friendship must u. shocks of
adversity 4218

UNDERGOES
Everything u. change 966

UNDERGROUND
easier to meet evil in open than u.
3381

UNDERLIES
His mercy u. 6916

UNDERMINE
scientifically proven that worry u.
health 5612

UNDERNEATH
death of Jesus goes u. deepest sin
2160
in some revolutions those u. get
on top 3785
proud put themselves u. 3785

will tunnel u. 2633

UNDERPRIVILEGED
People no longer sinful, only u.
10350

UNDERSATISFACTION
many curl up, die because of u.
3089

UNDERSTAND
Abraham's contemporaries could
not u. him 10877
among people whose language I
could not u. 7102
any greater need than that we u.
discipline of God 7485
because you cannot u. does not
cease to exist 4677
believe that you may u. 609
believes that he may u. 4910
best way to u. wrath of God 4999
blame what they do not u. 2081
by obedience we u. teaching of
God 8095
cannot always u. ways of God
4688
cannot u. how in presence of Lord
4853
children u. better than venerable
1216
children u. what parents have
rejected 12157
Christ never asks anyone to u. a
creed 6431
Confidence what you have before
u. situation 8361
content with what we can and
cannot u. 1820
dare to do our duty as we u. it
3755
devil does not come along lines
we u. 2702
do not u. digestive system but I eat
3733
do not u. immortality 6091
do not u. man until you have
learnt how he u. himself 7394
Do you fully u. power of words
12005
does not seek to u. that he may
believe 4910
don't u, trust me 2414
don't u. respiratory system, but I
breathe 3733
error to think can u. mysteries
11203
Everyone wants to u. painting
11608
everything I need to u. 6493
faith, either you don't u. or don't
believe 3741
Folks never u. folks they hate
5593
fools u. better than wise 1216
Friends who u. each other 4185
God made us hear and u. 7891
God seems careless whether men
u. him 11616
God whose ways you cannot u.
3684

Gold has no heart to u. 11813
hard to u. detours God takes us
  5423
have too much theology we don't
  u. 9552
He who has not experience will
  not u. 3535
helped me to u. failures, ruins
  10594
hidden because not in fit state to u.
  11609
Home not where you live, but
  where they u. you 5830
if u. grain of sand, u. everything
  1957
If we can u. mind of God 4135
illiterates u. better than learned
  1216
In age we u. 12191
intolerant toward person hasn't
  taken time to u. 11612
it, life no longer difficult 7012
Jesus spelling himself out in
  language men can u. 6445
looking to things you could not u.
  9650
Many see, few u. 8501
Men fear death, refuse to u. 2336
mind can remember, u, love its
  maker 7771
never u. the ego 9352
nor to u. pain, suffering 10876
not necessary to u. everything
  11611
not to despise, or oppose what we
  do not u. 9095
One may u. the cosmos 9352
only in God fully u. what you are
  8634
Our mind too limited to u. God
  4665
Sometimes I think I u. everything
  11615
suddenly u. I know nothing 6493
Theology attempt to u. the
  mystery 11206
to be understood as to u. 9086
to pray aright must u. what we
  are praying for 8824
To u. all makes one tolerant
  11398
to u. Christ intelligent faith 3801
To u. creep within, feel beating of
  heart 3078
To u. everything is to hate nothing
  11617
To u. is to complicate 11618
to u. part of Bible clearly 681
To u. the world and to like it 7069
unless he believed he would not u.
  4910
We do not u. 11620
When try to u. Christ's teaching
  6515
who does not u. your silence will
  probably not u. your words
  10251
whose ways I do not u. 11487

Why no attempt to u. song of
  birds 11608
without fearing to u. 4124
without need to u. why God does
  what he does 7697
world does not u. theology or
  dogma 7313
world man cannot u. 3495

UNDERSTANDABLE
Were the works of God readily u.
  4510

UNDERSTANDING
a person does not mean condoning
  11619
Because u. is earthbound 11606
can wait, obedience cannot 8114
collapsing world more conducive
  to u. truth 11491
Commandments contains formula
  for u. 701
complete u. absolutely impossible
  9455
Conversation enriches the u.
  10533
day when better u. among people
  3229
demands of another complete u.
  absolutely impossible 9455
does not mean condoning 3079
don't have time to achieve u. 7648
Don't try to reach God with your
  u. 11607
each generation makes own
  contribution to u. 9711
eternal truths do not depend upon
  human u. 11584
Failure to obey dulls spiritual u.
  8100
faith gives profound u. 7383
faith precedes u. does not follow
  3743
fear of God, source of u. 3993
finite 11606
God gives to every man u. 5387
God gives u. that lifts into life
  2617
God incomprehensible to man's u.
  4728
God's essence beyond human u.
  4670
If Christianity small enough for u.
  1202
imaginative u. and love 9094
incapable of u. one's condition
  7126
Jesus Christ, his peace passing all
  u. 6352
limited 11606
man who has u. has everything
  11946
means one does not accuse 11619
more u. when acquainted with
  own heart 10306
never comes quickly 7648
new u. of my truth 7123
new u. of their oneness 9093
no u. of long-faced Christian 6532

of redemption not necessary to
  salvation 9433
our u. is human to the core 11606
Peace can only be achieved by u.
  8452
prayer for u. 9065
prayer is a sort of u. 8748
religion small enough for our u.
  9538
reward of faith 609
Seeing God means u. 7547
Set a child to wondering, on road
  to u. 6691
skeptical about capacity to
  express u. of existence 3488
spring from your love to u. 7970
talk to straighten out u. 1882
True u. of God comes after ceased
  to reach to human beings 7548
When angry, my u. is sharpened
  408
with what little u. world is ruled
  5174

UNDERSTANDS
believing God u. everything 7560
Christian u. love in terms of God
  4494
Christian u. more than philosopher
  1326
friend u. where you've been 4169
friend u. your past 4172
Man knows more than he u. 6697
more he u. intuitively 8505
mother u. what child does not say
  7842
nature u. her business better than
  we do 3196
no happiness equal to heart that u.
  9504
no idea by which God u. things
  4986
No one u. me 6171
Only God u. universe 11635
only one who u. 6171
possessed to achieve ends he only
  vaguely u. 4399
use of life 4204
who u. his foolishness is wise
  11947
world u. love, sympathy 7313

UNDERSTOOD
a luxury to be u. 11610
Bible u. only by supernatural aid
  708
Freedom, fine word when rightly
  u. 4123
God u. only through his
  self-revelation 4738
have not u. the words of Christ
  10182
holier man is, less u. by world
  5760
Life is to be u. 3984
Life only u. backwards 6941
music u. by thousands 7905
our Lord u. human predicament
  6519

people have not yet u. command of Christ 7349

pure in heart who u. what life was about 5001

to be u. as to understand 9086

without feeling u. by at least one person 11613

UNDERTAKE
Love able to u. all things 7220
something that is difficult 2758

UNDERTAKER
if u. whistled at his work 2413
watching not for u. but uppertaker 9913

UNDERTAKES
God u. special protection of man 3999

UNDERTAKINGS
failure pioneer in new u. 3602

UNDESERVED
Grace overwhelming u. mercy 5221

UNDESERVING
Grace inclines God to bestow benefits upon u. 4652
Praise to the u. is severe satire 8736

UNDISCLOSED
what must God's mind be in u. resources 4675

UNDISCOVERED
great ocean of truth lay all u. before me 11508

UNDISTORTED
Only in quiet waters things mirror themselves u. 7718

UNDISTURBED
God judging men with u. compassion 4720
Reflected u. in me 7715
time to be alarmed is when things u. 7040

UNDO
No amount of falls will u. us 3609
O God! that it were possible to u. things done 9568
that which we have done amiss 9054

UNDONE
duty to leave u. that thou wouldst do 9667
Evil can never be u. 3354
It's the thing you leave u. 2502
What he leaves u. will rob him of peace of mind 11690
wrongdoer often has left something u. 6157

UNDOUBTING
pinnacle of spiritual life is u. trust 11480

UNEARNED
suffering is redemptive 10919

UNEARTH
gift of serenity 10553

UNEARTHLY
prayer closet scene of u. conflicts 8976

UNEASINESS
is denying wisdom of God 1569
more u. than destruction of millions 10035
Receive every u. with both thy hands 7698
understandable u. about the Uncreated 4614

UNEASY
conscience is hair in mouth 1662
Dark, u. world of family life 3886
manger as u. as his cross 6489
wants which make us u. to ourselves 2861

UNEDUCABLE
you have an Albert Einstein 161

UNEDUCATED
good for u. to read quotations 9383

UNENJOYED
something u. impairs enjoyment 2869

UNEQUAL
only in love u. made equal 3238

UNEVENTFUL
Goodness is u. 5067
years of u. duties 10190

UNEXAMINED
life u. not worth living 7032

UNEXPECTED
arrivals, departures of pleasure 8612
brightest blazes of gladness kindled by u. sparks 8606
ear shocked by u. 844
gives anticipation, surprise 4318
happiness lies in u. friendly word 3143
more quickly than u. guest 3879
not be upset when u. happens 2887
see good things in u. places 8575
see talents in u. people 8575
Unwelcomed visitors bring u. blessings 832

UNEXPLAINABLE
unoffended in face of the u. 7727

UNEXPLAINED
things in life more than explained 11616

UNFAILING
ingratitude the u. mark of a narrow soul 6251
regularity of the seasons 4643

UNFAILINGLY
God reveals himself u. to seeker 4907

UNFAIRLY
judged when we do good 187

UNFAITHFUL
if God is unchanging he could not be u. 4583

UNFAITHFULNESS
in keeping appointment dishonesty 2914

UNFALTERING
By an u. trust, approach thy grave 2203
greatest whose reliance on truth most u. 5297

UNFATHOMABLE
can never penetrate u. mysteries of God 3702
history of our Lord u. depth 6380
infinity of God not mysterious, only u. 4684

UNFATHOMED
Baby, u. mystery 805

UNFEELING
God not u. 7556
lust of gold, u. and remorseless 11858

UNFINISHED
Christ, Completer of u. people, work, times 6428
Let there be naught u, broken, marred 7519
life, a vast, obscure u. masterpiece 6904

UNFIT
Whenever visions of God u. us for practical life 5466

UNFOLD
God's plan, like lilies, u. 5403
Listened to, makes us u. 1857

UNFOLDED
soul on earth never to be u. 10649

UNFOLDS
meaning u. and strangeness vanishes 6145

UNFORGETTABLY
showed u. how deeply he must suffer 6506

UNFORGIVENESS
Take off all your u. 10787

UNFORGIVING
no torment like inner torment of u. spirit 9640
spirit refuses to be healed, refuses to forget 9640

UNFORTUNATELY
for the scientifically-minded 4739

UNFRUITFUL
who do not love fellow beings live u. lives 7321

UNFULFILLED
critics claim Bible has u. promises 679

UNGODLINESS
Grace can pardon our u. 5212

UNGODLY
hope God too kind to punish u. 4726

UNGRATEFUL
Hell full of the u. 5687
if ills irreparable, murmur u. 1563
never known man of ability to be u. 5255
No great mind ever u. 6251
to those teachers 5251

UNGUARDED
strength is double weakness 10765

UNHAPPIEST
more money than they know how to use 932
more time than they know how to use 932

UNHAPPINESS
blessedness makes joy possible in u. 6536
cause of man's u. is 5560
makes its very u. sublime 10676
search for happiness chief sources of u. 5559
the winter of our u. 10581
think, talk, act yourself into u. 3185
true u. is in doing injustice 6265
would decision bring world u. 2494

UNHAPPY
alcohol, made million homes u. 331
are they who are proud 379
can't be enthusiastic and u. at same time 3189
civilization is always gregarious 10515
Difficult child is u. 1125
Do not speak of own happiness to someone u. 3067
Half the world u. 2866
making one another u. 31
Men who are u. proud of the fact 5541
slaves, who are u. from lack of money 8681
take u. time bit by bit, hour by hour 5354
they who lose their cool 379
too proud to say, "I'm sorry" 379
virtuous men also most u. 6821
who marry to escape u. home 7660
without control young people u. 12178
worry about tomorrow, be u. today 11402

UNHEALTHY
Shrinking from death u. 2255

UNHEARD
by the world rises silent to thee 8778

The poor too often turn away, u. 8694

UNHESITATINGLY
To trust in God u. 6913

UNHOLY
make man holy, put him back into u. world 5759
No feelings u. in themselves 4016
O u. audacity 230
take u. man out of u. world 5759

UNHONORED
Unwept, u. and unsung 10088

UNIFORM
what is war but murder in u. 11777

UNIFORMITY
Christ provided unity, not u. 1451
not a colorless u. 6179
produces mediocrity 3244
science assumes permanence, u. of natural laws 9869
Selfishness aims at absolute u. 10079

UNIFYING
shall find God u. our thinking 3774

UNILLUMINATED
Lord has little good to say of u. mind 7776
mystery doctrine viewed on side u. 7937

UNIMAGINABLY
God speaks to us of plan u. bold 4900

UNIMPORTANT
no u. people 3233

UNINTELLIGIBLE
leave rest of Scripture u. 743
Philosophers take simplest, turn into u. 8591

UNINTERESTED
no uninteresting things, only u. people 868

UNINTERESTING
no u. things, only uninterested people 868

UNINTERRUPTED
heaven, u. communion with God 5644

UNINTERRUPTEDLY
Just walk on u. and very quietly 5427

UNINVOLVED
God not u. 7556

UNION
at variance not likely to be in u. 5045
between the Father and Son a live concrete thing 11425
church u. is external 1387
Death consummation of u. with God 2257

Happiness u. of ourselves with God 5520
Mysticism art of u. with reality 7956
Prayer means raised up into u. with God 8909
product of organizing activity 1387
through pain seemed more real, holy 8269

UNIQUE
All God's works u. 4993
Every man u. being 6173
God is the most u. being 4993
infinite describes what is u. 4706
Jesus Christ is u. 9741
Jesus leaps in a u. way across the centuries 6448
Man's u. agony as a species 7415
nothing found that is not u. 4993
reading the Bible encountered a person as u. as any 4491
traditions identify family as u. 3876
You are u. 3039

UNIQUENESS
Creativity identical with God's u. 1999
Recognition of individual affirms u. of each person 9952
that gives freshness, vitality to a relationship 6197
water down u, lose freedom 1635

UNIT
family, basic u. of government 3888
family, basic u. of human organization 3880

UNITARY
God has no parts, single in u. being 4610

UNITE
contemplation and action 1766
salvation and comfort u. 9812
Silence will u. you to God 10245

UNITED
Be u. with other Christians 4020
fear of God to be u. with love of God 9736
Happiness is being u. to God and each other 4120
iron most strongly u. by fiercest flame 4273
men animated by love of Christ feel u. 3081
not presume to separate what God has u. 6681
Weak things u. become strong 11624

UNITED NATIONS
delegates to U. not as important 11027

UNITES
by love soul u. to God 7967
Doctrine divides, service u. 10129
explore what u. 9093

UNITING
Love capable of u. living beings
7208
Silent worship is u. 12114

UNITY
bad never at u. with one another
or themselves 5045
Christ provided u, not uniformity
1451
Church u. is internal 1387
creates strength 11623
entered into u. 2989
God is U. 11429
Good makes for u. 5025
Holiest Trinity, perfect in U.
11424
In necessary things, u. 7196
man, diversity in u. 7374
man, picturesque piece of
diversity in u. 6173
no u. where there is but one
11622
of God, can neither conceive nor
divide 4580
prayer for u. 9093
religious persons knit into u. 1413
result of spiritual, organic growth
1387
soul acting as a u. 7948
Trinity, act in harmonious u.
11422

UNIVERSAL
become channels of God's u. love
4768
church, most u. body in world
1277
Death more u. than life 6884
God the u. intelligence 4692
Indifference to evil more u. than
evil itself 3379
Jesus teaches u. love 913
language of soul 10676
perpetual yes of u. acquiescence
1645
Psalms, timeless and u. 797
Silence the u. refuge 10266
The only cheap and u. cure 5932

UNIVERSALITY
Apply test of u. 2494

UNIVERSALIZES
Love u. its concern 7274

UNIVERSALLY
strange to be known u, yet be so
lonely 7130

UNIVERSE
all that is decayed, abortive in u.
4997
all the u. in a grain of sand 1957
Before God created u. 4879
believer special to the God of the
u. 9999
Beneath you and external to you
7370
Boredom, when lose contact with
u. 866
continues to deal in extravagances
1971

corpse of the u. 483
cross, open house for u. 2155
denier of God, alone in u. 483
divine power shining in
continuing state of u. 11652
do not feel I am speck of dust in u.
11124
does not know it exists 1984
Engineer of u. made me part of
design 4565
find nothing lowly in the u. 11651
fortuitous concourse of atoms
1989
functions best when God's laws
obeyed 1520
God not tucked away in far
corner of u. 7556
God will look after the u. 2780
handful of sand anthology of u.
11625
Holiness a fire whose warmth
pervades u. 5741
How play with building blocks of
the u, fail to be touched by awe
9866
If God has spoken, why is u. not
convinced 4963
If silent, an exception to the u.
7997
inheritance from God all the u.
4694
is centered on God 11647
is not hostile 11648
is simply indifferent 11648
Man the greatest marvel in the u.
7497
master tapestry of the u. 12
more we learn about wonders of u.
11644
mosaic in design of God's u. 4005
moved God to choose order of u.
4989
Night conceals world, reveals u.
8083
no neutral ground in u. 4918
not free to act 1984
not friendly 11648
of u. God is final end 4514
one of God's thoughts 11251
Only God understands u. 11635
only one corner of u. certain of
improving 9953
ordinary people are restoring u.
1285
penny will hide biggest star in u.
7795
planet ball-bearing in hub of u.
11633
Satan must be most frustrated
personality in u. 9858
seems designed by mathematician
1974
Sorrow reigns on thrones of u.
10613
swallows me up like a speck
11268
thoughts overwhelm when
contemplating u. 698
through thought I grasp u. 11268

under reign of God 1285
war in u. price worth paying 4132
when this great u. lay in mind of
God 4769
whole show on fire 1971
whose vigor hurled a u. 6139
widest thing in u. not space 5625
wonderful, vast 1984
Worship is a soul in awe before
mystery of u. 12132

UNIVERSITIES
stamp civilization with own ideas
3040

UNIVERSITY
of election and predestination
11192
People hurry to get out of u. 3027

UNJUST
Ah, how u. to nature and himself
is thoughtless, thankless, man
3190
Christ died to save us from being
u. 6365
God of all mercy a God u. 4723
just slips upon snow u. doesn't
clear away 9905
materialistic status quo 8696
sun shine upon just and u. 4129
To forbear replying to an u.
reproach 6281

UNJUSTLY
He who acts u. acts u. to himself
6262
strengthen all persons u. accused
9104

UNKIND
as u. as if he had refused 10148
God too good to be u. 4990
Have deaf ear for u. remarks 9456
Keep us from u. words, u. silence
9106
learned kindness from u. 5251
Rich gifts poor when givers u.
4372
Thou art not so u. 6249

UNKINDNESS
you will meet with u. 10159

UNKNOWABLE
minds emotionally speculate on u.
4704

UNKNOWN
All we know infinitely less than
remains u. 6677
Before us a future all u. 5376
Behind the dim u. 5377
Better to love God and die u.
10777
Christ alone qualified to guide
into vast u. 2323
Confession brings to light u. 1596
Death not journey into u. land
2249
Death opens u. doors 2264
element that makes an idea an idea
2013

Eve, rather than leave that one u. 11053

fear, taunt with u. 3971

God chooses base, lowly, u. 3861

I faced a future all u. 5413

I lean upon thy love u. 4977

not an u. country, Christ is there 5659

out of self, into u. regions 9930

puts adventure into life 4318

safely into the U. 5417

single event can awaken within stranger u. to us 6873

something to sharpen souls on 4318

suffering u. to all others 10873

Thank God for u. future 4318

The Pilot knows the u. seas 5448

Wisdom like dawn that comes up slowly out of u. ocean 11969

UNLAWFUL

Covetousness has for mother u. desire 5313

to teach theory that denies divine creation 1986

UNLEARN'D

he knew no schoolman's subtle art 11957

UNLEARNING

repentance means u. self-conceit 9577

UNLIGHTED

Unshared joy is u. candle 4295

UNLIKE

operate in dimension totally u. our Lord 11606

UNLIMITED

heart capable of u. extension in all directions 5625

No man to be trusted with u. power 8714

power of evil u. if on earth alone 3377

power of God, limited power of Satan 4917

succeed if u. enthusiasm 3176

UNLIVED

future, live yet u. 4325

UNLOADS

as one u. one's heart to a dear friend 8970

UNLOCKS

Obedience is key that u. door 8101

Spring u. the flowers 9895

UNLOVABLE

Grace loves the u. 5222

Love means to love that which is u. 11691

UNLOVELY

Grace loves the u. 5222

is solitude of soul without God 10573

UNMAPPED

great deal of u. country within us 8669

UNMARKED

can choose to be bag of marbles, u. 9524

UNMASKS

Fortune u. men 11807

UNMEASURED

by the flight of years 5633

UNMERCIFUL

going to meet u. good and bad people, institutions, organizations 7746

UNMET

future opportunity yet u. 4325

UNMISTAKABLY

respond with love when u. wronged 6278

UNNATURAL

appears as if God were u. 896

for Christianity to be popular 1209

UNNECESSARY

display of knowledge is weakness 6694

No person absolutely u. 3446

systematically ascetic in u. points 8546

UNNOTICED

In u. offices the Son of God grew 10190

When love u. came to earth 6458

UNNUMBER'D

worlds attend 4672

UNOBTRUSIVE

God's way often insignificant and u. 4664

UNOCCUPIED

the mind cannot be 7764

UNOFFENDED

Learn the blessedness of the u. in face of the unexplainable 7727

UNOFFICIAL

saints always among u. crowd 9786

UNORTHODOX

our theology has been profoundly u. 6604

UNPARDONABLE

forgiving means to pardon that which is u. 11691

UNPERFECTED

Flesh is Bible's word for u. human nature 9926

UNPERPLEXED

God judging men with u. certainty 4720

UNPLEASANT

Cynicism u. way of saying truth 2180

self-centered people live in u. surroundings 10077

things not interruptions 2750

things one's real life 2750

UNPOPULAR

Chastity the most u. of Christian virtues 10237

progress resulted from people who took u. positions 9308

Truth-teller always u. 11501

UNPREDICTABLE

works of the Holy Spirit u. 5791

UNPRODUCTIVE

near close of u. career 8661

UNPROFITABLE

history shows how u. pride is 9218

How u. seem all uses of this world 2603

intellectual world u. if we knew everything 9286

UNPUNISHED

Reading, polite, u. vice 858

seeing that evils go u. 3349

UNQUENCHABLE

love becomes as coals deep-burning, u. 7236

UNQUESTIONABLY

Bible u. greatest of books 701

UNQUESTIONING

Spirit of God will expect u. obedience 5776

UNRAVELING

Prayer preserves life from u. 8953

UNREADY

God is ever ready, we are so u. 4562

UNREAL

regard unseen world as u. world 3812

UNREALITY

most real shadowy u. 1399

worse misfortune u. of life for rich 11854

UNREALIZED

Independence is u. weakness 6414

UNREASONABLE

for preacher to please all 9151

hope is as u. as indispensable 5903

load will be as intolerable as it is u. 12064

man adapts world to himself 980

progress depends on u. man 980

who think no need of others become u. 9506

UNRECOGNIZED

obstacle often u. opportunity 2711

UNRECORDED

years of u. duties 10190

UNREDEEMED
social compulsions of an u. world 10003

UNREGARDED
command to repent goes u. 4726

UNRELENTING
steady, u. approach of him whom I desired not to meet 9829

UNRELIEVED
Rest and motion u. and unchecked equally destructive 9685

UNRELIGIOUS
Christ did things apparently u. 6501

UNREMEMBERED
His little, nameless, u. acts 6664 626

UNREMITTING
And u. Energy, pervades 4711

UNREPENTED
by u. sin cut off sense of God 4864
sin is continued sin 9575

UNRESERVEDLY
conforming u. to that of God 9835

UNRESOLVABLES
good marriage overlooks u. 7591

UNREVEALED
guarantees guidance in matters u. 5435

UNROLLED
themselves unto thine eye, ear 4708

UNRULY
Man's chief enemy own u. nature 3165

UNSAID
Discretion is leaving a few things u. 2892
Leave some things u. 10279

UNSCRAMBLE
cannot u. eggs 1744

UNSEARCHABLE
God's Book, u. 656

UNSEASONABLE
Pride, u, unfitting 9231

UNSEEING
that we pass heedless, u. 9064

UNSEEMLY
specific requests to God u. 8821

UNSEEN
best servant does his work u. 10191
Christ the u. guest at every meal 5823
gigantic celebration in u. world 3326
he has u. companionship 10567

Jesus offends because emphasis on u. life 6450
noblest service comes from u. hands 10191
object of faith, u. reality 3831
praying saint performs havoc among u. forces of darkness 9014
regard u. world as unreal world 3812
spiritual creatures walk earth 362
things u. are eternal 3746
Through faith u. world takes shape 3812

UNSELFISH
least-used words by u. person 11653
Self-sacrifice never entirely u. 9763

UNSELFISHNESS
letting other people's lives alone 11654
magnet that will attract friends 4282
not interfering with people's lives 11654
recognizes variety of types as delightful 9512
turns burdens into life 10083

UNSETTLES
church, like yeast, u. mass 1427

UNSHAKABLE
vision of world unshaken, u. 3292

UNSHAKEN
vision of world u, unshakable 3292

UNSHARED
joy is unlighted candle 4295

UNSKILLED
Waiting upon God beats all work to one u. in it 7724

UNSLIPPING
Knit hearts with u. knot 7625

UNSOIL'D
Time u. and swift 11345

UNSOLVED
many things lie u. 8394

UNSPEAKABLE
harmony of u. splendors 3648
it is joy u. 7964
out of soul God coins u. riches 10666
should no longer be called u. 9411
Thanks to God for u. gift 1372
were works of God understandable, would be neither wonderful nor u. 4510

UNSPEAKABLY
Christ, u. wise 6499

UNSPIRITUAL
Whenever nation becomes u. 12194

UNSPOKEN
Conduct, u. sermon 554
God reads the prayer u. in my heart 7478
word u, you are master 1835

UNSPREADING
a rumor, difficult 5163

UNSTABLE
imagine God emotionally u. 4579

UNSTAINED
They have left u. 4114

UNSTEALABLE
time is u. 11356

UNSUCCESSFUL
men with talent common 8555

UNSUNG
Unwept, unhonored, and u. 10088

UNSURE
imagine God u. of himself 4579

UNSYMPATHETIC
because tone of voice u. 9516

UNTAINTED
Bible u. by error 710
What stronger breastplate than a heart u. 6320

UNTASTED
let no pleasure pass u. 11375

UNTELL
To u. the days and to redeem these hours 9568

UNTENABLE
belief that God will do everything for man u. 3415
belief that man can do everything u. 3415

UNTHANKFUL
God's mercy, not witholding abundance from u. 4581
wants which make us u. to God 2861

UNTHINKABLE
God is u. if we are innocent 5493

UNTHINKING
God not u. 7556

UNTIE
Let Lord u. the knots 2802
Never cut what you can u. 8401

UNTIL
friends are dead 4223
he died 4199
satisfied with fellowship with God 4311

UNTILLED
ground will bring thistles, thorns 7774
mind will bring thistles, thorns 7774

UNTOLD
world is full of u. novelties 8507

UNTOUCHABLE
Christ touched the u. 6433

UNTRAINED
find you not u. to stand the test 8546
Prayer cannot be seized by u. hands 8914

UNTRAVELED
future, path yet u. 4325

UNTRIED
Christian faith found difficult, left u. 1220

UNTROD
A dream of the vast u. 2964
Before us a path u. 5376

UNTROUBLED
People born u. 9777

UNTUNE
music shall u. the sky 7925

UNUSED
truth as useless as u. muscle 11583

UNUTTERABLE
element in Christian experience 12120

UNUTTERED
God knows every u. secret 4881

UNVEILS
in his Son, Jesus, God u. his very face 9706

UNWANTED
Nor feel u. at close of day 8145

UNWELCOMED
visitors bring blessings 832

UNWEPT
unhonored and unsung 10088

UNWILLING
as though God u. to fill us 4785
heart u. will find thousand excuses 7871
if u. to accept righteous reign of God 8818
if u. to give up my own sovereignty 8818

UNWILLINGNESS
difficulty as Christians stems from u. 1304
Honesty, u. to lie to others 5873
maturity, u. to lie to oneself 5873

UNWISE
To judge wisely must know how things appear to u. 6595

UNWORTHINESS
may dismay thee 3047

UNWORTHY
idolatry thoughts about God u. of him 6075
which no u. affection may drag downwards 9057
which no u. purpose may tempt aside 9057

UNWRAP
hidden beauties in ordinary day 2201

UNWRITTEN
Baby: U. history 805

UNYIELDING
Jesus has so long been identified with conservatism of u. sort 6452

UP
cannot be an u. without a down 5357
God is above, but not raised u. 4848
God's path is u. 7529
God's restrictions hold us u. 9558
Look u, not down 8379
man drags man down, or man lifts man u. 9522
Play it down, pray it u. 2606
Reach u. as far as you can 7514
saints experienced u. and down 2593
Success, getting u. more times than you fall 10804
Treasures in heaven laid u. only as 9565
world a ladder for some to go u, some down 7047

UPHEAVED
mountains are God's thoughts u. 8048

UPHEAVES
His hand u. the billows 4505

UPHILL
Does the road wind u. all the way 6885
Every u. has its downhill 6890

UPHOLSTERER
tidiness the u. of a happy home 5848

UPLIFT
concern always to u, never to tear down 6519

UPLIFTING
In confession we open lives to u. grace 1602

UPLOOK
Faith makes u. good 3705
When outlook bad, try u. 9030

UPPERTAKER
watching not for undertaker but u. 9913

UPRIGHT
be sturdy, u. in thinking 836
Give me an u. heart 9057
life based on self-realization 10044
Love is u. 7246
man's dignity to stand u. 7395
satanically managed man is u. 10044

UPRIGHTLY
we reform others when act u. 3457

UPRISING
prayer beginning of u. against disorder of world 9001

UPROAR
Golden Rule would reconcile political u. 5005
of the restless 9070

UPROOT
less easy to u. faults 3959
no fear wind will u. tree 6307

UPROOTED
without warning u. from earth-born securities 7488

UPROOTING
nothing else but love 7329

UPS
Life a tumble-about thing of u, downs 6955

UPSET
not be u. when unexpected happens 2887
talk about God, nobody gets u. 6518
what happens when gospel preached 5105
whole course of life u. 7046

UPSETS
Bible deals with u. 696
God's providence u. your timetable 11370
gospel, grain of sand that u. world's machinery 5099

UPSIDE
God makes shoes u. down 4668

UPSIDE DOWN
Christians who have turned world u. 11735
knock themselves and their world u. 8850

UPSTREAM
swimming u. 4094

UPTIGHT
both u. about evangelism 3303
than u. brother who squeaks, whines 9529

UPWARD
Faith is blind, except u. 3683
glancing of an eye 8939
If u. you can soar 460
love forces its way u. 7283
men who are lifting world u. 3142
our hands reach always u. 7575
Temptation provokes me to look u. 11089
to thee 10247
Vision looks u, becomes faith 11738

URGE
God first put u. within us 4573
restless u. to create 4643

URGENT
Life is always u. 11388

URGES
confidence in Christ u. us on 1611
Grace u. us to change, grow 5221
Though Bible u. us on to
    perfection 9254

URN
A little u. will contain all that
    remains 2442
A penny in the u. of poverty 6070

US
It is for u. to make the effort 4945
Joy is in u. 6541
Life is the test of u. 6932
people like u. are We 454

USE
ain't no u. putting up umbrella till
    it rains 12065
All of creation God gives to u.
    3191
Almighty does make u. of human
    agencies 4949
Anxiety has its u. 3961
Bible, bread for daily u. 715
day to u. strength given us 6947
everything as if it belongs to God
    10740
fault which humbles of more u.
    3931
for passions stuff given to us for
    happiness 4359
God knows how to u. disordered
    actions 4644
God to get a job 7517
God will disappoint man
    attempting to u. him 4468
God will u. us as piece of mosaic
    4005
God will u. you to further his ends
    10141
great u. of life 10189
Greatness lies in right u. of
    strength 5284
have talent, u. in every way
    possible 10993
Holy Spirit lifts personality to
    highest u. 5798
hope, of good u. while traveling
    through life 5924
How to u. thy noble powers 8671
How we u. our money 10016
If do not u. mind God has given us
    6693
It ain't no u. 37
It's up to me to u. it 11303
Life consist in the u. 2338
make u. of suffering 10935
men u. physical power 8715
most u. small portion of soul's
    resources 8659
no u. going back for lost
    opportunity 8226
no u. mounting on stilts 9248
no u. to pray for old days 8377
not much u. if not in right
    direction 5409
not only all brains I have, but all I
    can borrow 6795

Nothing is ordinary if you know
    how to u. 2010
obey better expressed by word *u.*
    8111
ordinary situations 5058
pray for them that u. us 5001
sharp tongue grows keener with u.
    11406
Talent, u. it or lose it 10995
things and love people 9510
To handle others, u. your heart
    9508
To handle yourself, u. your head
    9508
To shape and u. 2599
tragedy is failure to u. talent
    10997
tyrannous to u. strength like a
    giant 8707
understands u. of life 4204
we can but u. for ourselves 6178
What's u. of hurrying when 5591
who has great power should u. it
    lightly 8704
Wisdom is right u. of knowledge
    11973
wise man more u. from enemies
    than fool from friends 9444
wise men u. studies 2996

USED
future isn't what it u. to be 4327
intellect given to be u. for God's
    glory 10708
Life u. to condition us for eternity
    6944
People u. to need rest after work
    3114
Prosperity an instrument to be u.
    9340
psychological secrets Hilter,
    Mussolini u. 12178
to ask God to help me 4994
Work can be u. as defensive shield
    3904
wrong instruments being u. for job
    4739

USED UP
replaced, forgotten. That's a lie
    945

USEFUL
charity, to be u. without
    recompense 1084
Don't try and be u. 10141
Every man serves u. purpose
    11805
God makes u. something broken
    885
Love enough to be u. 1809
Passions u. in a thousand ways
    10234
to reap praise sow u. deeds 1574
Youth would rather do noble than
    u. deeds 12181

USEFULNESS
God disciplines for u. 2845
Neither u. nor duty God's purpose
    197

result of acceptance, humilities
    1807
who feel their time of u. is told
    8145

USELESS
aim which thwarts happiness
    4411
discussion apt to become worse
    than u. 4124
Education u. without Bible 3003
fear makes u. 3965
hell, weeping u. 5700
Integrity without knowledge u.
    3013
many time-consuming activities u.
    115
miserable feeling that u. to strive
    anymore 4507
No man is u. while he has friend
    4257
No one is u. in this world 10175
no prayer life, u. to make child
    say prayers 8348
O Lord, let me not live to be u.
    7008
Slip u. away 2198
Stumblers who give up u. 3618
Theological truth u. until obeyed
    11205
to put best foot forward, drag
    other 11601
trial only stops when it is u. 5352
Unused truth as u. as unused
    muscle 11583
who means well u. unless does
    well 6335

USES
bad person loves things and u.
    people 5041
God u. chronic pain, weakness
    8256
God u. experience to teach us
    10306
God u. our sins to remind us of
    weakness 10306
good person loves people, u. things
    5041
How weary seem all u. of this
    world 2603
Is it progress if cannibal u. fork
    9313
saint u. commands of Lord 8111
spiritual power u. men 8715
war u. man's best to do man's
    worst 11763
Young people, why God u. them
    so often 12177

USHERING
in new age, new dimension of
    existence 5711

USHERS
Some churches train their u. to
    smile 6062

USING
So many are busy "u." God 7517
temptation in u. riches 11865

not in what one attains 11664
obtain too easy, v. too lightly 8563
of good works based on love of God 10115
of good works not based on number 10115
of marriage that children produce adults 7669
only one who can see v. of being humbled 6007
Reality has not news v. 9404
seldom known until lost 4292
submission will mean loss of all we v. 11768
teach me v. of my thorn 2099
to bring life to highest v. 5044
Vice a mistake in estimating v. 10410
we v. health, God values patience 11667
what you miss, not what you have 11669
When meaning goes, v. goes 4437
would be no v. in obedience 8091

VALUED
Children must be v. as priceless possession 1115

VALUES
believer makes his decisions on eternal v. 10707
Bible asserts spiritual v. 701
church often in conflict with v. 1385
Church, new order, new v. 1385
cleavage between truths we affirm, v. we live by 6068
difference between Christian love, and v. of world evident 6278
false v. brought into evangelical favor 11666
family established society's basic v. 3888
God v. not your deeds 7864
God wants to give new v. 7863
God's v. differ from ours 11667
into the soil of life's enduring v. 9111
kind of faith God v. 3789
live by same v. Jesus had 3313
one-sided v. never sufficient 8634
Only eternal v. give meaning to temporal ones 11311
religious v. into higher or lower case 11658
response to assault reveal v. by which you live 6288
single decade to lay foundation of v. 8314
television insinuates false v. 11031
warped view of God's v. 3861
we value health, God v. patience 11667
which Christ declared false 11666
wise lover v. love of the giver 7157
Worldliness accepting v. of man-centered society 12053
Worldliness twists v. by rearranging price tags 12054

VANGUARD
Christians should be in v. 1277

VANISH
comforts v. 7291

VANISHES
As soon as danger past, devotion v. 8788
Happiness v. when envy appears 3218
meaning unfolds and strangeness v. 6145
Sleep v. before house of care 10488

VANISHING
do not find v. acts amusing 2303

VANITIES
Love is not intent on v. 7246
Two v. can never love one another 9256

VANITY
asks, "Is it popular" 1679
can give no hollow aid 10530
creatures motivated by v. 9518
Criticism's child 2050
solitude without fellowship abyss of v. 10547
will end in v. 9467

VANQUISHED
Hell today is v. 2986
In war no victor and v. 11752
unless Reason v. way will not be open 7950

VAPOR
Fame is v. 1010

VARIABILITY
one of the virtues of a woman 7663

VARIABLE
people as v. as the wind 9521

VARIANCE
anything at v. with itself 5045

VARIED
life runs quick through v. range 973
where evil is v. and attractive 3347

VARIES
Civilization v. with the family 3868
concept of spirituality v. among groups 10713
family v. with civilization 3868

VARIETY
as landscapes their v. from light 103
Bible's v. like scenes of nature 680
outside home is adventure, v. 5842
Unselfishness recognizes v. of types as delightful 9512

VARIOUS
All revolutions v. parts of same scheme 4898
God, inexhaustibly v. 4503

VARY
Emotion may v. in religious experience 3052
truth does not v. because men ignore 11540

VASE
I am the v. of God 4852

VAST
A dream of the v. untrod 2964
And v. eternity 4676
Divinity, so v. all thoughts lost in immensity 4745
God speaks to us of plan v. in scale 4900
God's love a v. bottomless, shoreless sea 4750
In the v. and the minute we see 1963
life, a v. obscure unfinished masterpiece 6904
mind of God so v. and deep 4675
neurotic misery of world 4437
Spirit of God will enfold you in a love so v. 5776
truth being infinite is v. 11550
Would sink forever thro' the v. profound 4708

VASTLY
God is so v. wonderful 7463

VASTNESS
Bible's v. like bottom of sea 680
hint of the everlasting in v. of sea 3290

VEHEMENTLY
youth doing things excessively, v. 12181

VEHICLE
Bible, v. to express thoughts that overwhelm 698

VEIL
casting aside of v. after v. 4906
Humility is a divine v. 6005
I would not lift the v. 9072
made of living spiritual tissue 2097
of future woven by hand of mercy 4330
rending of v. 2097
revelation, casting aside of v. after v. 9706
Self the opaque v. that hides God 9945

VEILED
deep inner work v. to eye of man 10706

VEINS
twining through v. 6131

VENERABLE
children understand better than v. 1216
love of God v. as father's love for child 4792

VENGEANCE
Can v. be pursued further than
  death 9716
descending to their level in v. 9730

VENOM
legalism spreads paralyzing v.
  6823
When snake is dead, v. dead 3419

VENTILATOR
industry must be the v. 5848

VENTRILOQUIST
I wish I were a great v. 870

VENTURE
baptism of Holy Ghost does not
  mean put into great v. for God
  5789
Faith a terrific v. in the dark 3668
To those who v. into space 11628

VENTURES
where man never v. 1715

VENTURING
forth we know not where 9930

VERB
God, why not a v. 4520

VERBAL
Honesty, an absence of v.
  superficiality 5874

VERBS
Life in Christ string of action v.
  1235

VERDICT
kneeling awaiting his v. on us
  3333
makes Christ stand hat-in-hand
  awaiting v. 3333

VERIFIED
experience must be v. by Word of
  God 3550
If it can be v. we don't need faith
  3740

VERITCAL
Wisdom is v, comes down from
  above 11928

VERNACULAR
If you can't turn faith into v. 3741

VERSE
single v. of Bible may be dangerous
  642
some stab fingers at v. 693

VERSUS
will v. will, punch v. punch 1622

VESSEL
Do not look upon the v, but upon
  what it holds 6297
empty v. makes greatest sound
  4066
Moor the v. with a thread of silk
  9233
that grows as filled will never be
  full 10699
Unless v. clean what you pour
  turns sour 1054

VESSELS
Satan watches for v. that sail
  without convoy 2664
We are the v. 4537

VESTIBULE
world is v. of eternity 6670

VESTING
Without whose v. beauty 7109

VESTMENT
Hope will put on patience as a v.
  5912

VEX
if troubles large enough to v. 4789

VIBRANT
church intended to be v. 1414
Tune me, Lord, into one full v.
  chord 7928

VIBRATES
Every good deed touches chord
  that v. in heaven 6670

VICAR
Conscience, true v. of Christ 1673

VICE
acquired without a tutor 11725
After one v, greater follows 10293
Concealed goodness a sort of v.
  5056
essential v. is pride 9240
false moral arithmetic 10410
Hypocrisy homage v. pays to
  virtue 6051
In people's eyes I read malice, v.
  3571
is ignorance 11724
is its own punishment 10298
is sickness 11726
miscalculation of chances 10410
mistake in estimating value 10410
never an instant's truce between
  virtue, v. 11700
prefer comfortable v. to virtue
  that bores 3941
Pride leads to every other v. 9240
quickly creeps in 11725
Reading, polite, unpunished v.
  858
repeated like wandr'ing wind
  10411
Slander v. that strikes double blow
  10463
stings even in pleasures 10412
when one associates with v. 10326
who is kept from v. by punishment
  11723
wore v. like a garment 10320

VICES
bids others think of his v. 9207
creep in under name of virtues
  10413
denouncing people's v, faults 1162
familiar we pardon 10414
if we trample them underfoot
  10420
more apt to catch v. than virtues
  4286

more liable to catch v. than virtues
  9514
new ones we rebuke 10414
not so great a struggle with my v.
  6115
once v, now manners 3958
tempt by rewards they offer 11101
through indulgence in own v.
  10503
Virtue is not absence of v. 11709
virtues are frequently v. disguised
  6060
We make ladder of our v. 10420
wish to be saved from mischief of
  v, but not v. 10338

VICIOUS
one v. or thoughtless kick destroys
  7233
response to v. attack reveal values
  6288

VICTIM
fall v. to adult influences 1105
fall v. to mass entertainment 1105
Independent of God, v. of
  circumstances 1480

VICTIMS
God wants us victors, not v. 1608
man only animal on friendly
  terms with v. 7585
of philosophy of activism 130
people more easily fall v. to a great
  lie than to small one 7974

VICTOR
In war no v. and vanquished
  11752

VICTORIES
all eternity to celebrate our v.
  3293
destructive v. won over others
  1165
God's defeats of us are our v.
  11673
Little v. over temptations, silent
  threads of gold 6997
make efforts but win no v. 6813
most significant witness not v. but
  defeat 2518
one short hour to win v. 3293
over evil, self 1165
remember your v. 9270
some defeats more triumph than v.
  2514

VICTORIOUS
emerge lame but v. at dawn 9777
life is Christ's business 11672

VICTORIOUSLY
God brings us through v. 165

VICTORS
God wants us v, not victims 1608
If another war, no v. only losers
  11749
Neglect of prayer guarantee not v.
  8872

VICTORY
comes through defeat 2519

Defeat may serve as well as v. 2508

finds a hundred fathers 2516

first step to v. is to recognize enemy 11670

follows in justice's train 6628

found in Christ Jesus, not in some formula 7105

God does not promise final v. in this life 5385

good general knows when v. impossible 8485

good general sees way to v. 8485

He that perseveres makes every contest a v. 8542

Holiness is v. through conflict 5743

in service to be expected 10206

Jesus' v. lies in defeat 6443

never so near to v. as when defeated 2511

no packages of spiritual v. sent special delivery 1013

O grave! Where is thy v. 2389

of science reveals more clearly divine design 9866

other side pray, too, for v. 9021

praying to God to give v. 9021

Psalms, triumph of man's v. 798

saints have their v. 5301

smile of God is v. 11671

task with vision is v. 12006

Thou lover's v. 5932

to one who believes, life is v. 607

triumphant Christian celebrates v. already won 11672

triumphant Christian does not fight for v. 11672

twilight that knows not v. 1922

well to stop using terms v. and defeat 5753

VIEW

Darkness is my point of v. 7106

different v. of church, ministry 2987

event which Creator of world has in v. 4898

God does not v. the fruit 7864

God helps us v. world from new perspective 4735

hours with happy prospects in v. pleasing 3508

learn how to v. others with humility 10306

light is God's point of v. 7106

Man judges from a partial v. 6583

more reverent v. of God 4720

must scale mountain if v. plain 8562

natural v. and Bible v. of man different 7429

Others may v. results 10706

problems as opportunities 2726

temptation to be like God eclipsed v. of God 4419

totally new point of v. 9827

Transported with the v, I'm lost 4819

warped v. of God's values 3861

Worship to see world from point of v. of God 12133

your point of v. is everything 8517

VIEWED

mystery doctrine v. on side unilluminated 7937

revelation doctrine v. on illuminated side 7937

VIEWETH

sun with one eye v. world 11645

VIEWPOINT

desire to see everything from God's v. 10719

VIEWS

book that agrees with our v. 11216

less satisfied with superficial v. of Christ 6480

Religion is good v. 9545

VIGILANCE

When good people cease v, evil men prevail 7991

VIGILANT

over child lest frosts of May nip his blossoms 8282

over thy child in April of his understanding 8282

VIGOR

eccentricity proportional to v. 1007

inaction saps v. of the mind 6765

whose v. hurled a universe 6139

world without children, without v. 1104

VIGOROUS

Hope is a v. principle 5917

Love is v. 7246

VILE

God clothed himself in v. man's flesh 6126

To the v. dust from whence he sprung 10088

VILEST

tell God you prefer v. amusements 8830

VILLAGE

let it ring from every v. 4157

soon living in electronic v. 4332

VILLAIN

like v. with smiling cheek 5011

One may smile and smile and be a v. 6059

One murder makes a v. 11758

VILLAS

preaches from v. to slums about mansions in heaven 6065

VINDICATE

Truth ere long shall appear to v. 10448

VINDICATES

God never v. himself 4891

God scarcely v. his saints to men 11616

VINDICATING

deliver me from lust of v. myself 9722

VINDICTIVE

I don't believe in v. God 9354

VINDICTIVENESS

to triumph without v. 11775

VINEGAR

easier to catch flies with honey than v. 6643

Lord has given me v. and honey 2728

Lord has given v. with teaspoon 2728

men, some turn to v. 7419

truly tastes bitter 2147

VINEYARDS

performing quickly the slow miracle in v. 6513

VIOLATE

never v. laws of God without consequences 10336

VIOLATES

war v. order of nature 11751

VIOLENCE

a crime against humanity 11678

church, force for peace in world of v. 1433

Covetousness has for friend, v. 5313

cross a picture of v. 2145

defeats its own ends 11677

destroys dignity 11678

destroys fabric of society 11678

destroys freedom of human beings 11678

destroys life 11678

destroys what it defends 11678

done to us by others less painful 11676

goes against truth of humanity 11678

goes against truth of our faith 11678

is a lie 11678

less painful than v. we do to ourselves 11676

multiplies v. 11675

Perseverance more prevailing than v. 8552

what v. fails to accomplish 4403

who achieves power by v. 11674

Young men lose lives by v. 12197

VIOLENT

a v. injustice 6258

Christ's words provoked v. rejection 6377

God's often v. intrusions into history 9710

hatred sinks us below those we hate 5603

too v. rigor tempts chastity 3554

VIOLIN

Life like playing v. solo in public 6967

VIRTUOUSNESS
flee into sanctuary of private v. 11690

VIRUS
soul weakened by v. of pride 10436

VISIBLE
atheist without v. support 474
God knows all things v. and invisible 4881
heart transcends all v. things 4749
however small v. measure of our lives 6232
majority best way because v. 5191
Stronger, deeper roots less v. 7703

VISION
Ah! for a v. of God 7448
and a task is hope of world 11730
anything that dims my v. of Christ 7036
art of seeing things invisible 11737
attempt to communicate v. 6169
Beyond our v. weak and dim 10204
Christians with v. in hearts, Bible in hands 11735
encompasses vast vista 11736
Give us clear v. 11731
God leading world with v. of truth 4474
great man's world bounded by limits of v. 11728
high ecstasy of v. 2856
if had keen v. of all that is ordinary in life 8496
impaired by cataracts of sin 10436
Light'ning their eyes to v. and adoring 8454
look at Jesus to correct blurry v. 4489
looks inward, becomes duty 11738
looks outward, becomes aspiration 11738
looks upward, becomes faith 11738
man with v. of God devoted to God himself 11729
No masses of earth can block God's v. 4883
no v. of eternity, never get hold of time 3272
of holiness of God 4660
of world unshaken, unshakable 3292
outside realm of predictable 11736
poor v. limits deeds 11734
Sainthood gives v. that can find good in criminals 9778
sufficient v. left to lift eyes to hills 10436
task with v. is victory 12006
task without a v. a drudgery 11730
tears prepare for clearer v. of God 11024

Wesley communicated v. of King 9740
when mind not in v. of God 4989
which is muddied 6931
without task a dream 12006

VISIONARY
Christ, not v. 1154

VISIONS
Whenever v. of God unfit us for practical life 5466

VISIT
Christ will v. you often 5529
closet of prayer, more you v. more you will return 9039
God plans personal v. to his own world 6127
I stop in for a v. 1391
No one can be caught in place he does not v. 5484
only here for short v. 9530

VISITANT
Pleasure oft a v. 8271

VISITED
with deliberate purpose, God v. this planet 6144

VISITING
God is v. for consolation 4514

VISITORS
Fish, v. smell in three days 5956
Sorrows v. that come without invitation 10622
Unwelcomed v. bring blessings 832

VISITS
God often v. us 4546
Jesus Christ, v. frequent 6352

VISTA
Christ providing a v. 6434
higher the hill, wider the v. 3488

VISTAS
Vision encompasses vast v. 11736

VITAL
Brokenness, v. step toward revival 881
character v. to society's survival 3880
genuine Christianity has always v. throb of praise 6251
like God to make most v. thing easy 3737
Love for Lord most v. love 7221

VITALITY
uniqueness that gives v. to a relationship 6197

VIVACITY
smiles brighten by their spiritual v. 10500

VIVID
And v. lightings flash from pole to pole 4827
God asks for something v. 4507

VIXENS
To snap like v. at the truth 5048

VOCABULARY
add a word a day to v. 1853
most important words in v. 11994
word snob belongs to sourgrape v. 457

VOCAL
A God, a God! the v. hills reply 6138

VOCATION
Heaven is the Christian's v. 3095
sees greater in v. than bread, butter 3107

VOCATIONAL
Whenever v. activities develop qualities 5014

VOICE
A deeper v. across the room 3644
A v. in the wind I do not know 4962
Affliction able to drown out earthly v. 274
And that v. still soundeth on 6497
behind the thunder, still, small v. 1515
Being in right does not depend on loud v. 11905
can be heard, this v. within 274
Christian, v. through which Christ speaks 1248
Conscience v. that makes you feel smaller 1672
Deep within us, a speaking v. 1757
for which he listened 4965
give few men thy v. 1843
God draws us by v. in soul 7949
God's v. in response to mine 8932
God, the V. in my silence 6907
God, v. deafening in its thunderousness 4465
Has not the whole earth a v. 7997
heard your v. behind me telling me to return 9070
holy life a v. 5735
human v, the perfect instrument 7893
I hear his v. among the trees 7452
impulse of love is v. of God within 4278
In the valley God is tuning thy v. 10600
inner v. of God does not argue 4967
is a second face 1883
listen for v. of God, learn of him 4964
Love suffers as the v. sings 7953
Mine was the boat, his the v. 1147
Nothing is without v. 8029
nothing swifter in life than v. of rumor 5142
of eternity cannot drown 274
of forgiveness louder 4100
of God a friendly v. 4966
of God just speaks 4967
of God self-authenticating 4967

VOICELESS

of God, too still to be easily audible 4465

of intelligence soft and weak 6331

of parents is v. of gods to their children 5856

of sin is loud 4100

of subconscious argues 4967

Of v. uplifted from the sod 8926

prayer v. of man to God 9704

Reason's v. and God's 3813

revelation v. of God to man 9704

rises to heaven when you praise 8725

Silent worship enables us to hear v. of God 12114

spirituality an echo of God's v. 5981

that gentle, inward v. 8813

there came a v. 5415

This coward with pathetic v. 2583

through the darkness heard 7943

tone of v. unsympathetic 9516

very noise of the siege will drown still small v. 8854

Which binds us to the infinite, the v. 3700

within zone of God's v, profoundly altered 7540

Worship v. in night calling for help 12132

Yet 'tis thy v, my God, that bids them fly 4827

You know no disturbing v. 4969

VOICELESS

In v. prayer 10969

VOICES

are saying, "Let it all hang out" 9976

deaf cannot hear v. of dearest friends 9094

Earth with thousand v. praises God 2973

irrelevant v. brought to silence 274

lament our v. must be silent 7056

Of their great v. uttering endless love 4708

Raised v. lower esteem 9488

stillness of nature louder than choir of v. 8041

thousand v. clamor for attention 7447

VOID

Fall on the seeming v, and find 3767

let the illimitable v. of space 4712

Nothing v. of God, he fills his work 4860

VOIDS

sins attempts to fill v. 10295

VOLTAIRE

Mock on, mock on, V. 596

VOLUME

all mankind of one v. 5966

Every man is a v. 6172

How endless is v. God has written of world 6901

man a v. if you know how to read him 8490

VOLUMES

Jesus furnished themes for more learned v. 6449

VOLUNTARILY

happiness is v. united to God 4120

VOLUNTARY

cross, v. sacrifice 2118

how can v. act of self-surrender be involuntary 9799

VOLUNTEERS

God calls for v. to oppose evil 3378

VOTE

afraid of men who v. for everything 586

Man has the casting v. 9175

VOTES

Man v. breaks tie 1145

VOTING

devil v. against man 1145

Lord always v. for man 1145

VOUCHSAFES

God v. to speak to us one by one 6178

VOWED

never to marry until found ideal woman 7665

VOWS

greatness in adherence to v. given 5283

VOYAGE

as we v. along through life 4432

Death a v. home 2249

Life a v. that's homeward bound 6956

shall go on planned v. 5945

through time to eternity 3689

VULGAR

no desire, however v. we may not lay before God 7536

VULNERABILITY

darkness potential for v. 2612

God sides with poor because of v. 6630

nothing else but love 7329

VULNERABLE

cross hurts where disarmed v. 2092

W

WADE

Hope will w. through sea of blood 5912

What tho' we w. in wealth, or soar in fame 7088

Where reason cannot w, faith may swim 3821

WAGES

will serve devil for better w. 2646

WAGING

wars that cause blood to flow 4895

WAGON

God sometimes puts springs in w. 4808

worst wheel of w. that screeches 1562

WAGS

dog w. tail instead of tongue 9499

WAIF

man without purpose, a w. 4436

WAILING

of newborn infant mingled with dirge for the dead 7043

WAIT

All comes to him who knows how to w. 8391

also serve who only stand and w. 10202

and God will come 5460

assurance to w. patiently 3744

cross is everywhere in w. for you 2105

Do not w. for extraordinary circumstances 5058

Do not w. to do good actions 623

for wisest of counselors, time 11347

God alters things while we w. 8395

God never comes to those who do not w. 5460

if patient, can w. much faster 8400

in darkness long as necessary 2557

in quietness until light in darkness 3718

Love can w. and worship endlessly 7353

must w. for God 5460

My work is done, why w. 10942

Never w. for fitter time or place to talk to God 8874

on Lord in prayer as you sit on freeway 8424

opportunities to train ourselves to w. on the Lord 8421

Optimists do not w. for improvement 8238

Prayer is to w. till one hears God speak 8935

Rather than fighting w. 2556

Simply w. upon God 5440

so long as stationary, w. 5444

so long will I w. or look for mercy 2590

Still round the corner there may w. 8239

the great teacher death, and God adore 5913

the muffled oar 6916

Time too slow for those who w. 11333

to w. often harder than to work 8418

tragedy of life is we w. so long to begin it 7042

Understanding can w, obedience cannot 8114

upon Lord, renew strength 10764

upon men, dissipate energies 10764

when doubt, w. 5402

WAITING

All heaven w. to help 5373

angels are w. for me 2445

Do not keep me w. 2301

God is w. for me 2451

God w. for us to recognize him 8843

High Priest w. to receive me 716

in the Divine garage 8181

In w. the Son of God grew 10190

In working or in w, another year with thee 8077

jump from worship to w. to work 10716

Never become irritable while w. 8400

obtain the most precious gifts by w. for them 8425

Patience, w. without anxiety 8414

Patient w. often highest way of doing God's will 8416

Quiet w. before the Lord 8957

see God w. at the open door 7085

to come up flower in Gardener's time 5672

to hush our latest breath 2219

upon God not idleness 7724

upon God work which beats all work 7724

Whatsoever may be w. 10112

youth eagerly w. for play to begin 12168

WAITS

for chance never sure of dinner 8215

Hate w. only to be provoked 7265

he who w. to be righteous will never enter 10402

He who w. to do great deal of good at once 5071

How long God w. for us to learn lesson 7056

mosquito never w. for an opening 8223

only the completion of present task 9658

Though the fool w, the day does not 6780

who w. to be asked for help, unkind 10148

WAKE

at three, live an hour with God 8794

for shame, my sluggish heart 8671

One short sleep past, we w. eternally 2356

others w. from sermon refreshed 10094

To w. the morn, sentinel the night 11344

When people sleep in church, preacher should w. up 9171

when w. January 2 world will look same 8080

when we w. and when we sleep 362

WAKED

long ere echoes w. the solitudes 4769

WAKES

heart oft times w. when we sleep 2969

soul w. and grows 9940

to find God there 4847

WAKING

and finding it home 2399

in dreams act part learned in w. hours 2966

WALK

and told it to w. 1982

Angels guard you when you w. 356

as we w. tightrope of life 6715

At cool of day, with God I w. 7452

beside me, be my friend 4224

Do not w. through time without 11292

Don't w. behind me, I may not lead 4224

emerging will never w. alone 10567

Faith will lead you where you cannot w. 3716

friend will silently w. with you 4175

God cannot make us w. 1143

God will listen as you w. 8874

I do not ask to w. smooth paths 1927

I never w. back 82

I w. through the Lord's goodness almost with difficulty 4646

I wonder how I am ever to w. to the end 7090

I would rather w. with God in the dark 5419

I'd rather one should w. with me 10098

If head wax, don't w. in sun 11918

If we w. in the woods 1733

indicative of our w. with God 1331

Let thy soul w. slowly in thee 10256

like a child w. with thee down all my days 9051

Love asks us to w. many miles 7273

Man alone has capacity to w, talk with God 7497

man likes to go alone for w. 1639

Men who w. with God would not grieve enemies 3166

more depends on w. than talk 3443

need new strength to w. old paths 9554

O for a closer w. with God 7507

on uninterruptedly and very quietly 5427

ones who w. alone 179

Ride less and w. more 9281

see him w, know his thoughts 8494

So shall I w. aright 5412

softly 576

spend three years teaching child to w. 8336

take our Lord's hand and w. through things 5374

those who w. on well-trodden path throw stones 1643

to w. into nowhere 4982

To w. out of his will 4982

Truth may w. around naked 6869

When you w. with God, you get where he's going 5465

with the world, can't w. with God 12034

WALKED

a mile with Pleasure 10596

a mile with Sorrow 10596

Don't judge any man until w. in his moccasins 6574

hard flints to be w. over 10165

until I have w. in his moccasins for two weeks 9065

WALKER

I'm a slow w. 82

WALKING

Faith w. in dark with God 3714

God's way becomes plain when start w. 5404

I can't see my brother when he's w. past 5587

Life's but a w. shadow 6994

man without faith, a w. corpse 3791

ordained by God 7038

than man keep straight line w. in dark 6614

WALKS

Benighted w. under midday sun 1683

Christian who squeaks when he w. 9529

for all the w. I want to take 11301

God w. among pots and pipkins 5826

God w. everywhere incognito 4871

God w. with us as of old 7996

He w. with God, he lives like Christ 1015

man leaves footprints when w. through life 6231

Whosoever w. toward God one cubit 7573

WALL

bad to lean against falling w. 3380

will continue 11782

would end if dead could return 11774

Youth must inherit aftermath of w. 11757

WARD

to w. off bolts of divine wrath 4998

WARFARE

God himself fights for the soul 2734

Life is w. 6981

prayer not prattle, is w. 8871

Strength'ning their arms to w. glad and grim 8454

WARLIKE

best soldier is not w. 11784

WARM

can't get w. on another's fur coat 6782

hand on a cold morning 438

I'll wrap him w. with love 6134

if world seems cold, kindle fires to w. it 5959

in joy a w. effluence of love 6537

let us w. ourselves 43

One kind word can w. three winter months 6662

right temperature at home maintained by w. hearts 5855

Virtue, though in rags, will keep w. 11715

WARMED

home must be w. by affection 5848

WARMER

advancing in life whose blood w. 6898

If only I may grow w. 7688

WARMHEARTED

Holy Spirit will make man w. 1064

WARMING

in the fire feel God's heart w. 4858

WARMS

Forgiveness w. heart 4075

friend w. by his presence 4179

WARMTH

even for people blessed with w. of heart 7304

gospel w. which penetrates heart 732

Holiness a fire whose w. pervades universe 5741

love, like w. should beam forth 3839

Mother is w. 7853

stronger than force, fury 4296

with Christ, life and w. of full day head 7094

WARNING

friction with body w. 847

thorn of experience worth wilderness of w. 3540

without w. uprooted from earth-born securities 7488

WARNS

Conscience w. us as a friend 1677

Conscience w. us someone may be looking 1671

friend one who w. you 4171

WARPED

view of God's values 3861

WARPING

twisting, w. innocent family members 3873

WARRANT

for believing God cares 4779

is the Word of God, naught else is worth believing 9813

WARS

Gold does civil w. create 11811

If Christian nations were nations of Christians, would be no w. 11748

just which are ordained by God 11743

No kingdom with as many w. as kingdom of Christ 1215

No self-respecting wolf guilty of our w. 10361

souls are battlegrounds for civil w. 6068

waging w. that cause blood to flow 4895

within world, reflection of w. inside people 11764

world started with w, shall be destroyed with w. 11765

WAS

ain't what we w. 9825

From the wonderful w, by the wonderful is 4313

God is where he w. 4849

WASH

life like going through car w. on bicycle 7023

WASH'D

rose is sweetest w. with morning dew 7309

WASHED

guilt w. out by repentance 10419

Only eyes w. by tears see clearly 2555

there are feet to be w. 10165

WASHES

Music w. away dust of life 7912

WASHING

rainbow is ribbon nature puts on after w. hair 9391

WASHINGTON

discrimination and Booker T. W. 161

remarkable thing about W. 7981

snows of Valley Forge and George W. 161

task before me greater than that rested upon W. 5179

WASMS

isms of youth the w. of age 12174

WASTE

day is time no one wealthy enough to w. 2191

day too dear to w. a moment on yesterdays 8375

great haste makes great w. 5588

is to w. person you are 6217

Regret an appalling w. of energy 9440

Remind us not to w. your creation 9117

to ask God to do is to w. prayers 10199

to attempt to do is to w. efforts 10199

tragic w. of truth 3758

we lay w. our powers 12046

Without God life a shortless, trackless w. 7098

WASTED

As wholly w, wholly vain 3538

How I have w. half my day 9049

I will consider my earthly existence w. 6919

Sympathy never w. except when give to yourself 10981

WASTES

Satan w. no ammunitions on those in sins 9860

way will be made through w. 5444

WATCH

Be true to God, w. 1549

cannot dream w. exists and has no watchmaker 12038

frustrations melt into praise 8424

keeping w. above his own 5377

Love alone his w. is keeping 1123

must w. what we teach 5818

Plant love and w. what happens 7289

right, clocks in town wrong 2803

Stand aside and w. yourself go by 10009

takes little effort to w. man carry load 6160

that you do what you should do 9912

thing to w. is our strength 10760

Yet mine eyes the w. do keep 1514

WATCHES

God w. to see door move from within 4775

one who w. others suffering disbelieves in God 10936

Satan w. for vessels that sail without convoy 2664

WATCHFUL

And guard me with a w. eye 9350

in effort to be w. become suspicious 9502

Love is w. 7246

WATCHFULNESS

deep relationship requires w. 9446

WATCHING

elite would have looked to see if anyone w. 6147

not for undertaker but for uppertaker 9913

Snow is beautiful when w. other fellow shovel 9904

WATCHWORD

Now is w. of the wise 11361

WATER

able to make this w. calm 9098

as w. willing to flow into emptied channel 4785

believe in getting into hot w. 11435

Dirty w. does not wash clean 2462

Don't pour away w. because of mirage 2806

down God-given individuality 1635

drown by staying in w. 3636

fire quenched by w. 372

free for the taking 3838

Happiness the light on the w. 5527

heart of wise man lies quiet like limpid w. 11944

if longing heart finds living w, will be alone 10536

in the w. God's gentleness to refresh you 4858

into wine, performing quickly slow miracle in vineyards 6513

is cold, dark, deep 5527

life flowing like w. through fingers 8381

Little drops of w. 6659

man who never alters opinion like standing w. 9185

no more w. than a newborn puppy 446

no vacuum into which God's deep w. may rise 9938

One drop of w. for my soul 7003

Only a fool tests depth of w. with both feet 11936

shapes itself to vessel 1463

Sins like circles in w. 10383

Small drops of w. hollow out a stone 8556

stagnant w. loses its purity 6765

streams of living w. flowing 5810

trying to hold w. in hands 5519

virtues we write in w. 9619

well's dry, we know worth of w. 444

why green grass and liquid w. 12037

With the wonderful w. round you curled 8010

Works without faith like fish without w. 3826

You don't drown by falling in w. 3636

WATERED

But it is fed and w. 4625

Friendship plant which must often be w. 4231

WATERMELON

when you can explain mystery of w. 7939

WATERS

And I like a little fish in thy great w. 7492

cast bread upon w. while seasick 4373

Christ is living w. 6370

Only in quiet w. things mirror themselves undistorted 7718

other w. continually flowing 985

Still w. run deep 10267

Through quiet w, stormy weather 4281

until justice rolls down like w. 6629

we want still w. 229

would not part w. of sea 967

WAVE

can never ride on w. that went out yesterday 8372

Eternity is the ocean, time the w. 3267

impression like w. of electricity going through me 5797

little w. of emotion enough for many 4471

we often see only ebb of advancing w. 5944

WAVERING

Christian no respect from church, world 2771

WAVES

as w. make toward pebbled shore 2329

easy to hear music in w. 8034

Its w. no further swell 4813

need not always destroy 2798

of liquid love 5797

so well-controlled very few w. of glory 3184

WAX

If head w, don't walk in sun 11918

WAY

a man dies more important than death itself 2336

A wonderful w. is the King's Highway 4313

able to thank Creator for w. he made us 9993

Abraham did not know the w. 5372

afterwards we see we had to go that w. 5423

Almighty finds a w. of letting me know 5410

And Christ our Lord the w. hath trod 2219

and ways, and a w. 10679

anyone happier because you passed his w. 3136

best w. for child to learn to fear God 8327

best w. of living, suffering, dying 742

best w. to keep from stepping on toes 11286

best w. to keep is to let go 4733

better to ask w. ten times 5424

can do small things in great w. 10155

Can I discern my w. 5434

Christ as man is w. by which we go 6364

Christ offering a w. of release 6434

Christ the only w. to approach God 6372

Christ the W. unchangeable 6397

Christ will never strong-arm his w. into your life 6438

coming of Christ by w. of Bethlehem manger 6145

comparison game sure w. to poor self-image 6208

Death God's w. of giving life 2246

Death nature's way to slow down 2248

devil leads downward, fiddles all the w. 2697

discouragement when we insist on our own w. 2879

dispense wealth best w. to preserve it 11870

distasteful, w. which leads to himself 1717

Does the road wind uphill all the w. 6885

easiest w. to dignity is humility 6031

faith illumines the w. 3649

Faith sees the w. 2939

find w. to fundamental joy 10915

finding God's w. in suddenness of storms 1803

found by Jesus' will 7099

from God to human heart through human heart 3334

Go searching all the w. 7475

go through life afraid will miss the w. 3758

God cannot come in any w. but his own w. 4664

God found a better w. for woman . 1120

God has brought us on our w. 10953

God judges man by w. he is facing 4713

God makes it impossible to lose our w. 5397

God reached by w. of love, suffering 4802

God will reach down all the w. 7514

God's approval of our w. 5443

God's w. becomes plain when start walking 5404

God's w. contrary to common sense 1294

God's w. of answering the Christian's prayer 8804

God's w. often insignificant, unobstrusive 4664

good general sees w. to victory
8485

Great works do not always lie in
our w. 5068

grope w. through endless traffic
jams 5859

Had I gone my own w. 5594

happiness w. we look at the world
5538

Hell is enjoyment of your own w.
forever 5695

high soul climbs the high w.
10679

highest w. of doing God's will
8416

History endless repetition of
wrong w. of living 5713

Holy is the w. God is 5749

hope an easier w. to journey's end
5924

hope, cheering the lonely w. 5940

I am on the w. with you 4248

I don't know a blessing when it
comes my w. 5587

If all experience God same w.
6169

If but the w. be straight, cannot go
amiss 5471

in w. other than predetermined by
God 11082

Individuals as much right to act w.
they decide as we 6193

insist on your own w, will get it
5695

It is the w. the Master went 10133

joy, commit ourselves to God's w.
6566

Lead thou the w, thou guidest best
4977

Let God have his w. 460

Life has w. of prying loose grasp
11656

life of Jesus cannot be discussed in
same w. as any other man 6476

life, aimless comet till halts deadly
w. 6937

life, every inch of the w. is disputed
6947

look back over w. we have come
5392

love forces its w. upward 7283

love of God bars w. to hell 4781

majority best w. because visible
5191

man to make his w. best he can
3495

move through life in distracted w.
5590

must not find our own w. 5446

My w. is very simple 7953

never arrive, always on the w.
7035

no better w. to finish spiritual life
10705

no longer have to be treated
certain w. 9963

no other w. to express richness of
God, meagerness of men 9784

None goes his w. alone 919

not good advertisement for w. of
God 5474

not so much his will and w. 5443

of suffering witness soul bears to
itself 10866

on the w. to the grave 6986

One must do good in right w.
5075

only one w. to be born 2393

only one w. to heaven 11863

only w. can find ourselves is in
sorrow 10643

only w. to have friend is be one
4205

out of trouble never as simple as
w. in 11453

people learn w. to be made holy
9838

Prayer enabled to move ourselves
God's w. 8925

Prayer not to persuade God to
move our w. 8925

Prepare the w! A God, a God
appears 6138

prosper as we do common things
in uncommon w. 9344

safe w. to destroy enemy 3170

see no w. out of the world's misery
7099

shows greatness by w. he treats
little men 5272

sign means we're on the w. 5439

so determined to get own w.
writes diary in advance 10772

stick in hand not God's w. 6786

Suffering only w. some can learn
10897

surest w. to lose is to protect 4733

Teach him all the w. to heaven
8296

than merely tell the w. 3435

Thank God for the w. he made you
6206

that lead to everything 7869

the w. the Son of God went 10165

the w. you look at problems 507

There is no other w. but through
5407

There is no w. out, no w. back
5407

through valley of death on its w.
to greatness 5289

Thy w. not mine, O Lord 5456

to Babylon will never bring you to
Jerusalem 10403

to be humble is not to stoop 6037

to be nothing is do nothing 6778

to bliss lies not on beds of down
2112

To find that better w. 9067

to happiness 5561

to know is to will to do God's will
5447

To lead men in his w. 10122

to love is to realize it might be lost
7311

To order my onward w. 633

to read book of aphorisms 9387

To repent is to alter w. of looking
at life 9605

to the top in God's kingdom
10161

to trouble God is not to come at
all 8964

treat men the w. they are, will
never improve them 5971

treat men the w. you want them to
be 5971

trust cannot crowd its w. in 12081

We are all beggars, each in his
own w. 5986

we handle trials makes world
pause 10938

What better w. could you choose
356

What God throws my w. comes
5416

what seems hindrance becomes a
w. 10901

Which w. his soul shall go 1155

whichever w. God turns my feet, I
go 5416

will be made through oceans,
rivers, wastes, rocks 5444

Will show the w. 5434

will show you a w. to feed
thousands 10205

With merry company dreary w.
endured 4304

with my hand in thine just go thy
w. 9072

Without the w. is no going 6382

Worship a w. of living 12133

wrong w. always seems more
reasonable 5453

you will end in your own hell
9196

WAYS

A myriad homes, a myriad w.
4834

a thousand w. to die 2393

accept Christ's w. as our w. 3335

And justify the w. of God to men
7566

angels direct our w. 363

attempting to find new w. of
bettering things 9311

break through ordinary w. of men
10564

cannot always understand w. of
God 4688

Christ not one of many w. to
approach God 6372

God draws us in three w. 7949

God fulfills himself m. ways 978

God intrudes in myriad w. 7556

God meets needs in striking w.
3744

God whose w. you cannot
understand 3684

God's w. seem dark but soon or
late 11299

good sermon helps in different w.
10094

heart willing will find thousand w.
7871

impedes us in our natural outlook and w. 9821

In all the w. you can 10126

keeps us from giving in innovative w. to others 6825

Life lost in thousand, small uncaring w. 6972

must conclude God's w. are perfect 4443

of awakening inner reverence 9734

of Providence cannot be reasoned out 5450

Passions useful in a thousand w. 10234

People come to poverty two w. 4040

pessimist looks both w. crossing one-way street 8585

strange misunderstanding of God's w. 9840

Though my feet are set in silent w. 6917

thousand w. to wealth 11863

Through thorny w. lead to joyful end 1502

two w. of being rich 11864

two w. of spreading light 3455

two w. to handle difficulties 2753

we go our w. 2378

whose w. I do not understand 11487

wise and good were all God's w. 4904

WAYWARD

heart by sorrow rent 7917

WE

Individuals as much right to act way they decide as w. 6193

people like us are W. 454

say we must do all w. can 10980

then w. and ours will do for you 5009

When w. and ours have it in our power 5009

WEAK

a conscience to the w. 10130

acquiescence of indolence 4507

alcohol, destroy the w. 331

Beyond our vision w. and dim 10204

chains of habit too w. to be felt 5500

Faith knows itself w. 3702

For we are w. and need some deep revealing 9050

God takes w. and makes them strong 10745

God wanted weakness, who so w. as I 11787

God, w, powerless in the world 4899

grow on limbs too w. to bear 10611

If any be but w, how strong is Christ 6391

In celebration w, lowly receive new stature 3235

Integrity without knowledge w. 3013

Jesus proclaims w. are the strong 6447

made w. that he might obey 8806

mental reflection of God badly out of focus 4579

mind magnifies trifling things 7754

not a hand so w. and white 10201

not strong, were to be esteemed 5001

Obstacles in pathway of w. 10754

person is injured by prosperity 7683

persons cannot be sincere 10431

Private opinion is w. 8200

Quarrels are weapons of the w. 9362

Sarcasm weapon of w. 1770

Self can turn a powerful prayer into a w. one 10080

Seven days without prayer makes one w. 8960

so he might be w. enough to suffer 6126

so w. is man 8877

still our tongues of w. complainings 9090

strong or w. depending on knowledge of God 1321

That my love is w. and faint 9077

That we should ever w. or heartless be 8867

things united become strong 11624

thought too w. to be expressed simply 10285

to strengthen w. faith 3744

to the w. God is gentle 4649

too w. to cling to Christ 9022

Tough hope be w. or sick with long delay 8768

turn w. sin-battered life toward Great Physician 10436

voice of intelligence soft and w. 6331

We are not w. enough 10768

We kneel, how w. 8867

WEAKEN

alcohol, w. the strong 331

do not w. yourself by looking forward 9650

WEAKENED

soul w. by virus of pride 10436

WEAKENING

sin w. of power 10360

WEAKENS

To exaggerate w. what we say 3425

Whatever w. reason is sin 10424

WEAKER

become stronger only when become w. 10769

He who injured you either stronger or w. 6263

If w. spare him 6263

Unto my hand cling w. ones 179

we feel, harder we lean on God 10761

we feel, the harder we lean 8256

you make us stronger or w. 9522

WEAKEST

Bible within sight of w. 702

chain no stronger than w. link 10744

Christ in w. hour 2127

Christian, strongest when w. 1265

God in likeness of w. of all living creatures 6154

Man a reed, w. in nature 7406

place within possibility for w. 3737

Prayer the w. of all things 8940

saint can experience power 9563

The w. saint upon his knees 8959

WEAKNESS

bury w. of friend in silence 4183

Christ helps us by his w, suffering 4899

Christian mind has w. unmatched in Christian history 7768

Christianity not doctrine of w. 1165

cross revealed God in w. 6471

cruelty springs from w. 27

Day of Judgment to tell tragedies of w. 1055

death raises from w. into strength 2250

deepens dependence on Christ for strength 8256

deny God opportunity of working through w. 10407

doom ourselves to w. 2821

faith is weakness leaning on God's strength 3775

given w. that he might feel need of God 8806

God uses chronic pain and w. 8256

God uses our sins to remind us of w. 10306

God wanted w, who so weak as I 11787

God, author of human w. 230

I would be humble, I know my w. 1018

immediate neighbors of tolerance 11400

Independence is unrealized w. 6414

Ingratitude a form of w. 5255

irreverence indication of w. 9735

lie is refuge of w. 6845

Look for strength in people, not w. 5077

lust for power rooted in w. 8718

Man calls sin a w, God willfulness 4560

Meekness is not w. 7730

mistaking w. for strength defeats 10749

my greatest strength 11789

naive is man's w, child's strength 7977

Neutrality evidence of w. 8073

no unsuspected w. in our character 4884

noise evidence of w, not strength 10576

not likely Lord will bypass way of w. 11791

of the merely well-meaning 11779

or strength add to my life 1538

Pleasant w. after pain 5360

Prayer girds w. with divine strength 8912

Prayer is w. leaning on omnipotence 8949

Pride and w. are Siamese twins 9226

Reconciliation is not w. 9431

Samson's w. was showing off his strength 792

Sin is not w. 10371

Sin is w. 10363

Strength grows out of w. 10755

Strength made perfect in w. 8170

strength often as great a handicap as w. 10750

Stronger by w, wiser men become 7701

sympathizing with my strength not with my w. 3139

tears shed for self tears of w. 11026

Two things indicate w. 1887

Unguarded strength is double w. 10765

unnecessary display of knowledge is w. 6694

we think of gentleness as w. 4402

when matched beside w. of the Christian 10512

when strength is our own, only w. 10767

Whether w. or strength 1461

WEAKNESSES

assume God unable to work in our w. 3613

Bible, contains all human w, strength 701

excuse w. of others 1080

forget your w. 9271

make us appreciate God's strength 11790

necessary to purposes of life 11788

One of the w. of our age 5321

Our Father knows our w. better than we do 9832

our Lord saw people's w. 6519

remedy for w. in Scriptures 650

WEALTH

a good servant 11873

a very bad mistress 11873

abounding in w. yet miserable 249

amazing w. of the Bible 694

condemn w. who see no chance of getting it 11868

Contentment not w. but few wants 1780

dispense w. best way to preserve it 11870

enough to support needs 1809

even if called to give up w. 4615

goal not material w. 3113

Great w, content seldom live together 11818

Great w. implies great loss 11819

Health and w. wean us of need for Christ 5608

Health better than w. 5609

is his that enjoys it 11876

is like seawater 11875

is not elegance 11662

is not his that has it 11876

is of the heart, not the hand 11867

laid up in our heavenly banking account 3751

let neighbor bear the load of your w. 8689

lightens not heart and care of man 11877

like a viper 11874

Little w, little care 11833

loss of w. is loss of dirt 11857

lost w. lost trouble 1776

love of w. makes bitter men 7303

makes people worry about losing it 11859

man in evolution from poor to truer w. 9351

miser's w. is the devil's 11796

misers amass w. for those who wish their death 11837

more we drink, thirstier we become 11875

nature, extravagant w. of beauty 8046

no right to consume w. without producing it 5569

of soul measured by how much it can feel 10677

of the compassionate spirit 11841

only thing w. does for some people 11859

people mistake w. for happiness 8510

people who love God for w. 4801

perhaps the greater load 8689

prayed for w. that he might do greater things 8806

Success is neither fame, w. or power 10807

than die a slave to w. 10777

thou beggar's w. 5932

thousand ways to w. 11863

To be enjoyed, w. must be interrupted 443

to the needy, Christ is w. 6391

wanton w. foams high, and brave 4379

What tho' we wade in w. 7088

When w. is lost, nothing is lost 1066

Where there are friends, there is w. 4301

who condemn w. are those who have none 11868

will be swept away 3719

Wisdom is the w. of the wise 11974

Wisdom outweighs any w. 11976

Without thy presence, w. bags of cares 4877

WEALTHY

as good as anybody if had equal chance 3228

day is time no one w. enough to waste 2191

few have spiritual resources to be both w. and godly 11806

frequently rich w. because oppressed poor 6630

I don't look down upon the w. 3228

if w. call him father 3921

who can lose all he has 8637

WEAN

Health, wealth w. us of need for Christ 5608

WEANING

When God is w. a soul 10036

WEAPON

God sends w. to conquer 3418

Hope the major w. against suicide 5925

invincible w. against evils of earth 11841

most potent w. God has given man 4154

Music w. used to make perverse seem glamorous 7910

Sarcasm w. of weak 1770

sharp word cuts deeper than w. 2051

to fight with w. of prayer 8818

tongue can be dangerous w. 5118

tongue powerful w. of manipulation 1882

WEAPONLESS

He moves into the battle wholly w. 6124

WEAPONRY

hunger more explosive than atomic w. 8692

WEAPONS

Bible more powerful than w. 726

Christ did not conquer by w. 6389

fight devil with own w. overmatch 2647

people fret over nuclear w. 10503

Quarrels are w. of the weak 9362

tongue most dangerous of w. 11417

We grasp the w. we have given 10756

WEAR

a scowl, have wrinkles 10502

a smile, have friends 10502

better to w. out than rust out 6767

easier to w. mask 6057

Few minds w. out, more rust out 7756

In triumph w. Christlike chain 1299

Kind words don't w. out tongue
6646
our people out 115
which no tribulation can w. out
9057
who w. shoe know best where
pinches 8275
your expression the most
important 434

WEARER
Only the w. knows where shoe
pinches 3542

WEARIED
Comes sweet with music to thy w.
ear 10960
Though w. love is not tired 7283

WEARIES
sermon w. people by its length
10095

WEARINESS
heaven, w. no place there 5644
increased possession loads us with
new w. 8625
love's object removes its w. 6457
receive as from the Lord 1461
Talk to him in prayer of all your
w. in serving him 8968
The w, the fever, and the fret 7044
tongue registers no w. 11420

WEARING
more danger of rusting out than
w. out 8177
so accustomed to w. disguise 6067

WEARISOME
in company w. and dissipating
10572

WEARS
Faith w. everyday clothes 3715
it's day-to-day living that w. you
out 6876
Pain w. no mask 10583
reason polar bear w. fur coat 6213
The one who w. my face 9947
when eraser w. out ahead of pencil
3263
When you use life, it w. out 6905

WEARY
Along a rough, a w. road 7007
and ill at ease 7919
daily burden of a w. life 9683
eyes grown w. of the garish day
10481
heaven upon earth to w. head
10484
hope that God does not w. of
mankind 4896
How w. seem all uses of this world
2603
music bringest eternity nearer to
w. soul of man 7916
Not work, but worry makes us w.
12071
poverty is a w. thing 8684
Rest of the w. 6468
wants w. us in foolish anxieties
2861

WEATHER
atheist in fair w. 486
best to read w. forecast before
pray for rain 8851
can't beat the w. 9879
Don't knock the w. 7998
1841
God sorts out the w. 37
no such thing as bad w. 8005
no w. in space 11650
only different kinds of good w.
8033
Prosperity good campaigning w.
for devil 9338
Through quiet waters, stormy w.
4281
trouble like hot w. 11431
Who can see finger of God in w.
4961

WEAVE
We w. with colors all our own
3289
what tangled web do parents w.
8319

WEAVER'S
In the W. skillful hand 10606

WEAVES
sounds which Holy Spirit w.
together in heavenly harmony
5799

WEAVING
pain thread in pattern of God's w.
10915

WEB
Experience a kind of huge spider
w. 3524
of life is of mingled yarn 7045

WEBLIKE
Songs spring forth w. from mind
at peace 7920

WEBS
in asterisks her w. are spread 6118

WEBSTER
last words of Noah W. 2379

WED
Better half hang'd than ill w. 7604

WEED
And found itself a w. 2052
Anger is a w. 371
bouquet in chubby fist says it all
1102
plant whose virtues not yet
discovered 8646

WEEDING
man w. turnips also serving God
12146

WEEDS
always flourish 3417
call them w. and murder them
8577
he who loves w. may find w. 5140
Lilies that fester smell worse than
w. 5039

man of words and not deeds like
garden of w. 9319

WEEK
Day of all the w. the best 10953
In politics a w. is very long time
5180
Lord's Day firm foundation to
build six-story w. 10958
Safely through another w. 10953
Some people stay longer in hour
than others in w. 9492
Sunday clasp that binds together
the w. 10956
Sunday clears away rust of the w.
10954
Tomorrow must be longest day of
w. 9302
trite as multiplication table w. after
3911
Who could stand whole w. before
lived 4336

WEEKDAY
Sunday self and w. self not good if
detached 10949

WEEKDAYS
Christ, turn w. into Sundays 5529

WEEKEND
fight dandelions all w. 239
today call it the w. 10952

WEEKENDS
w. get into another box on wheels
5859

WEEP
Among those who laugh, do not w.
3064
Among those who w, do not laugh
3064
And w. away life of care 2882
better to w. with wise than laugh
with fools 9475
comes a time when love can only
w. 4781
comfort those who w. by weeping
1506
I w. for what I'm like when alone
10538
if world a changeless state 983
if you must 2412
man appears for a little while to w.
7372
no need that others w. for him
10877
not for me, but for yourselves
2455
not that world changes 983
though I w. because those sails are
battered 11470
To w. and sigh because I'm blind
1810
To w. is to make less depth of grief
5361
When house doth sigh and w.
1514
when you w, no one sees 10647
While some w. I'll fight 3342
without being taught man can
only w. 7412

WEEPING

a w. in world as though Lord were dead 2611

faith brings power, not w. 3748

hell, w. useless 5700

I would not bid you cease your w. 1509

Laughter, w. two intensest forms of human emotion 6728

Let me come in where you are w. 1509

World poverty is a hundred million mothers w. 8699

WEEPS

Better cottage where one merry than palace where one w. 5821

Man only animal that laughs, w. 7413

WEIGH

days when burdens w. us down 9059

having neither to w. thoughts 4260

no more wilt w. my eyelids down 10485

Read to w, consider 856

WEIGHED

down by obsessive fear 5474

power that measured, w. spanned world 4592

seldom w. in same scales 9495

WEIGHS

God w. intentions 6336

love w. actions in scales of his honor 6457

wisdom, awful wisdom which w. 11906

WEIGHT

and strain are gone 7486

burdened with the unbearable w. of ourselves 9917

Can ease this w. of sin 8451

cannot speak of w. and God 4680

Christ's words that carry w. 1536

God gives without w. his mercy 4451

God gives wrath by w. 4451

Ills have no w, tears no bitterness 7474

lends w. to one's opinions 9389

Lord's Prayer for w. of its petition 7154

more than man can bear 4319

oppress us with w. of the tomb 2611

Our portion of the w. of care 8863

People lose w. by keeping mouths shut 9972

WEIRD

Conceit w. disease 1586

However w. life's monody sounds 7895

WELCOME

all wonders in one sight 6153

But we could not see the w. 2217

depths as w. as surest heaven 9930

happy morning 2986

Love bade me w, yet my soul drew back 5481

No greeting like his w. 4208

Silence as w. after satiety as after disappointment 10266

WELCOMED

dark night of soul experience to be w. 2608

WELFARE

God's love disposes him to desire our w. 4754

God's sovereignty enables him to secure our w. 4754

goodness of God to desire our w. 7093

Is church ready to found w. societies 10086

love, causes us to seek w. of others 7304

power of God to achieve our w. 7093

the wisdom of God to plan our w. 7093

troubles large enough to endanger w. 4789

WELL

And all is w, tho faith and form 3644

Anything devil does always done w. 2640

as I'm able 6134

confidently hope that all will yet be w. 5179

do ordinary things extraordinarily w. 10137

Do you wish people to think w. of you 5996

Doctors called in when people were w. 6880

doing w. wisest and best 67

Don't speak w. of yourself 5996

done better than w. said 3459

Education enable man to put things w. 2998

frog in w. knows nothing of ocean 8665

God does w. what he does 4446

God is, all is w. 4935

God wants us to do ordinary things extraordinarily w. 7118

he himself is very w. 8142

if acted right has done w, though alone 5032

If w. thou hast begun 543

if we all did as w. today 3511

Is w. and best 4746

let few be w. tried 4218

Living w. is best revenge 9719

moments when everything goes w. 3998

My life is ending, I know that w. 7101

no profit to learn w. if neglect to do w. 3016

not how w. we have spoken, but how w. we have lived 6600

not w. for man to pray cream, live skim milk 8856

planning w. is wiser 67

playing it w. is what matters 9911

pray only as w. as we live 8885

prayer, mercy like two buckets in w. 8884

preaches w. who lives w. 9138

religious din assure everything is w. 12096

reputation easily cracked, never w. mended 9615

responsible for how w. we fulfill responsibilities 9660

Rest satisfied with doing w. 2785

roars the storm to those that hear 3644

saint comprehends that all is w. 10910

sweep streets so w. 2777

thanks God as much as he were sound and w. 9782

Thinking w. is wise 67

To pray w. better half of study 9007

What God does, he does w. 4996

what is, is w. 8243

What will be will be w. 8243

When one knows oneself w. 6597

who means w. useless unless does w. 6335

wish people to think w. of you 9614

work w. done never needs doing over 8579

worth doing at all, worth doing w. 96

WELL FILLED

A little house w. 5814

WELL LOVED

Beside us a friend w, known 5338

WELL TILLED

a little field w. 5814

WELL WILLED

a little wife w. 5814

WELL-ADJUSTED

not w. who makes world better place 6196

WELL-ATTESTED

Christian faith founded upon w. fact of history 6144

WELL-BEING

Agape love is concern for w. of another 7158

all equally responsible for w. of world 9678

temporarily lose sense of w. 2593

When consider w. of others 9520

WELL-CONTROLLED

so w. very few waves of glory 3184

WELL-DEFINED

happy religion is w. knowledge of Jesus Christ 6713

spiritual life most easily lived 1332

WELL-DOING
consciousness of w. ample reward 5069

WELL-DRESSED
turn away on grounds too w. to be honest 10086

WELL-EDUCATED
no matter how intelligent or w. 752

WELL-EXAMINED
prove hand of God 5454

WELL-GREASED
Time like w. string 11343

WELL-HANDLED
came about like a w. ship 11130

WELL-MEANING
weakness of the merely w. 11779

WELL-ORDERED
If your love pure, simple, w. 7193

WELL-PLACED
quotation sign of educated person 9389

WELL'S
When the w. dry 444

WELLS
Intellectual sophistication can dry up w. of creativity 6325

WELL-SPENT
evening of w. life brings lamps with it 8171

WELL-WORN
genius never travels on w. paths 4393

WENT
may be sorry you stayed or w. 6674
than he w. through before 5379

WEPT
Christ w. that thou mightest laugh 6393
he who has not w. in David 5224
When Jesus saw city, he w. 10522

WESLEY
communicated vision of King to countrymen 9740
in one generation, a Carey in next is inevitable 9740

WEST
East is east, w. is w. 915
In Christ there is no east or w. 911
Of east or w. 4746
One ship drives east, another w. 4432
We of the nervous w. 130

WESTMINSTER ABBEY
whether you preach in W. 3845

WET
must wait for God in the wind and w. 5460
One already w. 40

WETS
God w. you with his rain 4466

WHALE
However big w. may be 11071

WHAT
and where they be 2214
can never know w. we are 7438
legalist is a w. asker 6820
not w. a man does that determines sacred or secular 7865
Politics science of how who gets w, when, why 5186
that we may know w. to stand for 11731
Their names are W. and Why and When 6686
To w. shall I compare this life of ours 7070

WHATEVER
Freedom does not mean do w. I want 4122
placed in God's hands, still possess 8628
you fear most you will serve 4006

WHEAT
back of the mill is the w. and the shower 9345
We were chaff, now w. 1348

WHEEDLED
out of liberty 4115

WHEEL
is come full circle 1739
Keep your shoulder to the w. 3503
Let God put you on his w. and whirl 2849
like trying to make w. without hub 4632
quick revolving w. shall rest in peace 3288
that does the squeaking 8564
way we act behind the w. 1331
worst w. screeches loudest 1562

WHEELBARROW
Trust like getting into w. 3669

WHEELS
And w. his throne upon the whirling worlds 1963
at weekends get into another box on w. 5859

WHEN
And how and w. and where 1855
interpretation will come w, as God pleases 4885
is the time for love to be born 6155
Politics science of how who gets what, w, why 5186
Their names are What and Why and W. 6686
Wise men not always silent, but know w. to be 11977

WHERE
And How and W. and Who 6686
And how and when and w. 1855
is it, this present 11389

that we may know w. to stand 11731
venturing forth we know not w. 9930
What and w. they be 2214

WHEREVER
glance falls God turns to beauty 4463
God rules human heart as King 4736
I go—only thou 4518
I stand—only thou 4518
the Son of God goes 5810
we go, always find God present 4845
you are, be all there 3186
you are, friends make your world 4212
you go, go with whole heart 3187

WHETS
Misfortune w. 11808

WHIM
home where man can indulge in a w. 5842
marriage paper torn up at w. 2924

WHINE
if treat shabbily, no right to w. when he is dead 2317
If you have w. in you 10032
less 5604

WHINES
Christian who w. when he talks 9529

WHIPPED
father w. son for swearing, swore himself 3914

WHIRL
Let God put you on his wheel and w. 2849
of religious activity 4410

WHIRLING
And wheels his throne upon the w. worlds 1963

WHIRLWIND
God not in w. of activity 10747

WHISPER
can find its way to God 8849
elves reach to w. in ear 1122
even though that word be in a w. 6511
God can hear your faintest w. 8801
If wife small, stoop down and w. in ear 7620
Let not thy will roar when power can but w. 6800
when you pray, more a w. than a kiss 8801

WHISPERED
insinuations rhetoric of the devil 10478

WHISPERING
God is w. to us incessantly 10273

revelation secret w. of God in ear
of a soul 9705

WHISPERS
God w. to us in our pleasures
8257
the o'erfraught heart, bids it break
5333

WHISTLE
children w. to keep up courage
476

WHITE
angels, dressed in w. 359
don't want them to see my face is
w. 3229
feathers remain w. but heart
grows black 9517

WHITEN
who blackens others does not w.
himself 10451

WHITER
white than snow 1368

WHITEST
He whose garments are w. 6004

WHITEWASH
Knot in plank will show through
w. 2469

WHITEWASHED
crow shows black again 2462

WHO
And How and Where and W.
6686
can never know w. we are 7438
God quietly tells us w. we are
6830
has God, has all 4519
has put me here 4905
hath ought that is not thine 4954
Jesus tried for w. he was 6413
Politics science of how w. gets
what, when, why 5186
Situationist is a w. seeker 6820
will give me back days when life
had wings 12176

WHOEVER
must forgive w. has wronged you
4109

WHOLE
Adjusts, sustains, and agitates the
w. 4711
Forever shared, forever w. 6409
half truth is a w. lie 6843
Holy Spirit breaks the heart,
makes it w. 5794
Made man a perfect w. 5606
The eternal eye that sees the w.
6583
'Tis woman's w. existence 7278
to think we are w. and need no
help 10045
To yield is to be preserved w. 7071
Who saith, "A w. I planned" 8132

WHOLEHEARTEDLY
swallow w. any lie that flatters us
6870

WHOLENESS
Openness to w. as secrets to
sickness 5883

WHOLESOME
home where w. recreation enjoyed
5853
nights are w, no planets strike
1371
seldom w. home in absence of
religious inspiration 5858

WHOM
Of w. you speak, to w. you speak
1855
To w. would God go for
permission 4955

WHOSOEVER
elect are w. will 3046
nonelect w. won't 3046

WHY
and how is God to be loved 7574
But w. you did it 7862
comes temptation but for man to
meet 11122
do we dread ordeal 11459
do we fear trouble 11459
doesn't God do something 10922
flung without knowing how or w.
into world 3495
God himself is the reason w. God
is to be loved 7574
God is virtue's w. 11687
God knows, not I, the reason w.
11468
God never answers the w. 167
he does it determines sacred or
secular 7865
know w. man alone laughs 6742
no reason w. here rather than there
4905
now rather than then 4905
Politics science of how who gets
what, when, w. 5186
question about miracle not how it
happened, but w. 6500
saint does not know w. he suffers
10910
same thing makes us laugh, cry
10660
Their names are What and W. and
When 6686
worry? What can worry do?
12091
Young people, w. God uses them
so often 12177

WHYS
I lay my w. before your cross
12102

WICK
Life not the w. 6973

WICKED
afraid of everything 3996
afraid of God's creatures 3996
afraid of God, he is enemy 3996
afraid of himself, his own
executioner 3996

afraid of Satan, he is his tormentor
3996
All w. men are slaves 11881
always outnumber the good 5182
as restless as hen wanting to lay
egg 11886
Better poor than w. 8674
can't teach people how w. they are
4773
death is w. man's fear 2372
distance one should keep from w.
cannot be measured 11888
Flee the w, even when they are
charming 11882
flee when no man pursueth 11892
For never, never w. man was wise
11883
God permits the w, but not forever
11884
has blood like that of bed bug
11885
He injures good men who spare w.
6608
is a coward 3996
learn by experience how w. 4773
make better time when righteous
after them 11892
man is his own hell 11880
Man, I can assure you, a w.
creature 10333
men obey from fear 5053
night in which good rise, w. sink
10878
No man became very w. all at once
11889
not when conscious of faults most
w. 10329
practice virtue from self-interest
11710
repent not so much for evil deeds
of w. people 6285
shun the light as devil the cross
11893
Some w. people would be less
dangerous 11891
till we realize how w. we are 4773
What w. do should not disturb
good man's tranquility 11894

WICKEDNESS
always easier than virtue 11895
because world based on freedom
4149
No w. proceeds on reason 11890
takes shortcut to everything 11895
when acquainted with w. of own
heart 10306
whose future w. he foresaw 5020

WIDE
Bible, great and w. as world 750
door of suffering is w. 10900
grow so w, deep nothing human is
strange 10540
is our mouth 7575
narrow mind, w. mouth go
together 4059
The Infinite Goodness has such w.
arms 4645

You travel w. and far to scout, see, search 4926

WIDELY
How w. Jesus known difficult to judge 6395

WIDENESS
in God's mercy like the w. of the sea 7745

WIDENS
Scripture w. and deepens 685

WIDER
higher the hill, w. the vista 3488
nothing is w. than love 7283
Scripture far higher, w. 691

WIDEST
thing in universe not space 5625

WIDOW
care for his w. and orphan 5199

WIDOW'S MITE
she only gave 4379

WIDTH
can do something about life's w. and depth 7095

WIFE
a little w. well willed 5814
As would have a daughter, so choose a w. 7602
Choose neither w. nor linen by candlelight 7609
Choose w. by ear rather than eye 7610
deaf husband, blind w. happy couple 7589
get bad w, become a philosopher 7606
good husband makes a good w. 7590
good w. makes a good husband 7592
husband, w. one in honor, influence 3868
ideal w. has an ideal husband 7600
If w. small, stoop down and whisper in ear 7620
is but half a w. who is not a friend 7651
is nearest neighbor 7654
Let w. make husband glad to come home 7627
man too good for world, no good for his w. 7594
My w. is an angel 7649
not a guitar 7599
one good w. a spiritual harem 7663
should be his deepest love 7654
Try praising w. even if it does frighten her 7662
who does not honor w. dishonors himself 7616

WIFE'S
man forever criticizing w. judgment 7655

WILD
center of man a curious w. pain 7521
flowers on distant hills 8498
home, w. place in world of rules 5842
Human beings w. animals when born 7382
most dangerous of w. beasts, a slanderer 10472
no w. beast so ferocious as Christians 11212
tongue a w. beast 11415

WILDERNESS
Adam and Eve into far w. 365
born from depths of divine w. 5967
faith finds table in w. 3703
no w. like life without friends 4284
Promised Land always lies on other side of w. 5669
see world being turned into w. 8445
The world, it is a w. 11021
thorn of experience worth w. of warning 3540
To seek a barren w. 4118
today. Promised Land tomorrow 1935

WILDEST
God's promises beyond w. dreams 4458

WILDLY
rushed about w. searching for you 7473

WILL
accept with faith, resignation his holy w. 4688
all that God w. 9835
And the sun and the Father's w. 9345
And works his sovereign w. 4941
angels would leap to do his w. 12099
attach feeble w. to all-powerful w. 9835
Bible, redirects my w. 722
bring life under God's sovereign w. 4734
cannot say thy w. be done if 8818
cannot simultaneously w. sin and repentance 5210
center of God's w. is safety 4980
Christ release from fury of the w. 6434
Christian love an affair of the w. 4777
commonsense decisions are God's w. unless he checks 5464
conflict between conscience, w. 3367
conform my w. to thine 9101
controlled by other power than my own w. 4949
desire all my works be according to his w. 5411

devil no power to compel against w. 2679
devote w. to purpose of God 12124
do not want to agonize to find your w. 8820
do w. of another rather than thine own 8448
easy for God to do what he w. 4831
elect are whosoever w. 3046
endowed with a soul and a w. to be saved 9425
Evil people enamorment with own w. 3367
Evil that which God does not w. 3361
Faith believing God w. 3691
Father, set me free in the glory of thy w. 9052
Father, thy w. be done 8088
forced against you w. 183
Forgiveness a decision of the w. 4109
God concerned about keeping us in his w. 5390
God does his w. for the most part unconsciously to us 7690
God does what he w. 7495
God draws us when w. subdued 7949
God gives us w. to w. 11505
God governed all things by counsels of his w. 4904
God is omnipotent w. 4514
God's w. is man's home 1790
good w. got by many actions, lost by one 9611
Had bred but courage, love, valiant w. 4921
He that w. not when he may 8216
holiness depends on God's grace, our w. to be holy 5754
How does w. become sanctified 9835
I just want to do God's w. 4975
idea of our w. subjected to God's control 5467
If I w. nothing of my own 4977
if live in God and die to own w. 10047
In God's w. is our peace 4973
In life, in death, thy lovely w. 8098
In me thy blessed w. is wrought 4977
in our despair, against our w, comes wisdom 11919
is blind man who carries lame man 918
is power 2635
Let not thy w. roar when power can but whisper 6800
love, rather a condition of the heart and w. 7304
man convinced against his w. 9179
man to work out in world w. of God 3195

man who leaves money to charity
in w. 4377

man's business to do w. of God
566

Man's free w., God's sovereign w.
1149

Men who possess opinions and a
w. 6299

must be bathed in new element
880

must be reborn 880

must be reconsecrated to Maker
880

no disappointments in w. of God
2801

Not as I w. but as thou wilt 4976

not God's w. we see before or
around us 5397

not his w. that we neglect the mind
7758

not so much his w. and way 5443

nothing can ever come to pass
against our w. 9835

Nothing difficult to those who
have w. 8549

O W, that willest good alone 4977

Of an omniscient w. 4338

of God never leads to miserable
feeling 4507

only desire to do w. of his Father
9280

Our peace in his w. 4979

perversion of the w. turned aside
from thee 10317

Prayer from a living source within
the w. 8911

Prayer identifying oneself with the
divine w. 8922

Prayer the renunciation of one's
own w. 8922

preserve peace if w. firm,
submissive 8453

recognizing God's w. 5395

roots of achievement lie in the w.
92

saint has same w. with Christ
9766

shall not when he w. 8216

Sin an affair of the w. 10361

so that I w. only as thou willest
9052

surrender w. to God, discover
resources 10769

the w. to become the best 92

Thy joy to do the Father's w.
10133

Thy w. at once thy perfection and
mine 9052

thy w. be done in everything,
everywhere 9082

thy w. be done in father, mother,
child 9082

thy w. be done without a but, if,
limit 9082

thy w. be done without a reserve
9082

to neither strive nor cry 8430

To walk out of his w. 4982

too fond of our own w. 9679

'Twas his w, it is mine 7520

valiant w. to overcome 4643

versus w, punch versus punch
1622

way to know is to w. to do God's
will 5447

We do not pray to change his w.
9799

we ourselves must w. the truth
11505

What God w, no frost can kill
4959

what mattered was Father's w.
done 4425

What w. be w. be well 8243

whatever God may w, soul should
w. 4978

when God knows we meant to do
his w. 4810

when God's w. is done, we
grumble 8791

When the w. is ready, feet light
7870

where human w. leaves, divine
grace begins 5200

Where loves rules, no w. to power
7343

Whose w. is wiser than my own
8825

without us God w. not 7576

WILL OF GOD

cannot bend ourselves to w. 4984

devil categorically refuses to do w.
4915

devil has nothing to say about w.
· 4915

devil hates w. 4915

doing w. leaves no time for
disputing his plans 4970

each party claims to act in w.
4972

either burden we carry or power
which carries us 5451

end of life is to do w. 5554

forces of evil in opposition to w.
8762

have to be broken to w. 4984

help discover w. and do it 5373

holiness is conformity to w. 5758

I believe the w. prevails 5411

if cannot work out w. where God
has placed us 4974

knew w. before they prayed 8890

living in obedience to whatever
lies ahead 5370

need heart that wants w. more
than anything 5442

no disappointments if wills buried
in w. 4981

Nothing more, nothing less 7876

Obedience is submission to w.
8099

peace is adjustment of life to w.
8460

quiet mind merged into w. 7773

Self-will, pour into ocean of w.
4978

should spend efforts seeking to
know, do w. 5543

sometimes w. everything destroyed
5423

that we accept the w. 7485

To will the w. 4983

wish that w. be fulfilled in thee
8448

WILLED

creation, w. by God 1975

If God w, brooms would shoot
4944

WILLFUL

extraordinary w. people 3367

sin w. refusal to obey God 10387

WILFULLNESS

unlively dough of human w. 530

WILLING

as light w. to flood room 4785

as water w. to flow into emptied
channel 4785

Christ was w. to suffer 9448

Discouraged people need w.
someone 3066

door must be opened by w. hand
4775

goal for which w. to exchange
piece of life 4422

God w. to enter human
personality and change it 5777

heart w. will find a thousand ways
7871

If God not w. to forgive 4088

if w. to let go 9563

Least w. still to quit the ground
8174

May I be w. Lord, to bear 2098

my w. and hoping are optimistic
8247

Nothing impossible to w. heart
10797

someone else w. to trust him 4275

To be w. to accept crucifixion
with Christ 10048

to come as pauper, receive Holy
Spirit 5792

to go into debt for work of God
3297

to let your personality be taken
over 5776

to make ideas accessible 11007

to swallow, too lazy to chew 6758

to take one world at a time 6092

to use minds without prejudice
4124

truth where few are w. to search
3259

what God is w. to forget 4633

when wrong, make us w. to change
9119

WILLINGLY

If you carry the cross w. 183

whatever God allow, soul should
w. embrace 4978

WILLINGNESS

Being humble involves w. to be
reckoned failure 5993

must be free w. on our part 4128

Prayer is laying hold of God's w. 8933

risk God's w. to do miraculous 3669

thrill at God's w. 4135

Where w. is great, difficulties not great 2634

WILLS

ages of man: w. 7037

bring our w. into harmony with his 9799

conclude crimes committed because God w. 3349

Evil cannot be evil as it w. 3377

God w. a rich harmony 6179

God w. that man should be good 5060

God w. the development of all men 9351

God w. us to tread hidden paths 5397

Great souls have w, feeble ones wishes 8541

have patience, can have what he w. 8398

heart right when w. what God w. 2566

no disappointments if w. buried in will of God 4981

nothing can happen save that which God w. 9835

Nothing happens unless Omnipotent w. it 4828

Peace is rhythm of our w. with Jesus' love-will 8467

saint w. everything God w. 9790

WIN

All who joy would w. must share it 5505

better to w. glorious triumphs 1922

God knows who shall lose or w. 4887

I am not bound to w. 6303

make incredible efforts but w. no victories 6813

Man seeks to w. glory by sacrifice of others 2152

one short hour to w. victories 3293

smiles, kindness w. the heart 6656

Unless beaten within, bound to w. 3627

WIND

A voice in the w. I do not know 4962

Blow, blow thou winter w. 6249

blows it back again 596

braces up 8033

can w. check up again 8373

can't catch w. in a net 10722

cannot direct w. 4056

Crisis opportunity riding dangerous w. 2048

Does the road w. uphill all the way 6885

I heard without the night w. moan 5413

must wait for God in the w. 5460

no fear w. will uproot tree 6307

no w. is the right w. 4433

of God always blowing but must hoist sail 5452

of God's admonishment may burst doors, windows 4775

optimist expects w. to change 8249

people as variable as the w. 9521

pessimist complains about the w. 8249

The w. is passing by 8053

Vice repeated like wand'ring w. 10411

when great oak is straining in w. 2508

Who has seen the w. 8053

with an east w. 44

You throw the sand against the w. 596

WINDBAG

one-minute experience, two-hour description 3420

WINDOW

Bible w. in this prison-world 711

Bible w. to look into eternity 711

Christ a w. in dark dungeon of ego 6434

Habit cannot be tossed out w. 5495

humble receives praise way clean w. takes light 6033

Lord, make my life a w. 9079

The little w. where the sun 2588

through which world sees God 3438

When God shuts door, he opens w. 5462

you are w. through which you see the world 8573

WINDOWS

clouded with human fancies 2936

Doubt hammer that breaks w. 2936

ears, eyes doors, w. of soul 845

education to turn mirrors into w. 3019

few people are w. 3019

people would break God's w. 4480

Tears clean w. of the soul 11017

wind of God's admonishment may burst w. 4775

WINDS

angels, are w. 359

Christ Lion in majesty, rebuking w, demons 6425

Like the w. of the sea are ways of fate 4432

of G. are blowing 5810

roots grow deep when w. strong 212

songs in wild whispering of w. 8034

Temptations like w. that firmly root tree 11094

with the self-same w. that blow 4432

WINDWARD

sends down deeper root on w. side 2508

WINE

Christ is w. to feed his people 6370

first a friend, then an enemy 337

is a turncoat 337

Joy the w. that God is ever pouring 8454

Love the w. that gladdens heart of man 7256

make us broken bread, poured out w. as he chooses 9850

Men are like w. 7419

Mirth w. of human life 6739

must be crushed 2820

Night, more nourishing than bread, w. 2553

poured out wine to feed, nourish 887

water into w, performing quickly slow miracle in vineyards 6513

WINEBIBBER

Christ's life so social called a w. 6436

WINEPRESS

of cross, juice nourishes, strengthens 2095

WINES

the Lord's choicest w. 300

WING

Who gives its luster to an insect's w. 1963

WINGED

If slander be a snake, is a w. one 10456

time glides on 11354

WINGS

And the rush of winnowing w. 7943

Angel of Death, hear beating of his w. 2371

God hath two w, which he doth ever move 4812

Jesus gives truth carried on w. of love 6176

Knowing he has w. 11475

Lend, lend your w! 2389

Misfortunes come on w. 196

my freedoms grow, find w. 4125

not forced to take w. to find God 4924

On the w. of time grief flies away 5350

on w. of mysticism can spirit soar 7963

Pray not for crutches, but for w. 8895

Riches have w. 11849

Riches take w. 7291

Rigidity clips future's w. 6818

seemed to fan me like immense w. 5797

soul feels as though it had w. 9608
thank God for not having given
tiger w. 11140
Who will give me back days when
life had w. 12176

WINK

He never came a w. too soon 2588
When close eyes to devil, be sure
not a w. 2705

WINNERS

imitate w. when you lose 549

WINNING

Consistency, battle worth w. 1749
don't invest much w. not exciting
2629
friends meant most 4303
We are on w. side 1924
world to Christ means w.
individuals 3343

WINNOWING

And the rush of w. wings 7943

WINS

Christ in you that w. the crown
6381
Christianity w. great victories
1165
Strength that w. is calm 10757

WINSOME

grace, w. attractiveness of God
5227

WINSOMENESS

without curativeness 1315

WINTER

Blow, blow thou w. wind 6249
Christian, oak flourishing in w.
1249
church door locked in w. 1382
Every mile is two in w. 2544
Grace grows best in w. 5215
ideal occasion to slow down 9906
If only could sleep away w. time
9903
If w. comes, can spring be far
behind 9874
if we had no w. 182
In kingdom of hope there is no w.
5936
is a disease 9907
is not 9879
is on my head 8187
Laughter drives w. from the face
6735
Nature cannot jump from w. to
summer 9875
night is the w. 9877
No summer then shall glow, nor
w. freeze 3288
of sorrow, loneliness 968
One kind word can warm three w.
months 6662
Spring is w. defrosting 9893
Summer in w. Day in night 6153
to do job that was too cold last w.
9902

WINTERING

Think of yourself as seed w. in
earth 5672

WINTERS

All our w. are God's 10581

WIPE

Let it w. another's tears 6640

WIPES

Love w. out all sense of time 7229

WIRE

can have it all on the w. called
Jesus Christ 6521
We are the w. 7554
will never snap 6521

WISDOM

all w. gathered up in Bible 710
and virtue like two wheels of cart
11962
anger enters, w. departs 405
application of spiritual principles
11911
arranged by infinite w. 12
at proper times will forget 11963
attributes to the Son works in
which w. excels 11427
awful w. 11906
beginning of w. is to call things by
right names 11941
better to envy w. than riches
11921
bring to everyday living w. of God
3752
but folly 4877
by experience we learn w. 3530
By strides of human w. 11916
by-product of godly reactions
11911
by-product of right decisions
11911
cannot be wise with other men's w.
11958
casting doubt on God's w. 9993
Caution, eldest child of w. 11907
characteristic of w. not to do
desperate things 11922
comes by disillusionment 11964
comes by suffering 11965
comes from being faithful to small
tasks 11911
comes from the Lord 12127
comes not from trying to do great
things 11911
comes privately from God 11911
comes w. through the awful grace
of God 11919
Consideration, parent of w. 11909
Consideration, soil in which w.
may grow 11910
contemplate God's w. in
unchangeable order 4581
contrary to world 3752
creating w. which can enter men's
suffering 10884
deprive ourselves of royal display
of w. 4995
discrediting w. of God 6189
divine w. has given us prayer 8977

does not enter a malicious mind
11966
does not inspect but behold 11967
does this w. make me wiser 11933
Doubt, beginning not end, of w.
2934
dwells in minds attentive to their
own 6690
Every delay is hateful, but gives w.
11912
first step in w. is to question
everything 11935
first step of w. is to know what is
false 11943
from errors wise learn w. for
future 7794
get out of experience only w. in it
3551
give us w. to distinguish one from
the other 9060
God has all w. to direct you 4696
God in his w. gives self-knowledge
gradually 10006
God in his w. means to make
something of us 2887
God is perfect w. 9799
God is tempering for w. 4514
God's counsels in w. of world
stupidity 2809
God's essence beyond human w.
4670
God's w. for learning 5400
God's way contrary to w. on earth
1294
God, a seminary of w. 4698
God, w. is sublime 4477
good purchase though we pay
dear for it 11968
great w. to keep silent when
damaging words spoken 6271
grow in w, pardon more freely
4071
Heaven's eternal w. has decreed
9462
history contest between w. of God
and Satan 4916
Honesty first chapter of book of w.
5879
hope of nation not in w. of
executive 5190
if thinks he has found w, is a fool
11930
impossible for humans to
manufacture 12127
initiated into w. 10010
instead take infinite w. of God
3758
is honesty, knowledge applied
through experience 11972
is humble that he knows no more
6695
is knowledge of our own
ignorance 11942
is right use of knowledge 11973
is the wealth of the wise 11974
is to the soul what health is to the
body 11975
is vertical, comes down from
above 11928

keep secret is w. 1618
key to success 10799
knowing what to do next 11721
Knowledge and w. far from being
　one 6690
Knowledge comes, w. lingers 6692
　11926
leads from complex to simple
　11929
learn w. from failure 3630
lies in simplification 11927
like dawn that comes up slowly
　out of unknown ocean 11969
Man wise only while he searches
　for w. 11930
miser's money takes place of w.
　11795
Morality comes with sad w. of age
　7829
must sometime refuse what
　ignorance may ask 8971
my own w. insufficient for the day
　8822
My w. and my all 5456
nations have found w. in war
　11783
no w. like frankness 11952
no w. like silence 11953
not dispensed like a prescription
　11911
not dominant note in Jesus' life
　3848
not splashy and bold 11911
O w. of the world 10512
of God to plan our welfare 7093
oftentimes nearer when stoop
　than soar 6044
only a God who has infinite w.
　5438
outweighs any wealth 11976
Patience the companion of w.
　8412
perfected in w. 10010
Philosophy a longing after
　heavenly w. 8593
pray for w. yet 8827
Problems create courage and w.
　202
repudiate our own w. 3758
road to w. 11949
seeing life from God's perspective
　11971
Seizes the right, holds it to the last
　11906
short life with w. better than long
　life without it 11897
show want of faith in God by
　false w. 4322
Solomon famous for w. 795
Tears teach us w. 11019
Thine endless w, boundless power
　4659
Time converts knowledge into w.
　11323
to grow old master work of w.
　8178
to make stepping-stones out of
　stumbling blocks 9073

To seek w. in old age like mark in
　sand 11956
to seek w. in youth like inscription
　on stone 11956
trusting God's w. in dailyness of
　living 1803
uneasiness denying w. of God
　1569
wise man trusts w. of God 5459
wise men found their W. 1373
Worship brings w. 12127

WISE
Adversity makes a man w. 146
and good were all God's ways
　4904
art of being w. 11900
being w. is knowing what to
　overlook 11940
better to weep with w. than laugh
　with fools 9475
By nature honest, by experience w.
　11957
cannot be w. with other men's
　wisdom 11958
Christ, unspeakably w. 6499
competition of w. man with
　himself 1630
conversation with w. worth
　month's study of books 11898
easier to be w. for others than
　ourselves 11924
easier to look w. than talk wisely
　1856
Every scrap of w. man's time
　worth saving 11913
Every w. workman takes his tools
　163
fool wanders, w. travels 4058
fools understand better than w.
　1216
For never, never wicked man was
　w. 11883
From errors of others, w. man
　corrects his own 3257
from mistakes w. learn wisdom
　for future 7794
given poverty that he might be w.
　8806
God governed all things by w.
　counsels 4904
God guiding all that happens to
　w, holy end 5389
God hides in darkness from w.
　7709
God is too w. to make a mistake
　4461
God's designs infinitely w. 2545
good and w. lead quiet lives 9373
great man's foolish sayings pass
　for w. ones 5273
Hark, Hark, w. eternal Word
　6129
heart of w. man lies quiet like
　limpid water 11944
if evaluate things as really are
　8497
if evaluate things not as people
　report them to be 8497

If human beings as w. as animals
　5963
intellect of w. like glass 11945
Jesus proclaims fools are the w.
　6447
judge opinion 8205
lover values love of the giver 7157
man adapts to circumstances 1463
man cares not for what he cannot
　have 11899
man carries possessions within him
　11950
man does not grieve for what he
　has not 1793
man in storm prays to God 3997
man more use from enemies than
　fool from friends 9444
man prays for deliverance from
　fear 3997
man prays not for safety from
　danger 3997
man rejoices for what he has 1793
man seeks friend with qualities he
　himself lacks 4279
man sees a man's spirit 11896
man sees as much as he ought
　11902
man tells woman mouth beautiful
　when closed 2889
man trusts wisdom of God 5459
Man w. only while he searches for
　wisdom 11930
man will make more oppor-
　tunities than he finds 8210
man, even when he holds his
　tongue says more 11951
man, though slave, at liberty 4113
men change their minds, fools
　never 11978
men not always silent, but know
　when to be 11977
men ponder Bible 645
men say nothing in dangerous
　times 11979
men use studies 2996
Modest doubt is call'd beacon of
　the w. 2951
Money adds no more to w. than
　clothes to beautiful 7815
never w. to be cocksure 11923
never w. to underestimate enemy
　3163
No man ever became w. by chance
　11931
No man is born w. 11342
No man w. enough to be trusted
　with unlimited power 8714
Now is watchword of the w.
　11361
old owl sat on an oak 1832
Reproof never does a w. man harm
　11938
Riches serve a w. man, command
　a fool 7820
Said w. man to one in sorrow
　3076
sayings often fall on barren ground
　6672
Silence is foolish if we are w. 1869

Silence is w. if we are foolish 1869
Some w, some otherwise 4065
thinking well is w. 67
To know is not to be w. 11973
to let God hold you back 5422
to w. to let you pull wool over his eyes 3921
Too w. to err 4990
truly w. are color-blind 8245
truly w. if content 1820
We hate delay, yet it makes us w. 11959
When clouds seen, w. put on coats 11960
who understands his foolishness is w. 11947
Why aren't we like that w. old bird 1832
Wisdom is the wealth of the w. 11974
with merry, w. face 4195
words endure 11908
Yours the burden of w. guidance 8363

WISE MAN
If I were a w. 1376

WISE MEN
found their Wisdom 1373
saw light of star 1373

WISELY
accept old age w. 8158
Christ, w. speechless 6499
do duty w, leave issue to God 5176
easier to look wise than talk w. 1856
human to think w, act foolishly 5973
improve the present 8378
Much that may be thought cannot w. be said 2898
To judge w. must know how things appear to unwise 6595
to spend money w. most difficult 7823

WISER
admit wrong, w. today than yesterday 3249
After crosses, losses men grow humbler, w. 5990
be thankful God's answers are w. than your prayers 8861
does this wisdom make me w. 11933
foolish things of God w. 1294
get old, more foolish and w. 8127
have made one human being a little w. 6660
in the wrong, w. than yesterday 1593
left me none the w. 10596
man gets w, expects less 3497
never corrects mistakes, never w. tomorrow 8195
Now that I know I'm no w. than anyone 11933
planning well is w. 67

Satan now is w. than of yore 2690
Stronger by weakness, w. men become 7701
than you made feelings 4018
We become w. by adversity 245
Whose will is w. than my own 8825

WISEST
doing well w. and best 67
mind something yet to learn 3033
no life so meager w. can afford to despise it 7055
saints endure rather than escape pain 10847
thinks himself w, usually greatest fool 11917
Wait for w. of counselors, time 11347

WISH
And if for any w. thou dare not pray 8768
as we shall w. when we come to die 9120
But now, I often w. the night 2588
cannot make others as you w. 993
cannot make yourself as you w. 993
Death is godly man's w. 2372
Do you w. people to think well of you 5996
Do you w. to be great 5997
Dost thou w. to rise 6788
dream disguised fulfillment of w. 2968
Faith does not w. 3659
friend makes you w. to be at your best 4192
God had not given me what I prayed for 8879
I w. I were 870
If don't w. neighbor's good, you ask for your death 8067
If w. to be leader will be frustrated 10160
if w. to make everyone same 6189
large enough for a w, large enough for a prayer 8763
Let not that happen which I w. 9069
love is steady w. for loved person's good 7242
Man makes me w. for another world 8012
never w. for prizes of life 10875
no w. to see you loving anyone 10024
Prayer a w. turned Godward 8753
that will of God be fulfilled in thee 8448
Then pray to God to cast that w. away 8768
Those who w. to sing always find a song 5264
to be disappointed, look to others 6408
to be downhearted, look to yourself 6408

to be encouraged, look upon Jesus Christ 6408
to know the character of a love 7167
to pray a prayer in itself 8994
What you w. for your neighbor, ask for yourself 8067
When w. I am rich 11878
when we turn to God, our utmost w. is crowned 7451
Whence ability to w. evil, refuse good 5051
Why w. for privilege of living life again 7091

WISHED
take all things as if w, prayed for them 10926

WISHES
God knows how to use disordered w. 4644
Great souls have wills, feeble ones w. 8541
if man have half his w, double his trouble 2569
man has power to defy God's w. 4158
often be sorry if w. gratified 2573
people think with their w. rather than minds 7763
Selfishness asking others to live as one w. to live 10081
Selfishness not living as one w. to live 10081
when man w. impossible, he remembers God 7490

WISHFUL
not form of escapism or w. thinking 5629

WISHING
All our w. cannot change 38
Hope w. for a thing to come true 5927
to forestall God's arrangements 4322
Worldliness w. the forbidden possible to do 12054

WIT
Bible, where w. and reason fail 710
Converse makes sharp the glittering w. 10534
exchange most brilliant w. 4204
I have no w, no words, no tears 2587
of a nation discovered in its proverbs 9386

WITCH
No fairy takes, no w. hath power 1371

WITH
Thou wert w. me, I was not w. thee 4805

WITHDRAWN
live with ridicule, learn to be w. 1114

True dignity never lost when
honors w. 2765

WITHDRAWS
Christian, not one who w. 1251

WITHER
And flowers to w. at northwind's
breath 2324
does fruit of sin w. 10346
God will w. up every spring you
have 11689
Love neglected will soon w, die
7230

WITHERED
Man sees but w. leaves 8673
when sense of curiosity has w.
7829

WITHERS
heroes, contact w. them 8516
Hope w. away 7291
If spirit within w. 10694

WITHHELD
ever lurking disquiet in half w.
9683

WITHHOLD
Sometimes w. in mercy what we
ask 8877
to w. from child world's sorrows
8334

WITHHOLDS
who w. goods from his neighbor
10060

WITHIN
at rest w. himself 4307
before God can feel at home w. us
7450
Can give me peace w. 8451
capacity for change lies w. 3596
carry our worst enemies w. us
3157
Consider the nobility w. thee 9982
dark forces pent up w. 3165
Every man carries kingdom w.
6171
First keep peace w. yourself 8434
for healing men's lives must be
changed w. 5616
God at once w. and without his
works 4692
God is w, but not enclosed 4848
God is w. all things, but not
included 4612
God is w. filling 4848
God watches to see door move
from w. 4775
great deal of unmapped country
w. us 8669
Greatness w. reach of everyone
5283
have w. me the great pope, self
9929
Heart w. and God o'erhead 4331
Human improvement from w.
outward 1017
I feel the guilt w. 4642
I know God is w. me 5426
If spirit w. withers 10694

impulse of love is voice of God w.
4278
in hour of need faith born w. 3820
in quietness and turning w. 7725
interfering with God's working w.
us 10977
Jesus Christ, glory and beauty
come from w. 6352
keep w. own little sphere 4885
Let truth not shadows w. me speak
11515
looks for fault w. himself 9680
Lord, what a change w. us one
short hour 8867
man w. is angry 1706
moral law w. me 1709
Morality correct thinking w. 7832
more glorious world of God w. us
10535
multitude of words, empty w.
10245
my narrow heart 5788
my very soul 4795
no defeat save from w. 3627
not the shadows w. me 9070
O what may man w. him hide
2470
Only Christ can accomplish goal
w. us 8113
only enduring substance is w.
10654
Original sin malice ever flickering
w. 10347
Peace dwells w. the soul 8453
Peace w. makes beauty without
8463
person free even w. prison walls
4112
power of choosing good, evil w.
reach 5047
provided for from w. needs little
from without 5780
resources w. themselves 4286
rising of sap from w. 4160
seek solitude, look w. ourselves
4924
should act from w. with disregard
for opinions of others 6291
single events can awaken w.
stranger unknown to us 6873
storm w. that endangers 3997
There is a God w. us 7534
thou wert w. and I abroad 4805
Thought shows ugliness, beauty w.
11267
to be right w. where all concealed
6295
To understand any living thing,
creep w, feel beating of heart
3078
tumult of our passions w. 8800
Unless beaten w, bound to win
3627
Unless w. that which is above
11108
voice of a deep life w. 3700
What lies behind, before tiny
compared with w. 1058
When fight begins w. himself 6322

9940
wise man carries his possessions
w. him 11950
You were w. me and I was outside
7473

WITHOLDING
will take w. of honor quietly 5901

WITHOUT
all dangerous w. God's controlling
hand 4956
assistance of divine being cannot
succeed 5411
bigots, eccentrics, cranks, heretics
9318
body w. soul, a corpse 5088
building w. basis cannot stand
3826
can be no Christian life w. prayer
8938
can do nothing w. faith 3827
can do nothing w. grace of God
5207
can't hold a man down w. staying
down with him 10479
cannot be man I should be w.
times of quietness 7711
cannot learn w. pain 8276
cannot remain creative w. solitude
10579
Christ a hopeless end 5938
Christ life as twilight with dark
night ahead 7094
Christ, not one step 3822
Christianity rearing pagans 8308
consequences of action w. thought
11278
control young people unhappy
12178
debt, w. care 4044
Do not most moving moments find
us w. words 11986
Do w. the indispensible 6961
experience feeling led w. knowing
it 5392
faith impossible to please God
3823
faith in fatherhood of God 925
faith man becomes sterile, hopeless
3824
Faith w. thankfulness lacks
strength 11154
faith, society of indifferent 925
fatherhood of God 4632
fear w. love makes men desperate
9736
fearing to understand 4124
feeling understood by at least one
person 11613
first persevering through pain,
heartache, failure 6802
free will, man not in image of God
4158
Friendship w. self-interest rare,
beautiful 4238
frightful is solitude of soul w. God
10573
God at once within, w. his works
4692

God can no more do w. us 4533

God comes to see us w. a bell 4525

God in me, God w! Beyond compare! 4840

God in this life, w. him in next 1142

God is w. but not excluded 4848

God is w. growth, addition, development 4680

God w. whom one cannot live 4542

God we cannot 10221

God world maze w. clue 4522

God young people frustrated 12180

God, not over the threshold 5470

good example won't improve anybody 3436

goodness, no happiness 5060

gospel cannot live, fight, conquer w. prayer 9015

happy man's w. a shirt 11857

heretics world would not progress 9318

high pretensions to oppressive greatness 4204

history incomprehensible w. Christ 5709

hoped to be able to do w. God 5395

hypocrisy no new power can rise 8722

I am never w. God 4855

impossible for world to exist w. God 4597

impossible to rightly govern world w. God 5181

learning how to do w. the indispensable 7692

learning Jesus shed more light than scholars 6449

learning to be happy w. things we cannot have 8635

Life is to do w. 6980

Life lived w. forgiveness 4093

Life w. conflict impossible 6988

life w. purpose 4437

limit is how God is to be loved 7574

Lord's Prayer w. equal or rival 7154

love Maker w. hope of good 4807

Love rules kingdom w. sword 7270

love w. fear makes men remiss 9736

man w. courage, knife w. edge 1917

man w. faith, a walking corpse 3791

man w. prayer like tree w. roots 8752

man w. purpose like ship w. rudder 4436

many do w. things parents never heard of 8582

may be worship w. words 12121

may know there is a God w. knowing what he is 3814

Men seldom flatter w. purpose 4051

Morality w. religion 7833

neither is satisfied w. the other 4531

no gain w. pain 8273

no great genius w. mixture of madness 4398

no man can be a Christian w. morality 7830

No one rich enough to do w. neighbor 4258

no true love w. suffering 6506

no wilderness like life w. friends 4284

noise of the world w. 8800

None can live in love w. suffering 7246

nothing can exist w. God 4854

Nothing great done w. suffering 10875

Nothing great ever achieved w. enthusiasm 3178

Nothing so terrible as activity w. thought 6084

one single original thought 11237

Peace within makes beauty w. 8463

Power is to be able to do w. 8713

prayer, better heart w. words than words w. heart 8844

provided for from within needs little from w. 5780

road to hell w. signposts 5702

sacrifice no resurrection 4342

seeks applause from w. has happiness in another's keeping 5892

Seven days w. prayer makes one weak 8960

soul w. body, a ghost 5088

storm within that endangers, not storm w. 3997

task w. vision a drudgery 12006

than greatest of things w. meaning 7030

thy presence, wealth bags of cares 4877

thy sunshine and thy rain 11172

to be able to do w. is power 1818

to live w. prayer a foolish thing 8833

To think clearly w. hurry or confusion 6913

us, God will not 10221

using blatant tricks God brings suffering 10844

vision w. a task a dream 11730

What idea of God w. the sky 4512

Where marriage w. love will be love w. marriage 7668

whose vesting beauty 7109

Work w. love spells burnout 944

Works w. faith like fish w. water 3826

world of care w. 5817

worship of the heart 12131

worship w. seeing 4322

writing single line Jesus set more pens in motion 6449

WITHSTAND

friendship must undergo, w. shocks of adversity 4218

WITNESS

bear w. to mystery of God 7945

does not consists of propaganda 3336

evil soul producing holy w. 5011

glorifying God when no w. 1295

is not to what Jesus does, but to what he is 5790

means to live so life would not make sense if God did not exist 3336

not a w. to Jesus 11125

not stirring people up 3336

of church most effective when she declares 3796

The soul itself its awful w. is 3404

Truth is its own w. 11567

WITNESSES

baptism of Holy Ghost makes us w. to Jesus 5790

Conscience is a thousand w. 1667

eyes more exact w. than ears 3567

sin, two w. present to observe, our own selves and God 10418

two w: God, our own conscience 4872

WITNESSING

a quality of life 3344

not a once-a-week activity 3344

not a spare-time occupation 3344

You don't go w, you are a witness 3344

WITS

wise man trusts wisdom of God, not his own w. 5459

WIVES

Husbands in heaven whose w. chide not 7618

Husbands, w. should constantly guard against overcommitment 7617

not entering into conversation with w. 3904

try to tell husbands of troubles 3904

WOBBLE

don't get bent out of shape because you w. 6187

WOE

gave signs of w. 10314

Lord of himself, heritage of w. 9935

our w. is me pleases devil 2661

Teach me to feel another's w. 1552

WOES

No succor in my w. I want 8098

thoughtfulness for another's w. 1085

WOKE
That w. it unto day 4592
Until it w. one summer hour 2052

WOLF
Fear makes w. bigger 3969
foolish sheep makes w. his
 confessor 9473
Full many a sheep and lamb by w.
 is rent 8363
In front a precipice, behind a w.
 2733
madness for sheep to talk peace
 with w. 8446
No self-respecting w. guilty of our
 wars 10361
who feeds w. strengthens his y
 11064

WOLVES
Flatterers as w. resemble dogs
 4047
more dangerous than flies 11056
Where sheep, w. never far away
 8531
who goes with w. learns to howl
 9458

WOMAN
absurd to say a man can't love
 one w. all the time 7621
counsel a w. rather than bury 19
formed from beneath his arm to
 be protected 11982
formed from near his heart to be
 loved 11982
formed out of man's side to be his
 equal 11982
God found a better way for w.
 1120
golfer should marry w. who
 would rather shop than cook
 7656
I will not give a w. 21
ideal w. was waiting for ideal man
 7665
in biblical faith, w. is partner in
 ministry 11981
isn't sure she wants you to live 17
Man is fire, w. tow 10226
most important occupation for w.
 7856
To marry w. for her beauty 7661
twenty-nine much longer 312
under whose hands children grow
 up strong, pure 5857
Variability one of the virtues of a
 w. 7663
vowed never to marry until found
 ideal w. 7665
What would people of earth be
 without w. 11983
where w. equal with the man 3868
who creates, sustains home
 creator second only to God
 5857
with slop pail gives God glory
 1237

WOMANHOOD
not progress when w. lost its
 fragrance 7834

WOMAN'S
the Mighty, after submission to a
 w. pains 6142
'Tis w. whole existence 7278

WOMB
child in w. not lawful to destroy
 16
infinity walled in a w. until the
 next enormity 6142
into the virgin's w. 6150
of a woman who isn't sure 17

WOMEN
and men in the crowd meet,
 mingle 7150
are the church's strong rock 11980
commonest fallacy among w. 7854
God made w. to match the men
 3231
last at the cross, first at the altar
 11980
not denyin' w. are foolish 3231
spend money 7826
Whatever w. do must do twice as
 well 11984

WOMEN'S
know nothing of w. rights 3230

WON
destructive victories w. over others
 1165
Heaven is w. today 2986
may be sorry you w. or lost 6674
more battles w. by submitting
 11781
Peace w. by compromise
 short-lived 8464
triumphant Christian celebrates
 victory already w. 11672

WONDER
add word a day, friends will w.
 1853
As knowledge increases, w.
 deepens 6678
attention so concentrated no time
 to w. how we look 6056
Children listen to Bible with w.
 645
do not take time to w. if things
 worth doing 5590
every w. true 1290
greatest w. to find myself in heaven
 5655
Humility is to w. at nothing done
 to me 6010
I w. how I am ever to walk to the
 end 7090
In w, love and praise 4819
longer the shore line of w. 6702
mind dwells on w. of world 11301
need not w. whether God in
 receptive mood 4590
shall find God satisfying our sense
 of w. 3774
still they gazed, still the w. grew
 2994

stumble on w. upon w. 1290
television dulls w. 11031
that child of God should have sad
 heart 1096
the commonplace is full of w.
 6918
the more we know the more we w.
 4686
the starry heavens above me,
 moral law within me 1709
true knowledge of God result in
 sheer w. 6704
when our lives illumined by a w.
 4538
world will w. where they came
 from 9174
Worship is transcendent w. 12138
your body, what a w. it is 3039

WONDERED
he who has not w. in Isaiah 5224
I w. why, the years 179

WONDERFUL
A w. way is the King's Highway
 4313
Appreciation is a w. thing 437
believe in God, there will be w.
 surprises 4508
Each day is a w. gift 6524
earth, you're too w. to realize
 2974
From the w. was, by the w. is
 4313
God is so vastly w. 7463
God's love for sinners w. 4893
how much may be done 51
How w. is Death and his brother
 Sleep 2298
nothing more w. than alert, eager
 mind 7776
should no longer be called w.
 9411
To the still more w. is to be 4313
were works of God
 understandable, would be
 neither w. nor unspeakable
 4510
what a w. being the Lord Jesus
 Christ is 5782
What a w. world this would be
 3511
world w, inscrutable, magical
 12049
world's wonders, none more w.
 than man 7424

WONDERING
Knowledge begins with w. 6691
Set a child to w, on road to
 understanding 6691

WONDERS
Christ can do w. with broken heart
 10584
darkness has its w. 1788
Everything has its w. 1788
expect to find three w. in heaven
 5655
God does not need majority to
 work w. 1192

more we learn about w. of universe 11644

Numberless are the world's w. 7424

silence has its w. 1788

Welcome, all w. in one sight 6153

world, stage on which God displays many w. 12040

WONDER-WORKERS

baptism of Holy Ghost does not make us w. 5790

WONDER-WORKINGS

In w. or some bush aflame 8019

WONDROUS

is strength of cheerfulness 1099

Spirit of God will enfold you in a love so w. 5776

WON'T

fanatic w. change subject 3907

goes well, it w. last 3998

if you think too much of yourself, other people w. 9253

mistakes w. irreparably damage lives 3616

nonelect whosoever w. 3046

trouble is we w. let God help us 11454

unbelief is w. believe 2930

WOOD

cannot carve rotten w. 1070

cross is real w. 2147

If a man has good w. to sell 2776

To make a valentine God took two shafts of w. 2173

WOODLANDS

I to the w. wend, and there 8006

WOODS

though it be in the w. 2776

upon their summits wave in adoration 7997

with music ring 8039

would be very silent if no birds sang 7926

WOOED

to meeting with striped candy 1403

WORD

a balm or a bomb 12001

a kind w. never thrown away 6672

add w. a day, friends will wonder 1853

Anger quieted by gentle w. 372

Because they his deed and w. 2639

broadest w. is truth 11993

Christian more work than w. 1317

cross, God's last, endless w. 2153

cynic can chill with single w. 2176

darkest w. is *sin* 11993

dearest w. is *mother* 11993

deepest w. is *soul* 11993

difference between right w. and almost right w. 11992

embraces all heaven and earth 6511

even though that w. be in a whisper 6511

ever remember when regretted having said kind w. 6636

every suppressed w. reverberates 8528

Every w. for Christ away from discouragement 2940

friend, a w. when you're lonely 4174

God keeps his w. even when seems impossible 9321

God will have last w, will be good 4938

God's w. for my clearing 5400

good w. costs no more than bad w. 3128

Grace the final w. 5221

grasp mighty force behind things we say 12005

greatest w. is *God* 11993

happiness lies in unexpected friendly w. 3143

Hark, Hark, wise eternal W. 6129

He has but one w. 5872

He has no w. that gives hint of God 10274

his W. shall stand forever 9813

hope w. God has written on brow of every man 5947

how enduring w. God has spoken 730

if we took every w. at face value 9466

last deed done, last w. said 8082

longest w. is *eternity* 11993

love is a semantic confession 7312

love is a swampy one 7312

meanest w. is *hypocrisy* 11993

mind of God as discovered in W. and works 4675

mysticism, hard w. for "Kingdom of Heaven within" 7947

ne'er a w. said she 10596

nearest w. is *now* 11993

negative w. can defuse enthusiasm 12001

negative w. leaves you depressed 12001

never omitting speaking true w. 9491

no w. cross my lips that is not your w. 8748

Now it is his W. 6465

of parent fibre woven into character of child 8346

One greater than my heart whose W. cannot be broken 9813

One kind w. can warm three winter months 6662

One man's w. is no man's w. 6618

one small w. "to be" 3492

One w. can start a war 11759

out of season may mar a lifetime 2890

Plant w. of love heart-deep in a person's life 7289

positive w. becomes creative force 12001

positive w. makes you feel good 12001

positive w. releases positive energy 12001

primitive sound that is hardly a w. 11996

rashly spoken cannot be brought back 10681

remains unspoken, you are master 1835

Revelation is God's w. 4911

sharp w. cuts deeper than weapon 2051

single w. can turn you on, off 12001

Slander, at every w. a reputation dies 10468

snob belongs to sourgrape vocabulary 457

Speak that kind w. to sweeten a sorrow 6671

spirit is in every thought, w. and act 10697

strongest w. is *right* 11993

sweetest w. is *home* 11993

swiftest w. is *time* 11993

tenderest w. is *love* 11993

than speak reckless w. against servant of Christ 5143

the W. stern-sentenced to be nine months dumb 6142

to speak the difficult w. 6599

utter w, you are slave 1835

Was he ever ready with w. or good cheer 7423

When Jesus Christ utters a w. 6511

WORD OF GOD

accept or reject W. 686

gentle dogmatism that smiles while stands firm on W. 11188

Silence teaches us to speak W. 10562

still survives 730

when concur with promptings of Spirit, W. 5444

without illumination of Holy Spirit 752

WORDS

A thousand w. will not leave 101

Accept my thoughts for thanks; I have no w. 8792

accustomed to relying on w. to manage, control 10259

Actions don't always speak louder than w. 1833

an overdose may hurt 272

Apt w. power to asuage 3129

are but the shell 7726

are like medicine 272

are loaded pistols 11999

are slippery 11990

are things 12002

best prayers often have more groans than w. 8974

betray by speaking too many w. 628

bitter w. make people bitter 11985

born in the heart, not head 11997

breathe memories sweet as flutes 11998

call like a clarinet 11998

can sting like anything 12003

cannot express joy friend imparts 4269

cannot make you greater 1681

cannot speak for grief or ectasy 10274

charge like trumpets 11998

Charity is silence when w. would hurt 1085

Christ wrote no book yet w. counsel everywhere 6394

Christ's w. have same relevance 6359

Christ's w. never pass away 6523

Christ's w. pass into laws, doctrines 6523

Christ's w. pass into proverbs 6523

Christ's w. provoked acceptance or rejection 6377

Christ's w. simple, yet profound 6377

Christ's w. still not exhausted 6523

Christ's w. that carry weight 1536

Christianity condensed into four w. 1164

Cold w. freeze people 11985

contentious man will never lack w. 9357

Deeds are fruits, w. are leaves 2532

Do not most moving moments find us without w. 11986

Do you fully understand power of w. 12005

easier to swallow than eat angry w. 388

Emotion one of the w. that most deserve reverence 3054

emotionally loaded w. have their temporary effect 8845

essence of lying in deception, not w. 6859

fellowship without solitude void of w, feelings 10547

few w. will do 4302

fewer the w, the better the prayer 8978

Five w. cost Zacharias silence 11412

frantic stream of w. flows from us 1882

Friends speak with w. sweet, strong 4185

Give sorrow w. 5333

God cannot be comprehended in human w. 4682

God far exceeds all w. we can express 10249

Good w. worth much, cost little 11987

great w. to master are short 7000

harsh w. pierce the soul 373

healing w. not our own 10545

hot w. scorch people 11985

human voice gives you w. 7893

I have no wit, no w, no tears 2587

If only two tiny w. taken from them 4227

if receive not his w, they fly back and wound him 10447

ignorant uses w. for jargon 11998

Ill w. bellows to slackening fire 5145

immediate person uses many w. in his prayer 8981

Impure thoughts will not stand against pure w. 5028

in the world as w. in a book 7076

incarnation of emotions 12001

innocent in a dictionary 12004

instruments of music 11998

Into these two brief w. 8369

Jesus spoke w. never spoken before nor since 6449

Keep us from unkind w. 9106

Kind w. don't wear out tongue 6646

Kind w. music of the world 6645

Kind w. short, easy to speak 11988

Kind w. smooth, quiet, comfort 11985

Kind w. toward those you daily meet 6647

Kind w. echoes truly endless 11988

Kindness in w. creates confidence 6649

least-used w. by unselfish person 11653

Little passing w. of sympathy, silent threads of gold 6997

little w. of love 2503

Living is learning meaning of w. 7000

Lord's Prayer expressed in a few w. 7156

makes thousands, perhaps millions, think 12002

man of w. and not deeds like garden of weeds 9319

many great things expressed in single w. 10277

many w. expression of doubt 11991

may be worship without w. 12121

Men of few w. are best 1860

more power in silence than another by w. 3428

most important w. in vocabulary 11994

multitude of w, empty within 10245

murder when we destroy with w. 10683

music thousand times better than w. 7934

My thoughts, my w, my crimes forgive 9048

nails for fixing ideas 12000

need silence to recover from futility of w. 10556

never get to the end of Christ's w. 6523

never using two w. when one will do 12154

not just letters strung together 12001

not w. we have to look up in dictionary 7000

O God, hear these my final w. 9091

painful truth through loving w. 4289

People who have no secrets do not weigh their w. 8970

persist after meanings departed 1275

philosophy not best expressed in w. 1148

potent for good, evil 12004

potent who knows how to combine 12004

pour out millions of w, never notice prayers not answered 9019

powerless in a dictionary 12003

Prayer is more than w. 8923

prayer, better heart without w. than w. without heart 8844

Profanity fixes attention on w. rather than thoughts 9305

proverb much matter decocted into a few w. 9377

release energy 12001

rich as mother's answering back 11998

scarcely utters w. of humility 6041

seem so ambiguous 7934

Sharp w. dull respect 9488

Sharp w. make more wounds 393

should be measured with care 272

sigh can say more than many w. 8887

Silence more eloquent than w. 1870

silence of thoughts, w. 1767

Simple w. express great thoughts 11989

sound out like drums 11998

Speak approving, cheering w. 4223

Speak your kind w. soon 6663

stand by like impotent pale ghosts 10274

stimulators 12001

sweet as children's talk 11998

sweetest music in kind w. 11995

theology condensed into four w. 11195

Think not faithful who praise thy w. 3955

those luminous w. of Christ 6419

To God we use simplest shortest w. 9002

to reap praise sow gentle w. 1574

Treachery lurks in honeyed w. 4052

truth not w. but a life and being 11572

we shouldn't have said 3882

What power does anyone have to injure you with w. 6287

When w. leave off, music begins 7932

will probably not understand your w. 10251

wisdom to keep silent when damaging w. spoken 6271

wise w. endure 11908

With cryptic w, too strangely set 8049

with many w. convince of God's power 11991

wound caused by w. more painful 5119

wrathful w. make people wrathful 11985

WORDSWORTH

saw city, grew lyrical 10522

WORDY

abstains from giving w. evidence 1837

Silence prevents being suffocated by w. world 10562

unbelief that quenches the fire 11991

WORK

a blessing from God 12025

a way of life 3127

A workless worker in a world of w. 12016

all eating, none of the w. 3097

all have brains, what we need is w. 7755

ambition can drive you into w. 2862

among Christ's little ones, content 1802

An honest man's the noblest w. of God 5885

And life till my w. is done 12007

and play, artifical pair of opposites 12022

And scan his w. in vain 5378

anything that makes Christian w. difficult 7036

as if success depended upon ourselves 10791

as if you were to live a hundred years 12023

as though everything depended on you 8892

average person puts 25 percent into w. 2788

beginning most important part of w. 544

best play contains w. 12022

best servant does his w. unseen 10191

best w. God wants 941

Better to show up for w. at sunset 8141

Bible illustrates w. of God 737

By his first w. God gave me to myself 4528

by the next w. God gave himself to me 4528

can be defensive shield 3904

can sit and look at it for hours 12009

cannot choose our own w. 5446

Christ by first w. gave me to myself 6361

Christ must do your w. 1536

Christ, Completer of unfinished w. 6428

Christian more w. than word 1317

Christian w. crippled by blessings, traditions of past 10124

Christianity, not devotion to w. 1176

Christians don't w. to go to heaven 1356

Christians w. because they are going to heaven 1356

church, all one great w. 1447

cling to virtues sufficient to obscure w. of God 11701

cramping restrictions of hard w. 6386

create atmosphere of harmony, love 580

creation is God's w. 4911

day of worry more exhausting than day of w. 12056

day's w. will begin the next morning 2422

degree to which one's w. emblazon character of Christ 5306

Denying we can accomplish God's w. is worse kind of pride 9199

designed for eternity only done by Spirit 10181

dictionary only place where success before w. 3118

did ten times more w. 10825

do life's plain, common w. as it comes 12018

do with cheerful heart the w. God appoints 10150

Do your w. well 2355

don't show up until w. is done 6773

down to grave, shall have ended day's w. 11132

easy for those who like to w. 3126

ended up asking God to w. through me 4994

energy for w. advanced by prayer 8976

Every noble w. at first impossible 8536 2627

Everything born of God no shadowy w. 872

Evil is here? That's w. to do 3358

excuse for not entering into conversation 3904

expression of worker's faculties 12026

Faithless w. God never rewards 3825

fascinates me 12009

first w. after new birth 4537

for good of country gladly, as unto God 10525

For if thy w. on earth be sweet 5635

from early until late 12029

fulfill itself to glory of God 3127

get the w. of the Lord done 115

Give us the man who sings at his w. 3090

gives God glory 12013

go forth to w. till evening 6947

God able to w. failures into his plans 3613

God buries his workmen, carries on his w. 2286

God can w. through saints 126

God cannot w. in a vacuum 4824

God cannot w. with empty minds 4824

God cannot w. with prejudice 4824

God does best w. in difficult circumstances 3769

God give me w. 12007

God gives us ability to w. in his kingdom 4648

God has other w. for you 9658

God is at w. through the good 5014

God respects me when I w. 12008

God stooped to w. by, in his children 4467

God will find thee w. 10142

God's w. from beginning is revelation 4906

God, no lifeless, powerless w. 872

gospel of w. in Christian churches 130

Grace is God's energy at w. within his church 5219

Great sufferers do world's w. 10849

great word to master, w. 7000

greatest thing in the world 12027

Habits servants that regulate your w. 5498

Half the w. done to make things appear what they are not 2465

happy in w. three things needed 3101

hardest w. is to do nothing 6775

have not time for Christ whose w. it is 10117

Health enough to make w. pleasure 1809

heaven, w. is their rest, recreation 5644

holding nothing back 2774

Hope sets the head, heart to w. 5917

hope teaches w. with all energy 3834

Hunger a suitable comrade for w.-shy 6759

I like w. 12009

If cannot w. or rise from my chair 8135

if cannot w. out will of God 4974

if don't want to w. 3098

If God has w. for me to do 6921

if God took away your Christian w. 97

If interest in w. of others cool 7187

If w. for God because brings me good opinion 10158

If w. not going to communicate 9147

If w. of God be comprehended by reason 3841

If we w. upon marble, will perish 6796

if we w. upon men's immortal minds 6796

immortals whom we w. with 8483

Impossible to get exhausted in God's w. 940

In the morning of life, w. 6928

is man's great function 12024

Jehovah sharpens and prepares for w. 163

Jesus' w. was in marketplace 3331

journeymen cannot execute w. of prayer 8914

jump from worship to waiting to w. 10716

Kindness love in w. clothes 6652

Leave tomorrow's w. to tomorrow's time 12067

left my w. but just begun 9049

let us also w. for it 2791

let us strive on to finish w. we are in 5199

Lord calls to no special w. 1308

Lord, turn routines of w. into celebrations of love 12015

Lord, when thou seest my w. is done 12016

Love is not the w. of the Holy Spirit 7244

love of God persistent as artist's love for w. 4792

man appears for a little while to w. 7372

man to w. out in world will of God 3195

meat of life 12028

medium in which worker offers himself to God 12026

men bring w. home as excuse 3904

more interested in God than in w. for him 10141

Mundane w. sacred as parson's 3113

must be fit for w. 3101

must have success in w. 3101

must not be so lost in w. of earth 6108

must not do too much w. 3101

My w. is done, why wait 10942

necessary w. to arrive at solution 9009

no distinction between spiritual, material w. 6985

No great achievement without persistent w. 85

No leader ever did w. cheaply, easily 5289

No life dreary when w. delight 3106

No machine can do w. of one extraordinary man 8660

No person enthusiastic about w. 3108

no w. better than another 3123

No w. noble or good of emulation 2009

Nobody else can do the w. 6204

not a curse 12025

not a necessary drudgery 3127

not a thing one does to live 12026

not for purpose of making money 3127

not that we are at w. for God, he is at w. in us 5793

Not w. but worry makes us weary 12071

not what a man does that determines w. sacred or secular 7865

not your w. I want 351

Nothing is w. unless 12017 3111

Nothing void of God, he fills his w. 4860

nuisance knowledge acquired by hard w. 3014

of progress so immense 5944

Often assume God unable to w. 3613

on in despair 2601

one's self to death 344

Only when grief finds its w. done 5352

Opportunities usually disguised as hard w. 8221

out appreciation of redemption 11274

out what God has worked in 1012

Parents should w. together as two bookends 8322

People used to need rest after w. 3114

perfect w. God will accomplish 1468

power to w. under stress 8423

practice w. of forgiveness 4072

Prayer is a greater w. for God 8908

Prayer not a lazy substitute for w. 8924

presses and battle thickens 235

price is always w. 9759

problems opportunities in w. clothes 2726

productive w. must include play 12022

Religious w. done without gifts of the Spirit 10181

Satan is at w. through evil 5014

see devil's w. everywhere 2650

should find proper exercise, delight 3127

sing at w. like bird in wood 3084

small is the w. you have done 3174

so many forces at w. in, about us 5458

so taken up with Christian w. 10117

Strength of character may be acquired at w. 5849

supernaturally created for a supernatural w. 10206

takes hard w. to discipline 8335

temptation shows w. God has to do 11086

the divine w. in us 3766

The great Creator from his w. return'd 1967

the Lord of the w. 115

the w. will be completed 48

thing one lives to do 12026

three things needed to be happy in w. 12011

through handicaps found my w. 11147

Thy w. alone, O Christ 8451

to become, not to acquire 3124

to climb a mountain to pray 8860

To do his w. God must have cooperation 11269

To do his w. today 10122

to grow old master w. of wisdom 8178

To w. is to pray 7877

to wait often harder than to w. 8418

Today need exercise after w. 3114

Tomorrow day on which loafers w. 11404

too often w. is worshiped, not God 97

two great forces at w. in world today 4917

Waiting upon God w. which beats all w. 7724

We have hard w. to do 6881

well done never needs doing over 8579

What greater w. than training mind 3037

When his w. is done, his aim fulfilled 6803

When love, skill w. together 12020

when ought to be praying 9008

When you w. for the Lord 10217

When your w. speaks for itself 12021

When your w. speaks for itself, don't interrupt 6043

who has given me grace to w. 10208

Who love their w. 11686

Why is God at w. in me 3042

will do deep inner w. 10706

willing to go into debt for w. of God 3297

with fewer creaks, groans 1093

Without fantasy no creative w. comes to birth 2024

without love spells burnout 944

won't have to w. 3098

won't kill, worry will 12083

Worry less and w. more 9281

WORKED

Creatures that w. like machines 4120

God has w. in past history 5724

hard for him 46

I shall feel I have w. with God 1097

my best, subject to ultimate judgment 6591

not going to heaven because we've w. 5653

way from doubt to truth 2949

WORKER

Christian w. must be sent 10188

no royal road to becoming w. for God 9564

WORKERS

earn money 7826

God wants worshipers before w. 12099

only acceptable w. those who worship 12099

WORKING

Almighty w. on a great scale 8419

could add two hours to my w. day 9531

If a man gets money without w. for it 7800

in that position try w. 3503

In w. or in waiting, another year with thee 8077

interfering with God's w. within us 10977

Love is the Holy Spirit w. in us 7244

on a puzzle, pure and simple 9922

Salvation is worth w. for 9810

secret w. of the heart 4749

To pray when one ought to be w. 9008

until he starts w. 2772

When w. for others 3125

WORKLESS

faith God never regards 3825

WORKMAN

Every wise w. takes his tools 163

WORKMAN'S

hand hath toiled in vain 47

Passed by a man in w. guise 6458

WORKMANSHIP

Quality w. not expensive 3116

Quality w. priceless 3116

WORKMEN

God buries his w, carries on his work 2286

WORKS

accept Christ without knowing how it w. 1893

all God's w. unique 4993

Be not proud of good w. 9195

before w. can please God 5087

best awakening of reverence is contemplation of w. of God 9734

confession of evil w. beginning of good w. 5040

desire w. be according to his will 5411

difference between faith, w. 3786

Discipleship that God w. through us 2831

do right when offer faith, w. to God 3829

every moment we may do little w. excellently 5068

Faith root of w. 3699

For God, who loveth all his w. 5904

God at once within, without his w. 4692

God w. continually 6525

God w. in us the doing of the w. 10209

God w. powerfully, but gently, gradually 4814

God's great w. are silent 1956

Good w. never erase guilt 5061

grace given that we may do good w. 5209

Great w. do not always lie in our way 5068

greatest w. done by the ones 91

his sovereign will 4941

How, if we to be fittest, continue the same 981

Idolatry trust in one's own w. 6071

if separate faith and w. do wrong 3829

If thou wouldst taste his w. 4737

If w. of God easily comprehended 9411

If we miss seeing God in his w. 4995

love with which w. are done 7288

man most exalted of all God's w. 7395

mind of God as discovered in Word and w. 4675

miracles of Jesus ordinary w. of his Father 6479

more deeply he w. the mine 737

more skill, design than w. of man 1964

not based on number and excellence 98

not so much for importance of our w. 7288

Observe God in his w. 8031

of Holy Spirit not confined to institututional church 5791

of the Holy Spirit unpredictable 5791

patiently God w. to teach 7056

punishment w. with sense of justice 9355

sin death of good w. 10360

thanks God has vouchsafed me knowledge of his w. 11144

Thou changest thy w, purpose unchanged 4954

value of good w. based on love of God 10115

98

value of good w. not based on number 10115

We do the w. 10209

we try to do ourselves 3786

Were the w. of God readily understandable 4510

when faith is present, God w. through anyone 3723

When marriage w, nothing can take its place 7664

without faith like fish without water 3826

Written on thy w. I read 1966

WORKS OF GOD

transcendent greatness inspire awe 9734

WORKSHOP

Christian home is the Master's w. 5850

church is w. 1434

idle brain is devil's w. 6754

lazy man is w. for Satan 6749

than anything else in Lord's w. 10855

WORLD

a beautiful book 12039

a collection of cogs 9501

a great stage 12040

a jolly, kind companion 515

a ladder for some to go up, some down 7047

a mighty, interesting w. 2346

a searching for something beyond what the w. contains 7521

a strange time 525

a sure teacher 12052

a thought in God's eye 12044

a very nice place, an interesting place 6929

a weeping in w. as though Lord were dead 2611

able to know what everybody else in w. thinks 4332

Abounding sin terror of w. 5203

above man's head 11627

action might safely be made law for w. 3453

Adam introduced sin into w. 757

all equally responsible for w. 9678

All men whilst awake in common w. 2965

All revolutions from beginning to end of w. 4898

All the w. in grain of sand 1957

All the w. is a hospital 12030

All the w. suffers 6533

All's right with the w. 8233

alms money put to interest in other w. 11359

always apprehensive 10512

always restless 10512

always tumultuous 10512

ambitiously seek after w. while living 2344

angry with God for creating w. 481

another w, where wrongs are
corrected 5678
appears very little 4707
art, point the w. toward ultimate
truth 1998
as place of training w. not so bad
5535
asks, How much does he give
10735
at its worst, Christians must be at
their best 1353
bad w, an incredibly bad w. 1293
beating up thro' all the bitter w.
8911
beautifully serenaded at the start
7886
beauty, wonder, power 8054
believed in God, w. had meaning
7011
best thing in w. for you 138
better off without ignorance,
doubt 3778
Bible great and wide as w. 750
Bible shows how w. progresses
723
Bible walks ways of w. 645
Bible, compendium of human
experience in w. 701
Bible, most thought-suggesting
book in w. 719
bondage is with w. not saints 4159
breath of one eternal idea 4594
brilliance without conscience 1705
broad w. of man's voyage 3689
by existence proclaims God 1953
by those who suffered w. has
advanced 10858
can argue against Christianity as
institution 1307
can have both heaven and hell in
this w. 7078
can no longer revolve around you
1306
Can the w. exist 45
cannot add to peace of w. 580
centered in God is peace 8436
changes 6455
character formed in stormy
billows of w. 1042
charged with grandeur of God
8044
childhood earlier miniature w.
1126
childhood model of greater w.
1126
children manage homes 525
Christ directs us to the w. 12031
Christ enters w. to heal its wounds
6487
Christ Jesus came to w. clothed in
humility 5992
Christ lived in another w. 6436
Christ living at heart of the w.
6369
Christ passed through w. like
flame 867
Christ told w. truth about itself
11525

Christ's method of better w. alone
succeeds 6487
Christ's outward life immersed in
w. 6439
Christ, to tear your name from
this w. 6496
Christian has that which is
impossible to w. 10512
Christian's place is in the w. 1330
Christianity will change w. 1196
Christianity, no control over state
of w. 1188
Christians to cleanse, sweeten w.
1271
Christians who did most for this w.
5629
Christians who have turned w.
upside down 11735
church does not echo but
confronts w. 1428
church in w. bombarded with evil
1433
church in w. buried with hatred
1433
church in w. torn with violence
1433
church members direct churches
525
church most universal body in w.
1277
church to bring crucified Christ to
w. 1405
collapsing w. more conducive to
understanding truth 11491
coming of Jesus into the w. 6146
compulsive self-seclusion toward
our w. 7072
consecration is going out into w.
1721
continual looking forward to
eternal w. 5629
created w. small parenthesis in
eternity 3284
cross of Christ an offense to the w.
6317
crowded with God 4871
dark, uneasy w. of family life 3886
deaf live in silent w. so remote,
different 9094
Death is but crossing the w. 7319
delusions in w. that evils cured by
legislation 5184
depart without fear out of this w.
2338
devil man of the w. 2651
difference between Christian love,
values of w. evident 6278
difference which rouses contempt
of the w. 10917
Difficult child at war with w. 1125
disgracefully managed 3203
divine eternal drama 1981
division high, deep between
Christian, w. 1338
do not know when w. drama will
end 9911
does not have facts 8456
does not understand theology or
dogma 7313

Don't go around saying w. owes
you a living 9652
don't have to light all the w. 7107
don't want us free to express faith
creatively in w. 6824
dying for want of good hearing
9163
dying not for want of good
preaching 9163
early Christians so much in other
w. 5666
easy to believe in God in our little
w. 592
embarrasses me 12038
Enemy-occupied territory 1190
enter w. alone, leave it alone
10574
essential difference between you
and the w. 10917
Evangelism supernatural remedy
for w. 3304
event which Creator of w. has in
view 4898
every burned book enlightens the
w. 8528
Every man is a miniature w. 6487
Every step of progress w. has made
7673
Everyone thinks of changing w.
964
everything in it surprising 12037
existed before foundation of w.
3490
expect to pass through this w. but
once 10152
extending into ever-increasing
enormity 1975
Failure not worst thing in w. 3589
Farewell, vain w. 12032
fast becoming a madhouse 525
fight vigorously evils of the w.
6619
Filling the w. he lies in a manger
6122
finest cheating in w. done under
guise of honesty 5888
for all joys, riches of the w. 5652
For most men w. is centered in self
8436
For truth-teller w. has little liking
11501
forced to be good, happy 4149
friend comes in when w. has gone
out 4167
frown, it will look sour 515
full of care, sorrow 10639
full of faces 8995
full of two kinds of people 10198
full of wickedness and misery
4149
funny old w, man's lucky if gets
out alive 6936
genius sees w. at different angle
4389
getting on in w. chief object in life
10086
gigantic celebration in unseen w.
3326
given to man in trust 3195

glad of excuse not to listen to gospel 1334

Glorious the w. of God around us 10535

God compelled to conceal himself from w. 4657

God governs the w. 5176

God has a plan for this bankrupt w. 4902

God has taken w. upon his heart 10922

God has to take some people out of this w. 11809

God helps us view w. from new perspective 4735 4308

God is not saving w. 3308

God is the poet of w. 4474

God lets himself be pushed out of the w. 4899

God loved w, do likewise 7172

God passes through thicket of w. 4463

God pity the Christian w. gets best of 1330

God plans personal visit to his own w. 6127

God saying to w, "I love you" 7173

God wanted w. to have music 7886

God wants to come to his w. through man 4549

God with patience leading w. 4474

God would not permit evil in w. 5017

God's counsels in wisdom of w. stupidity 2809

God's epistle to mankind 8045

God's love can enfold whole w. 4760

God's strength worth more than w. 10768

God's w. balanced, calm, in order 420

God, not the w, can give peace 8456

God, weak and powerless in the w. 4899

going to have music at the last 7886

good heart better than all heads in w. 5054

Good-bye proud w! I'm going home 2291

gospel not made to dominate w. 5099

government cannot redeem w. 5177

Grace comes into soul as sun into w. 5213

great in resources 10512

great man's w. bounded by limits of vision 11728

great of w. those who loved God more 5295

Great thing in w. is 4434

great w. of facts 592

Great, wide, beautiful, wonderful w. 8010

guided by clocks that show wrong time 2803

had music at the start 7886

Half the w. unhappy 2866

Hamlet, not his w, that is wrong 7396

happiness way we look at the w. 5538

has disease called man 7432

has made marriage scrap of paper 2924

has many religions, one gospel 5106

has yet to see what God can do 2835

hated, crucified Jesus 2168

have no rock under your feet 10512

have not loved the w, nor the w. me 12033

have not peace 10512

He who gives most light to w. 6004

He who governed w. before I was born 10145

he worries about all the trash in the w. 7670

Heaven is our home, the w. our inn 7077

help the w. go around 9114

history of w. contest between God, Satan, fallen men 4916

holier man is, less understood by men of w. 5760

holy life is living above w. while in it 5736

home wild place in w. of rules 5842

honors of this w. puff, emptiness, peril 5898

hopeful in prospects 10512

horribly disordered 10521

hostile person lives in a hostile w. 9441

How endless is volume God has written of w. 6901

how much better this w. than hell 2592

How weary seem all uses of this w. 2603

I am a little w. made cunningly 7384

I am in love with this w. 8011

I don't belong here 6929

I had the w, it was nothin' 3855

ideal child would find no fitness in w. 8293

If 10 percent holy, w. converted before year's end 5750

if did duty, might be full of love 12041

if full of the w. no room for Spirit of God 5783

If God forget w, would cease to be 4597

If I hate or despise any one man in w. 5599

if spirit withers, so will w. we build around us 10694

if take pride in greats of w. 3861

If think of w. as place for happiness 5535

If this is God's w. 3233

if this w. were all man, would lose all hope 8012

if w. had refrained from evil 5031

If w. has knocked you out, get up 1024

If w. is cold, build fires 4250

immeasurable totality of energies, forms 1975

impossible for w. to exist without God 4597

impossible to rightly govern w. without God 5181

In a w. I never made 3978

In Christ church has enough to feed w. 6374

in constant flux 977

In faith, hope w. will disagree 1079

in the w. as words in a book 7076

In this w. I am a stranger 6929

In this w. only two tragedies 2570

In w. called tolerance 11394

in w. everything depends on taking initiative 5446

In w. not what we take makes rich 624

in w. ruled by cause and effect 11590

In w. what we give up makes rich 624

in which creatures do good or harm 4132

in which doubt so close to faith 7081

in which heartbreak so close to happiness 7081

in which sorrow so close to joy 7081

in with God, at outs with w. 12035

In youth w. began to exist when he was born 12169

infant w, wrapped in swaddling clothes of light 7886

inmates are trying to run asylum 525

intellectual w. stale, unprofitable if we knew everything 9286

Into the dangerous w. I leapt 808

into the real w, the real waking 5672

is a great sculptor's shop 9822

is a looking glass 436

is a net 12051

is big, its troubles still bigger 10520

is brimming with happy thoughts 2020

is divided into people 93

is drowned in sleep 1514

is full of beauty 12041

is full of educated derelicts 8555

is full of untold novelties 8507

is God's book 12042
is God's nursery for his upper
  rooms 12043
is God's w. still 3195
is made to mingled pattern 5052
is my Father's house 1310
is not a prison house 7530
is so empty 4280
is still a miracle 12049
is the land of the dying 7064
is too much with us 12046
is very lovely 7048
is vestibule of eternity 6670
is wrong side up 12047
it is a wilderness 11021
Jesus gave w. such mature insights
  6196
Jesus is risen, he shall the w.
  restore 9692
joy a secret spring w. can't see
  6529
kind of spiritual kindergarten
  7530
Kind words music of the w. 6645
knock themselves and their w.
  upside down 8850
know origin by name of God
  1977
land of dying 2400
Laughter is God's hand on
  troubled w. 6731
law of mutation belongs to fallen
  w. 4589
learn patience by going into
  hurly-burly w. 8422
leave the w. confessing 737
Leaving the w. their day 7475
Let him that would move w. move
  himself 3439
lie travels around w. 6846
lies down in sepulchre of ages
  3266
like robbing w. of sun 4299
lived not in one w. but in two
  3292
look on loveliness of w. 10592
look upon w. as my parish 3312
Lord of this w. also Lord of every
  other 6092
Lord's Prayer most fearful prayer
  in w. 8828
love beyond the w. cannot be
  separated 7319
                                  3291
Love is medicine for sickness of w.
  7250
Love one ingredient of which w.
  never tires 7251
love such as w. had never before
  seen 6419
love the panacea for ills of w.
  7203
Love the subtlest force in w. 7255
loving person lives in a loving w.
  9441
luxuries of w. cannot satisfy lonely
  7176
luxury being in the w. 3480

made significant mark on his w.
  8793
made to mingled pattern 4335
Magnificent, his six days' work, a
  w. 1967
make man holy, put him back into
  unholy w. 5759
makes human life tolerable in w.
  4999
Man cannot live all to this w.
  12109
man cannot understand 3495
man flung without knowing how,
  why into w. 3495
Man makes me wish for another
  w. 8012
man technically capable of
  destroying w. 9872
man to work out in w. will of God
  3195
man too good for w, no good for
  his wife 7594
man travels w. in search of what
  he needs 5815
Man's w. encompassed by anxiety
  420
Man's w. has become nervous 420
Man, the glory, jest, riddle of the
  w. 7417
manifold in methods 10512
many a battle fought w. knows
  nothing about 7061
men who are lifting w. upward
  3142
mind dwells on beauty, wonder of
  w. 11301
Mind w. less and God more 2443
more glorious w. of God within us
  10535
more we stir in w, more we are
  entangled 12051
most powerful influence in w.
  5766
moving toward w. of throwaway
  products 10524
must come under omnipotent
  surgery 10521
must conquer the w. or the w. will
  conquer you 7096
must turn back on one-half of w.
  9151
mystic too full of God to speak to
  w. 7965
name of Jesus plowed into history
  of w. 5727
natural w, impossible to be made
  over 873
needs changing 1333
neurotics suffered to enrich w.
  4390
neutrality in conflict of w. 4999
never feel God will cast evil out of
  w. 3415
never will w. know all it owes to
  neurotics 4390
new w. will arise from religious
  mists 637
next w. is land of the living 7064

Night conceals w, reveals universe
  8083
night without Christianity 1214
No God, no w. 4485
no great men in this w. 8668
No one is useless in this w. 10175
no such thing as freedom in w.
  4159
noise of the w. without 8800
noisy w. where people indifferent
  592
nor bow'd to its idolatries a
  patient knee 12033
not absolutely given to man 3195
not bound to make the w. go right
  10150
not enough darkness in w. to put
  out light of candle 8241
not sufficiency in w. for man's
  greed 3204
not that they might escape the w.
  8805
Not till we have lost w. do we
  find ourselves 10549
not w. out of joint that makes
  problem 7396
not well-adjusted who makes w.
  better place 6196
nothing certain in this w. 7062
nothing in w. more precious than
  person 2343
nothing in w. more squandered
  than human being 2343
Nothing in w. without meaning
  4903
nothing perfect in this w. 2085
Nothing that happens in w. by
  chance 4948
nothing you can rely on 10512
nothing, smoke, shadow, pain
  4412
O God, stand by me against all
  the w. 9109
O God, thy w. is dark 10878
O w, as God has made it 8030
O wisdom, strength of the w.
  10512
observing way we undergo trials
  3319
odds w. can throw against
  tortured soul 3736
Of all delights of this w. 10228
of automata, hardly worth
  creating 4120
of care without 5817
of little use who cannot read it
  12039
of love shut in 5817
of nice people as desperately in
  need as a miserable w. 7827
of nuclear giants, ethical infants
  1705
of strife shut out 5817
one family in love, forbearance,
  common joy 9093
only hope for w. 5094
Only in quiet mind is adequate
  perception of w. 7718
Open eyes, w. full of God 4861

Order governs the w. 2659

out of joint 10521

over the dead w. has no power 2395

owes onward impulses to men ill at ease 2875

owes you nothing, it was here first 9652

pain, God's megaphone to rouse a deaf w. 8257

painting 1981

parted by the hurrying w. and droop 10578

patients are writing prescriptions 525

peace which the w. cannot give 422

peace which the w. cannot take away 422

person down in w. ounce of help better 3146

plainer I hear immortal symphonies of w. to come 11132

plenty of other people occupied with affairs of w. 9261

poetry 1981

poverty a hundred million mothers weeping 8699

poverty-striken, starvation-ridden w. 10051

power to blow our w. to pieces 10087

prayer beginning of uprising against disorder of w. 9001

Prayer moves the arm which moves the w. 8950

prayers for evangelization of w. irony if lip service 3320

preferable to have w. against thee than Jesus offended 8525

present state of w. diseased 10271

Psalm 23 filled w. with melodious joy 801

rather that w. be at odds with me 6294

rationalism tries to find God in picture of w. 4495

reaction of w. is to get rid of him 6127

reads Christians more than Bible 575

Real goodness points to another w. 5079

real w. invisible spiritual realities 615

realize nothing is secular in w. 4732

reasonable man adapts to w. 980

reflection of man's face 436

reform thy w, beginning with me 9103

reformation of the w. 3230

regard seen w. as real w. 3812

regard unseen w. as unreal w. 3812

reject Christ's existence, w. inexplicable riddle 5728

representing in w. Order to come 2103

requires fat fee 12052

resolved that in this w. 1810

rushed about like some monster loose in your beautiful w. 7473

same Jesus as before w. began 6466

Satan tried Jesus Christ becoming King of w. 11082

says, "What can't be cured must be endured" 1335

schemes of w. reconstruction have failed 6487

science dragon capable of destroying w. 9870

sculpture 1981

see w. being turned into wilderness 8445

seeing truth lived through us 3317

sets course for how we live in seen w. 3812

Shall bid that w. decay 4592

shall take care of it when I am dead 11367

shown w. typical Christian a bore 867

sick of its business 10578

Silence prevents being suffocated by w. 10562

since ceased to think of other w. become ineffective 5656

since thou hast shut me up in this w. 7006

sixteen hours daily thinking about w. 7491

slaves to the spirit of this w. 3018

so extremely odd 12037

so kind, you leave with regret 2293

so rich in delusions truth is priceless 11523

So shines good deed in naughty w. 2499

social compulsions of an unredeemed w. 10003

something in Jesus rebuked w. 2168

soul of man like the rolling w. 10673

spirit lamp w. blows upon 10696

Spirit of God in sharp opposition to easy ways of w. 5776

spiritual w, Jesus Christ makes possible 873

stage on which God displays many wonders 12040

stars giving beauty to the w. 9116

started with wars, shall be destroyed with wars 11765

strike at the sin of which w. is full 10304

students threatening schools 525

sufficiency in w. for man's need 3204

sun with one eye vieweth w. 11645

Take prayer out of the w. 8967

take riches with you to other w. 11824

take unholy man out of unholy w. 5759

takes notion of God from Christians 575

Tears showers that fertilize w. 10625

tendency of w. is down 7529

Than this w. dreams of 8869

than to love the w. and be a hero 10777

Thank God for having created this w. 5678

that is yours; now cultivate it 3195

that they might learn to conquer w. 8805

The safety of the w. was lying there 6133

The w. confess its sin 4642

The w. is moving so fast 66

The w. recedes; it disappears 2389

The w. was built in order 1976

The w. would be nicer than ever 909

there I can read thy power, wisdom, love 12048

Things do not happen in w, are brought about 4953

things that hold in slippery w. 4643

Thou art not my friend, I'm not thine 2291

Thou didst create the w, 'twas thy proud mandate 4592

thought of one eternal God 4594

thought, willed, realized by God 1975

threat to stability of w. is hunger 8692

three hardest tasks in w. 7838

Through faith unseen w. takes shape 3812

tired of its pleasures 10578

To be honest as this w. goes 5867

To be nobody but myself in w. 6215

to die amid ringing blast of archangel's trumpet 7886

To forsake Christ for w. 6495

to know most satisfying thing in w. 5450

to live in neutral w. nightmare 4999

To make message interesting to w. 5109

to peep at such a w. 10529

to the faithful w. is a possession 11696

To understand the w. and to like it 7069

to you seems drained of sweets 5575

today doesn't make sense 8508

too dangerous for anything but the truth 11545

too small for anything but brotherhood 11545

tough in thousand cruel ways
1211

toy w. which moves when pulls
strings 4132

treadmill of rat-racing w. 350

trouble in w. caused by people
wanting to be important 9220

trouble with w. is 10518

truth belongs to heaven, not w.
8596

twilight in w. with Christianity
1214

two great forces at work in w.
today 4917

Unbelief makes w. moral desert
11595

understands love, sympathy 7313

Undulate round the w. 2237

Unheard by the w. rises silent to
thee 8778

unless meditation results in
changing conditions in w. 7725

unreasonable man adapts w. to
himself 980

unseen w. takes shape as real w.
3812

until kingdom of this w. is
kingdom of our Lord 6939

until the busy w. is hushed 9105

use leisure, happiest people in w.
5567

vast neurotic misery of w. 4437

vision and a task is hope of w.
11730

vision of w. unshaken, unshakable
3292

walk with the w, can't walk with
God 12034

want church that will move the w.
1452

wants geniuses just like other
people 4394

wars within w. reflection of wars
within people 11764

was in liquidation 784

wavering Christian no respect
from w. 2771

way we handle trials makes w.
pause 10938

We make w. miserable in
measuring by moral maxims
6826

weep not that w. changes 983

What a wonderful w. this would
be 3511

What God may do on w. scale
7564

What is this thing called the w.
3485

What w. calls virtue a name, a
dream 11720

what we have done for the w.
remains 10091

What you possess in w. will
belong to someone else 1062

When a true genius appears in w.
4400

when asleep in w. of his own 2965

when church different from w.
5096

When God makes the w. too hot
283

When God measures men in the
next w. 6112

When God thought, the w. was
born 11244

When the w. is still and dim 7927

when wake on January 1 w. will
look same 8080

Whenever sounds of w. die out in
soul 4968

where message is crazy tale 592

Whereto the w. beats time 2268

Wherever you are, friends make
your w. 4212

Who bathes in worldly joys swims
in w. of fears 8615

whole w. booby-trapped by devil
2701

whole w. is my native land 908

whole w. stands still 1369

whom w. esteems as good,
condemns as bad 5042

will always keep eyes on spot
where crack was 9612

will be peace in the w. 8441

will be restless with place in w.
4311

will find w. quite intolerable 5535

will never change w. until we are
changed 1333

will never outgrow need for love
7251

will satiate ourselves with crumbs
from w. 12050

will seem two hundred times more
real than God 7491

will wonder where they came from
9174

willing to take one w. at a time
6092

window through which w. sees
God 3438

window through which you see w.
8573

Winning w. to Christ means
winning individuals 3343

wisdom contrary to w. 3752

With doctrine w. taken apart, put
together 11213

with what little understanding w.
is ruled 5174

withdrawing into ever-decreasing
minuteness 1975

without children, w. without
newness 1104

Without God w. maze without clue
4522

Without heretics w. would not
progress 9318

wonderful, inscrutable, magical
12049

Work greatest thing in the w.
12027

Worship seeing w. in light of God
12133

Worship to see w. from God's
point of view 12133

would be far less angry feeling in
w. 9465

would have known little progress
9311

would keel over 6184

would shake it to its foundations
6496

Yet the light of the bright w. dies
7306

you are beautifully dressed 8010

You come into w. alone 7151

you go out of w. alone 7151

you've seen the w. 8054

youth a spirit of relating to the w.
12183

WORLDLINESS

accepting values of man-centered
society 12053

difference between w, godliness is
renewed mind 7769

excluding God from our lives
12053

mental slavery to illegitimate
pleasure 12054

not only doing what is forbidden
12054

twists values by rearranging price
tags 12054

wishing the forbidden possible to
do 12054

WORLDLY

may not put trust in w. thing 187

never set heart on w. success
10875

no w. gain with loss 1776

no w. loss without gain 1776

people imagine saints find it
difficult to live 4159

pure in heart, not sophisticated
and w. 5001

saints need no w. or intellectual
greatness 5301

spirit shuts Bible 683

Who bathes in w. joys swims in
world of fears 8615

WORLD'S

About the w. despair 2589

And the w. danger 6133

Christ great central fact in w.
history 5710

Christ turned w. standards upside
down 5001

death but a parcel of the w. life
2338

death but a piece of the w. order
2338

doctrine master key to w. problems
11213

easy to live after w. opinions 6195

God can make pieces of w. puzzle
fit 4735

gospel, grain of sand that upsets
w. machinery 5099

great men not commonly great
scholars 5302

Great sufferers do w. work 10849

has not rest at home is in w. hell 5828

Love like a lovely rose, the w. delight 7179

Most of w. great souls have been lonely 7138

No trembler in w. storm-troubled sphere 3765

Numberless are the w. wonders 7424

O'er the w. tempestuous sea 5428

one of w. greatest tragedies 5625

one, only remedy is cross 2169

see no way out of the w. misery 7099

share w. sorrow 10592

shortest sermon is traffic light 10109

Skepticism has not changed w. heart 5723

teachings of Christ can solve w. problems 6487

the w. great Shepherd now is born 6123

thy book 12048

to withhold from child w. sorrows 8334

toddler, w. opponent of law, order 1129

w. an inn, death the journey's end 2330

who fills w. unempty'd granaries 11138

Who see the w. great anguish and its wrong 426

WORLDS

A thousand w. which roll around us brightly 4592

And wheels his throne upon the whirling w. 1963

can send w. rolling in space 4951

love of God, love that made the w. 4792

Midst flaming w, in these arrayed 4719

no death, only change of w. 2391

no more difficult to make million w. than one 7940

room for ten thousand times ten thousand w. 4760

Unnumber'd w. attend 4672

WORLDWIDE

Only Jesus w. remembrance 1369

Spirit of God gives w. outlook 7786

WORM

Before the w. tore Eden 2123

difference between Almighty God and helpless w. 3786

God feeds even the w. in the earth 9347

God makes the glow w. and star 8008

Is man a god or a w. 3494

O senseless man who cannot make a w. 6073

saint does not call himself a w. 9784

WORMY

because he enjoys being w. 9784

WORN OUT

To be w. is to be renewed 7071

WORRIED

about future 8632

and now knowing God 7888

Lord cannot endure any who love him be w. 3986

Today the tomorrow you w. about yesterday 11383

WORRIES

about all the trash in the world 7670

eat you when you're alive 12084

forget the w. in your head 240

quiet mind one that nothing w. 7773

rid of fears, w, bad eating habits 12076

Splinters help you forget w. 240

Ten die of little w. 12061

WORRY

a species of myopia 12086

about tomorrow, be unhappy today 11402

absence of thought 12078

because you w. too much 12074

comes from humans 12127

day of w. more exhausting than day of work 12056

Do not w. may never happen 3500

does not empty tomorrow of its sorrows 409

Don't hurry, don't w. 9530

Don't tell me w. doesn't do any good 12060

don't w. about rumor, slander 6271

empties today of its strength 409

failure to think 12078

fills with gloom the days 12091

gives a small thing a big shadow 12085

gives indigestion 12091

gives sleepless hours 12091

Happy is man too busy to w. by day 12062

If I try to w. it out 1472

impossible for Lord to experience 12127

indication God cannot look after us 12087

interest paid by those who borrow trouble 12090

Keep mind free from w. 5561

less and work more 9281

like a rocking chair 12088

make my heart sit down 419

need not w. about consequences 6306

never keeps trouble from overtaking you 12091

never robs tomorrow of sorrow 12089

Not work, but w. makes us weary 12071

on big, broad, easy road ought to w. 2745

Only one type of w. correct 12074

only saps today of its strength 12089

proven that w. undermine health 5612

sand in machinery of life 3731

saps strength 10406

Tain't worthwhile to wear a day all out 12055

tendency to w. about things that cannot be changed 7793

that gets you, not loss of sleep 10483

Things I w. about don't happen 12060

too sleepy to w. at night 12062

wealth makes people w. about losing it 11859

When w. is present 12081

Why w? What can w. do 12091

won't have to w. about aches, pains 2346

Work won't kill, w. will 12083

Worship dispels w. 12127

yesterday's w. and tomorrow's anxiety 12092

WORRYING

about trash party will make 7670

faith means not w. 3805

hour w. on our knees is not prayer 9009

Life's too short for w. 12068

WORSE

always someone w. off than yourself 217

And to make bad matters w. 2589

Bad is called good when w. happens 153

bad man w. when pretends to be saint 6045

boredom of life for the rich is w. misfortune 11854

comfort things might have been w. 11439

discussion apt to become w. than useless 4124

Doth make fault w. by excuse 3934

excuse w. than lie 3474

fear of death w. than death 2376

Gossip w. than fighting 5134

governed by men w. than themselves 5193

grow neither better nor w. 8180

honest man not w. because dog barks at him 5866

if neighbor is w. for our Christianity 8065

is it to have eyes and not see 6289

Lilies that fester smell w. than weeds 5039

Marriage does not make us w. 7633

no better and no w. than I 4255

no charity, w. kind of heart trouble 1077

not w. person is somebody
  denigrates 1067
Nothing seems w. to man than his
  death 2342
pain of mind w. than pain of body
  8272
perhaps little praying w. than no
  praying 8889
poor man expects no change for w.
  8695
sin seems w. in consequences than
  intentions 10294
temptation leaves us better or w.
  11052
than flooded basement is flooded
  attic 8581
think divorce a panacea find
  remedy w. than disease 2927
to submit to dictation w. than war
  11768
tumble when fall over own bluff
  7587

WORSHIP
a way of living 12133
an adventure of the spirit 12119
And w. only thee 6074
aware of own limitations 12136
aware of task at hand 12136
aware of the Father 12136
aware of the Father's directives
  12136
begins in holy expectancy 12105
Bless all who w. thee 619
brings wisdom, dispels worry
  12127
But simply w. thee 12094
by refusing to w. God 4442
candle in act of being kindled
  12132
church community of w. 1414
clover leaves sleeping in attitude
  of w. 8000
concept of ineffable w. has been
  lost 12120
conclude w. must take place in
  church 12101
could planning w. save broken
  necks 767
ends in holy obedience 12105
erect houses of w, but our shrines
  are our places of business 6068
fellowship with God with our
  spirit 12139
First w. God 12097
Freedom in w. God 4114
giving to God best he has given us
  12134
God I w. too big for space to
  contain 11643
God in difficult circumstances 238
God not pleased with w. at
  Jerusalem 12101
God seeks w. of those trapped in
  moral ruin 12098
highest, noblest act 12137
Hospitality one form of w. 5958
I cannot adore enough. I cannot
  speak 12125

if all returned God identical w.
  6169
If person does not enjoy w. 5654
If w. does not change us 12105
immortal part of us meets with
  God 12139
in w. kneeling 12102
In w. we meet power of God
  12103
is a drop in quest of the ocean
  12132
is a soul in awe before mystery of
  universe 12132
is the Christian life 12135
is transcendent wonder 12138
isn't appreciating harmony of the
  choir 12139
isn't joining in singing hymns
  12139
isn't listening to a sermon 12139
isn't prayer 12139
jump from w. to waiting to work
  10716
Knowledge given to lead us to
  higher w. 6693
Life's mysteries for our w. 6995
Love and wait and w. endlessly
  7353
ludicrous for Christian to believe
  he is object of public w. 9217
man climbing altar stairs to God
  12132
may be w. without words 12121
means "to feel in the heart"
  12140
method of evil one to obscure
  himself behind object of w.
  2699
Mystery constitutes essence of w.
  12118
never knew how to w. until knew
  how to love 7185
No one can w. God on empty
  stomach 7152
of God become occupation of soul
  3987
of God not a rule of safety 12119
of himself: the more devoted, the
  fewer proselytes 9249
only acceptable workers those
  who w. 12099
only when begin to w, begin to
  grow 12107
pictured at its best in Isaiah 12136
renews the spirit 12141
requires only a man and God
  12142
seeing world in light of God
  12133
Silent w. is healing 12114
Some only hear God in public w.
  1477
stand in its strengthening 12103
substituted social control for
  family w. 5808
Success demands sacrifices from
  those who w. her 10801
thirsty land crying out for rain
  12132

time flowing into eternity 12132
to devote the will to purpose of
  God 12124
to feed the mind 12124
to purge the imagination 12124
to quicken the conscience 12124
to rise to higher level of existence
  12133
to see world from God's point of
  view 12133
To w. rightly is to love each other
  7284
too busy to learn to w. 12098
voice in night calling for help
  12132
was not as dangerous as should
  have been 12106
Whatever is outward in w. 12129
When men w, God is satisfied
  12137
When you w, you are fulfilled
  12137
who w. God from fear 12123
Who w. God shall find him 12130
without seeing 4322
Without w. of the heart 12131
would w. devil if he appear 12123
your heroes from afar 8516

WORSHIPED
Christian work is w., not God 97
Christians assume have w. because
  in church 12101
in silence w. best 10249
Prosperity not a deity to be w.
  9340

WORSHIPER
aware of no power, presence,
  reality 1399
cannot relate words to life 1399
dreamy numbness 1399
is no nearer to God than before
  8845
sits in suspended mentation 1399

WORSHIPERS
can tell you what dress pastor's
  wife wore 12111
cannot recall text of sermon
  12111
error, dies among his w. 11579
God is looking for w. 12098
God wants w. before workers
  12099
If haven't learned to be w. 12104
Jesus Christ came to make w. out
  of rebels 12137

WORSHIPING
almost w. the female bosom 10238
Beware of w. Jesus while you
  blaspheme him 3646
each member of w. congregation
  5799
heart needs no proof 600
realize I in knowing you don't
  need a why 12102

WORSHIPS
If w. not God, will have idols
  12109

WORST

and best both inclined 5048

bankrupt is lost enthusiasm 3183

best or w. in this life another matter 10789

carry our w. enemies within us 3157

corruption of best becomes the w. 10718

enemies can do is kill you 6158

Failure not w. thing in world 3589

friends can do is betray you 6158

get ready for the w. 5911

God estimates us at our best, not our w. 4650

hardship lack of sunglasses 3147

Hitting the ceiling w. 384

instead of harping on w. in people 5928

is not to try 3589

is that which persecutes the mind 7765

kind of bondage 4122

likely to believe w. about another 3412

Marriage unspeakably oppressive at its w. 7641

moment for atheist 488

not falling that is the w. 10318

of all modern notions w. is this 5842

People who cannot be alone w. company 10552

pleasures purely spiritual 10400

sin is not to hate, but be indifferent 6164

so much good in the w. of us 3953

Sometimes will have w. of it for doing right 4555

things present seem w. 8382

time is always the present 11387

war uses man's best to do man's w. 11763

we carry our w. enemies with us 9921

wheel screeches loudest 1562

wind up with nothing but w. 8324

World at its w, Christians must be at their best 1353

WORTH

A man's w. something 9940

a thousand thanks when things agreeable 11157

Acceptance of one's w. core of personality 9980

doing at all, w. doing well 96

friend you buy won't be w. what you pay 4176

God sums up man's w. by his character 11238

God's strength w. more than world 10768

good scare w. more than advice 3960

Good words w. much, cost little 11987
1844

guileless mind w. any price 5865

happiness in w, choice of friends 4293

I never knew the w. of him 4199

if memory have its w. 981

if only knew w. of suffering 10872

if things we do are w. doing 5590

if things we say are w. saying 5590

if things we think are w. thinking 5590

Is life w. living 6932

keep what is w. keeping 4260

knowledge of Bible w. more than college 640

least of things with meaning w. more 7030

life is w. the living 2978

life unexamined not w. living 7032

little thing in hand w. more 7116

Man w. as much as 11657

man's fight with himself w. something 1063

may hear a man say, Life is not w. living 6880

Nothing w. knowing can be taught 11932

Of a man as man, regardless of birth 7423

of an individual endowed by the Creator 10001

of an individual not ascribed by law 10001

of kind deed lies in the love 2506

of man measured by objects pursued 469

One cool judgment w. thousand hasty councils 6587

one day in Spirit w. more than thousand in flesh 5787

One example w. thousand arguments 3450

One father w. more than hundred schoolmasters 3923

One today w. two tomorrows 11376

only creed w. twopence 2031

Outside show poor substitute for inner w. 6061

Salvation is w. working for 9810

see men of w, become like them 1065

Things only w. what you make them w. 11665

This, I was w. to God 9981

thorn of experience w. wilderness of warning 3540

thoughts that come to us w. more 11250

To become like Christ only thing w. caring for 6494

To gain that which is w. having 4340

to God in public is what I am in private 6315

unable to distinguish what is w. reading 2997

we are w. more than results of our efforts 10545

well's dry, we know w. of water 444

What is outside yourself does not convey much w. 9626

with contentment crown the thought of w. 4505

WORTHIER

thing to deserve than to possess honor 5893

WORTHINESS

election depends not upon w. 3047

WORTHLESS

cannot treat human embryo as w. 24

conviction without action w. 3737

creed w. if it doesn't take us to Christ 2026

Doing things by halves w. 2770

everything else is w. 7195

God would never invest in w. property 9989

Let no one say we are w. 9989

Many people happy but w. to society 5539

not more w. if criticized 1681

Thou dost desire my w. heart 7456

WORTHWHILE

most w. form of education 3031

Tain't w. to wear a day all out before it comes 12055

WORTHWHILENESS

faith in w. of life 4005

WORTHY

by choosing us God makes us w. 3044

by justifying us God makes us w. 6631

desires honors, not w. of honor 9203

Few men w. of experience 3534

God did not choose us because w. 3044

God does not justify us because w. 6631

God is fitting to be w. of him 4514

God, no one more w. of our love 7533

Gossip lack of w. theme 5131

Lord, make me w. 8786

man who believes he is w. of heaven 5668

members of family whose father is in heaven 5001

more w. they are, more humility will be seen 5991

Nature shows something w. of a God 8026

without leaving w. evidence of your passage 11292

WOUND

caused by words more painful than w. caused by arrow 5119

Choose to heal, rather than w. 1138

Earth felt the w. 10314

fanatic, w. that never healed 3910

For Christian to do wrong is to w. Friend 1283

heals, but scar remains 10446

if receive his words, they fly forward and w. you 10447

if receive not his words, they fly back and w. him 10447

jests at scars that never felt a w. 10850

Looking at w. of sin will never save 9804

Music eases grief's smarting w. 7913

No w, no scar 10604

scar on conscience same as w. 1660

What can w. more deeply 4210

What w. did ever heal but by degrees 8399

WOUNDED

become the w. person 3071

Bind the hearts we have w. 9054

Error, w, writhes in pain 11579

Gold no balm to w. spirit 7798

Grace can heal us when w. 5212

oysters never w. fit only for stew 10883

see the w. and angry 7300

WOUNDING

Holy Ghost able to show wrong without w. 2078

Slander w. him that commits and him against whom committed 10463

WOUNDS

balm to fester'd w. 3129

blood that from Lord's w. flow 2142

Christ enters world to heal its w. 6487

Envy w. herself 3214

It heals his w. 1507

man who studies revenge keeps own w. green 9714

more w. than surgeons can heal 393

my soul flies through these w. 292

only in place of healing dare to show w. 10551

ready to suffer w, endure pain 9088

Sharp words make w. 393

shelter broken hearts 1443

through w. to seek thee 292

to bind up nation's w. 5199

to fight and not to heed the w. 9113

too many w. to heal 10211

WOVEN

silent threads of gold when w. together 6997

veil of future w. by hand of mercy 4330

WRANGLE

God allows man to w. about him 4673

WRAP

I'll w. him warm with love 6134

Man, w. yourself in God 2658

WRAPPED

in mortality 3482

infant world, w. in swaddling clothes of light 7886

that messiahs aren't found w. in rags 6147

you w. me in your splendor 7473

WRAPPINGS

Lies can be disguised in gorgeous w. 6853

WRAPS

Like one that w. the drapery of his couch 2203

WRAPT

All were w. in gloom 7109

WRATH

alternative to w. is neutrality 4999

best way to understand w. of God 4999

children of w, now sons of mercy 1348

God gives w. by weight 4451

God turns from w, never from love 4757

God's w. toward you burns like fire 4523

I told my w, my w. did end 386

I told not my w, my w. did grow 386

Jesus is to me all grace, no w. 6498

judgment of God not proof of his w. 4721

Lord abandoned to God's blazing w. 6383

love and w. obverse and reverse of same thing 4999

occasions for w. often leave us calm 3056

of God is pure 401

to ward off bolts of divine w. 4998

WRATH OF GOD

alternative to w. not love 4999

WRATHFUL

words make people w. 11985

WRECK

Sidon scarcely left w. behind 730

something has been saved from w. 11072

WRECKS

If, rising on its w. 3538

Towering o'er the w. of time 2133

WRESTLE

devil can w. with but not overcome 2673

WRESTLED

Christ w. with justice 6393

WRESTLES

devil w. with God 2691

He that w. with us strengthens our nerves 1623

WRESTLING

Life is w. with evil 6947

with evil, hand to hand, foot to foot 6947

WRETCH

concentrated all in self 10088

WRETCHED

can be as w. as you choose 10816

However w, still a member of common species 906

If God my friend, cannot be w. 7476

Is life so w. 6931

refuse of your teeming shore 7985

WRETCHEDNESS

O sad estate of human w. 8877

WRETCHES

poor w. saved from shipwreck 10386

To w. such as I 7007

WRINKLED

Character gives awe to w. skin 997

Time has w. my brow 11328

WRINKLES

If w. must be written upon brows 8137

let w. not be written upon the heart 8137

Old age puts more w. in minds than on faces 8162

should indicate where smiles have been 8188

time writes no w. on brow of eternity 3266

wear a scowl, have w. 10502

WRITE

Does not the lightning w. God's name in fire 7997

down advice of him who loves you 273

down advice though you do not like it 273

God did not w. solo parts 10135

injuries in dust, benefits in marble 9523

let lightning w. his name in fire 4712

Not without design does God w. the music of our lives 7056

nothing you cannot believe to be true 9871

Reach forth and w. upon the sky 8015

student used to w, now calls collect 3896

To w. the love of God above 4748

virtues we w. in water 9619

When angry, I can w. well 408

WRITER

a kind of evangelist 12155

have failed as Christian w. 12147

writes to teach himself 12148

WRITERS

God not interested only in Christian w. 12146
love quotations 9389

WRITES

if w. cultured papers call him Papa 3921
Man w. histories 5719
Sin w. histories 10380

WRITHE

under tyrannies of cruel master 6280

WRITHES

Error, wounded, w. in pain 11579

WRITING

as much dignity in tilling field as w. poem 2762
book nearest man gets to having a baby 12158
for half a century w. my thoughts in prose, verse 11132
God concerned with all kinds of w. 12146
if educated knows how to use colons in w. 12152
Jesus without w. single line set more pens in motion 6449
like w. on sand by seashore 3860
more exposure than quality of w. 12156
so difficult feel writers will escape punishment hereafter 12159
type of w. that causes crime 12156
Where desire to learn much w. 6711

WRITTEN

Be astounded God should have w. 644
Bible most human book ever w. 701
Every syllable already w. down in deeds 6482
figures w. by fingers of sunlight 4454
History, story w. by finger of God 5712
hope, word God has w. on brow of every man 5947
How endless is volume God has w. of world 6901
If faults w. on forehead 3943
in library, most books w. for him 6965
Infinite w. name on earth in flowers 4705
Infinite w. name on heavens in stars 4705
name of God may be w. upon that soul 10475
name of Jesus not so much w. as plowed into history 5727
on thy works I read 1966
Our lives are albums w. through 7017
perpetual must be w. on eternal shores 3860

personality w. and signed by God 6183
what man has w. man may read 8049
Why the best books haven't been w. 8230

WRONG

Absent always in the w. 10471
Accept Christ attitude likely w. 3333
admit you're w, you're right 9665
All truth to love, all w. to hate 7986
anything that ... is w. for me 7036
as if you alone had done the w. 9672
Authentic men aren't afraid to admit when w. 3916
Bearing w. part of fellowship of Christ's sufferings 6257
Beware of discernment of w. 2803
Bible, deals with right and w. 721
born in w. generation 12190
Both may be, one must be w. 4972
came over me that suicide was w. 10940
can change thing that is w. 3596
Christ could not afford to be w. 11509
Christian admits w. to be right 1265
concept of God leads to w. concept of sin 4568
Condemn the w, yet the w. pursue 10319
danger signals life is on w. track 5466
devil is sincere, but sincerely w. 10429
Dirt is matter in w. place 5121
Distinguish between right, w. burden-bearing 937
Doubt not always sign man is w. 2933
error proceeds in w. direction 3258
even people who have done us w. 7304
for Christian to do w. is to wound Friend 1283
free to make w. decisions 2486
Give them grace to pray for such as do them w. 9104
God puts right all that was w. 837
Hamlet, not his world, that is w. 7396
have chosen the w. day 10961
He who does w. does w. against himself 6262
History endless repetition of w. way of living 5713
Holy Ghost able to show w. without wounding 2078
Holy Spirit will put right what is w. 894
Honesty often in the w. 5877
I alone am responsible for w. I do 9661

I see the w. that round me lies 4642
if course is w. avoid though lose life as consequence 6291
if decisions w. God will always check 5464
If I am w, O teach my heart 9067
if souls not saved, something w. 1404
if w, sanction of mankind will not justify 5032
in effort to be right may go w. 9502
in the w, wiser than yesterday 1593
instruments being used for job 4739
irritable person like hedgehog rolled up w. way 9630
is w. even if everyone for it 1037
It matters not how deep intrenched the w. 6256
It were a hellish w. 6258
ladder of success leaning against w. wall 10777
life is stronger than w. 2985
looking in the w. place 7105
Lord does not tell us we are w. 8106
man condemned for continuing to do w. 6586
measure by which judged right or w. is love 7307
My country right or w. like saying 7980
never be ashamed to admit w. 3249
never turned w. to right 3174
No snowflake ever falls in w. place 8028
not to do w. never do anything 1636
not to speak w, never speak 1636
nothing w. with being individuals 9952
Of w. and outrage with which earth is fill'd 6273
One act of thanksgiving when things go w. 11157
One more w. to man 6275
Optimism maintaining everything right when w. 8236
part with him when he goes w. 6303
praying for rain with tub w. side up 8868
real always checked with w. 9498
regard as enormous little w. you did to others 4097
regard as trifling great w. done to you 4097
Right actions best apologies for w. actions 9598
rub w. way will bite, scratch 9482
separate faith and works w. 3829
Sin is energy in the w. channel 10364
Sin is not w. doing 10372

Sin is turning in the w. direction 10370

Sin is w. being 10372

television, nothing w. that not watching won't cure 11042

than take w. road once 5424

things w. with the country total of things w. with individuals 7989

Thou dost preserve the stars from w. 4598

time to be right is when everyone else is w. 6805

To forget a w. is mild revenge 9729

to mourn for sin because it is w. 9581

to right w. 9088

to say, "I was w." 7838

To w. the wronger till he render right 11344

trying to spell God with w. blocks 7530

unafraid whether right or w. 6216

was his who wrongfully complained 1565

way always seems more reasonable 5453

when conscious of being saint, something w. 10722

When everything goes dead w. 10493

When w, make us willing to change 9119

Whenever knowledge becomes dry something w. 6704

who quietly suffer w. 6274

Who see the world's great anguish and its w. 426

Why should we do ourselves this w. 8867

will have an explanation 7060

world guided by clocks that show w. time 2803

world is w. side up 12047

would have married the w. man 8797

your idea of love w. 4755

WRONGDOER

not always one who has done something 6157

often has left something undone 6157

WRONGDOING

kept from w. because of presence of others 1051

WRONGED

if w. do no one slight 1191

must forgive whoever has w. you 4109

respond with love when unmistakably w. 6278

WRONGER

To wrong the w. till he render right 11344

WRONGS

another world where w. are corrected 5678

By bearing old w. provoke new ones 9632

he that w. his friends w. himself more 1684

Satan tries to make us think w. spring from God 9859

to withhold from child world's w. 8334

While prayers to heal her w. move slow behind 6269

WROTE

Christ w. no book yet words counsel everywhere 6394

in library a few books he w. himself 6965

WROUGHT

In me thy blessed will is w. 4977

we tangle up the plans the Lord hath w. 6117

⅄

YARD

by the y. life is hard 6930

wish to run rescue mission within y. of hell 7783

YARDSTICK

futile as y. that will measure infinity 5718

give up measuring value with y. of others 10162

YARN

web of life of mingled y. 7045

YAWN

can choke God's Word with a y. 11349

YAWNING

Why does one man's y. make another yawn 6247

YEAR

Another y. is dawning 8077

Another y. of progress 8077

as I tread on another y. 8079

by y. better equipped 4439

can hardly make friend in y. 4305

day an epitome of the y. 9877

Each moment of y. has its own beauty 9873

if gives way to fault for y. or two 3935

importance to learn more every y. 3017

in a shroud of leaves dead, is lying 11321

In working or in waiting, another y. with thee 8077

is closed, record made 8082

never a thunderstorm to announce new y. 11329

Once in the y. 1369

One y. of self-surrender 10074

reminder of Resurrection at start of each new y. 8080

Sabbath, fifty-two springs in every y. 10950

The good Old Y. is with the past 8078

We turn to meet another y. 8082

who stood at the gate of the y. 5417

YEARNING

arises from image of God in nature of man 4744

for something better 470

for something holier 470

for something nobler 470

heart's y. for love 4643

no y. however trifling we may not lay before God 7536

peers yawning, Caleb y. 764

soul's moanings are y. for the Infinite 7516

to breathe free 7985

to comprehend the incomprehensible 4744

to know what cannot be known 7531
  4744

to touch, taste the unapproachable 4744

touching of God makes us hungry, and y. 5764

YEARNINGS

are homesickness for heaven 7516

precious thing God finds in us 10666

YEAR'S

If 10 percent holy, world converted before y. end 5750

YEARS

After two thousand y. of mass 11739

come to my door 11320

Don't let parenting y. get away 8294

During my many y. in the cabinet 5094

Elderly person is ten y. older 8124

Eternal y. lie in God's heart 3274

even if lasted for thousands and thousands of y. 5652

few y. we spend on earth only first scene 6106

fifteen y. teaching child to be quiet 8336

first hundred y. the hardest 6992

found myself as strong as forty y. ago 7104

he is curtailed who overflowed all skies, all y. 6120

How dread are thine eternal y. 4659

I think and think for y. 2775

If I only had three y. to serve the Lord 6687

immersion for y. in history of thought 3027

In early y. of Christian experience 3744

in y. of uneventful duties 10190

Let it travel down the y. 6640

love of life increased with y. 8174

more progress in silence than in y. of study 12112

No age can heap its outward y. on thee 4605

No matter how the y. go by 8122

not how many y. we live 6933

nothing more fleeting than y. 11354

of patience to tame young human beings 7382

One minute of patience, ten y. of peace 8404

power of Bible persists through y. 654

repent for y. to efface fault 4091

reputation of thousand y. determined by conduct of one hour 9625

riches of limitless time, endless y. 3274

Scripture widens, deepens with y. 685

sew people together through the y. 7608

simple record of three short y. 6483

Sixty y. ago I knew everything 3024

spend three y. teaching child to walk 8336

supported me through y. of exile 7102

Swift fly the y. and rise th' expected morn 6143

teach much days never knew 3546

than fourscore y. of selfishness 10074

than learn from man in thousand y. 4964

The pages of our y. 7017

The y. have flown 179

Thirty y. of Lord's life hidden 8112

three y. old, have done more than half 8306

through the y. using only small part of himself 8661

took God y. to teach me to say "Lord anything" 4892

Unmeasured by the flight of y. 5633

We live in deeds, not y. 1056

Will make them old before their y. 4003

Work as if you were to live a hundred y. 12023

would spend two y. studying, preparing 6687

YEAST
Beatitudes, y. of love 530

YELLOW
If the light is red or y. 5422

YELLOW-PETALLED
June 9886

YES
Answer Y. 6892

For all that shall be, y. 9055

I need your y. 1536

make it possible for him to say y. to what we ask 8924

most important words are y. to God 11994

perpetual y. of universal acquiescence 1645

say the y. of faith 1306

Saying y. to God means saying no to things that offend his holiness 5755

without saying y. to something far better 11110

YESTERDAY
admit wrong, wiser today than y. 3249

can never ride on wave that went out y. 8372

cannot change y. 3502

did and did-not of y. 1734

do it y. 2768

educate in what nobody knew y. 3035

God is not the God of y. 10124

how far we have progressed since y. 9832

I hung on cross 2121

I was buried with Christ 2121

I was dying with Christ 2121

I've shut the door on y. 11369

in the wrong, wiser than y. 1593

is a canceled check 11390

Learn from y. 11304

Lost, y. somewhere between sunrise, sunset 11306

love you more today than y. 5882

no road back to y. 7051

O God! that it were possible to call back y. 9568

Procrastination is keeping up with y. 9299

riddling the faith of y. 2953

Today is not y. 981

Today the tomorrow you worried about y. 11383

Tomorrow hopes we've learnt from y. 11403

we are dead to y. 11365

you really got on my nerves 5882

YESTERDAY'S
Today is y. pupil 11384 3547

today locks out y. nightmares 11382

worry and tomorrow's anxiety 12092

YESTERDAYS
day too dear to waste moment on y. 11366

fatuous, ineffectual y. 8370

God has lived our y. 11295

YIELD
bad tree does not y. good apples 986

God is aiding to y. fruit 4514

Lord asks us to y. to him 2490

nor does hope y. to cynicism 5928

Our part is to y. 2097

refusing to y. to depression, fear 2563

room for some little time to God 7708

To y. is to be preserved whole 7071

will y. to that about us 11108

YIELDING
old order y. place to new 978

Preserve us from y. to dejection 9092

to temptation is opening door, inviting devil in 11088

While y. to parental leadership 8338

YIELDS
noncomformist never y. to passive patience 6619

YOKE
Break off the y. and set me free 2583

gentle device to make hard labor light 2816

instrument of mercy 2816

men speak of y. of Christ as slavery 2816

not instrument of torture 2816

sanctification not a heavy y. 9842

seems difficult to put on y. of Christ 2824

what y. really for 2816

when put on y. of Christ becomes easy 2824

YONDER
hope ties itself y. 5919

not God away off up y. 8801

YOU
are special, distinct, unique 6206

aren't an accident 10004

aren't an assembly-line product 10004

cannot be everything 352

God already had y. in mind 4879

Nobody can be y. as effectively as y. can 9983

Nobody can be y. as efficiently as y. can 6203

Not your work, but y. 351

that y. alone are y. 6223

the work that God marked out for y. 6204

to do for y. and yours 5009

were deliberately planned 10004

were lovingly positioned on earth 10004

were not made from common mold 6206

were specifically gifted 10004

weren't mass-produced 10004

what y. and yours have done for us 5009

Where y. are, be all there 3186

YOUNG
And whom he finds y, keeps y. still 7264

aspirations that never come to pass 12195

But I had talked with God when y. 1817

By hope kept y. of heart 3834

can be y. and old at same time 11323

Death comes to y. men 2349

feel tired at end of action 313

grow y. as I leave my me behind 9920

heart that loves is always y. 7302

it was the y. people who flocked to Jesus 6452

Love makes those y. whom age doth chill 7264

men lose lives by violence 12197

men may die, old men must 2433

Men of 70, 80 often more youthful than the y. 12198

Next to the very y, very old most selfish 10072

no respect for youth when I was y. 9647

No y. man ever thinks he shall die 12171

not y. enough to know everything 6684

saint is ever y. 9785

so y, so strong, so sure of God 1609

Spring makes everything y. except man 9894

still disappointed, still y. 8126

too y. now, I will enjoy life 4886

training minds, forming habits of y. 3037

when y, sure of everything 956

When y. man no one had respect for youth 12190

When y. nine out of ten failures 10825

When y. passion marvelous thing 10229

When y. run into difficulties 12196

Whenever friends compliment about looking y. 8185

YOUNG PEOPLE

amazed how much y. know about sex 10222

built for God 12180

designate god with clay feet as devil incarnate 12179

do impossible before find out impossible 12177

need control, authority 12178

seem so cynical 12179

when learn a god has clay feet designate as devil incarnate 12179

who control what y. are taught 8360

why God uses them so often 12177

will respond if challenge tough enough 12180

without control y. unhappy 12178

without God frustrated, confused 12180

YOUNGER

Nothing so dates a man as to decry y. generation 12192

YOURS

all good things are y. 5604

to do for you and y. 5009

what you and y. have done for us 5009

YOURSELF

and me. I am sick of both 9958

Are you complete in y. 1450

Be patient with everyone, above all y. 8292

best to y. when good to others 6673

best way to cheer y. up 2559

betray somebody else, betray y. 631

Beware of no man more than y. 9921 3157

brief instant of time allotted to y. 7063

brilliant conversationalist talks to you about y. 5112

Brotherhood: helping y. by helping others 903

by devoting y. singleheartedly to God 10703

cannot make y. as you wish 993

Cast off everything not y. 995

change sitution or y. 2753

Control y. 375

deny y, favorite text of asceticism 467

deny y. sounds hard 8108

deny y. that you may give 4387

difference between glorify God, y. 3469

do not distract y. by looking forward 9650

Don't be ferocious with y. 9923

Don't sell y. short 10001

Don't speak well of y. 5996 9614

easy times, brace y. 969

experience something you give y. 10996

find y. loving any pleasure better than prayers 6925

find y. on easy road ought to worry 2745

First keep peace within y. 8434

Forget y. and think of those around 11284

friend, someone with whom you dare to be y. 4173

give respect to 511

give y, truly give 1725

hammer, forge y. into character 1071

Have some time for y. and God 9265

healthy self-image is seeing y. as God sees you 9978

Hope in the Lord, but exert y. 5914

If doubt y, on shaky ground 11599

if he is stronger, spare y. 6263

if you can accept poverty as God's will for y. 8678

If you find y. so loaded 4319

If you hate, you hate something that is part of y. 5600

if you think too much of y, other people won't 9253

If you want to hear truth about y. 8058

If you were someone else, could you stand y. 9990

In trouble go not out of y. for aid 2734

Insist on y, never imitate 6194

Judge y. by the friends you choose 4194

just try being y. 6191

Keep y. clean and bright 3438

keep y. clean, bright 8573

leave y. at the cross 10048

love y. in such a way 10024

Make most of y. that is all there is 2781

Make y. necessary to somebody 10172

Man, wrap y. in God 2658

Maturity, concern for others outweighing concern for y. 7693

never makes excuses for y. 3478

Only you can prove immortality to y. 6102

pray for another, will be helped y. 8838

Prepare y. for battle 9861

put y. in his shoes 11286

Remind y. God is with you 9983

repentance means killing part of y. 9577

right you claim for y. 11282

same zeal as if y. 3125

See failings in y. 2808

See not good in y. 2808

stand aside and watch y. go by 10009

Sympathy never wasted except when give to y. 10981

Think of what is faulty in y. 3939

Think of y. as "he" instead of "I" 10009

Think of y. as seed wintering in earth 5672

thought of y. never bothers you 2822

to be downhearted, look to y. 6408

to be miserable think about y. 10816

To handle y, use your head 9508

truest self-respect is not to think of y. 10000

try putting y. in their place 3073

turn y. upwards, inwards 2105

want to be respected, must respect y. 9642

What is outside y. does not convey much worth 9626

What you make of y. your gift to God 8560

What you wish for your neighbor, ask for y. 8067

when give y. you truly give 10219

When you empty y, God Almighty rushes in 9956

when you try to make y. more, you are diminishing y. 9941

when you've made a fool of y. 4213

you answer only for y. 74

you carry y. with you 2105

You have made us for y. 4312

YOURSELVES

Weep not for me, but for y. 2455

YOUTH

accent on y, stress on parents 8354

aspirations that never come to pass 12195

begins when objects to parents having own way 3905

begins when parents become retarded 3906

belief y. happiest time of life a fallacy 7026

believes everything exists for his sake 12169

cannot go back to his y. 12170

Character gives splendor to y. 997

Cheer the y. who's bravely trying 4217

defect of age to rail at pleasures of y. 12189

demand not for old age but for y. 12194

devil entangles y. with beauty 2677

Direct efforts to preparing y. for path 8291

do things excessively, vehemently 12181

Don't laugh at y. affectations 12163

eagerly waiting for play to begin 12168

exalted notions 12181

fades 7860

feeling of eternity in y. 12175

fifty y. of old age 307

Forty old age of y. 307

governed more by feeling than reasoning 12181

grace, force, fascination 12188

happy because capacity to see beauty 12182

has to do with spirit, not age 12198

hate too much 12181

I remember my y. 12165

ideal state if came later in life 12187

If y. be a defect 12167

in days of y. remembered God 8140

in y. just, generous, forbearing 8184

In y. we learn 12191 310

In y. world began to exist when he was born 12169

is a blunder 7097 12199

is y, age is age 12186

isms of y. the wasms of age 12174

large, lusty, loving 12188

looks forward 12200

love too much 12181

Memory controls y. 7735

must inherit aftermath of war 11757

no business to require head of age on shoulders of y. 12186

no respect for y. when I was young 9647

not definable by age 12183

not yet humbled by life 12181

not yet learned limitations 12181

one thing that never returns 12184

overdo everything 12181

person to carry on what you have started 12160

psychological secrets used to control y. 12178

serenity of age takes the place of riotous y. 7101

shows but half 8132

sins of y. paid for in old age 10401

spirit of daring, creating, asserting life 12183

spirit of relating to world 12183

spiritual life is unaging y. 10712

take over churches, schools, corporations 12160

think they know everything 12181

thinks nothing of health 5619

to seek wisdom in y. like inscription on stone 11956

use fires of y. to drive engines of age 11323

wants master, controller 12180

well to pay him attention 12160

When young man no one had respect for y. 12190

who must fight and die 11757

wholly experimental 12185

will assume control of cities, states, nations 12160

would rather do noble than useful deeds 12181

Young men lose lives by violence 12197

YOUTHFUL

Men of 70, 80 often more y. than the young 12198

YOUTH'S

when y. gone 305

Z

ZACHARIAS

Five words cost Z. silence 11412

ZEAL

God is enkindling with z. 4514

good deeds with same zeal 108

Kindness converted more sinners than z. 6648

Misplaced z. is z. for God rather than z. of God 7502

same z. as if yourself 3125

ZENITH OF POWER

if man compare all he can see, is at Z. 6698

ZERO

Life minus love equals z. 7206

ZEST

if in life you keep the z. 8122

Life will take on new z. 3185

ZESTFUL

Mirth offered sparkling with z. life to God 6739

ZOAR

is pointed out when God foretells Sodom's ruin 11432

ZONE

brought within z. of God's voice 7540

ZYME

last words of Noah Webster 2379

ZYMOSIS

last words of Noah Webster 2379

ZYMURGY

last words of Noah Webster 2379